THE REVELL BIBLE DICTIONARY

THE REVELL BIBLE DICTIONARY

Fleming H. Revell
A Division of Baker Book House Co
Grand Rapids, Michigan 49516

For illustration credits see pages 1154-56.

Library of Congress Cataloging-in-Publication Data

The Revell Bible dictionary
    p.   cm.
  ISBN 0-8007-1594-2
   1. Bible—Dictionaries.   I. Fleming H. Revell Company.
  BS440.R484   1990
  220'.3—dc20   90-33002
                                         CIP

Copyright © 1990 by Fleming H. Revell
a division of Baker Book House Company
P.O. Box 6287, Grand Rapids, MI 49516-6287

Second printing, February 1994

Printed in the United States of America

FOREWORD

Rightly called "the greatest book ever written," the Bible has captivated children and adults with its bold images of heroes and heroines and has comforted generations of believers with its warm affirmation of God's great love. Yet the Bible, reflecting a world thousands of years distant in time, also puzzles. Unfamiliar names and places, strange customs, and unknown words frequently discourage or confuse readers.

The Revell Bible Dictionary has been written to help. This is not a Bible dictionary for scholars, full of technical detail. It's a Bible dictionary for the home; for the person who wants concise, authoritative insights that will help him or her understand what the Bible says and what that means for contemporary Christian life.

I join the publisher in inviting you to explore the Bible in a fresh, new way. Through pictures and carefully crafted descriptions, we encourage you to discover the meaning of the Bible's words, of its institutions, of its customs and practices. We invite you to enter the world of Scripture: to visit the homes where Bible people lived, to join them at meals and at work, to understand the way they experienced life. Meet the great men and women of the Bible and learn from their relationship with God. Be present at sacred history's significant events, events that shaped the way we understand and know God today.

Thousands of articles provide the information you need to read and to understand the Bible today. And there's more. Unique feature after unique feature also help you to apply the Bible's message. In warm, devotional tones, this Bible dictionary helps you hear the Lord speak to you personally through the one Book believers are convinced is the Word of God.

In developing this Bible dictionary, we have remained committed to these principles: Each article must reflect the Bible's story as the Scriptures themselves tell it, must be trustworthy, drawing on insights from many disciplines, and must reflect the positive truths of Scripture with as little theological bias as possible. For this reason I deeply appreciate our panel of scholars, both men and women—experts in archaeology, in the Old and New Testament, and in Christian traditions from Roman Catholicism to the Protestant charismatic movement. While they are not to be held responsible for views reflected in the finished work, they have checked each article for accuracy and theological bias and offered many suggestions to help Revell provide a Bible dictionary that will be helpful to all—a Bible dictionary we trust will enrich your personal appreciation of the world's greatest Book.

Lawrence O. Richards, Ph.D.

Above: Solomon's Jerusalem.
It took seven years for King
Solomon to build the Temple
high on Mount Moriah (upper
right), but he spent thirteen
years building his elaborate
palace (center). David's
Jerusalem comprised only
twelve acres (left); Solomon
expanded the city northward
and more than doubled its
size.

**BIBLICAL PAINTINGS
BY LLOYD K. TOWNSEND**

C O N T E N T S

HOW TO USE
THIS DICTIONARY

This dictionary is divided into two major sections: (1) The A to Z dictionary —with about 2,000 entries on subjects ranging from atonement to ziggurats and including the most significant people and places of biblical times—will help you understand the Bible better, and (2) Identiquick™ (beginning on page 1049) will identify for you all the people and places mentioned in the Bible.

UNDERSTANDING THE PURPOSE

The Revell Bible Dictionary is published (1) to give you reliable information—both verbal and visual—that will help you understand the Bible and its teachings; (2) to give you guidance on how to apply the Bible in your own life; and (3) to give you a sense of wonder and appreciation about God's revelation to us, and in so doing to provide you with a rich and enjoyable devotional experience.

These are unique aspects of this Bible dictionary and, as a result, when you read it, you will sense a different "feel" from other reference works. This dictionary is intended, not only to help you to know, but also to help you to apply and feel.

MAIN SECTION

FINDING THE WORD YOU WANT

All the entries in the Revell Bible Dictionary are listed in strict alphabetical order, letter by letter. This applies equally to hyphenated entries and entries that consist of two or more words:

judge
Judges, Book of
judgment
judgment day

All entries are highlighted in boldface type. Those that are words taken directly from Hebrew, Greek, or other ancient languages are also italicized. Examples would be words like:

agape
corban
shekinah

PROPER NAMES

In the Identiquick™ section you will find all the proper names mentioned in the Bible. In addition, some 200 of the key people and places are treated fully in the main body of the text.

When a person is profiled in the main alphabetical section of this dictionary, a boxed paragraph contains a short biography for quick comprehension.

Lot (LAHT; "covering"). Nephew of Abraham, who traveled with him to Canaan and unwisely settled in Sodom. **Father:** Haran. Descendants: Moabites, Ammonites. Scripture: Gen. 11-14, 19.

DEFINITIONS

Each entry word or phrase is immediately followed by a brief definition. If the entry word has several meanings, or if its Old Testament and New Testament usages differ, multiple definitions are provided.

queen (1) The wife of a king, as in Esth. 1:9; (2) the mother of the reigning king, the "queen mother," as in 2 Chr. 15:16, and (3) infrequently, a woman sovereign, as in 1 Ki. 10:1.

CROSS-REFERENCES

This dictionary has three types of cross-references. The first immediately follows an entry and directs the reader to the entry word under which the definition is found.

Ingathering, Feast of *See* Tabernacles, Feast of.

The second type highlights entries with information related to a particular issue in a particular paragraph.

ordinance A statute, decree, judicial decision, or law; an authoritative command—used primarily as a synonym for the Law of God, but also of authoritative commands of a king. *See also* Law.

The third type is found under the Related Articles column in the Reading and Study Guide charts, which are supplied for each book of the Bible.

ACTS: A READING AND STUDY GUIDE		
Chapter	**Content Summary**	**Related Articles**
1	Jesus ascends into heaven. The disciples choose a replacement for Judas while waiting in Jerusalem for the Spirit.	Ascension of Christ Holy Spirit
2	The Holy Spirit comes on Pentecost, and Peter preaches the first gospel sermon.	Church Tongues of fire
3	Peter heals a cripple at the Temple gate, then preaches Christ to onlookers.	Peter Repent

BIBLE VERSIONS

This dictionary is primarily keyed to the New International Version of the Holy Bible. Because of the time-honored tradition of the King James Version, however, many entry words from that version are included. They are identified with the parenthetical abbreviation (KJV) and are usually cross-referenced to the equivalent word in the New International Version.

Occasionally, references are made in entries to other translations, including the New American Standard Bible, the Revised Standard Version, and the Jerusalem Bible.

ABBREVIATIONS

BIBLE VERSIONS

NIV	New International Version
KJV	King James Version or Authorized Version
RSV	Revised Standard Version
NASB	New American Standard Bible
NEB	New English Bible
JB	The Jerusalem Bible
ASV	American Standard Version
TEV	Today's English Version
NAB	New American Bible
LB	Living Bible

BIBLICAL BOOKS

OLD TESTAMENT

Gen.	Genesis
Ex.	Exodus
Lev.	Leviticus
Num.	Numbers
Deut.	Deuteronomy
Josh.	Joshua
Jdg.	Judges
Ruth	Ruth
1 Sam.	1 Samuel
2 Sam.	2 Samuel
1 Ki.	1 Kings
2 Ki.	2 Kings
1 Chr.	1 Chronicles
2 Chr.	2 Chronicles
Ezra	Ezra
Neh.	Nehemiah
Esth.	Esther
Job	Job
Ps./Pss.	Psalms
Prov.	Proverbs
Eccl.	Ecclesiastes
Song	Song of Songs
Isa.	Isaiah
Jer.	Jeremiah
Lam.	Lamentations
Ezek.	Ezekiel
Dan.	Daniel
Hos.	Hosea
Joel	Joel
Amos	Amos
Obad.	Obadiah
Jon.	Jonah
Mic.	Micah
Nah.	Nahum
Hab.	Habakkuk
Zeph.	Zephaniah
Hag.	Haggai
Zech.	Zechariah
Mal.	Malachi

NEW TESTAMENT

Mt.	Matthew
Mk.	Mark
Lk.	Luke
Jn.	John
Acts	Acts
Rom.	Romans
1 Cor.	1 Corinthians
2 Cor.	2 Corinthians
Gal.	Galatians
Eph.	Ephesians
Phil.	Philippians
Col.	Colossians
1 Th.	1 Thessalonians
2 Th.	2 Thessalonians
1 Tim.	1 Timothy
2 Tim.	2 Timothy
Tit.	Titus
Phlm.	Philemon
Heb.	Hebrews
Jas.	James
1,2 Pet.	1,2 Peter
1,2,3 Jn.	1,2,3 John
Jude	Jude
Rev.	Revelation

OTHER ABBREVIATIONS

Aram.	Aramaic
Gk.	Greek
Heb.	Hebrew
Lat.	Latin

OT	Old Testament
NT	New Testament
B.C.	Before Christ
A.D.	Anno Domini
ch./chs.	chapter/chapters
v./vv.	verse/verses
lit.	literally
fig.	figuratively

TRANSLITERATION

The following transliterations have been adopted in this dictionary:

Greek

$\alpha = a$		$\rho = r$	
$\beta = b$		$\sigma, s = s$	
$\gamma = g$		$\tau = t$	
$\delta = d$		$\upsilon = y$	
$\varepsilon = e$		$\varphi = ph$	
$\zeta = z$		$\chi = ch$	
$\eta = \bar{e}$		$\psi = ps$	
$\theta = th$		$\omega = \bar{o}$	
$\iota = i$		$\dot{\rho} = rh$	
$\kappa = k$		$' = h$	
$\lambda = l$		$\gamma\xi = nx$	
$\mu = m$		$\gamma\gamma = ng$	
$\nu = n$		$\alpha\upsilon = au$	
$\xi = x$		$\varepsilon\upsilon = eu$	
$o = o$		$o\upsilon = ou$	
$\pi = p$		$\upsilon\iota = \upsilon i$	

Hebrew

א $= '$		ל $= l$	
ב $= b$		מ $= m$	
ב $= b$		נ $= n$	
ג $= g$		ס $= s$	
ג $= g$		ע $= '$	
ד $= d$		פ $= p$	
ד $= d$		פ $= p$	
ה $= h$		צ $= s$	
ו $= w$		ק $= q$	
ז $= z$		ר $= r$	
ח $= h$		שׂ $= s$	
ט $= t$		שׁ $= sh$	
י $= y$		ת $= t$	
כ $= k$		ת $= t$	
כ $= k$			

x

IDENTIQUICK™

IDENTIQUICK™, PEOPLE, PLACES, AND MAPS

Specific information on how to use Identiquick™ is given on pages 1050 and 1105.

People and places that are treated fully in the main body of the text are highlighted in the Identiquick™ sections with asterisks.

A pronunciation guide for each proper name will help you pronounce it. The syllable that is capitalized is the one that is to be accented.

> **AARON*** [AIR-uhn] 1450 B.C. The older brother and companion of Moses during the Exodus, and Israel's first high priest. Ex. 4–40; Lev.; Num.; Deut. 9,10. **Parents:** Amram and Jochebed. **Siblings:** Moses and Miriam. **Wife:** Elisheba. **Sons:** Nadab, Abihu, Eleazar, Ithamar.
>
> **ABIGAIL** [AB-uh-gayl; "father rejoices"] **1.*** 1000 B.C. Wise wife of Nabal, who saved his household from David and later married David. 1 Sam. 25,27,30; 2 Sam. 2,3. **Son by David:** Kileab.
> **2.** 1000 B.C. A sister of David and mother of Amasa 1. 2 Sam. 17:25; 1 Chr. 2:16,17.

Places are coded to the map section to help you locate them. Each map is identified by a Roman numeral, and the grids within the map are coded by letters and numbers. Small villages and other geographic references are identified by giving their location in connection with a larger city or area. Thus, Abdon is listed as "about 15 miles (24 km) S of Tyre [**VII**, B1]. Since Abdon is too small a village to be listed on the map, you are directed to Tyre on map **VII**, quadrant B1.

> **ABDON** [AB-dahn; possibly "servile"] He-bron, KJV; Ebron, RSV. A Levitical town in Asher assigned to the Gershonites. Identified with the ruins of Abdeh, about 15 miles (24 km) S of Tyre [**VII**, B1]. Josh. 19:28; 21:30; 1 Chr. 6:74.

The map section on pages 1140–1153 is intended not only to supplement the simple maps used alongside articles in the main body, but also to provide historical and geographical background.

STAFF

ADMINISTRATION

Project Director: Robert G. Manley

Editorial Directors: William J. Petersen, Gary Sledge

Production Director: Joseph A. Repole

Controller: William O. Schubert

EDITORIAL

Project Coordinators: Timothy D. Westergren, Patricia S. Klein, Jean Pease, Rex Williams

Researcher: Tim Richards

Archaeological Consultant: Gordon Franz

Content Editors: J. Randall Petersen, Cynthia Rudder, Mark Boyer

Proofreaders: William de Plata, Roy Brown, Dale Winship, Lois Stück, Marina Marketos, Pamela Landfear

Secretaries: Edith Ley, Linda Higdon

GRAPHICS

Designer: James F. Brisson

Graphics Manager: Jo Haight

Special Art: Lloyd K. Townsend

Artists: James F. Brisson, Paul Richards, Jo Haight, Marge Tracy, and others.

Graphics Expeditors: Sue Lehmberg, Christine Babcock, Maureen Ruckdeschel

Photographers: Erich Lessing, Zev Radovan, Daniel Blatt, Gleason L. Archer, V. Gilbert Beers, Willem Van Gemeren, William Sanford LaSor, Herbert Turner, Bill Engel, Gordon Franz, and others. (*See* Photo and Illustration Credits for specific credits.)

Cartographers: R. R. Donnelley and Sons Company, James F. Brisson, Tim Richards

PRODUCTION

Assistant Production Manager: Carol Hough

Copywriter: Cindy Shaw

Typesetters: American–Stratford Graphic Services, Inc., Brattleboro, VT

Printers: Arcata Graphics Company, Kingsport, TN

THE REVELL BIBLE DICTIONARY

General Editor and Writer
LAWRENCE O. RICHARDS, Ph.D.

CONSULTING EDITORS

GLEASON L. ARCHER
Professor of Old Testament,
Trinity Evangelical Divinity School,
Deerfield, Illinois

JAMIE BUCKINGHAM
Late Editor-in-chief,
Ministries Today Magazine;
senior pastor, Tabernacle Church,
Melbourne, Florida

DAVID S. DOCKERY
Associate professor of New Testament
*   interpretation,*
Southern Baptist Theological Seminary,
Louisville, Kentucky

ARTHUR FARSTAD
Writer, editor;
formerly, executive editor, New King
*   James Version, Thomas Nelson Inc.;*
and professor, Dallas Theological
*   Seminary, Dallas, Texas*

CATHERINE KROEGER
Researcher;
section coordinator,
Society of Biblical Literature;
formerly, chaplain, Hamilton College.
Clinton, New York

G. HERBERT LIVINGSTON
Professor of Old Testament, emeritus,
Asbury Theological Seminary,
Wilmore, Kentucky

KAREN MAINS
Writer;
broadcaster, Chapel of the Air,
Wheaton, Illinois

JAMES G. SIGOUNTOS
Assistant professor of New Testament,
Alliance Theological Seminary,
Nyack, New York

BASTIAAN VAN ELDEREN
Professor of New Testament, emeritus,
Vreij Universiteit,
Amsterdam, Netherlands;
formerly professor, Calvin Theological
*   Seminary,*
Grand Rapids, Michigan

In addition to the consulting editors, several advisors—both Protestant and Roman Catholic—were of inestimable value for their counsel and direction.

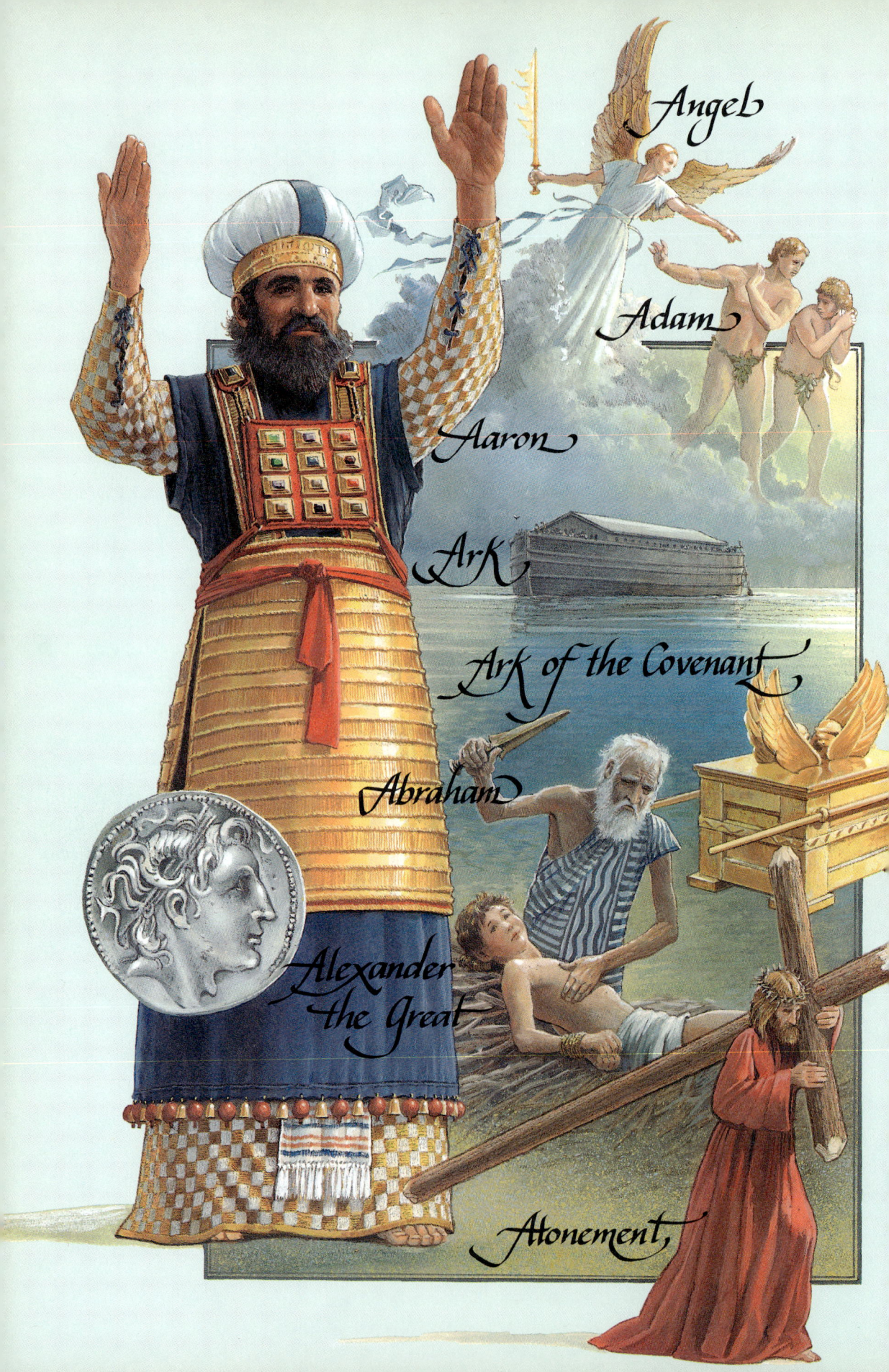

Angel

Adam

Aaron

Ark

Ark of the Covenant

Abraham

Alexander
the Great

Atonement

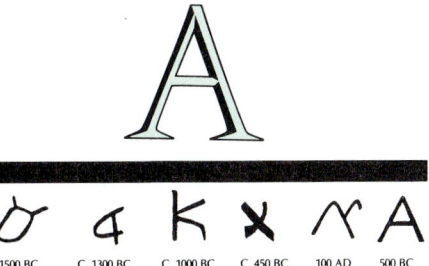

C. 1500 BC
PROTO-SINAITIC
C. 1300 BC
CANAANITE
C. 1000 BC
PHOENICIAN
C. 450 BC
ARAMAIC
100 AD
HEBREW
500 BC
GREEK

Aaron [AIR-uhn; meaning uncertain]. Older brother and companion of Moses during the Exodus and Israel's first high priest; about 1450 B.C. **Scripture:** Ex. 4–40; Lev.; Num.; Deut. 9, 10. **Parents:** Amram and Jochebed. **Siblings:** Moses and Miriam. **Wife:** Elisheba. **Sons:** Nadab, Abihu, Eleazar, Ithamar.

BACKGROUND

In the dramatic Exodus from Egypt and during the wanderings in the wilderness, Aaron assisted his brother Moses in leading the Israelites. Scripture consistently portrays Aaron as subordinate to Moses, but he was much more than an assistant. He served as Moses' spokesman and became Israel's first priest.

SIGNIFICANCE

1. *Prophet.* When Moses claimed to be "slow of speech and tongue" (Ex. 4:10), God allowed him to enlist Aaron as his spokesman—not only to Pharaoh, but also to the Israelites. Aaron could "speak well" (Ex. 4:14). In Exodus we frequently find a three-step process of communication: God tells Moses to tell Aaron to tell the people (Ex. 7:9; 8:5; 16:9).

*After their disobedience **Adam** and Eve are driven from Eden, its entrance guarded by sword-wielding cherubim, a type of **angel**. Generations later, God tells Noah to build an **ark** to escape a catastrophic flood that would wipe out sinful human civilization. More generations pass. **Abraham** is called by God to be the founding father of a special people; Abraham's faith, stretched when God commands him to sacrifice his only son, serves as a model for those of every race who believe in God. Four centuries later, Abraham's descendants dash from Egypt in their miraculous Exodus. **Aaron** is named high priest of the freed people. Annually, he pours sacrificial blood on the **ark of the covenant** on Yom Kippur, the **Day of Atonement**. Centuries pass. Israel settles in Canaan. Kingdoms rise and fall, as conquerors like **Alexander** shape human history. Then in the days of Augustus Caesar, a child is born in Bethlehem. As an adult, Jesus preaches and heals, but is sentenced to death by crucifixion and staggers under the weight of a cross on which he becomes the ultimate Atonement.*

Having the task of speaking God's words to God's people, Aaron might be called a forerunner of the prophets. His spokesman's role, defined in Ex. 4:14-17, illustrates God's relationship with his prophets: "It will be as if he were your mouth, and as if you were God to him" (Ex. 4:16). *See also* Prophet.

2. *Priest.* As high priest, Aaron also represented his people before God, and his descendants carried on this responsibility throughout Israel's history. Thus the OT refers to priests as "sons of Aaron" (Jdg. 20:27,28; 2 Chr. 13:10; 29:21) or "Aaronites" (1 Chr. 12:27 KJV); the NT speaks of the "order of Aaron" because he was the father of that branch of the tribe of Levi that served the altar. *See also* High Priest; Priest.

STRENGTHS AND WEAKNESSES

Two incidents illustrate Aaron's weaknesses. While Moses was on Mount Sinai receiving the Law from God, Aaron gave in to the urging of the people and made a golden calf for them to worship (Ex. 32). Aaron evidently lacked his brother's courage and commitment. *See also* Golden Calf; Idol.

Later Aaron and his sister Miriam showed their jealousy of their younger brother (Num. 12). God had spoken through them as well as Moses; why should Moses have priority? This aroused God's anger and Miriam was stricken with leprosy. Because leprosy would have disqualified him from the priesthood (Lev. 21:16-23), Aaron was not stricken. Though he had been given one of the most significant spiritual roles in OT faith, Aaron was dissatisfied and was jealous of what God was doing through his younger brother.

Usually, however, Aaron was Moses' faithful companion and supported him in crises. When the people rebelled against God and refused to enter the Promised Land, Aaron stood by his brother despite the people's threat to stone them both (Num. 14:1-10).

Each gemstone in Aaron's breastpiece was engraved with the name of an Israelite tribe and worn over his heart when the high priest approached God.

1

Because of their sin of striking the rock at Meribah (Num. 20:1-13), neither Aaron nor Moses was permitted to enter Canaan. Just before Aaron's death, his high priestly garments were removed and put on his son Eleazar (Num. 20:22-29).

LEARNING FROM AARON'S LIFE

Aaron's relationship with Moses is our key. Note how Aaron failed when Moses was absent (Ex. 32) but acted courageously when his brother was there (compare Ex. 8, 16; Num. 14). We all need supportive relationships. With such help we can take stands that we might lack the courage to take alone. In such relationships God also enables the weak to strengthen the strong (Ex. 17:8-13).

When Aaron's almond-wood staff sprouted overnight, all Israel recognized his family to be God's choice as priests. A woodcut from the Cologne Bible, A.D. 1470.

Aaron's staff (rod KJV**)** Following a rebellion against the leadership of Moses and Aaron, God commanded Moses to take a wooden staff from the leader of each of Israel's tribes, write the leader's name on it, and place each staff in the tabernacle (or Tent of Meeting, NIV; Num. 17). Aaron's name was written on the staff representing the tribe of Levi, and overnight that staff sprouted, budded, blossomed, and produced almonds.

This demonstrated to all Israel that God had chosen Aaron, his sons, and his father's family to be priests and that "only you and your sons may serve as priests" at the altar (Num. 18:1,7). Aaron's staff was preserved inside the ark of the covenant (or Testimony, NIV) in the tabernacle (Heb. 9:4). The description in Num. 17 makes it very unlikely that this rod is the same as Moses' staff or the "staff of God." See also Ark of the Covenant; Staff; Tabernacle.

abandon Various Hebrew and Greek words indicating "cast off," "leave," or "depart."

OLD TESTAMENT

In the rocky history of Israel's relationship with God, abandonment is an all-too-common theme. Two Hebrew words convey the idea. The stronger term, 'azab, is frequently used when the Bible speaks of forsaking God. It pictures a conscious decision to turn away from God, often to idols (see 1 Ki. 19:10). The weaker term, natash, is typically used when the OT speaks of God abandoning a particular generation to an enemy. Yet rejection of one generation does not mean that God forsakes his people as a whole (Ps. 94:14; 1 Sam. 12:22). For a graphic illustration of why God chose to withdraw from active involvement with some OT generations, see Isa. 5:1-7.

NEW TESTAMENT

Interestingly, the strongest NT references to abandonment come directly from the OT. On the cross, Jesus cried to his Father, "My God, my God, why have you forsaken me?" (Mt. 27:46), quoting David's lament in Ps. 22:1. Perhaps remembering Christ's grief, Peter quoted another psalm (16:10) on the day of Pentecost: "You will not abandon me [meaning the Holy One, Jesus] to the grave" (Acts 2:27). The Epistle to the Hebrews extends the promise to all Christians, citing Deut. 31:6, "God has said, 'Never will I leave you; never will I forsake you' " (Heb. 13:5).

Abba [AH-buh]. Aramaic for "dear father." This Aramaic word was one of the first that a child in first-century Palestine would learn. In the first century even adults called their fathers Abba, expressing a relationship that existed only within the family circle. Perhaps the best translation is "dear father." Abba is found three times in the NT (Mk. 14:36; Rom. 8:15; Gal. 4:6). Jesus introduced this intimate way of addressing God; nowhere in Jewish devotional literature is there a hint that the Hebrews felt free to address their awesome God as Abba. But Paul invites Christians to think of God in this warm, affectionate way, confident of our welcome as his children through Jesus Christ. See also Adoption; Father.

Abel [AY-buhl; possibly "breath" or "vapor"]. Godly second son of Adam murdered by his brother Cain. **Scripture:** Gen. 4. **Parents:** Adam and Eve. **Sibling:** Cain. No descendants recorded.

BACKGROUND

Abel is described as a righteous person who offered God an acceptable sacrifice, a lamb from his flock (Gen. 4:4; Mt. 23:35; 1 Jn. 3:12). When Cain's offering of fruit was rejected, the angry Cain murdered his unsuspecting brother. Many see in this story evidence that God had already introduced blood sacrifice as the only way sinful human beings might approach him. *See also* Cain; Sacrifices and Offerings.

LEARNING FROM ABEL'S LIFE

The events of Gen. 4 demonstrate one aspect of the Fall. God told Adam that he would "surely die" if he ate the forbidden fruit (Gen. 2:17). In Scripture, death is both physical and spiritual. The injustice of Abel's murder illustrates the effect of spiritual death and the corrupting power of sin. In every society injustice and oppression exist and the innocent still suffer because of the hostile or wicked acts of others. Abel's murder reminds us of the anguish caused by sin and of our own vulnerability. Yet it also reminds us that God sees the plight of his people, for Abel is listed among the heroes of faith and "commended as a righteous man" (Heb. 11:4). His life on earth was brief; his welcome by God is everlasting. *See also* Death.

abhor Several Hebrew words indicating emotional loathing. Each carries a strong sense of rejection or pushing away. God's people are urged to abhor idolatry (Deut. 7:26) and warned against abhorring God's laws (Lev. 26:14,15).

Abiathar [uh-BI-uh-thahr; "father (source) of abundance"]. Sole survivor when Saul massacred his father and 84 other priests; chaplain and later high priest under King David, about 1000 B.C. **Scripture:** 1 Sam. 22,23; 2 Sam. 15,17; 1 Ki. 1–4; 1 Chr. 15,18,24,27. **Father:** Ahimelech. **Son:** Ahimelech.

BACKGROUND

Abiathar was the only one to escape when King Saul massacred his father and 84 other priests who had innocently helped David (1 Sam. 21,22). Abiathar fled and joined David's fugitive band, serving as their chaplain. He had escaped with the high priest's ephod (1 Sam. 22:20-23), and used it to help David discern the will of God (1 Sam. 30:7,8). (*See also* Urim and Thummim.) When David became king, he made Abiathar high priest. Abiathar remained faithful to David during Absalom's rebellion (2 Sam. 15). But when David grew too old to rule effectively, Abiathar threw his support to David's son Adonijah rather than to Solomon (1 Ki. 1). Solomon became king, but spared Abiathar's life because he had "shared all my father's hardships" and because he had "carried the ark of God" (1

Ki. 2:26). Abiathar was removed from his priesthood and banished to Anathoth.

The reference in Mk. 2:26 to David's action at Nob taking place "in the days of Abiathar the high priest" has been called a historical error. Yet Mark does not say "*when* Abiathar was high priest" but rather "in the days of Abiathar [i.e., in the lifetime of Abiathar who became] the high priest."

LEARNING FROM ABIATHAR'S LIFE

Abiathar illustrates both forgiveness and faithfulness. David accepted responsibility for the massacre of the priests. Yet Abiathar held no grudge. Instead, he became a faithful ally of David, and remained loyal even after David named Zadok to share the high priesthood with Abiathar. In fact, Zadok may have been the more favored of the two since he is always named first wherever the two priests are mentioned together (2 Sam. 15:35; 17:15; 20:25; 1 Chr. 15:11). Abiathar stayed faithful to David even though Absalom's rebellion may have given him an opportunity to gain sole possession of the high priest's office.

The small city of Nob (just NE of Jerusalem) was a religious center. There Abiathar's family was massacred for aiding the fugitive David.

3

Abiathar's support of Adonijah was apparently innocent: When David, on his deathbed, advised Solomon on how to deal with certain enemies, Abiathar was not listed among them (1 Ki. 2:1-12).

Abib [AH-bib; "an ear of corn"]. The first month of the Hebrew ceremonial year, Abib falls during our March/April. The Israelites left Egypt in the miraculous Exodus during the month of Abib, and its 14th day has been commemorated ever since as the Passover. After the Babylonian captivity, the month became known as Nisan, a name the exiled Israelites borrowed from the Akkadian calendar of their captors. *See also* Calendar; Exile; Passover.

abide (KJV) In the NIV, often translated "remain," "dwell," "continue," or "live in."

OLD TESTAMENT

The several Hebrew words rendered "abide" in the KJV have the sense of settling down, remaining, or even passing the night. The word is not used as a theological term in the OT.

NEW TESTAMENT

The theological implications of abiding are emphasized particularly in the Gospel and the Epistles of John. John uses the Greek *menō*, also translated "be with" and "live in," to describe a mystical union. God the Father is "living in" Jesus the Son and working through him (Jn. 14:10). A similar union with Jesus enables the believer to bear spiritual fruit (Jn. 15:1-11). Believers abide in Jesus when they take his words to heart and obey them (Jn. 8:31; 15:10). "Whoever claims to live in [abide in] him must walk as Jesus did" (1 Jn. 2:6).

John's Gospel explains that as the branch bears fruit when it abides in the vine, so Christians bear fruit when they abide in (stay close to) Christ.

Abigail [AB-uh-gayl; "my father rejoices," or "source of joy"]. Wise wife of the brutish Nabal, who saved her husband's household from David and later married David about 1000 B.C. **Scripture:** 1 Sam. 25,27,30; 2 Sam. 2,3. **Parents:** unknown. **Husbands:** Nabal, David. **Son by David:** Kileab (Chileab), also known as Daniel.

BACKGROUND

David, though an outlaw pursued by Saul, had protected the flocks and herds of Nabal. At harvest time Nabal insulted David's messengers and refused to share from his abundance. Angry, David determined to wipe out Nabal's household. Abigail acted quickly. She met the marching David with provisions and urged him not to take bloody revenge. David accepted her advice and thanked her. When Nabal died ten days later, David invited Abigail to be his wife. She traveled with David during the difficult years while he fled from Saul, and she bore him one son (called Kileab, or Daniel).

LEARNING FROM ABIGAIL'S LIFE

Abigail is described in 1 Sam. 25 as "a beautiful and intelligent woman." The story reveals her to be quick-thinking, assertive, and willing to take responsibility. Her confrontation with David illustrates her wisdom. She not only pointed out the moral folly of "needless bloodshed" but subtly revealed the political folly as well. Anyone the Lord made leader over Israel might find that needless bloodshed made him vulnerable to future enemies (1 Sam. 25:30,31). David praised God, realizing the Lord had sent Abigail to save him from a tragic mistake.

Abigail makes a good character study for those who wonder what feminine virtues were valued in OT times; she certainly serves as a good biblical model for godly women today.

Abihu [uh-BI-hoo; "my father is he"]. Priest who was struck dead for approaching God's altar with "unauthorized fire" about 1450 B.C. **Scripture:** Ex. 6,24; Lev. 10; Num. 3. **Parents:** Aaron and Elisheba. **Siblings:** Nadab, Eleazar, Ithamar.

BACKGROUND

Along with his older brother Nadab, Abihu the priest offered "unauthorized fire" before the Lord. This suggests that they failed to burn the incense on coals taken from the altar of sacrifice (Lev. 10:1-5; 16:12). Fire from God then enveloped them, and they died. The text explains: God must be honored as holy by those who approach him. Violation of God's statutes dishonors him. This event, taking place as the OT priests began their ministry under the Mosaic Law, was a tragic but necessary lesson.

LEARNING FROM ABIHU'S LIFE

Abihu and his brother encountered both God's holiness and his grace. Exodus 24:1 tells us that at Sinai God called Moses, Aaron, "Nadab and Abihu, and seventy of the elders of Israel" to approach the mountain. There they caught a glimpse of their awesome God. God had singled out Nadab and Abihu and had given them a special revelation which should have instilled a deep respect for the Lord. Their disregard of his instructions despite this experience reveals much about their heart attitude. The injunction against drinking before entering to officiate in the Holy

A thirteenth-century French miniature tells Abigail's story. Above, she halts David and his men and brings them provisions before they can avenge the insult of her husband, Nabal.

Lower left, Abigail tells her proud husband what she has done; lower right, Nabal suffers a stroke. After Nabal's death, David took Abigail as his wife.

Place (Lev. 10:9) may suggest these brothers had been drinking before they committed their sacrilege.

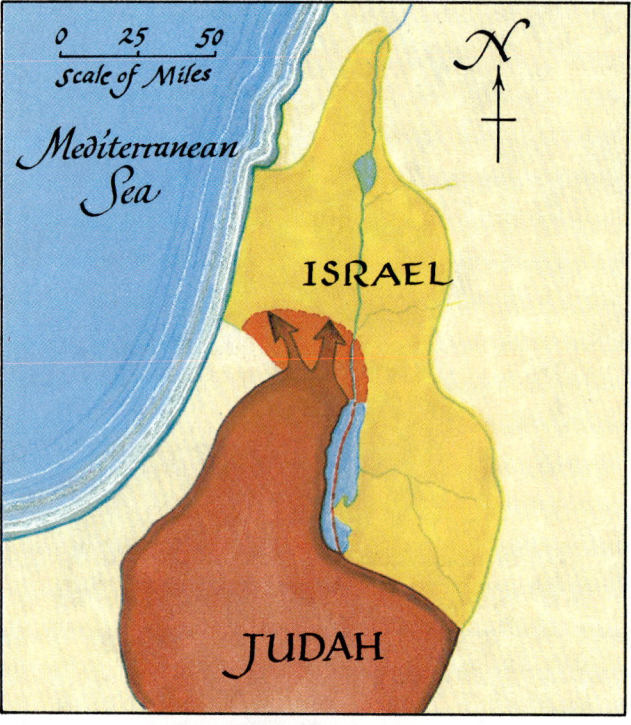

Though outnumbered, Abijah invaded Israel, seeking to reunite the divided kingdom.

Abijah [uh-BI-juh; "my father is Yahweh"]. King of Judah 913–910 B.C. For others with this name, consult IDENTI-QUICK: PEOPLE. **Scripture:** 1 Ki. 15; 2 Chr. 13. **Parents:** Rehoboam and Maacah, daughter of Absalom. **Wives:** 14. **Sons:** 22, including Asa. **Daughters:** 16.

BACKGROUND

King Abijah, also called Abijam, ruled Judah for three years (913–910 B.C.). The united Hebrew kingdom ruled by David and Solomon had been divided some 20 years earlier. Judah in the south and Israel in the north had remained hostile during this period, and full-scale war broke out during Abijah's reign. Abijah was not a godly person nor did he strive to keep Judah religiously pure (*compare* 1 Ki. 15:3 with 14:22-24). Yet when his forces were outnumbered two to one, Abijah called on God ("he is our leader") and relied on the fact that in Judah, the Lord was still worshiped according to the Law. Abijah's army decisively defeated Israel and recovered considerable territory (2 Chr. 13:3-18).

Identification of Abijah's mother as "a daughter of Uriel" (2 Chr. 13:2) and "of Abishalom" (1 Ki. 15:2) is no contradiction. The Hebrews typically used *son* and *daugh-*

6

ter in the sense of *descendant*. Abijah's mother, Maacah, was a granddaughter of both.

LEARNING FROM ABIJAH'S LIFE

Though Abijah relied more on ritual observance than on the Lord himself, his words before the battle stimulated faith in his men. The text says "the men of Judah were victorious because they relied on the Lord" (2 Chr. 13:18). First Kings 15 adds that God made Jerusalem strong "for David's sake" rather than because Abijah himself pleased God. God may give us victories not because we are right, but because we rely on him despite our misunderstandings and personal failures.

Abimelech [uh-BIM-uh-lek; "my father is king"]. This son of Gideon had 70 of his brothers murdered in an attempt to establish himself as king about 1100 B.C. **Scripture:** Jdg. 8–10.

Also a common name of Philistine rulers, as "Thutmose" or "Amenhotep" was of Egyptian rulers. The Abimelechs of Gerar play a significant role in the stories of Abraham (Gen. 20:1-18) and Isaac (Gen. 26:1-33). The Abimelech mentioned in Ps. 34 may possibly have been Achish, the ruler of Gath (1 Sam. 21:19–22:1). *See also* IDENTI-QUICK: PEOPLE.

BACKGROUND

After Gideon died, his 70 sons vied for his position as a ruling judge of Israel. Abimelech gathered support from his mother's clan in Shechem and, with their contributions, hired assassins who murdered his brothers—except for the youngest, Jotham, who escaped. As Abimelech was being crowned in Shechem, Jotham climbed Mount Gerizim, overlooking the town. From there he predicted that a kingdom founded on murder would soon be shattered. Within three years a group in Shechem rebelled. Abimelech defeated them and destroyed the city, but soon afterward was fatally wounded in the siege of another city (Thebez). "Thus God repaid the wickedness" of both Abimelech and the people of Shechem (Jdg. 9:56). *See also* Judge.

LEARNING FROM ABIMELECH'S LIFE

From the giving of the Law to the reign of Saul (about 1450–1050 B.C.), Israel was a theocracy. God was recognized as King; human leaders were called judges. (*See* Judges of Israel.) When Gideon won a great victory over the Midianites, the people clamored to make him king. He refused, saying, "The Lord will rule over you" (Jdg. 8:23). Yet in later life Gideon named a son "my father is king"! We cannot know for certain, but must wonder how much Abimelech's later ambition was stimulated by this name and by his father's apparent hunger for a throne (which the name may have suggested). Our influence on our children is both subtle and powerful.

The story of Abimelech illustrates another vital principle. We live in a moral universe. God does not permit us to enjoy anything won by wickedness. The person who seeks to benefit himself at the expense of others is on a path that leads to self-destruction.

Abishai [uh-BI-shi; meaning uncertain]. Loyal battle companion of David about 1000 B.C. **Scripture:** 1 Sam. 26; 2 Sam.; 1 Chr. 18. **Mother:** Zeruiah, a sister of David. **Brothers:** Joab, Asahel.

BACKGROUND

David's nephew was a fierce warrior, but unfortunately, he was rather one-dimensional. His response to every danger was to strike out and kill. Yet Abishai was fiercely loyal to David, whom he joined when David fled from Saul, and stayed with through Absalom's rebellion. Abishai also showed his loyalty by constantly deferring to David's more humane judgments.

LEARNING FROM ABISHAI'S LIFE

Look first at the incidents which reveal Abishai's fierceness (1 Sam. 26:6-9; 2 Sam. 2:18-30; 16:5-12; 19:11-21). Then note passages that show his importance to David (2 Sam. 10:9-14; 21:15-17; 1 Chr. 18:12,13). Abishai was God's gift to David. But David was also God's gift to Abishai, who permitted himself to be guided by the king. Often God brings us into fellowship with others whose strengths balance our weaknesses.

An Egyptian relief at Medinet Habu depicts Rameses II's battle against the Lybians in the twelfth century B.C., about the time of Abimelech and only a century before Abishai and Abner, all noted warriors. The Philistines used chariots against the Israelites in the time of Samuel. Chariots, useless in Palestine's highlands, did not become standard military equipment for the Israelites until the time of Solomon.

Abner [AB-nuhr; "father is Ner" (a lamp)]. Commander of Saul's armies about 1030 B.C. **Scripture:** 1 Sam. 17,20,26; 2 Sam. 2,3. **Father:** Ner, an uncle of Saul.

BACKGROUND

A cousin of King Saul, Abner commanded Israel's armed forces about 1030 B.C. After Saul's death he threw his support to Saul's son Ish-Bosheth. Though David became ruler of Judah, the most powerful of the twelve tribes, Ish-Bosheth ruled the others because of Abner's efforts.

Yet at one point Ish-Bosheth accused Abner of taking one of Saul's concubines. This act would have implied that Abner viewed himself as the real ruler. Angered by the accusation, Abner began negotiations to unite all twelve tribes under David's rule. However, he was soon treacherously murdered by Abishai and Joab, David's military leaders, to avenge the death of their brother, Asahel. David publicly mourned Abner, under whom he had served while in Saul's army. The mourning also demonstrated that David had no role in the murder.

abolish In English, "to do away with" or "put an end to." Also "to make irrelevant." Jesus did not come to abolish the OT Law but to fulfill it (Mt. 5:17). The Greek word is *katalyō*, "to tear down." But a different Greek word, *katargeō*, appears when Eph. 2:15 speaks of "abolishing" the Law. This word means to make irrelevant or of no effect. That OT law which called for strict separation between Jew and Gentile does not apply to those who through Christ have been reconciled to God and to each other. *See also* Fulfill.

abomination Something abhorrent to God. Behind the several Hebrew words translated "abomination" are two root words, *to'ebah* and *shiqqus*, both of which picture revulsion: such things make God sick. Idolatry and immorality are described as "abominations" to the Lord. So are homosexuality (Lev. 18:22) and the occult (Deut. 18:9-14). Proverbs 6:16-19 identifies other abominations that provoke God to anger.

Antiochus IV Epiphanes, shown on this silver tetradrachm coin, desecrated the Jerusalem Temple, an act foreshadowing a yet future "abomination of desolation."

abomination of desolation Jesus foretold a future "desolating abomination" and identified it as the act which initiates the great tribulation ("distress," NIV) of history's end (Mt. 24:15-25). Christ defined this event by referring to Daniel's prophecy (Dan. 11:31; 12:11). Most commentators see the "abomination of desolation" as the setting up of a false object of worship in Jerusalem (*compare* 2 Th. 2:3,4). A historical example is seen in the actions of Antiochus Epiphanes, who desecrated the Jerusalem Temple by building an altar to Zeus in 168 B.C., and offering pigs (ritually unclean animals) in sacrifice. *See also* Antichrist; Tribulation.

Abraham [AY-bruh-ham; "father of a multitude"]. Known as Abram [AY-bruhm; "exalted father"] until his name was changed by God. The key figure in Israel's history, about 2100 B.C.; the NT's prime example of faith. **Scripture:** Gen. 11:26–25:11. **Father:** Terah. **Brothers:** Haran and Nahor. **Wives:** Sarai (Sarah); Keturah. **Concubine:** Hagar. **Children:** by Sarah: Isaac; by Hagar: Ishmael; by Keturah: Zimran, Jokshan, Medan, Midian, Ishbak, Shuah.

BACKGROUND

Abraham was born nearly 4,100 years ago in the renowned Mesopotamian city of Ur, the center of the great Sumerian culture. There he rejected the worship of "other gods" (Josh. 24:2) to give himself to Jehovah alone, who summoned him to leave his homeland. Abraham's journey took him along well-established trade routes, first to Haran and then, after the death of his father, into Canaan.

For the next hundred years Abraham lived a nomadic life in this land which God promised his descendants would ultimately possess. *See also* Ur of the Chaldees; IDENTI-QUICK: PLACES.

SIGNIFICANCE

Genesis 1–11 describes God's dealings with the human race. In Gen. 12 the focus shifts to a single individual and his family line. Through the family of Abraham, God would reveal himself and his purposes; through the family of Abraham a Savior would be born to reconcile all humankind to God. Thus the bulk of the OT is the story of God's work in and through the descendants of Abraham, the nation of Israel. And the NT is the story of the Savior born from Abraham's family line (Mt. 1:2; Lk. 3:34).

This standard depicting peace comes from Abraham's home city of Ur. The mosaic, made of lapis lazuli and shell, was set in bitumen on wood and was discovered in the royal tombs.

8

Worshipers brought votive statues
to Sumerian temples to pay their vows
to the gods. A variety of gods were
worshiped, including four who controlled
the major elements
of the universe.

Sacred history is rooted in and flows from the story of Abraham as that story is found in Gen. 11:26–25:11.

THE ABRAHAMIC COVENANT

Abraham's role as the OT's key figure is crystallized in covenant promises that God made to him. A covenant (*berit*) was a binding statement of relationship. Between nations, a covenant was a treaty; between a ruler and those he ruled, it served as a constitution; between individuals, a covenant was a pact or contract. God made a formal contract with Abraham in which he pre-announced what he

would do for and through Abraham. The Book of Hebrews notes that God confirmed his promises to Abraham by an oath (covenant) ''so that by two unchangeable things in which it is impossible for God to lie, we [who believe] may be greatly encouraged'' (6:18). *See also* Covenant.

The elements of God's covenant with Abraham are first stated in Gen. 12 and then confirmed and expanded in Gen. 15 and 17. These are:

I will make you into a great nation
    and I will bless you;
I will make your name great,
    and you will be a blessing.
I will bless those who bless you,
    and whoever curses you I will curse;
and all peoples on earth
    will be blessed through you.   (12:2,3)

And

To your offspring I will give this land. (12:7)

This clay cuneiform
tablet from Ur was
inscribed during
Abraham's lifetime.
It lists the monthly
rations of barley for
17 gardeners.

9

SUMMARY

Abraham's life spanned 175 years and took him from Mesopotamia to Canaan, from one end of the Fertile Crescent to the other. The events of his life are both personal and national, involving the kings of neighboring nations as well as his own family. The NT uses several of these events to illustrate spiritual truths.

The chart (page 12) lists the chronological sequence of events of Abraham's life, and notes NT passages commenting on them. (Dates are approximate.) *See also* Chronology of the Bible.

CONTRIBUTIONS OF ARCHAEOLOGY

Unusual conditions existed in Canaan during the age of the patriarchs. During the Early Bronze Age (3150–2200 B.C.), Canaan was comprised of flourishing and powerful city-states. In the later Middle Bronze Age II (2000–1500 B.C.), urban civ-

ilizations again developed. But for 200–300 years between these two eras, for reasons still unknown to archaeologists, some of the cities of Canaan were abandoned or less populated and people took up a pastoral way of life.

Excavations at Ur, tablets found at Mari, and texts from Nuzi have illuminated many events reported in Genesis. Inheritance laws of that day permitted a childless man to adopt a slave as an heir (Gen. 15:2-4). Later Sarah gave her slave Hagar to Abraham as a concubine (Gen. 16). Was this immoral? Not according to contemporary laws and customs. One marriage contract found at Nuzi stipulates that if a certain woman named Giliminu does not give birth, she will get her husband a slave as a concubine and will have authority over any children produced by her. When Sarah gave Hagar to Abraham, she was acting in harmony with established social

Genesis traces Abraham's journey from the great city of Ur to Haran and on into Canaan. There he became a prosperous shepherd and cattleman. In a time of famine he fled to Egypt, but returned to pitch his tents in the area of Hebron and Beersheba in southern Canaan. Below, shepherds still watch their flocks near Beersheba, even as Abraham did 4,000 years ago.

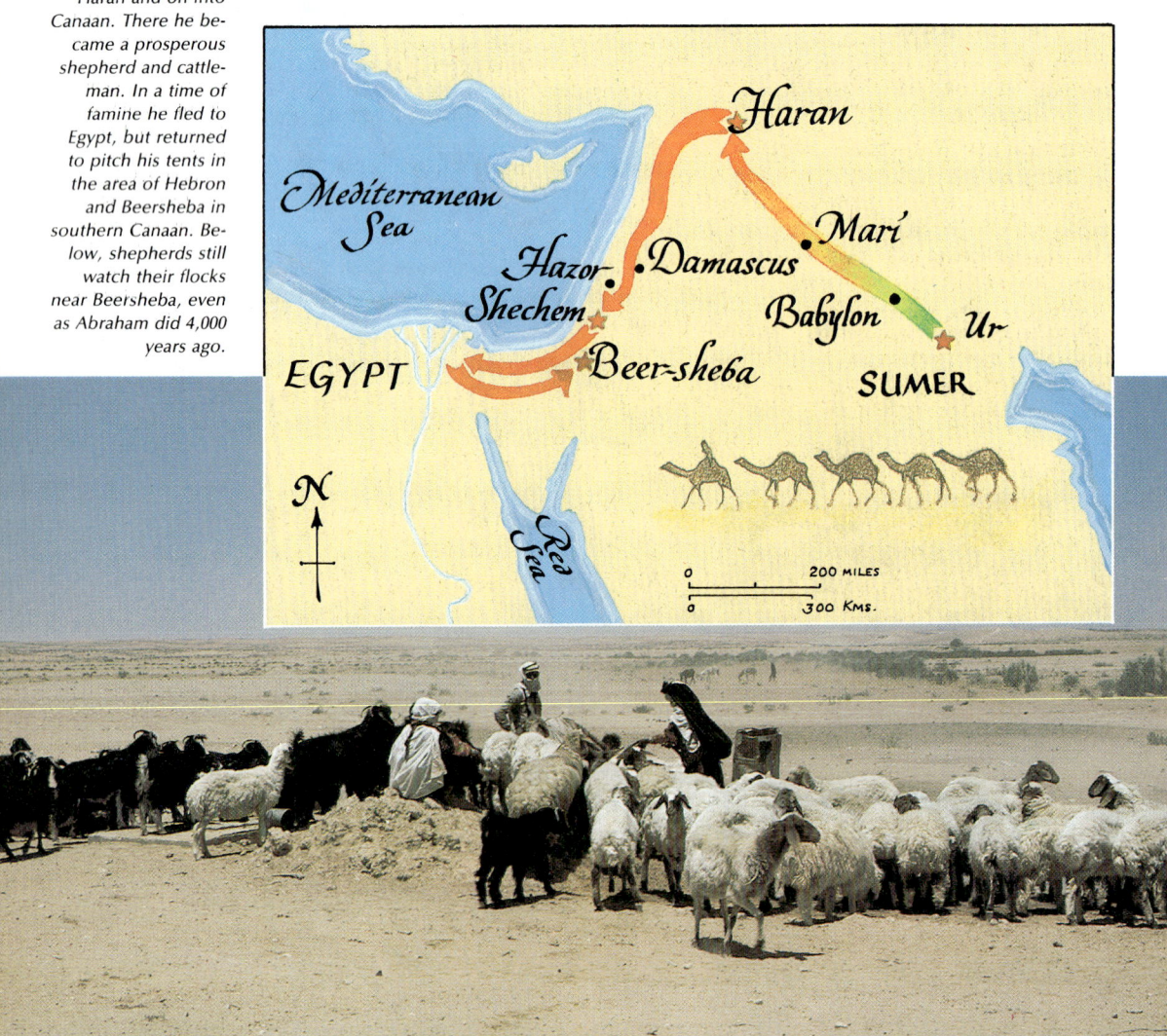

custom. But by those same customs Abraham had no legal right to send away Hagar and her son and therefore was reluctant to do so (Gen. 21:12-21). He took that step only when commanded to do so by God, who promised Abraham that Ishmael would become a great nation as well (v. 18).

In these and many other instances, the findings of archaeologists have provided fresh insights into the biblical text.

ABRAHAM'S SPIRITUAL JOURNEY

Genesis focuses attention on three great tests of Abraham's faith. But it does not hesitate to describe situations in which his faith wavered.

1. *Faith to risk* (*Gen. 12:1-5*). Abraham's great wealth suggests that he lived a comfortable life in one of the world's great cities when God spoke to him, telling him to "go to the land I will show you." Faith is willing to risk all on God's faithfulness, and to venture into the unknown.

2. *Faith to trust* (*Gen. 17:1-27*). Abraham was 99 and Sarah had long ceased menstruating when God promised that the two of them would have a child. Romans 4:19-21 says that Abraham "faced the fact that his body was as good as dead . . . and that Sarah's womb was also dead. Yet he did not waver through unbelief regarding the promise of God, but was . . . fully persuaded that God had power to do what he had promised." Faith is not limited to the evidence of the senses, knowing that God is more real than anything we can see or feel.

3. *Faith to surrender* (*Gen. 22*). Commanded to sacrifice his son Isaac, Abraham got up "early the next morning" and set out for Mount Moriah. On the third day, he went on with Isaac after telling his servants, "Stay here. We will come back to you." The NT explains that Abraham was ready to surrender his son to God, reasoning "that God could raise the dead" (Heb. 11:19) and would do so, for God had promised that Isaac would inherit God's

covenant promises. Faith surrenders all to God, sure that he will return even more than we can give.

But Abraham's spiritual journey, like our own, was marred by failures. Genesis 12:10-20 and 20:1-18 tell us that Abraham lied to protect himself, fearing he would be killed for his beautiful wife Sarah, who was also his half-sister or niece. Twice he begged Sarah to lie for him. Abraham thought "surely there is no fear of God in this place" (Gen. 20:11). In this Abraham failed to realize that, whether or not the people feared the Lord, God was present. Abraham responded with faith when God spoke to him, but when God was silent his faith faltered.

LEARNING FROM ABRAHAM'S LIFE

Both the OT and NT emphasize Abraham's faith in God. Note that in each Genesis incident faith (a) involved specific response to God's revelation and (b) was expressed through obedience. This pattern, in which God initiates and man responds, is seen throughout Scripture. Romans 4 contains the NT's commentary on Abraham as a man of faith.

While Abraham's faith provides a model for our own, Abraham's failures contain a seed of comfort. Rather than being discouraged when we fall short, we can take heart: Abraham's greatest act of faith (Gen. 22) followed his failures.

Another theme worth exploring is the role of prayer in Abraham's experience. His prayer is often linked with sacrifice (Gen. 12:8; 13:4). Abraham felt free to share his concerns with the Lord (15:2,3; 17:17,18), and even to intercede with God on behalf of Sodom and Gomorrah (18:16-33). It was on the basis of Abraham's prayer that God later spared Abimelech (20:7).

KEY VERSES

1. *Genesis 13:8,9.* Abraham surrenders his right as the elder to choose first in order to maintain peace with his nephew Lot.

This Egyptian mural from the tomb of Beni-Hassan shows a Semitic tribe with its possessions seeking permission to enter Egypt. The mural, from the time of the Patriarchs, is the best illustration of the clothing worn during this time.

A ram caught in a thicket? No, this statue found in a cemetery in Ur shows a ram and the tree of life, both common motifs in Sumerian art. It is dated about 500 years before Abraham.

2. *Genesis 18:19.* Abraham establishes a pattern of living that his descendants are to be taught to follow the Lord (*compare* Jn. 8:33-39 and Rom. 9:6-8).

3. *Genesis 18:32.* Abraham's prayer that Sodom might be spared if as few as ten righteous persons could be found is in harmony with God's heart, yet underestimates his grace. Only one good man could be found in the cities of the plain—and God removed him before he destroyed the rest.

4. *Genesis 22:3.* Abraham does not delay when told by God to sacrifice his son Isaac, but rises "early the next morning" to obey.

5. *Genesis 24:7.* Abraham reveals that at last he has learned to expect God to work in and through circumstances as well as on occasions of special revelation.

Biblically and theologically, Abraham is a towering figure, even though in some ways he was a very ordinary person. As a true believer, he struggled successfully with doubt, found comfort and strength in prayer, and met life's greatest challenges by acting on the conviction that God's Word is trustworthy, to be believed, and to be obeyed.

Abraham's side (bosom KJV) Intertestamental Jewish literature gives this name to Paradise (*see* 4 Maccabees 13:17). The NT uses the term only once. Jesus told of the poor beggar Lazarus being transported to the delights of Abraham's side at his death, while the uncompassionate rich man is tormented in hell (Lk. 16:19-31). *See also* Heaven; Hell; Paradise.

LIFE OF ABRAHAM

Event	Genesis Passage	New Testament Commentary	Abraham's Age	Approximate Date B.C.
Abram's birth.	11:26			2166
His call by God.	12:1-3	Heb. 11:8		
His entry into Canaan.	12:4-9	Acts 7:2-32	75	2091
Abram in Egypt says Sarai is his sister.	12:10-20			
Abram and Lot separate.	13:1-18			
Abram rescues Lot.	14:1-17			
Abram pays tithes to Melchizedek.	14:18-24	Heb. 7:1-10		
Abram given formal covenant: his faith is credited to him as righteousness.	15:1-21	Rom. 4:1-17 Gal. 3:6-25 Heb. 6:13-20	85	2081
Abraham fathers Ishmael by Sarah's maid, Hagar.	16:1-16		86	2080
Abraham given circumcision and promised a son by Sarah.	17:1-27	Rom. 4:18-25 Heb. 11:11,12	99	2067
Abraham pleads for Sodom.	18:1-33			
Sodom destroyed, Lot saved.	19:1-38			
In Gerar, Abraham again calls Sarah his sister.	20:1-18			
Isaac born.	21:1-7		100	2066
Abraham sends Hagar, Ishmael away.	21:8-34	Gal. 4:21-31	103	2063
Abraham challenged to sacrifice Isaac before the Lord.	22:1-24	Heb. 11:17-29 Jas. 2:20-24		
Sarah dies and is buried at Hebron.	23:1-20		137	2029
Abraham sends for a bride for Isaac (Rebekah).	24:1-67		140	2026
Abraham dies.	25:1-11		175	1991

BACKGROUND

Absalom was well aware that the northern tribes had not united under his father David at the beginning of his reign. In fact, the division between the northern and southern tribes had continued for more than seven years. Taking advantage of this earlier rift, Absalom plotted to seize his father's throne. By a combination of pretended sympathy for the concerns of the northerners and a flair for pageantry, Absalom "stole the hearts of the men of Israel" (2 Sam. 15:1-6).

With his northern power base established, Absalom went down to Hebron in the south to lead a revolt against David. His violation of his father's concubines (16:21,22) was a public proclamation that there could be no reconciliation between them. In the great battle that followed, fought in the forest of Ephraim (2 Sam. 18:6), Absalom was killed and the kingdom reunited. But Absalom's rebellion deepened the distrust between north and south which, on Solomon's death, led to permanent division of the kingdom.

ABSALOM, THE MAN

Absalom was a gifted and handsome individual. But his character made his name, "father of peace" (or "source of peace"), a mockery. When Amnon, an older half-brother, raped his sister Tamar, Absalom counseled her to be quiet—and then arranged Amnon's assassination two years later (13:20-30). Absalom then fled the country and lived in exile until, after three years, David recalled him. Later, after a public reconciliation with his father, Absalom began his carefully crafted four-year campaign to woo the northern tribes. When Absalom declared himself king, David fled east to Mahanaim (2 Sam. 17:24). Following the advice of Hushai, David's secret agent, Absalom took the time to assemble a great army and then pursued his father across the Jordan. In the battle that followed, thousands were killed, and the rebellion was suppressed. General Joab, despite his king's orders to spare his rebel son, put Absalom to death. Gifted but vain, ambitious but vengeful,

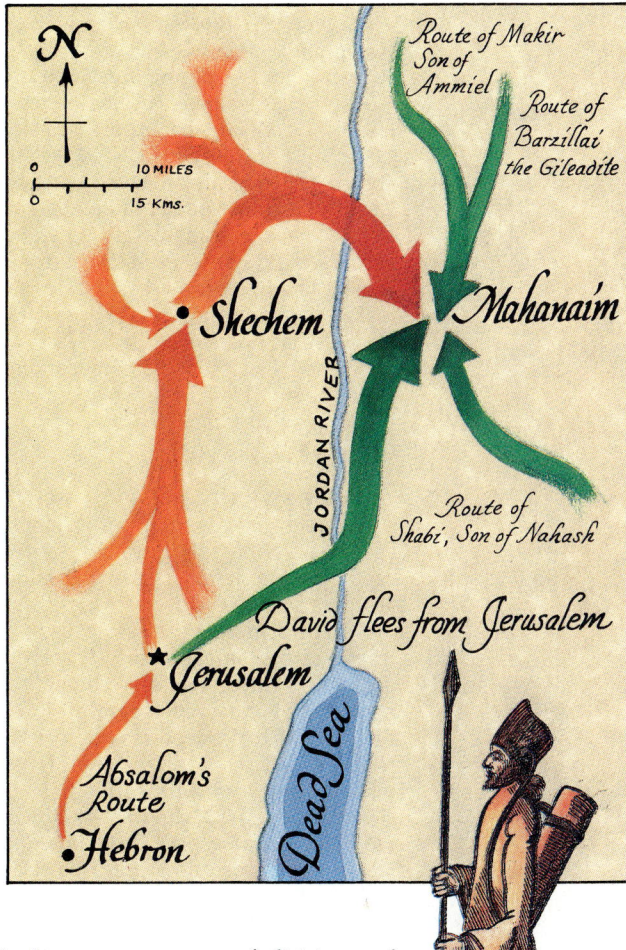

Absalom was a source of division and suffering rather than peace, to both his family and his land.

ABSALOM AND DAVID

The story of Absalom's rebellion reveals both David's great strengths and his weaknesses. David was furious when he heard Amnon had raped Tamar—but he did nothing about it. David's refusal to discipline Amnon opened the door for Absalom's revenge. Then, when Absalom committed murder, David again failed to act. He neither punished Absalom nor confronted him to demand public confession and repentance. It is apparent that David's weakness stemmed from unwise love. Rather than disciplining his erring sons, David held back. The result of withholding discipline was civil war for the nation and anguish for David, who could only weep disconsolately when Absalom's death was reported. "O my son Absalom! My son, my son Absalom!" he lamented, until finally Joab induced him to make an appearance to his troops (18:33; 19:5-8).

Rebellious Absalom, whose power base lay in the north, was crowned king in Hebron, where his forces threatened the capital, Jerusalem. David fled with a handful of loyal troops across the Jordan, where the fateful battle with Absalom took place.

13

The story also reveals David's strengths. According to their titles, David composed Psalms 3 and 4 during his flight from Absalom. He examines his own heart and failures (3:1,2), and then his thoughts turn to his relationship with God (3:3,4). Despite the enemies that now surround him, David finds inner peace: "I lie down and sleep; I wake again, because the Lord sustains me" (3:5). In Ps. 4, David considers the kingly glory he has just lost and realizes how meaningless it is. He says to God, "You have filled my heart with greater joy than when their grain and new wine abound. I will lie down and sleep in peace, for you alone, O Lord, make me dwell in safety" (4:7,8).

LEARNING FROM ABSALOM'S LIFE

Absalom is far from an exemplary character. Even his positive traits—a capacity for long-range planning and an acute political sensitivity—were twisted by selfish motives. He risked the consequences of avenging his sister's dishonor, yet this vengeance brought her not healing but despair (2 Sam. 13:20). Yet the focus of this extended story is not so much on Absalom as it is on David's relationship with his sons. In any family, especially one with children by different mothers, we can expect a certain amount of sibling jealousy and strife. Yet David worsened this situation in his family by his failure to discipline. A study of Absalom's life reminds us that we must not ignore the sins in our families.

The acacia tree provides durable wood ideal for cabinetmaking. It is still common in the Sinai.

abstain To refrain from, to avoid. "I urge you," says Peter, ". . . to abstain from sinful desires, which war against the soul" (1 Pet. 2:11). The word is *apechomai*, "to keep away from, refrain from." Paul uses it to say, "Avoid every kind of evil" (1 Th. 5:22).

Yet abstinence can be overdone. Paul warns against the "hypocritical liars" who order people to "abstain from certain foods, which God created to be received with thanksgiving" (1 Tim. 4:3). This is in harmony with Col. 2:16-23, where the apostle opposes those who would place ascetic prohibitions on believers. Some people saw such regulated abstinence as an aid to spiritual advancement, but Paul insists that human-based restrictions have no value in restraining the appetites of the flesh. True holiness is attained through the living Christ, not dead legalities.

The request of the early Jewish church that Gentile believers "abstain from food sacrificed to idols, from blood, from the meat of strangled animals and from sexual immorality" (Acts 15:29) has raised many questions. It seems best to understand these requests as a means of easing tension between Jewish and Gentile Christian communities. The reference to "sexual immorality" includes not only fornication but possibly such marriages as are prohibited in Lev. 18:6-18. Blood is intimately linked in the OT with sacrifice (Lev. 17:11), and strangled animals with the lifeblood still in them were not to be eaten (Gen. 9:4). The idea that these requests are an appeal by the Jewish church to their Gentile brothers to be sensitive to Jewish convictions is supported by the fact that similar regulations already existed in the first century for Gentiles who lived among Jews (*see* Rom. 14). *See also* Convictions; Drunkenness; Fast; Wine.

Abyss In Greek culture *abyssos,* meaning "bottomless," served as an image of the mysterious realm of the dead. The word occurs repeatedly in Revelation for the underground chasm where evil demonic beings are imprisoned (9:1-11; 20:1-3) and from which the beast arises (11:7; 17:8). The legion of demons which Jesus cast into a herd of pigs had begged him not to send them back to the Abyss (Lk. 8:31). *See also* Demon.

acacia wood [uh-KAY-shuh]. The hard, durable wood of the acacia tree was used in the construction of Israel's tabernacle and its furnishings (Ex. 25–27,30,35–38). The tree, called "shittah" in the KJV (Heb., *shittah),* is still common in the Sinai and Israel's southern desert regions.

accept, acceptance In ordinary speech, *accept* means to take or receive. But it has a special religious meaning as well: "favorably receive or welcome an act or individual." Because personal relationship with God and others is so important, the religious concept of acceptance is a critical one, expressed by a variety of Hebrew and Greek words.

ACCEPTANCE BY GOD

The key Hebrew terms *(rasah, rason)* mean "to be pleased with" or "to favor." Pagans tried to gain the favor of gods or goddesses by bringing them offerings.

Ritual offerings are important in the OT, but are not viewed as bribes. In fact, God only accepted the offerings of those whose faith and life-style already made them acceptable to him! This vital distinction was forgotten at times, and had to be re-emphasized by the prophets (Isa. 1:10-17; Mic. 6:6-8). Thus Israel is told,

"The multitude of your sacrifices—
   what are they to me?" says the Lord. . . .
"Stop bringing meaningless offerings!
   Your incense is detestable to me.
New Moons, Sabbaths and convocations—
   I cannot bear your evil assemblies. . . .
Take your evil deeds
   out of my sight!
Stop doing wrong,
   learn to do right.
Seek justice,
   encourage the oppressed.
Defend the cause of the fatherless,
   plead the cause of the widow." (Isa. 1:11-17)

The real message of the OT is that God accepts the person who makes a heart commitment to the Lord, and who expresses that commitment by doing justice and caring for the oppressed as well as by bringing offerings.

ACCEPTABLE LIVES

The OT emphasis is picked up in the NT and expressed by several different Greek words. *Dektos, euprosdektos,* and *euarestos* all mean "pleasing" or "acceptable." They are often used with descriptions of a Christian life that is moral, loving, and devoted to the service of others (*see* Rom. 12:1,2; 14:17,18; 2 Cor. 8:12; Phil. 4:18).

ACCEPT ONE ANOTHER

This expression uses the Greek word *proslambanō,* an important relational term in the Epistles found in Rom. 14:1,3; 15:7; and Phlm. 17. Here *accept* means "to welcome," and is an invitation to share fully in the lives of members of the community of faith. We must accept even a believer who is weak in the faith, Paul says, because "God has accepted [welcomed] him" (Rom. 14:3).

Thus the message of the Bible is that those who have a personal relationship with God already enjoy God's favor. It is our privilege to offer him in return a godly, loving life.

access The right of personal approach. Through Christ we "have gained access by faith" to a relationship with God characterized by justification, peace, and grace (Rom. 5:2). Ephesians 2:18 says that through Christ all believers "have access to the Father by one Spirit," while 3:12 adds that "in him and through faith in him we may approach God with freedom and confidence." The same Greek word, *prosagōgē,* appears in the three texts. These are its only NT uses.

Yet *access* carries great theological meaning. It portrays a dramatic new relationship that believers have with God. Reference to the Spirit in Eph. 2:18 focuses on prayer (*see also* Rom. 8:26,27). These verses remind us that we can pray with freedom and confidence, knowing that God hears even when we may not feel particularly close to him.

accord Harmony, with one mind. Between the time of Jesus' ascension and the day of Pentecost, his followers met for prayer "with one accord" (KJV, RSV). This is the first of eleven appearances of the Greek *homothymadon* in the Book of Acts (also found in Rom. 15:6). The NIV translates it "all together," but the KJV and RSV better capture the sense of harmony conveyed by this word.

The image is of an orchestra, in which many different instruments blend together to create music beyond the power of any one of them alone. What a picture of the Church as God intends it to be! He does not rob us of our individual differences, but calls us to "live in such harmony with one another, in accord with Christ Jesus, that together you may with one voice glorify the God and Father of our Lord Jesus Christ" (Rom. 15:5,6 RSV).

account The word is used in a variety of ways in the Bible: (1) as a report or description, e.g., "this is the account of Noah"; (2) as a cause or explanation, e.g., "on account of my name"; (3) for worth or importance, e.g., "even men of little account in the church." *Account* also has two important theological uses: (4) to furnish a reckoning or give an explanation, e.g., "give an account on the day of judgment"; and (5) to call to account, or to punish or reprimand, e.g., "call him to account for his wickedness." These two uses remind us that God is the supreme judge of his moral universe, and that each human being is ultimately responsible to God for his own choices. Hebrews 4:13 reminds us, "Nothing in all creation is hidden from God's sight. Everything is uncovered and laid bare before the eyes of him to whom we must give account." *See also* Judge.

accursed Peter calls false teachers "an accursed brood" or literally "children of a curse" (2 Pet. 2:14). The term not only suggests overwhelming revulsion but also implies that God is uttering the curse. The Greek word, *kataraomai*, is used for Jesus' cursing of the fig tree (Mk. 11:21) and the "curse of the law" (Gal. 3:10,13).

But *accursed* also translates the Greek *anathema*, which has a more specialized meaning of being banned, excommunicated, or shunned as an unholy thing. Paul said that if anyone taught a different gospel from his, "let him be accursed" (Gal. 1:8,9). *See also* Anathema; Curse; Devoted Things.

accuse, accusation Legal terms which indicate charging someone with breaking a human or divine law.

OLD TESTAMENT

The legal system of the OT relied heavily on the local administration of justice, and disputes were to be settled according to rules laid down in the Law. Deuteronomy 19:15-19 is the central passage of the rules on evidence and false accusation:

One witness is not enough to convict a man accused of any crime or offense he may have committed. A matter must be established by the testimony of two or three witnesses. If a malicious witness takes the stand to accuse a man of a crime, the two men involved in the dispute must stand in the presence of the Lord before the priests and the judges who are in office at the time. The judges must make a thorough investigation, and if the witness proves to be a liar, giving false testimony against his brother, then do to him as he intended to do to his brother. You must purge the evil from among you.

NEW TESTAMENT

The writers of the NT use several technical legal terms in speaking of accusations. The ordinary word for bringing criminal charges against someone *(katēgoreō)* is used in the Gospels and Acts of accusations made against Jesus and Paul. It is also used by Jesus, when he points out to the Pharisees that Moses (i.e., the OT Law itself) is their accuser.

However, 2 Pet. 2:11 and Jude 9 use a different term, *krisis*. This word means not only to bring a charge but to pass judgment as well. No one but God has the right to pass judgment.

But the most meaningful usage of legal terminology is found in Rom. 8:33, where Paul asks, "Who then will bring any charge against those whom God has chosen?" The word here, *enkaleō*, is not used of filing legal charges but of the simple threat of legal action. Because of Jesus, we have been cleared by God himself and not even the threat of condemnation exists.

Aceldama (KJV) *See* Akeldama.

Achan [AY-kuhn; possibly "troubler"]. Violated God's command and took loot from Jericho, causing a military defeat at Ai about 1400 B.C. **Scripture:** Josh. 7,8. **Father:** Carmi.

BACKGROUND

Victory at Jericho had come when the Israelites obeyed God's strange command to march silently around the city for seven days. The lesson was clear: the Canaanites would be defeated only if Israel remained obedient. But Achan violated God's command and took loot from Jericho even though that city had been put under a ban by God himself. Because of this sin the Israelites were defeated at Ai.

ACHAN'S DEATH

When found out, Achan and his family were executed. Many question the severity of the punishment. However, (1) the battles of Jericho and Ai underlined for Israel the necessity of absolute obedience. The effect of disobedience on the community at this critical time was so great that violators had to be executed. (2) Achan's disobedience led to the death of 36 of his countrymen. Execution was appropriate. (3) Some have noted that Achan hid his loot "in the ground inside my tent," where his family members would have known. They did not die merely for Achan's sin but for their own complicity as conspiring accessories.

LEARNING FROM ACHAN'S LIFE

Blessing under Law was contingent on obedience to God. Thus each individual's actions had an impact on the entire community of faith. Achan's personal tragedy emphasizes our need to consider how our actions affect others—in our families, churches, and communities.

acknowledge The Bible consistently calls us to acknowledge two things: our sin and our God. The Hebrew word is *yada'*, which regularly means "to know." The Greek NT uses *homologeō*, "to say the same thing."

ACKNOWLEDGING SIN

In Ps. 32:5, David prays, "Then I acknowledged my sin to you." Jeremiah urges Israel, "Only acknowledge your guilt" (Jer. 31:3). To step forward in one's relationship with God, one must recognize (know) the fact of one's sin, and its implications (separation from God). When John writes, "If we confess our sins, [God] . . . will forgive us our sins" (1 Jn. 1:9), he uses the Greek word for acknowledge, *homologeō*. We must agree with God that we are sinners and need his forgiveness.

ACKNOWLEDGING GOD

The OT calls on Israel to "acknowledge [*yada'*, "know"] and take to heart this day that the Lord is God in heaven above and on the earth below" (Deut. 4:39). As always in the OT, knowledge means much more than mental grasping. It involves a participation with the one known: the most striking example might be when "Adam knew Eve" (Gen. 4:1 KJV), referring to sexual union. Certainly to know or acknowledge God connotes a relationship at least as thorough. If we truly understand mentally who he is, that knowledge will result in a response of commitment. As Jer. 22:16 says of a godly king, " 'He defended the cause of the poor and needy, and so all went well. Is not that what it means to know [*yada'*, "acknowledge"] me?' declares the Lord."

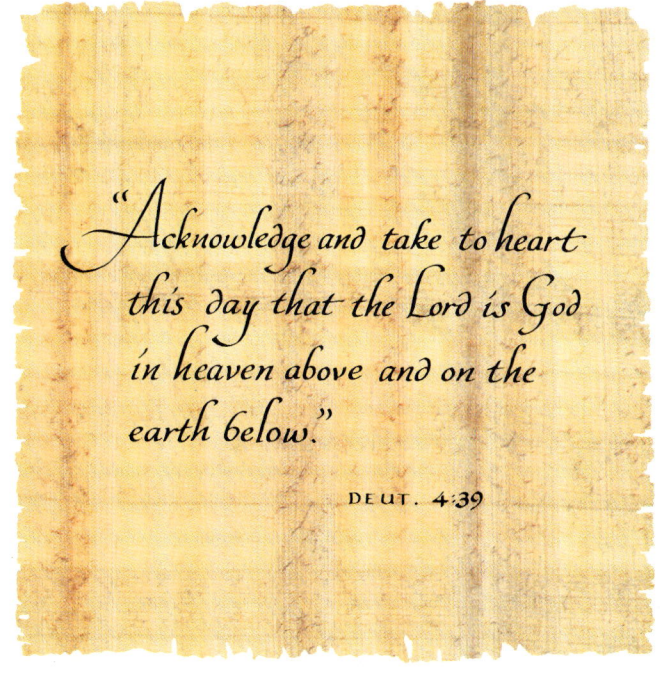

"Acknowledge and take to heart this day that the Lord is God in heaven above and on the earth below."

DEUT. 4:39

The NT speaks of acknowledging Christ (Lk. 12:8; 1 Jn. 4:3). In Greek, the word (*homologeō*) has a verbal sense: speaking out in support of someone. Jesus said, "Whoever acknowledges me before men, I will also acknowledge him before my Father in heaven" (Mt. 10:32). In legal usage, the word meant accepting a court order and abiding by it. Acknowledging Christ is to express publicly our personal commitment to Jesus and then to live out that commitment. *See also* Confess; Know.

Acknowledging God implies not only knowledge of him but our full commitment to him.

acre The word occurs only in 1 Sam. 14:14 and Isa. 5:10. It represents the amount of land that a yoke (pair) of oxen could plow in one day. So also the English acre was first determined by the amount of land a team of horses could plow in one day. *See also* Weights and Measures.

How much land could a yoke of oxen plow in a day? The answer would vary from country to country. The Egyptian Nile basin might be easier to plow than rock-strewn Canaan.

Acts of the Apostles

The Book of Acts draws us into the world of the first century, as it vividly tells the story of the explosive spread of Christianity in the first three decades after Christ's resurrection.

Acts focuses on the ministry of two men, Peter in Jerusalem and Judea (chs. 1–12) and Paul in the wider world of the Gentiles (chs. 13–28). This narrative history gives a background against which we can better understand the New Testament Epistles, and provides vital insights into the dynamic qualities of first-century evangelism.

AUTHORSHIP

Church records as early as the second century say that Luke wrote Acts. There is no good reason to doubt this tradition. The author, who proves himself a precise historian throughout the book, sometimes shifts his pronoun to "we," indicating that he was present with Paul on those occasions. In his Epistles to Philemon and the Colossians, Paul lists Luke, "the doctor" (Col. 4:14), among his companions. Through a process of elimination, checking the probable dates, and noting that the vocabulary of Acts would fit with that of a well-educated doctor, we can reasonably assume that Luke was the author.

HISTORICAL SIGNIFICANCE

Some ten books in the OT are narrative histories. In the NT, only Acts provides historical background for the growth of the Christian church. The author joined Paul's missionary team in Troas, and writes as an eyewitness in Acts 16:10-17, 20:5–21:18, and 27:1–28:16. His association

On the day of Pentecost, Jews from across the known world had gathered in Jerusalem. In response to Peter's sermon, 3,000 believed and subsequently returned to their native lands, taking their newfound faith with them.

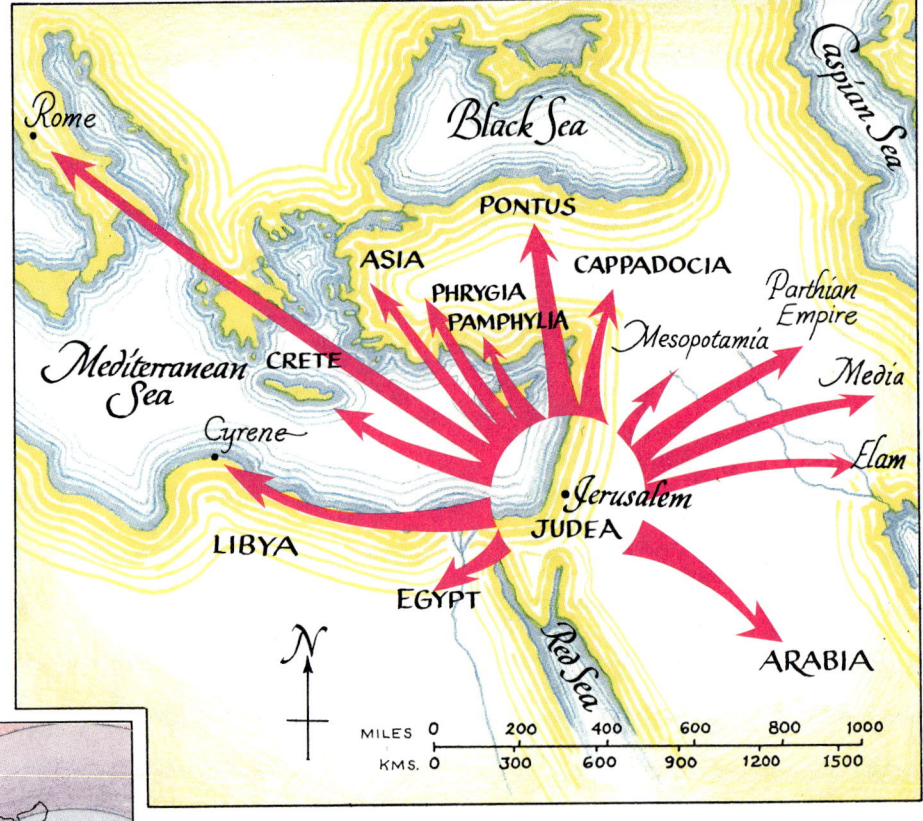

The Book of Acts describes the dynamic spread of the Gospel, (1) from its origin in Jerusalem, (2) to Judea and Samaria, (3) then up the Mediterranean coast from Caesarea to Antioch. Then this first Gentile church (4) launched Paul and Barnabas on their first missionary tour of Asia Minor, (5) followed by the penetration of Europe. Finally (6) Paul "appeals to Caesar" and is taken to Rome itself, to witness for Christ at the heart of the empire.

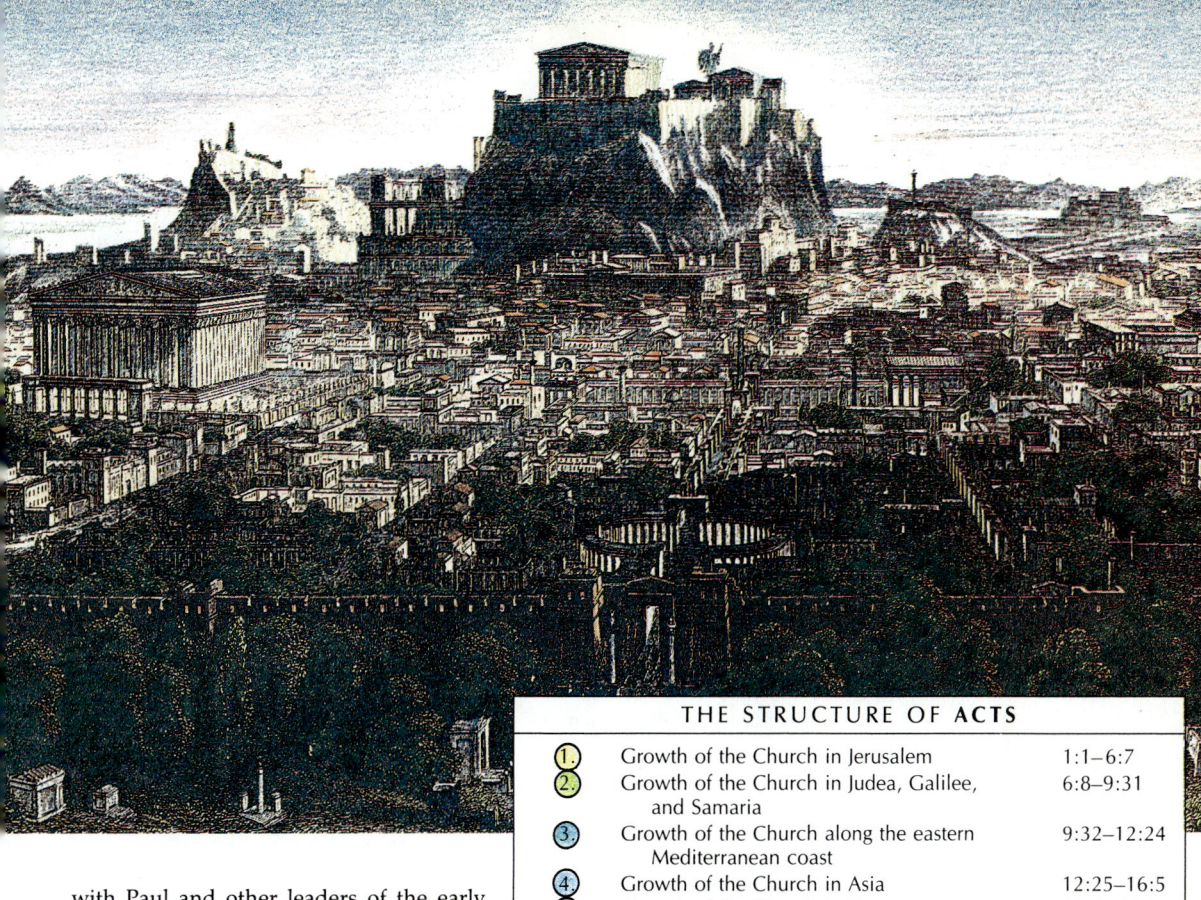

THE STRUCTURE OF ACTS

1.	Growth of the Church in Jerusalem	1:1–6:7
2.	Growth of the Church in Judea, Galilee, and Samaria	6:8–9:31
3.	Growth of the Church along the eastern Mediterranean coast	9:32–12:24
4.	Growth of the Church in Asia	12:25–16:5
5.	Growth of the Church in Europe	16:6–19:20
6.	Paul's imprisonment and witness in Rome	19:21–28:31

with Paul and other leaders of the early church provided additional sources for his narrative. Luke's use of appropriate titles for officials in different localities, once questioned by critics, has been supported by recent archaeological finds, adding to his reputation as a careful and accurate historian.

Luke takes up the story of the church from Christ's ascension from outside Jerusalem in A.D. 30, and ends abruptly at Paul's first imprisonment in Rome. Many date the writing of Acts to the time of this imprisonment, around A.D. 62.

STRUCTURE

Acts is the story of the new church, with each new movement in the church growing out of an earlier phase of expansion. Each transition point is clearly marked by a summary statement, as in Acts 6:7, "So the word of God spread. The number of disciples in Jerusalem increased rapidly, and a large number of priests became obedient to the faith." Other transitions occur at 9:31, 12:24, 16:5, and 19:20. The last verse in the book, 28:31, is a similar summary.

THEOLOGICAL CONTRIBUTION

As narrative, Acts does not teach, but rather tells a story. For this reason it's unwise to try to develop doctrine from the Book of Acts. Nevertheless Acts is a rich source of insight into the dynamics of early Christianity. In particular, Acts gives us unique insights into: early evangelistic preaching, church life and leadership, the role of the Holy Spirit, and the growing rift between Christianity and Judaism.

1. *Early evangelistic preaching.* Nearly one-fifth of Acts consists of speeches. Among them are lengthy summaries of how the Gospel was preached by both Peter and Paul (2:14-36; 3:12-26; 4:8-20; 13:16-41; and 17:16-34). In each sermon, an introduction establishes a point of contact with the listeners, and then each focuses clearly on the following points:

- Jesus was God's man.
- Jesus died and was raised again.
- Jesus will come again to judge the world.

This preaching of Jesus culminated in a call to the listeners to respond to the Gospel message. *See also* Evangelist; Faith; Resurrection.

2. *Church life and leadership.* The repeated use of the Greek word *homothymadon,* "of one accord" (1:14; 2:1,46; 4:24; 5:12; 15:25)

Majestic Athens was an intimidating city, its towering Acropolis set on a rugged hill. Undaunted, the apostle Paul climbed to its Areopagus to boldly argue "an unknown god" with the city's skeptical philosophers.

in descriptions of the Jerusalem church emphasizes its unity and harmony. These descriptions portray shared life—meeting together, eating together, worshiping together, studying together, even giving gladly to provide for each other's material needs (2:45; 4:32-37; 6:1). Often the early church is shown gathered together for prayer, revealing not only the believers' sense of need but also their total reliance on God (2:42; 4:31; 12:5; 13:3). *See also* Fellowship; Prayer.

Initially leadership was exercised by the apostles. Deacons were soon added to deal with practical matters such as the distribution of food to widows (6:1-6). As the church expanded beyond Judea, elders were appointed to provide local spiritual leadership (11:30; 14:23; 15:2; 21:18). Local prophets are also mentioned (11:27-30; 13:1). And throughout the early church era, itinerant teachers such as Apollos (18:24-28) and trouble-shooters such as

Timothy and Titus traveled frequently among the churches. Thus local congregations and their leaders had access to a whole network of leaders who could help them with special needs. *See also* Apostle; Deacon; Elder; Prophet.

Acts thus shows that the church, in both its local and international expressions, existed more as a warm community of caring persons than as a formal institution.

3. *The role of the Holy Spirit.* The Holy Spirit is mentioned over 50 times in Acts, a fact which has led many to think of this book as "The Acts of the Holy Spirit." The visible signs associated with the coming of the Spirit on the day of Pentecost (2:1-13; *compare* 8:17,18; 10:44-46; 19:6) have raised many questions about what modern Christians should expect to experience. There is no doubt that the Holy Spirit is presented here as the source of the early church's power (4:29-31), and that both Peter and

ACTS: A READING AND STUDY GUIDE

Chapter	Content Summary	Related Articles
1	Jesus ascends into heaven. The disciples choose a replacement for Judas while waiting in Jerusalem for the Spirit.	Ascension of Christ Holy Spirit
2	The Holy Spirit comes on Pentecost, and Peter preaches the first gospel sermon.	Church Tongues of fire
3	Peter heals a cripple at the Temple gate, then preaches Christ to onlookers.	Peter Repent
4	Peter and John are ordered to stop preaching Jesus, but join with the church in a prayer for boldness.	Salvation Prayer
5	Ananias and Sapphira lie to the Holy Spirit; the apostles are persecuted by the Jewish council.	Holy Spirit Sanhedrin
6	Deacons are appointed to see to the distribution of food. One of them, Stephen, is accused of blasphemy and seized.	Deacon Blasphemy
7	Stephen reviews history and demonstrates that Israel has consistently failed to be responsive to God. He is stoned.	Forgive Stephen
8	The Samaritans respond to the Gospel as preached by Philip. Philip is led away by the Spirit to witness to one man.	Samaritans
9	Saul is converted on the road to Damascus, and begins to preach Christ. In Judea, Peter raises Dorcas from the dead.	
10	Peter goes to the home of a Roman army officer, Cornelius, and preaches the first gospel sermon directed to Gentiles.	Gentile God-fearing
11	Peter reports Cornelius's conversion to the church. A Gentile congregation is established in Antioch.	Baptism of the Spirit
12	Peter, imprisoned in Jerusalem, is miraculously released.	Angel
13	On their first missionary journey, Paul and Barnabas visit Cyprus, preach to the Jews in Pisidian Antioch.	Barnabas
14	The missionaries travel on to Iconium, Lystra, and Derbe before returning to Antioch in Syria.	

Paul were enabled by the Spirit to perform miracles (Peter: 3:1-10; 5:15,16; 8:9-24; 9:36-41. Paul: 13:6-11; 14:8-16; 19:11,12; 20:9-12). Acts also portrays the Holy Spirit as actively directing missionary operations (8:29; 10:19; 13:2,4; 16:6,7).

4. *The growing rift between Christianity and Judaism.* Christianity began as a movement within Judaism and was known as "the Way" (9:2; 18:25,26; 22:4; 24:14,22). This was an advantage, as Judaism was a *licit* (officially recognized) religion in the Roman Empire and the early Christian missionaries were thus protected by law as they traveled and preached. Acts suggests that, despite some persecution (ch. 8), as long as the church was predominantly Jewish, it coexisted with traditional Judaism in Palestine. But as the number of Gentile Christians grew, some within the church felt Gentile believers must adopt the Mosaic Law and a Jewish life-style (15:1). This view was rejected by a council meeting in Jerusalem about A.D. 49. Paul continued to go first to Jewish synagogues when traveling, but Acts portrays a growing resistance on the part of the non-believing Jewish community to Paul's message (17:5-8,13-15; 18:12-17; 22:21,22).

MASTERY KEYS

The repeated reference to the Holy Spirit is important. Underline each and note specifically what the Holy Spirit does in and/or through believers.

Compare the evangelistic sermons in Acts (2:14-36; 3:12-26; 4:8-12; 13:16-41; 17:22-31) by listing themes in parallel columns. What do recurring themes tell you about personal or public evangelism?

SPECIAL FEATURES

While Peter and Paul are the dominant figures in Acts, this book contains vivid portraits of several other persons. Among the most attractive are Barnabas and Stephen, as well as Priscilla and her husband Aquila.

Chapter	Content Summary	Related Articles
15	A council is held in Jerusalem to determine whether Gentile converts are subject to Mosaic Law.	Law Circumcision
16	Paul crosses into Europe, wins converts and is imprisoned in Philippi.	House
17	The missionaries visit Thessalonica, Berea, and Athens, where Paul preaches to Greek philosophers.	Epicurean Stoic philosophers
18	Paul and his team settle for a time in Corinth. Apollos is instructed by the husband/wife team of Aquila and Priscilla.	Priscilla Aquila
19	Paul settles for three years in Ephesus until a silversmith incites a riot.	Demon
20	Paul travels through Macedonia and Greece, then turns toward Jerusalem.	Prophet
21	In Jerusalem Paul joins worshipers in the Temple, which causes a riot until he is rescued by Roman soldiers.	Temple, Jerusalem
22	Paul angers the crowd by telling of his call to go to Gentiles. Paul's Roman citizenship saves him from a beating.	Citizen
23	Paul addresses the Sanhedrin, claiming his Pharisee heritage. A plot to kill him is discovered, and an army escort takes him to the Roman governor at Caesarea.	Pharisees Sadducees Caesarea
24	Paul is tried before Felix, who puts off making any decision in the case for two years.	
25	Paul is tried before the new governor, Festus. Asked to go to Jerusalem for trial, Paul appeals to Caesar.	
26	Paul shares the Gospel with King Agrippa, whose advice Festus asked.	Agrippa
27	Paul sets sail for Rome, but his ship is wrecked.	
28	Paul winters on Malta, then goes on to Rome where he is allowed to live under guard in a rented house.	Paul

Adam [AD-uhm; "human being" or "humanity." Possibly derived from a word meaning "red soil" or the color "crimson"]. The first man, directly created by God in his own image and given dominion on earth. **Scripture:** Gen. 1–5. **Wife:** Eve. **Children:** Cain, Abel, Seth, and "other sons and daughters."

The OT uses the Hebrew term *'adam* over 500 times in the sense of "man" or "mankind." Only in Gen. 1–5 and 1 Chr. 1:1 is it the proper name of Adam, the first man. Yet this Genesis use is central, for it establishes the biblical view of human nature and Scripture's bold affirmation of the unique place given human beings in God's universe. (*Compare* Rom. 5:12-14; 2 Cor. 15:45.)

An illuminated Haggadah from Sarajevo, Yugoslavia tells the story of Adam and Eve. Upper left: tempted by the serpent; upper right: hiding from the Lord; below: the curse on man and serpent, and eviction from the Garden in shame.

22

ADAM'S CREATION

Genesis 1,2 report God's intention to "make man in our image, in our likeness, and let them rule . . . over all the earth" (Gen. 1:26). God then stooped to mold a body for Adam from the earth, and "breathed into his nostrils the breath of life" (Gen. 2:7). God thus created a being whose nature was both material and spiritual, who would live in this world yet whose life was not limited to the physical universe.

The creation of Adam in God's image and likeness is best understood as creation with all those qualities which make a being truly a person as God is a Person—with spiritual, aesthetic, rational, emotional, and moral capacities (*see* Eph. 4:24-32; Col. 3:8-16). Genesis 2 shows Adam using each of these capacities—in walking with God, in appreciating the beauty of Eden, in naming the animals and thus ordering God's universe, in experiencing a need for a "suitable helper," and in responding to God's command not to eat from the tree of the knowledge of good and evil. Thus Genesis introduces immediately the idea that human nature can be understood only by comparing human beings with God, not by comparing man with animal life. *See also* Image.

IMPLICATIONS OF "DOMINION"

In the same way, Genesis establishes a biblical view of mankind's place in God's universe. Human beings were given dominion over all the earth and all its living creatures (1:26). Here dominion must be understood not in the sense of a "right to use" but as "responsibility to care for." This also is reflected in Gen. 2, as Adam is placed in Eden "to work it and take care of it" (2:15). Thus man is "over" the physical universe but is "under" God and responsible to him. Placing the tree of the knowledge of good and evil in Eden shows that human beings are also morally responsible to God. *See also* Dominion; Tempt.

ADAM'S FALL

Genesis 1 and 2 define human nature and mankind's role in God's universe. Genesis 3 and 4 explain the failure of every human society to achieve the promise that shines so brightly in the creation account.

Eve has now been formed from Adam's rib, and is thus shown to be a full participant with him in all it means to be a human being. She is deceived by Satan and eats fruit from the forbidden tree. Adam, undeceived and knowing fully what he is doing, also eats (1 Tim. 2:13,14). In this, each represents an aspect of sin: Eve as one who falls short of doing God's will through human weakness, and Adam as one who consciously rebels against the known will of God. The consequences of this original sinful act are identified in Scripture as (1) the flawed character of human beings, who are centered on self rather than on God, a mind-set which expresses itself in selfish, thoughtless, and criminal acts, (2) the flawed nature of the physical universe, and (3) the deadness to God and godliness which humankind exhibits. *See also* Death; Earth; Eve; Sin; Woman.

ADAM AND CHRIST

The NT links Adam and Jesus Christ in two vital ways. First, the genealogy of Jesus given in Lk. 3 traces Christ's line of descent back to Adam. This is intended to establish Jesus, the Son of God, as one who is also a true human being. Second, in two major passages in the Epistles (Rom. 5:12-21; 1 Cor. 15:20-49), Jesus is presented as a "second Adam," whose impact on the human race is in dramatic contrast to the negative impact of the first Adam. Paul argues that every person is "in Adam" or "in Christ." That is, each person's essential inner character is rooted either in his relationship to Adam as a fallen sinner, or in a relationship with Jesus which brings inner spiritual renewal. Thus Adam stands as the source and prototype of fallen humanity, while Christ stands as the source and prototype of humanity redeemed.

HISTORICITY

Some have pointed to the powerful symbolism of the Genesis account of creation and argued that these stories should be viewed as myth. Whatever a person chooses to believe, there can be no doubt that Scripture itself treats Adam as a historic personality, and treats the Genesis account as a historical record of facts (so the Lord Jesus himself implies in Mt. 19:4-6).

adamant (KJV) A hard stone or substance viewed as unbreakable. In the face of harsh criticism, Ezekiel was assured by the Lord that he had been made hard-headed: "as an adamant harder than flint have I made thy forehead" (Ezek. 3:9 KJV). In Jer. 17:1 and Zech. 7:12, adamant (Heb., *shamir*) pictures the resistance of God's people to his Law. Though other versions prefer flint, diamond or "the hardest stone" to the KJV's *adamant*, the image still connotes impenetrable hardness.

Adar [AY-dahr]. Twelfth month of the calendar adopted by the Hebrews after the Babylonian captivity. It falls during our February/March. *See also* Calendar.

adder Several poisonous snakes are named in the Hebrew OT. English versions show no consistency in translating the Hebrew names, but render all or some of them as "adder," "asp," "cobra," "serpent," and especially "viper."

Poisonous snakes have two primary associations in Scripture, both of which are moral in nature. In passages such as Pss.

58:4 and 140:3, poisonous snakes serve as images of the violent and hostile relationship of wicked people with other human beings. In prophetic passages such as Ps. 91:13 and Isa. 11:8, they serve as images of those evils which God will stamp out and never again permit when he renews the earth. *See also* Serpent; Viper.

adjure (KJV) A term found in the KJV, where it means to solemnly command or to charge, often under oath.

administer, administration Where "administer justice" occurs in some modern translations of the OT, the Hebrew typically reads "do justice." The only "administrators" mentioned as such in the OT are Daniel and his associates (Dan. 6). The Persian title describing them indicates a post at the highest level of government.

In modern English versions of the NT, three different Greek words are at times rendered by "administration." (1) *Diakonia* literally means "service" or "ministry." This term is found in 2 Cor. 8:19,20; 9:1, 12, where Paul speaks of administering a gift to be sent to the needy. (2) *Oikonomos* means "household manager," a position often held by a slave in first-century society. The term, sometimes rendered "steward," is used at times of leaders or overseers who manage the church (1 Cor. 4:1,2; Tit. 1:7). (3) *Kybernēsis* is found in 1 Cor. 12:28 where Paul speaks of the spiritual gift of administration. The word (rendered "governments" in the KJV) is found only here in the NT. It is a term borrowed from seafaring, used to designate the steersman or pilot who holds the ship on course. *See also* Spiritual Gifts.

In any society, words like *administer* are general terms, defined by the view of leadership held within the culture. It is not possible therefore to develop a theology of church administration from the Greek words themselves. A person must examine the "culture of the church" and the way various leadership terms are used in the NT in order to determine the functional meaning of these words. *See also* Church; Leader.

admonish In common usage, "admonish" suggests a mild reproof or word of warning. In the NT, to admonish (*noutheteō*) is to perform a positive ministry, stimulated by genuine concern for others. The Greek root occurs eleven times, and is often translated "warn" or "warning." Yet this warning is not judgmental. It involves encouraging and instructing others to live godly and productive lives. Clothed with "compassion, kindness, humility, gentleness and patience," believers are called to "teach and admonish one another" as a loving and mutual ministry (Col. 3:12,16).

ADONIJAH
and his
Step~brothers
(PARTIAL LIST)

FATHER
DAVID

MOTHER
AHINOAM
SON
AMNON

MOTHER
ABIGAIL
SON
KILEAB

MOTHER
MAACAH
SON
ABSALOM

MOTHER
HAGGITH
SON
ADONIJAH

MOTHER
BATHSHEBA
SON
SOLOMON

> **Adonijah** [AD-oh-NI-juh; "Yahweh is Lord" or "Yahweh is my Lord"]. David's oldest surviving son, set aside when Solomon was proclaimed king by David about 970 B.C. **Scripture:** 1 Kings 1,2. **Parents:** David and Haggith. **Significant half-brothers:** Absalom, Solomon, Amnon.

In his old age, David delayed confirmation of his successor to Israel's throne. He had earlier designated Solomon as his successor (in 1 Chr. 22:5-17; 23:1) before the leading men of Israel. Adonijah, David's oldest surviving son, gained the support of many influential persons and began to behave as if he were co-regent. Supporters of his rival and half-brother, Solomon, urged David to publicly announce his choice. Solomon was thereupon anointed king (co-regent with David), and Adonijah's supporters quickly deserted him.

In an age when kings commonly executed family rivals, Solomon permitted Adonijah to live. But when Adonijah some time later asked to marry Abishag, David's beautiful young virgin nurse, Solomon immediately had him killed. To take a wife or concubine of the previous king was considered a claim to the throne, and Solomon saw that such a marriage would give Adonijah, who was Solomon's older brother, an even stronger claim that might well lead to a future civil war.

adoption No biblical laws regulate the process of taking a person into one's own family. Yet Paul uses the image of adoption to help believers grasp the exciting implications of the Christian's relationship with God.

OLD TESTAMENT
Ancient Near Eastern texts provide insights into adoption customs that are reflected in Genesis. Childless, Abram would have adopted his slave Eliezer in order to have an heir (Gen. 15:3). This practice was an element of ancient "social security," for the new son accepted the responsibility of care for his aged parents. Also, according to custom, Abraham should have adopted Ishmael, his son by Hagar (Gen. 16), and Jacob would have adopted his children by his concubines, Bilhah and Zilpah (Gen. 30). Moses was adopted by Pharaoh's daughter, according to Egyptian law (Ex. 2:10).

As noted, the Mosaic code makes no express provision for adoption, and there is no indication that adoption was widely practiced by the Jews.

NEW TESTAMENT
In Rom. 9:4, Paul says of Israel, "Theirs is the adoption [Gk., *hyiothesia*] as sons." The word is used five times in the NT, always by Paul. He borrows his imagery from the provisions of Roman law.

According to Roman law, an adopted person's old relationships and responsibilities were totally severed. The individual became a member of a new family, and was under the authority of the father of that family. In this new family relationship, the father was viewed as owner of all the adoptee's possessions and had the right to control his behavior. This was essential, because under Roman law the father was considered responsible for his children's actions and had a duty to discipline them, so that they might bring honor to his family name. But the adoptee also had benefits. The father committed himself and his resources to his heirs. An heir could draw on him for advice and help, sure of his support.

The image of adoption, then, appropriately symbolizes the Christian's changed estate. Believers are no longer slaves, either to OT Law or to sin. We are full members of God's family. We owe allegiance only to God our Father, and we can depend on him to support us with every resource at his command.

ADOPTION
WHAT IT MEANS FOR THE CHRISTIAN

Adoption passages	Application of Roman law to Christian experience
Rom. 8:15	Adopted, we are now God's children, free to address him intimately as "Dear Father." *See* Abba.
Rom. 8:23	We eagerly await the full benefits of our adoption in the coming resurrection.
Gal. 4:5	Adoption has transformed us from slaves to heirs of God. We are to claim the full rights of our sonship and no longer live as if we were slaves.
Eph. 1:5	Our adoption is at God's pleasure, according to the free exercise of his will and of his grace.

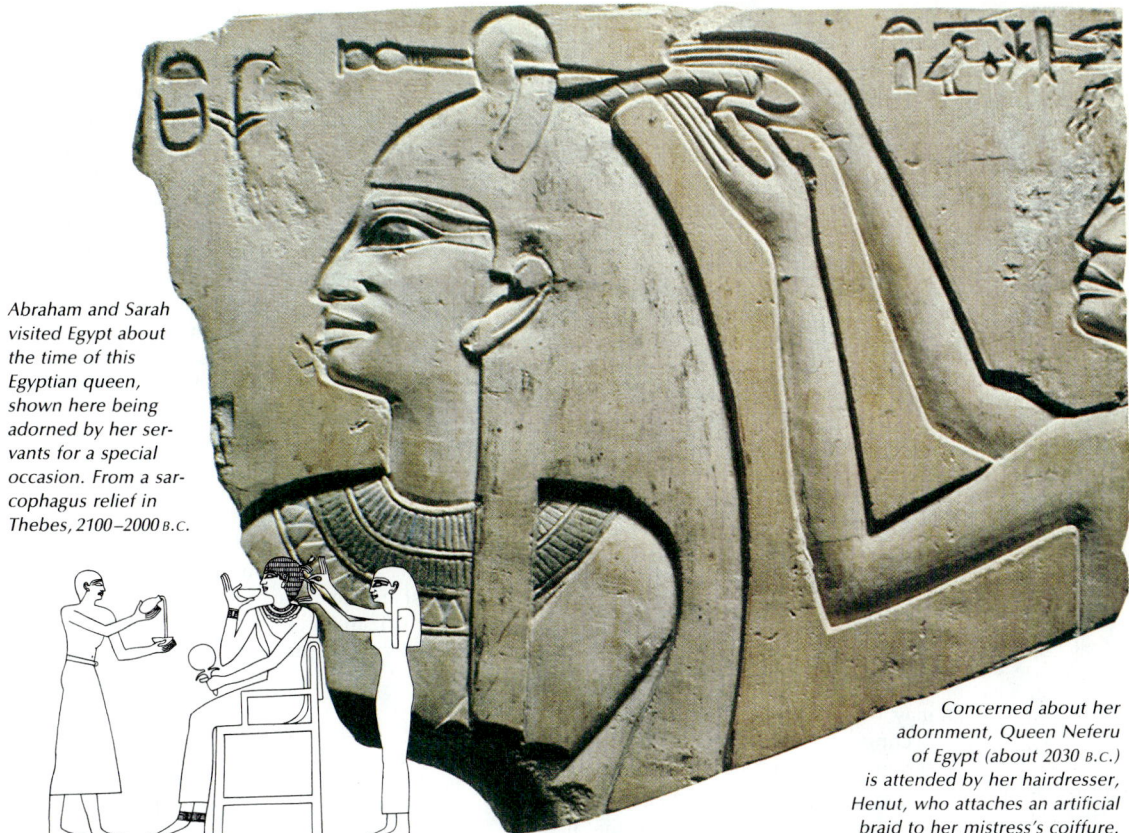

Abraham and Sarah visited Egypt about the time of this Egyptian queen, shown here being adorned by her servants for a special occasion. From a sarcophagus relief in Thebes, 2100–2000 B.C.

Concerned about her adornment, Queen Neferu of Egypt (about 2030 B.C.) is attended by her hairdresser, Henut, who attaches an artificial braid to her mistress's coiffure.

adorn [Gk., *kosmeō*]. To decorate or beautify. The NT primarily uses "adorn" when speaking of buildings or of women.

A house was adorned when cleaned and put in order (Mt. 12:44; Lk. 11:25). Tombs and the stunning Temple expanded by Herod were adorned with carvings and specially dressed stones (Mt. 23:29; Lk. 21:5). Revelation says the foundations of the heavenly Jerusalem will be adorned ["decorated," NIV] with every kind of precious stone (Rev. 21:19).

Peter describes how women in biblical times adorned themselves, mentioning "braided hair and the wearing of gold jewelry and fine clothes" (1 Pet. 3:3). Paul joins Peter in urging Christian women not to draw attention to their looks with braided hair "or gold or pearls or expensive clothes" (1 Tim. 2:9). But neither passage says it is wrong to be attractive. The point of each passage is to warn against dressing suggestively or focusing the attention of others on one's looks. Each passage urges instead that women and men value "the unfading beauty of a gentle and quiet spirit," expressed in good deeds. *See also* Beauty.

adultery Adultery (Heb., *na'ap*; Gk., *moicheia*) is a specific sexual sin forbidden in both Testaments. In the OT, the adultery often symbolizes spiritual unfaithfulness, as when God's people turned to idolatry (Jer. 3:1-10; Ezek. 23; Hos. 4). *See also* Idol.

ADULTERY AND OTHER SEXUAL SINS

In the Bible, sexual intercourse is considered appropriate only within marriage. A variety of sexual sins are mentioned in Scripture, ranging from premarital intercourse to prostitution, rape, homosexuality, and bestiality. In this list of proscribed behavior, *na'ap* (adultery) is clearly defined: Adultery is a sexual relationship with a married person who is not one's spouse. The OT Law specified the death penalty for adultery, indicating how seriously it is viewed (Lev. 18:20; 20:10; Deut. 22:22-24). *See also* Sex.

THE COVENANT OF MARRIAGE

The seriousness of adultery is rooted in the biblical view of marriage as a covenant between two persons that reflects the relationship of God with his people. Within the covenant relationship, each party owes the other complete and exclusive faithful-

25

ness. Only by remaining faithful to the covenant relationship can both partners be blessed. *See also* Covenant; Marriage.

ADULTERY AND DIVORCE

The OT does not identify adultery as grounds for divorce. While it is likely that unfaithfulness caused some to divorce, there is no biblical record of this either. Probably this was due to the law of Lev. 20:10, which established death by stoning as the penalty for adultery (*see also* Deut. 22:22-30). The OT Law decreed that a wife suspected of adultery be brought before the priest. A rigorous ceremonial procedure followed which would clear or condemn her (Num. 5:11-31). The solemn rite would set the mind of the suspicious husband at rest, renewing the marriage and reducing the likelihood of divorce.

In the NT, however, Jesus takes a much clearer stand on the issues of adultery and divorce: ". . . I tell you that anyone who divorces his wife, except for marital unfaithfulness, and marries another woman commits adultery" (Mt. 19:9; Mk. 10:10-12). The disciples express considerable dismay over this statement (Mt. 19:10), reflecting their understanding of the seriousness of adultery. *See also* Divorce.

JESUS AND THE ADULTEROUS LOOK

Jesus said, "You have heard that it was said, 'Do not commit adultery.' But I tell you that anyone who looks at a woman lustfully has already committed adultery with her in his heart" (Mt. 5:27,28). In this passage Jesus lists a series of "it was said . . . but I tell you" examples. Each "it was said" quotes an OT law or tradition which regulated behavior. With each contrasting "but I tell you," Jesus shifts the focus from acts to inner intent. Christ's point is that righteousness is not simply a matter of outward conformity to Law, but is a matter of heart attitude and of those inner motives which may or may not find expression in one's acts. Adultery is wrong, and a person committing this sin falls short of being righteous. But to fix one's gaze on another person and engage in sexual fantasies is also wrong, and shows just as clearly that the person who looks lustfully is not righteous either. *See also* Righteousness.

adversary The Hebrew word is *satan*, meaning a person who opposes or fights against another. The root is found 30 times in the OT; in 16 of these occurrences it is used as a proper name of the devil. *See also* Satan.

advocate (KJV) One who stands by and encourages, helps, counsels, or speaks in our behalf. John writes, "If any one does sin, we have an advocate with the Father, Jesus Christ the righteous" (1 Jn. 2:1 RSV).

The Greek word, *paraklētos*, which is used only by John in the NT, usually refers to a "helper" or "adviser." In 1 Jn. 2:1, *paraklētos* is used in a well-established legal sense, as a non-professional "helper in court" who defends another by offering evidence. The imagery in 1 John is clear: When a believer sins, Christ pleads the efficacy of his blood as the atoning sacrifice for all sin. On the basis of Christ's accomplished work, the believer is acquitted by God.

In John's Gospel Jesus refers to the Holy Spirit by the same Greek word: "I will ask the Father, and he will give you another Counselor" (14:16) and again "Unless I go away, the Counselor will not come to you" (16:7).

Even as Jesus is our *paraklētos* in heaven, so the Holy Spirit has come to be our *paraklētos* on earth. *See also* Confess.

affection All versions use *affection* in the OT to render several different Hebrew words for *love*. In modern NT versions, *affection* is exclusively a positive term, expressing deep concern for others in need. For an insight into the distinctive nature of Christian affection for others, *see* Compassion.

In this limestone relief (Egypt, about 1370 B.C.), Queen Nefertiti affectionately kisses her child.

Where the KJV uses *affection* in a negative sense, the Greek root means "feelings" or "passions." Passion itself is neutral, except where associated with man's sinful nature, as in Rom. 1:26 and Gal. 5:24. *See also* Flesh.

affliction Many Bible words describe the suffering and pain human beings experience in this life. *Affliction* is one of these special terms, but one which focuses our attention on a different aspect of suffering in each Testament.

OLD TESTAMENT

The afflicted person or nation lacks the food or funds or the power needed to defend against oppressors. The Hebrew word for affliction, *'anah,* emphasizes this helplessness.

In the OT, affliction is closely associated with sin. God is the one who afflicts not only Israel's enemies but his own people as well. Yet affliction is not necessarily intended for punishment. Affliction is a divine gift as well, for when a person realizes his helplessness he is most likely to turn to the Lord. The Psalmist cites God's gracious intent in afflicting his people in Ps. 119. "Before I was afflicted I went astray," he writes, "but now I obey your word" (v. 67). And "It was good for me to be afflicted so that I might learn your decrees" (v. 71). Personal experience had taught him to sense God's enduring love even in times of trouble: "In faithfulness you have afflicted me" (v. 75).

This perspective on affliction echoes throughout the Psalms. When we are humbled by situations that reduce us to helplessness, we are invited to turn to God and are given special promises. God will "defend the afflicted among the people" and "will deliver . . . the afflicted who have no one to help" (Ps. 72:4,12).

NEW TESTAMENT

The NT often views affliction not as vulnerability or punishment, but as a privilege. This is rooted in the fact that the source of most affliction (Gk., *thlipsis*) is external circumstance—the difficulties and the opposition Christians experience as they seek to live a godly life. When we choose to follow Jesus, we often find ourselves in conflict with a world whose beliefs and values caused Christ suffering, too. This conflict will cause us emotional pain and anguish, but such suffering is a privilege and not a punishment. As we suffer for choosing what is right, we follow in the footsteps of our Lord.

So affliction has two powerful messages for believers. The message of the OT is that, when God brings us low and we come to the end of our own resources, we are invited to turn to the Lord. The message in the NT is that we must expect pressures if we choose to obey God. Yet how good it is to know that in experiencing this kind of pain we draw closer to Jesus, for we participate in his sufferings (*compare* Col. 1:24). *See also* Suffer.

agape [ah-GAH-pay]. Self-giving love that is not merited. In the first century, the Greek language contained several different words for *love*. *Eros* expressed the sexual aspects of love between a man and a woman. *Philia* was the most common word, and suggested affection for friends and relatives, which was often expressed through acts of hospitality and concern.

The Greeks also had another word for love: *agapē*. But, generally, that word was colorless and weak with no fixed meaning. Before the New Testament was written, *agapē* was not often used as a noun. For example, the verb form appears commonly enough in the Septuagint, but the noun is used only 16 times. But when the NT writers adopted *agapē*, they infused it with stunning new meaning. In the NT, *agapē* is the word chosen to express both the love of God and the love that knowing God infuses into human relationships.

At times *eros* has been defined as love generated by passion, *philia* as love generated by natural affection or liking, and *agapē* as a love generated by the will. It seems best however to define *agapē* differently: This is love as God himself has expressed it in Christ. We understand such love only when we see in Jesus God's commitment to a lost humanity, a commitment so deep that "he sent his one and only Son into the world that we might live through him. This is love: not that we loved God, but that he loved us and sent his Son as an atoning sacrifice for our sins" (1 Jn. 4:9,10).

The Assyrians were known for brutality toward captives, pulling them with rings attached to their lips and putting out their eyes with spears. This drawing shows King Sargon II (about 710 B.C.) dealing with traitors.

When we define *agapē* by God's act in Christ, we realize that it is completely selfless. It keeps on caring despite the flaws in others; it acts for the benefit of the loved one even when an act of love costs the lover everything.

The most striking aspect of the NT's teaching on *agapē* is that God creates the capacity for this kind of love in each believer. John says, "We love because he [God] first loved us" (1 Jn. 4:19). This new capacity for love is to find expression in everything we do. "Be imitators of God," Eph. 5:1 says, "as dearly loved children, and live a life of love, just as Christ loved us and gave himself up for us." We now can model our relationships with others on God's relationship with us, and can choose to love them as he has loved us.

While Christ himself is the ultimate definition of *agapē*, the Bible also gives us other descriptions of the life of love that Jesus' followers are called to live. Perhaps the most beautiful description is found in 1 Cor. 13:4-7:

Love is patient, love is kind. It does not envy, it does not boast, it is not proud. It is not rude, it is not self-seeking, it is not easily angered, it keeps no record of wrongs. Love does not delight in evil but rejoices with the truth. It always protects, always trusts, always hopes, always perseveres.

If we lead this kind of life, we will come to know *agapē* not just as a theological concept, but as a reality—and through us others will begin to sense the indescribable love of God. *See also* Love.

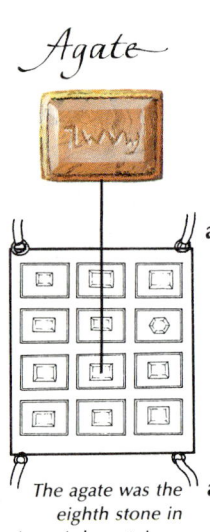

Agate

The agate was the eighth stone in Aaron's breastpiece. Long before Aaron, the Sumerians valued it in beads, rings, and cylinder seals.

agate One of the twelve stones set in the breastpiece of the Jewish high priest. An agate (Heb., *shebo*) is usually marked by uneven white and brown bands. The Bible mentions it only when referring to the high priest's breastpiece (Ex. 28:19; 39:12). The stone called an "agate" in the KJV of Isa. 54:12 and Ezek. 27:16 is a *kadekod,* or ruby. *See also* Breastpiece.

age, ages A period of time with no defined length, but with a distinct character. The Greek word, *aiōn*, is related to our "eon."

Jesus spoke about the "age to come," and contrasted it with "this age" (Lk. 18:30). The Epistles pick up this language, speaking of the human "rulers of this age" (1 Cor. 2:6-8) and calling Satan "the god of this age" (2 Cor. 4:4).

Consistently in the NT, "this age" stretches between Jesus' first and second comings. It is described as "evil" (Gal. 1:4), dominated by rulers who are ignorant of God's ways (1 Cor. 1:20-25); an age decorated with illusions woven by Satan, who is its god (2 Cor. 4:4). Perhaps the best portrait of the spiritual characteristics of this age is found in Eph. 2:1-3, which shows persons "dead in transgressions and sins" who follow "the ways of this world and of the ruler of the kingdom of the air." Such people gratify "the cravings of our sinful nature" and follow "its desires and thoughts."

According to Jesus, at the end of this age "the Son of Man will send out his angels, and they will weed out of his kingdom everything that causes sin and all who do evil" (Mt. 13:41). The "age to come" will be characterized by the rule of God on earth, where "the righteous will shine like the sun in the kingdom of their Father" (Mt. 13:43).

Perhaps most striking in the Bible's portrayal of these two contrasting ages is the fact that although believers now live in a present that is warped and twisted by sin, Christ gave himself "to rescue us from the present evil age" (Gal. 1:4). The death and resurrection of Jesus has not yet changed the world, but it has transformed his followers. Through Jesus, the believer is enabled to "say 'No' to ungodliness and worldly passions, and to live self-controlled, upright and godly lives in this present age" (Tit. 2:12).

age, old age Old age had its physical drawbacks in biblical times just as it has today. But in the biblical world, attaining old age was viewed as a blessing, and older persons were treated with respect. In addition, the old were honored for the wisdom they had gained through the years. The "elders" in both Jewish society and the Christian community were drawn from older members. Both OT and NT seem to set the age of 60 as the point at which a person is considered "old"—and thus worthy of special consideration (Lev. 27:3-7; 1 Tim. 5:9).

A GOOD OLD AGE

The writer of the Book of Ecclesiastes poetically describes the physical drawbacks of age (12:1-5). With age, pleasures decline (v. 1). The eyes dim (v. 2) and the back grows bent (v. 3). Teeth and hearing are lost (vv. 3,4), as is the ability to sleep through the night (v. 4). With age and debility, fears grow but desires are deadened (v. 5). And then, finally, death comes.

But this gradual loss of physical powers is not the dominant image in Scripture.

The Law says, "Rise in the presence of the aged, show respect for the elderly and [so] revere your God" (Lev. 19:32).

In addition, local leaders in Jewish society were older men. The key Hebrew term here is *zaqen*, which is rendered both as "old man" and "elder." Throughout the OT, phrases like the "seventy elders of the people" (Num. 11:16) and "your elders and judges" (Deut. 21:2) make it clear that age carried significant prestige. Even kings, whose rule was hereditary, disregarded the advice of older counselors at their peril (1 Ki. 12:6-17). The aged were expected to be wiser than the young. Proverbs reflects the attitude of the society, as Solomon writes:

Listen, my son, to your father's instruction
and do not forsake your mother's teaching.
They will be a garland to grace your head
and a chain to adorn your neck.
(Prov. 1:8,9)

The grey head *(sib)* in this society was a mark of honor, and a person whose hair was white when he died had lived to a "good old age."

Despite the respect that age merited, it was not the only criterion by which persons were evaluated. David says, "I have more understanding than the elders, for I obey your precepts" (Ps. 119:100). Only the person who had spent a lifetime learning and living by God's Law could take his place among the respected older ones of Israel.

AS FATHERS AND AS MOTHERS

The OT attitude toward the aged is clearly reflected in the NT. Paul tells Timothy not to rebuke an older man harshly, "but exhort him as if he were your father," and to treat "older women as mothers" (1 Tim. 5:1,2). The same chapter goes on to give directions concerning women who are to be placed on the "list of widows." These were widows who not only were supported by the church but also ministered by training younger women in Christian virtues (Tit. 2:3-5). Such a widow had to be over 60, and one who "has been faithful to her husband, and is well-known for her good deeds, such as bringing up children, showing hospitality, washing the feet of the saints, helping those in trouble and devoting herself to all kinds of good deeds" (1 Tim. 5:9,10). This emphasis on age plus demonstrated maturity in the faith is also seen in Paul's instructions on choosing elders for the church. While no age criteria are mentioned, the whole context of Scripture suggests that these leaders were older persons whose personal qualities revealed an appropriate, long-term commitment to godly living (Tit. 1:5-9). *See also* Elder; Leader.

Congregations which adopt the biblical perspective on age will come to view older members as important resources and find creative ways to involve them in interpersonal ministries. Individuals who adopt the biblical perspective on age may well feel more comfortable about growing older. Life will change, and our bodies will lose many of their powers, but all that we learn through years of following Jesus prepares us to help others.

agony An intense suffering that often goes beyond merely physical pain. The English word comes from the Greek *agōn*, denoting a contest or struggle. Jesus' spiritual conflict in Gethsemane is described in this way (Lk. 22:44). Other Greek words for agony involve both emotional and physical torment, particularly in passages which speak of the anguish of the damned (Lk. 16:24,25; Rev. 9:5; 14:11; 16:10; 18:7,10,15). *See also* Hell.

Near Eastern peoples viewed the elderly with respect and sought their advice.

Spades and shovels were used to remove stones from Israel's rocky fields (Isa. 5:1,2).

agriculture The Israelites were people of the land. Canaan was their heritage, given by God to Abraham and his descendants (Gen. 12:7). After Joshua led the Israelites into Canaan, he oversaw the apportionment of the land. Each family received its own property, property never to be sold but to be preserved for that family forever (Lev. 25:23-35). In the Israelite economy, life depended primarily on what could be grown, not on trade or manufacturing. Food, clothing, shelter—every necessity of life—came from the land.

To understand the life-style and even the faith of OT people, we must know something about the land and what it produced.

THE GEOGRAPHY OF PALESTINE

Palestine, a tiny land, stretches less than 150 miles north and south, with the Dead Sea lying barely 50 miles from the Mediterranean coast. This narrow strip of land sweeps gently up from the coast only to tumble suddenly into the deep Jordan Valley, nearly 700 feet below sea level. The result is a land of contrasts: tiny Palestine contains fertile plains and valleys; rugged mountains some 3,280 feet high; hot, arid lowlands and desolate deserts. In Bible times, this complex land contained fields where animals could graze, rich soils in which grain grew abundantly, high hillsides ideal for raising grapes, and thin, rocky soil where olive trees were grown. An agricultural livelihood was not easy in Palestine. Almost everywhere the ground was stony. But somewhere on the varied topography of this land nearly every crop—even oranges—can grow.

THE CLIMATE OF PALESTINE

The climate of Palestine also varies greatly in different areas. The coastal plain and the mountainsides facing the sea receive plenty of rain. Other areas receive much less. In some localities, crops depend on heavy dew during critical growing months.

The climate of Palestine is quite stable from year to year. What the Bible calls the "early rains" come in the autumn, when grain is planted. The "latter rains" fall in the spring and flesh out the crops. Summers, stretching from mid-May to mid-October, are hot and very dry. This pattern has continued, with minor fluctuations, over several thousand years.

Yet even minor fluctuations have caused terrible famines, for agriculture in Palestine depends completely on rainfall. Moses emphasized this dependence as he spoke to the Israelites before they entered the land.

The land you are entering to take over is not like the land of Egypt, from which you have come, where you planted your seed and irrigated it by foot as in a vegetable garden. But the land you are crossing the Jordan to take possession of is a land of mountains and valleys that drinks rain from heaven. It is a land the Lord your God cares for; the eyes of the Lord your God are continually on it from the beginning of the year to its end.

(Deut. 11:10-12)

This feature of Palestine's climate had great spiritual significance. Moses warned the people not to turn away and worship other gods, lest the Lord's anger burn, "and he will shut the heavens so that it will not rain and the ground will yield no produce, and you will soon perish from the good land the Lord is giving you" (Deut. 11:17). Throughout the OT, droughts in Palestine are associated with the apostasy of a particular generation (*see* 1 Ki. 8:35; Jer. 14; Amos 4:7). Israel is encouraged to view God as the lifegiver, who sends the rains that give the land its vitality (2 Chr. 7:13,14; Ps. 65:9-13; 135:7; Isa. 30:23-26; Amos 9:6).

CROPS: WHERE AND HOW THEY GREW

The complex geography and climate of Palestine created conditions in which a variety of crops could grow. Yet through-

Though annual rainfall in Israel varies, from nearly 50 inches in the north near Mount Hermon to 2 inches or less in some desert areas of the south, most rain falls between November and March, with virtually none in the summer months.

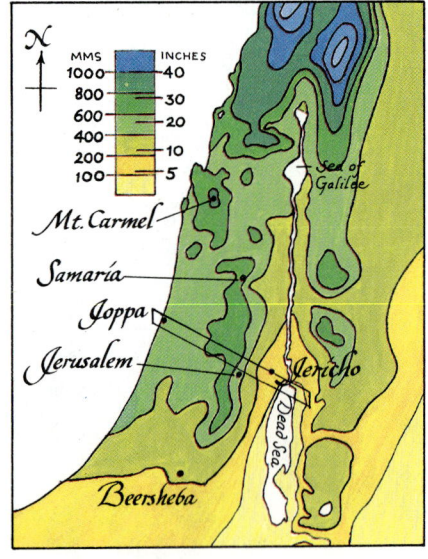

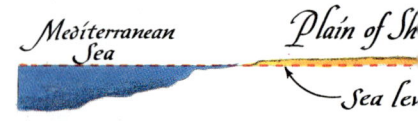

out Bible times three crops remained central: grains, grapes, and olives.

Wheat was the preferred grain in Palestine, for it gave the highest yield and was used in making bread. Galilee produced the best wheat. In the drier, hotter southeast, barley was grown, primarily as animal feed. Other minor grains, such as spelt (a primitive kind of wheat), were also grown. *See also* Bread; Wheat.

Grapes grew in the hill country. They were planted on terraced, rock-walled plots laboriously built along the hillsides. Some grapes were eaten fresh and others dried as raisins, but most of the crop was squeezed to make wine. *See also* Vine; Wine.

Olives were a very important crop, for their oil replaced animal fat in the Israelite's meat-poor diet. Olive trees need little water and grow well in shallow, rocky soil. But because they could not stand cold, most were grown in southern Palestine. Olives were eaten, of course. But their most important contribution was as a source of the light, rich oil used not only in cooking but also as fuel in lamps and in various medicines. *See also* Food; Oil; Olive.

Dates and figs were also important in the Israelite's diet. Both were pressed into cakes, and dates were probably heated to produce a sweetener that tasted much like honey. Other food crops ranged from cucumbers and onions to lentils and various beans. *See also* Fig.

The land also produced some of the clothing worn by Israelites. Though they often wore garments woven from wool, they also used a finer linen cloth made from flax. *See also* Clothing; Linen.

THE AGRICULTURAL YEAR

The land and its seasons shaped the life and work of Palestine's inhabitants. This fact is reflected in an early stone inscription, known as the Gezer calendar, which links each month to the agricultural needs of the land. This stone calendar reads:

Two months are [olive] harvest;
Two months are planting [grain];
Two months are late planting;
A month is hoeing up of flax,
A month is harvest of barley;
A month is harvest and feasting;
Two months are vine tending
A month is summer fruit.

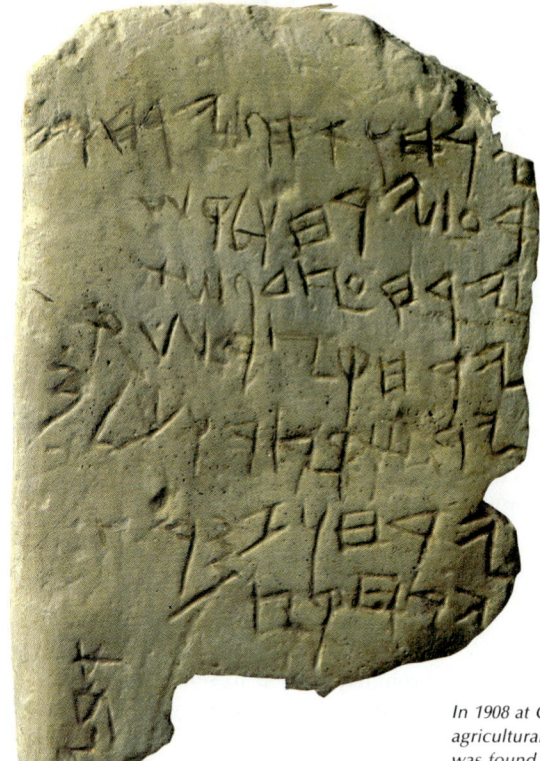

In 1908 at Gezer, this agricultural calendar was found, inscribed in old Hebrew script on a small, limestone block. It is probably a schoolboy's writing exercise and dates from the time of Solomon, about 950 B.C. It follows the civil year, rather than the agricultural year, which began two months later.

Daily life in Palestine thus followed the needs of the land. The pace and cycle of each year remained stable, and life on the land fell into a comfortable routine.

From mid-September to mid-October olives were harvested and pressed for their oil. With November's early rains planting began, and fields were plowed and seeded. With grain planting done, farmers tended garden plots from January to March. The latter rains came in March and April, filling out the grain. During those months flax was cut off close to the ground with a hoe, and its stalks were dried. Grain was harvested in April, May, and June, beginning with the barley crop and ending with the wheat crop. Once cut down, the crop was threshed and winnowed, and the grain placed in storage jars. From June through August the grape vines were cared for. Grapes, figs, and pomegranates were harvested in August and September with much joy and celebration. Then the farmer's yearly cycle began again. *See also* Calendar.

The cross section below shows altitude along the band marked on the map on left. Although the Mediterranean Sea and the Dead Sea are only fifty miles apart, the terrain between them includes mountains, plains, swamps and deserts.

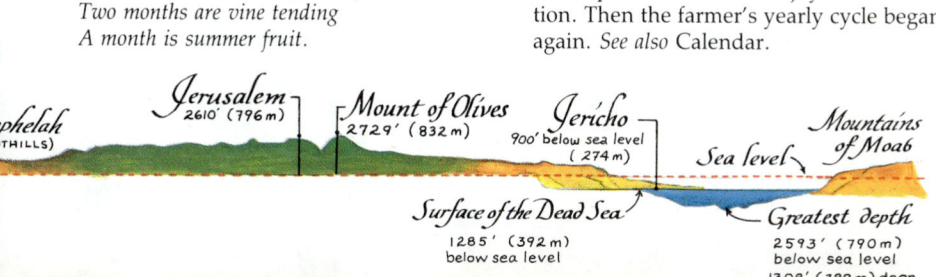

ephelah (FOOTHILLS)

Jerusalem 2610' (796m)

Mount of Olives 2729' (832m)

Jericho 900' below sea level (274m)

Sea level

Mountains of Moab

Surface of the Dead Sea 1285' (392m) below sea level

Greatest depth 2593' (790m) below sea level 1308' (399m) deep

In Israel today, wheat is winnowed in much the same way as it was 3,000 years ago.

Using a winnowing shovel or a wooden fork with broad prongs, the farmer tossed harvested grain into the wind. The heavier kernels fell straight down, while the chaff was blown away (Ps. 1:4).

While this agricultural cycle seems stable, it was far from secure. The farmer counted on God to send each rain in its season. Without rains at just the right time, crops would dwindle or die. If the season were too wet or too cold, vital crops might be ruined by mildew and blight (Amos 4:9; Hag. 2:17; 1 Ki. 8:37). The Middle East also knew plagues of locusts, grasshopper-like insects that would swarm into the land and devour every living plant for miles around (Deut. 28:42; Joel 1:4). *See also* Locust.

The farmer's life, and thus the life of all in Palestine, was at root insecure. Only if God provided what the land required each year could the Israelites survive and prosper. These people, so close to the land and so aware of their vulnerability, should have been particularly sensitive to their need for a close relationship with God, for not only had God given them the land but he also gave them the yearly rains which made it productive (Ps. 65:9-13; *compare* Mt. 5:45).

A FIRST-CENTURY B.C. FARM

Archaeologists have excavated many farms in Israel. One eleven-acre farm at Ein Yalu, developed during the first century B.C., illustrates the agriculture of Palestine in biblical times.

The farm is built on a steep hillside just below a spring. Its fields were created by constructing stone-walled terraces and filling them in with soil. The Ein Yalu farmers cut into the rock to find the water source, and then carved channels in the rock to direct its flow. They also cut several reservoirs into the rock, one of which held 3,500 cubic feet of water. Other channels were cut and plastered to guide the water to some of the terraces. About three of the farm's acres were irrigated in this way. Vegetables could be grown only on the irrigated terraces. Grains and grapes, as well as figs and olives, were grown on the other terraces.

Farms like the one at Ein Yalu help us realize how much toil was involved in wresting a living from the land. Untold hours and even years must have been spent constructing the terraced fields where crops could be planted. More years of back-breaking labor were spent cutting into the rock to develop any water source. Generation after generation would work to make improvements, and this was in addition to the regular labor of planting and harvest, of winnowing the grain and pressing the olives. How true God's explanation of the impact of sin proved to be: "through painful toil you will eat of [the fruit of the ground] all the days of your life. . . .By the sweat of your brow you

Plowing — Rainy Season — Olive Harvest — Planting — Cold Season — Almond Harvest — Flax Harvest

| September | October | November | December | January | February |

will eat your food until you return to the ground'' (Gen. 3:17,19).

CITIES AND THEIR FOOD SUPPLY

Many terraced farms were built around urban centers. It was impractical to transport a city's food supplies over any distance, so farms had to be established nearby. As city populations grew, networks of terraced farms were developed around them.

TERRACE CONSTRUCTION

Creating land by building terraces was necessary due to Palestine's steep, rocky slopes. Over the years, certain features of terraces have changed. Foundations of first-century B.C. terraces were laid with large, square-cut stones. Earlier terraces, built during the eighth- through sixth-centuries B.C., had triangular stones at their base. The age of a terraced farm can often be established by studying its construction.

Terrace construction involved as much skill as hard work. After the stone retaining wall was built, alternating layers of gravel, soil, and stones were laid. A well-made terrace would hold just enough water for crops to grow and pass the extra moisture on to the terrace below. Poorly constructed, a terrace might hold too much water or not enough.

Many thousands of these small terraced farms existed in ancient Israel and in the time of Christ. Israel truly was a land flowing with milk and honey. But that flow depended not only on the goodness of the God who gave Israel its well-timed rains, but also on the skill and labor of its people.

FAITH AND FARMING

The OT reminded Israel of an important fact: God has said, ''the land is mine and you are but aliens and my tenants'' (Lev. 25:23). From this basic fact flowed many aspects of Israel's faith: (1) God, the owner of the land, claimed the right to establish laws governing its use. (2) God, the owner of the land, claimed a tithe from it for the support of the priesthood and for the poor (Deut. 14:22-29). *See* Tithe. (3) And God, the owner of the land and giver of the rains, was worshiped in great religious festivals that celebrated the harvest.

Old Testament Law includes many regulations concerning the land and its use. Grapes were not to be picked from a vine for three years after planting (Lev. 19:23). Stone boundary markers defining each family's property were not to be moved (Deut. 19:14). The land was to be allowed to rest every seventh year, while the people lived from stored food (Lev. 25:1-7). No family could sell its land permanently, although it could sell the use of the land (Lev. 25:8-18). A visitor was free to eat ripened grapes or grains, but could not take away produce in a container (Deut. 23:24,25). Even oxen were not to be muzzled when led over cut sheaves to separate

The Israelites terraced their fields to conserve rainfall and prevent soil erosion. The photo above shows how terracing is still practiced in the Hebron hills.

Rainy Season — Citrus Harvest — March

Dry Season — Barley Harvest — April

Wheat Harvest — May

First Figs — Grape Harvest — June

Summer Heat — Date Harvest — July

Summer Figs — August

the chaff and grain kernels. The oxen were to be allowed to eat as they worked (Deut. 25:4). And when crops were harvested, no fruit or grain that fell to the ground was to be picked up. Instead, the poor and fatherless were to be invited into the fields to harvest for themselves what had fallen (Deut. 24:21).

A tithe (ten percent) of the land's produce was to be given by the farmer to support the priests and Levites who led Israel in worship and to help the poor (Deut. 26). In a moving ceremony each year, the worshiper brought a symbolic "firstfruit" portion. He briefly recited the history of Israel's release from Egyptian servitude and claim of the Promised Land, and then declared: "Now I bring the firstfruits of the soil that you, O Lord, have given me" (Deut. 26:10). *See also* Tithe.

Different religious festivals in Israel had different purposes. Some, like Passover, were intended to help God's people relive sacred history and experience divine deliverance as their forefathers had. Three had links with agriculture. On the first day of the week-long Feast of Unleavened Bread (Adar 15–21), associated with Passover (Adar 14), the first sheaf of ripened barley was presented to God (Lev. 23:9-14). This took place in early April. The one-day Feast of Weeks took place "seven weeks from the time you begin to put the sickle to the standing grain" and marked the grain harvest. Later the festival became known as Pentecost, and was held exactly 50 days after Passover, in late May or early June (Ex. 23:16; Lev. 23:15-21; Deut. 16:9-12). The last agricultural festival was called by several names: Ingathering, Tabernacles, and Booths. This seven-day celebration was held after the fruit crops had been harvested. The people camped out in huts made of branches to recall the years of wilderness wandering, which contrasted so greatly with the rich harvest they had just won from the land (Lev. 23:33-43). This festival fell in early October. *See also* Feasts, Festivals, and Fasts.

IMAGES OF SPIRITUAL TRUTHS

Just as Jesus drew on experiences that would be familiar to an agricultural people, the OT communicates spiritual truths by references to farming. Probably the clearest example of this is seen in Isa. 5:1-7. There the Lord is pictured constructing a farm terrace much like the one at Ein Yalu. God is like the farmer who has a vineyard "on a fertile hillside." He dug up the area and cleared it of stones, built a watchtower and cut a winepress out of the rock. All this work was done in expectation of a crop of good grapes. But despite all God's labor and care, his vineyard produced only sour grapes. Now all he can do is break down the terrace wall and take away its hedge, letting the vineyard become a wasteland. And then comes the explanation of this powerful image:

The vineyard of the Lord Almighty
* is the house of Israel,*
and the men of Judah
* are the garden of his delight.*
And he looked for justice, but saw bloodshed;
* for righteousness, but heard cries of*
*   distress.*   (Isa. 5:7)

A similar image is used in Ps. 80:8-19. Other fascinating analogies appear in Prov. 20:26; 24:30-34; and Job 24.

Agricultural images are also found in prophetic visions of future blessing. When God establishes his Kingdom on earth, "the reaper will be overtaken by the plowman and the planter by the one treading grapes" while "new wine will drip from the mountains and flow from all the hills" (Amos 9:13; *compare* Zech. 8:12,13).

In the NT, Jesus' image of the Gospel as seed sown on different kinds of ground is well known (Mk. 4:1-20). Yet Jesus used other agricultural illustrations. Jesus compared people to trees, which bring forth good or bad fruit according to their nature (Lk. 6:43-45). Jesus called himself the vine to which each believer must be united in order to produce fruit (Jn. 15:1-8).

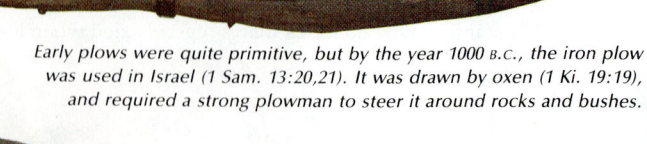

Early plows were quite primitive, but by the year 1000 B.C., the iron plow was used in Israel (1 Sam. 13:20,21). It was drawn by oxen (1 Ki. 19:19), and required a strong plowman to steer it around rocks and bushes.

The NT Epistles also employ agricultural images. Paul uses the image of grafting to illustrate the special new relationship between Jewish believers and Gentile believers (Rom. 11). Later Paul asks the Corinthians, who were so eager to develop personality cults around the early apostles, to see human leaders merely as workers employed in God's field. Paul may plant, and Apollos may water, but it is God who makes things [and people] grow (1 Cor. 3:5-9). James sees yet another implication in the concept of growth. To those who suffer, James urges patience, saying, ''See how the farmer waits for the land to yield its valuable crop and how patient he is for the autumn and spring rains. You, too, be patient and stand firm, because the Lord's coming is near'' (Jas. 5:7,8).

In a significant and perhaps surprising way, the agriculture—the land of Palestine, its climate, and its products—have shaped not only the people of the Bible, but the Bible itself.

The Tomb of Sennedjem, 1300 B.C., depicts an Egyptian farmer's agricultural paradise. The fields are irrigated by canals, the flax and wheat are tall and ripe, the trees in the orchards are laden with fruit, and the garden is lush with flowers.

Hand sickles, used by farmers to mow their fields (Deut. 16:9), have changed very little in 3,500 years. The cutting blade, made from flint at first, was made of iron after 1000 B.C.

Herod the Great and his descendants ruled Jewish Palestine for more than 100 years.

• Though an Edomite, Herod the Great was appointed king of the Jews in 40 B.C. He died in 4 B.C., shortly after the birth of ► Christ.

• Aristobulus, his son, was executed for treason in about ► 7 B.C.

• Herod Agrippa I stepped into his ► grandfather's position in A.D. 41.

• Too young to get the throne upon his father's death, ► Agrippa II worked his way up the political ladder, until A.D. 59, when he ruled much of northern Palestine.

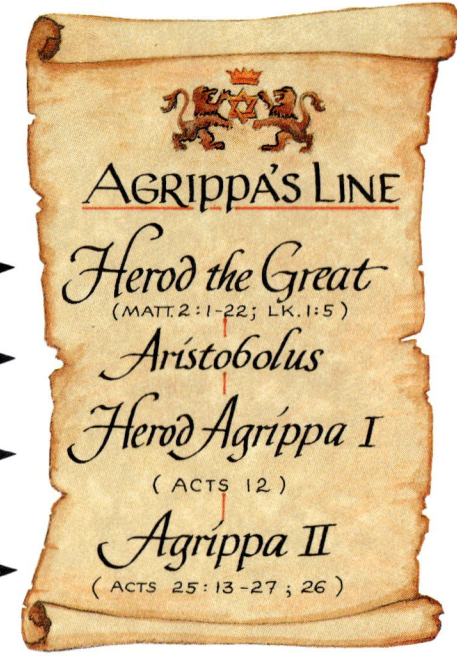

AGRIPPA'S LINE

Herod the Great
(MATT. 2:1-22; LK. 1:5)

Aristobolus

Herod Agrippa I
(ACTS 12)

Agrippa II
(ACTS 25:13-27 ; 26)

Agrippa [uh-GRIP-uh; meaning unknown]. Ruler of Galilee to whom the new Roman governor, Festus, turned for advice regarding an imprisoned Paul about A.D. 59. **Scripture:** Acts 25,26. **Great-grandfather:** Herod the Great. **Father:** Herod Agrippa I. **Sisters:** Bernice, Drusilla.

BACKGROUND

Great-grandson of the king who tried to kill the infant Jesus (Herod the Great), son of the king who killed James and imprisoned Peter (Herod Agrippa I), King Agrippa (Herod Agrippa II) is known for his interview with the apostle Paul (Acts 25,26).

Born in A.D. 27, Agrippa was a 17-year-old student in Rome when his father died suddenly (Acts 12:21-23). The Roman authorities considered him too young to rule effectively, but they soon gave him a small territory. Over the years, his domain grew larger. By the time he heard Paul's defense (about A.D. 59), Agrippa ruled Abilene, Iturea, Trachonitis, and part of Galilee. He remained loyal to his Roman superiors, although he often intervened on behalf of his Jewish subjects and tried to prevent the rebellion of A.D. 66–70. During his lifetime, Agrippa's close relationship with his sister Bernice was a constant scandal. Agrippa never married, and died about A.D. 100.

PAUL BEFORE AGRIPPA

Agrippa and Bernice made a courtesy visit to Caesarea to see the new Roman

A bronze coin (lepton), minted in Jerusalem, depicts Herod Agrippa I, king of Judea.

governor, Festus. The governor confessed his confusion about how to deal with his Jewish subjects' religious dispute with Paul, and asked Agrippa for advice. The next day Paul was given the opportunity to plead his own case before Agrippa, Bernice, and "all the leading men of the city." Paul apparently had a high opinion of Agrippa as one "well acquainted with all the Jewish customs and controversies" and as a person who truly believed the prophets (Acts 26:3,27), and so he spoke freely about his conversion and Christ's resurrection.

The old hymn "Almost Persuaded" was inspired by Agrippa's response to Paul (Acts 26:28). But Agrippa's statement "Almost thou persuadest me to be a Christian" (KJV) is better translated by the NIV: "Do you think that in such a short time you can persuade me to be a Christian?"

Afterward, Agrippa advised Festus that Paul could have been set free if he had not already appealed to Caesar's higher court in Rome. *See also* Appeal to Caesar; Herod.

LEARNING FROM AGRIPPA'S LIFE

Some see Agrippa's "almost persuaded" remark as the response of a cynic; others as the reaction of a man resisting conviction; still others as the cry of a person moved but pleading for more time to consider the claims of Christ. Does the text or what we know of Agrippa make any one of these interpretations more likely? What if Agrippa's relationship with Bernice was incestuous, as rumor then insisted? What if Paul's evident respect for Agrippa's religious understanding was not simply a polite introduction to his defense but a totally accurate evaluation of the man? It is valuable to think about questions like these, even if we can't answer them, because they encourage us to explore what is likely to help or hinder response to the Gospel by people of our own day.

Ahab [AY-hab; "father is brother"]. One of Israel's most wicked yet most successful kings, who ruled the Northern Kingdom 874–853 B.C. **Scripture:** 1 Ki. 16–22; 2 Chr. 18. **Father:** Omri. **Wife:** Jezebel. **Sons:** Ahaziah, Jehoram. **Daughter:** Athaliah.

BACKGROUND

Ahab inherited a powerful kingdom from his father, Omri. An aggressive and successful ruler himself, he fortified a number of cities bordering on Aram (Syria), with which he engaged in several wars (1 Ki. 20:1-34).

When the Assyrian conqueror Shalmaneser III invaded the area, Ahab joined with Aram and other Middle Eastern nations to resist him. An Assyrian monument commemorating the battle of Qarqar (853 B.C.) records Ahab's contribution of 10,000 soldiers and 2,000 chariots to the combined forces. This compares with only 1,200 chariots mustered by the Arameans, giving some measure of Ahab's relative strength. This monolith inscription, now in the British Museum, is the oldest secular record mentioning an Israelite king. *See also* Aram; Assyria.

Another stone monument from the period, the Moabite Stone, tells of the successful revolt of the Moabites against Ahab. The Moabites had been defeated by Omri, Ahab's father, and forced to pay a yearly tribute to Israel. Halfway through the reign of Ahab, Moab refused to pay tribute and took back lost territory. After Ahab's death a military expedition sent to subdue Moab failed, and Israel was forced to recognize Moab's independence (2 Ki. 3).

Ahab also did much to beautify his capital of Samaria. The Bible remarks on his use of expensive ivory as decorative material (1 Ki. 22:39). *See also* Ivory; Samaria.

Religiously, Ahab was dominated by his wife, Jezebel, who actively promoted the lewd form of Baal worship practiced in her homeland, Sidon. First Kings 16:30-33 says that Ahab "did more evil in the eyes of the Lord than any of those [kings] before him. He not only considered it trivial to commit the sins of Jeroboam son of Nebat, but he also married Jezebel, daughter of Ethbaal king of the Sidonians, and began to serve Baal and worship him." *See also* Baal; Jeroboam I.

The biblical account focuses on Ahab's spiritual life and on the ongoing struggle in Israel between Baalism and biblical faith. The great prophet Elijah was his primary opponent, although other prophets were active during the spiritually critical years of Ahab's reign. *See also* Elijah; Micaiah.

LEARNING FROM AHAB'S LIFE

Scripture focuses on three major events in Ahab's life:

1. *Elijah's great drought* (1 Ki. 17,18). Ahab sat back while Jezebel waged a campaign to wipe out the worship of Yahweh (Jehovah) by killing the Lord's prophets and importing hundreds of pagan religious teachers to promote Baal worship (1 Ki. 18:4,22). The situation became so desperate that Elijah thought of himself as the only worshiper of the Lord left in Israel (19:14). In consoling Elijah, God revealed the reassuring information that in all Israel some 7,000 had not bowed down to Baal or adored him (19:18).

Moses had warned Israel that, if Israel turned away from the Lord, God would withhold the rains (Deut. 11:16,17). Elijah was thus sent to confront Ahab and announce in God's name, "There will be neither dew nor rain in the next few years except at my word" (1 Ki. 17:1). For three and a-half years (Jas. 5:17) no rains fell in Israel, and Ahab became desperate to keep the horses of his chariot forces alive, not to mention his people (1 Ki. 18:5). *See also* Rain.

Then Elijah confronted Ahab again and announced that the drought had come because "you have abandoned the Lord's commands and have followed the Baals"

The Moabite Stone, dating to about 830 B.C., tells of the revolt of the Moabites during King Ahab's reign. The black basalt stone, about 40 inches (one meter) tall, contains a 34-line inscription in a language closely related to biblical Hebrew.

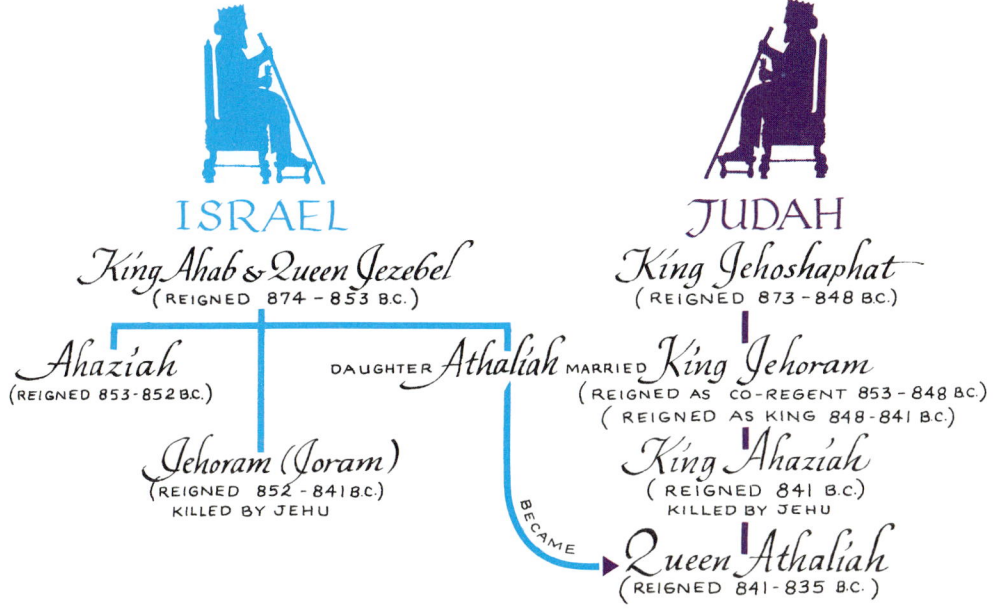

ISRAEL
King Ahab & Queen Jezebel
(REIGNED 874 - 853 B.C.)

Ahaziah
(REIGNED 853-852 B.C.)

Jehoram (Joram)
(REIGNED 852 - 841 B.C.)
KILLED BY JEHU

DAUGHTER *Athaliah* MARRIED

JUDAH
King Jehoshaphat
(REIGNED 873 - 848 B.C.)

King Jehoram
(REIGNED AS CO-REGENT 853 - 848 B.C.)
(REIGNED AS KING 848-841 B.C.)

King Ahaziah
(REIGNED 841 B.C.)
KILLED BY JEHU

BECAME

Queen Athaliah
(REIGNED 841-835 B.C.)

Above: Only ruins remain of Ahab's once-magnificent palace in Samaria; below: Ahab's marriage to Jezebel, princess of Tyre, gave him a political tie with the northwest, but in the northeast, the Arameans, with their capital at Damascus, were persistent foes.

(18:18). At Elijah's challenge, Ahab assembled Israel at Mount Carmel to witness a contest between Elijah and Baal's prophets. There, when Elijah prayed, fire from heaven consumed his sacrificial offering. Stunned, the people fell to the ground and cried, "The Lord, he is God!" (18:39). The 450 prophets of Baal were killed, and then the rains returned (18:41-46).

Ahab witnessed all these events. Yet he remained basically untouched. His wife's reaction was more direct. When Ahab told Jezebel, she sent a message to Elijah threatening his life.

In the drought and in the miracle at Mount Carmel, Ahab was given clear evidence that the Lord truly is God. Unlike his people, Ahab refused to acknowledge the Lord.

2. *The incident at Naboth's vineyard* (1 Ki. 21). Ahab wanted a vineyard owned by Naboth that lay close to his palace. He offered Naboth a fair price, but Naboth, following an OT law, refused (Lev. 25:23). Ahab sulked. Jezebel ridiculed her husband, but arranged in Ahab's name to have Naboth falsely accused of blasphemy and stoned to death. A delighted Ahab went immediately to take possession of the vineyard.

There Elijah again confronted him and told him that God would now bring disaster on Ahab. None of his children would survive, and the dogs would lick Ahab's blood in the same field where Naboth had died. Ahab had been given chance after chance to turn to the Lord. The murder of Naboth and Ahab's reaction showed how hard Ahab's heart had become.

3. *Ahab's wars with Ben-Hadad* (1 Ki. 20,22). Despite Ahab's apostasy and the Baal worship he promoted in Israel, God gave Israel two great victories in war with the Arameans (Syrians). The Lord sent a prophet to foretell the first victory, so that "you will know I am the Lord" (20:13), and to warn Ahab to prepare for a second Aramean invasion. Again Ahab was promised victory, both because of the Arameans' contempt for God and so that "you will know that I am the Lord" (20:28). But even in victory, Ahab proved unresponsive to God and was sullen and angry when rebuked by God's prophet (20:43).

Both of these victories must have taken place before the incident of Naboth's vineyard.

Prior to a third battle, Ahab's death was predicted by the prophet Micaiah (1 Ki. 22). In that engagement, Ahab was pierced by an arrow shot "at random." He died, and the blood on the floor of his chariot was later licked up by dogs in the place where Naboth had died.

From a secular point of view, Ahab was a successful and powerful ruler. From a spiritual point of view, he was an utter failure whose unwise choice of a pagan wife and whose rejection of the Lord brought his people great suffering and loss.

Ahasuerus [uh-HAZ-yoo-AIR-uhs; "ruling hero"]. Known in secular history as Xerxes I, who ruled Persia 486–465 B.C. and in Scripture as the ruler who married Esther. *See* Xerxes.

Ahaz [AY-haz; "he grasped" or "Yahweh holds him fast"]. Evil eleventh king of Judah 735–715 B.C., who burned a son as a human sacrifice. **Scripture:** 2 Ki. 16; 2 Chr. 28; Isa. 7. **Father:** Jotham. **Wife:** Abijah. **Son:** Hezekiah.

BACKGROUND

While Ahaz ruled Judah, two neighboring kingdoms—Aram (Syria) under King Rezin and Israel (the northern kingdom) under King Pekah—formed an alliance to withstand the superpower Assyria. Ahaz, however, refused to join them. So Rezin and Pekah invaded Judah, determined to set up the "son of Tabeel" as a puppet king. Judah lost 120,000 men and 200,000 captives in battle. Though Ahaz survived, his land was devastated. Both the Edomites to the east and the Philistines to the south and west took advantage of this opportunity to invade. Terrified, Ahaz stripped the Temple and capital city of their gold and silver and sent it as a bribe to the king of Assyria, Tiglath-Pileser III. The Assyrians did invade Aram, taking Damascus and killing Rezin. But then Tiglath-Pileser demanded more tribute from Ahaz. Ahaz paid as much as he could, but it was not enough. It soon became clear that Assyria intended to annex Judah too.

AHAZ'S SPIRITUAL LIFE

The biblical text focuses on Ahaz's relationship with God. Although preceded by

This wall relief from Tiglath-Pileser's palace shows tribute being brought from vassal states. King Ahaz sent gold and silver from Jerusalem about this time.

four relatively godly kings, the young Ahaz "walked in the ways of the kings of Israel and also made cast idols for worshiping the Baals. He . . . sacrificed his sons in the fire, following the detestable ways of the nations the Lord had driven out before the Israelites" (2 Chr. 28:2,3). According to Isa. 8:19, Ahaz also consulted mediums and spiritists. *See also* Topheth.

After the defeat of Rezin, Ahaz visited Tiglath-Pileser in Damascus. There he saw an altar whose design he liked, and commanded that it be duplicated to replace the Solomonic altar of sacrifice in the Jerusalem Temple (2 Ki. 16:10-14).

After the Assyrian intentions to invade Judah became clear, Ahaz became a complete apostate. He closed the Temple, stripped it of its holy objects, and openly worshiped the gods of Damascus.

Ahaz was so despised by his people that on his death he was refused burial with the other kings of Judah (2 Chr. 28:27).

LEARNING FROM AHAZ'S LIFE

An incident from Isa. 7 provides the key for a study of Ahaz. When word of the plans of Rezin and Pekah to attack Judah reached Ahaz, God sent Isaiah to meet him. Speaking in the name of Judah's sovereign Lord, Isaiah promised Ahaz, "It will not happen." The power of the two enemies would be utterly shattered "within sixty-five years" (7:8). Isaiah then commanded Ahaz to ask the Lord for a sign (miraculous event) as proof that this prophecy would come true. Ahaz refused, hypocritically claiming he was unwilling to "put the Lord to the test." *See* Sign.

An angry Isaiah then uttered the famous prophecy concerning the virgin birth of a child to be called Immanuel ["with us is God!"]. But he also uttered a short-term "sign" prophecy. Pointing forward to a son (Shear-Jashub) whom he would soon beget by a virgin prophetess he would shortly take in marriage (7:3), Isaiah promised that before his child would "know enough to reject the wrong and choose the right" both Israel and Aram would be laid waste by Assyria (7:16,17). And then Assyria, to whom Ahaz planned to appeal, would turn on Judah and bring years of intense suffering upon her (7:18-25).

In the confrontation Isaiah expressed a principle that is as true for us as it was for Ahaz: "If you do not stand firm in your faith, you will not stand at all" (7:9). But Ahaz rejected God and turned to Assyria as Judah's hope. In the disasters that followed, Ahaz's rejection of the Lord became even more decisive.

Ahaziah [ay-huh-ZI-uh; "Yahweh has grasped"]. The name of two biblical kings: (1) The evil ninth king of Israel who ruled 853–852 B.C. He consulted Baal-zebub rather than the Lord when he was injured. **Scripture:** 1 Ki. 22; 2 Ki. 1; 2 Chr. 20. **Parents:** Ahab and Jezebel. **Children:** none.
(2) The evil sixth king of Judah who ruled 841 B.C. **Scripture:** 2 Ki. 8,9; 2 Chr. 22. He is called Jehoahaz in 2 Chr. 21:16,17, where he is identified as the youngest son of Jehoram. **Parents:** Jehoram and Athaliah. **Grandparents:** Ahab and Jezebel. **Sister:** Jehosheba. **Surviving son:** Joash.

AHAZIAH, KING OF ISRAEL

When Ahaziah succeeded his father Ahab as king, he inherited an ongoing conflict with the Moabites. Formerly a subject state paying yearly tribute to Israel, Moab openly rebelled against Ahaziah, seizing several fortified cities on the border. Ahaziah could not put down the revolt. Later, he attempted to reopen a sea route to Tarshish used in Solomon's time. This effort also failed as a storm wiped out a joint Israel/Judah fleet anchored at Ezion Geber. *See also* Ahab; Moab.

In the second year of his reign, Ahaziah was injured in a fall from the roof of his palace in Samaria. He sent to ask a pagan deity if he would recover, but Elijah intercepted the messengers, and announced that the apostate king would die (2 Ki. 1). Ahaziah was succeeded by his brother, Jehoram.

AHAZIAH, KING OF JUDAH

This Ahaziah ruled Judah for less than a year. Encouraged in evil by his mother, Athaliah, he joined Israel in an ill-fated campaign against Hazael, king of Aram. Ahaziah then visited his uncle, Joram, who was king of Israel and had been wounded in the battle with Hazael. On that visit Ahaziah was killed by Jehu, a military commander who also murdered and supplanted Joram as king of Israel.

LEARNING FROM THEIR LIVES

Both of these kings died young. Each during his brief lifetime followed evil. It is no coincidence that each of these wicked rulers was a direct descendant of Ahab and Jezebel, the most evil pair portrayed in the Bible. God does not leave the guilty unpunished; "he punishes the children and their children for the sin of the fathers to the third and fourth generation" (Ex. 34:7). Yet this verse does not portray a vindictive God. Rather, it realistically assesses the impact of parents' evil choices on future generations. Ahab and Jezebel set a pattern which their children and

grandchildren chose to follow. This negative example underscores the importance of establishing patterns of godly living in our homes.

Ahithophel [ah-HITH-oh-fel; "brother of foolishness"]. The brilliant adviser of David, who joined Absalom's revolt about 980 B.C. **Scripture:** 2 Sam. 15–17. **Parents:** unknown. Some believe he is the grandfather of Bathsheba (*compare* 2 Sam. 23:34 and 2 Sam. 11:3) and joined Absalom because of David's adultery with his granddaughter (2 Sam. 11,12).

BACKGROUND

Ahithophel had an acute intelligence, so great that his advice "was like that of one who inquires of God" (2 Sam. 16:23). Word that Ahithophel had joined Absalom shook David, who prayed fervently that God would "turn Ahithophel's counsel into foolishness" (15:31). While fleeing from Absalom, David persuaded another loyal adviser, Hushai, to stay behind to counteract Ahithophel's influence.

Ahithophel's first advice was followed. When Absalom entered Jerusalem, he put up tents on the palace roof and publicly violated David's concubines. This act established his intention to supplant his father: there could be no compromise after such a public insult. Absalom and his followers were now totally committed.

Ahithophel then advised Absalom to pursue David immediately, to kill him before he could assemble a loyal army from Transjordan. But Hushai was able to delay Absalom by urging him to assemble a huge army of his own before crossing the Jordan. David thus gained time to escape and gather his loyal followers around him to resist the forces against him.

Ahithophel, however, realized exactly what delay would mean. When Absalom failed to pursue David immediately, Ahithophel knew all was lost. He returned to his home and hanged himself.

LEARNING FROM AHITHOPHEL'S LIFE

Ahithophel's penetrating analysis of the political situation was completely accurate. Yet ultimately that analysis did not help, for Ahithophel enlisted his intelligence in an evil cause, against the person God had appointed to the throne of Israel. All Ahithophel's wisdom was unable to thwart the intent of God to bless David.

No human ability, enlisted against God's purposes, can prosper.

Ai [AY-i; "heap" or "ruin"]. City at which Joshua's forces met defeat after the victory at Jericho about 1400 B.C.

BACKGROUND

The name Ai (literally, "heap" or "ruin") may suggest that even in biblical

In the first battle against Ai, Joshua's troops were routed; later, after the sin of Achan was dealt with, Ai was destroyed, and the king of Ai was hanged, as depicted in this medieval Bible illumination.

41

times this city was located by or near ancient ruins. The biblical account places Ai east of Bethel (Josh. 7:2) and near Jericho and Jerusalem. Most archaeologists place Ai at a site named Et Tell. Since the topography of the area hardly fits the biblical account, this identification has caused considerable debate. Excavations at Et Tell indicate that a large, prosperous city there was destroyed about 2200 B.C., long before Joshua's conquest of Canaan. After 2200 B.C. Et Tell seems to have been abandoned for a thousand years. Certainly there was no major city at Et Tell for Joshua to destroy at the time of the conquest, whether in 1405 or in 1250 B.C.

A variety of solutions have been suggested, ranging from dismissal of the biblical account as folklore, to the belief that Ai was little more than an outpost settlement, to the argument that Et Tell should not be identified as biblical Ai. More archaeological work needs to be done in the area.

BIBLICAL SIGNIFICANCE

The Book of Joshua sets Ai in counterpoint to Jericho. At Jericho, the Israelites obeyed God's command and marched silently around the city for seven days. On the seventh day, the people shouted and the city walls collapsed. The lesson of Jericho was that obedience brings victory. The text then tells of an expedition sent against the smaller city of Ai, where Israel was defeated. God revealed that the defeat was caused by the sin of one man who had violated God's command and taken spoil from Jericho. The lesson of Ai was that disobedience brings defeat. *See also* Achan; Jericho.

These two events, which occurred in the early stages of Israel's invasion of Canaan,

were vital object lessons for God's people. As surely as obedience brings blessing, disobedience leads to disaster.

air Two idiomatic uses of *air* occur in Scripture. (1) Paul says in 1 Cor. 9:26 that he does not "fight like a man beating the air." That is, he is not shadowboxing, but is in a serious struggle with a real opponent, seeking to win a real prize. (2) Paul in Eph. 2:2 describes Satan as "the ruler of the kingdom of the air." This image communicated powerfully with both Greeks and Jews, who viewed the air as the realm of demons and evil spirits. *See also* Demon.

The often-repeated phrase "birds of the air" is literally "birds of the heavens," or "birds of the sky." *See also* Birds.

Akeldama [ah-KEL-de-mah; "field of blood"]. (Aceldama, KJV.) When Judas tried to return the 30 pieces of silver he received to betray Jesus, the priests who paid it refused to accept the money (Mt. 27:3-10). Judas threw the coins on the Temple floor and left. As blood money, these coins could not be returned to the Temple treasury, so they were spent to buy a field outside Jerusalem to use as a burial ground for foreigners. Tradition says this field lay in the Valley of Hinnom.

alabaster A soft, semi-transparent stone, usually light-colored and sometimes banded. It is soft enough for carving yet capable of being polished, and is easily shaped into beautiful vases or boxes. Each of the synoptic Gospels tells of a woman who came to Jesus in Bethany "with an alabaster jar ['box,' KJV] of very expensive perfume," and anointed Jesus' feet.

Archaeologists have found many alabaster objects from biblical times. The most expensive alabaster was imported to Palestine from Egypt. Made of hard calcium carbonate or gypsum, Egyptian alabaster was especially valued for making perfume flasks and for use as "marble" facings on buildings. Palestinian alabaster was of softer calcium sulfate, and was also used to make vases and flasks.

Containers of all sorts were carved from alabaster and then polished. This collection found at Ein-Samya dates from the time of Joshua, well over 3,000 years ago.

BACKGROUND

For 200 years, city-states established by the Greeks along the Aegean Sea had been dominated by the great Persian Empire. Alexander's father, Philip of Macedon, forged a coalition of Greek cities in 338 B.C. with the expressed intent of invading Persia, but died in 336. The 20-year-old Alexander then became king of Macedon and leader of the anti-Persian cause. Two years later, with his authority firmly established in Europe, Alexander led 40,000 men across the Hellespont to invade the territory controlled by the Persians.

CONQUEST

Alexander's outnumbered forces won victory after victory. They defeated the Persians on the banks of the Granicus River, enabling Alexander to march south along the Aegean coast. By this maneuver he was able to relieve the Greek states there and also to threaten the bases from which the powerful Persian fleet endangered Greek shipping in the Aegean. But Persia's "great king," Darius, who worried that his subordinates would be unable to stop Alexander's invading force, now appeared with a massive army. Alexander fought, and in 333 B.C. defeated Darius at Issus. Alexander then continued south. He took Tyre, using a tactic prophesied by Ezekiel centuries earlier (Ezek. 26). Alexander then led his forces into Egypt, where he founded the most famous city that bears his name, Alexandria.

By 331 B.C., Alexander was again ready to challenge the might of Persia. He led his forces north, passing through Palestine. Then in a series of victories he crushed Darius and took Susa, the capital of the Empire; Persepolis, its treasury; and Babylon. When Darius was murdered by a subordinate, Alexander declared himself Darius's heir and ruler of the Persian Empire. Alexander retained the administrative structure of the Empire, but went about setting up Greek-style cities throughout it.

In 327 B.C., Alexander conquered Bactria (modern Afghanistan) and passed on into India. When his armies refused to go further, Alexander returned to Babylon. He died there at age 33, the victim of a fever after a period of heavy drinking.

After Alexander's death, his empire was

This bust of Alexander the Great was carved in Egyptian alabaster in the first century B.C.

divided among four of his generals. The prophecy of Daniel, particularly 8:8-12 and 11:2-4, accurately describes the course of the Persian Empire, Alexander's invasion, and the division of the empire after his death. *See also* Daniel.

ALEXANDER'S INFLUENCE

Alexander lived during the 400 years between the time of Malachi, the last OT prophet, and the coming of Christ. While Alexander's actions fit the prophetic vision of Daniel, and his conquest of Tyre is accurately described by Ezekiel, Alexander himself is named only in the Apocrypha. Yet Alexander's impact on sacred history was great.

Through his conquests, Alexander spread and firmly rooted Greek culture and language throughout the eastern world. The Hellenized cities attracted large Jewish communities. In time, there came to be about a million Jews in Egypt, with another two or three million in Greek-speaking regions such as Syria, Asia Minor, Libya, Greece, and Rome. Jewish members of these communities were affected by Greek thought and values, and many lost their ability to speak the Aramaic of their homeland. Their need of a Greek version of

43

the OT led Ptolemy II of Philadelphius (285–246 B.C.) to sponsor the translation known as the Septuagint. This made the OT available not only to Jews but also to the general population. A number of Jewish Hellenists (Jews who adopted aspects of Greek culture) even attempted to show that the nobler visions of Greek philosophers had their source in the Jewish Scriptures.

The availability of the OT in Greek and the efforts of Jewish apologists had an impact. One Jewish Hellenist, Philo (20 B.C.–A.D. 40), rejoiced because the laws of Moses "attract and win the attention of all, of barbarians, of Greeks, of dwellers on this mainland, of nations of the East and West, of Europe and Asia, and of the whole inhabited world from end to end." How striking this is, in view of the fact that the Book of Acts reveals that most churches founded by Paul had a core not of Jewish believers, but of Gentiles who had already been attracted to the synagogue and the purity of OT faith. *See also* God-fearing.

In two ways, then, Alexander's Hellenization of the eastern world prepared that world for the Christian message: (1) it provided a common tongue, Greek, in which the Gospel could be preached and spread abroad, and (2) through the activities of Hellenistic Jews, Gentiles were attracted to the OT's vision of God, and were thus readied to become the believing core of local churches everywhere.

algum tree *See* Almug tree.

alien A foreigner or outsider. Since Israel existed as a nation as well as a faith community, it needed laws governing the rights and treatment of aliens. The NT uses the term only in analogies designed to help Christians better understand their relationship with God and with the world.

OLD TESTAMENT

Three Hebrew words are translated "alien," "foreigner," or "stranger" in English versions. These words have different shades of meaning, but together convey the idea of a person who is not related, is unfamiliar, and who thus does not share the rights of community members. The OT Law detailed the rights, privileges, and obligations of any alien who visited Israel or settled there as a resident.

Several OT passages state general principles for dealing with aliens. "The same law applies to the native-born and to the alien living among you" (Ex. 12:49; Lev. 24:22). Applying this principle, the Law

Alexander the Great carved out an empire that stretched from Greece to the borders of India. He crushed the Persians under Darius twice before conquering the western Indian provinces. He died in 323 B.C. in Babylon. Inset: Silver coin with Alexander's likeness, minted in Thrace in Asia Minor about 300 B.C.

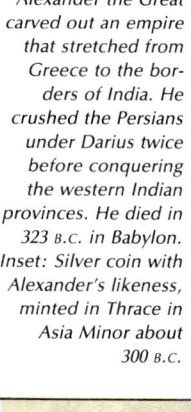

guaranteed foreigners justice (Deut. 1:16) and warned Israelites not to oppress them (Ex. 22:21; Lev. 19:33,34; Num. 15:15,16). While the Law did set out certain distinctions between an Israelite and a resident alien, the obligation to love and treat aliens like fellow-citizens is a striking aspect of the Mosaic code (Lev. 19:34; Deut. 10:19).

Although the Law commands a gracious attitude toward the alien, statements by the prophets and in the Gospels show that aliens were typically viewed and often treated with hostility (*compare* Jer. 7:5,6; Mal. 3:5; Acts 11:2,3; Gal. 2:11-14).

NEW TESTAMENT

The NT uses two Greek words, *parepidēmos* and *paroikos*, for people who are merely away from home. A third, *xenos*, emphasizes the differentness of a person, practice, or doctrine.

Unlike OT Law, Roman law observed a great distinction between citizens and other inhabitants of the Empire. All who lacked Roman citizenship were considered aliens, and were subject to the laws of their homeland even when in other countries. The NT thus draws an analogy for Christians. As citizens of God's Kingdom, we are subject to his laws even while we live as aliens in this world. *See also* Citizen.

Paul, who was a Roman citizen, tends to emphasize the rights of Christians as citizens of Christ's Kingdom. However, Peter (1 Pet. 2:11) and the writer of Hebrews (Heb. 11:13) see the Christian experience from the viewpoint of the alien, who was without protection or rights in the Roman Empire. No citizen could be beaten, but an alien commonly was tortured if suspected of a crime. A citizen could bring an alien into a Roman court, but an alien had no access to the Roman's justice system. Thus the Roman Empire for all its benefits was essentially hostile to the non-citizen. Peter reminds us that as "aliens and strangers in the world" we can expect to gain no benefit from the world or from its ways. Common sense demands that as aliens we "abstain from sinful desires, which war against your soul" (1 Pet. 2:11), and commit ourselves to doing the good which characterizes the eternal Kingdom of God.

alienate (1) To make unfriendly or hostile; (2) to cause to be withdrawn or detached. These two senses of the word can cause confusion for modern readers. But the three NT Greek words for alienation are distinctly defined.

ALIENATED NONBELIEVERS

Those who do not know Christ are de-

ISRAEL'S LAWS REGARDING ALIENS

Topic	Content	Scripture
Worship	Could offer sacrifices	Lev. 17:8
	Could celebrate some religious festivals	Deut. 16:11,13
	Forbidden to work on Sabbath	Ex. 20:10
	Forbidden to work on Day of Atonement	Lev. 16:29
	Heard Law read each Sabbatical year	Deut. 31:10-13
	Could not share in Passover unless circumcised	Ex. 12:43,48
	Must not eat leaven during Passover week	Ex. 12:19
	Not permitted to enter sanctuary unless circumcised	Ezek. 44:9
	Forbidden to eat blood	Lev. 17:12
	Not required to pay tithes	Deut. 14:28,29
Criminal Matters	Were stoned for blasphemy	Num. 15:30
	Were liable to same penalties as Israelites	Lev. 24:16
Morality	Were subject to Israel's sexual regulations	Lev. 18:26
Social Matters	Could sue and be sued	Deut. 1:16
	Could apply for welfare	Deut. 14:29
	Could glean at harvest time	Lev. 19:10
	Could use cities of refuge	Num. 35:15
	Alien employees must not be defrauded by Jewish employers	Deut. 24:14
	Must pay interest on money borrowed	Deut. 23:20
	Alien debts were not canceled on Sabbatical years	Deut. 15:3
	Alien slaves were not freed during the Year of Jubilee	Lev. 25:46

scribed in Ephesians and Colossians as "alienated" (*apallōtrioō*) from God. These are "enemies" who engage in "evil behavior" (Col. 1:21). They are "separate from Christ" (Eph. 2:12) and also from "the life of God" (Eph. 4:18). Blind and insensitive to spiritual things, the lost are hostile to God. Yet believers know that they were once like this, too, so even the alienated can be "brought near [to God] through the blood of Christ" (Eph. 2:13).

ALIENATED CHRISTIANS

Galatians 5:4 warns, "You who are trying to be justified by law have been alienated from Christ; you have fallen away from grace." The Greek word here is *katargeō*, which means "separated from" or "disconnected." Paul's point is that a person who looks to the Law as an aid to Christian living must look away from grace. Such a believer, who no longer relies on grace, is temporarily disconnected from the source of spiritual power, so that his relationship with Christ has no practical value for daily Christian living. *See also* Grace; Law.

Some versions also use "alienate" in Gal. 4:17, which describes some teachers who wanted the Galatians to be "shut out" (*ekkleiō*) of any relationship with Paul.

ALLEGORIES IN SCRIPTURE

The Bible uses the word *allēgoreō* only once, in Gal. 4:24. There Paul finds a hidden meaning in the OT story of Abraham's expulsion of his son Ishmael. Paul suggests that the historical events, when viewed allegorically, support his teaching that the Law and grace are contradictory and cannot coexist (*see* Gal. 4:21-31).

Many commentators view the Song of Songs as an allegory. They take this ancient love poem to speak of either the relationship between God and Israel, or the relationship between Christ and his Church. *See also* Song of Songs.

ALLEGORICAL INTERPRETATION

In Paul's day, some Jewish commentators, like later Christian interpreters, approached Scripture allegorically. They discounted the literal and historical meaning of reported events and looked for deeper, hidden intent. One rabbi roughly contemporary with Paul suggested that "as a hammer strikes many sparks, so does a single verse of Scripture have many meanings." Philo, the Jewish philosopher of 20 B.C.–A.D. 40, said that his method of looking for inner meanings had been followed by Jews in Alexandria for many generations.

The NT writers, while using various figures of speech freely, do not treat OT events as allegories, but as history. The meaning of the events is to be found in what actually happened, not in something else that the reported events are supposed to represent.

Despite the example of the NT, many early Christian expositors adopted an allegorical approach to interpreting the Bible. Origen (A.D. 185–254) used allegorical interpretation to read Platonic philosophy into the Bible. Augustine (A.D. 354–430) and even Thomas Aquinas (A.D. 1225–1274) are well-known church fathers whose sometimes fanciful interpretations rested on allegory. *See also* Interpretation of Scripture.

Unlike an allegory, in which each element has meaning, the point of a parable depends on a single major resemblance. In Jesus' parable of the sower, Christ focuses our attention on how different people respond to the Word of God.

allegory A story in which people, things, and happenings have a hidden moral or spiritual meaning. It is a description of one thing by talking of another.

It differs from a parable or a type, although parables and types may contain allegorical elements. A parable compares one thing to another but does not confuse them; in an allegory the qualities and relationships of one may be transferred to the other.

alleluia (KJV) A transliterated form of the Hebrew *Hallelu Yah*, meaning "Praise the Lord." *Hallelu Yah* is found in the OT only in Pss. 104–150, where it is used 23 times at the beginning or end of various psalms (*see* Ps. 106:1,48). Many believe it called the congregation to participate in reciting the psalm.

The form *alleluia* is found only in Rev. 19:1,3,4,6 (KJV; *hallelujah*, NIV). Here, all in heaven join to praise God for his culminating acts of judgment on the wicked at the end of history, and for the joy about to be experienced by his saints. The word *alleluia* is so meaningful that it was incorporated untranslated into Christian liturgy and has become an integral part of Christian worship. It is applied to the resurrection of Jesus Christ and to life in the spirit of the resurrection.

alliance A covenant or treaty between nations. The Mosaic Law commanded Israel, "do not make a covenant" (*berit*) with the people of Canaan or their gods. This principle, often violated in Israel's history, had at least two important purposes.

1. *Non-alliance would protect the purity of biblical faith.* In the biblical world, international treaties were typically ratified by marriage between royal houses. Such a marriage would dilute commitment to God and would probably introduce worship of the bride's pagan deities into Israel. This happened in two notable cases: (*a*) In the process of developing a network of international treaties, Solomon married many foreign wives. First Kings 11:4 reports, "As Solomon grew old, his wives turned his heart after other gods." He even built worship centers for them near Jerusalem. (*b*) Later, King Ahab of Israel married Jezebel, a daughter of the royal family of Sidon. As a result, he began to serve Baal and worship him (1 Ki. 16:31). In each case, violation of the principle of national non-alliance proved spiritually disastrous for the king and for the nation.

2. *Alliance would promote dependence on something other than God.* Joshua 23:10-12 suggests that to make an alliance is to "turn away" from the "God who fights for you." The only security Israel could know was to be found in God; to make international treaties was to transfer one's faith from God to men.

Prophets often warned against international alliances (Isa. 20; 28:15-18; 30:1,2; Jer. 2:18,36; Hos. 8:9). But the history of Israel and Judah abounds with examples of disastrous treaties (1 Ki. 20:34-43; 2 Ki. 22; 2 Chr. 18; Isa. 7:1-9).

The principle of non-alliance in the OT extended to other forms of international cooperation as well, for Jehoshaphat of Judah was rebuked by a prophet for joining in a trade venture with Ahaziah of Israel (*see* 2 Chr. 20:35-37). This OT principle of non-alliance with those who do not know or depend on God is helpful in understanding the reasons for Paul's instruction in 2 Cor. 6:14 not to be "yoked together" with unbelievers. *See also* Separate.

allotment The division of land among the tribes and families of Israel. Before the Israelites entered Canaan, God commanded Moses, "The land is to be allotted to them as an inheritance based on the number of names. To a larger group give a larger inheritance, and to a smaller group a smaller one." But, the passage continues, "be sure that the land is distributed by lot [*goral*]" (Num. 26:53-55).

Joshua 13–21 describes the division of Canaan after it was conquered, with each tribe given an area appropriate to its size, and the area then subdivided and distributed "by lot," a process perhaps analogous to modern "drawing straws." Each family's holding in Canaan thus became known as its "allotment" (*goral*), "portion" (*heleq*), or "inheritance" (*nahalah*). The Israelites did *not* view this as dividing the land "by chance." As Prov. 16:33 puts it, "The lot is cast into the lap, but its every decision is from the Lord." Thus the land assigned to each family group was viewed as a gift, given to them personally by God himself. *See also* Lots.

While an Israelite might sell the right to farm his land, the land itself could never be sold. Every fiftieth year, the rights to each family's portion would revert to its original owner. *See also* Jubilee.

ALLOTMENT AS A METAPHOR
David used the allotment of the Promised Land as a poetic image to express his deep sense of God's active involvement in his life:

Lord, you have assigned me my portion and
     my cup:
     you have made my lot sure.
The boundary lines have fallen for me
     in pleasant places;
     surely I have a delightful inheritance.
                              (Ps. 16:5,6)

David knew that all that had happened to him had not come about by blind chance. God had been at work in and through each of David's experiences and, despite his times of anguish, David realized that what God had given was good.

Almighty A name of God. In most versions of the OT, it translates the Hebrew *shaddai*. From a root *sadad* ("be violent, very powerful"), this word brings out God's transcendent power surpassing all human authority and all the adverse powers of nature.

The term appears to be a very old one. Even before God introduced himself to Moses as "Yahweh," he had manifested himself to the patriarchs as "the Almighty" (Ex. 6:2,3). The Book of Job accounts for 31 of the OT's 48 uses of *shaddai*, which seems to testify to the antiquity of that book. Early Jewish commentators suggested that *shaddai* emphasizes God's "all sufficiency" as well as his power.

In the NT, *pantokratōr*, which literally means "all powerful," is translated as "almighty." Nine of ten uses of this word are in Revelation, where it is almost always spoken *to* God in praise. It is used *of* God in Rev. 19:15 to describe him as he steps personally into history to execute final judgment on a rebellious humankind. *See also* God ("Names of God" Chart).

The pink blossoms of the early-blooming almond tree were a promise that other flowers would soon appear.

almond tree The almond tree of the Bible is the *amygdalus communis*, whose nuts were prized in Bible times as they are today for their unique flavor. The Hebrew name, *shaqed*, means "early," possibly due to the fact that the almond tree blossoms before its leaves appear.

The almond is mentioned eleven times in the OT. Two are of special interest: (1) Jeremiah 1:11,12 contains a play on words. God shows the prophet a branch, which Jeremiah identifies as an almond (*shaqed*). God then says, "You have seen well, for I am watching [*shoqed*] over my word to perform it" (RSV). This verb has the same sound as the "almond," but comes from a different root, actually meaning "be wakeful, watch over." (2) The staff that Aaron brought before the Lord to demonstrate to

48

the Israelites that God had called him to be their high priest was an almond branch (Num. 17:8). Overnight the staff not only budded, but also produced mature fruit.

almsgiving The practice of giving to the poor, literally "doing kind acts" (*eleēmosynē*).

OLD TESTAMENT

The Jewish attitude toward almsgiving was deeply rooted in the OT's expressed concern for the poor and needy in society. God had said: "There will always be poor people in the land. Therefore I command you to be openhanded toward your brothers and toward the poor and needy in your land" (Deut. 15:11). *See also* Poor.

Later, the prophets emphasized that it was not ritual observance that pleased God, but rather social justice. Through Isaiah God announced,

Is not this the kind of fasting I have chosen:
to loose the chains of injustice
and untie the cords of the yoke,
to set the oppressed free
and break every yoke?
Is it not to share your food with the hungry
and to provide the poor wanderer with
shelter—
when you see the naked, to clothe him,
and not to turn away from your own flesh
and blood?
Then your light will break forth like the
dawn,
and your healing will quickly appear;
then your righteousness will go before you,
and the glory of God will be your
rear guard. (Isa. 58:6-8)

Throughout the OT, almsgiving and righteousness go together. Job, portrayed as a "blameless and upright man," defended himself against his accusers by pointing out, "I rescued the poor who cried for help, and the fatherless who had none to assist him." In so doing, he says, "I was a father to the needy; I took up the case of the stranger. I broke the fangs of the wicked and snatched the victims from their teeth" (Job 29:12,16,17).

"He who oppresses the poor," says Prov. 14:31, "shows contempt for their Maker, but whoever is kind to the needy honors God." And Ps. 112:5 expresses this general truth: "Good will come to him who is generous and lends freely, who conducts his affairs with justice." In the best of rabbinic teaching, the wealth of the rich was something held in trust for the poor. The wealthy were God's agents on earth, whose mission was to be a blessing to others.

Understanding this deeply entrenched view, we gain some insight into the power of Jesus' story about the rich man who would not even share the crumbs that fell from his table with the beggar Lazarus, who lay outside his gate. This rich man had not listened to Moses' teaching on social justice; the torment the rich man felt after death was deserved (Lk. 16:19-31).

We can also understand why some of the wealthy in Christ's day made a great show of almsgiving. They not only, in their view, gained merit with God, but also won a reputation on earth as pious and righteous men.

In confronting this practice, Christ did not speak against almsgiving. Instead, he condemned the hypocrisy of a public donation intended primarily to win human applause rather than divine pleasure. When one gives to the needy, Jesus taught, it is to be a private transaction between the person, the poor, and the Lord (Mt. 6:1-5).

The Book of Acts mentions almsgiving in four passages. Acts 3 mentions a cripple who begged alms. Acts 9:36 tells us that Dorcas was known for her continual charity ("alms-deeds," KJV). Acts 10:1-6 describes the almsgiving of the Roman military officer Cornelius, whose generosity and religious commitment had won the favorable attention of the Lord. Acts 24:17 refers to Paul's visit to the Temple at Jerusalem, where he gave "gifts for the poor."

Although almsgiving is not mentioned in the rest of the NT, a concern for the needy infuses descriptions of early church life, and strong, direct commands to care for the poor are found throughout the teaching of the Epistles. *See also* Give.

The precious red wood of the almug tree was imported from Ophir for use in Solomon's Temple.

almug tree Probably the red sandalwood (*pterocarpus santalinus*). According to 1 Ki. 10:11, Solomon imported the bright red wood to decorate his palace and the Temple, and also to make stringed instru-

ments. This wood is still valued in the East for making musical instruments. The same wood is called "algum" in a parallel passage, 2 Chr. 9:10,11.

The 2 Chronicles text notes, "Nothing like them had ever been seen in Judah." This tree does not grow in Palestine, although smaller red sandalwood trees do grow in Lebanon.

aloe A fragrant wood used as perfume. Some doubt that the aloe (*'ahalot*) of the OT is the same as the aloe (*aloē*) of the NT.

Old Testament aloe is associated with expensive imported perfumes and fragrances. Many have suggested it was eaglewood (*aquilaria agallocha*), which when it decays releases a sweet fragrance that repels insects. This substance, mentioned along with myrrh in Ps. 45:8, may also be referred to in Jn. 19:39,40. There, Jesus' body was wrapped in linens and some 75 pounds of "a mixture of myrrh and aloes." This was "according to the burial customs of the Jews."

Some have argued that "aloes" in John refers to *aloe socotrina*, a somewhat bitter medicinal plant used in Egyptian embalming. Others believe that Jewish burial custom featured the more expensive, fragrant perfume.

In any case, the mixture of myrrh and aloes used to prepare Jesus' body for burial was expensive. It is significant that Nicodemus, a member of the Sanhedrin who had previously consulted with Jesus in private, made this contribution.

Alpha and Omega The first and last letters of the Greek alphabet, used in Revelation as a divine name. The phrase appears three times, each time in a similar formula spoken first by God the Father and then by Jesus:

"I am the Alpha and the Omega, and who is,
who was, and who is to come, the
Almighty." (1:8)
"I am the Alpha and the Omega, the
beginning and the end." (21:6)
"I am the Alpha and Omega, the first and
the last, the beginning and the end."
(22:13)

The text explains the imagery: God, and then Christ, are revealed to be both the source and the sum of all; both Creator and Culmination. Christ's primacy is expressed in other passages in the NT (Jn. 1:1-14; Col. 1:15-20; Heb. 1:1-3). Yet this announcement is reserved until history's end, when Christ can also say, "It is done" (Rev. 21:6). *See also* God.

Egyptian embalmers used pulp from the fleshy leaves of the aloe socotrina, a bitter medicinal plant with tubular red flowers.

The first and last letters of the Greek alphabet symbolize Jesus Christ, Creator and Culminator.

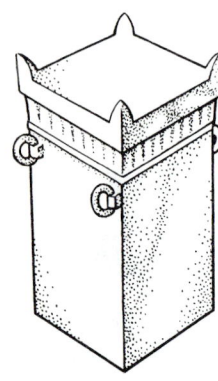

altar A raised platform or table on which a priest sacrificed a victim or offering to God. Altars have always had a place in biblical worship.

OLD TESTAMENT

The basic Hebrew word for altar (*mizebeha*) literally means "to slaughter and cut up for the purpose of sacrifice," and thus came to refer to the place where that occurred. Noah set up the first biblical altar upon leaving the ark (Gen. 8:20). Abraham worshiped at several altars (Gen. 12:7; 13:4; 22:9), as did Isaac (Gen. 26:25) and Jacob (Gen. 33:20; 35:1,3). These have been called "lay altars" to distinguish them from the altars commanded by God in the Law, which were to be served only by ordained priests. *See also* Priest; Sacrifices and Offerings.

1. *Classification of altars.* Altars may be classified as "natural," made of earth or a single rock (Jdg. 6:19-23; 1 Sam. 14:31-35) or of piled stones, and "fabricated" altars made of metal. Old Testament Law states, "If you make an altar of stones for me, do not build it with dressed stones, for you will defile it if you use a tool on it. And do not go up to my altar on steps" (Ex. 20:25,26). An altar-platform recently excavated on Mount Ebal, dating to at least 1000 B.C., follows this prescription. The design of the Mount Ebal altar is similar to that of the altar in the Jerusalem Temple at the time of Christ. The Temple altar is described by Josephus and in the *Middot*, a tract on altar construction found in the Mishnah, which preserves Jewish oral law.

The altar Israel used for burnt offerings in the centuries before Solomon's Temple, was made of bronze-covered acacia wood. It is described in Ex. 27:1-4.

Build an altar of acacia wood, three cubits high; it is to be square, five cubits long and five cubits wide. Make a horn at each of the four corners, so that the horns and the altar are of one piece, and overlay the altar with bronze. Make all its utensils of bronze—its pots to remove the ashes, and its shovels, sprinkling bowls, meat forks and firepans. Make a grating for it, a bronze network, and make a bronze ring at each of the four corners of the network.

Throughout the OT, bronze is associated with the altar, and thus with judgment on sin. *See also* Bronze.

In contrast, Israel's other fabricated altar was covered with gold. This altar was not used for sacrifice, but for burning incense.

2. *The altar in Israel's worship.* Just as Israel had one God, so the people were to sacrifice at one altar. Before the Temple was built, the altar was located at the tabernacle complex, just inside the only entrance to the courtyard. Note the placement. Any worshiper seeking to approach God would have to pass by the altar. There the blood sacrifice was made which God ordained "to make atonement for yourselves on the altar" (Lev. 17:11). The symbolism was clear: Only by means of an atoning sacrifice could a person draw near to God. In this function, the Jewish altar differed significantly from the altars of pagans: Sacrifices offered on pagan altars

The portable bronze altar of sacrifice used by Israel in the wilderness had four "horns" at the top. Carrying poles were thrust through the four rings attached to its sides.

Canaanite sacrifices were offered on this altar uncovered at Megiddo. It was approached by a flight of steps that are covered with animal bones and shattered pottery.

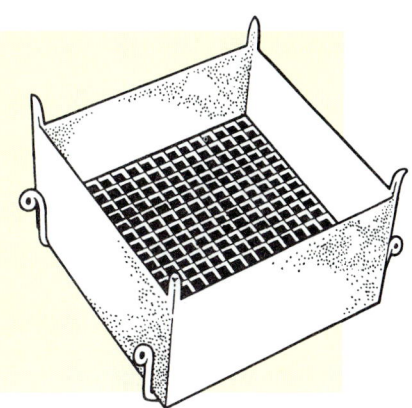

ISRAEL'S TWO ALTARS

Altar of Sacrifice	Altar of Incense
7½' x 7½' x 4½'	18" x 18" x 36"
Made of bronze	Made of gold
Burned sacrificial animals	Burned sweet-smelling incense
Located in open air at door of courtyard	Located within Temple or tabernacle
Served by priests	Served by priests
Symbolizes atonement	Symbolizes worship
Ex. 27:1-8; 38:1-7	Ex. 30:1-10

The fire that consumed sacrifices rested on a bronze grating set within the altar.

were viewed as food for the gods, whereas sacrifices on the Jewish altar were viewed as offerings of thanksgiving, celebration, or expiation for sin. So the altar of the Israelites was not a means of attracting gods or goddesses near enough to hear requests, but rather a means by which human beings might approach a holy God. *See also* Atonement.

Many, including the writer of the NT Book of Hebrews, have observed symbolic correspondence between the OT sacrificial system and the death of Christ on the cross. Hebrews says Jesus is the high priest of the new covenant whose sacrifice was his body (Heb. 7:27). Adopting this typology, the OT's emphasis on a single altar of sacrifice, placed strategically on the one avenue of approach to God, corresponds symbolically to Jesus' saying, "I am the way and the truth and the life. No one comes to the Father except through me" (Jn. 14:6).

The OT also notes other roles for altars. Altars might be erected as memorials to remind Israel of significant events (*see* Ex. 17:15; Josh. 22). Also, people could sometimes flee to the "holy ground" of the altar for refuge or sanctuary (1 Ki. 1:50,51; 2:28). Also, sacrifices of thanksgiving that featured offerings of grain or other produce were sometimes made on the altar of sac-

rifice. It was appropriate that the place of atonement should also be a place of worship and thanksgiving.

ALTARS FOR NATIONAL WORSHIP

There were five sacrificial altars associated with Israel's faith and worship: (1) the portable altar that traveled with the tabernacle (Ex. 27:1-8); (2) the altar built outside Solomon's Temple in Jerusalem (2 Chr. 4:1); (3) the altar built by the group that returned to Judah after the Babylonian captivity (Ezra 3); (4) the enlarged altar constructed when Herod beautified and expanded that Temple in the time of Christ; (5) the altar in the Temple which Ezekiel prophesied would be built in the age of the Messiah (Ezek. 43).

Even though Israel was to offer sacrifices only at the altar before the central sanctuary, from the time of Israel's entry into the land until the time of the Babylonian captivity there was a strong tendency to construct many local altars. Some of these local places of worship were dedicated to Baal or other pagan gods, but some local altars were dedicated to Yahweh, as well. Typically, during the periodic revivals led by Judah's godly kings, local altars were torn down and the king insisted that the people "must worship before this altar in Jerusalem" (2 Ki. 18:22; *compare* 23:8,9).

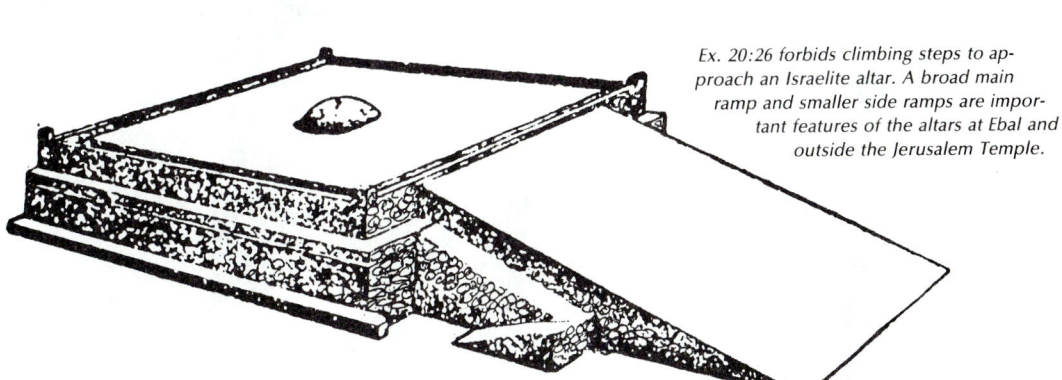

Ex. 20:26 forbids climbing steps to approach an Israelite altar. A broad main ramp and smaller side ramps are important features of the altars at Ebal and outside the Jerusalem Temple.

NEW TESTAMENT

The NT uses "altar" (Gk., *thysiastērion*) both literally and symbolically. Herod's Temple stood in Jesus' day, and Jesus referred to its altar on occasion. The person who brings a gift to the altar, but is alienated from his brother, should make peace first, Jesus said (Mt. 5:23,24). He also spoke against his opponents' hypocritical practice of distinguishing between non-binding oaths, sworn by the altar, and binding oaths, sworn by the gifts on the altar (Mt. 23:18-20). *See also* Oath.

Acts uses a different word for the altar to the Unknown God, which Paul encountered in Athens. It was a *bōmos*, a "high place" or raised platform (Acts 17:23).

In 1 Cor. 9,10 Paul looks back at the OT altar and draws principles for Christian behavior: (1) preachers should be fed and supported, as the OT priests were allowed to eat the sacrificial meat; and (2) Christians should not participate in the sacrifice-rituals of false gods.

The writer of Hebrews notes strong parallels between the OT altar and Christ (Heb. 7,9). "We have an altar from which those who minister at the tabernacle have no right to eat" (Heb. 13:10). Christ himself is that altar; he is the sacrifice. In this new era, the eating of the sacrificial meat—that is, participation with Christ—is reserved for those who have abandoned the old, and have come "outside the camp" (v. 13), to Jesus.

Revelation speaks of an altar in heaven, on which the prayers of the saints are offered like incense (Rev. 8:3). This is clearly analogous to the OT's altar of incense, with an angel in the role of the offering priest.

always (1) at all times, invariably; or (2) forever, perpetually. In the Bible, "always" is *not* associated with eternity, but rather with one's experience in *this* world.

OLD TESTAMENT

"Oh, that their hearts would be inclined to fear me and keep all my commands always [*kol-hayammim*, all their days], so that it might go well with them and their children forever [*le'olam*, to eternity]" (Deut. 5:29). This verse points up the contrast: We keep God's commands in this world, and we enjoy his blessings into eternity.

The Hebrew phrase "all the days" is the most common term for "always" in the OT. A second term, *tamid*, is best translated "continually." The Lord's eyes are said to be "always upon" the Promised Land, "from the beginning of the year even unto the end of the year" (Deut. 11:12, KJV). The one "always" term that does have a perpetual sense to it (*nesah*) usually appears in the negative. "The needy will not always be forgotten" (Ps. 9:18). God "will not always accuse" (Ps. 103:9), "nor will I always be angry" (Isa. 57:16).

NEW TESTAMENT

In Jesus' Great Commission, he promised, "I will be with you always, to the very end of the age" (Mt. 28:20). There he used "all the days," a common phrase in Hebrew, but not in NT Greek. Usually NT writers use simple adverbs, *pantote* or *aei*. All of these focus on our experience in this world and emphasize either stability over time or continuous experience in time. Because we know God is with us continually and for all time, we can "rejoice in the Lord always" (Phil. 4:4).

These hewn limestone altars from Canaanite Megiddo are only about two feet high. They were probably used to burn incense.

52

Amalekites A semi-nomadic people who ranged over a wide area south of Palestine, including the Sinai and Arabian peninsulas (Gen. 14:7; 1 Sam. 15:7). They were the first enemies to attack Israelites under Moses at the battle of Rephidim (Ex. 17:8-14). Because they attacked without provocation, God promised to have them completely destroyed some day in the future (later fulfilled by King Saul, 1 Sam. 15:2-9). In Gideon's day, the Amalekites dominated at least part of Israel's heartland (Jdg. 6:3,33), and even in David's time, Amalekite forces or raiding parties were capable of penetrating Philistine territory (2 Sam. 27:8,9).

Genesis 36:15,16 identifies the Amalekites as a clan descending from Esau. At the time of the Exodus (about 1450 B.C.), the Amalekites and the Canaanites attacked Israel as they retreated toward the desert after refusing to obey God at Kadesh (Num. 14:45). In Deut. 25:17-19, the Lord reminded Israel of the guerrilla tactics the Amalekites had used:

Remember what the Amalekites did to you along the way when you came out of Egypt. When you were weary and worn out, they met you on your journey and cut off all who were lagging behind; they had no fear of God. When the Lord your God gives you rest from all the enemies around you in the land he is giving you to possess as an inheritance, you shall blot out the memory of Amalek from under heaven. Do not forget!

This experience and Moses' command, along with Amalekite persecution during the time of the judges, provide a background against which we can understand the mission on which Saul, Israel's first king, was sent about 1030 B.C. He was to "attack the Amalekites and totally destroy everything that belongs to them" (1 Sam. 15:3). Saul attacked, but did not obey God's command to destroy them totally. He was subsequently rejected by God for his disobedience (15:18,19). *See also* Devoted Things.

It is ironic that an Amalekite soldier claimed he had killed Saul on Mount Gilboa at Saul's own request (2 Sam. 1:1-16). But this was a lie for which he was executed by David; we learn from 1 Sam. 31:4 that Saul actually committed suicide. In 1 Chr. 4:42,43, we learn that a few Amalekites may have survived until the time of Hezekiah (715–686 B.C.).

Amarna letters Ancient clay tablets written in Akkadian but discovered in Egypt. These letters from Canaan reveal numerous details of the politics of biblical times.

El-Amarna is the name given the ruins of the Egyptian city of Akhetaten, which was built some 200 miles south of modern Cairo by Pharaoh Akhenaton, who is thought to have ruled 1379–1352 B.C. Hundreds of clay tablets found there record diplomatic correspondence between the Egyptian Empire and other states in the biblical world.

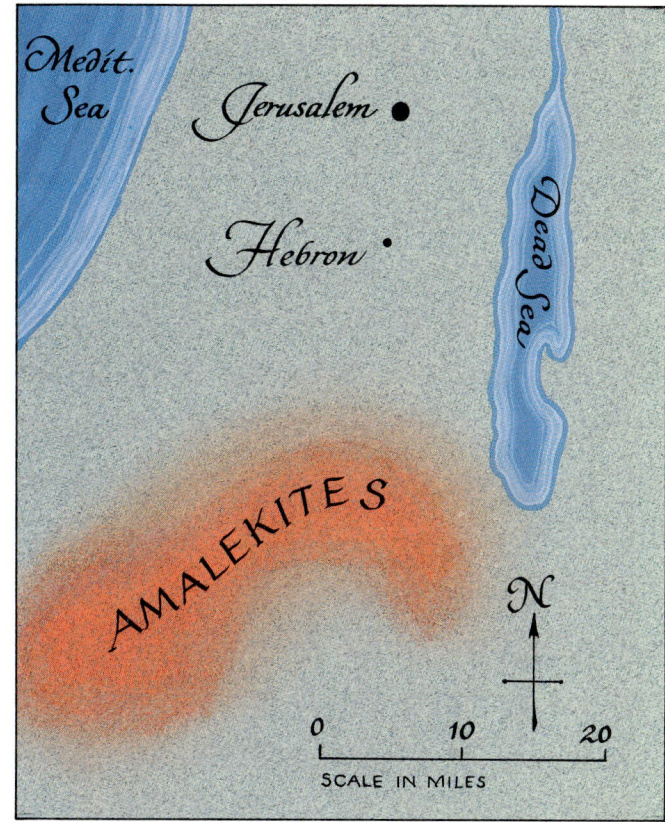

The Amalekites, who claimed rights to lands south of Palestine, attacked the Israelites during their wilderness wanderings.

One of the famous "Amarna letters," discovered at Tell el-Amarna, Egypt, in 1887. The letters include diplomatic correspondence from Mesopotamian rulers, to Pharaoh Akhenaton, and from Palestinian subject kings requesting aid against marauding "hapiru." The hapiru are often identifed with the Hebrew conquerors under Joshua, but such an identification is much debated.

53

These Egyptian carvings of kings' heads date from the time of Akhenaton, 1350–1334 B.C.

For some 200 years, Egypt had dominated the Syria/Palestine area, and most of the smaller states in that area were vassals and paid Egypt tribute. But by the time of Amenhotep (traditionally about 1412–1375 B.C.), Egyptian power had waned. The Amarna letters provide a fascinating picture of conditions in Palestine through letters exchanged with rulers of city-states in Beirut, Sidon, Tyre, Jerusalem, Hazor, Megiddo, and others, as well as letters exchanged with more distant powers such as Assyria and Babylon. These letters include frantic requests for military help, complaints from Egyptian commissioners that subject states are not supplying required food and laborers, and frequent mention of a people identified as the "Habiru" or "Hapiru," who were seizing territory in Canaan.

The Amarna letters thus picture a power vacuum in Canaan, which surely was significant in Israel's conquest of the land. But the letters also raise many questions. Does the Amarna correspondence reflect an Israelite invasion then taking place? Or does it simply establish conditions which help to explain Joshua's successful attack some years later? At the present time the answers to these questions are uncertain, for several reasons. First, there exist some questions about the dating of Egyptian dynasties, which would affect the dating of Ahkenaton and the letters written during his administration. Second, while the tablets on which the Amarna letters were written have been known since A.D. 1887, current translations remain poor.

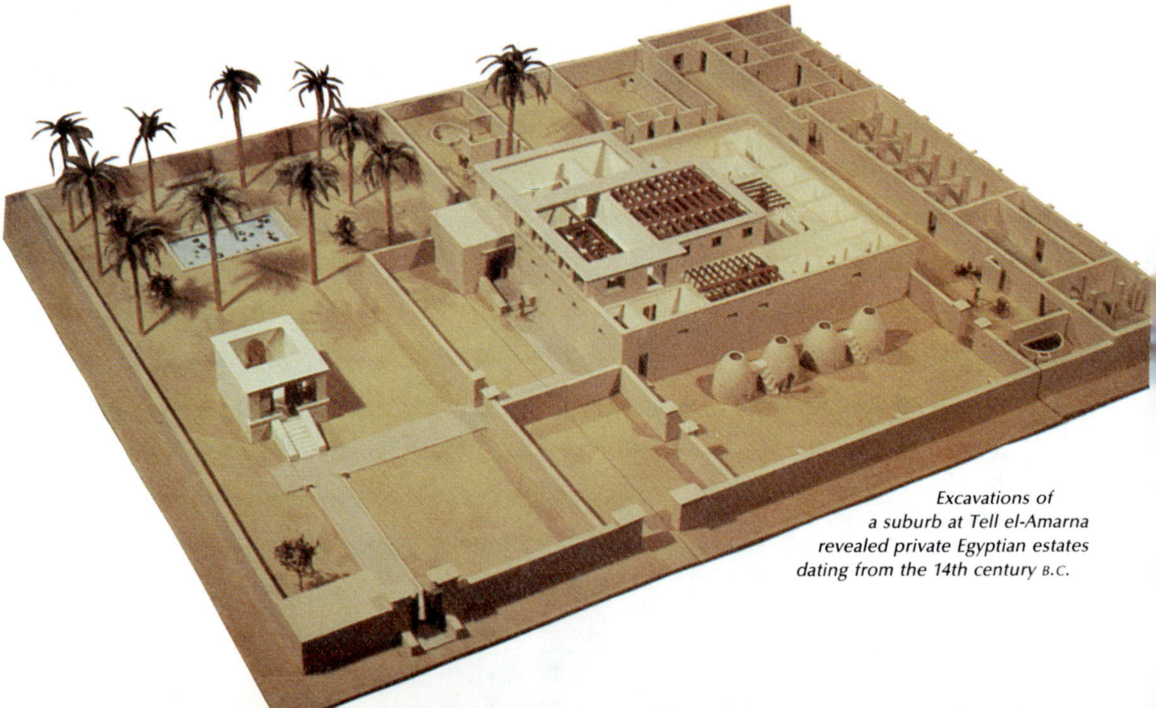

Excavations of a suburb at Tell el-Amarna revealed private Egyptian estates dating from the 14th century B.C.

While the Amarna letters do not answer many questions about the date of the Exodus, they do provide vital background about the political situation in Canaan around the time of Israel's conquest. They fully support Scripture's portrait of a land divided into separate city-states, without an effective alliance with any major world power.

amazement Full of wonder, fascination, or fear. The word typically describes the reaction of the crowds to Jesus' teaching and miracles (*see* Mt. 8:27; 13:54; 15:31; Mk. 1:27; 6:51; Lk. 5:26; Jn. 2:18; 4:32; 7:15). Four different Greek words are translated "amazed" or "amazement." These are synonyms, yet carry slightly different connotations. Comparing these shades of meaning, we get a fascinating picture of the reactions that Jesus stimulated: fear, mixed with amazement, mixed with wonder. There was also the "stunned amazement" that leaves a person unable to grasp what has just happened. Perhaps the most common theme is that of anxiety: a vague disquiet rooted in the fact that Jesus' words did not fit his hearers' expectations, and that his acts simply could not be explained by any known natural process. *See also* Miracle.

Amaziah [AM-uh-ZI-uh; "Yahweh is mighty"]. Eighth king of Judah 796–767 B.C., who began well but turned from God and ultimately was assassinated. **Parents:** Joash and Jehoaddin. **Son:** Uzziah. **Scripture:** 2 Ki. 14; 2 Chr. 25. The 29 years ascribed to his reign in 2 Ki. 14:1-20 probably include some years as co-regent (*compare* 1 Ki. 14:2 with 2 Chr. 25:1).

BACKGROUND

The united kingdom of David and Solomon had been divided into two nations for over 130 years when Amaziah began his reign. The balance of power between the two had often shifted during that time. When Amaziah took Judah's throne, both Israel and Judah seemed ready for military and economic revival. Amaziah raised an army and successfully attacked Edom. Following his victory, Amaziah turned his attention to Israel, and challenged King Jehoash.

This challenge came more out of anger and arrogance than from any military need. Amaziah had hired mercenary troops from Israel for his battle with Edom. When a prophet rebuked him for this alliance, Amaziah sent the northern troops home. (*See also* Alliance.) These troops were furious, and on their way back to

Israel, they attacked and sacked several of Judah's towns. In the battle that Amaziah forced, his army was defeated and he was taken captive. A 600-foot section of Jerusalem's city wall was broken down, and Temple treasures were taken to Samaria.

Amaziah's spirit was now broken. He turned completely from the Lord. Near the end of his reign, opposition to the king was so great in Jerusalem that he fled the city. The opposition party sent men after the king to Lachish, and they killed him there.

LEARNING FROM AMAZIAH'S LIFE

A disturbing pattern seen in other Bible persons is also apparent in Amaziah's life: He began well, but ended poorly. Amaziah is commended for abandoning the common practice of executing the entire family of those who murdered his own father, and executing only the killers as Deut. 24:16 instructs. Amaziah also listened to God's prophet and obeyed his command to release the mercenaries he had hired from Israel.

But then the victory Amaziah won over the Edomites was his undoing. Arrogantly Amaziah brought the gods (idols) of Edom back to Jerusalem and began to worship them. When a man of God rebuked him, Amaziah threatened the prophet's life. Amaziah's idolatry apparently alienated many people in Judah. "From the time that Amaziah turned away from following the Lord, they conspired against him in Jerusalem" (2 Chr. 25:27).

For many of us as well, success may hold more spiritual dangers than continued struggle.

ambassador (KJV) A representative of a nation or ruler, dispatched on special occasions. Typically, the ambassador held a position of high rank in the government (2 Ki. 18:17). Old Testament examples of ambassadorial missions include 2 Sam. 10:2-4; 2 Chr. 32:31; 35:21; and Isa. 30:4. (The RSV and the NIV use "envoy" rather than "ambassador.") In the NT, Paul identifies himself as "an ambassador in chains" (Eph. 6:20). More significantly, he calls each Christian to see himself as "Christ's ambassador," entrusted with the message of reconciliation. In that ambassadorial role, when we share Christ with others, it is "as though God were making his appeal through us" (2 Cor. 5:19,20).

amber (KJV) The original meaning of the Hebrew *hashemal* is uncertain. It occurs only in Ezek. 1:4,27; 8:2, where the RSV

Line drawing of a Syrian ambassador to Egyptian Pharaoh Tutankhamen, 1361–1352 B.C. The pose depicts worship in Egyptian art; Pharaohs were considered divine and would be greeted as such by foreign emissaries.

55

has "gleaming bronze" and the NIV has "glowing metal." While the root meaning remains uncertain, all scholars agree that the image, used to describe the visible glory of God, conveys the sense of brilliance.

amen A transliteration of a solemn Hebrew word describing something firm, true, or reliable. *Amen* has remained untranslated in Christian tradition.

In ordinary speech, *amen* expressed willingness to obey a superior (1 Ki. 1:36) or agreement with a speaker (Jer. 28:6). But it was typically used in worship ritual, to end a prayer (Rom. 15:33), or as a congregational response (Deut. 27:15-26; Rom. 16:27; Eph. 3:21; 1 Pet. 4:11). In such contexts, *amen* has the sense of "truly" or "let it be so."

John reports that Christ began some of his teaching with "Amen, Amen, I say to you." Modern versions tend to render this "truly, truly." Only Jesus used this phrase, which affirmed the trustworthiness of what he was about to say. The NT also portrays Jesus himself as *the* Amen, who confirms the promises of God and ensures the fulfillment of the Father's plans (2 Cor. 1:20; Rev. 3:14). *See also* Truth.

Amethyst

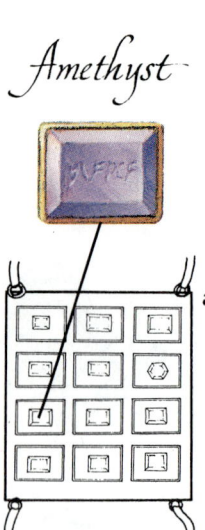

The wine-colored amethyst was highly prized in the Near East.

amethyst One of the twelve precious stones on the breastpiece of the high priest (Ex. 28:19; 39:12). The biblical amethyst (Heb., *'ahelameh,* which means "averting intoxication"; Gk., *amethystos*) was a form of corundum, ranging in color from pale violet to deep purple. It is also mentioned in Rev. 21:20 as a decorative material on the foundation of the new Jerusalem.

Ammonites A neighboring nation that frequently opposed OT Israel. The Ammonites inhabited territory that is now modern Jordan, and maintained a capital at Rabbah, modern Amman. They traced their ancestry to Ben Ammi, a son of Abraham's nephew Lot (about 1985 B.C.). Thus the Israelites initially viewed them as near relatives, and were prohibited from invading their territory (Deut. 2:19). However, the Ammonites joined Moab in hiring Balaam to curse Israel. This act of hostility led to their banishment from the assembly of Israel and to God's command, "Do not seek peace or good relations with them" (Deut. 23:3-6).

Conflict between Israel and Ammon persisted from the time of Israel's conquest of Canaan until the time of the Maccabees, two centuries before Christ. The Ammo-

This limestone statue of an Ammonite king dates from the 9th century B.C. age of Jehoshaphat, when Ammon joined with Moab and Edom to attack Judah.

nites aided Moab in the earliest oppression of Israel about 1370 B.C. (Jdg. 3:13). Saul defeated the Ammonites when they attacked Jabesh Gilead about 1050 B.C. (1 Sam. 11). David maintained friendly relations with Nahash, king of Ammon (2 Sam. 10:1,2). But when Nahash's successor, Hanun, provoked hostilities, David invaded Ammon and took Rabbah (2 Sam. 12:26-31). Through the era of David and Solomon, Ammon remained a client state, forced to pay yearly tribute to Israel.

Solomon took Ammonite wives, who influenced him to worship their idol, Molech (1 Ki. 11:1,5,7). Solomon's son and successor, Rehoboam, had an Ammonite mother (1 Ki. 14:21,31).

During Jehoshaphat's time (872–848 B.C.), Ammon once again aligned with Moab and Edom to attack Judah (2 Chr. 20:1-30), and this time was defeated. Still later, Uzziah (792–740 B.C.) and Jotham (750–732 B.C.) again exacted tribute from Ammon (2 Chr. 26:8; 27:5).

In Hezekiah's time (715–686 B.C.), the Ammonites became vassals of the Assyrians and their culture flourished. Prior to the Babylonian invasion of Judah in the early 600s B.C., Nebuchadnezzar sent Ammonite raiding parties against Judah (2 Ki. 24:2).

In view of the long history of enmity between the Hebrew people and the Ammonites, the prophets announced God's judgment on Ammon and predicted its ultimate destruction (Jer. 49:1-6; Amos 1:13-15; Zeph. 2:8-11).

Amorites An early Semitic people who settled in Palestine and Syria, and throughout western Mesopotamia. Ancient evidence indicates the Amorites (*Amurru*) had an extensive kingdom from the late third millennium B.C. to the mid-second. Its capital city, Mari, has given archaeologists a treasure trove of information. More than 20,000 clay tablets have been found there, providing important insights into the culture of the Middle East in the time of Israel's patriarchs.

Genesis 15 mentions the "Amorites" twice — as one of many nations inhabiting Palestine (v. 21) and as a blanket term including all those nations (v. 16). This may reflect the gradual division of the Amorite kingdom into city-states, ruled by local kings.

The Amarna letters, from about the time of the Exodus, include correspondence from a number of Amorite kings in Palestine and Syria. The Pentateuch describes a large Amorite kingdom east of the Jordan. The Israelites, on their way to Palestine, asked the Amorite king for safe passage through this land, promising to stay on the established highway and do the land no damage. But King Sihon refused them permission and mustered his army. In response, the Israelites totally destroyed the Transjordan Amorites (Num. 21:21-30). That land then became part of the inheritance of the tribes Reuben, Gad, and Manasseh.

After Israel's conquest of Palestine, the Amorites are never again presented in Scripture as a major military force, although they are mentioned as enemies of Israel during the time of the judges (Jdg. 1:34-36). A few survivors remained in the area as late as the time of David (2 Sam. 21:2).

The Amorites were not forgotten, however, and later references to them in Scripture recall evil practices associated with their religion (1 Ki. 21:26). *See also* Amarna Letters; Baal.

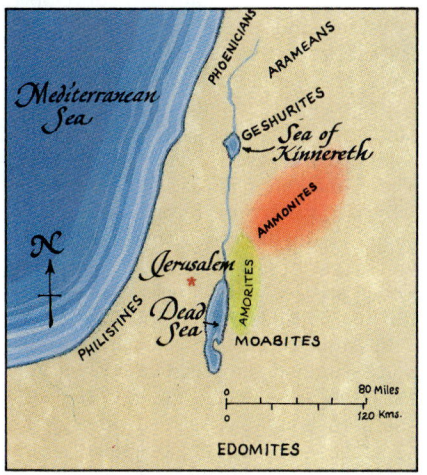

At the time of the Exodus, both Amorites and Ammonites controlled land east of the Jordan River.

This statuette from 2650 B.C., found in a Mari temple, depicts an early Amorite.

An Amorite woman is depicted in this steatite statuette from about 2500 B.C. It was found in the Temple of Ishtar at Mari.

Amos, Book of This book contains messages that the prophet Amos [AY-muhs; "burden"] uttered in Israel during the later part of the reign of Jeroboam II (793–753 B.C.). Most scholars date Amos's ministry, which lasted only a few months, to about 760 B.C. Amos spoke out against the empty ritualism of a people who, in a time of material prosperity, had lost sight of justice and were indifferent to the plight of the poor and the oppressed.

BACKGROUND

Politically and materially, the two last decades of Jeroboam II rivaled the golden age of David and Solomon. King Benhadad III of Syria died in 776 B.C., creating a power vacuum. Jeroboam II acted quickly and took Damascus (2 Ki. 14:28), gaining control of the region's lucrative trade routes. Soon a merchant class developed in Israel, and the population gradually shifted from the country to the cities. Land, the traditional source of wealth in Israel, was torn from the grip of individual families (in violation of OT Law) and consolidated into great estates for the rich. The Samaritan Ostraca, clay shards on which a variety of records were kept, suggest a highly centralized government and a system of heavy agricultural taxes. Other archaeological finds also attest to the luxurious life-style of the era.

In Amos's time, Jeroboam II expanded and beautified the religious centers built by Jeroboam I when the northern and southern kingdoms were divided (1 Ki. 12:26-33; see Amos 7:13). Religion was popular with the wealthy, and many had second homes near the worship sites at Bethel or Dan (3:14,15). New shrines were constructed at Gilgal and Beersheba (4:4; 5:5). The wealthy seem to have taken comfort in sacrificing to Yahweh at these centers, assuming that their prosperity was a sign of his blessing and approval.

Amos condemned the rich, who callously defrauded the poor for sandals and shekels.

Yet the gap between the rich and poor in Israel's society widened, and with it came social oppression. Amos indicted the people of Israel in powerful words: "You trample on the poor and force him to give you grain . . . You oppress the righteous and take bribes, and you deprive the poor of justice in the courts" (5:11,12). Israel had replaced sensitivity to human need with a brutal indifference. The people of Israel were ready to "sell the righteous for silver, and the needy for a pair of sandals. They trample on the heads of the poor as upon the dust of the ground and deny justice to the oppressed" (2:6,7).

Against this background of material prosperity, but moral and spiritual depravity, Amos rebuked the people of Israel.

AMOS, THE MAN

Apart from the sparse information given in his book, we know nothing about the author. Amos came from Tekoa in Judah, an area about ten miles south of Jerusalem and six miles south of Bethlehem. He is identified in 1:1 as a "shepherd." The word here is not the normal *ra'ah* but rather *noged*, a term found only here and in 2 Ki. 3:4. A related word found in Ugaritic texts suggests that Amos was not a poor shepherd, but rather a sheep rancher. Amos's bold, simple, and yet powerful literary style also suggests that he was a cultured man. It is likely that God called a wealthy but righteous individual, whose values had been shaped by the Law of the Lord, to speak to the wealthy of Israel who had abandoned divine values.

The brief biographical interlude in 7:10-17 underlines the fact that Amos was not a "prophet nor a prophet's son" (that is, not a minister, nor even a seminarian). Amos was simply a layman, called by God for a special mission, and willing to respond to that call. In doing so, he confronted the sin and injustice that had been institutional-

After a two-verse introduction, Amos pronounces judgments on eight nations, including Judah and Israel (1:3–2:16). In one case after another, he proclaims God's retribution for "three sins, even for four," a phrase meaning "for repeated sins."

Amos then records three sermons, each of which is introduced with the phrase "Hear this word" (3:1; 4:1; 5:1). These sermons spell out the reasons for God's judgment on Israel, and focus on the injustice and corruption of a society which had abandoned God's standards and scorned his values.

Amos then shares five visions of judgment (7:1–9:10). These visions emphasize God's grace in withholding judgment in the past (7:1-6), the certainty of the judgment about to fall (7:7-9; 8:1-14), and the totally devastating nature of the judgment (9:1-10).

But Amos ends on a note of hope (9:11-15). Like other OT prophets, Amos looks ahead to a day when God will restore his people under a Davidic ruler. This final vision expresses the divine commitment: "I will plant Israel in their own land, never again to be uprooted" (9:15).

MASTERY KEYS

Amos presents the timeless message of God to all materialistic societies where the desire for wealth and luxury blinds citizens to the needs of the poor and leads to institutionalized oppression. In such situations, Amos articulates God's cry for justice, a quality described in Amos 5:14,15:

Numerous ivory furniture inlays and decorative plaques, dating from the time of Amos, have been found at Nimrud.

ized in Israel. When commanded by Amaziah, the priest of Bethel, to leave the country, Amos boldly announced God's judgment on the priest himself: "Your wife will become a prostitute in the city, and your sons and daughters will fall by the sword. Your land will be measured and divided up, and you yourself will die in a pagan country. And Israel will certainly go into exile, away from their native land" (7:17).

STRUCTURE

Amos is organized simply and clearly.

Seek good, not evil,
  that you may live.
Then the Lord God Almighty will be with you,
  just as you say he is.
Hate evil, love good;
  maintain justice in the courts.

The sins that most disturb Amos, and

This ivory inlay decorated a chair in Samaria. It shows chariots and drivers in a battle scene. Amos prophesied, "The houses adorned with ivory will be destroyed."

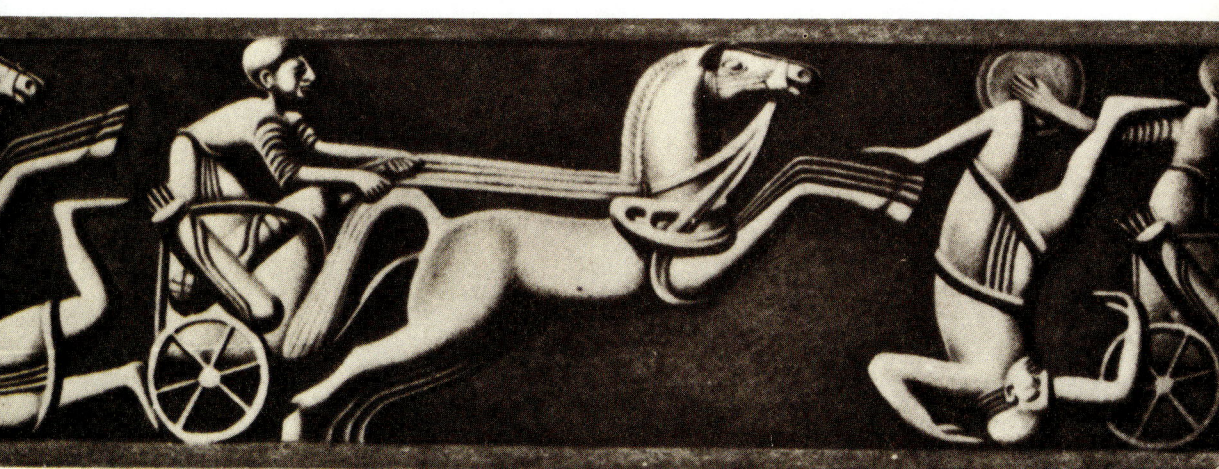

which best characterize the unjust society, are described in Amos 2:6-8; 5:10-13; 6:1-7; and 8:4-6. By studying these passages carefully, we can become more sensitive to that justice to which God's love for humankind calls all people everywhere.

SPECIAL FEATURES

1. Amos beautifully illustrates the OT concept of justice. Essentially, it rests on the conviction that God has established standards for interpersonal relationships, standards which express God's own character and his concern for human beings. Justice involves doing good to others and showing an active concern for their well-being. Amos reminds us that justice is not only a matter of private relationships but also of public policy. God calls us to do justice and also to seek to build a just, moral society. *See also* Justice.

2. Amos deals with the relationship between justice and religion. Several passages in Amos attack the practices of people who delight in ritual worship and sacrifice (4:2-5; 5:21-27). Amos does not reject the idea of sacrifice, but he points out two problems with the way it was done. First, Israel's worship took place at worship centers other than the single Jerusalem sanctuary where God had ordained that sacrifice should be made (Deut. 12:5,6). Second, the people who came to worship habitually violated God's moral law. The sacrifices were unacceptable because the persons offering them had ignored justice. Thus God says, "Away with the noise of your songs! I will not listen to the music of your harps. But let justice roll on like a river, righteousness like a never-failing stream" (5:23,24). No worship offered by a people comfortable with sin is acceptable to the Lord. *See also* Justice; Sacrifices and Offerings.

3. Amos speaks out concerning the coming Day of the Lord. This technical theological term identifies any time when God personally intervenes in the course of history, and particularly his intervention at history's end. The "chosen people" of Israel, blind to their own sins, actually expected God's intervention to benefit them. Amos makes it clear that the Day of the Lord is first of all a day of divine judgment. "That day will be darkness, not light" (5:18).

The devastating invasion by Assyria in 722 B.C., which swept Israel away and resulted in the deportation of her citizens, was an expression of the Day of the Lord.

Yet the Day of the Lord is also bright with hope. As "that day" ends, God will restore his people and bless them (9:11-15). *See also* Day of the Lord.

AMOS: A READING AND STUDY GUIDE

Chapter	Content Summary	Related Articles
1	Amos announces judgment on nations around Palestine for repeated sins.	Judge
2	Amos continues his announcement of judgment, but now includes Judah and particularly Israel.	Poor
3	Amos's first sermon announces the intention of Israel's Sovereign Lord to punish Israel for her sins.	
4	Amos's second sermon reviews disasters God has brought on Israel in futile attempts to encourage repentance.	Discipline Repent
5	Amos's third sermon identifies specific sins and again invites repentance. Amos then goes on to describe the Day of the Lord.	Justice Day of the Lord
6	Amos's third sermon continues with further descriptions of Israel's sins and the punishment for them.	Pride
7	Visions given to Amos indicate that judgment is being postponed. When ordered out of Israel, Amos announces the high priest's fate.	Jeroboam II
8	Additional visions emphasize the certainty and terror of the judgment coming on Israel.	
9	Amos describes the total destruction of the nation. Yet he concludes his prophecy with a promise of restoration.	Future

amulet *See* Sorcerer.

Anakites (**Anakim,** KJV) A tribal group from Hebron (Josh. 11:21; 21:11), feared for their unusual size and strength (Deut. 9:2). Egyptian execration texts, on which enemies of the pharoah were written as part of a ritual curse, mention a tribe of Anak living in Palestine around 2000 B.C., whose leaders have Semitic names. *See also* Giant.

Ananias [an-uh-NI-uhs; from the Hebrew Ananiah, "Yahweh has graciously bestowed"]. Member of the Jerusalem church who with his wife Sapphira was struck dead for plotting to deceive the church, about A.D. 35. **Scripture:** Acts 5:1-11. For others with the same name, *see* IDENTI-QUICK: PEOPLE.

Many in the early church gave generously to support the poor (Acts 4:32-37), following an OT tradition. Ananias and his wife, Sapphira, sold land and pretended to donate all the proceeds, while holding back part of the price. They were struck dead for this deceit, not for failure to give all. *See also* Give; Poor.

The incident may also illustrate Paul's talk of turning over a sinning Christian to Satan for physical death (1 Cor. 5:5) and John's reference to a "sin that leads to death" (1 Jn. 5:16).

LEARNING FROM ANANIAS'S LIFE

Ananias's sudden death had a great impact on the early church. "Great fear" here suggests a healthy awe of God. Christians can become too casual with the Lord, and fail to remember that the loving Jesus of the Gospels is also the Holy One of OT vision. The impact of this event on the young church might be compared with Isaiah's reaction when he first saw the Lord, realized his sin, was cleansed, and was then commissioned to serve God (Isa. 6).

anathema (KJV) [ah-NAH-thay-mah]. A Greek word typically translated "curse" in English versions, but merely transliterated in the KJV of 1 Cor. 16:22. The term is rooted in the OT view that the sacred objects of pagan religions are worthy only of complete destruction (*see* Deut. 7:25, 26). In Roman Catholicism, until the Second Vatican Council, the term is used in pronouncements against beliefs which Catholics reject as false, as well as against individuals who are to be excluded from the church for moral offenses or heresy. *See also* Curse.

While claiming to donate all they received from the sale of their property, Ananias and Sapphira had actually hidden part of their gain.

ancestor A person from whom an individual or family is descended. Both OT and NT generally use the word "father" (Heb., *'ab*; Gk., *patēr*) in this sense of "forefather."

Many cultures view dead ancestors as objects of fear or veneration. While the OT gives detailed accounts of the lives of Israel's patriarchs, there is no hint of ancestor worship. There is, however, a distinctive view of the relationship between past and living generations.

God chose Abraham, Isaac, and Jacob, and made a covenant with them—and, through them, with their descendants. Descent from these three men thus formed the foundation upon which each succeeding generation based its identity as the people of God. Each new generation of descendants inherited the covenant that the Lord had given their ancestors. It was vitally important to the Jewish people not only to be members of a current covenant community, but also to affirm solidarity with previous generations, whose unbroken line could be traced back through the centuries to Abraham. Thus the many genealogical lists found in the OT attest to Israel's appreciation of ancestry. *See also* Covenant; Genealogy.

This iron anchor dating from New Testament times was found near Haifa, Israel.

anchor A weight that keeps a ship from drifting. Ships on the Mediterranean typically traveled close to shore, and anchored along the coast at night. Several anchors were necessary to provide security. The earliest were made of stone, but by NT times, most were made of iron.

Anchors (*ankura*) are mentioned only in Luke's report of Paul's shipwreck (Acts 27) and in a figurative way in Heb. 6:19. There God's promises, "firm and secure," are viewed as "an anchor for the soul." The anchor is "firm" when deeply imbedded in the ocean floor, and "secure" because it is itself unbreakable. Note that Christians need only the single anchor of God's promise, in contrast to the many anchors carried by the ships of ancient days.

In Old Testament times, anchors were more crude and made of heavy stones.

Ancient of Days A distinctive name of God found only in Dan. 7:9,13,22. The context helps us sense its significance. God takes his place on a flaming throne, judging world empires which flicker into and out of existence in brief succession. Centuries pass, and then God, the Ancient of Days, the Source who precedes time itself, comes to pronounce final judgment "in favor of the saints of the Most High" (7:22). The name then emphasizes the eternal existence of God, and suggests the ultimate expression of his authority as he comes to judge humankind at history's end. *See also* God ("Names of God" Chart).

Andrew [AN-droo; "manly"]. One of Jesus' earliest followers and one of the twelve apostles. **Father:** John, also called Jonah (Mt. 16:17). **Brother:** Peter, with whom he operated a fishing business from their home in Capernaum, in partnership with James and John, who also became Jesus' disciples. The church historian Eusebius says Andrew later ministered in Scythia, an area in southern Russia north of the Black Sea.

References to Andrew in the Gospels help us to develop the following picture: When reports of John the Baptist's ministry reached Capernaum, Andrew left his nets to become one of John's disciples. The day John identified Jesus as the "Lamb of God," Andrew began to follow Christ, and later introduced Peter to the Lord (Jn. 1:35-42).

Andrew returned to the fishing business until a few months later when he, Peter, and their partners were all called to become Jesus' full-time disciples (Mk. 1:16-18; Mt. 4:18-22).

As a disciple, Andrew accompanied Christ during his three years of ministry on earth. Listed fourth among the twelve disciples of Jesus (Mk. 3:13-19), Andrew figures into several Gospel stories: Andrew found the boy with loaves and fishes for the feeding of the 5,000 (Jn. 6:8,9); Philip asked Andrew's help on behalf of some Greeks who wanted to see Jesus (John 12:20-22); and Andrew joined Peter, James, and John in questioning Jesus about the end of world (Mk. 13:3,4). *See also* Disciple.

LEARNING FROM ANDREW'S LIFE

Andrew was the first of the disciples to respond when John the Baptist called Israel to prepare for the coming of the Messiah. His spiritual sensitivity was matched by an unusual sensitivity to other people. He is portrayed as an introducer: he brought Peter to Jesus, and made friends with the boy who brought a lunch when he joined the crowds that trailed after Christ. The fact that Philip went to Andrew with the Greeks' request to see Jesus suggests that the other disciples also saw Andrew as an open, friendly person, ever ready to respond to needs and to offer help.

Andrew should be studied as a model of that very personal concern for individuals which is so fully expressed in Jesus' own relationship with others.

angel A messenger from God. Though the word itself (Heb., *mal'ak*; Gk., *angelos*) can refer to a human messenger, in the NT it usually means a heavenly being, one of a special class created by God to serve him. The NT describes angels as "ministering spirits sent to serve those who will inherit salvation" (Heb. 1:14).

MINISTRIES OF ANGELS

Both Testaments cast angels in similar roles: 1. Angels have communicated special messages to God's saints (Gen. 22:11; Jdg. 13:3-5; Zech. 1–6; Lk. 1:11-20; 2:8-14). 2. Angels have protected and aided God's saints (Gen. 19:15-17; 48:16; Ex. 23:20-23; 1 Ki. 19:5; 2 Ki. 6; Mt. 18:10; Acts 12:7-11,15). For generations, Jewish children have been taught this nighttime prayer:

In the name of the Lord, the God of Israel! May Michael be at my right hand and

Gabriel at my left, before me Uriel and behind me Raphael, and above my head—the Divine Presence of God.

3. Angels have served as God's agents in carrying out divine judgment (Gen. 19:12,13; 2 Sam. 24:16; 2 Chr. 32:21; Isa. 37:36; Ezek. 9:1,2). The NT associates them with the terrible punishments accompanying Christ's return (Mt. 13:41,49; 2 Th. 1:6-8; Rev. 8:5–9:15; 12:7; 14:9,10,14-19; 16:1-12,17-21).

In addition to their ministries to human beings, angels have served God as witnesses to his creative and redemptive acts (Job 38:7; Gal. 3:19; Heb. 2:2; 1 Pet. 1:10-12). In response, they constantly praise the Lord for who he is and what he has done (Ps. 103:20,21; Rev. 5:11,12).

NATURE OF ANGELS

The Bible leaves many questions about angels unanswered. The occasional references give us clues as to their nature, but there is still much we must deduce for ourselves.

This medieval statue at Saint Sebald's Church, Nürnberg, Germany, depicts the disciple Andrew, who introduced Peter to the Savior.

63

A medieval artist at Saint Lawrence Church, Nürnberg, Germany, conceived of angels as winged persons with musical instruments.

God created angels before he made the material universe (Job 38:7; Col. 1:16). Immortal, they neither die nor marry (Mt. 22:30). The term "sons of God" applied to angels indicates only that they were directly created by him. (*See also* Son.) Angels have appeared in human form, although this seems to involve some shielding of an essential brightness or glory (Jdg. 13:6; Dan. 10:5,6; Lk. 24:4). In human form, they invariably appear as male. None of these angels is described as having wings.

Some orders of angelic beings, however, bear strikingly unusual features, having characteristics of both human beings and of animals, including wings (Gen. 3:24; Isa. 6:2-6; Ezek. 1:4-28). *See also* Cherubs; Seraphs.

Three angels are given personal names in Scripture: Michael, the archangel (that is, "chief angel"); Gabriel; and Lucifer, who became Satan (Dan. 8:16; 10:13; Lk. 1:11-20; Isa. 14:12). *See also* Satan.

CHARACTER OF ANGELS

Angels can be categorized by character. Good angels have remained faithful to God. Their character is reflected in names such as "heavenly beings" (Ps. 89:6) and "holy ones" (Ps. 89:5,7; Dan. 4:13,17,23; 8:13). Evil angels followed Satan in his great rebellion against God (Mt. 25:41; Jude 6). Many believe that the "evil spirits" and "demons" of the NT are these fallen angels. *See also* Demon.

Several passages of Scripture suggest that there are distinctions of rank within the hosts of both good and evil angels. This is implied in Dan. 10:12-14, where an angel sent from God to explain Daniel's dream was delayed by one of Satan's angels, identified as "the prince of the Persian kingdom," until one of God's angels of even higher rank could come to help. In the NT, Paul used existing categories to rank "the spiritual forces of evil in heavenly realms" as rulers, authorities, and powers (Eph. 6:12; *see also* Rom. 8:38; 1 Cor. 15:24). Despite the unspecified powers of these forces of evil, the NT reassures us that Jesus, with whom we are united by faith, "has gone into heaven and is at God's right hand—with angels, authorities and powers in submission to him" (1 Pet. 3:22).

DESTINY OF THE ANGELS

Jesus bluntly stated that eternal fire, which we commonly refer to as hell, was "prepared for the devil and his angels" (Mt. 25:41; *see* Rev. 20:10). Paul says that believers will take part in the judgment of fallen angels (1 Cor. 6:3). *See also* Hell.

Perhaps even more significant is the prospect explained in Heb. 2: Humanity, though created "a little lower than the angels" (v. 7), will be raised to a glory that far exceeds that of the angelic hosts. As the writer says, "surely it is not angels he [Jesus] helps, but Abraham's descendants" (v. 16). In that statement he makes a vital point. The focus of God's concern, and the focus of Scripture, is not on angels, but on mankind. Christ took on human nature so that, in the world to come and throughout all eternity, we who trust in Jesus might be lifted far above the angels, to be "crowned with glory and honor" in him (v. 9).

angel of the Lord A heavenly messenger who appeared at especially critical times in the OT and transmitted pivotal OT revelations. Many commentators have speculated that God himself may have appeared as this angel, perhaps as a pre-incarnate manifestation of the Son of God (*see* Gen. 16:7-13; Ex. 3:2-6; 23:20,21; Jdg. 6:11-24). Yet in some passages the angel of the Lord is clearly distinct from God (2 Sam. 24:16; Zech. 1:12; Lk. 1:19).

The activities of the angel of the Lord include all those ministries typical of angels. It may be best to think of the angel of the Lord as Israel's guardian angel: the "angel of [God's] presence" who saved the chosen people from their distress (Isa. 63:9). *See also* Angel.

anger Hostility, rage. This strong emotion can take many forms, as seen in the range of biblical words for it. In Hebrew, *'ap* portrays flaring nostrils; *hemah* and *haron* indicate burning and heat; *qesep* is a violation of a relationship which causes heated anger; and *'ebrah* is fury. The Greek *thymos* is an outburst of anger, while *orgē* is a brooding, deliberate kind of anger.

ANGRY PEOPLE

Jonathan's anger with his father over Saul's treatment of David is one of a number of biblical examples of justifiable anger (1 Sam. 20:34), since Saul did treat David shamefully. On the other hand, Saul's anger at David, stimulated by jealousy, was not justified (1 Sam. 18:8). While we may distinguish between cases of justifiable and unjustifiable anger, Scripture clearly focuses on the issue of what we do with anger. Moral action, not emotion, is Scripture's primary concern. Two furious brothers tricked and wiped out the population of a town when one of the men there raped their sister (Gen. 34). Their anger was justified, but their actions were sinful (Gen. 49:5-7). The problem with human anger is that it affects moral choices. As Prov. 29:22 warns, a hot-tempered man "commits many sins." Psalm 37:8 warns that anger "only leads to evil." A person whose actions are motivated by anger is unlikely to choose a godly path (Jas. 1:19,20).

Jesus identified anger as a root of murder (Mt. 5:21,22), and the NT says, "Get rid of all bitterness, rage and anger . . . along with every form of malice. Be kind and compassionate to one another, forgiving each other, just as in Christ God forgave you" (Eph. 4:31,32).

AN ANGRY GOD

Some have thought that the concept of an angry God conflicts with the Bible's portrait of divine love, yet we need to note several teachings associated with the anger of God: (1) God's anger is never petty or personal. What arouses God's anger is taking "advantage of a widow or an orphan" (Ex. 22:22-24) or willful violation of a covenant relationship (Deut. 29:22-28). *See also* Covenant. (2) Expressions of God's anger benefit rather than harm his people (Ps. 76:10; 78:31-38; Jer. 32:37). God alone is able to balance his anger with love (Ex. 34:6,7). (3) God's anger is linked with his role as moral judge of the universe (Isa. 63; Mt. 3:7; Rom. 9:22). God, in righteous anger, will take responsibility for judging disobedience and punishing those who do evil (Isa. 13:9; 66:14,15; Jer. 21:5; Rom. 2:5-8).

In each of these respects God's anger differs from human anger, just as God himself is different from fallen human beings. Nine times in the OT God reveals himself as "slow to anger." Habakkuk 3:2 adds that "in wrath [God will] remember mercy."

MASTERING OUR ANGER

The story of David's anger at Nabal and Abigail's intervention (1 Sam. 25) reveals a strategy for dealing with our own anger. Note these principles: (1) David chose anger. He might have pitied Nabal or committed the outrage to the Lord. We need to accept personal responsibility for the way we respond to situations, rather than supposing that someone or something "made" us angry. (2) Abigail kept David from translating his anger into action. We may feel angry. But we can and must stop short of sinful acts. (3) Abigail asked David to forgive Nabal. We, too, are to forgive and, according to Jesus, to love even our enemies (Mt. 5:43-48). *See also* Forgive. (4) The story relates the death of Nabal, and implies that God acted to punish him. The NT teaches that, even when truly injured by another person, we are to leave vengeance in the hands of God, and to concentrate on doing good (Rom. 12:19-21). If we practice these biblical principles, we, too, can master anger.

In the ninth century B.C. the Assyrians pictured angels as bearded beings who guarded the king.

anguish An extreme mental and emotional distress caused by some painful situation or circumstance. Psalm 118:5 offers us guidance: "In my anguish I cried to the Lord, and he answered by setting me free."

animals In the Bible, ''animal'' typically refers to mammals as distinct from birds, reptiles, insects and fish. The Hebrew *behemah* indicates the larger four-footed animals. *Hayyah* is used of wild animals, while large domestic animals may be referred to as *miqneh* and smaller domestic animals as *son* or *soneh* (for example, sheep or goats). While the Hebrew people made a variety of distinctions between animals, they did not of course use the classification systems of modern biology, which have been developed in the last two centuries. For specific kinds of animals, see other entries listed by animal name or type.

The Bible offers special insight into the relationship between human and animal life, and the role of animals in the created order.

ANIMALS: OBJECTS OF GOD'S CONCERN

Psalm 104 portrays God's loving concern for animal as well as human life.

> He makes springs pour water into the
> ravines;
> it flows between the mountains.
> They give water to all the beasts of the field;
> the wild donkeys quench their thirst.
> The birds of the air nest by the waters;
> they sing among the branches. . . .
> He makes the grass grow for the cattle,
> and plants for man to cultivate—
> bringing forth food from the earth. . . .
> The trees of the Lord are well watered,
> the cedars of Lebanon that he planted.
> There the birds make their nests;
> the stork has its home in the pine trees.
> The high mountains belong to the wild goats;
> the crags are a refuge for the coneys.

The behemoth of the Book of Job was very possibly the hippopotamus.

This idyllic vision is balanced by more prosaic expressions of God's concern for animal life, as when God withheld judgment on Nineveh not only for the sake of its citizens, but also for the ''many cattle as well'' (Jon. 4:11). The Midrash, containing the comments of rabbis on OT Scripture, picks up this theme and calls upon the righteous to be compassionate toward animals, because ''as the Holy One, blessed be he, has compassion upon man, so has he compassion on the beasts of the field.'' Jesus taught that not even an individual sparrow can fall without God taking note (Mt. 10:29-31).

The creation account in Genesis establishes the basis for humanity's relationship with animals. Human beings, created in

God's image, were to "rule over the fish of the sea and the birds of the air, over the livestock, over all the earth, and over all the creatures that move along the ground" (Gen. 1:26). In this context, "rule" ("dominion," KJV) certainly includes a right to use animal creation. But more significantly, the Hebrew term, *radah*, implies a responsibility for animal creation. God has charged mankind with caring for the living things he created, a charge reflected in the command of the Law not to muzzle an ox while it is treading out grain (Deut. 25:4).

ANIMALS: DISTINCT FROM MANKIND

In Scripture, man's responsibility for animal creation rests squarely on the conviction that human and animal life are distinctly different. Man has dominion be-cause human beings, made in the image of God, are of an order that is higher than and superior to the animals.

This attitude, expressed consistently throughout the OT, directly confronts the evolutionist's view that man and an animal share a common heritage. The scriptural view is seen in these facts: (1) Adam and Eve were created in a manner different from the way animals were made, and only humans bear God's image and likeness (Gen. 1,2). *See also* Image. (2) Each "kind" (*min*) of animal has its own place in creation, and each can reproduce only according to its kind. *See also* Kind. (3) Human beings are strictly forbidden any sexual involvement with animals, and any who cross this boundary are considered

The Peaceable Kingdom *by Edward Hicks, about 1840, depicts the Messianic Age foretold in Isaiah 11, when little children will play safely with ferocious animals.*

67

worthy of death (Ex. 22:19; Lev. 18:23). (4) The animal "mind" is different from the human mind. It is apparently without self-awareness (Dan. 4:16,34; 5:21). Animals are described as "senseless and ignorant," suggesting that they are limited to present experience and are unable either to evaluate the present or reason about the future (Ps. 73:22). Peter and Jude liken false teachers to "brute beasts, creatures of instinct" and "unreasoning animals" (2 Pet. 2:12; Jude 10). (5) Paul in speaking of the resurrection points out that "all flesh is not the same: men have one kind of flesh, animals have another" (1 Cor. 15:39). While human beings will participate in a resurrection from the dead, there is no hint in Scripture that any animal will experience resurrection. (7) Animals were offered in sacrifice as symbolic substitutes for sinners. If animals were of comparable value, the right of an animal to live would not have been so violated.

Musing on what can be observed in this world, Solomon asked, "Who knows if the spirit of man rises upward and if the spirit of the animal goes down into the earth?" (Eccl. 3:21). But reasoning from the revelation of the rest of Scripture, we find a clear distinction between human and animal life—in origin, nature, characteristics, and destiny.

ANIMALS: SERVANTS AND SACRIFICES

The OT Law organized animals into two important ritual classes: clean and unclean. The clean could serve as food for the Jewish people. Sacrificial animals were also drawn from this class. Eating unclean animals, however, was strictly forbidden. Even touching the carcass of an unclean animal kept a person from participating in Israel's worship rituals. The principles for distinguishing between the clean and the unclean are found in Lev. 11.

Israel was told, "You must distinguish between the clean and unclean, between the living creatures that may be eaten and those that may not be eaten" (Lev. 11:47). Some have looked for a medical or health reason for the distinction, but "clean" and "unclean" are ritual categories. They reflect the divine concern to establish and maintain Israel's sense of separation from all other peoples, and her sense of separation unto the Lord. There is no reason to seek a health basis for these dietary laws, especially in view of the point made in Peter's NT vision (Acts 10:15) that it is simply God's Word that makes a thing clean or unclean for his people. *See also* Clean and Unclean.

The most significant of the clean animals were those used in sacrifice (Lev. 1). These were herd animals (young bulls, sheep, or

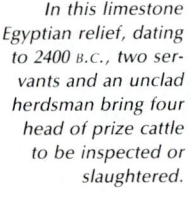

In this limestone Egyptian relief, dating to 2400 B.C., two servants and an unclad herdsman bring four head of prize cattle to be inspected or slaughtered.

goats) or birds (doves or young pigeons). The blood of these animals, representing their lives, would make "atonement for one's life" (Lev. 17:11). Yet, as noted above, there was no true correspondence between the value of an animal and a human life. Thus Hebrews argues, "The blood of goats and bulls and the ashes of a heifer sprinkled on those who are ceremonially unclean [merely] sanctify them so that they are outwardly clean." It took the blood of Christ to "cleanse our consciences" and thus to effect that inner transformation which enables us at last to "serve the living God" (Heb. 9:13,14).

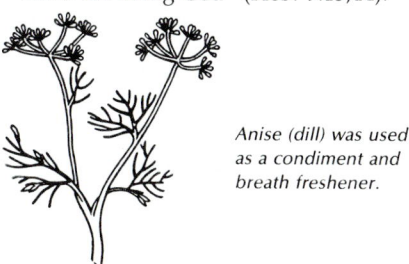

Anise (dill) was used as a condiment and breath freshener.

anise (KJV) An aromatic plant whose seeds were used as a condiment. Called "dill" in modern versions, anise (*anēthon*) is mentioned only in Mt. 23:23, where Jesus ridiculed those Pharisees who carefully counted every seed to make sure God received his ten percent, but "neglected the more important matters of the law—justice, mercy and faithfulness." *See also* Dill.

Anna [AN-uh; "grace," "favor"]. A prophetess who recognized the infant Jesus as the Messiah when he was presented to the Lord at the Temple. **Scripture:** Lk. 2:36-38. **Father:** Phanuel.

Anna appears in only three verses of Scripture, but this brief reference carries many implications. Anna was widowed after seven years of marriage. Considering the typical early age of marriage, Anna at 84 had probably been a widow for at least 60 years. Anna had chosen an unusual course. Rather than remarry (something the apostle Paul later advised for young widows, 1 Tim. 5:11-15), Anna committed herself to a life of prayer, worship, and fasting at the Jerusalem Temple.

LEARNING FROM ANNA'S LIFE
Perhaps most striking is that after six decades of dedication Anna was granted the privilege of viewing the infant Savior. Faithfulness like Anna's carries its own reward of an enriched relationship with God, and often wins a special blessing as well.

Annas [AN-uhs; "grace of Yahweh"]. Past high priest and most influential of the priests in the time of Jesus. **Father:** Seth. **Son-in-law:** Caiaphas, who presided at the trial of Jesus.

The first-century Jewish historian Josephus gives important background about Annas. Annas was sponsored as high priest by the Roman governor Quirinius in A.D. 6. He was deposed in A.D. 15 by Valerius Gratus. Yet he carried such clout that he placed five sons, one son-in-law, and a grandson in the high priesthood. This high priestly family was noted for vast wealth, materialism, and greed. Jesus' attacks during Passover celebrations on those who made God's house a "den of robbers" were undoubtedly directed against practices established by Annas and his family (Jn. 2:12-17; Mk. 11:15-19). The reputation of the family was so odious that the Jewish Talmud contains the curse, "Woe to the family of Annas!"

Yet Annas seems to have completely dominated the priesthood and thus the Sadducean party. *See also* Sadducees. Mention of the "high priesthood of Annas and Caiaphas" (Lk. 3:2) is unique, as the Jews did not have joint high priests and did not refer to former high priests by a courtesy title, as Americans refer to ex-presidents. The fact that Jesus was brought to the house of Annas before being taken to Caiaphas, who was then the official high priest, suggests that Annas was the prime mover in Jesus' arrest and execution (Jn. 18:15-24). Acts 4:6 says "Annas the high priest" was present with "the other men of the high priest's family" at the cross-examination of Peter and John after Peter's healing of a cripple.

This background on Annas helps us avoid the assumption that those who organized Jesus' trial and who pressured Pontius Pilate to execute him were truly motivated by a desire to protect the Jewish people (*see* Jn. 11:48-50). The priestly office in Jesus' time was exploitative, and the motivation of Annas and his family was intensely selfish. Since the hirelings who were supposed to care for God's flock were in fact "thieves and robbers," it is no wonder that the one who came not to exploit the sheep but to lay down his life for them was viewed as a threat by these rapacious "hired hands" (Jn. 10:1-3).

LEARNING FROM ANNAS'S LIFE
Extra-biblical sources describe the "booths of the sons of Annas" where animals and grain for offerings were sold at inflated prices to worshipers. This, with

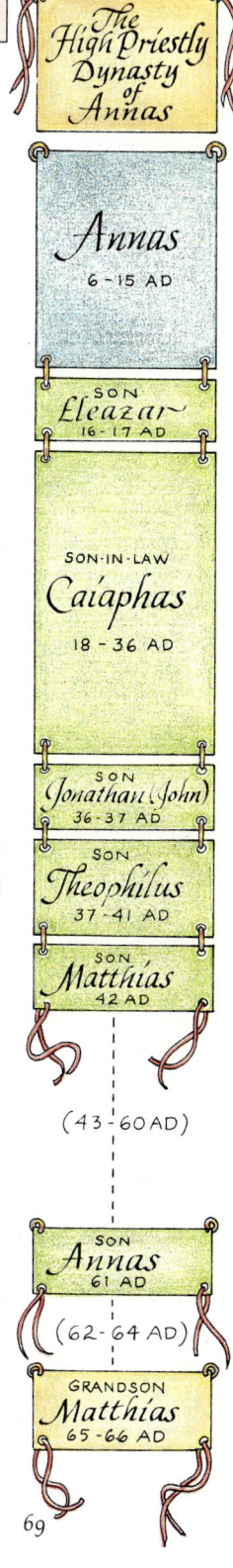

The
High Priestly
Dynasty
of
Annas

Annas
6 - 15 AD

SON
Eleazar
16 - 17 AD

SON-IN-LAW
Caiaphas
18 - 36 AD

SON
Jonathan (John)
36 - 37 AD

SON
Theophilus
37 - 41 AD

SON
Matthias
42 AD

(43 - 60 AD)

SON
Annas
61 AD

(62 - 64 AD)

GRANDSON
Matthias
65 - 66 AD

69

Jesus' blunt references to making the Temple a "den of thieves," does more than establish the values of this priestly family. It also places them in a category described by Peter and Jude, who warn against false teachers of the Christian era who "in their greed" will "exploit you" (2 Pet. 2:3). Jude speaks against those who rush for profit into Balaam's error (choosing wealth rather than God's will) and who are "shepherds who feed only themselves" (Jude 11,12). Whenever the Bible mentions Annas, we find him opposing the people and work of God. Perhaps Jesus' words sum it up best: "No one can serve two masters. Either he will hate the one and love the other, or he will be devoted to the one and despise the other. You cannot serve both God and Money" (Mt. 6:24). Annas served money, and he could not, would not, serve God. *See also* Money.

annunciation An announcing, in particular when Gabriel told the virgin Mary she would bear the Christ-child. Jesus' imminent birth was announced to three persons: Zechariah (Lk. 1:13), Joseph (Mt. 1:20,21), and Mary (Lk. 1:26-38). However, the Annunciation commonly refers to Gabriel's words to Mary. While the phrase "blessed are you among women" in Lk. 1:28 is not in several of the most important manuscripts, it fully harmonizes with the ancient, earnest desire of Jewish women to be the mother of the promised Messiah (*see* Dan. 11:37). Liturgical churches celebrate the Feast of the Annunciation on March 25. The *Ave Maria*, an eleventh-century prayer, incorporates Scripture from these verses in Luke. *See also* Mary, the mother of Jesus.

anoint To pour oil or rub ointment on a person or object.

SECULAR USES OF ANOINTING

Rubbing the skin with scented oils or ointments was common in OT times (Deut. 28:40; Ruth 3:2). This cosmetic use symbolized gladness (Ps. 45:7; 104:15), and was avoided when people were in mourning (2 Sam. 12:20; Isa. 61:3; Mt. 6:16,17). Guests were anointed with perfumed oils as a mark of special honor (Lk. 7:36-47). In Ps. 23:5 David praises God, saying "You anoint my head with oil." The Hebrew

Jan van Eyck's The Annunciation *depicts Mary hearing the words of Gabriel: "Greetings, you who are highly favored! The Lord is with you."*

word here, *dashen*, comes from a root that means to "make fat." David means simply that God has honored and blessed him to an unusual extent.

Anointing with soothing oils and unguents also was part of established medical treatment in biblical times. This is confirmed in both the OT (Isa. 1:6; Ezek. 16:9) and the NT (Mt. 6:17; Mk. 6:13). The NT word *aleiphō* used in such instances always indicates a literal rubbing. This word is used in Jas. 5:14 for anointing the sick. The choice of *aleiphō*, along with the text's specification of olive oil (*elaion*), suggests that James is prescribing both prayer and medical treatment for the Christian sick. Bodies would also be anointed with perfumed oils in preparation for burial (Mk. 14:8; Lk. 23:55,56).

ANOINTING IN THE OLD TESTAMENT

Religiously significant anointings in the OT typically use the root *m-sh-h*, which means to smear or rub with oil or ointment. By this act, objects as well as persons were consecrated for ritual use (Gen. 31:13; Ex. 30:26; 40:10). Persons who were anointed were in effect divinely ordained to a particular office or ministry.

Old Testament Law specifies a special, sacred anointing oil for ordaining priests. The formula calls for 12½ pounds of liquid myrrh, 6¼ pounds of fragrant cinnamon, 6¼ pounds of fragrant cane, 12½ pounds of cassia, to be mixed with 4 quarts of purified olive oil. This sacred substance could be used for no other purpose than anointing priests (Ex. 30:22-33).

While the OT mentions an instance in which a prophet was anointed (1 Ki. 19:16), the major religious use of anointing was in ordaining rulers (2 Sam. 2:4; 1 Ki. 1:39; 1 Chr. 29:22). By this act, a king became "God's anointed," who ruled by divine right (*see* 1 Sam. 10:1; 24:6-10). This was appropriate in Israel, where the one who held the office of king was considered a sub-ruler under God, ruling the people on God's behalf. (*See also* King.) The OT implies, although it does not specifically teach, that a person anointed for a task is also empowered by God's Spirit to carry it out successfully (1 Sam. 10:1-7; 16:13).

The practice of anointing rulers also has prophetic significance. The OT looks forward to a time when God's Messiah (literally, God's "Anointed One") will appear to reclaim the throne of David (Ps. 2:2; Isa. 61:1; Dan. 9:26). The NT identifies Jesus as the Messiah (Jn. 1:41; 4:25), and the title "Christ" is from the Greek word for "Anointed One." *See also* Christ.

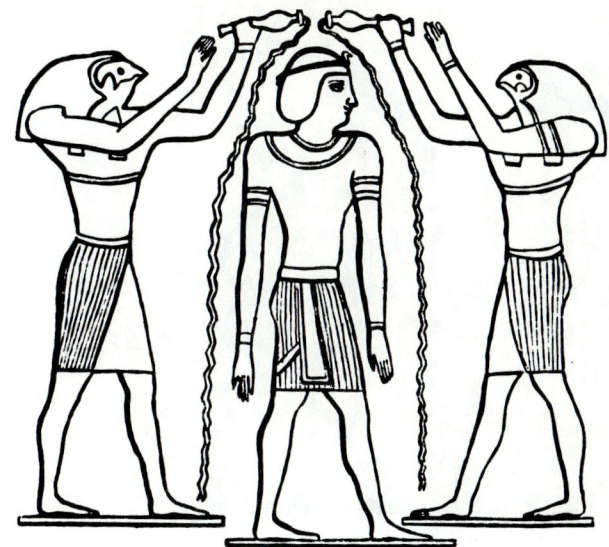

ANOINTING IN THE NEW TESTAMENT

Anointing, as a religious practice that sets apart or ordains persons to special service, does not occur in the NT. However, we do find anointing used figuratively. While *aleiphō* indicates a literal rubbing with oil, the NT uses the word *chriō*, also translated "anoint," to indicate special divine appointment (Lk. 4:18; Acts 4:27; 10:38; 2 Cor. 1:21; Heb. 1:9). Figuratively, every believer has been anointed, set apart to receive all God has promised. As evidence of this unique ordination, God has "set his seal of ownership on us, and put his Spirit in our hearts as a deposit, guaranteeing what is to come" (2 Cor. 1:22).

Another Greek word, *chrisma*, focuses on the substance with which one is anointed. *Chrisma* is found only three times in the NT (1 Jn. 2:20,27), where the writer describes an anointing for Christians that is from Christ, which remains "in you," and which teaches about all things. Because of John's earlier identification of the Holy Spirit as the Teacher whom Christ sends to be in believers (Jn. 16:12-16; *compare* 1 Cor. 2:6-16), commentators have understood the *chrisma*-anointing of 1 Jn. 2 to be the Spirit himself.

An Egyptian wall painting shows the anointing of a new ruler.

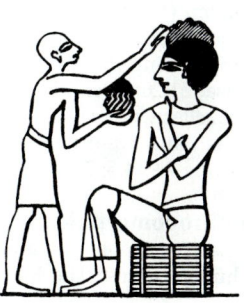

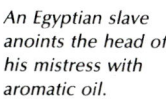
An Egyptian slave anoints the head of his mistress with aromatic oil.

ant A small, usually wingless insect known for its strength and industry. Solomon's reputation as a careful biologist (1 Ki. 4:33) is supported by the Bible's two references to ants, both found in Proverbs (6:6; 30:25). The first describes accurately the behavior of ants who, with "no commander, no overseer or ruler," go about storing provisions in summer and at harvest. Yet only two of the 104 types of ants in the East are harvester ants and behave in this way.

Solomon exhorts lazy humans to follow the example of the ants. But perhaps his appreciation for them has other roots. Solomon was an enthusiastic builder and, by necessity, a bureaucrat. To accomplish his goals, he used forced labor and erected several levels of supervisors to ensure that the work was done (2 Chr. 8:7-10). The constant, unsupervised activity of the ant must have seemed remarkable to Solomon in view of the effort it took to force human beings to do the work he wanted to accomplish.

antelope A deer-like, horned animal. Today only tiny, swift gazelles live in Palestine. Many believe larger antelopes, such as the addax or oryx, roamed there in Bible times. The antelope, called "roebuck" or "hart" in the KJV, was a ritually clean animal and had a place on King Solomon's menu (1 Ki. 4:23). Hunters would capture these speedy animals as they grazed, by frightening them into previously set nets (Isa. 51:20). Delicate and beautiful, young gazelles were valued as pets in the Middle East, and often mentioned in love poetry (Song 2:9; 4:5; 7:3).

anthropomorphism A literary device that speaks of God, animals, or objects in human terms. The Bible speaks of God's

hand, of his face, of God feeling jealousy, etc. The biblical language, however, is clearly figurative. Moses quotes God in Ex. 33:20, "You cannot see my face, for no one may see me and live," and 1 Tim. 6:16 describes the Lord as one "who lives in unapproachable light, whom no one has seen or can see."

Why then the use of anthropomorphic language for God? On the one hand, if we could not use language which described God in ways human beings can understand, very little could be said about him. But more importantly, the God of Scripture is personal rather than impersonal, a living being rather than an abstract force. We properly speak of God's eyes, not because he has two giant physical eyes, but because it is inconceivable that the one who formed the eye cannot see. The Hebrew people properly spoke of God's right hand, not because a giant arm appeared in the sky when God acted, but because the right hand in that culture symbolized power, and God's people knew the Lord as a living being who exerted his power on their behalf.

The anthropomorphic language of the Bible does not reflect a crude or primitive view of God. Instead it expresses an exalted concept, which honors God as a personal being, and which maintains the necessary balance between God's transcendence and his active involvement in the affairs of this world.

antichrist An opponent of Christ, or a substitute Christ. The name, coined by John and found only in his letters, is rooted in ancient biblical prophecies concerning an evil person who will appear at history's end to rally mankind against God.

John also speaks of "many antichrists," and of a spirit of antichrist which is active even before the end times (1 Jn. 2:18; 4:3). These antichristian false teachers can be recognized by their denial of Jesus as God in the flesh. Such persons are "deceivers" who may masquerade as Christians, but whose true character is revealed by their refusal to affirm the full deity of Jesus Christ.

The idea of the Antichrist has captured the imagination of many Christians. The *Didache*, a Christian instruction manual for new believers from the early second century, teaches that the Antichrist will perform miracles and present himself as the Son of God. By the end of the second century, Irenaeus had departed from a literal approach to interpretation and identified the Roman Empire as the Antichrist. Irenaeus reached his conclusion by assigning numerical values to letters, an approach suggested by Rev. 13:18, which refers to "calculating" the beast's name and gives his number as 666. Since Irenaeus, many have used the same approach and have variously identified Nero, Muhammed, Napoleon, Hitler, and others as the Antichrist. The multitude of obvious miscalculations shows the futility of this approach to dealing with the biblical material concerning the Antichrist.

Paul says simply that "at the proper time . . . the lawless one will be revealed, whom the Lord Jesus will overthrow" (2 Th. 2:6,8). Within the context of Scripture, divorced from centuries of fruitless speculation, the Antichrist is consistently presented as a person who, in league with Satan, will appear at history's end just prior to the Second Coming of Jesus Christ. *See also* Second Coming.

Antioch [AN-te-ahk]. Sixteen "Antiochs" were established by Seleucus Nicator around 300 B.C. in honor of his father. Two Antiochs are mentioned in the Bible: Pisidian Antioch lay in the province of Phrygia, and is mentioned in Acts 13:14; 14:19,21; 2 Tim. 3:11. Other NT references are to Syrian Antioch, which by the first century was the third largest city in the Roman Empire, with some 500,000 inhabitants.

Syrian Antioch was a focal point for the development of Christianity. This cosmopolitan city had many Jewish citizens who, over several generations, had developed good relationships with their Gentile neighbors.

After Stephen was martyred in Jerusalem about A.D. 33, many Jewish Christians fled to Antioch. There the Gospel message quickly spread beyond the Jewish community, and the Antioch church began to evangelize Gentiles intentionally (Acts 11:19-24). The most stunning innovation, however, was this church's acceptance of Gentile converts as full members of the church without requiring circumcision or adoption of a Jewish life-style.

When word reached Jerusalem, church leaders dispatched Barnabas to investigate the situation at Antioch. Barnabas recognized the work of the Holy Spirit and enthusiastically encouraged the brothers. He brought Paul to Antioch and, with others, they formed a team that guided this emerging experiment in cross-cultural Christianity (Acts 11:25,26; 13:1). It was here that the name "Christians" was first given to Jesus' followers.

Yet the Antioch church maintained its solidarity with the Jerusalem church. Antioch believers gave generously when a famine crippled Judea and impoverished the mother church (Acts 11:29,30).

The Antioch church also sent out Barnabas and Paul as the first team of Christian missionaries (Acts 13:2–14:28). As a result of this missionary journey many churches were established whose core groups were primarily Gentile believers.

Later, when some Christian Pharisees arrived in Antioch and taught that "real Christians" must accept circumcision and live by the Law of Moses, Paul led a delegation from Antioch to Jerusalem to

Two of the sixteen Antiochs of ancient times are mentioned in the Bible: Antioch of Pisidia, in central Asia Minor, and Antioch of Syria.

set the matter straight. There a council of apostles and elders agreed that Gentiles did not have to adopt a Jewish life-style or be circumcised. Thus they affirmed church unity founded on a relationship with Jesus rather than on cultural uniformity (Acts 15:1-21; Gal. 2:1-14). *See also* Council of Jerusalem.

While Jerusalem was the birthplace of the church, Syrian Antioch was the place where the church struggled through adolescence into vigorous young adulthood, and where circumstances forced Paul to think through the basic theological issues associated with the transition from OT to NT eras.

anxiety Intense worry or concern. Though generally cautioning against anxiety, the NT does present some positive insights.

Paul writes of his "concern" for the churches he has planted (2 Cor. 11:28) and of a person's legitimate concern to please his or her spouse (1 Cor. 7:32-34). In both cases he uses the Greek *merimnaō*, elsewhere translated "worry" or "anxiety."

But there is also a stressful anxiety; a worry that burdens us or may even come to dominate our lives. Most biblical occur-

rences of *merimnaō* thus focus on how to deal with the pressures that commonly cause human beings to be anxious or to worry.

Jesus' teaching on anxiety is repeated in Mt. 6:25-34 and Lk. 12:22-34. Christ portrays the pagan, who does not know God, as "running after" life's necessities (that is, concentrating his efforts on obtaining them), and in the process becoming anxious and distressed. In contrast, Jesus tells his listeners to remember that they are important to a God who clothes the grass of the field and feeds the birds. Because God is "your heavenly Father," and human beings are truly important to him, God will meet every need. Thus God's child is released from worry by trusting in God as a loving Father. More importantly, he or she is released to concentrate every effort on seeking God's Kingdom and righteousness. In Jesus' view, anxiety is not only painful, it is the enemy of complete commitment to the Lord.

The Epistles pick up the theme of trust and add practical advice. Paul says, "Do not be anxious about anything, but in everything, by prayer and petition, with thanksgiving, present your requests to God" (Phil. 4:6). When anxious feelings come, we are to express our trust in God through prayer. Then, the apostle promises, "the peace of God, which transcends all understanding, will guard your hearts and your minds in Christ Jesus" (Phil. 4:7). Peter adds, "Cast all your anxiety on him because he cares for you" (1 Pet. 5:7).

ape An animal of the primate family. The "ape" (*qop*) imported during the Solomonic era was probably a monkey or baboon (1 Ki. 10:22; 2 Chr. 9:21). The appearance of these exotic animals on the shipping invoice with silver and ivory makes it clear they were a luxury item, intended for purchase by the wealthy of Solomon's immensely prosperous kingdom.

apocalyptic literature Religious writings that claim to present a mystical revelation from God, generally in symbolic language, and usually involving the prospect of devastating supernatural intervention in human history in the end times. This literature, with its roots in OT prophetic vision, reflected a growing pessimism about life in this world. After the Babylonian captivity, Israel remained oppressed by a series of Gentile world-empires. Even the struggle during the 160s B.C. that led to limited independence fell far short of Israel's dreams. But why, after rejecting the

This four-inch linen baboon from 300 B.C., found in Saqqara, Egypt, represents an exotic imported animal greatly valued by the wealthy.

idol worship for which she was punished, was Israel not restored to her former glory? The apocalyptic literature that emerged between 200 B.C. and A.D. 100 attempted to explain the mystery of the silence of Israel's God.

Apocalyptic writings shared several important characteristics. They claimed to describe visions in which the writer was transported to astral realms, often to the very throne room of God. The reports of these visions are filled with symbolic language, sometimes powerful, but often trite. The authors usually took the name of some long-dead saint. Thus among Jewish apocalyptic writings are the Apocalypse of Abraham; the Apocalypse of Baruch; 2 Baruch; the Ascension of Isaiah; the Ascension of Moses; 1 and 2 Enoch; the Life of Adam and Eve; the Testament of Abraham; and many others. These apocalyptic writings typically review history in the form of prophecy, as if Abraham or Isaiah were writing it in his own time. Each writer tried to unveil those hidden cosmic reasons for Israel's failure to experience God's blessings. The apocalyptic writers generally explained things in terms of a cosmic struggle between God, with his angels, and Satan, with his demonic legions. The age in which the writers lived was the battlefield for this struggle. Ultimately the war would end and God would exercise his power to usher in a new age of righteousness.

It is important to distinguish between *apocalyptic writings*, which are a historic literary form, and an *apocalyptic view of the future*. The latter has its roots deep in the OT, for the prophets also foresaw God's personal intervention at the end of history to judge evil and to establish everlasting righteousness. Among the many OT examples of an apocalyptic view of history's end are Isa. 56–65 and Zech. 9–14, as well as Dan. 11,12. New Testament examples include Mt. 24 and 2 Th. 1,2. Of all the books in the Bible, however, only Daniel and Revelation can be considered primarily apocalyptic. *See also* Future.

The many apocalyptic writings that emerged from Judaism picked up themes present in the OT, but often carried them far beyond what Scripture revealed. The Jewish writers, and some early Christian apocalyptic authors, saw the present age as dark and evil, dominated by Satan and his demonic forces. Yet a new age lay ahead—a powerful Messiah would bring salvation to the world and establish God's Kingdom on earth. Then there would be

retribution and glory, as God would at last honor the saints who had suffered in ages past.

While Daniel and Revelation share characteristics of other apocalyptic writings, they differ in significant ways. Daniel served as a model for the non-canonical books, which often pick up the symbolism found there and in other prophetic writings. And while Revelation is an unveiling of heavenly events disclosed in a series of visions, it is the signed work of the apostle John, and is not ascribed to some deceased saint by an anonymous author. Most importantly however, the other apocalyptic writings were never considered Scripture or included on lists of canonical writings by the Jews or by the early church. *See also* Canon; Daniel; Revelation.

Interestingly, by the end of the first century A.D., rabbinical sages banned these apocalyptic works because so much of their viewpoint was reflected in the teaching of the early church, which identified Jesus as the Jewish Messiah and eagerly anticipated his Second Coming to establish the rule of God on earth.

Albrecht Dürer's famous woodcut from about A.D. 1500 depicts the Four Horsemen that Revelation associates with the end of the world.

Apocrypha Gk., "hidden" or "obscure." In current Christian usage, this term has come to mean "set aside" or "withdrawn" and therefore, non-Scriptural writings. The word *apocrypha* is applied to three distinct sets of writings. (1) 14 books from the Septuagint that are not included in the Jewish Scriptures; eleven of these books are fully accepted in the Roman Catholic canon but all are regarded by Protestants as non-canonical. These books are called "deuterocanonical" by Roman Catholics and "Old Testament Apocrypha" by Protestants. (2) In Roman Catholicism, those books from the Septuagint which were not accepted as canon, often called the "Pseudepigrapha." (3) Various non-canonical Christian writings whose origins are often falsely attributed to NT characters and which were omitted from the NT because they were not accepted as resulting from revelation, often called "New Testament Apocrypha."

ORIGINS OF THE OT APOCRYPHA

In the third century B.C., the ruling Ptolemy in Alexandria, Egypt, gathered Jewish translators together to translate the Jewish Scriptures into Greek. This Greek translation eventually became known as the Septuagint and was in common use by Greek-speaking Jews in the first century. The Septuagint included the Law, the Prophets, and the Writings of the Hebrew Scriptures, but gradually included with the Writings various works of a religious or historical nature which had emerged in Judaism between the time of Ezra and the destruction of the Temple (A.D. 70). These books were interspersed throughout the Writings but whether they were ever regarded as canonical is a matter of debate.

However, at Jamnia in A.D. 90, Hebrew rabbis affirmed the traditional Hebrew canon and denied status to the additional writings of the Septuagint. The extra-canonical religious writings were banned as dangerous, perhaps in part because these books were part of the Septuagint used by the new Christian church. Rabbi Akiba went so far as to say that "he who reads the outside books shall have no place in the world to come."

Although the early Greek-speaking church used the Septuagint and included some of the Apocrypha with the OT, Jerome (known for his Vulgate translation of Scripture), labeled them as apocryphal. He treated them as edifying but not to be used for doctrinal insights. In spite of Jerome, however, the broader canon of the Septuagint was tacitly accepted by many.

During the Protestant Reformation of the 16th century the books of the Apocrypha became involved in disputes about doctrine (especially purgatory, masses for the dead, and good works obtaining merit with God). Because of this, some Protestant movements—Lutheran and Anglican, in particular—placed them in a secondary position (to be used for ethical but not doctrinal teaching) while still printing them with their Scriptures. Other groups tended to set them aside completely as "of no authority in the Church of God" whatever. In response, the Roman Catholic church at the Council of Trent in A.D. 1546 declared all of them except for 1 and 2 Esdras and the Prayer of Manasseh as canonical. These books are now called "deuterocanonical" in the Roman Catholic Church. The Orthodox Church (Greek and Russian) includes all the books accepted as deuterocanonical by Roman Catholics plus 1 Esdras, the Prayer of Manasseh, 3 and 4 Maccabees and Psalm 151.

THE CONTENT OF THE OT APOCRYPHA

There are several types of Jewish apocryphal writings. First, Second, Third, and Fourth Maccabees are histories of the Maccabean revolt. The Prayer of Manasseh is liturgy, while 2 Esdras is an account of apocalyptic visions. Ecclesiasticus and Baruch are wisdom literature. The Epistle of Jeremiah is an attack on idolatry.

These and other writings emerged during the long silence that fell between the death of the last OT prophet, Malachi (about 400 B.C.), and the appearance of John the Baptist. To some extent these writings attempted to discern what God was saying to a nation that, though it had repudiated idolatry, still suffered under the dominion of a succession of pagan powers. *See also* Apocalyptic Literature.

These books were highly valued by some in the early church, although other church fathers discounted them in view of the clear distinction that was maintained between them and the books of the Hebrew canon. Even Luther thought them "useful and good reading," although not to be held equal to the sacred Scripture.

THE NT APOCRYPHA

The term "apocryphal" ("hidden") is also applied to numerous non-canonical books written during the early Christian era. Sometimes called the "lost books of the Bible," they are often presented as newly discovered works, yet none of them preserves an authentic tradition. Most Christian apocryphal works are imaginative tales of the supposed experiences of

Christ or one of the apostles. Often a Christian apocryphal book was written as propaganda for a particular sect or to stress a particular doctrine. Many even promote heresies. They can be categorized in roughly the same way as NT books:

1. *Gospels.* Arabic Gospel of the Infancy, Armenian Gospel of the Infancy, Assumption of the Virgin, Gospel of Bartholomew, Book of the Resurrection of Christ by Bartholomew, Gospel of Basilides, Gospel of the Ebionites, Gospel according to the Egyptians, Gospel according to the Hebrews, Protoevangelium of James, History of Joseph the Carpenter, Gospel of Marchio, Gospel of the Birth of Mary, Gospel of Matthias, Gospel of the Nazarenes, Gospel of Peter, Gospel of Philip, Gospel of Pseudo-Matthew, and Gospel of Thomas.

2. *Acts.* Apostolic history of Adbias, Acts of Andrew, Fragmentary Story of Andrew, Acts of Andrew and Matthew, Acts of Andrew and Paul, Acts of Barnabas, Ascents of James, Acts of James the Great, Acts of John, Acts of John by Prochorus, Martyrdom of Matthew, Acts of Paul, Passion of Paul, Acts of Peter, Passion of Peter, Preaching of Peter, Slavonic Acts of Peter, Acts of Peter and Andrew, Acts of Peter and Paul, Passion of Peter and Paul, Acts of Philip, Acts of Pilate, Acts of Thaddeus, and Acts of Thomas.

3. *Epistles.* Epistles of Christ and Abgarus, Epistle of the Apostles, Third Epistle to

OLD TESTAMENT APOCRYPHA

Name of Book	Roman Catholic Canon	Roman Catholic Apocrypha	Orthodox Canon	Description
1 Esdras		√	√	Historical account of return from Babylonian captivity; parallel to Chronicles, Ezra, Nehemiah
2 Esdras (4 Ezra)		√		Visions and revelations of early Jewish rabbis
Tobit	√		√	Didactic fiction of Tobit's trials living in 8th century B.C. Nineveh
Judith	√		√	Fictional exploits of a Jewish heroine who assassinated an Assyrian general
Additions to Esther	√		√	Five additions which give a more religious cast to Esther
The Wisdom of Solomon	√		√	A first century B.C. exhortation to wisdom
Ecclesiasticus (Wisdom of Sirach)	√		√	A collection of the writings of Joshua ben-Sera (about 180 B.C.) giving his advice for a successful life by combining personal piety with practical wisdom
Baruch	√		√	Allegedly written by Baruch, a friend of Jeremiah, meant as an encouragement to Jews in the Babylonian exile of 597 B.C.
A Letter of Jeremiah	√		√	An attack on idolatry in the form of a letter from Jeremiah, often appended to Baruch
The Song of the Three Children	√		√	Hymn of praise sung by Shadrach, Meshach and Abednego in the fiery furnace
Susanna	√		√	The story of a virtuous woman who was falsely accused of adultery and defended by Daniel
Bel and the Dragon	√		√	A folklore narration written to ridicule idolatry
The Prayer of Mannaseh		√	√	The prayer of the idolatrous king begging for forgiveness, as referred to in 2 Chr. 33:11-19
1 Maccabees	√		√	The struggle of Jews against Hellenistic rulers (175–134 B.C.), particularly the battle with Antiochus Epiphanes
2 Maccabees	√		√	A narrative of the Maccabean revolt
3 Maccabees			√	An account of life under Ptolemy IV (221–204 B.C.)
4 Maccabees			√	A tract about the rule of reason over passion
Psalm 151			√	

the Corinthians, Epistle to the Laodiceans, Epistle to Lentulus, Epistles of Paul and Seneca, and Apocryphal Epistle of Titus. 4. *Apocalypses.* Apocalypses of James, Paul, Peter, Thomas, the Virgin, and the Revelation of Stephen.

In addition to these works, a number of writings by Gnostics also gained some prominence. These include the Wisdom of Jesus, the Acts of Peter and the Twelve Apostles, the Dialog of the Savior, the Teachings of Silvanus, and Apocalypses of Dositheus, Messos, and Zostrianus. *See also* Gnostics.

We should never, then, suppose that the books we find in our OT and NT are there simply because no other religious writings existed in biblical times. Rather, the books of the OT and NT are unique in that they alone, among the many religious writings of both the Jewish and Christian era, have the stamp of divine authority, and have from the beginning been recognized by the believing community as the living and authoritative Word of God.

apostasy Defection or falling away from the faith. Paul was falsely accused of spreading apostasy (Gk., *apostasia*), teaching Jews to "turn away from Moses" (Acts 21:21). The only other NT occurrence of this word concerns a defection from Christian faith—2 Th. 2:3 predicts a time of apostasy or rebellion ("falling away," KJV) when the Antichrist is revealed.

The OT, while not using the term *apostasy*, often describes it, as Israel turns from the living God:

"Has a nation ever changed its gods?
 (Yet they are not gods at all.)
But my people have exchanged their Glory
 for worthless idols. . . .
Your wickedness will punish you;
 your backsliding will rebuke you.
Consider then and realize
 how evil and bitter it is for you
when you forsake the Lord your God
 and have no awe of me."

(Jer. 2:11,19)

The NT warns against turning from Christ back to Judaism (Heb. 6:1-8), and against becoming so discouraged that commitment wanes (Heb. 10:26-39). But there is no real parallel between the apostasy of Israel and the experience of an individual Christian. The NT does, however, warn of apostate movements in which "some will abandon the faith and follow deceiving spirits and things taught by demons" (1 Tim. 4:1). Leaders of such movements are described in 2 Pet. 2 and Jude 8-13. *See also* False Prophets and Teachers.

The large figure of the Canaanite god Reshef, from the thirteenth century B.C., holds a mace in his right hand. In the background are silver figurines of other Canaanite deities, dating from the eighteenth century B.C. Jeremiah said, "My people have exchanged their Glory for worthless idols" (Jer. 2:11).

ITE IN MVNDVM VNIVERSVM, ET PRÆDICATE EVANGELIVM OMNI CREATVRÆ·

SIMON PETRVS · ANDREAS · PHILIPPVS · BARTHOLOMÆVS · IOANNES · IACOBVS · SIMON CANANÆ · MATHIAS · PAVLVS · IVDAS THADDÆ · IACOBVS ALPHÆI · MATTHÆVS · THOMAS·

apostle One who is sent out; specifically applied to Jesus' twelve disciples, Paul, and other NT missionaries. By NT times, *apostle* meant an envoy, one sent on a mission as the personal representative of the one sending him. The word was used in the Greek OT for messengers who were sent by God and who spoke with his authority. In the NT, the word *apostle* serves both as a title and as a general description.

THE APOSTLES

As a specialized title, *apostle* designates Jesus' twelve original disciples, who had a unique role in the founding of the church. They were envoys with authority, personally trained by Jesus himself. Jesus also commissioned them to "go and make disciples of all nations, baptizing them in the name of the Father and of the Son and of the Holy Spirit, and teaching them to obey everything I have commanded you" (Mt. 28:18-20). The commission is restated in Acts 1:8: "You will be my witnesses in Jerusalem, and in all Judea and Samaria, and to the ends of the earth."

After Judas's betrayal and suicide, the assembled believers decided to choose a new apostle to replace him. Peter then gave the requirements: he must "have been with us the whole time the Lord Jesus went in and out among us, beginning from John's baptism to the time when Jesus was taken up from us. For one of these must become a witness with us of his resurrection" (Acts 1:21,22).

The apostles did give powerful witness of the risen Christ, first in Jerusalem and then beyond the region of Palestine (*see* Acts 5:12-16; 8:1; 13:1-3). Paul rightly speaks of God's household as "built on the foundation of the apostles and prophets, with Christ Jesus himself as the chief cornerstone" (Eph. 2:20; *compare* 1 Cor. 12:28). In the early church "Peter and the apostles" guided its organization and growth. *See also* Disciple.

In all this, the apostles functioned as unique individuals, filling a specific role which was never translated into a church office.

THE APOSTLE PAUL

In his writings, Paul claimed for himself an apostolic authority equal to that of the Twelve (1 Cor. 4:9; 9:1,2; Gal. 2). Paul too saw the risen Jesus (Acts 9:1-6; 1 Cor. 15:3-8). He was directly commissioned by the Lord (Acts 26:15-18) as "a herald and an apostle . . . and a teacher of the true faith to the Gentiles" (1 Tim. 2:7). The validity of Paul's claim is acknowledged in 2 Peter where the writings of Paul are classed with the "other Scriptures" (2 Pet. 3:14-16).

OTHER APOSTLES

But Scripture also calls others "apostles," apparently in a more general sense. Barnabas (Acts 14:14) may acquire the title through affiliation with Paul or the other apostles, but Andronicus and Junias (Rom. 16:7) are otherwise unknown. Paul also writes heatedly of false teachers who consider themselves "super-apostles" (2 Cor. 11:1-15).

In this sense, the word describes the first-century evangelists and traveling mis-

The Apostles, by Hans Holbein the Younger, included Paul (left) with the Twelve, and replaced Judas Iscariot with Matthias (Acts 1:26). According to early church historian Eusebius, all but John died a martyr's death.

79

sionaries who were actively carrying out Jesus' command to the Twelve to "go into all the world" as witnesses to Jesus.

Are there apostles today? In this general sense, yes. Every Christian is an envoy of Christ. As Christ commissioned the Twelve, so he has "committed to us the ministry of reconciliation" (2 Cor. 5:18). The modern missionary may fill the role closest to that of the NT apostle, but each believer remains a representative of our Lord.

apothecary (KJV) A pharmacist. This archaic term used in the KJV is usually rendered "perfumer" in modern versions. In biblical times, a perfumer mixed both cosmetics and medical ointments.

appeal to Caesar A legal right of a Roman citizen to judicial review. Under Roman law, a citizen had the right of *provocatio*—the right to be tried in Rome rather than in an inferior court. When Festus, the newly appointed Roman governor, suggested Paul be tried in Jerusalem on charges brought by Paul's Jewish enemies, Paul exercised this right and officially appealed his case to Caesar. This took his case out of Festus's jurisdiction, and he was sent under guard to Rome to be tried before Nero (Acts 25,26).

apple An edible fruit and the tree that bears it. While even modern versions translate the Hebrew *tappuah* as "apple," most agree a different fruit tree is intended. According to biblical references the tree offered shade, fragrance, a sweet fruit, and a beautiful appearance (Song 2:3,5; 7:8; 8:5). Oranges, apricots, and quinces have been suggested as the biblical fruit. While apricots fit the description, evidence from secular writings suggest this fruit was not introduced to Palestine until the first century B.C. The orange, a major export item for modern Israel, may be the most likely biblical "apple."

Scholars suggest the sweet tappuah *fruit of the Old Testament is an orange, not an apple. Oranges are a major Israeli export today.*

apple of the eye Figuratively, something precious. In Old English usage, the "apple of the eye" was its pupil, but the phrase was used figuratively of anything that was precious and to be carefully guarded. The English phrase translates three different Hebrew idioms, but all have the same meaning. Most common is the Hebrew phrase, "the *'ishon* of the eye" (Deut. 32:10 of Israel, Ps. 17:8 of David, and Prov. 7:2 of godly instruction). The word means "little man," and suggests the reflection one sees in another's eye.

This provides some fascinating theolog-

ical implications. We are precious to God because in us he sees his reflected image, while the Law is precious to believers because it reflects what we are called in God to become.

In the other idioms, Israel is the *babah* ("gate," Zech. 2:8) and *bat* ("daughter," Lam. 2:18) of the eye.

Aquila [AK-wih-luh; "eagle"]. An early Christian notable with his wife Priscilla as friend and faithful supporter of Paul. **Scripture:** Acts 18.

Acts 18 identifies Aquila as a Jew. Like other Jews living outside Palestine, he and his wife adopted Roman names in addition to their Jewish names, which are not given in Scripture. Expelled from Rome by edict of the Emperor Claudius (about A.D. 49), they settled in Corinth. Paul, who shared their trade of tentmaking (that is, leatherworking), stayed with Aquila and Priscilla there. *See also* Tentmaker.

Aquila was apparently well off: he owned property, and the couple was free to travel with Paul to Ephesus (Acts 18:24-26). According to 1 Cor. 16:19, a house-church was established in their home. Later, after Claudius's edict expelling Jews was revoked in A.D. 54, the couple apparently returned to Rome and became leaders of the Christian community there (Rom. 16:3-5a).

LEARNING FROM AQUILA'S LIFE

Three elements of the biblical account are worth special consideration. First, in the welcome given Paul, the invitation to Apollos, and the sponsoring of a house-church, Aquila and Priscilla demonstrate the hospitality which has traditionally been highly valued in the East. The pair remained loyal to Paul even when their guest's teaching roused serious opposition (Acts 18:9-17). Perhaps it was at this time that "they risked their lives" for Paul (Rom. 16:4). *See also* Hospitality.

Second, note the sensitive way in which Aquila and Priscilla instructed Apollos. This eloquent Jew, who knew only of the baptism of John, spoke fervently in the Ephesian synagogue about the coming of the Messiah. Rather than correcting Apollos publicly, the couple invited him to their home. There they quietly "explained to him the way of God more adequately" (Acts 18:26). The church leaders then "encouraged" Apollos, who later became one of early Christianity's important traveling teachers. This couple's sensitivity in sharing Christ can serve as a model for the ministry of modern Christians. *See also* Baptism; John the Baptist.

Third, note the interplay of names. When the couple is introduced in Acts, Aquila is named first. But in the six other NT references to the pair, Priscilla is named first. While this has led to much speculation, the obvious implication is that Priscilla, if not the dominant spiritual force in the home, made such an exceptional impression on the Christian community that Luke, Paul, and all others who knew them thought first of Priscilla. Today, when many women are concerned about their role in life, Priscilla's primacy shows that gifted women were recognized and valued in the early church. *See also* Woman.

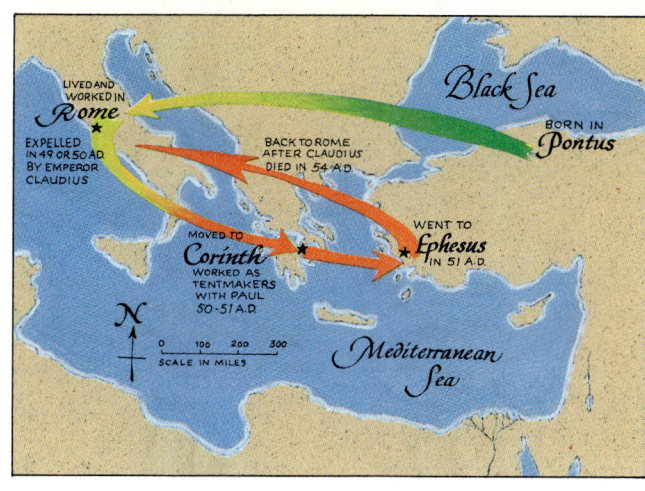

Arabah [AHR-ah-bah]. Generally, a desert or plain. Specifically, the arid valley between the Red Sea and Dead Sea.

In the KJV, *arabah* is regularly translated as "desert," "wilderness," or "plain." In contemporary versions, however, "the Arabah" appears as a proper name for a particular desert region, the desolate, 105-mile-long valley south of the Dead Sea. Dry and hot, with only about two inches of rainfall a year, the valley sinks to 1,298 feet below sea level and rises to a maximum height of 655 feet above sea level.

In biblical times, the Arabah incorporated the entire Jordan rift valley, from the Sea of Galilee south, including the "cities of the plain" around the Dead Sea. Important trade routes ran through the southern Arabah, and copper and iron mines were established there (*see* Deut. 8:9).

According to Gen. 13, the Arabah around the Dead Sea was beautiful and fertile in Abraham's time, until devastated by God's judgment on Sodom and Gomorrah. *See also* Sodom and Gomorrah. Although the region is dry and desolate now, the OT prophets speak of a time when waters will flow from Jerusalem to make the land around the Dead Sea rich again (Zech. 14:8; Ezek. 47:1-12).

Arabia The world's largest peninsula, Arabia is almost a third as large as the continental United States. It is a desolate area, hot and humid along the coast, and scorching hot in the desert interior during the summer. On the southern coast lies Mecca, the most holy city of Islam. Most scholars believe the Queen of Sheba once

Aquila and Priscilla, active leaders in the early church, illustrate the mobility of people in the first-century Roman Empire. They were born in Pontus and exiled from Rome by Claudius's edict against the Jews (A.D. 49). The couple worked as tentmakers and ministered alongside the apostle Paul in Corinth and Ephesus. When Claudius's edict was revoked in A.D. 54, they returned to Rome.

Below: Major trade routes crossed the Arabian peninsula. Gold, spices, and precious stones carried by camel caravans reached Israel through these routes.

Right: This eighth-century Hebrew ostracon (pottery fragment) bearing the inscription, "Gold of Ophir for Beth Horon, 30 shekels," was found in Israel near modern Tel Aviv.

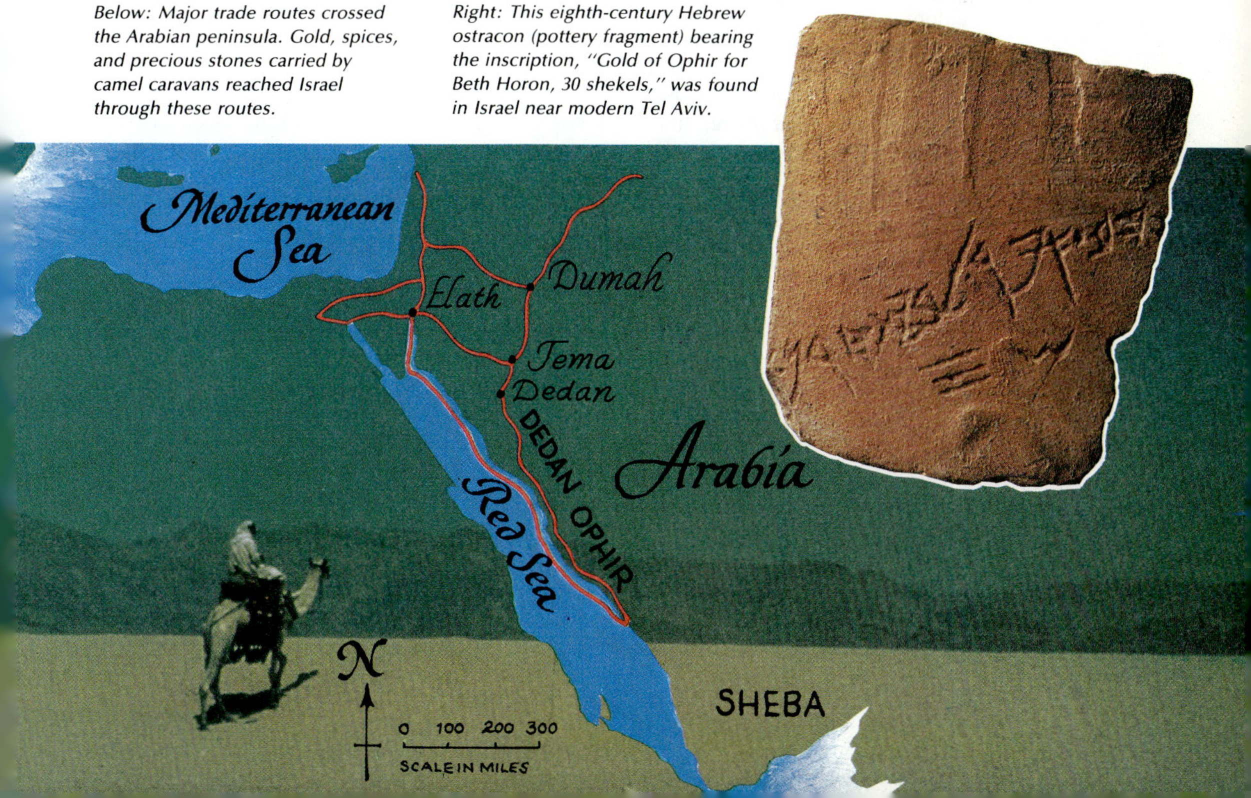

ruled near the southern tip of the peninsula (1 Ki. 10:1-10). We know it today as the oil-rich land of the Saudis, shared by Yemen, Oman, the United Arab Emirates, Qatar, and Kuwait.

The Bible mentions Arabia only 15 times. This is in part because the Bible, when referring to a particular geographical area, will often name the tribal groups which lived there. Another reason is that Arabia never played a significant role in Israel's history.

The two NT references to Arabia, probably following contemporary custom, refer to the land of the Nabateans, an Arab kingdom just west of Damascus.

Despite its rugged nature, the Arabian peninsula was crossed by several important trade routes in biblical times. On these routes, camel caravans transported gold, frankincense, and other goods produced in Arabia, as well as spices and expensive products from Africa and India. These trade routes were especially important to Israel during the economic boom of Solomon's time and just afterward.

Aram, Arameans A nation neighboring Israel on the northeast during much of the OT period. The Arameans, a Semitic people, spread throughout Syria and into Mesopotamia during the third millennium B.C. They are mentioned in numerous extra-biblical texts recovered by archaeologists. While the Arameans occupied much land, they divided themselves into small city-states and never united to form a dominant kingdom. Arameans are mentioned among Israel's enemies during the time of the judges (Jdg. 3:7-11; 10:6). Later Damascus emerged as the premier Aramean state, and proved to be a persistent enemy of Israel and Judah. A survey

Aramean sundial from the first century B.C. Throughout the era of the Hebrew kingdoms the Arameans were at odds with Israel. Biblical Aram comprises much of modern Syria.

of relationships between the Jews and Arameans from the time of David until the time of Jeroboam II puts the role of the Arameans into perspective.

1010–930 B.C.

An Aramean king, Hadadezer, established an extensive kingdom that briefly extended to the Euphrates River (2 Sam. 8:10). David defeated him and established Israelite authority over Syria (2 Sam. 8:5-12; 10). During Solomon's reign, Israel's authority in Syria was challenged by Rezon, who after years of insurgency finally established himself as king in Damascus (1 Ki. 11:23-25).

930–843 B.C.

After Rezon's death, Hezion took the throne and established the dynasty traced in 1 Ki. 15:18. Ben-Hadad (900–860 B.C.?) supported Judah when it was attacked by Israel (1 Ki. 15:18-20). Ben-Hadad II (860–843 B.C.?) proved to be the persistent enemy of Ahab, who defeated him only with God's help (1 Ki. 20). Later Ben-Hadad forged a coalition of states to oppose the expansion of Assyria. The coalition held off the Assyrian advance in a famous battle at Qarqar in 853 B.C. Ahab was part of this coalition, and provided the largest single military force.

843–732 B.C.

When Hazael murdered and replaced Ben-Hadad, the anti-Assyrian coalition fell apart. Furious, Hazael attacked Israel (2 Ki. 10:32,33). Relief came when Adad-nirari III of Assyria invaded Syria about 804 B.C. But Hazael's successor, Ben-Hadad III, continued to battle Israel although he was forced to surrender lands taken by Hazael to Jehoash of Israel (2 Ki. 13:25).

When Ben-Hadad's forces were crushed in a battle with a different enemy, Jeroboam II of Israel quickly acted to take Damascus (2 Ki. 14:28). The prosperity of Israel during Jeroboam's reign was largely due to control of the important trade routes that ran through Damascus.

After Jeroboam's death, Rezin became king in Damascus. He reconquered the lands across the Jordan and threatened Judah. The resurgence of Aramean power led Ahaz of Judah to appeal to Assyria. Tiglath-Pileser III gladly used the appeal as an excuse, and in 732 B.C. he invaded Damascus, killed Rezin (2 Ki. 16:5-9), and deported the Aramean population (*see* Amos 1:4,5).

The picture Scripture gives of hostility and tangled alliances is quite characteristic of life and politics in Bible times.

Aramaic language A Semitic language closely related to Hebrew. Aramaic became the trade language of the ancient East. During the Assyrian era (1100–538 B.C.), it became the language of diplomacy as well. Inscriptions from the tenth century B.C. contain the earliest surviving texts in the Aramaic language.

In 701 B.C., when an Assyrian general appeared outside the walls of Jerusalem to threaten Hezekiah, he was asked to speak in Aramaic, so the people listening from the city walls would not understand him. At that time, Aramaic was known only by officials, so far as the Jews were concerned (2 Ki. 18:26-28). After the Babylonian captivity, however, Aramaic had supplanted Hebrew as the common language of the people. Therefore, Ezra found it necessary to interpret (translate) the Scriptures when they were read to the populace (Neh. 8:8). Some of the latest OT writings (Ezra 4:8–6:18; 7:12-26; Dan. 2:4–7:28) are in Aramaic, and by about 300 B.C. Jewish rabbis were writing their biblical commentaries in Aramaic rather than Hebrew. Synagogue services were commonly bilingual as well: The Scriptures were first read in Hebrew and then repeated in the better-understood Aramaic.

The language persisted in Palestine beyond the first century A.D. Jesus and his disciples undoubtedly spoke Aramaic as well as Greek and some Hebrew, and a number of phrases in the Gospels can be best understood as Aramaisms.

Ararat A mountainous region in Asia Minor. When the waters of the Flood subsided, Noah's ark went aground in the mountainous region of Ararat (Gen. 8:4). The phrase "mountains of" may suggest the ark did not land on the peak known as Mount Ararat but in that general area.

The mountains of Ararat lie in present-day Turkey. Lake Van, the center of the district, is 6,000 feet above sea level, with mountains around it towering up nearly 17,000 feet. Tradition identifies the south slope of Mount Massis (Ararat) as the landing place of the ark. The Babylonian Gilgamesh Epic gives a story of the Flood which specifies Mount Nisir, a mountain about 9,000 feet high, as the resting place of Ut-napishtim's ark. A number of attempts have been made to locate the remains of Noah's ark. While fragments of wood have been found which some claim are from the ark, such claims have never been substantiated. The rough terrain, severe weather, and political tension of the region have prevented a careful survey of the area.

The altitude of this mountainous region is significant. In any local flood, the ark would have been swept along toward the sea. Only a cataclysm like that described in Gen. 6–9 could have lifted Noah's boat to such a height.

Aramaic (Elephantine)	Hebrew cursive 8th BC	Classical Greek	Latin (Roman)
א	א	A	A
ב	ב	B	B
ג	ג	Γ	G
ד	ד	Δ	D
ה	ה	E	E
ו	ו	φ	
ז	ז	Z	Z
ח	ח	H	H
ט	ט	Θ	
י	י	I	I
כ	כ	K	K
ל	ל	Λ	L
מ	מ	M	M
נ	נ	N	N
ס	ס	Ξ	
ע	ע	O	O
פ	פ	Π	P
צ	צ		
ק	ק		Q
ר	ר	P	R
ש	ש	Σ	S
ת	ת	T	T

Aramaic and Hebrew characters. During the exile (sixth century B.C.), Aramaic replaced Hebrew as the spoken language of the Jews. Jesus preached and taught in Aramaic.

The mountainous region of Ararat (Urartu) in northeastern Turkey includes Mount Ararat, elevation 16,945 feet (5,165 meters).

Black Sea

MT. ARARAT

Medit. Sea

archaeology The scientific study of ancient peoples and cultures by the recovery and interpretation of the remains of the past. As a special science, it is hardly 200 years old, and more careful modern methods of excavation have been in use for only some 50 or 60 years. Yet its accomplishments have often been spectacular. The discovery of the Rosetta Stone in 1798, on which the same text is engraved in hieroglyphic Egyptian, Demotic Egyptian and Hellenistic Greek, led to the deciphering of ancient Egyptian hieroglyphic writing in 1824. Next to this in importance was the discovery and recording in 1835 of the Behiston Rock inscription of Darius the Great with its three parallel versions of Old Persian, Babylonian, and Elamite cuneiform. After these were deciphered, the whole of post-Sumerian Mesopotamian literature was opened up to modern scholarship. In the 1840s and 1850s, excavations in Nineveh and other capital cities of Assyria uncovered the palaces of ancient kings, including innumerable clay tablets from the archives of Sennacherib and some 25,000 tablets from the library of Ashurbanipal. These tablets provided the basis for reconstructing the history of both Assyria and Babylon.

In 1877, files of diplomatic correspondence written in Babylonian cuneiform were uncovered in the ruins of Akhenaton's capital at Tell el-Amarna. These Amarna letters reveal much about the political situation in Palestine about the time of the Exodus. (*See also* Amarna Letters.) A 1925–1931 expedition at Nuzi uncovered 20,000 clay tablets written in Babylonian cuneiform that tell us much about the customs and laws of northern Mesopotamia from the time of Abraham to about 1500 B.C.

Workers at a typical "dig."

Stone steps lead past earthen rampart to the innermost arch (top center) of the massive defensive works of Laish. These 18th-century B.C. defenses protected the Canaanite city until it was conquered by the tribe of Dan in the twelfth century B.C.

Significant work began in Palestine in 1907 at Jericho and 1908 in Samaria. But it was the discovery in 1922 of the tomb of Tutankhamen in Egypt and Leonard Woolley's excavations at Ur that captured the imagination of the public and helped to popularize archaeology.

Despite continuing interest in archaeology in Bible lands, only around 200 of some 9,000 known sites in Palestine have been studied, and these are only partially excavated. Yet archaeology in Bible lands has provided fascinating information that often illuminates the biblical text, and has provided a knowledge of cultural background which enables us to better understand the experiences of Bible men and women.

ARCHAEOLOGICAL METHODS

Archaeologists seek to locate, date, and interpret all kinds of remains of past cultures. Human remains, objects of art, pottery, buildings, inscriptions, written documents, tools, weapons, coins, and cult objects are all carefully studied to develop a picture of the daily life, customs, politics, and beliefs of people of the past.

Much of the work of biblical archaeologists rests on the fact that many sites in Bible lands have been occupied for thousands of years. New generations built on and over the ruins of earlier generations. Over the centuries, as cities were repeatedly destroyed and reconstructed, mounds of debris have accumulated. These mounds, which modern-day archaeologists call *tells,* are a common land formation throughout Palestine.

Occupation of most of these cities was not continuous. Many cities were attacked and devastated by war; others were abandoned for hundreds of years at a time. As archaeologists unearth these sites, they can usually find distinguishable levels of occupation, which reveal a city's history. A layer of ash, for example, may mark the destruction of one settlement and the beginning of a new society that built upon it centuries later.

When an archaeological team digs into a *tell,* its members try to distinguish the levels, or strata, which mark each period of occupation. Obviously, a lower level is from an earlier period than the levels above it. The changing styles of pottery observable in the successive levels of a *tell* are of particular value in estimating the time of occupation. In general archaeologists attempt to date each stratum located in a dig, and then study the articles found in that stratum to learn more about the people and the society of that age. This procedure is called stratigraphic excavation.

While the basic approach of the archaeologist is straightforward, the work is difficult and must be done carefully. Archaeologists today plot a grid over their site, dividing it into fields that are typically two to five meters on each side. These fields are then subdivided into four smaller squares. The dirt is then carefully removed from selected squares and every item found is charted, sketched or photographed, and labeled as it is removed.

Cross-section of a typical "tell" (mound) excavation shows artifacts as they might occur in various strata. Analysis of finds in each stratum is the primary means of dating ancient cities. By studying the location of objects, archaeologists can determine the periods when a particular site was occupied and can learn much about its history.

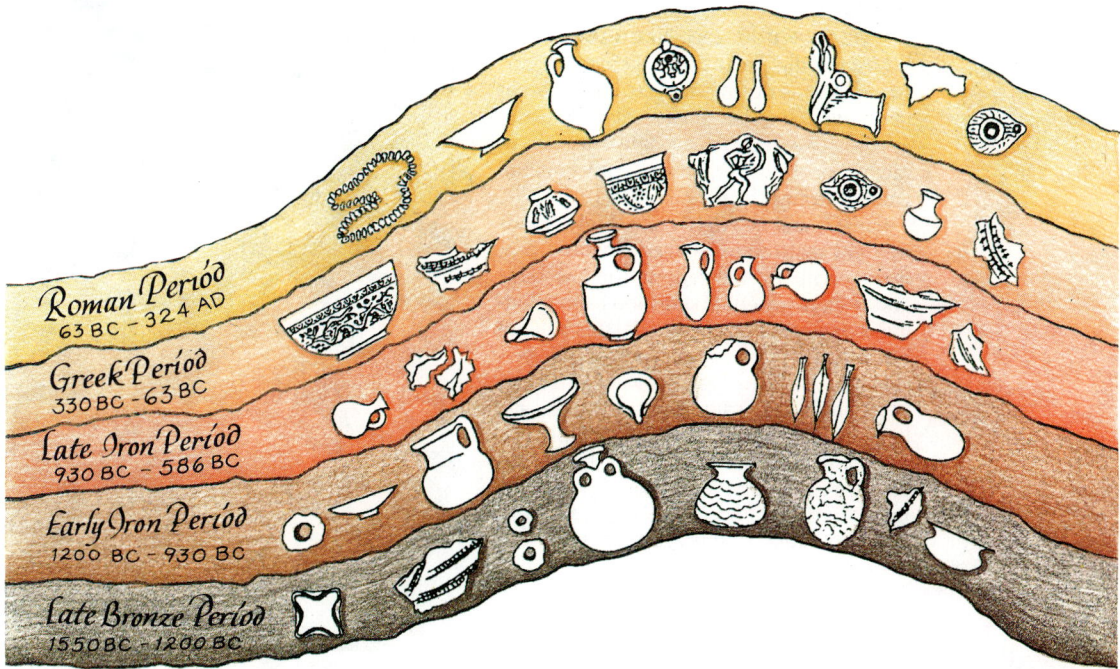

This excavation in Jerusalem revealed a tenth-century B.C. stepped-stone structure (center) probably used as a revetment wall. The wall is 50 feet (15 meters) high. Structures from the seventh century and the early Roman periods are also visible.

Below: worker removes earth and debris from pottery.

Volunteer worker cleans a Corinthian capital (top of column). Types of architecture provide important clues for dating excavated buildings.

Gradually a three-dimensional representation of the site is developed, based on exact measurements. Artifacts found in each stratum are studied to see what they reveal about life during that period.

VALUE OF BIBLICAL ARCHAEOLOGY

Despite the great care taken today, archaeology, as do all sciences, has inherent limitations. It is not always easy to distinguish between strata, to date strata accurately, or to interpret the information gained during the dig.

Earlier archaeologists in Bible lands thought that their discoveries would confirm specific events reported in the Bible and resolve unsettled questions about dating. For a number of reasons, this has not happened. For one thing, only a tiny percentage of all the potential sites have or ever will be excavated, and no single site in Israel has ever been studied completely. Also, only a tiny percentage of the articles of any period survive the passage of time. Even in dry biblical lands, wood will rot, and clothing, leather, and paper will decay.

Another problem lies in the fact that archaeologists must interpret what they discover. What is the meaning of the tiny bronze bull found on a hillside near a stone altar in the tribal area of Ephraim? Was this a Jewish high place? Or a place where Canaanites worshiped? In just which century was this particular city attacked and destroyed, and who was the enemy? The fact that archaeologists heatedly debate this kind of question, as well as such major issues as the date of the Exodus, makes it clear that archaeology is far from an exact science. Even the most confident pronouncements of the biblical archaeologist are made by fallible men and women, who are all too likely to be proven wrong.

Despite its limitations, archaeology can contribute much to our understanding of the Bible. First, archaeology provides knowledge of the cultural context in which biblical events took place. The deciphered languages of the past have helped us better understand biblical Hebrew. Recovered texts dealing with ancient laws and customs have helped us interpret specific Bible texts. For instance, "Jacob have I loved and Esau have I hated" is not an expression of God's antagonism toward Esau, but part of a legal formula expressing God's choice of Jacob as heir to the covenant promises and his rejection of any claim by Esau of a right to inherit. (*See also* Covenant.) Study of the Code of Hammurabi, recorded some 300 years before Moses, helps us see both the similarity and the difference between Israel's moral vision and that of their pagan contemporaries.

In addition, archaeology has helped us understand much about the daily life and experience of people in biblical times. For instance, the roof height of houses built during the time of the judges suggests the typical Israelite may have been only about five feet tall. Saul could have stood head and shoulders above his people at only some six feet, still far short of Goliath's nine-foot stature.

Through the discoveries of archaeology we know much about how people farmed, how they managed their limited water supplies, what they ate, how they defended their cities, and how they went to war.

Archaeology has also proven helpful in refuting some of the claims of critics of the Bible's historical accuracy. The Book of Daniel was once ridiculed for naming Belshazzar as king of Babylon—until an inscription was found that identified him as

ruling jointly with his father Nabonidus. Again and again, details such as the titles given officials, descriptions of court practices, the terminology used in poetry in cognate languages, and other minutiae, have refuted the critics and demonstrated the trustworthiness of the Bible.

As many have pointed out, the Bible is a record of God's revelation of himself to human beings. The truth of what the Bible teaches lies beyond the ability of archaeology either to prove or to disprove. Yet the Bible is also a human document, and its writers report the dealings of God with humankind in time and space. The spiritual and historical aspects of Scripture are so intertwined that any significant distortion of history by the writers of the Bible would bring its message into question. *See also* Inspiration.

The fact that the Bible has proven to be such a trustworthy report of history cannot help but reassure believers, and confirm our belief that Scripture truly is the Word of God.

A worker carefully reconstructs a pot unearthed at Deir el-Balah, near Gaza.

Top left: Volunteer surveys the results of hundreds of hours of digging by hand to uncover ancient structures.

Capitals were often laid on top of one another to achieve a desired height or effect.

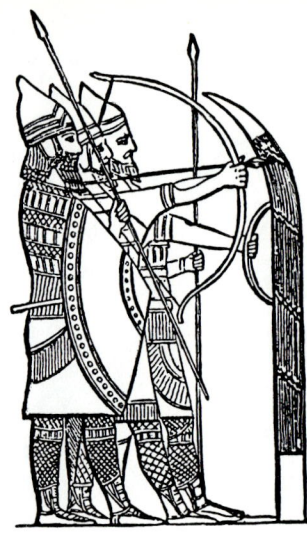

Line drawing from an Assyrian relief, about 690 B.C., shows two archers sheltered by a large reed shield. Assyrian army groups included large, organized corps of archers.

archangel See angel.

archer One who shoots with bow and arrow, usually in warfare.

Archers played an important role in ancient armies. Most armies included a corps of archers as their long-range threat. The composite bow widely used in the Middle East about 1500 B.C. proved effective at a distance of 300–400 yards.

Ancient drawings and carvings from Bible lands depict archers in battle. One representation of an attack on a fort about

The Areopagus as it looks today. "The Hill of Ares" later became known as Mars Hill. Ares was the Greek god of war and Mars was the Roman one. Map shows the relationship of the Areopagus to other landmarks in ancient Athens.

Panathenaic Way

Agora

Valerian Wall

Areopagus

MARS HILL

Parthenon

ACROPOLIS

0 ———— 300 yds
0 ———— 300 m

1900 B.C. shows the defenders firing arrows and throwing rocks.

While Hos. 1:5 speaks of the bow as symbolic of military force, Scripture gives no description of any Israelite corps of archers (*but see* 1 Chr. 8:40). However, Israelite archers appear in Assyrian reliefs that portray the defense of Lachish in 701 B.C. *See also* Arrow; Bow; Warfare.

Areopagus A small hill near the Acropolis in Athens, also known as Mars Hill. "Areopagus" also refers to the council of Athenian leaders that met there. In Athens, Paul preached in the open-air market. He was ridiculed by local philosophers and then brought "to a meeting of the Areopagus" (Acts 17:19).

Originally this council had advised the kings of Athens. It lost its political influence by the end of the fifth century B.C., but retained some judicial authority. In the first century A.D., it still exercised control over those who wished to lecture or teach in Athens. Acts 17 records a summary of what Paul taught there and the response of this council of leading citizens. Most scoffed, but others wanted to withhold judgment and hear Paul again. While no mention is made of a church founded in Athens, at least one council member and a leading Athenian woman, with a few others, were converted (Acts 17:34).

ark, Noah's The boat by which Noah and his family survived the great Flood. In describing Noah's ark, Genesis uses the Hebrew word *tebah*, which means "chest" or "vessel that floats" (Gen. 6–9). The term is used only here and in Ex. 2:3,5, where it describes the reed basket in which baby Moses floated on the Nile.

The Bible specifies the dimensions of the ark. Assuming Noah used an 18-inch cubit, the vessel was 450 feet long, 75 feet wide, and 45 feet high (140 by 23 by 13.5 meters). A vessel of this size, with three decks and numerous rooms (literally, "nests") would have a 20,000-ton displacement and about 1,396,000 cubic feet of interior space. If the larger 22.5-inch cubit was used, the ark would have displaced about 43,000 tons! Assuming that the animals hibernated, the ark could easily have accommodated as many as 35,000 different vertebrate "kinds" along with Noah and his family. *See also* Cubit; Kind.

The vessel described in Gen. 6:14-16 was made of "gopher wood" (KJV), most likely cypress. Light and durable, cypress wood was later used for shipbuilding by

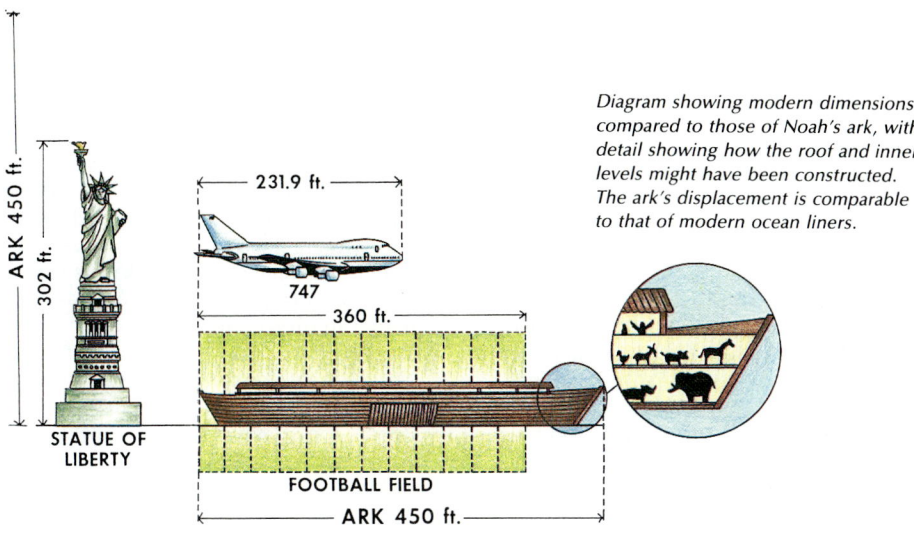

Diagram showing modern dimensions compared to those of Noah's ark, with detail showing how the roof and inner levels might have been constructed. The ark's displacement is comparable to that of modern ocean liners.

ARK 450 ft.
302 ft.
231.9 ft.
747
360 ft.
STATUE OF LIBERTY
FOOTBALL FIELD
ARK 450 ft.

the Phoenicians. The entire vessel was then coated with pitch inside and out to make it watertight. An 18-inch opening for light and air was apparently left between the hull and the roof. The proportions of the ark, an extremely stable design, are similar to those of modern cargo ships. This is in striking contrast to the vessel described in the Epic of Gilgamesh, a Sumerian flood tale. That ark was a cube that could never have floated. *See also* Ararat; Noah.

ark of the covenant The portable sacred chest which held the holiest relics of Israel's history and served as the place for the direct manifestation of the presence of God.

God gave Moses detailed instructions for building the ark of the covenant (Ex. 25:10-22), also known as "the ark of the Testimony" (Num. 4:5), "the ark of God" (1 Sam. 3:3), and poetically "the ark of your might" (Ps. 132:8). The ark measured 3¾ by 2¼ by 2¼ feet (1.1 by .07 by .07 meters), and was made of acacia wood, overlaid with gold inside and out. On top of the cover, two cherubim made of hammered gold sat at each end, facing each other and looking towards the cover. Their wings arched gracefully up, overshadowing the cover. *See also* Cherubs.

The ark had three main functions:

(1) It served as a container for the two stone tablets of the Law that Moses brought down from Mount Sinai (Deut. 10:2,5), a jar of the manna that God provided during the wilderness wanderings (Ex. 16:33,34), and the rod which budded to confirm Aaron's exclusive call to Israel's priesthood (Num. 17:10).

(2) The ark's cover was the place where sacrificial blood was spilled once a year on the Day of Atonement to make atonement "for all the sins of the Israelites" (Lev. 16:34). *See also* Atonement.

(3) The ark was viewed as the locus of God's presence with his people. God promised Moses that "there, above the cover between the two cherubim that are over the ark of the Testimony, I will meet with you and give you all my commands for the Israelites" (Ex. 25:22). Years later, although King Hezekiah did not dare to go into the Holy of Holies in the Temple where the ark lay, he prayed to the God of Israel who was "enthroned between the cherubim" (2 Ki. 19:15).

These functions made the ark of the covenant the most holy object in Israel's worship. When the shrine was carried, it was to be covered so that no one could see it (Ex. 40:5; Num. 4:5). This practice reminded the people to revere their holy God. Years later, in Samuel's time, God struck dead the inhabitants of Bethshemesh who looked into the ark, stimulating the response: "Who can stand in the presence of the Lord, this holy God?" (1 Sam. 6:20). *See also* Holy.

THE HISTORY OF THE ARK

The history of the ark can be traced for nearly a thousand years, from its construction to the time of the destruction of the Jerusalem Temple in 586 B.C. The ark was carried ahead of the Israelites as they traveled through the wilderness, as they entered Canaan (Josh. 3:6), and in the march around Jericho (6:6). After the conquest of Palestine, the ark was placed in the tabernacle, which was set up first at Shiloh, then at Bethel (18:1,8-10; 19:51; Jdg. 20:26, 27; 21:2). (*See also* Tabernacle.) Later the ark was moved back to Shiloh (1 Sam. 1:3; *compare* 3:3). David brought the ark to Jerusalem when he made that city capital of a united Israel (2 Sam. 6). When David's son Solomon constructed the Temple, he installed the ark in its innermost chamber (1 Ki. 8). There is no record of the ark surviving Nebuchadnezzar's final attack in which Jerusalem and its Temple were destroyed in 586 B.C. In fact, Jeremiah prophesied that the ark would be destroyed, for the prophet proclaims in God's name that in a future time "it will never enter their minds or be remembered; it will not be missed, nor will another one be made. At that time they will call Jerusalem The Throne of the Lord, and all nations will gather in Jerusalem to honor the name of the Lord" (Jer. 3:16,17).

The ark of the covenant was the most holy object in Old Testament religion, for here atoning blood was sprinkled once a year by Israel's high priest. This is one artist's interpretation of the lost ark.

LEARNING FROM THE ARK

No history of the ark would be complete without noting how it was misunderstood by Israel. The ark, which at first symbolized God's presence, came to be viewed by the general populace as the actual presence of God himself. Consider this incident from late in the time of the judges (1 Sam. 4–6): After a defeat by the Philistines, the elders of Israel said, "Let us bring the ark of the Lord's covenant from Shiloh, so that it may go with us and save us from the hand of our enemies" (1 Sam. 4:3). This essentially pagan religious concept was echoed by the Philistines who, when they learned that the ark had arrived, said, "A god has come into the camp" (1 Sam. 4:7).

But as it turned out, Israel lost the battle; the ark was captured and placed in the temple of the Philistine god Dagon. When the idol fell down before the ark, and the Philistines experienced a seven-month

plague of mysterious, painful tumors, they returned the ark to Israel (1 Sam. 6).

The same confusion between symbols of God's presence and the divine presence itself characterized the decades just before the destruction of Jerusalem. The people reasoned wrongly that because God's presence dwelt in the Temple when it was dedicated by Solomon, and the ark rested in the inner sanctuary (2 Chr. 5), God was committed to protect the Temple and its city. The prophet Ezekiel responded with a disclosure of a vision of the glory of God going up from between the cherubim as it abandoned the Temple and Jerusalem itself (Ezek. 8–11). The generation which placed its hope not in the living God but in a mere symbol of God's presence was crushed by the Babylonian armies, and the survivors were taken captive to a foreign land.

God may permit the use of material objects as symbols. Many Christian traditions, like ancient Israel, use material things as aids to worship. Such objects must never be confused or equated with God himself, nor must our confidence be placed in them. We must remember, as Solomon did when he addressed God at the dedication of Israel's Temple, "The heavens, even the highest heavens, cannot contain you. How much less this temple I have built!" (2 Chr. 6:18). It is in God, not symbols of his presence, that we trust.

arm Upper limb of the human body. In the ancient Middle East, the shoulder and arm symbolized strength or power. Thus, when God says he will redeem Israel from Egyptian slavery with "an outstretched arm" (Ex. 6:6), he is graphically describing his power over human affairs. To "break the arms of the wicked" was to destroy their strength and capacity to harm others (Ps. 37:17; Ezek. 30:24,25). The bared arm, like the outstretched arm, symbolized power being used, usually in warfare (Ezek. 4:7).

One's reaction to the revealed arm of God depends on his or her relationship with the Lord. For the believer, God's arm means comfort: "The eternal God is your refuge, and underneath are the everlasting arms. He will drive out your enemy before you, . . . So Israel will live in safety alone; Jacob's spring is secure in a land of grain and new wine" (Deut. 33:27,28).

Armageddon The place described in Rev. 16:16, where the demon-energized armies of the nations will gather for a final battle against the Jewish people.

kingdoms varied tremendously from king to king. Under Ahab, a strong and militarily successful ruler, Israel contributed 2,000 chariots to an allied force that resisted the Assyrians at Qarqar (853 B.C.). The rival kingdom of Damascus contributed only 1,200. About 150 years later, the Assyrians scoffed at King Hezekiah, offering to supply Judah with 2,000 horses if the king could find 2,000 cavalry troopers to mount them (2 Ki. 18:23). But in answer to Hezekiah's prayer, the angel of the Lord caused the death of 185,000 men in the Assyrian camp, and King Sennacherib returned to his own land without attacking Jerusalem (2 Ki. 19:35,36). *See also* Number; Warfare.

GOD AS LORD OF ARMIES

Hezekiah's prayer and its surprising answer illustrate an important OT concept. One of the names given God is "Lord of armies" ("Lord of hosts," KJV). Because Scripture emphasizes God's command of heavenly armies, the phrase is translated "Lord Almighty" in the NIV. Yet the name also reflects God's commitment to lead the armies of earthly Israel. A generation in Israel which honored God and kept his Law could count on the Lord's involvement in their wars, for God promised through Moses, "Do not be terrified by them, for the Lord your God, who is among you, is a great and awesome God. . . . The Lord your God will deliver them over to you, throwing them into great confusion until they are destroyed. . . . No one will be able to stand up against you; you will destroy them" (Deut. 7:21-24).

According to Scripture, it is the faithfulness of Israel's God, not the strength of Israel's armies, that accounts for the victories the nation has won. It was Israel's faithlessness that accounted for the tragic defeats she suffered.

Examples of such divine intervention can be seen in Israel's wars against Jericho (Josh. 5:13–6:27); the Amorites (Josh. 10:1-15); the Midianites (Jdg. 7); the Philistines (1 Sam. 7:2-14; 2 Sam. 5:17-25); Syria (Aram) (1 Ki. 20:13-30; 2 Ki. 6:24–7:20); Moab (2 Ki. 3); and Assyria (2 Ki. 18,19).

Relief shows second-century A.D. Roman soldiers of the Praetorian Guard in ceremonial helmets and breastplates.

armor Defensive covering worn in battle. During the patriarchal period (2100–1570 B.C.), soldiers seldom wore any armor. But as the composite bow, with its greater penetrating power, replaced the simple bow, the ancient armies had to develop defensive garments. Among their innovations: shields, helmets, and coats of mail

The cuirass protected the soldier from neck to waist. Shown here: (L-R) Roman Imperial Guard; Phrygian; Persian; Dacian; Greek.

Styles of
HELMETS

Egyptian

Assyrian

Philistine

Persian

Greek

(body armor made of metal scales). The metal scales, punctured by tiny holes, were sown onto garments with heavy thread. Equipment lists found in the Nuzi excavation classify coats of mail by the number of large and small scales on each. One of the coats listed had 1,035 metal scales.

Such armor was extremely expensive, and no military force could completely equip its troops with coats of mail. These were typically assigned to chariot soldiers and archers, who needed both hands for fighting and thus could not carry a shield. However, the coat of mail had weaknesses. Ahab was killed in battle when a random arrow struck him in the armpit, where sleeve and body armor were joined (1 Ki. 22:34).

While Goliath wore protective armor on his legs ("greaves"; 1 Sam. 17:6), this was not typical of the armies of the era.

armor-bearer The personal assistant of a champion warrior. The armor-bearer did more than carry weapons. Typically a younger man, the armor-bearer was responsible to follow the fighter he served and to kill any of the enemy his champion disabled (1 Sam. 14:13). The Bible mentions the armor-bearers of Abimelech (Jdg. 9:54), Jonathan (1 Sam. 14), and Saul (1 Sam. 31:4-6). Joab, David's general, had ten (2 Sam. 18:15). Both Abimelech and Saul, in hopeless situations, asked their armor-bearers to kill them.

armor of God The apostle Paul's figurative expression of the believer's spiritual defense against the devil (Eph. 6:11-18). Describing the equipment of the most heavily armed Roman infantry legions,

Assyrian soldiers, in helmet and breastplate, carry heads of vanquished foes, 750 B.C.

Paul instructed Christians to equip themselves with the "full armor of God so that you can take your stand against the devil's schemes" (Eph. 6:11).

In context, this exhortation stands as a summary of the whole Epistle. Thus, to interpret Paul's exhortation properly, we need to see how he applies the qualities associated with each piece of equipment to his discussion of the Body of Christ.

If a church is equipped with these armor-like qualities, its members will withstand all of Satan's efforts to destroy its witness and effectiveness.

aroma Scent, fragrance. In 2 Cor. 2:15, Paul says we are "the aroma of Christ," referring not to the aroma of an OT sacrifice, but to the incense burned during the victory procession customarily given a successful Roman general. Paul sees Christ as

AN INTERPRETATION OF THE ARMOR OF GOD

Equipment	Quality	Interpretation
Belt	Truth	Openness and honesty bind Christians together (4:15,25)
Breastplate	Righteousness	Morality and purity are to mark every life (5:3)
Sandals (shod feet)	Gospel of peace	Unity and harmonious relationships must be maintained (4:3)
Shield	Faith	Confidence and hope should be placed in God (3:20)
Helmet	Salvation	Awareness of our identity as members of Christ's Body brings assurance (3:6)
Sword of the Spirit	Word of God	Only this equipment has not been discussed previously in Ephesians, so it is defined now (6:17)

a conquerer, who leads the Church in a victory parade. The Gospel message itself, as it is borne in a believer's life, is the incense. Just as that aroma seemed fragrant to the fellow-citizens of the victor, the Gospel message is sweet to those who are saved. But to the captives of the victorious general who were led through the city in chains, the incense was the smell of death, for many would soon die in gladiatorial games. Similarly, the Gospel is the smell of death to those who refuse to believe Christ's good news, because they, too, will perish.

arrogance Unwarranted pride, haughtiness. Several Hebrew words are translated "arrogance" in English versions. Together they portray an attitude which is often linked in Scripture with sin and divine judgment (Deut. 1:42,43; Isa. 2:11,17). The arrogant person is self-important and self-confident. His insensitivity to others is matched by an unwillingness to submit to God. Psalm 73 depicts the character of arrogant people:

From their callous hearts comes iniquity;
the evil conceits of their minds know no
limits.
They scoff, and speak with malice;
in their arrogance they threaten oppression.
Their mouths lay claim to heaven,
and their tongues take possession of the
earth.
. . . .
They say, "How can God know?
Does the Most High have knowledge?"
(Ps. 73:7-11)

No wonder God says through Isaiah, "I will punish the world for its evil, the wicked for their sins. I will put an end to the arrogance of the haughty and will humble the pride of the ruthless" (Isa. 13:11).

arrow A pointed shaft shot from a bow. The shafts of early arrows were made from reeds or light wood (usually about 30 inches long), notched at one end. The tip of the arrow was often of flint, but sometimes bone, bronze, or iron. Sometimes the tip was dipped in poison to make the arrow more effective (Job 6:9), and sometimes combustible materials were used (Eph. 6:16). To keep the arrow from wandering off course during its flight, feathers usually adorned the tail of the arrow. Arrows were carried in quivers, which could hold 20 or 30 of them.

Arrows were used in hunting (Gen. 21:10; 27:3; Isa. 7:24), and in Babylon they were used for divination (Ezek. 21:21). They also played a major role in warfare in the ancient world.

Warfare changed as weapons became more sophisticated. The evolution of bows from simple to composite increased their effective distance and striking power. This in turn stimulated development of better shields and body armor. Arrowheads also changed shape, size, weight, and material. Ancient armies were equipped with arrows carefully matched to their intended use in warfare and to the makeup of enemy armies. Heavier arrows, for instance, were used for firing from city walls; lighter arrows, which traveled farther, were used in open-field fighting. *See also* Archer; Warfare.

art Clearly, God is the preeminent artist in this universe. He sculpted the Grand Canyon, designed the forms of all living creatures, and splashed the vivid colors of sunset across the sky. It would be surprising if human beings, created in God's image, failed to share their Maker's passion for creating beauty.

Even when we expand our concept of the arts to include dance, music, and literature, God himself has set the standard. The mating rituals of his creatures, as well as brightly colored leaves swirling on a crisp fall breeze, model the dance. The range and tone of the human voice and the songs of the birds are nature's instruments, while the heavens declare God's glory in a voice heard to the ends of the earth (Ps. 19:1-4). Given God's example, it may seem surprising that Israel was not a leader in the arts. While cultures in Egypt and Mesopotamia left many great works of art, Israel's contribution seems limited to literature and music.

ISRAEL AND THE ARTS
Traditionally the arts are classified as spatial (related to space) and temporal (related to time). Architecture, sculpture, and painting are the spatial arts. Music and literature are the temporal, with dance and theater overlapping both categories. For a number of reasons, Israel made no significant contribution to the spatial arts.

One reason was that Israel had no stable, lasting society to provide the context in which a distinctive artistic tradition might develop and flourish. In Egypt, Israel was a slave class, dominated by a culture whose traditions had already been established for over a thousand years. After its invasion of Canaan, the people of Israel continually struggled for their exis-

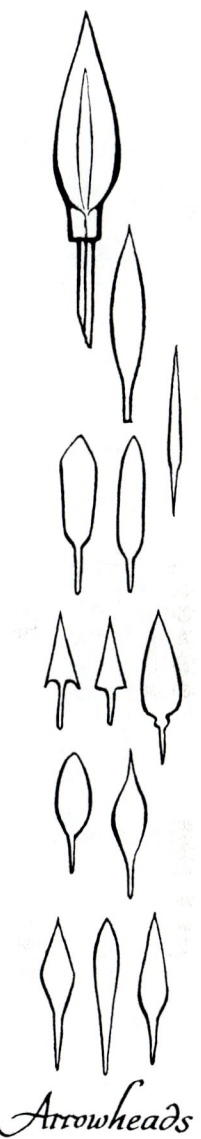

Arrowheads

Arrowheads from Palestine reflect the various materials, sizes, and shapes used in different eras.

95

EXAMPLES OF ART IN THE BIBLE

SPATIAL ARTS

ARCHITECTURE
Adopted Canaanite style.
In Solomonic era, building of
fortified cities, palace and
Jerusalem Temple (1 Ki. 9).

SCULPTURE
Skills present in the Exodus
generation (Ex. 32).
Misused in making idols in Israel's
later history (Isa. 40:18–20).

PAINTING
Egyptian-style wall paintings used
in idolatrous worship
(Ezek. 8:9–11).

TEMPORAL ARTS

DANCE
Associated throughout
history with religious
and other celebrations
(Ex. 15:20; Jdg. 11:34; 1 Ki.
18:26; Ps. 149:3).

MUSIC
Associated as early as 2000 B.C. with
family gatherings (Gen. 31:27).
Always an important part of worship in
Israel (1 Chr. 6:31,32; Ps. 33:2; Ps.
98:4–6) and other cultures (Dan. 3:5).
Associated with NT worship (Eph.
5:19) and celebration (Jas. 5:13) and
with worship in heaven to come
(Rev. 14:3; 15:3).

LITERATURE
Many literary forms found in
Scripture, including:
Poetry: Jdg. 5; Ps. 23
Narrative: Gen. 24; Jdg. 6
Short story: Ruth, Jonah
Liturgy: Ps. 118
Prophecy: Isa. 1; Amos 5
Apocalypse: Dan. 8; Rev. 8
Parable: Mt. 18; Lk. 15
Persuasion: Philemon
Didactics: Rom. 3

tence against neighboring nations. It was not until the time of David that Israel established itself as a united and powerful kingdom. Even when the Temple was built, Solomon had to borrow builders and artists, as well as many elements of the Temple's design, from Hiram, king of Tyre (1 Ki. 5–7).

Undoubtedly the most significant reason that Israel did not develop the spatial arts was the second commandment of the Decalogue: "You shall not make for yourself an idol in the form of anything in heaven above or on the earth beneath or in the waters below" (Ex. 20:4). This prohibition was not against art but against making idols. Yet the art of the ancient Near East was essentially religious in nature, and this led to a deep Jewish hostility toward all representational art.

On the other hand, Israel developed a rich and powerful language through which God's message to humankind was delivered in poetry, narrative history, wisdom literature, vivid imagery, and prophetic utterance. While discoveries in the Near East show parallels with Israel's literary forms, the power and beauty of the OT Scriptures clearly excel.

THE ARTS IN SCRIPTURE
Coming out of Egypt, the Israelites had artistic skills. God enhanced the existing talents of Bezalel and Oholiab to "make artistic designs for work in gold, silver and bronze, to cut and set stones, to work in wood, and to engage in all kinds of craftsmanship" (Ex. 31:4,5). This involved fashioning images of the cherubim that bent over the cover of the ark, the golden

lampstand and other furnishings of the tabernacle, as well as designing the garments for the priests. *See also* Tabernacle.

Others must have had the same talent, as seen in the story of the golden idol "cast in the shape of a calf" that Israel made while Moses was on Mount Sinai (Ex. 32:4). The process of casting involved carving or sculpting the figure, making a clay mold, and casting it in gold.

These skills, probably learned from the Egyptians, apparently vanished with the death of that generation. As noted, when Solomon built his Temple, he sent to Tyre for the skilled craftsmen needed to do the decorative work for his Temple (1 Ki. 7:13-15) and supervise its construction.

Music and dancing were also a part of Israel's worship. Many of the psalms were set to music, and many contain musical notations in their superscriptions. *See also* Music and Musical Instruments; Psalms; Selah.

While we have no scores of Hebrew music or information about their dance patterns, it is clear that both are linked not only with worship, but also with other times of celebration. The Israelites used dancing and music to celebrate God's triumph over Egypt at the Red Sea (Ex. 15:20), David's victory over Goliath (1 Sam. 18:7), and the ark's entry into Jerusalem (2 Sam. 6:14). The Lord promised his people in captivity, "Again you will take up your tambourines, and go out to dance with the joyful" (Jer. 31:4).

Yet it is the rich literature and language of the Bible that reveals the true genius of Israel, as God shaped a tongue and literary capacity uniquely capable of expressing his message to mankind. Nothing before or since has rivaled the power and beauty of that language, or its capacity for translation into the tongue of every tribe and nation.

Artaxerxes [ahr-tuh-ZERK-sees; "mighty king"]. Four Persian rulers in ancient history bore the name Artaxerxes, leading to speculation that it might be a title, like "Pharaoh" or "Abimelech." When the Books of Ezra and Nehemiah mention Artaxerxes, they are probably referring to two different rulers, Artaxerxes I (464–424 B.C.) and Artaxerxes II (404–358 B.C.). *See also* Persia.

Artemis [AHR-tuh-muhs] **of Ephesus** Called Diana in the KJV, Artemis of the Ephesians was a goddess of fertility modeled on the ancient Asian "earth mother" goddess Cybele or Ashtoreth. Statues and figurines depict her with many breasts, which represent fertility. *See also* Asherah.

Sometime after the Greeks settled in Asia Minor, they adopted this Asian goddess and gave her the name of their Greek goddess, Artemis. About 600 B.C., her followers built a massive temple in Ephesus where ancient shrines had previously been erected. This structure was destroyed in 356 B.C., and a rebuilt temple was completed about 250 B.C. The temple of Artemis of Ephesus, considered one of the seven wonders of the ancient world, contained an image of Artemis fashioned from a meteorite (Acts 19:35). The temple itself measured 425 feet by 225 feet (130 meters by 69 meters), and featured 127 decorated columns that stood 60 feet high (18 meters).

Worship of Artemis was widespread in Asia. Thousands of pilgrims visited Ephesus each year to worship at the temple (which was Artemis's major shrine) and to take part in the month-long festival dedicated to the goddess. In addition, the temple treasury functioned as a bank, ca-

Gold daric minted in Persia about 400 B.C. features the likeness of Artaxerxes II.

Statue of Artemis recovered at Ephesus shows multiple breasts, or possibly eggs. The worship of Artemis (Diana) at Ephesus fused Greek and Near Eastern cults.

pable of making massive loans. The economy of Ephesus depended on the flow of tourists, many of whom bought silver replicas of the shrine (Acts 19:25). *See also* Ephesians.

When the apostle Paul began preaching there, the impact of the Gospel was so overwhelming that it threatened the income of silversmiths and others who served the religious pilgrims. These craftsmen feared "not only that our trade will lose its good name, but also that the temple of the great goddess Artemis will be discredited, and the goddess herself, who is worshiped throughout the province of Asia and the world, will be robbed of her divine majesty" (Acts 19:27).

Asa [AY-suh; "healer"]. The third king of Judah, who ruled from 910–869 B.C., and was its first godly ruler. **Scripture:** 1 Ki. 15; 2 Chr. 14–16. **Maternal grandmother:** Maacah, a daughter of Absalom. **Father:** Abijah. **Wife:** Azubah. **Son and successor:** Jehoshaphat.

BACKGROUND

Just 20 years after Solomon's united kingdom was torn apart, Asa took the throne of Judah. A state of hostility still existed. Worse still, because Asa's father and grandfather had turned to idolatry, Judah was dotted with shrines to the gods and goddesses of the pagan peoples around them (1 Ki. 14:22-24). Yet, when Asa came to power, he "commanded Judah to seek the Lord, and to obey his laws and commands" (2 Chr. 14:4). God rewarded Asa's commitment with an exceptionally long 41-year reign.

EVENTS OF ASA'S REIGN

Asa apparently began his reign with immediate but incomplete reform efforts. Despite the tension that existed along the border, Judah experienced a time of building and prosperity. Sometime during these years a large army from Cush (southern Egypt) invaded Judah. Asa appealed to God for help, and the enemy was defeated.

On the return of the victorious army, the prophet Azariah encouraged Asa to "be strong and do not give up, for your work will be rewarded" (2 Chr. 15:7). The message stimulated Asa to complete the reforms begun earlier. He removed idols from the whole land, repaired the altar of the Lord, and then assembled all his people for a great ceremony of covenant renewal, or recommitment to the Lord. *See* Covenant Renewal. At this time, Asa removed his grandmother as queen mother because she refused to seek God and in-

Revivals under Asa and other godly kings of Judah featured destruction of "Asherim" and other persistent symbols of Canaanite religion

stead set up an Asherah pole (2 Chr. 15:12-16). (*See also* Asherah.) This time of renewal happened in the 15th year of Asa's reign (895 B.C.) and it apparently stimulated an unexpected hostile response from King Baasha of Israel.

In the 16th year of Asa's reign (rather than the 36th which is apparently a scribal error in 2 Chr. 16:1), Baasha acted to fortify the city of Ramah "to prevent anyone leaving or entering the territory of Asa king of Judah." Ramah lay just five miles north of Jerusalem, and Baasha's probable motive was not only to threaten his enemy but also to keep any of his own people from traveling south to participate in the religious revival.

Asa's faith failed, and rather than attack, he sent a bribe to King Ben-Hadad of Syria, urging him to attack Israel. Ben-Hadad did attack, Israel withdrew from Ramah, and Asa mustered his people to carry away the vast store of building material that Baasha had assembled. When another prophet, Hanani, rebuked Asa for relying on Syria rather than the Lord, the angry king imprisoned him and also "brutally oppressed" others who may have objected (2 Chr. 16:10).

In the 39th year of Asa's reign, he fell sick, probably with dropsy. After a two-year illness in which Asa sought help from physicians but not from the Lord, he died, and was succeeded by his son Jehoshaphat.

LEARNING FROM ASA'S LIFE

Both the Books of 1 Kings and 2 Chronicles share the divine evaluation of Asa: he "did what was good and right in the eyes of the Lord" (2 Chr. 14:2; *compare* 1 Ki. 15:11,14). This evaluation is based on his commitment to God's Law and his active opposition to idolatry. Yet two incidents in his life reveal an inner weakness. When challenged by Baasha, and again in his final illness, Asa failed to rely on the Lord. We need to consider the distinction between "doing what is right" and "relying on the Lord." There is no indication that Asa knowingly violated God's Law. Yet, when frightened, Asa had difficulty relying on the Lord. He did rely once, and was granted victory (2 Chr. 14:11). But Asa did not learn from this experience, and at critical times in his life he failed to turn matters over to the Lord.

The lesson for us is that while it is good to do what is right, God is more concerned with our relationship to him, demonstrated by our reliance upon him during the critical situations of our lives.

98

ascension of Christ Jesus' return to heaven 40 days after his resurrection. The Bible reports that after Jesus' resurrection, he spent 40 days teaching his disciples. Then, as they watched, he rose up bodily from the Mount of Olives until hidden by a cloud (Mk. 16:19; Lk. 24:50,51; Acts 1:9-11). Prophetic allusions to the ascension have been seen in Pss. 68:18 and 110:1 (*see* Eph. 4:8-10 and Heb. 1:13). Jesus taught his disciples that he came down from heaven, the spiritual realm which is symbolically "above" the material plane, and that when his work was complete, he would return there to his Father (Jn. 6:32, 33; 14:1-4). The Bible makes clear that Jesus ascended in his resurrected body, and that he will some day return bodily (Acts 1:9-11; 2 Th. 1:7-10). *See also* Heaven.

SIGNIFICANCE

1. The ascension symbolizes Christ's exaltation "to the highest place" in the universe (Phil. 2:9-11). Jesus is now "seated . . . at his [God's] right hand in the heavenly realms, far above all rule and authority, power and dominion. . . . And God [has] placed all things under his feet and appointed him to be head over everything for the church" (Eph. 1:20-22). This gives confidence to Christians today who share the Gospel. Jesus, who commands us to go and make disciples, says, "All authority in heaven and on earth has been given to me," and promises, "Surely I am with you always, to the very end of the age" (Mt. 28:18-20). *See also* Hand.

2. The ascension of Jesus shifts our attention from his finished work to his present ministry for believers. In his death and resurrection, Christ has completed the work of redemption, and thus he is seated [that is, at rest] at God's right hand (Heb. 10:11-14). While on the throne, Jesus intercedes for believers (Rom. 8:34; Heb. 4:14; 6:20; 7:25), serving as our advocate when we sin (1 Jn. 2:1). As head of his Body, the Church, Jesus guides and supervises our individual and corporate growth (Eph. 4:14-16). During this present age, Christ also is actively preparing the "place" we will occupy in eternity (Jn. 14:1-3). *See also* Head; High Priest; Lord.

3. The ascension is linked to the sending of God's Spirit to indwell believers (Jn. 14:15-18; 15:26–16:16). Jesus said, "Unless I go away, the Counselor will not come to you, but if I go, I will send him to you" (Jn. 16:7). All the present works of the Holy Spirit for believers thus hinge on the ascension. Ephesians 4:7-12 relates the as-

cension specifically to spiritual gifts that empower the leadership of the Church. *See also* Holy Spirit.

4. Finally, the bodily ascension of Christ is an implicit promise of his bodily return. The witnesses of the ascension were told by angels, "This same Jesus, who has been taken from you into heaven, will come back in the same way you have seen him go into heaven" (Acts 1:11). The Jesus who lived, died, and rose again in history past will come again, and his return will mark the beginning of history's end.

The ascension depicted in stained glass. The ascension is at once a symbol of Christ's exaltation, his present ministry, his giving of the Holy Spirit, and his future bodily returned to this world.

Asher *See* IDENTI-QUICK: PEOPLE; Israel, Tribes of.

Asherah [ASH-sher-ah]. Canaanite goddess of fertility and originally the consort of El, but, in biblical times, of Baal. Known   99

Cast metal figurine from Nahariyeh, dating to about 1900 B.C., probably represents the Canaanite goddess Asherah.

The Roman province of Asia corresponds roughly to the region of Anatolia in modern Turkey. Much of Paul's missionary effort took place in Ephesus, the provincial capital.

also in Scripture as Ashtoreth [ASH-tuh-reth] and by the plural form Ashtaroth [ASH-tuh-rahth]. Asherah is linked with other fertility goddesses of the ancient Near East such as the Sumerian Inanna, the Mesopotamian Ishtar, the Babylonian Ashratum, Phoenician Ashirat, and the Greek Astarte.

In biblical times, the people of Canaan and Syria worshiped Asherah as a fertility goddess. Her worship involved sexual excesses intended to stimulate rain and quicken the ability of animals and people to reproduce. Asherah figures were apparently made of wood (Jdg. 6:26), and the goddess is associated with sacred trees or groves of trees (*asherot*). Many believe that "asherah" in the Bible often means "sacred grove," as it is sometimes translated in the KJV. God commanded that the objects erected by Asherah's worshipers (1 Ki. 14:23; 2 Ki. 17:10) should be cut down and burned (Ex. 34:13; Deut. 12:3).

The depraved worship of Asherah and Baal held a fatal attraction for Israel, and many turned to it (Jdg. 2:13; 10:6; 1 Sam. 7:3,4; 1 Ki. 11:5). King Ahab and his wife Jezebel led a concentrated effort to make Baal and Asherah dominant in Israel (1 Ki. 18), and later Manasseh placed a carved Asherah pole in the Jerusalem Temple itself (2 Ki. 21:7).

The Babylonian captivity purged Israel of idolatry. After that time, the ancient worship of the fertility goddess was no longer found in Israel. *See also* Baal; Gods and Goddesses.

ashes The remains of a fire. In the powerful imagery of the OT, ashes carry several related meanings. Dust and ashes symbolize insignificance in Gen. 18:27 and Job 30:19, and ashes alone symbolize worthless things in Job 13:12 and Isa. 44:20. Ashes also speak of destructive judgments (Ezek. 28:18; Jer. 31:40; 2 Pet. 2:6). When linked with sackcloth, ashes convey the deep grief associated with personal and national tragedies (2 Sam. 13:19; Esth. 4:1, 3; Job 2:8). Finally, sackcloth and ashes are also associated with repentance (Job 42:6; Mt. 11:21; Lk. 10:13) and with urgent prayer (Dan. 9:3).

The biblical practice of putting on the roughest clothing and sitting in ashes or covering one's head with ashes symbolizes a deep sense of helplessness and anguish. In this way, the sufferer demonstrated his intention to plead for God's mercy and to abandon all efforts to help himself. *See also* Confess.

Asia In the NT, a Roman province which included the western part of Asia Minor and some of the coastal islands. Ephesus, the city where Paul stayed for two years on his third missionary journey, was the seat of Roman government in this province. From this strategic city Paul's message spread until "all the Jews and Greeks who lived in the province of Asia heard the word of the Lord" (Acts 19:10; *compare* 1 Th. 1:8). *See also* Missions.

The seven churches of Asia mentioned in Revelation were all in important cities.

Asiarch A title held by some prominent citizens of the province of Asia. "Asiarch" appears only in some versions of Acts 19:31. It is translated "official" in the NIV, "chief of Asia" in the KJV, and "dignitary of the province" in the NEB. However, "Asiarch" was undoubtedly an honorary rather than official rank. The title was given to wealthy and public-spirited men who underwrote the cost of religious festivals and public games, and who were recognized as leading citizens of the province. Archaeologists' discovery of the names of a number of Asiarchs inscribed on public buildings and cast on coins suggests how influential those carrying this title must have been.

Paul's teaching in Ephesus eventually led to a riot, incited by the silversmith Demetrius. In relating the incident, Luke mentions that some of the influential Asiarchs were "friends of Paul," and advised him to keep out of sight while the city officials handled the crowd. Although Paul once wrote that "not many" influential persons responded to the Gospel, it is clear from Acts 19:31 that some did.

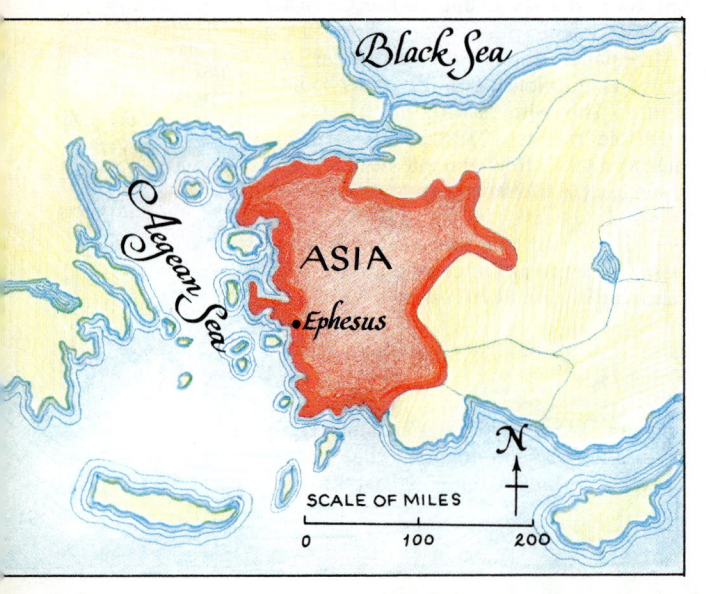

Black Sea

Aegean Sea

ASIA

•Ephesus

N

SCALE OF MILES

0   100   200

asp (KJV) A poisonous snake. The OT names several different poisonous snakes. English versions show no consistency in translating the Hebrew names, but render all or some of them as "adder," "asp," "cobra," "venomous serpent," and especially "viper." *See also* Adder.

ass (KJV) A beast of burden of the horse family. Inscriptions show that wild asses ("donkeys" in many modern versions) were domesticated by the early third millennium B.C. These animals, called *'aton* for their strength or *hamor* for their reddish brown color, were important in biblical Israel. They carried burdens (Gen. 42:26; 1 Sam. 16:20) and were also used in agriculture (Deut. 22:10; Isa. 30:24). Donkeys were also ridden by all classes of people (Ex. 4:20; Num. 22:21; Jdg. 10:4). The prophecy that Israel's Messiah would enter Jerusalem "riding on a colt, the foal of a donkey" (Zech. 9:9) emphasizes his peacefulness, in contrast to those who rode "war-horses from Jerusalem" (9:10). *See also* Messiah.

While the Greeks and Romans used asses as food, the donkey was considered unclean in Israel and could not be eaten (*see* Lev. 11:1-8; Deut. 14:3-8). On its death, a donkey's unclean body was hurriedly dragged away and thrown outside a city. When Jeremiah prophesied King Jehoiakim's death (about 598 B.C.), he revealed God's contempt for the evil king in the prediction that he would have the burial of a donkey (Jer. 22:19).

assembly Congregation, group of people. The entire nation of Israel assembled regularly for worship, but an assembly might be called for other purposes as well, from preparing for war (Jdg. 21:20; 1 Sam. 7:7) to crowning a new king (1 Ki. 17:20) or to see an army off to war (Jdg. 21:10). Throughout the OT, the assembly served as a religious and political focal point for Israel.

Two Hebrew words appear most frequently. One of these, *'edah* (often translated "congregation" or "community"), specifically describes an assembly of all Israelites, rather than an assembly of representatives and emphasizes the unity of the people in their covenant relationship with God.

In the NT no theological conclusions can be drawn from the use of the word. The word is used in Acts 7:38, referring to Moses in the assembly of the Israelites in the wilderness, and it is used in Acts 19 referring to a secular assembly of citizens in Ephesus.

Assur [AH-suhr]. An ancient name for the capital city, land, and chief god of Assyria (also Asshur). In the OT, this term refers to the land or the nation, and is appropriately translated "Assyria" in most modern versions. *See also* Assyria.

assurance Certainty, confidence. Much theological debate has swirled around the idea of assurance, which in theology means that a person not only possesses salvation, but knows that he or she is saved. Some teach that a person can never be certain that he or she is saved; others believe that the most one can enjoy is assurance at a particular moment; others hold that a person can know that he or she is irrevocably a child of God.

The ass was the most common means of transportation and heavy labor in biblical Israel. God enabled Balaam's ass to speak and rebuke him (Num. 22:28).

The differences cannot be settled by an appeal to Greek words that are sometimes translated "assurance" in NT versions. *Parrēsia* means "confidence" or "boldness." The Christian has "assurance in approaching God" in prayer, and church leaders gain "great assurance in their faith in Christ" (1 Jn. 5:14; 1 Tim. 3:13). *Plērophoria* often means "certainty," and because of Christ we can "draw near to God . . . in full assurance of faith" (Heb. 10:22). *Plērophoreō* often means "to achieve certainty." Abraham was "fully persuaded that God had power to do what he had promised" (Rom. 4:21).

None of these passages speaks directly to the question raised by theologians. Each focuses not on the believer's subjective experience, but on the utter trustworthiness of God and his Word, which awakens our faith and encourages continuing trust in his promises. We approach God with the assurance that he will welcome us on the basis of Christ's work for us. The "full assurance of faith" is not a conviction that we are saved, but that he is our Savior.

While the Greek terms themselves do not settle the question of assurance, Scripture does speak to this issue. The Bible says, "He who has the Son has life; he who does not have the Son of God does not have life. I write these things to you who believe in the name of the Son of God so that you may know that you have eternal life" (1 Jn. 5:12,13).

Above: Two winged bulls with human heads guarded the entrance to the palace at ancient Nimrud, built by Ashurnasirpal about 870 B.C.
Below: Layard's 1849 rendition of ancient Nineveh shows the Tigris flowing beneath the city walls.

Assyria The warlike nation that dominated the Middle East 911–609 B.C. and took the northern kingdom of Israel captive in 722 B.C. Mesopotamia, lying between the Tigris and Euphrates rivers, was the cradle of a series of powerful ancient empires. From this portion of what is known as the Fertile Crescent emerged the Sumerian Empire, in which Ur, Abraham's birthplace, was a foremost city. That Empire was supplanted in successive order by the Hurrian, Assyrian, and Babylonian empires.

The great Assyrian Empire originated in the second millennium B.C. along the upper Tigris, in what is now northern Iraq. Nineveh became its best-known city. For a 300-year period (911–609 B.C.), at the height of its power, Assyria was the greatest political power yet seen in the Near East. During this time Assyria's aggressive policies had a terrible impact on the two Hebrew kingdoms of Israel and Judah.

THE ASSYRIANS

The empires that emerged from the Fertile Crescent shared several characteristics. Society in the Tigris/Euphrates valley was structured around powerful cities. The cities, autocratically ruled by priest-kings, dominated the villages and agricultural land surrounding them. This domination was based on force, and those who lived outside the cities were essentially serfs in a feudal society.

While trade certainly had its place in the Assyrian Empire, warfare was an essential aspect of the Assyrian way of life. Annual campaigns were launched, not so much to add lands to the Empire as to seize the wealth and captives needed to carry out the grandiose building plans of its rulers, who constructed great palaces to celebrate their victories. Many of these massive palace ruins have been excavated, and they reveal the two artistic achievements of the Assyrians: in architecture and in the carved reliefs and statuary that decorated their buildings. These decorations invariably depicted the king as a favorite of the gods and a victorious warrior. Panel after panel shows the king's military campaigns in great detail.

Archaeologists have recovered from these palaces many volumes of Assyrian literature, written on clay tablets or cylinders. These volumes have enabled scholars to understand the life and beliefs of the Assyrians. The kingship dominated every aspect of Assyrian life and thinking, and rulers were considered sacred. The Assyrians worshiped a variety of gods and goddesses. These were thought of as kings, who lived in their temples as a king lived in his palace. Deities were more concerned with the king and the city than with individuals, and thus the private person had little contact with the gods. Instead, his life was controlled by *simtu*—a destiny established by his nature—which determined the way he fit into the cosmos.

Assyrian seal cylinders reveal a "science fiction view" of the universe, in which monsters, demons, gods, and heroes roamed the earth. Assyria's primitive medical texts rely heavily on magic and incantations. The daily life of the average citizen was especially devoid of meaning. Texts suggest a heavy use of alcohol, naming a great variety of beers and wines. The laws on their books make it clear that drunkenness was a severe social problem. Prostitution flourished, and sex was practiced openly in streets and parks, as well as in the privacy of established brothels, called "places of pleasure."

This, then, was the nation which, under a series of strong and aggressive rulers, built powerful military machines and, by sheer force, established a dominant position in the biblical world.

An Assyrian princess in full dress.

Left: The Assyrians, shown here impaling captives, were able to maintain their rule for over 300 years, in part by their oppressive treatment of conquered peoples. Right: A literal "head count." Scribes kept a tally of enemy dead in order to maintain accurate records of Assyrian campaigns.

ASSYRIA'S IMPACT ON BIBLE HISTORY

The three centuries of Assyrian dominance (911–609 B.C.) are called the Neo-Assyrian era, which can be divided into four distinct periods:

1. *911–824 B.C.* Under Adad-nirari II, Ashurnasirpal II, and Shalmaneser III, the Assyrians put great pressure on the Aramean states and attacked Palestine through Syria. Under Ahab, Israel temporarily suspended its war with the Syrians (Arameans) to join them in opposing Assyria at Qarqar in 853 B.C.

2. *824–744 B.C.* In the 800s, Assyria crushed Syria's military power. But then the Assyrians were forced to deal with an enemy to the north and with internal rebellions. With the Assyrians and Arameans now weakened, Israel under Jeroboam II, and Judah under Uzziah, expanded their territories.

3. *744–627 B.C.* Assyrian power was rebuilt by a series of strong rulers (Tiglath-Pileser III, Shalmaneser V, Sargon II, Sennacherib, Esarhaddon, and Ashurbanipal). These rulers sought not only spoil but to expand their empire. They instituted a policy of deporting defeated people from their homelands, and developed a complex bureaucracy to administer the empire. During this period, Israel (the northern kingdom) was invaded and her people deported from Palestine (722 B.C.). Judah (the southern kingdom) was re-

One of the few contemporary depictions of an Israelite king shows Jehu submitting to Shalmaneser III, while Israelite porters bearing tribute wait in line behind him. The images were found on the "Black Obelisk" at Nimrud, dated about 840 B.C.

duced to a vassal state during much of this period, but revolted in 704–701 B.C.

4. *627–609 B.C.* After Ashurbanipal's death, an internal power struggle weakened Assyria. The Chaldeans (Babylonians) took Assyria's capital cities in 614 and 612 B.C. and finally destroyed the last Assyrian army in 609 B.C. It was at this time that godly King Josiah of Judah was killed, battling an Egyptian force which was coming to the assistance of the Assyrians.

The Babylonian Empire now supplanted the Assyrian, and within a few short years, the Babylonians devastated Josiah's land, carrying the people of Judah into captivity.

ASSYRIA AS GOD'S INSTRUMENT

The Assyrians were a brutal people. Many of the reliefs celebrating their victories include scenes showing the torture of defeated enemies. Yet through Isaiah, God identified Assyria as "the rod of my anger, in whose hand is the club of my wrath" (Isa. 10:5). God brought Assyria against his people to punish them. As Isaiah says to Israel and Judah:

Woe to those who make unjust laws,
to those who issue oppressive decrees,
to deprive the poor of their rights
and withhold justice from the oppressed of
my people
making widows their prey
and robbing the fatherless.
What will you do on the day of reckoning,
when disaster comes from afar? (10:1-3)

The Assyrians were that disaster from afar that the Lord used to judge the wickedness and injustice of his people.

But Isaiah's prophecy went further: God will use the Assyrians as a rod, yet the Assyrian will be held responsible for

The Assyrian Empire

Mediterranean Sea

Nineveh ◉

Lachish

CASPIAN SEA

PERSIAN GULF

RED SEA

N

SCALE OF MILES
100   200   300

Relief from Sennacherib's palace at Nineveh celebrates the victory won at La-chish in 701 B.C. An Assyrian soldier pours water on a siege engine to protect it from torches thrown from the tower. At rear, Israelites leave Lachish for exile. Inset: Map shows Assyrian Empire at its greatest extent.

"what he intends." That intention is to destroy, not to discipline (10:7). Rather than acknowledge God and submit to him, the Assyrians take pride in their power and show only contempt for God, "as if a rod were to wield him who lifts it up" (10:12-15). Thus in time, says Isaiah, God will crush the Assyrians completely (10:16-34).

For centuries Assyria lay as a dark and threatening cloud to the north of the Israelites. The very existence of Israel and Judah, and the lives of all their citizens, might have been blotted out any time Assyria chose to invade. Isaiah, however, puts the evil empire's role in perspective. God will judge all sin. In the flow of history, one sinning nation will be judged by another, yet the judgment of the second nation is also sure. Israel and Judah would experience an Assyrian invasion, but only for their discipline. Therefore, God comforts Judah:

O my people who live in Zion,
  do not be afraid of the Assyrians,
who beat you with a rod
  and lift up a club against you, as Egypt
    did.
Very soon my anger against you will end
  and my wrath will be directed
    to their destruction.   (10:24,25)

God's people did continue to exist, long after Assyria was forgotten and her massive palaces lay buried. So will it ever be. Christians may also know God's discipline, inflicted through wicked persons. But, against his own people, God's anger ends "very soon," and they will experience his everlasting grace.

ASSYRIAN KINGS IN SCRIPTURE

Assyrian Ruler	Scripture	Summary
Pul (Tiglath-Pileser)	2 Ki. 15:19	Menahem of Israel paid him 37 tons of silver to "strengthen his own hold on Israel."
Tiglath-Pileser (745–727 B.C.)	2 Ki. 16 2 Chr. 28	Ahaz of Judah paid him to invade Damascus. Rezin of Damascus was killed, but Tiglath-Pileser "gave [Ahaz] trouble instead of help" and Ahaz was forced to strip his palace and the Temple of treasures as tribute.
Shalmaneser (727–721 B.C.)	2 Ki. 7	His vassal, King Hoshea of Israel, rebelled. Assyria invaded and deported the Israelites, and then resettled the land with foreigners. Hezekiah of Judah paid a vast tribute to bribe Shalmaneser to leave Judah alone.
Sennacherib (705–681 B.C.)	2 Ki. 18,19 Isa. 36, 37	He invaded Judah, taking 18 walled towns including the stronghold at Lachish. Before Jerusalem could be attacked, Hezekiah turned to God, who miraculously put to death a large number of Sennacherib's soldiers and forced his withdrawal to Assyria.

Sennacherib on his throne.

astonish To surprise, amaze, or shock. Four different Greek words are translated "amaze" or "astonish." These words usually describe the reaction of observers to things that Jesus taught or to the miracles he performed. When we combine the shades of meaning of the four Greek words, we have a portrait of how the people of Jesus' time experienced his ministry: Christ's teachings and works caused stunned amazement; the people could not take in what was happening; they felt anxious and uncertain; for they could not explain what they saw or heard. *See also* Amazement; Miracle.

astrology The belief that the positions of the sun, moon, planets, and stars influence the experience of individuals and nations. Astrologers study the heavens and offer advice based on their reading and interpretation of the heavenly bodies. The Bible scorns astrology with other occult practices, as in Isaiah's prediction of the fall of Babylon:

Keep on, then, with your magic spells
and with your many sorceries,
which you have labored at since
childhood. . . .
All the counsel you have received has only
worn out!
Let your astrologers come forward,
those stargazers who make predictions
month by month,
let them save you from what is coming
upon you. . . .
Each of them goes on in his error;
there is not one that can save you.
(Isa. 47:12-15)

Astrology is not listed with other occult practices condemned in Deut. 18 for the simple reason that the practice emerged in Mesopotamia, and was not known in Palestine in Moses' day. Mesopotamian documents from the middle of the third millennium B.C. list a variety of supposed effects linked with the new moon. Clay tablets from the library of Assyrian King Ashurbanipal (669–627 B.C.) indicate a highly developed astrological system, and list thousands of astrological omens. Yet astrology became known in the West only after Alexander the Great's conquest of the Persian Empire.

Understandably, most biblical references to astrology occur in Daniel, for Daniel held government posts in the Babylonian and Persian empires which, like the Assyrian Empire they supplanted, made much of astrology. In the Book of Daniel, the KJV translates *'ashap* as "astrologer,"

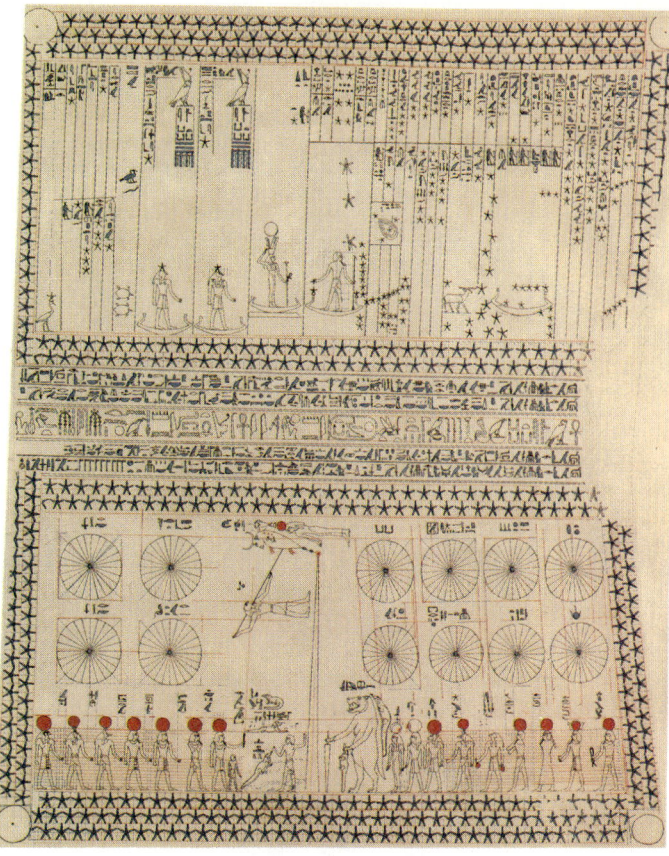

Astrological table from the Tomb of Senenmut, about 1500 B.C. Astrology, which provided a basis for several Near Eastern religions, was a snare to God's people (see Jer. 7:18; Amos 5:26).

but other versions render this word "enchanter." The word *kasedim* ("Chaldean," KJV) is rendered "astrologer" in the NIV. Actually, *kasedim* refers to a class of highly trained professional advisors and administrators in the Babylonian Empire. Knowledge of astrology was part of their training, yet this training did not help them interpret Nebuchadnezzar's dream (Dan. 2:10,11) or the writing that appeared on Belshazzar's wall (Dan. 5). Only Daniel, who relied on revelation from God, could discover the truth.

No wonder Jeremiah says, "Do not learn the ways of the nations or be terrified by signs in the sky, though the nations are terrified by them" (Jer. 10:2). The NT teaches us that we can find direction, not from astrology but from the Word of God, the indwelling Holy Spirit, the insights of the Church and the proper use of our renewed minds (Rom. 12:2).

Babylonian astrological calendar from the first millennium B.C. attributes earthly events to influences in the heavens.

Athaliah [ATH-uh-LI-yah; "Yahweh is great"]. An evil queen who murdered her own grandchildren to secure the throne. She was the only woman to reign over pre-exilic Judah (841–835 B.C.). **Grandfather:** Omri. **Parents:** Ahab and Jezebel. **Husband:** Jehoram, king of Judah. **Son:** Ahaziah. **Grandson:** Joash. **Scripture:** 2 Ki. 8,11; 2 Chr. 22,23.

BACKGROUND

Ahab and Jezebel, Athaliah's evil parents, had ruled the northern kingdom of Israel and promoted the worship of Baal there. In what was apparently a political alliance, Athaliah married King Jehoram of Judah, who had murdered his brothers when he came to the throne, and who shared her commitment to paganism. *See also* Ahab; Baal.

Ivory carving of a north Syrian woman at a window, eighth century B.C. Queen Athaliah heard the noise of her grandson's coronation from an open window. When she went to investigate she was put to death by the high priest's men.

When Jehoram contracted an incurable bowel disease and died at age 38, their 22-year-old son Ahaziah became king. Ahaziah was killed after ruling Judah for only one year.

Upon the news of her son's death, Athaliah acted quickly to destroy all male heirs to the throne, killing her own grandchildren and the whole royal house of Judah. Confident that no one with a claim to the throne remained, Athaliah proclaimed herself ruler of Judah. But Ahaziah's infant son Joash had been hidden in the Jerusalem Temple. When Joash was seven years old, Jehoiada the high priest enlisted the aid of the military and crowned Joash king, anointing him in a Temple ceremony. Athaliah heard the noise of the celebration and came to see what it was. On orders from the high priest, soldiers dragged the evil queen outside the Temple and executed her. Encouraged by Jehoiada, the people enthusiastically tore down altars to Baal in Jerusalem and killed Baal's high priest, Mattan.

LEARNING FROM ATHALIAH'S LIFE

First, Athaliah demonstrates the transmission of beliefs and values through the family. Her wicked parents, Ahab and Jezebel, clearly had an impact on her. She in turn "encouraged [her son Ahaziah] in doing wrong" (2 Chr. 22:3). Second, note the moral ramifications of her faith. The pagan Athaliah had no compunction about murdering the family of her own son in order to gain personal power, just as her pagan husband, Jehoram, had not hesitated to murder his brothers to consolidate his position. Third, consider Athaliah's fate. Her character caused others to fear and hate her. No one protested her execution, and on her death "all the people of the land rejoiced" (2 Chr. 23:21).

Athaliah's root problem was that she turned from God to embrace a counterfeit religion. Everything that happened to her hinged on that decision. That basic choice is still the essential one. The faith we choose shapes our character, governs our moral choices, and determines how others view us.

Athens The principal city in the Greek province of Attica. Ancient Athens gained fame as the home of philosophers and sculptors, and for its early experiments in democracy.

First-century Athens, however, had no real role in the spread of Christianity. The Bible mentions Athens only in Acts 17. That chapter summarizes a sermon which Paul gave there in defense of his teaching. The sermon shows how the apostle adapted his presentation of the Gospel to his audience without compromising basic truths. Thus, Paul does not start by quoting from the OT, as Peter did when speaking to Jews (Acts 2,4). Instead Paul reasons as one of the Greek philosophers might. He actually quotes a Greek poet (17:28), not to prove his point, but to establish common ground with his listeners. In this way, Paul leads his listeners to a logical conclusion about God's nature (17:24-31)—and then launches into a presentation of revealed truth. This God, whose existence can be demonstrated through reason, "has set a day when he will judge the world with justice by the man he has appointed. He has given proof of this to all men by raising him from the dead" (17:31). *See also* Areopagus.

No church was established in Athens at that time, but some of Paul's listeners did respond to the message and believe.

The Acropolis, seen from the Temple of Jupiter in modern Athens, retains traces of the majesty that made it one of the wonders of the ancient world. For centuries Athens was the cultural center of the West.

atheism The belief that God does not exist. Originally, the word "atheist" was applied to anyone who refused to acknowledge the gods of his society. Roman society viewed the early Christians as atheists because they would not honor pagan gods at state functions or during military ceremonies.

Throughout history, there have always been some who deny the existence of any deity. Yet Scripture teaches that from the beginning, God's existence has been "made plain to [literally, in] them" through creation. Therefore, the claim of atheism is no excuse, because those who argue that there is no God suppress the inner witness of conscience and the outer witness of creation that testify of God's existence (Rom. 1:18-21,28; 2:14,15).

Atheism as a philosophy is false, yet the Bible does suggest that there is a "practical atheism"—many people behave as if God did not exist. Asaph describes practical atheism in Ps. 73:6-11:

Pride is their necklace;
they clothe themselves with violence.
From their callous hearts comes iniquity;
the evil conceits of their minds know
no limits.
They scoff, and speak with malice;
in their arrogance they threaten oppression.
Their mouths lay claim to heaven,
and their tongues take possession of the
earth.
Therefore their people turn to them

and drink up waters in abundance.
They say, "How can God know?
Does the Most High have knowledge?"

It is practical atheism, not philosophical atheism, which marks so much of mankind and puts its adherents in the greatest spiritual danger. Psalm 14 makes this observation: "The fool says in his heart, 'There is no God.' " The Hebrew word for "fool," *nabal*, describes a person's inner disposition. The individual who closes his heart against God and morality, and who resists the inner conviction that he or she must make peace with God, will be drawn into a life of sin and ultimately, but too late, be "overwhelmed with dread" (Ps. 14:5). The practical atheist may choose a life-style which ignores God. But since God does exist, each human being must one day give an account to him.

athletics Sports, physical games or exercises. The Hebrew people were not sports-minded, and the OT makes only a few allusions to sports. But the Greeks held a different view of physical training and athletics. Their athletic games had been held in honor of the gods on Olympus since 780 B.C. And their notion of excellence, *aretē*, called for personal wholeness, including physical development. The Greeks' passionate interest in sports, like the rest of their culture, spread through the Middle East after Alexander's conquest. In some cities, arenas were built

Silver tetradrachm dated about 450 B.C., the height of Athenian influence and power. It bears the image of Athena, the patron goddess of the city.

109

Marble relief shows young Greeks posed in the stand-up manner of pankration wrestling.

Paul uses a related term, *agōn*, when he says, "I have fought the good fight, I have finished the race, I have kept the faith" (2 Tim. 4:7). Because of Paul's commitment to total effort, he is sure that "now there is in store for me the crown of righteousness, which the Lord, the righteous Judge, will award to me on that day" (2 Tim. 4:8). This image of God as the umpire, waiting to reward the believer who has run life's race well, recurs often in the NT (1 Cor. 9:25; Phil. 4:1; 1 Th. 2:19. *See also* 1 Pet. 5:4; Jas. 1:12; Rev. 2:10).

Perhaps 1 Cor. 9:24-27 best sums up what Paul himself learned about life from athletics, and what he wants us to take to heart:

Do you not know that in a race all the runners run, but only one gets the prize? Run in such a way as to get the prize. Everyone who competes in the games goes into strict training. They do it to get a crown that will not last; but we do it to get a crown that will last forever. Therefore I do not run like a man running aimlessly; I do not fight like a man beating the air. No, I beat my body and make it my slave so that . . . I . . . will not be disqualified. . . .

that could hold over 40,000 people (which may have exceeded the entire population of first-century Jerusalem).

Greek and Roman games were dedicated to pagan gods, and prizes often contained their images. For this reason, the Jewish community initially was opposed to sports. Yet the apostle Paul clearly knew about sporting events and, judging from the many illustrations in his Epistles, may have been an avid sports fan.

First, Paul praised the self-discipline of athletes. To win the prize, an athlete must train diligently and then compete by the rules (2 Tim. 2:5). Paul insisted that believers should put the same effort into being godly as the athlete puts into getting ready for competition (1 Tim. 4:7,8).

Paul was also aware of the pain that comes as an athlete extends himself in his struggle for victory. The pain and intensity are expressed in the athletic term *agōnizomai*, "to strive." Paul uses this word to describe Epaphras, who "is always striving for you in his prayers" (Col. 4:12, ASV). Paul portrays himself "striving with all the energy which he [God] mightily inspires within me" (Col. 1:29, RSV).

Bronze Roman copies of Greek originals, from Herculaneum.

Marble slabs from Imperial Rome list and illustrate prizes won by an athlete from Rhamnous, Greece: a vase, pine crown, shield, and wild celery crown. Greek and Roman victors were often honored by commemorative statues.

atonement The act of making amends, paying for a wrong, or restoring harmony between persons who have been at odds. This theological term has Anglo-Saxon roots, and means "to make at one."

In the OT, "to atone" (Heb., *kapar*, meaning "to purge, cleanse, purify," or "to cover and conceal") has to do with the cleansing of ritual and moral impurities, which was required before an Israelite could approach God.

The formula used in the OT ceremony of atonement, found in Lev. 4 and 14, helps us grasp the significance of atonement. A person came to the priest, acknowledged guilt, and presented an animal to be killed and burned on the altar as a sacrifice. "In this way the priest will make atonement for the man's sin, and he will be forgiven" (Lev. 4:26). Thus atonement in the OT is directly linked with sin, sacrifice, and God's forgiveness of the sinner. *See also* Forgive; Sacrifices and Offerings; Sin.

Yet it is only through the NT that we fully understand the OT ceremony. That ritual was God's visual aid—a drama, enacted again and again to help Israel understand the fact that sin erects a barrier between man and God, and to prepare Israel to grasp the meaning of the death of its Messiah. Later Paul explains the death of Christ in terms of atonement. "God presented him [Jesus] as a sacrifice of atonement, through faith in his blood. He did this to demonstrate his justice, because in his forbearance he had left the sins committed beforehand unpunished" (Rom. 3:25).

The OT sacrifices had provided no moral basis on which God could extend his forgiveness to sinners. Yet God had forgiven, and had done so justly, knowing that in the coming death of Christ, the moral foundation for forgiveness would be laid. Over the centuries, the church has struggled to define exactly how Christ's death makes forgiveness possible. Yet, no matter how it was accomplished, the NT unmistakably reports that Christ's death and resurrection have put us "at one" with God: "While we were still sinners, Christ died for us. Since we have now been justified by his blood, how much more shall we be saved from God's wrath through him!" (Rom. 5:8,9). "In him [Jesus] we have redemption through his blood, the forgiveness of sins" (Eph. 1:7). And, "Now in Christ Jesus you who once were far away have been brought near through the blood of Christ" (Eph. 2:13).

What the blood of goats and bulls could never do, the blood of Jesus has done, cleansing "our consciences from acts that lead to death, so that we may serve the living God" (Heb. 9:14).

Atonement, Day of The Jews' highest holy day, Yom Kippur [yome kip-PUR], occurring each autumn, ten days after the Jewish new year begins. Amid Israel's many festivals, marking various aspects of their relationship with God, the Day of Atonement stood out (Lev. 16; 23:26-32; Num. 29:7-11).

On that day and that day only, the high priest, wearing a simple linen robe, entered the inner room of the tabernacle, where he sprinkled the blood of two sacrificial animals. One of these was offered for his sins, and the other for the sins of the nation. The blood was sprinkled on the cover of the ark of the covenant and the ground in front of it. The cover of the ark, over which the golden cherubim bent, was the "mercy seat" or "place of propitiation," where God symbolically met his people. (*See also* Ark of the Covenant; Mercy Seat; Propitiation.) In honor of this special day, the Israelites were to fast—the only fasting day required in OT Law.

The sacrifice of the Day of Atonement was unique for much more than the solemnity of its annual repetition. The Law says of other sin offerings, "When anyone sins unintentionally," he is to bring a guilt offering (Lev. 4:2,13,22,27; 5:14) and make a blood sacrifice for atonement. But of the sacrifice offered on Israel's most holy day, the Bible says, "In this way he will make atonement for the Most Holy Place because of the uncleanness and rebellion of the Israelites, whatever their sins have been" (Lev. 16:16).

To symbolize God's forgiveness, the high priest laid his hands on a living goat and confessed the nation's sin. Then the goat was driven out into the desert.

The Book of Hebrews looks back to the Day of Atonement and views many of its elements as a mirror, or type, reflecting the meaning of the death of Christ (Heb. 8–10). Christ, our high priest, entered heaven itself carrying his own blood, the fruit of his self-sacrifice. Yet Christ's sacrifice stands in stark contrast to the repeated sacrifices of the OT era. Then the yearly repetition reminded the people of Israel of their sinful condition even as they promised forgiveness. But, the Bible teaches, now "we have been made holy through the sacrifice of the body of Jesus Christ once for all" (Heb. 10:10). There is no need

The ultimate, once-for-all atonement was won by Christ in his death on the cross of Calvary.

for Christ's sacrifice to be repeated, for on history's true Day of Atonement, as Jesus hung on the cross, by that "one sacrifice he has made perfect forever those who are being made holy" (Heb. 10:14).

After the destruction of the Jerusalem Temple by the Romans in A.D. 70, Judaism's sacrifices ceased. Yet observance of the Day of Atonement has continued down to our own time. Yom Kippur is marked by fasting and confession of sins, but there is no shedding of blood.

Glass bust of Augustus only 5 centimeters high, cast from a mold. Probably a copy of art commissioned to commemorate granting of the title princeps "first citizen," in 27 B.C.

Silver coin with likeness of Augustus. His politically motivated efforts to link himself with deity evolved into a cult of emperor worship fostered by later Caesars.

Augustus Caesar The first emperor of Rome, ruling 27 B.C.–A.D. 14. Mentioned only once in Scripture (Lk. 2:1), Augustus Caesar still did much to prepare the Roman world for the spread of the Gospel.

He was born Caesar Octavianus in 63 B.C., grandnephew of Julius Caesar, and was later named as the great general's heir. After Julius was assassinated in 44 B.C., it took Octavian over a decade to defeat his rivals and become sole ruler of the Roman Empire. He began his rule in 31 B.C. but officially became Emperor only when he was voted the title *Augustus* ("reverend" or "sacred") in 27 B.C. Augustus was careful to maintain the outward form of the Republican system, but since he retained control of the armies and gradually added other powers, he was, in effect, Rome's sole autocrat.

The era of Augustus was a time of unparalleled peace and prosperity. He put down the pirates and bandits that had infested the Empire, and interfered as little as possible in the self-governance of Rome's provinces. His policies were especially favorable to the Jewish communities which were established in all the major cities of the Empire. Both the existence of these scattered Jewish communities, and the freedom to travel without fear, were important to the Christian missionary effort initiated by the apostle Paul.

The impact of Augustus on the Empire and the respect in which he was held by his contemporaries are summed up in a birthday inscription honoring Augustus in 7 B.C.: "Everything was deteriorating and changing into misfortune, but he set it right and gave the whole world another appearance."

author Maker, creator. The Book of Hebrews calls Jesus the "author of salvation" (2:10) and the "author and perfecter of our faith" (12:2). The Greek word *archēgos* can mean "leader" or "prince" (Acts 5:31) but usually carries the stronger sense of "founder" or "originator." Thus Peter tells the Jerusalem crowd, "You killed the author of life—but God raised him from the dead" (Acts 3:15). In Heb. 5:9 (KJV), Jesus is called the "author of eternal salvation." The Greek word is *aitios*, properly translated "source" by modern versions.

authority Power, influence. One's view of authority is shaped by the system within which it operates. Authority takes on one shape in the military, another in a dictatorship, another in a democracy, another in the family, and yet another in the Church.

The Greek word *exousia*, "freedom of action," underlies the Bible's teaching on authority. It implies that a person with authority (1) has personal freedom to act, and (2) has the right or ability to limit that freedom in others.

GOD'S UNIVERSAL AUTHORITY

God has ultimate authority in his universe, total freedom of action. As the Lord says through Isaiah,

I am God, and there is no other;
I am God, and there is none like me.
I make known the end from the beginning,
   from ancient times, what is still to come.
I say: My purpose will stand,
   and I will do all that I please. . . .
What I have said, that will I bring about;
   what I have planned, that will I do.

(Isa. 46:9-11)

As Creator and Judge of his universe, God has a right to the allegiance of his creatures, and a right to establish the moral framework within which they are to live. Human beings "acknowledge and take to heart . . . that the Lord is God in heaven above and on earth below" by choosing to limit their own freedom of action in order to "keep his decrees and commands" (Deut. 4:39,40).

Because God's freedom of action (authority) is complete, he can determine how to respond to those who do acknowledge him, and to those who do not. He freely chooses when and how to punish, when and how to bless, and when and how to forgive. The Bible is not only a revelation of God's will to us, but also is the history of God's direct and providential control of events.

HUMAN AUTHORITIES

Romans 13 casts human rulers as servants of God, agents who have been established "to bring punishment on the wrongdoer." There is no divine authorization here of any particular form of government, or of any individual ruler. Paul argues that, because of the impact of sin on human beings, society must place re-

straints on individual freedom of action. And to carry out this function, human governments must use the coercive power necessary to enforce its laws.

In this context, Paul urges Christians to choose to submit to rulers, not from fear of punishment, but out of reverence for an institution which God has ordained. Peter makes the same appeal. Christians under secular authorities should willingly limit their freedom of action, even in extreme situations where the established authority is unjust. A Christian slave is to submit "for the Lord's sake" and "not only to those [masters] who are good and considerate, but also to those who are harsh" (1 Pet. 2:18).

Submission to any human authority which may be over us is "God's will," in order "that by doing good you should silence the ignorant talk of foolish men" (1 Pet. 2:15).

Peter then makes this significant statement: "Live as free men, but do not use your freedom as a cover-up for evil" (2:16). Christian freedom is not authority to do whatever one wishes, but rather the freedom to choose that which is right within the framework established by God's Law, and within the framework established by the laws of one's society.

SPIRITUAL AUTHORITY

We must take care to distinguish between different shades of meaning in the NT word translated "authority." The Gospels say that Jesus "has authority on earth" (Mk. 2:10). In fact, those who heard Jesus and saw his miracles were stunned

Map of the Roman Empire showing its extent at the death of Caesar Augustus in A.D. 14.

113

because he acted with authority (Mt. 7:29). Here we see a reflection of Christ's deity: Jesus demonstrated on earth that he had God's own unrestricted freedom of action. He exercised control over wind and wave, over hunger and disease, and even over demons.

Jesus taught with authority. That is, he communicated the will of God to human beings accurately and completely. And what Jesus taught was morally binding on his hearers: It was the very Word of God to mankind. Yet it is striking that, in the exercise of his authority, Jesus always preserved the freedom of his hearers to accept or reject his morally binding Word. Jesus neither compelled nor coerced response, but rather invited listeners to exercise faith and to freely choose response to God.

This same pattern is seen in the OT prophets, who also spoke an authoritative word from God. The prophet relied only on God, who again and again acted to discipline his people when they would not obey him. However, the authority of the prophet never implied a right to compel or coerce obedience from the people of God. The prophet might announce consequences of disobedience, but he could not enforce compliance. Listeners had to freely acknowledge the authority of the word spoken by the prophets, and freely choose to respond to it.

In the NT, Paul speaks of an apostolic "authority" given him by God (2 Cor. 10:8; 13:10). That authority, like the prophets', rested partially in the fact that he and the other apostles revealed the authoritative (morally binding) Word of God. But the NT also calls on Christians to submit to the "authority" of church leaders (Heb. 13:17).

THE GRANT OF SPIRITUAL AUTHORITY

God does place leaders in his church, and grant them spiritual authority. The Roman Catholic Church sees the grant of authority in Jesus' words to Peter in Mt. 16:19, "I will give you the keys of the kingdom of heaven; whatever you bind on earth will be bound in heaven; whatever you loose on earth will be loosed in heaven." This is reinforced by Jesus' words to Peter after the resurrection, "feed my sheep," Jn. 21:15-17. Authority was also granted to the other disciples who, with Peter, were commissioned to go and make disciples of all nations (Mt. 28:16-20). These passages mean much to Roman Catholic Christians and others, who see their bishops as successors of the apostles and heirs to the authority given to them by Jesus.

In most Protestant traditions leaders respond to a personal call to ministry. While one generation of leaders must entrust received truths "to reliable men who will also be qualified to teach others also" (2 Tim. 2:2), the grant of authority is not seen

THE MEANING OF "AUTHORITY" IN SCRIPTURE

SITUATION	MEANING
When used of God and of Jesus.	Absolute and unrestricted freedom of action. The right to limit the freedom of action of others by establishing a moral framework in which they are to live.
When used of human authorities.	The right to use forceful means to punish wrongdoers and to compel society's members to keep its laws.
When used of the Bible.	The right to limit the freedom of action of human beings by establishing the moral framework within which we are to live.
When used of spiritual leaders.	The right to influence others to choose to live within the moral framework which has been established by God and revealed to human beings in Christ and in the written Word.
When used alone.	Freedom of action itself, or the right to limit the freedom of action of others by (1) directly coercing desired behaviors, as governments do, or by (2) establishing a moral framework within which others are to live, as God does through the Word revealed by the prophets and apostles, or by (3) seeking to influence others to choose to live within the moral framework of God and society, as Christian leaders do.

as hierarchical but a response to the Spirit who enables those who are Christ's gift to his church in every generation (Eph. 4:11). The many warnings in the NT against false teachers, and exhortations to the church to test those who claim teaching authority, seem to Protestants to indicate that the person—what he is, what he does and what he believes—is more important than the position or the office he holds.

What is the nature of the authority of leaders? Essentially, God extends to church leaders the freedom to direct the people of God to respond to Christ's moral authority. Since even Jesus was careful never to claim a coercive authority over persons who are free moral agents, then mere humans in positions of spiritual leadership must be even more careful not to claim such an authority. It is, however, right and proper for secular governments to demand—and compel—obedience. But it is not now and never has been right for those in spiritual leadership to attempt to compel a response which, to be meaningful, must be a free choice. *See also* Leader.

Thus the exercise of spiritual authority in the church is intended to make others both responsible and free. Those under authority are responsible to respond. But they must be free to make their own choice. Those with spiritual authority should remember this fact, and always invite rather than coerce response. *See also* Discipline, Church.

DIFFICULT PASSAGES ON AUTHORITY

When we understand the basic meaning of *exousia*, we gain insight into a number of more difficult Bible passages. Only those who receive Jesus have the freedom ("authority") to become the children of God (Jn. 1:12). Pilate's own authority (freedom of action) was circumscribed by the fact that he derived that authority from Rome and had to act as Rome demanded rather than according to his personal convictions (Jn. 19:8-13). Women are told in 1 Cor. 11:10 to wear a veil as "a sign of authority on her head." Paul does not mean as "a sign of male authority," as the verse has sometimes been taken. Instead the veil is a sign that, in Christ, women have the freedom of action to participate actively in the life and worship of the church. *See also* Woman.

avenge To take revenge, to pay back for an injury. The OT says God "will avenge the blood of his servants; he will take vengeance on his enemies and make atonement for his land and people" (Deut.

32:43). This is appropriate, because God acts not out of vindictiveness, but as moral Judge (*see* Ps. 94). Because God is Judge, human beings are not to take vengeance into their own hands. The Mosaic Law says, "Do not seek revenge or bear a grudge against one of your people, but love your neighbor as yourself" (Lev. 19:18), and the NT reflects this theme: "Do not take revenge, my friends, but leave room for God's wrath, for it is written: 'It is mine to avenge, I will repay,' says the Lord" (Rom. 12:19). The one exception to this rule is when human beings are acting as God's agents to execute justice, as did the OT avenger of blood, and as do modern governments (Rom. 13:4). *See also* Avenger of Blood.

How are Christians to respond when injured by others? Romans 12:20 echoes Jesus' call to love our enemies (Mt. 5:43-48): " 'If your enemy is hungry, feed him; if he is thirsty, give him something to drink. In doing this, you will heap burning coals on his head.' Do not be overcome by evil, but overcome evil with good." *See also* Judge.

avenger of blood One given responsibility in the OT to seek out and execute a murderer. When the Mosaic Law was given, Israel had no central government. The administration of justice belonged to local authorities. *See also* Justice.

In Israel, the nearest male kinsman was responsible to watch out for family interests. This included redeeming family property or purchasing the release of a poor relative who had been sold into slavery (Lev. 25:25,47-49; Ruth 4). The nearest male kinsman of a person who was killed was designated the "avenger of blood," and was responsible to execute the murderer: "the avenger of blood shall put the murderer to death" (Num. 35:19).

The Chair of Moses was the seat of honor and authority in the synagogue at Chorazin, from the first century A.D. An Aramaic inscription identifies "Yudan, son of Ishmael" as the artisan.

Some have criticized this provision in OT Law, believing that it is in conflict with Christ's call to forgive and to love our enemies. But it is not. In this particular function, the avenger of blood acted as God's agent, even as state and local governments today are his agents. Both the avenger of blood and civil governments were commissioned by God to carry out the sentence which God had pronounced against murderers (Gen. 9:6; Rom. 13:3-5). *See also* Murder.

Yet the law that established the avenger's role also set up a number of safeguards, and made a clear distinction between intentional homicide and accidental death (Num. 35:6-34). *See also* Cities of Refuge.

Despite the fact that a victim's relative was charged with the duty of executing the murderer, this was clearly a judicial function, and not a matter of personal revenge.

awe Fear, terror, deep reverence. The several Greek and Hebrew words for awe in the Bible all share a sense of terror or fear. Generally, God is the object of that fear.

This provides a proper balance to the emphasis we rightly place on the love and gentleness of God as revealed in Jesus. God is a loving Person. But he is also glorious and awe-inspiring in his majesty. A healthy fear of God does not drive his people from him, but rather motivates a respect that results in obedience. *See also* Fear.

awl Pointed tools used by carpenters and leather workers for punching holes. Archaeologists have discovered many awls from biblical times. Most are about six inches long, and are usually made of bone or metal.

The only scriptural references to awls occur in descriptions of a solemn ear-piercing ritual (Ex. 21:6; Deut. 15:17). A Jewish person might sell himself or a family member into servitude to another Jew, but the transaction was closely governed. Such a servant must be well-treated, and must be freed after six years. When re-

leased, the servant was to be compensated generously for his years of service. However, a servant might choose not to accept freedom. In this case, the servant's ear was to be pierced with an awl, "and he will become your servant for life" (Deut. 15:17). *See also* Slave.

ax A tool for chopping or cutting. "Axes" in OT times were used for cutting down trees (Deut. 19:5; Jdg. 9:48) and as tools for working stone (1 Ki. 6:7). In times of war, these agricultural or building tools might also be used as weapons (1 Sam. 13:20). While armies in the biblical world used war axes, the term translated "ax" in the KJV of Jer. 51:20 is appropriately translated "war club" in the NIV. The Hebrew OT has nine different words for "ax." These terms probably represent different shapes of cutting and chopping tools, and there is no way to determine exactly what each term specifically meant.

Often biblical axes are described as "iron," meaning that the head was of iron, attached to a wooden shaft. The story of the lost axhead in 2 Ki. 6:5, and the illustration of accidental homicide in Deut. 19:5, which cites an axhead flying off and accidentally killing one's neighbor, indicate that there was no secure way of fastening the head to the wooden handle.

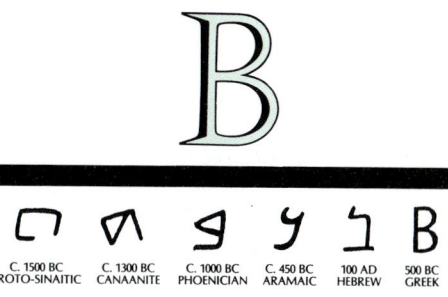

| C. 1500 BC PROTO-SINAITIC | C. 1300 BC CANAANITE | C. 1000 BC PHOENICIAN | C. 450 BC ARAMAIC | 100 AD HEBREW | 500 BC GREEK |

Baal [BAY-al; "lord," "owner," "husband"]. 1. As a common noun, rendered "lord" in the KJV, the owner of property, such as a house (Jdg. 19:22) or cattle (Ex. 21:28). 2. As a proper noun, the Canaanite deity Baal. 3. In addition, "baal" may indicate a deity other than the Canaanite Baal. Thus it appears in personal names, sometimes referring to the pagan deity, as in Jerub-Baal (Jdg. 6:32), and sometimes referring to God as "lord," as in Baal-Hanan ["the Lord is gracious"] (1 Chr. 27:28). The inclusion of "baal" in personal names suggests a weakening of the strict separation God's people were to maintain between the true God and the gods of the Canaanites. Biblical writers found this practice so repugnant that they sometimes replaced *baal* with *bosheth* ("shame") in people's names (2 Sam. 2:8). In place names, such as Baal Peor (Hos. 9:10) and Baal Tamar (Jdg. 20:33), "baal" may indicate local deities thought of as owners of the district, or a manifestation of the major Canaanite deity.

BAAL IN CANAANITE MYTHOLOGY

Literature recovered from Ras Shamra, dating to the 1400s B.C., contains a number of mythical stories about Canaanite gods, known as the Baal Cycle. These stories seem to suggest the gradual replacement of El by Baal as chief god of the Canaanites. The myths portray Baal as god of the sky and rain, struggling with Mot, who represents drought. Baal also is in conflict with Yamm, in a struggle between fertility and sterility. The annual pattern of early and later rains in Palestine, alternating with hot, dry summers, was explained in terms of the victories of one god over the other. As god of rain and fertility, Baal was of primary importance in agricultural Palestine. *See also* Agriculture.

In the myths Baal is also portrayed as bloodthirsty and highly sexed. The erotic element in Baal worship was intended to stimulate the god to mate with his consort (who in biblical times was called Asherah or Astarte), and so bring rain and fertility to the land. The Bible identifies ritual prostitution as one depraved element in Baal worship (Jdg. 2:17; Amos 2:7,8). *See also* Asherah.

BAAL AND ISRAEL'S HISTORY

Throughout Israel's pre-exilic history, the Hebrews were strongly attracted to the worship of Baal, and erected local "high places" where his cult rituals were practiced (Deut. 4:3; Jdg. 2:11; Jer. 2:8). This appeal may in part have been rooted in Baal's supposed control of the rain, upon which life in Palestine depended. But the sensual aspects of Baal worship, which seemed to justify sexual excess in contrast to the Law's strict regulations, appealed to many as well.

The greatest challenge of Baal to the worship of Yahweh came in the ninth century B.C., when Ahab and Jezebel actively promoted a virulent form of Baal worship

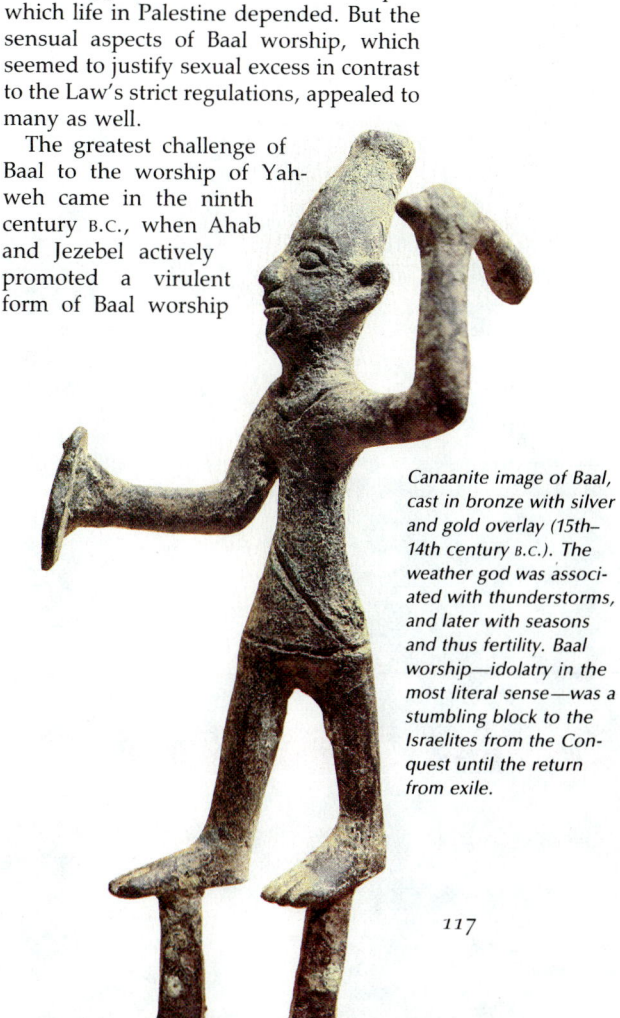

Canaanite image of Baal, cast in bronze with silver and gold overlay (15th–14th century B.C.). The weather god was associated with thunderstorms, and later with seasons and thus fertility. Baal worship—idolatry in the most literal sense—was a stumbling block to the Israelites from the Conquest until the return from exile.

117

imported from Phoenicia (1 Ki. 16–2 Ki. 10). In this period Elijah was God's primary proponent. The struggle culminated in a great contest with 450 prophets of Baal on Mount Carmel. Elijah's resounding victory stimulated a popular uprising against Baalism, caused the death of Baal's prophets, and laid the groundwork for Jehu's subsequent extermination of Baal worship in Israel. *See also* Ahab; Jehu; Jezebel.

The struggle continued in Judah, however. There Athaliah, a daughter of Jezebel, had married into the royal family. She usurped the throne of Judah and promoted Baalism until she was killed and replaced by her seven-year-old grandson, Joash (2 Ki. 11). *See also* Athaliah.

Despite the victory over Phoenician Baalism, traditional Canaanite worship of Baal persisted in Israel. Centuries after the Hebrew people had entered Canaan, as the Babylonian armies were advancing on Judah, one could find, on the very streets of Jerusalem and on the roofs of her houses, altars where incense was burned to honor Baal (Jer. 11:13; 32:29).

Babel [BA-buhl; "confusion"]. The site of the tower where God confused the languages of its builders; also an early name of Babylon. God commanded Noah's descendants to "fill the earth" (Gen. 9:1). Instead, they determined to build a city in Shinar (Babylonia). They also planned "a tower that reaches to the heavens" to "make a name" for themselves and to unify them so they would "not be scattered over the face of the earth" (Gen. 11:4). The building of the city and tower thus symbolizes human pride and rebellion against God. *See also* Babylon.

The tower of Babel probably was a terraced mound of brick and earth, and may have been like the later Sumerian and Babylonian temple structures known as *ziggurats*. The phrase "with its top in the heavens" may not refer to height but to a temple built on its top, intended as a point of contact with God.

The Lord suddenly caused the people to speak different languages. Unable to work cooperatively on the project, the people of the different language groups then spread out as God had originally intended.

"The Tower of Babel" by Pieter Bruegel, 1563. "Babel" in the language of Babylon meant "Gate of God;" in Hebrew it meant "confusion." Inset: one conception of what the Tower looked like, based on archaeological evidence. The biblical reference to the use of bitumen in its construction, virtually unknown in Israel, is evidence of historical accuracy.

Babylon [BAB-uh-lohn]. Capital of the Babylonian Empire. In Scripture "Babylon" refers to both the city and empire. In apocalyptic literature "Babylon the Great" represents human political, economic, and religious systems devoted to crass materialism and ungodly living in defiance of the holiness and sovereignty of God.

Ruins of the ancient city lie along the river Euphrates, about 50 miles south of Baghdad in modern Iraq. At its height, the city covered between 3.5 and 6 square miles (9 and 15.5 square kilometers). According to Herodotus, who wrote in the fifth century B.C., it was surrounded by 60 miles of walls up to 300 feet high and 87 feet wide. Archaeological expeditions between 1899 and 1917, and after 1958, have revealed much about this enormously wealthy city and its kings.

A BRIEF HISTORY

Babylon may be the oldest city in the world. The traditional site of the tower of Babel (Gen. 11:1-9), it was one of several cities founded by Nimrod (Gen. 10:10).

The oldest settlement at Babylon, established prior to 3000 B.C., was destroyed by Sargon of Akkad about 2400 B.C.

Near the end of the 2000s B.C., an Amorite dynasty adopted Babylon as its capital. This dynasty, the Old Babylonian, persisted until the city was sacked by the Hittites in 1595 B.C. The most famous king of this era was Hammurabi (1792–1750 B.C.), known for his codification of strict laws intended to correct social and economic ills. Features of these laws are similar to those found in the Mosaic code. *See also* Hammurabi, Code of.

During the last centuries of this period, Babylon became an educational and literary center. The city boasted a famous school for scribes, and scholars produced a vast library of materials. Detailed technical works in astronomy and astrology were written in cuneiform on clay tablets.

For the next four centuries (1570–1150 B.C.) a Kassite dynasty controlled the city and maintained close relationships with Egypt. Nebuchadnezzar I (1124–1103 B.C.) made Babylon his capital. The dynasty he founded lasted about a hundred years.

Although the city was incorporated into the Assyrian Empire about 1000 B.C., it resisted outside rule, and was alternately controlled by the Assyrians and the Chaldeans, an aggressive tribe of Viking-like raiders from northeast Arabia. In 698 B.C., the Assyrian ruler Sennacherib destroyed the city, but his successor Ashurbanipal

rebuilt it. *See also* Assyria; Chaldeans.

The Neo-Babylonian Empire was launched in 625 B.C. when the Chaldean Nabopolassar took the throne. Within two decades he, in league with the Medes under Cyaxares, crushed the Assyrian armies. Habakkuk may be referring to his phenomenal rise when he reports God's words, "Look at the nations and watch—and be utterly amazed. For I am going to do something in your days that you would not believe, even if you were told. I am raising up the Babylonians [Chaldeans]" (Hab. 1:5,6).

Under Nabopolassar's son, Nebuchadnezzar II (605–562 B.C.), Babylon reached the pinnacle of world power. In the process Jerusalem and its Temple were destroyed and the Jewish people were deported from their national homeland. Nebuchadnezzar II was a builder and master administrator as well as conqueror. He constructed several palaces, a massive ziggurat with a temple to the god Marduk on top, and the famous hanging gardens, a

The Ishtar Gate and Processional Way, from the reign of Nebuchadnezzar II. This king, who razed Jerusalem in 586 B.C., undertook many building projects in his capital, Babylon.

119

Portion of the Code of Hammurabi, 1790 B.C. This Babylonian legal code is older than Mosaic Law.

wonder of the ancient world. *See also* Nebuchadnezzar II.

The last Babylonian ruler Nabonidus 555–539 B.C.) retired to the Arabian city of Teima, leaving his son Belshazzar in charge as co-regent. Cyrus conquered Babylon in 539 B.C. and established the Persian Empire.

Under Cyrus and his successors, the city of Babylon retained its influence as a vastly wealthy commercial and intellectual center. Residing in it was a large and prosperous Jewish community, whose active involvement in study of the OT is reflected in the Babylonian Talmud, which established some of the traditions still followed in modern Judaism. The city continued to exert its influence in Mesopotamia for several centuries, even into the Christian era.

IMPACT ON BIBLE HISTORY

Envoys from Babylon visited King Hezekiah of Judah (715–686 B.C.) to congratulate him on his recovery from serious illness. Hezekiah showed them the nation's wealth, and earned Isaiah's rebuke (2 Ki. 20:12-18; Isa. 39). A century later, Babylonians were to carry those riches away.

Miraculously, Judah had been able to stay out of the clutches of the Assyrian Empire, even though the northern kingdom of Israel had been swept away. But the rise of Babylon marked the end of Judah's independence. Nebuchadnezzar II made Judah a vassal state in 605 B.C. Three years later, when King Jehoiakim rebelled, Nebuchadnezzar's armies invaded.

Jerusalem surrendered, and young King Jehoiachin was taken to Babylon with 10,000 artisans and all the Temple's treasures. A list of rations provided for Jehoiachin and his family has been found among the thousands of Babylonian records recovered by archaeologists.

Nebuchadnezzar installed Zedekiah as king of Judah. But this puppet ruler also rebelled. A final invasion culminated in the destruction of Jerusalem and Solomon's Temple in 586 B.C. At that time most of the nation's remaining population was taken to Babylon.

Several OT prophetic books relate closely to these events. Habakkuk, in Josiah's time (640–609 B.C.), foretold the coming Babylonian invasion as a divine discipline. Jeremiah futilely urged submission to the Babylonians during the reigns of Judah's last four rulers. Ezekiel, taken to Babylon with the first group of captives, had a vision of God's protecting presence departing from the Jerusalem Temple, and he also urged the same submission to Babylon as Jeremiah had. *See also* Ezekiel; Habakkuk; Jeremiah.

Although they urged submission, these OT prophets also predicted Babylon's final doom (Isa. 13,14,47,48; Jer. 25). Like Assyria, historic Babylon lay under the judgment of God.

The Book of Daniel also concerns the Babylonian captivity, telling of a young Jewish captive who rose to influence with Nebuchadnezzar and subsequent rulers. The Book of Lamentations (probably composed by Jeremiah) expresses the anguish felt by the Jewish people at being torn from their homeland. *See also* Daniel; Lamentations.

IMPACT OF THE CAPTIVITY

Moses had warned that if God's people sinned they would be uprooted from their land and scattered among the nations (Deut. 28:15-68). The Babylonian captivity partially fulfilled this warning. Yet the captivity proved a blessing. The Hebrew people were purged of idolatry in Babylon. Their religion was refocused on the

Right: Clay seal of Nebuchadnezzar II, 6th century B.C. God used the great Babylonian conqueror to punish his own idolatrous and disobedient people. Far right: Map showing Babylon's strategic position in the Fertile Crescent. Warlike peoples from the Tigris-Euphrates Valley periodically moved through Canaan to attack Egypt.

120

BABYLONIAN RULERS IN THE SCRIPTURE

Babylonian Ruler	Scripture	Summary
Merodach-Baladan II	2 Ki. 20; Isa. 39	His envoys visited Judah in 711 B.C., probably to spy out its wealth.
Nebuchadnezzar II	2 Ki. 24,25 2 Chr. 36 Daniel	The great conqueror, he deported the Jewish people and destroyed the city of Jerusalem. Many personal insights are found in Dan. 1–5.
Belshazzar	Dan. 5,7	Ruler of Babylon, but second to his father Nabonidus, who left him to run the kingdom.

Detail from the Ishtar Gate showing reconstructed lion. Babylon, which overthrew the Assyrian Empire in 605 B.C., was itself overthrown by Cyrus the Persian in 539 B.C.

Scriptures, and the synagogue was developed as a place of study and worship.

As predicted in Isa. 13:19,20, Babylon ultimately became a completely deserted site (partly because its soil had become saline through two millennia of irrigation) and totally abandoned except for the Jewish suburb of Hillah.

SYMBOLIC BABYLON

Symbolic, or "mystery," Babylon appears in the Book of Revelation (Rev. 14:8; 16:19; 17:5,18). In this apocalyptic setting "Babylon the Great" represents human achievement in a society constructed without due reverence for God. The theme of pride is introduced in Scripture's initial reference to Babel, a city founded so that men might "make a name for ourselves and not be scattered" (Gen. 11:4). Isaiah vividly describes the Lucifer-like arrogance of Babylon (Isa. 14:12-15). And the theme finds its full development in Revelation with "Babylon the Great," which is both a religious system hostile to God and morality (Rev. 17), and a monument to man's materialistic achievements (Rev. 18).

Symbolic Babylon lies under the judgment of God. Ultimately Christ will return to execute judgment on all our Babylons. As Isaiah foretold, "The arrogance of man will be brought low and the pride of men humbled; the Lord alone will be exalted in that day, and the idols will totally disappear" (Isa. 2:17,18).

backbite *See* Slander.

backslide Fall away from faithfulness to God. This word, found only in the OT, appears more often in the KJV than in modern versions. The primary Hebrew word, *meshubah,* means "disloyalty" or "a turning away." Another Hebrew root word, *sarar,* indicates apostasy. As used in the Bible, "backsliding" usually describes the spiritual and moral condition of the community, not of an individual believer. When backsliding, Israel abandoned her covenant commitments. She worshiped foreign gods (Jer. 3:12,13) and turned from "the way of the Lord, the requirements of their God" (Jer. 5:5,6).

badger skin (KJV) A material mentioned in the Bible only in connection with Israel's tabernacle (Ex. 25:5; 26:14; Num. 4:6,25)

Model of Egyptian bakery. Baked bread, leavened and unleavened, was used in the worship of several ancient Near Eastern religions.

and with making sandals (Ezek. 16:10). The Hebrew word, *tahash*, has been translated "badger skins" (KJV), "goatskins" (RSV), "hides of sea cows" (NIV), "tahas skins" (CONF), and "porpoise hides" (NASB and NEB). The most likely meaning for *tahash* is the skin of the dugong, a large aquatic mammal related to the manatee. At the time of the Exodus, dugong were plentiful in the Gulf of Aqaba, not far from where the instructions for constructing the tabernacle were most likely given. These mammals, which grew to be ten feet long, were valued in the Sinai area for their skin, which was used in sandal-making. See also Coney.

bag A pouch or container, usually made of leather. Small coin purses were the most common bags of biblical times (Isa. 46:6; Hag. 1:6; Jn. 12:6). Weights used to balance scales were also carried in small bags (Deut. 25:13; Prov. 16:11; Mic. 6:11). Larger bags served as knapsacks for carrying provisions (1 Sam. 17:40; Lk. 10:4; 22:35,36).

Two references to bags deserve special attention. Job 14:16,17 pictures God placing sins in a purse, tying it tightly, and then putting the purse out of sight. Job says:

A man rolling bread. Flat cakes were most common in ancient Israel, since the "oven" consisted of a jar with coals inside. The dough was pressed flat against its sides.

> Surely then you will count my steps
> but not keep track of my sin.
> My offenses will be sealed up in a bag;
> you will cover over my sin.

In Luke 10:4, Jesus commands his disciples not to take along "a purse or a bag [of provisions] or sandals" when on a preaching mission. They were to trust God completely to meet their needs, even as Jesus did during his time on earth.

baker One who prepares food, especially bread, by baking. Professional bakers (Heb., *'opeh*) worked only in cities (Jer. 37:21), since in small towns and in the countryside each family did its own baking of cakes and breads. Genesis 40 gives the title "chief baker" to one of Egypt's important officials. This is a court title and, like the title "cupbearer," does not necessarily reflect all of the holder's actual duties.

Balaam [BAY-luhm; "devourer"?]. Famous pagan practitioner of the occult who was hired by King Balak of Moab to curse Israel, about 1405 B.C. **Scripture:** Num. 22–24. **Father:** Beor.

BACKGROUND

At the end of their 40 years of wandering in the Sinai desert, the people of Israel approached Canaan from the east, and camped across the Jordan from Jericho on the plains of Moab. The terrified king of the Moabites, Balak, sent for Balaam to come and curse Israel.

Balaam is identified in Josh. 13:22 as one who practiced divination (*qesem*). He was not a prophet in the biblical sense, but combined a worship of Jehovah with practice of occult powers (which are condemned by God in Deut. 18:10-13). In this context, the "curse" Balaam was hired to utter was basically pagan in concept, because it was rooted in the notion that particular incantations could bind an enemy or drain the power of individuals and nations. See also Curse; Divination.

But when messengers arrived from Balak, God directly intervened, first telling Balaam not to go, then warning him, and finally causing Balaam to bless Israel. One of the most significant of Balaam's utterances applies to all who have a covenant relationship with the living God: "There is no sorcery against Jacob, no divination against Israel" (Num. 23:23). No occult power can harm God's own.

God would not permit Balaam to curse Israel, but rather at each attempt compelled him to utter words of blessing. Nevertheless, Balaam afterwards devised

BALAAM

The angel of the Lord bars Balaam's way, as in Num. 22:21-35. Balaam was famous in his day as a diviner with supernatural powers. In the NT, Balaam is disdained as a man motivated by greed.

a crafty scheme to get Israel in trouble with God, and thus satisfy Balak's malice. According to Num. 31:16, he advised Balak to send a number of attractive young Midianite women onto the plains, to seduce the Israelites into adultery and idol worship. Balaam reasoned that God himself might curse Israel as a punishment for such sins. The plot ultimately failed when Phinehas, a son of Aaron, acted to kill an Israelite and his Moabite paramour (Num. 25). There was a great loss of life on the part of the Hebrew men who had been seduced but after 24,000 had died of a plague, the nation was purged of this abomination and restored to God's favor (Num. 25:1-11).

Balaam was killed in Israel's subsequent invasion of Canaan (Num. 31:8).

LEARNING FROM BALAAM'S LIFE

Three NT writers refer to Balaam. Peter condemns the "way of Balaam" as he discusses the motives of false teachers who see religion as a means for gaining wealth (2 Pet. 2:15). Jude 11 speaks of the "error of Balaam," which is to be so dominated by greed that doing God's will seems unimportant. And John mentions the "teaching of Balaam," apparently a combination of immorality and religion (Rev. 2:14).

Note especially: (1) Despite a clear prohibition against accompanying Balak's messengers ("Do not go with them"), Balaam was so eager for his fee that he sought God again for permission to go (22:1-20). (2) The appearance of God's death angel served as a vivid warning to Balaam to "speak only what I [God] tell you" (22:21-41). (3) Nevertheless, Balaam tried three times to bribe God with sacri-fices to let him curse Israel. *See also* Sacrifices and Offerings. Balaam found himself compelled to pronounce God's blessing instead because (as he said) "I must do whatever the Lord says" (23:1–24:9); he had no choice in the matter. (4) When the furious Balak threatened not to pay Balaam "handsomely," Balaam thought of a clever maneuver by which Moab might corrupt God's people, supposing that the Lord would then have to curse Israel (Num. 24:10–25:18; 31:16). This advice reveals Balaam's basic attitude of opposition toward God, who had revealed his intention to bless Israel.

Some have taken the opening words of Balaam's third and fourth oracles (Num. 24:3,4,15,16) as evidence that Balaam was a prophet of God. Balaam here represents himself as "one who hears the words of God, who has knowledge from the Most High, who sees a vision from the Almighty." In view of the character of Balaam and the NT remarks, these words might also be taken as expressions of wonder by this practitioner of the occult, that God had actually spoken to and through him (*compare* 1 Sam. 28).

The story of Balaam raises many thought-provoking issues. When we know God's will, why do we keep asking him to change his mind? Balaam was motivated by greed to disobey God. What motivates us to disobey, and to obey? How does God communicate today to those who are not his people? Consider, too, how secure God's people are. Not only was Israel protected from Balaam's magic, but even his plot against Israel failed, although there was a heavy loss of life on the part of those seduced.

Detail of Egyptian tomb painting showing ten heavy metal rings weighed on a balance (1380 B.C.).

Alabaster balm amphora (vase) from Tutankhamen's tomb (14th century B.C.). Balm was used widely in ancient cultures, and in the Bible symbolizes healing.

balances Scales for weighing. The ancient world regularly used balances to weigh grain, money, and other items. A beam would be balanced on a stand or suspended at its center by a cord; a pan would hang at each end. The material to be weighed would be placed in one pan until it balanced the fixed weight in the other.

The weighing of food in balances often symbolizes scarcity and famine (Ezek. 4:15,16; Rev. 6:5,6), since only in hard times would rationing be necessary. Archaeologists have found pictures of balances in Egyptian wall painting, as well as actual balance pans and weights used more than 3,500 years ago.

Scripture also associates balances with social justice. The Mosaic Law decrees: "Do not use dishonest standards when measuring length, weight or quantity. Use honest scales and honest weights" (Lev. 19:35,36). Balance scales could easily be manipulated by slightly shortening one arm, or by using false weights. Proverbs 11:1 says, "The Lord abhors dishonest scales." Yet the words of the prophets condemning these dishonest practices suggest that cheating was common in Israel (Hos. 12:7; Amos 8:5; Mic. 6:11).

While Egyptian religious wall paintings show the heart of a deceased king, noble, or commoner weighed in a balance against the goddess Maat ("truth"), similar symbolism occurs in the Bible only in Job 31:6 and Dan. 5:27. (In the Egyptian concept of trial before Osiris, the king of the dead, the soul was supposed to deny he had ever committed any sin while still alive. The declaration he made would then be weighed against the symbol of truth.) But salvation in Scripture is never viewed as a matter of balancing a person's good acts against his sins.

bald, baldness Lack of hair on one's head. Though natural baldness may not have been common in the biblical Middle East, it was by no means unknown (*see* 2 Ki. 2:23). Leviticus 13:40-44 makes a dis-

tinction between normal hair loss and hair loss caused by a skin disease. The latter would make an Israelite unclean. A shaved head signified humiliation and shame. When David sent envoys of good will to Hanun, king of the Amorites, Hanun humiliated David's messengers by shaving off their hair and beards. This insult led to war (2 Sam. 10).

Shaving one's head was also a sign of mourning (Job 1:20; Isa. 15:2; Jer. 7:29; 47:5; 48:37; Ezek. 7:18; Amos 8:10). However, Deut. 14:1,2 forbids shaving one's head in mourning for the dead because this practice had pagan associations. Nazirites were to shave their heads upon the fulfillment of their vows (Num. 6:18). The image of baldness is found in the warnings of the prophets, who confronted unrepentant Israel with the prospect of a future in which "instead of fragrance there will be a stench; instead of a sash, a rope; instead of well-dressed hair, baldness; instead of fine clothing, sackcloth; instead of beauty, branding" (Isa. 3:24). *See also* Nazirite; Clean and Unclean.

balm A natural healing substance. No one today knows what the *seri* or *sori* (balm) of the Bible really was but it seems to have been a kind of gum secreted from an aromatic bush or tree, such as *Pistacia mutica*. All we know is that it was an expensive commodity often carried by camel caravans (Gen. 37:25; 43:11), valued as a medicine, and apparently effective in reducing pain (Jer. 51:8). Jeremiah associates balm with Gilead (Jer. 8:22; 46:11), but does not make clear whether it grew there, was processed there, or whether Gilead served as a transfer point on a caravan route.

balsam A tree of biblical lands. Balsam trees played a decisive role in one of David's battles against the Philistines (2 Sam. 5:23,24; 1 Chr. 14:14,15). God instructed David to circle behind his enemy and to attack when he heard "the sound of marching" in the tops of the balsam trees.

This is the only biblical reference to the balsam (Heb., *baka'*). It is difficult to pin down precisely what kind of tree the *baka'* was. The KJV calls it the "mulberry" tree. Some have suggested that the *baka'* is a species of poplar (perhaps the aspen), whose leaves shake noisily in a breeze. But since the word seems to be related to the verb "to weep" (Heb., *bakah*), it may refer to the *Euphorbia apios* or the *Pistacia lentiscus* which drip a milky aromatic sap.

banish [Heb., *nadah*]. To drive away. In the OT God's people are often likened to a flock of sheep. Even as sheep may be scattered by a wild animal (Jer. 50:17), God's flock may be driven away from him by false prophets (Deut. 13:5) or selfish shepherds (Ezek. 34:4). The OT warned that God would banish his own flock if they were unfaithful to him, and would drive them from the Promised Land, to be scattered among pagan nations (Deut. 30:17,18; Jer. 16:15).

Israelites who were diseased or unclean were confined outside the camp of Israel and were not permitted to take part in worship celebrations (Num. 12:14,15), but they were not banished. "Banish" is a much stronger term. The OT makes no legal provision for condemning an Israelite to exile. David was accused of banishing Absalom (2 Sam. 14:13), but actually Absalom fled after murdering his brother Amnon; he was not driven away by David.

banner A flag or identifying standard. As the Israelites wandered in the wilderness, each tribal group raised a *degel*, or banner. David says, "We will shout for joy when you are victorious and will lift up our banners in the name of our God" (Ps. 20:5). In warfare, such standards often identified different regiments. But the OT also uses the image in a decidedly non-military context: "His banner [i.e., his identifying flag] over me is love."

A second Hebrew word for banner, or standard, *nes*, carries the idea of a sign or signal flag, something that might call the whole nation together. While each tribe of wandering Israelites carried a *degel*, Moses lifted the bronze serpent on a *nes*, so that anyone in Israel could look at it and be healed (Num. 21:8,9). After the historic battle in which the Israelites defeated the Amalekites (Ex. 17), Moses built an altar and named it "The Lord is my banner" (*Yahweh-nissi*), as an acknowledgment that all strength comes from the Lord. Isaiah likes to use this word, promising that Messiah will stand as a banner (11:10) and will "raise a banner for the nations and gather the exiles of Israel" (11:12).

banquet A formal meal held in honor of a person or a special occasion. In biblical times, banquets were lavish affairs where guests would eat meat and drink wine. In fact, the Hebrew word for this secular feast, *mishteh*, is derived from the verb meaning "to drink." Amos 6:4-6 describes a typical banquet scene, condemned by Amos only because such celebrations had become the daily practice of Israel's rich at the expense of the poor:

Bronze Roman ensign fixed to a pole and borne by a soldier is representative of symbols of military units.

Limestone plaque from Sin Temple, Iraq, 25th century B.C., depicts various banquet scenes. Banquets marked special occasions such as marriages, births, and weanings. The frequent banquets held by the rich are viewed in Scripture as selfish excess. Below: This rendition of the Last Supper shows the disciples "reclining at table," the usual posture at a formal banquet or feast.

You lie on beds inlaid with ivory
and lounge on your couches.
You dine on choice lambs
and fattened calves.
You strum away on your harps like David
and improvise on musical instruments.
You drink wine by the bowlful
and use the finest lotions. . . .

But banquets were usually reserved for special occasions, such as the arrival of a guest (Gen. 19:3; 2 Sam. 3:20), the weaning of a child (Gen. 21:8), a wedding (Jdg. 14:10), or the completion of a harvest (1 Sam. 25:11; Jdg. 9:27).

The infrequency of these special meals made them important social occasions. The giver of a banquet carefully considered whom to invite and where to place his guests, since the seating arrangements communicated significant social messages. This lies behind Jesus' criticism of the Pharisees for their love of "the place of honor at banquets and the most important seats in the synagogues" (Mt. 23:6). Luke 14:7-10 reports that once, when Jesus observed some guests competing for the place of honor at the table, he recommended a policy of humility, suggesting that if they took the lowest place, and the host later said, "Friend, move to a better place," they would be honored in the presence of their fellow guests.

This dual significance—the joyous celebration and the social honor—made the banquet an appropriate image of divine favor. Isaiah looked forward to the messianic age, saying to Israel:

On this mountain the Lord Almighty will
prepare
a feast of rich food for all peoples,
a banquet of aged wine—
the best of meats and the finest of
wines.

(Isa. 25:6)

It is no surprise to find Jesus using the same imagery. In the Kingdom of heaven, believers from every nation will take their places at the feast with Abraham, Isaac, and Jacob (Mt. 8:11), while the wicked will be excluded. In one of Jesus' parables, the Kingdom of heaven is likened to a king who prepared a wedding banquet and sent out invitations. When the guests were too involved in their own affairs to come, and even mistreated the messengers, the king brought in strangers off the street (Mt. 22:1-14). The parable was easily understood by Jesus' listeners: Ignoring a banquet invitation conveyed a blunt and open rejection.

Banquets also played an important part in the social life of Gentiles in the Roman Empire. Friends met for private banquets. Most skilled workers belonged to guilds, which held regular guild banquets. Public banquets were common. It was the practice in the Roman world to dedicate such banquets to a god or goddess, and to spill out a cup of wine in the honored deity's name. This practice put pressure on Christians, reflected in Paul's warning that those who participate in Christ should not "drink the cup of demons" (1 Cor. 10:21) by sharing in such meals.

Despite the fact that some reject the King's invitation, God's banquet hall will be filled. Revelation pictures the glad union of Christ and his Church in heaven as a joyous wedding banquet.

"Hallelujah!
For our Lord God Almighty reigns.
Let us rejoice and be glad
and give him glory!
For the wedding of the Lamb has come,
and his bride has made herself ready. . . ."

(Rev. 19:6,7)

But Revelation portrays another, grimmer banquet. At this, the "great supper of God," the birds of the air are the guests. And the fare? The bodies of those who engage in mankind's last great rebellion against God (Rev. 19:17). *See also* Feasts, Festivals, and Fasts; Meat; Wine.

baptism A sacred rite involving water, symbolizing a purification from sin. Though baptism is a sacrament or ordinance practiced by almost all of Christendom, Christians have differed over the significance of baptism, the mode of baptism, and who should receive baptism. Before trying to understand the differences, we need to be clear on the Bible's use of this important term.

A BRIEF HISTORY

The Septuagint, the Greek translation of the OT completed about 200 B.C., uses *baptizō* for the cleansings and washing with water required by the Law for ritual purification (Ex. 30:17-21; Lev. 11:25; Num. 19:17).

In the time of Jesus, the Jewish people used ritual bathing pools for personal purification. Archaeologists have found such baths not only on the Temple Mount but also in the remains of wealthy homes in Jerusalem, and even at the Khirbet Qumran, the headquarters of the Dead Sea Scrolls sect. Each bath, or *mikvah*, had a reserve pool that was filled from rain wa-

Relief of child's baptism from a sarcophagus found in the Baths of Diocletian in Rome. Although Christians debate its mode and significance, baptism is almost universally practiced.

ter because rabbinic law dictated flowing ("living") water for use in purification.

John's baptism conformed to this law, since he baptized in the Jordan River (Mt. 3:6; Mk. 1:5). As Jewish purification rites usually involved immersion, John probably immersed his disciples as well. Yet John's practice transformed the meaning of immersion in water. John's baptism was no longer a private ritual of personal purifica-tion; John introduced baptism as a public act symbolizing repentance and recommitment to God's laws, in expectation of the Messiah's imminent coming. When the NT refers to "the baptism of John," it draws our attention to John's message of expectation, in contrast to the post-resurrection gospel meaning of salvation through Christ's completed work.

There is no evidence that Jesus himself baptized anyone. In Mt. 3:13-16, we are told that Jesus (in order "to fulfill all righteousness" as the sin-bearer of the redeemed) constrained John, despite his own protest, to baptize him also in the Jordan River. Then the Holy Spirit descended upon him, anointing him for his messianic ministry (*see* Mk. 1:9-11; Lk. 3:21-23; Jn. 1:32,33.) Just before his return to heaven, Christ commanded his followers to make disciples and to baptize them, not for repentance but "in the name of the Father, the Son, and the Holy Spirit" (Mt. 28:19). Subsequently the church consistently practiced water baptism, but with yet another, distinctively Christian meaning (Acts 2:38; 1 Cor. 1:13-17).

BAPTISM AS A SPIRITUAL REALITY
New Testament references to baptism, however, do not lay the principal emphasis on water, as such. "Baptism" is treated as a specialized theological term indicating the believer's identification and union with

Ritual bath, or mikvah, from first-century Jericho, illustrates emphasis placed by Jews on ceremonial cleansing. Among other purposes, mikvaoth were used for baptizing converts to Judaism.

Jesus Christ and participation in Jesus' death and resurrection. Romans uses *baptizō* in this way, in a passage that best expresses the doctrine:

Don't you know that all of us who were baptized into Christ Jesus were baptized into his death? We were therefore buried with him through baptism into death in order that, just as Christ was raised from the dead through the glory of the Father, we too may live a new life.

If we have been united with him like this in his death, we will certainly also be united with him in his resurrection. For we know that our old self was crucified with him so that the body of sin might be done away with, that we should no longer be slaves to sin—because anyone who has died has been freed from sin.

Now if we died with Christ, we believe that we will also live with him. (Rom. 6:3-8)

We find another key to the theological meaning of baptism in 1 Cor. 12:13: "We were all baptized by one Spirit into one body." Paul wants us to understand that the Holy Spirit is the one who unites us to Jesus and, through Jesus, to other Christians, in a work that is performed for all who believe thus. It is clear that baptism is a sign and seal of our ingrafting into Christ, our partaking of all the benefits of the covenant of grace, and of our engagement to be the Lord's.

In its theological sense, then, "baptism" expresses the spiritual reality of the believer's union with Jesus Christ and, through that union, one's identification with Christ in his death and resurrection. Because our union with Jesus is a spiritual reality, we are enabled by God's grace and power to overcome the pull of the sin nature and can live righteous lives.

PASSAGES ON BAPTISM

Many have suggested that "baptism" was selected as a term to describe union with Christ because the word was associated in the first century with dyeing. A piece of cloth dipped into a vat of dye would permanently take on the dye's color. Those who are united to Jesus participate in his death and resurrection, and as a result, they are changed, experiencing an inner transformation toward Christ's likeness (2 Cor. 3:18). Against this background, Christian water baptism is an appropriate symbol of the spiritual reality that occurs.

Even with this frame of reference, a number of Bible references need further explanation:

• *Matthew 3:11.* Baptism "with fire" is usually taken as a reference to the final judgment of those who will not believe. (*See* v.12.) Others, however, see it as a reference to the Holy Spirit's work in purifying believers, represented on the day of Pentecost by the "tongues of fire" that came to rest on the disciples (Acts 2:3). *See also* Baptism in the Spirit.

• *Matthew 3:14.* Jesus presented himself for John's baptism. John, who knew his cousin as a godly person, at first refused. Christ insisted. The phrase "it is proper for us to do this to fulfill all righteousness" (v.15) does not mean that Jesus had sins to repent of. Jesus meant that it was right for him to publicly take a stand with John's message in this way. *See also* John the Baptist.

• *Mark 10:38,39.* Jesus asked two followers, "Can you . . . be baptized with the baptism I am baptized with?" Christ was asking whether they could participate in his immersion in the suffering of the crucifixion he was about to experience.

BAPTISM IN THE NEW TESTAMENT

References to John's baptism	References to water baptism	References to spiritual baptism
Mt. 3:1-16	Mk. 16:16	Mt. 3:11
Mt. 21:25	Jn. 4:2	Mk. 1:8
Mk. 1:4-11	Acts 2:38-41	Lk. 3:16
Mk. 11:30	Acts 8:12-16	Jn. 1:26,33
Lk. 3:3-21	Acts 9:18	Acts 2:38,39
Lk. 7:29,30	Acts 10:47,48	Acts 8:16
Lk. 20:4	Acts 16:15,33	Acts 11:16
Jn. 1:26	Acts 18:8	Rom. 6:3,4
Jn. 3:22,23	Acts 19:5	1 Cor. 10:2
Acts 1:5,22	Acts 22:16	1 Cor. 12:13
Acts 10:37	1 Cor. 1:13-17	Gal. 3:27
Acts 13:24	Heb. 6:2	Eph. 4:5
Acts 18:25	1 Pet. 3:21	Col. 2:12
Acts 19:3,4		1 Pet. 3:21

- *1 Corinthians 10:2.* The Israelites who left Egypt in the Exodus were "baptized into Moses," meaning that they had been brought together as one people under Moses' leadership through God's miraculous acts. Paul may also have the water-image of the Red Sea in mind as he chooses his terminology (although no immersion was involved in this crossing).

- *1 Corinthians 15:29.* Paul does not lend support for the strange practice of being "baptized for the dead" which apparently had emerged in Corinth. Paul simply points out that a person who submits to baptism in response to the earnest admonition of a dying believer would be unable to meet with him in heaven were it not for the bodily resurrection of believers after death.

- *1 Peter 3:20–4:2.* In Peter's reference to "baptism that now saves you . . . by the resurrection of Jesus Christ," he draws an analogy between our spiritual baptism, by which we are united with Christ, and the experience of Noah. As the ark carried Noah through the waters of judgment and deposited him in a new world, so our salvation through our union with Jesus (signified and sealed through baptism) carries us safely beyond God's judgment and deposits us in a new spiritual realm in which we live by God's will rather than by "evil human desires" (4:2).

VIEWS IN CHRISTIAN TRADITIONS

Christians have developed differing traditions concerning the significance, participants, and mode of baptism. There is no decisive scriptural evidence for a preferred mode of baptism, and it is well known that in the early church Christians were baptized by sprinkling and by pouring of water as well as by immersion.

There are three major views of the significance of water baptism. 1. *The sacramental view* sees baptism as a means of grace, which by its performance brings remission of sins and new life (Catholic), or which implants a faith which will later be energized by preaching of the Word (Lutheran). 2. *The covenantal view*, held by Reformed Protestant churches, sees water baptism as a sign of a covenant relationship with God, as circumcision was in the OT. Vows are made by or for the person being baptized. Baptism not only initiates the individual into the Church, but it is also the sign and seal of God's grace unto redemption. 3. *The symbolic view* treats water baptism as a public confession of Christ as Savior, and an appropriate sym-

bol of the work God has already done in uniting the believer to Jesus. Those who hold the first two views practice infant baptism. Those holding the third view argue that baptism is appropriate only when a person is old enough to make a personal commitment to Christ.

Detail from Alessandro Magnasco's Baptism of Christ, *about 1730—a fantastic, almost surrealistic impression of the event.*

baptism of the Spirit John the Baptist told his listeners that the coming Messiah would baptize with the Holy Spirit and not just water (Mt. 3:11; Mk. 1:8). Jesus used the same language after his resurrection, telling his disciples to wait in Jerusalem, because "in a few days you will be baptized with the Holy Spirit" (Acts 1:5). Peter looked back on Pentecost and identified it as the time at which this promise was fulfilled (Acts 11:16). These passages establish that (1) the promised baptism of the Holy Spirit came on the day of Pentecost, and that (2) those who became Christians after Pentecost shared in that experience. Yet these passages do not explain what "baptism with the Holy Spirit" actually is.

In 1 Cor. 12:13, Paul defines it as that work of the Spirit by which all who believe are united to Jesus as members of his living Body. But the phrase "baptism of the Spirit" has another meaning in some Christian traditions. In Pentecostal and charismatic circles, the phrase expresses the belief that after salvation believers can look forward to a special experience of the

Holy Spirit, who will come to them and bring them power for holy living. In these traditions, speaking in tongues, as the disciples did on the day of Pentecost, is usually taken as evidence that a Christian has received this special gift and been "baptized by the Spirit." *See also* Baptism.

Barabbas [Buh-RAB-uhs; "son of Abba" or "son of his father"]. The prisoner released from jail in place of Jesus. **Scripture:** Mt. 27:16; Mk. 15:11; Lk. 23:18; Jn. 18:40.

Mark and Luke portray Barabbas as an "insurrectionist who had committed murder in the uprising" (Mk. 15:7). John calls him a robber. Each of these crimes called for the death penalty under Roman law, and Barabbas was awaiting execution when Jesus was tried by Pilate. In Pilate's effort to free Jesus, he offered the crowd a choice: he would release Barabbas or Jesus.

If Barabbas were a Zealot, a first-century "freedom fighter" who wanted to break Rome's hold on Palestine, then this offer would have been a tactical mistake. Crowds are all too ready to honor those who claim to kill in a cause. More likely, Barabbas was recognized as a vicious criminal, whose crimes were more against his own people than against Rome. Yet the chief priests "stirred up the crowds to have Pilate release Barabbas instead" (Mk. 15:11).

Many have speculated about what happened to Barabbas, since he is never mentioned again in the Bible nor in any known secular source. The practice of releasing a prisoner on the Jewish holiday is also unknown apart from the biblical reference.

Peter, however, may have had this incident in mind when he treated Christ's death as an injustice; a case in which the righteous died "for" the unrighteous (1 Pet. 3:18). The one who deserved execution was freed, and the innocent took his place. In this sense, the incident of Barabbas's release is a vivid image of redemption itself. Christ's death was from the standpoint of human responsibility a supreme injustice (*see* Acts 2:23; 3:14,15), nevertheless it proved to be the central element in the grand plan of God to release those who deserve punishment by taking on himself the stroke that justice decrees. In his death, Jesus was not simply a substitute for Barabbas, but for all who receive him by faith.

barbarian A non-Greek, a foreigner, one who is uncivilized. In the fifth century B.C., at the height of the golden age of Greek civilization, the Greeks coined this word to describe foreigners. *Barbaros* originally described a person speaking a foreign (non-Greek) language, and later came to mean any alien (non-Greek) race. By NT times, it was a term of contempt, meaning

While Hebrews grew full beards, Egyptians preferred to be clean-shaven (see Gen. 41:14). Scene from tomb of Userhat (Egypt, 18th Dynasty): Barber works while others wait their turn.

6arleycorn

Barley fields, shown here with Mount Tabor, were the source of "daily bread" for the poor. Upper classes ground wheat to make bread.

one who was backward, coarse, or uncivilized. Paul saw himself obligated to both the cultured Greek and the barbarian (Rom. 1:14), for he held the grand vision of a people of God who were united, not by a common culture or sophistication, but by a common faith in Jesus Christ (Col. 3:11; *compare* Eph. 2:19). *See also* Gentile.

barber One who shaves or cuts hair. We know that Jewish men were concerned about the looks of their hair, and kept their beards and mustaches trimmed (2 Sam. 14:25,26; 19:24). Yet only once does Scripture mention a "barber" (Heb., *gallab*) and that is just a passing reference to a "barber's razor" (Ezek. 5:1).

barley A grain grown in Palestine. Israelite farmers grew two staple grains, wheat and barley. Barley ripened about a month before wheat, in March or April, and cost about half as much (2 Ki. 7:1). It was fed to horses and cattle, and the poor used it in bread. In Ezekiel, barley symbolizes poverty and national disaster (4:9-12). Biblical references to barley may carry a note of scorn: Gideon's soldiers seemed like nothing but "a round loaf of barley bread" to the Midianites, but they would still win the battle (Jdg. 7:13).

It is significant that the five loaves Jesus multiplied as food for thousands were barley (Jn. 6:9). From this incident came Christ's presentation of himself as the "bread of life." Like barley, Christ was not highly valued by his own people. Yet he alone provides eternal life for the spiritually poor and needy. *See also* Agriculture; Bread.

BACKGROUND

A native of Cyprus, Barnabas may have been visiting Jerusalem as a pilgrim to observe the Feast of Pentecost the year Christ was crucified. He became an active Christian, quickly demonstrating his compassion by selling his own property and bringing the money to the apostles to be distributed to believers in need (Acts 4:36,37).

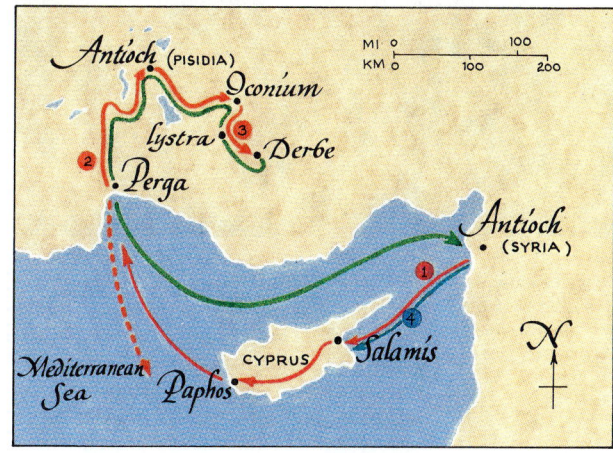

When Paul came to Jerusalem after his conversion, the Christians were afraid that this former persecutor intended to infiltrate their movement and destroy it. It was Barnabas who took the risk of bringing Paul into the fellowship, telling the leaders Paul's conversion story and relating how Paul had preached Christ in Damascus (Acts 9:26,27). Some years later, Barnabas was sent by the Jerusalem church to check out reports of Gentiles turning to God in Antioch. As a "good man, full of the Holy Spirit and faith," Barnabas was able to work effectively in this predominantly Gentile church. After a time, Barnabas went to Tarsus and sought out Paul, bringing him back to join the leadership team in Antioch (Acts 11:19-26). When a severe famine struck, Barnabas and Paul took the gifts of the Antioch church to the Christians in Judea (11:27-30).

Map shows route taken by Barnabas on his missionary journeys: 1) Barnabas, Paul and Mark sail to Cyprus, Barnabas' home. 2) Mark leaves the work and sails for home. 3) The people of Lystra assume Barnabas and Paul are gods. Barnabas is called Zeus; Paul, the "chief speaker," is taken for his messenger, Hermes. 4) After "sharp disagreement" with Paul, Barnabas gives Mark a second chance and returns with him to Cyprus.

Perga in Pamphylia, where John Mark deserted the missionary team (Acts 13:13).

(1) The nickname "Barnabas" which stayed with Joseph the Levite all his life is introduced with the report that he "sold a field he owned" and brought the money to be used for brothers and sisters in need (Acts 4:36,37). Barnabas was a loving, sensitive man, who was easily moved by the needs of others. He is a model of that practical and godly "pity" that demonstrates Christlike love (1 Jn. 3:16-24).

(2) The same trait is shown in Barnabas's willingness to risk contacting Paul when others were afraid (Acts 9:26,27). People's needs are not just material, but spiritual and social as well. Barnabas reached out to draw Paul into the Christian fellowship.

(3) In Antioch, Barnabas was able to overcome his natural Jewish prejudices, accept the idea of a predominantly Gentile church, and work harmoniously with non-Jews. Galatians 2:9-13 indicates how difficult this was. *See also* Gentile.

(4) When Barnabas left on the first missionary journey, he was the acknowledged leader (Acts 13:2,7). But almost immediately Paul took over that role, and the team became "Paul and his companions" (13:13,42,46). The generous and selfless Barnabas fit easily into this new role and continued as Paul's partner.

(5) Although Barnabas showed no concern for his own personal status, he took a strong stand when it came to young John Mark. Paul would not hear of taking John Mark on another missions trip; Paul was adamant because of Mark's earlier desertion. Yet Barnabas wanted to give Mark another chance. Barnabas was still willing to take a risk for the sake of another person, just as he had been when he stood in defense of a young Paul in Jerusalem!

While it is futile to argue over who was "right" in this bitter disagreement that separated two friends, Scripture adds a fascinating footnote. Many years later, in prison, Paul wrote to Timothy, "Get Mark and bring him with you, because he is helpful to me in my ministry" (2 Tim. 4:11). Barnabas had sacrificed an old and dear friendship to encourage young John Mark. But in the end, even Paul realized that the simple goodness of his compassionate companion had salvaged a young man for the ministry whom Paul would have lost. (*Compare* Col. 4:10,11; Phlm. 24.)

After the Holy Spirit called them to be the church's first missionary team, Barnabas traveled with Paul to Cyprus, his home, and on to other cities in Asia Minor. A later incident in Lystra suggests that Barnabas may have been a relatively large man, for when Paul healed a cripple there, Barnabas was taken for the god Jupiter and the smaller Paul for Mercury, his spokesman (Acts 13,14).

Both men were delegates to the Jerusalem council that debated the proper relationship between the Jewish church and the Gentile congregations then springing up throughout the Roman world (Acts 15). *See also* Antioch; Council of Jerusalem. But on their return, a "sharp disagreement" separated the two friends. Barnabas wanted to take young John Mark on their second mission. Paul refused, because Mark had "deserted them" on the first journey. Paul chose another partner, Silas, and left without Barnabas, while Barnabas took Mark and set out on a mission of his own (15:36-41). *See also* Paul.

LEARNING FROM BARNABAS'S LIFE

Many significant insights are woven into the framework of the story of Barnabas:

barren, barrenness A woman's inability to bear children. In the biblical world, the childless woman was not only sorrowful but ashamed and disgraced. Eliphaz, one of Job's friends, summed up the view of his day that "the company of the godless will be barren" (Job 15:34). Hannah's despair (1 Sam. 1) and Rachel's bitter plea, "Give me children, or I'll die!" (Gen. 30:1), express the impact of barrenness on women of their time. No wonder Proverbs lists among those things which can never be satisfied "the grave, [and] the barren womb" (Prov. 30:16).

Undoubtedly, one of the most important OT promises God gave to his covenant people was that, if they were faithful to him, "none will miscarry or be barren in your land" (Ex. 23:26).

Yet in the case of the Bible's four most famous barren women, this "curse" was a prelude to great blessing. Barren Sarah bore Isaac to Abraham, and thus founded the line from which Christ came (Gen. 21). Barren Rachel bore Joseph, whom God used to preserve his family in Egypt (Gen. 30). Barren Hannah's prayer for a child was answered and she bore Samuel, Israel's last and greatest judge (1 Sam. 1). And a barren Elizabeth gave birth to John the Baptist, who prepared the way for the ministry of our Lord (Lk. 1).

Bartholomew [Bahr-THOL-uh-myu; "son of Tolmai." *Tolmai* probably means "ploughman"]. One of the "unknown" among the twelve disciples of Jesus, who appears only in lists which name them all, in A.D. 30. Some suggest he is the Nathanael of John 1, but the evidence is not conclusive. **Scripture:** Mt. 10:3; Mk. 3:18; Lk. 6:14; Acts 1:13.

The view that Bartholomew is the family name of Nathanael developed because (1) Nathanael is found only in John's Gospel and Bartholomew only in the Synoptics, and (2) both seem to be mentioned in association with Philip (Mt. 10:3; Mk. 3:18; Lk. 6:14; Jn. 1:43-51; 21:2). The strongest support is that (3) "Nathanael" is named among the disciples in Jn. 21:2. *See also* Disciple; Nathanael.

Early traditions cast Bartholomew as an active missionary after Christ's resurrection, and sites in India, Armenia, Mesopotamia, and Persia have laid claim to his ministry.

Baruch [Bahr-RUKE; "blessed"]. Friend and secretary of the prophet Jeremiah, about 600 B.C. **Scripture:** Jeremiah 32,36,43,45. **Father:** Neriah. **Brother:** Seraiah, an official in the royal court.

BACKGROUND
Jeremiah prophesied in Judah during the last 40 years of that kingdom's existence. His emotional warnings were ignored, and the prophet was reviled as a traitor for his insistence that Babylon had been raised up by God to discipline Judah, and for his constant call for surrender to Nebuchadnezzar. Apparently near the mid-point of Jeremiah's ministry, in the reign of King Jehoiakim (608–597 B.C.), God gave Jeremiah a friend and supporter. Baruch, a member of a well-connected family, not only served as the prophet's scribe but also publicly read his prophecies to the people. Baruch thus suffered the same rejection as his mentor during the last years before Judah's exile.

In the end, Baruch was accused of having so much influence over the aged Jeremiah that he, not the prophet, was the source of Jeremiah's messages (43:3).

The OT does not say what happened to Baruch. One tradition says he was taken to Babylon, and another that he died in Egypt. Yet as the centuries passed, Baruch became more and more of a hero to the Jewish people. The great respect in which he was held is reflected in the large number of apocryphal writings which were given his name. *See also* Apocrypha.

LEARNING FROM BARUCH'S LIFE
Two passages give us insight into the character of Jeremiah's friend:

• *Jeremiah 36.* Jeremiah was under house arrest, so he asked Baruch to take the scroll of prophecies he had just dictated and read them aloud at the Temple on a special holy day when many would be present. Baruch "did everything Jeremiah told him to do." Baruch was then taken aside and asked to read the scroll to several officials, who advised Baruch to take Jeremiah and go into hiding before they brought the scroll to King Jehoiakim. The king coolly cut up the scroll as it was read, burned it, and then ordered the arrest of the prophet and his secretary.

After hearing of the scroll's destruction, Jeremiah dictated his prophecies to Baruch again, this time including words of God's judgment on King Jehoiakim personally.

• *Jeremiah 45.* Baruch was apparently appalled by what had happened. As a member of a well-connected family whose brother was a court official (*compare* Jer. 36:4; 51:59), Baruch had expected to win a

Below left: Baruch's own seal, dated late 7th century B.C. This spectacular find from Jerusalem reads, "Berechiah [Baruch] son of Neriah the scribe." This clay seal is one of very few artifacts referring directly to a specific biblical character or event.

Below: Hebrew scribe with writing kit. Scribes came from and were chiefly employed by the upper classes.

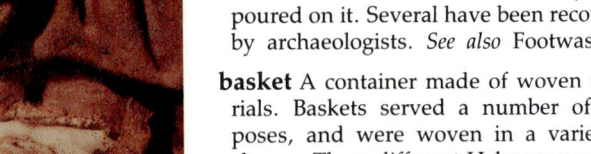

the disciples' feet (Jn. 13). These interesting basins had a molded bridge on which to rest the foot while water from a jar was poured on it. Several have been recovered by archaeologists. *See also* Footwashing.

basket A container made of woven materials. Baskets served a number of purposes, and were woven in a variety of shapes. Three different Hebrew words for "basket" convey the distinctions. The *sal* carried the flat loaves of bread baked in the Middle East, and probably was flat itself (Gen. 40:16-18; Lev. 8:2,26). The woven *tene'* was a large container used to store agricultural products (Deut. 28:5). The *kelub* was apparently used in gathering fruit. It resembled a net for trapping or caging birds (Jer. 5:27). All of these containers were commonplace in Bible times, and were essential to the people's way of life. Therefore, basket weaving, like pottery, was an important industry.

The miracle stories of Jesus use two different Greek words for "basket." In the feeding of the 5,000, the disciples used twelve *kophinoi*, large, hamper-like baskets, to collect the leftover food (Mt. 14:20). But after the feeding of the 4,000, they carried the even larger *spyris* (Mt. 15:37). This sturdy hamper was large enough to hold the apostle Paul as he was lowered from the city walls of Damascus in a dramatic escape from his enemies (Acts 9:25).

bastard (KJV) An illegitimate child or one born of a forbidden marriage. Such persons and their descendants were excluded from worship in the sanctuary of Israel for ten generations (Deut. 23:2). In Heb. 12:8, the writer points out that "illegitimate children" are more likely to be deprived the discipline and training provided by a father than would be true of his biological son. The person who is a legitimate offspring of God through new birth should therefore expect God to carry out a father's responsibility to discipline him or her when needed. *See also* Born Again; Discipline.

bath Israel's standard liquid measure. The bath was used to measure water (1 Ki. 7:26), wine (Isa. 5:10), and oil (2 Chr. 2:10). It represented approximately 5½ U.S. gallons or 21 liters. *See also* Weights and Measures.

bathing Cleansing one's body in water. Palestine is a dry land, virtually without rain for six months of the year. Archaeologists have discovered and studied the

Small wash basin shown at Peter's feet, in detail from relief on a marble sarcophagus from the 4th century A.D.

Below: Tile mosaic of a basket of fruit shaped to fit on a donkey recalls Amos's prophecy involving a "basket of ripe fruit" (Amos 8:1,2). Bottom: From tomb of Nakht (Thebes, Egypt), workers place threshed grain in large baskets, as the Egyptians did at Joseph's instructions when he was vizier of Egypt (Gen. 41).

high post in Judah's society. Now he was marked as an enemy of the king! Baruch groaned with self-pity. God rebuked him, informing him that he was about to tear down the kingdom of Judah itself and bring disaster on its inhabitants. "Should you then seek great things for yourself?" But the Lord added this promise: "Wherever you go I will let you escape with your life" (Jer. 45:5).

Several things about Baruch invite consideration. Given his ambition, the fact that Baruch not only recorded Jeremiah's message but read it publicly shows admirable commitment. It cost Baruch something important to obey God's prophet. Yet Baruch experienced regret and self-pity, so God spoke to him along lines Jesus would one day preach: "A man's life does not consist in the abundance of his possessions" (Lk. 12:15).

basin A shallow container for liquids. In biblical times, basins were often pottery, although they sometimes were made of gold (1 Chr. 28:17). The OT uses several different Hebrew words, probably indicating different kinds of basins. For an illustration of various shapes and styles, *see* Pottery.

The only basin (Gk., *niptēr*) mentioned in the NT was used by Jesus in washing

carefully constructed cisterns, designed to collect and save every drop of water, built by the Jewish inhabitants of Palestine from the time of the Exodus. Given the great need to conserve water in that area, we would hardly expect the Israelites to share modern notions about cleanliness and bathing. *See also* Cistern.

If we define "bathing" as washing the whole body, only some eight such instances occur in the OT. One of these refers to Pharaoh's daughter (Ex. 2:5), two to ritual occasions (Lev. 8:6; 2 Ki. 5:10-14), and two to preparation for visiting or receiving guests (Ruth 3:3; Ezek. 23:40). Two other bathings seem to have been for personal refreshment or cleansing (2 Sam. 11:2; 12:20), and one describes prostitutes bathing in a pool in Samaria (1 Ki. 22:38).

Yet various kinds of partial washings were important to the Hebrew people. A host or his servant normally washed the feet of a guest who walked to his home. Hands were washed before meals. In Jesus' time, the washing of hands had ritual significance, and was performed as much for religious purification as for cleanliness (Mk. 7:2).

Although this particular practice was traditional rather than prescribed, it was rooted in OT Law, which prescribes washing with water as part of many purification ceremonies (Lev. 15:5-27). In the time of Jesus, the homes of the wealthy in Jerusalem featured ceremonial immersion baths used in ritual purifications. *See also* Baptism.

Washing with water was clearly associated in Israel with moral purity and personal cleanliness. This standard of cleanliness was unusual for that era.

There is also a hint in the Gospels that people were more concerned about cleanliness than the few references to bathing in the Bible might suggest. At the Last Supper, Jesus noted, "A person who has had a bath (*louō*) needs only to wash (*niptō*) his feet; his whole body is clean" (Jn. 13:10). Both bathing the whole body and washing the dust off one's feet were familiar to these disciples, even though they came from "backward" Galilee.

But Jesus intended his remark as a parable. The person who has been completely cleansed through faith in the Savior will still figuratively find his feet stained as he lives in a sin-warped society. Although cleansed once for all, the believer still must return to Christ for continued purification from daily sins.

Bathsheba [Bath-SHEE-bah; "daughter of Sheba" or "daughter of oath or vow"]. The woman with whom King David committed adultery; he later married her and they had four sons, including his successor, King Solomon, about 990 B.C. **Scripture:** 2 Sam. 11,12; 1 Ki. 1,2. **Father:** Eliam (2 Sam. 11:3, called Ammiel in 1 Chr. 3:5). **Husbands:** Uriah, David. **Sons by David:** Shammua, Shobab, Nathan, Solomon.

BACKGROUND

Her story is one of the best known in the Bible. From his palace roof, David saw Bathsheba bathing. Inflamed by her beauty, David had her brought to him. When Bathsheba became pregnant, David first tried to hide his adultery by having her army officer husband, Uriah, brought back from the front. But Uriah refused to sleep with his wife while his men were on the field, so David arranged to have Uriah killed in battle. David then married Bathsheba. When confronted by Nathan the prophet, David finally confessed his sin. He made his confession public by

Woman bathing, clay figurine from 12th–10th century B.C., found at Achziv. Bathsheba was bathing at night when David saw her from his rooftop and desired her.

writing Psalm 51 and setting it to music for use in worship.

Although David had several wives, Bathsheba seemed to have been special to him and he had four sons by her. We see Bathsheba's continuing influence on David in the fact that he promised her that her oldest surviving son, Solomon (2 Sam. 12:24; 1 Chr. 3:5) would succeed him as king (1 Ki. 1:13; *compare* Song 3:11). Bathsheba and Nathan the prophet successfully urged the aged David to fulfill this promise when another of his sons, Adonijah, tried to proclaim himself as his father's successor. *See also* Adonijah; Solomon.

A mikvah or ceremonial bath in Jerusalem, 6th century B.C. These baths were used for ritual purification rather than daily bathing in water-scarce Palestine.

things suggest that Bathsheba was an unusual woman: (1) She did not let herself be destroyed by what was in effect a rape, and (2) she later recognized David's positive qualities and was able to develop a strong relationship with him.

Many of us have shattering experiences; many of us may even have been betrayed by those whose profession of faith, like David's, led us to trust them. Bathsheba suggests to us that, through repentance and forgiveness, something beautiful may grow from even the most terrible of failures.

battle *See* War.

bay tree (KJV) [Heb., *'ezrah*; literally, "native-born"]. Mentioned only in the KJV of Ps. 37:35, this is properly translated in modern versions as a "green tree" which flourishes "in its native soil," but it may well refer to *Laurus nobilis*, a dark evergreen which in Palestine towers to the height of 60 feet.

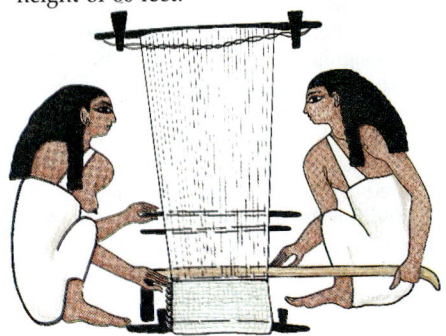

Bears like this one, from a Mesopotamian relief, roamed Palestine in the days of David and Elisha.

Goliath's spear had a shaft "like a weaver's rod" (1 Sam. 17:7). A long, thick warp, the weaver's beam, is shown at the top of the loom in this Egyptian tomb painting (about 2000 B.C.).

It is difficult to assess Bathsheba's role in the original seduction. Perhaps if she had been as assertive as another of David's wives, Abigail, David could have been dissuaded. Yet, other evidence suggests that Bathsheba was a resourceful person. It would take more than beauty to retain the interest of so unusual a person as David, and to influence him to select Solomon as the next king (although the choice of successor had actually been made by God himself, 1 Chr. 22:9). Nathan must have recognized Bathsheba's influence too, since he asked her to make the initial approach to David when Adonijah attempted to crown himself king (1 Ki. 1). *See also* Abigail; Beauty; Nathan.

Yet in another passage, Bathsheba seems politically naive. After Solomon was crowned, Adonijah (David's oldest surviving son who had earlier made a bid for the crown) begged Bathsheba to ask Solomon for permission to marry a young woman named Abishag. Abishag had been David's last concubine. Although Abishag had not had sex with the aged king, marriage to her in the ancient East would have symbolized Adonijah's right to royal "succession," and thus provided a potential challenge to Solomon's right to the throne. Solomon grasped the implications of this request, even though his mother did not, and ordered Adonijah's execution.

LEARNING FROM BATHSHEBA'S LIFE

The biblical text is careful to fix responsibility for the seduction on David: Bathsheba was bathing at dusk; David only happened to see her that evening because he was restless and unable to sleep. He then "sent messengers to get her." A woman of this society, whose husband was away and therefore unable to protect her, had no defense against a king. Two

beam A large timber or board, used in the construction of houses and buildings. Beams supported walls, ceilings, and gates in city walls (1 Ki. 6:9,36; 2 Chr. 3:7; Neh. 2:8; 3:3,6; Song 1:17). The "weaver's beam" (or "rod," NIV) was the heavy bar around which the warp cords were wrapped in a loom (1 Sam. 17:7; 1 Chr. 11:23). Jesus quoted a familiar proverb when he criticized those who found fault with others, saying that a judgmental attitude leads us to focus on every speck of sawdust in other people's eyes, while overlooking the beam ("log," RSV, NASB; "plank," NIV) in our own (Mt. 7:3-5).

bear (noun). A large, furry mammal. In early biblical times, light-colored bears ranged Palestine. Fierce predators, these bears often killed sheep and goats. Young David showed significant courage in fighting and killing a bear to protect his sheep (1 Sam. 17:34-37). The strength and ferocity of bears made them appropriate sym-

136

bols of aggressive powers in the visions of Daniel (Dan. 7:5) and of John (Rev. 13:2). These same qualities are replaced with meekness in Isaiah's vision: "The cow will feed with the bear, their young will lie down together" (11:7)—a striking image of the forces of nature at peace in the coming age. It is especially striking in light of the proverb that describes warfare and brutality in terms of the berserk rage of a "bear robbed of her cubs" (2 Sam. 17:8; Hos. 13:8).

Yet Prov. 17:12 reminds us that sin is even more dangerous to mankind: "Better to meet a bear robbed of her cubs than a fool in his folly." Here the "fool" is *kesil*, a person whose stubborn pursuit of wrong choices is often exhibited in sexual immorality. *See also* Fool.

Probably the most unusual incident in the Bible concerning bears is reported in 2 Ki. 2:23,24. Two she-bears mauled a menacing youth-gang (not "little children" as in the KJV) who ridiculed the prophet Elisha for his bald head and his pretensions to being the successor of Elijah.

bear (verb). (1) To produce, as fruit; (2) to carry; (3) to endure. The NT uses this common verb in several different ways. Jesus spoke of "bearing fruit." Figuratively, a Christian's good life is the natural fruit produced by an intimate relationship with Jesus (Mt. 7:15-20; Jn. 15:1-8). *See also* Fruit.

Christians are also encouraged to "bear" each other's unusually heavy burdens (*baros*), but are told to carry their own normal loads (*phortion*) (Gal. 6:2,5).

Finally, we are to "bear with" one another's faults. The Greek word here is *anechomai*, which literally means "to put up with" (Eph. 4:2). Actually, each of these meanings calls for a basic Christian virtue: patience. It takes patience to wait for fruit to ripen—even for the spiritual fruit God produces in our lives; it takes patience to carry more than our usual

The Egyptians (top) scrupulously shaved their faces and tied on ceremonial beards. In other Near Eastern cultures men grew long, free-flowing beards. God prescribed a definite style for Israelite men (Lev. 19:27).

burden; and it especially takes patience to bear with others who are immature or weak.

beard Facial hair on a man's chin and cheeks. Hebrew men were proud of their beards and tended them carefully (*see* 2 Sam. 19:24), but were not allowed to emulate pagan styles in cutting beard edges (Lev. 19:27; 21:5). Cutting off one's own beard was a symbol of great grief (Ezra 9:3; Isa. 15:2; Jer. 41:5; 48:37,38), while having one's beard cut off by another person meant shame and dishonor (2 Sam. 10:4,5; Isa. 50:6). Isaiah's prediction that God would use Assyria as a razor to cut off the hair and beards of his people makes it very clear that God intended the Assyrian invasion to bring disgrace on Israel for her many sins (Isa. 7:20). *See also* Bald; Barber.

beast Animal. Except where indicated by the context, "beast" (Heb., *behemah*; *hayyah*) does not imply a dangerous animal. (*See* 1 Cor. 15:32.) It can mean merely "cattle." Yet "beast" often does have a negative connotation, especially when human beings are portrayed as acting like "brute beasts" (Ps. 73:22; 2 Pet. 2:12; Jude 10). *See also* Animals.

In prophetic imagery, hostile powers are often seen as "beasts." We see this in Rev. 13, which describes two beasts. The first, from the sea (Rev. 13:1-10), combines the features of the world empires described in Daniel's vision (Dan. 7:3-7). Thus this beast is generally taken to represent political power. The second (Rev. 13:11-17) represents religious authority. Interpreters of the Bible have differed over whether these beasts represent historic political and religious institutions which are antagonistic to Christ or whether they describe particular individuals who will appear at history's end. *See also* Prophet; Revelation.

Hans Holbein the Younger's illustration of Dan. 7 depicts the "four beasts [that] came up out of the sea," which were interpreted by Daniel as "four kingdoms."

An Egyptian slave receives a beating, from a tomb drawing in Thebes. Mosaic Law permitted criminals to be given up to forty lashes (Deut. 25:3). The Jews gave "forty lashes minus one," to be sure they did not inadvertently break the Law (2 Cor. 11:24).

beat, beating Violent physical punishment. The Bible uses several words for physical abuse. A surprising number are directed against Jesus and his followers. Christ was slapped (*rapizō*) during his trial (Mt. 26:67). After he was condemned, he was beaten (*derō*) by the Roman soldiers (Lk. 22:63) and then flogged (*mastigoō*) with scourges (Jn. 19:1) in preparation for his crucifixion. This latter term describes especially severe punishment, and generally was linked to offenses that carried the death penalty. *See also* Scourge.

The apostle Paul underwent another kind of beating: *rabdizō*, being beaten with wooden rods (Acts 16:22; 2 Cor. 11:25). In one parable, Jesus spoke of the beatings (*derō*) God's people had meted out to the OT prophets (Mt. 21:35; Mk. 12:3). He also warned his disciples that they would receive even the most terrible of beatings (*mastigoō*) as they sought to follow him (Mt. 10:17; 23:34).

But the Book of Hebrews adds a special counterpoint to this theme. God is with us in every such experience. Even the beating that draws blood is the gift of a Father who cares, "because the Lord disciplines those he loves, and he punishes [*mastigoō*] everyone he accepts as a son" (Heb. 12:6). Our tragedies, like our joys, are evidence of the loving hand of God who shapes all things for our good. *See also* Discipline.

Beatitudes The sayings that introduce Jesus' Sermon on the Mount in Mt. 5:3-11, or the parallel passage containing four sayings in Lk. 6:20-22. The term *beatitude* is

THE BEATITUDES
(Matthew 5:3-10)

Jesus' Words	Kingdom Values	Human Values
Blessed are those who are: (v.3) poor in spirit	• self-abasement • humility • dependence on God • reliance on God's Word	• self-esteem • self-confidence • self-sufficiency • self-reliance
(v.4) mourn	• sensitivity to personal weaknesses • concern for others • contriteness • desire to forgive and be forgiven	• pleasure • personal comfort • entertainment • self-justification
(v.5) meek	• courtesy • obedience to God • willingness to serve • gentleness	• pride • power • self-importance • prestige
(v.6) hunger for righteousness	• desire to grow • moral purity • self-control • self-denial	• self-satisfaction • personal freedom • material success • moral relativity
(v.7) merciful	• compassion • generosity • forgiveness	• self-righteousness • personal rights • vengeance
(v.8) pure in heart	• moral sensitivity • separation from worldliness • integrity	• cosmopolitan attitude • sophistication • broad-mindedness
(v.9) peacemakers	• social concern • justice • reconciliation	• competition • defensiveness • assertiveness
(v.10) persecuted because of righteousness	• involvement in doing good • endurance • dedication • loyalty	• ability to compromise • popularity • "don't-rock-the-boat" • opportunism

Map: Location of the Mount of the Beatitudes in relation to cities that were scenes of Jesus' ministry. The most likely site is near Capernaum, but tourists are often taken to a location near Tiberias instead.

Photo: This low hill outside Capernaum is the most likely site where Jesus preached his "Sermon on the Mount."

taken from the Latin word for "blessed" or "fortunate"—the word that begins each of these sayings.

If we classified every "blessed are . . ." statement in the Bible as a "beatitude," we would find many. In the OT, the man whom God corrects (Job 5:17), all who do not walk in the counsel of the ungodly but delight in the Law of the Lord (Ps. 1:1,2), all who take refuge in God (Ps. 2:12), the person who has regard for the weak (Ps. 41:1)—all such are among those who are pronounced "blessed." Paul also uses the beatitude form in Rom. 14:22, as does James in his letter (Jas. 1:12) and John in the Book of Revelation (1:3; 14:13; 16:15; 19:9; 20:6; 22:7,14). Still, the words of Christ in Matthew and Luke are generally considered to be the Beatitudes.

While these sayings of Jesus have a traditional form, they radically challenged the tradition of his day. The OT takes the stance that blessings will come in this life to the person who keeps God's Law. This view is rooted in the Lord's commitment to his people, stated in the Mosaic covenant. Obedience will bring blessing and prosperity (Deut. 28:1-14); disobedience will bring punishment and national disaster (Deut. 28:15-68). Yet Jesus goes so far as to describe the poor as blessed and the rich as woeful, the hungry blessed and the well-fed as troubled!

Some commentators argue that Jesus is speaking eschatologically here. Jesus' forecast of blessing is associated with the coming of the "Kingdom of heaven." The blessedness of the godly life will not be experienced on earth, but awaits history's end. Thus they see Jesus redefining the OT's promise of divine reward in our immediate future, to teach that rewards will be delayed until the final triumph of righteousness.

But the Kingdom of God is not just future. Jesus spoke in the Sermon on the Mount and elsewhere about the moral and spiritual principles of his Kingdom, principles which would fill the lives of his followers on earth. While God's Kingdom will have a future expression at history's end, Jesus' Kingdom also existed when he spoke, and it exists now. Jesus is King, and wherever believers live out their allegiance to him, Christ's Kingdom has a present phase. So the Beatitudes describe a Kingdom life-style for believers here and now. *See also* Kingdom.

A second radical challenge appears in the Beatitudes' focus on basic attitudes and values. Old Testament Law looked at behavior, and promised rewards for conforming to God's revealed standards. But Jesus probes our innermost character, and announces that those who possess a godly outlook and values are blessed, for they are surely God's Kingdom people, both now and at history's end.

Third, these Beatitudes radically confront the basic attitudes and values which pervade human cultures. The poor, the meek, and the person who yearns for righteousness have little status in a society that values wealth, education, and personal achievement far more than a heart relationship to God and to his fellow man.

In stating his Beatitudes, Jesus sought to startle his listeners; his images of the wealthy poor, the happy mourner, and the persecuted peacemaker were intended to jolt his listeners into thinking about and questioning the traditional values and attitudes that shaped their lives. And the Beatitudes should have the same impact on us today. Men and women of every age need to examine themselves and to make sure that the things which are important to them are the things which are important to God. The Kingdom of God still exists, and his people are still called to renounce their allegiance to the values of this world in full commitment to the Kingdom of the Lord.

139

Clay model of a bed from Iraq, early 2nd millennium B.C.

Above: Woman reclining on bed shaped in dog's image. "Bed" in the OT often suggests a person's private, quiet, or intimate times or thoughts (see Ps. 4:4; 36:4; 63:6; Mic. 2:1).

beauty Pleasing appearance. Peter gives us insight into the beauty-enhancement practices of the women of his day when he shares this important piece of advice: "Your beauty should not come from outward adornment, such as braided hair and the wearing of gold jewelry and fine clothes. Instead, it should be that of your inner self, the unfading beauty of a gentle and quiet spirit, which is of great worth in God's sight" (1 Pet. 3:3,4).

A variety of complex ideas are associated with the concept of beauty in both OT and NT. In Hebrew, something beautiful is "good" or "pleasing" (*tob*). When applied to a woman, this word carries the idea of "desirable." Rebekah is described as "good of appearance" in Gen. 24:16; so also is Bathsheba in 2 Sam. 11:2. Sarah in Gen. 12:11 is said to be "lovely of appearance." In Gen. 29:17, Rachel is described as both "lovely of form" and "lovely of appearance." Abigail in 1 Sam. 25:3 is likewise "lovely of form," and even Joseph in Gen. 39:6 is, using the masculine form, "lovely or handsome of form."

In the Book of Esther, Queen Vashti appears as beautiful (*tob*) but insubordinate, so King Xerxes set up a beauty contest to select a replacement. He sent servants throughout the Persian Empire hunting for desirable young women, and eventually chose Esther, "lovely in form and features" (Esth. 2:7), as his new queen.

Proverbs warns against such an external view: "Charm is deceptive, and beauty is fleeting; but a woman who fears the Lord is to be praised" (Prov. 31:30). Many other proverbs remind us that there are more important traits to develop than physical desirability (Prov. 11:16,22; 12:4; 19:14; 27:15,16; 31:10-31).

The OT concept of beauty is not limited to evaluations of a person's looks. Scripture sees beauty in God's design of nature, and particularly in the splendid person of God, whose beauty is expressed in the Hebrew word *sebi*, often translated "adornment" or "glory."

The words *beauty* and *beautiful* do not occur often in the NT. The word *hōraios*, "beautiful," occurs four times (Mt. 23:27; Acts 3:2,10; Rom. 10:15). Yet one of the Greek words usually rendered "good" (*kalos*) has an aesthetic dimension, suggesting that the thing, person, or action it describes is both beautiful and pleasing. It is just this kind of thing and person that Paul has in mind when he writes, "Brothers, whatever is true, whatever is noble, whatever is right, whatever is pure, whatever is lovely, whatever is admirable—if anything is excellent or praiseworthy—think about such things" (Phil. 4:8). There is no more succinct definition of true beauty in the literature of any language or any time.

bed A place for sleeping or resting. The bed of the poor was a mat or simply a few folds of clothing spread out on the floor. Some homes had raised earthen benches or platforms built along a wall. During the day, the mat that served as a bed would be rolled up and put away (Jn. 5:5-8), and the platform could be used for sitting. Only the wealthy could afford a separate bed chamber or bedroom.

Some in biblical times had beds made of wooden frames and with nets of cords, on which clothing or mats could be spread (Lk. 5:18). Such a bed frame was recovered in archaeological excavations at Jericho and this type of bed may have been used by David (1 Sam. 19:15) about 1000 B.C.

The poor used only their outer garments as a covering at night. This is the reason for the biblical injunction, "If the man is poor, do not go to sleep with his pledge [something given the lender to guarantee a loan] in your possession. Return his cloak to him by sunset so that he may sleep in it" (Deut. 24:12,13).

It was different for those who were better off. The hard-working wife of Prov. 31 "makes coverings for her bed" (v. 22). And the wealthy might have prepared their beds as did the adulteress described in Prov. 7:16,17:

I have covered my bed
with colored linens from Egypt.
I have perfumed my bed
with myrrh, aloes and cinnamon.

The very wealthy lavished even more care on their beds, which also served as couches on which to recline when feasting. Esther 1:6 describes beds made of silver and gold used for feasting at the Persian palace. Amos speaks against the exploitative rich who "lie on beds inlaid with ivory" (Amos 6:4). Ivory inlays from the time of King Ahab, like the ones Amos mentions, have been recovered in excavations at Samaria. (*See* 1 Ki. 22:39.)

The uses of the bed mentioned in Scripture are nearly all familiar to us. It is the place of sleep or rest (2 Sam. 4:7; Ps. 132:3; Lk. 17:34); the place where the sick await recovery (Ex. 21:18; Ps. 41:3). It is the place where marital joys are shared (Heb. 13:4), but also the place where adultery can be committed (Gen. 49:4; Prov. 7:16-18). Isaiah describes the bed as a place where the apostate in Israel engaged in sex acts associated with pagan worship (Isa. 57:7-9; *compare* Ezek. 23:17). Yet another use, perhaps more familiar to us, may be seen in 1 Ki. 21:4, when Ahab retreated to his bed to sulk after Naboth refused to sell him a vineyard.

Beds had a role in death as well as life—on occasion beds served as funeral biers (2 Sam. 3:31; 2 Chr. 16:14).

Beelzebub [Bee-EL-zay-bub; "lord of flies"; in some manuscripts, Beelzebul, "lord of filth" or "lord of the house (of demons)." The form *Beel-zebub* may have been a scornful mockery of the pagan title, just as the Hebrews often substituted *Bosheth* "shame" for *Baal* "lord"]. Second Kings 1 mentions Baal-Zebub, and identifies him as the god of Ekron, one of the major Philistine cities about 850 B.C. In Jesus' time Beelzebub was regarded as the prince of demons (Mk. 3:22; Lk. 11:15—both of which spell the name Beelzebel in the earliest and best manuscripts).

All three synoptic Gospels report the desperate charge of Jesus' enemies that Christ drove out demons "by Beelzebub."

This was stimulated by the fact that "all the people" were wondering if Jesus could be "the Son of David," Israel's Messiah (Mt. 12:23). The Pharisees tried to counter Jesus' impact by claiming that his miracles were energized by Satan rather than by God, and implying that Jesus might himself be a demon. Jesus ridiculed this accusation. If Satan were in the business of fighting Satan, his kingdom would soon collapse (Mt. 12:26). The fact that Jesus confronted and drove out demons was evidence that our Lord was energized by the Spirit of God—and evidence that God's Kingdom had suddenly burst upon that moment of human history.

beer An alcoholic drink made from grain. The NIV translates the Hebrew *shekar* as "beer." Other versions tend to follow the KJV, which calls it "strong drink." The root verb, *shkr*, means "to be drunken." It seems to refer to any liquor made from grain or dates rather than from grapes. While distilling liquor was not known in biblical times, beverages with 7% to 10% alcoholic content were made from grains.

Although wine is associated with joyous celebration as well as excess, *shekar* is more closely linked with drunkenness. While this intoxicant may revive the dying (Prov. 31:6), Proverbs warns that "beer is a brawler" (20:1) and is not for rulers (31:4), who have a special need for self-control. *See also* Drunkenness; Wine.

Beer- [BEE-air]. In place names, the Hebrew word *beer* means "well." Thus Beersheba is "the well of Sheba" or "well of the oath." Wells were important sites in arid Palestine. Settlements would naturally spring up around them and sometimes take their names from them. When God appeared to the fleeing Hagar near a desert spring, she called the place Beer-Lahai-Roi, "the well of the Living One who sees me" (Gen. 16:14). A generation later, Isaac lived there (Gen. 25:11). *See also* Well.

Israelite beer jug has holes, visible at the base of the spout, to filter out husks of grain (normally barley) used in the brewing.

Wooden model of an Egyptian granary/ brewery, 2050 B.C., shows women grinding barley, kneading dough, and rolling it into loaves. After baking, the loaves were broken up and soaked with water to begin the beer-making process.

Silver tetradrachm (four-drachma) coin, 4th century B.C., with bee image. Bees symbolized enemy attack against Israel in Scripture.

bees Insects that swarm and sting, feeding on nectar and producing honey. Bees symbolize enemy attacks against Israel in three Scripture passages (Deut. 1:44; Ps. 118:12; Isa. 7:18). The only other biblical reference to bees links them with honey (Jdg. 14:8). There is no archaeological evidence of beekeeping in Palestine before about 300 B.C. However, the OT's many references to Canaan as a "land flowing with milk and honey" suggest that both products were cultivated from ancient times.

beetle A winged insect. The *haregol*, mentioned only in Lev. 11:22 among "clean" (edible) insects, is called a beetle by the KJV, but is more likely the cricket, as in the ASV, RSV, and NIV.

beget (KJV) An old-fashioned English term for fathering children, used often in the KJV. Modern versions tend to say Seth "became the father of" Enosh (Gen. 5:6, NIV), and so on. Note that these words for begetting *usually* indicate an immediate father/son relationship, but they sometimes describe ancestry, thus skipping a number of generations between the "father" and the "son." So when Matthew says Jehoram "begat" Uzziah (Mt. 1:8, KJV), he means he was his ancestor. We know from 2 Chr. 21–26 that Jehoram was actually Uzziah's great-great-grandfather. *See also* Genealogy; Only Begotten.

beggar One who asks for money or goods from others, and relies on this aid for subsistence. In Middle Eastern lands, begging has long been recognized as a profession. Yet the Bible has surprisingly few references to beggars.

Typically beggars were crippled by some obvious disease or disability. Bartimaeus was blind (Mk. 10:46-52; *compare* Mt. 20:29-34; Lk. 18:35-43), Lazarus covered with open ulcers (Lk. 16:19-21), and the beggar healed by Peter was lame from birth (Acts 3:1-10). Giving money to beggars was considered an important act of piety by the Jews of Jesus' time, in view of the OT's often-expressed concern for the poor and oppressed. But Christ and his disciples went to the root of the problem. They healed the beggars who appealed to them, combating the diseases which kept them from earning their own living. *See also* Almsgiving; Poor.

beginning Start, origin. Both Hebrew words for beginning (*re'sit, tehillah*) indicate the "first in a series," or initiation. These words help us understand something important about the biblical world view. The universe is ordered and orderly; all that exists can be traced back to beginnings, from which events have flowed in an orderly sequence governed by cause and effect. Thus, for the Hebrew, logic as well as revelation testified to the fact that "in the beginning God created the heavens and the earth" (Gen. 1:1). Before the material universe even existed, God was in being from beginningless eternity.

This sense of orderliness extends to the moral universe as well as the physical. Thus Scripture affirms, "The fear of the Lord is the beginning of wisdom" (Prov. 9:10). "Wisdom," as the ability and willingness to make right moral choices, is ultimately rooted in one's awe of God as a person who exists and who governs human affairs. Commitment to what is right flows naturally, and only, from one's sense of the reality of God.

The NT retains the OT outlook but adds a philosophical aspect. The "beginning" of any series of events has more than just moral or material importance. It provides a "basic principle" or the universal "first cause." Thus when the Bible says that Jesus acted "in the beginning," but before creation, Scripture clearly identifies Jesus as God and as the "first cause" of our existence (Jn. 1:1-5; Heb. 1:10; Col. 1:16).

behemoth [be-HE-muth]. A large beast. This creature appears only in Job 40:15-24. The description of its looks and habits has led most commentators to identify this animal as a gigantic species of hippopotamus. Another possibility is the water buffalo.

Egyptian hippopotamus, 18th century B.C., glazed ceramic with bird, reeds, and lotus-flower ornaments. Most scholars believe this is the mysterious biblical behemoth, whose "bones are tubes of bronze, his limbs like rods of iron" (Job 40:18).

Portion of one of the Dead Sea Scrolls, found in caves at Qumran, Israel, between 1947 and 1960. These scrolls are the oldest extant manuscripts of the OT.

Bezalel [BEZ-uh-lel; "in God's shadow (protection)"]. The craftsman gifted by the Holy Spirit to construct the tabernacle and its furnishings, about 1450 B.C.. **Scripture:** Ex. 31:1-11; 35:30–39:42.

The metallurgical, engraving, and jewel-cutting technology required for making the tabernacle existed in Egypt in the middle of the second millennium. While Bezalel may have been trained in such skills, the text emphasizes that his exceptional ability was a direct gift of the Holy Spirit.

The OT often speaks of the Holy Spirit "coming upon" persons to equip them for special tasks or callings. Yet Bezalel reminds us of two important things. (1) Whatever our natural talents, we need the Spirit's enablement to accomplish anything significant for the Lord. (2) God's gifts to his people are artistic as well as "spiritual." As Paul reminds us, "Whatever you do, whether in word or deed, do it all in the name of the Lord Jesus, giving thanks to God the Father through him" (Col. 3:17). *See also* Holy Spirit; Tabernacle.

Bible The sacred Scriptures of the Christian Church. The name "Bible" comes from the Greek *biblos*, "book," which derives from the papyrus reed (*byblos*) once used to make the paper on which documents were written. By the fifth century A.D., the collection of writings which had been known as "the books" (*biblia*) began to be called "the book," the Bible.

The Bible itself is the collection of Old and New Testament writings, which Christians recognize as authoritative in matters of faith and morals.

THE UNIQUENESS OF THE BIBLE

Other world religions have writings they hold sacred. These religious texts include the Veda and Upanishads of Hinduism, the Tripitaka of Buddhism, the Zend-Avesta of Zoroastrianism, and the Koran of Islam. Yet none of these writings compares with the Bible, and only the Koran, which was written by Mohammed, makes any claim of being direct divine revelation.

What makes the Christian Bible unique among the world's sacred texts? At least these eight characteristics:

• *Unity.* The Bible includes 66 books (more for Catholics and Orthodox believers), written over a span of some 1,500 years by at least 40 different authors. These authors include philosophers, kings, prophets, and shepherds; both highly educated and "unlearned" men. Yet the Bible is one book, which reveals one God and the gradual unfolding of his plan for humankind. The unity of the Bible, with the harmony of its books, testifies to its supernatural origin.

• *Authority.* The prophets as well as other writers of Scripture believed they were communicating the message of God. Over two thousand times OT writers affirm, "This is what the Lord says," or "The word of the Lord came to" the speaker. The Bible states that all Scripture

147

is given by God (or "God-breathed," 2 Tim. 3:16), and that "men spoke from God as they were carried along by the Holy Spirit" (2 Pet. 1:21). Thus the Bible claims for itself a unique authority, an authority which rests on the fact that the Judeo-Christian Scriptures are the very Word of God. *See also* Inspiration.

• *The Character of Revelation.* Empedocles, in the fifth century B.C., complained, "Weak and narrow are the powers implanted in the limbs of man. What they dream they know is but the little that each has stumbled upon in wandering about the world. Yet boast they all that they have learned the whole. Vain fools! For what that is, no eye hath seen, no ear hath heard, nor can it be conceived by the mind of man." Yet Scripture claims to express that "whole," for it reveals not only the meaning of life but the very thoughts, motives, intentions, and plans of God himself (1 Cor. 2:9-12). *See also* Reveal.

• *Historical Integrity.* Of all sacred writings, only the Bible is firmly rooted in history. God is not a mythical being, and stories about his acts are not merely symbolic tales. The Bible is a historical document, reporting events that actually happened in space and time. God's mighty acts and their meaning are tightly woven into the history of the people of Israel, and they culminate in the historic

Pottery jar with lid, in which were found several Dead Sea Scrolls. Also shown are two fragments from the scrolls, which date from between 200 B.C. and A.D. 70 and were found at seven separate sites.

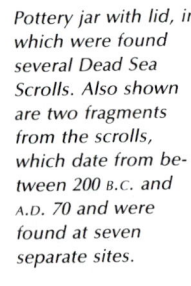

birth, crucifixion, burial and resurrection of Jesus Christ. Thus the Bible has a historical integrity which none of the sacred writings of the world's other religions share.

• *Verifiability.* The roots of Scripture in history make the Bible a uniquely verifiable book. First, archaeology can and has provided information which supports the trustworthiness of the Bible as a historical document. While no find can prove or disprove Scripture's religious statements, archaeology can speak to Scripture's historical reliability. And, again and again, the Bible has proven to be reliable as a historical document. *See also* Archaeology.

Of greater significance is prophecy. The fifth book of the Bible, Deuteronomy, gives this test to be used to verify any person's claim to speak for God: "If what a prophet proclaims in the name of the Lord does not take place or come true, that is a message the Lord has not spoken" (Deut. 18:22). Later God says through the prophet Isaiah, "I make known the end from the beginning, from ancient times, what is still to come" (Isa. 46:10). And Scripture holds many prophecies which can be adequately explained only by acknowledging its claim to be revelation from God. *See also* Prophet.

• *Testamentary Structure.* The Bible is unique among sacred writings for its testamentary structure. The word translated "testament" (Heb., *b'erit*; Gk., *diathēkē*) means "covenant," a formal contract which defines a relationship. Both Old and New Testaments extend God's invitation to human beings to enter a covenant relationship with him. Each Testament defines and explains the nature of that relationship; the OT explains history itself in terms of God's faithfulness to his covenant commitment to Israel—both to bless and to punish. Thus Scripture focuses on a unique relationship between God and human beings. And this focus, which gives Scripture its testamentary structure, also sets the Bible apart. *See also* Covenant.

• *Salvation Emphasis.* Most of the world's religions, and many secular philosophers, can be credited with a high moral vision. Even Confucius stated a form of Christianity's "golden rule." Yet Scripture alone portrays human beings as lost in sin, with an unbridgeable gap between moral obligation and moral ability. Where other religions insist that human beings work toward moral or spiritual achievements, the Bible calls on us to abandon our own efforts and, through

וְהַמֶּלֶךְ דָּוִד זָקֵן בָּא בַּיָּמִים וַיְכַסֻּהוּ
בַּבְּגָדִים וְלֹא יִחַם לוֹ וַיֹּאמְרוּ לוֹ עֲבָדָיו
יְבַקְשׁוּ לַאדֹנִי הַמֶּלֶךְ נַעֲרָה בְתוּלָה
וְעָמְדָה לִפְנֵי הַמֶּלֶךְ וּתְהִי לוֹ סֹכֶנֶת וְשָׁכְבָה
בְחֵיקֶךָ וְחַם לַאדֹנִי הַמֶּלֶךְ וַיְבַקְשׁוּ נַעֲרָה
יָפָה בְּכֹל גְּבוּל יִשְׂרָאֵל וַיִּמְצְאוּ אֶת
אֲבִישַׁג הַשּׁוּנַמִּית וַיָּבִאוּ אֹתָהּ לַמֶּלֶךְ
וְהַנַּעֲרָה יָפָה עַד מְאֹד וַתְּהִי לַמֶּלֶךְ סֹכֶנֶת
וַתְּשָׁרְתֵהוּ וְהַמֶּלֶךְ לֹא יְדָעָהּ וַאֲדֹנִיָּה
בֶן חַגִּית מִתְנַשֵּׂא לֵאמֹר אֲנִי אֶמְלֹךְ וַיַּעַשׂ
לוֹ רֶכֶב וּפָרָשִׁים וַחֲמִשִּׁים אִישׁ רָצִים
לְפָנָיו וְלֹא עֲצָבוֹ אָבִיו מִיָּמָיו לֵאמֹר מַדּוּעַ
כָּכָה עָשִׂיתָ וְגַם הוּא טוֹב תֹּאַר מְאֹד וְאֹתוֹ
יָלְדָה אַחֲרֵי אַבְשָׁלוֹם וַיִּהְיוּ דְבָרָיו עִם
יוֹאָב בֶּן צְרוּיָה וְעִם אֶבְיָתָר הַכֹּהֵן וַיַּעְזְרוּ
אַחֲרֵי אֲדֹנִיָּה וְצָדוֹק הַכֹּהֵן וּבְנָיָהוּ בֶן
יְהוֹיָדָע וְנָתָן הַנָּבִיא וְשִׁמְעִי וְרֵעִי
וְהַגִּבּוֹרִים אֲשֶׁר לְדָוִד לֹא הָיוּ עִם אֲדֹנִיָּהוּ
וַיִּזְבַּח אֲדֹנִיָּהוּ צֹאן וּבָקָר וּמְרִיא עִם

King David on throne with royal scepter, from 15th-century Kennicott Bible (in Hebrew). The Masoretes (a Jewish scribal school) added vowel markings (called "points") to the consonants of the Hebrew text around A.D. 1100.

faith in God, to rely wholly on his enablement. The Bible's concept of salvation, not simply blessedness after death but divine enablement of those who are spiritually helpless now, also sets the Scripture apart.

• *Philosophical Completeness.* The Bible alone answers all the basic questions that trouble humankind. Where did we come from? What gives life meaning? Why is there evil in the world? What is right, and what is wrong? How can I live a truly good life? What does the future hold, for the universe and for me as an individual? Who is God, and how can I know him? These and other questions are answered in a satisfactory and complete way only in the Word of God.

A BRIEF HISTORY

A firm tradition holds that the first books of the OT date back to Moses, perhaps 1,400 years before Christ. Other books were written in the course of time, with the OT's last book, Malachi, completed about 400 B.C. *See also* Biblical Criticism; Chronology of the Bible. The bulk of the OT was written in Hebrew, with smaller portions from the Persian period (in Daniel and Ezra) written in Aramaic. Ancient Hebrew was written only in consonants, and vowel signs were not added until the sixth century A.D. These authoritative writings were divided into three categories: (1) The Law (*Torah*), composed of the five books of Moses—Genesis, Exodus, Leviticus, Numbers, and Deuteronomy. (2) The Prophets (*Nebi'im*)— including both historical and prophetic books, and (3) The Writings (*Ketubim*)—Psalms, Proverbs, Job, Song of Solomon, Ruth, Lamentations, Ecclesiastes, and Esther, plus the Books of Daniel, Ezra-Nehemiah, and Chronicles.

Probably around 200 B.C. a translation of the Hebrew Scriptures into Greek was completed for those many Jews scattered throughout the world who no longer understood Hebrew. This translation, known as the Septuagint and often abbreviated as LXX, also served the early church. *See also* Septuagint.

In this version additional books appeared in the "Writings" section comprising much of what later became known as the Apocrypha. *See also* Apocrypha.

The NT was written in *koinē*, the common Greek spoken by ordinary people in the first century. Unlike the OT, which was written over many centuries, the NT was completed in the decades between Christ's resurrection and about the end of the first century. *See also* Chronology of the Bible.

These writings, by Jesus' apostles, Paul, and their close colleagues, were widely circulated in the churches. The present 27 books were generally accepted as Scripture within the next hundred years, although the authority of James, Jude, 2 and 3 John, and 2 Peter were disputed by some. Official acceptance of all 27 books came at church councils at Hippo and Carthage before A.D. 400. The NT also has its divisions. They are: (1) Gospels—of Matthew, Mark, Luke, and John. (2) History—Acts. (3) Epistles—of Paul and others. (4) Apocalypse—Revelation.

TRANSMISSION OF THE TEXT

Until the invention of movable type printing in A.D. 1455, all copies of the Bible had to be made by hand. Thus one would expect a good number of copying errors corrupting the original text of Scripture. Yet the Jewish people had an extremely high view of their Bible and took great care to copy the Bible accurately.

Our master text of the Hebrew OT is called the Masoretic text, and was standardized about A.D. 1100. The Dead Sea Scrolls, discovered in 1947, gave access for the first time to biblical texts dating from two or even three centuries B.C. And these scroll texts agree substantially with the Masoretic texts of a millennium later.

Additional evidence of the accurate transmission of the OT comes from the Septuagint. While the Septuagint is not considered a completely trustworthy rendering of the Hebrew, it still permits us to compare the Greek with our Hebrew versions. The same can be said of the Targums, which are Aramaic paraphrases of Scripture, and the Talmud, which records the comments of rabbis on the written text. The last line of evidence is the totally accurate preservation of the Masoretic text from A.D. 1100.

Great care was taken by the copyist to ensure accuracy. A scribe would count the words and letters in the original and in his copy. He would find the middle word and the middle letter in each to make sure they were the same. With such respect for the OT it is not surprising that its Hebrew text has been so very well preserved.

Transmission of the NT text presents different problems, for there are many different copies of ancient manuscripts available. Some of these have clearly been edited. These manuscripts have been studied, along with versions of the NT in Old Latin, Old Syriac, and Coptic (an Egyptian language), and scholars have attempted from the mass of evidence to recapture the original Greek text. This work has been so successful that one Greek scholar affirms that serious doubts about the original exist only for material which would cover a brief half page of a Greek New Testament —and even these textual questions do not affect a single NT passage that teaches a significant doctrine!

It is true that we do not have the *autographa* (the first written texts) of the Old or New Testaments. But there is sufficient evidence that our English versions are translations of accurate Hebrew and Greek texts, which do represent the originals.

OUR USE OF THE BIBLE

The Christian Scriptures are unique among the world's sacred writings. We can have confidence that the Bible truly is the Word of God, and that the Bible we read is essentially identical with the original writings themselves. Yet it is not enough to have a high view of Scripture. The Bible was given to us by God for a purpose. God wants us to *use* the Bible, so that we might come to know him and to rightly order our lives.

Perhaps the words of Jesus express these themes best. Christ corrected one group of questioners by saying, "You are in error because you do not know the Scriptures or the power of God" (Mt. 22:29). To others he said, "You diligently study the Scriptures because you think that by them you possess eternal life. These are the Scriptures that testify about me" (Jn. 5:39). We do not want to fall into error for lack of knowing the Word of God, yet we do not want to miss its central message—that Jesus Christ is the giver of eternal life.

After we have come to know Jesus, the Scriptures must play an increasingly important role in our lives. Again we hear Jesus' words: "Everyone who hears these words of mine and puts them into practice is like a wise man who built his house on the rock" (Mt. 7:24). As the people of God, we must build our lives on the solid foundation of hearing, and putting into practice, the Word of our God.

Bible versions Today many versions of the Bible are available in English. Most are careful attempts to express the meaning of the original Greek and Hebrew texts for contemporary readers. In one sense, we do not need so many versions: the differences among them are relatively minor. Yet in another sense the versions are important, helping us see familiar truths in

Codex Sinaiticus, one of the most significant Greek manuscripts used by scholars to determine the original text of the NT, was found on Mount Sinai in 1844. It has the entire Bible in Greek, and dates to the 4th century A.D.

fresh ways or clarifying ideas that may be difficult to understand.

Bible versions can be classified in various ways. The most helpful classifications are by origin, method, focus, and bias.

ORIGIN OF BIBLE VERSIONS

Some English versions are original translations. That is, scholars have gone back to the Greek and Hebrew texts in fresh attempts to express their meaning in contemporary English. The King James Bible (KJV) was such a version when it was produced in 1611 by a panel of scholars drawn from Oxford and Cambridge Universities. The New English Bible (NEB) of 1970 and the New International Version (NIV) of 1978 are modern examples of fresh translations from the best Hebrew and Greek texts now available.

The New American Bible, produced by the Catholic Biblical Association of America, is another good example; it is the first Catholic Bible in English translated from the original Hebrew and Greek. Other Catholic versions are revisions of existing translations, generally using more recent Greek and Hebrew texts than the original translations. The Catholic Confraternity Version of 1948, like the Douay Bible before it, was produced by translating from the earlier Latin Vulgate.

The American Standard Version (ASV) of 1901 was a helpful revision of the King James, and the Revised Standard Version

CONCISE OVERVIEW OF ENGLISH BIBLE VERSIONS

Version	Date	Translator(s)	Description
King James Version (KJV) (also known as the Authorized Version)	1611	50 scholars appointed by King James I	A translation based on Hebrew and Greek texts and on earlier English.
American Standard Version (ASV)	1901	American scholars	American version of the English Revised Version of 1885, which was a revision of the King James Version.
Revised Standard Version (RSV)	1952	Ecumenical committee of scholars for the National Council of Churches of Christ in the U.S.A.	Revision of the American Standard Version of 1901, using more recent Hebrew and Greek texts.
New Testament in Modern English	1958	J.B. Phillips	Paraphrase in contemporary language.
Amplified Bible	1965	Sponsored by the Lockman Foundation of California	Draws on all known texts and is intended to supplement other translations.
Jerusalem Bible (JB)	1966	Roman Catholic scholars	Translated from ancient texts following the interpretations of L'Ecole Biblique in its *Bible de Jerusalem*. Particularly noted for its literary quality.
The Modern Language Bible (Berkeley Version)	1969	Gerrit Verkuyl	Based on ancient texts and the King James Version.
New English Bible (NEB)	1970	Ecumenical committee of 50 scholars, sponsored by British denominations and the Bible Societies of Great Britain	A contemporary English version, using the most widely accepted Greek, Hebrew and Aramaic texts. Literary quality, as well as accuracy, was a major consideration.
New American Bible (NAB)	1970	Catholic Biblical Association of America	Sponsored by Confraternity of Christian Doctrine, this translation was prepared from oldest available texts and was first official Catholic Bible to depart from Latin Vulgate text.
New American Standard Bible (NASB)	1971	Sponsored by the Lockman Foundation of California	Revision of the American Standard Version of 1901.
Living Bible (LB)	1971	Kenneth N. Taylor	Paraphrase into contemporary American English.
Today's English Version (TEV) (Good News for Modern Man)	1976	American Bible Society	The Bible in very simple English, especially useful for those unfamiliar with the Bible and for those who speak English as a second language.
New International Version (NIV)	1978	Sponsored by the New York International Bible Society	Prepared by a "transdenominational" and international group of evangelical scholars, whose goals were accuracy, clarity, contemporary idiom, and dignity.
New King James Version (NKJV)	1982	A team of conservative scholars	A new translation based on the *textus receptus* of the NT and the *Biblia Hebraica* of the OT, but following the thought flow and cadence of the KJV.

(RSV) of 1952 was a revision of the ASV. The New King James Version (NKJV) of 1982 also follows the traditional text for its main body.

METHOD

What is the best way to translate from one language to another? Some early Bible versions were woodenly literal, simply replacing the words in the source with equivalent English terms. But, increasingly, translators recognized the need to express the meaning of the original in the language of their own time. Thus translators began using idiomatic English and seeking English synonyms that would express the range of meanings of words in the source.

Today we can find versions which take a more literal approach to translation (like the KJV, NASB, or ASV), those which seek a "dynamic equivalence" in modern English of the original (like NEB and NIV), and even paraphrases which actually interpret the original text for the reader (like the Living Bible, also known as *The Book*, and the Phillips Version of the NT). While paraphrases can provide fresh insights into Scripture, the reader should know their limits. The interpretive aspect of paraphrases makes them less reliable than versions which seek simply to express the meaning of the original in equivalent contemporary English.

FOCUS

While each of our versions has been produced with the intention of helping English readers better understand the Word of God, occasionally a certain translation has a unique focus. The Amplified Bible of 1965 uses parentheses and brackets to add several alternative readings that supposedly "amplify" the meaning of the text. *Today's English Version* (Good News for Modern Man) of 1976 is an attempt to simplify the Bible by replacing its more difficult terms.

One very helpful special-focus version is the *International Children's Bible* (ICB) of 1986, which is a fresh translation from the original into the idiom and vocabulary of children aged eight to thirteen.

BIAS

A final element to consider in evaluating English versions is the theological bias of the translators or revisers. In most cases the bias does not seriously impair the accuracy of the version. While the RSV was at first criticized for the "liberal" bias of the revisers, it is generally recognized as an outstanding English version. Typically a theological bias is more likely in a paraphrase. At times bias makes a version untrustworthy, as is the case with the *New World Translation* (1950) produced by the Jehovah's Witnesses. Sometimes bias is seen, not in the translation but in notes appended to the text.

CHOOSING A BIBLE VERSION

With so many versions available in English, which should you choose? As you try to answer this question for yourself, remember the distinction between translations and paraphrases and consider your own particular needs. For a basic Bible, select a translation that is reliable and comfortable for you to read. For study, you may wish your Bible to contain study helps such as cross references, maps, introductions, and concordance. It can also be helpful to have a second translation for comparative readings. Modern paraphrases are excellent for meditation and devotional readings, but are not recommended for study.

Biblical criticism Specialized study of the original biblical text or the historical context of biblical documents.

Textual criticism, called "lower criticism" because it is concerned only with the text, seeks to establish the accurate wording of the original writings. Other forms of criticism, called "higher criticism," examine the date, setting, authorship, original meaning, and other elements related to the composition of Bible books.

LOWER CRITICISM

Study of the text has greatly advanced our understanding of the Bible. In transmitting any text over the course of centuries, errors in copying or editorial changes are apt to creep in. Textual criticism studies existing sources in an attempt to establish the Bible's original text. A standard set of rules help the scholar to define and deal constructively with scribal errors, most of which are easily corrected when the factors leading to copyists' mistakes have been carefully analyzed.

In the case of the OT, the later Hebrew text has been compared with the early Greek translation made in the second century B.C. (the Septuagint), and with fragments of early biblical documents recovered among the Dead Sea Scrolls. Also, archaeologists have uncovered thousands of documents in languages closely related to Hebrew which help us understand obscure or isolated words in the biblical text. *See also* Dead Sea Scrolls; Septuagint.

Many different families of texts exist for the NT. These "families" are groups of manuscripts which were copied from the same source and thus reflect slightly different readings from those of other "families" of manuscripts. These groups are often named for the parts of the world where they are found (Alexandrian, Western, and Byzantine). Hundreds of Greek manuscripts of the NT from the first few centuries A.D. exist today. We also have many translations of the NT into Armenian, Syriac, Coptic, and other languages. By working with these sources, scholars have come to general agreement on the original text of most of the NT.

Textual criticism has enabled modern English versions to be based on Hebrew and Greek texts which are essentially the same as the original. Thus the work of textual critics has added both to our understanding of the Bible, and to our confidence that our versions express God's Word accurately.

HIGHER CRITICISM

A number of critical approaches have been used in an attempt to discern when and how the biblical documents were written. However, scholars disagree about the value of higher criticism in our interpretation of the Bible.

• *Form criticism* examines a book for ways of expression and linguistic structures which may identify divergent sources for specific elements.

• *Historical criticism* seeks to use historical, philological, and particularly archaeological analysis to establish the historical setting of a book. As practiced by rationalist scholars it tends to assume the account in the received text is not to be trusted as accurate unless corroborative evidence comes from archaeological sources or ancient pagan records.

• *Literary criticism* analyzes the structure, literary forms, style, vocabulary, point of view, repetition of words, and logic of a book. Any change in style or choice of words is evidence of a difference in authorship or time of composition.

• *Redaction criticism* attempts to determine the supposed process of initial writing, editing, and final composition of a Bible book or passage, in light of probable reworking of the earlier tradition to conform to later trends in the life of the believing community.

• *Source criticism* is an aspect of literary criticism, and tries to identify individual sources used in constructing a particular book or unit. Anything that savors of the supernatural or miraculous is thought to have been injected by the superstition of later generations.

Why the disagreement over the methods and results of higher criticism? One critical approach, called "source criticism," is rooted in the fact that some biblical books were composed using earlier sources. Genesis, for instance, surely relies on oral or written sources in telling the stories of Abraham and Isaac and Jacob which were not written down in their final form until a thousand or 1,500 years after the events which they record.

In some cases, the original sources actually exist. The writer(s) of 1 and 2 Chronicles occasionally refer to the previously written books of Samuel and the Kings. In the case of the NT, many scholars believe that Mark was an existing source used by Matthew and Luke. By comparing the later books with these earlier sources, scholars try to determine just how the writers of later biblical books used such sources in their own compositions.

However, much biblical source criticism assumes sources which no longer exist. The source critics speculate on what these assumed sources were. This approach is not only speculative, but its conclusions can never be verified, since we do not have the supposed source. Yet, some scholars have suggested major revisions in the framework of biblical history based on highly subjective speculation.

We find another reason for disagreement over the role and results of higher criticism when we compare assumptions about dating. Two types of evidence can be used in dating any document: internal and external. Internal evidence includes specific statements about authorship and events within the document itself, such as "these are the words of Amos, one of the shepherds of Tekoa—what he saw concerning Israel two years before the earthquake, when Uzziah was king of Judah and Jeroboam son of Jehoash was king of Israel" (Amos 1:1). There are other kinds of internal evidence as well. The Book of Job uses terms and language that suggest it may be one of the earliest of the OT books, and names found in Job are common in written documents of the early second millennium B.C.

External evidence also helps fix the date of a particular book. Archaeology has helped to establish the framework of culture and chronology for the world of the Bible. References have been found in secular sources to events described in the Bible, and often technical terms, details, and reflections of foreign customs have shown how accurately the Bible reflects the eras it purports to describe.

But the weight given to internal and external evidence often depends on the basic presuppositions of the critic himself. Much in Scripture is predictive in nature, and describes events which had not yet happened in the writer's time. Thus the Book of Daniel describes in detail international events which took place hundreds of years after the man Daniel died. Scholars who question whether prophecy could spell out in detail what would transpire centuries later will naturally date the Book of Daniel no earlier than the second century B.C. Yet those who believe biblical prophecy can be precise and accurate in its predictions usually accept the traditional date and authorship, which are supported by considerable internal evidence. *See also* Daniel.

While conservative scholars see some measure of value in some of the tools used in higher criticism, they consider these tools inadequate to reconstruct history with any kind of accuracy since they are manipulated by antisupernatural bias. Those who view Scripture as the miraculously revealed and preserved Word of God give full credence to the Bible's own testimony about itself.

bier A bed-like framework on which a corpse, sometimes in a coffin, was dis-

played and then carried to the place of burial (2 Sam. 3:31; Lk. 7:14, KJV).

bind To tie up or tie together. Thus this English word has both negative aspects—imprisonment or other restriction—and positive senses—healing or uniting in marriage. The meaning is understood from the context: "to bind up the brokenhearted" clearly expresses healing (Isa. 61:1) by the use of bandages, while "those who are bound" suggests the bonds of captivity or imprisonment (*see* Jdg. 15). The same range of meaning is found in the NT Greek term *deō*. However, *deō* is used in two contexts which have raised questions.

THE MARRIAGE BOND
(Rom. 7:1-6; 1 Cor. 7:15,39.) When is a once-married person free to remarry? These two passages indicate that the bond is broken on the death of one partner, or when one party (in this context, an unbeliever) refuses to live as a spouse with the other. *See also* Divorce; Marriage.

BINDING AND LOOSING
(Mt. 16:19; 18:18.) These passages report Jesus' words, first to Peter and then to all the disciples: "Whatever you bind on earth will be bound in heaven, and whatever you loose on earth will be loosed in heaven." The early church fathers saw in these words a reflection of a recognized rabbinic authority to expel persons from a congregation and to receive them back again. This view, which links the power of binding and loosing with church discipline, fits the context of Mt. 18:15-18. *See also* Discipline.

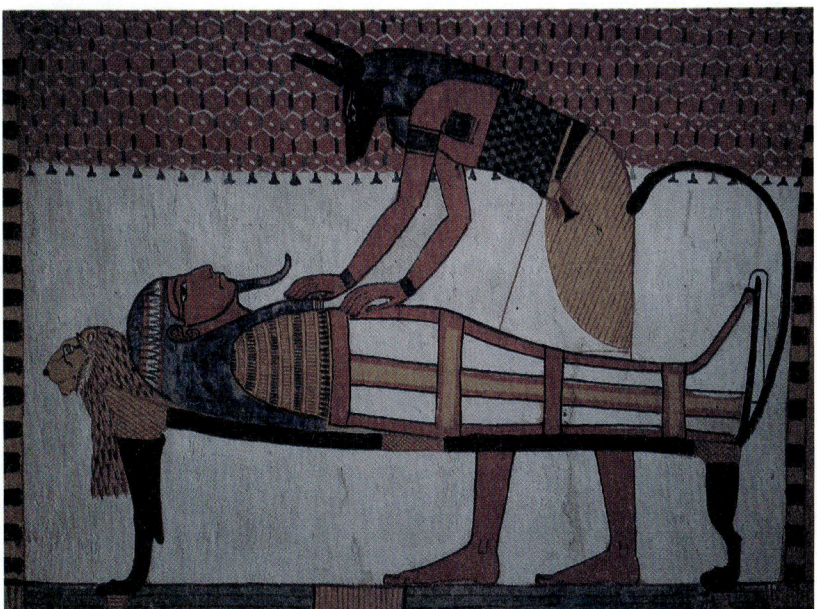

Bier portrayed on ceiling of tomb at Thebes, Egypt. Remains of Hebrews were buried the day of death, and not formally displayed.

155

birds Feathered or furred vertebrates which are able to fly. Nearly 400 different kinds of birds are found in Palestine. The Bible refers to 50 different kinds of birds, mentioning them in 45 of its 66 books. The Hebrews classified many of the birds of prey as "screamers," while sparrow-like birds were "twitterers." But more importantly, the Law classified birds as clean or unclean. *See also* Clean and Unclean.

Clean birds, which could be used for food, include the pigeon, partridge, and quail. Pigeons and turtledoves might also be offered to God in sacrifice by the poor.

A number of unclean flying creatures, which could not be used for food or in worship, are named specifically in Lev. 11:13-19 and Deut. 14:11-20. These are the eagle, vulture, kite, falcon, raven, owl, gull, hawk, cormorant, osprey, stork, heron, hoopoe, and bat.

Jesus reminded his hearers that a God who is concerned with each sparrow, and who has provided food for all the birds of the air, will surely watch over human beings (Mt. 6:25-27; Lk. 12:6). But Jesus also spoke of vultures gathering in the dread day of divine judgment (Mt. 24:28). Perhaps Christ's most touching reference is found in Mt. 8:20, in a saying that echoes the OT's imagery of a bird's nest as a place of security (Ps. 104:17; Prov. 27:8; Isa. 16:2). While "foxes have holes and

birds of the air have nests," Jesus himself had "no place to lay his head."

birthright Special inheritance rights given a firstborn son. Many documents recovered from the ancient Near East attest to the practice of granting birthrights. The firstborn received a double portion of the estate, and the family line was to be continued through him. While the OT specifically forbids setting aside the rights of a firstborn in favor of a younger son born to a better-loved second wife (Deut. 21:15-17), ancient tablets found in Nuzi record a transaction similar to the one between Jacob and Esau (Gen. 25:27-34)—the firstborn son selling his birthright to a younger brother. *See also* Firstborn.

By selling his birthright for a bowl of stew, Esau overtly expressed his contempt for God, for that birthright included the covenant promise which God made to Abraham, to be passed on to and through his family line. Esau's act showed how little he valued God or his promises. *See also* Covenant.

bishop (KJV, RSV) Overseer or guardian, an official church leader. The Greek word, *episcopos*, suggests close involvement and constant observation as well as authority. *Episcopos* appears five times in the NT (Acts 20:28; Phil. 1:1; 1 Tim. 3:2; Tit. 1:7;

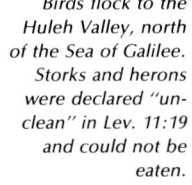

and in 1 Pet. 2:25 of Jesus). Paul spells out the bishop's qualifications in 1 Tim. 3:1-7 and Tit. 1:5-9.

Most think that "bishop" and "elder" were interchangeable titles of leaders of the early church. This view was held by a number of early church fathers, such as Irenaeus and John Chrysostom. However, as early as A.D. 117, Ignatius, a bishop in Antioch, set forth a hierarchical view which made the bishop the chief authority and representative of God in his area. *See also* Authority; Elder; Leader.

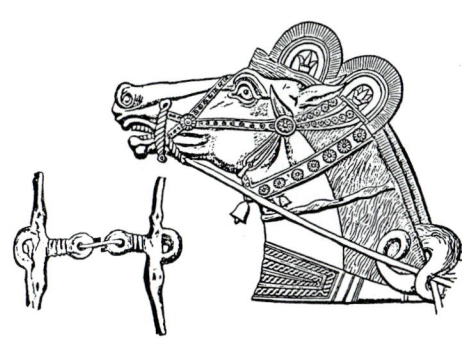

bit A horse's mouthpiece, attached to the bridle. The bit and bridle enable a rider to guide a resisting animal. The same Hebrew and Greek words can be translated either "bit" or "bridle"; each symbolically expresses response to God.

Promising to instruct and guide believers, God says, "Do not be like the horse or the mule, which have no understanding but must be controlled by bit and bridle or they will not come to you" (Ps. 32:9). The NT uses the image when urging believers to bridle themselves; that is, to exercise self-control (Jas. 1:26; 3:2,3).

What if a human being chooses not to respond to God? Isaiah 37:29 pictures God putting a bit in the mouth of the Assyrian conqueror Sennacherib and compelling him to lead his army home. *See also* Bridle.

bitter herbs Vegetables with an acrid taste, used in the Passover meal. The Bible prescribes that "bitter herbs" be eaten with the flesh of the Passover lamb (Ex. 12:8). These would represent the bitterness of Israel's slavery in Egypt before the Exodus. The original "bitter herbs" were probably a kind of lettuce or endive. In the modern Jewish celebration of Passover, the bitter herbs are represented by horseradish. *See also* Passover.

bitter, bitterness Unpleasantness, a resentful attitude. In the OT, tragedy and suffering cause "bitterness." In the NT, "bitterness" does not refer to pain as much as to the resentful and angry attitude that suffering may produce. Thus Heb. 12 warns us: Painful experiences must be seen and accepted as God's loving discipline (vv.5,6), lest a person "misses the grace of God" and a "bitter root grows up to cause trouble" (v.15). The key to avoiding bitterness is to remember that God is a loving Person, who not only deals with us in grace but who graciously provides us with the strength to endure our hardships and grow from them. *See also* Suffer.

bitumen Probably asphalt, which was available in Mesopotamia and Palestine. This material has three different Hebrew names, which have been variously translated as slime, pitch, and tar, as well as bitumen.

Bitumen was used to caulk Noah's ark (Gen. 6:14) and Moses' bulrush basket (Ex. 2:3). Rafts and rush boats used in ancient times along the Euphrates River were caulked with bitumen. Bitumen was also used as mortar to bind the burnt brick that covered the great Ziggurat found at Ur. Genesis reflects this use when describing construction of the tower of Babel (Gen. 11:3).

blameless The Hebrew *naqi* is equivalent to innocent of an offense, or pure, godly,

Detail of bronze bit from Nimrud, and side view of bit in horse's mouth. The bit symbolizes control in the Bible.

leading a life which pleases God. In neither Testament does "blameless" imply sinlessness. The blameless OT saint was eager to please God, and chose to live by God's known will (Job 1:1). The NT teaches a positional, judicial blamelessness: believers are forgiven because Christ died to pay for our sins (Eph. 1:4; Col. 1:22). Yet the forgiven saint is called to live in wholehearted purity. In 2 Peter believers are urged to live "holy and godly lives" and to "make every effort to be found spotless, blameless and at peace" with God (2 Pet. 3:11,14).

Stephen, unjustly accused of blasphemy, is stoned in this scene from a woodcut by Gustav Doré. The death sentence in Israel was carried out by stoning (Lev. 24:16).

158

blasphemy Slanderous or abusive speech, directed toward God or a fellow human being. Blasphemy against God, as treated in the OT, can involve cursing or reviling God or treating him with contempt.

In Deuteronomy Moses expresses the appropriate attitude of a human being toward God, calling on Israel to "acknowledge and take to heart this day that the Lord is God in heaven above and on the earth below" (Deut. 4:39). This attitude leads to thanksgiving and to obedience. The opposite of this attitude is expressed in the third commandment: "You shall not misuse the name of the Lord your God" (Ex. 20:7). Misuse here means to treat God's name with contempt by speaking lightly of him or by acting as if he were irrelevant to daily life. Essentially, then, "blasphemy" is contempt for God expressed in word or deed, especially by cursing, denying, or spurning him.

In Israel the penalty for blasphemy of God was death by stoning (Lev. 24:10-23; Acts 6:11; 7:58). While generally blasphemy was a sin committed by pagans, Paul notes that all too often Jewish hypocrisy stimulated pagan contempt for Israel's God (Rom. 2:24).

JESUS CHARGED WITH BLASPHEMY
Jesus was accused of blasphemy for "making himself equal with God" (Jn. 5:18). To those Jews who did not accept Christ's claim of deity, Jesus' teaching about himself seemed tantamount to bringing God down to mere human level. This would have been blasphemy—except that Jesus truly was God the Son.

BLASPHEMY AGAINST THE SPIRIT
Many have been disturbed by Jesus' mention of this "unforgivable" sin: "All the sins and blasphemies of men will be forgiven them. But whoever blasphemes against the Holy Spirit will never be forgiven; he is guilty of an eternal sin" (Mt. 12:30-32; Mk. 3:28,29; Lk. 12:10).

The context of Jesus' remarks helps us understand. Christ had performed notable and obvious miracles in the power of the Holy Spirit. But his desperate opponents rejected the evidence and claimed that the miracles were actually energized by Satan. This amazing charge showed how completely hardened to God they were. So Christ's statement may be taken to mean (1) that those who consciously reject the work of the Spirit of God cannot find forgiveness or, more likely, (2) that those specific individuals of Jesus' time who preferred to credit Satan with the work of the Spirit rather than acknowledge Jesus had hardened themselves beyond the possibility of repentance.

In either case, the very concern of anyone who worries that he or she might have committed an unforgivable sin is proof that he or she has not. A person truly contemptuous of God and his Spirit would not be concerned in the slightest about his or her relationship with God.

blemish Defect, flaw. In OT times, both animal sacrifices and the priests who offered them were to be without blemish. The two Hebrew words that express this concept (*mum*, and the negative of *tamin*, "perfection") have been variously translated as flaw, defect, fault, or disfigurement. The disqualifying blemishes are defined in Lev. 21:17-23; 22:18-25; and Deut. 15:21.

This provision of the Law (1) was intended to emphasize the honor due to God, who must be offered our very best (Mal. 1:6-8). Yet (2) it also has prophetic intent, for the OT sacrifices prefigured Jesus Christ, the perfect Son of God, "a lamb without blemish or defect" (1 Pet. 1:19).

Paul compares a husband's love for his wife to that of Christ, who gave himself up to help his Church reach her full potential "as a radiant church, without stain or wrinkle or any other blemish, but holy and blameless" (Eph. 5:27).

bless, blessed, blessing The speaking or doing of good things for another. The OT affirms that God is the source of the favor and well-being bestowed upon man it calls "blessing" (*berakah*). The concept is important: the Hebrew root translated blessing (*barak*) occurs 415 times in the OT.

Blessing is often contrasted with cursing, and both of these relate to obedience. God, who supervises human affairs, gave his Law partly to reveal how human beings might live happy and productive lives, and avoid misery and pain. Thus, after restating the Law in Deuteronomy, Moses tells Israel, "I am setting before you today a blessing and a curse—the blessing if you obey the commands of the Lord your God that I am giving you today; the curse if you disobey" (Deut. 11:26-28). Our personal well-being is directly connected with our walk with God.

Many OT statements link blessing in this life to personal relationship with God. In a series of "blessed are" statements, the psalmists pronounce those blessed who keep God's statutes (Ps. 119:1,2), and who through his discipline have made a commitment to do justice (Ps. 94:12; 106:3; *see also* Ps. 32:1; 40:4; 41:1; 146:5).

Jesus chose to introduce his Sermon on the Mount by introducing a radically new view of blessedness. Each Beatitude begins, like the psalms mentioned above, with the "blessed are" ("happy," or "fortunate") formula (Mt. 5:3-10; Lk. 6:20-22). Like the psalms, each focuses on an atti-

tude or action which brings blessing. However, the blessings envisioned in the OT are primarily material. In Jesus' Beatitudes the blessings are basically spiritual, and the reward is found in the relationships enjoyed with God himself and in his service. Only the poor in spirit, those who mourn, who are meek, who hunger and thirst for righteousness, who are merciful and pure in heart, are truly in tune with God's heart and will have a glorious inheritance in the coming age. Jesus' followers are called to find fulfillment in godliness rather than in material reward. *See also* Beatitudes.

The complexity of the biblical concept is seen in the many ways in which "bless" and "blessing" are used. Among them are:

1. *Blessing and cursing.* The story of Balaam (Num. 22–24) illustrates this. Balaam was hired by the pagan king of Moab to curse Israel, by magic, and thus to weaken its power. But instead God commanded Balaam to bless and thus enhance Israel's power. In Scripture, effectual blessing and cursing do not stem from magic, but rather from God himself. Both acknowledge the ability of God to lift up or to bring low, to strengthen or destroy.

2. *Parental blessing.* This served to affirm succession and pass benefits on to the next generation. Often in Scripture such blessings have a prophetic significance (Gen. 49:1-28; Deut. 33).

3. *Blessing other people.* In contexts where an individual "blesses" a superior, the phrase suggests honoring or showing respect (Gen. 47:7; 2 Sam. 14:22). The NT calls on believers to "bless" (*eulogeo*) others rather than to curse them. Such expressions mean that we are to wish for others and do to others only what is good, no matter how we are treated by them (Lk. 6:28; Rom. 12:14; 1 Cor. 4:12).

4. *Blessing God.* The phrase means to praise or thank God, and implies acknowledging him as the source of all good gifts. In some versions, such as the NIV, the Hebrew *barak* may be translated "praise" when used in this sense. The Bible expresses the same thought when it calls God "the Blessed One" (Mk. 14:61).

5. *The "cup of blessing."* In 1 Cor. 10:16, Paul uses this phrase to denote the Lord's Supper. The name comes from the third cup of wine, or "cup of blessing," drunk during the Jewish Passover celebration. This third cup accompanied a prayer of thanksgiving. The cup portrays Communion as a ceremony not only of remem-

brance but also of thanksgiving. It is a time to praise God who in Christ has "blessed us . . . with every spiritual blessing" (Eph. 1:3).

blind, blindness Inability to see. Eye diseases have historically been common in Palestine and other Middle Eastern countries. The usual cause is infection, which many times leads to blindness. The "blindness from birth" mentioned in the Bible was probably caused by an infection passed to an infant at birth.

The Hebrew word for blindness is '*ivver*, which means "closed," or "contracted." Blindness quite naturally came to symbolize a spiritual insensitivity. In Isaiah, the messianic age is portrayed as a time when God will heal physical and spiritual blindness. When the Messiah comes, "then will the eyes of the blind be opened and the ears of the deaf be unstopped" (Isa. 35:5).

Isaiah's predictions form a backdrop for Jesus' own claims. When some came asking if he were truly the Messiah, Jesus simply referred to miracles they had seen him perform: "The blind receive sight, the lame walk, those who have leprosy are cured, the deaf hear" (Mt. 11:5,6).

Later, even when Jesus gave sight to a man born blind, the testimony of that miracle was rejected by Israel's spiritual leaders, who claimed to have special insight into God's Word and ways. Theirs was the only blindness that Jesus could not cure: the spiritual blindness of those who refused to acknowledge their need, and who remained arrogantly confident of their own understanding (Jn. 9:1-41; 2 Pet. 1:9; Rev. 3:17).

blood The life-sustaining fluid in the veins and arteries of humans and animals. The Bible treats blood (Heb., *dam*) as sacred fluid, symbolic of life, which is itself the gift of God. The thought is best expressed in Lev. 17:11: "The life of a creature is in the blood, and I have given it to you to make atonement for yourselves on the altar." Since blood represented a creature's life, the Jew was forbidden to drink blood or use it in foods (Deut. 12:23).

Most of the 360 OT occurrences of *dam* (blood) fall into one of two categories. (1) Blood denotes violence, either in lawful war or by murder. Usually the plural is used in such cases; it may be rendered "bloodshed" or even as "bloodguiltiness" in some passages, like Ps. 51:14. (2) Blood expresses the essence of the OT sacrifice,

in which an animal substitute was killed to make atonement for human sins. *See also* Atonement.

In the NT *haima* (blood) also often refers to bloodshed, and at times to OT sacrifices. But 38 of the NT's 99 uses of the term refer to the blood of Christ. The "blood of Christ" conveys two major theological emphases. (1) The death of Jesus on the cross is viewed as instituting the new covenant, which God promised through the OT prophets (Jer. 31:33,34). In OT times the sealing of a covenant by sacrifice, a "covenant of blood" (illustrated in Gen. 15:8-21), made it the most binding of OT commitments. As a "covenant of blood," Christ's death expresses God's total commitment to forgive all who believe in his Son. *See also* Covenant.

(2) But the "blood of Christ" is also viewed as the fulfillment of all that the OT sacrifices foreshadowed. The sinless Son of God gave his life that human beings might be redeemed (Eph. 1:7); he himself became the sacrifice of atonement by which we have been reconciled to God. *See also* Sacrifices and Offerings.

New Testament passages which most clearly explain the significance of the blood of Christ are Rom. 3:24-26; 5:6-11; Heb. 8–10; and Rev. 5:6-14.

A number of other biblical expressions involving blood may call for explanation:
- *Of one blood* (Acts 17:26) affirms the unity of humankind. We humans share a common nature.
- *Bloodguilt* is incurred when a person kills another (Ps. 51:14). The term may also be used of any sin for which the OT prescribes the death penalty (Ezek. 18:13).
- *Avenger of blood* (Num. 35:19) identifies the nearest relative of a murdered person, who was responsible to carry out God's decree that "whoever sheds the blood of man, by man shall his blood be shed" (Gen. 9:6). *See also* Avenger of Blood; Murder.
- *"Drinking" Christ's blood* (Jn. 6:53-56) is a metaphorical expression indicating the way in which we, by faith, partake in the benefits of his sacrifice.

Boanerges [BOH-uh-NUHR-jeez; "sons of thunder"]. The nickname given James and John by Jesus (Mk. 3:17). This has been taken by some as a reference to their boldness and fervency. More likely, it denotes their quick temper, illustrated by the brothers' eagerness to call down fire on a Samaritan town that refused shelter to Jesus and his followers (Lk. 9:51-55).

boar [Heb., *hazir*]. A wild pig. Although the pig was domesticated before 3000 B.C., wild pigs ranged widely in the Middle East and throughout Europe. The Bible refers directly to them only in Ps. 80:13, where the fierce and evil-tempered animal stands symbolically for Israel's national enemies.

boast Brag, speak of one's own excellence or self-sufficiency. The Bible associates boasting with human arrogance. Boasting characterizes the person who fails to sense his or her dependence on God. The Lord described the proper human attitude in Jer. 9:23,24: "Let not the wise man boast of his wisdom or the strong man boast of his strength or the rich man boast of his riches, but let him who boasts boast about this: that he understands and knows me, that I am the Lord, who exercises kindness, justice and righteousness on earth, for in these I delight."

boat A small craft for water travel. Sturdy small boats (*ploion* or *ploiarion*) were used on the Sea of Galilee (Lake Tiberias) for fishing and for transportation of people and goods. These were powered by a single sail or by oar, and typically could hold ten or twelve people. Several of Jesus' disciples operated a fishing business using such boats (Mt. 4:18-22), and at times Jesus traveled by boat (Mt. 9:1; Lk. 8:22). The only ocean-going small boats mentioned in the Bible are skiffs (*skaphe*), usually dragged behind or carried aboard larger ocean-going ships (Acts 27:16,30,32). *See also* Ship.

Boaz [BOH-az; "strength," probably meaning "strength is in him"]. The "kinsman-redeemer" who married Ruth and became the forefather of King David, about 1100 B.C. **Father:** Salmon. **Scripture:** Ruth.

BACKGROUND

Boaz was a wealthy landowner who lived in Bethlehem during the time of the judges. In the Book of Ruth, he is portrayed as a kind man who had a great sense of responsibility to his family and his workers.

Limestone boar's head from Greco-Roman era.

The boar often symbolized unbridled anger.

The time of the judges was an era of spiritual and moral decline. Thus Naomi feared that her daughter-in-law Ruth might be raped or beaten if she tried to gather fallen grain in a stranger's field (Ruth 2:22). But Boaz's kindness demonstrates that even during this dark time godly individuals could still be found in Israel's small villages. *See also* Judges, Book of.

The story also shows the concept of the kinsman-redeemer (*go'el*). Under OT Law a near relative had the right to act on behalf of an enslaved or dispossessed kinsman (Lev. 25:47,48). When Boaz married Ruth, he redeemed the property lost earlier by Ruth's mother-in-law when her husband and sons had moved from Israel. But Boaz had to pledge their firstborn son to carry on the line of Ruth's dead husband. *See also* Kinsman.

LEARNING FROM BOAZ'S LIFE

Boaz lived quietly and honestly during the most difficult of times. He followed the Law in permitting Ruth to collect fallen grain in his fields (Lev. 19:9,10; Deut. 24:19-22). He also valued Ruth (who seems to have been attractive even though she is not expressly described in the text as "beautiful") for her sterling loyalty and noble character (Ruth 2:11,12; 3:11).

Strikingly, the book ends by identifying the son of Boaz and Ruth as the grandfather of David, Israel's greatest king. Often the significance of a quiet, godly life is difficult to evaluate. We should remember that the full significance of Boaz's life was understood only after his death, revealed in the towering figure of his great-grandson.

Ripe wheat on an Egyptian relief. Boaz owned many wheat fields. His first act of kindness to Ruth was to allow her to glean in his fields.

Boaz and Jakin outside the Temple entrance. The capitals held bowls, possibly for incense or fire.

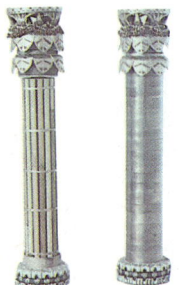

Boaz and Jakin from a model of Solomon's Temple.

Boaz and Jakin [BOH-az; "strength" and JAY-kin; "establish"]. Two free-standing hollow bronze pillars just outside the entrance to Solomon's Temple (1 Ki. 7:21; Jer. 52:20-23). Each was capped with a decorated, bowl-like capital, which may have been used for burning incense. The differences in height recorded in 1 Ki. 7:15 (27 feet or 8.2 meters) and 2 Chr. 3:15-17 (52.5 feet or 16 meters) may be due to a corruption of the Chronicles text, or perhaps Chronicles gives the combined height of the pillars when set in recessed bases.

No specific purpose for the pillars is stated in Scripture. Many have suggested that the pillars bore inscriptions whose key words were "strength" and "establish," commemorating God's commitment to the Davidic line.

The pillars were broken up when Nebuchadnezzar destroyed the Temple in 586 B.C. and the metal was taken to Babylon (2 Ki. 25:13).

body Physical self, corpse, a mass of people or things.

THE BIBLICAL PERSPECTIVE

In the OT, "body" (*basar* or *beten*) does not stand in contrast with "soul" and "spirit." Rather, the three terms all represent the whole human being, but from distinct perspectives. *Basar* presents human beings as persons who live in the context of a material universe. *See also*

Flesh. *Beten* basically means "belly" or "womb" and is always used in connection with childbirth or ancestry. A third term is *gewiyyah* (back, skeletal structure) which is used of bodies that have been slain in battle or that are subjected to hard labor; occasionally also of the body of heavenly beings such as a cherub.

Similarly, the NT teaches the significance of the physical body (Gk., *sōma*). We are not just "spiritual beings," trapped in bodies, whose real destiny is release from the material. In Colossians, Paul argues urgently against such an "otherworldly" view of faith. He reminds his readers that God "has reconciled you by Christ's physical body through death to present you holy in his sight" (Col. 1:22; *see* Heb. 10:10). The physical was both important and necessary in God's plan of redemption. Even so, the life we live in the body, what we do in this present universe, is important. That is why Paul so deeply desires that "now as always Christ will be exalted in my body" (Phil. 1:20). In word and deed, our bodily lives should be lived in the name of, and for the sake of, our Lord Jesus.

Thus the body does not stand in conflict with soul and spirit, but our bodily life is the vehicle through which soul and spirit find expression, to the glory of God. *See also* Colossians; Gnostics.

A TECHNICAL PERSPECTIVE

The NT also uses "body" in a number of specialized theological phrases. The body comes across as the vehicle through which sin was transmitted from Adam to all humanity. Various NT expressions reflect this:

• *mortal body (Rom. 6:12)*. The phrase highlights human weakness. Paul is not stressing the fact that this body is subject to biological death, but that we human beings are vulnerable to sin. Yet Christ offers hope: the Spirit who raised Jesus from the dead is able to bring spiritual vitality to us even in our mortality (Rom. 8:11).

• *body of death (Rom. 7:24; 8:10)*. "Death" here is spiritual rather than physical, and the phrase indicates sin's impact on human nature. Without divine enablement we cannot do what is truly good, nor please God. *See also* Death; Sin.

• *natural body (1 Cor. 15:44)*. The natural body is our biological, flesh-and-blood body. Paul describes it in 1 Cor. 15 as perishable and weak, corrupted by its inheritance from Adam. The "natural body" stands in contrast to the "spiritual body" believers will receive at the resurrection.

• *spiritual body (1 Cor. 15:44).* The resurrection body Christians will receive is called a "spiritual body," in that it will be under the control of the spirit and have powers and capacities transcending those of our present physical body. Paul describes the spiritual body as imperishable and powerful. *See also* Spiritual.

• *resurrection body (1 Cor. 15:35-49).* When Jesus returns, believers will be raised from the dead. The body to be received then is called the resurrection, or spiritual, body. *See also* Resurrection.

CHRIST'S BODY AND COMMUNION

Jesus spoke of the bread broken at the Last Supper as "my body" (Mt. 26:26). Christians have disagreed over the exact sense in which the bread of Communion "is" Christ's body. But all agree that broken bread at least represents Jesus' body in his sacrifice of himself on Calvary. *See also* Lord's Supper.

Body of Christ An image of the Christian Church. Among the many NT descriptions of the Church, the mystical "body of Christ" stands out as most prominent of all (*see* Rom. 12; 1 Cor. 12; Eph. 4).

ROMANS 12

Believers are united to one another in Christ—so intimately joined that the only appropriate image is that of a body with its various parts. Each member-part of this supernatural Body has different gifts which enable him or her to contribute to the well-being of others, and each is to serve others actively with his or her gifts. The chapter emphasizes the importance of intimate, loving relationships. These create the context in which parts of the Body can minister to one another.

1 CORINTHIANS 12

Christians are united to Jesus Christ and to each other, as parts of a body are united to their head and each other. Each Christian, like parts of a literal body, has his or her own role to play so that the Body may function as God intends. Each part is enabled (gifted) by God to carry out its function. The Church will be a healthy, vital Body as believers respect each other's role, and share in one another's sorrows and joys.

EPHESIANS 1:22,23

Christ is the living "head over everything for the church," which is his Body.

EPHESIANS 4:11-32

The Church grows toward spiritual maturity "as each part does its work." The passage again emphasizes the development of loving relationships between members of the Body, creating the context for mutual ministry.

SUMMARY

Taken together, these NT passages convey important truths about the nature of the Church, and suggest guidelines for congregational life (*see* chart). For the individual Christian, the teaching is both encouraging and exciting, reminding each of us that we are important, with a real contribution to make to the growth and well-being of others. And this teaching challenges each of us to reach out, to become more actively involved in the lives of others.

Job on His Dunghill, by Jean Bourdichon. Job was afflicted with boils "from the soles of his feet to the top of his head" (Job 2:7).

boil An inflamed swelling on the skin. Biblical "boils" (*shehin*) range from the painful but superficial sores that covered Job (Job 2:7) to the life-threatening abcess that afflicted Hezekiah (Isa. 38:1-21).

163

bold, boldness Confidence, assurance, or rash behavior. Boldness can be good or bad. Peter describes false prophets in 2 Pet. 2:10 as bold (*tolmētēs*) and audacious (*authadēs*). But Peter also prayed for boldness (*parrēsia*) in Acts 4:29. This term suggests a confidence that comes out in frank and courageous speech. The same word describes the assurance with which the Christian can approach God's throne (Heb. 4:16).

The incident in Acts 4 reveals the secret of Christian boldness. Peter and John had been beaten and commanded not to speak publicly of Jesus. They shared this with the church, and then the congregation turned to God in prayer. Together these believers acknowledged God as sovereign, and asked him to enable them to "speak your word with great boldness" (Acts 4:24-29). When we remember that God truly is sovereign, and depend on him for enablement, we too will find the courage to express our faith in Christ boldly. And we can trust his sovereign promises as we stand before his throne. *See also* Sovereignty of God.

bondage (1) Serfdom or slavery (Heb., *'abadim*), especially Israel's condition when slaves in Egypt (Ex. 1:14; 20:2). (2) In NT, subjection to some compulsion or influence (Gk., *douleia*)—to decay (Rom. 8:21), the Law (Gal. 5:1), or the fear of death (Heb. 2:15). Modern versions tend to use slavery where the KJV has bondage. *See also* Slave.

bondservant (KJV) A term used in the KJV for "servant" or "slave" (Heb., *'ebed*; Gk., *doulos*). Bondservants (also "bondmen") were those who subordinated their will to the wishes of another. *See also* Servant; Slave.

Egyptian statue of Semitic prisoner, 19th-18th century B.C. Bondage (slavery) was the usual lot of defeated foes.

book (Heb., *sepher*; Gk., *biblos* or *biblion*). A written document or collection of writings. The "book" of biblical times was not necessarily a bound volume. It might be simply a genealogical list (Mt. 1:1), a letter (1 Ki. 21:8), a memorial (Ex. 17:14), a written "bill" of divorce (Deut. 24:1), or a more extensive writing such as the first five books of our OT, the "book of Moses."

The ancients recorded information on many different materials. These included clay cylinders and tablets, stone, or waxed tablets. But usually "books" were written on "paper" or on treated animal skin. Paper was made by pressing and gluing together strips of the papyrus reed.

Initially the papyrus or skins were joined in rolls (scrolls) some 10 to 12 inches wide and 20 to 30 feet long. Later, in the second century A.D., single or folded written sheets might be stacked together in a "codex." *See also* Scroll.

The Bible mentions about 50 different "books," many of which have been lost. Most of these are chronicles of the various kings of Israel and Judah, such as the "book of the Acts of Solomon" (1 Ki. 11:41). They also include the very early "Book of Jashar" (Josh. 10:13).

Used figuratively, "book" also refers to a record maintained by God (Ex. 32:32,33). The "book of life" (Ps. 69:27,28) lists the company of the righteous who "share in your [God's] salvation." The NT also uses this phrase (Phil. 4:3; Rev. 20:12-15), and Malachi echoes the thought, referring to a "book of remembrance" that God maintains, listing those who fear the Lord and talk about him with each other. "They will be mine," God says, "in the day when I make up my treasured possession. I will spare them, just as in compassion a man spares his son who serves him" (Mal. 3:16,17).

booth Temporary shelter. After the harvest, during the annual Feast of Tabernacles, the Israelites were commanded to live outdoors in "booths" (Heb., *sukkot*) made of tree branches. The experience commemorated the years of homeless wandering in the wilderness, and emphasized by contrast the good gifts that God had provided in their Promised Land. *See also* Feasts, Festivals, and Fasts; Tabernacles.

Sometimes during military campaigns soldiers used such shelters (2 Sam. 11:11). Vineyard workers also made use of them. The booths not only provided shelter from the sun, but they also enabled the workers to protect ripening crops from birds and beasts (Isa. 1:8).

Booths, Feast of *See* Feasts, Festivals, and Fasts; Tabernacles, Feast of.

booty Spoils taken in war. Booty—which some Bible versions call "prey," "plunder," or "robbery"—includes not just gold and silver but also clothing, food, weapons, animals, and captives.

Numbers 31:21-24 gives rules for ritual purification of such spoils. Verses 25-54 establish principles for dividing booty among the Lord, the army, and the community of Israel. Subsequent generations followed these principles (Josh. 8:2,27). David clarified an important point: Every member of an army was treated equally in the division of the spoil, including those who had been assigned to guard the supplies (1 Sam. 30:23-25).

border Boundaries, limits of a certain territory. Israel's borders were set by God, and the boundaries of each tribe and family were established by him (Num. 34; Josh. 15–19). The fact that God himself not only gave Israel her land but personally allotted each family its place helps us understand how deeply rooted the Israelites' sense of place was—and remains today. *See also* Boundaries; Lots.

born again Regenerated by God. The phrase is found in Jesus' words to a Jewish leader named Nicodemus: "No one can see the kingdom of God unless he is born again" (Jn. 3:3). The imagery is rooted in the OT. Deuteronomy 32:18 speaks of God as figuratively giving Israel birth. The prophet Jeremiah foresaw a coming age when God would give his people a renewed heart and mind (Jer. 31:33,34). *See also* Covenant. Thus the image of spiritual rebirth should have been familiar to Nicodemus, and this "teacher of Israel" who could not grasp what Jesus meant deserved Christ's rebuke.

Simply put, one is born again when he or she receives Jesus Christ as Savior and becomes a child of God (Jn. 1:12,13). This spiritual rebirth leads to a moral transformation, for "no one who is born of God will continue to sin, because God's seed [nature] remains in him; he cannot go on sinning, because he has been born of God" (1 Jn. 3:9; *see* 3:6; 5:18).

The image is particularly helpful. No one can "see the kingdom of God" until

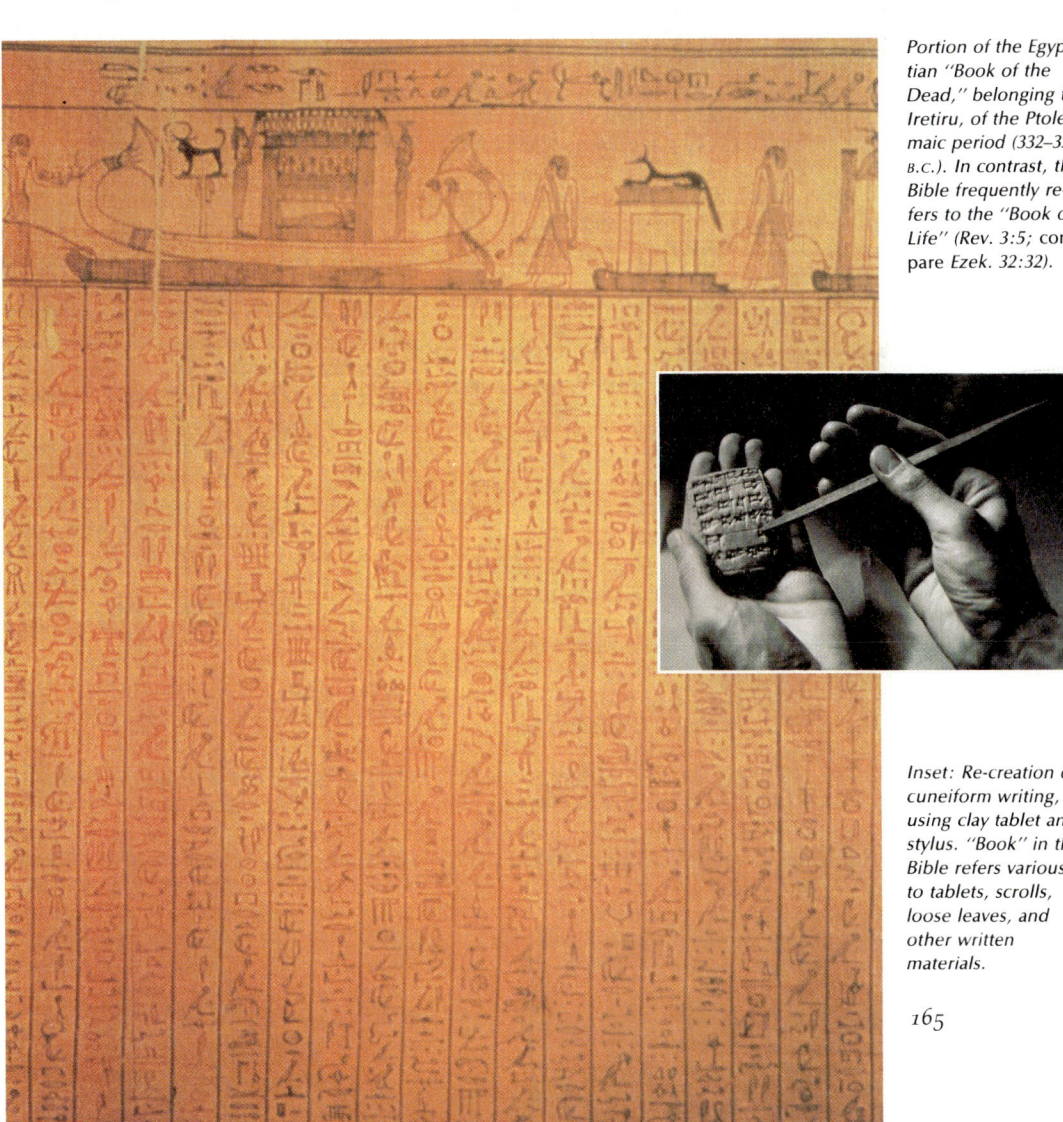

Portion of the Egyptian "Book of the Dead," belonging to Iretiru, of the Ptolemaic period (332–330 B.C.). In contrast, the Bible frequently refers to the "Book of Life" (Rev. 3:5; compare Ezek. 32:32).

Inset: Re-creation of cuneiform writing, using clay tablet and stylus. "Book" in the Bible refers variously to tablets, scrolls, loose leaves, and other written materials.

he or she is born again, just as no infant can see this present world until he or she is born into it. And, as infants are born with a potential that they can realize only through growth toward maturity, so those who come by faith into a personal relationship with God must grow as Christians.

Perhaps the clearest explanation of the change of heart resulting from regeneration is found in 2 Cor. 5:14,15—a constraining love of Christ which turns us from spiritual death (living for ourselves) to living for our blessed Savior himself as the most important person in our lives.

We may fail often as we stumble through spiritual infancy. But we have God's promise that, because God has shared his nature with us in a spiritual rebirth, we will grow; we will ultimately overcome our weaknesses, to become more and more like our Lord.

borrow To receive something with the intention of paying it back. Israel did not have a credit economy: A person did not borrow money in order to buy more things, but in order to survive. Thus borrowing and lending were treated more as moral than economic issues.

Old Testament Law encouraged lending to those in need. Such loans were to be made to fellow countrymen without charging interest (Ex. 22:25-27). The poor were to repay the loan, but if a person was unable to do so, the Law provided that every seventh year all debts should be canceled. Even if the seventh year was near, Israelites were to lend generously (Deut. 15:7-11). Thus Ps. 37:26 describes the righteous by saying, "They are always generous and lend freely." *See also* Poor; Sabbath Year.

While the OT acknowledges the possibility that "the wicked borrow and do not repay," nevertheless the godly man was to keep on giving generously (Ps. 37:21). Like many Mosaic laws, this was more often broken than kept (Neh. 5:1-12). Yet a sense of obligation to care for the needy is still felt in modern Judaism. *See also* Almsgiving.

However, the OT obligation to lend generously at no interest did not extend to the heathen (Deut. 15:6). One could lend at interest to a "stranger" (a non-Jew; *see* Deut. 23:20).

Exodus 22:7-15 discusses the loan of property or work animals, and tells how to deal with situations in which the lent goods are stolen or destroyed while in a borrower's possession.

One special note. The KJV speaks of the Israelites "borrowing" gold and silver from the Egyptians as they were about to leave that country (Ex. 11:2; 12:36). The Hebrew word should be translated "ask for," as it is in all modern versions. It has no connotation of later returning or paying back, as our word "borrow" has. The Egyptians, eager to be rid of this people whose God had punished them with devastating plagues, gave their wealth gladly.

By NT times, a commercial economy had largely replaced the agrarian economy of the OT. Two of Jesus' parables mention commercial loans and banking (Lk. 16:1-8; 19:12-27). Yet the old obligation to be generous is restated by Christ, and even extended to enemies (Lk. 6:32-36). *See also* Enemy.

While there may be no direct biblical guidance for us today as to how we should use credit, there is the continuing testimony of Scripture that generosity toward those in need remains pleasing to God: "I command you to be openhanded toward your brothers and toward the poor and needy in your land" (Deut. 15:11). *See also* Give.

bosom A person's chest; figuratively, one's affections. Isaiah speaks of God as one who "shall gather the lambs with his arm and carry them in his bosom [Heb., *hiq*]" (Isa. 40:11, KJV). The NIV nicely captures the figurative sense "in his bosom" with "close to his heart."

In Jesus' story, the beggar Lazarus is carried to "Abraham's bosom" (Gk., *kolpos*) after he dies (Lk. 16:22,23). The phrase represents not only what we would call "heaven," but also a place of honor close to the founding father of the Jewish faith.

In Jn. 1:18, Jesus is spoken of as "in the bosom of the Father." The symbolism again connotes intimacy, this time the intimate relationship of Jesus to God the Father. It affirms that the supreme place of honor "at the Father's side" (NIV) is reserved only for the Son.

bottle A container for liquid. The five Hebrew words translated "bottle" in the KJV were stone or clay jars, or animal skins sewn together and sealed to hold wine, milk, or water (Josh. 9:4; Jdg. 4:19; Ps. 33:7). The Greek word *askos*, translated "bottle" in the KJV, means wineskin. Modern versions typically translate the Hebrew and Greek words as jar or wineskin. *See also* Pottery; Wineskin.

166

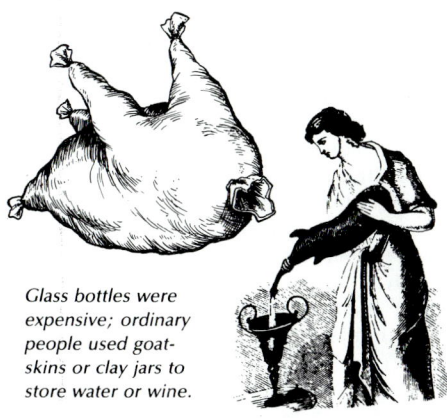

Glass bottles were expensive; ordinary people used goatskins or clay jars to store water or wine.

Tiny bottles, made of baked clay or glass, were in common use as perfume bottles, unguentaria, or tear bottles. These bottles were fragile and often decorated. Isaiah 3:20 describes a perfume bottle [Heb., *bet nepesh*; "house of breath"] in his list of the finery that God will take away from the women of Zion in judgment. Psalm 56:8 mentions a tear bottle, used to collect the tears of mourners. These bottles are known especially from Egyptian tombs.

boundaries Limits of territory. Israel's concern with boundaries rested on the conviction that God gave Palestine to Abraham's descendants, "from the river of Egypt [not the Nile, but the Wadi el'Arish] to the great river, the Euphrates" (Gen. 15:18). Just before the people of Israel invaded Canaan, specific national boundaries were established (Num. 34:1-12). Ezekiel describes similar boundaries as he prophesies about Israel's future (Ezek. 47:15-20).

Within the nation, each tribe was given its own territory, with boundaries clearly marked out. Then the territory of each tribe was divided by lot, clan by clan, and family by family (Josh. 13–19). *See also* Lots.

Because every homestead was viewed as God's allotment to a specific family, "no inheritance in Israel is to pass from tribe to tribe, for every Israelite shall keep the tribal land inherited from his forefathers" (Num. 36:7). An Israelite might sell the right to work his land, but he could never lose title to it. Leased fields were to be returned to the original owner every 50th year, the year of Jubilee (Lev. 25:1-34). Leviticus states, "The land must not be sold permanently." The people of Israel were tenants on property which ultimately belonged to the Lord (Lev. 25:23). *See also* Jubilee.

These property laws help us understand scriptural references to "boundary stones," which marked off each family's fields. The Law commanded, "Do not move your neighbor's boundary stone [Heb., *gebul*] set up by your predecessors in the inheritance you receive in the land the Lord your God is giving you to possess" (Deut. 19:14; *see* Prov. 22:28).

Naboth demonstrated commitment to God's Law when he refused to sell his vineyard to King Ahab, saying, "The Lord forbid that I should give you the inheritance of my fathers" (1 Ki. 21:3). The subsequent murder of Naboth and theft of his vineyard is a measure of the wickedness of Israel's most evil king and queen.

Bottles from various periods. From left: Terra cotta flask, about 1100 B.C., shaped to resemble a skin; Egyptian core-formed glass bottle, 1450–1350 B.C.; terra cotta bottle from Hebron, 8th century B.C.; Syrian bottle found in burial cave at Gezer. Jeremiah was ordered to break a "bottle" to symbolize Judah's coming destruction (Jer. 19, KJV).

oil could be poured. The wick itself was of flax fiber because of its fine capillary attraction.) *See also* Lamp; Pottery.

The bowls of biblical times could be beautiful as well as useful. Delicately painted, thin-walled "eggshell" pottery bowls were a specialty of Nabatea and were widely distributed over the extensive caravan routes. Delicate pottery dating from the first century A.D. has been excavated in Jerusalem.

bracelet An ornament worn around the wrist or arm. Both men and women of the ancient Near East wore bracelets and anklets. Most were bronze, but iron and even glass bracelets were not uncommon. The bracelets given to Rebekah were made of gold (Gen. 24:22). Gold bracelets that the children of Israel carried from Egypt were melted down and used in the construction of the tabernacle (Num. 31:50).

braids *See* Hair.

bramble A prickly shrub or vine. Some fifteen Hebrew names for thorny plants are found in the Bible. These have been variously translated as thorns, thistles, brambles, and briers. The exact plant indicated by a given term is impossible to establish.

The word most often translated bramble (*'atad*) probably indicates one of two prickly evergreen shrubs which grow near water. The "bramble" (*hoah*) of Isa. 34:13 is a thistle.

branch A limb or extension of the trunk of a tree or shrub. Biblical writers use a variety of vivid images involving branches. Prosperity is a fruitful vine "whose branches climb over a wall" (Gen. 49:22; *see* Ps. 80:11). Apostate Israel is cast out "like a rejected branch," discarded because of its unfruitfulness (Isa. 14:19). A similar image in Jn. 15:5,6 warns that believers who fail to remain in intimate fellowship with Jesus and draw strength from him will be fruitless. *See also* Vine.

Syrian relief of an archer (9th century B.C.). In the Bible the bow is often a symbol of military strength.

Line drawing from an Assyrian relief showing two men stringing a bow.

bow A curved, flexible device for launching arrows. The earliest bows were single pieces of wood, treated and shaped. But ancient carvings indicate that between 3000 and 1500 B.C. archers developed composite bows, made by gluing wood, bone, and sinew together. The composite bow became a powerful long-range weapon, effective at 300–400 yards. This innovation revolutionized the tactics of warfare. *See also* Archers; Arrow; Warfare.

bowl A shallow container for liquids, fruits, or condiments. Some ten different Hebrew words have been rendered "bowl" in English versions. These words can also mean "basin" and "cup." Bowls were commonly pottery, but sometimes wood, or even gold and silver. Shallow pottery bowls holding olive oil and a flaxen wick served as lamps in biblical times. (The wicks were confined in a pinched nose concavity at one end of the bowl. Later on the bowl itself was completely roofed over with a pottery covering, pierced only by a hole into which the

Below left: Israelite bowls and other pottery from the first century A.D. Amos chided Israel for her complacent luxury, including drinking "wine by the bowlful" (Amos 6:6). Below right: First-century Nabatean pottery found in Jerusalem exhibits delicate "eggshell" construction and fragile beauty that has survived the centuries.

But "branch" (*neser*, or *semah*) appears most prominently in the OT as a symbol of the coming Messiah. A Branch growing from the stump (the family line) of Jesse (the father of King David) will establish righteousness and bring peace to the earth (Isa. 11). Isaiah foresees a day when God will personally intervene and bring glory to the survivors of Israel. He says, "In that day the Branch of the Lord will be beauti-

Egyptian gold bracelet. The giving of a bracelet was a sign of affection in Bible times, as today.

ful and glorious" (Isa. 4:2). This thought is amplified in Jer. 33:15-18. The Branch from David's line will restore Israel and establish God's new covenant with all mankind.

Long before Jesus' birth, Jewish rabbis understood these Branch passages to refer to the coming Messiah. These Scriptures still give a good summary of the OT prophets' vision of the future. *See also* Future; Prophet.

brass In Scripture, any alloy of metal, but most commonly bronze, an alloy of copper and tin (Heb., *nehosheth*). When Paul mentioned "sounding brass" (*chalkos ēchōn*) in 1 Cor. 13, he was probably referring to a brass "sounding-vase." Such vases were arranged in Greek theaters to amplify the voices of actors. Thus Paul's imagery conveyed a powerful message to the Corinthians, where sounding-vases had been in use for over 100 years. Even though one speaks "in the tongues of men and of angels," without love he or she is merely an empty sounding-vase, hollowly echoing words, but tragically void within. *See also* Bronze.

As for brass in the modern sense, it is copper compounded with zinc rather than tin.

bread (1) A food made from a dough composed of a grain flour or meal mixed with water and, usually, yeast; (2) food generally.

The bread of the well-to-do was made of wheat, while the poor generally ate cheaper barley bread. In times of famine, grain might be mixed with "beans and lentils, millet and spelt" (Ezek. 4:9). *See also* Barley; Wheat.

To make bread, coarsely ground grain was mixed with water and leaven (Gen. 18:6; Mt. 13:33). Typically bread was baked daily. In 1 Ki. 19:6 and Isa. 44:19 we find bread baked "over hot coals"—dough would be pressed into flat cakes, spread on a hot rock, and covered with hot ashes. The Hebrew word for bread in 1 Chr. 9:31 suggests flat cakes cooked in a pan or griddle. Bread might also be shaped into loaves and baked in hive-like clay ovens. One Egyptian papyrus lists about 30 different kinds of loaves. The Bible also mentions various kinds of breads, some of which can be easily prepared today.

Two Bible Recipes for Bread

The bread that Sarah readied for Abraham's guests (Gen. 18:6) can be duplicated using this recipe:

Mix 3½ cups of whole wheat flour with ¾ cup of warm water, and 1 teaspoon of salt. Knead together for some ten minutes. Cover with a damp cloth and leave for 2 to 3 hours. Form the dough into eight flat, round pieces about 6" across. Cover again and let sit for half an hour, and then cook in a lightly oiled pan or outdoors on pieces of rock or tiles.

Barley cakes (Ezek. 4:12) can be made with 1½ cup of hot milk mixed with 3 cups barley flour, ¼ teaspoon of salt, ¾ cup of raisins, and 3 tablespoons of honey. These cakes can be flattened and fried in hot oil, or balls of the barley dough can be baked for 20 to 25 minutes in a 400° oven until browned.

Bread seal.

Several breads play special roles in the biblical drama.

• *Manna* was a crisp, sweet flake which God supernaturally provided for Israel during the years of wilderness wandering. *See also* Manna.

• *Unleavened bread*, bread made without yeast, was eaten during the Passover season to commemorate Israel's flight from Egypt. *See also* Unleavened Bread.

• *Shewbread* (or showbread) were special loaves of bread that were freshly baked daily and displayed before the Lord in Israel's tabernacle and later in its Temple. *See also* Shewbread.

Most significantly, Jesus spoke of himself as the "true bread" that came down from heaven and "gives life to the world" (Jn. 6:32-59). In his famous sermon on the Bread of Life, Christ pictured himself as the one on whom spiritual life depends. "I tell you the truth," Jesus said, "he who believes has everlasting life. I am the bread of life. . . . If anyone eats of this bread, he will live forever" (Jn. 6:47-51).

breastpiece A garment worn over the chest of Israel's high priest. The breastpiece (*hoshen*) of Israel's high priest ("breastplate" in the KJV) was a woven pouch nine inches square, attached by gold chains and rings to his ephod, an armless outer vest (Ex. 28:15-30). The breastpiece held twelve jewels, set in gold filigree and arranged in three rows. Each precious stone was engraved with the name of one of Israel's twelve tribes. The high priest wore the breastpiece when he performed any of his religious functions. The jewels symbolically represented the whole nation, carried into the presence of God close to the high priest's heart.

Israelite figurine kneading dough. The Passover "bread of affliction" was to be unleavened, and was eaten standing, to symbolize haste.

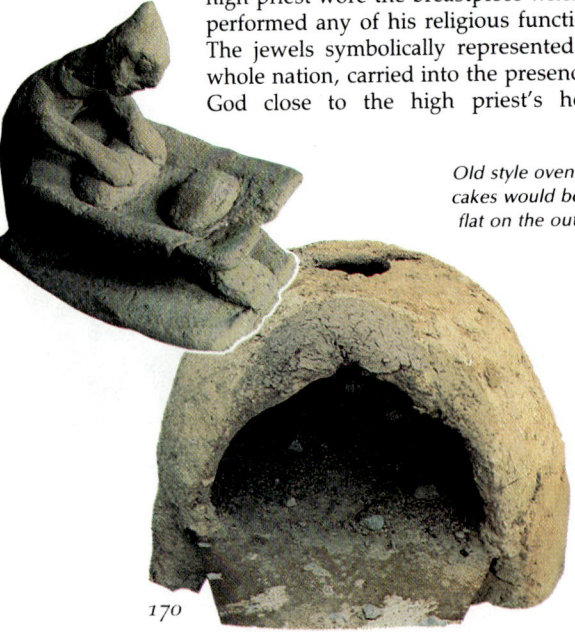

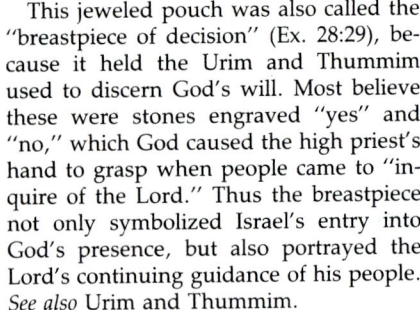

This jeweled pouch was also called the "breastpiece of decision" (Ex. 28:29), because it held the Urim and Thummim used to discern God's will. Most believe these were stones engraved "yes" and "no," which God caused the high priest's hand to grasp when people came to "inquire of the Lord." Thus the breastpiece not only symbolized Israel's entry into God's presence, but also portrayed the Lord's continuing guidance of his people. *See also* Urim and Thummim.

breastplate (1) OT: The high priest's breastpiece (KJV); (2) NT: metal or mail worn over the chest of a soldier. The breastplate (Gk., *thōrax*) of the NT (1 Th. 5:8; Rev. 9:9,17) protected the upper bodies of soldiers in battle. Paul used this image in describing the "armor of God." The Christian's vital heart area is best protected by personal righteousness (Eph. 6:14). *See also* Armor of God; Breastpiece.

breath of life A theologically significant phrase suggesting the distinction between animal and human life. According to Genesis, after God shaped Adam from the dust of the earth, he "breathed into his nostrils the breath of life, and the man became a living being" (Gen. 2:7). The Hebrew *ruah* means "wind," "breath," or "spirit." In Gen. 2 and in other contexts, *ruah* represents the vitalizing principle that marks the difference between living and non-living things (Gen. 6:17). Only God is able to cross this dividing line, to give and to maintain life (Job 27:3).

Yet there is something unique about human life which sets mankind apart from the animals. God gave biological life to all living creatures. But the breath of life God breathed into mankind "gives him understanding" (Job 32:8). As "living beings" (*nepes*), humans have been granted a self-conscious existence which extends beyond death into eternity. *See also* Animals; Life; Soul; Spirit.

Old style oven. The cakes would be laid flat on the outside.

Egyptian wooden model of persons making bread (2400–1800 B.C.).

Traditional representation of Aaron's breastplate. The Bible does not record the order of the names to be inscribed on the stones, so that identification of a tribe with a certain stone is guesswork.

1. Ruby
2. Topaz
3. Carbuncle
4. Turquoise
5. Sapphire
6. Emerald
7. Jacinth
8. Agate
9. Amethyst
10. Beryl
11. Onyx
12. Jasper

171

Nebuchadnezzar's name and title appear on this Babylonian brick, from about 600 B.C. Bricks were widely used in Mesopotamia, far less so in stony Palestine.

Brickmaking captives depicted on a wall painting from the tomb of Rekhmira at Thebes (1533–1450 B.C.) Bearded foreigners, under the supervision of an Egyptian (with stick far right), gather water and work mud and straw together into molds. At top left a worker lifts a mold from a sun-dried brick. At far right a worker carries cured bricks to building site. Israelite workers were making bricks in Egypt at the time this was painted.

brick Hardened clay molded into oblong blocks used in building. Mud or clay bricks were basic building material in Egypt. Bricks were sometimes used in Palestine too, despite the availability of stone. The bricks of ancient homes typically measured about 9 inches by 4½ inches by 3 inches (23 by 11.5 by 7.5 centimeters). In larger buildings bricks might be twice that size. In Egypt and Palestine mud was used as mortar, while bitumen ("tar") was used in Mesopotamia (Gen. 11:3). *See also* Bitumen.

As slaves in Egypt, the Israelites were forced to make bricks (Ex. 1:14). Numerous tomb paintings portray Egyptian brickmaking of that era.

Workers dug out mud, which they mixed with water. At times straw was added, as indicated in Ex. 5:1-21. The decomposing straw released an acid which made the mud bricks stronger and less liable to crack. After working the mud and straw to the right consistency, the workers pressed the mixture into wooden frames. The frames were then lifted off, and the bricks were usually left to dry in the sun. By NT times it was not uncommon to bake bricks in a kiln.

Egyptian records reveal the difficulty in making bricks. In one case some 600 workmen produced only 39,118 bricks a day, about 65 bricks per man. Today four men make about 3,000 bricks a day. It is no wonder that Israelite workmen in Egypt were frustrated when they were ordered to gather their own straw, yet their daily quota of bricks was left the same (Ex. 5:18).

Isaiah 65:3 condemns Israel's altars of brick. Altars used in the worship of Yahweh were to be made only of earth or uncut stone (Ex. 20:24-26).

bride and bridegroom A woman and man about to be married, or those recently married.

In biblical times, as now, weddings abounded with joy and fulfillment. One of the traditional Seven Blessings pronounced at a Jewish wedding says: "You did create joy and gladness, bridegroom and bride, mirth and exaltation, pleasure and delight, love, comradeship, peace and fellowship. Blessed are you, O Lord, who causes the groom to rejoice with the bride."

In many ways the wedding celebration was the culmination of the bride's and groom's life to date. Festivities typically lasted for a week (Jdg. 14:17), and during this time bride and bridegroom were dressed and treated as queen and king. Several of Jesus' illustrations give us insights into wedding customs (Mt. 22:2-14; 25:1-13; Lk. 12:35-38).

The eager expectation of a bride before her wedding, and the joy associated with the celebration, add special meaning to the NT's vision of the Church as the "bride of Christ" (2 Cor. 11:2; Rev. 19:6,7; 21:9; 22:17). Jesus, the bridegroom (Mt. 9:15), is coming for his bride. When Christ returns, all she has yearned for will be realized.

We may draw many parallels between the wedding practices of biblical times and Christian teaching. For instance, the groom came to the bride's house to escort her to his home; Jesus will return to earth to escort his Church to heaven (1 Th. 4:13-18). Again, the father of the groom selected the bride, but she had a right to refuse him (Gen. 24); God the Father "chose us in him before the creation of the world" (Eph. 1:4), yet only those who choose to receive the Son establish a personal relationship with him (Jn. 1:12).

Paul applies the image of bride and groom in a distinctive way. Christ "loved the church and gave himself up for her, to make her holy, . . . to present her to himself as a radiant church, without stain or wrinkle or any other blemish, but holy

Egyptian marriage contract, dated 172 B.C. wherein the groom, the priest Pagosh, agrees to pay his bride Teteimhotep a fixed sum within 30 days should they divorce. Jesus' stand against divorce was a departure from Near Eastern cultural norms.

and blameless" (Eph. 5:25-27; *see* 2 Cor. 11:2). The Church will find fulfillment when Christ comes for her. Until then she keeps herself pure for him. By remaining submissive to Jesus, Christians can prepare themselves for the joyful wedding feast which will take place when Jesus comes. *See also* Marriage.

bridle The part of a harness that attaches to the horse's head or mouth and permits a rider to guide the animal. In Scripture, the bridle and bit (the horse's mouthpiece) sometimes symbolize God's interactions with people. God promised godly King Hezekiah that he would put a bit in the mouth of the wicked Assyrian king Sennacherib, who had devastated Israel and was threatening Jerusalem, and make him go home (Isa. 37:29).

Believers are promised that God will instruct them, and are urged, "Do not be like the horse or the mule, which have no understanding but must be controlled by bit and bridle or they will not come to you" (Ps. 32:9). God yearns for his people to respond willingly, rather than to resist and force him to compel obedience.

The NT picks up the image and asks us to bridle ourselves; that is, to exercise self-control (Jas. 1:26; 3:2,3). *See also* Bit.

brier A prickly or thorny bush. Over a dozen Hebrew words name thorny plants, and have been variously translated in English versions as thorns, thistles, brambles, and briers. The exact identity of these plants is impossible to determine today. Scripture often associates briers with land which has become worthless, especially through God's judgments on sinning Israel. In a typical passage, Isaiah warns

that "where there were a thousand vines worth a thousand silver shekels, there will be only briers and thorns. Men will go there with bow and arrow, for the land will be covered with briers and thorns. As for all the hills once cultivated by the hoe, you will no longer go there for fear of the briers and thorns" (Isa. 7:23-25).

brimstone (KJV) Combustible sulfur. Brimstone lay in great deposits in the ancient Near East, particularly in the area of the Dead Sea. This soft yellow element melts at only 113°C. When it burns, melted streams of sulfur flow like lava, and give off suffocating fumes. Sodom and Gomorrah were destroyed by a rain of fire and brimstone, perhaps when an earthquake ignited oil and sulfur deposits on the plain on which they were situated. *See also* Sodom and Gomorrah.

Life-sized representation of man and woman at Thebes about 1350 B.C., holding hands in a display of affection. Marriage based on mutual love and submission is the biblical ideal.

173

Painting from Rekh-mira's tomb, Thebes, about 1475 B.C., shows casting of doors similar to Solomon's bronze-covered Temple doors. Workers pour molten bronze into a vented mold; plan for the doors is top right.

Top right: Bronze Israelite oil lamp (300–100 B.C.), decorated with pomegranates and bulls' heads. Bronze pomegranates formed part of the Temple's ornamentation (2 Ki. 25:17).

Bronze cat, sacred animal of the Egyptian goddess Bastet, (1550–1300 B.C.) Bronze preceded iron as material for implements, weapons, and cult objects.

The terror linked with fiery brimstone serves in both Testaments as an image of destruction and divine punishment (Gen. 19; Ps. 11:6; Lk. 17:29; Rev. 19:20; 20:10). *See also* Hell.

bronze An alloy of copper, zinc, and often tin. People of biblical times used bronze to make tools, weapons, cooking pots, and decorative jewelry. Palestinian bronze dating to about 1500 B.C. has been found to contain 23% zinc and 10% tin. This mixture, relatively soft and easy to work, was the dominant metal in Palestine until iron came into use around 1000 B.C.

Bronze tripod and vessels, possibly used in ceremonial washings before the altar; Megiddo, 900–800 B.C. Most of the tabernacle and Temple utensils were made of bronze, including the "basin for washing" and its stand (Ex. 38:8).

Bronze was used in the making of the tabernacle's altar of sacrifice, as well as the laver in which the priests washed (Ex. 35:16; 2 Ki. 16:14-17). Thus bronze frequently symbolizes divine judgment.

Archaeologists have found bronze cymbals in Palestine, dating to the fourteenth century B.C. These instruments are about four inches across, with holes in the center through which loops of iron wire were slipped to attach them to the fingers. David probably played cymbals like these as the ark was carried into Jerusalem (2 Sam. 6:5). *See also* Brass.

Bronze Age The historical era, about 3200–1200 B.C., when bronze was the primary metal used in weapons, tools, and other artifacts.

Bronze soon replaced copper as the dominant metal in the ancient world because of its hardness and its ability to maintain a keen cutting edge. It first appeared in the great city-states of Mesopotamia, such as Ur, and its use spread gradually into Syria and Egypt.

Archaeologists divide the Bronze Age into three major subdivisions, and commonly use these subdivisions to date various strata of their excavations. These are: Early Bronze Age (3200–2000 B.C.); Middle Bronze Age (2000–1500 B.C.); and Late Bronze Age (1500–1200 B.C.). The Iron Age followed.

bronze serpent The cast bronze image of a serpent, made by Moses. When the Israelites were punished by a plague of poisonous snakes, God told Moses to make a bronze serpent. This image was placed at the top of a pole in the middle of camp, and all who looked at it were promised immunity from the serpents' bite (Num. 21:4-9). The bronze serpent was preserved for some 700 years until the time of Hezekiah (715–686 B.C.). That king ordered it destroyed because it had become an idol to many of his people.

Jesus compared his coming crucifixion to the historic raising of the bronze serpent in Israel's camp. The Son must also be

Archaeological Age		Characteristics	Prominent Peoples
Early Bronze/ Canaanite 3160–2200 B.C.		Sumerians create bronze from an alloy of copper and arsenic then tin. 750-year urban age in Palestine; trading towns flourish.	City-states of Sumer, Ebla, and Akkad successively influence whole Fertile Crescent. Egyptians influential in Phoenicia.
Middle Bronze 2200–1550 B.C.		Powerful city-states that emerged now decline. Herders succeed towndwellers, only to move toward urban living themselves.	Semi-nomadic Amorites migrate into scrub lands between cities (2000 B.C.). Hyksos rule in Egypt/ Palestine (1730–1550).
Late Bronze 1550–1200 B.C.		Six different scripts found attest to diverse mix of cultures in Palestine. Old Canaanite culture comes to an abrupt end; Israelites live in towns.	Egyptians control trade routes. Israelites enter Canaan. Sea Peoples (Philistines) invade coastal plain (1200 B.C.).
Iron/Israelite 1200–332 B.C.		Philistines first to use iron in Palestine. Israelites adopt Syro-Phoenician architecture and art forms such as ivories.	Israel's monarchy established (1000 B.C.). Assyria (824–722), Babylon (625–539) and Persia (539–330) rule successively. Phoenician trade dominates the Mediterranean.

lifted up "that everyone who believes in him may have eternal life" (Jn. 3:14,15). The analogy is clear. Those in the Exodus generation who believed God's Word enough to look to the bronze serpent were delivered from death. All who believe God's Word about Jesus, and look to the Savior, who has been lifted up on Calvary's cross, will receive eternal life. *See also* Cross; Life.

brooch *See* Jewelry.

broom tree A desert shrub, large enough to provide some shade (1 Ki. 19:4). Its roots served as fuel (Ps. 120:4), but were bitter to eat (Job 30:4). The figurative use in Isa. 14:23 suggests that branches of the tree served as brooms to sweep the dust from tents or homes.

brother (1) A male sibling; (2) any relative or kinsman; (3) a close friend; (4) a fellow Christian. The OT presents an extended concept of brotherhood, beyond mere family ties. Jonathan was a "brother" to his friend David (2 Sam. 1:26). The Israelites were to look upon fellow Hebrews as brothers (Deut. 15:7-11). King Ahab made a treaty with Ben-Hadad of Syria and called him "brother" (1 Ki. 20:32,33)—thus arousing the anger of God.

Jesus introduced a special meaning of "brother," which later became established in the early church. Once, told that his mother and brothers were waiting to see him, Jesus responded, "Who is my mother, and who are my brothers? . . . whoever does the will of my Father in heaven is my brother and sister and mother" (Mt. 12:46-50). The ultimate family bond between human beings was to be founded not on blood but on shared relationship with God.

In the NT church, "brother" took on this new and deeper meaning. While all human beings are linked by their humanity and are God's creations, the Bible teaches that those who trust Christ come into special relationship with God and with each other. As fellow children of God through faith in Christ Jesus (Gal. 3:26), it was natural that Christians should think

of each other as brothers and sisters. Ephesians 3:14,15 provides the rationale. God is Father, "from whom his whole family in heaven and on earth derives its name [its identity *as family*]." John especially places great stress on the family relationship: "If anyone says, 'I love God,' yet hates his brother, he is a liar. For anyone who does not love his brother, whom he has seen, cannot love God, whom he has not seen. And he [God] has given us this command: Whoever loves God must also love his brother" (1 Jn. 4:20,21).

brothers of Jesus (1) Male children of Mary and Joseph (therefore, half-brothers of Jesus); or possibly (2) close relatives of Jesus. Since the OT often used "brother" for relatives and clan members, some have argued that the *adelphoi* (brothers) of Jesus named in the Gospels were perhaps cous-

Bronze Age, GAD (Generally Accepted Dates).

The Hebrew rotem, or broom "tree," a rare and welcome source of shade and fuel for the wilderness traveler.

175

ins of Jesus, but not children of Mary and Joseph. The pre-Reformation Christian Church developed a belief in the perpetual virginity of Mary, noting that the dying Jesus consigned his mother to John rather than to a relative. Thus, today, the Roman Catholic Church views the *adelphoi* as close relatives, not half-brothers.

However, other Christians feel that the NT does not support such an interpretation. The people of Jesus' hometown asked in amazement, "Isn't this Mary's son and the brother of James, Joseph, Judas and Simon? Aren't his sisters here with us?" (Mk. 6:3). John 2:12 again links Jesus' mother and brothers, and John 7:3-5 tells us that "even his own brothers did not believe in him" at one point in his public ministry. Protestant scholars feel that, not just the language, but the contexts in which Jesus' brothers are mentioned, suggest strongly that these were in fact children of Mary and Joseph who lived in the same home with them. They also point to Mt. 1:24,25 which tells us that Joseph took Mary home with him as his wife after she was pregnant with Jesus, but "he had no [sexual] union with her until she gave birth to a son."

Most commentators agree with an early tradition that James, author of the Epistle of James and leader of the Jerusalem church (Acts 15:13), was a half-brother of Jesus. Christ's brothers may have had their doubts about him at first, but after the resurrection they joined the company of faith (Acts 1:14), and at least one played a leading role in the early days of the church (Gal. 1:19; *compare* 1 Cor. 9:5). Jude, the author of the Epistle of Jude, has also been thought to be a brother of Jesus.

build (1) To construct; (2) metaphorically, to promote Christian growth. The OT pictures God as the builder of his redeemed people (Jer. 33:7-9). And the NT casts Christians as God's house, with Jesus as the master builder (Heb. 3:3-6).

Perhaps most significant for Christian experience is the concept expressed in the Greek word *oikodomeō*, which means to "build up" and (often "edify" in English versions). While the Church is God's building, and Christ himself both master builder and foundation (Mt. 16:18; 1 Cor. 3:9-15), God permits Christians a role as fellow builders, who work with him and contribute to the growth of other believers. Ephesians 4:12-16 describes the Church, its members bound together in a unity that is experienced through love, growing and building itself up, "as each part does its work." *See also* Church; Mature; Spiritual Gifts.

Bul *See* Calendar.

bull The adult male bovine. Cattle were among the "clean" animals identified in Israel's Law: they could be used for food

Egyptian sculptor's model of a bull, in limestone, 3rd century B.C., displays its grace, strength, and fearlessness so admired by the ancients.

176

and offered to God in sacrifice. Male cattle are called bullocks (KJV), steers or oxen (RSV) in English versions, as well as bulls. The bull, noted for its strength in biblical times, was represented in Solomon's Temple. Twelve bronze bulls served as the pedestal for the great bronze washing basin that stood outside the Temple doors.

In the Bible, the bull symbolizes strength and sometimes fierceness. In the Psalms, bulls represent Israel's enemies (22:12; 68:30).

Prominent in the religions of the ancient Near East, bulls served as symbols of fertility and power. In Egypt, the Apis bull was under the patronage of Ptah, the creator and fertility god whose temple was at Memphis. In Sumeria the storm god Ishkur was shown as a bull. The Canaanite neighbors of Israel envisioned their primary god as a bull, or pictured their god Baal as standing on the back of a bull. These associations with pagan religions help us sense how serious it was when the Israelites worshiped a golden calf (Ex. 32). That apostasy recurred in the time of Jeroboam I, who set up golden calves at Bethel and Dan and announced, "Here are your gods, O Israel, who brought you up out of Egypt" (1 Ki. 12:28).

bulrushes (KJV) Fast-growing papyrus reeds, which grew along the Nile and in Egypt's delta lakes and backwaters. Bound bundles of papyrus reeds were woven to build ships that plied the great river of Egypt, while strips of papyrus pounded flat and glued together served as writing material. *See also* Papyrus.

burden (1) A load; (2) a worry or responsibility; (3) in prophetic contexts, a message from God. In the OT, burdens can be literal, like the load carried by a donkey (Ex. 23:5), or psychological, like a deep concern (Job 7:20). In the prophets, a burden is a divine message, often one heavily laden with warnings of divine judgment (Isa. 15:1; Jer. 23:34; Hab. 1:1; Zech. 12:1; or Mal. 1:1—translated "oracle" by the NIV, this is the same Hebrew word, *massa'*, used for "burden").

"Burden" has a similar range of meaning in the NT. But two passages are worth special note. Galatians 6:2 urges believers to "carry each other's burdens." Yet in Gal. 6:5 the Bible says "each one should carry his own load." Is this a conflict? No, for in 6:2 "burden" is *baros*, an unusually heavy load. In 6:5 the word is *phortion*, the normal load carried by a soldier on duty.

We need to help brothers and sisters with unusually heavy burdens to bear. But at the same time each of us needs to be willing to carry our own normal load of troubles and obligations.

Jesus extended an invitation to all who are weary and burdened: "Come to me . . . and I will give you rest. . . . For my yoke is easy, and my burden [*phortion*] is light" (Mt. 11:28-30). When we are yoked to Jesus, even the "normal load" we each are called to carry becomes easier to bear. *See also* Yoke.

burial Interment of a corpse underground or in a tomb. Archaeologists have found burial practices extremely significant for understanding the beliefs and cultures of ancient peoples. Most ancient burial practices demonstrate some belief in an afterlife. The dead were provided with food, weapons, tools, cookwear or jewelry for use in the beyond. Yet the burial practices of the Hebrew people differed strikingly, suggesting a powerfully distinctive belief system from those of the peoples around them. No ancient Hebrew tomb has yet

Moses' mother wove bundles of bulrushes (papyrus plants) like these to build the floating "ark" to hold her baby until Pharaoh's daughter found him (Ex. 2, KJV).

been found intact; all of them have been robbed. But there is no evidence that food or equipment intended for life beyond the grave was ever buried with the corpse. At most there might be a few precious adornments which survivors of the family might have interred with the deceased. But even of this there is no positive proof.

EGYPTIAN BURIAL PRACTICES

Wealthy Egyptians prepared carefully for the afterlife. Egyptians believed that the existence of the soul was linked to the existence of the body, and thus they mummified corpses to preserve them forever. The Bible indicates that Jacob and Joseph, who both died in Egypt, were embalmed (mummified) according to Egyptian practice (Gen. 50:2,3,26).

The mummy body was buried in a cave or pyramid. The walls were typically decorated with scenes of daily life and religious texts. The tomb chamber was filled with items the dead person would need in the world beyond. Carved ships with rowers, food, jewels, and chariots were provided for the dead. It was thought that spiritual counterparts of all of these persons and conveniences would be available for the deceased provided the proper incantations had been recited by the priests at the time of burial.

There was, however, no hope held out to the poor. They were buried in the sands. As their bodies decayed, their souls were thought to be lost forever.

MESOPOTAMIAN BURIAL PRACTICES

Leonard Woolley's excavations at Ur showed similar preparations for the afterlife. One king and queen from the 1st Dynasty of Ur were found buried in a great excavation—along with the bodies of the male and female attendants who had served them in life. The remains suggest that the servants had dressed in their best finery, had taken their places in the entourage of the rulers they had served, and then had taken poison.

BURIAL PRACTICES IN PALESTINE

The earliest bodies recovered from Palestine date from before 4000 B.C. Some of them were buried in a seated position, with knees drawn up to the chest. Often the bodies were buried wearing necklaces and anklets of shell or stone, and some had been painted with red pigment. Later, in the Early Bronze Age (3200–2000 B.C.), bodies were buried in shallow pits along with cooking pots, and the pits were filled with stones.

In the Middle Bronze Age (2000–1500 B.C.), some bodies were laid upon stone platforms built on the ground. Jars and grinding stones, used in preparing food, were placed beside them, and more earth and stones were heaped over the body. In some cases during this era, warriors were buried with their mounts.

In the Late Bronze Age (1500–1200 B.C.), the usual tomb was a cave or chamber cut into the ground. Again pottery vessels were placed near the dead for their use in the beyond. Thus the ancients demonstrated their belief in an afterlife.

HEBREW BURIAL CUSTOMS

The Bible describes a variety of burial customs, but none of these provided the corpse with material possessions for the next world. Bodies of the dead were not embalmed (except those of Jacob and Joseph in Egypt and very possibly the rest of Jacob's twelve sons as well), but buried quickly, on the day of death or within twenty-four hours, with no attempt to preserve them. God had announced,

"Dust you are and to dust you will return" (Gen. 3:19). Surely a body, whose destiny was dust, had no need for pots or jewelry. In fact, the pagan practice of placing food by the body of the dead is expressly forbidden in Mosaic Law (Deut. 26:14). It was commonly believed that, in contrast to the spirit of an animal, which went down into the earth with the body, the spirit of a man rose upward (Eccl. 3:21). One day the body would be raised and reunited with the spirit (Dan. 12:2). *See also* Resurrection.

Burial was important to the Jews. Dead bodies were ritually unclean, as were those who touched them (Num. 5:2). The judgment on Jezebel, to be eaten by dogs and not buried, was considered to be the ultimate disgrace (2 Ki. 9:10).

In Israel, a dead body was prepared for burial by washing (Acts 9:37). It was then wrapped in cloth, with a square of linen wrapped around the head (Jn. 11:44; 20:6,7). Rabbinic writings tell us that the chin was bound so it did not sink lower. Perfumes might also be wound into these wrappings (Lk. 23:55,56).

The body was then carried to the burial site on a wooden bier. It was accompanied by friends and relatives, who wept and wailed loudly as a sign of respect for the dead person (Mk. 5:38; Acts 8:2). All who saw the procession were expected to join it out of respect for the family. In OT and NT Israel professional mourners were hired to weep loudly outside the home and to accompany the mourners to the grave (Mt. 9:23). While Moses and Aaron were mourned for 30 days (Num. 20:29; Deut. 34:5-8), the typical period for mourning, well established by Jesus' time, was seven days.

Archaeologists have found many tombs (all of them rifled) from the first century A.D. in and around Jerusalem, providing insight into the burial of Jesus. *See also* Burial of Jesus; Mourn.

burial of Jesus Tombs built in Jerusalem and Judea between 40 B.C. and A.D. 135 are distinctive. Many have been excavated, giving us a good idea of burial practices of the era.

Burial chambers of the well-to-do were cut into rock. Beyond the small, square opening, a large chamber was hewn out of Palestine's soft limestone, containing one or more benches on which the body was laid for preparation. The bodies were then laid in long, narrow chambers called *kokhim*, which were cut into the walls. First-century tombs typically held several generations of a family. The bones of the decomposed bodies were placed in stone boxes (ossuaries), which were stored in the *kokhim*. These tombs were often sealed with large round stone slabs which rolled down to cover the entrance. Often the tombs were placed in gardens.

The Gospels give us a similar description of Jesus' burial place. The tomb was that of the wealthy Joseph of Arimathea, which he had "cut out of the rock" and sealed with a large rolling stone (Mt. 27:57-60). The garden in which the tomb was being constructed lay close to the place of crucifixion (Jn. 19:38-42). Even the picture of John bending down to look into the tomb through a low-cut entrance to discover that Jesus' body was no longer there (Jn. 20:5), is a detail that fits the well-known pattern of first-century Judean tombs.

While we know the kind of tomb in which Jesus' body was buried, the exact site is a matter of debate. Early testimony lends support to the traditional Roman

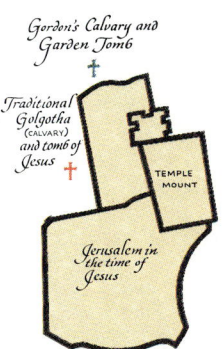

Map shows the two most likely sites of Jesus' burial. Golgotha and Church of the Holy Sepulchre, dating from a 4th-century tradition, at left; Gordon's Calvary and the Garden tomb, featuring a skull-like outcropping outside the city walls, at top. No tradition is associated with the garden site.

179

Exterior of the Garden Tomb, Jerusalem, showing bench, low entrance, and stone that could be rolled to cover the entrance and sealed in place. While this tomb has been proposed as the burial site of Jesus, it has little support among modern archaeologists. It does show the way Jesus' tomb was probably constructed.

Catholic site, under the Church of the Holy Sepulchre. While the site is now covered by marble panels, a description dating from about A.D. 670 seems to fit the pattern of first-century tombs. Since its rediscovery in the 19th century, the Garden Tomb has been preferred by many evangelicals as the place where Jesus was buried. But few contemporary archaeologists agree.

burning bush The plant in which God appeared to Moses at the foot of Mount Horeb (Ex. 3:1-6). The bush was one of a

Moses, having gone to see the "strange sight" of a bush that burns without being consumed, has taken off his sandals as the Lord commanded, in this fresco from the synagogue at Dura Europus on the Euphrates River, early 3rd century A.D.

number of "thorny plants" found in that region that cannot be identified with certainty. *See also* Bramble. However, the event was clearly miraculous, one of several appearances of God in Scripture that are associated with fire (Ex. 13:21; 19:18; 2 Th. 1:7). *See also* Angel of the Lord; Miracle; Shekinah.

Here, as in other settings, fire signifies the holiness of God. Thus Moses is told to take off his sandals, for "the place where you are standing is holy ground." Later Moses led the children of Israel back to this location, for "Horeb" (Ex. 3:1) is the name for the range to which Mount Sinai belonged, where God gave Israel his Law (Ex. 19,20).

burnt offering A sacrifice required by Israel's Law, in which an animal was consumed by fire. Most offerings and sacrifices in Israel's worship system were burned. However, "burnt offering" in English versions usually translates the Hebrew 'olah ("the ascending one"). In this offering the entire animal, except for the skin, was burned on the altar and its smoke ascended skyward.

The "burnt offering" was not an offering for a specific sin, but rather for the sinful heart or sin-nature which required an atonement if the worshiper was to have access to God for his subsequent offerings at the time of worship. It also symbolized total commitment of the worshiper to the Lord. The animals used in this offering were the young bull, ram, or male goat.

The poor could offer turtledoves or young pigeons (Lev. 1:3,10,14).

The Law required the priests to present a burnt offering on behalf of the whole nation at the entrance to the tabernacle or Temple each morning and evening (Ex. 29:38-42; Num. 28:3-8), with double the offering on Sabbath (Num. 28:9,10). Burnt offerings were also made at each new moon and at a number of Israel's worship festivals (Num. 28:11–29:39). Special 'olah offerings were required at the consecration of priests (Ex. 29:15-18), the purification of women after childbirth (Lev. 12:6-8), and on other occasions.

While the whole burnt offering symbolized commitment to God, the Lord was concerned with reality rather than ritual. Thus God cried out to a sinning Israel through Isaiah:

"The multitude of your sacrifices—
what are they to me?" says the Lord.
"I have more than enough of burnt offerings,
of rams and the fat of fattened
animals. . . ."

(Isa. 1:11)

David puts God's attitude in perspective when he pleads for forgiveness in Ps. 51, and says:

You do not delight in sacrifice, or I would
bring it;
you do not take pleasure in burnt offerings.
The sacrifices of God are a broken spirit;
a broken and contrite heart,
O God, you will not despise.

(Ps. 51:16,17)

Yet David went on to acknowledge that, when the heart of God's people was right, "Then there will be righteous sacrifices, whole burnt offerings to delight you" (51:19).

The message for us is an important one. Only when we are fully committed to the Lord will we be able to fully please him.

bushel A dry measure about ¼ of a U.S. bushel or 8.5 liters. The Greek *modios* ("bushel," KJV; "bowl," NIV) was large enough to cover and hide a burning lamp (Mt. 5:15). *See also* Weights and Measures.

butler (KJV) A high administrative post in ancient empires. The Egyptian official so identified in Gen. 40 was actually Pharaoh's cupbearer (Heb., *shoqeh*, from *shaqeh*, "give to drink"). The importance of the post is shown by the privilege granted the holder to fill the ruler's drinking vessel. Nehemiah later held a similar post in the Persian Empire (Neh. 2:1). *See also* Cupbearer.

butter Thickened milk or cream. Fresh milk did not keep in the heat of the Middle East before the days of refrigeration, but it was easily transformed into nutritious by-products. What the KJV calls "butter" was not churned cream but thickened milk, except possibly in Prov. 30:33. Modern versions typically call it "curds," but it was probably very much like yogurt and soft white [farmer's] cheese.

Ancient Israelite butter churn. The art of hand churning butter has gone relatively unchanged for millennia.

Milk is poured into a churn in which butter will be made, in this temple relief from Tell el-Obeid, near Ur, early third millennium B.C.

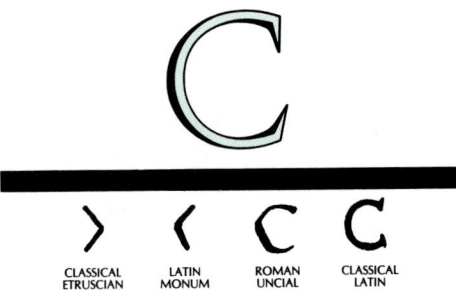

cab A dry measure, slightly more than 1 U.S. quart (1.2 liters). It is mentioned only in 2 Ki. 6:25. *See also* Weights and Measures.

Caesar A title of Roman emperors and, in Scripture, a symbol of secular authority. "Caesar" was derived from the family name of Julius Caesar (101–44 B.C.), who was the uncle of Rome's first emperor, Augustus. The name was perpetuated into the 20th century in the titles of Russia's Czar and Germany's Kaiser.

Jesus once showed his critics a coin and said, "Give to Caesar what is Caesar's, and to God what is God's" (Mt. 22:15-22). His meaning was clearly understood. Earthly rulers have a claim to our taxes and our submission, but God alone deserves our total allegiance.

The NT mentions several Caesars. Augustus Caesar ruled when Christ was born (Lk. 2:1). Tiberius Caesar (A.D. 14–37) held power in Rome during Christ's adult life (Lk. 3:1). The fanatic Caligula, whom Scripture does not mention, succeeded Tiberius and ruled for a few years. His successor, Claudius Caesar (A.D. 41–54), gave an order deporting all Jews from Rome (Acts 18:2), forcing Priscilla and Aquila to move to Corinth. Nero (A.D. 54–68), although unnamed in the Bible, was Caesar when Paul exercised his right as a Roman citizen to appeal to the emperor (Acts 25:1-12). Nero was the first emperor to distinguish between Christians and Jews. Blaming the Christians for a disastrous fire in Rome in A.D. 64, he launched the first official Roman persecution against the church. Tradition holds that both Paul and Peter were executed in Rome near the end of Nero's reign. Vespasian (A.D. 69–79) was in the middle of a war against Judean rebels when his troops proclaimed him the new Caesar in A.D. 69. He left his son Titus to destroy Jerusalem (as Jesus prophesied in Mt. 24) and crush the rebellion. Titus (A.D. 79–81) succeeded his father as emperor and was followed by his brother, Domitian (A.D. 81–96). Domitian launched the second major persecution against the Christians, and was responsible for exiling the apostle John to Patmos, which is the setting for the Book of Revelation. *See also* Appeal to Caesar; Augustus Caesar; Nero.

Caesar's household Most probably a reference to the civil service of the Roman Empire. During Paul's imprisonment in Rome he sent greeting to the Philippians from the saints who "belong to Caesar's household" (Phil. 4:22). Who were these saints? In NT times one's "household" included not only relatives but also servants living with the family. Caesar's household would extend even further to all those in Rome in his service, those civil servants who administered the Empire.

The Early Caesars of Rome

Top: Silver denarius from rule of Julius Caesar, 54–48 B.C.

Middle: Augustus Caesar shown on this coin minted during his rule, 31 B.C.– A.D. 14.

Bottom: Gold aureus from reign of Nero, A.D. 54–68.

	BIBLICAL REFERENCE
Julius Caesar 49-44 BC	
(Second Triumvirate) 44 - 31 BC	
Augustus 31 BC - AD 14	Lk. 2:1
Tiberius AD 14 - 37	Lk. 3:1
Caligula AD 37 - 41	
Claudius AD 41 - 54	Acts 11:28; 17:7; 18:2
Nero AD 54 - 68	Acts 25:11; Phil. 4:22

But Acts 28:16 tells us that, during Paul's first imprisonment in Rome, when Philippians was written, the apostle lived in a rented house "with a soldier to guard him." Some commentators believe that these palace guards, drawn from the emperor's own elite Praetorians, were the saints of "Caesar's household," who had been converted as they guarded the apostle (Phil. 1:13).

Caesarea A city built on the Mediterranean coast of Judea by Herod the Great between 22 and 10 B.C. The beautiful marble city, just 65 road miles from Jerusalem, served as Judea's major seaport and as the Roman administrative center. The Roman governor, customs collector, and provincial finance officer were all headquartered in Caesarea, along with numerous troops. They often called the city Caesarea Maritima ("of the sea") to distinguish it from the inland Caesarea Philippi to the north, and from other cities in the Empire named in honor of Augustus Caesar.

Five major roads led to Caesarea, including the great seacoast trade route between Tyre and Egypt, and the fields on the plains surrounding it were famous for their fertility. Some 50,000 people lived there in the A.D. 40s and 50s. Fresh water was supplied to the city by a six-mile-long tunnel cut through the rock of Mount Carmel to channel water from underground springs. The water was carried another six-and-a-half miles by an aqueduct constructed along the shore.

The most stunning achievement at Caesarea Maritima was the construction of a sheltered harbor. Herod's engineers built a circular breakwater of huge stones, each measuring 50 by 18 by 9 feet (15.5 by 5.5 by 2.75 meters).

The breakwater, some 200 feet (61 meters) wide on the south, was laid in water as much as 140 feet (43 meters) deep. Not only was this man-made harbor as large as the famous Piraeus harbor in ancient Athens, but its engineers also built channels that permitted them to flush out the harbor, thus keeping it from silting up.

The Book of Acts records a number of events occurring in Caesarea. Cornelius, an officer in the cohort of Roman citizens stationed there, became the first Gentile to respond to the Gospel (Acts 10). Philip the evangelist, one of the Jerusalem church's first deacons, later settled in Caesarea (Acts 21:8). And Paul, sent to Caesarea from Jerusalem in protective custody, spent two years imprisoned there before he appealed to Caesar's higher court and was sent on to Rome (Acts 23:23–25:12).

After the NT era, Caesarea remained an important city. A famous rabbinic academy was established there in A.D. 250, and it was home to the church fathers Origen and Eusebius. Caesarea was taken by the Muslims in A.D. 641, and destroyed in A.D. 1291. *See also* Cornelius.

Above: This aqueduct brought water into Caesarea in the days when Philip and Peter preached the Gospel there.

Left: The seat of the Roman Empire's government in Palestine for over 600 years, Caesarea featured a man-made harbor from which Paul sailed for Rome.

183

Caiaphas [KAY-uh-fuhs]. The high priest who presided at Jesus' trial before the Sanhedrin in A.D. 33. **Father-in-law:** Annas. **Scripture:** Jn. 18:13-24; Mt. 26:57-68.

Caiaphas was the son-in-law of Annas, who for many years dominated the priesthood and the Sadducean party. Extrabiblical sources establish this family's greed and its exploitation of the Jewish people. At that time, the high priesthood was no longer hereditary—the eldest son of Aaron's family—but was a Roman political appointment given because of graft. Christ's remarks about "thieves and robbers" who pretended to be shepherds but who stole from God's flock (Jn. 10:8-10) would have been clearly understood by

Steps dating from the first century, which Jesus probably trod, lead up from the Kidron Valley near the traditional site of Caiaphas's house, where Jesus was brought at night for an illegal pretrial hearing.

his hearers—and by the family of Annas. This vindictive and selfish motive for Jesus' capture and trial before Caiaphas's court is reflected in a discussion held after Jesus raised Lazarus. The Jewish leaders expressed fear that, if Jesus sparked a popular uprising, the Romans might come and take away "both our place and our nation." Then Caiaphas remarked how expedient it would be for just one man to die, rather than the whole nation! And from that day the leaders began to plot Jesus' death (Jn. 11:48-53). *See also* Annas; Sadducees; Sanhedrin.

LEARNING FROM CAIAPHAS'S LIFE

The Gospels portray Caiaphas as a manipulative, dishonest man who was willing to break the divine Law he was sworn as high priest to uphold, in order to achieve his own goals. After being taken

184

to Annas for a preliminary examination, Jesus was brought at night to the Sanhedrin, chaired by Caiaphas (Mt. 26:57-68). A night trial was illegal under Jewish law. Even false witnesses were unable to provide the evidence required for the death penalty—but that was the punishment the tribunal had already decided to inflict (26:59). Caiaphas then administered a binding oath and asked Jesus whether he was the Son of God. Jesus responded, "Yes." Hypocritically tearing his clothes to indicate righteous horror at this "outrage," Caiaphas announced that Jesus had spoken blasphemy, a crime that merited death under OT Law. Caiaphas now had a basis for the Sanhedrin's verdict, but the Roman governor still had to confirm the Sanhedrin's sentence.

The Sanhedrin met again in the morning, to confirm the illegal nighttime verdict (Jn. 18:28). Then Christ was taken to Pilate, who alone could order Jesus' death. Rather than stating the charge under which the Sanhedrin had convicted Jesus, the Jewish leaders accused Christ of claiming to be a king, and thus a rival to Caesar.

We may at times be frustrated by people like Caiaphas, who are so hardened that nothing we do can affect them. In such situations, we need to remember Jesus' words to Caiaphas and the Sanhedrin. "In the future you will see the Son of Man sitting at the right hand of the Mighty One and coming on the clouds of heaven" (Mt. 26:64). No matter how much power a person may have in this world, God's day of reckoning will surely come.

An illuminated Bible from the late 12th century pictures Jesus before Caiaphas. Earlier this high priest had unwittingly prophesied that Jesus' death would be "for the people" (Jn. 11:50).

> **Cain** [KAYN; "to acquire" or "metal worker, smith"]. The farmer son of Adam and Eve who killed his brother Abel when his own offering of produce was rejected by God. **Scripture**: Gen. 4.

While the Bible does not explain why Cain's offering was rejected, the fact that God urged Cain to "do what is right" (Gen. 4:7) makes it clear that Cain knew his offering was unacceptable. The best suggestion is that, as Scripture consistently portrays God's call for blood sacrifice, Abel's offering of a lamb was acceptable while Cain's bloodless offering was not (Gen. 4:4). *See also* Atonement; Sacrifices and Offerings.

Yet frustration at God's rejection of his offering hardly explains Cain's murder of Abel. Coming immediately after the story of the Fall of Adam and Eve (Gen. 3), the story of Cain murdering his brother simply demonstrates the devastating impact of sin on humanity, and its corruption of natural affections. *See also* Death.

Cain's subsequent flight and founding of a civilization east of Eden have raised questions. Where did Cain get his wife? The answer is in Gen. 5:4. Adam lived for over 800 years after this event, and "had other sons and daughters." Why did God spare Cain, though he later commanded that murderers be put to death (Gen. 9:6)? Perhaps for the same reason he spared peoples of Abraham's day (Gen. 15:16): Sin had not yet achieved its full expression, and divine judgment was withheld until it might be seen as justified.

Cainite civilization developed beyond a subsistence level, for Cain's descendants developed both music and metallurgy (Gen. 4:19-22). Yet, as the story of Lamech demonstrates (Gen. 4:23,24), Cain's descendants not only mimicked their forefather in doing evil, but also tried to justify sin. Ultimately the sin within humanity was fully expressed, as "every inclination of the thoughts of [the human] heart was only evil all the time" (Gen. 6:5). When that time came, God did judge—with the great Flood. *See also* Flood.

LEARNING FROM CAIN'S LIFE

Cain showed no remorse when God confronted him about Abel's murder—only sorrow at his severe punishment (Gen. 4:13,14). Cain models a worldly sorrow that leads to spiritual death, not a godly sorrow that causes repentance (2 Cor. 7:10).

John says that Cain "belonged to the evil one" (1 Jn. 3:12) and hated his brother because his own acts were evil and his brother's righteous. Jude 11 speaks of the "way of Cain" taken by false teachers, whose own evil leads them to strike out at others who are righteous.

> **Caleb** [KAY-leb; "dog"]. One of two spies who urged Israel to obey God and attack Canaan, about 1440 B.C. He survived the wilderness wanderings and fought valiantly during the conquest of Canaan 40 years later. **Father**: Jephunneh. **Daughter**: Acsah. **Nephew and son-in-law**: Othniel, Israel's first judge. **Scripture**: Num. 14; Josh. 14,15; Jdg. 1:12-20.

The Israelites who experienced God's miraculous deliverance from Egypt proved sullen and unresponsive to God (Ex. 15:22-27; Num. 11,12). This attitude hardened into open rebellion at God's command to enter and take Canaan (Num. 14). Only four leaders—Moses, Aaron, Joshua, and Caleb—expressed their belief that God could help them defeat the powerful peoples of Canaan. When God sent the rebellious generation back into the wilderness, he promised that of the whole assembly only Joshua and Caleb would live to see Israel settled in the Promised Land. *See also* Canaan.

LEARNING FROM CALEB'S LIFE

The Bible says Caleb followed the Lord "wholeheartedly" (Num. 14:24). What qualities did this commitment build into his character? Primarily, Caleb represents courage. While the other spies were terrified at the size and military strength of the Canaanites, Caleb remained confident: ". . . the Lord is with us. Do not be afraid of them" (Num. 14:9). Forty-five years later Caleb asked Joshua for a fortified district that was still occupied by some of its giant inhabitants (Josh. 14:6-15). *See also* Anakites.

Caleb had courage of a special sort. He evaluated the strength of the enemies and

Cain and Abel, by Moutier St. Jean, 12th century A.D., shows the two brothers bringing their sacrifices to the altar. Abel's sacrifice of a lamb was accepted; Cain's sacrifice of fruit was not.

Clay tablet bearing the inscription "Caleb" in proto-Canaanite characters dates from the time of the biblical Caleb or earlier.

185

Though all the spies brought evidence of the Promised Land's fertility, only Caleb and Joshua returned unafraid for Israel to take possession.

fully understood their military superiority. But Caleb was far more impressed with the overarching superiority of God. When we, like Caleb, are fully aware of how great God is, we will gain Caleb's courage to obey, whatever the apparent odds.

calendar A reckoning of the passage of time according to natural cycles. The two natural cycles that dominated the calendars of ancient peoples were the solar year, with its flow of seasons, and the monthly cycles of the moon. Most early societies structured their calendars on the lunar year, assuming 12 months of 29 or 30 days. However, a lunar year contains only 354¼ days. It had to be corrected to coincide with the solar year (365¼ days) to assure that the agricultural seasons would fall in about the same months each year. The Babylonians invented a complicated system for adding an extra, or intercalary, month in seven of every nineteen years. The ancient Hebrews, who also used a lunar calendar, probably followed the Babylonian example and added an extra month of Adar when necessary.

THE HEBREW CALENDAR

Sequence Sacred/Civil		Month (Pre-Exilic)/Post-Exilic	Weather Conditions	Agricultural Conditions	Feasts and Festivals
1	7	**(Abib) Nisan** *March-April*	Spring or "latter" rains; melting mountain snows.	Barley and flax harvests begin.	• *14* Passover • *15–21* Feast of Unleavened Bread • *16* Day of Firstfruits (barley)
2	8	**(Ziv) Iyyar** *April-May*	Dry season begins. Sky usually cloudless throughout the summer.	Barley harvest completed.	
3	9	**Sivan** *May-June*	Hot winds blow from southern deserts.	Wheat harvested; almonds ripen; honey gathered in Jordan Valley.	• *5* Pentecost (Feast of Weeks)
4	10	**Tammuz** *June-July*	Intense heat with heavy morning dews.	Early figs ripen.	
5	11	**Ab** *July-August*	Heat and heavy dews continue.	Grapes, olives, walnuts ripen.	
6	12	**Elul** *Aug.-Sept.*	Hot; lightning storms with little rain.	Figs and olives processed; wine-making begins. Dates, summer figs, pomegranates ripen.	
7	1	**(Ethanim) Tishri** *Sept.-Oct.*	Fall ("former" or "early") rains begin; nights cool.	Soil is plowed and planting begins.	• *1* Rosh Hashanah (Feast of Trumpe • *10* Yom Kippur (Day of Atonemer • *15–21* Sukkoth (Feast of Tabernacle • *22* Solemn Assembly
8	2	**(Bul) Heshvan** *Oct.-Nov.*	Rainy month.	Wheat and barley sown.	
9	3	**Kislev** *Nov.-Dec.*	Cold and stormy, with heavy rainfall.	Flocks moved to the plains.	• *25* Hanukkah (Feast of Dedication)
10	4	**Tebeth** *Dec.-Jan.*	Coldest month of the year; rain continues; hail and snow on highest hills.		
11	5	**Shebat** *Jan.-Feb.*	Gradually warms to most pleasant season of the year.	Almond and peach trees blossom.	
12	6	**Adar** *Feb.-March*	Spring rains begin.	Citrus fruit harvest.	• *14* Feast of Purim

The Jewish calendar had two primary functions. It structured the agricultural year, beginning in the fall with the olive harvest. *See also* Agriculture. But the Hebrew calendar also structured the religious year, which set the time for divinely ordained feasts and festivals. The religious new year began in the spring, with the first day of the month of Abib (Nisan).

A unique feature of the Jewish calendar was its seven-day week, which recalled the six days of creation and the seventh (the Sabbath) on which God rested. Other ancient cultures tended to have three ten-day weeks in each 30-day month with intercalary days every few years to conform the lunar year to the solar year.

calf worship *See* Idol.

call, calling (1) To demand or request one's presence; (2) to name; (3) to appoint to a specific duty; (4) to invite response.

People call to one another (Gen. 19:5) or call on God when in need (Ps. 116:4). But when God does the calling, something more is implied.

THE GOD WHO NAMES

To call someone by name implies some kind of relationship. In Scripture, one's name is a crucial part of one's identity. Thus, when God said to Israel, "I have called you by name; you are mine" (Isa. 43:1, RSV), he expressed deep intimacy.

When God gives a name to someone or something, he continues the creative process. God created by speaking ("Let there be light"—Gen. 1:3; *see* John 1:3), so when "God called the light 'day' and the darkness. . . 'night' " (Gen. 1:5), he was shaping these newly created elements, molding them to his use. Similarly, when God calls a person by a new name, as he did Abram and Sarai (Gen. 17:5,15), he indicates that he is at work within that person, establishing a new identity. *See also* Creation; Name; Word.

THE GOD WHO COMMUNICATES

We call to people to get their attention, to initiate a conversation. So does God. He called to Adam in the Garden of Eden (Gen. 3:9), because Adam and Eve were hiding. He also called to Moses from the burning bush (Ex. 3:4) and to the sleeping Samuel (1 Sam. 3). In each case he had something very important to say. The emphasis is on God's message. The proper response is simply, "Here I am."

THE GOD WHO APPOINTS

Calling also carries the sense of commissioning, appointing someone to a specific task. After God called to Moses and Samuel to get their attention, he gave them jobs to do. Jesus called people to follow him, to be his disciples (Mt. 4:21; Mk. 3:13). Paul identified himself as one "called to be an apostle" (Rom. 1:1; 1 Cor. 1:1).

THE GOD WHO INVITES

In the Gospels, we see a slightly different kind of divine call. Jesus tells of people being called to a feast (Mt. 22:1-14). It is an invitation freely offered. The emphasis has shifted from the message to the response. Amazingly, many refuse to respond to the gracious invitation! The parable, of course, depicts God's invitation to human beings to enter into a relationship with him—an invitation presented in the very person of Jesus Christ. Yet, as John reminds us, Jesus came to his own, "but his own did not receive him. Yet to all who received him, to those who believed in his name, he gave the right to become children of God" (Jn. 1:11,12).

THE GOD WHO SAVES

In the Epistles, the emphasis shifts again. The "called" are those who have responded to the Gospel message. God's "calling" is the entire work of salvation, from the plan he conceived "before the creation of the world" (Eph. 1:4) to the final glorification of his people (Rom. 8:29,30). *See also* Predestine; Salvation.

As we survey the OT and NT, then, we see in this simple word a progressive unveiling of who God is. God names his creation, shaping its identity with his powerful Word. He calls out to his people, revealing himself and appointing some to specific tasks. In Jesus, God invites all people to a joyous feast of fellowship with him. Those who respond enjoy that fellowship now and look forward to even fuller glory to come.

Calvary (KJV) The place outside Jerusalem where Jesus was crucified.

The name Calvary never appears in the Greek NT, but only in the KJV and NKJV of Luke 23:33. It comes from a Latin word for "skull," *calvarium*, which the Latin Vulgate used to translate the Greek *kranion* (which does appear in all four Gospels).

According to Jewish law, public executions had to take place outside the city. Therefore, a conspicuous location outside of Jerusalem was used for that purpose. Appropriately, it became known as "The Skull" (in Aramaic, *Golgotha*), possibly because it resembled a human skull. *See also* Golgotha.

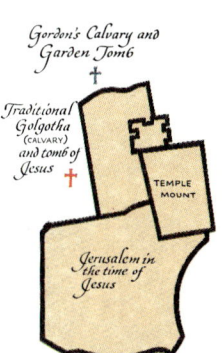

Map shows the traditional site of Calvary, outside of Jerusalem.

187

Above: Relief from Ashurbanipal's palace at Nineveh, about 640 B.C., shows armored Assyrians routing ill-equipped Arabs, atop camels. Through Gideon and his small army God delivered Israel from the camel-riding Midianites (Jdg. 6:5).

Left: Neo-Assyrian cylindrical seal and its impression: horseman pursues camel rider. As shown, the "camel" of the Bible is the one-humped dromedary.

camel The one-humped dromedary, a common beast of burden in the ancient Middle East. Caravans of camels, each burdened with up to 400 pounds and traveling 8 to 10 miles (13 to 16 kilometers) per hour, carried spices and other goods along established trade routes in biblical times. The camel, domesticated as early as 2500 B.C., is mentioned a number of times in the OT. Abraham and Job owned herds of camels, testifying to their great wealth (Gen. 12:16; Job 1:3). Swift riding camels were used in warfare by the Midianites around 1175 B.C. (Jdg. 6:1-6).

These fascinating animals seem uniquely designed for their role as desert beasts of burden. Broad feet carry their weight over desert sands; thick coats serve as insulation. Camels can carry some five gallons (23 liters) of water in each of their three stomachs, and go without drinking for three days. The hump of the camel stores fat which is used when food is scarce. And the camel thrives on the sparse, bitter vegetation found in desert regions.

The camel, which lives for 40 to 50 years, served desert peoples in many ways. Its hair was woven to make tents and rough clothing (Mt. 3:4). Its milk was drunk and used in making cheese. Camels were "unclean" by OT Law and could not be eaten by Israelites, but camels served other nations as food.

One of the most memorable references to camels in the Bible is Jesus' enigmatic comparison of the difficulty of a camel passing through the eye of a needle to the difficulty of a rich man entering heaven (Mt. 19:24). *See also* Eye of a Needle.

Jesus also used a camel image to express his scorn for the Pharisees' legalism (Mt. 23:24). These Pharisees strained their wine to make sure that not even an "unclean" gnat would be eaten. Yet they figuratively swallowed camels, which were also unclean! The expression summarizes Christ's contempt for those who carefully counted the leaves of tiny plants used to flavor food to be sure God received his tithe, but paid no attention to the most important matters with which God's Law deals justice, mercy, and faithfulness toward other human beings.

camphire A KJV term for henna, a shrub whose leaves were ground into an orange cosmetic paste. *See also* Henna.

Canaan, Canaanites Ancient name of the land along the eastern shore of the Mediterranean, stretching from Sidon in the north to Gaza in the south, and reaching inland at least as far as the Jordan Valley (Gen. 10:19). A number of Semitic peoples, including the familiar Hittites and Amorites, are called Canaanites in the OT (Gen. 10:18).

Archaeologists have recovered texts from the ancient Canaanite city-state of Ugarit, discovered in 1928 in modern-day Syria. These documents reveal details of the political and religious life-style of the Canaanites, and fully support the Bible's portrait of these tribes.

The material remains found by archaeologists testify to the high level of sophistication of Canaanite society. By 3000 B.C. they had settled the land of Canaan and as early as 2000 B.C. they had written records, correspondence, and a complex religious mythology in a language that contains over 30 different consonants. Politically the Canaanites were organized into independent city-states, each with its own ruler and aristocracy (Josh. 12). The great majority of people in and around each city were politically powerless farmers and workers.

The religion of the Canaanites focused

Above: Canaanite clay coffins from Deir el-Balah bear distorted human images. The OT forbade the Hebrews to fashion any objects in human form.

Right: Map shows location of major Canaanite cities and tribes identified in the Bible.

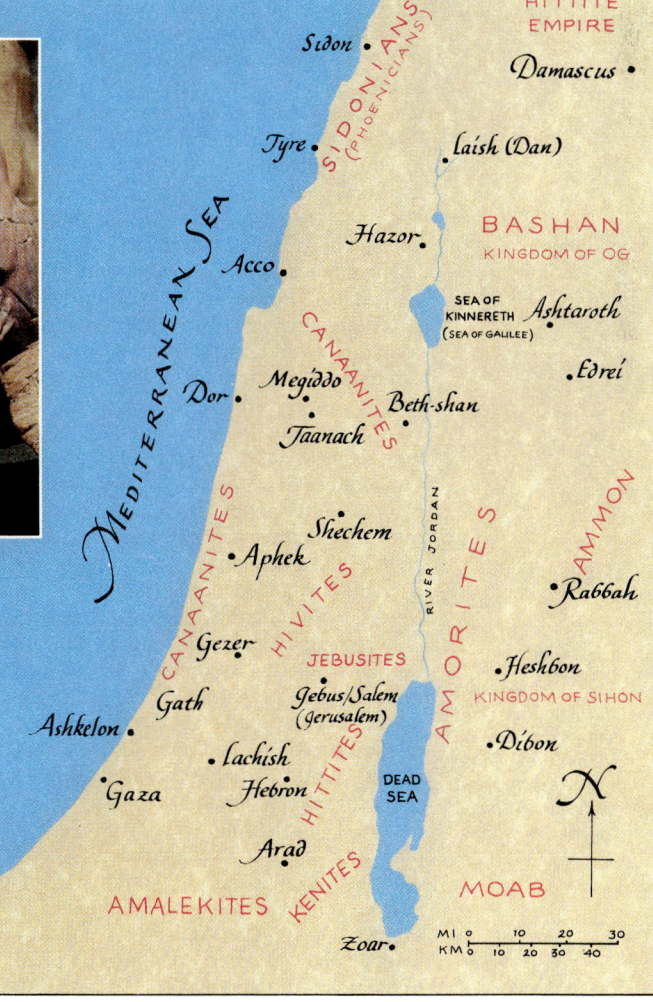

on fertility, and its myths were structured around the agricultural cycle. The gods of the Canaanites were brutal and highly sexed. One myth actually portrays Baal having intercourse with a young cow. Religious rites employed sex between persons not married to each other in order to stimulate the gods and goddesses to grant fertility to the land and to their livestock. Possibly some of the Semites believed that the fertility of the land depended on the deities' sexual activity. The Canaanites even designated homosexual priests and priestesses as their "holy ones." These were employed as cult prostitutes.

The OT shows total revulsion for these and other Canaanite practices. The Law commands, "No Israelite man or woman is to become a shrine prostitute" (Deut. 23:17), and establishes the death penalty for homosexuality (Lev. 20:13) and bestiality (Lev. 20:15).

Deuteronomy describes other practices of the Canaanites and strictly forbids Israel from adopting them. "Let no one be found among you who sacrifices his son or daughter in the fire, who practices divination or sorcery, interprets omens, engages in witchcraft, or casts spells, or who is a medium or spiritist or who consults the dead. Anyone who does these things is detestable to the Lord" (Deut. 18:10,11).

The moral and religious depravity of the Canaanites, portrayed in Scripture and revealed even more clearly in the materials recovered from Ugarit, explains why God commanded Israel to totally destroy these people within the borders of the Promised Land. The war of extermination was a long-delayed divine judgment on the Canaanites (Gen. 15:16). God also wanted to protect his people from degeneration; thus the depraved world view and lifestyle of the Canaanites was to be purged from the earth. God warned Israel through Moses, "Completely destroy them. . . . Otherwise they will teach you to follow all the detestable things they do in worshiping their gods" (Deut. 20:17,18).

The contrast between the moral and religious vision of the Canaanites and that of the Scripture could hardly be more pronounced. The issue at the time of the conquest, and through much of OT history, was whose view of morality, and whose concept of God, would survive. Seen in this perspective, the command to exterminate the Canaanites was not only justified, but necessary for the good of all humanity in the coming ages. *See also* Baal; War.

This incense burner from Taanach, decorated with cult figures, was used by Canaanites, whose rites opposed Hebrew worship at nearly every point.

candle (KJV) A small bowl filled with olive oil (Gk., *lampas*) which served as a lamp in Bible times. *See also* Lamp.

The seven-branched menorah *of Jewish tradition is translated "candlestick" in the KJV and "lampstand" in modern versions.*

candlestick (KJV) The golden lampstand (*menorah*) within Israel's tabernacle, and later in the Jerusalem Temple. *See also* Lampstand.

cankerworm (KJV) Most likely the larva (caterpillar) stage of the locust. Some modern versions render the Hebrew word (*yeleq*) as "young locust."

Swarms of locusts often devastated the ancient Middle East and Africa. The crushing weight of this ancient plague is reflected in Joel's description: "What the locust swarm has left the great locusts have eaten; what the great locusts have left the young locusts have eaten; what the young locusts have left other locusts have eaten" (Joel 1:4).

canon A collection of writings considered authoritative. The English term comes from the Greek *kanon*, which originally referred to a builder's rule or level. In the Christian church, it refers to the body of writings regarded as Holy Scripture.

Most of the OT canon (the Law and Prophets) was established long before the time of Christ. (The Writings section was fixed perhaps only after the fall of Jerusalem in A.D. 70.) The Scriptures were clearly distinguished from the many other Hebrew religious writings that existed then. Jesus and the early church accepted the OT canon as God's Word. *See also* Apocrypha.

But in Judaism an extensive tradition had also developed around the Scriptures. This "oral law," or *Mishnah*, preserved the interpretations of generations of rabbis, and was viewed by many Jews as an authority equal to that of the written Word. Indeed, the Pharisees held that the oral traditions of Judaism had been given by Moses at the same time he gave the written Law! Yet Jesus solidly rejected this view (Mt. 15:3; *compare* Mk. 7:6-13). The written Word of God alone was to be faith's rule and guide, not any human interpretation of that Word.

As the books that make up our NT were written, some were acknowledged to be Scripture almost immediately. For instance, 2 Peter mentions Paul, "who wrote you with the wisdom that God gave him," and notes that some try to distort Paul's writings "as they do the other Scriptures" (2 Pet. 3:15,16).

Individual churches throughout the Roman world developed their own lists of writings approved for use in public worship. These lists were essentially the same. The four Gospels and Paul's Epistles were already being placed in collections of Christian writings in the first half of the second century. Church fathers from the second century quoted these and other NT works as authoritative. *See also* Chronology of the Bible.

Still, it took the heretic Marcion to push the churches into developing a "canon" of Scripture. This second-century Gnostic devised his own canon, containing certain letters of Paul and a severely edited version of Luke. Church leaders like Irenaeus (A.D. 130–202) and Tertullian (A.D. 160–220) rallied to defend the proper Scriptures, and suddenly churches were paying more attention to what belonged and what did not.

Sometime before A.D. 180 Melito of Sardis wrote of the "books of the old covenant" and the "books of the new covenant," a clear indication that the churches were placing their own Christian writings on a par with the OT canon. In 1740 an Italian scholar published a Latin list of NT books he discovered from the church at Rome, now called the Muratorian Fragment, which dates to about A.D. 190 and lists its approved canon. It lists nearly all of the present NT books but mentions only two Epistles of John, an Apocalypse of Peter and no Epistles of Peter. Hebrews is also omitted.

Over the next two centuries, the process continued. Several church fathers list the books considered canonical in their churches in their times. Both Origen (about A.D. 185–255) and Eusebius (about A.D. 260–340) surveyed the churches to see

what books were recognized. There was general agreement, but James, Jude, 2 Peter, 2 and 3 John, Revelation and Hebrews were in one way or another questioned. But, through time, the Holy Spirit guided the Christians to sift through these works and select the authoritative Scriptures. The first official determination of a church-wide canon was made in the eastern church in A.D. 367 with the 39th Paschal Letter of Athanasius. The western church approved the same canon in A.D. 397 at the Council of Carthage, establishing our present NT.

Capernaum An important first-century city at the northern end of the Sea of Galilee. When Jesus began his public ministry, he moved from Nazareth to Capernaum. A major city of the area, Capernaum contained a permanent tax office (Mk. 2:14), was home to a royal official (Jn. 4:46), and was garrisoned by a detachment of Roman soldiers. The centurion of this detachment was commended by Jesus for his great faith in the true God (Mt. 8:5-13), which he had earlier demonstrated by building the Jewish population a synagogue (Lk. 7:5).

Small boats have plied the rich fishing waters south of Capernaum since before the time of Christ.

191

Capernaum was a center of the Galilean fishing industry and the home of many of Jesus' fishermen disciples. Jesus worked many miracles there (Mt. 8:14,15; Mk. 2:1-12; Lk. 7:1-10; Jn. 4:46-54) and delivered some of his most significant sermons nearby (Jn. 6). But Capernaum was also a proud city, most of whose people refused to respond to Christ's ministry. Jesus pronounced a curse on this city for its unbelief (Lk. 10:15).

Remains of the house in Capernaum traditionally identified as Peter's (Mt. 8:14).

Recent excavations have uncovered a first-century synagogue under these fourth-century ruins, suggesting this may be the site of Jesus' preaching and miracles. The original synagogue may have been financed by the centurion of Lk. 7:5.

Archaeologists have been exploring the site of ancient Capernaum (Tell Hum) for over 100 years now. A fourth-century limestone synagogue was an early find, but beneath it a 1981 excavation discovered a first-century synagogue of basalt—possibly the one the centurion built (Lk. 7:5) and in which Jesus preached.

Also, a fourth-century house-church appears to incorporate the remains of a first-century house, which some have identified as Peter's house (Mt. 8:14).

captain Officer in charge of small units of troops; in KJV, founder or originator.

From the time of the Exodus, the Israelites identified subgroups within their army as "thousands" and "hundreds" (Num. 31:48,52). A captain (Heb., *sar*) would command such a unit. Thousands and hundreds seem to have continued as the basis of Israel's military organization (2 Sam. 18:1), though there are later references to groups of 50 (2 Ki. 1:10). Modern versions sometimes use "commander" to translate *sar*.

In Heb. 2:10, the KJV calls Jesus the "captain of [our] salvation." The Greek word is *archēgos*, which modern versions translate as "author" or "pioneer." Greeks would use *archēgos* for the founder of a city or school. In this context it identifies Jesus as the one whose experience of death opened the way to salvation for his human brothers.

captivity Being seized and held against one's will; specifically in Scripture, the exile of the Jewish people from their homeland.

As the Israelites prepared to enter the Promised Land, God warned them against straying from his commands. In Deut. 28:15-68, he predicted the drought, plagues, and military defeats that would result from disobedience. Worst of all, "You will be uprooted from the land you are entering to possess" (v. 63).

The prophecy was sadly fulfilled in the history of both the Northern Kingdom (Israel) and the Southern Kingdom (Judah).

ISRAEL'S CAPTIVITY

The Northern Kingdom strayed into idolatry and corruption and faced pressure from the mighty Assyrian Empire for some 150 years, culminating in Israel's final defeat in 722 B.C. The Assyrians, knowing that people torn from their homelands and local gods were less likely to revolt, employed a policy of mass deportation. About 730 B.C. Tiglath-Pileser (745–727) deported the Transjordan tribes and the people of Galilee (1 Chr. 5:26; 2 Ki. 15:29). Later, Shalmaneser V (727–722 B.C.) invaded Israel and besieged Samaria, the capital city (2 Ki. 17:3-5), but died before taking the city. Finally, Sargon II (722–705 B.C.) destroyed Samaria and took the rest of Israel's citizens captive. His annals report that he carried away over 27,000 Israelites. His successor, Sennacherib (705–681 B.C.), later threatened Judah, and claimed to have captured more than 200,000 (2 Ki. 18:13). The Bible reports no return of the thousands who were deported by the Assyrians. *See also* Assyria; Israel.

192

JUDAH'S CAPTIVITY

The Southern Kingdom miraculously weathered the Assyrian threat and continued to exist as a nation until its final destruction by the Babylonians over a century later. Jews were deported to Babylon in three separate waves—in 605 B.C., 597 B.C., and 586 B.C. with the final fall of Jerusalem (2 Ki. 24:10-16; 25:8-12; 2 Chr. 36:20; Jer. 52:28-30).

Several books of the OT (Jeremiah, Ezekiel, Habukkuk) deal with the years just before and during the Babylonian captivity; others tell about the subsequent resettlement of Judah many decades later (Ezra, Nehemiah).

BABYLONIAN CAPTIVITY

It would be wrong to think of the Babylonian captivity as either imprisonment or as a holocaust. It was in fact resettlement, and the captives most likely had the status in Babylon of *mushkenu,* a free person of the lower classes.

Many of the Jews were settled near the city of Babylon by the "river" Kebar, a major irrigation canal in a district named Tel Aviv. Modern Israel's port city Tel Aviv commemorates that name.

Many captives worked on the king's projects. Recovered Babylonian records indicate that some became successful businessmen. Biblical allusions suggest that many exiles owned their homes and had land on which to raise crops (Jer. 29:4-7; Ezek. 8:1; 12:1-7). The Jewish community also maintained its own elders, priests, and prophets, and apparently enjoyed a measure of self-government.

Despite the relatively comfortable conditions in Babylon, the captivity was still painful to the godly Jew, who remembered Jerusalem and yearned for the land God had promised to Abraham's children. That pain is powerfully expressed in the mournful dirges of the Book of Lamentations:

My eyes will flow unceasingly,
  without relief,
until the Lord looks down
  from heaven and sees.
What I see brings grief to my soul
  because of all the women of my city.
                    (Lam. 3:49-51)

THEOLOGICAL FERMENT

The crisis years that led up to the Babylonian captivity, and the captivity itself, were times of theological ferment. Many in Judah had formerly relied on the mere existence of God's Temple in Jerusalem to protect them from the Babylonian enemy. Surely God would not forsake the city that contained the Temple which Solomon had built for him (2 Chr. 6:40-42; Jer. 7:2-11)! Ezekiel, ministering in Babylon, was given a vision from the Lord in which he was shown the sins of the people of Jerusalem

Mournful Judeans deported into exile from Lachish are depicted on a stone relief found in Sennacherib's palace in Nineveh. Assyrian records say 200,150 Jews were taken in the invasion about 700 B.C.

Drawing from a palace relief shows the torture of bound captives in time of Sennacherib. The Assyrians often brutalized captives before enslaving or killing them.

and watched as the glory of God departed from the Temple (Ezek. 8–11). No protection for God's people could be found in a building emptied of God's sanctifying presence.

The destruction of the city not only shattered this misplaced confidence but also raised basic questions about Judah's relationship with God. Did deportation from the Promised Land mean that God had abandoned his sinning people forever? Jeremiah addressed the question of God's intentions. The captivity was a divine judgment. Yet God remained committed to his people and to his covenant promises. Jeremiah predicted that the captivity would last for only 70 years (Jer. 25), and God said through his prophet,

"I have loved you with an everlasting love;
I have drawn you with loving-kindness.
I will build you up again
and you will be rebuilt, O Virgin Israel."
(Jer. 31:3,4)

This bas relief shows captive Judeans mounting carts for their trip into exile. The Assyrians deported defeated foes from their homeland to ensure against uprisings.

Jeremiah then expressed perhaps the key promise of the OT. True, Israel and Judah had been unfaithful to God, and the captivity was a just judgment. Yet in some future day God intended to make a new covenant with the house of Israel. The new covenant is described as "not like"

the Mosaic covenant, in which God's Law was engraved on stone. In the future God would engrave his law on the very hearts of his people. Then "they will all know me, from the least of them to the greatest" (Jer. 31:33,34). *See also* Covenant.

The captivity did underline the failure of Israel and Judah to be responsive to their God. But the captivity in no way meant that God would break his commitments to Abraham and abandon Judah.

The story is told of Rabbi Akiba, who laughed happily when he saw a fox emerge from the ruins of Jerusalem's devastated Second Temple (the temple built after the return from Babylon, and after being gloriously enlarged and rebuilt by Herod, devastated by the Romans in A.D. 70). Akiba's companions, who wept at the sight, asked how he could possibly laugh. He replied by quoting a prophecy found in Micah 3:12, "Zion will be plowed like a field," and then a prophecy of Zechariah, written while the Second Temple still stood, "Once again men and women of ripe old age will sit in the streets of Jerusalem" (Zech. 8:4). Rabbi Akiba said that, as long as the earlier prophecy of devastation had not been fulfilled, he might have doubted Zechariah's prophecy of blessing. But since the earlier prophecy had been fulfilled so literally, he could be quite certain that the prophecy of blessing would be fulfilled just as literally.

This surely is one of the major messages of the captivity. Deportation to Babylon was evidence that God remained faithful to what he had promised. The God who in Moses' time promised that sinning Israel would be deported also promised she would be regathered. And this same God promised that one day the old covenant, marred by human failure, would be replaced by a covenant that is gloriously new.

BENEFITS OF THE CAPTIVITY
The prophets understood the captivity as divine discipline. Like all God's disciplinary acts, the captivity had a number of positive outcomes. *See also* Discipline.

Cut off from the Temple, the focus of Jewish faith shifted from religious ritual to a study of the Word of God. This deep concern for the Word of God has characterized Judaism through the centuries.

In Babylon a class of men called scribes emerged, who dedicated themselves to study, live, and teach the Scriptures. The practice of meeting each Sabbath to study, pray, and praise was also initiated in Babylon. Thus the captivity experience led to development of the synagogue, which has been vital in the history of Judaism and of Christianity. *See also* Scribe; Synagogue.

And, after the captivity, the Hebrew people never again were attracted to that idolatry which had plagued their forefathers from the Israelites' first entry into the Promised Land to the day when Jerusalem fell.

Carbuncle

carbuncle (KSV, RSV) A green gemstone. The KJV and RSV use this name for the *bareqet,* one of the gems in the first row of the high priest's breastpiece (Ex. 28:17). Other versions translate it as beryl (NIV), green felspar (NEB), or emerald (NASB). The Hebrew root suggests a "shining stone," but no one can be sure just which gem is indicated.

It is probably best to take the phrase *eben eqdah,* translated "carbuncle" in the KJV of Isa. 54:12, as the NIV does: "I will make your battlements of rubies, your gates of *sparkling jewels*, and all your walls of precious stones."

carnal (KJV) Fleshly, bodily, or material. Paul regularly contrasts the flesh (*sarx*) and fleshly (*sarkikos*) pursuits with things of the Spirit. "Carnal" appears in the KJV and other translations for *sarkikos*. Modern versions often use "unspiritual," "worldly," or say that individuals are behaving "like mere men." Twice the NT has *ta sarkika* with the sense of "material things" (Rom. 15:27; 1 Cor. 9:11).

The distinction between "carnal" and "spiritual" in the NT is a significant theological concept. Carnal people are dominated by their own desires. They cut themselves off from the guidance of God's Spirit and thus become the willing captives of thoughts, desires, and values that are contrary to God's nature and will.

In Romans 7:4–8:11, Paul argues that the person who acts in his or her own strength falls short of pleasing God because of the corrupting power of the carnal

(fleshly) nature. Only by relying on the Holy Spirit for divine enablement are we lifted beyond ourselves and empowered to live a fresh, new kind of life that is in fullest harmony with God. *See also* Flesh; Holy Spirit; Spirituality.

carpenter A skilled craftsman who works with wood or metal. This occupation holds special interest for Christians because the Bible identifies Jesus as a carpenter (Mk. 6:3).

The main OT term for carpenter is *harash*, which indicates any craftsman working with wood or metal. At times the word occurs with *'es* ("wood, tree"), to denote a person specially skilled in woodworking. About 975 B.C. Israel had to import carpenters from Tyre (2 Sam. 5:11). Nearly four centuries later Jewish craftsmen were taken captive to Babylon (Jer. 29:2). In his derisive portrayal of idolaters (Isa. 44:9-20), Isaiah describes how the craftsmen of his time (700 B.C.) worked with metal and wood.

This sparkling green jewel was third in the top row of Aaron's high priestly breastpiece.

Ivory relief of a carpenter at work, from Roman Alexandria, third or fourth century A.D.

What did these woodworkers make in biblical times? Wood was generally scarce in Palestine, and most homes were constructed of stone, but roof beams and often doors were made of wood. The many fishing boats that crossed the Sea of Galilee were wooden, and fashioning them called for special skills. Probably Joseph and Jesus, working in Nazareth some miles from the water, made farm tools like plows and sickles, and furnishings for the homes of their neighbors: chairs, tables, and bedframes.

Above: These crude copper tools with wood handles date to the 18th century B.C. The tool box has owner's name inscribed at left, list of tools at right.

Top: Scene from an Egyptian tomb shows (from left): carpenters tapping chisel with a mallet; sawing with a copper saw; completing a couch frame; operating a bow drill.

Jesus' neighbors found it difficult to grasp the fact that the carpenter who had made yokes for their animals was in fact the Messiah. It is easy to lose sight of God in the commonplace. We too may fail to realize that our Lord most often reveals himself in the simple things of daily life.

cart A wheeled vehicle. In Scripture, the context determines whether the word indicates a heavier, four-wheeled wagon or the more common two-wheeled cart.

Reliefs make it possible to trace the development of these vehicles in biblical lands, from the unwieldy, solid-wheels of ancient Egypt and Mesopotamia, to the spoke-wheeled carts shown bearing loot and captive women from Lachish to Assyria. In Israel both carts and wagons were pulled by oxen or cows (1 Sam. 6:7; 2 Sam. 6:3). Carts were also driven over sheaves of wheat or barley to thresh out the grain (Amos 2:13; Isa. 28:27,28).

The only other wheeled vehicle men-

tioned in the Bible is the chariot. *See also* Chariot.

cassia A cinnamon-like spice (Heb., *qiddah*) made from the bark of the cassia tree.

caterpillar (KJV, RSV) A form in the life cycle of the locust, which terrified the ancient world by its capacity to destroy all vegetation. Some modern versions translate the Hebrew word, *hasil,* as "locust."

cattle Bovines, such as bulls, cows, and oxen. In the KJV, "cattle" may include other large domesticated animals, such as donkeys, goats, and sheep.

Cattle were a form of wealth in Abraham's time (Gen. 12:16). Throughout the biblical era they were valued not only for their meat and the milk, cheese, and leather they produced, but also as work animals. Cattle were used to pull carts, for plowing, and at harvest time for treading on sheaves of wheat and barley to separate the kernels of grain. Young cattle were also offered in sacrifice. The "fatted calf," a delicacy of the wealthy, was eaten at festival times by the common people.

Cattle need better grazing than was

available in much of Palestine. Through most of the biblical era large herds of cattle were limited to the lands across the Jordan and to the hill country of upper Galilee.

Mosaic Law shows great sensitivity to these animals, which contributed so much to the well-being of God's people. Like their owners, cattle rested on the Sabbath (Ex. 23:12), though it was permissible for a cattle owner to water his herd. Oxen were not to be muzzled when treading out grain (Deut. 25:4). Nothing comparing to this concern for animal welfare existed in most early civilizations, nor did it characterize our own society until the 19th century. *See also* Bull; Golden Calf; Ox.

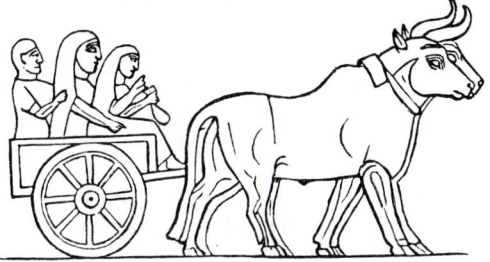

Oxen draw captive women in cart; from palace relief in Nimrud, Assyria, 745–727 B.C.

cauls (KJV) An archaic term for the fat of the inner organs of sacrificial animals.

cave A hollow opening in the earth, usually in a hillside.

The geological make-up of Palestine—its porous sandstone, limestone, and chalk—has caused the formation of many natural caves, some of them very large. Thus caves played an important role in the daily life and political intrigue of the Israelites.

Caves, either natural or hewn out of the rock, served as burial chambers (Jn. 11:38). Abraham had to haggle with Ephron the Hittite to buy a proper burial cave for Sarah (Gen. 23). Since caves were also used as stables, it is possible that Jesus was born in a cave.

The OT often refers to caves as hiding places (1 Ki. 18:13; Jdg. 6:2; 2 Sam. 17:9). Some of these were quite large: The cave of Adullam (1 Sam. 22:1) served as headquarters for David's band of 400 men. When David hid out from the jealous Saul in the caves of En Gedi, his men could hide "far back" in one as he crept up on an unknowing Saul (1 Sam. 24:1-4). This was the same area where, a millennium later, scribes would hide the Scriptures from the invading Romans (A.D. 69). These "Dead Sea Scrolls," discovered in the 20th century, are the oldest copies of the Hebrew Scriptures we have, preserving most of Isaiah's prophecy and parts of other OT books.

It was Isaiah who predicted a terrible day of God's judgment, when "men will flee to caves in the rocks and to holes in the ground from dread of the Lord and the splendor of his majesty" (Isa. 2:19). In the NT, Rev. 6:15-17 picks up the theme, showing humanity hiding in caves, calling on mountains to fall on them and to hide them from the wrath of the returning Christ.

cedar Large evergreen tree of Lebanon, prized for its use in the construction of public buildings; generally, any evergreen, including the juniper bush.

Cedars once covered Lebanon's western slopes, 4,500–5,700 feet above sea level. When Solomon contracted with the local king to use those cedars to construct the Temple, his palace, and other buildings,

Tomb scene (about 1420 B.C.) shows cattle of an Egyptian police captain, so-called "Nebamun," being bound and branded as he, seated right, supervises.

The righteous will flourish like a palm tree,
    they will grow like a cedar of Lebanon;
planted in the house of the Lord,
    they will flourish in the courts of our God.
                                    (Ps. 92:12,13)

Not every reference to "cedar" in the Bible is to the cedars of Lebanon. The Hebrew *'erez*, rendered "cedar" in all English versions, is most likely a generic word for the pine family. "Cedars" that grow beside waters (Num. 24:6) and the "cedar wood" of Lev. 14:4, found on the hot, low Sinai peninsula, are probably the scented juniper, which was more a shrub or bush than a tree.

celebration Participation in a joyous festivity; particularly (in Scripture) the religious festivals of Israel. Although weddings and other occasions were marked by joyous parties, the translators of our English versions link "celebrate" to Israel's three great religious festivals: Passover and Unleavened Bread; Weeks (Harvest, or Firstfruits); and Booths (Tabernacles). This is appropriate, for in Israel God was recognized as the source of all good gifts which enrich human life. The religious festivals which remembered his goodness and expressed his people's praise were to be celebrations in the fullest possible sense. *See also* Feasts, Festivals, and Fasts; Passover; Tabernacles, Feast of; Weeks, Feast of.

celibacy The state of being unmarried, or abstaining from sexual relations. The Hebrews viewed marriage as the normal state of human beings. In Israel men and women expected to marry, and hoped to have many children. The NT introduces celibacy as a valid option for the Christian.

Jesus spoke of some who "renounced marriage because of the kingdom of heaven" (Mt. 19:12). Paul develops this theme in 1 Cor. 7, where the apostle notes

Above: Syrian woodcutters felling cedars of Lebanon, from a wall relief in the Great Hall of Pharaoh Sethos I (about 1300 B.C.). Inset: The stately cedar of Lebanon, whose wood was prized for its beauty, fragrance, and durability, was used in building Solomon's and Ezra's temples.

he employed 10,000 lumberjacks at a time to cut them down (1 Ki. 5:13,14). Five hundred years later, when the Temple was being rebuilt, the builders sent to Lebanon for more cedars (Ezra 3:7). Many noted buildings of the ancient world, such as the temple of Diana at Ephesus, used the famous cedars of Lebanon in their construction.

The wood was prized for various reasons. The trunk is tall, with the typical tree growing to a height of 70 to 80 feet (21 to 24 meters) and a girth of 30 to 40 feet (9 to 12 meters). The fragrance of the Lebanon cedar's wood is attractive to human beings, but repels insects. The warm red wood is solid, unmarred by knots, and is very slow to decay. These qualities made it ideal for the construction of important buildings and also ships.

Poetic references to Lebanon's cedars emphasize the strength and beauty of this most prized of ancient trees. Ps. 92 says,

the advantages of the single state. A married person naturally (and rightly) is concerned with the affairs of this world and with pleasing his or her spouse. An unmarried person is free to be totally devoted to the Lord. Also the married "face many troubles in this life" (v. 28) that single people avoid.

Celibacy was Paul's personal choice, yet the apostle was careful not to suggest that those who marry are less spiritual. Both marriage and singleness are matters of gift: God grants marriage to some and singleness to others.

Despite his personal preference, Paul upholds the right of the apostles to "take a believing wife along" on their travels (1 Cor. 9:5). Paul calls forbidding marriage a doctrine "taught by demons," passed on by "hypocritical liars" who only masquerade as Christian teachers. Marriage was "created to be received with thanksgiving by those who believe and who know the truth" (1 Tim. 4:1-5). The NT thus urges believers to consider the celibate life as an option, but it guards against the view that celibacy is "more spiritual" than marriage.

censer A container in which incense was burned. According to Ex. 27:3, bronze censers ("firepans," NIV) were among the holy instruments used in worshiping the Lord. Hot coals were placed in the censer, and sweet-smelling incense was added. Most visualize the censer (Heb., *mahetah*) as a shallow pan, but some see it as a small, portable shovel-like tool. Many hand-held censers have been found by archaeologists in Middle Eastern cult centers.

On two occasions, the rite of incense-offering involved God's dramatic judgment on rebellious Israelites. Fire consumed Nadab and Abihu when they offered "unauthorized fire before the Lord" (Lev. 10), and Korah and his followers were swallowed up by the earth shortly after God rejected their incense

offering (Num. 16). *See also* Abihu; Incense; Korah.

census Counting the population and appraising their property, generally for tax purposes. In biblical times, population counts were taken to establish the tax base and number of men of military age. Moses numbered Israel to collect an "atonement tax" used to support ministry in the tabernacle (Ex. 30:11-16). Around 1445 B.C. a military census of Israelites at Sinai registered 603,550 men (Num. 1:46). Forty years later, the new generation mobilized 601,730 (Num. 26). This latter census also was used as a basis for dividing Canaan among Israel's tribes, clans, and families.

At some unspecified time during the latter part of David's rule (1010–970 B.C.), he ordered a count of men of military age. This census displeased God and brought divine punishment in the form of a devastating plague (2 Sam. 24; 1 Chr. 21). The account in these two passages has raised several questions. Why was this census sinful? The text records that David's army commanders opposed his plan as showing a reliance on mere numbers rather than on the grace and power of God.

Who was responsible for David's decision? In 2 Sam. 24, it says the Lord incited David; 1 Chr. 21 says Satan incited him. Yet David accepted responsibility for his decision. The solution lies in the Hebrew concept of causation. Each person in a moral sequence is responsible for his or her own acts. While an individual may be influenced by outside forces, he remains personally responsible for his choices. No one forced David to take the census. Da-

This censer, found near Masada, is typical of the hand-held devices used to carry hot coals on which incense burned during religious ceremonies.

Famous "Goose Census" from Theban tomb painting, about 1400 B.C. Livestock as well as people were valued assets. Ancient rulers insisted both be numbered regularly.

vid was free to choose, and chose to do wrong.

Why the discrepancy in the results of David's census [2 Sam. 24 lists 1,300,000 men; 1 Chr. 21 lists 1,100,000]? Various explanations have been offered. The text of one passage may have been corrupted in copying. The number in 2 Samuel may not include Levi and Benjamin, which Joab would not number (1 Chr. 21:6). Or the smaller number may omit Israel's standing army. Whatever the solution, this "error" in the Bible is more apparent than real.

The Book of Ezra reports a census of those who returned to Judah from Babylon in 539 B.C. The purpose was to make sure that all who returned really were members of God's covenant people, and to authenticate the lineage of those who claimed to be priests.

The NT mentions two censuses (Lk. 2:1-5; Acts 5:37). These were taken to establish property values so that Rome could assess taxes on its provinces. The date of the census associated with Jesus' birth is uncertain, in part because it probably was not completed the year it was initiated. We do know that the Roman system called for a count of Empire residents every 14 years. The method is illustrated in this notice, published in A.D. 104 by the chief prefect of Egypt, Gaius Vibius. It reads in part:

Because of the approaching census it is necessary for all of those residing for any cause away from their own districts to prepare to return at once to their own governments, in order that they may complete the family administration of the enrollment.

How striking that a policy established by the Roman government was instrumental in assuring that Jesus was born, as prophesied in Mic. 5:2, in the city of Bethlehem. For Bethlehem was the home district of David's family, and both Joseph and Mary were of his line.

The census mentioned in Acts 5:37 took place in A.D. 6, and set off a revolt led by Judas of Galilee. It was brutally put down. The Zealot party, which called for armed rebellion against Rome, probably developed out of this revolt. Later Simon the Zealot became one of Jesus' disciples (Mt. 10:4).

centurion A Roman officer commanding 100 soldiers. The Roman army was organized into legions, each with a full-strength complement of 6,000 men. Each legion was made up of six cohorts, with 60 "centuries" of 100 men, each led by a centurion.

Centurions were the working officers on whom the effectiveness of the Roman army depended. Intelligent, well paid, and highly motivated, they typically stayed in the army beyond the normal 20-year enlistment. On discharge a centurion received a large bonus. Many became influential citizens of the cities in which they retired.

The NT displays a strikingly positive attitude toward these military men. Jesus was deeply impressed by the faith of a centurion posted in Capernaum. His piety was recognized by the Jewish community, which urged Jesus to help him, saying that the centurion "loves our nation and has built our synagogue" (Lk. 7:1-10).

The centurion in charge of Jesus' execution reacted very differently than did the

Bronze Roman statuette of a legionary or praetorian guard, second century A.D. A centurion would command a unit of 100 such legionaries. For a centurion's armor, see Armor.

chief priests and other onlookers, who mocked Christ on the cross (Mk. 15:31, 32). Seeing how Jesus died, the centurion said, "Surely this man was the Son of God!" (Mk. 15:39).

The first Gentile to hear and respond to the Gospel was another centurion, Cornelius (Acts 10). Acts describes him as a man who "gave generously to those in need and prayed to God regularly." The reference to Cornelius and his family as "devout and God-fearing" (v. 2) indicates a serious interest in the Jewish faith and a commitment to keep parts of the Law. *See also* God-fearing.

Another centurion, Julius, was detailed to escort Paul from Caesarea to Rome. When the ship was about to be wrecked, Julius refused to let his soldiers kill the prisoners because he "wanted to spare Paul's life" (Acts 27:43).

chaff (1) Hulls and dust-like particles blown away when grain is threshed; (2) stubble left in the field after grain is harvested; (3) the straw left after threshing. In biblical times wheat and barley were "winnowed" at harvest. Sheaves were spread on an open hillside. The area was called a "threshing floor." The sheaves were then trampled, often by oxen, to break up the stalks. The residue was tossed in the air. The heavy kernels of grain fell to the ground, while lighter pieces of straw were blown to one side. The chaff (*mos*), made up of hulls and tiny dust-like particles, was blown completely away.

In the OT, "chaff" represents the wicked, whose acts merit divine judgment. The first Psalm contrasts the long-term security of the righteous ("a tree planted by streams of water") with the instability of the wicked: "They are like chaff that the wind blows away" (Ps. 1:4).

In the Middle East the process of separating wheat from chaff has not changed for thousands of years. When tossed in the air, the light chaff blows away while the kernels fall to the ground.

Other Hebrew words translated "chaff" actually mean stubble left in a field after the grain has been harvested.

In the NT, John the Baptist described a threshing-floor scene in which the coming Messiah would gather the wheat into the barn and burn up the chaff "with unquenchable fire" (Mt. 3:12). In this case the chaff (Gk., *achyron*) is the straw which falls alongside the good grain. Those without moral substance will face fiery judgment when God gathers up his own.

chaff

chain Joined links of metal. In Scripture, chains represent both luxury and deprivation, privilege and punishment. Then, as now, gold chains were worn as jewelry, around the neck, wrist, or ankle (Isa. 3:20). For Joseph and Daniel, gold chains served as symbols of high office (Gen. 41:42; Dan. 5:16). A gold chain was also part of the high priest's attire (Ex. 28:14).

Yet chains also indicate imprisonment or captivity (2 Ki. 23:33; Jer. 40:1,4). Peter and Paul were both chained while imprisoned (Acts 12:6; 26:29). The Romans often

Detail of relief from palace of Ashurnasirpal II, 883–859 B.C., shows defenders on wall attempting to snag a battering ram with chains. In Scripture, chains symbolize bondage as well as finery and the mark of high office.

chained a prisoner to a guard or jailer. Thus Paul, writing from prison, regularly referred to his chains, not just as physical weights, but as a metaphor for his imprisonment. He hailed Onesiphorus, who "was not ashamed of my chains" (2 Tim. 1:16), and said his chains had encouraged other believers to speak out (Phil. 1:14).

One fascinating use of chains is suggested in Ezek. 7:23,24: "Prepare chains [Heb., *rattoq*], because the land is full of bloodshed and the city is full of violence." The Lord threatens to bring "the most wicked of the nations" to attack his people. Ancient reliefs show defenders of a walled city using heavy chains in an attempt to unseat a battering ram. Through Ezekiel, God calls Israel to forge such chains for defense of the homeland: a defense that is futile because Israel's sins cry out for judgment.

Chaldeans (1) A tribe from southern Babylon; (2) a term for all Babylonians; (3) an educated class of advisers and administrators in Babylonian and later empires of the Middle East. The Chaldeans were a fierce tribal people who originally lived in a small district in southern Babylonia, along the Persian Gulf in what is now part of Iraq. Through the first quarter of the first millennium B.C. they waged persistent guerrilla warfare within the dominant Assyrian Empire.

Glazed tile head of a Chaldean warrior, second millennium B.C.

Around 720 B.C. a Chaldean ruler gained control of the city of Babylon. Isaiah thus uses "Chaldeans" as a synonym for "Babylonians" (Isa. 23:13; 43:14). The Assyrians put down this rebellion, but a century later another Chaldean, Nabopolassar, took the throne of Babylon and launched the Neo-Babylonian Empire. The sudden rise of this new empire may be reflected in God's revelation to Habakkuk:

Look at the nations and watch—
  and be utterly amazed.
For I am going to do something in your days
  that you would not believe,
  even if you were told.
I am raising up the Chaldeans,
  that ruthless and impetuous people,
who sweep across the whole earth. . . .

(Hab. 1:5,6)

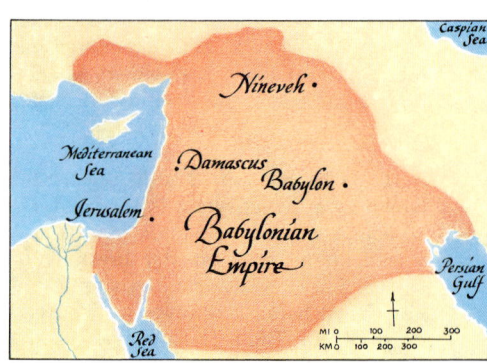

Area of Chaldea, in lower Mesopotamia. Abraham came from "Ur of the Chaldeans."

By 605 B.C. the Assyrian armies were crushed, and the Assyrian Empire was supplanted by the Babylonian. In some English versions the more familiar "Babylonian" is used where the original reads *kasdim* ("Chaldean"). *See also* Babylon.

In Daniel we find the ethnic use of "Chaldean" in two passages: 1:4 and probably 5:30. But the predominant use of *kasdim* in Daniel is to identify a class of astrologer and astronomer priests. Long before the development of accurate measuring instruments, these "Chaldeans" of Babylon had calculated the length of the solar year as 365 days, six hours and 41 seconds—an error of less than 30 minutes!

Daniel himself was counted among the Chaldeans, for he had been trained with other promising Hebrew youths to serve as administrators of the Babylonians' vast empire. Many think that the Magi (the "wise men" of Mt. 2) who came from the East to see the Christ child, were members of this highly educated class.

While KJV and RSV retain "Chaldean" in Daniel, the NIV replaces it with "astrologer" (Dan. 2:4,5,10; 4:7).

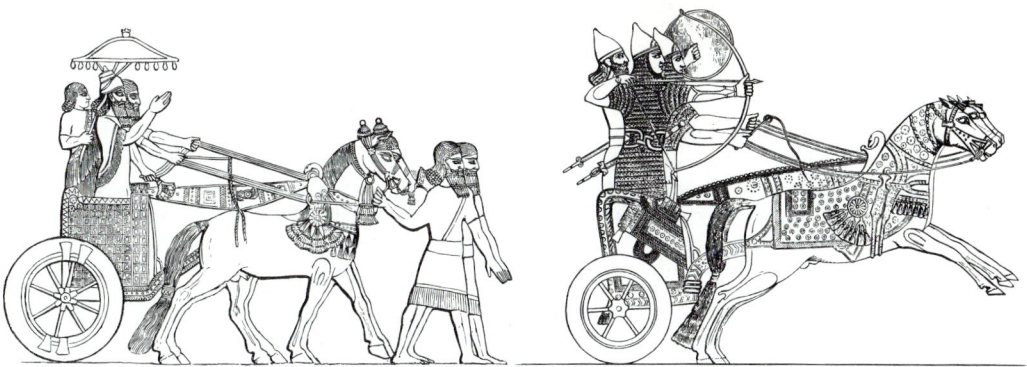

chamberlain (KJV, RSV) An official in a royal court.

The English word denotes someone in charge of the king's chamber, and thus the KJV uses it for the seven officials who oversaw Xerxes' (Ahasuerus's) harem (Esth. 1:10). Since such attendants were often castrated, the word "eunuch" is used elsewhere. Both words translate the Hebrew *saris,* which has a broader meaning as well, including any trusted official in a royal court. So, Potiphar is described as a *saris* ("officer," KJV) of the Pharaoh (Gen. 39:1), as are the butler and baker (Gen. 40:2). Various "eunuchs" or "officers" appear in OT accounts of royal retinues.

In the NT, the KJV calls both Blastus (Acts 12:20) and Erastus (Rom. 16:23) chamberlains. Blastus was literally, in the Greek, "in charge of the bedroom" of King Herod. Erastus served as *oikonomos* in Rome, literally a "household manager," but here an official status as "the city's director of public works" (NIV). *See also* Eunuch.

charge A formal accusation of a criminal offense, or the threat of legal proceedings.

The NT often uses technical first-century legal terms. Usually, "charge" denotes an indictment (*katēgoria*), a formal accusation of a criminal offense. Such charges were brought against Jesus and Paul at their trials. Jesus said that the Law of Moses itself indicts Israel (Jn. 5:45). Paul notes that the conscience of pagans charges them with sin (Rom. 2:15).

A different kind of charge appears in Jude 9 and 2 Pet. 2:11. There, God's angels do not presume to make "slanderous accusations" against the devil or other celestial beings (in contrast to false teachers, who make all sorts of blasphemous charges). The legal term used here for "accusation" refers to charges that have been proven—and their judgment handed down. Only God has the right to pass final judgment.

On the other hand, *enkaleō* as a law term implies a preliminary hearing, a threat of further legal proceedings. Paul uses this word to assure us that no one can even threaten to bring charges against those whom God has chosen and justified (Rom. 8:33). God has already pronounced us innocent. *See also* Accuse.

chariot A two-wheeled horse-drawn vehicle. Light chariots, usually drawn by two horses, transformed warfare in the ancient world. Chariots were first used as mobile firing platforms for archers; early war chariots carried a driver and archer.

The first chariots mentioned in the Bible were ceremonial vehicles used by Egyp-

tian royalty and high officials (Gen. 41:43). Egyptian chariots of painted wood and leather were very light and could be easily carried on a man's shoulders. When the Pharaoh of the Exodus pursued the Israelites, God destroyed Egypt's chariot army in the Red Sea (Ex. 14).

The Hittites developed heavier, paneled chariots which carried a driver, a warrior who fought with spear and sword, and a shield-bearer. Canaanite chariots were apparently of this type, with iron-studded

Above left: Tiglath-Pileser II, king of Assyria, 745–727 B.C., in his chariot in this line drawing of a wall relief discovered at Calah (Nimrud). Above right: Assyrian war chariot from an earlier period. Its wheels had only six spokes in contrast to the eight-spoked ones common later.

The light and speedy Egyptian war chariot carried two men. Six hundred of Pharaoh's chariots were lost in the surging Red Sea in an attempt to recapture the fleeing Israelites (Ex. 14).

203

sides. War chariots were in use in Canaan before the Israelites arrived, and even after the Israelites had conquered most of the land, Canaanite "iron chariots" limited Israelite control to mountainous sections of Palestine (Jdg. 1:19).

Solomon built a large chariot army, which he was never forced to use in warfare. In the era of the divided kingdom, Israel maintained a chariot army whenever possible. Assyrian records say that King Ahab of Israel contributed 2,000 chariots and 10,000 men to the coalition that battled the Assyrians at Qarqar in 853 B.C.

The vital role of chariots in ancient warfare clarifies the grief of King Jehoash at the death of Elisha: "The chariots and horsemen of Israel!" the king lamented (2 Ki. 13:14). That is, this prophet was a national treasure, a spiritual defense more valuable to Israel than its cavalry and chariot forces. The lament reflects an insight expressed by Moses centuries before. Moses said, "When you go to war against your enemies and see horses and chariots and an army greater than yours, do not be afraid of them, because the Lord your God, who brought you up out of Egypt, will be with you" (Deut. 20:1). The security of God's people rests not on military might but on relationship with the Lord.

The phrase "chariots of the sun" in 2 Ki. 23:11 (KJV) is a reference to items associated with a pagan sun-worship cult which Josiah purged from Judah during his revival, about 620 B.C.

The only NT references to chariots occur in Revelation and in Acts 8, where Philip stepped into the chariot of the Ethiopian eunuch to explain the Scriptures. The chariot indicates the Ethiopian's rank, a high position in the court of Queen Candace (Acts 8:27). In Rev. 9:9, the awesome locusts sound like the thundering of many chariots. Later, merchants mourn the fall of Babylon because there is no one to buy their chariots ("carriages," NIV) or other wares (Rev. 18:13).

charisma A gift graciously given by God, usually involving some special divine enablement for service. This Greek word is the source of "charismatic," often used today of those who speak in tongues. Charismatic persons and churches tend to emphasize the work of the Holy Spirit and the more spectacular spiritual gifts mentioned in the Bible: tongues, healing, miracles, etc. *See also* Spiritual Gifts; Tongues, Gift of.

charity (KJV) *See* Love.

charm (1) A magical formula; (2) an amulet engraved with a magical formula. The Hebrew *lahash* means "secret speech," and indicates a magical formula spoken to gain some end or to ward off evil. A charm was usually chanted, and its efficacy supposedly depended on using the correct words and also on how they were spoken. "Secret speech" might also be engraved on an object, such as an amulet, which was then called a charm (*compare* Isa. 3:20).

Ezekiel decries the practice of women sewing "magic charms" (Heb., *kesatot*) on their wrists (Ezek. 13:18,20). Scripture condemns all attempts to influence events by an appeal to any supernatural power other than God. *See also* Magic.

Bottom right: Stone sheep amulets from Iraq (before 2900 B.C.) were worn about the neck. Similar amulets had raised designs on the bottom and were used as personal seals.
Below: Charms or amulets (19th–18th centuries B.C.) were relied on for protection and good luck. The Israelites were forbidden to practice such superstitions.

Broken eighth-century ivory panel from Nimrud, Assyria, bears sphinxes carved in Phoenician style. Some identify these figures with the biblical cherubim, which also have a guardian's role. The line drawing (left) represents two cherubim on the ark of the covenant.

chasten, chastise (KJV, RSV) To discipline, correct. While "chastise" implies punishment in English, the Hebrew word (*yasar*) has to do with "correction intended to contribute to one's growth and learning." Thus Proverbs says, "My son, despise not the chastening of the Lord, neither be weary of his correction: For whom the Lord loveth he correcteth; even as a father the son in whom he delighteth" (Prov. 3:11,12, KJV). *See also* Discipline; Punish.

cheese Pressed, dried curds of milk. In Bible times cheese was made by pressing curds of milk into balls (*see* Job 10:10). Milk would not keep in the heat of Palestine, so most milk was used to make cheese or yogurt. Although not often mentioned in the Bible, cheese was an important food in a land where meat was seldom eaten. In the first century, one district in Jerusalem was known as "Cheesemakers' [Tyropoeon] Valley." *See also* Butter.

cherub, cherubim (KJV, RSV) A specific class of angelic beings. First mentioned as guardians of the way to the tree of life (Gen. 3:24), cherubim are later associated with the throne of God (Ezek. 10). Golden statues of cherubim adorned the cover of the holy ark, their wings overarching it and meeting (Ex. 25:17-22; 1 Ki. 6:23-28). Figures of cherubim were embroidered in curtains within the tabernacle (Ex. 26:31), and were engraved with trees and flowers on the gold-covered panels within Solomon's Temple (1 Ki. 6:29).

Ezekiel saw these guardians of the divine throne in two visions (Ezek. 1,10). He clearly struggled to describe these strange creatures, noting four wings, four faces, and mixed human and animal characteristics.

Archaeologists have suggested that carved figures of winged lions with human faces, which guarded important buildings in Mesopotamia, may have served as models for representations of cherubim in Israel's tabernacle and Temple. *See also* Angels; Ark of the Covenant.

chicken A domesticated farm bird. When Jesus wept over Jerusalem, he said he longed to gather her children "as a hen gathers her chicks under her wings" (Lk. 13:34). Not long afterward, a rooster's crow signaled Peter's betrayal of Jesus (Mt. 26:34,74).

Those are practically our only biblical glimpses of this bird species. Proverbs does compare a king to a "strutting rooster" (Prov. 30:31), and the "choice fowl" provided daily for Solomon's table (1 Ki. 4:23) may have included chickens—but they were probably geese.

Roman bronze cock evokes the image of the rooster in Caiaphas's courtyard, whose crowing reminded Peter that Jesus had predicted his denial.

205

Roman child's marble sarcophagus shows children playing. In Jesus' teaching, children represent trust and dependence (Mt. 18:2-4).

Roman limestone relief shows two midwives attending a woman giving birth. Jeremiah frequently uses the sharp pains of childbirth ("labor," NIV) to suggest the terror that will grip the world as God's judgment draws near.

chief seats Places of honor in a synagogue or at a banquet. The "chief seats" in a synagogue faced the congregation and were placed in front of the "ark," an alcove or shrine which contained the sacred scrolls of Scripture (*see* Synagogue). Chief seats at a banquet were often raised on a dais, and placed close to the host.

Jesus rebuked the religious leaders of his day for craving places of honor at religious and social events. Their attitude was in sharp contrast with that of Jesus, who told his disciples, "Whoever wants to be first must be your slave—just as the Son of Man did not come to be served, but to serve, and to give his life as a ransom for many" (Mt. 20:27,28).

childbirth A woman's act of bringing forth a baby. Jewish women passionately desired to bear children, even though it was dangerous and painful. Of the 80 times the OT mentions childbirth (Heb., *yalad*), in 60 it speaks of the pain. Several different Hebrew words for mental anguish and physical agony are found in these contexts. The prophets refer to intense birthpains to convey the seriousness of the coming divine judgment (Jer. 6:24; Mic. 4:9,10; *see also* Mt. 24:8).

The NT picks up the image of childbirth, but applies it differently. Paul compares his concern for the Galatians to the pangs of childbirth "until Christ is formed in you" (Gal. 4:19). In Romans he describes the creation itself "groaning as in the pains of childbirth," waiting in "eager expectation" for Christ's return and for the full revelation of all that it means for us to be sons of God (Rom. 8:18-25).

The Romans passage adds a positive note about the pain of childbirth, a note which infuses the Bible's view of suffering. Childbirth's pain may be intense, but it results in the emergence of new life. A mother-to-be suffers her pain in hope, knowing the pain will pass and she will soon joyfully hold an infant in her arms. Christians too suffer in hope. We believe that God in his goodness will redeem our pain, ultimately using it for his glory and our good. *See also* Timothy, First and Second Epistles to.

child, children (1) Offspring; (2) immature persons.

Psalm 128 beautifully expresses the Hebrew attitude toward children:

Your wife will be like a fruitful vine
  within your house;
your sons will be like olive shoots
  around your table.
Thus is the man blessed
  who fears the Lord.

May the Lord bless you from Zion
  all the days of your life;
may you see the prosperity of Jerusalem,
  and may you live to see your children's
  children.

(Ps. 128:3-6)

Interest in children is reflected in the Hebrew language itself, which has a number of words for boys and girls that, like our "toddler" or "preschooler," define stages of development from infancy. The Israelites saw children as a gift from God (Ps. 127:3,4), and childlessness caused intense grief (1 Sam. 1:1-16). The family's firstborn son belonged to God and was "redeemed" by payment of a special Temple fee (Ex. 13:1,2,11-13). Some parents dedicated their children to God even before birth (Jdg. 13:3-5; 1 Sam. 1:11).

A child's progress toward maturity was marked by religious rites and celebrations. Sons were circumcised the eighth day as a sign of their solidarity with God's covenant people (Gen. 17:12-14). Weaning was celebrated with a feast (Gen. 21:8). The faithful Jew, whose goal was to see his children grow in godliness, took personal responsibility for the nurture of children. The bar mitzvah—a ceremony in which a son becomes a "son of the Law" or an individual fully responsible to keep God's Law—remains a high point of religious education in modern Judaism. *See also* Discipline.

The Greek language also has quite specific terms for speaking of children. These often have special theological significance in the NT. The *nepios* was a very young child, weak and totally dependent. Paul says in 1 Cor. 3:1-4 that the Corinthians, divided and quarreling over favorite leaders, are "mere infants in Christ." Their behavior marked them off as spiritual weaklings.

Paidion is a child past infancy but not older than seven. This is the term Jesus used when he taught that only when adults change and become like little children can they enter God's Kingdom (Mt. 18:2-4). In context, Christ's later statement that the Kingdom belongs to little children (19:14) is a clear rejection of adults' self-effort and attempts to earn their own salvation. Even the most zealous of the

Pharisees did not imagine that a young child's relationship to God depended on his or her efforts to keep God's Law.

Pais is a term for children between the ages of 7 and 14. *Teknon*, another theologically important word in the NT, expresses a relationship within a family. Believers are no longer simply God's creations but, through Christ, have become members of God's family. John uses *teknon* to express his wonder at the Christian's privileged position: "How great is the love the Father has lavished on us, that we should be called children [*tekna*] of God! . . . Dear friends, now we are children of God, and what we will be has not yet been made known. But we know that when he appears, we shall be like him, for we shall see him as he is" (1 Jn. 3:1,2). *See also* Children of God; Fatherhood of God.

A related word, *teknion*, is a warm and affectionate "dear child" or "little child." Jesus used this word with his disciples at

Christ Blessing Children *by Nicholas Maes.* "Jesus said, 'Let the little children come to me . . . for the kingdom of heaven belongs to such as these' " (Mt. 19:14).

207

the Last Supper (Jn. 13:33). Paul (Gal. 4:19) and John (1 Jn. 2:1) also referred to their converts in this way.

children of God (1) Human beings as God's creations; (2) those who have become members of God's family by faith in Jesus. In modern thought all human beings are children of God. In one sense this view is accurate. Paul, arguing in Athens that God should be recognized as Creator, says, "We are his [God's] offspring" (Acts 17:28,29).

But the phrase "children of God" also has a more limited application. It describes persons who, although once alienated from God by sin, have through Christ become members of the family of the redeemed. The biblical concept of "children" (Gk., *tekna*) or "sons" (Gk., *huioi*) of God generally indicates this deeply personal relationship with God.

In the powerful imagery of the NT, Christians are strangers to God who have now been adopted as family members (Eph. 1:5) or who have been spiritually reborn (Jn. 3:1-18). Those who believe in Christ have been born again and "given God's own indestructible heredity" (1 Pet. 1:23, PHILLIPS). *See also* Adoption; Born Again; Child.

This special use of "children of God" to designate believers in no way implies a lack of concern for the rest of humanity, nor does it deny the infinite worth and value of every person. Instead "children of God" is a technical theological phrase, a joyous affirmation of the unique personal relationship with God which Christians enjoy through Jesus Christ. *See also* Fatherhood of God; Son.

children of Israel The physical descendants (Gk., *huioi*) of Israel (Jacob), from whose twelve sons the Hebrew people came. It is usually used in the sense of "Israelite," and some modern versions translate the phrase in this way. *See also* Israel, Tribes of.

child sacrifice The practice of killing one's children as an offering to a pagan god. The nations that inhabited Palestine prior to the Israelites practiced child sacrifice in the worship of their pagan deities. These rituals continued even after Israel conquered the land—both in neighboring nations and at times in Israel itself.

For instance, King Mesha of Moab sacrificed his oldest son when his city was under siege by an Israelite army (2 Ki. 3:27). A text recovered from Ugarit con-

tains the ritual prayer to be used on such an occasion. It reads in part:

O Baal:
Drive away the force from our gates,
The aggressor from our walls.
We shall sacrifice a bull, O Baal,
A votive-pledge we shall fulfill:
A firstborn, Baal, we shall sacrifice,
A child we shall fulfill.

This terrible rite is depicted in various pictorial records of ancient warfare, like one showing Ramses II's attack on Ashkelon.

Some Baal cults encouraged the sacrifice of children in normal times. When the OT mentions sacrificing children to Molech, it refers to the pagan practice of burning young children alive (Lev. 20:2-5; 2 Ki. 23:10; Jer. 32:35). In Jeremiah's day the people of Judah had established a *topheth* —a high place where young children were sacrificed to pagan deities and their ashes buried in jars (Jer. 7:31,32; 19:11-15). *See also* High Place; Topheth.

The OT condemns human sacrifice. God's command to Israel to exterminate the Canaanites was intended to punish such sins and to wipe out the practice.

Chisleu (KJV) *See* Calendar; Kislev.

choir *See* Music and Musical Instruments.

chosen people The Jews. The term "chosen people" reflects the sovereign choice of Israel by God. Moses says in Deut. 7:6-8, "The Lord your God has chosen you out of all the peoples on the face of the earth to be his people, his treasured possession. The Lord did not . . . choose you because you were more numerous than other peoples, for you were the fewest of all peoples. But it was because the Lord loved you and kept the oath he swore to your forefathers. . . ."

Israel was to be a worshiping and serving community (Deut. 18:5; Isa. 41:8,9). God intended to bless all people through Israel, not to bless Israel alone (Gen. 12:3). And Israel has blessed mankind. The Hebrew people have been the agents through whom God gave the OT Scriptures and the channel through which he revealed himself in Jesus.

God's choice of Israel implies responsibility as well as privilege. A people called by God's name must reflect his character. The chosen people were "the children of the Lord your God" and thus were to be holy, displaying a resemblance to their Lord (Deut. 14:1,2).

Votive stele (third century B.C.) from topheth at Carthage shows a priest carrying a child about to be sacrificed. 'Topheth' means roughly "fire-place," a place set apart for these horrible rites.

Funerary inscription of Livia Primitiva (Rome, third century A.D.) affirms her Christian faith with symbols representing Christ as the Good Shepherd, a fisher of men, and an "anchor for the soul" (Heb. 6:19).

Thus the idea of a chosen people emphasizes (1) God's freedom to select, and (2) the responsibility of those whom God chooses to the rest of humanity and to the Lord. These same emphases are preserved in the NT, and expressed in the doctrine of election. *See also* Elect.

Christ The Anointed One, or Messiah. Christ (*christos*) is the Greek translation of the Hebrew *meshiah* ("Messiah"). It is not a name but a description, "anointed one." In biblical thought, anointing is intimately associated with divine commission to a royal, priestly, or prophetic ministry. Thus to acknowledge Jesus as "the Christ" was to affirm that the carpenter from Nazareth was the Messiah foreseen by OT prophets —the person whom God would commission to deliver his people. *See also* Anoint.

A number of incidents indicate that the Jewish people were well aware of God's promises and looked forward to Messiah's coming. Even a Samaritan woman with whom Jesus talked said, " 'I know that Messiah' (called Christ) 'is coming' " (Jn. 4:25). The high priest showed that the Jews viewed the coming deliverer as God himself when he asked Jesus, "Are you the Christ, the Son of the Blessed One?" (Mk. 14:61). *See also* Jesus Christ; Messiah.

Christian A person who has a personal faith relationship with Jesus Christ. Believers were first called Christians in Antioch (Acts 11:26) and the word appears only two more times in the NT (Acts 26:28;

1 Pet. 4:16). The Greek word, *christianos*, means "belonging to Christ."

Today "Christian" is often used in a secular way to distinguish Westerners from those born in cultures dominated by other religions. But the origin and meaning of the term limits its most appropriate use to those who have a personal faith in Christ, and who thus truly belong to him.

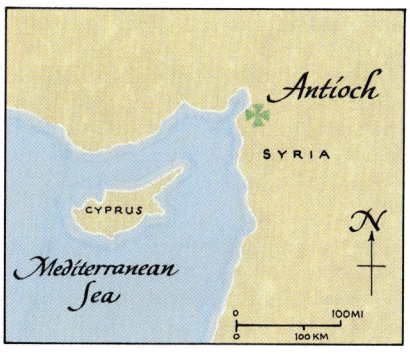

Map locates Syrian Antioch, where "the disciples were first called Christians" (Acts 11:26).

Christmas The traditional celebration of Christ's birth (Christ + Mass). There is no evidence in Scripture that the early church celebrated the birth of Christ. In fact, early traditions differ about the time of year in which Jesus was born. Some suggest mid-April; others early January. Observance of December 25th became common by the A.D. 330s, when this date was chosen to replace a Roman celebration commemorating the sun's climb following the winter solstice.

Assyrian soldiers sack the Judean city of Lachish in the invasion described in 2 Chr. 29–32. These vivid images of soldiers carrying curved swords, spears, shields, a throne, and incense burners, decorated the palace walls of the conqueror Sennacherib.

Chronicles, First and Second Books of

The Chronicles are a religious history of the Jewish people, from creation to the return of the exiles from Babylon in 539 B.C. In the Hebrew Bible the two books form a single unit. (They were divided in the Septuagint, the Greek OT of the second century B.C.) The history of Judah is continued for another hundred years by the books of Ezra-Nehemiah, which also are treated as a single unit in the Hebrew OT.

Jewish tradition identifies Ezra as the author of all four books. Contemporary scholars agree, and believe these books were written by or put into their final form by Ezra about 440 B.C. *See also* Ezra.

BACKGROUND

The few thousand Jews who returned to Judah from Babylon were motivated by their faith. They were determined to rebuild God's Temple and eager to live again in the land the Lord promised to Abraham's descendants. But once in Judah, the struggle to make a living gradually drained their dedication. The Jewish community soon ignored Sabbath law and violated the prohibition against marrying pagans (Ezra 9; Neh. 13:23-28). The well-to-do oppressed the poor (Neh. 5). The tithes intended to support those who served the Temple were withheld, so that priests and Levites were forced to leave Jerusalem and work their fields.

Against this background, a loss of religious focus, the chronicler reviews the history of Israel, to demonstrate that only a people who worship and serve the Lord can expect to experience his blessing.

HISTORICAL SIGNIFICANCE

In the tiny land of Judah, a speck in the vast Persian Empire, God's chosen people seemed insignificant and powerless. The Chronicles were written to help this people recall its roots and to regain perspective. The writer carefully organized his material to achieve this end.

• *1 Chronicles 1–9.* A genealogical record traces Judah's roots from Adam to the restoration. History demonstrates that God has worked with the chosen people from the beginning.

• *1 Chronicles 10–29.* A review of David's reign emphasizes his religious commitment and military successes. History demonstrates that godliness is the key to national success.

• *2 Chronicles 1–9.* A review of Solomon's reign emphasizes the building and dedication of the Temple. History demonstrates that worship of God brings national prosperity.

• *2 Chronicles 10–36.* A review of the reigns of Judah's kings shows that godly kings, who led Judah to worship and obey God, were blessed with supernatural aid and success.

In the context of its own time, the Book(s) of Chronicles both pointed out the rewards of dedication to God, and called the people of Judah to recommit themselves.

SPECIAL FEATURES

The emphases found in Chronicles help us grasp the writer's purposes. These emphases include: establishing Jerusalem as Judah's religious center (*see* 1 Chr. 11, 13–17,21–27); building the Temple and worshiping God there (1 Chr. 22–26; 2 Chr. 2–7); and revivals led by godly kings, which feature keeping Passover and other required festivals in Jerusalem (2 Chr. 14–20,23,24,29–32,34,35).

There are other notable characteristics. The author quotes a wide variety of sources for the information in his history. Some 40 passages are parallel to those found in the Samuels and Kings. In addition, the author refers to several sets of records of royal reigns (1 Chr. 27:24; 2 Chr. 16:11) and to a number of collected sayings of various prophets (2 Chr. 9:29; 12:15). Thus Chronicles is a carefully researched, although selective, history.

1 CHRONICLES: A READING AND STUDY GUIDE

Chapter	Content Summary	Related Articles
	Genealogies	
1	The line of Judah is traced from Adam to Israel.	Genealogy
2	The family line of Judah is traced onward from the time of the patriarchs to that of David.	Israel Judah
3	The family line of Judah is traced through David and Solomon.	David Solomon
4–8	The family line of the each tribe is traced, with Judah again emphasized.	
9	The family lines of those who returned to Judah from Babylon are traced.	Captivity Remnant
	The Reign of David: 1010–970 B.C.	
10	King Saul dies because he was "unfaithful to the Lord," making way for David to become king.	King Saul
11,12	David, supported by a corps of "mighty men," becomes king and takes Jerusalem, making it his capital city.	Mighty Men Jerusalem
13	David fails in his first attempt to move the ark of God to Jerusalem.	Ark of the Covenant
14	David does "as God commanded him" and so wins military victories over the Philistines.	Philistines
15	David succeeds in moving the ark of God to Jerusalem, thus making his city the religious as well as political center of his kingdom.	
16	David praises God, and begins to organize divine worship.	Praise Levites
17	David is told not to build a temple, but is promised that his family will continue forever as Israel's royal line.	Covenant Messiah
18–20	David's victories over foreign enemies are summarized.	
21	David unwisely counts Israel's fighting men. The place where David builds an altar of sacrifice becomes the site of the future Temple of God.	Census Sacrifices and Offerings
22	David stockpiles materials and money to be used in building a temple, and urges Solomon to complete the work.	Temple, Jerusalem
23–26	David completes the organization of the Levites and priests to supervise work on the Temple and to lead worship there.	Music Priest
27	David's organization of the army and the kingdom is reviewed.	
28	David urges his people and Solomon to complete the Temple, and delivers plans he has drawn up.	
29	David solicits gifts from the people to finance the Temple. Leaders and people respond gladly, and David publicly praises God.	Give

2 CHRONICLES: A READING AND STUDY GUIDE

Chapter	Content Summary	Related Articles
	The Reign of Solomon: 970–930 B.C.	
1	Solomon becomes king at David's death. He asks God for wisdom to lead his people.	Solomon Wisdom
2	Solomon contracts with Hiram of Tyre for lumber and skilled workmen to supervise construction of the Temple.	Carpenter Cedar
3,4	The Temple and its furnishings are carefully described.	Holy of Holies Cherub; Altar
5–7	Solomon brings the ark of God to the Temple, and offers his great prayer of dedication. God's presence enters the Temple, and God appears to Solomon to emphasize the need for faithfulness.	Ark of the Covenant Prayer; Obey Glory
8,9	Solomon's achievements and the splendor of his kingdom are summarized.	Wealth
	Reigns of Selected Kings of Judah	
10–12	Solomon's son Rehoboam (931–913 B.C.) loses the allegiance of the ten northern tribes. They set up a rival kingdom called "Israel" under Jeroboam I.	Rehoboam Jeroboam I Israel
13	Abijah (913–910 B.C.) trusts God and defeats an army sent against Judah by Jeroboam.	Abijah
14–16	Asa (910–869 B.C.) purges the land of idols and recalls Judah to wholehearted worship.	Asa Idol
17–20	Jehoshaphat (872–848 B.C.) also urges faithfulness to God. Through trust in God he defeats powerful enemies and brings prosperity to Judah.	Jehoshaphat Ahab
21	Jehoram (848–841 B.C.) refuses to follow God's Law, and as a result his armies are defeated and he himself dies of an agonizing disease.	Sickness
22	Ahaziah (841 B.C.) and Queen Athaliah (841–835 B.C.) worship Baal. Each comes to a bad end.	Ahaziah Athaliah

Interestingly, the writer fails to mention the sins of David and Solomon. This may be because the data is irrelevant to his purpose. Some have suggested that the omissions support the view that Chronicles is God's commentary on the Samuels and Kings. In a divine commentary it would be appropriate to omit such sins, for when God forgives he forgets: "I will forgive their wickedness and will remember their sins no more" (Jer. 31:34).

MASTERY KEYS

Read Chronicles against the background of Judah's humble situation. Note the emphasis on the Temple and on worship. How stunning it must have been for Judah's struggling few to realize that, despite appearances, they truly were the chosen of God, whose first calling was to faithfully worship and serve the Lord. As you read, note common characteristics of the revivals reported in 2 Chronicles. *See also* Revival.

About 1730 a Dutch scholar constructed a model of Solomon's Temple, from which this facade has been preserved. Although 2 Chronicles records many details of the Temple, the exact design is unknown.

2 CHRONICLES: A READING AND STUDY GUIDE *CONT.*

Chapter	Content Summary	Related Articles
23,24	Joash (835–796 B.C.) is crowned king at seven. He repairs the Temple, and follows the Lord as long as his adviser, the priest Jehoiada, lives. Later Joash abandons God, and Judah is devastated by enemies.	Joash
25	Amaziah (796–767 B.C.) follows God half-heartedly but obeys before a critical battle, thus winning the day.	Amaziah
26	Uzziah (790–739 B.C.) follows the Lord until success makes him proud. When he becomes arrogant, Uzziah is stricken with leprosy.	Leprosy
27	Jotham (751–736 B.C.) "grew powerful because he walked steadfastly before the Lord his God."	
28	Ahaz (742–728–725 B.C.) worships Baal and even sacrifices his children in the fire. As a result he is defeated and his reign troubled.	Ahaz Baal
29–32	Hezekiah (728–725–697 B.C.) leads his people back to God. He restores Temple worship and leads a Passover festival. When Judah is invaded by Assyria, Hezekiah relies on God, who miraculously destroys the Assyrian forces.	Hezekiah Assyria
33	Manasseh (697–642 B.C.) proves to be the most evil of Judah's kings. But when taken prisoner by Assyria he turns to God, who brings him back to Judah. The repentant king urges all to serve the Lord. His son Amon does evil. He is assassinated after a two-year reign.	Manasseh Repent
34,35	Josiah (640–609 B.C.) institutes many reforms. He purges the land of idolatry, restores the Temple, finds and publishes the lost book of God's Law, and celebrates Passover.	Josiah
36	Several wicked kings are mentioned briefly. The book concludes with an accusation. God's people have mocked his messengers, despised his words, and scoffed at his prophets. Exile to Babylon is just punishment for a disobedient people.	Captivity Babylon Discipline

Chronology of the Bible

OLD TESTAMENT

Accurate dating of OT events is extremely difficult. Efforts at dating are complicated by a lack of cross-references to established dates in secular history prior to the battle of Qarqar in 853 B.C. But chronological problems are not peculiar to Hebrew history. There are similar problems in establishing dates for any ancient civilization. Even the dates of well-known Egyptian dynasties, documented by many existing artifacts and written records, remain uncertain.

Yet there are special complications related to dating biblical events. For instance, (1) the Bible sometimes gives the number of years between significant events—but some of these may involve rounding off odd numbers. Repetition of the number 40 suggests that 40 may be used figuratively, to represent completeness. If so, it is unlikely that Saul, David, and Solomon each reigned exactly 40 years. (2) The era of the judges cannot be calculated by adding up the years of rule given there. Many judges ruled only a few of the twelve tribes, and several probably overlapped. (3) The divided kingdoms Judah and Israel used different methods to calculate the length of a king's reign—and co-regencies often complicate our knowledge of how long an individual spent on the throne.

Simply put, there are too many unknowns, and too many uncertainties in our interpretation of the biblical data, to claim absolute certainty for any chronology of the OT, although many dates have been established beyond a reasonable doubt.

These difficulties are further complicated by those liberal scholars who view the OT as a reconstruction of history. For instance, one group holds that forerunners of the Hebrew people drifted into Palestine in the 1300s B.C., to unite later as a nation. They suppose the Exodus account to be a late invention, or a mere fable intended to provide the nation with a sense of identity.

Persons who discount the essential accuracy of the biblical account rely heavily on archaeology. But the archaeological evidence does not compel anyone to abandon the Bible's internal chronology for any modern reconstruction. *See also* Jericho.

There is another reason to build our chronology of the OT on internal evidence. If we are to understand the story of the Bible, we must hear that story as the Bible tells it. Thus, the chronology of this Bible dictionary relies primarily on the internal evidence—on what the Bible itself says. The OT chronology presented here reflects the best attempts of conservative scholars to solve the many dating problems which admittedly do exist.

The extent and nature of these problems differ from era to era, so it is helpful to look at Bible chronology from age to age.

Creation to Abraham. One striking feature of the early chapters of Genesis is the genealogy found there, which lists the number of years pre-Flood patriarchs lived and the age at which eldest sons were born. This detailed listing led Bishop Ussher, working from the chronological data given in the Bible, to set the date for creation at 4004 B.C.

The problem with this approach is that Hebrew genealogies characteristically list important persons in a family line, but not all persons. Counting up the years does not necessarily tell us the number of years that elapsed from the birth of the first in line to the death of the last.

There is no sure way to establish the date of any event recorded in Gen. 1–11 from either internal or external evidence. The time frame of early Genesis, whether it involves thousands or hundreds of thousands of years, must be left open to further investigation.

• *Abraham to Moses.* A number of specific chronological notes in the OT enable us to construct a chronology of this period. The basic data is: Abraham was 75 when he entered Canaan (Gen. 12:4), 100 at the birth of Isaac (Gen. 21:5). Isaac was 60 at the birth of Jacob (Gen. 25:26). Jacob was 130 when he entered Egypt (Gen. 47:9,28). Exodus 12:40 says the children of Israel spent 430 years in Egypt. Between the Exodus and the dedication of the Temple (in Solomon's fourth year), 480 years elapsed (1 Ki. 6:1). The date of Solomon's fourth year can be fixed from external evidence (966 B.C.). Working back from this date, using the time spans mentioned in Scripture, gives us the approximate dates for the patriarchs and for the Exodus.

• *Conquest to Monarchy.* The primary difficulty in setting dates for the period of the judges is the fact that the years given for their rule do not seem to run consecutively. Apparently the various judges governed different tribal groups, and some surely overlapped. Thus the dates assigned to this period are more speculative than those assigned in any other period of biblical history.

A CHRONOLOGY OF THE BIBLE

Old Testament

WORLD EVENTS DATES

COPPER/STONE AGE 4000-3150 B.C. Jericho protected by a high wall and moat. 7000 B. C.

First date on Egyptian calendar. 4236 B.C.

Oldest long-distance road built in Mesopotamia. 3500 B.C.

Tin first combined with copper to make bronze.

First date on Mayan calendar. 3372 B.C.

EARLY BRONZE AGE 3150-2200 B.C. First Egyptian dynasty established. 3100 B.C.

Hieroglyphic writing used on Egyptian monuments.

Wheeled vehicles come into use in Mesopotamia.

Oldest papyrus (paper) book produced in Egypt. 3000 B.C.

Earliest known dam built across Nile at Kosherh. 2900 B.C.

Egyptian reed warships appear on the Nile.

First Egyptian physician, Imhotep, designs the first step pyramid.

Paved streets with drains in several cities in India. 2750 B.C.

In China, Shen Nung writes book on medicinal plants and herbs. 2735 B.C.

First formula for ink developed. 2697 B.C.

First emperor establishes dynasty in China.

Glass beads created in Babylon. 2500 B.C.

Gold necklaces, jewelry used in Ur.

First Sumerian empire founded. 2350 B.C.

Horses first used in Mesopotamia.

Ancestors of Greek people move into Mediterranean area.

Babylonians draw maps on clay tablets.

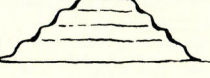

WORLD EVENTS	DATES	BIBLICAL EVENTS
MIDDLE BRONZE AGE 2200-1550 B.C.	2200 B.C.	
Pottery introduced in pre-Inca South America.	2166 B.C.	Abram born.
Ur-Nammu law code published in Ur.		

Bronze Age begins in Europe.	2100 B.C.	
Wooden ships developed in Crete.	2091 B.C.	Abram enters Canaan.
	2080 B.C.	Ishmael is born.
Cinnamon brought to Arabia from China.	2066 B.C.	Isaac is born.
	2029 B.C.	Sarah dies.
Powerful Middle Kingdom in Egypt begins.	2026 B.C.	Isaac marries Rebekah.
	2006 B.C.	Jacob is born.

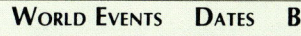

Maize (corn) grown throughout Central America.	2000 B.C.	
	1929 B.C.	Jacob goes to Haran.
	1915 B.C.	Joseph born.
Pictograph writing develops in China.	1909 B.C.	Jacob returns to Canaan.

HARAN

	1900 B.C.	
	1898 B.C.	Joseph taken to Egypt.
Sumerian Epic of Gilgamesh compiled.	1883 B.C.	Joseph appointed vizier.
	1876 B.C.	Jacob and his family migrate to Egypt.
	1859 B.C.	Jacob dies.
	1805 B.C.	Joseph dies.

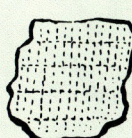

Stonehenge constructed. 1800 B.C.

First systematic astronomy developed in Babylon.

Bellows used in smelting metal.

Silk trade well established in China. 1700 B.C.

Law Code of Hammurabi published in Babylon.

Hyksos enter Egypt.

First all-glass vessels used. 1600 B.C.

First log roads built in Europe.

A CHRONOLOGY OF THE BIBLE

Old Testament (continued)

WORLD EVENTS	DATES	BIBLICAL EVENTS	BOOKS
LATE BRONZE AGE 1550-1200 B.C.	1527 B.C.	Moses born.	
	1500 B.C.		
	1486 B.C.	Moses flees to Midian.	
Thutmose III rules Egypt			
Hindu scriptures	1446 B.C.	The Exodus begins (April).	Genesis
(Vedas) begun.	1445 B.C.	Law given at Sinai.	Exodus
Amenhotep II rules Egypt			Leviticus
(1450-1423 B.C.)	1406 B.C.	Moses dies.	Numbers
		Conquest of Canaan begins; Jericho falls.	Deuteronomy
	1400 B.C.	Land divided among twelve tribes (from 1400 B.C.).	
	1399 B.C.	Canaanites power broken.	
			Joshua
	1375 B.C.	Joshua dies.	
Tutankhamen king	1374 B.C.	Othniel (judge from 1374-1334 B.C.).	
in Egypt (1361 B.C.).			
	1316 B.C.	Ehud (judge from 1316-1235 B.C.).	
	1300 B.C.		
Chinese put highway commissioner in charge of maintaining roads.	1235 B.C.	Oppression by Jabin and Sisera begins.	
Philistines settle Canaan's coasts.	1216 B.C.	Victory of Deborah and Barak.	
IRON AGE 1200-300 B.C.	1200 B.C.		
The Greeks destroy Troy.	1176 B.C.	Midianite oppression begins.	
Phoenicians import tin	1169 B.C.	Victory of Gideon.	
from the British Isles.			
Philistines begin to			
oppress Israelites.	1120 B.C.	Eli serves as Israel's high priest until 1080 B.C.	
	1100 B.C.		
China develops	1095 B.C.	Samson's career against the Philistines (1095-1075 B.C.).	Ruth
postal relay system.	1085 B.C.	Jephthah's victory of Ammonites.	Judges
	1080 B.C.	Battle of Shiloh.	
Phoenicians build trading	1063 B.C.	Samuel comes to office.	
colonies around the	1043 B.C.	Saul becomes king of Israel.	
Mediterranean.	1040 B.C.	David born.	
	1010 B.C.	Death of Saul and Jonathan.	
		David made king of Judah.	
Greeks adopt Phoenician	1003 B.C.	David crowned king of all Israel.	
alphabet.		David takes Jerusalem.	
	1000 B.C.		
	970 B.C.	Death of King David.	Proverbs
		Solomon becomes king.	Song of
	966 B.C.	Temple construction begins.	Solomon
Libyan pharaohs rule Egypt.	959 B.C.	Temple dedicated.	Ecclesiastes
	930 B.C.	Solomon dies.	
		Kingdom divided.	

	Rulers of Judah	**Rulers of Israel**	
	Rehoboam (931-913 B.C.)	Jeroboam I (930-910 B.C.)	
	Abijam (913-910 B.C.)		
		Nadab (910-909 B.C.)	
	Asa (910-869 B.C.)	Baasha (909-886 B.C.)	

	DATES	Rulers of Judah	Rulers of Israel	BOOKS
	900 B.C.		Elah (886-885 B.C.)	
			Zimri (885 B.C.)	
			Omri (885-874 B.C.)	
Carthage founded.		Jehoshaphat (872-848 B.C.)*	Ahab (874-853 B.C.)	
			Ahaziah (853-852 B.C)	Obadiah
		Jehoram (853-841 B.C.)*	Jehoram (852-841 B.C.)	

*Indicates co-regency with predecessor.

A CHRONOLOGY OF THE BIBLE

Old Testament (continued)

World Events	Dates	Biblical Events		Books
			Jehu (841-814 B.C.)	Joel
		Ahaziah (841 B.C.)		
Homer composes Iliad, Odyssey.		Athaliah (841-835 B.C.)	Jehoahaz (814-798 B.C.)	
		Joash (835-796 B.C.)		
	800 B.C.		Jehoash (798-782 B.C.)	
		Amaziah (796-767 B.C.)	Jeroboam II (793-753 B.C.)*	Jonah Amos
First Olympic games held in Greece (776 B.C.).		Azariah/Uzziah (790-739 B.C.)*	Zechariah (753-752 B.C.)	
Tiglath-Pileser III rules			Shallum (752 B.C.)	
Assyria (774 B.C.).		Jotham (751-736 B.C.)*	Menahem (752-742 B.C.)	Micah
Traditional date for		Ahaz (742-728 B.C.)*	Pekahiah (742-740 B.C.)	Hosea
founding of Rome			Pekah (752-732 B.C.)*	
(753 B.C.).			Hoshea (732-723 B.C.)	
Sargon II rules Assyria		Hezekiah 728-697 B.C.)*		Isaiah
(722-705 B.C.).	722 B.C.		**Samaria falls to Assyria; Israelites exiled.**	
	700 B.C.	Manasseh (697-642 B.C.)*		
Sennacherib builds 50-mile water canal for Nineveh. Phoenicians make and sell soap. Quill pens invented.		Amon (642-640 B.C.) Josiah (640-609 B.C.)		Nahum Habakkuk Zephaniah
Nineveh falls.	612 B.C.		**Babylonian Empire**	Jeremiah
Battle of Megiddo	609 B.C.	Jehoahaz (609-608 B.C.) Jehoiakim (608-597 B.C.) Jehoiachin (597 B.C.)	Nebuchadnezzar (605-562 B.C.)	Ezekiel
Invention of coinage by	600 B.C.	Zedekiah (597-587 B.C.)	Reign of Nabonidus	
Lydians.	587 B.C.	**Judah falls to Babylon: Jerusalem and the Temple are destroyed; the last Jews are sent into exile.**	(555-530 B.C.) Belshazzar viceroy (550-539 B.C.) Babylon falls (539 B.C.)	Daniel
Buddha born.	563 B.C.		**Persian Empire**	
Confucius born.	551 B.C.		Darius the Mede	
Pythagorus invents geometry.	538 B.C.	Jews return to their land under Zerubabel.	(539-538 B.C.) Cyrus crowned in Babylon	Haggai Zechariah
Book publishing begins in Greece.	536 B.C.	Foundations for the new Temple are laid.	(538 B.C.) Cambyses rules (529-523 B.C.)	
	516 B.C.	Temple completed and	Darius the Great	
	509 B.C.	dedicated.	(522-485 B.C.)	
Romans found Republic.	500 B.C.		Xerxes (Ahasuerus) (485-424 B.C.)	
Democracy established in Athens.	457 B.C.	Ezra comes to Jerusalem.	Esther made queen (478 B.C.) Artaxerxes I (464-424 B.C.)	Esther Ezra
The Torah (Law)	445 B.C.	Nehemiah serves as governor.	Darius II (423-406 B.C.)	Nehemiah
is codified.	429 B.C.		Artaxerxes II (404-359 B.C.)	Malachi
Plato born.	400 B.C.			

Alexander the Great conquers the Persian Empire. **332 B.C.**
The Hebrew Scriptures are translated into Greek (Septuagint) **250–50 B.C.**
Greeks adopt Phoenician alphabet. **200 B.C.**
Antiochus IV (Epiphanes) desecrates the Temple. **167 B.C.**
Judas Mattathias and his sons, the Maccabees, revolt against Antiochus.
Rededication of the Temple by Judas Maccabeus (Hanukkah). **165 B.C.**
Paper invented in China. **105 B.C.**
Julius Caesar campaigns in Britain. **55, 54 B.C.**
Herod the Great rebuilds the Temple in Jerusalem. **20 B.C.**

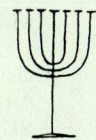

A CHRONOLOGY OF THE BIBLE

New Testament

World Event	Dates	Biblical Events	Book
Death of Herod the Great.	4 B.C.	Birth of Jesus Christ and John the Baptist.	
15th year of Tiberius. *Pontius Pilate, Roman*	A.D. 26	Jesus begins his public ministry. Death of John the Baptist.	
procurator (A.D. 26-36).	A.D. 30	Crucifixion and resurrection of Jesus. The ascension of Jesus; the Holy Spirit comes at Pentecost.	
Aretas in authority in	A.D. 34	Saul (later called Paul) converted on Damascus road.	
Damascus.	A.D. 37	Paul's first visit to Jerusalem.	
	A.D. 40		
Death of Herod Agrippa I.	A.D. 44	James (the brother of John) martyred. Paul's second visit to Jerusalem.	*James*
Josephus reports famine in			
Palestine.	A.D. 46		
	A.D. 47	Paul's first missionary journey (A.D. 47-49).	
	A.D. 50	The Council meets at Jerusalem.	*Galatians*
Gallio proconsul of Achaia.	A.D. 51	Paul's second missionary journey (A.D. 51-53).	*Mark* *1,2Thessalonians*
	A.D. 54	Paul's third missionary journey (A.D. 54-57).	*Romans* *1,2 Corinthians*
Festus replaces Felix as	A.D. 58	Paul arrested in Jerusalem, held in Caesarea.	*Luke*
Judean governor.	A.D. 60	Paul appeals to Caesar.	*Matthew*
	A.D. 61	Paul a prisoner in Rome.	*Ephesians*
	A.D. 62?	James (the Lord's brother) martyred.	*Colossians*
Rome burned under Nero.	A.D. 64		*Philemon*
	A.D. 66	Paul's second imprisonment in Rome.	*Phillippians*
	A.D. 67?	Paul and Peter executed in Rome.	*Acts; 1,2 Peter* *1,2 Timothy*
Jerusalem falls to the			*Titus; Jude*
Roman army under Titus.	A.D. 70		*Hebrews*
Fall of Masada, the last			
Jewish stronghold.	A.D. 73		
	A.D. 80		
Persecution of Christians	A.D. 90	The apostle John exiled to Patmos.	
under emperor Domitian.			*John*
(A.D. 81-96)	A.D. 96		*1,2,3 John*
	A.D. 98?	The last of the apostles, John, dies.	*Revelation*

• *The Divided Kingdom.* Much secular and biblical data help us establish the dates of the kings of Judah and Israel. Yet here too there are problems. The kings of Judah and Israel used different systems to calculate years of rule: In Judah, the year of accession to the throne was reckoned as the king's first year. In Israel, however, the following year after a king took the throne was considered his first year. Co-regencies were quite common (especially in Judah), and thus one king's reign might overlap that of another. While such factors complicate the development of a chronology, the dates of most kings are sure within a small margin of error.

• *Exile and Return.* There is much secular data available for this era, so the dating of events reported in the Bible after 605 B.C. is relatively sure. In some cases we know not just the year, but even the month and day. For instance, we know the days on which Haggai preached the sermons that stimulated the people to finish building the Jerusalem Temple.

NEW TESTAMENT

It is not possible to date all events reported in the NT precisely. The Romans used a solar calendar much like ours, introduced by Julius Caesar. But there was no system for numbering years consecutively. Luke uses the common system for fixing dates when he speaks of a census decreed "while Quirinius was governor of Syria" (Lk. 2:2), and dates the ministry of John the Baptist by saying he began to preach "in the fifteenth year of the reign of Tiberius Caesar—when Pontius Pilate was governor of Judea, Herod tetrarch of Galilee, his brother Philip tetrarch of Iturea and Traconitis, and Lysanias tetrarch of Abilene—during the high priesthood of

Annas and Caiaphas" (Lk. 3:1,2). While these converging conditions may have had meaning for first-century readers, it is somewhat uncertain 2,000 years later to relate them to our calendar.

The problem of dating is complicated by the fact that the Jews used a lunar calendar of twelve 29- or 30-day months, which was adjusted to fit the solar year by following the Babylonian practice of adding extra months in seven of every 19 years. *See also* Calendar.

In addition, Hebrew references to time are imprecise. To say that Jesus was "about thirty years old" when he began his public ministry means only that he was probably between 28 and 32 years of age. According to first-century custom, a reference to three years conceivably might indicate only 26 or 27 months, and Jesus' reference to being raised "after three days" (Mt. 27:63) might just as well mean "the day after tomorrow" as "72 hours."

To further complicate NT dating, secular writers paid little attention to the young religious movement called Christianity. So there are few references relating sacred history to secular events whose dates are known.

Despite such problems, scholars who have studied first-century records have furnished us with a framework within which to fit the NT story. Herod's death almost surely took place in 4 B.C. This is very important for establishing the year Jesus was born. An inscription discovered at Delphi almost certainly dates Gallio as proconsul of Achaia in A.D. 52–53 (*see* Acts 18:12-17). This places Paul's visit to Corinth at that time. Festus succeeded Felix in Judea about A.D. 60. This date helps us determine when Paul was arrested in Jerusalem and what years he spent in prison in Rome. By working with these and other dates, we can attempt to reconstruct the chronology of early Christianity. The accompanying chart matches known and estimated dates in secular history with the likely dates of key events reported in the NT.

church (1) Christians of all times and places, the mystical Body of Christ; (2) the interdependent ministering community of believers world-wide; (3) Christians in a particular city or province; (4) a group of Christians meeting together regularly, a local congregation.

NEW TESTAMENT USAGE

The word translated "church" in the NT is *ekklēsia*. It means a "called-out assem-

This mosaic portrays a fifth-century church. God's Church is not a building, though believers are likened in Scripture to "living stones . . . being built into a spiritual house" of which Christ is the "chosen and precious cornerstone" (1 Pet. 2:5,6).

bly." The secular Greek *ekklēsia* was a political but never a religious assembly, but in the Greek Septuagint it is regularly used for the Hebrew *qahal*, "congregation," especially in the Pentateuch. In the first century the Jewish religious assembly was called the *synagōgē* ("synagogue"). As a NT theological concept, "church" describes a new community, called out in the Gospel and set apart to God.

The word *ekklēsia* occurs in the Gospels only in Mt. 16:18 and 18:17. In Mt. 16:18, after Peter's remarkable confession of faith, Christ announces the future building of his Church. In the other reference, the Jewish synagogue may be referred to by the word *ekklēsia*. The use of "church" to identify the Christian community developed only after Christ's death and resurrection, for God's new community is founded on those events. Built on the foundation of the apostles and prophets, the Church came into existence as first Jews and then Gentiles established a personal relationship with God through faith in Christ and the blood he shed to redeem humankind (1 Cor. 3:11; Eph. 2:20-23). As a community of those who have made a faith response to God's promise of salvation in Christ Jesus, the *ekklēsia* of the NT began on the day of Pentecost (Acts 2), following Jesus' resurrection. *See also* Baptism; Pentecost.

The apostolic character of the Church is affirmed by all Christians. Some understand this to mean that the New Testament, written by the apostles or by writers directed by the apostles, gives guidance to the Church. Others in the Catholic and Episcopal traditions emphasize the apostolic teaching authority of the church hierarchy, as passed down from the apostles themselves.

BIBLICAL IMAGES OF THE CHURCH

	As the Body of Christ	As the Family of the Father	As the Temple of the Spirit
We relate to	Jesus Christ	God the Father	The Holy Spirit
He is our	Living Head	Loving Father	Wise Builder
We are	Living members of Christ's Body on earth	Beloved brothers and sisters in God's own family	Living stones in God's holy temple
God gives us	Spiritual gifts	The capacity to love one another	Spiritual priesthood
We are to	Be responsive to Christ our living Head	Experience the love of God for us	Worship God
	Use our spiritual gifts to build up one another	Be rooted and established in love for one another	Be joined together as a holy, priestly community
	Represent Christ in the world	Live a life of love as God's dear children	Live holy lives in this present world
As a result, we in the community	Grow towards maturity	Experience the reality and the power of God	Become more and more holy
Key Scriptures	1 Cor. 12:12-31; Eph. 1:22; 4:1-16; Col. 1:18	Jn. 13:33,34; Eph. 3:14-21; 5:1,2; 1 Jn. 5:1,2	Eph. 2:21,22; 1 Pet. 2:4-10
Related Articles	Body Head Spiritual Gifts	Family Fatherhood of God Love	Holy Holy Spirit Priest

The NT consistently portrays the church as persons, not as an institution and never as a building. In Acts and the Epistles, "church" refers 92 times to local or provincial assemblies of God's new community: "the church that meets at their house," the "church at Antioch," or "the Galatian churches" (Rom. 16:5; Acts 13:1; 1 Cor. 16:1). Twenty more times *ekklēsia* speaks of the whole community of believers, as in the statement that Christ is "head over everything for the church, which is his body" (Eph. 1:22,23). In these cases, the term represents all Christians of every time and place bound together in a universal spiritual union.

THE NATURE OF THE COMMUNITY

The NT uses three powerful images to help us grasp the nature of the church as people in community.

1. *The Church is the Body of Christ*. As in a body, each member is linked to its head (Jesus Christ), and each member is linked to other members of the living organism. As each member of Christ's Body performs his or her function, using spiritual gifts to minister to others, the Body grows and matures. Jesus Christ continues to minister through his maturing Body on earth, and through his Body continues his incarnation in this world. *See also* Body.

2. *The Church is the family of God*. As family, believers relate to God as Father, and to other believers as brothers and sisters. As members of God's family love and care for each other, intimate fellowship develops. Community members experience the love of God together, and can witness to his transforming power in this world. *See also* Family; Fellowship.

3. *The Church is God's holy temple*. As a holy temple, believers are building stones, linked to the Holy Spirit, who uses them to construct God's edifice on earth. Each stone in the divine construction is to exercise his or her priesthood, helping the community and individuals to grow in holiness. *See also* Priest.

THE DESTINY OF THE CHURCH

The Church's destiny is expressed in another image: the bride of Christ. As Christ's beloved, believers are destined for resurrection, at which we will experience fully our union with the Lord, a union as intimate as that of human marriage (Rev. 19,21). *See also* Bride and Bridegroom.

Each NT image of the Church universal gives us important data about who we are as the community of believers. Yet perhaps just as important is the tone of warmth and intimacy found in each. As Christians, we are bonded to Jesus so intimately that the image of a body, in which each member is directly linked to the head, is required to express the reality. We are so deeply loved by God that the image of a family, in which children are treasured and are to treasure each other, is required to express the nature of the affection that binds us to God. And we are so perfectly sealed by the Spirit that the image of a holy temple, in which each stone is carefully laid and bonded together, is required to describe the worshiping, serving people God has called to express his character in the world.

cinnamon A spice made from the bark of a tree that grows in tropical countries. This familiar spice was valued in biblical times not only as a flavor for foods but also as an ingredient in perfume (Prov. 7:17). It was also mixed in the sacred anointing oil used in Israel's worship rituals (Ex. 30:22-33). In biblical times cinnamon was imported from Asian countries, primarily through Arabia.

circumcision Cutting off the fold of skin (foreskin) at the end of the penis. An Israelite boy was circumcised on the eighth day of his life as a symbol of his inclusion among God's covenant people, the descendants of Abraham through Isaac and Jacob. As a symbolic act, circumcision was an affirmation of faith in the God who had given promises to Abraham and his posterity. But the symbol, while a necessary expression of faith (Gen. 17:14), was not sufficient in itself. Thus Moses called on the Israelites to "circumcise" their hearts, and so be responsive to the Lord (Deut. 10:16; see 30:6; Lev. 26:41; Jer. 4:4; 9:25,26). This spiritual challenge summed up what God asked of Israel:

To fear the Lord your God, to walk in all his ways, to love him, to serve the Lord your God with all your heart and with all your soul, and to observe the Lord's commands and decrees that I am giving you today for your own good.

(Deut. 10:12,13)

The emphasis on personal response to God in the OT makes it clear that a relationship with God does not and cannot rest on physical descent alone, nor on carrying out the ritual requirements of religion. *See also* Covenant.

The apostle Paul argues this point in several passages. Abraham was credited by God with righteousness before circumcision was introduced. Thus the "sign of circumcision" was a "seal of the righteousness that he [already] had by faith while he was still uncircumcised" (Rom. 4:11). It is faith, of which circumcision was only a sign, that makes a person righteous in God's sight. This argument cuts two ways. (1) The Jew who bore the sign of circumcision must have an Abraham-like faith in God if the sign is to have any value. And (2) a Gentile, who is not descended from Abraham and who does not bear in his flesh the sign of the Abrahamic covenant, must be considered righteous if he or she has an Abraham-like faith in Jesus Christ.

The Christian church did not carry over circumcision as a sign or symbol. Early attempts by Jewish Christians to impose this OT symbol on the new faith community were rejected by the Council of Jerusalem (Acts 15:1-29). This decision affirmed the fact that the new faith must always be viewed as a matter of the heart; efforts to require physical rituals for salvation must be rejected. So Paul says of those who have turned their hearts to God through faith in Jesus, "It is we who are the [true] circumcision, we who worship by the Spirit of God, who glory in Christ Jesus, and who put no confidence in the flesh" (Phil. 3:3).

While circumcision as a religious rite is not practiced in the Christian community, the Bible's teaching concerning circumcision serves as a healthy reminder. We too have symbols which represent aspects of our faith. But the symbols are not the reality. The open secret of personal relationship with God is vital faith in Jesus Christ: Salvation is a matter of faith from first to last (Rom. 1:17).

cistern A reservoir for collecting and storing water. Much of Palestine is hot, rocky land, and very dry during the six months in which rain seldom falls. Israelite settlements, usually built on the tops of hills, had to have a stable water supply. They solved the problem by carving cisterns (Heb., *bor*)—bell-shaped hollows—in the rock, in which rainwater was collected.

Cisterns served both individual households and entire communities. Household systems were often quite sophisticated. In a typical system, a rock channel led to a trap filled with rocks, designed to strain impurities. The water then flowed into a series of interconnected cisterns. Each trapped more impurities, and channeled water into a larger cistern which opened inside the house. About the time the Israelites invaded Canaan, a method of sealing cisterns was developed, so even areas with porous rock could be settled.

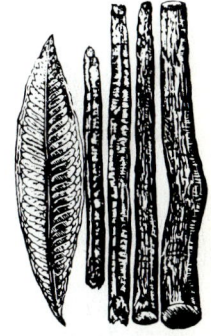

Ground bark of the cinnamon tree was used as an ingredient in perfume as well as a spice.

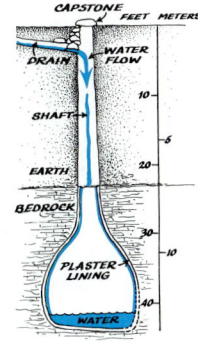

Typical cistern construction. Jeremiah, who was imprisoned in a cistern, likened Judah's interest in foreign deities to forsaking "springs of water" in favor of "broken cisterns that cannot hold water" (Jer. 2:13).

Archaeological study of a number of hilltop settlements suggests that most household cistern systems held 20 to 30 cubic yards (15.3 to 23 cubic meters) of liquid, and provided enough water annually to support six to twelve people.

Cities in Palestine often had larger artificial reservoirs. One cistern near Jerusalem's Temple mount held nearly three million gallons of water. Such public cisterns were especially important in ancient cities which were besieged in time of war and needed a source of water within their walls.

It is interesting that in a society which had no jails, larger cisterns were sometimes used as temporary prisons (Gen. 37:22; Jer. 38:6-13). They may also have served as grain storage pits.

Jeremiah referred to cisterns to make a spiritual point. When Israel forsook God for idols, he said, it was like abandoning a vital, bubbling spring to dig "broken cisterns that cannot hold water" (Jer. 2:13). God, the source of living water, is the only one who can sustain the believer. Turning away from him leads only to dryness, desolation, and death.

Spiral stone staircase leads down into a large cistern at Gibeon. Plastered cisterns varied greatly in size and were essential for water storage in arid Palestine.

cities of refuge Designated cities in Israel where a person who accidently killed another might flee for safety. Old Testament Law required that a murderer be put to death. As there were no police in Israel, a near relative of the victim was charged with this responsibility. He was designated the "avenger of blood."

But OT Law makes a clear distinction between intentional murder and accidental homicide. To protect those who might slay accidentally, the Law designated six of the 48 Levite cities as "cities of refuge." The six were so distributed that no Israelite lived more than 30 miles from refuge. The cities of refuge are identified in Josh. 20:7,8 as Kedesh, Shechem, Kiriath Arba (Hebron), Bezer, Ramoth Gilead, and Golan.

Regulations governing refuge are found in Num. 35 and Deut. 19. A person who slew another accidentally was to flee immediately to the nearest city of refuge. He was protected there until a public trial could determine whether the victim had been intentionally slain. If the death was judged accidental, the killer was allowed to remain in the city of refuge, where he

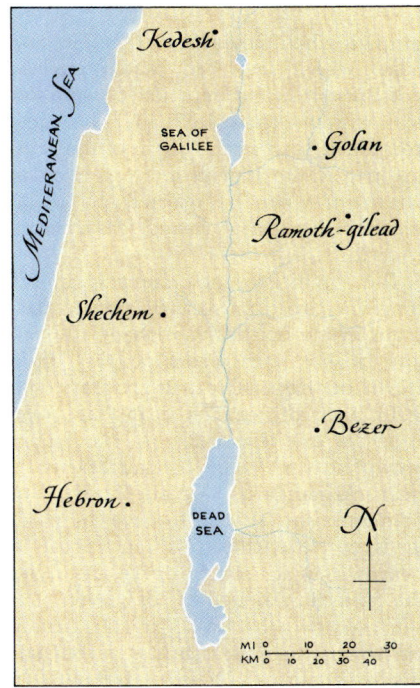

mitigating circumstances. The thoughtful and repeated regulations concerning cities of refuge contradict this distorted portrait of the Mosaic code, and reveal its balanced concern for the rights of individuals as well as for righteousness in the community.

cities of the plain Five cities that lay in a fertile plain at the south end of the Dead Sea in Abraham's time—Sodom, Gomorrah, Admah, Zeboiim, and the smaller Zoar (Gen. 10:19; 13:12; 14:8). Abraham's nephew Lot settled in the region of Sodom, known for its wickedness. When the Lord destroyed the four larger cities of the plain—probably about 2065 B.C. in a fiery earthquake that released explosive gases—Lot and his daughters found refuge in Zoar (Gen. 19:20-26). Many scholars believe that the remains of the destroyed cities lie under the Dead Sea at its shallow southern end. *See also* Sodom and Gomorrah.

lived until the death of the current high priest. Then he was free to return home, safe from the avenger of blood. However, if the verdict was intentional homicide, no refuge was allowed. The killer was executed by the avenger of blood.

Old Testament Law is sometimes portrayed as rigid and cruel, demanding an eye for an eye without consideration of

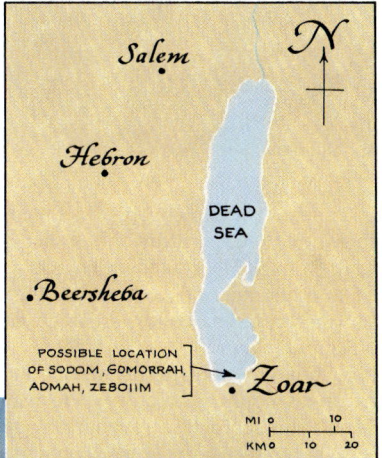

Genesis tells us that the Lord destroyed four of these ancient cities, including Sodom and Gomorrah, which probably lay in the southern end of the Dead Sea.

The western shore of the Dead Sea as viewed from the air.

citizen A person with the personal and civil rights of living in his own land. English versions of the Bible often use "citizen" in the sense of inhabitant, to indicate a person who lives in a particular town or province. But "citizen" carries other important meanings.

In OT times citizenship was racial and religious. A citizen of Israel had to be a descendant of Abraham, and thus one of

Roman military patent in bronze, dated to our calendar Dec. 2 A.D. 76. Such documents gave soldiers, on their retirement, title to lands and often conferred Roman citizenship.

God's covenant people. This fact, not whether one lived within the nation's boundaries, fixed Hebrew identity. A person of another race or faith, even if he lived in the Promised Land, remained an alien. *See also* Alien.

In NT times a person was deemed a citizen of his country of origin. He was considered subject to its laws wherever he might travel. Thus Saul (Paul) could be given authority by the Sanhedrin in Jerusalem to arrest Jews who followed Christ in Damascus (Acts 9:1,2).

In the Roman Empire citizenship was a political concept. A person with Roman citizenship was treated as if he were a resident of that great city, Rome. Wherever in the Empire a citizen might be, he or she was subject only to Roman courts and laws. A Roman citizen could not be examined by torture or imprisoned before trial. Citizenship conferred the right to travel freely, and protection by the local Roman garrison.

Artist's representation of the city of Babylon during the reign of Nebuchadnezzar, 605–563 B.C. The Euphrates River flows past the Temple of Marduk and the seven-stage ziggurat. Jewish exiles were urged to "seek the peace and prosperity of the city" during their captivity (Jer. 29:7).

The value of Roman citizenship is shown by several incidents reported in Acts. The magistrates in Philippi, itself a Roman colony whose inhabitants had been granted citizenship, were literally terrified when they learned that Paul and Silas, whom they had beaten publicly without a trial and imprisoned, were Roman citizens (Acts 16:37-40). The same concern is seen in the alarm of the commander of the Roman army garrison in Jerusalem when he realized that Paul, whom he had put in chains, was a citizen (Acts 22:25,26).

The significance of citizenship in NT times helps us understand several passages in the Epistles. Christians are "fellow citizens with God's people" (Eph. 2:19); "our citizenship is in heaven" (Phil. 3:20). Such affirmations mean that (1) we believers are responsible to the higher laws of heaven. We are obligated to live by heaven's standards, and not those of humankind. But (2) we also have the privileges of citizenship. We can appeal to heaven's higher court, for we are under the protection of the King of heaven himself. We may be proud of our earthly citizenship, as Paul clearly was. But our first allegiance is to heaven, and our sole ground of confidence is that, through Christ, heaven is our home.

city A large or important population center, usually (especially in the OT) walled or fortified. The walled cities of Palestine were distinct from the unfortified villages. Behind the walls of the Palestinian cities, houses and people crowded together on streets that were little more than narrow, wandering alleys.

To picture the biblical world accurately,

This model reconstructs Jerusalem as it would have looked at the time of Jesus. The refurbished Temple, which was not finished until A.D. 62, is at the top right, overlooking the densely populated lower city.

Terra-cotta tablet with map of the city of Umma in Mesopotamia.

we also need to distinguish between the giant city-states of ancient Mesopotamia, the tiny, scattered cities of Israel, and the Hellenistic cities of NT times.

MESOPOTAMIAN CITY-STATES

In Mesopotamia great city-states dominated surrounding areas. One of the most important, the "great city" of Nineveh (Jon. 1:2) with an estimated population of 175,000, was enclosed within some eight miles of city wall. The city contained crowded residential districts, which featured many taverns and brothels. Temple and governmental districts, with the ruler's palaces, were also within the walls. But the entire metropolitan area of Nineveh incorporated within some 60 square miles a population of more than 600,000. Other great Mesopotamian cities include Ur and Babylon.

CITIES AND TOWNS IN ISRAEL

The typical city or walled town in Israel was much smaller than the cities of Mesopotamia. Even in Canaanite times, no giant city-state developed there. Instead, each small city was independent, linked to others by ethnic affiliation or temporary political expediency. In the centuries of Hebrew domination, smaller cities were the rule. The population of Jerusalem in David's time has been estimated at only 3,500 to 5,000. Even in the time of Christ, only 35,000 to 50,000 lived there.

Most cities of Palestine covered only five to ten acres, and were situated at the top or on the side of a hill. Although the typical city might be surrounded by walls 20 feet (6 meters) thick, it would hold only some 100 to 150 houses.

Palestinian cities typically had a "high place," where an altar was constructed in Canaanite or idolatrous times. There was a broader, open area by the city gate where the elders met and business was conducted. Some cities featured a tower or citadel as a last line of defense. *See also* City Gate.

Inside the walls of OT cities narrow unpaved alleys led, helter-skelter, to slightly wider courts on which the doors of a half-dozen or more homes opened. Refuse, sheep or goats, and small hive-like ovens for cooking might all be seen in these courtyards. There was no plumbing or water-borne waste disposal. Most of the one-story homes had a common room in which the whole family lived and slept. *See also* House.

Palestine's cities and towns were largely agricultural rather than trade or manufacturing centers. Most of the inhabitants worked in fields around the city, and during the growing and harvest seasons they sometimes slept there. A larger or more important city was called a "mother," and nearby unwalled villages of ten or a dozen houses were called "daughters" (Heb., *banot*—Num. 21:25; Josh. 15).

HELLENISTIC CITIES OF NT TIMES

The cities mentioned in the NT differ from both the Mesopotamian metropolis and the OT city. Hellenistic cities featured a number of public buildings—theaters, temples, baths, and gymnasiums—and a large central marketplace. The theater at Philippi, a city visited by the apostle Paul, was laid out on a mountainside and could hold up to 50,000 people.

Cities were different in function as well. The Hellenistic cities of the Roman Empire were centers of trade, transportation, and government. Districts were set aside for important trades—bakers, cheesemakers, leatherworkers, carpenters, metalworkers, potters, etc. Streets were paved, and many cities had complex systems for distributing water and removing wastes. But even Hellenistic cities were crowded, and most residents were poor. Despite the luxury displayed in the design of homes for the rich, most of the city population lived in what we would consider slum conditions.

Yet when viewed from the perspective of the people of biblical times, cities had a powerful appeal. In Mesopotamia the metropolis was symbolic of power and glory. In Palestine the walled city spoke of security. In the NT era the Hellenistic city spoke of culture, comfort, and pride. Even the apostle Paul felt pride in his home city, expressed when he called Tarsus "no ordinary city" (Acts 21:39). The lasting appeal of the city underscores the faith of the patriarchs, who abandoned the cities of their time to live in tents as wanderers, because they looked for a new and different city: "the city with foundations, whose architect and builder is God" (Heb. 11:10). In that yet unseen city and in its Maker the believer finds real security; in that city alone we take pride.

city gate The entrance to a walled city, often used as a city's business center. The focus of community life in biblical times was the city gate. Crowded with shops and stalls, it served as the business center. It was also the legal center, where transactions were witnessed (Ruth 4:1) and disputes were brought to the city elders for judgment (Amos 5:15, KJV). A person "seated at the city gate" was an acknowledged elder, among the most respected members of the community (Gen. 19:1; 34:24). Here too the prophets often cried out the Word of God (1 Ki. 22:10). Crowded, noisy, and alive with activity, the gate was unquestionably the center of city life in Palestine. *See also* City.

The city gate had another important function. As an opening in the high walls that surrounded an ancient city, the gate was the weakest point in city defenses. The gate area thus had to be strengthened, often with towers and by designing the entry with sharp turns and multiple doors. Yet the gate was also an opening through which local forces might be launched to attack the enemy, so this too had to be considered in its construction.

city of David Jerusalem. David captured a strong walled city from the Jebusites, and made it the religious and political center of his kingdom (2 Sam. 5:7,9). For a time it was called the "City of David," though it soon became known as Jerusalem. In David's time, the city grew to hold a population of 3,500 to 5,000.

The NT makes reference to a "town of David" (Lk. 2:4,11; Jn. 7:42). The town is Bethlehem, where David as well as Jesus was born. *See also* Jerusalem; Zion.

clan An undefined group of persons related through a common ancestor. Old Testament clans were groups of related families within one of Israel's twelve tribes. The exact nature of the relationships implied by "clan" is uncertain, as difficult to define as are other Hebrew kinship terms. The basic Hebrew word rendered "clan" is 'elep, "thousand."

Clay figurines excavated from the City of David bring to mind Isaiah's vision of people and nations as malleable clay in the hands of a sovereign God (Isa. 45:9).

Some believe this implies that each clan was expected to provide a thousand soldiers in time of war.

clay Fine-grained earth, workable when wet, used to make pottery and bricks. Clay was so important in biblical times that the Hebrews used three different words for dry clay, and two for wet. Scripture also has a number of technical words for clay that has been fired, as was pottery, and yet another word for worked clay used by brickmakers.

What made clay so important in the biblical world was its many and varied uses. The pottery vases and dishes used in every home—even the toys of the children—were made of clay. Clay was the major component in sun-dried and fired brick. Brick, with stone, was the primary building material in Egypt, Mesopotamia, and Palestine. Clay was used to plaster wall and floor surfaces, and was packed over layers of branches to make waterproof roofs. *See also* Brick; Pottery.

In Mesopotamia, clay served as writing material. Hundreds of thousands of fired or sun-dried clay tablets from pre-biblical times have been discovered at archaeological sites in the region. The relatively few that have been translated have given scholars crucial data on the social, religious, and political life of ancient civilizations. Later, when ink was developed, people commonly wrote on broken pieces of clay pottery (potsherds). Archaeologists have also discovered many impressions of official seals, pressed into clay to establish ownership or to verify a ruler's commands. (Job 38:14 poetically describes God stamping his seal on the earth's clay.) *See also* Writing.

Clay also aided the developing science of metalworking. Crucibles of fired clay held the molten metal, and it was poured into clay molds. When cooled, the clay molds could easily be broken off and the sturdy metal would remain. This iron-clay relationship is expressed in Nebuchadnezzar's vision (Dan. 2:31-45). He saw an image with its toes "partly iron and partly baked clay," so, as Daniel interpreted it, the kingdom they represented would be "partly strong and partly brittle. . . . the people will be a mixture and will not remain united, any more than iron mixes with clay" (vv. 42,43).

Pagan idols were often made of clay, as were many incense stands and altars used in their worship.

The commonness of clay and its pliability made it a rich image for biblical writers.

This Roman oil lamp (above) and amphora or jar from the Hellenistic period (below) were both found in Israel. Clay was used as commonly as we use plastic today.

The area to the southeast, below the Temple Mount in Jerusalem, is the site of the ancient City of David, known earlier as Salem and as Jebus.

227

Job calls his friends' arguments "defenses of clay," denoting their worthlessness (Job 13:12). Isaiah indicates that human beings are clay in the hands of God the potter (Isa. 64:8), and thus we have no right to complain about how God has made us (Isa. 45:9; see 29:16; Jer. 18:6; Rom. 9:21).

In the NT, Jesus made clay ("mud," NIV) by spitting on the ground, and he placed this on a blind man's eyes to heal him (Jn. 9:6). His reasons are unclear. Perhaps he was making some sort of curative salve from the clay. Or perhaps it was symbolic of creation: God had made man from the earth's clay (Job 10:9; 33:6; see Gen. 2:7); now Jesus was remaking this man born blind. Whatever the reason, claymaking involved "work," according to Sabbath law, and thus Jesus quite deliberately aroused the ire of the Pharisees.

clean and unclean Ritual terms used in OT religion to identify persons, places, animals, and things which could or could not have a role in the worship of God.

The OT concept of cleanness is rooted in the holiness of God. Priests, places, sacrificial animals, and objects used in worship were "holy" or "set apart" for God. For the worship of an utterly holy God to be done properly, all of these elements needed to be thoroughly "clean." Uncleanness was an affront to God's holiness.

A person became unclean through contact with an unclean thing (for example, a dead body); by menstruation, seminal discharge or childbirth; by contracting certain skin diseases; or by eating unclean food. In OT times a believer had to be in a "clean" condition to participate in community worship of God.

In the NT the old categories of clean and unclean things are set aside, and the focus of relationship with God shifts from externals to heart attitude.

CLEAN AND UNCLEAN IN THE OT
Some scholars have tried to explain rit-

ual uncleanness by suggesting the regulations dealt with matters of sanitation. Thus unclean animals were thought of as those which might carry disease. But this explanation misses the point. When the distinction between clean and unclean animals was introduced, Moses portrayed God as saying,

Do not defile yourselves by any of these creatures. Do not make yourselves unclean by means of them or be made unclean by them. I am the Lord your God; consecrate yourselves and be holy, because I am holy.

(Lev. 11:43,44)

Clean and unclean were holiness issues, reminders to the Israelites that they were God's own people and must set themselves completely apart to him.

A close examination of those things the OT identifies as unclean reveals that they focus on the central experiences of human life: on birth and death, sex, food, and health. In establishing the clean and unclean, God showed Israel in a graphic way that every issue of life must be related to him, and that in every way God's people must be set apart from others.

Ceremonial uncleanness did not cancel a believer's relationship with God, although uncleanness did temporarily disrupt participation in community worship. The Law provided steps a person could take to become "clean" again. These steps involved (1) a period of time during which the individual remained unclean and could not participate in worship rituals, and (2) purification, either by washing with water or by offering a blood sacrifice. Persons set apart to God (as were the priests) and objects dedicated to God's service were cleansed by blood.

While the early OT books pay most attention to ritual uncleanness, the concept of clean and unclean had moral im-

CLEAN AND UNCLEAN ANIMALS

Category	Classification Principle	Examples
Land animals	If it has a split hoof *and* chews the cud it is clean. Animals with paws or that travel in any other way are unclean.	Camel, badger, pig, weasel, rat, lizards of all types are unclean.
Water creatures	If it has fins *and* scales, it is clean.	Catfish, eels, shellfish are unclean.
Birds	Specific birds are restricted.	Eagle, vulture, hawk, raven, owls, gull, cormorant, osprey, stork, heron, hoopoe, bat are unclean.
Insects	Flying insects that walk, *except* those with jointed legs, are unclean.	Locusts, katydids, crickets, grasshoppers are clean.

plications. Sinful acts made a person "unclean" in God's sight. The sacrifice of the Day of Atonement was offered to cleanse [literally, to make the people of Israel clean] from "all your sins" (Lev. 16:30). The later prophets drew this analogy when condemning the sins of God's people. The psalmist describes the idolatry of the forefathers and says, literally, they "made themselves unclean by what they did" (Ps. 106:39; see Jer. 2:23; Ezek. 20:30,31; Mic. 2:10). This is the theme Jesus emphasized, as he explained the inner meaning of Mosaic Law, and taught that ultimately clean and unclean had always been matters of the heart. See also Atonement, Day of.

CLEAN AND UNCLEAN IN THE NT

In Jesus' time the Pharisees emphasized external, ritual performance. This led them to criticize the failure of Jesus' disciples to go through a ceremonial washing before they ate, thus (according to them) eating "with unclean hands" (Mk. 7:1-23). Jesus later explained, "Nothing outside a man can make him 'unclean' by going into him. Rather, it is what comes out of a man that makes him 'unclean' " (v. 15).

Jesus' statement seems to contradict the ritual concept of clean and unclean. In fact, however, it did three very different things:

1. Jesus challenged the right of the rabbis to extend the concept by calling things unclean which Scripture did not identify as such.

2. Jesus focused attention on the moral thread which was always present in the Law. "From within, out of men's hearts, come evil thoughts, sexual immorality, theft, murder, adultery, greed, malice, deceit, lewdness, envy, slander, arrogance and folly. All these evils come from inside and make a man 'unclean' " (vv. 21-23).

3. Jesus acted, as was his right as the Son of God, to annul the Law's ritual regulations, making them of no effect. Thus, Mark comments, "In saying this, Jesus declared all foods 'clean' " (v. 19).

The young church struggled with this change, as with the other revolutionary changes in life-style introduced by Jesus. The vision of Peter, in which he was called on to kill and eat "unclean" animals, is significant. Revolted at the very thought, Peter refused, only to hear the voice say, "Do not call anything impure that God has made clean" (Acts 10:15). This vision was intended to jolt Peter's preconceived notion that Gentiles were unclean and that Jews were the only "clean" people with

Traditionally designated house of Simon the tanner in Joppa where God prepared Peter to minister to the Gentile Cornelius by giving Peter a vision of ceremonially unclean animals that he now "declared clean" (Acts 10).

access to God. But it also did more. The vision affirmed the belief that ritual cleanness and uncleanness does not rest merely in an object or thing. A thing is unclean only because God calls it unclean. When God removes this designation, the thing becomes clean again.

Paul makes the vital point that "no food is unclean in itself" (Rom. 14:14). Only a violation of God's Word or one's own conscience can interrupt fellowship with God. God is concerned about what is in our hearts.

cloak An outer garment. In biblical times, this important garment was typically a large square of cloth with armholes. It fell to or below the knees. Even though other clothing was worn under the cloak, and the cloak might be taken off when working in the heat, a man without his cloak was spoken of as "naked" (1 Sam. 19:24, KJV). The cloak also served as a covering at night. There are several different Hebrew and Greek words for cloak in Scripture. These are sometimes translated as garment, wrapper, robe, coat, or merely clothes.

The average person in Palestine had only one cloak, and it was his most important possession. This explains a particularly thoughtful provision in the Mosaic Law: "If you take your neighbor's cloak as a pledge, return it to him by sunset, because his cloak is the only covering he has for his body. What else will he sleep in? When he cries out to me [against you], I will hear, for I am compassionate" (Ex. 22:26,27).

Like other familiar things, the cloak has a place in Scripture's imagery. God, about to execute judgment, wraps "himself in zeal as in a cloak" (Isa. 59:17).

Jesus used the cloak in a powerful illustration. Revenge is not for Jesus' followers: Someone who sues to take your tunic should be given the cloak too (Mt. 5:40). God's nature is not expressed in resistance and revenge but in love, even for one's enemies. See also Clothing.

Drawing shows the flowing, comfortable cloak or outer garment worn by both men and women in biblical times.

1. *Assyrian king wearing a tassled tunic, cloak, and* cidaris *(conical cap).*

2. *A Semitic group is depicted on this wall mural from the tomb of the Egyptian nobleman Khnumhotep (about 1890 B.C.). This is how the biblical patriarchs probably dressed.*

3. *Examples of Assyrian dress (left to right): a commoner, court official, and nobleman.*

4. *Sculpted Sumerian woman wearing a tunic of overlapping "leaves" of leather (3rd millennium B.C.).*

5. *Median nobility from the time of the Babylonian Exile.*

6. *The adornments on these Judean women—from headbands to ankle chains — sparked God's judgment in Isa. 3:16.*

7. *Painted tiles of Syrian peoples were found at Thebes in Egyptian tombs (1550–1300 B.C.).*

8. *A Judean king.*

9. *The captives on this Egyptian frieze represent subject nations —Libya, Babylonia, and Nubia—each attired in native costume (about 1380 B.C.).*

10. *An Egyptian official, wearing a loin cloth, leads a captive woman carrying two naked children. Her "flounced" tunic is actually wrapped in spiral fashion.*

11. *Linen clothing, made from flax, was was worn by everyone from fan bearer to pharaoh.*

12. *A pleated wool and linen tunic from an Egyptian tomb (1785–1680 B.C.). It would have originally been a striking off-white color.*

Continued on page 232.

closet (KJV) An inner room, providing some degree of privacy. There were few such places in the typical house of OT times. Yet the bride and groom were provided with a private space (Heb., *huppah*) for marital intimacy (Ps. 19:5). New Testament houses provided more private areas (Gk., *tameion*). Jesus said, "When you pray, go into your room [an inner room, *tameion*], close the door, and pray to your Father, who is unseen" (Mt. 6:6). Our personal prayer relationship with God involves such an intimate transaction that the most private of rooms is called for.

clothing Garments worn for modesty, comfort, and adornment. The clothing of all the lands of the Bible was similar—practical for areas which might be very hot one time of year and very cold in another. Then, as now, clothing communicated many social messages. In Israel clothing distinguished a person's sex, and might indicate occupation, economic situation, social status, and even one's emotional state. Unlike today, however, special clothes were marked more by color and embroidery than by widely varying styles.

BASIC CLOTHING

In cooler weather, men wore an undershirt-like garment of wool or linen which came to the loins or knees. Everyday outer wear was a one-piece tunic, a lined, long-sleeved garment which came to or below the knees. This garment might be briefer for workmen, or might be pulled up between the legs and tied when working. (This was described as "girding" oneself—a term used to indicate being ready for work or action.) A long, folded sash of cloth or leather, called a "girdle" in the KJV, was wrapped around the waist. Its folds served as pockets. Atop all of this, a loose-fitting cloak or robe was worn for warmth or on social occasions. The richly decorated *me'il* (Heb.) cloak conveyed the wearer's status, while the ordinary *simelah* (Heb.) cloak was the working garment of the common man.

Headdresses, which might be turban-like or simply a square of cloth held by a headband, protected wearers from the sun. Sandals were strapped to the feet. On occasion, some would wear shoes with soft uppers.

Though the dress of women was very similar, it was so decorated and designed that it could not be confused with men's dress. Women's tunics fell to the feet; the headdress differed, and their sleeves were usually pointed. Often a woman wore a brief jacket over her outer robe.

Our knowledge of the styles of garments in various periods of Bible history comes from paintings and relief carvings recovered in Egypt, Mesopotamia, and Palestine. Yet the basic clothing worn in the ancient Middle East remained essentially the same over several millennia.

MATERIALS AND COLORS

Several materials were used in clothing. Leather was common, and the hair of goats and camels was woven into rough but warm garments. Flax was grown in Egypt and some parts of Palestine, and its fibers were treated and woven to make the linen garments mentioned in Scripture. Cotton clothing was also known, although cotton fibers were much harder to separate and weave than were the fibers of flax. Silk, which was imported, was very rare. The most common material used in making clothing in Palestine was wool, which excelled in warmth. It came in several natural colors (white, yellow, brown, black) and was more easily dyed than linen. The garments worn in biblical times were generally colorful. Biblical references to "blue, purple and scarlet" (Ex. 25:4; 28:6, etc.) illustrate the wide range of colors available in textiles.

SOCIAL AND SPIRITUAL MESSAGE

The theological message of clothing appears in Gen. 3, where God gives clothes of animal skin to Adam and Eve to cover their nakedness. God's act conveys two messages, both of which were institutionalized in Israel. (1) Human sin can be covered only at the price of a life. And (2) nakedness is to be covered, for a race marred in the Fall will not appreciate the beauty of the human form in a holy way. This last message is emphasized in the contrast between the ever-modest clothing adopted by the Hebrews and the often revealing clothing worn in other cultures.

Another spiritual message comes through in the clear distinction between men's and women's clothes. Deuteronomy 22:5 says, "A woman must not wear men's clothing, nor a man wear women's clothing, for the Lord your God detests anyone who does this." The statute is not a sign of discrimination, but an affirmation of the intrinsic worth of each sex. Each person is to wear clothing that proclaims his or her sexual identity.

Many items of dress are indicated by Hebrew words whose meanings are uncertain. We find a cluster of such terms in Isaiah's warning to the haughty women of the 700s B.C., whose ostentatious wealth was gained by plundering the poor. Their bangles and headbands, their crescent necklaces, earrings, bracelets, and veils, their headdresses and ankle chains and sashes, their fine robes and capes and cloaks and purses and shawls, all testified to their haughty unconcern for the exploited of the land (Isa. 3:18-26).

Jesus had a similar view of some Pharisees who, to advertise their religious zeal and piety, "make the tassels of their garments long." By such ornamentation, probably on their prayer shawls, these men were showing off. As Jesus said: "Everything they do is for men to see" (Mt. 23:5).

Clothing communicated other social messages as well. Certain patterns in dress designated trades or professions. Embroidery and other subtle signs, with quality of cloth, identified social status. Even emotional states were indicated by clothing choice. People wore bright clothing and finery when celebrating, but expressed mourning and repentance by donning sackcloth—coarse material from which sacks were made (Gen. 37:34; Jer. 4:8).

cloud A visible mass of condensed water vapor suspended in the atmosphere.

Like other natural elements, clouds often appear in the figurative language of Scripture. A king's favor is "like a rain cloud in spring" (Prov. 16:15). God has "swept away your offenses like a cloud, your sins like the morning mist" (Isa. 44:22). False teachers are useless "clouds without rain" (Jude 12). A "cloud of witnesses" (Heb. 12:1) is a common classical expression suggesting a crowd gathered for a theater or sporting event.

But clouds are also closely connected with those times when God reveals himself (Ex. 19:9; Deut. 5:22; 1 Ki. 8:10; Ezek. 1:4; Mt. 17:5, etc.). The most significant cloud in Scripture is the bright cloud/fiery pillar that accompanied the Israelites from Sinai to the Promised Land (Ex. 33:9; Num. 9:15-23; 1 Cor. 10:1,2). That cloud was a visible representation of God, seen by all the Israelites of the Exodus era. Day and night the brightly shining cloud stood over the tabernacle in the center of Israel's camp, evidence of his constant presence. The cloud also affirmed God's guidance, for only when it moved was Israel to break camp, and the nation would travel only where the cloud led. No other generation in history was given such unmistakable evidence that God was present and guiding his people. See also Pillar.

Yet despite such evidence, the Exodus generation refused to obey God when the cloud led to the borders of Canaan (Num. 14). The majority of Israelites were afraid to enter the Promised Land. No amount of proof can move an untrusting heart to respond to God. No evidence can by itself produce or take the place of faith.

coat of many colors (KJV) A special garment given to Joseph by his father, Jacob, indicating his favoritism. It is better translated by modern versions as "a richly ornamented robe" (Gen. 37:3), although it also possibly refers to a long-sleeved garment. See also Embroidery.

cock crow (KJV) Peter denied Jesus just before "cock crow." The phrase indicates an undetermined time before dawn. Chickens probably became common in Palestine only in Roman times, although they may have been imported as a delicacy and served at Solomon's table (1 Ki. 4:23). See also Chicken.

coins Stamped or inscribed pieces of metal with fixed weight or value that are issued by a governmental authority identified by the design or symbol on the coin. Early OT references to denominations of money, such as a half shekel or shekel of silver, do not refer to coins but to a particular weight. See also Money.

The first minted coins were issued by the Kingdom of Lydia in Asia Minor (western Turkey) about 650 B.C. By 450 B.C. most major Greek city-states were minting coins, and some of the provinces and merchant cities of Asia Minor and Phoeni-

Below: A mold for minting coins, found in Jerusalem, illustrates part of the process. The Jews issued coins infrequently, such as during revolts or with foreign rulers' permission.
Bottom: Hoard of bronze Judean perutot from about A.D. 60 found in an oil lamp at En Gedi. Each peruta weighed about 1 gram and was equal to the two lepta the poor widow mentioned in Mk. 12:42 contributed to the Temple treasury.

cia had produced local currencies. The "darics" referred to in Ezra were a standard gold coinage introduced by Darius I about 510 B.C.

The New Testament refers to several different coins, including the silver denarius, which was equivalent to a day's wages, and the "mite" offered to God by a widow, which was worth perhaps a tenth of a cent (Mk. 12:42).

collection A gathering of funds. What the KJV calls a "collection" in 2 Chr. 24:6 is, in the NIV, a "tax imposed by Moses" for the upkeep of the tabernacle, and later the Temple (Ex. 30:12,16). The NT "collection" (Rom. 15:25-27; 1 Cor. 16:1-4) was a voluntary gift, intended for the relief of the needy. *See also* Give; Tithe.

colony A city or region in a subservient, sometimes privileged, relation to a more powerful empire. Acts 16:12 identifies Philippi as "a Roman colony." Philippi had been granted this status in 30 B.C. Following normal practice, many Roman army veterans were settled there, and the residents were then granted citizenship. Corinth was established as a Roman colony in 44 B.C.

Colony cities had special status within the Roman Empire. They were self-governing, exempt from the control of the governors of the provinces in which they lay. Colonies were also exempt from many taxes. *See also* Philippians.

color Pigment, hue. No specific term for the word "color" is found in the Hebrew or Greek Scriptures. When colors are mentioned, more concern is shown for the brightness or muted character of the color than for its specific hue.

Artificial colors were made from a variety of substances, ranging from sea shells to insects to vegetation. In biblical times it was impossible to control the quality of manufactured colors, so no standard range of hues was developed in Palestine.

Even when used symbolically, color terms may focus on some factor other than hue. For instance, Isa. 1:18 speaks of sins being "like scarlet" and "red as crimson." Scarlet and crimson are mentioned here because crimson/scarlet dye was the most difficult to bleach from any material. Isaiah's point is that God can cleanse a repentant people from even the most permanent stains of sin.

Colossians, Epistle to the Colosse was a cosmopolitan city, lying in the Lycus River valley in what is now Turkey, on the major trade route between Ephesus and the Euphrates River. Paul did not establish the church in Colosse; apparently the Gospel was carried there by local people who heard Paul in Ephesus (Acts 19:10).

The Epistle to the Colossians was written by Paul probably during his imprisonment in Rome, about A.D. 62. Paul learned of serious doctrinal misunderstandings in Colosse when a member of the Colossian congregation, Epaphras, visited him in Rome (Col. 1:7,8). Paul had already determined to send a converted runaway slave, Onesimus, back to his master in Colosse (Col. 4:9). So Paul took the opportunity to pen this brief but powerful message to the church, intending it to be circulated to

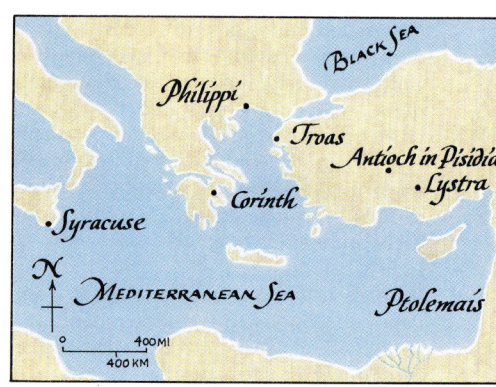

Map shows location of several Roman colonies that figured prominently in Paul's ministry.

other congregations as well (4:16). The link between the letters to the Colossians and to Philemon is well established, and attested by references in each letter to the same individuals (Col. 4:9-14,17; Phlm. 23,24). *See also* Philemon.

BACKGROUND

The population of Colosse was mixed, with Greek, Jewish, and native Phrygian residents as well as Roman army veterans. Many believe the doctrinal errors which crept into the Colossian church reflect a philosophical Judaism; others see the errors as an early form of a heresy known as gnosticism. While Colossians does not define the false doctrines held by some in the Colossian church, three elements are clear: (1) the error involved an exaltation of elemental spirits ("angels," or planetary lords) who were thought of as necessary intermediaries between people in the material world and a transcendent God (Col. 1:16,20; 2:15). Ultimately this view denied Jesus either his deity or his humanity, and thus robbed him of his essential place in Christianity; (2) the error emphasized ascetic and liturgical practices, which were

WHITE
milk Gen.49:12
wool Rev. 1:14

PURPLE
purple-dye
dress Jer.10:9

BLUE

GREEN

GREEN-YELLOW
grass 2 Ki.19:26
grass Mk 6:39

YELLOW

RED
blood 2 Ki. 3:22
worm Ex.16:20
lips Song 4:3
curtain 2 Chr. 3:14
paint Ezek. 23:14
sky Mt. 16:2
robe Mt. 27:28

RED-PURPLE
robe Esth. 8:15
robe Lk.16:19

BLACK
raven Song 5:11
ink 2 Cor. 3:3

thought to produce spirituality (Col. 2:11,16-23); and (3) those in error claimed a special knowledge of spiritual reality, thought to be deeper and more perfect than that found in the simple Gospel of Christ (Col. 2:4,8,18). *See also* Gnostics.

THEOLOGICAL CONTRIBUTIONS

Against this background the apostle Paul presents positive teaching about the person of Christ and about the true nature of Christian spirituality.

• *Who is Jesus?* Colossians insists there is no chasm between the transcendent God and his material creation, and thus no need for a hierarchy of angelic powers. Jesus is himself the "image" [*eikōn*, "exact expression"] of God. He is Creator of both the material and spiritual dimensions of the universe. All existing angelic powers are subject to Christ (Col. 1:15-17). What is more, God's fullness dwells in the human Jesus; in Christ God brings the earthly and heavenly into full harmony (Col. 1:19,20). This letter makes clear that God has chosen to reconcile us "by Christ's physical body through death" (Col. 1:22). God actually used and worked through the ma-terial to accomplish spiritual ends. And further, "In Christ all the fullness of the Deity lives in bodily form, and you have been given fullness in Christ" (Col. 2:9,10). Any effort to approach God through angelic intermediaries is thus both foolish and wrong, a denial of Christ and a retreat from true Christian faith.

• *What is Christian spirituality?* The ascetic assumes that by denying needs associated with his physical (material) body, he will develop his spiritual (immaterial) nature. In Colosse this view was linked with legalistic demands. Paul says, "Such regulations indeed have an appearance of wisdom . . . but they lack any value in restraining sensual indulgence" (Col. 2:23). The Colossian approach to spirituality stimulates an unspiritual pride (Col. 2:18,19).

How then should Christians understand spirituality? By looking to Christ, who took on human form, and did God's will in this world. In the same way, the spiritual Christian does God's will here and now, in and as part of the material creation.

Paul's prayer in Col. 1:9-12 introduces this viewpoint. Exercising spiritual wis-

COLOSSIANS: A READING AND STUDY GUIDE

Passage	Content Summary	Related Articles
1:3-14	Paul praises the Colossians for their faith and love. Paul shares a prayer which expresses his vision of spiritual growth.	Spirituality Wisdom
1:15-23	Paul defines the nature and role of Christ. He affirms the essential link between Jesus and the material universe, in Christ's role as Creator and Reconciler.	Firstborn Creation Reconciliation
1:24–2:5	The message of Christ is the "word of God in its fullness." Full knowledge of the mystery of God is found in Christ and in Christ alone.	Mystery Know
2:6-15	Philosophies based on human tradition are worthless. Our fullness is found in Christ, in whom "all the fullness of the Deity lives."	Philosophy Baptism
2:16-23	Worship of angels and ascetic self-denial, along with legalistic ritualism, have no spiritual value.	Angel Legalism
3:1-11	The earthly nature and its sinful desires are to be denied, and Christians are to act in harmony with their new, God-like self.	
3:12-17	True spirituality is expressed in loving acts that build unity; worship is summed up in shared and spontaneous praise.	Love Worship Peace
3:18–4:1	Love must be shown in every family relationship including that between masters and their household slaves.	Submission Slave; Family
4:2-6	In conclusion, Paul encourages the Colossians to pray, and to be wise in their dealings with non-Christians.	Prayer
4:7-18	Paul adds a number of greetings from Christians who are with him in Rome.	

Right: Site of ancient
city of Colosse.
Inset: Location of
Colosse and
neighboring towns
in the Lycus Valley.

dom and insight, the believer is to apply God's revealed will as a guide in daily life (v. 9). He or she will thus live a life worthy of the Lord, demonstrated in all kinds of good works (v. 10). In this way alone believers can come to know God better in a personal, experiential way. *See also* Will; Wisdom.

Christians are to "put on the new self, which is being renewed in knowledge and in the image of its Creator" (Col. 3:10). Thus clothed, the believer will live a life of "compassion, kindness, humility, gentleness and patience" (Col. 3:12). This kind of life, not one of ascetic self-denial or legalism, involves the true spirituality.

MASTERY KEYS

Colossians is a Christological letter. That is, it centers on the question of who Jesus is. It will help you understand this letter if you make a list of what it says about Jesus and what he has accomplished. The letter also provides a firm foundation for Christian ethics. As those who are being renewed in God's image (Col. 3:10), we are to express God's character in our every act and relationship. Make another list, this time of the actions which express our ethical duty as God's people.

SPECIAL FEATURES

Paul blends warm personal expression with his corrective teaching. In 1:3-14, he expresses praise and a loving concern that has led him to pray daily for the Colossians. In 1:24–2:5, he explains his motives—his deep desire to share Christ. In 4:7-18, the apostle sends personal greetings to and from various believers. Each of these sections helps us sense the relational context of Christian correction. If we confront others, it must be done as an act of love. We need to communicate that love along with our correction.

colt The foal of a donkey. The "colt" (Heb., *'ayir*; Gk., *polos*) of the Bible was not a young horse, but the foal of a donkey. One such colt became a powerful symbol of Jesus' Messiahship. As he entered Jerusalem before the Passover festival, shortly before his death, Jesus rode on a colt (Mt. 21:1-11; Mk. 11:1-11; Lk. 19:28-44; Jn. 12:12-19). About 500 years earlier, Zechariah had prophesied: "See, your king comes to you, righteous and having salvation, gentle and riding on a donkey, on a colt, the foal of a donkey" (Zech. 9:9). Jesus' "triumphal entry" can thus be understood as a final affirmation that he was indeed the promised King. The people of Jerusalem apparently recognized the symbolism of the Christ's entry on the colt. In their cry of "Hosanna to the Son of David!" they hailed Jesus as the Messiah.

Comforter Jesus' term for the Holy Spirit. Four times in the Last Supper discourse, Jesus describes the Holy Spirit as the Comforter (KJV) or Counselor (NIV). The Greek word is *parakletos*, a warm and supportive term for someone who comes alongside, to give comfort and encouragement, or else to invite or to exhort. In context, the Comforter is the living presence of God with believers (Jn. 14:16), sent to teach and guide (Jn. 14:26). As the agent of God the Father, the Spirit whispers the message of Jesus within us (Jn. 15:26).

The Spirit's activity is so important to our lives that Jesus told his disciples, "It is for your good that I am going away. Unless I go away, the Comforter [Counselor, NIV] will not come to you; but if I go, I will send him to you" (Jn. 16:7). *See also* Counsel.

commandment An order or statute. A number of Hebrew terms stress the fact that, when God speaks, not just human beings but all creation must respond (Ps. 33:9; Isa. 45:12). The most common Hebrew word for commandment, *miswah*, is a technical religious term that defines the responsibilities of people who are in a covenant relationship with the Lord. Because the relational element is always implied, God's commandments cannot be viewed as cold, impersonal law. God's commands are a living expression of God's own nature and character. Thus, to respond obediently to God's commandments is to respond personally to the Lord himself. *See also* Covenant.

Some view God's laws, edicts, and statutes in a cold, legalistic way or as a method of earning merit. But the Scriptures set forth the commandment as a guideline intended for our own benefit as well as the honor of God. The new covenant involves a personal relationship marked by a mutual commitment—of people to God and of God to his people. *See also* Law.

Commandment, New Christ's command, "As I have loved you, so you must love one another" (Jn. 13:34).

In Scripture, a commandment defines the responsibilities of a person in covenant relationship with God. The new commandment defines what is expected of those who relate to God through the new covenant established by Jesus Christ.

The new responsibility is in complete harmony with the commandments of the OT, for Paul writes, ". . . Whatever other commandment there may be, [is] summed up in this one rule: 'Love your neighbor as yourself.' Love does no harm to its neighbor. Therefore love is the fulfillment of the law" (Rom. 13:9,10).

Commandments, Ten Ten rules given at Mount Sinai which summed up the responsibilities of those who related to God through the covenant of the Law. The Ten Commandments were given to Israel by God at Mount Sinai, probably about 1450 B.C. These "ten words" from Sinai were engraved by God on two stone tablets, which were later placed in the ark of the covenant, the most holy object in OT religion. *See also* Sinai.

The Ten Commandments appear twice in the OT (Ex. 20:2-17; Deut. 5:6-21), and express the core of what God requires of people who have been called to live in covenant relationship with him. The Ten Commandments also reflect the moral character of the giver. Thus we know more of what God is like by examining the way of life he requires. *See also* Covenant; Law.

As an expression of God's character, the Ten Commandments speak not only to Israel, but to all persons of every age. With the exception of the command to keep the Sabbath, each of the ten is restated in some form in the NT.

DIVISION OF THE TEN

The commandments are not numbered in the OT text. The Jews took God's preamble, "I am the Lord your God, who brought you out of Egypt," as the first commandment calling for faith. Then they combined the "no other gods" and "no idols" statements as their second commandment. Roman Catholics and Lutherans also unite those two commandments, and then divide the prohibition against coveting. Most Protestants, however, list the following as the Ten Commandments.

First stone tablet: relationship with God

1. No other gods.
2. No idols.
3. No vain use of God's name.
4. Keep the Sabbath holy.

Second stone tablet: relationship with people

5. Honor father and mother.
6. No murder.
7. No adultery.
8. No stealing.
9. No false testimony.
10. No coveting.

POSITIVE ASPECTS

Although the Ten Commandments are expressed negatively as "thou shalt nots," they are essentially positive. (1) The Ten Commandments are positive in intent; they are intended to guide God's people into a rich and fulfilling way of life. As Moses said, "Walk in all the way that the Lord your God has commanded you, so that you may live and prosper" (Deut. 5:33). Each human being needs divine moral guidance to avoid choices which harm himself and others, and which bring divine judgment. (2) The Ten Commandments are positive in impact. Each has powerful positive implications for relation-

Sixteenth-century illustrated manuscript shows Moses holding the tablets of the Law atop Mount Sinai while awed Hebrews watch.

ship with God and other human beings. Whenever an evil is forbidden, the opposite good is implied. Thus, Jesus summed up the commandments by saying that they call for love of God and for love of neighbor (Mt. 22:37-40). (3) The Ten Commandments are positive in application. All but one is restated in some form in the NT as a principle of Christian living.

WHAT THE COMMANDMENTS TEACH

What does each of the Ten Commandments teach us? Briefly:

• *"You shall have no other gods before me"* (Ex. 20:3). We owe our allegiance to God alone. Indeed, he is the only one worthy of our loyalty—he cares for us even as we worship him.

• *"You shall not make for yourself an idol"* (Ex. 20:4-6). The Israelites' neighbors worshiped a variety of false gods through physical images. By contrast, God emphasized his transcendence. He revealed himself through his Word and his powerful miracles. Only one physical image would ever be able to perfectly capture the essence of the true God—Jesus Christ, God-in-the-flesh. *See also* Idol.

• *"You shall not take the name of the Lord your God in vain"* (Ex. 20:7, RSV). To take God's name in vain is to use his holy name unworthily or to no good purpose, which

Gustav Dore's classic representation of Moses breaking the original tablet of the Law after discovering his people worshiping a golden calf (Ex. 32:19).

is in turn to consider "God" an empty or meaningless word. God's revealed name is Yahweh, which means, "The One Who Is Always Present" or "He who is"—or, "He who has eternal and unconditional existence"—in contrast to all of the created universe. We are to be constantly aware that God is real, and that he is with us.

Some versions read, "Do not misuse the name of the Lord your God." The translators here assumed that the command was prohibiting the use of God's name in magical formulas or incantations. *See also* Name; Yahweh.

• *"Remember the Sabbath day by keeping it holy"* (Ex. 20:8). The command originally kept the Israelites from working on the seventh day. The early Christians substituted Sunday, the day of Jesus' resurrection, for the Sabbath as their holy day. We can still observe the spirit of this command, however, as we set time aside to remember the Lord, to worship him, and to rejoice in him. *See also* Sabbath.

• *"Honor your father and your mother"* (Ex. 20:12). Respect for parents leads to knowledge of God. Parents often introduce us to God and, to the young child, mother and father represent God's authority. Thus the family is a sacred institution and the home should have a central role in the nurture of children.

• *"You shall not murder"* (Ex. 20:13). The life of every human person has worth and value. We are to actively protect and guard one another. *See also* Murder.

• *"You shall not commit adultery"* (Ex. 20:14). Each person must be loyal to his or her spouse, thus mirroring the covenant commitment that exists between God and his people. *See also* Adultery.

• *"You shall not steal"* (Ex. 20:15). Concern for others extends to honoring their property. We are to love others, not "use" them for material gain. *See also* Thief.

• *"You shall not give false testimony against your neighbor"* (Ex. 20:16). We are to guard others' reputations as well as their lives and property. *See also* Lie.

• *"You shall not covet"* (Ex. 20:17). We are to place the highest value on people, not on possessions. It is not what others have that is to be important to us, but they themselves, for all persons are important to God. *See also* Covet.

The Ten Commandments are far more than ten rules to live by. They reveal the structure of our faith relationship with God, and the structure of our moral relationship with others. Today as in OT times the Ten Commandments reveal God, and they continue to guide us into loving, healthy relationships with the Lord and with one another.

commerce *See* Trade.

communion *See* Lord's Supper.

compassion Pity or loving concern, which often moves a person to provide help. David, at a moment when he was overwhelmed by a sense of sin, cried out to God for mercy. He begged the Lord to forgive "according to your great compassion" (Ps. 51:1).

Knowing that God was compassionate changed David's life. God's revelation of his compassionate nature should bring us comfort and hope.

COMPASSION IN THE OT

Two different Hebrew words are rendered "compassion" in English versions. *Hamal* emphasizes one's emotional response to a person in need. It is also translated "to have pity." *Raham* means "to love" and "to have mercy" as well as "to be compassionate." Nearly three-quarters of the occurrences of *raham* in the OT refer to God's love or his compassion for human beings. While God remains free to respond compassionately or to withhold compassion (Ex. 33:19), Scripture portrays him as one who cares deeply for us, and whose love moves him to help.

COMPASSION IN THE NT

Three different Greek words are sometimes translated "compassion" in the NT. *Eleos* means "mercy." *Oiktirmos* is pain at the sight of suffering. *Splanchnizomai* means to feel a wrenching pull on the emotions. This word generally describes Jesus' feelings when confronted by a person in need (Mk. 1:40-42; 6:34). Moved by compassion, Jesus acted to meet the need which moved him. God truly is moved by our needs—so moved that he acts, and by acting changes our lives. Compassion as "mercy" is described in Rom. 12:8 as one of the motivational gifts given by the Holy Spirit.

compel (1) To force compliance; (2) often in Scripture, to create or invite response. When the NT speaks of compulsion, it generally does not mean forced compliance. Instead the compulsion comes from within, as a response to other persons or to the Gospel.

In one of Jesus' parables, a king's servants were to compel passersby to come to a banquet (Lk. 14:16-24). This does not mean that they were to force guests to attend. Rather, they were to issue a compelling invitation. The invitation would create a response in the outsiders who received it (*compare* 2 Cor. 5:14).

God carefully guards our freedom. He forces no one to respond to him against his or her will.

concubine A secondary wife, with inferior social and legal standing. Middle Eastern law and custom in OT times permitted men to have secondary wives, called concubines. A concubine did not have all the rights of a primary wife. But a concubine did have legal status. Her rights, and the rights of any children the concubine might bear, were well defined. These are all well documented from secular sources, such as the Code of Hammurabi (1750 B.C.).

The handmaidens that Rachel and Leah gave to Jacob became his concubines, legal but secondary wives (Gen. 30:3-13). While the OT holds up the ideal of monogamy, OT Law recognized long-established customs. The Mosaic code goes beyond other codes in guarding the rights of a Hebrew girl who might be sold into servanthood and possibly become a concubine (Ex. 21:7-11). *See also* Marriage.

The colored portion of this line drawing of a wall relief from 'Ey's tomb at Amarna (14th century B.C.) shows two houses reserved for his concubines and their children. The front rooms show women eating, dancing, and playing instruments. The bedrooms at far left contain lyres, lutes, and other articles.

concupiscence (KJV) Strong evil desires or sexual passions. Three times in the KJV this archaic word translates the Greek *epithumia*, "desire" (Rom. 7:8; Col. 3:5; 1 Th. 4:5). *Epithumia* usually indicates evil desires, which originate in man's sinful nature. Modern versions use phrases like "evil desires" and "passionate lust." *See also* Desire.

condemn (1) To declare guilty; (2) to pass sentence on; (3) to strongly disapprove. Though not a pleasant matter, condemnation is a crucial part of the story of God's dealings with humanity. Because of his holiness, God condemns human sin. That condemnation implies punishment —eternal separation from God.

Fortunately, that is not the whole story, as Jesus made clear: "God did not send his Son into the world to condemn the world, but to save the world through him" (Jn. 3:17).

BASIS OF DIVINE CONDEMNATION

In the OT, the words most often translated "condemn" are from roots which mean "to act wickedly" or "to be guilty." God holds human beings responsible for their wicked acts. As moral judge of his universe, God will punish those who sin. *See also* Judge.

In the NT, "condemn" is from a family of Greek words which share the basic meaning of "to decide, distinguish, or judge." The wicked are distinguished by a failure to respond to the requirements of OT Law, or by a failure to respond to the words of Jesus. Both OT Law and Christ's words "condemn" the sinner by testifying against his actions or attitude (Rom. 3:19,20; Jn. 12:47-50).

FAITH AND CONDEMNATION

Jesus said that a person who believes in the Son "is not condemned, but whoever does not believe stands condemned already because he has not believed in the name of God's one and only Son" (Jn. 3:18; *see* 5:24). The passage does not suggest that persons are condemned for the sin of unbelief, but rather that only faith in Christ which shows itself in godly living allows us to escape condemnation. The person who trusts Christ receives forgiveness. The person who does not trust Christ must answer for his or her sins and, because all have sinned (Rom. 3:9-19), is "condemned already." *See also* Faith; Forgive.

One of the most freeing statements of Scripture is this: "There is now no condemnation for those who are in Christ Jesus" (Rom. 8:1; *see* v. 34). Christians, like other human beings, do fall short and sin. We too feel the pangs of guilt. At such times we recall the forgiveness which is ours in Christ, shake off the deadening grip of guilt feelings, and make a fresh start on righteous living. *See also* Confess.

While Christ assures us of forgiveness, he also calls us to live holy lives. If we keep on obeying God's commands and doing what pleases him, not even our hearts will have occasion to condemn us (1 Jn. 3:21-24).

DEMONSTRATED GUILT

English versions of the NT frequently use "condemn" in another sense. At times "condemn" means "to demonstrate guilt." Thus, Jesus says that the people of Nineveh who repented under Jonah's preaching will condemn the Jews of his time, for they did not repent at the preaching of Jesus, one far greater than Jonah (Mt. 12:41,42; *see* Heb. 11:7). The repentance of Nineveh demonstrated how the people of Jesus' time should have responded to Christ.

CONDEMNING ONE ANOTHER

Another sense of "condemn" is "to consider guilty" or "to charge with guilt." Christians are to recognize acts which God has condemned as sin, and are to discipline sinning believers. But the Bible warns against charging one another with guilt over issues on which God has not spoken. Jesus said, "Do not condemn and you will not be condemned" (Lk. 6:37). Romans examines this common problem carefully, and insists that we must neither look down on nor condemn fellow believers whose convictions differ from our own in matters of diet or of traditional custom (Rom. 14:1–15:7). *See also* Convictions; Discipline.

SUMMARY

God has already judged the wicked acts of human beings and condemned (pronounced judgment on) the whole human race as sinners. But Jesus came to release the condemned and to provide forgiveness. The one who puts his trust in Jesus "has eternal life and will not be condemned" (Jn. 5:24). Awareness of the fact that we are forgiven frees us to approach God confidently, and enables us to put aside our feelings of guilt and live in God's grace. Because we acknowledge God alone as the perfect and unerring Judge of moral beings, we do not condemn others and are careful not to burden them with continual feelings of guilt after they have already put their trust in Christ's atoning blood. *See also* Guilt.

coney The Syrian rock hyrax (Heb., *shapan*). This quick, rabbit-sized animal lives in hilly areas, primarily in Africa, although they are also found in Israel even today. A timid animal, the coney seldom ventures far from the rocky crevasses to which it scurries when frightened. These "creatures of little power" that "make their home in the crags" (Prov. 30:26) are eaten in Africa. They are classified as unclean animals by OT Law. *See also* Animals; Clean and Unclean.

confess, confession (1) To openly declare one's faith; (2) to admit one's guilt. The words translated "confess" in the OT and NT are powerful terms. The Hebrew *yada'* has the basic meaning of "to know." In certain contexts, though, *yada'* goes further: it means "to know and to respond to what one knows." Thus, someone knows God's goodness and declares or "confesses" it. Or, someone knows the seriousness of his or her sin and confesses it.

The Greek *homologeō* means literally "to say the same." It also served as a legal term in the first century. In Roman law *homologeō* meant to accept an official decision or legal order, and to abide by it. *See also* Acknowledge.

When translated "confess," both the *yada'* and *homologeō* portray the believer in action, boldly declaring his or her faith, or openly acknowledging failure and sin.

BOLDLY DECLARING FAITH

Jesus called on the people of his time to confess him openly before men (Mt. 10:32; Lk. 12:8). This required boldness, because the Jewish leaders had decided that anyone who acknowledged Jesus as the Christ should be excommunicated (Jn. 9:22). Later Paul says that saving faith must take this kind of risk: "For it is with your heart that you believe and are justified, and it is with your mouth that you confess and are saved" (Rom. 10:9,10).

Early Christian doctrinal statements took the form of confessions, which boldly stated the essence of the faith Christians professed. One of the earliest and most powerful was penned by Irenaeus, a missionary and church leader of A.D. 190.

> #### CONFESSION OF IRENAEUS
> The church, though dispersed throughout the whole world, even to the ends of the earth, has received from the apostles and their disciples this faith: [She believes] in one God, the Father Almighty, Maker of heaven, and earth, and the sea, and all things that are in them, and in one Christ Jesus, the Son of God, who became incarnate for our salvation, and in the Holy Spirit, who proclaimed through the prophets the dispensations of God, and the advent, and the birth from a virgin, and the passion, and the resurrection from the dead, and the ascension into heaven in the flesh of the beloved Christ Jesus, our Lord, and His [future] manifestation from heaven in the glory of the Father "to gather all things in one," and to raise up anew all flesh of the whole human race, in order that to Christ Jesus, our Lord, and God, and Savior, and King, according to the will of the invisible Father, "every knee should bow, of things in heaven, and things in earth, and things under the earth, and that every tongue should confess" to Him, and that He should execute just judgment towards all; that He may send "spiritual wickedness," and the angels who transgressed and became apostates, together with the ungodly, and unrighteous, and wicked and profane of men, into everlasting fire; but may, in the exercise of His grace, confer immortality on the righteous, and holy, and those who have kept His commandments, and have persevered in His love, some from the beginning [of their Christian course], and others from the date of their repentance, and may surround them with everlasting glory.

OPENLY CONFESSING SIN

Both Testaments portray confession as the avenue through which a sinning believer can be restored to fellowship with God. Psalms 32 and 51 explore the experience of the sinning saint, and portray the relief that confessing sin to God brings.

When I kept silent,
my bones wasted away
through my groaning all day long.
For day and night
your hand was heavy upon me;
my strength was sapped
as in the heat of summer.
Then I acknowledged my sin to you
and did not cover up my iniquity.
I said, "I will confess

The "coney" of Scripture is the Syrian rock hyrax, which lives among mountain crags in Palestine (Ps. 104:18).

241

my transgressions to the Lord''—
and you forgave
  the guilt of my sin.   (Ps. 32:3-5)

The OT often describes a public confession of sins. This may involve a leader or group of leaders confessing the sins of the whole community. Nehemiah prayed, ''I confess the sins we Israelites, including myself and my father's house, have committed against you'' (Neh. 1:6). This kind of confession is incorporated in the liturgy of some denominations.

Public confession may also take the form of an open admission by an individual of personal fault. David even penned Psalm 51 for use in public worship, in effect confessing his adultery publicly (*compare* 51:1). Because David's sin was public knowledge, public confession was required. This too is incorporated in the discipline of some denominations.

In Roman Catholicism, private confession of sins to a priest, made for forgiveness, is considered a sacrament. In Jas. 5:16, we are advised to ''confess your sins to each other and pray for each other so that you may be healed.''

HEALING POWER OF CONFESSION

The Bible's central passage on confession of specific sins is 1 Jn. 1:5–2:2. The passage warns us against pretense in our relationship with God. We must evaluate ourselves and our actions honestly, and face up to our shortcomings. When we acknowledge our sins to God, ''he is faithful and just and will forgive us our sins.'' But the passage goes on. He will also ''purify us from all unrighteousness'' (1:9). Confession offers more than forgiveness. Confession restores fellowship with God and introduces hope. After confession, God again works within us, so we can hope to avoid failures in the future.

A person unwilling to acknowledge his faults and sins, to himself or to God, closes his life to this cleansing work of God's Spirit.

confirmation (1) A ceremony admitting a person to full membership in the church; (2) a course of study leading to membership. Confirmation is not a biblical term, but it has deep roots in church history. Very shortly after the apostles died, the church adopted the practice of giving converts a special course of instruction before baptism. In Catholicism this evolved into the sacrament of confirmation administered by a bishop. The sacrament of confirmation is understood to strengthen the gift of the Holy Spirit, given at baptism, as an aid to Christian living. Catholic boys and girls usually receive the sacrament after a period of instruction in Catholic faith.

The Reformation rejected the sacramental view of confirmation. But the Reformers did affirm the importance of instructing young people. Many Protestant churches today conduct confirmation classes as a prelude to church membership.

confound (KJV) To put to shame. The Hebrew terms for ''confound'' or ''confounded'' portray a visible change in a person's appearance, as he or she turns pale or blushes when publicly humiliated (2 Ki. 19:6; Ps. 22:5). The Hebrew word, as in Ps. 25:1-3 and Joel 2:27, emphasizes the objective state of someone whose hopes and expectations are revealed to be empty, such as those defeated by an enemy or those who have put their faith in a false god. Modern versions tend to use ''shame'' or ''ashamed.'' *See also* Shame.

congregation An assembly of people. In the OT, ''congregation'' describes the Israelites gathering together, usually for worship, but also to prepare for war (Jdg. 21:10) or to crown a king (1 Ki. 12:20). Modern versions tend to use ''assembly'' or ''community'' where the KJV has ''congregation.'' *See also* Assembly.

Conquest The invasion of Canaan about 1400 B.C. by the Israelites. The story of the Conquest is described in the Book of Joshua.

Joshua first led his people across the Jordan River to Gilgal, where all the males were circumcised (Josh. 3–5). Jericho fell first (ch. 6), then Ai (ch. 8). The southern campaign was provoked by five local kings. Joshua routed their forces at Gibeon and then captured their cities (chs. 9,10). The northern campaign also was triggered by Canaanite kings, who gathered at the Waters of Merom. Joshua again surprised the enemy and chased the fleeing armies (ch. 11).

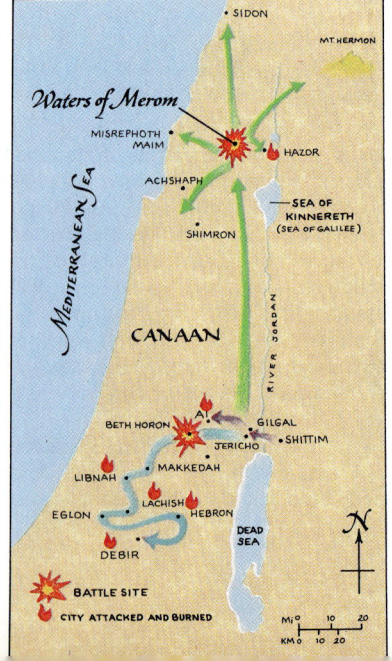

Detail of a French illuminated manuscript from about A.D. 1250 depicts Joshua with his arm raised to halt the sun and moon during a battle with five kings of Canaan. While Joshua destroyed the major Canaanite armies, the Conquest was a gradual and incomplete process, as the Book of Judges attests (Jdg. 1:19–3:6).

HISTORICAL RELIABILITY

The Bible portrays an invasion of Palestine by the Israelites, during which the most powerful of the existing Canaanite city-states were destroyed. However, some scholars view the biblical account as a much later, and inaccurate, reconstruction of history.

Yet the famous Jewish archaeologist Yigael Yadin says flatly that "in its broad outline the archaeological record supports the narrative in Joshua and Judges."

DATING THE CONQUEST

Even those who hold to the essential reliability of the Bible's account disagree concerning the date of the Exodus and the conquest of Canaan. Most archaeologists currently assume that the Israelites entered Canaan about 1230–1220 B.C. This dating hinges on two beliefs: (1) that the Late Bronze Age extended from about 1550 to 1200 B.C., and (2) that the archaeological evidence found in cities like Jericho does not "fit" with dates given in the OT for the Exodus and Conquest.

However, conservative scholars have challenged the view of the majority because the later date for the Conquest has its own set of archaeological problems. Furthermore, pottery remains and scarabs from the time of Jericho's destruction have been found. These date no later than the 15th century B.C., indicating that the city was destroyed around 1400 B.C.—which fits perfectly with the conservative view.

While debates about the nature and date of the Conquest will continue, those who trust the historical reliability of the Bible can do so on the basis of reasoned evidence as well as on the basis of faith. *See also* Exodus; Jericho.

conscience Moral standards, a sense of right and wrong. Conscience is a complicated NT concept. No parallel word is found in the OT, although the "heart" at times displays some of the function of conscience. Thus the expression, "David's heart smote him" (KJV), is appropriately translated by the NIV, "David was conscience-stricken" (1 Sam. 24:5; *compare* 1 Sam. 25:31).

Since the idea of conscience is not strong in the OT, we must look for roots of the concept in the Greek culture. In that culture the word *syneidēsis*, "consciousness," (or literally, "shared knowledge"), came to mean consciousness of one's moral standing. Someone gained moral self-knowledge by contemplating his or her own past deeds. The Greek found this moral self-knowledge distinctly unpleasant. Again and again conscience is portrayed in Greek literature as the dark accuser of humanity, a storehouse of knowledge of one's failures and sins.

The NT builds on this foundational meaning, but defines conscience more clearly, and explains the role God has given to this unique human capacity for moral self-knowledge.

243

CONSCIENCE AND THE PAGAN

In Rom. 2:12-16 Paul argues that the activity of the pagan conscience is proof that all people lack righteousness. Moral law is engraved in human nature. The pagans' opinions about which acts are right and wrong may not always match the moral ideal revealed in God's Law, but this is irrelevant. God will not judge the pagan by divine standards which the pagan does not know. Instead God will use the pagan's own moral code in judging him. And, even by his own code, the pagan is proven a sinner. Conscience itself demonstrates the proof of Paul's argument, for conscience accuses, showing each of us that we have done what we ourselves hold to be wrong.

Besides serving as a witness to humanity's moral nature, conscience also is a witness against each individual. The fact that each person is accused by his conscience proves that all have sinned.

CONSCIENCE AND THE CHRISTIAN

While conscience is a good witness against us, it is a poor moral guide.

Conscience does judge actions, but there is no guarantee its evaluations are correct! Only a conscience fully informed by divine revelation can hope to evaluate choices and actions correctly. But even then conscience is fallible. Christians also should severely limit the area in which they permit their conscience to function. The sole role of conscience is to evaluate our own actions. We must never evaluate or judge the actions of others by the standard of our own conscience. Several NT passages contribute to our understanding of these important points.

• *1 Corinthians 8–10*. The Corinthians disagreed about eating meat sacrificed to idols. This action bothered the consciences of some, but not those of others. Clearly, even the Christian consciences of the Corinthians were not reliable guides in this matter. Paul asks the "strong" (who feel it is all right to eat such meat) to respect the position of the "weak" (who feel eating the carcass of an animal sacrificed to a pagan god is wrong). Paul does not make this request because the "weak" brother's conscience is correct, but because weak believers might be harmed if they ate meat in violation of their own conscience. Acting against conscience defiles, and introduces a corrupting element into our lives (1 Cor. 8:7; *compare* 1 Tim. 1:5).

In Corinth each party needed to extend freedom to the other to follow the dictates of individual conscience. We must learn not to judge, or to be judged by, another's conscience.

With this principle established, Paul goes on to urge the Corinthians to avoid idolatry and the practices associated with it.

• *Romans 14,15*. Believers are to stop passing judgment on others in matters of personal conviction. We must neither condemn nor look down on those whose convictions are different from our own. Paul says, in essence, "Whatever you believe about such things keep between yourself and God." Conscience is an inner voice, not a public standard to be imposed on a Christian community.

• *Hebrews 9*. This passage deals with bondage to our feelings of guilt over past sins. Psychologically, the accusations of conscience drag us down and rob us of that confidence in God which enables us to meet the future with faith and hope. In the words of Hebrews, unresolved guilt traps us in "acts that lead to death" (v. 14). But Christ's blood cleanses the believer's conscience from such acts: In Christ we are forgiven. Cleansed by Christ's blood, we are to accept release from the burden of our past and look forward to a new and different future (Heb. 8:12; 9:28).

• *1 Corinthians 4:4,5*. Several times the Bible mentions the value of a clear conscience. While God, not conscience, is our ultimate Judge, we should always do what we believe to be right, and so keep our consciences clear.

SUMMARY

The Bible presents a distinct view of human nature. We are moral beings, with inner standards of right and wrong. Our moral nature is demonstrated by the conscience, which evaluates our acts by whatever standards we hold, and convicts us when we do something we believe to be wrong.

We must not violate conscience by doing something believed to be wrong. But we must also realize that conscience is not an infallible guide. Each of us needs to study God's Word to better inform our consciences. And we must rely on the guidance of the Holy Spirit and seek advice from the spiritually mature. *See also* Convictions.

consecrate, consecration To set apart or dedicate to the worship and service of God. In OT times consecration of persons and things typically occurred through religious ritual (Ex. 29,40; 2 Chr. 29). The recurring OT phrase "consecrate yourself" means to prepare for worship or service (1) by meeting the ritual requirements of OT faith (Lev. 11:44), but also (2) by obeying the moral decrees embodied in OT Law (Lev. 20:7,8).

In its few NT occurrences, "consecrate" generally refers back to OT ritual practices. In the RSV, consecrate is used where other English versions have "dedicate" or "sanctify." *See also* Sanctify.

consume To eat up; figuratively, to burn or destroy. This word usually appears in its figurative sense in Scripture. Fire frequently "consumes" things, whether a forest (Ezek. 20:47), a burnt offering (1 Ki. 18:38), or a rebellious nation (Ezek. 15:7; Heb. 10:27). But the mystery of the burning bush Moses encountered was that it was not consumed by the fire—it just kept burning (Ex. 3:2). The Lord described himself as a "consuming fire" (Deut. 4:24), and at Sinai the Israelites feared that God's fiery presence would consume them (Deut. 5:25). The prophets often depicted the fiery judgment of God consuming his enemies or his sinful people (Isa. 10:17-19; Jer. 5:14-17).

But one can also experience emotional consumption. David spoke of standing up for God against his enemies and said, "Zeal for your house consumes me" (Ps. 69:9). John quotes this verse after telling how Jesus drove the moneychangers from the Temple (Jn. 2:17). The Lord's passion for the purity of his Father's house made him burn with anger against those who were misusing it.

contempt Scorn, despising, or neglect. To have contempt for someone or something is to value it so lightly that we pay no attention to it when making choices. Esau had contempt for the covenant promise God had given his grandfather Abraham, and so he willingly traded his birthright for a bowl of stew (Gen. 25:33,34). Job muses, "Men at ease have contempt for misfortune" (Job 12:5). That is, they don't even think about things going wrong.

On the other hand, God is shown as one who "pours contempt on nobles. . . . But he lifted the needy out of their affliction" (Ps. 107:40; *see* Job 12:21). When it comes to meeting human needs, God seems to neglect the wealthy in favor of those who truly need him.

David complains about the wicked: "With pride and contempt, they speak arrogantly against the righteous" (Ps. 31:18). And Proverbs succinctly adds, "When wickedness comes, so does contempt" (Prov. 18:3). This probably means that wickedness is contemptible, that by being wicked, you demean yourself.

The lesson for believers is this: When we fail to obey the Lord, refusing to take his Word into account when we make our decisions, we show contempt for him. And by doing so, we undermine our own value. When we show the Lord that we truly value him, we can be lifted up by Jesus' great love for us. *See also* Despise.

contentment Satisfaction of one's needs; control of one's desires. The Greek verb *arkeō* conveys a sense of freedom from reliance on other people or things. This is not simply a passive acceptance of our situation in life, but a positive assurance that because God supplies all our needs we are freed from unnecessary desires.

The fundamental importance of contentment to people of God is evidenced in the tenth commandment which forbids coveting (Ex. 20:17), as well as in the teaching of the Proverbs (Prov. 15:17; 17:1), and the exhortation of the prophets (*for example,* Mic. 2:2). Contentment is also an essential element of the teaching and life of Jesus Christ, who challenges his followers to learn contentment by relying on God to supply all their needs (Mt. 6:25-32) and to avoid greed of any sort (Lk. 12:13-21). Paul places contentment opposite the love of money which leads to a variety of moral problems; the Christian life should be marked by "godliness with contentment" (1 Tim. 6:6-10; *also compare* Phil. 4:11).

convert, conversion To change one's beliefs and/or behavior. When Peter urged his hearers to "repent and turn to God" ("be converted," KJV), he was echoing OT calls for recommitment (Acts 3:19). The

Moses consecrates his brother Aaron as high priest. In Ex. 29:29 God instructs: "Aaron's sacred garments will belong to his descendants so that they can be anointed and ordained in them."

prophets frequently implored the Israelites to abandon their sinful ways and turn (Heb., *shub*) back to God. By NT times, the noun form indicated a Gentile who made a commitment to Jewish faith—a *prosēlytos* (Acts 6:5). The Christian church quickly adopted this term for anyone who turned to Christ from either a Jewish or pagan background (Rom. 16:5; 1 Tim. 3:6).

In neither the OT nor NT does conversion suggest a mere change of religious opinion. Conversion implies a change of both attitude and behavior. The prime example of conversion is, of course, the transformation of Saul from a persecutor of Christians into Paul, the apostle who dedicated his life to spreading Christ's Gospel across the Roman Empire. But conversion need not be as dramatic as Paul's. It may be very quiet, like the conversion of Lydia (Acts 16:13-15), whose beliefs and behavior underwent a more subtle change. Perhaps Paul's words of praise for the Christians at Thessalonica best sum up the NT implications of conversion: "You turned to God from idols to serve the living and true God" (1 Th. 1:9).

Conversion still involves more than a verbal profession of faith. It means abandoning empty objects of faith. It means committing one's entire life to the service of the living God. In this sense, the believer is continually being converted.

convict To convince or reprove of sin. Jesus said the Holy Spirit would "convict the world of guilt in regard to sin and righteousness and judgment" (Jn. 16:8). In this ministry the Spirit uses Scripture (Acts 2:37; Jas. 2:9), general revelation (Rom. 1:18-20), and human conscience (Rom. 2:14,15). While the Spirit persuades human beings of guilt and convinces them of judgment to come, conviction alone does not produce conversion. Conviction is best understood as God's gracious preparation of individuals for salvation. Each person who becomes aware of his or her need must then personally repent and place his or her hope in God (1 Th. 1:5). *See also* Conscience; Repent.

convictions Deeply held personal beliefs about what behavior is appropriate for Christians, particularly in matters not directly forbidden or commanded in Scripture. Disputes over personal convictions arose in the early church as they do in our own day. In Rome some believers felt that certain days were especially sacred; others considered "every day alike" (Rom. 14:5). Some were vegetarians; others ate meat (Rom. 14:1,2). In Corinth some bought meat at temple markets. Others were shocked, because such animals had been sacrificed to a pagan deity (1 Cor. 8). In modern times, convictions in various Christian communities have condemned or condoned dancing, various hair styles, the use of cosmetics, attending the theater, popular music, etc.

The word "convictions" is not found in the Bible. Yet, in every society, Christians will have strong opinions about what is or is not appropriate behavior. By extending to others the freedom to differ in matters of conviction, Christ's Church develops a "spirit of unity among yourselves as you follow Christ Jesus, so that with one heart and mouth you may glorify the God and Father of our Lord Jesus Christ" (Rom. 15:5,6).

cooking Heating food in preparation for eating. In biblical times, the women of the home did the cooking. They baked the breads that were the staple of every diet, as well as vegetable dishes and other foods.

The grain for breads was ground daily. So the stone mill, with its upper and lower grindstones, was essential household equipment. Bread might be baked in flat cakes by laying the dough on heated stones, but most OT homes had rounded, hive-shaped ovens just outside. A fire burned within, heating the plaster-covered bricks of this hollow structure, which stood 2 to 3 feet (1 meter) high. Flat

First-century clay stove in Jerusalem has three openings or "burners." Niches at the rear were for utensils and spices.

cakes of dough were then stuck to its sides, or rounded cakes might be placed inside after the ashes were scraped away.

In Jesus' day, many women cooked on

Women in Jesus' day cooked in kitchens much like this one, re-constructed in the famous "burned house" in upper Jerusalem which dates to the Roman destruction of the city in A.D. 70.

clay stoves. On the rare occasions when they served meat, they would roast it or boil it in a pot. Various clay or metal pots were used in cooking: large, lidded casserole dishes called *ilpas* for slow-cooked vegetables or stews of fish or meat; shallow pans (like modern skillets) for frying; deeper pans for deep-frying. Well-equipped first-century kitchens might also have a matched pedestal and ceramic jar. A fire would be kindled within the pedestal, and water would be boiled in the jar above.

Food was served in large bowls and trays. During the meal the family and guests dipped into these dishes with their fingers. Drink was carried in jugs or pitchers, and individuals had their own cups of clay or colored glass.

Many first-century women took pride in their arrays of cooking and serving utensils. Marriage contracts usually stipulated that, in the case of divorce, the woman would retain the items in her kitchen.

Egyptian shepherds prepare and cook game over an open fire, from time of the Old Empire (2686–2040 B.C.). Portions of most OT sacrifices were to be cooked and enjoyed by those offering them as part of the ceremony.

copper A common metal, reddish-brown and malleable. Copper was the first metal mined, smelted, and worked by human beings. The necessary processes were probably developed in the fifth millennium B.C. Within a thousand years they were widely known throughout the ancient world. It was not until about 2000 B.C. that bronze, an alloy of copper and tin, supplanted copper as the metal of choice. Deposits of copper existed in Palestine in OT times (Deut. 8:9; Job 28:1-5). Copper coins were in circulation in NT times (Mt. 10:9). *See also* Bronze; Metals.

coppersmith (KJV) A general term for any metalworker or smith. The KJV identifies an opponent of Paul in Ephesus as "Alexander the coppersmith" (2 Tim. 4:14). The Greek word, *chalkeus*, literally means "worker in bronze."

In Ephesus the metalworkers' guild made medallions containing the image of an ancient shrine of their goddess, Diana (Artemis). Paul's preaching had such an impact in Ephesus that people no longer bought the medallions, and thus the livelihood of the metalworkers was threatened (Acts 19:23-41).

cor *See* Weights and Measures.

coral *See* Jewelry.

corban An offering dedicated to God. The OT uses this word for the many offerings a person might make to God (Lev. 1:2; 22:27; Num. 7:25). By NT times, however,

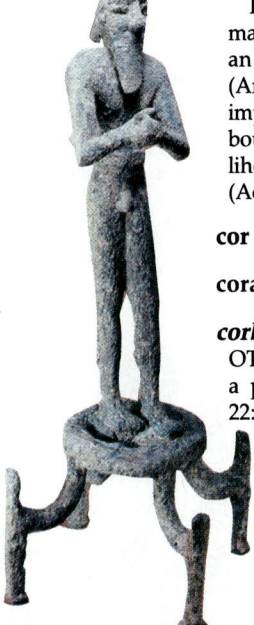

Copper stand designed to support a bowl, from the Temple Oval at Khafaje, Iraq (2600–2350 B.C.).

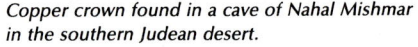

Copper crown found in a cave of Nahal Mishmar in the southern Judean desert.

corban indicated something dedicated to God, but held in trust by the offerer during his lifetime. Thus a person might declare property *corban*, but continue to use the profits it generated for his own benefit. In Christ's time *corban* served some as a legal loophole, used to avoid giving financial aid to parents.

Jesus condemned the argument that it would not be right to take something dedicated to God and use it to feed and house one's parents (Mt. 15:1-9; Mk. 7:9-13). This legalistic application of *corban* nullified God's command to honor father and mother! Jesus added, "And you do many things like that" (Mk. 7:13).

Christ's criticism unveils the essential flaw in legalistic religion. By shifting attention from God's intentions to our own rules, we sooner or later misuse the rules and violate God's intentions. Believers must always seek to understand and follow the divine intention, and avoid the use of regulations in a way that violates the spirit of the Word.

cord A thin rope. Cords or ropes were made from a variety of fibers in biblical times: goat or camel hair, fiber from date trees, hemp, papyrus, pine needles. Woven flax fiber made strong and durable cords, and these were commonly used in making fish nets. The Bible also mentions ropes or cords ("chains," NIV) of gold (Ex. 28:24,25) and silver (Eccl. 12:6).

In biblical times people used cords and rope as bowstrings, to tie down tents, to bind captives, in fishing, to make snares for hunting, to suspend lamps, to bind sacrificial animals, to measure objects, to produce rigging for ships, etc.

Cords, like other everyday objects, are often used figuratively in the OT. Proverbs 5:22 warns, "The evil deeds of a wicked man ensnare him; the cords of his sin hold him fast." In contrast, God says to Israel through Hosea, "I led them [my people] with cords of human kindness, with ties of love" (Hos. 11:4). Today, too, we can respond to each tug on the delicate threads of love by which God binds us to him, or we can break away, only to find ourselves tangled in the unbreakable snare of sin.

coriander A bush whose ripe seeds were prized as a flavoring. The coriander grows wild in Palestine but is also planted in vegetable gardens. The manna God supplied the Exodus generation was the size and shape of coriander seeds (Num. 11:7). *See also* Manna.

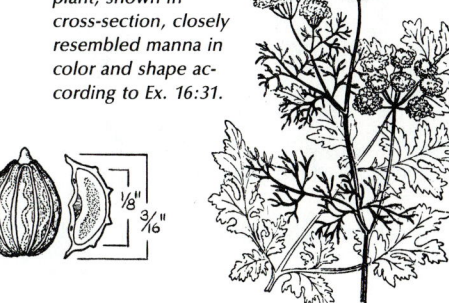

The seed of this plant, shown in cross-section, closely resembled manna in color and shape according to Ex. 16:31.

Corinthians, First Epistle to the Paul's first letter to the Corinthians is often called "the problem epistle." Here the apostle deals with a series of sins and errors in the Corinthian church. He often introduces new problems with the Greek words *peri de*, "now concerning." This recurring phrase helps us outline the book.

BACKGROUND

Corinth was built on a narrow isthmus of land which tied the Peloponnesian peninsula to the Greek mainland. To avoid a dangerous sea journey around the peninsula, cargoes and even small ships were transported over the five land miles between the Aegean Sea and the Gulf of Corinth. In the first century, Corinth was the capital of Achaia, and the seat of the Roman proconsul who governed southern and central Greece. At the height of its prosperity this busy commercial center had a population estimated at 200,000 freemen and 500,000 slaves.

The city had been destroyed by the Romans in 146 B.C., but re-established as a Roman colony in 44 B.C. The earlier city had gained a reputation for sexual excess, but the rebuilt Corinth of Paul's day (A.D. 51–52) probably had the morality of any other major city of the Empire.

One fascinating archaeological find is an

	STRUCTURE OF **1 CORINTHIANS**	
I.	Concerning the lack of unity	1–4
II.	Concerning sin in the church family	5,6
III.	Concerning marriage and divorce	7
IV.	Concerning doctrinal disputes	8–10
V.	Concerning women and worship	11
VI.	Concerning spirituality	12–14
VII.	Concerning resurrection realities	15
VIII.	Parting encouragement	16

inscription commemorating the gift of a paved roadway to the city by its treasurer, Erastus. Most believe this is the same person Paul won to Christ there (Acts 19:22; Rom. 16:23; 2 Tim. 4:20).

HISTORICAL SIGNIFICANCE

Paul founded the church in Corinth during the year and a half he taught there on his second missionary journey (Acts 18). In A.D. 57, some five years later, he wrote his first letter to Corinth from Ephesus. In this brief time many disputes and problems had emerged in the congregation. Paul's first letter to the Corinthians helps

This first-century jar, inscribed with two doves and the Hebrew word corban, *was found near the Temple wall in Jerusalem. Literally translated "sacrifice,"* corban *came to mean anything consecrated to God.*

Temple of Apollo at Corinth, 6th century B.C. The flat-topped mesa or Acrocorinth in the background contained a temple of Aphrodite. This cosmopolitan trading city offered a wide range of popular religions and gods.

This Corinthian inscription refers to the macellum (Gk., makellon) or meat market mentioned by Paul in 1 Cor. 10:25, where meat sacrificed to idols would have been sold.

1 CORINTHIANS: A READING AND STUDY GUIDE

Chapter	Content Summary	Related Articles
1	Factions in the church destroy the unity of what is one body. They display foolishness, not wisdom.	Unity Wisdom
2	God has revealed spiritual wisdom in words, but those who possess his Spirit must apply them.	Reveal Spirituality
3	Applying God's wisdom, we realize human leaders are simply servants. Jesus alone is the focus of faith.	Leader Worldly
4	The Corinthians need the humble and sacrificial attitude of their spiritual leaders rather than to "take pride in one man over against another" (v. 6).	Servant
5	Open immorality in the church is to be disciplined by expelling the sinning person.	Discipline Judge
6	Lawsuits should be settled within the church, not in pagan courts. Sexual immorality must be avoided.	Immorality
7	Single people have an advantage—fewer distractions in serving the Lord. But it is also good to marry. If an unbelieving spouse deserts a believer, he or she is free to remarry but should consider celibacy.	Marriage Sex Celibacy
8	Doctrinal disputes must be resolved in love, not by argument. Each must consider how his acts affect others.	Idol Conscience Convictions
9	Having rights does not mean we must demand them. Paul surrendered many rights for the sake of the Gospel.	Rights
10	Idolatry is linked with immorality and demonic powers. Christians should not participate. When eating with unbelievers, they need not ask from where meat came.	
11	Women are to worship as women. The Lord's Supper is to be celebrated in a worthy manner.	Authority Woman
12	One does not prove one's spirituality by spiritual gifts. These are given to all believers to build Christ's Body.	Spirituality Spiritual Gifts
13	The true measure of spirituality is love, for love displays Christian maturity.	Love
14	Meetings of the church should be orderly, but give all opportunity to exercise their spiritual gifts.	Church Tongues, Gift of
15	Christ experienced a bodily resurrection, as will all who believe in him.	Resurrection
16	Paul adds personal notes and encourages the collection of money for the needy.	Give

us sense the struggles of a predominantly Gentile church as its members attempted to grasp the implications of the Christian message and to live Christian lives. The fact that many of the same problems trouble churches today gives this letter practical importance as well as great historical interest.

THEOLOGICAL CONTRIBUTIONS

First Corinthians contains the Bible's clearest exposition of the doctrine of bodily resurrection (ch. 15). The doctrine of spiritual gifts is also carefully explained (chs. 12–14). But the focus of 1 Corinthians is not on doctrine but on practical theology. Here we learn how to deal with a fellow Christian who sins (ch. 5), about sexuality in marriage and divorce (ch. 7), about how to deal with doctrinal disputes (chs. 8–10). And here we gain insights into the place of women in the church (ch. 11).

Yet one of the most valuable contributions of 1 Corinthians appears in Paul's approach to all kinds of interpersonal and church problems. Carefully and graciously Paul defines each issue, and then lays out basic principles which can be applied to resolve them. What we learn from the apostle's approach to church problems is perhaps as important as the specific solutions he gives. The lectionary used by several major Christian denominations reads 1 Corinthians at the beginning of each liturgical year, because of the lessons in this letter for church living in our times.

MASTERY KEYS

Several steps will help us understand the teaching of this letter, and also develop an effective problem-solving approach we can apply in any situation. (1) Read through a section (see outline). Then write down a clear definition of the problem. (2) Make a list of the biblical principles or truths that Paul applies to find his solution. (3) Write out how applying the listed principles or truths will change attitudes or actions, and thus solve the problem.

Corinthians, Second Epistle to the

This letter was written by the apostle Paul from Macedonia, probably within a year or so of the first Epistle. It needs to be read in the wider context of Paul's relationship with this troubled and troublesome church.

In 1 Corinthians Paul answered a number of questions raised by the Corinthian Christians and gave instructions for dealing with several divisive issues. Many in the church refused to listen. So Paul made a "painful," and unsuccessful, visit to this flock (2 Cor. 2:1; 13:2). Later Paul tried again, and wrote a blunt letter of rebuke. This letter, which has been lost, caused the Corinthians sorrow—but a majority did respond to the apostle's authority (2 Cor. 7:5-8). When word of their repentance reached Paul, he sat down to write the letter we know as 2 Corinthians.

HISTORICAL SIGNIFICANCE

This is the most revealing of Paul's letters. Paul shares his feelings, explains his motives, and states the convictions on which his ministry is based. Second Corinthians is unmatched as a source of insight into the apostle himself and, more importantly, insight into the nature of a Christian ministry which has its roots in God's new covenant.

THEOLOGICAL CONTRIBUTIONS

The death of Christ instituted what the Bible calls the new covenant. In biblical times, a "covenant" defined relationships between individuals or groups. The "old covenant" or Mosaic Law defined the relationship between God and Israel. The new covenant superseded it and defined the new relationship with God which became possible through the death and resurrection of Jesus.

While the Book of Hebrews explores new covenant theology, 2 Corinthians explains new covenant ministry. Thus it is a very important book for all believers. Parents can apply these principles to help

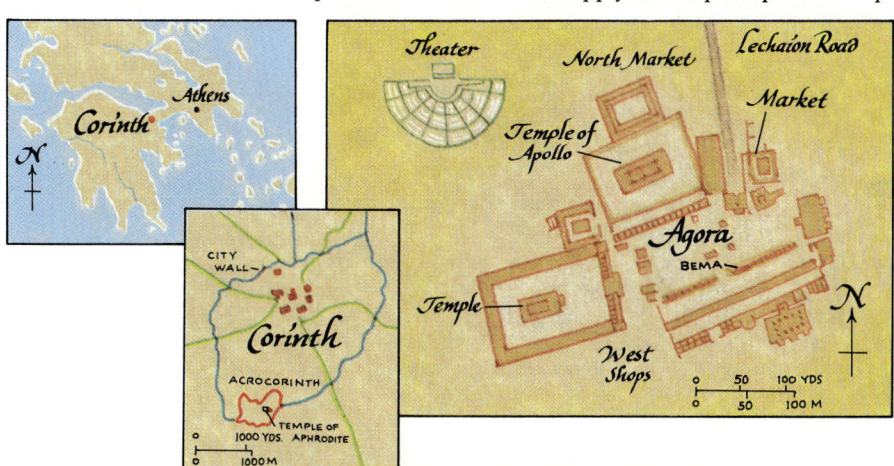

Left: First-century Corinth was situated on the isthmus between central Greece and the Peloponnesian peninsula. It was a burgeoning seaport and capital of the Roman province of Achaia.
Center: The city controlled both the crossroads and the two ports on either side of the isthmus.
Right: Layout of the agora or marketplace of Corinth as unearthed by archaeologists.

The bema or judgment seat at Corinth. Probably that of Gallio, the proconsul who refused to hear the Jews' accusations against Paul A.D. 51 or 52.

their children grow. And laypersons as well as pastors can apply them to minister effectively to others.

MASTERY KEYS

Prepare to study 2 Corinthians by reading articles on New Covenant and Leadership. Note that Paul often uses "we" and "our" in the sense of "I" and "my."

For personal enrichment, make a three-column chart. Work through the book paragraph by paragraph. For each paragraph, list in column one what Paul believes; in column two, how Paul feels; in column three, what Paul does. Then look for patterns of belief, feelings, and actions that may help you be a better

parent or minister more effectively to friends and neighbors.

SPECIAL FEATURES

What was the apostle Paul really like? This book tells us. Read 1:3-11; 1:23–2:17; 4:1-18; 6:3-13; 7:5-16; and 11:1–12:10. If you add just two other passages (1 Th. 2; Phil. 3), you will come to know Paul in a very personal way.

corn A grain crop. American corn, elsewhere known as maize, is native to North America and did not exist in ancient Palestine. The word translated "corn" in the KJV and NEB is best rendered "grain," and refers to all the cereal crops (wheat, rye, etc.).

2 CORINTHIANS: A READING AND STUDY GUIDE

Chapter	Content Summary	Related Articles
1	Troubles enable us to comfort others who suffer. Though delayed, Paul hopes to visit Corinth soon.	
2	The repentant sinner is to be forgiven and restored.	Discipline
3	New covenant ministry is rooted in the hope of individual transformation into Christ's likeness.	Hope Transformation
4	Disappointments cannot discourage, for all visible things change, while the unseen is eternal.	
5	Christ's reconciling work will succeed: believers will be brought into harmony with the Lord.	Reconciliation Compel
6	Paul has suffered for the sake of his ministry. Christians are not be yoked with unbelievers.	Suffer Yoke
7	Paul is moved by and rejoices at the Corinthians' positive response to his earlier letter of rebuke.	Repent
8	Christian giving is God's way of meeting the needs of all Christians as they occur.	Tithe Give
9	Christian giving is to be a free response to God and to others, not a duty or matter of compulsion.	
10	Paul's ministry is not based on worldly skills but on an authority given him by Christ.	Authority
11	False apostles take from the churches. Paul not only serves without charge but suffers for the sake of the churches.	False Prophets and Teachers
12,13	Paul has learned that when he is weakest God works through him most powerfully. He warns those who have not repented to do so before he visits again.	Weakness

Cornelius [kohr-NEEL-ee-uhs]. A Roman centurion posted in Caesarea about A.D. 40–50. The first recorded Gentile convert to Christianity. **Scripture:** Acts 10,11.

BACKGROUND

Inscriptions verify that the "Italian Regiment" in which Cornelius served was posted to Caesarea Maritima around A.D. 50. As a centurion, he would have led a unit of about 100 soldiers. Cornelius was respected in the Jewish community for his generosity and devotion to prayer (Acts 10:2). He had associated himself with Judaism, but as a God-fearer who retained his Gentile identity rather than as a convert. While respected by the Jews, Cornelius would not have been accepted as a member of the covenant community, or permitted to worship God with them. In fact, a pious Jew would not have willingly entered Cornelius's house. *See also* Caesarea; Centurion; God-fearing.

This explains why, before God sent Peter to Cornelius's house, he gave Peter a vision. In the vision Peter was told to kill and eat animals which were unclean. When Peter refused, he was told, "Do not call anything impure [unclean] that God has made clean." *See also* Clean and Unclean.

Responding to the vision, Peter went to the home of Cornelius the Gentile and shared the Gospel. Cornelius and his household believed, and they all received the Holy Spirit, which was evidenced by audible signs that had been given the disciples at Pentecost. Peter went back to the church at Jerusalem and reported what had happened. The amazed believers praised God, saying, "God has granted even the Gentiles repentance unto life" (Acts 11:18).

LEARNING FROM CORNELIUS'S LIFE

Theologically, Cornelius represents a turning point in sacred history. The OT told of a day when God would include Gentiles among his people (Isa. 49:6). Now that day had come!

Practically, Cornelius presents us with a study in relationships:

1. *Relationship to God.* Cornelius was a good and religious man who honestly tried to please God. God did not accept Cornelius because of his good works, but God did reveal himself further through Peter. God will reveal himself to those who seek him, who respond to what they do know of the Lord.

2. *Relationship to the faith community.* Cornelius is the classic "outsider." He was respected, perhaps even admired, but no one in Israel thought of him as "one of us." We may be just as hesitant to share the Gospel with admired people as with the openly wicked. Christians need to see everyone within the circle of God's love, and be willing to welcome anyone into the community of faith.

Peter baptizes the Roman centurion Cornelius, the first Gentile Christian, in this relief on the "Sarcophagus of the Miraculous Source," fourth century A.D., Arles, France. The salvation of Cornelius convinced the early church that God intended to bless the entire human race through Jesus Christ (Acts 11).

Above: The cornerstone (keystone) of an arch holds the structure together.

Right: Cornerstones (foundation stones) at the southwest corner of Jerusalem's Temple Mount anchored the structure. Peter speaks of Jesus as the "chosen and precious cornerstone" of our faith (1 Pet. 2:6).

Below: Line drawing of Egyptian lady applying rouge. In her left hand she holds a mirror. Biblical texts emphasize the value of a gentle and quiet spirit over "outward adornment" (1 Pet. 3:3-5).

Right: Cosmetic jars and implements from Masada. Esther was given beauty treatments and trained for six months in the use of perfumes and cosmetics before she was allowed to appear before King Xerxes (Esth. 2:12).

cornerstone The keystone in a structure, either the corner of the foundation (Job 38:6; Jer. 51:26) or the final stone (capstone) of an arch (Ps. 118:22). In both testaments, the cornerstone (the first or last stone placed) serves as an image of the Messiah, God's alpha and omega, his first and last. New Testament writers seem fond of Ps. 118:22, "The stone the builders rejected has become the capstone," quoting it five times (Mt. 21:42; Mk. 12:10; Lk. 20:17; Acts 4:11; 1 Pet. 2:7). Despite rejection by his own people, Jesus is precious to those who acknowledge him as the cornerstone of their salvation.

In Ephesians, Paul pictures the Church as a building, a "holy temple," built on the ministry of the apostles and prophets, "with Christ Jesus himself as the chief cornerstone" (2:20).

cornet (KJV) A musical horn or perhaps the Egyptian sistrum, a kind of rattle. In 2 Sam. 6:5 the "cornets" are actually castanets. *See also* Music and Musical Instruments.

cosmetics Substances applied to beautify the face or hair. A number of Egyptian wall paintings portray women applying cosmetics. The discovery in Palestine and Syria of scores of personal cosmetic palettes used to prepare colored powders, of perfume dishes, bottles, flasks, boxes, tweezers, spoons, and applicators called "kohl sticks" makes it clear that women of that age were concerned with beauty.

Both men and women, living in those dry climates, used perfumed ointments and oils to moisturize the skin (Ruth 3:3; Ps. 133:2; Song 1:13). Bright orange henna was mixed with oil and applied to the palms of the hands, the feet, nails, and sometimes the hair. Dark black kohl was used to outline the eyes. Rouge and various colored powders were made by grinding minerals and mixing them with gum or water. The Bible mentions 18 different kinds of perfume. *See also* Apothecary; Perfume.

While we know from archaeology that cosmetics were widely used in biblical cultures, there are relatively few references to them in Scripture. The earliest appears in the name of Job's daughter Keren-Happuch, which means a "horn of eye paint" (Job 42:14). Later references to eye paint are critical of women who advertise their sexuality by overusing this beauty aid (Jer. 4:30; Ezek. 23:40; *compare also* Isa. 4:14-24).

council (1) In the Gospels and Acts, usually the Jewish Sanhedrin, a group of 71 that served as the highest religious and legal authority in Judaism, with authority over all Jews throughout the Roman Empire. (2) Local groups of elders which served as minor courts to settle disputes (Mt. 10:17; Mk. 13:9). (3) In Acts 25:12, the *symboulion,* a group of advisers assembled by Roman governors.

Council of Jerusalem The gathering reported in Acts 15, also known as the First Apostolic Council. This crucial meeting took place after the first missionary journey of Paul and Barnabas, during which several predominantly Gentile churches were established.

As the number of Gentile converts increased, many Jewish Christians were troubled. Could Gentiles become Christians without becoming Jews first? Some maintained, "Unless you are circumcised according to the custom taught by Moses, you cannot be saved" (Acts 15:1). Paul and Barnabas resisted this doctrine fiercely. Finally, the church at Antioch, a pioneer in reaching the Gentiles, sent a delegation to Jerusalem to discuss the issue with the church leaders there.

When Paul and Barnabas reported the results of their mission, some of the believing Pharisees insisted on requiring the Gentiles to keep the Law and be circumcised—in essence, to convert to Judaism. After much discussion, the council rejected this view. The critical argument, advanced by Peter, was simple. God had accepted Gentiles who had simply believed in Jesus, and shown his acceptance by giving them the Holy Spirit. Faith in Christ, by Jew and by Gentile, was the one requirement for divine acceptance. What right then did the council have to add other conditions?

James the Just, the acknowledged leader of the Jerusalem church, pointed out that the OT prophets foresaw a day when Gentiles would bear God's name. If Gentiles were to be saved as Gentiles, it was not necessary for them to become Jews or to take on responsibilities which were uniquely Jewish. In this the council affirmed that salvation is by faith alone.

However, the council did request that Gentile Christians be sensitive to certain convictions held by their Jewish brothers. Specifically mentioned are:

1. *Food sacrificed to idols.* In the first century most meat was purchased at temple markets. When an animal was offered to a pagan deity, most of the carcass was then sold. Some Christians, particularly the Jews, considered it wrong to participate in pagan idolatry by buying such meat (1 Cor. 8).

2. *Consuming blood.* Pagans also considered the eating of blood, separately or in a strangled animal, a delicacy. This seemed horrible to the Jews (Lev. 17:11).

3. *Sexual standards.* The council asked Gentile Christians to adopt the sexual standards of the Jewish community, which were significantly higher than those of pagan society.

The Council of Jerusalem is historically significant for the prayerful and peaceful way in which a serious dispute was settled. The council is theologically significant for affirming that Mosaic Law is uniquely Jewish, a yoke Gentile Christians should not be required to bear. God's grace, expressed in Jesus Christ, is the foundation on which salvation rests, for Jew and Gentile alike. Nothing beyond a faith-response to the Gospel can be required of those seeking to participate in the Christian community, for salvation is by faith alone. *See also* Faith; Judaizers.

counsel, counselor Advice, direction; one who offers it. Biblical terms for advice or counsel vary in their emphasis. In the OT, counsel (*ya'as*) given by advisers typically takes the form of a plan to deal with a specific situation (2 Sam. 17; 1 Ki. 12). The role of the counselor was to suggest options, particularly to the king. Proverbs 15:22 states a common theme: "Plans fail for lack of counsel, but with many advisers they succeed." Human beings need to explore many options before acting.

However, when the OT speaks of God's counsel, it is not one option of many. God's direction is rooted in his purposes: What God says to us reveals what he intends to do. Following God's counsel leads us into his good purposes. The promise of Ps. 32:8 is especially precious: "I will instruct you and teach you in the way you should go; I will counsel you and watch over you."

In the NT, the counsel or advice given by human beings is best understood as mature, considered opinion. But here too the Christian has the promise of divine guidance.

Jesus introduced the Holy Spirit as Counselor (Comforter, KJV) in his Last Supper discourse (Jn. 14–16). Christ told the disciples that, though he was going away, he would send them "another" Counselor (Jn. 14:16). The Greek word means "another of the same kind." The Spirit continues to teach and guide as Jesus did (Jn. 14:26).

The Greek word translated Counselor is *paraklētos*, one who comes alongside to comfort, encourage, invite or exhort. Jesus promised that the Counselor, the living presence of God, would "be with you forever" (Jn. 14:16). Because the Holy Spirit is present in Jesus' people, we are never left without guidance or help. *See also* Comforter.

Cuneiform tablet from Hazor (1800–1600 B.C.) records an ancient lawsuit. The earliest mention of court proceedings in the Bible is found in Ex. 18, which reports that Moses heard the disputes of the Israelites and ruled on them.

court A judicial assembly, or the societal structure in which justice is decided. The Mosaic Law established the basic religious, civil, and social customs to be followed in Israel. However, OT Law established no police force or judicial system such as we now know. Responsibility for enforcing the laws of God and for settling disputes between individuals was distributed, with most cases being resolved in the local community. The city gate, where the elders of the community sat, generally served as the local court, and all cases were tried in public. There witnesses were called, and each party was questioned closely. Some believe that, where there was no clear proof in civil cases, the litigants cast lots (Prov. 16:33; 18:18).

Like all other justice systems, this one could be abused. The OT speaks of judges taking bribes (Deut. 16:19; Isa. 5:23), and also warns against witnesses giving false testimony (Deut. 5:20; Isa. 29:21). Clearly this legal system required that the majority in every community be persons of honesty and good will. All too often in Israel's history this was not the case. Thus Habakkuk complains, "The law is paralyzed,

and justice never prevails. The wicked hem in the righteous, so that justice is perverted" (Hab. 1:4).

While the local court system functioned throughout Israel's history, higher courts did exist at various times. In the wilderness, Moses divided Israel into groups of tens, fifties, hundreds, and thousands, with officials over each unit. Cases which could not be settled in the smaller units might be appealed to a larger unit, and serious problems were brought to Moses himself (Ex. 18).

Exodus also speaks of persons appearing "before God" in certain cases (Ex. 22:8,9). This phrase, which is rendered "before the judges" in the NIV, probably calls for appearance before the priests at the central sanctuary.

During the centuries that judges governed Israel, these military and political leaders also heard and decided difficult legal cases (Jdg. 4:5; 1 Sam. 7:15; 8:1-3). *See also* Judge.

After the monarchy was established, the king himself served as a sort of supreme court in difficult cases and heard appeals from local courts. Absalom undermined the allegiance of the northern tribes to David by meeting those who came to David for justice and saying that, if he were judge, he would decide in their favor (2 Sam. 15:4). Perhaps the Bible's best known legal case was brought before King Solomon, who was asked to decide which of two prostitutes was the mother of a surviving infant (1 Ki. 3:16-28). When Solomon ordered the live infant cut in two, the real mother cried out in protest.

After the Babylonian captivity, governors like Nehemiah served as the highest court. By the time of Christ, the Sanhedrin, a group of 71 men in Jerusalem, was the supreme governing body in Judaism, responsible to settle difficult cases and to enforce the religious law which governed the lives of Jewish people everywhere. As from the beginning, local councils of the synagogue in each community continued to deal with local disputes (Mt. 10:17; Mk. 13:9). *See also* Council; Justice.

covenant A formal, binding agreement defining relationships and responsibilities between two or more parties. The ancient concept of covenant undergirds both Testaments. The Hebrew word for covenant is *berit*. Between nations a *berit* was a treaty (1 Ki. 15:19). Between individuals it might be a business contract, or pledge of friendship (1 Sam. 18:3). Between a ruler and subjects, a *berit* served as a constitution, spelling out the rights and responsibilities of each party. Because the *berit* was a formal, legally binding instrument, God chose to express his commitments to human beings in the readily understood covenant form. So biblical covenants define the relationship between God and his people, and give binding expression to statements of his plans and purposes.

There are four major biblical covenants. Under each of these covenants God revealed certain of his purposes and made certain commitments to human beings.

1. *The Abrahamic Covenant* (about 2080 B.C.). God had spoken to Abraham and told him to go to a land the Lord would show him. At that time God gave Abraham several specific promises.

> *"I will make you into a great nation*
> *and I will bless you;*
> *I will make your name great,*
> *and you will be a blessing.*
> *I will bless those who bless you,*
> *and whoever curses you I will curse;*
> *and all peoples on earth*
> *will be blessed through you."*
>
> (Gen. 12:2,3)

The same chapter adds, "To your offspring I will give this land [Canaan]" (v. 7).

These promises were confirmed by the most binding of all ancient covenants, a covenant of blood. Parties to a covenant of blood passed between the divided halves of animals, symbolically pledging their own lives if either should violate the covenant's stipulations. But in the covenant of blood described in Gen. 15, the Lord alone passed between the halves. The promises God made to Abraham were unconditional: God would keep them no matter how Abraham or his offspring might fail!

Looking back on this incident, the writer of Hebrews says, "Because God wanted to make the unchanging nature of his purpose very clear to the heirs of what was promised, he confirmed it with an oath" (Heb. 6:17).

In the case of the Abrahamic covenant, then, the covenant served as an oath, a formal and legally binding commitment to keep promises which God had already made to Abraham.

2. *The Mosaic (Law) Covenant* (about 1445 B.C.). After Moses led the people of Israel out of Egypt to Sinai, God proposed that "out of all nations you will be my treasured possession . . . a holy nation" (Ex. 19:5,6). When Israel heard this proposal, "the people all responded together, 'We will do everything the Lord has said' " (Ex. 19:8).

Many commentators have noted that the Law given at Sinai, as stated in Exodus and as restated in Deuteronomy, took the form of an ancient Middle Eastern suzerainty (rulership) treaty. Mosaic Law was a constitution for the nation-to-be, and God himself was the nation's ruler. Specifically, such suzerainty covenants:

- Identify the ruler and give his titles (Ex. 20:1,2; Deut. 1:1-5).
- Tell the deeds of the ruler for his people (Ex. 19:4,5; Deut. 1:6–4:49).
- State the principles that govern the relationship between the parties (Ex. 20:2-7; Ex. 21:1–23:19; Deut. 5–26).
- State blessings to be won by obedience, and punishments due upon disobedience (Ex. 23:20-33; Deut. 27–30).
- Record acceptance of the covenant by the governed (Ex. 24:1-8; Deut. 31–33). (*See also* Deuteronomy, Book of.)

When we understand the Law's nature as a national constitution, we can see why

FOUR BIBLICAL COVENANTS

Covenant Name	Made with	Its Nature	God's Stated Purposes	Benefits for Believers Today
Abrahamic	Abraham	Promise	To bless Abraham and his family, and through them all people.	Through Abraham's descendants we have received the Scriptures and Christ.
Mosaic or Old *(the Law)*	Nation of Israel	National Constitution	To teach Israel how to live as subjects of God the King.	Through the Law we discover God's moral character and his moral will for us.
Davidic	David	Messianic Promise	To produce a divine Ruler and Savior from David's family line.	Christ was born of David's family. By faith we enter the Kingdom of God's Son (Col. 1:13).
New	Israel and Judah	Messianic Fulfillment	To forgive sins and transform human beings from within.	We who believe in Christ receive all the benefits promised under the new covenant.

the Mosaic code includes statutes on civil and criminal law as well as religious and moral rulings.

Given the special nature of this covenant as a suzerainty *berit*, a contract between God as divine Ruler and the Israelites as his people, we must note important differences between the Mosaic and Abrahamic covenants.

God's original promises to Abraham were unconditional (Gen. 12:2,3). In these, he stated what he intended to do for Abraham and his offspring. God confirmed these promises with a covenant which was, in effect, an oath.

God made promises to the new nation of Israel, too. But the promises expressed conditions. If Israel would keep his laws, God would protect and bless the nation. If Israel did not obey, God would discipline and punish the nation. In the relationship between the nation Israel and God, God's treatment of the nation was contingent on Israel's obedience.

It is also important to note that the Abrahamic covenant is, in a sense, timeless. The blessings promised to Abraham look forward not only to a future in which his family will grow into a nation, but to an even more distant future in which "all peoples on earth will be blessed through you."

The Mosaic covenant, on the other hand, functioned in the "here and now" of each generation of Israelites. If in a given generation the nation turned to God and obeyed his laws, the nation would be blessed. The OT bears this out; stories of revival under various judges and kings are accompanied by reports of the blessings which followed. The sacred history also bears out the other aspect of the covenant. When a generation turned away from God and disobeyed, decline and disaster resulted.

But God's OT Law was never presented as, or intended to be, a way of salvation for individuals. The covenant of Law was the constitution of the nation Israel, a *berit* between God as Israel's ruler, and his people as a nation.

It is also important to realize that the Mosaic covenant, which is called the "old" covenant in contrast to the new covenant, was intended to be temporary. Jeremiah said the old covenant was to be replaced by the new (Jer. 31:31-34), and Paul argues that the Law covenant was in effect only until Christ came (Gal. 3:15-25).

3. *The Davidic Covenant* (about 990 B.C.). After David had been confirmed as king of Israel's twelve tribes, and had defeated foreign enemies, he wanted to build a mag-

nificent temple to honor the Lord. God refused David permission. But through the prophet Nathan, God gave David a promise, which is identified in Ps. 89:2-4 as a covenant. According to this promise, "Your house and your kingdom will endure forever before me; your throne will be established forever" (2 Sam. 7:16). It is clear that David too viewed this commitment as an unbreakable oath (2 Sam. 7:28).

The Jewish people of Jesus' day understood the Davidic covenant to mean that the Messiah foretold by the prophets would be a descendant of David. The genealogies of Jesus, found in Mt. 1 and Lk. 3, are significant because they establish Christ's descent from David and thus support the claim of Jesus of Nazareth to be the OT's promised Savior. *See also* Messiah.

Like the Abrahamic covenant the Davidic covenant is timeless, in that it looks ahead to a day when God will keep his promise and Christ will rule all as King. But the covenant also had "here and now" implications. David's line was preserved until the promised ruler was born.

4. *The New Covenant.* Predicted by Jeremiah (ch. 31) and Ezekiel (ch. 36), this was instituted by Jesus Christ. God's people failed tragically under the old (or Mosaic) covenant. As a consequence of persistent idolatry and sin, the people of the Northern Kingdom, Israel, were crushed by the Assyrians and taken into captivity in 722 B.C. A century and a quarter later, the Southern Kingdom, Judah, was under terrible pressure from the Babylonians. The prophet Jeremiah warned that Judah too would soon be destroyed and her people deported. But among Jeremiah's dark announcements of doom there was a lightning-bright flash of hope. "The time is coming," Jeremiah cried in God's name, "when I will make a new covenant with the house of Israel" (Jer. 31:31).

The prophet went on to explain that the new covenant "will not be like" the Mosaic covenant, which God's people broke. Instead, under the new covenant,

"I will put my law in their minds
   and write it on their hearts.
I will be their God
   and they will be my people.
No longer will a man teach his neighbor,
   or a man his brother, saying, 'Know the
      Lord,'
because they will all know me,
   from the least of them to the greatest,"
            declares the Lord.
"For I will forgive their wickedness
   and will remember their sins no more."
               (Jer. 31:33,34)

This covenant was not instituted in Jeremiah's day. Jeremiah only foresaw it. The new covenant was sealed on Calvary, about A.D. 30. The night of his arrest Jesus clearly identified his death by crucifixion as the making of the new covenant. He offered his disciples a cup of wine and said, "This is my blood of the covenant, which is poured out for many for the forgiveness of sins" (Mt. 26:28). As Luke records it, "This cup is the new covenant in my blood" (Lk. 22:20).

The death of Christ was a culmination of the imagery present in the covenant of blood, that most solemn of ancient oaths. God's certain promise of forgiveness for humankind was sealed with the shed blood of his Son.

The new covenant promise was originally given to "the house of Israel and the house of Judah" (Jer. 31:31). Yet it is under the new covenant that salvation is offered to all. That salvation provides not only forgiveness of sins but also an inner transformation, expressed by Jeremiah as putting God's Law in our minds and writing it on our hearts. Through Jesus Christ all the benefits of the new covenant are now made available to those who put their trust in him.

COVENANTS AND SALVATION

Covenants are essentially formal announcements by God of his purposes and intentions. Most define how God's people are to relate to him.

God gave formal legal expression to promises made to Abraham by a covenant (Gen. 15:8-19). But God had previously pronounced Abraham righteous on the basis of his faith, before the formal covenant was made (Gen. 15:6).

In the Mosaic covenant, God as Israel's ruler announced the blessings and punishments he would bring upon Israel, depending on how the nation responded to his Law (Ex. 20–24). But before this covenant was introduced, the Israelites were already a redeemed people. God had delivered them from slavery (Ex. 12–15).

God announced to David that he intended to establish an eternal kingdom through one of his descendants (1 Sam. 7). But long before this promise was made, David had developed a deep faith in God, and fully grasped the fact that salvation depends on God's grace rather than human works. As is written in the Psalms:

Blessed is he
whose transgressions are forgiven,
whose sins are covered.

Blessed is the man
whose sin the Lord does not count
against him.   (Ps. 32:1,2)

God committed himself in Christ to forgive sins and to transform hearts. The Bible says that the way of faith, which brought salvation to Abraham and David, remains the one way individuals can experience salvation today (Rom. 4).

No OT saint was saved by keeping the Law. It revealed what God commanded and in particular how he intended to relate to the people of the covenant.

Today Christians relate to God under the new covenant, not the old. We are saved by faith, and once faith has brought us into personal relationship with God, all the benefits and promises of the new covenant— promises of forgiveness of sins and transformation into Christ's likeness—are ours.

covering the head A practice of women in NT times, worshiping with a scarf or veil on one's head. In 1 Cor. 11:2-16 Paul wrote that women at worship should have

Warriors embrace, sealing a covenant of peace, in basalt relief on a ritual basin from Ebla, 2200–1550 B.C. At right a god looks on. The Old Testament casts God's relationship with Israel in a distinctive covenant context.

their heads covered with what most versions call a veil. Apparently some women had abandoned this item of apparel, perhaps to affirm that in Christ they were equal with men. Paul says that women should wear the veil to show that as women they have divine authority (v. 10) to pray and prophesy in church services (v. 5).

Some commentators have suggested that in Greek culture only prostitutes went bareheaded. According to this view, Paul is simply concerned that Christian women act with modesty when the congregation gathers for worship. Nevertheless, it is possible to see this passage as Paul's affirmation of a woman's right to approach God through Christ. Women do not need to become like men in order to pray or prophesy. *See also* Authority; Veil; Woman.

covet, covetous To desire another person's possessions. The tenth commandment states that we are not to look longingly on another's wealth or his wife.

God expects his people to care about other persons and to use things. Often this order is reversed, so that human beings care about things and use people. We are never to care so much about things

Terra-cotta figurine of late first century B.C. shows a woman draped in a shawl, followed by a child holding her train. Paul expected first-century Christian women to dress appropriately when they prayed (1 Cor. 11:13).

that we violate the rights of another person. In fact, the biblical ideal is that we freely share our material possessions with those in need. *See also* Give.

In every case of covetousness in Scripture the passionate desire for material possessions brings personal and spiritual disaster. Among the best examples to use in teaching are Achan (Josh. 7), Ahab (1 Ki. 21), and Gehazi (2 Ki. 5:20-27). *See also* Achan; Ahab; Gehazi.

Because covetousness involves focusing one's desire on some material object, it tempts a person to put that object above God himself. Jesus warned that no one can serve two masters. Ultimately a choice must be made between them (Mt. 6:24). The covetous person has made his choice. He has given a mere thing the place in his life that rightfully belongs to God. For this reason Paul calls the greedy individual an idolater. The thing he wants so badly becomes like a god to him, for his desire for it determines the choices he will make (Eph. 5:5).

What is the cure for covetousness? Only a sincere love for God and for other people can inculcate the right perspective: that material possessions are a matter of temporary stewardship for which we are accountable to God.

cows of Bashan Amos's unflattering term for the rich women of Israel. Bashan was a rich grazing area, noted for its fat cattle. The prophet compares the wealthy women of Israel, who showed no concern for the poor in Israel, to fat, complacent cows (Amos 4:1). Amos goes on to describe the life-style of these women: They rested on ivory-inlaid couches, drinking wine and eating sweets, while their impoverished neighbors starved. *See also* Amos; Cattle.

crane (KJV, RSV) A bird. The *sus,* identified as a crane in the KJV and RSV, is more likely the swift, of which three species are found in Palestine. It is mentioned only in Isa. 38:14 and Jer. 8:7.

create To make or cause. "In the beginning, God created. . . ." Appropriately, the Bible starts with the act of creating. The Hebrew word, *bara',* does not just refer to God's fashioning the world out of nothing. It emphasizes God's role as initiator, first cause, the one who makes things happen.

Scripture continues to portray God as a creator and initiator. God originated human life, making Adam and Eve in his own image (Gen. 1:27; 5:1,2). He brought into being moral law (Gen. 2:15-17). He initiated the process which brings human beings forgiveness and cleansing (Ps. 51:10; 2 Cor. 5:17). And, at history's end, God will create a new heaven and earth (Isa. 65:17,18).

creation God's initiation, out of nothing, of all that is. The biblical view of creation stands in stark contrast to the myths of the ancient world, and to modern "scientific" theories of origins. According to the Bible, a personal God created the heavens and the earth and all living things.

GENESIS ACCOUNT OF CREATION

Several debates have raged over the first two chapters of Genesis. Some maintain that this creation account is an artificial presentation designed to teach a religious lesson, while others say it is completely historical. The fact is that the Bible itself treats these chapters as history, but history which, like myth, presents a distinctive world view.

Another debated question is whether the "days" of Gen. 1 were seven consecutive 24-hour days, or longer periods of time, or perhaps 24-hour days separated by geologic ages. Persons with a high view of Scripture differ on this issue. *See also* Day.

Another debate focuses on whether the Gen. 1,2 events took place millions of years ago, or only ten or fifteen thousand years ago. It is enough to note that there simply is no direct biblical evidence as to the age of the earth.

According to the Babylonian Atrahasis Epic, *recorded on this cuneiform tablet from the 17th century* B.C., *the gods created humanity to till the soil. The Genesis account affirms that God created man and woman in his image, for his glory, and to have fellowship with him.*

But far more important than these debates is the view of the universe which these chapters establish. They summarize

WHAT WERE THE SEVEN DAYS OF CREATION?

Theories	Description
Myth theory	The Genesis account has no historical foundation, but was devised to express the Hebrew view of God and his relation to the universe.
Seven-day theory	God created in seven consecutive 24-hour days, but an unknowable period of time ago.
Gap theory	God's original creation was ruined when Satan fell (Isa. 14:13-15). Genesis describes repair of the ruin. Fossils, etc., belong to the original creation.
Indefinite age theory	Each "day" is actually an indefinite, geological age. There is no conflict of Genesis with science.
Day-age theory	During a 24-hour day God created, and then permitted a geologic age to pass for the development of what he had made (vegetation, sea life, animals, etc.).
Revelatory day theory	The "days" in Genesis are not days of creation but the days on which God showed Moses what he had done.
Revelatory device theory	The author of Genesis simply used days to organize his material.

A 1635 edition of Miles Coverdale's English Bible portrays the six days of creation.

the biblical answer to humanity's most basic questions.

According to Gen. 1, our universe is not the product of chance, but the purposeful creation of a living being. This being, God, created Earth as a home for humankind. He placed the earth in a universe marked by stability, regularity, diversity, and beauty. God filled the earth with living creatures and then, in the culminating act of creation, he stooped to shape human beings. He himself made the first male and female, and gave them the breath of life. *See also* Breath of Life.

The so-called "two creation accounts" found in Gen. 1 and 2 are better understood as a common literary device in ancient Semitic and Egyptian literature. After giving an overview of creation, the writer returns to focus on the most significant event. In this case, that event is the creation of humans, shaped in the very image and likeness of God.

The Genesis account of creation, although brief, expresses Scripture's most basic understandings of the origin and meaning of life:

• *The Creator is a person.* Thus the universe itself is essentially personal, not impersonal; random chance does not rule.

• *The material universe is not eternal, but created.* All pagan creation narratives assume the pre-existence of matter without accounting for its origin.

• *Life was created, mature, by God.* It did not spring by chance from non-living matter.

• *Many of God's attributes can be known through the universe he created.* As Rom. 1:19,20 points out, God's eternal power

and divinity should be recognizable by any reasonable observer. The universe has regularity; therefore, God is perceived as trustworthy. It is rich in diversity; God is creative. It is marked by beauty; God is the source of beauty.

• *Human beings are special.* We may share biological life with earth's animals, but human beings are distinct from other living creatures. *See also* Animals.

• *Human beings are the special object of divine concern.* God not only shared his image and likeness with Adam and Eve, but also gave them dominion over what he had made. *See also* Dominion.

These fundamental understandings concerning the origin and nature of the universe, and concerning the nature of human beings, pervade Scripture.

METHOD OF CREATION

The Genesis account simply states, "God said . . . and there was." This repeated expression, which suggests that God simply spoke the universe into existence, recurs throughout the OT. The psalmist says, "He spoke, and it came to be; he commanded, and it stood firm" (Ps. 33:9). The prophets poetically portray the universe as the work of God's hands, an expression meaning "that which God has personally accomplished" (Isa. 45:11,12). Yet the awe-inspiring reality taught in Scripture is that God needed no pre-existing material, nor mechanical means, but was able to call the universe and its contents into being simply by giving voice to his thoughts. As Heb. 11:3 puts it, "By faith we understand that the universe was formed at God's command, so that what is seen was not made out of what was visible."

262

The fourth dayes worke. The fifth dayes worke. The sixte dayes worke.

ADDITIONAL TEACHINGS

A number of passages outside Genesis present God as Creator. Among the most powerful: Job 38–41; Ps. 33:6-9; 90:2; 102:25-27; Isa. 40:21-31; Jn. 1:1-10; Rom. 1:18-23; Col. 1:15,16; Heb. 1:10-12.

The Bible also portrays each person of the Trinity as active in the work of cre-ation. Creation is the work of the Father (Ps. 33:6; Isa. 44:24; 45:12), of the Son (Jn. 1:3,10; Col. 1:16), and of the Holy Spirit (Gen. 1:2; Job 26:13).

SUMMARY

Because we are so familiar with the biblical account of origins, we may not realize how unique it is. The world view

CONCEPTS OF ORIGINS

	Mesopotamian	Greek	Modern	Judeo-Christian
Source	*Enuma Elish* myth	Mythology	Evolutionary theory	*The Bible*
Origin of the Universe	Universe formed from corpse of goddess Tiamat	The material universe has always existed	Universe began in un-explained "Big Bang" 15 billion years ago	God spoke and caused the universe to come into existence
Origin of Human Life	Mankind sprang from blood of murdered god Kingu	Origin of human life a mystery	Humans evolved with other animals from spontaneously gener-ated single-cell life	God created all ani-mal life and created humans in a separate, special act of creation
View of Deity(s)	Many competing gods and goddesses	Many competing gods and goddesses	God is unknown and unknowable	One personal and knowable God exists
Relation of Deity(s) to the Universe	Gods populate the universe, but do not fully control it	Gods populate the universe, but do not fully control it	God is irrelevant as the universe is subject only to natural law	God is beyond the universe, but sustains it and can act upon and within it
Relation of Man to Deity(s)	Men inferior and sub-ject to whims of un-caring gods	Man subject to fate and whims of capri-cious and selfish gods	Has no statement to make about man's re-lationship to the su-pernatural	God created humans in his own image and granted them domin-ion over the earth. God loves humans actively
Destiny of Man and the Universe	No certainty of eter-nal life for man, only for the gods; yet gifts are buried with the dead for their use be-yond the grave	The dead go to Hades where all are misera-ble, although the mer-itorious go to the Elysian Fields.	Second law of ther-modynamics indi-cates that the universe will cool and die. Death is extinction for every individual	God will destroy this universe, create a new and righteous one. Human beings will be raised to bless-edness or punishment

expressed in Genesis simply did not exist elsewhere in the ancient world. In fact, it conflicted sharply with other ancient views (*see* accompanying chart).

The Genesis account also conflicts with the modern secular view, which holds that the universe came into existence by chance through an uncaused explosion billions of years ago. It further supposes that life sprang by chance from non-living matter and, across millions of years, earth's complex creatures evolved from one-celled organisms. According to Scripture, the universe is a carefully designed creation and human beings have been created in the image and likeness of God.

creation, new Individuals remade by God or the future universe that God will create at history's end. The basic meaning of "create," established in the Hebrew term *bara'*, is "to originate or bring something new into existence." When the Bible speaks of a new creation, then, it indicates a new beginning. *See also* Create.

Scripture portrays the present universe as ruined by sin, with nature itself warped out of its intended shape (Gen. 3:17,18; Rom. 8:19-21). This universe will be destroyed in cataclysmic judgment (2 Pet. 3:10-12). But the Bible's message of judgment stands beside a message of hope. God announced through Isaiah, "Behold, I will create new heavens and a new earth." In this new creation, humanity will "be glad and rejoice forever" (Isa. 65:17,18).

But not only the material creation cries out for a new beginning. Human beings too have been devastated by sin. And unlike objects in the physical universe, each person is destined for eternal, self-conscious existence. *See also* Eternal Life

Both Testaments affirm that God intends to give human beings a new beginning, by forgiving sins and implanting fresh spiritual life. In the OT the image is that of a new heart (Ezek. 36:26-28; Jer. 31:31-34). The NT links this inner transformation to Jesus. Those who establish a personal relationship with God through Christ are granted a new spiritual beginning, which will culminate in a full restoration of the human pattern intended at the original creation. In the language of the NT, "If anyone is in Christ, he is a new creation; the old has gone, the new has come" (2 Cor. 5:17). And, "We are God's workmanship, created in Christ Jesus to do good works" (Eph. 2:10).

creature A living being, whether animal, human, or angelic. The various Hebrew and Greek words for "creature" generally emphasize the fact that these beings are living rather than the fact that God created them.

creed An affirmation of faith or statement of doctrine. The word "creed," from the Latin *credo*, "I believe," does not appear in the Bible. But various NT references suggest a well-defined body of core truths held by the early church. Paul's instructions to Timothy are significant: "What you heard from me, keep as the pattern of sound teaching" (2 Tim. 1:13), and "The

Creeds serve as concise statements of Christian faith. The earliest creeds were interrogatory (below)—confessional questions asked of a baptismal candidate—rather than declaratory, such as the Apostle's Creed.

And [when] he [who is to be baptized] goes down into the water, let him who baptizes lay hands on him saying:
"Do you believe in God the Father almighty?"
And he who is to be baptized shall say, "I believe."
Let him baptize him at once, having his hand laid upon his head. And after this let him say:
"Do you believe in Christ Jesus, the Son of God,
Who was born of Holy Spirit and virgin Mary,
Who was crucified in the days of Pontius Pilate,
And died,
And rose the third day living from the dead,
And ascended into the heavens,
And sat down at the right hand of the Father,
And will come to judge the living and the dead?"
And when he says, "I believe," let him baptize him the second time and again say:
"Do you believe in the Holy Spirit, in the holy Church,
And the resurrection of the flesh?"
And he who is being baptized shall say, "I believe." And so let him baptize him the third time.

—St. Hippolytus, *Apostolic Tradition* (A.D. 215)

things you have heard me say in the presence of many witnesses entrust to reliable men who will also be qualified to teach others" (2 Tim. 2:2).

One early summary of the core of Christian teaching is the Apostles' Creed, which in some form probably dates to shortly after the close of the NT.

creeping things Small insects and animals. Two Hebrew words are found where English versions have "creeping things." *Remes* includes reptiles, insects, and probably small mammals. *Sheres* means swarming creatures, which in Lev. 11:44,46 include mice and lizards. The class of creeping things is thus very broad and, while distinct from birds, fish, cattle, and larger animals, it is not a true biological division. The name indicates simply creatures that appear to us to live close to the ground.

crime and punishment In modern society a crime is a violation of the laws of the state and a criminal's offense is considered to be against society or the state. After trial the convicted criminal is usually punished by being sent to prison. This system of criminal justice generally ignores any losses suffered by the victim.

The biblical view of crime and punishment is different. In the OT, crime is sin against God as well as an offense against an individual and/or the community. The criminal must answer to God for his sinful acts and seek forgiveness. And, in the biblical system, a convicted criminal must also restore social harmony by compensating the victim or, with certain offenses, by undergoing punishment.

The differences in these two approaches to crime and punishment are significant. In the biblical system, (1) the needs of the victim are compassionately addressed, and (2) the criminal is quickly restored as a contributing member of the community

(unless he has committed a capital crime). Neither the criminal (who is seldom imprisoned) nor the victim (whose injury or loss is compensated)—nor the family of either—must be supported at the expense of society.

If we understand crime as an offense against an individual or the community, we can classify the kinds of crime identified in OT Law, and the punishments that were considered appropriate.

CRIMES AGAINST THE COMMUNITY

Certain acts were crimes against the whole society, for they jeopardized the existence of Israel as a holy community. Failure to deal with these crimes would bring the whole community under the judgment of God (Deut. 17:12,13; 19:13-21). Among such crimes were murder, idolatry, blasphemy, witchcraft and the like. Certain sexual crimes such as adultery, homosexuality, and rape were also considered destructive to the whole community (Lev. 20:10-16), as was kidnapping (Ex. 21:16). These crimes were considered so heinous and such a threat to the well-being of the community that the death penalty was appropriate.

The death penalty was also intended to deter: "The rest of the people will hear of this and be afraid, and never again will such an evil thing be done among you" (Deut. 19:20).

It is important to note that OT Law distinguishes between intentional homicide, accidental killing, and justifiable homicide. The Law established procedures to determine the category of a particular killing (Deut. 19:11-18). The death penalty for homicide is reserved for intentional homicide alone. Justifiable homicide is not treated as punishable. *See also* Cities of Refuge; Murder.

CRIMES AGAINST PERSONS

A variety of crimes involve injury to

These ballot disks (fourth century B.C.) were dropped anonymously into a box by Athenian jurors. Disks with solid hubs indicate acquittal, hollow hubs a guilty verdict. In Israel the Law defined crimes and set punishment. The elders among God's people were responsible to hear witnesses publicly and determine guilt or innocence.

  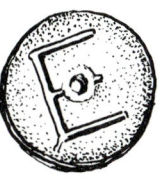  

individuals. Rape and seduction injure the entire family. The bridal price must be paid the father, and in the case of rape the man must marry the woman. She is protected against being divorced later (Ex. 22:16,17).

A person injured by accident is to be compensated for lost income and the cost of treatment (Ex. 21:18,19). A person injured purposely could demand a ransom (a money payment) as compensation for his loss.

Talion law, or the "law of equivalent retribution," which demands an "eye for an eye" in the case of serious intentional injury, was intended to provide just compensation for the injured party (Ex. 21:24-26; Deut. 19:21). But it also limits the amount of revenge an injured party or his family may seek. No one could justify a crime against another by arguing that he was injured first. And no feud, involving a series of increasingly serious injuries, would be permitted to erupt among the families of Israel. If an injury done to one person by another was matched by exactly the same injury imposed on him, there would be an obvious deterrent to injuring yet another person, and harmony could be restored.

CRIMES AGAINST PROPERTY

Old Testament Law also prescribed compensation for various property losses caused by neglect (Ex. 22:12-14). In the case of theft, simple restitution was not enough. The owner of a slaughtered animal was to be repaid three or four times over (Ex. 22:1). A living animal had to be returned with another like it. Double value of any other stolen property was due the victim from the thief (Ex. 22:7). If the thief had nothing and could not make restitution in any other way, he was to be indentured until he had repaid his victim by his labor.

While some of the penalties exacted under OT Law may seem harsh by modern standards, they are in fact far less harsh than those stated in other ancient Middle Eastern law codes. They are also unique in their two primary concerns: Victims of crimes deserve compensation; and the community must be kept from the undermining effect of unavenged injustice. Crime enjoyed no tolerance in the ideal community envisioned in OT Law, and members of the community were called on to act decisively when crimes occurred.

crimson One of several shades of red mentioned in the Bible. Red dye was obtained from the crushed bodies of the *coccus ilicis* and other bark-infesting insects. The dye

was permanent; once fixed, it would not wash out. Isaiah 1:18 refers to the indelible quality of this color, as God invites his people to return to him. "Though your sins are like scarlet, they shall be as white as snow; though they are red as crimson, they shall be like wool."

cross (1) An instrument used by the Romans to execute some classes of criminals; (2) a Christian symbol expressing the meaning of Christ's death. The cross was a literal instrument of execution (Mt. 27:32-44). But the cross also became a symbol, the most powerful in the Christian faith, representing the redemption won for us by Jesus' death.

THE CROSS OF CHRIST

Paul speaks of "the message of the cross" (1 Cor. 1:18), and proclaims the wonderful news that Jesus has reconciled both Jew and Gentile to God through the cross (Eph. 2:16). Those who were "enemies of the cross of Christ" (Phil. 3:18) rejected the Christian message and refused to submit to Christ as Lord.

In all of these cases, the cross stands for something more: the astonishing fact that God's Son died a humiliating death in order to bring humankind back to God. Crucifixion was not only gruesome, it was a shameful death, reserved for slaves and the worst criminals. Thus the cross would be a stark image—a total absurdity to those who did not understand but a powerful expression to the faithful of the extent of God's love. *See also* Crucifixion.

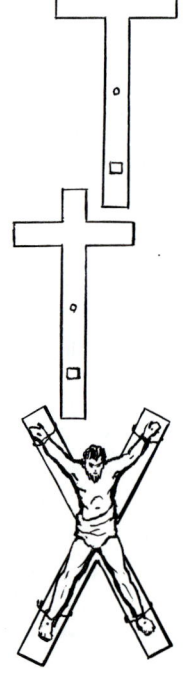

The "cross" originally was a long stake to which a body was bound. During Roman times a transverse bar was added to form a T, later called St. Anthony's cross (top), or the familiar Latin cross (center). Later the diagonal St. Andrew's cross was also used (bottom). Crucifixion was such common punishment inflicted by Roman authorities that any pains or troubles were dubbed "crosses."

THE BELIEVER'S DAILY CROSS

Jesus claimed that anyone who sought to be his disciple must deny himself and "take up his cross daily and follow me" (Lk. 9:23; *see* Mt. 16:24; Mk. 8:34). He said this after announcing that he would go to Jerusalem and die there. Jesus had made it plain that this was God's will for him. In context, Christ was not asking his disciples to die, or even to suffer physically. Jesus simply said that a person who seeks to be a disciple must share Christ's total submission to the will of God. A disciple will set aside his own desires and choose to do the will of the Father. Figuratively, the believer's daily cross represents the personal will of God for each individual, whatever that may be.

crow *See* Raven.

crown (1) A headpiece indicating royalty or priesthood; (2) a symbol of authority; (3) a symbol of victory or reward.

ISRAEL'S CROWN

The crown (Heb., *nezer*) of the high priest was a plate of gold inscribed with the words, "Holy to Yahweh." This was fastened to his turban with a blue cord (Ex. 39:30,31).

Scripture mentions a crown worn by Israel's kings (2 Sam. 1:10), but does not describe it. Two other Hebrew words refer to the crowns worn by rulers of other nations. The shapes of many of these are carved on reliefs of ancient monuments.

In OT poetry, the crown often serves as a symbol of glory, as in Prov. 12:4, "A wife of noble character is her husband's crown." And when God made man, he "crowned him with glory and honor" (Ps. 8:5).

THE CROWN OF POWER

In the NT, the Greek word *diadēma* is used where the crown is intended to suggest the power either of evil beings (Rev. 12:3; 13:1) or Christ, whose ultimate authority is symbolized by "many crowns" (Rev. 19:12).

THE CROWN OF VICTORY

In Greek athletic games, winners would be crowned with wreaths of leaves. This *stephanos* had no cash value, but it guaranteed an athlete praise and honor in his community.

The crown of thorns woven for Jesus before his crucifixion is called a *stephanos* (Mt. 27:29). The soldiers mocked what they thought to be the defeat of this King of the Jews, never dreaming that in dying

Christ would win the ultimate victory over sin and death.

The NT also uses *stephanos* for the crowns that await believers. Paul looks forward to the resurrection and says, "There is in store for me the crown of righteousness, which the Lord, the right-

eous Judge, will award to me on that day—and not only to me, but also to all who have longed for his appearing" (2 Tim. 4:8). In Revelation, believers under persecution are told, "Be faithful, even to the point of death, and I will give you the crown of life" (Rev. 2:10; *see* Jas. 1:12).

These crowns should not be viewed as rewards for unusual Christian accomplishment. Rather they are God's promise to all of us that in the resurrection we will share in the victory Christ has won. The crown of righteousness symbolizes complete victory over sin, and the crown of life victory over death.

In another striking image, Peter—after urging Christian leaders to serve God's flock rather than lord it over them—promises them that "when the Chief Shepherd appears, you will receive the crown of glory that will never fade away" (1 Pet. 5:4). When Christ, whose own suffering and servanthood were so misunderstood, appears, then that humility which humans despise will be seen as glorious indeed.

Assyrian King Ashurbanipal (669–627 B.C.) wearing an embroidered headdress reserved for royalty in this detail from a hunting scene on palace walls at Nineveh. Crowns in many forms have symbolized high position in ancient cultures.

Andrea Mantegna's
The Calvary, *painted on wood for an altar in 1477, presents a different mode of crucifixion for Christ from the two thieves.*

The significance of the crucifixion, however, does not lie in the form of execution or even the anguish but in its meaning as an atoning sacrifice.

crucifixion A barbaric method of execution developed in the East but adopted by the Romans to punish crimes such as rebellion, piracy, murder, and violent robbery.

The *stauros* (cross) was typically a pole imbedded in the earth, a little taller than a person. This was topped by a portable crossbar. In view of the scarcity of wood near Jerusalem in the first century, the poles on Golgotha were undoubtedly permanent. It was probably the crossbar that Jesus was forced to carry.

By the first century the Romans had perfected this form of punishment. As an official known as the *carnifix serarum* supervised, the victim was beaten with a leather whip containing shreds of metal or bone that tore the flesh. Weakened by the pain and loss of blood, the victim was then forced to carry the crossbar to the place of execution. The crossbar was fixed to the top of the imbedded pole, and the victim

The ankle bone of a young man crucified outside Jerusalem in the first century A.D. still contains the metal spike used to nail this foot to a cross.

Romans increased the strain on the body by breaking the leg bones of the victim. When they wanted to prolong the agony, they nailed a wooden block called a *sedile* to the front of the pole, on which the buttocks might rest.

This, the agonizing death of a criminal, the ultimate in shame and humiliation, was what Jesus endured for our sake. *See also* Cross.

cruse *See* Pottery.

crystal Transparent quartz. *Krystallos*, used in the Greek OT and in Revelation, means "clear ice." The name reflects the Greek belief that the mineral was formed by freezing mountain waters.

cubit A measure of length used by ancient peoples that represents the distance from a man's elbow to the tip of his middle finger. While this distance would vary from person to person, a standard cubit was used in building. Working from an eighth-century B.C. inscription in the Siloam tunnel in Jerusalem, which gives its length as 1,200 cubits, and computing the capacity of the gigantic bronze bowl that stood outside Solomon's Temple (1 Ki. 7:23-26), the length of the standard cubit works out to about 17.5 inches (44.5 centimeters). *See also* Weights and Measures.

The fact that the Bible speaks of a common cubit (Deut. 3:11) suggests that another cubit was also used. In Egypt there were two cubits, an ordinary measure and a "royal cubit," measuring about 20 inches (51 centimeters) long. If the royal cubit was intended in the description of Noah's ark, that vessel was over 500 feet (152.5 meters) long, but if the standard cubit is used, the ark was 430 feet (131 meters).

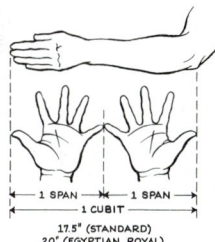

A cubit was originally measured as above. Later cubits were standardized for construction purposes.

was either tied or nailed with his arms stretched along it.

In Jesus' case, nails were probably driven through the palms near the fleshy part of the thumb, the only part of the hand that could bear the body's weight (if indeed the wrist and forearm are not included in "hand"). Archaeologists have discovered remains of a young man crucified in Jerusalem in the first century; these show that the victim's feet were probably nailed to the sides of the fixed post by spikes driven through the heel.

Suspended in this awkward position, the victim died slowly, from extreme shock or from the gradual weakening of the two sets of muscles used for breathing. When it was desirable to hasten death, the

cuckoo (KJV) Most likely the sea gull though no positive identification is possible (Lev. 11:16; Deut. 14:15).

cucumber Edible member of the gourd family. The cucumber was widely grown in Egypt and Palestine, where it served as a prized staple in the daily diet.

cummin A small plant in the parsley family, whose seeds were used to season food in Jesus' day. The seeds were also used in medicine, and crushed for use in some perfumes. Jesus chided those Pharisees who labored to separate every tiny seed in order to give God his tithe, but who overlooked the Law's call to do justice and to be merciful (Mt. 23:23).

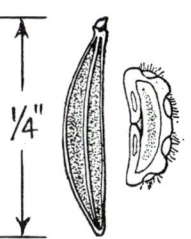

This garden herb, used to spice stews and cakes, was meticulously tithed by legalistic Pharisees.

Above: Combat scenes adorn a Roman "gladiator cup" made of mold-blown glass (first century A.D.).
Left: Glass measuring cup, found in Israel (first century A.D.).
Right: Clay cup for measuring grain, found in the Negev (2200–1900 B.C.).

cup A small container for liquids. Rulers often used elaborate cups of silver or gold, with handles. Common citizens drank from shallow cups of clay.

In ancient times, the cup came to symbolize one's lot in life. Each individual has a limited life span—one cup, you might say, in the great ocean of history. That cup might be filled with God's blessing or his wrath (Ps. 11:6, KJV; 16:5; Isa. 51:17). The OT pictures God "pouring out" favor or disfavor upon individuals and nations. In Ps. 23:5, David exults that "my cup overflows," that is, his life is full of God's blessing.

Jesus spoke on several occasions of his "cup" (Jn. 18:11), but the symbol changes slightly. Previously, one's cup was one's fate—you had to drink what was poured out for you. But Jesus speaks as one who decides his own fate—he may or may not drink from that cup. When James and John angled for seats of honor in his Kingdom, Jesus asked whether they also were willing to drink from his cup (Mk. 10:38); the context makes clear that it was a cup of suffering. Later, in Gethsemane,

Jesus prayed that the cup might be taken away, but he agreed to drink it if the Father so willed (Mt. 26:42).

The imagery of the cup enriches our understanding of the Passover meal and the Lord's Supper. The Passover service included four cups of wine. In drinking, participants celebrated the blessings God had poured out on them, reliving them and returning thanks to God. *See also* Passover.

In the NT, Paul calls the communion cup the "cup of thanksgiving" (1 Cor. 10:16). This was the name of the third cup of the Passover service, which was accompanied by a prayer praising God for delivering his people from slavery. Paul's comparison fits, because in communion Christians celebrate and express thanks for God's deliverance from sin. We can drink the cup of God's blessing because Jesus drank the cup of suffering. *See also* Lord's Supper.

In the ancient world, the cup also represented friendship and acceptance. A host would offer a cup of wine to a guest, who would accept it in a gesture of friendship. Certainly, we can see the communion cup as an offer of friendship and acceptance from Christ (our host) to us.

But Paul also draws a negative inference from that custom. The person who has accepted "the cup of the Lord," he says, must not accept "the cup of demons." In that day worshipers of pagan deities often held feasts, dedicating the cup to their gods. These were open social affairs in many cities and Christians would be tempted to participate. But Paul warns that taking part in such meals would symbolize fellowship with pagan deities (demons). We are to take the cup of Christ, and give him our exclusive allegiance (1 Cor. 10:14-22).

cupbearer A high official in the royal courts of Egypt (Gen. 40:1), Israel (1 Ki. 10:5), and Persia (Neh. 1:11). Cupbearers were not servants but persons of high rank, who served the king wine at his table. This access to the ruler made the cupbearer very influential, as reflected in the story of Nehemiah, cupbearer to Artaxerxes Longimanus. In the twentieth year of Artaxerxes' reign Nehemiah asked for and received an appointment as governor of Judah. His personal wealth was so great that he personally paid all the expenses of the 150 officials on his staff (Neh. 5:17,18).

curse (1) To call down evil or injury on someone or something; (2) to conjure the gods magically to cause injury or harm; (3) the evil or injury caused by a curse.

In the ancient world, a curse was viewed as a magical thing. A curse not only expressed a desire to harm, but actually was believed to have destructive power. So when the king of Moab hired the seer Balaam to curse Israel, he wanted Balaam to use magic incantations to weaken God's people (Num. 22). *See also* Magic.

In Scripture, however, "curse" is a moral rather than a magical concept. It was not to be viewed in the pagan way. We see this in a curious episode from Leviticus. A man, half Egyptian, half Israelite, "blasphemed the name of the Lord with a curse" and was executed (Lev. 24:10-16). He had probably used God's name in a magical incantation. God's purpose was clear: Under no circumstances should the Israelites treat their God like the gods and goddesses of the pagans, who could be manipulated by magic.

But some similarities exist between pagan and biblical curses. Curses of the Bible bind and weaken. The fig tree that Jesus cursed withered immediately, its strength drained (Mk. 11:21). In the same way,

God's curse upon the earth drained the ground of its vitality, and the land brought forth thorns and thistles (Gen. 3:17-19). But these are God's curses—not the curses of men seeking to use God to harm others.

Several different Hebrew words are translated "curse" in English versions. Among them is *'alah,* which indicates a solemn oath. This "curse" is a firm statement of what God will do if his people persist in sin; *'arar* has a similar emphasis—to bind under a penalty or curse. Another word, *qelalah,* carries the idea of treating someone lightly, with contempt or rejection. When a person curses something, he makes it of little importance. (Remember that the Hebrew word for "glory," *kabod,* comes from the word for "heavy" or "of great importance." Thus we might see this kind of curse as "deglorifying" someone or something.)

Deuteronomy 29:20 warned the Israelites, "If you do not obey the Lord your God and do not carefully follow all his commands and decrees I am giving you today, all these curses will come upon you

A Persian cupbearer, carved in limestone on palace walls in Persepolis during the reign of Xerxes I (486–465 B.C.). Two decades later Nehemiah was cupbearer to his son Artaxerxes. The king's cupbearer was a trusted friend and important government official.

and overtake you." There follows a list of specific curses on the city, country, people, and animals.

Against this background we can understand the meaning of several fascinating NT verses. The Bible calls upon Christians to "bless those who persecute you; bless and do not curse" (Rom. 12:14). We must not seek to harm even our enemies. Instead we are to seek the good of all enemies, and wish them well.

In Galatians Paul says that "all who rely on observing the law are under a curse" (Gal. 3:10-14). Built into the Law is a blessing for those who obey, but a curse upon those who break it. Since all fall short, any who count on their own efforts and seek to keep the Law are lost. Only persons who rely on Christ rather than on keeping the Law can escape the punishment which the Law decrees.

curtain of the Temple The thick, colorful, woven curtain that separated inner and outer rooms of Israel's Temple. The inner room, called the Holy of Holies, was the place of the divine presence. It could be entered only by the high priest, once a year, when he brought sacrificial blood on the Day of Atonement. *See also* Day of Atonement; Temple.

According to Heb. 9:8, the heavy curtain symbolized the fact that "the way into the Most Holy Place [i.e., God's presence] had not yet been disclosed." Three of the Gospels report that, at the moment of Jesus' death, "the curtain of the temple was torn in two from top to bottom" (Mt. 27:51; Mk. 15:38; Lk. 23:45). The symbolism is clear. The death of Jesus opened the way into the very presence of God, providing believers with an access which simply was not possible during OT times. The writer of Hebrews says that, "since we [now] have confidence to enter the Most Holy Place by the blood of Jesus, . . . let us draw near to God with a sincere heart in full assurance of faith" (Heb. 10:19,22).

The torn curtain is a witness that because of Christ nothing stands in the way of our reconciliation to God.

cutting (one's self) A practice in many ancient cultures expressing grief or mourning. Some pagan worshipers also tried to attract the attention of their gods in this way. Religious epics discovered at Ugarit describe the chief god, El, cutting his face, arms, chest, and back in mourning over the death of the god Baal. Jere-

miah reports that the practice was followed by the people of Judah as late as the sixth century B.C., even though OT Law said, "Do not cut your bodies for the dead or put tattoo marks on yourselves" (Lev. 19:28; *compare* Jer. 16:6). God's people might grieve at the death of a loved one, but should not express the despair with pagan rituals.

The OT also tells how the prophets of Baal cut themselves in their confrontation with Elijah on Mount Carmel, "as was their custom" (1 Ki. 18:28). In Canaanite mythology Baal was a violent as well as highly sexed deity. These pagan prophets probably intended the smell of fresh blood to arouse Baal, and draw attention to his worshipers.

Jesus' exhortation, "If your hand or your foot causes you to sin, cut it off and throw it away" (Mt. 18:8), is not a call for self-mutilation. Jesus uses this figure of speech to emphasize the seriousness of sin. Temptations to sin must be decisively rejected, even if rejecting them seems as painful as the loss of part of our own body.

These bronze cymbals from Megiddo (about 1400 B.C.) were worn on finger and thumb. Cymbals were used in Hebrew worship (1 Chr. 15:16) as Ps. 150 evidences.

cymbals Small metal plates struck together to make music. Metal cymbals (Heb., *mesiltayim,* and *selilim*) dating as far back as the 14th century B.C. have been found in the Middle East. Pairs of the bowl-like bronze instruments range between 4 and 6 inches (10 to 15 centimeters) in diameter. Each cymbal was fitted with an iron finger ring. From ancient reliefs it appears that cymbals were played by striking them against each other with an up-and-down rather than side-by-side motion.

Cymbals are not mentioned in Israel's history until the time of David, when they are used in public worship of the Lord (1 Chr. 13:8; *see* Ps. 150:5).

cypress A tree yielding long-lasting hardwood, especially prized in Egypt, where it was used to make the coffins in which mummies were placed. Isaiah 44:14 lists cypress among woods chosen by idol makers. Most scholars believe that the "gopher wood" used by Noah to make the ark was cypress (Gen. 6:14, KJV). *See also* Gopher Wood.

Cyrus II [SI-ruhs]. King of Persia from 558–530 B.C. Also known as "the Great." Unified the empires of Media and Persia in 549 B.C. and continued his conquests, finally marching into Babylon on October 29, 539 B.C., to take the throne of that ancient empire. **Scripture:** 2 Chr. 36:22,23; Ezra 1:1-8; 3:7; 4:3,5; 5:13,14,17; 6:3,14; Isa. 44:28; 45:1-4; Dan. 1:21; 6:28; 10:1. **Grandfather:** Cyrus I. **Parents:** Cambyses I and Mandane, the daughter of Astyages, the king of Media. **Son:** Cambyses II.

When Cyrus incorporated the Babylonian Empire into his territories, he instituted an unusual policy. Cyrus granted permission to peoples who had been deported to return to their homelands, and he encouraged the rebuilding of their houses of worship. Ezra 1:2-4 contains a copy of the decree concerning Judah and the Jews; a decree that was duplicated for other peoples that had been deported by the Babylonians. The famous Cyrus Cylinder, a 10-inch (25-centimeter) clay cylinder inscribed with cuneiform writing, reports the policy, saying "I [Cyrus] gathered all their inhabitants and returned [to them] their habitations."

Ezra quotes Cyrus referring to the Lord as "God of heaven," and giving him credit for having "given me all the kingdoms of the earth" (Ezra 1:2). This does not mean that the great ruler knew the Lord; more likely, it reflects Cyrus's political acumen. In similar proclamations reinstating other peoples, Cyrus claimed he had been chosen by the gods of those nations. Thus he was shrewdly using the religious piety of his subject nations to gain their loyalty.

However, the Bible says that Cyrus was raised up by God as an instrument of his will. The appearance of Cyrus was predicted by Isaiah, who wrote of the Jews' Exile and subsequent return to Judah. Through Isaiah, God said of Cyrus:

"He is my shepherd and will accomplish all that I please; he will say of Jerusalem, 'Let it be rebuilt,' and of the temple, 'Let its foundations be laid.' "

God goes on to call Cyrus his "anointed . . . , whose right hand I take hold of to subdue nations before him" (Isa. 44:28–45:1).

Cyrus the Great established an effective system of administration throughout his empire. He was killed in battle in 530 B.C., and succeeded by his son, Cambyses II. *See also* Persia.

The stately cypress tree provided the wood with which Noah constructed the ark (Gen. 6:14, NIV).

Below: Sixth-century marble head of a Persian king, possibly Cyrus the Great. Cyrus's less oppressive Persian kingdom ruled the Fertile Crescent for over 200 years, from the fall of Babylon to the invasion of Alexander the Great.

Below left: The Cyrus Cylinder (536 B.C.) documents the decree, recorded in Ezra 1, permitting the Jews to return to Judah and rebuild the Temple. Like Nebuchadnezzar, Cyrus is identified as an agent to carry out God's will for the Jewish people.

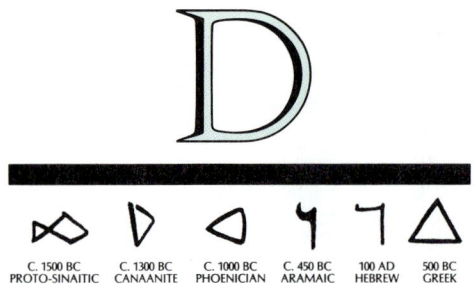

dagger A short sword. The same Hebrew word (*hereb*) is translated both "dagger" and "sword." *Hereb* means a "destroying weapon."

Daggers were usually flat and triangular, and often had one or more raised ribs to add strength. Archaeologists have recovered ceremonial daggers made of gold as well as functional bronze and iron blades.

Dagger, chain, and pronged spearhead from the period of the Philistine invasion of the coast of Canaan, about 1275 B.C. (see Amos 9:7). The dagger's handle is bronze and its blade iron. The Philistines were a consistent threat to Israel during the time of the judges because of their sophisticated weapons.

Dagon [DAY-gon; "corn"]. The principal god of the Philistines. Near the end of the era of the judges, the Philistines captured the ark of God and brought it to the temple of Dagon in Ashdod (1 Sam. 5). Their celebration was short-lived. The idol representing Dagon was found shattered and fallen on its face before the ark.

The name Dagon goes back to at least 2500 B.C. In the original Canaanite pantheon, Dagon seems to have been next to El in power. Little is known of Dagon's specific role in the mythology of Canaanite peoples. Ancient documents suggest he was originally a god of crops and fertility. The notion that Dagon was represented as part fish is not supported by archaeology.

In Canaanite mythology Dagon was the father of Baal, a god who gradually took over his role as god of fertility. By the time of Israel's monarchy (1000–600 B.C.), Baal had become the primary Canaanite deity. *See also* Baal; Philistines.

Damascus For over 4,000 years Damascus, today the capital of Syria, has been an important city in the Middle East. Situated about 60 miles (100 kilometers) east of the Mediterranean, and watered by two rivers, Damascus controlled caravan routes over which vast amounts of wealth were carried in ancient times. Its location made it a rich as well as strategic city.

Damascus first appears in the story of Abraham (Gen. 14:15). David placed an Israelite garrison there, but later a series of Aramean kings made Damascus their capital. Damascus's greatest impact on Israelite history took place during the divided monarchy. Between the 900s B.C. and the destruction of Israel in 722 B.C., kings of Damascus conducted persistent warfare with both the northern and southern Hebrew kingdoms. *See also* Aram.

Right: Damascus is located about 60 miles (100 kilometers) from the Mediterranean coast, due east of the city of Sidon. Below: Plan of the city highlights Straight Street, where Ananias found the blinded Saul in the house of Judas, healed, and baptized him (Acts 9:10-19).

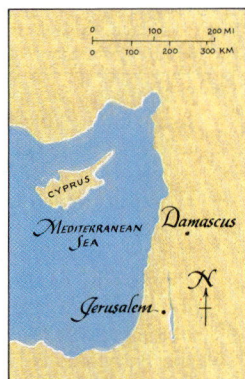

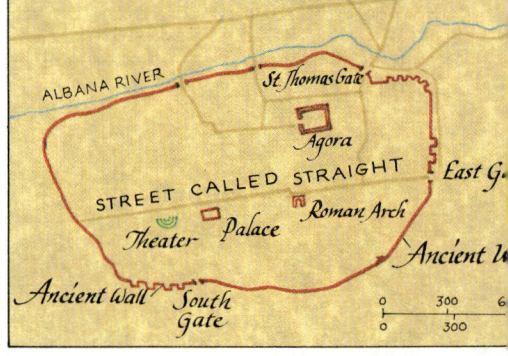

Above: A house perches on a portion of Damascus's ancient walls. Paul was let down through an opening probably like those at the left.
Left: Paul escaping from Damascus in a basket, depicted on an 11th-century enamel plaque. His fearless preaching provoked the city's Jews to conspire to kill him (Acts 9:19-27).

After the Assyrian conquest of the 700s B.C., Damascus served as an administrative center for the various empires that ruled the Middle East.

By the first century A.D., a number of Jews had settled in Damascus. Paul was converted on the road from Jerusalem to Damascus, while traveling there to arrest Jewish followers of Jesus.

From the fourth century, Damascus was a stronghold of Christianity until Islamic armies overran it in A.D. 639.

dance Rhythmic movement of the body, usually to music. Dancing was a joyous experience for God's OT people, associated with celebration and worship. The various Hebrew words for dance are descriptive: they portray the dancer enthusiastically leaping and skipping, twisting and whirling. Throughout Scripture, dancing stands in contrast with mourning. Psalm 30:11 says, "You turned my wailing into dancing; you removed my sackcloth and clothed me with joy."

A vivid sense of the meaning of dance is conveyed in the story of the prodigal son (Lk. 15). When the prodigal returned, his father cried out, "Let's have a feast and celebrate. For this son of mine was dead and is alive again; he was lost and is found" (vv. 23,24). The passage goes on to tell how the older brother, returning home, "heard music and dancing." Every joyful occasion, such as a wedding feast, had its share of music and dancing.

What specific occasions stimulated dancing? The Israelites danced with joy after crossing the Red Sea (Ex. 15:20). Later, military victories were typically celebrated in this way (1 Sam. 18:6).

Worship was a joyful experience in Israel. David danced before the Lord as the ark was brought to Jerusalem (2 Sam. 6:14). Psalm 149:2-5 expresses what David must have felt:

Let Israel rejoice in their Maker;
let the people of Zion be glad in their King.
Let them praise his name with dancing
and make music to him with tambourine
and harp.
For the Lord takes delight in his people;
he crowns the humble with salvation.
Let the saints rejoice in this honor
and sing for joy on their beds.

"David . . . danced before the Lord with all his might" (2 Sam. 6:14). Dancer with long-necked stringed instrument; fragment of a relief from the 14th century B.C., found at the Canaanite city of Laish, renamed Dan.

Scripture also associates dancing with God's ultimate restoration of his people. Jeremiah proclaims God's everlasting love for Israel and, in a time marked by despair, promises, "Again you will take up your tambourines and go out to dance with the joyful" (Jer. 31:4).

The sensuous dance of the daughter of Herodias (Mt. 14:6; Mk. 6:22) was not in the biblical tradition, but was entertainment in the manner of the Greeks. In ancient Jewish culture men and women danced in separate groups.

275

Daniel, Book of The Book of Daniel relates the experiences and visions of a Jewish captive, taken to Babylon as a youth in 605 B.C. and trained to become an administrator in Nebuchadnezzar's vast empire. For some 60 years Daniel remained influential in the government of Babylon and of the Persian Empire that supplanted it. Daniel's last recorded vision is dated to the third year of Cyrus, 536–535 B.C.

The book divides naturally into two sections. Chapters 1–6 relate events which took place in the Babylonian and Persian courts. Chapters 7–12 report apocalyptic visions given to Daniel.

DATE AND AUTHORSHIP

Liberal scholars view Daniel as a legendary figure, even though he is named three times by his contemporary, Ezekiel (Ezek. 14:14,20; 28:3). They see the Book of Daniel as a composite work, written about 165 B.C., that is, after the events prophesied in Daniel's visions.

Conservative scholars, however, view Daniel as a historical person, and believe the book was completed by Daniel before his death about 532 B.C. Conservatives believe that God revealed future events through the prophets, so the accuracy of Daniel's predictions is hardly evidence of a late date. They also note that many of the "historical problems" cited by 19th-century critics have been resolved by archaeological finds, which have demonstrated how accurately the author of Daniel portrays details of empire history and court life. For instance, the ethnic denotation "Chaldean" is also used correctly to designate a class of astrologer soothsayers or "wise men" (NIV). Belshazzar, long scoffed at as an invention, has been identified as the son and co-regent of Nabonidus (he offered to make Daniel "third highest ruler in the kingdom" [Dan. 5:16], because he himself was second). The change in punishments from fire (Dan. 3) to the lions' den (Dan. 6) reflects a change from Babylonian to Persian practices. "Darius the Mede" has not

FULFILLED PROPHECIES OF DANIEL 2,3,7 & 8				
	Babylon	**Medo-Persia**	**Greece**	**Rome**
Daniel 2:32-45 **Dream Image** **603 B.C.**	Head of Gold (2:32,37,38)	Chest and Arms of Silver (2:32,39)	Belly and Thighs of Bronze (2:32,39)	Legs of Iron, Feet of Iron and Clay (2:33,40,41)
Daniel 7 **Vision of the** **Four Beasts**	Lion (7:4)	Bear (7:5)	Leopard (7:6)	Strong Beast (7:7,11,19,23)
Daniel 8 **Vision of the** **Ram and Goat**		Ram (8:3,4,20)	Goat with One Horn (8:5-8,21) Four Horns (8:8,22) Little Horn (8:9-14)	

yet been identified by cuneiform records. But "Darius" was a title assumed at coronation, just as Roman emperors became Caesar upon accession. The name might well be an alternate title of Cyrus himself, or perhaps a reference to a man named Gubaru, whom secular sources identify as ruler under Cyrus of Babylon and the "regions beyond the river." *See also* Prophecy.

THEOLOGICAL CONTRIBUTIONS

The Book of Daniel portrays God as absolute Sovereign. This theme is developed in three ways. First, Daniel's experience in the courts of Nebuchadnezzar and Cyrus reveals the Lord's power over the rulers of human empires. According to Daniel 4:37, even the great king confessed, "Now I, Nebuchadnezzar, praise and exalt and glorify the King of heaven."

Second, in a series of detailed prophecies, God revealed the future to Daniel. His visions describe the emergence of successive world powers, culminating in Rome's domination of the known world.

Third, evidence of God's sovereignty is found in the prophecy of the "seventy weeks," which dates the appearance of God's Messiah from the issuance of a then-future decree to rebuild Jerusalem. *See also* Seventy Weeks.

MASTERY KEYS

Read the first six chapters of Daniel for personal spiritual enrichment. Ezekiel 28:3 commends Daniel for wisdom. In what ways was Daniel wise? How can his choices serve as a model for today? Note: Daniel was probably about 13 years of age in chapter one. When cast into the lions' den (ch. 6), he was in his 80s.

The later chapters of Daniel are prophetic. (*See* the articles on prophecy and apocalyptic literature.) Note that the prophecies in chs. 7,8 have been fulfilled. Chapter 9 contains a key messianic prophecy, while chs. 11,12 contain obscure prophecies of events associated with history's end. *See also* Future.

SPECIAL FEATURES

Daniel 10 gives unique insight into the unseen world. Good and evil angels are ranged against each other in conflict. Angels have differing ranks and power: The angel messenger sent to Daniel could not pass Satan's angel ("the prince of the Persian kingdom") until Michael, a chief angel, came to help. This, with Job 1 and 1 Ki. 22, is one of the few chapters in the

DANIEL: A READING AND STUDY GUIDE

Chapter	Content Summary	Related Articles
1	Young Daniel, in training in Babylon, determines to keep God's Law; enters Nebuchadnezzar's civil service.	Dietary Laws Exile
2	Daniel interprets Nebuchadnezzar's dream of future world empires.	Nebuchadnezzar Kingdom
3	Shadrach, Meshach, and Abednego refuse to worship an idol; are rescued from fiery furnace by God.	Idol
4	Nebuchadnezzar is punished with madness for his pride. When restored, he acknowledges and worships God.	Gentiles Worship
5	Daniel interprets an inscription which appears at King Belshazzar's feast and warns of Babylon's imminent fall.	Babylon
6	Daniel, now a high official in the Medo-Persian Empire, is delivered by God from a den of lions.	Persia Darius
7	Daniel dreams of four beasts who represent successive world empires. An angel interprets the dream.	Angels Sovereignty
8	Daniel dreams of a ram and a goat, whose horns represent rulers of Medo-Persia and Greece.	Greece
9	The angel Gabriel gives Daniel a time frame for the appearance of God's promised Messiah.	Messiah Seventy Weeks
10	Another angel appears to explain "what will happen to your people [Israel] in the future."	Future Israel
11	The angel describes war raging in the Middle East, and an invasion of Israel by "the king of the North."	Antichrist Abomination of Desolation
12	After a time of terrible tribulation, to last 1,290 days, blessing and resurrection will come.	Tribulation Resurrection

Bible that penetrates the veil between seen and unseen worlds.

Daniel 12:2 contains the OT's clearest reference to resurrection.

daric A thick, gold coin introduced into Persia by Darius I. It weighed about .3 ounces (8.4 grams). *See also* Money.

Darius [dah-RI-uhs]. The name of three Persian rulers mentioned in the OT, the most notable being Darius the Mede in Dan. 5,6.

DARIUS THE MEDE (DAN. 5,6)

No person of this name is found in Babylonian texts, but Daniel refers to him as ruler after Belshazzar. Some take Darius to be a man named Gubaru, whom Cyrus appointed governor of Babylon. Others take "Darius the Mede" to be a name or title of Cyrus himself. Since Cyrus ruled the united Medo-Persian Empire, it is possible that he might bear a Median name as well as a Persian one. *See also* Daniel.

DARIUS THE GREAT (522–485 B.C.)

His lengthy rule was marked by military conquest, magnificent constructions at Susa, his capital, and effective administration of the Persian Empire. He is best known in history for his unsuccessful invasion of Europe, which was stopped by the Greeks at Marathon. *See also* Esther.

This Darius confirmed the earlier decree of Cyrus and ordered that Empire funds be used to rebuild the Jerusalem Temple (Ezra 5,6). Haggai and Zechariah prophesied during his reign (Hag. 1:1; Zech. 1:1).

DARIUS II (424–405 B.C.)

He ruled Persia and Babylon, and was called "Darius the Persian" in Neh. 12:22, possibly to distinguish him from "the Mede." *See also* Persia.

dark, darkness (1) The entire or partial absence of light; (2) metaphorically, (a) the hidden, (b) terror and divine judgment, (c) the realm of sin. In every society, darkness and light serve as powerful, contrasting symbols. It is not surprising that darkness should be a powerful theological metaphor in both Testaments. *See also* Light.

OLD TESTAMENT

In the OT, God is associated with brightness and glory. Yet from man's perspective, God is hidden, masked by clouds and darkness (Ex. 20:21; Ps. 18:11). While no darkness can hide us from God (Ps. 139:11,12), God himself is shrouded in mystery apart from his self-revelation.

Darkness in the OT also communicates a

sense of terror, associated with divine judgment. Looking ahead to God's intervention in history, Amos warns, "Why do you long for the day of the Lord? That day will be darkness, not light. It will be as though a man fled from a lion only to meet a bear. . . . Will not the day of the Lord be

darkness, not light—pitch-dark, without a ray of brightness?" (Amos 5:18-20; *see* Joel 2:2,31; Zeph. 1:15).

NEW TESTAMENT

In the NT, darkness again expresses the terror of judgment. Jesus warns that those without faith "will be thrown outside, into the darkness, where there will be weeping and gnashing of teeth" (Mt. 8:12).

But in the NT darkness and light take on a powerful moral aura. Light is characteristic of the realm of God, where all is pure and holy. Darkness is characteristic of a realm where sin reigns (Eph. 5:11; 6:12). Jesus' coming revealed that humanity is not simply blind to God and goodness, but has chosen the dark. Jesus said, "This is the verdict: Light has come into the world, but men loved darkness instead of light because their deeds were evil" (Jn. 3:19).

Conversion to Christ is like moving out of spiritual darkness into light. But with conversion comes the necessity of living in the light. "For you were once darkness, but now you are light in the Lord," Paul wrote. "Live as children of light (for the fruit of the light consists in all goodness, righteousness and truth) and find out what pleases the Lord. Have nothing to do with the fruitless deeds of darkness . . ." (Eph. 5:8-11; *see* Jude 6).

John uses light and darkness in another distinctive way. "Walking in the light" in John is maintaining fellowship with God, while walking in darkness is an image of losing touch with God, and thus losing one's moral way (1 Jn. 1:7).

date The sweet, oblong fruit of the date palm. Dates hang in large clusters from the top of the tree and are harvested in late summer or early fall. Like figs, dates could be dried or made into small cakes for long-term storage. Their fruit was a staple food for many desert tribes in Arabia and North Africa. *See also* Fruit; Palm Tree.

daughter (1) A female child; (2) any female descendant; (3) a female member of a community; (4) a town close to a major city. Some take the repeated prophetic address to the "daughter of Jerusalem," or "the daughter of Zion," etc., as a reference to the inhabitants of the named city. However, "daughter" may also refer to towns associated with major population centers (Josh. 15:45,47, Heb.).

David [DAY-vid; meaning unknown]. King of Israel 1010–970 B.C. Israel's greatest king, who wholeheartedly loved the Lord. David defeated Israel's enemies, expanded the nation's borders, and established Jerusalem as its political and religious center. His military, political, and religious innovations initiated Israel's golden age, and unified the Hebrew people as never before. David is Scripture's ideal king; the model for God's Messiah, who was to be born of David's family line and ultimately to rule God's never-ending Kingdom. **Scripture:** 1,2 Sam.; 1 Chr.

BACKGROUND

Under Israel's first king, Saul, the Hebrew people remained a loose association of tribal groups. Saul's spiritual shortcomings were even more serious than his weaknesses as a leader, and God determined to give Israel a ruler who would be a man "after his own heart" (1 Sam. 13:14). *See also* Saul.

Young David was introduced into the royal court as a harpist, whose music soothed the moody Saul. After defeating the giant Philistine, Goliath, David was given military command and married one of Saul's daughters. David proved so successful that Saul became jealous. Forced to

flee, David gathered a team of fighting men around him, who later became the core of his army. But David refused to fight Saul, whom God had appointed king.

After Saul's death David was crowned king by the tribe of Judah. The northern tribes crowned a son of Saul. Seven years later David became king of the united tribes. He established Jerusalem, lying on the border between the northern and southern tribes, as his capital and brought the ark of God there. *See also* Jerusalem.

David then organized the army, the

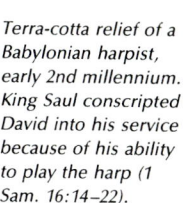

Terra-cotta relief of a Babylonian harpist, early 2nd millennium. King Saul conscripted David into his service because of his ability to play the harp (1 Sam. 16:14–22).

worship system, and the administration of his kingdom. In a series of wars, David greatly extended the nation's borders.

David's later years were relatively peaceful, except for strife within his own family. During the last decade of his life, David dedicated himself to gathering resources for the construction of a temple. He wrote many psalms for use in public worship, which give insight into his deep love for and trust in God. *See also* Psalms.

David is honored in Scripture not only for what he accomplished, but for what he represents. As David was founder of the model Hebrew kingdom, his greater descendant, Christ, is founder of God's spiritual and eternal rule. *See also* Covenant; Kingdom.

279

LEARNING FROM DAVID'S LIFE

The Bible contains more stories about David than about any other person except Jesus. Rather than reading or teaching story by story, it is helpful to look for unifying themes.

• *David as warrior.* The story of Goliath (1 Sam. 17) displays David's physical courage, and also his military creativity. No one but David thought of using the sling, a long-distance weapon, against the giant Philistine. Most important, however, the story reveals the source of David's confidence: "It is not by sword or spear that the Lord saves; for the battle is the Lord's, and he will give you into our hands" (17:47). David surely was a military genius, but his courage came from his dependence on God.

• *David as friend.* David demonstrated a capacity for friendship and loyalty. The prime example is his relationship with Jonathan, who as Saul's oldest son would expect to succeed Saul as king (1 Sam. 18,20). Jonathan surrendered personal am-

bition to help his friend, and when David did become king he took Jonathan's crippled son Mephibosheth into his inner circle of friends (2 Sam. 9). Perhaps David's greatest demonstration of loyalty was to Saul, who tried to kill him. David honored Saul's appointment to the kingship by God, and would not harm Saul despite repeated opportunities to do so (1 Sam. 24,26). The loyalty that so many showed to David was undoubtedly won by the loyalty that David himself modeled.

• *David as ruler.* An able administrator and organizer, he began to organize his army while still a fugitive (1 Chr. 11,12,27). He organized the worship system for the central sanctuary he established in Jerusalem (1 Chr. 23–26:19). David set up an effective central government with administrators responsible for tribal areas (1 Chr. 26:20-28). The fact that the First Book of Chronicles devotes so many chapters to these issues reminds us that practical abilities as well as spiritual commitment are necessary for accomplishment.

• *David as psalmist.* David's psalms reveal not only his deep love for God, but also his own very human emotions. The freedom of David to share his thoughts and feelings with the Lord helps us realize that God cares for us, and is eager to listen as we express our needs, fears, anger, joys, and even despair. David's psalms serve as a model of truly meaningful, very personal prayer.

Many psalms are linked to David's experiences. For instance, Psalm 3 relates David's thoughts as he fled during Absalom's rebellion (2 Sam. 15,16). Studying such psalms with the linked passage in 1,2 Samuel or 1 Chronicles can be very enriching.

• *David as parent.* Although David ruled his country well, he failed to rule his sons. When one son, Amnon, raped a half-sister, David failed to act (2 Sam. 13).

SOME OF DAVID'S WIVES AND SONS

Michal (1 Sam. 18:27)	Abigail (1 Sam. 25:42)	Ahinoam (1 Sam. 25:43)	Maacah (1 Chr. 3:2)	Haggith (1 Chr. 3:2)	Abital (1 Chr. 3:3)	Eglah (1 Chr. 3:3)	Bathsheba (1 Chr. 3:5)
	Kileab or Daniel (1 Chr. 3:1)	Amnon (1 Chr. 3:1)	Absalom (1 Chr. 3:2)	Adonijah (1 Chr. 3:2)	Shephatiah (1 Chr. 3:3)	Ithream (1 Chr. 3:3)	Shimea/Shammah Shobab Nathan Solomon (2 Sam. 5:14; 1 Chr. 3:5)

The Valley of Elah in SW Judah, where David killed Goliath (1 Sam. 17:2,19; 21:9). The Philistines had already taken the nearby city of Azekah and were seeking to command Socoh (17:1).

After another son, Absalom, took revenge and murdered Amnon, David failed to either punish or forgive his son (2 Sam. 14). David's mourning for the slain Absalom after Absalom had brought about a civil war (2 Sam. 18:32,33) reveals David's father-love for his wayward child. Yet that love apparently blinded David to the need for discipline. If David had only acted decisively, he might have saved one or both of these sons. *See also* Absalom.

• *David as sinner.* David's failures as a parent illustrate human frailty: David fell short as a father. But David's adultery with Bathsheba, and his arrangement for the death in battle of her husband Uriah, portray David as subject to lust in rebellion against God and godliness (2 Sam. 11). An honest love for God fell prey to the pride of power, which led to gross sin. *See also* Sin.

But the story does not end here. When David was confronted by the prophet Nathan, he acknowledged his sin (2 Sam. 12). David not only confessed his sin to God, but because the sin must have become public knowledge, David also made his confession public. That public confession is recorded as Psalm 51, where it served Israel and serves us as an example of how to restore interrupted relationship with God. *See also* Confess.

• *David as a worshiper of God.* David's last years were spent establishing and organizing public worship, and making preparations for building a temple to the Lord (1 Chr. 23–26,28,29). His personal life was marked by private worship, expressed so honestly in many of his psalms.

Perhaps we best capture the spirit of David by listening, with the people of Is-

rael, to David's rejoicing as he and his people responded wholeheartedly to the Lord:

"Praise be to you, O Lord,
God of our father Israel,
from everlasting to everlasting.
Yours, O Lord, is the greatness and
the power
and the glory and the majesty and
the splendor,
for everything in heaven and earth
is yours.
Yours, O Lord, is the kingdom;
you are exalted as head over all.
Wealth and honor come from you;
you are the ruler of all things.
In your hands are strength and power
to exalt and give strength to all.
Now, our God, we give you thanks,
and praise your glorious name."
(1 Chr. 29:10-13)

day (1) A 24-hour period; (2) any period of time during which certain events take place; (3) the time, as opposed to night, when the sun shines, and metaphorically a symbol of light and goodness.

THE LITERAL 24-HOUR DAY

The Hebrew day was measured from sunset to sunset (Gen. 1:5; Lev. 23:32). In early times it was loosely divided into three major parts: evening, morning, and noon (Ps. 55:17). Other divisions of the day may be represented in phrases such as the "heat of the day," the "cool of the day," etc. The use of a sundial as early as the 8th century B.C. indicates that the day was further divided (Isa. 38:8). By Jesus' time, daylight was divided into twelve

Line drawing of an Assyrian slingman from a wall relief. David, an unlikely warrior in his people's eyes, surprised them and the Philistines with his skill when he killed Goliath with one shot (1 Sam. 17).

hours between sunrise and sunset, the night into watches. *See also* Hour, Watches of the Night.

Only the seventh day in the Hebrew week had a name, Sabbath. The others were indicated by numbers: the first day, second day, etc.

The familiar saying in 2 Peter, "With the Lord a day is like a thousand years, and a thousand years are like a day" (3:8), simply affirms that, unlike human beings, God is not bound by time. As humans, we live within the space-time universe, but God is free to act without those constraints.

THE FIGURATIVE DAY

"Day" is also used in the Bible in figurative and metaphorical ways. The expression "day of," with a descriptive term such as "wrath" (Job 20:28), "salvation" (2 Cor. 6:2) or even "small things" (Zech. 4:10), indicates a period of time during which certain events take place. The length of time in these expressions is indefinite. While the "Day of Atonement" was a specific 24-hour day, the "day of salvation" extends from Christ's resurrection to his Second Coming. In this case "day" represents an entire epoch in sacred history, the Christian era.

The NT also uses "day" and "night" as contrasting symbols. Day represents light and goodness; night, darkness and evil (Rom. 13:13). As Christians we are "sons of the light and sons of the day. We do not belong to the night or to the darkness" (1 Th. 5:5). Day also represents that time during which human beings are awake and active, while night represents quiescence and sleep (Jn. 9:4).

THE DAYS OF CREATION

Many have questioned the meaning of "day" in the Genesis description of creation. Is a 24-hour day intended? Or is "day" used in its figurative sense as an indefinite period of time during which certain events took place? Various interpretations have been suggested, many of which have been held by persons who maintain a high view of Scripture. Is the view that Genesis describes seven consecutive 24-hour days most consistent with the text? Each Genesis "day" is marked by evening and morning, and this seems to describe the daily cycle (Gen. 1:5,8,13,19, 23,31). Also Ex. 20:8-11 seems to treat the days literally. On the other hand, the seventh day lacks the "evening and morning" phrase, which led the Jewish rabbis to suggest that God's Sabbath is still being celebrated and therefore cannot be a literal 24-hour day. *See also* Creation.

Day of Atonement *See* Atonement, Day of.

day of the Lord A time when God acts decisively in human history to implement some aspect of his redemptive plan.

Three events are usually associated with the day of the Lord: (1) The OT prophets speak of judgment upon unbelieving Israel. "The cry on the day of the Lord will be bitter. . . . That day will be a day of wrath, a day of distress and anguish, a day of trouble and ruin, a day of darkness and gloom, a day of clouds and blackness" (Zeph. 1:14,15). The fall of Israel and Judah to the Assyrians and Babylonians partly fulfilled such dire predictions of God's anger (Isa. 22; Joel 1,2; Amos 5).

(2) Both OT and NT point to Christ's Second Coming to judge the world at history's end as "the day of the Lord" (Zech. 14; 1 Th. 5:12; *see* Mt. 24:43,44). (3) At a climactic "day" still further in the future, the earth itself will be renovated by fire (2 Pet. 3:10-13). *See also* Day; Judgment; Millennium; New Heavens.

daysman (KJV) An arbitrator in a dispute between two persons (Job 9:33).

deacon, deaconess A church officer. The Greek word for deacon (*diakonos*) means "servant." It is clear from Acts 6 and 1 Tim. 3 that "deacon" was a recognized office or position of leadership in the early church. What is not clear in our English versions is that women as well as men may have held this office. In Greek, Rom. 16:1 calls Phoebe a deaconess of the church of Cenchrea. The word *gunaikas* in 1 Tim. 3:11, often understood as "the deacons' wives," may also be taken as "the women deacons."

The Bible gives us no complete job description, but does indicate some aspects of the office. (1) Acts 6 describes a situation in which the daily distribution of food to the congregation's needy was committed to seven deacons "known to be full of the Spirit and wisdom" (v. 3). (2) The Greek word *diakonia* means "service" or "ministry." The word focuses attention on loving action undertaken in the service of others. (3) In several contexts, the NT shows Christian service (*diakonia*) toward people in prison (Mt. 25:44), in financial need (2 Cor. 9:1), and in need of supportive relationships (1 Cor. 12:5). Thus, deacons appear to have been godly believers chosen to supervise the helping ministries of the church. *See also* Servant.

A portion of the scroll of Isaiah—the oldest manuscript of a complete book of the OT (about 100 B.C.). The leather scroll was found in so-called Cave I (below) at Qumran in 1947.

Left: Some of the manuscripts found near the Dead Sea were stored in unique pottery jars, which may have been produced specifically to store scrolls. When the Roman army overran the Qumran community, its library was hidden and saved from destruction.
Below: The most important scrolls were found in eleven caves in and around Wadi Qumran on the northwestern edge of the Dead Sea.
Bottom: Aerial view of Khirbet Qumran, the excavated building complex believed to have housed an ascetic Jewish community of Essenes from 2nd century B.C. to the Temple's destruction in A.D. 70. The ruins are perched on a spur overlooking a landscape little changed since Jesus' day.

Dead Sea Scrolls A group of ancient manuscripts written on papyrus and leather parchment, found, beginning in 1947, hidden in caves near the Dead Sea. The manuscripts were written or copied between 250 B.C. and A.D. 68, and had been part of the library of a Jewish religious sect called the Essenes. Among some 500 manuscripts which have been identified are fragments of every OT book except Esther, including all of Isaiah and fine portions of the Psalms. These biblical scrolls, which are more than 1,000 years older than any other known Hebrew texts, demonstrate the reliability of the Hebrew Bible. *See also* Bible.

The Dead Sea Scrolls also contain other types of literature: fragments of apocryphal books, books describing rules for living in the Essene community at Qumran, and portions of commentaries and histories.

Some of the scrolls that have been published led to fanciful identification of Jesus with the Essene sect—a view largely rejected by responsible critics. Nevertheless, these documents provide important information on the history of Israel and its religious situation between the second century B.C. and the first century A.D.

One of the grim facts of human existence is that "no one has power over the day of his death" (Eccl. 8:8). Jesus, however, promised life after death: "I am the resurrection and the life. He who believes in me will live, even though he dies" (Jn. 11:25). Painted terracotta coffin dated about 500 B.C., found near Smyrna.

death (1) The end of a biological life; (2) the moral and spiritual state of human beings separated from God.

DEATH VIEWED BIOLOGICALLY

All living things die. Thus, persons must come to grips with the reality of biological death. Those granted a brief 70 or 80 years of life must say with the psalmist, "Teach us to number our days aright, that we may gain a heart of wisdom" (Ps. 90:10,12).

For believers, biological death marks the end of trials and the entry into a new and better world. Isaiah observes:

The righteous perish,
and no one ponders it in his heart;
devout men are taken away,
and no one understands
that the righteous are taken away
to be spared from evil.
Those who walk uprightly
enter into peace;
they find rest as they lie in death.

(Isa. 57:1,2)

The most hopeless word in the Greek tongue, *nekros* ("corpse"), indicates the state of the dead. But in over half of its 133 occurrences in the NT, *nekros* is contrasted with resurrection. Death is not the end for the believer—it is the doorway to endless life.

Despite the hope-filled view of death which pervades both Testaments, death remains a terrible distortion of what God intended for our race. In biblical perspective, biological death is *un*natural, and the whole universe strains toward liberation from that bondage (Rom. 8:20,21). *See also* Hades; Sheol.

STATE OF THE DEAD

The Bible makes it clear that each person is destined to exist as a self-aware individual throughout eternity. However, what happens to a person before final judgment has been debated.

Some have argued from the use of "sleep" as a euphemism for death that persons remain unconscious after dying until the resurrection (1 Th. 4:13-15; 1 Cor. 15:51,52). However, the euphemism is obviously drawn from the similarity of the sleeping and dead body. "Sleep" says nothing about the personality or self-awareness of the soul.

Other passages strongly indicate that death does not interrupt self-awareness. Paul expects at the end of his life in the body to "depart and be with Christ, which is better by far" (Phil. 1:23). In another passage Paul seems to suggest that death does not launch us into eternity as naked souls, but that God has prepared a "heavenly dwelling" with which our personality will be clothed at death (2 Cor. 5:1-5).

In a very striking parable found in Luke's Gospel, Jesus described what happened after the death of two men, a rich man and a beggar named Lazarus. Each went to a place in which he was fully self-aware, able to experience pleasure and pain. Each could see, feel, think, and converse. But one was in torment, and the other in a place of blessing (Lk. 16:19-31).

Human beings, made in God's image, cannot simply cease to exist. Each of us will retain our own individual identity, conscious and self-aware throughout eternity. *See also* Eternity; Heaven; Hell.

DEATH VIEWED MORALLY

In Scripture, death is an ethical as well as biological concept. It stands as a symbol of the moral distortion which sin injected into the world. In Eph. 2:1-5, Paul describes mankind as morally "dead in your transgressions and sins." The passage goes on to describe human beings moved not by high moral vision but by the cravings, thoughts, and desires of sinful human nature (*see* 1 Jn. 3:14). Moral death is an insensitivity to the life of God's Spirit, and to the love and holiness which the Spirit offers. Yet here, too, there is hope.

The believer, who finds new life through faith in Christ, can be freed from the bondage of moral death. The Spirit of God, who raised Jesus from the dead and who is living within us, "will also give life to your mortal bodies" (Rom. 8:11). Even in our present mortality, God's Spirit enables us to do and be good (*see* Col. 3:1-4).

DEATH VIEWED SPIRITUALLY

Scripture also uses death as an image of lost relationship with God. The close fellowship of Eden disintegrated after Adam and Eve sinned. Ever since, humanity has been thoroughly alienated from God. This alienation is expressed in various ways, including active antagonism toward God. Romans 1:18-32 describes how humans, in general, have reacted to the way God reveals himself in creation.

Like Adam after the Fall, instead of loving God, men are afraid of him. Instead of seeking forgiveness, men try to hide or minimize their guilt. And in it all, rather than seeking to please God, a lost mankind wants only to please itself. The implications of spiritual death are finely drawn in Jesus' images of those who refuse the invitation of a king, and are thrown "outside, into the darkness, where there will be weeping and gnashing of teeth" (Mt. 22:13).

Excluded from personal relationship with God, and under divine condemnation (Rom. 5:16,17), there is no hope for a spiritually dead human being apart from God's gift of a new and eternal spiritual life (Jn. 3:16-18). *See also* Eternal Life; Hell; Second Death.

SUMMARY

The biblical concept of death is complex and significant. Biological death is not "natural," but a distortion of God's original plan, introduced into the universe as a consequence of human sin.

Death as an ethical term portrays humanity so distorted by sin that its desires and choices are constantly at odds with God's will and holiness. Death as a spiritual term portrays man as insensitive and unresponsive to the spiritual universe. In a state of spiritual death, human beings are alienated from God, isolated from relationship with him (Eph. 2:12,13).

In every aspect, then, death is the enemy of humankind: an enemy that will be destroyed when Jesus returns (1 Cor. 15:26).

death, second In rabbinic writings and the NT, a metaphor for eternal punishment or hell. According to Rev. 20:14, "The lake of fire is the second death." *See also* Hell.

death of Christ The end of Christ's biological life, by crucifixion, but also the sacrifice for sin and the spiritual redemption that resulted. The Bible teaches that the death of Christ was the means by which human beings were freed from bondage to every aspect of death—biological, moral, and spiritual (Heb. 2:14). Romans 4:25 says, "He [Jesus] was delivered over to death for our sins and was raised to life for our justification." *See also* Crucifixion.

THE BENEFITS WON

Scripture clearly defines the benefits which Christ's death won for us:

• Human beings must die biologically. But those who belong to Jesus will be raised, inheriting eternal life, never to die again (1 Cor. 15:12-57). *See also* Resurrection.

• Believers will still sense the pull of sin within, but the death of Jesus has made it possible for "the righteous requirements of the law" to be "fully met in us" (Rom. 8:3,4). Christ's death is the basis for the believer's moral renewal. *See also* Forgive; Redeem.

• Through the death of Christ, a harmonious relationship with God can be restored. Believers are no longer alienated, but have been reconciled to God "through the death of his Son" (Rom. 5:10). *See also* Atonement.

"Deborah, a prophetess, the wife of Lappidoth, was leading Israel at that time. She held court under the Palm of Deborah . . . and the Israelites came to her to have their disputes settled" (Jdg. 4:4,5). Ivory head of a woman, from Megiddo, 13th–12th centuries B.C.

Deborah [DEB-uh-ruh; "bee"]. About 1200 B.C., a prophetess who led Israel during the era of the judges. **Scripture:** Jdg. 4,5.

BACKGROUND

Between the death of Joshua (about 1375 B.C.) and the emergence of the monarchy (about 1043 B.C.), the Israelite tribes were led by charismatic leaders called judges, whom God raised up in times of need. The judges, usually military leaders, delivered God's people from foreign oppressors. Afterward the victorious judges helped the

At Deborah's command Barak charged down Mount Tabor and routed the Canaanite forces under Sisera by the Kishon River (Jdg. 4:14-16).

people maintain their commitment to God. They also settled disputes too difficult for local courts. Deborah is the only woman on the OT's roll of twelve judges. *See also* Courts; Judges, Book of.

LEARNING FROM DEBORAH'S LIFE

The text calls Deborah a prophetess, a person through whom God spoke to his people. According to Jdg. 4:5, she was a judge even before the battle which shattered the power of the Canaanites who oppressed the north-central tribes. The Jdg. 4:4 phrase translated "wife of Lappidoth" possibly is descriptive: Deborah was "a spirited woman."

Deborah clearly was far more assertive and confident than her general, Barak. She issued the call to battle (4:6); Barak was unwilling to go into battle unless Deborah accompanied him (4:8). While this was undoubtedly because Deborah, as a prophetess, represented the presence of God, Barak's stand also suggests Deborah's forceful personality and unbounded faith. Deborah finally consented to go with Barak, and the battle began at her command, "Go!" (Jdg. 4:14).

The poem, "The Song of Deborah" (Jdg. 5), has been called one of the most beautiful literary works in any language. What is striking in this biblical story is the fact that Deborah lived in a patriarchal society. In OT culture, women had limited roles. Yet Deborah was acknowledged as a leader. Her personal qualities and her prophetic gift overcame cultural resistance to leadership by a woman. Today, too, closeness to God and outstanding personal qualities can overcome limitations imposed by the conventions of society.

Even more important is what Deborah's story shows us about God's attitude toward women. The Lord could have chosen a man for her role. But instead he selected Deborah, a spirited woman who trusted him, to lead his people. Being a woman did not disqualify her from a leadership role usually held by men. God is not bound by human stereotypes; historically, God has not given leadership or prophetic gifts to men alone.

deceit Misleading, lying, or promise-breaking.

When Eve tried to avoid blame for the first sin, she said, "The serpent deceived me" (Gen. 3:13). That word comes from the Hebrew root *nasha'*, which means "to lead astray." A number of other Hebrew words have related meanings.

Ramah indicates trickery. "Why have you deceived me?" is a common biblical complaint: Jacob said it to Laban after learning he had married Leah, not Rachel (Gen. 29:25); Joshua to the Gibeonites, who pretended to be pilgrims from far away (Josh. 9:22); Saul to his daughter Michal after she had smuggled David safely away (1 Sam. 19:17); and the witch of Endor to Saul when he came in disguise to seek Samuel's spirit (1 Sam. 28:12).

When Proverbs, in its description of the virtuous wife, says, "Charm is deceptive" (Prov. 31:30), it uses yet another Hebrew word, *sheqer*. This means simple falsehood, something that has no basis in reality. It is the same word used in the Ten Commandments for "false witness" (Ex. 20:16).

The psalmist adds another word when asking for rescue from foreigners, "whose mouths are full of lies [*shaw'*], whose right hands are deceitful [*sheqer*]" (Ps. 144:8,11). *Shaw'* means "empty."

In the NT, the word most closely associated with deceit is *planaō*, which means to lead astray by words or behavior.

Against this background the NT command, "Do not lie to each other" (Col. 3:9), becomes far more complex than it first appears. God's people are to eliminate any words or actions that paint a false portrait of reality, or are intended to mislead and thus to harm others. John spares no words in condemning false teachers, "who do not acknowledge Jesus Christ as coming in the flesh. Any such person is the deceiver and the antichrist" (2 Jn. 7). Satan, who seeks to mislead and harm humanity, is called "a liar and the father of lies" (Jn. 8:44). In contrast, God is always open and honest with us and seeks our good. We must be just as open and honest with others. *See also* False.

decree A binding order or proclamation from a ruler. A decree expresses the fixed purpose or command of the authority issuing it. Several of the Hebrew words translated "decree" suggest carving or cutting such statements into rock.

Some versions of the OT use the word "decree" only in connection with official proclamations of such rulers as Cyrus (Ezra 6:3) and Nebuchadnezzar (Dan. 3:10). Other English versions use "decree" in reference to nature, as in, "He set them [the heavenly bodies] in place for ever and ever; he gave a decree that will never pass away" (Ps. 148:6; *see* Job 28:26; Prov. 8:29, KJV). In such contexts God's "decree" expresses what we would call a "natural law."

The NIV often uses "decree" to mean the revealed will of God. God's will was carved not just on stone tablets on Mount Sinai but is "carved" also in God's own unchangeable moral character and fixed purposes.

If we respond to the decrees of human rulers, how much more should we pay attention to the decrees of God. David says,

your servant will meditate on your decrees.
Your statutes are my delight;
they are my counselors.

(Ps. 119:23,24)

In the NT, decree (Gk., *dogma*) is used of royal proclamations of Roman emperors (Lk. 2:1; Acts 17:7) and of divine moral judgments (Rom. 1:32).

dedicate To set apart as holy, for the service of God. Articles and sacred objects in ancient Israel were dedicated by a religious ritual (Ex. 29; Num. 7; 2 Chr. 29). Persons might also be dedicated by a service initiating them into office (Lev. 21:12). The OT also speaks of persons dedicating themselves to the Lord (Num. 6:12) as an act of special personal commitment. *See also* Consecrate; Devotion.

Dedication, Feast of Hanukkah, the Jewish Festival of Lights, which falls on the 25th of Kislev. Its eight days of rejoicing commemorate the rededication of the Jerusalem Temple by Judas Maccabeus in 164 B.C., three years after its altar had been defiled by the sacrifice of unclean animals, ordered by Antiochus Epiphanes. The festival, mentioned only in Jn. 10:22, was not instituted by OT Law. *See also* Calendar; Festivals, Feasts, and Fasts; Hanukkah; Maccabees.

deer General name for any of the family *cervidai*, hoofed, cud-chewing animals. Bones of three type of deer have been unearthed in Palestine. While some think the deer of Scripture were the larger red deer, they probably were the small fallow deer, a spotted animal about 39 inches (1 meter) high, and the even smaller roe deer. A number of Hebrew terms whose specific meaning cannot be determined indicate deer.

defile To make ceremonially unclean, or, especially in the prophets, morally unclean (*see* Lev. 11:24; 17:15; Isa. 59:3, RSV).

In OT times ritual uncleanness disqualified a person from participating in the community's worship of God. The concept of ritual cleanness and uncleanness underlined the importance of complete dedication of God's people to the Lord. Many ritual and ceremonial regulations in the

Branched lampstands (menorahs) carved on stone in a synagogue in Corinth (4th century A.D.). The Feast of Dedication, which features lighting one lamp or candle successively each of eight nights (see Hanukkah), helped to make these the symbol of Judaism.

Law had no moral or social purpose. Rules that limited diet or prohibited a farmer from plowing with two kinds of animals, and many other such regulations, were simply intended to remind the Israelite daily that God's people were different— that in every aspect Israelites were to conduct lives separated to the Lord.

The prophets used the language of ritual and ceremony to show that sin defiled God's people morally and cut off their fellowship with the Lord. *See also* Clean and Unclean.

deity God, the divine nature, the state of being God. In OT Israel, God was a person, more than an abstract concept. But the Greek world of the NT was used to pondering "deity" as an idea. Thus, in discussing the nature of God and the identity of Jesus, the NT writers (particularly Paul) had to employ three distinct but closely related Greek terms.

To theion referred to the quality of deity itself apart from any particular god. In Athens Paul challenged his listeners to think more deeply—and more personally —about the nature of "the Deity" (Acts 17:29). *Theiotēs* was another abstract term exploring God's nature. Paul uses it in Rom. 1:20 to argue that the "Godness" of the Creator is evident from what has been made. *Theotēs* suggests God's essential being, and is the least impersonal of the three.

Paul refers to Jesus (Col. 2:9), saying that "in Christ all the fullness of the Deity [*theiotēs*] lives in bodily form." In using this Greek word, Paul speaks of all that God is in his unique and essential being. Because Jesus is fully and completely God in the flesh, "You have been given fullness in Christ" (Col. 2:10). *See also* God; Jesus Christ.

deliver (1) To rescue or save; (2) to give, surrender, or hand over.

OLD TESTAMENT

One person may rescue another, but mostly in the OT we read of God rescuing his helpless people. Well over half the uses of this term occur in cries from God's people to the Lord, begging for his help, or in praise offered to him for deliverance.

What does God deliver his people from? In most OT instances, the threat is immediate and earthly, rather than spiritual. God rescues from the foreign oppressor and from natural disaster. But, by analogy, God also delivers his people from sin.

What we call salvation is taught in the OT, although it is not emphasized there. Personal salvation is reflected in such cries of the psalmist as:

Help us, O God our Savior,
  for the glory of your name;
deliver us and atone for our sins
  for your name's sake. (Ps. 79:9)

NEW TESTAMENT

The NT emphasizes spiritual deliverance. While Jesus did save many from disease and demonic influence during his earthly ministry, the NT focuses on the saving effect of his sacrificial death and resurrection.

The Greek word *sōzō*, "save," appears over 100 times (the related words *sōtēr*, "Savior," and *sōtēria*, "salvation," occur another 70 times), describing Jesus' work of delivering believers from the penalty and power of sin. Through Jesus, God has delivered us from wrath and brought us into his own Kingdom (Col. 1:13).

The concept of deliverance reflects the biblical view of humanity as helpless before external and internal forces over which we have no real control. The disasters which threaten us may be physical, such as war or illness or poverty. They may be spiritual, the consequences of our sin. In either case our only recourse is to cry out with the psalmist to the only one who can help: "Deliver me, O my God" (Ps. 71:4). *See also* Salvation.

The second meaning of deliver, "to give, surrender, or hand over" (Gk., *paradidōmi*), appears many times in Scripture. One of its common uses refers to Jesus being "delivered up" to be crucified. The Jews delivered Jesus up to Pilate (Mt. 27:2) and Pilate delivered him to the soldiers (Mt. 27:26). But earlier Jesus spoke of being "delivered into the hands of men" (Mk. 9:31, KJV), implying that God himself was handing Jesus over for the punishment of our sins (Rom. 4:25).

The NT also speaks of God's message being "delivered unto the saints" (Jude 3; *see* 1 Cor. 11:23; 15:3; 2 Pet. 2:21). The language implies that the Bible's teaching and the Church's doctrine did not originate with Paul or Peter, but was merely being "passed on" by these leaders.

demon An evil spiritual being, hostile to God and to humanity. Both Eastern (Babylonian) and Western (Greek) cultures believed in the existence of spiritual beings somewhat less powerful than their gods. While the Babylonian spirits were more or

less neutral, the Greeks saw demons as hostile beings bent on doing mischief. Although the Greek word for such beings (*daimonion*) appears in the Gospels, it would be a mistake to assume that this reflects a pagan world view. The Bible presents a unique view of such supernatural beings.

OLD TESTAMENT

The OT mentions demons directly only twice (Deut. 32:17; Ps. 106:36,37). But other OT passages suggest that evil spirits lie behind occult practices, such as spiritism, which the Bible condemns (Deut. 18:9-12; 1 Sam. 28:13; Isa. 8:19).

From various biblical texts, we can piece together the ancient Hebrews' view of the devil and the demons associated with him. Isaiah 14:12-15 seems to tell the story of Satan's fall. Jesus himself referred to fallen angels, who followed Satan in his primeval rebellion (Mt. 25:41). Daniel 10 portrays such beings struggling against God's forces. According to Jude 6, these angels "did not keep their positions of authority but abandoned their own home." *See also* Satan.

So the knowledge of evil spiritual beings was apparently well-ensconced in Jewish thinking long before Jesus began casting out demons in first-century Palestine.

THE GOSPELS AND ACTS

The Gospels give us the clearest portrait of demonic beings, in reporting their confrontations with Jesus. Here we see demons function as living beings with the ability to speak, hear, think, feel, and act (Mt. 8:31; 17:18; Mk. 1:34; 5:12; Lk. 8:32; 10:17).

The demons of the Bible are unhesitatingly hostile to human beings. They oppress men and women, causing disease (Mt. 4:24; 12:22; 15:22; Lk. 4:35) and madness (Mk. 5:2-20; Lk. 8:27-39). Wherever Jesus found demon-possession, he drove the demons out and delivered the person from his or her suffering.

The Book of Acts also describes exorcisms. Demons were cast out of afflicted

persons in the name of Jesus, but only by those who had a personal relationship with the Lord (Acts 19:13-16).

THE EPISTLES

The NT Epistles also refer to spiritual powers that war against God and his people. Paul says, "Our struggle is not against flesh and blood, but against the rulers, against the authorities, against the powers of this dark world and against the spiritual forces of evil in heavenly realms" (Eph. 6:12). These titles refer to orders of evil spirits, not impersonal evil influences.

Certainly Paul and other writers of the NT affirm the reality of demons (1 Cor. 10:20,21; Jas. 2:19). Paul and John both indicate that false teaching will be introduced into Christianity by demons (1 Tim. 4:1; 1 Jn. 4:1-3). Yet we find no instruction on exorcism in the Epistles and no apparent concern that demons might take control of or oppress believers. Instead, John says believers "have overcome them, because the one who is in you is greater than the one who is in the world" (1 Jn. 4:4).

CONTEMPORARY DEMONOLOGY

The flurry of demonic activity reported in the Gospels and the surprising silence of the Epistles on this subject leave many confused. Some today ignore the demonic, while others tend to blame demons for every personal problem or sin.

On the one hand, the Bible clearly teaches that evil spiritual beings do exist.

Above: The demon called Legion leaves the possessed man from the Gadarene region at Christ's command (Mk. 5:1-20). Detail of an ivory tablet, Milan, Italy, A.D. 970.
Above left: Terracotta mask of the monster Humbaba (Babylon, 7th century B.C.) portrays supernatural evil. The reality of demonic powers, often called "evil spirits" in the Bible, is attested by every ancient culture known.

Medieval woodcut from the 15th century A.D. depicts the moment Peter denied, for the third time, any acquaintance with Jesus. The rooster is crowing (top left) as Jesus looks at Peter through a window (Lk. 22:60,61).

Yet it is not at all clear that the demonic activity we read of in the Gospels is normative. Some have suggested that evil spirits were unusually active then as Satan marshaled his forces to oppose Christ. The Pharisees' charge that Christ cast out demons by the power of the prince of demons may rest on the Pharisees' awareness that demons were most active wherever Christ traveled (Mt. 12:22-29)! Jesus answered the charge easily. He drove demons out. Satan would hardly drive out Satan.

What about demonic activity today? From all we can tell from the OT and the Epistles, demons did not concentrate on afflicting individuals. Certainly they can. But if this were a common experience, the relative silence of Scripture concerning how to deal with demons would be difficult to explain.

Rather than focusing our attention on demons, the Bible draws our attention to God. We are to concentrate on loving and serving him, and on loving one another for Jesus' sake. The Holy Spirit of God, who has taken up residence within us, will guard us from the spirit, and spirits, of evil. Nevertheless, we are authorized and empowered to expel or repel them in the name of Jesus (*see* Acts 16:18; 19:13-16).

denarius A silver coin issued by the Romans representing a day's wages for a workman in NT times. In the KJV the denarius is called a "penny." Some modern versions identify the denarius simply as a "silver coin." *See also* Money.

On one side this denarius bears the laureate head of Tiberius Caesar, who ruled during most of Jesus' life (A.D. 14–37). The reverse shows a seated woman with staff and branch—probably the personification of the Pax Romana or "Roman Peace."

deny To reject, to disown.

When the apostle John writes of "antichrists" who "deny that Jesus is the Christ," he means persons who reject the true identity of our Lord. This apparently means more than just disputing some fact: it means denying (disowning, NIV) Christ himself (Mt. 10:33; Lk. 12:9).

But Peter's "denial" of Jesus was different (Mt. 26:69-75). In the context of his faith, Peter's denial was not rejection but unfaithfulness. Later the repentant disciple returned—ashamed of his failure but eager to renew his fellowship with the Lord.

The words of 2 Tim. 2:11-13, though troublesome at first, may actually clarify the matter. "If we disown [deny] him, he will also disown [deny] us" does not imply God's final rejection of a believer. We know this because the passage continues: "If we are faithless, he will remain faithful, for he cannot disown [deny] himself." The saying is intended to remind believers that if we turn away from God after conversion we will lose fellowship with Jesus. But even then he remains faithful in his commitment to us. The door remains open for our return.

In another puzzling passage Jesus calls on disciples to deny themselves, to take up their cross daily, and to follow him (Mt. 16:24; Mk. 8:34; Lk. 9:23). Jesus means we are to reject our own self-centered desires or any personal desires that conflict with God's will. Rather, we must choose the will of God as Jesus did. *See also* Cross.

deposit (1) A down payment made on a purchase; (2) something left in another's care.

According to the NT, the Holy Spirit has

been given to believers as a deposit, a down payment guaranteeing God's commitment. On three occasions (2 Cor. 1:22; 5:5; Eph. 1:14), Paul borrowed this Greek business term (*arrabōn*) to reassure his readers of God's plans to bring them safely through this world to final redemption.

Another Greek word translated "deposit" (*parakatathēkē*) means something left in another's care. God entrusted Timothy with leadership, and Paul encouraged him to be faithful to that trust (1 Tim. 6:20; 2 Tim. 1:12,14).

depravity In Christian thought, the corruption and perversion of the human nature by sin.

Total depravity is understood differently in various Christian traditions. But it does not imply that an unconverted human being can do nothing praiseworthy. Jesus once commented, "If you, then, though you are evil, know how to give good gifts to your children, how much more will your Father in heaven give good gifts to those who ask him!" (Mt. 7:11). Human beings can do good, if we measure goodness by human standards.

But such commendable conduct does not save us from the guilt and curse of sin, for God measures goodness against his own utter perfection. The doctrine of total depravity affirms that human nature is corrupted by sin, so that in no thought or action can anyone do that perfect good which God requires. In truth, fallen humanity shows a strong tendency to actively pursue evil (Rom. 1:28-32; 3:9-20).

Once we realize that we are unable to please God by what *we do*, we can repent and receive God's grace—relying on what *he has done* for us.

depths A literal or metaphorical reference to deep waters.

Some ancient peoples envisioned the earth as the entire realm of life, and the world beyond and beneath as a vast underground sea. One could peer into the ocean, and glimpse shapes flashing there, but nothing could be seen clearly.

The OT is less clear than the NT about the hereafter. To OT saints, what happened after death must have seemed as obscure and unknowable as the ocean depths. So the OT frequently uses "depths" or "the deep" metaphorically, to suggest the unknown and the unknowable in the life to come (*see* Pss. 63:9; 86:13; Prov. 9:18; Amos 9:2).

deputy A subordinate ruler or officer representing one of higher authority. In the KJV, the term often refers to an officer or governor appointed by a ruler to oversee areas within his realm. In the NT, the Greek word *anthypates*, which the KJV translates "deputy," usually indicates a person in charge of a Roman province. Thus modern versions often render it "proconsul."

desert An arid, infertile, unpopulated area. The hot, dry climate of the Middle East has created various desert areas. The Isra-

About five miles east of Jerusalem the wilderness of Judea begins—a genuine, rocky wasteland that stretches south from Jericho down the western side of the Dead Sea. Jesus was tempted by the devil in this desolate place (Lk. 4:1,2).

elites wandered through the deserts of the Negev and Sinai before moving north to settle in Canaan's more fertile areas. Occasionally, marauding nomads would sweep in from the Arabian desert in the east, just as the fierce desert wind would blow westward, drying up the Judean air. The great desert of Israel was the Negev (meaning "dry") in the south of Judah, between the Arabah and Sinai Peninsula. Another desert, the Judean wilderness, lay between Jericho and Jerusalem, north and west of the stagnant Dead Sea. David hid out from Saul in these rocky canyons; John the Baptist preached here; and the Good Samaritan cared for the victim of a highway robbery. This is probably where Jesus went to be tempted.

Rains fall in the desert each year during a brief rainy season, but the water courses quickly through a network of stream beds, and seldom sinks into the parched ground. Sometimes grasses will spring up quickly, but die in the heat of day. Yet this grass occasionally provided pasturage for flocks. Amazingly, recent advances in irrigation have enabled modern inhabitants to cultivate much desert land; it has proven quite fertile.

The Bible regularly reflects the conditions and terrain in which it was written. Thus desert images figure prominently in its poetry. From the Judean desert, David wrote:

O God, you are my God,
earnestly I seek you;
my soul thirsts for you,
my body longs for you,
in a dry and weary land
where there is no water. (Ps. 63:1)

The OT prophets look forward to a day when God will come, and transform the desert.

The desert and the parched land will be glad;
the wilderness will rejoice and blossom.
Like the crocus, it will burst into bloom;
it will rejoice greatly and shout for joy.
The glory of Lebanon will be given to it,
the splendor of Carmel and Sharon;
they will see the glory of the Lord,
the splendor of our God. (Isa. 35:1,2)

desire (1) To wish for, long for; in a descriptive sense, an expression of the capacity to evaluate, make choices, feel pleasure; (2) to crave, a dominating wish for; in a negative sense, an expression of man's sinful nature; covetousness; (3) to want sexually.

God, who himself has desires and makes choices, has gifted us with these capacities. So desire is not intrinsically wrong. The Stoic or Buddhist notion that to be spiritual a person must achieve a state in which he or she desires nothing is foreign to Scripture. In many OT passages "desire" is a morally neutral term, and carries no hint of condemnation. Only when desire extends to what is unlawful or ungodly is it condemned (Ex. 20:17).

But some words for desire are strongly

292

negative. The Hebrew word *hamad* portrays objects as desirable, but often so desirable that they stimulate covetousness. Our capacity to desire and to take pleasure can be misdirected. And misdirected desire can motivate ungodly choices.

The NT picks up this negative emphasis. With very few exceptions it uses "desire" (*epithymia*) in a negative sense. Desire springs from and expresses man's sinful nature. Human beings are driven by sinful passions. Lost humanity is bent on "gratifying the cravings of our sinful nature and following its desires and thoughts" (Eph. 2:3).

As a NT ethical term, however, desire is not morally neutral. In this context, desires are evil, expressions of a human nature warped and twisted by sin. That ethical insight in the NT is intended to warn us against the evil within. We cannot safely do whatever we want, arguing that our desires are "natural." Instead we are called to evaluate our desires, and to choose not what seems pleasant but what God says is truly good.

In the words of Eph. 4:22-24, we are "taught, with regard to your former way of life, to put off your old self, which is being corrupted by its deceitful desires; to be made new in the attitude of your minds; and to put on the new self, created to be like God in true righteousness and holiness."

desolation The devastation caused by a natural disaster or, especially in the OT, by divine judgment. *See also* Abomination of Desolation.

despise To view or to treat with contempt; to place little value on; to fail to consider when making decisions.

When Esau sold his right as eldest son to the covenant promises God had given his grandfather and father, he "despised his birthright" (Gen. 25:34). According to 2 Sam. 12:10, a person who willfully sins shows this same kind of contempt for God.

In the NT, the Greek words translated "despise" mean to think little of, or to place no value on. The NT warns us not to look down on [regard as of no value] fellow Christians whose views differ from our own (Rom. 14:3,10). Other believers, like God himself, are to be highly valued. *See also* Contempt.

destroy, destruction To kill, put an end to, tear down; violent death or devastation.

When Paul urged believers to consider the effects of their actions on other believers, lest they destroy their faith (Rom. 14:15), he used a Greek word (*apollymi*) that means "to bring ruin to, to tear down." Christians are to encourage and build others up, not to tear them down.

In 1 Cor. 15:26, death is portrayed as an enemy yet to be destroyed by Jesus. This Greek word (*katargeō*) means "to nullify, to make inoperative."

John says that Christ came to "destroy the devil's work" (1 Jn. 3:8). The Greek word means "to undo." The harm that Satan caused by deceiving Eve, and all that he has done since to harm humanity, is being undone by Jesus.

This sampling suggests that "destroy" has many shades of meaning in the NT. Similarly, the OT employs more than 30 different Hebrew words for "destroy" or "destruction."

Deuteronomy, Book of The fifth book of the OT, the last of the five books of Moses. The name comes from the Greek for "second law." (The Law was first given at Mount Sinai. Deuteronomy covers the second major expression of God's Law, given on the plains of Moab before Israel's entry into Canaan.) The Jews, however, generally title a book by its opening phrase. Thus Deuteronomy's Hebrew name is *'eleh hadebarim*, "These Are the Words," which is a fitting caption for this collection of sermons given by Moses shortly before his death.

The book explicitly claims Moses as its author (Deut. 1:1; 31:9,24,26), and so Jewish and Christian traditions have always supported Mosaic authorship, although many modern scholars have questioned this. A number of clues in the text indicate that Deuteronomy was in fact written in Moses' time. Whenever Deuteronomy refers to events surrounding the Exodus from Egypt, it speaks in the past tense, but it repeatedly (70 times) mentions the entry into Canaan as future. The surrounding nations named in Deuteronomy are those of Moses' time (Canaanites, Ammonites, Moabites, etc.). Of special note is the treaty structure of Deuteronomy. Archaeology has shown that this particular format was used only in the age of Moses (1500–1200 B.C.).

BACKGROUND

Some 40 years before giving the sermons recorded in Deuteronomy, Moses had led a slave people out of Egypt. At Sinai the delivered slaves were given God's Law, 293 and had committed themselves to obey it. But that generation had rebelled at Kadesh Barnea. As a result they were condemned to wander the Sinai peninsula until everyone who was then over 20 died (Num. 14:29). As Deuteronomy opens, a fresh new generation waits just outside the Promised Land, eager to enter. Moses, now about 120 years old, challenges them to make a complete commitment to their God and to enjoy the fruit of obedience.

way modified the covenant promises given Abraham ages before. Rather it defined how each generation of Jews could live in fellowship with God and be assured of his blessing. The treaty format helped Israel understand that the nation was to be a theocracy, a community whose ruler was God. Deuteronomy is such a complete summary of the relationship between God and Israel that the Jewish rabbis referred to the book as "five fifths of the Law." *See also* Covenant.

HISTORICAL SIGNIFICANCE

Deuteronomy is more than a series of sermons. It is structured as a *suzerainty treaty*, which in Moses' time defined the relationship between a ruler and his subjects. See the chart on page 296.

This treaty between God and Israel in no

THEOLOGICAL CONTRIBUTIONS

Deuteronomy is the clearest OT exposition of life under the Law covenant. It emphasizes God's love in choosing Israel and in giving his people the Law. Law is a love gift because it shows human beings how to live in harmony with God and his

DEUTERONOMY: A READING AND STUDY GUIDE

Chapter	Content Summary	Related Articles
1	Israel rebelled earlier at Kadesh Barnea when God urged his people to enter Canaan.	Unbelief
2	Yet God cared for Israel during 38 years of wilderness wandering, and enabled them to defeat their enemies.	
3	Now Israel has defeated the peoples east of the Jordan. It is time to enter the Promised Land, but without Moses.	
4	The key to victory is acknowledging God, by giving him complete allegiance and keeping all his commandments.	Idol Obedience
5	The Ten Commandments, given earlier and accepted then by Israel, express the Law's core principles.	Ten Commandments
6	Love for God, communicated from generation to generation, will produce obedience as God's goodness is recalled.	Love Education
7	Love also motivated God to choose Israel, and love will move him to bless if only his people will obey.	Miracle
8	God's love was demonstrated even in the wilderness years, and must not be forgotten when prosperity comes.	Wealth
9	When that blessing comes it will be a gift of grace, not deserved by a nation which once worshiped a golden calf.	Grace
10	The Ten Commandments, now preserved in stone, must be taken to heart, for God "is your praise; he is your God."	Heart
11	Obedience and love for God, then, are the door to blessing; disobedience the door to disaster. The choice is clear.	Bless Curse
12	Specific now, Moses calls Israel to establish one worship center and to worship God in the way he requires.	Worship Offering
13	The worship of other gods is forbidden; the apostate is to be put to death to protect the community.	Crime and Punishment
14	Clean and unclean foods are defined, with tithes to be collected to support God's service and the needy.	Clean and Unclean
15	Every seventh year debts are to be canceled and Hebrew slaves are to be freed.	Borrow Slavery
16	The Passover and other established religious festivals are to be carefully observed.	Feasts, Festivals, and Fasts

creation. Thus again and again Deuteronomy urges doing what is right in God's sight, "that it may go well with you" (Deut. 5:16; 6:18; etc.). If Israel would love God wholeheartedly and respect their neighbor, God would guarantee both material and spiritual blessings. *See also* Law.

Deuteronomy also contains the key to understanding the exhortations and warnings of the OT prophets. First, the prophets reflected a spiritual and moral vision which Deuteronomy expresses impressively: God alone is to be worshiped; he demands exclusive allegiance; his laws embody a concern for others that must be maintained by individuals and by society. Second, both the prophets' warnings of expulsion from the Promised Land, and their promises of subsequent regathering, are rooted in the warning sections of Deuteronomy (chs. 27–29). Thus Deuteronomy lays a foundation for interpreting sacred history. God is actively involved in Israel's experiences, shaping events according to principles of righteousness and reward established here. *See also* Prophecy.

More than 80 times the NT quotes from Deuteronomy, further underscoring its importance. When Jesus was tempted by Satan (Mt. 4; Lk. 4), three times he quoted from this OT book (Deut. 6:13; 6:16; 8:3).

MASTERY KEYS

Deuteronomy uses the word "love" [loved, loves] 31 times; "obey" [obedience] 31 times; and the phrase "this law" or "this book of the law" 24 times. Underline

DEUTERONOMY: A READING AND STUDY GUIDE *CONT.*

Chapter	Content Summary	Related Articles
17	Justice is to be administered locally and fairly, and rules for a future monarchy are laid down.	Justice Kings
18	Priests are to be supported by offerings. Israel is not to turn to the occult for guidance; God will send prophets.	Witchcraft Prophet
19	Cities of refuge are to be established for those who kill without premeditation, and rules of evidence are given.	Cities of Refuge
20	Rules governing war establish who can serve in the army and humane consideration of the enemy.	War
21	Various rules tell how to deal with an unsolved murder, marrying captives, children's and parents' rights.	Murder
22	Various laws are listed, including a number of regulations regarding marriage violations.	Marriage Adultery
23–25	More miscellaneous laws are stated, including laws on divorce.	Divorce
26	Tithes are to be given as an expression of thanks to God.	Give
27	The new generation now formally commits itself to the terms of the Law covenant, to obey and to love God.	
28	Now the blessings God will give the obedient and the punishments he will send on the disobedient are detailed.	Bless Curse
29	In a final sermon Moses looks ahead, and warns of the disasters which will come when future generations rebel.	
30	When a rebellious Israel returns to God, he will bring them back to the land and bless. So each generation must face the fact that it has a life-or-death decision to make.	Prophecy
31	Joshua is identified as Moses' successor, but the old leader sadly predicts future rebellions of Israel against God.	
32	Moses teaches Israel a poem-song which sums up the message of Deuteronomy. It is to be memorized and taken to heart.	
33	Just before his death, Moses blesses each tribe.	Bless
34	Moses is then given a glimpse of the Promised Land, across the Jordan. He dies, and God himself digs the grave.	

Structure of Suzerainty Treaty

Preamble Deut. 1:1-5	Setting the context of the treaty.
Prologue Deut. 1:6–4:43	History of prior relationship between ruler and subjects.
Stipulations Deut. 4:44–11:32	General statement of principles to govern the relationship being formally entered.
Stipulation details Deut. 12:1–26:19	Explanation of specific rules to be followed by the subjects.
Document clause Deut. 27:1-26	Call for treaty's ratification by subjects.
Blessings Deut. 28:1-14	Explanation of benefits of keeping the treaty.
Cursings Deut. 28:15-68	Warning of punishments if treaty is broken.
Recapitulation Deut. 29:1–30:10	Reviewing and summarizing the treaty.

View of the Promised Land from Mount Nebo, where Moses stood. Before he died (Deut. 34), Moses repeated the Law of God to the Israelites on the plains of Moab (lower right) east of the Jordan, the setting of the Book of Deuteronomy.

each and note the relationship of these three words or phrases in the text.

Read carefully the "stipulations" section of Deuteronomy (Deut. 4:44–11:32) and identify the underlying themes which explain the nature of God's relationship with his covenant people.

SPECIAL FEATURES

The Book of Deuteronomy introduces the idea of a father/son relationship between God and Israel (Deut. 1:31; 8:2-5; 14:1,2; 32:6). God's feeling for his people is not that of a distant ruler for strangers, but of a father for his sons. Even the punishments Israel experienced must be understood in the context of a father's loving discipline.

devil A name for Satan, the powerful angel who rebelled against God. The Greek word *diabolos* means "slanderer" or "accuser."

The term "devil" reflects both Satan's character and the strategy he uses against human beings. As to his character, Jesus said, "There is no truth in him. When he lies, he speaks his native language, for he is a liar and the father of lies" (Jn. 8:44). As to his strategy, the devil used lies to draw Eve into sin (Gen. 3:1-5), and twisted the truth when tempting Jesus (Mt. 4:6). *See also* Satan; Tempt.

In view of Satan's strategy of deceit, Christians are urged to "put off falsehood and speak truthfully" to one another, and thus "not give the devil a foothold" (Eph. 4:25-27). Believers are to instruct those who reject and oppose Christianity, "in the hope that God will grant them repentance leading them to a knowledge of the truth, and that they will come to their senses and escape from the trap of the devil, who has taken them captive to do his will" (2 Tim. 2:25,26). *See also* Deceit.

The KJV uses the term "devils" for other Hebrew and Greek words, which are better translated as pagan gods or demons. *See also* Demon.

devoted things Anything dedicated irrevocably to the Lord. Anything a man owned might be so dedicated (Lev. 27:28). Once committed, a devoted thing could not be sold or reclaimed. Devotion put an object beyond the possibility of common use.

During the conquest of Canaan, several of the most powerful cities of the land were devoted to the Lord (Josh. 6:17), meaning that they were to be utterly destroyed, with their entire populations. Objects from such cities that might survive burning, such as precious metals, could be placed in the treasury of the Lord's house.

A variety of words and phrases are used to translate the Hebrew root *herem*, which expresses this concept. Older versions speak of cities being placed "under a ban." Modern versions often use phrases like "totally destroy" or "set apart for destruction" to communicate the thought (Num. 21:1,2).

diadem A symbol of royal authority, a jeweled band or golden plate worn on the cloth headdresses of Near Eastern rulers. *See also* Crown.

dial (KJV, RSV) An instrument for measuring the passage of time. The only mention of anything that might serve as such a mechanism is found in 2 Ki. 20:5-11 and Isa. 38:8. The Hebrew word means "steps of a stairway," as in the NIV. Apparently some object was placed so that the afternoon sun cast its shadow, and one step after another was darkened. This timepiece is identified with the rule of Ahaz, and was probably constructed in the 720s B.C.

Diana *See* Artemis.

dietary laws Rules in Mosaic Law which distinguished between clean (edible) and unclean (not to be eaten) foods, and regulated food preparation (Lev. 11; Deut. 14). Jews through the millennia have followed the dietary laws of the Bible, distinguishing between kosher and *terefah* (forbidden) foods. Daniel refused to "defile himself with the royal food and wine" provided in Babylon (Dan. 1:8). Peter was unwilling to kill and eat unclean animals, even after a voice from heaven ordered him to eat. Shocked, Peter objected. "Surely not, Lord! I have never eaten anything impure or unclean" (Acts 10:9-14).

The dietary code was intended to heighten the awareness of the Israelites that they were set apart from other peoples. The dietary laws transformed eating itself into a religious experience.

Dietary laws also made it unlikely that Jews and Gentiles would eat together, thus limiting social relationships. Centuries later, the Talmud, a collection of rabbinical books discussing and debating the meaning and application of OT laws, observed: "We should not eat their bread because we may be led thereby to drink their wine. We should not drink their wine because we may be led thereby to intermarry with them, and this will only lead us to worship their gods." *See also* Clean and Unclean.

dill *See* Anise.

discerning of spirits One of the gifts of the Holy Spirit; according to 1 Cor. 12:10, the ability to distinguish between true and

Though disk-shaped sundials were used by ancient peoples, the account of Hezekiah's healing features "the stairway of Ahaz," whose steps told time by gradual shadows cast across them by an object set up nearby (2 Ki. 20:1-11).

false prophets. False prophets troubled the early church (1 Jn. 4:1-3), and so the church needed people who were gifted to discern the nature of messages spoken in God's name.

disciple A learner or student. The Greek word *mathētēs* was fairly common in the Judaism of Jesus' day. So it was no surprise that it came to identify the followers of Jesus. But, amazingly, the term does not appear at all in the Epistles. Possibly

297

Dutch woodcut (1488) depicts three disciples plucking wheat kernels on the Sabbath while Jesus defends their actions to two Pharisees (Mt. 12:1-8; Mk. 2:23-28; Lk. 6:1-5).

this designation became obsolete once their divine teacher ascended to heaven. Those who had been *mathētai* now became *apostoloi*. But according to Luke, members of the early churches were known as disciples (Acts 6:1).

DISCIPLESHIP IN JUDAISM

In first-century Judaism, religious leaders received their training through a well-defined system. Recognized rabbis attracted disciples, who lived and studied with them. The rabbi provided support for his students; they devoted full time to serving the rabbi and learning from him. The goal of discipleship was that the learner would not only master what his teacher knew, but also become like him in piety (Lk. 6:40). The people of Jesus' time were amazed when Christ began to teach, for he displayed learning "without having studied" with a rabbi in this traditional manner (Jn. 7:15).

JESUS' DISCIPLES

When Jesus began his ministry, the Bible says he "appointed twelve . . . that they might be with him" (Mk. 3:14). Jesus' twelve disciples, listed in this passage, are:

Simon (to whom he gave the name Peter); James son of Zebedee, and his brother John (to them he gave the name Boanerges, which means Sons of Thunder); Andrew, Philip, Bartholomew, Matthew, Thomas, James son of Alphaeus, Thaddaeus, Simon the Zealot and Judas Iscariot, who betrayed him.

(Mk. 3:16-19)

298   In the tradition of the time, these twelve

disciples literally lived with Jesus. They traveled with him, watched all he did, and listened to all he said. When Christ was finished with a day of public ministry, he taught his disciples privately, asking them questions and explaining what they had observed.

When the Gospels speak of "the disciples" or "the twelve," this small group of men is intended.

OTHER USES OF "DISCIPLE"

The Gospels also use "disciple" in two non-technical senses:

• *A person who followed a particular movement or school of thought.* Thus both the Pharisees' school of strict interpretation of the Law (Mt. 22:16; Lk. 5:33) and John the Baptist's revival movement (Mt. 11:2; Mk. 2:18) had disciples.

• *One who believes in Jesus.* But the kind of belief suggested by this use is not necessarily marked by commitment. As Jn. 6:66 points out, many early "disciples" who had been attracted by Jesus' teaching turned away when that teaching became more difficult. The true disciple was and is the person so committed to Jesus that he will "obey everything" Christ commanded (Mt. 28:20).

DISCIPLESHIP TODAY?

The word "disciple" is not in the vocabulary of the NT Epistles, as either a technical or general term, although Paul often took younger persons with him on his missionary journeys. But the discipleship approach used by the rabbis to train leaders tended to produce a religious elite, and Christ specifically warned his followers against this (Mt. 23:8-12). In contrast, Christian leaders were to be servants. They matured within the fellowship of the church and were affirmed as leaders only when their character and gifts were recognized by the local congregation.

discipline Correction or punishment which makes a positive contribution to one's growth in righteousness. While punishment is a part of discipline, we must remember that discipline is a very positive term. Moses said to Israel, "Know then in your heart that as a man disciplines his son, so the Lord your God disciplines you" (Deut. 8:5). The NT makes the point even more strongly. "The Lord disciplines those he loves, and he punishes everyone he accepts as a son" (Heb. 12:6). Discipline is an act of love, a parent's gift to a child.

OLD TESTAMENT

The loving nature of divine discipline is emphasized in such passages as Deut. 8:1-5 and 11:1-7. The prophets later interpreted Israel's history in terms of divine discipline. History demonstrated God's commitment to bless righteous generations, and to discipline the rebellious until they turn back to God. This perspective is powerfully expressed in Hosea 11–14, which concludes,

Who is wise? He will realize these things.
Who is discerning? He will understand them.
The ways of the Lord are right;
the righteous walk in them,
but the rebellious stumble in them.
(Hos. 14:9)

NEW TESTAMENT

The NT concept of discipline parallels that of the OT. To discipline is to instruct, train, and guide development.

Hebrews 12:4-13 draws together the biblical vision with the following points: (1) Divine discipline is evidence of God's love, not of anger or abandonment. Hardships serve to remind us that God is simply treating us as sons. (2) God disciplines for our good. His specific goal is that we might become holy. (3) Disciplinary experiences are painful, but produce righteousness and peace. (4) To profit from discipline, we need to endure it, neither making light of it nor becoming discouraged by it. We are to remain committed to holiness. We are to remain aware of God's grace, even when we hurt, so we do not become bitter.

Parents who follow the divine example will not draw back from disciplining their children. But they will guard against discipline that is an expression of anger rather than love, and discipline that has no goal other than retribution.

discipline, church Correction or punishment carried out by the church.

Church discipline, like God's own, is intended to bring about a return to righteousness. It is to be applied only in the case of continuing moral fault. Those who continue in sin should be accountable to the church body. *See also* Confess.

Many view Mt. 18:15-17 as a description of the process to be followed in discipline cases. The person at fault is to be confronted by one believer, then several, and finally by church elders. If he or she refuses to confess and repent, the matter should be brought before the entire church. If the sinner remains obstinate, the church should "treat him as you would a pagan or a tax collector" (Mt. 18:17), apparently a reference to expulsion from membership. Paul encountered such a case in the Corinthian church. A church member was involved in an immoral relationship with his father's wife. Paul urged the church to put him out of the fellowship (1 Cor. 5). Not that Christians should stay away from sinners; on the contrary. But one who calls himself a believer and yet openly indulges in sin threatens to infect the church—as yeast spreads throughout dough. For its own good, and for the good of the offender, the church must stand true to its identity as a body of repentant believers.

And, though it seems harsh, expulsion from fellowship has a theological basis. The Bible teaches that sin separates human beings from God, so that believers who persist in sin are out of fellowship with the Lord. By expelling the member who refuses to repent, the church acts out this spiritual reality. This should make it very clear to the offender what his or her spiritual condition is.

Rightly understood, church discipline is an act of love. There is no place in church discipline for a judgmental or condemning attitude (Gal. 6:1). When the sinner does repent, as the man in Corinth did, Paul says, "You ought to forgive and comfort him, so that he will not be overwhelmed by excessive sorrow" (2 Cor. 2:7).

disease Illness; departure from a state of health. People in biblical times had little medicine to combat disease. The OT, however, presents God as Healer, and stresses the importance of a close relationship with the Lord.

DISEASES DESCRIBED IN THE BIBLE

Many of the more common diseases of the ancient Middle East are listed in Deut. 28 among the punishments destined to strike Israel if that nation turned from God. In this catalog are: wasting disease (probably tuberculosis), fever (including malaria, typhoid, typhus), inflammation, boils and tumors, festering sores and itch (probably scabies, caused by a tiny burrowing insect), madness (such as Saul's paranoia [1 Sam. 16:14-23] and Nebuchadnezzar's insanity [Dan. 4]), blindness and confusion of the mind, and plagues (including bubonic).

Leprosy, mentioned often in each Testament, served as the general name for a variety of skin conditions. *See also* Leprosy. Blindness was common, and is mentioned some 60 times in Scripture. In hot, dusty Palestine, eyes were especially susceptible to a variety of infections.

The Gospels mention a woman with a serious menstrual disorder which caused her to hemorrhage chronically for years (Lk. 8:43-48). Other physical problems described there are paralysis (Mk. 2:1-12), and epilepsy (Mt. 17:14-18).

DISEASE AND GOD

Old Testament Law gave the priests the task of diagnosing infectious skin diseases. The Law prescribed both washing and isolation until the condition was cured (Lev. 14).

The OT also outlines a relationship between spiritual and physical health. People in right relationship with God and others are less likely to become ill. Israelites who lived by the Law knew inner and interpersonal peace (*shalom*). This inner harmony was destroyed by sin, and the resultant stress made persons more susceptible to sickness (*see* Ps. 32:3,4; Isa. 57:19-21).

Both the OT and NT also suggest a more direct supernatural involvement in disease. Under the Law covenant, God offered to keep his people "free from every disease" (Deut. 7:15). And God announced to the Exodus generation, "I am

IDENTIFYING DISEASES IN THE BIBLE

Bible Name	Probable Diagnosis	References
Ague (KJV)	See Fever	Lev. 26:16; Deut. 28:22
Blains (KJV)	Anthrax? See Boils	Ex. 9:9,10
Blemish (KJV)	See Defect	Ex. 12:5; Lev. 21:16-24
Blindness	Trachoma, gonorrheic infection, or birth defect	Gen. 27:1; 48:10; 1 Sam. 4:15; Mt. 20:30-34; Mk. 8:24; Jn. 9:1-41
Bloody Flux (KJV)	See Dysentery	Acts 28:8
Boils	Generic term for inflamed skin ulcers	Ex. 9:9,10; Job 2:7; 2 Ki. 20:7
Consumption	Tuberculosis? Cancer?	Lev. 26:16; Deut. 28:22
Deafness	Congenital or effect of aging	Lev. 19:14; Lk. 1:20; Mk. 7:32; 9:32
Defect	Any impairment such as humped back, broken bones, dwarfism	Ex. 12:5; Lev. 21:16-24
Dropsy	Edema	Lk. 14:1-4
Dumbness	Aphasia or effect of deafness	Ezek. 33:22; Lk. 1:20-22
Dysentery	Intestinal infection	2 Chr. 21:15-19; Acts 28:8
Emerods (KJV)	See Tumors	1 Sam. 5:6
Fever	Symptom of typhus, typhoid, or malaria	Lev. 26:16; Deut. 28:22; Lk. 4:38; Jn. 4:52; Acts 28:8
Flow of blood	Menorraghia	Lk. 8:43-48
Lunatick (KJV)	See Seizures	Mt. 4:24; 17:15
Lameness		Mt. 15:30,31; Acts 3:2-11
Leprosy	Various skin conditions, including odd pigmentation and Hansen's Disease (NT)?	Lev. 13:1-46; Lk. 5:12,13; 17:11-19
Madness	Mental disorder or erratic behavior	Deut. 28:28; 1 Sam. 16:14-23; Dan. 4:28-37; Lk. 6:11; 2 Tim. 3:9
Palsy, Paralysis	Various causes	Mt. 4:24; 8:6; Mk. 2:3; Lk. 5:18,24; Acts 8:7; 9:33,34
Plague, pestilence	Generic for any epidemic	Ex. 7–10; Num. 11:33; 14:37; 16:46,47
Seizures	Epilepsy	Mt. 4:24; 17:15; Mk. 9:17-19
Skin disorders	Itch (scabies), ringworm, eczema, cysts, sores	Lev. 13:30-37; 14:54; 21:20; 22:22; Deut. 28:27
Tumors	Bubonic plague? Hemorrhoids?	1 Sam. 5:6-12
Wen (KJV)	Warts; see Defect	Lev. 22:22
Withered hand	Polio myelitis?	Mt. 12:10; Lk. 6:6,8
Worms	Various parasites	Isa. 14:11; 51:8; Acts 12:23

On his way to Rome, Paul showed the power of God over disease by healing the father of the chief official of Malta, who lay "sick in bed, suffering from fever and dysentery" (Acts 28:8).

the Lord who heals you" (Ex. 15:26). But divine protection against disease was contingent on Israel's obedience. Disobedience made Israel vulnerable.

This vulnerability may in part have involved such things as sexually transmitted diseases, which can gain no foothold in a holy society. But sin also made Israel vulnerable to hostile spiritual forces, such as the spirit who crippled a woman for 18 years (Lk. 13:11) and the legion of demons who infested the madman of Gadara (Mk. 5).

DISEASE AND GOD TODAY

In NT times, many Jews commonly believed that every sickness was a punishment for sin or a result of demonic oppression. But when Jesus' disciples sought a theological explanation for a man's being born blind, Christ corrected this impression. They asked, "Who sinned, this man or his parents, that he was born blind?" Jesus answered, "Neither" (Jn. 9:1-3). Disease is a natural consequence in a world corrupted by sin, and all human beings who live here are susceptible to sickness.

Instead of explaining why this man suffered, Christ announced that his blindness was an opportunity to display the glory of God. Jesus gave the man sight, and by healing he revealed both the power and compassion of God.

Disease is still a grim reminder of sin's grip on our universe. God is able to heal, but sometimes, in sickness, we have an opportunity to experience, and display, the glory of God.

The apostle Paul suffered from some unnamed affliction. He prayed, but was not healed. God revealed to him that his "thorn in the flesh" was a gift; a reminder of human weakness intended to encourage greater reliance on the Lord (2 Cor. 12:1-

10). Paul's affirmation of faith in this situation remains a model for us all: "I will boast all the more gladly about my weaknesses, so that Christ's power may rest on me" (v. 9).

Disease is an enemy. One day God will purge it entirely from his universe (Rev. 21:4). *See also* Healing; Medicine; Sickness.

disgrace Shame, reproach, dishonor. A person in "disgrace" (Heb., *kelimmah*) has been publicly humiliated, with appropriate damage to his or her reputation (*herpah*).

Both sinning and serious errors in judgment may lead to disgrace (Prov. 18:3), but the person who confesses and turns to God finds hope.

dish A container used to prepare or serve food. Archaeologists have unearthed a wide variety of pottery jars, bowls, and dishes. Two of the four Hebrew words translated "plate" and "dish" refer to golden vessels used in tabernacle worship (Ex. 25:29; Num. 4:7).

In the NT, the dish into which Jesus dipped bread at the Last Supper was a *tryblion*, a large bowl of bronze or pottery that held a main dish (Mt. 26:23; Mk.

Shallow, glass dish manufactured during Roman ascendancy, first century B.C.

Above: Israelite terra-cotta bowls from 8th century B.C. The smaller of these shallow dishes are like one mentioned in Lk. 11:39.

This early Roman plate beautifully illustrates the widespread dependence of the Greco-Roman world on seafood. It shows one each of red mullet, bass, small torpedo, sargus (unknown today), and cuttlefish. Campania, Italy, 350–300 B.C.

14:20). In contrast, the *pinax* of Lk. 11:39, Mt. 14:8,11 and Mk. 6:25,28 was not a platter, but a small, shallow bowl used by individuals. *See also* Cooking; Pottery.

dishonesty Lack of integrity; deceit; fraud. The Hebrew root, *batsa'*, is related to the verb "to cut off." Dishonesty in business (Prov. 20:23) as well as hypocrisy in religion is strongly denounced. The honest man does right by others, and shows more concern for persons than for their possessions.

dishonor *See* Honor.

disobedience Refusal or failure to comply with an expressed wish or command. In Scripture, obedience and disobedience often describe human response to God's Word. The obedient do what God says; the disobedient refuse or neglect.

Sin entered the world through Adam's disobedience (Gen. 3; Rom. 5:12,19). And disobedience continues to mark unregenerate humankind; Paul characterizes unbelievers as "those who are disobedient" (Eph. 2:2). The OT warns that disobedience brings harm as well as judgment, for God's laws are intended to show us what is beneficial as well as holy.

What lies at the core of disobedience? Hebrews 3,4 analyze disobedience from the perspective of faith. Persons with a "sinful, unbelieving heart" (3:12) will turn away when they hear the voice of God. Disobedience thus is an expression of unbelief.

On the other hand, obedience is linked with love. "Whoever has my commands and obeys them," Christ said, "he is the one who loves me" (Jn. 14:21).

Faith and love are both relational terms. And, apart from a close personal relationship with God through Jesus, true obedience is impossible (Heb. 11:6). On the other hand, those who are growing in their love for God will become more obedient to him. "If anyone loves me," Jesus promised, "he *will* obey my teaching" (Jn. 14:23). *See also* Faith; Love; Obey.

disown To reject or be unfaithful in a relationship. In the context of decision, "disown" means to decide against, or reject. In the context of faith, "disown" suggests a temporary loss of fellowship.

Jesus spoke of decision when he said, "He who disowns me before men will be disowned before the angels of God" (Lk. 12:9). But 2 Tim. 2:11-13 uses "disown" in the context of faith. There the issue is one of fellowship with the Lord. We may turn from God for a time, and during that time we will lose out on the benefits of a close relationship with Christ. But such turning away is not an absolute rejection, for the 2 Timothy passage goes on to say, "If we are faithless, he will remain faithful, for he cannot disown himself." Consider the example of Peter, who disowned Jesus in a time of crisis (Mt. 26:69-75), but was later restored to fellowship with the risen Christ (Jn. 21:15-19). *See also* Deny.

dispensation (1) A system by which anything is administered; (2) specifically, a particular era in which God deals with humans in a certain way.

The Greek word translated dispensation in many English versions is *oikonomia*, from which we get "economy." It refers to the management or supervision of a household (1 Cor. 9:17; Eph. 1:10; 3:2; and Col. 1:25). In three passages *oikonomia* refers to Paul's calling as a steward, responsible for carrying out the divine plan unveiled in the Gospel. In Eph. 1:10 *oikonomia* refers to the divine plan of salvation itself.

When theologians speak of "dispensations," they generally mean the different ways God has related to human beings in various eras. Abraham had no Mosaic Law to follow. The NT introduces an era in which the OT rituals have been set aside, and no animal sacrifices are required.

Different Christian traditions hold different dispensational views. Most theologians tend to limit the number and importance of dispensations. But American "dispensationalism," reflected in the Scofield Reference Bible, sees seven distinct periods defined in Scripture:

Innocence (Creation to the Fall), *Conscience* (Adam to the Flood), *Human Government* (Noah to Abraham), *Promise* (Abraham to Moses), *Law* (Moses to death of Christ), *Grace* (resurrection to Second Coming of Christ), *Kingdom* (the establishment of Christ's visible rule).

While we may note some changes in how God has related to human beings throughout history, we should also recognize an underlying unity. In every age, salvation has been a gift of grace, beyond the capacity of any human being to earn. In every age, a faith-response to God's self-revelation has been the only avenue to personal relationship with God.

dispersion of Israel The scattering of the Jewish people from their homeland. Through much of history, a majority of Jews have lived in nations far from their homeland. This scattering among Gentile nations has been called the *Diaspora*, or Dispersion of Israel.

OLD TESTAMENT BACKGROUND

From the time of their first patriarch, Abraham, the Jews have been "people of the land." Jacob's family migrated to Egypt, where their descendants became slaves. But God led Israel back to the Promised Land through a miraculous sea crossing and a generation of desert wanderings.

The Law, transmitted through Moses, gave detailed instructions about the land the Israelites would inhabit. It was a "land of milk and honey" (Num. 13:27), full of blessing and peace—if the Israelites were true to the Lord. But the Law also predicted what would happen to an unfaithful Israel. After listing terrible punishments God would bring on his people if they violated their covenant with him, Moses recorded the ultimate:

Then the Lord will scatter you among all nations, from one end of the earth to the other. There you will worship other gods—gods of wood and stone, which neither you nor your fathers have known. Among those nations you will find no repose, no resting place for the sole of your foot. There the Lord will give you an anxious mind, eyes weary with longing, and a despairing heart. You will live in constant suspense, filled with dread both night and day, never sure of your life. (Deut. 28:64-66)

HISTORICAL DISPERSIONS

The Jewish people remained concentrated in Palestine until the Assyrian invasions of the late 700s B.C. The Northern Kingdom, Israel, was defeated and its people taken captive in 722 B.C. The people of the Southern Kingdom, Judah, were removed by the Babylonians in a series of deportations ending in 586 B.C.

When Cyrus, the Medo-Persian ruler, conquered Babylon in 539 B.C., he gave the Jews permission to return to Judah. But most of the Jews stayed in the major cities of the Babylonian and Persian Empires. Only a tiny minority returned to resettle Judah. Outside of Palestine, Babylonia was the part of the world most densely populated by Jews.

According to the first-century Jewish historian Josephus, Syria had large numbers of Jews in every city. By then a number of Jews had also settled in Egypt's greatest city, Alexandria. Some Jews had been carried to Egypt as captives by Shishak as early as the tenth century B.C. Others fled there at the time of the Babylonian invasion. Philo, another first-century writer, says there were a million Jews in Egypt in his day.

Jewish communities also existed in cities throughout Asia Minor. There is some evidence that large groups of Jews were transplanted to mixed-population cities by the Seleucid rulers 200 years before Christ. A few small Jewish districts existed in cities in Greece as early as the second century B.C., and a large Jewish population lived in Rome. Many of the Jews in the West were descendants of captives brought to Rome as slaves after the invasion of Palestine by Pompey in 63 B.C.

Soon after Judah's exile to Babylon, families of those who murdered the appointed governor, Gedaliah, fled to Egypt, taking the prophet Jeremiah with them (2 Ki. 25:22-26; Jer. 40-44). There they founded a Jewish military colony on Yeb or Elephantine Island on the Nile River, at which this 5th-century papyrus deed in Aramaic was found.

Extent of Jews under United Monarchy

Assyrian exile of Northern Kingdom, Israel

Babylonian exile of Judah

Flight into Egypt

Jews in the Persian capital

Gradual dispersion in the Hellenized world (300 B.C.–A.D. 100)

Under Ptolemaic kingdom

Under Seleucid kingdom and Romans

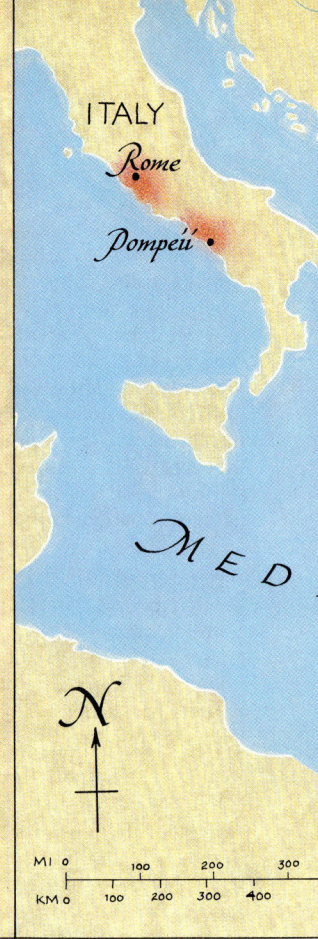

ITALY
Rome
Pompeii

MED

N

MI 0   100   200   300
KM 0   100   200   300   400

The forced exile of Israel in 712 B.C. (2 Ki. 17:6; 1 Chr. 5:26) and Judah, 597–582 B.C. (2 Ki. 24:11-16; Jer. 52:28-30; Ezek. 3:15), initiated a "dispersion" that continued under the Persian, Hellenistic, and Roman empires. Some scholars believe that one of every ten persons in the first-century Roman Empire was a Jew.

Part of a stone lintel found in Corinth bearing the inscription, "Synagogue of the Hebrews." Paul's outreach, focused initially on Jewish communities in Asia Minor, used the synagogue as his "platform" (Acts 13:5, 13-15; 14:1).

The final great dispersion of the Jews took place after the Roman general Titus conquered Jerusalem in A.D. 70, destroying the Temple.

There is no evidence that life was unusually hard for the Jews of the dispersion. In many cities they were granted unusual privileges, and prospered. However, most Jews remained members of the lower classes, and were often the object of anti-Semitic feelings. Yet most of them not only remained orthodox, but actively sought proselytes. The literature of the first century suggests that many Gentiles responded positively to the orderliness, discipline, and monotheism of OT Law. *See also* God-fearing.

Thus, while the OT views the dispersion of the Jews as divine judgment, God used that scattering for good. When the early Christian missionaries began to spread the Gospel, the many Jewish communities and their proselytes proved fertile ground for Christian evangelism.

304

REGATHERING

Although it predicted the dispersion of the Jewish people, the OT still ties the destiny of Israel to the Promised Land. The prophets foresaw a day when the Jews would return to Israel (Isa. 11:11-13; 35; Jer. 31:16,17). Zechariah, who wrote after the return under Cyrus, shares this word from the Lord:

Though I scatter them among the peoples,
yet in distant lands they will
remember me.
They and their children will survive,
and they will return.
I will bring them back from Egypt
and gather them from Assyria.
I will bring them to Gilead and Lebanon,
and there will not be room enough
for them.

(Zech. 10:9,10)

One of the wonders of history is that God's ancient people, although torn from their roots, have continued for some 4,000 years to remember the Lord "in distant lands." Many students of prophecy look at the founding of the nation Israel in 1948 (over 2,000 years after the last independent Jewish state was destroyed by the

Major cities with a Jewish community

Babylonians) as a landmark event which may indicate approaching fulfillment of the ancient promises. *See also* Prophecy.

distress Pressure, dismay, tribulation. The Hebrew and Greek words portray the person in "distress" as someone in a narrow place, pressured by difficult circumstances which cause emotional stress. While distress is often the result of external forces, such as enemy armies or economic disaster, distress can also be internal, caused by sinful or unwise choices.

In NT prophetic passages, "distress" is used in some English versions to translate *thlipsis* (Mt. 24:21: "For then there will be great distress"). In such passages, "distress" is a technical theological term, indicating the time of great tribulation which the prophets associated with history's end. *See also* Tribulation.

divination An attempt to learn about the future by observing omens in nature or consulting supernatural sources. Distinct from magic, which is an attempt to manipulate or control events through supernatural forces, divining seeks information in order to guide decision-making.

The Mesopotamians looked for omens in the livers of sacrificial animals. The shape and texture of each section of the liver was studied carefully by *baru*-priests, guided by written texts on interpretation. In some periods, diviners were attached to army corps.

In other ancient civilizations sticks or arrows were thrown in the air, and the pattern in which they fell was studied. The Greeks and Romans watched the flight of birds or examined their entrails. A desperate Saul consulted a medium, hoping to gain help from the dead Samuel (1 Sam. 28). Acts 16:16-19 tells of a demon-possessed slave girl in Philippi who earned her owners much money by divining.

The use of Urim and Thummim to discern God's will resembled divination, as did casting lots to determine the distribution of land in Canaan after the conquest. But God commanded the use of these two means, and he used them to communicate with his people in special situations. *See also* Urim and Thummim.

Yet divination was strictly forbidden in the Law, along with other occult practices of the Canaanites (Deut. 18:9-13). Israel 305

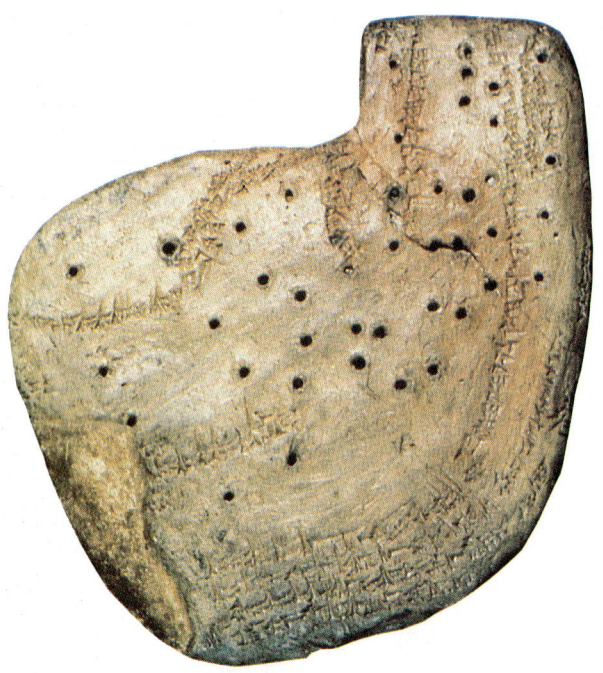

Clay model of a sheep's liver inscribed with omens for use by a Babylonian diviner (1830–1530 B.C.). Widely consulted in Bible times, diviners drew God's condemnation (Deut. 18:9-13).

divorce The legal dissolution of a marriage. Old Testament Law permitted issuing a "certificate of divorce" that dissolved a marriage, and freed divorced persons to remarry (Deut. 24:1-4; *see* Lev. 21:7,14; Ezek. 44:22). An example of such a certificate may be seen in Hos. 2:2: "She is not my wife, and I am not her husband."

Yet God's ideal was and is a life-long marital relationship marked by mutual commitment and love. Jesus explained that divorce was permitted by the Law "because your hearts were hard" (Mt. 19:8).

There has always been considerable debate over grounds for divorce. The OT has the husband initiating divorce because he "finds something indecent about" his wife. Even the rabbis of Jesus' time could not agree on just what this phrase meant. Some held that only adultery provided valid grounds. But the OT penalty for adultery was stoning, not divorce (Lev. 20:10). Other rabbis in Jesus' day held that anything which displeased a husband constituted grounds for divorce.

Jesus himself refused to be drawn into the argument over grounds, even though the "easy divorce" position treated marriage lightly and was a gross distortion of God's original intent. Instead Jesus stated that God had joined husband and wife, and no human was qualified to separate them (Mt. 19:6).

Matthew records Jesus' assertion that remarriage after divorce was adultery, except in the case of *porneia*. Debate has raged throughout church history over what this Greek word includes. The NIV

was to look to God alone for aid. God would guide his people by the written Word and, when more guidance was needed, by sending prophets (Deut. 18:14-22). In the context of the covenant, any appeal to the occult displayed a lack of faith in God.

Today, too, God is committed to lead us. We have no need of the occult, for God has given us his Word and the Holy Spirit to guide us into his will.

SOME ANCIENT METHODS OF DIVINATION		
Name	**Explanation**	**Scripture**
Inductive		
Astrology	Relation of heavenly bodies to the zodiac	Isa. 47:13; Jer. 10:2
Hepatoscopy	"Reading" sheep or goat's liver	
Hydromancy	Various methods using water	Gen. 44:5,15
Lots	Casting lots for group decision	Lev. 16:8; Num. 26:55,56; Josh. 18,19; 1 Chr. 24:5; Esth. 9:24-26; Jon. 1:7; Mt. 27:35; Acts 1:26
Rhabdomancy	Studying thrown sticks or arrows	2 Ki. 13:14-19; Ezek. 21:21; Hos. 4:12
Intuitive		
Necromancy	Consulting with the dead	Lev. 19:31; 20:6; Deut. 18:11; 1 Sam. 28:8; 2 Ki. 21:6; 2 Chr. 10:13; Isa. 8:19,20
Oneiromancy	Seeking out guidance through dreams	Gen. 40:1-40; Jer. 23:25-27; Dan 4:1-18
Oracles	Divine pronouncements from special places	Acts 16:16

The terms of this Aramaic marriage contract from Elephantine, Egypt, 449 B.C., include payment and disposition of property in the event of divorce or death. Divorce was uncommon among Jews, even though a man could divorce his wife simply by giving her a written notice (Deut. 24:1-3).

translates it "marital unfaithfulness" (Mt. 19:9). Some have held that Jesus meant adultery, and that adultery constitutes grounds for divorce. But a different Greek word (*moicheia*) means adultery; in fact, that word is used in this same verse.

Perhaps it is best to take *porneia* as parallel to hardness of heart, meaning here unfaithfulness to the marriage covenant itself. Such unfaithfulness may take other forms beside sexual promiscuity.

The Bible clearly states that God hates divorce (Mal. 2:13-16), and he affirms marriage. Scripture also upholds the ideal of life-long marriage, and offers hope to every couple that, through mutual love and a willingness to forgive, the ideal *can* be achieved (1 Cor. 7:15). *See also* Marriage.

doctrine The authoritative teaching of truths to be believed. The Greek words translated doctrine (*didachē* or *didaskalia*) simply mean "teaching." The earliest teachings of the church focused on Jesus, and are reflected in the sermons of Peter and Paul recorded in Acts. These sermons present the historical Jesus as God's Messiah, who died for our sins, was raised from the dead, and became the means of salvation for all who trust in his name (*see* Acts 2,3).

As the apostles continued to teach, and as the NT Epistles were written, a body of accepted truth developed around this core. Thus later letters of the NT speak of "the truths of the faith and of the good teaching that you have followed" (1 Tim. 4:6). It was the responsibility of the next

generation of Christian leaders to "hold firmly to the trustworthy message as it has been taught" and thus be able to "encourage others by sound doctrine and refute those who oppose it" (Tit. 1:9; *see* Jude 3). This body of truth, preserved for us in Scripture, has been affirmed by the church through the centuries.

However, Christian doctrine is more than a set of propositions. In 1 Tim. 1:8-11, Paul lists a variety of sins and notes that they "are contrary to the sound doctrine that conforms to the glorious gospel of the blessed God." Christian teaching calls on believers to live lives of holiness, as well as believe a set of revealed truths. *See also* Creed; Teach.

dog A carnivorous four-footed mammal, sometimes domesticated. The dog was semi-domesticated early in history, and was valued in Mesopotamia as a hunting companion. But the dogs of Palestine were hardly man's best friend. Scripture portrays them as fierce scavengers; eaters of unclean animals (Ex. 22:31), who are likely to turn on anyone who touches them (Prov. 26:17). Evil Queen Jezebel suffered the ultimate degradation when her dead body was eaten by a pack of wild dogs (2 Ki. 9:30-37; *compare* 1 Ki. 22:38).

Stylized Egyptian drawings of domesticated dogs. This jackal-headed breed symbolized the god Anubis. The Israelites, on the other hand, viewed the wild, scavenger dogs of Palestine with disgust.

307

A saluki—a tall, slender Asiatic hunting dog—chases down a hare in this Byzantine mosaic (5th century A.D.) from a church in Syria.

The Jews' contempt for dogs comes out in many ways in the Bible. Goliath was furious that David came against him with only a staff in his hand. "Am I a dog," he said, "that you come at me with sticks?" (1 Sam. 17:43). Deuteronomy 23:18 calls male prostitutes dogs. The psalmist characterized his enemies as vicious dogs, dangerous but contemptible (Ps. 22:16,20). Isaiah pictures Israel's spiritual leaders as mute dogs, too concerned with satisfying their own appetites to warn God's people of coming judgment (Isa. 56:9-12).

This negative attitude toward dogs carries over into the NT. Paul calls false teachers who twist the Gospel "those dogs, those men who do evil" (Phil. 3:2). Excluded from God's holy city, according to Rev. 22:15, are "the dogs, those who practice magic arts, the sexually immoral, the murderers, the idolaters and everyone who practices falsehood."

Against this background, we can understand Jesus' brief conversation with the Canaanite woman who begged him to heal her daughter (Mt. 15:21-28; Mk. 7:24-30). Jesus refused her request at first, saying he had been sent to Israel's lost sheep, and it was "not right to take the children's bread and toss it to their dogs." Jesus portrayed the people of Israel as valued animals, sheep, while the pagan Canaanites were represented by the worthless dog. The woman responded in faith, and some humility: "But even the dogs eat the crumbs that fall from their masters' table."

Jesus *did* heal the woman's daughter, because of her faith. The ministry of the

Jewish Messiah, who came to redeem God's ancient people, has overflowed, bringing healing and forgiveness to all who turn to him.

dominion Authority, power to rule, responsibility. Psalm 22:28 says, "Dominion belongs to the Lord and he rules over the nations."

Several Hebrew words are translated "rule" or "dominion." The most fascinating of them, *radah*, describes only the rule of human beings under God. The 25 uses of this word in the OT indicate two primary expressions of human dominion: over creation and over other humans.

DOMINION OVER CREATION

The creation story tells us that God made man in his likeness, and then gave humanity rule over all living creatures (Gen. 1:26,28). This dominion is not a right to exploit, but rather a responsibility to govern wisely for the benefit of those ruled. God's gift of dominion over nature is the theological base for Christian concern for ecology. The good gifts God has provided are to be guarded and preserved.

DOMINION OVER OTHER PERSONS

The same sense of caring occurs when *radah* is used of man's dominion over other men. Old Testament Law commanded owners not to misuse their legal authority over slaves. Even though a slave was legally considered the property of the owner, God's people were told, "Do not rule over them ruthlessly, but fear your God" (Lev. 25:43).

This same view, that authority must be

exercised for the benefit of the ruled, is expressed in Psalm 72. There Solomon describes the ideal king:

For he will deliver the needy who cry out,
*   the afflicted who have no one to help.*
He will take pity on the weak and the needy
*   and save the needy from death.*
He will rescue them from oppression and
*   violence,*
*   for precious is their blood in his sight.*
(Ps. 72:12-14)

While the right to rule may be vested in a human being, dominion carries responsibility. Under God's dominion, a ruler must care for those ruled. Thus in Scripture even authority is, in essence, servanthood.

"DOMINIONS" IN THE NT

When Eph. 1:21 and 6:12 mention rulers, authorities, dominions, and powers, these terms identify "spiritual forces of evil" (6:12, NIV). Paul exults in the fact that Jesus, an ideal Ruler who is concerned for our welfare, is far greater than any evil spirits. *See also* Authority.

donkey Small, horse-like animal with longer ears and a shorter mane. Donkeys were domesticated and used in Mesopotamia to draw wheeled carts as early as 3000 B.C.

When Jesus entered Jerusalem riding a donkey's colt (Mt. 21:1-11), he carried with him the fulfillment of various prophetic and historical images.

Texts from the 17th century B.C. indicate that in times of peace royalty was expected to ride a donkey rather than a horse, which was associated with warfare. This may have been in Zechariah's mind as he prophesied, "See, your king comes to you, righteous and having salvation, gentle and riding on a donkey" (9:9). Christ came to Jerusalem in peace, presenting himself as Israel's long-awaited King. *See also* Ass.

Stone door on a Greek funeral stela, second century A.D. It hints at the wealth of the deceased, whose house may have had such ornate doors.

door An entryway; a movable barrier that closes an entryway. In Bible times most doors were made of wood or stone. The heavy slabs were not hung from hinges, but pivoted inward on upper and lower sockets. Wide openings were hung with double doors, which would be bolted with bars of wood or metal. Doors were also locked by wooden slides inserted in a hole in the doorpost, which could be opened by wooden keys.

Doors in ancient times were often ornamented. Many Jewish homes featured Scripture verses carved into the doorposts (Deut. 6:4-9).

The "doors" to tents and to the OT tabernacle were simply cloth flaps or openings through which a person entered.

Medieval painting of Christ's entry into Jerusalem, riding on a donkey's colt (Mt. 21:1-11; Mk. 11:1-11; Lk. 19:28-38; Jn. 12:12-15). This action fulfilled Zech. 9:9: "See, your king comes to you . . . gentle and riding on a donkey, on a colt, the foal of a donkey."

Left: The donkey was the major beast of burden for the Israelites—a basic item of personal property (Ex. 22:8,9; 23:4,5). Terra-cotta figure carrying firewood, 6th century B.C.

Low, narrow doorways of a building ruin in Capernaum. Jesus spoke symbolically of the "narrow door" as the passage to eternal life (Lk. 13:24).

BACKGROUND

Since no family is mentioned in the story, it seems likely that Dorcas was a well-to-do widow, "always doing good and helping the poor" (Acts 9:36). This help included the making of clothes. Dorcas's death so disturbed the church in Joppa that its members sent to Peter, asking him, "Please, come at once!" After prayer, Peter called on Dorcas to return to life, and she did. The miracle stimulated a revival in Joppa.

LEARNING FROM DORCAS'S LIFE

Dorcas is the only woman specifically identified in Scripture as a disciple (Acts 9:36). Yet her commitment was expressed by helping the poor rather than in leadership. She reminds us that "religion that God our Father accepts as pure and faultless is this: to look after orphans and widows in their distress and to keep oneself from being polluted by the world" (Jas. 1:27).

The impact of such service is seen in the tears of those who knew Dorcas's love. Dorcas was no Deborah or Priscilla. She was not a leader or teacher. But her quiet ministry to others may have borne greater fruit. Even today "Dorcas societies" in many churches model their activities on her good works.

Christians of both sexes can learn from Dorcas the importance of wise priorities. We do not need some highly visible, public ministry to be significant in the Church of Christ. All we need is to love others and to serve them as Dorcas did.

The Bible uses "door" in various figures of speech. Jesus "stands at the door and knocks" (Rev. 3:20). This suggests nearness, eagerness to enter our lives, and also the freedom God gives individuals to welcome the Savior or shut him out. A door opened wide is an opportunity (1 Cor. 16:9). When Jesus calls himself "the door" in the Good Shepherd context of Jn. 10:9, he is referring to the entryway into an enclosed pasture. Jesus is the only way we, like sheep, can enter eternal life.

doorkeeper A servant posted beside the gates of a city, the doors of public buildings, such as Israel's Temple, or the entrances to the homes of the wealthy (Jn. 18:16,17). In Israel's religion, priests served as doorkeepers for the ark (1 Chr. 15:23,24). The doorkeepers of the Temple were apparently responsible for collecting gifts offered by worshipers (2 Ki. 22:4). Although doorkeeping was a low-status occupation, a psalm celebrates the privilege of those who served as doorkeepers at God's Temple.

Line drawing of an ancient Egyptian door illustrates what archaeologists have found in numerous places—that doors were hung in sockets with door pins like the metal one shown.

> Better is one day in your courts
>   than a thousand elsewhere;
> I would rather be a doorkeeper in the house of
>   my God
>   than dwell in the tents of the wicked.
>   (Ps. 84:10)

doorpost Part of the frame of a doorway.
Doorposts played two important roles in Israel's faith. (1) The blood of the Passover lamb was sprinkled there just before the Israelites' departure from Egypt (Ex. 12:7-23). (2) Deuteronomy 6:9 and 11:20 tell God's people to write his words on the doorposts of their houses and on their gates to remind them of God's commands each time they enter or leave home.

"In Joppa there was a disciple named . . . Dorcas who was always doing good and helping the poor" (Acts 9:36)—which meant in part that she made clothing for them (v. 39).

310

double-minded A term used by James (1:8; 4:8) to describe an uncommitted person, a doubter. The Greek word, *dipsychos*, means literally to be "of two minds." The uncommitted individual has no reason to expect divine guidance. Only those who are determined to do what God says will be given the wisdom to know what they should do (Jas. 1:5-8).

doubt Uncertainty, hesitation to commit oneself, unbelief. In a secular context, doubt may indicate a healthy skepticism. But in the NT doubt is a religious concept. It is typically expressed by the Greek word *diakrino*, "to judge or evaluate" (*see* Mk. 11:23; Rom. 4:20; 14:23). The NIV captures the basic idea when it translates this word, "to have hesitation" (Acts 10:20; 11:12). Essentially, religious doubt is uncertainty about what God has revealed. Such doubt seriously weakens relationship with God and blocks a full experience of his grace (Mt. 21:21; Jas. 1:6).

What is the opposite of doubt? Simple trust: the conviction that God has power to do all that he has promised in our lives.

dove A bird in the *Columbidae*, or pigeon, family. A ritually clean bird, the dove or pigeon was eaten by the Hebrews and accepted by God as a sacrifice offered by the poor (Lev. 12:8). The fact that Mary offered a pigeon for her purification after Jesus' birth is evidence that the couple was poor despite Joseph's work at his trade (Lk. 2:22-24). *See also* Pigeon.

Noah released a dove in an attempt to find out whether it was safe to open the door of the ark (Gen. 8:8,9). In Song of Solomon, the dove represents the lover. Hosea compares Israel to a dove, "easily deceived and senseless," as it flitted between Assyria and Egypt seeking an ally, rather than depending on the Lord for protection.

The most familiar appearance of the dove is in the story of the baptism of Jesus. The Holy Spirit descended on him in a form "like a dove" (Mt. 3:16).

dowry (KJV; variously translated in other versions) (1) A gift or payment (Heb., *mohar*) to the bride's father from the groom; (2) a gift (*shilluhim*) to the bride from her father. In the Middle East, a man was expected to make a gift to his bride's father (Ex. 22:17). Such compensation to the father was not always paid in money. Jacob worked for seven years in order to marry Laban's daughter Rachel (Gen. 29:18). King Saul urged David to marry his daughter, saying he wanted "no other price for the bride"

than evidence that David had killed a hundred of Israel's Philistine enemies (1 Sam. 18:25).

Yet it would be a mistake to conclude that women were merely property to be purchased. The bride was also given gifts by her father, which she brought into the marriage. But these remained hers if there should be a divorce. Laban, for instance, gave each of his daughters a servant woman when they married Jacob (Gen. 29:24,29). When Caleb's daughter married Othniel, she urged her groom to ask Caleb for a field as a marriage gift. Then this assertive young woman begged her father for additional springs of water "as a special favor" (Josh. 15:17-19).

In NT times the gift given the bride by her father often took the form of coins, with holes drilled in them so they could be worn on a string. It is likely that the woman in Jesus' parable who was distraught when she lost one of the ten silver coins was so upset because the coins were her dowry (Lk. 15:8-10).

Against this background we can better understand Hebrew marriage. Marriage called for an exchange of gifts. The gift to the father acknowledged the importance of the daughter to him, and also symbolized her value to the groom. The fact that the resources a woman brought into the marriage as a bridal gift remained hers is significant. The wife was never mere property. She was a property owner, an independent person who came into the relationship as a valued and valuable partner to her husband. *See also* Marriage; Woman.

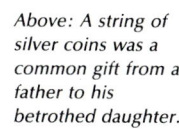

doxology An expression of praise. The most familiar doxologies used in Christian worship are: (1) The *Gloria Patri*, "Glory be to the Father, and to the Son, and to the Holy Ghost, world without end, Amen." (2) The hymn stanza, "Praise God, from whom all blessings flow; Praise him, all creatures here below; Praise him above, ye heavenly hosts; Praise Father, Son, and Holy Ghost." (3) The angels' praise at Jesus' birth, often called the Greater Doxology, "Glory to God in the highest, and on earth peace to men on whom his favor rests" (Lk. 2:14).

Many phrases found in the OT and NT have served God's people as doxologies. These phrases often take the form of blessings, such as "Blessed be the God and Father of our Lord Jesus Christ" (Eph. 1:3, KJV). *See also* Praise.

Reverse of a silver tetradrachm, a four drachma coin from the 4th century, bearing a stag, palm tree and the Greek name BOIOTOS.

drachma A silver coin, in NT times worth about one day's wages for a common laborer. Silver coins from Persia and Babylon as well as Greece were called *drachma*, which means "handful" (that is, a handful of six bronze spits which could be purchased with that amount of silver). A common world-wide value for silver coins was gradually fixed after Alexander's conquest (330 B.C.). By the first century the drachma was about equivalent to the Roman denarius, which served as the standard for a day's wages. *See also* Money.

dragon (KJV) A strange, fearsome, or mythical beast. The mythical flying beast that breathes fire is not actually mentioned in the Bible. The KJV uses "dragon" for two Hebrew words. The first, *tan*, is actually a jackal, as in modern English versions. The second, *tannin*, refers to some large water creature. It has been variously translated as whale, sea monster, and crocodile.

Only one dragon (Gk., *drakōn*) rears its ugly head in the NT. It appears in Rev. 12,13, where it symbolizes Satan. There Satan, "that ancient serpent" who deceived Eve in Eden, is fully revealed as a powerful and terrifying being who strikes at God by making war against his saints.

dram (KJV) The *daric. See also* Money.

dreams A series of thoughts, images, and sensations, passing through one's mind when asleep. Many ancient cultures were preoccupied with dreams, viewing them as supernatural messages. Books on how to interpret dreams were written in Egypt and Mesopotamia. Royal advisers were expected to interpret the dreams of rulers. We see the significance ascribed to dreams in Pharaoh's reaction to his dreams of cattle and crops (Gen. 41), and by Nebuchadnezzar's reaction to his dream of a giant image (Dan. 2).

AS A SOURCE OF REVELATION

While the Hebrew culture tended to emphasize dreams less than pagan cultures, Scripture does record some significant dreams. Yet most messages conveyed in scriptural dreams come directly from God or an angel, not shrouded in symbolism which required interpretation (Num. 12:6; *but see* Gen. 37:1-11). God spoke plainly to Abraham about his descendants while Abraham was in a deep sleep (Gen. 15). God apparently spoke just as directly to the pagan king Abimelech after he had innocently taken Sarah into his harem (Gen. 20). And while Joseph's dreams were very symbolic, he plainly understood the meanings and his brothers had no doubts about their validity (Gen. 37:5-11).

While dreams were an avenue of revelation, the mere fact that a person dreamed was no guarantee that his dream contained a word from God. According to Deut. 13:1-5, what the dreamer dreamed had to be tested against written revelation. No dream that called God's people away from the life-style portrayed in Scripture could be from the Lord. Jeremiah records God's perspective on false prophets who based their messages on false dreams:

"They say, 'I had a dream! I had a dream!' How long will this continue in the hearts of these lying prophets, who prophesy the delusions of their own minds? They think the dreams they tell one another will make my people forget my name, just as their fathers forgot my name through Baal worship. Let the prophet who has a dream tell his dream, but let the one who has my word speak it faithfully." (Jer. 23:25-28)

In OT times God's revelation sometimes came through dreams. As Heb. 1:1 says, "In the past God spoke to our forefathers through the prophets at many times and in various ways." But the passage continues, "In these last days he [God] has spoken to us by his Son" (Heb. 1:2).

AS A SOURCE OF GUIDANCE

The NT portrays dreams not so much as an avenue of revelation but as a mode of divine guidance. An angel appeared to Joseph in a dream and told him to take Mary as his wife (Mt. 1:20,21). Later Joseph

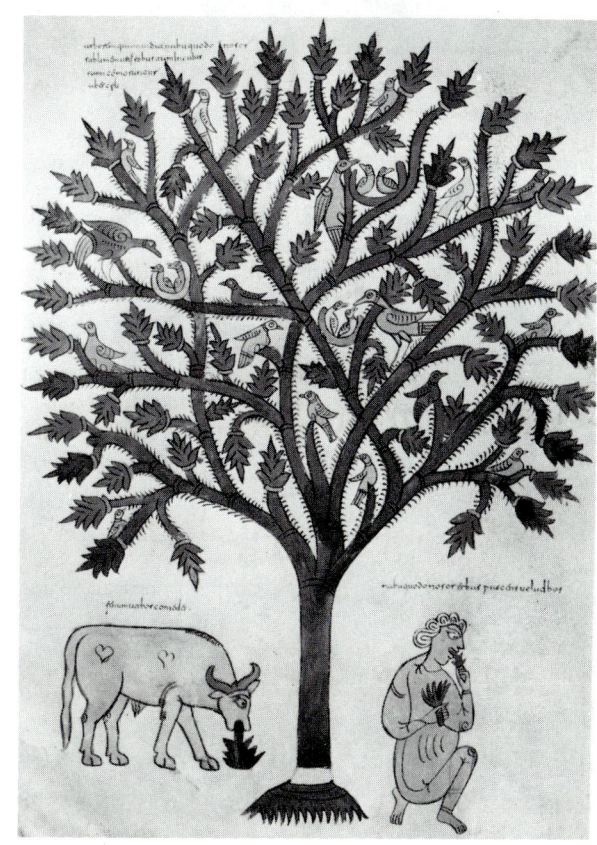

Above: Pharaoh's dream (Gen. 41) of seven cows and seven lean cows was interpreted by Joseph to indicate years of plenty and of famine. The Cologne Bible (A.D. 1479) depicts the sleeping monarch and the cattle along the Nile.

Right; Nebuchadnezzar's dream (Dan. 4) color-fully illustrated in a 10th-century Spanish manu-script. The large tree represented this king who had created a vast, powerful empire (vv. 19-22). Below it, however, he eats grass like cattle— God's judgment of madness for his pride (vv. 23-27).

was warned in a dream to flee to Egypt (Mt. 2:13). The wise men were told in a dream not to return to Herod (Mt. 2:12). Pilate's wife apparently had a nightmare that convinced her of Jesus' innocence (Mt. 27:19). And Paul had a "vision" one night of a man from Macedonia pleading for help. Yet dreams are not prevalent in the NT, and the Epistles seem to ignore them.

drink offering Wine offered in connection with certain OT sacrifices (Ex. 29:40; Lev. 23:13,18). These drink offerings always accompanied a meal offering, and were expressions of thanksgiving and dedication.

Paul used the image of wine poured on a sacrifice in Phil. 2:17. Writing from prison, in danger of execution, Paul suggested his death would serve as an added expression of thanks to God, which could only enhance the sacrificial service that faith had stimulated in the Philippian congregation.

A drunken worker is supported by two satyrs, in this bronze artifact found south of Rome. The Scriptures emphatically condemn drunkenness as "doing what pagans choose to do" (1 Pet. 4:3).

drink, strong (KJV) Any intoxicating beverage other than wine. The Hebrew *shekar* is often translated "beer" in modern English versions but it may have included liquor from fermented dates or other fruits or grains. Except for Num. 28:7, *shekar* is always linked with wine, as in Prov. 20:1: "Wine is a mocker and beer a brawler; whoever is led astray by them is not wise." *See also* Beer; Drunkenness; Wine.

Egyptian laborers lift a crucible of molten metal in order to pour off dross from its surface. Tomb of Rekhmira, about 1475 B.C.

dross The impurities that rise to the surface and are skimmed off when metal is heated to a liquid state. The prophets used dross figuratively. Sin had transformed Israel's silver into dross. Divine judgment was a blast of fire intended to separate dross from silver, so that it might be poured off (Ezek. 22:18-22).

drunkenness An impaired condition caused by alcoholic beverages. The Bible expresses its negative view of drunkenness in various ways. Those who drink are likely to "forget what the law decrees" (Prov. 31:4,5). Drunkenness is associated with personal injury, a loss of judgment and personal property (*see* Isa. 28:1,7,8). The OT warns that "drunkards and gluttons become poor" (Prov. 23:21). The NT contrasts drunkenness with self-control (1 Th. 5:7-9), and warns, "Do not get drunk on wine, which leads to debauchery" (Eph. 5:18).

While neither Testament forbids the use of intoxicants, each makes it clear we are not to drink to excess. Christians are to surrender control of their lives to God's Spirit (Eph. 5:18), not to alcohol.

The Bible does not comment on alcoholism as a disease. But it does hold that each human being is a morally responsible individual. In every situation choices exist. No person is forced to choose against his or her will and we must assume responsibility for our choices.

The contemporary Dung Gate of Jerusalem was built in the 16th century; the original was part of the wall Nehemiah rebuilt in the 5th century B.C.

duke (KJV) Leader of a tribal group or clan. The various Hebrew words translated "duke" in the KJV are usually rendered "chief man" or "leading man" in modern versions.

dumb Unable to speak. As a physical defect, the inability to speak is often associated with deafness. Jesus healed a number of dumb individuals (Mt. 15:30; Mk. 7:37; Lk. 11:14). Zechariah was struck dumb by God for expressing doubt when an angel promised him a child (Lk. 1:20-22).

There are several important figurative uses of dumbness in Scripture. Isaiah compares the Messiah to a sheep, dumb before her shearers (Isa. 53:7). The image suggests submission, and is usually taken to portray Jesus' refusal to defend himself at his trials.

Dumbness can indicate a psychological state, as when David felt such intense pressure that he cried, "I am like a deaf man, who cannot hear, like a mute, who cannot open his mouth" (Ps. 38:13).

For Paul, dumbness is a spiritual state (Rom. 3:19). God's Law serves as a standard for self-evaluation as well as divine evaluation, "so that every mouth may be silenced and the whole world held accountable to God."

dung Human or animal waste. Modern versions tend to use "offal" rather than dung. Excrement was never burned with sacrificial animals (Ex. 29:14; Lev. 8:17). But dried animal dung was often used as fuel in the hot, dry lands of the Bible (*see* Ezek. 4:10-15).

Dung Gate The entry at the southwest corner of the wall around Jerusalem. It is mentioned only in the Book of Nehemiah. The gate led to the Valley of Hinnom, where city refuse was disposed of in Nehemiah's time.

dust Loose or dry earth. In the OT, dust, the source from which God shaped man's physical body (Gen. 2:7), often stands for human frailty. God is compassionate; "he remembers that we are dust" (Ps. 103:14).

When a person dies, the body returns to dust (Gen. 3:19). The statement that Satan will "eat dust" (Gen. 3:14) suggests that his influence over God's people is limited to this present life. *See also* Eternal Life.

dye A substance used to give color, usually to cloth. Throughout the Middle East wool and linens were dyed a variety of colors. Just as in the modern world, people of biblical times liked colorful clothing.

Red dye was produced from insects or the roots of the madder plant. Purples were extracted from the *murex* and *purpura* mollusks. To obtain it, their shells were

Above: The naturally extracted scarlet or crimson dye produces intense, permanent color—a perfect poetic picture for Isaiah: "Though your sins be as scarlet, they shall be as white as snow; though they are red as crimson, they shall be like wool" (1:18). Inset: Metal vat from 1st century B.C. Dye was stored in such containers for use in large stone baths where woolen yarn was dyed.

crushed and their glands were boiled in a salt solution. Yellow and orange dyes were extracted from various plants.

Archaeologists have excavated a number of buildings in Palestine where dyeing was done in 10-by-30-foot rooms. Generally, these rooms included two small vats, with covers designed to catch drops of dye and direct them back into the vat. The size of the vats suggests that thread was dyed before being woven into cloth. Small containers for holding fixing agents, such as potash or lime, were also in the room. The way such buildings were clustered together suggests that families engaged in the industry may have formed a sort of guild and lived in a common district.

315

Eden

Elijah

Egypt

Eagle

Esther

Eating

Ephesus

✗	Ϥ	Ⴘ	Ϟ	Ⴈ	E
C. 1500 BC	C. 300 BC	C. 1000 BC	C. 450 BC	100 AD	500 BC
PROTO-SINAITIC	S. ARABIAN	PHOENICIAN	ARAMAIC	HEBREW	GREEK

eagle A large bird of prey. The Hebrew *nesher* includes the largest members of both eagle and vulture families. Both birds eat carrion and hunt prey. They are similar in size, nesting patterns, flight, and lifespan. Most modern versions use both eagle and vulture to translate *nesher*, letting the context determine which bird is intended.

The *nesher* heads the list of unclean birds in the OT (Lev. 11:13; Deut. 14:12). Other references to eagles are illustrative or metaphorical. The flight of these magnificent birds captured the imagination of the Hebrews. One of the three things thought "too amazing for me" is "the way of an eagle in the sky" (Prov. 30:18,19). The effortless flight of the eagle serves Isaiah as an image of believers whose hope is in the Lord: they "will soar on wings like eagles" (40:31).

The prophets also used vultures as symbols of judgment. Circling above the battlefield, they await the chance to feed on the dead (Hos. 8:1; Mt. 24:28).

Both eagle and vulture build their nests high on mountain crags, and protect their young. These characteristics make the eagle an appropriate symbol of security, as in Moses' description of God who is "like an eagle that stirs up its nest and hovers over its young, that spreads its wings to catch them and carries them on its pinions" (Deut. 32:11; *see* Job 39:27-30).

The eagle appropriately represented the regal power of Babylon in Nebuchadnezzar's dream (Dan. 7:4). It also represents its part of the animal kingdom as one of the faces on the living creatures who guard God's throne (Ezek. 1:10). *See also* Bird.

ear The organ of hearing. Figuratively, the ear is far more. In the Bible the ear stands for the whole process of receiving God's message, understanding it, and responding to it. To "hear" in Scripture implies a favorable response.

Thus Jeremiah complains about his generation, "Their ears are closed so they cannot hear. The word of the Lord is offensive to them" (6:10). These people were unwilling to respond to the Word of God. They rejected it, and thus did not "hear" what the prophet was preaching.

The eagle on this silver coin from Tyre (dated to 97–96 B.C.) captures the regal power its majesty represents.

On this 13th-century stela found at Memphis, Egypt, rows of ears were carved on either side of a prayer to the god Ptah (in hieroglyphics) to ensure that it would be heard. In contrast, the psalmists assure worshipers of the true God that he both hears and responds to them (Pss. 65:2; 94:9).

Scripture's earliest chapters tell of the Garden of **Eden** *and how that idyllic spot became polluted by sin. In Exodus, God reaches down to redeem his people from bondage in* **Egypt**. *Later, prophets like* **Elijah** *called God's people to repentance and boldly confronted evil monarchs. Lovely* **Esther** *herself was called upon to plead for her people before a mighty ruler. Through the prophets God promised that he would renew his people so that they could "soar on wings like* **eagles.**" *In the New Testament Jesus called himself the living bread and invited his disciples to* **eat**. *After Christ's resurrection the Gospel spread to key cities of the Western world like* **Ephesus** *in Asia Minor. In Paul's majestic letter to the Ephesian Christians, he prays that their eyes might be enlightened and that they might live with God's eternal purpose in view.*

The Bible often draws a distinction or makes a connection between having physical ears and "hearing" (understanding and accepting) God's Word. Quite simply, ears are supposed to hear. The psalmist mocks the idols which "have ears, but cannot hear" (Ps. 115:6). The true God, who shaped the ear, both hears and responds when his people call on him (Ps. 94:9). When people pray in Scripture, they often ask the Lord to "give ear" or to "turn his ear" to them.

The Lord gave Isaiah the frustrating task of prophesying to people whose ears were dull (Isa. 6:9,10). Jesus himself turned that frustration around with his parables and challenged his audience repeatedly, "He who has ears, let him hear" (Mt. 11:15; 13:9,43; *see* Rev. 2:7,11,17).

Paul predicted that someday people would have "itching ears," and would find teachers who taught what they wanted to hear. Thus they would "turn their ears away from the truth" (2 Tim. 4:3,4).

In the story of Peter cutting off the ear of the high priest's servant at Jesus' arrest, a diminutive form of the word for "ear" is used, perhaps referring to the outer part of the ear or even the ear lobe. *See also* Hear.

ear, pierced The physical symbol of slavery or servanthood.

In Israelite culture, a bond-servant would serve only six years (perhaps to pay off a debt) and then go free. But the servant could choose to stay in his master's service for life. An ear-piercing ceremony would symbolize this choice (Ex. 21:5,6; Deut. 15:16,17). The master would take an awl and thrust it through the servant's ear lobe into his door. This act represented the opening of the servant's ear for a lifetime of obedience. *See also* Ear.

In Isa. 50:5 the Messiah indicates his eternal obedience to the Father, saying, "The Sovereign Lord has opened my ears, and I have not been rebellious." Many believe this phrase reflects the ancient pierced ear ceremony of commitment to a lifetime of obedience.

earnest (KJV) *See* Deposit.

earrings Ornaments attached to the ear lobe. Women in biblical times often wore earrings to enhance their appearance (Isa. 3:19; Ezek. 16:12; Hos. 2:13). Some men also sported earrings (Num. 31:50; Jdg. 8:24). Earrings mentioned in the Bible were usually made of gold or silver. Archaeologists have also recovered many earrings dating from OT times made of copper and bronze, and some inset with jewels. Pagan cultures often considered earrings magic charms which would protect the wearer from spirits who might enter through the ear and cause disease. *See also* Jewelry and Precious Stones.

earth (1) The known world; (2) the soil. The Hebrew word *'eres* means earth or land, and is used in various ways. The phrase "heaven and earth" stands for the entire material universe. *'Eres* may encompass the known world, or simply a national/political unit, such as the "land of Egypt." The word also refers to the planet's surface, to the soil, or to dry land, as opposed to sea.

The OT affirms that, in every sense, God is Lord of the heavens and of the earth. He created the earth, and superintends what happens here (Ps. 47). Although the original harmony of God's creation has been shattered by sin, God has not abandoned this planet. God's Messiah "will not falter or be discouraged till he establishes justice on earth" (Isa. 42:4).

Bottom: Earrings have adorned humans for centuries. The two examples in gold, Egyptian (right) and Greek (left), hint at the large size common in the ancient world. Earrings were a valued gift (Job 42:11), and an offering for the tabernacle (Num. 31:50).
Below: Assyrian earrings drawn from wall reliefs.

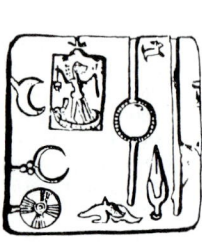

Above: Assyrian earrings and mold.
Left: Egyptian earrings from wall reliefs.

Yet the prophet's vision for the future extends beyond this present universe. In a time beyond history's end God promises, "I will create new heavens and a new earth. The former things will not be remembered, nor will they come to mind" (Isa. 65:17). *See also* Creation; Dust; World.

earthly A technical theological term, indicating something which originates in this universe and is thus temporary, severely limited, or morally tainted. In most of its seven occurrences, the "earthly" is contrasted with the "heavenly," which is characterized by strength, purity, and goodness, coming from the realm of God (Jas. 3:14-17). *See also* Heaven.

earthquake A shaking or trembling of the earth's surface. Palestine is relatively unstable geologically, lying near one of earth's main earthquake belts. While Scripture specifically mentions only a handful of Middle East quakes (1 Ki. 19:11; Amos 1:1; Zech. 14:5; Mt. 27:54; 28:2), the area averages nearly one major quake each century. Other earthquakes or quake-like events include the opening of the earth to swallow Dathan and Abiram (Num. 16), the shaking of the ground that caused a Philistine army to panic (1 Sam. 14), and, in Macedonia, the disturbance that opened the prison doors in Philippi for Paul and Silas (Acts 16). Many feel that an earthquake contributed to the destruction of Sodom and Gomorrah (Gen. 19).

Both OT and NT prophecies forecast a future time of earthquakes. Isaiah depicts the Lord routing Israel's enemies with a storm and an earthquake (Isa. 29:6). In a sermon, Jesus predicts "earthquakes, famines and pestilences in various places, and fearful events and great signs from heaven" (Lk. 21:11). And the Book of Revelation describes several quakes, associating them with the outpouring of God's wrath (Rev. 6:12; 8:5; 11:13,19; 16:18).

east The direction from which the sun rises. "East" in the Bible means east of Palestine. The eastern sea (Ezek. 47:18) is the Dead Sea; easterners, or "children of the east" (Gen. 29:1; Jdg. 6:3; 1 Ki. 4:30), are inhabitants of any land lying east of the Jordan River.

The east wind mentioned in the Bible is the sirocco, a wind which blows into Palestine from the desert in May and October. While God used an east wind to drive back the waters of the Red Sea (Ex. 14:21), this scorching and destructive wind is more often associated with divine judgment (Isa. 27:8; Jer. 4:11,12; Jon. 4:8).

One of Scripture's finest promises is that, when God forgives us, he removes our transgressions "as far as the east is from the west" (Ps. 103:12). Since the two concepts are diametrically opposed, this is an infinite distance.

Easter The annual Christian festival celebrating the resurrection of Jesus Christ.

Above: One of the world's major earthquake zones lies along the 2,000-mile Afro-Arabian Fault, which stretches into Palestine. The Scriptures record that God used earthquakes or quake-like events to mete out judgment— a supernatural use of a natural phenomenon.
Above left: NASA satellite photograph of the earth. Our ability to view the earth from this perspective only increases our awe of God, who made the universe (Ps. 148).

"Banquet in the Vine-arbor," a relief from the 7th century B.C. in which Assyrian king Ashurbanipal (reclining) feasts with his wife. This scene reflects the feasting described in Amos 6:4-6 with ivory-inlaid couches, musical accompaniment and the choicest food and drink.

The earliest mention of Easter occurs in correspondence between the bishops of Rome and Smyrna, dating to A.D. 154. It is clear from these letters that a holy day was widely celebrated at the time.

The date of Easter roughly matches that of the Jewish Passover. But Easter is now celebrated on the first Sunday after the full moon following the spring equinox, so it falls each year between March 22 and April 23.

The name "Easter" is of later origin. It was apparently taken from the name of the Germanic goddess of spring, Eostre.

The KJV uses "Easter" to translate the Greek *pascha* in Acts 12:4. Modern versions properly render this "Passover." *See also* Passover; Resurrection of Jesus.

eating Consuming food. In the Middle East eating was (and still is) a joy, a social event, a shared experience that bonded guest and host together.

Genesis 18 tells of Abraham's reaction when, sitting by his tent in the heat of the day, he noticed three strangers standing nearby. He hurried out to meet them, saying, "Let me get you something to eat." Abraham then personally selected a choice calf to serve them, and Sarah prepared bread.

The story portrays the typical hospitality of the Middle East, and also suggests the importance of food. Even in the heat of the day, when food was not generally prepared, strangers must be welcomed with a meal.

EATING CUSTOMS

The Hebrews normally ate two meals: a light breakfast of bread, fruit, and cheese served between nine and noon, and a heavier supper eaten in the evening. In most homes the "table" was a circular leather or skin mat. The family and guests sat on the ground or floor, dipping their fingers in the large dishes which contained the food (Mt. 26:23; Ruth 2:14). Only the wealthy or those at banquets ate from low tables while reclining on couches (Amos 6:4; Mt. 8:11, NASB).

Because they ate with their hands, people generally washed their hands before meals. In Jesus' day the Pharisees had converted such washing into a religious ritual that was without foundation in God's Law (Mt. 15:1,2; Mk. 7:1-5).

It was customary to thank God before eating (1 Sam. 9:13; Mt. 15:36; Jn. 6:11). One prayer common in the first century was: "Blessed art Thou, Lord God, King of the Universe, Who bringeth bread forth from the earth." A second prayer was generally said after the meal, for Deut.

These line drawings show Egyptians eating in typical fashion, seated around short tables. Joseph probably served his brothers in a similar way, though he did not eat with them (Gen. 43:31-35).

8:10 said, "When you have eaten and are satisfied, praise the Lord your God for the good land he has given you."

But it was not only these blessings that made eating a religious experience. Old Testament Law carefully regulated what God's people might eat, and how it should be prepared. Even the foods the Israelites enjoyed reminded them that they were called to be a people set apart to their God. *See also* Clean and Unclean.

EATING AT FEASTS

Feasts were very important social occasions in Bible times. Amos describes feasting in the eighth century B.C.

You lie on beds inlaid with ivory
and lounge on your couches.
You dine on choice lambs
and fatted calves.
You strum away on your harps like David
and improvise on musical instruments.
You drink wine by the bowlful
and use the finest lotions.   (Amos 6:4-6)

Feasting usually took place at night, in brightly lit rooms. Jesus often used these joyous occasions as an illustration of God's Kingdom. He warned that in the day of judgment those who reject God's invitation will be excluded from the brightness of that celebration and "thrown outside, into the darkness" (Mt. 8:12; 22:13; *see* Isa. 25:6-9).

In NT times the guests at a feast usually reclined on pillows or couches. The nearer a guest was to his host, the more highly he was honored. Jesus' story of the rich man and the beggar Lazarus pictures the dead beggar at "Abraham's side" (Lk. 16:22; "bosom," KJV). The imagery was clear to Christ's hearers: The beggar was an honored guest in glory, while the rich man was cut off from the blessed state.

The Gospels highlight one other feasting practice. At the Last Supper, Jesus gave Judas Iscariot a "sop" (Jn. 13:26; "piece of bread," NIV). The sop was a piece of bread which the host dipped in the common dish, or an especially tender bit of meat he chose from it. Giving a guest such a morsel was not only an honor, but an expression of warmth and friendship. How striking that Jesus knew the traitor, and extended

this one last evidence of his love. What clear evidence of the hardness of Judas's heart, that even this expression of friendship did not move him to repent.

EATING AS PARTICIPATION

Eating in the Bible is a powerful symbol of participation. Agreements which settled some dispute were often celebrated by a shared meal (Gen. 31:54). The meal was an expression of renewed trust, and to violate such trust would be an especially repulsive act (Mk. 14:18). Exodus 24:9-11 portrays the elders of Israel eating and drinking on Mount Sinai in God's presence, a symbol of mutual trust and celebration of Israel's acceptance of the covenant of Law. *See also* Covenant.

When Paul describes church discipline, he tells Christians not to associate with anyone who calls himself a brother but adopts a sinful life-style. When we realize that in the biblical world even visiting enemies were fed (2 Ki. 6:22,23), Paul's final words indicate how complete the isolation of this sinning brother was to be: "With such a man do not even eat" (1 Cor. 5:11). The unrepentant brother cannot participate in the fellowship of Christ's Church.

Peter's refusal to eat with Gentile Christians in Antioch while Jewish brethren were visiting was a theological rather than merely social statement (Gal. 2:11-21). Paul realized this at once, and confronted Peter. Through faith in the Gospel, Jew and Gentile alike participate in Christ. Peter's refusal to eat was a symbolic but very real denial of the doctrine of salvation by faith.

Eating served as a powerful symbol in Israel's sacrificial system. In connection with the three peace-offerings, after choice parts of an animal had been burned and set aside for the priests, the offerer and his family feasted on the rest of the meat. The meal displayed full identification of the

Three children crouch and eat off one dish in this scene on a Roman funeral monument. As shown here, most people in the ancient world sat on the floor and ate without utensils.

worshiper with the act of sacrifice, and celebrated the divine forgiveness. This significance is underlined in the Exodus prohibition against anyone but an Israelite taking part in the Passover feast (Ex. 12:43).

When Jesus spoke of eating his flesh and drinking his blood (Jn. 6:48-58), he was calling for just such a complete identification of the believer with his own sacrifice at the cross. The Lord's Supper, instituted by Jesus, is also a symbolic participation; it is a meal by which Christians express and experience their union with Jesus in his death. Thus Paul says, "Is not the cup of thanksgiving for which we give thanks a participation in the blood of Christ? And is not the bread that we break a participation in the body of Christ?" (1 Cor. 10:16; *see* Mt. 26:17-30).

In the Greek world, social gatherings were often dedicated to a pagan god. Because taking part in such a feast involved symbolic participation, Paul called on the Corinthians not to eat these meals (1 Cor. 10:14-22). According to Ps. 106:28, those who ate sacrifices offered to lifeless gods "yoked themselves" to them.

FIGURATIVE USES OF EATING

The Hebrew word for eat (*'akal*) also has the sense of consuming or devouring, and is used of disasters which consume the resources of the nation.

The prophets speak of "eating" God's Word as a figure for identifying completely with the Lord and practicing his will. Thus Jeremiah cried, "When your words came, I ate them; they were my joy and my heart's delight, for I bear your name, O Lord God Almighty" (Jer. 15:16).

Throughout Scripture, then, eating has special significance. It is one of the most enjoyable experiences of our life on earth, not only for the delights of taste and smell, but also because it is an occasion which friends and family share. Yet the religious significance of eating overshadows the social. In the world of the Bible, eating expressed union with and participation in that which the food symbolized. How great a privilege then to share today in the Lord's Supper, and to realize that this act expresses our faith in Jesus, and affirms our union with him in his death.

Ebla An ancient city recently excavated in modern Syria. Some 2,400 years before the birth of Christ, and at least two centuries before Abraham, the kings of Ebla governed a Canaanite empire that stretched at times from the Mediterranean Sea to the Persian Gulf. About 260,000 people lived in the capital city, with 11,000 officials employed in government service.

Although Ebla is not mentioned in the Bible, excavations there have proven very important to students of the OT. Excavation of the city in 1974–1977 powerfully refuted the charge that the early chapters of Genesis were not historically reliable. Some 20,000 tablets written in Sumerian and Eblaite, a language related to Hebrew, mention cities named in the patriarchal narratives. They also use personal names similar to those in the OT. They even

Marching warriors, armed with lances and boomerang-like throwing sticks, tread on four crouching lions in this relief from an Eblaite sacrificial basin (second millennium B.C.). At its peak the city of Ebla was inhabited by some 260,000 people.

furnish a certain background to the development of the cult of Baal, to which the Israelites later proved so vulnerable.

Although most of the written records found in Ebla have not been translated or published, the texts we do have show us a Middle Eastern culture accurately reflected in the patriarchal narratives.

Ecclesiastes, Book of This OT book adopts philosophical discourse to report a search for life's meaning. In this search, the writer strictly limits himself. He will rely only on human reason ("explore by wisdom," 1:13). And he will consider only data available within the framework of the created universe ("under the sun," 1:14). While the doctrine of inspiration guarantees accurate expression of what the book is intended to convey, inspiration does not mean that this writer's conclusions are correct. The despondent view that life is "meaningless," repeated again and again, is *not* the view of Scripture. It is, however, a conclusion that even the wisest of human beings must come to—if life in this world is all there is.

BACKGROUND

The author identifies himself as "the *kohelet* [Preacher, KJV; Teacher, NIV], son of David, king of Jerusalem." Tradition holds that the author was Solomon, who wrote the book near the end of his reign, after his pagan wives had turned his heart from the Lord (1 Ki. 11:9-13). Then, with his spiritual bearings lost, and unwilling to follow his father's example of repentance, Solomon began a desperate and useless search for meaning.

Some have argued that the style and vocabulary of the book suggest a later origin than Solomon, who reigned 970–940 B.C. They say that the philosophical orien-

tation suggests a Greek influence. These points are hardly decisive.

Ecclesiastes apparently contains a diction peculiar to philosophical discourse originally developed in Phoenicia. Among other linguistic features are the many commercial terms found in Ecclesiastes, which fit Solomon's ties with Phoenicia. Certainly the writer's description of himself and his activities (Eccl. 1:12-18; 2:4-9) strongly support the ancient rabbis' conviction that this book was written by King Solomon himself.

THEOLOGICAL DISTINCTIVES

Ecclesiastes purports to be a book that reflects the best human reasoning about the meaning of life. It is important not to mistake Solomon's provisional conclusions ("under the sun") for divine truth. Such sayings as "man's fate is like that of the animals" is a conclusion Solomon drew from observing that "as one dies, so dies the other" (Eccl. 3:19). When Solomon says, "Who knows if the spirit of man rises upward and if the spirit of the animal goes down into the earth," he simply means no human being can tell the difference by earthly observation (Eccl. 3:21).

The Book of Ecclesiastes, then, cannot be used to establish biblical doctrine. Instead, the musings of this wisest of men establishes the limits of human reason. And Solomon's despair reflects the conclusions of many philosophers of our age, such as Camus and Sartre.

What conclusions did Solomon reach? First, he realized that human beings have an ethical sense, for Solomon speaks of good and evil, righteousness and wickedness, the virtuous and the sinful. But nowhere does Solomon define his moral terms. Second, he concluded that each

Left: Pillar and offering slab of the "Great Temple" on the acropolis of Ebla (second millennium B.C.). Records of Baal worship found here have helped scholars to understand this cult that rivaled worship of Israel's God.

Right: One of some 20,000 tablets discovered in 1975 in the royal archives of Ebla (2400 B.C.). These tablets contain names similar to ones found in the Book of Genesis.

person should enjoy the pleasures this life affords (Eccl. 2:24,25; 3:12,13; 6:1,2; 8:15). Third, he decided that life is basically unfair. "There is something else meaningless that occurs on earth," Solomon writes, "righteous men who get what the wicked deserve, and wicked men who get what the righteous deserve" (Eccl. 8:14). Fourth, Solomon concluded that God exists, but is so remote as to be unknowable (Eccl. 5:2; 8:17). God is to be remembered and honored as Creator. But Solomon cannot by wisdom discern God as Redeemer. Even in his concluding exhortation to fear God and keep his commandments, Solomon cries out in despair, " 'Meaningless! Meaningless!' says the Teacher. 'Everything is meaningless!' " (Eccl. 12:8).

This clay oil lamp (third century B.C.), found in northern Palestine, is shaped like a schoolmaster reading a scroll. A teacher reading a book of wisdom such as Ecclesiastes would roll and unroll the scroll as he read.

MASTERY KEYS

To master the Book of Ecclesiastes, read through it and underline the recurring phrases, "under the sun" and "by wisdom." These establish the limitations the author placed on himself in writing this book, and help us understand it as a expression of the best of human reasoning rather than divine revelation. Note: (1) where Solomon looked for, and could not find, meaning; (2) comparisons Solomon makes in trying to determine which of life's ultimately meaningless choices are better; (3) statements made in this book which do *not* reflect truths taught in other Bible books.

SPECIAL FEATURES

Read this book to develop sensitivity to the emptiness felt by persons who have no personal relationship with God. Unbelievers who read Ecclesiastes often identify with the emptiness felt by the writer. The book can be a help in making such persons aware of their need for God.

Eden The area where Adam and Eve lived before their sin. Eden seems to have been the early name for a large geographical area, including Mesopotamia and perhaps

The word "Eden" written in Sumerian cuneiform, the earliest script known (third millennium B.C.). Sumerian also contains the word "Adam," but not "Eve."

the entire Fertile Crescent. The name probably comes from the Hebrew word for "delight," or perhaps is derived from a root word for a steppe or high plain. The

ECCLESIASTES: A READING AND STUDY GUIDE		
Chapter	**Content Summary**	**Related Articles**
1	Solomon states his theme: All is meaningless. His intellect and devotion to study has brought despair.	Wisdom Reason
I. Demonstration of Solomon's Theme		
2	Solomon has sampled sensual pleasures and succeeded with great projects. Yet the prospect of death has robbed him of satisfaction.	Death Sex
3	Life is controlled by cycles. These cycles repeat again and again. There is nothing new. Life itself is unfair, and death the end.	
4	Human suffering, isolation, and ambition all demonstrate the meaninglessness of life.	Suffer
5	God's existence is self-evident, but he cannot be known. Riches cannot satisfy for even when a person is rich he remains insecure and frustrated.	Creation
6	Better to be a stillborn child than a man of a hundred with many children. For who can tell what is good for him now, or what will happen on earth after he dies.	
II. Solomon's Deductions		
7	Some ways are better than others; extremes should be avoided.	
8	Submission to human authorities and to God is to be preferred, as is enjoying the good things of life.	
9	Since death awaits, enjoy life while you can.	
10	It is better to be wise than foolish in this life.	
11	Prepare for the future as well as you can, even though you cannot control it, and remember God.	
12	Because we grow old and die, all is meaningless. All we can do is to fear God and keep his commandments.	Commandment

garden God planted was in the eastern part of this area (Gen. 2:8). Four rivers flowed through the garden, and it contained many trees, including the tree of life and the tree of the knowledge of good and evil (Gen. 2:9-14). The two most likely locations lie in the mountains of Armenia and at the head of the Persian Gulf, but no theory of the garden's location is without difficulties.

Genesis treats the Garden of Eden as a historical place, and describes the care with which God designed it for Adam and Eve. It was in Eden that humanity fell, and from this garden Adam and Eve were expelled. Bible students who take Ezek. 28:11-19 as a description of Satan's fall note that he is described in his unfallen state as "in Eden, the garden of God" (v. 13). Where Satan turned to sin, God created a pure humanity and established an ideal environment, only to see man choose Satan's path.

Symbolically, Eden has always represented the idyllic state, where beauty and peace reign. The prophets refer to Eden when speaking of the blessings God will give his people (Ezek. 36:35; Joel 2:3). As Isaiah says,

The Lord will surely comfort Zion
  and will look with compassion on
    all her ruins;
he will make her deserts like Eden,
  her wastelands like the garden of the Lord.
Joy and gladness will be found in her,
  thanksgiving and the sound of singing.
(Isa. 51:3)

Paradise was lost. But the Bible assures us that paradise also lies ahead.

edify, edification To build up; building up. The Gospels use the verb form of the Greek *oikodomeō* in a literal sense: One man built his house on a rock (Mt. 7:24); another built bigger barns (Lk. 12:18). But Paul uses both verb and noun forms figuratively. To Paul the Church is God's building (1 Cor. 3:9; Eph. 2:21). Christians are to build each other up, and thus work with God on completing the unique spiritual structure that is Christ's Church (1 Cor. 14:26; Eph. 4:16). *See also* Build.

Edom, Edomites A nation descended from Esau (Gen. 36). The name Edom means "red," a nickname for Esau after he traded his birthright for some red stew (Gen. 25:30). His descendants took this name and settled southeast of Canaan. Their land extended from the south end of

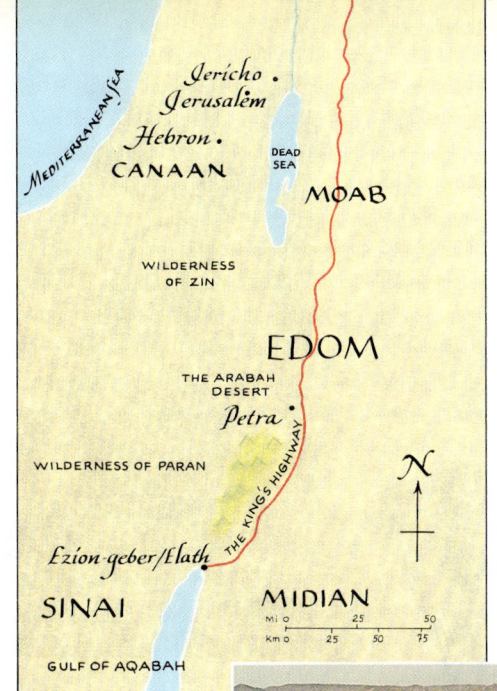

Above: The King's Highway, a major trade route in biblical times, afforded the Edomites a strategic place in trade and travel. They used their influence, for example, to bar the wandering Israelites from passage (Num. 20:14-21).

the Dead Sea to the Gulf of Aqaba, including both the low-level desert (*see also* Arabah) and the mountains to the east. This was a strategic area, for in biblical times a major trade route called the King's Highway traversed Edom (Num. 20:17).

When the Israelites left Egypt, they asked the Edomites for permission to travel this route toward Canaan. The request was refused, but because of the ancient relationship between the brothers Jacob and Esau, from whom the two peoples sprang, Israel would not fight against Edom (Num. 20:14-21; Jdg. 11:17,18).

Later the Edomites showed persistent hostility against the Jews. David conquered Edom (1 Ki. 11:15,16), and Solomon built a port on the Gulf of Aqaba (1 Ki. 9:26). But the following centuries saw a series of rebellions, invasions, and counter-invasions, until Edom became a vassal state of Assyria about 736 B.C. Many of the prophets predicted that God would judge the Edomites for their hatred of the Jewish people (Jer. 49:7-22; Ezek. 25:12-14; Joel 3:19; Amos 9:12; Obadiah).

Arid mountains of Edom, east of the Dead Sea.

Above: A teacher and two students in a schoolroom scene carved in stone (A.D. 200–300). For those parents who could afford it, their children's education was a personal affair: the teacher would come to the student's home and might even serve as a guardian or trustee (see Gal. 4:1,2).

CLASSROOMS

courtyard

doorkeeper

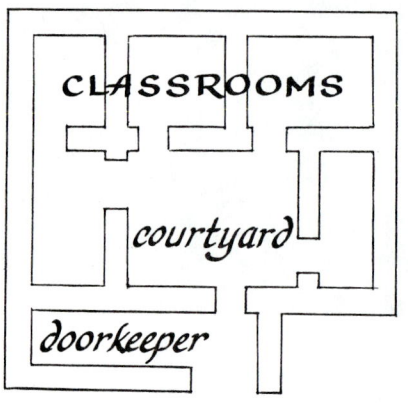

Floor plan of a Babylonian school or "tablet house" in Ur (about 2000 B.C.). Here children learned to write some 600 cuneiform symbols on soft clay tablets with a wooden stylus. Above left: This scene of a teacher and his student is one of several painted around the center of a shallow Athenian bowl (5th century B.C.).

education Instruction, learning. Modern educators make a helpful distinction between formal and non-formal education. Formal education is schooling, the teaching and learning of a distinctive body of information or skill in a special setting. Non-formal education is more closely linked with everyday experience. It involves the learning of a way of life, and its undergirding beliefs, by participating in that way of life with other members of a community.

In biblical times, as in our own, both formal and non-formal education took place. Yet, in matters of faith, Scripture seems to emphasize non-formal education. We see this as Moses urges parents to impress God's commands upon their children: "Talk about them when you sit at home and when you walk along the road, when you lie down and when you get up" (Deut. 6:7). We see it in the

festivals Israel used to relive its history, and in the "memorials" scattered through the land (Gen. 28:18-22; Ex. 24:4; Josh. 4:4-24). We even see non-formal education in the sacrificial system, and in the psalms sung by God's people (Ex. 15). In essence, the total way of life shared by the people of God was designed to nurture children and adults in the faith. *See also* Nurture.

FORMAL EDUCATION IN OT TIMES

Schools for the training of scribes, those professionals who wrote documents and maintained government records, were established early in Egypt and Mesopotamia. Daniel was enrolled in such a school for government officials after he was deported to Babylon (Dan. 1). While there is no record of such schools in Israel, a scribal class did develop there. Seraiah served as a scribe (secretary, NIV) for David (2 Sam. 8:17), and Baruch for Jeremiah (Jer. 36:27). There is even a hint in 1 Chr. 2:55 that scribes were grouped into "clans" and trained (or employed) at Jabez.

The priests and Levites had their responsibilities in Temple worship, but were sometimes called on to teach God's Law as well. In 686 B.C. Jehoshaphat sent out priests and Levites who "taught throughout Judah, taking with them the Book of the Law of the Lord; they went around to all the towns of Judah and taught the people."

The clearest evidence of a trained scribal class emerges after the Exile (about 460 B.C.). Ezra, who was from a priestly family, is introduced as "a teacher well versed in the Law of Moses," who "devoted himself to the study and observance of the Law of the Lord, and to teaching its decrees and laws in Israel" (Ezra 7:6,10). Later we find Ezra standing with a number of Levites, instructing the people in the Law. These educators "read from the Book of the Law of God, making it clear and giving the meaning so that the people could understand what was being read" (Neh. 8:8).

The resurgent scribal movement was closely connected with the development of the synagogue. Held captive in Babylon, separated from the Temple, the Jews developed a form of worship that centered on God's Law, rather than ritual sacrifice. Instruction became a crucial part of this worship. Thus the synagogue service opened with a recitation of Deut. 6:4-9 and various prayers, moved to a reading and explanation of a passage of the Law and a passage from the prophets, and closed with a benediction. The synagogue became a center for adult education and for the study of the Scriptures. It reflected the developing ideal that the laborer in Israel should be a scholar, and every scholar should work at a trade. To achieve that ideal, by the first century B.C. primary schools had been established throughout Judah where young boys learned to read, write, and memorize major portions of Scripture. Those who showed special promise went on to study the Law more thoroughly with some well-known rabbi (Acts 22:3).

There is another thread which may suggest a formal education. The OT often

speaks of bands of prophets, or "sons of the prophets" (1 Sam. 10:5; 19:20; 2 Ki. 2:3). Many take these phrases to indicate that some kind of training process was used to prepare individuals for the prophetic ministry.

By the first century, the process of training spiritual leaders was well defined. It involved a period of discipleship, during which the learner lived with and served his teacher, while learning all he could

from the teacher's instruction and from his way of life. This process clearly involved both formal and non-formal education. *See also* Disciple.

EDUCATION IN THE CHURCH

Members of the early church met weekly to praise, pray, and learn from traveling teachers and prophets, from local leaders, from the letters of the apostles, and from each other, but there is no indication in the NT that the church developed formal religious schooling. Leaders of the local church emerged from the congregation, identified by their character as well as their grasp of the truths of the faith. Those called to a wider itinerant ministry, like Titus and Timothy, were trained on the job, accompanying an apostle or other mature leader on his missions.

Early meetings of the church were no doubt similar to meetings in the synagogue. Yet there was a new spirit of involvement, as every believer exercised his or her gift to build up others. There was instruction. But far from being formal, the meetings of the church were vital, alive, filled with sharing and caring—the very essence of the non-formal approach to teaching and learning in community.

Perhaps the most important conclusion we can draw from this survey is that, in the teaching and learning of faith, we should not rely on formal teaching/learning alone. We do need the disciplined study which formal education provides. But for growth in Christ and in community, we need to communicate our faith in a framework which nurtures not only the understanding, but the whole person as well.

A student's wooden writing board (about 1450 B.C.) on which is inscribed in hieratic script a list of names of people of Keftiu (Crete and SW coast of Asia Minor). The training of scribes was an important endeavor in the ancient Near East.

Terra-cotta dish with Aramaic alphabet written twice, probably for practice by a pupil. This fragment was found in a small synagogue in the Herodium, a fortress southeast of Bethlehem built by Herod the Great.

327

Egypt The nation that developed in ancient times around the Nile River. The Nile River valley and delta cradled one of earth's most ancient and fascinating civilizations. That civilization, marked by great building and literary achievements, was concentrated in a green belt watered by the Nile, a strip that today constitutes only 4% of Egypt's land area but holds 96% of its population. This land, watered for millennia by annual flooding of the 4,000-mile-long Nile, produced abundant crops and supported a population large enough for Egyptian rulers to undertake great building programs and maintain large armies.

Between 3100 and 2686 B.C. Egypt's "two lands," its delta and upper river, were united under rulers of her first two dynasties. Egypt experienced alternating periods of strength and weakness, but remained one of the dominant powers of the ancient world.

ART AND ARCHITECTURE

Egypt's towering buildings and sculptured works of art have aroused the wonder of the world. Hundreds of years before Abraham was born, Egyptian pharaohs oversaw construction of the pyramids, intended to preserve their remains for eternity. One of these, the Great Pyramid, stood 492 feet (150 meters) high. It was 782 feet (238 meters) square at the base, and covered nearly 13 acres. Some 2,300,000 limestone blocks, weighing 2½ tons each, were used in its construction.

Along with the pyramids, the land contains silent recumbent figures (sphinxes) cut into living rock. Temples, composed of rows of massive pillars that are open to the air, also stand on the red sands. Inside the tombs, the works of long-dead artists capture scenes of daily life and work, and portray the souls of the dead facing Egypt's gods. Religious texts, written in the picture-language (hieroglyphics) of the ancients, offer advice and magical formulas that are supposed to guarantee acceptance in the afterlife.

The sheer size, age, and beauty of human works preserved over the millennia awaken awe and capture the imagination.

THE RELIGION OF EGYPT

Egypt was a land of many gods and religious concepts. Each locality seems to have emphasized its local deity. Because of these diverse deities, much syncretism was employed by civil and religious leaders to cement political unity.

Over the centuries, several emerged as primary gods: Re, the sun god; Ptah, the patron of craftsmen; Osiris, god of the underworld; and his wife, Isis. Yet there were dozens of others, many representing the powers of nature, such as fertility, illness, the rise and fall of the Nile. Often the gods of Egypt were represented as half-human, half-beast, such as Anubis who had the head of a jackal, and Sobek, with that of a crocodile. The pantheon of Egypt was further confused by the fact that over the centuries the gods and goddesses traded attributes and functions, making a religion so complex that no one today really understands ancient Egypt's faith.

Certain aspects of that faith do stand out, however. Everything in Egypt was considered the act of some god. This underlies God's statement in Ex. 12:12, that in the final plague "I will bring judgment on all the gods of Egypt." God's acts judged Egypt's gods, for they demonstrated that those gods were powerless before the Lord, the God of the Hebrew slaves.

Worship of the gods of Egypt was actually conducted by the priests. They alone, with royalty, had access to temples. There the idols representing Egypt's gods were awakened in the morning, bathed and dressed, fed their morning sacrifice, consulted, fed again, and finally put to bed. What a contrast between the dependent gods of Egypt and the powerful God of Scripture!

Because religious records and writings were maintained by the priests, we know much about the official religion of the elite, and almost nothing about popular faith. Yet thousands of recovered figures representing Osiris make it clear that the people, like their rulers, were obsessed with concern over what happened after death. The Egyptians were convinced that the body was the material abode of the soul, during life and after death as well. This explains the months-long embalming process used to preserve the bodies of royalty and the rich, and the tombs they so carefully prepared. It also explains the presence in these tombs of the many beautiful artifacts: jewels and golden plates, chariots and model ships and carved figures of servants, all intended for use by the soul in the world beyond. Again and again the skills of Egypt demonstrate how much material progress human beings can accomplish in this world—and how little they know of spiritual realities without revelation from God.

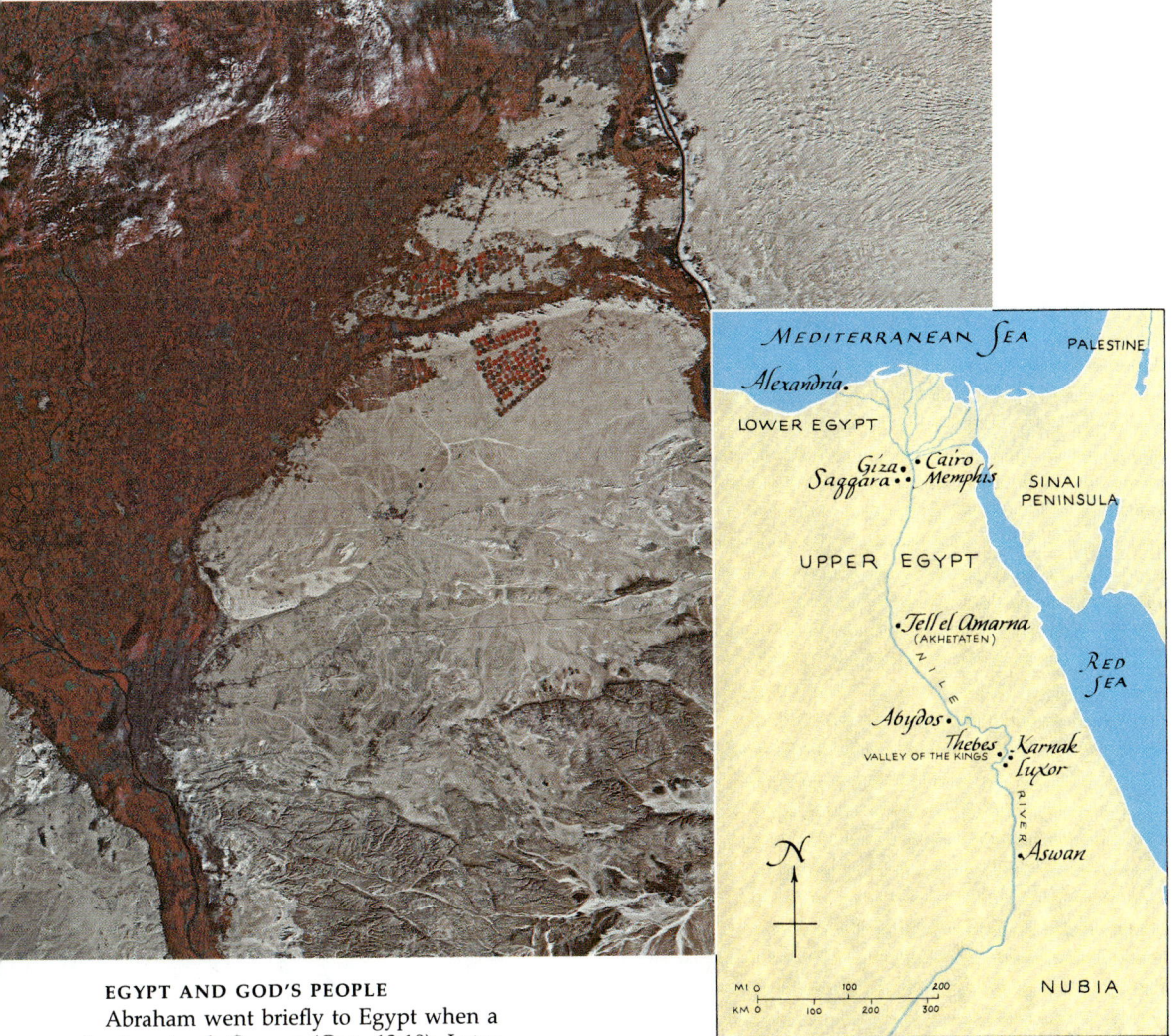

EGYPT AND GOD'S PEOPLE

Abraham went briefly to Egypt when a famine struck Canaan (Gen. 12:10). Later his great-grandson, Joseph, rose from slavery to become second-in-command of that great land (Gen. 39–50). The Book of Genesis contains many authentic details of life in Egypt and at the royal court. Joseph brought his family to Egypt, and settled them in the land of Goshen. For some 400 years the Israelites remained in Egypt, where they were at last enslaved. Yet in secure Egypt the Israelites multiplied rapidly (Ex. 1:6,7), something that could never have happened in Canaan, which at this time was divided into warring city-states. *See also* Genesis; Joseph.

When the time was right, God sent Moses to bring his people out of Egypt and lead them back to Canaan. Now a people of some two to three million, with 603,550 men over twenty (Num. 1:46), Israel had the population base necessary to establish a nation in Canaan. The Jews' deliverance from Egypt by God's intervention stands not only as a turning point in history, but also as a dramatic revelation of God. The God of the Bible, the God of Israel, is a redeeming God, who has power to act in this world, and who remains ever faithful to his people. *See also* Exodus.

In the centuries that followed, Egypt had a continuing impact on life in Israel. Solomon married one of Pharaoh's daughters. A later pharaoh harbored Jeroboam after his revolt against Solomon (1 Ki. 11:26-40), and invaded Judah after Solomon's death (1 Ki. 14:25,26; 2 Chr. 12:1-9). Later kings of Judah had skirmishes with Egypt. In 610–609 B.C., when the Egyptians hurried to assist an Assyrian army threatened with annihilation by the Babylonians, godly King Josiah of Judah fought them, and was killed.

Despite the anguish of years of oppression in Egypt, and the uneasy relationship between the Hebrew kingdoms and Egypt, the Bible remains surprisingly positive toward the Egyptian people. The prophets do warn that Egypt will be punished for her sins (Isa. 19; Jer. 46). But they

Satellite photo of Nile River delta, including modern-day Cairo, captures only a portion of the long, snake-like terrain of ancient Egypt that hugged the Nile's banks (map).

329

1. *Sculptor's study of a quail chick, the Egyptian hieroglyph for the w-sound (332–330 B.C.). The ancient Egyptians caught and pickled large numbers of quail during their southern migration, so the wandering Israelites would have been familiar with this food that God provided (Ex. 16:13).*

2. *Gold statue of the god of Thebes, Amon-Re. Before the reign of Amenhotep IV (also called Akhenaten, 1379–1361 B.C.), Egyptian worship of this god had gained prominence. But soon after the young pharaoh ascended the throne he began to worship only Aten, the divine sun disk (part of Amon's headpiece) as the only god, source of all life and love.*

3. *Gilded mummy mask of a woman (first millennium B.C.) reveals the earthly wealth and glory that once was Egypt.*

4. *The cross-like symbol of life, the ankh, was a popular amulet and decorative motif. This ankh dates to 750 B.C.*

5. *Three Egyptian deities (from left to right): Osiris, the judge of the dead, king of eternity; Isis, wife of Osiris, goddess of motherhood and fertility; Horus, falcon-headed god of the rising sun, son of Osiris and Isis.*

6. *This copy of an original tomb painting (1275 B.C.) beautifully details the sculptor Ipuy and his wife receiving offerings from his children for the afterlife.*

7. *Ancient Egyptians are known for monumental architecture, much of it for temples or "homes" for their gods. These ruins were once the temple of the crocodile-headed Sebek, god of fertility and creator of the world.*

8. *View across fruit trees and date palms to the famed pyramids of Giza, which proclaim the grandeur of three ancient pharaohs of the Old Kingdom. These were*

continued on page 332

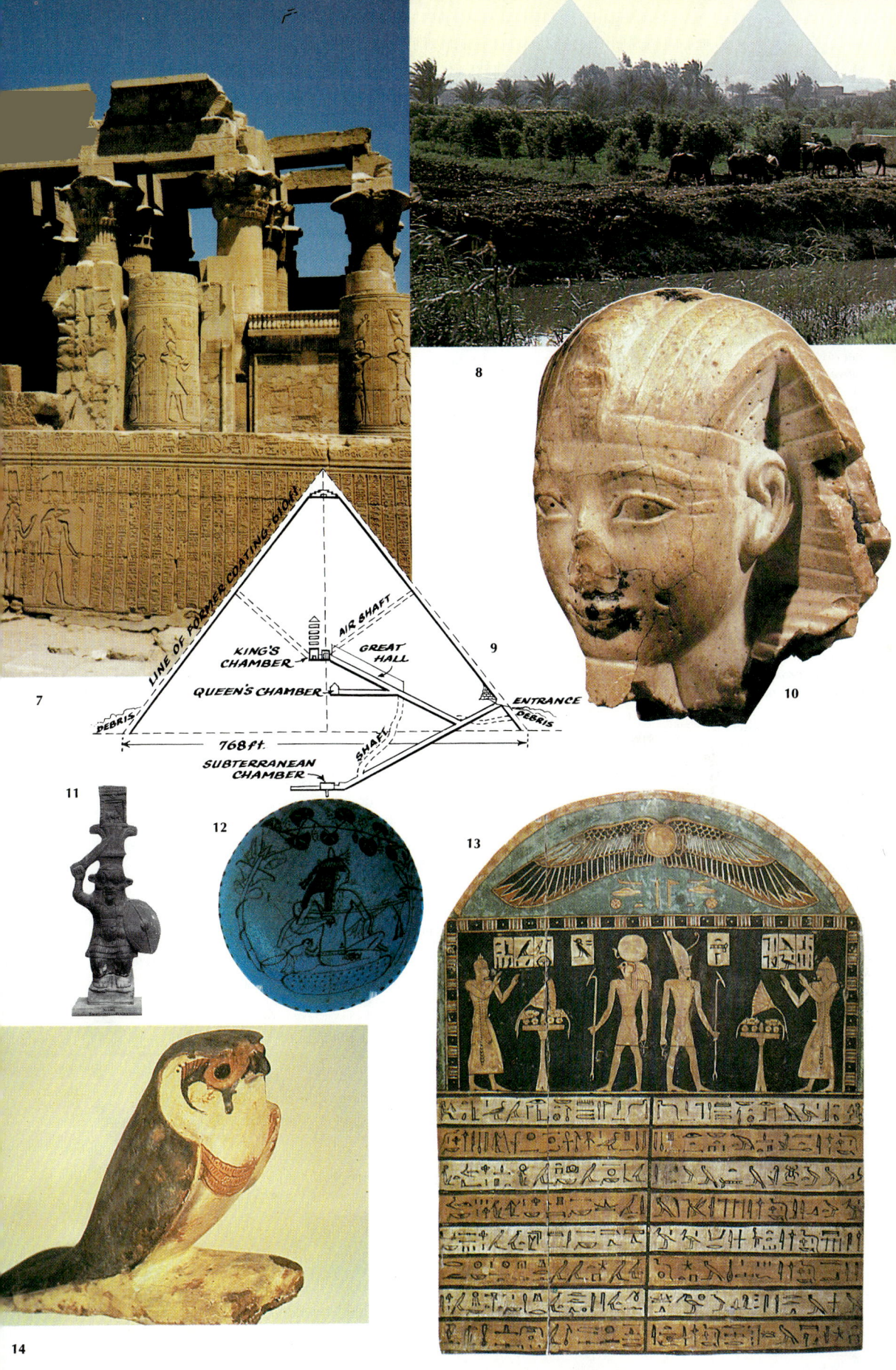

7

8

9

10

LINE OF FORMER COATING 810ft

AIR SHAFT

KING'S CHAMBER

GREAT HALL

QUEEN'S CHAMBER

ENTRANCE

DEBRIS

DEBRIS

768 ft.

SHAFT

SUBTERRANEAN CHAMBER

11

12

13

14

already hundreds of years old when Joseph first came to Egypt.
9. Cross-section of the pyramid of Pharaoh Cheops at Giza. The complex design of ancient Egyptian tombs often hindered archaeologists' explorations. Cheops's funeral chamber was walled in granite 137 feet (41.8 meters) above ground level.
10. This head of Amenhotep II (1436–1411 B.C.) is the earliest known portrait in glass. Its original blue color protrudes on the right side though 3,400 years of burial have turned it tan.
11. Household god Bes, a dwarf with lion's features. He protected the house from evil and, despite his grotesque appearance, also brought happiness and music to the home.
12. Earthenware bowl decorated with blue glaze (1300 B.C.). The woman is playing a long-necked, stringed instrument with a monkey at her side. The Egyptians excelled in arts of all kinds.
13. Wooden prayer stela depicting the priest Harsiese worshipping the gods Re-Horakhtu (left) and Atum (right).
14. Painted wooden falcon statuette from the 19th Dynasty (1293–1185 B.C.).

paint a picture of ultimate blessing and reconciliation. Isaiah predicts, "The Lord Almighty will bless them, saying, 'Blessed be Egypt my people, Assyria my handiwork, and Israel my inheritance' " (Isa. 19:25).

Egypt, River of The stream that marked the southwestern boundary of Judah (Num. 34:5; Josh. 15:4,47). Most scholars identify this boundary as a seasonal stream that flows through the Wadi el-Arish. In Gen. 15:18, the Lord promised to give Abraham's descendants the land between the Euphrates and the "flowing river" (*nahar*) of Egypt, which may possibly indicate not the wadi (*nahal*) but the easternmost branch of the Nile River itself (*but see* 1 Ki. 8:65; 2 Ki. 24:7; 2 Chr. 7:8).

El (1) The generic name for "god" in ancient Semitic languages; (2) the proper name of the chief god in the Canaanite pantheon; (3) in Scripture, a designation of the one true God.

By the time Israel was established in Palestine, Baal had replaced El as the primary god of the Canaanites.

In Scripture the word *El* is often combined with other nouns and adjectives to indicate the true God (*El Shaddai, El Olam*) in the same way that we capitalize God to distinguish the Lord from other gods. *El* probably comes from a root that means "to be strong." *See also* Baal; Elohim; God, Names of.

elder (1) An older person; (2) an ecclesiastical term designating a leader of the faith community in both OT and NT. In biblical times older persons were given special respect. Age and experience were associated with wisdom and understanding.

ELDERS IN THE OLD TESTAMENT
The Hebrew word for elder, *zaqen*, often serves as a political term, identifying a leader of tribes, of towns, or of the nation.
Elders led the Israelites during their

EGYPT'S HISTORY IN BRIEF

Date (B.C.)	Period	Features
4000–3100	Predynastic	Independent towns
3100–2686	Early Dynastic	"Two lands" united under Dynasties 1,2
2686–2180	Old Kingdom Dynasties 3–6	Effective administration; capital at Memphis; Major pyramids built; Religious literature
2180–2040	1st Intermediate	Division of "two lands" in political upheaval; Philosophical literature
2040–1786	Middle Kingdom Dynasties 11–13	Reunion of "two lands"; capital near Memphis; Strength and prosperity; Expanding trade; Much influence in Canaan; Story literature and flourishing arts and crafts; Hebrews move to Egypt
1786–1550	2nd Intermediate	Hyksos (Asiatics) take control of the delta region
1550–1070	New Kingdom Dynasties 18–20	Hyksos expelled; capital at Thebes; Palestine dominated; Moses born (1527? B.C.); Exodus (Amenhotep II Pharaoh); 150 years of waning power
1070–664	3rd Intermediate	Support for David's, Solomon's enemies; Shishak (Sheshonq) invades Judah (925 B.C.); Antagonistic to Assyria; Armies crushed by Assyria in 25th dynasty
664–525	Late Dynastic	Re-emerges as a power during 26th dynasty; Crushed by Babylon (605 B.C.); Promises but does not help Judah against Babylon
525–332	Persian	Persian Empire dominates
332–30	Ptolemaic Dynasty	Alexander the Great conquers; Alexander's general establishes dynasty
30–	Roman	Cleopatra dies; Egypt made part of Roman Empire

slavery in Egypt (Ex. 3:16) and, after the Exodus, they participated in leadership under Moses. Elders also functioned during the centuries when Israel was governed by judges and then kings. During these eras, local elders gathered at city gates to discuss public affairs (Deut. 21:19; 22:15), to witness business transactions (Ruth 4:9,11), and to try criminal cases (Deut. 19:12; 21:1-9). The Jewish people also had elders during the Babylonian Captivity (Jer. 29:1) and after the return to Palestine (Ezra 10:8).

While the specific duties of elders probably varied over the centuries, the institution itself seems to have been quite stable. Throughout Jewish history, responsibility for the local community rested on a group of men—predominantly senior citizens —who had acquired a reputation for good leadership and wise counsel. The concept of shared rather than individual leadership thus has deep roots in Scripture, as does the direct participation of the elders in the life of the community. Their decisions flowed not only from a knowledge of the Law, but also from an intimate knowledge of the persons who might be involved in disputes or charged with crimes.

ELDERS IN THE GOSPELS

When the Gospels speak of elders, they usually refer to members of the Sanhedrin, the council of 70 that was responsible for administering Jewish law. This supreme court of Israel had been granted administrative as well as judicial authority by the Roman government. In the phrase "the traditions of the elders," however, elder is not used politically, but religiously, and means those of earlier times whose interpretations of the Law had been accepted by contemporary Judaism.

ELDERS IN THE NEW TESTAMENT

The Christian church gradually grew distinct from Judaism, but it retained the principle of shared leadership by older, respected members of the community (Acts 14:23; 15:2-23; Tit. 1:5). Most scholars feel that the terms "elder" (*presbyteros*) and "bishop" (*episcopos,* "overseer") were just different names for the same office in the early church. (*Compare* Acts 20:17 with 20:28; and Tit. 1:5 with 1:7.)

The NT's teaching on elders makes two main points. First, elders are to be chosen on the basis of their personal and moral character. Demonstrated growth as a Christian enabled the elder to serve his community as an example of the Christian way of life (1 Tim. 3; Tit. 1). Elders were apparently selected by their congregations, and later confirmed by the apostles or their representatives (Acts 14:21-23; Tit. 1:5).

Second, the ministry of elders was essentially pastoral. Their ministry involved teaching and "directing the affairs of the church" (1 Tim. 5:17; 2 Tim. 2:2). Other passages which suggest a pastoral role for elders include Rom. 12:8; 1 Th. 5:12,13; 1 Pet. 5:1-4; Jas. 5:14. *See also* Leadership.

The 24 elders mentioned in Revelation seem to represent the believers of OT and NT eras.

elect Chosen, selected; an individual or group called by God to a particular ministry or relationship.

The OT speaks of the people of Israel as God's chosen ones (1 Chr. 16:13; Ps. 105:43). The term (Heb., *bahar*) presents a picture of one small group selected out of a field of many—and selected for a purpose. "Out of all the peoples on the face of the earth, the Lord has chosen you to be his treasured possession" (Deut. 14:2).

But God also chose smaller groups (the priests, Deut. 21:5) and individuals (Abraham, Gen. 18:19; Saul, 2 Sam. 21:6; David, 2 Chr. 6:6; Solomon, 1 Chr. 28:5). These "elect," or chosen ones, all bore a special responsibility to serve the God who chose them. Isaiah 42:1 speaks of the coming Messiah as a servant, "my chosen one in whom I delight."

The NT continues this theme, but takes it a step further. The Greek word, *eklektos,* means literally, "picked out." Out of the broad field of all Israel, God has picked out a few who will be faithful to him. Jesus said, "Many are invited, but few are chosen" (Mt. 22:14). Thus Paul mourns the Jews' futile attempts to earn God's favor through the Law, but says, "There is a remnant chosen by grace" (Rom. 11:5). This chosen remnant is the company of those who have trusted Christ. "What Israel sought so earnestly it did not obtain, but the elect did" (Rom. 11:7).

Later Paul speaks of the elect as those —Jews and Gentiles—who *will* trust Christ, but haven't yet. He tells Timothy he is willing to endure imprisonment and suffering "for the sake of the elect, that they too may obtain . . . salvation" (2 Tim. 2:10).

Subsequently, "the elect" became synonymous with "the Christians." Peter addressed his first Epistle to "God's elect, strangers in the world" (1 Pet. 1:1). Is he implying that being chosen by God results in a certain estrangement from the world? In the next chapter he assures his readers that Christ himself was "rejected by men but chosen by God and precious to him" and reminds them, "You are a chosen people" (1 Pet. 2:4,9). *See also* Chosen People; Election.

election The sovereign choice of God.

Because the Bible speaks so often of God's choices, theologians have sought to understand the relationship between human and divine choice. This study has often focused on the issue of individual salvation: Did God choose certain individuals to be saved and reject others? Do individuals have free choice when the Gospel is presented, or can only the elect respond with faith?

The answers to such questions have tended to divide Christians. Yet our theologies often fail to reflect an important feature of Scripture itself: the equal affirmation of truths which, on the surface, appear to be contradictory. What we need to ask is, "What, within the context of Scripture, is affirmed by the language of election?" And then we need to be careful not to go beyond what is affirmed as we construct our theologies.

" *You did not choose me, but I chose you and appointed you to go and bear fruit — fruit that will last.* "

JOHN 15:16

GOD'S FREEDOM TO CHOOSE

The Bible clearly teaches that God is free to act as he chooses. This is reflected in God's selection of Israel to be his people (Deut. 7:6; Isa. 14:1), and in his selection of Jerusalem as the site for the Temple (Deut. 12:5; 15:20; Josh. 9:27). We see God's freedom to choose in his selection of Abraham to receive his covenant promises (Gen. 12:1; 18:19). God also selected Moses to deliver his people (Ps. 106:23) and David to rule over them (1 Sam. 16:9-13).

Why did God choose Israel? The simple answer comes through again and again in Scripture: because he wanted to. God did not choose Israel because of any quality in them, "but it was because the Lord loved you and kept the oath he swore to your forefathers" (Deut. 7:7-9). Paul develops this theme in Romans 9. He acknowledges that God chose to favor Isaac rather than Ishmael, and Jacob rather than Esau, but argues that God's choice "does not . . . depend on man's desire or effort, but on God's mercy" (Rom. 9:16).

Such passages emphasize the fact that no human act or attitude influences God to act as he does. When God chooses to provide salvation, he does so freely (Eph. 1). When God selects individuals to play a role in salvation history, he is motivated only by his own love and grace.

Thus in Scripture, election is not evidence of favoritism, but proof of God's love and mercy. God's choices make no statement about the persons who are chosen. But his choices do tell us everything about his own loving heart, as he reaches out to touch the lives of persons who in no way merit his favor.

We need to understand all statements about election in this way. Jesus told his disciples, "You did not choose me, but I chose you . . . to go and bear fruit" (Jn. 15:16). By this, Jesus was not belittling the disciples' choice to follow him, but rather he was emphasizing the fact that God is the initiator. It was God who reached out in love to draw the disciples into a relationship with Christ which would make their lives fruitful.

HUMAN FREEDOM TO CHOOSE

God's freedom to choose and act is unlimited. Human beings, however, have freedom only within the context of options that God makes available.

In OT times, God's Law set forth a way of life which was pleasing to him. Israel was then challenged to choose (Deut. 30:19). As the recipients of divine revelation, God's people were freed by their knowledge to "reject the wrong and choose the right" (Isa. 7:15,16). Israel might choose to follow false gods as other nations did, but they also had the option of fearing the Lord, and living according to God's statutes (Ps. 119:173).

In this context, we see that God's choices did not limit the choices of human beings, but instead they provided his people with the opportunity to choose between good and evil.

In the same way, God's saving acts and the proclamation of the Gospel do not take away human freedom to choose, but expand it. The Gospel message expands the freedom of the unsaved by giving them a totally new choice. A human being can respond to the Gospel and be saved, or he can reject Christ and continue in his unsaved state.

FREEDOM TO CHOOSE

The Bible makes it clear that God is a free, sovereign person, whose decision to provide salvation is influenced only by his own love and grace. Even where the Bible speaks of election as God's choice of a specific individual, the choice is based solely on God's grace.

The Bible also affirms the human freedom to choose, but human choice carries a commensurate responsibility. Election by God does not rule out human choice; rather, God's revelation of salvation expands human freedom to choose by providing a real alternative between good and evil, between God and false gods. Thus divine election and human freedom are twin themes in Scripture, neither of which denies the other. In fact, most NT passages on election focus not on God's choice of individuals for salvation, but on his choice of the believing community (Eph. 1:1-11).

From first to last, salvation is a divine undertaking, motivated by unimaginable love and grace. God conceived the plan of salvation; his Son died to provide salvation; and his Spirit lives within us that we might experience salvation's benefits even now. *See also* Chosen People; Elect; Predestine; Salvation.

Eli [EE-lie; "exalted"]. The high priest who trained the child Samuel, 1125 B.C. **Sons:** Phinehas and Hophni. **Scripture:** 1 Sam. 1–4.

BACKGROUND

During the era of the judges, the tabernacle and the ark of the covenant were kept at Shiloh. Eli, an aged descendant of Aaron, served there as high priest. He is significant in sacred history, not for himself, but because he raised and trained Samuel, Israel's last and greatest judge. *See also* Ark of the Covenant; Tabernacle.

LEARNING FROM ELI'S LIFE

Although Eli was successful and sensitive in nurturing young Samuel (1 Sam. 3:8,9), Scripture portrays Eli as a weak person. His flaw lay in his attitude of indulgence toward his sons, whom Eli "honored" more than he honored God (2:29). The word translated "honor" comes

from a root word that means "to be heavy, or weighty." The idea is that Eli gave more weight to his sons' wishes than to God's. Eli knew his sons "slept with the women who served at the entrance to the Tent of Meeting" (1 Sam. 2:22). Eli also permitted them to violate the ritual rules of sacrifice (2:29). "His sons made themselves contemptible, and he failed to restrain them" (1 Sam. 3:13). Eli's two sons were subsequently killed in battle by the Philistines, who also captured the ark. When Eli heard the news, he fell from his chair and broke his neck.

The high priest Eli receives Samuel from Hannah in this medieval illuminated manuscript.

One principle illustrated by the story of Eli is stated in 1 Sam. 2:30: "Those who honor me will I honor, but those who despise me will be disdained." Failure to put God first has disastrous results.

Parents should find a warning in Eli's story. In that culture the father had authority even over grown children, but Eli was unwilling to exercise it. Parents must not neglect the godly discipline of their children. *See also* Discipline; Rebuke.

Elijah's whirlwind ride to heaven (2 Ki. 2:11,12) dramatically depicted in baroque style by Giovanni Piazzetta (1682–1754). Elisha, awestruck by the event, cries out "My father, my father!" (v. 12).

Elijah [ee-LI-juh; "my God is Yahweh"]. The most prominent prophet of his time, 875–850 B.C., Elijah confronted the evil King Ahab and Queen Jezebel when they tried to establish Baal worship as Israel's religion. **Scripture:** 1 Ki. 17–19,21; 2 Ki. 1,2.

BACKGROUND

Elijah lived at a critical time in Israel's history. Ahab, ruler of the Northern Kingdom, had married Jezebel, the daughter of Ethbaal, king of Sidon. She influenced Ahab to adopt the virulent form of Baal worship then practiced in Sidon. While Ahab's years were marked by political and military successes, they were also the focus of a fierce religious struggle between Baalism and the worship of Yahweh.

This struggle is summed up in three powerful stories. (1) Elijah finds Ahab and, in the name of the Lord, announces a terrible drought upon the land (1 Ki. 17). This judgment was a direct confrontation between the Lord and Baal, for Baal was a god of nature and fertility, whose worship was intended to ensure the rains needed to produce a good crop. *See also* Baal. (2) Three years later, Elijah confronts 450

prophets of Baal in a contest on Mount Carmel (1 Ki. 18). Fire falls from heaven and consumes a sacrifice in answer to Elijah's prayer. The people kill Baal's prophets, and the rains return at Elijah's announcement. (3) Elijah confronts Ahab, who has gladly taken possession of a vineyard he had coveted. Jezebel had arranged the death of the previous owner (1 Ki. 21). *See also* Ahab.

Interspersed among these three episodes are two very personal stories. (1) After the victory at Carmel, Elijah falls victim to fear and depression, and retreats into the wilderness to Mount Horeb (1 Ki. 19). There God speaks to him and meets his personal needs. (2) Elijah, his work done, is taken up directly into heaven while his companion and successor, Elisha, looks on (2 Ki. 2).

Note the prominent place given to miracles. Elijah is fed by ravens, multiplies a widow's food, brings the widow's son back to life, calls down fire from heaven, and restores the rains. Scripture reports only a few periods marked by multiple miracles: the age of the Exodus, the time of Elijah and Elisha, the years of Christ's

337

ministry on earth, and the early days of the Church. *See also* Miracle.

Malachi, the last of the minor prophets, looks toward history's end and promises, "I will send you the prophet Elijah before that great and dreadful day" (4:5). *See also* Day of the Lord. The prophet views future conditions as similar to those in Elijah's time, when the true faith was threatened by an aggressive counterfeit. Jesus indicated that John the Baptist was, in a sense, Elijah, preparing the way for God's salvation, as Malachi had predicted (Mt. 17:10-13). Some believe that Malachi's prophecy awaits even greater fulfillment, and that Elijah is one of the two witnesses spoken of in Rev. 11.

LEARNING FROM ELIJAH'S LIFE

Each of the Elijah stories is significant. First Kings 17 introduces the drought, but focuses on the way that God met the needs of Elijah himself. God cares for his own, even in times of national disaster.

First Kings 18 demonstrates Elijah's great faith in God. He was confident that God could and would act in response to prayer. Elijah's faith was honored, and the visible answer to his prayer convinced the people that "the Lord, he is God." We too can pray confidently. Answers to our prayers are still visible evidence of the reality of our God.

First Kings 19 is the most personal and revealing of the chapters, both of Elijah as a man and of his God. In spite of Elijah's victory at Mount Carmel, he became fearful and deeply depressed. The tender way in which God dealt with Elijah suggests positive ways that we can help those who experience depression. Note that (1) God supported Elijah with food, even when he ran away (1 Ki. 19:6-9). (2) God spoke to Elijah in a "gentle whisper" (19:12). (3) God gave Elijah a task to do, and (4) reassured him that there really were others faithful to the Lord (19:15-18). (5) God gave Elijah a companion, Elisha, to share his ministry (19:16).

Elisha [ee-LI-shuh; "God is salvation"]. The successor of Elijah and leading prophet in Israel, the Northern Kingdom, during the reigns of Joram, Jehu, Jehoahaz, and Joash (850–800 B.C.). **Father:** Shaphat of Abel Meholah. **Scripture:** 2 Ki. 1–9, 13.

BACKGROUND

The preceding quarter-century had been marked by open conflict between Baalism, introduced by Ahab and Jezebel, and the worship of the true God, promoted by

Elijah the prophet. After the death of Ahab and Jezebel, Jehu killed the devotees of the Baal cult. Elisha's 50-year ministry was one of healing, demonstrating God's concern both for individuals and for the nation.

The chapters on Elisha report 14 miracles, twice as many as are attributed to Elijah. They are (1) separating the Jordan waters (2 Ki. 2:14); (2) healing a spring (2:21); (3) cursing several jeering young men (2:24); (4) filling ditches with water to win a battle (3:15-26); (5) multiplying a widow's oil (4:1-7); (6) promising a pregnancy (4:14-17); (7) raising the Shunammite's son from the dead (4:32-37); (8) rendering poisonous stew harmless (4:38-41); (9) multiplying loaves (4:42-44); (10) healing Naaman's leprosy (5:1-19); (11) cursing Gehazi with leprosy (5:19-27); (12) making an iron axhead float (6:1-6); (13) blinding an Aramean (Syrian) army (6:8-23); (14) showing his servant an angelic army (6:15-17).

LEARNING FROM ELISHA'S LIFE

The stories of Elisha focus on the miracles he performed. These fall into two classes: works done on behalf of ordinary people, and miracles performed on behalf of the nation. *See also* Miracle.

The miracles for ordinary people demonstrate God's concern for individuals and thus prefigure the miracles of Jesus. Most of these were performed during the reign of Joram, a few short years after Ahab's death. God, through Elisha, was showing that he could forgive his people and could meet their needs.

Elisha's miracles for the nation were also vivid lessons. For the sake of Jehoshaphat of Judah, who had remained faithful to God, God gave Israel and Judah victory over Moab. Naaman, the general of the fierce Syrian army, was healed of leprosy to demonstrate that "there is a prophet in Israel" (2 Ki. 5:8). Elisha provided his king with information about Syrian army movements, and even led a "blinded" enemy force into Samaria, Israel's capital city, where they were captured (2 Ki. 6). Each of these miracles served to demonstrate

Aerial view of Dothan, located in Samaria 13 miles north of Shechem. A band of Syrians besieged Elisha here (2 Ki. 6:8-23).

Reconstructed room from the kings' period contains storage jars. In Dothan archaeologists found several thousand of these pottery vessels, the kind the widow in 2 Ki. 4 borrowed and filled with oil at Elisha's command.

God's ability to protect his people, if only Israel would rely on him.

Elisha's ministry thus contrasts strikingly with that of Elijah. Elijah confronted. He called for a punishing drought and called fire down on Ahaziah's soldiers (2 Ki. 1). Elisha comforted. He met the needs of ordinary people and protected his nation.

God's grace, like his discipline, is intended to draw us toward faith.

Elohim A general Hebrew term for God, found over 2,500 times in the OT. Elohim is plural in form, but when indicating the God of the Bible, it is used with singular verbs and adjectives. Most linguists believe the plural indicates majesty or magnitude. Some suggest it implies the trinity of the Bible's one God.

When the word refers to pagan gods (Gen. 35:2; Ex. 18:11), it is plural in sense. It is used also in referring to angels and judges as God's representatives (Ps. 8:5; Ex. 21:6; 1 Sam. 2:25).

There is no agreement on the root from which Elohim is derived. One possible root emphasizes "strength," the other "being in front," and thus preeminent.

Elohim, nevertheless, remains a general name in the sense that it stands for God as Creator and supreme being. In contrast, God's personal name, Yahweh, is associated with his saving work and covenant relationship with his people. *See also* El; Names of God; Yahweh.

Eloi, Eloi, lama sabachthani The cry of Jesus from the cross, Aramaic for "My God, my God, why have you forsaken me?" (Mt. 27:46). Jesus was quoting Ps. 22:1, the first verse of a messianic psalm associated with the suffering of God's Anointed One.

The cry is theologically significant. It captures that timeless moment when the Son of God "became sin" for lost humanity (2 Cor. 5:21); the perfect fellowship of the persons of the Godhead was severed as the Holy Father turned away from the Son. The transaction that took place in that moment is perhaps the central mystery of Christian faith.

embalm Treatment of a dead body to preserve it from decay. This process was used in Egypt to preserve the bodies of important persons. After organs were removed from the body, the corpse was dehydrated by a complicated process that took up to 70 days. This treatment, intended to pre-

serve the body forever, reflects the Egyptian belief that existence of the soul depended on existence of the body.

The Jewish people never attempted to preserve the body. The Bible reports the embalming of only Jacob (Gen. 50:2,3) and Joseph (Gen. 50:26), who both died in Egypt. *See also* Burial.

embroider To ornament by appliqueing or weaving in colored threads, or by weaving designs into cloth. Ornamented clothing was valued in Mesopotamia and Egypt, even before Abraham's time. The Bible indicates a similar appreciation for embroidered cloth. The vestments of the high priest and the curtains of the tabernacle were decorated with fine embroidery (Ex. 26,28,29). Embroidered goods were valued as spoils of war (Jdg. 5:30) and trade goods (Ezek. 27:16,24).

Joseph's "coat of many colors" is appropriately rendered in the NIV as a "richly ornamented robe" (Gen. 37:23).

Embroidery probably employed a variety of techniques. It certainly involved

Above: Mummy of an Egyptian priestess at Thebes (about 1050 B.C.). In the Bible only Jacob and Joseph are reported to have been embalmed (Gen. 50:2,3,26). Top: Drawing of a mummified dog. Animals symbolized certain gods. Thousands of animal mummies —ibis, cats, fish, snakes, cattle, rams, crocodiles, and hawks—have been found in Egyptian tombs.

needlework, in which colored threads were worked into cloth (Ex. 26:36; 27:16; 28:39). In some garments even gold thread was used (Ex. 39:3; Ps. 45:13). *See also* Dye.

Different patterns woven into cloth may also have been considered embroidery. An example is Aaron's "checkered work" ["woven tunic," NIV] (Ex. 28:4). Additional techniques may be suggested in references to "cunning work" (KJV) or "skilled work" (Ex. 26:1,31 RSV).

Dyed wool embroidery in a fine design on linen cloth found in southern Egypt. Joseph's "multicolored coat" may well instead have been heavily embroidered (Gen. 37:23).

Emerald

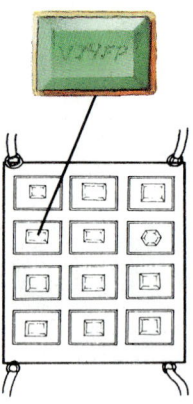

emerald A green gemstone. The emeralds of the ancient Middle East were mined in Egypt near the Red Sea.

The emerald was the third stone in the second row of gems in the breastpiece of the high priest (Ex. 28:18). It will also decorate one of the foundations of God's new Jerusalem (Rev. 21:19). *See also* Breastpiece; Jerusalem, New.

emerods (KJV) Tumors or boils. In 1 Sam. 5,6, God afflicted the Philistines with these tumors "in their secret parts" (5:9, KJV). Thus they were probably hemorrhoids.

The Hebrew word for the emerald, bareket, means "glittering," which aptly describes the stone's beauty. As today, emeralds were rare and extremely precious in ancient times.

Alexander the Great, here sculpted in stone (second century B.C.), initiated the policy of Hellenization, which had a pervasive influence on the culture of New Testament times.

emperor Ruler of an empire; in Scripture, especially Rome. Direct references to the Roman emperor occur in Acts 25:21,25. In 1 Pet. 2:13,17, the Greek has *basileus*, "king." Peter uses it to mean simply any supreme human ruler; in NT times this was the emperor. Peter calls on Christians to submit to human authorities "for it is God's will that by doing good you should silence the ignorant talk of foolish men" (1 Pet. 2:15). *See also* Caesar; King; Roman Empire.

enchantment (KJV) Any occult or magic practice intended to influence events or the gods by casting spells. Several Hebrew words are translated "enchantment" or "enchanter" in English versions. These include words for astrology, sorcery, and exorcism.

Scripture clearly forbids every occult practice (Deut. 18:9-13). God's people must rely on God alone for guidance. He will supervise the events of their lives.

Numbers 23 suggests that God will protect those who are in covenant relationship with him against the practice of magic. The passage tells of Balak, king of Moab, who hired the seer Balaam to curse Israel. But that pagan practitioner of the occult was led instead to announce,

God is not a man, that he should lie,
nor a son of man, that he should
change his mind.
Does he speak and then not act?
Does he promise and not fulfill?
I have received a command to bless;
he has blessed, and I cannot change
it. . . .
The Lord their God is with them;
the shout of the King is among them. . . .
There is no sorcery against Jacob,
no divination against Israel.
(Num. 23:19-21,23)

God was, and is, mightier than any occult power. *See also* Magic.

enemy A hostile person, nation, or force. The biblical words for "enemy" are strong and active. They portray a hostility and hatred expressed in acts intended to harm.

OLD TESTAMENT

In the OT, the Hebrew words for enemy often refer to the national enemies of Israel. At other times, hostile individuals are referred to as enemies, as in Ex. 23:4,5, where God's people are told, "If you come across your enemy's ox or donkey wandering off, be sure to take it back to him. If you see the donkey of someone who hates you fallen down under its load, do not leave it there; be sure you help him with it."

While the psalmist called for divine judgment on political and national enemies (Ps. 137:8,9), the OT clearly agrees with the NT that the righteous should treat personal enemies graciously. Saul acknowledged that David was righteous for returning good for evil (1 Sam. 24:17-19). And Proverbs 25:21 says,

If your enemy is hungry, give him food to
eat;
if he is thirsty, give him water to drink.
In doing this, you will heap burning coals on
his head,
and the Lord will reward you.

NEW TESTAMENT

The NT takes a more personal approach. Paul describes the one-sided enmity of the unsaved toward God: "When we were God's enemies, we were reconciled to him through the death of his Son" (Rom. 5:10;

340

see Phil. 3:18; Col. 1:21). In this, God himself provides the supreme example of the way of life Christ calls for in his Sermon on the Mount: "Love your enemies and pray for those who persecute you" (Mt. 5:43,44).

Romans 8:7 tells us that "the sinful mind [lit., 'the mind-set of the flesh'] is hostile to God. It does not submit to God's law, nor can it do so." Yet through personal relationship with Christ we can experience a change not only in our attitude toward God but also in our attitude toward other human beings. Aware of God's love for us, we can extend love even to those who choose to be our enemies.

engrave To cut letters or designs in hard materials such as wood, clay, metal, or stone. Jeremiah cries out to his people, "Judah's sin is engraved with an iron tool, inscribed with a flint [possibly diamond] point" (Jer. 17:1). But elsewhere the Lord says he cannot forget his people: "See, I have engraved you on the palms of my hands" (Isa. 49:16).

The OT refers often to engraving, using different Hebrew words depending on the material engraved. The words "Holy to the Lord" were engraved on the golden plate worn on the turban of Israel's high priest (Ex. 28:36), and the names of the tribes of Israel were engraved on the various gemstones he wore on his ephod (Ex. 28:9). Designs were engraved on the inner walls of the Temple (1 Ki. 6:29), and on the bronze stands used in Temple worship (1 Ki. 7:29).

One of the most common and important uses of engraving was in making the personal seals of officials and individuals, with which they authenticated decrees, letters, or business papers (Ex. 28:11).

Archaeology has revealed many engraved or carved objects from biblical times. These include signet rings, ivory carvings and inlay work, inscriptions on metal and pottery, carvings on stone monuments, etc. According to Ex. 31:1-9 and 35:30-35, at the time of the Exodus, Bezalel and Oholiab were skilled craftsmen who trained other Israelites and supervised the work on the tabernacle and priestly garments. They were probably trained in Egypt, where engraving skills were highly developed.

Tools used by engravers in later biblical times included steel chisels and diamond-tipped drill bits attached to a stick which was spun by the back-and-forth motion of a bow.

The bow drill this carpenter uses in this wall painting differs from an engraving drill only in the type of bit employed. Tomb of Rekhmira (1475 B.C.).

In a NT reference to engraving, Paul emphasizes the permanence of God's work in Christians. The words that were once engraved on tablets of stone are being carved into our very hearts by his Holy Spirit, so that our lives will be a letter from God, easily read by all (2 Cor. 3:1-3).

Enoch, Book of One of a number of religious writings that appeared in Judaism in the centuries before and after Christ. Although these popular writings were not regarded as authoritative Scripture, they were read for their many valuable spiritual insights.

One of the most popular of these works, the Book of Enoch, was actually a lengthy compilation of various religious writings. The contents were ascribed to Enoch, perhaps because the Jews, noting that the Enoch of Genesis had been taken directly into heaven, felt he must have had special knowledge of divine secrets.

It is likely that Jude 14,15 either quotes from or paraphrases a familiar passage from this popular work, much as Paul quoted a well-known pagan poet in his sermon on Mars Hill (Acts 17:28). In each case, an insight from a non-inspired source is woven into Scripture and validated as true. *See also* Apocalyptic Literature; Apocrypha.

Stone seal (8th century B.C.) engraved with a man reaping with a sickle. The task of engraving seals was an important trade in biblical times.

envoy [ON-voy]. The personal representative of a ruler, sent on a special mission; an ambassador. Paul uses the image to describe not just the mission of the apostles, but also the mission of every believer.

As Christ's envoy, each believer is entrusted by God with the Gospel message of reconciliation. When we, as God's personal representatives, share Christ with others, it is "as though God were making his appeal through us" (2 Cor. 5:19,20). *See also* Ambassador.

Ephesians, Book of The Epistle to the Ephesians was written by the apostle Paul from Rome during his first imprisonment, probably in A.D. 62–63. Christ is the focus of this letter, but its theme is the Church of Christ. Ephesians presents Jesus as a living leader, the powerful head of his Church. Christ's people are bonded together as his Body, a living organism which is both a family and a holy temple.

BACKGROUND

Ephesus lay just four miles from the Aegean Sea, which was accessed by an inland harbor off the nearby Caÿster River. Besides being ideally situated for sea trade, Ephesus was connected by highways to all the important trade routes. In Paul's day it was the fourth largest city in the Empire, with a population between 200,000 and 500,000. The Roman governor of Asia resided in Ephesus. A large colony of Jews also made their home there. Ephesus was a wealthy city, with a 24,000-seat theater carved into one of its rock hillsides. But the city's real claim to fame, and the mainstay of its economy, was the magnificent temple of Artemis (Diana, KJV).

This temple, four times the size of the Parthenon in Athens, was a cultic center visited by pilgrims from all over the Mediterranean world. The temple itself was 150 feet (46 meters) wide and 377 feet (115 meters) long, with 117 columns 60 feet (18 meters) tall. It housed the figure of Artemis, a local fertility deity, which some believe was cast from a meteorite (Acts 19:35).

The temple's beauty was legendary, as was its wealth. The temple treasury served Asia as a bank, to which even kings applied for massive loans. Hundreds of tradesmen—like the silversmiths mentioned in Acts 19 who made souvenir images for tourists, as well as innkeepers and restaurateurs—prospered because of the multitudes who flocked to Ephesus each year to visit the temple.

Though institutional religion was a great success in Ephesus and a source of both pride and profit, it failed to meet the deepest needs of the population. Acts 19:13-20 suggests that many Ephesians were involved in sorcery and witchcraft, and that demons were active in this center of pagan faith.

Paul spent over two years in Ephesus (Acts 19:8,10), and his ministry had a tremendous impact. Practitioners of magic burned their books, and idol worshipers

This silver denarius from the reign of Emperor Hadrian (A.D. 117–138) bears the statue of Artemis (Diana) enshrined within her huge temple, the Artemision, in Ephesus. The ritual worship of this goddess enhanced the prosperity of Ephesus for some 500 years.

The great Hellenistic theater at Ephesus, where the mob scene of Acts 19 took place. The theater measures almost 500 feet (152.5 meters) in diameter and could hold 25,000 people—only 10 percent of the city's population at its zenith under the Romans.

threw away their idols. In fact, so many people turned to Christ that the silversmiths' business was threatened (Acts 19:23-28). The vibrant, living church that Paul founded contrasted sharply with the dead, sterile stones forming the magnificent temple of the Ephesian religion.

AUTHORSHIP

Some dispute Paul's authorship of this letter on the basis of literary style or content. They point to the use of unusual words and sentences that are longer than those typically found in Paul's letters. The letter, then, could have been written by a disciple of Paul who expressed the teachings of the apostle. Questions have also been raised about why so few personal references are included, since Paul knew the Ephesians so intimately. Others point to theological distinctions that separate the letter from undisputed Pauline epistles. However, the book specifically states Pauline authorship (1:1; 3:1), its teachings are consistent with the material in Paul's other letters, and the early church universally accepted this letter as genuine.

THEOLOGICAL CONTRIBUTIONS

In his letter to the Ephesians, the apostle Paul presents the Bible's clearest picture of the Church as a living organism.

To describe the Church, Paul uses three analogies: (1) The Church is a body, of which Christ is the living Head. As a body, members of the Church draw strength from the Head, who has been exalted above every spiritual power (Eph. 1:20-22; 2:14-18; 4:1-6). *See also* Body; Church; Head.

(2) The Church is also a holy temple, built of living stones by the Holy Spirit. As such, we worship God and honor him by living holy lives (Eph. 2:19-22). *See also* Holy; Temple.

(3) The Church is a family, an identity derived from each believer's relationship with God as Father. As Christians grow in

View down the Street of the Kuretes in Ephesus. Both sides are lined with inscribed statue bases and excavated structures dating to the first and second centuries A.D. This street boasted three official temples for emperor worship, which earned Ephesus the title neokoros ("temple warden," Acts 19:35) three times over. Paul had friends among the Asiarchs (Acts 19:31), city officials whose duties included overseeing these imperial temples.

343

family love, we experience together the love of Christ, and are filled with God's fullness (Eph. 3:14-19). *See also* Family.

Ephesians emphasizes other vital truths as well. (1) It identifies the role of each person of the Godhead in bringing us salvation (Eph. 1:3-14). (2) It enhances our understanding of God's grace by describing the depths of mankind's lost condition (2:1-10). (3) It lays the basis for reconciliation of hostilities based on racial or cultural differences (2:11-22). (4) It affirms the spiritual union experienced by all Christians, and calls for mutual involvement in ministry to one another (4:1-16). (5) It explains the husband's true role as "head" of the wife by pointing out how Christ, the Head of the Church, gave himself up that his "bride" might reach her full potential (5:22-33). (6) It describes the "armor of God," which enables Christians to withstand spiritual enemies (Eph. 6:10-18).

With all this, the Book of Ephesians is eminently practical, for it shows Christians how to "live a life of love, just as Christ loved us and gave himself up for us" (4:17–6:9).

MASTERY KEYS

The book focuses our attention on the Church as people in relationship with Jesus and with each other. In view of this, underline words or phrases that teach who Christ is and what relationship with him means. Next, circle words or passages that speak of relationships among Christians. From this study, describe an "ideal" local church. Consider: what can you do to help draw your own congregation nearer to the ideal?

SPECIAL FEATURES

The Book of Ephesians incorporates two prayers of Paul for this church (Eph. 1:15-19; 3:14-19). These prayers might serve as model prayers for ourselves and others. The book also includes one of Scripture's most beautiful benedictions (Eph. 3:20,21).

ephod A sleeveless vest, worn by priests when worshiping God. Ordinary priests wore ephods of linen (1 Sam. 22:18). Even David, though not a priest, wore an ephod when bringing the ark of the covenant into Jerusalem (1 Chr. 15:27).

The ephod of the high priest was highly ornamented (Ex. 28), embroidered with gold, scarlet, purple, and blue threads. The ephod was fastened at the waist with a woven belt, or girdle, and was connected at the top by shoulder pieces. These shoulder pieces were set with two onyx stones, engraved with the names of the tribes of Israel. A gem-studded breastpiece was attached by gold rings set in the high priest's ephod. *See also* Breastpiece.

While each element of the high priest's vestments may have had symbolic mean-

---

EPHESIANS: A READING AND STUDY GUIDE

Chapter	Content Summary	Related Articles
1	Each person of the Godhead works together to provide salvation. Paul prays that his readers might realize how important they are to God and perceive the power that God has made available to us through the resurrected Christ.	Trinity Salvation Predestine Resurrection
2	God has formed his Church from those who were spiritually dead. He has given them life and bonded them together in a single body, making peace by the death of his Son.	Death Grace Unity
3	The Church in which Jew and Gentile are bonded together is a mystery hidden in past times, but now revealed. Paul prays that Christ's people will live together in love, for in this way they will experience Christ's love.	Mystery Love Family Father
4	The Church, as a unified body, grows as its members minister to one another. For such ministry, believers must commit themselves to put off the "old self" and live lives of love and holiness together.	Spiritual Gifts Leader Holy
5	The life of love and holiness is further described, with exhortations to encourage each other in faith. The relationship of husbands to wives is to be modeled on the relationship between Christ and the Church.	Light Church Husband Submission
6	Believers are to submit to human authorities, even as those in authority are responsible to God. God has provided spiritual armor to enable us to live victorious Christian lives.	Authority Slave Armor of God

ing, the splendor of his apparel indicates his significance in the religion of Israel and foreshadows, as well, the ministry of Jesus, who serves as the believer's high priest. *See also* High Priest.

Epicurean A Greek philosophic school mentioned only in Acts 17:18. The Epicureans took their name from Epicurus, who lived and taught in Athens 342–271 B.C. According to Epicurus, the goal of human existence was to find happiness, which he identified with pleasure. But Epicurus defined pleasure broadly. "By pleasure we mean the absence of pain in the body and trouble in the soul." Intellectual pleasures were superior to sensual pleasures. Since over-indulgence in fleshly pleasures results in pain (e.g., drunkenness produces a hangover), Epicurus encouraged a "golden mean"—a balanced life in which excesses were avoided by means of reasoned discrimination. Contentment was found in limiting desires and securing a peace that could be maintained regardless of circumstances.

Epicurus's view of pleasure was based on a mechanistic and materialistic view of the universe. He believed that only matter (atoms) and space (void) existed eternally and that the universe was created through motion. Thus all life ended with the dissolution of the body. The immortal gods who existed were of a finer material nature and lived in a state of tranquility and indifference to this world.

Epicureanism was still popular in the first century. When Paul preached in Athens, he flew in the face of popular beliefs, presenting a God who not only created the world, but intervened in history by becoming a man, dying, and rising from death. Paul pointedly referred to Christ's bodily resurrection (not dissolution) and warned that Christ would return to judge humanity by his standard of justice (not human pleasure).

epistle A written message, a letter. Twenty-one of the 27 books of the New Testament are identified as epistles: the Pauline Epistles—Romans; 1,2 Corinthians; Galatians; Ephesians; Philippians; Colossians; 1,2 Thessalonians; 1,2 Timothy; Titus; Philemon—and the General Epistles (so-called because they are addressed to no specific church)—Hebrews; James; 1,2 Peter; 1,2,3 John; Jude.

In NT times, letters were written on papyrus or leather parchment, which was then rolled, tied, and sealed. Private letters, like those of the NT, were carried by

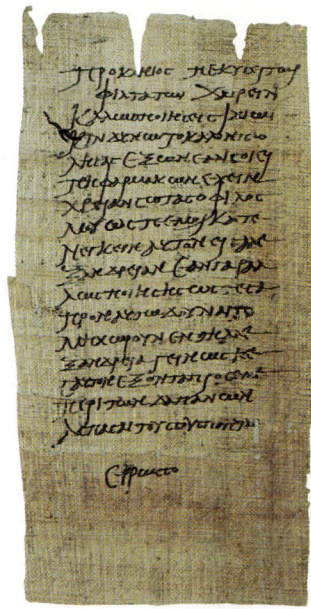

In this papyrus letter written in semicursive Greek script, an Alexandrian, Procleius, asks a man named Percusis to send some medicine by way of his friend Sotas. As with the NT Epistles of the same era, the sender's name begins rather than ends the letter, as is customary today.

private persons. Only official documents were carried by the Roman postal service.

Letters were often dictated to a secretary. The author would then add a few words in his own handwriting to authenticate the epistle as genuine (Gal. 6:11).

First-century epistles typically followed the form observed in NT letters. An introductory greeting named the sender and recipient and expressed thanksgiving. Then followed the body, which communicated the purpose of the letter. The letter ended with a farewell, accompanied by various closing remarks.

In the Greek and Roman world, letters became more than personal communication. They sometimes took on a high literary quality and were reproduced and distributed. Scholars have debated whether the NT Epistles were intended as personal letters or more literary works. The truth probably lies between the two.

Some NT Epistles are very personal, such as 1,2 Timothy, Philemon, Galatians, and Philippians. Others, like Hebrews, Ephesians, and Colossians, are less personal and seem more like theological works or sermons. But, with the possible exception of Philemon and 3 John, all the NT Epistles seem to have been written for public use of some kind.

Paul specifically asked the Colossians to share their Epistle with the Laodiceans (Col. 4:16). In this way churches probably collected copies of the various epistles. Peter's mention of Paul's letters among "the other Scriptures" (2 Pet. 3:15,16) indicates that his Epistles were recognized as Scripture by that time. *See also* Canon; Writing.

Esau had reason to be angry, his bitterness turned into contempt for God. This is seen in his plot to kill Jacob as soon as Isaac died (Gen. 27:41).

Jacob fled to Paddan Aram. When he returned some 20 years later, Esau was no longer angry. The text suggests why. Esau politely rejected Jacob's gifts of flocks and herds, saying, "I already have plenty" (Gen. 33:9). Esau had been angry because he feared that Jacob's theft of the blessing would impoverish him. But God had blessed him with riches and so Esau was completely satisfied.

STUDYING THE LIFE OF ESAU

Esau is typical of all materialists who can see no further than this present world and find the meaning of life in their possessions. Esau did not value God's promise because he had little regard for a god he could not touch or see. He married idolatrous Gentiles regardless of his family's covenant relationship with Yahweh (Gen. 21:46). Esau is like many people today who ignore spiritual concerns in their pursuit of material gain.

Malachi 1:3 provides a divine commentary: the Lord says, "I have loved Jacob, but Esau I have hated." This phrase reflects an ancient inheritance formula. The claim of Jacob to God's covenant promises is confirmed (he is "loved"), while any claim of Esau's is decisively rejected (he is "hated"). A materialistic attitude which rejects God must lead, in principle, to divine rejection.

Note that God gave Esau the riches he yearned for, but according to Ps. 73, this is not an unmixed blessing! Materialists are "on slippery ground." Possessing everything they desire, materialists never sense their need for God until "suddenly they are destroyed" (Ps. 73:18-20).

In Rom. 9:10-13, Paul refers to the birth of Esau and Jacob. Before the boys were born, God told Rebekah that the older twin, Esau, would serve the younger. This demonstrates the freedom of God to choose, for his announcement came before they "had done anything good or bad." Thus, God's choice does not depend on human works, but is a totally free exercise of his grace. *See also* Election.

Illustration from a 16th-century Hebrew commentary tells the story: Esau hunts game for his stew while Rebekah dresses Jacob in hairy clothing in order to deceive Isaac (Gen. 27).

Esau [EE-saw; "hairy"]. The older twin brother of Jacob, who "despised his birthright" and traded away the Abrahamic covenant for a bowl of stew, about 2000–1900 B.C. **Father:** Isaac. **Mother:** Rebekah. His descendants, through his six wives, later became known as the Edomites. **Scripture:** Gen. 25–27,36. *See also* Edom.

BACKGROUND

In patriarchal times the eldest son became head of the family upon the death of the father and received at least twice the inheritance of any other child. Esau, as the oldest son in the line of Abraham and Isaac, possessed the "birthright" and, in the normal course of events, would have inherited not only the bulk of his father Isaac's wealth, but also the covenant promises given to Abraham by God.

Genesis 25 pictures Esau as a hearty outdoorsman, a man's man, who took delight in the good things of this world. But Esau was unconcerned about spiritual fulfillment—so unconcerned that one day, when he was especially hungry, he traded his birthright to his brother Jacob for a bowl of stew. The OT says, "So Esau despised [literally, showed contempt for] his birthright." *See also* Despise.

Later, Esau was furious when his brother and his mother conspired to deceive his aged father, Isaac, and "steal" the blessing which Isaac had intended to give his older son (Gen. 27). Although

Essenes A strict sect of Judaism that existed from the middle of the second century B.C. until the destruction of Jerusalem by the Romans in A.D. 70. The Essenes insisted on strict observance of OT Law, which they expanded and interpreted in their own commentaries. Some of this

346

material was included in the Dead Sea
Scrolls, documents that probably came
from the library of an Essene community
at Qumran. *See also* Dead Sea Scrolls.

Both Philo and Josephus describe the
Essenes as a sect, with adherents in most
towns of Judea, whose members lived
frugally and practiced communal ownership of property. While they did not condemn marriage, many Essenes practiced
celibacy and maintained their sect by
adopting very young children, although
they limited their contacts with those outside the brotherhood.

The Essenes looked to the future and
expected an apocalyptic battle between
good and evil. There is also evidence of
messianic expectations in their writings.
While some have suggested that Jesus or
John the Baptist were Essenes, the extreme
strictness of the sect in ritual matters, and
their isolationism make this extremely unlikely.

Esther, Book of The book that tells the
dramatic story of a plot to exterminate the
Jewish people during the Persian period,
and of their deliverance through the providential marriage of a young Jewish orphan to the king of Persia. This
deliverance is still celebrated by Jews in
the Feast of Purim.

*Above: A 19th-century painting of
the story of Esther and Mordecai.*

*Below: Aerial view of
the excavations at
Khirbet Qumran near
the Dead Sea. These
buildings are
believed to have
been inhabited by an
Essene community.
The monastery-like
enclosure reflects the
sect's ascetic "Order
of Community,"
which governed
members' lives.*

Archaeologists have not yet found secular references to the book's major characters—Vashti, Esther, Mordecai, and Haman—though the Persian name Mardukaya was prominent in this period. This Hebrew story is rich in authentic details about practices in the Persian court and it contains many Persian names and loan words. Most scholars agree that the book was written during or shortly after the reign of Xerxes, the "Ahasuerus" of the KJV and other versions. The author of the book is not known.

HISTORICAL BACKGROUND

The Persian ruler of Esther is usually identified as Xerxes (486–465 B.C.). The time gap between the banquet in Xerxes' third year (1:3) and Esther's introduction into his harem in his seventh year (2:16) is explained by the fact that Xerxes had led an unsuccessful invasion of Greece (483–480 B.C.). The family of Mordecai, the cousin who raised Esther, had been brought to Mesopotamia about a hundred years earlier, after the Babylonians had invaded Judah and taken her people captive (2:5,6). Although some Jews had returned to Judah in the time of Cyrus (536 B.C.), many stayed in Babylon and other large cities of Mesopotamia. *See also* Captivity.

THEOLOGICAL CONTRIBUTIONS

Although the Book of Esther is the only book in Scripture that contains no mention of God, it certainly shows God at work. (1) God does not need to perform miracles to deliver his people, but can work through circumstances. Many "coincidences" worked together to thwart the plot of Haman, the king's most esteemed prince, against the Jewish people. (2) Haman's hatred of the Jews, and his ultimate downfall, illustrate God's faithfulness to the covenant promise given to Abraham: "I will bless those who bless you, and whoever curses you I will curse" (Gen. 12:3). *See also* Providence.

ESTHER THE WOMAN

Esther's name comes from the Persian word for "star." The text indicates that she was a "star" in our modern sense, "lovely in form and features" (2:7), rising to prominence in the king's harem.

Esther's Hebrew name was Hadassah ("Myrtle"), but, for a time at least, she hid her Jewish identity. As in so many times and places throughout history, the Jews were a distinct minority, and their distinction drew opposition from people in power. Wisely, Mordecai instructed Esther to keep quiet about her Jewish heritage, and she dutifully obeyed.

We know little concerning Esther's feelings about her relationship with Xerxes. Her position was one of honor, but also considerable danger. Xerxes was noted for his temper and unpredictability, as well as his rampant sexual appetite. The previous queen, Vashti, had suddenly fallen out of the king's favor. The same could happen to Esther. That is why she originally balked when Mordecai asked her to approach the king. To appear uninvited could mean death, especially if the king didn't like her anymore—and he hadn't summoned her for a month.

But apparently Esther realized that God had made her queen of Persia in order to save his people from this threat. (Mordecai, however, had reminded her that God could and would find someone else to deliver them if she refused—4:14.) After asking her people to join her in fasting (an activity Scripture associates with prayer), she approached the king—with a shrewd plan of her own. Her courage saved her people, doomed the rascal Haman, and exalted her cousin Mordecai.

Esther's story encourages us when we find ourselves, unexpectedly, in positions of influence, but feel hindered by our inadequacies. God, who arranges the circumstances of our lives, is able to work through us as we risk taking a stand in his Name.

MASTERY KEYS

First, read through the book as a story. Then, go back over each chapter and underline references which may illustrate God's providential control of events.

eternal, eternity That which is outside of and not limited by time. The eternal has no beginning and no end. Like God and his purposes, the eternal exists forever (Eph. 3:11; Rom. 1:20). As Paul said in 2 Cor. 4:18, everything in the material universe is subject to change, "but what is unseen is eternal."

In these and other passages, "eternal" does not possess only a future dimension. That is, the believer through Christ participates in the eternal now, not just after death.

What else is eternal—immune from the corroding effect of change? The redemption that Christ secured for us on Calvary is eternal (Heb. 5:9; 9:12), and so is the new, spiritual life that results from faith in Christ (Jn. 17:3). Nothing that happens during our lifetime can alter the pronouncement of God, that whoever believes in Jesus has been given eternal life (Jn. 3:15-18; 1 Jn. 5:11-13).

And, as Peter promises, faithfulness to

ESTHER: A READING AND STUDY GUIDE

Chapter	Content Summary	Related Articles
1	Xerxes divorces Vashti for publicly refusing to obey him.	Xerxes; Persia
2	Esther pleases Xerxes more than any other and is made queen. Mordecai, her cousin, saves Xerxes from a plot against his life.	Harem; Mordecai
3	Haman, a high official of Xerxes, is angered because Mordecai will not bow down to him. He determines to kill Mordecai and exterminate his race.	Haman
4	Mordecai persuades Esther to speak to Xerxes.	
5	Esther invites Xerxes and Haman to a banquet. Haman builds a gallows on which to hang Mordecai.	
6	A sleepless Xerxes has the record of his reign read to him and discovers nothing has been done to reward Mordecai for thwarting the plot against his life. Xerxes orders Haman to honor Mordecai.	
7	Esther begs for the life of her people. Haman is hung on the gallows he had built for Mordecai.	
8	Xerxes gives the Jews the right to kill anyone who might attack them under Haman's earlier decree.	
9	The Jews destroy their enemies throughout the Persian Empire. Haman's sons are hung. A thanksgiving feast, called Purim, is established.	
10	Mordecai serves Xerxes as his prime minister and uses his influence for the good of his people.	

our calling will ensure us a "rich welcome into the eternal kingdom of our Lord and Savior Jesus Christ" (2 Pet. 1:11). *See also* Everlasting; Life.

Ethiopian eunuch An official in the court of the Queen Mother (the Candace) of Ethiopia, converted through Philip's ministry (Acts 8:27-40). The title "eunuch" was sometimes granted to high military officials, but this minister's assignment to the Candace indicates that he was a personal attendant who had been castrated. Still, such servants often rose to power within royal courts, and Acts mentions that this eunuch controlled the treasury.

Ethiopia (called Cush in the Hebrew OT) was not the same region as modern Ethiopia. It lay along the upper Nile, extending from Aswan south to Khartoum. It had a history of power struggles with its neighbor Egypt. One Ethiopian king even marched to aid the Jewish king Hezekiah against Assyria about 700 B.C. (Isa. 37:9). Isaiah had warned Hezekiah against depending on Egypt and "Cush," but many Jews apparently fled to the Nile regions for safety (Isa. 20:6).

These Jews may have formed the beginnings of a Jewish community in Ethiopia that grew in the following centuries. Archaeologists have found evidence of Jewish dispersion throughout the ancient world in the several centuries before Christ. The eunuch's acquaintance with Isaiah suggests that he may have attached himself to the Jews in Ethiopia as a God-fearer, a Gentile attracted to the OT's moral and religious vision. *See also* God-fearing.

Isaiah had spoken of the Ethiopians as "a people tall and smooth-skinned, . . . feared far and wide, an aggressive nation of strange speech" and had predicted a day when Ethiopians would bring gifts to the Lord in Jerusalem (Isa. 18:2,7). This eunuch-treasurer had probably brought a gift as he came to Jerusalem to worship, fulfilling Isaiah's prophecy, but he received a much greater gift on the way home.

As a eunuch and a foreigner, he would have been prevented from participating fully in Temple worship (Lev. 22:24; Deut. 23:1). But Isaiah had also predicted that eunuchs and foreigners would someday be welcomed by God (Isa. 56:3-7). This was fulfilled as the Spirit brought Philip near the eunuch's chariot. Fittingly, the Ethiopian was reading Isaiah. After Philip explained the Gospel, the eunuch, in the aggressive manner his race was known for, asked to be baptized. Philip agreed, and the door of faith swung open: those who were excluded from Judaism were welcomed into Christ's new covenant. *See also* Eunuch; Philip.

Although Cornelius (Acts 10) is generally considered the first Gentile convert to Christianity, the honor really belongs to the Ethiopian eunuch. According to tradition, the eunuch returned to Ethiopia and spread the Gospel throughout his homeland. *See also* Eunuch.

eunuch [YOO-nuk]. A castrated male servant or royal official. In biblical times male servants who served among the women of a ruler's harem were often castrated (2 Ki. 9:32). Often these male servants gained positions of influence. The Greek historian Xenophon says that Cyrus the Great of Persia believed that eunuchs made better servants and officials, not only because castration supposedly made them more docile, but also because they would not be distracted by family ties.

Old Testament Law prohibits castration (Deut. 23:1), and eunuchs were not permitted to participate in the worship of God. However, Isaiah 56 looks forward to a day when all those who are excluded under the Mosaic code will be welcome to worship—a day when God will "bring [them] to my holy mountain and give them joy in my house of prayer" (56:7). *See also* Ethiopian Eunuch.

Euphrates River [yoo-FRAY-teez]. The longest river in western Asia, flowing 1,780 miles (2,890 kilometers) from Turkey, through Syria, and into the Persian Gulf. The Euphrates, along with its sister river, the Tigris, has always been important in the history of the region.

Genesis identifies the Euphrates as one of four rivers that ran through the Garden of Eden. Perhaps more importantly, this river is one boundary of the land that God promised Abraham and Israel (Gen. 15:18; Josh. 1:2-4). Revelation also mentions the Euphrates in its descriptions of cataclysmic warfare (9:14; 16:12).

Euroclydon [yoo-RAHK-lee-don] (KJV). The Greek name of a violent, springtime wind that sweeps into the Mediterranean from the northeast. This wind, rendered "Northeaster" in RSV and NIV, wrecked Paul's ship as he was being taken to Rome (Acts 27:14).

evangelist, evangelism, evangelize

One who announces good news, especially the Gospel of Jesus Christ. In Greek, the verb *euangelizō* literally means "to announce or bring good news." This and related words were used occasionally by secular writers for a marriage announcement or news of military victory.

But Christians quickly adopted these words for their own activity of spreading the good news of Jesus. Acts 8:4 tells us that the Christians who were driven from Jerusalem by persecution "preached [Gk., *euangelizō*] the word" wherever they went. This ministry of evangelism, sharing Christ with others, continues to be the privilege of all believers everywhere.

The noun "evangelist" appears only three times in the NT, describing people with a special role in the church. Philip "the evangelist" (Acts 21:8) carried on significant ministry in Samaria and with the Ethiopian eunuch (Acts 8). The title may have served to distinguish this Philip, one of the seven deacons chosen in Acts 6, from the apostle Philip.

Timothy, an itinerant teacher, is also exhorted to "do the work of an evangelist"

(2 Tim. 4:5). "Evangelists" are also listed among the leaders (apostles, prophets, pastors, and teachers) whom Christ has given as a gift to his Church.

These uses indicate that "evangelist" identifies those specially gifted by God to communicate the Gospel.

In the third century A.D., Christian writers began to speak of the writers of the four Gospels as "the evangelists." However, this does not reflect any biblical usage of the term. *See also* Apostle; Gospel.

The Euphrates River winds its way through the mountains of Anatolia (Turkish Armenia) before bending eastward toward the Persian Gulf.

Medieval woodcut depicting the creation of Eve from a rib taken from Adam's side while he sleeps. God created Eve to meet Adam's deepest need for companionship (Gen. 2:20-25).

Eve [EEV; "life giver"(?)]. The first woman, wife of Adam, who was deceived by Satan and disobeyed God by eating from the tree of knowledge. **Children:** Cain, Abel, Seth, and "other sons and daughters" (Gen. 5:4). **Scripture:** Gen. 2,3.

BACKGROUND

The story of the creation of Adam and Eve is particularly important, for it lays the foundation of the biblical view of human nature and the relationship between men and women. Of particular note is the fact that Eve is created as a "suitable helper" (Heb., 'ezer) for Adam (Gen. 2:18-22). The word does not imply subordination or inferiority, but identity, for only a being with the same personal capacities and capabilities as Adam could have related to him (God himself is called a "help" ['ezer] in Ps. 46:1 and elsewhere). Some believe the word means a "helper comparable to" Adam—an interpretation supported by Adam's reaction, "This is now bone of my bones and flesh of my flesh" (2:23). *See also* Woman.

Genesis presents Eve as more than the representative female. She was a flesh-and-blood woman, appreciative of beauty and eager to grow and learn (3:6). She was also deceived by Satan. While Eve knew that it was wrong to eat the forbidden fruit, she was all too easily convinced to question God's motives and doubt the consequences of disobedience (3:1-5). Paul

raises this point in 1 Tim. 2:14 as an explanation for not allowing women authoritative teaching roles in the church.

Eve lived many years after this event and gave Adam a number of sons and daughters (Gen. 5:4).

LEARNING FROM EVE'S LIFE

1. Eve is the prototype woman, and we must seek the biblical view of woman's identity in what is said of her in Gen. 2. Nothing there suggests anything other than that women share fully in the same image and likeness of God as Adam and are fully men's equals.

2. Eve helps us define the relationship between husbands and wives. The relationship became hierarchical only after sin was introduced in Gen. 3. It is the Gospel that restores to women their full value as persons and heals the damage done by men who have often perceived them merely as servants and personal property. *See also* Authority; Marriage; Submission.

everlasting Eternal, continuing without limit into the future.

God called his covenants with Abraham and David "everlasting" (Gen. 17:7; 2 Sam. 23:5). This was possible because, as Moses sang, "from everlasting to everlasting you are God" (Ps. 90:2). God himself has no limit of time or place, and thus his promises last forever.

In the OT, "everlasting" generally refers only to God, his purposes and commitments. But there is one reference to humanity's eternal destiny. Daniel 12:2 mentions a resurrection in which some will awake "to everlasting life, others to shame and eternal contempt."

The NT builds on the OT concept. The eternal stands outside of time, uncorrupted by its passage. Everything in this present world is changeable; it will pass away. The eternal stands secure forever.

Thus God's gift of everlasting life takes on added meaning. Our new life extends endlessly into the future—even beyond the future, into eternity. *See also* Eternal; Life.

evil Wickedness, hostility, moral deficiency; the misery caused by wicked acts.

Philosophers have pondered the existence of evil for centuries. And many ordinary people, stricken by tragedy or victimized by the sins of others, have cried out, "Why?"

THE NATURE OF EVIL

There are no easy answers, for philosophers or for sufferers, but the Bible does take a clear position on evil. Scripture presents human sin as the source of evil in this world. Sin has flawed fallen humanity, so that evil is both a lack in human character (an absence of good) and rebellion against God and his standards. Humanity's sinful actions are "evil," both because they violate the moral standards established by God and because they do harm to other humans.

In the OT, evil (ra') is a complex term, indicating both evil acts and the consequences of those acts. Thus, where the OT suggests that God does evil, it means that as moral ruler of his universe God brings disaster or distress to those who do wrong. Such statements do not suggest that God himself performs any morally evil acts.

In the NT, the OT concept is further refined. Human beings are and do *kakos* (evil). Such acts flow from the fact that humanity is flawed. The term suggests an absence of good. Human beings also are and do *ponēros* (evil). These are rebellious acts, acts intended to violate God's standards and harm others. Evil is not only a lack of good; it is also energy actively channeled toward evil (Mt. 15:18,19).

According to Scripture, the evil we see in society—the crime, the injustice, the indifference to the suffering of others—is rooted in human nature itself. We live in a society where people are committed to "following the ways of this world and the ruler of the kingdom of the air [Satan]," seeking always to gratify "the cravings of our sinful nature and following its desires and thoughts" (Eph. 2:2,3). As long as the world is peopled with sinful human beings, there will be victims, and the innocent will suffer. *See also* Satan; Suffering.

GOD AND EVIL

Scripture relates God to evil in a variety of ways:

(1) God has revealed standards of right and wrong. Deuteronomy 30:15 sums up the impact of this revelation: "See, I set before you today life and prosperity, death and destruction." The passage continues, "Now choose life." God's moral revelation guides us to make choices which will help us avoid evil actions and their terrible consequences.

(2) God has established human government to restrain the expression of evil in society (Rom. 13).

(3) God acts to punish evil, often by bringing disaster on persons and nations who violate his standards and harm others (Isa. 45:7; Jer. 18:11; Amos 3:6). Even those who seem to prosper experience God's

judgment within their hearts (Hab. 2). *See also* Habakkuk.

(4) God acts to repair the damage sin has done to human beings. The Gospel carries with it the promise of ongoing transformation now, so that we are enabled to do and be good, despite our flaws (2 Cor. 3:18; Rom. 8:1-4).

(5) God will, in the future, replace this present universe with a new heaven and earth (Isa. 65; 2 Pet. 3:8-13; Rev. 20,21).

(6) At our resurrection God will complete the transformation begun in believers so that we will bear the likeness of Christ himself (1 Cor. 15).

(7) God will punish those who persist in doing evil and fail to respond to his offer of salvation (2 Th. 1:3-10; Rev. 20:11-15).

GOD'S PARTICIPATION WITH US

Perhaps the most striking theme in the NT is that God does not view evil from a distance, nor does he stand aside from our suffering. In Jesus, God actually participated with us in the terrible and tragic impact of evil on human experience. The writer of Hebrews points out that Jesus "had to be made like his brothers in every way. . . . Because he himself suffered when he was tempted, he is able to help those who are being tempted" (Heb. 2:17,18). In his humanity, Christ felt every pressure, every hurt, and every injustice that evil makes us heir to.

Engraved glass plaque of Adam and Eve with the serpent (A.D. 1650–1675). The German text quotes Gen. 3:6, which records the act of their disobedience that introduced sin into creation.

We can never really explain the existence of evil. It is difficult to comfort those who suffer innocently, but we can affirm that God will deal with evil in his own time. And we can remember that God loved us so much that he refused to remain aloof. He stepped into our world to share our pain. However much we hurt, we can know that God understands and cares.

evil spirits Hostile spiritual beings, demons. New Testament references to "evil [*ponēros*] spirits" depict them as hostile beings who seek to do harm to humans. In Scripture, "evil spirits" is another name for demons, those angels who followed Satan in his rebellion against God. *See also* Angel; Demon; Evil; Satan.

ewe [yoo]. A female sheep or lamb. *See also* Sheep.

example A pattern which can serve as a model. The NT focuses our attention on living models: persons whose lives or actions set examples for God's people to follow.

The most important example for Christians is Christ himself. When Christ took the role of a servant and washed his disciples' feet, he said, "I have set you an example that you should do as I have done for you" (Jn. 13:15). Peter calls believers to do good, even when it may lead to pain and unjust suffering. "To this you were called, because Christ suffered for you, leaving you an example, that you should follow in his steps" (1 Pet. 2:19-21).

These and other passages (1 Jn. 2:6; Eph. 5:1) call us to pay the closest attention to Jesus, not only as Savior but also as the best example of how to please God.

God has also provided other examples for us. Peter calls on elders to be "examples to the flock" (1 Pet. 5:3). Christians are to notice the godly among themselves,

Ewe with its lamb, carved in relief on a marble fountain basin found near Rome (first century A.D.). Isaiah, prophesying comfort for Israel, describes God as a shepherd who "gently leads those that have young" (40:11).

those whose lives harmonize with their doctrine, and to model their lives after those examples (1 Tim. 4:12; Phil. 4:9). *See also* Leaders.

exile In Scripture, expulsion of the Hebrew people from the Promised Land. The most extreme national punishment for violation of the Mosaic Law was to "be uprooted from the land you are entering to possess" (Deut. 28:63). The Northern Kingdom of Israel was shattered and its people deported by the Assyrians in 722 B.C. Many thousands were also taken from the Southern Kingdom, Judah, at that time. Yet Judah continued as a nation until it was finally crushed by the Babylonians in 586 B.C., when the remnant of its population was exiled to Babylon or fled to Egypt. *See also* Captivity.

Eleven disciples cluster tightly around Jesus as he washes the feet of a twelfth (probably Peter) in this 15th-century woodcut from Germany. The example of servanthood Jesus set has rarely been matched by his followers.

Jewish families with cattle and baggage traveling into exile in Assyria. This scene is detail of a massive wall relief of the Siege of Lachish (701 B.C.) found in Sennacherib's palace in Nineveh.

Exodus God's rescue of the Hebrew people from slavery in Egypt, and their subsequent journey to Canaan.

Several debates focus on the Exodus story, found in the second book of the OT, the Book of Exodus. (1) Is it historical? Some scholars have argued that the story was made up centuries after it was supposed to have happened. They theorize that the ancestors of the Jews were nomads who drifted into Canaan. There is no real archaeological support for this view, and it clearly contradicts the biblical account.

Thus most scholars believe the Exodus story has its roots in actual events. *See also* Conquest.

(2) When did the Exodus take place? Two dates are generally argued: an early date of about 1450 B.C., and a late date of about 1290 or even 1230 B.C. While more archaeologists tend to support the late date, there is sufficient biblical and archaeological evidence to accept 1450 B.C. as the date of the Exodus. *See also* Chronology of the Bible.

(3) What was the route of the Exodus? Three different routes have been suggested by scholars. The northern route is impossible to harmonize with any possible location of Mount Sinai. The central route assumes Mount Sinai is in Arabia, which hardly is tenable. Only the southern route fits the biblical account and the generally accepted identification of Mount Sinai with Jebel Musa. *See also* Sinai.

In and through the Exodus, God revealed himself to Israel in many unique ways. During this period, God revealed his name, Yahweh; instituted the Passover; gave the Mosaic covenant of Law; and established the priesthood and sacrificial system. All this makes the time of the Exodus one of the most important periods in all of sacred history. *See also* Exodus, Book of.

Exodus, Book of The second book of the Old Testament. The title "Exodus" means "a going out." The second of the five books of Moses, Exodus tells of the great numerical growth of the Israelites during their enslavement in Egypt (ch. 1). It introduces Moses (chs. 2–4), and records the terrible plagues God brought upon Egypt to secure his people's release (chs. 5–13). It records the story of Israel's march to Mount Sinai (chs. 14–18) and the proclamation there of the covenant of Law (chs. 19–24). The book concludes with a description of the OT worship center, the tabernacle ("tent of meeting", NIV), where the Israelites would meet and worship God (chs. 25–40).

AUTHORSHIP AND DATE

Many modern scholars hold that Exodus is a patchwork composition created during Israel's kingdom age, but this view rests on conjecture. The Bible itself identifies Moses as the author of Exodus (Ex. 24:4; 34:27; Josh. 8:30-35; Mk. 1:44; 7:10); this view was universally held in Judaism and

355

by the early church. If we accept an early date for the Exodus, the events reported here took place shortly after 1450 B.C. *See also* Chronology of the Bible; Conquest.

BACKGROUND

Around 2100 B.C., God promised Abraham that he would give the land of Canaan (Palestine) to Abraham's descendants (Gen. 12:7; 13:15; 15:18). Abraham's son and grandson lived in Canaan as nomads, but the family moved to Egypt about 1875 B.C. Within Egypt's protective environment the Israelites multiplied, so much so that the foreign-led Hyksos Dynasty and the Egyptians began to see them as a threat. They eventually enslaved the Israelites and took steps to cut their birthrate. *See also* Egypt.

Under this oppression, the Israelites cried to God for deliverance. Exodus tells the story of that deliverance, and of Moses, the man God chose to lead this new nation. It also tells of the giving of the Law, which became Israel's constitution as they journeyed toward their Promised Land and settled there.

THEOLOGICAL CONTRIBUTIONS

Exodus introduces several themes that are vital to our understanding of OT theology and faith: (1) God's personal name, Yahweh; (2) Miracle; (3) Passover; (4) Law; and (5) Tabernacle.

MASTERY KEYS

Before reading Exodus, read background articles in this dictionary on each of the five themes mentioned above. Then read Exodus carefully, noting how each theme is developed.

Moses is one of the most significant figures in Scripture, commended in the NT as "faithful as a servant in all God's house" (Heb. 3:5). Mark the passages in which Moses communicates with God, with Pharaoh, or with his people. Then explore these passages. What can Moses teach us about servanthood and faithfulness?

SPECIAL FEATURES

God reveals the name Yahweh to Moses. The name means "The One Who Is Always Present." Exodus illustrates the importance of this name. God's presence was revealed in the miracles that forced Pharaoh to release his Hebrew slaves. It was demonstrated in the manna that was given daily to meet Israel's need for food. It was expressed in the Law, given by God to structure healthy relationships with God and with other persons. It is good to know that God is present with us, too—to protect, provide for, and guide us.

Right: This small bronze bull is a prayer offering from a temple at Byblos (in Lebanon), and dates to the second millennium B.C. It is gilded in gold, reminiscent of the golden calf (Ex. 32:4).

Desert of Midian at southwestern part of the Sinai peninsula with Mount Sinai in the distance. The way to this region from the oasis of Marah (Ex. 15:23) follows an ancient caravan route which hops from oasis to oasis.

The Exodus

Jericho
MEDITERRANEAN SEA
Jerusalem · MT. NEBO
Dibon
Raamses
Succoth ·
BITTER LAKES
Kadesh Barnea
SINAI PENINSULA
MT. HOR
· Memphis
NILE RIVER
Marah · Ezion Geber
Elim
Dophkah
Rephidim · · Hazeroth
MT. SINAI
N
0 20 40 60 80 MILES
RED SEA

EXODUS: A READING AND STUDY GUIDE

Chapter	Content Summary	Related Articles
	I. Deliverance from Egypt	
1	The Israelites are enslaved in Egypt, Pharaoh orders Hebrew male infants thrown into the Nile.	Egypt Israelites
2	Moses is born, adopted by Pharaoh's daughter, but as an adult he identifies with the Israelites and flees to Midian after killing an Egyptian foreman.	Moses
3	Forty years later God calls Moses to return to Egypt and deliver Israel. God reveals his name, Yahweh.	Yahweh
4	Moses returns, with Aaron his brother assigned to assist him. The Israelites greet him joyfully.	Aaron Circumcision
5	Pharaoh rejects Moses' request to release Israel and increases the work required from his slaves. Moses turns to God.	Brick
6	God promises "mighty acts of judgment" which will help Israel "know that I am the Lord your God."	Miracle Genealogy
7	Moses calls on God to turn the life-giving waters of the Nile to blood. Pharaoh breaks promise of release.	Heart
8	Plagues of frogs, gnats, and flies shake the confidence of a wavering Pharaoh, but still Pharaoh will not let Israel go.	
9	Plagues strike livestock, the Egyptians themselves, and their crops. Pharaoh admits sin, yet will not let Israel go.	
10	Locusts and darkness strike Egypt. Pharaoh threatens to kill Moses, and will not let Israel go.	
11	God tells Moses of the final plague, death to every firstborn Egyptian son and firstborn of their cattle.	Firstborn
12	The Passover meal is instituted. The lamb's blood on Jewish doorposts protects those within from death. That very night Pharaoh expels the Israelites, laden with gifts.	Passover Blood
13	The commemorative Passover meal is instituted. God leads the Israelites into the desert.	Pillar of Cloud and Fire
14	God opens the sea for his people, then closes the waters on a pursuing Egyptian army, drowning them.	Red Sea
15	Moses teaches the people a song of praise for Israel's deliverance from Egypt. The people now journey toward Sinai.	Psalms Praise
	II. The Journey to Sinai	
16	God provides manna to feed the Israelites on the journey.	Manna
17	God provides water for a now angry and quarreling people. An Amalekite army is defeated by the Israelites.	Rock Amalekites
18	Moses' father-in-law suggests appointing elders and officers to reduce the responsibilities borne by Moses.	Judge
	III. The Law Given at Mount Sinai	
19	The Israelites come to Mount Sinai, which is shrouded in awesome clouds and lightning.	Sinai Holy
20	God gives the Ten Commandments, which summarize his moral Law. Moses is instructed on construction of altars.	Law Commandments, Ten
21	Various laws concerning servants and personal injury apply principles implicit in the Ten Commandments.	Slave
22	More laws concerning property rights and other issues.	Justice Neighbor
23	After stating these laws, God promises that an angel will guard his people and enable them to defeat their pagan enemies.	Sabbath Feasts, Festivals, and Fasts
24	The people agree to obey God's Law. The elders share a commemorative meal. Moses climbs Sinai to stay 40 days.	Eating

continued

Chapter	Content Summary	Related Articles
	IV. The OT Worship System is Instituted	
25	God instructs Moses to make a tabernacle and furnish it "exactly like the pattern I will show you."	Ark of the Covenant
26	Specifications for the tabernacle proper.	Tabernacle
27	Specifications for the altar, courtyard, and lampstand fuel.	Altar Lampstand
28	Specifications for garments of the high priest.	High Priest
29	Instructions for the consecration of the priesthood.	Consecrate Atonement
30	Specifications for the altar of incense, basin for washing, anointing oil, and incense.	Anoint Incense
31	Two Israelites are gifted with the skills needed to construct the tabernacle and its furnishings.	Gifts
32	In the valley, Aaron casts an idol in the form of a golden calf. Moses returns, breaks the tablets of stone, has 3,000 idolaters executed, and intercedes for the people.	Idol Golden Calf
33	Moses begs for relief from the burden of leadership. God promises Moses his sustained presence.	
34	Moses receives new stone tablets on Sinai, with further instructions concerning worship. Moses veils his face.	Veil
35	The Israelites contribute materials to be used in construction of the tabernacle.	Tabernacle
36	The skilled workers use the contributed material to fashion the tabernacle proper.	Gifts
37	The ark of the covenant, lampstand, and altar of incense are constructed.	Ark of the Covenant Lampstand
38	The altar of burnt offering and courtyard are constructed. The cost is summarized.	Shekels Talents
39	The priestly garments are woven. Moses inspects the work and finds all has been done as God commanded.	
40	The tabernacle is set up, and the glory of God fills this tent of meeting between God and his people.	Glory

exorcise [EK-sor-size]. To drive out an evil spirit or spirits. Magic charms and incantations were commonly used in ancient Mesopotamia and Egypt to help persons supposedly possessed or oppressed by evil spirits.

Often the magic spells featured a special word or phrase thought to be especially powerful. Apparently, some Jewish exorcists tried to use the name of Jesus in this way in Ephesus. They failed, and were beaten by the demon-possessed man (Acts 19:13-16; *compare* Mt. 12:27).

The Bible does not use the term exorcism to describe Jesus' ministry of casting out demons. Jesus used no magic and spoke no incantations. Instead, Christ simply commanded evil spirits to leave the persons they troubled and the spirits obeyed (Mt. 8:16; Mk. 1:25; 5:8). Jesus also gave his disciples authority over evil spirits. They exercised this authority simply by commanding the spirits in Jesus' name (Mk. 16:17; Acts 16:18). *See also* Demons.

expiation [EK-spee-AY-shuhn]. Making amends or satisfaction for wrongdoing. Some versions use this English word at times to translate the Hebrew *kippur*, "atonement." The RSV and some other versions also use "expiation" to translate the Greek *hilastērion;* other versions use "propitiation." *See also* Atonement; Propitiation.

The choice of words is significant, for in this case word choice reflects a theological viewpoint. *Expiation* focuses attention on how the guilt of the original violation might be removed. *Propitiation* focuses attention on the personal reaction of God to sin, and on sin's impact on our relationship with him.

Those who favor the use of *propitiation* see sin as something which arouses the righteous anger of God and which places human beings under his wrath. Those who prefer *expiation* see sin as an offense that requires punishment, satisfaction. As a whole, Scripture presents both ideas.

To say, as the NT does, that the death of Christ was a *hilastērion* for our sin (Rom. 3:25; Heb. 2:17; 9:5; 1 Jn. 2:2) affirms that in his death Christ bore our sins. In so doing, he fully satisfied the righteous demands of God that sin be punished, enabling God to deal graciously with lost human beings.

Whichever emphasis one wishes to give to *kippur* and *hilastērion*, the NT makes it clear that we are saved "from God's wrath" (Rom. 5:9) by the death of his Son, and now "we have peace with God through our Lord Jesus Christ, through whom we have gained access by faith into this grace in which we now stand" (vv. 1,2).

eye The organ of sight, the ability to see, literally or figuratively. Scripture uses "eye" in both literal and figurative senses. Women in biblical times often painted their eyes, as did Jezebel (2 Ki. 9:30; Jer. 4:30). Egyptian women used different colors of eye paint, obtained by grinding various stones and ores. Archaeologists have found cosmetic palettes on which affluent women would grind their eye paint.

Figuratively, the eyes represent a capacity to perceive. References to God's "eyes" simply affirm that God has the ability to perceive everything that happens on earth. The psalmist asked those who assumed God was ignorant of their actions, "Does he who formed the eye not see?" (Ps. 94:9).

While eyes may also represent the spiritual perception of human beings (Gen. 3:5,7; Mt. 6:22,23; Eph. 1:18), the ear and hearing are far more important images. We cannot actually see God, but we can hear his Word—the testimony of those who have received covenant promises or have seen the Father in the person and life of his Son.

eye of a needle The hole in a needle in which thread is inserted. The Greek word for the needle in Jesus' sayings of Mt. 19:24, Mk. 10:25, and Lk. 18:25 indicates a literal sewing needle. Some scholars have speculated that Jesus was referring to a low, narrow gate in a city wall, through which individuals could pass after the main gates had been closed for the night. To enter this gate, a camel, some 6 to 8 feet (1.8 to 2.4 meters) tall, would have to be unloaded and literally kneel and crawl through. This presents an enticing picture of how a rich person might enter heaven, but there is no solid evidence that this was what Jesus had in mind.

More likely, Jesus' saying, which has parallels in rabbinic writings, indicates the utter impossibility of the situation—apart from the power of God (Mt. 19:26). Thus Jesus by this hyperbole was saying that a person who trusted in riches was totally missing the OT's message, that salvation comes through dependence on God. *See also* Almsgiving; Wealth.

Above: Contrary to common understanding, there is no historical evidence that a pedestrian gate was the "needle's eye" of Jesus' famous saying. Above left: Roman sewing needle made of bone (second century A.D.).

Below left: Eye-salve stick with seal that reads, "Q[uintus] Valerius Sextus and his recipe: balm against failing eyesight." The Lord Jesus warned the church in Laodicea to buy eye-salve in order to see clearly their pitiful spiritual condition (Rev. 3:18).

The udjat-eye of the god Horus was a popular Egyptian amulet. It warded off the "evil eye," a widespread superstition that the glances of an ill-disposed person could cause personal harm.

Ezekiel, Book of

Ezekiel, Book of A major prophetic book that records the warnings of Ezekiel to the captives in Babylon just before the destruction of Jerusalem in 586 B.C.—and his later words of hope to these exiles.

BACKGROUND

Near the end of the sixth century B.C., the mighty Babylonians subdued Judah and made her a vassal state. In Jerusalem the prophet Jeremiah urged his king and people to submit to the Babylonians as God's judgment for their apostasy, but Judah persisted in rebelling. At the same time, in Babylon a young prophet named Ezekiel, who had been taken into captivity earlier with most of Judah's aristocracy (597 B.C.), echoed Jeremiah's warnings. But God's prophets were ignored. Then in 587 B.C. the Babylonian army under Nebuchadnezzar sacked Jerusalem, destroyed Solomon's majestic Temple, and carried most of the remaining population of Judah into captivity. *See also* Captivity; Jeremiah.

Ezekiel, who had spoken out boldly between 593 and 586 B.C., fell silent (Ezek. 1:1,2; 29:17). But about 13 years later he began to prophesy again (32:17). This time his words were not of judgment, but of hope. These two themes, judgment and hope, are each associated with a different period of Ezekiel's ministry and make a natural division to this powerful book of prophecy.

AUTHOR AND DATE

Ezekiel [ee-ZEE-kee-uhl; "God strengthens"] was from a priestly family. He was 25 when taken to Babylon, and began his prophetic ministry at age 30 (Ezek. 1:2). The book can be dated confidently by specific months and years mentioned within the book, as well as by its content. Thus, we are able to determine that Ezekiel was a contemporary of Daniel and Jeremiah during the darkest era of OT history.

Deeply aware of his calling, Ezekiel saw himself as a divinely compelled watchman who cried out to warn his people of impending danger (Ezek. 33). Ezekiel's distinctive expression, "the hand of the Lord was upon me," expresses the powerful sense of urgency that impelled him to deliver his message, whether God's people would listen or not.

HISTORICAL SIGNIFICANCE

The book gives much information about the experience of the Jewish captives in Babylon. A fascinating passage of Scripture on the ships of Tyre (Ezek. 27) provides antiquity's clearest picture of merchant shipping. Like the Book of Jeremiah, Ezekiel gives us many insights into the beliefs, attitudes, and religious practices of God's people just prior to Babylon's final invasion of Judah. Ezekiel's indictment of Israel explains the basis on which God decreed her exile—the ultimate national punishment under the Mosaic code (Ezek. 20:1-38; Deut. 28:64-68).

THEOLOGICAL CONTRIBUTIONS

The Book of Ezekiel makes a number of contributions to God's progressive revelation of himself and his purposes. (1) Ezekiel sees visions of God enthroned in glory (Ezek. 1,8). As in the vision of Isa. 6, God is "high and lifted up," outside the material universe and sovereign over it. Many images found in Ezekiel are reflected in the Book of Revelation. (2) Ezekiel associates the glory of God with holiness. In a critical vision, after seeing God's people practice idolatry in the Temple itself, he observes the glory of God withdrawing from Solomon's magnificent edifice (Ezek. 8–11), signifying God's unwillingness to remain among a people who persist in perversity and wickedness. (3) Some 50 times God, through Ezekiel, repeats the phrase, "You shall know that I am the LORD [Heb., Yahweh]." This name means "The One Who Is Always Present." Israel had abandoned the Lord to worship idols and broken the covenant. Now God, who had yearned to show himself present with his people in blessing, would show himself present by his judgments! Through the terrors of invasion and exile, the people of Judah would realize at last who God is and abandon idolatry forever. See also Idol; Yahweh.

Other theological emphases in Ezekiel concern human responsibility and destiny. The theme of Israel's corporate responsibility to obey God is deeply imbedded in OT Law. Ezekiel emphasizes individual responsibility. In the coming judgment on the nation, Ezekiel sees that God will distinguish between the righteous and wicked individual, and the "soul [person] who sins will die" (Ezek. 18). This emphasis does not deny the theme of corporate responsibility, but stresses the personal responsibility of each individual to respond to God, regardless of what others do. Within the context of a national judgment, God will still "judge each of you according to his own way" (Ezek. 33:1-20). Since the captive people would lose their corporate national identity, it was necessary for Ezekiel to emphasize individual responsibility.

Ezekiel also focuses on a theme found in Jeremiah. He looks forward to a time when God will work within the individual to transform the heart and make each believer truly responsive to the Lord (Ezek. 11:19,20; 36:26,27).

MASTERY KEYS

Ezekiel's messages before the fall of Jerusalem focus on God's judgment of his people (chs. 1–32). The rest of the book (chs. 33–48) contains messages of hope, given some 13 years later. Theological themes are central to each section. Color coding can help your study of Ezekiel. Use a different color for those passages that reveal God, define personal responsibility, and state God's plans for the future. Use yet another color to mark the expression, "you will know that I am the LORD," mentioned more than 50 times. In what ways does God reveal his identity as Yahweh to Israel—and to us?

SPECIAL FEATURES

Ezekiel makes a significant contribution to the OT's prophetic vision of history's end. Even though Israel's national hope might be dashed and her people scattered, God promises to shepherd his people, give them a new national life (Ezek. 37) in their homeland (Ezek. 34,35), and raise a Temple in Jerusalem even more magnificent than Solomon's (Ezek. 40–48).

"On the fifth of the month—it was the fifth year of the exile of King Jehoiachin— the word of the Lord came to Ezekiel the priest . . . in the land of the Chaldeans" (Ezek. 1:2,3).

Chapter	Content Summary	Related Articles
	I. Books of Judgment	
	Ezekiel's call: Chs. 1–3	
1	In his fifth year among the captives in Babylon, Ezekiel sees a stunning vision of God.	Living Creatures Vision
2	Ezekiel is called to minister to God's rebellious people whether they listen or not.	Prophet Hear
3	Ezekiel is warned that Israel is hard and obstinate. Yet, as a watchman, he is responsible to warn them.	Watchman Righteous
	Judgments on Judah: Chs. 4–24	
4	For over a year Ezekiel acts out the coming siege of Jerusalem and rations the food and water he consumes.	Siege
5	Ezekiel shaves his head, and burns and scatters his hair to foretell the fate of those who remain in the homeland.	Captivity
6	The centers of idol worship in Israel will be destroyed and those who have worshiped there will die.	High Place Idol
7	Ezekiel announces disaster and doom, as God turns away from his people and his "treasured place."	Day of the Lord Temple
8	Ezekiel is transported to Jerusalem in a vision and sees that the holy city and Temple are desecrated by idolatry.	Spirit Tammuz
9	Ezekiel sees those who grieve over idolatry marked for deliverance, but the idolaters are killed without pity.	Cherub Remnant
10	Ezekiel sees the glory of the Lord, the sign of the divine presence, depart from the Temple.	Glory
11	Ezekiel hears the leaders of Judah condemned, but is promised that one day the scattered will be regathered.	Flesh Heart
12	Ezekiel dramatizes the coming exile. Daily he packs a few belongings and leaves his house.	Exile
13	Ezekiel condemns the prophets who lead God's people astray by falsely declaring that there will be peace.	False Prophets Peace
14	Idols in the heart are as terrible as wooden idols. Judgment is inescapable; Jerusalem must fall.	Judgment
15	Jerusalem is likened to a useless vine that has no value except as fuel for the fire.	Vine Face
16	Jerusalem is likened to an abandoned child, loved and cared for by God, who matured into a beautiful but promiscuous woman. Yet God will restore her.	Prostitute Sodom Covenant
17	Images of two eagles and a vine portray Judah's apostasy. Those breaking God's covenant will be punished.	Branch
18	Ezekiel announces that each person will live or die according to his own righteousness or sin in the coming invasion.	Soul Death
19	Ezekiel utters a lament over the uprooting of his nation.	
20	Ezekiel states God's charge against Israel—rebellion from its very beginning as a nation.	Rebellion Restore
21	Ezekiel identifies Babylon as a sword in God's hand, which he will use to punish Israel for her sins.	Babylon
22	Ezekiel identifies the sins of violence the people of Judah have committed against one another.	Justice
23	Ezekiel condemns Judah for committing the same sins as her sister Israel. Judah now must bear the consequences.	Adultery Lust

Ezra, Book of The 15th book of the OT. In the Hebrew Bible the books of Ezra and Nehemiah originally formed a single unit. Together they tell the story of the return of the Jews to Judah after the Babylonian Captivity. *See also* Captivity.

BACKGROUND

The two Hebrew kingdoms, Israel in the north and Judah in the south, had fallen to two great Mesopotamian empires—Israel to the Assyrians in 722 B.C. and Judah to the Babylonians, following a series of in-

Chapter	Content Summary	Related Articles
24	Ezekiel announces that the fire of judgment will now purify Judah. Ezekiel's wife dies, but cannot be mourned.	Fire Mourn
	Judgments on Foreign Nations: Chs. 25–32	
25	Ezekiel prophesies against the nations considered to be his people's enemies.	Ammonites Moab
26	Ezekiel prophesies against Tyre, predicting destruction.	Tyre
27	Ezekiel laments for Tyre, in the ancient world's clearest portrait of shipping and trade routes.	Ship Trade
28	Ezekiel prophesies against the "ruler of Tyre," and a "king of Tyre" whom many take to represent Satan.	Satan Eden, Garden of
29	Ezekiel prophesies against Egypt: it is to be given to the Babylonians.	Egypt
30	Ezekiel laments over Egypt and predicts her crushing defeat.	
31	A cedar of Lebanon symbolizes the glory of Egypt about to be brought down.	Cedar
32	Ezekiel pens a lament to be chanted on Egypt's downfall.	
	II. Books of Hope	
33	Ezekiel has been commissioned a watchman, to warn Judah to practice, and not just listen to, God's Word.	Watchman
34	Human shepherds who have failed Israel will be judged, and God himself will shepherd his flock with justice.	Shepherd Justice
35	God will judge Edom for its hostility against Israel.	Edom
36	God will again favor the mountains of Israel. He will remove centers of idol worship and repopulate his land.	Mount
37	Scattered Israel, dry bones in a valley, will be restored to become one nation under a Davidic king.	Covenant
38	Gog will invade Israel from the north at a time when everyone seems secure. God will then judge Gog.	Gog and Magog
39	Destruction of Gog's army will display God's glory, and Israel will again "know that I am the Lord your God."	Future
40	With Israel reestablished in the land, the area for a new Temple will be laid out.	Temple
41,42	Ezekiel describes the Temple itself and the rooms to be prepared for the priests who will offer sacrifice there.	Sacrifices and Offerings
43	God's glory will return; the Lord will again take up residence with his people. Daily sacrifices are ordained.	
44	The ministries of the priests and Levites who serve at the Temple are described.	Levites
45	The city will be redivided, justice will rule, and special offerings will be made to the Lord.	Justice Sacrifices and Offerings
46	Sacrifices and offerings are described in more detail.	
47	A river will flow from the Temple to the sea, and Israel's borders will be expanded.	
48	The land will again be divided among the tribes of Israel; each will have its portion around the city, whose new name will be "The Lord Is There."	

vasions that culminated with the destruction of Jerusalem and Solomon's Temple in 586 B.C. Both of these empires followed a policy of exiling conquered races from their homelands and resettling them elsewhere in their empires. The Bible views deportations as divine judgments on the Israelites for persistent idolatry and violation of their covenant with God. *See also* Covenant.

Yet Scripture foretold that any exile would be temporary. God's people were

CHRONOLOGY OF THE RETURN

Persian Kings	Dates B.C.	Events in Jerusalem
Cyrus the Great	539–530	Return under Zerubbabel (538 B.C.); Temple foundations laid, work stops
Cambyses	530–522	
Darius I	522–486	Temple restarted, completed under preaching of Haggai, Zechariah
Xerxes	486–465	
Artaxerxes I	465–424	Ezra sent to Jerusalem (458 B.C.)
		Nehemiah, as governor, rebuilds walls (445–? B.C.)
		Nehemiah governor again (433–430 B.C.)

Ezra reading the Law. The Book of Ezra is a unique window on the increased study of the Law among Jews during the Babylonian Captivity.

spiritually purified during the Babylonian Captivity, and after their release, the Jews were never again tempted by idolatry. The synagogue movement, with its emphasis on local community worship and the study of the Holy Scriptures, had begun during the Captivity and became a vital part of everyday life from that time onward.

When Cyrus the Great toppled Babylon and consolidated his great Persian Empire in 539 B.C., he reversed the deportation policy and issued decrees permitting captive peoples to return to their homelands. Once there, they were encouraged to re-establish their temples and offer sacrifices for his success. The Jews were one of the first peoples to respond to this opportunity. Yet, of the estimated two million Hebrews who had found homes in the cities of the pagan empires, only about 50,000 chose to return to Palestine! Still, those who did return were those "whose heart God had moved" (Ezra 1:5). The motive for the return was religious; the goal—a revival of worship at a new Temple to be built in Jerusalem.

AUTHORSHIP AND DATE

The traditional author of Ezra/Nehemiah is Ezra. Ezra, whose name means "help," was a priest who traced his line back to Aaron's son, Eleazar (1 Chr. 6:3-15; Ezra 7:1-5). Ezra is described as a scribe who "had devoted himself to the study and observance of the Law of the Lord, and to teaching its decrees and laws in Israel" (Ezra 7:10). Ezra was sent to Judah in 458 B.C., 80 years after the first group returned, with a magistrate's commission to enforce God's Law as the official law of the land (Ezra 7:25,26). Ezra continued to teach the Law during the revival initiated by Nehemiah, who was appointed governor of Judah in 445 B.C. and again in 433 B.C. The Books of Ezra and Nehemiah were probably completed some time after 430 B.C. Many scholars believe that Ezra also wrote 1 and 2 Chronicles.

HISTORICAL SIGNIFICANCE

The narrative in Ezra/Nehemiah gives us insights into the political, social, and religious context of the small group of Jews who returned to repopulate a tiny portion of their homeland. These books also provide the background for an understanding of the messages of the prophets Haggai, Zechariah, and Malachi.

The form of the decree of Cyrus (Ezra 1:2-4) fits the pattern of similar decrees discovered by archaeologists. Cyrus's acknowledgment of God was not an expression of personal faith but a standard formula showing respect for the gods of all peoples in his empire. The phrase "the God who is in Jerusalem" reflects the pagan view that gods and goddesses were headquartered or even limited to the particular locality which they "owned."

The supposed conflict between Ezra 3:8-10 and Hag. 2:18 concerning when the Temple foundation was laid is easily reconciled by noting that the first attempt to rebuild had been stopped and that a new "ground breaking" ceremony probably launched the later, successful effort to complete the Temple.

THEOLOGICAL CONTRIBUTIONS

Ezra adds little to the OT's revelation of God, but the book does reveal the special emphasis on the study of Scripture which emerged during the Captivity.

MASTERY KEYS

Ezra is not a continuous narrative. The flow is interrupted by the insertion of documents, out of historical sequence, that relate to local opposition to the Jews (4:6-23). Official documents (4:7–6:18; 7:12-26) are written in Aramaic, the common speech and language of diplomacy, while the rest of the book is written in Hebrew. The rebuilding, stimulated by Haggai and Zechariah, began in 520 B.C., 16 to 18 years after the work was first begun. A gap of nearly 60 years should be noted between Ezra 6:22, which records the Temple's completion and dedication in 516 B.C., and the following verse, 7:1, which records Ezra's arrival in Jerusalem in 457 B.C.

SPECIAL FEATURES

The Book of Ezra reveals much about the character of its author. Note Ezra's concern for the king's impression of God and Ezra's faith, demonstrated by the fact that he took considerable wealth to Jerusalem without military escort (8:21-23). Note also his sensitivity to sin and his willingness to confess the sins of the people. This was expressed by his concern about intermarriage between Jews and pagans in a beautiful prayer of confession which stimulated public confession and recommitment to God (9:5–10:16). We must never doubt the influence one person can have on a whole community of believers.

EZRA: A READING AND STUDY GUIDE

Chapter	Content Summary	Related Articles
1	Cyrus permits a return to Jerusalem (538 B.C.), sends back articles taken by Nebuchadnezzar from the Temple.	Temple Cyrus
2	Genealogies of the leaders of the 50,000 who went back to Judah.	Genealogy
3	The altar of sacrifice is rebuilt, and the foundation stone of the Temple is laid and dedicated.	Altar
4	Jewish leaders reject help from foreigners the Assyrians had resettled in Israel. Later opposition (460 B.C.) illustrates their hostility toward the Jews and their Temple.	Samaritans
5	Two prophets stimulate renewed work on the Temple, 520 B.C. Letters are sent to Darius, who confirms the project.	Haggai Zechariah
6	Darius orders the Temple completed at public expense. The Temple is completed and dedicated; Passover is kept.	Passover
7	In 458 B.C. Ezra is commissioned to go to Judah to teach and administer God's Law.	Scribe Justice
8	Ezra returns with some 5,000 persons and great treasures donated to the Temple.	
9	Ezra confesses to God the sin of intermarriage practiced by many men in Judah.	Intermarriage Confess
10	The men confess their sin and divorce their foreign wives.	

F

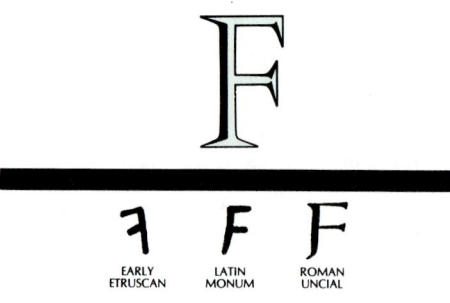

face The front of one's head; a person's features. Each person's face is unique, and thus suggests his or her identity as an individual. As such, "face" often stands for the person himself and/or his presence. When God's OT people spoke of seeking or seeing God's face, they meant coming into God's presence, either for ritual worship at the tabernacle or in prayer (2 Sam. 21:1; Pss. 24:6; 119:58).

Cain's "downcast" face expressed anger (Gen. 4:6). A shining face, turned toward a person, expresses favor (Num. 6:25,26; Ps. 80:3). To hide one's face from another means to withdraw favor (Deut. 31:18).

In ordinary speech, meeting "face to face" indicated the direct experience by each person of the other. Although Jacob felt that he had seen God "face to face, and yet my life was spared" (Gen. 32:30; *see* Jdg. 6:22), Jacob was wrong. He had not experienced the full and complete presence of God, which is so overwhelming that God told Moses, "You cannot see my face, for no one may see me and live" (Ex. 33:20). Later, when Moses writes of God speaking to Israel "face to face" from Mount Sinai, he means a personal experience with God, but not a complete experience of God.

The writer of Hebrews says that in the past God spoke in various ways, "but in these last days he has spoken to us by his Son" (Heb. 1:2). In the human face of Jesus we, at last, meet God as he really is, "full of grace and truth" (Jn. 1:14,15). As Jesus told his disciples, "Anyone who has seen me has seen the Father. I am in the Father, and . . . the Father is in me" (Jn. 14:9,10). The long-hidden face of God is unveiled in the person of God's Son.

faith Belief, confidence, trust, reliance. In the Bible, religious faith is a life-shaping attitude toward God. The person with faith considers God's revelation of himself and of truth to be certain and sure. The person with faith then responds to God with trust, love, and obedience.

God made promises to Abraham, and the Bible says, "Abraham believed the Lord, and he [God] credited it to him as righteousness" (Gen. 15:6). God gave Israel a Law that revealed his moral character and guided the believer's faith-response (Deut. 4:5-8). In the NT, the object of faith is Jesus. Only twelve times does the NT speak of "faith in God" rather than faith in the Lord Jesus Christ, because Jesus is now the one in whom God has fully expressed himself.

Biblical faith, then, has two aspects: on God's part there is an act of revelation that calls for a response; on man's part there is a response of faith that evaluates God's revelation as trustworthy and responds wholeheartedly to the Lord.

Thus God presents Jesus as his Son, whose death wins us forgiveness, and we, by faith, rely completely on Jesus for our salvation.

BIBLICAL EXAMPLES OF FAITH

Perhaps the best way to understand religious faith is to look at significant NT passages describing it.

• *Romans 4.* This chapter looks back to Genesis, focusing on Abraham's response to God's promise of a child. Abraham "did not waver through unbelief regarding the promise of God, . . . being fully persuaded that God had power to do what he had promised" (vv. 20,21). Abraham's faith was in God himself and in God's power to do what he promised. So also, we who believe in Jesus have confidence.

"By faith Abraham, when God tested him, offered Isaac as a sacrifice . . . even though God had said to him, 'It is through Isaac that your offspring will be reckoned' " (Heb. 11:17,18). Jewish haggadah (narration) from 15th century A.D.

These two Greek warriors dramatically demonstrate the value of their large shields in close combat. The apostle Paul likens faith in God to these protective pieces of armor, with which a Christian can "extinguish all the flaming arrows of the evil one" (Eph. 6:16). Stone relief from Nereid Monument, 4th century B.C.

We may not understand the how or why, but we are persuaded that God can do for us what he has promised.

• *Hebrews 11.* This great chapter begins, "Faith is being sure of what we hope for and certain of what we do not see." The chapter continues by listing men and women whose faith in God was expressed by actions. Noah built an ark long before he saw the rains that God warned would flood the earth. Abraham believed God's promise of a child long before he saw the signs of his wife's pregnancy. Joseph, dying in Egypt, looked ahead and spoke of the time four centuries later when his family's descendants would return to the land God had promised them.

In each case, faith shaped the believer's perception of the future and made a difference in the choices that he made.

Faith should shape our perspective, too, transforming the way we live our lives. We who believe in Jesus can be sure of what we hope for, even though we cannot yet see it.

• *James 2.* "Faith" can be ineffectual in at least two ways. A person who places his confidence in false or empty objects of faith is believing in vain. In this case, faith's object is invalid. Or, a person can "believe" intellectually, without a personal commitment to what is believed. In this case, faith's response is inadequate. James illustrates this second problem with the observation that even demons believe that God exists—"and shudder." A "faith" that exists simply as an agreement that something is true, without that wholehearted response which motivates action, is a futile faith. The faith in God to which we are called in Jesus engages our total response to the Lord. We consider God trustworthy, and because we believe, everything we think and do is shaped by that conviction.

THE BENEFITS OF FAITH

Faith, biblically understood, has life-transforming effects. When we place our faith in Jesus, the Bible affirms that we have "eternal life and will not be condemned" but have "crossed over from death to life" (Jn. 5:24). Moreover, this faith expresses itself presently in a love for God and for others that, through the Holy Spirit, produces love, joy, peace, patience, kindness, goodness, faithfulness, gentleness, and self-control (Gal. 5:1-23).

Faith in Christ is our guarantee of eternal life. But faith brings us even more. Like the heroes described in Heb. 11, we who believe in Jesus find our lives reshaped and renewed. *See also* Believe.

faithful, faithfulness Reliable, trustworthy, loyal. The biblical words for "faithfulness" express certainty. That which is faithful is steady, true, and established. The supreme example of faithfulness is God: He can be trusted, for he is completely trustworthy.

GOD'S FAITHFULNESS

The OT views faithfulness as one of the most wonderful of God's qualities. We are secure because he will never betray our confidence in him. Deuteronomy 7:9 sums up the OT emphasis: "Know therefore that the Lord your God is God; he is the faithful God, keeping his covenant of love to a thousand generations of those who love him and keep his commands." *See also* Covenant.

367

Psalm 89, which celebrates the faithfulness of God, begins:

I will sing of the Lord's great love forever;
with my mouth I will make your
faithfulness known through all
generations.
I will declare that your love stands firm
forever,
that you established your faithfulness in
heaven itself. (Ps. 89:1,2)

This foundational understanding also pervades the NT, and is expressed in such remarks as "The Lord is faithful." Our faithful God does not permit us to be tempted beyond our capacity to overcome (1 Cor. 10:13); he strengthens us and protects us from the evil one (2 Th. 3:3); he forgives us and keeps on cleansing us as we confess our sins to him (1 Jn. 1:9).

The same sense of security is expressed in the formula, "This is a faithful saying" (KJV), or "Here is a trustworthy saying" (NIV), *see* 1 Tim. 1:15; 3:1; 4:9; 2 Tim. 2:11; Tit. 3:8. In each text, Paul states foundational truths which believers of every age can fully count on.

FAITHFULNESS IN THE BELIEVER

All of sacred history has testified to God's faithfulness. But Scripture also points to the importance of the believer's faithfulness to God. God is completely loyal to us. How appropriate then that we should be loyal to him.

Loyalty to God is expressed practically. God, in the OT, defines a "faithful priest" as one "who will do according to what is in my heart and mind" (1 Sam. 2:35). The writer of Hebrews commends Moses as one whose life proved him to be "faithful as a servant," and points us to Jesus, who was "faithful as a son" (Heb. 3:5,6).

Perhaps we best sense the importance of faithfulness in Jesus' familiar story of the talents (Mt. 25). Christ told of individuals who were given different resources and told to use those resources for their master's benefit. Each servant who used his resources wisely received the same commendation: "Well done, good and faithful servant" (Mt. 25:21,23). God does not evaluate us by how much we have, but rather how faithfully we use what we have in his service.

Fall, the In Christian theology, Adam and Eve's disobedience in Eden, described in Gen. 3, with the consequent loss of innocence and its disastrous effects on the human race.

THE SETTING

The early chapters of Genesis define humanity as the crowning creation of God, formed by him in his own image. The first pair, Adam and Eve, enjoyed innocence; they had no first-hand or experiential knowledge of sin. God placed a tree in Eden, the "tree of the knowledge of good and evil," and commanded Adam not to eat of it. By this, God acknowledged the first pair's moral nature, and gave them the opportunity to choose what was good. But the existence of the tree also created the possibility that they might choose evil. Despite God's stern warning, Eve and then Adam disobeyed.

Although this act of disobedience, with its far-reaching consequences, is what Christians usually mean by "the Fall," biblical evidence suggests that Satan and his angels also "fell" from an original sinless state (Jude 6).

THE OCCASION

After some undisclosed period of time, during which Adam and Eve lived in intimate fellowship with God and each other, Satan tempted Eve by challenging God's motives and the integrity of his Word. Both Eve and Adam disobeyed God and ate the forbidden fruit. *See also* Tempt.

CONSEQUENCES OF THE FALL

Adam and Eve "died" spiritually, and passed on a deadened spiritual nature to their descendants. Scripture describes fallen human beings as morally, intellectually, and emotionally corrupt, hostile toward God and one another (Eph. 2:1-3; Rom. 1:18-32; 3:9-18). In addition, nature itself was twisted out of its original design (Gen. 3:17-19; Rom. 8:19-22). *See also* Death.

Scripture's description of the Fall is the key to a biblical understanding of the origin of both sin and evil. Sin was admitted into the world by Adam's act of disobedience and a corrupt nature was transmitted through Adam to the whole human race (Rom. 5:12-19). Evil, as an active bent of fallen human nature producing the pain and suffering men cause one another, is the consequence of that first act, amplified by the multitude of sins which it had generated. *See also* Evil; Sin.

RESULTANT RELATIONSHIP

The Fall radically affected man's relationship with God. Genesis 3 pictures Adam and Eve, who had once walked with God in the Garden of Eden in the cool of the evening, now hiding from him in terror. The knowledge of good and evil flooded their awakened consciences with

"Then the eyes of both of them were opened, and they realized they were naked; so they sewed fig leaves together and made coverings for themselves" (Gen. 3:7).

guilt, and guilt produced fear, shame, and a profound alienation from God.

The rest of the Bible explores the failure of sinful humanity to respond to God. Yet God, now morally responsible to punish the beings he had created in his own image, continued to love. He revealed himself and his will. To bridge the alienation, God established sacrifice as an avenue of approach. Ultimately, God came to earth in the person of his Son, Jesus, to take upon himself the burden of our sin and restore individuals to a harmonious relationship with himself. Jesus died, the righteous on behalf of the unrighteous, and by his death he restores our union with God (1 Pet. 3:18).

Thus, the Bible speaks of two Adams. The first, history's original man, disobeyed and severed the bonds that united man to God. The second Adam, Christ, was obedient even to the point of death, and in his self-sacrifice he restored all who trust him

Adam and Eve on this green-tinted Roman dish (about A.D. 350) show signs of the Fall's curse: Eve's hand covers her genitals in shame and Adam carries a stalk of wheat in his left hand to indicate working the soil (Gen. 3:6–19). The serpent is wrapped around the tree (right).

to a loving, intimate relationship with God. *See also* Adam.

DID THE FALL REALLY HAPPEN?
Some theologians have described the story of the Fall as a myth. Most who use this language assume the story is a fictional

THE USES OF "FALL" IN THE NEW TESTAMENT

Passage	NIV Translation	Greek Word	Topic of Passage	Meaning of "Fall"
Rom. 14:21	"cause your brother to fall"	*proskoptō*, "stumble"	personal convictions about matters not called sin in the Bible	act against own conscience
1 Cor. 10:12	"be careful that you don't fall"	*piptō*, "fall"	avoiding or overcoming temptations to sin	give in to temptation
Heb. 4:11	"fall by following their example of disobedience"	*piptō*, "fall"	failure to find God's best by disobeying the Lord	fail to trust and obey God
Heb. 6:6	"fall away"	*parapiptō*, "fall aside"	temptation of Jewish Christians to return to Judaism	abandon Christian community
Gal. 5:4	"fallen away from grace"	*ekpiptō*, "fall down from"	contrast between relying on one's own effort to keep God's Law and relying on grace	self-effort that cuts Christians off from daily grace
2 Pet. 3:17	"fall from your secure position"	*ekpiptō*, "fall down from"	false teachers who turn believers away from full reliance on Jesus	follow such false teachings and fail to rely fully on Jesus
1 Tim. 6:9	"fall into temptation"	*empiptō*, "fall into"	becoming ensnared by worldly desires	give in to temptation

Each of the passages above focuses on Christian experience after salvation. None deals with salvation or saving faith in Christ. Thus the "fall" involved is not the loss of salvation but a failure to rely daily on God's grace and to experience the full benefits of salvation. *See also* Salvation.

drama, but one that powerfully expresses basic elements in the biblical perspective of reality.

Yet the NT, as well as the OT, treats the Genesis account of the Fall as history (Mt. 19:5,6; Mk. 10:7,8; Rom. 5:12-19; 1 Cor. 15:45,47,49; 1 Tim. 2:13,14). Thus other scholars have asserted that the Fall is a historical event. In this view, early Genesis and the story of the Fall validate the biblical understanding of man's nature, of sin, of evil, and of the need for redemption precisely because these events actually took place in history. *See also* Adam; Eve.

fall Metaphorically, in Scripture, (1) to stumble, fail; (2) to yield to temptation, to sin; (3) to come to ruin; (4) to come to a lower or lesser condition. The theological use of "fall" to describe Adam's sin and its consequences has affected the way that some scholars interpret the meaning of this word in various NT passages. At times, this has led to unnecessary worry about personal salvation.

Most of the Greek words translated "fall" in English versions are forms of *piptō*, with prepositions added to indicate falling down, falling away, falling aside, etc. "Fall" is used in the NT in a literal sense to describe a person stumbling or a building torn down by a flood (Mt. 7:27). But "fall" is often used figuratively, as in the phrase "fallen away from grace."

The specific meaning of "fall" must be determined by the context of the passage. The accompanying chart examines passages that frequently cause concern and suggests the most probable meaning of "fall" in each context.

false, falsehood (1) Misrepresenting reality; (2) breaking a trust, being false in a personal relationship.

Various Hebrew words portray falsehood and deceit in the OT. Deceit purposely misleads others. The Hebrew words for falsehood emphasize four aspects: (1) The false has no basis in reality. (2) The false is empty, unreal. (3) The false violates commitments. (4) The false is undependable; the false person harms others by failing to live up to the most basic requirements of personal relationships. *See also* Deceit; Lie.

Thus the "false prophet" mentioned so often in the OT is a person whose proclamations are not divinely revealed. His undependable teachings deceive others and do harm. *See also* False Prophets and Teachers.

Some 15 different Greek words express the idea of falsehood in the NT. Most are built on the root *pseudō*. In the NT, falsehood draws our attention to the difference between reality and illusion. Since only God knows reality as it truly is, we depend on his revelation for our own understanding of what is true and trustworthy. *See also* Truth.

God's revealed Word is the standard by which we measure what is true and false. God also calls us to be true in our own lives and relationships. This starts in our relationship with God. We must honestly confess our sins and failures, for "if we claim we have not sinned, we make him [God] out to be a liar and his word has no place in our lives" (1 Jn. 1:10). We must also be honest in our relationships with other Christians. As Eph. 4:25 says, "Each of you must put off falsehood and speak truthfully to his neighbor, for we are all members of one body."

false prophets and teachers (1) Persons who misrepresent themselves as God's spokesmen; (2) those whose teachings cannot be depended on because they have no basis in reality. *See also* False.

Moses promised that God would speak to his people through prophets, and gave Israel various ways to determine which prophets are true and which are false.

According to Deut. 13:1-5, any prophet who advocates worship of other gods is a false prophet. According to Deut. 18:14-22, the true prophet will (1) be an Israelite, (2) speak in the name of Yahweh rather than that of some other god, and (3) make predictions which come true. Any prophet who "proclaims a message in the name of the Lord that does not take place or come true, that is a message the Lord has not spoken."

The NT describes false prophets and teachers. (1) Doctrinally, they can be recognized by their denial that Jesus is the Christ, the Son of God (2 Pet. 2:11; 1 Jn. 4:1-3). (2) Morally, they are marked by arrogance, a love for money, antagonism to authority, and sexual corruption (2 Pet. 2:10,12,15; Jude 3,4,8,11-13,16,19). (3) Their ministries are marked by an appeal to the "lustful desires of sinful human nature" and by the promise of "freedom" (2 Pet. 2:18,19).

False prophets and teachers plagued Israel throughout the OT era. They were also present in the apostolic age, and they continue to trouble the modern church.

familiar spirit An occult term for the "ghost" or spirit being summoned by a medium. A person with a familiar spirit is a medium or spiritist (Heb., 'ob) in communication with the dead.

The notion of making contact with someone or something in the spirit world is common in modern times, although the beings contacted are not usually identified as demons. The contemporary practice of "channeling," the activity by which the supposed spirit of a long-dead person speaks through a living, human channel, is undoubtedly the same practice described by the Hebrew 'ob.

While many so-called mediums rely on trickery, some make contact with actual demonic beings. The OT takes this possibility seriously and strictly prohibits such occult practices: "A man or woman who is a medium or spiritist among you must be put to death. You are to stone them; their blood will be on their own heads" (Lev. 20:27).

family (1) The nuclear unit of a husband, wife, and their children; (2) a larger group of persons linked by common descent; (3) all those dependent on the head of a family.

THE FAMILY IN OT TIMES

The family was most commonly referred to as a "house" or "household." Archaeological remains of houses and water cisterns in Israel indicate that most nuclear families consisted of six or seven members. At times, close relatives may have lived in houses next to one another. Quite char-

acteristically, sons would build or select a dwelling in the same compound as their parents once they married.

The pattern for the nuclear family is established early in Genesis and supported in Mosaic Law by strict regulations prohibiting adultery and other sexual deviations which weaken the family structure (Ex. 20:14; Lev. 18). Divorce and remarriage, although permitted in OT times, were not common or looked on favorably. *See also* Polygamy.

The Israelite family was ruled by the father. While some rights of family members were protected by law (Ex. 21:7-11; Deut. 21:10-18), the father was legally responsible for his wife and their children. Wealthy families often had slaves, concubines, and hired foreign workers living with them. These persons submitted to the authority of the father and were considered members of the larger household, although they did not have the right of a child to address the father familiarly.

The nuclear family in Israel was linked both to the clan and the tribe. The clan included several families that shared a common ancestor and generally lived close to each other. Clan members had the right and duty to redeem the property of a near relative whose homestead had been sold to pay a debt, and to redeem members who had been sold into slavery. *See also* Kinsman.

The tribe was an even larger unit whose

Attended by his family, the royal scribe Nakht enjoys fowling with snake-headed throw sticks and fishing with a spear (missing). Tomb painting from Thebes, about 1425 B.C.

Greek funeral slab with six family portraits dating from the second century A.D. The inscription below the bust identifies them as a well-respected family from Apollonia, a city through which Paul passed on his way to Thessalonica (Acts 17:1).

though not necessarily living in the same house. The household of the Roman centurion Cornelius probably included "his relatives and close friends" (Acts 10:24). The "house" of the Philippian jailer may even have consisted of the jailers he supervised, as well as his children and servants (Acts 16:31-34). *See also* House.

FAMILY RESPONSIBILITIES

Members of the family were bound together in a covenant-like relationship. Husband and wife were committed to one another, and each worked to meet the family's need for food and shelter. The father was primarily responsible for the religious training of children, although the mother's influence is mentioned often in the Bible (Prov. 31; 2 Tim. 1:5; 3:15). Parents were to provide for their children, to discipline and guide them wisely, and to communicate God's Word to them effectively (Ex. 12:26; Deut. 6:6,7; Eph. 6:4; 1 Tim. 5:8). In return, children owed their parents respect, obedience, and support in their old age, if necessary (Ex. 20:12; Eph. 6:1; Col. 3:20; 1 Tim. 5:8). The family was an intimate sphere of mutual love and duty—a womb which protected and nourished each new generation as it grew to godly maturity. *See also* Nurture.

THE CHURCH AS FAMILY

The NT casts the Church as God's family. How appropriate, then, that "brother" becomes the most common form of address between Christians. Paul urged Timothy to treat members of the Body of Christ as fathers, mothers, brothers, and sisters (1 Tim. 5). He advised that, if no members of a person's natural family remained, the church family should support those widows and orphans in need (1 Tim. 5:16).

Similarly, James counsels "look[ing] after orphans and widows in their distress." This familial caring, the apostle says, is part of the religion which "God our Father accepts as pure and faultless" (1:27).

members traced their ancestry back to one of the twelve sons of Jacob (Israel). The numerous genealogies in the Bible show how important the family line was.

After the land of Canaan was distributed to the Israelites by tribe, the tribe functioned as a political unit and as a basis for army units (Num. 1). Not until the time of David did the tribes unite under strong, national leadership. Later, tribal jealousies led to the shattering of David's kingdom after the death of his son Solomon.

THE FAMILY IN NT TIMES

Although family responsibilities and clan relationships varied little between the Testaments, tribal identity became less important. Nevertheless, the Jews continued to keep careful genealogical records (Mt. 1; Lk. 3).

In the NT Epistles, however, references to "house" and "household" tend to reflect the Roman concept of family. In addition to parents, children, and servants, the household included employees and others who were dependent on the father's estate

famine A lack of food due to drought, war, insect plagues, or other disasters.

Agriculture in Palestine depended on two seasons of rain. When either the early or latter rains failed, the land faced potential famine. Other natural disasters threatened the food supply as well. Hailstorms might destroy grain fields, or swarms of locusts and caterpillars might consume all vegetation. Biblical famines could also be precipitated by armies who lived off crops found in the lands they invaded.

The best-known biblical famine was foretold in Pharaoh's dream (Gen. 41). Joseph's interpretation of this dream led to his rise to power in Egypt and prepared the way for his family to enter that great land, where they multiplied and prospered. While this famine was used by God to bless his people, the Bible most often associates famine with divine judgment (Deut. 32:24; Jer. 14:12; Ezek. 5:16).

fan (KJV) A long wooden fork used in winnowing grain. *See also* Winnow.

farming *See* Agriculture.

farthing (KJV) A small coin worth only a few cents. Modern versions use the word "penny" as a translation for both *assarion* (Mt. 10:29; Lk. 12:6) and *kodrantēs* (Mt. 5:26; Mk. 12:42). *See also* Coins; Money.

fast, fasting (1) Going without food and/ or water; (2) consuming only water and simple foods.

Many biblical fasts lasted for a day, from sunrise to sunset; some continued for several days. Individuals often fasted when in the grip of some crisis or strong emotion (1 Sam. 1:3-7; 2 Sam. 12:15-18; Dan. 6:18). Old Testament Law legislated fasting only on the Day of Atonement (Lev. 16:29; Jer. 36:6). Public fasting was associated with national repentance (Neh. 9:1) and crisis (Jdg. 20:26; 1 Sam. 7:6; 2 Chr. 20:3). These fasts were typically accompanied by confession and by earnest appeal to God in prayer. *See* Atonement, Day of; Feasts, Festivals, and Fasts.

When fasting expressed true repentance and grief, God responded with acts of deliverance (Jon. 3:5-10; Esth. 4:3,16; 9:31). At other times, however, fasting was little more than a hypocritical attempt to manipulate God. In the time of Isaiah, for example, the people complained that they had fasted, but God had not seemed to notice (Isa. 58:2,3). Isaiah's response is significant. God cares more about righteousness than fasting:

"Is not this the kind of fasting I have chosen:
*   to loose the chains of injustice*
*   and untie the cords of the yoke,*
*   to set the oppressed free*
*   and break every yoke?*
Is it not to share your food with the hungry
*   and to provide the poor wanderer with*
*   shelter—*
when you see the naked, to clothe him,
*   and not to turn away from your own flesh*
*   and blood?*
Then your light will break forth like the
*   dawn,*
*   and your healing will quickly appear . . ."*
                                    (Isa. 58:6-8)

After 586 B.C., the destruction of Jerusalem was commemorated with four annual fasts, mentioned only in Zech. 7:1-7 and 8:19. Again, God questioned the motive for these fasts, saying that Israel fasted for themselves rather than for him. And again the Lord returned to the central issue: "Administer true justice; show mercy and compassion to one another. Do not oppress the widow or the fatherless, the alien or the poor. In your hearts do not think evil of each other" (7:9,10).

Criticism of ritual fasting is also found in the NT. Jesus dismissed those who paraded their piety on the two traditional fast days, Tuesday and Thursday. On those

The farthing (KJV) or penny (NIV) of Mt. 10:29 was actually the Roman as (Gk., assarion), a bronze or copper coin worth 1/16 of a denarius. The as shown here bears the portrait of Tiberius Caesar (A.D. 22–23).

373

days they looked somber, disfiguring their faces to make sure everyone knew they were fasting. Dryly, Jesus commented, "They have their reward" (Mt. 6:16-18).

Jesus criticized the misuse of fasting, not fasting itself. He himself fasted for 40 days before beginning his public ministry (Mt. 4:2), yet he noted that fasting was not appropriate for his disciples while he was present with them. Rather, it was a time for rejoicing (Mt. 9:14,15; Lk. 5:33-35). The reference in Mk. 9:14-29 to fasting and prayer to cast out demons, like that in 1 Cor. 7:5, is not in the oldest Greek manuscripts and may be an addition to the original text. The NT Epistles contain no encouragement to fast.

Yet believers did fast in the apostolic age, when ordaining elders and teachers (Acts 13:2,3; 14:23) and occasionally in times of special need (compare Acts 12:5; Acts 27:1-38). Soon after the apostolic age, Christian leaders called for fasting before baptism, at Easter, and as a weekly habit on Wednesdays and Fridays.

It is clear that fasting is an appropriate expression of grief or deep religious need, but fasting is no substitute for a heartfelt commitment to righteousness and justice. Fasting is no meritorious act, nor a way to win a "more spiritual" rating from God or from others.

Some Christians today fast as a spiritual discipline: to develop proper control over bodily desires or to prepare for a special task or decision.

fat (1) The greasy tissue of animals; (2) the richest part of something. The fat of sacrificed animals was burned on the altar and prohibited by the Mosaic Law from the Hebrew diet (Lev. 3:17).

Used figuratively, "fat" may suggest prosperity and fertile lands. Yet there is a negative overtone, for the person grown fat is self-satisfied, and apt to abandon God (Deut. 32:15).

father (1) A male parent; (2) any ancestor; (3) God; (4) the creator or originator of something; (5) a polite form of address to a superior.

FATHER AS A PARENT

The father in the patriarchal family of Bible times had a number of special responsibilities. He was the spiritual leader of the home (Gen. 12:8; Ex. 12:3), responsible, with his wife, for the education of his children (Prov. 22:6; Deut. 6:7-9). He was to discipline his children wisely and lovingly (Prov. 13:24; Eph. 6:4; Heb. 12:5-

11). He was to provide for his family (Prov. 6:6-11; 1 Tim. 5:8) and defend their rights in court (Deut. 22:13-19). When Job aided widows and orphans, he assumed the role of a father (Job 29:16).

According to the Jewish Talmud, the father's duties to his son can be summed up in five responsibilities. The father was to circumcise his son, to "redeem" him from God if he was the firstborn (Num. 18:15,16), to teach him the Law, to teach him a trade, and to find him a wife (Gen. 24:4).

While the father had great authority over his children, and even was able to sell them into temporary servitude in order to pay debts, the OT clearly admonishes fathers to have compassion for their children (Ps. 103:13). This loving, caring father-child relationship was so common in Israel that God used this image to describe his love for Israel. See also Fatherhood of God.

FATHER AS AN ANCESTOR

The term "father" is often used of grandfathers and more remote ancestors (Gen. 32:9; 1 Ki. 15:11; Mt. 1:1-16). This use makes it difficult to determine the time gaps in most Hebrew genealogies. Generations may have passed between a "father" and the son he "begat." Even in NT times, Jews referred to Abraham and David, their most renowned ancestors, as "father" (Jn. 8:39; Mk. 11:10).

FATHER AS CREATOR/ ORIGINATOR

Often when God is spoken of as Father in the OT, the emphasis is not on relationship but on origin. Israel traced its beginnings as a nation back to its being chosen and redeemed by God. So Malachi cries out, "Have we not all one Father? Did not one God create us?" (Mal. 2:10). In a similar way, Genesis speaks of Jubal as "the father of all who play the harp and flute" (Gen. 4:21), crediting Jubal with the invention of musical instruments.

This usage helps explain Jesus' charge that the Jewish religious leaders who opposed him so violently were descendants of "your father, the devil" (Jn. 8:44; compare Rom. 4:11). Satan is identified as "a murderer from the beginning . . . [and] a liar." Because Satan is the father (originator) of lies, those who denied the truth that Jesus spoke identified themselves with Satan rather than God.

FATHER AS A TITLE OF RESPECT

Calling an older person or one in authority "father" was a polite form of address in biblical times (Jdg. 17:10; 1 Sam. 24:11; 2 Ki. 5:13). In these passages a Levite, a king, and a commander are addressed respectfully as "my father."

In his scathing rebuke of the Pharisees, Jesus said, "Do not call anyone on earth 'father,' for you have one Father, and he is in heaven" (Mt. 23:9). Jesus was not prohibiting us from treating people with respect; he was, however, clearly accusing the Pharisees of setting up systems of authority that replaced the authority of God.

fatherhood of God "God the Father" distinguishes the first person of the Trinity from the Son and Holy Spirit. God's fatherhood (1) affirms God's role as Creator; (2) portrays his compassion; (3) affirms his unique relationship with Jesus as his Son; and (4) in the NT expresses the intimacy of the personal relationship made possible for us with God through Jesus Christ. *See also* Father; Trinity.

GOD AS CREATOR OR ORIGINATOR

Just as a human father is viewed as the source of life for his descendants (*compare* Gen. 17:5; Rom. 4:11), many references to the fatherhood of God portray him as Creator. He is called the "Father of the heavenly lights [i.e., the stars]" (Jas. 1:17), of "our spirits" (Heb. 12:9), and of humanity, which was created in God's image (Acts 17:26). In this same sense, God is spoken of as the Father of the Hebrew people, whom he chose and ultimately planted as a nation in the Promised Land (Jer. 31:9). As Moses taught Israel,

Is he not your Father, your Creator,
who made you and formed you?

(Deut. 32:6)

It is right and proper to affirm the universal fatherhood of God in this sense of Creator and source, for all humanity springs from him.

GOD'S FATHERLY CHARACTER

Often Scripture portrays God's character and role as that of a loving father. Moses uses the image in Deut. 1:31: "You saw how the Lord your God carried you, as a father carries his son." The frequent use of this image reminds God's people of the Lord's compassion (Ps. 103:13) and his tender love (Hos. 11:1), as well as his loving discipline (Prov. 3:11,12). *See also* Discipline.

GOD AS THE FATHER OF JESUS

Against the background of the OT's concept of God's fatherhood, Christ's claim that God was his Father caused great consternation because Jesus was clearly using the term to affirm a unique, personal relationship with Israel's God. John 5 records one instance of both Jesus' claim and the people's response. "For this reason the Jews ['Jews' is John's term for the religious leaders who opposed Christ] tried all the harder to kill him; not only was he breaking the Sabbath, but he was even calling God his own Father, making himself equal with God" (Jn. 5:18). This equality continues to be affirmed in the NT Epistles where God is identified as "the Father of our Lord Jesus Christ" (Eph. 1:17; 1 Cor. 8:6; 1 Pet. 1:3).

GOD AS FATHER OF BELIEVERS

Even more striking is the fact that the NT teaches believers to look to God as their Father. Yet believers do not share Jesus' unique relationship with God the Father as an equal. Jesus consistently made a distinction by referring to "my Father" and "your Father." Yet, through Jesus, Christ's followers have been drawn into a far more intimate relationship with

Moses reminded the new generation of Israelites about to enter Canaan that God had carried them out of bondage, "as a father carries his son" (Deut. 1:31). Detail from a stone relief on a child's sarcophagus, second century A.D.

375

God than anyone had imagined possible. The theology of this new relationship is developed in the NT teaching on sonship, but the practical implications of having God as a Father infuse both Gospels and Epistles. *See also* Son.

Christ taught his disciples to pray, "Our Father" (Mt. 6:9). He encouraged them to rely so completely on God's Father-love that they would be released from worry, even over necessities of life (Mt. 6:25-34). God the Father, who is completely good, can be counted on to give good gifts to his children (Mt. 7:9-12).

Experience of the new relationship we have with God as Father brings us peace (Rom. 1:7; 1 Cor. 1:3; Eph. 1:2). We now have immediate access to the Father in prayer (Eph. 2:18), and even the freedom to address the Creator as a child would his loving father (Rom. 8:15). *See also* Abba.

God, then, is the Father of all in the sense of being Creator of all humanity. God is also Father in his essential attitude toward all mankind, for he loves and has compassion for everyone. He is the Father of Jesus in a special sense, for in nature Jesus and God the Father are equal and one. In a more restrictive sense, God is the spiritual Father of those who, through faith in Christ, have become members of God's own family. *See also* Family.

fatherless Persons who have no father to provide for or defend them. The images of the alien, the widow, and the fatherless in the OT stand as symbols of the powerless and disadvantaged in human society. *See also* Alien.

Under Mosaic Law the third year's tithe was to be stored, so that "the aliens, the fatherless and the widows who live in your towns may come and eat and be satisfied" (Deut. 14:29; 26:12). In addition, the part of the crop that fell to the ground was to be left there by the farmer, so that it could be gathered freely by the alien, the fatherless, and the widow (Deut. 24:19-21). Furthermore, the Law states, "Cursed is the man who withholds justice from the alien, the fatherless or the widow" (Deut. 27:19); the Law obligates the godly to protect them from oppression (Deut. 10:18; 24:17; 26:12,13).

God places himself squarely on the side of the oppressed in society, and declares himself their defender (Ps. 10:14), "a father to the fatherless, a defender of widows" (Ps. 68:5).

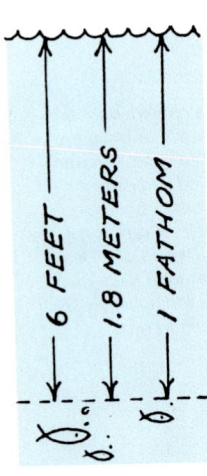

fathom (KJV, RSV) A nautical measure of depth equivalent to about 6 feet (1.8

meters). It is mentioned only in the account of Paul's shipwreck (Acts 27:28).

fear Terror, dread; reverence, awe. Fear can paralyze or weaken us. It can lead to flight or foolish action. When Belshazzar saw the writing on the wall, "his face turned pale and he was so frightened that his knees knocked together and his legs gave way" (Dan. 5:6). Yet for the believer, the fear of God leads to freedom, love, and worship.

REASONABLENESS OF FEAR

Fear is a reasonable emotion. It was reasonable for Jacob to be afraid of his brother Esau, whom he had wronged (Gen. 32:7). It was reasonable for Job, terrified by the unexplained disasters that befell him, to fear what lay ahead (Job 3:25; 21:6). Throughout biblical times it was reasonable for men and women to fear famine, invasion, and disease. Even today it is not unreasonable to be afraid. Fear is a natural, although painful, emotion.

FEAR AS AN ENEMY

Fear is a foe when it robs us of strength or motivates us to make wrong choices. This kind of fear might be called a fear of anticipated evil. We look ahead and, realizing how vulnerable we are, we fear those things that may go wrong.

In the days of Saul, the Israelites "hid in caves and thickets, among the rocks, and in pits and cisterns" rather than face a Philistine army (1 Sam. 13). Their fear of anticipated evil robbed them of courage and faith.

Saul violated God's command to destroy the flocks of an enemy people, because "I was afraid of the people and gave in to them" (1 Sam. 15:24). His fear of an anticipated evil led him to disobey God.

The Gospels tell us that many who believed in Jesus were unwilling to acknowledge him publicly (Jn. 9:22; Acts 5:13). Their fear of anticipated evil made them timid and unwilling to act.

Even more tragically, human beings are often terrified of God. Adam and Eve hid from God after eating the forbidden fruit because they were afraid (Gen. 3:10). Sin alienates us from God and creates anxiety about our relationship with the Lord. Moses was terrified that an angry God would destroy Israel for worshiping the golden calf at Mount Sinai (Ex. 32). Sinners anticipate punishment at the hand of an angry God. In fact, our sins may create a constant state of unease. "The wicked man flees though no one pursues" (Prov. 28:1).

In one sense the sinner's fear of God is appropriate because God will punish sin. The Bible often describes the Day of Judgment in terms of terror (Ps. 48:2-5; Isa. 13:6-8). But the tragedy is that so many, in their terror, flee from God rather than turn to him. There is an alternative to punishment—forgiveness. When fear of anticipated evil drives us from God, rather than to him, fear is our enemy.

FEAR AS A FRIEND

Fear can also be a friend. A child who is afraid of being burned will avoid fire. An adult who is afraid of the consequences will avoid sin. Fear of anticipated evil protects us from harmful choices. There is also a more subtle value to fear. David expresses it this way in Psalm 56:3,4:

When I am afraid,
 I will trust in you.
In God, whose word I praise,
 in God I trust; I will not be afraid.
 What can mortal man do to me?

Fear of anticipated evil can cause us to recognize our vulnerability and to realize how completely we must depend on God for all things. Scripture reminds us of God's love and his trustworthiness: "Do not be afraid, for I am with you" (Isa. 43:5).

Fear is positive when it causes us to turn to the Lord; it can lead us to reevaluate our relationship with God, and perhaps to make a fresh commitment to trust him. Through trust in God, we gain victory over our fear, and we anticipate good from his loving hand.

fear of God, fear of the Lord A reverential awe which leads the believer to love and obey God.

When the Bible says that the "fear of the Lord is the beginning of knowledge" (Prov. 1:7; *compare* Ps. 36:1-4), it means that a healthy respect for the living God is the foundation of religious faith and morality. Thus the phrase, "those who fear the Lord," which appears throughout the OT, refers to believers or religious people. In the first century A.D. Gentiles who did not convert to Judaism, but who worshiped Israel's God and lived by Scripture's moral Law, were appropriately called "God fearers" (Acts 13:16, JB). *See also* God-fearing.

The nature and outcome of a reverential awe of God is most clearly expressed in the words of Deut. 10:12,13. God admonishes Israel to fear him, describing that fear in terms of the life-style and attitudes it creates. "And now, O Israel, what does the Lord your God ask of you but to fear the Lord your God, to walk in all his ways, to love him, to serve the Lord your God with all your heart and with all your soul, and to observe the Lord's commands and decrees that I am giving you today for your own good?"

The NT also views a reverent awe of God as a motive for holy living (1 Pet. 1:17; 2:17). More importantly, Jesus taught that fear of God frees us from other fears. Jesus contrasted the anxiety of the pagan, who worries about food and clothing, with the freedom experienced by the believer who knows God's fatherly love. Fear of God offers us freedom from worry and release from other concerns that block us from seeking first God's Kingdom and righteousness (Mt. 6:25-34). Jesus comforted his disciples by reminding them that God notes even the sparrow's fall, and "you are worth more than many sparrows" (Lk. 12:7). The person who stands in awe of God considers God the ultimate reality. He or she cares more about God's approval than what others will think or do (Mt. 10:28-31).

The person who fears the Lord and has an awareness of God's power and authority will live a godly life out of respect for God. As the writer of Heb. 12:28,29 says, "Let us be thankful, and so worship God acceptably with reverence and awe, for our God is a consuming fire."

feasts, festivals, and fasts Religious observances which punctuated the Jewish year. The terms "feast" or "festival" [Heb., *hag* or *mo'ad*] convey joyful celebration.

The distinct ritual of the Feast of Booths (Sukkot) is the requirement to "dwell in booths" (sukkah) like this one in commemoration of God's protection of the wandering Israelites (Lev. 23:39-43).

Jewish Feasts, Fasts and Festivals

Nisan
- **14** **Passover** (Ex. 12; Lev. 23:5)
- **15–21** **Feast of Unleavened Bread** (Lev. 23:6-8) Both commemorate God's deliverance of Israel out of Egypt; feast includes a day of firstfruits for the barley harvest (Lev. 23:9-14)

Iyyar
- **14** Second Passover (Num. 9:9-13; 2 Chr. 30:2,3) Limited to those ritually unclean or unavoidably absent from Passover

Sivan
- **6** **Feast of Weeks or Harvest (Pentecost)** (Ex. 34:22; Lev. 23:15-21) Commemorates giving of the Law at Mount Sinai; also a day of firstfruits for the wheat harvest (Ex. 23:16)

Tammuz
- **17** Fast of the fourth month (Zec. 8:19) Mourns the breach of Jerusalem's walls in 586 B.C. and A.D. 70

Ab
- **9** Fast of the fifth month (Zec. 8:19) Mourns destruction of Solomon's and Herod's Temples
- **15** Fifteenth of Ab (Mishnaic) Day of rejoicing in post-exilic times

Elul

Tishri
- **1** **Feast of Trumpets (Rosh Hashanah)** (Lev. 23:24,25) Day of blowing trumpets to begin civil new year
- **3** Fast of Gedaliah (Zec. 7:5; 8:19) Commemorates his assassination (2 Ki. 25:25; Jer. 40–41)
- **10** **Day of Atonement (Yom Kippur)** (Lev. 23:26-32; Ex. 30:10) Fast day; high priest makes atonement for the nation's sin
- **15–22** **Feast of Tabernacles or Ingathering (Sukkot)** (Lev. 23:33-43; Num. 29:12-40) Commemorates 40 years of wandering
- **23** Simhat Torah; finish of the Law's annual reading cycle

Heshvan

Kislev
- **25–30** **Feast of Dedication (Hanukkah)** (Jn. 10:22) Commemorates purification of the Temple by Judas Maccabeus in 164 B.C. (1 Maccabees 4:59); also known as the Festival of Lights

Tebeth
- **1–2** **Feast of Dedication** (cont.)
- **10** Fast of the tenth month (Zec. 8:19) Commemorates beginning of siege of Jerusalem by Nebuchadnezzar (2 Ki. 25:1)

Shebat
- **13** Fast of Esther: (see Esth. 3:13) Date of Haman's planned execution of Jews; first observed in 8th century A.D.
- **14** **Feast of Esther (Purim)** (Esth. 9) Commemorates deliverance of the Jews in Esther's day
- **15** Shushan Purim; traditional day walled cities in Israel celebrate Purim

Adar

Legend
- ▢ Important biblical day
- ▢ Pilgrimage festival
- ▢ Fast or extrabiblical observance

Specific activities and ritual varied from festival to festival but they all included sacrifices, prayers, special meals, ceremonies and customs. Current customary Hebrew greetings during such holy days—*Hag sameah* ("May you have a joyful festival") and *Moadim le-simhah* ("Festivals of rejoicing for you")—capture the Jewish sense that commitment to God is compatible with enjoying his temporal gifts (Lev. 23:40; Deut. 16:14). In fact, three feasts combine religious celebrations with seasonal events.

Unlike other religions of the ancient Near East, however, the origins of seasonal rituals were subservient to the greater purpose of acknowledging God's forgiveness, favor, and provision (Ex. 10:2; 12:8-14; Lev. 22:31–23:2; Deut. 16:1-17). These events drew God's people together to worship and to remember their heritage. They also provided a vital means of deepening Israel's faith. God expressed displeasure with the Israelites when, despite their external observance of feasts, they were unjust and disobedient to God's Law (Isa. 1:10-20).

Fasts, by their nature, were times of mourning or reflection on one's sin. Many fast days were noted on the religious calendar of Israel, but only one fast day was ordained by Mosaic Law—the Day of Atonement. *See also* Atonement, Day of; Fast.

ORDAINED FEASTS

Old Testament Law established five yearly religious festivals (Lev. 23:4-44). By NT times, others had been added to the calendar (*see* accompanying chart).

Three of the five ordained festivals—the feasts of Unleavened Bread, Weeks, and Tabernacles—were "pilgrim festivals," which required adult males to participate at the sanctuary (Ex. 23:14,17; Deut. 16:16,17). *See also* Passover; Pentecost; Tabernacles, Feast of.

Each of these five main feasts included "holy convocations," involving the sacrifice of animals. Passover and the Feast of Tabernacles, both week-long events, were marked by solemn assemblies on the first and last day. The people shared communal meals, eating the meat of the sacrificial animals. These convocations were times of joy, for while the sacrifices reminded Israel of sin, they also affirmed God's forgiveness. *See also* Sacrifices and Offerings.

An important aspect of the feasts and fasts is their commemoration of historic events. In a sense, the festivals allowed the Hebrew people to re-live history. Only

the Day of Atonement and Feast of Trumpets were purely occasions of atonement and reconciliation with God.

Subsequent festivals added to the calendar also commemorated important events of God's deliverance of Israel. The most significant of these were the Festival of Lights (*Hanukkah*), called "Dedication" in the Gospel of John (10:22), and Purim, the Feast of Esther.

OTHER WORSHIP TIMES

In addition to the annual festivals, there were other times of worship; these were organized by sevens.

Every seven days a Sabbath was set aside for rest and remembrance of God as Creator. Every seventh year debts were canceled, and the land was given a rest from cultivation. The people and the land itself were to be relieved of their burdens, even as God himself had lifted Israel and carried her to the Promised Land. God promised sufficient crops in the sixth year to carry the people through the seventh year.

After a cycle of seven sevens of years, the fiftieth year was celebrated as a year of Jubilee. During that year any land which had been sold was returned to the family which originally held it, and all slaves were freed. The fiftieth year thus mirrored the freedom which God himself had won for Israel, delivering them from the slave quarters in Egypt to land of their own in Canaan.

It is no wonder, then, that Israel's worship calendar was marked by joy and celebration. Each calendar event reminded godly Israelites of what God had done for them.

The Christian calendar year is also designed to stimulate a sense of joy and wonder. It, too, commemorates God's great acts for his people. Sunday has replaced the Sabbath, and each week Christians gather to remember that Jesus, who was raised the first day of the week, lives. At Christmas we recall with wonder that God became flesh and lived among us. On Good Friday we re-live the crucifixion, remembering that Jesus suffered for our sins. And on Easter we rejoice, not only in Jesus' resurrection, but in the new life that the living Christ gives to all who believe in him.

Rightly understood, then, times of worship in both OT and NT eras were times for joy and celebration. In each era God's people had occasion to remember all God had done for them and to respond to God's goodness with thanksgiving and joyful praise. *See also* Worship.

fellowship (1) A community, an intimate association; (2) a mutual sharing; (3) a participatory relationship. The Greek term, *koinōnia*, is translated by a variety of words in English versions, including "sharing," "partnership," "contribution," and "fellowship."

Koinōnia is used in three significant theological ways in the NT. First, Paul states that God has called us into fellowship with his Son (1 Cor. 1:9). The positional use of *koinōnia* reflects our bonding to Jesus by faith—this union with Jesus is the source of power for Christian living (Jn. 15:1-5).

Second, John's letters use this word to describe the believer's experience with Christ (1 Jn. 1:3,7). The experiential use of *koinōnia* teaches us that in order to live in partnership with a holy God we must be completely honest with him. We must not deny sin but confess it, so that God can continually cleanse and purify us.

Third, Acts and the Epistles use *koinōnia* to describe relationships in the Christian community (Acts 2:42; Rom. 15:26; Gal. 2:9; Phil. 1:5). The relational use of *koinōnia* is especially powerful because it portrays the Christian community as close-knit and loving. Acts 2 describes beautifully the warm bond among believers in the early church, who freely gave to anyone in need. "Every day they continued to meet together in the temple courts. They broke bread in their homes and ate together with glad and sincere hearts, praising God and enjoying the favor of all the people" (Acts 2:46,47).

Left: Mosaic floor from a synagogue in Tiberius (5th century A.D.) includes elements from Israel's festivals: a menorah *or candlestick for Hanukkah, a* shofar *or ram's horn trumpet for Rosh Hashanah, and an* arbaah minim, *a wand made of four different plants, for Sukkot.*

What is perhaps most striking in this relational use of *koinōnia* is that this word, rather than "giving," is used to describe the contributions Christians might give to others in need (*see* Rom. 15:26; 2 Cor. 8:4; 9:13). Christian giving is a sharing of possessions within the Body of Christ, an expression of love and solidarity. *See also* Give.

In the Greek-speaking world, *koinōnia* was sometimes used to describe an ideal secular society in which harmony and good will would reign. That ideal has never been realized among men, but this dream of intimacy and harmony becomes possible in the Church, where a shared relationship with Jesus generates Christian love among believers.

fetters Chains or shackles normally fastened on the legs of captives or prisoners (2 Sam. 3:34; Pss. 2:3; 149:8; Lk. 8:29). "Fetter" is used in some English versions to indicate any kind of bond or chain, though "shackles" is more common in the NIV (Jdg. 16:21; Ps. 105:18; Jer. 39:7; Nah. 1:13). Job described his suffering figuratively—being shackled by God (13:27; 33:11).

Above: Assyrian-style ankle shackles. King Zedekiah was bound with similar ones made of bronze when he and the people of Judah were exiled to Babylon (2 Ki. 25:7). Right: An Egyptian official drags a fettered Semitic prisoner in this relief from the tomb of Horemhab, viceroy under Amenhopis IV (1350–1315 B.C.).

fever High body temperature. The various biblical words for "fever" often refer to different stages of malaria, a disease common in the north of Israel and in the Jordan Valley. Peter's mother-in-law (Mt. 8:14) and the nobleman's son (Jn. 4:52), both of whom lived in Capernaum, probably suffered from malaria.

Other diseases similar to malaria that may be indicated by the word "fever" are yellow fever, blackwater fever, and undulant fever. High fevers are also associated with dysentery (Acts 28:8). Heat stroke, often raising the body temperature as high as 107°, was also a problem in Palestine during summer (Deut. 28:22; 2 Ki. 4:19).

fig A fruit tree common in the Middle East. Its fruit was one of the most important food crops of Palestine. Fig trees grew about 15 feet (5 meters) high. Dried figs, high in sugar content, were pressed into cakes and served as a staple in the Hebrew diet (1 Sam. 25:18). Poultices of figs were also applied to boils (2 Ki. 20:7; Isa. 38:21).

Fig trees were valued for their shade as well as for their fruit. These two contributions make fig trees an appropriate biblical symbol of peace and prosperity (1 Ki. 4:25; Isa. 36:16; Hag. 2:19).

The leaves of the fig tree appear in two important biblical stories. Adam and Eve tried to cover themselves by making aprons of fig leaves (Gen. 3:7). God replaced the leafy aprons with clothing of animal skins. Some scholars have pointed out that this constituted history's first sacrifice, a symbolic representation of the fact that sin can be covered only by blood.

The Gospels tell us that Jesus cursed a barren fig tree whose leafiness suggested fruitfulness (Mk. 11:13,14,20,21). Most scholars view this fig tree as a symbol of Israel, which in Jesus' day appeared to be vital but was actually barren of righteousness (*compare* Mk. 11:15-19; Isa. 5:1-7).

filling with the Spirit A special act of God's Spirit in the believer. This phrase has special theological significance in the NT. The Greek verbs meaning "fill" (*plēthō*, and *plēroō*) always occur in the passive voice when the Spirit is involved (Lk. 1:15,41,67; Acts 2:4; 4:8,31; 9:17; 13:9; Eph. 5:18). Other passages use the passive participle or adjective "full" (Lk. 4:1; Acts 6:3,5; 7:55; 11:24). Both the passive voice and the use of the adjective make it clear that it is God who acts to fill us. We do not fill ourselves; we receive the filling of the Spirit as his gracious gift.

Various Christian traditions have differing interpretations of the phrase "filling with the Spirit," or "Spirit-filled." Yet two aspects of the Spirit's filling are clearly defined in Scripture. First, the Spirit's filling involves empowering for ministry. John the Baptist was filled to prepare him for his mission (Lk. 1:17). The first deacons were required to be men who were filled

with the Spirit (Acts 6:1-6). This emphasis is consistent with the Spirit's historic role in equipping individuals to serve God (Jdg. 6:34; 11:29; 14:19).

The first deacons also illustrate a second aspect of the Spirit's filling: spiritual maturity. They were noted for their wisdom and their faith (Acts 6:3,5). Being filled with God's Spirit is vital for Christian maturity. It leads to growth and personal transformation marked by qualities described in the Bible as "fruit" of the Spirit, such as "love, joy, peace, patience, kindness, goodness, faithfulness, gentleness and self-control" (Gal. 5:22,23).

Paul highlights a third aspect of the Spirit's filling in Eph. 5:18-21. The Spirit aids Christians in corporate encouragement, praise, thanksgiving, and submission. *See also* Holy Spirit.

finger A digit of the hand. When "finger" is used figuratively it indicates someone's direct involvement in an activity. Analyzing the plague of gnats, the Egyptian magicians confessed, "This is the finger of God" (Ex. 8:19), meaning simply that the plague could not be dismissed as magic but could only be an act of God. To say that the stone tablets given to Moses on Sinai were "inscribed by the finger of

God" (Ex. 31:18) does not imply that God wrote with a physical hand; it simply asserts that God himself gave the Ten Commandments (*compare* Lk. 11:20).

fir tree A general term, as in Isa. 41:19 and 60:13, for an evergreen such as cypress, juniper, and pine. Its specific designation in many passages is most likely the Aleppo pine. *See also* Pine Tree.

The wood, imported mainly from Lebanon, was used in the floor and ceilings of Solomon's Temple (1 Ki. 6:15,34), in the construction of ships (Ezek. 27:5), and for making musical instruments (2 Sam. 6:5).

fire The flames or hot coals of anything burning. Fire played a role in the worship and imagery of the OT, as well as in the daily life of God's people.

Fire, kindled by a fire-drill or by striking flint on iron pyrite, was used to cook food, to harden pottery, and to refine metals. But fires could be dangerous in dry Palestine. Old Testament Law stated that anyone who built a fire which then spread to damage another's grain had to pay for his neighbor's loss (Ex. 22:6; Jdg. 15:4,5; 2 Sam. 14:30).

In Israel's ritual worship, fire consumed sacrificial offerings and purified objects used in worship (Num. 31:21-23). The fire

Two men pick and pack figs in baskets in this copy of a painting from the tomb of Khnumhotpe (about 1875 B.C.). Their tame baboons help themselves to the ripe fruit.
Inset:
The common fig (Ficus carica) is mentioned more than 50 times in the Bible and was one of the Israelites' most important foods. Hebrew has four different words for the fig: the green or unripe figs pictured here are called pagehim.

A stone carving from Nineveh (640 B.C.) depicts the destruction and burning of the city of Hamanu by the Assyrians. The Babylonians would do the same to Jerusalem some 60 years later (2 Chr. 36:19).

that burned on the altar of sacrifice outside the tabernacle and the fire kindled within the Temple on the altar of incense were themselves sacred. These fires were to be kept burning at all times and could be used only in ritual worship. Two of Aaron's sons were killed because they made an incense offering with "unauthorized fire" (Lev. 10:1,2; Num. 3:4).

Fire in Scripture is often associated with appearances of God. God appeared to Moses in the burning bush (Ex. 3:2), and to all Israel from atop Mount Sinai (Ex. 19:18). A pillar of fire stood over the tab-

Egyptian wooden model of a man fanning a charcoal fire (about 1900 B.C.). Most biblical peoples cooked on open fires of some sort (see Lk. 21:9).

ernacle in the wilderness, symbolizing God's presence with his people (Ex. 13:21,22). Fire, falling from heaven to consume the sacrifice Elijah offered on Mount Carmel, convinced the people of Israel that "the Lord, he is God" (1 Ki. 18:36-39).

Fire is often a symbol of God's glory or holiness (Deut. 4:24; Ezek. 1:4,13). To remind believers of the awe that we should have for God, the writer of Hebrews says, "Let us be thankful, and so worship God acceptably with reverence and awe, for our God is a consuming fire" (Heb. 12:28,29).

An expression of God's glory and holiness, fire is also an appropriate symbol of divine judgment. Isaiah warns that "with fire and with his sword the Lord will execute judgment upon all men" (Isa. 66:15,16). Paul uses similar terms to describe the judgment that lies ahead. He writes of the time when "the Lord Jesus is revealed from heaven in blazing fire with his powerful angels" to take vengeance on those who have not responded to God's grace (2 Th. 1:7,8). This association makes it likely that John the Baptist's mention of a "baptism with fire" refers to judgment (Mt. 3:11,12). What we call hell, the eternal state of the lost, is described in Revelation as the fiery "lake of burning sulfur" (Rev. 20:10,14,15; compare Jude 7).

Fire is also associated with purification and renewal. Peter writes of the great value of trials here on earth, even though they may bring temporary grief. These

382

ordeals test our faith and, like the refiner's fire, prove it to be as genuine as gold.

Peter informs us that this present universe will "be destroyed by fire" and "the elements will melt in the heat" (2 Pet. 3:10-12). Yet the old is purged in order to be replaced by "a new heaven and a new earth, the home of righteousness" (2 Pet. 3:13; *compare* Isa. 65:17). At that time, the believer's works will also be tested by fire, even as the sacred vessels of the first Temple were passed through the fire at their dedication. The purpose of this fiery test is not to punish but to reveal the quality of our lives in Christ and to qualify us for reward (1 Cor. 3:10-15).

firkin (KJV) A unit of liquid measure equivalent to 10.8 U.S. gallons (41 liters). It is used in Jn. 2:6 to translate *metrētēs*, which equaled 10.4 gallons (39.4 liters). *See also* Weights and Measures.

firmament (KJV) The universe beyond earth's envelope of air. The Hebrew word, *raqia'*, means simply "expanse." It is best to take the Gen. 1 creation account in its simplest sense: Above the envelope of air and water which surround our earth is a great expanse in which God has placed the moon and stars.

According to some modern scholars, the ancient Hebrews thought the earth was flat, covered by a polished, metal-like dome—the "firmament"—which had stars attached to it, and window-like openings through which rain fell. But this view of Hebrew cosmology rests on the assumption that "firmament" means something solid. It also takes OT references to the "windows" of heaven too literally. Israelite writers often spoke in poetic images; why not here?

It is unwise to try to develop any diagram of the universe from Scripture. The Bible is not a science textbook. Yet, if one were to choose texts from which to construct diagrams, it would perhaps be just as valid to select Isa. 40:22 and Job 26:7. These verses give a surprisingly modern picture of the earth. "He [God] sits enthroned above the circle of the earth" (Isa. 40:22), and "He [God] spreads out the northern skies over empty space; he suspends the earth over nothing" (Job 26:7). Certainly a circular earth suspended in space has no resemblance to the primitive flat-earth view that the critics suppose the ancient Hebrews held.

firstborn The first male offspring of humans or animals. The firstborn was considered sacred in OT times, and belonged

to God in a special way, as did the firstfruits of the earth.

God's claim to the firstborn son in Israel rested not only on his right as Creator but on his deliverance of Israel's firstborn when the firstborn of Egypt were struck dead (Ex. 13:1-16). Later, the tribe of Levi was accepted as a substitute for the firstborn of the Israelites. That tribe was set apart to serve God forever at Israel's worship center (Num. 3,8). As a constant reminder of God's deliverance, Jewish fathers were to appear at the worship center 30 days after the birth of their firstborn and pay five shekels to redeem their sons from Temple service (Num. 18:15,16).

Firstborn animals also belonged to the Lord. The firstborn of clean animals were to be sacrificed. The firstborn of unclean

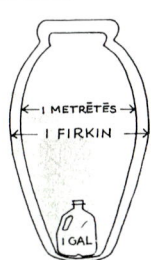

One firkin equals 10.8 U.S. gallons (41 liters). One metrētēs equals 10.4 gallons (39.4 liters).

In keeping with the Law of Moses, Mary and Joseph consecrated Jesus, her firstborn, to the Lord (Lk. 2:22). She then offered a pair of doves for ritual purification in accordance with Lev. 12:8. Greek grave stela dated about 450 B.C.

animals, such as the donkey, would either be redeemed by payment of a fixed price or killed.

In Hebrew culture the firstborn son was the legal successor of his father as head of the family or clan. He also received a double portion of his family's wealth upon the father's death. Scripture has this favored treatment in view when describing Israel as God's firstborn (Ex. 4:22). The Hebrew people, chosen in their forefather Abraham, were special objects of God's love and care.

A different aspect of the firstborn's privilege is intended by NT passages that speak of Jesus as "firstborn of creation" and "firstborn among many brothers" (Rom. 8:29; Col. 1:15; Heb. 1:6). These texts do not suggest that Jesus is a created being, as some sects have argued. Instead, they affirm Christ's superior position. To call Christ "firstborn" acknowledges his supremacy over all creation and supremacy over the brothers and sisters whom his sacrifice enabled to become members of God's family. This use of "firstborn" to indicate supremacy is found in some rabbinical commentaries, which speak of God as "firstborn of the world."

"Firstborn" does have a temporal meaning, however, when it describes Jesus as the very first person in human history to be raised from the grave in a resurrected body. In his humanity Jesus was in fact the "firstborn from the dead" (Col. 1:18; Rev. 1:5).

Restored painting of fish-drying and net-making. Dried fish were a staple for many ancient peoples, including the Israelites.

first day of the week Sunday. The Jews gave a name, the Sabbath, only to the seventh day of the week. All other days were identified by number. Christian worship gradually shifted from the Sabbath to the first day of the week as the influence of the Hebrew Christian churches declined, largely because it was on the first day that Jesus rose from the dead (Jn. 20:1) *See also* Sunday.

firstfruits The first grain or fruit harvested each year. This produce, in addition to the firstborn of farm animals, was considered sacred. It was offered to God in thanksgiving and celebration in a special ceremony held on the Day of Firstfruits, which took place during the festival of Pentecost (Num. 28:26; 2 Chr. 31:5). *See also* Pentecost.

fish, fishing Catching fish by net or hook and line. Fish were an important source of protein in the Hebrew diet, which seldom included animal flesh. Fishing was an important industry, and some 330 fishing boats worked the Sea of Galilee in the first century. Seven of Christ's disciples were fishermen: Peter, Andrew, Philip, James, John, Thomas, and Nathanael (Lk. 5:7,10; Jn. 21:2).

Under OT Law only fish with scales and fins were "clean," or acceptable for the Hebrew diet. These included ocean fish, taken from the Mediterranean coast and the Gulf of Aqaba, and the staple freshwater fish, especially carp and tilapia, harvested from the Sea of Galilee (Lake Gennesaret).

Most fishermen worked at night from small wooden boats. Most often they used dragnets (Jn. 21:8) or cast nets (Mt. 4:18),

The Calling of the Apostles Peter and Andrew *by Duccio di Buoninsegna (14th century) illustrates Mt. 4:19: " 'Come, follow me,' Jesus said, 'and I will make you fishers of men.' "*

although at times they fished with hook and line (Mt. 17:27; Amos 4:2). Spear fishing, illustrated in a painting on the wall of an Egyptian tomb from Thebes (dating about 1500 B.C.), is alluded to only in Job 41:7.

Fishing was arduous work. Rowing the sturdy wooden boats and hauling in the heavy nets demanded strength and stamina. After the fishermen worked most of the night, they still had to mend the nets and dry, salt, or pickle the fish for transportation to distant markets. Nevertheless, fishing was profitable. Peter and his partners had moved from the village of Bethsaida to the important governmental center of Capernaum. Peter owned a large home there, where he maintained his own family and his wife's mother (Mk. 1:30). The best fishing on the Sea of Galilee, in NT times as today, lay at the north end of the lake in the area of these two cities.

Several of Jesus' miracles are associated with fish and fishing. Christ multiplied a few pieces of bread and some dried fish to feed thousands, and demonstrated his power over nature by guiding his followers to unusual catches (Lk. 5:1-9; Jn. 21:1-14).

The Bible story of Jonah features a "great fish" (not necessarily a whale, as the KJV translates Mt. 12:40) which swallowed the disobedient prophet. The text makes it clear that this was a miracle and that God had acted to "provide" [*manah*] a great fish for this purpose (Jon. 1:17). *See also* Jonah, Book of.

This fish-shaped dish cover (A.D. 50–100) is cast in glass and would have come from an upper-class home. Though dried fish was a cheap food, the wealthy enjoyed the best species freshly prepared.

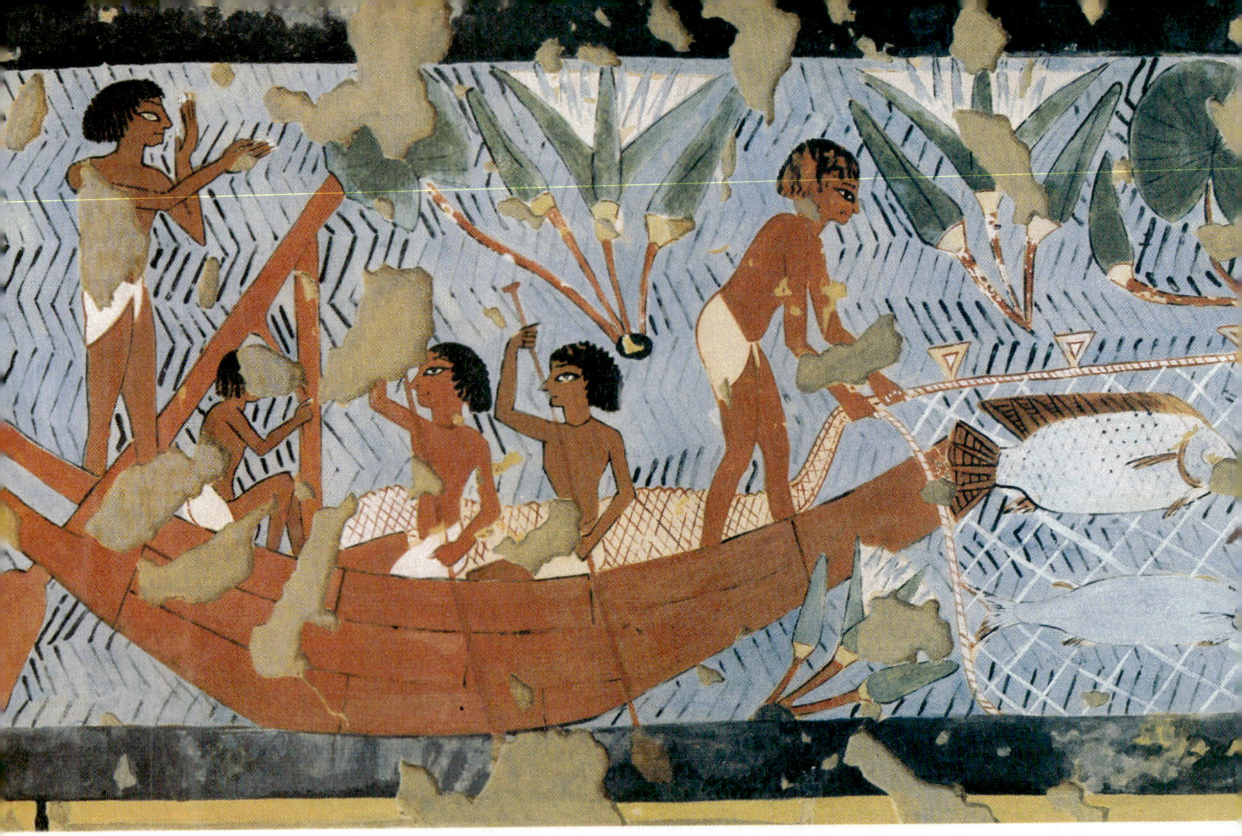

Among lily- and papyrus-covered marshes Egyptian fishermen have made a large catch in their dragnet—not large, however, when compared to the netful Jesus' disciples towed to shore according to Jn. 21.

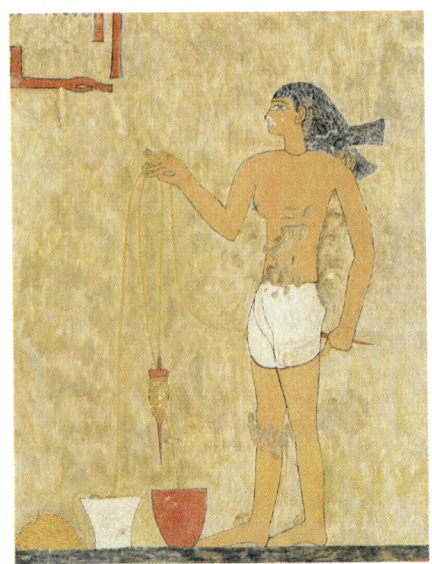

In the NT, when confronted by the collectors of the annual Temple tax, Jesus told Peter to catch a fish: In its mouth he would find a coin to pay the tax for Jesus and himself (Mt. 17:27). Jesus used this incident to illustrate a truth that the rabbis of his day had overlooked. Rulers did not collect taxes from their own family but from strangers. The very fact that God ordained a Temple tax was evidence that his chosen people were not yet truly his sons and daughters.

Images from fishing are also used symbolically in Scripture. When the OT speaks of catching people in nets, the purpose of the "fishermen" is always to do them harm (Hab. 1:14-17). Yet Jesus' own disciples left their nets and boats to become "fishers of men." Only God can enable us to "catch" others for their good (Mt. 4:18,19).

The early church used the fish as an identifying symbol. Drawings of fish have been found on the walls of Roman catacombs, used by early Christians for funeral services. This was because the Greek word for fish, *ichthus,* served as an acronym for *Iēsous Christos Theou Huios Sōtēr* ("Jesus Christ, God's Son, Savior").

Fish Gate One of the gates in the city wall of Jerusalem (2 Chr. 33:14; Neh. 3:3). The name apparently reflects the use of this gate to bring dried or salted fish into the city for sale. Some scholars argue that the gate was on the eastern wall, but others prefer the northwestern.

flax Fine fibers drawn from the stem of the flax plant and woven to make linen cloth.

There were different grades of linen, from coarse (Ezek. 9:2; Dan. 10:5) to especially fine (Gen. 41:42; Rev. 18:12). The linen clothes of the wealthy were often

Flax is the oldest known source of textile fibers. Here an Egyptian worker spins loosely twisted flax into threads used to weave linen cloth. The Egyptians perfected its use and became catalysts for its spread in the ancient world. The plague of hail that destroyed Egypt's blooming flax (Ex. 9:31) probably pushed up clothing prices since the Egyptians generally abhorred wool.

embroidered, as were the garments of the high priest. *See also* Embroidery.

To make linen, ripened flax plants were pulled up by the roots and left out to dry. This often took place on the flat roofs of the houses in Palestine, as seen in the story of the Israelite spies in Jericho who hid under a pile of flax plants drying on Rahab's roof (Josh. 2:6).

Next, the dried stalks were split, and a comb was used to separate the threads. These threads were then spun together and woven into linen cloth. *See also* Linen.

fleece The wool coat of a sheep cut in a single piece, before it is carded and drawn into threads. Like other "firstfruits," this first coat of wool was dedicated for the use of the priests.

The common phrase, "putting out a fleece," comes from the story of Gideon, who placed a fleece on the ground overnight (Jdg. 6:36-40). He wanted to be sure that the Lord had indeed chosen him to save his people, so he asked God to confirm his choice by making the fleece wet with dew while keeping the ground dry. The next night, for further confirmation, Gideon asked that the fleece be dry but the ground wet. Many Christians, wisely or unwisely, have taken Gideon's act as a model, asking God to confirm a course of action by a certain sign.

Scripture gives no explicit approval or disapproval to Gideon's tactics, though the Lord did grant these particular miracles and Gideon went on to defeat the Midianites. Other Bible passages speak against "testing" the Lord (Mt. 4:7; 12:38-42), but these seem to be cases of unbelief. Elsewhere, Isaiah begged the faithless Ahaz to ask for a sign from God (Isa. 7:10-17). Apparently Gideon was asking in faith. *See also* Sign.

Reconstruction of an Israelite wool carder's shop from pre-Roman times. An uncarded fleece similar to that laid out by Gideon (Jdg. 6:36-40) hangs from a hook (top left).

flesh (1) The soft body parts of living creatures; (2) the person as an individual self (Ps. 16:9,10); (3) all living creatures; and also (4) family or other relationships, as in the expression, "my own flesh and blood." In the OT, "flesh" (*basar*) symbolizes mortality and human life in this world. In the NT, "flesh" (*sarx*) is further represented as the sin nature of humankind.

FLESH IN THE OLD TESTAMENT

All OT terms that speak of human nature, such as "heart" and "soul" and "spirit," as well as "flesh," denote human beings as a unified whole. Each, however, focuses on a specific aspect of the whole being. "Flesh" depicts persons as mortal —participants for a time in the affairs of this passing world. Although mankind was created by God in his image, we have a physical nature. Our bodily life has limitations, and our experiences take place in a material universe. Theologically, "flesh" in the OT focuses our attention on life and experience in this world.

When we understand this meaning of "flesh," we can grasp the unique implication of God's statement concerning marriage in Gen. 2:24. In saying that the man and woman become "one flesh," Scripture implies more than sexual union. The married couple, as one, are to share together all the joys and trials of their life on earth until they are parted by death.

Yet the most powerful implication of "flesh" is one of weakness and mortality. Our life on earth is brief. Our powers are weak. Thus the psalmist says,

As for man, his days are like grass,
 he flourishes like a flower of the field;
the wind blows over it and it is gone,
 and its place remembers it no more.
                                   (Ps. 103:15,16)

Since God knows that we are flesh, he is both merciful and patient (Ps. 78:39). He calls us to acknowledge our weakness and refuse to trust in "the arm of flesh," relying, instead, solely on the Lord (Ps. 56:4; Jer. 17:5).

FLESH IN THE NEW TESTAMENT

The range of meanings of *sarx* in the NT parallels the meanings of *basar* in the OT. Flesh is used literally to indicate the physical body (1 Cor. 15:39; Gal. 2:20), and figuratively to mean "human being" (Rom. 3:20), living in the material universe (1 Cor. 7:28), or family relationship (Rom. 9:3; 1 Cor. 10:18). But Paul gives *sarx* new theological content. While the Hebrew *basar* views human beings as mortal—frail and limited—the Greek *sarx* presents human beings as fatally flawed. In Paul's letters, "flesh" implies sin's corruption.

THE STRUGGLE

Since *sarx*, like *basar*, regards a person as a whole, the NT teaching implicit in "flesh" is that sin has infected every human capacity. Our emotions, desires, intellect, and will are all corrupt, so Paul can say, "I know that nothing good lives in me, that is, in my sinful nature [*sarx*]" (Rom. 7:18). Therefore, living according to the flesh, expressing and responding to its sinful urgings, is the way to disaster. God calls us to live according to the Spirit of God, by responding to and expressing his desires and his will, thus finding life and peace (Rom. 8:1-9).

The contrast Paul draws in Rom. 7,8, between life according to the flesh and life according to the Spirit, has led some to the teaching that believers have two natures. There is in each of us a sin nature, inherited from Adam, and a new nature, given to us by God. Christians can overcome the inner pull of sin only by consciously surrendering to God and by relying on him to energize the new in us.

FLESH AND SPIRIT IN CONTRAST

In Gal. 5:16-26, Paul describes acts that flow from and express the flesh, that is, the sinful human nature. These acts include sexual immorality, fits of rage, jealousy, drunkenness, "and the like." In contrast, the Spirit produces such fruit as love, joy, peace, kindness, and goodness. Paul says we must choose to "live by the Spirit"; he promises that, if we do, "you will not gratify the desires of the sinful nature [the *sarx*]."

In another passage (1 Cor. 3:1-4), Paul calls believers in Corinth "fleshly" (*sarkikos*). He means that by their bickering and jealousies they show that they are controlled by their sin natures rather than by God.

SUMMARY

As an ordinary word, "flesh" in the Bible conveys all the meanings suggested by our English term. But as a theological term, "flesh" means far more. In the OT, flesh emphasizes human frailty, without negative moral overtones. In fact, the expression in Ezek. 36:26, "a heart of flesh," indicates a heart that is responsive to God, in contrast to an unresponsive heart of stone.

In the NT, however, flesh has strong

moral overtones. It stands for a sinful human nature which the believer can overcome only through reliance on the Holy Spirit. *See also* Holy Spirit.

flock A group of sheep cared for by one or more shepherds. In both Testaments, believers are called the flock of God and the Lord is presented as a shepherd (Isa. 40:11; Lk. 12:32; 1 Pet. 5:2,3). *See also* Sheep; Shepherd.

Flood The great deluge, described in Gen. 6–8.

THE GENESIS ACCOUNT

Genesis presents the Flood as divine judgment on a humanity that rejected God and whose "every inclination . . . was only evil all the time" (Gen. 6:5). Righteous Noah was given 120 years in which to build a great boat (Gen. 6:3). When the boat was finished and supplies had been stored, Noah took animals into the ark. God sealed Noah and his family inside. For 40 days it rained, and the torrential rains, along with upsurging subterranean waters, scoured earth's surface of all air-breathing life (Gen. 7:21-23). After about a year, the flood waters subsided enough for the ark to rest on one of the mountains of Ararat. *See also* Ararat; Ark, Noah's.

FLOOD INTERPRETATIONS

Some interpreters view the Flood as a mythical story without roots in history.

Conservatives hold the traditional view that the Genesis account reports historical events. Strikingly, flood stories are found in the traditions of peoples in America, Australia, and the Pacific Islands, in addition to those traditions found among the peoples of the biblical world. There are many parallels between the biblical account and the flood story told in the Sumerian *Epic of Gilgamesh*, although the perception of God in each differs radically. It seems reasonable to believe that the events reported in Genesis are the historical origin of the memory of a great flood,

This 7th-century tablet, inscribed with part of the Assyrian version of the Epic of Gilgamesh, *records an ancient Sumerian account of the Flood. The cuneiform poem shares similarities with Gen. 6–9, which supports the view that the Flood was a historical event.*

The ark floats atop the rising flood in this 10th-century Spanish manuscript. "Every living thing on the face of the earth was wiped out. . . . Only Noah was left, and those with him in the ark" (Gen. 7:23).

This painting, attributed to American artist Joseph Henry Hidley (1830–1872), portrays pairs of animals docilely entering Noah's ark. It originally served as part of an enclosure for a fireplace and was intended to amuse children.

preserved in so many parts of the world.

Those who believe the Genesis account to be accurate do differ, however, on whether the Flood was local or worldwide. (1) Those scholars holding a local flood theory believe that humankind had not yet spread far from Eden, so a local flood would have accomplished God's purpose. They also view biblical statements about the Flood covering the earth's high mountains as phenomenological, indicating only high ground in the relevant locality.

(2) Those who argue for a worldwide flood believe that the cataclysm reshaped the surface of our planet. The mountains that were covered to a depth of 20 feet (Gen. 7:20) were not earth's present mountains. These were thrust up by the weight of the flood waters as earth's present sea beds were depressed. Support for this view comes mainly from the language of Genesis itself, although some attempt to prove a universal flood from geologic and other scientific data.

Neither the local nor universal flood theories resolve the problem of dating the

Flood. Those who view the Flood as a historical event have suggested dates ranging from 10,000 to 60,000 years ago.

Despite problems of interpretation and dating, both OT and NT treat the Flood as a historical event (Mt. 24:36-39; 1 Pet. 3:18-21; 2 Pet. 3:3-7).

THEOLOGICAL SIGNIFICANCE

The flood account contributes significantly to the unfolding revelation of God in Genesis. Genesis 1–3 reveals God as the Creator. In the story of the Flood, God is revealed as moral Judge of his universe. Spiritual death is not the only consequence of sin (Gen. 3). Sin arouses the wrath of God and leads to divine judgment.

Yet in the story of the Flood, God the Judge is also God the Savior. The Lord found one righteous man, Noah, in that age and told him of his intentions to judge the earth. He also provided a way of escape, commanding him to build an ark. In the great boat Noah and his sons constructed, God preserved their lives.

In the aftermath of the Flood, God appears as Covenant-maker, a role he would later assume with Abraham, Moses, David, and (through Jesus) all humanity. Noah and his family were to fill the earth, observing certain basic rules (Gen. 9:1-7). God, in turn, promised that he would never again destroy the world with a flood. As a sign of his covenant, he gave the rainbow (Gen. 9:8-17). *See also* Covenant; Noah; Rainbow.

THE FLOOD IN THE NT

The NT has three major references to the Flood. Christ likens the unexpectedness of his Second Coming to the days before the Flood, when people went about life's normal activities totally unaware that judgment was imminent (Mt. 24:36-44).

Peter, in an extended analogy, portrays salvation by likening it to the Flood (1 Pet. 3:19–4:2). Union with Christ, as the ark, carries us through the waters of divine judgment to deposit us in a new world where we are called to live the rest of our lives by the will of God.

In his second letter, Peter again refers to the Flood. Those who assume that "everything goes on as it has since the beginning" of the world "deliberately forget" that long ago God acted to judge the sin of humanity. The Flood stands as a dreadful reminder that God truly is the Judge of humanity and that this present world is also being "kept for the day of judgment and the destruction of ungodly men" (2 Pet. 3:3-7). *See also* Judgment.

flowers The blossoms or petals of seed-bearing plants.

The spring rains of Palestine stimulate a bursting forth of colorful flowers. Delicate blossoms of pink, white, blue, and red tint the landscape, giving way as summer comes to other, predominantly white and yellow, blossoms. Undoubtedly, as Jesus

taught in the fields of Galilee, he was surrounded by nature's beauty and delighted to look upon the lilies of the field and the colorful blossoms on flowering shrubs and trees.

Yet the Bible seldom mentions flowers and rarely identifies flowering plants by name. This, perhaps, is because flowers were not cultivated in garden plots or brought indoors for decoration. Nevertheless, Jesus' comments about flowers show that their beauty was appreciated in Israel (Mt. 6:28,29). Their blossoms were crushed to obtain fragrances for perfumes, and women also wove flowers into garlands for festive occasions. According to 1 Ki. 7:19,26, the blossom of the lily served as a model for the top of the pillars that stood before Solomon's magnificent Temple. *See also* Lily.

Figuratively, flowers usually symbolize the fragility of life on earth. Like the spring flowers that suddenly burst into bloom and just as suddenly are gone, our time on earth is also short.

All men are like grass,
and all their glory is like the flowers of the
field.
The grass withers and the flowers fall,
because the breath of the Lord blows on
them.

(Isa. 40:6,7)

By analogy, Isaiah reminds us that, in contrast to our transitory nature, "the word of our God stands forever" (40:8).

Jesus notes the beautiful appearance of flowers that last only a short time. He asks his hearers, "If that is how God clothes the grass of the field, which is here today and tomorrow is thrown into the fire, will he not much more clothe you?" (Mt. 6:30).

Thus, the flowers of the field remind the believer of life's transitory nature, and yet, at the same time, they convey a message of hope. Life is short, and life's glories are fleeting, but the God with whom our lives are now intertwined exists forever.

flute A long, slender, high-pitched wind instrument. Two different kinds of wind instruments are translated "flute" or "pipe" in modern versions. One instrument was a single tube of reed, wood, bone, or ivory. The other consisted of two separate tubes of equal length joined with cloth and resin. The more complex double pipes often had twin mouthpieces, each of which usually held a single reed. The double pipes, properly called a double clarinet or double oboe, depending on length and pipe size, were played at the same time.

Female musician playing the double reed flute, the type mentioned in 1 Sam. 10:5. It was a common instrument in many ancient cultures. This terra cotta figurine was found in the ruins of Carthage in Tunisia.

Spring rains deck Palestine—despite its dry climate—with wild flowers.

391

Above: Bone flute excavated from the City of David (about 1000 B.C.).

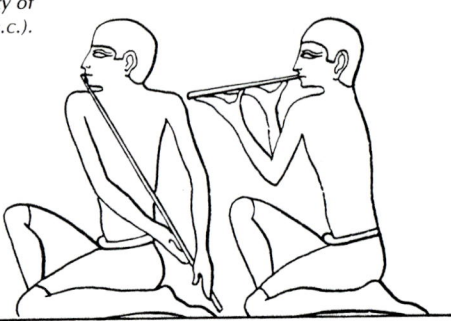

Right: Line drawing from a tomb relief of the Old Kingdom (2nd millennium B.C.) shows two musicians with flutes of different lengths.

that horned beasts have one voice when they live, but seven when they are dead. "Its two horns [are made into] two trumpets; its two legbones, two flutes; its hide, a drum; its large intestine is for harps [strings]; and its small intestines are used for citherns [instruments like guitars]."

food Edible material consumed for sustenance, nutrition, and pleasure. The Hebrews ate two main meals a day, one around noon and one in the evening (Ex. 16:12; Ruth 2:14; Acts 10:9,10). It is likely they also snacked earlier in the morning (*compare* 1 Ki. 17:6; Jn. 21:12).

Once Israel settled in the Promised Land, the people enjoyed a varied diet. The grains of Canaan included wheat, barley, millet, and spelt. These were either ground into coarse flour and baked into bread, or the grain was eaten parched. Bread was so basic to the diet that it often stood for "food" in the Bible, as in Jesus' saying, "Man does not live by bread alone" (Mt. 4:4).

Vegetables mentioned in the Bible include cucumbers, beans, onions, herbs [greens], garlic, and lentils. A number of small garden plants served as condiments: mint, dill, and cummin are mentioned in Mt. 23:23.

Israel's varied topography made it possible to cultivate a great variety of fruits and nuts. The Bible mentions figs, apples, pomegranates, grapes, olives, pistachios, and almonds. Melons are grown in modern Israel and shipped to European markets. Figs and raisins were dried and pressed into cakes. Olives were pressed to produce a light and tasty cooking oil. It is

Each instrument had several holes cut in the tube that could be blocked by the musician's fingers to change the notes he played.

Shepherds in the fields made simple reed flutes to play while caring for their sheep; they may have also used them to call their flocks (Jdg. 5:16). Some flutes were used for secular purposes, while others were used exclusively for worship (1 Sam. 10:5; Isa. 30:29). Flutes were also played at weddings and at funerals, a practice mentioned in the description of the mourning for Jairus's twelve-year-old daughter (Lk. 7:32).

Most flutes of Bible times were made of materials that easily deteriorate, so few examples have lasted. But a section of one flute made from a cow's foreleg, dating to Jerusalem's destruction in A.D. 70, has been recovered by archaeologists. This illustrates a comment from the Talmud,

Food in ancient art is most frequently represented as offerings to gods or royalty, as in this tomb painting from Thebes, Egypt (18th Dynasty, about 1425 B.C.).

likely that the date, although not named in Scripture, also made an important contribution to the daily diet. Other fruits grown in ancient or modern Israel include apricots, pears, quinces, peaches, and oranges. *See also* Agriculture.

Milk products provided essential protein in the Hebrew diet. Seven ritually-clean wild animals are mentioned in the Bible, and these undoubtedly were hunted in patriarchal times (antelope, deer, gazelle, ibex, mountain sheep, roebuck, and wild goat). Sheep and cattle were typically killed only for sacrifice and eaten only on special, festive occasions. Birds supplied eggs and were also eaten; these included the hen, quail, partridge, pigeon, turtledove, and even the sparrow. Several types of locusts were also eaten.

Both ocean fish and freshwater fish, caught in the Sea of Galilee (Lake Gennesaret), were an important food. The fish were dried, pickled, or salted for preservation and shipped to cities such as Jerusalem.

Honey provided a delightful element in the Hebrew diet and was apparently abundant during OT times.

Another essential ingredient, salt, was also easily obtained. *See also* Salt.

Not all these foods, however, were available to all the people or at all times. Nevertheless, the land God gave to his people was truly rich in agricultural resources. It was a productive land, "flowing with milk and honey." As long as God's people lived in harmony with the Lord, they enjoyed the land's bounty and had all they needed for a healthy and prosperous life.

fool An ignorant person. In the OT, "fool" and "folly" indicate moral rather than intellectual deficiency. Each of three Hebrew words translated "fool" emphasizes a different moral fault. The folly that Prov. 22:15 says is "bound up in the heart of a child" is an insistence on having his or her own way. Children need the "rod of correction" to teach them not to rebel impulsively. With the firm guidance of parents, children can overcome this foolishness.

The fool who says in his heart, "There is no God," has shut God out of his life (Ps. 14:1). His evil character is likely to be expressed in gross sins (Jdg. 19:23,24; 2 Sam. 13:12). Such a person is so twisted that he or she is open neither to reason nor to God.

In the NT, three different Greek words are translated "fool." Each portrays a person who lacks understanding because he

or she has not adequately taken God into account. One good example is the wealthy farmer in Jesus' parable, who thought life consisted in the riches he could store up in his barns, unaware that one night he must die and face God's judgment (Lk. 12:16-21).

Christians also can be foolish if they fail to evaluate life's issues from God's perspective. Paul points out in 1 Cor. 1:20-24 that God's wisdom is very different from the wisdom of this world. Only when we adopt his perspective, revealed in the written Word, can we hope to avoid foolish choices and become truly wise. *See also* Mind.

Below: Assyrian King Sennacherib seated on a throne with footstool at the siege of Lachish (701 B.C., 2 Chr. 32:9). A footstool was necessary because the throne was raised to keep the king's head higher than his standing subjects.

Right: Detail from an Egyptian wall painting (18th Dynasty) graphically illustrates Ps. 110:1: "The LORD says to my Lord, 'Sit at my right hand until I make your enemies a footstool for your feet.'"

footstool A low support for the feet of a royal person. When used symbolically in the Bible, the footstool suggests the exalted position of God or Jesus over human beings or over earth itself (Isa. 66:1; Heb. 10:13).

393

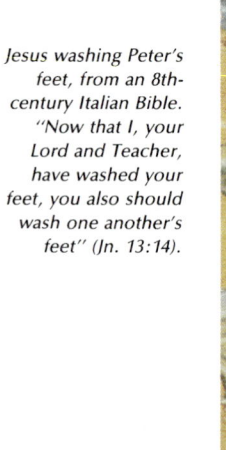

Jesus washing Peter's feet, from an 8th-century Italian Bible. "Now that I, your Lord and Teacher, have washed your feet, you also should wash one another's feet" (Jn. 13:14).

Clay foot bath found at Beersheba. Washing dusty feet was a common courtesy in Hebrew culture. Jesus noted the failure of a Pharisee to extend this to him as a guest (Lk. 7:44).

footwashing Pouring water over the feet to remove the dust of travel. The Hebrew people wore open sandals, so traveling along the dusty roads of Palestine caused feet to become dirty quite quickly. When a guest came to a home in Palestine, his or her feet might be washed by a servant or by the woman of the house. At the least, the guest was provided with water for footwashing (Gen. 19:2; 24:32; Jdg. 19:21). Jesus rightly criticized a Pharisee who had invited him to his home but failed to extend even this minimum courtesy (Lk. 7:36-50).

The most significant biblical incident involving footwashing took place at the Last Supper the night before Jesus was crucified. Taking the servant's role, Christ himself washed his disciples' feet. He was teaching two lessons through this action. First, his washing of the disciples' feet symbolized the continual cleansing that would be available to them through his death (Jn. 13:6-10). Second, his washing of the disciples' feet provided an example for Christian leaders, who are to see themselves as servants of God's people (Jn. 13:12-17).

Some Christian groups observe a ritual of footwashing, taking literally Jesus' words, "I have set you an example that you should do as I have done for you" (Jn. 13:15). This practice, however, has never been widely adopted by the church. In fact, the only reference to footwashing in an Epistle is an example of hospitality (1 Tim. 5:10).

forbearance Patient withholding of judgment. The Greek word means literally "to hold back." It suggests mercy rather than tolerance, as in the case of God's withholding punishment to give mankind opportunity to repent (Rom. 2:4; 3:25; 2 Pet. 3:9). The same thought is expressed in Col. 3:13, which calls on God's people to "bear with" the weaknesses of others as well as to forgive them. *See also* Forgive.

foreigner (1) A non-Jew, who may have lived in Israel as a resident alien; (2) any person not a member of the covenant community. Old Testament laws protected the rights of aliens who became residents of Israel. The NT uses the idea of the foreigner ("alien" or "stranger') to help Christians understand their relationship to God and to the world.

The OT provided that resident aliens should live under the same Law as Jews (Ex. 12:49). This protected them from injustice, just as the Law protected God's own people. Resident aliens were even granted some of the privileges reserved for Israel. *See also* Alien.

The NT draws analogies from Roman

394

law, which discriminated against all in the Empire who were not citizens of Rome. Both Heb. 11:13 and 1 Pet. 2:11 remind believers that we are strangers in this world, citizens of God's Kingdom. Our expectation and our hope must be fixed above. *See also* Citizen.

foreknow To know beforehand. God knows what will happen before it occurs (Acts 2:23), and knows believers before they make the personal choice of faith (Rom. 8:29; 11:2; 1 Pet. 1:2). Believers may know the future too, but only as it has been revealed by God (2 Pet. 3:17).

While "foreknow" does not appear in the OT, the concept of God as one who knows all things before they come to pass is undoubtedly there. God says through Isaiah,

"I am God, and there is no other;
I am God, and there is none like me.
I make known the end from the beginning,
from ancient times, what is still to come."

(Isa. 46:9,10a)

This text clearly associates God's foreknowledge with his sovereignty. God knows what will come to pass, for he has ordained it.

"I say: My purpose will stand,
and I will do all that I please. . . .
What I have said, that will I bring about;
what I have planned, that will I do."

(Isa. 46:10b,11)

Different theological traditions have viewed foreknowledge from slightly different perspectives. One tradition emphasizes the fact that "foreknow" means only "to know beforehand." Its proponents argue that this is all that is implied; that God does not act directly to affect the course of history or, more specifically, the choices of any given individual. Another theological tradition views foreknowledge as so intimately associated with God's sovereignty that it implies that God acts to determine what will happen. In this tradition, foreknowledge is understood to imply foreordination or predestination.

In such disputes we need to keep two seemingly contradictory truths in balance. God is actively involved in the flow of history, as well as in individual lives. Yet at the same time, human beings are free to make responsible choices. While it is true that "those God foreknew he also predestined to be conformed to the likeness of his Son" (Rom. 8:29), it remains true that "if you confess with your mouth, 'Jesus is Lord,' and believe in your heart that God raised him from the dead, you will be saved" (Rom. 10:9). *See also* Election; Predestine.

forerunner A military term used for a soldier sent ahead to scout or to prepare for the arrival of the main force. In Heb. 6:20 Jesus is pictured as the forerunner who has entered heaven to make everything ready for us (Jn. 14:1-4).

foreskin The skin covering the end of the penis, which the Jews removed by circumcision as a sign of participation in the covenant God made with Abraham (Gen. 17:9-14).

This practice distinguished the Hebrews from other peoples in the ancient world. Saul's request that David present him with a hundred Philistine foreskins as a wedding gift was logical, for it would assure the king that David had actually killed a hundred of Israel's pagan enemy (1 Sam. 18:25-27). *See also* Circumcision; Covenant.

forget To lose knowledge of someone or something.

To forget God is to fail "to observe his commands, his laws and his decrees" (Deut. 8:11; *see* Deut. 4:31; Ps. 119:61). Those who forget God turn to sin, and God will judge them (Ps. 50:22). The NT urges Christians not to forget [neglect] to do good (Heb. 13:16).

Many of the 102 occurrences of the Hebrew word for "forget" contain promises. God says to his people,

"Can a mother forget the baby at her breast
and have no compassion on the child she
has borne?
Though she may forget,
I will not forget you!"

(Isa. 49:15)

forgive (1) To pardon or absolve of wrongdoing; (2) to cancel a debt; (3) to give up resentment.

The Christian doctrine of forgiveness explains how God deals with our sins. The Hebrew and Greek words for forgiveness convey a variety of images: to cover or atone (Heb., *kapar*); to carry or take away (Heb., *nasa'*); to pardon (Heb., *salah*); to be gracious (Gk., *charizomai*); to dismiss or send away (Gk., *aphiēmi*); remission (KJV), release, or freedom (Gk., *aphesis*). Of all the world's religions, only Judaism and Christianity portray God as forgiving. Human beings have sinned and deserve punishment, yet God in love finds ways to forgive and to restore a harmonious relationship.

FORGIVENESS AND SALVATION

The Old and New Testaments bluntly portray all human beings as sinners, who fall short of God's requirements and willfully violate them. As sinners, human beings are alienated from God and hostile to him (Rom. 5:10; Col. 1:21; Eph. 2:1-3).

Before a harmonious relationship can be reestablished, the sin which caused the alienation must be dealt with. Again both Testaments agree: (1) God is willing to forgive because of his love for us. As Daniel cried in his prayer of confession, "We do not make requests of you because we are righteous, but because of your great mercy" (Dan. 9:18). (2) God's forgiveness is associated with sacrifice. The sacrifices of atonement in the OT prefigured Christ's ultimate sacrifice of himself. God acted in his Son, and "now he has

reconciled you by Christ's physical body through death to present you holy in his sight, without blemish and free from accusation" (Col. 1:22). As the NT repeatedly affirms, in Christ "we have redemption, the forgiveness of sins" (Col. 1:14). (3) God's forgiveness is received by faith. There is nothing that human beings can do to merit forgiveness. We can only gladly receive, by faith, that which God offers us as a free gift (Eph. 2:8-10). *See also* Faith; Sacrifices and Offerings.

Sins which have been forgiven, and in fact carried by Christ to the cross and paid in full there, can never be held against the believer again. No charge can be brought against the believer, for God has justified—declared righteous—those whose sins Christ has taken away.

CHRISTIAN EXPERIENCE

Acceptance of God's forgiveness transforms the attitude of the believer. (1) The

"But while [his son] was still a long way off, his father saw him and was filled with compassion for him; he ran to his son, threw his arms around him and kissed him" (Lk. 15:20).

NT links forgiveness to love for God. Jesus taught that the person who has been forgiven much loves much (Lk. 7:36-50). (2) The NT links forgiveness with release from guilt feelings. Hebrews 9:11-14 speaks of Christ's blood cleansing our consciences, setting us free to serve God. We can forget the past, and look ahead confidently. (3) The NT links receiving forgiveness and extending it. We are to model our relationships with others on the way God relates to us. "Be kind and compassionate to one another, forgiving each other, just as in Christ God forgave you" (Eph. 4:32).

FORGIVENESS OF SINS

The NT teaches that a believer's sins interrupt his or her fellowship with God. Though the Christian is a forgiven person —with all sins past, present, and future paid for in Christ's one sacrifice (Heb. 10:14)—yet the Christian who sins will experience a loss of present fellowship with God, and will feel again the pangs of guilt.

John makes clear that sins will occur in the believer's life, but these should be confessed to God (1 Jn. 1:5–2:1). Then the Lord "is faithful and just and will forgive us our sins and purify us from all unrighteousness" (v. 9). With confession, harmony with God is restored, and God is able to continue his purifying work in the believer's life. *See also* Confess.

DIFFICULT PASSAGES

While the Bible's basic teaching on forgiveness is clear, some passages have raised questions.

(1) Is God's forgiveness contingent on our forgiving others? The Lord's Prayer does say, "Forgive us our debts, as we also have forgiven our debtors." And Jesus said, "If you forgive men when they sin against you, your heavenly Father will also forgive you. But if you do not forgive men their sins, your Father will not forgive your sins" (Mt. 6:12,14,15). How can this be reconciled with the Gospel's announcement of forgiveness to anyone who believes in Jesus?

The best way to understand this saying is to realize that receiving and extending forgiveness can never be separated. The hardness of an unforgiving person prevents him from accepting forgiveness as well as from extending it. Another way to interpret this would be as a warning: The person who fails to forgive will be exposing himself to temporal judgment by God (*compare* Mt. 18:21-35).

(2) Is God's forgiveness contingent on repentance? Many passages promising for-

giveness call for repentance, which is a change of heart and mind (Lev. 26:14-45; Ps. 32:3-5; Isa. 1:27,28; 59:20; Mt. 4:17; Acts 5:31). Yet many other passages offering God's forgiveness do not mention repentance (Ps. 65:3; 86:5; Jer. 31:31-34; Mic. 7:18-20; Eph. 1:7; Col. 1:14; 2:13; 1 Jn. 2:2). The answer is found in the complexity of the salvation God offers us in Christ. The person who receives salvation by faith is forgiven, and released from the guilt incurred by his or her acts of sin. But sin is a rebellious attitude as well as wrongful acts. In Christ God not only forgives, but works within the heart to change the sinner's attitude and orientation. The Bible rightly links repentance, as an inner change of heart and mind, to forgiveness, not because one is contingent on the other but because they are both elements in the one "package" of salvation. *See also* Repent.

(3) Is any sin unforgivable? Jesus identified one unpardonable sin (Mt. 12:31; Mk. 3:28,29; Lk. 12:10) when the Pharisees accused him of performing his miracles by the power of Satan. Christ called this blasphemy against the Holy Spirit. He said that the persons who so blasphemed "will never be forgiven" but were "guilty of an eternal sin." *See also* Unpardonable Sin.

SUMMARY

Christianity offers total and complete forgiveness to those who place their trust in God's Son, Jesus. The Bible shows humanity in desperate need of forgiveness, and portrays God as a loving and merciful person. In Christ we receive a forgiveness that awakens our love for God, releases us from the burden of past guilt, and helps us develop a forgiving attitude toward others as well.

fornication (KJV) Sexual relations between unmarried persons. The Bible makes a distinction between fornication and adultery, which is sexual intercourse of a married person with someone not his or her own spouse.

The OT term for fornication (*zanah*) is often translated "prostitution." While fornication is forbidden by God (Lev. 19:29), it does not always call for the death penalty, while adultery does (Lev. 20:10). Like adultery, fornication is used figuratively to represent spiritual and moral unfaithfulness to God (Jer. 2:1-9; Ezek. 23:1-45; Hos. 4:10-19; *see* Rev. 17). The Greek term (*porneia*) seems to indicate sexual immorality in general and, while still distinct from adultery, includes "marital unfaithfulness" (Mt. 19:9).

There seem to be three underlying reasons why all sex outside of marriage is both wrong and harmful. (1) God intends sex to serve a sacramental role in bonding husband and wife together as one. Engaging in casual sex trivializes an act intended to deepen an intimate relationship, and robs the sex act of its sacramental meaning. (2) Marriage is a covenant commitment, and like other covenants calls for complete and utter faithfulness. Unfaithfulness in human relationships is linked in Scripture to unfaithfulness in our relationship with the Lord. (3) Sex outside of marriage is using others for self-gratification. "The prostitute reduces you to a loaf of bread, and the adulteress preys upon your very life" (Prov. 6:26). God calls us to value others as persons and to serve them, not use them for selfish purposes. We cannot view others as sex objects and at the same time see them as God does. *See also* Adultery; Marriage; Sex.

forsake To abandon, leave, or give up on someone or something.

Scripture gives us two pictures of forsaking: God's people abandoning God; and God turning away from his people. But two different Hebrew words are used, offering insight into these relationships.

The stronger, *'azab*, depicts people spurning God to worship idols. God says, "I will pronounce my judgments on my people because of their wickedness in forsaking ['azab] me" (Jer. 1:16). The weaker term, *natash*, is typically used for God forsaking his people. This word pictures a farmer leaving his land unplowed, or a shepherd leaving his flock uncared for. God forsakes only when his people sin, and then by withdrawing his protection, to let them suffer the consequences of their acts. Yet, as Moses announced to Israel, "The Lord himself . . . will never leave you nor forsake ['azab] you" (Deut. 31:8).

The NT uses several different Greek words for "forsake." Some are mild, suggesting simply a departure from a particular place. One, *enkataleipō*, is stronger. Jesus used it to cry out to God, "Why have you forsaken me?" (Mt. 27:46). Because Jesus suffered abandonment when he bore our sins on Calvary, we have received a marvelous commitment from the Lord. The Book of Hebrews renews the OT promise, putting it in God's own words: "Never will I leave you; never will I forsake you" (Heb. 13:5). *See also* Abandon.

fortifications Stone walls with towers, gates, and bars, intended to defend a city or garrison against attack.

Walled cities were built in Syria-Palestine from the third millennium B.C. The spies Moses sent to explore Canaan about 1445 B.C. reported that "the people who live there are powerful, and the cities are fortified and very large" (Num. 13:28). A generation later, with Joshua as commander, the Israelites took many of these cities, usually by first destroying their armies in the open field. Walled cities were not built by the Israelites until the time of David and Solomon. Solomon constructed a number of fortified cities in-

An Assyrian fortified camp during the siege of Lachish (701 B.C.). The artist presented a bird's-eye view of the fortifications and a frontal view of elements in the camp.

Right: Aerial view of the citadel of Arad, a southern royal border fortress built during Israel's golden age (10th century B.C.).

A steep, isolated hill, such as this one on which Samaria once stood, provided an excellent, naturally defensible site for a city. Omri, the king of Israel, bought the hill and transferred the capital there about 880 B.C. (1 Ki. 16:24). It was the capital of the Northern Kingdom until its conquest by the Assyrians in 723 B.C. (2 Ki. 17:6).

tended to serve as defensive strongholds in case of foreign invasion (1 Ki. 9:15). Solomon's successors also fortified cities and towns against attack (2 Chr. 11:5-12).

Typical fortifications might include two or more walls of rough stone, 15 to 25 feet (4.5 to 7.5 meters) thick and 35 or more feet (10.5 meters) high. A trench might be dug around the walls. The lower part of a wall might feature a gradual slope, sometimes covered with plaster, making it difficult to attack with a battering ram. Towers were often built at the corners or along the wall. These extended out over the wall so the defenders could fire arrows or missiles down on the attackers. Entrances to the city were protected by these towers and often by a series of gates. *See also* City Gate.

Even fortified cities could be taken by a determined enemy. Sometimes a protracted siege was used to starve a city into submission. At other times direct assault might be used. The Assyrians typically built ramps of earth against the walls of a fortified city, and used battering rams to dismantle the upper walls. In Roman times catapults and mobile towers were used in attacks on walled cities.

The fortresses that men built on earth were impressive. But they were vulnerable to a determined enemy. Longing for a surer defense, the psalmist cried out, "The Lord is my rock, my fortress and my deliverer; my God is my rock, in whom I take refuge" (Ps. 18:2).

foundation The base on which a structure is erected. While used literally in the OT (1 Ki. 5:17; 16:34), foundation is more often used in Scripture as a figure of speech.

The Hebrew word *yasad*, to lay a foundation, emphasizes immovability and solidity. Thus, to say God "laid the

The view from a fortified city sets the scene for 2 Ki. 6:15: "When the servant of [Elisha] went out [to the walls] early the next morning, an army with horses and chariots had surrounded the city. 'Oh, my lord, what shall we do?' he asked."

399

The servants of a court official pull the ropes of a clapnet snare full of birds in this tomb painting (about 1425 B.C.). David used fowling imagery to describe God's protective character: "Surely [the Lord] will save you from the fowler's snare" (Ps. 91:3).

foundations of the earth" (Job 38:4; Ps. 102:25) suggests not only that God created the physical universe, but also that he established the immutable laws by which it operates.

Praying to his Father, Jesus said, "You loved Me before the foundation of the world" (Jn. 17:24 NKJV). The same phrase is used to indicate when Jesus was chosen as our sacrifice (1 Pet. 1:20) and Paul says we believers were chosen by God before the world's foundation. The Greek word they use, *katabolē*, emphasizes the act of founding, thus the NIV translates the phrase "the *creation* of the world."

But the NT also paints the picture of a building's foundation (Gk., *themelios*) to make several important points. Paul told Timothy to urge rich Christians to be "rich in good deeds and to be generous and willing to share. In this way they will lay up treasure for themselves as a firm foundation for the coming age" (1 Tim. 6:19).

Paul described the Church as a holy temple "built on the foundation of the apostles and prophets, with Christ Jesus himself as the chief cornerstone" (Eph. 2:20). There is no conflict here with 1 Cor. 3:11: "No one can lay any foundation other than the one already laid, which is Jesus Christ." For the Corinthians, already disputing about personalities, Paul intentionally downplays the role of Christian leaders. But for the Ephesians, he describes the way God builds his Church —solidly on the teachings of the apostles and prophets. And even though false teachers may try to topple the structure, "God's solid foundation stands firm" (2 Tim. 2:19). *See also* Building; Cornerstone; Creation.

A branch of the frankincense tree, source of the aromatic gum used in compounding the special incense used in Hebrew worship (Ex. 30:1,7-9,30).

fountain (KJV) A spring, water flowing from the ground.

Because of its geological structure, Palestine is a land of many springs (Deut. 8:7). Modern versions use "spring" and sometimes "well" to translate the several Hebrew terms that the KJV calls fountains. Some versions retain "fountain" in poetic expressions, such as "The fear of the Lord is a fountain of life" (Prov. 14:27; *see* Ps. 36:9; Song 4:12; Jer. 9:1).

fowler A bird catcher. Fowlers used nets and snares to trap their prey. In Jer. 5:26 they represent enemies who try to destroy the godly. *See also* Snare.

fox Small members of the dog family, common in Syria-Palestine. The Hebrew and Greek terms, *shu'al* and *alōpēx*, were probably used for both foxes, which dig dens and usually live alone, and jackals, which live in packs. Jesus certainly meant foxes when he referred to animals that lived in holes (Lk. 9:58). The 300 animals Samson caught were more likely jackals (Jdg. 15:4). *See also* Jackal.

The fox was symbolic of slyness in biblical imagery. Jesus called Herod Antipas a fox (Lk. 13:22).

frankincense The aromatic dried resin collected from the bark of several trees in the *Boswellia* family.

The Israelites prized frankincense as an ingredient in perfume (Song 3:6; 4:6), but even more as part of the sacred incense used in worship (Ex. 30:9,34-38). Frankincense was never added to sin offerings (Lev. 5:11) but did accompany several other sacrifices (Lev. 2:1-12; 6:14-18). God also commanded Moses to place frankincense "as a memorial portion" beside the showbread in the tabernacle and Temple (Lev. 24:7).

The *Boswellia* trees grew in Arabia, Ethiopia, and India. When their bark was cut, resin would ooze out and harden into whitish beads. These would be collected and processed, then exported by camel caravan throughout the known world (Isa. 60:6; Rev. 18:13). It makes sense that the Magi "from the east" brought frankincense to honor the newborn Jesus (Mt. 2:1,11). *See also* Incense.

free, freedom Released or exempted from restrictions; acquitted; independent.

In the Greek-speaking world of the first century, "freedom" indicated citizens' rights in a community. This political sense is not found in Scripture, nor is the idea that "freedom" is a license to do whatever one pleases. Instead, the Bible views freedom against a background of bondage, both literal and spiritual.

THE MODEL

The scriptural approach goes back to the Exodus. God's people were slaves in Egypt, helpless under their oppressors. God intervened through Moses, and by powerful acts forced the Egyptians to release his people. God himself then taught the Israelites how to live righteously, and continued to intervene against their enemies, giving them a land where they could live, free from every oppressing power.

Each element in the biblical concept of freedom is present in this experience of Israel. (1) Mankind is oppressed and helpless. (2) God acts to redeem, winning his people's release. (3) The freed people live righteous lives. (4) God continues to act for his people to preserve their freedom from oppressing powers.

SPIRITUAL FREEDOM

The NT follows the same paradigm in its teaching on Christian freedom. (1) Humanity is in bondage to sin, and no one can free himself from its chains. (2) God has acted in Christ to redeem, setting us free from both sin and the Law. (3) Freed

from sin's bondage, we can live truly righteous lives. (4) God, through his Holy Spirit, acts within us to enable us to remain free of the oppressing power of sin and the Law. (Major biblical passages which explore the nature of Christian freedom include: Jn. 8:31-36; Rom. 6:1-23; 8:1-11; and Gal. 5:1-26.) *See also* Law; Sin.

We must keep this entire biblical context in mind as we study relevant passages. For instance, when Paul writes, "For freedom . . . Christ has set us free" (Gal. 5:1), he is *not* saying that we are free to do whatever we please, but that we are free to do God's will. The Christian is freed by Christ to be righteous and do righteous-

The apostle Paul argued ardently for freedom in Jesus Christ from the Law. This enamel plaque from the 11th century A.D. shows him "disputing with the Greeks [Grecian Jews]" and "refuting the Jews" (see Acts 9:22,28).

THE BIBLICAL CONCEPT OF FREEDOM

Theme	Background	God's Freeing Actions	Freedom's Expression	God's Helping Actions
The Exodus	Israel enslaved in Egypt (Ex. 1,2)	Plagues force Pharaoh to release slaves (Ex. 7–11)	Israel taught God's will; led to Canaan (Ex. 19–Deut.)	God enables conquest of Canaan (Joshua)
Christian freedom from sin	Mankind enslaved by sin (Rom. 7:14-24; 8:5-11; Eph. 2:1-3; Gal. 5:19-21)	Union with Christ in his death and resurrection brings freedom (Rom. 6:1-10)	Do not let sin reign; offer members to God as instruments of righteousness (Rom. 6:11-13; 8:3,4; Gal. 5:13,22, 23)	The Spirit enables a righteous life (Rom. 8:3-11; Gal. 5:22, 23)
Christian freedom from the Law	Mankind enslaved by Law (Rom. 7:1-6; 8:3; Gal. 3:1-14; 1 Cor. 15:56)	Through Christ we are not under Law but under grace (Rom. 6:14-23; 8:1-4; Gal. 3:13-25; 4:4-7, 21-31)	Live righteously as the Law demands (Rom. 8:4; Gal. 5:13-26)	The Spirit enables a righteous life (Rom. 8:10,11; Gal. 5:16-26)

ness, and so to avoid the harmful consequences which always come from doing wrong. Thus Christian freedom, while a release from the oppression of sin, is not found in independence. Rather, Christian freedom is found in choosing to serve God. Only by taking a new master, Christ, can we truly be released from the power of our old masters, sin and the Law. According to 2 Pet. 2:19, false teachers promise a freedom to follow the desires of the sinful human nature, but "they themselves are slaves of depravity." Christian freedom is found in the disciplined doing of good, not in the wanton exercise of human license.

FREEDOM AND SLAVERY

Slavery was institutionalized in biblical times. The OT Law permitted the temporary enslavement of a Hebrew, but after six years the slave was to be freed. There were only two exceptions: out of love for the master, a servant might choose not to be freed; and a servant-woman who became a secondary wife could not be resold but had to be treated as a member of the family (Ex. 21:1-11). *See also* Concubine. Because the Israelites were a redeemed people, destined for freedom, no Israelite was to be sold into permanent slavery or to a foreigner. *See also* Slave.

In NT times, under Roman law, slaves were regarded as property and had few rights. Even a freed slave, who possessed some rights, could not advance to high rank in the military or hold public office. Freed slaves also continued to be obligated to their former masters. Many analogies in the NT are built on the status of slaves, freedmen, and those who were born free.

For instance, Paul bases his argument in Rom. 6:17-23 on the fact that a person freed by an old master (sin) could still be obligated to him. The only way to experience true freedom was to offer oneself as a slave to a new master (righteousness), to whom a person will owe total allegiance. Only by committing ourselves to God, and by doing his will, can we be truly free.

freedman One released from slavery. A slave might purchase his or her own freedom or be set free by the master.

In the Roman Empire a slave had no personal rights, a free-born citizen full rights, and a freedman limited personal rights. Acts 6:9 mentions a "Synagogue of the Freedmen" in Jerusalem. It probably was founded by Jews who had been taken elsewhere in the Roman Empire as slaves, won their freedom, and had returned to their homeland. *See also* Citizen; Free.

friendship A bond of liking and trust, marked by companionship and some degree of intimacy.

In the OT David and Jonathan (1 Sam. 20), and Ruth and Naomi (Ruth 1:16-18; 2:11), model close friendships and the loyalty friendship implies. At times the OT uses "friend" for one who is politically loyal (1 Sam. 30:26; 2 Sam. 15:37).

The Book of Proverbs contains many sayings about friends. "A friend loves at all times" emphasizes loyalty (Prov. 17:17). "Faithful are the wounds of a friend" (Prov. 27:6 RSV) suggests a level of intimacy that permits total honesty. Moses' identification as a "friend of God" is rooted in his loyalty to the Lord and reflected in God's willingness to speak directly to him "as a man speaks with his friend" (Ex. 33:11).

Jesus used the term "friend," perhaps lightly at times, as a form of address (Mt. 20:13; Lk. 5:20). The angry charge of the Pharisees that Jesus was "a friend of tax collectors and sinners" (Lk. 7:34; Mt. 9:11) simply meant that he associated freely with them, and that they responded to him with liking and trust. The zealously religious of Jesus' day were careful to have nothing to do with such persons.

When Jesus spoke of his disciples as friends he had in mind a far greater commitment. Jesus demonstrated his loyalty by laying down his life for his friends (Jn. 15:13). Disciples show loyalty to Jesus by doing what Christ commands (Jn. 15:14). Friendship with God is expressed by complete loyalty to him (Jas. 4:4).

The phrase "dear friends" appears in some modern versions, translating a Greek word that means "beloved" (2 Cor. 7:1; 1 Pet. 2:11; 1 Jn. 2:7).

fringe (KJV) A tassel, with a thread of blue, or a blue cord, hanging from the four corners of the hem of the outer cloak. *See also* Tassel.

frog A tail-less amphibian mentioned in the OT only in connection with the plague of frogs God brought on the Egyptians (Ex. 8:1-15).

The three-inch animals which infested Egypt were associated with the Egyptian goddess Heqt, who was thought to aid women in childbirth. The rotting bodies of the frogs, who quickly died on the land, thus served as a judgment of the one true God on another of Egypt's many deities (Ex. 12:12). The frog-like demons of Rev. 16:13 call up images of the Exodus judgment. They may also suggest repulsion and disgust, since the frog is unclean (Lev. 11:10,41).

frontlet (KJV, RSV) An ornament or headband worn on the forehead. Headbands were the simplest and most common form of headdress in OT times.

The rites of the Passover Feast were instituted by God to serve as a consistent reminder that God brought the Israelites out of Egypt—"as frontlets [symbols, NIV] between your eyes" (Ex. 13:9,16). In two other places the Law exhorts that God's commands be tied as frontlets, emphasizing their constant presence (Deut. 6:8; 11:18).

God sent hoards of frogs into Egyptian homes as the second plague against Pharaoh (Ex. 8:1-15). Woodblock print from the Cologne Bible, A.D. 1479.

Right: Egyptian sculptor's rendering of a frog, a common amphibian in Palestine and Egypt.

This command, which may have been intended metaphorically, was taken literally by the Jews starting in the first century B.C. They wrote four passages of the Law on bits of parchment (Ex. 13:1-10; 11-16; Deut. 6:4-9; 11:13-21), placed these in small boxes, and tied the boxes to the arm and forehead for morning prayers. *See also* Phylacteries.

fruit (1) The edible product of a tree or woody plant, surrounding its seeds; (2) the entire produce of a land; (3) the results of one's actions or character.

FRUIT FROM TREES

Fruit was an important part of the diet in Palestine. Even in war fruit trees were not to be cut down and used to construct siege works (Deut. 20:19,20). The three most important fruits of Palestine were grapes, olives, and figs. Other fruits mentioned in Scripture include pomegranates, melons, mulberries, sycamore figs, and several varieties of nuts. *See also* Agriculture; Almond Tree; Fig; Olive; Pomegranate; Wine.

FRUIT AS A PRODUCT

The word "fruit" appears in a number of expressions suggesting produce in general ("fruit of the land") or the product of human or divine actions. Thus the "fruit of the righteous" (Prov. 11:30) is the bless-

fruitfulness In Scripture, a metaphor for the righteous and loving acts which God expects from human beings.

The image expresses the concept that actions are a product of character. The NT makes it clear that fruitfulness is only possible through a personal and sustained

Above: Dates hang in a cluster among the top fronds of a date palm. This fruit aptly illustrates the word "fruitfulness" because its flesh, seed, and even its flower yielded useful products for the people of Israel. Above right: God commanded that fruitbearing trees be regarded as unclean for three years from planting and as holy to the Lord in their fourth year. In the fifth year their fruit could be eaten. "In this way," said the Lord, "your harvest will be increased" (Lev. 19:23-25).

ing the righteous person receives by pleasing God, while the "fruit of the Spirit" (Gal. 5:22) is the product of the Spirit's work in the believer's heart.

FRUIT AS A MORAL PRODUCT

Jesus said, "No good tree bears bad fruit, nor does a bad tree bear good fruit" and went on to explain that good and evil acts flow from a person's essential character (Lk. 6:43-45; Mt. 12:33-37). Fruitfulness often serves as a metaphor for moral righteousness. Note especially the analogy in Isa. 5:1-7, where the prophet pictures Israel as a vine planted by God. But the nation had yielded only the bad fruit of bloodshed in place of justice, and cries of distress in place of righteousness.

The NT makes it clear that believers should live fruitful moral lives. Jesus spoke of his followers as branches, in vital union with the central vine (Christ), the source of nourishment and strength. Only by living in intimate fellowship with Jesus, and obeying his commands, can the Christian produce the fruit God desires (Jn. 15:1-17).

Other passages also develop the theme of dependence on God. Romans 7:4-8 argues that only those who are energized by God's Spirit can bear "fruit to God." Galatians 5:16-26 contrasts the fruit of human nature with the fruit produced by God's Spirit in human lives. This fruit, displayed both in basic attitude and in relationships with others, is described as "love, joy, peace, patience, kindness, goodness, faithfulness, gentleness and self-control."

A fuller washed newly woven cloth in a mixture of water and alkaline clay to remove its remaining natural oils. The man pictured supports himself on rails while he treads the cloth with his bare feet. Detail from a stone stela found in Roman Gaul, second century A.D.

404

relationship with Jesus Christ. While some have taken fruitfulness to suggest success in bringing others to faith in Christ, the image in both Testaments is directly linked to Scripture's moral vision for humankind. *See also* Fruit.

fulfill (1) To meet the requirements of law or custom; (2) to accomplish a vow or complete an act; (3) to make a prediction come true; (4) God's accomplishment of his purposes.

Jesus announced that he had not come to destroy the Law but to fulfill it (Mt. 5:17). This is often taken in the first sense mentioned above, meeting all the Law's requirements. But Jesus' statement has also been taken to mean that he is the end of the Law, that is, he brings to completion all that the Law looked forward to. However, in rabbinical idiom to "fulfill the law" was to give a complete and accurate explanation of it. It was the desire of every rabbi to so "fulfill the law." If intended in this sense, Jesus was saying that his teaching explained the true meaning of God's Law.

fuller (KJV) A person who treats wool or newly woven cloth, and cleans clothing. In biblical times fullers used ashes and other alkalis to remove the gummy substances found on raw fibers. The process involved dipping, beating, washing, and then sun-bleaching the cloth. Because of the odors associated with this occupation and the need for water, fullers' shops were usually found outside city walls (2 Ki. 18:17; Isa. 7:3).

At Jesus' transfiguration, "his garments became glistening, intensely white, as no fuller on earth could bleach them" (Mk. 9:3 RSV). Malachi 3:2 pictures God's Messiah "like a refiner's fire or a launderer's [fuller's] soap." Each image is one of purification, and should be associated with Christ's second rather than first coming.

fullness (1) That which fills; (2) full measure [the whole]; (3) completeness; (4) maturity.

Fullness (*plērōma*) is an important theological term in Christological passages of the NT. Paul writes, "God was pleased to have all his fullness dwell in him [Christ]" (Col. 1:19), emphasizing the complete expression of God through Jesus. Later Paul reiterates, "In Christ all the fullness of the Deity lives in bodily form," but adds, "and you have been given fullness in Christ" (Col. 2:9,10). Paul was writing to people who looked for spiritual fulfillment in ritual religion (Col. 2:16-23). But everything they needed for growth and maturity was already theirs through personal relationship with Jesus.

In Ephesians Paul portrays the Church as "the fullness of him who fills everything in every way" (Eph. 1:23). The thought here is that in some sense the Church completes Christ, who from the beginning was intended to express God through members of his Body. Later Paul prays for the Ephesians, "that you may be filled to the full measure of all the fullness of God" (Eph. 3:19). God wants us to find our completion by being filled with his presence. And, as believers love and minister to each other, God works within individual and community to enable each to "become mature, attaining to the whole measure of the fullness of Christ" (Eph. 4:13).

funeral A ceremony associated with the disposal of the dead.

Burial customs varied in the biblical world. The Hebrew people did not embalm, but buried the dead within a few hours after death. The body was washed. Sometimes spices were placed in the graveclothes in which the corpse was

Funeral procession of the vizier Ramose (about 1375 B.C.). Servants carry furnishings to his tomb while female relatives of all ages mourn. Joseph, also a vizier in his own day, probably had an elaborate funeral because he saved Egypt from famine's devastation (Gen. 50:26).

405

furlong
(220 YARDS / 201 METERS)

stadion
(202 YARDS/185 METERS)

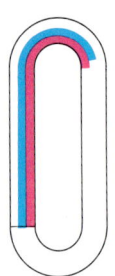

A furlong is about half-way around a running track. In the KJV it is a rendering of the Greek word stadion.

Scenes drawn in Roman catacombs by early Christians often featured Old Testament stories, like Daniel's three friends in the fiery furnace (Dan. 3). As Christians buried and mourned their dead, who were often victims of Roman persecution, they took comfort in the triumphs of others who had suffered.

wrapped (Jn. 19:39,40). The body was carried on a wooden frame, a bier, and was accompanied by relatives and friends. People who observed the procession were expected to join it out of respect for the dead person (Lk. 7:12). In NT times, professional mourners shrieked and wailed to mark a death, and led the procession to the grave site. There is no indication in Scripture that a religious service was performed before or after interment. The word "funeral" does not occur in the Bible. *See also* Burial.

furlong (KJV, RSV) A measure of distance, about one-tenth of a mile. "Furlong" translates the Greek *stadion,* which measured 202 yards (185 meters). An English furlong is 220 yards.

furnace (1) An enclosed chamber or structure for producing heat; (2) any extremely hot place.

Furnaces were not used in biblical times to heat homes. They were used primarily for smelting metals or as kilns for firing bricks and ceramics. Kilns were dome-shaped and looked much like the ovens used in baking bread. The furnace for rendering metals was made of clay bricks. In some texts, the "furnace" is only the smelting pot in which metals were heated, not the whole installation.

In biblical imagery, the furnace is associated with divine judgment, which may be intended to purify (Isa. 48:10,11) or to punish (Ps. 21:9,10). Jesus uses this imagery in one of his clearest statements about eternal punishment. When Christ returns, "everything that causes sin and all who do evil" will be rooted out, and God's angels "will throw them into the fiery furnace, where there will be weeping and gnashing of teeth" (Mt. 13:41,42; *compare* Rev. 9:2). *See also* Judgment; Judgment Day.

furnishings, furniture Movable objects in a home that equip it for living. The broader word "furnishings" (NIV), rather than "furniture," is used for the equipment of the tabernacle and Temple (Ex. 25:9; 40:9; 1 Chr. 9:29) as well as that of a person's dwelling (Num. 19:18; Neh. 13:8).

When a wealthy woman prepared a room for the prophet Elisha, she furnished it luxuriously. She "put in it a bed and a table, a chair and a lamp" (2 Ki. 4:10). Even these sparse furnishings were luxurious when compared to the possessions found in the homes of the poor. There a low, 12-inch (30-millimeter) stone or mud ledge generally ran along one or more sides of the room for seating. At night an animal skin was thrown on the floor as a

mattress; a goat skin, stuffed with feathers or wool, served as a pillow. The outer robes worn during the day functioned as blankets. Somewhere in the room, a clay lamp filled with olive oil was kept burning at night.

Homes of the wealthy might feature a bench, covered with cushions, on two or three sides of a room. At night an elevated section of the bench served as a bed. Some of the very wealthy had bedsteads made of wood or bronze, or couches that might even be inlaid with ivory (*compare* Amos 6:4). The affluent slept on thick, woven mattresses at night. Proverbs describes a bed covered with colored Egyptian linens, perfumed with myrrh, aloes, and cinnamon (7:16,17). Other furnishings in the rich man's home might include stools, a low table or two, and a brazier for heating. In addition there were lamps, of bronze or other metals.

future (1) A time to come, (2) what will happen or is to be. Theologians refer to the study of the future as "eschatology," a term derived from the Greek word *eschatos*, meaning "last." Just as Scripture tells of God's interaction in the past, tracing historic events from creation and the Fall to the redemption offered through the cross of Christ, so it also reveals God's involvement in the present, shaping events to fulfill his intended purpose.

The Lord says through Isaiah,

"I am God, and there is no other;
I am God, there is none like me.

I make known the end from the beginning,
from ancient times, what is still to come."

The statement continues,

"What I have said, that will I bring about;
what I have planned, that will I do."

(Isa. 46:9-11)

Some of God's future plans have been revealed through the Bible's many prophecies. Hundreds of these have already been fulfilled. Others deal with things still to come, such as the Second Coming of Christ.

Christians differ on whether certain prophecies should be taken literally. However, if biblical prophecy is taken in a literal sense, this is the future it portrays.

FUTURE ACCORDING TO THE OT

Nearly all the OT prophets look into the distant future and portray history's end. All see God fulfilling at that time his ancient covenant promises to Abraham and to the nation Israel. Major elements associated with that fulfillment are:

1. *A regathering of Israel.* As history draws to a close, God's OT people are recalled to their land, regathered by the Lord himself (Isa. 11:11,12; 14:1-3; 27:12, 13; 43:1-8; 66:20-22; Jer. 16:14,15; 23:3-8; 30:10,11; 31:31-37; Ezek. 11:17-20; 20:33-38; 34:11-16; 39:25-29; Hos. 1:10,11; Joel 3:17-21; Amos 9:11-15; Mic. 4:4-7; Zeph. 3:14-20; Zech. 8:4-8).

2. *A time of tribulation and conflict.* At history's end, the nations assemble to invade and crush Israel. The coalition is led by a great northern power. The invasion is

407

a judgment that purifies Israel. However, despite the horrors of those days, a Jewish remnant survives the destruction (*the invaders:* Ezek. 38,39; Dan. 11:40-45; Joel 2:1-17; *the tribulations:* Deut. 4:25-31; Isa. 2:12,19; 13:6-9; 24:1-3,19-21; 26:20,21; Jer. 30:7; Ezek. 13:5; 30:3; Dan. 11:40; Joel 1:15; 2:1,2; 3:14; Amos 5:18-20; Zeph. 1:14,15; Zech. 14:1; *the survivors:* Isa. 4:3,4; 6:12,13; 26:20; 65:13-25; Jer. 15:11; 33:25,26; Ezek. 14:22; 37:21,22; Hos. 3:5; Amos 9:11-15; Zech. 13:8,9; Mal. 3:16,17).

3. *God's intervention.* The Messiah appears and supernaturally crushes the enemy. A great spiritual conversion takes place among both Jews and Gentiles, and the Messiah, a ruler from David's family line, establishes an earthly kingdom (Isa. 2:1-4; 4:2-6; 9:6,7; 11:1-13; 24:1-23; 32:1-5; 33:17-24; 35:1-10; 52:7-10; 60:1–61:6; 66:15-23; Jer. 31:1-27; 33:14-26; Ezek. 20:33-42; 34:20-31; Dan. 2:31-45; 7:1-28; 9:20-27; Hos. 3:4,5; Joel 2:28–3:2,17-21; Amos 9:9-15; Obad. 15-21; Mic. 4:1-5; Zech. 2:1-13; 14:1-21; Mal. 3:1-5; 4:1-6). *See also* Day of the Lord.

4. *Cataclysmic destruction and universal re-creation.* At some subsequent time God destroys the present universe, to replace it with new heavens and a new earth (Isa. 51:6; 65:17; 66:22-24).

FUTURE ACCORDING TO THE NT

Prophecy in the Gospels reflects OT teachings. However, in the Epistles, prophecy focuses on the Church rather than on Israel.

1. *The Second Coming of Christ.* Jesus will return bodily to earth. His Second Coming will be marked by terrible judgments on the lost and by the resurrection of believers (Mt. 24:36-44; Mk. 13:26,27; Jn. 14:1-3; Acts 1:11; Rom. 8:18,19; 1 Cor. 15:12-58; Phil. 3:20,21; 1 Th. 4:13-18; 2 Th. 1:3-10; Jas. 5:7,8; 1 Jn. 3:1-3; Rev. 19). *See also* Day of Christ; Day of the Lord; Resurrection.

2. *The final judgment and creation of a new universe.* At some time after Christ's return, final judgment will take place. At that time all who have not trusted themselves to God will be condemned to eternal punishment. Then God will destroy the present universe and create a new one in which only righteousness dwells (Rom. 8:18-25; 2 Pet. 3:1-13; Rev. 20–22). *See also* Hell; Judgment Day.

COMMON ELEMENTS

While images of the future in the two Testaments differ in focus, they do not conflict. Several common elements exist.

1. *The Resurrection.* The OT says little about the eternal destiny of the individual. Yet what is said does not deny bodily resurrection. Both affirm that "multitudes who sleep in the dust of the earth will awake: some to everlasting life, others to shame and everlasting contempt" (Dan. 12:2; *compare* Jn. 5:28,29). *See also* Death; Judgment Day; Resurrection.

2. *Salvation for Gentiles.* While the OT predicts glory for the nation Israel, it holds out hope that Gentiles will one day share in God's salvation. When Messiah comes he will "stand as a banner for the peoples; the nations will rally to him, and his place of rest will be glorious" (Isa. 11:10).

3. *The Restoration of Israel.* In the NT, Paul argues that God's creation of the Church does not mean he has abandoned the nation Israel. The apostle writes that when the deliverer comes again "all Israel will be saved, as it is written," for "God's gifts and his call are irrevocable" (Rom. 11:26,29).

4. *Period of Universal Blessing.* Both Testaments look forward to a future age in which God will establish his personal reign on earth, through the promised Davidic king. This period is seen by some as the time when the promises given to Israel will be fulfilled.

Thus, common elements in prophecy of OT and NT suggest that the Bible's vision of the future is harmonious and whole. Yet only when Jesus returns will we know how the elements fit together.

MAJOR ESCHATOLOGICAL SYSTEMS

Throughout history, Christians have proposed three major frameworks in which to fit the future events predicted in Scripture: premillennialism, amillennialism, and postmillennialism.

1. *Premillennialism.* Modern premillennialism holds the following beliefs:

• The Antichrist will rise to power amid great tribulation and will subsequently persecute the Jews. *See also* Antichrist.

• Christ will return bodily to earth *before* the millennium.

• Christ will reign on earth for 1,000 years, thus fulfilling his covenant promises to Israel.

• Satan will lead a rebellion at the end of the millennium, which Christ will crush.

• After the final battle will come the Day of Judgment, the destruction of the earth, and the creation of a new heaven and earth.

A form of premillennialism called *chil-*

iasm was held by most of the early church fathers until the third century A.D. Polycarp, Clement of Rome, Ignatius, Justin Martyr, Irenaeus, Tertullian, and Cyprian were some of its early proponents. Between A.D. 140 and 160, Justin Martyr wrote that "I, and as many as are orthodox Christians, do acknowledge that there shall be a resurrection of the body, and a residence of a thousand years in Jerusalem, adorned and enlarged, as the prophets Ezekiel, Isaiah, and others do unanimously attest" (*Dialogue with Trypho* 80). The same view is reflected in the *Didache*, written about A.D. 100, and in the writings of other church fathers up to about A.D. 300.

2. *Amillennialism.* After the first three centuries of the Christian era, a shift in understanding took place. Instead of a literal interpretation of OT prophecy, a spiritualized view came to be accepted, resulting in the following doctrines:

• Satan is bound during the inter-Advent or Church age.

• There will be no literal 1,000-year reign of Christ on earth.

• The covenants promised to Israel are spiritually inherited by the Church. *See also* Covenant.

• The millennium itself is either spiritually represented in the Church or is presently taking place in heaven.

• Christ's return brings judgment; the earth is then destroyed, and a new heaven and earth are created.

Amillennialism was supported by such theologians as Tyconius, Clement of Alexandria, Origen, and Augustine. Around A.D. 390, Tyconius wrote a commentary on Revelation, using an allegorical rather than literal method to interpret the Scripture and making no attempt to relate Revelation to the predictions of OT prophets. However, it was Augustine's *City of God* that heralded the downfall of premillennialism by its assertion that the Church was God's kingdom on earth—a theme endorsed by the Roman Catholic Church, which added that papal authority represented Christ's earthly rule.

Other things influenced the shift from a premillennial to an amillennial view: 1) the emphasis some premillennialists placed on earthly rewards and carnal pleasure, 2) the influence of asceticism and gnosticism, 3) the antagonism toward anything "Jewish," and 4) the increasing use of allegorical exegesis, which encouraged Christians to seek a spiritual rather than historical fulfillment of these texts. However, it was the powerful teachings of Augustine that succeeded in subduing the premillennialist view. *See also* Gnostics.

3. *Postmillennialism.* The amillennial position was held by the church through the Reformation. However, in the post-Reformation period, a new millennial view was developed, postmillennialism. This view proposed a literal millennium coming through the Church. Its tenets are:

• The preaching of the Gospel and the spread of Christian morals will bring in the millennium.

• Christ's kingdom is not political, but spiritual.

• Christ will return after the millennial period and will bring judgment; then, the earth is destroyed, and a new heaven and earth are created.

Within the postmillennial movement, there arose two camps: one conservative, believing God's power would direct the millennium; the other liberal, believing man's natural progress would cause an earthly utopia. However, after World War I, when it was obvious the world was not getting better, postmillennialism faded in popularity. Nevertheless, this view is enjoying a resurgence in some circles.

4. *Millennialism today.* The Reformation brought a return to a more literal interpretation of Scripture, laying the groundwork for the reemergence of premillennialism. In the 19th century, premillennialism continually gained ground until, now, it is held by most Dispensational theologians, while amillennialism retains its place in Covenant or Reformed theology.

Though Christians today differ concerning details of what the future holds, there are some things on which all agree. The Bible does promise that Christ will return. At that time, his saints will be resurrected. At that time, too, God will judge sin and sinners. And, after all God's purposes for this universe have been fulfilled, we will share eternity with God on a new and perfect heaven and earth. Then, what Revelation promises will come true:

Now the dwelling of God is with men, and he will live with them. They will be his people, and God himself . . . will wipe every tear from their eyes. There will be no more death or mourning or crying or pain, for the old order of things has passed away.

(Rev. 21:3,4)

As he who was seated on the throne said to John in his vision, "I am making everything new!" (Rev. 21:5). *See also* Prophecy, Interpretation of.

409

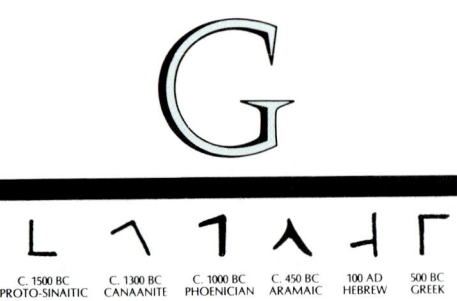

G

L ٦ ٦ ٨ ╕ Γ

C. 1500 BC PROTO-SINAITIC   C. 1300 BC CANAANITE   C. 1000 BC PHOENICIAN   C. 450 BC ARAMAIC   100 AD HEBREW   500 BC GREEK

The Angel of the Annunciation *by Simone Martini (*A.D. *1284– 1344). "[Gabriel] said to her, 'Do not be afraid, Mary, you have found favor with God. You will be with child and give birth to a son, and you are to give him the name Jesus'* " (Lk. 1:30,31).

Gabriel [GAY-bree-el; "strength of God," or "man of God"]. One of two angels named in Scripture. Each of Gabriel's four appearances is associated with revelation about the coming Messiah: 1) He explains Daniel's vision (Dan. 8:16). 2) He reveals the prophecy of the 70 weeks (Dan. 9:21). 3) He proclaims the birth of John the Baptist (Lk. 1:11-20) and 4) the birth of Jesus (Lk. 1:26-38).

Gabriel is also portrayed in Jewish intertestamental literature as one of the four angels of highest rank, an archangel, and his introduction in Lk. 1:19 testifies to this: "I am Gabriel. I stand in the presence of God." Furthermore, Jewish folklore credits Gabriel with the role of an intercessor on behalf of God's people and as an angel of power who destroys the wicked (*compare* 2 Chr. 32:21). Often, Jewish writings attribute the deeds of unnamed OT angels to Gabriel. Christian tradition has also developed legends concerning Gabriel, one of which is that he will blow the trumpet to announce Christ's return (*compare* 1 Th. 4:16). However, except for his high rank, none of these traditions has biblical support. *See also* Angel; Michael.

Gad *See* Israel, Tribes of.

Galatia In the first century, (1) a large Roman province, and (2) specifically the north-central part of that province originally invaded by Gauls from Europe about 275 B.C.

Biblical scholars have debated for hundreds of years whether the Galatia referred to in the NT was the northern area originally settled by the Gauls or the southern area added in 25 B.C when the Romans made Galatia a province. A number of arguments seem to favor the south Galatia theory: 1) There is no record in Acts of a visit by Paul to the north, and 2) Acts 13,14 give a careful account of church planting in the south Galatian cities of Derbe, Lystra, Iconium, and (Pisidian) Antioch (*compare* Acts 16:6; 18:23; 2 Tim. 4:10; 1 Pet. 1:1).

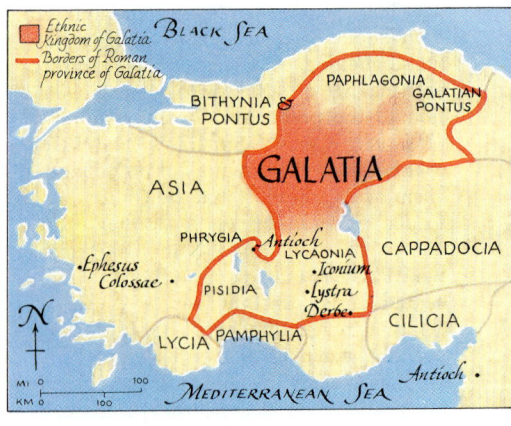

The Roman province of Galatia included parts of Pontus, Paphlagonia, Phrygia, Lycaonia and Pisidia, as well as the Gallic kingdom of Galatia. Biblical scholars dispute how large an area Paul had in mind when he wrote "to the churches in Galatia" (Gal. 1:2).

eye of believers from Jerusalem illustrates pressure to hold to the old ways (Gal. 2:11-21).

During the first century A.D., this aqueduct channeled water to the Roman town of Pisidian Antioch, Paul's first stop in Galatia (Acts 13:14-50; 14:19,21). The city probably had a small Christian community since he returned on his second and third journeys (16:6; 18:23).

THEOLOGICAL CONTRIBUTIONS

Paul focuses here on the relationship between Law and grace. He shows that OT Law is irrelevant to salvation and to living the Christian life. Both salvation and the Christian experience are received by faith. The believer must rely on God's Holy Spirit, who produces an inner righteousness, rather than on human efforts to keep the Law. The outline lists Paul's arguments for the insufficiency of the Law.

Galatians, Epistle to the

This brief but powerful Epistle was written by the apostle Paul, possibly as early as A.D. 49 or 50. Along with the Epistle to the Romans, Galatians was a keystone of the Protestant Reformation, because of its powerful affirmation of justification by faith alone. Today, Galatians remains one of the Bible's clearest statements concerning the relationship of the Gospel, Law, and righteousness.

BACKGROUND

Shortly after Paul and Barnabas traveled in south Galatia (Acts 13,14), the churches they founded were approached by Jewish Christians who called on Gentile converts to adopt Jewish customs. The teaching of these Judaizers was probably similar to that summed up in Acts 15. They said that "unless you are circumcised according to the custom taught by Moses, you cannot be saved," and that Gentile Christians were "required to obey the law of Moses" (vv. 1,5). Paul recognized this as a serious distortion of the Gospel message and acted immediately. He wrote this letter to circulate among the churches he had just revisited (*see* Gal. 1:6). He then led a delegation to Jerusalem, where a council of church leaders affirmed Gentile converts' freedom from Mosaic Law (Acts 15). *See also* Council of Jerusalem.

HISTORICAL CONTRIBUTIONS

Galatians 1:11–2:10 provides vital data for a chronology of Paul's life. The entire book gives insight into the early struggle to relate OT and NT faiths and the difficulty of establishing an integrated Jewish-Gentile church. Peter's hesitation to eat with Gentile Christians under the critical

---

THE STRUCTURE OF GALATIANS

I. The Law is opposed to life. This is demonstrated by: **3:1-18**
  A. Experience: The Galatians received life through faith (3:1-5).
  B. Example: Abraham received spiritual life through faith (3:6-9).
  C. Scripture: The just shall live by faith (3:10-18).

II. The Law's role is severely limited: **3:19–4:7**
  A. In duration: It is temporary (3:19,20).
  B. In ability: It cannot give life (3:21,22).
  C. In function: It is only a supervising servant (3:23,24).
  D. In relevance: It is nullified today, since believers are "in Christ" and are now sons of God (3:25–4:7).

III. The Law is an inferior way, bringing to the believer: **4:8–5:12**
  A. Dissatisfaction: It robs us of joy (4:8-19).
  B. Bondage: It robs us of freedom (4:20–5:1).
  C. Powerlessness: It drains us of faith by turning our attention to useless self-effort (5:2-12).

Against this background, Paul calls believers to "live by the Spirit," for nothing produced in the human personality by God's Spirit will violate any part of the divine Law (5:16-26). *See also* Freedom; Fruit; Grace; Law; Righteousness; Son.

MASTERY KEYS

Use the outline above to trace the central argument; then study the related dictionary articles. Make lists contrasting the characteristics and products of the "sinful nature" and the "Spirit" (Gal. 5). Then write an explanation of the significance of (1) the statement, "Against such things there is no law," in Gal. 5:23, and (2) the concepts expressed in Gal. 6:15.

SPECIAL FEATURES

Paul's reference to Sarah and Hagar in Gal. 4:21-31 is a clear example of allegorical

411

interpretation of OT events in the NT and is typical of rabbinic typology of the time. *See also* Allegory.

Furthermore, several vital doctrines are summed up in various verses of Galatians: 2:20, Christ in us; 4:28, spiritual adoption; 5:6, faith; 5:13, freedom in Christ.

Galilee included land originally given to the tribes of Asher, Issachar, Naphtali, and Zebulun. Tiberias was its capital at the time of Jesus' ministry.

galbanum *See* incense.

Galilee A small region in northern Palestine which, until the Romans made it an administrative district in 63 B.C., had no fixed boundaries.

From the Assyrian assimilation of the Northern Kingdom (734–722 B.C.) until the Maccabean period (80 B.C.) the *galil* [Heb., "ring, circle"] was not governed by Jews. The term "Galilee of the nations [or Gentiles]" in Isa. 9:1 reflects this fact, highlighting its mixed population. Jews were the minority.

In the first century Galilee was about 44 miles (70 kilometers) long and 25 miles (40 kilometers) wide and, according to Josephus, contained around 204 villages. This beautiful region, rich in lush hills and fertile plains, was the scene of most of the events reported in the first three Gospels. Twenty-five of Christ's 33 recorded miracles took place in Galilee, and most of his parables were told here. Many of the events occurred near Capernaum, which Jesus adopted as his home (Mt. 4:13).

Galilee, along with Judea and Samaria, contained the largest concentrations of Jews in the Greco-Roman world. This

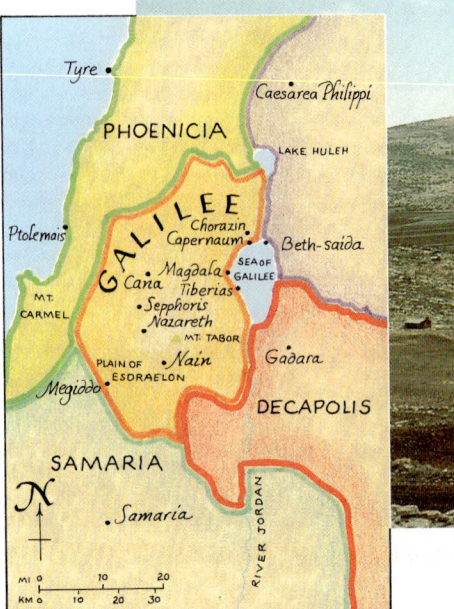

northern province, however, was somewhat isolated, and its more rustic inhabitants were considered ignorant by the people of Judea. This was partly because they spoke with a broad accent (Mt. 26:73) and because Galilean customs differed slightly from those of Judea. (The Pharisees even considered Galilean olive oil ritually impure!) This attitude of contempt is reflected in the Jewish leaders' easy dismissal of Jesus: They were sure no prophet could arise from Galilee (Jn. 1:46; 7:52; *compare* Mt. 2:23).

GALATIANS: A READING AND STUDY GUIDE		
Chapter	Content Summary	Related Articles
1	The Galatians are deserting the true Gospel for a different gospel. Paul reviews his credentials.	Gospel Paul
2	Paul's authority from God was affirmed by the original apostles. His confrontation with Peter shows how vital the issue of Law vs. grace is.	Law Grace Apostle
3	Observing the Law offers neither salvation nor spiritual growth. The righteous live by faith, not by the Law which from the first served a temporary purpose.	Righteousness Faith
4	Christ redeemed us and granted us, through the Holy Spirit, full rights as sons. Even OT history illustrates that God's inheritance is for sons, not slaves.	Holy Spirit Sons
5	Christians are granted freedom so we might live righteous, loving lives. This experience can be produced only by the Spirit; we are to live by his presence and power.	Free Flesh
6	Believers are called to do good to all and must rely only on the grace brought to us in Christ's cross.	Works, Good

הסירה העתיקה
THE ANCIENT BOAT

Galilee, Sea of The large, fresh-water lake in the district of Galilee in northern Palestine.

This body of water is called by a variety of names in Scripture: Sea of Kinnereth (Josh. 12:3), Lake of Gennesaret (Lk. 5:1), the Sea of Tiberias (Jn. 6:1; 21:1), or simply "the sea" or "the lake." It lies approximately 700 feet (211 meters) below sea level, and in some places is 150 feet (46 meters) deep. Set between two ranges of high hills, the Sea of Galilee is subject to sudden fierce winds and violent storms, as reported in Mt. 8,14; Mk. 4,6; Lk. 8; and Jn. 6. The northern end of the lake was a rich source of fish in biblical times, and Josephus says that some 330 fishing boats operated on the body of water in the first century. Much of Christ's ministry took place on the shores and in the cities surrounding the Sea of Galilee. *See also* Fish.

The fertile valleys of Galilee were the "breadbasket" of Israel. In Jesus' time, Galilean wheat was a major export, although most of it was sent to Rome to pay taxes. Left: Cradled in mud for 2,000 years, this 27-foot (8.2 meters) boat was recently excavated from the shore of the Sea of Galilee. It fits one of at least two classes of boats that plied the lake in Jesus' day and is the type referred to in the Gospels. Below: A fishing boat heads for shore on the Sea of Galilee. Gospel accounts report that Jesus and his disciples crossed these waters regularly.

Overleaf: "Jesus went out of the house and sat by the lake. Such large crowds gathered around him that he got into a boat and sat in it, while all the people stood on the shore" (Mt. 13:1,2).

gall (1) A bitter and possibly poisonous extract from a plant or plants native to Palestine, and (2) bile from the liver, which has an extremely bitter taste if mistakenly cooked with an animal.

The wine mixed with gall that was offered to Christ on the cross was intended to deaden his pain (Mt. 27:34). Evidence suggests that this gall may have been the bitter juice of the poppy or the spongy pulp of the colocynth gourd fruit, which was mixed with water or wine (*compare* Jer. 9:15). Furthermore, gall serves as a metaphor in Scripture for bitter and extremely painful experiences.

Assyrian soldiers impale Judean captives on tall stakes. The "gallows" Haman built for Mordecai (Esth. 5:14) probably refers to a similar mode of execution.

416

gallows An instrument of execution mentioned only in the Book of Esther. The Hebrew *'ets* of Esther simply means a tree or post. Hanging, however, was not common in Persia. The usual mode of execution was impaling the body on a sharpened pole or stake, which was probably the fate Haman intended for Mordecai. *See also* Hanging.

Gamaliel [guh-MAY-lee-uhl; "reward of God"]. Notable as the rabbi who trained the apostle Paul, and president of the Sanhedrin who counseled the release of the apostles from prison, A.D. 40. **Father:** Simeon. **Grandfather:** Hillel. **Scripture:** Acts 5:34-40; 22:3.

BACKGROUND

Gamaliel was a Pharisee, who served the Sanhedrin during the reigns of Tiberius, Caligula, and Claudius. He is said to have died about A.D. 62. Rabbinic literature identifies him as Gamaliel I or Gamaliel the Elder, a teacher of the moderate school of Hillel.

Gamaliel resisted those who wanted to put the apostles to death. On his advice, they were released by the Sanhedrin, even though the apostles boldly announced they would continue to preach Christ.

SIGNIFICANCE

Despite his identification with the Pharisee party, Gamaliel seems to have been a moderate. He was "honored by all the people" (Acts 5:34), and was able to influence even zealous members of the Sanhedrin. He won the apostles' release by arguing that "if their purpose or activity is of human origin, it will fail. But if it is from God, you will . . . find yourselves fighting against God" (Acts 5:38,39).

LEARNING FROM GAMALIEL'S LIFE

Gamaliel represents many influential and well-respected individuals who are paralyzed from making a decision for Christ by their position. Though Gamaliel reasoned moderately and soundly in defense of the apostles, in years to come he did not ever recognize the divine origin of Christian faith. Unlike his student Paul, he did not convert (contrary to some early traditions). In light of Christ's resurrection, the preaching of the Gospel, and the apostles' signs and wonders, his readiness to withhold judgment may eventually have served as a way to avoid the claims of Christ and his followers.

games (1) Forms of play or amusement; (2) sports or competitions. Few games are mentioned in the OT. Our information about games basically comes from the findings of archaeologists.

CHILDREN'S GAMES

Archaeologists working in Palestine have found a variety of toys: tiny clay pots and furniture, wooden dolls and rattles. Some of these date from 900 B.C. Older boys undoubtedly played with slings, while younger boys and girls acted out weddings and funerals (*compare* Zech. 8:5;

The entrance to the tomb of Gamaliel the Elder in Beth Shearim, a famous burial place for important Jews. Gamaliel was held in such high honor that he was designated Rabban ("our teacher"), a title reserved for leading scholars.

Mt. 11:16,17). Very probably, children also played out stories of Bible heroes and events.

INTELLECTUAL GAMES

Riddles were popular with adults. These were intended not only to entertain but often to instruct. (*See* Num. 12:8; Jdg. 14; Ps. 49:4; Prov. 1:6; Dan. 5:12.)

BOARD GAMES

While no board games are mentioned in the Bible, archaeologists have recovered a variety of them from Mesopotamia and Egypt. Several involved moving pieces on boards divided into squares or placing pegs in a sequence of holes. The moves in most of these games were determined by throwing dice or knucklebones. Game boards recovered from Palestine date as early as 1500 B.C. Gambling was also common in the Middle East. Each Gospel reports that the Roman soldiers cast dice and gambled for Jesus' robe, as predicted in Ps. 22:18 (*compare* Mt. 27:35; Mk. 15:24; Lk. 23:34; Jn. 19:23,24). However, the Jews so disapproved of playing games for money that no gambler was considered fit to testify in court.

ATHLETIC GAMES

Little is known of athletic games in ancient Israel. Genesis 32:24,25 mentions wrestling. Other passages allude to belt-wrestling, in which the holds are made on an opponent's belt. Isaiah 11:5 refers to this distinctive wrestling belt when speaking of the Messiah: "Righteousness will be his belt and faithfulness the sash around his waist." The Messiah comes prepared to contend, not for glory and honor, but for righteousness and justice.

The NT has many allusions to the athletic games popular in the Greek and Roman world. Though these contests were despised by the orthodox Jew, Herod sponsored these games in Jerusalem itself. Paul, whose letters are addressed to Gentile churches, often mentions athletic games to make a spiritual point. The NT refers to:

1. *Boxing.* "I do not fight like a man beating the air" (1 Cor. 9:26). Boxers wore metal-studded leather straps on their hands, so opponents tried to evade rather than block blows. Paul concentrated on landing telling blows for the sake of the Gospel and did not "beat the air" (*compare* 2 Tim. 4:7).

2. *Foot racing.* "Throw off everything that hinders . . . run with perseverance the race marked out for us. Let us fix our eyes on Jesus" (Heb. 12:1,2). The racer stripped off all extra weight and kept to the course that had been laid out. In the Greek games, a square pillar marked the finish line. The runner kept his eyes on that goal, for reaching it was all that counted. So, according to this illustration, the Christian keeps his eyes fixed on Jesus, the goal toward which his life flows. (*See* Gal. 2:2; Phil. 2:16; 2 Tim. 4:7.)

3. *Chariot racing.* "Forgetting what is behind and straining toward what is ahead, I press on" (Phil. 3:13). Paul may have been referring to the charioteer who leaned forward, straining as his horses sped toward the finish line. A backward look could be disastrous in this dangerous sport; the only safety lay in reaching the goal and claiming the prize.

Other images from Greek games occur in Paul's writings. He speaks of the herald who calls competitors to the starting line but cannot compete in the race himself (1 Cor. 9:27). He speaks of the strict training regime followed by the athletes, who practiced endlessly and carefully watched their weight (1 Cor. 9:24,25). Furthermore, Paul brings up images of the judges who reward the victor a crown fashioned of wild olive, parsley, pine, laurel, or celery, which "will not last." In contrast, Paul speaks of the lasting crown God will award believers who live this present life victoriously (1 Cor. 9:24,25; 2 Tim. 2:5; 4:8; *compare* 1 Pet. 5:4).

In one passage Paul even alludes to the *venatio*, a Roman "game" in which wild animals were baited and then matched against criminals or trained hunters. "I fought with wild beasts in Ephesus," Paul says in 1 Cor. 15:32. *See also* Dance; Song.

1,2 Senet, an Egyptian board game from predynastic times, popular among all classes of Egyptians. A tomb painting (1300–1200 B.C.) shows Queen Nefertari playing.

3. Stone dice from Ptolemaic Egypt. Dice as we know them (right) did not appear until the Greco-Roman period.

4. Egyptian game of "Hounds and Jackals" with ivory playing pieces and ivory and ebony veneer.

5. Ivory board for the so-called "55 Holes" game found in a Canaanite palace at Megiddo (1300 B.C.). It is one of few games excavated in Palestine.

6. Deep-cut relief from a Roman marble sarcophagus shows a group of children playing a game. In Zechariah's prophecy, streets filled with playing children symbolized God's future blessing (8:1-4).

7. This 5,000-year-old game board is one of the oldest in the world. Found in a royal tomb of the city of Ur in Mesopotamia, it is inlaid with shell, lapis lazuli, red limestone, and black shale.

8. Egyptian game piece in the form of a Semitic prisoner. It is contemporary with the Israelite oppression (New Kingdom, 1580–1200 B.C.).

9. Roman figurine of girls playing knucklebones, originally a Greek game that used sheep or goat joints (Taranto, Italy, about 330 B.C.).

10. Painting on marble from Pompeii presents the mythical Niobe and her daughters absorbed in knucklebones. These pieces were used in a variety of games and for gambling too. The Roman soldiers who "cast lots" for Jesus' clothes may have thrown knucklebones (Mt. 27:35; Mk. 15:24; Lk. 23:34; Jn. 19:24).

11. Greek vessel bearing scenes of three events of the pentathlon: javelin, discus, and vaulting. Paul illustrated 1 Corinthians with athletic metaphors (9:24-27).

12. Ivory gaming pieces from Megiddo (14th–12th century B.C.). The bottom piece bears an ibex and a palm.

13. The flagstone floor of Antonia Fortress, Jerusalem, where Jesus faced Pontius Pilate, is carved with game "boards." The small square (left) is called "The Mill." Players sought to place stones on three intersections in a row.

14. Ivory toy dog with movable mouth. Though the Bible never refers to toys, Israelite children probably played with ones similar to many uncovered in the Near East.

1

2

3

4

5

6

7

8

9

10

11

12

13

14

garden (1) A walled enclosure where flowers, vegetables, vines, or fruit trees were cultivated; (2) a broad public or private park.

Peoples from Mesopotamia to Egypt viewed gardens as places to relax in and enjoy. The privacy afforded by high walls or thick hedges, the rich smell of growing things, and the tastes of fresh fruits were valued by all peoples of Bible lands. Gardens served as outdoor living areas in the summer, as places for banqueting, even as locations to build shelters where the owner might sleep at night. The author of Ecclesiastes "made gardens and parks and planted all kinds of fruit trees in them" (2:5). The Song of Solomon poetically describes the beloved as a locked garden, filled with choice fruits and spices (4:12-16).

Three gardens play prominent roles in sacred history. (1) Adam was placed in the parklike Garden of Eden, in Gen. 2,3. There he and Eve were united, disobeyed God, and were exiled from this paradise. (2) The night before his crucifixion Jesus prayed in Gethsemane, a garden planted with olive trees, in Mt. 26:36-46. Here Jesus expressed his anguish and his full submission to the Father's will. (3) Christ's resurrection took place from a garden tomb, in Jn. 19:41. It was common practice for the rich, such as Joseph of Arimathea in whose tomb the body of Christ was placed, to lay out a garden just outside their last resting place.

Egyptian physicians prescribed garlic for headaches, throat disorders, and lethargy. The Israelites, newly liberated from Egypt, seemed to have appreciated garlic for its culinary properties (Num. 11:5).

Throughout human history, the garden has symbolized a place of beauty, peace, and rest. Thus, the significance of the garden made it an appropriate image of the blessing promised the righteous, who are destined to be "like a well-watered garden, like a spring whose waters never fail" (Isa. 58:11; *compare* 51:3; Jer. 31:12). Furthermore, the garden image is used eschatologically in describing the eternal bliss of the righteous. Revelation 22:1-6 describes God's heavenly Kingdom in terms of a garden, and just as earthly gardens offer a sanctuary of rest, so God's heaven will provide a place of peace and rest for believers. In heaven, the lost paradise of Eden will be restored. *See also* Eden, Garden of; Gethsemane; Paradise.

garlic [Heb., *shûm*]. The bulbous root of the lily family, the shallot, or our common garlic. While mentioned only in Num. 11:5, the garlic was certainly used in Palestine to flavor foods. Garlic was also used in the Middle East to aid digestion and as a diuretic. Externally, its juice was employed as an antiseptic.

garrison (1) A military post, an outpost (1 Sam. 14:1); (2) a fort manned by soldiers.

When the Philistines dominated Israel they placed garrisons as far east as the Jordan Valley (1 Sam. 14). Later David and other Hebrew rulers put garrisons in subdued lands and fortified their own cities (2 Chr. 17:2). *See also* Fortifications.

Right: Plan of the garden villa of an Egyptian noble of the Old Kingdom (2600–2200 B.C.). It reflects aspects of gardens Solomon built (Eccl. 2:5): high walls, fruit and spice trees, ponds, and a grape arbor (center). Below: Grecian and Roman courtyards within the house, like this peristyle (court enclosed by covered columns) of a Roman house in Pompeii (A.D. 79), often featured fragrant plants. The line drawing shows it decorated with marble seats, statues, and fountains.

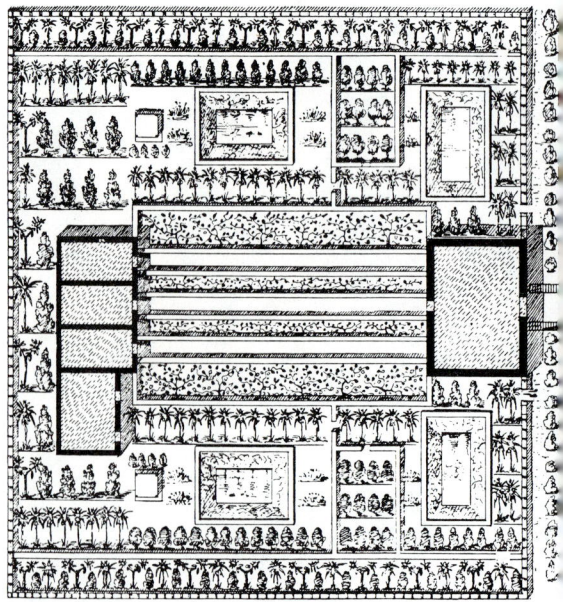

Reconstructed mud-brick gate of the Canaanite town of Laish from the Middle Bronze Age (1800–1550 B.C.). Men from the tribe of Dan captured the town and renamed it Dan (Josh. 19:47), which then became the northernmost city of Israel (Jdg. 20:1).

gate (1) The entrance to any structure, but especially (2) the fortified entrance to a walled city. City gates were especially strong, usually made of heavy wood reinforced with bronze or iron and strengthened with extra walls and towers for defense (*compare* 2 Sam. 18:24). *See also* City Gate.

The open area just inside the gates served as the city's civic center. There the elders held court—the Hebrew expression indicating courts of justice is "judges of the gate"—and there they witnessed business transactions (Amos 5:15; Ruth 4:1-11). In addition to providing a place for legal proceedings, the city gates served as the general market place (2 Ki. 7:1,18; Neh. 13:15,16) and the place to hear and announce news. Therefore, prophets often came to the busy gates to deliver messages from the Lord (Jer. 17:19,20).

The city gates named in the OT refer to various gates in the wall of Jerusalem. And most of these and their locations are mentioned only in the Book of Nehemiah, which records accounts of the inspection, rebuilding, and dedication of Jerusalem's walls after the Exile (Neh. 2:12-15; 3:1-32; 12:31-43). Nehemiah also provides a clue to how they were named—or nicknamed: The Fish Gate (3:3; 12:39) probably got its

name from a fish market run by men from Tyre who lived in Jerusalem (13:16). In the NT the "Beautiful Gate" of Acts 3 is probably the eastern gate in Herod's Temple leading from the Court of the Gentiles to the Court of Women. *See also* Temple.

Gates are often used as symbols of security and strength in Scripture. The prophecy that in the future Jerusalem's gates will remain open forever is an image of universal peace (Isa. 60:11). However, when Jesus spoke of the "gates of Hades" (Mt. 16:18), his listeners understood him to mean "the powers of death" since death was the entrance or gate to Hades. This is the way the phrase was used in Jewish writings of the intertestamental period.

gatekeeper A guard or attendant posted at the gates of a city, public buildings, or the homes of some wealthy person. Also called doorkeeper, porter, guard, or simply one on duty at the entrance.

Keepers of city gates were probably soldiers. They supervised traffic, watched who entered, and closed the gates in time of danger (2 Ki. 7:10-20). Soldiers might also be posted to guard the gates of the Temple (2 Ki. 11:4-9).

Temple gatekeepers were "priests who guarded the entrance" (2 Ki. 12:9). They

The Golden Gate, protruding from Jerusalem's eastern wall, faces the Kidron Valley. The present gate and wall, built by Suleiman the Great in the 16th century, was constructed directly above an earlier gate and wall dating to the 7th century. When in use, both led onto the Temple Mount.

Drawing of Solomonic gate of Megiddo, a fortified city located in the Valley of Jezreel on the trade route between Syria and Egypt. Solomon chose to garrison this city, along with Hazor and Gezer, with chariots and horses (1 Ki. 9:15-19).

421

also collected money offerings made by the worshipers. Temple gatekeepers may have been a special order of priests, responsible to maintain the Temple and its grounds and to ensure ritual purity. Whether they were priests or not, they were Levites and had special duties (*compare* 1 Chr. 9:22; 15:23,24; 2 Chr. 31:14-18; Neh. 12:25,26).

Another function of gatekeepers was to provide personal security for important people. The reference in Esther to officers who guarded the king's doorway suggests that they served as royal bodyguards (Esth. 2:19-21).

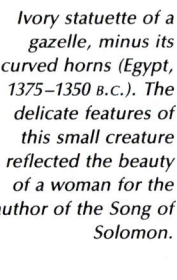
Ivory statuette of a gazelle, minus its curved horns (Egypt, 1375–1350 B.C.). The delicate features of this small creature reflected the beauty of a woman for the author of the Song of Solomon.

gazelle ("roe," "roebuck" KJV). A small tan antelope, common in Syria and Palestine in OT times. The adults of the two species of gazelle prevalent in Palestine were about 2 feet (60 centimeters) high and 3 feet (1 meter) long. The gazelle was a clean animal and was hunted for food (Deut. 14:5). The graceful creature was also appreciated for its delicate beauty (Song 4:5; 7:3) and speed (2 Sam. 2:18).

A small lump of clay from the 6th century B.C. bears the impression of a seal: "Belonging to Hananiah, son of Gedaliah." The same "Gedaliah" may well have been Judah's puppet governor, appointed by Nebuchadnezzar but treacherously murdered two months later. The Jewish fast on the third day of Tishri commemorates his death (Zech. 7:5; 8:19).

> **Gedaliah** [ged-uh-LI-uh; "Yahweh is great"]. Governor of Judah for two months in 586 B.C. **Father:** Ahikam; **Grandfather:** Shapan—both officers in Judah's royal court (2 Ki. 22:3). **Scripture:** Jer. 40,41.

BACKGROUND
When Nebuchadnezzar destroyed Jerusalem, he deported all but the poorest of the land. He appointed Gedaliah as their governor and left a small Babylonian garrison to support him. Gedaliah promised he would serve the Babylonians and urged the few Jews who remained to work their farms, all of which received the endorsement of Jeremiah, the prophet of God (Jer. 40:5,6). However, Baalis, the Ammonite king, enlisted Ishmael, son of another prominent Jewish family, to assassinate Gedaliah. Gedaliah would not believe those who warned him of the plot, and he was murdered at a meal he served in honor of Ishmael and his men.

LEARNING FROM GEDALIAH'S LIFE
Gedaliah seems a very attractive character. He was to govern only the poorest of the land (Jer. 40:7). (The Hebrew word here means the lower classes or those who lack material wealth.) Yet he acted quickly to reassure them (40:9), promised to represent them to the Babylonians, and set them to work harvesting crops in accordance with God's will (40:10). When informed of the plot against his life, Gedaliah could not credit Ishmael, a person of royal blood, with such evil (40:14). Therefore, when urged to permit one of his officers to assassinate Ishmael to save his own life, a horrified Gedaliah refused. In this Gedaliah was perhaps naïve, but he showed himself to be a truly good man.

> **Gehazi** [guh-HAY-zi; "valley of vision"]. The servant of Elisha who was cursed by God with leprosy, 850–825 B.C. **Scripture:** 2 Ki. 4,5,8.

BACKGROUND
Elisha had an active ministry in Israel after the death of Elijah. Baal worship had been put down, and Elisha's many miracles demonstrated to Israel's kings and her people the power and compassion of the Lord. Gehazi accompanied his master everywhere, and witnessed all that Elisha did. However, Gehazi tragically fell into the snare of greed, bringing upon himself and his heirs God's curse. When an Assyrian army commander, Naaman, was healed of leprosy, Elisha refused any payment or reward. However, prompted by greed, Gehazi pursued Naaman and asked for about 75 pounds (34 kilograms) of silver and clothing. But Gehazi had not deceived Elisha. Upon Gehazi's return, the prophet cursed his servant with Naaman's leprosy and sent him away. Nevertheless, Gehazi continued to testify of God's miracles done through Elisha, even gaining an audience with the king of Israel (2 Ki. 8).

LEARNING FROM GEHAZI'S LIFE
Elisha's foolish servant had good qualities. He was sensitive to others' needs (4:11-14), and protective of his master (4:25-27). Yet Gehazi lied to Naaman when, in the name of Elisha, he asked for money and garments (5:19-25).

In his choice, Gehazi perhaps represents all whose judgment is distorted by a desire for money. Jesus warned that a man cannot serve God and money, for he will invariably make a choice for one that spurns the other (Lk. 16:13). Gehazi made such a choice when he ignored Elisha's refusal to take gifts from Naaman, choosing instead to make a profit from God's gracious miracle.

Gehenna [geh-HEN-nuh]. A popular expression from intertestamental times meaning hell or hellfire.

The word is derived from the Hebrew *ge-hinnom* or "Valley of Hinnom," which is also known in the OT as the "Valley of Ben ['sons of'] Hinnom" (NIV). This valley ran southwest of Jerusalem, where there was a Topheth, a site for child sacrifice (2 Chr. 28:3; Jer. 7:31; 32:35). Josiah destroyed the unholy site (2 Ki. 23:10). *See also* Child Sacrifice; Molech.

Jeremiah declared that when God judged Judah, the Valley of Ben Hinnom would be filled with bodies left unburied, associating the place with judgment (Jer. 7:30-33; 19:1-13). Later, the valley was used as a place to burn refuse and the bodies of criminals and animals.

Thus, by NT times, Gehenna became a synonym for hell, which English versions use to translate the Greek word (Mt. 5:22,29,30; 23:33; Mk. 9:45; Lk. 12:5). In Jesus' sayings, Gehenna always indicates the place of final punishment, described in Mt. 13:42,50; 25:41; and Mk. 9:43 as unquenchable fire or a fiery furnace. *See also* Hell; Judgment Day; Sheol.

genealogy An orderly list of names recording the ancestry of an individual, family group, tribe, or nation. Bible genealogies (1) trace descent from the patriarchs, and thus the right of a family or individual to membership in the covenant community; (2) provide the basis of Israel's early military organization, Num. 1:2-4; (3) establish the basis for religious taxation, Num. 7:11-82; (4) trace descent from Aaron, and thus the right to serve as a priest; and (5) trace descent from David, and thus the right of royal succession in Judah. As the Messiah was to be of David's line, this record became increasingly important.

The genealogies of the Hebrews and other early Middle Eastern societies are designedly incomplete, listing significant ancestors, not all ancestors. Thus in Scripture "became the father of" means "was an ancestor of," and "the son of" simply means "a descendant of." In some cases "son of" indicates legal succession rather than actual parentage. Because genealogies are intentionally incomplete, it is not possible to calculate dates using these lists. *See also* Son.

This cuneiform clay prism listing Sumerian kings is the oldest known genealogy from the ancient Near East (1800 B.C.). It includes a blank area (lower left) which shows the gap in royal descent caused by a devastating flood—perhaps the *Flood*.

genealogy of Jesus Orderly lists tracing the human ancestry of Jesus the Messiah, found in Mt. 1:1-17 and Lk. 3:23-38.

Each genealogy of Jesus is intended to establish Jesus as a descendant of David. However, Luke goes further, tracing Christ's line to Adam to establish Jesus' identity with the human race. Each purpose is theologically significant: The promised Messiah was to emerge from David's line, and only one who was truly human could represent humanity as high priest and as sacrifice (Heb. 2:14-18). *See also* Messiah.

Biblical genealogies characteristically include only selected ancestors. This is illustrated by Luke's list of some 20 ancestors between David and the Exile, while Matthew has only 14. A significant difference between the two is that Matthew traces Jesus' line through Solomon and Judah's kings, while Luke traces the line through Nathan, another son of David by Bathsheba (1 Chr. 3:5). The two primary explanations assume (1) that Matthew traces the legal line and Luke the biological line of Joseph, or (2) that Luke gives the genealogy of Mary, while Matthew lists the genealogy of Joseph. This second view is supported by Jeremiah's curse on Jehoiachin, a king in Solomon's line, whose descendants were never to occupy Israel's

throne, even though the legal right was theirs (*compare* Jer. 22:30; Mt. 1:11). If this second explanation is correct, Jesus' legal right to the throne is established through Joseph, while his biological descent from David is established through Mary. This view may be reflected in Rom. 1:3, which affirms that Jesus "as to his human nature was a descendant of David."

Two other features of these genealogies are of note: (1) Each genealogy guards the doctrine of the virgin birth. Christ was the son, "so it was thought, of Joseph" (Lk. 3:23; *see also* Mt. 1:16); (2) Matthew includes four women in Jesus' genealogy, which is contrary to Hebrew practice, and even more unusual are the women selected: Tamar (Mt. 1:3), who became pregnant by her father-in-law, Gen. 38; Rahab (Mt. 1:5), who was the believing prostitute who survived the destruction of Jericho, Josh. 2; 6:25; Ruth (Mt. 1:5), who was a Moabitess; and Bathsheba (Mt. 1:6), who was the adulterous wife of Uriah, a victim of David's passion, 2 Sam. 11,12. God's grace not only reached out to save these women but also placed them in the line of the Redeemer.

Thus, the genealogies show both that Jesus fulfills Israel's messianic expectations and that, through the incarnation, the redemption Christ won is for all of humanity.

generation [Heb., *dor*]. (1) The period of time between the birth of a man and his firstborn son. This length of times varies, but OT writers seem to assume that 30 to 40 years constitute a generation, Deut. 2:14; Ps. 95:10; (2) all persons living in a particular era; (3) a class of persons sharing a characteristic, such as righteousness, Ps. 14:5 (KJV); (4) Heb., *toledot*, a genealogical record, which translates "generations of" in the KJV, but "the account of" in the NIV. This term is used to organize the Book of Genesis and is associated throughout Scripture with genealogical lists. *See also* Genealogy.

The Greek words rendered "generation" in the NT have the same range of meanings as *dor*. The specific meaning is usually clear from the context, but Mt. 24:34 is less easy to interpret. After describing signs of his coming "with power and glory," Jesus said, "I tell you the truth, this generation will certainly not pass away until all these things have happened." Possible interpretations of "this generation" are (1) the predicted events associated with the Second Coming will take place within forty years or (2) the Jewish people will be preserved until history's end.

Genesis, Book of The first book of the OT. The name "Genesis" is derived from a Greek term meaning "beginnings" or "origins." The Hebrew title is *bere'shit*, from Gen. 1:1, "in the beginning."

There are several ways to analyze Genesis:

1. *By focus.* Genesis 1–11 traces God's dealing with the human race, while Gen. 12–50 introduces God's covenant with Abraham's line.

2. *By literary structure.* There are ten occurrences of "this is the account of" ("generations of," KJV) in the book. Each section preserves a historical account: of the heavens and earth (2:4), of Adam's line (5:1), of Noah (6:9), of the sons of Noah (10:1), of Shem (11:10), of Terah (11:27), of Ishmael (25:12), of Isaac (25:19), of Esau (36:1), and of Jacob (37:2).

3. *By function.* Genesis 1–11 sets man in God's universe; Gen. 11–23 tells the story of Abraham, 24–26 the story of Isaac, 27–36 the story of Jacob, and 37–50 the story of Joseph.

AUTHORSHIP

Though no explicit claim is made in Genesis, Jewish and Christian traditions hold Moses to be author of the first five books of the OT. While a few explanatory verses may have been added in later years (*see* 12:6; 14:7), nothing in Genesis requires post-Mosaic origin. Moses' direct contact with God accounts for material that must have been received by revelation (*compare* Ex. 33:11; Num. 12:8). It is also probable that by the time of Moses much of the historical fact revealed in Genesis was preserved in written form and/or oral tradition, which Moses, under God's direction, faithfully recorded. Genesis dates, therefore, near the end of the Exodus period, about 1400 B.C.

HISTORICAL SIGNIFICANCE

Details in the stories of the patriarchs accurately reflect social conditions and customs of 2100–1800 B.C., as excavations of thousands of clay tablets in the Middle East, especially at Mari and Nuzi, amply testify. For instance, the names found in Genesis were common during that period, as were adoption customs, the possession of household gods as evidence of the right of inheritance, the possibility of negotiating for a birthright, an infertile wife's gift of a servant maid to her husband, and other practices reported in Genesis—all of which fit perfectly into the historical setting. Furthermore, details in the Egyptian background of Joseph's story are just as

This fanciful "Tree of Jesse" illuminates a medieval psalter and highlights some of the ancestors of Jesus: Jesse, at bottom in blue; David directly above him; then Solomon with a scepter; Mary with her son Jesus; and finally Jesus.

425

authentic. Thus, archaeological finds assure us that the biblical account is ancient, for it is filled with details which could hardly have been invented many hundreds or even thousands of years later, as critics of Genesis once affirmed.

THEOLOGICAL CONTRIBUTIONS

The greatest significance of Genesis is found in its theology. The book is truly foundational to a biblical understanding of God, the universe, and of ourselves.

Genesis 1–11 functions as an overture to an opera or prologue introducing a drama. The great themes to be expressed as history unfolds are stated clearly in these passages: (1) God exists, and he is Creator of the universe (Gen. 1). (2) Human beings are a direct, special creation of God (Gen. 1,2). (3) Adam and Eve rebelled and became sinners (Gen. 3), a perversion which infects the entire race (Gen. 4). (4) Sin brings punishment, for God is moral Judge of his universe. Yet God acts to rescue those who trust him (Gen. 6–9). (5) Humankind, scattered across the earth, is a fallen race of sinners in need of salvation (Gen. 10,11).

Genesis 12–50 introduces the dominant theme of the OT. God chose Abraham and gave him promises which he confirmed by covenant. Through Abraham's seed, all peoples are destined to be blessed (Gen. 12:3).

Thus, Gen. 1–11 looks backward and affirms that God is the source of the universe, of humanity, of moral standards, and of redeeming grace. Genesis 12–50 looks ahead and affirms that God has a loving purpose which he intends to achieve in history. Therefore, Genesis answers the most significant questions phi-

losophers can ask: Who are we? Where did we come from? And, where are we going?

MASTERY KEYS

Study Gen. 1–11 and 12–50 as separate units. For Gen. 1–11, list verses which speak of beginnings. For instance, Gen. 2 speaks of the first man (v. 7), the first work (v. 15), the first recorded words spoken to man (v. 16), the first divine command (v. 17), the first woman (vv. 21-25), and the institution of marriage (v. 24). When you have listed such Genesis "firsts," think about the significance of each in its context. Before reading Gen. 12–50, read the article on covenant. Then focus your study on the life of each of the succeeding major characters, using the dictionary articles on each.

SPECIAL FEATURES

Genesis does not deal with many of the questions that concern moderns, such as the age of the universe or the date of the Flood. However, Genesis does directly confront evolutionary theory by teaching that human beings are the direct, special creation of God. The account of the Flood also seems to challenge the uniformitarian assumptions of modern science (*compare* 2 Pet. 3:5-7).

Right: Vellum fragment containing an Old Latin translation of Genesis 5:29–6:2. Oxyrynchus, Egypt, probably late 5th century A.D.

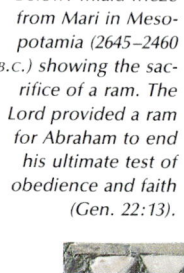

Below: Inlaid frieze from Mari in Mesopotamia (2645–2460 B.C.) showing the sacrifice of a ram. The Lord provided a ram for Abraham to end his ultimate test of obedience and faith (Gen. 22:13).

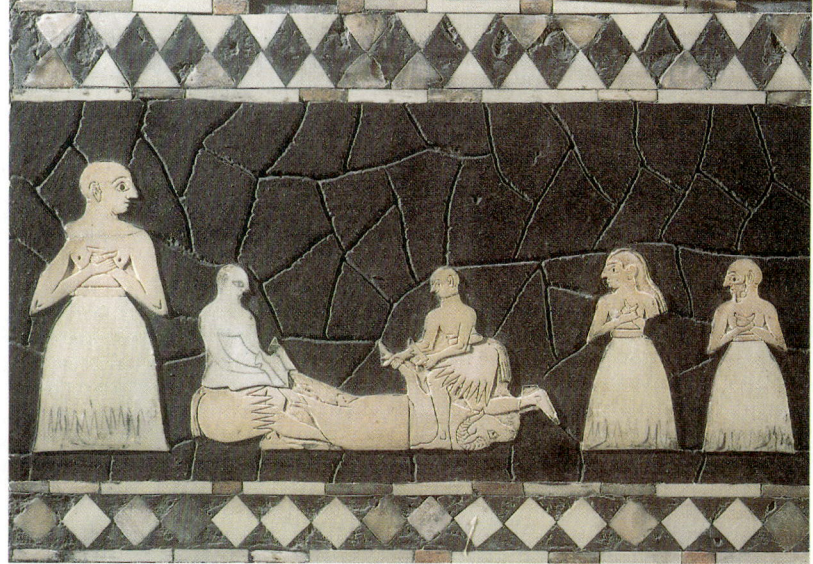

GENESIS: A READING AND STUDY GUIDE

Chapter	Content Summary	Related Articles
1	God creates and fashions the physical universe. He determines to make man in his image and likeness.	Creation Image of God
2	God creates Adam and places him in Eden. God then creates Eve from Adam's rib.	Adam Eve
3	Eve is tempted. Both eat the forbidden fruit. God announces judgment on Adam, Eve, and the serpent.	Tempt Sin; Death
4	Cain kills his brother Abel and is exiled. Lamech illustrates other expressions of sin in society.	Cain Abel
5	Adam's line is traced to Noah.	Genealogy
6	God determines to judge the sin that is rampant on earth. Righteous Noah is told to build an ark.	Flood Noah
7	The Flood destroys all air-breathing life.	
8	The waters dry up. Noah and his family leave the ark and worship God with a burnt offering.	Ararat Sacrifice
9	God makes the rainbow the sign of his promise never to cause another cataclysmic flood. Ham violates his father Noah's privacy.	Rainbow Naked
10	Lines of Japheth, Ham, and Shem are traced.	Nations, Table of
11	Languages are introduced at Babel. Shem's line is traced to Abram.	Babel
12	Abram is given promises by God and moves to Canaan. He goes briefly to Egypt and lies concerning Sarai.	Canaan Sarah
13	Abram and Lot separate. Abram gives Lot his choice of where to settle. Lot chooses the Jordan plain.	Lot
14	Lot and the people of the plain are captured by invading forces. Abram rescues them and is blessed by Melchizedek.	Melchizedek
15	God confirms his promises by making a binding "covenant of blood" with Abram. God predicts bondage in Egypt.	Covenant Faith
16	Sarai gives her maid, Hagar, to Abram as a secondary wife. Sarai mistreats Hagar. Ishmael is born.	Concubine Ishmael
17	God promises Abram he and Sarai will have a child. Their names are changed to Abraham and Sarah. Circumcision is established as a sign of the Abrahamic covenant.	Circumcision Abraham
18	Angelic visitors foretell Sodom's destruction. Abraham prays for any righteous among the people of the plain.	Prayer Angel
19	Sodom and Gomorrah are destroyed. Lot escapes, but fathers the Moabites and Ammonites by his daughters.	Sodom and Gomorrah
20	Abraham again lies about his relationship with Sarah. God protects Sarah and Abraham.	Prophet
21	Isaac is born to Abraham and Sarah. Hagar and Ishmael are sent away.	Isaac Ishmael
22	Abraham shows his willingness to obey God, even to offering Isaac as a sacrifice.	Test; Obey Faith
23	Sarah dies and is buried. Abraham buys land for a burial plot.	Hittite
24	Abraham sends an unnamed servant to find a bride for Isaac. The servant brings Rebekah back to Canaan.	Rebekah
25	Abraham dies. Ishmael's sons are listed. Jacob and Esau are born.	Jacob Esau

continued

Chapter	Content Summary	Related Articles
26	Isaac repeats the sin of Abraham and lies about his wife. Isaac makes a treaty with Abimelech.	Abimelech
27	Jacob obtains Esau's birthright and tricks Isaac into giving him the firstborn's blessing.	Birthright Firstborn
28	Jacob goes to Paddan Aram for a bride. God confirms the Abrahamic covenant with Jacob in a dream.	Dreams
29	Jacob works seven years for his uncle Laban for the hand of Rachel, is tricked into marrying Leah, but is given Rachel as wife too, for another seven years of labor. The handmaids Zilpah and Bilhah accompany Leah and Rachel.	Dowry Concubine
30	Jacob's family increases. God multiplies Jacob's flocks at Laban's expense.	Laban
31	Jacob flees Laban with his family and flocks. Laban pursues. The two make a treaty.	Teraphim Idol
32	Jacob prepares to meet Esau by sending gifts. Jacob wrestles with God; his name is changed to Israel.	Gift Israel
33	Jacob meets Esau. The two are reconciled.	
34	Jacob's daughter Dinah is raped at Shechem. Her brothers trick and then kill the men of the city.	
35	Jacob purges his camp of pagan gods at Bethel. God extends the covenant to his sons. His father and his wife die.	Idol
36	Esau's descendants are listed.	Genealogy
37	Joseph, Jacob's favorite son, stimulates jealousy by his dreams. He is sold into slavery by his brothers.	Joseph Egypt
38	Judah fathers twins by Tamar, wife of his deceased son. She is in the line of the Messiah (Mt. 1:4).	Levirate Marriage
39	Joseph refuses to be seduced by his master's wife. He is thrown in prison.	
40	Dreams of Pharaoh's cupbearer and baker are interpreted by Joseph.	Dreams Pharaoh
41	Pharaoh's dream of a coming famine is interpreted by Joseph. Joseph is made governor of Egypt to prepare for the famine.	Famine
42	Joseph's brothers come to Egypt to buy food, but Joseph does not disclose himself to them; he secretly returns their money.	
43	Joseph's brothers return to Egypt. Again Joseph does not tell them who he is.	
44	Joseph has his cup hidden in their baggage. His men make them return to Egypt.	Divination
45	Joseph reveals himself to his brothers, and tells them to bring the entire family to Egypt. Jacob learns Joseph is alive.	
46	The 66 Israelites who entered Egypt are named.	Genealogy
47	Pharaoh meets Jacob and permits the family to settle in Goshen. Joseph purchases all Egypt's land for Pharaoh.	
48	Jacob blesses Joseph and his two sons, Ephraim and Manasseh.	
49	Jacob blesses each of his twelve sons appropriately; then he dies.	Blessing
50	Joseph has Jacob embalmed and returns to Canaan to bury him. Joseph reassures his brothers. Joseph dies.	Canaan

Gentile A non-Jewish individual or people; a pagan nation.

God's covenant with the descendants of Abraham through Isaac and Jacob set the Israelites apart from all other peoples. Their separation was emphasized in the Law, which forbade intermarriage (Ex. 34:15,16; Deut. 7:1-5) and established a variety of dietary and other laws intended to maintain that separation (Lev. 11; Deut. 4). By the first century, such laws were considered "walls," protecting the Jew from contamination by his unclean Gentile neighbors (*compare* Acts 10:1-29). *See also* Dietary Laws.

Despite its emphasis on separation, the OT does not view Gentiles with hostility. Old Testament Law guarded the rights of resident aliens, and God's original promise to Abraham says that "all the peoples of the earth" will be blessed through his covenant people, a theme repeated by the prophets (Isa. 2:2-4; 45:22-24; 51:4,5). Therefore, by the first century, many Jews living in foreign countries actively sought to convert Gentiles to Judaism. They also recognized the special status of Gentiles who believed in the Lord and followed the moral precepts of the Law without being circumcised or obeying Israel's dietary laws. *See also* Alien; God-Fearing.

Many OT stories display God's concern for the non-Jew: God sent Jonah to Nineveh out of compassion for the innocent in that great Assyrian city (Jon. 4:11); Ruth of Moab was not only accepted into the covenant people, but became an ancestress of King David and the Messiah; Naaman, commander of the Syrian army (2 Ki. 5), was a prominent Gentile who came to know the Lord without converting to Judaism.

Despite these examples of God's concern for Gentiles, and despite the missionary zeal of some Jews, there was a marked hostility toward non-Jews in first-century Judaism. The zealous Jew was contemptuous of Gentile idolatry and immorality and considered Gentiles unclean. As Paul notes, Gentiles were "excluded from citizenship in Israel and foreigners to the covenants of promise, without hope and without God in the world" (Eph. 2:12). When Gentiles began to respond to the Gospel message, tremendous tension was created in the then-predominantly Jewish church. Paul responded by affirming that the blood of Jesus had "destroyed the barrier, the dividing wall of hostility" and had made of the two groups one unified Church. Since Jew and Gentile alike are reconciled to God through the cross and have the same access to the Father, the old distinctions are irrelevant (Eph. 2:11-22). This position had been previously affirmed in a council of the church held in Jerusalem about A.D. 50 (Acts 15). *See also* Council of Jerusalem.

New Testament Epistles, however, reflect continuing tension, as first-generation Christians tried to work out the unity the apostles affirmed. The Book of Galatians is directed primarily to Gentile believers, who had been told by Jewish Christians that they must become Jews to be good Christians. Galatians sums up Paul's view that neither salvation nor spiritual growth are to be found in OT Law. Also, the Epistle to the Hebrews, directed to Jewish Christians, urges them not to return to Judaism. Hebrews argues that everything symbolized in the OT faith is fulfilled in Jesus. Therefore, Gentile and Jew alike experience spiritual reality in the new Christian faith.

Gentiles, Court of the The outer court of Herod's Temple compound. Gentiles could enter this courtyard, but were warned that death awaited any non-Jew who entered the next. *See also* Temple.

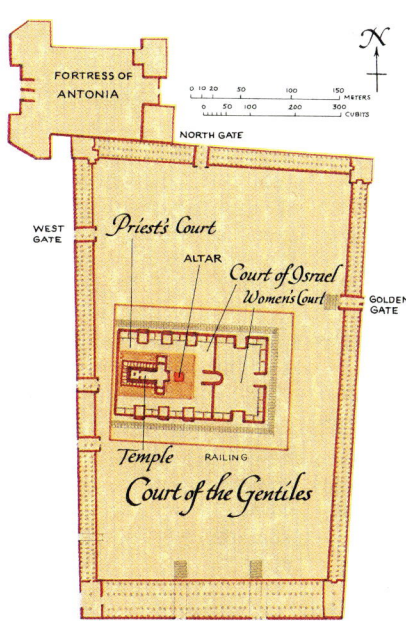

Left: Plan of Herod's Temple shows the large Court of the Gentiles, surrounded by a covered colonnade. Paul was almost killed here because some Jews accused him, saying, "He has brought Greeks into the temple area and defiled this holy place" (Acts 21:29).

Far left: This tablet, inscribed in Greek, is one of several in Greek and Latin set up on a railing in the Court of the Gentiles to warn Gentiles against going any farther on pain of death.

FORTRESS OF ANTONIA

NORTH GATE

WEST GATE

Priest's Court

ALTAR

Court of Israel

Women's Court

GOLDEN GATE

Temple   RAILING

Court of the Gentiles

HULDAH GATES

gentle, gentleness [Gk., *epieikēs, prautēs*]. (1) Thoughtful, calm, considerate; (2) mild, yielding, soothing.

Gentleness is perhaps best understood by its opposites. A gentle person does not selfishly insist on his or her own way. A gentle person is not angry or arrogant. He is not rigid and does not demand his rights or strict justice, but makes allowances for others. The calm, reasonable, caring spirit associated with gentleness is a mark of inner beauty and is "of great worth in God's sight" (1 Pet. 3:4).

Jesus himself is described as a gentle person (2 Cor. 10:1), and Christian leaders are required to cultivate this attribute (1 Tim. 3:3; Tit. 3:2). Gentleness is produced in the human personality by the Holy Spirit (Gal. 5:22,23).

gestures Physical movement or action. The Middle Easterner makes extensive use of gestures—more so than his Western contemporary. Besides recording the natural reactions to given circumstances (*compare* Jn. 11:35), the Scriptures provide numerous examples of cultural and symbolic gestures. Gestures of hospitality include kissing (instead of handshaking) (Gen. 27:27; 33:4; Ex. 4:27; 18:7; 1 Sam. 20:41; Lk. 7:45; Acts 20:37); bowing or prostrating oneself as a sign of worship or respect (Gen. 18:2,3; 23:7,12; Mt. 18:26; Acts 10:25; Rev. 19:10); greeting with words of peace (Lk. 10:5,6; Jn. 20:19,21); washing a guest's feet (Gen. 18:4; 1 Sam. 25:41; Lk. 7:44; Jn. 13:4,5); and anointing an honored person's head with oil (Ps. 23:5; Lk. 7:46). Other actions may include wagging the head and grimacing in scorn (Ps. 22:7); striking hands in a bargain (Prov. 6:1); shaking dust off one's feet as a sign of rejection (Lk. 9:5); and tearing one's clothes and placing ash or dust on one's head in strong emotion or repentance (2 Sam. 13:19,31; 2 Ki. 5:7; Jer. 6:26; Lk. 10:13).

Both the OT prophets and Jesus used symbolic gestures in their ministries. Ezekiel made extensive use of symbolic actions (*compare* Ezek. 3:24; 4:1-15). When Christ touched lepers (Lk. 5:12,13), he showed he had the power to make the unclean clean, just as he has the power to make the unrighteous righteous (2 Cor. 5:21). Therefore, the use of cultural and symbolic gestures play an important role in biblical records.

Gethsemane [geth-SEM-ah-nee; "oil press"]. An olive grove or garden located somewhere on the Mount of Olives across from Jerusalem. Luke 22:39,40 and Jn. 18:1 in-

Olive trees filled Gethsemane (Heb., gat shemen), which means "oil press." All four Gospels indicate that Jesus and his disciples frequented this garden (Mt. 26:36; Mk. 14:32; Lk. 22:39; Jn. 18:1).

dicate Jesus went there regularly with his disciples. Furthermore, it was in this garden that Christ poured out his anguished prayer the night before his crucifixion. The word used to describe the Lord's experience, *agōnia*, expresses extreme stress. Some set Christ's struggle in the

garden of Gethsemane in contrast with Adam's temptation in the garden of Eden. Jesus overcame temptation by prayer and by conscious commitment to the known will of God, and thus qualified himself to undo the damage done by Adam's sin (Rom. 5:18,19). *See also* Adam; Garden; Temptation.

ghost (KJV) [Heb., *repaim*; Gk., *phantasma*]. (1) Any disembodied spirit; (2) the disembodied personality of a dead person.

In the KJV, "ghost" is often used to translate words which mean a person's "spirit" in contrast to his or her body. Modern versions avoid this confusion and use "ghost" in a contemporary sense. *See also* Spirit.

People of the ancient Middle East feared ghosts. They believed that the dead could take vengeance on persons who had harmed or neglected them while they were living. This view is not reflected in the OT, which teaches that while there is consciousness after death, the dead are limited to Sheol. *See also* Sheol.

While the OT views the dead as powerless, unable to affect the world of the living for good or evil, the popular view in the first century probably was infused with the pagan's superstitious awe. The NT tells us that when Jesus' disciples saw him walking on the water one night "they were terrified. 'It's a ghost,' they said, and cried out in fear" (Mt. 14:26). *See also* Medium; Spirit.

430

giant An unusually tall and powerful person. Four Hebrew words are translated "giant" in the KJV, some inappropriately. Mistranslations are corrected in modern versions.

(1) *Gibbor* (Job 16:14) means a warrior or military hero. (2) The meaning of "Rephaites" [Heb., *rephaim*] is uncertain (Deut. 2:11,20; 3:11,13). Some think it indicates a military guild, a class of men wealthy enough to provide themselves with chariots and armor. (3) The "sons of Anak" were members of a powerful clan or race beside which the Israelites felt themselves as insignificant as grasshoppers (Num. 13:33). The KJV translates Anakim by "giants," while modern versions retain the Hebrew word as a name. (4) A final term taken to mean giants is *nephilim*. According to Gen. 6:4, Nephilim were first produced by the union of "sons of God" and the daughters of men. This is often understood to mean sexual union between fallen angels and women. Others understand Gen. 6:4 to describe intermarriage between the line of Seth and that of Cain. Modern versions tend simply to read "Nephilim," without interpretation.

There are persistent traditions among Middle Eastern peoples of an early race of giant men and women, but to date archaeologists have found no evidence of such a race. Nevertheless, the Bible does identify several unusually large individuals. The most famous is Goliath, the Philistine warrior slain by David. Using the normal length of the cubit and span, the biblical text gives Goliath's height as 9 feet, 9 inches (3 meters) tall. Other notable individuals include a huge man with extra fingers and toes (2 Sam. 21:20) and a 7½ foot (2.3 meters) tall Egyptian (1 Chr. 11:23).

Gibeon (1) A Canaanite city 5½ miles (9 kilometers) northwest of Jerusalem (Josh. 9); and later (2) the same city allotted to the tribe of Benjamin and set apart for the Levites (Josh. 18:25; 21:17).

The original Gibeonites were Hivites. They tricked the Israelites into making a peace treaty with them. Because the treaty was ratified in the name of the Lord, the Israelites were bound by it when the deception was discovered. The Gibeonites were spared, therefore, but became "woodcutters and water carriers for the community and for the altar of the Lord" (Josh. 9:27).

The Gibeonite community continued through the era of the judges. Then Saul set out to destroy them, which violated the original treaty, and also the Mosaic Law governing relationships with resident aliens. In David's time, God punished Israel with a famine, which was relieved only when David permitted the Gibeonites to execute seven members of Saul's family (2 Sam. 21:1-14). *See also* Alien.

"When the people of Gibeon heard what Joshua had done to Jericho and Ai, they resorted to a ruse" (Josh. 9:3). In this medieval Bible illumination, the disguised Gibeonites implore Joshua at Gilgal: "We have come from a distant country; make a treaty with us" (v. 6).

Other references indicate that a Gibeonite was among David's military heroes (1 Chr. 12:4), and that Gibeonites helped rebuild Jerusalem's walls after the Exile (Neh. 3:7). However, these may have been Israelite inhabitants of Gibeon, which was set aside as a Levitical city within the territory of Benjamin (Josh. 18:25; 21:17). Thus, for some time the tabernacle was set up at Gibeon (1 Chr. 16:39; 21:29; 2 Chr. 1:3,13). See also Tabernacle.

Gideon [GID-ee-uhn; "cutter down"]. The fifth judge in Israel, notable for delivering the central Israelite tribes from Midianite oppression, about 1170 B.C. Also known as Jerubbaal, "let Baal contend." **Father:** Joash. **Sons:** Jether, Abimelech, 68 others who are not named. **Scripture:** Jdg. 6–8.

BACKGROUND

Israel had no hereditary leader in the era of the judges (about 1375–1100 B.C.). The period was marked by cycles of apostasy, foreign oppression, and the subsequent appearance of deliverers raised up by God. These deliverers defeated the oppressors and ruled as judges during their lifetime. However, the title "judge" can be misleading. While the judges did dispense justice, they were also rulers in the fullest sense of the term.

The Midianites and Amalekites in the Gideon story were semi-nomadic peoples who crossed the Jordan River into central Canaan at harvest time to plunder and destroy, causing famine conditions in Israel. Therefore, when the people of Israel cried out to God, he raised up Gideon to fill the deliverer's role. See also Judge; Judges, Book of.

LEARNING FROM GIDEON'S LIFE

The life of Gideon can be studied from different perspectives.

1. *Gideon's self-doubt.* Gideon's initial image is that of a defeated man. We meet him trying to thresh wheat while hiding in a winepress. When called a "mighty warrior," Gideon pleads his insignificance.

Later, however, he does tear down an altar to Baal erected by his father, but he does it at night because he is "afraid of his family and the men of the town" (Jdg. 6:27). Despite evidence of God's favor, Gideon tests God twice by setting out a fleece and asking God to keep it alternately wet with dew or dry. Yet note that though Gideon felt he was insignificant, he trusted God enough to tear the altar down, to call out Israel's military forces, and to pare his army down at God's command. Gideon's request for proof that God was with him did not show lack of faith; it expressed his own self-doubt. Nevertheless, Gideon's faith is clearly demonstrated in his willingness to reduce his forces from 32,000 to just 300 men at God's command. The person who obeys God even when he is afraid and uncertain can perhaps be credited with greater faith than the man who obeys and never doubts.

2. *Gideon and God.* God fully understood Gideon and provided the reassurance he needed by: (1) miraculously burning Gideon's offering (6:19-22), (2) answering Gideon's requests concerning the fleece (6:36-40), and (3) letting Gideon hear two of his enemies talk about a dream that signified Gideon's coming triumph (7:8-14). Note that each of these revelations is preceded and followed by obedience on Gideon's part. Thus, Gideon's example shows that while God is sensitive to the needs of his children, only obedience keeps us close enough to him to hear the reassurance he offers.

3. *Gideon's temptation.* Gideon showed admirable restraint after the victory over the Midianites. He willingly let others take credit for the victory (8:1-3), and he refused the opportunity to be crowned king, saying, "The Lord will rule over you" (8:22,23). Yet two elements of the story tell us that Gideon did not retain his original humility. (1) Gideon made a golden ephod, the short vestlike overgarment worn by priests. This was apparently intended to be a reminder of his victory. However, it soon became more: an object of worship for Gideon's family and for all Israel. (2) Gideon named one of his many sons Abimelech. In Hebrew this name means "my father is king"! Although Gideon had rejected the crown of Israel, he eventually came to think of himself as Israel's rightful ruler. Later, the boy that Gideon named "my father is king" murdered his brothers and tried to establish himself as king in Israel (Jdg. 9)!

Gideon's life reveals how difficult it is to

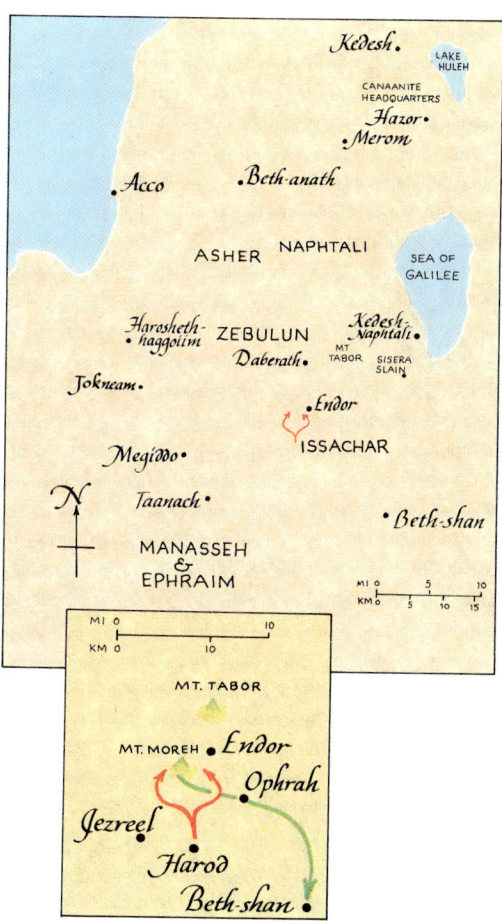

Gideon camped at the spring of Harod with his army—32,000 men drawn from the tribes of Asher, Manasseh, Naphtali, and Zebulun (Jdg. 6:35). After God "pared down" Gideon's troops to 300 they surrounded the Midianite forces and sent them fleeing in confusion (7:1-22).

Dowry; Feasts, Festivals, and Fasts.

In the social hierarchy, inferiors gave gifts to superiors. Many ancient reliefs show subject rulers bringing gifts to their overlord. In return, the overlord was expected to be generous to his subjects. It is likely that the gifts Jacob sent ahead to Esau expressed subservience to the brother whose birthright and blessing he had stolen 20 years before (Gen. 32).

The practice of balancing relationships by a mutual giving of gifts was easily distorted. Hebrew words for "gift" at times are correctly rendered "bribe." Exodus 23:6-8 warns against denying justice to the poor in their lawsuits, and adds, "Do not accept a bribe [gift], for a bribe blinds those who see and twists the words of the righteous" (compare Ps. 15:5).

The OT also urges believers to give freely to the poor, who can give nothing of value in return. However, the OT casts God as the protector of the poor. Giving to the poor, therefore, creates an obligation which God himself will balance by blessing the giver. Proverbs 19:17 expresses this succinctly: "He who is kind to the poor lends to the Lord, and he will reward him for what he has done." Thus, "He who gives to the poor will lack nothing" (Prov. 28:27). See also Almsgiving.

2. *Gifts and Relationship with God.* The cultural view of gift-giving is reflected in several aspects of OT faith. The Mosaic Law is written in the form of a Middle Eastern suzerainty treaty. This kind of treaty defined the relationship between a ruler and his subjects. See also Covenant; Deuteronomy.

In casting God as Israel's King, the Law defined the obligations of the people to God and the blessings of God to the people (compare Deut. 28). Among the obligations the people owed God were loyalty, obedience, and offerings (gifts). The prophet Malachi charged the people of his time with offering God crippled and diseased animals. "Try offering them to your governor," Malachi says sarcastically. "Would he be pleased with you?" The prophet then announced God's word: "Cursed is the cheat who has an acceptable male in his flock and vows to give it, but then sacrifices a blemished animal to the Lord. For I am a great king" (Mal. 1:6-14).

The interchange of gifts is seen in various aspects of OT faith. For instance, the Levites were given to God in exchange for the firstborn sons whom God spared in Egypt. Yet, at the same time, priests and Levites were God's gifts to Israel, in that

maintain a balance between trust and self-confidence. Nevertheless, Gideon is listed among the heroes of the faith (Heb. 11:32) as one whose humble trust and obedience is a worthy example for others to follow.

gift (1) The giving of something of value to another person, typically in exchange for something else of value; (2) an expression of submission and respect presented to a superior by an inferior; (3) in the NT, a free gift expressing God's love for human beings or man's love for God; (4) an enablement of the Holy Spirit in and through believers for effective ministry to others.

OLD TESTAMENT

1. *Gifts and Interpersonal Relationships.* The exchange of gifts was an important social mechanism. Marriage gifts to and from the father of the bride established harmonious relationships between old and new family units.

Gift-giving also marked other festive occasions (Esth. 9:22; Ps. 45:12). See also

Semitic envoys bring gold and silver gifts to the Egyptian court (1400 B.C.). Ancient peoples presented gifts as tribute to royalty (2 Sam. 8:2), on festive occasions (Ps. 45:12; Esth. 9:19), or as part of a dowry (Gen. 34:12). Jacob sent a massive gift of livestock ahead of him when he went to meet Esau, out of fear that Esau still bore a grudge against him (Gen. 32:13-21).

they represented the others before the Lord and were responsible for Israel's spiritual well-being. Furthermore, the tithes and offerings the Israelites gave to God were in turn given by God to the Levites and the priests. The Levites were given as a gift to the priestly family of Aaron to aid them in the tabernacle and Temple. Throughout the system a delicate balance was maintained. The giving of gifts honored God and at the same time was the means by which God in turn blessed his people.

NEW TESTAMENT

1. *Gifts and Interpersonal Relationships.* Mutuality is retained in some NT teaching on giving. Mutuality is seen in 2 Cor. 8,9, where Paul urges the Corinthians to give generously to relieve destitute fellow believers, "that there might be equality." Paul further explains: "At the present time your plenty will supply what they need, so that in turn their plenty will supply what you need. Then there will be equality" (8:13,14). *See also* Give; Tithe.

The element of mutuality is also seen in the NT's teaching on spiritual gifts. God gives each believer a spiritual gift "for the common good." As each person exercises his or her gift to serve others, the whole body is built up. *See also* Spiritual Gifts.

Yet the NT introduces a new basis for giving: Believers are urged to give freely when there is no expectation of return. The motive for such giving is not that God will repay, but that the giver will be like God. Jesus taught love even for enemies. He pointed out that God himself "causes his sun to rise on the evil and the good." Christ's followers are to give, not because

giving produces an obligation and repayment, but to "be perfect, therefore, as your heavenly Father is perfect" (Mt. 5:45-48).

Looking back with the perspective provided by Jesus, we realize that from the beginning God has given freely to humankind, often without an adequate return or even thanks (Rom. 1:21). Even Israel's relationship with God was originally established simply because "the Lord set his affection on your forefathers and loved them, and he chose you, their descendants, above all the nations" (Deut. 10:15). Thus relationship with God is itself always a gift, freely granted without considering any balancing gift that might be given in return!

This spirit of free giving, which flows from love, is to characterize the Christian's personal relationships with others: We do not give to establish or to repay an obligation, but we give freely to express love.

2. *Gifts and Relationship with God.* The common NT word for giving is *dōron,* which is often translated "free gift" when used of God's gifts to man in Christ. Even more significant is *dōrea,* a formal endowment by God to believers. Justification, righteousness, and all else that God bestows on the believer come as free gifts without reference to human works (Rom. 3:24; 5:17; Eph. 2:8; 3:7). *See also* Salvation.

Rather than the pattern of reciprocity seen in the Law, God's example of giving now becomes the standard for Christians. We offer ourselves to God, not because of any benefit we may receive, but simply because we love the One who has given himself for us. We offer ourselves to others

434

too, not because of what we may receive from them, but because we are followers of Jesus (*compare* Jn. 13:1-17). We give because God gives, and we are to be like him.

gifts of the Spirit *See* Spiritual Gifts.

girdle (KJV) A garment worn around the waist or lower body. A number of Hebrew words are translated girdle in the KJV (called "belt" in the NIV). Among them

Loincloth on an Egyptian laborer. The word "girdle" could also signify sash or belt.

are words for: (1) the ornamented sash or belt worn by the high priest, Ex. 28:4,8,27,28 (*see also* Isa. 22:21); (2) a loincloth, typically a square yard of cloth folded and worn between hips and ribs, Jer. 13:1-11; (3) a belt, ornamented or leather, used to support a sword (2 Sam. 20:8) or to tuck clothing in as one worked.

give, giving To contribute; the contribution of money by believers. New Testament principles of giving supersede the principle of the tithe imposed in OT Law. The OT established a percentage of income to be given for the support of Israel's priesthood and the poor. The NT, however, describes a different approach to giving, appropriate to the believer's new covenant relationship with God through Jesus. *See also* Gift; Tithe.

The characteristic word used in the NT to portray Christian giving is *koinōnia*, sharing. Those involved in full-time ministry have a right to be supported by the persons they serve (1 Cor. 9:7-12; 1 Tim. 5:17,18). However, most NT giving is not to support ministry, but to meet the basic needs of destitute fellow Christians (Acts 4:32-37; 1 Cor. 16:1-3; 2 Cor. 8:1-13; 1 Tim. 6:17-19). There was organized giving within local churches to care for believing widows and orphans who had no other family (Acts 6:1-4; 1 Tim. 5:1-16).

Second Corinthians 8,9 teaches that a Christian is to evaluate the needs of others

and to give as he is able to meet them. No percentage guidelines are provided. Rather, each Christian is to give cheerfully "what he has decided in his heart to give" (9:7). While there is no compulsion to give, awareness of four things should stimulate Christian giving: (1) Those who sow generously reap generously; (2) God's grace abounds so that all our own needs will be met, enabling us to share generously; (3) giving stimulates praise to God and prayers for the giver; and (4) giving is an acceptable expression of thanks to God for his own inexpressible gift to us of Jesus Christ.

Other NT passages provide insight into giving. First Corinthians 16:1-3 encourages weekly systematic giving in keeping with income. First Timothy 6:17-19 suggests that riches have value only to the extent that the wealthy use them to do good deeds. First John 3:11-20 makes it clear that love for God compels Christians with material possessions to share with others in need.

The basic NT view of giving thus reflects its perspective on material possessions themselves. Christians are to be a people with unusual values. We care about people, not things, and so use our possessions to serve people, rather than using people to add to our personal wealth. Christians who have this perspective will realize that they are simply stewards charged with the wise distribution of the material things God has entrusted into their care. Therefore, all we have, not just a tenth, belongs to the Lord.

A woman gives coins as an offering, on this floor mosaic from a 6th century A.D. Byzantine church in the Negev. Jesus stressed the importance of right motivation in his teaching on giving (Mt. 6:1-4; Mk. 12:41-44; Lk. 6:30,38; 12:32-34).

glass (KJV) A brittle, translucent or transparent substance made by heating silicates with soda or potash and lime. Glass was unusual and expensive in Palestine until Roman times. Therefore, the "glass" (i.e., mirror) mentioned in OT and NT was not true glass but a flat, polished bronze surface (Isa. 3:23; Jas. 1:23). *See also* Mirror.

Glass was used for ornaments and small bowls or bottles in northern Mesopotamia and in Egypt by 1400 B.C. The substance was also used as a glaze over pottery or brick walls. Nevertheless, glass played only a small role in Palestine until the first century B.C. Until that time glass vessels were formed in molds, an expensive process. However, the invention of glass blowing resulted in more quickly manufactured and less expensive products.

The earliest known glass factory where both molded and blown glass were mass produced was in Jerusalem and dates to the time of King Herod.

gleaning The gathering of grain that fell to the ground during harvesting or of fruit that was not ripe at first picking.

Old Testament Law establishes the right of the poor to glean the staple crops of grain, olives, and grapes (Lev. 19:9,10; Deut. 24:19-22). This important social mechanism helped meet the needs of the poor without robbing them of the self-respect associated in Scripture with honest toil. Ruth 2 provides an excellent example of gleaning. Here, the young widow picks up loose grain behind harvesters in the fields of Boaz, making full use of the generous law. *See also* Poor.

glory Of men, (1) their power, reputation, or importance; of God, (2) the manifestation of his essential character or qualities; or (3) his brightness or visible splendor.

Above: This reclining lion rested on the lip of a small vessel and served as a kind of decorative glass appliqué. Egypt, New Kingdom, after 1320 B.C.

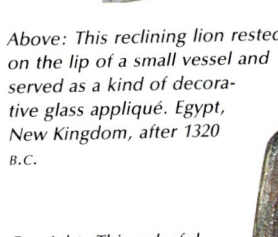

Right: Glass inlay figure with hands raised, from the Ptolemaic period (3rd–1st century B.C.). By the 14th century B.C. glass was used for architectural embellishments in Mesopotamia and furniture inlay in Egypt.

Below: First-century Roman glass bottle and bowl excavated in Palestine. The invention of glass-blowing methods made glass tableware cheap and easy to mass-produce in Roman times.

Far right: This colorful, Phoenician-style amphora from the Hellenistic era (330–60 B.C.) was made by winding strands of molten glass around a core-formed vessel. Hundreds have been found all over the Mediterranean area, including Palestine, from as early as the 8th century.

GLORY IN THE OT

The KJV renders 25 Hebrew words "glory." The basic OT term, *kabod*, means "heavy," thus weighty or important. Riches (Ps. 49:16), power (Isa. 8:7), or reputation (Phil. 2:29) may be sources of glory in human society. Yet the true importance of humankind is found in the fact that God gave man his own image and dominion over creation, thus crowning humanity with glory and honor (Ps. 8:5).

God's glory is rooted in his essential nature and is displayed in his acts in this world (Ex. 14:4; 29:43; Ps. 19:1). The glory of God was given visible expression in the fiery cloud that covered Mount Sinai, the fiery cloud that accompanied the Israelites, and the glowing cloud that filled the tabernacle and Temple (Ex. 24:16-18; 40:34-38; 1 Ki. 8:10,11). Isaiah and Ezekiel had visions in which God's glory was expressed as visible, blinding splendor (Ezek. 1:4,14; Isa. 6:1-5). Furthermore, the OT predicts that at history's end God will display his glory in and through a restored Israel (Isa. 24:23; 60:1,2; 66:18,19; Zech. 2:4,5).

Throughout the Scriptures, there is only one adequate response to God's revelation of his glory: worship. By recognizing God's presence and praising his qualities, we "glory in his holy name" (1 Chr. 16:10, 28; Ps. 29:1).

GOD'S GLORY IN THE NT

According to the NT, God's glory (Gk., *doxa*) is displayed in his manifestation of himself in Jesus Christ. God's glory flared briefly into visible splendor at Jesus' transfiguration (Luke 9:31,32). Yet in the fourth Gospel, "glory" is primarily the display of God's essential character in Jesus' life and works: his ministry, death, resurrection, and ascension (Jn. 17:22,24; Rom. 6:4). John 1:14 says, "The Word became flesh and lived for a while among us. We have seen his glory, the glory of the one and only Son, who came from the Father, full of grace and truth."

The glory manifested in Christ at his advent was visible only to the eyes of faith. At the Second Coming, Christ's splendor will be displayed to all (Col. 3:4; 2 Th. 1:6-10; Tit. 2:13). At that great eschatological unveiling of the true God, every knee will bow, and "every tongue confess that Jesus Christ is Lord, to the glory of God the Father" (Phil. 2:11).

THE BELIEVER AND GOD'S GLORY

The NT says that "all have sinned and fall short of the glory of God" (Rom. 3:23). Because of sin, we fail to reveal God in our character or actions. Yet Christians can

Jean Millet's The Gleaners (1857) beautifully illustrates the centuries-old practice of picking clean the harvested fields, which set the scene for the story of Ruth.

"reflect the Lord's glory, [for we] are being transformed into his [Christ's] likeness with ever-increasing glory, which comes from the Lord, who is the Spirit" (2 Cor. 3:18). Jesus also said that bearing fruit "is to my Father's glory" (Jn. 15:8). The thought expressed in such passages is that God now actively displays himself through the lives and actions of people in whom his Spirit dwells. Because God is present in us, he is able to reveal his qualities and character through us (*compare* 1 Cor. 10:31; Eph. 1:12,14; Phil. 1:11; Col. 1:27). We glorify God, therefore, by responding with faith and praise to his self-revelation in Jesus and by living godly lives here and now.

glossolalia [GLOS-uh-LAL-yuh; "speaking in tongues"]. This term, coined from the Greek in the 19th century, refers to speaking in a foreign or unknown language under the influence of the Holy Spirit. The phenomenon is reported in Acts 2:4; 10:46; 19:6 and is treated extensively in 1 Cor. 12–14. *See also* Tongues, Gift of.

gnash teeth To grind the teeth. In the OT, gnashing of teeth expresses hostility and anger (Ps. 35:16; 37:12). This rage is also expressed in the Sanhedrin at Stephen's trial. Those whom Stephen accused of murdering God's Christ "were furious and gnashed their teeth at him" (Acts 7:54). In the Gospels, grinding the teeth expresses the frustration and pain of those condemned to eternal torment (*compare* Mt. 8:12; 13:42,50; 24:51; 25:30; Lk. 13:28). *See also* Gestures.

gnats A general term for tiny insects, such as lice, mosquitoes, or biting sandflies. Clouds of gnats were the third plague God brought on the Egyptians (Ex. 8:16-18). In

437

the NT, Jesus remarked that the Pharisees carefully screened the tiniest two-winged creatures out of their drink, while swallowing a camel (Mt. 23:24). Both the gnat and the camel were unclean and could not be eaten. The Pharisees often concentrated so much on the tiny issues of the Law that they missed the truly important issues of justice, mercy, and faithfulness.

Gnostics, gnosticism A complex and varied philosophical/religious movement of the first few centuries A.D., strongly opposed by early church fathers. Gnosticism promised salvation from the grip of the material universe through special knowledge or *gnōsis*.

Gnosticism came to be known as a particular system of thought primarily from writings of church fathers who opposed it. Several Gnostic texts have been found, the most important assembled within the Nag Hammadi Library, a collection of thirteen codices discovered in upper Egypt in 1945.

Scholars debate whether there is any reflection of gnosticism in Scripture. Some see Colossians as a polemic against early Gnostic beliefs. They also point to 1 Tim. 6:20, which urges Timothy to turn away from "the opposing ideas of what is falsely called knowledge [*gnōsis*]." *See also* Colossians.

The basic tenets of gnosticism are clear from existing sources. The Gnostics were strict dualists; they saw the material universe as inherently evil and the immaterial (spiritual) as good. The material universe was created by an inferior being, not by God. A spark of the immaterial or divine is held captive within human beings. Knowledge, imparted by a mythic redeemer fig-

ure, who was sometimes identified with Christ, awakens the individual to his or her true nature. Those awakened will then escape to the realm of the spirit at death.

Morally, some forms of gnosticism called for asceticism, to strengthen the self by punishing the body. Other Gnostics encouraged sensuality, arguing that what the body did could not affect the true self imprisoned in it. Gnostic beliefs were essentially anti-Christian.

The Scriptures, on the contrary, cast God as Creator of a "good" world and as ruler of the universe, one who is directly involved in space-time events. Jesus is a historic, not mythical, figure. He was born into this world, blending in himself true human nature and full deity. Jesus lived, died, and was raised in a physical body. Through his death, Jesus won salvation for those who put their faith in him. When Christ returns, all believers will be resurrected, to live embodied for eternity.

There is no dualism in these Christian doctrines, nor is there any isolation of material and spiritual realms. Salvation is not found in some secret knowledge, but in the historic Jesus, who offers forgiveness of sins and eternal life to all who trust in him. *See also* Salvation.

goad A long, sharpened pole used to guide oxen. This sturdy shaft was sometimes eight feet long. Its end was often sheathed in metal and used to clear mud from the plowshare. Shamgar used the ox goad as a weapon to kill 600 Philistines (Jdg. 3:31). The common expression "to kick against the goad" meant to resist what was right or obvious (*see* Acts 26:14).

This bas relief depicts the use of asses to tread grain (Old Kingdom, about 2500 B.C.). The man to the left, armed with a goad, prevents them from escaping, while another threatens them with a stick to stop them from eating. Shamgar, a judge of Israel, smote hundreds of Philistines with a goad (Jdg. 3:31).

438

goat Sheep-like, cud-chewing mammals, with hair and hollow horns. Remains found near Jericho date to 9,000 years ago and suggest that goats may have been the first domesticated beast.

In early biblical times, goats were valued for their meat, milk, and cheese. Young kids were considered choice meat (Deut. 14:4; Jdg. 6:19). Goat skins were used to make water or wine bottles, and their hair was woven into ropes and fabric. The tabernacle had a covering woven of goat hair (Ex. 26:7). Goats were acceptable sacrificial animals (Lev. 1:10; 4:28). Symbolically, the animals often represented sin and condemnation (Lev. 16:8-26; Mt. 25:31-46).

Goats are hardy and able to survive in arid regions. However, they overgraze, eating even the roots of plants. Some believe goat herds were a factor in making so much of modern Palestine an arid desert.

God [Heb., *'el, 'eloah, 'elohim*; Gk., *theos*]. Generic term for the deity, used in Scripture of the true God and of the gods and goddesses worshiped by other peoples. The meaning of the word "god" depends on the attributes and qualities ascribed to God in the culture where the word is used. *See also* El; Elohim; Gods. The meaning of "God" in the Judeo-Christian tradition is defined by his self-revelation recorded in Scripture.

God's self-revelation involves: (1) his acts in history, as they are recorded and interpreted in Scripture; (2) the qualities or attributes ascribed to him; and (3) the names by which he has chosen to be known. Although God can never be fully comprehended, each of these sources is important for the development of an adequate concept of God.

GOD'S HISTORIC ACTS

God is not remote from his creation but is an active participant in the scheme of history. God created the heavens, earth, and all living things, and in a special act, he created Adam and Eve in his own image. He established a moral standard and warned Adam of the consequences of disobedience. After the Fall, when sin dominated the earth, God brought a destroying Flood. Yet he saved Noah and his family. Later, God gave promises to Abram, which he confirmed with an oath (covenant). God was faithful to his covenant and redeemed Israel from slavery by mighty acts. He gave Israel his Law, thus establishing a minimum standard of behavior and revealing something of his own moral character, and he remained faithful to his covenant through the centuries, blessing obedient generations and disciplining the disobedient. Finally, God entered the world in the person of his Son, Jesus, who lived among us, displaying God in his words and actions. Jesus went to the cross in order that, through his death, human beings might be redeemed. Then, he rose again and returned to heaven with the promise he would come again to take his own with him.

Our understanding of God is shaped first by seeing his acts and listening to the interpretation of each act in the Bible. By what God has made, we see "his eternal power and Godhead" (Rom. 1:20, KJV). That is, we know that he exists and that he

The detail of a relief on a 4th-century sarcophagus of a Christian portrays the Last Judgment in Jesus' graphic terms—separating the sheep from the goats (Mt. 25:31-46).

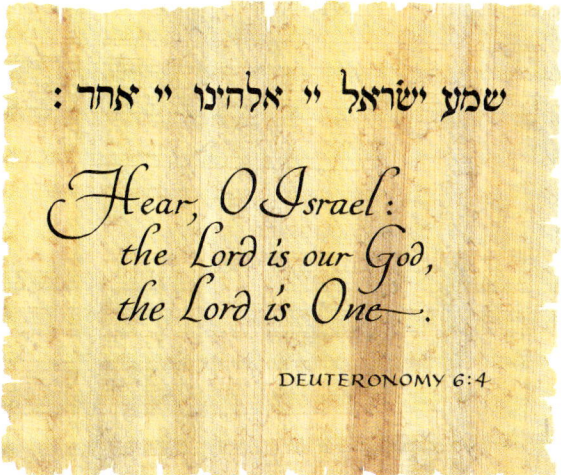

שמע ישראל יי אלהינו יי אחד :

Hear, O Israel: the Lord is our God, the Lord is One.

DEUTERONOMY 6:4

is all-powerful. In the Flood, we see God as moral Judge. In the covenant God made with Abraham, we learn that he seeks relationship with human beings. In the deliverance God won for his people from Egypt, we see both his faithfulness to his promise and his role as Redeemer of the helpless. And in Jesus, we see the ultimate demonstration of his love and grace.

GOD'S ATTRIBUTES

When interpreting God's historic acts, Scripture ascribes appropriate qualities or attributes to him. According to Scripture, God is Spirit. He is one, yet exists in three Persons as Father, Son, and Holy Spirit. He is Creator and Sustainer of the universe. He is loving, holy, just, and good. He is angry and jealous. He is Judge and

NAMES OF GOD

Name	Meaning	Significance
Hebrew		
El Elyon Gen. 14:18-20	Most High	God is sovereign, the maker of heaven and earth.
Shapat Gen. 18:25	Judge	God is righteous. He is the moral authority in his universe.
El Olam Gen. 21:33	The Eternal God	God continues to exist beyond the life span of any man. His existence guarantees our security.
Yahweh-jireh Gen. 22:14	The Lord Provides	God meets our needs and provides a substitute that we may live.
El Elohe-Yisra'el Gen. 33:20	God, the God of Israel	Relationship with God brings a new name and identity to his people, even as Jacob's name was changed to Israel.
El Shaddai Gen. 49:25	God of Mountains	God is all-powerful, high.
Yahweh-nissi Ex. 17:15	The Lord My Banner	God gives us victories.
Yahweh-shalom Jdg. 6:24	The Lord Is Peace	God makes us whole. He brings us inner harmony and peace.
El Berit Jdg. 9:46	God of the Covenant	God makes and keeps his covenants.
Yahweh-seba'ot 1 Sam. 17:45	God of Armies	God is all-powerful. He is present to fight for his people.
Adonai Ps. 2:4	Lord, Master	God has authority, dominion.
Qedosh Yisra'el Isa. 1:4	The Holy One of Israel	God is holy. By his acts of judgment and redemption, he makes his people holy.
Yahweh-tsidkenu Jer. 23:6	The Lord Our Righteousness	God is righteous. By his acts he both declares and makes his people righteous.
Yahweh-shammah Ezek. 48:35	The Lord Is There	God will be uniquely present with his people at history's end.
Aramaic		
Attiq yomin Dan. 7:9	Ancient of Days	God has ultimate authority to judge the world.
Illaya Dan. 7:18	Most High	Again, God has ultimate authority.
Greek		
Logos Jn. 1:1	The Word	Jesus expresses and communicates God to human beings.
Sōtēr Jn. 4:42	Savior	Jesus rescues us from sin and helplessness.
Theos ho Patēr Eph. 3:14	God the Father	God is Father in his authority over all and in his love for members of his family.
Kyrios Phil. 2:9-11	Lord	Jesus is now exalted as supreme.
Alpha kai Omega Rev. 1:8	The Beginning and the End	Jesus is the source of life. He initiates history and is its culmination.

Avenger. He is righteous, forgiving, full of mercy, full of pity. He purposes and carries out his purposes. He is wise, immortal, eternal. He is all-powerful, a refuge, a help in time of trouble. He is a Father to those who trust in him. God is one who hears and answers prayer. He delivers and rescues. He is Law-giver and Life-giver. He is our rock, our shield, our fortress, our strong tower, our glory. He is the author of time and of eternity. He is our Redeemer, our guide, our enabler. He is Savior, brother, friend.

These and dozens more terms are used in Scripture to describe God. They express who God is in himself and who God is for his people. Through terms like these, we come to sense what "God" means when that word is used of the One who reveals himself through the Word.

GOD'S NAMES

A third source of God's self-revelation is the names given him. Most biblical names have meaning. In Hebrew culture, a name expressed something about the essential nature or character of the thing or person named. Scripture gives many different names to God (*see* accompanying chart). These names, too, reveal God's character.

The one name not found on the chart is Yahweh or Jehovah. Yahweh is the personal, not descriptive, name of the God of the Old Testament. It is his covenant name by which he chooses to be known by those to whom he has made commitments. Yahweh means, "The One Who Is Always Present." It is the name God's people are always to remember. The God who has made himself known to us in so many ways *is* with us now. He is not limited to sacred history nor to the Second Coming for which Christians wait. He is present with us, committed now and forever, not only to be God, but to be our God.

God's historic acts, his attributes, and his names provide rich material for devotional meditations, giving us insight into the person, works, and motivations of our Redeemer and Lord.

God-fearing [*phoboumenos*; "fearing one"]. The description of pious Gentiles, closely associated with the synagogue in cities throughout the Roman Empire, but also of converts to Judaism. In Jewish writings, "heaven-fearing" has the same force as "God-fearing."

Between 300 B.C. and A.D. 70, the Jews actively sought converts. The number of references in first-century B.C. Roman writers to Jewish sympathizers suggests that many were attracted to Judaism. But most of these pagans appear to have "turned Jew" without undergoing circumcision or strictly observing Jewish laws.

Such persons, who adopted the beliefs and some of the practices of Judaism without becoming Jews, were among the first to turn to Christ when the apostles visited various cities and spoke in synagogues (*compare* Acts 10:2; 13:26,50; 17:4,17).

godly, godliness [Heb., *hasid*; Gk., *eusebēs*]. (1) OT, those who have received and responded to God's grace; (2) NT, those whose faith in God is expressed by obedience. Godliness is thus summed up in worshiping God and putting one's religion into practice (1 Tim. 5:4), which includes demonstrating such virtues as righteousness, holiness, and the "fruit of the Spirit" (*compare* Gal. 5:22,23). The NT emphasizes the Christian's call to live a godly life in an age that is essentially evil (*compare* 1 Tim. 4:7; Tit. 2:12; 2 Pet. 3:11).

gods, goddesses (1) The deities and idols worshiped by ancient peoples; (2) in Ps. 82:1,6, human judges appointed to exercise on earth a prerogative of God, the ultimate Judge. However, this verse does not ascribe deity to human beings.

The religions of the ancient world were complex. Most featured hosts of gods and goddesses. These deities were much like human beings, but on a grander scale. Although they possessed the virtues common to humanity, the gods were also untrustworthy, sexually immoral, and often displayed the least attractive of human traits. The deities of the pagans were not really concerned with humankind but had to be bribed or manipulated by magic to grant blessings. Often gods were thought of as "owners" of localities where they were worshiped. Persons moving to a new area would worship the local god as well as any gods of their own people.

Papyrus certificate (libellus) dating to A.D. 250 states that a certain Aurelius Horion had officially sacrificed to the emperor as a god. Every Roman citizen at that time, no matter what his religion, was obliged to possess such a certificate.

This Babylonian tablet commemorates King Nabu-apla-iddina's endowment of the temple of the sun god Shamash at Sippar (about 870 B.C.).

Pagan religions had several characteristics in common: (1) Some gods and goddesses were associated with forces of nature. A specific god or goddess was thought to control the sea, the storm, the rains, the fertility of the earth, etc. Religious rites were based on the yearly cycle of nature and often featured sex acts designed to stimulate the gods to copulate, thus supposedly guaranteeing a good crop. The priests and priestesses of these gods often served as ritual prostitutes. (2) Some gods and goddesses were associated with activities that concerned human beings. There were gods and goddesses of war, of love, of hunting, of childbirth, of education and literature, etc. Gods were also adopted as the deity of a particular nation, as Marduk was by Babylon, and thus were concerned with its politics and conquests. (3) Whereas Christianity presents itself in a historical context, the cults of the pagan gods were rooted in mythological tales cast in an imaginary past. Many of the pagan rites sought to reenact these stories.

Pagan religions, with their hosts of selfish gods and goddesses, stand in stark contrast to the religion of the Bible. Scripture affirms the existence of one God, who created and controls all of nature. He is the God of the whole earth—of the past, present, and future. And this God truly cares for humankind. He calls us to a personal relationship with him despite our sins and failures. He loves us so much that he gave his own Son that we might know forgiveness and eternal life. This God sums up in himself all that is right and good and calls his worshipers to moral and loving lives. He is as far removed from the pagan deities as light is from darkness.

Gog A far northern ruler of people identified in Ezek. 38,39 as an invader who will ravage Israel and then miraculously be destroyed by God. Historically, Gog may be identified as Gyges, king of Lydia. However, the Ezekiel passage most likely refers to future events rather than historical figures.

PAGAN GODS NAMED IN THE BIBLE

Name (NIV)	Worshipers	Reference	Description
Adrammelech	Sepharvaim	2 Ki. 17:31	Demanded child sacrifice
Anammelech	Sepharvaim	2 Ki. 17:31	Demanded child sacrifice
Artemis	All Asia	Acts 19:28	Many-breasted fertility goddess; called "Diana" in some versions.
Asherah	Canaanites	2 Chr. 24:18	Wife of Baal; symbolized by a pole
Ashima	Hamathites	2 Ki. 17:30	A god of the Hittites
Ashtoreth	Sidonians	1 Ki. 11:5	Goddess of sex, fertility; Astarté in Greek
Baal	Canaanites	Jdg. 2:13	Chief god of Canaan until the Exile; the name Baal is often linked with place names, such as Gad, Peor, etc.
Baal-Zebub	Philistines	2 Ki. 1:2	God of Ekron consulted by Ahaziah
Bel	Babylonians	Jer. 51:44	Alternate name of chief god, Marduk
Castor, Pollux	Greeks	Acts 28:11	Twin sons of Zeus
Chemosh	Moabites	1 Ki. 11:7	Chief god of Moab and perhaps Ammon
Dagon	Philistines	1 Sam. 5:27	God of rain or agriculture
Destiny	Canaanites	Isa. 65:11	God of fate; "Meni" in some versions
Fortune	Canaanites	Isa. 65:11	God of luck; "Gad" in some versions
Hermes	Greeks	Acts 14:12	Messenger god, god of cunning, theft
Marduk	Babylon	Jer. 50:2	God of war; patron god of Babylon
Molech	Ammonites	Zeph. 1:5	Worshiped with child sacrifice
Moloch	Ammonites	Acts 7:43	With Milcom, another name for Molech
Nebo	Babylonians	Isa. 46:1	God of wisdom, literature, arts
Nergal	Cuthites	2 Ki. 17:30	Medo-Persian god of war
Nibhaz	Avvites	2 Ki. 17:31	
Nisroch	Assyrians	Isa. 37:38	God worshiped in Nineveh
Rephan	Israelites	Acts 7:43	Possibly another name for Moloch
Rimmon	Assyrians	2 Ki. 5:18	God of thunder, lightning, rain
Succoth Benoth	Babylonians	2 Ki. 17:30	Mistress of Marduk
Tammuz	Babylonians	Ezek. 8:14	Babylonian fertility god
Tartak	Avvites	2 Ki. 17:31	
Zeus	Greeks	Acts 14:12	Chief god in Greek pantheon

On etymological grounds, some have identified the peoples and the places named in this passage with Russia, and thus expect Russia to invade modern Palestine. However, the identification is far from sure. Nevertheless, the OT prophets agree that God will use an enemy from the far north to purify his people as history comes to a close (see Jer. 1:14; 4:6; 10:22; 13:20; Dan. 11) and that this enemy will be destroyed by an act of God on Israel's mountains (Isa. 14:24,25; 31:8,9; Joel 2:20; Zech. 14).

This eschatological passage was understood by the rabbis to describe events taking place at history's end after the days of the Messiah. Revelation 20:7-9 agrees with the rabbinical understanding, relating John's vision of the future:

When the thousand years [of Christ's reign] are over, Satan will be released from his prison and will go out to deceive the nations in the four corners of the earth—Gog and Magog—to gather them for battle. . . . They marched across the breadth of the earth and surrounded the camp of God's people, the city he loves. But fire came down from heaven and devoured them.

gold A precious metal. In its native state, gold is often alloyed with silver or other metals. It is easily worked by beating and was used liberally to decorate Israel's tabernacle and Temple (Ex. 25:11; 28:2-30; 1 Ki. 6:14-35). However, gold was also used in idolatrous worship (Ex. 32:2-4; 1 Ki. 12:28). *See also* Bull.

Listed 385 times, gold is the most frequently mentioned metal in the Bible. Some 13 Hebrew words describe different grades and forms of the metal. However, gold was not native to Palestine but was imported from places whose exact locations remain unknown (*compare* Gen. 2:11; 1 Ki. 10:1,2; Jer. 10:9; Ezek. 27:22). Archaeologists have found golden vases and bowls, jewelry, and many other objects scattered throughout Bible lands. Solomon's control of trade routes and his aggressive merchandising brought large amounts of gold into Israel during his reign. The Bible gives Solomon's personal income as 666 talents of gold annually. At a rate of $450 an ounce, Solomon's yearly income in gold would have been $360,000,000.

While gold was the standard by which material things were valued, writers of the Bible consider many things of far greater worth: Wisdom (Prov. 3:13,14), God's Law (Ps. 119:72), and faith itself (1 Pet. 1:7)

should be treasured far more than the precious metal.

golden calf An idol of gold cast by Aaron while Moses was on Mount Sinai receiving the Ten Commandments (Ex. 32:1-5). In the ancient Near East, pagan deities were often represented as bulls or were envisioned riding on the backs of bulls. *See also* Bull; Idol.

Golden Rule The common name given Jesus' summary statement of the OT Law and prophets: "In everything, do to others what you would have them do to you" (Mt. 7:12; Lk. 6:31). This concept was known in Judaism before Christ but was expressed negatively as "What you hate, do not do to anyone." Similar expressions are found in Confucianism, Hinduism, Buddhism, and Islam.

Christianity makes no exclusive claim to high moral vision, but only a personal relationship with Christ provides the divine enablement needed to achieve the ideals which good men hold in common. *See also* Good.

Below: Gold from the mines of Nubia is offered as a gift to Pharaoh on this wall painting dated about 1400 B.C. It was cast into rings for ease of transport. Gold, not found in Palestine, was imported to Israel from Ophir—possibly Africa or India.

Gold-leafed, Canaanite idol of the goddess Ashtoreth, found in Palestine (14th–13th century). The Israelites quickly turned to her worship after conquering Canaan (Jdg. 2:13; 10:6). Even the aging Solomon joined in her worship (1 Ki. 11:5; 2 Ki. 23:13).

Egyptian goldsmiths in this line drawing, taken from a wall relief of an Old Kingdom tomb (2625–2475 B.C.), weigh, melt, and shape gold into jewelry. Goldsmiths in Israel were rebuked by Jeremiah for aiding idolatry (Jer. 10:14; 51:17).

goldsmith A craftsman who refined gold, cast golden objects, and/or worked the metal into desired shapes. While Hebrew goldsmiths probably specialized in jewelry, in times of apostasy they used their skills to cover idols with a thin sheet of beaten gold nailed in place (Isa. 41:7). This same process was also used extensively in Solomon's Temple (1 Ki. 6:14-35). In the time of Nehemiah, a guild of goldsmiths had workshops in Jerusalem (*compare* Neh. 3:31,32).

Golgotha [Heb., "skull"]. The public execution ground where Jesus was crucified.

The exact location of Golgotha is uncertain. It lay outside Jerusalem's walls (Heb. 13:12) by a major roadway (Mt. 27:39). It was near the city (Jn. 19:20) and easily visible from a distance (Mt. 27:55; Mk. 15:40). This last fact has led some to believe

This hill is believed by some to be Golgotha because of its skull-like rock formation (detail).

that Golgotha was a hill. *See also* Calvary; Cross.

Gomorrah *See* Cities of the Plain; Sodom.

good [OT: Heb., *tob*]. (1) Beautiful, attractive, desirable; (2) useful, profitable, excellent; (3) morally right, loving. [NT: Gk., *agathos*]. (1) Useful, profitable; (2) morally right. [Gk., *kalos*]. Beautiful, ideal.

"Good" is a complex concept, expressed by several different Hebrew and Greek words, primarily *tob*, *agathos*, and *kalos*. Original creation, a beautiful woman, an attractive child, a fertile field, the married state are all described in Scripture by "good."

In an absolute moral sense, only God is truly good. Goodness is a divine attribute (Ps. 25:9; 106:1), which is expressed in God's relationship with Israel (Ps. 73:1) and with all mankind (Ps. 145:9; Mt. 5:43-45). James insists that God neither tempts nor is tempted by evil but that "every good and perfect gift is from above, coming down from the Father of the heavenly lights, who does not change" (1:17).

Some have puzzled over Jesus' response to the wealthy young man who greeted him as "good teacher" (Mk. 10:17). Jesus replied, "Why do you call me good? No one is good—except God alone." This was no denial of deity, but a challenge to the speaker. A person must either acknowledge Jesus as God or refrain from calling him "good."

To speak of something or someone as "good" begs evaluation. On a human level some people are more moral than others. Jesus himself noted that we, though evil, "know how to give good gifts to [our] children" (Mt. 7:11). But when the standard of comparison is God, "there is no one who does good, not even one" (Ps. 14:3; Rom. 3:12).

God, who is good in an absolute moral sense, has revealed "what is good" to humankind. Micah sums goodness up as "to act justly and to love mercy and to walk humbly with your God" (6:8). God's commandments are good and mark out a pathway which is morally right. They are also attractive and beneficial, for doing good keeps us from harm and guides us to our benefit.

Both Testaments call on God's covenant people to "trust in the Lord and do good" (Ps. 37:3). The NT lays great stress on doing good. Believers are "to do good, to be rich in good deeds, to be generous and willing to share" (1 Tim. 6:18; *compare* 2 Cor. 9:8; Gal. 6:9,10; Eph. 2:10; Col. 1:10; 2 Tim. 2:21; Tit. 3:1,14; Heb. 13:16; 1 Pet. 2:15).

Good works are not a way persons can earn salvation, but are a product of salvation. Salvation is "not by works, so that no one can boast." Yet, God's salvation so renews human beings that they become "God's workmanship, created in Christ Jesus to do good works, which God prepared in advance for us to do" (Eph. 2:9,10). *See also* Works, Good.

Good Samaritan Popular name for the Samaritan in Jesus' parable who had mercy on a robbery victim (Lk. 10:23-37). Through this story Jesus taught that the OT command to "love your neighbor as yourself" is a call to show concern for any human being in need. *See also* Samaritans; Neighbors.

gopher wood (KJV) [Heb., *gōper*]. The wood from which Noah's ark was constructed. The Hebrew word is found only in Gen. 6:14. Several modern versions take the wood to be cypress. *See also* Cypress.

Gospel [Gk., *euangelion,* "good news"]. (1) As a noun, all that God has done, is doing, and will do in his risen Son, Jesus Christ; (2) as an adjective, various aspects of that work; (3) a name applied to each of the first four books of the NT. *See also* Gospels, The.

"Gospel" appears 75 times in the NT. When it appears alone, "the gospel" stands for the whole of the Christian message. At times the Gospel is further defined. "The gospel of the kingdom" is the good news that Jesus of Nazareth is the long-awaited messianic King. The "gospel of God" identifies the origin of the good news, while "the gospel of Christ" and "the gospel of his Son" focus attention on the content of the good news.

John 3:16 has been called "the gospel in a nutshell." A more complete summary of the good news Christians believe is found in Paul's statement of "the gospel I preached to you" (1 Cor. 15:3-6). The passage reads,

For what I received I passed on to you as of first importance: that Christ died for our sins according to the Scriptures, that he was buried, that he was raised on the third day according to the Scriptures, and that he appeared to Peter, and then to the Twelve. After that, he appeared to more than five hundred of the brothers at the same time, most of whom are still living, though some have fallen asleep.

Other biblical summaries of the core Gospel are found in Peter's sermons in Acts 2:14-41 and 3:12-26, in Rom. 1:1-6, and in Phil. 2:6-11.

The Book of Romans is a carefully reasoned and detailed presentation of the Christian Gospel against the background of OT faith and life.

Gospels, The Four narratives proclaiming the one Gospel of Jesus Christ that begin the NT. Though Matthew and Mark used the noun "Gospel" (*for example,* Mt. 4:23; Mk. 1:1), not until the mid-second century A.D. were the four identified as a literary group by the plural form "Gospels" (*euangelia*). Even then, however, their traditional titles highlighted the recognition of only one Gospel in a fourfold record: "The Gospel According to Matthew," etc. (*compare* Rom. 1:1-3).

The first three Gospels, called the synoptics, have much material in common. Of Mark's 661 verses, 606 are similar to verses in Matthew and 380 are similar to verses in Luke. This has led to speculation that the three drew on a common written source, or that two of the three were dependent on the other. Others have noted the material most often repeated in Matthew and Luke consists of sayings of Jesus. They propose a written compilation of Christ's sayings, from which these two writers drew.

It may not be necessary to assume sources. Each Gospel is ascribed to a person who either witnessed the events described or who obtained eyewitness accounts. First-century preaching must have involved telling familiar stories again and again, and repeating the words of Jesus over and over. It would hardly be

surprising if, after thousands of retellings, stories took on patterned form.

Despite similarities in the material included in the synoptics, these three Gospels do vary significantly. Each of the authors shaped his telling of the story of Jesus to accomplish specific purposes. Each writer organized and cast his material to fit his audience. Matthew, writing to the Jews, shaped his material to show that Jesus was the Messiah the prophets foretold. Matthew often quotes or alludes to the OT. Sequences of events show Jesus as king, but a servant king. And Matthew takes care to show what has happened to the promised messianic Kingdom. Mark writes for the Romans, and shows Jesus as a bold man of action. Luke writes for the Greeks. This most human of the Gospels displays Jesus as a perfect man, who surpasses the ancient Greek ideal of aretē, excellence.

John uses a different approach to organize his book. He relates seven miracles, and reports Jesus' major discourses at length. John's is a universal Gospel, writ-

Facing page: These scenes and parables from the life of Christ come from an English manuscript with no text. They served the same purpose as stained glass windows—to teach biblical events to illiterate people. Left-hand portion of a full leaf, Canterbury, mid-12th century A.D.

A BRIEF HARMONY OF THE FOUR GOSPELS

	MATTHEW	MARK	LUKE	JOHN
BIRTH AND CHILDHOOD (4/5 B.C.)				
Genealogy of Jesus	1:1-17		3:23-38	
Jesus' Birth Foretold	1:18-25		1:26-38	
The Birth of Jesus	2:1-12		2:1-39	
Childhood and Visit to Temple			2:40-52	
PREPARATION FOR PUBLIC MINISTRY (A.D. 29)				
Jesus Is Baptized	3:13-17	1:9-11	3:21,22	
Jesus Tempted in the Wilderness	4:1-11	1:12,13	4:1-13	
BEGINNING OF JESUS' MINISTRY				
John Points Out Jesus				1:19-34
John's Disciples Attracted				1:35-51
The First Miracle: Water to Wine				2:1-12
Jesus Explains "Born Again"				3:1-21
GREAT GALILEAN MINISTRY				
Jesus Arrives in Galilee	4:12-17	1:14	4:14	4:43-45
Calls First of the Twelve	4:18-22	1:16-20	5:1-11	
Jesus Performs Many Miracles	8:1-4 9:1-17	1:40—2:12	5:12—6:19	
The Sermon on the Mount	5:1—7:29		6:20-49	
Jesus Speaks in Parables	13:1-53	4:1-34	8:4-18	
Jesus Performs a Series of Miracles	8:23—9:8 9:18-26	4:35—5:43	8:22-56	
Jesus Feeds 5,000	14:13-21	6:33-44	9:11-17	6:1-14
Jesus Walks on the Sea	14:22-33	6:45-52		6:15-21
Jesus Affirmed as Christ and Son of God	16:13-26	8:27—9:1	9:18-27	
Jesus Transformed	16:27—17:13	9:2-13	9:28-36	
Jesus Predicts His Death and Resurrection	17:22,23	9:31,32	9:43-45	
Jesus' Last Galilean Ministry	17:24—18:34	9:33-50	9:46-50	7:1-9
JUDEAN AND PEREAN MINISTRY				
Journey to Jerusalem	19:1,2	10:1	9:51-62	7:10
Jesus Claims Deity				8:12-59
Jesus Claims to Be the Good Shepherd				10:1-21
Story of the Good Samaritan			10:25-37	
Jesus in Mary and Martha's Home			10:38-42	
Jesus Teaches a Prayer			11:1-13	
Jesus Raises Lazarus				11:1-44
JESUS TRAVELS TOWARD JERUSALEM				
The Rich Young Ruler	19:16—20:16	10:17-31	18:18-30	
Jesus Predicts His Death	20:17-19	10:32-34	18:31-34	
Jesus Arrives at Bethany				11:55—12:11

continued

	MATTHEW	MARK	LUKE	JOHN
JESUS' LAST WEEK (PASSOVER, A.D. 33)				
Sunday				
The Triumphal Entry	21:1-9	11:1-10	19:29-40	12:12-19
Monday				
Jesus Cleanses the Temple	21:12,13	11:15-19	19:45-48	
Tuesday				
The Widow Gives Her Mite		12:41-44	21:1-4	
Jesus Teaches on History's End	24,25	13:1-37	21:5-38	
Wednesday				
Thursday				
The Passover Meal Held	26:17-29	14:12-25	22:7-30	13:1-30
Jesus Predicts Peter's Denial	26:31-35	14:27-31	22:31-38	13:31-38
The Last Supper Teaching				14–16
Prayer at Gethsemane	26:36-46	14:32-42	22:39-46	18:1
Jesus Arrested	26:47-56	14:43-52	22:47-53	18:2-12
On Trial before Annas				18:12-14; 19-23
On Trial before Caiaphas	26:57-68	14:55-65	22:54-65	18:24
Peter Denies the Lord	26:69-75	14:66-72	22:54-62	18:15-18; 25-27
On Trial before the Sanhedrin	27:1	15:1	22:66-71	
Suicide of Judas	27:3-10			
Friday				
On Trial before Pilate	27:11-14	15:2-5	23:1-5	18:28-38
Taken to Herod			23:6-12	
Returned to Pilate	27:15-26	15:6-15	23:13-25	18:39–19:16
Led to Calvary	27:31-34	15:20-23	23:26-32	19:16,17
Jesus' Crucifixion	27:35-56	15:24-41	23:33-49	19:18-30
Jesus' Body Buried	27:57-60	15:42-46	23:50-54	19:31-42
Saturday				
Women Visit the Tomb	27:61	15:47	23:55,57	
Sunday				
The Women Return	28:1-8	16:1-8	24:1-12	20:1-10
RESURRECTION APPEARANCES	28:9-20	[16:9-18]	24:13-49	20:11–21:25
AT THE ASCENSION		[16:19,20]	24:50-53	

ten to demonstrate to all that Jesus is the Son of God.

The different purposes of the authors explain some of the so-called discrepancies in Gospel accounts. The Gospels accurately report events. But sometimes the sequence of events is restructured to better fit the author's special purpose.

Other assumed discrepancies may be explained in other ways. For instance, Jesus traveled and taught in Palestine for three to three-and-a-half years. In that time he must have told his parables again and again, in different settings and to different audiences. He must have healed hundreds. Where details in the Gospel accounts differ, at least some of the differences may be due to authors' relating similar but not necessarily the same events.

Because of the differences in purpose, each Gospel must be studied on its own. Much can be learned from characteristics that are distinctive to each. *See also* John,

Gospel According To; Luke; Mark; Matthew.

Despite their differences, the good news the Gospels tell is the one "gospel about Jesus Christ, the Son of God" (Mk. 1:1). The earliest attempt to harmonize the events reported in all four Gospels was made by Tatian, a disciple of Justin, in about A.D. 170. It was called the *Diatessaron.*

gossip (1) To whisper tales about a person behind his or her back; (2) maliciously to slander another.

Proverbs 11:13 says, "A gossip betrays a confidence." The gossip's whispering destroys the harmonious relationship God desires between people (Prov. 16:28; 26:20). In the NT, gossip appears on lists of "every kind of wickedness" characterizing sinful human beings—in the same context as murder and hating God (Rom. 1:29-32; 2 Cor. 12:20).

gourd Inedible relatives of the squash. Because of their hard rinds, gourds were used as dippers or cups in the Middle East, though this use is not illustrated in Scripture. The gourd is mentioned in the OT several times. First, the Temple and the bronze basin outside it were decorated with an alternating gourd ("knop," KJV) and flower design (1 Ki. 6:18; 7:24; 1 Chr. 4:3). The fruit of a "wild gourd" poisoned a stew which Elisha miraculously cleansed (2 Ki. 4:39). Finally, the word the KJV translates "gourd" in Jonah 4 is better rendered "plant" (RSV) or "vine" (NIV).

government, human The system by which a political unit or society is administered.

The original commission God gave human beings to rule over his creation (Gen. 1:26,27) did not include a right to rule one another. The Fall, however, distorted interpersonal relationships. Therefore, God announced to Eve: Adam "will rule over you" (Gen. 3:16). Yet this statement falls short of instituting human government. The next chapters of Genesis picture a state of anarchy, a society in which "every inclination of the thoughts of his [man's] heart was only evil all the time" (Gen. 6:5). God acted to judge that society and, after the Flood, uttered words to Noah which many take as a formal institution of human government.

Whoever sheds the blood of man,
by man shall his blood be shed.

(Gen. 9:6)

In making mankind responsible for the enforcement of justice, God implies the entire range of governmental functions.

After Gen. 11, the focus of Scripture shifts from the human race in general to God's covenant people. Within that context, a series of governmental systems has existed.

The initial system for the covenant people was patriarchal or tribal. This situation persisted up to the time of Moses. At Sinai, God was constitutionally established as Israel's King. *See also* King; Law. The Law given by the King provided the structure for the society of God's people. However, the laws God established had to be administered. And the administration of laws is the province of governments.

Under Moses, governmental functions were distributed to leaders of thousands, hundreds, fifties, and even tens (Ex. 18). This distribution was formalized in the Law, which relied on local elders to see

that God's commands were carried out and that justice was administered. The distribution of many governmental and most judicial functions to local elders characterized Israel even when centralized governmental structures were later imposed. *See also* Elder. The ages of the judges and of the monarchy added new layers of government. But effective administration of the divine Law still depended on godly local elders and on a committed people willing to practice God's commandments.

During and after the Babylonian Captivity, God's covenant people were ruled by pagan empires. In this era of subservience, Israel was responsible to obey foreign rulers. At the same time, they remained responsible to obey the laws of God. Again, local leaders and elders were responsible for administering divine Law, while foreign governors saw to administration of secular law. In the time of Jesus, a Sanhedrin, or court of seventy elders, governed the Jewish people under Jewish law, which Rome allowed to function. *See also* Citizen.

As the NT era began, the church found itself in a new situation. Israel had been not only a covenant people but a nation. The church was a covenant people living within many nations. Christians were still self-governing in a spiritual sense. Each congregation was led and guarded by local elders. Yet individual Christians were also citizens of their country and of the Empire. At this point, a new definition of the relationship between God's people and human governments was required. That definition is found in Christ's teaching, is illustrated in Acts, and is made explicit in the Epistles.

GUIDING PRINCIPLES

Jesus said, "Give to Caesar what is Caesar's, and to God what is God's" (Mt. 22:21). The believer was responsible to be

Cup made from a half of a dried gourd.

On this tablet, inscribed in Sumerian cuneiform, King Uruinimgina of Lagash (24th century B.C.) describes his attempts to reform bureaucratic abuses in his government. God declared his own reform principle through the prophet Jeremiah: " 'The days are coming,' declares the Lord, 'when I will raise up to David a righteous Branch, a King who will reign wisely and do what is just and right in the land.' "

Nebuchadnezzar's appointed governor of Suhi and Mari prays to the gods Adad and Ishtar on this relief from the palace in Babylon (605–562 B.C.). Gedaliah was appointed governor of the remnant left in Judea after the Exile in 587 B.C. (2 Ki. 25:22; Jer. 40:7).

Bronze coin minted in A.D. 54 under Felix Antonius, who was procurator (governor) of Judea from 52–59, and before whom Paul was brought for trial in Caesarea (Acts 23:23,24).

a good citizen of both earthly and heavenly kingdoms. Later, Peter wrote, "Submit yourselves for the Lord's sake to every authority instituted among men." He instructs submission even when a human authority is unjust (1 Pet. 2:13-25).

There is one exception to the rule of submission. When Peter and John were commanded by the Sanhedrin, the governing authority in Judah, to stop preaching Christ, they replied, "Judge for yourselves whether it is right in God's sight to obey you rather than God" (Acts 4:19). When human and divine authority conflict, the Christian must obey the higher authority.

Two principles sum up the NT's teaching on the relationship between believers and human government: (1) Be good citizens; and (2) when human and divine authorities conflict, obey God.

RATIONALE

Romans 13:1-7 calls rulers God's servants, agents of God's wrath empowered to punish the wrongdoers. A secular ruler may not act from religious motivation, but restrains evil out of self-interest, for if injustice and crime flourish, a society and its government will fall. Government must maintain a semblance of law and order, or it will be unable to maintain itself. So God uses the self-interest of rulers to achieve his good purposes.

governor A subordinate ruler appointed to administer a country, province, or smaller territory.

The powers and responsibilities held by "governors" in OT and NT cannot be determined from the title alone. For instance, Pilate, as governor (actually, prefect) of Judea, had the power of life or death over its citizens (Mt. 10:18; Lk. 21:12).

The KJV uses "governor" in archaic senses for the master of ceremonies at a wedding feast (Jn. 2:8,9) and for the pilot of a ship (Jas. 3:4).

grace Theologically, (1) God's free and spontaneous action taken to meet human need, especially in providing salvation and in enabling the believer; (2) man's response of gratitude to God's gracious acts, thanksgiving. In secular Greek, (1) an attractive charm or beauty, as in Prov. 1:9; (2) a kindly or favorable attitude, as in Lk. 4:22; (3) appreciation for a favor or some kindness.

OLD TESTAMENT

The Hebrew has no single word that is equivalent to the Greek word for grace, *charis*. The closest term is *hen*, the favor shown to an inferior by a superior. However, while the concept of grace is not developed in the OT, grace surely is displayed there, especially in God's choice of Abraham and Israel and in his patience with his people. A clear expression of grace is found in God's revelation of himself to Moses: "The Lord, the Lord, the compassionate and gracious God, slow to anger, abounding in love and faithfulness, maintaining love to thousands, forgiving wickedness, rebellion and sin" (Ex. 34:6,7).

NEW TESTAMENT

In the New Testament, grace [*charis*] is summed up in God's provision of salvation. The theological concept is expressed most clearly in Eph. 2:1-10. We were "dead in . . . transgressions and sins," controlled by "the cravings of our sinful nature." Although we deserved God's wrath, he was moved by "his great love for us" to make us "alive with Christ." God's response to human helplessness was an act of pure grace—"it is by grace you have been saved." But grace does not stop here. God has also "raised us up with Christ." Through this spiritual resurrection, God provided the inner resources that enable us to "show the incomparable riches of his grace." Therefore, God's gracious action in our lives constitutes a re-creation. Through grace we are able to "do good works, which God prepared in advance for us to do."

This passage emphasizes the fact that all man can do to experience the saving and re-creating grace of God is to trust the Lord. Salvation is in every respect a gift of God, accepted by faith and independent of all human works or merit "so that no one can boast." *See also* Faith; Love; Mercy.

GRACE AND LAW IN THE NT

A number of NT passages contrast grace and Law. Romans 3:10–4:25 argues that Law requires men to be righteous. However, since no one is righteous, Law in essence is an agent of condemnation. It makes humanity conscious of sin and guilt but provides no means of escape. On the other hand, grace meets man in his wickedness and offers righteousness as a gift. Thus Law, while what it requires is good, constitutes a call to works that no man can perform. Grace, however, makes men good and enables them to perform righteous acts.

This contrast is restated in Gal. 3. Law and grace operate on different premises. One demands; the other gives. One requires; the other promises. From the beginning, relationship with God was rooted in God's promise of grace rather than on our own self-efforts. *See also* Law.

GRACE IN THE BELIEVER'S LIFE

The Christian, who has exercised faith in Christ, now has free access to God's grace (Rom. 5:1,2). The believer can "approach the throne of grace with confidence" and receive "mercy and find grace to help" in time of need (Heb. 4:14-16). Yet grace is accessible only through faith. A believer who struggles to keep the Law, rather than rely on the work of God within, has "fallen away from grace" (Gal. 5:4). That is, he or she has ceased relying on God's enablement to rely instead on self-effort, thus ensuring failure.

A number of times "grace" is used of the gifts given by God's Spirit. These "grace gifts" enable believers to minister effectively to the needs of others (Rom. 12:3; 2 Cor. 1:12; Gal. 2:9; Eph. 4:7). Of giving, Paul says that God makes "all grace abound" to us, so that we in turn may "abound in every good work" (2 Cor. 9:8). Our confidence that God's gracious provision extends to our material as well as spiritual needs frees us to give generously to others.

Thus, grace is a key theological term in the NT. The concept uniquely expresses all that God has chosen to do for us in Christ, the nature of the relationship God seeks with believers, and the loving relationship God calls believers to establish with one another in this present world.

graft The process by which branches from one plant are inserted into branches of another.

In the Middle East, branches from cultivated olive trees might be grafted into wild trees to improve the fruit. In Paul's analogy, the process is reversed. Gentile Christians are branches of a wild olive tree, grafted on to Israel, the tree that God has so lovingly cultivated (Rom. 11:11-24). The analogy is intended to emphasize the importance of faith, to encourage humility, and to promote awareness of Christianity's roots in Judaism.

grain (1) Cereal grasses such as wheat, barley, rice, or oats; (2) the small, hard seed of the cereal grasses.

Grain was the most important food crop in Israel. It is usually found first in any list of the three primary products of the land: grain, grapes, and olives. The most important grains grown in Palestine were wheat and barley. A poor quality wheat, called "spelt" in some versions, was also grown. However, no corn grew in Palestine: When the KJV was published, "corn" was a general term for all grains. *See also* Barley; Wheat.

Grain was planted in October at the beginning of the rainy season and harvested between April and June. Stalks of ripe grain were cut with a hand sickle. The stalks were laid out on clear, flat ground where they were trampled by heavy farm animals to break up the stalks and separate the kernels of grain. The trampled piles were then tossed into the air, and the

Olive crops could be improved by grafting branches from a cultivated tree into wild stock. Paul used the image in reverse: Gentiles are wild stock that God has grafted into the root and trunk of Israel (Rom. 11:22-24).

One laborer carries a sack of grain while a scribe makes notes on a writing board, in a wooden model of a granary found in an Egyptian tomb (about 1400 B.C.). To avoid impending famine, "Joseph stored up huge quantities of grain, like the sand of the sea; it was so much that he stopped keeping records because it was beyond measure" (Gen. 41:49).

Cuneiform-inscribed tablet from Ur (2900–2600 B.C.) records deliveries of barley and meal to a temple. The priests and Levites of Israel received their grain as a portion of the offerings Israelites brought for various sacrifices (Lev. 27:30; Num. 18:21,27).

wind blew away the lighter material, the heavier kernels falling to the ground. The grain was then cleaned and stored, usually in pottery or stone jars. Women daily took out the grain needed for bread and crushed it into coarse flour. *See also* Bread; Threshing.

Grain also has a role in the imagery of the NT. For instance, God's Word is like wheat seeds cast by the sower, only some of which take root and grow to maturity (Mt. 13:1-23). Furthermore, the Kingdom of heaven is compared to a field sown with both wheat and weeds, which grow together. But at harvest, the two will be separated, and God's Messiah will gather his wheat (the saved) into his barn, while the chaff (the unsaved) will be burned up (Mt. 3:11,12; 13:24-30).

Christ himself is like a kernel of wheat. Only by falling to the ground and dying could he produce a harvest of many like himself (Jn. 12:24). Similarly, the believer must be willing to give up rather than hold on to his life, for the Christian becomes his true self only by dying to self and following Jesus (Jn. 12:25,26).

Thus, grain, so vital to those living in the biblical world, is an appropriate symbol of those who are important to God. And the familiar images of planting, growing, and harvesting are effective vehicles for expressing spiritual truths.

grape (1) A fruit that grows in clusters on woody vines; (2) the vines themselves. One of the three basic crops, with grain and olives, on which life in Palestine depended. Grapes were eaten fresh, dried to become raisins, and squeezed for their juice, which was made into wine. *See also* Vine; Wine.

grass Plants with long, narrow leaves and jointed stems, including in Scripture (1) various green plants that grow low to the ground and are eaten by grazing animals, (2) various grains, such as wheat, rye, etc.,

or (3) green plants as a whole, as Mt. 6:30.

Grass is frequently used in Scripture as a symbol of the transitory nature of life. In Palestine's hot season, "the sun rises with scorching heat and withers the plant [i.e., grass]; its blossom falls and its beauty is destroyed" (Jas. 1:11). This natural phenomenon, so obvious in the dry areas of the Holy Land, reminds the biblical writers of the brevity of human life. The psalmist says, "As for man, his days are like grass, he flourishes like a flower of the field; the wind blows over it and it is gone" (Ps. 103:15). The NT picks up the same imagery, drawing from Isa. 40:6-8, and says, "All men are like grass, and all their glory is like the flowers of the field; the grass withers and the flowers fall, but the word of the Lord stands forever" (1 Pet. 1:24).

Each of these images emphasizes the transitory nature of life and vulnerability to forces beyond our control. Jesus preserved this tone, but transformed the image when he spoke of the lilies of the field (Mt. 6:28-34). Grasses do perish after momentary life. Yet the beauty in which they are clothed testifies to God's loving care: A God who takes such pains to clothe grasses will surely take care of human beings, who are far more precious to him. Our very vulnerability leads us to trust in God, for we have no other hope. The brevity of our days on earth helps us realize that the meaning of life must be found in God and his Kingdom.

grasshopper An insect with long hind legs suitable for jumping, many species of which are destructive to crops. *See also* Locust.

In most contexts, grasshoppers represent a destructive force that strips the land of its crops. Thus, grasshoppers are typically agents of divine punishment or discipline (1 Ki. 8:37; Ps. 78:46). Ironically, these destructive creatures were one of the few ritually clean insects that Israelites might eat if they chose (Lev. 11:22). *See also* Dietary Laws.

gratitude Thankful awareness of that which has been received. The concept is best summed up in the use of *charis* in the NT to express the believer's response to God's grace, as well as God's gift of grace in Jesus Christ. *See also* Thanks.

grave (1) Literally, the place of interment of dead bodies, the tomb; (2) euphemistically, the realm of death, used in expressions meaning "to die," as in "go down to the grave"; (3) symbolically, as in Ps. 5:9, "their throat is an open grave," to suggest (moral) corruption. *See also* Burial; Funeral; Sheol.

grave clothes [Gk., *keiria*, "winding sheet"]. A linen cloth, or strips of cloth, in which a corpse's trunk, and sometimes its limbs, were wrapped for burial. When Lazarus was raised by Jesus, he stumbled from the grave encumbered by his grave clothes (Jn. 11:44). When Jesus was resurrected, the strips of linen still lay where his body had been. The implication is that the resurrected Christ passed through the grave clothes, leaving them lying empty where he had been (Jn. 20:6,7).

graven image (KJV) [Heb., *pesel*, "carved figure"]. The carved representation of a god or goddess. The worship ritual of every ancient deity except Israel's God included such figures. Modern versions generally translate *pesel* by "idol" or "image" (*compare* Lev. 19:4; Deut. 27:15). *See also* Idol.

great Of much more than ordinary size, quality, quantity, or degree. The English word effectively expresses the shades of several different Hebrew and Greek words translated "great" or "greatness."

Two biblical themes are important. First, "great" is often used to emphasize the unusual in God's character or actions. The Exodus miracles were great acts (Deut. 10:21). The psalmists overflow with praise for God's great mercy (Ps. 5:7) and great love (Ps. 17:7). God exercises great patience (Rom. 9:22), great power (Eph. 1:19), and has provided a great salvation (Heb. 2:3). Jesus is a great high priest (Heb. 4:14) and our great Shepherd (Heb. 13:20). God himself is a great God (Tit. 2:13).

The second important theme is seen in Jesus' teaching about greatness. When asked, "Who is greatest in the kingdom of heaven?" Jesus responded, "Whoever humbles himself like this child" (Mt. 18:1-5). Unlike many, "this child" had responded when called by Jesus and came to stand where Jesus directed (v. 2). Those who seek spiritual greatness must be obedient to the voice of the Savior. A little later, the mother of James and John begged Jesus to give her sons authority in

his coming Kingdom (Mt. 20:20,21). The incident created jealousy among the disciples, and Jesus gave further instruction in true greatness. In human society, "greatness" is authority over others. In Jesus' Kingdom, greatness is servanthood. Christ said, "Whoever wants to become great among you must be your servant, and whoever wants to be first must be your slave—just as the Son of Man did not come to be served, but to serve, and to give his life as a ransom for many" (Mt. 20:24-28).

Greatness in God's sight is a matter of response to God's Word and to the needs of others. Because each Christian can obey God and serve others, each has the opportunity to be great. *See also* Servant.

Detail of Benozzo Gozzoli's The Raising of Lazarus *shows the artist's impression of grave clothes of NT times. Biblical and extrabiblical descriptions seem to suggest both linen garments and wrappings in burial preparations.*

This tombstone, decorated with menorahs and inscribed in Greek, was found in the Jewish catacombs in Rome. Many Jews in the Roman Empire spoke only Greek.

Grecian Jews [*Hellēnistai*; only in Acts 6:1; 9:29]. (1) Jews who spoke only Greek; (2) Greek-speaking Jews who had immigrated to Judea; (3) assimilated Jews who had adopted Greek culture and ideals and did not conform to the rigid Judaism of the homeland. *See also* Hellenists.

453

THRACE
Philippi
Thessalonica
Berea
MACEDONIA
ASIA MINOR
AEGEAN SEA
BOEOTIA
Athens
Ephesus
Corinth
N
PELOPONNESUS
Sparta
RHODES
CYCLADES ISLANDS
CRETE
MI 0 100
KM 0 100
MEDITERRANEAN SEA

Above: The columns of the Temple of Athena in Athens, the Parthenon, hint at the cultural greatness of Greece in her golden age.

Greece Home of the Greek people and culture, lying along the Aegean Sea. The origin of the Greek people is uncertain, but their influence on the world of the first century and subsequently on Western culture was great.

In the eighth century B.C., the Greeks were settled in independent city-states along the Aegean. However, population growth stimulated an era of colonization. So, between 750–550 B.C., independent Greek cities were established along the shores of the Mediterranean and Black seas. Politically, this era saw a transition from local monarchy, through aristocracy and dictatorships, to democracy. Intellectually, the era saw spectacular developments in language, literature, philosophy, and the arts, heralding a cultural metamorphosis that spread throughout the Mediterranean world. However, because the Greek city-states and their colonies failed to unite and develop great political power, they fell prey to stronger political forces.

After Cyrus overcame Babylon in 539 B.C., the Persian Empire spread westward. Persia soon controlled the Greek city-states on the eastern shore of the Mediterranean. In 490 B.C., Darius I invaded Europe. The Persians were thrown back by the Greeks then, and again in 480 B.C. in battles that preserved the West. But war among Greece's city-states took its toll, and the weakened Greeks were vulnerable to the developing great powers, Rome and Carthage.

In 338 B.C., Philip of Macedon defeated the Greek armies and proclaimed himself Greece's protector. His son, Alexander, imbued with Greek ideals, later invaded Persia to retake the Greek city-states. What Alexander did was to conquer the entire Empire, including Asia Minor, Syria and Palestine, Egypt, and Mesopotamia, to the border of India itself. Alexander's conquest spread the Greek language, ideals, and culture throughout most of the known world. When Alexander died young, the lands he had conquered were divided among his generals, who actively promoted Hellenism in order to unify the diverse peoples they ruled.

Although the Romans soon imposed their stern political structure on Europe and most of Alexander's old territories, the underlying culture of the Roman world was Greek. Nearly everyone spoke Greek and had adopted Greek ways of thinking. When Christianity emerged in tiny Judea, the Greek language provided the vehicle by which the Gospel could be spread to all peoples.

Doric
Corinthian
Ionic

Details of columns from the three famous orders of Greek architecture.

greed The desire to acquire and keep more than one needs; avarice, covetousness.

Scripture portrays greed as an unmixed evil, against which Jesus' followers are to be on their guard (Lk. 12:15). Greed is no minor sin. It is found on lists with murder, adultery, and malice (Mk. 7:22); with sexual immorality, theft, and drunkenness (1 Cor. 5:11; 6:10). Because desire for wealth or possessions takes first place in the greedy person's heart, greed is equated with idolatry (Col. 3:5). Therefore, church leaders must "not [be] greedy for money, but eager to serve" (1 Pet. 5:2).

In essence, "greed" defines a person's character. The person motivated by love for God will sacrifice possessions to serve others. The person motivated by love for self will sacrifice others—and God—to possess things.

Greek [*Hellēn*]. (1) A person who lives or whose ancestors lived in Greece, as in Acts 16:1; (2) in the NT, a synonym for Gentile, any non-Jew, as in Rom. 10:12. The phrase "Jew and Greek" means all humankind, as everyone fits one of these categories.

The distinction between the Jews as God's covenant people and all other human beings was important in first-century Judaism. Therefore, Paul often uses the phrase "Jew and Greek" to emphasize the universal nature of Christian faith. Christ died for all. Through faith all of humanity now has access to the Father. The old distinctions are no longer relevant, for "you are all one in Christ Jesus" (Gal. 3:28).

Bronze head representing Sophocles, famous Greek dramatist, exemplifies Hellenistic portraiture in third century B.C. Hellenistic culture and language spread through the empire established by Alexander the Great.

The earliest Greek inscriptions yet known are scratched on pottery. Some of these date back to 730 B.C.

Greek language One of two highly distinctive languages in which the bulk of the Scriptures was written. *See also* Hebrew Language. Unlike Hebrew, Greek is an inflexional language. That is, meanings are communicated by adding prefixes, suffixes, or making internal changes in word stems. Inflections show such things as subject, object, direct object, and possession, as well as indicate direct address, origin, instrumentation, and other functions. A single Greek verb theoretically might appear in over 600 separate forms! While this may seem complicated, such a sophisticated language has the advantage of being able to communicate delicate nuances of meaning.

The most complex forms are limited to classical Greek, which flowered in the fifth century B.C. In the mid-fourth century B.C., dramatic change was introduced. Alexander the Great's army, drawn from all parts of Greece and speaking many dialects, set out to conquer the Persian Empire. In order to unify the various dialects and facilitate the influence of Hellenism, the Greek language was modified, simplified, and spread throughout the conquered lands. By the first century, nearly everyone in the Roman Empire spoke both his own language and *koinē*, a common Greek variant. When the first Christian missionaries preached or wrote, they were able to communicate their message clearly through this universal language.

While less complex than classical Greek, the *koinē* variant was direct, powerful, and clear. Today, over 50,000 papyrus texts in *koinē* from the early Christian era have been published. Many thousands more have been read by scholars. The manuscripts include all types of documents—legal papers, personal letters, business inventories, children's writing exercises, etc. These finds have helped NT scholars

English equivalent	Classical Greek (IONIA)	New Testament Greek (KOINE)
a	ΛΑ	ΛΑ
b	Β	Β
g	Γ	Γ
d	Δ	ΔΔ
e	ΕΕ	ΕΕ
z	Ι	ΖΖ
ē	ΘΗ	Η
th	⊗⊙Θ	ΘΘ
i	Ι	Ι
k	Κ	Κ
l	ΛΛ	ΛΛ
m	ΜΜ	Μμ
n	Ν	Ν
x	Ξ	Ξ
o	Ο	Ο
p	ΓΠ	Π
q	φ	
r	ΡD	Ρ
s	Ξ	ΣΣϹ
t	Τ	Τ
u	VY	ΥΥ
ph	Φ	Φ
kh	Χ	Χ
ps	ΨV	ΨΨ
ō	ΩΣ	Ωω

develop a precise understanding of the meaning of many biblical terms and phrases. The recovered papyri demonstrate conclusively that the NT was written with ordinary words, to communicate effectively to the common person.

greeting A salutation (1) on meeting another person, or (2) placed at the beginning of a letter.

The traditional Hebrew greeting is *shalom*, which is often translated "peace." The word actually suggests health and wholeness, an internal and external harmony that is reflected in the deepest meaning of our word "peace" (*compare* 1 Sam. 25:5; 2 Sam. 8:10). *See also* Shalom.

Greetings between the Hebrews were often expressive and emotional, and involved hugging and kissing.

The warmth reflected in this emotional greeting is also seen in the early church (*compare* Gen. 27:26; 1 Sam. 1:10; Lk. 7:38; Rom. 16:16). The NT letters typically begin with a formula greeting. The author identifies himself and the intended recipients, and then expresses his best wishes for them, such as "Grace be to you and peace from God our Father and the Lord Jesus Christ" (2 Cor. 1:2). This pattern is not unique to the NT, but follows the normal conventions of first-century correspondence. *See also* Gestures.

grief (1) Intense emotional suffering, often caused by some loss or disaster; (2) the loss or disaster which causes the suffering.

In modern thought, "grief" is a purely psychological term. However, the OT use of "grief" draws attention to the total situation, including the cause as well as the emotional state.

The NT indicates that Christians are subject to added stress as they seek to follow Jesus, for commitment often brings persecution. Yet the NT links grief with grace. First Peter 1:3-9 presents truths that bring Christians comfort in times of grief. (1) We have an inheritance. What happens to us now can never rob us of that which God has reserved for us in heaven. (2) We have a perspective. We know that suffering reveals the genuine character of our faith and results in praise, honor, and glory. (3) We have a love for Jesus. This fills us with an inexpressible joy, which exists despite our circumstances.

Christians are not exempt from suffering or grief. But God's grace provides us with the strength, and even joy, to see us through. *See also* Joy; Suffering.

Assyrian guard escorts two captive Judeans to King Sennacherib. Detail of the Battle of Lachish (701 B.C.) relief at Nineveh. Elite corps of guards figure importantly in several biblical events (see 2 Ki. 11:4-8; 25; Jer. 52; Mt. 27:62–28:14; Lk. 22:4,52; Phil. 1:13).

grove (KJV) [Heb., *asherah*]. A group of trees, usually oak, where pagan practices were performed. The Hebrew word for "grove" indicates the pagan goddess Asherah. The NIV typically translates this word "Asherah pole." This reflects the pagan practice of setting up altars in or by groves of trees and of using the tree trunk as a cult symbol. The OT forbids planting or setting up any such symbol near God's altar (Deut. 16:21). *See also* Asherah; Gods; Idol.

grudge (KJV) A lingering anger. Several Hebrew words are translated as "grudge" or "grumble" in the KJV and other versions. This complaining, angry spirit is forbidden in Lev. 19:18. *See also* Anger; Complain.

guarantee (1) Gk. *engyos*, a legal term, the bond pledged as security for fulfilling a business commitment. Jesus is the pledge guaranteeing God's promise of forgiveness, Heb. 7:22. (2) Gk. *arrabōn*, a downpayment or deposit ensuring that full payment will be made, 2 Cor. 1:22; 5:5; Eph. 1:14. (3) Gk. *bebaios*, certain, firm, or established, and in this sense guaranteed.

In context, each word reassures the believer that God himself guarantees what he has promised in his Word.

456

guard (VERB) (1) To keep confined, imprisoned, as in 1 Ki. 20:39; (2) to protect, as in 1 Sam. 26:15; (3) to be watchful, alert, as in Mt. 16:11.

While we wait for Jesus to return, we can take to heart scriptural admonitions to "be on guard" against the "yeast [teachings] of the Pharisees" (Mt. 16:6), against all kinds of greed (Lk. 12:15), against those who distort the truth (Acts 20:30,31), and against error (2 Pet. 3:17).

As we commit all things to the Lord, his peace "guards" our hearts and minds (Phil. 4:7)—we are "shielded [guarded] by God's power" until complete salvation is revealed (1 Pet. 1:5).

guard (NOUN) (1) Heb., *tabbah*, "slaughterer," a member of a king's bodyguard, as in Gen. 37:36; (2) *rus*, "runner," a member of a military unit close to the king, perhaps including his staff, as in 1 Ki. 14:27; (3) *mishmar, mishma'at*, "watchman," "posted guard," as in Neh. 4:9. Also, the NT speaks of the Temple Guard (Lk. 22:52). This was composed of Levites who policed the Temple area.

guardian A person who supervised the affairs of children in wealthy Greek or Roman families until they reached the age of 16. The apostle Paul used this word to describe the function of the Law (Gal. 3:23-25).

guest chamber (KJV) In Mk. 14:14 and Lk. 22:11, simply a room in which to eat. In modern versions, a "guest room." *See also* Hospitality.

guidance *See* Lead.

guilt [Heb., *'asam*, "to commit an offense," "to be guilty"; Gk., *enochos*, "to be liable for punishment"]. With other Hebrew and Greek words translated "guilt," these indicate that guilt involves (1) a wicked or sinful act, (2) a resultant condition of being guilty, and (3) liability for punishment. A particular verse or passage may emphasize any one of these three aspects, but guilt itself implies all three. The modern notion that "guilt" is a psychological state of remorse or the torment produced by a bad conscience is foreign to Scripture.

OBJECTIVE GUILT

The Bible treats guilt as an objective rather than subjective reality. This is especially clear in Paul's argument in Rom. 1:18–3:20, which demonstrates that "the whole world" is "held accountable to [that is, 'guilty before'] God." *See also* Conscience.

The OT teaches that individuals are responsible for unintentional as well as intentional sins. When an Israelite became aware of a sin of commission or omission, he was to bring a guilt offering and to make restitution. He would be forgiven, and his sin covered (*compare* Lev. 5:14-16). This requirement taught responsibility for one's actions and their consequences and also assured that God was ready to forgive. The NT corollary is found in 1 Jn. 1:9, which calls on Christians to confess sins of which they become aware. *See also* Confess; Reconciliation; Sin.

In each Testament, God forgives sin, not guilt. That is, God deals with our guilt by forgiving the sin that made us guilty. Through Christ's sacrifice, sins are "sent away" to be remembered no more. With forgiveness of the sin, guilt no longer exists except as a memory (Heb. 9:11–10:18). *See also* Atonement; Forgive.

GUILT FEELINGS

While the language of Scripture focuses attention on objective guilt, there are clear biblical references to guilt feelings. In Ps. 32:3,4, David graphically describes the emotional trauma associated with guilt, a trauma which also he hints at in Ps. 51:8-11. These same psalms express the "joy and gladness" that come with confession of sin and reconciliation: "The bones that you [God] have crushed rejoice" (51:8).

guilt offering [Heb., *'asham*]. A sin offering, required for depriving God or another person of that which was rightfully his or hers. Acts requiring a guilt offering include: desecrating holy things (Lev. 5:14-19), cheating, robbing or failing to report lost property, swearing falsely in court, seducing a slave girl (Lev. 6:1-5; 19:20-22), failing to remain ritually clean during a Nazirite oath (Num. 6:9-12). The cleansed leper also made this offering, for his disease had deprived God of his worship by excluding him from Israel's annual worship festivals (Lev. 14:12-18).

Every guilt offering required confession of sin, restoration of the full value of what had been taken plus a 20-percent fine and the sacrifice of an animal. This ritual strongly affirms the biblical concept of guilt. Each person is responsible for his actions and their consequences. His or her responsibility is both to God and to the offended party. God can and will forgive, but restitution is required.

gum resin *See* Incense.

C. 1500 BC PROTO-SINAITIC   C. 1300 BC CANAANITE   C. 1000 BC PHOENICIAN   C. 450 BC ARAMAIC   100 AD HEBREW   500 BC GREEK

Habakkuk, Book of Internal evidence suggests this brief book of the OT was written in the later part of the reign of Josiah (620–612 B.C.), just before the emergence of the Chaldeans (Babylonians) as a world power. Habakkuk raises the question of how a holy God can permit evil to triumph and gives God's surprising answer.

BACKGROUND

For over 150 years, Assyria had been the dominant world power, a constant threat to Judah. In Judah, King Josiah had led a religious revival. He destroyed the high places where pagan deities were worshiped, restored Temple worship, and recalled the priests and Levites to their ancient service. But the revival was apparently superficial, and Habakkuk complains of injustice in Judah, for "the wicked hem in [surround] the righteous" (1:4). In Israel, courts were led by unjust elders, who took bribes, listened to lies, and perverted justice. Against this wickedness Habakkuk cried out to the Lord. How could Israel's holy God permit such conditions?

The book is structured as a dialog. Habakkuk expresses his complaint, and the Lord responds. These dialogs are recorded in 1:1-4; 1:5-11; 1:12–2:1; 2:2-20; 3:1-19.

Commentary on Habakkuk 1:1–2:20, one of the so-called Dead Sea Scrolls hidden by Qumran community. It is not a biblical commentary in the modern sense: the anonymous writer interprets the prophecy only to reveal allusions to the Essene sect. This copy dates to the end of the first century B.C.

AUTHORSHIP

Not much is known about the prophet Habakkuk except what can be discerned from his writings. Tradition suggests Habakkuk [Huh-BAK-kuhk, "wrestler" or "embracer"] was a Levite. This view is supported by the musical notations found in 3:1,3,9,13, and 19, which are similar to those found in worship psalms.

THEOLOGICAL CONTRIBUTIONS

Habakkuk makes two theologically significant points.

1. The history of nations incorporates divine judgment. Therefore, the rise and fall of empires has moral as well as political and military explanations (*compare* Isa. 10:5-11). Habakkuk sees that soon God will bring the Babylonians sweeping down on his sinning people as punishment.

2. God is judging the wicked now. Habakkuk 2 explains and lists five "woes" God brings on the wicked even as they seem to prosper: (1) They are never satisfied, 2:4,5; (2) the wicked create the hostility that will destroy them, 2:6-8; (3) the wicked will never be secure, 2:9-11; (4) the accomplishments of the wicked will not last, 2:12-14; and (5) the things the wicked do determine the way they will be treated, 2:15-17. The chapter concludes with the

HABAKKUK: A READING AND STUDY GUIDE

Chapter	Content Summary	Related Articles
1:1-4	Habakkuk complains of injustice in Judah. He cannot understand God's failure to judge the wicked.	Justice Judge
1:5-11	God answers that he is raising up the Babylonians (Chaldeans) to invade Judah.	War Babylon
1:12–2:1	Habakkuk accepts Babylon as an instrument of judgment, but he questions how God can allow the wicked Babylonians to prosper.	Holy Wicked
2:2-20	The Babylonians will only appear to succeed. God is actively judging them with terrible "woes."	
3:1-19	Habakkuk asks that Judah's judgment come soon. God gives Habakkuk visions of past acts of judgment. Despite Habakkuk's terror, the prophet expresses personal faith.	Faith

familiar, "The Lord is in his holy temple; let all the earth be silent before him." This is no call to worship. It is a statement that the holy God is active now, as Judge of the wicked, even though they seem to prosper.

In chapter three, Habakkuk acknowledges God's righteousness and begs God to judge Judah speedily. But the prophet is then given a vision of God's past acts of judgment. Crushed by the realization of what God's judgment will mean to him and his people, the prophet trembles. Then, in a great leap of faith, Habakkuk determines to rejoice in the Lord, trusting that God will enable him to safely negotiate the dangerous years, vv. 18,19.

MASTERY KEYS

Twice Habakkuk addresses God as "Holy One." This vision of God led Habakkuk to the conviction, "Your eyes are too pure to look on evil." As you read, be alert for answers to the question of how a holy God can permit the wicked to prosper, much less exist. Note also the judgment theme, as it is worked out in human history (ch. 1), within the personality of the wicked (ch. 2), and in God's personal interventions (ch. 3).

SPECIAL FEATURES

Paul quotes Hab. 2:4, "The righteous will live by his faith [or, faithfulness]," in Rom. 1. It is the capstone of his assertion that God provides the believer with a righteousness that "is by faith from first to last" (Rom. 1:17). This verse opened Martin Luther's eyes to the Gospel and, in that sense, launched the Protestant Reformation.

Hades [HAY-deez]. Greek name for the god of the dead, also known as Pluto. In Judaism, Hades was identified, along with Sheol, as a place where the dead await judgment. Through the second to first centuries B.C., Jews believed the wicked dead went to one compartment of Hades and the righteous to another compartment called "paradise" or "Abraham's bosom." Jesus' story of a rich man and the beggar Lazarus (Lk. 16:19-31) adopts this image to the extent that the rich man is seen in a place of torment, called Hades, while the poor beggar is "by Abraham's side." Between these two locations a great gulf is fixed, so none can pass from one side to the other.

The term Hades occurs in the Greek NT in Mt. 11:23; 16:18; Lk. 10:15; 16:23; Acts 2:27,31; 1 Cor. 15:55; Rev. 1:18; 6:8; 20:13,14. English versions often render Hades as "hell." However, unlike Gehenna, Hades is never used of the place of final punishment, which *we* call "hell." The "gates of Hades" (Mt. 16:18) represent the rallying point of Satan's forces, as the city gate was the rallying place of a city's army. *See also* Hell; Sheol.

Hagar [HAY-gahr; "flight"]. The servant of Sarah, given by her to Abraham as a secondary wife. **Son:** Ishmael. **Scripture:** Gen. 16:1-16; 21:8-21; Gal. 4:21-31.

BACKGROUND

Hagar was Sarah's Egyptian slave. Custom permitted childless Sarah to give Hagar to Abraham as a secondary wife in order to bear him children. When Hagar conceived, this gave evidence that Sarah

459

was barren rather than Abraham sterile, and Hagar showed contempt for her mistress. In response, Sarah so mistreated Hagar that the slave girl fled in terror. However, an angel instructed Hagar to return and promised that her son would prosper.

Sarah later had a son, Isaac, whom the Lord decreed would be Abraham's heir. But Ishmael cruelly teased his younger half-brother, and Sarah insisted Hagar be sent away. This violated custom, which assigned definite rights to the offspring of a secondary wife. Only when God intervened and promised to care personally for Ishmael did Abraham send his son and Hagar into the desert. When the two seemed about to die of thirst, an angel appeared and reaffirmed God's promise to Hagar, and her eyes were opened and "she saw a well of water." Thus, her son lived and grew up to be a hunter in the wilderness of Paran. He married an Egyptian woman and fathered a mighty nation, fulfilling God's promise to Abraham and to Hagar.

LEARNING FROM HAGAR'S LIFE

Certainly Hagar was mistreated. Sarah "took" Hagar and "gave her to her husband." Hagar had no say in the matter; she was powerless. We should hardly be surprised when the powerless show their frustration at injustice by hostility. The Hebrew term describing Hagar's attitude toward Sarah is *qalal*, "to be slight" or "to curse." Yet Hagar's actions were self-defeating. They led to harsh treatment by her mistress and apparently infected Ishmael with her attitude. Nevertheless, God was gracious to Hagar and gave her an independent life with her son, Ishmael.

Hagar's life illustrates the fact that mistreatment begets hostility, but that hostility stimulates even more severe mistreatment! Is there a way out of the tragic cycle of injustice, hostility, and more injustice? Peter points to that way (1 Pet. 2:13-25). Do good and bear up under the pain of unjust suffering as Jesus did. If we "entrust ourselves to him who judges justly," we can expect him to break the tragic cycle and bring us freedom in the end.

Haggai, Book of This brief book contains four sermons Haggai delivered in 520 B.C. (1:1). Haggai [HAG-ay-i; "festival"] prophesied to the few who returned to Judah from Babylon, exhorting them to finish the Temple whose foundation they had laid 18 years before. The people responded, and the Temple was completed in 516 B.C.

BACKGROUND

Only some 50,000 Jews returned to Judah in 539 B.C., when Cyrus permitted captive peoples to return to their homelands. They erected an altar and laid the Temple foundation. But soon, their efforts were diverted into clearing the once-fertile fields, building houses, and trying simply to survive—yet as Haggai said, "you have planted much, but have harvested little. . . . You earn wages, only to put them in a purse with holes in it" (1:5,6). Haggai urged Zerubbabel the Jewish governor of

The desert surrounding the well of Beer-sheba in the Negev. Here Abraham sent his maidservant Hagar and son Ishmael into the desert (Gen. 21:8-21).

Second Year of Darius II (520 B.C.)

DAY 1	DAY 24	DAY 21		DAY 24
Hag. 1:1	Hag. 1:15	Hag. 2:1		Hag. 2:10
Elul (6)	Ethanim (7)	Bul (8)	Kislev (9)	
August	September	October	November	December

the Persian province of Judah, Joshua the high priest, and the whole population to put God first and complete the Temple.

The messages of Haggai are carefully dated: the first sermon, Hag. 1:1-11, the 1st day of the 6th month (Aug./Sept.); the second, Hag. 2:1-9, the 21st day of the 7th month (Sept./Oct.); the third and fourth sermons, Hag. 2:10-19; 2:20-23, the 24th day of the 9th month (Nov./Dec.).

HISTORICAL CONTRIBUTION

Haggai helps us appreciate the problems faced by the few who returned to Judah from Babylon. Furthermore, his description is helpful background to the prophecies of his contemporary, Zechariah.

THEOLOGICAL CONTRIBUTIONS

Haggai's call to rebuild the Temple has theological foundations:

(1) While God is faithful to the terms of his covenant, economic disasters came because the people failed to honor God and obey God's covenant (1:7-11). The people responded to the rebuke and returned to work on the Temple. Through Haggai, God promised, "From this day on I will bless you" (2:19).

(2) Haggai refers to "shak[ing] the nations," and to the "desired of the nations" (2:7, compare 2:21,22). Each phrase refers to the days of the Messiah. According to the earlier prophets, the Messiah would enter God's Temple in Jerusalem (compare Isa.

2:2-4; Ezek. 43:1-5; Mic. 4:1-4). Therefore, the Temple must be rebuilt in expectation of the Messiah's arrival. While the Temple which the remnant could afford might not compare with Solomon's for splendor, Haggai promises "the glory of the present house will be greater than the glory of the former house." It was. This Second Temple lasted for nearly 500 years, longer than either Solomon's or Herod's Temples. See also Temple, Jerusalem.

Haggai's appeal to ritual theology in 2:10-19 is also significant. He asks the priests to clarify a point of law concerning clean and unclean. Their answer establishes the fact that when something unclean touches a thing that is clean, the clean is polluted. However, the touch of something clean never cleanses the unclean. Before the Exile, the Jews supposed that the existence of the Jerusalem Temple guaranteed their safety. Haggai warns against such thinking. The mere presence of God's Temple cannot cleanse an unclean people. God blesses because of his grace, not because of the righteousness of the Temple builders. See also Clean and Unclean.

MASTERY KEYS

Examine each of the four sermons as a separate unit. Note particularly how each exhorts or encourages God's discouraged people.

The book of Haggai is unique because it records the exact dates on which Haggai delivered his prophecies.

HAGGAI: A READING AND STUDY GUIDE

Chapter	Content Summary	Related Articles
1:1-15	Judah is poor because her people have not honored God. The people respond and prepare to finish the House of the Lord.	Temple Covenant
2:1-9	The new Temple, though less splendid than the first, will be more glorious because of Messiah.	Messiah
2:10-19	Ritual law proves the rebuilt Temple will not purify the people. Yet God will bless.	Clean and Unclean Wealth
2:20-23	Pagan empires will be overthrown by God; Judah will be great in Messiah's time.	

SPECIAL FEATURES

Haggai and Zechariah both refer to Zerubbabel. Mathew 1:12 identifies him as a descendant of David and ancestor of Christ. In Hag. 2:23 Zerubbabel is symbolic of, or represents, Jesus the Messiah.

hail Pellets of ice, associated with violent thunderstorms. Hailstorms can destroy crops and cause injury.

God can control the hail, as he can all natural phenomena (Job 38:22; Ps. 148:8). He exercised that control to bring a devastating hailstorm on Egypt (Ex. 9:23-26) and to defeat an Amorite army (Josh. 10:11). In the prophets, hail serves as a symbol of divine judgment (Isa. 30:30; Ezek. 13:13; Hag. 2:17; Rev. 8:7; 11:19; 16:21). *See also* Judgment; Plague.

hair Threadlike growth covering the human body, especially the head. Hair styles have meaning in every culture. This was true of the Hebrews and of the first-century world in which the Church began.

OT CUSTOMS AND THEIR MEANING

In ancient Israel, both sexes let their hair grow long. Men notable for their hair are Esau, whose entire body was ''hairy'' (Gen. 25:25; 27:11); Samson, whose hair was associated with his strength (Jdg. 13:5); and handsome Absalom, whose very long hair was much admired (2 Sam. 14:26). In contrast, Elisha's baldness made him vulnerable to insults (2 Ki. 2:23).

The hair of both sexes was carefully dressed. The Talmud speaks of hairdressers who plaited the hair or braided it. Samson's hair was plaited in seven distinct locks or bands (Jdg. 16:13,19). Often sweet-smelling ointments were worked into the hair (Ruth 3:3; Ps. 23:5; Eccl. 9:8). The ''barber,'' mentioned only in Ezek. 5:1, trimmed the hair and beard but generally did not cut it. Carefully dressed hair was a sign of well-being and joy, while unkempt hair represented mourning or shame.

Hair style also had religious significance. The hair at the sides of the head and the beard of the Jewish man were not to be cut. The hair at the front of the head was not to be shaved, for this practice was associated with pagan rites (*compare* Lev. 19:27; 21:5; Deut. 14:1). A person who took a Nazirite vow was to let his hair grow untrimmed (Num. 6:5-18). When the vow was completed, the Nazirite's hair was to be shaved and offered to God as a sacrifice.

Funeral portrait of a bearded Egyptian man from the time of the Roman Empire. His hairstyle was common among Gentiles and non-Romans in the New Testament world.

An elaborate hairstyle worn by Roman women of the late first and early second century A.D. illustrates a biblical admonition written about that time: "Your beauty should not come from outward adornment, such as braided hair" . . . (1 Peter 3:3).

Grey hair is spoken of with respect, as a person so old was thought to be experienced and wise.

NT CUSTOMS AND THEIR MEANING

By NT times, men cut their hair short, although the Jews continued to let the locks of hair at the sides of the head grow long. Length of hair was a mark of distinction between the sexes, a fact which Paul mentions in 1 Cor. 11:14-16. Both Paul and Peter seem critical of braided hair for women (1 Tim. 2:9; 1 Pet. 3:3). Some believe that braids were then a mark of prostitutes. However, in context, each apostle's remark seems more directed against Christian women relying on beauty aids rather than on character.

Anointing the head with ointment was still practiced (Mt. 6:17), and offering to anoint a guest's head was a mark of hospitality (Lk. 7:46).

EXPRESSIONS REFERRING TO HAIR

A number of sayings concerning hair are found in both Testaments. David's complaint that his sins and troubles are "more than the hairs of my head" means that they are "without number" (Ps. 40:12; 69:4). The expression "not a hair of his head will fall to the ground" means that one is totally safe and secure (1 Sam. 14:45; 1 Ki. 1:52). Jesus used this idiom to assure his disciples of God's care in times of persecution (Lk. 21:18). The saying "the very hairs of your head are numbered" implies that God knows everything about the situation of his children and that he cares deeply (Mt. 10:30; Lk. 12:7).

half-shekel tax A payment made yearly by Jewish males over twenty toward upkeep of the Jerusalem Temple. A half-shekel in NT times was worth two drachma, or two days' pay. This payment is generally identified as the "Temple tax" or "tribute money" in modern versions (*compare* Mt. 17:24).

The basis for this tax was "atonement money" that the Lord told Moses to collect from the Israelites whose lives he spared in Egypt. That money was to be used "for the service of the Tent of Meeting" (the tabernacle), and was a memorial reminding each Israelite that God spared him personally when his ancestors were delivered from slavery (*see* Ex. 30:11-16; 38:13).

After the destruction of the Temple in A.D. 70, Vespasian forced the Jews to pay taxes to the temple of Jupiter Capitolinus.

hallelujah (NIV) [hal-uh-LOO-yuh; "praise the Lord!"]. An ecstatic call to worship, found in the later psalms (Pss. 104–150). While typically associated with public worship, perhaps the listeners' response to liturgical readings, it is also found in individual expressions of praise (*compare* Ps. 111:1; 116:19; 146:1).

"Hallelujah" conveys a sense of the joyous exultation shared as the community of faith gathers to worship the Lord.

Silver half-shekel from the time of the first Jewish revolt against Rome (A.D. 66–70). In Jesus' day the Jews paid this amount for the annual Temple tax with the Greek didrachmon or 2-drachm coin.

463

That same sense of exultation overflows in Rev. 19, the only NT chapter in which "hallelujah" is found. There the multitude in heaven praises God because of his triumph over earthly "Babylon" and because Christ himself is about to lead the armies of heaven against the wicked on earth.

"Hallelujah" has been adopted in many Christian traditions, especially in Eastern Church liturgy. *See also* Alleluia.

hallowed (KJV) To be set apart or treated as holy. In the KJV and other older versions, "hallowed" is often used to indicate that which God himself has set apart, such as the Sabbath (Gen. 2:3). In modern English versions, "hallowed" is retained only in the Lord's Prayer, "Hallowed be your name" (Mt. 6:9; Lk. 11:2). In Hebrew thought, the "name" represents and expresses the thing named. Thus this phrase in the Lord's Prayer expresses the worshiper's respect for God and his or her commitment to demonstrate this respect by living a holy life. *See also* Holy.

Ham The second(?) son of Noah. **Brothers:** Shem, Japheth. **Scripture:** Gen. 9:18–10:20.

BACKGROUND

Ham's sons are progenitors of populations which settled in major geographical areas: Cush (Ethiopia), Mizraim (Egypt, including Africa), Put (Libya), and Canaan (Palestine). In Scripture, Egypt is sometimes spoken of as "the land of Ham" (Ps. 78:51; 105:23,27). While there is no distinct Hamitic race, modern scholars speak of a Hamitic family of languages. *See also* Nations, Table of.

Genesis 9:20-27 describes an incident in which Ham showed disrespect for his father. The reason why Noah awakened and cursed Canaan, one of Ham's sons, continues to puzzle Bible students. One suggestion is that Canaan was tainted with his father's weakness. Or possibly the two incidents are not related in a cause/effect sense—biblical curses do at times have a predictive dimension. *See also* Curse.

LEARNING FROM HAM'S LIFE

The Ten Commandments state, "Honor your father and your mother" (Ex. 20:12), a principle reiterated throughout both the OT and NT (*see* Prov. 6:20; Eph. 6:1,2; Col. 3:20). Thus, when Ham showed disrespect toward his father, he brought upon himself and his heirs swift judgment. Whenever this principle is broken, it brings strife and disharmony to the family, breaking the fellowship between the individual members and creating bitterness. This, in turn, brings dishonor to the Lord who created the family unit and who chose to illustrate his relationship to believers in terms of a "heavenly" family (Eph. 2:19; 3:14,15). It is important, therefore, that we avoid the sin of Ham and properly "honor" our parents, providing models for our own children to follow. (*See* Eph. 6:1-4; Col. 3:20,21.) *See also* Honor; Obey.

Haman [HAY-muhn; meaning unknown]. Notable as the Persian noble whose plot to destroy the Jewish people was thwarted by Mordecai and Esther, about 457 B.C. **Father:** Hammedatha. **Scripture:** Esther.

BACKGROUND

Haman was prime minister of Persia under Xerxes. His pride was wounded when Mordecai, a minor government official, refused to kneel when he passed. Furious, Haman determined to wipe out Mordecai's race, the Jews. Through a series of events, Haman's plot was thwarted and he suffered the fate intended for Mordecai—he was hanged on the gallows he had built to punish the Jew. *See also* Gallows; Hanging; Purim.

LEARNING FROM HAMAN'S LIFE

Haman illustrates the destructive impact of pride. He was honored by Xerxes (Esth. 3:1,2) and immensely wealthy (3:9), and he boasted about both (5:10-12). Yet he revealed, "All this gives me no satisfaction as long as I see that Jew Mordecai sitting at the king's gate" (5:13). Haman's pride stimulated anger and hatred of those who would not flatter him, and so distorted his perspective that he was willing to wipe out an entire race because of one person's slight. However, when Haman acted on his anger, he set in motion of series of events that destroyed not Mordecai, but himself.

Pride is as destructive today. The proud man boasts but finds no satisfaction. His pride stimulates destructive emotions that, if acted upon, bring troubles to others and, ultimately, to himself. It is no wonder Scripture says that "God opposes the proud but gives grace to the humble" (Jas. 4:6).

hammer (1) A wooden-headed mallet used to drive tent pegs, as in Jdg. 4:21; (2) a tool, usually with a stone or infrequently metal head, used by stonemasons or metalworkers, as in 1 Ki. 6:7; Isa. 44:12; (3) a weapon, such as a war club or battle ax, as in Jer. 51:20. Symbolically, the hammer represents great, destructive power (Jer. 23:29; 50:20-23).

Hammurabi, Code of [Hahm-oo-RAH-bee]. The systematic legal code of Babylon inscribed on a black dionite pillar measuring 8 feet (2.4 meters) in height. The pillar also includes a prologue and epilogue which glorify Hammurabi, the powerful ruler of Babylon from 1792–1750 B.C. While Hammurabi is not mentioned in the Bible, his name and times are known from texts recovered by archaeologists. The Code of Hammurabi is a lengthy inscription which reveals the legal provisions of a culture that existed around the age of the patriarchs, in particular regulations regarding commercial, social, domestic, and moral life. It, with other ancient law codes, gives insight into customs reflected in Gen. 12–50. Furthermore, specific laws from Hammurabi's code are often compared and contrasted with the way parallel issues are presented in the Mosaic code, which dates from some 300 years later. *See also* Law.

This basalt stela contains the legal code of Babylonian king Hammurabi (1792–1750 B.C.): 282 laws which parallel Israel's covenant code in some respects. In the scene at the top of the stela (left) the king worships the enthroned sun god Shamash.

hand The fingers, thumb, palm, and (in Hebrew usage) the wrist. The hand is mentioned some 1,600 times in the OT, often symbolically or in idiomatic expressions, frequently serving as a symbol of power or ability. For example, the "hand of God" indicates both sovereignty and divine action. *See also* Gestures.

handbreadth *See* Weights and Measures.

handmaid (KJV) (1) A female slave or servant; (2) when used by a person of herself, an expression of humility (Ruth 3:9; 1 Sam. 1:11; Lk. 1:38). *See also* Servant; Slave.

hands, laying on of A significant symbolic act described in both OT and NT, the meaning of which depends on the context.

HAND EXPRESSIONS AND THEIR MEANINGS

Expression or Act	Meaning
To offer hand	Give help or aid
To raise hand against	Attack or rebel
To be at the right hand of	Have authority
To place in the hand of	Be subject to
To lay hands on	Ordain, bless
To lay hands on	Injure or kill
To stretch out hand	Punishment of wicked, help for God's own
To relax the hand	Fail in a duty
To bury the hand	Be lazy
To drop the hands	Weakness
To strengthen hand	Make strong, resolute
To lay hand on mouth	Be silent
To put hand on head	Display grief
To wash hands	Express innocence, cleanse ritually
To put hand to	Go to work at
To lift hands	Bless, pray, ask help
To kiss one's hand	Act of worship
To kiss another's hand	Act of respect
To fill the hand	Consecration, commitment
To require at hand of	Liability for
To put hand under thigh	Take a solemn oath
Hand is with	Take sides with
Hand of the Lord upon	Utter prophecy
Hand not reach	Power limited
Hand of the Lord heavy	Punishment experienced
Hollow of the hand	Place of security
At your hand	From you

Above: Syrian envoys to Egypt raise their hands to ask for help from Pharaoh Tutmose IV (1425–1417 B.C.); detail of a tomb painting at Thebes. In ancient Near Eastern cultures, lifting an open palm was a gesture of supplication (Ex. 9:33; 17:11; Ps. 28:2).

Right: Women and children clap their hands as they follow musicians celebrating the accession of Elamite prince Ummanigash; relief from the palace of Ashurbanipal, Nineveh, about 640 B.C. In Scripture, the Psalmist exhorted, "Clap your hands, all you nations" (47:1).

Laying on of hands may indicate identification, transferrence of a gift or a curse, and/or ordination.

1. *Sacrifice.* Anyone bringing a sacrifice laid hands on the head of the animal before it was killed (Lev. 4:4,24). This act identified the offerer with the substitute about to die for the offerer's sins. This relationship is important. The NT calls us to identify ourselves with Christ, who died as a sacrifice for our sins (Rom. 6:1-14; 2 Cor. 5:20,21). *See also* Sacrifice; Scapegoat.

2. *Blessing.* A person blessing another laid hands on the one receiving the blessing (Gen. 48:14). For example, Jesus laid hands on children to bless them (Mt. 19:15), and in two cases, the Holy Spirit was given by the apostles to new converts by laying on of hands (Acts 8:17; 19:1-7). In the first instance, the act of transferring the gift of the Holy Spirit authenticated the authority of the apostles over the Samaritan as well as the Jewish church. *See also* Bless.

3. *Healing.* In many cases, healers laid hands on the sick or disabled (*see* Mk. 5:23; Lk. 4:40; Acts 9:12). Here the act clearly indicates transferrence of God's healing power.

4. *Testifying.* Witnesses who testified against a blasphemer were to place their hands on his head when he was about to be executed, thus placing all the guilt of his deed upon him and absolving the community (Lev. 24:14).

5. *Ordination.* Old Testament priests and Levites were ordained by laying on of hands (Lev. 8:14; Num. 8:12), as was Joshua as Moses' successor (Num. 27:23). Furthermore, laying on of hands was

adopted for ordination in the NT church (Acts 6:6; 13:3). The ordination ceremony seems important primarily to affirm before the faith community the divine gifts and calling of the leadership. Only in Timothy's case is laying on of hands associated with imparting a spiritual gift (1 Tim. 4:14; 2 Tim. 1:6).

hanging [Heb., *talah*]. (1) Exhibition of a corpse after execution (Deut. 21:22,23); (2) execution on the "gallows" (such as those erected by Haman), probably a sharpened pole for impaling the victim. [Heb., *hanaq*]. (3) used of the suicide by strangulation of Ahithophel (2 Sam. 17:23; *compare* Mt. 27:5). [Gk., *kremannumi*]. (4) used of Jesus' crucifixion (Lk. 23:39; Acts 5:30; *compare* Gal. 3:13).

The method of execution used in Israel was stoning, not strangulation (Josh. 7:25). However, hanging the corpse of an executed criminal served as a visible reminder to the community of the penalty for heinous crimes. Nevertheless, the body was to be buried before evening (Deut. 21:22,23; Josh. 8:29; *compare* Mt. 27:57). Pharaoh's baker was hanged, but whether this indicates the method of execution in Egypt or the exposure of his dead body is unknown (Gen. 40:18-22).

hangings (KJV) [Heb., *qela'im*]. (1) The curtains or tapestries of the tabernacle (Ex. 36:37); (2) drapes used in pagan cult worship (2 Ki. 23:7); and (3) curtains hung in the garden of Xerxes' palace (Esth. 1:6). · *See also* Tabernacle.

Hannah [HAN-uh; "grace," "favor"]. The mother of Samuel, Israel's last judge, 1095 B.C. **Husband:** Elkanah. **Son:** Samuel. **Scripture:** 1 Sam. 1:1–2:11.

BACKGROUND

Hannah lived in the days of the judges. She was childless, taunted by her husband's second wife. One year, when Israel gathered to the tabernacle at Shiloh, Hannah bargained with God. If he would give her a son, the child would be dedicated to the Lord. God heard her prayer, and the child Hannah bore, Samuel, became Israel's last judge, who anointed both Saul and David king.

LEARNING FROM HANNAH'S LIFE

Hannah's anguish over her childlessness motivated fervent prayer (1:10). Her vow to God is unique, for Hannah was willing to give up to the Lord what God gave to her (1:10). Unlike many, Hannah was careful to praise God when her prayer was answered (2:1-10), and she faithfully kept her vow to surrender Samuel to the Lord's service (1:22). In all these, Hannah models important aspects of the believer's prayer life.

The story of Hannah also illustrates God's grace: (1) God had given Hannah a supportive and loving husband (1:4,5,8); (2) the son she gave God grew into a godly man; and (3) Hannah later bore three more sons and two daughters (2:21). Thus, God answered Hannah's petition beyond her original expectations. Paul declares God is able "to do immeasurably more than all we ask or imagine" (Eph. 3:20).

Hannah's anguish over her childlessness motivated fervent prayer, which Eli mistook for drunkenness (left). She was faithful to her vow and presented Samuel to God's service under Eli (right). Detail of an illuminated manuscript, 12th century A.D.

467

Hanukkah [HAHN-uh-kuh; "dedication"]. The eight-day festival celebrating the completed cleansing of the defiled Temple in 164 B.C. after the victory of Judas Maccabaeus over the Seleucids in 167 B.C. The festival is mentioned only in Jn. 10:22, where it is called the "Feast of Dedication." Hanukkah is still celebrated annually by the Jewish people. Today it is called the Festival of Lights, commemorating the story of the flame which burned for eight days in the Temple lampstand despite the fact there was only one day's supply of oil. *See also* Calendar; Maccabees.

Hanukkah lamps traditionally had eight receptacles for oil, one for each day of the festival, but after the destruction of Jerusalem the seven-branched lampstand gradually became the symbol of Judaism and displaced the hanukiot in its own feast.

happy (1) A condition of well-being which comes with divine blessing or as a consequence of righteous living; (2) in modern versions, a feeling of pleasure, contentment, joy.

Hebrew and Greek words translated "happy" in older versions and the RSV mean "blessed." The NIV and some modern paraphrases use "happy" in the contemporary sense of feelings of pleasure. *See also* Beatitudes; Bless; Contentment; Joy.

hardening of the heart Stubborn, willful resistance to the will of God. A number of Hebrew verbs are translated "harden" in English versions. Among them are words that mean "to be obstinate," "to make the heart strong against," "to be stubborn," "to resist," "to be closed, insensitive, or blind to."

Often persons are portrayed as hardening their own hearts (Ex. 8:32; 9:34,35; Deut. 15:7). However, God also hardens human hearts (Ex. 4:21; 7:3; 14:4; Deut. 2:30; Isa. 63:17). There is no contradiction here. The OT views each person as responsible for his own choices, so that

Line drawings of harp players depicted in Egyptian tomb paintings.

God's action does not lessen human responsibility.

The case of Pharaoh clarifies this. God did not harden Pharaoh against his will. God hardened Pharaoh's heart in direct consequence of Pharaoh's stubborn rebellion. God simply revealed more of himself and his power through the succeeding plagues, revelation against which Pharaoh fought all the harder. As the heat of the sun hardens clay but softens wax, so the light of divine revelation hardens those who resist the Lord but softens those who are responsive to him (*compare* Rev. 9:20, 21; 16:10,11).

harlot (KJV) [Heb., *zonah*]. (1) A woman who exchanges sex for money. Two other Hebrew terms are used in Proverbs of the common prostitute. [Heb., *qedeshah*]. (2) A woman who serves as a cult prostitute in a fertility religion, as in Gen. 38:21; Deut. 23:17; and Hos. 4:14; (3) figuratively, a symbol of idolatry.

Warnings that Levites must not marry prostitutes or have daughters who are prostitutes (Lev. 21:7,9) and that money earned by prostitution must not be used to pay a vow (Deut. 23:18) suggest that prostitution was not uncommon in Israel. Archaeology has shown it was very common in other ancient cultures. While OT Law prescribes the death penalty for harlotry, the penalty was seldom exacted (Gen. 38:24; Lev. 21:9; Deut. 22:21). *See also* Prostitute.

harp [Heb., *kinnor*]. A hand-held stringed instrument. The *kinnor* was probably not a harp, as in many versions, but a lyre. This musical instrument was common in Israel by the time of King David. David played the lyre to calm King Saul (1 Sam. 16), and it was one of the musical instruments used in Israel's worship (1 Chr. 15:16; 25:6). Representations of the *kinnor* suggest it was an instrument composed of a sound box and two curved arms connected by a crossbar at the top with twelve attached strings. *See also* Lyre.

Many consider the *nebel*, rendered "psaltry" in the KJV, a true harp. Metal parts of standing harps have been recovered from Ur, and wooden Egyptian harps have been preserved. However, no known image of the *nebel* exists, and its exact nature is uncertain.

hart (KJV) A male deer. *See also* Deer.

harvest (1) To gather in a crop; (2) the time of year when crops mature and are gathered. Several of Israel's festivals are associated with thanksgiving for harvests. *See also* Agriculture; Thresh; Winnow.

Figuratively, harvest is the time of fulfillment. As the actions of people and nations mature, those who do evil will reap punishment (Prov. 22:8; Hos. 10:13-15; Rev. 14:15), while those who sow righteousness will reap reward (Hos. 10:12; *compare* Gal. 6:8). In one parable, Jesus identifies God's harvest time as the end of the age (Mt. 13:36-43). *See also* Judgment; Judgment Day.

The harvest has other symbolic meanings in Scripture. Jesus spoke of fields ready for harvest when he sent his disciples out to preach (Lk. 10:2; Jn. 4:35). These fields represent men and women ready to respond to the Gospel message. Furthermore, divine discipline produces a "harvest of righteousness" (Heb. 12:11), as do the efforts of peacemakers (Jas. 3:18).

hate (1) To reject decisively; (2) to have a strong negative emotional response or antagonism toward a person or thing.

DECISIVE REJECTION

In our culture, hatred is perceived primarily as an emotion. However, in Scripture, the emphasis is often on volition. One who hates decisively rejects something. This fact helps us understand biblical statements about God's hatred. Scripture affirms that God hates evildoers (Ps. 5:6), pagan worship (Deut. 12:31), practices like lying and perjury (Prov. 6:16-19), injustice (Mic. 3), and even the worship of his sinning people (Isa. 1:14; Amos 5:21). This means that God detests and rejects each of these things. Thus, the godly person will love what God loves, and hate, in the sense of detest and decisively reject, what God hates (Ps. 119:128; 139:21).

The famous statement that God loved Jacob and hated Esau (Mal. 1:3; Rom. 9:13) means that God, in his electing love, chose Jacob to receive his covenant promises, while decisively rejecting any claim of Esau to them. The statement does not mean God was actually antagonistic toward Esau. Far from cursing Esau, God blessed him. Genesis tells us that when the two brothers met after twenty years, Esau grandly refused Jacob's gifts, saying, "I already have plenty, my brother. Keep what you have for yourself" (Gen. 33:9).

Scenes of harvest activity on an estate supervised by Menna, the overseer of government lands, who watches from a papyrus shelter; from his tomb, about 1420 B.C.

469

Jesus' call to hate one's family (Mt. 10:37; Lk. 14:26) and even to "hate [one's] life in this world" (Jn. 12:25) is a command, not to hate emotionally, but to reject anything which might claim a higher allegiance than God.

ACTIVE ANIMOSITY

There is also an element of active animosity in hatred. God detests what he rejects and will act to punish the evildoer. Yet God's hatred is distinctive from human hatred: (1) It is always directed against evil, and (2) God's hatred is not an overpowering emotion, but is always balanced by his love, compassion, mercy, holiness, and other attributes.

When human hatred is addressed in Scripture, it is portrayed as a destructive emotion to be avoided. Hatred as active animosity flows from man's sin nature (Gal. 5:20), and it is associated with violence (Prov. 29:10). Jesus explains that the divine law against murder is a condemnation of hate-filled anger, for anger motivates violence and revenge (Mt. 5:21,22; compare 1 Jn. 3:15).

Man's active animosity and rejection is often directed against God as well as other people. "Those who hate him [God]" are persons who turn from God to idols and fail to keep his covenant (Deut. 7:10). Jesus was greeted with such active animosity that he was crucified, demonstrating the truth of his statement that the world hated him (Jn. 15:25). Christ further warned the disciples, "All men will hate you because of me" (Mt. 10:22). Another passage explains, "Everyone who does evil hates the light" (Jn. 3:20).

The NT calls Christ's followers not to hate but to love others. The worldly wisdom of Jesus' time counseled, "Love your neighbor and hate your enemy." But Jesus himself said, "Love your enemy and pray for those who persecute you" (Mt. 5:43-48). Vengeance belongs to God, who alone can punish justly. By rejecting hatred in favor of love, the believer will "not be overcome by evil, but overcome evil with good" (Rom. 12:17 -21).

Hawk statue carved from serpentine stone with restored metal parts originally fashioned in gold (1550–1070 B.C.). Hawks are still common in Palestine, though they migrate south in the fall (see Job 39:26).

hawk [Heb., *nes*]. A small bird of prey, listed among unclean birds in Lev. 11:13-19 and Deut. 14:11-18; *nes* was used of any of the many different species of this keen-eyed, swift predator which were native to Palestine.

head [Heb., *ro'sh*; Gk., *kephalē*]. The top part of the body, containing the brain, the eyes, ears, nose, and mouth. The Hebrews did not think of the head as the seat of intellect but did associate it with personal identity. Thus, to swear by one's head (Mt. 5:36) was to make an oath guaranteed by his or her life itself.

Metaphorically, the head has many meanings in the OT. These include (1) the source or beginning, as of a river; (2) the top, as of a mountain; (3) a chief or ancestral head of a family or clan; or (4) high rank in the military, judicial, or other hierarchy.

In the NT the Church is viewed primarily as an organism, and "head" is used in an organic rather than organizational sense.

The organic context helps us understand three theologically significant uses of "head" in the NT.

1. *Christ is head of the Church* (Eph. 1:22; 4:15; 5:23; Col. 1:18; 2:10,19). These passages describe Jesus as the one who sustains, protects, and guides the Church to whom he himself gives life.

2. *The husband is head of the wife* (Eph. 5:22-33). Here the emphasis is on the role of an organic head in nourishing life. This is seen in the parallels Paul draws. As Christ gave himself up for the Church, so the husband should be willing to help the wife achieve her spiritual potential (5:26,27). He "feeds and cares for" his wife "just as Christ does the church" (5:29). *See also* Submission.

3. *Man is head of woman* (1 Cor. 11:1-16). In this controversial passage, Paul says that "the head of every man is Christ, and the head of the woman is man, and the head of Christ is God" (11:3). Here head may be used primarily in a historic sense rather than in an organic or hierarchical sense. We know that inherent superiority/inferiority is not at issue; for, as Paul argues, the order of creation established by God indicates that "woman is not independent of man, nor is man independent of woman" (11:11)—their roles are interdependent and complementary.

headband A strip of cloth or leather commonly used in the ancient Near East to secure a headcovering or to keep hair in place. The Hebrews used squares or strips of cloth to cover their heads in summer and winter. While some headcoverings were turban-like, often a simple square of cloth was draped over the head. It was held in place by a headband. *See also* Covering the Head.

healing, gift of One of the *charismata*, or "grace gifts," given to some for the benefit of the church (1 Cor. 12:9,28,30). In Scripture, God identifies himself as the healer of his people (Ex. 15:26), and Jesus performed many notable healings in his public ministry (Mt. 8:14-17; Lk. 5:17). The early ministry of the apostles was also marked by healings (Acts 5:12-16). Yet the healings performed by Jesus and the apostles served as signs authenticating them as God's messengers, which is not the case with the gift of healing Paul mentions in 1 Corinthians.

While God at times does act to heal his people, he does not always heal. Paul exercised this spiritual gift (Acts 28:8,9); yet he did not heal Epaphroditus (Phil. 2:25-28), nor Timothy whom he advised to take medicinal wine for his chronic stomach problem (1 Tim. 5:23). In addition, Paul himself suffered from what was probably a chronic sickness which God chose not to heal (2 Cor. 12:1-10). *See also* Health.

James places healing within the context of the church and its elders. By the laying on of hands, the elders have a specific role to play for anyone seeking divine healing (Jas. 5:14,15). *See also* Elder.

health Total well-being—physically, spiritually, and psychologically. A close association of sin and sickness is established in (1) the covenant promise of God to maintain the health of his obedient people, Ex. 15:26; (2) the symbolic use of sickness to represent sin, Isa. 1:5,6; and (3) the fact that one purpose of the Messiah's suffering is to bring total healing to his own, Isa. 53:5. That the healing won in the atonement is physical as well as spiritual is attested by Mt. 8:17. The truly healthy person has a harmonious relationship with God, with others, and with his own body.

RELATIONSHIP WITH GOD

The Bible affirms that God is the source of spiritual and physical health. He "forgives all your sins and heals all your diseases" (Ps. 103:3). Modern medicine is currently rediscovering the relationship of

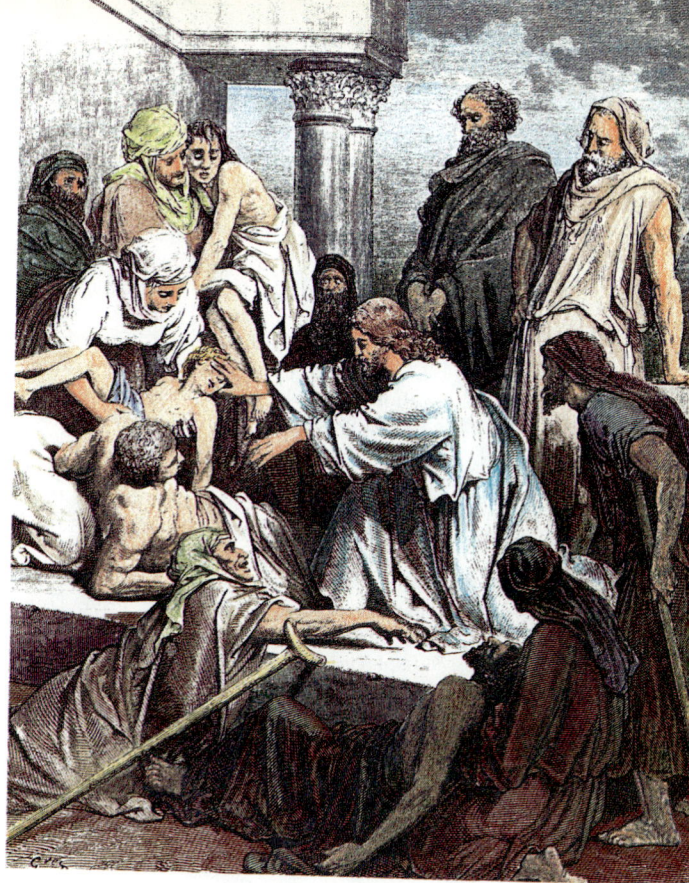

spiritual and psychological well-being to physical health. To be physically healthy, therefore, it is important to maintain a close relationship with God and to appropriate his spiritual forgiveness.

While loss of health is associated in Scripture with sin, sins are not the direct cause of most physical illness. Paul and other godly members of the NT church suffered from illnesses (*compare* 2 Cor. 12:7,8; 1 Tim. 5:23), and we can hardly view their health problems as punishment for personal sins. Jesus corrected his disciples when they expressed this view and asked him whose sin caused a man to be born blind. Jesus said, "Neither this man nor his parents sinned, but this happened

Engraving by Gustav Doré depicts a common event in Jesus' ministry: "Great crowds came to him, bringing the lame, the blind, the crippled, the dumb, and many others, and laid them at his feet; and he healed them" (Mt. 15:30).

An example of Roman hygiene, these marble latrines from Ephesus have a channel for running water to carry away waste. Roman cities in New Testament times were probably healthier than most.

471

Marble thank offering for the cure of a leg. The inscription reads: "Tyche [dedicated this] to [the deities] Asklepios and Hygieia [as a] thank offering." Jews could present sacrifices as thank offerings for healings, among other things.

so that the work of God might be displayed in his life" (Jn. 9:1-3).

Nor can every loss of physical health be repaired by sufficient faith. Again, Paul, Timothy, and others, whose faith we can hardly doubt, struggled with ill health. While a study of Jesus' healing miracles shows that a measure of faith was often a condition of healing (*see* Mt. 9:29; Lk. 17:19; 18:42), other healings give no indication that faith had a direct role (*see* Lk. 13:11-13; 14:4; 22:51). God is our healer, but in his wisdom he may choose not to restore physical health and well-being. In such cases, we need to hear, with Paul, the words which assure us of God's presence and his continuing love: "My grace is sufficient for you, for my power is made perfect in weakness" (2 Cor. 12:9). Thus, the grace and power of God are at times displayed in maintaining a whole, healthy spirit within a weak or even powerless body.

MAINTAINING PHYSICAL HEALTH

Maintaining fellowship with God is one aspect of maintaining physical health. Scripture offers other prescriptions as well.

Moral prescriptions include self-control

Statue of a sick Egyptian man (1580–1200 B.C.). For the Israelites, dust, dirt, sewage, insects, rodents, and farm animals were constant "companions" and effective disease carriers, often thwarting the Law's provision for good health practices.

in eating and drinking. Believers are to view their bodies as temples of the Holy Spirit and to care for them. Prohibition of homosexual and promiscuous heterosexual acts clearly has a positive impact on health.

Several of the provisions of Mosaic Law had public health impact. Deuteronomy 23:12,13 tells Israel to set up latrines outside their camp and to carefully cover excrement. Persons with communicable diseases were quarantined (Lev. 13,14), and those with possibly infectious discharges were isolated (Lev. 15:2-8). Special cleansing was required after touching the dead (Num. 19:11-22), and washing with running water was often prescribed in ritual cleansings (Lev. 15:6-13). If the laws given Israel by Moses some 1,400 years before Christ had been followed in European cities in the Middle Ages, many of the plagues that devastated medieval Europe might have been avoided.

While little is said in the Bible of physicians (Gen. 50:2; 2 Chr. 16:12; Jer. 8:22; Mk. 5:26; Col. 4:14), it is clear there were those who treated the sick. Jesus himself said, "It is not the healthy who need a doctor, but the sick" (Lk. 5:31).

Similarly, little is said of medicines. Yet references to local treatment with salves and plasters are found in the OT (Isa. 1:6; 38:21; Jer. 8:22). Furthermore, Paul actively encouraged Timothy to use wine medicinally (1 Tim. 5:23), and the Greek word for the oil with which the sick were to be anointed when prayed for suggests medicinal intent (Jas. 5:14-16).

CONCLUSIONS

Taken together, various biblical passages suggest a total approach to physical health. The peace that comes with a close personal relationship with God is vital to our well-being. Making good moral choices and following good health practices are also important. In addition, when one is sick, it is important to receive treatment. None of these practical steps denies God his role as healer, but instead recognizes the fact that God works through natural as well as supernatural means to bring good health to his people. *See also* Disease; Sickness.

hear [Heb., *shema'*]. (1) The physical act of hearing, listening; (2) to understand a message; (3) to respond to the message heard, to obey. [Gk., *akouō*]. (4) To hear and process a message. [Gk., *hypakouō*]. (5) To respond, to obey.

The Hebrew verb is found some 1,050 times in the OT and is generally translated "hear" or "listen to." The context determines whether the emphasis should be on the act of hearing, on processing what is heard, or on responding to it. Typically, when the speaker is God, to "hear" his Word is to understand and obey it. For this reason several newer English versions accurately translate *shama'* as "obey," as in Ex. 19:5 and Jer. 32:23. Similarly, appeals asking God to "hear" the worshiper's prayer assume that when God hears he will act (*compare* 2 Chr. 6:21-30).

The NT is more analytical in its approach to hearing. At times to "hear" God's Word means to grasp or understand the divine perspective. In one parable, Jesus says the Word that God shares is like seed cast by the sower. It takes root in good soil, that is, the person who "hears the word and understands it" (Mt. 13:23). However, many closed their minds to the message of Jesus (Mt. 13:15). Thus, he said that many who listened to him could not "hear" what he said (Jn. 8:43).

We must accept the perspective God communicates to us. Yet the divine Word is not spoken simply to provide perspective. There is in any Word from God an imperative call to act. Jesus' story of two builders illustrates this fact. The man who built on solid rock represents "everyone who hears these words of mine and puts them into practice" (Mt. 7:24). Likewise,

the man who built on shifting sand symbolizes those who disregard God's revelation. If one fails to act on what he understands, he will lose even his initial grasp of God's truth (Jas. 1:25).

The key NT passage which analyzes hearing is Heb. 3,4. These chapters recall the experience of Israel as it was poised to enter Canaan. When God told his people to go up into the land, they understood his Word. But the people refused to obey. This refusal, Hebrews explains, was due to unbelief. Only a living trust in God will enable a hearer to obey (Heb. 4:2).

Truly "hearing" God's Word is not a matter of the intellect but of the heart. When we trust God with our whole heart, we put what we understand of his will into practice, and in obedience, we find rest.

heart [Heb., *leb*; Gk., *kardia*]. (1) The true inner self; (2) rarely, the physical organ.

In Hebrew thought, the heart was the center of each person's being and intellect. It is with the heart that a man feels, perceives, and makes moral choices. It is also with the heart that one seeks and responds to God.

Many expressions in Scripture illustrate this. As the organ of feeling, the heart despairs (Deut. 28:65), grieves (1 Sam. 2:33), is filled with terror (1 Sam. 28:5), is sad (Neh. 2:2), joyful (Ps. 119:111), or cheerful (Prov. 17:22). Discouragement is to "lose heart" (1 Sam. 17:32), and anger makes the heart "grow hot" (Ps. 39:3).

As the center of man's perceptual life, the heart acknowledges (Deut. 4:39), knows (Deut. 8:5), discerns (1 Ki. 3:9), and has wisdom (1 Ki. 10:24). The heart is the place where God's Word is to be hidden (Ps. 119:11), so that by understanding God's way the believer might not sin against him. With the heart we treasure either God's Kingdom or worldly goods (Mt. 6:21).

As the organ of moral choice, the heart inclines toward evil (Gen. 8:21), prompts action (Ex. 25:2), is deceitful (Jer. 17:9), and devises injustice (Ps. 58:2). In explaining the moral nature of uncleanness, Jesus said that "out of the heart come evil thoughts, murder, adultery, sexual immorality, theft, false testimony, slander" (Mt. 15:19). But the heart can also be upright (Ps. 97:11), steadfast (Ps. 108:1), and full of integrity (1 Ki. 9:4).

The heart also responds, or fails to respond, to God. We are to love God with all our heart (Deut. 6:5). The heart can be

Scene from the Egyptian "Book of the Dead" illustrates the weighing of a dead man's heart against the feather of Maat, symbol of truth. Below the scale sits a monster to whom the heart would be thrown should the judgment be unfavorable. In the Bible, the cleanness and purity of the human heart is God's ultimate concern (Ps. 51:10; Mt. 5:8).

hard (Ex. 8:32) or fully committed (2 Chr. 15:17). *See also* Hardening the Heart. The heart can be set on seeking God (2 Chr. 19:3), or it can be "enticed" away from him (Job 31:9). The heart can be proud (Ezek. 28:2) and stone-like (Ezek. 36:26); yet God can give a new heart of responsive flesh (Ezek. 36:26). A heart can be unrepentant (Rom. 2:5) and unbelieving (Heb. 3:12) or sincere in full assurance of faith (Heb. 10:22).

Thus, whenever we read in Scripture of the human heart, we know that a statement is being made about the very essence of our being.

heave offering (KJV) [Heb., *teruma;* "dedicated gift"]. The *teruma* is not an offering but any sacred contribution transferring ownership of something to God. Such gifts were given to the Levites and priests for their livelihood (Lev. 7:32-34; Num. 18:24-32), were used to help in building the tabernacle and Temple (Ex. 25:2,3) and for support of the Temple generally (2 Chr. 31:10-14). "Heave offering" is a mistranslation not carried over into most mod-

ern English versions. It is generally translated "present" or "contribution" in the NIV.

heaven [Heb., *shamayim;* Gk., *ouranos*]. (1) The created universe beyond earth; (2) the spiritual realm, the home of God; (3) in the phrase, "the heavens and the earth," the whole material universe.

THE UNIVERSE BEYOND EARTH

The rich imagery of the Hebrew language describes the heavens in a variety of ways: They are a gauze curtain (Ps. 104:2 KJV); a tent (Isa. 40:22); a garment (Ps. 102:25,26); the firmament, which some have mistakenly taken to suggest a polished and hammered metal dome (Gen. 1:6-8 KJV; Ps. 150:1 KJV). Other images suggest there are sluice-gates in the heavens through which the rains are released (Gen. 7:11; Isa. 24:18), and the clouds that hold water are wineskins (Job 38:37).

All too often this imagery is used to argue that the Hebrews had a "primitive cosmology." Yet other images, which amazingly reflect modern scientific views,

474

are ignored. For instance, only recently has science proven that the earth exists in the shape of a circle (Isa. 40:22) and hangs in empty space; suspended over nothing (Job 26:7)—concepts presented clearly in the Scriptures millennia ago.

Despite our uncertainty about the details of ancient Hebrew cosmology, we know it affirms two realms: The heavens include the atmosphere and all the space beyond it; the earth is the surface of the planet on which we live. The Hebrews may not have foreseen the development of high-powered telescopes or space probes. Nevertheless, the psalmist "consider[ed] your heavens, the work of your fingers, the moon and the stars. . . ." (8:3a), and Job was a careful observer of heavenly constellations (9:9). Nothing in the Bible conflicts with space exploration and the thrust of science to explore the universe.

THE SPIRITUAL HOME OF GOD
Heaven is often spoken of as the realm of God in the NT (Mt. 3:17; 6:1,9; 7:11; Lk. 11:13; Heb. 1:3; 8:1; 9:24). This use maintains the dualism seen in Hebrew cosmology. God says through Isaiah, "As the heavens are higher than the earth, so are my ways higher than your ways and my thoughts than your thoughts" (Isa. 55:9). Mankind has no access to the thoughts of a transcendent God, except as God reveals them.

Yet God is not limited to the heavens. God's mighty acts in history demonstrate his control over what happens on earth (*compare* Isa. 40:10-31). His Word comes from the realm of heaven and accomplishes his purposes on earth, even as the rain that comes down from the heavens waters the earth and makes it bud and flourish (Isa. 55:10,11). One day the will of God will be done as perfectly on earth as it is now done in heaven (Mt. 6:10).

The NT, using the same metaphorical language, affirms that Jesus "came down from heaven" (Jn. 6:4 KJV), and after the resurrection, Christ returned to heaven (Acts 1:11; Col. 4:1). Yet heaven is not so much a location as the spiritual realm itself, a timeless dimension that touches earth while remaining distinct from it. Paul says that our citizenship is in heaven, implying that we live according to God's laws and values (Phil. 3:20). Furthermore, our treasures are to be in heaven (Mt. 6:20), our true home (Eph. 3:19; Heb. 12:22). Because our lives are oriented to heaven rather than earth, we eagerly look forward to the day

Christ will return from heaven to take us to himself (Acts 1:11; 1 Th. 4:16; 2 Th. 1:7). *See also* Kingdom of God.

THE TOTAL MATERIAL UNIVERSE
The phrase "the heavens and the earth" is often linked with statements of God's cosmic purposes. God, who created the heavens and the earth, has a plan for the universe. At history's end, this present universe will be set aside (Isa. 51:6), and God will create new heavens and a new earth as the home of righteousness (Isa. 65:17; 2 Pet. 3:10-13). Yet the language of "heaven *and* earth" is absent from Revelation. Why? Because finally, at history's end, the ancient separation of heaven and earth will be no more, for "the dwelling of God [will be] with men" (Rev. 21:3).

COLLOQUIAL USE OF "HEAVEN"
While the Bible does not use heaven in the colloquial sense as the place where

Medieval mystic Hildegard's illumination of the new heaven and new earth pictured with three rings: the triune God fills the top one; the middle ring contains the people of God, who "possess the brightness of eternity and seek celestial joys in great glory"; the lower one symbolizes the new world's elements.

475

Early Hebrew (ABOUT 586 B.C.)	Later Hebrew (1ST CENT. A.D.)	Hebrew name
𐤀	א	'alep
𐤁	ב	bet
𐤂	ג	gimel
𐤃	ד	dalet
𐤄	ה	he
𐤅	ו	waw
𐤆	ז	zayin
𐤇	ח	het
𐤈	ט	tet
𐤉	י	yod
𐤊	כ	kap
𐤋	ל	lamed
𐤌	מ	mem
𐤍	נ	nun
𐤎	ס	samek
𐤏	ע	'ayin
𐤐	פ	pe'
𐤑	צ	sade
𐤒	ק	qop
𐤓	ר	res
𐤔	ש	shin
𐤕	ת	taw

believers go after death, that usage is not inaccurate. At death, the believer does come into the presence of God (2 Cor. 5:6-8). There, the dead wait with Christ for history's grand denouement. Then God "will bring with Jesus those who have fallen asleep in him" to receive their resurrection bodies (1 Th. 4:14). If, then, by "heaven" we mean the continuing personal experience of eternal life in the presence of God, our colloquial understanding of heaven is a biblical concept indeed. *See also* Hell.

Hebrew [Heb., *'ibri*]. An ethnic term used of Abraham and the Israelites by foreigners and by the Israelites of themselves (Gen. 39:14; Ex. 2:6,7; 5:3). Later books identify the Hebrews with all Israel (1 Sam. 13:3,4).

The origin of the name is unknown. However, it may have been derived from the patriarchal ancestor, Eber (*compare* Gen. 10:21; 11:16-26). Attempts to identify the Hebrews with *hapiru*, a Near Eastern designation for stateless wanderers and marauders, have been abandoned; there is no linguistic relationship between the two terms.

Hebrew language A member of a family of Semitic languages, which includes Aramaic and Arabic. Hebrew is very similar to ancient Ugaritic and Phoenician. Documents written in these languages have helped us understand some obscure Hebrew words. Once critics claimed that many words and phrases in Genesis were of much later origin than the patriarchal era. However, comparison with other Canaanite tongues has shown the antiquity of the Genesis account.

The oldest example of written Hebrew is the Gezer Calendar, written on a child's exercise tablet in the time of Solomon (970–931 B.C.).

The Hebrew alphabet has 22 characters, all of which are consonants. Vowels were not written originally; they were added to the biblical text about A.D. 1000. Hebrew words are constructed on roots of three consonants.

The language itself is complex. Hebrew verb tenses do not specify time, as English tenses do, but portray action. Tenses show whether action is completed (perfect tense) or incomplete, repetitive, or continuous (imperfect tense). There are verb forms for infinitives and participles as well as imperatives. In addition, verbs may appear in one of seven stems.

Thus, the complex Hebrew verb system permits graphic portrayal of action without a need to rely on adverbs.

The language also tended to shape the perception of its speakers. While there are ways in Hebrew to place action in the past, present, or future, the thrust of the language is to describe events as if they are presently happening. Therefore, God's historic acts for his people did not seem lost in the distant past. Each retelling made the events vividly present. The language itself helped Israelites of every era

Glazed tile head of a Semitic man, from the temple of Rameses III, 12th century B.C. The Hebrew people, tribes descended from Abraham, were Semites—that is, ultimately descendants of Noah's son Shem (Gen. 10).

to personally experience what God did for his people.

Hebrew thought was also concrete. Rather than use abstract expressions, Hebrew tends to use metaphors. For instance, "breaking the arm of the wicked" means to make them impotent. "Bitter of soul" means to be miserable. "Lifting up another's head" means to strengthen him. This quality of the language gives it a peculiar power, which is not lost in translation. What, for instance, could more powerfully portray the Messiah's loving humility than Isa. 53:7:

He was oppressed and afflicted,
yet he did not open his mouth;
he was led like a lamb to the
slaughter,
and as a sheep before her
shearers is silent,
so he did not open his mouth.

Imagery is important in translating Hebrew poetry. Hebrew poetry does not rely on rhyme or rhythm but on parallelism of thought. This means that Hebrew poetry alone can be translated into other languages without loss of meaning or power. *See also* Poetry.

Not all the OT was written in Hebrew, nor did Hebrew remain the language of God's people. Ezra 4:8–6:18; 7:12-26; Dan. 2:4–7:28; and Jer. 10:11 are written in Aramaic. Aramaic is the Semitic tongue which became the international language of the Persian Empire. Nehemiah 8:8 may indicate that soon after the Babylonian captivity some Jews were unable to speak their native tongue. However, evidence indicates that Hebrew remained the language of theological discourse and was even used in some correspondence at the time of Christ. Jesus undoubtedly spoke Hebrew and Aramaic as well as *koinē* Greek.

Most Jews did not return to Judah after Babylon's fall. Thousands remained in that city or settled in other major population centers. A hundred and fifty years before Christ, there were so many Jews who could not understand Hebrew that a Greek translation of the OT, called the Septuagint or the LXX, was prepared for them. However, when the Septuagint was adopted as the OT of the Christian church, its use was dropped by the Jewish community. *See also* Septuagint.

Hebrews, Epistle to the

This NT letter was written to Hebrew Christians by an unknown author to demonstrate the superiority of Christ's new covenant to the old covenant (Mosaic Law) under which Israel had lived. References to OT worship ritual suggest Hebrews was written prior to the destruction of the Jerusalem Temple by the Romans in A.D. 70.

BACKGROUND

Severe tensions existed in the early church between Jewish and Gentile Christians. Many, whose roots were in Judaism, insisted Gentile converts adopt a Jewish life-style and abide by OT Law. This teaching stimulated Paul to write to the Galatians. It also precipitated the first council of the young church (Acts 15). *See also* Council of Jerusalem. That council affirmed the freedom of Gentiles from the unbearable "yoke" of the Law, and announced that God by his grace saves through faith alone (15:10,11).

Yet the tension continued to be felt in the Jewish Christian community. Many were drawn to the familiar practices God had ordained for their forefathers. These Christians needed a clear vision of the

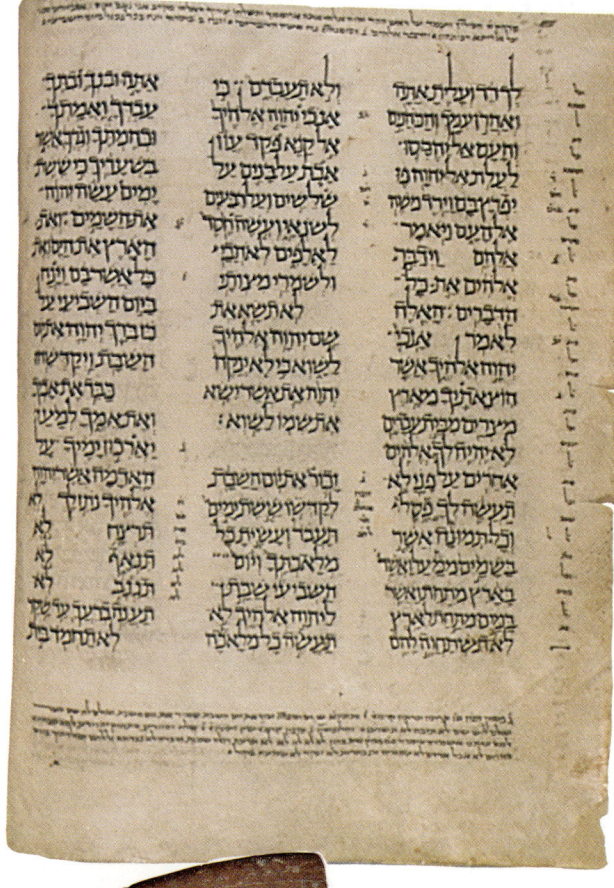

Hebrew "Square Script," familiar as the printed form in modern Hebrew Bibles. Though it was adopted during the exile, the development and inclusion of vowel "points" did not begin until the 5th century A.D. This 9th-century text contains Exodus 19:24–20:17, which includes most of the Ten Commandments.

Eighth-century B.C. Hebrew inscription on an ostracon (pottery fragment) found at the city of Samaria. It shows the flowing script of pre-exilic Hebrew.

relationship of Christianity to OT faith. They particularly needed to see in Christ the reality that OT practices merely foreshadowed. Hebrews was written to meet that need.

This commonly accepted view of Hebrews is supported by a number of facts. (1) The book is sharply focused on critical elements of the OT system, such as priesthood and sacrifice. (2) The author uses terms and forms of argument typical of Alexandrian rabbis of the same period. (3) The author constantly compares and contrasts Christ with elements of the OT system to show how Christ is superior. (4) The need for this Epistle is illustrated by the fact that at least five million Jews lived in various cities outside of Judea in the first century. Some estimate that as many as one person in ten in the Roman Empire was a Jew or an adherent to Jewish religion.

AUTHORSHIP

The author of Hebrews is unknown. The sophisticated Greek writing style and rabbinic arguments suggest he was an Alexandrian Jew, which has led many to

STRUCTURE OF HEBREWS

I. Jesus: God's Final Word	1–4:13
A. Superior to the angels (1,2)	
Parenthesis: 2:1-4	
B. Superior to Moses (3)	
C. Superior to Joshua (4:1-11)	
Parenthesis: 4:12,13	
II. Jesus: High Priest in the Order of Melchizedek	4:14–7:28
Parenthesis: 5:11–6:8	
III. Jesus: The Perfect Sacrifice	8:1–10:18
A. In a new covenant (8)	
B. Of a spiritual tabernacle (9)	
C. Once for all (10:1-18)	
IV. Jesus: Object of Faith	10:19–13:17
A. Faith's perseverance (10:19-39)	
Parenthesis: 10:26-29	
B. Faith's hope (11)	
C. Faith's discipline (12:1-11)	
D. Faith's charges (12:12–13:17)	
Parenthesis: 12:25-29	
V. Epilogue	13:18-25

suppose Hebrews was written by Apollos (Acts 18:18-28). Others argue for Barnabas. The style seems to rule out Paul. Ultimately, as Origen aptly wrote, "God [alone] knows the truth of the matter."

THEOLOGICAL CONTRIBUTIONS

Hebrews is a theological gold mine.

1. *Christ's Superiority.* Hebrews affirms the deity and superiority of Jesus. As the "exact representation" of the Deity, Jesus is God, superior to angels and to Moses as a source of revelation (Heb. 1–4). As high priest of a new order, Jesus is superior in every way to the Aaronic priesthood, and he guarantees salvation. As a living high priest, Jesus provides believers with immediate access to God (Heb. 5–8). Finally, as a sacrifice, Jesus' blood is more efficacious than the blood of OT bulls and goats (Heb. 9,10).

Thus, in every way, Jesus fulfills the "shadow" of the OT and brings us into a relationship with God that is superior to that offered by OT faith (Heb. 8:5; 10:1).

2. *Old and New Covenants.* Hebrews clarifies the nature of the old and new covenants. It shows the limits of the old and the superiority of the new, under which God not only forgives our sins but writes his law on our very hearts (*see* Heb. 8:7-13).

3. *Priesthood.* Hebrews examines the role and nature of priesthood, and shows what it means for believers to have a living high priest.

4. *Sacrifice.* Hebrews defines the meaning of Christ's sacrifice, which perfects the believer and cleanses the conscience.

5. *Christ's Humanity.* Hebrews uniquely affirms the human nature of Jesus and examines what this meant for Christ and means for his people in terms of his qualifications to be our high priest (2:14-18; 5:1-8; 12:3).

6. *Faith.* Hebrews illustrates the value of faith by showing how those with faith respond actively to God (Heb. 11).

MASTERY KEYS

The author writes to show how Christ is superior to OT faith. To understand Hebrews, we need a grasp of the OT. (*See* related articles listed in the Study Guide.) Furthermore, the author's argument is often interrupted by warnings. Trace the main line of argument by initially skipping the warnings (Heb. 2:1-4; 4:12,13; 5:11–6:8; 10:26-29; 12:25-29).

SPECIAL FEATURES

The warnings in Hebrews are addressed to believers to encourage deeper commitment to Christian faith and life.

hedge [Heb., *mesuka*]. (1) A thorn hedge of cut branches or living plants. [Heb., *gedera*]. (2) A fence, usually made of loose stones (KJV). [Gk., *phragmos*]. (3) Any kind of partition, a fence or, as in the NIV, a wall. Hedges protected vineyards (Isa. 5:5; Mk. 12:1) and marked off fields (Lk. 14:23 KJV).

Figuratively, God plants a hedge around his own to protect them (Job 1:10). Also, man's limitations mean that each individual is "hedged in" by his or her inability to know or control the future (Job 3:23).

hedgehog (KJV) Small porcupine-like animals about a foot long, covered with short spines. In Isa. 14:23; 34:11; and Zeph. 2:14,

the habitation of the hedgehog symbolizes desolation. *See also* Owl (NIV).

Hedgehog pendant unearthed at the ancient city of Elam (3000–2900 B.C.), located in modern-day Syria.

heifer A young cow. Heifers were clean animals and were often sacrificed (Num. 19:1-10; Deut. 21:1-9; 1 Sam. 16:2). They were esteemed for their milk (Isa. 7:21, 22), as plow animals (Jdg. 14:18), and were used to thresh grain (Deut. 21:3; Hos. 10:11). Furthermore, since heifers were considered beautiful animals, some women were named "Eglah" after the creatures. A trained heifer symbolized obedience (Hos. 10:11), while a stubborn heifer represented disobedience (Hos. 4:16).

HEBREWS: A READING AND STUDY GUIDE

Chapter	Content Summary	Related Articles
1	God has now spoken to us by Jesus, who is himself God.	Word
2	We must pay close attention to this revelation. Through Jesus' incarnation, God will lift us above angels.	Incarnation Angel
3	Jesus is greater than Moses. We must hear and respond to his voice.	Voice Unbelief
4	When we hear and respond to God's voice, we enter into his Sabbath rest.	Sabbath Rest
5	Jesus is the sinless high priest who has won us eternal salvation. We must build on these foundational truths.	High Priest Maturity
6	We grow to maturity not by questioning, but by counting on God's promises.	Fall Oath
7	Christ's priesthood is of Melchizedek, not Aaron. As our ever-living high priest, he saves completely.	Melchizedek Intercession
8	Christ's priesthood indicates a transition from an old, inadequate covenant to a new, superior covenant.	Covenant
9	OT sacrifices did not provide access to God. Christ's blood cleanses us inwardly so we may serve God.	Blood Sacrifices and Offerings
10	Christ's one sacrifice perfects believers forever. God both forgives and writes his law on our hearts.	Holy
11	Faith, as an active commitment to do God's will, leads to changed behavior.	Faith
12	God is actively involved in our lives, applying discipline to make us more holy. We must not refuse or resist him.	Discipline
13	God calls us to love and serve others together. He will equip us with all we need to do his will.	

heir [Heb., from *yarash*, "to possess, succeed"; Gk., *klēronomos*, "one who receives a portion"]. An heir receives property upon the death of another. Old Testament inheritance law is found in Num. 27:1-11 and Deut. 21:15-17. *See also* Firstborn; Inheritance.

In the NT, "heir" has deep theological significance, indicating a unique right to possess. The appointment of Christ as "heir of all things" establishes the Son's right to the universe which he himself created (Heb. 1:2). Christians are co-heirs with Christ and will share his glory (Rom. 8:17). Paul says, "If you belong to Christ, then you are Abraham's seed, and heirs according to the promise" (Gal. 3:29) *See also* Adoption; Inheritance.

hell [Heb., *she'ol*]. (1) Translated "hell" only in KJV; actually means death or the grave. [Gk., *hadēs*]. (2) The grave in the OT sense, as in Mt. 11:23; (3) the place where the dead await final judgment, as in Lk. 16:23-28. [Gk., *gehenna*]. (4) The place of final punishment, as in Mt. 5:22; Mk. 9:43. *See also* Gehenna; Hades.

THE NT CONCEPT OF HELL

Abaddon	"Destruction" (Rev. 9:11).
Abyss	An adjective, "bottomless," used for a place of smoldering fire and captive demons (Lk. 8:31; Rom. 10:7, "deep"; Rev. 9:1,2).
Gehenna	Greek word derived from Hebrew *ge hinnom*, "Valley of Hinnom," the garbage dump outside Jerusalem which had once served as place for child sacrifice by fire. In the NT it symbolizes the place of eternal fire and final punishment (Mt. 5:22,29, 30; 23:15-33; Mk. 9:43-47; Lk. 12:5; Jas. 3:6).
Hades	Realm of the dead derived from a Greek god by that name (Mt. 16:18; Rev. 1:18; 6:8; 20:13). NT equivalent of OT *she 'ol* "the grave" or "death" (Mt. 11:23; Lk. 10:15; Acts 2:27,31; 1 Cor. 15:55). Not usually a place of punishment, but see Lk. 16:23,24.
Lake of fire	Graphic image used in Rev. 19:20; 20:10,14,15.
Tartaros	Place of eternal punishment in Greek mythology; from verb *tartaroō*, "to confine in Tartaros," only in 2 Pet. 2:4.

The OT speaks of a resurrection for the righteous and the wicked (Dan. 12:1-3), but does not deal with the question of what happens to the individual after death. While the NT does speak of eternal destiny, only *gehenna* shares today's popular meaning of "hell."

Jesus himself associates *gehenna* with fire that burns eternally, and he stated that fiery punishment has been prepared "for the devil and his angels" (Mt. 25:41). Revelation gives us the clearest picture of the eternal destiny of the lost. Describing Satan's doom, Rev. 20:10 says, "The devil, who deceived them, was thrown into the lake of burning sulfur, where the beast and the false prophet had been thrown. They will be tormented day and night for ever and ever." The passage goes on to describe a final judgment: anyone whose name was not found in Christ's book of life "was thrown into the lake of fire" (20:15). *See also* Judgment Day.

This vision of hell is rejected by some who feel hell is inconsistent with the God of love revealed in Jesus. Yet Jesus himself spoke more often of hell than of heaven. Several biblical concepts may help the believer put hell in perspective.

When God created human beings, he shared his own image and likeness with us. This gift makes each individual far too significant to live a brief, solitary life, then simply cease to exist. Each human being will exist beyond his or her physical death, to find a destiny in eternity. The gift God gave man also brought with it personal responsibility. Man was given the capacity to choose, and with that capacity came the possibility of making wrong, and even disastrous, choices. When Adam fell, his sin brought spiritual death. Sin also brought mankind under God's wrath, for justice demands that sin be punished. Yet human beings were too precious to God to be abandoned, so through Jesus' suffering and death, God provided salvation for everyone who responds with faith to God's self-revelation. *See also* Fall, the; Salvation.

When Jesus said that God created *gehenna* for Satan and his angels, he made a most significant statement. God did not create hell for humanity. Actually, God has acted, at great personal cost, to free us from the threat of eternal punishment. Jesus said, "God did not send his Son into the world to condemn the world, but to save the world through him" (Jn. 3:18). Only willful, continuing refusal to respond to God's revelation of himself can now condemn an individual; the choice of each person's destiny is his or hers alone.

Hellenists Persons who adopted Greek thought, customs, and life-style. The generals who divided Alexander the Great's empire actively promoted Hellenism as a way of unifying diverse peoples. However, Hellenization was resisted by most Jews, who rebelled when the Seleucid rulers of Palestine tried to stamp out Judaism. Nevertheless, Acts 6:1 and 9:29 speak of Hellenistic ("Grecian") Jews. These may have been repatriated Jews, who spoke only Greek, or more liberal Jews who had chosen a Hellenized way of life.

helmet A protective head covering worn by soldiers, usually made of hardened leather or metal. Ancient reliefs show a variety of helmet styles. Assyrian soldiers are shown with conical helmets that have ear flaps or with crested helmets. Roman legionaries wore rugged, close-fitting helmets. Early Israelite forces lacked armor but by the later monarchy were equipped with helmets.

Symbolically, Christians struggling with evil spiritual forces are encouraged to put on the "helmet of salvation" (Eph. 6:17; *compare* 1 Th. 5:8), for assurance of salvation will protect the mind against assaults of doubt and fear. *See also* Armor.

helpmeet A word inaccurately compounded from the KJV translation of Gen. 2:18, which describes Eve as a "help meet for" Adam. This old English phrase translates the Hebrew *'ezer kenedgo,* which means "a helper suitable for" him. Both the context and the Hebrew phrase suggest that Eve was "suitable" because she was Adam's counterpart—a being like, rather than unlike, him, so that she could fully share his life.

helps [Gk., *antilēmpsis;* "burden bearing," "acts of aid"]. The noun occurs only in 1 Cor. 12:28, in the list of *charismata* or spiritual grace gifts given believers by the Holy Spirit. The root of this verb is found in Acts 20:35 and 1 Th. 5:14. This spiritual gift encompasses any helpful act a person can perform to aid another, especially acts that encourage the weak. *See also* Spiritual Gifts.

hem The often embroidered border or fringes on outer garments worn by ancient peoples. Texts from Mesopotamia indicate that the ornamented hem served to identify a person's social role and status, thus representing the person himself.

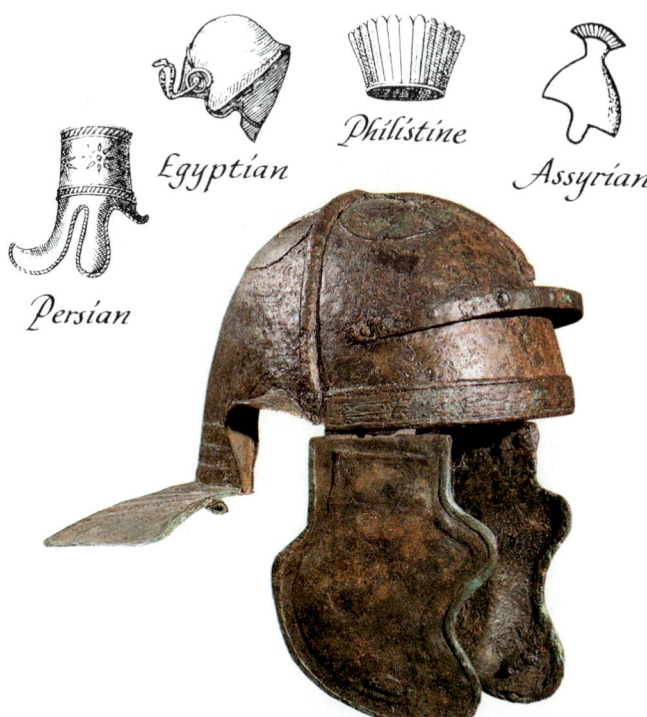

Egyptian

Philistine

Assyrian

Persian

The significance of the hem is illustrated in three biblical incidents. (1) When David cut a piece from the hem of Saul's garment, he was conscience-stricken, 1 Sam. 24:5. David had not harmed Saul, but in cutting off some of his hem, he had in effect assaulted the monarch. (2) The sick woman of Lk. 8:40-48 came up behind Jesus and touched the "edge of his cloak." She touched the hem purposely. In so doing she "touched him"—the person of Christ—and drew healing from Christ. (3) Jesus criticized the Pharisees for making the "tassels on their garments long" (Mt. 23:5). Tassels were to be worn on the hem of the Israelites' garments to remind them of their identity as God's people. Making the tassels long was a claim to spiritual importance.

hemlock (KJV) *See* Gall.

henna A shrub whose leaves are powdered and made into a reddish yellow cosmetic paste used to color fingernails and even the palm of the hand. Henna is called camphire in some English versions.

herald One who brings news. In the OT, the herald is (1) the representative of a ruler, who brings good news, as Isa. 40:9,

Above: Bronze helmet of the type worn by Roman soldiers stationed in first-century Judea. Paul probably had this in mind when he enjoined the metaphorical "helmet of salvation" for the Christians in Ephesus (Eph. 6:17).
Top: Helmets (left to right) for Persian and Egyptian royalty, Philistine and Assyrian soldiers.

Left: A wide, tasseled fringe on the hem of a garment worn by an Assyrian official of King Sargon II (about 710 B.C.). An Israelite's fringe was distinguished by a tassel on each of his cloak's four corners (Num. 15:38; Dt. 22:12).

Below: Excavated theater at Caesarea. With his wealth, Herod, who was an admirer of all things Roman, planned his own "Rome," a port city that became the Roman administrative center of Palestine. Bottom: Herod spent money lavishly on palaces and fortresses for himself and his family. This one, the Herodium, is located in the hills southeast of Bethlehem. Walls with four towers (inset) protected fortress retreat where Herod was buried.

or (2) one who announced the king's presence or will.

In the NT, the Greek equivalent, *kērux*, is translated as teacher or preacher, and the herald's activity, *kērussein*, as evangelizing or preaching the good news of Jesus.

herbs Small plants used to flavor food (2 Ki. 4:39) or gathered for their odor or medicinal use. Bitter herbs were served with the passover meal (Ex. 12:8). Because of uncertainty concerning the specific plants designated by various Hebrew words, a number of terms are incorrectly translated "herb" in the KJV. *See also* Spices.

herder, herdsman A person who cares for flocks or herds of any domesticated animal. Herders were men who worked directly with the animals, as in Mt. 8:33;

Mk. 5:14; Lk. 8:34. Jesus contrasts his commitment to his sheep with the act of a "hired hand" who abandons the sheep when he sees the wolf coming (Jn. 10:11-13). *See also* Shepherd.

heresy [Gk., *hairesis*]. (1) Sects or parties with special doctrines, as the Pharisees (Acts 15:5) or, from an outsider's view, the Jerusalem church (Acts 24:5); (2) parties or factions within the Church (1 Cor. 11:19; Gal. 5:20); (3) false teachings which deviate from revealed truth or promote an ungodly life-style (only in 1 Pet. 2:1). In time, this third sense dominated in the Church, so that in theology "heresy" means erroneous or false doctrine.

Herod [HAIR-uhd]. The family name of several rulers mentioned in the Gospels and Acts. Four generations of Herods were involved in the government of Palestine. *See* IDENTIQUICK: PEOPLE.

Herod the Great The Idumean king of Judea, 37–4 B.C., who beautified the Jerusalem Temple, and ordered boy children in the Bethlehem area killed in an effort to destroy Jesus. **Father:** Antipater. **Scripture:** Mt. 2; Lk. 1:5.

BACKGROUND

Herod became governor of Galilee in 47 B.C., at the age of 25. By ingratiating himself with a series of Roman rulers, through a series of bloody civil wars, and by murdering rivals, Herod achieved kingship in 37 B.C.

The first dozen years of Herod's rule were dedicated to consolidating his power. These years too were marked by bloodshed, including the execution of his favorite wife, Mariamne I, and all her male relatives. At the end of this period, no

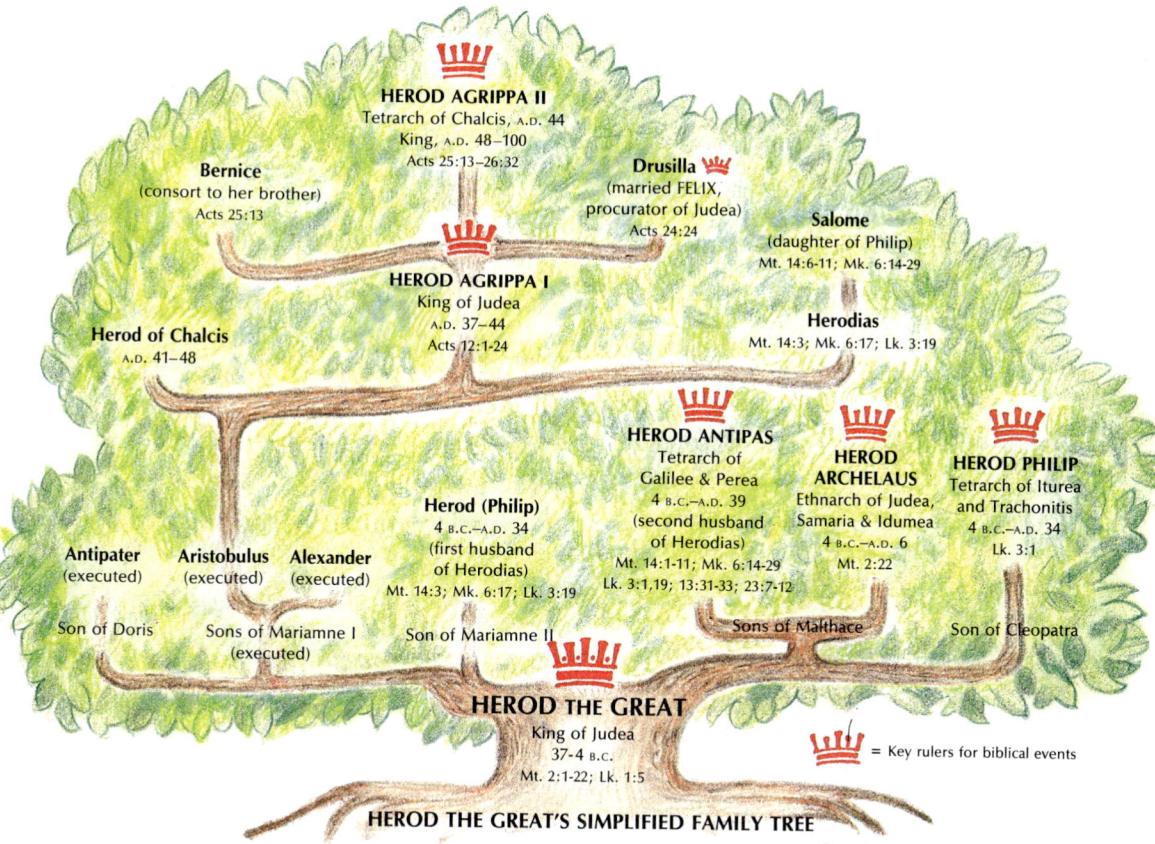

HEROD AGRIPPA II
Tetrarch of Chalcis, A.D. 44
King, A.D. 48–100
Acts 25:13–26:32

Bernice
(consort to her brother)
Acts 25:13

Drusilla
(married FELIX,
procurator of Judea)
Acts 24:24

Salome
(daughter of Philip)
Mt. 14:6-11; Mk. 6:14-29

HEROD AGRIPPA I
King of Judea
A.D. 37–44
Acts 12:1-24

Herod of Chalcis
A.D. 41–48

Herodias
Mt. 14:3; Mk. 6:17; Lk. 3:19

HEROD ANTIPAS
Tetrarch of
Galilee & Perea
4 B.C.–A.D. 39
(second husband
of Herodias)
Mt. 14:1-11; Mk. 6:14-29
Lk. 3:1,19; 13:31-33; 23:7-12

**HEROD
ARCHELAUS**
Ethnarch of Judea,
Samaria & Idumea
4 B.C.–A.D. 6
Mt. 2:22

HEROD PHILIP
Tetrarch of Iturea
and Trachonitis
4 B.C.–A.D. 34
Lk. 3:1

Herod (Philip)
4 B.C.–A.D. 34
(first husband
of Herodias)
Mt. 14:3; Mk. 6:17; Lk. 3:19

Antipater
(executed)

Aristobulus
(executed)

Alexander
(executed)

Son of Doris

Sons of Mariamne I
(executed)

Son of Mariamne II

Sons of Malthace

Son of Cleopatra

HEROD THE GREAT
King of Judea
37-4 B.C.
Mt. 2:1-22; Lk. 1:5

= Key rulers for biblical events

HEROD THE GREAT'S SIMPLIFIED FAMILY TREE

rivals of this cruel, paranoid ruler remained.

The years 25–14 B.C. saw unmatched prosperity in Judea. Herod undertook great building projects. He constructed Caesarea Maritima, a retreat at Masada, and most importantly, began his project to enlarge and beautify the Jerusalem Temple. *See also* Temple, Jerusalem.

Family troubles dominated the years 14–4 B.C. Rumors of plots by his various wives and their children led Herod to execute many of his sons, including his two favorites born to Mariamne I. Hostile, impulsive, dominated by morbid fears, the evil Herod lived out his last years hated by family and people alike. While dying from his last illness, Herod ordered the execution of boy children in the vicinity of Bethlehem in a futile effort to destroy one he was told had been born King of the Jews. However, Joseph, warned in a dream, had taken Mary and the young Jesus to Egypt (Mt. 2).

Just five days before Herod died, he executed another son, Antipater, whom he earlier had designated as his heir. As the end drew near, Herod ordered prominent Jews from every part of the nation to appear in Jerusalem. When they arrived, he had them imprisoned, and left orders that they be killed the moment he died. Herod knew that only in this way could he ensure national mourning rather than joy.

LEARNING FROM HEROD'S LIFE

The Bible makes no observation about Herod. None is needed. Herod stands in stark contrast to the other King presented in Matthew's Gospel—Jesus, the servant King. Herod dedicated his life to gaining power but found no peace. He gained not love but hatred and fear. Today, Herod is only a footnote in history, while Jesus, who gave life rather than took it, is known, loved, and worshiped.

Herodians [Her-OH-dee-uhnz]. A political group mentioned in the Gospels who joined the Pharisees in opposing Jesus (Mk. 3:6; 12:13). The term most likely designates those who were political supporters of Herod Antipas. Their concern was probably to maintain the political status quo, which Jesus appeared to threaten, rather than with the religious issues that alienated the Pharisees from Jesus.

Herod's simplified family tree highlights those who ruled in Palestine after his death in 4 B.C. (see Mt. 2:15).

483

heron Any of the seven Palestinian varieties of wading birds with long necks and legs who subsist on fish and aquatic animals. The term is found only on lists of unclean birds in Lev. 11:19 and Deut. 14:18.

Hezekiah [HEZ-uh-KI-uh; "Yahweh is my strength"]. Godly 14th king of Judah, 728–686 B.C. Notable for contrast with his evil father, Ahaz, and wicked son, Manasseh. **Scripture:** 2 Ki. 18–20; 2 Chr. 29–32; Isa. 36–39.

This mosaic from the ruins of a 4th-century church depicts a heron feeding on a lotus flower.

BACKGROUND

Hezekiah became sole ruler of Judah in 715 B.C. and immediately instituted religious reforms. He reopened and repaired the Jerusalem Temple and reestablished rituals of worship there. Hezekiah aggressively shut down local worship centers ("high places") throughout Judah and destroyed cult objects, such as Asherah poles. Second Kings 18:5,6 says, "Hezekiah trusted in the Lord, the God of Israel. There was no one like him among all the kings of Judah, either before him or after him. He held fast to the Lord and did not cease to follow him."

Hezekiah is portrayed in Assyrian records as the leader of a rebellion against that empire. In preparation for an Assyrian invasion, Hezekiah had a tunnel cut through 1,748 feet (533 meters) of solid rock to provide Jerusalem with access to water (2 Ki. 20:20). An inscription in the tunnel reports that teams of workers began at each end and met in the middle.

Sennacherib led the Assyrian army against Judah. According to Assyrian accounts, that army took 42 cities and some 200,000 prisoners. When a messenger called for Jerusalem's surrender, Hezekiah turned to the Lord. In answer to his prayer, God caused the death of 185,000 of the invaders, and the city was spared.

Near death, Hezekiah appealed to God, who extended his life 15 years. Then, when a delegation from far-away Babylon came to congratulate Hezekiah, the king showed them all the treasures of Jerusa-

When invading Assyrians threatened to cut off Jerusalem's water supply, King Hezekiah ordered a tunnel (right) dug from the Spring of Gihon outside the city walls to the Pool of Siloam within them. Armed only with simple tools, workers began at both ends and hewed through 1750 feet of solid limestone. At the entrance to this passage, dubbed "Hezekiah's Tunnel," the king placed a commemorative inscription, of which the stone on the left is a cast.

lem. Isaiah rebuked the king, seeing the delegation as spies and knowing that the time would come when everything would be taken away to Babylon (1 Ki. 20:12-18).

The sequence of events in Hezekiah's life is unclear in the OT text. However, the following chronology accounts for most biblical and extra-biblical data.

LEARNING FROM HEZEKIAH'S LIFE

The key to understanding Hezekiah is the phrase, "Hezekiah trusted in the Lord" (1 Ki. 18:5). That trust explains the king's vigorous cleansing of Judah and his personal commitment to keep God's Law. Hezekiah exhibited trust in bringing Sennacherib's challenge to the Lord, and his brief prayer is a model for all believers (2 Ki. 19:14-19). Hezekiah exhibited trust even when despondent from his near-terminal illness (2 Ki. 20:1-3), and he expected the sign of healing promised by Isaiah (20:8), not because he doubted God but because he trusted him. Though Hezekiah was imperfect—failing to consult God about the Babylonian envoys and showing a lack of concern for his descendants (20:19)—yet his trust in God is exemplary and worthy of the praise given to him in 2 Ki. 18:5,6.

---

higgaion A notation found in certain psalms indicating how the words should be sung or the melody played. English translations vary from "solemn sound" (KJV) to "melody" (RSV), from "sounding chords" (NEB) to "muted music" (JB). *See also* Psalms.

THE LIFE OF HEZEKIAH

Date	Event
740 B.C.	Hezekiah born
728 B.C.	Hezekiah co-regent with Ahaz
723 B.C.	Samaria conquered by Assyria
722 B.C.	Sargon king of Assyria Northern Kingdom deported
715 B.C.	Ahaz dies; Hezekiah sole king
705 B.C.	Sennacherib king of Assyria
701 B.C.	Hezekiah sick, recovers Deliverance from Assyria Babylonian delegation visits
697 B.C.	Manasseh made co-regent
689 B.C.	Sennacherib destroys Babylon
688 B.C.	Sennacherib fails to take Jerusalem
686 B.C.	Hezekiah dies

high place (1) In rural areas, usually an elevated or hilltop site set aside for cult worship; (2) in cities, a platform or altar.

Old Testament high places were sanctuary sites, set aside by the Canaanites as places to conduct religious rites. These places often featured symbolic stones (Heb., *massebot*), altars for sacrifice or burning incense, a wooden Asherah pole, along with graven or molten images, various vessels, and sometimes a raised platform. The rites conducted at high places often involved immorality and even child sacrifice.

God commanded Israel to drive out the Canaanites, to destroy their idols, and to "demolish all their high places" (Num. 33:52). God was to be worshiped only at the tabernacle, and later the Temple (Deut. 26:2,3). But this command was not carried out. At times the Israelites worshiped God at local high places (*compare* 1 Sam. 9:12-27; 2 Chr. 33:17). But more often these sites served as sanctuaries for Canaanite rituals, and the people worshiped Ashtoreth, Chemosh, Molech, Baal, and other pagan deities (Jdg. 6:25-28; 1 Ki. 11:5-8; 2 Ki. 23:13). These places of unauthorized or pagan worship proved a recurring stumbling block for Israel. Even Solomon, the king who built the Temple of the Lord, fell prey to the lure of these unholy spots when late in his reign he built high places outside Jerusalem dedicated to the gods of his foreign wives (1 Ki. 11:7,8).

After Solomon's death, rulers of the Northern Kingdom (Israel) actively promoted worship at high places in an effort to wean the northern tribes away from religious allegiance to Jerusalem (1 Ki. 12:25-33; 2 Ki. 17:9-12). In the south, the reform movements of godly kings refocused worship at the Temple and involved efforts to stamp out the high places (*see* 2 Chr. 31:1; 34:3-7). Unfortunately, these attempts often failed. Throughout this age of the monarchy, the prophets cried out against worship at Israel's high places. Ezekiel 20:28-31 sums up the religious significance of the high places and their terrible impact on the spiritual life of Israel:

"'When I brought them [Israel] into the land I had sworn to give them and they saw any high hill or any leafy tree, there they offered their sacrifices, made offerings that provoked me to anger, presented their fragrant incense and poured out their drink offerings. Then I said to them: What is this high place you go to? . . .' Therefore say to the house of Israel: 'This is what the Sovereign Lord says: Will you defile yourselves the way your fathers did and lust after their vile images? When you offer your gifts—the sacrifice of your sons in the fire—you continue to defile yourselves with all your idols to this day.' "

As a result, God announced, "I will execute judgment upon you" (Ezek. 20:35; *compare* Jer. 17:3; Ezek. 43:7-9; Mic. 1:5).

However, the Jews turned from idolatry during the Babylonian Captivity: Postexilic prophets do not mention cultic high places in their warnings and exhortations.

These ten large stelae at Gezer may have been a Canaanite high place in the Middle Bronze Age (see 2 Kings 18:4).

high priest (1) The only OT priest qualified to carry out the priesthood's full mediatorial function; (2) Jesus, who serves as the only and eternal high priest of the new covenant.

THE PRIESTHOOD

The functions of the OT priesthood are outlined in Deut. 33:8-10. Priests, drawn from the tribe of Levi and the family of Aaron, (1) guard God's covenant by (2) teaching God's precepts and Law, and (3) offer incense and sacrifice on God's altar. In teaching God's Law, the priests spoke to men on God's behalf. In presenting sacrifices and offerings, the priests spoke to God for men. Thus their role was mediatorial, intended to bond God's covenant people to him. *See also* Priest.

THE HIGH PRIEST OF THE OT

Any of the priests could teach God's written Law and offer sacrifices on behalf of those who committed unintentional sins. But the high priest was unique. The high priest alone bore on his chest, in a sacred pouch, the Urim and Thummim. Through the Urim and Thummim, God gave specific guidance concerning his will in situations not covered in the written Word. Furthermore, the high priest alone could enter the Holy of Holies on the Day of Atonement. There he offered the blood of a sacrifice which made atonement for all the sins of God's people, both unintentional and willful (Lev. 16). In these two ministries, the high priest was the sole mediator of the covenant that God made with Israel. Thus, in these functions, the high priest was a type, or living portrait, of Jesus Christ.

JESUS AS HIGH PRIEST

Hebrews presents Jesus as the High Priest of the new covenant, which was ratified by his death on Calvary. Key passages that deal with Christ's high priesthood are Heb. 4:14-16; 5:1-10; 7:1–8:13.

Christ fulfills the mediatorial role given to the OT high priest. Christ communicates God's will to us, for under the new covenant which Christ administers, God puts his laws in our minds, and writes them on our hearts (8:10). Christ guarantees salvation and the forgiveness of all sins, being "able to save completely those who come to God through him, because he always lives to intercede for them" (7:25).

Hebrews 7:26-28 sums up the significance of Christ's high priesthood in these words:

Such a high priest meets our need—one who

Artist's rendering of the high priest's garments. God specified their design in Ex. 28.

is holy, blameless, pure, set apart from sinners, exalted above the heavens. Unlike the other high priests, he does not need to offer sacrifices day after day, first for his own sins and then for the sins of the people. He sacrificed for their sins once for all when he offered himself. For the law appoints as high priests men who are weak; but the oath, which came after the law, appointed the Son, who has been made perfect forever.

hin A Hebrew unit of liquid measure, of approximately 1 gallon (3.7 liters). The *hin* is most often mentioned in ritual prescriptions of oil and wine added to offerings made to God (*compare* Ex. 30:24; Ezek. 45:24). *See also* Weights and Measures.

hind (KJV) A female deer. *See* Deer.

Hinnom, Valley of *See* Gehenna.

The Hittites were an Indo-European people who settled in what is now northern Turkey. They derived their name from the Hatti, earlier inhabitants of the area. At its height in the 14th century B.C. their kingdom encompassed the whole region of Syria (see Josh. 1:4).

hired man, hireling A worker, typically hired by the day. Old Testament Law protected the workman's rights. Deuteronomy 24:14,15 says, "Do not take advantage of a hired man who is poor and needy, whether he is a brother Israelite or an alien living in one of your towns. Pay him his wages each day before sunset, because he is poor and is counting on it."

Joshua's distribution of the land to tribal and family groups provided property for all Israelites, and provisions in the Mosaic Law preserved the property rights of each family. However, the laws governing sale of land were not enforced, and gradually some families were displaced from their property. Isaiah, in the 8th century B.C., cried out against those who "add house to house and join field to field till no space is left and you live alone in the land" (Isa. 5:8).

This dispossession created a class of landless poor and fostered social injustice. On one hand, because of the large worker pool, the wealthy were able to keep wages low and to defraud laborers (*see* Mal. 3:5). On the other hand, the hireling had little motivation to work hard or take risks for his employer's property (*compare* Jn. 10:13). *See also* Poor.

hiss (KJV) To audibly expel breath between the teeth. In OT times the sound indicated (1) scoffing, derision, contempt, or horror, as in Jer. 19:8; Lam. 2:15; or (2) signaling or calling to, as in Zech. 10:8.

Hittite (1) A great northern empire, which at its height included all of Syria, as in Josh. 1:4; (2) an ethnic group, widespread in Canaan by patriarchal times, as in Gen. 15:20.

The Hittite Empire developed in northern Anatolia (modern Turkey) around 1800 B.C. By 1650 B.C. Hittite armies sacked Babylon. After a decline, the Hittites became a major power again under Suppilulimas around 1350 B.C. At that time the empire included all of Syria. But by 1200 B.C. the empire had been shattered by the aggressive Sea Peoples, among whom were the biblical Philistines. The Hittite Empire was gone, but Hittite culture was preserved in Syrian city-states. Although the empire never included Canaan proper, later Assyrian and Babylonian records refer to the northern fertile crescent area, extending into Syria and Palestine, as the "land of the Hatti [that is, Hittites]."

By Abraham's time, groups of migrant Hittites were already settled in Canaan. Most biblical mentions of Hittites refer to these ethnic groups rather than the Hittite Empire. Abraham purchased a cave from

A late Hittite relief of a cavalryman (10th–9th centuries B.C.).

487

Ephron the Hittite as a tomb for Sarah (Gen. 23). Exodus identifies Canaan as the land of the Hittites, Amorites, Perizzites, Hivites, etc. Bathsheba's husband was Uriah the Hittite (2 Sam. 11).

Scholars have shown that the Sinai covenant follows the form of a Hittite suzerainty treaty such as was used in the 14th or 13th century B.C. Hittite influence may also be seen in the literary form of Deuteronomy. *See also* Deuteronomy. The writing of Deuteronomy in a Hittite literary form known in Moses' time demonstrates the unity of the book.

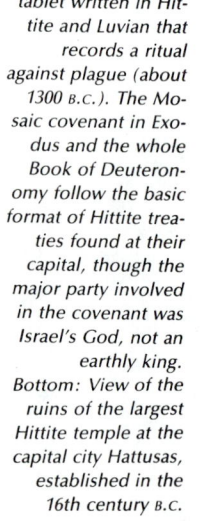

A bilingual tablet written in Hittite and Luvian that records a ritual against plague (about 1300 B.C.). The Mosaic covenant in Exodus and the whole Book of Deuteronomy follow the basic format of Hittite treaties found at their capital, though the major party involved in the covenant was Israel's God, not an earthly king. Bottom: View of the ruins of the largest Hittite temple at the capital city Hattusas, established in the 16th century B.C.

Hivites One of seven peoples who inhabited Canaan from the time of the patriarchs until the Conquest. Scattered communities of Hivites seem to have existed in various parts of Canaan (Gen. 34:2; Josh. 11:3,19). A remnant of this group remained in Palestine in Solomon's time (2 Chr. 8:7). Some scholars believe the Hivites and Horites are the same people, but this identification has virtually no evidence in support. *See also* Horites.

holy, holiness (1) God himself in his essential nature; (2) persons, places, things, and times set apart or consecrated to God and therefore sacred; (3) a quality of character and actions that is in harmony with God's nature and expressed will.

GOD AS HOLY

Scholars debate the meaning of the Hebrew root *q-d-sh*. Etymologically it has been related to glory, to separateness, to purity and brightness, and to "terrible shining."

While the root may be arguable, the Bible teaches that God's essential nature is holy. Both the Hebrew word *qodesh* and the Greek word *hagios* refer to separation from what is temporal or impure. God is Israel's Holy One (Isa. 1:4), and the NT proclaims, "You alone are holy" (Rev. 15:4). The demons' claim to know Jesus as "the Holy One of God" is likely an explicit acknowledgment of Christ's deity (Mk. 1:24; Lk. 4:34) as well as of his messiahship (*compare* Ps. 16:10).

In biblical imagery, God's holiness is associated with fire (*compare* Ezek. 1:4-28; 2 Th. 1:6-10). The very brilliance of the light surrounding God reveals he is awesomely "other." Ezekiel's vision powerfully expresses this sense of awe and "otherness." God approached his prophet in "an immense cloud with flashing lightning and surrounded by brilliant light. The center of the fire looked like glowing metal. . . ." Squinting, the prophet peered deep within the brightness and saw, high on a throne, a manlike figure who "looked like glowing metal, as if full of fire . . . brilliant light surrounded him. Like the appearance of a rainbow in the clouds on a rainy day, so was the radiance around him" (Ezek. 1:4,26-28).

God's holiness is also intimately linked with righteousness. Isaiah says, "The Lord Almighty will be exalted by his justice, and the holy God will show himself holy by his righteousness" (Isa. 5:16). Where there is human moral failure, the brightness of God's righteous anger manifests itself like a purging fire (Lev. 10:1-3; Ezek. 38:18-23; Zeph. 1:14-18).

CONSECRATION

In the OT, that which is associated with God becomes holy. Although associated holiness is different from God's essential holiness, it does set the holy apart from nonholy things. Sacred objects were to be treated with special respect. Thus, God told Moses at the burning bush to take off his shoes, for he was standing on holy ground (Ex. 3:5,6). Among the holy in Israel's religion were places, such as Mount Sinai (Ex. 19:23); persons, such as the priests and Levites (Lev. 21:7); times, such as the weekly Sabbath (Ex. 20:8-11); and all things associated with Temple worship, such as the holy incense, the altar, altar utensils, etc.

The Hebrew people themselves, because God chose them to be his people, were holy in this distinctive, "set-aside" sense (Ex. 19:4-6; Deut. 7:6). Certain cultic rules defined what the Israelites could and could not do as a people associated with God. These cultic rules were often symbolic rather than moral in character. There is nothing inherently dirty about animals designated unclean, nor is eating a kid cooked in its mother's milk an overtly moral issue. Such laws were intended to remind the Hebrew people of their unique relationship with God. And these cultic rules were important. The priests were told, "You must distinguish between the holy and the common, between the unclean and the clean, and you must teach the Israelites all the decrees the Lord has given them through Moses" (Lev. 10:10,11).

HOLY LIVING

The so-called "holiness code" (Lev. 18–26) includes a number of moral as well as cultic commands. Leviticus 19:2 calls Israel to "be holy because I, the Lord your God, am holy." The passage then goes on to denounce idolatry, theft, lying, fraud, slander, revenge, and other moral faults, and, on the positive side, to command love of neighbor.

The NT sets aside cultic holiness, but re-emphasizes moral holiness. Peter says, "Just as he who called you is holy, so be holy in all you do; for it is written, 'Be holy, because I am holy'" (1 Pet. 1:15,16). This compelling argument, on which morality in both OT and NT is based, is a simple but powerful one. God is holy. Therefore all who are associated with him must be holy and reflect him in their character and actions (*compare* Col. 3:5-14).

In the OT, the concept of holiness leans toward separation. Holy sites and objects were rigorously kept separate from the common, and interaction between Israel and surrounding peoples was discouraged.

In the NT, holiness leans toward dynamic involvement. God's people are saints [Gk., *hagioi;* literally, "holy ones"] (Rom. 1:7; 1 Cor. 1:2). The body of the believer has itself become the temple of the Holy Spirit, who lives within (1 Cor. 6:19). The Christian has been set apart to God—but not set apart from involvement with unbelievers. Paul says, "I have written you in my letter not to associate with sexually immoral people—not at all meaning the people of this world who are immoral, or the greedy and swindlers, or idolaters. In that case you would have to leave the world" (1 Cor. 5:9,10).

New Testament holiness is not a matter of isolation but a moral dynamic—the power of the indwelling Spirit of God (Rom. 12:2; Gal. 3:20)—which enables the believer to live a truly good and loving life in a society marred by evil, selfishness, and sin. By living a life which reflects the essential nature of God, the believer both glorifies the Lord and serves as a beacon, attracting others to Christ.

The beauty and attractiveness of true holiness shines through in a brief description of God's "chosen people, holy and dearly loved." According to Col. 3:12,13, God's saints are a people who clothe themselves with "compassion, kindness, humility, gentleness and patience"; who "bear with each other and forgive whatever grievances [they] may have against one another"; and who "forgive as the Lord forgave you."

SUMMARY

God alone is holy in essence. His holiness is both an awesome "otherness" and moral perfection. In OT faith and worship, consecrated persons, places, times, and things were invested with associated holiness. Cultic rules inculcated respect and awe for the sacred. Moral rules expressed the behavior God expected from persons who were associated with him.

In the NT, ceremonial holiness is set aside, and the moral is emphasized. Christians are themselves set apart as God's holy ones through a personal relationship with Jesus. Christians are also indwelt by the Holy Spirit, who expresses the positive dynamic of God's essential holiness through Christians. The holiness of God requires that we who are associated with him live good and self-giving lives daily in this present world. *See also* Sanctify.

holy kiss *See* Kiss.

Holy Land *See* Palestine.

Holy of Holies (KJV) The inner room of the tabernacle (Ex. 26:34) and later of the Jerusalem Temple (1 Ki. 6:16), called "Most Holy Place" in some versions. This inner room, which contained the ark of the covenant, was most holy because it was the focus of God's living presence with his OT people. Only once a year, on the Day of Atonement, was the high priest

allowed to enter the inner room, and then with the blood of an animal sacrificed for the willful and the unintentional sins of the people. *See also* Tabernacle; Temple, Jerusalem.

holy place The tabernacle and Temple, each of which was set apart in its era as the sole place where Israelites could offer sacrifices to God. More specifically it refers to the first chamber of the tabernacle, which contained the lampstand, table of shewbread, and the golden incense altar. *See also* Tabernacle; Temple, Jerusalem.

Holy Spirit The third person of the Trinity. Known in the OT as the Spirit, the Spirit of God, the Spirit of the Lord [Yahweh]. In the NT identified primarily as the Holy Spirit, but also called the Spirit of Jesus, the Spirit of Christ, the Spirit of his [God's] Son.

PERSONALITY OF THE SPIRIT

The Spirit acts as a person rather than an impersonal force. He creates (Gen. 1:2; Ps. 33:6), gives life (Ps. 104:29,30), understands and communicates (1 Cor. 2:9-12). Men can rebel against or grieve the Spirit (Isa. 63:10-14; Acts 5:3,9), and can resist him (Mt. 12:31,32; Acts 7:51). The Spirit is a distinct personality (Mt. 3:16,17; Jn. 14:16,17; 15:26). Both Testaments call the Spirit "God" (Isa. 6:9; Acts 5:3,4), and Jesus identified the Spirit as "another" Comforter (*allos*, "of the same kind or nature") like himself (Jn. 14:16). The formula of Mt. 28:19 clearly ranks the Spirit with the Father and Son as God, in whose name Christian baptism is performed.

RELATION TO FATHER AND SON

Each person of the Trinity is fully and equally God. Yet each is distinct, and each has a distinct role in carrying out the plan

Below right: A priest offers incense in front of the curtain of Holy of Holies. Only the high priest could enter the Most Holy Place, and only then once a year, dressed in white (Lev. 16).

of salvation. In performing his role, the Spirit is said to be sent by both the Father (Jn. 14:26) and the Son (Jn. 15:26). In performing his ministry, the Spirit is committed to exalting Christ rather than himself (Jn. 16:13-15). As Jesus submitted to the will of the Father (Mt. 26:39), so the Spirit submits himself to the Father and the Son. *See also* God; Trinity.

WORK OF THE SPIRIT IN THE OT

The Spirit is identified as an agent of creation (Gen. 1:2; Ps. 33:6) and giver of physical life (Ps. 33:6). Most references to his activity, however, have to do with human beings. The Spirit of God endowed the artisans who built Israel's tabernacle with perfect skill (Ex. 31:3), and endowed Israel's heroes with extraordinary strength (*compare* Jdg. 3:10; 14:6; 1 Sam. 16:13). The Spirit gave the prophets their wisdom and understanding (Gen. 41:38; 2 Sam. 23:2; Mic. 3:8). References to the Spirit "coming upon" any OT individual usually indicate special, temporary, divine enablement for a specific task or mission.

In prophecy, the Spirit is associated with the ministry of the Messiah (Isa. 42:1) and with a future transformation of earth into a home for righteousness (Isa. 32:15; 59:21; Ezek. 36:27). The relationship of the Spirit to righteous living is also expressed in Ps. 51:10,11, as David cries:

Create in me a pure heart, O God,
 and renew a steadfast spirit within me.
Do not cast me from your presence
 or take your Holy Spirit from me.

WORK OF THE SPIRIT IN THE NT

The Spirit of God empowered Christ for his ministry (Mt. 1:18,20; 3:13-17; 12:28; Mk. 1:9-11; Lk. 3:21,22; 4:14-21; Jn. 1:32,33). Furthermore, Jesus outlined the Spirit's ministry to believers in Jn. 14–16. The Spirit would be in believers and with them forever (14:16,17). The Spirit would teach and remind Christ's disciples of all Jesus had said (14:26). He would testify within all believers the truth about Jesus (15:26,27), convict the world of sin (16:8-11), guide his followers into all truth, reveal what is to come, and make known Christ's will (16:13-15).

After the resurrection of Jesus, the Spirit created the Church as a living organism by bonding believers to Christ and to one another (Acts 2; 1 Cor. 12:13). Visible flames and speaking in foreign languages prompted by the Spirit marked the birthday of the Church at Pentecost. The NT continues to describe the works of the Spirit in and through believers. He fills

believers, empowering them for service (Acts 2:4; 4:31). He indwells believers, enabling godly living (Rom. 8:1-27). The Spirit produces the fruit of good character (Gal. 5:22,23). He assists us in our prayers to the Father (Rom. 8:26,27). The Spirit's permanent, indwelling presence makes the body of the believer a temple (1 Cor. 6:19), and he is a constant source of inner strength (1 Jn. 4:1-6). The Spirit gives gifts which enable Christians to minister to others (Rom. 12; 1 Cor. 12). In brief, the Holy Spirit is the active agent in every Christian's life, the Person through whom the Godhead presently works out the divine will in this world.

THE HOLY SPIRIT'S MINISTRY

The NT Epistles emphasize two aspects of the Holy Spirit's ministry in Christians.

1. The Spirit enables us to live a holy life. In the OT, the Spirit is called "holy" only in Ps. 51 and Isa. 63. In the NT, he is called the Holy Spirit nearly 90 times! The adjective "holy" is not merely a reference to the Spirit's essential holiness, but to his ministry. The Spirit is the Holy Spirit

The Spirit's coming at Pentecost is depicted on the closed panels of a medieval, three-paneled altar (triptych). Tongues of fire descend from the hands of God on the twelve apostles (Acts 2:1-4).

"As soon as Jesus was baptized, he went up out of the water. At that moment heaven was opened, and he saw the Spirit of God descending on him like a dove . . ." (Mt. 3:16; compare Mk. 1:10; Lk. 3:22).

because he is the one who transforms believers and enables the living of a holy life. While this theme is seen throughout the NT, three passages are basic.

Most scholars think Romans 7 expresses the frustration of the believer who struggles to obey God's Law and finds himself failing. Romans 8 introduces God's solution. The "righteous requirements of the law" can be "fully met in us, who do not live according to the sinful nature but according to the Spirit" (8:4). As we commit ourselves to the Spirit's control, we discover that "if the Spirit of him who raised Jesus from the dead is living in you, he who raised Christ from the dead will also give life to your mortal bodies through his Spirit, who lives in you" (8:11).

Second Corinthians 3 portrays the Spirit of God as the one who writes righteousness in human hearts (3:3). Paul says that we "reflect the Lord's glory [for we] are being transformed into his likeness with ever-increasing glory, which comes from the Lord, who is the Spirit" (3:18).

Galatians 5 contrasts the character and experience of those who live by their human nature with the character and experience of those who "live by the Spirit" (5:16) and "keep in step" with him (5:25). Paul says that the "fruit of the Spirit is love, joy, peace, patience, kindness, goodness, faithfulness, gentleness and self-control" (5:22,23). The adjective "holy" associated with the Spirit is a constant reminder that God calls us to live, and enables us to live, a holy life. *See also* Holy.

2. The Holy Spirit gives each believer spiritual gifts. These gifts are specifically related to building up the body of Christ "until we all reach unity in the faith and in the knowledge of the Son of God and become mature, attaining to the whole measure of the fullness of Christ" (Eph. 4:13; *compare* 1 Cor. 12:7). This too is related to holiness, for as we grow toward maturity we "put on the new self, created to be like God in true righteousness and holiness" (Eph. 4:23,24). *See also* Spiritual Gifts.

SUMMARY

The Spirit is a separate and distinct person within the Godhead. In the OT era, he is an agent of creation, and he temporarily empowered individuals for specific tasks. In the NT era, the Spirit permanently indwells believers, and produces holiness by transforming believers from within. While the focus of Christian faith is Christ, the Spirit is God's active agent in our lives today. His presence assures us of the strength we need to do God's will and promises an inner spiritual transformation and growth toward Christlikeness.

Terra-cotta figurine of donkey laden with two baskets, which if life-size would equal the Hebrew measure of 1 homer.

homer An ancient unit of measure, a donkey load. Estimates place the homer between a little over five U.S. bushels to nearly eight U.S bushels. In liquid measure, the homer is estimated between 50 and 55 gallons (227.3 to 250 liters). *See also* Weights and Measures.

homosexuality Sexual intercourse with a person of the same sex. Contemporary use of "homosexual" to describe those who experience sexual "desire" for others of the same sex is not primary in Scripture. Nearly every reference is to actual performance of sex acts with a person or persons of the same sex.

Homosexual acts are condemned in the strongest terms in both Testaments. The moral character of Sodom was revealed in its inhabitants' intent on homosexual rape (Gen. 19:1-25; *compare* Jdg. 19:13–20:48). Old Testament Law says, "Do not lie with a man as one lies with a woman; that is detestable" (Lev. 18:22), and later adds, "If a man lies with a man as one lies with a woman, both of them have done what is detestable. They must be put to death" (Lev. 20:13). In contrast, Canaanite religion promoted homosexual prostitution (1 Ki. 14:24; 22:46).

In Rom. 1, Paul describes both lesbian and homosexual behavior. They are "unnatural"—"indecent acts" motivated by "shameful lusts," "perversions." First Timothy 1:9,10 lists homosexuals ("perverts," NIV; "sodomites," RSV) among the "ungodly and sinful, the unholy and irreligious." First Corinthians 6:9 includes "homosexual offenders" with the wicked who "will not inherit the kingdom of God."

The Scriptures in no way support the notion that homosexuality is a morally acceptable alternative life-style. Rather, the Bible labels homosexual acts sin, even as it identifies heterosexual acts outside of marriage as sin.

Yet Scripture offers a word of hope. In 1 Cor. 6, Paul concludes his list of wicked acts by observing, "And that is what some of you were. But you were washed, you were sanctified, you were justified in the name of the Lord Jesus Christ and by the Spirit of our God" (6:11). No repentant person is beyond redemption. No perversion is beyond cure. And no homosexual sin puts a person beyond the reach of God's transforming grace.

honesty *See* Dishonesty.

honey, honeycomb (1) The sweet, thick substance produced by bees from the nectar of flowering plants; (2) sometimes, a date or grape syrup.

As the standard of sweetness in biblical times, honey was highly valued (Ps. 19:10; 119:103). Canaan was described as a land flowing with milk and honey (Ex. 3:8,17) because of its fertility. Wild honey was gathered by the Israelites (Deut. 32:13; Ps. 81:16).

Later, it was listed among firstfruits brought to the Temple for the use of priests and Levites (2 Chr. 31:5), which suggests that bees had been domesticated. However, honey was not to be used in any offering presented to God (Lev. 2:11).

honor (1) To be elevated in the eyes of others on the basis of rank, reputation, status, or character; (2) to show respect to a person in appropriate ways. *See also* Disgrace; Glory.

THOSE HONORED
God himself is, of course, worthy of ultimate honor. Parents are also to be honored (Ex. 20:12; Eph. 6:2). Kings and masters deserve respect (Rom. 13:7; 1 Tim. 6:1; 1 Pet. 2:17). Within the community of

faith, special honor is due church elders and others whose godly character or ministry elevates them in the eyes of the Lord and his people. In Proverbs, traits worthy of honor are: wisdom, which in Scripture means seeing and taking the righteous path (3:35); openness to correction (13:18); humility (18:12); peacefulness (20:3); and lowliness (29:23). In the NT, Rom. 2:10 promises "glory, honor, and peace for everyone who does good."

SHOWING HONOR
We honor God by worshiping him, by respecting his Word, and by putting it into practice. Jesus honored the Father by doing always the things that pleased him (Jn. 8:49-51; Rom. 15:3).

The command to honor parents is found twice in the OT (Ex. 20:12; Deut. 5:16) and six times in the NT. Children honor parents by obedience (Eph. 6:1). Adult children honor their parents by providing needed financial support (Mk. 7:9-13; 1 Tim. 5:8).

Both Testaments also tell believers to honor rulers. In OT times, persons might bow down (2 Sam. 9:6) or even fall on the ground to express respect for a king (2 Sam. 14:4). Believers show respect for employers (masters) by working hard, and for government by paying all taxes due (Rom. 13:6,7; 1 Tim. 6:2).

A Median envoy raises his hand to his lips as a sign of honor for King Darius I; from the treasury at Persepolis, 521–486 B.C.

Within the community of faith, Christians are to honor leaders (Phil. 2:29; 1 Tim. 5:17). Respect is shown by listening to leaders and remaining open to their persuasion (Heb. 13:7,17).

493

Believers are also to honor one another, viewing each brother or sister as more important than oneself (Rom. 12:10). Peter goes further: "Show proper respect for everyone" (1 Pet. 2:17). God himself created humankind and "crowned him with glory and honor" (Ps. 8:5). We express the honor due every person by being sensitive and caring, showing both concern and respect as we seek to help individuals.

The concept of "honor" in a unique way expresses a basic Christian attitude toward God, society, and others as persons. The Christian works within and supports the social order. Yet the Christian never forgets that people, not the social role, are the true focus of God's concern.

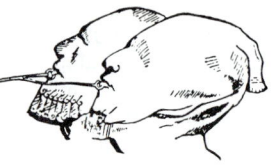

Above: An Assyrian meat hook.

Right: Hooks through the lower lip hold two prisoners on a leash. Judah's king Manasseh was taken to Babylon with a hook in his nose (2 Chr. 33:10).

hook Several kinds of hooks are mentioned in the OT. (1) The curtains in the tabernacle were hung on hooks (Ex. 26:32). (2) Pruning hooks, small, sickle-shaped knives, were used to trim vines and trees and at times were used as weapons in wartime (Isa. 2:4; Mic. 4:3). (3) Hooks or rings were put in the sensitive noses of animals to control or lead them (2 Ki. 19:28; 2 Chr. 33:11). The Assyrians used such hooks to control captives. Isaiah uses this image to assert God's sovereign control over Sennacherib of Assyria (Isa. 37:29). (4) Hook and line were used in fishing (Job 41:2; Mt. 17:27). (5) Double-pronged hooks were meat-hooks on which parts of sacrificed animals were hung (Ezek. 40:38-43).

Called the lapwing in the KJV, the hoopoe nests in holes along paths (where travelers pack the earth firmly) in order to prevent invasion by predators.

hoopoe An insect-eating bird, related to the kingfisher, noted for its crest and distinctive plumage. Hoopoes shown in a scene painted 3,800 years ago in Egypt look just like the hoopoes seen today.

hope (1) An ordinary desire and confidence for something, as in Ruth 1:12; Lk. 6:34; (2) an eager, confident expectation that sustains a person while he or she is waiting patiently for future fulfillment. The Hebrew words are often translated "wait" in modern versions. Paul interrelates hope with faith and love—things that remain (1 Cor. 13:13).

HOPE IN GOD

At times, the OT identifies a specific object of hope, such as a return of the exiles to the Promised Land (Jer. 31:16,17). Most often, however, "hope" expresses reliance on the Lord. "Lord," the psalmist says, as he looks to God for deliverance from his transgressions, "what do I look for? My hope is in you" (Ps. 39:7). The same is true when enemies surround us. "The Lord preserves the faithful," David writes. "Be strong and take heart, all you who hope in the Lord" (Ps. 31:23,24). Whatever the problem, whatever the need, the exhortation comes:

O Israel, put your hope in the Lord,
for with the Lord is unfailing love
and with him is full redemption.
(Ps. 130:7)

Clearly, hope and faith are intimately related. God has entered into a covenant relationship with Israel. Within that relationship the believer has hope. The future is uncertain, yet God will remain faithful to his commitments.

HOPE EXPLAINED

In the NT our faith and hope remain fixed in God (Rom. 15:13; 1 Pet. 1:13). Yet now believers are invited to look ahead with confidence. We are invited to hope for a personal transformation, associated with resurrection. This hope, which is made real to us by the Holy Spirit (Rom. 5:5), has two aspects.

1. We hope for our future resurrection itself (Acts 2:26; 24:15; Rom. 8:20-24; 1 Cor. 15:19-28; 1 Th. 4:13-18). At our resurrection, we will know the full experience of the eternal life God has given us through Christ's own resurrection (Tit. 1:2; 1 Pet. 1:3-9). *See also* Resurrection. Because the ultimate fulfillment of the Christian's future will be realized when Jesus returns, the Second Coming is itself called the "blessed hope" (Tit. 2:13).

494

2. *We hope for a partial experience of the promised transformation now.* Christians have been called to a present hope, rooted in God's incomparably great power. That power, which God exerted in raising Christ from the dead, is now active in all who believe, as the Spirit of God gives vital new life even to our mortal bodies (Rom. 8:9-11; 2 Cor. 3:12; Gal. 5:5; Eph. 1:18-23). *See also* Transformation.

These two aspects of the Christian's hope are summed up in 1 John 3:2,3. The apostle says that "what we will be has not yet been made known. But we know that when he appears, we shall be like him, for we shall see him as he is." Then he adds, "Everyone who has this hope in him purifies himself, just as he [Jesus] is pure."

IMPACT OF HOPE

In the OT, hope directs the believer's eyes toward the future and calls for patient waiting. While we wait, hope in God provides present strength and encouragement (Ps. 31:23,24). Hope also comforts. "You have given me hope," David says. "My comfort in my suffering is this: Your promise preserves my life" (Ps. 119:49,50).

In the NT, the impact of hope is spelled out even more clearly. The Christian's identity is redefined by hope. We no longer see ourselves primarily as sinners, but realize that God has destined us to be holy. Individually we begin to live not as the person we were, but as the person we can become in Christ. This is the thought in John's mind when he says, "He that has this hope in him purifies himself" (1 Jn. 3:3).

The hope of transformation does even more. It fills us with joy despite present trials (Rom. 5:2), frees us to be honest with ourselves and others (2 Cor. 3:12), stimulates our faith and love (Col. 1:5), inspires endurance (1 Th. 1:3), and enables us to have such a positive attitude despite sufferings that unbelievers beg an explanation (1 Pet. 3:15).

The Christian hope of transformation in a coming resurrection is not escapism, but a powerful motivation for faithful, godly living now. We, like the saints of the OT, know the Person in whom we hope. Therefore, as the Scriptures exhort: "Let us hold unswervingly to the hope we profess, for he who promised is faithful" (Heb. 10:23).

Horites [HOHR-ites; Heb., *hori;* "hole," "cave dweller"]. An ethnic group, inhabitants of Edom in patriarchal times (Gen. 14:6) with scattered communities in central Palestine (Gen. 34:2; Josh. 9:6,7). The descendants of Esau displaced the Horites in Edom and occupied their stronghold at Mount Seir. Some identify the Horites with the Hivites of the OT. *See also* Hivites.

The theory that the Horites were actually Hurrians, a dominant people displaced by the Hittites about 1800 B.C., has little archaeological support though it is commonly assumed by many secular scholars.

Terra-cotta bull found in Israel. The Mosaic code included case law concerning a bull goring a person with its horns (Ex. 21:28-31).

horn (1) The bone-like growth on the head of animals. Removed, the animal horn might serve as a container for oil or for cosmetics (1 Ki. 1:39).

(2) The extension on each of the four upper corners of the altar of sacrifice. The significance of these projections is uncertain, but the blood of sacrifices was sprinkled on them (Lev. 4:7), and persons seeking refuge might grasp them (1 Ki. 1:50-53). They may have served to secure the ropes that tied the animal to the kindling wood on the altar.

(3) A symbol of strength, power, and often aggression (*compare* Zech. 1:18-21). In Dan. 7 and 8, as well as Rev. 13 and 17, animal horns represent individual rulers of great empires. Psalm 75 uses horns to symbolize arrogant human power, and concludes, "I will cut off the horns of all the wicked, but the horns of the righteous will be lifted up" (v. 10).

"Horned" altar found at Beersheba (10th–9th centuries B.C.) probably typifies the altars of the tabernacle and Temple. The blood of a sacrificed animal was smeared on these projections (Lev. 4:7).

(4) A wind instrument made from an animal's horn and used to transmit signals. The deep, mournful sound of the ram's horn (*shophar*) called Israel to arms and launched battle (Jdg. 6:34; Jer. 4:19-21). It announced the Day of Atonement and the new year (*Rosh Hashanah*).

(5) A metal horn or trumpet. English Bible versions typically fail to distinguish between the animal horn and metal instruments. Different blasts on silver trumpets served as signals when Israel traveled in the wilderness (Num. 10:2-10). These trumpets were sounded on joyous occasions (Ps. 98).

hornet A large, stinging insect of the wasp family. The species found in Palestine is about 1½ inches (3.9 millimeters) long, with a venomous, painful sting. A wasp colony may hold as many as 10,000 insects. Each mention of hornets in the Bible is associated with God's promise to aid his people in battle, to "send the hornet in front of you" (Ex. 23:28; Deut. 7:20; Josh. 24:12) to disrupt the enemy forces.

horse A large, strong, four-legged animal with solid hooves and long mane and tail. Horses are among the OT's "unclean" animals, not to be used as food. Of some

Left: Horses with richly ornamented harnesses await the king in this relief from Nineveh. King Solomon is reported to have had stables for four thousand horses at his garrison cities (2 Chr. 9:25).

Below: Assyrian king Ashurbanipal hunts lions on horseback; relief carving of a lion hunt from his palace in Nineveh (about 640 B.C.).

Right: Unique frontal view of a horse on a wall relief in a temple built by Rameses II (about 1370 B.C.). The Pharaoh of the Exodus lost an army's worth of horses and chariots by drowning when he attempted to re-enslave the Israelites (Ex. 14:23-31).

150 references to horses and horsemen in the Bible, 90 are figurative or prophetic in character.

Horses were probably domesticated in central Asia around 3000 B.C. These powerful animals were used in warfare, hunting, and the pulling of chariots. There is no indication that horses were used in farming. The first explicit Bible reference to horses tells of Joseph accepting horses and other livestock from the breadless Egyptian citizenry in exchange for grain during the seven-year famine (Gen. 47:17).

By the time of the Exodus, the city-states of Canaan possessed chariot armies (Josh. 11:4-9). However, OT Law forbad Israel's king to "multiply horses" (Deut. 17:14-16). As the primary biblical association of horses is with warfare (compare Zech. 9:9,10), this can be taken as an injunction against Israel building a military machine. God's people were to depend on the Lord rather than on their own strength (Ps. 33:17; Ezek. 17:15). Saul and David largely obeyed this prohibition. However, Solomon assembled thousands of horses and built a large chariot army (1 Ki. 4:26; 2 Chr. 9:25). Whenever possible, later kings of Israel and Judah also maintained chariot armies. Assyrian records say that Ahab contributed 2,000 chariots to a coalition that stopped Shalmaneser's forces at Qarqar in 853 B.C.

Symbolically, horses portray status, might, and honor. The horse was reserved for kings, high government officials, and the military (compare 2 Sam. 15:1; 1 Ki. 1:5; Acts 8:26-29). Thus, Haman could think of no higher honor than being permitted to ride through Persia's capital on a horse the king himself had ridden (Esth. 6:9).

The most graphic portrayal of a warhorse in Scripture (Job 39:19-25) pictures the horse pawing fiercely, then charging in frenzied excitement into battle. The association of horses with warfare makes them appropriate biblical symbols of judgment and death in prophetic passages. The terrible destructive forces unleashed on the earth at history's end are pictured as four horsemen (Rev. 6:2-5; compare Zech. 6:2-7). See also Warfare.

hosanna [hoh-ZAN-uh; "Save now!"]. A cry of expectant praise associated with Israel's messianic hope. The Hebrew expression appears in the joyful Psalm 118:25 followed by the phrase: "Blessed is he who comes in the name of the Lord." Psalm 118 was sung on each of the seven days of the Feast of Tabernacles, and verses 25 and 26 were chanted as a worship response by the people, who waved myrtle and palm branches.

By Jesus' time, "he who comes in the name of the Lord" was understood to be the Messiah himself. The use of this familiar shout of praise to greet Jesus when he entered Jerusalem on Palm Sunday (Mt. 21:9; Mk. 11:9,10; Jn. 12:13) as well as shouts welcoming him as the son [descendant] of David make it clear that the

497

Large, gold Hebrew letters announce "Hosanna" or "Save now!" on an illumination from the 15th-century Rothschild manuscript.

crowds expected Jesus to bring the deliverance they associated with the OT's messianic prophecies. *See also* Messiah.

Later, "hosanna" was adopted by the Church as an expression of praise.

Hosea, Book of The first of the minor prophetic books of the OT. Written by Hosea [hoh-ZAY-uh; "he has saved"], this book reveals the depth of God's love and pain for the rebellious Northern Kingdom of Israel—a rebelliousness symbolized by Gomer, the unfaithful wife of Hosea.

BACKGROUND

Hosea wrote during the later years of Jeroboam II of Israel, sometime between 786–748 B.C. Under this powerful monarch, Israel had expanded its borders and experienced explosive prosperity. But the nation was bankrupt spiritually. Just a few years before Hosea's ministry began, Amos visited Israel and cried out against the ungodliness and injustice that festered in the superficially religious society. *See also* Amos. Hosea, too, touches on social conditions (6:7–7:7). But Hosea looks deeper and exposes the root of Israel's immoralities.

Except for brief moments in their earliest history (2:15; 11:1), God's people had been rebellious and unfaithful. Now the people of the Northern Kingdom ridicule God's prophets (9:7,8), ignore the divine laws (4:6), consecrate themselves to vile idols (9:9,10), and even dedicate their daughters as religious prostitutes to conduct the pagan rites of the Canaanites (4:10-15). As Hosea says, "Ephraim has surrounded me with lies, the house of Israel with deceit. And Judah is unruly against God, even against the faithful Holy One" (11:12).

Against this background and the background of his own agonizing experience with his unfaithful wife, Gomer, Hosea delivers his unique and deeply moving message.

AUTHORSHIP

While the Book of Hosea gives no detailed information regarding the place of Hosea's birth or his upbringing, the evidence given in the passages would indicate that Hosea, the son of Beeri, was a citizen of the Northern Kingdom, a land he dearly loved.

Chapters 1 and 3 of this book tell Hosea's personal story, and the passages are best understood as sequential. Hosea's unfaithful wife, Gomer, leaves and becomes a prostitute (ch. 1). Finally, her youth gone and beauty dissipated, the prophet finds her, purchases her back, and brings her home as God had directed him to do (ch. 3). The remainder of the book contains a number of messages directed to the nation Israel.

THEOLOGICAL CONTRIBUTIONS

Hosea provides deep insights into both the heart of man and the heart of God. Neither Gomer nor Israel respond to kindness and love (*compare* 11:4). Each is arrogantly unfaithful, Gomer with human lovers and Israel with pagan gods.

The course chosen by Gomer and Israel leads each to disaster. Both are ultimately betrayed by their lovers. Each is enslaved, Gomer by an unnamed master and Israel by Assyria (3:2; 9:1-4).

Hosea's experience with Gomer allows him to feel God's anguish over his unfaithful people. Knowing that nothing can force Gomer to love her husband, Hosea permits her rebellion to reap its tragic consequences, just as God must do with Israel (10:13). Until then Hosea and God must wait: "I will go back to my place until they admit their guilt" (5:15).

But oh, the anguish! In one of Scripture's most beautiful passages, God looks back and says,

"It was I who taught Ephraim to walk,
taking them by the arms;
but they did not realize
it was I who healed them.

498

I led them with cords of human kindness,
  with ties of love;
I lifted the yoke from their neck
  and bent down to feed them. . . .
How can I give you up, Ephraim?
  How can I hand you over, Israel?"

(Hos. 11:3,4,8)

Despite the pain, God remains committed to Israel. In the coming disaster, "They will seek my face; in their misery they will earnestly seek me" (5:15). Then, God declares, "I will . . . speak tenderly to her" (2:14), and "I will show my love to the one I called 'Not my loved one.' I will say to those called 'Not my people,' 'You are my people'; and they will say, 'You are my God' " (2:23).

In this brief book we see powerfully displayed the deceitfulness of the human heart and the redemptive love of God.

MASTERY KEYS

Hosea 2 summarizes the message of the book. Chapters 1,3 tell the story of Hosea. The rest of the book contains messages directed to Israel, exposing the nation's sin, warning of coming judgment, and yet revealing God's continuing love. To grasp the extent of God's love for humankind, first make a list of Israel's sins; then next to it list the divine promises intended to encourage repentance.

Hosea himself deserves careful study. He remains a simple man, untouched by the corruption of his society. His wife is unfaithful, but rather than becoming hardened, Hosea becomes more sensitive. Rather than insulating himself from suffering, he opens himself to more suffering by continuing to love Gomer. At the end, Hosea even finds the grace to bring her back into his home. In the prophet Hosea, we see our own calling to reflect God's steadfast love, even in the most painful of personal circumstances.

SPECIAL FEATURES

Hosea gives his children symbolic names. Jezreel ("God will scatter") was the valley where Jehu wiped out King Omri's line. Now Jehu's own line is to be cut off and with it the nation. Lo-Ruhama ("Not loved") and Lo-Ammi ("Not my people") foreshadow the coming invasion of Israel and the population's deportation to Assyria.

hospitality [Gk., *philoxenia;* "love to strangers"]. The practice of welcoming, feeding, and sheltering travelers.

No single word for hospitality is found in the OT. Yet the practice is deeply rooted in custom and is illustrated in many OT stories, such as Abraham's entertainment

HOSEA: A READING AND STUDY GUIDE

Chapter	Content Summary	Related Articles
1	God tells Hosea to marry Gomer, who will be unfaithful to him. God gives their children symbolic names.	Jeroboam II Amos
2	A brief message introduces the theme of Israel's punishment and restoration.	Adultery Husband
3	God tells Hosea to find and restore his adulterous wife.	
4	Israel's idolatry is portrayed as prostitution.	Prostitute
5	God decrees judgment on arrogant Israel.	Arrogance
6,7	Israel's unfaithfulness and unrepentant attitude are described further.	Covenant Repent
8	Israel has sown the wind. She will reap the whirlwind and be punished for wickedness.	Judgment
9,10	Punishment is decreed "because your sins are so many, your hostility so great."	Sin
11	Despite Israel's sin, God continues to love his people.	Love
12	If Israel will not return to God and maintain love and justice, God will expel his people from their land.	Justice Exile
13	God's people must "acknowledge no God but me" or face destruction. The rebels must bear their guilt.	Guilt
14	Repentance will bring blessing when Israel at last appeals to God to forgive all their sins.	Forgive

Abraham is the gracious host and Sarah the astonished eavesdropper in Antonio Guardi's portrayal of the three angels visiting Abraham (Gen. 18:1-15).

of three angelic strangers (Gen. 18). A host who welcomed a stranger became responsible for the welfare of his guest (Gen. 19:8; Jdg. 19:24,25). Typically, a traveler would stop at a city gate or community well to await an invitation (Gen. 19:1; 24:11-33). In recent times, Arab and Bedouin cultures have viewed hospitality as a religious as well as social duty.

In the NT, when Jesus sent his disciples out to preach, he told them not to bring money or even extra clothing. Instead, they were to rely on the hospitality of someone in the communities where they ministered. On entering a town, they were to preach their message and heal the sick. The message and miracles would establish who the disciples were. If they were then offered hospitality, they would stay. If hospitality were refused, it would indicate rejection of the message as well as messenger, and the disciples were to leave that town (Mt. 10:1-15; Mk. 6:7-11).

The NT further exhorts Christians to extend hospitality to other believers (Rom. 12:13; 1 Pet. 4:9; 3 Jn. 8). Elders and deacons particularly were to be hospitable (1 Tim. 3:2; Tit. 1:8). This was especially important in the early church, when many teachers and leaders had itinerant ministries.

Yet the warm welcome offered strangers who came to town in Christ's name made the church vulnerable. So the NT guards against the abuse of hospitality. Those who come must be orthodox believers. "If anyone comes to you and does not bring this teaching [that Christ is God, come in the flesh], do not take him into your house or welcome him" (2 Jn. 10). And, idlers who imposed on others without working to support themselves were also to be expelled (2 Th. 3:11-13).

host of heaven (1) The stars and other heavenly bodies (Gen. 2:1; Deut. 4:19); (2) angelic beings (Ps. 103:20,21; Lk. 2:13).

God is described as "God of hosts" or "God of the armies of Israel" (1 Sam. 17:45). The name expresses the conviction of God's people that the Lord has all power in heaven and on earth, and aids his own. *See also* Angel; Star.

hour (1) A one-twelfth division of daylight; (2) an indefinite future moment when a significant event will take place, such as the "hour" of Christ's return (Mt. 24:36); (3) a critical or pivotal moment in the life of a person or race (Jn. 12:23; Rom. 13:11).

The hour is not used as a measure of time in the OT. The day was simply divided into morning, noon, and evening. In the NT, the hour is one-twelfth of the daylight period (Jn. 11:9). The Hebrews divided the hours of daylight, so the third hour would be approximately 9 A.M. This system is used in the Synoptic Gospels and early Acts (Mt. 20:1-16; 27:45,46; Acts 2:15). It is possible that John adopts the Roman system, which, like ours, counts 12 hours from midnight and 12 from noon (Jn. 1:39; 4:6,52). *See also* Time.

house, household (1) Any dwelling, from a tent to a palace. Thus, the OT Temple was the "house of God" because it was uniquely the focus of his presence with Israel. *See also* Housing. (2) A term used for a variety of social units based on relationship. In both Testaments, "house" expresses basic concepts of relationship and social structure. Generally, the "house" or "household" is a relatively small unit made up of relatives and servants living together and functioning as an economic unit. But the "whole house of Israel" includes all members of the OT faith-community, just as the NT "household of God" indicates all believers.

HOUSE AS BASIC SOCIAL UNIT

In OT times, the household was the basic unit of society. Generally, the household included all members of the extended family. Jacob's household included some 71 persons—wives, sons, daughters-in-law, and grandchildren—when that patriarch entered Egypt (Gen. 46:1-27). However, "house" could be extended further. The wealthy Abraham's house included not only family but also servants "born in his household" (Gen. 14:14).

In biblical times, the household had true corporate identity. When the son of a local ruler violated Dinah, a daughter of Jacob, two of her brothers murdered all the men of the city. All were assumed to be responsible for the act of a community member. Jacob was angry with his sons, for he feared that other Canaanites would "join forces against me and attack me, [and] I and my household will be destroyed" (Gen. 34:30). Thus, Jacob and his household might, in turn, be held responsible for the act of two of its members. In the same vein, Rahab's act in hiding the Israelite spies won not only her life but the lives of her "father and mother, brothers and sisters, and all who belong to them" (Josh. 2:13). Likewise, Achan's sin at Jericho was expiated only by his execution —with all his family (Josh. 7:24).

Religion was also a family matter in OT times. Abraham was chosen by God and charged to "direct his children and his

Jewish hourly divisions of day and night in NT times. The length of the hours varied as they were calculated according to sunrise and sunset. The Romans began their first hour at midnight and noon.

Noon
6
5   7
4   8
3   9
2   10
1   11
Sunrise 12 -   - 12 Sunset
                        JEWISH DAY BEGINS
11   1
10   2
9   3
8   4
7   6   5
Midnight
ROMAN DAY BEGINS

household after him to keep the way of the Lord" (Gen. 18:19). Instruction of children in God's Word was a family responsibility under the Law (Deut. 6:6-9), and many of Israel's religious festivals were celebrated in and by the family unit (compare Ex. 12:3,4,31-49; Lev. 16:17; Num. 18:31; etc.).

In Acts and the Epistles, "house" and "household" reflect the Roman rather than Hebrew view of the unit. The household included not only family members with their slaves and servants, but also persons who were under some obligation to the head of the family. Theoretically, the head of the family had absolute power over its members, owning all members' property.

The extended nature of the NT household is reflected in several key passages. The Roman centurion Cornelius had "called together his relatives and close friends" to hear Peter (Acts 10:24). The household of the Philippian jailer (literally, in Acts 16:33 "his all" rather than "his family," as in the NIV) may have included the jailers under him as well as close relatives. "Caesar's household" in Phil. 4:22 is often understood as soldiers in the emperor's own Praetorian Regiment, not necessarily relatives of the Emperor Nero.

Often conversion was experienced by family units, following the lead of the head of the family. This is illustrated in the experience of Cornelius (Acts 11:14), as well as those of Lydia (16:15), the Philippian jailer (16:31-34), Crispus (18:8), and possibly Stephanas (1 Cor. 1:16). None of these passages imply that a family member is saved by the faith of its head. Rather, it suggests that family members in OT and NT society were motivated by the decision of the head of the family.

The influence of the head of the family on its members is reflected in Paul's instructions that elders and deacons must manage their households well (1 Tim. 3:4,12). In NT society, a person who could not influence his family members to live godly lives could hardly be trusted with leadership in the church.

The bond that existed between family members is reflected in the NT's teaching on responsibility for one's family. In Paul's view, "anyone [who] does not provide for his relatives, and especially for his immediate family . . . has denied the faith and is worse than an unbeliever" (1 Tim. 5:8).

THE HOUSEHOLD ACROSS TIME

The OT and NT view the household as a social unit with a corporate identity as real as the individual identity of its members.

This sense of identity not only bound members of living generations together but also extended through time. God's promise to build David a house was a promise to maintain David's family line so that he always had a descendant qualified to sit on Israel's throne (2 Sam. 7:25-29). This use reflects a sense of identity of the living with past generations—an identity that finds frequent expression in the OT.

House and household, then, reflect a view of corporate identity and mutual responsibility that is far stronger than exists in our individualistic Western society. While the Bible does teach the responsibility of each individual for his or her own acts, it also strongly affirms a parallel corporate responsibility of the family.

house church A congregation, usually small, that met regularly in a private home (Acts 16:40; Rom. 16:5; 1 Cor. 16:19).

Early Christians did not erect special buildings for worship but met in homes. This limited the size of the group that could meet together. At times, Christians in a city might assemble for shared worship, but Christian life was essentially a small group experience. This smaller size enhanced the intimacy of early Christian relationships (compare Eph. 4:29-32; Col. 3:12-14). The close relationships created the context in which mutual ministry could take place and spiritual gifts be fully exercised.

The role of elders and other leaders in the early church must have been affected by this meeting structure. Whether elders supervised a number of smaller congregations or functioned within a house group is uncertain. See also Church; Worship.

household gods See Teraphim.

housing Permanent shelter erected for occupation by settled populations. While the wealthy of each biblical era could afford relatively comfortable housing, most people in Bible times lived in simple, small structures.

PALESTINIAN HOUSING

Most people in Bible times lived either in small walled cities, which typically enclosed six to eight acres, or in small unwalled villages of a few clustered houses. City houses were packed close together. Usually, residences of several families opened on a common court. The houses themselves might have just a single room or two at most, though some houses were two stories high. In two-story houses the family often slept on the upper floor. In the villages, small houses were typically built with a four-room plan. The four-room house had a room running across the back with three long rooms, which could be further subdivided, running perpendicular to it. The center room, which might be open or covered, served as a common courtyard.

Houses in Palestine were typically made of stone or mud brick, often built on sturdy bedrock foundations. Inside walls were coated entirely or partially with waterproof plaster, while the floors were clay. Roofs were quite low, often being only six feet (1.8 meters) from the floor. The roof, generally made with wooden beams that held layered branches and packed mud, was usually reached by an outside stairway and was walled around the edges (Deut. 22:8).

Doorways were low and framed by wooden or stone doorposts, a lintel, and threshold. Doors were not hung on hinges, but rotated inward on pivots and could be barred from inside. The few windows were simple openings, generally placed high up in the wall and kept small to help control winter and summer temperatures.

Houses were sparsely furnished. Most homes simply contained cooking utensils and raised areas for sleeping. However, village houses often had cistern systems, and some houses contained firepits for cooking. Braziers were also used for heating. All homes contained food storage jars or sunken storage pits. By NT times, most homes also contained small clay stoves, about one foot high and two feet wide

(30.48 by 60.96 centimeters). *See also* Cistern; Furniture.

The homes of wealthier people were larger and had more rooms than their poorer contemporaries. Several downstairs rooms of one Jerusalem home, destroyed when the Romans sacked the city in A.D. 70, have been uncovered by archaeologists. This part of the house had a small paved courtyard, a kitchen, a ritual bath, and three other small rooms.

Outside of Palestine, the wealthy, who constituted less than one percent of the population, lived in spacious villas or large city homes featuring rooms built around an open inner garden chamber (*atrium*).

Shopkeepers and artisans typically lived in rooms above or behind their place of business. In Rome most of the population lived in multistory apartment houses, occupying only a single room, in constant danger from fire or the building's collapse.

HOUSING AND LIFE-STYLE

In Israel's agricultural society, city dwellers often lived outdoors in their fields during the harvest and other seasons, the houses providing shelter during inclement weather and a place to store one's food and other possessions. In addition, houses often served as a workshop for those engaged in a trade. The rooftop provided living and work space during much of the year. Flax was dried on the roof, as were raisins and dates, and the family often slept on the roof during the hot season. Daily use of the roof explains the OT's command to "make a parapet around your roof so you may not bring guilt of blood-

The furniture and pottery excavated in a tomb at Jericho (inset) have been used in the reconstruction at the right, which represents a wealthy Canaanite family and household in the Middle Bronze Age at Jericho (2200–1550 B.C.).

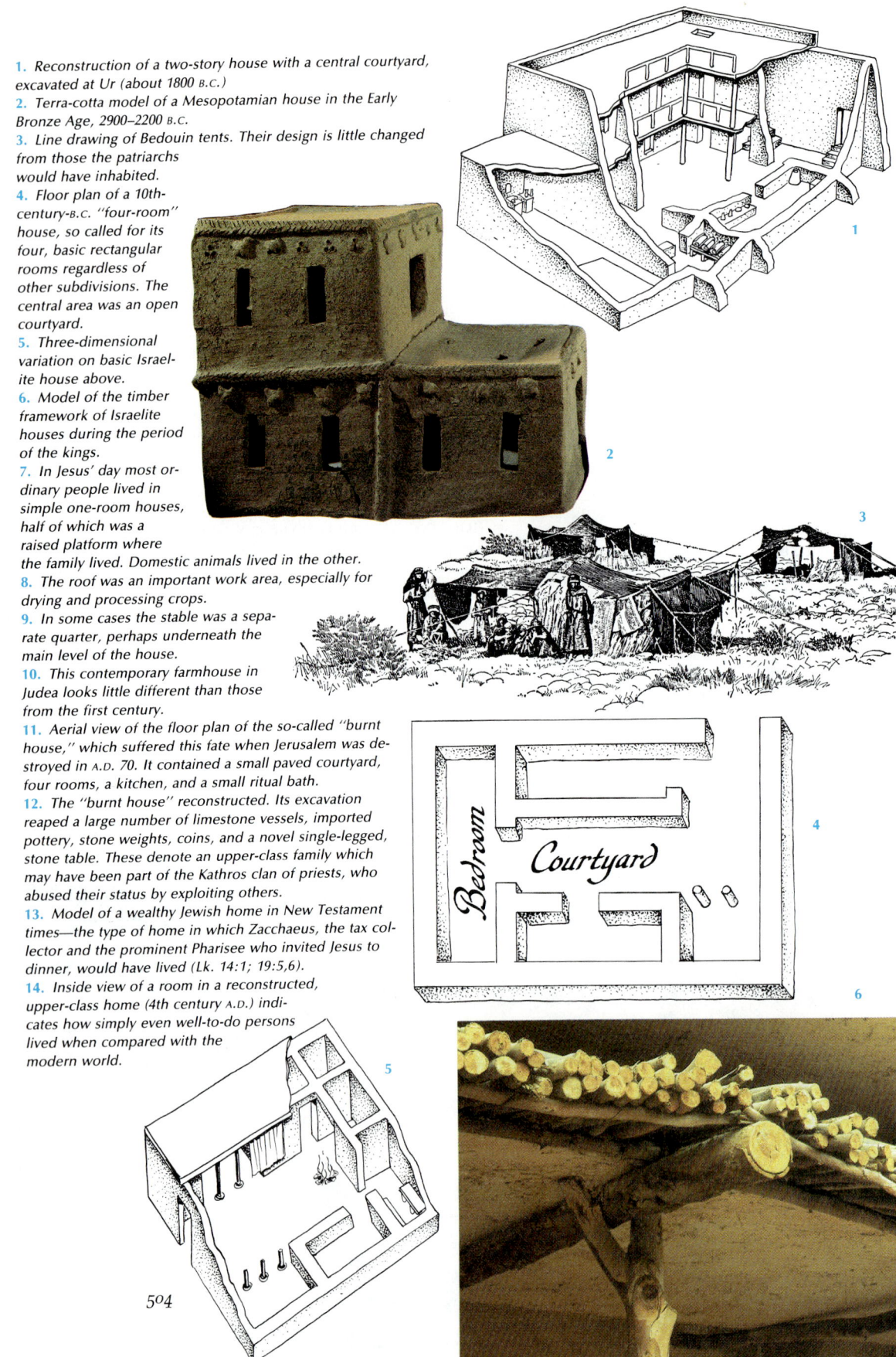

1. Reconstruction of a two-story house with a central courtyard, excavated at Ur (about 1800 B.C.)

2. Terra-cotta model of a Mesopotamian house in the Early Bronze Age, 2900–2200 B.C.

3. Line drawing of Bedouin tents. Their design is little changed from those the patriarchs would have inhabited.

4. Floor plan of a 10th-century-B.C. "four-room" house, so called for its four, basic rectangular rooms regardless of other subdivisions. The central area was an open courtyard.

5. Three-dimensional variation on basic Israelite house above.

6. Model of the timber framework of Israelite houses during the period of the kings.

7. In Jesus' day most ordinary people lived in simple one-room houses, half of which was a raised platform where the family lived. Domestic animals lived in the other.

8. The roof was an important work area, especially for drying and processing crops.

9. In some cases the stable was a separate quarter, perhaps underneath the main level of the house.

10. This contemporary farmhouse in Judea looks little different than those from the first century.

11. Aerial view of the floor plan of the so-called "burnt house," which suffered this fate when Jerusalem was destroyed in A.D. 70. It contained a small paved courtyard, four rooms, a kitchen, and a small ritual bath.

12. The "burnt house" reconstructed. Its excavation reaped a large number of limestone vessels, imported pottery, stone weights, coins, and a novel single-legged, stone table. These denote an upper-class family which may have been part of the Kathros clan of priests, who abused their status by exploiting others.

13. Model of a wealthy Jewish home in New Testament times—the type of home in which Zacchaeus, the tax collector and the prominent Pharisee who invited Jesus to dinner, would have lived (Lk. 14:1; 19:5,6).

14. Inside view of a room in a reconstructed, upper-class home (4th century A.D.) indicates how simply even well-to-do persons lived when compared with the modern world.

Bedroom

Courtyard

504

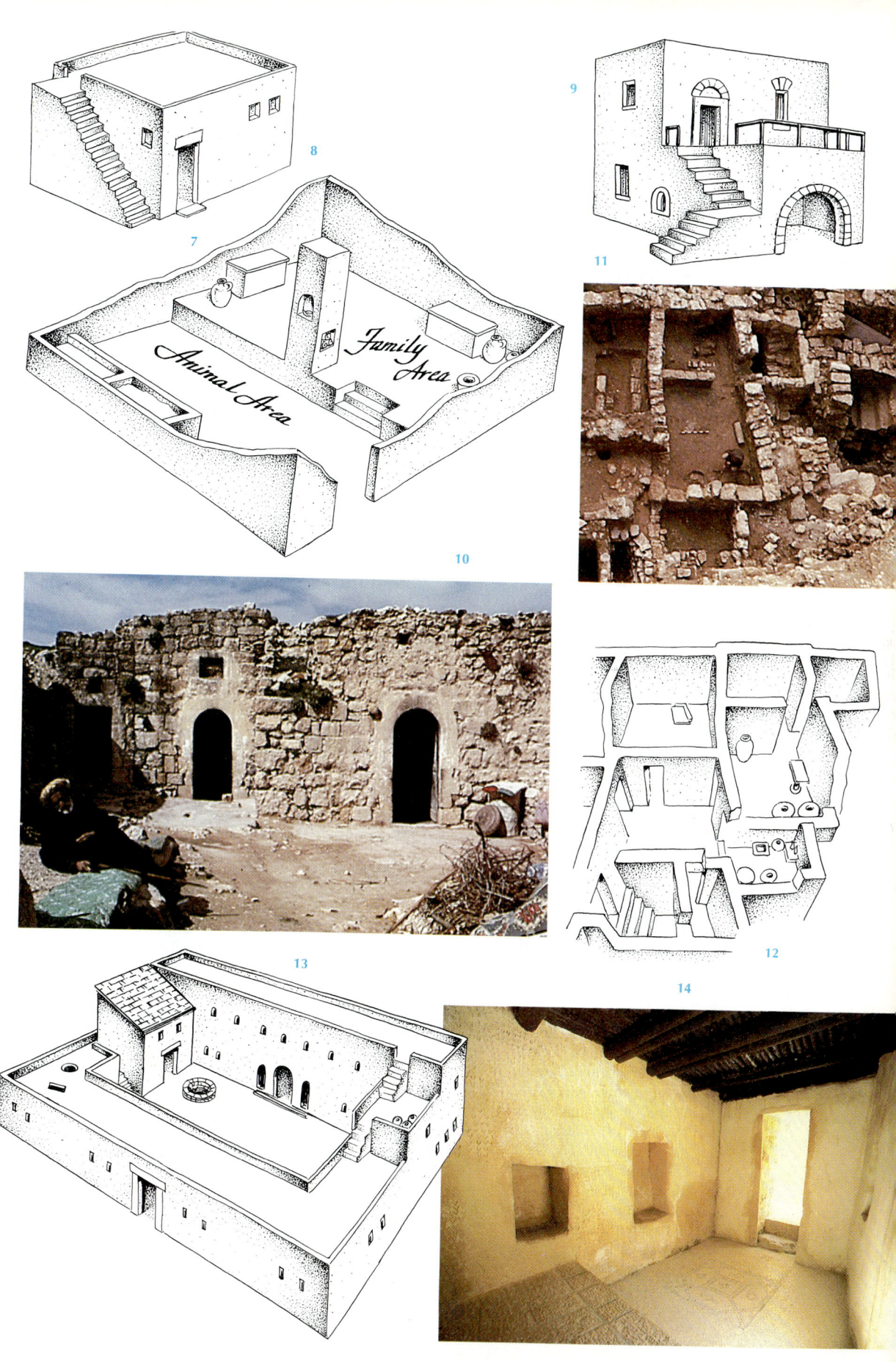

8

9

7

11

Family
Area

Animal Area

10

13

12

14

shed on your house if someone falls from the roof" (Deut. 22:8).

We would consider these houses tiny, bare, and crowded. Typically, seven or eight family members lived and slept together in a single home, and in time of war or severe weather, not only the family but also livestock found shelter in the courtyard or even inside the house. Yet the house provided the shelter and support the family group required.

humble, humility (1) OT: poor, afflicted, lowly; (2) theologically, dependent on God and truly pious; (3) NT: free of pride, dependent on God and concerned for others.

HUMILITY IN THE OT

The Hebrew terms originally described persons who were economically and socially powerless, but gradually the focus shifts in the OT from the state of the poor to the utter dependence forced upon them. The poor call upon God because he is their only hope. The wealthy and powerful become arrogant, and depend not on God but on their social status. In Deut. 8:10-20 Israel is warned against the pride often associated with success. Once a person says, "My power and the strength of my hands have produced this wealth for me," he tends to forget the Lord. Such persons will "surely be destroyed."

Humility, thus, is transformed from the condition of poverty to the attitude of the believer who acknowledges total dependence on God. In the Psalms and prophets, humility is the mark of the pious and righteous man and stands in contrast to the arrogance of the wicked. Psalm 147:6 says, "The Lord sustains the humble but casts the wicked to the ground." And Micah says to an arrogant generation, "[God] has showed you, O man, what is good. And what does the Lord require of you? To act justly and to love mercy and to walk humbly with your God" (6:8).

HUMILITY IN THE NT

In the Gospels, some of Christ's references to humility have a distinct OT flavor. The person who exalts himself will be brought low. Arrogance will bring social as well as spiritual disaster (Mt. 23:13; Lk. 14:11; 18:14). Christ's rebuke to the religious leaders in Lk. 13:17 not only silenced but humbled, in the sense of humiliated, his opponents. Yet Christ speaks of himself as humble, using the theological sense of that word to express his responsiveness to God and to human need.

In the secular world of the first century,

tapeinos described a social powerlessness, which to the Greek was deplorable and shameful. Yet the NT Epistles consistently portray humility as a major Christian virtue. This reversal of values rests on two great realities.

First, the Greeks tended to view man as the measure of all things. To be humble was to be low on the social scale, and thus a failure as a human being. But in the Judeo-Christian tradition, God is the measure of all things. To be humble is to be totally dependent on God and thus in right relationship with him. Humility enables human beings to fulfill their destiny as persons created for fellowship with God. But this attitude of dependence must be directed toward God. Colossians 2:18-23 speaks of a false humility, which is defective because it depends on beings other than God.

Second, Christ himself powerfully modeled humility. Christ "made himself nothing" in his incarnation, and then "humbled himself and became obedient to death" (Phil. 2:7,8; *compare* Mt. 11:29; 2 Cor. 10:1)—the fullest display of humility possible.

The Christian virtue of humility affects relationships with others as well as reflects personal dependence on God. The humble person is not concerned with his or her prestige. Philippians 2:3,4 captures this concept perfectly: "Do nothing out of selfish ambition or vain conceit, but in humility consider others better than yourselves. Each of you should look not only to your own interests, but also to the interests of others" (*compare* Rom. 12:10-16). Freedom from a sense of one's own importance, with honest concern for others and personal dependence on God, makes humility one of the most mentioned and encouraged of Christian virtues (Col. 3:12; Tit. 3:2; Jas. 3:13; 4:6; 1 Pet. 3:8; 5:5).

hunger (1) Serious deprivation of food, famine; (2) figuratively, to desire something strongly, as necessary for life itself.

Hebrew words for hunger are often translated "famine," and describe a desperate lack rather than simple appetite. *See also* Famine. God used hunger to discipline his people and to demonstrate to them their need for right relationship with him (Deut. 8:3; 28:47,48; Isa. 49:10). At the same time, Scripture portrays God as the one who supplies food for hungry animals and for mankind. He is the one who "fills the hungry with good things" (Ps. 107:9; *compare* 146:7).

The believer is urged to follow God's example and show concern for the hungry. Only the morally deficient leaves the hungry without food (Isa. 32:6). The godly man relieves the needs of the hungry (Isa. 58:6,7; Mt. 25:34-40) and even feeds a hungry enemy (Prov. 25:21; Rom. 12:20).

The seriousness of hunger as an acute lack rather than simple appetite is reflected in its figurative uses. Thus, the person who hungers after righteousness is blessed because he is acutely aware of his need. He simply must have that righteousness which God alone can supply (Mt. 5:6). *See also* Righteousness.

Christ presented himself as the bread of life and promised, ''He who comes to me will never go hungry'' (Jn. 6:35). In portraying himself as bread, the staple food of Palestine and a symbol of life itself, Christ promised to meet every spiritual need—and satisfy the spiritual hunger—of those who put their trust in him (Jn. 6:31-58).

hunting The pursuit of wild animals for food, sport, or in defense of one's herds.

Hunting for sport is frequently portrayed in the material remains of some ancient cultures. A wall painting from the tomb of Pharaoh Amenhotep (about 2000

Above: Egyptian police chief, the so-called Nebamun, hunts birds in Egyptian marshes; detail of a tomb painting at Thebes, 1422–1411 B.C. Below: Ashurbanipal lances a wounded lion in this detail of a relief from his palace in Nineveh, about 645 B.C. Some early Assyrian kings clearly enjoyed lion hunting, a sport reserved for them in enclosed grounds.

B.C.) shows him hunting with bows and arrows. A relief of Ashurbanipal of Assyria (about 640 B.C.) depicts the ruler firing arrows at lions, while guarded by hunting dogs and their handlers. Yet there is little mention of hunting in Israel, and none that suggests hunting was viewed as a sport.

Both Nimrod (Gen. 10:9) and Esau (Gen. 25:27) are called hunters. We know that Esau used bow and arrows, and that he sought deer as game (Gen. 27:3). Later biblical passages mention trapping birds in nets (Pss. 91:3; 124:7; Isa. 19:8), setting traps (Amos 3:5), and even digging pits into which animals might fall (Ps. 35:7; Ezek. 19:1-4). This hunting was done for food, and a number of wild animals, especially from the deer family, were "clean" according to OT Law and could be used for food (Deut. 14:5).

Wild animals were also hunted to protect flocks of sheep and goats. Most notable in the OT is David's killing of a bear and lion who attacked the sheep he guarded (1 Sam. 17:34-36; *compare* 2 Sam. 23:20).

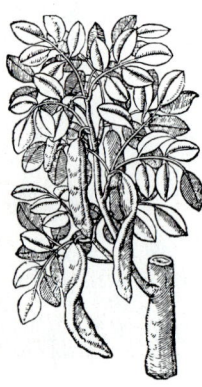

The bean pods of the carob tree may have been the "husks" the prodigal son fed pigs (Lk. 15:16).

husband A man viewed in relationship to his wife. Rabbinical teaching on the relationship between husband and wife is rooted in Ex. 21:10, which says that a husband must "not deprive" a wife of "her food, clothing and marital rights." From this the rabbis concluded that a husband was responsible to provide his wife with all the material necessities of life and to meet her sexual and emotional needs.

While some teachers focused on the role of husband as provider and assigned him the sole right to use the family's resources, other rabbis focused on the quality of the marriage relationship. They saw the couple as two candles: the love of each was constantly to rekindle the love of the other. However, because women had fewer rights and responsibilities in ancient cultures, the husband had the primary responsibility to love and cherish his wife.

In the NT, Paul goes beyond the rabbis to teach that wives like husbands "own" their partner's body. Thus, the sexual needs of women as well as men are to be met within the marriage (1 Cor. 7:3,4). Furthermore, as head, the husband is to imitate Christ and accept responsibility for his wife's nurture (Eph. 5:22-33). Three times in this passage Paul emphasizes Christlike love as the means of a fulfilling headship. The husband is to love his wife

Pharaoh Akhenaten, unique for his monotheistic worship of the sun disk, wrote a hymn to the sun that uses language similar to Hebrew poetry in the Psalms: "How manifold are your works, mysterious to our eyes! O sole god, like whom there is no other! You created the world according to your desire. . ." (see Psalm 104:24).

508

as his own body and to nurture and care for her (*compare* 1 Pet. 3:7, which calls on husbands to respect or honor their wives). *See also* Bride and Bridegroom; Head; Submission; Wife; Woman.

husbandman (KJV) Archaic term for a farmer. *See also* Agriculture.

husbandry See Agriculture.

husks (KJV) Bean pods of the carob tree, used in the Middle East as animal fodder, as in Lk. 15:16. In difficult times, the beans were also eaten by the poor. The Greek word is translated "pods" in most modern versions of the NT. The two Hebrew words translated "husks" in the KJV OT are each used only once (Num. 6:4; 2 Ki. 4:42). Their real meaning remains uncertain.

hyena A large, striped carnivore with powerful head and shoulders. The hyena feeds at night, often on refuse and dead animals. The precise meaning of the Hebrew word is uncertain although hyenas roamed Palestine in biblical times. Some modern versions render the Hebrew word as wolf, wild beast, or even as bird of prey.

hymn Any poetic composition or song in praise of God, used in worship. Hymns might be recited or sung and were part of the shared worship experienced by NT congregations. In OT times, many psalms were used in this way by the Jews.

Hymns became essential elements in NT worship and served not only as expressions of praise but also as affirmations of basic doctrines. Passages of Scripture which may have been based on or used as hymns in the NT church include Phil. 2:6-11; Col. 1:15-20; the doxologies found in Lk. 2:14; 1 Tim. 1:17 and 6:15,16; Rev. 4:8; 5:12,13; and poetical passages such as Lk. 1:46-55 and 2:10-14. *See also* Psalms; Song.

hypocrite, hypocrisy [Gk., *hypokritēs;* "an actor playing the part of another"]. When Greek actors performed, they used masks which represented the character each portrayed. This suggests that the hypocrite is a person whose real self and motives are masked, perhaps even from himself (Mt. 7:21-23).

In Matthew 23 Jesus identifies the Pharisees and teachers of the Law as hypocrites and describes the actions that merit that term. These teachers of the Law do not practice what they preach (23:3). They put great effort into winning converts and then corrupt them (23:15). They concern themselves with the minor details of God's Law and ignore its more important issues (23:23). They are concerned with externals and ignore the heart (23:25). They try to appear to others as holy but inwardly are wicked (23:27). They build the tombs of the prophets but display the attitude of those who murdered them (23:29-32). Based on Jesus' scathing denouncement,

hypocrisy describes a state of spiritual blindness, self-righteousness, and wickedness.

hyssop A small bush, with thin branches and unremarkable leaves and flowers. In Hebrew tradition, the hyssop symbolized humility and was contrasted with the proud cedar of Lebanon (1 Ki. 4:33).

Hyssop is associated with sacrifice in the OT. A bundle of hyssop served as a brush with which the blood of the sacrificial lamb was sprinkled on the doorpost during the first Passover in Egypt (Ex. 12:22). Hyssop was also used to sprinkle cleansing blood on the people of Israel (Ex. 24:6-8; Lev. 14:4) and various holy objects (Lev. 14:49-52). David referred to sacrifice symbolically when he cried to God for forgiveness and said, "Cleanse me with hyssop, and I will be clean" (Ps. 51:7).

Above: The "humble" hyssop bush, or Syrian marjoram, belongs to the mint family. Its hairy stems, bunched together with its leaves and flowers, hold fluid well and make an excellent "sprinkler" (Ex. 12:22 and others).

Left: Poet Menander and theatrical masks, first-century marble copy of a third-century B.C. original. "Hypocrite," a Greek word transliterated, originally referred to an actor who performed behind a mask. This relates easily to the popular English idea of pretense or gap between outward expression and inward motivation (see Mt. 23).

I

ㄴ ᚴ Ꮗ ㇇ ㄱ |

C. 1500 BC   C. 1300 BC   C. 1000 BC   C. 450 BC   100 AD   500 BC
PROTO-SINAITIC   CANAANITE   PHOENICIAN   ARAMAIC   HEBREW   GREEK

I AM The divine name, revealed to Moses when God spoke to him from the burning bush, Ex. 3:14. The name "I AM," like Yahweh (Jehovah), is the first person form of the Hebrew verb "to be."

The name "I AM" is often expanded to mean "I am (who I am)." In context, the name is better understood as an affirmation by God of his eternal presence with each generation of his people: God is the One who is always present (*compare* Lev. 26:12). *See also* Jehovah.

Jewish scholars who heard Jesus say, "Before Abraham was, I am," understood immediately that he was claiming identity with the I AM of the OT. They "picked up stones to stone him" (Jn. 8:57-59), the penalty for blasphemy (Lev. 24:16).

Persian ibex ornament crafted in bronze (700–400 B.C.).

Ibex and other mountain goats once thrived in rocky Palestine: "The high mountains belong to the wild goats" (Ps. 104:18). Today they are protected on reserves like this one at En Gedi.

ibex A variety of wild mountain goat with large, backward curving horns. The ibex is mentioned only in Job 39:1; Ps. 104:18; and 1 Sam. 24:1,2. However, each use reveals keen observation of the traits of this shy, agile cliff dweller. Most English versions translate the Hebrew word as mountain goat or wild goat.

idol, idolatry (1) Any object one shapes or uses as an object of worship; (2) all rites and practices associated with the worship of objects.

Over 15 Hebrew terms are used of idols. Specific terms have such meanings as "a likeness," "a form," "a representation," "an appearance," and "a human construction." More descriptive terms portray an idol as "a nothingness," "a falsehood," "a shameful thing," "an abomination," or a mere "helpless log."

In biblical times, idols were shaped in human and animal forms. A stone or tree trunk might serve as an idol. At times, idols were treated as if they were themselves gods (Isa. 44:17-20). However, most idols probably represented the god or goddess, with the likeness between the image and the deity serving as a link between material and spiritual worlds. As male Canaanite gods are often portrayed riding on a bull, many believe the golden calf of Ex. 32 and the calves or bulls Jeroboam I erected at Bethel and Dan were intended to serve as thrones for an invisible deity (1 Ki. 12:25-33).

Idolatry constantly tempted the people of Israel up to the time of the Exile (Ex. 32; Josh. 24:14; 1 Ki. 18; 2 Ki. 21:7). Thus, idolatry was not an evolutionary step towards monotheism but just the opposite—a turning away from the worship of the "one true God." The Exile experience, however, purged God's OT people of their yearning for idols. Nevertheless, idolatry remained dominant in surrounding cultures. It was well entrenched in the first-century world when the Christian church exploded out of tiny Palestine.

The OT takes a strong stand against idolatry. The Ten Commandments state, "You shall not make for yourself an idol in the form of anything in heaven above or on the earth beneath or in the waters below. You shall not bow down to them or worship them" (Ex. 20:4,5). Important reasons are given for this command.

1. *Idolatry distorts the concept of God.* Deuteronomy 4:15,16 says, "You saw no form of any kind the day the Lord spoke to you at Horeb out of the fire. Therefore watch yourselves very carefully, so that you do not become corrupt and make for yourselves an idol, an image of any shape." God is Spirit. Any attempt to represent him in material form will distort his essential nature.

2. *Idolatry represents human arrogance.* Idolatry is essentially reliance on human ideas of religion rather than on divine revelation. Man becomes the measure, and gods are created in man's image. In contrast, Scripture defines mankind as created in the image of God. It is utter arrogance to create gods in man's image, rather than acknowledge God as the one who created man. This theme is developed in Isa. 2:8-22, where the futility of idolatry is set against the repeated warning, "The arrogance of man will be brought low and the pride of men humbled." Isaiah further says, "The Lord alone will be exalted . . . and the idols will totally disappear" (vv. 17,18).

3. *Idolatry leads to immorality* (Hos. 9:10). Ancient religion focused on cycles of nature. Gods and goddesses were thought to control fertility, and many rites were intended to stimulate deities sexually. In Rom. 1:18-32, Paul argues that immorality is a natural consequence of idolatry. The idolater abandons knowledge of the true God (1:18-23), and this, in turn, cuts him off from knowledge of his own moral nature and leads to a "morality" that simply expresses sinful human desires (1:24,25). The consequence is an immoral life-style (1:26,27) marked by sinful attitudes and actions (1:28-31)—a view repeated in Paul's first letter to the Corinthians (10:6-10).

4. *Idolatry serves as a point of contact with the demonic.* Idols themselves are nothing, as Isaiah and the other prophets argue. "But," as Paul says, "the sacrifices of pagans are offered to demons, not to God, and I do not want you to be participants with demons" (1 Cor. 10:20). This opens up the possibility that people in ancient times did receive supernatural aid from idols, which may help explain why idolatry was deeply rooted in many societies. But any supernatural power channeled through idols was demonic in nature. God's own are to have nothing to do with the demonic but to rely wholly on the Lord (*compare* Deut. 12:1-3; 18:9-14). *See also* Demon.

Scripture, then, condemns idolatry because it distorts the truth and leads people away from God. Thus, idols need not be only graven images; they may be money (Col. 3:5), sexual desires (Eph. 5:5), covetousness (Gal. 5:19,20), etc.—whatever serves to turn our attention away from God.

ignorance (1) In the OT (KJV): a sin committed in ignorance, an error for which the violator remained culpable, as Ezek. 45:20. *See also* Sin. (2) A lack of knowledge, as in Ps. 73:22; Rom. 11:25; Heb. 5:2. (3) In the NT, as a religious term, a failure to perceive or respond to truth, as in Acts 13:27; Rom. 2:1-4.

Leviticus 4 details sacrifices to be offered when an individual or the community sins unintentionally. In each case, a person who commits such a sin is guilty. Intentional sin is more serious, yet guilt is

Israelite calf found in Samaria (12th century B.C.). The Israelites struggled with idolatry from the very start of their special relationship to God, as Ex. 32:4 clearly shows: "[Aaron] took what they handed to him and made it into an idol cast in the shape of a calf. . . .Then they said 'This is your god, O Israel, who brought you up out of Egypt.' "

MAN IN THE IMAGE OF GOD

Genesis links two Hebrew words, *selem*, "image," and *demut*, "likeness," to make a distinctive statement about human nature: God made mankind in his own image-likeness (Gen. 1:26,27; 5:1-32; 9:6). It is this image-likeness that sets humanity apart from all other created beings and that makes human life so precious that no compensation can be offered for taking another person's life (Gen. 9:6).

Some have historically tried to make a distinction between "image" and "likeness," but it is best to take the two terms as nearly synonymous, paired to form a technical theological expression. This expression affirms that God is the original to whom human beings must be compared if we are to know our true nature.

Like God, each human being can think, choose, feel, respond, initiate, act, etc. It is just such traits which remain a mystery to those who seek to explain human existence by aeons of evolution from single-celled life, generated spontaneously in some ancient cosmic accident. The Genesis doctrine of image-likeness affirms that we can only grasp humanity's identity when we look to God and see in human beings a dim reflection of God's personality.

The image-likeness of God is not clear in humanity today. The image-likeness of God in the first man and woman, Adam and Eve, was even then only a reflection. In Adam's Fall, even that reflection was distorted, as sin warped man's intellect, emotions, values, and will. But even then the image was not totally lost (Jas. 3:9). Individual human beings remain significant and important to God because each of us continues in some measure to reflect our Creator and each of us has an eternal destiny. Thus, it is significant that the NT views conversion as a renewal. Through God's work in our lives, we are "being renewed in knowledge in the image of" our Creator (Col. 3:10).

CHRIST IN THE IMAGE OF GOD

The OT states that human beings are made in the image of God. In contrast, the NT affirms that Christ *is* the image of God. The two Greek words used in such statements are *eikōn* and *charaktēr*. The first means a perfect reflection of the prototype and establishes identity with the prototype. Thus, Christ "is the image of the invisible God" (Col. 1:15; *compare* 2 Cor. 4:4). The second is a term that suggests a cast image, as of a coin, which is an exact representation of a mold. Hebrews 1:3

Terra-cotta figurine and mold found at the mines of Timnah. Idol-making was quite a business in Bible times, even among wayward Israelites (Isa. 44:9-20).

implicit in the deed, intentional or not. Ignorance of the Law is, thus, not a valid excuse.

In the NT, "ignorance" is often used as a theological term to portray the state of the unsaved. Here, ignorance is an inability to perceive or respond to spiritual truth, a state shared by all the unsaved. This spiritual state in part explains why human beings, ignorant of God's righteousness, aggressively attempt to establish themselves as righteous (Rom. 10:3). Again, ignorance does not excuse sin. At best, ignorance explains why man so often acts against his own best interest and against the divine will.

Yet, Paul also says that he obtained mercy because he "acted in ignorance and unbelief" (1 Tim. 1:13). The same thought is expressed in Acts 17:30. The state of sin described by this ignorance is not willful rejection of known truth but a blind failure to respond to truth. The antidote to such ignorance is not just knowledge but an act of faith that opens the mind and heart to God.

image (1) OT: an idol—wood or metal shaped to represent an object or being; (2) in the OT, used with "likeness" to make a statement concerning human nature; (3) in the NT, a statement about the nature of Christ.

says that Christ is the "exact representation of his [God's] being."

These terms are even more significant when compared with words used to express Christ's relationship to humankind. When the NT speaks of Christ as "like his brothers," it uses *homoioō*. This word asserts similarity but falls short of affirming complete identity. However, Christians are currently being transformed into Christ's likeness (2 Cor. 3:18). Here, strikingly, *eikōn* is used! While God will never bear our likeness, for he remains the eternal standard, yet, in Christ, the redeemed will be "conformed to the *eikōn* [perfect reflection] of his Son" (Rom. 8:29).

Philippians 2 is another significant passage. Jesus, who existed in the form (*morphē*) of God, took on the form (*morphē*) of a servant. Here *morphē* means "the mode of existence which most closely conforms to the essence of what it represents." Jesus existed as God and, without any loss of that essence which made him God, became a human being and adopted our mode of existence in this material world. *See also* Incarnation. Though not stated in Philippians, a significant analogy is suggested. Death will change our *morphē*, our "mode of existence," but there will be no loss of personhood or of the essence that makes each of us unique. Instead, shedding our mortal bodies, we will put on immortality—we will truly be "like" Christ (1 Cor. 15:50-57; 1 Jn. 3:1-3).

Immanuel [Heb., *'immanu'el;* "with us is God"]. The name given in Isaiah's prophecy to a child to be born of a virgin, who will serve as a sign to God's people. Matthew 1:23 identifies Jesus as the child who fulfills this prediction.

The term is first found in Isa. 7:1-17, in the context of an event which occurred in 753 B.C. Isaiah, carrying his infant son Shear-Jashub, meets King Ahaz. The king is frightened because a coalition of Israel and Syria threatens Judah. Isaiah promises deliverance and tells Ahaz to ask God for a sign. The king, one of Judah's most wicked rulers, refuses. Isaiah then announces that God will give "you" a sign. The plural "you" in Hebrew indicates the sign is for God's people rather than for Ahaz. "The virgin will be with child and will give birth to a son, and will call him Immanuel" (7:14). Isaiah then goes on to say that within the span of time it takes a child to learn the difference between right and wrong, "the land of the two kings you dread will be laid waste" (7:16).

Interpretation of this passage is much debated, with many denying that Isaiah suggests either a virgin birth or the coming of the Messiah. However, (1) Mt. 1:23 establishes the messianic link. Jesus is specifically said to fulfill Isaiah's prophecy. (2) The virgin birth is established by Matthew's use of *parthenos* (virgin) to render the Hebrew *'almah; 'almah* itself is the only Hebrew term always applied to an unmarried woman. (3) Two children are in view in the original Isaiah text: the Immanuel yet to be born and Shear-Jashub, then on Isaiah's arm. It is best to take 7:15-17 as a reference to Shear-Jashub, perhaps held up by Isaiah as the prophet promised the quick demise of Ahaz's enemies. (4) The continuing context picks up the name Immanuel and culminates in the promise that a child to be born, a son given, will bear divine names and establish an endless kingdom (9:6,7)—prophecies only the Messiah can fulfill.

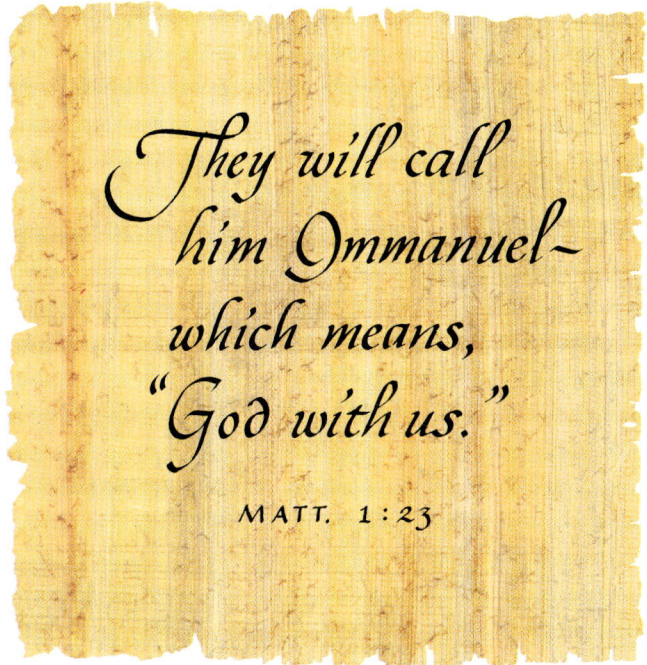

They will call him Immanuel—which means, "God with us."

MATT. 1:23

immorality [Gk., *porneia*]. In Scripture, unlawful sexual intercourse. Because our concept of immorality is broader, contemporary English versions often use a defining phrase, "sexual immorality," to render the single Greek term. *See also* Adultery; Fornication; Prostitute.

immortal, imperishable Immune to decay, incorruptible. In Scripture, these two synonyms portray immunity to all the

Alabaster cup bears a wish of immortality for Tutankhamun: "May you spend millions of years . . . sitting with your face to the north wind"; tomb of Tutankhamun (about 1342 B.C.).

forces that cause change and decay in the material universe. God himself has this immunity (Rom. 1:23; 1 Tim. 1:17), and he gives believers an "incorruptible heredity" (1 Pet. 1:23 PHILLIPS). In the resurrection, believers will be "raised imperishable" (1 Cor. 15:42) to live forever immune to the power of death (1 Cor. 15:50-55). *See also* Resurrection.

imposter *See* Magic.

impure *See* Clean and Unclean.

incarnation To become flesh. The term refers to the Christian doctrine that the eternal Son of God became a true human being in Jesus Christ.

GOSPELS: INCARNATION AFFIRMED
The nativity stories given in Mt. 1 and Lk. 1 describe Jesus' supernatural conception. Made pregnant by the Holy Spirit without the agency of a human father, Mary bears a son called Immanuel—"God with us" (Mt. 1:23). Furthermore, Jn. 1 speaks of Jesus as the eternal Word, who was God, and was with God in the beginning. The pre-existing Word, himself the Creator, "became flesh and lived for a while among us" (1:14). In other passages, John's Gospel identifies Jesus as the one who came from heaven (Jn. 3:13-15; 6:33-39) and who existed before Abraham as the I AM of the OT (Jn. 8:57,58). *See also* I AM; Immanuel; Jesus Christ; John, the Gospel According to.

EPISTLES: INCARNATION EXPLAINED
The NT Epistles teach that Jesus is both fully God and fully man. Key passages are Phil. 2:6-8; Col. 1:15-20; and Heb. 1.
• *Philippians 2:6-8.* Christ left his mode

of existence (Gk., *morphē*) as God to take on the mode of existence of a human being. In making this transition, Christ did not abandon his deity but rather took on true humanity in addition to it. At history's end, the God-Man, Jesus Christ, will be acknowledged as Lord by all.
• *Colossians 1:15-20.* All the fullness of God dwells in Jesus. He is a perfect reflection (Gk., *eikōn*) of the invisible God, and in Christ "all the fullness of the Deity lives in bodily form" (Col. 2:9).
• *Hebrews 1.* As Son of God, Christ is the "exact representation" (Gk., *charaktēr*) of God's being. In the OT, God himself calls the Son "God" (Heb. 1:8,9; *compare* Ps. 45:6,7).
These and other passages establish the Christian doctrine that One who existed eternally with the Father as a distinct but equal Person took on humanity and lived a human life on earth. The Son was both fully human and fully God, at one and the same time, bonding both natures in the single person of Jesus Christ.

INCARNATION IN CHURCH HISTORY
The mystery of the union of deity and humanity in Jesus has challenged theologians from the first. Orthodox Christians have resisted the tendency to emphasize either Christ's deity or his humanity at the expense of the other.

Some groups have viewed Christ as a "God-filled" man, as if the Jesus *persona* were a puppet shell which God filled and activated. Other groups viewed the Son as a creation, not as God. Some have tried to explain the union of God and man as a fusion of the two natures, creating something new, while others spoke of the human nature being absorbed into the divine. The final orthodox formulation was expressed by the Council of Chalcedon in A.D. 451. It affirms one Christ, in whom the natures of God and man exist together, without either nature being confused, diminished, mutilated, absorbed, or in any other way distorted by the union.

This understanding of Jesus' identity is foundational. Only one who was God as well as man could pay the infinite price of humanity's sin. Only a person who was tempted as we are, and yet sinless, can understand and help us in our own spiritual struggles (Heb. 2:18; 4:14,15; 5:7-10; *compare* 2 Cor. 5:21; 1 Pet. 2:22).

INCARNATION IN THE OT
The OT does not expressly teach the incarnation, but what the OT does teach implies it and is in full harmony with this

doctrine. The incarnation explains how an infant born of a virgin could be Immanuel, "God with us" (Isa. 7:14). It also explains the declaration of Isa. 9:6, which speaks of a child to be born, a son to be given, and then goes on to proclaim him as God Almighty. Micah 5:2-4 also takes on fresh meaning in light of the NT's teaching on the incarnation. We now understand how the ruler to be born in Bethlehem can be one "whose origins are from of old, from ancient times," and how this one will shepherd his flock "in the majesty of the name of the Lord his God."

Taken together, overwhelming biblical evidence asserts that Jesus Christ is both divine and human. He is God the Son and yet a child of Mary. The true "historical Jesus" was not simply a man of his time but also the God of all eternity.

incense Aromatic compounds burned on special occasions, especially as part of the worship rituals of nearly all peoples of the ancient world. *See also* Frankincense.

According to OT Law, incense was to be burned inside the tabernacle morning and evening (Ex. 30:1-10; *compare* Lk. 1:8-11), burned on a small golden altar, always on coals carried on shovel-like censers from the larger altar outside where animal sacrifices were burned. Once a year, on the Day of Atonement, the high priest carried a censer of incense into the Holy of Holies with sacrificial blood (*compare* Eph. 5:2). *See also* Censer.

Exodus 30:34-38 gives the formula for the holy incense—made of galbanum, onycha, and stacte—which was to be used only in worship rituals. Other formulas were used for the incense burned at celebrations and funerals (*compare* 2 Chr. 16:14; Prov. 27:9). Incense was costly (Isa. 60:6), and in Rev. 18:13 it stands for luxury. Symbolically, incense represents prayer (Ps. 141:2; Lk. 1:10; Rev. 5:8; 8:3).

incest Sexual relations between persons so closely related that a marriage is forbidden.

Leviticus 18:6 says that "no one is to approach any close relative to have sexual relations." The chapter goes on to define "close relatives" as one's mother, one's father's wife, sister, half-sister, grandchild, aunt, daughter-in-law, and sister-in-law. Those committing incest were to be cut off from Israel (Lev. 18:29) or executed (Lev. 20:11-13). Such a person would also be childless (Lev. 20:21). In the NT, Paul calls on the Corinthians to expel an incestuous brother from their congregation (1 Cor. 5:2-5).

Ingathering, Feast of *See* Tabernacles, Feast of.

inheritance (1) The rights of a child or adopted heir to the tangible or intangible property of his father on the father's death; (2) one's heritage, especially the land given to Israel by the Lord as a permanent heritage, as in Ex. 32:13; Deut. 4:21; Ps. 37:11; (3) NT: the rights in one's father's estate enjoyed under Roman law by any child by right of birth.

INHERITANCE IN THE OT

Passages in Genesis reflect inheritance customs, a number of which are formalized in the Mosaic Law. Inheritance laws covered such issues as the rights of the firstborn, the rights of children born to a concubine and acknowledged by the father (Deut. 21:15-17; *compare* Gen. 35:23-26), the rights of daughters (Num. 27:1-11), the transfer of property should a man die childless (Deut. 25:5-10), etc. Because the land each family occupied in Canaan was viewed as a direct gift by God to that family, it was important that property remain in the family (Ruth 3:9-13; 4:1-12; 1 Ki. 21:3).

Incense was commonly burned during Canaanite worship rituals on incense stands such as these. In Israelite worship a special incense and its burning were set apart for priests alone. Its offering to other gods was apostasy (Jer. 1:16; Ezek. 8:33).

515

HERITAGE IN THE OT

God's gift of the land of Canaan to Israel as an inheritance, or heritage, is stated in Gen. 12:7; Ex. 32:13; Josh. 1:6; 22:19, and many other passages. Israel saw itself as a people of the Promised Land, and Israel's understanding of God's purposes for his people was intimately linked to this land. The view that Canaan is Israel's permanent possession by right of divine gift is deeply rooted in the OT. Actual possession of the territory could be temporarily forfeited, however, if Israel turned its back on the Lord (as happened in 587–586 B.C. and in A.D. 70).

But in the theology of the OT, "inheritance" takes on additional significance. The landless tribe of Levi was to be supported by the tithes and gifts paid by the other tribes to the Lord. Thus, God himself was Levi's inheritance (Deut. 18:1,2). By extension, God was the inheritance not only of the Levites but also of all Israel (Ps. 16:5,6). In return, Israel was God's heritage—his property and his special possession (Ps. 79:1; Jer. 10:16).

INHERITANCE IN THE NT

In the Epistles, the concept of inheritance is shaped by Roman rather than Hebrew law. Under Roman law, one's inheritance was the total of all tangible and intangible assets one possessed. While the head of the family managed his inheritance, his children were considered co-owners. Thus one came into his or her inheritance rights at birth, although actual possession would be deferred until the death of the parent. So Rom. 8:17 says, "Now if we are children, then we are heirs—heirs of God and co-heirs with Christ"—in contrast to the wicked who "will not inherit the kingdom of God." Their acts demonstrate they have nothing of his heredity (1 Cor. 6:9,10; Eph. 5:5).

The legal point Paul makes in passages on inheritance is that as God's heirs, we share now in all that is his. As Father, God uses his resources to benefit us, his children (Rom. 9:6-8; Gal. 3:6,7,28,29). In the resurrection, we will fully possess our inheritance. But even now, God uses his tangible and intangible possessions to meet our every need (1 Pet. 1:4).

iniquity The Hebrew word (*'awon*) suggests a willful twisting of, or deviation from, the divine standard (Ps. 73:7; Isa. 61:8). The Greek word (*adikia*) suggests conscious human acts that cause harm to others in violation of the divine ideal (Rom. 1:18,29). *See also* Sin.

ink A fluid or a solid which could be moistened and used by scribes to write on several different materials.

Ink pot identical to those found in the scriptorium at Qumran where the copies of the Dead Sea Scrolls were made.

Ink is mentioned in Jer. 36:18; 2 Cor. 3:3; 2 Jn. 12; 3 Jn. 13, and alluded to in a number of other passages, such as Ex. 32:33 and Num. 5:23. Commonly, ink was made of soot mixed with gum or oil. Metallic inks were made by mixing iron sulfate in tannic acid and water. Inks were applied with a brush or pen to parchment, papyrus, or clay shards. Archaeologists have recovered Hebrew correspondence written in ink on clay potsherds dating from about 586 B.C. (the Lachish Letters).

The Bible also mentions an "inkhorn" (KJV) or "writing kit" (NIV). These kits, carried by scribes, held several reed pens and containers for solid or liquid ink (Ezek. 9:2,3,11).

inn (1) OT: initially, any place along the road where travelers camped; (2) later, a walled structure providing shelter for travelers and their animals; (3) NT: at times, a spare room in a private home, as in Lk. 2:7.

Travelers in biblical times tended to rely on the hospitality of locals when they traveled. *See also* Hospitality. The use of *katalyma* in Lk. 2:7 suggests that Joseph and Mary were looking for a guest room in Bethlehem rather than room in an inn.

In time, walled buildings were constructed along trade routes. These provided shelter and water. However, travelers were responsible for food for themselves and their animals. One of the best-known inns of biblical times lay on the barren road between Jerusalem and Jericho and is mentioned by Jesus in his story of the Good Samaritan (Lk. 10:34).

inquire (1) To seek information, to ask, to investigate, as in 2 Sam. 11:3; (2) in the OT, to seek divine guidance, as in 1 Sam. 14:37; 28:6.

Several Hebrew terms mean to "ask," "inquire," "seek," or "search." These are used interchangeably. In religious contexts, persons inquired of God for some specific purpose, especially for guidance in a particular situation. The most frequent inquiries reported in the historical books concern going to war or how to conduct a battle (Jdg. 20:18; 1 Sam. 14:37; 2 Sam. 2:1; 5:19).

The OT describes two primary ways through which God's people sought his guidance. (1) They might inquire of God by having the high priest use the Urim and Thummim (Num. 27:21; 1 Sam. 22:9-15). This seems to have involved drawing lots from within the breastpiece he wore over his heart. *See also* Urim and Thummim. (2) By David's time, this mode of inquiry was largely replaced by seeking guidance from one of God's prophets (1 Ki. 14:5; 2 Ki. 3:11; 8:8; 2 Chr. 11:2-4; Ezek.

20:1-3). In either case, God could and did refuse to respond to the inquiries of those who had turned away from him (Ezek. 20:1-3; *compare* 1 Sam. 28:1-7).

The religious sense of "inquire of the Lord" is not found in the NT. Yet the NT reports instances of special divine guidance (Acts 9:10-15; 10:9-29; 13:1-3; 16:6-10; 20:22-24).

insects Loosely, any of the many small invertebrate animals. With the exception of such insects as locusts and grasshoppers, swarming creatures were unclean, and the Hebrews were not to eat them (Lev. 11:20-23).

Various insects had an economic impact on agricultural Palestine. But the locust is the only insect mentioned extensively in the OT. References to honey suggest that both wild and domesticated bees were highly valued.

inspiration [Gk., *theopneustos;* "God-breathed"]. The Christian doctrine stated in 2 Tim. 3:16 that "all Scripture is God-breathed and is useful for teaching, rebuking, correcting and training in righteousness."

The term *theopneustos* is significant. It indicates a "breathing out" by God: The Lord was active in the process, so that what the writers penned in Scripture were words "taught by the Holy Spirit" (1 Cor. 2:13).

The Inn of the Good Samaritan, today's Khan Hathrour, lies halfway between Jerusalem and Jericho. It is the traditional site for the lodging place of Lk. 10:34.

INSPIRATION DEFINED

The doctrine of revelation holds that God has acted to disclose both himself and his will to humanity. The doctrine of inspiration holds that in some way God's Spirit so participated in or guided the writers of the Scriptures that the original documents communicate what he intended. It is the Scriptures, not the writers, who are inspired—a distinction which is sometimes lost or confused.

While *theopneustos* occurs only in 2 Tim. 3:16, the Bible is replete with expressions which communicate the fact that God has spoken supernaturally through its writers. David affirmed, "The Spirit of the Lord spoke through me; his word was on my tongue" (2 Sam. 23:2). Over 2,500 times the prophets and other OT writers use expressions such as "thus says the Lord" or "the Lord says." Men of God were carried along by the Spirit, so what they wrote was both their own words and words God "spoke by the Holy Spirit" (Acts 4:25).

The biblical documents themselves bear the mark of each writer's personality and his linguistic habits. Inspiration does not block out individuality. Rather, the doctrine of inspiration affirms that the words the writers chose were used by God to convey his message to humanity.

PAUL'S INTERCESSORY PRAYERS

For Christians in Rome	Rom. 1:8-10
For Israel	Rom. 10:1
For the Corinthian church	1 Cor. 1:4-9; 2 Cor. 13:7-9
For Christians in Ephesus	Eph. 1:16-23; Eph. 3:14-19
For Christians in Philippi	Phil. 1:3-11
For the Colossian church	Col. 1:3-14
For Christians in Thessalonica	1 Thess. 1:2,3; 2:13; 3:9-13; 5:23
	2 Thess. 1:3; 2:13,16,17; 3:16
For Timothy	2 Tim. 1:3,4
For Philemon	Phlm. 4-6

intercession Addressed to God, prayer for another person, usually to obtain God's help. *See also* Prayer.

Intercession is embedded in the OT concept of the priesthood, especially in the ministry of the high priest (Heb. 5:1). The NT says that because our high priest Jesus lives forever, "he is able to save completely those who come to God through him, because he always lives to intercede for them" (Heb. 7:25). In addition, the Holy Spirit "himself intercedes for us with groans that words cannot express" (Rom. 8:26). The fact that both Christ and the Spirit pray for each believer provides great encouragement to us.

Both Testaments contain notable examples of intercession. Abraham pleaded with God for any righteous who might live in Sodom (Gen. 18:16-33). Moses pleaded with God not to abandon Israel, even though the people had consistently disobeyed his commands (Num. 14:10-19). Significant intercessory prayers are found in Paul's letters (Eph. 1:17-20; 3:14-19; and Col. 1:9-13). These prayers provide important models to guide us in our prayers for others.

The NT writers felt that intercessory prayer was particularly important. Paul often mentions his prayers for believers in the young churches he founded and also asks the churches to pray for him (Eph. 6:19; Col. 4:2-4). James urges Christians to pray for one another's healing and notes that "the prayer of a righteous man is powerful and effective" (Jas. 5:16). Paul urged Timothy to teach the churches "first of all, that requests, prayers, intercession and thanksgiving be made for everyone" (1 Tim. 2:1). Through intercessory prayer, believers uphold and encourage one another before the Lord—touching each other's lives across the span of time and space.

interest A fee charged on a loan. The Israelite economy was agricultural, not commercial. Thus, commercial loans, while widely practiced in surrounding nations, were uncommon in Israel. It was the poor who borrowed, and they did so to obtain the necessities of life. Therefore, OT laws concerning borrowing should be seen as elements of Israel's social justice system rather than basic elements in its economic system. Charging interest was regarded as unworthy and improper between citizens of Israel—as a violation of brotherhood.

Under OT laws, the well-to-do were called on to lend to the poor without charging interest and, under certain conditions, to forgive loans that could not be repaid (Ex. 22:25; Deut. 15:1-11). The prophets who condemn the practice of charging interest do so because the wealthy have violated the rights of the poor (Neh. 5:1-11; Jer. 15:10; Ezek. 18:8). *See also* Borrow.

The Bible, however, establishes the fact that lending money at interest is not wrong in itself. Old Testament Law permitted Israelites to loan money to foreigners at interest (Deut. 23:20). And two parables of Jesus propose making such loans (Mt. 25:27; Lk. 19:23).

Loan agreement in Greek between the "rancher" Euboulos and the city of Orchomenos (third century B.C.). It includes provisions for payment of interest, a practice forbidden between Israelites out of compassion for the poor (Lev. 25:35-38).

intermarriage In the OT, marrying a non-Israelite, and thus creating family bonds between Hebrews and pagans.

Israel was called to an exclusive relationship with God as his people (Lev. 26:12). Intermarriage with other groups would lead to a loss of this identity (Gen. 34:8-10) and provide temptation to adopt pagan religious practices (1 Ki. 11:2). By the time of Ezra and Nehemiah, intermarriage was clearly recognized as unfaithfulness to the Lord and a most serious sin (Ezra 9; Neh. 13:23-28).

This view of intermarriage did not prevent individuals from marrying foreign women captured in war (Deut. 21:10-14) or foreign women who had settled down within Israel. The distinction seems to be that such marriages formed no family bond with pagan social groups but rather brought a bride without family ties into the faith-community.

In the NT, 2 Cor. 6:14 ("Do not be yoked together with unbelievers") prohibits marriage between Christians and non-Christians. This application of Paul's teaching is supported by his statement that a Christian widow is "free to marry anyone she wishes, but he must belong to the Lord" (1 Cor. 7:39).

interpretation of Scripture The process by which the meaning of the Bible is understood.

In practice, interpretation has two distinct but related aspects. (1) Interpretation tries to determine, "What does this mean? What is being said?" (2) The interpreter then tries to determine, "What does this mean to me? What is God saying to me personally?"

The Scripture is intended to communicate God's message to us. Thus we expect the Bible to be understandable. We may not understand all we read. But if we read carefully and intelligently, we will understand most of what we read.

The NT says that Scripture is profitable "for teaching, rebuking, correcting and training in righteousness, so that the man of God may be thoroughly equipped for every good work" (2 Tim. 3:16,17). When we approach the Bible reverently, read it intelligently, and respond obediently, we can expect the Word of God to have a transforming impact on our lives.

READING THE BIBLE INTELLIGENTLY

There are several elements to intelligent reading of Scripture. Some of these may seem scholarly to the untrained reader, but numerous Bible study tools are available to fill in whatever knowledge we may lack.

1. Be aware of historical setting. The books of the OT were written over a span of a thousand years. Knowing the history of Israel and the specific setting of each OT book is important if we are to understand its message to the original readers. Similarly, an understanding of the first century helps us better interpret the Gospels and NT Epistles. *See also* Chronology of the Bible.

2. Observe literary form. The Bible contains historical narrative, poetry, proverbs, parables, letters, sermons, prophecy, and apocalyptic visions. We cannot interpret poems as we do narratives or letters of instruction. To interpret the Bible accurately we need to know characteristics of Hebrew poetry, the use of symbolism in apocalyptic literature, various rules for interpreting prophecy, etc. *See also* Apocalyptic Literature; Epistle; Parable; Poetry; Prophecy, Interpretation of; Proverb.

We also need to be aware of literary devices. Hyperbole, which is exaggeration for the sake of effect, helps us understand Jesus' saying, "If your hand or your foot causes you to sin, cut it off" (Mt. 18:8). Other literary devices in Scripture include metaphor and anthropomorphism (ascribing human parts or motives to God).

3. Interpret in context. Bible verses and phrases always appear in the larger context of a paragraph, chapter, and book. We need to understand what we read within that larger frame of reference.

Interpreting in context means being aware of such things as to whom a passage is addressed; what issue the writer is addressing; any special circumstances when the passage was written; whether promises or warnings are conditional; etc.

4. Check unfamiliar terms. Many things in the Bible reflect a culture very different from our own. We may not understand the role of institutions, such as the priesthood or Passover. We may not understand the meaning of such terms as "grace," the OT's use of "save," or the NT concept of "house." It is important to look up unfamiliar terms, or words whose use in the passage we are reading seems unusual.

5. Seek confirmation. From the beginning, Christians have looked to the Bible for an understanding of their faith. Their witness testifies to the fact that the plain message of Scripture can be, and has been, understood. Various Christian traditions do differ on some doctrines. But there is a vast body of common understanding.

We can find confirmation of our understanding of Scripture by comparing passages with other Scripture passages, by seeking the opinions of mature Christians, and by checking our views against beliefs held in common by Christians through the centuries.

None of these principles for reading the Bible intelligently is unique. Intelligent reading of the Bible follows the same rules of interpretation we would use in seeking to understand any other literature, for God has spoken to us in human language.

APPLICATION TO LIFE

The Holy Spirit illuminates Scripture for the believer, not only clarifying what it means, but also pointing out how it applies to one's life. Several principles help us.

1. Maintain an appropriate attitude. We are to read the Bible expectantly. The living God meets us in his Word. His purpose is not to condemn us for our failures, but to unveil life's possibilities. Whatever Scripture shows that God expects from us, his Spirit, living within, gives us the strength to achieve.

2. Seek God's general will. First we look for principles of faith and life-style that apply to believers everywhere. When we read a passage like Rom. 12:9-21, we are moved to consider ways to honor others, be more patient in affliction, be faithful in prayer, practice hospitality, or share with others in need.

3. Seek God's specific will. We look for principles that may guide us in specific situations. We need to be especially aware of any problems we need to solve, emotions we need to deal with, or decisions we need to make. As we read prayerfully, we can expect the Holy Spirit to give us insight and guidance.

4. Consciously respond. We can respond by taking some specific overt action. We can respond with worship. We can respond by confessing a sin, expressing thanksgiving, becoming aware of an attitude, exploring an emotion.

If we try to apply Scripture to our lives, we find that the Bible really does speak to us.

iron A common metallic element, used in the ancient world in farm implements and weapons, and valued for its hardness.

Bronze, an alloy of copper and tin, was the dominant metal in the ancient world from 3200 to 1200 B.C. Iron objects were used during this era, but these were few, hammered from free iron or meteorites.

The melting point of iron is 1540° C. This temperature could not be achieved in furnaces of that time. The "chariots of iron" used by the Canaanites about 1390 B.C. may have been studded with iron, but would scarcely have been cast from iron or plated with it (Josh. 17:18; Jdg. 1:19).

Depletion of copper deposits stimulated the development of iron-smelting technologies. Most scholars today believe iron-working was brought into the biblical world by the Sea Peoples (groups from the Greek islands and Crete), of whom the Philistines were a branch. In the time of Saul the Philistines maintained a monopoly on working iron. The Israelites even had to go to Philistine smiths to have their iron tools sharpened. Only Saul and his son had iron weapons when Israel rebelled against their Philistine overlords (1 Sam. 13:19-22). Archaeologists have found iron tools from this era in both Israel and Philistia, but iron weapons only in Philistine territories.

Later David broke the power of the Philistines, and the secrets of working iron passed to the Israelites (*see also* 2 Chr. 2:14). During the monarchy, iron became more common and was used in all kinds of tools and weapons.

Iron is used figuratively in Scripture to suggest strength and often destructive power (Ps. 2:9; Ezek. 22:18-22; Dan. 7:7).

Iron Age A term used by archaeologists to indicate the era when iron became the metal of choice for agricultural implements and weapons. The Iron Age is generally divided into three periods: Iron Age I, 1200–1000 B.C.; Iron Age II, 1000–586 B.C.; Iron Age III, 586–332 B.C.

A Greek amphora depicting an ancient blacksmith shop. In Isaiah, God says, "See, it is I who created the blacksmith who fans the coals into flame and forges a weapon fit for its work" (54:16).

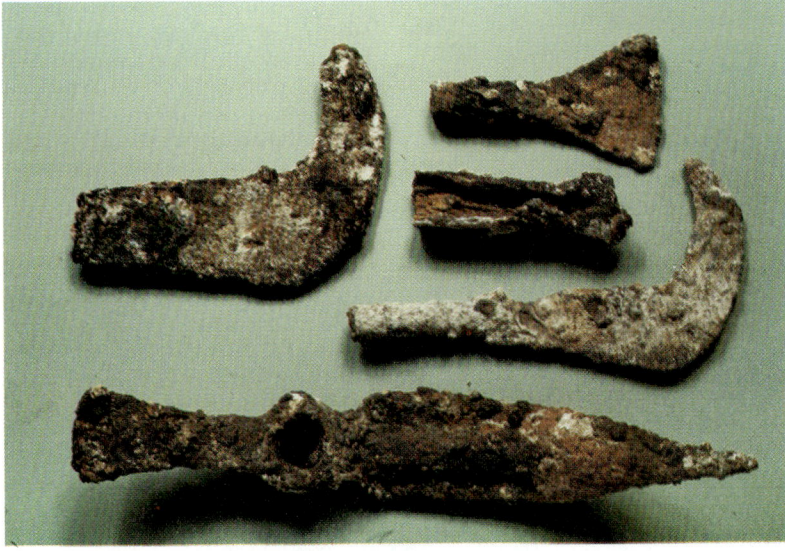

Israelite iron tools from Samaria. Iron-working technology came to Israel from the Philistines, whose iron weapons proved a constant nemesis through the period of the judges.

Contemporary stained-glass rendering of the akedah or "binding" of Isaac (Gen. 22:9). This experience in Isaac's life is one of many in Genesis where the promised line of Abraham seems to be in jeopardy.

Isaac [I-zik; "he laughs"]. The son of Abraham who inherited the covenant promises. **Born:** about 2066 B.C. **Mother:** Sarah. **Wife:** Rebekah. **Children:** Esau, Jacob. **Scripture:** Gen. 21–28.

BACKGROUND

When Abraham was a hundred years old and Sarah had ceased menstruating, God told him they would have a son. Abraham believed God, and a year later Isaac was born. On Abraham's death, the covenant promises God had given Abraham passed to this son. *See also* Abraham; Covenant.

Like Abraham, Isaac lived a semi-nomadic life in Canaan. At that time, parts of Canaan were settled by various ethnic groups in small independent city-states. Much of the land was open, with room for Isaac to grow crops on the southern plains during the rainy season and move to higher pasture lands in summer.

The biblical story focuses on a few events in Isaac's life: his birth (Gen. 21); his nearly being offered as a sacrifice (Gen. 22); obtaining his wife, Rebekah (Gen. 24); his uneasy relationships with the Philistines (Gen. 26), and his blessing of Jacob (Gen. 27).

LEARNING FROM ISAAC'S LIFE

Isaac appears as a somewhat passive individual, dependent on his father and especially his mother (21:8-10; *see* 24:67). Isaac trustingly went with Abraham to Mount Moriah, where Abraham had been commanded to sacrifice his son. He noted they brought no sacrificial lamb (22:7) but trusted his father enough to permit himself to be bound and laid on the altar (22:9). At 40, Isaac took no active role in obtaining a wife but left the search in the hands of Abraham's servant (Gen. 24).

After Abraham's death, Isaac showed timidity in dealing with the people of Canaan. Fear led him to lie about his relationship with Rebekah (26:1-11). When disputes arose over wells Isaac's own servants had dug, Isaac abandoned them to the Canaanites. Only after God appeared to Isaac and said, "Do not be afraid" (26:24), did Isaac take a stand and work out a treaty with his adversaries (26:25-33).

Like many who have depended too much on parents, the adult Isaac found it difficult to accept responsibility or act decisively. It took a personal experience with God to change Isaac. After this experience, no further failures of Isaac are mentioned in the text.

The next act of Isaac which Genesis reports is the blessing of Jacob and Esau. Isaac preferred his son Esau and intended to pass the intangible benefits of his special relationship with God to him. God, however, wanted Jacob to carry on the covenant line (Gen. 25:21-26). Jacob eventually obtained the blessing Isaac planned for Esau, first by persuading his older brother to give him the birthright in exchange for a bowl of stew (Gen. 25:33), and then by pretending to be Esau after Esau had been promised his father's blessing (Gen. 27). The key to the story is found in Isaac's remark when he realized he had been deceived: ". . .—and indeed he [Jacob] will be blessed!" (27:33). Isaac recognized God's hand in the event. Hebrews 11:20 says that the blessing Isaac gave his sons was an act of faith. Rather than willfully withdraw his blessing from Jacob, Isaac submitted to the will of God.

In many ways Isaac deserves our admiration. Except for Joseph, he is perhaps the only one of the patriarchs to remain monogamous. Rather than condemn Rebekah, he prays on behalf of his childless wife (25: 21). He was a man of peace, who praised God when peace prevailed (26:19-32).

In Galatians 4, Paul uses Isaac as an image of the Christian. He reminds his readers that Abraham had also had a son by Hagar, his slave-wife. So if ancestral lines were all that mattered, this son, Ishmael, and his descendants would be considered heirs of Abraham. But God made clear in Genesis that Isaac, the child of promise, would inherit Abraham's covenant.

Paul tells the Christians in Galatia, "Now you, brothers, like Isaac, are children of promise" (Gal. 4:28). Through Christ, we are heirs of the covenant. As Christians, free from sin and the Law, we are like Isaac. *See also* Ishmael.

Isaiah, Book of The first of the major prophetic books of the OT. This majestic book contains bold prophetic warnings, mixed with towering visions of future blessing. Isaiah is especially notable for its striking prophecies of the Messiah, and for its exceptional literary style.

BACKGROUND

Isaiah [i-ZAY-yuh; "Yahweh is salvation"] ministered during the rule of Kings Uzziah, Jotham, Ahaz, and Hezekiah. Isaiah was called to prophetic ministry in 739 B.C., the year Uzziah died. His last dated ministry took place in 701 B.C., although most of chs. 40–66 must have been written in the reign of Manasseh before his martyrdom around 680 B.C.

Little is known of Isaiah's personal life. He lived in Jerusalem (7:1-3; 37:2), was married to a prophetess (8:3), and had two sons, each of whom was given a symbolic name (7:3; 8:3). Isaiah wrote lost biographies of Uzziah and Hezekiah (2 Chr. 26:22; 32:32). A political activist of sorts, Isaiah spoke out strongly against foreign alliances of any kind (7:1-18; 20). Jewish tradition holds that Isaiah was martyred under Manasseh, by being sawed in two (*compare* Heb. 11:37).

Just before Isaiah began his prophetic ministry, both Israel and Judah had experienced great prosperity. Syria was weak,

Isaac dug wells throughout southern Palestine (Gen. 26:12-32), becoming wealthy, but making his neighbors envious.

The Isaiah scroll from the caves at Qumran is 1,000 years older than any other copies of the Hebrew Bible. Yet there are few differences in the text, which gives good ground for confidence about the reliable transmission of the Old Testament.

and during the reigns of Uzziah and Jotham (792–735 B.C.), Assyria was inactive in the area.

But Assyria became aggressive again under Tiglath-Pileser III (745–727 B.C.). Syria and Israel tried to force Ahaz of Judah to join them in an anti-Assyrian alliance. Against God's command through Isaiah, Ahaz called on Assyria for aid (Isa. 7). Assyria took Damascus in 732 B.C. and invaded the area east of the Jordan. Judah became a vassal of Assyria. In 722 Sargon II of Assyria captured Samaria, capital of Israel, and deported the ten northern tribes.

Jerusalem, however, was spared, and in chs. 36 and 37 Isaiah tells how God turned the Assyrian threat away in 705 or 701 B.C. Yet the incipient warfare with Assyria devastated much of Judah and brought the period of prosperity to an end.

During the early years, Isaiah warned Israel and Judah that God would judge his people's sins. After the Northern Kingdom of Israel had been taken into captivity in 722 B.C., Isaiah looked beyond the judgment, which descended on Judah in 587 B.C., to describe the blessings God has in store for his people at history's end.

THE UNITY OF ISAIAH

The Book of Isaiah divides naturally into two parts, separated by a historical interlude. The message and viewpoint of these two parts of Isaiah are dramatically different. Yet before the 18th century, no one questioned the unity of Isaiah.

Today many scholars think Isaiah was written by two, or even three authors. Two types of evidence are presented. (1) Isaiah 1–35 reflects pre-exilic conditions.

Isaiah 40–66 has a post-exilic viewpoint. It describes the fall of Babylon, and Isa. 44, 45 even names its conqueror, Cyrus. (2) Linguistic analysis shows differences in vocabulary and style between the two major sections of Isaiah.

Most conservative scholars do not view this evidence as conclusive. Biblical prophets often speak as if witnessing the future events they describe. The linguistic differences can be explained by the difference in subject matter between the two sections. In fact, many distinctive stylistic traits are found in both parts of Isaiah.

There is much evidence against the notion of two Isaiahs. No early tradition supports it. New Testament authors quote Isaiah some 50 times, and treat both sections as the work of Isaiah (Mt. 4:14; Lk. 4:17; Jn. 12:38-41). Manuscripts of Isaiah found among the Dead Sea Scrolls, dating to about 150 B.C., show no division of the book. Major sections of Isa. 40–66 are addressed to Jerusalem, which according to the critical theory did not exist at the time this section was written (40:2; 41:27). It seems best to take Isaiah as it is presented in Scripture: a unified work by one of the greatest of the OT prophets.

THEOLOGICAL CONTRIBUTIONS

Isaiah's vision exalts God as the "Holy One of Israel." This phrase occurs 26 times, 13 in each half of the book. God's righteous character is demonstrated in words of judgment (chs. 2,5). Matchless passages affirm God's transcendence (Isa. 40), and affirm his control of events taking place on earth (chs. 10,37). Isaiah draws a number of clear pictures of the Messiah

ISAIAH: A READING AND STUDY GUIDE

Chapter	Content Summary	Related Articles
1	Judah's worship is detestable to God, for the people practice injustice.	Justice; Righteousness
2	Destruction is coming because of Judah's idolatry and arrogance.	Day of the Lord Arrogance
3	God takes his place in court and pronounces judgment on the wicked.	Judgment; Wicked
4	When Messiah appears, the Lord will cleanse the survivors of Judah.	Branch; Remnant
5	Judah is a vineyard that produced bitter fruit. God will be exalted by their just punishment.	Vine
6	Isaiah has a vision of God, who sends him as his messenger to his people.	Holy
7	Isaiah predicts the collapse of the Syria/Israel coalition and the birth of Immanuel.	Ahaz; Immanuel
8	Assyria is God's instrument to punish Israel for turning to other gods and to mediums.	Assyria; Medium
9	Isaiah predicts the birth of a child with divine names who will reign forever.	Messiah
10	God will send Assyria to punish Judah for social injustice. A remnant will survive.	Assyria; Remnant
11	A descendant of Jesse [David's father] will bring peace to the peoples of earth.	Messiah; Banner
12	Isaiah praises God, who is the salvation, strength, and song of true believers.	Salvation
13	God will judge the Babylonians in his own time.	Babylon
14	Judah and Israel will return to their land. God will judge Assyria and the Philistines.	Exile; Philistines
15,16	God will ruin Moab.	Moab
17	Damascus, the capital of Syria, will be destroyed.	Aram
18	The aggressive people of Cush [upper Egypt] will be cut off.	Ethiopia
19	Egypt's power will be broken. Ultimately the Egyptians will worship the Lord.	Egypt
20	Assyria will defeat the forces of Egypt and Cush.	
21	Babylon and Edom will fall.	Edom
22	Jerusalem will be crushed by enemies and her people slaughtered.	Jerusalem
23	The rich seacoast city of Tyre will be destroyed.	Tyre
24	God will lay waste to the earth. He will shatter its cities to punish the wicked.	Covenant
25	Isaiah praises God, refuge for the needy. One day he will "swallow up death forever."	Poor
26	A song of salvation will be sung by those who trust God, and the dead will rise.	Resurrection; Salvation
27	Israel will become a fruitful vineyard, her guilt atoned for.	Atonement; Guilt
28	God will lay the cornerstone for a righteous society in Zion.	Cornerstone
29	Though Israel has been deaf to God's words, one day they will hear and rejoice in God.	Scroll Heart
30	God longs to be gracious to his people and will judge their enemies.	Grace
31	Judah must not rely on Egypt for military help.	Egypt
32	God will establish a righteous kingdom, but only when his Spirit is poured out from above.	Kingdom Holy Spirit
33	Despite present distress, the righteous will see the King and know peace.	Righteousness
34	The Lord will exact vengeance on the nations that have oppressed his people.	Vengeance
35	When God has restored his people, they and their land will rejoice.	
36	Sennacherib's commander threatens Jerusalem.	Hezekiah *continued*

Chapter	Content Summary	Related Articles
37	Hezekiah prays for help. As Isaiah said, thousands of Sennacherib's soldiers die.	
38	Hezekiah falls ill. He begs God for recovery. He is healed and praises the Lord.	Hezekiah
39	Hezekiah shows envoys from Babylon Judah's riches. He is rebuked by Isaiah.	Babylon
40	Isaiah comforts God's people with the promise that the Sovereign God himself will shepherd them.	Comforter Sovereign
41	God has chosen Israel and will not reject them. Their Redeemer controls the future.	Redeem; Prophet
42	A Servant of the Lord will become a Covenant for those in darkness.	Servant; Covenant
43	God, who created Israel, is its Savior. God will blot out Judah's sins.	Forgive
44	The Lord is in control, not dumb idols. He has decreed that Cyrus will order Jerusalem rebuilt.	Idol Cyrus
45	God has chosen Cyrus to release Judah from captivity. God has sworn it.	
46	God will sustain his people. He is God, and Babylon's gods will fall to him.	
47	Babylon will fall. No powers to which Babylon looks can help.	Babylon
48	God foretold this future, but Judah did not listen. If they had, no judgment would have fallen.	Prophet
49	God's Servant will restore Jacob. God will not forget his own children.	Gentile; Child
50	God's Servant will be obedient, unlike Israel. The Sovereign Lord will help him.	Servant
51	God will provide an everlasting salvation for his people and defend them against their enemies.	Salvation
52	God's power will save Judah. God's Servant will act wisely but will suffer.	Servant
53	God's Servant will bear sins and be cut off from the land of the living.	Sheep; Sacrifices and Offerings
54	God's unfailing love will not be shaken. His people will know peace.	Love
55	The thirsty are invited to seek God and find their needs met by a merciful Lord.	Mercy
56	God announces blessing for those who maintain justice and states his charges against the wicked.	Bless Justice
57	God continues to detail the sins of the wicked and returns to the theme of blessing for the contrite.	Humble
58	True fasting is not a matter of food but of doing justice.	Fast; Justice
59	Iniquities separate the people from God, but the Redeemer will come to Zion.	Redeemer; Zion
60	Zion [Jerusalem] will again be glorious. Nations will bow down to it or perish.	Zion
61	The year of God's favor is coming, when God will comfort those who mourn. God's people will be clothed in righteousness.	Comforter Righteousness
62	Jerusalem will know peace. God will rejoice over his redeemed people.	Peace
63	God is praised as Redeemer as Israel's rebellion is reviewed.	Vengeance
64	God is acknowledged as Father, the Potter who has the right to shape his people.	Father Potter
65	After God judges this earth, he will create a new heaven and earth marked by righteousness and peace.	Create Future
66	God will honor the humble. In his new world, peace will flow like a river.	Peace

(chs. 9,53), and predicts his virgin birth (Isa. 7). Isaiah gives the clearest vision found in the OT of the distant future, describing a new heaven and earth that God will create to become the home of righteousness (chs. 65,66). Nearly every chapter contains some fresh and vigorous image that helps us to know God better or to better understand his dealings with humanity.

MASTERY KEYS

Focus on chapters which are characteristic of Isaiah's ministry, and sum up his message. Chapters to read carefully are: 1, 6,9,13,32,40,44,53,57,65,66.

SPECIAL FEATURES

The "servant songs" of Isaiah are vivid pictures of a coming "servant of the Lord," usually to be identified with the Messiah. These are found in 42:1-4; 45:5-7; 49:1-6; 50:4-11; 52:13–53:12. Other pictures of the Messiah, which make Isaiah the OT's "evangelist" [teller of good news], are found in chs. 4,7,9,11,12, and 32.

Ishmael [ISH-may-uhl; "God heard"]. The son born to Abraham and Hagar, Sarah's maidservant, about 2080 B.C. **Scripture:** Gen. 16,17,21,25; 1 Chr. 1.

BACKGROUND

When Sarah continued barren, she followed contemporary custom and urged Abraham to impregnate her maid, Hagar, as her proxy. Sarah could then legally claim this child as her own. *See also* Hagar.

Hagar became pregnant, proving Abraham was potent, and she began to show contempt for Sarah. Sarah resented this and treated her harshly. Abraham's "permission" for Sarah to treat her this way (Gen. 16:6) simply stated her legal rights; it did not mean Abraham approved of her harshness. Archaeological discoveries show that in this era a wife had authority to treat her servant as she wished. When Hagar fled, an angel told her to return.

Ishmael was Abraham's legal heir until the birth of Isaac, by Sarah. The son of a primary wife had legal precedence.

When Ishmael was 16 and Isaac was 2, Sarah urged Abraham to send Ishmael away. This was strictly against custom. Abraham loved his son and refused until God told him to do as Sarah said. God promised to bless and care for Ishmael. As Hagar and Ishmael wandered away, they were about to die of thirst when God again intervened, revealing a well of water. According to Gen. 25:13-16, Ishmael fathered

STRUCTURE OF ISAIAH

I.	Visions of Judgment		1–35
	A. The Holy One	1–6	
	B. Book of Immanuel	7–12	
	C. Oracles of judgment	13–24	
	D. God's good purpose	25–35	
II.	Historical Interlude		36–39
III.	Visions of Splendor		40–66
	A. Beyond the Exile	40–48	
	B. God's servant	49–55	
	C. Redemption required	56–59	
	D. Restoration	60–66	

The imperial guard of the Assyrian king Sennacherib, whose army threatened to capture Jerusalem during Hezekiah's reign. The king of Judah received and followed the counsel of Isaiah during that time (Isa. 36–39). Relief from Nineveh, 704–681 B.C.

a dozen sons, each of whom became a tribal patriarch. Ishmael lived a long life and participated with Isaac in the burial of his father (25:9).

LEARNING FROM ISHMAEL'S LIFE

Ishmael is the classic victim of others' acts. The hostility between his mother and Sarah must have affected his early years. His apparent rejection at 16 by a father whom Ishmael thought loved him must have hurt him deeply. To this was added the trauma of near death in the desert. Everyone who has grown up in a difficult family situation or who has experienced rejection can identify with Ishmael.

Against this background, four things in the biblical account are particularly important. (1) Ishmael was circumcised at 13 (Gen. 17:25). While the Abrahamic covenant would be transmitted through Isaac, Ishmael was covered by God's covenant love. (2) God intervened directly on behalf of Ishmael before his birth and after he was expelled by Abraham (Gen. 16,21). Ishmael would have heard stories of the first intervention from his mother. He experienced the second intervention himself. Despite the actions of the people around him, Ishmael had evidence that God was guarding him. (3) Ishmael was successful as an adult. This was not because he had an ideal childhood, but because "God was with the boy as he grew up" (Gen. 21:20). He had a large family of his own and prospered. (4) Ishmael participated in the burial of Abraham (Gen. 25). As an adult he was apparently reconciled with his father and half-brother. With maturity came perspective. Perhaps Ishmael was better able to understand his father's motives and to sense Abraham's very real love.

We cannot change the network of relationships into which we were born, but we can learn from Ishmael that an unhappy childhood does not indicate that God has rejected us. Through faith in God, our future can hold personal success, understanding, and even reconciliation with those who have hurt us.

After the death of Solomon, Israel's tribal allegiances divided the weakened nation into two kingdoms, Israel and Judah. (1 Ki. 12:16,17).

island, isle An ambiguous term in the OT, used to designate (1) habitable land, as in Isa. 42:15; (2) coastlands along the Mediterranean, as in Isa. 11:11; 20:6; (3) land surrounded by water, as in Ezek. 26:18; (4) any region across the waters from Palestine, as in Jer. 25:22.

Often the use of "islands" in the OT suggests a great distance between those lands and Palestine, as in Isa. 41:5 and 66:19. Thus it refers to Gentile nations.

Sometimes the prophets express the magnitude of God's majesty by saying that even the "islands" [that is, distant lands] will be aware of his greatness.

In the NT, "island" is used in the normal, literal sense, as in Acts 13:6; 28:11; Rev. 1:9.

Israel [IZ-ree-uhl; "God perseveres," or "he perseveres with God"]. This name is used in seven distinct senses in Scripture:

(1) As a personal name, given by God to Jacob (Gen. 32:28). *See also* Jacob.

(2) To designate the covenant community as a religious entity, made up of the physical descendants of Abraham, Isaac, and Jacob (Ex. 1:1; Deut. 1:38).

(3) As the name of the nation formed by the covenant community after the Exodus (Jdg. 19:1; 1 Ki. 9:5). In this use, Israel can stand either for the national territory or for the people who are citizens of the nation.

The covenant community did not in fact function as a united nation for the first 400 years of its existence in Canaan. Unification of the tribes under a central government was attempted by Saul, but only accomplished by David.

(4) As the name of the northernmost of the two kingdoms established when the nation was divided after the death of Solomon (1 Ki. 12:16,17; 14:16; 15:9). This kingdom encompassed the area of the ten northern tribes. The Southern Kingdom, Judah, retained areas occupied by the two southern tribes (Judah and Benjamin). "Israel," the Northern Kingdom, was also known as Samaria (for its capital) and Ephraim (for its largest tribe).

(5) For the religious and political entity re-established in Judea after the Exile (Ezra 7:13; 9:1).

(6) As true believers within the larger community. Paul argues in Rom. 9:6-8 that not all who were physically descended from Abraham, Isaac, and Jacob (Israel) had a meaningful spiritual relationship with God. Thus "not all who are descended from Israel are Israel." This view is reflected in the OT doctrine of a remnant and is clearly illustrated in Israel's long history of rebellion against the Lord (1 Ki. 19:14-18). *See also* Remnant.

(7) As a prophetic entity. The Israel spoken of by the prophets is composed of true believers (sense 6) who are descendants of Abraham, Isaac, and Jacob (sense 2), and who will be re-established in the Promised Land as a national entity (sense 3).

Israel, kings of *See* Chronology of the Bible.

Israelites bring gifts of tribute to Shalmaneser III, king of Assyria: silver and gold articles as well as a staff for the king and some hunting spears. From the Black Obelisk, 841 B.C.

Israel, tribes of The large family groups descended from the twelve sons of Jacob (Israel), which became the fundamental divisions of the Hebrew people and nation. Each tribal group retained its own identity, and each was given its own district to occupy when the land of Canaan was conquered by Joshua.

A BRIEF FAMILY HISTORY

Jacob, the son of Isaac and grandson of Abraham, had children by two wives and two concubines. Among them were twelve sons, who became the ancestors of what we call the "twelve tribes" of Israel.

However, the number twelve is complicated by the fact that Joseph's two sons, Manasseh and Ephraim, took his place as tribal ancestors, thus giving him the double portion of the firstborn son (Gen. 48:22). This would have brought the number of tribal groups to thirteen, except that Levi, set apart to serve God, received no land but was given portions of the sacrifices and offerings the others made to the Lord. (In Rev. 7, Dan is omitted from the list of tribes that contribute 12,000 preachers each for ministry during the tribulation. This helps to explain why Dan is not represented on the twelve foundations of the holy city in Rev. 21.)

The biblical account suggests that Jacob's family went to Egypt about 1876 B.C. Each tribal group grew explosively during the next few centuries. When the Israelites left Egypt some 400 years later, a census tallied up 603,550 men of military age. The largest tribe, Judah, contributed 74,600 men and the smallest, Manasseh, 32,400. In Egypt the tribes were subdivided into clans and households. Elders of tribal subdivisions functioned as administrators and judges (Ex. 3:18; 12:21). Moses may have integrated this existing system with a new one he imposed (Ex. 18:13-26). During the Exodus and through the period of the judges, units in Israel's army were organized along tribal and clan lines (Num. 32; Jdg. 1).

DIVISION OF THE LAND

One of the most significant OT events is the division of Canaan, described in the Book of Joshua. God promised Abraham that his descendants would possess Canaan. Centuries later God delivered those descendants from Egypt. God brought them to Canaan, where the Jews broke the military power of the city-states established there. Then Joshua "allotted" land to each tribe and, within the tribal territory, to clans and households.

The process of "allotment" involved the literal casting of lots. As God controlled the outcome of each cast (Prov. 16:33), each family viewed its land as a direct gift of God, to be held in trust for him (Lev. 25:13-55). Land passed from generation to generation. Much of the social legislation in the Mosaic Law is intended to maintain the family's original holdings, whatever financial reverses a given generation might experience. *See also* Allotment; Poor.

Thus the tribes of Israel, whose separate

529

identities were carefully maintained, stamped that identity on the territories given to them. For centuries after the Conquest, the tribes lived on their own land, and functioned more as a loose confederation than a nation. Even after the tribes were welded into a unified whole by David and Solomon, tribal identities remained strong. These identities played a role in the splintering of the kingdom at Solomon's death.

Several historic events broke down the identity between tribe and territory. (1) When the kingdom divided after Solomon's death, Jeroboam I established a counterfeit religious system and ordained non-Levitical priests. Many families migrated to Judah from the ten northern tribes rather than be unfaithful to God. (2) Social and economic changes in Israel and Judah in the eighth century B.C. led to the dislocation of many from their land and the unification of many family holdings into large agricultural estates. (3) In 722 B.C., the Assyrians deported the ten northern tribes from Israel and resettled foreign people there. (4) In 586 B.C., the last residents of Judah were deported to Babylon or fled to Egypt. All the tribes of Israel had been torn from their land. A remnant did return to Judah in 538 B.C., but most never regained ancestral lands. Later on, however, Jews filtered northward towards Galilee where they mingled with the small remnant of the northern tribes whom the Assyrians had not deported.

The sons of Jacob (Israel) began the twelve tribal groupings of the Israelite nation, the "children of Israel."

Yet throughout OT history, genealogies were carefully maintained. The Jewish people continued to be proud of their tribal heritage. These genealogies documented Christ's descent from David through both Mary and Joseph. And they enabled Saul of Tarsus to boast of his descent from Benjamin. *See also* Genealogy.

SKETCH OF THE TWELVE TRIBES

From the biblical documents we can develop brief histories of each of the twelve tribes. Some are more extensive than others, for some tribes played a greater role in the Bible's story.

• *Asher* [ASH-uhr; "happy"]. A son of Jacob and Zilpah (Gen. 30:12,13).

This tribe occupied the Mediterranean coasts and western Galilee, which contains some of the most fertile land in Israel (Gen. 49:20; Deut. 33:24,25). The names of the cities given to Asher are found in Josh. 19:24-31.

Asher was apparently affected by the Midianite raids during the age of the judges, and responded to Gideon's call for armed resistance (Jdg. 6:35).

• *Benjamin* [BEN-juh-min; "son of my right hand," or "son of the south"]. Benjamin was the youngest son of Jacob, by Rachel, who died giving him birth (Gen. 35:16-20).

This tribe occupied central Palestine, a mountainous area between Jerusalem and Bethel. Cities belonging to Benjamin are listed in Josh. 18:11-28. In the judges' era

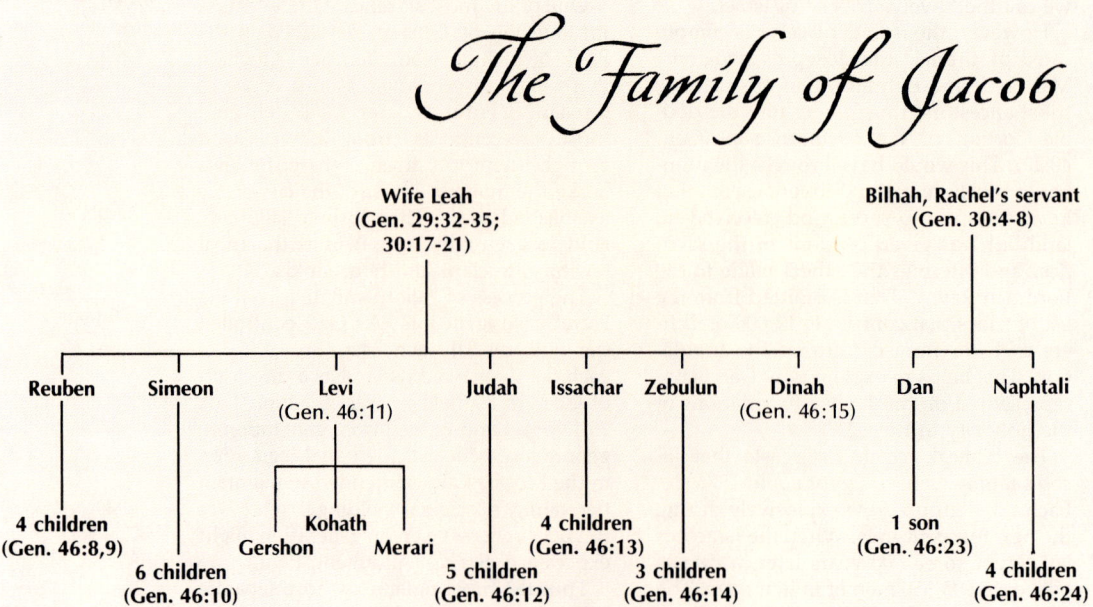

The Family of Jacob

Wife Leah (Gen. 29:32-35; 30:17-21)							Bilhah, Rachel's servant (Gen. 30:4-8)	
Reuben	Simeon	Levi (Gen. 46:11)	Judah	Issachar	Zebulun	Dinah (Gen. 46:15)	Dan	Naphtali
4 children (Gen. 46:8,9)	6 children (Gen. 46:10)	Gershon / Kohath / Merari	5 children (Gen. 46:12)	4 children (Gen. 46:13)	3 children (Gen. 46:14)		1 son (Gen. 46:23)	4 children (Gen. 46:24)

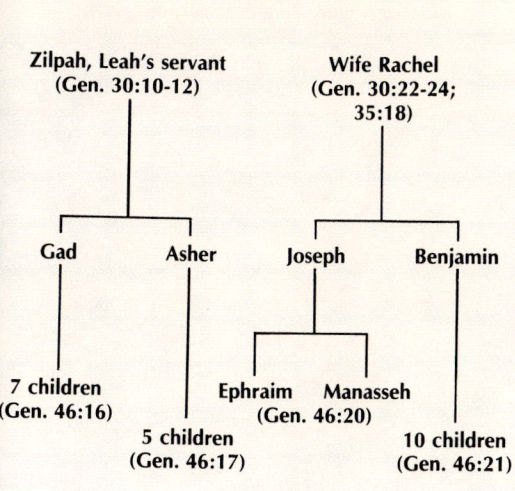

this tribe was almost wiped out by the others after a gang of men in one Benjamite village raped and killed the concubine of a traveling Levite who sought shelter there. The rest of the Benjamite communities refused to allow any punishment of Gibeah, and this resulted in the near extinction of the entire tribe (Jdg. 19–21).

When the nation of Israel demanded the establishment of a monarchy, Saul, a Benjamite, became its first king (1 Sam. 10–12). The Benjamites were fiercely loyal to Saul, and the tribe resisted David's succession (2 Sam. 16,21). Yet later Benjamin allied with Judah and remained loyal to David's grandson, Rehoboam.

• *Dan* ["he has vindicated"]. The older of the two sons of Jacob by Bilhah (Gen. 30:1-6).

The territory given Dan lay along the Mediterranean coast, bounded by Ephraim, Judah, and Benjamin (Josh. 19:40-48). But later on the Danites were forced back toward the highlands by pressure from the Amorites and Philistines. During the era of the judges most of the tribe left its homeland and migrated north. They settled in a valley near the headwaters of the Jordan, where they were isolated from the other tribes. They took the city of Laish and renamed it Dan (Jdg. 18). Thus the phrase "from Dan to Beersheba" is often used in Scripture to indicate the extent of the land, from northern to southern borders.

A worship center was established at Dan by Jeroboam I when Solomon's king-

Drawn uniquely with the west at the top, Sebastian Muenster's map of the Holy Land (1544) shows the last ten stations of the wilderness wandering and the division of the land among the tribes of Israel (Josh. 14).

531

dom splintered into Israel and Judah (1 Ki. 12:29). The city of Dan remained the site of this shrine until its people were deported by Tiglath-Pileser III, in 732 B.C.

A remnant of the tribe of Dan seems to have remained in the original homeland in the south. Samson was a Danite from this group, and his story reflects the tension between the Danites and the Philistines (Jdg. 13–16). This southern remnant was apparently absorbed by the tribe of Judah.

Dan is not among the tribes listed in Rev. 7. No explanation is given for the omission. The reason may be that Dan alone abandoned the land it had been allotted and settled elsewhere. However, Ezek. 48 predicts that Dan will have a portion along Israel's northern frontier in the messianic age. This confirms Jacob's prophetic blessing, "Dan will provide justice for his people as one of the tribes of Israel" (Gen. 49:16).

• *Ephraim* [EE-free-uhm; "fruitful"]. The younger of the two sons born to Joseph in Egypt (Gen. 41:50-52).

Ephraim's allotment of land encompassed the fertile valleys and hill country between the Mediterranean Sea and the Jordan Valley (Josh. 16:5-10). The tribe itself became extremely prominent. Joshua was an Ephraimite (Num. 13:8). The tabernacle stood in Shiloh, in the territory of Ephraim, during Joshua's lifetime and the age of the judges (Josh. 18:1; Jdg. 18:31; 1 Sam. 3). The judges Deborah, Tola, and Abdon were all associated with Ephraim (Jdg. 4:5; 10:1; 12:15). Samuel was also an Ephraimite (1 Sam. 1:1). After the death of Solomon, Jeroboam I, an Ephraimite, became the first ruler of the Northern Kingdom, Israel (1 Ki. 11:26).

In the Chronicles and the prophets the name "Ephraim" is often used to desig-

View of land in the tribe of Benjamin's allotment, which lay in the Judean hills between Jerusalem and Bethel. When the tribes clamored for a king, Samuel anointed Saul, a Benjamite (1 Sam. 10).

nate the Northern Kingdom. Ezekiel 37:15-28 predicts that Judah and Ephraim will be reunited as one nation under a Davidic king.

• *Gad* ["fortunate"]. The first son of Jacob by Zilpah (Gen. 30:10,11).

The Gadites were cattle herders, who asked for the rich pasturelands east of the Jordan as their inheritance (Num. 32:1-5). These lands extended from the southern shore of the Sea of Galilee to the northern tip of the Dead Sea (Josh. 12:1-6; 13:8-13). The land was given to them with the provision that they take part in the Conquest of Canaan (Num. 32:28-32; Josh. 1:12-18).

Some Gadites joined David in his struggle with Saul. These were "brave warriors, ready for battle and able to handle the shield and spear" (1 Chr. 12:8). Their warlike character is reflected in Jacob's prophetic blessing on the tribe (Gen. 49:19).

Later, in the eighth century B.C., the Syrians occupied much of the Gadite territory east of the Jordan. The land was won back by Jeroboam II, but not long afterward it was overrun by the Assyrians under Tiglath-Pileser III in 732 B.C. and its people deported (1 Chr. 5:26).

Ezekiel 48:27 sees Gad restored in the messianic age and given a portion in Canaan proper.

• *Issachar* [IS-uh-kahr; "hired worker"]. The fifth son of Jacob by Leah (Gen. 30:14-18).

Issachar's tribal territory was the fertile land that lay between the Jezreel and Jordan valleys (Josh. 19:17-23; 17:10,11). Deborah may have come from this tribe, and the battle against Sisera described in Jdg. 4 took place in Issachar's territory. The battle at Mount Gilboa in which Saul and Jonathan were killed also took place

here (1 Sam. 31). In David's time the men of Issachar were respected for their military skill. Their leaders are described as men "who understood the times and knew what Israel should do" (1 Chr. 12:32).

• *Judah* [JOO-duh; "praise"]. The fourth son of Jacob by Leah (Gen. 29:35). Judah was one of the most influential of the twelve brothers, as shown often in the story of Jacob (Gen. 37:26,27; 43:3-10; 44:16-34).

Jacob's prophetic blessing of Judah predicts that his descendants will be leaders, blessed by their brothers for a significant role in subduing Israel's enemies (Gen. 49:8-12). The prediction, "The scepter will not depart from Judah, nor the ruler's staff from between his feet" (Gen. 49:10), is usually taken as a messianic prophecy, while its more immediate reference was to the future royal line of David.

Judah's territory extended from the south end of the Dead Sea to Jerusalem and included both the coastlands and mountains (Josh. 15:1-12). The tribe was unable to occupy the coastlands permanently because of the Philistines, and gradually surrendered parts of its territory to other tribal groups (Jdg. 1:4-19).

Famous members of this tribe include Caleb, the faithful spy (Num. 14). Only he and Joshua of the Exodus generation lived to enter the Promised Land (Josh. 14:6-15; Jdg. 1:20). The city Caleb took over, Kiriath Arba, or Hebron, became the major city in Judah. Later David, also of Judah, was crowned king by his own tribe at Hebron, where he ruled for seven years before being acknowledged by the rest of the tribes.

Solomon was from Judah, as were all of Judah's kings between 730 B.C. and the Babylonian Captivity in 586 B.C. Jesus, too, was descended from David, and thus from the tribe of Judah.

Judah is mentioned first among the twelve tribes in the Rev. 7:5 listing of the 144,000.

• *Levi* [LEE-vi; "joined"]. The third son of Jacob and Leah (Gen. 29:34). The only significant event involving Levi was his conspiracy with his brother Simeon to murder the inhabitants of Shechem in revenge for the rape of their sister, Dinah (Gen. 34:25-29).

Alone of all the tribes, Levi received no allotment of land after the Israelites conquered Canaan. Instead, the tribe was given scattered cities in the territories of the other tribes.

The reason is rooted in Levi's special religious status. God spared the firstborn of Israel when he struck down those of Egypt (Ex. 11–13). God later laid claim to the firstborn males of the Israelites but took the Levites in their place (Num. 3:11-13). The entire tribe was thus set apart to the Lord and became sacred. The priests were drawn from the Levite family of Aaron. The other clans and families were given the task of transporting and caring for Israel's house of worship, the tabernacle (Num. 3,4). In return for this service, God set aside portions of sacrificed animals and grain offerings as food for the priests and Levites.

Later the Law defined other important tasks of the Levites. They were to transmit and to administer the divine Law (Deut. 17:18; 33:10). Once Israel entered Canaan, the Levites were given cities within the territories of the other tribes. Living in these cities facilitated their teaching ministry, and provided the Levites with permanent homes and fields.

The Levites rotated between service at the tabernacle and their homes. Later, when a central sanctuary was established, this rotation plan was continued. Responsibilities of the Levites were carefully defined. These involved caring for the ark of God (1 Chr. 15:11-15), providing worship music (1 Chr. 15:16-22), and continuing the ministry of teaching and administering God's Law (2 Chr. 17:7-9; 19:8-11). When the Temple was built, Levites were made responsible for its repair and the storage of offerings and gifts to the Lord (*see* 1 Chr. 23–26).

• *Manasseh* [muh-NAS-uh; "one who causes forgetfulness"]. The elder son of Joseph, born in Egypt (Gen. 41:51).

His tribe's territory lay on both sides of the Jordan River. One portion occupied

The Valley of Rephaim formed part of the boundary between the tribes of Judah and Benjamin. In the KJV it is called the Valley of the Giants (Josh. 15:8).

say of a man who had excelled in honor and power, "You will no longer excel" (Gen. 49:3,4).

During the Exodus period, the tribe of Reuben was given priority (Ex. 6:14; Num. 1:5). Yet the Reubenites Dathan and Abiram led a brief rebellion against Moses and were destroyed (Num. 16).

The tribe of Reuben asked for and received some of the rich pastureland east of the Jordan as its inheritance (Num. 32:33-38; Josh. 13:15-23). They were strong militarily in the days of Saul (1 Chr. 5:10). But there is no mention of Reuben after the deportation by Tiglath-Pileser III of Assyria in 732 B.C. However, Ezek. 48:7 reserves a portion of Palestine for Reuben during the messianic age.

• *Simeon* [SIM-ee-uhn; "one who hears"]. The second son of Jacob by Leah (Gen. 29:33). He conspired with his brother Levi to wipe out the population of the town of Shechem in revenge for the rape of their sister, Dinah. Joseph chose to keep Simeon in Egypt as a guarantee that his brothers would bring Benjamin the next time they came to buy food (Gen. 42:18-24). Simeon's violence is mentioned in Jacob's prophetic blessing of the tribes of Simeon and Levi, "I will scatter them in Jacob and disperse them in Israel" (Gen. 49:7).

The tribe of Simeon was given land in the far south of Canaan, within the territory assigned to Judah (Josh. 19:1-9; *see* 1 Chr. 4:24-33). In the time of King Asa (910–869 B.C.), Simeonites were among those who participated in Judah's religious revival (2 Chr. 15:9). In the days of Hezekiah (729–697 B.C.), the Simeonites took territory from the Hamites and Amalekites (1 Chr. 4:34-43). Some scholars suggest that this move indicates they left their southern lands, perhaps because of a drought that dried up their pastureland. However, this might indicate only a subduing or expulsion of foreign invaders.

The tribe of Simeon is to have its own territory in the messianic kingdom (Ezek. 48:24) and is mentioned in Rev. 7:7.

• *Zebulun* [ZEB-yoo-luhn; "exalt" or "honor"]. Zebulun was the sixth son of Jacob and Leah (Gen. 30:19,20).

This tribe was given a large segment of southern Galilee (Josh. 19:10-16). An important trade route passed through the territory controlled by Zebulun, and the land was fertile because of its stable rainfall pattern. The relative wealth and power of the tribe is reflected in the comment that Zebulun provided David's army with

the northernmost region east of the Jordan. The rest occupied the north central hill country on the west bank (Josh. 17:1-13).

Both Gideon (Jdg. 6–8) and Jephthah (Jdg. 10–12) were members of this tribe.

• *Naphtali* [NAF-tuh-li; "wrestler"]. The second son of Jacob and Bilhah (Gen. 30:7,8).

This tribe settled in eastern and central Galilee. Its territory included the upper Jordan and part of the shoreline of the Sea of Galilee. Cities included in the land are identified in Josh. 19:32-39. Judges 1:33 indicates that Naphtali "lived among the Canaanites." This close association may suggest the early religious pollution of this tribe.

A person of note from Naphtali is Barak, who led the troops with Deborah (Jdg. 4,5). As a frontier district, Naphtali suffered first when Israel was attacked by Syria (1 Ki. 15:20). Later Naphtali was the first tribe west of the Jordan to be invaded by Assyria (2 Ki. 15:29). But Isaiah promised that the land of Naphtali (and its neighbor tribe Zebulun) would one day be blessed above all others (Isa. 9:1,2). This was fulfilled centuries later as Jesus preached on Galilee's shores (Mt. 4:13-16).

• *Reuben* [ROO-ben; "behold, a son"]. The eldest son of Jacob, by Leah (Gen. 29:32). Reuben tried to rescue Joseph from his brothers (Gen. 37:21-30). Later he pledged his own two sons as a guarantee that he would guard Benjamin, now his father's favorite, if Jacob allowed young Benjamin to go with his brothers to Egypt (Gen. 42:37). Yet years before Reuben had lost his honor and his father's trust by sleeping with Jacob's concubine, Bilhah (Gen. 35:22). This act of incest led Jacob to

50,000 experienced soldiers prepared for battle "with every type of weapon" (1 Chr. 12:33).

Well-known men of Zebulun include the judge Elon (Jdg. 12:11) and the prophet Jonah (2 Ki. 14:25). Nazareth, where Jesus grew up, falls within the territory given to Zebulun, fulfilling Isaiah's prophecy of blessing on this area (Isa. 9:1,2; Mt. 4:13-16).

The territory of Zebulun was devastated by the Assyrians in 732 B.C. and the land incorporated into the Assyrian Empire. A few members of this tribe participated when Hezekiah reinstituted the Passover festival (2 Chr. 30:10,11; *but see* 31:1).

issue of blood (KJV) A chronic menstrual hemorrhage (Mk. 5:25; Lk. 8:43,44). According to Levitical law, such an issue of blood made a woman unclean (Lev. 15:25-28). *See also* Unclean.

Italian Band (or Cohort or Regiment)

A unit of the Roman army made up of troops enlisted in Italy and holding Roman citizenship. Acts 10:1 mentions Cornelius as a centurion in the Italian Regiment.

The standing Roman army included 25–30 legions of 4,000–6,000 soldiers each. Each legion was divided into ten cohorts, although there were auxiliary cohorts which did not belong to any particular legion—the Italian Cohort was probably one of these. Each cohort included six "centuries" of about 100 men. Thus Cornelius would have been one of six centurions in his regiment.

Archaeologists have established the presence of the Cohort II Italica in Caesarea between A.D. 69 and 157. It may have been there as early as the 40s—Cornelius's time. However, it was common practice in the Roman army to assign centurions to detached duty. *See also* Centurion; Cornelius.

ivory The hard, white dentine tusks of elephants, hippopotamuses, walruses, and some other animals.

Ivory was prized in the ancient world. Carved and polished, it was used as jewelry. Furniture inlaid with ivory was also popular among the wealthy. Archaeologists have found carved ivory pieces from nearly every ancient culture of the Middle East.

Solomon's trading fleets imported ivory from distant lands, along with gold and other treasures (1 Ki. 10:22; 2 Chr. 9:21). His own throne was inlaid with ivory (1 Ki. 10:18). Two centuries after this wise and wealthy king, the prophet Amos decried the decadence of Israel's well-to-do, who squandered their wealth on ivory-inlaid couches and houses (Amos 6:4; 3:15). As the Assyrian kings conquered the nations of the Middle East, the treasures they exacted as tribute frequently included ivory.

Large numbers of ivory artifacts from the Late Bronze Age (1550–1200 B.C.) have been uncovered at Megiddo, a major trading city on the Great Trunk Road through Canaan. Found in the palace, these figurines and inlaid plaques aid in reconstructing the life of Canaanite kings.
Below and left: Plaques decorated with papyrus and lotus blooms, distinctly Egyptian motifs employed by Phoenician artisans.
Left: Female figure carved on both sides and with glass eyes (12th century B.C.).
Bottom: Engraved ivory knife depicts the celebration of a king's triumph (about 1180 B.C.).
Inset: Duck-shaped lid of a cosmetic box found in Judah (12th century B.C.).

J

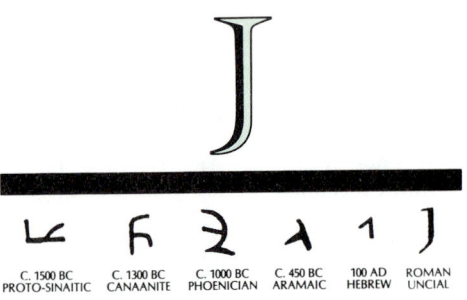

C. 1500 BC PROTO-SINAITIC | C. 1300 BC CANAANITE | C. 1000 BC PHOENICIAN | C. 450 BC ARAMAIC | 100 AD HEBREW | ROMAN UNCIAL

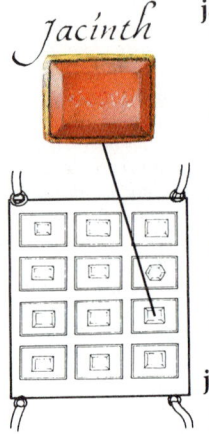

jacinth

The jacinth of the OT was probably a variety of zircon, a brilliant stone with an intense inner fire.

jacinth The first stone in the third row of the high priest's breastpiece (Ex. 28:19). The jewel cannot be identified with certainty. NIV and RSV take the Hebrew *leshem* to be an orange or reddish zircon, while the NEB and some other versions call it turquoise. Its color is reflected in the armor worn by mounted troops unleashed on mankind at history's end. (The "dark blue" of Rev. 9:17 in the NIV is actually hyacinthine, or jacinth.) Jacinth also decorates one of the foundations of the new Jerusalem (Rev. 21:20).

jackal A member of the dog family. A jackal is a scavenger, smaller than a wolf but similar in features. It travels in packs and nearly always appears in the OT in the plural. Jackals are nocturnal. They feed on grapes and vegetables as well as carrion and smaller animals. Jackals prefer a desert habitat and once ranged widely in the ancient Middle East and Mesopotamia. Some jackals are still found in modern Palestine.

Nearly all biblical references to jackals are symbolic and suggest desolation and abandonment. A land which has been visited by divine judgment will become "a haunt for jackals" (Ps. 44:19; Isa. 34:13; Jer. 9:11; etc.), or will lie desolate, "with jackals prowling over it" (Lam. 5:18).

The KJV sometimes mistranslates the Hebrew word for jackals (*tannim*), as "dragons" or "foxes." Other versions render it as "sea monsters" or "sea serpents."

Jacob [JAY-kuhb; "supplanter"]. The younger son of Isaac and Rebekah; about 2006–1859 B.C. Inheriting the covenant promise initially given Abraham, he passed it on to his twelve sons. Jacob's name was changed by God to Israel. **Wives:** Rachel, Leah. **Concubines:** Bilhah, Zilpah. **Scripture:** Gen. 25–49.

BACKGROUND

Jacob, the younger of twin sons, purchased the birthright of his brother Esau for the price of a savory stew (Gen. 25). Later Jacob conspired with his mother to steal the blessing the twins' father intended for Esau (Gen. 27). Jacob then fled to relatives in Paddan Aram. On that trip God met him in a dream at Bethel, confirming the passage of Abraham's covenant to Jacob (Gen. 28). *See also* Birthright; Covenant.

In Paddan Aram Jacob fell in love with his cousin Rachel. He worked seven years to earn the dowry for his bride, but on the wedding night Rachel's older sister, Leah, was substituted for Rachel. After seven more years of labor, Jacob was given Rachel as a wife also (Gen. 29). In a competition motivated by jealousy, each wife gave Jacob a maidservant as a secondary wife (Gen. 30). The twelve sons that Jacob had by these four women became the ancestral heads of the tribal groups into which the Jewish people were divided.

In a final, six-year period Jacob built up a large flock of sheep, and God caused Jacob's flocks to multiply more than those of his father-in-law, Laban, stirring up enmity. So Jacob and his family moved out, toward Canaan (Gen. 30,31). Laban angrily pursued them, but a truce was worked out (Gen. 31). As an anxious Jacob prepared to meet his brother Esau (who had promised to kill him 21 years before), he was confronted on Mount Peniel by someone described both as a man and as God. After a nocturnal wrestling match, Jacob was given the name Israel (Gen. 32). *See also* Israel; Laban.

The meeting with Esau went well (Gen.

33), and Jacob returned to a nomadic life in Canaan. Appearing to Jacob again, God reconfirmed transmission of the Abrahamic covenant to and through him (Gen. 35).

The biblical story then follows one of Jacob's sons, Joseph, whom God used to bring the family of Jacob to Egypt. Secure in this fertile land, the family multiplied.

Theologically significant, the story of Jacob establishes the right of his descendants to the covenant relationship that God first granted to Abraham. Through the covenant people, descendants of Abraham, Isaac, and Jacob, God uniquely revealed himself and his plans for humankind. And through this people, humanity's Redeemer, Christ Jesus, was born.

LEARNING FROM JACOB'S LIFE

Many incidents in his life have application for us:

1. Purchasing the birthright (Gen. 25:19-34). At first, we blame Jacob for taking advantage of his brother's hunger. But, on the other hand, we should note that Jacob valued the intangible, spiritual benefits of God's covenant, which Esau "despised" (see Heb. 12:16,17).

2. Stealing Esau's blessing (Gen. 27:1-

Miniatures from a 13th century Bible, depicting the life of Jacob. Upper left, Jacob meets Rachel at well near Haran (Gen. 29). Upper right, Jacob seals covenant with Laban at Gilead (Gen. 31). Lower left, Jacob wrestles at Peniel (Gen. 32). Lower right, Jacob is reunited with Esau (Gen. 33).

46). It was unnecessary for Jacob and his mother to conspire to steal the blessing. God had spoken to Jacob's mother Rebekah when she was pregnant, and predicted that Jacob would be pre-eminent (Gen. 25:19-26). The pair's trickery and deceit obtained something God would have provided freely had they behaved morally. Their actions rightly provoked Esau's anger. Fear of what Esau might do forced Jacob to flee and robbed Rebekah of the company of her favorite son, whom she never saw again.

3. God's appearance at Bethel (Gen. 28:10-22). Jacob's vow is a model for believers today. He sought only the basics from God, not luxury. Jacob asked that God would: (1) be with him and watch over him on his journey; (2) give him food to eat and clothes to wear; and (3) return him safely to his father's house. In gratitude for this basic provision, Jacob committed himself to God and committed a tenth of all he possessed as an expression of thanks.

4. Jacob's wives (Gen. 30:1-24). Jacob's marriages were moral within the context of the society in which he lived. Yet the jealousy and tension exhibited in the text serve as a powerful reminder that God's ideal, of one man and one woman committed to each other alone for life, is not only right but is also good for both husband and wife.

5. Jacob's flocks increase (Gen. 30:25-43). Laban had broken many commitments to Jacob. The story of the increase of Jacob's flocks is an example of poetic justice, as God tricks Laban the trickster. Practicing deceit makes us all susceptible to deception.

6. Giving gifts to Esau (Gen. 32). The giving of gifts by one seeking another's favor was established practice in the ancient Middle East. Jacob's actions were culturally correct and did not necessarily reflect a lack of trust in God. There is no need to "prove" trust in God by violating what our culture considers common courtesy.

7. Return to Bethel (Gen. 35). Jacob's return to Bethel, where God had first spoken to him, is significant. He was to settle there (35:1). And there God spoke to him again (35:10-13). We too can return spiritually to the place where God first spoke to us. We can settle there spiritually, and keep our hearts open to hear God's voice.

8. Fatherly failure (Gen. 37:1-11). Jacob was spiritually sensitive, but not particularly wise in dealing with family relationships. His obvious favoritism toward Joseph provoked the jealousy of his older sons.

9. Jacob's death (Gen. 48–50). Although the family had moved to Egypt, Jacob instructed his sons to bury him in Canaan with his father Isaac and grandfather Abraham. Jacob's confidence that God would be faithful to his covenant is reflected in the words of Gen. 48:21, "I am about to die, but God will be with you and take you back to the land of your fathers."

Jacob's well A well near Sychar which Jn. 4:4-6 says was situated on land Jacob gave to his son Joseph (Gen. 48:22). The well remains today, still over 75 feet deep, under the floor of a Greek Orthodox church.

Jakin and Boaz Two bronze pillars which stood at the entrance of Solomon's Temple. Their names in Hebrew mean "establish" and "strength." *See also* Boaz and Jakin; Temple.

James, Book of An Epistle often regarded as the earliest of the NT books, filled with practical advice on Christian living. It was probably written by James, the brother of Jesus, to instruct Jewish/Christian congregations outside of Palestine (1:1).

BACKGROUND
In the early years after the resurrection, the church was composed of Jewish believers. The persecution reported in Acts 8:1-3 scattered many believers from Jerusalem. These generally went to relatives and neighbors outside Judea, for in the first century Jewish quarters existed in most of the Roman Empire's major cities. The Book of James is traditionally viewed as a general epistle, circulated to Jewish/Christian congregations established within these scattered Jewish communities. The traditional view is that James was written be-

"The sons of Israel carried their father Jacob and their children and their wives in the wagons which Pharaoh had sent to transport him" (Gen. 46:5). Terra-cotta model of a wagon from the time of the patriarchs (2200–1550 B.C.).

538

fore A.D. 62, as early as the mid-40s, by James, the Lord's brother, who played such a significant role in the first council of the church, held in Jerusalem about A.D. 49 (Acts 15).

Some have speculated that the book might be a pre-Christian Jewish work, or that a Galilean could not have written in such an excellent Greek style. Others have said it must have been written later because James 2:14-26 seems to challenge Paul by affirming the importance of works.

Yet a number of features suggest the Epistle was written in Palestine (Jas. 5:4,7,17,18). The book reflects emphases of OT Judaism and of Jesus' Sermon on the Mount (*compare* 2:13 with Mt. 5:7; 3:12 with Mt. 7:16; 3:18 with Mt. 7:20; 5:2 with Mt. 6:19; 5:12 with Mt. 5:34-37). Paul himself emphasized good works as an expression of faith, so assuming a conflict with Paul is hardly necessary. With no compelling reason to assign James a late date, it seems best to accept the traditional view.

THEOLOGICAL CONTRIBUTIONS

James reflects many themes found in the OT Law and prophets and in Jesus' own teaching. James calls on believers to love their brothers and care for the poor and helpless (Jas. 2:14-26; 1:27). The believer is to show no partiality to the rich (2:1-13), and is to be ruled by God's peaceable wisdom rather than by worldliness (4:1-6) or human passions (4:13–5:6). Each practical exhortation is appropriate for a people whose Scripture was still the OT, and who saw faith in Christ as a fulfillment of OT promises.

While the practical theology of James is in complete harmony with the OT and with the teachings of Christ, James's teaching on works has troubled many later theologians. Luther called James an "epis-

Faith by itself, if it is not accompanied by action, is dead.

JAMES 2:17

tle of straw," thinking that James was contradicting the Pauline doctrine of salvation by faith alone. The supposed conflict is resolved when we understand that James and Paul deal with different issues. Paul taught the basis of salvation; James explored the life appropriate to salvation. Neither Paul nor James believed that saving faith could exist apart from a significant change of life. In fact, James uses the word "faith" more often than Paul does in the Book of Galatians.

MASTERY KEYS

We read James as a personal exhortation to practice our faith in Christ. Almost every paragraph suggests a way to test our attitudes toward others or relationships with them.

The author of James expressly forbids showing favoritism to the rich, who could easily be recognized with "a gold ring and fine clothes" (2:2).

JAMES: A READING AND STUDY GUIDE

Chapter	Content Summary	Related Articles
1	God intends trials to bless us. We must put God's Word into practice rather than just hear it.	Trial Tempt
2	Believers are not to show favoritism, but to love all. A "faith" that exists without deeds is a dead faith.	Neighbor Faith
3	Faith challenges us to control our tongues. We are to live by the pure and peaceable wisdom of heaven.	Perfect Wisdom
4	Faith calls us to submit to God, to refrain from judging others, and to depend on God for the future.	Submission Judge
5	Faith commits us to wait for future blessing, to exercise patience, and to pray together expectantly.	Patience Healing

The ibis-headed god, Thoth, was among other things a magician who knew secrets of healing. The patron deity of Egyptian magicians, however, was Isis, who would have been appealed to for the power to copy Moses' miracles (Ex. 7).

Jannes and Jambres [JAN-ez, JAM-brez]. Two Egyptian magician-priests who mimicked the initial miracles of Moses in Pharaoh's court (Ex. 7:11,12,22). The names, given only in 2 Tim. 3:8, are also found in Jewish legends popular among both Jews and Gentiles. Pagan writers of the early Christian era, such as Pliny the Elder and Apuleius, also identify Jannes and Jambres as scribes and magicians of Egypt.

Paul tells Timothy that the "last days" will see people opposing the truth just as these magicians opposed Moses. And just as Jannes and Jambres eventually (and publicly) failed to match the Lord's miracles (Ex. 8:18,19), so these people's "folly will be clear to everyone" (2 Tim. 3:9). *See also* Magic.

jar *See* Pottery.

Jashar, Book of [JAH-shur; "upright"]. A lost writing mentioned in Josh. 10:13 and 2 Sam. 1:18, which contained accounts of significant events in Israel's history, probably in poetic form.

jasper The twelfth jewel in the breastpiece of the high priest (Ex. 28:20). A silicon dioxide gemstone closely related to chalcedony, jasper occurs in a variety of colors. Gem quality jasper is rare.

Because jasper is opaque, its description in Rev. 21:11 as "clear as crystal" is unusual. Some resolve the conflict by noting that the gold of the new Jerusalem is also described as "like transparent glass" (21:21). Obviously, the holy city will have features unlike anything we have seen. Others take the Greek term, *iaspis*, as a crystalline quartz rather than true jasper.

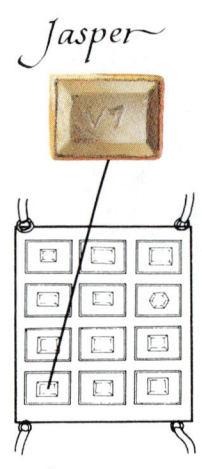

Jasper

The final stone in the high priest's vestments, jasper was also used in seals and signet rings.

540

javelin The javelin of biblical times was more like a large arrow than a spear. Soldiers carried several javelins, which they hurled by hand. Sometimes a cord was wound around the shaft of the javelin, with a loop held in the hand. When the javelin was thrown, the cord unwound, causing the shaft to spin.

The javelin had a metal head attached to a wooden shaft. Often the base was also weighted with metal, which improved the weapon's balance. *See also* Warfare.

Detail of the "Stela of the Vultures" that commemorates the victory of King Eannatum of Lagash, 2450 B.C. The king's chariot is equipped with a quiver full of light javelins.

jealousy A powerful emotion relating to the object of one's passionate desire. In the OT, (1) negatively, jealousy or envy is stimulated by a desire for something that rightly belongs to another, as in Gen. 30:1; Prov. 3:31. (2) Positively, jealousy can mean full commitment or intense love, as in Joel 2:18; Zech. 1:14. In the NT, (3) negatively, an emotion which stimulates hostile acts, as in Acts 7:9 and 13:45. The NT links jealousy with quarreling in 1 Cor. 3:3 and with anger in 2 Cor. 12:20.

THE JEALOUSY OF GOD

When the OT describes God as jealous, the word is used in its positive sense. God cares deeply for his people. His commitment is emotional as well as volitional. God demonstrated his passion both by showering blessings on Israel when that nation was obedient and punishing them when they turned away. Yet in the context of covenant, even punishment is positive, for it is designed to turn God's people back to him. God's jealousy also led him to punish nations that unjustly attacked Israel (*see* Isa. 42:13; Zech. 1:14,15).

The classic OT expression of divine jealousy is found with the commandment against idolatry (Ex. 20:5,6). Israel was not to bow down to pagan idols, "for I, the Lord your God, am a jealous God."

Jebusites [JEB-uh-sites; "trampled down"]. An ancient tribal group established in Canaan in the time of the patriarchs, 2100 B.C. (Gen. 10:16; 15:21). They controlled the hills around Jerusalem when it was called Jebus.

The Jebusites resisted Joshua's invasion (Josh. 9:1). Although defeated, they continued to hold their mountain territory through the era of the judges (Jdg. 1:21; 19:11). David conquered their city and made it his political and religious capital (2 Sam. 5:6-10; *see* 1 Chr. 21), effectively ending the Jebusites' existence as an independent people. *See also* Jerusalem.

Jehoshaphat [juh-HAHSH-uh-fat; "Yahweh has judged," or "Yahweh establishes justice"]. Godly fourth king of Judah, 872–848 B.C. His "heart was devoted to the ways of the Lord" (2 Chr. 17:6). **Father:** Asa. **Son and successor:** Jehoram. His other sons were executed by Jehoram. **Scripture:** 1 Ki. 22; 2 Chr. 17–20.

BACKGROUND

Jehoshaphat was the godly son of a godly father, Asa. Jehoshaphat ruled Judah while Omri and his heirs (Ahab, Ahaziah, and Jehoram) ruled Israel. Historically, Judah and Israel had been involved in chronic warfare since the division of Solomon's kingdom in 931 B.C.

Jehoshaphat garrisoned the border between the two states (2 Chr. 17:1,2) and developed a strong citizen army (2 Chr. 17:12-19).

Continuing the religious reforms of his father, Jehoshaphat commissioned priests to teach God's Law on an itinerant basis, going around "to all the towns of Judah." God blessed his efforts with peace and prosperity (2 Chr. 17:7-11).

Once secure, Jehoshaphat became less hostile toward Israel. He married a son to Ahab's daughter (2 Chr. 18:1). He then joined Ahab in a military venture against Ramoth Gilead (2 Chr. 18:2-34) and later engaged in a joint trading venture with Ahaziah of Israel (2 Chr. 20:35-37). Because of Israel's wickedness, the Lord was not pleased with these alliances. He sent prophets to rebuke Jehoshaphat (2 Chr. 19:1-3; 20:37).

Despite his mistakes, Jehoshaphat remained a godly man. His charge to his appointed judges shows a deep sensitivity to God's living presence and to the Lord's concern for justice (2 Chr. 19:4-10). When Judah was invaded by the forces of Moab and Ammon, Jehoshaphat completely and openly relied on God (2 Chr. 20:1-29).

The final years of Jehoshaphat's 25-year reign were peaceful. But despite his example and his efforts at religious reformation, "the people still had not set their hearts on the God of their fathers" (2 Chr. 20:33).

The Kidron Valley is traditionally identified with the prophet Joel's "Valley of Jehoshaphat," the place of God's final judgment (Joel 3:2,12).

LEARNING FROM JEHOSHAPHAT'S LIFE

Even the best people fall short of being perfect. Jehoshaphat was an unusually godly individual who nevertheless made serious mistakes. We can learn as much from his failures as from his many fine qualities.

1. The error of alliance with unbelievers (1 Ki. 22; 2 Chr. 18). The prophets who confronted Jehoshaphat expressed a principle that can guide us in our closer relationships with others. "Should you help the wicked and love those who hate the Lord?" The answer clearly is no. Jehoshaphat's every alliance with kings of Israel was disastrous. His son and successor, Jehoram, married to a daughter of Ahab, turned from the Lord to worship Baal (2 Chr. 21:6). Many died uselessly in the indecisive invasion Jehoshaphat and Ahab mounted against the Arameans. And the ships involved in the joint trading venture of Jehoshaphat and Ahaziah were all wrecked in a severe storm. Alliances between those who love God and those who reject him do not prosper.

2. The power of example (2 Chr. 19). Jehoshaphat's name means, "The Lord establishes justice." Jehoshaphat had a God-like concern for justice and a deep awareness that he ruled not as an autocrat but as a servant of God. When Jehoshaphat appointed itinerant judges to administer justice according to God's Law, he gave them a charge which reflected his own personal commitment: "Consider carefully what you do, because you are not judging for man but for the Lord, who is with you whenever you give a verdict" (19:6).

3. Humility and prayer (2 Chr. 20). The invasion of Judah by a strong force led an alarmed Jehoshaphat to call for fasting and prayer. The king himself led the assembly, expressing his own sense of weakness and dependence: "O our God, will you not judge them? For we have no power to face this vast army that is attacking us. We do not know what to do, but our eyes are upon you" (20:12).

Promised victory by the prophet Jahaziel, Jehoshaphat led his forces out "early in the morning." His expectant faith is revealed in his last challenge to his people: "Have faith in his [God's] prophets and you will be successful" (20:21).

The invading armies fell to fighting among themselves and annihilated each other. The army of Judah arrived in time to carry off the spoil, and to thank God.

Jehoshaphat again modeled for his people that sense of humility matched with an expectant faith which characterize effective prayer.

Jehovah An incorrect anglicization of the personal name of Israel's God, represented in Hebrew by the four consonants YHWH. *See also* God, Names of; Yahweh.

The personal name of God was so sacred to the Hebrews that it was not uttered. When someone reading the Scriptures publicly would come to "YHWH," he would say instead, *"Adonai"* (the common term for "lord").

For centuries Hebrew was written with consonants only. The proper pronunciation of words—putting in the right vowels—was passed on by oral tradition, not written down. But in the Middle Ages, Jewish scribes, the Masoretes, began adding "points," tiny notations above or below the consonants to indicate the vowels. Coming to the name YHWH, they added the vowels of *Adonai* to remind the reader to say, *"Adonai,"* instead.

When English translators, centuries later, examined God's name in the Masoretic text, they found the letter *Y* (the Hebrew *yod*, which was often read as *J*), with the first indefinite vowel of *Adonai* (which they read as *e*); the consonant *H* (*he*) with the second vowel *o*; the consonant *W* (the Hebrew *waw*, often read as a *V*), with the third vowel of *Adonai*, *a*; and the final consonant *H*. Thus what the Hebrews pronounced as "Yahweh" or "Yahveh" (when they pronounced it) became "Jehovah" in early English Bibles.

Yet, following Hebrew custom, the name was most often translated as "the Lord." Most English versions employ small capital letters (LORD) to indicate "Yahweh" and an initial capital (Lord) to identify *Adonai*.

Jehu [JAY-hoo; "he is Yahweh"]. The army commander whose coup wiped out the line of Omri and Ahab and ended Jezebel's efforts to establish Phoenician Baal-worship in Israel. **Father:** Jehoshaphat, son of Nimshi. **Son and successor:** Jehoahaz. **Scripture:** 2 Ki. 9,10.

BACKGROUND

The prophet Elisha sent a young prophet to anoint Jehu, then commander of Israel's army, as next king of Israel. The prophet commissioned Jehu to destroy the house of Ahab completely. Jehu acted quickly. He killed the current king, Joram, and his mother, Jezebel. Jehu then arranged for the murder of all members of the royal family (2 Ki. 9:14–10:17).

Jehu called all worshipers of Baal together on the pretext of holding a religious festival. In an obvious effort to wipe out the religious support base of the previous dynasty, he then murdered them all and announced himself a worshiper of the Lord.

However, Jehu's religious "commitment" was political rather than personal. He did demolish the centers where Baal had been worshiped. But he ignored the divine Law and continued the religious system Jeroboam I had established when Israel was founded. This system featured a non-Aaronic priesthood, substitute religious festivals, and worship centers at Dan and Bethel rather than Jerusalem. This last measure was intended to isolate the Israelites from Jerusalem, which was not only the site of the Temple, where the Lord had told his people to worship him, but also the political capital of rival Judah.

God rewarded Jehu for wiping out the house of Ahab and the worship of Baal. Jehu ruled as king for 28 years, and the dynasty he founded lasted for four more generations. Yet the years of Jehu's rule were difficult, and the king lost territory to Hazael of Syria.

LEARNING FROM JEHU'S LIFE

Jehu is an example of the person who seeks to use God for his own ends, rather than submit to God for his use. Jehu said he was concerned for God's honor (2 Ki. 10:16). Actually he saw religion as a means he could use to justify his acts and help him gain what he wanted—royal authority. When Jehu achieved his ends, his true attitude toward God was revealed, and he "was not careful to keep the law of the Lord" (2 Ki. 10:31).

What counts is not what we say about our commitment to God when we want the support of others, but how our commitment is expressed in daily life when we have nothing to gain except God's approval.

Jephthah [JEF-thuh; "he opens"]. The eighth of Israel's judges, an illegitimate son who delivered his people from the Ammonites, about 1085 B.C. **Parents:** Gilead and a harlot. **Child:** an unnamed daughter. **Scripture:** Jdg. 10:6–12:7.

BACKGROUND

During the era of the judges no central government united the Israelite tribes, and frequently foreign enemies oppressed various tribal territories.

Jephthah was born in this uncertain age. When his father died, Jephthah was expelled from the family by his half-brothers. He settled outside Israel's tribal lands, probably in Syria, and became the captain of a band of other unemployed outcasts.

After 18 years of Ammonite oppression, the Israelites on the east side of the Jordan decided to resist. They turned to Jephthah and begged him to command their forces, promising that if he did he would be recognized as their permanent leader.

Jephthah accepted. But before leading his people against the enemy, Jephthah

Jehu, king of Israel, or his ambassador, bowing before Assyrian king Shalmaneser III. The cuneiform text details the tribute of gold and silver that he offered as a vassal. Detail of the Black Obelisk set up in Nineveh about 841 B.C.

Jephthah's Return
was painted by an
anonymous American
about 1812. Jephthah,
returning home victo-
rious over the Am-
monites, is greeted
first by his
tambourine-playing
daughter.
(Jdg. 11:30-40).

vowed to offer God "whatever comes out of the door of my house to meet me when I return in triumph . . . and I will sacrifice it as a burnt offering" (Jdg. 11:31).

Jephthah was successful in subduing the Ammonites. But when he returned home in triumph, his daughter was the first to meet him! The text says that, after granting his daughter two months to mourn the fact that she would now never marry, Jephthah "did to her as he had vowed" (Jdg. 11:38,39). Biblical scholars have disagreed over whether she was sacrificed or redeemed for money and dedicated to a celibate life of service to the Lord.

The second alternative is more likely, for several reasons. (1) OT Law, with which Jephthah was familiar (11:15-27), forbids human sacrifice (Lev. 18:21; 20:2-5; Deut. 12:31; 18:10). (2) No priest would have officiated at such a sacrifice, and Jephthah was not qualified to serve as a priest. (3) The OT establishes an alternative, by which a person or thing dedicated to the Lord might be set aside for a lifetime of service (see Lev. 27; 1 Sam. 1:28; Lk. 2:36,37). (4) The text indicates that the girl was mourning the fact she could never marry, not her coming death (Jdg. 11:37).

LEARNING FROM JEPHTHAH'S LIFE
Jephthah's deep faith in God is striking.

Despite rejection by his family and by God's people, he continued to trust the Lord. His words and actions reveal the depth of his commitment (Jdg. 11:9,14-27,30,31,35). His faith is also reflected in his daughter's understanding that Jephthah must keep his word to the Lord (Jdg. 11:36).

Jephthah's mistreatment by his family and people might well have made him bitter. He might have cursed them for their hypocrisy in defrauding him of his share of the family inheritance (Jdg. 11:2) and might have rejected the God they claimed to worship. Yet Jephthah looked beyond the faults of human beings to sense the reality of God.

God's people are called to reflect God's character. But we often fail. Even when we suffer from others' failures, we must maintain a faith like Jephthah's, anchored in God himself rather than those who represent him.

Jeremiah, Book of A major prophetic book of the OT, containing messages directed to the people of Judah from 627 B.C. until the destruction of Jerusalem in 586 B.C. Jeremiah thus reports God's final words of warning to a nation determined not to hear or heed the Law of the Lord.

Yet this book also contains words of promise. One day God will make a new covenant with his people, under which they will be redeemed and restored to their land.

BACKGROUND

The 40 years of Jeremiah's ministry were marked by stunning change. Assyria, which had dominated the international scene for centuries, was challenged and then crushed by Babylon. At first, this struggle between Mesopotamian superpowers reduced external pressure on Palestine. This led to a religious and political revival during the reign of King Josiah. But the decisive battle of Carchemish in 605 B.C. left Babylon the dominant world power. Babylon's expansionist policy meant that Judah was again endangered. Between 605 and 586 B.C. the prophet Jeremiah called on the Jews to submit to Babylon. He announced that Babylon was God's instrument, chosen to punish God's

JEREMIAH: A READING AND STUDY GUIDE

Chapter	Content Summary	Related Articles
	I. Jeremiah's Mission	
1	Jeremiah is called to prophesy and promised divine protection despite hostility.	Prophet
2	God brings charges against Judah for forsaking him and running after idols.	Baal; Sin
3	Judah has been an unfaithful "wife," committing "adultery." Yet God invites her to return.	Adultery
4	Jeremiah announces disaster from the north, an invader who will ruin the land.	Babylon; North
5	Judah's people love prophets who tell lies and priests who reject the Law's authority.	Priest; Authority
6	Soon Jerusalem will be under siege. The people stand at a crossroads, yet will not walk in God's way.	Warfare
7	Jeremiah stands before the Temple and denounces worshipers who do not forsake their sins. He is forbidden even to pray for them.	Temple, Jerusalem Prayer; Worship
8	Those charged with ministering God's Law handle it falsely, promising peace where there is no peace.	Law Peace
9	God will scatter his people and punish all whose religion is superficial.	Exile
10	The living, eternal God cannot be compared with idols. God is the maker of all things.	Idol
	II. The Broken Covenant	
11	Judah had promised to obey the Lord but has broken the covenant made at Sinai. God has decreed disaster. Jeremiah's life is threatened if he preaches more.	Covenant
12	Jeremiah cries about injustice. God answers, "I will give the one I love" to enemies.	Justice; Enemy
13	A linen belt and smashed wineskins serve as images of the coming captivity.	Symbol
14	God will send drought, famine, and war. Again Jeremiah is told not to pray for Judah.	Punish Intercession
15	God has fixed the destiny of the nation and of individuals, yet all are invited to repent.	Repent
16	God has withdrawn his love and blessing from Judah because they worship idols.	Love; Idol
17	God searches the heart and mind, and rewards men according to their deeds. A curse rests on those who put their confidence in men rather than God.	Reward Curse
18	Jeremiah observes a potter. The sovereign Lord controls nations as a potter his clay.	Potter
19	Jeremiah breaks a pottery jar, symbolizing God's intention to smash Judah beyond repair.	Topheth
20	Jeremiah is beaten and put in stocks by a priest, Pashur. God will judge Pashur, but Jeremiah laments he is ridiculed.	Judge
	III. Judgment Nears	
21	King Zedekiah asks if God will help against Babylon. Jeremiah predicts disaster.	Justice
22	Wicked sons of King Josiah have betrayed their father's righteousness.	King; Poor
23	One day a righteous descendant of David will take the throne. Now God rejects Judah and its lying prophets.	Messiah Dreams

continued

people for generations of unfaithfulness. But Jeremiah's warnings were rejected, and the prophet himself was viewed as a traitor.

Jeremiah [JAIR-uh-MI-uh; possibly "Yahweh lifts up"] felt the rejection by his people deeply. He suffered intensely as he witnessed his homeland gradually crushed. The strong sense of despair that the prophet often conveys (4:19-21; 12:6; 14:8,9; 16:8,9) has earned Jeremiah the nickname, "the weeping prophet." Yet Jeremiah remained true to his calling. This man, born into a priestly family (Jer. 1:1), faithfully announced the Word of his God to a people whose sins had made them totally insensitive to the Lord, to justice, and to morality (Jer. 3). Particularly impressive are the brief confessions of personal faith interwoven with Jeremiah's messages. Only his awareness of who God is enabled the prophet to go on (10:23,24; 11:18–12:6; 15:10-21; 17:9-18; 18:18-23; 20:7-18).

THEOLOGICAL CONTRIBUTIONS
Jeremiah shows us a God who is exalted,

JEREMIAH: A READING AND STUDY GUIDE *CONT.*

Chapter	Content Summary	Related Articles
24	Two baskets of figs symbolize those who will die in Jerusalem and those who will survive in exile.	Nebuchadnezzar
25	Jeremiah predicts a 70-year captivity. Then God's wrath will pour out on the nations.	Anger
26	King Jehoiakim threatens Jeremiah with death and executes other prophets of the Lord.	
27	Jeremiah fashions a yoke to symbolize the surrender to Babylon.	Yoke
28	The false prophet Hananiah breaks the yoke and promises freedom. Jeremiah makes a yoke of iron and predicts the imminent death of Hananiah.	False Prophets
29	Jeremiah writes those already in Babylon to prepare for a lengthy captivity.	
30	Judah will be disciplined but then restored to its land. The people will find fresh faith in God.	Discipline
31	God's love is everlasting. Judah's mourning will turn to joy. God will make a new covenant providing forgiveness and transformation.	Love; Covenant Forgive
32	Jeremiah buys a field in enemy territory to show his confidence in Judah's restoration.	
33	God promises a day when Judah will call, and he will answer to keep the Davidic covenant.	Covenant Messiah
34	Zedekiah warned privately by Jeremiah. He frees Hebrew slaves but only temporarily.	Slave
35	The Recabite clan obeyed an ancestral command against drinking wine, while Judah disobeyed God.	Recabites Wine
36	Jehoiakim burns a scroll containing Jeremiah's words. Jeremiah dictates another.	Scroll
37	Nebuchadnezzar is outside the city walls. Jeremiah is imprisoned for "desertion."	
38	Jeremiah is thrown in a muddy cistern to die but is rescued by a royal official. Zedekiah again questions the prophet and hears a message of doom.	Cistern
39	Jerusalem falls. The king is captured. Jeremiah protected on orders of Nebuchadnezzar.	
V. Jerusalem Fallen		
40	Jeremiah is released and remains in Judah. Gedaliah is appointed governor by Nebuchadnezzar.	Gedaliah
41	Gedaliah is assassinated, and the remnant is afraid.	
42	The remaining Jews beg Jeremiah to tell them God's will.	
43	Jeremiah tells them to submit and remain in Judah. He warns against going to Egypt.	Egypt
44	The people reject Jeremiah's words. They are determined to head south.	
45	Baruch, Jeremiah's secretary, is told he will be spared. He is to be satisfied with this.	Baruch
46–51	The judgment of the Philistines, Moab, Ammon, Edom, Syria, Babylon, and other nations is announced. God will avenge his people.	
52	Fall of Jerusalem reviewed; a list made of items taken from the Temple to Babylon.	Temple, Jerusalem

and who is to be honored by men. Awed by his commission to communicate the Word of God (20:7-9), Jeremiah had only contempt for the false prophets who lightly shared their dreams as divine revelation or who simply lied in their pronouncements (23:9-40). He was deeply aware of God's activity in his own life. As God said to him,

"Before I formed you in the womb I knew you,
    before you were born I set you apart;
    I appointed you as a prophet to the
        nations." (Jer. 1:5)

God had also worked in the history of his covenant people. Yet they had rejected his glory (2:11,12). They were faithless children (3:19,22-25), servants who had broken the bond with their master (2:20). Judah was disobedient (3:13), unfaithful to her marriage vows (3:20). In consequence God, who is sovereign over all the nations, would call the nations against his people. This scenario, common to Isaiah and many of the other prophets, is a major emphasis in the Book of Jeremiah.

Yet Jeremiah's most striking and theologically significant contribution is the prediction of a new covenant, which God will one day make with his people (Jer. 31). Under the new covenant, God says,

"I will put my law in their minds
    and write it on their hearts.
I will be their God,
    and they will be my people.
No longer will a man teach his neighbor,
    or a man his brother, saying, 'Know the
        Lord,'
because they will all know me,
    from the least of them to the greatest,"
        declares the Lord.
"For I will forgive their wickedness
    and will remember their sins no more."
            (Jer. 31:33,34)

Along with this spiritual transformation, God also promises a complete restoration of Judah to her land (23:1-8; 30:10,11,18-21; 31:1-14,23-25) under a Davidic ruler (23:5,6).

Jeremiah's message builds on the conviction that God is faithful to his covenant—and more. God will punish his people for their wickedness, as the old covenant demands (Deut. 28). But because the old covenant has failed, and God continues to love his own, the conditions of that first covenant will be set aside. One day God will act to establish a relationship with human beings based on a forgiveness and inner transformation. That new cove-

nant was instituted on Calvary and provides the basis by which believers today know God. *See also* Covenant.

MASTERY KEYS

To sense the central thrust of this powerful OT book, study several key chapters before reading it through. (1) To meet Jeremiah, whose faith remained steadfast despite depression and emotional turmoil, read Jer. 10:23,24; 11:18–12:6; 15:10-21; 17:9-18; 18:18-23; and 20:7-18. (2) To sense the spiritual condition of Judah, read Jer. 2:1–3:5, with chs. 23 and 35. (3) To understand the situation as the end draws near, read Jer. 37–44. (4) To discover the eschatology of Jeremiah and its relationship to the new covenant, read Jer. 30–33.

Left: Pottery fragment found at Lachish bears part of a letter that contains an intriguing reference to "the prophet," which may have been Jeremiah. Its other contents clearly show that it was written "while the army of the king of Babylon was fighting against Jerusalem and . . . Lachish and Azekah . . . the only fortified cities left in Judah" (Jer. 34:7).

Below: King Jehoiakim burns part of the scroll on which Jeremiah's prophecy against Judah is written (Jer. 36:21-24). Inset: Clay seal impression of "Gemariah, son of Shaphan," a scribe in the court of Jehoiakim who was present at the burning of Jeremiah's scroll (Jer. 36:25).

Jericho [JAIR-ih-koh]. A city six miles (ten kilometers) north of the Dead Sea, along the Jordan River. Jericho lies on a fertile plain, the low-altitude rift valley through which the Jordan rolls. The tropical climate and flowing springs make Jericho a green oasis in a desert region. In ancient times, it was called "The City of Palm Trees" (Deut. 34:3). To the west, the arid canyons of the Judean Desert climb toward the hills of Jerusalem, 16 miles (27 kilometers) away.

We know Jericho best as the city conquered by Joshua's army when "the walls came a-tumblin' down." But the city has a substantial history, beginning long before that conquest.

Studying the various layers of debris from the excavated site of the city, archaeologists have concluded that Jericho was first settled sometime before 9600 B.C. Those first inhabitants even built a shrine there.

By 8000 B.C., walls were built, establishing Jericho's claim as "the oldest walled town in the world." Jericho prospered from 3200 B.C. until the settlement was destroyed in 2300 B.C.

But the city was rebuilt, and it flourished again in the patriarchal period (1900–1500 B.C.). Tombs near Jericho have yielded remains of tables, stools, pottery, bedsteads, jewelry, weapons, and foodstuffs. These have enriched our understanding of daily life during the time of Abraham, Isaac, and Jacob.

At some later date Jericho, again a strong walled city, was violently overthrown. Archaeologists have disagreed on the date of this destruction, which carries great implications for the dating of Joshua's conquest (*see* below).

For several centuries there was no walled city at the Jericho site. In the time of Ahab (874–853 B.C.), the city was rebuilt

by Hiel of Bethel, who lost two sons in the process, fulfilling a curse uttered by Joshua (1 Ki. 16:34; Josh. 6:26). This new city figures into several biblical stories. Its location made it a logical place for a transfer of prisoners between the northern and southern kingdoms (2 Chr. 28:15). And the invading Babylonians captured King Zedekiah near Jericho as he fled from Jerusalem (2 Ki. 25:5).

In NT times, Jesus dined with Zacchaeus in Jericho (Lk. 19:1-10) and healed two blind men (Mt. 20:29-34). The Good Samaritan in Christ's parable traveled the desert road between Jericho and Jerusalem (Lk. 10:30-37).

THE DATE OF JERICHO'S FALL

The Jericho site was examined first by Charles Warren in 1868, and again by a German expedition between 1907 and 1911. The first significant investigation to delve into the site's history was conducted by John Garstang between 1930 and 1936. He concluded that "City IV" (the fourth city established on the site) fell in the late 15th or early 14th century B.C., and linked its destruction with the Israelite invasion. Kathleen Kenyon worked in Jericho between 1952 and 1958, and reached very different conclusions. She believed City IV was destroyed about 1550 B.C. by Egyptian forces. This would mean that Jericho was unoccupied in 1400 B.C., the traditional date of Joshua's invasion. Kenyon's conclusions have influenced the opinions of many modern scholars who believe the

Left: Map locating the city of Jericho in different eras. Right: This excavated mound (Tell es-Sultan) clearly shows from the air all that is left of ancient Jericho.

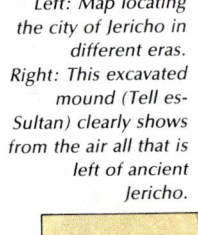

Israelites did not enter Canaan until about 1310 B.C. Yet even then Jericho, according to Kenyon's analysis, was not the strong walled city that we read of in the Bible.

Recently Garstang's and Kenyon's work has been re-analyzed by Bryant G. Wood. Relying on firmly established methods of pottery dating, supported by carbon-14 dating of debris from City IV, Wood argues that the archaeological data from pottery, stratigraphy, scarab data, and the carbon-14 reading, all show that City IV fell at the end of the 15th century B.C. His study supports Garstang's original conclusions, and harmonizes not only with the Bible's picture of the destruction of Jericho by Joshua's forces, but also with the Bible's internal chronology, which places the fall of Jericho about 1400 B.C. and the conquest of Canaan between 1400 and 1390 B.C.

Jeroboam I [JAIR-uh-BOH-uhm; "may the people multiply"]. The rebel who founded the Northern Kingdom of Israel, and ruled 931–913 B.C. He set up a counterfeit religious system to keep his citizens from going to Jerusalem to worship the Lord. **Father:** Nebat. **Son and successor:** Nadab. **Scripture:** 1 Ki. 11–14.

BACKGROUND

As a promising young official in Solomon's service, Jeroboam was told by the prophet Ahijah that God would give him

Above: Aerial view of the northern wing of Herod the Great's winter palace at Jericho. A bridge led across a river in the foreground to a sunken garden. Inset: Neolithic tower (8500–4500 B.C.) at the ancient ruins of Jericho has shown that Jericho is one of the oldest cities in the world.

ten of Israel's twelve tribes to rule, but would reserve two for Solomon's son. Solomon subsequently tried to kill Jeroboam, who fled to Egypt. On Solomon's death, Jeroboam won the allegiance of the ten tribes promised him and established a northern splinter kingdom, which took the name Israel.

Jeroboam then fortified his borders against the southern kingdom, Judah. Ac-

549

cording to OT Law, all Israelites were to travel to Jerusalem to worship the Lord. To prevent this, Jeroboam established worship centers at Bethel and Dan. He supplied these with golden calves, altars for sacrifice, and a priesthood drawn from families other than that of Aaron. He also established festivals that paralleled those commanded in OT Law but were held on different dates. This counterfeit system was maintained by every succeeding king of Israel. Because of this, the OT often says Israel's kings "walked in the ways of Jeroboam," and accuses Jeroboam as the man who "caused Israel to sin."

Jeroboam ruled for 22 years. His reign was marked by continual skirmishes with Judah, including one pitched battle with Abijah in which Jeroboam was defeated (2 Chr. 13:1-19).

LEARNING FROM JEROBOAM'S LIFE

The life of this king illustrates how a leader's failure to trust God affects not only himself, but the history of a nation.

When the prophet told Jeroboam God would give him ten of Israel's tribes, he also conveyed a promise. God would be with Jeroboam and establish his dynasty— if "you do whatever I command you and walk in my ways and do what is right" (1 Ki. 11:38). When Jeroboam became king, however, he "thought to himself" that permitting his people to worship in Jerusalem according to God's Law might turn their allegiance to Solomon's son and successor, Rehoboam. This fear led Jeroboam I to disregard God's Word, and to set up a separate worship system in Israel. Theoretically, the Israelites still worshiped the Lord, who was probably envisioned as standing, invisible, on the back of the golden bulls Jeroboam commissioned. But every element of Jeroboam's worship system violated the pattern provided in God's Law. *See also* Golden Calf.

The day the altar at Bethel was dedicated, a prophet from Judah cried out against Jeroboam's acts (1 Ki. 13:1-5). This prophet then himself disobeyed God and was killed by a lion (1 Ki. 13:6-34).

The object lesson was clear: Disobedience brings death. Yet "even after this Jeroboam did not change his evil ways" (1 Ki. 13:33). His actions led to the downfall of his own house. His son ruled only two years before he was assassinated along with the rest of Jeroboam's family. Jeroboam's actions also led to the eventual fall of the kingdom itself. Those Israelites not killed in the Assyrian invasion of 722 B.C. were deported from their homeland.

Jeroboam II [JAIR-uh-BOH-uhm; "may the people multiply"]. The politically and militarily successful 13th king of Israel, who ruled in the days of Jonah and Amos, 793–753 B.C. **Father:** Jehoash. **Son and successor:** Zechariah. **Scripture:** 2 Ki. 14:23-29.

BACKGROUND

Very little is said about this powerful king, who ruled Israel for 41 years. Yet his reign saw a resurgence of prosperity in Israel. Jeroboam II conducted successful wars against Syria. He retook territory Israel had not held since the time of David.

Military success brought much wealth to Israel, as did control of trade routes. An upper class quickly developed. The wealthy began to buy out family farms to develop great estates. The displaced poor were forced to work as hired labor and were oppressed by the rich. The corruption and injustice now deeply rooted in Israel's society is graphically described by the prophet Amos. The wealthy, drunk with wine and luxury, valued their poor brethren less than a pair of fashionable sandals (Amos 2:6; 8:6).

Ritual religion seems to have flourished in Jeroboam II's reign. The wealthy built vacation homes near the worship centers at Bethel and Dan, and offered endless sacrifices (Amos 4:4,5). This empty ritual worship was decisively rejected by the Lord (Amos 5:18-27). God refused to hear a people whose ways were corrupt (Amos 5:10-13).

LEARNING FROM JEROBOAM II'S LIFE

Jeroboam II was undoubtedly one of Israel's most able rulers. Yet almost nothing is said of his 41-year reign, except that "he did evil in the eyes of the Lord." Judged by human standards, Jeroboam II was an unqualified success. By God's standards, he is hardly worth mentioning. The silence of Scripture on the decades that Israel was led by this powerful man is perhaps the most significant commentary that can be made on his values.

Jerusalem [jeh-ROO-sah-lehm; "city of peace"]. The central and most significant of the cities in ancient Israel. Jerusalem was established about 1000 B.C. as Israel's political and religious center by King David. Solomon built the Temple there as the sole location for the national worship of Israel's God. After Solomon's kingdom split, Jerusalem continued to serve as the capital of the southern kingdom of Judah between 931 B.C. and the city's destruction by the Babylonians in 586 B.C. A remnant of Jews returned to Palestine from Babylon in 538 B.C. and rebuilt the Jerusalem Temple. During the centuries of Gentile domination that followed, Jerusalem remained the center of Jewish life and worship. Herod the Great beautified and expanded the Jerusalem Temple, and Christ preached in its courts. Jesus entered Jerusalem in triumph, ate the Last Supper there with his disciples, and was crucified outside the city's walls. After his resurrection, Jesus appeared to the disciples in a sealed room. The Spirit's miracle of Pentecost took place in Jerusalem, launching the Christian Church. In A.D. 70, putting down a Jewish rebellion, the Roman army under the command of Titus destroyed the city and its Temple. Yet the OT proph-

ets predict a central role for Jerusalem at history's end. The Book of Revelation calls the heavenly city the new Jerusalem.

JERUSALEM'S LOCATION

The city lies on Palestine's mountainous central ridge, some 33 miles (55 kilometers) from the Mediterranean Sea. Dry and windy at 2,500 feet (762 meters) above sea level, and 3,700 feet (1,128 meters) above the Jordan River, Jerusalem is not suited for agriculture. In biblical times it lacked an easily accessible water supply, and the limestone rock on which it stands held no minerals of value. Yet Jerusalem lay on a major trade route, and in David's time it straddled the border between northern and southern tribes. It served as a unifying location for the new nation, accessible to all who would come up to the heights to worship God at the temple David envisioned there.

PRE-KINGDOM HISTORY

Jerusalem (then "Salem") was already settled in the time of Abraham, who gave tithes to its priest-king, Melchizedek (Gen. 14:18-20; Ps. 76:2). When Joshua led the invasion of Palestine, Jerusalem was held by a Canaanite tribal group, the Jebusites. The city is often referred to in the Amarna Letters, Egyptian diplomatic correspondence dating to the 14th century B.C. The Jebusites held the city throughout the era of the judges (Jdg. 1:21). *See also* Jebusites.

IN DAVID'S TIME

After being recognized as king by the ten northern tribes as well as by Judah and Benjamin, David attacked the hilltop fortress of the Jebusites, then located on the southeastern hill (Zion), which lay beyond the walls of present-day Jerusalem. The city may have then held some 2,000 people. David established his capital there and brought the ark of God to the city. He also laid plans to build a temple at the very spot where, according to tradition, Abraham offered up his son Isaac (Gen. 22; 2 Sam. 24:18-25; 1 Chr. 21:18-28).

DURING THE KINGDOM ERA

During the reign of Solomon, the city and Temple held vast wealth. This was stripped in 917 B.C. by Shishak of Egypt, who invaded Judah unopposed (1 Ki. 14:26; 2 Chr. 12:9). In the following centuries Jerusalem was plundered seven more times, until it was finally destroyed by Nebuchadnezzar in 586 B.C.

AFTER THE RETURN

The Jews who returned to Judah from Babylon struggled to re-establish them-

This Babylonian chronicle records events from 605 to 594 B.C., including Nebuchadnezzar's capture of Jerusalem in March of 597 B.C. (2 Ki. 24:10-17).

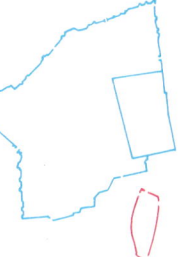

JEBUS (11ᵗʰ CENT. B.C.)
THE CITY OF DAVID

SOLOMON'S ADDITIONS
(10ᵗʰ CENT. B.C.)

8ᵗʰ - 7ᵗʰ CENT. ADDITIONS
(POSSIBLY HEZEKIAH)

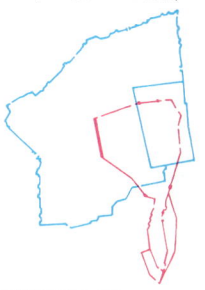

NEHEMIAH'S RECONSTRUCTION
(5ᵗʰ CENT. B.C.)

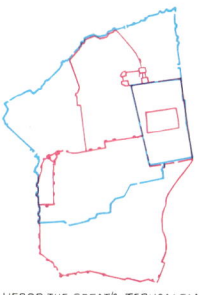

HEROD THE GREAT'S JERUSALEM
(1ˢᵀ CENT. B.C. – 1ˢᵀ CENT. A.D.)

―― PRESENT WALL OF OLD CITY

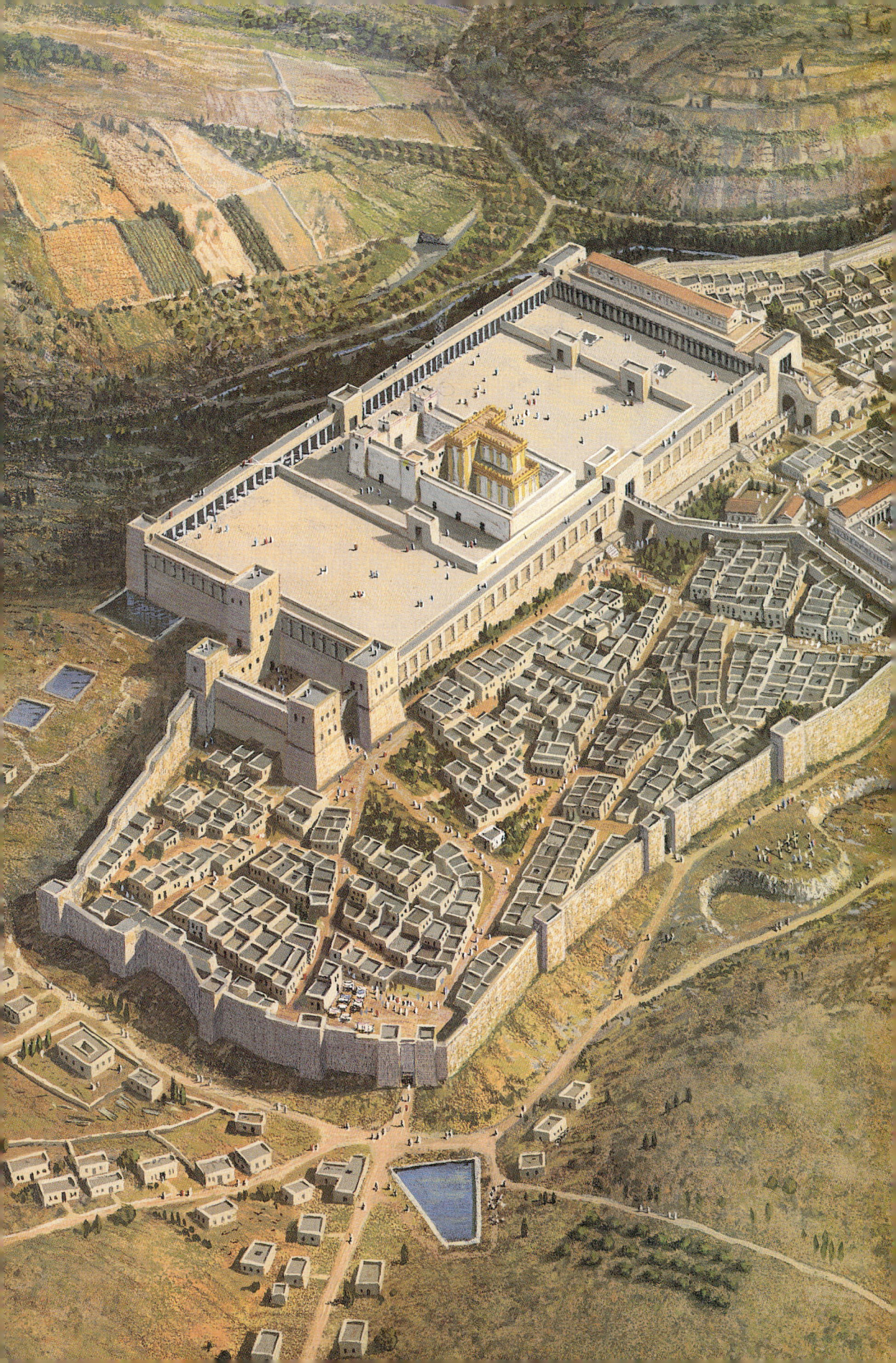

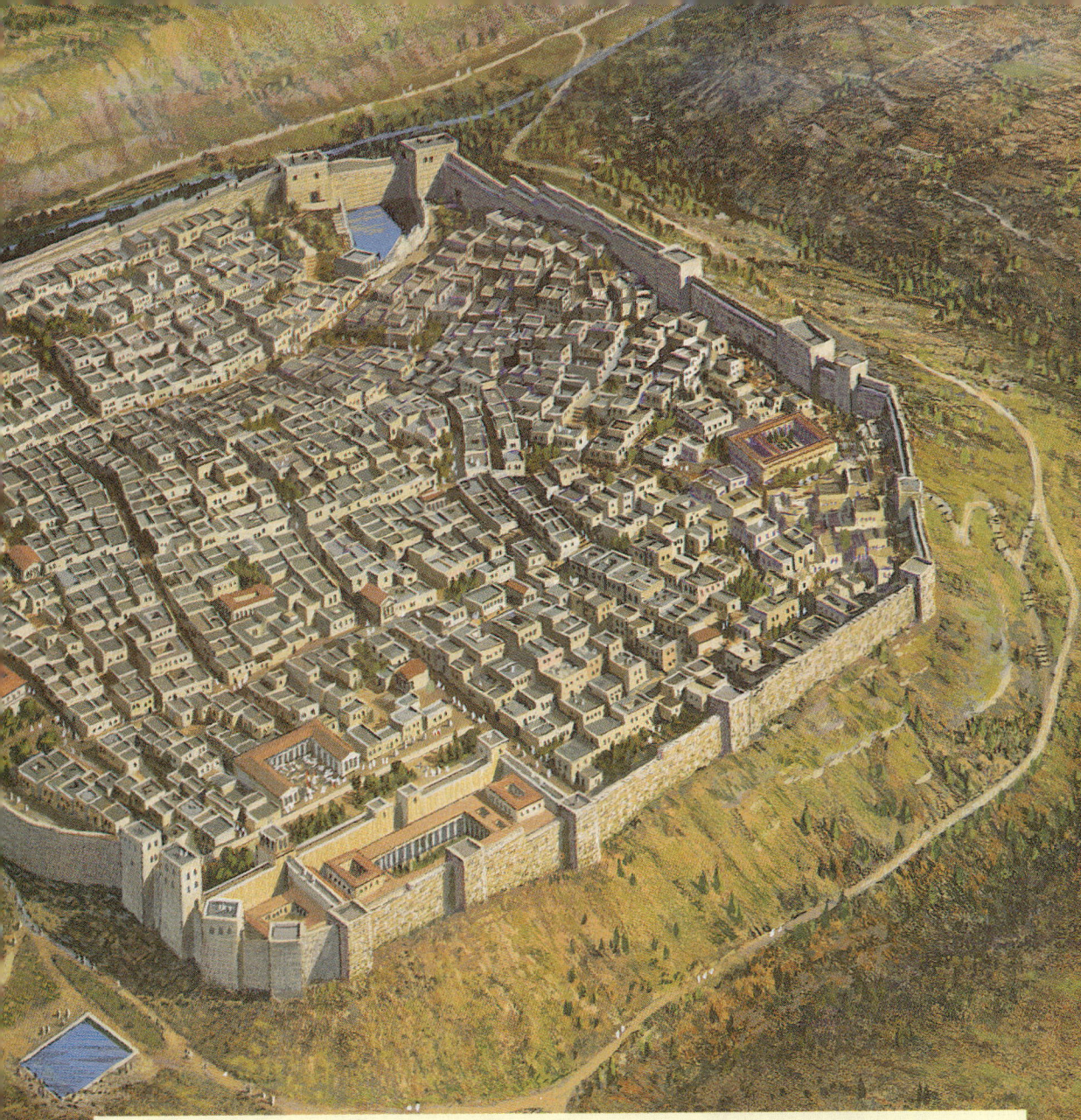

Jerusalem

This view of first-century Jerusalem looks southeast toward the Temple, where Jesus taught during Passion Week. Then, the evening before his Crucifixion, Jesus came with his disciples from Bethany to the Upper Room for the Last Supper. Jesus' steps during his final hours can be traced by following the numbered locations on the map at the right.

1 Upper Room
2 Gethsemane
3 Caiaphas's House
4 Praetorium (Antonia Fortress)
5 Herod's Palace
6 Pilate's Judgment
7 Via Dolorosa
8 Golgotha

Right: Aerial view of the Old City of Jerusalem. The former site of the Temple has been the home of the Dome of the Rock since the 7th century A.D.
Below: The wall of the Temple Mount clearly shows the latest three periods of construction. At the bottom are the huge, beautifully cut stones or ashlars of Herod's building; the next two reflect the repair of damaged walls by the Ommayid rulers of the 16th century A.D.
Lower right: Mosaic map of Jerusalem during the Byzantine era (6th century A.D.). A large colonnaded street, called the Cardo, ran through the center of the city. Floor of St. George's Church, Medeba, Jordan.

Preceding page: Artist's rendering of Jerusalem in Jesus' day. Precise reconstruction is impossible and archaeologists differ widely on the placement of the city walls.

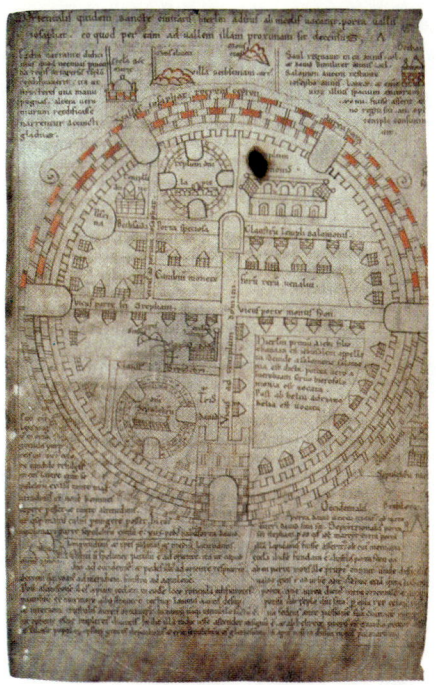

selves on the land. They gradually rebuilt the Jerusalem Temple and, about 80 years after the first group came home, reconstructed the city walls. At that time Jerusalem probably held some 4,500 persons.

During the next centuries Jerusalem failed to prosper, although it continued to be the center of Jewish faith and worship. Jerusalem was alternately crushed and restored, its walls torn down and rebuilt, on into the Roman era.

THE JERUSALEM OF JESUS' DAY

Herod the Great was made king of the Jews in 37 B.C. He brought to Judah not only cruel determination but also a passion for building. He began an expansion of the Jerusalem Temple in 20 B.C. which was not completed until A.D. 62, 58 years after his death. In Christ's day, too, Jerusalem was the center of Jewish faith and worship. The Sanhedrin, the ruling council of the Jews, met in Jerusalem. The Temple flourished there, with its sacrifices and rituals. Pilgrims from all over the world swelled the normal population of 60,000 to a quarter of a million during religious festivals.

JERUSALEM AND THE CHURCH

The first Christian converts were made in Jerusalem (Acts 2). Perhaps as many as 20,000 Christians resided in Jerusalem a decade or so after the resurrection. Persecution then scattered these believers and launched the spread of the Gospel to the outside world (Acts 8). The first council of the church was held in Jerusalem (Acts 15), and years later Paul was arrested there (Acts 21,22).

Jerusalem was besieged by the Romans and destroyed in A.D. 70. Some 600,000 Jews were killed in the Roman invasion, and thousands more carried away captive. Tradition tells us that prophets warned the Christian community, which escaped to safety before the Romans came.

After another rebellion in A.D. 134, the Romans leveled the ruins of Jerusalem in order to build a new city on its site. For two centuries no Jews were permitted to enter it.

JERUSALEM IN PROPHECY

The prophetic visions of the future contained in the OT place the people of Israel in their land at history's end. Jerusalem is not only mentioned in such prophecies, but is often the focal point. The people will return to their land, to worship at Jerusalem (Isa. 27:13). In the millennial age Jerusalem will be "a delight" (Isa. 65:18). When Messiah comes to take David's throne, "in those days Judah will be saved and Jerusalem will live in safety" (Jer. 33:16). Ezekiel describes a great temple to be built in Jerusalem in that era (Ezek. 40–48). Joel describes an enemy invasion that precipitates God's intervention at history's end, when he will "restore the fortunes of Judah and Jerusalem" (3:1; see Joel 2:9-12; Isa. 29:1-8; Zech. 14:1-3) and will again dwell in Zion, making Jerusalem truly holy (Joel 3:17).

Ultimately established as the capital of the Messiah and graced with the Temple of God, Jerusalem will be the political and religious center not only of Israel but of the whole world (Ps. 102:21,22; Isa. 2:2-4; 62:2). See also Future.

JERUSALEM AND ARCHAEOLOGY

Jerusalem has long fascinated archaeologists, although access to its buried remains has been difficult because of continued inhabitation of the walled city. Excavations on Mount Zion have uncovered elements of the fortress captured by King David from the Jebusites. Part of the enclosure walls supporting the Temple Mount may have been Solomon's work. The shaft of a tunnel hewn through a southeastern hill by Hezekiah to bring water within the city walls in 705 B.C. has been accessible since then. Israelite houses that were destroyed by the Babylonians in the late sixth century B.C. have been excavated. The complex system of pools and aqueducts that brought water to Jerusalem in the first century B.C. has been traced. These, with many fascinating artifacts from pottery shops and even glass factories, enrich our appreciation for this ancient city.

Crusader map of Jerusalem done by a monk of the Voormezeele Abbey, about A.D. 1150. Highly schematic, the map places the east of the city, the Temple Mount, at the top.

The Gospels are our primary source of information about Jesus' life on earth, while the Epistles show us how to interpret his life and death. Yet the NT's testimony is amply supported by the stunning impact of Christ on the world of the first century.

Within a few brief decades of Christ's death and resurrection, secular writers commented on the Christian movement. The Roman historian Tacitus, writing about Christians of Nero's time (A.D. 64), observes that "Christ from whom they took their name had been put to death as a punishment during the reign of Tiberius at the hands of one of our procurators, Pontius Pilate, and a most mischievous superstition, thus checked for the moment, again broke out not only in Judea, the first source of the evil, but even in Rome." A few decades later, the Christian movement was so strong that sporadic persecution broke out across the Empire in the time of the emperor Trajan. In another century or so, the church father Tertullian (about A.D. 160–220) wrote that Christians were "all but a majority" in the cities of North Africa.

THE PERSON OF JESUS

• *His humanity.* Jesus was born in Bethlehem of Judea, a few miles south of Jerusalem. His mother was a young woman named Mary, a virgin, who was pledged to be married to Joseph, a carpenter. As was common among the Jews, Jesus' genealogy was carefully recorded. That genealogy authenticated the later claim of his followers that Jesus was a descendant of King David. When Jesus was about two, the family hurriedly left Judea and fled to Egypt to escape Herod's slaughter of male infants in Bethlehem. Two or three years later they returned and settled in Galilee, in Nazareth. Little is known of Jesus' childhood, beyond the fact that he "grew in wisdom and stature, and in favor with God and men" (Lk. 2:52).

Jesus is about 30 years old when the Gospels pick up his story. He is baptized by John the Baptist, fasts for 40 days, undergoes temptation by Satan, and then begins a public ministry. For three or four years he travels throughout the cities and villages of Galilee and Judea. The Gospels show him as truly human. Jesus suffers hunger and thirst (Mt. 4:2; Jn. 4:7; 19:28). He knows exhaustion (Mk. 4:38; Jn. 4:6). Sensing a deep need for fellowship with God, Jesus often slips away from his followers to pray (Mt. 14:23; Lk. 6:12; 9:28). He is deeply moved by the suffering of others (Mt. 9:36; 20:34; Mk. 1:41), and his anger flares at those who are insensitive to God and human need (Mk. 11:12-17; Mk. 10:14). As Jesus approaches the end, he is "overwhelmed with sorrow to the point of death" (Mt. 26:38). After being beaten, and suffering massive loss of blood, Jesus staggers under the weight of his cross (Mt. 27:32). On Calvary, he cries out—and dies (Mt. 27:50). In all this Jesus is revealed to be a human being, heir to humanity's physical weaknesses and limitations.

• *His deity.* While the Gospels demonstrate Jesus' humanity, the Gospel writers also present Jesus as more than a man. They saw him walk on water (Mt. 14:22-33) and quiet a violent storm with a word (Mt. 8:23-27). They observed his miracles of healing (Mt. 8:8-17; Mk. 2:1-12; Lk. 5:17-26; Jn. 9:1-12), his authority over demons (Mk. 1:21-28; 5:1-20; Lk. 4:31-37), and even saw him raise the dead (Mt. 9:18-26; Lk. 8:40-56; Jn. 11:1-44).

The Gospels report the indignation of

MESSIANIC PROPHECIES IN MATTHEW

Event in Jesus' Life	Matthew Reference	Old Testament Reference
His virgin birth	Mt. 1:23	Isa. 7:14
His birthplace	Mt. 2:6	Mic. 5:2
Return from Egypt	Mt. 2:15	Hos. 11:1
Healings	Mt. 8:17	Isa. 53:4
Servanthood	Mt. 12:18-21	Isa. 42:1-4
Use of parables	Mt. 13:34	Ps. 78:2
Triumphal entry	Mt. 21:5	Zech. 9:9
His rejection	Mt. 21:42	Ps. 118:22
His deity	Mt. 22:44	Ps. 110:1
His abandonment	Mt. 26:31	Zech. 13:7
His return	Mt. 26:64	Dan. 7:13
Crucifixion details	Mt. 27:34,48	Ps. 69:21
	Mt. 27:35	Ps. 22:18
	Mt. 27:39,40	Ps. 22:7
	Mt. 27:43	Ps. 22:8
	Mt. 27:46	Ps. 22:1
His burial	Mt. 27:57-60	Isa. 53:9

the religious leaders when Jesus exercised a divine prerogative and forgave sin (Mk. 2:1-12). The Gospel writers carefully record Jesus' claim to have existed before Abraham's day, and the words he used to identify himself with the "I AM" of the OT (Jn. 8:52-59). John notes Jesus' claim that God sent his Son into the world, not to condemn the world but to save it (Jn. 3:16-18). In the fourth Gospel we find Jesus claiming that he has come from heaven (Jn. 6:31-38), and that he is so completely united with God the Father that any who have seen Jesus have seen God (Jn. 14:8-12). *See also* Deity.

The Gospels also record the conviction of the disciples. The man Jesus was, at one and the same time, a true human being and "the Christ, the Son of the living God" (Mt. 16:16).

The Epistles report a formula by which the early church affirmed its faith in the mystery of Jesus:

He appeared in a body,
was vindicated by the Spirit,
was seen by angels,
was preached among the nations,
was believed on in the world,
was taken up in glory.

(1 Tim. 3:16)

JESUS AND THE OLD TESTAMENT

• *The essential harmony of Jesus with the message of the OT.* Jesus was born a Jew, a member of a people chosen by God millennia before. Through the centuries the purposes of God for and through the Jewish people had been gradually revealed in a series of covenants, whose implications were developed by the Hebrew prophets. God's intent to redeem man and to establish a righteous Kingdom on earth are clearly expressed in the OT, as is his commitment to accomplish his purposes through a descendant of David, qualified to sit on the throne of a restored Israel. Thus it was that the Jewish people looked forward expectantly to the coming of God's Anointed One (Messiah), and the fulfillment of all God's promises through him.

The OT contains two distinct lines of teaching concerning the Messiah. According to one line of teaching, the Anointed One would be a conqueror, destined to restore an independent and regathered Israel to her rightful place as the premier nation on earth. As King of the restored Israel, the Messiah's reign would extend to the nations beyond Palestine. An era of peace would follow as the nations acknowledged and worshiped Israel's God. *See also* Future; Messiah.

According to the second line of teaching, the Anointed One would be a deliverer, destined to restore humankind to

"The Apostles in Pain," an artistic interpretation of Jn. 16:17-22 done in high relief on a sarcophagus from the 4th century A.D. After some three years of following Jesus, the twelve disciples were understandably distressed when Jesus announced that he would soon leave them.

Jesus the Good Shepherd was a favorite symbol of early Christians, as with this 4th-century A.D. statue from Constantinople (Istanbul, Turkey). Jesus said, "I am the good shepherd. The good shepherd lays down his life for his sheep. . . . I know my sheep and my sheep know me" (Jn. 10:11,14).

comes again, he will establish righteousness and reign over all humanity as David's greater son.

In their identification of Jesus as the Messiah, the NT writers affirm an essential unity between the OT and NT. The NT is rooted in and founded on the OT. Rather than being a new and radically different revelation, the NT explains and expands themes introduced in the OT. Thus the mission and ministry of Jesus was in fullest harmony with the OT Scriptures, which Jesus acknowledged to be the Word of God, and by which Jesus chose to live.

• *Specific prophecies concerning Jesus in the Old Testament.* Matthew is especially careful to document his identification of Jesus as God's Messiah. He quotes 53 times from the OT, and alludes to the OT on 76 other occasions. Most of the quotes are clearly messianic, and are intended to demonstrate that Jesus is the one foretold by the prophets.

Taking a slightly different tack, the author of Hebrews shows that Jesus is the reality foreshadowed in the OT's primary religious institutions. Jesus is God (Heb. 1), yet truly human (Heb. 2). The Word he brings from God is authoritative, and promises rest to those who respond to it (Heb. 3, 4). Jesus is like the high priests of the OT, offering sacrifices for the salvation of the people. But since Jesus, unlike the priests, lives forever, he is able to save completely (Heb. 5–7). And the covenant which Jesus administers is superior to the code of Moses, which failed to change human hearts. Jesus has introduced a new covenant which provides both forgiveness and transformation (Heb. 8). The tabernacle and Temple of the OT did reflect heavenly realities, but Christ is the reality they portrayed (Heb. 9). The blood of animal sacrifices covered sin, but Christ's blood cleanses from sin and clears the conscience (Heb. 9). In the one sacrifice of himself Christ accomplishes what the repeated sacrifices of the OT could never do for humankind (Heb. 10). *See also* Hebrews, Epistle to the.

In taking this line, the writer of Hebrews does not reject the OT or its teachings. Rather he argues that the entire OT system of faith and worship witnesses to Jesus. He fulfills perfectly everything the OT foreshadowed about sin, redemption, and man's relationship with God.

THE LIFE OF JESUS

Jesus lived almost his entire human life in tiny Palestine. Most of his years are wrapped in obscurity. Through Matthew

right relationship with God. Here the theme of suffering is introduced, particularly in Isa. 52:13–53:12, where the death of the Messiah as an offering for sin is most clearly unveiled. Through his work as God's Servant, the Anointed One would lay a foundation for the transformation of human hearts, so that a forgiven humanity would at last respond with love and devotion to the Lord. *See also* Covenant; Servant.

While elements of each purpose shine brightly in the biblical covenants and in the visions of the prophets, exactly when and how each mission was to be accomplished in history remained unclear. Then, the NT writers announce that the Anointed One did appear—Jesus of Nazareth. In his life, death, and resurrection Jesus Christ accomplished the most difficult messianic mission and provided for the salvation of lost humanity. When Jesus

558

and Luke we know something of his birth. Almost nothing is known of the next two decades, although we can assume that Jesus took up the trade of Joseph and worked as a carpenter (*see* Mk. 6:3). Then, for three or four years, Jesus carried on a public ministry of preaching, teaching, and healing.

• *Jesus' miracles.* The miracles of Jesus performed two primary functions. First, they authenticated Jesus as one who had been sent by God. Relatively early in Jesus' ministry Nicodemus, a member of the ruling council that later would agitate for Jesus' execution, told Jesus, "We know you are a teacher who has come from God. For no one could perform the miraculous signs you are doing if God were not with him" (Jn. 3:2; *see* Jn. 9:1-3,33).

The range of miracles reported in the Gospels demonstrates the authority of Jesus over nature (Mk. 4:35-41; 6:30-44, 45-52), over illness (Mk. 1:40-45; 2:1-12; 5:21-34), over demonic powers (Mk. 1:21-28; 3:20-30; 5:1-17), and over death itself (Mk. 5:35-43; Jn. 11). These miracles caused fear and consternation in observers. Jesus was acknowledged as a great prophet, but the miracles led few to lasting faith or discipleship.

The miracles are important in another aspect, however. Every miracle of Jesus that involved another person was performed for human benefit. The hungry were fed, the demon-possessed were freed, the sick healed. In no instance did Jesus exercise his power to punish or to harm. Thus the miracles of Jesus served as vivid evidence of the love of God that Jesus proclaimed.

• *Jesus' teaching.* Jesus stated that his teaching was not intended to abolish (Gk., *katalyo;* "to tear down, destroy") the Law and the prophets. Instead, Jesus intended his teaching to "fulfill" them. In Judaism a rabbi had the task of "fulfilling" the Law: a phrase which meant "to explain the true and full meaning." Jesus' teaching might conflict with the understanding of many religious leaders. But his teaching was in total harmony with previous revelation, and in fact revealed the true meaning of what God had said in ages past.

Jesus used a variety of teaching methods. He gave discourses, like the Sermon on the Mount (Mt. 5–7) and the sermon on the bread of life (Jn. 6). He told parables and stories (Mt. 13; Mk. 12; Lk. 15–18). He entered into dialogues (Lk. 14:1-14; Jn. 3), and asked probing questions (Mt. 16:13,15). Through each Jesus challenged

his listeners to rethink their concept of God and to re-evaluate their own relationship with the Lord and his Kingdom.

Although Jesus used many of the same methods as did the rabbis of his day, his teaching still set him apart, as Mt. 7:28,29 indicates: "The crowds were amazed at his teaching, because he taught as one who had authority, and not as their teachers of the law."

• *Opposition to Jesus.* The Gospels report a growing opposition to Jesus. His primary opponents, the Pharisees, were intensely dedicated to keeping not only God's written Law but also many additional regulations. The Gospels portray those Pharisees who opposed Jesus as self-righteous men, more concerned with legalistic details than with human need (Mt. 12:1-14), and more interested in what other people thought of them than in what God thought (Mt. 23:1-39).

We must be careful to distinguish between the godly Pharisees of Christ's day and the more visible members of this group portrayed in the Gospels. Not all Pharisees were hypocrites. Yet many members of this group felt threatened by Jesus and his teachings and were openly hostile.

Later, as the movement associated with Jesus seemed likely to have a political impact, the Sadducees joined the Pharisees in opposition to Jesus. This group, which included many priestly families, had adapted well to Roman rule and was intent on maintaining the status quo. The opposition of the priests had already been stimulated by Jesus' physical attacks on those who bought and sold in the Temple—a source of income for the high priest and his family (Mt. 21:12-17; Jn. 2:12-16).

When slander (Mt. 12:22-37), threats (Jn. 9:22), and direct attempts to discredit Jesus (Mt. 19:1-12; 22:15-46) all failed, Jesus' opponents determined to see Christ dead

The name of Jesus inscribed in Hebrew on stone. Jesus is the Greek form of Yeshua, a common Hebrew name that is also transliterated as Joshua and means "savior" (see Mt. 1:21).

(Mk. 3:6; Jn. 8:40; 11:50). *See also* Pharisees.

• *Jesus' disciples.* At the beginning of his public ministry, Jesus chose twelve men to be his disciples. Here the word "disciple" is used in a technical sense, well-established in first-century Judaism. Jesus would train these twelve, who traveled everywhere with him, and so prepare them for the leadership of his movement when he was gone.

THE TEACHING OF JESUS

Jesus came to a religious people, to a people intimately familiar with their history and heritage. His listeners shared a fundamental knowledge about God and his commands. So Jesus taught those who knew, not those who were ignorant. His methods were not intended to communicate the unknown, but to bring fresh and often surprising insights.

At the same time, certain recurring themes called for a complete reorientation of the listener's beliefs and convictions. These themes lay at the heart of Jesus' message.

• *Jesus' teaching about God as Father.* The OT speaks of God as "father" of the nation, in the sense of its source or originator (Deut. 32:6), and as one who treated Israel "as a father" (Deut. 1:31). Jesus took this idea even further, teaching that God is Father to those who trust him. This realization brings a new intimacy in prayer. His people can now confidently approach God Almighty as "Our Father in heaven" (Mt. 6:9). It brings new freedom. Because our heavenly Father will faithfully care for our basic needs, we are free to "seek first his kingdom and his righteousness" (Mt. 6:33). Because God is our Father, we look to him as our example and enabler, and model our relationships with others on his love and grace (Mt. 5:45-48). *See also* Father.

Yet this new intimacy with God as Father is mediated through Jesus himself, and Jesus alone. Only Jesus truly knows the Father (Mt. 11:27). Anyone coming to God as the Father must come through Jesus (Jn. 14:6). Only those who love the Son are loved by the Father, for the Father lives and expresses himself in his Son (Jn. 14:10-23).

• *Jesus' teaching on the Kingdom of God.* The re-establishment of a Hebrew kingdom on earth, under a descendant of David, was central to the Jewish messianic hope. Jesus did not reject this vision, but spoke of a final day when the prophesied kingdom would arrive in all its glory (Mk. 9:1; Lk. 19:11; 22:18).

But Jesus did redefine the kingdom. In biblical thought a kingdom is not only a particular geographical area but also a population governed by the will of a king. In one sense, the universe is God's kingdom, for ultimately his will is sovereign. The OT prophets speak of a time when God's Anointed One will rule Israel, and enforce God's will in Israel and all the nations of the earth.

Yet when Jesus began to preach, announcing "The kingdom of God is near," he did not have that physical kingdom in view (Mk. 1:15). Jesus called on his listeners to enter, or receive, God's kingdom now (Mt. 12:28). Jesus taught that God's sovereign authority over all things is to be experienced as well as affirmed; that God's kingdom is a present reality for his people as well as a future promise. Those who live by God's will in this present world will experience the Sovereign God working in their lives and circumstances.

But again, while Jesus affirmed truths intrinsic to OT revelation, he added a new dimension. Jesus warned that no one could even glimpse this kingdom without being "born again" (Jn. 3:3). An experience of the Kingdom of God in its present form demands an inner renewal, which is possible only through the spiritual rebirth Jesus came to provide.

• *Jesus' ethical teachings.* The ethical teachings of Jesus naturally mirror those of the OT, for the OT moral vision is itself rooted in the nature and character of God. Christ's contemporaries found his ethical principles novel, not because of new content, but because of a new approach to the issues.

The Pharisees approached ethics legalistically. Life was to be lived by rules. The ethical quality of an act was measured by its conformity to the rules, whether those were rules prescribed in the Law or expanded by tradition.

Jesus powerfully attacked this approach. The rules the Pharisees counted on led them to ignore human need and actually kept them from doing righteous deeds (Mt. 12:1-14). The rules disguised or distorted truths that God intended to express (Mt. 15:10-20). The rules became ends in themselves, so the legalist was unable to distinguish important moral issues from the less significant details (Mt. 23:23,24).

In place of an ethic based on rules, Jesus called for an ethic of love. The first and great commandment is to love God, he said, and the second is to love one's neigh-

law in their minds and write it on their hearts" (Jer. 31:33). This transaction, which Jesus called a new birth (Jn. 3:3), is an essential element in Jesus' ethical vision.

This transaction is also central to Christ's understanding of his mission. Jesus came not because humanity is good, but because it is lost. Only by giving his life as a ransom for sinners could the Son of Man make possible for his followers a life that approximates his ethical ideal (Mt. 20:28).

• *Jesus' claims about himself.* In all of Jesus' teachings, he reserved a central role for himself. God is Father, but Jesus mediates one's personal relationship with God (Jn. 14:6). Jesus not only announces, "The kingdom of God has come," but claims to be the decisive agent in the inauguration of the Kingdom (Mt. 12:28). Jesus announced an ethic of inner transformation but said that transformation could be achieved only by a new birth through faith in Jesus himself (Jn. 3:3-16).

Jesus claimed to exist before Abraham as the "I AM" (Yahweh) of the OT (Jn. 8:58; *see* Ex. 3:14). Jesus claimed, "I and my Father are one" (Jn. 10:30). This was so clear a claim of deity that many listeners "picked up stones to stone him," citing him for "blasphemy, because you, a mere man, claim to be God" (Jn. 10:30-33).

Jesus said that his hearers must put his words into practice (Mt. 7:24-27). He promised eternal life to those who believed in him and warned that whoever does not believe "stands condemned already" (Jn. 3:16-18). Jesus claimed that the Father had placed the judgment of humanity into his hands (Jn. 5:22). When Peter acknowledged Jesus as "the Christ, the Son of the Living God," Jesus commended him (Mt. 16:16,17). Later, when the Jewish court that condemned him asked Jesus if he were the Son of God, Christ answered, "You are right in saying I am" (Lk. 22:70).

This ultimately became the central issue. While other elements of Jesus' teaching lay within the broad framework of first-century Judaism, what Jesus said about himself was truly radical. Either his listeners acknowledged Jesus to be the Son of God, or they held back, unwilling to accept a "mere man" as the incarnation of their God.

• *Jesus' teaching about the future.* Jesus did not reject the OT's view of the future. He affirmed it. But again, Jesus gave himself a central role. He spoke of the time of the end, and linked it to his own return from heaven (Mt. 24:1-35). He urged his follow-

bor as oneself (Mt. 22:37-40). The OT Law and prophets "hang on these two commandments" because all these writings aim to teach Israel how to love both God and others.

An ethic of love does not abandon rules, which serve to identify and prohibit unloving acts, but it shifts the focus of attention from acts to intentions. Thus, in the Sermon on the Mount, Jesus shifts attention from murder to the anger and hatred which lead to it (Mt. 5:21-26), and from adultery to the lustful attitude of the one who commits it (Mt. 5:27-30). Because Jesus' ethics are concerned with inner motivation and not just deeds, Jesus told his listeners, "Unless your righteousness surpasses that of the Pharisees and the teachers of the law, you will certainly not enter the kingdom of heaven" (Mt. 5:20).

But this approach to ethics raises another issue. A person may control his acts. But how can one control thoughts and motives?

Christ's answer is to call these issues of the heart (Mt. 15:16-20). From the heart of man come evil thoughts, murder, immorality, theft, and other sins. The solution, expressed ages ago by Jeremiah, is to experience an inner transformation, an act of God by which, he said, "I will put my

ers to remain faithful while he was gone, to be ready for his coming at any moment (Mt. 24:36–25:31). He spoke of judgment to take place "when the Son of man comes in his glory, and all the angels with him" (Mt. 25:31-46). He warned the council that assembled to condemn him, "In the future you will see the Son of Man sitting at the right hand of the Mighty One and coming on the clouds of heaven" (Mt. 26:64). In his first coming Jesus was the servant who suffered for the sins of humankind. Jesus said he would come again, but as conqueror. Thus in his two comings, Jesus would fulfill both aspects of the prophets' messianic vision.

The issue in the first century was not so much what Jesus taught, but Jesus himself. Jesus had such a central role in all he said that his words demanded a decision —and they still do.

JESUS' DEATH AND RESURRECTION

The life and teaching of Jesus rightly draw much attention. But the writers of the Gospels clearly focus on Christ's death and resurrection. Approximately a third of the Gospel accounts (30 of 89 chapters) is devoted to the time between Jesus' triumphal entry into Jerusalem and his resurrection. The events of this single week give meaning to Jesus' ministry. Here we find the Jewish people decisively rejecting their Messiah. Jesus' teaching about himself had been heard, the issues drawn. And the verdict of that generation was against him.

The Gospels portray Jesus as quietly

TITLES OF JESUS

Title	Significance
In the Gospels	
Christ	The Greek word meaning "Anointed One," or Messiah.
Jesus	His personal name, meaning "Yahweh saves."
Lamb of God	A title indicating Christ's self-sacrifice in payment for sins.
Lord	A title of respect in most Gospel occurrences, like our "sir." In religious use, a title affirming deity and ultimate authority.
Master	A mark of respect used typically by those who were his followers.
Messiah	The Hebrew term for the "Anointed One" whom God would send to establish his Kingdom on earth.
Prophet	A person authorized to speak the Word of God to man.
Rabbi	"My great one," a mark of respect like our "Reverend."
Shepherd	Jesus is the "good shepherd" who lays down his life for the sheep.
Son of David	A messianic title reflecting OT prophecies that the expected ruler would be of David's line.
Son of Man	A title used by Jesus of himself, reflecting his human identity, his role as man's representative before God. Also reflects Dan. 7's implication of deity.
Son of God	A title affirming Jesus' unique relationship with the Father.
Teacher	A mark of respect extended to one who taught the Scriptures.
Word	*Logos* in Greek, a term John uses to show Jesus' unity with God and his role as a revealer of the Father.
In the Early Church	
Christ	The Savior, shown by his resurrection to be the Son of God.
Head of the Church	A title expressing Jesus' organic relationship to his Church and each member of it.
Lamb	A title in Revelation uniting Jesus' work of redemption and judgment.
Lord	The one with ultimate authority, an affirmation of Christ's deity, his present and future rule.
Son of God	A title affirming Jesus' pre-existence and full deity.

Christ's Head *by Leonardo da Vinci, Antwerp, Belgium, 16th century* A.D.

committed to the course that led to his crucifixion (Mt. 16:21-23). Jesus saw his death as something God willed, and he suffered it voluntarily (Jn. 17:1-4; Mt. 26:39,53). Only at the moment of death could Jesus cry out, "It is finished" (Jn. 19:30).

Each Gospel then reports the resurrection event, and the stunned realization by the apostles that Jesus lives again, not simply as a man but as "my Lord and my God" (Jn. 20:28).

The meaning of these events is explored in the Epistles. Jesus' death was "a sacrifice of atonement" (Rom. 3:25; *see* Heb. 10:1-18; 1 Pet. 1:18,19; 2:21-24). His blood was the basis for our reconciliation to God, who "by Christ's physical body through death" is able "to present you holy in his sight" (Col. 1:22). Jesus' resurrection was an affirmation and a guarantee. By the resurrection Jesus was "declared with power to be the Son of God" (Rom. 1:4). His resurrection foreshadows our own and guarantees it (1 Cor. 15:12-28). And the resurrected Jesus lives forever, interceding for us. His permanent priesthood assures us of eternal salvation (Heb. 7:25-28).

The NT writers did not realize many of these aspects of Jesus' identity and the importance of his death and resurrection

564

until after the fact. But their insights are thoroughly consistent with OT teaching and Jesus' own words.

THE OFFICES OF JESUS

From the early days of the church, Christians have summed up Christ's ministry under the biblical offices of prophet, priest, and king (Deut. 18:15; Ps. 110:4; Zech. 6:13).

• *Jesus as prophet.* A prophet conveys God's message to human beings. John's Gospel begins by presenting Jesus as the Word, who expressed God's truth not only by participating in creation, but also by becoming a human being and radiating God's glory (Jn. 1:1-14). In his days on earth, Jesus' words carried an authentic authority that was acknowledged by his listeners (Mt. 7:29; Mk. 1:22). Christ, as "the one whom God has sent," fulfills the prophet's role and "speaks the words of God" (Jn. 3:34; *see* 7:14-19).

• *Jesus as priest.* A priest represents humanity before God. He works to restore and to maintain fellowship between the two, by offering sacrifices and praying for sinners.

Christ functioned as a priest when he offered himself to God as a sacrifice for our sins (Heb. 8–10), and continues his priestly ministry by making intercession for us (Heb. 7:25).

While this element of Jesus' ministry was not understood by his followers during Christ's years on earth, Jesus himself spoke of it. He came to earth "to give his life as a ransom for many" (Mt. 20:28).

• *Jesus as king.* As Son of God, Jesus has sovereign authority over the universe. At the same time, Jesus exercises a unique authority over believers. By faith we have become citizens of God's earthly but invisible Kingdom, whose constitution is expressed in Christ's Sermon on the Mount (Mt. 5–7). In the future, when Christ returns, he will rule openly as "Lord of lords and King of kings" (Rev. 17:14).

JESUS IN THE EPISTLES

His intimate followers had known that Jesus was the Christ, the Son of the living God. But it was only after the resurrection that their awareness of Jesus' identity grew.

We find that awareness powerfully expressed in the Epistles. Jesus is Lord (Rom. 1:4). All things are placed under Jesus' feet, and he is head of his Church (Eph. 1:22). Jesus "being in very nature God" became a man, and after dying for us was exalted "to the highest place" and given the name "Lord" (Phil. 2:5-11). Jesus is the creative source of the universe, who even now holds that universe together by his own incredible power (Col. 1:15-18). As the "radiance of God's glory," Jesus is "the exact representation of his being, sustaining all things by his powerful word" (Heb. 1:3). When Jesus comes again he will be "revealed from heaven in blazing fire with his powerful angels" (2 Th. 1:7). Even the apostle John, who was especially close to Jesus during his life on earth, "fell at his [Jesus'] feet as though dead" when he saw Christ in a vision on Patmos, no longer veiled by flesh but stunning in his essential splendor (Rev. 1:9-18).

Some have suggested that NT authors are engaged in myth-making. The early church took the simple man Jesus, they say, and made him larger than life. They are sure that Jesus himself would be horrified to see these developments.

But this view fails to take into account the clear force of Jesus' own statements about himself. Jesus knew, and clearly announced, who he was. Yet Christ's humanity veiled as well as revealed his glory. The early church learned to view Jesus not only as the gentle, suffering servant of God, but at the same time as the awesome, splendid, and eternal God. The comfortable love Christians sense in and for the incarnate Son of God must be matched by awed worship of God the Son. The founder of Christian faith is both the "Jesus loves me" of children's songs, and the "Holy, Holy, Holy, Lord God Almighty" of our hymns.

Jew A person descended from the biblical Hebrews, or one whose religion is Judaism. This designation was originally derived from Judah, the name of the southern Hebrew kingdom, which was again used of this territory in the Babylonian and Persian Empires. The term became common only after the Exile in 586 B.C., referring both to inhabitants of the area (Ezra 5:1; Neh. 1:2; Jer. 32:12) and to any person who was Hebrew by birth (Esth. 2:5; 5:13; Dan. 3:8,12). In the Gospel of John, "the Jews" is occasionally used to indicate the religious leaders who were Christ's enemies, in contrast to the general populace (*compare* Jn. 7:1,11).

Throughout the Bible, "Jew" stands in contrast to "Gentile" (or non-Jew) and identifies both a race of people and their religion (Jn. 2:6; Acts 14:1; Gal. 3:28). In the NT, the term "Greek" is often used as a synonym for "Gentile." The use of the word "Jew" in the NT may vary. It is helpful to remember when reading the NT that Jesus was Jewish and conducted his ministry almost entirely among his Jewish people. Virtually all of his followers were Jewish, and in the beginning Christianity was considered merely a sect of Judaism. These believers continued attending synagogue and worshiping in the Temple.

As Gentiles began joining the ranks of believers, two problems arose. The first: should Gentile believers be required to convert to Judaism and therefore adopt the traditions and conform to the legal standards of the OT? This is the issue addressed in Galatians, and the Jews to whom Paul refers in Gal. 2:13 are Jewish believers whom Paul rebukes for removing themselves from Gentile believers. The second problem was that Gentiles were prohibited by the Law from participating in organized Jewish worship, and their increased visibility in the company of Jewish Christians led to considerable unrest in the non-believing Jewish community (Acts 21:28,29).

Paul's writing, particularly in Romans, draws distinctions between the religious and the racial dimensions of Jewishness. Birth into God's covenant community gives the Jewish people great spiritual advantages (Rom. 3:1,2), but Jewishness is not only outward, it is spiritual as well. Paul writes, "A man is not a Jew if he is only one outwardly, nor is circumcision merely outward and physical. No, a man is a Jew if he is one inwardly; and circumcision is circumcision of the heart, by the Spirit, not by the written code" (Rom. 2:28,29).

In the NT, Jews are sometimes enemies of the Gospel (Jn. 10:31; Acts 20:3; 1 Th. 2:14). But also, the earliest believers were Jews and the writers of the NT were all Jews, with the possible exception of Luke. They carried the message of Messiah to their own people, and extended it to the Gentiles as well. Paul yearned that his people, the people of Israel, would know Jesus as Messiah (Rom. 9:1-5). He beautifully illustrates the shared blessings and responsibilities of Jews and Gentiles alike with the image of the grafted olive tree (Rom. 11). Paul rejects the notion that Jews have been disowned by God, and emphasizes the fact that in Christ both Jew and Gentile have access to God (Eph. 2:18). Thus, while Jews sometimes participated in negative situations (just as Gentiles have), Scripture in no way supports Christian antagonism towards the Jewish people.

Above: Faience or ceramic necklaces with vegetable motifs, Egypt.
Left: Assorted jewelry in gold from the large hoard found at Tell el-Ajjul in Philistine territory, second millennium B.C.
Bottom: Egyptian jewelers at work about 1400 B.C.
Bottom left: Gold funeral crown from the Etruscan culture on the island of Crete, first millennium B.C.

jewelry Personal ornaments made of precious metals and precious or semi-precious stones and worn on various parts of the body.

Shortly after the Exodus the children of Israel contributed jewelry which they had obtained in Egypt in order that the tabernacle might be richly adorned: "All who were willing, men and women alike, came and brought gold jewelry of all kinds: brooches, earrings, rings and ornaments" (Ex. 35:22). But in Ezek. 16:11-13 we find God bestowing gifts of jewelry. He pictures Jerusalem as a beautiful, but unfaithful, woman: "I put bracelets on your arms and a necklace around your neck, and I put a ring on your nose, earrings on your ears and a beautiful crown on your head. So you were adorned with gold and silver." These descriptions give us some sense of the items of personal jewelry prized by men and women in biblical times.

Archaeologists have made spectacular finds in Egypt and Mesopotamia of beautifully crafted gold jewelry set with precious stones. Jewelry has also been recovered from ancient Israel, but this jewelry is made of less expensive metals, is set with more common stones, and shows less expert workmanship than jewelry from other, wealthier ancient cultures.

Particular jewels appear in this dictionary under their individual names. But translation of the original words, especially from Hebrew, has always been difficult. The various gems often draw their names from root words meaning "shining" or "radiant," and only occasionally even hint at a particular color. That explains the broad disagreements among translations.

Scripture consistently affirms the beauty and value of jewelry but warns against over-emphasis on external appearance. So Zechariah celebrates the beauty of a redeemed Israel: "They will sparkle in his land like jewels in a crown" (Zech. 9:16). But Proverbs sets proper priorities: "She [wisdom] is more precious than jewels" (Prov. 3:15 RSV). And the Lord complains about his errant nation: "She decked herself with rings and jewelry, and went after her lovers, but me she forgot" (Hos. 2:13).

In the NT, Peter urges Christian women to express an inner beauty:

Let not yours be the outward adorning with braiding of hair, decoration of gold, and wearing of robes, but let it be the hidden person of the heart with the imperishable jewel of a gentle and quiet spirit, which in God's sight is very precious.

(1 Pet. 3:3,4 RSV)

King Ahab's wife Jezebel actively promoted the perverse worship of Baal in the kingdom of Israel. The "woman in the window" motif is a popular one in Phoenician ivories, and many scholars believe it to represent sacred prostitution associated with the fertility cult of Baal.

Jezebel [JEZ-uh-bel; possibly "the prince returns," an exclamation linked to Baal worship]. The Phoenician wife of Ahab, eighth king of Israel, dedicated to replacing worship of the Lord with worship of Baal, 874–843 B.C. Jezebel was the active opponent of Elijah and murderer of many prophets. **Father:** Ethbaal, king of Sidon and Tyre. **Children:** Ahaziah and Joram, kings of Israel, and Athaliah, who married Jehoram of Judah and on his death became Judah's ruler. **Scripture:** 1 Ki. 16–22; 2 Ki. 9,10.

BACKGROUND

The marriage of Ahab and Jezebel sealed a treaty between Israel and Tyre. Jezebel influenced Ahab to worship Baal (1 Ki. 16:29-33; 21:25). With support from Ahab, she organized the murder of prophets of the Lord (1 Ki. 18:4,13), while importing hundreds of prophets of Baal from Phoenicia (1 Ki. 18:18-20). When Elijah triumphed over the prophets of Baal on Mount Carmel, Jezebel boldly threatened his life (1 Ki. 19:1-3).

Jezebel's strong personality comes through in the story of Naboth's vineyard. While Ahab sulked because Naboth would not trade the vineyard the king wanted, Jezebel arranged to kill Naboth and seize his property (1 Ki. 21).

After Ahab was killed, Jezebel exercised power through her royal sons for about ten years (1 Ki. 22:52). Jezebel was killed in the rebellion of an army commander, Jehu, who wiped out Ahab's family and proclaimed himself king of Israel (2 Ki. 9,10). *See also* Ahab; Jehu.

567

LEARNING FROM JEZEBEL'S LIFE

Jezebel is a vivid, dramatic person. She acts decisively and boldly. Even in her defeat at the hands of Elijah, Jezebel appears unshaken, immediately threatening Elijah's life. Her bold initiative is also seen in the story of Naboth's vineyard. Ahab sulked when Naboth refused to trade away his land. Jezebel contemptuously said to her weaker husband, "Is this how you act as king over Israel?" and promised, "I'll get you the vineyard" (1 Ki. 21:7). Unconcerned about morality, Jezebel quickly arranged Naboth's execution on false charges.

Although we might admire some of her traits—strength, confidence—Jezebel remains a classic scriptural example of the evil woman. She is cruel to those who stand in her way. She is cunning and devious, undeterred by moral considerations. She is domineering and arrogant, unwilling to submit to God even when his reality is proven. Elijah accurately predicted that dogs would eat Jezebel's body in the streets. "Like refuse [garbage]" her bones were scattered on the ground, "so that no one will be able to say, 'This is Jezebel' " (2 Ki.9:37; *see* 1 Ki. 21:23).

In Revelation, her name symbolically identifies a self-styled "prophetess" who led the church of Thyatira into idolatry and immorality (Rev. 2:20). Whatever her real name was, this Jezebel was no isolated case. Overconfident, assertive people are often insensitive to others and to God and susceptible to heretical extremes. Contrast Jezebel's traits with those of "the blessed" in Jesus' Sermon on the Mount (Mt. 5:1-12). God rewards the meek, merciful, humble person, while cutthroat go-getters like Jezebel reap the results of their enmity with God.

Joash [JOH-ash; "Yahweh has given"]. Ninth king of Judah, 835–796 B.C. Crowned at seven, Joash remained pious until the death of his mentor, the high priest Jehoiada. **Parents:** Ahaziah and Zibiah. **Wife:** Jehoaddin. **Son:** Amaziah. **Scripture:** 2 Ki. 11,12; 2 Chr. 22–24. **Note:** Joash is sometimes called Jehoash, a variant name, but he is distinct from King Jehoash of Israel, who ruled 801–785 B.C. (2 Ki. 13,14).

BACKGROUND

Athaliah, a daughter of Israel's evil King Ahab and Queen Jezebel, married into Judah's royal house. When her son, Ahaziah, was killed by Jehu, Athaliah took the throne. She immediately set about to exterminate the royal family. Only one infant escaped, and was hidden in the Temple. Six years later, the seven-year-old Joash was crowned king by the priests and the military, who remained loyal to the Davidic dynasty. Athaliah was killed, and the temple she erected to Baal was torn down (2 Ki. 11).

Under the influence of Jehoiada the priest, Joash repaired the Temple of the Lord and reinstituted active worship there. But when Jehoiada died, Joash turned away from God to worship Canaanite deities. This stimulated a flurry of prophetic activity throughout Judah, but to no avail. When Zechariah, the son of his old adviser, Jehoiada, confronted Joash in the name of the Lord, the king had Zechariah killed. This act turned many against the king, and some of his officials assassinated him in bed as he was recuperating from wounds received in battle.

LEARNING FROM JOASH'S LIFE

Joash illustrates both the value and danger of being too easily influenced. Friends can encourage a compliant person to make good choices, as Jehoiada helped the young king. But bad companions can just as easily influence a compliant individual to do wrong, as did those who swayed Joash toward pagan worship (2 Chr. 24:17). Ultimately each of us must be strong enough to take personal responsibility for our choices and actions. We can and should be willing to hear advice. But we must choose what is right no matter what others may say.

Job, Book of The first poetic book of the Bible, relating the anguish of righteous Job as he and his friends struggle to explain unparalleled disasters which have stripped him of his wealth, his children, and his health. In a dialogue format, this book powerfully expresses the doubts and fears of men whose concept of God is too limited to permit them to deal with the fact that righteous people as well as sinners experience suffering.

BACKGROUND

The author of Job is anonymous. Both the date of writing and the era reflected in the book's content are much debated.

One school views Job as a late construction, rooted in the covenant concept, and arising from the Babylonian Captivity. But this position is difficult to maintain. The language of Job is archaic, suggesting an early date. There is no mention in Job of a covenant, of the Law, or of any event in the history of Israel. The name "Job" is not found in later biblical periods but was common in the second millennium B.C. The life-style portrayed in Job is nomadic,

and references to raiding Chaldean tribesmen fit the patriarchal age but not post-
exilic periods. For these and other reasons,
the setting is probably the patriarchal age,
roughly 2100–1700 B.C.

However, some suggest that the book
may have been recorded in its present
form during the time of Solomon (970–930
B.C.), along with most of the Bible's wisdom literature.

Job himself is a timeless figure, a good
man who experiences various kinds of
severe suffering and struggles unsuccessfully to understand why. The problem is
universal, and the Book of Job remains one
of the most penetrating examinations of
the thoughts and emotions of sufferers.

THE THEME OF JOB

The author immediately establishes the
fact that Job was "blameless and upright,"
a person who "feared God and shunned
evil" (1:1). God draws Satan's attention to
Job, whereupon Satan insists that he can
make Job curse God. Satan is allowed to
engineer disaster after disaster, but "in all
this, Job did not sin in what he said"
(2:10). Satan is defeated. But Job's suffering goes on.

Three friends come to comfort Job, but
they soon find themselves debating the
cause of his misfortune (chs. 3–31). All
three believe God punishes the sinner only,
never the innocent. They conclude that,
since Job is suffering so intensely, he must
have sinned. Job denies the charge, but has
no other explanation for his calamities. In
the dialogue which takes up the bulk of the
book, Job expresses his feelings of betrayal
by the God he served so carefully.

Then a younger man, Elihu, enters the
discussion (chs. 32–37). He points out that
God may use suffering to teach. Elihu does
not offer this as an explanation for Job's
suffering, but to suggest that his elders
have been wrong to assume the only purpose God might have in permitting human
suffering is to punish. Elihu does rebuke
Job for his accusation of God's unfairness
or abandonment.

At this point God himself enters the
discussion (chs. 38–41). He offers Job no
precise explanation for his pain. He simply
challenges Job to consider God's greatness
and to realize how foolish it is for mortal
man to claim to understand God's purposes.

Humbled, Job recognizes his folly in
demanding to know God's reasons, and
submits to the Lord (42:1-6). God then
restores Job's health, doubles his wealth,
and gives him a long and blessed life.

In review, the book's solution to the
problem of suffering is straightforward.
God uses suffering for his own purposes,
which are ultimately to the benefit of the
sufferer. When tragedy comes, we need
not assume we are being punished.
Rather, we are to remember the steadfast
love of our sovereign God and patiently
submit to his will. James sums this up,
saying, "You have heard of Job's perseverance and have seen what the Lord finally
brought about. The Lord is full of compassion and mercy" (Jas. 5:11).

THEOLOGICAL CONTRIBUTIONS

We find a fascinating concept of God in
this book. The men of Job's era gained their
knowledge of God through tradition, visions, and dreams. These sources portray
God as transcendent, beyond nature, but in
control of the created universe. God involves himself in human affairs, requiring
human beings to help rather than injure
one another, and to worship him faithfully.
He actively punishes the wicked and rewards the good in this life. Yet God is gracious. He accepts sacrifice, and will forgive
the one who turns from his sin.

There is no reference in Job to a divine
covenant made with Abraham's children.

*Job is counseled by
two of his friends in
this sarcophagus re-
lief from Rome, 4th
century A.D. Job's
friends' unhelpful
conventional wisdom
takes up two-thirds of
the book.*

569

Chapter	Content Summary	Related Articles
	I. Introduction	
1	Satan engineers a series of disasters intended to make righteous Job curse God. Satan fails.	Satan
2	Satan strikes Job with painful boils all over his body. Job still refuses to curse God. Friends come to see Job.	Sickness
	II. Dialogue between Job and Three Friends	
3	Job curses the day of his birth and expresses the anguish he is feeling.	Suffer
4,5	Eliphaz argues that the innocent do not perish. Job should appeal to God, who restores those he disciplines.	Discipline
6,7	Job despairs and calls on God to remember his frailty. He asks why he has not been pardoned.	Pardon
8	Bildad is shocked at the suggestion that God is perverting justice in Job's case. God does not reject a blameless man.	Justice
9,10	Job agrees theoretically but complains that, though innocent, he is being punished.	Guilt
11	Zophar urges Job to repent. If Job will put away his sin, God will surely restore him.	Repent; Evil
12–14	Job affirms God's greatness but complains that his friends are unfairly against him. He begs for a chance to confront God and have God reveal his offense and his sin.	Wisdom
15	Eliphaz charges Job with undermining piety. The wicked suffer despair and anguish, not the good.	Wicked
16,17	Job claims he is an [undeserved] target of God's anger and again expresses despair.	
18	Bildad joins in attacking Job, reciting the punishments the wicked can expect from God.	
19	Job insists he has been wronged. He asks for pity, not attacks.	
20	Zophar is disturbed by Job's words. He reiterates terrible punishments for the wicked.	
21	Job feels terror as his experiences force him to question his beliefs about God: Often the wicked do *not* suffer, but prosper. His friend's platitudes are false!	Fear
22	Eliphaz takes Job's remarks as proof of wickedness. He demands that Job submit to God.	
23,24	Job expresses frustration at not being able to argue his case before God. Many who are truly wicked go unpunished. Job is terrified: Why would God oppose a righteous man?	
25	Bildad ignores the issue, and affirms God's greatness.	
26–31	Job charges God with denying him justice. He lists his good works and recalls others' respect. Now everyone mocks him. Though he cries out to God, there is no answer. Job has nothing more to say.	Works
	III. Elihu Speaks	
32	Elihu has remained silent while his elders spoke. Now he must speak out.	Elder
33	Job is wrong to claim innocence and also to think God must be punishing him. God may in fact use suffering to teach, and help a person *avoid* punishment.	Punish
34	God cannot and will not do evil. Job's claim to unjust punishment must be rejected.	
35	Job's insistence on a hearing before God is foolish; God need not answer mere humans.	
36	God is mighty, but he does not despise [ignore] men. Each experience teaches, although God's purposes are beyond human understanding.	Teach
37	If Job considers God's majesty, he will see that it is man's place simply to revere him.	
	IV. God Speaks to Job	
38,39	God calls on Job to consider natural wonders which display God's wisdom and power.	Wisdom
40,41	God directs Job's attention to animals so powerful men dare not hunt them. God created all these.	Create
	V. Job Responds	
42	Job submits to God unconditionally. God restores Job's wealth, health, and family.	Restore Submission

Here God is the ruler of humanity and is not identified as the God of Abraham, Isaac, and Jacob. Men are aware they owe a duty to God—a duty rooted in the fact that God is their Creator. Yet God is a distant and mysterious figure in Job. Humans know something of his moral will and acknowledge his power, but they cannot understand his actions.

MASTERY KEYS

The book finds Job and his friends trapped by their thinking about God. Each dialogue section reflects the conviction that God punishes sinners, and the conclusion that God must be punishing Job for some sin. But because Job knows he has not sinned, he is gradually forced to a conclusion he is unwilling to draw—that God is acting unjustly. The closer Job's reasoning brings him to this conclusion, the more violent the verbal attacks of Job's friends become.

SPECIAL FEATURES

Job's raw anguish has been shared by people throughout the ages. The great contribution of this book is not only its philosophical inquiry into suffering, but also the release it offers to moderns who similarly fear that their suffering is punishment and torment themselves over unknown or imagined sins.

Why do the godly suffer? There is no simple answer. But there is comfort here in the towering truth that, though we may not understand why, we need never doubt the love of our God.

Joel, Book of One of the minor prophetic books of the OT. The first half describes an invasion of locusts which took place in Joel's day. The second half describes events associated with a coming "day of the Lord."

BACKGROUND

No one knows when Joel [JOH-uhl; "Yahweh is God"] penned his brief but powerful prophecy. Suggested dates range from 870 to 200 B.C. An earlier date is most likely, not only because it is traditional, but because the nations Joel identifies as enemies are not Assyrians or Babylonians, but the much earlier Philistines and Phoenicians (3:4), Egyptians and Edomites (3:19).

The date, however, is not as significant as the circumstances that caused Joel to prophesy. Ancient Palestine was vulnerable to great swarms of locusts, which occasionally swept into the land and ate every green plant. The locusts also buried

eggs, which hatched into larvae, which then ate the regenerating plants. Joel interpreted the locust invasion in his day as divine judgment, and called on his people to repent (1:1–2:27).

But then Joel was catapulted into the future. He sees a great northern army swarm into Palestine with devastating, locust-like effect. This, the prophet says, is what will happen in the coming Day of the Lord (2:18–3:21).

THEOLOGICAL CONTRIBUTIONS

Joel shares the view of other OT prophets that repentance can turn aside divine judgment. "Even now," Joel declares in God's name, "return to me with all your heart" (2:12) and "then the Lord will . . . take pity on his people" (2:18).

Most significant is Joel's contribution to the OT concept of "the day of the Lord." In Isaiah this phrase consistently identifies events at history's end, when God will intervene to judge and then restore Israel. Joel sees the current locust plague as a harbinger of that day (1:15; 2:11). In Joel, "the day of the Lord" is a day when God acts decisively in history, personally or through an agent. While the focus of the day of the Lord in Scripture is on future judgment, that coming day closes with blessing and restoration (3:17-21).

SPECIAL FEATURES

At Pentecost, Peter quoted Joel 2:28-32 to explain the miraculous arrival of God's Spirit (Acts 2). Rules for interpreting prophecy include the "law of double reference" and the "law of partial fulfillment." These reflect the fact that some prophecies seem to refer to more than one future event, or even to several similar events. Thus Joel's vision of the outpouring of the Spirit can refer both to Pentecost and to a still-future outpouring at history's end. *See also* Prophecy, Interpretation of.

JOEL: A READING AND STUDY GUIDE		
Chapter	**Content Summary**	**Related Articles**
1	Joel describes the devastation caused by locusts and calls for a national day of mourning.	Locust Fast
2:1-27	The destruction is a divine judgment, a call to repent and experience God's blessing.	Repent Heart
2:28-32	After Israel returns, God will pour out his Spirit and offer salvation to all who call on him.	Holy Spirit Salvation
3	God will judge the nations and be a refuge for his people. God will pardon their sins and bless them.	Holy Pardon

John the Apostle [JAHN; "Yahweh is gracious"]. A disciple of Jesus who, with Peter and James, was especially close to the Lord. Author of five NT books. **Parents:** Zebedee and Salome. **Brother:** James. **Scripture:** the Gospels; Acts; 1,2,3 John; Revelation.

BACKGROUND

John came from a well-to-do fishing family, with a home in Capernaum (Mk. 1:20,21; Mt. 4:21-23). John was one of the twelve original disciples selected by Jesus (Lk. 5:10,11; 6:14). With Peter and James, John was a member of Jesus' inner circle of three which shared several special experiences with Jesus (Mt. 17:1; 26:37; Mk. 5:37; 14:33; Lk. 8:51). In Gal. 2:6-10 he is called a pillar of the Jerusalem church. Most commentators believe that John is the "disciple whom Jesus loved," modestly mentioned in Jn. 13:23; 19:26; 20:2; and 21:7,20-24.

Insights into John's personality come from three sources: incidents reported in the Gospels, John's later biblical writings,

and traditions preserved by the early church. According to tradition, John outlived the other disciples and died near the turn of the century. His Gospel and other books were written near the end of the first century A.D. A very early tradition, reported by writers who knew people who were taught by John, says that John settled in Ephesus. He was briefly exiled to the Isle of Patmos, where he probably wrote Revelation, but returned to Ephesus and died of old age. Irenaeus reports that, when John became too weak to walk, he was carried to church meetings. There he whispered, again and again, "Little children, love one another."

LEARNING FROM JOHN'S LIFE

Three incidents in the Gospels give a surprising picture of this "apostle of love." Luke 9:49 reports that John wanted to stop a man driving out demons in Jesus' name because "he is not one of us." When Samaritan villagers refused to give shelter to Jesus' disciples, James and John asked Jesus if they should call fire down from heaven to avenge the insult (Lk. 9:51-55). This sort of behavior earned these brothers the nickname "Sons of Thunder" (Mk. 3:17). Finally, Mt. 20:20-28 suggests that John and James had their mother ask Jesus for places of special authority in Christ's coming Kingdom. In each of these portraits, John seems to be an aggressive, self-centered individual.

In light of this, John's later emphasis on love gains greater significance. The mature John has learned that in Jesus' Church neither pride nor position are important. The mark of Christ's presence in the believer's life is love.

In a beautiful passage in his first letter, John conveys this truth he has learned so well: "Dear friends, let us love one another, for love comes from God . . . since God so loved us, we also ought to love one another" (1 Jn. 4:7,11).

John the Baptist [JAHN; "Yahweh is gracious"]. The bold prophet who prepared the way for Christ's ministry by preaching repentance, about 30 A.D. **Parents:** Zechariah and Elizabeth, a relative of Jesus' mother, Mary. **Scripture:** Mt. 3,11; Mk. 1,6; Lk. 1,3; Jn. 1,3,5.

BACKGROUND

The birth and ministry of John the Baptist were announced to John's father by an angel (Lk. 1). As an adult, John lived a solitary life in the desert until he began to preach. Then, like the prophets of old, John confronted the Jewish people with their need to repent (Mt. 3; Lk. 3). His strict ethical views correspond completely with OT Law (Lk. 3:10-14).

Yet in some ways John was unique. (1) John identified himself as forerunner of the promised Messiah and announced that God's Kingdom was near (Lk. 3:15-18; Jn. 1:19-28). (2) John introduced baptism as a visible sign of confession and repentance, Mk. 1:4. His baptism undoubtedly reflected the Jewish practice of washing in running water for ritual cleansing. Yet John transformed the meaning of this traditional act. *See also* Baptism.

John was a contemporary of Jesus, and their implied relationship is significant. John's initial reluctance to baptize Jesus was apparently based on the fact that he knew his relative to be a godly person (Mt. 3:13-15). But Jesus insisted. Publicly identifying himself with John's message by undergoing baptism was the right thing to do. When God's Spirit descended on Jesus during the baptism, John realized that his relative from Nazareth was the Son of God (Jn. 1:32-34).

As Jesus launched his own public ministry, many of John's followers drifted away to follow the new prophet. John expressed joy over this, saying, "He must become greater; I must become less" (Jn. 3:30).

Later on, John was imprisoned by Herod Antipas. After languishing there for a long time John became concerned. Jesus had not set up the earthly Kingdom which John and other pious Jews expected. John sent disciples to question Jesus. "Are you the one who was to come, or should we expect someone else?" (Mt. 11:3). Jesus told John's disciples to report back to him the healings they witnessed. Christ then told the crowds that John was the greatest of God's prophets. John fulfilled Malachi's prediction that another Elijah would come just before the Messiah (Mt. 11:7-19). Shortly after this, John was beheaded by Herod Antipas (Mk. 6:14-29).

LEARNING FROM JOHN'S LIFE

John was bold, yet humble. He fearlessly confronted rulers and religious leaders as well as ordinary men (Mt. 3:7-12). Rather than feeling jealousy at Jesus' growing popularity, John was filled with joy. He was ready to slip into the background to promote Christ (Jn. 3:29,30).

Yet John had doubts. He watched with growing puzzlement as Jesus went about teaching and healing. Why hadn't he established the expected Kingdom? We can identify with John's uncertainty. All of us have been puzzled at times when God

Ivory pulpit plaque from Ravenna, Italy, captures John the Baptist in the act of declaring, "Behold, the Lamb of God, who takes away the sin of the world" (Jn. 1:29). Note the symbolic lamb in a medallion.

failed to act as we thought he surely must. Though the NT does not tell us, John was probably satisfied with Jesus' answer. In healing and teaching, Jesus was doing the work of God. John might not know God's plans, but he could recognize God's loving hand.

John, the Epistles of Three concise, warmly pastoral letters by the apostle John written, probably late in the first century A.D., to encourage and guide churches. Each letter calls on Christians to lives of love and obedience, and two warn against false teachers—"antichrists."

BACKGROUND

By the end of the first century, Christian congregations were established in cities throughout the Roman Empire. Congregations were linked by the circulated letters of the apostles and by itinerant teachers. Unfortunately, some traveling teachers promoted heresy. This serious problem is reflected in the later NT letters, especially 2 Timothy, Jude, and the letters of John. Some believe John is concerned with the inroads of a specific heresy, Gnosticism. This dualistic philosophy dismissed the notion of sin and denied the deity of Jesus Christ. *See also* Gnosticism.

The three letters which bear John's name were almost certainly written by the apostle John. His authorship is attested about A.D. 140 by Papias, and about A.D. 180 by Irenaeus. This early tradition is supported by similarities between John's letters and his Gospel. Like the Gospel, 1 John contrasts light and darkness, truth and error, God and the devil, righteousness and sin, love and hate, life and death. And the stylistic resemblance between the letters

and the Gospel is unmistakable, despite some distinctiveness, such as 1 John's use of rhetorical questions.

There is less certainty about the date and destination of John's letters. According to early reports, John lived in Ephesus until he was exiled to the Isle of Patmos in the late 90s. His letters were probably written during the last decade and a half of the first century A.D.

First John lacks the characteristic greeting and farewell of first-century letters. It may have served as a tract, written for the Ephesian Christians, but copied and circulated to other churches. Second and Third John are personal letters, just long enough to fit a single sheet of papyrus.

THEOLOGICAL CONTRIBUTIONS

First John is pastoral rather than didactic. It lacks clear, logical organization, and relies on cycles of repeated thoughts and ideas. This makes the letter particularly difficult to outline. Even so, John's emphases are clear.

The first chapter encourages confession of sins, and rejects the notion that human beings can be sinless. Yet the book goes on to show that the true believer will seek to obey God's Word and will show love for other believers. John warns against false teachers, who can be recognized by their denial of Christianity's pivotal doctrine—that Jesus is the Son of God, God come in the flesh (1 Jn. 2:22; 4:2,3,15; 5:5; *see* 2 Jn. 7-11; 3 Jn. 9,10). In this, 1,2 and 3 John reflect the emphasis of John's Gospel, which sets out to demonstrate the deity of Jesus.

MASTERY KEYS

See the entry on Gnostics before reading John's Epistles. Then look for repeated words and themes, particularly love, obedience, and faith. Compare these with similar themes in John's Gospel. Note the role John sees for each of these in our Christian experience.

John, the Gospel according to The last written and most theological of the four Gospels. The fourth Gospel early won recognition as the "spiritual gospel" for its clear presentation of Jesus as the Son of God. Unlike the other three, this Gospel is not structured chronologically. Instead the author reports miracles and discourses in which Christ confronted his listeners with a clear claim to be God in the flesh. A key word in John is "witness." John reports historical events which witness to Christ's deity. He states his purpose clearly:

"These [things] are written that you may believe that Jesus is the Christ, the Son of God, and that by believing you may have life through his name" (20:31).

BACKGROUND

Matthew, Mark, and Luke wrote their Gospels within several decades of Jesus' death and resurrection about 30 A.D. Each writer shaped his account of Jesus' life for a particular first-century audience.

John's Gospel was probably written in the 90s. Tradition, language study, and the many references to "the disciple whom Jesus loved" all indicate that John the apostle wrote this book.

John writes as a witness to Jesus. Again and again the reader is confronted with claims that demand a verdict. John draws contrasts between life and death, faith and unbelief, and the reader is urged to choose.

DISTINCTIVE FEATURES

• *While the other Gospels focus on brief sayings or stories told by Jesus, John recounts lengthy sermons*. These take up 342 of the 877 verses in his book. The major discourses in John are:

1. On the new birth (3:1-21).
2. On the water of life (4:4-26).
3. On resurrection and life (5:19-47).

This detail of an illuminated manuscript shows "the disciple whom Jesus loved," traditionally John, leaning against Jesus as described in Jn. 13:22-25. Athens, Greece, 12th century A.D.

THE EPISTLES OF JOHN: A READING AND STUDY GUIDE

Chapter	Content Summary	Related Articles
	1 John	
1	John is eager for his readers to experience fellowship with God. This requires Christians to walk in the light and to confess sins to God, claiming Christ's forgiveness.	Fellowship Light Confess
2	Obedience and love for the brothers are evidence that a person has come to know God. Antichrists who deny Jesus will try to lead believers astray.	Obey Love Antichrist
3	True believers will not keep on sinning because they have been born of God. Love for others gives us confidence in our relationship with God, but love must be practical.	Sin Born Again Give
4	Those who deny Jesus Christ has come in the flesh are not from God. We love because God loved us first.	Incarnation Atonement
5	Those who believe Jesus is the Christ are born of God and have eternal life. Believers are to restore those who sin.	Believe; Faith Testimony; Death
	2 John	
1	The "elect lady" is to love and follow the truth and be on guard against deceivers.	Truth
	3 John	
1	Gaius should follow the truth and continue to show hospitality to itinerant teachers, but be on guard.	Hospitality

575

Wooden panel of a 5th-century A.D. book cover depicts the marriage feast at Cana, where Christ turned water into wine (Jn. 2:1-12); Milan, Italy.

4. On the bread of life (6:26-59).
5. On Jesus' deity (8:12-59).
6. On the good shepherd (10:1-21).
7. On Jesus' deity (10:22-38).
8. On Jesus' role (12:20-50).
9. On Jesus' departure (13:31–14:31).
10. On union with Jesus (15:1–16:33).
11. On Jesus' glorification (17:1-26).

• *John reports unmistakable claims of Jesus' deity.* Among these are seven "I am" statements. The phrase "I am" reflects the distinctive personal name of Israel's God, Yahweh, the "I AM" of Ex. 3:13-15.

1. I am the bread of life (6:35).
2. I am the light of the world (8:12).
3. I am the gate [door] for the sheep (10:7).
4. I am the good shepherd (10:11).
5. I am the resurrection and the life (11:25).
6. I am the way, truth, and life (14:6).
7. I am the true vine (15:1).

• *John's language is richly symbolic.* He fills common words with deep theological meaning, and uses these words again and again. Key words in John's writings are:

1. *Belief* An active, enduring trust (3:16,18; 8:31,32) based on a personal appropriation of Jesus (1:12).
2. *Darkness* Morally, sinfulness; spiritually, the domination of evil (3:19; 8:12; *see* 1 Jn. 1:5-7).
3. *Death* The spiritual condition of those separated from God (5:16-26).
4. *Falsehood* Deceit, or human illu-

sions, in contrast to reality as God reveals it (8:44; *see* 1 Jn. 1:6-10).
5. *Glory* The splendor of God, his beauty, power, love, goodness (1:14; 17:4,5).
6. *Hate* The intense antagonism to Jesus felt by nonbelievers (3:20; 15:18-25).
7. *Know* A term indicating both the personal relationship with God established through faith in Christ, and continuing fellowship with God maintained by obedience (8:31,32; 10:4,14,15; *see* 1 Jn. 4:15,16).
8. *Life* A spiritual dynamic which enables a believer to live righteously now, and guarantees future resurrection (3:15-36; 5:21-26; *see* 1 Jn. 2,3).
9. *Light* While implying holiness, John's emphasis is on spiritual illumination, understanding, and guidance (1:4-9; 3:19-21; *see* 1 Jn. 1:5-7).
10. *Love* A conscious choice to care for God and others, awakened in human beings by God's expression of love in Jesus (3:16; *see* 1 Jn. 4:7-21).
11. *Truth* That which corresponds with reality. Truth is known and revealed by God, and can be experienced by those who obey Jesus' words (8:31,32; *see* 1 Jn. 1:6-10).
12. *Unbelief* Not doubt, but refusal to respond to God's revelation in Jesus (3:16-21).
13. *Word* A title of Jesus, portraying him as the source and substance

576

of divine revelation (1:1-14; *see* 1 Jn. 1:1,2).

THEOLOGICAL CONTRIBUTIONS
John speaks of life vs. death, light vs. darkness, belief vs. unbelief, truth vs. falsehood, love vs. hate. By the use of these powerful images, John communicates spiritual realities in a universally appealing and understandable way.

THE GOSPEL OF JOHN: A READING AND STUDY GUIDE

Chapter	Content Summary	Related Articles
	I. Jesus' Ministry	
1	Jesus is introduced as the Word-become-flesh. John the Baptist identifies Jesus as the Lamb of God.	Word Incarnation
2	Jesus turns water to wine at a wedding in Cana. Then he drives merchants from the Temple.	Miracle
3	Jesus tells Nicodemus every man must be "born again." John the Baptist affirms that Jesus is the Son of God.	Born Again Son of God
4	Jesus teaches the Samaritan "woman at the well." Many Samaritans believe. He heals an official's son.	Samaritan Healing
5	Jesus heals on the Sabbath. He announces the gift of eternal life through belief in the Son.	Life Belief Faith
6	Jesus feeds 5,000 on five loaves and two fishes. He presents himself to the crowds as the Bread of Life.	Bread Disciple
7	Jesus teaches at the Feast of Tabernacles. He stimulates debate as to whether or not he is the Messiah.	Christ Messiah
8	Jesus forgives a woman taken in adultery. He presents himself as God, and his opponents as Satan's children.	Father Devil
9	Jesus heals a man born blind. The Pharisees' refusal to accept the evidence demonstrates their blindness.	Pharisee Blind
10	Jesus presents himself as the Good Shepherd. Those who do not believe try to stone him.	Shepherd
11	Lazarus dies. Jesus announces himself as the "resurrection and life" to Mary and Martha, and raises Lazarus.	Resurrection Death
12	Jesus makes a triumphal entry into Jerusalem, yet predicts his death. His opponents still will not believe.	
	II. Jesus in the Upper Room	
13	Jesus washes his disciples' feet to teach servanthood and predicts Judas's betrayal and Peter's denial.	Servant Peter
14	Jesus presents himself as the way to the Father and promises his disciples the Holy Spirit.	Holy Spirit Obey
15	Jesus presents himself as the vine, believers as branches. The Spirit will aid believers though the world hates them.	Vine World
16	Jesus explains more of the work of the Holy Spirit. He promises that God will answer his disciples' prayers.	Convict Prayer
17	Jesus prays for his disciples and all believers.	Unity
	III. Jesus' Arrest and Execution	
18	Jesus is arrested. Peter denies Jesus. Jesus is tried before the high priest and Pilate.	Pilate
19	Jesus is sentenced to crucifixion and dies on the cross.	Crucifixion
20	Jesus' tomb is empty. Jesus appears to Mary of Magdala, to his disciples, and to doubting Thomas.	Resurrection Doubt
21	Jesus meets his disciples at the Sea of Galilee. He reinstates Peter. John concludes his testimony about Jesus.	

John demonstrates that Jesus unmistakably presented himself to Israel as the Son of God. Jesus' listeners understood this as a claim of equality with God (5:18). Jesus affirmed his deity by identifying himself with the OT's "I AM" [Yahweh] (8:58). He claimed to exist with the Father "before the world began" (17:5), and stated, "Anyone who has seen me has seen the Father" (14:9). Similar claims are reported in the other Gospels (Mt. 26:63-65; Mk. 14:61,62), but John shows that this theme was woven through all Jesus' teaching about himself.

MASTERY KEYS

The key word in John is "belief" or "faith." To explore this theme, underline each appearance of these or related words (you may find nearly 100) and read each context carefully. What characterizes Christian belief? How is this faith expressed? What comes to us through belief in Jesus Christ? *See also* Believe; Faith.

SPECIAL FEATURES

John's use of the phrase "the Jews" is distinctive. In most cases this phrase does not include all the Jewish people, but indicates those religious leaders who opposed Jesus.

Jesus' upper room discourse (Jn. 13–16) is of special interest. In private conversation, the Lord prepares his disciples for his departure. This passage shows us how the gift of the Holy Spirit, the choice of obedience, and the privilege of prayer can enrich the lives of all Christians in every age.

John Mark *See* Mark, the Gospel According to.

Jonah, Book of One of the minor prophetic books of the OT. It tells the familiar story of the prophet Jonah's call to preach at Nineveh, his flight, recommitment, and the subsequent repentance of the Assyrian capital.

BACKGROUND

Jonah [JOH-nuh; "dove"], the son of Amittai, is identified in 2 Ki. 14:25 as a prophet who ministered in Israel during the reign of Jeroboam II (793–753 B.C.). He was a popular prophet, who predicted the victories by which Jeroboam expanded Israel's borders.

Some view the Book of Jonah as a parable or allegory, written as late as the fourth century B.C. If we take the book as historical, 760 B.C. is a reasonable date for the events it portrays. In this case, the book could certainly have been written by Jonah. Third-person narrative by the author about himself does appear in other ancient literature. Since no insurmountable arguments have been advanced for the late date, the historical interpretation is preferable. This view is supported by Jesus' comments on Jonah (Mt. 12:39-41), by tradition, and by a fascinating relationship between Jonah and Amos.

Jonah's story is well known. The prophet was commanded to go north to Nineveh and warn the Assyrians of imminent judgment. But Jonah, reluctant to see Nineveh spared, took a ship bound for Tarshish. After the Lord compelled the ship's crew to cast Jonah overboard to stop a violent storm, Jonah was swallowed by a great fish. Finally, he surrendered to the Lord and preached in Nineveh. The entire city, with a population of 600,000, repented. A disgruntled Jonah sat on a distant hilltop to see if Nineveh really would be destroyed. When Nineveh survived, Jonah complained bitterly. The patriotic prophet had refused the first commission because he understood the divine compassion and feared that God's grace would extend to a people who later threatened Israel's existence (4:1-3).

In historical context, the adventure of Jonah provided a powerful object lesson to

JONAH: A READING AND STUDY GUIDE

Chapter	Content Summary	Related Articles
1	Jonah flees from the Lord rather than preach in Nineveh. God brings a great storm. Jonah is thrown overboard.	Nineveh Ship
2	Within a great fish, Jonah surrenders to God and praises the Lord for deliverance.	
3	Jonah goes to Nineveh. The Ninevites believe God and repent.	Believe Faith; Repent
4	Nineveh survives. Jonah is angry, but God tells him to have compassion on the innocent children and animals in the great city.	Love Compassion

A Byzantine artist renders the casting of Jonah into the sea on the concave surface of a ritual cup (3rd–4th century A.D.). A stylized wave encloses the scene.

Israel. Jonah preached to a people who had no covenant relationship with God. Yet when they believed God and repented, the Lord withheld his judgment. Jonah's contemporary, Amos, came to Israel. He preached repentance and warned God's covenant people of judgment to come. Surely if God withheld the punishment due Nineveh, he would restore and bless a repentant Israel. The object lesson was clear.

But Amos's life was threatened, his message was rejected, and he was expelled from Israel. The coming judgment on God's people would not be set aside.

THEOLOGICAL CONTRIBUTIONS

The Book of Jonah illustrates God's concern for Gentiles as well as for Jews during the OT era. Jonah also shows that many statements of divine intention are conditional in nature. There was no "unless" in Jonah's message, "Forty more days and Nineveh will be destroyed" (3:4). Yet when the people of Nineveh repented, destruction was avoided. The conditional character of such pronouncements is implicit, not in Jonah's statement of it, but in the character of God himself. As Jonah said, "You are a gracious and compassionate God, slow to anger and abounding in love, a God who relents from sending calamity" (4:2).

MASTERY KEYS

Read Jonah first as a story. Then consider what the book tells us about the prophet, about the king and people of Nineveh, and about God. The divine compassion shown to the wicked city of Nineveh can serve as a model for our relationships with those who may seem beyond redemption.

SPECIAL FEATURES

The story of Jonah and the whale has always attracted attention. Some have made much of the fact that a Mediterranean sperm whale can swallow a man whole, and that its laryngeal pouch might hold enough air for a person to survive on. But the Hebrew words translated "whale" literally mean "great fish," a more general designation. And we need not seek a natural explanation: The text says God "provided" a great fish to swallow Jonah. The event is portrayed as a miracle, and should be understood that way.

Jonathan [JAHN-uh-thuhn; "Yahweh has given"]. The son and heir of King Saul, Jonathan was an inspirational military leader as well as loyal friend of David, about 1020 B.C. **Scripture:** 1 Sam. 14,18–20.

BACKGROUND

As oldest son and heir of King Saul, Jonathan was expected to succeed his father on Israel's throne. Scripture portrays Jonathan as a worthy prince—a bold, inspirational, and pious military leader in Israel's struggle with the Philistines.

Jonathan's essential character is revealed most clearly in his relationship with David (1 Sam. 18–20). When David entered Saul's service, the two became close friends, and formalized the bond between them by making a covenant of total commitment to one another's families. Jonathan supported David even as David's growing popularity and military success aroused the jealousy of King Saul. Jonathan at times openly defended David before his father. He also secretly helped David by keeping him informed of Saul's intentions.

Soon it was clear that David, despite his loyalty to the king, was a threat to Jonathan's succession (20:31). To Jonathan this threat was irrelevant: David was innocent of plotting to gain the throne, and Saul's vendetta against a loyal subject was shameful. Finally David fled for his life from Saul, but not before he and Jonathan reaffirmed their sworn oath.

After the death of Jonathan and Saul in battle at Mount Gilboa, David initiated a search for Jonathan's offspring. The only survivor, Jonathan's crippled son Mephib-

579

Right: Jonathan climbed up these two cliffs, called Bozez and Seneh, to reach and rout a Philistine outpost at the top (1 Sam. 14:4–14).

Below: View of the Jordan River as it winds its way from the Sea of Galilee to the Dead Sea. It covers some 200 miles (320 kilometers) when the direct distance is merely 70 miles (113 kilometers).

osheth, was given his father's lands and a place of honor at David's table for life.

LEARNING FROM JONATHAN'S LIFE

Jonathan is one of a handful of Bible characters who are wholly admirable. His relationship with David sets a truly high standard for friendship. Saul was jealous of David's successes; Jonathan was glad even though his succession was affected. Saul saw David as a threat; Jonathan recognized David's loyalty. Saul sought to take David's life by treachery; Jonathan openly defended him and risked his father's anger. Saul tried to kill David to prevent him from taking the throne; Jonathan worked to save David even though he himself was heir to that throne.

Jonathan models the principle of Prov. 17:17, "A friend loves at all times." Meditating on Jonathan's life gives us deep insights into the nature and responsibilities of friendship.

Jordan River [JOR-duhn; "flowing downward"]. The lowest river in the world, and the eastern boundary of biblical Canaan. The Jordan spills from Lake Huleh in northern Palestine, seven feet above sea level, and carries cool, fresh water into the fish-rich Sea of Galilee. From there it flows down into a deep rift valley. Dropping lower and lower, the Jordan empties into the Dead Sea, 1292 feet (394 meters) below sea level. The Jordan, typically about 90 to 100 feet wide and from three to ten feet deep (30 by 1-3 meters), twists and turns so often below the Sea of Galilee that, although only 70 miles (113 kilometers) separate the Sea of Galilee and the Dead Sea, the river itself is some 200 miles (322 kilometers) long.

Just south of Galilee, the area around the Jordan is relatively fertile for some 25 miles (40 kilometers). A major trade route crossed the Jordan in this region. But farther south, in ancient times the river bottom was a marsh. Jeremiah called the thickets there a "jungle" (Jer. 12:5, RSV), where lions prowled (Jer. 49:19; Zech. 11:3).

Just north of the Dead Sea, near Jericho, the Jordan Valley is a lush oasis. This was the territory which Abraham ceded to his nephew Lot (Gen. 13). It was also where Joshua led the Israelites into Canaan, as God miraculously held back the Jordan's waters (Josh. 3:9-17).

References to the Jordan in the period of the judges highlight battles fought at its fords, showing that the Jordan was an important line of defense (Jdg. 3:28; 7:24,25; 12:5,6; *see* 2 Sam. 2:29). Elijah passed over the Jordan into a wilderness area where he was taken up to heaven by

God (2 Ki. 2:7,8). Naaman, the leper commanding the Syrian army, felt contempt for the muddy Jordan but washed there seven times as commanded by Elisha and was healed (2 Ki. 5:1-14).

In the NT, we find John the Baptist preaching beside the Jordan. He baptized Jesus in its waters, and saw the Spirit descend on him, launching Christ on his earthly mission of teaching and healing (Mt. 3; Mk. 1; Lk. 3; Jn. 1:29-34).

Joseph, husband of Mary [JOH-suhf; "may God add"]. The carpenter of Nazareth. **Father:** Jacob. **Children:** James, Joseph, Simon, Judas, unnamed daughters. **Scripture:** Mt. 1,2; Lk. 2.

BACKGROUND

In NT times betrothal was a legal commitment almost as binding as marriage itself. So Joseph planned to take legal steps to set aside his engagement to Mary when he learned she was pregnant. *See also* Marriage.

Yet Joseph was a man of faith. When an angel appeared to him in a dream and informed him that the child in Mary's womb had been conceived by the Holy Spirit, Joseph went through with the wedding (Mt. 1:18-25). Later, when the child was probably about two years old, Joseph again responded to divine guidance given in a dream and fled with his family to Egypt (Mt. 2:13-15).

Little more is said of Joseph in the NT. We know that Joseph took twelve-year-old Jesus to Jerusalem for a required festival. But his absence at the crucifixion (Jn. 19:26) and in the upper room (Acts 1:14) suggests that Joseph had died before Jesus had begun his public ministry.

LEARNING FROM JOSEPH'S LIFE

Joseph is one of Scripture's quiet men: nothing he said is quoted. Yet, like many other quiet men, Joseph practiced his faith with dedication. He accepted the angel's testimony concerning Mary. Joseph married her, despite the certainty of whispered accusations. Joseph fled to Egypt to protect the Christ-child. He raised Jesus as his own, and taught Jesus his own trade (Mt. 13:55).

Joseph reminds us that silent people as well as the verbal can be persons of faith, whose righteousness is demonstrated by simple obedience to God's commands. Like Joseph, men and women of quiet faith are seldom celebrated. But they have an important role in carrying out God's plans for his people.

Joseph, son of Jacob [JOH-suhf; "may God add"]. As a youth Joseph was sold into slavery in Egypt, where he rose to be second only to Pharaoh, about 1880 B.C. **Parents:** Jacob and Rachel. **Sons:** Ephraim, Manasseh. **Scripture:** Gen. 37–50.

BACKGROUND

As the favorite of his father, Jacob, the first son of the beloved Rachel, Joseph aroused the jealousy of his brothers. They sold him to some Midianite slave-traders of the Ishmaelite nation, who in turn sold him in Egypt to Potiphar, captain of the royal guard (Gen. 37). Even as a slave Joseph distinguished himself so outstandingly that his master promoted him to the status of chief steward of the household. But after he had refused the advances of Potiphar's adulterous wife, she vengefully accused him to her husband as having attempted to rape her. This resulted in his confinement in state prison. Yet even there Joseph was appreciated by his jailer and promoted to supervisor of the entire prison (Gen. 39). There Joseph interpreted the dreams of a prisoner who later told Pharaoh of Joseph's ability (Gen. 40). *See also* Dreams. Joseph interpreted Pharaoh's dream and warned of a coming famine following seven years of surplus. Pharaoh followed his advice and put Joseph in

Albrecht Dürer portrays Joseph as an older man in his altarpiece "The Birth of Christ" (A.D. 1498) from St. Lawrence Church, Nürnberg, Germany. This assumption is probably correct.

With emotional gestures foreigners implore a royal Egyptian servant—an illustration perhaps of Gen. 42:6: "When Joseph's brothers arrived, they bowed down to him with their faces to the ground" (see Gen. 43:26-28).

charge of preparing Egypt for the coming disaster (Gen. 41). When the famine struck, Joseph's brothers came to Egypt to buy grain. After some trickery, Joseph revealed himself to them and brought his whole family to Egypt (Gen. 42–47).

HISTORICITY OF JOSEPH

The events in the life of Joseph have been assigned anywhere between 2000 and 1500 B.C. If we adopt the OT's internal chronology, Joseph probably was born about 1915 B.C. and became vizier of Egypt around 1880 B.C.

Many details of the biblical account vouch for the authenticity of the story. Joseph was given a signet ring and gold chain by Pharaoh (Gen. 41:42). Archaeologists have discovered that the chain signified control over the food supply, while the signet ring signified the role of vizier, who bore the title "Sealbearer of the King of Lower Egypt." Other details are also authentic for that period. The Egyptians did allow Asiatic peoples to graze their flocks in the delta region (Goshen) during famines. The "butler" of the KJV was Pharaoh's cupbearer, an important official and adviser in his own right. He would have been present when Pharaoh called on his wise men to interpret his dream (Gen. 41:8), and thus would have been in a position to recommend Joseph. The note that priests could not be forced to sell their land is also accurate (Gen. 47:22), and Egyptian records speak of seven-year cycles of plenty and famine.

A number of parallels to the story of Joseph are found in Egyptian literature. The

Autobiography of Idri-mi (about 1480–1450 B.C.) tells of Idri-mi's reconciliation with older brothers. The *Tale of Two Brothers* tells of an adulteress who turns against her handsome, young brother-in-law, who spurns her. The Amarna Letters (1490–1435 B.C.) mention Rekh-me-Re, a vizier during the reign of Thutmose III, whose duties were very similar to those of Joseph.

LEARNING FROM JOSEPH'S LIFE

Several incidents in the life of Joseph call for our consideration.

• *Jacob was unwise to show open favoritism toward Joseph* (Gen. 37). But Joseph too was unwise. He must have sensed the hostility of his brothers, yet he told them not only one but two dreams which predicted his ascendancy over them. The dreams came true, but Joseph would have been wise to keep them to himself.

• *Joseph's steadfast refusal to be seduced by Potiphar's wife is admirable* (Gen. 39). His reasoning is even more so. Joseph asked, "How could I do such a wicked thing and sin against God?" God remained the moral arbiter of his universe. The wise individual sees sin as sin, and chooses to obey God.

• *Joseph wisely hesitated to make himself known to his brothers* (Gen. 43–45). Instead Joseph tested them. He listened to their conversation when they thought he could not understand their language. Joseph also led his brothers to reconsider their earlier betrayal of him. What a contrast this was with the younger Joseph, who blurted out his dreams with no thought of how others might be affected.

• *After Joseph and his brothers were reconciled, he forgave them freely* (Gen. 45). Joseph saw God's hand in what had happened, and that insight relieved him of any anger he might have felt. His brothers were responsible for a terrible act. "But God sent me ahead of you to preserve for you a remnant on earth and to save your lives by a great deliverance" (Gen. 45:7).

• *After the death of Jacob, Joseph's brothers feared he would take revenge* (Gen. 50). They could not understand the forgiveness which Joseph extended. Joseph again cited God's purpose in sending him to Egypt. Belief in God's sovereignty freed Joseph from bitterness. God intended to preserve many lives from hunger through this one man's suffering.

Joseph remains one of the OT's beautiful people. He was steadfast in his righteousness, yet forgiving and non-judgmental. Believers today should seek that same blend of commitment and tenderness.

Josephus, Flavius A Jewish general who led a Galilean army against the Romans (A.D. 66–67). Taken captive in A.D. 67, Josephus survived by predicting that his captor, the general Vespasian, would become emperor. When this occurred, Josephus was released and served the Roman army as an interpreter and counselor in Jewish affairs.

After the fall of Jerusalem, Josephus spent the rest of his life in Rome, where he wrote a number of important books attempting to explain Jewish beliefs and traditions to the Graeco-Roman world. The most important of these, *The Jewish War* and *Jewish Antiquities,* supply most of the information we have about political and religious events during the 200-year span prior to the destruction of Jerusalem in A.D. 70. While Josephus's descriptions of such projects as the building of Caesarea Maritima were once ridiculed, archaeologists have proven him to be amazingly accurate.

Joshua, Book of The sixth book of the OT. Joshua tells the story of the conquest and occupation of Canaan by the Israelites, about 1390 B.C., under the leadership of Joshua, Moses' successor. Events reported in the Book of Joshua probably took place over 20–25 years.

BACKGROUND

The adult Israelites who escaped from Egypt had all died during their 40 years in the wilderness—all but the two faithful spies, Joshua and Caleb (Num. 13,14). Moses then led the new generation north, east of the Jordan, paralleling the Promised Land. On that journey the Israelites were rebuffed by the Moabites and Ammonites, who refused Israel passage through their lands. God had forbidden Moses to war with them because they were descended from Lot. Two kingdoms to the north, however, that of Heshbon and Bashan, were defeated, and their lands given to three Israelite tribes. Camped by the Jordan across from Jericho, Moses restated God's covenant. Then he himself went up on a high hill to glimpse Canaan, and died (Deut. 32–34).

Joshua [JAHSH-oo-uh; ''Yahweh is salvation''], who had been Israel's military leader (Ex. 17:10-14) and Moses' aide (Num. 11:28; Deut. 1:38), succeeded Moses (Num. 27:18-23; Deut. 34:9). When Joshua took command, God told him, ''Be strong and very courageous. Be careful to obey all the law my servant Moses gave you; do not turn from it to the right or the left, that you may be successful wherever you go'' (Josh. 1:7). This verse establishes the theme of the Book of Joshua.

Following page: The moment of truth in Jericho. The city's walls crumble when the trumpets sounded and the people shouted, just as God had promised (Josh. 6:20).

Upper left: A line drawing from Thebes showing a worker bringing grain to a granary. Three silos have already been filled.
Lower left: A model of an Egyptian granary from the time of Joseph. Grain was stored in large silos, surrounded by a walled courtyard. ''Joseph stored up huge quantities of grain, like the sand of the sea; it was so much that he stopped keeping records because it was beyond measure'' (Gen. 41:49).
Right: A bumper crop is recorded by an Egyptian scribe of Thutmose IV (15th century, B.C.)

JOSHUA: A READING AND STUDY GUIDE

Chapter	Content Summary	Related Articles
I. The Conquest of Canaan		
1	God promises to be with Joshua and summons the new leader to courage and obedience.	Obey Canaan
2	Spies sent across the Jordan are hidden by Rahab in Jericho. They promise to spare her life when the city falls.	Jericho Rahab
3	The Jordan's waters are held back so Israel can cross into Canaan.	Jordan River; Ark of the Covenant
4	The miracle establishes Joshua as leader. Joshua orders erection of a monument to commemorate crossing the Jordan.	Memorial
5	The men of Israel are circumcised. An angelic messenger meets Joshua to take command of God's army.	Circumcision
6	The Israelites obey God and march in silence around Jericho. They shout on the seventh day, and the walls fall.	
7	Achan takes and hides forbidden loot. As a direct result, Israel is defeated at Ai. Achan and family are stoned.	Covenant
8	Ai is attacked and destroyed. Joshua reads God's Law to the assembled people.	Law
9	The neighboring Gibeonites trick Joshua into a treaty. Because Israel swore in God's name, the treaty must stand.	Inquire Gibeon
10	God causes the sun to stand still, ensuring an Israelite victory. The central and southern campaign is summarized.	
11	Joshua defeats a northern coalition of Canaanite kings and destroys Hazor.	
12	The author lists kings of the city-states that Joshua and the Israelites have defeated.	
II. Division of the Land		
13	The land Moses assigned to the Reubenites, Gadites, and part of Manasseh east of the Jordan is confirmed to them.	
14,15	The land allotted to Judah is defined.	Allotment; Lots
16,17	The land allotted to Ephraim and Manasseh is defined.	
18	The allotment process is explained, and Benjamin's territory is defined.	
19	The allotments of Simeon, Zebulun, Issachar, Asher, Naphtali, and Dan are defined.	
20	God assigns cities of refuge so the person who kills another unintentionally can find safety until a fair trial.	Murder; Cities of Refuge
21	Special towns are given the Levites within the territory of the other tribes.	Levites
22	Men of the eastern tribes recross the Jordan, where they build an altar to symbolize their unity with the tribes now in Canaan.	Altar
III. Joshua's Farewell		
23	An aged Joshua exhorts Israel to continued obedience and faithfulness to the Lord.	Idol
24	Joshua calls on Israel to renew its commitment to God and to promise to live by his covenant. The people respond. Joshua dies.	

Joshua did obey God completely. He also used brilliant military strategy. After taking Jericho, Joshua attacked Canaan's central highlands, dividing the northern and southern city-states. Joshua then used night marches and other strategies to devastate the stronger walled cities. In this way, Joshua effectively destroyed the Canaanites' power of organized resistance. With enemy forces neutralized, Joshua went about dividing the land by lot. Each tribe was then responsible to mop up Canaanite resistance within its territory.

Joshua's leadership was moral as well as military. This is illustrated in the service of covenant renewal which Joshua led after his armies had conquered Jericho, Ai, and Bethel and were in control of Shechem (Josh. 8). Again at the end of his career he led his countrymen to recommit themselves to a life of obedience and complete loyalty to Yahweh (Josh. 24). Even after Joshua's death his godly influence continued for at least another generation, for "Israel served the Lord throughout the lifetime of Joshua and of the elders who outlived him" (Josh. 24:31).

HISTORICAL CONTRIBUTION

The Book of Joshua gives us the only written account of the Israelites' entry into Canaan. Rabbinic tradition ascribes authorship of major sections to Joshua himself, as does the book itself (Josh. 24:26). Other portions were clearly written later.

If we treat the book as an authentic document, its references to Jerusalem as a Jebusite stronghold (Josh. 15:8; 18:28), along with other internal features, indicate a date of writing or compilation during the age of the judges, prior to the time of David and probably before 1200 B.C. *See also* Chronology of the Bible; Conquest; Exodus; Jericho.

Historically, the conquest of Canaan and the distribution of the land by lot served as one basis for the Hebrew conviction that God gave Israel the Promised Land. The Joshua account suggests that God even assigned each family its own land. This apportionment also established the sites of Levitical cities and cities of refuge.

THEOLOGICAL CONTRIBUTIONS

The successful conquest demonstrates the covenant theme that obedience to God brings victory (as at Jericho—chs. 5,6), but disobedience ensures defeat (as at Ai—chs. 7,8).

The conquest narrative also raises the issue of the legitimacy of wars of extermination. The OT plainly says God commanded the Israelites to destroy the Canaanites utterly (Josh. 11:20; *see* Deut. 7:1-5; 20:16-18). The explanation lies in the clear biblical teaching that God can and does use human agents to bring judgment on those who refuse to repent and submit to the Lord. God delayed Canaan's judgment in Abraham's day because the ungodliness implicit in Canaanite religion

According to some archaeologists, this may be the actual stone erected by Joshua at Shechem more than 3,000 years ago to commemorate the Israelites' renewal of their covenant with the Lord (Josh. 24:1,26,27).

had not yet corrupted the entire society beyond hope (Gen. 15:16). In Joshua's day Canaanite culture was marked by a depravity that, like Sodom and Gomorrah, cried out for judgment. Extermination was also a painful necessity for the spiritual protection of the Israelites, who later were corrupted by Canaanite religion and immorality when they failed to utterly destroy the Canaanites they supplanted. *See also* Baal; Canaan.

MASTERY KEYS

The book is divided into three sections: Campaigns in the conquest (chs. 1–12), the distribution of the land (chs. 13–22), and Joshua's call to covenant commitment (chs. 23,24).

Josiah [joh-SI-uh; "Yahweh supports"]. Pious 17th king of Judah, notable as leader of Judah's last spiritual and political revival before the Babylonian Captivity, 640–609 B.C. **Father:** Amon. **Grandfather:** Manasseh. **Sons:** Jehoahaz, Eliakim/Jehoiakim, Zedekiah. **Scripture:** 2 Ki. 21–24; 2 Chr. 33–35.

BACKGROUND

For over 60 years Judah had been ruled by two aggressively wicked kings, Manasseh and Amon. During those years the little kingdom was also dominated by Assyria. Josiah came to the throne at the age of eight. As he neared manhood, Josiah "began to seek the God of his father [forefather] David" (2 Chr. 34:3). This personal quest grew into a commitment that affected national policy. Four years later, at age 20, Josiah initiated a nationwide purge of idolatry, tearing down the altars and

idols that filled his land. Josiah also began repairs on the Jerusalem Temple.

During the repairs, a fine copy of the lost Law of the Lord was found in the Temple. Scholars debate whether the book was the entire Pentateuch or just Deuteronomy. The original loss is not really surprising. Each copy of ancient documents had to be painstakingly made by hand. And most likely Manasseh and Amon, deeply hostile to the Lord, tried to purge Judah of its sacred books (*see* Jer. 36).

When Josiah learned the Law's requirements, he was deeply shaken. Clearly, Judah had failed to obey the Lord. It had fallen into the disobedience and ungodliness predicted in Lev. 26 and Deut. 28.

Recovery of the Law led to further reforms. Josiah was 26 when he called Judah together to hear God's Word read aloud publicly and led his people in renewing their covenant commitment to the Lord. For the first time in many generations, the whole nation of Judah celebrated Passover.

The religious revival led by Josiah was matched by political resurgence. The grip of Assyria had weakened, enabling Josiah to act more independently. But little Judah remained vulnerable to the rivalry of greater powers. Near the end of Josiah's reign, the Babylonians won a series of stunning victories over the Assyrian forces. When Pharaoh Neco of Egypt moved north to assist Assyria, Josiah tried to block the Egyptian advance. Josiah's motive is uncertain. Perhaps he felt Egypt threatened his country, or he may simply have wanted to keep Neco from aiding Josiah's traditional enemy. Whatever his reason, Josiah led his forces against Egypt and was fatally wounded at the battle of Megiddo.

LEARNING FROM JOSIAH'S LIFE

Those who assume that heredity or environment determines character find little support in the case of Josiah. His grandfather, who ruled Judah for 55 years, had led Judah astray "so that they did more evil than the nations the Lord had destroyed before the Israelites" (2 Ki. 21:9). Josiah's father, Amon, followed suit (2 Ki. 21:21). But Josiah turned his back on all the idolatry and moral corruption which filled Jerusalem, and at 16 began to seek the Lord. We should certainly understand the difficulties of those who were not brought up in a home with biblical values, but Josiah's example assures us that whatever a person's background, anyone can seek —and find—the Lord.

When Josiah learned through the newly discovered copy of the Law how short of God's standards Judah had fallen, he "tore his robes." This act symbolized deep despair and repentance. God's response is instructive: "Because your heart was responsive and you humbled yourself before the Lord . . . your eyes will not see all the disaster I am going to bring on this place" (2 Ki. 22:19,20). We too should take our failures seriously. But we need to remember that God honors those who humble themselves before him.

The biblical text focuses on Josiah's efforts to purge Judah of idolatry. The king systematically and completely cleansed his land. He also desecrated the idolatrous worship centers, so polluting them that they could not be used again even for pagan worship. When we turn to the Lord with our whole heart, everything which once led us away from him must go.

jot and tittle (KJV) Brush strokes used in forming Hebrew letters. The "jot" is the smallest Hebrew letter, *yod*, while the "tittle" is a stroke that distinguishes such Hebrew letters as *dalet* from *resh*, and *bet* from *kap*. The NIV appropriately translates Matthew 5:18, "Not the smallest letter, not the least stroke of a pen, will by any means disappear from the Law until everything is accomplished." Jesus' teaching does not abolish the Law or the prophets, but is in full harmony with them. Everything contained in the OT will be fulfilled, for it is God's Word.

joy (1) In the OT, essentially a sense of exultation rooted in God and God's acts for his people, which typically is expressed in exuberant public worship. (2) In the NT, an inner sense of exultation and confidence in God, which the Holy Spirit works in the lives of believers and which we experience despite present sufferings.

OLD TESTAMENT

The OT uses 27 different words built on 12 Hebrew roots to express joy. Three patterns emerge: (1) Joy is experienced

Left: The smallest letter in the Hebrew alphabet is yod, *the "jot."*
Right: The "tittle" is a stroke added to the letter resh *to distinguish it from* dalet.

Bottom: King Josiah fought Pharaoh Neco on the Plain of Jezreel (below) where he was shot by Egyptian archers and died, ending the religious reform he had recently begun in Judah (2 Chr. 35:20-24).

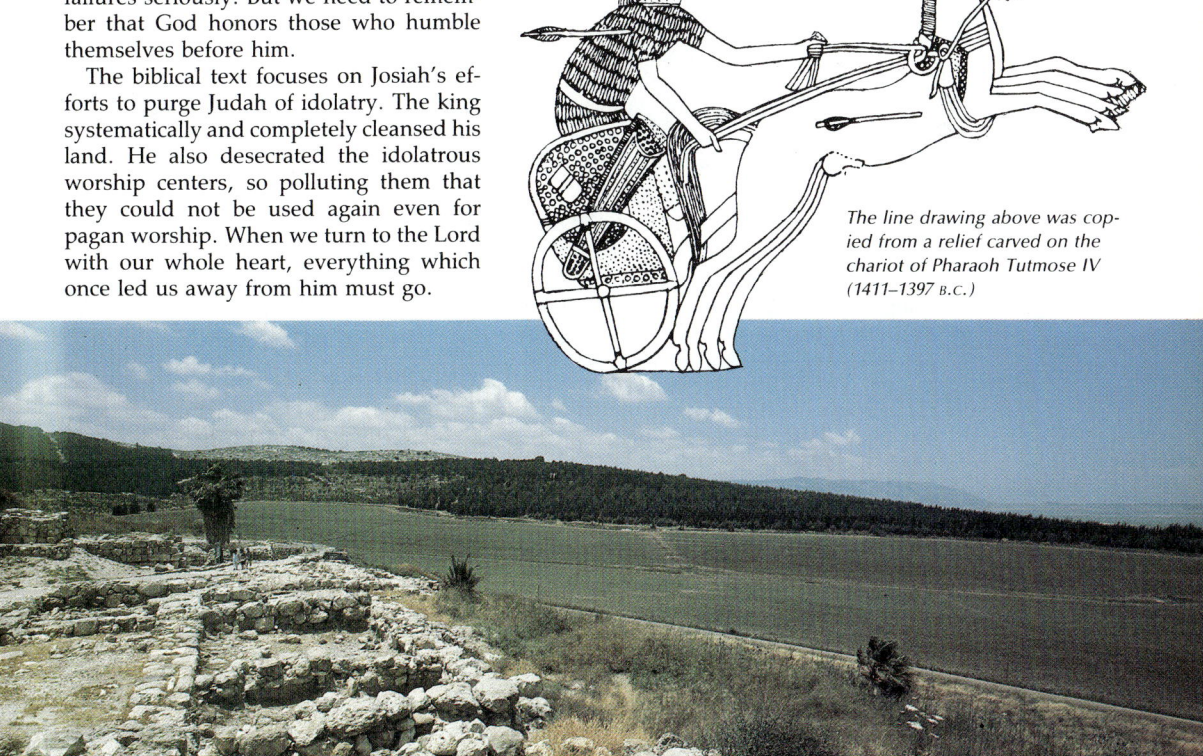

The line drawing above was copied from a relief carved on the chariot of Pharaoh Tutmose IV (1411–1397 B.C.)

The hills of Judah stretch into the distance southwest of Jerusalem. Because of Jerusalem, the tribe of Judah's territory would play the major role in the history of Israel.

when God acts for his people. Harvest time, military victories, and other evidences of God's faithfulness all provoke this emotion. (2) Joy is a shared experience, closely linked to the worship of the faith-community. (3) Joy is an expressive emotion, provoking glad shouts, dancing, and song. The text often conveys a sense of the enthusiasm and excitement which God's OT people brought to their worship of the Lord.

The OT also refers to joy found by individuals in their personal relationship with the Lord (Ps. 16:11; 19:8). Confidence in God is expressed not only in expectant hope, but in a pervading sense of joy when our thoughts turn to the Lord.

NEW TESTAMENT

Joy clearly comes from the Holy Spirit (Rom. 14:17; Gal. 5:22; 1 Th. 1:6). The believer finds joy in obeying Christ's commands (Jn. 15:10,11; 16:24). Even though we "suffer grief in all kinds of trials," we can be "filled with an inexpressible and glorious joy" (1 Pet. 1:6-9). A number of NT passages also link joy to serving fellow Christians (Rom. 16:19; Phil. 1:4,25; 2 Tim. 1:4; 1 Jn. 1:4; etc.).

The NT uses three words for joy. *Euphrainō* carries the sense of merrymaking and has both secular ("Eat, drink, and be merry"—Lk. 12:19) and religious ("Rejoice, O Gentiles, with his people"—Rom. 15:10) uses. *Chairō*, the most common word, connotes an inner feeling of pleasure, satisfaction, or well-being. *Agalliaō* comes closest to the OT sense of jubilation or public exultation. It often intensifies *chairō*, as if taking the inner

feeling and exploding it outward. In Mt. 5:12, Jesus warned his disciples of persecution and slander, but urged, "Rejoice [*chairō*] and be exceeding glad [*agalliaō*] because great is your reward in heaven."

Scripture usually sets joy apart from mere happiness. Even the joy of OT saints in material blessings is rooted not in the things themselves but in the evidence they provide of God's covenant love. In the NT joy often wells up in the most painful and desperate situations. Such joy, known by those who are obedient to Jesus, is supernaturally produced as we look ahead with confidence, to reaffirm our faith in the goodness and ultimate triumph of our God.

Jubilee, Year of In OT Israel, every 50th year, after seven cycles of seven years (Lev. 25:8-55). This was to be a year of rejoicing and celebration in ancient Israel. It was a time to "proclaim liberty throughout the land to its inhabitants" (Lev. 25:10). No crops were to be planted in the Year of Jubilee. Most significantly, any person who had been forced to sell his family property to another was to recover those lands that year. The fact that there could be no permanent sale of land in Israel was part of the unique social justice system of the OT, which if followed by God's people would have eliminated or significantly reduced poverty. *See also* Poor.

Judah [JOO-duh; "praise"]. In the OT, (1) the name of Jacob's fourth son by his first wife, Leah; (2) the name of the Israelite

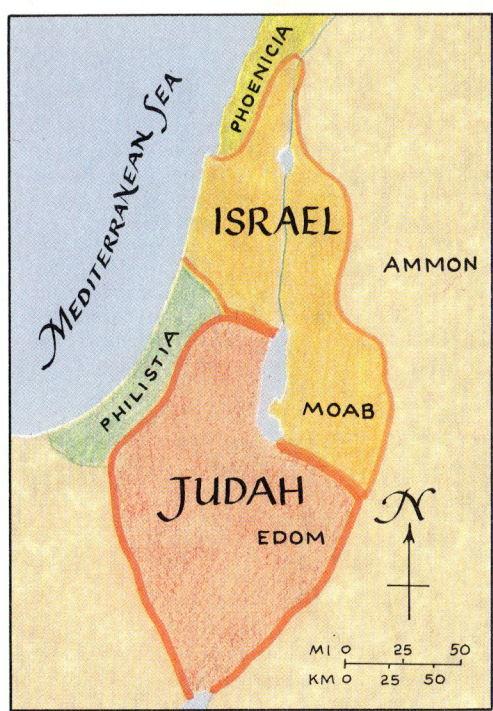

tribe descended from Jacob's fourth son; (3) the name by which the southern Israelite kingdom was known, 730–586 B.C.; (4) the tiny Jewish administrative district established in the Persian Empire after the return of the captives from Babylon in 538 B.C.; (5) at times "Judah" refers to God's covenant people as a whole, as in Zech. 10:3.

THE KINGDOM OF JUDAH

After Solomon's death the united kingdom he and David had ruled was shattered by rebellion. Only two tribes (Judah, Simeon, and the southern half of Benjamin) remained faithful to Solomon's son, Rehoboam, and to David's line. Ten tribes followed the charismatic Jeroboam, who set up a rival kingdom and also a rival religious system. *See also* Israel.

The northern kingdom took the name Israel, while the southern kingdom was known as Judah. Judah existed as an independent nation until 586 B.C., when its people were taken captive to Babylon. During the nearly three-and-a-half centuries of its existence Judah had 27 rulers, all of whom were descendants of David. Of these 27, some were godly men, who actively encouraged worship of the Lord. But many of the kings promoted idolatry and other practices forbidden in Scripture. Ultimately, borne down by the weight of repeated cycles of sin, the nation fell to Babylon in a culminating disaster which Scripture describes as divine judgment. *See also* Babylon; Captivity.

One may analyze the history of the kingdom of Judah by its relationship with its major enemies. Three periods emerge. During the first, from Rehoboam to Jotham (930–735 B.C.), Judah's primary enemies were Israel and Syria. During the second period, from Ahaz to Josiah (735–609 B.C.), Judah's primary enemy was Assyria, with Egypt lurking to the south. During the third period, from Jehoiakim to Zedekiah (608–586 B.C.), Judah's primary enemy was Babylon.

Another way to analyze the history of the kingdom of Judah is by cycles of religious revivals led by its more godly kings. These revivals took place during the reigns of Asa (about 895 B.C.), Jehoshaphat (about 870 B.C.), Joash (about 830–810 B.C.), Hezekiah (725 B.C.), and Josiah (about 625–612 B.C.). *See also* Chronology of the Bible.

THE DISTRICT OF JUDAH

The Jews who returned from Babylon to their homeland did not regain their independence. Instead, they became a small administrative district within the Trans-Euphrates province of the Persian Empire.

Judah, tribe of *See* Israel, tribes of.

Judaism The religion and culture of the Jewish people, as these have developed since the intertestamental period. The word "Judaism" appears in the time of the Maccabees (166–63 B.C.), when it summed up the commitment of the Jewish people both to the divine Law and to Jewish nationalism.

Pharisees	Sadducees	Herodians
[Heb., "separate ones"]. Group of strictly observant and popularly influential Jews concentrated in and around Jerusalem (Mt. 5:20; Lk. 11:42); some were Jesus' bitterest opponents. Scribes, or teachers of the Law, were specialists in the study of the Law; many Scribes were Pharisees (Lk. 20:46).	[Heb., "righteous ones"]. Largely hellenized religious faction containing some priests and leading members of the Sanhedrin (Acts 4:1; 5:17; 23:6). They were at odds with the Pharisees—rejecting oral law and doctrines such as the resurrection of the dead and the existence of angels/spirits (Mk. 12:18; Acts 23:8).	Party who favored the Herodian dynasty, especially Herod Antipas. They helped to plot Jesus' death (Mk. 3:6; 12:13; Mt. 22:16).

Essenes

[Aram., "healers"?]. Highly ordered sect of men who lived communally, such as at Qumran, near the Dead Sea. They believed the Jerusalem Temple had been improperly run since 152 B.C.

Zealots

Those opposed to foreign (Roman) rule in the spirit of the Maccabeans 200 years earlier (Acts 5:37). The "Assassins" of Acts 21:38 were among the most fanatical.

Jewish religious/ political parties.

HISTORICAL ROOTS

The Jewish religion is rooted in the OT revelation and in the traditions associated with it. Traditional Judaism focuses on serving God by keeping his Law.

Judaism divides the OT into three libraries: the *Torah* (the Law), the *Nebi'im* (the Prophets), and the *Ketubim* (the Writings). Together the whole OT is called *Tanakh*, which is an acronym of the three parts' initials—TaNaKh. In Judaism the five Mosaic books (the *Torah*) are considered the core books, with later books of the Bible viewed as valuable commentary on them, revealing the heart and soul of the life to which believers in God are called.

Gradually many interpretive works developed in Judaism. Many of these contain rules for living that are intended to protect the believer against violating any of the *Torah*'s basic commandments. Together the interpretive works make up the Talmud, a library of treatises on law, customs, and ceremonies. Religious Jews view the Talmud as Judaism's authoritative code.

The literature in the Talmud includes the *Mishnah*, a codification of ancient oral traditions relating to agriculture, festivals, marriage, civil and criminal law, sacred things, and purification. The Talmud also contains the *Gemara*, which is rabbinic commentary on the *Mishnah*, and the *Midrash*, which expounds on the precepts and ethical values of the Scripture.

MODERN JUDAISM

In the past 2,000 years Judaism has spawned a number of sects with distinctive doctrines or practices, such as the modern ultra-orthodox and the Hasidim. Today Judaism in the United States is divided into four major branches.

Orthodox Jews are traditionalists who accept the Law's statutes and commandments, as well as oral traditions about the Law recorded, for example, as fixed and authoritative for all times in the Mishnah. Reform Jews are more liberal, ready to reinterpret Judaism in view of modern issues, and also willing to break with many traditions, such as separating men and women in the synagogue or covering the head there. Conservative Judaism lies somewhere in the center, but is marked by a commitment to Jewish festivals and fast days and is most closely associated with Zionism. A fourth major group, here and in Israel itself, is non-religious. The non-religious, even atheistic, view themselves as members of the ancient culture, and may prize some of the traditions which set Jewish culture apart. But the non-religious Jew is less likely to be involved in the synagogue or concerned with keeping biblical laws.

Judaism, like Christianity, is a multifaceted faith, with many different branches and expressions. Yet Judaism remains essentially a racial faith, whose roots are anchored in God's ancient covenant with Abraham, Isaac, and Jacob. Christianity is essentially a faith of choice, as men and women from every tribe and tongue and nation respond to God's invitation, and establish a personal relationship with God through faith in Jesus Christ.

Judaizers This word is not found in Scripture, but is used today to describe the believers in the early days of the church who insisted that following Jesus required converting to Judaism. Conversion included circumcision and obeying the laws

592

of Moses. This thinking reflects the Jewish nature of the early church. The issues raised by these believers were addressed by the Council of Jerusalem (Acts 15:1-21). In his letter to the Galatians, Paul also responded to the Judaizers, chastising them for their failure to recognize that both justification and the Christian life are rooted in faith. Judaizers are sometimes known as legalists. *See also* Council of Jerusalem.

Judas Iscariot [JOO-duhs is-KAIR-ee-uht; "praised man of Karioth"]. The disciple who betrayed Jesus Christ with a kiss, and then committed suicide, about A.D. 30. **Father:** Simon Iscariot. **Scripture:** Mt. 26,27; Mk. 14; Lk. 22; Jn. 13,18; Acts 1.

BACKGROUND

Like the other disciples, Judas was cho-sen at the beginning of Christ's public ministry and accompanied our Lord for about three years. Like the others, he saw Jesus' miracles, heard him teach the crowds, and sat in on Jesus' intimate, personal instructions to the Twelve. Judas held a position of trust as the treasurer of the little band, though John tells us he stole from those funds (Jn. 12:5,6). *See also* Disciple.

We know Judas, of course, as the one who betrayed where Jesus could be ar-

Right: Bronze pyxis or coin box with two kinds of silver shekels, probable currency of Judas's payment for the betrayal of Jesus (Mt. 26:14-16).

Left: Jews praying at the Western Wall of the Temple Mount, which has been the physical focal point of orthodox Judaism in Jerusalem since the destruction of the Temple in A.D. 70.

593

Judas, full of remorse for betraying innocent blood, threw his payment into the Temple and hanged himself (Mt. 27:3–5).

rested privately in exchange for 30 silver coins. It is likely that for this price Judas agreed not only to identify Jesus, but also to testify against him. *See also* Coins.

Some have suggested Judas had a good motive for his betrayal. Perhaps he was only trying to get Jesus to reveal himself as the Messiah, or even to aid Jesus in his stated purpose of dying. But Jesus portrayed Judas's action as a betrayal (Jn. 13:18-21). And Mk. 14:21 makes it plain that Judas's decision to turn Jesus over to his enemies was accursed. Instead of a redemptive motive, Judas's terrible act was more likely done for money (Mt. 26:14-16); from a misunderstanding of Jesus' messianic ministry (Mk. 14:3-9); because of outright satanic influence (Jn. 13:27); out of some personal hurt; or because of some combination of these.

After Jesus was condemned, Judas was filled with remorse. He threw the blood money down in the Temple and went out and hanged himself (Mt. 27:1-10). Combining the accounts in Matthew and Acts, it seems that the rope or limb broke, and Judas fell into a ravine where "his body burst open and all his intestines spilled out" (Acts 1:18).

LEARNING FROM JUDAS'S LIFE

Judas offers a stark warning against a too-easy familiarity with Jesus Christ. Judas misread the love and grace he must have seen in Jesus' relationships with others. He stole despite the months and years he spent in Christ's company. When Judas at last faced the fact of his sin, he cut himself off from repentance. It is not enough to know about Jesus. We must be personally committed to him to guard us against our own sinful tendencies.

Jude, Epistle of One of the general Epistles of the NT. This one-chapter book sharply attacks false teachers within the Church.

Jude (JOOD; from "praise") is usually identified as the brother of Jesus and of the Epistle-writer James (Jude 1; *see* Mt. 13:55; Mk. 6:3). Many assume the book is of a relatively late date, A.D. 80–90, because of its subject matter. However, its contents parallel 2 Peter, written before the apostle's death in A.D. 67, so Jude may have been penned as early as the 60s.

BACKGROUND

Jude intended to write a letter of encouragement, but was led instead to pen a forceful letter urging believers to contend for the faith against false teachers. In the early church, teaching was given by local elders, from the writings of the apostles, and also by itinerant teachers. According to several Epistles, false teachers presented a significant problem for the young church. This issue is raised in 2 Timothy, 2 Peter, and 1,2 John as well as in Jude. Each letter warns against false teaching and provides some guidelines for distinguishing between the true and the false. *See also* False Prophets and Teachers.

THEOLOGICAL CONTRIBUTIONS

Jude gives several distinguishing marks of false teachers. They transform grace into license and deny Jesus Christ. They reject authority and are motivated by greed. They criticize others but "follow their own evil desires." They are users, not servants, who "boast about themselves and flatter others for their own advantage" (v. 16).

Three OT personalities give insight into the character of false teachers (v. 11). Like Cain, they hate their brethren. Like Balaam, they use religion to gain wealth. Like Korah, they rebel against those God has appointed leaders. Such individuals will share the fate of the unbelieving in

Israel who fell in the wilderness, of the angels who followed Satan, and of the people of Sodom and Gomorrah who "gave themselves up to sexual immorality and perversion" (vv. 5-7).

Yet Jude's main contribution is his word to believers who must deal with counterfeit Christians. The antidote to poisonous false teaching is not conflict, but commitment to the simple things that promote Christian growth. "Build yourselves up in your most holy faith and pray in the Holy Spirit. Keep yourselves in God's love as you wait for the mercy of our Lord Jesus Christ to bring you to eternal life. Be merciful to those who doubt; snatch others from the fire and save them; to others show mercy, mixed with fear—hating even the clothing stained by corrupted flesh" (vv. 20-23).

MASTERY KEYS

This brief letter uses bold imagery drawn from both Scripture and nature to portray teachers who distort Christian faith. Note phrases that give insight into the character, motivations, and methods of false teachers. But focus on those things which preserve us from falling into error.

SPECIAL FEATURES

Jude draws from well-known Jewish apocalyptic writings in vv. 9 and 14. Other allusions in vv. 6,14, and 15 are from 1

JUDE: A READING AND STUDY GUIDE

Verses	Content Summary	Related Articles
1,2	Jude greets his readers. He assures them of God's love and continuing care.	Love
3,4	Jude calls his readers to an intense struggle against those who threaten the faith from within.	Grace
5-7	Jude recalls divine judgments on history's sinners.	Judgment
8-10	Jude characterizes the false teachers as rebels against spiritual authority.	Authority
11	Jude illustrates the errors of the false teachers by alluding to Cain, Balaam, and Korah.	Animals
12,13	Jude uses images from nature to describe the worthlessness and futility of the false teachers.	Balaam Rebellion
14-16	Jude describes the judgment to fall when the Lord comes.	Apocrypha
17-23	Jude encourages believers. He calls on us to build ourselves up in the faith.	Mercy Holy Spirit
24,25	Jude concludes with a doxology. God is able to keep us from falling, and preserve us until Jesus comes.	Fall

Enoch, a pseudepigraphic work. Jude does not quote these works as authorities. Rather he intends to show that even these texts, which were misused by the false teachers, actually support an orthodox understanding of the OT. *See also* Apocalyptic Literature.

Judea [joo-DEE-uh]; "Judaea" KJV. (1) OT, the tiny Jewish district around Jerusalem in the Palestinian province of the Persian Empire (Ezra 5:8). (2) Intertestamental, the independent Jewish state established by the Maccabees. (3) NT, under Roman rule, the region that included Jerusalem, one of three divisions of the Jewish homeland (with Galilee and Samaria). In a political sense, Judea was the territory ruled over by Herod the Great (Mt. 19:1; Lk. 1:5; Acts 10:37). Later, Judea was made part of the Roman province of Syria.

Judea in Christ's day was a small district, partly mountainous, partly parched desert. Judea lacked the rich agricultural lands of Galilee, and no major trade route passed through Judea. The Judeans did keep sheep, and raised olives and grapes. They also mined salt from the Dead Sea. But the economy depended on revenues raised in Jerusalem from the half-shekel tax paid by Jews the world over, and money spent by Jewish pilgrims who came

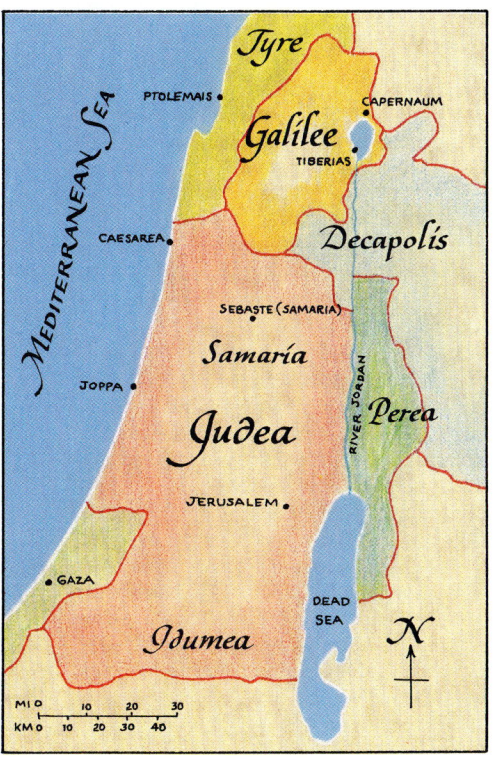

595

When the Romans put down the Jewish revolt in A.D. 70, Emperor Vespasian authorized the issue of commemorative coins with the Latin inscription Judea capta, "Judah is captured."

to Jerusalem to worship. Of the 200,000 people estimated to live in Judea in the first century, probably about 100,000 lived in or immediately around Jerusalem.

judge To rule, to condemn, to decide legal matters, or to evaluate moral matters. As a noun, one who rules or makes binding decisions. The Hebrew and Greek verbs show different shades of meaning. In Hebrew, to judge (*shapat*) is to establish or uphold justice. In Greek, to judge (*krino*) means to decide or evaluate, and in many instances does not have any legal or judicial sense. Therefore, the OT shows us various rulers "judging" Israel, that is, advancing the cause of justice in society. But the NT invites all believers to make moral decisions based on God's Word.

GOD AS JUDGE

God, as creator and ruler of the universe, acts as judge, punishing and rewarding the people of earth (Ps. 96:10-13). He is the ultimate standard of justice. In the NT sense as well, since God knows us inside and out, he alone is able to evaluate our deeds accurately and decide our fate wisely (Rom. 3:6; Heb. 10:30; Jas. 4:12).

GOVERNMENTAL AUTHORITY

God has delegated to human beings, in a limited way, authority to judge. This took various forms in OT Israel. The patriarchs judged their own households, but when the Israelites slaved away in Egypt, a system of tribal elders developed. Moses further organized this system, giving limited magisterial authority to leaders of groups of 10, 50, 100, and 1000 (Ex. 18:13-26). After the Israelites settled in Canaan, a series of "judges" emerged. These char-

ismatic leaders executed justice mostly in military ways, defeating various foreign oppressors so that Israel could live in peace and order. Certain judges, such as Deborah and Samuel (Jdg. 4:5; 1 Sam. 7:16), had magisterial duties as well.

Once the monarchy was established, the kings took on some judging duties. We remember Solomon's wise judgments (1 Ki. 3:16-28; 7:7); probably he was acting as a "supreme court." David had established a system of Levite judges (1 Chr. 23:4) and the elder system was still in place to judge civil disputes and criminal acts in local communities.

Later, the prophets decried the corruption of the judicial system: "The ruler demands gifts, the judge accepts bribes, the powerful dictate what they desire—they all conspire together" (Mic. 7:3). Isaiah berates the judges for forgetting justice: "They do not defend the cause of the fatherless; the widow's case does not come before them" (Isa. 1:23). This is the sort of "unjust judge" Jesus mentioned (Lk. 18:1-8), who would yield only if you badgered him enough.

During most of the OT, the faith-community (Israel) was also a political unit. But since Pentecost, the faith-community (now the Church) has been scattered among the nations. What sort of interaction should God's people have with their judges when those judges don't care about God's standards of justice? The NT says that God establishes even secular governments, giving them the authority to establish and enforce laws for the good of the people. Christians should submit to this authority as a way of honoring God (Rom. 13:1-7; 1 Pet. 2:13-17).

JUDGING WITHIN THE CHURCH

To judge or not to judge . . . Scripture can seem confusing on this matter. But we must distinguish between two kinds of judging.

1. *To judge against, to condemn.* One sense of the Greek word *krino* is quasi-legal. We set ourselves up as judges and evaluate other people, finding them guilty on some point—they don't measure up to our standards. Jesus warned against this kind of judging (Mt. 7:1,2; Lk. 6:37,38). Paul too calls on Christians to give each other freedom to live by personal convictions, without condemning or looking down on anyone for behavior which Scripture does not clearly identify as sin (Rom. 14:1-18). James says that adopting a critical attitude toward fellow Christians is the same as slandering them (Jas. 4:11,12).

Such warnings against judging express two vital truths. God alone is competent to judge, and Christians are to relate to others in a loving, not judgmental, way.

Similar passages encourage Christians who are judged by others. Paul says, "I care very little if I am judged by you or any human court" (1 Cor. 4:3). Christ is Lord. We are ultimately responsible to please him, not other human beings. In Col. 2:16-23, Paul points out that judging within the Christian community creates pressure for conformity, and blocks development of personal responsibility to Christ as Lord (see Rom. 14:5-9).

2. To evaluate. While the Bible speaks against condemning others, it also calls us to exercise good judgment and to discern. The spiritual person is able to "make judgments" about God's will for himself or herself (1 Cor. 2:15). The Corinthians were told to settle legal disputes between Christians by bringing them to a panel of believers rather than before pagan courts. Christians are certainly able to judge such "trivial cases" (1 Cor. 6:2-5). Paul also invites believers to "judge for yourselves" matters of Christian truth and conviction (1 Cor. 10:15; 11:13).

We are also to judge ourselves, to evaluate our own actions, distinguishing between those which involve sin and those which are pleasing to God (1 Cor. 11:31,32).

Some have argued that confronting sinning brothers and, if they persist in sinful behavior, expelling them from the church (1 Cor. 5) is inconsistent with biblical commands not to judge others. The apparent conflict is easily resolved. Church discipline is to be practiced only when a brother or sister habitually and willfully engages in acts which Scripture clearly identifies as sin. In such cases, Christians take a stand with God, who in his Word reveals his judgment of what constitutes sin. This process of discipline for the sake of restoration is to be done in a spirit of meekness as we recognize that we ourselves are susceptible to temptation (Gal. 6:1). See also Discipline, Church; Elder.

Judges, Book of One of the historical books of the OT, covering the years between the Israelites' conquest of Canaan and their first kings. It features stories of those charismatic leaders called "judges" who appeared periodically to deliver various tribal groups from foreign oppressors, and to rule these groups.

BACKGROUND

According to Scripture's internal chronology, the Israelites swept into Canaan under Joshua about 1400 B.C. and, in an extended campaign, broke the military power of the city-states there. See also Chronology of the Bible; Joshua.

The Israelite tribes then dispersed to the territories which Joshua had assigned them, with each tribe responsible to continue the struggle against any enemy remaining in its lands. Yet the Canaanites were not driven out. Archaeological evidence shows that Canaanite settlements remained in the richer valley areas, while the Israelites held the higher, less desirable ground (Jdg. 1:19,27). Even when an Israelite tribe defeated its enemies, the Canaanites were usually not destroyed but put to work as slaves.

From Joshua's death (about 1375 B.C.) until Saul's coronation (about 1040 B.C.), the Israelite tribes were little more than a loose confederation, bound together only

THE PERIOD OF THE JUDGES

JUDGE or Oppressor(s)	Scripture Reference	Years of Oppression	Years of Rule
Cushan, king of Aram	3:8	8	
OTHNIEL	3:11		40
Eglon, king of Moab	3:14	18	
EHUD	3:30		80
SHAMGAR	3:31		?
Jabin, a king of Canaan	4:3	20	
DEBORAH	4:4;5:31		40
Midianites	6:1	7	
GIDEON	8:28		40
Abimelech	9:22	3	
TOLA	10:1,2		23
JAIR	10:3		22
Ammonites	10:7,8	18	
JEPHTHAH	11:32;12:7		6
IBZAN	12:8-10		7
ELON	12:11,12		10
ABDON	12:13-15		8
Philistines	13:1	40	
SAMSON	15:20		20
ELI	1 Sam. 4:18		40
SAMUEL	1 Sam. 7:15		?
JOEL/ABIJAH	1 Sam. 8:1,2		?

by their shared language and traditions. From time to time, foreign enemies would invade various tribal territories, but not all of Palestine, and control them. The judges whom God raised up to drive out these enemies served their own and sometimes neighboring tribes, but not all of Israel.

The "judges," who give the book its name, were not simply civil magistrates, but rulers in the fullest sense. God raised these individuals up in times of crisis. With notable exceptions, the judges first defeated foreign enemies and then ruled for the rest of their lifetimes.

HISTORICAL SIGNIFICANCE

The Book of Judges provides the only written account of the period between the Conquest and monarchy. Though elements, such as the Song of Deborah (Jdg. 5), were written at the time of the events described, the Book of Judges as a whole must have been composed no earlier than the time of Samuel, about 1050 B.C.

The author of Judges clearly organized his material to make a theological point: A close walk with God is essential to national prosperity. A pattern begins in Jdg. 1,2. After Joshua died, the next generation intermarried with the Canaanites and turned to idolatry. God then disciplined his people at the hand of enemies, until in desperation they turned to the Lord.

The next 14 chapters (3–16) tell the stories of twelve judges in chronological order: Othniel (Jdg. 3:9-11); Ehud (3:15-30); Shamgar (3:31); Deborah (4:5–5:31); Gideon (6:11–8:35); Tola (10:1,2); Jair (10:3-5); Jephthah (10:6–12:7); Ibzan (12:8-10); Elon (12:11,12); Abdon (12:13-15); Samson (13:1–16:31). Each story follows the same pattern:

Sin	The Israelites turn from God.
Servitude	A foreign enemy oppresses.
Supplication	The Israelites turn to God.
Salvation	God raises up a deliverer.
Silence	The land has peace for a time.

JUDGES: A READING AND STUDY GUIDE

Chapter	Content Summary	Related Articles
I. The Dark Days of the Judges		
1	The tribes fail to drive out Canaanites left in their territories. Those defeated are pressed into forced labor.	Canaan
2	New generations of Israelites are attracted to Canaanite worship, and turn to idolatry and immorality.	Idol Baal
(3:1-6)	Intermarriage between the Israelites and Canaanites also promotes idolatry.	Marriage
II. Stories of the Judges in Chronological Sequence		
3	The cycle of sin, suffering, supplication, salvation, and silence is seen in the rules of Othniel and Ehud.	Judge
4	The judge Deborah and her general Barak defeat Canaanites.	Deborah
5	Deborah celebrates her victory in song.	Song; Poetry
6–8	Gideon defeats the Midianites with a mere 300 men.	Gideon
9	Gideon's son, Abimelech, fails to establish himself as king.	
10–12	Jephthah wins a victory over the Ammonites, and keeps his vow to offer his daughter to the Lord.	Jephthah Ammonites
13–16	Samson uses his strength to gain personal revenge on the Philistines, but fails to deliver Israel from oppression.	Samson Philistines
III. Illustrations of Corruption		
17,18	Micah and the Danites ignorantly violate laws related to worship, demonstrating corruption of religion.	Priest Worship
19	Wicked men threaten a Levite with homosexual rape, and he surrenders his concubine instead, both acts demonstrating moral corruption.	Sex Levites
20,21	The Benjamites defend the rapists, demonstrating civil corruption, and are attacked by the other tribes.	Israel, tribes of

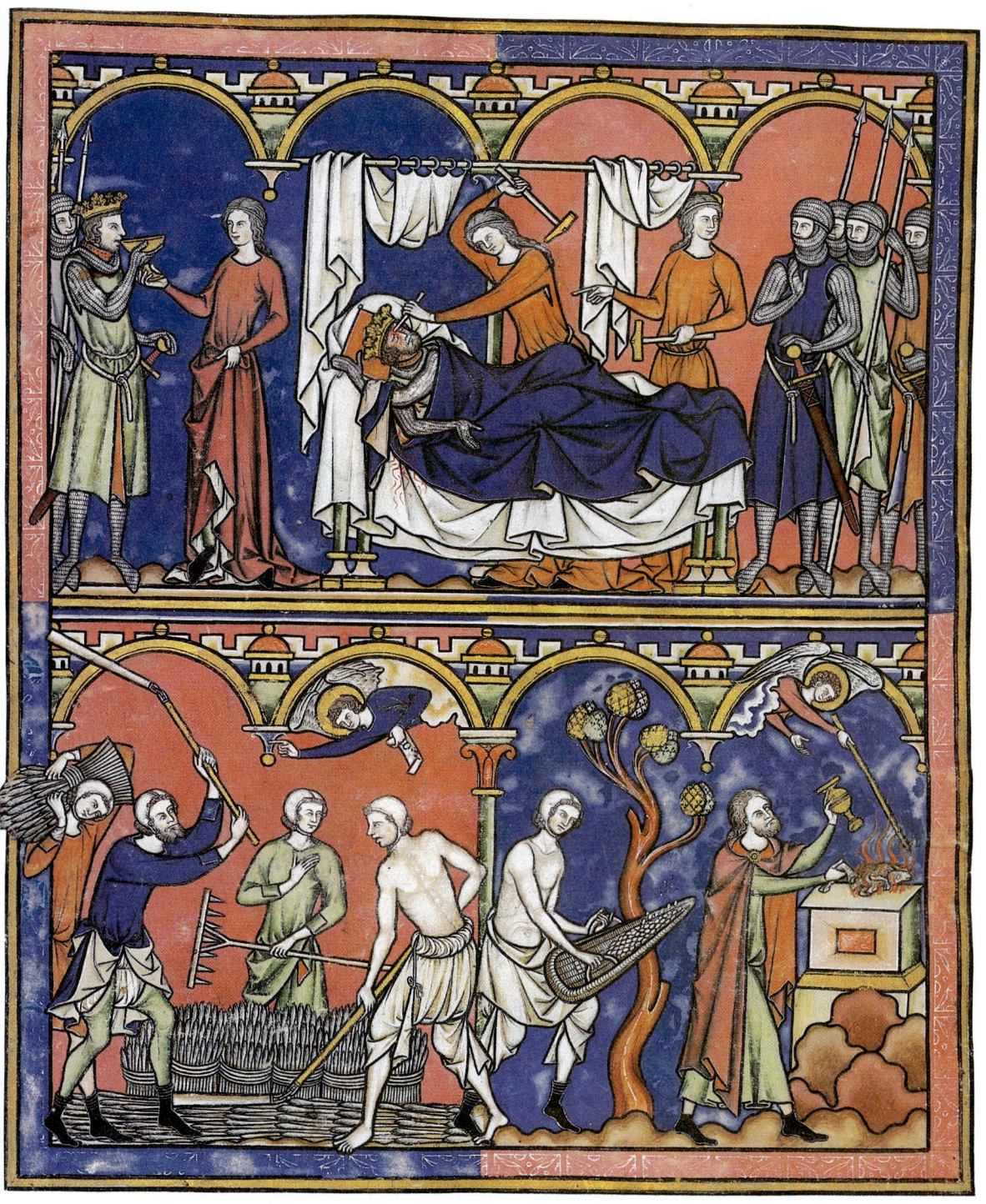

Scenes from the Book of Judges: In the upper panel Jael greets General Sisera from Hazor but then murders him with a tent peg as he sleeps. She then shows Barak her deed (4:17-22).

The lower panel shows the angel of the Lord appearing to Gideon as he threshes wheat (left) and igniting Gideon's sacrificial offering (6:11-22).

The book concludes (chs. 17–20) with stories told out of chronological sequence, which illustrate how far Israel departed from an obedient life-style during this period.

While not mentioned in the Book of Judges, events outside of Canaan strongly influenced the Israelite experience during this period. Egypt's authority in Palestine waned between 1400 and 1320 B.C. In the north, the Hittites encouraged anarchy in Syria-Palestine. This left the Israelites free of pressure from major world powers, but subject to the incursions of local enemies. Despite Egyptian invasions of Galilee and Phoenicia in 1318 B.C., Egyptian influence remained weak in Palestine. A hundred years later Egypt was challenged by the Sea Peoples. Many of this race, possibly from Crete, were driven back from Egypt to their colonies already established along Canaan's Mediterranean coasts. These people, the Philistines, then became Israel's chief enemy from the days of Samson well into David's reign.

THEOLOGICAL CONTRIBUTIONS

The Book of Judges demonstrates a basic theme of the OT: Those who keep covenant with God are blessed, while those who violate covenant relationship will be disciplined.

The book is also important for its dark view of humanity, contrasted with its bright vision of God. Human beings are warped and twisted, and quickly turn away from God (Jdg. 2:19; 17:6). God, though he punishes sin, is ever eager to restore his people when they repent (2:11,14; 3:1-4).

MASTERY KEYS

The reasons for the spiritual and political disasters of the period appear in Jdg. 1,2: incomplete obedience and open idolatry. The last five chapters (17–21) report incidents that demonstrate how far the Israelites departed from God's desires. Read these chapters as background to the stories in Jdg. 3–16.

Four of the twelve judges are given extensive treatment: Deborah, Gideon, Jephthah, and Samson. Follow the emphasis of the text, and concentrate on lessons to be learned from their lives. *See also* articles on each in this dictionary.

SPECIAL FEATURES

Note the repeated emphasis on the Spirit of the Lord coming upon the judges to empower them (Jdg. 3:10; 6:34; 11:29; 13:25; 14:6,19; 15:14).

judgment In the OT (1) a condemnation or punishment decreed by a ruler (often God). In the NT (2) a judge's decision, usually (but not always) suggesting condemnation; (3) an individual's decision on any matter (1 Cor. 7:40). *See also* Judge.

Old Testament examples of judgments imposed by God include the Genesis Flood (Gen. 6–8) and the Exodus plagues (Ex. 6:6; 7:4; 12:12). Because of God's commitment to justice, he will bring sinners to judgment whether they are his own people or outsiders (Ps. 1:5; Ezek. 11:11; 14:21).

The NT often speaks of divine judgment. John the Baptist portrayed the coming Messiah as one who would execute judgment in Israel (Mt. 3:11,12). Judgment, as God's condemnation of the wicked, was a major theme in Jesus' teaching (Mt. 5:22; 24:50,51; 25:41-46). The Father, he said, committed this awesome responsibility to him (Jn. 5:22-27). Paul speaks of a coming day of judgment (Rom. 2:1-11), and graphically portrays Christ's return as a time for divine vengeance on those who persecute his people (2 Th. 1:5-10). Revelation describes final judgment in fateful terms, portraying lost human beings cast into a lake of fire where Satan, too, will be confined (Rev. 20:11-15). *See also* Hell.

It is important to understand that human beings are judged on the basis of their acts. God's Law provides the standard of behavior for those who know it, while conscience provides a standard for those without the divine revelation (Rom. 2:12-16). *See also* Conscience.

By either standard, all human beings fail, "for all have sinned and fall short of the glory of God" (Rom. 3:23). Thus we all deserve God's judgment. But belief in Christ lifts us out of the arena of judgment, for our sins are forgiven through him. John writes, "Whoever believes in him is not condemned, but whoever does not believe stands condemned already because he has not believed in the name of God's one and only Son" (Jn. 3:18).

Judgment Day An expression often used by Christ of the time at history's end when God will sentence evildoers to eternal punishment (Mt. 10:15; 11:22-24; 12:36-42; Lk. 10:14).

judgment hall (KJV) The place where Pilate tried Jesus, according to Jn. 18:28; from the Greek transliteration of the Latin word *praetorium*, which other translations use as its name—the Praetorium (Mt. 27:27; Mk. 15:16). It generally refers to the

residence of a Roman governor. *See also* Praetorium.

judgment seat [Gk., *bēma*]. A raised platform used for public proclamation. Winners of athletic games were announced from a *bēma*. Civic officials pronounced judicial sentences and public commendations from such a platform. Paul's statement, "We must all appear before the judgment seat of Christ" (2 Cor. 5:10), would have stirred not only fear but also enthusiasm. The judgment seat in Corinth was a large, centrally located platform. When someone appeared before the *bēma*, it was sometimes for condemnation, sometimes for commendation.

With the Christian's sins paid for by Christ and no longer an issue, appearance at Christ's judgment seat will be to receive rewards (*see* Eph. 6:8; Rev. 22:12). *See also* Reward.

justice Righteousness, action which is in harmony with moral and ethical norms.

God is just, both in the sense that he defines the moral and ethical norms of the universe, and in that he acts in harmony with the standards he has revealed (Neh. 9:33). God is known by his justice (Ps. 9:16), and loves justice in his people (Ps. 99:4; Isa. 61:8). The biblical concept of justice includes divine retribution (2 Th. 1:6-9). *See also* Wrath of God.

The OT calls for strict legal justice. Elders in Israel were to judge disputes and criminal cases honestly. Their legal system included rules of evidence and even a system of appeals to higher courts (Deut. 16:18-20; 17:2-7). Distinctively, that system of justice emphasizes restitution for the victim, rather than punishment for the perpetrator.

But biblical justice also involves a responsibility to the poor and disadvantaged. It means more than merely refraining from oppressing others; the just person takes the initiative to relieve the poor and oppressed in society (Isa. 58:2-10; Jer. 22:15-17). *See also* Righteousness.

justification A declaration of innocence or righteousness. Paul argues in Romans that all people have sinned, falling short of God's standard of righteousness (chs. 1–3). Christ's death for our sins provides the basis on which God can justly declare the believer to be righteous (3:21–4:25). Paul makes it very clear that we are justified by faith (5:1), not by our actions.

Justification is essentially a legal concept, yet entails more in spiritual terms. God not only declares the believer to be righteous; God infuses new spiritual life—a righteousness actually *experienced* through faith in Jesus Christ (Gal. 3:21-26). *See also* Righteousness.

This fact helps us put the argument of James 2 in perspective. Both Paul and James write about faith. But Paul focuses on the object of faith, Christ, while James focuses on the life of authentic faith. In this context James argues that works are a natural expression of biblical faith. Abraham was justified by "what he did when he offered his son Isaac on the altar" (Jas. 2:21). Not that his actions earned him any favor with God, but they did indicate that his faith was sincere and deep. "His faith and his actions were working together, and his faith was made complete by what he did" (Jas. 2:22).

Justification, then, is God's judicial act in counting the believer righteous, by faith not works, on the basis of the redemptive work of Jesus in his death and resurrection (Rom. 4:18–5:11).

The bēma, a ceremonial platform used for official public speeches, at the marketplace of Corinth. Christians there would have immediately grasped Paul's reference to a metaphorical platform for Christ's final judgment (2 Cor. 5:10).

City gates in Israel were a place where business and legal matters were settled. The 8th-century B.C. prophet Amos condemned injustice "in the courts" (literally, "gates"; 5:10,12,15).

K

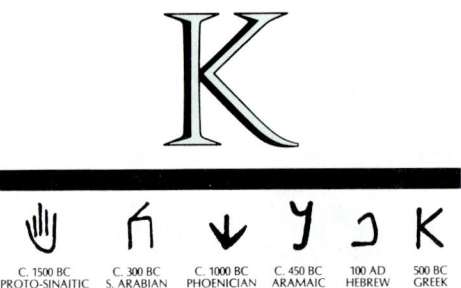

C. 1500 BC PROTO-SINAITIC   C. 300 BC S. ARABIAN   C. 1000 BC PHOENICIAN   C. 450 BC ARAMAIC   100 AD HEBREW   500 BC GREEK

I QT. + 1/16 QT. = I KAB

kab (RSV) A unit of dry measure equal to slightly more than 1 U.S. quart (1.2 liters), mentioned only in 2 Ki. 6:25.

Kadesh Barnea [KAY-desh bahr-NEE-uh; "holy" or "consecrated"]. An area in the Sinai Desert, just across the southern border of Canaan, best known as the encampment from which the Israelites sent twelve spies into the Promised Land. Kadesh lies in that section of the wilderness of Paran called the wilderness of Zin. Used as a reference point in Abraham's time (Gen. 16:14; 20:1), Kadesh also proved to be a significant site for the wandering Israelites. Ten of the twelve spies brought back a grim report of the strength of the Canaanite cities. This led the fearful nation to disobey God's command to attack (Num. 13,14). The Israelites were then doomed to wander

for 38 more years in the wilderness, until that generation died. The Book of Hebrews analyzes the events at Kadesh to show the relationship of faith, obedience, and rest in the Christian life (Heb. 3,4).

Kenites A tribe or clan of semi-nomadic metalworkers, whose name is derived from the Hebrew word for "smith." Genesis 15:19 lists them with the Canaanites and others as inhabitants of Israel's Promised Land. Moses' father-in-law, Jethro, was a Kenite whose descendants settled in a copper-rich district of the Sinai (Jdg. 1:16; 4:11).

The Kenites maintained a comfortable relationship with Israel. Jael, wife of Heber the Kenite, killed Israel's enemy Sisera in the time of Deborah (Jdg. 4:11,17-22). Saul warned the Kenites to leave Amale-

Nestled between barren hills in the western Negev, the oasis at Kadesh Barnea was to be the last stop on the Israelites' Exodus trek. Here, however, they were condemned to wander in the wilderness for a generation for their unbelief (Num. 13,14).

Left: Bronze axe and spearhead found in Israel, 11th–10th cent. B.C.

Jerusalem

CANAAN

DEAD SEA

Arad

THE NEGEV

THE ARABAH

Feinan
• (PUNON)

• Petra

NORTHERN
SINAI

EDOM

Timnah

N

☒ = MINES

0   20   40 MI
0 20 40 60 KM

GULF OF AQABAH

MIDIAN

kite territory before he invaded that land (1 Sam. 15:6). David sent gifts to Kenite cities while he was exiled from Israel in Saul's day (1 Sam. 30:29). According to 1 Chr. 2:55, the Recabites, praised later by Jeremiah for their obedience to an ancestor's decree (Jer. 35), may have been Kenites.

kenosis [Gk., "an emptying"]. A term used in Phil. 2:8-11 and by some theologians to express Christ's incarnation.

The magnificent words of Phil. 2:8-11 probably come from a hymn sung by the early church, praising Christ for the attitude he exhibited in his incarnation and death. The Greek term *kenosis* used there has been translated "made himself of no reputation" or "made himself nothing," and has stimulated speculation over the relationship between the divine and human natures of Christ.

Some 18th-century scholars proposed a Kenosis Theory, suggesting that Jesus voluntarily laid aside the very attributes of deity in order to experience life as a limited, ordinary human being. The theory in essence claims that Jesus stopped being God during the incarnation, to take up deity again after his resurrection. This notion is not supported by exegesis of the text or by an orthodox understanding of the incarnation, which holds that Jesus was at the same time fully God and truly human. *See also* Creed; Incarnation.

Instead, Phil. 2:8-11 teaches that Jesus abandoned the visible expression and prerogatives of deity, to live a truly human life, obediently subjecting himself to the human condition, even to death on the cross.

kerygma A Greek term for "proclamation" or "that which is preached." Found eight times in the NT (Mt. 12:41; Lk. 11:32; Rom. 16:25; 1 Cor. 1:21; 2:4; 15:14; 2 Tim. 4:17; Tit. 1:3), the word generally denotes the preaching of the basics of the faith—Jesus' saving death and resurrection, and the need for personal repentance. Theologians see the development of the Christian *kerygma* in the early chapters of Acts, where successive sermons proclaim the central aspects of Jesus' identity and his work. This is the heart of Christian preaching. *See also* Preach.

key An instrument for locking and unlocking doors, as in Jdg. 3:25. Symbolically, the key is a sign of authority. In Isa. 22:22, the "key to the house of David" involves the expression of royal authority. In Lk. 11:52, Jesus alludes to the practice of giv-

The Kenites are commonly thought to have been a tribe of metalworkers and miners. They lived in the northern Sinai, known in ancient times for its copper mining and smelting.

603

ing a Hebrew scribe a key as part of his ordination, implying a spiritual authority to interpret the faith. Jesus charged that the scribes had misused their authority. Rather than opening the Word to the masses, they threw away the key of knowledge.

Jesus gave the "keys of the kingdom of heaven" to Peter (Mt. 16:19). This act must be interpreted in view of the symbolic significance of keys.

Reconstructed pre-Roman lock and key. In Old Testament times, some keys were curved pieces of wood with pins that corresponded to holes in a hidden sliding bar (the long piece).

Christians of various traditions have understood the gift of the keys differently. The Roman Catholic Church believes that the act affirms Peter's spiritual authority on earth, and teaches that the keys are held today by the Pope, whom they trace as Peter's successor. Protestants generally hold one of two views: (1) Peter "used the keys" when he preached at Pentecost and in the house of Cornelius (Acts 2,10). The door of salvation is now open to all, so there is no further need for the keys. (2) Peter represents the other disciples (Mt. 18:18; Jn. 20:22,23) and all Christians. Now any believer may open the door of salvation to others by sharing the Gospel with them.

Whatever Jesus intended, Rev. 1:18 states that Christ retains "the keys of death and Hades." Peter, the other disciples, and Christians today are but stewards of Jesus, responsible to him to share the good news of salvation with all (1 Cor. 3:1-9).

Isaiah prophesied that even such a vulnerable animal as a young goat would be safe from natural enemies when God establishes his kingdom on earth (Isa. 11:6; compare Jdg. 14:6).

kid (KJV) A young goat. Since goats were clean animals, according to Jewish law, they could be eaten. At smaller feasts, a kid might replace a fattened calf (Gen. 27:9; Jdg. 6:19; 1 Sam. 10:3; Lk. 15:29). It could also serve as a sacrifice for Passover or other rituals (Ex. 12:5; Num. 15:11-16; 2 Chr. 35:7). *See also* Clean and Unclean.

The OT three times forbids cooking a young kid in its mother's milk (Ex. 23:19; 34:26; Deut. 14:21). Although some evidence suggests this prohibition was directed against a religious practice of the Canaanites, the statute is the basis for the modern Orthodox Jewish rule against cooking meat and milk foods in the same set of dishes.

kidneys Organs which separate water and waste products from the blood. Scripture refers to the literal kidneys of sacrificial animals, as in Ex. 29:13; Lev. 3:4; Isa. 34:6. But it also uses the Hebrew word for kidneys metaphorically, of the mind, emotions, or conscience, as in Ps. 16:7; Jer. 11:20; 12:2. In English versions metaphorical uses of kidney are generally rendered by "reins" (KJV) or "mind," "heart," or "inward parts" (RSV, NIV).

kill To end a life. Old Testament Hebrew makes a distinction between killing in general (*haraq*) and murder (*rasah*). The commandment reads, "You shall not murder [*rasah*]," rather than "You shall not kill [*haraq*]" (Ex. 20:13; Deut. 5:17). *See also* Murder.

kind [Heb., *min*]. A general term used in the OT to classify living creatures. *Min* occurs only 31 times in the OT. In each context Scripture affirms God's creation order. God has created living creatures with distinctive identities: "Let the land produce living creatures according to their kinds: livestock, creatures that move along the ground, wild animals, each according to its kind" (Gen. 1:24).

kindness Love expressed in charitable acts. The OT accents God's kindness (sometimes "lovingkindness") toward his people. The Hebrew term, *hesed*, indicates faithfulness in a relationship.

The NT sees kindness (*chrēstos*, *chrēstotēs*) as a moral goodness expressed in acts of friendship. God's overwhelming kindness comes through in his willingness to do good even to those who are his enemies (Rom. 2:4; Eph. 2:7; Tit. 3:4). Christians are exhorted to imitate God's kindness in their relationships with others (Gal. 5:22; Eph. 4:32; Col. 3:12). *See also* Covenant; Grace.

king A ruling magistrate, responsible for governing a city, nation, or other political unit.

The Hebrew word translated "king" (*melek*) is also rendered "governor," "ruler," and "chief." It is a general word for a person with civil authority, whatever the form of government or size of the unit governed.

In the ancient world, the king exercised all the functions of a modern government, including legislative, executive, and judicial, and held the power of life and death over his subjects.

In Israel the establishment of the monarchy created tension between the role of God and the role of the human ruler. In demanding a king, the people of Israel rejected God as their invisible ruler and protector, to depend on a mere human being (1 Sam. 12:12-17). Yet God worked through Israel's godly kings, who often led the nation to deeper dependence on him. *See also* Hezekiah; Josiah.

The prophets declared that God remained Israel's King as well as her Creator and Redeemer (Isa. 43:15; Mal. 1:14). They taught that one day God would visibly establish his now hidden authority over the whole earth (Zech. 14:9,16). Strikingly, that visible authority is to be exercised by a human descendant of David: the Messiah. *See also* Messiah.

The NT identifies Jesus as the promised Messiah, the one from David's line destined to be King (Mt. 1:1–2:6). The name "Christ" means "anointed one," and thus indicates Jesus' royal destiny. Yet "king" is most often associated in the Gospels with Jesus' death. Jesus' enemies accused him of claiming royal authority, and thus being a potential rival to Caesar. Jesus admitted his kingship, but said, "My kingdom is not of this world" (Jn. 18:36). Pilate affixed to the cross a plaque that read "King of the Jews" (Mt. 27:37; Jn. 19:19,21). *See also* Kingdom.

kingdom A ruler's sphere of authority. In human terms, this may be a geographical or political unit, such as the kingdom of Judah or the "divided kingdom." Theologically, the universe can be seen as God's kingdom, under his sovereign authority, as in Pss. 103:19; 145:11-13. But the OT prophets predicted a future kingdom which God would set up on earth (Isa. 9:6-8; Dan. 2:44). While the NT maintains that sense of expectation, it adds the idea that God's Kingdom is present wherever and whenever people acknowledge him as King.

THE GOSPEL OF THE KINGDOM

In Jesus' time, the Jews lived under Roman rule. Sustained by a passionate

Pottery jar handle bearing an imprinted seal with the Hebrew words "[belonging] to the king." Such impressions were stamped on standard-sized containers for oil, grain, and wine, which were delivered full to royal storehouses in payment of taxes from the rural population.

desire for freedom and for the triumph of their God, the Jewish people hoped fervently for fulfillment of the OT promises of an earthly kingdom set up by God.

This burning hope was fanned into flames by the appearance of John the Baptist who, in preaching his "gospel of the kingdom," announced that the Messiah was about to appear: "The kingdom of heaven is near" (Mt. 3:2).

When Jesus began his public ministry, he picked up John's theme (Mt. 4:17,23; Mk. 1:15). But Jesus went beyond John, to announce that "the kingdom of God has come upon you" (Mt. 12:28). Each of Jesus' acts of healing reinforced his claim, for the prophets had predicted that the coming King would bring peace and healing (Mal. 4:2; Mt. 9:35; Lk. 4:43).

Yet Jesus did not establish a political kingdom as the Jews expected, and his early popularity waned. Against the background of rejection, Christ spoke instead both of a present, spiritual kingdom that had come near (Mt. 4:17; Mk. 1:15) and of a future time when the Son of Man would come with great power and glory (Mt. 24:30; 25:31; Mk. 13:26). Reflecting this and the Jews' eager expectation, the disciples even asked the resurrected Jesus if he would "at this time restore the [earthly] kingdom to Israel?" Jesus replied that it was not for them to know the times or dates the Father had set (Acts 1:6,7). The physical, glorious kingdom remains an element in God's eternal plan. But in this present age, Christ's followers are commissioned "to be my witnesses in Jerusalem, and in all Judea and Samaria, and to the ends of the earth" (Acts 1:8).

GOD'S PRESENT KINGDOM

In thinking biblically about God's present Kingdom, we must remember the basic concept from the OT. A kingdom is not in essence a land distinguished by its own language, laws, and customs. A kingdom is the sphere in which a ruler exercises authority over the hearts and lives of his subjects. Thus God's present Kingdom is that sphere in which his authority is acknowledged by men and women who are committed to him and committed to do his will.

When we understand that God's present Kingdom exists wherever men and women choose to submit to God's authority, we understand the condition that Christ laid down for citizenship. Jesus said that unless a man is born again "he cannot enter the kingdom of God" (Jn. 3:5). A spiritual rebirth through personal faith in Jesus Christ is basic to human acknowledgment of the authority of God, an essential first step in expressing commitment to him.

Given this starting point, the NT adds many insights into what it means for the believer to live as a citizen of God's Kingdom.

1. *Insights from the Gospels.* The Beatitudes (Mt. 5:3-12) establish the values a citizen of Jesus' Kingdom will adopt. Jesus' Sermon on the Mount (Mt. 5–7) shows how people of every age live when fully committed to God's will. Jesus' parables in Mt. 13 contrast aspects of the present Kingdom with the earthly kingdom expected by his Jewish listeners. The Lord's Prayer sums up the commitment of the citizen of God's heavenly Kingdom: "Your will be done on earth as it is in heaven" (Mt. 6:10). *See also* Beatitudes; Lord's Prayer; Sermon on the Mount.

2. *Insights from the Epistles.* Believers have been rescued from the realm of darkness and brought "into the kingdom of the Son he loves" (Col. 1:13). As sons we inherit the Kingdom (Gal. 3:29; 4:7). Under Roman law heirs shared in their father's possessions while he still lived, rather than having an interest in them only after he died. All the benefits of living in the realm where God rules are now ours in Christ. *See also* Adoption; Heir.

THE REALM OF GOD'S ACTION

Much in the NT emphasizes how citizens of God's Kingdom respond to the one

THE KINGDOM OF GOD IN PARABLES (MT. 13)

Messianic Kingdom's Expected Form	Some OT Sources	Present Kingdom's Unexpected Form	Parable in Matthew 13
The Kingdom will subdue nations	Pss. 2; 18:43-50; 72:8-11; 110; Isa. 9:7; Mic. 5:4; Zech. 9:10	Individuals respond or fail to respond to the Kingdom's message	Soils (vv. 2-9,18-23)
The Kingdom is launched in power and glory	Pss. 2; 18; 45:4,5	The Kingdom produces results out of proportion to its insignificant start	Mustard Seed (vv. 31, 32); Yeast (v. 33)
The Kingdom brings peace and blessings to Israel as an act of God	Pss. 72:6,7; 132:13-18; Isa. 11:6-9; Jer. 23:6; Amos 9:13; Joel 4:18	The Kingdom must be sought for diligently and is worth all costs	Hidden Treasure (v. 44); Pearl (vv. 45,46)
The Kingdom begins with the separation of the good from the evil	Pss. 21:8-12; 72:1-4, 12-14	The Kingdom ends with the separation of the good from the evil	Weeds (vv. 24-30, 36-43); Net (vv. 47-50)

they acknowledge as King. But there is another implication of Scripture's teaching on God's present Kingdom. A person who lives as a citizen of God's Kingdom can expect the King to act on his behalf. Obedience places the believer within that sphere where God exercises direct control of the circumstances of life.

Thus Jesus tells his hearers not to be anxious even about necessities, because "your heavenly Father knows that you need them." Released from concern by our confidence in God, we believers are freed to "seek first [God's] kingdom and his righteousness" (Mt. 6:25-34).

Our confidence that God sovereignly controls the circumstances of our lives means that even if we suffer harm for doing what is good, we need not be discouraged (1 Pet. 3:8-18). We are at peace, assured that "in all things God works for the good of those who love him" (Rom. 8:28). Jesus taught frequently about the Kingdom of God, and he often used parables. In these simple stories and word pictures, he challenged many of his hearers' assumptions about the coming Kingdom.

Kingdom of God, Kingdom of heaven

Phrases used in the Gospels to express the idea of the rule of God on earth. The Bible speaks of different aspects of this rule from God's hidden rule over all things to the visible rule of God on earth through David's descendant, the Messiah. A third aspect of the Kingdom of God is the relationship of believers to the King.

Most see Matthew's use of "kingdom of heaven" as a reflection of the tendency in Judaism to avoid the direct use of the name of God. The two phrases are used synonymously throughout the Gospels. *See also* Kingdom.

Kings, First and Second Books of Two

of the historical books of the OT, considered one book in Jewish tradition. The two Books of Kings contain the history of the Hebrew monarchy from the death of David (about 970 B.C.). to the Babylonian conquest (586 B.C.).

BACKGROUND

David, Israel's second and greatest king, forged a loose confederation of Israelite tribes into a powerful, united people. David centralized Israel's worship, organized a powerful army, and created a bureaucracy that efficiently managed the entire nation. He defeated Israel's enemies and extended the nation's borders. Sol-omon, his son and successor, further strengthened the united kingdom, primarily by diplomatic means, and brought the nation immense wealth by his trading ventures. But on Solomon's death, an old rivalry between northern and southern tribes was exploited by Jeroboam, who won the allegiance of the ten northern tribes away from Solomon's son, Rehoboam.

The nation was thus broken into two: "Israel" in the north and "Judah" in the south. The two kingdoms struggled against each other and against neighboring nations. Despite occasional resurgence of power, and the ministry of many prophets, neither kingdom achieved the power or glory of the Davidic-Solomonic era.

Israel, led by an unbroken series of evil kings, survived just over 200 years before its population was deported in 722 B.C. by Assyrian conquerors. Judah, blessed with a number of godly kings who stimulated revivals of the biblical faith, survived until 586 B.C., when Jerusalem was destroyed and much of Judah's population was deported to Babylon. Each of the national disasters is portrayed in Scripture as divine judgment on peoples who failed to live the religious and morally pure life that their covenant with God required. *See also* Israel; Judah.

AUTHORSHIP AND DATE

The Books of Kings were written some time after the events described, possibly 600–550 B.C., but perhaps later. The author or authors drew on existing sources for data concerning political and military conditions and building activities during the reign of the kings. The text mentions the annals of Solomon (1 Ki. 11:41), makes 17 references to the annals of the kings of Israel (*see* 1 Ki. 14:19), and 15 to the annals of the kings of Judah (*see* 1 Ki. 14:29). These documents, and other records which may have served as background for 1 and 2 Kings, are not available today.

There are difficulties in dating the reigns of the various Hebrew kings, because of different ways in Judah and Israel of counting a king's first year; because of co-regencies, during which a king ruled jointly with his son; and because of other factors. Yet historians have established links with known dates in secular history, so the dating shown on the chart is a reliable approximation. *See also* Chronology of the Bible.

THEOLOGICAL CONTRIBUTIONS

The author of Kings intended not to   *607*

First and Second Kings serve as selective commentaries on material recorded in the "annals of the kings" of Israel and Judah, which are mentioned in 1 Kings 14:19 and other passages. This tablet contains the annals of the kings of the first dynasty of Babylon. As the partial translation at the right shows, each successive year in the reign of Sumu-abu (1894–1881 B.C.) is marked by one major event.

[Translation]

Reign of Sumu-abu

YEAR

1 [The year in which Sumu-abu became king. . . .].

2 [The year in which. . . . .].

3 The year in which the wall of [. . . . .].

4 The year in which the temple of Nin-sinna was built.

5 The year in which the great temple of Nannar was built.

6 The year after that in which the great temple of Nannar was built.

7 The second year after that in which the great temple of Nannar was built.

8 The year in which the great door of cedar was made for the temple of Nannar.

9 The year in which the wall of the city of Dilbat was built.

10 The year in which the crown of the god Ni of the city of Kish was made.

11 The year after that in which the crown of the god Ni of the city of Kish was made.

provide a political history of the kingdom era, but rather to demonstrate the politics of God, expressed in and through the history of Israel and Judah. He argues that the disasters which struck both Hebrew kingdoms are not evidence of divine abandonment but of divine faithfulness to a covenant which promises both blessing and discipline. *See also* Covenant.

Despite Judah's frequent rebellions, God remained faithful to his promise to David (1 Ki. 11:32-39; 2 Ki. 8:19; 19:34). Each king of Judah was of David's line, and from that line the promised Messiah would arise. *See also* Messiah.

MASTERY KEYS

Note the pattern used to describe the kings of northern and southern nations (*see* 1 Ki. 16:15-20; 22:41-50). A major departure from that pattern is found in 1 Ki. 17–2 Ki. 8, the story of Elijah and Elisha. These prophets ministered in a time marked by an aggressive royal attempt to replace the worship of the Lord with the worship of Baal. *See also* Ahab; Baal; Elijah; Elisha.

SPECIAL FEATURES

The history of Judah is marked by a series of revivals, stimulated by godly kings. Study of their lives is recommended. *See also* Asa; Hezekiah; Joash; Josiah.

1 KINGS: A READING AND STUDY GUIDE

Chapter	Content Summary	Related Articles
1	Adonijah attempts to take the throne. David, urged by Bathsheba and Nathan, acts to make Solomon king.	Bathsheba Nathan
2	David charges Solomon to deal with his old enemies. Solomon has Adonijah executed.	Solomon
3	Solomon pleases God by asking for wisdom to guide God's people. He displays wisdom dealing with two prostitutes.	Wisdom
4	Solomon reorganizes the bureaucracy. He composes poems and proverbs, studies botany and zoology.	Proverbs
5	Solomon completes preparations for building the Jerusalem Temple. He brings materials and craftsmen from Tyre.	Temple Temple, Jerusalem
6	Solomon completes construction of the Temple in seven years of concentrated effort.	
7	Solomon constructs his palace in 13 years. He continues work furnishing the Temple.	Altar Sea
8	Solomon brings the ark into the Temple, and dedicates the Temple with a prayer.	Ark of Covenant Prayer
9	God promises to answer the prayers of an obedient or repentant Israel. Other activities of Solomon are listed.	Obey Repent
10	The Queen of Sheba visits Solomon and is impressed by his wealth and wisdom.	
11	Solomon's foreign wives lure him away from God in his old age. Enemies then arise, including Jeroboam, destined to split the kingdom.	Edom Aram
12	Solomon dies, and ten tribes rebel against his son. In Israel Jeroboam sets up a false worship system.	Rehoboam Jeroboam I
13	A prophet from Judah predicts desecration of Jeroboam's altar. The prophet disobeys God, and is killed.	Prophet
14	Ahijah prophesies disaster on Jeroboam's line. Temple treasures are taken by Shishak of Egypt.	Egypt
15	Asa of Judah is committed to the Lord, but makes an alliance with Aram. Nadab, then Baasha, rule Israel.	Asa Aram
16	Baasha, Elah, Zimri, Omri, and Ahab continue the string of Israel's evil kings.	Ahab
17	Elijah the Tishbite calls for a three-year drought as punishment on Israel. Elijah is fed by ravens and a widow.	Elijah
18	Elijah reappears. On Mt. Carmel he confronts 450 prophets of Baal. Elijah's victory establishes the Lord's supremacy.	Baal
19	Elijah, suddenly terrified and depressed, flees Jezebel. God ministers to Elijah; gives him a companion, Elisha.	Jezebel
20	Ben-Hadad of Aram attacks Israel, but is defeated by Ahab with the prophet Elijah's help. Elijah condemns Ahab.	Samaritan
21	Ahab and Jezebel murder righteous Naboth for his vineyard. Their fate is pronounced by Elijah.	
22	Micaiah predicts Ahab's death in a coming battle against Aram. Godly Jehoshaphat becomes king of Judah.	Jehoshaphat

2 KINGS: A READING AND STUDY GUIDE

Chapter	Content Summary	Related Articles
1	God brings death to an injured Ahaziah of Israel for seeking help from a pagan deity.	Idol
2	Elijah is taken up to heaven. His prophetic mantle passes to Elisha, as demonstrated by three miracles.	Elisha Miracles
3	God brings Israel and Judah victory over Moab through the prophet Elisha.	Moab
4	Elisha multiplies a widow's oil, restores life to the son of a Shunammite woman, and does other miracles.	
5	Elisha heals Naaman, commander of the Aramean army, of leprosy. His servant Gehazi sins and becomes a leper.	Naaman Gehazi
6	Elisha makes an axhead float, and blinds an Aramean army. Samaria is besieged, and Elisha is threatened by his king.	Ahab Samaria
7	Elisha predicts the lifting of the siege, with plenty of food for starving Israel.	
8	Elisha predicts Hazael will rule Aram, and will cause intense suffering in Israel. Hazael kills King Ben-Hadad.	Aram, Arameans
9	Elisha sends a prophet to anoint Jehu king of Israel. Jehu kills Joram of Israel, Jezebel, and Ahaziah of Judah.	Jehu
10	Jehu kills Ahab's family, and acts to wipe out the worship of Baal in Israel. His motive is political, not religious.	Baal
11	In Judah, Athaliah murders the royal family and takes power. One child, Joash, survives and later becomes king.	Athaliah Joash
12	King Joash repairs the Temple and leads Judah in a revival. Later Joash bribes Hazael with Temple gold.	
13	Jehoahaz and Jehoash rule Israel. God helps them against the Arameans, but the prophet Elisha dies of old age.	
14	Amaziah of Judah, a godly king, defeats Edom, but is crushed by Israel. Jeroboam II becomes king of Israel.	Amaziah Jeroboam II
15	The reigns of Azariah, Zechariah, Shallum, Menahem, Pekahiah, Pekah, and Jotham are covered briefly.	Assyria
16	Ahaz of Judah appeals to Assyria for help against Aram. He adopts Assyria's gods, and strips God's Temple.	Ahaz
17	Hoshea, Israel's last king, is deported with his people "because the Israelites had sinned against the Lord." Israel's territory is resettled with foreigners.	Captivity Samaritans
18	Hezekiah, a man who trusts God, becomes king of Judah. But Assyria threatens Jerusalem with destruction.	Hezekiah
19	Hezekiah turns to God in prayer. Isaiah prophesies Judah's deliverance and Sennacherib's failure.	Isaiah
20	Hezekiah, mortally ill, appeals to God and is healed. He shows Babylonian envoys Judah's treasures, and is rebuked by Isaiah.	Healing Babylon
21	Evil king Manasseh rules for 55 years, followed by his evil son, Amon.	Manasseh
22	Young King Josiah seeks God and leads a great revival stimulated by recovery of a lost book of God's Law.	Josiah Law
23	Josiah leads Judah in a ceremony of covenant renewal. The king purges his land of idolatry.	Covenant
24	The last kings of Judah, Jehoiakim, Jehoiachin, and Zedekiah, are all evil.	Jeremiah
25	Rebellion against Babylon leads to the destruction of Jerusalem and of God's Temple.	Nebuchadnezzar Ezekiel

King's Highway A major international trade route, running along the highlands east of the Jordan River from Damascus to the Gulf of Aqaba on the Red Sea. Archaeologists have dated forts along the route to the time of Abraham (2300–2000 B.C.). The force led by Kedorlaomer against Sodom and Gomorrah probably came from the north along this road (Gen. 14).

The route was again fortified between 1400 and 600 B.C. Toward the beginning of this period, Moses asked the kings of Edom and Ammon for safe passage through their land, promising to keep his people on the King's Highway and not to invade their land (Num. 20:17; 21:22; Deut. 2:27).

This trade route was controlled by Israel during the reigns of David and Solomon. A hundred years after Christ it was known as the *Via Nova*. In the Turkish era it became the Tariq es-Sultan. Today a modern Jordanian highway closely follows the ancient route.

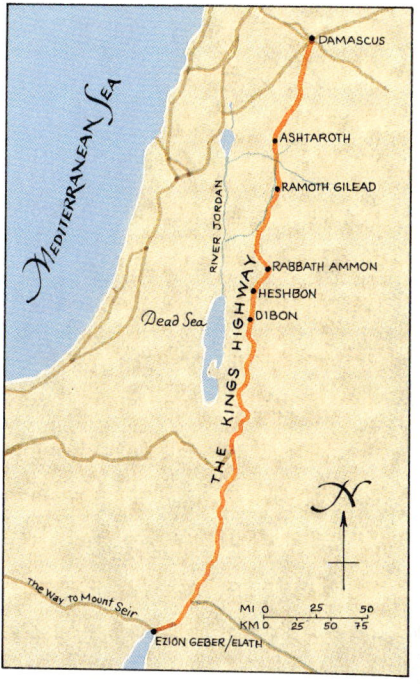

The route of the ancient "King's Highway." A modern highway follows part of the 5,000-year-old track.

King's Pool (Neh. 2:14). A reservoir in Jerusalem's royal garden. It was probably also the Pool of Siloam of the NT. *See also* Cistern.

kinsman, kinsman-redeemer In its broadest sense, one of the same race, tribe, or family. But the Hebrew term *go'el* has an important specialized meaning as well. Under OT Law, a near relative was obligated to avenge murder. If a member of his family was wrongfully slain, it was the duty of the *go'el* to enact God's justice, putting the murderer to death. If he pos-

sessed the financial resources, a near kinsman could also redeem a poor relative from slavery by paying the required debt. The kinsman could even redeem a relative's "sold" property by paying what the relation owed. For this reason some English versions, in appropriate contexts, translate *go'el* as "kinsman-redeemer" (Ruth 3:9 NIV).

Boaz emerges as the classic OT example of the kinsman-redeemer. Closely related to the family of Naomi (Ruth's mother-in-law), he "purchases" the family property by taking Ruth as his wife, so that their first son can be counted in the line of

French illuminated manuscript (A.D. 1250) depicts Ruth lying down at the feet of her kinsman Boaz at the barley harvest (Ruth 3:1-5). This action was a sign that Ruth, a widow, wished herself and her land to be bought back or "redeemed" by this relative.

The most famous kiss in the Bible, Judas's kiss of betrayal, is depicted on a panel from an altar by Nicholas of Verdun, Klosterneuberg Abbey, A.D. 1180.

Two porters kiss the ground as a sign of submission. A bas relief from Hermopolis, Egypt.

shared in their humanity so that by his death he might destroy him who holds the power of death—that is, the devil—and free those who all their lives were held in slavery by their fear of death.'' Indeed, ''he had to be made like his brothers in every way . . . that he might make atonement for the sins of the people'' (2:14-17). *See also* Avenger of Blood; Boaz; Redeem.

Kislev The ninth month in the Hebrew calendar, corresponding to November/December; called Chislev or Chisleu in some English versions. *See also* Calendar.

kiss A touch of the lips to another person's lips, face, hands, or feet.

The kiss is most often mentioned in Scripture in a family context, and is often accompanied by a warm embrace (Gen. 29:13; Lk. 15:20). The significance of the kiss depends on the relationship of the parties involved. Typically (1) a kiss served relatives and friends as an affectionate greeting or farewell (Gen. 33:4; Ruth 1:14; Rom. 16:16). (2) A kiss also served a ceremonial purpose, indicating respect (1 Sam. 10:1; 2 Sam. 15:5). (3) Kissing the hands or feet of a superior was an act of submission or worship (1 Ki. 19:18; Ps. 2:12). Much less common are (4) the seductive kiss (Prov. 7:13), and (5) the romantic kiss between lovers (Song 1:2).

In the NT the ''holy kiss'' with which Christians greeted one another (1 Cor. 16:20; 2 Cor. 13:12; 1 Pet. 5:14) reflects the fact that the early Christians saw each other as family, and developed loving personal relationships.

It is striking that Judas betrayed Jesus with a kiss (Mt. 26:48,49). His unnecessary perversion of this sign of affection and respect suggests much about the character of Judas Iscariot (*compare* 2 Sam. 20:9).

knee, kneel The joint between the thigh and the lower leg; to bend one's knees and rest on them.

In various scriptural phrases, the knees express important aspects of how a person feels or the person's relation to others. For instance, fear causes knees to ''give way'' (Isa. 35:3) or ''knock together'' (Dan. 5:6). Weak people are those with ''faltering knees'' (Job 4:4).

When enemies are vanquished, they are forced to their knees in submission (Ps. 20:8). But loyal subjects fall to their knees willingly, which may explain why kneeling is a posture of prayer (Dan 6:10). *See also* Prayer. People frequently knelt before

Ruth's dead husband, rightful heir to the family land.

Perhaps most important is the theological implication of kinsman-redemption. Only a near relation is qualified to pay the price that frees an individual from slavery, or to buy back what he or she has lost. In his incarnation, Christ became our kinsman by taking on human nature, that he might be qualified to pay the awesome price of our salvation.

In the words of Heb. 2, ''Since the children have flesh and blood, he too

Jesus (or "fell down" before him) in order to worship him and to ask him for healing or other favors (Mt. 17:14; Mk. 1:40).

Scripture also predicts a day when "every knee shall bow" before Jesus, acknowledging his Lordship (Phil. 2:10). Presumably, for some this will be the kneeling of devotion and worship, for others the kneeling of forced submission.

knife A short, sharpened tool used for cutting or stabbing.

Many of the same Hebrew words are used for knives and swords, but the OT has a specific term for knives used to slaughter sacrifices (Gen. 22:6; Jdg. 19:29). The OT mentions flint knives used by Moses and Joshua for circumcisions (Ex. 4:25; Josh. 5:2,3). While knives must have served a variety of important purposes, they were not mealtime utensils, since meat was generally cut into small pieces before being served. Many ancient knives have been recovered in Palestine, from short six-inch flint knives used as tools, to larger bronze and iron knives used as weapons. Other cultures have yielded beautifully worked knives inlaid with ivory or precious metals.

know, knowledge (1) To understand, to be well informed about; (2) to be acquainted or familiar with; (3) to possess information about; (4) to have mastered a subject by study or practice; (5) to recognize a person or thing. In Scripture, "know" and "knowledge" also serve as special relational terms. (6) To know God is to meet him in his self-revelation, to respond to that self-revelation with trust and obedience, and thus to establish or maintain a personal relationship with him. (7) To know one's spouse serves as a euphemism for sexual intercourse.

THE HEBREW AND GREEK WORDS

The Hebrew *yada'*, "to know," is used of all types of knowledge mentioned above. The religious use of *yada'* is most significant, for it describes seeing God in his Word or mighty acts and responding to him with faith. One who truly knows God takes to heart the fact that he is Lord, and demonstrates his knowledge by keeping God's decrees and commands (Deut. 4:39,40).

The Greek *ginōskō* and *oida/eidon* can denote either understanding facts or truths or perception and discernment. They reflect the Greek view that knowledge is intelligent comprehension. But the theological use of "know" in the NT is rooted in the OT's concept of knowing God. Religious knowledge is no mere philosophical or speculative grasp of truth. It is a personal, responsive relationship with the living God.

INSIGHT FROM NT PASSAGES

Many NT passages deal with the issue of religious knowledge. Key ones are:

• *John 8:19-47.* Those who hear Jesus but fail to respond to him with faith do not

Bronze figurine of a kneeling Egyptian man, possibly a priest (4th century B.C.). In biblical times the act of kneeling down indicated respect, submission, worship, or prayer.

Bronze embalmer's knife from Egypt (1580–1200 B.C.).

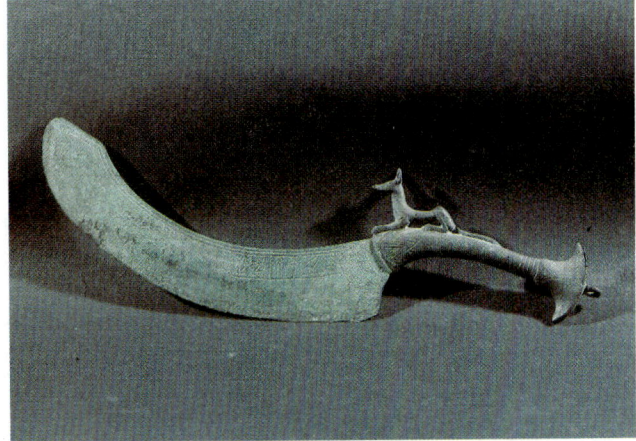

know God. To know truth experientially, one must hear Christ's words and put them into practice.

• *Romans 1:18-32.* God has revealed himself in creation. But mankind, thus

613

confronted by God, has refused to glorify or thank him. This has plunged humanity into religious and moral darkness.

• *1 Corinthians 2.* Philosophers attempt to comprehend reality by observation and rational thought. But God alone knows reality, and he communicates it to us in words the Spirit both inspires and interprets.

• *Ephesians 1:17-23; 2:14-18.* Paul prays that believers will know God better, not by engaging in rational thought, but by deepening that personal relationship with God which gives fresh perspective.

• *Colossians 1:9-12.* Paul prays that believers will exercise wisdom and insight, and apply what God has revealed of his will to their daily lives. Guided by revelation, the obedient Christian will bear fruit in every good work and, in the process, will come to know God better and better in a personal, experiential way.

• *1 John.* Obedience to God's commands (2:3-6,29) and love for others (4:7) demonstrate that we do know God. The Holy Spirit enables us to grasp and respond to God's Word (2:20-23; 4:13).

Medieval woodcut depicting the rebellion of Korah recorded in Numbers 16. The ground swallows up Korah's followers and their tents as Moses and Aaron watch.

Korah [KOHR-uh; "baldness"]. A Levite who led a rebellion against the leadership of Moses and Aaron in the wilderness, about 1448 B.C. **Father:** Izhar. **Sons:** Assir, Elkanah, Abiasaph. **Scripture:** Num. 16.

BACKGROUND

At Kadesh Barnea, Israel rejected God's command to attack Canaan (Num. 14).

The people, unwilling to accept responsibility for their sin and unbelief, criticized Moses. Korah led a group that challenged Moses on three grounds: (1) Since all the people of God are holy, no human leaders are necessary (16:1-3). (2) The privileges of the priesthood should be for all (16:39,40). (3) The failure to take Canaan was the fault of Moses, the leader (16:13,14). *See also* Leader; Priest.

Moses proposed a test. Korah and 250 followers appeared before the tabernacle the next day with censers, to offer incense to God. If God approved of their rebellion, he would accept their offering. But fire from God consumed the 250 who stood before the tabernacle, and the earth opened to swallow the tents and all the possessions of the rebels.

Apparently some sons of Korah did not follow their father in his rebellion. Korahite clans later served God as music leaders in the Jerusalem Temple (1 Chr. 6:37).

LEARNING FROM KORAH'S LIFE

It is a natural human tendency to grumble and to blame leaders when things go wrong. Yet Israel had godly, exceptional leaders in Moses and Aaron. This time the fault was in the people, who stubbornly refused to submit to God and to the leaders God gave them. Before we follow Korah's example and seek some theological excuse to challenge our leaders, we need to examine our own attitudes and personal relationship with God. All too often the fault lies not in our leaders but in ourselves.

L

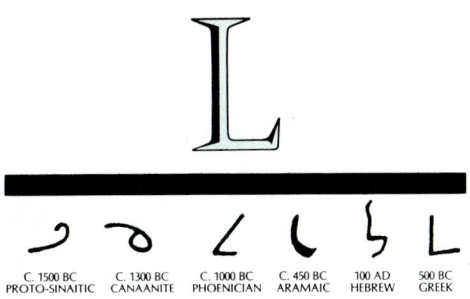

C. 1500 BC PROTO-SINAITIC   C. 1300 BC CANAANITE   C. 1000 BC PHOENICIAN   C. 450 BC ARAMAIC   100 AD HEBREW   500 BC GREEK

Laban [LAY-buhn; "white," "pale"]. The greedy and deceitful uncle and father-in-law of Jacob, whom Jacob served in Haran for 20 years, about 1930–1910 B.C. **Grandfather:** Nahor, Abram's brother. **Sister:** Rebekah, Isaac's wife and mother of Jacob. **Scripture:** Gen. 29–31.

BACKGROUND

Abram's brother Nahor had stayed in Haran while Abram, following God's call, continued on to Canaan. In Haran, Nahor's family assimilated into Aramean culture (Gen. 28:5), taking up their language (Gen. 31:47) and also adopting the local religion (Gen. 31:19; *but see* v. 53). The two branches of the family kept in contact, however, and both Isaac and Jacob sought wives among these relatives.

Laban, the great-nephew of Abraham, was a grasping, selfish man. Scripture's first image of Laban portrays his excitement at rich gifts Abram's servant brought when seeking a bride for Isaac (Gen. 24:29-32). Years later Laban welcomes his nephew Jacob, but makes him work seven years to win the hand of his daughter Rachel in marriage. He then deceitfully puts his older daughter, Leah, into the bridal chamber, so he can claim seven more years of service from Jacob in exchange for Rachel. Laban continues to trick and to cheat his nephew by breaking agreements and changing Jacob's wages ten times (Gen. 31:41).

Ultimately God tricks the trickster (Gen. 30:25-43), and gives Jacob the larger portion of the flocks he supervised for Laban. Convinced that he will never be treated fairly by his father-in-law, Jacob quietly flees the country with his wives, children, and herds.

Laban pursues. By custom Laban owned Jacob's family and flocks and had a right to claim them. And Rachel had stolen the household gods, possession of which represented a legal claim to inheritance of family property. But God warned Laban in a dream against harming Jacob. Laban must have watched in great anguish as Jacob went on toward Canaan with flocks and herds Laban had recently counted his own.

The OT reports no further contact between the two branches of Terah's family.

LEARNING FROM LABAN'S LIFE

Like many people today, Laban used people and valued possessions. This is the reverse of God's value system, which calls us to value people and use possessions.

The biblical text shows us the results of a Laban-like value system. (1) The user, who puts gain first and persons second, loses the affection of those who are closest to him. When Jacob consulted Rachel and Leah about fleeing to Canaan, they spoke bitterly of Laban. "Do we still have any share in the inheritance of our father's estate? Does he not regard us as foreigners? Not only has he sold us, but he has used up what was paid for us" (Gen. 31:14,15).

(2) The user, who seeks his own advantage at the expense of others, so violates trust that no one will deal honestly with him. Jacob explained his decision to flee secretly: "I was afraid, because I thought you would take your daughters away from me by force" (Gen. 31:31).

(3) In the end, the user loses rather than gains. In this case, God showed Jacob how to trick the trickster, and Jacob was able to legally transfer most of Laban's wealth to himself (Gen. 30:25-43). A person who relies on fraud or deceit not only loses the love and loyalty of others, but will not even keep the wealth for which he sacrificed them.

labor Usually toil, difficult or exhausting work in contrast to productive, satisfying work. Several Hebrew words for work suggest productive and meaningful exertion that satisfies the worker and serves others, but other Hebrew words portray a dark aspect of toil.

Work is never fun when it is pointless,   *615*

Laban's relationship with his nephew Jacob disintegrated because Jacob's speckled and spotted flock increased greatly through his shrewd breeding practices (Gen. 29).

and *'amal* captures this sense. When the psalmist declares, "Unless the Lord builds the house, its builders labor in vain" (Ps. 127:1), he uses *'amal*. The pessimistic Preacher of Ecclesiastes uses the word regularly to express the meaninglessness of all human pursuits "under the sun" (*see* Eccl. 2:10,11).

Labor can wear you out. The Hebrew *yaga'* could be translated "wearying effort" or "toil." The Lord told the Israelites, "I gave you a land on which you did not toil" (Josh. 24:13), reminding them that they did not have to slave over the land to eat from its crops. Proverbs uses *yaga'* to say, "Do not wear yourself out to get rich" (Prov. 23:4).

The regular words for labor, work, or service are *'abad* and *'abodah*. Although these words can refer to any work, including the work of priests in the tabernacle or Temple, or any form of serving the Lord, they are also used for "hard labor." Often when an enemy was conquered, its citizens were forced into compulsory labor. The Israelites' work in Egypt is described this way (Ex. 1:13,14).

The Greek NT also has several root words for labor. When Paul laid down the law against Thessalonian freeloaders—"If a man will not work, he shall not eat" (2 Th. 3:10)—he used the verb form of the most common—*ergon*. But two verses earlier he used two stronger words: "We worked night and day, with labor [*kopos*] and toil [*mochthos*] so that we would not be a burden to anyone" (2 Th. 3:8). While *ergon* denotes any kind of work or service, *kopos* and especially *mochthos* indicate the exertion involved. Paul encourages the Corinthians, "Always give yourselves fully to the work [*ergon*] of the Lord, because you know that your labor [*kopos*] in the Lord is not in vain" (1 Cor. 15:58).

In general, both OT and NT recognize that labor can be difficult, and sometimes pointless. Yet they urge believers to labor for what is good, and not to grow weary (Gal. 6:9,10). *See also* Work.

"Labor," in English, also refers to birth pangs, though entirely different Greek and Hebrew words are used. It is an important scriptural image. Isaiah speaks of labor pains on several occasions, usually describing the immensity of physical pain. Paul brings out the sense of waiting—labor pains hurt, but they also precede a good thing about to happen. He tells the Galatians he is "in the pains of childbirth until Christ be formed in you" (Gal. 4:19). And he says that all creation "has been groaning as in the pains of childbirth," awaiting the full revelation of God's glory (Rom. 8:22). *See also* Travail.

Lachish [LAY-kish]. An important city during Canaanite and Israelite times, about 25 miles (40 kilometers) southwest of Jerusalem. The ruins of Lachish (Tell ed-Duweir) have produced more evidence relating to literacy in ancient times than any other site in Palestine. The ancient city is also mentioned in archaeological finds from Egypt and Assyria.

In Egypt, archaeologists have found a substantial collection of diplomatic correspondence from the reign of Pharaoh Akhenaten, dating to the 14th century B.C. This includes letters from two kings of Lachish. The Canaanite city was destroyed by Joshua (Josh. 10:31-33), and lay in ruins through the times of the judges. *See also* Amarna Letters.

King Rehoboam of Judah rebuilt and fortified Lachish in the 920s B.C. as a defense against Egypt (2 Chr. 11:5-10). Archaeological evidence suggests the city was taken by Pharaoh Shishak, who successfully invaded Judah about 925 B.C. (2 Chr. 12:1-12). In 701 B.C., during the reign of Hezekiah, Lachish was taken by Sennacherib of Assyria. The siege of Lachish is the theme of decorations carved into the walls of a palace Sennacherib later constructed to celebrate his victories.

Later the city was rebuilt to serve as a defensive stronghold against the Babylonians. It was destroyed with Jerusalem, the only other fortified city remaining in Judah, in the 590s B.C. (Jer. 34:7). The famous "Lachish Letters" date from this period. These 21 documents are written in black ink on fragments of pottery jars. Most are addressed to the military commander of the city, Ya'osh. They give insight into the political and military situation during the Babylonian invasion of Judah. They also provide important information on the development of Hebrew writing.

Above: One of the Lachish letters, from about 590 B.C. Letter 4, written from an outpost of Lachish, ends, "We are looking for the signals of Lachish. . . . We do not see Azekah." Left: When Nebuchadnezzar besieged Jerusalem in the days of Jeremiah, Lachish and Azekah were the only fortified towns left in Judah (Jer. 34:6,7).

Above: This Lachish inscription, Bat Melek ("king's daughter"), dates from the 8th century B.C.

Left: Aerial view of Tell ed-Duweir, which archaeologist William Albright identified as the site of ancient Lachish.

Stained glass rendering of Jesus' famous parable in Lk. 15:3-7 depicts the lost sheep as a helpless lamb.

Egyptian warriors mounted on a two-wheeled scaling ladder. Saqqara, Egypt, 2750–2625 B.C.

ladder, Jacob's (KJV) The steps between earth and heaven which Jacob saw in a vision (Gen. 28:12). The Hebrew word *sullam* comes from a word for "piling up." It was sometimes used for the steps alongside a building which led to the roof. Thus many modern versions translate it "stairway." Perhaps Jacob, resting on the rocky terrain, envisioned a step-like heap of stones on which angels were ascending and descending.

Ladders were, however, used in the ancient Middle East, from Mesopotamia to Egypt. Farmers used them to pick fruit, builders to work on tall buildings, and soldiers to scale walls of besieged cities.

lake of fire (KJV) An image of eternal punishment found in Rev. 19–21. The Bible often associates fire with God's judgment (Dan. 7:10), sometimes emphasizing purification, but often just the awful pain of such punishment. By Jesus' time, Jewish writings had depicted a place of eternal judgment, where the fires could not be quenched. The word they used was Gehenna, derived from the name for the Valley of Hinnom, where children had been sacrificed in fiery pagan rituals (2 Chr. 28:3). The memories of such depravity burned into the consciousness of the Jews, so that, generations later, they would say, "The judgment of God is like that valley of fire, Gehenna, only worse."

Jesus described the punishment of the lost as the eternal fire of Gehenna, or hell (Mt. 5:22; Mk. 9:43). Revelation further sharpens the image, speaking of hell as a smoldering lake of burning sulfur. Into it, at the end of the age, are thrown all God's enemies. "This is the second death," the text repeats, indicating ultimate separation from God (Rev. 20:10,14). *See also* Fire; Hell.

lamb A young sheep, regularly used in OT sacrifices. In the first Passover, each Israelite household was to kill a lamb and eat its meat (Ex. 12:3). Its blood was put on the doorframes of their houses, to identify the homes of the faithful. The Lord's judgment would "pass over" the houses marked with the lamb's blood.

The lamb thus became a symbol of salvation for Israel. As the Law set out its system of sacrifices, the lamb was to be offered regularly for the sins of the people (Ex. 29:38-41; Lev. 3:7; Num. 29:13-38).

Isaiah 53 enriches the image. This towering messianic prophecy pictures the Servant who wins release for others by suffering as a sheep under the slaughterer's knife.

He was led like a lamb to the slaughter,
and as a sheep before her shearers is silent,
so he did not open his mouth. . . .
because he poured out his life unto death,
and was numbered with the transgressors.
For he bore the sin of many,
and made intercession for the
transgressors. (Isa. 53:7,12)

The NT presents Jesus as the fulfillment of this prophecy (Acts 8:32-35). John the Baptist introduced him, saying, "Look, the Lamb of God who takes away the sin of the world!" (Jn. 1:29). He was slain at Passover, though he was innocent. He was silent before his accusers; prayed for the murderers; and no bones were broken. Peter wrote later that believers are redeemed "with the precious blood of Christ, a lamb without blemish or defect" (1 Pet. 1:19).

The helplessness of lambs underscores a couple of biblical references. Jesus sent out his disciples "like lambs among wolves" (Lk. 10:3) and later urged Peter to provide leadership: "Feed my lambs" (Jn. 21:15).

But in the person of Jesus, this helplessness undergoes a marvelous turnaround. The Book of Revelation calls Jesus "the Lamb" 28 times, but not as a sufferer. This Lamb is the Lord of history, conqueror of all his foes. The one who bent his back and silently suffered a humiliating death is now fully revealed, clothed in splendor and might (Rev. 5:6-14), about to pour out the divine wrath on a rebellious humanity (6:15,16), and welcoming believers to his triumphant wedding feast (19:9).

> **Lamech** [LAY-mek; "strong youth"]. A significant descendant of Cain; his sons founded metalworking and musical guilds, and launched the nomadic life-style, prior to the Genesis Flood. **Father:** Methushael. **Sons:** Jabal, Jubal, Tubal-Cain. **Daughter:** Naamah. **Scripture:** Gen. 4:18-26.

BACKGROUND

Little is known of individuals who lived between the time of Adam and Eve and the Flood. Stories are told only about Cain, Lamech, and Noah. In each case the story develops the theme of sin introduced in Gen. 3. The impact of spiritual death, our heritage from Adam and Eve, is demonstrated in Cain's murderous rage at his brother. It is further seen in Lamech, whose children represent strides in the development of civilization, but who violates the divine ideal of monogamous marriage and engages in a twisted attempt to justify the murder of a man who did him some unnamed injury.

LEARNING FROM LAMECH'S LIFE

In Lamech's time civilization, represented by metalworking and music, and by new social inventions like the nomadic life-style, developed and became more complex. Yet the quality of life deteriorated; morality declined.

The true measure of a society is not material, but moral. Any civilization that disregards biblical morality will, despite its other accomplishments, fall.

lament To mourn, to express deep sorrow, grief, horror, or contrition. A dozen different Hebrew words are translated "lament" in English versions. Some of these words convey vivid visual impressions, of beating the breast or sitting in the dirt wearing unwashed mourning garments. Amos 5:16,17 portrays God's people lamenting in the coming day of his judgment:

"There will be wailing in all the streets
and cries of anguish in every public square.
The farmers will be summoned to weep
and the mourners to wail.
There will be wailing in all the vineyards,
for I will pass through your midst,"

> *says the Lord.*

Public lamentation was common in Hebrew life. It was stimulated by a variety of happenings, such as death or national calamity, war, plague, or national conviction of sin. Against the background of Israel's deeply emotional and open response to such events, it is not surprising that the Hebrews wrote dirge poems, such as are found in the Book of Lamentations, and even developed a special musical rhythm (*qinah*) for use with laments. *See also* Mourn.

Lamentations, Book of This short book, whose title means "Funeral Songs," expresses in five poetic dirges or laments the anguish experienced by the Hebrew exiles in Babylon.

BACKGROUND

In 586 B.C. Nebuchadnezzar put an end to the rebellious little kingdom of Judah.

The Hebrew word for lament literally means "howl" or "wail." This Philistine cult figurine from Hazor (11th century B.C.) displays a posture of lament in ancient times.

He attacked Jerusalem, destroyed the holy city and its Temple, and transported most of the remaining population of Judah to Babylon.

Stunned, the Jews at last realized how much they had lost. The city and Temple of their God lay in ruins, and they themselves were cut off from the land the Lord had promised the descendants of Abraham, Isaac, and Jacob.

The author of Lamentations expresses the despair felt by Jewish captives as they contrasted the former glory of Zion with its present state, and mourned their loss.

Lamentations was probably written shortly after the events it bewails. The realistic description of conditions during the siege of Jerusalem suggests an eyewitness account, and the book's tone of intense mourning suggests a grief which has not yet been resolved.

Written from the perspective of a witness to the fall of Jerusalem, Lamentations itself names no author. One tradition holds that the prophet Jeremiah journeyed to Babylon sometime after being taken to Egypt by the Jews following the death of Gedaliah, and there Jeremiah wrote this book. Arguments in support of this view mention linguistic similarities between Lamentations and the Book of Jeremiah, and the emotional congruity between Lamentations and the character of the man often called Scripture's "weeping prophet."

THEOLOGICAL CONTRIBUTIONS

The Books of Ezekiel and Jeremiah, as well as the writings of the earlier prophets, explain the deportation of the Jews as a divine judgment. They also offer the exiles hope for a future restoration of their relationship with God and return to their homeland. Theological questions and doubts about the meaning of God's apparent abandonment are thus resolved in the prophetic books.

But theology is more than a matter of the head. It is also a matter of the heart. The Jews needed to work through the recent disaster emotionally as well as intellectually. They needed to admit responsibility, recognizing the immensity of the problems their sin had caused. Only then could the Jews rebuild their confidence in God and experience a resurgence of hope. As Lamentations says,

O Daughter of Zion, your punishment will
*   end;*
* he will not prolong your exile.*
But, O Daughter of Edom, he will punish
*   your sin*
* and expose your wickedness.*   (Lam. 4:22)

Lamentations is essentially theology of the heart. It is an aid, in dirge or lament form, to help the people of Judah emotionally process the destruction of their homeland and confess their own sin, so that through this experience they might recover hope.

MASTERY KEYS

Feel the deep sense of loss and the grief of the exiles in Babylon. Note the contrast between the Zion that was, and the Zion that is. Note, too, the way the poem helps readers to confess sin and accept responsibility for the disaster that has stricken the homeland (Lam. 5:15,16).

SPECIAL FEATURES

Each chapter is a separate poem. The first four are acrostic poems: Each succeeding verse begins with the next letter of the 22-consonant Hebrew alphabet. Chapter 3 gives three verses to each of the 22 letters. This is a feature common in Hebrew poetry, and may have been used to aid memorization or simply for visual effect.

The recurring phrase "daughter of Zion" or "daughter of Jerusalem" refers to the cities of Judah and their entire populations.

LAMENTATIONS: A READING AND STUDY GUIDE

Chapter	Content Summary	Related Articles
1	Jerusalem is destroyed. All her splendor has departed. The city has sinned greatly, and now she weeps.	Exile Jerusalem
2	God has been angry with Jerusalem. The city weeps over the suffering of her people, whose hearts cry out to God.	Lament Suffer
3	The eyewitness remembers his affliction, but remembers that the Lord redeems, and will judge Judah's enemies.	Redeem Enemy
4	Life seems empty and meaningless in view of the suffering of the people of Jerusalem.	Sin Judgment
5	In disgrace, dependent on others, Judah must call on God to remember his people, to strengthen and restore them.	Remember

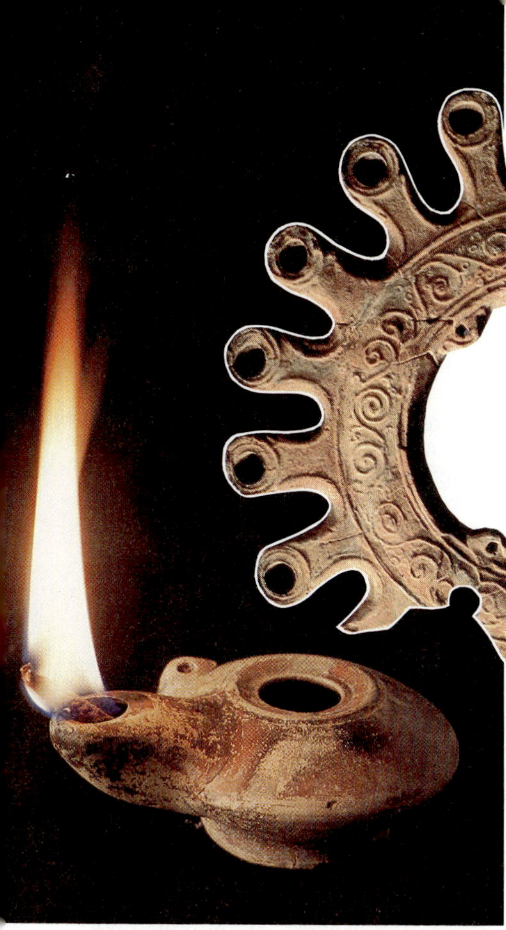

Left: Oil lamp from the era of Greek or Hellenistic ascendancy.

Left: This Roman, multi-spouted lamp would have hung in a great hall or palace.

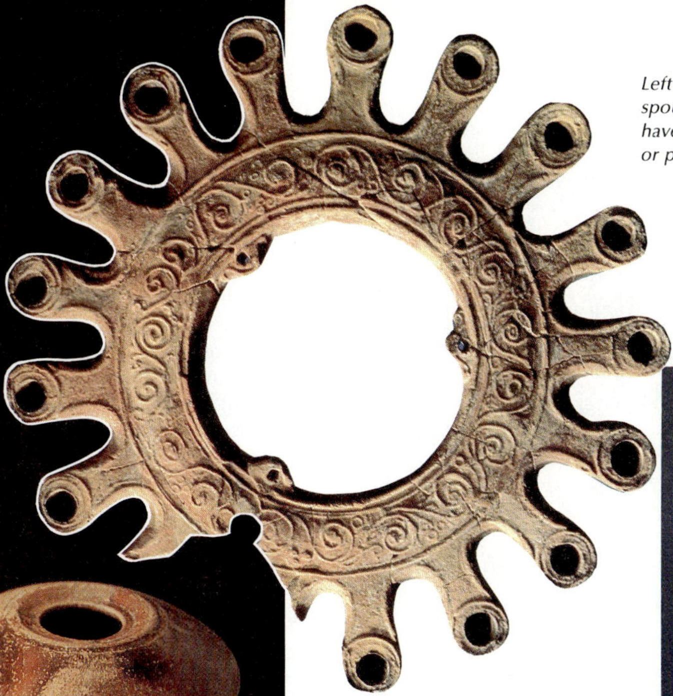

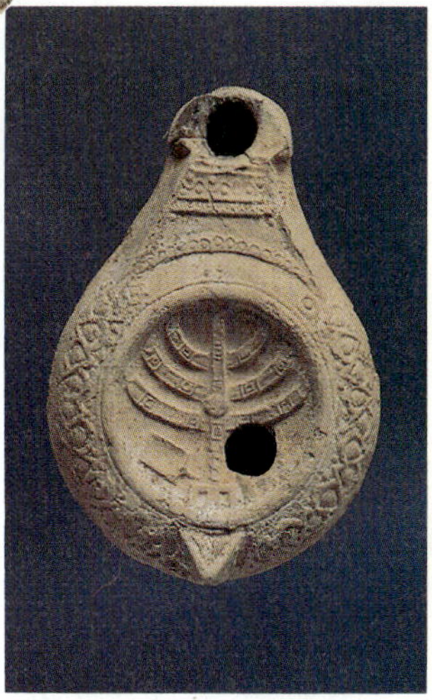

Above: This lamp from the Roman period (second-third centuries B.C.) is decorated with the Jewish menorah *or branched lampstand.*

lamp A small oil-burning vessel like a cup or deep saucer, with one or more wicks, used to light homes and other buildings. The familiar "candle" of the KJV is actually the common pottery lamp.

Lamps were kept burning at night in Hebrew homes, and a darkened residence indicated abandonment (Job 18:5,6; Prov. 31:18). Lamps were placed in niches in walls, or sometimes on stands.

Archaeologists have unearthed thousands of ancient lamps, some going back to the third or fourth millennium B.C. Because the form of lamps changed over the centuries, lamps from Bible times can be dated accurately.

In Scripture, God's Word is called a "lamp to my feet and light for my path" (Ps. 119:105). Lamps also stand for life itself (Prov. 24:20) and even for David, whom his men saw as the "lamp of Israel" (2 Sam. 21:17).

Jesus speaks of the "lamp of the body" as the eye—it allows light to give us sight (Mt. 6:22,23; Lk. 11:34-36). The ten virgins in Jesus' parable about his Second Coming were to bring lamps filled with oil to light the way of the wedding procession (Mt. 25:1-13). Five brought along jars of oil, while five expected to fill their lamps from someone else's store. The five who were unprepared for the bridegroom's appearance were locked out of the celebration and represent those who are not watching for the Lord's joyous return.

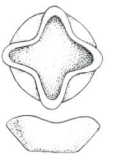

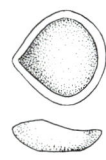

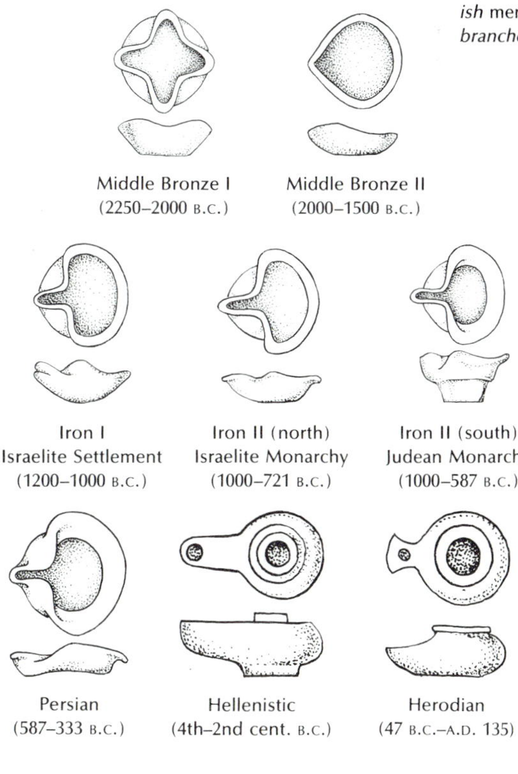

Middle Bronze I
(2250–2000 B.C.)
Middle Bronze II
(2000–1500 B.C.)
Iron I
Israelite Settlement
(1200–1000 B.C.)
Iron II (north)
Israelite Monarchy
(1000–721 B.C.)
Iron II (south)
Judean Monarchy
(1000–587 B.C.)
Persian
(587–333 B.C.)
Hellenistic
(4th–2nd cent. B.C.)
Herodian
(47 B.C.–A.D. 135)

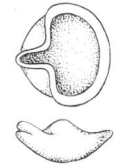

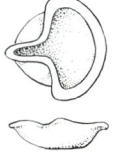

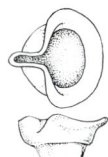

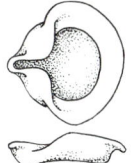

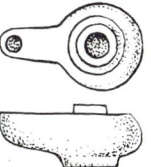

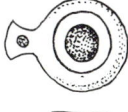

lampstand [Heb., *menorah*]. The branched golden stand placed in the tabernacle, and later the Temple, to support lamps. In 2 Ki. 4:10, a household lampstand is intended.

Exodus 25:31-40 describes the tabernacle lampstand as having six branches, three on each side of a central shaft. Seven oil lamps of pure gold were placed on the stand, to light the outer room of the tabernacle. The ten golden lampstands placed in Solomon's Temple are not described (1 Ki. 7:49). When the Temple was rebuilt after the Babylonian Captivity, a single golden lampstand with seven lamps was again used (Zech. 4:2). A famous illustration on the Arch of Titus in Rome shows a branched *menorah* being carried from Jerusalem.

Seven golden lampstands appear in John's vision of Christ, reported in Revelation. These represent seven churches in Asia to whom the Lord sends instruction by John (Rev. 1:20). Later in Revelation, the two faithful witnesses who preach in Jerusalem during the days of divine judgment are likened to lampstands (Rev. 11:4).

lascivious (KJV) Wanton, licentious. The Greek word means unrestrained greed, or an animal-like indulgence in any passionate desire. Lasciviousness appears in several lists of immoral behavior (Mk. 7:22; Gal. 5:19). Paul describes its nature well: "Having lost all sensitivity, they have given themselves over to sensuality [lasciviousness, KJV] so as to indulge in every kind of impurity, with a continual lust for more" (Eph. 4:19).

last days The final era of human history. When NT Epistles say that the readers were living then in the "last days" (2 Tim. 3:1; Heb. 1:2; 2 Pet. 3:3; 1 Jn. 2:18), the expression is used in the metaphorical sense of "epoch" or "era." Paul, Peter, John, and the writer of Hebrews all see the Christian era as the last great epoch before God brings history to an end. *See also* Day.

Last Supper The meal Jesus shared with his disciples the night before his crucifixion, reported in Jn. 13–17. *See also* Lord's Supper.

latchet (KJV) The leather strap which fastened the sandal to the foot (Gen. 14:23; Isa. 5:27). *See also* Sandal.

laughter In biblical times laughter did not indicate amusement, but expressed (1) mockery, or derision (Gen. 38:23; Mt. 9:24); (2) joy (Gen. 21:6; Ps. 126:2); and even (3) embarrassed uncertainty or doubt (Gen. 17:17). At times (4) individuals are portrayed as laughing at danger, an image of fearlessness (Job 5:22; 39:18).

Both Abraham and Sarah laughed when God announced they would have a son together (Gen. 17:17; 18:12). Yet only Sarah was rebuked (Gen. 18:13-15). The most likely explanation is that Sarah's laughter was mocking while Abraham's was an embarrassed expression of his uncertainty and surprise.

While the wicked ridicule God and believers with derisive laughter, the Lord laughs derisively at them (Ps. 2:4). They will awake too late to the reality of their plight (Lk. 6:25).

laver (KJV, RSV) A large bronze basin filled with water, in which the priests who ministered at the altar washed themselves (Ex. 30:17-21). Ten lavers plus a larger molten "sea" of water stood in the courtyard of Solomon's Temple (1 Ki. 7:27-39). These highly decorated lavers rested on wheeled stands and were movable.

The symbolic meaning of lavers is suggested in Eph. 5:26 and Tit. 3:5, which speak of cleansing and renewal. Old Testament priests washed themselves outwardly, and were physically pure. Christians are to be purified and cleansed within.

law In the OT [Heb., *torah*], divine instruction, given by God to show Israel how to live in covenant relationship with the Lord. The word "law" in the OT may indicate (1) God's revelation in general, including historical narrative and interpretation as well as statutes, ordinances, precepts, and commandments; (2) the five books of Moses; (3) specific instruction, such as the law governing the Passover or the conduct of war; (4) ceremonial rules for the conduct of worship; and (5) social and moral standards. For information on civil law in biblical times, *see* Government, Human; Hammurabi, Code of.

In the NT [Gk., *nomos*], fundamental principles. Although the NT usually uses "law" in an OT sense, referring to the specific revelation or commands of God, Paul occasionally expands it to include the general Greek meaning of a principle of nature (Rom. 7:21). Paul also uses "law" in a very specific sense, setting it apart from "grace" or "spirit." In this sense he means the Mosaic system as a way of earning favor with God (Rom. 6:14).

COVENANT CONTEXT OF OT LAW

God's covenant with Israel provides the framework within which we must read and understand all OT concepts, including that of law. A "covenant" is a formal commitment or contract defining the relationship between two or more parties. Old Testament revelation is rooted in God's decision to establish a special, redemptive relationship with human beings, and to

formalize that choice in legal, covenant form. *See also* Covenant.

God revealed himself to Abraham and made a covenant with him (Gen. 12). The covenant was passed on to his descendants and powerfully ratified in the events of the Exodus.

At Sinai, on the way to their Promised Land, the Israelites were given a "law"—a well-defined moral, social, and religious code of action, specifying how God expects those in covenant relationship with him to live.

This Law of Moses, or Law covenant, must be interpreted in relation to the existing Abrahamic covenant. Mosaic Law did not show Israel how to gain relationship with God. A covenant relationship between God and Israel already existed. Mosaic Law simply showed Israel how to experience fellowship with God within that existing relationship. Mosaic Law also specified what God would do when his people were obedient, and what he would do if they disobeyed. *See also* Deuteronomy.

In the OT, the salvation of individuals was a matter for faith, not for Mosaic Law. Abraham had believed God, and his faith was counted for righteousness (Gen. 15:6). Paul shows in Rom. 4 that the faith response to God has always been the way to salvation for the individual, whether a person is one of the covenant people or not. In OT times, people of faith responded positively to God's Law, and obeyed it out of love for God. With David, OT saints could cry,

Praise be to you, O Lord;
  teach me your decrees.
With my lips I recount
  all the laws that come from your mouth.
I rejoice in following your statutes
  as one rejoices in great riches.
I meditate on your precepts
  and consider your ways.
I delight in your decrees;
  I will not neglect your word.
                          (Ps. 119:12-16)

Conversely, the person in Israel without a saving faith turned his back on God and the Law, viewing it as a burden rather than a delight.

ANALYSIS OF MOSAIC LAW

Some Mosaic material is stated in the form of general principles, like the Ten Commandments. Other material is in the form of "case law." That is, a specific situation is described and a ruling given: "If a man uncovers a pit or digs one and

The famous Code of Hammurabi (1792–1750 B.C.) contains 282 laws, which are engraved on this black basalt stela found at Susa.

Archaeologists are uncertain about the design of the ten bronze lavers or basins used in the Temple sacrifices. The stands they sat on, however, may have resembled this Phoenician-style stand from Cyprus.

623

Pentateuch scroll case (Heb., tik) from Baghdad, Iraq, 1852. In each local synagogue the Law scroll is kept in such a case and placed at the foot of the sanctuary in an alcove called the "ark."

aspect of religious, personal, social, and national life. Generally, however, it is helpful in thinking about OT Law to break it down into codes and categories.

CODES OF OT LAW

The "codes" are large, distinct blocks of legislation.

1. *The Ten Commandments,* the fundamental code in Mosaic Law, state principles which lie at the heart of a healthy relationship with God and with others (Ex. 20:1-17; Deut. 5:6-21). *See also* Commandments, Ten.

2. *The Covenant Code* or the *Book of the Covenant* (Ex. 20:22–23:33) contains a variety of regulations concerning the way Israel is to live when settled in Canaan, and often takes a case law approach.

3. *The Deuteronomic Code* is an extended description of God's way of life for Israel (Deut. 12–26). It sums up law and history in view of covenant love, reviews elements of earlier codes, and discusses issues they omit.

4. *The Priestly Code* deals with such ritual issues as the offering of sacrifices by the priests and their inspection of the land and people for physical and ritual uncleanliness (Lev. 1–16).

5. *The Code of Holiness* gives detailed instructions on many technical matters relating to ritual cleanliness (Lev. 17–26). Holiness in this code is both moral and cultic. The passage is often punctuated with the command, "Be holy because I, the Lord your God, am holy" (Lev. 19:1).

JESUS CHRIST AND MOSAIC LAW

As a Jew, Jesus lived under the Law that God had given his covenant people. He supported and obeyed that Law, insisting that "not the smallest letter, not the least stroke of a pen, will by any means disappear from the Law until everything is accomplished" (Mt. 5:18). In the same context Jesus insisted that he came to "fulfill" the Law and the prophets (5:17).

To understand this claim we need to review his contemporaries' view of Moses' Law. Over the centuries various interpretations of the Law had been added to the religious literature of Judaism. These often-added regulations were intended to protect the pious Jew from unintentionally violating any Mosaic statute or ruling. By Jesus' time this "oral law" was considered to be as binding as Scripture itself. Some even argued that God had given both oral and written law to Moses at Sinai.

Jesus came into conflict with the Pharisees and teachers of the Law because he

fails to cover it and an ox or a donkey falls into it, the owner of the pit must pay for the loss" (Ex. 21:33,34). In most instances, case laws are drawn from previously established principles; for example, the case law ruling "Do not have sexual relations with your father's sister" is a direct application of the principle prohibiting all marital unfaithfulness.

Typically neither principle law nor case law is rigidly organized in the OT, so that rules for sexual behavior, for judging civil cases, for dealing with foreigners, for making a sacrifice, etc., may all be found in a single passage (Lev. 19).

Another aspect of Mosaic Law which makes analysis difficult is the fact that it does not easily fall into categories like civil or criminal law. The OT views life holistically, so Law quite naturally covers every

rejected the authority of this tradition, and proceeded to give his own, sometimes striking interpretation of the OT. When Jesus said that he came to "fulfill" the Law, he used that term as any rabbi would. Jesus intended to give a full and accurate explanation of the true meaning of the divine revelation! Since Jesus' exposition of the Law contradicted many notions held by the current religious leadership, conflict was inevitable.

In reading the Gospels, we need to remember that in them "law" sometimes means the entire OT revelation, as in Jn. 10:34; 12:34. Sometimes it means the Law given by Moses, as in Jn. 7:19,23. And sometimes "law" means the system of governing society adopted by the Jews of Jesus' day, which mixed both divine guidelines and mere human traditions, as in Jn. 7:51; 18:31 (see Jn. 8:15).

The main point made by Jesus in reinterpreting the Law for his generation is simple: God is not only concerned with a person's behavior but also with a person's heart. Any righteousness the legal zealot might achieve is insignificant. So, "Unless your righteousness surpasses that of the Pharisees and the teachers of the law, you will certainly not enter the kingdom of heaven" (Mt. 5:20). God cares not only about the act of murder, but also about the anger that stimulates it (Mt. 5:21,22). God is concerned not only with the act of adultery, but with the lust that precedes it (Mt. 5:27,28). The righteousness God requires thus demands inner transformation, to make the angry compassionate and the lustful loving. The Law, far from being a highway to holiness, is a mirror that reflects man's need for God's forgiveness and his purifying work within. So the Pharisee in Jesus' parable, confident in his self-righteousness, who thanks God that he is "not like other men—robbers, evildoers, adulterers," leaves the Temple a stranger to the Lord. But the tax collector, grieved by his failures, appeals for mercy and leaves the Temple justified before God (Lk. 18:9-14).

In essence, then, Jesus sought to restore an emphasis that shines so clearly in Deuteronomy. Law guides the response of a person who already loves God, but Law cannot help a sinful person win the approval of Israel's Holy One.

Jesus' reinterpretation of Law, restoring a perspective lost by many in Judaism, led to a thorough rethinking of the nature and function of Law in the early church, especially by the apostle Paul.

Ezra reading the Law, painted on the wall of a third-century synagogue in Syria.

SEVEN CATEGORIES OF MOSAIC LAW

I. Leadership Law

Qualifications	Deut. 23:1-3
Royalty	Deut. 17:14-20
Civil, religious judges	Deut. 17:8-13
Court system	Ex. 23:6-9; Deut. 16:18-20
Witnesses	Ex. 23:1-3; Deut. 17:6; 19:15-19
Enforcement	Deut. 13:9,10; 17:12,13
Prophets	Deut. 18:14-22

II. Military Law

Military service	Num. 31:3-6; Deut. 17:16; 23:9-14
Exemptions	Num. 1:48,49; Deut. 20:5-8; 24:5
Enemies outside Palestine	Deut. 20:10-15
Enemies within Palestine	Deut. 20:16-18

III. Criminal Law

Crimes against God	
Idolatry	Ex. 22:20; Deut. 13:1-18
Occult practices	Deut. 18:9-14
Human sacrifice	Lev. 20:2-5
Blasphemy	Lev. 24:16
Sabbath-breaking	Ex. 35:2,3
Sexual crimes	
Fornication	Deut. 22:13-21
Adultery	Lev. 20:10-12; Deut. 22:22-24
Homosexuality	Lev. 20:13
Prostitution	Lev. 19:29; 21:9
Incest	Lev. 20:11-14
Bestiality	Ex. 22:19; Deut. 27:21
Personal injury crimes	
Murder	Ex. 21:12-14; Num. 35:16-34
Assault	Ex. 21:18-27; Deut. 25:11,12
Rape	Deut. 22:25-29
Oppression	Ex. 22:21-24; Deut. 27:18,19
Kidnapping	Ex. 21:16; Deut. 24:7
Perjury	Ex. 23:1; Lev. 19:16
Property-related crimes	
Theft	Ex. 22:1-3; Lev. 19:35,36
Fraud	Lev. 6:1-7; Deut. 25:13-16

continued

IV. Laws of Humane Treatment

Of land and animals

Crop rotation	Ex. 23:11,12; Lev. 25:3-7
Feeding and care	Deut. 25:4; Ex. 20:8-11

Of persons

The helpless	Ex. 22:21-23
The poor	Lev. 25:35-37; Deut. 24:10-13
The elderly	Lev. 19:32
Travelers	Deut. 23:24,25
Servants	Lev. 19:13; Deut. 24:14
Slaves	Ex. 21:2-6,20-32
Aliens	Num. 15:13-16,29-31

V. Laws Governing the Family

Marriage

General laws	Lev. 18:6-18; Deut. 27:20-23
Of priests	Lev. 21:7,13-15
Wife's rights	Deut. 21:10-14
Husband's responsibilities	Num. 30:6-15
Divorce	Deut. 24:1-4

Children and parents

Parents' responsibility	Num. 18:15,16; Deut. 6:6,7
Child's responsibility	Ex. 20:12
Parents' authority	Num. 30:3-5

VI. Laws Concerning Property Rights

Damaged property	Ex. 22:7-15
Hazards	Ex. 21:28-36; Deut. 22:8
Land ownership	Lev. 25:1-34
Inheritance	Deut. 21:15-17; Num. 36:1-12

VII. Cultic Law

Concerning priesthood	Lev. 21
Concerning sacrifice	Lev. 1–7
Concerning ritual cleanliness	Lev. 11–15
Concerning the Sabbath	Ex. 20:8-11
Concerning religious festivals	Lev. 23
Concerning other religions	Deut. 7,13
Concerning giving	Deut. 14:22-29
Concerning vows	Lev. 27
Concerning place of worship	Ex. 35–38; Deut. 12
Concerning religious years	Lev. 25

LAW RECONSIDERED IN EPISTLES

The NT's use of *nomos* (law) for a variety of concepts is one reason for confusion about its teachings on this important subject. At times "law" simply means divine revelation. At times "law" is the Mosaic code. At times "law" means a universal principle, as in Paul's description of the principle ("law") of sin and death at work within his personality (Rom. 7:21). At times "law" is a spiritual principle, as in the cry of joy at Paul's discovery that God's Spirit enables him to live a holy life despite his sinfulness (Rom. 8:2). At times "law" represents the Mosaic system as an attitude, or approach to relationship with God. The Mosaic system fails in this last aspect, not because God's moral code is faulty but because human flesh is weak (Rom. 8:3).

If we are to understand the NT's teaching about "law," we must be aware of these various meanings of the word, and carefully trace the thought of the NT writers. As we do, we find three major concepts shape the NT perspective.

1. *Mosaic Law as Revelation: Its Glory.* As revelation, the Mosaic system successfully displays the love, holiness, and grace of God. In its emphasis on justice, the Law displays God's loving concern for every human being. In the Law's provision of sacrifice we see God's grace, inviting the guilty sinner to turn to him for forgiveness and restoration. In its promises, we see God as one who is truly caring, and whose rules are intended to help human beings live whole, happy, and holy lives. The Mosaic Law is successful in its revelatory purpose, for it is an expression of the character of God. As such, Paul affirms Law as "holy, and the commandment is holy, righteous and good" (Rom. 7:12).

The Mosaic Law is also successful in its function of revealing sin. Those who look at the life-style required by the Law's moral code, and reflect honestly on their own attitudes and behavior, are pointed away from works to faith. As Paul observes, "No one will be declared righteous in his sight by observing the law; rather, through the law we become conscious of sin" (Rom. 3:20). The Law which successfully reveals the character of God also successfully reveals the sinful character of human beings.

2. *Mosaic Law and Righteousness: Its Limitations.* There is much Mosaic Law cannot do, and was never intended to do. The apostle Paul pinpoints a number of flaws in contemporary Judaism's understanding of the Law as a moral and religious code.

• *The moral and religious code was never intended to replace faith as a way of salvation.* Abraham and David demonstrate the fact that OT saints were justified by faith. The Mosaic Law was introduced some 400 years after Abraham found a personal relationship with God simply by believing God's promise. Thus the "promise" nature of relationship with God has precedence (Rom. 4; Gal. 3).

• *The Law's moral and religious code is*

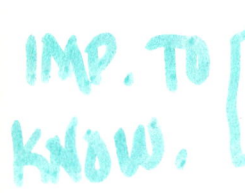
IMP. TO KNOW.

associated with sin, not with righteousness. Paul's statement that the Law is "not for the righteous but for lawbreakers" (1 Tim. 1:9) seems mysterious unless its function of revealing human sinfulness is understood. Just as a child's desire for cookies is increased when Mother says, "Don't touch," so "sinful passions [are] aroused by the law" (Rom. 7:5; see 1 Cor. 15:56). Law's definition of what is right simply cannot produce the righteousness it demands, and in fact stimulates mankind's sinful nature.

So Mosaic Law was intended to point human beings to grace, and bring about the realization that only through some loving, decisive act of God could salvation come (Rom. 3:21-25).

3. *The Old Covenant vs. the New: Law's Replacement.* The Mosaic system was introduced as a temporary expedient, destined to be replaced in God's good time. So says the author of Hebrews, citing Jeremiah as support.

"The time is coming," declares the Lord,
    "when I will make a new covenant
with the house of Israel,
    and with the house of Judah.
It will not be like the covenant
    I made with their forefathers
when I took them by the hand
    to lead them out of Egypt. . . .
This is the covenant I will make with the
        house of Israel
    after that time," declares the Lord.
"I will put my law in their minds
    and write it on their hearts.
I will be their God
    and they will be my people.
No longer will a man teach his neighbor,
    or a man his brother, saying,
        'Know the Lord,'
because they will all know me,
    from the least of them to the greatest,"
                    declares the Lord.
"For I will forgive their wickedness
    and will remember their sins no more."
                    (Jer. 31:31-34; see Heb. 8)

The NT understands the death of Christ as the making of that promised new covenant. The "new" stands in contrast to Mosaic Law and replaces it. Christ's death introduced a new approach to working out the believer's faith-relationship with God, so Paul can say we are "not under law, but under grace" (Rom. 6:14).

Here again we have one of those subtle shifts in the meaning of "law" that makes this teaching so hard for many to understand. Here "law" does not mean the fundamental moral or religious standards expressed in the Mosaic Law, but rather the Mosaic system. To say that we are not under law does not mean that Christians are released from the obligation to live a righteous life, but rather that we will not find righteousness through attempts to keep the detailed instructions of Moses. Paul argues that the death of Christ releases believers from any obligation to the Mosaic system, which failed to produce righteousness. For Christ, by making us alive to God, has made possible a truly righteous life that makes the old system irrelevant (Rom. 6:11-13).

The believer who tries to relate to God through the old system will fail (Rom. 7:1-25), but the believer who relates to God in the new covenant way will discover that "the righteous requirements of the law" are being "fully met" in his life (Rom. 8:1-4).

As Paul explains it, the new covenant way to relate to God is to consciously yield to the Holy Spirit, who will enable us to resist our sinful passions and will empower us to do the will of God (Rom. 8:5-15). The Spirit brings to our lives "love, joy, peace, patience, kindness, goodness, faithfulness, gentleness and self-control." Paul notes, "Against such things there is no law" (Gal. 5:22,23).

Law and the Prophets The OT revelation as a whole. The phrase reflects the Jewish division of the OT into Law, Prophets, and Writings. *See also* Judaism.

lawlessness The active violation of moral principles.

A lawless person is not someone who lacks moral guidance, but one who breaks known laws. The reference in 2 Th. 2:8 to "the lawless one" who will appear prior to Christ's return is generally understood to indicate the Antichrist. *See also* Antichrist.

lawyer A person trained in the law, specifically in the Law of Moses (except perhaps Tit. 3:13). Some modern versions tend to use the phrase, "expert in the law." Luke tends to use "lawyer" where other Gospel writers say "scribe." It is not surprising that Jesus faced opposition from lawyers, since he regularly rebuked them for neglecting justice and hindering those who sought God's Kingdom (Lk. 7:30; 11:45,46; 14:3). *See also* Scribe.

laying on hands *See* Hands, Laying on of.   627

Lazarus [LAZ-uh-ruhs; "God has helped"].
The friend Jesus raised from the dead days after
his burial in Bethany, about A.D. 30. **Sisters:**
Mary, Martha. **Scripture:** Jn. 11,12.

BACKGROUND

Jesus was a good friend of Lazarus,
Mary, and Martha, who lived in Bethany,
a small town less than two miles from
Jerusalem (Mt. 21:17; Lk. 10:38-41; Jn.
11:5,36). When Lazarus became sick, his
sisters sent an urgent message to Jesus.
Jesus did not go to Bethany immediately
and when he finally arrived there, he was
met by a tearful Martha, who told him
Lazarus had been in his tomb for four
days. Jesus spoke of himself as the resurrection and the life, went to the tomb, and
called out to Lazarus. Revived, Lazarus
came out of his tomb, still wrapped in the
linen clothes with which his body had
been prepared for burial.

Although this stunning miracle produced faith in some, it created a sense of
urgency in Jesus' enemies. "If we let him
go on like this," they exclaimed, "everyone will believe in him" (Jn. 11:48). John
adds, "From that day on they plotted to
take his [Jesus'] life" (v. 53).

LEARNING FROM LAZARUS'S LIFE

We know nothing of Lazarus as a person
beyond the fact that Jesus had a deep
affection for him. One tradition suggests
he was 30 when he died, and lived 30
years more after being restored to life.

Yet Lazarus's death became an opportunity for Jesus to display his power, and
Lazarus became a silent but powerful living witness to his Lord. That display of
Jesus' power made Lazarus a catalyst,
deepening the faith of some and the antagonism of others.

We can expect something like this if God
acts in some unusual way in our lives. Our
witness to what God has done will
strengthen the faith of some. But others
will be hardened in unbelief or even opposition. In such cases our mission, like
that of Lazarus, is simply to live out our
witness, and through that witness confront others with the reality of Jesus Christ.

lazy Unwilling to work or exert oneself, slothful. Various proverbs sum up the OT's attitude toward laziness. "Lazy hands make a man poor, but diligent hands bring wealth" (Prov. 10:4). In the NT, laziness is associated with various forms of wicked behavior (Mt. 25:26; Tit. 1:12). Paul instructs the Thessalonians to avoid idleness, establishing a simple rule: "If a man will not work, he shall not eat" (2 Th. 3:10). *See also* Work.

lead, guide (1) Literally, to show the way by going before or with; to conduct, direct. (2) Theologically, God's indication to his people of a course of action, by influencing or providing direction. "Leading" and "guidance" have to do with practical decisions of individual or community life for which there is no clear, determining expression of God's objective will in Scripture.

OLD TESTAMENT

God's active involvement with his people in a leading, guiding role is expressed in a number of Hebrew words: *Nahah* means "to conduct along the right path," as in Ex. 13:21. *Nahag* suggests shepherding, as in Ps. 80:1. *Nahal* means "to lead with care," again suggesting a shepherd's tender supervision of his flock, as in Isa.

The traditional tomb of Lazarus in Bethany.

40:11. *Darak* is active instruction in righteous ways, as in Ps. 25:4,5.

Besides portraying God as one who gives personal guidance to his people, the OT calls for the individual and the nation to actively seek God's guidance. This is expressed in the Hebrew words *darash*, which means "to seek with care," and *sa'al*. The act of inquiry is important. It is an expression of faith that God is (exists) and that he rewards those who earnestly seek him (Heb. 11:6). However, faith must include a willingness to do what God directs in order for guidance to be given (Jn. 7:17; Jas. 1:6,7; *compare* Jer. 42:1–43:13).

Israel was forbidden to use occult methods, such as were practiced by the Canaanites, to obtain supernatural guidance (Deut. 18:9-13). King Saul, for example, was specifically condemned for seeking guidance from a witch at Endor (1 Sam. 28:7-14; 1 Chr. 10:13). Instead, they were to rely on God, who guided in a variety of ways. When Israel acted without God's guidance, trouble and upheaval ensued as when the Gibeonites deceived Israel during the Conquest (Josh. 9:14).

NEW TESTAMENT

The NT reports incidents of guidance by dreams (Mt. 1:20; 2:12,13; Acts 16:9,10) and by prophets in the early church (Acts 11:27; 21:10). Several passages say simply that the Holy Spirit provided guidance, without mentioning the means (Lk. 4:1; Acts 13:2,3; 20:22; Rom. 8:14). Yet, it is clear that individuals are expected to seek and receive divine guidance. *See also* Dreams.

Many aspects of life which were regulated under OT Law are left to individual discretion in the NT. The OT specified clean foods and established holy days. In Rom. 14, Paul argues that such things are now matters of personal conviction and that Christ was raised from the dead to function as Lord in each individual's life. Thus, each person must "be fully convinced in his own mind" as to how he should please God (v. 5). A similar freedom and responsibility is implied in Paul's teaching on giving. The set tithe of the OT is replaced by encouragement to give generously. Yet, "Each man should give what he has decided in his heart to give, not reluctantly or under compulsion" (2 Cor. 9:7,8). Release from a law-ruled life of restrictions and obligations does not release the believer from the obligation to do God's will. Indeed, with freedom comes added responsibility to seek God's guidance for every significant decision in life. 629

SEEKING GOD'S GUIDANCE

There is, however, no easy answer to the questions we typically have concerning guidance. The NT suggests no formula and provides no specific steps for finding the will of God. At the same time, there are guiding principles:

1. *God's objective will is revealed for all persons in the moral teaching of the OT and NT.* No individual will be guided by the Holy Spirit to act contrary to the clearly revealed will of God for all. Accordingly, the better we grasp the nature and moral will of God revealed in the Scriptures, the more we will sense direction in our personal decisions.

2. *Believers are actively to seek God's will.* Prayer is associated with many biblical examples of guidance. Clearly looking to God for guidance is an essential element in experiencing his leading.

3. *Individuals are responsible to discern God's guidance.* While we are to seek advice from spiritual friends and leaders in those personal matters where there is no objective Word from God, each of us is responsible to Christ as our personal Lord and Savior. His Spirit is within us, and he will make God's will known (*compare* Jn. 14:26; 16:13,14; 1 Cor. 2:9,10).

God has promised to take an active part in leading his followers. As he led the children of Israel through the wilderness with a cloud by day and a pillar of fire by night (Ex. 40:36-38), so he promises to lead us.

"I will instruct you and teach you in the way
   you should go;
 I will counsel you and watch over you."
                                  (Ps. 32:8)

leader A person who (1) guides by going before to show the way, (2) has authority to command, (3) guides by influence or persuasion, or (4) is at the head, the first or foremost.

LEADERSHIP IN THE OT WORLD

The Hebrew terms *sar* and *nasi'* indicate anyone elevated to secular or religious influence, as in Lev. 4:22; Num. 7:11. Hebrew *shapat*, "judge," and *melek*, "king," best express the concept of leadership in the OT world—leadership is governmental authority vested in a single person. Even though kings and judges in Israel were subject to God's Law, these leaders had personal authority to command. *See also* Judge; King.

LEADERSHIP IN THE NT WORLD

Rome dominated the world of the NT, and final authority resided in the emperor. The Roman centurion could "tell this one, 'Go,' and he goes; and that one, 'Come,' and he comes" because he was a man "under authority" (Mt. 8:8,9). That is, as one in the military chain of command, the centurion was a representative of Caesar and was obeyed because the emperor had authority. Peter also reflects the view that ruling authority is vested in the person of the leader when he calls for submission to

---

OLD TESTAMENT ILLUSTRATIONS OF GUIDANCE

Genesis 12	God speaks to Abram (possibly in a dream) and sends him to Canaan.
Genesis 24	God leads Abraham's servant by shaping circumstances in answer to prayer.
Genesis 31:10-14	God shows Jacob how to acquire the best of Laban's flock for his own.
Exodus 13:21	God leads with supernatural manifestation of fiery cloud.
Numbers 27:21	Joshua is to obtain guidance by having the high priest use the Urim and Thummim.
Deuteronomy 18:6, 14-19	God promises to give guidance by sending prophets who will speak his Word.
1 Samuel 14:8-10	Jonathan seeks a sign to indicate whether God wants him to attack a Philistine outpost.
1 Samuel 14:41-43	Saul casts lots to determine who is at fault for breaking his vow regarding communal fasting.
1 Samuel 24:4-6	David finds guidance in God's Word and refuses to harm Saul (*compare* Pss. 19:7-14; 119).

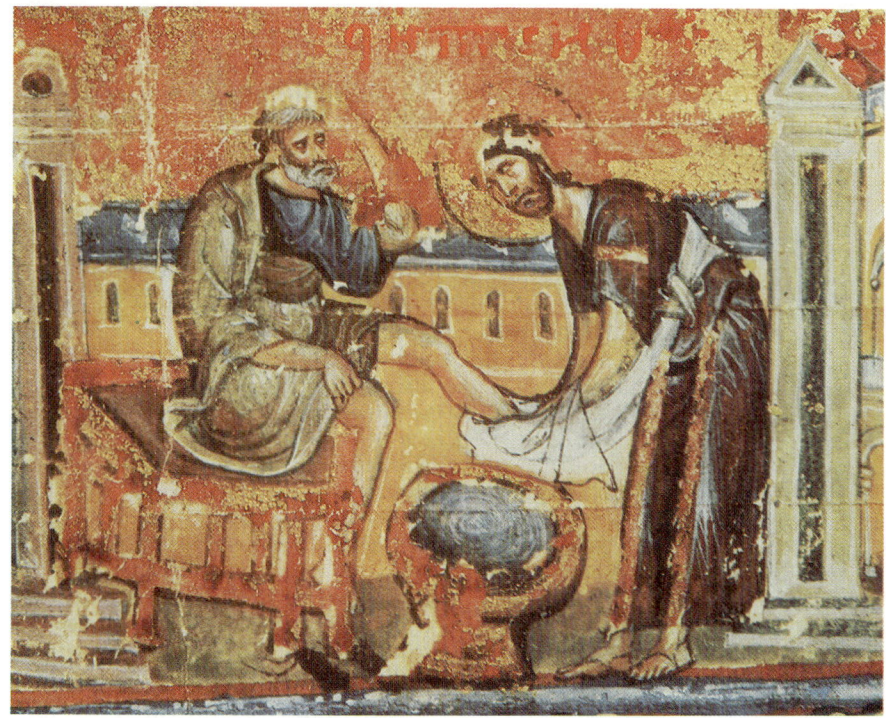

Jesus washes Peter's feet, in this 8th-century illuminated manuscript. The action graphically demonstrates Jesus' teaching on servant leadership.

the king "as the supreme authority, or to governors, who are sent by him to punish those who do wrong" (1 Pet. 2:13,14).

LEADERSHIP IN THE CHURCH

Jesus' teaching about spiritual leadership is striking in view of the cultural concept. Christ said:

"You know that the rulers of the Gentiles lord it over them, and their high officials exercise authority over them. Not so with you. Instead, whoever wants to become great among you must be your servant, and whoever wants to be first must be your slave—just as the Son of Man did not come to be served, but to serve, and to give his life as a ransom for many." (Mt. 20:25-28)

While the religious leadership of Judea claimed authority to command and demand respect as Israel's foremost, Jesus told his disciples:

"You are not to be called 'Rabbi,' for you have only one Master and you are all brothers. And do not call anyone on earth 'father,' for you have one Father, and he is in heaven. Nor are you to be called 'teacher,' for you have one Teacher, the Christ. The greatest among you will be your servant. For whoever exalts himself will be humbled, and whoever humbles himself will be exalted." (Mt. 23:8-12)

These images of spiritual leadership are in stark contrast with secular symbols of elevation and power. The spiritual leader is a servant, not a king; a shepherd, not a commander. The leader seeks "to prepare God's people for works of service" (Eph. 4:12) by providing an example and by teaching (1 Tim. 3:1-12; 4:11-16; 2 Tim. 3:10,14; Tit. 1:5-9; 1 Pet. 5:1-4). In essence, the Christian leader influences others to volunteer to follow Christ. The leader leads in a way to promote commitment to Christ rather than to gain compliance to him or to an institution. *See also* Authority.

While Christian leaders are responsible to lead as servants, believers have responsibilities to their leaders. These include the financial support of full-time leaders (1 Cor. 9:7-14) and treating leaders with respect (1 Th. 5:12,13). Hebrews 13:7 calls on believers to consider the example of leaders and imitate their faith, while Heb. 13:17 calls on believers to respond to the guidance leaders give. *See also* Obey.

> **Leah** [LEE-uh; "wild cow"]. First wife of Jacob, mother of six of his twelve sons, about 1900 B.C. **Father:** Laban. **Sister:** Rachel. **Sons:** Reuben, Simeon, Levi, Judah, Issachar, Zebulun. **Daughter:** Dinah. **Scripture:** Gen. 29–31.

BACKGROUND

Jacob journeyed from Canaan to Paddan Aram to find a wife among his relatives. He fell in love with his cousin Rachel, and contracted with his uncle Laban to work

631

seven years as her bridal price. On the wedding night Laban substituted Rachel's older, unattractive sister, Leah. When the substitution was discovered, Laban promised a furious Jacob he could wed Rachel, too—for another seven years of service.

The marriages predictably led to rivalry between the two sisters, who competed not only for Jacob's affection but for sons with which to win that affection. Both, following established custom of that time, urged Jacob to take their servant girls as secondary wives, so they could claim any children the servants bore as gifts to their husband.

LEARNING FROM LEAH'S LIFE

Leah was a plain girl with a beautiful sister. She must have been deeply sensitive about her looks. Her sense of inferiority was heightened by Jacob's choice of Rachel, and his understandable reaction to the wedding night substitution (Gen. 29:25). Leah also must have felt used by her father, who arranged the substitution not out of concern for her but to wring seven more years of service from Jacob (29:27). After Rachel was also given to Jacob, it was plain that Jacob "loved Rachel more than Leah" (29:30).

At the birth of her sons, Leah expressed her pathetic eagerness to be loved. When her eldest, Reuben, was born, she thought, "The Lord has seen my misery. Surely my husband will love me now" (Gen. 29:32). She viewed her second son, Simeon, as compensation from God, because "I am not loved" (29:33). At the birth of Levi, she still hoped. "Now at last my husband will become attached to me, because I have borne him three sons" (29:34). Finally with Judah she said, "I will praise the Lord" (29:35).

But then childless Rachel, jealous of Leah's fertility, provoked more ill will between them (Gen. 30:1-24), and Leah was again gripped by the jealousy and sense of worthlessness that had tormented her for so many years.

Several elements in Leah's story are instructive. Her misery was caused by comparing herself with her sister. Her family and Jacob must have made beauty seem the be-all and end-all of existence. Yet Leah must have had qualities in which she could have taken pride. We should not accept society's view of what makes us valuable.

Yet it seems no one was sensitive to Leah's feelings or her situation. We need to develop a sensitivity to people like Leah. In time Leah reconciled herself to the fact that Jacob would always love Rachel more and she began to take joy in the children God gave her. We too should find joy in what God has given us, and not be miserable because of what he has withheld.

leather The tanned skin of animals, typically cattle, donkeys, goats, oxen, and sheep. In some English versions, "skins" indicate leather articles.

Leather was widely used in biblical times. Various articles of clothing were made of leather (*compare* Lev. 13:48; 2 Ki. 1:8; Ezek. 16:10; Mt. 3:4), and in early centuries, hardened hides were used in the armor and shields of soldiers. Leather was also used in making tents, as in the coverings of the tabernacle (Ex. 35:7). In addition, leather could be used for household items: Whole tanned skins of small animals were used to carry water, milk, and wine (Gen. 21:15; Josh. 9:4; Jdg. 4:19), and parchment (Gk., *membrana*), made of treated leather, served as writing material (2 Tim. 4:13). However, because leather deteriorates so rapidly, few leather items have survived from biblical times.

During the patriarchal period, families probably tanned hides for their own use, but by the first century, tanning was a specialized occupation. As a tentmaker, Paul would have been skilled in making leather articles (Acts 18:3). The tanning process Paul would have used took several steps. First, hides were soaked in vats. All

Traditional Israelite leather workshop reconstructed from ancient times.

flesh and hair was scraped off. Then the hides were rubbed and oiled to make them smooth, and finally, various substances were used to preserve them. The greenish or reddish spots that made leather articles ritually unclean probably resulted from improper tanning. According to Lev. 13:47-59, such articles were contaminated and had to be destroyed.

leaven (KJV) A fermenting agent such as yeast added to a dough to make it rise. The leaven mentioned in the Bible is a piece of fermented dough left over from previous baking.

The Passover festival was celebrated with unleavened bread in memory of the haste with which Israel left Egypt, not even waiting for bread dough to rise (Deut. 16:2-4; Ezra 6:19-22). *See also* Passover. Leavened bread was excluded from any burnt offering made to the Lord (Ex. 29:2,23; Lev. 2:1-16; Num. 15:1-21) but was permitted in several offerings that were not burned (Lev. 2:11-13; 7:13-15).

In rabbinic literature, leaven is a symbol of evil and corruption, a concept echoed in several NT texts, where it represents Jewish legalism (Mt. 16:6,12; Gal. 5:9) or fleshly corruption (1 Cor. 5:6-8). The meaning of Mt. 13:33, in which Jesus describes the Kingdom of God as leaven placed in a large amount of dough, is much debated. Since the parables of Mt. 13 contrast the present form of Jesus' Kingdom with the earthly kingdom expected by the Jewish people, leaven may represent the slow yet permeating process by which Christendom would spread, in contrast to a powerful kingdom dramati-

cally imposed on an unsuspecting earth. *See also* Kingdom; Parable.

leek A popular food plant with bulbous root and edible leaves, similar to onions and garlic. The Exodus generation grumbled over the manna God provided, longing for the leeks and onions—and by implication, the former life—of Egypt (Num. 11:15).

lees (KJV) Sediment that settles to the bottom of a liquid, especially of wine. Modern versions read "dregs." Wine left on its lees tastes stronger. Symbolically, lees represent those who remain unresponsive to God, whose strengthened resistance will win them more severe judgment (Jer. 48:11; Zeph. 1:12).

legalism An attitude of strict and rigid adherence to Mosaic Law, expressed in Scripture as: (1) reliance on observing the Law as a means to salvation, as in Rom. 10:2,3; (2) reliance on observing the Law as a means of spiritual growth, as in Gal. 3:1-3; (3) insistence on observing the Law as a criterion of acceptance in the Christian community, as in Gal. 2:11-14. *See also* Law.

The Scriptures teach us that our standing with God is dependent on his grace rather than on our works. Salvation is a gift of God through the death of Jesus on Calvary. To depend on observance of the Law for salvation rather than on the grace God extends to us in Christ is to misuse the Law and to fall into legalism.

According to the apostle Paul, even our growth as Christians is dependent on

Tanners preparing leather: One takes a soaked hide from a jar, another scrapes a hide with a stone, a third stretches a skin over a trestle, and two men cut leather on a sloping board. Tomb of Rekhmira, Karnak, Egypt.

Leek plant and flower.

lentil A legume widely used for food, the first vegetable named in the Bible (Gen. 25:34).

The nutritious seeds harvested from pods on the small 8-inch (20.32-centimeter) plants were used in stews and sometimes ground and added to flour to bake breads (*compare* Ezek. 4:9). Lentils were a cultivated crop in David's time (2 Sam. 23:11).

Ivory leopard found at Ebla. A few leopards still live on a game preserve in Israel.

Above: "A man with leprosy came to him and begged . . . 'If you are willing, you can make me clean.' " (Mk. 1:40,41). Illuminated manuscript, 12th century A.D.

Inset: This tablet, dating from the first century A.D., reads: "Here were brought the bones of Uzziah, king of Judah. Do not open."

Tile bearing the stamp of the Roman Tenth Legion, "LEGX̄FR" or Legio X Fretensis, which razed Jerusalem in A.D. 70.

God's grace. Paul told the Galatian believers that they were foolish if, having been given God's Spirit upon responding with faith to the Gospel message, they expected to attain their goal of spiritual growth by human effort (Gal. 3:3).

At the same time, God's moral will as expressed in the Old and New Testaments remains normative for believers of every era. Christians, as well as God's OT people, are called to live righteous lives and to perform good works, thus honoring the biblical revelation of right and wrong. Although we are no longer obligated to live according to the specific regulations of the OT code, we must honor God's moral will.

The crucial factor in this obedience to God, however, is still our reliance on Christ. We can never rely on righteous living or the scrupulous keeping of biblical commands as the basis of our righteousness or salvation. Legalism, then, is any distortion or misuse of the Law through which the Christian is drawn away from the basic spiritual principles of reliance on Christ to adopt a works-oriented approach to living the Christian life.

legion The major unit of the Roman army. Under Augustus, the full complement of a legion was 6,000 infantry with an equal number of less heavily armed auxiliaries. In Jesus' time, three or four of Rome's 26 legions were stationed in Syria. However, in the NT, "legion" is not used in its technical sense but represents a great multitude, as in Mt. 26:53; Mk. 5:9; and Lk. 8:30.

leopard A great spotted cat. Some two dozen Sinai leopards, like those of biblical times which were once thought extinct, still live in Israel. The leopard is known for his fierceness (Jer. 5:6; Hos. 13:7), which makes Isaiah's vision of a future in which the leopard will lie down in peace with its prey more striking (Isa. 11:6).

leprosy (1) Used of a wide variety of skin rashes, scales, sores, or eruptions, not just clinical leprosy (the NIV appropriately translates this as "infectious skin diseases"); (2) used of mildew, mold, or decay found in houses and clothing, as in Lev. 13:47-59; 14:33-57.

In Israel, leprosy made a person ritually unclean. Priests were charged with diagnosis of these diseases according to careful descriptions provided in Lev. 13. The priests also performed ritual purification of a recovered leper, as specified in Lev. 14. During the course of an infectious skin disease, the leper was to be isolated from the community. Leviticus 13:45 says the leper "must wear torn clothes, let his hair be unkempt, cover the lower part of his face and cry out, 'Unclean! Unclean!' " This regulation makes the incident reported in Mk. 1:40-42 especially poignant. Jesus, who often healed with a word, healed the leper, the outcast, with a loving touch.

Levi *See* Israel, Tribes of; Levites.

leviathan In Job 41:1 and Ezek. 29:3-5, probably the crocodile; in other, poetic passages, chaotic forces personified as sea monsters and associated with the mythology of pagan religions. Isaiah 27:1 pictures

God's appearance to judge evil and deliver Israel by saying:

> In that day, the Lord will punish
>   with his sword,
>   his fierce, great and powerful sword,
> Leviathan the gliding serpent,
>   Leviathan the coiling serpent;
> he will slay the monster of the sea.

levirate marriage A provision in Mosaic Law that calls for a man to marry a childless brother's widow and make their first child the dead brother's heir (Deut. 25:5-10; *compare* Ruth 4).

Levites Members of the tribe of Levi who descended from Jacob's third son by Leah. During the Exodus, this tribe was set apart to serve God (Num. 3:39-51) as representatives of the 22,273 "firstborn" of Israel that God spared when he struck Egypt with his final plague (Ex. 11). To the family of Aaron was given the priesthood; other Levite clans assisted them in maintaining the worship center (Num. 3,4), preparing offerings (Num. 1:50; 1 Chr. 23:28-32), and as worship leaders (1 Chr. 15:16-22).

Only males between the ages of 25 and 50 were allowed to serve God at the tabernacle and, later, at the Jerusalem Temple (Num. 8:23-26). Duties of the Levites at the mobile tabernacle are outlined in Num. 3,4. Temple duties assigned by David and later kings are described in 1 Chr. 23 and 2

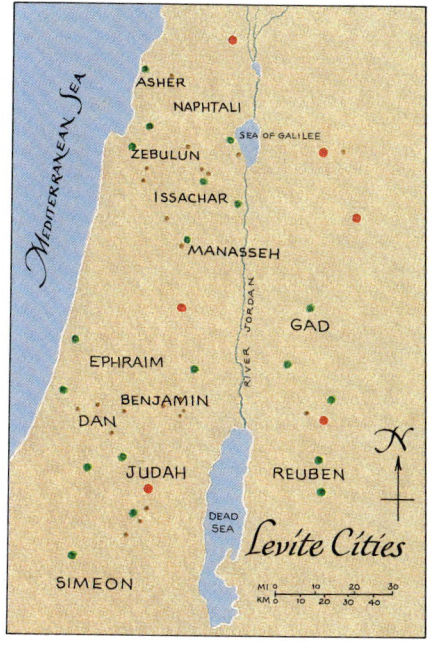

Chr. 23,29,31. Later, the Levites were assigned roles teaching and interpreting the Law (Deut. 33:10; 2 Chr. 17:7-9; 35:3).

When Israel conquered Canaan, no major territory was given to Levi. Instead, the Levites were given 48 cities scattered throughout the districts belonging to the other tribes. This facilitated the teaching of the Law and the distribution of tithes to the Levites (Deut. 33:10). Six Levitical cities were designated cities of refuge for those who accidentally committed homicide. *See also* Cities of Refuge. In addition to crop lands surrounding their cities, the Levites were to be supported during their time of service at the Temple by a share in the offerings and by tithes paid by the other tribes (Num. 18:21-32). This, then, was the Levites' inheritance.

Levites bore differing responsibilities in various eras of OT history. In David's day, Levites filled important administrative as well as liturgical posts. They alone could carry the ark of the covenant (2 Chr. 15:11-15), and the Temple musicians led in worship (1 Chr. 6:31-46). Levites also played important roles during times of national revival under Hezekiah (2 Chr. 29:11-17) and Josiah (2 Chr. 35).

The only NT references to Levites are (1) as members of a delegation from Jerusalem that went to listen critically to John the Baptist (Jn. 1:19), (2) as a character in the Parable of the Good Samaritan (Lk. 10:32), and (3) as one of Barnabas's titles (Acts 4:36).

Leviticus, Book of The third of the traditional five books of Moses. *See also* Pentateuch. The Jews knew this book as the "priests' book" and the "law of offerings." Leviticus contains detailed instructions to the priests and people concerning offerings, ritual cleanness, the Day of Atonement, personal and ritual holiness, and the religious calendar.

On this plaque (about 2450 B.C.), the Sumerian god Ninurta battles with a seven-headed monster—a mythical creature some identify with the Leviathan mentioned in Job, Pss. 74 and 104, and Isa. 27.

Map shows the distribution of Levitic cities in Israel (Josh. 21). The descendants of Levi did not receive territory as Jacob's other sons did; instead cities were placed under their control.

Line drawing of high priest and two Levites. God chose Levi's clan to be set apart for service at the tabernacle and then the Temple.

BACKGROUND

At Sinai, Moses was given a moral and social Law and instructions for building a tabernacle as Israel's worship center, as recorded in Ex. 19–40. Leviticus follows logically, instructing Israel in sacrifices to be made at the tabernacle and in the role of the priests who were to minister there. In essence, Leviticus provides a detailed explanation of how Israel is to fulfill its calling as "a kingdom of priests and a holy nation" (Ex. 19:6).

AUTHORSHIP

Some critics assume that Leviticus was compiled after 500 B.C. However, the book clearly places itself in the context of God's revelation to Moses at Sinai (*compare* Ex. 40:1; Num. 1:1). Some 38 times Leviticus quotes the Lord's words to Moses, and while Moses is not directly identified as the book's author, Mosaic authorship is implied. Practices analogous to those commanded by Moses in Leviticus existed long before the Mosaic era and there is no significant reason not to assume Mosaic authorship.

THEOLOGICAL CONTRIBUTIONS

The word "holy" is found 87 times in the book. "Sacrifice," if we include refer-

LEVITICUS: A READING AND STUDY GUIDE

Chapter	Content Summary	Related Articles
	I. Offerings	
1	What animals can be offered to the Lord as a voluntary sacrifice expressing dedication or thanksgiving.	Sacrifices and Offerings
2	How the grain offerings brought to the Lord expressing dedication or thanksgiving are to be prepared.	Grain Incense
3	What parts of "peace" or "fellowship" offerings brought to God are to be burned and which parts eaten.	Eating Fellowship
4,5	What sacrifices are to be made when a priest, individual, or the community sins unintentionally.	Sin Guilt
6	What restitution must be made before a thief can bring a sacrifice. How priests are to prepare and dispose of sacrifices and offerings.	Restitution
7	What portions of sacrificed animals are to be given to the priests for the support of their families.	Tithe
8	What qualifies a person for the priesthood, and how the family of Aaron is to be ordained to this ministry.	Priest Aaron
9	What sign from God occurs at the offering of the first sacrifices as the priests follow God's instructions and begin their ministry.	
10	Aaron's sons Nadab and Abihu die for their sin.	Obey
	II. Ritual Cleanness	
11	What animals are ritually clean and may be eaten in Israel, and what animals are unclean and not to be used for food.	Clean and Unclean Dietary Laws
12	What ritual regulations govern childbirth.	Childbirth
13	What is to be done if an Israelite breaks out with an infectious skin disease or if mildew infects clothes.	Leprosy
14	What is to be done to ritually cleanse a person who has recovered from a skin disease.	
15	What bodily discharges cause a person to be ritually unclean, and how the person may be cleansed.	

ences to "offerings" and "oblations," is found over 300 times and "atonement" 49 times. These important concepts give insight into Israel's relationship with God and help us better grasp the nature of our own relationship with God through Jesus Christ.

The Epistle to the Hebrews in the NT examines the parallels between the system of faith and worship established by Moses and the "better" system established by Christ, which both fulfills and supplants the older one. *See also* Covenant; Hebrews, Book of.

MASTERY KEYS

The Book of Leviticus is organized logically. Within most sections, the author speaks alternately to the priests and to the people. Following the headings of the Content Summary section in the Reading and Study Guide will clarify the instructions given in Leviticus.

SPECIAL FEATURES

Leviticus 19:18 commands, "Love your neighbor as yourself." The significance of

KEY TERMS IN LEVITICUS	
atonement	A covering of sin which makes possible a harmonious relationship with God and with others in the faith community.
clean	Ritually and morally pure, and thus qualified to participate in the community's worship of God.
guilt	The liability for punishment incurred when a person commits an act of sin.
holy	Separated to God, evidenced by obedience to the moral and ritual obligations expressed in God's Law.
priests	Members of the family of Aaron who served as mediators of the OT Law, offering sacrifices for sin and instructing Israel concerning God's will.
sacrifice	The ritual offering of the blood of an animal as the rightful penalty for the sin of the offerer.
sin	An intentional or unintentional violation of the will of God expressed in the Mosaic Law.

this call to love, which sums up the second tablet of the Ten Commandments, is underlined five times in the NT, in Mt. 19:19; Mk. 12:31; Lk. 10:27; Rom. 13:9; and Gal. 5:14.

LEVITICUS: A READING AND STUDY GUIDE *CONT.*

Chapter	Content Summary	Related Articles
	III. The Day of Atonement	
16	How the priests are to conduct the unique annual sacrifice that makes atonement for the intentional as well as the unintentional sins of Israel.	Atonement
17	What the significance is of the blood of sacrificial animals.	Blood
	IV. Holiness	
18	What sexual practices and relationships are forbidden to God's people.	Sex Homosexuality
19	What different ways God's own show respect for the various groups of people that make up society.	Poor Justice
20	What punishments are appropriate for various violations of the moral requirements of God's OT Law.	Judgment
21	In what ways standards for priests are higher than those established for the people in general.	
22	How the priests and people are to show their respect for the sacrifices and offerings commanded in the Law.	
	V. Worship Calendar	
23	What special days and seasons are sacred and to be celebrated in special ways by Israel.	Calendar; Feasts, Festivals, and Fasts
24	What is to be done to a blasphemer. How murder is to be dealt with.	Blasphemy Murder
25	What the sabbatical year is. How the year of Jubilee protects Israelite society against poverty.	Sabbath Jubilee
	VI. More Regulations	
26	How God will bless if the nation is obedient, and how he will punish if the nation disobeys.	Obey Discipline
27	What rules govern voluntary dedication of persons or property to the Lord. How vows are redeemed.	Vow Redeem

libation *See* Drink Offering.

liberty (1) Removal of or exemption from restrictions; (2) release, freedom from physical bondage; (3) independence from others. Modern versions tend to translate the Hebrew and Greek words rendered "liberty" in the KJV by "freedom." *See also* Free.

Just as the OT Israelites were liberated from bondage to Egypt, so, in a theological sense, Christians are liberated from bondage to Satan (Heb. 2:14), from the power of sin (Jn. 8:31-36), from obligation to the OT code of law (Rom. 6:14; Gal. 3:21-25), and from the fear of death (Heb. 2:15). Christian liberty, however, is essentially a freedom for rather than a freedom from: Christians are freed from the power of sin for God's service. The apostle Paul writes, "You, my brothers, were called to be free. But do not use your freedom to indulge the sinful nature; rather, serve one another in love" (Gal. 5:13).

Above: The ancient Egyptians fought the problem of lice by shaving their heads. Tomb of Nebamun and Ipuky, about 1380 B.C. Right: Ivory comb from Egypt decorated with a lion (5th century B.C.). Two-thousand-year-old remains of lice and their eggs have been found on some excavated combs.

lice (KJV) Any of a number of small, wingless, parasitic insects that feed on the blood of humans and some other mammals. The same Hebrew word is used of sand flies.

Lice were common in the hot, dusty Nile Valley; therefore, Egyptian priests and nobles shaved off their hair to give lice no holding place on their bodies—a precaution that availed little when God sent Egypt a plague of lice in preparation for the Exodus (Ex. 8:16-18). In some modern versions, the plague insects are called gnats. *See also* Gnats.

lie, lying To deceive or lead astray by falsehood. Lying is condemned in Scripture as a violation of the trust called for in personal relationships. Lying often is intended to harm others, and it invariably involves some distortion of truth. The NT calls on Christians to "put off falsehood and speak truthfully" to others (Eph. 4:25; *compare* Col. 3:9,10).

OLD TESTAMENT

Key Hebrew words translated deceit and falsehood are: (1) *Ramah,* to mislead, as in Ps. 10:7 which describes the wicked, "His mouth is full of curses and lies and threats." (2) *Saqar,* to tell a falsehood or deceive, a verb which suggests breaking a promise or commitment. A derivative, *seqer,* is used of false prophecies that have no basis in reality, as in Ex. 20:16, "You shall not give false testimony against your neighbor." (3) *Saw'* suggests presenting something unreal as real, as in Deut. 5:20's repetition of the above commandment. (4) *Kahash* is lack of dependability in a relationship. (5) *Patah* is active enticing to do wrong. All these words portray violations of trust, which are intended to harm the person to whom or against whom the lie is told.

NEW TESTAMENT

Greek words include: *planaō,* to lead astray; *apataō,* to entice; and *doloō* or *dolioō,* to treacherously trick or trap another person. Falsehood is expressed by some 15 Greek terms built on a single root. One of these words, *pseudomai,* means "to deceive by lying." All these terms are set in contrast to God's revelation of truth as an accurate portrayal of reality. Man's rejection of divine revelation has led humanity into a world of falsehood and illusion.

LYING AND MORALITY

The practice of lying destroys trust which is so vital in developing significant personal relationships. Lies are viewed negatively in Scripture: God himself does not lie at all (Tit. 1:2; Heb. 6:18), while Satan is called a liar and the father (originator or source) of lies (Jn. 8:42-47). If we model our behavior on God's example, we will surely rely on speaking the truth.

Yet, Scripture does report what seem to be commendable "lies." First, midwives in Egypt protected the Jewish infants they delivered, despite Pharaoh's decree that newborn males should be killed. They lied and told Pharaoh that the more vigorous Israelite women gave birth before the midwives arrived. The text says, "So God was kind to the midwives" (Ex. 1:20). Next, Rahab saved the Israelite spies by telling the king of Jericho that they had already left the city, when actually they were hidden on her roof (Josh. 2:1-7). However, God does not commend the midwives or Rahab for their lying. He commends the midwives because they feared him, and he commends Rahab because of her faith.

life (1) Personal existence, enjoyed by God and granted by him to his creatures, as in Jn. 1:4; (2) the principle which animates living beings; biological existence; one's life-span, as in Lev. 17:11; (3) one's manner of living or life-style, as in 2 Tim. 3:10; (4) the positive experience of a person who enjoys God's blessing, health, and fulfillment, as in Deut. 30:15,16; (5) the material things and ordinary experiences associated with daily living, as in Lk. 8:14; and (6) the spiritual principle which enables humans to have a personal relationship with God and self-conscious existence after biological death —eternal life, as in Jn. 3:16. Throughout the Bible, life in each of its aspects is contrasted with death. *See also* Death.

Genesis 1 and 2 present human life as a unique gift from God. The OT considers the quality of life as well as mere physical existence. Thus, a pleasant life is a gift of God, granted to those who respond to him in obedient faith. Proverbs 14:27 sums up the OT viewpoint: "The fear of the Lord is a fountain of life, turning a man from the snares of death." Health, prosperity, and personal fulfillment are all qualities associated with life, while sickness, disaster, and other debilitating events are expressions of death. For this reason, the Hebrews saw life as the most precious of gifts, to be protected and cherished. That belief is reflected in the modern Hebrew toast, *l'chaim*—"to life."

Few references to eternal life are found in the OT, and even these are debated. However, passages suggesting life after biological death include Pss. 16:11; 21:4-6; 30:5; Prov. 12:28; 15:24; and Dan. 12:2.

NEW TESTAMENT

Greek *bios*, seldom found in the NT, is used when speaking of peripheral issues, such as possessions, which may claim a person's attention or stimulate his pride, as in Lk. 8:14 and 1 Jn. 2:16. *Psychē*, often translated "soul," frequently means an

KEY NEW TESTAMENT PASSAGES ON *ETERNAL LIFE*

John 3:15,16,36	The gift of God is eternal life. It is given to all who believe in Jesus. Any who reject Jesus "will not see life."
John 5:21-26	Jesus, who has "life in himself," gives eternal life to those who hear and believe Jesus' words about himself.
John 10:10-28	Jesus lays down his life for us. He says, "I give them eternal life, and they shall never perish; no one can snatch them out of my hand."
John 11:1-43	Jesus claims to be "the resurrection and the life." He shows his power by raising Lazarus from the dead.
Romans 5:12-19	Jesus as the second Adam brings the gift of life to those ruined by the first Adam's disobedience and original sin.
Romans 6:1-10	Union with Christ in his death and resurrection is the basis of our death to sin and the basis of the new, righteous life lived by those who are alive to God.
Romans 8:1-11	The vitalizing principle of new life through Christ energizes our mortal bodies and enables us to be righteous.
1 Corinthians 15	Our mortal bodies will die, but the dead in Christ will be raised again, immortal and imperishable.
Galatians 2:19,20	Christ lives in believers, who "live by faith in the Son of God."
Ephesians 2:1-10	Believers were once dead in trespasses and sins, but have now been made alive in Christ. This life is a gift, not based on human effort, and is rooted in God's matchless grace.
1 John 2,3	Life from God will be expressed in the obedience and love shown by those who possess this life.
1 John 5:10-12	"God has given us eternal life, and this life is in his Son. He who has the Son has life; he who does not have the Son of God does not have life."

individual's life or personal existence. Thus in Lk. 12:22,23, Jesus tells his disciples that life is "more than food, and the body more than clothes." Because God cares for the individual, the believer is freed from constant anxiety about the necessities of life in order to seek God's Kingdom.

Zōē has a biological emphasis in classical Greek, referring to natural life—the opposite of death. In its theological context in the NT, however, it includes a spiritual dynamic that supersedes the natural end of life in death. *Zōē* calls attention to God's gift of eternal life. "Eternal" speaks to the nature as well as the extent of the life God gives to believers. *See also* Eternal.

Eternal life enables us to share God's nature and his values. Eternal life is so powerfully at work in believers that "no one who is born of God will continue to sin, because God's seed remains in him; he cannot go on sinning, because he has been born of God" (1 Jn. 3:9; *compare* Rom. 8:11; Eph. 2:1-10). Eternal life is found only in Jesus Christ, who "raises the dead and gives them life" (Jn. 5:21-24). It guarantees the believer's resurrection and personal existence in the presence of God forever (1 Cor. 15). *See also* Heaven; Resurrection.

life, book of God's list of those who escape the final judgment to enter his new heavens and earth; called the "Lamb's book of life" in Rev. 21:27, since faith in Jesus as the Lamb of God is the criterion for entry. This record, mentioned in the last book of the NT, is parallel to the "scroll of remembrance" mentioned in the last book of the OT, Malachi. There God says of those found written on its pages, "They will be mine . . . in the day when I make up my treasured possession. I will spare them, just as in compassion a man spares his son who serves him" (3:16,17).

light Literally, visible electromagnetic radiation either (1) natural, as from the sun, Gen. 1:16, or (2) artificial, as from a lamp, Mt. 25:1. Figuratively, of a spectrum of concepts ranging from (3) the essential nature of God, as in 1 Tim. 6:16, to (4) holiness, as in Isa. 5:20; Rom. 13:12; (5) revelation and spiritual illumination, as in Ps. 119:105; Jn. 3:19-21; Eph. 5:14; and (6) a life lived in harmony with God's revelation of reality, as in 1 Jn. 1:5-7.

The imagery of light and darkness is found frequently in both Testaments, with a variety of associations and applications. For example, God's presence, made visible

in a cloudy or fiery pillar, guided Israel in the wilderness (Ex. 13:21; *compare* Ps. 89:15). God's people are called to walk in the light provided by the Lord (Isa. 2:5), which comes from his Word (Pss. 43:3; 119:130). Finally, when God's new day dawns, "The Lord will be your everlasting light, and your days of sorrow will end" (Isa. 60:20).

In the NT, "light" is linked to Jesus. As Creator, Redeemer, and Revealer, Jesus is "the true light that gives light to every man" (Jn. 1:9). The believer, who responds to Jesus with faith, is transported "out of darkness into his wonderful light" (1 Pet. 2:9). As children of light (Eph. 5:8), Christians are expected to walk in the light (1 Jn. 1:7) and to "let your light shine before men, that they may see your good deeds and praise your Father in heaven" (Mt. 5:14-16).

lightning An electrical discharge causing a bright light in the sky. In Palestine, lightning flashes brightly during the spring and fall thunderstorms.

In the OT, lightning is associated with God, especially with revelations of his power, judgment, or glory (*compare* Ex. 9:23; 19:16-18; 2 Sam. 22:13; Ezek. 1:13,14; Zech. 9:14). In the NT, Jesus' Second Coming is compared to the sudden, unexpected flash of lightning that brightens the horizon (Lk. 17:24). In Revelation, flashes of lightning are associated both with God's essential glory (4:5; 11:19; *compare* Mt. 28:3) and with his judgments (8:5; 16:18). *See also* Glory.

lily A flower or a variety of flowers. The specific flower or flowers identified by these terms is unknown. Suggestions have ranged from madonna lilies to hyacinths. The word may be a general term indicating any brightly colored flower. The lilies and "lily-work" that decorated Solomon's Temple are thought to be modeled after the lotus, or water lily, which was a common architectural motif in Assyria and Persia as well as Egypt (1 Ki. 7:19-26). In the NT, the "lilies of the field" Jesus referred to were most likely wild *Anemone coronaria*, which still blanket the hillsides where Jesus spoke (Mt. 6:28; Lk. 12:27).

linen Cloth woven from fibers of the flax plant. A number of Hebrew words are translated flax, many of which distinguish between grades or quality of the cloth. Rough linen clothing was preferred to wool in the hot season and might be worn

KEY NEW TESTAMENT PASSAGES ON *LIGHT*

John 1:4-9	Jesus is the "true light." He is God, and he reveals God. He is the source of spiritual illumination for all in his creation.
John 3:19-21	When light shines, those who do evil react with hate. Lost humans prefer darkness, fearing light will expose their sin.
2 Corinthians 4:4-6	Satan as well as sin blinds the lost to the light of the Gospel. Only a creative act of the God who brought natural light into being can give us "the light of the knowledge of the glory of God in the face of Christ."
Ephesians 5:8-11	Children of light are to show the fruit of light, which "consists in all goodness, righteousness and truth." The holy life of believers will contrast with "deeds of darkness" and thus expose the true nature of disobedience.
1 John 1:5-7	Here "walking in light" is not sinlessness, but rather seeing our acts as God sees them, confessing any sins so that we can remain in fellowship with him. Here darkness means living in illusion and pretense.
1 John 2:8-11	No one who hates his brother lives in the light, for God, who is light, is also love.

by ordinary men and women. Fine linens were a luxury item worn by the rich (Isa. 3:23; Lk. 16:19).

The remarkable whiteness of fine, bleached linen is reflected in several of the Hebrew terms. White may have symbolic relationship to the role of linens in Israel's worship. Fine linens were used in the tabernacle (Ex. 26:1) and to make the clothing of the priests (Lev. 6:10). Linen was worn by the boy Samuel as he ministered at the tabernacle (1 Sam. 2:18), by David as he danced before the Lord (2 Sam. 6:14), and by the Levitical singers who led Israel in worship (2 Chr. 5:12). Furthermore, Revelation portrays the redeemed dressed in white linen (19:8).

Flax was grown in the Jordan Valley and in Galilee (Josh. 2:6). The plants were pulled up by the roots, dried, and then pounded to separate the long, thin fibers. These were bleached and spun and then woven into cloth. The process might be done by the women of the family; however, producing fine linen called for a high degree of skill, and as early as the time of Solomon guilds of textile workers produced fine linen in Israel (1 Chr. 4:21).

lintel (KJV) The beam laid over the top of a doorway to support the wall above it. Lintels in Palestine were often stone rather than wood. Both lintel and doorposts were marked with blood at the first Passover (Ex. 12:22,23).

After stalks of flax dried on the flat roofs of Israelite houses, they were pounded into the fibers used to make linen cloth.

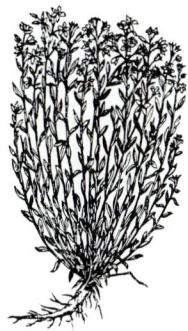

A dead lion (above) and wounded lioness (below) are both part of Assyrian King Ashurbanipal's "Lion Hunt" relief from his palace at Nineveh, about 640 B.C. The Asian lion, Panthera leo persica, once inhabited the biblical world.

lion A large carnivorous cat, currently found in Africa. Up to the 14th century A.D., an Asiatic subspecies of lion ranged Palestine and Syria.

In OT times, lions were a threat to herds and to humans (Jdg. 14:5,6; 1 Sam. 17:34-36; 1 Ki. 13:24-28). The legendary fierceness of the lion is reflected in the proverb, "A king's wrath is like the roar of a lion; he who angers him forfeits his life" (Prov. 20:2). Furthermore, God's judgments fall upon his people "like a lion" (Hos. 13:7,8), and God will chase his enemies "like a lion coming up from Jordan's thickets" (Jer. 50:44). Thus, Isaiah's prediction of a day when "the calf and the lion and the yearling [will live] together, and a little child will lead them" (11:6) is striking compared to Scripture's portrayal of the lion as a frightening and dangerous beast.

In the NT, the "mouth of the lion" symbolizes great danger (2 Tim. 4:17; *compare* Rev. 9:8; 13:2). Satan is portrayed as a roaring lion prowling in search of someone he can devour (1 Pet. 5:8). *See also* Devil; Satan.

At the same time, the lion is recognized as king of the beasts and can serve as a positive symbol of power and authority. A lion is represented as one of the faces of the "living creatures" who surround God's throne (Ezek. 1:10; Rev. 4:7). In Rev. 5:5, Jesus is announced as the "Lion of the tribe of Judah," a messianic image of power from Gen. 49:9 that surprises John, who then sees Christ as "a Lamb, looking as if it had been slain" (Rev. 5:6).

listen *See* Hear.

livestock *See* Cattle.

living As an adjective, (1) the possession of life, as in Gen. 1:24; 1 Pet. 2:4,5, or (2) the capacity to give life, as in references by Jesus to living water (Jn. 7:37-39; *compare* Jer. 2:13) and living bread (Jn. 6:51). As a noun, a general reference to humanity. *See also* Life.

living creatures (1) In a general sense, of animals, as in Gen. 1:24, and (2) in a special, technical sense, of the cherubim of Ezekiel's visions, as in Ezek. 1,3, and 10.

The four living creatures described by Ezekiel had a human form, each with the facial features of a man, lion, ox, and eagle. These are identified in Ezek. 10 as cherubim. The symbolism of the four faces is obscure but was taken by the Jewish rabbis to represent the pinnacle of human, wild animal, domestic animal, and bird creations. The creatures are found again, in slightly different form, in Rev. 4:6-9. *See also* Cherub.

lizard The common name of a slender, tailed reptile with four legs and scaly skin, such as the crocodile and chameleon. Lizards have some 1,700 species in 20 different families. Eighteen of the species have been found in Palestine. Most believe that several of the unclean animals that "move about on the ground" ("swarming creatures," KJV) are types of lizards (Lev. 11:29,30; Prov. 30:28).

loan *See* Borrow.

lock The device used to secure the door of a room (Jdg. 3:23), a house (Lk. 11:7; Jn. 20:19), or a prison (Acts 5:23). Figuratively, of unrevealed truth (Gal. 3:23). In homes, locks were usually bolts of wood that slid into slots in the doorframe and were secured with a wooden peg. The locks on city gates and prisons were often metal and could be opened with a large wooden or metal key. *See also* Key.

locust An insect related to the grasshopper. Swarms of them plagued the biblical world and Africa, eating every green thing and laying eggs. When these hatched, the larvae fed on whatever vegetation remained, causing famine as food crops were lost. Hebrew terms translated caterpillar, palmerworm, and cankerworm in older English versions of the OT most likely represent stages in the life cycle of this insect.

A locust invasion was one of the judgments God brought on Egypt through Moses (Ex. 10:12-20). In Deut. 28:42, God warns Israel that he will bring locusts upon them if the nation strays. Joel's prophecy of destruction on the Day of the Lord was stimulated by a swarm of locusts that swept into Israel in his day. *See also* Joel. However, despite their destructive nature, these insects did possess one favorable quality—locusts are among the few clean insects that Lev. 11:21,22 permits Israelites to eat (*see* Mk. 1:6).

log *See* Weights and Measures.

logos A Greek term commonly meaning "word," "explanation," "discourse," "book," or "saying."

In the OT Septuagint, *logos* usually represents the Hebrew *dabar*, which can indicate a word or event. *Dabar* is often used of God's speech and is closely identified with his person. As a technical term in Greek philosophy, *logos* indicates the rational principle or pattern which gives the universe its structure. (*See also* Stoic Philosophers.) When used as a theological term in the NT, *logos* served as a bridge for the Jewish concept of Wisdom in Proverbs into a Hellenistic culture.

In Jn. 1:1-18 "the Word [*logos*]" is identified as being God and being with God from the beginning. The *logos* is the Creator, through whom all things were made. Yet the *logos* "became flesh and lived for a while among us," and while "no one has ever seen God, . . . God the only [Son], who is at the Father's side, has made him known" (1:14,18).

This linkage of creation and God's revelation of himself is significant. John claims that in the historic person of Jesus Christ, the Creator-God became a man. Through the life and death of Jesus the *logos*, God's grace and truth have been revealed. In creation and incarnation, Jesus unveils God to humanity, being both the Messenger and the Message (Word). *See also* Incarnation; Revelation; Word.

These concepts are beautifully expressed in the first chapter of Hebrews:

In these last days [God] has spoken to us by his Son, whom he appointed heir of all things, and through whom he made the universe. The Son is the radiance of God's glory and the exact representation of his being, sustaining all things by his powerful word. (Heb. 1:2,3)

The locust, which swarms in ravenous, vegetation-eating hordes, symbolized utter destruction in the Bible (Joel 1:4; 2:25).

Left: Egyptian ivory lizard from the Old Kingdom (2700–2200 B.C.).

Left: Bronze lock and key, first or second century A.D.

The catacombs, the "underground" of Rome, are filled with evidences of early Christian faith. This fresco near the burial niches of St. Calixtus portrays Christ's ultimate lordship as the Ruler of the world.

loins (1) Literally, the part of the body between the ribs and hip bones; (2) figuratively, in older versions, the source of reproductive capacity, as in Gen. 35:11, and of physical strength, as in Nah. 2:1. The flowing robes worn by men and women in biblical times were typically worn loose when the people relaxed; otherwise, they were belted around the waist, or loins. *See also* Clothing; Girdle. "Girding up the loins" meant simply to tuck one's cloak into his belt so the person would be more free to act (*compare* 1 Ki. 18:46; Eph. 6:14).

long-suffering A quality of patience displayed in God's willingness to delay punishment in order to give human beings the opportunity to repent. In the OT, long-suffering is demonstrated in God's slowness to anger, as in Ps. 86:15. In the NT, long-suffering is displayed in God's tolerance and patience, a kindness that moves him to give men occasion to repent, as in Rom. 2:4; 2 Pet. 3:9. *See also* Patience.

644 **Lord** In the OT, Heb., *'adon;* (1) in common

speech, "master," "owner," and even "husband," as in Gen. 18:12; (2) a form of courteous address, much like our "sir," as in Gen. 19:2; (3) with its intensified form, *'adonay,* rendered "Lord" in English versions. (4) Heb., *ba'al,* "owner" or "overlord," as in Ex. 21:28, seldom used of God because of its use to designate Canaanite deities. *See also* Baal. (5) Heb., *yahweh,* the personal name of Israel's God, found 5,321 times in the OT, rendered "Lord" in English versions.

In the NT, Gk., *kyrios;* (6) in ordinary speech, a term of respect or courteous address; (7) of God and, especially after the resurrection, of Jesus, equivalent to the OT's divine name. In the Gospels, Jesus is often addressed as "lord" in the courteous rather than religious sense.

THE DIVINE NAME: YAHWEH

The divine name is formed from four consonants, YHWH, and is thought to be a form of the Hebrew verb "to be" or "to become." This name was revealed to Moses at the burning bush (Ex. 3:13-15).

There God identified himself as "I AM" and added, "This is my name forever, the name by which I am to be remembered from generation to generation."

This name is best taken as a redemptive statement rather than a philosophical affirmation of God's existence. Through Moses, God revealed himself to Israel (who had known of him through stories passed down through generations) by a name meaning "ONE WHO IS ALWAYS PRESENT." In that name God would soon strike Egypt with devastating plagues, and the Exodus generation would experience God as a living reality in a unique and powerful way. From this time on, God's people were to identify him by a name that affirmed his living presence with each generation of the covenant people, a name that calls each generation to renewed faith in God's redemptive power.

The pronunciation of YHWH is uncertain. The name was considered so sacred by the Jewish people that it was not to be spoken. Instead of pronouncing YHWH, a person would say " *adonay*," and the "o" and "a" vowels of that name were added to YHWH in the 12th century A.D. to produce "Jehovah." The best approximation of the original vocalization is probably Yahweh.

JESUS AS LORD

The simplest and one of the most common affirmations of the early church was "Jesus is Lord." By this expression the early church proclaimed the deity of Jesus of Nazareth and identified him with Yahweh of the OT. In this, the church followed Jesus himself, who claimed deity by announcing that "before Abraham was born, I am" (Jn. 8:58). While many uses of "lord" addressed to Jesus during his life on earth indicate nothing more than common courtesy (*compare* Lk. 6:46; Jn. 20:15), others reflect the realization of the disciples that Jesus was "Lord" and "God" (Jn. 20:28).

The most powerful affirmation of Jesus' Lordship is found in Phil. 2:6-11, which traces Christ's original possession of the divine nature (v. 6), his incarnation (v. 7), obedience even to death on the cross (v. 8), and subsequent exaltation by God to the "highest place" (v. 9). That exaltation grants Jesus "the name that is above every other name." Ultimately, believer and unbeliever alike will confess that "Jesus Christ is Lord" (v. 11).

Christian conviction that Jesus is Lord does not rest on Phil. 2 alone. The Lordship of Christ is one of the pervasive themes of NT revelation, as reflected in the constant linkage of the title "Lord" to "Jesus" and "Christ." Today, the Lord Jesus Christ is "at [God's] right hand in the heavenly realms, far above all rule and authority, power and dominion, and every title that can be given, not only in this present age but also in the one to come."

Besides the passages that speak specifically of Christ's active Lordship in believers' lives and the future expression of his Lordship in judgment, Christ's Lordship is implied in a variety of ways. Jesus is sovereign in the spiritual universe. He is over all "rule and authority"—"angels, authorities, and powers" are "in submission to him" (Eph. 1:21; 1 Pet. 3:22). Jesus is sovereign in his Church. He is "head over everything for the church, which is his body" (Eph. 1:22,23). Jesus is sovereign in the physical universe (Heb. 1:3; 11:3). In all things, he "works for the good of those who love him," continuing the exercise of God's providential care (Rom. 8:28). Ultimately, the Lordship of Christ will find its full expression on earth, when he rules the nations "with an iron scepter" and is acknowledged as "KING OF KINGS AND LORD OF LORDS" (Rev. 19:15,16).

Lord's Day The first day of the week, Sunday, which the early Christians adopted as their day of worship. While the phrase "the first day of the week" occurs several times throughout the NT, the term "Lord's Day" appears only in Rev. 1:10.

The OT Sabbath, the seventh day of the week, commemorated creation (Ex. 20:8-11). Sunday, however, is not a continuation of or replacement for the Sabbath, but instead commemorates Jesus' resurrection on the first day of the week (Jn. 20:1). While Sunday observance was not binding (Rom. 14:5,6; Col. 2:16), it was the practice of the early church to meet weekly on the Lord's Day (Acts 20:7; 1 Cor. 16:2). *See also* Sabbath.

There is little in Scripture to indicate how the first Christians celebrated the Lord's Day. The early practice of sharing an evening meal at which the Lord's Supper was celebrated was outlawed by the Emperor Trajan, who forbade dinners for "unlicensed clubs or societies." There are references to meetings before dawn at which songs, prayers, and instruction played a part. However, there was no transfer of the concept of a day of rest from Sabbath to Sunday. In the first century, the first day of the week was a normal workday. Yet the tendency to transfer elements of Sabbath observance to Sunday soon appeared and is reflected in the pronouncement of the fourth century Council of Laodicea that while "Christians must not Judaize by resting on the sabbath," they should, if possible, rest on the Lord's Day.

Essentially, the Christian Lord's Day is a day of rejoicing and celebration, for it commemorates the fact that Jesus Christ arose and that in him we too are raised to new life.

Lord's Prayer The popular name of the prayer Jesus taught his disciples in Mt. 6:9-13 and, in slightly different form, in Lk. 11:2-4. It is generally taken both as a specific prayer to be offered by Christians and as a model, summing up essential elements of all prayer. Matthew's version is:

Our Father in heaven,
hallowed be your name,
your kingdom come,
your will be done
*   on earth as it is in heaven.*
Give us today our daily bread.
Forgive us our debts,
*   as we also have forgiven our debtors.*
And lead us not into temptation,
but deliver us from the evil one.

An analysis of each phrase in the Lord's Prayer yields rich meaning for the Christian's prayer life.

• *Our Father.* Prayer relies on a personal relationship with God whose love is father-like. Prayer is an expression of the conviction that God is concerned about us and our needs. *See also* Father; Fatherhood of God.

• *In heaven.* Prayer acknowledges the transcendence of God. *See also* Heaven.

• *Hallowed be your name.* Prayer confesses the living presence of one whose name through all generations is I AM (Ex. 3:14,15). *See also* Lord.

• *Your kingdom come.* Prayer affirms God's right to rule in our lives now, and expresses the believer's desire that God establish his Kingdom on earth. *See also* Kingdom of God.

• *Your will be done on earth as it is in heaven.* Prayer defers to God's will and expresses submission to God, not an attempt to manipulate or use him.

• *Give us today our daily bread.* Prayer expresses dependence on God, not only for the necessities of life but for life itself. *See also* Bread.

• *Forgive us our debts, as we also have forgiven our debtors.* Prayer expresses con-

sciousness of human weaknesses. Prayer is an approach to God which acknowledges that forgiveness alone can provide the basis for a harmonious relationship with God and with others. *See also* Forgive.

• *Lead us not into temptation, but deliver us from the evil one.* Prayer recognizes spiritual vulnerability and expresses dependence on God to guard our heart.

The Lord's Prayer focuses attention on the underlying attitudes we adopt in approaching God. In Matthew, the context gives several illustrations showing that the believer's relationship with God is not to be a hypocritical public expression of piety, but a sincere reflection of our love and devotion through true prayer (Mt. 6:1-8, 16-18). *See also* Prayer.

Lord's Supper The celebration of communion or the Eucharist, instituted by Jesus at his last meal, a Passover *seder*, with the disciples the night before his crucifixion.

The Lord's Supper is a significant service in all Christian traditions. In Roman Catholic, Lutheran, Anglican, and some Reformed traditions, the Lord's Supper is viewed as a sacrament, a means of conveying God's grace to the participant. In the Roman Catholic and Eastern Orthodox view, the bread and wine of the sacrament become the actual body and blood of Christ when the words of institution are spoken by the priest. This is known as *transubstantiation*. In the others' view, the body and blood of Christ are present in, with, and under the bread and wine, a doctrine called *consubstantiation*. Evangelical Christians typically see the bread and wine as *symbolic* of Christ's body and blood and view the Lord's Supper as a witness to Christ but not a means of grace.

The events of this last meal are described in Mt. 26:17-30; Mk. 14:12-25; Lk. 22:7-20. Jerusalem's population expanded during Passover week and most homes were opened to accommodate guests who needed rooms in which to celebrate the Passover meal. Jesus sent John and Peter into Jerusalem to find "a certain man" and make arrangements with him to use his guest room. The two disciples made the preparations, which would have included going to the Temple to have a lamb slaughtered, and the disciples gathered in the upper room with Jesus. Against this vivid picture of sacrifice and redemption, Jesus spends these final private hours with his disciples, worshiping God and remembering his faithfulness. John's Gospel focuses on the conversations held during this meal, filled with grief and sadness, and notes particularly the Comforter Jesus promised to send (Jn. 13–16). *See also* Passover.

Using the key elements of the Passover meal, Jesus gives the significance of the bread and wine new dimension.

While they were eating, Jesus took bread, gave thanks and broke it, and gave it to his

Even the controversial and erratic surrealist painter Salvador Dali was drawn to the dramatic scene in the upper room with his painting of The Sacrament of the Last Supper.

disciples, saying, "Take and eat; this is my body."

Then he took the cup, gave thanks and offered it to them, saying, "Drink from it, all of you. This is my blood of the covenant, which is poured out for many for the forgiveness of sins." (Mt. 26:26-28)

Luke adds Jesus' words of institution, "Do this in remembrance of me" (Lk. 22:14-20; *compare* Mk. 14:22-25).

The meaning of the Lord's Supper is expanded in 1 Cor. 11:23-26. There Paul quotes Jesus' words and adds, "For whenever you eat this bread and drink this cup, you proclaim the Lord's death until he comes."

In this passage, Paul contrasts the Lord's Supper with the selfish and indulgent way in which some members of the Corinthian church celebrated their fellowship feast. What was meant to be an expression of Christian unity and fellowship brought instead division, in which the rich indulged themselves to excess while the poor went without. This behavior expressed an attitude unworthy of the Lord's Supper, which followed after the feast.

The significance of the Lord's Supper is understood in three ways. (1) In "pro-claiming the Lord's death," the Lord's Supper serves as what Augustine called a "visible word"; it is a testimony to Christ's redemptive work for all mankind. (2) In the Christian community, which finds its basis for unity in a common faith in Jesus, this ceremony is an occasion for fellowship. (3) Most importantly, the Lord's Supper is an occasion for "remembrance."

The phrase "in remembrance" is the key to understanding the significance of this Christian celebration. The last meal that Jesus shared with his disciples was the Passover meal, a festival that was designated a Hebrew *zikkaron*, or memorial festival. *Zikkaron* festivals and objects provided an occasion for the believer to relive the experience of God's saving grace to an earlier generation. Thus, on Passover, the Jewish people relived the deliverance of the nation of Israel from bondage (Ex. 12:14), just as the stones Joshua had brought from the Jordan River when Israel crossed into Canaan were intended to cause future generations to sense their participation in the Conquest (Josh. 4:7).

Building on this vital aspect of OT faith, we better understand Jesus' command to celebrate the Lord's Supper "in remembrance of me." His words are a call to experience our union with him in his

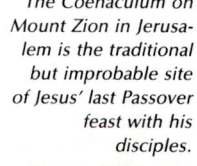

The Coenaculum on Mount Zion in Jerusalem is the traditional but improbable site of Jesus' last Passover feast with his disciples.

death and resurrection. In a very real sense, Christians were present with and in Jesus at his death (Rom. 6:1-7). Just as the Jews were to visualize their personal deliverance from Egypt in their ancestors, so we are to visualize our presence in Jesus' sacrifice of himself for us. In the communion service, the Christian is present again at the cross. Thus, Paul in 1 Cor. 10:16 says, "Is not the cup of thanksgiving for which we give thanks a participation in the blood of Christ? And is not the bread that we break a participation in the body of Christ?" Thus, the Lord's Supper is a repeated experience of God's redemptive love and grace.

Lot [LAHT; "covering"]. Abraham's nephew, who traveled with him to Canaan and unwisely settled in Sodom. **Father:** Haran. **Descendants:** Moabites, Ammonites. **Scripture:** Gen. 11–14, 19.

BACKGROUND

Lot traveled to Canaan with his childless uncle, Abraham. The two stayed together until their two growing herds strained local resources and led to fighting between their herdsmen. They then separated, and Abraham granted Lot first choice of where to go. Lot chose to settle in the verdant Jordan Valley near Sodom and Gomorrah (Gen. 13).

The OT relates three incidents concerning Lot. (1) The cities of the plain were attacked by raiders from the north under Kedorlaomer, and their populations were taken prisoner. Abraham then rescued Lot and the others (Gen. 14). (2) Two angelic messengers visited Sodom to warn Lot the city was about to be destroyed. Lot attempted to defend the messengers from homosexual gang rape by the men of Sodom, but the angels were compelled to strike them with blindness. Lot then fled the city with his family, but his wife defied the angels' warning; she looked back and was turned into a "pillar of salt" (Gen. 19). (3) Lot hid in a cave with his two daughters. They encouraged him to get drunk, and then they became pregnant by him, fearing "There is no man around here to lie with us." This incest produced the founders of two peoples with whom Israel struggled later, the Moabites and Ammonites (Gen. 19).

LEARNING FROM LOT'S LIFE

Lot is portrayed as a moral but weak man. Second Peter 2:7 calls him "a righteous man," reflecting on his refusal to participate in the "wicked thing" the Sodomites intended (Gen. 19:3,7). Yet Lot chose "for himself" the rich plain of the Jordan and pitched his tent "near Sodom," even though the "men of Sodom were wicked and were sinning greatly against the Lord" (Gen. 13:10-13). Later, Lot moved into the city and arranged for his daughters to marry men of Sodom (Gen. 19:12-14)!

Lot may have been a moral man personally, but he chose material comfort at the cost of constant distress over the "filthy lives of lawless men" (2 Pet. 2:7). Lot even mortgaged the character of his grandchildren by betrothing some of his daughters to men of Sodom. Significantly, when Sodom was destroyed, Lot was forced to flee, leaving the wealth he so valued behind, incinerated in the fires of God's judgment.

Above: Pen and ink drawing of Lot and his family, by Rembrandt van Rijn (1606–1669).
Above left: Salt pillars in the Dead Sea. When Lot's family fled God's wrath on Sodom and Gomorrah, Lot's wife, looking back at the destruction, turned into a pillar of salt.

Perhaps what we learn from Lot is that it is not enough to be a moral individual. We must actively avoid association with evil. Lot's choice of the creature comforts found in Sodom was the pivotal decision of his life. As Lot discovered, the cost of compromise is always high, and the benefits for which we sacrifice our integrity are fleeting.

lots (1) Small stones or other devices used to make choices, much like our drawing straws or throwing dice; (2) that which is determined by casting lots, an "allotment," as in Ps. 16:5. *See also* Urim and Thummim. Lots were used in many cultures in attempts to determine the will of the gods or to obtain supernatural guidance, as in Esth. 3:7; Jon. 1:7. Lots were also used in gambling, as in Mt. 27:35.

The OT reports many instances in which the Hebrews used this method to determine the will of God (Lev. 16:8; Josh. 7:14,15; 1 Chr. 24:5; Neh. 10:34). Most notably, lots were cast to determine the territory given to each of Israel's tribes in Canaan (Num. 26:55; Josh. 18:10). Lots were also cast to determine the sequence in which shifts of priests would serve in the Temple (1 Chr. 24:3-19; *compare* Lk. 1:5-9).

The biblical use of lots was not superstition but reflects the conviction that God exercises sovereign control over all things. Thus, "The lot is cast into the lap, but its every decision is from the Lord" (Prov.

16:33). Reflecting this conviction, each Israelite family perceived the land they received in Joshua's distribution as a divine gift, personally given to them by the Lord himself, and to be held in perpetual trust by the family. *See also* Jubilee.

The last biblical use of lots was to choose between two candidates for the post of Judas as a twelfth disciple (Acts 1:26). There is no suggestion in the NT Epistles that this practice was to be carried over into the Church, whose members are guided by the indwelling Holy Spirit of God (*compare* Acts 13:1-3). *See also* Holy Spirit; Lead.

love A powerful relational term, used of (1) the deep affection or liking one has for another person or persons; (2) the passionate affection one has for a person of the opposite sex, also used of sexual intercourse; (3) the commitment one makes to the best interests of other persons, as expressed in actions that benefit them. While love has this wide range of meanings in Scripture, the controlling concept when Scripture portrays divine or Christian love is that of commitment.

OLD TESTAMENT

Three Hebrew words are theologically significant. (1) *'Aheb.* The intensity of this word varies from "like" (as for food in Gen. 27:4) to deep love (as God's constant love for his people in Jer. 31:3). The intensity of the emotion generally depends on its subject and object. (2) *Hesed.* Often translated "loving-kindness," this term describes the bond of loyalty that exists between persons within the family or within other special relationships. *See also* Loving-kindness. When the OT describes the loyalty God exhibits to the people with whom he has established his covenant, it

Right: Lots found at the fortress of Masada, the final refuge of Jews in the rebellion against Rome, A.D. 63–70. Each is inscribed with a name. Josephus reports that such lots were used there to determine who would kill the others to avoid capture. Below: Roman figurine of girls playing knucklebones—a game handed down from the Greeks that used sheep or goat joints or pieces shaped like them. (Taranto, Italy, 330 B.C.)

uses this word. It is found in such powerful statements as Ex. 34:6,7: "God, slow to anger, abounding in love and faithfulness, maintaining love to thousands, and forgiving wickedness, rebellion and sin." (3) *Raham.* This word means "compassion" and portrays the response of a person who cares deeply about the needs of his or her loved ones.

The OT word that best reflects God's love for human beings is *hesed.* Focused uniquely on those whom God has redeemed, such love moves the Lord to forgive (Ps. 86:5), to deliver (Ps. 17:7), and to protect (Ps. 32:10) his own. In this covenant-love, God answers prayer (Ps. 66:20), communicates his Law (Ps. 119:124), and redeems his people (Ps. 130:7). Ultimately, this love will move God to restore Israel and to re-establish his Kingdom on earth (Isa. 55:3; Jer. 31:3,4).

Love (*'aheb*) motivated God's choice of Israel (Deut. 4:37,38) and his supervision of every historic event that affected his people, including their discipline (*compare* Deut. 7; Prov. 3:12; Hos. 11:1). God's compassionate love (*raham*) is another theme found often in explanations of the unique continuing relationship the Lord chose to maintain with Israel (*compare* Ex. 33:19; Mic. 7; Zech. 1:16). The OT, with a solitary exception in Jer. 2:2, reserves *hesed* to speak of God's love for human beings and not of man's love for God. Yet, the OT does call on men to love (*'aheb*) "the Lord your God with all your heart and with all your soul and with all your strength" (Deut. 6:5). The context makes it clear that the OT believer displayed love for God by obedience to his commands (Deut. 10:12,13; 20:16-20; Ps. 119:113,163-167). Furthermore, our love for God can be measured by our response to the initiating love of God.

NEW TESTAMENT

Two Greek words are translated with the English word "love." *Philia* suggests the warm, caring relationship appropriate to friendship and family. There are many compound words in the NT constructed on this root. These include Greek words that mean "brotherly love" and even "love for good."

The key word for love in the NT is *agapē.* A little-used term in classical Greek, *agapē* is transformed in the NT into the most powerful word imaginable for love. This transformation was accomplished when the Christian community used this word to portray the love of God in Christ. "This is love," the apostle John affirmed, "not that we loved God, but that he loved us and sent his Son as an atoning sacrifice for our sins" (1 Jn. 4:9,10). By this association, *agapē* was lifted from the realm of natural affection to become the affirmation of the ideal. The love human beings have yearned for has at last appeared in Christ. In him, we discern God's love, which is sacrificial, redeeming, unmerited, an expression of the character of the lover rather than dependent on qualities in the beloved.

Yet, the love of God does produce a love response in the believer. "We love [him]," John writes, "because he first loved us" (1 Jn. 4:19). In both Testaments, love is a volitional term, expressed in obedience to God (Jn. 14:21,23; 1 Jn. 5:3) and in the experience of a growing commitment to Christian brothers and sisters (Jn. 15:12; 1 Jn. 3:11-15). This spirit of love is the foundation of ethical behavior in the NT (1 Cor. 13).

The words on this fresco in a catacomb of Rome indicate that this is an agapē *("love") feast, a fellowship meal shared by early Christians (see 2 Pet. 2:13).*

651

The love which God has shown us, thus, is intended to provoke our love for him and to motivate a life-style of love toward others.

love feast An *agapē* or fellowship meal shared by members of the early church, as mentioned in 2 Pet. 2:13 (KJV, RSV) and Jude 12. Meals shared by members of clubs or brotherhoods were common in first-century Jewish and Gentile societies (*compare* Acts 2:46). Thus, it was natural for the early Christians, encouraged in their faith to love one another, to meet together for dinners as well as for worship. Acts 20:7-12 and 1 Cor. 11:17-33 suggest that the Lord's Supper was often celebrated at the end of these fellowship meals. *See also* Lord's Supper.

loving-kindness [Heb., *hesed*]. (1) When used of God, denotes God's love for his people, actively expressed as loyalty to his covenant promises and as mercy; (2) when used of man, generally expresses kindness or mercy toward others and devotion or piety towards God.

Translators have struggled to express God's *hesed* in English. Suggestions range from "solidarity" to "covenant love." The RSV tends to use "steadfast love" while the NIV leans toward "faithful love." *See also* Love.

Lucifer (KJV) [Latin, "light bearer"]. A name commonly ascribed to Satan.

The name is taken from the Latin translation of the Hebrew in Isa. 14:12: "How you have fallen from heaven, O morning star, son of the dawn!" Isaiah 14:12-15 is understood by many as a description of Satan's motivation for his original rebellion against God. The early church linked this passage with Christ's words in Lk. 10:18 concerning Satan's "fall like lightning from heaven" and adopted Lucifer as a name for Satan. However, others understand Isa. 14:12-15 as no more than ridicule directed against the pride and pretensions of the human king of Babylon and, thus, consider "Lucifer" as a traditional, yet misapplied name for Satan.

Luke, Gospel according to The third Gospel of the NT, Luke is the longest and most literary of the four NT portraits of Jesus' life on earth. The author intended to "draw up an account" of Jesus' life based on interviews with those "who from the first were eyewitnesses and servants of the word" (Lk. 1:1-4). His book is rich in detail and filled with sensitive portraits of individuals who came in contact with our Lord.

AUTHORSHIP

The author is identified by Irenaeus in A.D. 180 as Luke ["light"], Paul's "beloved physician" and companion (Col. 4:14, KJV; *compare* 2 Tim. 4:11; Phlm. 24). This early tradition is supported by strong arguments for Luke's authorship of Acts. As Luke and Acts share the same polished literary style, a common focus on such themes as evangelism (Lk. 1:19; 2:10; 4:18; Acts 5:42; 8:4; etc.), and careful descriptions of sicknesses, almost all commentators agree the two books were written by the same person. *See also* Acts. Furthermore, there is general agreement that Luke was a Gentile Christian (Col. 4:10-17). If so, he is the only Gentile to write a NT book.

BACKGROUND

Luke writes with the Hellenistic world in mind. The book's dedication to Theophilus hints at its relevance to a wider Gentile Christian audience (Lk. 1:1-4), and its similarity to Greco-Roman historical and literary works strongly suggests this. Moreover, the presence of "God-fearers" in his book and his alteration of some

"Our dear friend Luke, the doctor" (Col. 4:14) was Paul's companion and probably provided him medical care, especially during Paul's imprisonment.

Palestinian Jewish terms into Hellenistic ones (*for example*, "lawyer," *nomikos*, for "scribe," *grammateus*) also might indicate the intended readers. *See also* God-fearing; Grecian Jews; Hellenists.

THEOLOGICAL CONTRIBUTIONS

Luke's powerful portrait of Jesus emphasizes his compassion and perfect humanity. It challenges Greco-Roman cultural values of personal achievement and self-fulfillment by portraying the ideal Man, who served and cared for the lowest people in society. Luke gives many illustrations of Jesus ministering to social outcasts—like tax collectors and Samaritans—to women, to children, and to the poor. These manifest qualities set Jesus apart from the religious leaders who are hostile to him and make him accessible to the common man. Luke's portrait gives us the best insight of any of the Gospels into Jesus' humanity.

In this context, Luke's emphasis on the Holy Spirit, on prayer, and on evangelism is significant. Christ's birth was accomplished by the work of the Holy Spirit (Lk. 1:15,35). The Holy Spirit descended on Jesus at his baptism (3:22). Christ was filled with the Spirit as he performed every earthly ministry (4:1,34; 10:21). Because Jesus relied on the Spirit, Jesus' followers can live a Christ-like life, for God gives the

same Spirit to those who trust his Son (11:13; 12:12; 24:49; *compare* 6:40).

Furthermore, Luke's Gospel presents Jesus as a man of prayer. He prays at his baptism (3:21), before he predicts his death and resurrection (9:18), at the Transfiguration (9:28,29), and in many other instances recorded only in Luke (*compare* 5:16; 6:12; 10:21; 11:1; 22:31,32; 22:39-46; 23:34,46).

Above: Aerial view of the ruins of Caesarea, where Paul was imprisoned for two years. Here Luke had ample opportunities to do research on Jesus' life in preparation for writing his Gospel.

Luke's inclusion of Jesus' Parable of the Prodigal Son epitomizes his Gospel's emphasis on God's compassion (Lk. 15:11-32).

LUKE: A READING AND STUDY GUIDE

Chapter	Content Summary	Related Articles
1	The births of John the Baptist and Jesus are foretold by an angel. Mary and Zechariah praise God.	John the Baptist Incarnation
2	Jesus' birth is announced to shepherds by angels. Twelve-year-old Jesus goes to the Temple.	Angel
3	John the Baptist calls on the Jews to repent. Jesus is baptized, and his genealogy is recorded.	Repent Baptism
4	Jesus overcomes Satan's temptations. He is rejected in Nazareth but performs miracles in Capernaum.	Satan Tempt
5	Jesus calls his disciples. He heals a leper and a paralytic. He answers questions about fasting.	Healing Fast
6	Jesus announces his Lordship over the Sabbath. He teaches the Beatitudes and love for enemies.	Lord Judge
7	A Roman centurion displays faith, while John the Baptist expresses his doubts.	Centurion
8	Jesus tells the parable of the sower. He heals a possessed man and an infirm woman and raises a dead girl.	Demon Death
9	Jesus feeds 5,000. Peter confesses him as the Christ. Jesus is transfigured before three disciples.	Christ Transfiguration
10	Jesus sends out 72 disciples to preach. He talks about the Good Samaritan and visits Mary and Martha.	Disciple Woman
11	Jesus teaches on prayer. He is charged with being in league with Satan. He pronounces "woes" on his religious foes.	Prayer Woe; Pharisees
12	Jesus encourages his followers not to fear. He tells the story of the rich fool and urges disciples not to worry, but to be watchful and ready for his coming.	Fear Anxiety Second Coming
13	Jesus calls for repentance. He heals on the Sabbath and weeps over Jerusalem.	Sabbath
14	Jesus eats at a Pharisee's house and tells the parable of a Great Banquet. He states the cost of discipleship.	Parable Hate
15	Jesus tells the parables of the lost sheep, the lost coin, and the prodigal son.	
16	Jesus tells the parable of the shrewd manager and the story of the rich man and Lazarus.	Hell
17	Jesus commands forgiveness, heals ten lepers, and speaks of his Second Coming.	Forgive Second Coming
18	Jesus tells the parables of the persistent widow, and the Pharisee and the tax collector. He meets a rich young ruler, predicts his own death, and heals a blind beggar.	Wealth
19	Jesus visits Zacchaeus, tells the parable of ten minas, and enters Jerusalem in triumph.	
20	Jesus' authority is challenged. He tells the parable of the tenants and avoids two traps set by his enemies.	Authority
21	Jesus tells his disciples signs marking the end of the age.	Age, Ages
22	Judas plans to betray Jesus. The disciples meet for the Last Supper. Jesus prays in Gethsemane and is arrested. Peter denies Jesus while Jesus is on trial.	Judas Iscariot Trial
23	Jesus is condemned and crucified. He dies and is buried.	Crucifixion Burial
24	Jesus is raised from the dead. He meets two disciples on the Emmaus Road and later appears to all the disciples before ascending to heaven.	Resurrection Ascension

madness Insanity, mental illness, derangement. The terms used in Scripture are not clinical, but imply states ranging from mental unsoundness to complete irrationality.

In most ancient cultures, madness was assumed to be caused by a supernatural being or force. *See also* Lunatic.

The OT warns Israel that if the nation did not keep God's commands "the Lord will afflict you with madness, blindness, and confusion of mind" (Deut. 28:28). As King Saul slipped rapidly into depression and paranoia, it became increasingly clear that "the Spirit of the Lord had departed from Saul, and an evil spirit from the Lord tormented him" (1 Sam. 16:14).

When David pretended insanity in Gath, he "acted like a madman, making marks on the doors of the gate and letting saliva run down his beard" (1 Sam. 21:13). Nebuchadnezzar's insanity caused him to be driven away from people, to eat grass like cattle, his hair growing long and his uncut nails resembling birds' claws (Dan. 4:33).

In first-century Judaism, a connection between insanity and demon possession was firmly established in popular thought. The demon-possessed man of Gadara exhibited great strength, and "night and day among the tombs and in the hills he would cry out and cut himself with stones" (Mk. 5:5). Jesus drove out the legion of spirits who possessed the man, leaving him "in his right mind" (5:15).

Yet, the notion of madness is far broader than implied in such passages. When the serving girl, Rhoda, rushed in to report to the group praying for Peter's release from prison that the apostle was standing outside the door, their reaction was, "You're out of your mind!" (Acts 12:15). When Paul witnessed to King Agrippa and Festus, Festus became agitated and finally cried out, "You are out of your mind, Paul! Your great learning is driving you insane" (Acts 26:24). Clearly, according to first-century judgment, telling someone, "You're crazy," might indicate nothing more than refusal to accept what that speaker was saying. A far more serious charge was made against Jesus by the religious leaders when they argued, "He is demon-possessed and raving mad. Why listen to him?" (Jn. 10:20). Their unbelief is very evident in their scornful remarks. Thus, depending on the context, "madness" in Scripture can either indicate true insanity or disbelieving scorn for the one to whom the term is applied.

magi In the OT: (1) a scholarly, priestly class that served as advisers and astrologers to Babylonian and Persian rulers, as in Dan. 2:10; 4:7. *See also* Chaldeans. In the NT: (2) origin of the title "Magus," used often with contempt of traveling magicians or entertainers, but at times implying supernatural powers, as in Acts 13:6,8; (3) the name given visitors from the East who came to Herod in search of the child "born king of the Jews" (Mt. 2:1-12).

It is not possible to identify the Magi of Matthew's account. However, a class of magi persisted in Persia proper and at times was influential in the Parthian kingdom that lay east of Palestine and which successfully resisted Roman incursions, even mounting attacks on Roman territory.

The basis on which these particular Magi identified the Messiah's star remains a mystery. Some have suggested their insight was based on possession of the text of Num. 24:17, "A star will come out

This miniature from a Latin missal (prayer book) portrays the Magi following the star to Bethlehem and then presenting their expensive gifts to Jesus. Weingarten Abbey, Germany, A.D. 1200–1232.

659

of Jacob; a scepter will rise out of Israel.'' It is quite possible that the Magi would have had access to a copy of the OT and even to Jewish speculative writings. Daniel served as one of the magi, and the large Jewish community in Babylon continued to actively explore and write about the OT for centuries beyond the time of Nebuchadnezzar.

The notions that the Magi were kings and that there were three of them are very late inventions, as are their supposed names. Some have theorized the ''kingship'' of the Magi comes from such passages as Ps. 72:10; Isa. 49:7; 60:3; and that there were three of them because there are three recorded gifts, but this is at best

speculation. Nevertheless, it is significant that these Gentile ''wise men'' were among the first to recognize and worship Jesus.

magic The use of charms, spells, or rituals to influence persons or events or to control the supernatural beings thought to influence events. All occult practices to some extent involve the use of magic.

OLD TESTAMENT

Some eight different Hebrew roots identify magicians and their practices, ranging from sorcery or witchcraft to spiritism, from enchanting to divining. An early reference to magic in the OT is the ''earrings'' in Gen. 35:4, which were most likely charms worn by Jacob's wives. The magicians of Pharaoh's court whom Moses confronted also provide an early example of ancient Eastern magic (Ex. 7,8). Deuteronomy 18:9-13 calls all such practices ''detestable'' and forbids them to God's OT

people. Mosaic Law condemns the practice of any kind of magic and prescribes the death penalty for it (Ex. 22:18; Lev. 19:26,31; 20:6). The persistence of these practices despite their prohibition is seen in Isa. 3:20's reference to charms (''amulets,'' KJV) and in Micah's pronouncement that in Messiah's day, ''I will destroy your witchcraft and you will no longer cast spells'' (Mic. 5:12). Among the visions given to Ezekiel to explain why God must abandon Jerusalem and his Temple is a graphic image of the women of Judah sewing magic charms on their wrists with intent to harm others (13:17-23).

NEW TESTAMENT

Five terms in the NT are linked with magic, including metaphorical references in Gal. 3:1 and 2 Tim. 3:13 and the title ''Magus'' assumed by persons pretending to have supernatural powers (Acts 8:9; 13:6,8). In the Book of Revelation, those who practice any magic arts are condemned (21:8; 22:15). *See also* Magi.

Most significant is the Acts 19:19 reference to the burning of books on magic by believers in Ephesus who had earlier ''practiced sorcery.'' This incident suggests something of the prevalence of magic in the first century. A variety of early documents demonstrate that many relied on magic in the Roman world. The average person turned to magic for protection against illness and when making important decisions. Love potions and spells were used in attempts to gain power over others. Finally, certain types of magic were used to harm or destroy enemies. A surprising number of spells and incantations from this period show Jewish influence, both in a number of "names of power" invoked and in Jewish endings on words found in incantations.

MAGIC VS. CHRISTIAN FAITH

A study of a number of magic spells dating from the second century B.C. to the fifth century A.D. suggests that concepts of how magic works have changed little over the centuries. What is most significant, however, are the number of spells that deal with ordinary issues of life. People turned to magic for everything from warding off fever to help for getting along with others or for enhancing sexual performance. There are even spells to enable a person to eat garlic and not stink and to drink alcohol without getting drunk.

The Bible's strong anti-magic stance grows out of a distinctive and consistent world view. To the believer, God is the basic and universal reality. A person who maintains a covenant relationship with God relies on him for all things. To rely on magic is to abandon God. To practice magic is to turn to supernatural powers which are less than, and essentially hostile to, God and his Word. Thus, the Gospel of Christ necessarily challenged first-century men and women not only to turn to God, but also to turn away from idols and from the world view that idolatry represents (1 Th. 1:9). *See also* Charm; Divination; Sorcerer; Witch.

Magnificat The liturgical name given to Mary's song of praise (Lk. 1:46-55). It is the first word in the Latin translation. This song was shared with Elizabeth before the birth of Jesus. It resembles Hannah's praise song found in 1 Sam. 2:1-10. The Magnificat expresses Mary's joy at being chosen to become the mother of the Messiah (Lk. 1:46-49) and moves on to celebrate God's faithfulness and mercy to Israel (1:50-55).

Magog *See* Gog.

mahalath Possibly, a musical or literary term, found only in the titles of Pss. 53 and 88. *See also* Psalms.

Two maidservants pour water over their mistress and rub her arms, while a third holds a flower for her to smell and another a collar. Drawing of a tomb wall-painting from Thebes, 1580–1150 B.C.

maid, maiden, maidservant A woman. Some five Hebrew terms are translated "maid" in English versions. While some of the Hebrew words have specific meanings, the English "maid" does not identify a woman by her age, or social or marital status. Frequently, the maid or maiden is a bondservant, as in Lev. 25:6 and Deut. 15:12. *See also* Slave.

When used by a woman of herself, as by Abigail when she intercepted David on his way to kill Nabal, "maidservant" is a polite expression of humility (1 Sam. 25:41). Nevertheless, it referred to a real servant status in most cases (Gen. 16:1; 35:25,26; Ex. 20:10; Acts 12:13).

Malachi, Book of The last of the minor prophets, Malachi reflects conditions in Judah a century after the return of the Jewish exiles from Babylon. In 47 of Malachi's 55 verses, God speaks directly to his people, urging a renewed vision of himself as their living Master, King, Creator, and Judge.

BACKGROUND

Some 50,000 Jews returned from Babylon in 538 B.C. They immediately laid the foundation for rebuilding the Jerusalem Temple. However, the struggle to farm the long-abandoned land was more difficult than expected, and work on the Temple stopped. Then, motivated by the preaching of Haggai and Zechariah, the people completed the Temple in 520 B.C.

As the decades passed, the religious enthusiasm of the little community in Judah again waned. Ezra arrived in 457 B.C., commissioned to apply OT Law in the province. A few years later, in 444 B.C., Nehemiah was sent to Judah as its governor. Nehemiah oversaw the rebuilding of Jerusalem's walls, returned briefly to the Persian capital, and then came back to Jerusalem in 431 B.C. for a second term as governor.

The Books of Ezra and Nehemiah help us understand the conditions with which Malachi [MAL-uh-ki; "my messenger"] is so deeply concerned. Priests and people had lost their enthusiasm for God. Worship seemed routine and boring. The wealthy took advantage of the poor. Even the priests and elders of Judah took foreign wives. The Sabbath was violated as buyers and sellers swarmed on the day of rest to a marketplace set up just outside Jerusalem's walls.

It is not possible to pinpoint the exact date Malachi was written. Yet Temple worship had been re-established for some time, and a Persian governor (*pehah*; 1:8) resided in Judah. Some argue Malachi must have been written before Nehemiah's reforms. But the argument is hardly compelling, in view of how quickly the people of Judah reverted to their old ways between Nehemiah's first and second governorships. Most likely Malachi was written between 465 and 430 B.C.

AUTHORSHIP

Not much is known about Malachi. One view states that "Malachi" is a title taken from Mal. 3:1 and not the real name of the prophet. However, it is just as logical to assume "Malachi" is the prophet's name according to 1:1. The only information we have concerning Malachi is what we can glean from the book. He was probably born in Judah, and he undoubtedly prophesied in Jerusalem itself. He was zealous for the Law and exhorted the people to live righteous and moral lives, which would show their loyalty to God's covenant.

THEOLOGICAL CONTRIBUTIONS

Centuries before Malachi wrote, God revealed the name Yahweh to Moses, and said, "This is my name forever, the name by which I am to be remembered from generation to generation." The name, which means "One Who Is Always Present" or I AM, is a call to an intimate relationship with the Lord rooted in the awareness that he is (exists) and that he is active in the lives of his people (Heb. 11:6). It was just this reality that the people of Malachi's time had forgotten. Thus, through the prophet, God reveals himself again as Lord Almighty (1:4), Judah's Father and Master (1:6), her Great King (1:14), her Creator (2:10,15), and her Judge (3:17,18; 4:1). *See also* Yahweh.

The book is structured around six tests of our relationship with God as a living, present reality in our lives: (1) awareness of God's love, 1:1-5; (2) honoring God in our actions, 1:6–2:9; (3) faithfulness in our social relationships, 2:10-16; (4) fear of God expressed in our commitment to justice, 2:17–3:5; (5) serving God with our material resources, 3:6-14; and (6) meeting with others to talk about our Lord, 3:15-18.

MASTERY KEYS

Read the entry on Nehemiah for more historical background. Study each section dealing with a test of one's relationship with God to see what can be applied to your own life.

MALACHI: A READING AND STUDY GUIDE

Chapter	Content Summary	Related Articles
1:1-5	God demonstrated his love for Israel by sovereignly choosing Jacob; Esau's descendants are judged.	Love Esau
1:6-14	God the Great King is dishonored by people who find worship a burden and offer unworthy sacrifices.	Worship Sacrifices and Offerings
2:1-9	God the Lord Almighty is dishonored by priests who neither teach God's way nor walk in it.	Priest Law
2:10-16	God is spurned by those who faithlessly divorce their wives and marry pagan women. He will not accept the offerings of faithless persons.	Divorce Marriage
2:17–3:5	God is wearied by the "worship" of impure persons, whose failure to fear God is reflected in personal and social immorality.	Justice Fear
3:6-15	God is robbed by those who think so little of serving him that they withhold gifts and tithes.	Tithe Give
3:16-18	God is pleased by those who fear him and meet together to speak about him. The Lord will spare the righteous when he comes.	Righteousness Name
4:1-5	The Day of the Lord's judgment is coming, but first Elijah will come to prepare God's people.	Day of the Lord Elijah

Malachi promises that God will send Elijah to his people before the day of divine judgment comes. Christ said that, had Israel accepted him as Messiah, John the Baptist would have fulfilled this prediction (*compare* Mt. 11:7-14; 17:9-13).

malefactor (KJV) A term used in Lk. 23:32,33,39 of the thieves who were crucified with Jesus (Gk., *kakourgos*; "worker of evil"), and used by Christ's enemies in Jn. 18:30 when they accused him before Pilate (Gk., *kakopoios* or *kakov poiōs*; "doer of evil").

mammon (KJV) An Aramaic word meaning "riches" or "wealth." The word is found in the NT only in two sayings of Jesus.

In Mt. 6:24 (*compare* Lk. 16:13), Jesus warns that commitment to God and commitment to gaining wealth conflict. God and money are competing masters, in that we make decisions on the basis of our desire to serve the one or gain the other.

The other mention of mammon is found in Jesus' parable of the unjust steward (Lk. 16:9,11), where modern versions tend to interpret "unrighteous mammon" as "worldly wealth." Christ's teaching in this parable is often misunderstood. Jesus commended the dishonest steward, not for his acts but because he clearly understood that money is a resource to be used to prepare for the future. The believer must have this same perspective: We are not to "love money" as the Pharisees did (16:14), but rather view it simply as something we can use in the service of God and thus store up treasures in heaven (*compare* Mt. 6:19-21).

man Human being. In the OT, Hebrew *'adam* ("man") is the name of the first man, the basic Hebrew word for humanity or mankind. *'Ish* ("man") and *'ishah* ("woman") view each person as an individual who, as a human being, has worth and value. *'Enosh* ("man") contrasts the mortality of man in his present state with the eternality of God, as in Ps. 103:13-16. In its generic sense, it is sexless and is used throughout the Bible to indicate both men and women. *Basar* ("flesh") views man in relation to the experience of life on earth, as in Gen. 2:24, and in relation to his frailty, as in Ps. 73:26. *Nepesh* ("soul") pictures man in relation to each person's self-identity and self-awareness. *Ruah* ("spirit") portrays man in relation to his awareness of the supernatural and spiri-

tual. *Leb* ("heart") describes man in the totality of the emotions, motives, values, and perceptions that find expression in individual character and actions, as in Gen. 6:5.

In the NT, most Greek terms have meanings influenced by their Hebrew counterparts; thus, for the most part, their definitions should not be sought in meanings established in Greek culture or philosophy. Exceptions are "flesh" (*sarx*) and "soul" (*psychē*), which in Paul's writings take on a distinctive moral character and represent man's nature as distorted by the Fall.

The biblical view of humanity expressed in Scripture's use of these and other terms is distinctive. It stands in bold contrast to the common assumption that man is a biological accident. Instead, man is presented as a divine invention, a unique and culminating creation of God. To understand humanity, and ourselves as human beings, we must consider human nature from the viewpoints adopted in Scripture.

• *Origin*. Man is derived from a direct creative act of God.

• *Identity*. Man was created in the image of God.

• *Place*. Man has a place in the created order between animal and angel.

• *Destiny*. Each human being is destined for self-conscious awareness forever.

• *Structure*. Man is flesh, spirit, soul, heart, moral will, and more.

• *Relationships*. Man has capacities that involve him in relationships with God, with the self, with others, and with nature.

• *Fall*. The normal expression of human nature is corrupted by sin.

• *Autonomy*. Man is a responsible moral agent, aware of moral issues and capable of moral choice.

• *Redemption*. Ideal humanity is exemplified by Jesus Christ and is being restored in believers by virtue of the redemption Christ won.

• *Purpose*. Man was created to glorify God and to enjoy him forever.

ORIGIN

Genesis 1 and 2 portray the creation of the first man and woman. God shaped the dust of the earth into human form and breathed into that form his own "breath of life." The living being God created shares characteristics with the animals (Gen. 2:19) but is lifted above them by the unique gift of God's image (Gen. 1:26). Eve was then created from Adam's rib to establish her essential human identity with him. This

Genesis story is foundational to the biblical view of man.

The creation account implies more than divine concern with an abstract humanity. Implicit in God's careful shaping of the first humans is divine concern for each individual person. In Ps. 139:13-16, David describes God supervising his development in the womb, ordaining from the moment of conception all his days, "before one of them came to be" (*compare* Ps. 8). Jesus assured his hearers that "even the very hairs of your head are all numbered" (Mt. 10:30).

IDENTITY

In the creation story, God says, "Let us make man in our image, in our likeness" (Gen. 1:26). Linkage of the two Hebrew terms *selem* and *demut,* "image and likeness," occurs only where Scripture makes a distinctive statement about human nature (Gen. 1:26,27; 5:3,4; 9:6). It is best to take these terms as a reference to personhood. Like God, each human being has capacities essential to personhood—the capacity to think, to remember, to feel, to choose, to act, to respond, to communicate in language, etc. *See also* Image.

Taken as a whole, these capacities set man apart from the animals and require any search for human identity to begin with an examination of man's relationship to God rather than to any created being. The image of God, persisting despite the Fall, is the basis for Scripture's statement that "whoever sheds the blood of man, by man shall his blood be shed" (Gen. 9:6). The image of God, which each human being bears, makes him or her infinitely precious. *See also* Murder.

PLACE

The Genesis story gives man dominion over the animals, a concept that incorporates superiority and responsibility. Psalm 8 defines man's place more clearly: "You made him a little lower than the heavenly beings," and yet "you made him ruler over the works of your hands." The writer of Hebrews quotes this psalm and argues that God's ultimate intention in Christ is to bring "many sons to glory," that is, to lift human beings above the angels, to stand at Jesus' side (Heb. 2:5-13). The writer then adds, "Surely it is not angels he helps, but Abraham's descendants [that is, human beings with faith]" (2:16). *See also* Dominion.

This sense of place is important. In biblical times, nearly every society, whether Greek, Egyptian, or Canaanite, blurred the distinction between gods, men, and animals. Man imagined gods in his image, ascribing human traits and motives to them, yet at the same time often pictured his gods in animal form. A similar blurring of the distinction between man and animal characterizes modern evolutionary theory, which considers human beings no more than advanced animals. The OT's stern prohibition against creating idols of animal and human form is related to the necessity of maintaining an awareness that man is a being with a distinctive place in the created order.

DESTINY

The existence of the human personality after death is implied in the Genesis account but not developed in the OT. Even references to "forever," as in Ps. 23:6, probably imply no more than a continual, life-long experience. At the same time, some references in the OT do seem to suggest life after death (*compare* Pss. 16:11; 21:4-6; 30:5; Prov. 12:28; 15:24). Clearer statements are found in Dan. 12:2 and Isa. 26:19, the latter affirming, "Your dead will live; their bodies will rise. You who dwell in the dust, wake up and shout for joy.

Your dew is like the dew of the morning; the earth will give birth to her dead."

New Testament teaching on man's eternal destiny is developed in Jesus' words and in the Epistles. Jesus' story of the rich man and the beggar Lazarus portrays the dead as self-conscious, aware, able to feel and remember (Lk. 16:19-31). The Epistles teach that at death the believer goes to be with the Lord (2 Cor. 5:6-8), awaiting Christ's Second Coming when the personality will be united with a resurrection body (1 Cor. 15; 1 Th. 4:13-17). At history's end, the saved will be forever with the Lord (Rev. 21,22), while the lost are committed to a lake of fire (Rev. 20:11-15). Man thus has his origin and his destiny in eternity. No anthropology that focuses only on man's experience in this world can adequately determine the nature of man. *See also* Heaven; Hell; Judgment; Resurrection.

STRUCTURE

Attempts to describe the structure of human nature have tended to see man as a dual (body, soul) or tripartite (body, soul, spirit) being. Such attempts reflect the Greek analytical approach to the question of human nature, perhaps reading Greek philosophical concepts uncritically into biblical terms. In fact, the OT view of man is not analytical, and the Hebrew terms are not intended to divide human nature into parts. Instead, these terms view man as a whole, but look at particular aspects of the whole man's experience.

Basar ("flesh") looks at the whole person in relation to his experiences in this world. In this relationship, the flesh is weak, for human beings are subject to aging, sickness, death, and to forces in nature over which they have no control. Understanding the basic meaning of *basar* helps us see

that the Gen. 2:24 pronouncement, "They shall be one flesh," implies a marital unity found not simply in the sex act but in sharing the joys and sorrows of life on earth. Other biblical terms have similar broad rather than analytical meaning. *Nepesh* ("soul") looks at the whole person as a self-conscious individual, a "self" or "I." *Ruah* ("spirit") examines the whole man in his relationship to the unseen spiritual realm. *Leb* ("heart") analyzes the inner man and the complex networks of emotions, thoughts, motives, perceptions, and desires that find expression in action. Thus, Jesus said that "the things that come out of the mouth come from the heart" (Mt. 15:18).

This complex unity we call a human being can relate, think, feel, choose, and function in the material universe and relate to the unseen. Thus, rather than dividing human nature into separate and isolated components, it is best to adopt a holistic view.

RELATIONSHIPS

We need to study man by looking at the relationships human beings establish with God, self, others, and the physical universe. The image of God, which establishes man's personhood, makes personal relationship with God a possibility. As beings of "spirit" (Heb., *ruah*; Gk., *pneuma*), human beings are aware of and seek some kind of relationship with the supernatural. As beings of "self-awareness" (Heb., *nepesh*; Gk., *psychē*), human beings are conscious of and seek to actualize the self, by growth, achievement, etc. As beings of "inner complexity" (Heb., *leb*; Gk., *kardia*), human beings respond to and seek relationships with one another on multiple levels. The emotions, thoughts, perceptions, motives, drives, and desires within us demand a social

665

context, for they are stimulated by and directed toward our relationships with others. As beings of "body" or "flesh" (Heb., *basar;* Gk., *sōma, sarx*), human beings live in the physical universe and have capacities that enable them to manipulate the universe to provide food, clothing, shelter, and to develop complex material cultures fully. Thus, to understand human nature, we must view human beings in the complex relationships within which man exercises his God-given capacities.

FALL

The Christian understanding of human nature must begin with the affirmation of Scripture that God made man in his own image. While that image has been marred, it has not been lost (*compare* Gen. 9:6). The various capacities of human beings that enable men and women to relate to the supernatural, to self, to others, and to the material universe are witnesses to the continuing existence of the original image of God. It is clear, however, that the expression of the image of God in man has been corrupted, and each capacity distorted.

The biblical explanation for this corruption is the Fall, an act of sin committed by Adam and Eve. The Fall introduced death and so corrupted the first pair that they transmitted a marred image to their descendants. Because of the Fall, man's capacity to relate to the supernatural has been twisted and, thus, he finds expression in empty philosophies, ranging from the rawest paganism to the most sophisticated secular humanism. Because of the Fall, man's capacity to relate to self has been damaged, and finds expression in selfishness, pride, and psychological disorders. Because of the Fall, man's capacity to relate to others has been marred, and finds expression in hostility, injustice, faithlessness, oppression, and unconcern. Because of the Fall, man's capacity to master the material creation has been corrupted and finds expression in the rape of earth's resources.

Despite this dark picture of corruption, the image of God remains in man, giving each person value.

AUTONOMY

One of the distinctive capacities possessed by man is the awareness of moral issues and the ability to make moral choices. In the OT, it finds expression in the Mosaic covenant in the responsibility of each member of the community for the quality of the community's relationship with God. In the prophets, the emphasis is increasingly laid on the moral responsibil-

ity of the individual to love God and to love one's neighbor. Ezekiel 18 carefully fixes moral responsibility. Each individual is free to choose and is responsible for every moral choice, whatever the parental or societal influences. In the NT, the new covenant is rich in exhortations directed to God's "dear children" to imitate him and to "live a life of love, just as Christ loved us and gave himself up for us" (Eph. 5:2). Here, the Christian is challenged to be holy, as God is holy (1 Pet. 1:15).

To some philosophers, the biblical "ought" seems to imply "can." Thus, the very fact of moral responsibility has been taken as evidence against the biblical pronouncement that human beings are lost, spiritually "dead in your transgressions and sins" (Eph. 2:1-4). However, the overwhelming "oughts" of Scripture and the clear affirmation of individual responsibility are intended to make us conscious of our moral failures. Such consciousness of sin may motivate a search, both for forgiveness and for enablement. *See also* Law.

REDEMPTION

In Christ, the second Adam, we discover what each of us might have been. Moreover, we discover what we can ultimately become through faith in Jesus.

The Bible portrays human beings as lost. Yet each person is retrievable. Man is spiritually dead. Yet individuals can respond to the Gospel's call and experience a present, inner resurrection as well as be assured of a future resurrection of the body (*compare* Rom. 8:11). That human beings are redeemable is one of the great themes of Scripture and one of the most important aspects of the Bible's portrayal of human nature. Through faith in Jesus Christ, an individual establishes a personal relationship with God, experiences inner spiritual renewal, and can gradually counter, through the power of the Holy Spirit, many of the effects of original sin on the human personality. In the language of the NT, the redeemed begin to reflect the Lord's glory, for they "are being transformed into his likeness with ever-increasing glory, which comes from the Lord, who is the Spirit" (2 Cor. 3:18; *compare* Col. 3:10). *See also* Transformation.

Because every individual is redeemable, the deepest yearnings of the human heart can be realized. Through faith in Jesus, who purchased our redemption with his blood, and through the empowering work of the indwelling Holy Spirit, those who walk by faith are enabled to live holy, righteous, and loving lives (Rom. 8:3,4), and, thus, the Church is enabled to become a loving, worshiping fellowship. *See also* Holy Spirit; Redeem.

PURPOSE

Within God's created universe, each individual is: given the gift of life, urged to live wisely, encouraged to recognize his or her inadequacies, challenged to accept personal responsibility for failures and sins, offered forgiveness and a new life, and then enabled to become truly righteous through reliance on the One who has provided redemption. By living that truly righteous life, the believer glorifies God and enjoys fellowship with him. Ultimately, in the resurrection, each individual who has appropriated by faith the redemption Christ has provided will be totally cleansed from sin. Then and throughout eternity, the redeemed individual will both glorify God and enjoy fellowship with him forever (*compare* Rev. 21,22).

Manasseh [muh-NAS-uh; "one who causes forgetfulness"; *compare* Gen. 41:51]. Evil 14th king of Judah, who "led Judah and the people of Jerusalem astray," so that during his 55-year reign, 697–642 B.C., "they did more evil than the nations the Lord had destroyed before the Israelites" (2 Chr. 33:9). Manasseh experienced conversion while imprisoned by the Assyrians. Later returned to his throne, Manasseh failed in his efforts to undo the harm his earlier apostasy had caused. **Parents:** Hezekiah and Hephzibah. **Son:** Amon. **Scripture:** 2 Ki. 21; 2 Chr. 33.

Also the name of the first-born son of Joseph. *See also* Israel, Tribes of.

BACKGROUND

During most of Manasseh's reign, Judah was a vassal state, subject to Assyria. Despite the freedom of worship Assyria permitted in subject states, Manasseh refused to follow his father's reforms and worship Yahweh. Instead, he actively promoted foreign gods, including the old Canaanite deities. Manasseh "sacrificed his sons in the fire in the Valley of Ben Hinnom, practiced sorcery, divination and witchcraft, and consulted mediums and spiritists" (2 Chr. 33:6). Second Kings 21:16 says that Manasseh "shed so much innocent blood that he filled Jerusalem from end to end." Tradition says that Isaiah was executed by Manasseh, who ordered him cut apart with saws.

Late in his reign, Manasseh was taken as a captive to Babylon, where the Assyrian king frequently stayed after 648 B.C. It is likely he was suspected of supporting the rebellion of Egypt, which had broken

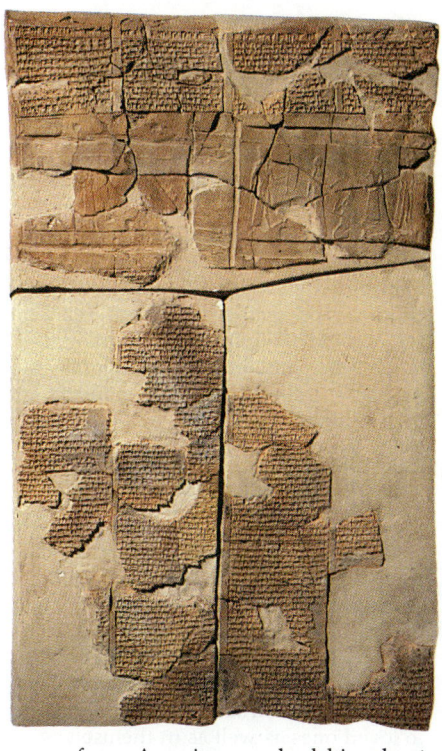

On this clay prism, the name "Manasseh, king of Judah" is listed among various rulers who were forced by Esarhaddon of Assyria to send materials for his new palace in Nineveh (about 673 B.C.).

away from Assyrian overlordship about 650 B.C., or the revolt of Shamash-shum-ukin, viceroy of Babylon. Manasseh was eventually restored to his throne and immediately began strengthening the defenses of Judah. It is likely that the Assyrians, now assured of Manasseh's loyalty, released him on the condition that Judah serve as a buffer state against possible Egyptian incursions into Assyrian territories.

While in Babylon, Manasseh experienced a religious conversion (2 Chr. 33:12,13). Back home, he devoted his few remaining years as king trying to undo the spiritual damage he had done to his nation. He restored Temple worship and rid the land of foreign gods.

Three Iron-Age idols of Astarte found in Judah. King Manasseh actively promoted worship of foreign deities (2 Chr. 33).

LEARNING FROM MANASSEH'S LIFE

Manasseh vividly demonstrates several biblical themes. (1) God's grace extends even to the "chief of sinners." No individual who is willing to turn to God is beyond redemption, whatever his or her past sins. (2) Individuals truly are responsible for their own choices. Hezekiah was devoted to God all his life, despite the fact that his own father, Ahaz, was a wicked man. Manasseh, the son of godly Hezekiah, chose to rebel against the pattern Hezekiah set and devoted himself to doing evil. Parents may influence their children, but parents are not ultimately responsible for their children's choices. We should not claim the credit if our children turn out well or feel guilt if they choose unwisely. (3) Consequences of past acts remain with us. Forgiveness offers the individual a new start but cannot change the past. Manasseh's religious reforms were real but fleeting. Under his son Amon, the people of Judah quickly reverted to the sinful ways Manasseh had promoted most of his earlier life. Thus, those who put off being reconciled to God risk doing terrible harm to loved ones as well as to themselves.

mandrake A plant of the potato (*solanacae*) family that produces a sweet, pulpy yellow fruit the size of a plum. The mandrake is valued in the East for its supposed aphrodisiac properties and because it is thought to stimulate fruitfulness in women. This view is reflected in two popular names for the fruit, "love apple" and "devil's apple."

The supposed relationship of this plant to fertility explains why childless Rachel was so eager to have some of the fruit found by her sister Leah's son, Reuben (Gen. 30:14-22). The text, however, states that it is God, not the fruit of this plant, that opens the womb (30:17,22).

The mandrake, whose roots were a purported aphrodisiac, played a role in the competition between Jacob's wives, Rachel and Leah (Gen. 30:14-18).

manger The feed box or trough used for domesticated animals, as in Lk. 2:16, also translated "stall" (*see* Lk. 13:15).

Many ancient feed boxes of hewn stone have been found in biblical lands. Luke tells us that the baby Jesus was laid in one of these boxes after his birth. Animals were often kept in the many natural caves found near Bethlehem, and it is likely that the manger where Jesus was placed was in one of these caves, which had been converted to a stable. Thus, the Christ-child was born in the most humble of places, surrounded by domestic animals and cared for by his new, tired parents, Mary and Joseph.

668

manna The food God provided for the Israelites after they left Egypt and before they entered the Promised Land, about 1440–1400 B.C. The name means "what?" and reflects the initial uncertainty of the Israelites about the sweet, white, seed-like particles that appeared like dew six days each week during the wilderness years.

Manna appeared when the Israelites exhausted the supplies brought with them from Egypt and disappeared when the people entered Canaan and had access to normal foods (*compare* Josh. 5:10-12). Other major OT passages that mention manna are Ex. 16:14-36; Num. 11:7-9; Ps. 78:24-31.

A number of attempts have been made to identify manna with natural products of the Sinai area, such as the sugar-rich secretions of various insects. The biblical account, however, makes it clear that manna appeared by the direct action of God, and none of the "natural" candidates fully fits the biblical description.

Manna has great spiritual significance and application in Scripture. As bread, manna speaks of sustaining life. As bread "from heaven," manna illustrates God's continuing presence with his people and of his concern for their well-being. As daily bread, which must be used the day it is gathered, manna portrays man's need to depend on God moment by moment and on God's faithfulness. As fleeting, destined to spoil if kept beyond the day it was gathered, manna speaks of the futility of our attempts to provide for our future

The stables excavated at Megiddo contained hollowed-out limestone blocks, which probably were feeding troughs or mangers.

apart from God. Yet on the day before the Sabbath, enough manna for two days was gathered, and on the Sabbath it would not spoil. Here, manna served to underline the sacred and special nature of the day of rest God established for his OT people.

Jesus drew on the complex spiritual significance of manna when he spoke of himself as the true bread from heaven, an enduring source of nourishment able to provide eternal life to those who participate in him (Jn. 6:25-59). Christ's association of himself with the manna God provided in the wilderness alienated many of Jesus' listeners, who found what he had said a ''hard saying.''

The Gathering of the Manna *by Bacchiacca, about A.D. 1540. The Israelites were instructed to gather each morning only as much as was needed for the day (Ex. 16:13-17).*

man of sin, man of lawlessness The person in prophecy who leads a great rebellion at history's end and even "sets himself up in God's temple, proclaiming himself to be God" (2 Th. 2:4). The association of this person with the return of Christ and the desecration of God's Temple has led many students of prophecy to identify him with the Antichrist. *See also* Antichrist.

Detail of Elijah Fed by the Ravens *shows Giovanni Battista Piazzetta's impression of Elijah's mantle, which became his legacy to Elisha (2 Ki. 2:11-15).*

man, old and new The unregenerate and regenerate aspects of human nature respectively. "Old man" refers to whatever in human nature and experience is tainted by sin. "New man" refers to that in human nature and experience which has been renewed and revitalized by the saving touch of Jesus Christ.

The Greek term *palaios* used in the phrase "old man" has a strong negative connotation in the NT and suggests corruption, obsolescence, and decay. Thus, the corrupt "old man" is put to death by being crucified with Christ (Rom. 6:6). It is to be "put off" along with the old, sinful way of life (Eph. 4:22; Col. 3:9). *See also* Old.

The Greek term used in the phrase "new man" (*kainos*) presents a powerful contrast. This word emphasizes quality: The "new" is not just the latest, but is also vastly superior. In Christ, human beings are recreated to live vital individual and corporate lives that glorify God (2 Cor.

5:17; *compare* Gal. 6:15; Eph. 2:15). This new man or "new self," as the NIV renders the phrase, has been "created to be like God in true righteousness and holiness" (Eph. 4:24). *See also* New.

mansions Probably rooms or apartments within a single home, not private estates. Accurate translation is important, for in Jn. 14:2 Jesus wants us to envision a future life of intimacy with God and other members of his family, shared in the one spacious home provided by the Father for his own (*compare* Jn. 14:23).

Man, Son of *See* Son.

mantle An outer garment, often sleeveless, worn by both men and women in biblical times.

Some eleven different Hebrew words indicate outer garments and are often translated as "robe." The precise garment indicated by many of these terms is uncertain. Some mantles or robes were used for protection from harsh weather, while others were decorated to indicate the wearer's status. *See also* Clothing.

marble Typically, a metamorphic ("transformed by heat") limestone. At times, words for "marble" in ancient documents are used of any carbonate rock that takes a polish.

Its attractive veins and colors made it a choice material for expensive public buildings and palaces in the ancient world. Marble was among the stones used in constructing Solomon's Temple (1 Chr. 29:2), and it was used extensively by the Persians (Esth. 1:6). In Rev. 18:12, it is among the valued objects traded by merchants of Babylon.

Marduk *See* Gods.

mark (1) A target at which arrows are shot or stones thrown, as in 1 Sam. 20:20; Job 16:12; (2) a goal toward which racers strain, as in Paul's metaphor of Phil. 3:14 KJV, "I press toward the mark"; (3) an incision, tattoo, or other artificial mark made on the body to serve as a sign or symbol. The OT prohibits cutting the body or beard for religious reasons, as the pagans of that era often did.

In Scripture, among the significant "marks" of this third sense are: (1) the "mark of Cain," an unspecified mark that God placed on Cain to warn others not to kill him (Gen. 4:15). (2) The mark of circumcision, which identified a Jewish man

670

as a member of the OT covenant community (Gen. 17:10-14). (3) The mark of voluntary servitude, made by an awl in the ear lobe of a Hebrew slave who chose to remain with his or her master more than the seven-year limit established in OT Law (Ex. 21:6). (4) The "marks of Jesus" that Paul carried in his body, probably the scars from floggings and beatings he received during his active missionary career (Gal. 6:17; *compare* 2 Cor. 11:23-25). (5) The "mark of the beast," an unspecified sign on the hand or forehead of followers of the Antichrist, required for anyone to do business in his realm (Rev. 13:16,17; 14:9-11). (6) The imprint of the "seal of the living God" on the foreheads of God's servants, to protect them from harm during the cataclysmic events described in Revelation (7:2,3).

Mark, Gospel according to The second and shortest Gospel in the NT, Mark is believed by most scholars to be the earliest of the biblical accounts of Christ's life. Mark is characterized by a fast-paced narrative, punctuated by the repeated use of "immediately" or "straightway" (*euthys*). The writer vividly describes the scenes he portrays, as when he pictures the demoniac of Gerasa pacing "night and day among the tombs and in the hills" where he "would cry out and cut himself with stones" (Mk. 5:5). Mark's focus on Jesus as a man of action makes this brief Gospel one of the easiest to read and most attractive of NT books.

BACKGROUND AND AUTHORSHIP
Early tradition says that the Gospel of Mark was written in Rome sometime between A.D. 65 and 70 by John Mark. This view is supported by the inclusion of a number of Latin words and by the author's habit of explaining Jewish customs, as if speaking to a Gentile audience (2:18; 7:3,4; 12:18). According to Papias (A.D. 140), Mark was the "interpreter of Peter" and wrote down Peter's teachings after the apostle was martyred in Rome. Irenaeus (A.D. 175) calls Mark "the disciple and interpreter of Peter," and affirms the apostolic source of the Gospel of Mark. Details are included by Mark that would be known only by an eyewitness, and several incidents reported by Mark were witnessed only by Peter and one or two others (5:21-24,35-43; 9:2-13).

While "Mark" was a very common name in the first century, tradition holds that the writer is the same John Mark who is frequently mentioned in the NT (Acts 12:12,

25; 15:37,39; Col. 4:10; 2 Tim. 4:11; Phlm. 24; 1 Pet. 5:13). Mark's story is fascinating in itself. This young cousin of Barnabas had gone along on Paul and Barnabas's first missionary journey, but left the others at Perga and returned to Jerusalem. Paul viewed this as desertion, and when Barnabas wanted to take Mark along on a second missionary venture, Paul adamantly refused. After an intense argument, the long-time friends parted company. Paul replaced Barnabas with Silas, while Barnabas took Mark and started out on a mission of his own. Later references to Mark in the Epistles indicate that the rift was healed. Paul writes of Mark as one who is "helpful to me in my ministry" (2 Tim. 4:11), and Peter calls Mark "my son" (1 Pet. 5:13).

Like the story of Jonah in the OT, Mark's experience brings encouragement. Early failures need not dismay us. God is rich in grace, and grace holds out the promise of that second chance.

THEOLOGICAL CONTRIBUTIONS
Mark brackets his document by the distinctive phrase "Son of God." He introduces his readers to "Jesus Christ, the Son of God" (1:1) in the hope that after reading about what Jesus has done they will conclude, with the centurion who witnessed the crucifixion, that "surely this man was the Son of God" (15:39).

Mark develops this theme throughout his book. He not only repeats the phrase "Son of God" (1:1,11; 3:11; 9:7; 12:6; 13:32; 14:36,61; 15:39), but demonstrates through his description of Jesus' acts that Christ has divine authority. Mark reports few of Jesus' parables but most of his miracles. Only chapter 13 contains any extended discourse, while five incidents of early conflict with the Pharisees establish Christ's authority to speak and act as God (2:1-12,15-17,18-22,23-28; 3:1-6). The narrative then continues with the report of a series of miracles which prove that Jesus' claim is founded in reality. The works Christ performs show him to be the Son of God.

Mark's Gospel divides naturally into two equal parts. Chapters 1–9 describe Jesus' ministry in Galilee. The works and wonders Jesus performed in Galilee provide a basis on which the reader can affirm Peter's confession that Jesus is not just another prophet but the Christ (8:29). Chapters 10–16 then focus on the major work of Jesus: his passion, death, and resurrection. Mark calls on his readers to see that Jesus died, not because he was powerless, but because it was his purpose to die. In fact, Jesus predicted his own death (8:31-33; 10:32-34; 14:1-10,24,25). The resurrection then demonstrates that Jesus is the Son of God and also that the purpose in his dying has been achieved.

MASTERY KEYS

Read Mark through at one sitting to sense the urgency and power of the narrative. Review chs. 1–9 and note every incident that demonstrates Christ's deity.

SPECIAL FEATURES

Mark 13, the only extended discourse of Jesus recorded in this Gospel, focuses on future events. Christ identifies signs that will precede his return (Mk. 13:5-31), but he emphasizes that his coming will be sudden and unexpected (13:33,35). Consequently, the believer is to be watchful and remain prepared for that moment (13:32-37).

The ending of Mark (16:9-20) is suspect. As early as A.D. 325, Eusebius rejected these verses because they were not present in certain Greek manuscripts available to him. Today, most scholars believe they were not in the original text.

MARK: A READING AND STUDY GUIDE

Chapter	Content Summary	Related Articles
1	John the Baptist introduces Jesus. After Jesus is baptized and tempted, he calls his disciples and performs healing miracles.	John the Baptist Baptism Miracle
2	Jesus heals a paralytic, calls Levi (Matthew) to discipleship, and answers questions about fasting.	Heal Fast
3	Jesus teaches and heals on the Sabbath, appoints twelve apostles, and is accused of being in league with Satan.	Pharisees Satan
4	Jesus teaches in parables and exercises his power to calm a storm at sea.	Parable
5	Jesus heals a demon-possessed man, heals a chronically ill woman, and raises a young girl from the dead.	Demon Death
6	Jesus is rejected in Nazareth but sends out the twelve to preach. John the Baptist is beheaded. Jesus feeds 5,000 and walks on the water.	Synagogue Disciple
7	Jesus is criticized for not following tradition. A Syrophoenician woman exercises faith. Jesus continues to heal.	Clean and Unclean Faith
8	Jesus feeds 4,000 and warns against the "yeast" of the Pharisees. Peter confesses Jesus is the Christ, and the Lord predicts his own death.	Leaven Christ Life
9	Jesus is transfigured and returns to heal a demonized child. His disciples argue about greatness, and Jesus warns against causing others to sin.	Transfiguration Great Hell
10	Jesus teaches on divorce, blesses children, and challenges a rich young man. He again predicts his death and warns against the wrong kind of spiritual leadership.	Divorce Kingdom Death of Christ Leadership
11	Jesus makes a triumphal entry into Jerusalem, clears the Temple of traders, and refuses to answer questions about his authority.	Temple, Jerusalem Authority
12	Jesus tells the parable of the tenants. He avoids traps set by his enemies and affirms the greatest commandment in OT Law.	Taxes Resurrection Commandment
13	Jesus speaks about his return at history's end.	Second Coming
14	Jesus is anointed with perfume at Bethany, holds a last supper with his disciples, and prays in Gethsemane. He is arrested and tried before the Sanhedrin and denied by Peter.	Anoint Last Supper Prayer Sanhedrin
15	Jesus is tried by Pilate, mocked by Roman soldiers, and crucified. He dies, and is buried.	Pilate Crucifixion
16	Jesus is raised from the dead and seen alive by women followers.	Resurrection

Above: The flooded marketplace of the ancient Roman harbor city, Puteoli, Italy. Right: Market scene cut in stone. The two little monkeys were used to attract customers.

market, marketplace (1) In the OT and Gospels, an area outside or within a city set apart for buying and selling. *See also* Gate. The oriental market or bazaar is filled with small shops and stands. It is an active, noisy place where people gather to gossip and be seen as well as to shop (*compare* Mt. 11:16; 20:3; Mk. 12:38; Lk. 11:43). (2) In Acts, a park-like area (*agora*) with paved paths and statues, usually surrounded by temples and other public buildings. This Greco-Roman marketplace served as the social and intellectual center of city life, where public trials and debates were often held (16:19; 17:5,17).

marriage A relationship between a man and woman in which society judges it is legitimate for them to live together. However, what a given society judges legitimate may vary significantly from the divine ideal portrayed in Scripture.

BIBLICAL CONCEPT OF MARRIAGE

Genesis 1 and 2 lay the foundation for a biblical concept of marriage. God created humanity male and female, and Scripture announces that "a man will leave his father and mother and be united to his wife, and they will become one flesh" (Gen. 2:24). "Leave father and mother" suggests that human beings are intended to live in close personal relationship with others and that the family is the nurturing unit in which a person grows to adulthood. Yet, when adulthood comes, ties are to be transferred from parents to the spouse.

"Be united to his wife" suggests that no extended period during which an individual is without "family" relationships is envisioned. A person leaves one relationship only in order to establish a new relationship. However, *see also* Celibacy.

"They will become one flesh" suggests the close bonding of individuals who love one another as equals and who can relate on every level of the human personality. "Flesh," while it implies sex, means far more. The Hebrew term looks at the total person in relation to his or her life on earth. "One flesh" thus implies that husband and wife will experience the joys and sorrows of this life, meeting life's challenges together. Thus, the married become

673

''no longer two, but one'' (Mt. 19:6). *See also* Man.

Nothing in Scripture contradicts the Genesis vision of the ideal, and much in both Testaments enriches our understanding of marriage. The bonding of two persons in marriage is covenantal, which God uses to illustrate the depth of his own commitment to Israel (*see* Isa. 62:4,5; Jer. 31:32). Husbands are to love their wives ''as Christ loved the church and gave himself up for her'' (Eph. 5:25), while wives respond to their husbands' love by freely submitting (Eph. 5:21-24). Covenant commitment provides the framework for marriage, and this reality is experienced as husband and wife each respond with deepening love to the other. *See also* Submission.

The basic purpose of marriage is found in the bond it creates and the context for mutual growth it provides. When Eve was brought to Adam, he knew that she shared his identity as a being made in the image of God, for she was ''bone of my bones and flesh of my flesh'' (Gen. 2:23). *See also* Woman.

Two other purposes in marriage are stated in Scripture. Genesis 1:28 (KJV) reports God's commission to ''be fruitful and multiply,'' thus providing the context for procreation. Furthermore, 1 Cor. 7:1-5 states that husbands and wives are to meet one another's sexual needs, thus guarding each other against temptations that are rooted in their sexual nature.

The biblical concept of marriage, then, is that of lifelong covenant relationship established between one man and one woman, which is to be nurtured by love and intimacy, enabling the couple to experience life in this world together and creating a healthy climate in which to bring up children.

ALTERNATE CONCEPTS

The OT describes other forms of marriage, specifically polygamy and concubinage, which do not match the ideal. In the context of their times, the relationship that Abraham established with Hagar (Gen. 16) and that of Jacob with Rachel and Leah (Gen. 29) were valid marriages, for that society judged it legitimate for them to live together, though their multiple marriages were out of the pattern that God intends for humanity. Similarly, the multiple marriages of Solomon, many of which were political in nature and were entered into as a way of ratifying treaties with other nations, were valid marriages from a sociological standpoint, even though in marrying as he did Solomon directly violated God's command (Deut. 17:16,17) and thus damaged his relationship with God. *See also* Concubine.

God's marital ideal is intended to guard us from alternate forms of marriage that society may invent, forms which are ultimately harmful to human beings. We need only review the anguish that Abraham and Jacob experienced and the spiritual idolatry into which Solomon fell as a direct result of their multiple marriages to sense the destructive potential of alternate forms of marriage. The farther a society strays from the ideal presented in Scripture, the greater the social and personal dangers involved.

PROHIBITED FORMS

The OT, while permitting ancient societies some latitude in marriage patterns, does prohibit certain marriages. These are implied in the list of unlawful sexual relationships described in Lev. 18; 20:17-21; and Deut. 27:20-23. Briefly, these passages prohibit sex with any close relative, by birth or marriage. Furthermore, along with incest and bestiality, lying with a man as "one lies with a woman" is identified as "detestable," thus ruling out any possibility of homosexual marriage (Lev. 18:22).

SPECIAL SITUATIONS

The Hebrew people placed great stress on producing children. This was not simply because children were deeply loved and valued but because children were vital if the family name was to be carried on. Thus OT Law legitimizes a special form of marriage called levirate marriage (Deut. 25:5-10; Ruth). In case a husband died before producing a child, his wife was to be given to the husband's brother. A child born to this couple would be considered the child of the first husband and would carry on his family line.

HEBREW MARRIAGE CUSTOMS

In most societies, marriages are recognized by some public rite of passage. In biblical times marriage customs were far different from and more formal than modern courtship, which involves dating, falling in love, and then a public wedding ceremony.

In biblical times, the parents of the groom typically chose and then negotiated for the bride (Gen. 34:11,12; Jdg. 14:1-4). Probably, the bride was asked to give her consent (Gen. 24:58; Jdg. 19:2,3), but this was not essential. Love in OT times was generally viewed as something that began at marriage, not something that led to marriage.

After a period of negotiation, the groom agreed to pay the father of the bride a price to compensate him for the loss of his daughter (Gen. 29:18-20; 34:12; Ex. 22;16,17). The payment of the bride price formalized the oral or written contract between the families, and the young couple was then betrothed. The groom also gave gifts to his bride (Gen. 24:53). Later, the father gave a dowry to his daughter.

The dowry might be a gift of money, of slaves (Gen. 24:59; 29:29), or of land (Jdg. 1:15; 1 Ki. 9:16). *See also* Dowry.

Betrothal was considered an initial, binding step in marriage. During the engagement period, the groom was exempt from military duty (Deut. 20:7). The bride remained at home, but her status had changed so that should she be raped, the act was considered adultery and the rapist would pay the penalty for this crime (Deut. 22:23-29).

The length of the betrothal varied considerably. During this time, the groom prepared a home for his bride, and the bride busied herself preparing her trousseau. Then, when it came time for the marriage to be consummated, the groom escorted the bride to their new home, accompanied and met by celebrating friends of the two families (Jdg. 14:20; Mt. 25:1-13). There, a wedding celebration took place that might last an entire week (Gen. 29:27; Jdg. 14:12-18; Jn. 2:1-11). During the festivities, the bride and groom dressed and were treated as king and queen.

The marriage was consummated during

In a Roman marriage the bride and groom shared a sacred wheat cake and then clasped hands as a sign of union while the marriage contract was read.

the festal week in the bridechamber, or *huppa*, while the guests waited outside. In some periods, a bloody sheet was exhibited to show that the bride was a virgin (Deut. 22:13-21). Then, with the wedding celebration over, the newly married husband and wife settled down to know each other better and to build a home.

DIVORCE AND REMARRIAGE

The OT does not clearly define grounds for divorce but recognizes the fact that marriages sometimes fail. Deuteronomy 24:1-4 commands that a written "bill of divorce" be provided for the wife. Divorced persons were free and were thus expected to remarry. Only two situations are stated in the OT where a husband could not obtain a divorce: (1) if he wrongly accused his wife of premarital sex (Deut. 22:13-19), or (2) if he himself had premarital sex with her and had been forced to marry her (Deut. 22:28,29).

There is no question that God hates divorce. It is a violation of the divine ideal and the breaking of a covenant commitment (Mal. 2:13-16). At the same time, Jesus implicitly recognized this option when he explained to the legalistic Pharisees that God permitted divorce in the Mosaic era "because your hearts were hard" (Mt. 19:8). Permission did not make divorce "right," but simply acknowledged that because human beings are sinners, the marriage relationship which God intended to enrich life might in fact become destructive.

In first-century Judaism, "hard" and "soft" positions had developed on divorce and remarriage. Some held that the only valid basis for divorce was unfaithfulness. Others argued that divorce should be granted if anything at all made the couple incompatible. The debate has continued through the Christian era, with some holding that Christ established a "no divorce" standard and others opting for a less restrictive view based on 1 Cor. 7:10-16. *See also* Divorce.

In summary, marriage is a relationship ordained by God. Its major purposes, of mutual support and the nurture of children, can be realized only when two people make a lifelong commitment to one another, intending "till death us do part" to share lovingly whatever their life on earth together may bring.

Mars Hill (KJV) The site in Athens where Paul preached Christ to local philosophers (Acts 17:16-34). *See also* Areopagus.

"Martha, Martha," the Lord answered, "you are worried and upset about many things, but only one thing is needed. Mary has chosen what is better and it will not be taken away from her" (Lk. 10:41,42). Christ in the House of Martha and Mary by Jan Vermeer.

Martha [MAHR-thuh; "lady"]. The sister of Mary and Lazarus of Bethany, whose distraction with preparations for Jesus' meal earned his gentle rebuke, about A.D. 30. **Scripture:** Lk. 10:38-42; Jn. 11; 12:1-3.

BACKGROUND

In Lk. 10:38-42 Martha was busy preparing food for Christ and his disciples. She felt distracted and harried and more than a little upset because her sister Mary left the work to listen to Jesus teach. When Martha complained to Jesus, Christ gently pointed out that Mary had made a wise choice—listening to him was more important than food preparation.

We next meet Martha in Jn. 11, where the text says, "Jesus loved Martha and her sister and Lazarus" (11:5). Lazarus had died, and Jesus finally arrived in Bethany after a long, unexplained delay. Martha, ever the activist, rushed to meet him, saying, "Lord, if you had been here, my brother would not have died," and openly confessing her faith in Jesus, identifying him as "the Christ, the son of God, who was to come into the world." Martha then went to get Mary, and the two led Jesus to the tomb, where he called Lazarus back from the dead.

The third incident, reported in Jn. 12:1-3, is a dinner given in Jesus' honor, at which Mary anointed Christ's feet with expensive ointment. The text says simply, "Martha served" (12:2).

LEARNING FROM MARTHA'S LIFE

We can understand Martha's frustration with Mary who simply sat and listened. But we can also understand Jesus' rebuke. Sometimes the activist becomes too busy, so busy that he or she has no time to commune with God.

Yet when Jesus' love for the little family at Bethany is stated in Jn. 11, Martha is named first. And it is Martha who hurries to meet Jesus and first expresses her faith in him as Lord. The busy among us may at times need to re-evaluate priorities, but when activity is motivated by faith in Jesus and by love for him, we can be sure of God's approval.

The last mention of Martha in the NT sums up her life in two simple words: "Martha served" (Jn. 12:2).

martyr [Gk., *martys*, "witness"]. One killed for his or her faith. As persecution of the early church developed, those who gave active witness to their faith in Christ often forfeited their lives, as in Acts 7:54-60; 22:20 (*compare* Rev. 2:13; 17:6).

OTHER MARYS OF THE NEW TESTAMENT

Mary of Bethany	With her sister Martha and brother Lazarus, a close friend of Jesus, whose feet she anointed with perfume. Lk. 10:38-42; Jn. 11:1-46; 12:1-3; *compare* Mt. 26:7; Mk. 14:3.
Mary, mother of James and Joseph (Joses)	A Galilean woman who, after being healed, followed Jesus and supported his ministry financially. Mt. 27:56; 28:1; Mk. 15:40,41,47.
Mary Magdalene	Another Galilean woman whom Jesus healed, and who helped to support Jesus' ministry. Mt. 27:56,61; 28:1; Mk. 15:40,47; 16:1,9; Lk. 8:2; Jn. 20:1,2,11-18.
Mary, mother of John Mark	A relative of Barnabas; her home was a gathering place for the Jerusalem church. Acts 12:12,13; Col. 4:10.
Mary of Rome	A woman commended by Paul in Rom. 16:6.

Above: Contemporary Russian Orthodox icon, The Virgin Eleousa, *by Vladislav Andreyev (1989).*

Mary, the mother of Jesus [MAIR-ee; Greek form of Miriam; meaning unknown]. The young Jewish virgin chosen by God to bear the Savior; her faith is beautifully expressed in words to her kinswoman, Elizabeth (Lk. 1:46-55). *See also* Magnificat. **Husband:** Joseph. **Cousin:** Elizabeth. **Scripture:** Mt. 1,2; Mk. 3:31-35; Lk. 1–3; 11:27,28; Jn. 2:1-11; 19:25; Acts 1:14.

BACKGROUND

Mary lived in Nazareth, where Joseph was a carpenter. Like Joseph, she was descended from David (*compare* Acts 2:30; Rom. 1:3; 2 Tim. 2:8). *See also* Genealogy of Jesus.

Mary was likely very young when she was betrothed to Joseph. In that culture, an older man might pledge to marry (pay the bride price for) an underage girl but not consummate the marriage until she reached maturity (generally, age 12). In such a case, the girl might even live in his home and, in the case of Joseph, accompany him on his journey to Bethlehem, although she was at the time only "pledged to be married to him" (Lk. 2:4,5). If such a girl was found pregnant, the future husband might demand return of the bridal price and "divorce" her, returning her to her family.

The text of Luke is most illuminating concerning Mary's faith and character (1:26-56). It portrays Mary's courage as she expressed her willingness to bear the "Son of the Most High," even though her pregnancy would surely be misunderstood and would put her future at risk (1:38). The text also portrays Mary's joy at the realization she was destined to bear the Messiah (1:46-55).

A contemplative Mary is seen in Luke 2, where on the first Christmas, she "treasured up all these things and pondered them in her heart." Subsequent events, also in Luke 2, must have given Mary more to ponder. In the Temple, elderly Simeon told her that "a sword will pierce your own soul too" (v. 35), and twelve years later, her son, also in the Jerusalem Temple, reminded her that his heavenly Father had priority (v. 49).

Other NT passages provide only brief glimpses of Mary. We see her at the wedding in Cana, appealing to her son and then telling the servants, "Do whatever he tells you" (Jn. 2:5). However, Mary is notably absent from Jn. 7:5, which says, "Even his own brothers did not believe in him." We meet Mary again at the foot of the cross, as Jesus commends this "dear woman" to the care of the disciple John (Jn. 19:26). We are given one final glimpse of Mary, praying with the disciples, other women, and Christ's brothers in an upper room (Acts 1:12-14). While extra-biblical stories about Mary abound, only brief references such as those noted above are found in Scripture.

The Bible references have been differently applied in Roman Catholic and Protestant traditions. Roman Catholic dogma sees Mary as a perpetual virgin, with the "brothers" of Jesus being cousins or possibly children from an earlier family of Joseph. Mary's appeal to Jesus at Cana gives Catholics reason to believe that she has influence with her Son, and so they seek her intercession with Jesus for them today. Protestants emphasize the believer's direct access to God in prayer and assume that the brothers of Christ are children of Mary by Joseph.

LEARNING FROM MARY'S LIFE

Possibly in reaction to Roman Catholic veneration of the Virgin, Protestants have often failed to honor Mary sufficiently. Mary is one of Scripture's most beautiful examples of a pure, unspoiled faith. Though she was fully aware of what people would think if she were found pregnant, she risked the personal shame and even the anger of Joseph and her own family. Her words, "I am the Lord's servant" (Lk. 1:38), remind us that a true faith in God is expressed by submission to his will.

Right: Masons cutting and dressing blocks of stone in a quarry. Cutting was done by chipping out a line of holes or a deep notch into which wooden wedges were driven. Soaking with water caused the wedges to swell and split the stone along the cut line.

maschil, maskil A Hebrew word of uncertain meaning found in the title of Psalms 32, 42, 44, 45, 52–55, 74, 78, 88, 89, and 142. Most believe the word indicates some special musical accompaniment or the use of the psalm in one of Israel's annual religious festivals. *See also* Psalms.

mason A stonecutter, a craftsman who builds with stone. Palestine abounds in soft limestones that harden when exposed to the air. *See also* Stone.

David and Solomon imported master masons from Phoenicia to work stone for their palaces and the Jerusalem Temple (1 Ki. 5:17,18; 1 Chr. 14:1). Through Solomon's extensive building programs, stoneworking skills seem to have been developed among the Israelites as well.

Herod the Great later used stones up to 25 feet (7.62 meters) long in his reconstruction of the Jerusalem Temple. They were cut from quarries near Jerusalem. Working in these quarries, masons would drill a series of holes in the bedrock, drive wooden pegs into the holes, and then pour water over the pegs. The wood absorbed the water, expanded, and broke each block away from its stratum. The blocks were then smoothed so perfectly that they fit together with no need of a binding mortar.

Left: The southwestern corner of the Temple Mount shows clearly the huge blocks with finished edges or margins that Herod used to enlarge it.

679

master In the OT, (1) the owner of persons or property, as in Gen. 24:9; Ex. 21:4; (2) the husband of a wife or concubine, as in Gen. 18:12; Jdg. 19:27; (3) a ruler or anyone exercising authority, as in 2 Sam. 2:5; 2 Ki. 5:4; and (4) God as the owner and ruler of Israel, as in Mal. 1:6. In the NT, all of the above, but also (5) a polite form of address, as in Lk. 8:24; 9:49. *See also* Leader.

St. Matthew Inspired by an Angel, by Rembrandt van Rijn (1606–1669).

Matthew, Gospel according to The first of the NT's four accounts of Jesus' life on earth. Written for Jewish Christians, it serves as a bridge between OT and NT. Matthew demonstrates that Jesus truly is the OT's messianic King, but a Servant King, whose present Kingdom is ethical and moral and is rooted in redemption.

AUTHORSHIP AND BACKGROUND

Tradition identifies Matthew, one of the original disciples (Mt. 10:2-4; Mk. 3:16-19; Lk. 6:14-16; Acts 1:13), as the author of this Gospel. Matthew [MATH-yoo; "gift of God"] is frequently identified with Levi, the converted tax collector of Mk. 2:13,14 and Lk. 5:27,28. Papias (A.D. 130) said that Matthew "wrote down the oracles [sayings] in the Hebrew [Aramaic] language, and each interpreted them as best he could." Most who accept the traditional authorship date this Gospel sometime prior to A.D. 70.

Matthew's Gospel was directed to Jewish Christians and intended to demonstrate that Jesus is the OT's Messiah as well as the Son of God. Matthew quotes some 50 times from the OT, and alludes to OT passages at least 70 more times, to show that Jesus' identity can be established beyond a doubt. The birth of Jesus is foretold in the OT (*compare* Mt. 1:23 with Isa. 7:14; Mt. 2:6 with Mic. 5:2; Mt. 2:15 with Hos. 11:1; Mt. 2:16-18 with Jer. 31:15; Mt. 3:3 with Isa. 40:3), and even the details of his death are predicted there (*compare* Mt. 26:15 with Zech. 11:12; Mt. 26:31 with Zech. 13:7; Mt. 26:38 with Ps. 42:6,11; Mt. 27:9 with Zech. 11:12,13 and Jer. 18:2-12; Mt. 27:34 with Ps. 69:21; Mt. 27:35 with Ps. 22:18; Mt. 27:39 with Ps. 22:7; Mt. 27:46 with Ps. 22:1). Thus, not only is Jesus seen to be the Messiah but his death and resurrection are shown to be elements of God's plan from the beginning. In hesitating about and then rejecting Jesus, his contemporaries rejected their Messiah and the very Son of the Living God (Mt. 12:23; 13:55,56; 14:2; 16:14).

Yet, even the Scriptural proof would fall short of answering all the questions of Matthew's Jewish readers. They would wonder what happened to the victorious Messiah portrayed in the OT and to the Kingdom the prophets said he would establish. Matthew is conscious of this objection and some 51 times speaks of the Kingdom of God, the Kingdom of heaven, or simply the Kingdom. Matthew also calls on his readers to look ahead. He portrays Jesus at history's end and teaches that when Jesus returns, the prophets' vision will be fulfilled. Jesus will judge evil and punish the wicked, demonstrating at last the full meaning of the rule of God over the earth and his universe (*compare* Mt. 13:24-30,36-43; 20:1-16; 22:1-14).

THEOLOGICAL CONTRIBUTIONS

Matthew's Gospel—with its interweaving of OT passages with events related to Jesus' birth, ministry, and death—demonstrates the essential unity of the OT and NT. The Christ of the New Testament is the Messiah predicted in the Old Testament. The person of Jesus is the unifying element between old covenant and new covenant, the OT community of faith and the new community established after Christ's death and resurrection. In this context, several themes found in Matthew are theologically important. These themes are Christology, Kingdom, ethics, discipleship, and eschatology.

1. *Christology.* This study focuses on the

person of Christ. In Matthew, we see Jesus Christ as the Son of God (1:21,23; 11:25-27; 26:28,29) and as the messianic King (1:17; 2:2,4; 11:2,3). However, Immanuel ("God with us") is portrayed as a Servant King, come to die in order that he might bring those who believe into his Kingdom.

2. *Kingdom*. This "kingdom" speaks of the rule of God over the universe and on earth. Matthew, especially in chapter 13, shows that Jesus established an unexpected expression of God's Kingdom, unlike the earthly kingdom of OT prophecy, but nevertheless a valid expression of God's rule on earth. The present form of God's Kingdom is expressed not in earthly rule but in personal relationships, demonstrated not by force of arms but by the moral transformation of its citizens. *See also* Kingdom.

3. *Ethics*. These are expressed in the Sermon on the Mount (chs. 5–7) and reflect a vision of Jesus' present Kingdom as God's rule within human hearts. The Law forbids murder and adultery, but Jesus calls for a people free even from the hate and lust that lead to these sins. The ethics of Jesus are rooted in the moral transformation which Christ lived, died, and rose again to make possible.

4. *Discipleship*. This is defined in Mt. 16:24-27 and is illustrated throughout the book. Citizens of God's Kingdom express their allegiance to Jesus by obeying his Word.

MATTHEW: A READING AND STUDY GUIDE

Chapter	Content Summary	Related Articles
1	Jesus' genealogy establishes his right as a descendant of David to rule. The virgin birth is described.	Genealogy
2	Wise men from the East worship Jesus. The family flees Herod. Later, they return and settle in Nazareth.	Immanuel Magi
3	John the Baptist calls Israel to repent and prepare for the Messiah. Jesus is baptized by John.	John the Baptist Baptism
4	Jesus overcomes Satan's three temptations. He begins to preach, calls the twelve disciples, and heals many people.	Satan Disciple
5	Jesus' Beatitudes launch his Sermon on the Mount. Jesus shows that the righteousness God requires exceeds that called for by OT statutes.	Beatitudes Sermon on the Mount Law
6	Jesus speaks of the believer's personal relationship with God as heavenly Father.	Lord's Prayer Father
7	Jesus condemns legalistic judging, encourages believers to pray, and calls for obedience.	Judge Obey
8	Jesus heals a leper and a centurion's son. He cures a demon-possessed man and calms a storm at sea.	Healing Demon
9	Jesus heals a paralytic and raises a dead girl. He calls Matthew as a disciple.	Sin
10	Jesus instructs the twelve and sends them out to preach and teach.	Gentile
11	John the Baptist asks if Jesus is the Messiah. Jesus pronounces woe on unrepentant cities.	Miracle Woe
12	Jesus claims to be Lord of the Sabbath. He refutes the charge that he is in league with Satan and warns of an unforgivable sin.	Sabbath
13	Jesus' parables present aspects of his present Kingdom.	Kingdom Parable
14	John the Baptist is beheaded. Jesus continues to teach, feeds 5,000, and walks on the water.	Herod
15	Jesus confronts the legalism of the Pharisees. He continues to perform authenticating miracles.	Clean and Unclean Legalism

continued

STRUCTURE OF MATTHEW

I.	Introduction: Jesus' birth	1,2
II.	Early Ministry in Galilee	3–7
	Narrative:	3,4
	Discourse:	5–7
III.	Ministry of Healing	8–10
	Narrative:	8:1–9:34
	Discourse:	9:35–10:42
IV.	Second Ministry in Galilee	11–13
	Narrative:	11,12
	Discourse:	13
V.	Mission and Miracles	14–18
	Narrative:	14–17
	Discourse:	18
VI.	Ministry in Judea	19–25
	Narrative:	19–22
	Discourse:	23–25
VII.	Death and Resurrection	26–28

5. *Eschatology.* A fifth major theme in Matthew is the future, which Jesus graphically portrays. Christ will come again at history's end. He will appear in power and glory, to judge the earth and openly establish God's rule (Mt. 13:24-30; 20:1-16; 22:1-14; 25).

MASTERY KEYS

Be alert for the word "kingdom" in Matthew's Gospel and for references to the OT. The Sermon on the Mount summarizes the moral and ethical structure of Jesus' Kingdom. The parables of Mt. 13 contrast the present form of God's Kingdom with that envisioned by the prophets. The Olivet discourse (Mt. 24,25) contains Christ's most extensive teaching on the future and urges believers to be ready for his return.

MATTHEW: A READING AND STUDY GUIDE *CONT.*

Chapter	Content Summary	Related Articles
16	The religious leaders demand a sign. The people waver concerning who Jesus is. Peter identifies Jesus as the Christ, the Son of God.	Christ Sadducees Son
17	Jesus is transfigured before three disciples. He heals an epileptic boy and pays Temple tax.	Transfigure Taxes
18	Jesus teaches about greatness in his Kingdom in three stories about relationships between believers.	Great Love
19	Jesus reaffirms the ideal of lifelong marriage and challenges a rich young man to total commitment.	Marriage Divorce
20	Jesus compares God to the gracious owner of a vineyard. James and John seek power in Jesus' coming Kingdom.	Grace Servant
21	Jesus makes a triumphal entry into Jerusalem and drives merchants from the Temple. His authority challenged, Jesus uses parables against the Pharisees.	Donkey Authority
22	Jesus tells the parable of the wedding banquet. He avoids traps set by his enemies and identifies the Law's greatest commandments.	Taxes Commandment
23	Jesus pronounces woes on Pharisees and teachers of the Law, and weeps over unresponsive Jerusalem.	Hypocrite
24	Jesus teaches about the end of the age and warns that his appearance will be unexpected.	Age, Ages Second Coming
25	Parables warn believers to live their lives in preparation for Jesus to return and judge mankind.	Talent Judge
26	Jesus' last days are summarized: his last supper, Gethsemane, his trial before the Sanhedrin, and Peter's denial.	Lord's Supper Sanhedrin Peter
27	Judas hangs himself. Jesus is tried by Pilate and condemned. He is mocked, crucified, and buried.	Judas Iscariot Pilate Crucifixion
28	Jesus is raised from the dead. He meets his disciples and commissions them to evangelize the world.	Resurrection Evangelism

SPECIAL FEATURES

Note Matthew's frequent use of the formula, "This was to fulfill that which was spoken through the prophet." Matthew's point is that every key event in Jesus' life happened in accord with God's specific will. The King of kings was in total control, even as he hung on the cross.

mattock An agricultural digging tool with a double-bladed metal head. It was used to loosen the soil. Though the KJV uses "mattock" in three passages—1 Sam. 13:20,21; 2 Chr. 34:6; and Isa. 7:25—other English translations use it only in 1 Samuel. *See also* Agriculture.

mature, maturity Spoken of persons who achieve the goal of Christian growth, who are "grown up" spiritually.

Maturity is a relative rather than an

reasoning like children, to "put childish ways behind" (13:11).

Maturity is possible for all believers, but is not automatic (*compare* Heb. 5:11–6:12). To grow, Christians need to be involved in the church (Eph. 4:12,13), to persevere in their faith despite trials (Jas. 1:4), and to apply Scripture obediently to daily life (Col. 1:9-11; Heb. 5:14).

meal Coarse or fine flour obtained by grinding grain. Bread made from various kinds of meal was the staple food in biblical times.

meal offerings *See* Sacrifices and Offerings.

meals Customary times for eating. In biblical times, people usually ate two meals. These were a light breakfast of bread or

absolute concept in the NT. No individual achieves sinless perfection in this life (1 Jn. 1:8-10). Instead, the mature Christian is one who by obedience to God has trained himself to distinguish good from evil (Heb. 5:14). The mature Christian presses on toward the goal of knowing Christ and becoming more like him (Phil. 3:10-15) and makes a full commitment to do the will of God (Col. 4:12).

Paul uses a child/adult analogy to explain maturity. When the Corinthians indulged in disputes, they were behaving like "infants in Christ," not like Christians (1 Cor. 3:1-3). Similarly, Corinthians who overemphasized the gift of tongues were "thinking like children" (1 Cor. 14:20). To Paul, evidence of true spirituality was love that "always protects, always trusts, always hopes, always perseveres" (13:7). Paul called all believers to follow his own example and to stop talking, thinking, and

fruit, often eaten at midmorning, and a large meal about sunset. The evening meal was shared by the family and generally featured a main dish served in a common bowl, into which each person dipped with his hands or with pieces of bread. *See also* Eating; Feasts, Festivals, and Fasts; Food.

meat The flesh of clean animals that the Hebrew people were permitted to eat, as distinct from fish and poultry (Lev. 11; Num. 11:4; Deut. 12:15). Generally, in OT times, meat was eaten only on special occasions, such as a religious festival, family celebration, or a feast to honor guests. *See also* Clean and Unclean.

The NT reports three disputes in the church concerning meat. 1. The Jerusalem Council, which determined that Gentile Christians were not subject to Jewish Law, asked Gentile brothers not to eat the meat of strangled animals (Acts 15:20,29). This

Elamite prisoners eat a meal while guarded by an Assyrian soldier. Wall relief from Ashurbanipal's palace in Nineveh, about 640 B.C.

Above: Butcher working in his shop as portrayed on a second-century A.D. sarcophagus. Right: Limestone statuette of a butcher slaughtering a trussed ox; tomb of Ny-kau-inpu, 2500–2300 B.C.

respected the Jewish revulsion for eating blood, which represents the life of the animal (*compare* Lev. 17:10-12).

2. The church in Rome was divided by a dispute between vegetarians and meat eaters (Rom. 14:2). Paul points out that this is a matter of personal conviction rather than theological substance. Neither group is to judge or look down on the other, but rather to extend freedom to do what each believes is pleasing to Christ as Lord (Rom. 14:3-11). *See also* Liberty; Lord.

3. The church in Corinth was divided by a theological dispute concerning meat (1 Cor. 8–10). In NT times, meat that had been sacrificed to a pagan deity was later sold in temple markets. Also, social gatherings were often dedicated to a pagan deity, and the meat eaten there symbolized participation in pagan worship. Paul establishes two rules for dealing with this problem. First, don't participate in any activity that is publicly identified with idolatry (10:14-21). Second, if invited to a meal, don't make an issue of where the meat was purchased unless the host announces it was sacrificed to such and such a god. In that case, don't eat—not because of your conscience, but for the sake of your host's conscience (10:23-30). Two principles emerge: Do all to the glory of God and guard others from stumbling (10:31-33).

meat offering *See* Sacrifices and Offerings.

Medes A powerful ancient people who occupied the mountainous region that is now northwestern Iran.

The Medes were first mentioned in As-

syrian records in 836 B.C. They were alternately subject people and fierce independent enemies of Assyria, eventually capturing Nineveh in 612 B.C. In about 550 B.C., the Medes were conquered by Cyrus the Great, who then became king of the Medes as well as the Persians. The two peoples, who are closely related linguistically, are often mentioned together in Scripture. Many Medes were brought into the Persian administration and with them many Median customs and laws. The Medes took part with the Persians in the overthrow of Babylon (Isa. 13:17; Jer. 51:11,28; Dan. 5:28). Unfortunately, little archaeological work has been done in ancient Media itself, so the history and accomplishments of this people are not well known.

mediator One who seeks to establish a relationship and understanding between two parties. In the OT, priests offered sacrifices on behalf of sinful human beings and instructed them in God's Law. However, the OT system was unable to take away sins or to bring about a true reconciliation (Heb. 10). Consequently, God through Jeremiah promised that he would one day establish a new covenant with human beings.

According to the NT, the new covenant was put into effect on the death of Jesus. Paul wrote that there is "one mediator between God and men, the man Christ Jesus, who gave himself as a ransom for all men" (1 Tim. 2:5,6).

Jesus alone is qualified to serve as mediator, because (1) as truly human and at the same time fully God, he alone is able to represent both sides in God's dispute with sinful human beings (Heb. 5:1-10); and (2) the blood of Christ not only established the new covenant but is the cleansing agent that wins forgiveness for our sins and brings us an inner moral transformation "so that we may serve the living God" (Heb. 9:14,15; *compare* 8:6-12). *See also* High Priest; Intercession; Reconciliation; Sacrifices and Offerings.

medicine A substance used to treat disease, relieve pain, or promote healing. Ancient medical texts from Mesopotamia and Egypt describe a variety of medical treatments and magical incantations. No similar Israelite medical texts have been recovered, and the OT flatly rejects any use of magic. *See also* Magic.

Right: A column from an Egyptian medical textbook, the oldest known. Edwin Smith Papyrus, 17th century B.C.
Left: Bronze surgeon's saw. It has fine teeth and was used for cutting through bones in amputations.
Below: Roman medical instruments (left to right): hammer, tweezers, scalpel, spoons, bowl, pliers.
Inset: The art of healing, with its semi-magical invocations to supernatural powers, became the science of medicine. This coin from Selinus depicts the local river-god sacrificing at the altar of the god of healing, Asclepius (the rooster).

Below : Trepanning, the technique of drilling or cutting a hole through the skull to relieve pressure, was widespread in the ancient world.

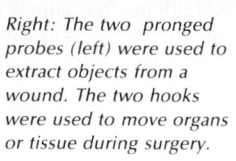

Right: The two pronged probes (left) were used to extract objects from a wound. The two hooks were used to move organs or tissue during surgery.

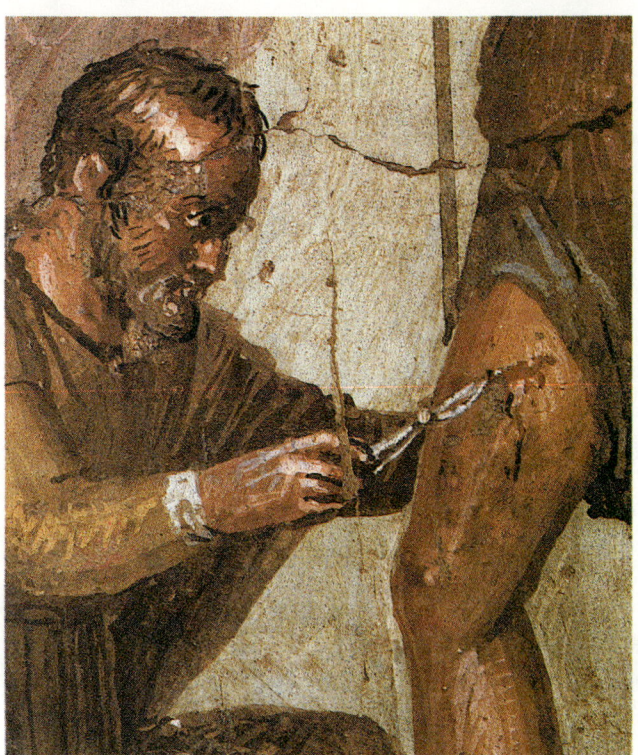

Surgeon tending to the hero Aeneas; detail of a fresco from Pompeii.

The Bible refers to medicines only a few times. When childless Rachel begged Leah for some of her son's mandrakes, she was following an Eastern folk or herbal medicine tradition regarding the mandrake's supposed ability to promote fertility in women (Gen. 30:14). Isaiah 1:6 and Lk. 10:34 mention ointments and healing balms used to treat wounds. Isaiah applied a poultice of figs to King Hezekiah's boil (Isa. 38:21). Gall and myrrh mixed with wine served as an anesthetic to lessen intense suffering (Mk. 15:23), and Paul encouraged Timothy to take a little wine for his chronic stomach problems (1 Tim. 5:23).

While the Israelites apparently did not develop a distinct medical science, physicians are mentioned in both Testaments. Jesus' references to physicians imply that doctors were relatively common in first-century Palestine (Mt. 9:12; Lk. 4:23). Luke, the companion of Paul, is identified in the KJV and RSV versions of Col. 4:14 as the "beloved physician."

At the same time, the Israelites seem to have been aware of the relationship between mental attitude and health (*compare* Prov. 17:22). Furthermore, the godly Jew exercised faith in God, who is the healer of his people (Ex. 15:26). However, faith did not rule out the use of medicine, as is illustrated in the Scripture's criticism of King Asa, who sought help "*only* from the physicians" (2 Chr. 16:12, italics added).

meditate To actively consider or reflect, especially on God (Ps. 48:9) or his Word (Josh. 1:8). Meditation is mentioned most often in the OT and is expressed in Hebrew words that mean "murmur," "mutter," "whisper," or "sigh." The words suggest the common Hebrew practice of speaking aloud under one's breath even when alone (*compare* Gen. 24:63) or when thinking inwardly, "in the heart" (*compare* Ps. 19:14).

In Ps. 119, the Psalmist refers frequently to meditation on God's Word. He says, "With my lips I recount all the laws that come from your mouth. I rejoice in following your statutes as one rejoices in great riches. I meditate on your precepts and consider your ways" (vv. 13-15). In this psalm, the writer credits meditation with giving him wisdom, insight, and unmatched understanding (vv. 98,99), and with enabling him to obey God (*compare* Ps. 1:1-3).

Meditation may also be reflected in Paul's advice to the Philippians, that "whatever is true, whatever is noble, whatever is right, whatever is pure, whatever is lovely, whatever is admirable—if anything is excellent or praiseworthy—think about such things" (Phil. 4:8). Thus, biblical meditation is a conscious act of reflecting on the Lord and his revelation of himself in his Word, as opposed to the concept of "losing oneself" in a mystic experience.

Mediterranean Sea The large body of water west of Palestine, commonly identified in the Bible simply as "the sea" (Num. 13:29) or the great or western sea (Deut. 11:24; 34:2; Joel 2:20; Zech. 14:8). Although Israel's land included a coastal area, it had no natural harbors. Thus the Hebrews remained an agricultural rather than a seafaring people.

In about 1200 B.C. the so-called Sea Peoples invaded coastal Palestine from the Mediterranean Sea. Scripture calls them the Philistines, and depicts them dominating the Israelites from Samson's time until David's. In the NT era the Mediterranean was vital to the Roman Empire, which depended on grain shipped from Egypt and the east. Of course, the apostle Paul traveled the Mediterranean frequently and experienced at least one shipwreck in his voyages. *See also* Philistines; Ships; Trade and Travel.

medium A person through whom the dead are thought to communicate with the living. Mosaic Law condemns seeking information from mediums or from any other occult sources (Deut. 18:11). The "witch of Endor" (KJV) was actually a medium (*compare* 1 Sam. 28). *See also* Magic; Sorcerer; Witch.

meek, meekness The quality of having a patient and gentle attitude. The KJV OT often translates the Hebrew *'anawah* ("suffering," "oppressed," and thus "humble") by the word "meek." But this is not quite the same as the NT concept. *See also* Humble.

In the NT, meekness is the opposite of arrogance. It suggests dependence on God and a gentle, nonthreatening demeanor toward others. Far from being weakness, meekness requires great inner strength, both in faith and self-control.

Megiddo An elevated area dominating the Plain of Esdraelon, the site of a series of fortified cities from 3500 B.C. through the era of Israel's kingdoms.

Megiddo controlled not only the fertile Galilean plains but also two of the area's most important trade routes: the north/south route that linked Egypt with the Fertile Crescent, and the east/west route that connected central Palestine with the coast. Its strategic location assured the prosperity of those occupying the city, and caused many fierce battles. Archaeological evidence shows that the city was taken in battle and destroyed many times.

Joshua defeated a coalition of forces that included the men of Megiddo, but the strong, fortified city itself was not taken "for the Cananites were determined to live in that region" (Josh. 17:12; Jdg. 1:27). Solomon, however, was able to rebuild it, fortify it and make it the capital of one of a dozen administrative districts (1 Ki. 4:7,12). Later, it was a keystone in the defensive plans of rulers of the northern kingdom, Israel. In Roman times the site was no longer occupied.

Megiddo is one of the most thoroughly excavated sites in Palestine. Excavations there have helped trace the pre-history of the area and have provided many insights into ancient life. Ruins once thought to have been stables established there for the powerful chariot army Solomon maintained at Megiddo are now believed to have been storehouses.

Left: View of the Mediterranean Sea from the ruins of Caesarea Maritima, the Roman administrative center of Judea in NT times. Below: Aerial view of the excavated site of Megiddo, a powerful city in OT times because it lay along the major trunk road and trade route between Egypt and Syria.

BACKGROUND

The Genesis account states that Melchizedek blessed Abraham after Abraham defeated the coalition of kings who had captured his nephew Lot and that Abraham paid Melchizedek a tithe. Further references to Melchizedek are found in the Psalms and in the Epistle to the Hebrews. The messianic Psalm 110 predicts that David's greater son will be ordained by God to an eternal priesthood "in the order of Melchizedek" (v. 4). Historically, this prediction is rooted in David's capture of Jerusalem and thus his right by conquest to the role of its priest-king. Theologically, the writer of Hebrews sees in Melchizedek the basis for a priesthood which antedates the Aaronic priesthood of Israel and, by implication, is superior to it.

The Babylonian mina (mene in Aramaic) was a small stone weight equivalent to 60 Persian shekels (Aram., tekel).

SIGNIFICANCE

Using typical rabbinic arguments, the author of Hebrews argues that the Melchizedekian priesthood is superior to the Aaronic priesthood because biblically (1) Melchizedek is "without father or mother, without genealogy, without beginning of days or end of life," and thus has a timeless priestly authority (Heb. 7:3); (2) the priestly line of Aaron, then present in the loins of Abraham, acknowledged Melchizedek's superiority in Abraham's act of paying a tithe (Heb. 7:4-10); (3) God's oath ordains an eternal priesthood for the one who takes up Melchizedek's role, while the Aaronic priesthood is destined to be set aside (Heb. 7:11-28).

While the whole argument may seem obscure to modern readers, it was compelling to first-century Jewish Christians, who were struggling to justify their abandonment of Judaism and who could see in this discussion evidence that the high priesthood of Jesus is biblically defensible and demonstrably superior to that of the OT.

memorial An object or activity intended to help God's people identify with God's historic acts or words.

Throughout the OT and NT, ceremonies, words, acts, and physical objects were used to commemorate various ways in which the Lord and his people interacted. Examples of memorials are: (1) the heap of stones Joshua set up by the Jordan to remind Israel of how God opened the river for their passage (Josh. 4:7); and (2) the Passover festival, designed to remind Israel of how God redeemed them from Egyptian captivity (Ex. 12:14). These memorials were intended to help each succeeding generation feel its participation with their ancestors in those acts God undertook to benefit his people. Memorials helped them to see that God had acted not only for their fathers, but for them as well.

The Eucharist (the Lord's Supper) can also be understood in this light. Jesus said, "Do this in remembrance" (Lk. 22:19; 1 Cor. 11:24,25). As we partake, we are to sense our participation in Jesus' death, realizing afresh that he died in our place.

"Mene, mene, tekel, parsin" Words miraculously written on a wall at Belshazzar's feast (Dan. 5:25). These words are names of Babylonian weights or coins. Each coin has a lesser value than the preceding. In English, the saying might be, "Dollar, dollar, quarter, dime."

Daniel did not translate the words literally but rather explained the meaning of the saying as a whole, based upon the Aramaic roots of the measurements meaning "to number," "to weigh," and "to divide."

Mene: God has numbered the days of your reign and brought it to an end.
Tekel: You have been weighed on the scales and found wanting.
Peres: Your kingdom is divided and given to the Medes and Persians.

(Dan. 5:26-28)

BACKGROUND

When David established himself as king he searched for some descendant of his friend Jonathan. He found Mephibosheth, who had been crippled at age five (2 Sam. 4:4). David confirmed Saul's family lands to Mephibosheth and went on to treat him as one of his own sons (9:1-11).

During Absalom's rebellion, David was forced to flee Jerusalem. Mephibosheth's family servant, Ziba, hurried to aid David, but lied about Mephibosheth in order to gain Mephibosheth's estate for himself (2 Sam. 16). Later, Mephibosheth explained that Ziba had betrayed him when he had attempted to follow David into exile. David, unwilling to decide between the two accounts, decreed that the fields be divided between Mephibosheth and Ziba (19:24-30).

LEARNING FROM MEPHIBOSHETH'S LIFE

Mephibosheth's story seems to tell us more about David than about Mephibosheth. In that age, families of deposed dynasties were usually killed by their successors (1 Ki. 16:11; 2 Ki. 10:1-17). David's act of granting Mephibosheth Saul's lands and bringing the crippled prince into his own family circle is a clear example of the grace toward others that recipients of God's grace are called to display.

Mephibosheth, as a recipient of David's grace, displays gratitude, loyalty, and a touching freedom from materialism. Abandoned by Ziba in Jerusalem during Absalom's rebellion, Mephibosheth openly displayed his loyalty to David by going into mourning (2 Sam. 19:24). This act of loyalty surely put him at risk with Absalom and his followers. Later, although he had been betrayed and slandered by his servant Ziba, Mephibosheth was more concerned about David's safety than about revenge. He accepted David's less-than-fair command to divide his fields with Ziba, for the fact that "my lord the king" had arrived home "safely" was more important to him than his wealth (19:30).

Mephibosheth's example reminds us to show our gratitude by open loyalty to the Lord, and to value our relationship with him far more than any earthly wealth or rights.

merchant A person whose business is buying and selling goods, locally or internationally.

International merchants traveled in caravans or by ship throughout the ancient world (Gen. 37:25-28; Prov. 31:14), transporting a variety of trade goods. Solomon brought much wealth into his kingdom by initiating trade in horses and chariots (1 Ki. 10:28,29) and by establishing a trading fleet (1 Ki. 9:26-28). Throughout most of the OT era, Israel maintained an agricultural economy, and did not develop an international merchant class. In fact, one major Hebrew word for trader is "Phoenician," because commerce was considered an activity for foreigners. *See also* Trade.

Originally, most families in Israel created the goods they used. Farmers and craftsmen traded extra goods in markets set up within or outside nearby cities, and fishermen salted or dried their catch and brought them to market. However, Nehemiah 3:8 (430 B.C.) mentions guilds of goldsmiths and perfume-makers, occupations that could hardly have been supported by the small Jewish community alone (*compare* Neh. 3:32).

Following the Babylonian Captivity and later during the Roman period, Jewish communities developed in the major cities of the world, and members of these communities engaged actively in trade. Not until NT times, however, did merchants

Greengrocer's stand carved into a stone slab (A.D. 200–250). Lydia, a traveling merchant who sold luxurious purple cloth, was Paul's first convert in Europe (Acts 16:12-15).

become as common as farmers in Judea (Mt. 22:5). Archaeological finds suggest that Palestine developed its own distinctive pottery and that some of the finest glass of the ancient world was created there. *See also* Glass.

[Jesus] took her hand and said to her . . . "Little girl, I say to you, get up!" (Mk. 5:41). In this way he showed mercy to Jairus and his family by raising a daughter to life.

mercy, merciful A compassionate response that moves a person to help one who is helpless and in need. In the OT: (1) Heb., *raham,* a feeling of compassion, normally translated as "love"; (2) *hanan,* the active help, motivated by love, that is offered to a person in need, often rendered "to be gracious" or "to show mercy." In the NT: (3) Gk., *eleos,* originally the deep emotion of concern aroused by suffering, which in the NT implies the giving of active help. The biblical use of *eleos* portrays God as one who is deeply moved by human suffering and who has chosen to come to our aid despite the sin that makes us his enemies. *See also* Grace; Love.

Mercy is especially visible in the Gospels and the NT Epistles. Whenever a person appealed to Jesus for mercy (Mt. 9:27; 15:22; 17:15; Mk. 10:47,48; Lk. 18:38,39), Jesus responded and met that person's need. Jesus taught that mercy is basic to God's very nature (*compare* Mt. 5:43-48), and he announced, "Blessed are the merciful, for they will be shown mercy" (Mt. 5:7). One of the faults of Israel's religious leaders was that in their emphasis on the details of God's OT Law they overlooked its roots in "justice, mercy, and faithfulness" (Mt. 23:23; *compare* 12:7).

The Epistles indicate that salvation itself has its roots in God's mercy (Eph. 2:4; 1 Pet. 1:3). Because we are spiritually helpless, we must rely for salvation not on our

own efforts but wholly on God's mercy (Rom. 9:16). Furthermore, Christians are dependent on God's mercy day by day, and we are advised to "approach the throne of grace with confidence, so that we may receive mercy [in our failures] and find grace to help [us not to fail again] in our time of need" (Heb. 4:16).

mercy seat A theological name given to the lid of the ark of the covenant ("ark of the Testimony" NIV), where once a year in OT times, on the Day of Atonement, Israel's high priest sprinkled sacrificial blood. Specifically, the "mercy seat" was the space on the lid between the cherubim. *See also* Atonement; Propitiation.

Mesopotamia [MES-oh-poh-TAY-mee-uh]. (1) OT name for the land lying between and around the Tigris and Euphrates rivers, as in Gen. 24:10 (KJV, RSV); (2) the area extended by the Greeks and Romans in NT times to include the whole Tigris-Euphrates valley, as in Acts 7:2.

The area is covered by the modern state of Iraq and was dominated by a series of ancient empires, including Assyria and Babylonia. Writing and literature developed early in this region, and it was through this ancient civilization that Abraham journeyed to the Promised Land, later sending his servant back to Nahor of Mesopotamia to find a wife for Isaac.

An early Mesopotamian king, Naram-Sin of Akkad (about 2280 B.C.), is portrayed climbing a mountain, with his army behind him. He wears the horned tiara reserved for gods.

TIME LINE FOR
Mesopotamia

3000 BC	
	SUMERIAN 3000 - 2371 BC
2500 BC	
	AKKADIAN 2371 - 2191 BC
	SUMERIAN 2191 - 2006 BC
2000 BC	**ISIN - LARSA** 2006 - 1894 BC
	AMORITE 1894 - 1595 BC
1500 BC	**KASSITE** 1595 - 1174 BC
	ARAMEAN 1174 - 950 BC
1000 BC	
	ASSYRIAN 950 - 612 BC
	BABYLONIAN
500 BC	**PERSIAN** 539 - 331 BC

Messiah [Heb., *mashiah*, "anointed one"]. By NT times, a title associated with the OT prophets' vision of a ruler from David's family line who would lead Israel to greatness. The Greek word for anointing, *christos*, supplied the title "Christ," which the NT applies to Jesus of Nazareth.

OLD TESTAMENT

The practice of anointing persons called by God to some special ministry is well established in the OT and in other ancient cultures. Priests (Ex. 30:30), prophets (1 Chr. 16:22), and kings (1 Sam. 15:17) were anointed. Even Cyrus, the Persian, is spoken of by Isaiah as God's anointed because he was ordained to carry out God's judgment on Babylon (Isa. 45:1). In time, the eschatological vision of the prophets focused on an individual who would become Israel's ideal King and fulfill the promises God had made to his people.

NEW TESTAMENT

Jesus acknowledged the title "Christ" when used by his disciples but did not make a public announcement of his Messiahship because of the public's misconceptions regarding the role of the "anointed one" (*compare* Mt. 16:16,17 with Mk. 8:29,30; *see also* Mt. 26:63,64; Mk. 14:61,62; Lk. 22:67-70; Jn. 11:27). However, after the resurrection, the church increasingly applied the title "Christ" to Jesus, using it as a personal name and associating it with the salvation that Jesus won for humankind in his death (*compare* Acts 2:31; 1 Cor. 1:23,24). *See also* Christ; Millennium; Savior; Son.

Time line showing the successive peoples and/or dynasties that controlled the large area called Mesopotamia.

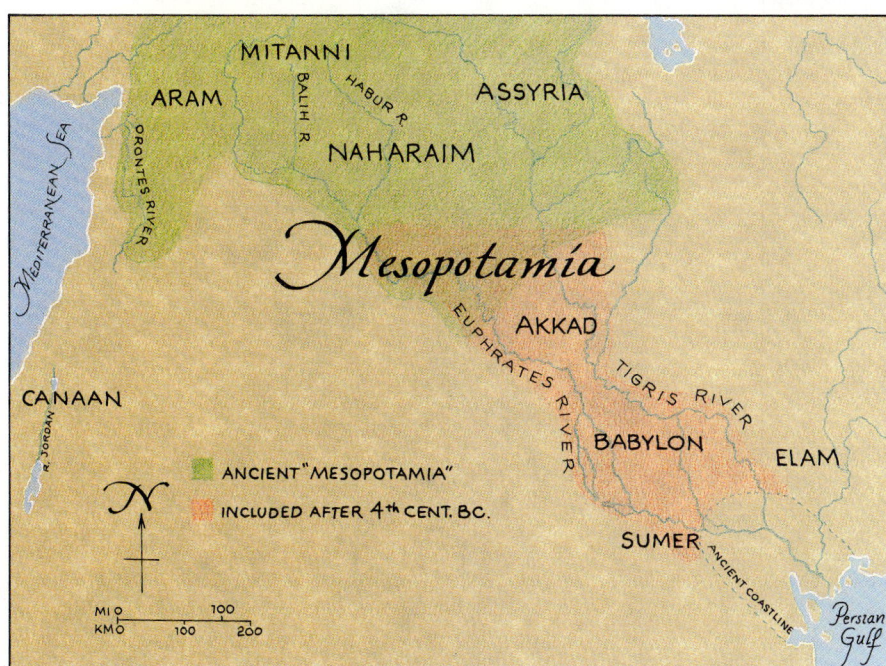

By NT times "Mesopotamia" referred to the whole length of the Tigris-Euphrates valley.

691

MESSIANIC PROPHECIES

Messiah Was to Be:	Old Testament Reference	Fulfilled in Jesus
The woman's seed would bruise Satan's head	**Gen. 3:15**	**Gal. 4:4; 1 Jn. 3:8**
Of Abraham's seed	**Gen. 17:7** *See also* 12:1-3; 21:12; 22:18; 28:14.	**Gal. 3:16** *See also* Jn. 11:51,52; Heb. 11:17-19.
Of the house of David	**2 Sam. 7:12,13** *See also* Gen. 49:10; Pss. 2:12; 89:3,4; 110:1,2; 132:11; Isa. 11:1; Jer. 23:5; 33:17,20,21.	**Acts 13:32** *See also* Mt. 1:1; 22:42-45; Mk. 11:9,10; 12:35-37; Lk. 1:31-33; Acts 2:29,30; Rom. 1:3,4; Rev. 5:5; 22:16.
Preceded by a messenger	**Mal. 3:1** *See also* Isa. 40:3.	**Lk. 1:17** *See also* Mt. 3:1,3.
Born of a virgin	**Isa. 7:14**	**Mt. 1:18** *See also* Mt. 1:21-23.
Born in Bethlehem	**Mic. 5:2**	**Mt. 2:1**
The Shepherd	**Isa. 40:11** *See also* Pss. 23:1-4; 80:1; Ezek. 34:23,24; Zech. 13:7.	**Jn. 10:11-16** *See also* Mt. 15:24; Mk. 14:27; Jn. 10:27,28; 1 Pet. 2:25; Heb. 13:20.
The Prophet	**Deut. 18:15**	**Acts 3:20-22**
The Priest	**Ps. 110:4** *See also* Zech. 6:13.	**Heb. 5:5,6** *See also* Heb. 4:14-16.
The King	**Zech. 9:9** *See also* Ps. 2:6; Jer. 23:5,6.	**Jn. 18:33,37** *See also* Mt. 28:18; Lk. 1:32,33; Jn. 1:49; Rev. 11:15.
The Redeemer	**Isa. 59:20** *See also* Isa. 19:20; 44:22,23; 45:15; 49:6-10; Hos. 1:7; Jer. 33:16.	**Lk. 2:11** *See also* Mt. 1:21; Jn. 3:14,15; Acts 4:12; 13:23; Rom. 11:26,27; Gal. 4:4; Heb. 9:12; 1 Pet. 1:18-21; Rev. 5:9.
The Sacrifice		
A stranger	**Ps. 69:8**	**Jn. 1:11; 7:3,5**
A stumbling stone	**Isa. 8:14**	**Rom. 9:32,33**
Hated	**Isa. 49:7** *See also* Pss. 2:1,2; 69:4.	**Jn. 15:24,25** *See also* Acts 4:27.
Reproached	**Ps. 69:9**	**Rom. 15:3**
Mocked	**Ps. 22:7,8**	**Mt. 27:39-44** *See also* Mt. 26:67,68; Mk. 15:14,19.
Smitten	**Mic. 5:1** *See also* Isa. 50:6; 53:4; Lam. 3:30; Zech. 13:6,7.	**Mt. 27:30** *See also* Mt. 26:67,68; Mk. 14:27; 15:19; Lk. 22:63; Jn. 1:3.
Spit upon	**Isa. 50:6**	**Mk. 14:65**
Crucified	**Ps. 22:16**	**Jn. 19:18** *See also* Jn. 20:25.
Counted with transgressors	**Isa. 53:12**	**Mk. 15:27,28**
Our sin-bearer	**Isa. 53:4-6** *See also* Isa. 53:8,12; Dan. 9:26.	**Jn. 1:29** *See also* Mt. 20:28; Heb. 9:28; 10:10; 1 Pet. 3:18.
Resurrected	**Pss. 16:10** *See also* Pss. 49:15; 71:20; Isa. 25:8.	**Lk. 24:6,31,34** *See also* Acts 2:31; 1 Cor. 15:5-9.

metals A class of chemical elements characterized by malleability, fusibility, and conductivity of heat and/or electricity. Of the 78 metal elements, only gold, silver, copper, tin, lead, iron, and mercury were known in biblical times.

Several of these metals were basic to the development of any ancient civilization's material culture, particularly those used in tools and weapons. Metals were also used as mediums of exchange and in jewelry. In addition, pagan worshipers cast idols, and many objects used in Israel's worship were cast or overlaid with precious metals.

Archaeologists generally identify historic ages by the principal metal in use. Each successive stage required advances in smelting and refining technology to produce and focus the intense heat required to render ore. While there is some debate over the beginning and ending of the various ages in Palestine, the following dates are generally accepted:

Copper-Stone Age	4000–3150 B.C.
Early Bronze Age	3150–2200 B.C.
Middle Bronze Age	2200–1550 B.C.
Late Bronze Age	1550–1200 B.C.
Iron Age	1200–332 B.C.

Other terms are used to identify periods after 332 B.C. *See also* Jericho.

The first mention of metals and metalworking is found in Gen. 4:22, where Tubal-Cain is identified as the first metalworker and credited with working in both bronze and iron in the days before the Genesis Flood. *See also* Bronze; Copper; Furnace; Gold; Iron; Silver.

Micah, Book of One of the minor prophetic books of the OT, Micah contains some of the most powerful and beautiful language to be found in the OT. Its parallel pronouncements of judgment and promises of restoration warned the wicked and offered hope to the godly among God's OT people.

BACKGROUND
Micah [MI-kuh; "who is like Yahweh!"]

was a contemporary of Isaiah, and prophesied during the last quarter of the eighth century (725–700 B.C.). During those decades, Assyria crushed the Northern Kingdom of Israel, whose capital was Samaria, and carried its people into captivity. Then, Judah and Jerusalem were threatened. Only God's intervention enabled the Southern Kingdom of Hezekiah to survive (Isa. 36–38). Nevertheless, the deferred Assyrian threat foreshadowed the destruction and exile of the Babylonian Captivity, which took place 100 years later, in Jeremiah's time. At that time, Judah's leaders recalled Micah's prophecy regarding the destruction of the Temple and Jerusalem (Jer. 26:18,19).

Micah, like Isaiah, confronted the two Hebrew kingdoms with the sins that made judgment certain. Therefore, it is not surprising to hear Micah's words about sin, repentance, and renewal echoed in the pronouncements of Isaiah (*compare* Mic. 4:1 with Isa. 2:2; Mic. 4:4 with Isa. 36:16). Yet, in addition to these basic themes, Micah constantly returned to the theme of the future restoration of exiles to their homeland. God must judge, but he will ultimately save his people. We see these alternating themes in each of Micah's collections of sermons: 1:2–2:13; 3:1–5:15; and 6:1–7:20.

THEOLOGICAL CONTRIBUTIONS
Micah presents a God who is personally involved in history. Although the invading forces may be Assyrian, it is "I" (God) who "will make Samaria a heap of rubble" (Mic. 1:6). Micah carefully details the sins that make divine judgment certain (2:1,2; 3:1-7; 6:9–7:6). However, Micah also reminds Israel and Judah that God is compassionate and loving. "Who is a God like you," the prophet asks, "who pardons sin and forgives the transgression of the remnant of his inheritance? You do not stay angry forever but delight to show mercy" (7:18). Because God is compassionate, the prophet looks to the future with hope and strongly emphasizes the messianic theme.

A wall painting from the tomb of Rekhmira, Thebes (about 1480 B.C.), depicts Egyptian metal workers. Bellows (upper left), worked with the feet, fan the flames; metal is melted in a crucible (lower left) held over the fire between two rods; workmen (center) carry tongs and blowpipes; molten metal is poured into molds; and a basket of fuel, probably charcoal, is emptied; vessels (right) are beaten into shape by stones on anvils, then are polished smooth by pebbles and ornamented with incised decoration.

693

"But you, Bethlehem Ephrathah,
though you are small among the
clans of Judah,
out of you will come for me
one who will be ruler
over Israel."

MICAH 5:2

Judean hills near Bethlehem, the small Judean town mentioned in Micah's prophecy.

God will send his people a ruler, to be born in Bethlehem, who will "stand and shepherd his flock in the strength of the Lord" (5:1-5). In his day, peace will reign. "Nation will not take up sword against nation, nor will they train for war anymore. Every man will sit under his own vine . . . and no one will make them afraid" (4:1-5). Together these passages constitute one of the clearest images of the Messiah and his ministry to be found in the OT. *See also* Messiah.

MASTERY KEYS

Read through the Book of Micah with particular attention to the many passages devoted to the themes of judgment and restoration. Study each passage carefully to see what you can discover about the nature of divine judgment and renewal.

SPECIAL FEATURES

Micah 6:1-8 portrays God facing his people in a court of law. The scene includes one of the OT's clearest statements of the religious and moral foundations of OT Law: "He has showed you, O man, what is good. And what does the Lord require of you? To act justly and to love mercy and to walk humbly with your God" (6:8).

MICAH: A READING AND STUDY GUIDE

Chapter	Content Summary	Related Articles
1	Micah warns that God is about to judge Samaria and Jerusalem, causing his sinful people to weep and wail.	Judgment Idol
2	Though the prophets remain silent, God intends to bring disaster on his people. Yet, a remnant will be saved.	Prophet Remnant
3	Israel's leaders and false prophets lead the people astray. God has given Micah power to declare the people's sin.	Sin
4	In the last days, God will bring peace to the earth. He will regather his exiled people to their land.	Peace Exile
5	The expected ruler will be born in Bethlehem. He will shepherd his people and will save the remnant.	Prophecy Assyria
6	God formally states his case against his people. He will punish the guilty.	Mercy Guilt
7	Israel will experience misery but will rise again. God will pardon and shepherd his people as in the past.	Evil Pardon

Micaiah [mih-KAY-yuh; "who is like Yahweh!"]. A prophet of the Lord who predicted the death of King Ahab in battle, about 853 B.C. **Father:** Imlah. **Scripture:** 1 Ki. 22; 2 Chr. 18.

BACKGROUND

King Ahab and his wife Jezebel actively promoted Baal worship in Israel. Before launching, with King Jehoshaphat of Judah, a joint military venture against the Syrians, Ahab inquired of his four hundred prophets, who all predicted a Hebrew victory. Jehoshaphat hesitated and asked if there were not a prophet of the Lord in Israel. Reluctantly, Ahab called for Micaiah, whom he hated because "he never prophesies anything good about me" (1 Ki. 22:8). Asked to predict the outcome of the Syrian venture, Micaiah at first repeated the words of Ahab's prophets, but with obvious sarcasm. Micaiah then revealed that a "lying spirit" spoke through Ahab's prophets. The combined Hebrew forces would be defeated, and Ahab would be killed in the coming battle. Micaiah was slapped by one of Ahab's prophets and jailed by the king until the king should return safely (22:27). However, the king did not return. God had spoken through Micaiah, and what he predicted came to pass. *See also* Prophet.

LEARNING FROM MICAIAH'S LIFE

Micaiah deserves thoughtful consideration. He was the lone representative of true religion in a land committed to the false. Micaiah had spoken out often against the evils done by Ahab (1 Ki. 22:8), and his words were met with open hostility and anger, and even blows (22:24).

Yet, Micaiah displayed a quiet confidence in God. As he was being taken to prison to await the king's return, Micaiah declared, "If you ever return safely, the Lord has not spoken through me. . . . Mark my words, all you people" (1 Ki. 22:28). Micaiah's courage grew out of the conviction that he represented God and that what he said was in full accord with God's will.

It is good to remember Micaiah when we find ourselves outnumbered by persons whose values and ideas are popular but wrong. We too can speak out with courage, if we know that what we believe is founded on the revealed will of God.

Michael [MI-kuhl; "who is like God?"]. A high-ranking angel (archangel) named in Dan. 10:21 and 12:1. Daniel identifies Michael as the "great prince who protects" the Jewish people. He is seen again in Rev. 12:7 at the head of warring angels fighting against Satan and his hosts. Michael is a prominent figure in many of the Jewish religious tracts written in the period between the OT and NT (*compare* Jude 9). *See also* Angel.

Michal [MI-kuhl; "who is like God?"]. Younger daughter of Saul, who married, then later despised David, about 1000 B.C. **Children:** none. **Scripture:** 1 Sam. 18,19; 2 Sam. 3,6.

BACKGROUND

After David established himself as a popular and successful military leader, Saul became jealous and fearful. When he learned his younger daughter Michal loved David, Saul offered her to David and asked David to kill a hundred Philistines as the bride price, hoping David would be killed in doing so. David survived and married Michal (1 Sam. 18). Later, Michal helped David escape an assassination plot (1 Sam. 19). David was forced to flee and live in exile. *See also* David.

Saul then married Michal to a man named Paltiel (1 Sam. 25:44). After Saul's death, David demanded and obtained the return of Michal, a demand that may have been motivated more by politics than by love. Some time later, David, dressed in the simple linen ephod often worn for worship, led the procession that brought God's ark to Jerusalem, dancing with joy and abandon. *See also* Ephod.

Michal, watching from a window, "despised him in her heart" (2 Sam. 6:16). When David came home, Michal scornfully confronted him over his "undignified" behavior. However, David rejected her rebuke. The text adds, "and Michal daughter of Saul had no children to the day of her death" (6:23), which in that culture was a sign of divine judgment.

LEARNING FROM MICHAL'S LIFE

Michal is one of those tragic women who find themselves used by men. Her father cruelly tried to use her fresh love for David to end David's life. After David fled, Saul, in an act intended to insult David as well as perhaps serve other political ends, married Michal to another man. While Michal freely chose to help David escape her father's assassins, David himself later used her for his political ends, demanding she be returned as a pre-condition for reconciliation with the tribes that had remained loyal to Saul's family after the king's death. In none of these situations did men with power consult Michal or consider her desires.

We can hardly blame Michal if, with such treatment, she became cynical. Yet, Michal's reaction as the ark of God was carried to Jerusalem shows the danger of cynicism. Michal could no longer rejoice in God and felt no excitement at all as the ark, the holiest object in Israel's religion, was carried to its new home. Instead, her bitterness finally welled up, and all she felt was disgust that David, a king, should appear before his people as a simple worshiper, stripped of his royal glory.

We can and should feel sympathy for Michal, and for all people who have been so used by others that they grow hard and cynical. Yet others have been used too—as Joseph was used by his brothers and by Potiphar's wife—without becoming bitter or losing their faith. The tragedies of Joseph's life deepened rather than destroyed his capacity to love and honor God. When we are manipulated and used by others, we can choose either to seek the good that God intends to bring to us through our suffering, or we can choose like Michal to let our faith wither and die. Tragically, those who make Michal's choice end as she did—bitter and alone.

michtam, miktam *See* Psalms.

middle wall The barrier wall that separated the inner court of the Jerusalem Temple from the outer "court of the Gentiles." Posted signs threatened death to any non-Jew who crossed this line.

Paul sees this physical barrier as an image of the spiritual barriers Judaism erected between Jew and Gentile (Eph. 2:14). The Law made a clear distinction between God's covenant people and others and was intended to serve as a witness of God in the world. But instead of drawing outsiders to God, the Law had created hostility between Israel and the rest of the world. Now, Paul argues, that ancient barrier to unity is gone, for in his death Christ has reconciled both Jew and Gentile to God apart from the Law and in effect made of the two a single, united family of faith (Eph. 2:11-22). *See also* Law.

Midianites [MID-ee-uhn-ites]. A people descended from Abraham by his concubine Keturah. They appear in the biblical account in the time of Moses (1527–1406 B.C.) and again as an oppressor in the time of Gideon (around 1100 B.C.).

The Midianites were a nomadic people whose territory at times included northwestern Arabia and part of the Sinai peninsula. Archaeologists consider the Midianites to have been traders, miners, and metalworkers as well as herdsmen (*compare* Num. 31:22,32-34). No modern ethnic group can be identified with the Midianites of biblical times.

Moses fled from Egypt to Midian, where he married Zipporah, daughter of the priest of Midian (Ex. 2:15-21). Moses' Midianite relatives were helpful during the first stage of the Exodus (Ex. 18). However, some 40 years later, the Midianites, allied with Moab, opposed passage of the Israelites through their land (Num. 22). Midianite women, following the advice of Balaam, enticed many Israelite men into idolatry and immorality, an act that led to war with Israel (Num. 25). Furthermore, in the time of Gideon, Midianite raiders riding camels dominated much of Canaan, bringing poverty and starvation to the Israelites (Jdg. 6). However, the Midianite forces were crushed in the uprising led by Gideon. Several later passages look back on these events (Ps. 83:9; Isa. 10:26; Hab. 3:7).

midwife A woman skilled in helping during childbirth. Ezekiel 16:4 describes some of their duties: The midwife cut the umbilical cord, bathed the baby, rubbed it with salt, and wrapped it in cloth. Egyptian reliefs show pregnant women squatting on a birthstool as midwives assist. *See also* Childbirth.

Midwives attended Rachel (Gen. 35:17, 18) and Tamar (Gen. 38:28) in the patriarchal period. The best-known midwives in Scripture are those who failed to carry out the command of Pharaoh to kill all male children born to the Israelites (Ex. 1:15-21). The only two midwives named in this passage have Egyptian names; it is likely they were heads of a guild of midwives who served both Israelites and Egyptians. *See also* Lie.

The middle wall of the Temple, the barrier between the Court of the Gentiles and the inner courts of the Temple. See Eph. 2:14.

mighty men A biblical phrase simply meaning "war heroes." While the word first appears in Gen. 6:4, it is best known as a designation for the outstanding warriors who became David's early followers and later the core of his military (2 Sam. 23:8-39).

mildew [Heb., *yeraqon*, "yellow" or "pale"]. The growth of fungi on organic matter. Mildew on clothing or household articles rendered those objects unclean (Deut. 13:47–14:57). Mildew is consistently associated with divine punishment (Deut. 28:22; 1 Ki. 8:37; 1 Chr. 6:28; Hag. 2:17; Amos 4:9).

mile (1) Latin, *milion*, only in Mt. 5:41, a Roman measure of 1,000 double paces, equal to 1,618 yards or 1,477.5 meters. (2) Gk., *stadion*, sometimes translated "furlong," about one-eighth mile or 200 meters, as in Lk. 24:13; Jn. 6:19. Some versions compute the distance into miles for the English reader's convenience.

milk The fluid drawn from the mammaries of cattle, sheep, and goats—a staple food in biblical times. Whole milk did not keep well in the warm climate of Palestine and was a luxury provided for guests (Gen. 18:8; Jdg. 5:25). Most milk was made into soft cheese or a soured, yogurt-like food. *See also* Butter; Cheese.

The description of Palestine as a land flowing with milk and honey suggests rich pasturage, suitable for flocks and herds (Ex. 3:8; Num. 13:27; Deut. 6:3; Josh. 5:6; Jer. 11:5).

Milk is also symbolic in the OT of abundance (Isa. 7:22) and of beauty (Gen. 49:12;

Song 4:11). In the NT, milk represents basic truths of the Word of God (1 Pet. 2:2; *compare* Heb. 5:12,13).

The obscure command in Deut. 14:21 against cooking a kid in its mother's milk has long been considered a reference to a Canaanite religious practice. However, review of the Ugaritic text on which this interpretation is based has shown the earlier translation to be in error. Whatever the rationale, Deut. 14:21 is the basis for the strict separation of milk and meat dishes in Jewish cooking. *See also* Dietary Laws.

mill, millstone A simple machine for grinding grain into flour, typically a flat, rectangular lower stone and a smaller, rounded upper stone.

Grain was placed on the lower stone and crushed with back-and-forth motions of the upper. Grinding grain was a daily chore of women or servants throughout the biblical era (Ex. 11:5; Isa. 47:2; Mt. 24:41). While larger rotary millstones were turned by animals or prisoners (Jdg. 16:21), each family normally used its own millstones to grind grain into the coarse flour from which bread was made. The "sound of the millstones and the light of the lamp" were the daytime and nighttime

Left: Roman milestone from the Via Maris or "Way of the Sea." Jesus said, "If someone forces you to go one mile, go with him two miles" (Mt. 5:41).

Below: Two hand mills from Israel (third century B.C.). The lower stone was firmly anchored, and the upper was turned either with an upright handle (bottom) or with a horizontal handle (top). Grain was poured into the center hole where it ran between the grinding stones.

The millstone Jesus referred to in Mt. 18:6; Mk. 9:42; and Lk. 17:2 was a huge, circular type powered by animals or water. Inset: Millet is a cereal grass whose seeds are the smallest of all grains. It was grown in ancient Babylonia and Assyria.

evidences of habitation, the absence of which symbolized desolation (Jer. 25:10).

Because the mill was a basic necessity in each household, Mosaic Law forbade a lender to hold a millstone as security for a loan (Deut. 24:6).

millennium Latin for a "thousand years." The millennium is a 1,000-year period, specifically mentioned in Rev. 20. According to this chapter, Satan will be bound for a thousand years (20:2,3). Afterwards, he will be released and lead the nations in a final war against God (20:7,8). After God defeats this coalition, the final judgment will take place (20:11-15).

Although the millennium is mentioned only in Rev. 20, the early church believed with Papias (A.D. 130) that there would be a literal 1,000-year period after the resurrection of the dead, during which "the kingdom of Christ will be set up in material form on this very earth." This view was largely abandoned by Christians after Augustine (A.D. 400), in favor of spiritualizing OT prophecies and Revelation. Belief in the millennium is not permitted by the Roman Catholic Church, whose scholars view this as a doctrine of the Jewish apocalyptic movement. *See also* Prophecy, Interpretation of.

Renewed interest in prophecy in the nineteenth century led to a revival of the early church's view of the millennium. Today, Christians generally take one of three positions. (1) Amillennial: The thousand years symbolize Christ's present rule from heaven. (2) Postmillennial: The thousand years represent the spiritual victory of the Gospel over forces of evil in our world. Christ will come after that spiritual victory is won. (3) Premillennial: Christ will return to set up his Kingdom for a literal 1,000-year period, during which OT prophecies, such as Isa. 11:3-9, Jer. 33, and Zech. 14, will be fulfilled on earth. *See also* Future.

millet A grass-like plant grown for its stalks and grain. Millet served as food for animals and for the poor. Ezekiel 4:9 suggests it was mixed with other grains and beans and ground to make flour when wheat and barley were in short supply.

mina A unit used in weighing precious metals and thus a unit of value. The weight of a mina apparently varied in the ancient world. In early times, the mina was equal to 50 shekels, and 50 minas constituted one talent. However, Ezek. 45:12 refers to a mina of 60 shekels.

The mina weighed about 500 to 550 grams. It is impossible to estimate the actual value of the ancient silver or gold mina at any given time, as we have no way today to measure its purchasing power. *See also* Mene, Mene, Tekel, Parsin; Money; Weights and Measures.

mind In the OT: the intellect, with all its capacities, represented by no specific Hebrew word, but implicit in the meaning of a variety of Hebrew terms variously translated "heart," "spirit," "soul," and "inner parts." In the NT: specific aspects of intellectual activity represented by distinctive terms. There (1) *phroneō, phronesis* indicate thought, judgment, or a way of thinking; (2) *nous* indicates one's perspective or capacity to perceive and is typically used in contexts where a NT author considers a person's spiritual judgment or insight; (3) *dianoia* represents the faculty used to organize or make sense of perceptions and experiences. *See also* Heart.

Modern translations often use "mind" in completely ordinary ways, such as "changed his mind" (Mt. 21:29), "make up your mind" (Lk. 21:14), and "keep in mind" (Jn. 15:18). However, each Greek term translated "mind" is used in theologically significant contexts.

Paul says of the human way of thinking (*phroneō*), "The mind of sinful man is death, but the mind controlled by the Spirit is life and peace; the sinful mind is hostile to God. It does not submit to God's law, nor can it do so" (Rom. 8:6,7). In the same book, Paul says that natural man understood (*noeō*) through the witness of creation that God exists but rejected that

698

knowledge. As a consequence, God "gave them over to a depraved mind [*nous*]" (Rom. 1:28). The inability of the natural mind to grasp the nature of reality is further emphasized in Eph. 4:17; 1 Tim. 6:5; and Tit. 1:15. In this same vein, the very organ with which human beings organize their perceptions and draw conclusions (*dianoia*) is darkened by sin, so that natural men are alienated from God and "enemies in [their] minds because of [their] evil behavior" (Col. 1:21). *See also* Conscience.

This dark picture of the human capacity to grasp spiritual realities provides the background for a vital aspect of Christ's redemptive work. Under the new covenant, God promised, "I will put my laws in their hearts, and I will write them on their minds" (Heb. 10:16; *compare* Jer. 31:33). Even with this new capacity, however, believers are exhorted to "be made new in the attitude of your minds; and to put on the new self, created to be like God in true righteousness and holiness" (Eph. 4:23,24; *compare* Rom. 8:6). Full commitment means we will not "conform any longer to the pattern of this world, but be transformed by the renewing of your mind. Then," the passage promises, "you will be able to test and approve what God's will is—his good, pleasing and perfect will" (Rom. 12:2).

minister, ministry In the OT: (1) Heb., *sarat*, persons who provide significant personal service to someone of high rank, in contrast to a menial servant or slave. The term is often used of the priests who "ministered to the Lord" at the tabernacle or Temple. In the NT: (2) Gk., *leitourgia*, referring to ministry in the religious sense, and (3) Gk., *diakonia*, an active use of one's gifts and resources to meet the material and spiritual needs of others, as in Mt. 25:44; Acts 6:2; 1 Cor. 12:5; 2 Cor. 9:1; Eph. 4:12. Ministry then is two-fold: to the Lord and to our fellow believers.

Ministry in this last NT sense is the calling of every Christian, not just of the ordained. Each of us is to respond to the challenge of ministry as we follow "the Son of Man [who] did not come to be served [*diakoneō*] but to serve" (Mt. 20:28). *See also* Deacon.

Minor Prophets The name given to the group of twelve shorter prophetic writings within the OT. The minor prophets are Hosea, Joel, Amos, Obadiah, Jonah, Micah, Nahum, Habakkuk, Zephaniah, Haggai, Zechariah, and Malachi. *See also* Prophecy; Prophet.

minstrel (KJV) Archaic term meaning musician. In the OT, it is used of a harpist (2 Ki. 3:15), while in the NT, it refers to a piper or flute player (Mt. 9:23).

mint An herb, used both to flavor cooked foods and as a stomach palliative. Mint and other small herbs were grown in household gardens. Jesus criticized the Pharisees, who carefully separated one out of every ten dried mint leaves to tithe but neglected the "more important matters of the law—justice, mercy and faithfulness" (Mt. 23:23).

miracle An event that so overrides what observers understand of natural law that it creates wonder and serves as evidence of God's active intervention in this universe.

Mint.

THE LANGUAGE OF MIRACLES

The Hebrew and Greek words used for miracles focus our attention on several implications of miraculous events. In the OT, (1) *pala'* means "to be marvelous, wonderful" and highlights the awe created by God's acts, as in Ex. 3:20; Ps. 118:23. (2) *Mopet*, "wonder," "sign," focuses attention on the miracle as evidence that God punishes and protects, as in Ex. 4:21; Deut. 7:19-24. (3) *'Ot*, "miraculous sign," emphasizes the fact that miracles are linked to the special revelation of God and his purposes, as in Deut. 4:34; Isa. 38:7. The plagues God brought on Egypt during the Exodus period illustrate each OT emphasis. They created awe in Hebrew and Egyptian alike. They showed that God exists (Ex. 7:5) and that he acts on behalf of

Sunset over the Valley of Aijalon, where God miraculously delayed nightfall and gave Joshua victory over the Amorites (Josh. 10:1-15).

Magnasco's Christ at the Sea of Galilee *captures the moment after the miracle of Peter walking on the water (Mt. 14:30).*

Fifth-century mosaic commemorates Jesus' miracle of multiplying loaves and fishes (Mt. 14; Mk. 6; Lk. 9).

his people (Ex. 6:7). The miracles also served to judge the gods of Egypt, revealing their powerlessness (Ex. 12:12).

In the NT, (4) *dunamis,* "act of power," expresses the conviction that the miraculous act cannot be explained by any natural process, but only as an expression of God's power, as in Mk. 6:2; Acts 2:22. (5) *Sēmeion,* "sign," indicates that miracles serve as a sign to authenticate as God's messenger the person who performs them, as in Mt. 12:38; Jn. 20:30. (6) Less frequently, *teras* appears and is used only with *sēmeion* in the phrase "signs and wonders," as in Mt. 24:24; and lastly (7) *ergon,* "work," as in Jn. 7:3; 10:32. Part of the significance of Jesus' miracles is summed up in the admission of Nicodemus, "Rabbi, we know you are a teacher who has come from God. For no one could perform the miraculous signs you are doing if God were not with him" (Jn. 3:2).

THE MESSAGE OF MIRACLES

The OT message of miracles is intimately linked to God's revelation of his covenant name, Yahweh (Jehovah), a name that means "I AM," or "One Who Is Always Present" (Ex. 3:14). *See also* Lord.

God had spoken to Abraham and given him great covenant promises. Yet, at the time the name "Yahweh" was revealed, Abraham's descendants were slaves in Egypt. In the miracles of the Exodus, God showed himself to be present with his people in power, and at the same time, authenticated Moses as an agent by whom his Law would be revealed to Israel. The greatest miracles of the OT era took place in the four brief decades of Moses' leadership.

It was half a millennium before another outburst of miraculous works occurred.

Ahab and Jezebel vigorously attempted to make Baal Israel's official deity. In response, Elijah and Elisha, the prophets of Jehovah God, performed 21 reported miracles. Through their ministry, Baalism was discredited and the people of Israel were called back to the realization that "the Lord—he is God" (1 Ki. 18:39).

The next and last period during which an increased number of miracles are reported lies in the first century. For a few brief years, Jesus Christ and his apostles performed miracles in their ministries.

Each of these three periods was significant in the history of revelation. The age of Moses saw the introduction of the old covenant. The age of Elijah saw the preservation of Israel's covenant relationship with the Lord, and the age of Jesus saw the introduction of the new covenant and the founding of the Church. Each period of miracles is linked to a fresh, powerful revelation of God.

While most biblical miracles can be grouped in one of these periods, miracles cannot be restricted to them, reminding us that God is not limited in when or how he chooses to intervene in his creation.

THE IMPACT OF MIRACLES

It would be wrong to suppose that miracles produce faith. Pharaoh's heart was hardened by the miracles of Moses, and he became even more antagonistic to God and his people (Ex. 8:19). Ahab and Jezebel failed to repent despite Elijah's miracles. Many who witnessed the wonders Christ performed rejected the Lord's claims (Jn. 9:28-34). Christ's enemies accused him of being in league with Satan (Mt. 12:22-27).

But the miracles forced those who observed them to make a choice. Obviously, supernatural events served to focus the issue. Pharaoh could not ignore the God of his slaves. The Israelites of Ahab's time could not slide unaware into idolatry. The people who heard Jesus speak could not ignore his words, for his works compelled attention. Miracles did not create belief, but they did create a situation in which each person was forced to choose faith or unbelief.

The NT mentions miracles among the spiritual gifts (1 Cor. 12:10,27,29), but it also predicts a coming age of miracles associated with the Antichrist, who will perform "all kinds of counterfeit miracles, signs and wonders" (2 Th. 2:9). These too will create a situation in which persons are confronted with the necessity of personal choice. According to the apostle Paul,

these counterfeit miracles will deceive only "those who are perishing" (2:10), not men and women whose faith is in Christ. *See also* Antichrist.

Today, biblical miracles serve to remind us how great our God is. As David cried, "Tell of all his wonderful acts. . . . Remember the wonders he has done, his miracles. . . . Declare . . . his marvelous deeds among all peoples" (1 Chr. 16:9,12,24). The God we worship is all-powerful. He can, has, and surely will, act in our world of space and time.

Miracles also remind us of God's character. The OT miracles show that God is loyal to his covenant commitments. And in the NT, almost all of Jesus' miracles benefited some human being and so served as evidence of God's love.

Detail of a 12th-century miniature shows Miriam leading the Israelite women in praise to God for their deliverance (Ex. 15:20).

Miriam [MEER-ee-uhm; "loved by Yahweh"]. The sister of Moses and Aaron, identified as a prophetess, who was stricken with leprosy for speaking against Moses, about 1450 B.C. **Father:** Amram. **Brothers:** Moses, Aaron. **Scripture:** Ex. 2,15; Num. 12.

BACKGROUND

Miriam was Moses' sister, old enough to watch the basket-boat in which he was placed as an infant (Ex. 2:4). Later, she served with Moses and Aaron as a leader during the Exodus, with special responsibility for the women (Ex. 15:20,21; Mic. 6:4). During the wilderness wanderings, she became unhappy with her role and jealous of Moses (Num. 12). She was rebuked by God and stricken with leprosy for seven days.

LEARNING FROM MIRIAM'S LIFE

Miriam is one of many women of the Bible who demonstrate that spiritual leadership is not reserved only for men. However, Miriam also illustrates the danger of dissatisfaction with our roles. Though she was a leader, she was jealous of Moses, *the* leader. Each of us can find fulfillment in the spiritual role God has given us in life, and Miriam's experience indicates that it is both self-defeating and wrong to yearn for a role God has chosen to give someone else. *See also* Aaron.

Bronze mirror with a handle in the form of a papyrus plant and two falcons. The metallic disk would have been highly polished.

mirror In biblical times, a polished metal surface used to reflect the image of a person who looks into it. Archaeologists have recovered a number of round bronze mirrors from Palestine and from other regions in the Middle East, many with carved handles. Glass mirrors were probably not introduced until the first century A.D.

Paul refers to the distortion in the best of ancient mirrors when he observes that our most accurate knowledge of spiritual things is but a "poor reflection" of reality (1 Cor. 13:12). In context, Paul is urging the Corinthians to emphasize love in their church rather than claim superior knowledge, a practice which had led to divisions and disputes.

James refers to a mirror to make an important point about our use of Scripture (Jas. 1:22-25). A person who simply glances in a mirror and then goes away, forgetting what he saw, misuses the mirror. The person who uses a mirror appropriately looks at himself or herself carefully and then combs back the stray hair or washes off the discovered smudge. A person who looks into the Word of God and fails to apply it for personal correction and self-improvement misuses the Word of God. Misused, neither a mirror nor Scripture will be of any benefit.

missions The sending of representatives, often to foreign lands, by a religious community to spread their faith.

PRE-CHRISTIAN MISSIONS

In a pagan missionary effort Jezebel imported hundreds of prophets of Baal from Sidon and actively persecuted the prophets of the Lord, seeking to shift the religious allegiance of Israel (1 Ki. 18).

In the intertestamental period, Judaism was itself a missionary religion. Active efforts were made to win converts to Judaism in the East and the West. Jesus referred critically to the missionary zeal of the Pharisees, who "travel over land and sea to win a single convert, and when he becomes one, you make him twice as much a son of hell as you are" (Mt. 23:15). Acts mentions converts (proselytes, KJV) to Judaism, many of whom responded enthusiastically to the Gospel (Acts 2:11; 6:5; 13:43).

MISSIONS IN THE EARLY CHURCH

The initial spread of the Gospel seems almost accidental. Jews from many parts of the world had come to Jerusalem to celebrate Pentecost. Many who heard the Gospel there from Peter were converted, and carried the new faith back to the Jewish quarters that were established in most cities of the Roman Empire. At home, growing persecution forced many believers to flee Jerusalem. Wherever they went, these scattered Christians spoke of their faith, leading to a great revival in Samaria (Acts 8).

In Antioch, the Gospel was shared with Gentiles, who responded in great numbers. To check on this phenomenon, the church at Jerusalem sent a delegation led by Barnabas. Realizing that God was at work, Barnabas stayed to teach and guide the rapidly growing congregation (Acts 11:19-30). It was this church that initiated an intentional missions program, sending out a team led by Barnabas and Saul to preach the Gospel and establish churches elsewhere. That became the first of three missionary journeys recorded in the Book of Acts.

From the Book of Acts as well as from the Epistles, one can understand the early church's missionary strategy.

• The missionary team went to major cities: provincial, political, population, and trade centers.

• The missionary team went first to the group most oriented to biblical faith: Jews and God-fearers. *See also* God-fearing.

• The missionary team concentrated on teaching those who responded to the Gospel, while not neglecting general evangelism.

• The missionary team moved on, often because persecution developed, to repeat the planting process in another key city of the Empire.

• The missionaries maintained contact with the young churches through letters, return visits, and visits by itinerant teachers.

• The church that was founded in each

population center developed its own leadership and undertook evangelization of the surrounding province (*compare* 1 Th. 1:4-8).

mist (1) Heb., *'ed*, an obscure word found only in Gen. 2:6 and Job 36:27, which describes the source of water before the Flood. Some believe the word indicates a stream or spring. (2) A fog, or low-lying cloud; a "morning mist," as in Hos. 6:4. Figuratively, mist suggests the shortness of human life (Jas. 4:14) or blindness, literal or spiritual (Acts 13:11; 2 Pet. 2:17).

mite (KJV) [Gk., *lepton*]. The smallest coin in use in Palestine in NT times. These small bronze coins were "worth only a fraction of a penny" (Mk. 12:41-44; Lk. 21:1-4). Both Mark and Luke tell of a widow whose gift of two mites Jesus considered more valuable than the large donations of the rich because she gave all she had (Mk. 12:42). As Paul later notes, "The gift is acceptable according to what one has, not according to what he does not have" (2 Cor. 8:12).

mitre (KJV) A turban, worn on the head by the high priest. On the turban was attached a gold plate which bore the words, "Holy to the Lord" (Ex. 39:28-31). *See also* Crown.

mixed multitude (KJV) (1) Slaves of different racial groups who fled Egypt with the Israelites in Ex. 12:38; (2) a pejorative meaning "rabble" applied to the Israelites who complained despite God's deliverance, Num. 11:4; (3) foreign wives and their offspring, Neh. 13:23,24; and (4) foreign nations to be overcome by Babylon, Jer. 25:20. Underlying each use of the phrase is the concept that the group described does not have, or acts as if it does not have, a covenant relationship with the Lord.

Moab, Moabites [MOH-ab; "from my father"]. (1) The name of the land occupied by the Moabites. (2) A people who occupied the land east of the Dead Sea at the time of the Exodus in what is now Jordan. The Moabites were descended from Moab, a son of Lot by the elder of his two unmarried daughters (Gen. 19:30-38). The name is found in Assyrian records as well as in Scripture. Archaeologists have shown that the high, well-watered plains of Moab supported an advanced civilization, its boundaries protected by a series of small but strong forts. However, the territory of Moab has not been as thoroughly surveyed or excavated as has Israel.

Moab is mentioned often in the OT. Moab's king, Balak, hired the prophet Balaam to curse Israel and, when this failed, attempted to turn God against his people by luring the Israelites into idolatry and immorality (Num. 22–25). At that time, God did not permit Israel to war with them (Deut. 2:9), although Israel crushed other Transjordan kingdoms.

Early in the age of the judges, Eglon of Moab dominated the Israelites east of the Jordan for 18 years, until Ehud assassinated him (Jdg. 3:12-30). Later David defeated Moab, the original land of his great-grandmother Ruth, and made the nation a subject state, which it remained until after the death of Solomon (2 Sam. 8:2,12).

Omri of Israel subdued the Moabites, who remained subject until the end of Ahab's reign (2 Ki. 3:4-27). Independence was finally won by Mesha, king of Moab, after the death of Ahab in 853 B.C. This independence was celebrated by the erection of what is known as the Moabite Stone, discovered in Jordan in 1868. However, hostilities persisted between the Hebrew kingdoms and Moab (2 Ki. 24:2; 2 Chr. 20:1-30; Isa. 15,16). *See also* Ahab.

Moab is mentioned often in both major and minor prophets as a people God would judge for their sins against Israel (*compare* Isa. 15,16; Jer. 48; Ezek. 25:8-11; Amos 2:1-3; Zeph. 2:8-11). Thus, the Moabites were conquered by Assyria and subsequently by Babylon, and by the time the Jews returned from captivity in Babylon, Moab no longer existed as a nation.

This bronze coin of minute value was probably the "widow's mite." It was issued by Pontius Pilate in A.D. 30 and bears the name of Tiberius Caesar.

Molech, Moloch A pagan deity, the national god of the Ammonites (1 Ki. 11:7; Acts 7:43). The name is similar to the Hebrew word for king (*melek*). Some scholars suggest that the Hebrews merged the consonants of *melek* with the vowels of *boshet*, their word for "shame." Thus, they may have labeled the Ammonite royal deity "the shameful king."

Several times the OT speaks of sacrificing children "to Molech" (Lev. 18:21; 20:2-5; 2 Ki. 23:10; Jer. 32:35). Yet it may be that not all of these references actually name the god Molech. Recently discovered inscriptions from Carthage suggest that the "mlk" in the Hebrew text of these verses may refer to a *molk* sacrifice. This involved burning young children alive in order to receive some benefit from a god. Jeremiah associates these *molk* sacrifices with an-

Stone relief of a Moabite warrior (8th century B.C.). A series of fortresses protected the boundaries of Moab, east of the Dead Sea.

These burial urns from Carthage contained the ashes of children burnt alive in sacrifice, a practice also followed by apostate Israelites in homage to Baal and other pagan gods.

other god, Baal, and expresses the Lord's horror at a practice that "I never commanded, nor did it enter my mind, that they should do such a detestable thing" (Jer. 32:35). *See also* Child Sacrifice.

molten sea (KJV) A giant bowl of cast bronze in Solomon's Temple. It held the water which priests used for ceremonial washing (2 Chr. 4:2-6).

The molten sea, some 15 feet (4.6 meters) in diameter and 7½ feet (2.3 meters) deep, rested on the backs of a dozen bronze oxen. It was placed between the altar of sacrifice and door into the Temple, the same position held by the bronze laver in the court of Israel's tabernacle. When the Babylonians conquered Jerusalem in 586 B.C. and raided the Temple, they broke up the molten sea and carried off its bronze. *See also* Basin; Laver.

Reconstruction of the "molten sea," the KJV's name for the huge bronze basin used for ritual washing at the Temple.

money A portable medium of exchange generally accepted in a society as a measure of value.

In early biblical times, wealth was measured in land, animals, or crops (Gen. 12:16). Barter was common. Vassal nations paid tribute in sheep and rams (2 Ki. 3:4), and individuals paid tithes and taxes in grain, oil, or wine (Deut. 14:22,23). But as early as Abraham's time, silver was the most common medium of exchange (Gen. 23:15,16). In fact, "silver" frequently

means "money" in both the OT and NT. Thus, Deut. 14:24,25 suggests that if it is too difficult to transport a tenth of one's crops to the place of worship, the crops may be exchanged for silver.

OLD TESTAMENT

At first silver and gold were weighed out on scales. The different values of money we read about in the Bible—the talent, shekel, mina, and gerah—refer to units of weight. But even these weight units were not standardized in early times. Thus, the shekels Abraham paid for Sarah's burial field were computed "according to the weight current among the merchants" (Gen. 23:16). And later, when governments attempted to standardize weights, there were still "heavy" and "light" weight systems.

Coins were not invented until about 600 B.C. The Persian Empire first put them to widespread use in the 500s B.C. Soon other nations and cities began creating their own coins. In each case, coins were stamped by the issuing authority, but their value was determined by the weight of the metal they contained. *See also* Coin.

Today we can estimate accurately the weight of silver in most units of ancient money. Although we cannot determine the purchasing power of these units at any given biblical period, we do have some hints. In the Mosaic era, a prime ram was valued at two silver shekels (Lev. 5:15), and six bushels (220 liters) of barley at 50 shekels (Lev. 27:16). Solomon bought chariots for 600 shekels and war horses for 150 shekels (1 Ki. 10:29). Yet we have no idea how a ram, or barley, was valued against olive oil, a woven robe, or against a mill for grinding grain. And we cannot measure the value of these basic commodities against a war horse.

NEW TESTAMENT

By NT times, Persian, Greek, and Roman coins of bronze and silver mingled with Jewish coins in the markets of Judea. The Roman denarius, quinarius, and sesterce; the Greek drachma, didrachma, tetradrachma, and assarion; shekels and half-shekels from Tyre; and coins minted by Herod the Great all circulated in Palestine and surrounding regions.

The coin most often mentioned in the NT is the Roman denarius. Its value, a laborer's pay for one day, remained fixed for most of the first century (Mt. 20:2,9). In Jesus' time, the Greek drachma and the Jewish or Tyrian shekel had about the same value as the denarius. This helps us understand the power of Jesus' parable of the unmerciful servant (Mt. 18:21-35). The servant intended to jail a fellow servant who owed him the significant sum of 100 denarii, perhaps a third of his yearly earnings. But the first servant had just been forgiven a debt of 10,000 talents. That debt was equivalent to 30 million days of labor—or 1,175 lifetimes of 70 years. The king, who represented God in Jesus' story, had forgiven his servant a debt that was literally unpayable.

A BIBLICAL VIEW OF MONEY

The NT presents three important insights on money: (1) Money has no ultimate value. In Jesus' parable, the rich fool was confident about the future because he had "plenty of good things laid up for many years." But that very night, the rich man died—and he was not ready to meet God (Lk. 12:13-21). Thus, for eternal purposes, all his wealth was worthless.

Jesus went on to remind his disciples that God knows our needs and will meet them. Thus, the believer need not set his heart on things that unbelievers desire but should seek God's Kingdom instead (Lk. 12:22-31).

(2) A love of money distorts relationships with God and others. Paul warns that the love of money leads to evil behavior (1 Tim. 6:3-10). "People who want to get rich fall into temptation and a trap and into many foolish and harmful desires that plunge men into ruin and destruction" (1 Tim. 6:9; *see* Acts 5:1-5). More significantly, the desire for money wars against our desire to serve God. A person cannot serve God and money, but must choose to make one or the other the highest goal in his life (Mt. 6:24).

This is the point of Jesus' instruction to the rich young ruler to sell all that he had and give the proceeds to the poor. The young man had honestly tried to treat others well, but Jesus revealed that the young man had substituted confidence in his wealth for confidence in God (Mt. 19:16-21).

In view of this perspective on money, it is not surprising that an important qualification for Christian leadership is that a person be free from a love of money (1 Tim. 3:3; 1 Pet. 5:2; *see* Heb. 13:5). Furthermore, James, sensitive to the way money distorts human relationships, warned members of the Jerusalem church not to show favoritism toward the rich (Jas. 2:1-13).

(3) Money is to be used, not valued for itself. Scripture does not suggest that it is

wrong to be wealthy. In OT times, wealth was correctly seen as one indication of divine blessing. The NT makes it clear, however, that money is to be valued only for what one can do with it.

Paul instructs Timothy, "Command those who are rich in this present world

WEIGHT OF OT MONETARY UNITS*

Unit	Equivalent	Weight (in silver)	
Talent	3,000 shekels	75.60 pounds	34.27 kilograms
Mina	50 shekels	1.26 pounds	571.20 grams
Shekel		.40 ounce	11.42 grams
Pim	2/3 shekel	.20 ounce	7.62 grams
Beka	1/2 shekel	.13 ounce	5.71 grams
Gerah	1/20 shekel	8.71 grains	.57 gram

*These weights are approximations at best.

A cache of gold Roman coins. Coins of many lands were in circulation in Palestine during NT times.

. . . to put their hope in God . . . [and] to do good, to be rich in good deeds, and to be generous and willing to share. In this way they will lay up treasure for themselves as a firm foundation for the coming age" (1 Tim. 6:17-19). This is the point of the troublesome parable of the unjust steward (Lk. 16:1-15). Jesus did not commend him for his dishonesty but did commend him for realizing that money is to be used to prepare for the future.

It is difficult in any age to maintain a healthy and balanced attitude toward money. However, if we realize that money is no measure of ultimate value, if we make God rather than wealth the focus of our desires, and if we then use our money in the service of God, we will find a contentment and inner peace which escapes those whose lives are spent in the pursuit of wealth. *See also* Coin; Silver.

Christ Driving the
Money Changers
from the Temple *by
Rembrandt van Rijn,*
A.D. 1635.

money changers Businessmen who
served as bankers in NT times, exchanging
currency and sometimes taking deposits
and making loans—with interest, which
was contrary to Mosaic Law.

Many money changers did business in
the outer court of the Temple. The rabbis
decreed that Temple taxes and the
price of sacrificial animals (Deut. 14:24,25)
be paid in silver didrachmas or tetra-
drachmas ["shekels of Tyre"]. Thus,
worshipers were forced to change any
of the many coinages current in Palestine
into "acceptable money"—at a charge
ranging from four to eight percent.
Money changers often cheated their
customers, and certain priestly families
shared in the proceeds, a fact established
by first-century documents as well as by
Jesus' charge that the money changers
were making God's house "a den of
robbers" (Mt. 21:13).

706 **months** *See* Calendar.

moon Earth's satellite, which revolves
from west to east around the earth once
each 29½ days.

In many ancient cultures, the moon was
identified with a god or goddess. In Abraham's Ur, the principal god was Nanna
(Sin) the moon god. But Moses warned
the Hebrews, "When you look up to the
sky and see the sun, the moon and the
stars—all the heavenly array—do not be
enticed into bowing down to them and
worshiping things the Lord your God has
apportioned to all the nations under
heaven" (Deut. 4:19). Thus, the heavenly
bodies in their regularity and array are not
gods but witnesses to the glory of their
Creator (Ps. 19:1-4; Rom. 1:20).

According to Genesis, the moon and
other heavenly bodies "serve as signs to
mark seasons and days and years" (1:14).
The Hebrew religious calendar was based
on lunar months. Religious festivals were
held on days calculated from the new
moon. The Jewish people also celebrated

the beginning of a lunar month with a New Moon festival, including sacrifices and feasts (1 Sam. 20:5-24; 2 Ki. 4:23; Neh. 10:33; Isa. 1:13,14; Hos. 5:7; Amos 8:5). Without criticizing OT practices, Paul in Col. 2:16 warns against those who would make Christianity a religion of ritual observances.

Symbolically the moon, with the other heavenly bodies, stands for permanence. The psalmist says that God's covenant with David and his family line "will be established forever like the moon, the faithful witness in the sky" (Ps. 89:37). Furthermore, the moon is often mentioned in eschatological passages, and a darkened moon is associated with the Second Coming of Jesus (Mt. 24:29; Mk. 13:24; Lk. 21:25). These NT predictions reflect earlier statements by the OT prophets about history's end (Isa. 13:10; Joel 2:10; 3:15).

Mordecai [MOR-duh-ki; "related to Marduk"]. Persian name of a minor Jewish official in the court of Xerxes who thwarted a plot to exterminate the Jews and became vizier of the Persian Empire, about 475 B.C. **Father:** Jair, a Benjamite. **Cousin:** Esther. **Scripture:** Book of Esther.

BACKGROUND

Mordecai, a minor official in the capital of Persia, persistently refused to get on his knees before the arrogant vizier, Haman. Haman was so incensed that he determined to destroy not only Mordecai, but Mordecai's entire race, the Jews. About this time, the ruler, Xerxes, was searching for a new queen. Mordecai enrolled his beautiful cousin Esther in the competition,

and she won. But Esther had kept her racial identity secret.

Meanwhile, Haman obtained permission to condemn the Jewish people. As the fatal day approached, a sleepless Xerxes learned from a reading of court records that Mordecai earlier had saved his life —and had not been rewarded. In a sudden and unexpected turn of events, Xerxes ordered Haman to honor Mordecai. The next day Xerxes learned from Esther that the race Haman had plotted to exterminate was the queen's own. Haman was hanged, and Mordecai received permission from Xerxes to grant the Jews the right of self-defense against their enemies. Finally, Mordecai became vizier in Haman's place. There he "worked for the good of his people and spoke up for the welfare of all the Jews" (Esth. 10:3).

LEARNING FROM MORDECAI'S LIFE

Mordecai's conviction that a man should worship God alone prevented him from bowing down to Haman, the powerful Persian noble (Esth. 3:3-5). This commitment to his faith brought intense pressure.

Yet throughout the ordeal Mordecai seems to have remained a man of faith. When he urged Queen Esther to intervene, Mordecai said, "If you remain silent at this time, relief and deliverance for the Jews will arise from another place" (4:14). God would still keep his covenant commitment to Israel, no matter how dark the situation appeared. And, events proved Mordecai right. God worked providentially to bring Haman down and to make Mordecai "second in rank to King Xerxes" (10:3).

Mordecai was the courageous Jew who challenged his cousin Esther to risk her life for her people. His deed is depicted on this scroll containing an illustrated Book of Esther.

Mordecai's life teaches us two vital lessons: (1) It is important to stand for what we believe, even when this might be unpopular or even dangerous, and (2) it is important to continue trusting God even if the stand we take creates problems. Our God retains sovereign control over every circumstance.

morning star *See* Lucifer.

morsel (sop, KJV) (1) A bit of bread torn from a flat loaf, used to dip food from the main dish set before diners, or (2) a choice bit of meat or food dipped from the main dish.

It was a distinct honor, and a special mark of friendship, when a host dipped a bit of bread into the dish for a guest (or selected a choice bite for him). This makes Jesus' act of offering such a morsel to Judas at the Last Supper especially poignant. Christ, even at the last moment, again expressed friendship to the man who had determined to betray him (Jn. 13:26-30). *See also* Bread; Eating.

mortal, mortality (1) That which is weak and must eventually die (Gen. 6:3; Ps. 56:4); (2) deadly, causing death (Ps. 17:9); (3) theologically, that aspect of human nature which is corrupted by sin (Rom. 6:12).

No single Hebrew word has the express meaning of mortality. Yet the OT shows a great awareness of human vulnerability in such passages as Ps. 103:15,16:

As for man, his days are like grass,
he flourishes like a flower of the field;
the wind blows over it and it is gone,
and its place remembers it no more.

In contrast, the Greeks had a specific word for mortality, *thnētos,* "subject to death." Writing to the Corinthians, Paul contrasts our present mortality with the immortality we will put on at the resurrec-

tion (1 Cor. 15:53,54; 2 Cor. 5:4). At that point, those who are in Christ will be beyond the power of every force associated with death and decay. Perhaps the most exciting use of this term is in Rom. 8:11. Although we have been corrupted by sin (Rom. 6:12), even now God the Holy Spirit, who lives within us, can "give life to [our] mortal bodies," releasing us from sin's grip, that we might serve the living God.

mortar (1) A bowl-shaped stone in which grain, spices, or cosmetics were crushed and finely ground (Num. 11:8; Prov. 27:22); (2) any substance used to bind brick or stone together (Gen. 11:3).

Ancient builders used a variety of substances as mortar. These included asphalt, or bitumen (rendered "tar" in Gen. 11:3); moistened clay, or cement, which hardened when it dried (called "mortar" in Gen. 11:3); and plaster (rendered "clay" in Lev. 14:42). However, ancient stone workers were so skilled that the stones in many larger buildings, such as Solomon's Temple, fit together perfectly without the need of any binding substance.

Moses [MOH-zuhs; Heb., "drawn out"; Egyptian, "child"]. Israel's great hero, who delivered God's people from Egypt, gave them God's Law at Sinai, and led them to the borders of the Promised Land before his death, about 1400 B.C. Moses is credited with the authorship of the first five books of the OT. **Parents:** Amram and Jochebed. **Siblings:** Aaron, Miriam. **Wife:** Zipporah. **Sons:** Gershom, Eliezer. **Scripture:** Exodus, Leviticus, Numbers, Deuteronomy.

The life of Moses divides into three 40-year periods: birth and training (Ex. 2:1-10), isolation in Midian (Ex. 2:11-25), and achievements as Israel's deliverer and lawgiver (Ex. 3–Deut.). When Moses was

born, the people of Israel were slaves in Egypt. When Moses died, Israel was strong and disciplined, poised for the conquest of Canaan, governed by a complex code of just laws, and worshiping God in a manner the Lord himself devised to testify of the ultimate salvation God would provide in Christ.

BIRTH AND TRAINING

The high birth rate of the Israelites so frightened the Egyptians that the Pharaoh ordered their male infants killed. Baby Moses was placed in the Nile in a papyrus reed basket. Pharaoh's daughter found him and brought him up as her child (Ex. 2:10). Thus, Moses would have been given typical royal family training (Acts 7:22). His education might well have included reading and writing in the 20-letter alphabet of the Canaanites, widely used in Egypt as early as 1500 B.C. and known by at least some Egyptian officials. Moses would also have had contact with people from Syria-Palestine, as persons from Asia often held high administrative posts in Egypt.

Somehow during these years Moses developed a strong sense of identity with his own Hebrew people. The writer of Hebrews says, "By faith Moses, when he had grown up, refused to be known as the son of Pharaoh's daughter. He chose to be mistreated along with the people of God rather than to enjoy the pleasures of sin for a short time" (11:24,25).

ISOLATION IN MIDIAN

Moses so identified with his people that one day, when he saw an Egyptian taskmaster beating a Hebrew, he killed the Egyptian. When the act became known, Moses was forced to flee. He settled among Midianites then living in the Sinai peninsula, married the daughter of a priest named Jethro, and spent the next 40 years of his life as a shepherd.

Although we read of other leaders withdrawing to the desert to prepare for later ministry (Elijah, Jesus, Paul), the Bible gives no specific statements on the importance of these years for Moses. Still, we can speculate that his own experience as a nomad in Sinai gave him knowledge that later helped him lead his nation through that same general area. *See also* Sinai.

DELIVERER AND LAWGIVER

Moses' great accomplishments were reserved for the last 40 years of his life, as recorded in the last four books of the Pentateuch. The man who had dreamed of helping his people was given that very

mission by God, who spoke to him from a burning bush (Ex. 3:4). Armed with a new revelation of God's name and with divine promises, Moses set out on a journey back to Egypt.

1. *Conflict with Pharaoh* (Ex. 5–15). In Egypt, Moses and his brother Aaron confronted Pharaoh and demanded the release of the Israelite slaves. Moses was led by God to announce a series of ten devastating plagues, which finally shattered the arrogance of Pharaoh and led to the Israelites' release. When Pharaoh changed his mind and sent a chariot army in pursuit, Moses, through the power of God, opened the Red Sea for his people to pass through, and destroyed the Egyptians when they tried to follow. *See also* Exodus; Plague; Red Sea.

2. *Conflict with the Israelites* (Ex. 16–18). Despite this miraculous deliverance, the Israelites failed to trust God or respond to

Moses receiving the Law from God on Mount Sinai as depicted in a 6th-century mosaic in the Monastery of St. Catherine, Sinai.

709

Moses' leadership. The journey from Egypt was marked by grumbling, complaining, quarreling, and rebellion. This mob of people, who had so recently been slaves, desperately needed to grow in faith and obedience. Thus, on the way to Mount Sinai, Moses, urged by Jethro, took steps to give organization to the Israelite camp (Ex. 18).

3. *Communication of the Law* (Ex. 20–Num. 10). Moses climbed a cloud-shrouded Sinai, where he received from God the Law which was to govern Israel. This was a total, interwoven system, intended to structure the moral, social, and religious life-style of the nation God intended to plant in Palestine. *See also* Covenant; Justice; Law; Priest; Sacrifice.

The Book of Exodus contains statements of the basic principles underlying the Law, as well as illustrations showing how specific principles were to be applied in Israel. Leviticus contains detailed instructions on sacrifices and the responsibilities of the priests and people, in view of the fact that

God had called Israel to be his holy people. *See also* Commandments, Ten; Holy.

After a year at Sinai, Moses further structured the camp for an organized march to Canaan, the land God had promised centuries earlier to give to Abraham's descendants (Num. 1–10).

Although he was intimately familiar with the southern Sinai, he had not traveled through the northern region nor into Canaan. He persuaded his brother-in-law Hobab, an expert guide and scout, to go with them as they traveled north toward Canaan.

4. *Continuing conflict and rebellion* (Num. 11–25). The journey toward Canaan revealed how undisciplined the Israelites remained. But now the Law formed a basis on which to deal with rebellion. Each rebellious act of the Israelites was met with immediate discipline, from plagues to fire from the Lord that consumed those who complained about their "hardships."

Yet at Kadesh Barnea, on the southern edge of Canaan, the people rebelled directly, fearfully refusing to obey God's command to attack and claim the Promised Land (Num. 14). As a consequence, all the adults present (except for Joshua and Caleb) were doomed to wander in Sinai for the rest of their lives. It would be 38 years before Israel would stand on the brink of the Promised Land again. Incidents during these years continue to reveal the unreadiness of Israel to submit to God. Finally, the last of the old generation died off and was replaced by a new generation ready to follow God.

5. *Call to commitment* (Num. 26–Deut. 34). Moses led the new, disciplined generation of Israelites along the east bank of the Jordan, defeating the peoples who lived there. Camped across the Jordan from Jericho, Moses reviewed the Law, casting it in the then-familiar form of a treaty between a ruler and his people, which we know now as Deuteronomy.

In this highly structured sermon, Moses emphasized the love that had moved God to rescue his people and to give them his Law. Moses concluded his great sermon by announcing the blessings that could be won by obedience and punishments that would follow disobedience. After leading the new generation in a service of covenant renewal, Moses climbed Mount Nebo and, after gazing across the Jordan at the land God was about to give Israel, died. The anonymous author of the postscript to Deuteronomy, after reporting Moses' death, concludes,

MOSES: KEY PASSAGES FOR STUDY

Ex. 3,4	Moses, sensing his weakness, hesitates to accept God's call to deliver the Israelites from Egypt.
Ex. 5:22–6:12	Moses expresses frustration and despair when Pharaoh increases his slaves' workload.
Ex. 7–11	Moses boldly confronts Pharaoh again and again to announce plagues God will bring on Egypt.
Ex. 16	Moses experiences frustration as the Israelites refuse to pay attention to him.
Ex. 32	Moses is furious when he returns from Mount Sinai and finds many Israelites involved in pagan worship.
Ex. 33	Moses begs for a special revelation of the Lord's glory.
Num. 11	Moses deals with more Israelite complaints and expresses his doubts to the Lord.
Num. 14	Moses attempts to stem the rebellion at Kadesh Barnea, and then intercedes for Israel.
Num. 16	Moses becomes angry and asks God to punish Korah for his rebellion.
Num. 27	Moses seeks God's guidance and shares some of his authority with Joshua.
Deut. 3:21-29	Moses recalls the sin that will keep him from entering the Promised Land.
Deut. 11	Moses reveals God's motives in calling for his people to obey the Law.
Deut. 32	Moses teaches a song intended to strengthen Israel's faith.

Since then, no prophet has risen in Israel like Moses, whom the Lord knew face to face, who did all those miraculous signs and wonders the Lord sent him to do in Egypt. . . . For no one has ever shown the mighty power or performed the awesome deeds that Moses did in the sight of all Israel. (34:10-12)

BIBLICAL EVALUATIONS OF MOSES

In a verse apparently added to the text of Numbers, an unnamed writer states, "Moses was a very humble man, more humble than anyone else on the face of the earth" (Num. 12:3). That is, Moses was characterized by complete and willing submission to God.

The author of Hebrews says Moses "was faithful in all God's house" (3:2), and presents him as a man of faith, whose trust in God enabled him to identify with his own oppressed race. He continued to demonstrate his faith by keeping the first Passover and leading Israel through the Red Sea (Heb. 11:24-29).

Moses stands in Scripture as the ideal prophet, the model for all later prophets through whom God revealed himself and his will to humanity (Deut. 18:18-22). Israel confidently relied on Moses as a trustworthy religious authority, and every pious Jew would state unhesitatingly, "We know

that God spoke to Moses" (Jn. 9:28,29).

Yet the Law Moses delivered to Israel was not God's final word. Moses himself was a type of the greater Prophet, Jesus, who appeared in history to reveal at last the full measure of God's love and grace (Jn. 1:17,45).

LEARNING FROM MOSES' LIFE

Moses lived with tremendous stress, burdened with the leadership of a people who constantly complained and often openly rebelled against him and his God. Nevertheless, a man of prayer, who often interceded for Israel, Moses faithfully kept on course despite discouragement and occasional despair. Far from being a mythical hero, drawn larger than life, Moses appears in Scripture as a true human being, an heir to all our weaknesses, yet a man who performed great deeds in the strength that only God can provide.

Most High *See* God.

mote (KJV) An archaic term meaning a speck of dust or other tiny particle. Jesus notes the irony of someone who tries to pluck the tiny mote from another's eye when the person has a huge log in his own (Mt. 7:3-5).

In Joachim Uytewael's canvas, Moses Striking the Rock, *Moses angrily hits the rock with his staff (right) as the Israelites and their animals rush in to drink (Num. 20:1-13).*

711

moth A destructive nocturnal insect. In Scripture the word refers to the clothes moth, whose larvae feed on wool, furs, and other dried animal matter. The moth symbolizes the destruction of precious things. In Ps. 39:11, the Lord's chastisement is compared to the insect's destruction, "You consume their wealth like a moth." And in Mt. 6:19, Jesus instructs us to store our treasures in heaven rather than on earth, "where moth and rust destroy."

God said through Isaiah, "As a mother comforts her child, so will I comfort you" (66:13). Portrait from a Roman funeral monument.

mother The female parent. Women had greater rights in Israel than in other ancient societies. Children owed a debt of respect to both father and mother (Ex. 20:12; Deut. 5:16; Mt. 15:4), and a person who attacked either his father or his mother was to be put to death (Ex. 21:15). The wife in Israel was viewed as more than a childbearer and, indeed, was an important partner with her husband in providing for the family (Prov. 31:10-31; *compare* Gen. 2).

We sense something of the tenderness associated with motherhood among God's covenant people in both Testaments. God expresses his love for Israel by saying through Isaiah,

*Can a mother forget the baby at her breast
and have no compassion on the child
she has borne?
Though she may forget,
I will not forget you!* (Isa. 49:15)

Paul uses the image of a mother "caring for her little children" to remind the Thessalonians of the love he showed when he founded their church (1 Th. 2:7).

Although the father had primary responsibility for training children, the mother participated significantly (Prov. 1:8; 6:20; 30:17; 31:1). As a child, Jesus obeyed both parents (Lk. 2:51), and as an adult, he showed concern for his mother's welfare (Jn. 19:26,27). As a child, Timothy received instruction in the Scriptures from both his mother Eunice and grandmother Lois (2 Tim. 1:5; 3:15). Among the people of God, a mother's impact on her children was great.

Symbolically, the term "mother" is used in various ways in Scripture. For instance, Isaiah alludes to the maternal instinct to illustrate God's deep love and compassion: "As a mother comforts her child, so will I comfort you" (Isa. 66:13). Yet Scripture, which portrays God as the Father, never describes him as mother. However, "mother" sometimes stands for the nation Israel (Jer. 50:12,13; Ezek. 19:1-14; Hos. 2:2-13). Also, in Rev. 17:5, symbolic Babylon is called the "mother [that is, nourisher] of prostitutes and of the abominations of the earth." In another metaphorical use, "mother" is applied to larger walled cities in Israel, and "daughter" to smaller, unwalled towns surrounding them (2 Sam. 20:19).

mount, mountain A high, mounded land mass that projects above the surrounding territory. In the Bible, "hill" and "mountain" are used interchangeably, apparently without a distinction between lower and higher mounds. "Mountain" may refer to a single mount, to a mountainous area, or to a mountain range.

The mountains of Palestine have great impact on its climate and contribute to the land's capacity to produce a wide variety of crops. Mountains also have religious significance. God revealed his name and his Law to Moses on Mount Sinai (Ex. 3,19). Mount Zion was chosen as the site of Solomon's Temple, and on a mountainside in Galilee, Jesus gave the sermon which set forth the moral foundation of his spiritual Kingdom (Mt. 5–7). The Mount of Olives is prominent in Jesus' later life: It was the site of Gethsemane,

MOUNTAINS OF PALESTINE

Mount	Height in feet (meters)	Reference	Biblical Significance
Sinai (Horeb)	7,500 (2,286)	Ex. 3,19	God revealed his name and his Law to Moses
Ebal	3,100 (945)	Deut. 11:29	Moses reminded Israel of the Law's blessings and curses
Gerizim	2,900 (884)		
Nebo	2,700 (823)	Deut. 32:49	Where Moses died
Halak	1,640 (500)	Josh. 11:17	Southern boundary of Joshua's conquest
Hermon	9,100 (2,774)	Josh. 11:17	Northern boundary of Joshua's conquest
Tabor	1,900 (580)	Jdg. 4:6	Deborah's forces battled Sisera
Gilboa	1,700 (518)	1 Sam. 31:1	Saul killed in his final battle
Carmel	1,750 (535)	1 Ki. 18:20	Elijah defeated prophets of Baal
Moriah		2 Chr. 3:1	Early name of Mount Zion
Zion		Ps. 48:1,2	Site of the OT Temple
Samaria		Amos 4:1	Capital of Israel, the Northern Kingdom
Temptation		Lk. 4:5	Jesus was tempted by Satan
Beatitudes		Mt. 5–7	Jesus' Sermon on the Mount
Transfiguration		Mt. 17:1	Jesus was transfigured
Olives	2,600 (811)	Zech. 14:4; Mt. 26:30	Site of Bethany, Gethsemane, Jesus' ascension, his predicted return

and of Christ's post-resurrection ascent into heaven (Acts 1). Not only did mountains play a significant role in Hebrew and Christian history, but the pagan peoples of Palestine preferred to worship their gods in mountain sanctuaries (Deut. 33:29; Jer. 17:2,3). *See also* High Place.

Because the mountainous regions of Palestine receive plenty of rain, mountains often serve as symbols of fertility (Deut. 33:15; Jer. 50:19). They also are associated with security (1 Sam. 14:22; Mt. 24:16) and, because of their impressive bulk, they suggest permanence (Isa. 54:10).

mourn, mourning Visible expression of grief or despair, associated with death (Gen. 23:2) or national disaster (Josh. 7:6; Esth. 4:1).

Mourning in biblical times was openly expressed by shrieking, weeping, and wailing (Gen. 50:10; 2 Sam. 13:36), by tearing one's clothes and rubbing dirt into the face and hair (2 Sam. 1:2; 15:32; Mic. 1:10), and was often accompanied by fasting (Ezra 8:21). While Lev. 19:28 prohibits the self-mutilation commonly practiced by pagans, Israelite mourning rites did call for loud expressions of grief, not only from family members but also from neighbors and, if possible, from professional mourners who were hired to add to the din.

Clay figurines of mourners found at Azor, 7th century B.C. Loud vocal expressions of grief characterized mourning in ancient Israel.

The period of most intense mourning began when a person died and ended when he or she was buried. The mourning period for the family (or for everyone when a national leader died) generally lasted an additional week, but could continue for up to 30 days (Num. 20:29). During these first days of mourning, the bereaved did not work but sat on the ground in torn clothing, waiting to be comforted by others in the community. *See also* Burial; Funeral; Grief.

mouse (KJV) A general term referring to any small rodent found in Palestine. The NIV uses "rat." The Philistines made five gold statuettes of rats as a guilt offering when they sent the ark of the covenant back to Israel (1 Sam. 6).

mouth The oral cavity, including lips, tongue, teeth, etc. In Scripture, the human mouth is the source of speech and self-revelation. Figuratively, "mouth" is used for the openings of caves and wells, the point at which rivers enter into larger bodies of water, and the edge of swords. Symbolically, placing a hand over the mouth indicates awe or shame (Job 40:4; Mic. 7:16).

The phrase "mouth of God" does not mean the Hebrews visualized God as having a human body, but emphasizes the fact that God has personally communicated with humankind. The idiomatic Hebrew expression "according to the mouth of the Lord" usually appears in our versions as "God commanded" or "God said" (Ex. 17:1). The essential meaning of the Hebrew expression is "according to God's express revelation" (*see* Deut. 8:3; Jer. 9:12; Mt. 4:4).

Since the human mouth is a source of revelation, it reveals not only people's thoughts but also their characters (Ps. 36:3; 59:12). Jesus said, "Out of the overflow of the heart the mouth speaks. The good man brings good things out of the good stored up in him, and the evil man brings evil things out of the evil stored up in him" (Mt. 12:34,35). While Col. 3:8 exhorts Christians to watch their speech, Jas. 3:1-12 notes how difficult this is. Yet James stresses that only good and constructive words are appropriate in the mouth of a person whom God has cleansed.

In Rom. 10:8-13, Paul links salvation to the act of confessing with the mouth, "Jesus is Lord." What Paul calls for here is an open declaration that publicly affirms a legally binding relationship. *See also* Confess.

mulberry tree (1) OT (KJV), the "mulberry tree" of 2 Sam. 5:23,24 and 1 Chr. 14:14,15 is actually the balsam or aspen. (2) NT, Lk. 17:6 (*sykaminō*) is the only biblical reference to the true "black" mulberry, which was common to Palestine and produced a small, dark, juicy fruit. *See also* Balsam.

mule A sterile animal produced by mating a horse with a donkey.

Mosaic Law stated, "Do not mate different kinds of animals" (Lev. 19:19), so it is likely that mules were imported and thus expensive. Most OT references portray mules in Israel as mounts for royalty (2 Sam. 13:29; 18:9; 1 Ki. 1:38), though they were valued in other societies for their ability to carry heavy burdens (2 Ki. 5:17; Ezek. 27:14).

Right: Clay figurine of a woman carried by a mule (Lemnos, Greece, first century B.C.). Mules were prized as beasts of burden.

murder The personal, intentional killing of another human being, in contrast to accidental homicide or causing the death of another person in war or in defense of one's property.

THE BIBLICAL WORDS FOR KILLING

We must distinguish between Hebrew words for personal killings (*rasah*), and other killings (typically *harag*). The commandment "You shall not kill" (*rasah*) prohibits only personal killing. It does not refer to war or capital punishment.

The Greek language makes a similar distinction. *Anaireō* and *apokteinō* are general terms, simply affirming that someone has been deprived of his or her life. But *phoneuō* means murder. Jesus chose this word in berating the Pharisees as "descendants of those who murdered the prophets" (Mt. 23:31). Wherever this word occurs, the act of killing is viewed as wicked and intentional (Mt. 5:21; 15:19; 19:18; Jas. 2:11).

THE OT LEGAL SYSTEM

God's Law makes careful distinctions regarding personal killing. It may be an accident. An accidental killing is treated differently from a premeditated or intentional killing. To exact the death penalty in ancient Israel, the judges had to establish a motive (hostility, intent) and determine that the means used (the weapon, the method) led directly to the victim's death (Num. 35). As a further safeguard, these elements were to be proven "on the testimony of witnesses. But no one is to be put to death on the testimony of only one witness" (Num. 35:30).

The person convicted of intentional *rasah* under these standards was to be put to death. "But if without hostility someone suddenly shoves another or throws something at him unintentionally or, without seeing him, drops a stone on him that could kill him, and he dies, then since he was not his enemy and he did not intend to harm him . . . the assembly must protect the one accused of murder" (Num. 35:22-25).

By NT times, only the Roman governor of Palestine had the authority to command execution. *See also* Avenger of Blood; Cities of Refuge; Hate; Kill; Revenge.

murrain (KJV) Any of a number of diseases likely to cause death in animals or persons. Modern versions say "plague." *See also* Plague.

music and musical instruments Vocal and instrumental sounds, combined in

Woodcut artist Albrecht Dürer portrays the violence of the first murder —Cain attacking Abel (Gen. 4:8).

patterns of melody, harmony, and rhythm.

Music's role in the ancient world is attested by the many pictures of instruments and their fragmented remains recovered by archaeologists from Egypt to Mesopotamia. One actual piece of music, a "hymn of [to] the gods," with both words and notes written in cuneiform, has been found on a tablet dating from about 1400 B.C. So-called "theory tablets" with instructions on tuning musical instruments have been found from as early as 1800 B.C.

OLD TESTAMENT

Music permeated Israel's daily life. Instruments were played at family parties (Gen. 31:27; Lk. 15:25). Song and dance celebrated the return of war heroes (Jdg. 11:34; 1 Sam. 18:6). Kings were enthroned to music (1 Ki. 1:39,40; 2 Ki. 11:14), and music was played as armies marched off to war. Music provided entertainment at the royal court (2 Sam. 19:35) and at the banquets of the wealthy (Isa. 5:12; 24:8,9). Workmen sang as they performed their tasks, and many occupations apparently used music to pace their work (Isa. 16:10; Jer. 25:30). Even sorrow was expressed in the slow, mournful notes of dirges and laments (2 Sam. 1:17,18; Mt. 9:23).

The archaeological evidence matches the OT portraits of Israelites making music —on the banks of the Red Sea, for instance, celebrating their deliverance in songs led by dancing women with tambourines (Ex. 15:20). It was apparently not until David's time, however, that a professional orchestra of musicians and singers was established to lead the Israelite worship (1 Chr. 15:16-23).

1. Prisoners from Phoenicia or Palestine play lyres in lament. Sennacherib's palace, Nineveh, 700 B.C. *See* 2 Sam. 1:17,18; Mt. 9:23.

2. Crescent-shaped harp decorated with a sphinx head that wears the crowns of Upper and Lower Egypt. Greco-Roman (332 B.C.–A.D. 324).

3,4. A main source of employment for ancient musicians was performing at banquets. Top: Hand-clapping and double flute accompany dancing girls. Bottom: Three musicians play stringed instruments. Paintings from the tombs of Nebamun and Rekhmira, about 1480 B.C.

5. Three instruments from Bible times: the sistrum, a metallic rattle of Egyptian origin (2 Sam. 6:5); the *shophar* or ram's horn (Ps. 81:3); a metal trumpet (Ps. 150).

6. Terra-cotta figurine of two female musicians riding a camel; Hama, Syria, second century A.D.

7. Woman playing a hand drum (KJV, timbrel); Shikmona, Israel, late 9th century B.C.

8. Philistine ritual stand from Ashdod (10th century B.C.) decorated with musicians (inset) playing cymbals, a double pipe, a drum and a lyre.

9. Cymbals were widely played in religious rites throughout the ancient Near East. The limestone fragment shows a participant in the dedication of a new temple in Ur, 2112–2095 B.C. The cymbals come from Anatolia, Turkey, about 2100 B.C.

10. Musicians from Elam play harps, a double pipe, and dulcimer to celebrate the enthronement of an Elamite prince; Nineveh, 640 B.C. *See* 1 Ki. 1:39,40; 2 Ki. 11:14.

11. David formed a choir and orchestra from the Levites, the assistants to the priests. *See* 1 Chr. 15,16.

continued

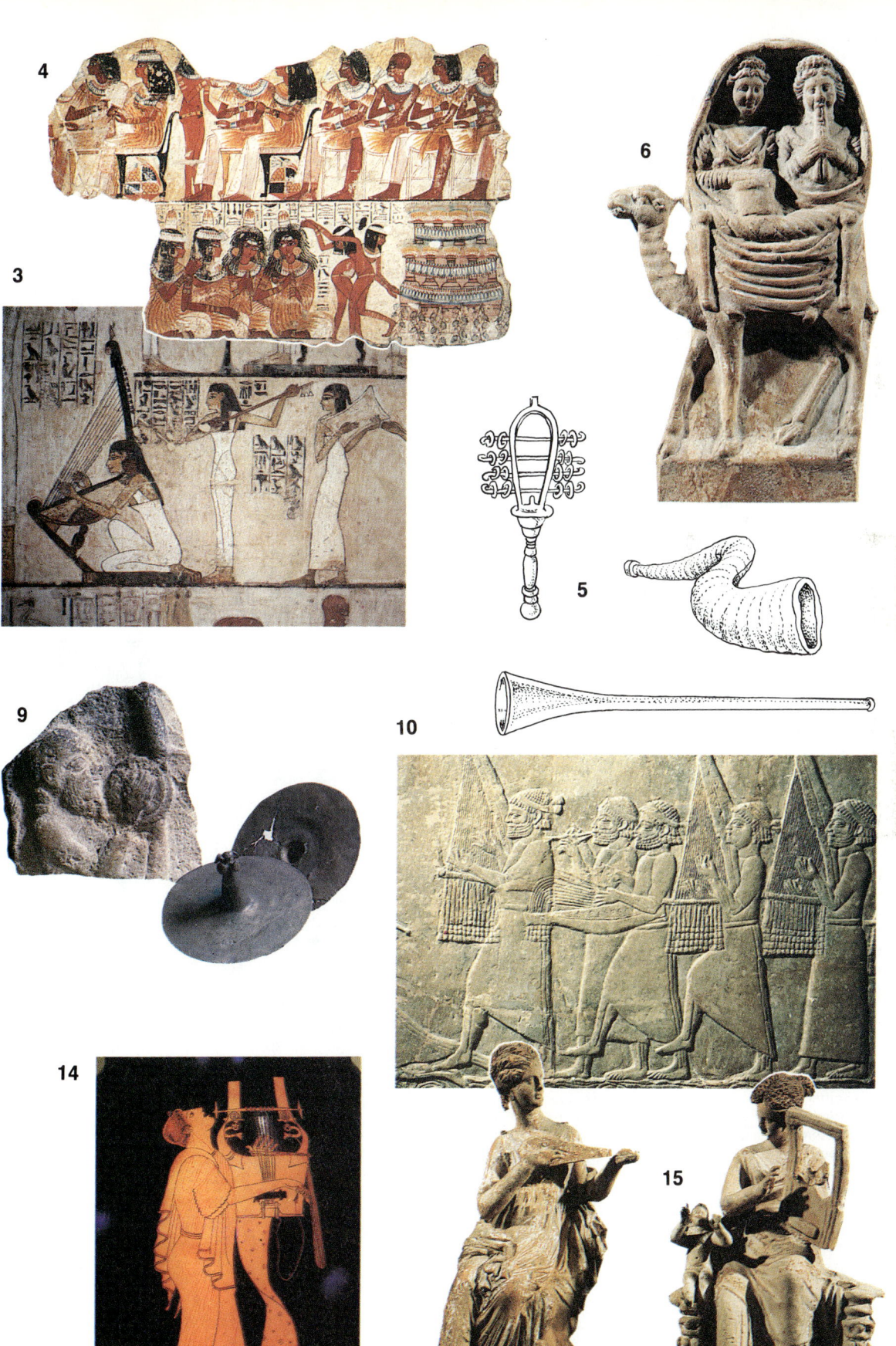

3

4

5

6

9

10

14

15

David's careful organization of Temple musicians and singers reflects the importance of music in Hebrew worship. Most scholars also believe the superscriptions of the Psalms contain musical notations. Psalm 4 tells the "director of music" that this work of David calls for accompaniment by stringed instruments, while Psalm 5 is "for flutes." Other directions, such as *sheminith* (Ps. 6) and *shiggaion* (Ps.

MAJOR MUSICAL INSTRUMENTS OF THE BIBLE

Instrument	Hebrew Word	Selected Scriptures
Wind		
Ram's Horn	*shophar, yobel*	Ex. 19:13; Ps. 81:3
Trumpet	*hasoserah*	Num. 10:2-10; Ps. 150:3
Flute	*'ugab*	Job 21:12; 30:31; Lk. 7:32
Double Pipe	*halil*	1 Ki. 1:40; Isa. 5:12
String		
Lyre	*nebel*	2 Sam. 6:5; Ps. 33:2
Harp	*kinnor*	Gen. 31:27; Ps. 43:4
Percussion		
Tambourine	*toph*	Ex. 15:20; Ps. 149:3
Cymbals	*selselim, mesiltayim*	1 Chr. 13:8; Neh. 12:27; Ps. 150:5

12. Harp and trumpets stamped on a coin from the Jewish revolt of Bar Kochba, A.D. 135.
13. While four bakers knead dough, a flutist plays in rhythm to their movements; Boeotia, Greece, 625–600 B.C. Isaiah 16:10 and Jer. 25:30 mention work songs.
14. Greek youth singing and playing a *kithara*. Detail of an Athenian amphora (490 B.C.).
15. Third-century B.C. Grecian figurines: young woman sitting on a rock playing a lyre (left); woman strumming a *kithara* (right) with a small figure of the god Eros at her side.

718

7), may indicate the melodic pattern, choreography, or special instructions to the singers. The familiar "selah" may well have been a direction to the conductor, calling for a sudden clash of cymbals or for an interlude played quietly on stringed instruments while the congregation meditated on the preceding thoughts.

NEW TESTAMENT

There is no evidence from NT times of a highly developed Christian musical tradition. This is not surprising, since the NT only documents the first few decades of the Christian era. In that span, the church did not have time for the gradual weaving of faith and music that took place over the centuries of the OT era. The Gospels' references to music fit the OT pattern (Mt. 24:31; Mk. 14:26; Lk. 7:32; 15:25), while in the Epistles, some references to music reflect its role in Greek culture (1 Cor. 13:1; 14:7,8). Other references clearly show that music had a role in the more intimate worship of Christians, who usually met together in small groups in private homes: "When you come together, everyone has a hymn, or a word of instruction, a revelation, a tongue or an interpretation" (1 Cor.

14:26). Paul encourages the church at Ephesus, "Speak to one another with psalms, hymns and spiritual songs. Sing and make music in your heart to the Lord" (Eph. 5:19). We find similar instruction to the Colossians: "Let the word of Christ dwell in you richly as you teach and admonish one another with all wisdom, and as you sing psalms, hymns and spiritual songs with gratitude in your hearts to God" (Col. 3:16; *see* Heb. 2:12; Jas. 5:13).

SUMMARY

Music in biblical times, as in our own, enriched the daily life of ordinary people. It captured the deepest emotions of the heart, celebrated national and personal joys and sorrows, and expressed the values shared by members of God's covenant community. Perhaps most of all, music was a vital element in worship, lifting the heart to God, celebrating his goodness, and calling to mind his mighty acts. In a most significant way, the thoughts of the men and women of faith were guided and shaped by music, so that, to a large extent, believers became what they sang.

Field of mustard and avocado (above) and mustard blossom (inset).

mustard Probably the black mustard (*Sinapis nigra*), a plant which was grown in Israel for its aromatic, oily seeds. The plant could grow up to 15 feet (4.6 meters) high, and its seeds attracted birds.

The rabbis of Jesus' day used the mustard seed as a symbol of anything tiny or insignificant. In each of the five references to the mustard seed in the NT, Jesus mentions this seed in the familiar rabbinical way (Mt. 13:31; 17:20; Mk. 4:31; Lk. 13:19; 17:6). Thus, the Kingdom of God looks insignificant to the world but holds within it the power of transforming growth. Even an insignificant faith can move mountains, because the power of faith is not in the strength of our belief but in the strength of the one in whom we believe.

muzzle A leather restraint placed over the mouth of an animal to prevent it from eating or biting, used metaphorically in Ps. 39:1 to suggest enforced silence.

The Law states, "Do not muzzle an ox while it is treading out the grain" (Deut. 25:4). Paul twice refers to this verse to support his ruling that church leaders have a right to be paid for their labor (1 Cor. 9:9; 1 Tim. 5:18).

myrrh A plant whose expensive, aromatic gum was used in perfume (Ps. 45:8; Prov. 7:17; Esth. 2:12) and incense (Ex. 30:23), as well as in preparing bodies for burial (Mk. 15:23; Jn. 19:39). Myrrh was imported from Arabia and India. Its status as a luxury item made it an appropriate gift equal to the frankincense and gold brought to the Christ child by Magi from the East (Mt. 2:11). *See also* Herbs; Perfume; Spices.

myrtle An evergreen native to Palestine that grows beside streams and in well-watered areas in Galilee. The myrtle reaches a maximum height of about 30 feet (9 meters). Its small, dark leaves, its delicate flowers, and its berries have a rich, fresh scent. Both the flowers and berries were used in making perfume, and cut myrtle branches were used to make the lean-tos in which Israelites lived outdoors during the week-long Feast of Tabernacles (Booths) (Neh. 8:15).

mystery (1) In the OT, only in Daniel, an obscure or symbolic communication from God that requires an interpreter to explain (Dan. 2:18,19). This same sense is found in Revelation, but only events at history's end will explain the meaning of these symbols (Rev. 10:7). *See also* Future.

(2) In Greek culture, a secret to be shared only with the initiated. Many religions in the first century took the form of secret societies, with special initiation rituals, and thus were called "mystery religions."

(3) In the NT and especially in Paul, a technical theological term, designating an aspect of God's eternal plan that was hidden or disguised in the OT but that has been revealed in the NT.

Specific revelations that Paul in his Epistles calls mysteries are:

• *Rom. 11:25* "Israel has experienced a hardening in part until the full number of the Gentiles has come in."

• *Rom. 16:25* "My gospel and the proclamation of Jesus Christ" (*see* Eph. 6:19).

• *1 Cor. 2:7; 4:1* "God's secret wisdom" displayed in the cross.

• *1 Cor. 15:51* "We will not all sleep [die], but we will all be changed."

• *Eph. 1:9* "The mystery of his [God's] will. . . , which he purposed in Christ."

• *Eph. 3:2-11* "The administration of God's grace."

• *Eph. 5:32* The union of "Christ and the church."

• *Col. 1:26,27* "Christ in you, the hope of glory."

• *Col. 2:2; 4:3* "Christ."

• *2 Th. 2:7* The "power of lawlessness is already at work," that is, the demonic influence Satan exerts in human society.

• *1 Tim. 3:16* "The mystery of godliness . . . He [God, in Christ] appeared in a body, was vindicated by the Spirit, was seen by angels, was preached among the nations, was believed on in the world, was taken up in glory."

The "mysteries" of the NT have always been part of God's plan and are prefigured in the OT but not explained there. With the coming of Christ, the obscure has been made clear. Yet, the mysteries of the Gospel, while accepted and understood by faith, remain hidden from those who lack God's Spirit. In the end, when the full meaning of each mystery has been worked out in history, all will see what God has done and bow in awe and wonder.

myth, mythology (1) In the NT, a story or belief that is false and misleading; (2) in modern thought, stories about pagan gods, goddesses, ancient heroes, or beliefs; (3) stories embodying fundamental or societal principles; or (4) stories that encompass certain principles of the spiritual world (such as C. S. Lewis's fictional writings).

Paul warns against myths of the first type in his Epistles. A person who accepts a myth turns away from the truth (2 Tim. 4:4) and promotes controversy rather than godliness (1 Tim. 1:4). Christians are exhorted to pay no attention to and have nothing to do with religious myths (1 Tim. 4:7; Tit. 1:14).

Because of the various meanings and connotations of the word "myth," it is unwise to use this term in reference to the Scriptures.

The gum from the myrrh plant was prized for its aroma (Ps. 45:8; Prov. 7:17).

Boughs of myrtle were the primary material for the booths built for the Feast of Tabernacles.

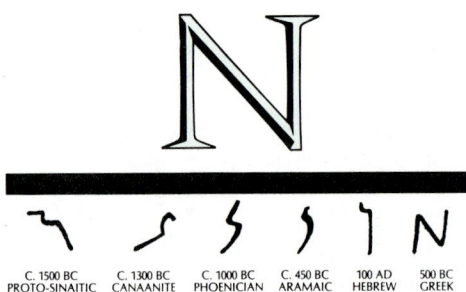

N

C. 1500 BC	C. 1300 BC	C. 1000 BC	C. 450 BC	100 AD	500 BC
PROTO-SINAITIC	CANAANITE	PHOENICIAN	ARAMAIC	HEBREW	GREEK

Naaman [NAY-uh-muhn; "pleasant"]. A leper commanding Syria's army, who came to Israel seeking a cure in the time of Elisha, about 825 B.C. **Scripture:** 2 Ki. 5.

BACKGROUND

In a time of uneasy peace between Syria (Aram) and Israel, a young Israelite captive told Naaman's wife of a prophet in her country who could cure Naaman's leprosy. Naaman carried a letter from King Ben-Hadad to Israel's king, who believed the Syrians were trying to create an incident in order to resume active warfare. Elisha sent a message to the king: "Have the man come to me and he will know that there is a prophet in Israel" (2 Ki. 5:8). Naaman visited Elisha but became furious when the prophet's servant told him to go dip seven times in the Jordan. However, on the urging of his own servants, Naaman finally decided to try the prophet's remedy and was miraculously cured.

He returned to Elisha, committing himself from that time on to worship the Lord only. He also sought a dispensation for times when his position in court would require him to accompany his king to worship Syria's national deities.

LEARNING FROM NAAMAN'S LIFE

Naaman's willingness to go to Israel for help suggests something of his desperation. Still, Naaman became incensed when Elisha failed to act as he thought a prophet should (2 Ki. 5:11,12). Many of us experi-

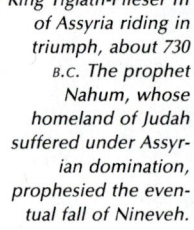

King Tiglath-Pileser III of Assyria riding in triumph, about 730 B.C. The prophet Nahum, whose homeland of Judah suffered under Assyrian domination, prophesied the eventual fall of Nineveh.

ence an inner struggle between our sense of need and our pride. Naaman's decision to wash in the Jordan was a victory of need over pride. Like Naaman, we need to abandon pride when we come to God and be willing to do what he truly requires, not what we think he should require.

Nahum, Book of One of the OT minor prophets. This short, undated prophecy is a poetic oracle of judgment, directed against Nineveh, the capital of Assyria. It predicts the destruction of the city and describes the method of overthrow to be used by Nineveh's conquerors.

BACKGROUND AND AUTHORSHIP

For many decades an aggressive Assyria exerted pressure on Syria-Palestine, ultimately conquering the region, and in 722 B.C. not only crushed the Northern Kingdom of Israel but also carried some 200,000 of Israel's citizens into captivity. All we know of the prophet Nahum [NAY-hum; "comforter"] is that he was from Elkosh, a town in Judah. His prophecy was uttered sometime between the 663 B.C. fall of Thebes (3:8) and the 612 B.C. fall of Nineveh. Nahum picks up a theme repeated in Isaiah: God will judge Assyria; the great empire will pay for its many sins (Isa. 10:5-19; 14:24-27; 18:4-6; 30:27-33; 37:21-35).

THEOLOGICAL CONTRIBUTIONS

Nahum begins with an acrostic poem that celebrates God's power, his role as

Judge, and his commitment to his covenant promises (ch. 1). Nineveh will be destroyed, and God's people will know peace.

The prophet then goes on to describe the fall of Nineveh in detail. Her fate will conclusively demonstrate the truth of everything Nahum has said about God and his intention to bless his people, Israel, once again (chs. 2,3).

MASTERY KEYS

While Nahum is a bold expression of God's anger against Nineveh, it is intended to comfort God's people. As you read, put yourself in the place of a people who have been dominated by a fearful enemy all their lives, and try to sense the joy and release from intolerable oppression that Nahum's ministry must have brought. Compare this book with the encouragement Paul gave the Thessalonians in 2 Th. 1:5-10.

nail (1) The hard plate that grows at the end of a human finger or toe (Deut. 21:12; Dan. 4:33). (2) A pointed fastener made of wood or metal (1 Chr. 22:3; Isa. 41:7).

Victims of crucifixion at times were tied to the cross bar. In Jesus' case, his hands and feet were nailed to the wooden posts (Jn. 20:25). Figuratively, OT Law was canceled by being "nailed" to Jesus' cross (Col. 2:14); then, Jesus' resurrection introduced the vital new principles of spiritual life and righteousness.

naked, nakedness Unclothed; poorly or partially clothed. Before they sinned, Adam and Eve were naked, without shame (Gen. 2:25). But after their fall, they realized they were naked and made clothing (Gen. 3:7). In another example, though his first wife, Michal, accused him of "disrobing," David was wearing a simple linen ephod, a garment associated with worship, when he led the procession bringing the ark into Jerusalem (2 Sam. 6:16-20).

When used to describe the condition of the poor or defeated people, "nakedness"

NAHUM: A READING AND STUDY GUIDE

Chapter	Content Summary	Related Articles
1	Nahum affirms God's great power and expresses the Lord's anger with Nineveh.	Assyria Judge
2	Nahum describes the enemy advance, his use of Nineveh's river system against her, and the sack of the city.	Nineveh War
3	Nahum returns in another powerful poem to view the destruction. Mockingly he ridicules Nineveh's futile efforts at self-defense.	

implies inadequate clothing and may or may not mean total exposure (Mt. 25:38; Mk. 14:52).

A puzzling passage in the OT says that Ham exposed the nakedness of his drunken father, Noah (Gen. 9:22-24). There is no consensus on just what Ham did. Though the Genesis text may imply no more than seeing Noah naked, the Hebrew expression "uncover the nakedness of" is a euphemism for having sexual relations, as in Lev. 18,20.

name A word or words by which a particular person, place, or thing is distinguished from other persons, places, or things.

In biblical times, names were more than mere labels. Many biblical names make statements about character. Abigail said of her husband, "He is just like his name —his name is Fool, and folly goes with him" (1 Sam. 25:25). Naomi, "pleasant," changed her name to Mara, "bitter," when she returned to Bethlehem bereft of her husband and sons (Ruth 1). Barnabas, "son of encouragement" or "comforter," was given his distinctive name by the apostles, who had come to value his compassionate nature.

Many compound names in Scripture make extended statements about their bearers. Immanuel, the unique name given the coming Messiah in Isa. 7:14, means "with us is God," a powerful affirmation of the deity of the coming Savior. Often compound names contain a fragment of the divine name in their first or last syllables—a "Ya" or "Ja" or less frequently "el"—indicating the parents' pious hope. *See also* God, Names of.

Actually, in biblical times the name was considered an extension or expression of

The ankle bone of a young man still contains the metal spike used to nail him to a cross in the first century A.D.

This 7th-century B.C. seal found in Mizpah reads, "Belonging to Jaazaniah, servant of the king." He is probably the official mentioned in 2 Ki. 25:23 and Jer. 40:8.

the person himself. To speak "in the name of" was to express the thoughts, or speak with the authority, of the named individual. The "name of the Lord" is exalted, because in his name God himself is suddenly present with the hearer, revealing both truth and his very self. To "take the name of the Lord in vain" (that is, to treat it as if "God" were an empty, meaningless term or expletive) is serious, for God's name is an aspect of his essence, and God must be treated with honor and respect.

This helps us understand what Jesus meant when he instructed his disciples to pray "in my name" (Jn. 14:13,14; 15:16; 16:23,24,26). Jesus was concerned not with the form of prayer but with its essence. In prayer we are to identify ourselves completely with Jesus, so that both the content and the motivation of our prayers are in full harmony with Jesus' values and his known will. We pray in Jesus' name with

complete confidence, for he whose name is above every other name is able to grant our request.

Naomi [nay-OH-mee; "pleasant"]. Ruth's mother-in-law, whose despair was finally turned to joy by her loyal daughter-in-law. **Husband:** Elimelech. **Sons:** Mahlon and Kilion. **Daughters-in-law:** Orpah, Ruth. **Grandson:** Obed, the grandfather of King David. **Scripture:** Ruth.

BACKGROUND

When famine struck Judah, Naomi's family moved to Moab. Her husband and two sons died there. Heartbroken and bitter, Naomi returned home accompanied by her loyal daughter-in-law, Ruth. There Naomi changed her name to Mara, "bitter." But Naomi was comforted by Ruth, whom Naomi guided into a marriage with an older relative, Boaz. According to levirate marriage law, the first child of Ruth and her husband was considered a member of Naomi's husband's family. Rejoicing in a daughter-in-law who loved her, and a baby to care for, Naomi found renewal and took back her original name. *See also* Levirate Marriage.

LEARNING FROM NAOMI'S LIFE

Many of us experience tragedies which might make us bitter. We learn from Naomi that there is hope—and that God may comfort us through a caring person. Naomi urged her daughters-in-law to stay in Moab when she set out for home. Perhaps she was motivated, like many of us, by a determination not to burden others with her sorrows. How fortunate that Ruth insisted on accompanying Naomi, no

Twelfth-century French miniature depicts scenes from Naomi's life: On the left, Naomi, seated, receives Ruth's threshed gleanings (Ruth 2:17-19); on the right, she counsels Ruth how to win Boaz for a husband (3:1-5).

722

matter what. It may seem noble to suffer alone, but each of us needs others. Through others whom the Lord brings to us, we too may find comfort and renewal.

Naphtali, Tribe of *See* Israel, Tribes of.

napkin (KJV) A small square of cloth, used to wrap small bundles (Lk. 19:20) or to cover the head (Jn. 11:44). The NIV uses "cloth" or "burial cloth."

Just such a small cloth was used to cover the head of Jesus when he was buried. Discovery of the napkin, carefully folded and placed beside the empty graveclothes in Christ's tomb, showed the disciples that he had risen as he said (Jn. 20:7).

nard A fragrant ointment derived from the spikenard plant (*Nardostachys jatamensi*).

Nard was produced in the Himalayas and sealed in clay or alabaster bottles or boxes. The container was broken and its expensive contents then used to anoint a guest or a person being honored (Song 1:12; 4:13,14; Mk. 14:3; Jn. 12:3). *See also* Hospitality; Ointment; Perfume.

"You are the man!" the prophet Nathan accused, rebuking David for his murder of Uriah and adultery with Bathsheba (2 Sam. 12:7).

David, "No." From this we learn it is valid to make decisions based on what we understand of God's nature and will, but at times God will give us special guidance through his Spirit.

Later, Nathan pointedly accused David of the sin he committed in sleeping with Bathsheba and in arranging the death of her husband, Uriah (2 Sam. 11). David might have had Nathan killed, as later kings of Israel did when prophets dared to displease them. Instead, David confessed his sin, repented, and was restored, but not before Nathan announced the penalty God would exact (12:10-14). It is not easy to rebuke the powerful. Nathan reminds us that our prophetic call is to stand against evil wherever it is found, in the hope that God will bring change.

Toward the end of David's life, Nathan, aware of David's pledge to make Solomon king, warned the aged king that another son was about to preempt the kingdom. Nathan did not assume any royal prerogatives. He merely acted to enable David to carry out David's own purposes. Today, too, the best ministry is a ministry that enables others to do what is in their best interests.

An alabaster flask like this one found at Masada (first century A.D.) probably held the expensive perfume made from nard used by a woman at Bethany to anoint Jesus (Mk. 14:3).

Nathan [NAY-thuhn; "gift"]. An influential prophet who ministered at David's royal court, about 975 B.C. He boldly confronted David after the king sinned with Bathsheba. **Scripture:** 2 Sam. 7,12; 1 Ki. 1.

BACKGROUND

Prophets often ministered to Hebrew kings, rebuking and guiding these rulers who held the power of life and death. Nathan, court prophet to David, is one example of a courageous man who risked his life to communicate the word of the Lord.

Three incidents involving Nathan appear in the OT. Nathan (1) advised David about building a temple to the Lord (2 Sam. 7), (2) confronted David about his sin with Bathsheba and announced God's judgment (2 Sam. 12), and (3) in a time of crisis appealed to David to fulfill his pledge and appoint Solomon as his successor. The OT also suggests that Nathan kept an official record of events during his years at court (1 Chr. 29:29; 2 Chr. 9:29) and worked closely with David to organize Israel's worship services (2 Chr. 29:25).

LEARNING FROM NATHAN'S LIFE

When David asked Nathan about his plan to build a temple in Jerusalem, the prophet gave his unqualified approval. David's plan was in harmony with what Nathan knew of God's will. Then God corrected Nathan and sent him to tell

---

Nathanael [nuh-THAN-yuhl; "gift of God"]. A "true Israelite," Nathanael was the second person to acknowledge Jesus as Son of God and King of Israel, about A.D. 30. Nathanael may be another name of Bartholomew, one of the twelve disciples. **Scripture:** Jn. 1:43-51; 21:2.

BACKGROUND

Three days after Jesus was baptized by John, the disciple Philip found Nathanael

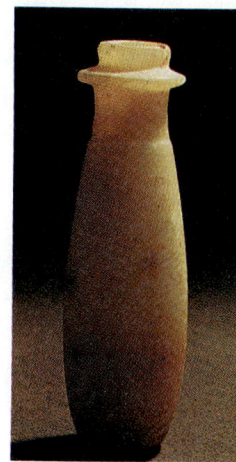

and reported that he had met the promised Messiah. Skeptical, because no OT prophecy suggested the Messiah would come from Nazareth, Nathanael went to see Jesus for himself. Jesus called him a "true Israelite, in whom there is nothing false." In surprise, Nathanael asked how Jesus could possibly know him. Jesus answered, "I saw you while you were still under the fig tree before Philip called you." In a leap of faith, Nathanael confessed, "Rabbi, you are the Son of God."

Many believe Nathanael became one of the Twelve, but under his other name, Bartholomew. The evidence: (1) John does not name Bartholomew, while the other Gospels do not mention Nathanael; (2) the other Gospels link Bartholomew with Philip, and in John 1 Nathanael appears as Philip's friend.

LEARNING FROM NATHANAEL'S LIFE

In calling Nathanael a "true Israelite," Jesus was not ascribing sinlessness to him, but recognizing his honest and complete commitment to God. Nathanael was no curiosity seeker. He had come from Cana in Galilee to Judea, where John was baptizing, moved by an honest hunger for God. In John's Gospel, Nathanael stands for all "true Israelites" who, like Nathanael, responded with faith to Jesus' works and words.

nation, nations A group of people defined by geography or a political or racial unity. In Scripture, the plural, "nations," usually indicates all non-Jewish peoples (Mt. 25:32).

nations, table of The genealogical record in Gen. 10, which lists then-known peoples and nations descended from the three sons of Noah: Ham, Shem, and Japheth.

Analysis of the table of nations is difficult. The criteria used to define a nation (racial characteristics, language, land area occupied) are not used consistently within the chapter—some nations are defined by language group, others by locale. Over the millennia, languages have changed and peoples have moved from one area to another. Nevertheless, many of the names in the table of nations have been found on other ancient inscriptions, so all the information given in Genesis was available to Moses as early as the 15th century B.C.

Generally accepted connections between the names in the table of nations and ancient nations or peoples:

HAM

Cush = Ethiopia
Sheba = Saba (S. Arabia)
Dedan = Dedan (N. Arabia)
Mizraim = Egypt
Ludites = Lydia
Philistines = Philistines
Caphtorites = Cretans
Put = Lybia
Canaan = Canaan
Sidon = Sidon
Heth = Hittites
Amorites = Amorites
Hivites = Hurrians
Hamathites = Hamathites
Shinar = Babylonia

SHEM

Elam = Elam
Asshur = Assyria
Hazarmaveth = Hadramaut
Sheba = Saba
Lud = Lydia
Aram = Arameans

JAPHETH

Gomer = Cimmerians
Ashkenaz = Scythians
Madai = Medes
Meshech = Muski
Javan = Ionia
Elishah = Alashia (Cyprus)
Rodanim = Rhodes
Tubal = Tabalians
Kittim = Cyprians

The location of the major nations or ethnic groups in the so-called "table of nations" (Gen. 10).

Descendants of Japheth
Descendants of Shem
Descendants of Ham

Above: View of the town of Nazareth from the Church of the Transfiguration on Mount Tabor.
Right: As a Nazarene, Jesus lived in a small town in lower Galilee.

nature (1) The essence, character, or innate instincts and tendencies of a person or thing (Rom. 1:20; 8:8); (2) the condition or state of a person or animal inherited from ancestors (Eph. 2:3); (3) the condition or order of things in the natural or social world (Rom. 1:26; 1 Cor. 11:14).

In modern use, "nature" is the sum total of all that exists in the material universe and the forces that order all phenomena. The way we talk about nature may imply that it is independent of the God who created it and, thus, free from his moral demands. People often wrongly assume that anything "natural" is "right."

This view of the universe is foreign to Scripture. Both OT and NT see "nature" in the context of creation. God formed our universe, ordained the laws which order it, and actively supervises its affairs. Thus, when Paul argues in 1 Cor. 11:14 from "the very nature of things," he means that a particular pattern found within nature has been ordained by God and testifies to a truth unveiled by revelation. For instance, human conscience which moves society to establish moral standards is evidence of a universal moral law, even though human standards may fall short of God's and will never move an individual to consistently do even what he himself

believes is right (Rom. 2:12-15). *See also* Conscience.

While "nature" is an avenue of revelation, it is inadequate because the universe, like human beings, has been corrupted by sin (Rom. 8:19-21). Thus, no one can argue for the rightness of any act on the basis of its being "natural." And, while certain truths are revealed in the natural world, such as the existence and power of God (Rom. 1:19,20), nature does not reveal God's love, his purposes for humankind, or his own standards of right and wrong.

Nazarene (1) A person from Nazareth, applied to Jesus in all four Gospels (Mt. 2:23; Mk. 14:67). (2) After the resurrection, one of the names by which early Christians were known (Acts 24:5).

Nazirite A person under a "special vow, a vow of separation to the Lord" (Num. 6:1). During the period of this vow, the Nazirite was not to cut his hair, touch a dead body, drink any fermented beverage, or consume any product of the grapevine. Requirements and procedures of this vow appear in Num. 6:1-21. Samson is probably the best-known Nazirite of the Bible (Jdg. 13:1-5), though Samuel (1 Sam. 1:11) and John the Baptist (Luke 1:15) were similarly dedicated.

725

B.C., taking the king and many other Jews with him to Babylon and setting his own candidate on Judah's throne. Within a decade, Judah rebelled again. This time Nebuchadnezzar commanded the destruction of Jerusalem and its Temple, and deported most of Judah's remaining population.

Records giving the details of the first 13 years of Nebuchadnezzar's reign have been recovered by archaeologists. One notable tablet records the allowance of supplies provided for the support of the captive king of Judah, Jehoiachin, along with his five sons and retainers, providing dramatic corroboration of 2 Ki. 25:27-30 and Jer. 52:31-34. The records of Nebuchadnezzar's last 30 years are incomplete, so we know much less about this period.

Nebuchadnezzar gained fame throughout the world not only as a conqueror but also as the beautifier of Babylon. He built temples to his gods, strengthened the city defenses with great walls, and erected the famous hanging gardens which were reckoned among the seven wonders of the ancient world.

The Books of Jeremiah and Ezekiel re-

King Nebuchadnezzar II was Babylon's most dazzling builder, as these three examples show: detail of a facade (above) from the walls of his throne hall; reconstruction of the massive, glazed-brick Ishtar Gate (inset), the processional gateway into Babylon; kiln-fired brick (right) stamped with an inscription commemorating the rebuilding of the temples of Marduk and Nabu.

> **Nebuchadnezzar II** [NEB-uh-kuhd-NEZ-uhr; "Nabu has protected the boundary stone," that is, "the succession"]. Ruler of Babylon, 605–562 B.C. He commanded the deportation of the Jewish people from their land and ordered the destruction of Jerusalem in 587 B.C. His accomplishments are known from extensive ancient records beside the Bible, but the Book of Daniel provides our greatest insight into his character. **Father:** Nabopolassar, founder of the Neo-Babylonian Empire in 625 B.C. **Son and successor:** Evil-Merodach. **Scripture:** Daniel.

BACKGROUND

Nebuchadnezzar ruled the most powerful empire of his era and followed an aggressive, expansionist policy. His defeat of Pharaoh Neco at Carchemish in 605 B.C. established Babylonian dominance of Syria-Palestine, and Judah became a vassal state. At that time, Nebuchadnezzar deported many members of Judah's upper class, including Daniel and Ezekiel.

Judah remained a center of discontent, especially after a temporary defeat of the Babylonians by Egypt in 601 B.C. But Nebuchadnezzar invaded Judah again in 597

flect conditions in Israel during Nebuchadnezzar's early rule. The Book of Daniel takes us into Nebuchadnezzar's court, enabling us to meet this powerful world-ruler who, through a series of revelations interpreted by Daniel, finally acknowledged the sovereignty of God.

LEARNING FROM NEBUCHADNEZZAR'S LIFE

Most instructive is Daniel's repeated portrait of Nebuchadnezzar as "angry and furious" (Dan. 2:12; 3:13,19). The king was also characterized by pride (Dan. 4:37). The most powerful man on earth controlled an empire but could not control himself.

God spoke to Nebuchadnezzar through Daniel and three other Jewish captives. Daniel revealed and explained a dream that had frightened Nebuchadnezzar, leading the king to admit, "Surely your God is the God of gods" (Dan. 2:47). When Daniel's three companions survived being thrown into a fiery furnace, the king decreed that no one in his empire should "say anything against the God of Shadrach, Meshach and Abednego" (Dan. 3:29). Finally, Daniel warned Nebuchadnezzar that God would humble him if he persisted in his pride. When the king's pride continued, God struck him with madness. After his recovery, Nebuchadnezzar experienced what some consider a true conversion. His kingdom was restored, and he announced, "Now I, Nebuchadnezzar, praise and exalt and glorify the King of heaven, because everything he does is right and all his ways are just. And those who walk in pride he is able to humble" (Dan. 4:37).

Neither history nor Scripture's portrayal of Nebuchadnezzar is sympathetic. He was by all accounts cruel, self-centered, and proud. His absolute power over others clearly corrupted him. And yet, even Nebuchadnezzar was not beyond the reach of God's grace.

neck The part of the body joining the head to the shoulders. Depending on the Hebrew term used, "neck" in the OT may refer to the back of the neck, the throat, or the entire neck.

The word has both literal and metaphorical uses in Scripture. A yoke or chain on the neck is a metaphor of national defeat and bondage (Gen. 27:40; Hos. 11:4; *see* Josh. 10:24). Bowing the neck symbolizes submission or surrender (Jer. 27:11). A millstone around the neck weighs down a person and plunges him into destruction

(Mt. 18:6). A hardened or stiff neck portrays spiritual rebellion and obstinacy (Deut. 31:27; Isa. 48:4). An outstretched neck expresses arrogance, an unwillingness to submit to God (Ps. 75:5).

necromancer (KJV) One who inquires of the dead, a spiritist.

Necromancy is one of several occult practices forbidden by Deut. 18:10,11. The "witch of Endor" was such a spiritist, who claimed ability to contact the dead for information and advice (1 Sam. 28:7-25). *See also* Wizard.

Negev (**Negeb** RSV) ["dry"]. The desert regions in the southern part of Canaan. Major trade routes ran through this desolate country, and Israel's southern border was protected by a series of forts erected here.

Nehemiah, Book of Last of the OT's narrative histories. Nehemiah describes the rebuilding of Jerusalem's walls after the Babylonian Exile, and records the religious reforms instituted by Nehemiah.

BACKGROUND

After King Cyrus of Persia conquered the Babylonian Empire, he issued a decree permitting captive peoples to return to their homelands (539 B.C.). While some 50,000 Jews trekked back to tiny Judea, far more remained, prospering in major cities of Persia's far-flung Empire. By 444 B.C. Nehemiah, a Jew whose family remained behind, had achieved the influential post of cupbearer to King Artaxerxes I (464–424 B.C.). When Nehemiah learned from a Jewish delegation that Jerusalem lay unwalled and underpopulated, he was deeply moved.

Nehemiah "mourned and fasted and prayed" for some four months. He then requested that Artaxerxes send him to his people's homeland. Nehemiah was given

Twelve-foot (3.7-meter) statue of the Babylonian god Nabu, Nebuchadnezzar's namesake.

The Negev Desert forms nearly half of present-day Israel.

full authority as a royal commissioner (*tir-sata*). Back in Judah, Nehemiah then faced a number of obstacles. The Jews were initially indifferent. A coalition of three major enemies (Sanballat the Samaritan, Tobiah the Ammonite, and Geshem, an Arab) first ridiculed and then threatened the small Jewish population. Many Jews were hamstrung by poverty, and many had abandoned trying to keep God's Law. Leaders had married foreign wives, tithes were no longer paid for the support of worship, and the people bought and sold on the Sabbath.

Nehemiah acted decisively. He united the Jewish community behind the rebuilding project despite the external opposition. Then Nehemiah acted aggressively to bring about spiritual reforms. He served as Judah's governor from 444 to 433 B.C. and also served a later term, which cannot be dated accurately.

The Book of Nehemiah remains popular today, primarily because of Nehemiah's

One of the most memorable of Nehemiah's actions was a secret night ride around Jerusalem, during which he surveyed the walls he was determined to rebuild (Neh. 2:11-20).

NEHEMIAH: A READING AND STUDY GUIDE

Chapter	Content Summary	Related Articles
1	Nehemiah is devastated at a report of conditions in Judah. He spends four months in prayer and confession.	Prayer Fast
2	Nehemiah asks Artaxerxes to send him to Judah. He examines the fallen walls and enlists Jewish support for rebuilding.	Cupbearer Wall
3	Nehemiah assigns sections of the wall to various groups.	Gate
4	Nehemiah arms his workmen when enemies threaten to attack.	Weapon
5	Nehemiah forces Jews who exploited their poor countrymen to relent and sets a personal example.	Borrow Oath
6	Nehemiah refuses to be frightened despite threats against his life. The wall around Jerusalem is completed.	
7	Nehemiah reviews the genealogical records of families that returned to Judah in 539 B.C.	Genealogy
8	Ezra reads and explains the Book of the Law to the people of Judah, who celebrate the Feast of Tabernacles.	Ezra Feasts, Festivals, and Fasts
9	The Israelites publicly confess their sins and the sins of their fathers.	Confess Covenant
10	The leaders of the people commit themselves in writing to keep God's Law and support Temple worship with tithes.	Marriage Tithe
11	Nehemiah resettles one-tenth of the population in Jerusalem.	Jerusalem
12	Nehemiah examines the genealogy of the priests and dedicates the newly built walls of Jerusalem.	Priest Dedicate
13	Nehemiah returns to Jerusalem after reporting to the king. He is appointed governor for a second term but finds the people of Judah have returned to their old sins. He again confronts and purifies the people.	Sabbath Holy

728

strengths as a leader. While uncompromising, Nehemiah was also totally courageous. He boldly confronted his opposition (Neh. 4,5,13) and rallied his supporters. He was sensitive to the needs of the poor, and angry with those who exploited them (5:1-13). Nehemiah set a personal example of the commitment he demanded (5:14-18). The moral force of his leadership succeeded in recalling the Jews to observance of God's Law during his term of office. Through it all, Nehemiah remained a man of prayer (1:5-11; 2:4; 4:4,5; 6:9,14).

HISTORICAL CONTRIBUTIONS

Nehemiah is the only OT first-person narrative written by an important Jewish leader. The book is a formal record of Nehemiah's administration and provides important insights into political, social, and religious conditions in post-exilic Judah. Interestingly, Sanballat and his sons are known from other fifth-century B.C. documents, the Elephantine Papyri.

In the Hebrew OT, Nehemiah and Ezra were combined on a single scroll. Some believe that Neh. 8–10 reports events associated with Ezra's return to Judah in 457 B.C., some 13 years before Nehemiah became governor.

MASTERY KEYS

Read the book through quickly to get an overview of the situation Nehemiah faced as governor. Then go back and isolate the different challenges Nehemiah faced, noting how he met each. See what principles you can apply to meet challenges in your own life.

SPECIAL FEATURES

Nehemiah frequently lists his good deeds and says to God, "Remember me" (5:19; 13:14,22,31). The phrase means "reward me." While some might see this as a presumption, it is in fact an expression of Nehemiah's deepest values. He did not strive for rewards in this world or he might have retained his influential post in the Persian court. Nehemiah was motivated only by the thought of pleasing his God.

nehiloth (KJV) A direction in the superscription of Ps. 5 calling for musical accompaniment with flutes. *See also* Psalms.

neighbor A close friend; an acquaintance; a fellow member of a community. In some covenant contexts, "neighbor" conveys as powerful a sense of relationship as "brother" or "sister." The word itself might be extended to include everyone a

Jesus told the parable of the Good Samaritan to illustrate his universal application of the word "neighbor" (Lk. 10:25-37).

person came in contact with, but in the OT it usually means "fellow Israelite."

When OT Law spelled out the mutual obligations of Israelites to each other, it frequently used the term "neighbor" (Heb., *rea'*). For instance, no Israelite was to give false testimony against his neighbor (Ex. 20:16) or covet his neighbor's wife or possessions (Ex. 20:17). Rather than defraud a neighbor (Lev. 19:13), a member of the covenant community was to share his property (Ex. 22:7-9), lend to his neighbor without charging interest (Deut. 15:2), and in every way show that he loved his neighbor as himself (Lev. 19:18).

The NT restates the command, "Love your neighbor," no less than nine times (Mt. 5:43; 19:19; 22:39; Mk. 12:31,33; Lk. 10:27; Rom. 13:9; Gal. 5:14; Jas. 2:8). One day, Jesus was questioned about the implications of this command by an "expert in the law" (Lk. 10:25-37). Jesus immediately affirmed the most extended use of the word "neighbor" in the story of the Good Samaritan. Jesus chose as his hero a member of a neighboring race that the Jews viewed with contempt. When a Jewish traveler was robbed and beaten, it was no priest or Levite who stopped to help the victim. It was a Samaritan. In Jesus' story, race did not count: Neighborliness was a simple matter of humanity, a matter of a relationship between one person in need and another able to assist him. When

Bronze flute player from Byblos, Lebanon, second millennium B.C.

the "expert in the law" admitted that the Samaritan had fulfilled a neighbor's obligation by helping the injured man, Jesus simply said, "Go and do likewise." Our neighbor, whom we are obligated to love, is anyone we know who may be in need.

Nephilim *See* Giant.

Nero [NEER-oh]. Emperor of Roman Empire, A.D. 54–68. **Parents:** Claudius Caesar and Agrippina, his fourth wife. **Wives:** Octavia, Poppea.

Nero Claudius Caesar is not named in Scripture, but his reign of terror significantly affected NT events and the development of the early church. It was to Nero's court that the apostle Paul appealed his case (Acts 25:10,11) and in which he was probably acquitted. However, in A.D. 64, Nero accused the Christians of starting a fire that destroyed much of Rome. He instituted a brutal local purge, which seems to have served later as a precedent for Empire-wide persecution. One tradition, probably authentic, says that both Paul and Peter were put to death in Rome during Nero's reign.

The young Nero had ruled well under the guidance of his tutor Seneca, his mother, and another advisor, Burrus. However, in A.D. 59, Nero had his mother put to death. When Burrus died and Seneca retired, there were no remaining checks on Nero's egocentric and paranoid tendencies, and Nero quickly added his wife and others to his list of victims. Nero

Bust of Nero Claudius Caesar, Roman emperor, A.D. 54-68.

was an ineffective ruler, who squandered the Empire's riches and was unable to quell revolts in Britain, Gaul, or Spain. The vicious and brutal emperor soon became unpopular at home and with the army. He committed suicide in A.D. 68 after being deposed and sentenced to death by the Roman Senate.

nest A structure in which birds lay eggs and shelter their young.

Scripture sometimes speaks of literal nests (Deut. 22:6; Ps. 104:17), but the word was also employed in numerous metaphors and poetic comparisons. Jesus described his own itinerant life-style by saying that, although the birds of the air had nests, the Son of Man had no place (of his own) to lay his head (Mt. 8:20).

As modern people speak of building a "nest egg" for their financial future, so in Scripture "nest" can be a metaphor for security. Habakkuk cries, "Woe to him who builds his realm by unjust gain to set his nest on high, to escape the clutches of ruin" (Hab. 2:9).

net A loosely woven, open fabrication of cords or strings, used to catch fish, birds, or other animals.

Nets used for each of these purposes are mentioned in the Bible. Fowlers often used clap nets, shaped something like an open clamshell, that closed suddenly when a bird touched the bait placed inside it (Prov. 1:17). Hunters might cast nets at their game (Job 19:6), spread nets that would tangle around animals' feet (Ps. 57:6), or stretch large nets along a trail and drive game into them. Fishing was often done with cast nets (Mt. 4:18) or by drag-

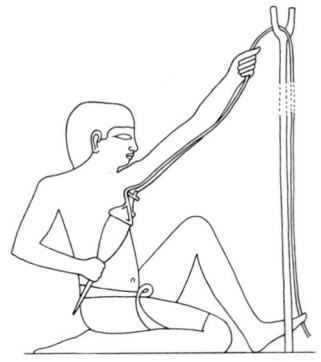

Line drawings copied from wall paintings in two Egyptian tombs depict the process of making fish nets (left to right): spinning twine, loading the shuttle, hand weaving the net.

nets and seines that were lowered from small boats (Mt. 13:47; Jn. 21:8).

The net serves OT writers as a symbol for the deceit of an enemy against a believer (Pss. 9:15; 140:5; Mic. 7:2). Habakkuk uses the net to describe the military might of Babylon, scooping up other nations into its empire (Hab. 1:15-17). *See also* Fish, Fishing.

nettle [Heb., *harul; qimmosh.*] Not the familiar nettle weed of the U.S. or U.K., but any of a number of thorny plants native to the Middle East. *See also* Briers.

new (1) Recent in time; (2) the modern, the youthful, the newly arrived or recently appearing; (3) better, superior to the old.

Two Greek words are translated "new." There is a slight but significant distinction between the two. *Neos* means "recent in time." *Kainos* can mean the same thing but often carries the additional implication of "new and improved." In the NT, *kainos* often describes aspects of the new covenant in Christ.

Christ said, "No one tears a patch from a new garment and sews it on an old one. If he does, he will have torn the new garment, and the patch from the new will not match the old. And no one pours new

THE "NEW" IN THE NEW TESTAMENT

The New	Reference	Significance
New covenant	Lk. 22:20; 1 Cor. 11:25; Heb. 8:8,13; 9:15	The new covenant established by Jesus replaces the Mosaic one. Unlike the old, the new produces righteousness by writing God's Law on human hearts rather than on stone tablets.
New commandment	Jn. 13:34; 1 Jn. 2:7,8; 2 Jn. 5	Jesus introduces a new standard: We are to love one another as he has loved us, sacrificially. This is a higher standard than the OT's "Love your neighbor as yourself."
New creation	2 Cor. 5:17; Gal. 6:15	Christ does not just reform sinners, but renews by giving those who believe new, spiritual life (*see* Rom. 6:4; 7:6).
One new man	Eph. 2:15	Christ unites all humanity in a single family by making the OT Law, which created hostility between Jew and Gentile, irrelevant.
New self	Eph. 4:24	Christ gives the believer a spiritual capacity for righteousness that counters our "old self" capacity for sin.
New heaven and new earth	2 Pet. 3:13; Rev. 21:1	God will dismiss this old, corrupted universe and create a new universe, to be the home of righteousness.
New Jerusalem	Rev. 21:2	God's capital city on earth will come down from heaven. It will need no natural or artificial light, for God will brighten it with his presence.
New song	Rev. 5:9; 14:3	The redeemed sing a song of praise to Christ as the full meaning of the redemption he has won for us and the universe becomes clear at history's end.

Christ and Nicodemus *portrayed on a 16th-century bronze medallion made by a German master.*

wine into old wineskins. If he does, the new wine will burst the skins, the wine will run out and the wineskins will be ruined. No, new wine must be poured into new wineskins. And no one after drinking old wine wants the new, for he says, 'The old is better' " (Lk. 5:36-39; *see* Mt. 9:16,17; Mk. 2:21,22).

The new cloth represents God's revelation in Jesus, which must not be torn apart and patched onto the old system. The old wineskins also represent the old system, which cannot contain new wine. Old wineskins no longer have the capacity to swell with the fermenting process, and as the new wine ages, the skins will split. Israel's reaction to the new wine is understandable but wrong. The old wine has aged, and its familiar taste seems better. But the old wineskins are empty. The fresh crop must be stored in new wineskins, where it can age and its own unique flavor can develop. Thus God's grace is now, in Christ, being poured into the new and better wineskin of the Gospel, where as it ages, its superiority becomes increasingly evident.

732

Nicodemus [NIK-uh-DEE-muhs; Gk., "conqueror of the people"]. A Pharisee who came to Jesus for secret instruction and was told that he "must be born again." Later, he became a secret disciple. **Scripture:** Jn. 3; 7:50-52; 19:38-42.

BACKGROUND

Little is known of Nicodemus. He was a Pharisee. Jesus called him "Israel's teacher" (Jn. 3:10), suggesting that he held an important role in the Sanhedrin, the Jewish ruling council. Both his hesitant defense of Jesus (Jn. 7:45-52) and his contribution of 75 pounds of vastly expensive spices to wrap Jesus' body for burial indicate that Nicodemus became a believer. An unsubstantiated tradition reports that Nicodemus was later baptized by Peter, was driven from the Sanhedrin, stripped of his wealth, and forced to leave Jerusalem.

LEARNING FROM NICODEMUS'S LIFE

When Nicodemus first came to Jesus, he said, "We know you are a teacher who has come from God" (3:2). Yet Nicodemus was unwilling to act on this knowledge.

His only wise course would have been

to submit to this teacher. Instead, he relied on his own limited grasp of the OT. Although "Israel's teacher," he failed to see any implication of spiritual rebirth in the OT promise that God would give men new hearts (Ezek. 18:31; *see* Jer. 31:31-34).

Later, Nicodemus hesitantly tried to defend Jesus, saying, "Does our law condemn anyone without first hearing him?" But Nicodemus was silenced by the immediate attack of his fellow Pharisees (Jn. 7:45-52). Finally, we see another tentative expression of faith. Nicodemus contributed an expensive amount of spices in which to wrap Jesus' body (Jn. 19:38-42).

Perhaps each incident in the Gospels that features Nicodemus traces another step along his road to faith. But if these acts of Nicodemus were hesitant expressions of a true faith in Jesus, how tragic his story is. The Pharisees accused Jesus of appealing only to the ignorant mob and argued, "Has any of the rulers or of the Pharisees believed in him? No!" If Nicodemus had been willing to stand openly with Jesus, he would have negated this powerful argument of Christ's opposition and perhaps encouraged others to commit themselves to Christ.

Nicolaitans An unknown group whose doctrines corrupted first-century churches in Ephesus (Rev. 2:6) and Pergamum (Rev. 2:15).

Early church fathers identified the group with Nicolas of Antioch (Acts 6:5) and say its teaching promoted compromise with paganism. Some see "Nicolaitan" as a Greek form of the name Balaam and view the heresy as sexual licentiousness.

night The period of darkness between sunset and sunrise.

Most uses of "night" in Scripture have a normal, temporal sense. In OT times, the night was divided into three watches; the NT generally follows Roman custom and divides the night into four watches. *See also* Watches of the Night.

At times night has symbolic implications. When Judas slipped away to betray Jesus, John adds, "And it was night" (Jn. 13:30). This sense of darkness persists until the first day of the week, when Jesus' disciples came and saw, in the first rays of the morning sun, that Christ's tomb was empty (Jn. 20:1-9).

In OT imagery, night is sometimes associated with suffering and sorrow (Ps. 30:5). In the NT, it is a time of secret, hidden action (Jn. 3:2) and a time for prayer (Lk. 6:12). In the Epistles, night is associated with the reign of sin in society (Rom. 13:12) and in individual life (1 Th. 5:5-7). The promise in Rev. 21:25 and 22:5 that there will be no night in God's new creation picks up the imagery of both Testaments. Because God will be present with his people, the believer will know neither sorrow nor sin, for joy and righteousness will at last prevail.

Nile The "great river of Egypt" that flows some 4,000 miles (6,500 kilometers) from central Africa to spill its waters into the Mediterranean Sea.

Below: The course of the river Nile.
Left: Boats on the Nile, the "roadway" of ancient Egypt.
Inset: The Egyptians personified the Nile in the river god Hapi, who ruled over fertility and sustained life. Bronze statue, 525-333 B.C.

The Nile was viewed by the ancient Egyptians as the source of their life. Its waters overflowed each year, bringing fertile new soil to Egypt's croplands. Because drought seldom interrupted the annual floods, the river freed the people from dependence on local rainfall. Thus Egypt provided the most secure living available in the ancient world. Its delta region, called "lower Egypt," stretched over 150 miles (240 kilometers) wide near the coastline.

The Nile also served as Egypt's highway, along which boats traveled north and south. Papyrus reeds grew along its banks, providing raw material for mats and baskets, paper, and other necessities. Its waters were filled with fish, and its backwaters teemed with waterfowl.

The Egyptians personified the Nile in the god Hapi, who was credited with the ability to produce and support life. When God turned the waters of the Nile blood-red, killing its fish, he demonstrated his superiority to this key Egyptian deity (Ex. 7:14-24).

Prophecies against Egypt often portray God acting against the Nile, as in Isa. 19:5, "The waters of the river will dry up" (*see* Ezek. 29:3-12; Zech. 10:11).

Nimrod [NIM-rod; meaning unknown]. A prominent figure in Mesopotamian leg-

ends, identified in Gen. 10:8 as a descendant of Cush. He is called a "mighty hunter before the Lord" (that is, "on earth") and is credited with establishing a kingdom that united the major cities of Babylon, Erech, Akkad, and Calneh. He also founded Nineveh and other cities. The "land of Nimrod" (Mic. 5:6) is Assyria.

Nineveh [NIN-uh-vuh]. One of the oldest cities in Mesopotamia. Nineveh lay on the bank of the Tigris River in what is now Iraq. It served as the capital city of Assyria from 705 B.C. to its fall in 612 B.C. Jonah traveled to Nineveh to announce divine judgment, possibly about 760 B.C., leading its people to repent. Referring to the repentant men of Nineveh, Jesus said that they would rise up and condemn the disbelievers of his day, for "one greater than Jonah is here" (Mt. 12:41;Lk.11:32). About a hundred years after Jonah, Nahum foretold Nineveh's destruction and predicted the strategy used by its attackers in 612 B.C.

Archaeologists have uncovered the parks, palaces, and administrative buildings that beautified the city. Enclosed by a 50-foot-high inner wall some 8 miles (13 kilometers) in circumference and extending another 2½ miles (4 kilometers) along the river, Nineveh easily held a population of more than 175,000. Within these walls lay the palace of Sennacherib, which contained nearly two miles of bas-reliefs carved in the walls of 71 halls, chambers,

Below: Nineveh was Assyria's capital at the height of its power (681–626 B.C.), when its empire reached into Egypt.
Left: Head of a gateway-guardian statue from Nineveh, from the days of King Sennacherib (704–681 B.C.), who laid siege to Jerusalem and exacted tribute from Hezekiah (2 Ki. 18; Isa. 36,37).

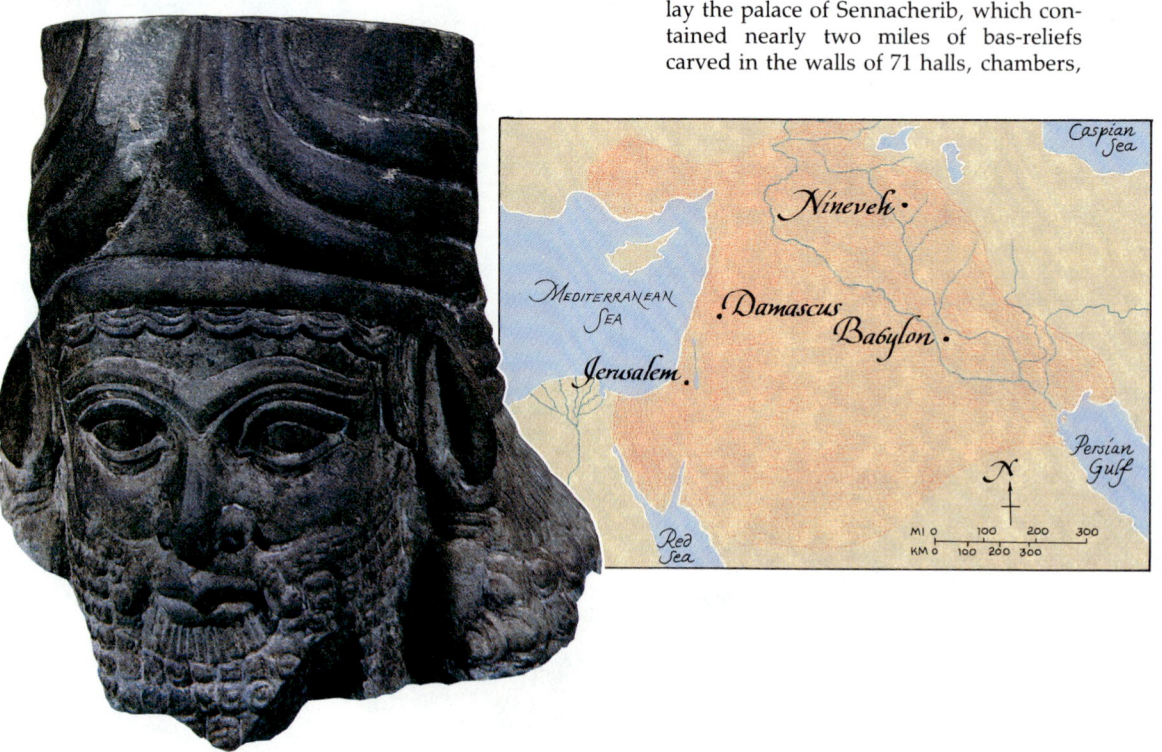

and passageways. The palace and library of Ashurbanipal have also been excavated. Libraries of these two kings contain census and tax records, summaries of legal decisions and business contracts as well as literary, medical, religious, and other treatises. Many tablets dealing with magic have been found, revealing that even the powerful rulers of all-conquering Assyria lived in fear of demonic and occult forces.

Nineveh was sacked by the combined forces of the Babylonians and the Medes in 612 B.C., and has lain in ruins to this day. *See also* Assyria; Jonah; Nahum.

Nisan The first month in the Hebrew religious year, corresponding to March/April. *See also* Calendar.

Noah [NOH-uh; "rest," "comfort"]. A righteous man in the wicked era before the Genesis Flood. Noah obeyed God and built a great ark in which his family and breeding stock from the animal kingdom were saved. **Ancestor:** Lamech. **Sons:** Shem, Ham, Japheth. **Scripture:** Gen. 6–9.

BACKGROUND
Noah was the only righteous man remaining in a culture characterized as so wicked that "every inclination of the

Above: Detail of the siege of Lachish reliefs unearthed at Nineveh shows the defeated Jewish inhabitants being led into exile by the Assyrian troops of King Sennacherib (about 701 B.C.).
Left: The fall of Nineveh is recorded in this Babylonian chronicle for the years 616 to 609 B.C.

Medieval miniature illumination of Gen. 6:1–9:17 (left to right): God directs Noah to build an ark; the Flood; leaving the ark; Noah's sacrifice and God's promise.

thoughts of [man's] heart was only evil all the time" (Gen. 6:5). Noah responded to God's warning of coming judgment and, with his three sons, spent some 120 years building a great, land-locked ship and filling it with supplies for himself and representatives of each "kind" of animal. Noah and his family were carried safely through the waters of the Flood and deposited on newly dried land to give humanity a fresh start. *See also* Ark, Noah's; Kind.

SIGNIFICANCE

Several aspects of Noah's story are theologically significant. (1) The Flood stands throughout Scripture as evidence that God

is moral Judge of his universe and that God can and will act to punish sin (2 Pet. 3:3-7). (2) The covenant God made with Noah, marked by the rainbow, commits God to refrain from destroying the world again by a flood (Gen. 9:8-17). (3) God's covenant with Noah delegates responsibility for punishing sin to human beings. All the functions of human government are implied in Gen. 9:6, "Whoever sheds the blood of man, by man shall his blood be shed." (4) Noah's deliverance symbolizes salvation in Christ. Jesus not only carries us safely through the waters of judgment but also deposits us in a new world, where we are to live by the will of God (1 Pet.

3:17–4:6). (5) Jesus warns that the end of this present age will be characterized by signs similar to those "in the time of Noah" (Mt. 24:36,37).

LEARNING FROM NOAH'S LIFE

Hebrews 11 ranks Noah among the heroes whose actions grew from faith. Noah, "when warned about things not yet seen, in holy fear built an ark to save his family" (Heb. 11:7). Day after day, year after year, he and his sons labored to build a vessel some 450 feet (137 meters) long. Noah withstood the taunts of neighbors and finally completed his course. The frame of the great vessel that rose against the plains gave silent witness to Noah's generation of the judgment to come. Hebrews adds, "By his faith he condemned the world and became heir of the righteousness that comes by faith" (Heb. 11:7).

From Noah we learn the value and the power of persistence. Noah's persistent faith not only saved his family from the Flood but was a witness to the people of his generation. Our actions as well as our words give testimony and are a channel through which the Spirit speaks to humankind (1 Pet. 3:19,20).

noon (1) The midpoint between sunrise and sunset, and (2) the brightest time of day. The context will suggest whether a given usage emphasizes time or brightness.

north The direction to the left when facing the rising sun.

Most of Israel's major enemies approached from the north (Arameans, Assyrians, Babylonians). Thus, north often has an ominous connotation in biblical prophecy (Isa. 41:25; Jer. 6:1; 25:9). Predictions of a great cataclysm at history's end include the appearance of a northern enemy to devastate a peaceful and seemingly secure Israel (Ezek. 38,39; Dan. 11; Zech. 6).

nose, nostrils The prominent part of the face between eyes and mouth.

The Hebrew word for "nose" sometimes stands for the whole face. It also appears in expressions of anger (flaring nostrils), as in Job 39:20. In our versions, these are typically translated into English idioms that eliminate reference to the nose.

Women in biblical times sometimes wore nose rings as jewelry (Gen. 24:22; Isa. 3:21). The OT pictures captives led into exile by ropes attached to hooks or rings inserted through their noses (Isa. 37:29). *See also* Hook.

number A symbol or word designating quantity or order.

The Hebrews, like most other ancient peoples, used a decimal system (based on tens) in counting. Originally, the words for numbers were written out. Later, some symbols were used. But by 150 B.C., scribes had adopted the Greek system and used letters of the alphabet to represent numbers.

Some of the uncertainty about the larger numbers given in the OT is caused by the transcription system. For instance, compare 1 Chr. 19:18, which speaks of 7,000 charioteers, with the parallel passage in 2 Sam. 10:18, which gives 700; or consider the 40,000 stalls of Solomon mentioned in 1 Ki. 4:26 (Hebrew text) with the parallel reference to 4,000 in 2 Chr. 9:25. Some scholars are particularly critical of the great number of soldiers given for ancient armies and of the census count of 600,000 Israelite men of military age who left Egypt in the Exodus (Num. 11:21).

Another difficulty is in understanding just what the writer intended to convey when using a particular number. Are biblical numbers intended to be definite or approximate? For instance, at times ten is not used in a definite way, but simply to indicate "quite a few" (Gen. 31:7). The number 40 occurs in contexts that suggest it represents a generation or symbolizes completion: Israel wandered for 40 years; David and Solomon each reigned for 40 years; Jesus was tempted in the wilderness for 40 days; etc. We live at such a distance from Hebrew culture that we cannot be sure whether the writer intended a literal 40 years or days, or if he intended—and his readers understood—a symbolic meaning.

Other numbers, while normally used in a definite sense, are also clearly symbolic. For instance, one is the number of the unique; six is the number of man; and seven the number of perfection. Jesus told his followers to forgive, not seven times, but seventy-seven times.

The rabbis were aware that numbers sometimes had significance beyond their common meaning. One school carried this observation to an extreme. Using an interpretive method called *gematria*, its members calculated the numerical value of key words in Scripture and searched for hidden, mystical meanings.

It is best to assume that numbers given in Scripture are generally accurate and definite, as well as to be aware that some may be intended to be approximate or symbolic.

Right: The oasis at Kadesh Barnea, where the Israelites camped while twelve men spied out the land and where they rebelled against Moses and Aaron. (Num. 14).

Above: The Book of Numbers is arranged around the "travel itinerary" of the Israelites' wilderness wanderings, which this wood-engraved map portrays (Lyon, France, A.D. 1468).

Numbers, Book of The fourth book of the Pentateuch; one of the historical books of the OT. Known to the Jews as "In the Wilderness," Numbers tells of the rebellion of the Israelites who had escaped Egypt, their wilderness wanderings, and the travels of a new, obedient generation of Israelites to the borders of the Promised Land. The book derives its title from the fact that the people were "numbered" in a census recorded in the early chapters.

BACKGROUND

Moses successfully led the Israelites, then a slave people, out of Egypt. They traveled deep into the Sinai Peninsula. There, camped before Mount Sinai, Israel made a covenant with God, agreeing to keep the Law he revealed to them through Moses. Biblical tradition affirms that Moses wrote the bulk of Numbers prior to 1400

B.C. Yet it must have been given final form at a later date, after the Conquest was complete (*see* Num. 12:3; 15:32; 21:14,15; 32:34-42). *See also* Chronology; Exodus.

The book is divided chronologically into three sections, although material within the sections does not follow strict chronological order. Part One (Num. 1–9) describes the organization of the camp and preparations for the march to Canaan. Part Two (Num. 10–20) describes the journey to Canaan, the rebellion at Kadesh Barnea, and the 38 years of wandering in the wilderness. Part Three (Num. 20–36) describes the slow journey of the new Israelite generation toward Canaan, where obedience would produce victory.

THEOLOGICAL CONTRIBUTIONS

These chapters reveal a God who is faithful to his covenant. As God promised, he blesses those who obey his laws and punishes the disobedient.

Numbers presents God as holy, one who is gracious and yet will punish sin. But punishment purified Israel, so God would not have to reject the entire nation for the sins of the guilty. Relationship with God demands complete commitment (Num. 1:47-54; 9:15-23; 20:12).

The theme of punishment is reflected in the contrast between consequences of disobedience now (Num. 10–14) and consequences of disobedience prior to receiving the Law (Ex. 16–19). The same acts are committed, but now they are violations of the Law and receive punishment. What a clear illustration of a principle Paul ob-

NUMBERS: A READING AND STUDY GUIDE

Chapter	Content Summary	Related Articles

I. Camped at Sinai

Chapter	Content Summary	Related Articles
1	Moses takes a census. He counts 603,550 Israelite men of military age.	Census Moses
2	Moses organizes the Israelite camp around the tabernacle.	Tabernacle
3,4	Moses assigns duties to the Levites.	Levites
5	Moses provides a test for a wife thought to be unfaithful.	Jealousy
6	Moses explains requirements for the Nazirite vow.	Nazirite; Vow
7	The leaders of each tribe bring offerings to God.	Sacrifices
8	Moses cleanses and dedicates the Levites to God.	Dedicate
9	Moses and the Israelites celebrate Passover. A fiery cloud appears over the tabernacle to guide Israel.	Passover Cloud

II. The Wilderness Wanderings

Chapter	Content Summary	Related Articles
10	As the priests blow silver trumpets, the Israelites leave Sinai, led by God's ark.	Priest Ark of God
11	God sends fire and quail whose flesh brings plague and death to punish the ungrateful Israelites.	
12	Miriam is stricken with leprosy for challenging the leadership of Moses.	Leprosy Humble
13	Moses sends twelve spies to explore Canaan.	Caleb
14	The Israelites are terrified at reports of Canaanite strength and refuse to obey God's command to attack. God condemns the rebel generation to die in the desert.	Canaan Rebellion
15	Moses transmits instructions on offerings for unintentional sins. A Sabbath-breaker is executed.	Sin Atonement
16	The earth opens to swallow up Korah's rebellious Levites. Afterward plague strikes the people when they accuse Moses of killing the Lord's people.	Korah Plague
17	Aaron's staff buds, confirming his call to the priesthood.	Staff
18	Moses defines the responsibilities of the priests. He affirms their right to tithes and the meat of sacrifices.	Priest Tithe
19	Moses tells how to cleanse the ceremonially unclean.	Clean and Unclean
20	Moses disobeys God. The Edomites refuse to give Israel passage through their lands. Aaron dies.	Edom Aaron

III. The Journey to Canaan

Chapter	Content Summary	Related Articles
21	Moses sets up a bronze snake to counter a plague of poisonous vipers. Israel defeats the Ammonites.	Serpent
22	King Balak of Moab summons Balaam to curse Israel. Balaam comes, despite being warned by God.	Balaam Curse
23,24	Balaam is forced to bless rather than curse Israel.	Bless
25	The Moabites attempt to corrupt Israel, causing 24,000 to die in a subsequent plague.	Idol Adultery
26	Moses takes a census of the new generation, counting 601,730 men of military age.	Census
27	Moses establishes the right of women to inherit property. Moses is told that Joshua will succeed him as leader.	Joshua Inheritance

continued

Chapter	Content Summary	Related Articles
28,29	Moses commands daily, weekly, and monthly offerings and reviews the special religious holidays Israel is to keep.	Sacrifices Feasts
30	Moses gives rules for making and keeping vows.	Vow
31	Israel defeats the Midianites and takes their land in the Transjordan.	Midianites War
32	Two Israelite tribes ask permission to settle the captured lands after Canaan is subdued.	Transjordan
33	Israel's journey from Egypt to the borders of Canaan is recapped.	Exodus
34	Moses defines the boundaries of the land in Canaan that God has given to Israel.	
35	Towns are given to the Levites in the territories of the other tribes. Cities of refuge are established where those accused of murder can flee.	Cities of Refuge Murder
36	The claim of Zelophehad's daughters to a homestead in Canaan is confirmed.	

serves in Gal. 3:21—the Law cannot impart life. The Law given at Sinai did not change the behavior of the Exodus generation; they remained rebellious and unwilling to respond to the Lord. What the Law did was to condemn the rebellious. Knowledge of right and wrong through the Law gave God a basis on which to punish sins.

SPECIAL FEATURES

Numbers contains several prayers of intercession offered by Moses (11:2, 11-15; 14:13-25). Also, the story of Balaam (chs. 22–24) contains some of the oldest and most powerful Hebrew poetry known.

MASTERY KEYS

Note particularly the spiritual condition of the Exodus generation (Num. 11–14,16), which led to the wilderness deaths of nearly all adults who left Egypt with Moses. Compare that generation with their children (Num. 30,31).

The decision to disobey God and refuse to enter Canaan is often referred to in the NT. Hebrews states that the refusal to obey was caused by a failure of faith. The person who truly trusts God will do what the Lord says (Heb. 3,4). *See also* Faith; Obedience.

nurse (1) The act of breastfeeding a child (Gen. 21:7); (2) a woman who breastfed another's child until the child was weaned, about age three (Gen. 35:8; Ex. 2:7); (3) a servant who supervised and cared for a young child (2 Sam. 4:4).

The spies return from Canaan and report to Moses and the people: "We went into the land to which you sent us, and it does flow with milk and honey! Here is its fruit" (Num. 13:27).

Old nurse sits on a cushioned bench and holds a naked baby on her lap. In Bible times, a "nurse" was a woman who breastfed another woman's baby. A fourth-century B.C. terra-cotta figurine from Greece.

nurture The process of rearing or promoting the development of children.

The OT outlines a distinctive yet complex nurture pattern woven through the lifestyle that the Law imposed on ancient Israel. Although most generations fell tragically short of implementing this pattern, OT Law nevertheless helps us grasp the principles and ideals of proper nurture.

Major elements in the OT nurture system are the community of faith, participation in community life, and parents as models who teach.

1. *The community of faith.* Under the Law, Israel was to be a nation and a family, bound together by loving concern and shared commitment to justice. Children in this just and moral community were to be surrounded by models of godly behavior. In this way, the community provided a context that supported moral and spiritual training.

2. *Participation in community life.* Children are viewed in the OT as active participants in the spiritual experiences of the community. The religious calendar was vital in effective nurture. Each Sabbath reminded all in Israel of God's creative work and provided time for talk and worship. In the Passover meal, children relived, with their mothers and fathers, the first Passover when God acted to deliver Israel from Egypt. During the Feast of Tabernacles, the whole family lived outdoors in leafy booths, remembering the journey through the desert when God fed their ancestors with manna. In sacrifice and celebration, children as well as adults were reminded of God's mighty acts on their behalf.

3. *Parents as models who teach.* The just, loving, and worshiping community of Israel provided the context in which more specific religious education took place. Parents were to be the true teachers of their children, explaining God's laws and applying God's laws in daily life (Deut. 6,11). To be effective, the parents must themselves love God and keep his commandments. They must then impress God's words on their children by talking about those words daily "when you sit at home and when you walk along the road, when you lie down and when you get up" (Deut. 6:7).

The Book of Proverbs offers many pithy sayings regarding verbal instruction (1:8; 6:20,23), modeling (13:20; 20:7; 23:26), discipline (3:11,12; 19:18; 22:15; 29:15), motivation (2:6; 3:5,6; 9:10; 23:19-21), and individual responsibility for acting on what has been taught (3:1; 4:10; 20:11).

The NT adds little about the nurture of children, but generally reaffirms OT principles. Community, participation, and parental instruction are still central to nurture (2 Tim. 1:5). However, now the community that provides the context for growth is the church, an intimate fellowship of believers who live in cultures that are often hostile to Christian values.

A family has gathered around a table for a meal in this carving from a funeral stone (A.D. 100–300). In the Bible, parents are primarily responsible to rear and guide the development of their children.

741

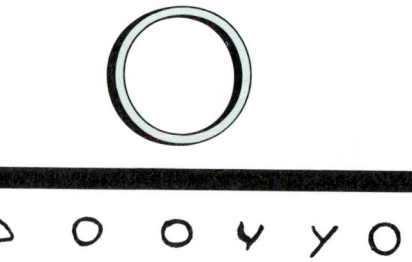

C. 1500 BC
PROTO-SINAITIC

C. 1300 BC
CANAANITE

C. 1000 BC
PHOENICIAN

C. 450 BC
ARAMAIC

100 AD
HEBREW

500 BC
GREEK

oak A large, acorn-bearing tree, a symbol of strength in the OT (Isa. 2:13; Amos 2:9; Zech. 11:2).

Among the two dozen varieties of oak found in Palestine are evergreen oaks that grow at elevations above 1,000 feet (305 meters) and deciduous oaks in the lowlands. Oak trees are often associated with pagan worship (Isa. 1:29; Ezek. 6:13; Hos. 4:13).

oath A sacred, unbreakable promise made as conclusive evidence that a person will or will not do a certain thing. An oath (1) was taken by witnesses in court cases, committing them to tell the truth (Ex. 22:11); (2) was given as a pledge of loyalty (Neh. 6:18); and (3) was made to God in the form of a vow to perform specific acts (Josh. 2:17,20).

In OT times, binding oaths were sworn "by the Lord" or by using God's name (Deut. 6:13; 1 Ki. 1:17). The Israelites under Joshua made such a commitment not to attack the Gibeonites, a people they thought lived far beyond the borders of Palestine. Even though Joshua later learned the Gibeonites had deceived him and were, in fact, neighbors, the vow remained binding because it had been made in the name of the Lord (Josh. 9:19).

GOD'S COVENANT

The most significant sacred promise, which cannot be broken, is the covenant God made with his people. God swore by himself to keep the promises he made to Abraham and Israel (Gen. 22:16; Ps. 89:35; Isa. 45:23; Jer. 44:26; Amos 6:8). The NT reminds us that God's promises were confirmed by an oath (Lk. 1:73; Acts 2:30; Heb. 7:20-25). Hebrews explains:

Men swear by someone greater than themselves, and the oath confirms what is said and puts an end to all argument. Because God wanted to make the unchanging nature of his purpose very clear to the heirs of what was promised, he confirmed it with an oath. God did this so that, by two unchangeable things in which it is impossible for God to lie, we who have fled to take hold of the hope offered to us may be greatly encouraged. (Heb. 6:16-18)

"SWEAR NOT AT ALL"

Despite the long tradition of swearing oaths, Jesus told his followers, "Do not swear [oaths] at all: either by heaven, for it is God's throne; or by the earth, for it is his footstool; or by Jerusalem, for it is the city of the Great King. . . ." Jesus concluded, "Simply let your 'Yes' be 'Yes,' and your 'No,' 'No'; anything beyond this comes from the evil one" (Mt. 5:33-37).

These words reflect criticism of the Pharisees, who argued over the exact form that made an oath binding and what forms "mean nothing" (Mt. 23:16). Christ teaches that form is irrelevant. A person who

Forests of deciduous Tabor oaks once covered much of lower Galilee (see Isa. 33:9; 35:2). This stand in the Gonen Forest is but a remnant.

Aerial view of territory in the Arabah inhabited by the Edomites in Bible times. Obadiah prophesied against Edom for its participation in an attack on Jerusalem.

makes a promise should keep it whether or not he takes an oath. In the fellowship of honest people, a person's word is as binding as a sacred oath. *See also* Covenant; Swear.

Obadiah, Book of A one-chapter prophetic book portraying in vivid poetry God's displeasure with Edom and his intention to judge that nation.

BACKGROUND AND AUTHORSHIP

Nothing is known of Obadiah [OH-buh-DI-uh; "servant of Yahweh"] beyond his name. Even the date of his prophecy is debated. The book describes a violation of Jerusalem by the Edomites (vv. 10-14). Jerusalem was in fact attacked several times, first in the ninth century B.C. (2 Ki. 8:20-22; 2 Chr. 21:16,17), again in the eighth century (2 Chr. 28:16-18), and lastly in the early sixth century B.C. by the Babylonians. Any or all of these occurrences could have been the background against which Obadiah speaks. Jewish tradition fixes on the earliest date, about 844 B.C., while many modern scholars prefer the later date, noting the bitterness toward Edom that other

prophets expressed about this time (Jer. 49:7-22; Lam. 4:21; Ezek. 25:12-14; 35:1-15).

Whatever the date, Obadiah announces God's judgment on the Edomites, a people descended from Esau, for their delight in the fall of Jerusalem and their attacks on fleeing Jews.

The Edomites remained persistent antagonists of Israel from the ninth century B.C. onward. After the fall of Jerusalem in 586 B.C., the Edomites migrated heavily into southern Judah. Their territory became known as Idumea, the Greek form of Edom. They remained under foreign domination through the periods of the Persians, Maccabeans, and Romans. The Edomites disappeared as a people after the destruction of Jerusalem in A.D. 70. *See also* Edom.

THEOLOGICAL CONTRIBUTIONS

Like most of the prophets, Obadiah portrays a God who is sovereign over the nations of the world. The Lord gives people and nations the freedom to make choices, but he also holds them responsible for the decisions they make. According to Obadiah's prophecy, Edom, which had

OBADIAH: A READING AND STUDY GUIDE		
Verses	**Content Summary**	**Related Articles**
1-9	God will bring disaster on Edom, a nation descended from Esau.	Edom
10-14	Edom will be punished for violence against Israel at a time when foreigners invade her.	Covenant
15-21	In a future "day" when God acts to judge, all nations who have been Israel's enemies will be punished, and Israel's exiles will possess the land in peace.	Day of the Lord Future Peace

743

shown itself an enemy to its "brother" Israel, would be judged and have no survivors (v. 18).

Obadiah, like most of the prophets, leaps from the specific (Edom) to the general (all nations, v. 15): God will confirm his special relationship with Israel. In a coming "Day of the Lord," all Israel's enemies will be destroyed. Then "on Mount Zion will be deliverance; it will be holy, and the house of Jacob will possess its inheritance" (v. 17). *See also* Day of the Lord.

SPECIAL FEATURES
Obadiah speaks in the confident awareness that he relays the words of the Lord (vv. 1,4,8,18). The message of the prophets was not their own but God's.

Elamites bow in obeisance before their new puppet king, presented to them by an Assyrian soldier at the end of a bitter war. From a limestone relief at Nineveh, about 650 B.C.

obeisance (KJV) Bowing low, especially on one's knees, even prostrating oneself on the ground. Modern English versions typically have "bow down" or "bow to the ground."

In Hebrew culture, making obeisance served as (1) an expression of respect for an equal (Gen. 23:12), or more often as (2) an expression of honor or submission to a superior (Ruth 2:10; 2 Sam. 24:20). Obeisance also appears frequently as (3) an act of worship or submission offered to a pagan deity (Lev. 26:1; Josh. 23:7).

obey, obedience To act in accord with what is commanded by an authority. In both Hebrew and Greek, the word "obey" is essentially the same as "hear" (Heb., *shema'*; Gk., *hypakouō*). This implies that, when one hears—or pays attention to—a superior (especially God), obedience is the proper response. Another Greek word (*peithō*) adds the sense of mental agreement. It literally means "to be persuaded." Note that obedience is a relational term: The hearer, who responds to the expressed will of another, is in some rela-

tionship with him or her that makes submission appropriate.

As children, we owe obedience to our parents (Eph. 6:1). As employees or servants, we owe obedience to our employers or masters (1 Pet. 2:18). As citizens, we owe obedience to the government (Rom. 13:1,2). Most importantly, as creatures, as members of a covenant community, as his children, and as his redeemed we owe obedience to God.

Jesus "humbled himself and became obedient unto death" (Phil. 2:8 RSV). Christ's willingness to "learn obedience from what he suffered" demonstrated Jesus' integrity as a true human being (Heb. 5:8). He was not only our holy sacrifice, but also a model for us of obedience to God.

To understand the nature of obedience to God, we need to note the close relationship of obedience to faith, love, and blessing.

OBEDIENCE AND FAITH

James argues that any "faith" unaccompanied by deeds (that is, obedience) is a dead faith. Even demons have that kind of faith, for they know that God exists. Saving faith must be expressed in acts and, indeed, is "made complete" by what one does (Jas. 2:18-26). Obedience is the visible aspect of true faith in God.

The writer of Hebrews goes back in history to make the same point. The Israelites who rebelled and failed to enter Canaan at God's command hardened their hearts. They refused to obey "because of their unbelief" (Heb. 3:19). Those who trust God will respond to him and will do his will (3:7–4:7). Hebrews 11 takes great pains to show that faith in God lies at the root of active obedience. Only because they had faith were Abraham, Sarah, Moses, Rahab, and others able to accomplish great things. *See also* Faith.

This intimate link between obedience and faith is further illustrated by the NT's use of the word "obey" to mean a faith response to the good news of salvation (Rom. 15:18; 16:26; 2 Th. 1:8).

OBEDIENCE AND LOVE

There is also an essential link between love and obedience. The Law's prime commandment is: "Love the Lord your God with all your heart and with all your soul and with all your strength." The passage adds, "These commandments that I give you today are to be upon your hearts" (Deut. 6:5,6).

The repetition of "heart" is significant. Fear or a desire for personal advantage may move a person to comply with another's wishes. But the obedience God seeks flows from a spontaneous heart response to him; it is a joyful willingness to do God's will. No mere sense of obligation can move anyone to obey from the heart.

Jesus made this very clear at the Last Supper. "If you love me, you will obey what I command. . . . Whoever has my commands and obeys them, he is the one who loves me. . . . If anyone loves me, he will obey my teaching" (Jn. 14:15,21,23). Love for Christ is the motivation which stimulates the believer to obey.

"*If anyone loves me, he will obey my teaching.*"

JOHN 14:23

OBEDIENCE AND BLESSING

Both Testaments affirm that obedience to God results in divine blessing: "Hear, O Israel, and be careful to obey so that it may go well with you and that you may increase greatly in a land flowing with milk and honey" (Deut. 6:3). Many other passages pick up this theme (Lev. 25:18,19; Deut. 4:30,31; 11:26-28; Deut. 28,30). The thought is not that the believer is bribed to obey, but rather that God is eager to bless his covenant people. Disobedience takes the believer out of the path of blessing. Obedience takes us into the path of blessing, where God is able to do for us all that he yearns to do.

Obeying God is intimate and personal. It grows out of our relationship with the Lord, and it exists only where there is faith in and love for God.

oblation (KJV) An offering or gift presented to God; usually an object (food or land) in contrast to an animal sacrifice (Lev. 2:4,12; Ezek. 48:9). *See also* Sacrifices and Offerings.

odor An airborne scent; in Scripture, used most frequently in the liturgical phrase describing sacrifices and offerings made to God as a "pleasing odor" or "an aroma pleasing to" the Lord.

In this context, the phrase serves as a technical theological statement, meaning simply that the offering or sacrifice was acceptable to the Lord. The sacrifices of the wicked are unacceptable. God is not concerned with mere ritual, and offerings made by those who do evil have a "detestable" aroma. God says through Isaiah, "I have no pleasure in" such meaningless offerings (Isa. 1:10-17; *see* Amos 5:21).

In the poetry of Revelation, aromatic incense represents the prayers of God's saints (5:8). In another figurative application, Paul points us to the sacrifice of Christ, which has been accepted by God. Knowing Christ, Paul says, is a "fragrance," and we who share the Gospel are the "aroma of Christ." To those who reject Christ, the message seems laden with the stench of death. But those who believe the Gospel find it to be the very fragrance of life (2 Cor. 2:14-17).

Noah and his family offer burnt sacrifices to God after the Flood, as depicted on a 9th-century A.D. ivory plaque from Salerno, Italy. The odor pleased God, who promised never again to destroy the earth with a flood (Gen. 8:20-22).

In Gal. 5:11, Paul refers to the "offense of the cross," using offense in the second sense above. Those who try to be justified by keeping the Law are insulted and angry at the Gospel message. They cannot believe their own works have no value and that "the only thing that counts is faith expressing itself through love" (Gal. 5:6).

offering *See* Sacrifices and Offerings.

Above: A life-sized relief from the palace walls of Sargon II, king of Assyria, shows two officers of his court (about 710 B.C.). One claps his hands to gain attention while the other raises his hand to introduce tribute bearers.

officer A general term in Scripture identifying subordinate officials of the king, the army, or the Temple.

The Hebrew or Greek words translated "officer" are not sharply defined and do not themselves imply any specific duties. Often, however, the duties of officers can be determined from the context in which the word is used.

offspring The progeny of a person or animal, but typically in Scripture, "descendants" (Gen. 3:15; Ruth 4:12).

One special use of the term is significant. In Athens, Paul quotes the Cilician poet Aratus, "We are his [God's] offspring" (Acts 17:24-31). Originally the phrase carried a Stoic, pantheistic mes-

offal The waste parts of a butchered animal; the entrails and other parts which were not burned as an offering or eaten. (Ex. 29:14; Lev. 4:11; 8:17; 16:27; Num. 19:5; Mal. 2:3).

offense (1) A sin, crime, or transgression (Ezek. 18:30); (2) an act that creates hurt feelings or resentment (Prov. 17:9); (3) in the KJV, something that causes a person to sin or stumble (Mt. 18:7; Rom. 9:32,33).

sage. But Paul reads new meaning into the familiar poet, supporting his argument that we humans are created by God and shaped in his image.

oil A greasy, combustible liquid obtained from animal or vegetable sources. In the Bible, "oil" in nearly every case is olive oil, obtained by crushing the fruit of the olive tree. *See also* Olive.

Oil, with grain and wine, was one of three staples in the Hebrew diet. Thus olives were also a valuable cash crop at home and abroad (Num. 18:12; Deut. 7:13; 2 Chr. 32:28). Solomon made payments in oil to the king of Tyre for his help in building the Temple (1 Ki. 5:11), and later, part of the payment for help in constructing the second Temple was made in oil (Ezra 3:7).

Olive oil was the butter and cooking oil of biblical times. It was the main source of fat in the diet (1 Ki. 17:12-16; 2 Ki. 4:2), and it was mixed with meal to make bread.

Olive oil was the fuel used in the lamps that were burned after dark in Hebrew homes (Ex. 25:6; 2 Ki. 4:10; Mt. 25:3-8).

The oil was poured into shallow clay bowls into which a flax wick was placed. Fine oil was the fuel for the seven-branched lampstand that provided the only light within the tabernacle and Temple (Ex. 27:20).

Wounds were treated with oil (Isa. 1:6; Mk. 6:13), sometimes with other substances added (Lk. 10:34). The reference in Jas. 5:14 to anointing the sick with oil is no doubt instruction to provide medical treatment along with prayer.

Olive oil was the base of most of the perfumed ointments and cosmetics used in the ancient world. In the heat of summer, oil was rubbed on the skin to keep it soft and supple (Ps. 104:15). Oil was usually applied to the body after bathing (Ruth 3:3; 2 Sam. 12:20). Honored guests were anointed with oil when they arrived at a banquet (Ps. 23:5; Amos 6:6), a courtesy refused Christ by Simon the Pharisee (Lk. 7:46). *See also* Ointment.

Oil also served as a preservative and was rubbed on such items as soldiers' leather shields (Isa. 21:5).

Those chosen by God for special roles often received an anointing with oil in a religious ritual. Kings (1 Sam. 10:1; 2 Ki. 9:3), priests (Lev. 8:30), and prophets (Isa. 61:1) were anointed. The furnishings of the tabernacle were anointed to consecrate them to God's service (Ex. 30:22-33). Many of the burnt and whole grain offerings made at the Temple included oil (Ex. 29:40; Lev. 2:4-6).

The pervasive role of olive oil in the daily life and economy of Israel made it an appropriate symbol of prosperity (Deut. 32:13; 33:24; Joel 2:24). Oil is also a symbol of joy (Ps. 45:7; Isa. 61:3) and brotherly love (Ps. 133).

Edge-runner oil press from the Hellenistic period. The slant-edged upper wheel was turned by human or donkey power, pushing the pits of the olives outward as the skins and pulp were separated.

Terra-cotta figurine of a young woman breastfeeding her offspring; Lemnos, Greece, first century B.C.

747

ointment A salve; an oily substance rubbed on the skin for cosmetic or medical purposes.

A wide variety of ointments was used in the ancient world. Olive oil served as the base of most ointments. Various spices and other substances were ground and mixed in the oil, which was sometimes then boiled to fix the fragrance (Job 41:31). Ointments were prepared by perfumers or pharmacists (Ex. 30:35; 2 Chr. 16:14) and kept in small, sealed vials or boxes. Alabaster vials were preferred for the more expensive ointments.

Psalm 133:2 probably describes a practice adopted from the Egyptians, who placed a small amount of thickened, perfumed ointment on the forehead of guests. As it melted, the sweet smelling substance ran down the face onto the clothing (*see* Mt. 6:17; Lk. 7:46).

old (1) Aged or in existence for some time; (2) associated with the past; (3) worn out, passing away (2 Cor. 5:17); (4) corrupt, defective, or obsolete.

Hebrew culture had great respect for elderly people and ancient traditions. The NT reflects this but also presents the "new" truth of Christ, which supplants many of the old traditions.

Where the NT uses "old" as a theological term, it nearly always is placed in contrast to the "new." The old covenant instituted through Moses has been replaced by the new covenant instituted in Christ (2 Cor. 3:14; Heb. 8:13). The old man, corrupted by sin, is re-created in Christ (2 Cor. 5:17; Col. 3:9,10). The "old way of the written code" is abandoned for the "new way of the Spirit," by which believers now relate to God (Rom. 7:6). The old heaven and earth are to be set aside, replaced by a new creation which will be the home of righteousness (2 Pet. 3:13; Rev. 21).

The use of "old" in the OT often conveys a sense of nostalgia, as believers recall the mighty acts God performed for Israel. There is none of this in the NT. Since the new has come, God is vitally at work now in every believer through his Spirit. *See also* Age; New.

olive A slow-growing, hardwood tree, and its oval, oil-bearing fruit. In biblical times, olive trees were common in Palestine, with many plains famous for verdant olive groves. Although the tree develops slowly, a cultivated olive tree can produce fruit for hundreds of years.

Olives were harvested in November. Some of the fruit was eaten, but most of the crop was pressed to obtain oil, which was used in preparing every meal, as fuel for the small lamps that lit Hebrew homes, or was mixed with spices or other substances to produce ointment and perfumes. A single tree can produce about 20 gallons of oil. *See also* Oil; Ointment.

To obtain oil, olives were spread on a circular stone basin and crushed under a heavy, rotating stone wheel. The first oil obtained from the crushed fruit was the most valuable and is spoken of in Scripture as "fine oil." After the olives were crushed and the fine oil extracted, the pulp was pressed by a stone-weighted beam. A pressure of hundreds of pounds squeezed out sediment, oil, and water. The lighter oil rose to the surface and was skimmed off by the farmer. Archaeologists have discovered many olive presses from biblical times.

The fruitfulness and beauty of the tree make it an appropriate symbol of strength and blessing, as in Ps. 52:8: "I am like an olive tree flourishing in the house of God; I trust in God's unfailing love for ever and ever."

omega The last letter of the Greek alphabet. Revelation portrays Jesus as the "Alpha and Omega," a phrase meaning the beginning and end—the one who sums up all things in himself (Rev. 1:8; 21:6; 22:13). *See also* Alpha and Omega.

omer A dry measure equaling one-tenth of an *ephah* or about 2 quarts (2.2 liters). It also can refer to the wave offering of the first sheaf of barley harvested in the spring (Lev. 23:9-15).

Onesimus [oh-NES-ih-muhs; "profitable"]. A runaway slave who converted to Christ under Paul and whom the apostle sent back to his owner, Philemon, about A.D. 62/63. **Scripture:** Col. 4:9; Philemon.

BACKGROUND

Onesimus was the slave of Philemon, a Christian leader in Colosse. He apparently stole money from his master (Phlm. 18) and fled to Rome. There he somehow came in contact with Paul, who was imprisoned (v. 10), and Onesimus was converted. Paul sent him back to his master with a letter appealing to Philemon to take him back, not as a slave but "as a dear brother" (v. 16).

One tradition holds that this young slave is the person referred to some 50 years later by the church father Ignatius as "a man of inexpressible love and your bishop."

LEARNING FROM ONESIMUS'S LIFE

We know very little about Onesimus as a person. Yet Paul's play on his name is suggestive. "Formerly he was useless to you," Paul says (v. 11). Not only useless, Onesimus was a burden, who stole from his master and, by running away, deprived Philemon of his rightful property. Conversion made a radical difference in this rebellious slave. At last Onesimus began to live up to his name, and "now he has become useful both to you and to me" (v. 11). Just how useful is suggested in Paul's letter to Colosse, where Philemon lived. In Col. 4:9, Paul calls Onesimus "our faithful and dear brother."

Onesimus reminds us that no matter how useless any human being seems to be, he or she has the potential to live a significant and useful life through the transforming power of Christ.

onion A plant whose bulbous root is prized for its pungent flavor. Onions grew in large quantities near the Nile River. They were eaten raw, used in soups and stews, boiled, and roasted. Onions are listed in Num. 11:5 among the vegetables of Egypt that the Israelites missed while journeying in the wilderness.

only begotten (KJV) Unique. The Greek word *monogenēs* appears in Jn. 1:14,18; 3:16,18; Heb. 11:17; and 1 Jn. 4:9. The term literally means "one of a kind," a sense captured nicely by the NIV translation, "one and only." Jesus is truly unique, both in his ministry of revelation and in the redemption he won for us as "God made flesh."

onycha [AHN-i-kah]. One of the ingredients in the sacred incense used only in worship of the Lord (Ex. 30:34). Onycha is a powder made from the horny lid that closes to protect certain Red Sea mollusks when they withdraw into their shells.

onyx A semi-precious variety of agate, with variously colored layers.

Biblical onyx was a softer chalcedony with black and white bands. Mounted on the shoulder of the high priest's ephod were onyx stones engraved with the names of Israel's tribes. An onyx also served as the middle stone in the bottom row of precious stones on the high priest's ephod (Ex. 25:7; 28:9; 35:9,27; 39:13).

Onyx was also among the precious stones David assembled for Solomon to use in building the Jerusalem Temple (1 Chr. 29:2).

oracle A message delivered with divine authority; a message directly from God rather than through a messenger.

In chapters 13–23, Isaiah delivers oracles of God against the various nations surrounding Judah. The Hebrew word used, *masa'*, can also mean "burden." These prophetic oracles were usually messages of judgment and, thus, not easy for the prophets to carry.

Ne'um is a more general word for an utterance or declaration. It is sometimes translated "oracle," especially in the account of Balaam's prophecy (Num. 24).

The KJV incorrectly renders *debir*, which indicates the inner room of Solomon's Temple, as "oracle." The misunderstanding is rooted in the Greek practice of sleeping in a sacred place in hopes that some god would speak through dreams.

Older versions sometimes translate the Greek *logia* by "oracle," while modern English versions retain its normal sense as a "message" from God (Acts 7:38; Rom. 3:2; Heb. 5:12).

Jeremiah records God's anger at false prophets who claim to have oracles from God:

The Greek capital letter omega, *which represents the long o-sound.*

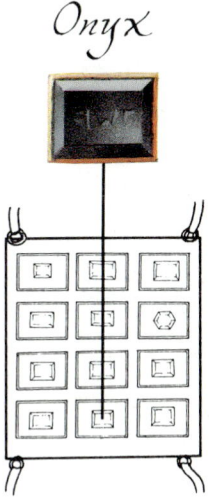

Onyx

Onyx was very precious in ancient times, but Job said it was not worth as much as wisdom (28:16).

749

Left: Small potter's oven from the Kings period. Potters also used larger kilns.
Below: Oven in a reconstructed Israelite house. Most homes had these clay, bread-baking devices in an open courtyard or near a doorway.

"I am against the prophets who steal from one another words supposedly from me. . . . every man's own word becomes his oracle and so you distort the words of the living God."
(Jer. 23:30,36)

ordain, ordination (1) To establish or determine—as God's sovereign decision to establish a covenant with Israel (Ps. 111:9) or to use the Babylonians to punish his rebellious people (Hab. 1:12). (2) To officially install or appoint religious leaders, just as Aaron and his sons were ordained to the OT priesthood (Ex. 28,29; Lev. 7,8; 21:10; Num. 3:3). (3) To set apart for ministry through prayer and the laying on of hands (Acts 6:6; 13:3).

While every NT believer has a spiritual gift and is called to minister (1 Cor. 12:7; Eph. 4:12,13), the NT does describe spiritual leaders whose gifts and character qualified them for their roles within the Church (1 Tim. 3; Tit. 2). These leaders were set apart by the apostles and the congregation they served (Acts 14:23; Tit. 1:5). Appointment to such leadership seems to have been accomplished in a service that featured prayer and a laying on of hands by the body of elders. Timothy was one such gifted and appointed leader (1 Tim. 4:14; 2 Tim. 1:6).

ordinance A statute, decree, judicial decision, or law; an authoritative command—used primarily as a synonym for the Law of God, but also of authoritative commands of a king. *See also* Law.

organ (KJV) *See* Flute.

ornaments Decorative articles used for personal adornment. *See also* Jewelry.

orphan A child without living parents, or without a father. The Hebrew term means "fatherless." Under OT Law, children of a widow were considered orphans. In Scripture, the widow and orphan frequently represent the powerless in society, and many provisions in the Mosaic Law reveal God's special concern for them. *See also* Fatherless; Poor.

ostrich The largest living bird, which cannot fly and stands up to 8 feet, 6 inches (2.59 meters) tall. Job 39:13-18 contains a graphic description of the ostrich.

Ostriches roamed the Sinai and Israel in biblical times and have been extinct there only since the early 1940s.

Bottle made from an ostrich eggshell (second millennium B.C.). Ostriches were not extinct in Palestine in Bible times.
Inset: This silver four-drachma coin from Athens bears an image of an owl (about 450 B.C.). Several species of owl are mentioned in the OT (Ps. 102:6; Isa. 34:11; Zeph. 2:14).

oven A compartment, in which heat is retained, used for cooking food.

The earliest ovens used in Palestine were hive-shaped mounds of clay, open at the top, some 2 or 3 feet (1 meter) in diameter. Pieces of broken pottery were pressed into the outside of the hollow mound. A fire made with straw and twigs or dried animal dung burned inside the oven on a bed of pebbles. Small loaves of bread were then placed inside, and the opening was covered with a stone or fragment of pottery. Alternatively, flattened pancakes of bread might be spread on the heated pottery pieces on the outer surface. In larger cities, bread might be prepared by commercial bakers using larger, hive-shaped ovens (Neh. 3:11; 12:38).

By the first century, women cooked on pottery stoves that featured an oven compartment. *See also* Cooking; Furnace.

overseer (1) A supervisor, foreman, or other officer responsible for some activity; (2) within the church, a bishop or elder.

The Greek word for "overseer," *episkopos,* seems interchangeable with *presbyteros* ("elder") and *poimēn* ("shepherd") in NT usage. Each term suggests a person who is responsible to watch over and care for the Christian community and its members (1 Tim. 3:1,2; 1 Pet. 2:25). *See also* Elder; Shepherd.

owl A nocturnal bird of prey, several species of which are found in Palestine. All owls were ritually unclean and could not be eaten by the Jewish people (Lev. 11:16; Deut. 14:15).

ox, oxen A bull; an adult, domesticated male bovine.

Oxen (bullocks, KJV) were important work animals in Israel, and herds of oxen represented great wealth. Oxen were used for plowing (Deut. 22:10), threshing (Deut. 25:4), and pulling wagons (2 Sam. 6:6). Because of their size and strength, oxen were to be carefully controlled by their owners (Ex. 21:28-36). As clean animals, oxen could be offered in sacrifice (Ex. 20:24; Lev. 22:23). Because of their great value, they were slaughtered for food only for special occasions (1 Sam. 14:31-34; Isa. 22:13; Mt. 22:4).

The leaders of the twelve Israelite tribes gave to the Levites six carts and twelve oxen to assist them in transporting the tabernacle (tent of meeting) across the wilderness (Num. 6). The ancient Egyptian model shows a stylized cart and oxen from about that time.

The ox symbolizes strength. The face of an ox was seen on the cherub in Ezekiel's vision (Ezek. 1:5-10) and on one of the living creatures by the throne of God (Rev. 4:6-11).

oxgoad *See* Goad.

Egyptian model of a peasant plowing with a pair of oxen (Middle Kingdom, about 2000 B.C.). Oxen were the most valued possession of an Israelite farmer.

C. 1500 BC
PROTO-SINAITIC

C. 300 BC
S. ARABIAN

C. 1000 BC
PHOENICIAN

C. 450 BC
ARAMAIC

100 AD
HEBREW

500 BC
GREEK

palace The residence of a king or other high official.

Typically, palaces served as administrative centers and treasuries as well as royal homes. About 20 Assyrian palaces have been excavated. The palace of Sargon II at Khorsabad extended over some 24 acres (9.7 hectares). Sennacherib's palace, covering only 5 acres (2 hectares), featured nearly 2 miles (3.2 kilometers) of sculptured stone reliefs lining the walls of its 70 rooms and halls. By comparison, Saul's fortress-palace at Gibeah (1 Sam. 15:34), excavated in 1922–23 and again in 1964, was only 171 by 115 feet (52 by 35 meters).

However, later Jewish kings had more wealth and built more elaborate palaces. Solomon's palace, described in 1 Ki. 7:1-12, took 13 years to build. The luxurious palace of Ahab in Samaria, "inlaid with ivory" (1 Ki. 22:39), has been excavated. Jeremiah describes the extravagance of Jehoiakim's palace—large rooms, wide windows, cedar paneling—and warns, "Woe to him who builds his palace by unrighteousness" (Jer. 22:13-19).

In the first century, Herod the Great, one of the most prolific builders of ancient times, constructed a number of palaces.

The most spectacular of Herod's homes was a multilevel retreat built on the mesa of Masada, later captured by Jews in their resistance against Rome.

Palestine One of several names for the land lying along the southeastern Mediterranean. Other names of this area, extending roughly from the Sinai Peninsula to Mount Hermon and from the Jordan to the Mediterranean, include Canaan, the Promised Land, and the land of Israel.

The Romans first named this area Palestine in A.D. 135 following the Jewish Bar-Kochba revolt—a change from its previous provincial name, Judea. The name derived from that of the Philistines, early inhabitants of the territory and enemies of Israel. The name "Palestine" was revived after World War I by the British, who governed the area under a League of Nations mandate. "Palestine" is typically used in biblical studies to designate the larger geographical area and in this context has no political implications.

palm *See* Weights and Measures.

palm tree In Scripture, the date palm, a tree reaching up to 90 feet (27.5 meters) tall, easily identified by its long, straight trunk topped with bunched, feathery branches.

In bibical times, the date palm provided a fruit valued for its sweetness. The leaves were used for roofing; its crown was woven to make rope; and its sap was drawn to produce a potent liquor, possibly the "strong drink" mentioned often in the OT. Palms take three decades to mature but may live 200 years. First-century writ-

Date palms on the eastern shore of the Sea of Galilee.

ers tell of forests of palms in Palestine at that time.

Palms provided the branches that joyful crowds waved to welcome Jesus to Jerusalem just before his crucifixion (Jn. 12:12,13), giving the name "Palm Sunday" to the first Sunday before Easter on the Christian calendar.

palmer worm (KJV) A stage in the life cycle of the locust—a swarming, grasshopper-like insect which has devastated the agriculture of Africa and Palestine from biblical to modern times. *See also* Locust.

paper Thin sheets manufactured in ancient times from the pulp of the papyrus reed.

Papyrus paper was made in Egypt by 2000 B.C. and was the primary writing material in the Greek and Roman world from about 500 B.C. to A.D. 400. Many papyrus manuscripts containing part or all of different OT and NT books have been recovered in Egypt, preserved by the dry climate.

To manufacture the paper, the stem of the mature papyrus reed was cut into sections about 12 inches (30.5 centimeters) long. The pithy core was extracted and then sliced into thin strips. These strips were laid side by side and then a second

Left: At the summit of the rock mesa of Masada, Herod the Great built a 43,000-square-foot palace on the western part and a private three-tiered retreat on the north. Herod also built palaces at Jerusalem, Machaerus, Jericho, and in his fortress of Herodium.

Top Left: The Hasmonean Palace as depicted in a model of Jerusalem. This is where Herod Antipas interviewed Jesus, hoping to see him perform a miracle (Lk. 23:6-12).

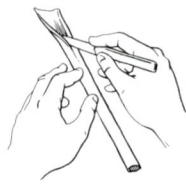

The process of making "paper" from the pith of papyrus stalks was a labor-intensive task.

Right: Heads of the aquatic plant Cyperus papyrus. *The pith from its stem was valued for making many useful goods in ancient Egypt. Below: Line drawing of a papyrus-gathering expedition copied from the walls of a royal Egyptian tomb (Saqqara, about 2400 B.C.).*

layer was placed at right angles to the first. These layers were pressed or glued together, pounded flat, and then sanded smooth. The resulting sheet of paper was slightly thicker and stiffer than modern brown wrapping paper.

There were several qualities of paper, depending on the width of the paper, thickness of the strips from which it was constructed, and the care taken in smoothing the finished product. Even the cheaper grades of paper were relatively expensive.

At first, up to 20 sheets of this paper were glued together and rolled up. For longer works, several rolls might be joined together to form a scroll as much as 30 feet (9 meters) long. By the second century A.D., sheets were commonly kept separate and laid atop each other, like the pages in a book, called a *codex*. The oldest NT manuscript presently in our possession, a fragment of John's Gospel copied a few years after the original was written, is in the form of a codex. *See also* Papyrus.

papyrus A marsh plant. Scholars agree that the plant called "bulrush" in many English versions is the papyrus, which grew in marshy areas along the upper Nile. According to Isaiah, the stem of this tall reed-like plant was used in making sea-going boats (Isa. 18:2). Undoubtedly, the "papyrus basket" in which the infant Moses was placed was a miniature boat, coated, like the larger ships, with tar and pitch (Ex. 2:3).

Papyrus was an impressive plant and a valuable resource. It grew 10 to 20 feet (3 to 6 meters) tall, and the stem of a mature plant was as much as 3 inches (8 centimeters) in diameter. Not only was the plant used in the construction of boats, but its sap was used as a sweetener and in making medicines. Paintbrushes were made by fraying the end of a small plant. Papyrus could be burned as fuel, and strands taken from it were woven to make fishing line.

Most important, the soft pithy interior was extracted, flattened, and glued together to make the paper used in ancient times. While Ezekiel's description of "eating" a scroll given him by God is symbolic (Ezek. 3:1-3), the papyrus pith used in making scrolls was in fact edible. *See also* Paper.

A medallion of a young man reading a scroll. A fresco from Herculaneum, a city destroyed by the eruption of Vesuvius, A.D. 79.

parable A saying, proverb, story, simile, or metaphor intended to communicate truth by comparison. Although parables exist in the OT (Hos. 12:10), the most familiar parables are those stories Jesus told to express aspects of God's Kingdom.

PURPOSE OF JESUS' PARABLES

Jesus' parables use familiar images to communicate spiritual truth. Leaven, lost sheep, wheat and weeds, bridesmaids waiting to escort the bridegroom and bride, lost coins, and prodigal sons were all woven into the context of daily life in first-century Judea.

Jesus told most of his parables after the religious leaders of Israel rejected him (Mt. 12:22-45). When asked why he then adopted this particular teaching method (Mt. 13:10), Jesus told his disciples, "The knowledge of the secrets of the kingdom of heaven has been given to you, but not to them." Christ went on to explain that

Jesus' parable of the sower features birds that feasted on exposed seed (Mt. 13:3,4). This relief from El Amarna, Egypt (1365 B.C.), shows men and boys scaring birds away from crops by clapping and banging on a metal pan.

PARABLES OF JESUS

Candle under a bowl (bushel)	Mt. 5:14-16	Pearl of great price	Mt. 13:45,46
	Mk. 4:21,22	Persistent widow	Lk. 18:1-8
	Lk. 8:16,17	Pharisee and the tax collector	Lk. 18:9-14
Fig tree, barren	Lk. 13:6-9	Prodigal son	Lk. 15:11-32
Fig tree, young leaves	Mt. 24:32-35	Rich fool	Lk. 12:16-21
	Mk. 13:28-31	Rich man and Lazarus	Lk. 16:19-31
	Lk. 21:29	Sheep and the goats	Mt. 25:31-46
Fishing net	Mt. 13:47-52	Sower, seed, and soils	Mt. 13:3-9,
Friend at midnight	Lk. 11:5-8		18-23
Good Samaritan	Lk. 10:25-37		Mk. 4:3-20
Great banquet	Lk. 14:16-24		Lk. 8:4-15
Growing seed	Mk. 4:26-29	Talents	Mt. 25:14-30
Hidden treasure	Mt. 13:44	Tares (weeds)	Mt. 13:24-30,
House built on the rock	Mt. 7:24-27		36-43
	Lk. 6:48,49	Tenants	Mt. 21:33-41
Laborers in the vineyard	Mt. 20:1-16		Mk. 12:1-9
Lost coin	Lk. 15:8-10		Lk. 20:9-16
Lost sheep	Mt. 18:12-14	Ten minas (pounds)	Lk. 19:12-27
	Lk. 15:3-7	Ten virgins	Mt. 25:1-13
Marriage feast (of the king's son)	Mt. 22:1-14	The tower/counting its cost	Lk. 14:28-33
Master and servant	Lk. 17:7-10	Two debtors	Lk. 7:36-50
Mustard seed	Mt. 13:31,32	Two sons	Mt. 21:28-32
	Mk. 4:31,32	Unjust steward	Lk. 16:1-13
	Lk. 13:18,19	Unmerciful servant	Mt. 18:21-35
New cloth on old garment	Mt. 9:16	Watch for his coming!	Mk. 13:32-37
	Mk. 2:21	Watchful servants	Lk. 12:35-40
	Lk. 5:36	Wise steward	Lk. 12:42-48
New wine and old bottles	Mt. 9:17	Yeast (leaven)	Mt. 13:33
	Mk. 2:22		Lk. 13:20,21
	Lk. 5:37,38		

his stories about the Kingdom of heaven would be understood by those with faith but remain obscure to those who did not believe (Mt. 13:11-17).

INTERPRETING JESUS' PARABLES

We need to keep several things in mind when reading Jesus' parables. (1) As "kingdom" in Scripture speaks of the rule exercised by a king rather than a geographical or national entity, so Christ's parables of the Kingdom concern the way God is at work in history and in believers' lives. (2) Parables were told to answer questions or illuminate issues raised by Jesus or others. A study of the context will define the issue with which a parable is concerned. (3) Unlike allegories, in which every part of the story has significance, only the elements in a parable which focus on the issue under discussion carry the point of Jesus' story. (4) To see the point of the parable, it is necessary to understand the

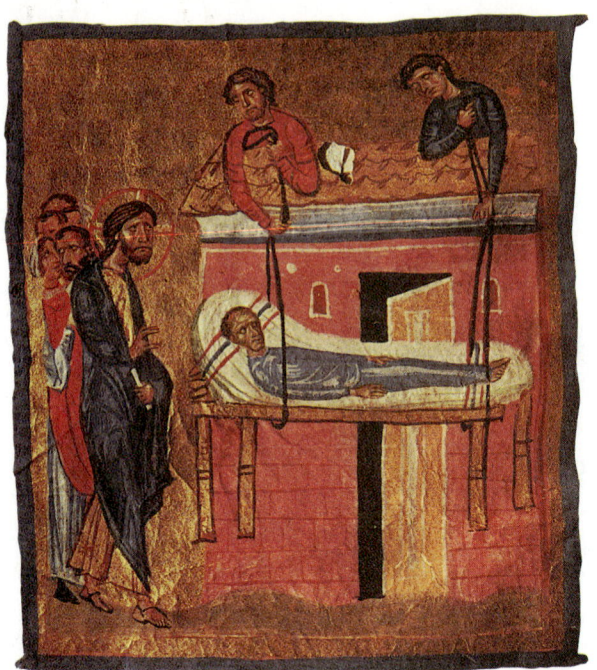

The paralytic brought by his friends to be healed had to be lowered through the roof because of the crowds around the house where Jesus taught. Illuminated Greek manuscript from The Four Gospels *(A.D. 1250–1300).*

customs and cultural peculiarities of its central element. For instance, to sense the panic felt by the woman who lost one of her ten coins (Lk. 15:8,9), we need to know that women in Bible times often wore their dowry of coins on a string as a necklace. This dowry was vitally important to women for more than monetary reasons. *See also* Dowry.

Paraclete [Gk., "one who is called alongside"]. A name given the Holy Spirit, variously translated in English versions as Helper, Comforter, and Counselor. *See also* Holy Spirit.

When Jesus promised his disciples that "another" Paraclete would come (Jn. 14:16,26; 15:26; 16:7), he described a twofold ministry of the Spirit. (1) The Spirit ministers to Jesus' disciples. He remains with them forever, to teach and remind them of what Christ has said. The Spirit guides disciples into all truth and will glorify Jesus by communicating what he hears from the Father. He will also predict things to come. (2) The Spirit ministers to the world through the disciples in whom and through whom he works. He convicts the world of sin, convinces the world of Christ's righteousness, and demonstrates the fact that divine judgment has already begun.

paradise (1) A loan word from the Persian, which originally meant "park" or "enclosed garden" (Neh. 2:8; Eccl. 2:5; Song 4:13). (2) In first-century Judaism, the lo-

cation of the righteous dead (Lk. 23:43). (3) The present location of Christ, where the personality (self) of the believer goes to upon his or her death (2 Cor. 12:3,4). (4) An eschatological reference to the new heaven and new earth God will one day establish (Rev. 2:7).

Paradise captured the interest of the Jews in the intertestamental period, and many fanciful descriptions of this home of the dead are found in extrabiblical Jewish writings. *See also* Abraham's Side; Hades; Heaven; Sheol.

paralytic A person who has suffered partial or complete loss of the ability to move some part of his or her body, especially the legs and/or arms. Three Gospels report the healing of paralytics by Jesus (Mt. 4:24; 9:2-6; Mk. 2:3-10; Lk. 5:18-26). Acts 8:7 says the apostles continued this ministry.

parapet A low wall or railing built around the edge of a roof.

Houses in Bible times were built with flat roofs. An outside stairway often led to the roof, which was used as an extra room during much of the year. Old Testament Law required a parapet to prevent children or adults from falling off the roof and injuring themselves (Deut. 22:8).

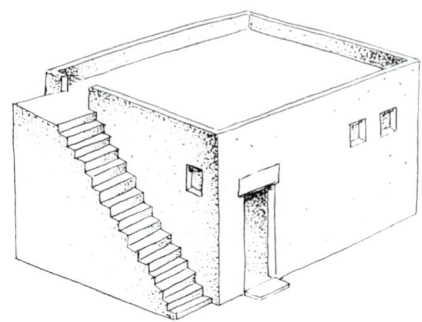

Ordinary people in Jesus' day utilized their simple houses to fullest advantage by having flat roofs accessible by a staircase. The parapet around the edge made it safer for the family as they worked.

pardon The act of an appropriate authority releasing a guilty party from punishment.

Theologically, pardon is a judicial act of God, rooted in his character and based on the blood Jesus shed for the forgiveness of our sins (Mic. 7:18,19; Mt. 26:28; 1 Cor. 11:25). *See also* Atonement; Forgive; Justification.

parousia [Gk., "coming," "personal presence"]. In ordinary speech, this Greek

756

word meant a visit or the arrival of an important visitor (2 Cor. 7:6,7; Phil. 1:26). Theologically, *parousia* refers to Christ's Second Coming. In this context, it may reflect both major classical usages: an official visit by a person of high rank and the sudden appearance of a hidden deity. *See also* Second Coming.

partition *See* Middle Wall.

partridge A quick, shy, quail-like bird that lives in rocky areas and, when pursued, scurries along the ground.

David likened Saul's efforts to catch him to a partridge hunt (1 Sam. 26:20). To make a prophetic point, Jeremiah quoted a familiar proverb that reflected a common but mistaken notion that partridges stole the young of other birds. "Like a partridge that hatches eggs it did not lay is the man who gains riches by unjust means. When his life is half gone, they will desert him, and in the end he will prove to be a fool" (Jer. 17:11).

Passover (1) The historic meal shared by Hebrew families on the night God passed over the Jewish community but struck the firstborn of Egypt dead (Ex. 12,13). (2) An annual commemorative meal shared by Jewish families, which re-creates the meal eaten by the Jews in Egypt on the original Passover (Ex. 12:24-30). (3) The seven-day annual festival, celebrated by public sacrifices and private sharing of the Passover meal, continued for a week by eating only unleavened bread and concluded with another day of sacrifices and celebration (2 Chr. 30:1-27).

The significance of Passover is reflected in the fact that the month in which it occurs (Abib/Nisan) is the first month in the Hebrew religious calendar, and that Passover was one of three festivals for which all Jews were to come to Jerusalem to celebrate (Deut. 16:1,5-7). *See also* Feasts, Festivals, and Fasts.

THE HISTORIC EVENT

Moses commanded each Hebrew family to take a lamb into the household between the 10th and 14th of the month. On the evening of the 14th, the lamb was to be slaughtered and its blood sprinkled on the doorpost of the home. The meat was to be roasted and eaten, with any leftovers burned. On the night of the 14th, every firstborn son in Egypt died, but within the blood-marked homes, the Israelites were safe. That very night Pharaoh, his arro-

gance stripped away at last, summoned Moses and Aaron and, with all the Egyptians, "urged the people to hurry and leave the country" (Ex. 12:33).

God's action that first Passover night was the final stroke that shattered the chains of slavery forged by the Egyptians. Thus, the Passover (Heb., *pesah*) celebration today is rightly known as a "festival of freedom."

THE COMMEMORATIVE MEAL

Moses established the Passover as a "lasting ordinance for you and your descendants" (Ex. 12:24). Each Jewish family is to eat unleavened bread between the 14th and 21st. On the 14th, the family shares a meal like that eaten at the first Passover and observes the simple ritual found in Ex. 13:14-16 (*see* Ex. 12:26,27):

When your son asks you, "What does this mean?" say to him, "With a mighty hand the Lord brought us out of Egypt, out of the land of slavery. When Pharaoh stubbornly refused to let us go, the Lord killed every firstborn in Egypt, both man and animal."

Most significantly, Ex. 12:14 calls the people to "commemorate" (Heb., *zikaron*) the annual Passover meal. Thus, the meal is an invitation for each new generation to identify with what God did for their forefathers. Each new generation is to realize through this rite that they were in fact present in their ancestors when God acted

The partridge is an elusive game bird that lives in rocky terrain (see 1 Sam. 26:20).

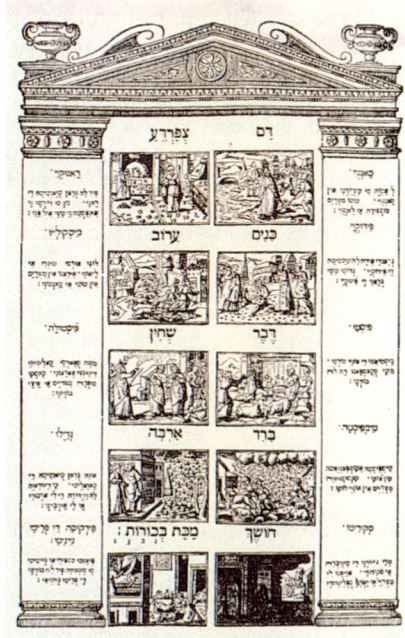

Page from a Venetian Haggadah ("narration"), printed in A.D. 1609, which displays the 13 symbols of the Feast of Passover in Ex. 12.

to make possible the freedom from slavery they now enjoy. *See also* Memorial.

THE PUBLIC FESTIVAL

The Law established Passover as a national as well as family festival (Deut. 16:2,5-7). The first and last days of Passover (the 14th and 21st) were to be marked by public celebration and sacrifice.

The OT mentions eight different Passover celebrations: (1) The original Passover (Ex. 12,13); (2) That of the second year of the Exodus (Num. 9:1-14); (3) Joshua's Passover at Gilgal (Josh. 5:10-12); (4) Celebrations during the late judges' period in Samuel's time (2 Ki. 23:22; 2 Chr. 35:18); (5) Solomon's Passover (1 Ki. 9:25; 2 Chr. 8:13; 30:26); (6) Hezekiah's Passover (2 Chr. 30:1-27); (7) Josiah's Passover (2 Ki. 23:21-23; 2 Chr. 35:1-19); (8) Zerubbabel's Passover (Ezra 6:19-22).

Each report of a Passover celebration conveys something of the sense of joy felt by the people of God as they recalled his mighty acts on their behalf and realized that they experienced freedom now only because of him.

PASSOVER IN THE NT

Passover was scrupulously observed in the first century, and thousands of Jews from all over the Roman world traveled to Jerusalem each year to celebrate there. The Last Supper that Jesus shared with his disciples was a Passover meal (Mt. 26:17-30; Mk. 14:12-26; Lk. 22:7-23). The symbolism is significant. A new "Passover lamb" was about to be sacrificed (Jn. 1:29; 1 Cor. 5:7), and through his death, Christ would win our ultimate freedom—freedom from the power and consequences of our sin. Just as the death of the first Passover lambs purchased safety for the Jews whose homes were marked by blood, so Jesus has purchased safety for all who rely on the merits of his sacrifice. *See also* Blood; Sacrifice.

pastor [Gk., *poimēn*, "shepherd"]. A leader of the church. "Pastor" occurs only in Eph. 4:11 and then in the plural. The verb, meaning "feed" or "take care of," is found twice: where Jesus tells Peter to "feed my lambs" (Jn. 21:15) and where Peter tells church elders to "be shepherds of God's flock" (1 Pet. 5:2).

Pastoral Epistles A name given in the early 18th century to three of Paul's letters: 1 and 2 Timothy and Titus. These three share much common vocabulary and address similar issues. They are also distinctive in that they were written toward the end of Paul's life to guide two younger leaders whom Paul had trained. *See also* Timothy; Titus.

patience In Greek, the capacity to remain self-controlled despite difficult circumstances or actions by others that might be expected to cause anger or upset.

God displays "kindness, tolerance, and patience" by withholding punishment in order to give unbelievers the opportunity to repent (Rom. 2:4; 9:22; 1 Tim. 1:16; 2 Pet. 3:15). This godly capacity is produced in believers by the Holy Spirit (Gal. 5:22). Patience is given priority in Paul's classic description of Christian love (1 Cor. 13:4) and is commended in no less than twelve of the NT Epistles. Taken together, NT references show that patience is a basic Christian attitude to be practiced in our relationships with others and exercised in difficult situations.

patriarch A "father" or chief ancestor of a tribe or race. The name is applied in the NT to David (Acts 2:29), the twelve sons of Jacob (Acts 7:8,9), and to Abraham (Heb. 7:4). However, "the patriarchs" were understood by the Jews to be Abraham, Isaac, and Jacob. Thus, the "patriarchal age" is the period from the birth of Abraham to the death of his grandson, Jacob. *See also* Chronology of the Bible.

> **Paul the Apostle** A zealous Pharisee who on conversion became Christianity's chief theologian and committed missionary to the Gentiles, A.D. 40s/50s. Paul's letters constitute about one-fourth of the New Testament. **Scripture:** Acts 8:1; 9,13–28; and the Pauline Epistles.

BACKGROUND

Paul was a Jew, born in the city of Tarsus, but trained in Jerusalem as a Pharisee under the most famous rabbi of his time, Gamaliel. Out of misplaced zeal, Paul actively persecuted followers of Christ, until he himself was converted by a direct confrontation with the risen Christ on the road to Damascus. According to his own testimony in Gal 1:17, he then "went immediately into Arabia and later returned to Damascus." This covered a period of three years.

Paul proved as zealous a Christian as he had been a persecutor. However, in Damascus and then in Jerusalem, Paul's presence stirred up so much opposition that he was forced to leave. "The brothers" escorted him to a ship and "sent him off to Tarsus" (Acts 9:30). Thus, Paul spent a

The apostle Paul, as depicted on the tomb of a Roman child named Asellus (about A.D. 313).

number of years—as many as ten—isolated from the main Christian movement in Palestine.

Later, Paul was invited by Barnabas to join the leadership team that guided the Gentile church at Antioch. After a time there, Barnabas and Paul were called by God to missionary service and set out to spread the Gospel in the Mediterranean world. As many responded eagerly to the Gospel, a number of predominantly Gentile churches were established throughout the empire. The mass movement among the Gentiles raised questions in the Jewish Christian community concerning the relationship of these Gentile Christians to OT Law. A church council held in Jerusalem determined that, since salvation was a matter of faith rather than works, Gentile believers were under no obligation to live by the Law God gave Israel or to adopt a Jewish life-style as a condition of acceptance into Christian fellowship.

Paul returned to the life of an itinerant missionary, breaking new ground and continuing to guide the congregations he had established. He wrote letters that are now part of our New Testament; he made personal visits; and he trained younger men like Timothy and Titus whom he sent to the churches as his personal representatives.

After nearly two decades of missionary work, Paul returned to Jerusalem. His presence caused a riot, and Paul's life was barely saved by the intervention of Roman soldiers. Paul defended himself against accusations made by the Jews but was kept under arrest by the Roman governors in Caesarea for some two years. Finally, Paul exercised his right as a Roman citizen and appealed to Caesar. After an eventful journey, Paul arrived in Rome. The Book

of Acts concludes at this point. However, suggestions in Paul's later Epistles and tradition indicate Paul was released, to be rearrested later and martyred during the reign of Nero. *See* Chronology of the Bible.

No review of the bare events of Paul's life can suggest how significant this one man was in the development of Christianity as a world religion. Even less can a review help us understand Paul as a human being. Yet in reading his Epistles, we gain insight into Paul as a person, and we sense the stunning impact of his thought and life in the early, critical decades of the Christian era.

PAUL AS A MISSIONARY

Physically, Paul was unremarkable. A second-century writing describes Paul as "a man of small stature, with bald head and crooked legs . . . with eyebrows meeting and nose somewhat hooked." Paul tacitly admits that his critics were right to say, "His letters are weighty and forceful, but in person he is unimpressive and his speaking amounts to nothing" (2 Cor. 10:10). Yet Paul developed an effective missionary strategy that enabled the new faith to penetrate multiple levels of first-century society, and he personally spearheaded the effort to communicate the faith to all in the Roman world.

Paul's strategy was to take a partner or a team to major cities, the political and economic hubs of the Roman provinces. There Paul first presented his message in the synagogue, reaching the Jews and the many Gentile "God-fearers" who had been attracted to the Jewish religion. From this group, Paul drew a core of believers. While he went on to evangelize the general population, Paul spent the bulk of his time teaching the new Christians. Then Paul

Facing profiles of Peter and Paul seem to reflect Paul's description of their conflict of Gal. 2:11: "I opposed him to his face, because he was in the wrong." Unfinished relief, 4th century A.D.

Roman city gate of Tarsus, birthplace of Paul. His family probably had lived there for a few generations as the Roman citizenship of Tarsian Jews dates to General Pompey's settlement, 65–64 B.C.

Christ, died to pay for human sins and was raised again to bring new life to believers; and he (2) developed close and loving personal relationships with the new believers. Later, Paul could remind the Thessalonians, "We were gentle among you, like a mother caring for her little children. We loved you so much that we were delighted to share with you not only the gospel of God but our lives as well, because you had become so dear to us" (1 Th. 2:7,8). (3) When demonic opposition was strong, Paul demonstrated the power of Christ through healing and other signs (Acts 19:11-20).

Paul's life as a missionary was a hard one, with little monetary help. In fact, Paul often worked at his tentmaking trade to pay his own way in the cities where he ministered. The great apostle recounted the personal cost of his commitment to spreading the Gospel:

I have worked much harder, been in prison more frequently, been flogged more severely, and been exposed to death again and again. Five times I received from the Jews the forty lashes minus one. Three times I was beaten with rods, once I was stoned, three times I was shipwrecked, I spent a night and a day in the open sea, I have been constantly on the move. I have been in danger from rivers, in danger from bandits, in danger from my own countrymen, in danger from Gentiles; in danger in the city, in danger in the country, in danger at sea; and in danger from false

and his missionary team moved on, leaving the new local congregation to build on the foundation he had laid. It would be the responsibility of this young church to reach out to others in the city and to reach the province at large (1 Th. 1:4-10).

Paul often revisited the churches he founded. He wrote circular letters of instruction and sent itinerant teachers and prophets to visit. But essentially each new congregation, led by local leaders, learned to rely on the Holy Spirit as it worked out local problems, guided by the OT, the apostolic letters, and local prophets and teachers.

In carrying out this strategy, Paul: (1) preached a simple Gospel, proclaiming forgiveness and reconciliation to God available to all because God's Son, Jesus

brothers. I have labored and toiled and have often gone without sleep; I have known hunger and thirst and have often gone without food; I have been cold and naked. Besides everything else, I face daily the pressure of my concern for all the churches. Who is weak, and I do not feel weak? Who is led into sin, and I do not inwardly burn?

(2 Cor. 11:23-29)

PAUL AS A THEOLOGIAN

At first, faith in Jesus seemed to fit easily within the framework of Judaism. Christ was, after all, the Messiah promised in the OT and the subject of many OT prophecies. Hebrew Christians, confident that God had spoken both in Moses and Christ, simply maintained the life-style commanded in the Mosaic Law while worshiping Jesus as Lord. For many years, Christianity was known as "the Way" and was viewed by the general populace and by Roman officials as a sect of Judaism, and thus a "licit" (officially sanctioned) religion.

However, as more and more Gentiles were converted and predominantly Gentile churches were established outside Palestine, questions arose. Was a Gentile Christian responsible to keep the Mosaic Law and, thus in effect, to become a Jew in order to be a Christian? What would become of Moses and the old order?

As apostle to the Gentiles, Paul fought to keep the Gospel uncluttered and resisted the efforts of some Christian Pharisees to impose Mosaic Law on new converts. Paul was a delegate to the Jerusalem Council, which considered this issue and which determined that the Law was "a yoke that neither we nor our fathers have been able to bear." The Council determined that "we should not make it difficult for the Gentiles who are turning to God" (Acts 15:10,19) and that in essence a person need not live like a Jew to be a good Christian. *See also* Council of Jerusalem.

Yet the determination of the Jerusalem Council did not explain why the Christian is free from Law, nor did it explain the inner workings of the new faith. It is here that Paul made his unique contribution. Paul, more than any other, presents a distinctive Christian theology, one that is consistent with and yet supplants the theology of the OT. Paul says this Gospel came to him directly "through a revelation of Jesus Christ" (Gal. 1:11,12; *see* Rom. 16:25,26; Eph. 3:2-12), and yet it was in full harmony with the teaching of the other apostles (Rom. 6:17; 1 Cor. 11:23; 15:3-5,11; Gal. 2:6-10).

1. *Christology.* Paul's exalted view of Jesus dominates his Epistles. Jesus is God made flesh (Phil. 2; Col. 1). The resurrected Jesus is Lord, the ultimate power in the universe (1 Cor. 15; Eph. 1). Christ provides salvation and power for righteous living to those who have a personal relationship with him through faith (Rom. 6–8; Gal. 2,3).

2. *Salvation.* Human beings are sinners who merit and are under the judgment of God. Yet God's love moved him to send his Son Jesus to die in our place. God offers salvation as a free gift to all who entrust themselves to Jesus. Salvation is thus a matter of grace, not of works. Those who trust Jesus as Savior are not only forgiven but are also given new, spiritual life (Rom. 5; Eph. 2).

3. *Righteousness.* God's saving work does more than impute righteousness to the sinner. God through his Holy Spirit actively operates in the believer to make him or her a righteous person. This work of God is best understood as a transformation of character toward Christ's own likeness; a transformation that will be complete only in the resurrection that Christ guarantees to those who believe in him. For this reason, those who are Christians are to "live a life of love" (Eph. 5:2) and to be "eager to do what is good" (Tit. 2:14; *see* Rom. 6,8; 1 Cor. 3).

4. *The Law.* The function of OT Law was

View of the NT harbor city of Miletus, where Paul bid an emotional farewell to the elders of the church in Ephesus before setting out for Jerusalem (Acts 20:13-38).

the OT. Paul's pattern of faith and life is designed not for a nation but rather for scattered colonies of God's people in a hostile world.

PAUL AS A HUMAN BEING

In some circles, it remains popular to portray Paul as a narrow, chauvinistic zealot, an idealogue more concerned with theology than with people. The image could hardly be more distorted.

As a zealous Pharisee and as a new Christian, Paul was undoubtedly abrasive, arousing such passions in his enemies that more than one group was determined to murder him (Acts 9:23,29). While he later mellowed, Paul never lost the boldness that made him willing to confront a rioting mob (Acts 19:30), fellow Christians (Acts 15; Gal. 2:11-21), the Jewish ruling council (Acts 23:1-10), or the powerful men who administered the Roman Empire (Acts 25,26). And Paul could be harsh, expecting others to show his own total commitment (Acts 15:36-41).

Yet Paul was tender and loving in dealing with the churches. He expressed his concern in constant prayers and in person, finding time to deal "with each of you [new believers] as a father deals with his own children, encouraging, comforting and urging you to live lives worthy of

Above: In this painting by Rembrandt van Rijn, Paul sits at his writing desk, deep in thought.

not to make a person righteous but to reveal man's need for salvation. Anyone who seeks to win God's favor by works falls into a trap and misuses Law. However, a person who follows the promptings of the Holy Spirit and relies on Christ rather than his or her own efforts will live the godly kind of life the Law describes (Rom. 8; Gal. 5).

5. *The Church.* The Church is the mystical Body of Christ, first a living organism and secondarily an organization. Each believer is united to Christ and, through him, to every other believer. Spiritual growth takes place as Jesus ministers through the spiritual gifts given to believers. Active participation in a local assembly is vital in order for the Body of Christ to be built up and to have unity (Rom. 12; 1 Cor. 12; Eph. 4).

6. *The Future.* Christians are to live godly lives in this present world, looking expectantly for the return of Christ. When Christ does return, he will take believers to be with him, punish sinners, and establish righteousness (1 Th. 4; 2 Th. 1,2).

Paul's teachings provide a framework within which Christian faith and life are seen to be in harmony with, yet distinct from, the system of faith and life found in

Previous page: In the daylight after the night's storm, the ship carrying Paul to Rome was wrecked on a sandbar of a small bay on Malta, but not one person on board was lost (Acts 27:27-44).

Below: The apostle Paul is led by soldiers to his execution as depicted in a relief from the sarcophagus of Junius Bassus (4th century A.D.).

764

Left: The great theater at Ephesus, where the craftsmen whose wealth depended on the sale of religious medals of Artemis rioted in protest of Paul's preaching (Acts 19:23-41).

Above: The Appian Way, one of the main roads out of Rome. Paul traveled on one of its branches from the port of Puteoli to Rome for his trial (Acts 28:11-16).
Left: Ruins of the Mamertine Prison, the state jail in Rome where, according to tradition, Paul was imprisoned a second time.

God" (1 Th. 2:11,12). Even when writing to the rebellious congregation at Corinth, where many openly challenged his authority, Paul displayed a striking openness and vulnerability while still challenging the Corinthians over their wrong attitudes (2 Cor. 1:3-11; 4:7-18; 12:11–13:10).

Paul's relationships with his fellow workers were close and intimate. Paul calls Timothy his "dear son" (2 Tim. 1:2), Titus his "true son in our common faith" (Tit. 1:4), Luke a "dear friend" (Col. 4:14), Epaphroditus "my brother, fellow worker and fellow soldier" (Phil. 2:25), and Philemon a "dear friend and fellow worker" (Phlm. 1). Paul commends "our sister Phoebe, a servant of the church in Cenchrea" who "has been a great help to many people, including me" (Rom. 16:1,2). In fact, among the people Paul asks to be remembered to are many women—a rather strange thing if Paul were the confirmed chauvinist many suppose. *See also* Women.

Personally, Paul was committed to the goal of taking hold of "that for which Christ Jesus took hold of me" (Phil. 3:12). He lived for Christ and unstintingly gave himself for others, not for personal gain or glory. Paul was not without his faults. However, the man we meet in Paul's letters is more than a towering intellect and missionary statesman: He is a warm and very human man, a friend who loved and who earned the love of others in return; a person who modeled, not just preached, Jesus' transforming love.

pavilion A tent, booth, or canopy. The Hebrew term, *sukah,* refers to any temporary shelter, such as tents used by an army on the march (1 Ki. 20:12) or the lean-to of branches constructed during the Feast of Tabernacles. Figuratively, the expanse of heaven is compared to a pavilion God erected for the sun (Ps. 19:5; *see* Job 36:29).

pattern *See* Type.

peace (1) Wholeness, unity, harmony; (2) prosperity, health, and fulfillment; (3) theologically, inner harmony and harmonious interpersonal relationships with others made possible by a personal relationship with God.

OLD TESTAMENT

In the narrative books of the OT, "peace" (Heb., *shalom*) is a lack of interpersonal or international strife and the well-being this brings (Gen. 26:29; Josh. 10:1-4). This meaning is well illustrated in 1 Ki. 4:24,25: With peace on all sides, Israel "lived in safety, each man under his own vine and fig tree."

The prophets and the Book of Psalms extend the concept of *shalom*. Because of David's relationship with God, he was able to "lie down and sleep in peace" despite imminent danger from the forces of his rebel son, Absalom (Ps. 4:8). In contrast, the wicked are in constant inner turmoil. They are "like the tossing sea, which cannot rest, whose waves cast up mire and mud. 'There is no peace,' says my God, 'for the wicked'" (Isa. 57:20,21). Here peace is not an absence of external strife but an inner calm, a sense of security that does not depend on external circumstances. In the Psalms and prophets, this peace is found by living in accord with God and his Word (Pss. 37:35-37; 119:165).

The OT also describes the price to be paid for inner peace. Isaiah 53:5 portrays the work of the Messiah, saying, "He was crushed for our iniquities; the punishment that brought us peace was upon him, and by his wounds we are healed."

In addition to inner peace, the prophets foresee an era of international and interpersonal peace on earth. The Messiah, who will establish this peace, is called the "Prince of Peace." One day his rule will be established, and "of the increase of his government and peace there will be no end" (Isa. 9:6,7).

NEW TESTAMENT

The conviction that "peace" depends on relationship with God is carried over into the NT. In Greek society, *eirēnē* was originally the state of order and prosperity made possible by the absence of war. Only later did philosophers extend the concept to one's psychological state.

The NT writers use "peace" in broad, inclusive ways. God is "the God of Peace." God is the source of a total peace that believers can experience now through a personal relationship with Christ (Rom. 15:33; 16:20; 1 Cor. 14:33; Phil. 4:9; Heb. 13:20). The peace that Christ brings has various aspects:

1. *It is peace with God (Rom. 5:1-11).* We are no longer God's enemies, but in Christ we have been reconciled to him.

2. *It is an inner peace, independent of external circumstances.* Jesus said, "Peace I leave with you; my peace I give you. I do not give to you as the world gives. Do not let your hearts be troubled and do not be afraid" (Jn. 14:27).

3. *It is a harmonious relationship among believers.* Paul describes this aspect of God's peace as "compassion, kindness, humility, gentleness and patience," with a mixture of forbearance and forgiveness, motivated by love. This peace binds a church together in "perfect unity." The apostle urges, "Let the peace of Christ rule in your hearts, since as members of one body you were called to peace. And be thankful" (Col. 3:12-15).

4. *It is relative harmony with the non-Christian world around us.* James describes the God-given wisdom we are to apply daily as "peace-loving" (3:17,18). And the writer of Hebrews urges, "Make every effort to live in peace with all men" (12:14; *see* Rom. 14:19).

5. *Peace in the NT is **not** international.* There is no promise of harmony between nations. In fact, Jesus warned that throughout this age "nation will rise against nation, and kingdom against kingdom" (Mt. 24:6,7). Not until the God of peace crushes Satan will the world know final rest from war (Rom. 16:20).

The biblical concept of "peace" is total and profound. It touches on our relationship with God, with our inner self, with other believers, and with the world at large. Biblically, peace is no mere absence of strife but the active experience of a harmony that promotes total well-being. Peace is always the product of God's active involvement in our lives, and God's intervention is essential, for sin has so marred individuals and society that strife is our constant companion. Only God's saving work can bring us an experience of his peace.

peace offering An offering made following a sacrifice for sin. Part of the offering (Heb., *shelem*) was burned and part was eaten by the offerer. Participating in the sacrificial meal symbolized the fellowship the now-forgiven worshiper experienced with God. Some versions call this a "fellowship offering." *See also* Fellowship.

peacock (KJV) A beautifully feathered bird native to India and Ceylon. Peacocks were imported into Egypt prior to the age of Solomon, but most believe the Hebrew word translated "peacock" in 1 Ki. 10:22 and 2 Chr. 9:21 (KJV) actually means "baboon." The bird called a peacock in Job

39:13 (KJV) is actually an ostrich. *See also* Ape; Ostrich.

pearl The only gem taken from the sea or formed within a living organism. Pearls are lustrous, milky-white or black objects formed when oysters coat irritating grains of sand or other foreign objects with layers of a protective secretion.

In the NT, pearls are found in lists of valuables and luxuries (1 Tim. 2:9; Rev. 17:4; 18:12,16). Each of the twelve gates of the New Jerusalem is "a single pearl" (Rev. 21:21). Jesus likened the Kingdom of heaven to a priceless pearl, for which a person will surrender all he or she has.

peg A short, pointed item used as a fastener. The ropes of tents were attached to the ground with tent pegs (Ex. 27:19). Isaiah records God's promise regarding the civil servant Eliakim: "I will drive him like a peg into a firm place." This may depict a peg pounded into a wooden wall as a support, perhaps for a shelf. Isaiah continues: "All the glory of his family will hang on him" (22:23,24).

pelican (KJV) A large water bird with webbed feet and a pouched lower beak. The bird called a pelican in the KJV of Lev. 11:18 and Deut. 14:17 was more likely a type of owl, hawk, or vulture.

pence, penny (KJV) The Roman *denarius*, a silver coin, representing a day's wages for a common laborer. The KJV sometimes calls this a "penny." However, modern versions use the word "penny" for smaller copper coins of little value. *See also* Money.

Pentateuch The first five books of the OT, called "the Book of the Law" or simply "the Torah" by the Jews. These books are the primary authority in Judaism, taking

Pearl-laden, ivory bust of a Jewish woman of the 9th–8th centuries B.C. Her adornment exemplifies the decadent affluence that Isaiah, Amos, and others prophesied against.

priority over all later works in the OT canon.

Moses is the traditional author of all five of the books, with the exception of brief sections such as Deut. 34:5-8, which describes his death. Both Testaments ascribe authorship to him (2 Chr. 25:4; Neh. 8:1; Mk. 12:26; Acts 15:5).

Mosaic authorship was not questioned until the 18th century, when liberal scholars challenged the historical accuracy of the OT. They asserted that these books could not possibly have been written before about 850 B.C. For instance, they said that no sophisticated written language existed in Moses' time. But more recent archaeological finds have revealed hundreds of documents in a script related to the later Hebrew script that were written about 2500 B.C., a thousand years before the traditional date of Moses and the Exodus. Archaeology has further demonstrated that OT customs and laws accurately reflect the culture of the periods the Pentateuch portrays.

However, the view that the books of Moses are later reconstructions from a variety of earlier documents persists among critical scholars. Theological conservatives consider these theories speculative. Most conservatives continue to believe that the Pentateuch in its present form is essentially the work of Moses, but do agree that Moses had access to both oral and written material from earlier times. The conservative conviction is supported by internal evidence and by the unbroken early tradition of Mosaic authorship. *See also* Interpretation of Scripture.

This Samaritan Torah scroll, which contains the Pentateuch in Samaritan script, dates to the 12th century A.D. The Pentateuch was the only Scripture accepted by the Samaritans.

Pentecost The OT "Feast of Weeks" (Ex. 34:22), which was held 50 days after Passover (Pentecost in Greek means "fiftieth"). By the first century A.D., it had become largely a celebration of God's giving of the Law to Moses. The Holy Spirit came visibly upon Jesus' disciples during the Pentecost after Christ's resurrection, an event generally understood to mark the birthday of the Church.

OLD TESTAMENT FESTIVAL

The Feast of Weeks marked the end of the grain harvest. It was a joyful thanksgiving festival acknowledging God as the source of blessing. A sheaf of wheat was waved before the Lord, representing the grain harvested throughout Israel; specified sacrifices were offered; and the Israelites were encouraged to make voluntary offerings from the surplus of their harvest (Lev. 23:15-22; Num. 28:26-31; Deut. 16:9-12).

Pentecost was one of three pilgrim festivals that every adult male in Israel was expected to attend. Other names given this harvest festival include the "day of firstfruits" (Num. 28:26) and "Feast of Harvest" (Ex. 23:16). *See also* Feasts, Festivals, and Fasts.

THE ACTS 2 EVENT

Acts 2 describes an event that took place on the Pentecost immediately following Christ's resurrection.

Jesus had told his disciples, "Do not leave Jerusalem, but wait for the gift my Father promised . . . in a few days you will be baptized with the Holy Spirit" (Acts 1:4,5). The promise was fulfilled on Pentecost:

When the day of Pentecost came, they were all together in one place. Suddenly a sound like the blowing of a violent wind came from heaven and filled the whole house where they were sitting. They saw what seemed to be tongues of fire that separated and came to rest on each of them. All of them were filled with the Holy Spirit and began to speak in other tongues as the Spirit enabled them.

(Acts 2:1-4)

While the wind and fire have OT parallels (1 Ki. 18:38; 19:11-13; Ezek. 37:9-14), tongues-speaking was a new, though possibly predicted, phenomenon (Isa. 28:11). *See also* Tongues.

These signs attracted a crowd, which was amazed because "each one heard them speaking in his own language" (Acts 2:6). This provided Peter with the opportunity to preach Christianity's first evangelistic sermon (Acts 2:14-41).

THE MEANING OF PENTECOST

Peter explained that what the stunned observers had witnessed was the outpouring of the Spirit promised by the prophet Joel (2:28-32). Other references, such as Acts 11:15 and 1 Cor. 12:13, suggest that the Spirit's coming marked the birth of the Church as the Body of Christ. At this point, the Holy Spirit, who empowered Jesus, became the living source of supernatural power for believers as well.

Charismatic Christians, who emphasize the importance of the ministry of the Holy Spirit to and through the believer, have emphasized the necessity of a "personal Pentecost" for each believer. Some view speaking in tongues as *the* sign of the Holy Spirit's presence in the Christian's life (*but see* 1 Cor. 12). *See also* Holy Spirit.

perdition (KJV) Destruction. Judas, called the "son of perdition" in Jn. 17:12 (KJV), is described as "the one doomed to [eternal] destruction," a term otherwise reserved for the Antichrist and his followers (2 Th. 2:3; Rev. 17:8,11).

perfect, perfection Wholeness and completeness. When used to describe any creature, "perfect" emphasizes the achievement of whatever level of maturity or morality can be expected, given the nature of a plant, animal, or person.

"PERFECTION" IN THEOLOGY

The call of Jesus to "be perfect, therefore, as your heavenly Father is perfect" (Mt. 5:48) has challenged and concerned Christians. Does Christ demand that the believer live a sinless life?

In the Wesleyan tradition, which defines "sin" as conscious and willful disobedience of the known will of God, the call to perfection is understood as an invitation to total submission to God's will. Even

though all fall short of complete Christlikeness through ignorance or natural limitations, the believer is "perfect" if he or she is not willfully disobedient.

In other traditions, sin is understood to include unintentional as well as willful failures. These traditions deny the possibility of a sinless perfection, noting that the NT says, "If we claim to be without sin, we deceive ourselves and the truth is not in us" (1 Jn. 1:8), and, "We all stumble in many ways" (Jas. 3:2).

Thus one's theological concept of Christian perfection may depend on which tradition he or she holds.

"PERFECTION" IN THE NT

The Greek word for "perfect," used by Jesus and the NT writers, is *teleios*. When applied to people, it means "fulfilled, mature, or fully equipped for a task" (*compare* Col. 1:28). Most NT passages use "perfect" and "perfection" in the sense of a potential to be experienced or of a maturity to be achieved.

There are exceptions. Some eschatological passages use "perfection" in an absolute sense (1 Cor. 13:10). John speaks of "perfect love," meaning a love that completely fills the believer and thus leaves no room for fear (1 Jn. 4:18). Hebrews speaks of Christ being "made perfect" (Heb. 5:9). Here the meaning is simply that Jesus' obedience qualified him fully for the role of Savior. The OT Law "made nothing perfect" in that it was unable to bring to completion the ministry of salvation symbolized in its sacrifices. But Jesus accomplished this task in his one sacrifice, making believers "perfect forever" (Heb. 7:28; 10:1,14).

Yet when Paul says, "Our prayer is for your perfection," and urges his readers to "aim for perfection" (2 Cor. 13:9,11), the focus is placed squarely on Christian maturity and hope—hope, because personal relationship with Jesus Christ opens the door to a better future, a future in which we can grow to become more like the Savior, more like the good and loving person each of us yearns to be.

perfume A compound in the form of powder, liquid, incense, or ointment formulated and valued for its sweet scent. *See also* Incense; Ointment.

In Bible times, people used perfumes of every kind, sometimes carrying dried spices in bags worn under clothing as sachets (Song 1:13) or in bottles (Isa. 3:20). Liquids and ointments were contained in flasks and jars (Mk. 14:3; Lk. 7:37).

Panel from the Verdun Altar gives a highly stylized view of the tongues of fire resting on each of the apostles; Klosterneuburg Abbey, Austria, A.D. 1180.

Egyptian perfume production techniques recorded in relief on a 17th-century B.C. sarcophagus. In Bible times, perfumes and scented oils were used to counteract body odors. Inset: Typical perfume vial (Gk., alabastron) from NT times with a long, narrow neck and lobed body.

Perfumed ointment served as a sacred anointing oil (Ex. 30:22-33) and perfumed incense had an important role in Israel's rituals of worship (Ex. 30:34-38). The formula for these fragrances was sacred and could be used only in ritual settings.

Perfumed oils were put on the body to soften the skin and mask unpleasant odors (Ruth 3:3; Ps. 45:8; Ezek. 16:9; Lk. 7:38). Then as now perfumes were worn as an aid to love-making (Esth. 2:12; Prov. 7:17; Song 1:12-14; 5:5). Perfumed oil was often poured on the feet or heads of banquet guests, and even dead bodies were wrapped in spices (2 Chr. 16:14; Jn. 19:39,40).

A number of different spices are mentioned as ingredients in perfumes. Among them are aloes, bdellium, calmus, cassia, cinnamon, frankincense, myrrh, nard, onycha, and saffron.

Preparing perfumes called for special skill. The Bible suggests that some who fled Egypt in the Exodus were perfume-makers (Ex. 30:25,35). There were perfumers in Israel when the monarchy was established (1 Sam. 8:13) and among those who returned to Judea after the Babylonian Captivity (Neh. 3:8). The mention of perfumers at every stage of OT history testifies to the significant role perfumes played in the life of men and women in ancient times.

perfumery See Apothecary.

perish (1) To be destroyed (Heb., 'abad), physical death rather than eternal punishment (2 Ki. 9:8). (2) To experience final loss (Gk., apollumi). The Greek word can mean merely physical death but often has to do with eternal judgment (Rom. 2:12). Yet 2 Pet. 3:9 reminds us that God is patient and withholds judgment, "not wanting anyone to perish, but everyone to come to repentance." (3) To vanish (Gk., aphanizō). Earthly treasures are not simply lost, but disappear completely (Mt. 6:19, 20; Acts 13:41; Jas. 4:14).

perjure, perjury (1) To lie while under an oath to tell the truth; (2) to break any oath (1 Tim. 1:10).

The Law of Israel stated, "If the witness [in a civil or criminal case] proves to be a liar, giving false testimony against his brother, then do to him as he intended to do to his brother. . . . The rest of the people will hear of this and be afraid, and never again will such an evil thing be done among you" (Deut. 19:18-20).

persecution Formal or widespread hostility directed against a particular group; harassment or injury, especially for reasons of religion or race.

There are many examples of persecution in the OT, dating from the oppression of the Israelites in Egypt to Haman's attempt during the Persian period to exterminate the Jews (see also Esther). It was not unusual in the second and first centuries B.C. for Jewish communities in major cities of the Roman Empire outside of Palestine to experience persecution.

After a few peaceful early years (Acts

770

2:47; 5:12-16,33-39), the Christian church began to experience persecution from the Jews. The death of Stephen (Acts 6,7) marks the hardening of the opposition. Christians were driven out of Jerusalem (Acts 8:1-3), and arrest orders were issued by the Sanhedrin for Jewish Christians in other cities (Acts 9:1,2). In A.D. 44, King Herod Agrippa "arrested some who belonged to the church, intending to persecute them," and executed James, the brother of John. This greatly pleased his Jewish population (Acts 12:1-3). Jewish opposition continues through the Book of Acts, and hostile Jews frequently followed the apostles on their missionary ventures, "agitating the crowds and stirring them up" (Acts 17:13).

At first, the Roman government treated Christianity as a sect of Judaism. As such, Christianity was a "licit" (legal) religion, and Christians were even protected from mob action by the government (Acts 19:23-41; 21:30-32). However, with the growing recognition that this sect was not Jewish but something radically new, tolerance was gradually replaced by hostility. Nero blamed the Christians for the fire that devastated Rome in A.D. 64, but the general population was already growing hostile toward them. By A.D. 112, a person who refused to recant his Christian faith and demonstrate his patriotism by burning incense at a government shrine could be executed. Though Christianity became "outlawed" under a general ban on unauthorized organizations, the governors of the various provinces could not actively search out Christians, so the intensity of persecution varied throughout the Empire.

It was clear by the middle of the first century that intensified persecution lay ahead. Jesus had warned, "If they persecuted me, they will persecute you also" (Jn. 15:20), and Paul taught believers not to "be unsettled" by such trials, knowing "quite well that we were destined for them" (1 Th. 3:1-5). Full commitment to God may arouse hostility in any society whose values are contrary to his will (Mt. 5:11,12; Lk. 11:49; 21:12).

Several NT passages instruct Christians on how to respond to persecution. Believers are to endure (1 Cor. 4:12) and also to love and pray for their persecutors (Mt. 5:44; Rom. 12:14). Peter reminds readers not to be surprised at fiery trials, "but rejoice that you participate in the sufferings of Christ, so that you may be overjoyed when his glory is revealed" (1 Pet.

4:13). When believers do right and persecution still arises "because of the name of Christ," the persecuted "should commit themselves to their faithful Creator and continue to do good" (4:19).

perseverance Enduring hardships with patience and persistence. In the NT, perseverance is a character trait, the strength to keep on despite disappointments and difficulties. In theology, the "perseverance of the saints" is the doctrine that those who have experienced salvation will not subsequently be lost. However, the word "perseverance" is not used in this theological sense in the NT.

As a character trait, perseverance is desirable, even though it comes through painful experiences. As the apostle Paul says, "Suffering produces perseverance; perseverance, character; and character, hope" (Rom. 5:3,4; Jas. 1:3,4). The writer of Hebrews reflects the NT perspective that, while this world is important, the only true measure of things is eternity. Thus he says, "Do not throw away your confidence; it will be richly rewarded. You need to persevere so that when you have done the will of God, you will receive what he has promised" (Heb. 10:35,36).

A Roman oil lamp stamped with the word PAX ("peace") sits in front of a painting of the martyrdom of Florian, a Roman officer under Emperor Diocletian (A.D. 304). While the Roman Empire generally afforded its citizens peace, there was widespread hostility toward Christians and this frequently flared into persecution.

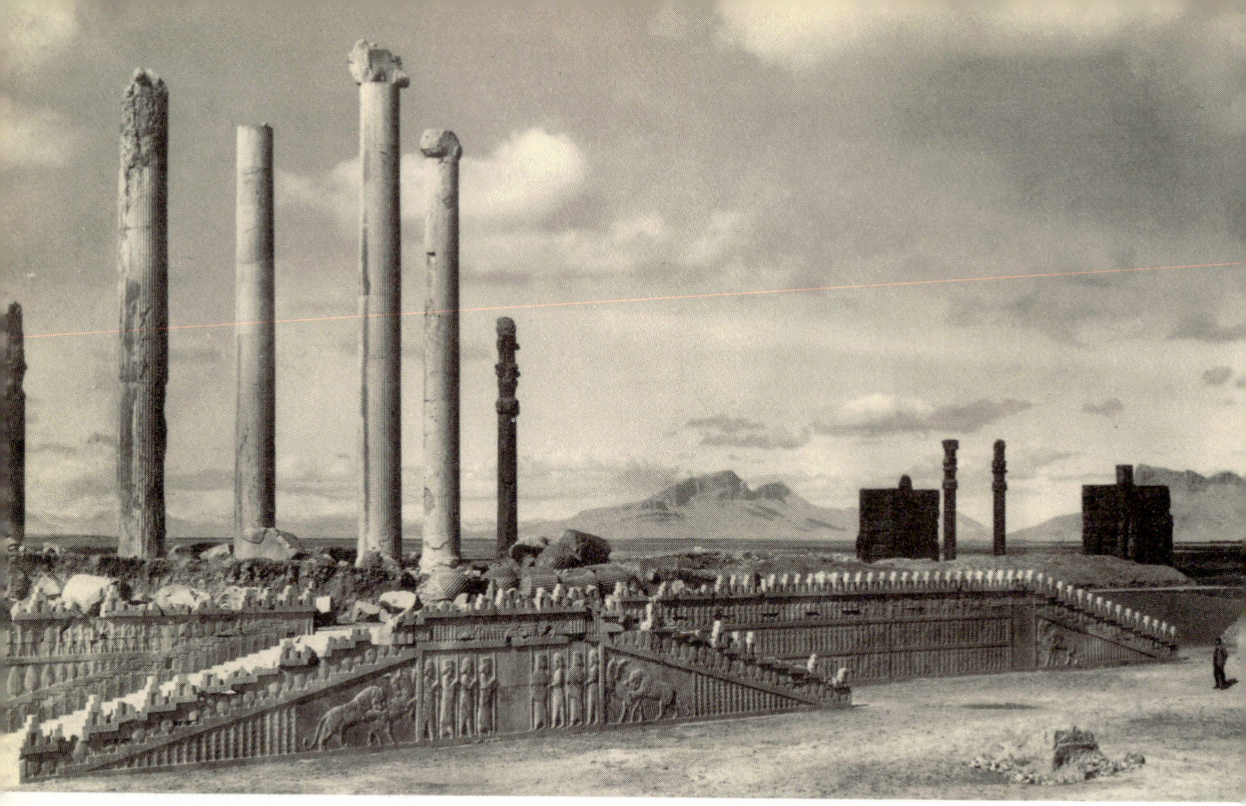

Above: Panoramic view of the platform on which the royal buildings of the Persian capital, Persepolis, were constructed. King Darius I, "the Great," began building at the end of the 6th century B.C. with a massive audience hall (Apadana) to the right of the equally large double staircase shown at center.

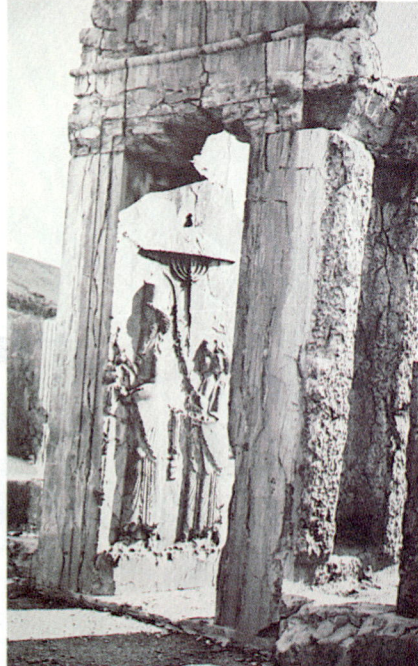

Persia An empire dominating the ancient world between 550 and 330 B.C. Along with the Medes, the Persians carved a mountain kingdom in what is now northwestern Iran. The Medes cooperated with the Babylonians in the sack of Nineveh in 612 B.C., and a Median princess married Nebuchadnezzar. For this princess, Amytis, Nebuchadnezzar built the famous hanging gardens.

A gateway into the Persian winter palace at Persepolis. The summer capital of Susa is the setting for the story of Esther, but very little has survived from the brick palace there.

In 549 B.C., Cyrus became king of Persia and revolted against his Median overlord. He succeeded in uniting the two powers, and in a series of campaigns, Cyrus extended authority over most of Asia Minor. He then attacked Babylon, and with surprising ease defeated the city in 539 B.C. He took over the vast Babylonian Empire, and for the next 200 years, Persia dominated the East.

Cyrus the Great was an enlightened and diplomatic ruler and a good administrator. Among his other reforms, Cyrus permitted the peoples deported by the Babylonians to return to their homelands. While some 50,000 Jews returned to Judea, many more remained in Mesopotamia, and vigorous Jewish communities existed in most of its major cities throughout the Persian period. The religion of the Persians was Zoroastrianism, a faith which promised blessing in this life to those who worshiped Ahura Mazda, the good god of light, who was opposed by an opposite, evil deity. Yet the Persians tolerated a number of other religions, including those of India as well as Judaism, within their Empire.

Cyrus was followed by other talented rulers. Darius (522–485 B.C.) further extended the Empire, created a network of roads, and devised an effective administration for his many provinces. The ruins of his palace at Persepolis are some of the region's most spectacular. Xerxes I (486–465 B.C.) is most probably the ruler of

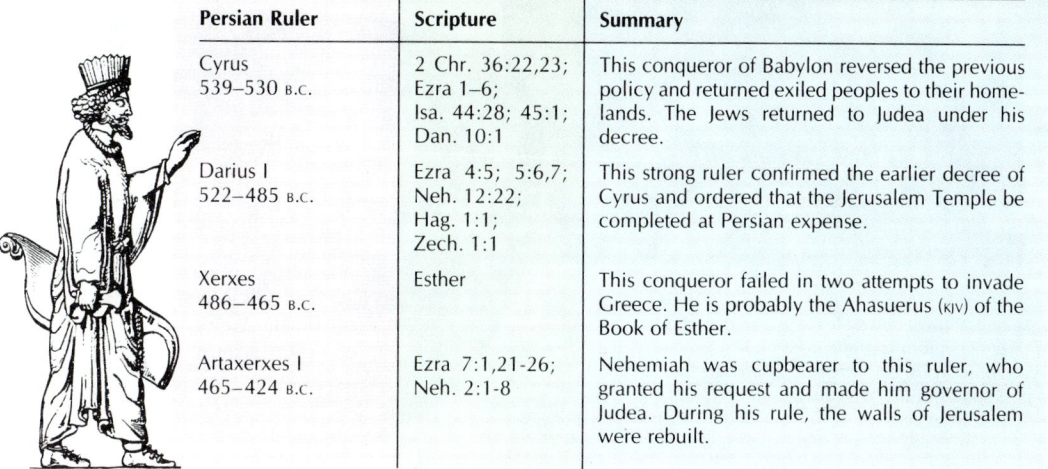

Right: The Persian Empire at the height of its extent under Darius the Great (522–485 B.C.). Below: Satellite photograph of the Persian Gulf. The Persian Empire had its center in the east in an area still called Parsistan.

ATHENS •
• PERGAMUM
• TARSUS
JERUSALEM •
BABYLON
• SUSA
MEMPHIS •

MI 0   200   400
KM 0   200   400

PERSIAN RULERS IN THE SCRIPTURES

Persian Ruler	Scripture	Summary
Cyrus 539–530 B.C.	2 Chr. 36:22,23; Ezra 1–6; Isa. 44:28; 45:1; Dan. 10:1	This conqueror of Babylon reversed the previous policy and returned exiled peoples to their homelands. The Jews returned to Judea under his decree.
Darius I 522–485 B.C.	Ezra 4:5; 5:6,7; Neh. 12:22; Hag. 1:1; Zech. 1:1	This strong ruler confirmed the earlier decree of Cyrus and ordered that the Jerusalem Temple be completed at Persian expense.
Xerxes 486–465 B.C.	Esther	This conqueror failed in two attempts to invade Greece. He is probably the Ahasuerus (KJV) of the Book of Esther.
Artaxerxes I 465–424 B.C.	Ezra 7:1,21-26; Neh. 2:1-8	Nehemiah was cupbearer to this ruler, who granted his request and made him governor of Judea. During his rule, the walls of Jerusalem were rebuilt.

Two guards, a Persian (right) and a Mede (left), from the bas relief of the palace stairway at Persepolis in Iran. Though Cyrus II overthrew Median domination in 549 B.C., Persia continued to be strongly influenced by the Medes.

the Book of Esther, best-known in secular history for his failed invasions of Greece in the 480s B.C. Several ineffective rulers followed Xerxes, and despite its immense size and resources, Persia was crushed by Alexander the Great and his small army in the 330s B.C.

IMPACT ON BIBLE HISTORY

In Isa. 45:1, Cyrus is called God's anointed, a term indicating God's specific choice of Cyrus to perform a task that would benefit God's people. Calling Cyrus by name, the Lord says, "He is my shepherd and will accomplish all that I please; he will say of Jerusalem, 'Let it be rebuilt,' and of the Temple, 'Let its foundations be laid' " (Isa. 44:28).

In 539 B.C., the year Cyrus took Babylon, he issued just such a decree, leading to the return of many Jews to Judea (Ezra 1–7). Later, Darius I confirmed this decree and encouraged completion of the Temple in 516 B.C., the time of Haggai and Zechariah.

While individuals like Daniel and Esther lived at the center of Persian power, little Judea was relatively unaffected by what happened within the larger empire, exceptwhen Nehemiah served as Persian governor (430s B.C.) and actively promoted the welfare of Jerusalem.

persuade To convince (Gk., *peithō*). In the NT, the process of persuasion is usually an attempt to influence others to believe in or obey the Gospel (Acts 18:4; 19:8). The same process may be used against Christianity (Gal. 5:8). In the passive voice, "to be persuaded" logically means "to believe" (Lk. 20:6; 2 Tim. 1:5). A different Greek word, *plērophoreō*, emphasizes complete conviction, like that of Abraham, who thoughtfully considered his and Sarah's advanced age and yet was "fully persuaded that God had power to do what he had promised" regarding Isaac's birth (Rom. 4:21).

pestilence (KJV) A disastrous epidemic. Such devastating events are generally viewed in the OT as a punishment reserved for rebellion in Israel or for Israel's enemies (Deut. 28:21; Ezek. 38:22). *See also* Plague.

Above: A bronze lion from Susa, the summer capital of Persia, 5th century B.C. Daniel, thrown into a Medo-Persian den of lions, praised God for shutting "the mouths of the lions" (Dan. 6:22).
Right: A silver bowl with gold inlay. The archers depicted on it were perhaps members of the royal guard of the "10,000 immortals." The Jews returned from captivity with "410 matching silver bowls" from Cyrus, king of Persia (Ezra 1:10). From Susa, about the 5th century B.C.

BACKGROUND

We know that Peter was a successful commercial fisherman before he became a disciple. He made a move that would have been possible only for a successful man, from Bethsaida to Capernaum, the administrative center of Galilee. The city was situated on a narrow plain where the cost of land was high. Peter was probably a partner in his business with Andrew and the two sons of Zebedee, James and John.

During Jesus' years of active ministry, he trained twelve disciples to take active leadership of the Church after his resurrection. Peter was foremost in this band of disciples. He is mentioned first in every listing of the Twelve and, with James and John, was a member of an inner group of three who accompanied Jesus on the Mount of Transfiguration (Mt. 17) and at Gethsemane (Mk. 14). Peter is consistently portrayed as taking the lead: He asks Jesus questions; gives unsolicited advice; boldly leaps into the sea to go to Jesus; affirms his conviction that Jesus is the Christ, the Son of God; expresses willingness to die with Jesus; and, on the night before the crucifixion, draws his sword to protect the Lord. While Peter's eagerness led him to go too far at times, his enthusiasm is attractive and compelling.

Yet Peter was more than an enthusiast. He was respected by the other disciples and accepted as their leader. After the resurrection, Peter was a spokesman for the Christian movement, preaching the first evangelistic sermons. Peter exhibited courage before the Sanhedrin (Acts 4) and confronted the Hebrew Christians who objected to his preaching at the house of the Roman centurion Cornelius (Acts 10,11). He is the one Paul went to Jerusalem "to get acquainted with" long before that apostle became an acknowledged Christian leader (Gal. 1:18).

Firm tradition places Peter in Rome in the A.D. 60s, where he and Paul were martyred under the reign of Nero.

THEOLOGICAL SIGNIFICANCE

Peter was a central figure at critical events that mark historical passages in the ministry of Jesus and the Church.

1. *Matthew 16: Transition from kingdom to the cross.* While the people of Israel hesitated over the identity of Jesus, Peter boldly spoke for the disciples, "You are the Christ, the Son of the living God." This confession moved Jesus to say,

Blessed are you, Simon son of Jonah, for this was not revealed to you by man, but by my Father in heaven. And I tell you that you are Peter, and on this rock I will build my church, and the gates of Hades will not overcome it. I will give you the keys of the kingdom of heaven; whatever you bind on earth will be bound in heaven, and whatever you loose on earth will be loosed in heaven.

(Mt. 16:17-19)

In historical context, this event marks a dramatic shift in Jesus' ministry. From this point on, Christ began to teach in parables and to speak to his disciples concerning his coming crucifixion. The nation to whom Christ had come did not recognize

Peter being arrested by two Roman soldiers. Tradition based on the Book of First Clement holds that Peter died during Emperor Nero's persecution (A.D. 64–68).

775

him for who he was. Now Jesus would minister to those like Peter who would acknowledge him as Lord. *See also* Parable.

Matthew 16:17-19 is central in the Roman Catholic Church's teaching that Christ gave Peter primacy over the entire church. Peter is considered the first of an unbroken line of bishops of Rome—the pope. As such, Peter is the Church's foundation, possessor of the keys to bind and loose on earth and in heaven.

Protestants generally understand the "rock" on which the Church will be built to be the truth Peter confessed: that Jesus is the Christ, the Son of the living God. Some do feel that Jesus granted Peter authority but then extended it to the whole Christian community (Mt. 18:15-19). While Peter is undoubtedly the most significant of the twelve apostles, Protestants do not agree that he was given ultimate authority.

2. *Acts 2,3: Transition from Christ's life on*

After praying, Peter simply said, "Tabitha, get up," and raised this disciple of Jesus from the dead (Acts 9:36-43). Relief from a column capital from the time of the Crusades.

earth to the post-resurrection Church. Peter preached the first Gospel sermons on and after the day of Pentecost. These sermons present Jesus as a historical person who was unjustly put to death and later raised by God's power. The resurrection proves Jesus is both Lord and Christ. In view of these historical facts, Peter called on his hearers to repent (change their minds about Jesus) and be baptized in Christ's name, "for the forgiveness of your sins. And you will receive the gift of the Holy Spirit" (Acts 2:38). These early sermons of Peter establish the core content of the Gospel and the thrust of apostolic preaching.

3. *Acts 10,11: Transition from a Jewish to universal message.* Of all the apostles, Peter first preached the Gospel message to a Gentile household. He was specially prepared for this ministry by a vision that set aside his natural prejudices against Gentiles. Later, Peter testified that God "gave them [Gentile believers] the same gift as he gave us [Jewish believers], who believed in the Lord Jesus Christ" (11:17). His evidence was accepted, and the early church praised God that he "has granted even the Gentiles repentance unto life" (11:18).

Thus, in each of these transition situations, Peter had a central and vital role.

LEARNING FROM PETER'S LIFE

Every incident involving Peter is rich in personal and devotional insights.

1. *Mt. 14:22-33: Peter walks on water.* When the disciples saw Jesus walking on the sea in a storm, Peter left the boat to walk to him. Then, suddenly aware of the wind and waves, Peter began to sink. Yet though his faith wavered, his courage to step out onto the water is commendable and speaks well of his character.

2. *Mt. 16:21-28: Peter rebukes Jesus.* Peter did not like it when Jesus spoke of going to the cross. Christ silenced him and warned, "You do not have in mind the things of God, but the things of men." If we acknowledge Jesus as the Son of the living God, we must submit our understanding as well as our will to him.

3. *Mk. 14:27-31: Jesus predicts Peter's denial.* Peter "insisted emphatically" that he would die before disowning Jesus. Yet all too soon, Peter did deny the Lord. Peter learned, as we all must, that we truly are weak. We must rely on God rather than ourselves.

4. *Jn. 21:15-25: Jesus restores Peter.* Peter had denied Jesus three times, and three times Jesus asked Peter, "Do you love

me?" Peter did love Jesus and was not only forgiven but was commissioned to "feed [Christ's] sheep" and to "feed [Christ's] lambs." If we truly love Jesus, God can use us despite our failures.

5. *Acts 4: Peter confronts the Sanhedrin.* The same Peter who had been so frightened of mere servants that he denied his Lord, boldly called the rulers of his people to account for murdering Jesus. Peter bore the beating that was decreed and refused to stop preaching about Jesus. Peter had failed before. He did not fail again but showed inner strength and courage. Despite our past failures, God is able to make us stand.

6. *Acts 11: Peter welcomes the Gentiles.* Peter was attacked by certain Jewish believers for going to the house of the Gentile Cornelius. He carefully related what had happened and explained not only how God had led him but also how God had accepted these Gentile Christians. Peter did not become defensive but showed wisdom as well as courtesy in explaining his actions. Peter had matured as a leader and as an individual, a prospect that God holds out to all of us.

7. *Gal. 2:11-21: Paul berates Peter for discrimination.* Despite his strengths and his leadership position, Peter remained an imperfect human. In Antioch, Peter ate with Gentile Christians until some Christians from Jerusalem, who retained the old Jewish prejudices against Gentiles, came to visit. Peter was influenced to separate himself from the Gentile brethren. Paul confronted him about this behavior because Peter was wrong. No matter how important we may be, we need others to rebuke us when we stray from the truth.

As Christians, we honor Peter as one of the heroes of our faith. We respect him as a leader whose character we admire, whose words—inspired by God—we obey, and whose example we gladly follow. And we realize, as did Peter, that God can use us despite our failures and make us victorious ministers of the Gospel.

Above: The remains in Capernaum of what is thought to be Peter's house. Mark 1:29-34 records Jesus' healing ministry there ("The whole town gathered at the door"), and the Gospels identify Capernaum as the center of his itinerant preaching in Galilee. Excavation has shown that the home served as a house church for some 300 years and that a Byzantine church building was erected over the main meeting room.

Unusual terrain in Cappadocia. Christians in this and four other Roman provinces of Asia Minor were the recipients of the Book of First Peter (1:1).

Peter, First Epistle of A letter circulated among the Christians of five provinces in northern Asia Minor, reaffirming the joy and hope available to Christians despite the suffering many must surely experience.

BACKGROUND

The letter was universally accepted by the early church as the work of the apostle Peter. Quotes from this letter are found in tracts just a generation away from the apostles, and by A.D. 150, churches in many countries accepted it as Peter's work. Critics who argue for a later date point to the book's skillful use of the Greek language, which would have required an education a fisherman like Peter would have been unlikely to receive. However, any force in this argument is diminished

1 PETER: A READING AND STUDY GUIDE

Chapter	Content Summary	Related Articles
1:1-12	Christians have been given salvation, though their faith may be tested now by various trials.	Salvation Trial
1:13–2:3	Christians who have been redeemed by Christ's blood and born again are called to be holy.	Born Again Holy
2:4-12	Christians are living stones in God's house, a royal priesthood, called to live good lives among pagans.	Church Priest
2:13–3:7	Living a good life calls for submission, even at great personal cost, as Christ modeled for us.	Submission Example
3:8-22	Christians may suffer for doing good, as Christ did, but God will use such suffering for his purposes.	Suffer Baptism
4:1-11	Christians are to abandon pagan ways and live clear-minded, self-controlled, and loving lives.	Will
4:12-19	Christians who suffer according to God's will must commit themselves to God and do good.	Good
5:1-13	Within the church, submission, humility, and alertness are all required.	Humble Shepherd

by 1 Pet. 5:12, which says Peter wrote "with the help of Silas." This implies that Peter's message was put in appropriate written form by this "faithful brother."

The letter was probably written about A.D. 64/65 from Rome (the symbolic "Babylon" of 5:13) shortly before Peter was martyred under Nero. The word *diaspora* (dispersion) in 1:1, along with references in 2:11,12 and 3:6, have led some to suppose Peter was writing to Jewish believers. However, 1:14 and 4:3 suggest a Gentile background for his readers. In view of Peter's influence in the predominantly Gentile church at Corinth (1 Cor. 1:12) as well as his leadership in the Jewish church, it seems best to take this as a letter intended equally for all Christians.

THEOLOGICAL CONTRIBUTIONS

Peter's message of hope is cast against a dark background. Emperor Claudius had been eager to revitalize the old Roman state religion and was hostile to all foreign faiths. The unstable Nero would soon torture and kill thousands of Christians in Rome. It was clear from growing official and popular hostility to Christianity that persecution and suffering lay ahead. Peter reminds his readers of what being born again means to them, warns them of the suffering they will experience, calls for a life-style of submission, and holds up Jesus Christ as their example.

1. *The New Birth.* Through God's gift, Christians have been born again "into a living hope through the resurrection of Jesus Christ from the dead, and into an inheritance that can never perish, spoil or fade" (1:3,4). In a series of contrasts, Peter explains in detail the wonderful transitions that have been accomplished for the believer. In view of all that God has done, therefore, the believer should aim to live a holy life whatever painful experiences may lie ahead (1:15).

2. *Submission.* Christians are to be responsive to those with secular authority, for servants of God must "show proper respect to everyone" (2:17). Even harsh authorities must be respected and obeyed (2:18). Submission also is appropriate in marriage (3:1-7) and within the church (5:5).

3. *Suffering.* In general, a person who does what is right will not suffer for it (3:13). Nevertheless, Christians living in a world that crucified Jesus must expect some injustice and suffering (2:18-21; 4:12-19). However, Christians should be sure they are not suffering because of any wrongdoing, but "because of the name of Christ." To endure this kind of suffering "is commendable before God" (2:20).

4. *Christ, our Example.* Peter constantly returns to the theme that Jesus, who was unjustly crucified, suffered for us and left "an example, that you should follow in his steps" (2:21; *see* 4:1-3).

MASTERY KEYS

In 1:1–2:12, note what God has done for believers and what he expects from us. In the rest of the book, study the twin themes of submission and suffering. What does submission involve? How are Christians to perceive and respond to suffering?

SPECIAL FEATURES

Peter gives detailed advice on how to deal with unjust suffering (1 Pet. 3:14-18). The believer is (1) not to be frightened, (2) to remember and trust in Christ as Lord, (3) to maintain a positive attitude, which may need to be explained to those who cannot understand it, and (4) to keep a clear conscience by continuing to do right.

Peter, Second Epistle of A circular letter written to instruct Christians on how to recognize and deal with false teachers.

BACKGROUND

The author is clearly identified as "Simon Peter, a servant and apostle of Jesus Christ" (1:1), an eyewitness to the transfiguration of Jesus (1:16-18), and friend of Paul (3:15). Doubts about these claims appear as early in church history as Origen (A.D. 217–251), and Eusebius described 2 Peter as "disputed, but familiar to the majority."

While the evidence for 2 Peter is weaker than for any other book in the NT, it is much stronger than for those books that have been excluded from the canon. Second Peter was accepted from the Council of Carthage in A.D. 397 to the Reformation, when Calvin expressed uncertainty about its Petrine authorship though Luther readily accepted it. It remains one of the most controversial books of the NT.

If we assume that 2 Peter is what it claims to be, the book serves as Peter's Testament—a common first-century literary form, containing the last authoritative words of a person expecting to die. As such, Peter foresees more danger to the church from false teachers within than from persecution without.

The change in subject of 2 Peter explains other significant differences between the two letters, differences that have been used as arguments against Petrine authorship. At the same time, there are many

2 PETER: A READING AND STUDY GUIDE

Chapter	Content Summary	Related Articles
1:3-11	Everything necessary for Christian life and godliness is ours. We should seek to grow.	Election Righteousness
1:12-21	Scripture is a sure and trustworthy guide, for its authors "spoke from God."	Bible Prophecy
2:1-22	False teachers follow "the corrupt desire of the sinful nature." They will be punished and the righteous saved.	False Arrogance
3:1-18	Jesus will come and this universe be destroyed by fire.	Future

Below: Two of four colossal statues of Rameses II (1290–1224 B.C.) at Abu Simbel. Each is 67 feet (20 meters) high and weighs 1,200 tons. Some scholars believe this self-glorifying and oppressive pharaoh reigned during the time of the Exodus. Below right: Bust of Thutmose III (1504–1450 B.C.). According to conservative scholars, he was the pharaoh who oppressed the Israelites (Ex. 1,2). If so, his successor Amenhotep II would have reigned during the Exodus (5–12).

similarities between the two letters, such as certain terms used only in 1 and 2 Peter and the similarities in the introductions and salutations.

THEOLOGICAL CONTRIBUTIONS

Peter makes several important points about judgment and false teachers. He refers back to the OT to illustrate God's deliverance of the just and punishment of the wicked (2:5-9; 3:10-13). Furthermore, Christ's coming will lead to the destruction by fire of this present universe (3:1-13). Finally, Christians are to be alert to recognize false teachers (2:1-22), but the best way to deal with the challenge is to continue in scriptural truths and to "grow in the grace and knowledge of our Lord and Savior Jesus Christ" (3:18).

MASTERY KEYS

Note the pointed advice on the personal commitments that guard Christians from the influence of false teachers (1:3-21; 3:14-17). List characteristics that reveal false teachers (2:1-22). Then note how knowing the events associated with Jesus' return should shape Christian attitudes.

SPECIAL FEATURES

Peter's comparison of Paul's writings to "the other Scriptures" is evidence of how quickly the authority of some NT letters was accepted in the Church.

Pharaoh Ruler of Egypt. The Egyptian word originally meant "the great house." But by about 1500 B.C., it became the title of the person inhabiting the palace, Egypt's king. In biblical times, "pharaoh" was used both with and without a proper name to indicate Egypt's ruler.

According to Egyptian dogma, the pharaoh was a god while in office; he owned the lands and the people; in early times, he also commanded Egypt's army. But through the centuries the pharaohs grew

isolated. Their functionaries ran the country, while they remained mere figureheads.

As one of the great powers of the ancient world and a close neighbor of Israel, Egypt exerted significant influence on God's people. It is not surprising then that a number of different pharaohs are mentioned in Scripture, although over half of them are not actually named.

Pharisees [FAIR-uh-sees; "separated ones"]. A small but extremely influential lay fellowship of men committed (1) to strictly observe all the ordinances of Judaism concerning ritual purity, as defined by tradition, and (2) to scrupulously carry out religious duties, such as tithing and the performance of ceremonial washings. The Gospels portray the Pharisees as antagonists of Jesus, although a number were later converted and joined the Christian

Lid of alabaster canopic with boy-pharaoh Tutankhamen's features painted in blue, red, and black (about 1342 B.C.). He is the best known Egyptian ruler because of his tomb's excavated treasures.

PHARAOHS IN THE BIBLE

Reference	Biblical Name	Secular Name	Significance
Gen. 12:14-20	Pharaoh	Likely a ruler of 12th Dynasty	He temporarily added Sarah to his harem.
Gen. 37–50	Pharaoh	Likely a Hyksos king of 15th Dynasty	Joseph was made vizier of Egypt by this pharaoh.
Ex. 1,2	King of Egypt; Pharaoh	Thutmose III (?) (1504–1450 B.C.)	He oppressed the Israelites.
Ex. 5–12	Pharaoh	Amenhotep II (?) (1450–1425 B.C.)	Moses confronted this Pharaoh of the Exodus.
1 Ki. 3:1; 7:8; 9:16,24; 11:1	Pharaoh	(Probably) Siamun (978–959 B.C.)	He attacked the Canaanite city of Gezer and gave it as a dowry when his daughter married Solomon.
1 Ki. 11:18-22	Pharaoh, king of Egypt	Amenemope (or Siamun) (993–984 B.C.)	He gave asylum to young prince Hadad during David's destruction of Edom.
1 Ki. 11:40 (see 14:25,26) 2 Chr. 12:1-12	Shishak	Sheshonq I (945–924 B.C.)	He invaded Judah and sacked the Temple during Rehoboam's reign.
2 Ki. 17:4	So, king of Egypt	Osokorn IV (?) (727–716 B.C.)	Hoshea, last king of Israel, allied with him against Assyria.
2 Ki. 19:9 Isa. 37:9	Tirhakah	Taharqa (690–664 B.C.)	This Cushite king of Egypt fought Sennacherib unsuccessfully.
2 Ki. 23:29 2 Chr.35:20-24	Pharaoh Neco	Neco II (610–595 B.C.)	He killed Josiah in 609 B.C. and briefly gained control of Judah.
Jer. 44:30 (see 37:5-11); Ezek. 17:11-21; 29:1-16	Pharaoh Hophra	Waibre (589–570 B.C.)	Jeremiah predicted his defeat by Nebuchadnezzar; Ezekiel prophesied against him also.

movement (Acts 15:5; 23:6; Phil. 3:5). Information about the Pharisees comes from three sources: the NT, the writings of the first-century Jewish historian Josephus, and later rabbinic writings that reflect conditions four decades after Christ's death.

BACKGROUND

The first mention of the name Pharisee occurs in the Maccabean period, about 135 B.C. While its origins are uncertain, Pharisaism was clearly a lay rather than priestly movement. Nurtured in the synagogue rather than the Temple, it was an outgrowth of the return-to-Scripture movement initiated during the Babylonian Captivity.

According to Josephus, there were only about 6,000 Pharisees in Jesus' day. These Pharisees were not necessarily scholars, although there were rabbis among them (Acts 5:34). Instead, these zealous and dedicated men relied on the existing interpretations and applications of OT Law formulated by earlier rabbis. Their concern for accuracy in interpretation of the Scriptures became an insistence on maintaining the tradition of the elders (Mt. 15:2; Mk. 7:3-5). Unfortunately, their rules of life cut them off from the ordinary Israelites, who, according to the Pharisees, lacked knowledge of and commitment to the Law. The contempt felt for the great mass of their fellow Jews is expressed in Jn. 7:48,49, in the Pharisees' retort to the Temple guards when they did not arrest Jesus because of the authority of his voice: "Has any of the rulers or of the Pharisees believed in him? No! But this mob that knows nothing of the law—there is a curse on them!"

Although the number of Pharisees was small and they displayed contempt for ordinary Israelites, Pharisaism was the leading sect in Jesus' day. The Pharisees were even influential enough to set the form of prayers and religious services in synagogues dominated by the Sadducees, a competing sect. Their influence was rooted in two things: (1) the great respect the common people had for these men who were committed to the most strict observance of their religion; and (2) the presence of a number of Pharisees on the Sanhedrin, the Jewish ruling council. As Jesus noted, the "teachers of the law and Pharisees sit in Moses' seat" (Mt. 23:2). *See also* Sadducees.

It is not surprising then that delegations of Pharisees from Jerusalem came to check out the activities of John the Baptist and of Jesus (Mt. 3:1-12; 9:1-13). The Pharisees

felt that they had the truth and, with the truth, the right to stand in judgment on other religious teachers.

Doctrinally, the Pharisees were orthodox. They were supernaturalists who believed in the existence of angels. They believed in immortality and expected the righteous dead to be resurrected and rewarded. They believed the testimony of the Scriptures that God would one day send a Messiah to restore freedom in Israel. They argued that both God's sovereign will and human free will operate in the world, a conviction expressed in Rabbi Akiba's later saying, "All is foreseen, but freedom of choice is given." Most significantly, the Pharisees believed that the OT Scriptures were the Word of God but also that Moses had communicated an oral law of equal standing and that this oral law was found in their traditions.

JESUS AND THE PHARISEES

The Gospels explain the conflict that developed between Jesus and the Pharisees. The problem was not doctrinal: In fact, Jesus clearly sided with the Pharisees on basic doctrinal issues (Mt. 22:23-32). The conflict grew because Jesus denied the validity of the oral traditions on which the Pharisees relied and, in so doing, challenged the Pharisees' outlook on life.

In his Sermon on the Mount, Jesus repeatedly used the expression, "You have heard that it was said . . . but I tell you." The reaction to this statement shows the impact of such words. "The crowds were amazed at his teaching, because he taught as one who had authority, and not as their teachers of the law" (Mt. 7:28,29).

Soon this man who acted and spoke with such assurance was observed violating some of those traditions that the Pharisees viewed as God's authoritative and binding Word. When Jesus' disciples picked heads of grain on the Sabbath, an action that the rabbis defined as "work," Christ defended his disciples. Jesus himself healed on the Sabbath, which again the Pharisees defined as "work" and therefore unlawful. Jesus' verdict, "It is lawful to do good on the Sabbath," so infuriated these religious zealots that "the Pharisees went out and plotted how they might kill Jesus" (Mt. 12:12,14).

The hostility of the Pharisees to Jesus continued to grow. This led to open criticism by Jesus, as in Mk. 7:1-13: "You have let go of the commands of God and are holding on to the traditions of men," and, "You nullify the word of God by your tradition that you have handed down. And you do many things like that." Near the end of his ministry, Jesus said, "You give a tenth of your spices—mint, dill and cummin. But you have neglected the more important matters of the law—justice, mercy and faithfulness. You should have practiced the latter, without neglecting the former. You blind guides! You strain out a gnat but swallow a camel" (Mt. 23:23,24; *compare* Mt. 9:9-13).

This last saying sums up Jesus' personal critique of Pharisaism. In its emphasis on performance and its preoccupation with details, the sect missed the true meaning of the OT. Holiness cannot be summed up in ritual observance but must be expressed in a commitment to justice, mercy, and faithfulness. Furthermore, true spirituality demands a love for the very people whom the Pharisees held in such contempt and from whom they isolated themselves.

NEGATIVE NT VIEWS

The view of the Pharisees found in the Gospels is more negative than that in either Josephus or rabbinical sources. Passages such as Mt. 15:1-9; 23; Mk. 2:15–3:6; 7:1-13; and Lk. 11:37-52 introduce us to Pharisees who are self-righteous and often hypocrites, whose public piety is practiced in order to gain the praise of the common people they so despise. They condemn Jesus not only for his friendship with "tax collectors and sinners" but also for his loving concern for the sick and demon-possessed. Their antagonism toward Jesus is so great they accuse him of being in league with Satan and actively plot to have him killed.

Yet these Pharisees do not necessarily represent all Pharisees! In rabbinical writings, the hypocrisy of some Pharisees is admitted and condemned even more harshly than in the Gospels. Undoubtedly, some in this movement, like Gamaliel (Acts 5:34) and the apostle Paul himself (Phil. 3:5), were motivated by an honest love and true zeal for God.

Yet the NT reflects a basic conflict with Pharisaism itself, not just with those Pharisees who led the opposition to Jesus and whose approach to religion Christ so strongly condemned. Ultimately, the Pharisees' belief that one could please God by keeping rules led them to a self-righteousness that had no need either to seek forgiveness themselves or to make allowances for human weaknesses in others. In contrast, Jesus revealed that God is a loving Father, fully aware of human weak-

Jesus told the story of a Pharisee and a tax collector (Lk. 18:10-14) to convict those who, like the Pharisees, were "confident of their own righteousness and looked down on everybody else" (v. 9).

nesses, and he encouraged a simple reliance on God. Where the Pharisees separated themselves from those less self-righteously rigorous, Jesus reached out to heal and to pronounce forgiveness of sins. And when the Pharisees expressed shock that he would associate with sinners, Christ quoted the OT and said, "Go and learn what this means: 'I desire mercy, not sacrifice.' For I have not come to call the righteous, but sinners" (Mt. 9:13).

Such vastly different approaches to religion must always come into conflict. That conflict became so fierce and the distinction between Jesus' teaching and Pharisaism so clear that the leading Pharisees resolved to bring about Christ's death.

The conflict persisted even within the apostolic church when converted Pharisees were unable to shake off their old mind-set and insisted that even Gentile Christians must be circumcised and keep the Mosaic Law (Acts 15:5). In taking a stand against this position, the first church council affirmed that Christianity is a religion of grace. Faith in Jesus Christ purifies the heart, making the believer truly good. Legalism had brought about no inner transformation: It was a burden Israel was never able to bear (Acts 15:6-11).

The continuing conflict led to a clear definition of the issue in Paul's Epistles, especially in Romans and Galatians. A Pharisee-like legalism leads no one along the road to salvation (Gal. 2:15,16) and, indeed, can make no contribution to living a truly spiritual life. Spiritual life depends not on observing the Law but on living by faith (Gal. 3:1-5). *See also* Faith; Law; Legalism.

Philemon, Epistle to A personal letter written to a convert of Paul on behalf of a runaway slave.

BACKGROUND

Philemon (fi-LEE-muhn; "friendship"), who had been converted by Paul (Phlm. 19), was the wealthy host of a house-church in Colosse. He had owned a slave named Onesimus (oh-NES-ih-muhs; "profitable"), who had apparently stolen

Roman servant portrayed among jugs and drinking cups (second century A.D.). Philemon's runaway slave, Onesimus, became a Christian under Paul's ministry.

from him and then run away (Phlm. 11,18). Somehow, Onesimus came into contact with Paul while the apostle was imprisoned in Rome (vv. 1,9,10,13,23), and Onesimus was then converted.

Paul sent Onesimus back to Philemon in the company of the messenger carrying his NT letter to the Colossians and a personal letter to Philemon himself (Col. 4:10-14). In Paul's note to Philemon, the apostle urges his convert to welcome Onesimus back—"no longer as a slave, but better than a slave, as a dear brother" (v. 16). The meaning of this phrase has been debated; some believe Paul subtly suggests that Philemon release Onesimus so the latter could return to Paul (vv. 12-14), while others do not see any such implication (vv. 15,16).

HISTORICAL SIGNIFICANCE

The letter is significant in two ways. First, it reflects the NT's consistent attitude toward slavery. The NT accepts slavery as a reality in the Roman Empire and does not call for its abolition (1 Cor. 7:20-24; 1 Pet. 2:18-25). Instead, the Christian slave is urged to serve his master wholeheartedly, while the master is instructed to view his slaves not as objects, but as persons of worth and value (Phlm. 16; Eph. 6:9)—a view that eventually led to the dissolution of slavery. *See also* Slave.

Second, the letter is significant as a model of Christian persuasion. Recognizing Philemon's personal right to be angry and his legal right to punish Onesimus, Paul carefully goes about changing Philemon's view of Onesimus and of their relationship. He reminds Philemon that he is known as one who loves the saints and whose love "has given me great joy and encouragement" (vv. 4-7). Paul appeals to this quality and asks Philemon to act out of love and accept Onesimus back (vv. 8-11). Paul assures Philemon that his slave has been changed by his conversion—and that as a "dear brother" he now merits welcome (vv. 12-17). Finally, Paul asks Philemon to charge any debt Onesimus may owe to Paul's account—knowing that Philemon owes Paul his very life in Christ (vv. 18,19). In essence, Paul's strategy is to

PHILEMON: A READING AND STUDY GUIDE		
Verse	**Content Summary**	**Related Articles**
1-3	Paul greets Philemon as a "fellow worker" who hosts a church in his house.	Fellowship Church
4-7	Paul thanks God for Philemon's love for the saints and his active involvement in sharing the Christian faith.	Love Saint
8-22	Paul appeals to Philemon to welcome his runaway slave Onesimus back as a Christian brother.	Slavery Authority
23-25	Paul adds greetings from several of his fellow workers.	

appeal to Philemon's better self—to remind him that Philemon is a man who loves, and to ask Philemon to reestablish his relationship with Onesimus, not on the basis of what the former slave might deserve, but on the basis of a love that reflects God's own attitude toward the undeserving.

Philip the Apostle *See* Disciple; IDENTI-QUICK: PEOPLE.

Philippians, Epistle to the In this letter, written in the early 60s A.D. to the church at Philippi while the apostle was imprisoned at Rome, Paul expresses his view of his imprisonment, encourages full commitment to Jesus, and shares the secret of lasting joy and inner peace.

BACKGROUND

By the middle of the first century, Philippi was an important city. As a Roman colony, Philippi had a number of political privileges, and as a major city on the Via Egnatia, Philippi had become the most important city in eastern Macedonia. *See also* Colony.

Paul founded the church in Philippi on his second missionary journey about A.D. 50. The city was apparently without a Jewish synagogue, and Paul's first convert was a cloth merchant named Lydia whom he found worshiping with other women outside the city on a riverbank. Although Paul's visit was brief and marred by a flogging and an overnight stay in jail (Acts 16:12-40), this first church he founded in Europe remained dear to the apostle. The affection was reciprocated: Repeatedly, the Philippian church sent gifts to help Paul with his ministry (Phil. 4:14-19).

When Paul was on trial at Caesarea for causing a disturbance in Jerusalem, he exercised his right as a Roman citizen and requested to be tried in Rome (Acts 24–26). He was then taken to Rome and spent two years in a rented house awaiting his hearing (Acts 28:30). Most commentators agree that Paul wrote Philippians and other "prison Epistles" from Rome during this two-year period (*compare* Phil. 1:13; 4:22; with 1:7,13,14,16).

Paul's warm and very personal letter was carried to Philippi by Epaphroditus, who had come to Rome with a monetary gift for Paul from the Philippian church. In Rome, Epaphroditus became ill. When he recovered, Paul sent him back to his anxious friends and used the opportunity to send this letter as well.

THEOLOGICAL CONTRIBUTIONS

Perhaps the most outstanding feature of this letter is the hymn of praise to Christ, which proclaims Christ's pre-existence, his incarnation, and his exaltation as Lord

Ruins of ancient Philippi, "a Roman colony and the leading city of that district in Macedonia" in Paul's day (Acts 16:12).

PHILIPPIANS: A READING AND STUDY GUIDE

Passage	Content Summary	Related Articles
1:1-11	Paul gives thanks for the Philippians' partnership in the Gospel and expresses his love.	Paul Day of Christ
1:12-30	Paul's imprisonment has actually advanced the spread of the Gospel.	Gospel Suffer
2:1-18	Paul exhorts humility and holds Jesus up as an example to follow.	Kenosis Humble
2:19-30	Paul intends to send Timothy and a recovered Epaphroditus to his friends in Philippi.	Timothy Healing
3:1-11	Paul himself has abandoned confidence based on works in order to know Christ and find righteousness in him.	Righteousness Resurrection
3:12—4:1	The mature Christian constantly seeks to become what Jesus can help him be and lives as a citizen of heaven.	Mark Mature Citizen
4:2-9	Paul exhorts interpersonal and inner peace, a quiet mind, and the practice of truths he has taught.	Peace Obey
4:10-23	Paul expresses his appreciation for the love and concern always shown by the Philippians.	Contentment Give

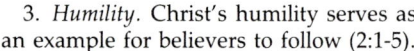

following the resurrection. *See also* Deity; Incarnation; Kenosis; Resurrection.

The letter is also notable for its practical theology of a Christ-centered life.

1. *Fruit*. Through Christ, believers produce the "fruit of righteousness" (Phil. 1:11).

2. *Preaching*. Preaching Christ is so significant that Paul could even rejoice in his imprisonment because of the opportunity to preach to Caesar's household and because his incarceration spurred others to preach Christ more enthusiastically (1:12-14).

A Roman-period crypt in Philippi that became known after the 5th century as the "Prison of St. Paul."

3. *Humility*. Christ's humility serves as an example for believers to follow (2:1-5).

4. *Power*. Knowing Jesus and experiencing the power of his resurrection is the most important thing in life (3:7-11).

5. *Perseverance*. With Paul, mature Christians should "press on toward the goal to win the prize for which God has called [us] heavenward in Christ Jesus" (3:12-15).

Thus, the practical application of Christ-centered principles helps us to understand better the person of Jesus Christ and his impact on our lives.

MASTERY KEYS

The apostle mentions the words "joy" and "rejoice" repeatedly. Mark each occurrence, and see what it is that can provide the Christian with joy (*see also* Joy). Also, trace the practical impact of a Christ-centered life. How is our relationship with Jesus to affect our values, attitudes, and behavior? What role is Jesus to play in the life of the Christian?

SPECIAL FEATURES

Paul shares two vital Christian secrets: (1) To be free of anxiety, "In everything, by prayer and petition, with thanksgiving, present your requests to God. And the peace of God . . . will guard your hearts and your minds in Christ Jesus" (Phil. 4:6,7); and (2) to develop a Christian outlook, "Whatever is true, whatever is noble, whatever is right, whatever is pure, whatever is lovely, whatever is admirable—if anything is excellent or praiseworthy—think about these things" (Phil. 4:8,9).

Philistines An aggressive Sea People whose mass invasion of the eastern Mediterranean coast resulted in the settlement of coastal Palestine by 1200 B.C. The Philistines were Israel's principal enemy from the time of Samson until their devastating defeats at the hands of David around 980 B.C. The Philistine best known from Scripture is the giant Goliath, who was killed by David.

Archaeology and Scripture agree that the Philistines originated in Caphtor, ancient Crete (Gen. 10:14; Jer. 47:4; Amos 9:7). Apparently, a large trading colony of the Minoans (whose culture flourished on Crete from about 2800 to 1400 B.C.) was established at Gerar in the time of Abraham (Gen. 21:22-34).

Some centuries later, when both the Hittites to the north and Egyptians to the south were relatively weak, a major invasion of the eastern Mediterranean was launched. Inscriptions of Pharaoh Merneptah (1236–1223 B.C.) tell of an attempted invasion by Sea Peoples launched from Libya. A hieroglyphic account of a later invasion in the eighth year of Rameses III (1198–1166 B.C.) tells of a massive land and sea invasion of the Nile Delta. Rameses threw the invaders back but permitted them to settle on Palestine's coastal plain. There the Philistines established five major cities: Ashdod, Ashkelon, Ekron, Gath, and Gaza. From these cities, the Philistines penetrated deep into Israelite territory. Remains of Philistine outposts have been found as far north as Hazor and Tel Dan, and as far west as Beth Shan in Galilee, and Bethel and Jerusalem in Judea.

Politically, the Philistines were led by the rulers or lords of their five major cities. Each Philistine lord ruled his own city and its surrounding villages. But together, these five functioned as a ruling council (Jdg. 16:5,8; 1 Sam. 29:1-7). They also served as military leaders (1 Sam. 7:7; 29:1-7) in time of war. This ability to coordinate the efforts of their people gave the Philistines a significant advantage over the basically leaderless Israelites in the era of the judges.

The warlike Philistines dominated the Israelites in the time of Samson. Samuel and Saul led Israel to notable victories that held the Philistines back, but not until David's time was the Philistines' military dominance ended. One reason for their dominance was their ability to work iron (1 Sam. 13:19; 17:7), a secret they withheld from Israel until forced by David to surrender it. Archaeologists have discovered that iron tools or weapons in Israel dating from before 1000 B.C. are invariably at sites occupied or controlled by the Philistines.

The crushing defeats administered by David did not destroy the Philistines as a people. They remained in their coastal cities and continued to harass the Israelites when able. The Bible portrays the Philistines offering tribute to Jehoshaphat of Judah (872–848 B.C.; 2 Chr. 17:11), but later invading the country in the time of Jehoram (853–841 B.C.; 2 Chr. 21:16). Uzziah (780–741 B.C.; 2 Chr. 26:6) and Hezekiah (715–687 B.C.; 2 Ki. 18:8) fought the Philistines, and both Amos and Isaiah predicted

The Philistines defeated Saul's army at Mount Gilboa in a rare attack on the northern part of Israel (1 Sam. 31:1-6). From the period of the judges until David's reign, they frequently dominated Israel's territory.

Two fettered Philistine soldiers, wearing their feathered helmets, in a relief commemorating the victory of Rameses III over this sea-faring people (Thebes, Egypt, 12th century B.C.).

God would judge these persistent enemies of his people (Amos 1:6-8; *compare* Isa. 9:12).

Philistine cities are mentioned in Assyrian annals. The Assyrians dominated the area from about 715 B.C. to their collapse around 609 B.C. The Philistines then joined Egypt in an unwise anti-Babylonian alliance. Acting decisively, Nebuchadnezzar invaded and deported the rulers and the population of Philistia (Jer. 25:20; 47:1-7; Zech. 9:5,6).

The Philistines had a high level of material culture, as illustrated in their distinctive and colorful pottery, their temple architecture, and the many figurines recovered despite the relatively few archaeological digs at Philistine sites. The religion of the Philistines is closer to that of the other Canaanites than to the original Minoan faith, which was dominated by the "Great Mother." While early examples of cult objects found in Ashdod reflect worship of the Mycenaean female goddess, soon the Canaanite deity Dagon headed the Philistine pantheon (1 Chr. 10:10)—thus showing the assimilation of the Philistines into Canaanite culture. The only Philistine religious practice reflected in the Bible is the giving of a "guilt offering" to the Lord when the Philistines, terrified by the plagues that struck them after capturing the ark of the Lord, returned the ark to Israel (1 Sam. 6:4).

Clockwise from above: Philistine beer pitcher; ritual worship objects; figurine found in recent excavations at the Philistine city of Ekron; Philistine temple at Tell Qasile, which showed signs of being burnt down (possibly by David).

philosophy By NT times, any system of thought attempting to explain the meaning and/or nature of the universe and of human experience. This included not only the various schools of thought developed in the Hellenistic world, such as the Stoic and Epicurean that flourished in Athens (Acts 17:18) —traditionally known as philosophies —but also Gnosticism and the pagan mystery religions. In this wider sense, Josephus refers to the schools of the Pharisees, Sadducees, and Essenes as the three *philosophai* of the Jews.

The common element in all such philosophies, whether it is obtained by an intellectual search or by other means, is a claim to fundamental knowledge about life and reality. Yet a sharp distinction separates the Scriptural view of human wisdom from the view of wisdom held in the world. The OT portrays wisdom as the application of God's revealed guidelines, so that a person lives a good and holy life. Such wisdom begins with the fear of God—that reverential awe through which the true believer remains aware of the Lord as an ever-present reality. The NT exults in the revelation of a truth that no human mind could conceive (Rom. 11:33-36). Although the philosophers whom Paul confronted in Athens were "very religious" and "spent all their time doing nothing but talking about and listening to the latest ideas," they remained ignorant of the "true Lord of heaven and earth" (Acts 17:21-24). As a result, all their learning was as empty and useless as the idols that abounded in their city.

According to Scripture, then, a reliance upon God's revelation of himself is foundational in any search for truth. Rather than "words taught us by human wisdom," Christian truth is expressed in "words taught by the Spirit," who knows the very mind of God (1 Cor. 2:6-16). Thus, Paul reminds the Corinthians, "I did not come to you with eloquence or superior wisdom as I proclaimed to you the testimony about God" (1 Cor. 2:1). Paul did not seek to persuade through oratorical skill, which characterized the method of the worldly wise, but through the dynamic spiritual power of the Gospel.

It is not surprising, then, that Paul asks scornfully, "Where is the philosopher of this age? Has not God made foolish the wisdom of the world? For since in the wisdom of God the world through its wisdom did not know him, God was pleased through the foolishness of what was preached to save those who believe" (1

Cor. 1:20,21; *see* 1 Tim. 6:20). And it is not surprising to catch the strong negative tone in Paul's warning, "See to it that no one takes you captive through hollow and deceptive philosophy, which depends on human tradition and the basic principles of this world rather than on Christ" (Col. 2:8).

Thus, any philosophy, based on human ideas about the world or not rooted in the fundamental truth of God's revelation of himself through Jesus Christ, is merely learned ignorance and cannot provide humankind with a grasp of ultimate reality.

Roman bust of a philosopher done in Greek style; found in Samaria, first century B.C. In Athens Paul disputed with a group of Stoic and Epicurean philosophers (Acts 17:16-34).

Phinehas [FIN-ee-uhs; "mouth of brass"]. A zealous priest who ended a plague by executing a sinning Israelite during the wilderness wandering, about 1425 B.C. **Grandfather:** Aaron. **Father:** Eleazar. **Scripture:** Num. 25.

BACKGROUND

Balak, the Moabite king, attempted unsuccessfully to have the prophet Balaam curse Israel (Num. 22-24). The ruler then followed Balaam's advice and attempted to corrupt God's people by sending pagan women to entice Israelite men into adultery and idolatrous worship. The device was all too successful, and as a result God struck the Israelite camp with a devastating plague that killed some 24,000.

When Phinehas saw an Israelite man bring one of the Midianite cult prostitutes into the Hebrew camp, Phinehas leaped up and followed them into the man's tent. There with a single thrust he drove a spear through them both. This act of Phinehas

789

stopped the plague, and Phinehas was promised that his descendants would never lack a man in the priesthood of Israel. The event is celebrated in Ps. 106:30,31:

Phinehas stood up and intervened,
and the plague was checked.
This was credited to him as
righteousness
for endless generations to come.

Phinehas went on to play a significant role in the conquest of Canaan (Num. 31:6) and led the anxious delegation that questioned the erection of an altar by the Transjordanian tribes (Josh. 22:9-34).

LEARNING FROM PHINEHAS'S LIFE

The OT's comment on Phinehas's action is revealing. The text reports God's statement: "He was as zealous as I am for my honor among them" (Num. 25:11). Zeal can be misplaced, but in this case, idolatry and immorality were corrupting God's people, and God's Law ordained the death penalty for both. Phinehas was determined that the penalty God had ordained should be carried out.

In our society, where police forces and courts are responsible to enforce the law, we cannot act as Phinehas did. However, this does not mean we are to shrug our shoulders and ignore evil. Moral outrage and the willingness to take a stand against evil are still godly characteristics. God is still pleased with those who are zealous for his honor and who care about the things that are important to him.

Phoebe [FEE-bee; "radiant"]. A woman Paul commends in the last chapter of Romans, about A.D. 57.

BACKGROUND

Nothing is known of Phoebe beyond Paul's commendation in Rom. 16:1,2. Yet the brief note is particularly significant. It reads, "I commend to you our sister Phoebe, a servant of the church in Cenchrea. I ask you to receive her in the Lord in a way worthy of the saints and to give her any help she may need from you, for she has been a great help to many people, including me."

Cenchrea was a town situated on the east harbor of Corinth. Phoebe is not only called a sister but "a servant." The word in the original is *diakonon,* meaning "servant" or "deacon." It is quite possible that Phoebe filled a definite office in the church and thus shows, with Lydia and Priscilla, that women did have significant leader-

ship roles in the apostolic church. *See also* Woman.

The phrase "great help to many" includes a word in Greek that suggests Phoebe was a patroness of the community. She was possibly a businesswoman who could protect Christians through her public influence. The request to "receive her in the Lord" is probably an indication that Phoebe herself carried this letter that Paul wrote to the church at Rome.

LEARNING FROM PHOEBE'S LIFE

In a day when women express deep concern about their role in the modern church, it would be easy to become involved in arguments about whether the word *diakonon* here indicates a church office or is used in a nontechnical way to indicate general social services rendered to others. But another phrase in these verses may better serve as Phoebe's epitaph, and for our encouragement. Paul says, "She has been a great help to many people." It is in the simple giving of ourselves to aid others, not in any office we may or may not hold, that we find the deepest meaning of our life in Christ.

Phoenicia, Phoenicians ["red purple"]. In Scripture, the narrow strip of land stretching some 185 miles (300 kilometers) along the eastern Mediterranean coast between Mount Carmel in the south and Mount Cassius in the north, in what is now Lebanon and Syria.

Phoenicia was settled in the fourth millennium B.C. by the same peoples who occupied the rest of Canaan. The Phoenicians, however, are generally considered

The Phoenician goddess Tanit, who demanded child sacrifice, was worshiped throughout the Mediterranean region. The sign of Tanit is seen in relief on the base of this terra-cotta statue (4th–2nd century B.C.).

as a distinct people from about 1200 B.C. onward.

The Phoenicians were daring traders and established sea trading posts throughout the Mediterranean (Ezek. 27,28). They were famed for the red-purple dye they extracted from the Murax mollusk. They introduced the alphabet in Greece and developed mathematical techniques needed for trading, including the invention of the *abacus*. However, only a few random quotations from their literature have survived.

Later, David developed strong ties with Hiram, king of Tyre, and used Phoenician raw materials and skilled workmen to construct his palace (1 Chr. 14:1,2). Solomon turned to Hiram and contracted for "a man skilled to work in gold and silver, bronze and iron, and in purple, crimson and blue yarn, and experienced in the art of engraving, to work in Judah and Jerusalem" on the Temple. Solomon added, "Send me also cedar, pine and algum logs from Lebanon, for I know that your men are skilled in cutting timber there. My men will work with yours" (2 Chr. 2:7,8).

During the Assyrian period, Phoenician cities lost their independence but remained flourishing commercial centers. They were semi-independent during the Babylonian and Persian years, but in the end they were denied the opportunity to trade by the powerful city-state of Carthage, itself Phoenician in origin. The aggressive Punic peoples of Carthage planted colonies in Algeria, Spain, and Morocco, and in 525 B.C., they closed the Mediterranean to Phoenician traders. In addition, the two chief Phoenician cities were later destroyed, Sidon in 351 B.C. after a rebellion against Persia, and Tyre in 332 B.C. in the invasion of Persia by Alexander the Great.

All in all, the picture of Phoenicia gained from both Scripture and archaeological digs is that of an industrious, highly cultured, and adventurous people, blessed with a productive homeland.

Yet, religiously, the Phoenicians displayed some of the most corrupt tendencies of Canaanite worship. In the ninth century B.C., it was Jezebel, the daughter of a king of Sidon, who influenced Ahab to attempt to replace Yahweh with Baal as Israel's god. The goddess Tanit, who demanded child sacrifice and was the dominant goddess in Carthage (where a district containing acres of remains of children burned alive has been discovered), was worshiped in Phoenicia as early as the seventh century B.C.

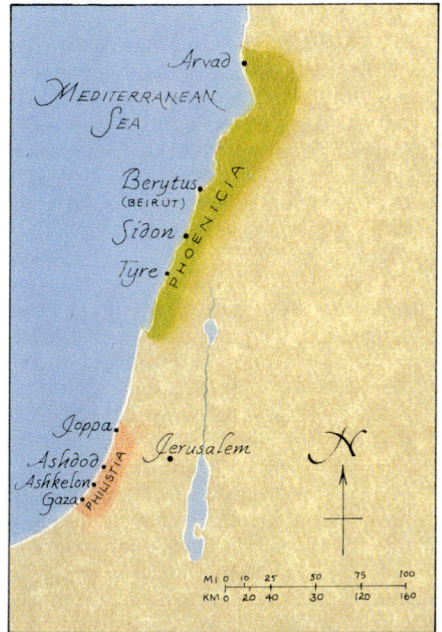

This ivory plaque with gold leaf and stone inlays is probably the work of a Phoenician craftsman, who used Egyptian motifs for the Assyrian king Ashurnasirpal II (Nimrud, 9th century B.C.).

Phoenician trading ship (below) shown in relief on the end of a sarcophagus. The Phoenicians were adventuresome traders based in city-states on a 150-mile (240-kilometer) stretch of the northern coast of Palestine.

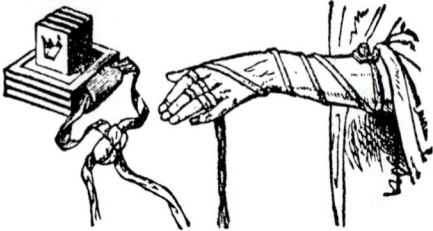

Phylacteries are strapped on in a prescribed manner to form the three letters of the divine name Shaddai ("Almighty").

Right: Jewish man at morning prayer, wearing phylacteries on his left forearm and forehead. Above: First-century A.D. head phylactery found in one of the so-called Qumran Caves near the Dead Sea. The rolled parchments each contain one of the passages that enjoin the wearing of a "sign" (NIV) or "frontlet" (KJV).

In NT times, many of the coastal cities still flourished. Jesus healed the daughter of a Syrophoenician woman when he visited the region near Tyre (Mk. 7:24-30). Early Christians, scattered by persecution, evangelized as far north as Phoenicia (Acts 11:19), and Paul passed through the region on his way to the Jerusalem Council (Acts 15:3).

phylactery Small boxes containing verses of Scripture that pious Jews wear strapped to the forehead and left hand during prayers.

The passages of Scripture placed in these small leather boxes are Ex. 13:1-10; 13:11-16; Deut. 6:4-9; and Deut. 11:13-21. Each passage speaks of a "sign on your hand and a reminder on your forehead that the law of the Lord is to be on your lips." The literal interpretation of this injunction led to the introduction of phylacteries, probably in the first century B.C. They were in common use in Judaism by the end of the second century A.D. and are worn by Orthodox Jews today.

In Scripture, phylacteries are mentioned only in Mt. 23:5, where Jesus criticizes some Pharisees because "everything they do is done for men to see: They make their phylacteries wide and the tassels on their garments long."

physician A person skilled in healing arts —in most ancient cultures, a priest or magician. *See also* Healing; Medicine.

pieces of silver *See* Money.

piety Faithfulness in fulfilling one's religious and social duties. *See also* Godly.

pig An animal with a flat snout and a stout body covered with bristles. Pigs were raised for their meat by many ancient peoples but were ritually unclean according to Mosaic Law (Lev. 11:7). Ancient Israel, lacking modern cooking appliances, was protected by this prohibition from exposure to the tapeworm causing trichinosis, which spends one stage of its life in the pig's muscles and can only be killed by thorough cooking.

God through Isaiah condemns his obstinate people "who continually provoke me to my very face, offering sacrifices in gardens and burning incense on altars of brick; who sit among the graves and spend their nights keeping secret vigil; who eat the flesh of pigs, and whose pots hold broth of unclean meat" (Isa. 65:3-5).

The repugnance the Jew felt for pigs helps us sense how low the prodigal son in Jesus' parable had fallen, for in desperation he went to work for a man "who sent him to his fields to feed pigs" (Lk. 15:15). In 2 Pet. 2:22, false teachers are compared to pigs.

pigeon A small, ritually clean bird slightly darker but otherwise indistinguishable from doves. These birds were domesticated in Israel (Isa. 60:8) and could be offered as sacrifices in place of the more expensive sheep or cattle, so that the poor could make required sacrifices (Lev. 5:7; *compare* Lev. 12:6,8; 14:21,22,30; 15:14,29; Num. 6:10). That Joseph and Mary brought only a pair of these birds when the infant Jesus was presented at the Temple indicates their poverty.

Pilate, Pontius [PON-shuhs PI-luht; "javelin-carrier"]. Roman governor of Judea A.D. 26–36, who condemned Jesus to death about A.D. 33. **Scripture:** Mt. 27; Mk. 15; Lk. 23; Jn. 18,19.

BACKGROUND

Pilate served first as prefect and then procurator of Judea. As such, he had vast authority, including command of the military forces that occupied the little land. He alone could order the death sentence. He appointed the Jewish high priest and even exercised control over funds in the Temple treasury. His service in Judea is attested not only in the Gospels, but also by first-century historians Flavius Josephus and Philo Judaeus and by recently discovered inscriptional evidence in Caesarea Maritima, the Roman administrative seat.

The Jewish sources that report on Pilate's decade in the Holy Land portray him as a hostile, insensitive person. One of Pilate's first acts was to antagonize the Jews by setting up image-bearing standards in Jerusalem considered idolatrous by the Jews. Due to determined demonstrations by the populace, Pilate was forced to take down the standards. Josephus and Philo also accuse him of slaughtering hundreds of Jews (*compare* Lk. 13:1), as well as misappropriating Temple funds in order to pay for an aqueduct to bring water to Jerusalem from a distant spring. Yet Pilate served in Judea for ten years rather than the normal three or four, evidence that the Emperor Tiberius considered him an effective administrator. Interestingly, the only known mention of Pilate in pagan writings is a

Terra-cotta pigeon, 9th–8th centuries B.C. Three varieties of the small pigeon, commonly called "turtledove," are found in Palestine.

passing reference in Tacitus to Pilate's service at the time of the execution of Christ.

Each of the Gospels adds something to the portrait of Pilate as Christ's judge. In the Gospels, Pilate is reluctant to order Jesus' crucifixion, for he is aware that Jesus had done no evil. Pilate actively sought to release Jesus, especially when he learned that Christ claimed to be the Son of God (Jn. 19:7). Finally, Pilate gave in, but only when the "Jews" (John's term for the religious leaders of Judea) kept shouting, "If you let this man go, you are no friend of Caesar. Anyone who claims to be a king opposes Caesar" (Jn. 19:12).

The Jewish evaluation of Pilate is reflected in the writings of Philo, which speak of "his corruptions, his acts of insolence, his rapine, his habit of insulting people, his cruelty, and his continual murders of people untried and uncondemned, and his never-ending, gratuitous and most grievous inhumanity." Surprisingly, early Christian writers were much more sympathetic. Though Eusebius reports that Pilate committed suicide in Gaul, other Christian

The names of Pontius Pilatus (Pilate) and Tiberius Caesar are inscribed on a dedication stone (left) from Caesarea Maritima. Bronze coins (below) were issued by Pilate in A.D. 29–31 for use in the province of Judea. Both of these archaeological finds confirm the historical reliability of the Gospels.

legends suggest that he and his wife became Christians. The Coptic church honors Pilate on June 25th as a saint and holds that he was ultimately converted and became a martyr for his faith.

LEARNING FROM PILATE'S LIFE

The Gospel accounts clearly state that he was convinced of Christ's innocence, made a few weak attempts to free him, but ultimately surrendered his convictions un-

Pilate washing his hands before declaring himself innocent of Jesus' blood (Mt. 27:24); detail of the Melker Altar by Jorg Breu, A.D. 1502.

der pressure from the Jewish leaders.

John tells us that Pilate asked Jesus, "What is truth?" We can almost see Pilate shrug his shoulders as he dismisses the concept. Yet "truth" is one of the most basic concepts of Scripture. The Bible claims that reality has a solid foundation—that God and righteousness exist and that "everyone on the side of truth listens to me [Jesus]" (Jn. 18:37-39). When we are convinced that objective truth exists and are committed to live by it, we will find the moral courage that Pilate lacked to act on our convictions.

Matthew tells us that Pilate "took water and washed his hands in front of the crowd." Declaring himself "innocent of this man's blood," Pilate told the crowd calling for Christ's death, "It is your responsibility" (Mt. 27:24-26). Of course, Pilate lied—not so much to them as to himself. As procurator, only Pilate had authority to pronounce the death sentence. Condemning or freeing Christ was Pilate's responsibility alone. No matter how intense the pressure on any of us to act against our conscience, we remain responsible for what we choose to do. We cannot shift the blame for our own moral choices to others.

pilgrimage (1) A metaphor for the human life span, rooted in the view that during one's time on earth, he or she is a stranger settled only temporarily in a foreign land, as in Gen. 47:9. In the OT and NT, this thought is also expressed by the term "sojourn." (2) A journey undertaken for religious purposes, such as to make a visit to the Jerusalem Temple, as in Ps. 84:5. Three of Israel's religious feasts were pilgrim festivals, which called for all Jewish men to assemble in Jerusalem. *See also* Feasts.

pillar An architectural support, a column, a heap of stones, or an erect stone slab. Several Hebrew words are translated "pillar" in English versions. They refer to a variety of wood or stone constructions with distinct roles in OT culture:

1. *Architectural columns.* Used as supports or for decoration, as in Jdg. 16:25-29; Esth. 1:6. Two highly decorated freestanding columns named Jakin and Boaz stood in front of Solomon's Temple (1 Ki. 7:15-22). *See also* Boaz and Jakin.

2. *Sacred stone slabs.* Served as symbols of a deity in Canaanite worship. Canaanite shrines frequently featured a stone pillar and wooden post or tree, symbolizing male and female sexuality and the deities whose intercourse Canaanite religion linked to the fertility of the land, as in Deut. 12:3; 2 Ki. 3:2. This type of pillar is often translated "image" in the KJV. The OT commands Israel to destroy the Canaanite worship centers (Deut. 7:5) and says, "Do not make idols or set up an image or a sacred stone for yourselves, and do not place a carved stone in your land to bow down before it" (Lev. 26:1).

3. *Heaps of stone.* Erected to serve as a memorial or reminder. Such memorials were used to mark graves, as in Gen. 35:20; to mark the site of personal religious experiences, as in Gen. 28:22; and to mark the site of an act God performed on behalf of his people, as in Josh. 4:4-9; 1 Sam. 7:12. The memorial use of pillars by the Israelites should not be confused with the Canaanite practice of using sacred slabs to symbolize their deities. *See also* Memorial.

4. *The miraculous cloud/fiery pillar.* Served as visible evidence of God's presence with the Exodus generation, by which he guided Israel from Egypt to Sinai and then during their years in the wilderness (Ex. 14:24; *compare* 14:19,20; 33:7-9; 34:5). While some have tried to explain this pillar by suggesting that Moses followed a practice of Persian armies and mounted a burning bowl of pitch on a pole, what the OT describes is clearly supernatural.

5. *Figurative pillars*. Served in the OT as symbols of support or strength, as in 1 Sam. 2:8; Job 26:11; Prov. 9:1. In the NT, Paul speaks of Peter, James, and John as "pillars" of the church (Gal. 2:9), and the Church is called the "pillar and foundation of the truth" (1 Tim. 3:15).

pillow (KJV) Any object used as a headrest. NIV uses the word "cushion." Jacob placed a stone under his head to serve as a pillow (Gen. 28:11). The "pillow" Jesus rested on in the small boat he shared with his disciples (Mk. 4:38) was a *proskeph-alaion*, probably a sandbag used for ballast, called a "balance pillow" (Arabic, *mehadet sabura*).

pim A measure of weight equal to about 7 grams, slightly over two-thirds of a shekel. *See also* Weights and Measures.

pine tree One of the family of conifers that includes the fir and the cedar. The Hebrew word translated "pine" is a general one, and the specific tree intended in any passage, except when reference is made to the cedars of Lebanon, is uncertain. *See also* Fir Tree.

pinnacle (KJV) In architecture, the highest point of a building or construction. In Mt. 4:5 and Lk. 4:9, the term translated "pinnacle" often indicated a tower or rampart.

Josephus says that the pinnacle of the Jerusalem Temple was the southeastern corner of its outer wall, which fell sharply away into the depths of the Kidron Valley. It was probably on this high point that Satan challenged Jesus to throw himself down to prove that he truly was the Son of God.

pipe (KJV) (1) A class of musical instruments, usually a flute, as in Dan. 3:5. *See also* Flute; Music. (2) One of two hollow tubes carrying golden olive oil to a lampstand seen in a vision of Zechariah (4:12).

pit (1) A natural or artificial cavity in the earth, especially a cistern or grain storage pit. In Palestine, cisterns were dug to collect rainwater. These were frequently large enough to serve as prisons, as in Jer. 38. Pit openings were to be carefully covered, so that no person or animal could fall in, as in Ex. 21:33,34; 2 Sam. 23:20; and Mt. 12:11. (2) A metaphor for danger, whether from the plots of the wicked, as in Ps. 35:7, or the sensual attractiveness of the prostitute, as in Prov. 22:14. However, because God is sovereign, setting traps for others is dangerous: "He who digs a hole and scoops it out falls into the pit he has made. The trouble he causes recoils on himself; his violence comes down on his own head" (Ps. 7:15,16). (3) A reference to the grave or to death, serving as a synonym for Sheol in the OT expression "the pit" (Ps. 30:3). *See also* Sheol.

pitch (1) In older versions, any thick, sticky substance, such as bitumen, tar, or mortar, used for caulking or waterproofing, as in Gen. 6:14 (*see also* Bitumen). (2) As a verb, to set up a temporary shelter, as in the phrase "to pitch one's tent," in Gen. 12:8; 1 Chr. 15:1.

pitcher (1) A pottery jar used to carry liquids, as in Gen. 24:14; Jdg. 7:16. The water jar typically had a rounded lip and one or two handles, although women

Sacred pillars from a Canaanite cult center at Gezer still stand today. The Israelites were forbidden to set up these stone slabs, which represented a male deity's sexuality (Ex. 23:24; Deut. 16:22).

Public grain storage pit at Megiddo.

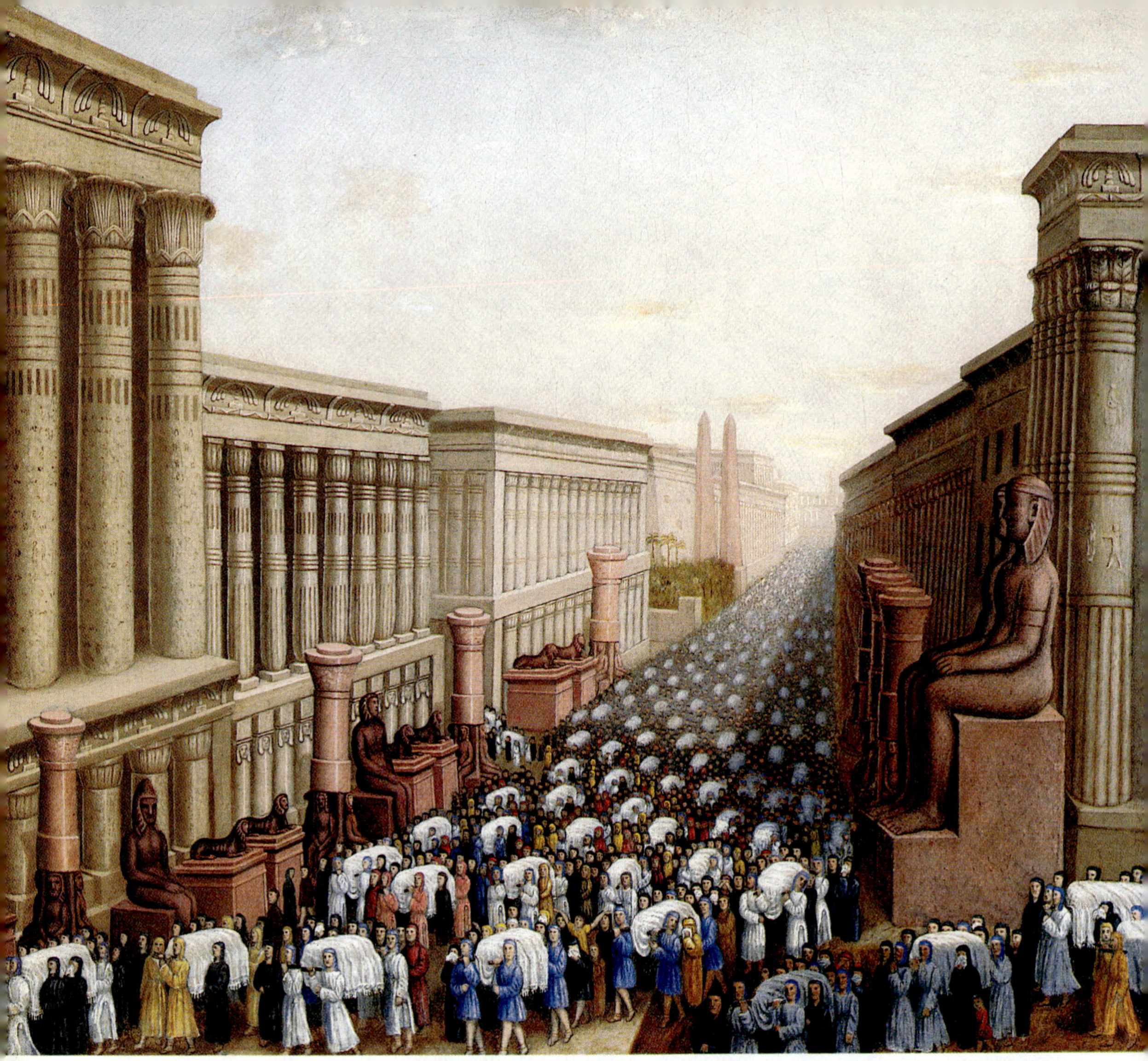

Burial of the First Born *by Erastus Salisbury Field (1805–1900). This American folk artist took the Exodus account of the tenth plague to its probable conclusion, portraying an imaginative mass funeral procession (Ex. 12:23-30).*

would usually carry these jars on their heads. (2) One type of sacred gold vessel associated with "pouring out of offerings," indicated in some modern versions, including the New King James.

In Eccl. 12:6, death is symbolized by a broken pitcher. *See also* Pottery.

pity A feeling of concern for the plight of another, which often moves a person to offer help. *See also* Compassion; Mercy.

Hellenistic-period water pitcher found in Israel. David stole King Saul's water jug as a sign that he had spared Saul's life the previous night (1 Sam. 26:12).

The Hebrew words most often translated "pity" are *hamal* and *raham*, which indicate both the emotion and the help offered as an expression of the emotion, as in 2 Sam. 12:6; *compare* Jer. 13:14. In the NT, pity is conveyed by three terms: *eleos*, which means "mercy"; *oiktirmos*, which is a cry of pity and concern and is often translated "compassion" or "mercy"; and *splangchnizomai*, which is usually found where the Gospels describe Jesus' feeling of compassion or pity for a person in need. That emotion is beautifully conveyed in Mk. 1:40-42, which describes Christ's response to a leper who appealed to him for healing. The NT says that, "filled with compassion [pity], Jesus reached out his hand and touched the man" and healed him. God calls on us as his chosen people to "clothe" ourselves with "compassion [pity]" and, in imitation of Christ, to reach out to others with loving concern (Col. 3:12).

plague An epidemic of infectious disease or some other calamity leading to significant hardship or loss of life. Plagues occur naturally, but in Scripture many are identified as God's punishment for sin. The character of certain recorded plagues as divine judgment is authenticated by their unusual severity, by their pre-announcement and timing, or by a prophet's later linkage of the plagues to sin.

God used a plague to protect Sarah when she was taken into Pharaoh's harem (Gen. 12:17). He sent plagues to punish the Israelites when they worshiped the golden calf (Ex. 32:35), murmured against the manna he provided (Num. 11:33,34),

THE TEN PLAGUES ON EGYPT

Plague	Scripture	Significance
Water to blood	Ex. 7:14-25	The Nile turned to "blood." Possibly red dirt or algae clogged the Nile and killed the fish, making the river the Egyptians personified as the source of life reek with death. Each of the first six plagues seems to proceed from the Nile and demonstrates God's power over that pagan deity. *See also* Nile.
Frogs	Ex. 8:1-15	Frogs, a symbol of fertility associated with the goddess Heqit, overwhelmed the land and when they died, polluted Egypt.
Gnats	Ex. 8:16-19	Some small stinging insect, such as the sand flea, is probably intended here. Egypt's magicians could not replicate this miracle and informed Pharaoh it was "the finger of God."
Flies	Ex. 8:20-32	Swarms, possibly of biting swamp flies or of stableflies, infested Egypt. The diseases they carry may well have been the source of the illnesses described as the fifth and sixth plagues.
Anthrax	Ex. 9:1-7	Many believe that the "very serious plague" that struck the cattle of Egypt was anthrax. The Israelite cattle were immune, showing that God made a distinction between his people and their oppressors.
Boils	Ex. 9:8-12	Probably skin anthrax, carried by the bites of the flies, which fed on the rotting carcasses of the frogs.
Hail	Ex. 9:13-35	The storm ruined the barley and flax, but again spared the land of Goshen occupied by the Israelites. Egyptians who had come to respect God were able to shelter their animals and slaves before the storm struck.
Locusts	Ex. 10:1-20	These voracious feeders stripped the land of any crops and greenery that remained. Following the other plagues that devastated the economy of Egypt, this plague was truly disastrous.
Darkness	Ex. 10:21-29	The sun, representing the Egyptian god Ra, was darkened, and for three days no one could see his hand before his face. Some suggest this was a *khamsin*, an intense wind that filled the air with dirt even as it drove the locusts out to sea. The text, however, indicates an even deeper and more terrifying darkness.
Death of firstborn	Ex. 11:1–12:36	This final plague took the firstborn of every Egyptian household, while leaving the Israelites untouched. This plague caused such terror that Pharaoh finally urged Moses to lead Israel out of his land to freedom. The pantheon of Egypt, through which their worshipers hoped to find everlasting life, was proven powerless before the God of the freed slaves (*compare* Ex. 12:12).

followed the rebels led by Korah (Num. 16:46-50), and committed idolatry at Baal-Peor (Num. 25:9; Ps. 106:29,30). A plague of locusts stimulated the prophecy uttered by Joel.

The most familiar of biblical plagues are those associated with Israel's release from Egypt. While each of the first nine plagues of the Exodus is a scourge known to have occurred naturally in Egypt in ancient times, the severity, the focus on Egyptian territory while leaving the Israelite area untouched, the beginning and end at Moses' command, and the concentration of all nine plagues within the span of a single year, mark these as mighty works or miracles performed by God on behalf of his covenant people. The Exodus plagues were intended (1) to help Israel know the Lord, as in Ex. 6:7; (2) to teach the Egyptians that "I am the Lord," as in Ex. 7:5; and (3) to exercise "judgment on all the gods of Egypt," as in Ex. 12:12.

plain Level or flat terrain. Several Hebrew words, which designate different kinds of flatlands, are translated "plain" in English versions.

The major types of plains referred to in the OT are: (1) *biq'ah*, "broad valley," plains found in a valley, as in Gen. 11:2. (2) *kikkar*, "a round thing," such as the relatively flat lands found in mountain valleys, as in Gen. 13:10-12. *See also* Cities of the Plain. (3) *mishor*, "level place," tableland found at a higher elevation, as in 1 Ki. 20:23. (4) *shepelah*, "lowland," usually of the fertile plains along the Mediterranean west of Canaan's mountains, as in 1 Chr. 27:28. (5) *'arabah*, "flat desert," especially of the hot dry lands sweeping down

from the upper Jordan Valley toward the Sinai, as in Num. 22:1; Deut. 1:1. Often modern versions use the original Hebrew word rather than "plain" to designate specific areas. Thus, the RSV speaks of the Shephelah, and the NIV calls the southern desert areas the Arabah.

plants Living organisms that possess cellulose cell walls and synthesize food from carbon dioxide. Rugged Palestine has a wide variety of climates and elevations that support a rich and varied plant life. Specific plants named in the Bible are discussed by name in separate articles. *See also* Agriculture.

pleasure, pleasing A feeling of enjoyment, delight, satisfaction. Many OT and NT words indicate pleasure and gladness, because God "richly provides us with everything for our enjoyment" (1 Tim. 6:17).

Among the words translated "pleasing" and "pleasure" are: Heb., *simhah*, pleasure or gladness; *rason*, from a root that means to be pleased with or favorable to; *hapesh*, expressing great delight or favor; Gk., *aresko*, indicating something from which a person derives great pleasure; *eudokeia*, used to indicate a choice that reflects a state of mind, as in Paul's statement that God "was pleased to reveal his Son in me so that I might preach him among the Gentiles" (Gal. 1:15,16). The NT also uses several words sparingly. Some imply "sinful pleasures" (*hedone; philedonos*), as in Heb. 11:25; 2 Pet. 2:13, while another word group (*euarestos, euaresteo*) focuses attention on how we can please God.

While the Bible encourages us to take

pleasure in the good things of life, it also emphasizes that no one can find life's meaning or personal satisfaction in pleasures alone. A concentration on pleasure is both destructive (Prov. 21:17) and futile. The writer of Ecclesiastes describes his search for life's meaning, and says:

I thought with my heart, "Come now, I will test you with pleasure to find out what is good." But that also proved to be meaningless. "Laughter," I said, "is foolish. And what does pleasure accomplish?" I tried cheering myself with wine, and embracing folly [immorality]—my mind still guiding me with wisdom. I wanted to see what was worthwhile for men to do under heaven during the few days of their lives. . . .
I denied myself nothing my eyes desired;
*   I refused my heart no pleasure.*

(Eccl. 2:1-3,10)

And the writer concludes, "Everything was meaningless, a chasing after the wind" (2:11).

While humankind is intended to enjoy God's good gifts, the meaning of life can never be found in the mere experience of pleasures. As Augustine pointed out, God made humans for fellowship with himself, and our hearts are restless until we find our rest in him. However, in the context of fellowship with God, human beings are free to enjoy and find satisfaction in the many positive pleasures God has designed—as the psalmist says, "At thy [God's] right hand there are pleasures forevermore" (Ps. 16:11, KJV).

pledge (1) An obligation, vow, or commitment, as in Gen. 19:14; Deut. 20:7; 1 Tim. 5:12. (2) More often, personal property of a debtor given as security for a loan or an obligation, as in Gen. 38:17-20; Deut. 24:10.

Old Testament Law carefully protects the poor, who were most likely to borrow and be forced to leave a pledge guaranteeing repayment. No creditor could enter a debtor's house to seize a pledge (Deut. 24:10,11). Certain items, such as one of the millstones used daily to grind grain for bread, or a widow's clothing, could not be taken in pledge (Deut. 24:6,17,18). If a person's outer cloak was surrendered as a pledge, it must be returned each night, for these robes were also used as blankets (Ex. 22:26,27; Deut. 24:12,13). *See also* Borrow.

Pleiades Bright constellation of seven stars, generally accepted as the group intended in Job 9:9; 38:31; and Amos 5:8. Each time this highly visible cluster is mentioned, it is to contrast the wonder of God's power with man's impotence, as in Job 9:8,9: "He alone stretches out the heavens and treads the waves of the sea. He is the Maker of . . . the Pleiades and the constellations of the south."

plow, plowshare A tool used to scratch the surface of the ground in preparation for sowing (Isa. 28:24,25). In biblical times, plows did not turn the ground over, as modern plows do.

The typical plow was made from the forked trunk of a small tree. One branch was shortened and sharpened so that it would dig into the ground when dragged by oxen. When possible, the digging branch was sheathed in metal. This metal sheath was the "plowshare." It was proverbial in Israel that in times of war the plowshare was beaten into the shape of a sword and that when peace came, the sword was re-forged into a plowshare (Isa. 2:4; Joel 3:10; Mic. 4:3).

Typically, a farmer walked behind his ox or oxen, using his left hand to guide the plow. His right hand held a long-shafted goad used to direct his animals. The

A deity plows behind a lion and a dragon, on a cylinder seal and in its impression, from Tell Asmar, Iraq (2350–2200 B.C.). Mesopotamian plows had a seed drill to distribute the grains evenly.

wealth of Elisha's family is indicated in that, when he was called to follow Elijah, he was plowing his family fields with twelve yoke of oxen (1 Ki. 19:19).

Plowing, a common sight in Israel, is often used symbolically. Referring to future devastation, the prophets spoke of populated areas as "plowed like a field" (Jer. 26:18; Mic. 3:12). Jesus' enigmatic illustration of the need for total dedication—"No one who puts his hand to the plow and looks back is fit for service in the kingdom of God" (Lk. 9:62)—was easily grasped by his hearers. A plowman visually marked a goal and headed for it. If he looked back, the furrow would not be straight and the field poorly prepared. Jesus simply meant that discipleship, like plowing, calls for complete concentration on the task ahead.

Plumb line.

plumb line A simple tool used by builders to determine the perpendicular. The plumb line was a cord with a stone or metal weight (called the plummet) tied to one end. Symbolically, the plumb line speaks of God's measurement of the righteousness of his people (2 Ki. 21:13; Isa. 28:17; Amos 7:7,8).

Right: Pods of the carob or locust tree, Ceratonia siliqua. When ripe, these pods are filled with a dark, honeylike syrup.

pod The fruit of carob or locust trees, which was used as animal feed and eaten by the very poor. Some suppose that the "locust" eaten by John the Baptist was this pod rather than the insect itself (Mt. 3:4). This is certainly the food the prodigal son fed to the pigs when destitute in a foreign land (Lk. 15:16). These pods are called "husks" in the KJV. *See also* Husk.

poetry An arrangement of words in a form appropriate to express thoughts and feelings in more emotional, powerful, connotative, and imaginative ways than in everyday or narrative speech, or prose. In many languages, poetry is identified by its rhythmic and rhymed character.

ROLE OF POETRY IN THE OT

Important in Hebrew society, poetry was closely linked with song. Many of the psalms, the prime example of Hebrew poetic expression, have superscriptions identifying them as *shir*, a song sung with or without instruments; *mizmor*, a hymn sung with instrumental accompaniment; *tehilla*, a hymn of praise, etc. Although secular songs have not been preserved in Scripture, undoubtedly these as well as the sacred songs played a significant role in the life of the Hebrew people.

Another indication of the importance of Hebrew poetry is the number of OT books that contain poetic expression. Poems are preserved in narrative books, as the hymn sung on crossing the Red Sea (Ex. 15), Deborah's song of triumph (Jdg. 5), and David's song of praise after being delivered from Saul's murderous attacks (2 Sam. 22). No less than 6 of the 39 OT books consist almost entirely of poetry (Job, Psalms, Proverbs, Ecclesiastes, Song of Songs, Lamentations). In addition, large sections of the major and minor prophets are in poetic form.

CHARACTER OF HEBREW POETRY

Hebrew poetry is often difficult to distinguish from prose. The Hebrew language itself is almost poetic in its nature, being rich in imagery, alliteration, and other devices. Moreover, Hebrew poetry does not rely on any obvious meter or on rhyme. Rhythm was originally conveyed in the accent or stress placed on various syllables of Hebrew words, but we are unable to recapture the pronunciation, much less the stress patterns of 3,000 years ago, so this identifying characteristic remains something of a mystery. We do know, however, that the rhythm in Hebrew poetry is found in patterns or arrangement of thoughts and concepts rather than in rhyme schemes.

The structure found in Hebrew poetry is called "parallelism," which simply means that a parallel or close relationship exists between the thought expressed in an initial phrase and the thought appearing in the next phrase. The simplest form of parallelism is "synonymous," in which the second phrase restates the thought of the first. Examples of synonymous parallelism abound, as in Ps. 103:8 and Ps. 9:4:

800

The Lord is compassionate and gracious,
  slow to anger, abounding in love.

You have upheld my right and my cause;
  you have sat on your throne, judging
    righteously.

It is important when reading the Bible to understand the parallel character of its poetry. For instance, Zech. 9:9 pictures Christ's entry into Jerusalem on Palm Sunday, and says:

See, your king comes to you,
  righteous and having salvation,
  gentle and riding on a donkey,
  on a colt, the foal of a donkey.

Some might take this to portray the Savior riding two beasts rather than the one the NT says Christ rode as he entered the Holy City. But when the OT text is read as poetry, the final phrase is understood simply as a synonymous repetition of the phrase above, so only one animal is intended.

Another type of parallelism is "antithetical." Here the thought in the second phrase strengthens the first by stating a contrast. Illustrations of antithetical parallelism are found throughout Scripture, as in Ps. 1:6 and Prov. 14:20:

For the Lord watches over the way of the
    righteous,
  but the way of the wicked will perish.

The poor are shunned even by their
    neighbors,
  but the rich have many friends.

A third basic type of parallelism is called "synthetic." Here the first phrase is followed by several others that build on and expand the original thought expressed. The classic example of synthetic parallelism is Ps. 1:3, which describes the righteous person who delights in God's Law:

He is like a tree planted by streams of
    water,
  which yields its fruit in season
and whose leaf does not wither.
  Whatever he does prospers.

BEAUTY OF HEBREW POETRY

Hebrew poetry is capable of capturing the most delicate of impressions, as in Deborah's description of the family of an oppressor, waiting hopefully for his return after a battle with Israel:

Through the window peered Sisera's mother;
  behind the lattice she cried out,
"Why is his chariot so long in coming?
  Why is the clatter of his chariots
    delayed?"

The wisest of her ladies answered her;
  indeed, she keeps saying to herself,
"Are they not finding and dividing the
    spoils;
  a girl or two for each man,
  colorful garments as plunder for
    Sisera,
  colorful garments embroidered,
  highly embroidered garments for my
    neck—
all this as plunder?"   (Jdg. 5:28-30)

At the same time, Hebrew poetry is capable of expressing the most powerful condemnation of evil, the most exalted vision of God, and the most uplifting images of hope.

Isaiah chooses the image of a vineyard to convey poetically God's disappointment in Israel:

The vineyard of the Lord Almighty
  is the house of Israel,
and the men of Judah
  are the garden of his delight.
And he looked for justice, but saw
    bloodshed;
for righteousness, but heard cries of
    distress.   (Isa. 5:7)

Isaiah also turns to poetry to describe God and to hold out the hope of what we can find only in him:

Do you not know?
  Have you not heard?
The Lord is the everlasting God,
  the Creator of the ends of the earth.
He will not grow tired or weary . . .
Even youths grow tired and weary,
  and young men stumble and fall;
but those who hope in the Lord
  will renew their strength.
They will soar on wings like eagles;
  they will run and not grow weary,
  they will walk and not be faint.
                              (Isa. 40:28-31)

Readers of the Bible owe an unpayable debt to Hebrew poetry, whose distinctive nature makes it possible for those of every tongue and tribe to sense, translated in their own language, the wonder and the joy of faith in Israel's God.

NEW TESTAMENT POETRY

In general, the writers of the NT do not weave Greek poetic forms into their own compositions, but Paul does quote from pagan Greek poets (Acts 17:28; 1 Cor. 15:33; Tit. 1:12; compare 1 Cor. 2:9) (see also Philosophy). The NT writers also draw into the text phrases that reflect the powerful poetic devices of the OT. Thus, in the NT we find:

1. *Liturgical poetry*. The best example of this type of poetry, which seems also to have served the early church as a confession of faith, is Phil. 2:5-11. Other passages identified as liturgical include 1 Tim. 3:16; 2 Tim. 2:11-13; and possibly Eph. 5:14. Eight poetic passages in Luke clearly follow the pattern established in the OT and were also used liturgically in the early church. These are Lk. 1:14-17,32,33,35,46-55,68-79; 2:14,29-32,34,35.

2. *NT quotations of OT poetry*. There may be as many as 200 such quotations, only a few of which are extensive. Most of the longer quotations are found in the Epistle to the Hebrews.

3. *Passages with poetic power*. Several NT passages are reminiscent of Hebrew poetry in their intensity or imagery. Among them are Mt. 23:37-39; Jn. 1:1-18; and 14:1-7. At times, Jesus' utterances reflect the parallelism of OT poetry, especially in the Sermon on the Mount (Mt. 5:3-12; 6:25-34). Poetic passages that are reminiscent of Greek rhetorical style are Rom. 8:35-38; 1 Cor. 13; and Heb. 11:33-36.

4. *Apocalyptic passages*. Such passages deal with history's end and adopt language that throbs with obscure imagery. Certainly within the Book of Revelation we find some of the most powerful praise songs of the NT, such as Rev. 1:7; 4:11; 5:9-13; 7:10,12,15-17; 19:1-3,5-7. *See also* Apocalyptic Literature.

In the NT, as in the OT, poetry lifts our hearts and expands our vision, leading us with the writers of the Scripture to praise "him who loves us and has freed us from our sins by his blood, and has made us to be a kingdom and priests to serve his God and Father—to him be glory and power for ever and ever! Amen" (Rev. 1:5,6).

poison Any substance that has a debilitating or deadly effect when introduced into the body.

Two major sources of poison are mentioned in Scripture: (1) poisonous reptiles (Deut. 32:24,33; Ps. 58:4), which also serve as a metaphor of the wicked, as in Pss. 58:4; 140:3; and Rom. 3:13; (2) poisonous plants, such as hemlock (Hos. 10:4) and the gourds that introduced "death in the pot" (2 Ki. 4:39). Some have incorrectly assumed that poison was used in the procedure employed to test the purity of a wife suspected of unfaithfulness by her jealous husband (Num. 5:11-31). Drinking a "deadly poison" is mentioned in Mk.

16:18. James 3:8 warns that the tongue "is a restless evil, full of deadly poison," and remarks that a person who is never at fault in what he says is truly mature.

politarch The title of city magistrates in Thessalonica, correctly used in Acts 17:6,8. For many years, this was considered a mistake, as the title was not known from other sources. Now, however, the title is attested by over a dozen inscriptions and has become evidence of Luke's careful and accurate portrayal of the first century A.D.

pollution Either (1) ritual uncleanness, as in Num. 9:6; 19:14, or (2) moral or spiritual impurity, as in Acts 15:20; 2 Pet. 2:20. Both disqualified a person from fellowship with God. In the OT, pollution is closely linked with the important concept of uncleanness. *See also* Clean and Unclean.

Modern versions tend to reserve the term for the serious offenses of murder and idolatry, as in Num. 35:33; Acts 15:29, and the moral corruption that characterizes the world, as in 2 Pet. 2:20. *See also* World.

pomegranate A slightly acidic, seed-filled yellow or red fruit that grows on a bush-like tree in Palestine.

The pomegranate was a symbol of the fruitfulness of Canaan (Num. 13:23; 20:5;

Top: Ripened pomegranates hanging from the tree (Punica granatum). Bottom: Pomegranate-shaped vase from Cyprus (about 1400 B.C.). This fruit was a popular decorative motif in Israel.

influence. In the OT, poverty implies vulnerability to oppression and exploitation by the rich.

NATURE OF POVERTY IN THE OT

A variety of Hebrew words are translated "poor" in the OT. *Dal* is a social term indicating the lower classes. *'Ani* emphasizes the powerlessness of the poor and is often best understood as "financial distress." *'Ebyon* indicates desperate need, while *rush* suggests the destitution that characterized the lower classes. Taken together, these words convey a picture of the poor as persons whose lack of financial resources condemns them to a lower quality of life and makes them vulnerable to those who take unfair advantage of their situation. Poverty robs the poor of their rights, of respect, and of any role in shaping the society.

Though the OT makes it clear that some poor are to blame for their own situation, poverty remains symptomatic of entrenched sin in the society as a whole. While "lazy hands make a man poor" (Prov. 10:4) and "drunkards and gluttons become poor" (Prov. 23:21), at the same time, "A poor man's field may produce abundant food, but injustice sweeps it

This ivory pomegranate is possibly from Solomon's Temple. The Hebrew inscription on its neck dates it to the kings' period and reads, "Belonging to . . . , holy to the priests." It could have been a finial on a throne or scepter, a hanging ornament or an altar decoration.

The pool of Siloam at the mouth of Hezekiah's tunnel, which this Israelite king ordered dug to bring water from the Gihon spring inside the city walls.

Deut. 8:8; *compare* Hag. 2:19). The fruit, or possibly the flower, was a decorative motif woven into the high priest's garments (Ex. 28:33-35; 39:24-26) and hammered into the brass work in Solomon's Temple (1 Ki. 7:18-20; 2 Chr. 3:16; 4:13).

The pomegranate fruit was eaten and its tart, refreshing juice was drunk or made into a sweet wine. The skin, rich in tannin, was used in tanning leather. Pomegranates ripened in mid-October and could be stored for use throughout the winter.

Pontius Pilate *See* Pilate, Pontius.

pool A natural or artificial reservoir for holding water. The term is used of natural ponds, as in Ps. 107:35, as well as of reservoirs and larger storage cisterns, as in Isa. 36:2; Neh. 3:15. Isaiah pictures the coming age of God's blessing as a time when "the burning sand will become a pool" (35:7), and God "will turn the desert into pools of water" (41:18). *See also* Cistern.

poor, poverty The state of possessing few if any material resources and little social

away" (Prov. 13:23). The constant cries of the prophets against injustice and oppression demonstrate that poverty in Israel could not be explained away by charging all the poor with laziness (Isa. 58:6,7; Zech. 7:9-12).

The same point is made by the many Hebrew words for oppression: *'ashaq,* the misuse of power to crush those of low status; *dak,* crushing oppression; *lahas,* the "squeezing" of the vulnerable in society; *nagas,* intense, painful pressure; *rasas,* the crushing weight of mistreatment. Each of these is associated in the OT text with poverty, despite the biblical injunction that "he who oppresses the poor shows contempt for their Maker, but whoever is kind to the needy honors God" (Prov. 14:31).

REMEDIES TO POVERTY IN OT LAW

The OT is filled with expressions of God's concern for the poor and with exhortations addressed to the wealthy to aid the less fortunate. In addition, social legislation in Mosaic Law includes a number of mechanisms designed to relieve the poor and to reduce poverty.

1. *Justice.* The legal system specifically prohibited showing favoritism to either the rich or the poor in court cases (Lev. 19:15). Instead, cases were to be decided strictly on their legal merits (Ex. 23:3,6).

2. *Gleaning.* Agricultural law gave the poor the right to gather any crops left in another's fields after the owner completed his harvest. Everything the harvesters missed or that fell to the ground was to be left for the poor (Lev. 19:10; 23:22). In addition, the poor of the land were to have access to any crops that grew spontaneously during the Sabbath year when no crops were to be planted. *See also* Sabbath Year.

3. *Loans.* The wealthy were encouraged to make interest-free loans to the poor (Lev. 25:35-37; Deut. 23:19,20). In addition, every seventh year any outstanding debts were to be cancelled. The OT is very specific in stating that the financially stable are obligated to show concern for the poor by lending, as Deut. 15:7-11 exhorts, "I command you to be openhanded toward your brothers and toward the poor and needy in your land." The Israelites understood this provision of the Law to imply an obligation on God's part, expressed in Prov. 19:17: "He who is kind to the poor lends to the Lord, and he will reward him for what he has done." *See also* Borrow; Debt; Interest; Pledge; Usury.

4. *Tithes.* Tithes of produce were to be collected every third year and stored locally (Deut. 14:28,29). This food was not only to be distributed to Levites but also to "the aliens, the fatherless and the widows."

5. *Property Rights.* Land laws were designed to protect Israelites against poverty. Each family was given permanent title to its own plot of land at the time of the Conquest. This land could not be sold, although it could be rented out for an amount equivalent to the projected value of the crops it would produce. Every fiftieth year, the year of Jubilee, any land that had been so rented was to be returned to the original owner. As wealth in ancient Israel was measured in land, this law guaranteed the preservation of a family's capital. Even if one person was lazy or unfortunate, he could not lose the land that held security for future generations (Lev. 25:23,24).

6. *Voluntary Servitude.* Old Testament Law also contained provision for voluntary servitude, wherein a poor person could sell his services for seven years to a wealthier fellow countryman (Deut. 15:12-18; *compare* Lev. 25:39-54). This provided money to the poor person to pay back his debts, and also gave him seven years of apprentice training for future success. At the end of the seventh year, the servant was to be released and supplied "liberally from your flock, your threshing floor and your wine press" (Deut. 15:14). Thus, the now-trained servant was given the resources needed to make a fresh start possible.

The variety and number of these social mechanisms demonstrate God's concern for the poor. One of the tragedies of sacred history is that with a few exceptions, the spirit as well as the letter of the poverty laws was systematically violated by society (Isa. 3:14,15; Jer. 5:28; Amos 5:11,12).

POVERTY IN THE NT

In the NT, the responsibility to help the poor is placed primarily upon the individual and local congregation. Unlike Israel, the Church is not a nation. It is a community existing within the wider secular society. Thus, while OT legislation might possibly serve as a model for modern social legislation, such legislation has no direct counterpart in the NT.

The NT does mention class differences. Paul says that "not many influential" but rather the "lowly" were found in the church at Corinth (1 Cor. 1:20-30). James

Two Egyptian tomb artifacts: Craftsman decorates a pottery vase (above), tomb of Rekhmira, 15th century B.C.; limestone figurine of a potter at his wheel (inset), tomb of Ny-kau-inpu, 2500–2300 B.C.

to him by God, as in Josh. 19:49. By extension, one's portion is his or her spiritual inheritance obtained through personal relationship with God, as in Pss. 16:5; 73:26; and 119:57. Also (3) the tithe Israel was to pay to the priests, as in Num. 18:28.

possession, demon *See* Demon.

Inscribed potsherds or ostraca that bear the names of Zealots who held out in Herod's fortress at Masada during the second Jewish revolt (A.D. 135).

806

post (1) Any place of assignment, as in Isa. 21:8, or an office with distinct responsibilities to be fulfilled, as of the watchman in Isa. 62:6. (2) In building, the vertical beam from which a door or gate was hung, as in Jdg. 16:3, but especially the poles used in erecting the curtains that surrounded the courtyard of the tabernacle, as in Ex. 38:15; Num. 3:37. Additionally, in some English versions, (3) runners who carried official messages from the king are called ''posts'' in the KJV (2 Chr. 30:6; Esth. 3:13,15).

pot A vessel, generally of clay. Pots were made in a variety of shapes and forms and were used for carrying water, storing food, cooking, and dozens of other daily household tasks in ancient Israel. *See also* Pottery.

potsherds Broken pieces of clay pots. Such remains have been of great value in dating various strata of excavations in Palestine. Also, potsherds were used in OT times as a material on which brief messages were written. These inscribed potsherds, called ''ostraca,'' are valuable to archaeologists. Job used these sharp clay fragments to scrape his boils (Job 2:8).

Model of Herod's Temple shows the large, covered porch, called Solomon's Portico or Colonnade. The first believers in Jerusalem met there (Acts 5:12).

warns against showing favoritism to the rich in the church (Jas. 2:1-9), and Paul urges the believers at Rome to "be willing to associate with people of low position" (Rom. 12:13-16). Brotherly love and respect for one another's spiritual gifts are expected to make class distinctions irrelevant in the Christian community.

The NT maintains an important balance within the local congregation. Regarding brothers who are unwilling to work, Paul writes, "If a man will not work, he shall not eat" (2 Th. 3:9-15). On the other hand, Christian love must find practical expression where real needs exist. According to the NT, each believer is responsible to meet the immediate needs of the destitute with whom he or she is in contact (Jas. 2:14-16; 1 Jn. 3:16-18). Apparently, some organized efforts for the poor characterized the early church throughout the NT era (Acts 2:45; 6:1-7; 1 Tim. 5:1-16). And the NT's major teaching on giving was stimulated by the need of Christians in an area experiencing disaster conditions (2 Cor. 8,9). Contributions were solicited, not to expand an institution, but to meet the very real need of the destitute. While Christians are encouraged to "do good to all people," there is a special obligation to help those in need "who belong to the family of believers" (Gal. 6:10).

Both Testaments call for those who have a covenant relationship with God to recognize the Lord's deep concern for the poor and oppressed and to reflect that concern in practical ways. The Bible calls us to take responsibility for the condition of the poor and to do all that we can—individually, through the church, and in society—to alleviate poverty.

poor in spirit Those who recognize their spiritual poverty and as a result rely on God rather than self-effort (Mt. 5:3; *compare* Lk. 18:9-14). *See also* Beatitudes.

poplar tree A tree within the willow family that was valued for the dark shade it cast and that Hos. 4:13 associates with pagan worship.

porch, portico The broad, pillared veranda in front of the Jerusalem Temple constructed by Solomon (1 Ki. 6:3) and of the future Temple described in Ezekiel's vision (Ezek. 40). Private homes could have porches (Jdg. 3:23; Mk. 14:66), as did the throne room of the king (1 Ki. 7:6,7).

porter (KJV) An archaic term for gatekeeper or doorkeeper, an official on guard often with responsibility for entry into cities or such public buildings as the Temple. *See also* Doorkeeper.

portion That part of a whole which is allotted to an individual. In Scripture, "portion" is often used to indicate: (1) that part of a family estate inherited by an heir, as in Gen. 31:14. In OT times, the oldest son received twice the amount given any other heir. Thus, Elisha's request for a double portion of Elijah's spirit was a request that he might succeed the older man as Israel's chief prophet (2 Ki. 2:9). (2) Especially, the land owned by an Israelite, which he realized had been allotte

pottage (KJV) A soup or stew made with vegetables and sometimes seasoned with meat (Gen. 25:29-34; 2 Ki. 4:38-41). Throughout Bible times, stews served as main dishes and were typically eaten with the fingers or by dipping into them with a fragment of bread. Bread, stew, and drink constituted a complete meal.

potter A person who makes vessels from clay. Because a variety of pottery was needed in every Hebrew home, each village generally had its own potter (Jer. 18:3,4). In time, guilds of potters developed in larger cities, and districts were set aside for this occupation (*compare* 1 Chr. 4:23).

The ancient potter needed to develop several skills. He had to find good clay, mix it with water and grit, and then work to remove any pockets of air. Isaiah describes this process when likening God's judgment to "a potter treading the clay" (Isa. 41:25). The worked clay was then fashioned by hand.

Throughout the Israelite period (1400–600 B.C.), potters worked with the "slow wheel," a stone bowl with a rounded projection below and a flat top. This was placed on a base featuring a depression into which the upper projection fit. Olive oil was probably used as a lubricant to help the wheel turn more easily. The potter slowly turned the upper wheel with his hand or feet as he shaped the clay vessel. Later a "fast wheel," like that used by modern potters, was introduced. This featured a flat top fixed to a long shaft and a heavy lower wheel that was turned by foot.

After the pots were shaped, they were then coated with a watery wash of clay or occasionally decorated with a thin red or black stripe. Finally, they were heated in a closed kiln for several days to form the finished product.

Because the skills of a potter were difficult to master, pottery making was generally a family affair, and each family's traditions were passed from generation to generation.

potter's field A plot of land purchased as a burial ground for indigents with the money Judas received for betraying Jesus (Mt. 27:7). *See also* Akeldama.

pottery Fire-hardened clay objects. When clay objects are subjected to temperatures between 700° and 900° Fahrenheit (420° and 530° Celsius), chemical changes take

Right: The shir *was a wide-mouthed cooking pot made in various sizes.*
Below: Several sizes of a handled pot called the parur, *used for heating liquids (Jdg. 6:19).*

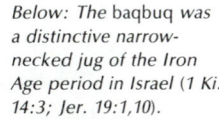

Right: The mahabat *was a clay or metal baking tray some 12–14 inches (30–35 centimeters) in diameter (Lev. 2:5; Ezek. 4:3).*

Left: Terra-cotta perfume flasks, called alabastroi, *from Herodian Jerusalem.*

Below: The baqbuq *was a distinctive narrow-necked jug of the Iron Age period in Israel (1 Ki. 14:3; Jer. 19:1,10).*

Above: Large storage jar (nebel) for oil, wine, or grain, found in King Ahab's excavated palace at Samaria (9th century B.C.). It held about 6 gallons (23 liters).

Right: Water pitcher (kad) from the kingdom of Judah (8th century B.C.). One of the handles is formed into a base for a small jug (Gen. 24:14; Jdg. 7:16).

Right: Israelite drinking cup, called kos in Hebrew, made in the shape of a pomegranate (Hebron, 8th century B.C.)

Above: Among the household pottery found at Masada was this tryblioi, a large deep dish from which all the family could take food (see Mt. 26:23).
Below: Large, valuable banquet bowl with cover, called a sepel (Jdg. 5:25; 6:38).

place that give them many of the characteristics of stone.

Pottery vessels of all shapes were needed in ancient households. Giant jars stored water and olive oil, jugs carried water, juglets served wine, and small vials held perfume. Clay storage jars held the household's supply of grain and other foods. For cooking, housewives used clay pots, and, by the first century, clay ovens. At meals, shallow pottery bowls served as both platters and dishes. The lamps that lit the Hebrew home at night were of pottery too. Even altars of incense found at Canaanite worship centers were made of pottery. Because so many pottery objects were in constant use in biblical times, untold numbers of whole vessels or their fragments have been found at archaeological sites throughout Syria and Israel.

These pottery vessels and potsherds (that is, pottery fragments) are valuable archaeological finds. By looking at the shape of a pottery vessel, the design of its base or spout, the shape of its lip, the curve of its handles, the style of burnishing, or the decorative motifs, an archaeologist can usually determine to the century and often to the quarter-century the date it was made. Thus, pottery remains found at an archaeological site help determine when the site was occupied, and often when the city suffered sudden destruction; they may even fix the date of the particular period when occupation ended.

Symbolically, pottery-making and pottery itself is used in Scripture to illustrate God's power and sovereignty (*compare* Gen. 2:7; Ps. 2:9; Isa. 29:16; 45:9; 64:8; Jer. 18:1-10; 19:10,11; Rom. 9:20-24; Rev. 2:26-29).

pound (KJV) A *mina*, a monetary unit and unit of weight in Mesopotamia, weighing between 1.2 to 1.3 pounds (550 to 600 grams). *See also* Money; Weights and Measures.

power The ability to do, act, or accomplish something.

OLD TESTAMENT

Used (1) primarily of God's power, ability, and strength, but also (2) of military might and positions of authority within society, as in Isa. 17:3; Dan. 11:6, and (3) of anyone or anything that dominates or endangers, as in Dan. 6:27.

God alone has the unfettered ability to accomplish whatever he wills (Job 12:13; Ps. 147:5). God made the earth by his power (Jer. 10:12) and rules forever by his power (Ps. 66:7). God, however, graciously stoops to use his power to help his people (2 Chr. 25:8; Ps. 68:35). The power of human beings is insignificant in comparison, and Israel was to remain conscious that she was redeemed "by [God's] great power" from Egypt (Deut. 9:29) and to remain dependent on the Lord (Dan. 2:23).

The OT also speaks of the "power of the Lord" coming upon individuals or of the Spirit of the Lord coming upon them "in power." These phrases indicate a special grant of supernatural strength or ability needed by an individual to perform a task assigned to him or her by God (*compare* 1 Sam. 10:10).

NEW TESTAMENT

Several different Greek words are translated "power" in the NT. *Kratos, dynamis,* and *ischys* indicate strength and ability to act. *Exousia* expresses the authority or freedom of a person with power to do as he or she chooses. Jesus, endowed by God with both strength and authority, serves as an example of how God exercises his power on behalf of human beings. The God of the OT who gave power to the weak (Isa. 40:29) reached out through Jesus to cleanse and to heal. In the resurrection, Jesus was "declared with power to be the Son of God" (Rom. 1:4). Through the resurrection, he became the source of spiritual power for those who believe in him.

Because of its ability to transform those who believe, the "cross of Christ" is spoken of as having power (1 Cor. 1:17). Christ himself is "the power of God" (1:24). He has "all authority in heaven and on earth" (Mt. 28:18). In his Second Coming, that power will be fully revealed (Mt. 24:30).

Acts and the NT Epistles emphasize empowerment of believers by the Holy Spirit (Acts 1:8; 4:33; 10:38; Phil. 3:21). Since "the Spirit of him who raised Jesus from the dead is living in you, he who raised Christ from the dead will also give life to your mortal bodies through his Spirit" (Rom. 8:11). This power is often associated with divine healing and authority over demonic forces (Acts 3:1-10; 5:12,16; 14:8-18; 20:7-12). *See also* Holy Spirit.

Believers can expect great things because of "his power that is at work within us" (Eph. 3:20) and because of "his incomparably great power for us who believe. That power is like the working of his mighty strength, which he exerted in

Christ when he raised him from the dead and seated him at his right hand" (Eph. 1:19,20).

powers The hierarchy of fallen angels or supernatural beings who, although enemies of God and man, are subordinate to Christ's authority and power (Rom. 8:38; Eph. 6:12; Col. 1:16; and 1 Pet. 3:22). *See also* Angel; Demon.

Praetorium A technical Latin term that originally referred to the command tent of a Roman army group, but by the first century had a number of different meanings. The word occurs in the Greek NT in (1) Mt. 27:27; Mk. 15:16; Jn. 18:28; 19:9, the temporary military headquarters or palace in Jerusalem that housed the Roman governor, where Jesus was tried before Pilate; (2) Acts 23:35, Herod's headquarters; (3) Phil. 1:13, of the "palace guard." Here the term may indicate an elite guard of Roman soldiers responsible directly to the emperor, or it may be extended to include the larger corps of civil servants in Rome who administered the Empire.

WORDS FOR PRAISE IN SCRIPTURE

Term	Meaning
Hebrew	
halal	To acclaim, boast of, glory in; satisfaction in exalting the one whose works and self we praise.
yadah	To praise, give thanks, confess; acknowledging God's works and character, recounting his acts.
zamar	To sing praises, to make music; using instruments of music to express praise to God.
sabah	To praise, commend; adoration for God's wonderful works for us.
Greek	
aineō	To praise, with God alone being the object of praise in the NT.
epaineō	To commend; commending God for his works, qualities, himself.
eulogeō	To bless, speak well of.
doxazō	To glorify, give glory to.
megalynō	To magnify, to "declare the praises of" (1 Pet. 2:9).

praise An expression of admiration or appreciation. Praise is essentially a response to God, who meets us through revelation. Revelation, whether in nature, in the Scripture, or in the incarnation, makes us sensible of who God is and of his qualities. The appropriate response to God's self-revelation is not only faith but also praise.

In praise, we reflect back to God that which he has revealed to us about himself, with expressions of our admiration and appreciation. Praise may be expressed in private prayer or public worship, in words or in song. Undoubtedly, the best models for our praise are found in the psalms, hymns (see Rev. 4:11; 5:9,10; 19:1-8), and prayers recorded in Scripture.

Psalm 145 demonstrates many of the characteristics of praise. It is addressed to God; it contemplates his works and his character; and it blesses God and his name—that is, it expresses appreciation to God for who he is by nature. In the process, the psalm not only ascribes worth to God but deepens our innermost sense of what he means to us.

Praise springs from our fellowship with God and the joy his goodness toward us brings (Ps. 107:8,9). Praise is a characteristic of those who follow God, even as the absence of praise marks the lost (1 Pet. 2:9; compare Rom. 1:21) or those out of fellowship with the Lord.

prayer Speaking to or communicating with God. Many different words are used in Scripture to describe various aspects of prayer, but in its purest and simplest sense, prayer is talking with God. See also Confess; Intercession; Praise; Supplication; Thanks; Worship.

For a person to pray, there must be (1) an acknowledgment of God's existence, (2) hope that God knows and cares about us, and (3) expectation that God is able and willing to respond to us. Prayer as described in Scripture is an expression of covenant relationship. According to the OT, God established a special relationship with Abraham and his descendants. According to the NT, God in Christ reached out beyond Israel to establish a personal bond with all who accept his offer of salvation. In the context of these relationships, prayer is not petitioning a distant deity but coming to a known and trusted friend. In the NT, it is likened to a child drawing close to his or her loving and dearly loved father. Paul captures the wonder of this relationship when he says that through the Holy Spirit we utter the cry of the littlest Hebrew child, holding out its arms in delight at the nearness of its father. "Abba," we cry, uttering a word which literally means, "Daddy!" (Rom. 8:15; Gal. 4:6).

NT PATTERN OF PRAYER

The NT describes a specific pattern in prayer that reflects the roles of the Father, Son, and Holy Spirit.

Prayer is addressed to the Father, not in any ritualistic sense but as an expression of trust. Jesus taught his disciples to say, "Our Father in heaven" (Mt. 6:9-13). In this model prayer, we sense how completely we can depend on God and how fully we are to surrender to his will. Jesus concluded this teaching with the promise that "your heavenly Father knows" your needs. Moved by Father-love, God will surely meet our needs (Mt. 6:32). See also Lord's Prayer.

Prayer is offered in the name of Jesus. Christ presented himself as the way, the truth, and the life, and said, "No one comes to the Father except through me" (Jn. 14:6). In his death for us, Jesus fully opened the way to God. To come to God in Christ's name is to come having accepted the salvation Jesus died to provide—and identifying ourselves with his values and character. Because of Jesus we can, in the words of Heb. 4:16, "approach the throne of grace with confidence, so that we may receive mercy and find grace to help us in our time of need."

The Holy Spirit is the living bond between the believer and God and, according to Scripture, is a participant in our prayers. Romans 8:26,27 says that "the Spirit himself intercedes for us with groans that words cannot express," and "the Spirit intercedes for the saints in accordance with God's will" (compare 1 Cor. 14:13-15).

This NT pattern does not suggest that any particular ritual is to be followed in prayer. Instead, it affirms prayer as an aspect of relationship with God, an intimate engagement with each Person of the Trinity.

COMMONLY ASKED QUESTIONS

Questions that are commonly asked about prayer include:

1. *What is the best time to pray?* Paul says, "Pray continually" (1 Th. 5:17; 1 Tim. 5:5). By this, he means to maintain constant awareness of God and express thoughts and desires to him. However, the Bible also contains examples of persons who set aside specific times to meet with God (Dan. 6:10; Mk. 1:35). Furthermore, Jesus advised finding a private place where one could pray "in secret," undistracted by others (Mt. 6:5,6).

2. *What position should we adopt while praying?* No special position is com-

manded. Solomon prayed standing and "spread out his hands toward heaven" (1 Ki. 8:22). First Timothy 2:8 also speaks of praying with upraised hands; Gen. 24:26 describes prayer with head bowed; Dan. 6:10 and Eph. 3:14 picture prayer while kneeling; Josh. 7:6 and Rev. 1:17 portray praying while prostrate before the Lord.

3. *Are there conditions we must fulfill to have our prayers answered?* God does not answer prayers because we have met his conditions, but because he is gracious and merciful.

We can have confidence in prayer when we reject disobedience (Deut. 1:43-45), spiritual indifference (Isa. 58:7-9), and injustice (Isa. 1:15-17). God actively encourages us to pray by urging us to ask, seek, and knock (Mt. 7:7-11). We are to pray in Jesus' name, harmonizing our requests with his work, character, and purposes (Jn. 14:13,14). God promises that when what we ask is within the framework established by his known and specific will, we can be sure that our request will be granted (1 Jn. 5:14,15). Such passages should be viewed as affirmations of our privileges in approaching God rather than as conditions we must meet.

4. *Does God always answer prayer?* He does hear and respond to every prayer of the believer. However, his answer is not always "Yes." Paul prayed that God would remove a "thorn in the flesh" that troubled him deeply. God said "No," but promised Paul so much grace that the Lord's own strength would be manifested through Paul's weakness (2 Cor. 12:9,10). Furthermore, James makes it clear that selfish prayers will not be answered—not because God is angry when we ask, but because receiving such things would be spiritually detrimental (Jas. 4:1-4). Therefore, recognizing that God is committed to what is best for us, the wise Christian makes every request in the spirit Christ demonstrated in Gethsemane, when he said, "Yet not as I will, but as you will" (Mt. 26:39).

5. *Are there things for which we should not pray?* We should not pray for anything that is clearly contrary to God's will as expressed in Scripture.

6. *Does prayer change God's mind?* The way in which prayer is woven into the plan and purpose of God is shrouded in mystery. God is sovereign and has knowledge of the end of things from their beginning. At the same time, we have been commanded to pray, and Scripture says that often "you do not have because you do not ask God" (Jas. 4:2). James adds, "The prayer of a righteous man is powerful and effective" (5:16). We do not need to understand the mystery of prayer and how it affects God's sovereignty. We need only to pray.

7. *Should we bother God with little things?* Paul says, "In everything, by prayer and petition, with thanksgiving, present your requests to God" (Phil. 4:6). Because God truly cares about us, he is never "bothered" by any situation we may find ourselves in, no matter how insignificant it may seem.

8. *Should we keep on praying if no answer comes?* While Jesus warned his disciples not to "keep on babbling like pagans" who "think they will be heard because of their many words" (Mt. 6:7), Christ also told stories that encourage persistence in prayer (Lk. 18:1-8). Delay in an answer to prayer is not a rebuff but an invitation to continue bringing that concern to God (*see* Dan. 10).

9. *What is the role of corporate prayer?* While Christians are urged to pray privately, Jesus also encouraged Christians to pray with others (Mt. 18:19). The Book of Acts gives many examples of corporate prayer which demonstrate its power (Acts 1:14; 2:42; 4:23-31; 13:1-3).

"May the lifting up of my hands be like the evening sacrifice," wrote the Psalmist (141:2). Here Noah is depicted, after the Flood, praying to God with upraised hands. From a marble bas relief on an early Christian sarcophagus.

811

JESUS AND PRAYER

Prayer was important in the life of Jesus. Three of the Gospel writers speak of Jesus withdrawing to pray in private (Mt. 14:23; Mk. 1:35; 6:46), and Luke tells us that Christ "spent the night praying to God" (Lk. 6:12). If Christ himself needed to spend time alone with his Father, how much more do we!

The Gospels also contain Jesus' specific teaching on prayer. Matthew 6 reports Jesus' contempt for those who made a public show of their piety, and instead calls for prayer "in secret" to God the Father. Against this background, Jesus taught his disciples how they should pray (*see also* Lord's Prayer). According to the parallel passage in Lk. 11, Jesus told his disciples to ask, seek, and knock. If human

MODEL PRAYERS

Of Intercession	Gen. 18:16-33 Ex. 32:11-20
Of Confession	Ps. 32; Ps. 51 Ezra 9:5-15
Of Dedication	2 Chr. 6:14-42
Of Complaint	Num. 14:11-19
For Blessing	Ps. 90
For Healing	Isa. 38:3,9-20
In National Crisis	2 Ki. 19:14-19
Of Thanksgiving	1 Sam. 2:1-10 Ps. 16
Of Trust	Ps. 23
In Despair	Ps. 73
Of Dependence	2 Chr. 20:6-12
Of Recommitment	Jon. 2:2-9
For Deliverance	Isa. 37:14-20
For Restoration	Dan. 9:4-19
Of Praise	Lk. 1:46-55
Lord's Prayer	Mt. 6:5-13 Lk. 11:2-4
For Unity	Jn. 17
Of Petition	Acts 4:23-30
For Believers	Eph. 1:16-23 Eph. 3:14-21

fathers give good gifts to their children, he said, "how much more" will God the Father shower good things on his own. Luke also contains two parables on prayer, one of which encourages persistence (Lk. 18:1-8), while the other deals with the need for a humble attitude as we approach God (Lk. 18:9-14).

We do not know what Jesus said in his most private moments with the Father. However, two of Christ's personal prayers are recorded in the NT. Both of them were offered the night before Christ's crucifixion. The first is Jesus' high priestly prayer in Jn. 17. This prayer concludes the report of what Jesus said during the Last Supper. In it, Jesus first asks, now that his work of bringing eternal life to men is nearly complete, to be restored to the glory he shared with the Father "before the world began" (17:1-5). Christ then prays for those who accept God's words and "believe that you sent me" (17:6-12). The prayer asks that while those who believe remain in this world, they will be protected from the evil one and sanctified (made holy) through God's Word (17:13-19). Christ also prayed that believers might experience "complete unity." This request can be understood in two ways—first as unity in the Church, a theme prevalent in the Epistles, and second as unity with God, even as Jesus is one with the Father (17:20-23). Christ concludes by expressing his desire for believers to "be with me where I am, and to see my glory" (17:24), committing himself to continue to make the Father known to his own (17:25,26).

The second example of Christ's personal prayers is his prayer of submission in Mt. 26; Mk. 14; Lk. 22. Each of these writers describes Jesus' anguish at Gethsemane as he cried out to the Father, asking, "If you are willing, take this cup from me." Yet Jesus expressed submission by adding, "Not my will, but yours be done." These words have been a continual reminder to Christians that prayer is not a matter of manipulating God but of expressing our requests and praise in the conviction that God's will is best.

Thus, with the apostle Paul, Christians know that "in all things God works for the good of those who love him, who have been called according to his purpose" (Rom. 8:28).

preach (1) *kēryssō,* to proclaim or announce a message as a herald, (2) *euangelizomai,* to announce "good news." Jesus' own ministry involved "preaching and teaching," with no division made between these activities (Mt. 4:23; Lk. 20:1).

THE PREACHER

In biblical times, the role of the *kēryx,* "preacher" or "herald," was of great significance. This person was an individual of good character, charged with the important responsibility of delivering a message entrusted to him by some important personage. In both Testaments, this image is used to underline the importance of the message delivered by those who serve as God's spokesmen: It is not the preacher who is important but the content of his message, a message from God himself.

Peter speaks of Noah as a preacher of righteousness, whose action in building the ark was a symbolic sermon to the people of his time (2 Pet. 2:5). Jonah, who delivered God's message to Nineveh is another example of an OT preacher (Jon. 3:2). In fact, in the context of heralding, most of the OT prophets can be considered preachers.

THE MESSAGE

In the Gospels, both John the Baptist and Jesus emphasize the message of God's "kingdom," a declaration of God's sovereignty and spiritual principles rather than immediate earthly rule. In the rest of the NT, the emphasis of the message is Christ himself, for he is the embodiment of God's Kingdom. The death, burial, resurrection, and ascension of the Lord are all essential features of the NT message. *See also* Kerygma.

predestine, predestination To determine beforehand; that which God has determined will happen. Christian theological traditions differ on exactly how God has predestined individuals for salvation.

BIBLICAL USE

The Greek word occurs only six times in the NT (Acts 4:28; Rom. 8:29,30; 1 Cor. 2:7; Eph. 1:5,11). Acts 4:28 teaches that God predetermined the events that culminated in Jesus' crucifixion. Romans 8 teaches that those who love God are "predestined to be conformed to the likeness of his Son." First Corinthians 2 speaks of God's plan of redemption and says it was "destined for our glory before time began." Ephesians 1:5 speaks of believers being predestined to "be adopted as his sons through Jesus Christ" and 1:11 adds that we were chosen "in him . . . having been predestined according to the plan of him who works out everything in conformity with the purpose of his will."

PREDESTINATION AND ELECTION

In Christian theology, predestination is intimately related to the concept of election. The Greek root translated "election" simply means "to choose." In Scripture,

"election" speaks of God's sovereign and free choice of places and especially of persons. *See also* Sovereignty of God.

The OT portrays God making a number of significant choices. For a place, he chose Jerusalem as the site of his Temple. For a nation, he chose Israel from all the peoples of the world (Gen. 15; Deut. 7:6; Ps. 33:12; Isa. 14:1; 45:4). For individuals, God chose Abraham (Gen. 18:19; Neh. 9:7), Moses (Ps. 106:23), and David (1 Ki. 8:16; 1 Chr. 28:4). In each case, the choice was free, motivated only by God's love and purpose. As Deut. 7:7,8 says, "The Lord did not set his affection on you and choose you because you were more numerous than other peoples. . . . It was because the Lord loved you and kept the oath he swore to your forefathers."

In the NT, Paul develops this theme and argues against those who try to find a reason for God's choice (Rom. 9). God chose Isaac but rejected Ishmael. Jacob and Esau were twins, but God chose Jacob to receive the covenant promises (Rom. 9:6-13). Paul's point is not, however, that God chooses individuals for salvation but that God's purposes rest on and proceed from grace. God did not choose Isaac and Jacob because of their merit but as a free expression of his love and will (Rom. 9:14-16).

PREDESTINATION AND SALVATION

The Bible teaches that salvation is entirely of God, an expression of his sovereign and free decision to redeem human beings, and was carried out by him in the life, death, and resurrection of Jesus. This is the concept that both election and predestination emphasize.

Yet the Bible also teaches that salvation involves the exercise of individual free will in making a faith response to the divine offer. Whatever one may believe about predestination, John 3:16 remains true: "God so loved the world that he gave his one and only Son, that whoever believes in him shall not perish but have eternal life."

We may never be able to balance Scripture's affirmation of God's sovereignty and its invitation to all to believe. But Martin Luther suggested an approach that might well be taken by those who worry about whether or not they are predestined. Luther wrote, "I believe in Jesus Christ. What does it concern me, whether or not I am predestined? He has given us ground to stand on, that is, Jesus Christ, and through him we may climb to heaven."

Preparation, Day of The day before the Sabbath and all other Hebrew religious festivals. Because no work could be done on the Sabbath, Preparation Day was especially busy. Extra grain must be ground and extra bread baked (Ex. 16:4,5), clothes must be washed, and many Jews would take a ceremonial cleansing bath. Even more preparation was necessary on the day before a major festival.

The Preparation Day mentioned in the Gospels was the day before the Passover festival (Mt. 27:62; Jn. 19:14,31). The city of Jerusalem would be packed with people, many thousands of lambs would be carried to the Temple and sacrificed, and women would rush to assemble the special foods eaten with the Passover meal.

presbyter *See* Elder.

press (1) Winepress, a cavity carved into rock, or a very large tub-like construction, in which men and women trampled

Below: Small winepress at Tell Qasile from the period of the kings (970–586 B.C.).
Left: Olive press from the Roman period in Israel. In order to keep the olive pits from being crushed while separating the skin and pulp from the pits, the vertical stone had to be suspended, either from the central column on which it turned or on wedges in the trough.

grapes to squeeze out the juice. In both Testaments, the overflow of the wine-press serves as an image of judgment. The most graphic language is found in Rev. 14:19,20: "The angel swung his sickle on the earth, gathered its grapes and threw them into the great winepress of God's wrath. They were trampled in the wine-press outside the city, and blood flowed out of the press, rising as high as the horses' bridles for a distance of 180 miles" (300 kilometers) (compare Isa. 63:3; Joel 3:13).

(2) Olive press, one of two kinds of olive press, a round stone wheel used to crush the ripe fruit or a stone-weighted boom used to put pressure on baskets filled with the crushed fruit. See also Olives.

prick (KJV) "Thorn," "splinter." The noun is used of the slender, pointed goad used to control animals. To "kick against the pricks" portrays an animal who resists guidance from its owner, as Paul at first resisted the Gospel of God (Acts 9:5 KJV).

pride (1) Negatively, arrogance, overween-ing self-confidence, resulting in an unwill-ingness to submit to God and an insensi-tive disregard for others, as in Ps. 10:2,4. (2) Positively, delight in the accomplish-ments of others or of oneself, as in 2 Cor. 7:4. See also Arrogance.

Both Testaments tend to use "pride" in the negative sense. Isaiah 14:13,14 and Ezek. 28:11-19 are often taken as descrip-tions of Satan's fall. In each case, pride, which motivated this powerful angel to set his will against God's, is portrayed as the culprit (compare 1 Tim. 3:7; 2 Tim. 2:26). That same rebellious attitude, which can corrupt even the godly (2 Chr. 26:16,17), brings human beings under the judgment of God (Isa. 2:11).

In the NT, Paul warns against several expressions of pride. Pride is particularly dangerous in the non-Christian who seeks to earn salvation. Because salvation is and must be a work of God for human beings rather than a work of human beings for God, reliance on one's own efforts distorts the Gospel message. Paul shows that not even Abraham can take pride or glory in his salvation (Rom. 4:1,3; compare Eph. 2:8,9; Phil. 3:4-11). Salvation is a gift of God, ours through faith in Jesus Christ, not of self-achievement.

Paul also shows that pride distorts Christian interpersonal relationships. He urges believers in Rome, "Do not be proud, but be willing to associate with people of low position" (Rom. 12:16). Paul rebukes the Corinthians for being proud of themselves while permitting a man liv-ing in open sin to remain in their fellow-ship (1 Cor. 5:2). Paul also notes that pride has so puffed up participants in a doctrinal dispute in Corinth that they cannot relate to one another in love, and thus have closed their hearts to the ministry of the Holy Spirit (1 Cor. 8:1-3). Pride, thus, is the enemy of relationship with God and the enemy of healthy relationships within the Christian fellowship.

Another particular form of pride (authadēs; "self-will" or "stubbornness") is a mark of false teachers who infiltrate Christ's church (Tit. 1:7; 2 Pet. 2:10).

It is not wrong to find joy in what God is doing in our lives. In that sense, we can "take pride in" our accomplishments or those of others. But, as the OT warns, "When you have eaten and are satisfied," there is a danger that "your heart will become proud and you will forget the Lord your God" (Deut. 8:10,14). This kind of pride is arrogance, and as such, a source of sin.

priest, priesthood In Israel, a male de-scendant of the family of Aaron of the tribe of Levi, charged with responsibility to supervise Israel's worship center and to offer the sacrifices called for in the Law of Moses. See also High Priest.

OLD TESTAMENT

In the earliest times, the father of the household served as family priest (Gen. 8:20-22; 12:6,7). With the introduction of the Mosaic Law, a hereditary priesthood became one of the most important ele-ments of OT religion. The Hebrew word kohen ("priest") occurs over 700 times in the OT. This priestly order is often called the "levitical priesthood" because only those descended from Aaron the Levite could serve in it (Ex. 28:1; Lev. 21,22). The priests performed ritual functions only be-tween the ages of 25 and 50.

Deuteronomy 33:9,10 summarizes the duties of the priests in a poetic statement about Levi:

He watched over your word
and guarded your covenant.
He teaches your precepts to Jacob
and your law to Israel.
He offers incense before you
and whole burnt offerings on
your altar.

In addition to teaching God's Law (Lev. 10:11; compare 2 Chr. 17:9) and offering sacrifices to atone for the sins of God's people (Lev. 1–4,16), the priests diagnosed diseases that made worshipers ceremonially unclean (Lev. 13,14) and ritually purified those who had recovered (Lev. 14) (*see also* Leprosy). Priests examined all sacrificial animals to make sure they were unblemished and healthy (Lev. 22:17-21), and they established the value of all goods donated to God (Lev. 27). Priests supervised the tabernacle and, later, Temple

Model of the high priest of Israel wearing his special garments, which are described in detail in Ex. 28 and 39:1-31.

grounds and its repairs (Num. 3,4; 2 Chr. 29). They announced the beginning of religious festivals (Lev. 25:9). Priests served as judges in special cases (Deut. 17:9,12) and were called on to discern God's will by the use of Urim and Thummim or by casting lots (Num. 27:21; 1 Sam. 10:20-24). Priests who accompanied the army cried out before a battle, calling on Israel not to be fainthearted or afraid, "for the Lord your God is the one who goes with you to fight for you against your enemies to give you victory" (Deut. 20:1-4).

In view of the special role of the priests in serving God, priests were required to maintain a special standard of purity. They were to keep the Law as it applied to all Israel but had additional responsibilities themselves. No priest could minister before the Lord if he had a physical defect or when he was ritually unclean or drunk

(Lev. 21:17–22:8). No priest could marry a woman defiled by prostitution or divorced from her husband (Lev. 21:7). The high priest could not even marry a widow (Lev. 21:14). (*See also* Clean and Unclean.)

It would be easy to misunderstand the role of priests by focusing on the ritual aspects of their duties. At heart, Israel's religion was relational, and the responsibilities of the priests were designed to guard and preserve an intimate relationship between God and his people. Thus, the priests in Israel's religion served as mediators. In performing sacrifices and offerings, the priests atoned for Israel's failures and thus restored a harmonious relationship with God. In teaching and administering God's Word, the priests guided Israel into the holy way of life that their calling required, a holiness that would permit God to shower his blessings on them. *See also* Holy.

NEW TESTAMENT
References to priests in the Gospels and Acts are clearly to persons in Israel who held the established OT office.

In the Epistles, however, the OT system, with its sacrifices and priesthood, is set aside in Christ. Jesus' one sacrifice has accomplished our salvation, and Jesus himself has been ordained as our high priest in a tradition going back to Melchizedek rather than to Levi. *See also* High Priest; Melchizedek.

With the shift in high priest comes the announcement that God's Word to Israel in Ex. 19:6 is now fulfilled in his NT people: "You will be for me a kingdom of priests and a holy nation" (*compare* Isa. 61:6; Rev. 5:10). Peter says that we are "being built into a spiritual house to be a holy priesthood, offering spiritual sacrifices acceptable to God through Jesus Christ" (1 Pet. 2:5; *compare* Rev. 20:6). The context defines these spiritual sacrifices as worship, declaring "the praises of him who called you out of darkness into this wonderful light." Thus, the priesthood of believers is more closely related to worship than to any public ministry.

However, the NT portrays all Christians functioning in ways that are analogous to the functions of OT priests (*see* 1 Pet. 2:5,9). Under the new covenant instituted by Christ, God has planted his Word in all our hearts, and we are to minister to each other and thus stimulate spiritual growth (1 Cor. 12:7-11; Eph. 4:11-16). We are also to pray for one another, representing each other before God.

While the NT fails to identify any Christian as a "priest," in A.D. 107 Ignatius of Antioch spoke of a triple division of the ordained ministry as bishop, priest, and deacon. By A.D. 200 Christian ministers were commonly identified as priests.

prince Not just (1) the heir of a king; but also (2) a title of a person with significant royal, military, or other authority, as in Num. 22:15; (3) a form of courteous address to a person with significant wealth, as in Gen. 23:6; (4) in Daniel and the NT, a ranking angel in the spiritual realm, as in Dan. 10:13; 12:1; Mt. 12:24.

"Prince" is frequently used in English versions to translate more specific foreign titles, as in Dan. 1:3; 3:2. It is also used to translate as many as five different Hebrew words that have the general meaning of "leader," "captain," "overlord," or "judge."

princess Generally, a woman of royal rank, but in Esth. 1:18 simply of nobility.

principalities (KJV) Particularly powerful rulers, either (1) human, as in Tit. 3:1, or most often (2) of demonic origin, as in Rom. 8:38; Eph. 6:12; Col. 1:16; 2:15. *See also* Demon; Powers; Prince.

Prisca, Priscilla [prih-SIL-uh; "simplicity"]. Always mentioned with her husband Aquila, Priscilla was an active Christian commended by Paul as a fellow worker. **Scripture:** Acts 18:2,18-28; Rom. 16:3-5; 1 Cor. 16:19.

BACKGROUND

Aquila and Priscilla let Paul share in their tentmaker trade. Although sufficiently wealthy to have a home large enough to host a church group (Rom. 16:5), the couple seems to have relocated often, having met Paul in Corinth probably after being expelled from Rome in one of Emperor Claudius's proscriptions against Jews (Acts 18:2). The couple then had a distinctive ministry in Ephesus (Acts 18:24-26) before later moving back to Rome (Rom. 16:3).

Their active involvement with Paul seems to have endangered them, for Paul says, "They risked their lives for me" (Rom. 16:4). Acts 18 portrays them as particularly sensitive in the way they invited an enthusiastic evangelist, Apollos, to their home to "explain to him the way of God more adequately."

LEARNING FROM PRISCILLA'S LIFE

Of the seven references to this couple, only the first places Aquila's name before

his wife's. In the others, it is "Priscilla and Aquila." The order surely suggests that Priscilla was an exceptional woman. Some hypothesize Priscilla was a church leader; others say she held a higher social status than her husband. Nevertheless, the fact that she is always mentioned with her husband tells us that the couple worked together as a team and that Aquila was unthreatened by his wife's strengths. This provides impressive evidence that women were truly valued in the apostolic church and that their partnership in ministry was readily accepted (*compare* Rom. 16:6,12,15).

prison A facility or room used to hold persons awaiting trial or the execution of a judicial proceeding.

IMPRISONMENT IN ISRAEL

The OT legal system did not impose terms of imprisonment as a penalty. In Israel, a person who committed a crime against property was to make restitution, often several times over (Ex. 22:1-15). The "eye for an eye" penalty invoked when crimes were committed against persons typically involved the payment of a money settlement (Ex. 21:12-36). Whipping was also a common punishment in Judaism, with the offender receiving up to 39 stripes (Deut. 25:1-3; 2 Cor. 11:24).

However, persons who were awaiting trial or sentencing were often imprisoned (*compare* Gen. 39:19–41:14; Lev. 24:12; 1 Ki. 22:26,27; Ezra 7:26; Acts 4:3; 12:3,4; 23:35; Phil. 1:7-26). Jeremiah's confinement in the house of Jonathan the secretary (Jer. 37:15,16) and later in an empty cistern (Jer. 38:6-10) clearly show the hostility of Judah's leaders to this prophet who counseled surrender to the invading Babylonians. Yet Jeremiah was not imprisoned as punishment but was held to keep him from influencing the people of Jerusalem. Nevertheless, during the monarchy, kings of Judah and Israel seem to have set aside rooms in their administrative buildings to serve as prisons for notable political or religious figures (1 Ki. 22:26,27; 2 Chr. 16:10; Jer. 32:2).

While imprisonment was not a typical Hebrew punishment, OT Law did establish a form of confinement for a person who killed another accidentally. Such persons were confined to a city of refuge until the death of the high priest. If a person guilty of involuntary manslaughter left the city of refuge before that time, he or she could be executed by the kin of the person he or she had killed (Num. 35:6-34; Deut.

Right: Traditional site for the "prison of Christ," in what is now the Sisters of Sion Convent, Jerusalem. It would have been a part of the Antonia Fortress, one of two places where Jesus could have been kept while awaiting Pilate's verdict. Traces of stocks can still be seen.

Left: The agony of a Lybian prisoner bound at the elbows is captured in this bronze and silver figurine from Egypt (1580–1200 B.C.). Egyptian prisons were generally forced-labor compounds rather than dungeons (Gen. 39:20-23).

4:41-43; 19:1-10). Solomon adapted this concept when he ordered Shimei, who had insulted his father David, not to leave Jerusalem on pain of death (1 Ki. 2:36-45). *See also* Cities of Refuge.

IMPRISONMENT IN OTHER NATIONS

In Egypt, Joseph was imprisoned in a facility maintained to confine prisoners of Pharaoh (Gen. 39:20). Undoubtedly, ordinary criminals were set to forced labor rather than imprisoned. In the era of the judges, Samson was blinded, shackled, and forced to work for the Philistines (Jdg. 16:21,25). During the Babylonian Captivity, Nebuchadnezzar maintained rooms for captive kings such as Jehoiachin (2 Ki. 24:15) and Zedekiah (2 Ki. 25:2-7; Jer. 39:1-7). Each of these persons was, however, a special political prisoner, and their imprisonment does not imply that any of these ancient civilizations maintained an extensive prison system.

The Greeks and Romans also used prisons for those awaiting trial. John the Baptist, Peter, and Paul were all held at one time or another in such a facility in Jerusalem. Peter was not only kept behind locked and guarded iron doors but was also chained to two soldiers (Acts 12:1-11). The best NT description of a Roman prison is of the city jail at Philippi (Acts 16:16-28). Paul and Silas were flogged and put in an "inner cell," where their feet were fastened in stocks. Such inner rooms had no windows or circulation. Prisoners' feet were locked in place in stone or wooden stocks, with holes spread far enough apart to be painful. In addition, the prisoners were often chained to the prison walls. Again, such jails served as holding pens for those awaiting trial or for those condemned and awaiting punishment. Later, when Paul was imprisoned in Rome awaiting trial in the emperor's court, he lived in a private house but remained under military guard (Acts 28:16,30).

Three uses of "prison" in the NT call for comment. Matthew 18:21-34 speaks of a debtor being thrown in prison "until he could pay the debt." However, his imprisonment was not long term. A person who could not raise the needed money was sold into servitude, with his wife and children, and the sale price applied to his debt (18:25). Peter speaks of "spirits in prison who disobeyed long ago'' (1 Pet. 3:19,20). The reference may be to those who lived before the Genesis Flood and who failed to respond when the Spirit of God spoke to them through Noah. These are now ''in prison'' in the typical cultural sense of being confined and awaiting judgment. Finally, Rev. 20:7 speaks of the release of Satan from a confinement of 1,000 years during which Christ will have reigned on earth. Again, the ''prison'' is a place where Satan will be held while awaiting final punishment.

The modern penitentiary has no parallel in Scripture, for other mechanisms were relied on to deter crime and punish criminals (*see also* Crime and Punishment). Yet to be imprisoned in biblical times was as devastating an experience as it often is today. How significant, then, that Jesus encouraged his disciples to visit those in prison (Mt. 25:36-44), and that the writer of Hebrews says, ''Remember those in prison as if you were their fellow prisoners, and those who are mistreated as if you yourselves were suffering'' (Heb. 13:3).

prize (1) Something given to the winner of a contest, as in 1 Cor. 9:24; (2) in some English versions, property taken by force or captured in war, as in Jer. 21:9.

Paul often turns to the popular athletic contests held throughout the Hellenistic world for metaphors that communicate spiritual truths. One of the metaphors Paul uses is that of the prize, typically a wreath of laurel, parsley, or other greenery. While the prize lacked intrinsic value, the victor in an important race was often richly rewarded by the city he represented.

Paul uses the metaphor to make a single point: Christian faith demands concentrated dedication to Christ. In 1 Cor. 9:24-27, Paul reminds his readers that before the race athletes dedicate themselves to training. In Phil. 3:14, he pictures the race in progress, the athlete's eyes fixed on the goal, refusing to look back and break stride. A similar note is sounded in Col. 2:18, where Paul describes turning aside from Christ to follow mere ceremonialism and the worship of angels as leaving the race course and thus being disqualified from winning the prize. In Paul's words, the prize is taking hold of that ''for which God has called me heavenward in Christ Jesus'' (Phil. 3:14).

proconsul In NT times, the title of the Roman officer who governed a province or district outside of Rome.

The proconsul held both judicial and military power. While a proconsul's behavior might be examined after he was out of office, during his term of office he held complete authority over his district. Proconsuls mentioned in the NT are Sergius Paulus, who governed Cyprus and became a Christian during Paul's first missionary journey (Acts 13:4-12), and Gallio, proconsul of Achaia, who refused to listen to the Corinthian Jews' accusations against Paul, since their complaint involved ''questions about words and names and your own law'' (Acts 18:15).

procurator In the first century, a general term for various officials of the Roman Empire who looked after the interests of the emperor; also, in NT times, the title of the governors of minor provinces who had the same authority in their districts as did proconsuls who ruled major provinces. While the governors of Judea held this rank, Pilate (Mt. 27:11), Felix (Acts 23:24), and Festus (Acts 24:27) are simply called *hēgemōn*, ''governors.''

Stone slab set up by the council of Miletus. It records the honors rewarded Loukios of Miletus as prizes for his athletic victories. The apostle Paul anticipated receiving the crown of righteousness as his prize for finishing his ''race'' (1 Tim. 4:7,8).

faned the name of the Lord Almighty (Mal. 1:12).

The ritual aspects of Israel's religion were not carried over into the Church age. Nevertheless, God is holy, and Christians are his people, his ambassadors. What they do and say can either honor God or "profane" his name before those who do not believe.

promise A statement of one's intent to do or not to do something.

Any word from God stating his intent is by nature a promise. Thus, the OT speaks of God's promises to Abraham (Gen. 18:19), of his promise of good things for Israel (Num. 10:29), and of God's promise of the land of Canaan to Abraham's descendants (Deut. 6:18,23), etc. Typically, the OT promises have an eschatological focus: They will be fulfilled at history's end when God acts to bring to pass all he has preannounced. *See also* Prophecy.

In the NT, "promise" may be a synonym for salvation, emphasizing the gracious nature of God's expressed intent to save and bless mankind in Christ, as in Gal. 3:14; 2 Tim. 1:1. In Christ, the Christian receives a number of specific promises that are fulfilled now, such as the promise of eternal life (1 Tim. 4:8), of the Holy Spirit (Acts 1:4; Eph. 1:13), the promise of rest (Heb. 4:1), and the promise of spiritual freedom (Jn. 8:32-36). At the same time, many of God's promises in Christ have an eschatological focus, such as the promise of a crown of life (Jas. 1:12) and of Christ's return (2 Pet. 3:9,13).

PROMISE AND COVENANT

No specific term for "promise" occurs in Hebrew. Instead, words meaning "to speak," "to say," etc., are sometimes translated as "promise." Despite this, the thread of promise runs through the entire Old Testament. God made specific promises to Abraham, expressed in a series of "I will" statements (Gen. 12:1-3,7). These statements express clearly what God intends to do for Abraham and his progeny through Isaac and Jacob and were confirmed by a formal covenant (Gen. 15), a binding agreement with full legal force in Abraham's culture. *See also* Covenant.

In Rom. 4 and Gal. 3, the apostle Paul bases an important theological concept on the fact that God's covenant commitment to Abraham is in essence a promise. Romans 4 notes that Abraham's faith-response to God's statement of intent was credited to Abraham as righteousness. Abraham, Paul

The Return of the Prodigal *by the 17th century Spanish painter Murillo depicts the beloved parable (Lk. 15:11-32) as the son says, "Father, I have sinned against heaven and against you."*

prodigal son The popular name given the younger son in Jesus' parable about a youth who asked for and then foolishly wasted his share of his father's estate (Lk. 15:11-32). The story illustrates not only the forgiving love of the father but pointedly exposes the attitude of the older brother, who was angry when his father celebrated the prodigal's return. With the two other parables of Lk. 15, this story illustrates God's own unquenchable love for the lost and heaven's joy over "one sinner who repents" (15:10).

profane (1) As applied to an object or person—unholy, not consecrated to God; (2) as a verb, to defile a holy thing by using it in a common, ordinary way.

The OT made a sharp distinction between the secular and the sacred. That which was set aside for God's use was holy and had to be treated in accordance with rules laid down in the OT Law. A violation of any rule regarding the treatment of a holy person or thing not only profaned that person or thing but also showed disrespect for God, to whom the person or thing was dedicated (Lev. 22:32; Isa. 48:11). This thought is frequently expressed in warning Israel, a people set apart to God, that any failure to exalt God by complete obedience profaned his holy name. As Lev. 19:12 says, "Do not swear falsely by my name and so profane the name of your God." Furthermore, Israel's priests were to treat the holy offerings with deep respect, "so they will not profane my holy name" (Lev. 22:2). And, Malachi warns that the attitude of the people who despised worship pro-

notes, "did not waver through unbelief regarding the promise of God, but was strengthened in his faith and gave glory to God, being fully persuaded that God had power to do what he had promised" (Rom. 4:20,21). Today, human beings "who believe in him who raised Jesus our Lord from the dead" and thus trust the promise of God in Christ, have this faith credited to them for righteousness as well (4:23,24).

PROMISE AND SALVATION

In Gal. 3, Paul argues that the Mosaic Law, which was introduced hundreds of years after God made his promises to Abraham, could not annul the divine promise. Historic precedents demonstrate that human beings have always been saved by faith in God's promise. Since salvation is found in relying on God's promise, it cannot depend on keeping the Law. The Law's limited role has always been to demonstrate that human beings are trapped in sin, in desperate need of a righteousness that can be found only in faith. Thus, "promise" underlines the gracious nature of salvation and emphasizes the impossibility of establishing a relationship with God through personal merit or good works.

Promised Land An ancient designation for Canaan—later known as Israel—which God granted to the children of Abraham through Isaac and Jacob (Gen. 12:6,7).

Moses described Canaan as the land God promised Israel "on oath" (Num. 14:15,16).

prophecy, interpretation of Much in the writings of the OT prophets is predictive in nature. Yet Christians differ on how to interpret many of the passages that contain far-term prophecies.

BASIC APPROACHES

In general, three approaches are taken to interpret OT prophecy.

1. *Denying predictive elements.* Those who take this approach assume that the "predictions" were actually made much later than the date suggested by internal evidence, after the event prophesied had occurred.

2. *Spiritualizing predictive elements.* Those who take this approach assume that the blessings promised to Israel as God's covenant people are intended for Christians under the new covenant. Such specific blessings as restoration to the land and peace and prosperity under the rule of the Messiah are taken as symbolic of the inner peace and spiritual prosperity that Christians find in Christ and the blessedness awaiting all believers.

3. *Assuming literal fulfillment of all predictions.* Those who take this approach believe that the yet-unfulfilled prophecies of the OT will be fulfilled as they were understood by the prophets and by those

The Valley of Eshcol, north of Hebron in the hill country of Judah. Here the twelve spies sent to explore the Promised Land gathered a cluster (Heb., eshcol) of grapes as evidence of the land's fruitfulness (Num. 13:23,24).

to whom they spoke. In interpreting the unfulfilled prophecies of the OT, those who take a literal approach are guided by studying prophecies that already have been fulfilled.

EXAMPLE OF FULFILLED PROPHECY

Fulfilled prophecy may serve as a model in developing an approach to the yet-unfulfilled prophecies of Scripture. If so, the most striking feature of fulfilled prophecy is its concrete, literal nature. If Daniel is taken as prophecy, its vision of future world empires is stunning in its accuracy (*see also* Daniel). Even more so are prophecies concerning Jesus. Hundreds of years before Christ's birth, the OT predicted he would come from David's line (Isa. 9:6,7; 11:1), be born of a virgin (Isa. 7:14) in Bethlehem (Mic. 5:2), and spend his early years in Nazareth of Galilee (Isa. 9:1,2). His death is described in detail, from his execution with criminals (Isa. 53:9,12) and burial with the rich (Isa. 53:9), to the offer of vinegar while he hung on the cross (Ps. 69:21) as soldiers gambled for his clothing (Ps. 22:18). His dying words are recorded nearly a thousand years before Calvary (Ps. 22:1; 31:5), and while his side would be pierced (Zech. 12:10), not a bone of his body would be broken (Ps. 34:20). Assembled together, these prophecies are amazing in their accuracy, and each was fulfilled, not in a symbolic or spiritual way, but literally in history.

Yet if the pattern seen in fulfilled prophecy suggests a literal approach to interpreting unfulfilled prophecy, it also reminds us how difficult it is to develop a clear picture of the future from prophetic material.

SPECIAL CHARACTERISTICS

The accuracy of fulfilled prophecies concerning Christ is striking. Yet such prophecies are scattered, found not in a single location but in different books written at different times. Only by looking back with the perspective provided by history can we tell for certain that they speak of a single person and are fulfilled in the span of that person's life. Thus, Peter pictures the prophets themselves peering "intently" into their own writings, not to understand what they had said, but to puzzle over "the time and circumstances" of their fulfillment (1 Pet. 1:10-12). Prophecy provides glimpses of the future but does not provide the details in such a way that one can be positive about the exact time and circumstances of fulfillment. As the prophets gave descriptions of

Roman *sestertius issued by Vespasian, emperor of Rome (A.D. 69–79), who razed Jerusalem in A.D. 70. Jesus prophesied the destruction of Jerusalem and the Temple (Mt. 23:37–24:3; Lk. 21:20-24; 23:28-31).*

what they saw in visions of the future, they were limited to their own time, experience, and vocabulary. In addition, prophecy often has multiple references; that is, a predicted event may foreshadow a series of events rather than a single event, just as Ezekiel's prophecies of the imminent invasion of Judah by Babylon mirrors another, greater invasion launched from the north at history's end (*compare* Jer. 38,39). In addition, some prophecies may be partially fulfilled in an event, while still awaiting complete fulfillment in the distant future. For example, Joel's prophecy of the Day of the Lord was partially fulfilled when the Spirit came on the day of Pentecost (Acts 2:14-21), but other elements of this prophecy have yet to happen.

These and other problems, such as whether a particular prophecy is conditional or unconditional or whether a time break occurs within a paragraph or even a sentence (*compare* Lk. 4:18,19 with Isa. 61:1,2), make even the literal approach to biblical prophecy an uncertain and difficult task.

What, then, can we conclude about the interpretation of predictive biblical prophecy? First, unfulfilled predictive prophecy provides a broad outline of the future. That outline is continuously repeated in the prophets and is consistent with the future envisioned in the NT. Second, we should remain cautious of those who speak confidently about their particular, detailed vision of the future distilled from biblical prophecy. Even if OT and NT prophecies are to be fulfilled literally, only the unfolding of the events themselves will enable us to know the full circumstances surrounding their fulfillment. Third, and perhaps most importantly, we can share with the prophets and the apostles the conviction that God is in charge of history. God does know the end from the beginning. He who loves us exercises sovereign control over the course of world events. Whatever he has planned for the future, history's end will prove a complete and glorious fulfillment of the purposes of our God. (*See also* Future.)

prophet, prophecy One who communicates or interprets messages from God. A prophet is a person authorized to speak for God. The prophet's message was called in Hebrew a *nebu'ah*, "prophecy;" sometimes it was also termed a vision, oracle, or burden, but most often it was identified as "the word of the Lord." Prophets and prophecy play a major role in the devel-

opment of the OT faith and in the early years of the Christian era.

MOSES, THE PROTOTYPIC PROPHET

Moses' ministry defines the characteristics of the true prophet, and Moses' message is the foundation on which all the OT prophets build. The characteristics of the prophet in Israel are defined in Ex. 3, which describes Moses' meeting with God before the burning bush.

First, in Ex. 3:1-9, God revealed himself and his purposes to Moses. While the mode of revelation would vary, prophets were the first of all men and women to whom God revealed not only himself but his purposes as well. The prophets spoke with the deep conviction that what they said was not their message but a message from the Lord.

Second, God called and commissioned Moses (3:10). The priesthood and monarchy in Israel were hereditary, but prophets received a special call to their office from God himself (Isa. 6; Jer. 1:4-19; Ezek. 1–3; Amos 7:14,15).

Third, God told Moses to deliver his message in the name of Yahweh (that is, "I AM" or "the Lord" (3:13-15). All future prophecy to Israel was to be delivered in the name of the Lord and in his name alone (Deut. 18:19,20). *See also* Lord.

Fourth, God gave Moses authenticating signs that Israel would accept, and God promised that he would perform miracles that would compel the Egyptians to release Israel. The authenticating sign, often taking the form of a prediction that comes true, was a mark of a prophet whose word was to be respected as God's own (3:16-20).

Fifth, God told Moses what the future would bring (Ex. 3:16-22). While not all prophecy is predictive, a marked predictive element is found in the ministry of Israel's prophets.

In a pivotal passage in Deut. 18, Moses assures Israel that God would provide guidance to his people after Moses' death. Each of the elements seen in Ex. 3 is repeated in this key paragraph.

The Lord said to me: . . . "I will raise up for them a prophet like you from among their brothers; I will put my words in his mouth, and he will tell them everything I command him. If anyone does not listen to my words that the prophet speaks in my name, I myself will call him to account. But a prophet who presumes to speak in my name anything I have not commanded him to say, or a prophet who speaks in the name of other gods, must be put to death."

You may say to yourselves, "How can we

The birth of Jesus in the town of Bethlehem fulfilled Micah's prophecy: "But you, Bethlehem Ephrathah, though you are small among the clans of Judah, out of you will come for me one who will be ruler over Israel" (5:2; compare Mt. 2:6).

823

know when a message has not been spoken by the Lord?'' If what a prophet proclaims in the name of the Lord does not take place or come true, that is a message the Lord has not spoken. (Deut. 18:17-22)

Thus, Moses defines the role of the prophet by example and by the Deut. 18 exhortation. His message also serves as the foundation on which all later prophets build. The Law given through Moses established the moral and religious framework of Hebrew society. When the later prophets spoke out against idolatry or injustice, they recalled Israel to its national origins in Mosaic legislation.

Even the prophets' visions of Israel's future break no new ground, although they often add previously unrevealed details to Scripture. Visions of the future restate a view of history and of eschatology already established in Moses' writ-

Roman road, lined with columns, at Tyre, the principal seaport of Phoenicia. This proud, powerful city was the focus of much OT prophecy.

ings. Succeeding generations in Israel are blessed or punished depending on their observance of Moses' Law (Deut. 28). The graded punishments, each intended to call Israel to repentance and renewal, culminate in exile from the land (Deut. 29), a frequent theme in the prophets. Yet, at history's end Israel will be restored to faith and to her land, and the promises made to Abraham will be fulfilled (Deut. 30:1-10). This view of history and history's end, firmly established in the books of Moses, provides the framework within which OT prophets speak.

TRUE AND FALSE PROPHETS

The Deut. 18 passage foresees the rise of

false prophets. Thus, Israel is given certain tests by which the prophet called by God can be distinguished from the person who imagines or feigns divine inspiration. The true prophet will be an Israelite (18:15), will speak in the name of the Lord (18:19,20), and his message will be authenticated by the accuracy of his statements about the future: "If what a prophet proclaims in the name of the Lord does not take place or come true, that is a message the Lord has not spoken" (18:22).

The confrontation between Jeremiah and Hananiah illustrates this (Jer. 28). Hananiah announced in the name of the Lord that Babylon's yoke would be broken in two years and that the Jews currently captive there would return home. Shortly thereafter, the word of the Lord came to Jeremiah, and he announced that Babylon would become stronger, not be broken. Jeremiah also announced, "The Lord has not sent you. . . . Therefore, this is what the Lord says: 'I am about to remove you from the face of the earth. This very year you are going to die, because you have preached rebellion against the Lord'" (28:15,16). In less than two months, Hananiah was dead (28:1,17), and Jeremiah's message was authenticated, for what he announced in God's name had come true.

Strikingly, this evidence did not convince Jeremiah's contemporaries to obey his message—nor did the authenticating signs produced by other prophets generally win acceptance of their message. The rebellious are not interested in evidence. If they had been sensitive to God's voice, the words of Scripture would have been enough without the special signs.

Several other passages describe characteristics of false prophets. Deuteronomy 13 teaches that false prophets will lead the people after other gods and will rebel against God's previously revealed will. Both Jer. 23 and Ezek. 12–14 emphasize that false prophets preach peace regardless of social injustice and immorality, which true prophets of God seek to correct.

The OT names many of the prophets of God who ministered in Israel. Among them are several women, including Miriam (Ex. 15:20), Deborah (Jdg. 4:4), Huldah (2 Ki. 22:14), Isaiah's unnamed wife (Isa. 8:3), and in the NT, Anna (Lk. 2:36). Samuel functions as a prophet as well as judge. Nathan was court prophet to David, and many different prophets ministered to rulers in the age of the monarchy. During the Captivity, Daniel served as a prophet, and after the return from captivity, Haggai, Zechariah, and Malachi had prominent prophetic ministries in Judea. Jesus identified John the Baptist as the greatest of the OT prophets, but Christ himself fulfilled the specific prediction of Moses that God would raise up "a prophet like me" to whom Israel must listen.

PROPHETIC INSPIRATION

Scripture does not tell us how the prophet heard the Word of the Lord. The Hebrew phrase "The word of the Lord came" simply implies that God's Word became evident to the prophet. He or she knew that a particular message was from God and was to be delivered in God's name.

Despite the attempts of some to suggest that a prophetic ecstasy like that characterizing the *prophētēs* and oracle of the Hellenistic world, whose babblings and obscure sayings, delivered in a deep trance characterized by loss of awareness, were interpreted by others, no such behavior is normative for the Hebrew prophet. There are instances of ecstatic behavior, as in Num. 11:25-29; 1 Sam. 10:6,10; 19:20,23. But the prophets of the OT neither relied on trances to receive their messages nor exhibited erratic behavior when delivering them.

The means by which the message from God was communicated to the prophet might be as direct as the words spoken to Moses at the burning bush, or later, when God spoke to Moses "face to face" (Deut. 12:8). The message might come through dreams and visions (Num. 12:6,7; 1 Sam. 28:6,15; Jer. 31:26) or even through symbols (Jer. 18; Amos 8:1-3). Whatever the means, both Testaments credit prophetic revelation to the Spirit of God (1 Ki. 22:24; 1 Chr. 12:18; 2 Chr. 20:14; Mic. 3:8; 1 Cor. 2:6-16; 1 Pet. 1:10-12).

The prophets adopted various means when delivering their message. The most common was proclamation: The prophet simply spoke God's message to his generation. The first five books of Moses are didactic, but contain prophecies (*for example,* Deut. 31:24-29; 32). Other prophetic utterances are framed in vivid and powerful poetry as is, for instance, much of Isaiah and Habakkuk.

More difficult to interpret are prophetic visions, such as Daniel's visions foretelling the future (Dan. 7–12). Yet some visions, such as the withdrawal of the glory of God from the Jerusalem Temple before the Temple's destruction by Nebuchadnezzar (Ezek. 8–11), are overwhelmingly powerful and clear. Zechariah contains a whole series of visions, and most of the Book of Revelation is the description of a single vision given to the apostle John on the Isle of Patmos. The prophets also communicated God's message by symbolic actions, such as Elisha's command to Joash to shoot arrows representing victories over Syria (2 Ki. 13:15-19) and the many symbolic acts of Jeremiah and Ezekiel, which vividly communicated God's intention to judge his people (Jer. 13,32; Ezek. 12).

Whatever the form of the prophetic ministry, the forms of communication selected by the prophet were intended not to obscure but to express God's warnings, invitations, and intent to Israel. Thus, whether couched in plain speech, in poetry, in reports of visions, or in symbolic actions, the meaning of the prophet's message was understandable to his or her contemporaries. In any study of the OT, it is important to ask first of all what message the prophet was communicating to the men and women of his own generation, before emphasizing the sometimes fascinating images of the future woven through so many of their words.

THEMES OF THE PROPHETS

When we look at the message of the prophets to the people of their own time, we note a number of recurrent themes. The prophets spoke as those entrusted with a word from God. They spoke to a people whose identity had been established by covenant—Israel was God's chosen, and as such the nation was to be holy. Yet God's people were rebellious, having turned from God to idolatry and from compassion to injustice. Because of Israel's sins, God would surely visit his people with terrible judgments and the certain destruction of their hopes. Nevertheless, God's love for his people remained unshaken. Because of that love, God would ultimately restore his people to himself and to the Promised Land.

Generation after generation, the prophets in Israel preached faithfulness, urged justice, confronted sin, warned of coming judgment, offered hope to all who would turn to God, and maintained the vision of a God whose unshaken love for his people would triumph in the end.

THE ROLE OF THE PROPHET

The prophet served as the contemporary voice of God to his generation. As the voice of God, the prophet pointed out religious and social sins and called for repentance. But the prophet also was a source of specific divine guidance. Prophets confronted and counseled kings and even directed battles. Incidents reported in the OT give us fascinating insight into the significant national role of the prophet:

- Nathan rebukes David for his sin with Bathsheba, leading David to repent (2 Sam. 12).
- An unnamed prophet confronts Jeroboam I as he institutes counterfeit religion in Israel (1 Ki. 13).
- Elijah defeats prophets of Baal in contest on Mount Carmel and has all Baal's prophets killed (1 Ki. 18).
- An unnamed prophet directs Ahab's army to victory over Syria. Later he condemns Ahab for releasing the king of Aram (1 Ki. 20).
- Elijah condemns Ahab for the murder of Naboth and theft of his vineyard (1 Ki. 21).
- Elisha predicts the end of the siege of Samaria (2 Ki. 7).
- Elisha sends a prophet to anoint general Jehu king of Israel, stimulating Jehu's murder of all in Ahab's family (2 Ki. 9).
- Isaiah predicts the retreat of Assyrian forces and the death of Sennacherib (2 Ki. 19).
- Hanani rebukes King Asa, who is so angry he imprisons the prophet (2 Chr. 16).
- Micaiah predicts Ahab's death in battle and the defeat of the combined armies of Judah and Israel (2 Chr. 18).
- Jeremiah is cursed and imprisoned for predicting the fall of Jerusalem to Babylon and counseling surrender (Jer. 37,38).
- Daniel interprets Nebuchadnezzar's dreams (Dan. 2,4).
- Amos confronts the religious authorities in Israel and condemns the people for exploiting the poor (Amos 7,8).

In addition to these dramatic images of Israel's prophets as independent watchdogs through whom God spoke to the rulers of his people, the prophets also had a ministry to the common man. Saul consulted Samuel about lost donkeys (1 Sam. 9:6-10). Elisha miraculously multiplied a poor widow's jar of oil (2 Ki. 4) and made a lost axhead float (2 Ki. 6). Such simple miracles prefigure the ministry of Christ and demonstrate God's love for the individual as well as the nation. Not only the

miracles but also the preaching of the prophets served the people. Even in their most dire warnings, the prophets provided Israel with a theocratic interpretation of contemporary events and of history itself. The godly Israelite would hear in the words of the prophets what Habakkuk himself heard when God revealed through him the imminent danger to Judah from Babylon: "O Lord, you have appointed them to execute judgment; O Rock, you have ordained them to punish" (Hab. 1:12). Even disasters demonstrated, not God's abandonment of Israel, but his commitment to purifying those whom he loved.

PREDICTIVE PROPHECY

Woven through the message of the OT prophets are many predictions about future events. Perhaps as much as one-third of the material found in the OT prophets is predictive.

Predictive prophecy falls into one of two categories: near-term or far-term. Near-term predictions tell what is about to be experienced by those in the prophet's own generation. Jeremiah's announcement that Hananiah would die within a year is a near-term prediction, and within two months Hananiah was dead. Habakkuk's prediction of a coming invasion by the Babylonians probably took place within two decades, even though its fulfillment called for the unexpected overthrow of Assyria by the Babylonians and the emergence of a new, vast empire. The fulfillment of near-term predictions served to authenticate the prophet as God's messenger. As God says of near-term prophecy through Isaiah, speaking to a generation that resisted his Word,

Remember this, fix it in mind,
    take it to heart, you rebels.
Remember the former things, those of
        long ago;
    I am God, and there is no other;
    I am God, and there is none like me.
I make known the end from the beginning,
    from ancient times, what is still
        to come.

I say: My purpose will stand,
  and I will do all that I please. . . .
What I have said, that will I bring about;
  what I have planned, that
    will I do.   (Isa. 46:8-11)

Much of the OT predictive prophecy is far-term; that is, the things predicted by the prophet would be fulfilled long after his death and the deaths of his contemporaries. A number of far-term prophecies, such as predictions concerning Christ's first coming, have now been fulfilled. However, many more of the predictive prophecies found in the Bible have not yet been fulfilled or have been fulfilled only partially. Christians differ as to how this predictive material in the OT should be understood. Yet all recognize the significant place assigned to prediction in the older Testament. *See also* Prophecy, Interpretation of.

While most of the predictive material of Scripture is found in the OT, the NT also contains predictive prophecy. Notable predictive passages include Mt. 24; Mk. 13; 1 Th. 4; 2 Th. 1,2; 2 Pet. 3, and Rev. 4–22. *See also* Revelation, Book of.

PROPHETS IN THE NT

Several prophets are identified in the Gospels. Prophetic utterances are made by John the Baptist's father Zechariah and by Mary, Anna, Simeon, and John the Baptist (Lk. 1:46-55,67-79; 2:26-38; *compare* Mt. 11:13,14). Jesus himself is the ultimate prophet, who fulfills or shows the true meaning of the revelation granted through Moses, filling it with grace, and correcting Israel's misunderstanding with truth (Jn. 1:1-18). *See also* Fulfill.

Actually, Christianity as a faith is firmly rooted in the ministry of Israel's prophets, whose vision of a Messiah Jesus completes. Thus, Paul says that the Church, a holy temple in the Lord, is "built on the foundation of the apostles and prophets, with Christ Jesus himself as the chief cornerstone" (Eph. 2:20).

The challenging question, however, is whether the ministry of prophets as sources of divine revelation and guidance continues into the fully developed NT era.

Through the period represented by the Book of Acts, roughly A.D. 30–60, certain persons in the church had ministries much like those of OT prophets and are identified as prophets. Philip the evangelist had four daughters who prophesied (Acts 21:9). A prophet named Agabus predicted a famine during the reign of Claudius and that if Paul returned to Jerusalem he would be imprisoned because of the Jews (Acts 11:28; 21:10,11). Timothy's spiritual gift came to him through a prophetic message (1 Tim. 4:14). Prophecy is also identified as a spiritual gift in Rom. 12:6 and 1 Cor. 12–14. The late books of the NT, 2 Peter, Jude, and 1 John, all warn against false prophets, who can be recognized by their denial of Christ's incarnation, their materialistic motives, and their appeal to the selfish motives of those they lead astray. *See also* False Prophets.

Such references should make us hesitate to dismiss the possibility of prophets in the contemporary church. At the same time, we must remain cautious, remembering that Christ himself brought and is the full revelation of God (Heb. 1:1-3). Whatever a modern "prophet" may say, it will not contradict the full written revelation we now have in Scripture. In addition, the specific guidance that God provided to Israel through the prophets is now granted every individual Christian through the indwelling Holy Spirit. Thus, the revelatory functions of the prophet in OT times, and even in the first decades of the Church age, are personalized through the written Word and the indwelling Spirit in the lives of present-day believers.

propitiation (KJV) [from Gk., *hilaskomai*, "to avert anger by the offering of a sacrifice"]. Although several versions translate the Greek term as "expiation" (RSV) or "atonement," the word *hilaskomai* means "propitiate" and always denotes the removal of wrath.

The Bible teaches that God is so unalterably opposed to sin that he is obligated to judge sinners. Thus, Eph. 2:1-3 says that all of us "were by nature objects of wrath." Yet the Ephesians passage continues on and describes God's great love for us. He showers unmerited favor on us by making us "alive with Christ even when we were dead in transgressions" (2:4-10).

The teaching explicit in "propitiation" is that God's righteous anger has been turned aside by Christ's sacrifice. The key NT passage explaining this doctrine is Rom. 3:21-26. It says that we are

justified freely by his [God's] grace through the redemption that came by Christ Jesus. God presented him as a hilastērion [propitiating sacrifice], through faith in his blood. He did this to demonstrate his justice, because in his forbearance he had left the sins committed beforehand unpunished—he did it to demonstrate his justice at the present time, so as to be just and the one who justifies the man who has faith in Jesus.

Simply put, God demonstrated his justice by punishing sin—but by punishing himself in the person of God the Son, serving as our substitute. Now that our sins have been punished in Jesus, our substitute, God has taken upon himself the penalty for the sins of humanity, and thus is able to pronounce us righteous in his sight, no longer objects of his wrath. *See also* Atonement.

Greek words meaning "propitiation" or "place of propitiation" occur in Lk. 18:13,14; Rom. 3:25; Heb. 2:17; 9:5; 1 Jn. 2:2; and 4:10.

proselyte (KJV) By the first century, a Gentile who had adopted the Jewish religion. *See also* God-fearing. In NT times, many Gentiles were drawn to the Jewish religion because of its monotheism and ethical moral standards. The Jews of the Diaspora were especially open to proselytes.

The Greek word, *prosēlytos,* is found only four times in the NT. Jesus charged the scribes and Pharisees of his day with going to great lengths to make one proselyte (convert), only to make him "twice as much a son of hell as you are" (Mt. 23:15). Acts 2:11 says that many Jews and proselytes were in Jerusalem for Pentecost. Acts 6:5 identifies one of the seven deacons of the Jerusalem church as a proselyte. And Acts 13:43 reports that after Paul preached in the Antioch synagogue, many Jews and devout proselytes were converted to Christ there.

prostitute (1) [Heb., *zonah*], an ordinary prostitute; a woman who exchanges sex for money, as in Gen. 34:31; (2) [Heb., *qedeshah*], a cult prostitute, male or female; a person whose sex acts were part of a religious ritual intended to stimulate pagan deities and thus ensure the fertility of the fields and herds, as in Gen. 38:21; Deut. 23:17,18; (3) [Gk., *porne*], one who engages in immoral sexual acts; (4) symbolically, a representation of idolatry, as in Num. 15:39, or materialism, as in Rev. 17.

PROSTITUTION IN ISRAEL

In many ancient societies, prostitution was accepted behavior. In Assyria, prostitution was so common that couples openly engaged in intercourse on the streets and in taverns. Assyrian law required only that a prostitute identify herself by not wearing a veil.

Ordinary prostitution was apparently practiced in Israel throughout the biblical period. Tamar dressed as a prostitute to draw the attention of Judah (Gen. 38:14). Rahab the harlot was accepted into Israel (Josh. 6). The women who came to Solomon with their dispute over a baby were both prostitutes (1 Ki. 3:16). In the first century, "prostitutes and tax collectors" responded to the Gospel message (Mt. 21:31,32). Further evidence of the ubiquity of ordinary prostitution is found in various descriptive phrases. Prostitutes looked for customers by frequenting public places (1 Ki. 22:38; Prov. 7:12). They dressed seductively (Prov. 7:10-12; Isa. 3:16), calling and reaching out to attract attention (Prov. 7:11,13; Jer. 2:23-25). Isaiah 23:16-18 suggests that entertainers typically earned most of their income by prostitution. Married women as well as the unmarried were likely to work as prostitutes (Prov. 7:16-19).

While ordinary prostitution was tolerated in Israel, it clearly was not sanctioned. The half brothers of Jephthah succeeded in disinheriting him because his mother was a prostitute (Jdg. 11:1,2). No Israelite was to permit his daughter to become a prostitute (Lev. 19:29), nor were the wages of a prostitute acceptable as a gift to God (Deut. 23:17,18). The unmarried daughter of an Israelite who did turn to prostitution was to be stoned (Deut. 22:21). Priests, set aside as holy to the Lord, were to have no contact with prostitution (Lev. 21:7,14). If the unmarried daughter of a priest became a prostitute, she was to be burned (Lev. 21:9). In the NT, the linkage of prostitutes with tax collectors reflects the negative evaluation of both occupations in first-century Judaism (Mt. 21:31,32).

The NT, which rules out all forms of sexual immorality, expresses shock that a Christian would go to a prostitute, as the act would pollute the believer, who is Christ's living temple (1 Cor. 6:15,16).

CULT PROSTITUTION

Cult prostitution is viewed even more seriously in the OT. The fertility religions of Canaan assumed that the sex acts of their gods and goddesses were responsible for the fertility of fields and herds. When male or female cult prostitutes engaged in sex, the intention was to sexually stimulate their deities.

Cult prostitution was an abomination on three counts: (1) It gave immorality religious sanction; (2) it was associated with pagan religions; and (3) it involved an express reliance on magic (*see also* Idol; Magic). Yet the Canaanite religions held a

dark attraction for ancient Israel, and cult
prostitution is mentioned repeatedly
throughout the OT up to the end of the
monarchy (1 Sam. 2:22; 1 Ki. 14:23,24;
15:12; 22:46; 2 Ki. 23:7; Jer. 3:2; Ezek. 8:14;
23:27; Hos. 4:13). Moses and the prophets
speak in the strongest terms against these
practices, and the revivals held under the
few godly kings of Judah characteristically
involve purifying the land of cult prostitutes and prostitution.

PROSTITUTION AS A SYMBOL

The association of cult prostitution with
Canaanite religions and with marital unfaithfulness makes it a powerful image of
breaking covenant with God. Hosea, who
uses the symbol of harlotry throughout his
prophecy to portray Israel's rejection of
the Lord, charges idolatrous Israel with "a
spirit of prostitution [that] leads them
astray; they are unfaithful to their God"
(Hos. 4:12). As a result, society brimmed
over with immorality and injustice. Hosea
says:

"I will not punish your daughters
    when they turn to prostitution,
nor your daughters-in-law
    when they commit adultery,
because the men themselves consort
        with harlots
    and sacrifice with shrine prostitutes—
    a people without understanding will
        come to ruin!"   (Hos. 4:14)

Here symbol and reality are closely
linked, for the heart that turns from God
will surely turn to sin, and ultimately
experience judgment (Rom. 1:21-32).

proverb Essentially a popular saying that
tersely sums up some truth gleaned from
experience, such as "like mother, like
daughter" (Ezek. 16:44), or the cynical
"Physician, heal yourself" (Lk. 4:23). Proverbs were also used in "taunt songs" and
riddles (Isa. 14:4-23; Hab. 2:6).

While the Book of Proverbs is a library
of such sayings, bits of proverbial wisdom
are scattered throughout the OT and NT.
They are found in poems, as short stories
and allusions, and as probing questions
and pungent replies. Some entire psalms,
the "wisdom psalms," draw heavily on
proverbs (Pss. 1,32,34,37,49,73,112,127,
128,133), as does the Book of Ecclesiastes.
Jesus incorporated proverbs in his teaching, in such expressions as "Where your
treasure is, there your heart will be also"
(Mt. 6:21); "Wide is the gate and broad is
the road that leads to destruction, and
many enter though it" (Mt. 7:13); and "The
Sabbath was made for man, not man for the
Sabbath" (Mt. 2:27). The use of memorable,
pithy sayings contributed to the effectiveness of Jesus' teaching and preaching.

Proverbs, Book of A collection of pithy
statements summing up truths learned

from life's experience. Proverbs is classified as "wisdom literature." It is intended to help the reader, envisioned as a young person just starting out in life, make prudent and sensible choices. *See also* Wisdom.

BACKGROUND AND AUTHORSHIP

Both tradition and internal evidence ascribe most of the Book of Proverbs to Solomon (1:1; 10:1; 25:1). Two other contributors are mentioned by name, Agur (Prov. 30:1) and Lemuel (31:1). The idea that Solomon contributed many if not most of the sayings in this book is supported by 1 Ki. 4:32, which reports that among many other accomplishments, Solomon "spoke three thousand proverbs." At the same time, there is no doubt that the collection we have was compiled some 250 years after Solomon's time, by scribes working under the direction of King Hezekiah (728–697 B.C.), as stated in Prov. 25:1. Proverbs from several different sources were probably included at that time.

THEOLOGICAL CONTRIBUTIONS

Nontheological in character, the Book of Proverbs makes no mention of covenant or sacrifice. It does not distinguish Israel from the rest of humankind nor does it present a grand eschatological vision. Instead, the Book of Proverbs turns a practical eye on daily life and makes a variety of observations on sensible living.

Several things must be remembered when applying the proverbs this book contains: (1) The proverbs state general principles. They are not promises that God has made to his people to be claimed by faith. (2) The general principles stated here have exceptions. While it is usually true that "a soft answer turns away wrath," this is not always the case. (3) These proverbs have universal application. They are true not only for God's covenant people but for all mankind. A person in any society who follows these guidelines will live a better and happier life than one who does not. (4) Yet, "The fear of the Lord is the beginning of knowledge" (Prov. 1:7). Awareness of and respect for God as a moral ruler underlies sensible living in every society and every age.

MASTERY KEYS

The Book of Proverbs is not arranged by topic, but certain themes recur, scattered throughout the book. The Topical Guide thus does not outline chapters but rather lists proverbs according to the major topics explored in the book. Use this study guide to examine observations on poverty, work,

TOPICAL GUIDE TO PROVERBS

Topic	References
Adultery	5:1-6 / 6:24-29 / 6:30-32 / 7:6-27 / 22:14 / 23:26-28 / 29:3 / 30:20.
Alcohol	20:1 / 23:20,21,29-35 / 31:4-7.
Business	6:1-5 / 11:1,13-15,26 / 14:15 / 15:22 / 16:11 / 17:18 / 18:17 / 19:20 / 20:10,14,16,18,23 / 22:26,27 / 24:27 / 27:12,13.
Cheerfulness	12:25 / 15:13,15,30 / 17:22.
Crime	6:30,31 / 10:9,16 / 13:11 / 15:6,27 / 16:8,19 / 17:15,23 / 18:5 / 19:5,9 / 20:17 / 28:6,8 / 29:24.
Discipline	3:11,12 / 5:12-14,23 / 6:23 / 9:7-10 / 10:17 / 12:1 / 13:18,24 / 15:5,10,32 / 19:18 / 22:15 / 23:13,14 / 27:5 / 29:15,17.
Doing good	3:27,28 / 11:27 / 12:2 / 14:19,22 / 20:22 / 22:1 / 25:21,22.
Evil	8:13 / 11:19,27 / 14:22 / 17:11,13 / 24:19,20 / 28:5,13 / 30:32.
Fools	1:22 / 3:35 / 10:23 / 12:15,16,23 / 13:16,19 / 14:3,7-9 / 15:5 / 16:22 / 17:12,16,28 / 18:2,6,7 / 20:3 / 23:9 / 26:1,3-12 / 27:22.
Friendship	1:10-19 / 12:26 / 13:20 / 16:28 / 17:17 / 18:1,24 / 19:7 / 22:10 / 27:6,10.
Giving	3:9,10 / 11:24,25 / 18:16 / 22:9,16 / 25:14 / 28:25,27.
Gossip	11:13 / 16:28 / 18:8 / 20:19 / 26:22.
Government	8:15,16 / 13:17 / 14:28,34,35 / 16:10,12-15 / 17:26 / 18:17 / 20:8 / 21:28 / 24:24,25 / 25:5 / 28:2,3,15,16 / 29:2,4,12,14.
Jealousy/Envy	3:31,32 / 6:34,35 / 14:30 / 23:17 / 24:1,2,19,20 / 27:4.
Laziness	6:9-11 / 10:4 / 12:24,27 / 13:4 / 15:19 / 19:15 / 20:4,13 / 24:30-34 / 26:13-16.
Lies	6:16,17 / 10:18 / 12:17-19,22 / 14:5,24 / 17:4,20 / 19:22 / 24:28,29 / 25:9,10,18 / 26:24-28 / 30:8.
The Lord	1:7 / 3:5-8,11,12,25,26 / 5:20,21 / 8:13 / 9:10-12 / 10:3,22,27,29 / 11:20 / 12:22 / 14:2,16,26,27,31 / 15:3,8,9,33 / 16:2-5,7,9,20,33 / 18:10 / 19:3,17,18,23 / 20:24 / 22:2,12,22,23 / 24:21,22 / 25:2,21,22 / 28:14,25 / 29:26 / 30:5-9.
Love	10:12 / 15:17 / 16:6 / 17:9,17 / 19:22 / 20:6.
Neighbors	3:29,30 / 6:16-19 / 11:9 / 14:20,21 / 26:17-20 / 29:5.
Parent/Child	1:8,9 / 4:1-4 / 6:20-23 / 10:1 / 13:1 / 15:20 / 17:6,21,25 / 19:13,18,26 / 20:7,11,20 / 22:6 / 23:13,14,22,24 / 28:24 / 30:17.
Poverty/The Poor	6:10,11 / 10:4,15 / 13:8,18,23 / 14:20,31 / 17:5 / 18:23 / 19:1,4,7,17,22 / 22:2,7,9,16,22,23 / 24:30-34 / 28:6,8,19,22 / 29:7 / 30:11-14 / 31:8,9.
Prayer	15:29 / 28:9.
Pride/Arrogance	6:16,17 / 8:13 / 11:2 / 13:10 / 15:25 / 16:5,18 / 17:7 / 18:12 / 25:6,7 / 27:2 / 29:1,23.
The Righteous	10:7,16,28,30 / 11:5,10,18,23,31 / 12:3,5-7,10,12,13,21,28 / 13:5,6,9,21,25 / 15:9 / 20:7 / 24:16 / 29:7.
Temper	14:17,29 / 15:1,18 / 16:32 / 19:19 / 22:24,25 / 29:11,22.
The Tongue	6:16,17 / 10:11,18,21,31,32 / 11:12 / 12:18 / 13:2,3 / 15:1,2,4,7 / 18:21
Wealth	10:2,4,15,22 / 11:4,28 / 13:8,21,22 / 14:24 / 15:16 / 18:11 / 19:4 / 20:21 / 22:4 / 23:4-8 / 28:8,20,25.
The Wicked	1:10-19 / 2:12-15,22 / 3:33-35 / 4:14-19 / 5:22,23 / 6:12-15 / 10:3,6,16,24,25,28,30 / 11:3,5-7,10,18,21,23,31 / 12:3,5-7,12,13,21 / 13:6,9,21,25 / 14:11,19 / 15:9,26 / 17:4 / 22:5 / 24:1,2,19,20 / 28:1,11,12.
Wisdom	1:2-7 / 2:1-22 / 3:1-4,13-18 / 4:7-9 / 8:1-36 / 9:10-12 / 12:8 / 16:16 / 24:5,14 / 28:26.
Women	11:22 / 12:4 / 14:1 / 18:22 / 19:14 / 25:24 / 27:15,16 / 31:10-31.
Work	12:11,14,24,27 / 14:23 / 16:26 / 18:9 / 22:29 / 27:18,23-27.

(1:20-33; 8:1-3; 9:1-6). The Book of Proverbs also identifies four kinds of fools. One is ignorant but teachable (1:4,22; 7:7; 21:11). Another is hardened and obstinate (1:7; 10:23; 12:23; 17:10; 20:3; 27:22). A third fool is arrogant, an attitude that keeps him from learning (3:34; 21:24; 22:10; 29:8). A fourth fool is warped morally (17:21; 26:3; 30:22). *See also* Fool.

providence The continuous active involvement of God in the created universe; his supervision of all things from the creation to eternity.

The word "providence" is not found in Scripture. Yet the concept is clearly taught. It is illustrated in the OT in the Book of Esther and in the NT by events leading up to the crucifixion of Christ. The Book of Esther reports a series of apparent coincidences through which the ruler Xerxes (Ahasuerus, KJV,RSV) deposed the enemy of the Jews, Haman, and saved the Jews from extinction. The unfolding coincidences suggest that God, although not named in the book, worked through natural cause-and-effect sequences to protect his covenant people. Furthermore, in the NT, Acts 4:27,28 states that while Jesus' enemies acted freely as morally responsible beings to bring about his death, "they did what your [God's] power and will had decided beforehand."

These two incidents support the Christian conviction that God is so great that he is able to weave together the free choices of myriad human beings and the patterns of cause and effect that link events throughout history and accomplish his purposes through them. God's providential workings are hidden. They do not violate a person's free will, nor do they normally violate natural cause and effect by introducing the miraculous.

The doctrine of providence is dramatically different from the belief of the ancients that humanity is subject to impersonal fate or, according to modern perception, subject to chaotic chance. The Christian sees the universe as subject to God's will and thus looks to the future with hope rather than fear. While we accept responsibility for our personal choices, we remain convinced that "in all things God works for the good of those who love him" (Rom. 8:28).

Passages that invite believers to trust in the providential care of God include: Deut. 32:7-43; Pss. 74:12-17; 104:27-30; Mt. 6:25-33; 10:29-31; Rom. 8:28-39; 2 Cor. 4:11-18; 1 Pet. 1:3-9.

God "sits enthroned above the circle of the earth" (Isa. 40:22) in this world map attached to a Latin manuscript of the Psalms (about A.D. 1275).

friendship, business decisions, etc.

The proverbs exhibit the parallelism that is characteristic of Hebrew poetry. Read the article on poetry to learn how to interpret statements in this form.

SPECIAL FEATURES

The author or compiler of the first nine chapters personifies wisdom as a woman

STRUCTURE OF PROVERBS		
I.	Treatise on Wisdom	1–9
II.	Proverbs of Solomon (1)	10:1–22:16
III.	Sayings of the Wise (1)	22:17–24:22
IV.	Sayings of the Wise (2)	24:23-34
V.	Proverbs of Solomon (2)	25:1–29:27
VI.	Words of Agur	30
VII.	Words of Lemuel	31:1-9
VIII.	In Praise of a Good Wife	31:10-31

pruning hook Semicircular blades used by farmers in Israel to prune vines and tree branches.

The inner edge of the pruning hook was sharpened; the outside of the blade was blunt. To beat a pruning hook into a spear (Joel 3:10), the outer rather than inner edge was sharpened, and the tool was fastened to a shaft. To beat such a spear back into a pruning hook (Isa. 2:4; Mic. 4:3), all that was required was to rework the blade, putting the edge back on the inside.

Psalms, Book of A collection of 150 poems and songs, many of which were used in public worship in ancient Israel. It was called by the Hebrews *sepher tehillim,* the "book of praises." Martin Luther called it a work through which we are shown the heart of all the saints. It is perhaps best understood as a celebration of, and guide to, intimate relationship with God. As such, the Psalms is one of the most significant, most personal, and most rewarding of the books of the Bible.

BACKGROUND AND AUTHORSHIP

The psalms collected in this book were written by a number of different persons over the span of hundreds of years. Psalm 90 is attributed to Moses (about 1450 B.C.), some 73 psalms are attributed to David (about 1000 B.C.), others to Temple musicians (Asaph, Ethan, the sons of Korah), and some were written after the Exile (74,79,89,107,137). While some critics once claimed that none of the psalms could have been written as early as David, archaeological finds of poetic literature in parallel cultures show that some of the psalms might well be among the earliest biblical literature. There is certainly no reason now to doubt that David, the psalmist of Israel (2 Sam. 23:1), personally penned many of these worship songs and poems. Moreover, Davidic authorship of several psalms is authenticated by references in the NT (*compare* Mk. 12:36; Lk. 20:42,43; Acts 2:25-35; Rom. 4:6-8).

Psalms is organized into five "books," with a doxology closing each book. The division reflects the addition of new collections to the psalter at various times. Book 1 (Pss. 1–41) was probably compiled in the time of David. Book 2 (Pss. 42–72) was probably added in the time of Solomon. Books 3 (Pss. 73–89) and 4 (90–106) date from the time of the Exile; and the strongly liturgical Book 5 (Pss. 107–150) is thought to have been added in the time of Ezra after the return from Babylon. Even if this theory is correct, many of the psalms in the later collections probably were used in worship long before being added to the official psalm book.

1. *Poetic structure.* Psalms is one of three OT poetic books. Hebrew poetry does not depend on rhyme or the arrangement of sounds, but on "parallelism," the arrangement of thought. In synonymous parallelism, the second line repeats the thought of the first. In antithetical parallelism, the thought of the first line is emphasized by a contrasting statement in the next. In syn-

---

STRUCTURE OF THE PSALMS

Book	1	Mostly psalms attributed to David and that use "Yahweh" for God's name. Contains introductory psalms (1,2), ones with allusions to David's life (7,18,34), and those used in Temple worship (24,30,34,38).	1–41
Book	2	Psalms attributed to the Sons of Korah (42–49); Asaph (50); David (51–65; 68–71); Solomon (72). This group uses "Elohim" for God's name. Contains psalms with allusions to David's life (51,52,54, 56,57,59,60, 63), and ones used in Temple worship (48,70).	42–72
Book	3	Psalms attributed to Asaph (73–83); the Sons of Korah (84,85,87,88); David (86); Ethan (89). This group uses both "Elohim" (73–83) and "Yahweh" (84–89) for God's name. Contains psalms used by Levites in Temple worship (81,82).	73–89
Book	4	Psalms attributed to Moses (90); David (101,103). "Yahweh;" employed for God's name. Contains psalms for Temple worship (92–94), ones that celebrate God's kingship (93–99), and "Hallelujah" psalms (104–106).	90–106
Book	5	Some attributed to David (108–110;138–145). This group uses "Yahweh" for God's name. Contains the "Egyptian" Hallel (113–118), Songs of Ascent or Pilgrim Psalms (120–134), and "Hallelujah" psalms (146–150).	107–150

Carved ivory cover of the Dagulfe Psalter (8th century A.D.) portrays King David dictating a psalm and playing a harp (right side), and scenes from the life of Jerome (left), who translated the Psalms into Latin.

thetic parallelism, the second or succeeding lines build on the thought expressed in the first. In Hebrew poetry, many complex patterns can be formed by mixing these basic forms. It is important in reading or trying to interpret the psalms to understand this characteristic of Hebrew poetry. Several of the psalms are acrostics, with each line or set of lines starting with a different letter of the Hebrew alphabet (*compare* 9,10,25,34,37,111,112,119). *See also* Poetry.

2. *Musical structure.* Many of the psalms

are songs, intended for use in liturgical settings. This is reflected in many of the superscriptions that accompany all but 34 of the book's 150 psalms. Some of these contain technical musical notations, such as "with stringed instruments" (Ps. 4), or "for flutes" (Ps. 5), and "according to *gittith*," which possibly means "instrumental music" (Ps. 8). Some superscriptions also identify the literary type of the psalm, such as a song (Ps. 30) or a psalm (Ps. 23).

3. *Classification.* A number of ap-

proaches have been taken in attempting to classify the various psalms. One system is based on supposed liturgical use. In this system, psalms are classified as hymns (8,29,33,64,111,115), as individual songs of thanksgiving (30,34,66,116,138), as individual laments (6,13,31,39), as communal laments (12,14,44,74,79), as royal psalms (2,18,20,35,40,45), as wisdom psalms (1,32, 37,49,119), etc.

Another system classifies psalms by their content. Using content as the criterion, psalms have been classed as: historical, rooted in Israel's common experience (14,44,46–48,53,66,68,74,76,78–80,83,85, 87,105,106,108,122–126,129); imprecatory, calling out for vindication against one's own and God's enemies (5,7,28,35,54, 55,58,59,69,79,83,101,109,137); messianic, concerning the coming deliverer (2,8,16, 22,24,40,45,69,72,89,102,109,110,132); and penitential, expressing a sense of sorrow and seeking reconciliation after having sinned (6,32,38,51,102,130,143). Many psalms, of course, simply sing God's praise (33,103,139).

THEOLOGICAL CONTRIBUTIONS

The psalms make many exalted affirmations about God. He is celebrated as Creator (33:6-9; 95:3-7), as faithful (18:25,28; 89:5-8; 145:13-16), as loving (36:5-7; 63:3-5; 108:3-5), merciful (28:6,7; 30:8,10; 86:15-17), as righteous (11:4-7; 145:17-21), as sovereign (47:7-9; 96:10-13), as acting on behalf of his covenant people (77:11-15; 111:2-4,6-9). Yet the psalms fail to mention many themes repeated so often in the OT. There is little reference to sacrifice, and although God is expected to deliver his saints, that expectation is focused on this present life rather than on the next. The eschatological vision of the future so clear in the prophets is reflected in the psalms in visions of the Messiah, as in Ps. 2, but eschatology is hardly dominant.

Essentially, the theology of the psalms is relational. The psalms draw attention to the relationship with God experienced by his people as they pass through this life. As such, the psalms are of great value to believers of every age. The psalms model intimacy with God and show us how to relate any situation in which we may find ourselves to the Lord.

1. *Life experiences.* The psalms draw from life and relate life to God. David was devastated as he fled from his son Absalom, seriously considering whether his failures had caused God to set him aside. The historical background given in 2 Sam.

David plays a harp in this mosaic floor design from a 6th-century A.D. synagogue in Israel.

TOPICAL GUIDE TO THE PSALMS

Anger	4 / 17 / 28 / 36 / 109.
Anxiety/fear	3 / 11 / 12 / 27 / 46 / 49 / 59 / 64 / 91 / 121 / 139 / 146.
Decision-making	1 / 25 / 26 / 37 / 62 / 101 / 119.
Direction	13 / 25 / 37 / 89 / 119 / 146.
Disappointment	16 / 92 / 102 / 130.
Discouragement	12 / 42 / 55 / 86 / 107 / 142.
Injustice	7 / 9 / 10 / 17 / 35 / 52 / 56 / 94 / 109.
Insignificance	8 / 23 / 86 / 119 / 139.
Joy	33 / 47 / 63 / 84 / 96 / 97 / 98 / 100 / 148.
Knowing God	8 / 18 / 19 / 29 / 65 / 89 / 103 / 105 / 111 / 136 / 145 / 147.
Loneliness	3 / 13 / 17 / 25 / 27 / 69 / 91.
Patience	4 / 5 / 37 / 89 / 123.
Reassurance	1 / 15 / 18 / 23 / 26 / 112 / 121 / 128.
Safety/security	34 / 84 / 91.
Sickness	22 / 23 / 41 / 116.
Sorrows/grief	6 / 31 / 71 / 77 / 94 / 123.
Stress	12 / 24 / 31 / 34 / 43 / 56 / 84.
Thankfulness	30 / 33 / 34 / 40 / 66 / 89 / 96 / 113 / 136.
Troubled spirit	10 / 86 / 90 / 94 / 126 / 138 / 142.
Weakness	4 / 23 / 62 / 70 / 102 / 138.

14–17 reveals the mortal danger David faced at that time. Psalm 3, whose superscription reads, "when he [David] fled from his son Absalom," expresses David's feelings of fear and abandonment (3:1,2). Nevertheless, David remembered how God had protected and strengthened him, and so David prayed (3:3,4). Comforted, David then describes his ensuing experience of inner peace:

I lie down and sleep;
I wake again, because the Lord
sustains me.
I will not fear the tens of thousands
drawn up against me on every side.
(Ps. 3:5,6)

A number of David's psalms are linked in this way with historical situations, which enables us to sense the circumstances that caused the emotions David expressed to God. These psalms are: Ps. 7 with 1 Sam. 24:11,12; Ps. 18 with 2 Sam. 7:1 and 2 Sam. 22; Ps. 30 with 2 Sam. 24:25 and 1 Chr. 22:1-6; Ps. 34 with 1 Sam. 21:10-15; Ps. 51 with 2 Sam. 12:13,14; Ps. 52 with 1 Sam. 22:6-23; Ps. 54 with 1 Sam. 23:19; Ps. 56 with 1 Sam. 21:3-15; Ps. 57 with 1 Sam. 24:3; Ps. 59 with 1 Sam. 19:11,12; Ps. 60 with 2 Sam. 8:13,14; Ps. 63 with 2 Sam. 16:2; and Ps. 142 with 1 Sam. 24:1-6.

2. *Universal experiences.* The psalms reflect universal experiences. For instance, Pss. 32 and 51 are prime models of penitential psalms. They show how an attempt to mask guilt affects us:

When I kept silent,
my bones wasted away
through my groaning all day long.
For day and night
your hand was heavy upon me;
my strength was sapped
as in the heat of summer. (Ps. 32:3,4)

And they teach us how to appeal to God:

Have mercy on me, O God,
according to your unfailing love;
according to your great compassion
blot out my transgressions.
Wash away all my iniquity
and cleanse me from my sin.
For I know my transgressions,
and my sin is always before me.
Against you, you only, have I sinned
and done what is evil in your sight.
(Ps. 51:1-3)

The psalms express universal emotions and show us how to deal with them in healing, healthy ways. Our situations may differ in detail from those of the psalmists, but the emotions—stress, fear, uncertainty, etc.—are common to human beings of every age. A good example is found in Ps. 73, which illustrates the emotion of envy or jealousy. The writer, Asaph, confesses that his feet almost slipped because he envied the arrogant (Ps. 73:1-3). The wicked seemed healthy and strong, "free from the burdens common to man" (v. 5). Comparing his life to what he saw of the carefree wicked, Asaph was bitter, feeling that "in vain have I kept my heart pure; in vain have I washed my hands in innocence" (v. 13). But "I entered the sanctuary of God," and "then I understood their final destiny" (v. 17). Then, in God's house, the poet realizes that the very prosperity he envied has made the wicked feel so safe and secure that they sense no need for God (vv. 18-20). His envy was foolish, because the very prosperity that Asaph yearned for was not a gift from God, but "slippery ground" on which the wicked would fall to ruin. Suddenly, understanding it all, Asaph rejoices:

Yet I am always with you;
you hold me by my right hand.
You guide me with your counsel,
and afterward you will take me into
glory.
Whom have I in heaven but you?
And earth has nothing I desire
besides you. (Ps. 73:23-25)

Many of the psalms meet us where we are, in the grip of destructive emotions, and lead us through a healing process. They show us how to relate our emotions and experiences to God and how to find inner peace. Certainly, one enriching way to read these poems is to look inward, identify a troubled emotion, locate that same emotion in the psalms, and then let these ancient poems guide us into peace.

3. *Meditation.* The psalms encourage us to meditate on God. As we read the psalms and glimpse the images they cast, we are drawn to think deeply about what our relationship with God means. There is no better Psalm to illustrate this than the familiar 23rd. Generations of Christians have experienced comfort and peace as they quoted, "The Lord is my shepherd, I shall not be in want. He makes me lie down in green pastures, he leads me beside the still waters."

In these and many other vital ways, the psalms trace the strands of life that tie us so closely to the Lord. Because of this unique quality, the Book of Psalms truly has become one of the most precious of the spiritual resources in God's Word.

MASTERY KEYS

Read the various psalms with your heart as well as your head. Open your heart to the emotions expressed by the writers. Feel with them the meaning of a personal relationship with God. Also use the Topical Guide here, which links many of the psalms to experiences shared by human beings of every time and every place.

You might also read through the psalms guided by the categories discussed under Theological Contributions.

SPECIAL FEATURES

Many unknown words from the superscriptions of the psalms are believed to be musical or choreographical instructions for liturgical use. The best known, *selah*, may indicate a pause, an increase in volume, or some other instruction. Perhaps it is best to read *selah* as if it is a call for a musical rest, as if saying to the listener, "Think about it!"

publican (KJV) A tax or toll collector, a class scorned in Jesus' time for serving the interests of the Romans and for frequently charging much more than what was due. However, Jesus commended the publicans for their willingness to believe him—unlike the self-righteous Pharisees (Mt. 9:9-13; 11:19; 21:31,32; Mk. 2:13-17; Lk. 5:27-32; 7:29-35; 15:1,2; 18:9-14; 19:1-10). *See also* Taxes.

pulse (KJV) A dish of meal and legumes. It was eaten by Daniel and his companions, who were determined to abide by Jewish dietary laws while in Babylon (Dan. 1:12,16). Both RSV and NIV read "vegetables."

punish (1) To impose a penalty on a wrongdoer for his or her offense; (2) to cause a wrongdoer to suffer for his crime or offense.

OLD TESTAMENT

As Creator of all, God is also responsible to be the Judge of all. This view is reflected in the stories of the Genesis Flood (Gen. 6–8) and of the destruction of Sodom and Gomorrah (Gen. 18,19). It is also expressed in such statements as "I will punish the world for its evil" (Isa. 13:11).

More significantly, in the OT, God accepted special responsibility for Israel when he established the Abrahamic covenant (*see also* Covenant). Under the Abrahamic covenant, God committed himself to act against those who mistreat Abraham's descendants (Gen. 12:3; *compare* Isa. 10:5-12; Jer. 25:8-12; Ezek. 30:14). In the later Mosaic covenant, God promised to bless his people when they obeyed but

Roman tax collector receives money from four people in this relief from a funeral stela (100–300 A.D.).

Pharaoh Sahure of the Old Kingdom punishes a Semitic enemy with death; drawing from a relief in the quarries of Sinai.

also to punish them when they disobeyed, for the wicked acts of Israel violated their special relationship with God (Deut. 28; Jer. 5). *See also* Law.

According to the OT, acts of sin make a person guilty and subject to divine punishment. Yet, while there are hints of eternal punishment (Isa. 66:24; Dan. 12:2), the punishments presented in the OT are essentially administered in this life.

NEW TESTAMENT

Several Greek words develop the concept of punishment in the NT. Among them are *dike*, "justice," *ekdikeō*, "to do justice, avenge," and *kolasis*, which portrays punishment as a painful experience. Closely related are the ideas of rebuke (*timoria, epitimia*) and discipline (*paideia*). These words are used within the framework established in the OT, that is, punishment is a divine act that justly and appropriately causes the guilty to suffer for their sins.

The NT teaches that God has now given human government the responsibility of punishing crimes and evil in this life (Rom. 13:4,5). God will act to punish those who cause his saints to suffer; however, as Paul teaches, "This will happen when the Lord Jesus is revealed from heaven in blazing fire with his powerful angels." Then God "will punish those who do not know God and do not obey the gospel of our Lord Jesus. They will be punished with everlasting destruction and shut out from the presence of the Lord" (2 Th. 1:7-10).

Two elements of the divine punishment portrayed in this passage are important. First, the punishment due the wicked is delayed until history's end (Rom. 2:1-16). Second, punishment is no longer primarily suffering in this life but rather "everlasting destruction." According to Jesus, the wicked will "go away to eternal punishment," which he describes as "the eternal fire prepared for the devil and his angels" (Mt. 25:46,41). *See also* Hell; Judgment; Resurrection.

pure (1) Of substances, unadulterated, such as "pure gold," as in Ex. 25:11, or even "pure joy," as in Jas. 1:2. (2) In a cultic sense, ritually clean, as in Ezra 6:20 (KJV); Lk. 2:22 (*see also* Clean and Unclean). (3) In a moral sense, characterized by blamelessness; a habit of making right and good choices, as in Job 8:6; Phil. 1:10 (*see also* Blameless). No one can literally say, "I am pure and without sin" (Job 33:9), but in a limited sense, one's conduct can be "pure and right" (Prov. 20:11). God himself is "too pure to look on evil" (Hab. 1:13). (4) In a spiritual sense, characterized by wholehearted commitment to God, as in Ps. 51:10; Mt. 5:8.

The image of a pure heart is especially important in both Testaments. The pure in heart will be blessed by the Lord (Pss. 24:4,5; 73:1). Jesus says the pure in heart are blessed, for "they will see God" (Mt. 5:8). Wholehearted commitment to God enables the believer to focus his attention on the Lord and so become aware of God's presence in his daily life. Also, love flows from a pure heart, undivided by conflicting loyalties (1 Tim. 1:5).

purge (KJV) To extricate impurities from, to rid of what is wrong or undesirable, as in 2 Chr. 34:3; Ps. 51:7.

purification (1) The ceremonial cleansing of a person who is ritually unclean. (2) The preparation of persons or objects to be dedicated to God, as of the Levites (Lev. 8:12) and of the altar of sacrifice and other sacred objects (Lev. 8:15; *compare* 1 Chr. 23:28).

The Law of Moses established rites of purification (1) for mothers after the birth of a child, as in Lev. 12; Lk. 2:22-24; (2) for those who had contact with a dead body, as in Num. 19; (3) for those who recovered from infectious skin diseases, as in Lev. 13,14; (4) for those preparing to worship God, as in Acts 21:18,21; (5) and for many other circumstances, as in Lev. 11,15,17. *See also* Clean and Unclean; Law; Leprosy.

Purim A religious holiday celebrated the 14th and 15th days of the month before Passover (Esth. 9:24-32). It commemorates the deliverance of the Jews through Esther and Mordecai from the plot of Haman to exterminate their race. *See also* Esther; Feasts, Festivals, and Fasts.

purple A deep crimson color, shading from blue to red, associated in the ancient world with high rank and great wealth, as in Jdg. 8:26; Dan. 5:29; Lk. 16:19. Lydia, a merchant in Philippi, was a "dealer in purple" (Acts 16:14).

Purple dye was obtained from the murex shellfish of the eastern Mediterranean. Some hypothesize that the name Canaan meant "the land of purple" because of its trade in purple dye and products. The color, mentioned frequently in the OT, always suggests power or riches.

Purple remained the mark of highest distinction in the Roman Empire. In the first century, the emperor merited a purple cloak, senators a broad band of purple down the front, and the next lower class a narrow band. In later Roman times, it was considered treason for anyone outside the emperor's own court to wear clothing dyed with pure purple.

Because purple was difficult to produce, it was very expensive and consequently a symbol of importance. An Austrian chemist in the early 1900s demonstrated that some 12,000 murex shells were needed to produce just one and one-half grams of dye. The Roman writer Pliny indicates that most of the shells needed to make this dye were gathered by divers, each "offering his person as bait to sea monsters while he hastens to snatch his booty and exploring a bottom that no anchor yet has touched."

Distinctive purple dyes, called "Tyrian," were extracted from mollusks of the genus Murex. The Phoenicians maintained a monopoly on this expensive product in Bible times.

purse Typically, a leather bag used to carry coins, as in Prov. 7:20; Lk. 10:4; 22:35,36. The "purse" in Mt. 10:9 (KJV) is a belt (*zōnē*). Coins were carried in the folds of cloth belts, while leather or camel hair belts featured slots into which coins could be placed.

Detail of a temple statue shows a pilgrim clutching a leather purse or money pouch. Jesus instructed 72 disciples not to take "purse or bag" on a short-term mission in Galilee (Lk. 10:4).

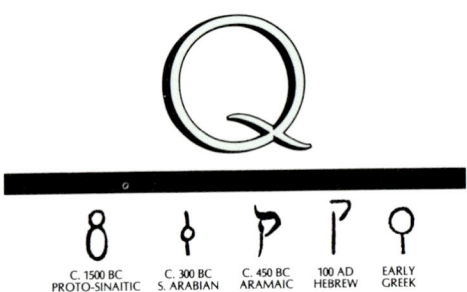

Q

C. 1500 BC
PROTO-SINAITIC

C. 300 BC
S. ARABIAN

C. 450 BC
ARAMAIC

100 AD
HEBREW

EARLY
GREEK

quail A brown, migratory game bird about 7 inches (17.78 centimeters) long. As late as the 1900s, millions of the now regionally scarce bird crossed the route of the Exodus twice yearly, on migrations between Europe or Asia and Africa.

The quail is mentioned in Ex. 16:13; Num. 11:31; and Ps. 105:40. The description in these passages, of birds flying just a few feet above the earth, fits the fact that quail are assisted in their migration by the wind and often forced to the ground when the winds shift.

Below: Medieval woodcut portrays God's provision of quail (right) as well as manna for the wandering Israelites (Ex. 16).

Above: A quail sits in foliage on this woven tapestry from a Coptic church in Egypt (third or fourth century A.D.).

queen (1) The wife of a king, as in Esth. 1:9; (2) the mother of the reigning king, the "queen mother," as in 2 Chr. 15:16; and (3) infrequently, a woman sovereign, as in 1 Ki. 10:1.

In Israel, the wife of the king had less importance than his mother, though neither had any official function or authority. Thus, the influence of a queen on her husband depended on her strength of character. Queen Jezebel even acted in her husband's name and showed little of the humble obedience expected from a king's consort (1 Ki. 19:1-3; 21:5-16). While some nations were legitimately ruled by queens, as was Sheba in Solomon's time and Ethiopia in the NT, the only woman ruler of Israel was Athaliah (2 Ki. 8:26; 11:1-4). Athaliah, the queen mother, seized the throne of Judah after the death of her son. She murdered all but one of her grandchildren, missing only the one hidden from her, and ruled for seven years until the surviving child was revealed and crowned.

Queen of Heaven Title of a female deity actively worshiped in Judah prior to its fall to Babylon in 586 B.C. (Jer. 7:18-20; 44:17-25).5

The identity of this deity is uncertain. A prominent mother-goddess is found in many ancient religions. Isis of the Egyptians, Anat and later Ashtoreth of the Canaanites, and Ishtar of the Mesopotamians were all at times titled "Queen of Heaven." Writing about the same time, Ezekiel mentions "wailing for Tammuz" (8:14), a rite associated with worship of these goddesses, and especially with Ishtar. The references in Jeremiah and Ezekiel to worship of the Queen of Heaven demonstrate how seriously Judah was polluted by pagan fertility religions.

quench (KJV) [Gk., sbennumi, "put out, extinguish"]. The Greek word is used liter-

quiver A leather container for arrows. It was carried, usually slung over the shoulder, by hunters (Gen. 27:3) and soldiers (Isa. 22:6). The simile in Jer. 5:16, "Their quivers are like an open grave," suggests the prowess of the Babylonians whom God would bring against his people. A more positive figure portrays the family as a man's quiver and his children as the arrows it contains (Ps. 127:3-5).

Above: Solomon meets the Queen of Sheba (2 Chr. 9) in this painting by an unknown 15th-century painter from Siena, Italy.
Left: Statue of Hatshepsut (15th century B.C.), possibly the Egyptian princess who found baby Moses floating in a reed basket and raised him (Ex. 2:5-10).

ally of putting out fire in Mt. 12:20 and figuratively of extinguishing the "flaming arrows" of Satan in Eph. 6:16. In 1 Th. 5:19 (KJV), where Paul warns, "Quench not the Holy Spirit," the NIV reads, "Do not put out the Spirit's fire." The ministry of the Holy Spirit in our lives is to be encouraged. We are not to dampen it by ignoring or resisting the Spirit's promptings.

Life-size Elamite archer with quiver and spear; part of a frieze in enameled brick from the palace of Darius I at Susa, Persia, about 515 B.C.

R

C. 1500 BC PROTO-SINAITIC   C. 1000 BC PHOENICIAN   C. 450 BC ARAMAIC   100 AD HEBREW   EARLY W. GREEK   500 BC GREEK

Painting of a rabbi by Rembrandt van Rijn (A.D. 1606–1669). Though he had no formal training, Jesus was called a rabbi because of the authority with which he taught (see Mt. 7:28,29).

rabbi, rabboni A title of respect used to address a person recognized as an expert in the Law of Moses. John 1:38 describes rabbi as "teacher" (*compare* Mt. 23:7,8), and Jn. 20:16 (KJV) portrays it as "master." Use of the term "rabbi" to address Jesus may not indicate the speaker had faith (Mt. 26:25; Jn. 3:2); it may merely indicate respect or acknowledgment of position.

In NT times, a rabbi was not an ordained person, as he is in modern Judaism. However, most rabbis had been trained by a well-defined apprenticeship process. *See also* Disciple. Jesus was set apart from other rabbis in first-century Judaism by more than his lack of traditional training. The NT says, "The crowds were amazed at his teaching, because he taught as one who had authority, and not as their teachers of the law" (Mt. 7:28,29).

Jesus warned against calling anyone "rabbi" (Mt. 23:8,9). In context, this is a clear prohibition against his followers establishing any superior/subordinate relationships within Christianity. Jesus defined true greatness for his followers: The truly great believer will humble himself and serve others (23:11,12).

raca Found only in Mt. 5:22, an insulting expression of contempt, in Aramaic, probably meaning "fool."

In the Sermon on the Mount, Jesus calls his listeners to look beyond the letter of the Mosaic Law. The Law takes a stand against murder, but the act of murder originates in anger and in contempt for others—of which name-calling, like *raca*, is a symptom. Thus, the Law expresses God's concern with motives, not just with acts, and implies that God will judge the root as well as the fruit of sinful acts.

We cannot be content with obeying the letter of the Law. We must let God transform us from within, to release us from the emotion of anger and the attitude of contempt, which God hates as much as the physical act of murder. *See also* Sermon on the Mount.

race (1) An athletic contest; a footrace, emphasizing either speed or endurance; (2) an ethnic division or classification of peoples.

THE FOOTRACE

Competitive racing seems to have played no significant role in ancient Israel, although it may be mentioned in a few passages (Ps. 19:5; Jer. 12:5). In contrast, racing and other athletic contests were highly valued in the Hellenistic culture. Thus, Paul, writing to a predominantly Gentile audience, makes a number of allusions to races and other contests (1 Cor. 9:24-27; Phil. 1:27-30; 3:13,14; 2 Tim. 4:7,8). The writer of Hebrews also portrays the Christian life as a race and pictures the saints of all the ages past cheering on the believer (Heb. 12:1,2).

Formal elements of the first-century footrace included (1) a set course, with a square pillar that served as the goal; (2) a herald, who announced each competitor and called out the name and family of the winner; (3) a prize, which was a wreath of greenery, as in 2 Tim. 2:5 (*see also* Crown); and (4) judges, who identified the winner and presented the prize, as in 2 Tim. 4:8. Each of these elements is alluded to in NT references.

THE RACES OF MAN

Today, "race" is normally thought of in terms of skin color. In biblical times, however, the concept of "race" was far less specific. Peoples were distinguished from one another by language, by geographical location, possibly by customs, and at times by some distinguishing physical characteristic that developed as a result of inbreeding.

While there was undoubtedly a pride in race in a national or ethnic sense, there is no suggestion in Scripture of racial superiority. And certainly the Bible makes no negative allusions to dark skin color (*compare* Job 30:30; Lam. 5:10; Song 1:5, KJV).

Rachel [RAY-chuhl; "ewe"]. The best-loved wife of Jacob (Israel), about 1900 B.C. **Father:** Laban. **Sister:** Leah. **Sons:** Joseph, Benjamin. **Scripture:** Gen. 29–35.

BACKGROUND

When he fled Canaan and took refuge in Haran, Jacob fell in love with the beautiful Rachel, the younger daughter of his uncle Laban. Jacob agreed to work for seven

Bound prisoners represent races subject to Egypt about 1380 B.C.: Bedouins, Nubians, Libyans, Cretans, and Babylonians. Detail of a painting in the tomb of Anen, Thebes.

These figurines from Syria may have served as protective house gods. Similar ones have been found in northwest Mesopotamia, where Rachel stole her father Laban's household gods when she and Jacob fled (Gen. 31:19,34).

years as a bride price for Rachel. However, when Jacob's term of service was complete, Laban substituted Leah, Rachel's older, unattractive sister as the bride. Laban then agreed to marry Rachel to Jacob, in return for seven more years of service. *See also* Dowry.

The relationship between Rachel and Leah and their common husband was strained. Jacob loved Rachel more, but Leah proved more fertile, and produced several sons. Desperately jealous, Rachel followed the established custom and insisted that Jacob accept her slave girl, Bilhah, as a secondary wife. Bilhah's sons would be considered Rachel's, and Rachel exercised her prerogative by naming both sons of this union, Dan and Naphtali (Gen. 30:1-8). Not to be outdone, Leah pressed her slave Zilpah on Jacob, too. The competition did nothing to quiet Rachel's heart, but only stimulated her desperate desire to bear Jacob a child of her own. Finally, Rachel did bear a son, Joseph. Joseph, like Rachel, became Jacob's favorite, a fact which stimulated the jealousy of Joseph's brothers.

When Jacob determined to leave his uncle's service, Rachel stole Laban's household gods, perhaps intending to use them to establish the right of her own child to the possessions of her father. *See also* Teraphim. Later, Rachel died giving birth to a second son, Benjamin. The traditional site of Rachel's grave lies about four miles south of Jerusalem, within a mile of Bethlehem.

LEARNING FROM RACHEL'S LIFE
Jeremiah uses a phrase that seems to sum up the tone of Rachel's life: "Rachel weeping for her children . . . because they are no more" (Jer. 31:15). The reference uses Rachel as a symbol of Judah's suffering at the time of the Babylonian invasion and also serves as a prophecy, fulfilled by the first-century Bethlehem mothers who grieved for their own infants, executed in Herod's frantic attempt to destroy the newborn messianic King (Mt. 2:16-18).

Though Rachel was beautiful and loved, she found no satisfaction in these gifts from God, nor in the favor showed her by Jacob. Instead, she focused on her childlessness and cried out to Jacob, "Give me children, or I'll die!" (Gen. 30:1). Though blessed in many ways, she focused instead on what she lacked and was thus doomed to discontentment.

Rachel died young, while giving birth to Benjamin: The children she expected to give meaning to her life instead brought her death.

Later, Rachel's child, Joseph, played a vital role in God's plan for his OT people. He was the agent of their safe entry into Egypt. However, the honor of being the mother of the line through which Christ was born belongs to Leah, the mother of Judah. Ultimately, none of us can find fulfillment in our children. We must seek the meaning of our life in serving God wholeheartedly and find contentment in the good gifts God has given us, without yearning for what we do not have.

Rahab [RAY-hab; "spacious," "broad"]. A prostitute living in Jericho, who as an act of faith in God helped two Israelite spies escape the city, about 1400 B.C. Rahab and her family were brought into the people of Israel, and she became an ancestress of Christ. **Scripture:** Josh. 2,6; Mt. 1:5.

BACKGROUND

The OT knows two kinds of prostitutes: the ordinary prostitute, who sold sexual services, and the ritual prostitute, whose sex acts were elements in idolatrous worship. Rahab was the former, very possibly operating an inn in her home, with sex just one of the services sold. *See also* Prostitute.

When the Israelites approached Jericho, all in the city were terrified at reports of the power of Israel's God, but only Rahab made a decision to commit herself to the Lord. She hid the two Israelite spies and made them promise to spare her when they took the city. Hebrews lists her with the heroes of faith (Heb. 11:31), and James eulogizes her choice, pointing to her act of commitment as a demonstration of her faith in God (Jas. 2:25).

Her full integration into the people of Israel is witnessed in that she became the wife of Salmon, an ancestress of King David and, through David, of Jesus Christ (Ruth 4:20,21; Mt. 1:5).

LEARNING FROM RAHAB'S LIFE

Second Corinthians 5:17 says, "If anyone is in Christ, he is a new creation." Rahab is an example of a person who, through faith, was truly renewed. This Canaanite prostitute, the immoral worshiper of pagan deities, responded with faith to what she heard of the true God. By her act of commitment, Rahab turned her back on her old life and identified herself completely with the people of God. Transformed, Rahab became a wife and mother in Israel, one of the few women who are honored by being listed in the genealogy of Jesus Christ.

Rahab teaches us that we can never narrow the circle of God's grace to exclude any individual or class. That circle opens wide to welcome any who, like Rahab, demonstrate a personal faith in God.

"Joshua spared Rahab the prostitute, with her family and all who belonged to her, because she hid the men Joshua had sent as spies to Jericho" (Josh. 6:25).

845

rain (1) Noun: water falling from the sky, providing the moisture needed to grow crops and quench the thirst of animals and man. (2) Verb: to pour out or pour upon, as in the judgment of fire and brimstone to be rained upon God's enemies (*compare* Ex. 9:18).

The OT celebrates God as the person who controls the rains (Ps. 104:10-15). In the covenant God established with Israel through Moses, the Lord promised to bless the Israelites with abundant rain when they were obedient (Deut. 28:12) but to hold back the rain if they turned away from him (Deut. 28:22-24). The three-year drought announced by Elijah when Ahab was king (1 Ki. 17) is the classic biblical example of this judgment (*compare* Jer. 3:3; Amos 4:6,7).

Rainfall varies in different parts of Palestine, but everywhere it is essential for crops and thus for survival. The rainy season usually begins in mid-October (the early rains) and ends by April or May (the latter rains). Rain seldom falls during the summer. *See also* Agriculture.

In Scripture, rain usually signifies blessing and abundance (Ps. 72:6,7). In Isa. 55:8-11, the ability of rain to cause the land to produce crops makes it an appropriate symbol of God's Word, which also "will accomplish what I [God] desire and achieve the purpose for which I sent it."

rainbow The arched spectrum of colors seen in the sky as light, refracted through water vapor suspended in the air.

Genesis 9:11-17 establishes the rainbow as the sign of God's covenant with Noah and, through Noah, with all life on earth. This covenant is God's commitment that "never again will all life be cut off by the waters of a flood; never again will there be a flood to destroy the earth."

Strikingly, the rainbow is later mentioned in Scripture only in descriptions of God's awesome appearances in prophetic visions, through which divine judgments are announced (Ezek. 1:28; Rev. 4:3; 10:1). The same rainbow that testifies to God's grace also witnesses to God's judgment on mankind in the past and his future judgment (2 Pet. 3:3-13).

raisins Grapes soaked in oil and water and dried in the sun.

In biblical times, sun-dried raisins were pressed into cakes (1 Chr. 12:40) and carried by travelers and soldiers. Raisins are high in sugar and resist spoiling. Sometimes they were eaten alone, sometimes

with other dried fruit, and sometimes they were cooked with cereal grains in a nourishing gruel.

ram (1) A mature male sheep. The ram was a popular sacrificial animal (Lev. 5:15; *compare* Gen. 22:1-19; 1 Sam. 15:22; Isa. 1:11; Mic. 6:7,8). Rams were also a source of meat in the OT diet (Gen. 31:38). (2) A weighted pole, a battering ram, used by ancient armies to weaken the wall or gate of a fortified city (Ezek. 4:2).

Persian rhyton (drinking vessel) with a ram's head (about 500 B.C.). The two-horned ram of Daniel's vision symbolized the kingdoms of Media and Persia (Dan. 8:3,4).

ram's horn A ritually significant instrument formed from the curved horn of a ram. *See also* Music; Shophar.

ransom [Heb., *kophar, ga'al*; Gk., *lytron*]. A price paid to obtain release from some obligation. *See also* Redeem.

In OT times, ransom money might be demanded from a person whose animal killed or injured another or whose own acts caused injury (Ex. 21:30; 22:6-12). The price paid to obtain release of a slave could also be considered a ransom (Lev. 19:20). Furthermore, the OT calls those who survive divine judgments on Israel and are restored to fellowship with God "the ransomed of the Lord" (Isa. 35:10).

The NT uses the concept to explain the purpose of Christ's death. Jesus came "to give his life as a ransom for many" (Mt. 20:28; Mk. 10:45; 1 Tim. 2:6). Hebrews 9:15 declares that believers can serve the living God, "now that he has died as a ransom to set them free from the sins committed under the first covenant."

Some early Christian theologians mistakenly promoted the idea that Christ's death was a purchase price paid to Satan. Despite this early misconception, the NT teaches that a price had to be paid if sinful human beings were to be restored to a right relationship with God. In dying for us on the cross, Jesus paid the penalty for our sins. The price both freed us of our debt and satisfied God's justice, opening the way for him to welcome us into his family.

Rapha, Raphaites *See* Giant.

rapture A word referring to Christians being caught up (from the Latin, "rapio") in the air and united with Christ at his Second Coming. The view is derived from 1 Th. 4:15-17. Those who hold to the premillennial return of Jesus Christ are divided as to whether the rapture will occur prior to, in the middle of, or at the conclusion of the great tribulation which precedes Christ's return in power to establish his reign on earth. *See also* Eschatology; Second Coming.

Ras Shamra The archaeological name of the *tell* (mound) that stands at the site of ancient Ugarit. This city, lying on the

Syrian coast opposite Cyprus, was important in the 15th and 14th centuries B.C. Ugarit's importance to biblical studies lies in the extensive library recovered there. The myths and legends recorded on clay tablets provide important background information on the Canaanite gods and goddesses mentioned in the Scriptures. The language of Ugarit, which contains parallels with Hebrew, helps us interpret the biblical text and demonstrates the antiquity of OT literary forms. *See also* Baal; Canaan; Gods.

Raven sitting on the roof of Noah's ark (Gen. 8:6,7). Detail of a 9th-century ivory plaque in the Cathedral of San Matteo, Salerno, Italy.

Bronze statuette from Ras Shamra depicting one of the Ugaritic gods (13th century B.C.). The artifacts excavated there have increased our understanding of Canaanite deities mentioned in the Bible.

raven A large, black scavenger bird of the crow family, considered unclean by OT Law and which thus could not be sacrificed or eaten.

The OT chooses the raven, in spite of its unclean status, to illustrate God's providential care of living creatures (Job 38:41; Ps. 147:9). It is even more striking that Jesus specifically named the raven as a creature for whom God cares and went on to say, "How much more valuable you are than birds!" (Lk. 12:24). The contrast of this unclean bird with God's people, who were "clean," having been chosen and set apart by the Lord, magnified the impact of Christ's teaching. If God cares for the lowly, how much more will he care for those who have great value as his own covenant people!

A similar lesson is seen in God's use of ravens to bring food to Elijah (1 Ki. 17). Even the lowly of this world are given the privilege of serving God.

847

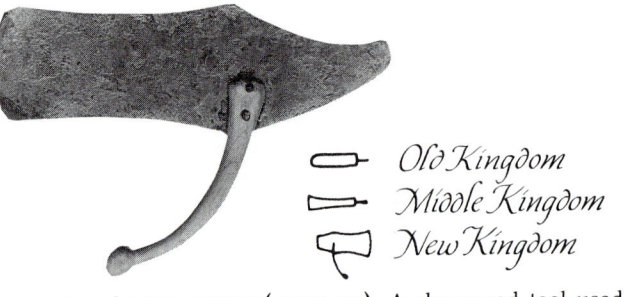

Old Kingdom
Middle Kingdom
New Kingdom

razor (rasor KJV) A sharpened tool used for cutting the hair or beard. The earliest razors were of flint. In biblical times, razors were usually made of bronze.

While the Egyptians shaved their faces (*compare* Gen. 41:14), Hebrew men let their beards grow. No razor was to touch a person who took a Nazirite vow (Num. 6:5).

reap To gather grain by cutting the stalk with a sickle, or flax by pulling it up by the roots. Reaping was hard labor. The worker bent double, grasped a handful of stalks, and cut them off near the ground with a hand sickle. *See also* Agriculture; Glean; Harvest.

In both Testaments, reaping also serves to illustrate the fact that every act has consequences, whether for good or evil (Job 4:8; Hos. 8:7; Rom. 6:22; 2 Cor. 9:6). Galatians 6:7,8 summarizes, "A man reaps what he sows. The one who sows to please his sinful nature, from that nature will reap destruction; the one who sows to please the Spirit, from the Spirit will reap eternal life." *See also* Judgment Day.

Genesis 24 recounts how Abraham's servant traveled to Nahor to find a wife for Isaac and how, in answer to prayer, he found Rebekah at the town well.

Rebekah [ruh-BEK-uh]. Isaac's only wife, who plotted with her younger son Jacob to obtain the blessing that would normally have gone to his older brother, Esau, about 1900 B.C. **Father:** Bethuel, Abraham's nephew. **Brother:** Laban. **Scripture:** Gen. 24–28.

BACKGROUND

Abraham, unwilling to take a wife for his son Isaac from the Canaanites, sent his

chief servant to his relatives in Paddan Aram to find Isaac a wife. The romantic story of how Rebekah proved to be the answer to the servant's prayer and chose to take the long trip to Canaan to marry Isaac is told in Gen. 24.

Years later as she was about to give birth, God told Rebekah that she would have twins and that "the older will serve the younger" (Gen. 25:23). As the two boys grew, Jacob, who was the younger, became Rebekah's favorite, while Esau was preferred by Isaac. When Isaac grew old, Rebekah plotted with her favorite son to steal the blessing that custom said belonged to Esau. The plot succeeded, but Esau was so furious that he determined to kill Jacob after Isaac died. Terrified, Rebekah sent Jacob to her family, some 500 miles away, supposedly to find a bride.

Stone seal (8th century B.C.) engraved with a man reaping with a sickle. The sage said, "He who sows righteousness reaps a sure reward" (Prov. 11:22).

LEARNING FROM REBEKAH'S LIFE

The Rebekah we meet in Gen. 24 is characterized by innocence. A beautiful girl, she spontaneously offered to draw water not only for Abraham's servant but also for his camels. Attracted by the notion of marrying a rich and distant husband, the young Rebekah willingly left home and accompanied the servant back to Canaan. We can suppose she was not disappointed, for Gen. 24:67 says, "She became his [Isaac's] wife, and he loved her."

Yet the Rebekah we meet some years later is a different woman. She had lost her innocence, and despite being told by God that her older son (Esau) would serve the younger (Jacob), she led Jacob to deceive her husband and trick him into giving Jacob the blessing he intended to give Esau. This act totally alienated the two brothers. Rebekah was forced to send her favorite son away to save his life—and she never saw Jacob again.

People like Rebekah who abandon innocence find it hard to trust God. Instead, they may, like Rebekah, turn to deceit to gain what they feel they must have. What a tragedy! The final, lonely years of Rebekah's life remind us that a simple, innocent trust in God may not be so foolish after all.

rebellion Technically, the refusal of a subordinate to fulfill his responsibilities to a superior (*see also* Sin). In Scripture, rebellion is viewed as a serious violation of obligations, breaking the personal relationship between the superior and subordinate. *See also* Covenant.

Most significant in Scripture is the use of "rebellion" to describe the violation by God's people of their covenant relationship with the Lord. Unlike unintentional sins, rebellion is conscious and willful disobedience. The classic example of rebellion is Israel's refusal to obey God's command to enter Canaan (Num. 14), after promising at Mount Sinai to be obedient (Ex. 24:7). The frequency with which words for rebellion are found in the OT testifies to the great tragedy of sacred history: Generation after generation of Israelites proved unfaithful, turning aside to worship other gods and violating the laws and statutes that God decreed through Moses.

The writer of Hebrews warns Christians, "Today, if you hear his voice, do not harden your hearts as [Israel] did in the rebellion" (3:15). The warning is appropriate, for rebellion is also a sin of NT believers. Only those who have a personal relationship with God can violate it. A trusting attitude toward God and a faith that prompts us to respond positively to what he says will guard us against the rebellion that brought such suffering to Israel of old.

Recabites A Kenite tribe, whose members obeyed their founder's command to live a nomadic life and refrain from drinking wine. Their faithfulness was in marked contrast with Judah's refusal to obey the commands of God. God promised through Jeremiah to bless this family for its faithfulness (Jer. 35).

receive [Gk., *dechomai*, "to receive"; *lambano*, "to reach out and take hold of," usually in an active, but sometimes in a passive sense]. Compounds containing these two Greek words have specialized meanings.

"Receive" is often used in an ordinary sense, but three uses of the term have great theological significance.

1. *Receive Christ.* John 1:11,12 says that those who receive Christ are given "the right to become children of God." The Greek word translated "receive," *paralambano*, means "to actively welcome into one's life or fellowship" and is equated in the text with believing in Christ. Thus, to receive Christ is to reach out and, by faith, to accept the gift God offers us in his Son.

2. *Receive the Word.* The phrase is figurative, a technical theological saying that simply means to exercise faith in Jesus (*compare* Lk. 8:13; Acts 8:14; 1 Th. 1:6; 2:13; Jas. 1:21).

3. *Receive the Holy Spirit.* In this phrase, found in Jn. 20:22; Acts 1:8; 2:38; 8:15,17,19; 10:47; 19:2; Rom. 8:15; 2 Cor. 11:4; Gal. 3:2, the NT always uses *lambano* but emphasizes the passive aspect of that term. Paul argues that the Galatians did nothing to merit the Holy Spirit but "received the Spirit" because they believed (3:2). The various references to receiving the Spirit stress no human act but rather emphasize the gift that God gives. Christians, however, differ on whether the Spirit is received by a separate act of faith or upon one's initial exercise of saving faith. *See also* Holy Spirit.

reconciliation To bring about a change that restores harmony between persons, or more significantly, between human beings and God.

RECONCILIATION WITH GOD

Pagan religions frequently viewed the gods as hostile to human beings and called for offerings designed to reconcile the deities to their worshipers. The Bible teaches that while the justice of God must be satisfied, it is human beings who must be reconciled to God (*see also* Propitiation). Objectively, sin disrupted the harmonious relationship between human beings and God (*see also* Atonement). Psychologically, the alienation sin caused made human beings hostile toward God. These elements are united in Rom. 5, which describes Christ's death for the ungodly and says, "If, when we were God's enemies, we were reconciled to him through the death of his Son, how much more,

Silver shekel from Judah was issued during the first rebellion of the Jews against Rome (A.D. 66–70).

849

having been reconciled, shall we be saved through his life" (5:10).

This passage delineates three key elements in biblical doctrine: (1) It is humanity that needs reconciliation to God. Man's sinful attitude toward God must change. (2) God acted in Christ to accomplish reconciliation. (3) In receiving Christ, we experience a spiritual change, which transforms our hostile attitude toward God and makes us love and "rejoice in God through our Lord Jesus Christ" (5:11).

Reconciliation with God is both positional and practical; that is, through Christ the believer is harmoniously related to God, yet the Christian is also responsible to "be reconciled to God" (2 Cor. 5:16-21). In this passage, Paul sees Christians as ambassadors, not just to the unsaved but to other believers. We are to urge one another to live a righteous life, demonstrating that we are truly in harmony with a holy God.

RECONCILIATION WITH OTHERS

The death of Christ also lays the foundation for interpersonal reconciliation. Mankind typically seeks to bond groups together by selecting others "like us," and then by setting "us" against "them." Typically, hostility develops between "us" and "them" and is supported on the basis of such distinctions as color, social status, and wealth.

In Eph. 2:11-22, Paul points out that such a "we"/"them" hostility existed between the Jew and Gentile in the first century. However, through the cross, Christ "destroyed the barrier, the dividing wall of hostility." Paul's point is that through the cross Christ brought both Jew and Gentile into a new, distinctive relationship with God. It is this personal relationship with God that now defines the Christian and makes all other distinctions irrelevant. We are one in Christ, who "himself is our peace." Having God as our common Father, we are now brothers, fellow citizens in the Kingdom of our God. No wonder Paul writes, "There is neither Jew nor Greek, slave nor free, male nor female, for you are all one in Christ Jesus" (Gal. 3:28). *See also* Peace; Unity.

Thus, by understanding what Christ has done for us, each Christian is responsible to live in harmony with other members of the Body of Christ and, when strains occur, to take the initiative in seeking personal reconciliation (Mt. 5:23,24).

redeem, redemption To pay a purchase price, with a view to releasing another

from some significant danger or bondage. *See also* Redeemer.

redeemer A person who intervenes and pays a necessary price to win the release of another from some bondage or danger. The metaphor of redemption, so clearly established in the OT, is applied in the NT to explain the meaning of Christ's death and its implications for those who believe in him.

OLD TESTAMENT

Hebrew, (1) *padah,* to transfer ownership by payment of an appropriate price, as in Lev. 19:20. (2) *Ga'al,* to act as kinsman, that is, to intervene on behalf of a relative who is in trouble, as in Lev. 25:47-55. Only a near relation had the right to buy another person out of slavery or to pay whatever price was necessary to restore property to a member of his family. (3) *Kapar,* to ransom, to atone by making a substitutionary payment, as in Ex. 30:11-16.

The language of redemption was applied to the ordinary things of life—the payment of a price to free a slave or the payment of a debt to return property to its owner. However, the significance of the biblical terms is found in their application to God's relationship with his people. Because God redeemed the forefathers "from the oppressor, the day he displayed his miraculous signs in Egypt" (Ps. 78:42,43), he established his claim to the allegiance of Israel. Israel was his own purchased possession (Deut. 14:2; Ps. 74:2). The very fact that God chose to redeem Israel is evidence that a very special relationship existed: God considered this people his family; he was bonded to them by the covenant he established with Abraham (Ex. 6:5,6).

Awareness of God's commitment to Israel and Israel's belonging to the Lord provided the OT saints with both a sense of assurance and a powerful motive for holy living. The psalmist cried out to God, "My Rock and my Redeemer" (Ps. 19:14), and Isaiah repeatedly comforted his generation with a vision of God as Israel's redeemer (Isa. 41:14; 43:14; 44:6,24; 47:4).

While the vision of God as redeemer serves as an anchor for Israel's faith, redemption in the OT was essentially deliverance from dangers in this life. Only in Ps. 130:7,8 do we find the doctrine of spiritual redemption which bursts into prominence in the NT: "With the Lord is unfailing love and with him is full redemption. He himself will redeem Israel from all their sins."

NEW TESTAMENT

Greek, (1) *lytroō, lytrōsis,* "to redeem or ransom." (2) *Exagorazō,* intensive, "to purchase." The use of these words in the NT is not defined by their application in Greek culture or in Roman law. Rather, the concept of redemption is carried over from the OT. Reflecting the OT understanding, a person who qualified to redeem must be a near relation. Thus, Christ became a human being, and in establishing his identity with mankind, he established his right to act as our redeemer (Heb. 2).

Also reflecting the OT concept, the one who redeems must pay the price required to free the one he seeks to deliver. The NT focuses our attention on our spiritual deliverance rather than our physical deliverance. Israel was often oppressed by foreign enemies, but all mankind is oppressed by sin. In fact, human beings are slaves to the sinful tendencies rooted in fallen human nature. All humanity is trapped in a spiritual slavery, with eternal death the only wages we can expect (Rom. 5:12-21; 6:15-23). The redemption that man desperately needs is redemption not from human oppressors but from sin.

We are redeemed "from all wickedness," Paul writes, so that we might become "eager to do what is good" (Tit. 2:14). Christ's sacrifice of himself broke the grip that sin had established on our race. Those who respond to the good news of Christ are not only forgiven but are brought into the family of God and are freed to live good and holy lives. *See also* Atonement; Propitiation; Sacrifice.

red heifer A young cow, whose ashes were mixed in water with other substances and used in certain OT purification rites, for uncleanness caused by contact with the dead (Num. 19). No explanation is given in the text for any symbolism intended by the sacrifice of the red heifer.

Red Sea (1) The narrow sea that divides Africa from Arabia, extending some 1,300 miles (2,100 kilometers) from the Gulf of Aden to the Suez. (2) The name given in

"Moses stretched out his hand over the sea, and at daybreak the sea went back to its place. The Egyptians were fleeing from it and the Lord swept them into the sea" (Ex. 14:27).

The current Red Sea and possible location of the Israelite crossing at its northern reaches at the time of the Exodus.

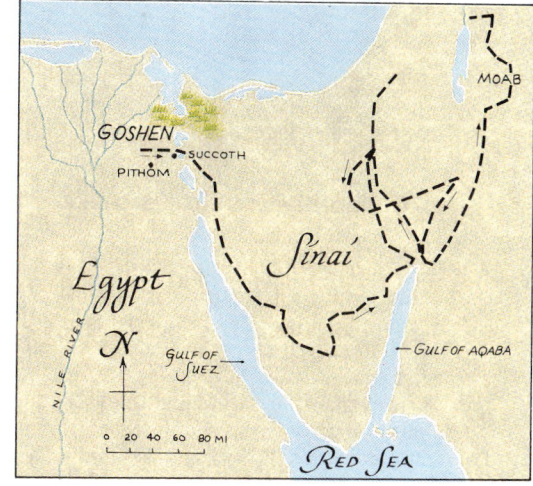

This medieval wood-cut depicts Moses bringing the Israelites to safety. Shortly afterward both Moses and Miriam led the people in praise, "I will sing to the Lord, for he is highly exalted" (Ex. 15:1, 21).

many English versions to the body of water that God miraculously divided during the Exodus, so that the Israelites might escape a pursuing Egyptian army (Ex. 14).

There is little doubt that the translation of *yam suph* in Ex. 14 as "red sea" is in error. The Hebrew means "reed sea" or "papyrus marsh." Depending on one's view of the route of the Exodus, various bodies of water have been nominated as the Reed Sea, ranging from an area known as the Bitter Lakes if the Israelites followed the traditional southern route, to Lake Timsah if they followed the less likely central route. *See also* Exodus.

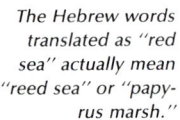

The Hebrew words translated as "red sea" actually mean "reed sea" or "papyrus marsh."

reed *See* Papyrus.

refine, refining The process of removing impurities from metal ore by heating at high temperatures, as in Isa. 1:25. *See also* Furnace; Metals.

Metaphorically, refining refers to the purification of God's people (Ps. 66:10; Jer. 9:7; Zech. 13:9). Such purification is accomplished by suffering and affliction, a fact that recasts suffering as a positive rather than negative experience. Thus, Peter urges Christians to remember that the trials that have caused them to suffer grief have come "so that your faith—of greater worth than gold, which perishes even though refined by fire—may be proved genuine and may result in praise, glory, and honor when Jesus Christ is revealed" (1 Pet. 1:7). *See also* Smith.

refuge, cities of Cities established as refuges for those who killed a person unintentionally. *See also* Cities of Refuge; Murder.

regeneration (KJV) [Gk., *palingenesia*; "renewal," "restoration"]. The Greek word occurs only in Mt. 19:28, which speaks of the "renewal of all things" at history's end, and Tit. 3:5, which speaks of individual "renewal by the Holy Spirit."

While no term for regeneration is found in the OT, and the NT use of *palingenesia* is limited, the visions of a renewal of this present universe and a transforming renewal of the human personality are woven throughout Scripture. Isaiah sums up the first theme in reporting God's promise:

Behold, I will create
   new heavens and a new earth.
The former things will not be
   remembered,
   nor will they come to mind.
But be glad and rejoice forever
   in what I will create,
for I will create Jerusalem to be a delight
   and its people a joy.

(Isa. 65:17,18)

The theme of personal renewal is found in Jeremiah's prediction of a new covenant, under which God will give his people a new heart (Jer. 31:23-34). This promise, kept in Israel, underlies the NT's teaching that those who trust in Jesus are granted spiritual rebirth (1 Pet. 1:23). *See also* Born Again.

Rehoboam [REE-huh-BOH-uhm; "welcome the people"]. The son of Solomon whose arrogant attitude led to the division of his father's united kingdom into two antagonistic nations, about 930 B.C. Rehoboam then ruled Judah, the Southern Kingdom, for some 17 years. **Father:** Solomon. **Mother:** Naamah, an Ammonite. **Wife:** Maacah, who was committed to paganism, 1 Ki. 15:10. **Scripture:** 1 Ki. 12,14,15; 2 Chr. 10–12.

BACKGROUND

Despite prosperity, Solomon taxed his people heavily to carry out his ambitious building programs. On Solomon's death, the people demanded that his son and successor reduce the burden. The arrogant Rehoboam foolishly followed the advice of his young contemporaries and threatened to increase taxes. The northern ten tribes rebelled and set up a rival kingdom under Jeroboam I. Rehoboam failed in an attempt to force the rebels to return and fell into a pattern of military skirmishes with the North. Although he tried to strengthen Judah militarily, Rehoboam fell spiritually by permitting or perhaps encouraging the establishment of a number of pagan worship centers in his land. As punishment, God permitted Shishak of Egypt to suc-cessfully invade Judah. Confronted then by the prophet Shemaiah, Rehoboam repented and humbled himself.

LEARNING FROM REHOBOAM'S LIFE

Rehoboam illustrates well the folly of pride. His unreasonable assertion of what he felt were his rights as king led to the loss of half his kingdom. His insensitivity and disobedience to God in permitting the development of pagan worship centers led to even more crushing losses. However, Rehoboam did repent, and the divine permission to retain his throne illustrates God's grace to those who abandon their pride. Nevertheless, the most important lesson to learn from Rehoboam is that the arrogant man will make unwise choices that will ultimately harm himself as well as others. *See also* Arrogance.

"In the fifth year of King Rehoboam, Shishak [Sheshonq I] king of Egypt attacked Jerusalem. He carried off the treasures of the temple of the Lord and . . . of the royal palace" (1 Ki. 14:25,26). These two reliefs at Thebes commemorate this victory (about 930 B.C.). Above: Shishak grabs Israelites by the hair; (left) close-up shows the heads of his captives.

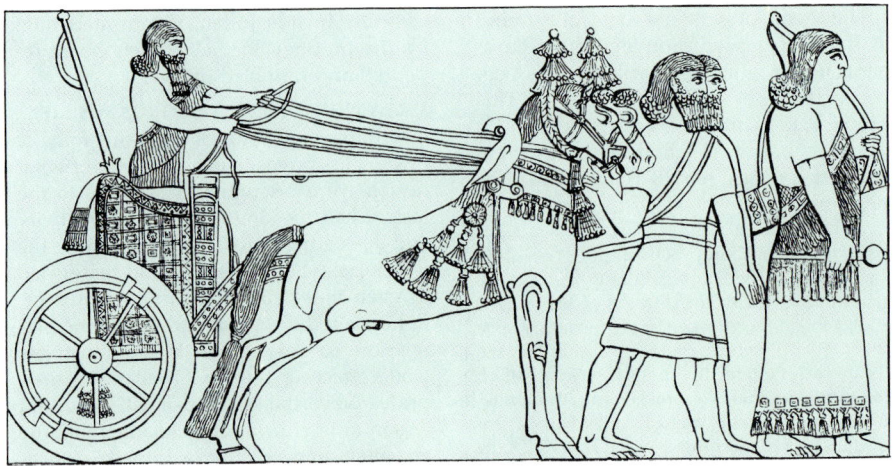

reins (1) KJV, the kidneys. Used figuratively in the OT to indicate the inner, emotional self ("the righteous God trieth the hearts and reins," Ps. 7:9). (2) Lines attached to an animal's bridle by which a rider turns the animal's head and steers its course. A "tight rein" indicates firm control (Jas. 1:26). A "free rein" indicates release of control (Job 10:1).

remarriage *See* Marriage.

remember (1) To think about, meditate on, keep in mind; (2) to be guided by, to act in accord with, as in "remember the covenant" or, in appeals to God, "remember your great mercy." In addition, the NT adds specialized religious uses: to remember in prayer (1 Th. 1:3) and to teach by reminding (2 Pet. 1:12-15).

God called Israel to "remember that you were slaves in Egypt" (Deut. 5:15) and to "remember well what the Lord your God did to Pharaoh and to all Egypt" (Deut. 7:18). Such exhortations call new generations of Israelites to identify with God's historic acts. In remembering, a person stands with the forefathers; he realizes that what the Lord did for them was done for him as well. In this sense, remembering is an act of faith, which brings a believer into the living presence of God.

The same God who saved Israel commanded his people to live holy lives, as holiness is defined in Moses' Law. Thus remembering involves more than identifying oneself with God's saving acts. It means to accept one's obligations as a member of God's covenant people (Num. 15:40). A generation that "did not remember" the Lord failed to view themselves as his people and as a result failed to obey his commands (Jdg. 8:34).

Israel belonged to God, and so the nation could count on God to act on their behalf. In the OT, we repeatedly find cries addressed to the Lord, asking him to remember his people in perilous times. Here "remember" means simply to act and thus fulfill the promises woven into the covenant which bound Israel to God and God to Israel. Even an individual believer could appeal to God to "remember me and care for me" (Jer. 15:15).

Thus "remember" is a significant word in the OT vocabulary of faith. To remember God and his acts is to affirm our trust in him. To call on God to remember is to appeal to him to act as deliverer. And to remember God's commands is to obey them. *See also* Memorial.

remission (KJV) *See* Forgive.

remnant Survivors; that portion of a nation that escapes an event which destroys the majority. The remnant may then serve as the nucleus through whom the group is renewed.

The OT frequently speaks of a remnant that survives divine judgment on sinning Israel. This recurring pattern teaches us two things. First, God will not hesitate to judge sin. When Israel turned away from God, the Lord acted to purge the evil, often at the cost of many lives. But the second lesson is that God will preserve the faithful and never totally destroy Israel. The devastating character of the divine judgments—and the place of the remnant —is graphically portrayed by Isaiah. The great prophet predicts that God will soon bring Assyria down upon sinning Israel:

In that day the remnant of Israel,
the survivors of the house of Jacob,

will no longer rely on him
  who struck them down
but will truly rely on the Lord,
  the Holy One of Israel.
A remnant will return, a remnant of Jacob
  will return to the Mighty God.
Though your people, O Israel, be like the
    sand by the sea,
  only a remnant will return.
Destruction has been decreed,
  overwhelming and righteous.
The Lord, the Lord Almighty, will carry out
  the destruction decreed upon the whole
    land.   (Isa. 10:20-23)

Ancient Israel was subjected to a series of such judgments, and sacred history reports a number of new beginnings. Yet the prophets also apply the concept of the remnant to history's end. Then, as in the past, God will judge his people, but the faithful will survive to enter an eternal kingdom he will establish. *See also* Future; Kingdom of God.

The apostle Paul applies the concept of the remnant in two ways. First, he points out that in welcoming Gentiles and setting Israel to one side, God has not been inconsistent. Throughout history, the majority in Israel was often unfaithful and thus was set aside through divine judgments (Rom. 9:22-33). Second, the Church established by Christ contains many Jewish believers. These Hebrew Christians are "a remnant chosen by grace" (Rom. 11:5), proof that God has not rejected his ancient people.

repent, repentance A deep, radical change of both perspective and commitment, resulting in a moral and spiritual transformation.

The OT frequently uses the word *shub*, "to turn," in a spiritual sense, indicating a turning from idols to God or turning from evil to obey God's commandments. John the Baptist demanded a similar act of repentance. In his early ministry, Christ too made this demand. John and Jesus called the people of Israel to abandon evil and return wholeheartedly to the holiness described in Moses' Law (Mt. 3:2; 4:17). Later, when Christ himself became the issue, to repent meant to change one's mind about Jesus and commit oneself fully to him, the Son of God (Lk. 13:3,5; Acts 2:38; 3:19).

In the NT Epistles, "repentance" (Gk., *metanoia*; lit., "change of mind") describes a personal decision that changes the direction of a person's life. While repentance is linked with "godly sorrow" in 2 Cor. 7:10, it is more than an emotion; it is a life-transforming choice. Furthermore, while repentance often stands for salvation itself in the Epistles (Rom. 2:4; 2 Tim. 2:25; 2 Pet. 3:9), it is faith, the faith that causes us to repent, that saves us. True faith in God will always be expressed by turning from evil as one turns to the Lord. *See also* Faith; Salvation.

reproach Public exposure of sins or weaknesses, which causes harm to a person's reputation and brings him or her ridicule. Often, divine judgment is described as exposing a person or nation to reproach.

Psalm 44 powerfully expresses the emotions felt when an individual or nation suffers reproach:

You have made us a reproach to our
    neighbors,
  the scorn and derision of those around us.
You have made us a byword among the
    nations;
  the peoples shake their heads at us.
My disgrace is before me all day long,
  and my face is covered with shame
at the taunts of those who reproach and revile
    me,
  because of the enemy, who is bent on
    revenge.   (Ps. 44:13-16)

The NT states that Christian leaders must be "above reproach" (1 Tim. 3:2): Leaders must have—and deserve—good reputations.

reprobate (KJV) [Gk., *adokimos*; "disapproved"]. Rejected or disqualified, having failed the test. A "reprobate mind" (Rom. 1:28) is corrupt, unfit for its task of evaluating. A person who is reprobate is one in whom Christ does not dwell (2 Cor. 13:5,7).

rescue To deliver; to save. In the OT, rescue refers to deliverance from the danger of death or human enemies. In the NT, rescue refers primarily to deliverance from sin and its consequences. *See also* Salvation.

respect To esteem; to treat with due regard. The NT calls us to treat others with respect. We show respect for the government by obeying its laws (Rom. 13:7). A slave shows respect for his master by submissiveness and hard work (Eph. 6:5-8; 1 Pet. 2:18). The Christian shows respect for God by worshiping and obeying him. But respect is not always linked to one's position in society. A person becomes "worthy of respect" by living a moral and decent life (1 Tim. 3:8,11; Tit. 2:2).

However, Scripture says that we must not be "respecters of persons" (KJV), meaning that we must not show unfair favoritism. In any judicial proceeding, the judge must render a verdict based solely on the law and never show partiality to either litigant (Lev. 19:15). Neither should a church show special favor to the rich (Jas. 2:1-7; *see* Lk. 20:21).

Priests of the Egyptian sun god Aten bow in respect (El Amarna, about 1340 B.C.).

rest (1) The remainder. *See also* Remnant. (2) Peaceful repose; an end to labor or release from a burden.

The OT sets aside the seventh day of the week as a day of rest. The day commemorated God's creative activity (Ex. 20:8-11) and served as a powerful image of Israel's covenant relationship with the Lord (Ex. 31:12,13). In addition, the OT day of rest was associated with redemption, for it was a day on which Israel was to "remember that you were slaves in Egypt and that the Lord your God brought you out of there with a mighty hand and an outstretched arm. Therefore the Lord your God has commanded you to observe the Sabbath day" (Deut. 5:15). These aspects of the Sabbath were intended to provide Israel with the inner peace that comes from awareness that God is (exists) and that God is committed to care for his people.

The OT day of rest also had a humanitarian aspect, for it provided for physical as well as spiritual rest. In Jesus' statement that God made the Sabbath for man (and not man for the Sabbath), we find an indication of God's concern for our total being and his desire to meet our physical as well as spiritual and psychological needs (Mk. 2:27; *see* Ex. 23:10-12). *See also* Sabbath.

In the NT, the writer of Hebrews returns to a pivotal moment in OT history to make a point vital to Christian living (chs. 3,4). He reminds his readers that the Exodus generation heard God's voice telling them to invade Canaan but refused to obey. As a result, they were turned away from the promised Jewish homeland and doomed to wander in the wilderness until nearly all adult members of that rebellious generation died. The writer concludes that the Exodus generation could not enter the "rest" God was eager to provide because of unbelief, expressed as disobedience.

The writer then argues that this OT "rest"—a settled, secure life for Israel on its own land—is a symbol of the spiritual rest to be found by believers today. That rest is not inactivity. It is, however, release from the burdens of fruitless struggle. To find rest, we need only to listen for and heed God's voice as he speaks to us through his Word today.

While the argument of Heb. 3,4 is complex, its point is simple. God rested when he completed the work of creation. God remains active, but in his activity, he is at peace. In creating and organizing the universe, God shaped all things according to his plan and purpose. He who knows the end from the beginning can never be surprised as history unfolds: Everything is on course to achieve his appointed ends. So, nothing that happens to us can surprise God. God has a solution for every difficulty we face, every decision we must make, every temptation we need to overcome.

Hebrews teaches that we "rest from our own work" by recognizing our limitations and relying on God. Because "nothing in all creation is hidden from God's sight," the person who hears and obeys God's voice knows true rest.

restitution Repayment for things stolen or damage caused. Old Testament Law called for the victim of criminal acts to be repaid, often with punitive damages added, for the harm done. Two Hebrew words express the concept: *shub*, "to turn back or return" (Num. 5:7-9); and *shalem*, "to make complete," which indicates a restoration of social harmony by compensating the victim for his losses (Ex. 22:3).

English criminal law treats theft and assault as crimes against society for which

criminals must be punished. Yet, in this process, the victim is often ignored and is not compensated for his or her losses. In biblical law, theft and assault are treated as crimes against the victim, and primary attention is given to compensating the victim. A thief not only had to pay for what was stolen but, in some cases, was required to repay the victim four or five times over (Ex. 22:1,4; 2 Sam. 12:6). For example, a person who cheated a neighbor was to repay him and add an extra 20 percent (Lev. 6:1-7).

The OT law of restitution is reflected in the promise of the tax collector Zacchaeus, who said after meeting Jesus he would repay fourfold anyone he had cheated (Lk. 19:1-10).

restore (1) In ordinary use, to renew, heal, make alive. (2) In the prophets and in some NT contexts, a technical term for the political restoration of Israel by God (Jer. 15:19; Acts 1:6). The use of "restore" in Acts is significant, for it reveals the conviction of Jesus' followers even after his resurrection that Christ must one day fulfill the promises God gave Israel through the prophets.

The conviction is clearly expressed in Peter's early preaching. Jesus "must remain in heaven until the time comes for God to restore everything, as he promised long ago through his holy prophets" (Acts 3:21). *See also* Future; Second Coming.

resurrection (1) The bodily raising of the dead to life (Mt. 22:23). (2) Analogically, the transition of believers to a new state of being at the time when the dead are raised (1 Th. 4:16). (3) Figuratively, the vivifying effect of the Holy Spirit's work in the Christian, enabling the believer to live a holy life now (Phil. 3:10,11).

It is important to make a distinction between resurrection and resuscitation. The latter is restoration to earthly life, and those so restored do die eventually (1 Ki. 17:17-24; Mt. 9:18-26; Jn. 11). Resurrection comes at history's end, restoring those who have died to transformed bodies in which they will spend eternity.

Several distinctive Christian doctrines on resurrection emerge: (1) Every human being continues self-conscious existence after biological death. (2) Every individual will be raised from the dead and embodied. However, only the bodies of the saved will be clothed with immortality and cleansed from every taint of sin. (3) Every human being will exist, embodied, throughout eternity. *See also* Heaven; Hell.

The Christian doctrine has no parallels in pagan thought. Other religions have assumed the continuation of the personality in an afterlife, often in some other "world" much like this one. But the belief that the personality (or soul) will be reunited with the body is distinctive of the Judeo-Christian faith.

OLD TESTAMENT

The doctrine of resurrection is suggested

Jesus appears to Mary Magdalene at his tomb while two Roman guards sleep, in this stained-glass presentation of the resurrected Christ (Jn. 20:10-18).

in the OT but not emphasized (Job 14:14; Pss. 17:15; 49:7-20; 73:23-26). Isaiah promised, "Your dead will live; their bodies will rise" (Isa. 26:19). The clearest OT expression is found in Dan. 12:2: "Multitudes who sleep in the dust of the earth will awake: some to everlasting life, others to shame and everlasting contempt." There was enough evidence of a resurrection in the OT for the Pharisees to hold firmly to this belief, and Jesus rebuked the Sadducees who denied a resurrection. "You are in error," he said, "because you do not know the Scriptures or the power of God" (Mt. 22:29).

NEW TESTAMENT

The NT makes a distinction between the resurrection of the believer and the unbeliever. The believer alone will experience resurrection as transformation to a new state of being (1 Th. 4:13-18). Revelation 20:5,6 distinguishes between this "first" resurrection and the resurrection of the unsaved to face judgment for their sins (see 20:11-15).

Rather vague descriptions of the resurrected body are given in several NT passages. John says that when Jesus appears, "we shall be like him" (1 Jn. 3:1,2). Paul confesses uncertainty about the exact nature of the resurrection body, but contrasts it with our present bodies in several key respects. Our risen bodies will be imperishable, not mortal. We will be vessels of glory, not dishonor. We will be filled with power, not weakness. Significantly, the resurrected body is characterized as spiritual rather than natural. At last, the domination of sin will be broken and the spirit will be in control (1 Cor. 15).

RESURRECTION AND EXPERIENCE

Paul makes much of the fact that the Holy Spirit was the agent of Christ's resurrection. "If the Spirit of him who raised Jesus from the dead is living in you, he . . . will also give life to your mortal bodies through his Spirit, who lives in you" (Rom. 8:11). Though sin maintains a grip upon us, the Spirit of God can lift us beyond the limitations imposed by our mortality, enabling us to live righteous lives here and now. This is what Paul refers to in Phil. 3:10,11. He yearns to "know Christ and the power of his resurrection" in the sense of experiencing the vivifying power of the Spirit in his daily life.

resurrection of Jesus The historic act in which God raised Jesus' body from the dead three days after Christ's death on the cross.

From the very beginning, belief in Jesus' bodily resurrection has been a keystone of Christian faith. It is an essential element in apostolic teaching (Acts 2:24-36; 3:15-26; 4:10; 5:30; 10:40; 13:34-37; 17:18-32). It is so important that Paul writes, "If Christ has not been raised, your faith is futile; you are still in your sins" (1 Cor. 15:17).

WITNESSES TO THE RESURRECTION

The immediate post-crucifixion proclamation of Jesus' resurrection is powerful evidence that Christ actually was raised from the dead. If Jesus had not been raised, the simplest way to stop the Christian movement would have been to produce his body. Jesus' enemies did plant a rumor that Christ's disciples had stolen his body (Mt. 28:11-15), but still the conviction spread through Jerusalem and then the world that Jesus had in fact been raised.

There were several reasons for this conviction. First, there was the powerful preaching of the disciples. These men claimed to have seen the risen Jesus, and their ministry was authenticated by miracles of healing. Surely their commitment cannot be accounted for if they consciously tried to build a religion—one in which the disciples themselves were severely persecuted—on a lie.

Second, there were many witnesses to authenticate the claim of resurrection. These persons were so convinced they had seen Jesus that they willingly suffered the loss of their positions and even their lives to follow the risen Savior.

A final and compelling line of evidence is noted by Paul in 1 Cor. 15:4. Christ was

WITNESSES TO JESUS' RESURRECTION	
Peter	Lk. 24:34
	1 Cor. 15:5
Mary of Magdala	Jn. 20:10-18
Two disciples at Emmaus	Lk. 24:13-31
The apostles,	Lk. 24:36-45
except Thomas	Jn. 20:19-24
with Thomas	Jn. 20:25-29
Seven by Lake of Tiberias	Jn. 21:1-23
Some 500 in Galilee	1 Cor. 15:6
James	1 Cor. 15:7
Many at the ascension	Acts 1:3-11
Stephen	Acts 7:55
Paul,	1 Cor. 15:8
near Damascus	Acts 9:3-6
in Jerusalem	Acts 22:17-21
	Acts 23:11
John on Patmos	Rev. 1:10-19

raised on the third day "according to the Scriptures." The resurrection of Jesus was pre-announced in the OT (Acts 2:24-32), God's sure and unbreakable Word.

No event in ancient history is as thoroughly documented as the resurrection of Christ. And few events have had such widespread impact on the shaping of an entire society as the Gospel message proclaiming a resurrected Christ was carried throughout the Roman world.

JESUS' RESURRECTION BODY

While the NT says little about the resurrection body, there are hints in post-resurrection descriptions of Christ. His body is "flesh and bones," not "flesh and blood" (Lk. 24:39). The distinction is significant, for Lev. 17:11 says that "the life of a creature is in the blood." While he could be touched and he could eat, Jesus supernaturally appeared among his disciples in a locked room (Jn. 20:26). The limitations imposed on human beings by their physical nature do not seem to exist for the resurrection body.

THEOLOGICAL SIGNIFICANCE

There are several theological points made by Christ's resurrection:

Jesus talks with two disciples at Emmaus (Lk. 24:13-35), as depicted in a painting by Rembrandt van Rijn. They were among the many witnesses to Jesus' resurrection.

• *Proof of Jesus' deity.* Paul says that Jesus was "declared with power to be the Son of God by his resurrection from the dead" (Rom. 1:4). All that Jesus claimed for himself is verified by the fact of his resurrection.

• *Guarantee of our own resurrection.* Paul calls Jesus the "firstfruits of those who have fallen asleep" (1 Cor. 15:20). Because Christ was raised, those who believe in him are assured of a personal resurrection.

• *Guarantee of our salvation.* The ever-living Jesus has a permanent priesthood and "is able to save completely those who come to God through him, because he always lives to intercede for them" (Heb. 7:24,25).

• *Source of present power for holy living.* Christians are united with Jesus in his resurrection (Rom. 6:5). Through this union and enablement by the Spirit who raised Jesus from the dead (Rom. 8:11), believers are able to live Christlike lives now, despite the limitations imposed by sin (1 Pet. 3:21).

• *Key to the fulfillment of OT and NT promises about the future.* God's purposes will be achieved, and his plans carried to fruition, when the risen Jesus returns to earth. *See also* Future; Resurrection.

Reuben, Tribe of *See* Israel, Tribes of.

reveal/revelation God's acts of disclosure, making known to human beings through natural and special means both his own nature and other relevant truths.

REVELATION IN BOTH TESTAMENTS

The Bible affirms that God has taken the initiative to make known to human beings things that otherwise would remain hidden. In the OT, "reveal" is *galah*, Hebrew for "to uncover" and "to be open, visible." Deuteronomy states, "The things revealed belong to us and to our children forever, that we may follow all the words of this law" (Deut. 29:29). The God of the OT, who spoke to Abraham, who spoke to Moses, and who continued to speak to his people through the prophets (Amos 3:7), is unquestionably a God of revelation.

This conviction is developed more fully in the NT. Two Greek words for revealing—*phaneroō*, "to make plain," and *apokalyptō*, "to uncover"—convey the same basic idea. Revelation in the NT is: (1) the means through which we have current knowledge of God's plans, whether previously unveiled by the OT prophets (1 Pet. 1:12) or unveiled in the Gospel (Rom.

1:17,18; Gal. 1:12; Eph. 3:3,4); and (2) the culminating act at history's end (the apocalypse) in which God will make Jesus visible to all in the universe as Lord and will also make believers visible as his children (Rom. 2:5; 8:18,19; 2 Th. 1:7; 1 Pet. 1:5,7,13).

THE MEANS OF REVELATION

Christians have primarily been concerned with understanding revelation as the means by which we have current knowledge of hidden truth. The Bible identifies two sources of revealed truth: general revelation and special revelation. General revelation is communication of relevant truths about God through natural means, such as the creation and man's moral nature or conscience. Special revelation is the communication of relevant truths about God through supernatural means, specifically through God's acts in history and through Jesus. Each of these sources of revelation, general and special, is interpreted by and understood through the written Word of God.

Through general revelation, all human beings are given some knowledge of God. The creation shows us that God exists and has ultimate power (Rom. 1:18-20; Ps. 19). God's moral nature is also revealed through the creation, specifically through human beings who, formed in God's image, have a moral conscience (Rom. 2:14-16). While the knowledge of God granted through general revelation is limited, it is enough to give each person the opportunity to respond appropriately to the Lord (Rom. 1:20,21; *compare* Acts 14:17).

Special revelation includes all those acts of God by which he has communicated to human beings. These include the words spoken to Abraham, visions granted the prophets, the miracles performed in Egypt, the Law given through Moses, the fiery sermons of the prophets, and ultimately the incarnation, miracles, teachings, death, and resurrection of Jesus. Strikingly, we can only be sure of the meaning of these acts of special revelation through their interpretation in the Bible. The Scriptures are both an authentic record of what God has revealed to human beings and an accurate interpreter of the meaning of his acts.

The apostle Paul develops this truth in 1 Cor. 2:6-16. That which no eye can see nor mind conceive has been revealed to us by God's Spirit, who expresses the very "thoughts of God." While the Spirit must serve as our inner interpreter of the words he inspired, it remains true that we have in the Scriptures an objective revelation from God of relevant truth, through which God himself meets with us. *See also* Bible; Inspiration.

Some theologians have attempted to make a clear distinction between personal and propositional revelation. They assert that God reveals himself, not information. But God makes himself known through the information he reveals. God as a Person meets his people in every word he speaks. Thus, the two forms of revelation are essentially one. This truth is dramatically realized in the person and message of Jesus Christ, the Word made flesh, who shall always be the ultimate revelation of God to humankind. And so, as we respond in faith to God's revelation, we in fact respond to *him*. As Jesus told his disciples, "Whoever has my commands and obeys them, he is the one who loves me. He who loves me will be loved by my Father, and I too will love him and show myself to him" (Jn. 14:21).

Revelation, the Book of The last book of the NT, also called the Apocalypse. The book, filled with vivid symbols, bold images, and mystic numbers, has been variously interpreted by Christians. Yet all agree that Revelation makes a powerful statement concerning the ultimate triumph of God.

BACKGROUND

Early Christian writers certify the book's own testimony that it is the work of the apostle John. According to tradition, John wrote Revelation near the end of the reign of the Emperor Domitian, about A.D. 95 or 96, while in exile on the Isle of Patmos. In the book, John reports his vision of the glorified Christ (Rev. 1) and communicates a message from Jesus to seven contemporary churches in Asia Minor (Rev. 2,3). The rest of the book reports an extended vision, in which John is transported to heaven and watches events unfold there and on earth (Rev. 4–18). The vision culminates in the return of Christ, the doom of Satan, final judgment, and establishment by God of a new creation (Rev. 19–22).

A BRIEF HISTORY

For the first 200 years of church history, Christians integrated the OT and NT pictures of the future and interpreted both literally. Revelation, which refers or alludes to the OT in 278 of its 404 verses, was seen as a prophetic vision of that future.

In A.D. 390, Tyconius, a leader of the African church, wrote a commentary on Revelation that spiritualized events described there. His allegorical approach was adopted, and his method of interpreting Revelation was followed by Augustine (A.D. 354 – 430), Primasius (about A.D. 550), Alcuin (A.D. 735–804), Maurus (A.D. 775–836), and Strabo (A.D. 807–859).

Joachim of Fiore (A.D. 1130–1202) rejected this approach and introduced chronological divisions. He broke history into three ages: the age of the Father (creation to Christ), the age of the Son (Christ to Joachim's own day), and the age of the Spirit (Joachim's time to final judgment).

A chronological approach was adopted during the Reformation by Luther, Calvin, and others. The Antichrist-beast (Rev. 13) and the harlot (Rev. 17,18) were interpreted as the papacy and as Rome, while historic events that took place in Europe were identified with the various seals and trumpets of the book. Catholics responded with a commentary on Revelation in which Francisco Ribera (A.D. 1537–1591) argued that the Antichrist was an individual who would appear at some future time, not the pope. Other Catholic writers held that Revelation applied only to events before the fall of Rome in A.D. 476. No medieval, Reformation, or Catholic scholar followed the lead of the early church and attempted to relate Revelation to the writings of the OT prophets.

INTERPRETIVE SYSTEMS TODAY

Revelation is difficult to read and understand. Its images and symbols are often obscure. Even when John appears to give straightforward descriptions of what he sees, he must struggle with the limitations imposed by the vocabulary of the first century to describe things that were unfamiliar to citizens of that time.

Given these and other difficulties associated with apocalyptic literature, and the differing theological viewpoints of interpreters, it is not surprising that Christians hold varying views of this powerful NT book. The five major views of Revelation are:

1. *Preterist.* Revelation describes conditions existing when John wrote the book. Christians were persecuted under the Emperor Domitian. John uses symbolism to disguise what is essentially a polemic against the Roman Empire and an effort to encourage Christians.

2. *Historicist.* Revelation previews the Christian era. The trumpets, seals, and bowls of judgment are different periods of history. The Reformers attempted to identify the events of chapters 4–16 with a

Contemporary painting by Paul Richards visualizing the judgments of the seven seals in Rev. 6.

chronology of the Western church from the first through 18th centuries.

Modern historicists see Revelation as a nonchronological panorama of history. Seven separate parallel visions portray, from slightly different viewpoints, the age between Christ's first and second comings. Modern historicists are found among Christians of Reformed background, Mennonites, Southern Baptists, and others.

3. *Idealist.* Revelation has no relationship to history, but rather uses symbols familiar to first-century readers to portray the timeless conflict between good and evil.

4. *Futurist.* Revelation 4–16 is a portrait of future events that will take place at history's end. The events described are the same as those found in OT and Mt. 24 descriptions of a great tribulation to take place prior to the establishment of God's Kingdom.

5. *Apocalyptic.* Revelation was composed following the established tradition of Jewish apocalyptic writings, of which some 100 are known to exist, characterized by complex symbolism and cryptic language. *See also* Apocalyptic Literature.

THEOLOGICAL CONTRIBUTIONS

Whatever approach is taken, Revelation remains a powerful affirmation of the ultimate triumph of God. The blessing promised those who read and take the words of this book to heart (Rev. 1:3) is realized in the fresh awareness we gain of the majesty of God and the merits of the one whom we worship. The unexcelled power of Revelation's poetry lifts us, with the writer and the worshipers in heaven, to cry

You are worthy, our Lord and God,
to receive glory and honor and power

(Rev. 4:11)

and moves us to look forward to the day when the vision of John becomes reality, when

The kingdom of the world has become
the kingdom of our Lord and of
his Christ,
and he will reign for ever and ever.

(Rev. 11:15)

REVELATION: A READING AND STUDY GUIDE

Futurist Interpretation	Chapter	Modern Historicist Interpretation
The prologue and greeting move quickly to a vision of the glorified Jesus.	1	John's vision of Christ features repetition of the number seven, which stands for completeness. This is the key to understanding the book.
The seven churches represent stages of church history: apostolic (Ephesus), early persecutions (Smyrna), hierarchical (Pergamum), Dark Ages (Thyatira), Reformation (Sardis), the "true church" of every age (Philadelphia), the luke-warm 20th-century church (Laodicea).	2,3	John writes to historical churches, which represent churches of every age. We are to study the letters to identify our own situations and then listen to what Christ says to us.
John is called to heaven (raptured?) to see "what will take place later" (1:19).	4	The 24 elders represent the twelve patriarchs and twelve apostles, as the vision unites OT and NT saints in the worship of Scripture's one God.
Jesus, the Lamb, opens a scroll which represents his title to the messianic Kingdom of Dan. 7:13,14. This unleashes preliminary judgments on the earth.	5	The scroll symbolizes redemption. Christ, returned to heaven after dying for humankind, symbolically opens the way of salvation to all and begins his rule over all from heaven.
The tribulation judgments of Mt. 24:5-8 are unleashed. The martyrs are believers killed during this period.	6	Christ, the first rider, comes to win his victory on earth through the Gospel message. A struggle follows, culminating in God's final victory over his enemies and vindication of martyred believers.
God sends out 144,000 Jewish converts to preach Christ during the tribulation period, and multitudes are saved.	7	The number 144,000 is symbolic of perfection and represents the church of all ages. (Mention of the tribal identities is discounted.)
Further judgments come as the tribulation deepens.	8	The first of seven parallel sections of Revelation, this chapter suggests that God uses natural disasters to warn mankind of final judgment.
Demonic enemies of mankind are unleashed, but the unconverted refuse to repent.	9	The vision represents the existence of demonic, anti-Christian influences in the world today and shows why believers must put on the whole armor of God (Eph. 6:11,12).
Earth is quiet, waiting, as an angel announces history is about to close "just as he [God] announced to his servants the prophets."	10	This interlude reminds believers that though God is silent, he is poised to execute judgment at time's end.
Two persons, often identified as Moses and Elijah (Mt. 17:1-5), preach for 3½ years in Jerusalem until they are finally killed by the Antichrist.	11	The 3½-year period is symbolic of periods of affliction. The witnesses represent the whole church, while their deaths symbolize its silence in times of persecution. That they are raised shows that God will triumph in the end.
Israel, represented by a woman, is preserved during the last half of the tribulation (1,260 days) foretold by Daniel, as Satan directs the world's hostility against the Jews.	12	The woman is Israel, the church of the OT. The war in heaven was won by Jesus on Calvary. Despite Satan's hatred, the church will be preserved.
The Antichrist (represented by a first beast) unites European countries (the ten horns), reviving the old Roman Empire. He is aided by a second beast (the false prophet).	13	The first beast represents anti-Christian governments, while the second represents false religion. The number 666 means that the counterfeit falls far short of the true, while the 42 months are the entire church age.
The overthrow of Babylon the Great, a symbol of both political and religious power, is previewed.	14	The chapter contains another image of final judgment. Babylon is all that is ungodly in this world. Other elements represent the purity of the true church.

continued

Futurist Interpretation	Chapter	Modern Historicist Interpretation
Terrible, devastating judgments strike the followers of the Antichrist as the tribulation comes to an end.	15,16	These chapters contain symbolic rather than realistic descriptions of final judgment
"Mystery Babylon," representing a worldwide religion, is overthrown, to be replaced by worship of the Antichrist.	17	The woman stands for pseudo-spiritual powers operating in the world today.
Babylon, representing secular, military, and political power as consolidated under the Antichrist, is destroyed by God.	18	"Babylon" is a symbolic representation of past, present, and future centers of materialistic human culture. All Babylons will be destroyed by God.
Christ appears to lead the final battle, which is predicted in such OT passages as Ezek. 38,39; Dan. 11; and Zech. 14. His victory initiates Christ's rule on earth.	19	The chapter uses apocalyptic symbolism to portray the final victory of Christ and the complete overthrow of God's enemies. The beast and false prophet are personifications of Satan's evil powers, but not individuals.
Christ rules for a thousand-year period (the Millennium), fulfilling many OT prophecies. Satan is released but crushed by Christ and thrown into the lake of fire. The unsaved dead are raised and judged.	20	The chapter begins the last parallel vision. It too portrays the entire period between first and second comings. The thousand-year period is symbolic of the believer's present exaltation in Christ. The last part of the chapter describes a general resurrection for all, to take place at history's end.
God destroys this present universe (2 Pet. 3) to create a new heaven and earth as the home of the redeemed, and he himself lives among men.	21,22	John gives a picture of the new heavens and earth, but the elements are to be taken symbolically rather than literally. Thus, the "new Jerusalem" is the Church Triumphant, not a city.

MASTERY KEYS

Read for the overall impact of John's vision. A quick reading, without pausing over puzzling passages, fills the heart with awe, wonder, and worship. This book is intended to communicate the certainty of God's ultimate triumph, rather than the details of how that triumph is to be accomplished. This is Revelation's most important contribution to Christians today.

Then use the two reading and study guides provided to see how the book is understood by using the most common interpretive approaches taken today—futurist and modern historicist.

SPECIAL FEATURES

The book is filled with symbols, many of which are explained within the context (1:20; 4:5; 5:8; 7:13,14; 12:9; 17:9,12,15,18). Some can be understood from other passages in Revelation. The descriptions of Jesus in each of the letters to the seven churches in chs. 2,3 come from John's vision in 1:9-20. The rewards Jesus promises in each case are seen fulfilled in John's heavenly visit:

- Eating from the tree of life (2:7) in 22:2.

- Receiving the crown of life and protection from the second death (2:10,11) in 4:4 and 20:6.
- Being given the morning star and authority over the nations (2:26,28) in 5:10 and 22:16.
- Wearing white robes and having their names written in the book of life (3:5) in 7:9 and 20:15.
- Having Christ's new name written on them (3:12) in 22:4.
- Receiving the right to sit with Christ on his throne (3:21) in 22:3.

Other symbols are drawn from the OT, and their meaning can be traced with a concordance. Among them are the tree of life (2:7; 22:2; *see* Gen. 2:9), the iron scepter (2:27; *see* Ps. 2:9), the morning star (2:28; *see* Dan. 12:3), the key of David (3:7; *see* Isa. 22:22), and others. It is possible to trace some of the symbolism in Revelation to Jewish apocalyptic literature of the time, and thus scholarly research can help to illuminate the meaning of various passages. However, the meaning assumed for each symbol varies with the interpretive school. *See also* Apocalyptic Literature; Future; Second Coming; Tribulation.

revenge Vengeance; a judicial concept associated with God's righteousness and his responsibility to judge evildoers. While judicial vengeance is justified, personal revenge is forbidden in Lev. 19:18 and Deut. 32:35. *See also* Vengeance.

revile To use abusive language in speaking to or about another; to show contempt for. Generally, when the wicked revile, it is an act directed against the godly or against the Lord (Pss. 10:13; 55:3).

reward The return one receives for his acts, especially repayment for doing good (Prov. 11:31; Ps. 19:11); a wage paid for one's labor.

The basic biblical idea is that God as a moral person rewards good and punishes evil. In this way, God maintains balance and harmony in the moral universe by treating all persons fairly. "The Lord will reward everyone for whatever good he does, whether he is slave or free" (Eph. 6:8).

Paul, however, carefully guards against the notion prevalent in Judaism that salvation is a matter of service and reward. Paul quotes Gen. 15:6, reminding his readers that Abraham was considered righteous not because of his works but because of his faith in God. Paul then argues that "when a man works, his wages are not credited to him as a gift, but as an obligation. However, to the man who does not work but trusts God who justifies the wicked, his faith is credited as righteousness" (Rom. 4:3-5). Thus, salvation is a gift, not a reward for good works.

riddle A saying whose meaning is hidden; a puzzle to be solved. The Hebrew word, *hidah*, means "something tied in a knot," suggesting that it must be untied to be understood.

The classic example is the saying Samson challenged the Philistines to explain, "Out of the eater, something to eat; out of the strong, something sweet" (Jdg. 14:14).

right hand *See* Hand.

righteousness OT: (1) An absolute quality of God, who always acts in harmony with his moral nature (Ps. 4:1; Jer. 12:1). God's character is the standard by which righteousness is measured. (2) Conformity to the moral and ethical norms revealed in God's Law (Deut. 6:25; Ps. 119:121). In the OT, righteousness is not an abstract quality or sinlessness but rather acting in har-

mony with one's obligations to God and to other persons (1 Sam. 24:17). In this limited sense, individuals in the OT are called "righteous." This sense of righteousness is sometimes found in the Gospels (Mt. 1:19; Mk. 6:20).

NT: (3) Imputed righteousness: the declaration by God that a person is righteous in God's sight, not by virtue of that person's acts but by virtue of his faith in Jesus (Rom. 1:17; 3:21; *see* Gen. 15:6). (4) Actual righteousness: inner moral conformity of one's character to the character of God, and the acts that flow from a righteous moral character (Rom. 8:4; Eph. 4:24).

OLD TESTAMENT

In God's case, righteousness is an absolute quality, an aspect of God's intrinsic character. He establishes righteous moral standards (Ps. 119:75,164), reveals his righteousness in acts of judgment (Pss. 9:8; 98:9), and exhibits righteousness in his saving acts (Ps. 31:1; Isa. 45:21).

In the case of mankind, righteousness has a much more limited meaning. No human being is righteous in an absolute sense (Ps. 143:2). Yet OT believers whose acts conformed with the standards revealed by God are frequently called righteous. However, the OT shows that even this limited righteousness is rooted in the believer's intimate relationship with God (Pss. 33:1; 64:10; 140:13; Mal. 3:18).

The person who chooses to live by God's standards will be blessed (Ps. 5:12) and upheld (Ps. 37:17), will flourish (Ps. 92:12) and be remembered (Ps. 112:6).

The limited righteousness of the believer who was committed to obeying God brought great rewards. Yet the OT makes it clear that human righteousness is not the basis of God's favor. God did not choose Israel because the nation was righteous, but "because the Lord loved you and kept the oath he swore to your forefathers" (Deut. 7:7-9). The basis of the OT relationship with God was the Lord's covenant commitment to Abraham, not human obedience to Mosaic Law. *See also* Covenant.

NEW TESTAMENT

The NT significantly expands the OT concept. Jesus called for a righteousness that exceeded that of the "Pharisees and the teachers of the law," who expected to achieve salvation by zealously obeying the letter of OT statutes (Mt. 5:20). Jesus went on to give a series of illustrations showing that, while the Law deals with external actions, it also reveals God's concern with the attitudes and motives that generate those actions. Later, Christ said plainly, "Out of the heart come evil thoughts, murder, adultery, sexual immorality, theft, false testimony, slander" (Mt. 15:19). The righteousness with which God is concerned is inner righteousness: a character which is God-like in nature, without which a person "will certainly not enter the kingdom of heaven" (Mt. 5:20). This inner righteousness will naturally and necessarily lead to a righteous life.

Paul develops this teaching of Jesus: "No one will be declared righteous in his [God's] sight by observing the law" (Rom. 3:20). The function of the Law is not to help man become righteous but to demonstrate man's sinfulness.

A dilemma then exists. A person must be righteous within to be accepted by God. But nothing a person does can make him righteous. Paul resolves the dilemma by returning to the OT and fixing on a principle expressed in Gen. 15:6. Abraham was not righteous in any absolute sense. But Abraham believed God, and faith "was credited to him as righteousness." Thus, Abraham was granted the standing of a righteous person by God, despite the fact that he was a sinner! God chose to impute or credit to Abraham a righteousness that Abraham did not intrinsically possess.

Paul argues that God did the right thing to grant an imputed righteousness to those in the OT era who responded to him with faith, just as he is right today when he offers imputed righteousness to any who respond with faith to the good news of Jesus Christ. The death of Christ for sinners shows that God does punish sin, and as Christ died for all, God is free to declare those who believe in him legally guiltless and to impute righteousness to them.

The NT teaches that a person who exercises faith in Christ experiences an inner moral transformation toward Christ-likeness that will culminate in total righteousness at the resurrection.

The foundation for the believer's transformation is laid: (1) in the new birth, through which Christians are given a "new self, created to be like God in true righteousness and holiness" (Eph. 4:24); (2) in the believer's vital present union with Jesus—raised with Jesus to experience a new dimension of life, Christians can offer themselves to God and use their bodies as instruments of righteousness (Rom. 6:1-14); and (3) in the presence of the Holy Spirit, whose supernatural power

can give life even to the mortal body, so that those who follow the Spirit's promptings fully meet "the righteous requirements of the law" (Rom. 8:4,11).

In these and other passages (Gal. 2,3; Phil. 3:1-11; Jas. 2:20-26), the NT makes it clear that the Christian is expected to live a truly righteous life and is equipped for righteousness by the work of God within.

rights (1) Legal rights; that to which a person is entitled by the divine Law (Ex. 21:10; Prov. 31:5; Gal. 4:5). (2) Personal rights; the freedom of a believer to follow his or her conscience in areas where Scripture does not define sin (1 Cor. 9:15). Two NT passages focus attention on the Christian's exercise of his or her personal rights.

Romans 14 examines the right of a believer to follow his or her conscience in "disputable matters," such as what a person eats or what days he regards as sacred. Paul teaches that Christians must not judge one another on such issues. Each individual must be responsible to Christ as Lord and do what he believes is pleasing to God, while, at the same time, considering the needs of others: "It is better not to eat meat or drink wine or to do anything else that will cause your brother to fall" (v. 21). However, ideally, no Christian will make an issue of debatable things, so each person can keep whatever he or she believes about these things "between yourself and God" (v. 22).

First Corinthians 8,9 also deals with "personal rights." Some Corinthians were arguing that it was wrong for Christians to participate in social events where the food was dedicated to an idol. Others protested that since idols have no real existence participating was no problem. In 1 Corinthians, Paul enters the fray. However, before dealing with the doctrinal question in ch. 10, Paul discusses personal rights in ch. 9. Paul himself had the "right" to be financially supported and the "right" to marry and travel with a wife. Paul, however, chose not to exercise these and other "rights" (9:12). He chose to give up his rights in order to serve those to whom he ministered.

The contrast is striking, for each side in Corinth insisted on exercising its rights, without concern for any impact on others.

Both Rom. 14 and 1 Cor. 9 assume the existence of personal rights. Christians are not asked to surrender rights simply to live in harmony with others. But Christians are asked to care about believing brothers and sisters and to consider carefully the impact that exercising their rights will have on others' spiritual well-being.

ring (1) A metallic circlet worn by men and women as jewelry (Gen. 24:47; Ex. 32:2; Jas. 2:2), or engraved with an individual's identifying mark to serve as an official seal or signature (Esth. 3:10; Jer. 22:24). (2) A metallic circlet used as a fastener in the construction of the tabernacle (Ex. 25:12-15; 26:24-30) and on the garments of the high priest (Ex. 28:23-28).

Above: Hittite ring seal exemplifies how important a ring could be when used as an official identification (see Gen. 41:41-43).
Far left: so-called "horse ring" of Rameses II, pharaoh of Egypt, in the 13th century B.C.
Left: Line drawings of styles of ancient rings. Three Egyptian rings in the shapes of a snake, scarab-beetle, and eye; and two Roman rings, one bearing horses.

river A stream of water flowing into some greater body of water, typically fed by smaller streams.

In Mesopotamia and Egypt, great civilizations developed along major rivers, the Nile, Euphrates, and Tigris. Flooding by these rivers kept the land fertile, and great irrigation canals extended the farmable region. The rivers thus supported the large, stable populations required for conquest. The Jordan, Israel's major river, lies in a deep valley, limiting the flat land available for irrigation.

Rivers frequently served as borders in the ancient world, marking off the territory of one group from that of another.

River of Egypt *See* Egypt, River of.

The River Jordan north of the Sea of Galilee. On the plateau overlooking this river basin stands the excavated site of Hazor, the largest Canaanite city of its day.

road A path or route. Well-established trade routes linked the major civilizations of OT times. Later, the Romans built highways along many of these routes to speed communication or to move armies from one part of their Empire to another.

ROADS IN OT TIMES

In OT times, roads outside of cities were unpaved but well-worn caravan tracks, slightly improved in rocky or rough terrain. Hebrew has a number of specific terms for roads, which are variously translated by road, path, highway, ramp, passage, trail, etc.

The most important OT roadways were the international trade routes and their various branches, which linked the great civilizations lying to the north and south of Palestine. Long before the age of Abraham and well past the time of Christ, caravans of goods and invading armies followed these established routes. The most significant was the King's Highway, stretching over the high plateau east of the Jordan from the Gulf of Aqaba to Damascus. In the south this route then cut across the Sinai to Memphis in Egypt. In the north it continued up to Aleppo and then paralleled the Euphrates River to Babylon and Ur. After the domestication of the camel, this route was shortened for cara-

vans, which could cut across the desert to Tadmor and Mari. This road served as the major route along which spices were transported from Arabia.

The Great West Road lay along the seacoast, linking Egypt's delta with the major coastal cities of Megiddo, Tyre, Byblos, and Ugarit. In Roman times, this route was known as the Via Maris (Way of the Sea).

Branches of these roads passed through Canaan, following the natural contours of the land. The same internal routes were followed by Abraham and the patriarchs, by Joshua and his army, and by the worshipers who trekked three times each year to Jerusalem to worship at the Temple established by Solomon. A new network of internal roads had been developed in Galilee by the first century.

ROADS IN NT TIMES

By the first century A.D., major roads radiated from Rome to every part of the far-flung Roman Empire. These roads were so well-constructed that most can be traced today.

Major Roman highways were constructed by laying a foundation of large stones, then a layer of smaller stones cemented with lime. Above this was a third layer of smaller stones, and the whole was capped with flat blocks of flint paving stones. The surface of Roman roads was slightly arched, and gutters along the side helped to carry off rainwater. The whole construction was two to three feet (60 to 90 centimeters) deep. The Romans also set up distance markers along the roadsides and built regularly spaced posthouses where relay horses were kept ready for imperial messengers.

This system of roads was the key to the excellent system of communications that linked the Roman Empire and increased the mobility of Rome's armies. It also

Below: Map of roads and trade routes in the OT world.
Right: The Via Egnatia near Neapolis. This Roman road was a crucial land route from the west coast of Macedonia to Asia Minor in the east. Paul probably traveled this highway between Neapolis and Thessalonica (Acts 16:11–17:1).

aided the rapid spread of the Gospel message. Missionaries like Barnabas, Silas, Timothy, Titus, and the apostle Paul traveled freely on Roman highways, putting them to a use never imagined by the men who ordered their construction.

robbery The taking of property that rightfully belongs to others.

In some OT passages, robbery is associated with violence (Jdg. 9:25), but the biblical term does not itself imply it. However, robbery does imply the serious violation of an individual's rights as a person, not just the taking of his property. Thus, Isaiah lashes out against those who make unjust laws "to deprive the poor of their rights and withhold [rob] justice from the oppressed of my people, making widows their prey and robbing the fatherless" (10:2). God charges Israel with robbing him of his tithes and offerings (Mal. 3:8), not because he is dependent on them but because Israel's failure shows contempt for his person. The serious nature of robbery is further suggested by its association in Isa. 61:8 with iniquity, a sin of willful rebellion.

In the NT, the Greek word *harpagmon*, which the KJV translates "robbery" in Phil. 2:6, can also mean the thing that is stolen, or plunder. In the Philippians context, the wording of modern versions— "something to be grasped"—works well. Jesus had not stolen his equality with God. It was part of his very nature. And so he could freely give up his divine privileges in order to save us.

robe An outer garment worn by men and women. *See also* Cloak; Clothing.

rock Literally, a stone, slab of stone, or a stone mass or cliff. Figuratively, a place of shelter or safety (Ps. 18:2). Canaan is a rocky land, and the people of the Bible were familiar with its many caves and the rocky crags that provided hiding places in times of danger.

There are two significant "rocks" mentioned in Scripture. First, a stream flowed from the slab of rock that Moses struck, providing water for the Exodus generation (Ex. 17:6). The NT views this rock as a symbol of Christ, the source of spiritual drink for God's children (1 Cor. 10:1-6).

Second, the name Jesus gave to Simon (Peter, from the Greek *petros*) means "rock" (Mt. 16:18). Roman Catholics understand the statement of Jesus, "On this rock I will build my church," as Christ's

Roman street in the city of Ostia, the principal harbor for Rome in the first and second centuries A.D.

Rocky wilderness on the approach to Mount Sinai (also called Horeb). Somewhere in this area Moses struck "the rock at Horeb" to provide water for the Israelites (Ex. 17:1-7).

The Egyptian god Osiris, judge of the dead, holds the symbols of his authority: a rod with a crook and a flail. Pharaohs employed these two as their royal scepters.

32:10; Mk. 6:8); (2) a club used for defense (Ex. 21:19; Ps. 23:4); (3) a shepherd's crook (Lev. 27:32); (4) a small switch used to punish children (Prov. 22:15) or a heavier pole used to beat adults (2 Sam. 7:14; Mt. 27:30) or used symbolically by God to discipline nations (Isa. 10:5); (5) a symbol of authority, or a scepter (Jdg. 5:14; Ps. 125:3); (6) a staff used to thresh by pounding sheaves of grain (Isa. 28:27); or (7) a measuring stick (Ezek. 40:3; Rev. 11:1). *See also* Aaron's Staff.

roebuck (KJV) *See* Gazelle.

Roman Empire The territory of Western Europe and the Mediterranean that the city of Rome ruled from the first century B.C. to the fifth century A.D.

The Empire bound together a variety of peoples and cultures, maintaining itself not only by military power but by efficient and generally lenient provincial administration. Another unifying factor was the nearly universal use of the Greek language and a general acceptance of Greek culture and values. In addition, a complex of major land and sea routes linked major cities of the Empire, permitting the easy movement of people and goods as well as armies.

The Empire offered its population of some 54 million persons (of which probably 5 million were Jews) prosperity, security, and many freedoms in return for reasonable taxes and loyalty to the Roman emperor. For instance, through the first century there was little inflation. Bankers paid lenders 5 or 6 percent on investments, and the maximum interest rate on ordinary loans was set at 12 percent. Regarding freedom, while Roman law imposed harsh penalties for criminal acts and for any activity that might be considered treasonable, most national groups were permitted to follow their own customs and religions. Self-government by each national group, under its own laws and courts, was encouraged, although Roman laws and courts were supreme.

Religious toleration also characterized the Empire during most of the first century. The austere official Roman cult had little spiritual appeal for the masses. Before Christianity exploded out of little Palestine in the A.D. 40s and 50s, many in the Empire had turned to Eastern mystery religions and to magic in an effort to satisfy their spiritual hunger. Foreign cults were, however, viewed as dangerous superstitions by the Romans themselves. By the end of the first century, Christianity was considered dangerous to the state,

granting primacy to Peter over the church and other apostles. Protestants generally say the "rock" was Peter's confession of faith (v. 16), and that this faith in Jesus' true identity would serve as the foundation stone for his Church.

rod (KJV) A wooden staff, either straight or with a crook on one end, that served a variety of purposes in biblical times. The Hebrew words translated "staff" can also be translated "rod."

Depending on the context, the rod is (1) a walking stick used by travelers (Gen.

ROMAN RULERS IN THE NEW TESTAMENT

Term (Greek)	Meaning
Caesar (*kaisaros*)	Family name of Julius Caesar taken by Augustus and used as a generic title for the emperor from that time on (Lk. 2:1; 3:1)
Proconsul (*anthypatos*)	"Governor" of a province administered by the Senate (Acts 13:7; 18:12)
Procurator (*hēgemōn*)	Imperial financial agent in a Senate province or "governor" of a minor province under an imperial legate (Mt. 27:11; Acts 23:24; 24:27)
Tribune (*chiliarchos*)	High-ranking military officer in charge of up to 1,000 men (Acts 21:31)
Centurion (*hekatontarchos*)	Officer in charge of 100 men (Mk. 15:19; Acts 10:1)

and Christians had begun to be persecuted.

The Empire, which gave the varied peoples of Europe and the Mediterranean a common language and permitted free movement of persons and ideas, was essential to the spread of Christianity. Christians preached and wrote in Greek, the language understood by nearly everyone. Missionaries freely crossed borders that in later nationalistic ages would have blocked their passage. Everywhere Christians found a spiritual hunger unsatisfied by the existing philosophies, religions, superstitions, and belief in magic. The gradual expansion of Roman power, culminating in the establishment of a unified empire by Augustus, is evidence that God was at work, preparing the world for the birth of his Son and the spread of the Gospel. *See also* Augustus Caesar; Caesar.

Romans, Epistle to the

Romans, Epistle to the The longest and most theological of Paul's NT letters. Written to the church at Rome about A.D. 57, Romans is a closely reasoned exposition of the doctrines of righteousness and of salvation by faith alone. The book has had a significant impact in church history, stimulating the conversion of St. Augustine, of Martin Luther, and through Luther's commentary on Romans, of John Wesley.

ROME

When Paul wrote his letter, this city, the nerve center of the widespread Roman Empire, held about one million of the Empire's 54 million persons. Augustus had constructed magnificent public buildings there and the rich inhabited luxurious villas. But most of the city's population were squeezed into four- or five-story tenements, called *insulae*. The first floor of these buildings contained shops that opened onto narrow, crowded, and dirty streets. People lived in the smaller, higher rooms, none of which had running water or sanitary facilities. The tenements, made of wood or sometimes brick, were all too likely to collapse or to be destroyed by fire.

Like many modern cities, Rome had an urban police force and firefighters, and prostitutes, who registered with the courts and paid their tax, wandered the streets in identifying clothing. Many foreigners had settled in Rome, most clustering together with others of their ethnic background in one or another of the city's 14 administrative districts. A rather large population of Jews lived in Rome, and the church to which Paul wrote was undoubtedly made up of both Jewish and Gentile Christians. Although there is no record of how the church at Rome was established, a large Christian community existed there. Its first members may have been converted in Jerusalem on the day of Pentecost (Acts 2). That community was later persecuted under Nero in the A.D. 60s. Tradition tells us that both Paul and Peter were martyred in Rome during Nero's reign.

BACKGROUND

As the Christian movement became more deeply rooted in the Gentile world, the sharp division between OT and NT eras was made ever more clear. In Romans, the great apostle assembles evidence to explain the apparent divide, while affirming God's consistency in his dealings with humankind.

Paul does this by demonstrating that God's purpose is not summed up in the OT Law, on which Israel had fixed its attention, but in the underlying issue of righteousness. With bold strokes, the apostle shows that both Jew and Gentile fall short of the righteousness God demands (Rom. 1–3). Yet the OT testifies that God, from the beginning, has been willing to impute righteousness to sinners

This inscription at Corinth contains the name of Erastus, commissioner of public works, who may have been the city treasurer mentioned in Rom. 16:23.

1. *Two Roman soldiers carved on a column from the praetorium of Mogontiacum (Mainz, Germany). The well-trained and disciplined legions kept the Roman Empire intact for some 450 years.*

2. *Glass hand basin and container (first century A.D.). Techniques of glass blowing were perfected in Italy, so that glass products gradually became common household items.*

3. *Scene of census registration from the sarcophagus of Domitius Ahenobarbus (Rome, about A.D. 100). The taxation of Roman provinces was determined on the basis of census information.*

4. *Arch of Titus, erected by Emperor Domitian at the forum in Rome (A.D. 81) in commemoration of the conquest of Jerusalem by Titus in A.D. 70.*

5. *War elephant trampling a Galatian warrior.*

6. *Seats of a Roman theater at Shechem, Israel. The Romans were extensive builders, and remains of public buildings are found all over Europe and the Middle East.*

7. *Bronze kettle with three lion's paws for legs. Hundreds of expensive items were uncovered at Pompeii, a wealthy Roman city destroyed by a volcanic eruption in A.D. 79.*

8,9. *Two frescoes from Stabiae, Italy, display Roman architecture: typical villa design with colonnades (pillared porches) and view of a harbor.*

10. *Still-life painting with a hare, a fresco from Herculaneum. The art of painting on fresh, moist plaster was largely a Roman development.*

11. *Roman ruins at Gerasa (Jerash, Jordan).*

3

4

7

8

10

11

who have faith in him (Rom. 4). Paul then shows that Christ, who died for our sins to satisfy the justice of God, is now set forth by God as the one in whom we are to believe (Rom. 5).

But God in Christ has done more than provide forgiveness. Through believers' union with Jesus, and by the power of the indwelling Holy Spirit, Christians who rely on God rather than on themselves are enabled to live righteous lives (Rom. 6–8).

Paul then turns to the question of God's dealings with Israel and demonstrates that God has been consistent—and thus righteous—in his historical and present dealings with his covenant people (Rom. 9–11). *See also* Righteousness.

In the final chapters, Paul returns to the theme of righteous living, this time not to the question of how an individual can live a good life, but how the church is intended to function as a just and moral community (Rom. 12–16).

THEOLOGICAL CONTRIBUTIONS
Romans is an extended treatise on imputed and practical righteousness and the

ROMANS: A READING AND STUDY GUIDE

Chapter	Content Summary	Related Articles
1	Paul introduces the theme of righteousness (v.17) and traces the results of man's failure to have faith in God.	Righteousness Anger
2	Both the Jews who have God's Law and the Gentiles who do not have fallen short of righteousness and merit judgment.	Law Conscience
3	Scripture proves that all have sinned. But the death of Christ demonstrates the rightness of God's gracious offer of justification to all who have faith in Jesus.	Sin Grace Justification
4	The OT shows that God has always accepted faith in place of righteousness and that righteous standing is thus a gift.	Faith Promise Gift
5	Faith in Jesus, who died for sinners, brings peace with God and also brings the believer new life.	Peace Life
6	Faith unites us to Jesus: Believers, who died in his death and live through his life, can live righteous lives.	Death Holy
7	Although we are legally free of the Law, if we try to follow it in our own strength, we will keep on falling short.	Law Flesh
8	Controlled by the Spirit, we can live righteous lives now even as we look ahead to the ultimate transformation that Christ guarantees.	Holy Spirit Predestine Transformation
9	History shows that God is not unrighteous or inconsistent in his present dealings with Israel.	Israel Works, Good
10	All must submit to God's righteousness rather than attempt to establish their own righteousness, as the Jewish people sought to do.	Confess
11	Even so, a remnant of Israel (converted Jews) remains. And one day, all the prophets' promises to Israel will be fulfilled.	Remnant Covenant Future
12	Christians are now called to unite in a single body, to use their gifts to serve one another, and to grow in a just and moral community.	Church Spiritual Gifts Good
13	Members of God's righteous community will obey civil laws and concentrate on loving one another.	Government, Human Love
14	Members of a righteous community will not judge each other but each will be responsible to Christ for his or her choices.	Judge Lord
15	Members of a righteous community will show concern for the convictions of others and promote unity.	Strong Unity
16	Paul extends personal greetings to many believers in Rome.	Woman

relationship of each to faith in Jesus Christ. The best way to understand the doctrine is by carefully tracing the book's argument using an outline.

MASTERY KEYS

Read Romans thoughtfully, guided both by the outline and the Reading and Study Guide. A good way to study Romans is to try and sum up each paragraph in a single sentence.

SPECIAL FEATURES

Many key biblical terms are woven throughout Paul's argument. Among them are Law, grace, flesh, justification, Holy Spirit, and especially righteousness. Reading the articles on these topics will give you important background for understanding Paul's argument in Romans.

STRUCTURE OF **ROMANS**		
I. Introduction		1:1-17
II. Universal Need of Righteousness		1:18–3:20
III. God's Gift of Righteousness (Justification)		3:21–5:21
IV. Righteous Living Now Possible through		6:1–8:39
A. Union with Christ	6:1-14	
B. Slavery to Righteousness	6:15-23	
C. Release from Law	7:1-25	
D. The Spirit within	8:1-17	
E. Final Glorification	8:18-39	
V. Righteousness in Israel's History		9:1–11:36
VI. Righteousness in the New Community		12:1–15:13
VII. Personal Notes		15:14–16:27

roof (1) The top of a house or building; (2) idiomatic of a house or home (Mt. 8:8).

Nearly all buildings in Israel had flat roofs. They were typically constructed of clay packed tightly by stone rollers on top of a mat of branches that was laid over wooden beams. Mark writes quite literally when he describes friends of a paralyzed man "digging" a hole in the roof of a house so they could lower the man down to Jesus (Mk. 2:4).

During the summer season people often slept on the roofs of their houses—thus, the OT law requiring a parapet around the roof (Deut. 22:8)—or they spent the evenings there talking (2 Sam. 11:2). Rahab used the roof as a place to lay out stalks of flax to dry (Josh. 2:6).

room A separate section within a building. Houses in Bible times typically had few rooms. *See also* House.

root That part of a plant which is underground, anchoring the plant and drawing the nourishment and moisture it needs to flourish.

Nearly all references to roots in the Bible are symbolic. In most cases, the symbol-ism is clear, reflecting the vital role of the root in relation to the other parts of the plant. Thus, being "rooted" means to be firmly established (Eph. 3:17). In the OT, uprooting symbolizes national destruction (Jer. 1:10). Other images symbolize sin: roots that rot (Isa. 5:24) and dry up (Hos. 9:16). John's warning that an axe lies at the root of the tree means that judgment is near (Mt. 3:10).

In the OT, "root" is also an important image of the Messiah. He is the source as well as the descendant of Jesse (David's father) and of David (Isa. 11:10; Rev. 5:5). As a "root out of dry ground," the Messiah is the source of life unexpectedly appearing in a lifeless landscape (Isa. 53:2).

The eagle, depicted here on a round base (A.D. 100–300), was the symbol of the Roman Empire. In his letter to the Christians in Rome, Paul urges Christians to submit themselves to the governing authorities, "for there is no authority except that which God has established" (13:1).

In an extended analogy, Paul pictures God as a root that makes those who are connected with him (branches) holy. Paul goes on to portray the nation Israel as branches of a domesticated olive tree temporarily broken off so that Gentiles, growing on a wild olive tree, can be grafted in (Rom. 11:16-24).

In the NT Epistles, a root may also indicate the source of a spiritual condition. Thus, a love of money is a root from which all kinds of evil grow (1 Tim. 6:10), while a root of bitterness causes trouble and defiles many (Heb. 12:15).

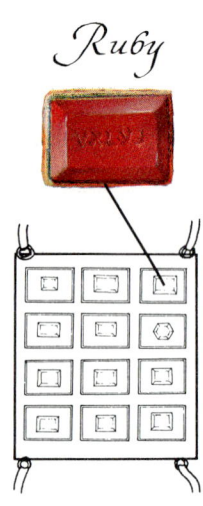

Far right: Roman ropemaker depicted in relief on a sarcophagus from Rome.
Right: A ropemaking method which required a team of three: One twirled the weighted strands, another controlled the tautness of the rope with spikes, and a third twisted the strands in the opposite direction to form the finished product.

rope A woven strand of twisted plant fibers, hair, or animal hide. Hebrew words make no distinction between a thick rope and a thin cord. *See also* Cord.

rose A flower, named only in Song 2:1 and Isa. 35:1 (KJV).

The "rose" of Scripture is not the flower called by that name today. In Isa. 35:1, the flower is probably the crocus (as in the NIV), which bursts into bloom after an infrequent desert rain. Most take the "rose of Sharon" in Solomon's great love poem as the narcissus or perhaps a tulip. Both these plants grow in the highlands around Sharon and are valued garden plants.

Rosh Hashanah [rahsh hah-SHAH-nah]. The Hebrew new year festival, celebrated each autumn. The phrase means literally "head of the yearly cycle."

Ruby

ruby A transparent, deep red precious stone. The true ruby is probably not intended in any biblical reference. No ruby dating earlier than the third century B.C. has been found at any excavated Middle Eastern site.

Several different Hebrew words have been translated "ruby" in English versions. The first gem in the first row of the high priest's breastpiece, an 'odem (called a ruby in the NIV), is probably a sardius, a red carnelian used in jewelry in OT times. *Peninim*, also identified as rubies by the NIV (Job 28:18; Prov. 3:15; 8:11; 20:15; 31:10; Lam. 4:7), most likely are pearls or red coral.

A wife of noble character "is worth far more than rubies" (Prov. 31:10). The deep red stone was highly valued in Old Testament times.

rudiments (KJV) Basic principles. In Col. 2:8,20, Paul refers to the world's empty approach to religion, based on strict regulations.

ruler A person with authority. "Ruler" describes those with many different kinds of authority, including (1) Egypt's vizier (prime minister) (Gen. 45:26); (2) heads of tribes (Gen. 25:16); (3) kings (1 Ki. 11:34); (4) princes (Jer. 30:21); (5) members of the Jewish Sanhedrin in NT times (Acts 4:5); (6) the master of ceremonies at a feast (Jn. 2:9); (7) local city magistrates (Acts 17:6,8); (8) powerful spiritual beings (Eph. 6:12); and (9) God himself (1 Tim. 6:15).

ruler of the synagogue An important position, typically held by a wealthy and generous member of the congregation. The ruler supervised the upkeep of the building and also oversaw the worship services. The ruler of the synagogue was probably also responsible for distribution of funds to meet special needs in the congregation. A study of some 19 Greek and Latin inscriptions ranging from the first century B.C. to the sixth century A.D. shows that women as well as men held this post.

In Israel, rulers of the synagogue seem to have had authority to discipline members (Jn. 9:22; 16:2). Rulers of synagogues named in the NT include Jairus (Mk. 5:22; Lk. 8:41); Crispus, who became a Christian (Acts 18:8); and Sosthenes (Acts 18:17).

rush *See* Papyrus.

Ruth, Book of The brief, heartwarming story of the faithful daughter-in-law of Naomi, whose loyalty and personal qualities were rewarded by her marriage to Boaz, Naomi's relative, about 1100 B.C.

BACKGROUND

The events reported in this book take place at the end of the age of the judges, a dark era when the Israelite tribes were weak and divided and frequently abandoned the religion established through Moses. Against this background, the Book of Ruth [ROOTH; "friendship"] is far more than a love story. It shows that even during Israel's darkest time individuals like Boaz trusted God and lived upright lives. In times of national decline, God preserved a remnant who could serve as the core of a future revival. *See also* Judges, Book of; Naomi; Remnant.

While the book portrays conditions about a hundred years prior to the time of David, it was written after he became king (4:16-22). The author is unknown.

THEOLOGICAL CONTRIBUTIONS

The simple story has several theological implications. First, the book provides the clearest OT example of the kinsman-redeemer. Mosaic Law established the right of a near relative to help a destitute individual by paying the price to redeem him or her from slavery, or by buying back land he or she had been forced to sell. As a near kinsman, Boaz chose to marry the widow Ruth. Their first child was considered the son of Ruth's dead husband, and the child inherited his family name and property.

The kinsman-redeemer principle is important, since it foreshadows the incarnation of Christ. To redeem a lost and helpless humanity, God himself became human, so that from the position of a near kinsman he might pay the price that redeems humankind.

Second, the book illustrates God's concern for Gentiles in OT times. Ruth, a Moabite, was not only welcomed into the covenant people but became an ancestor of King David and thus of Jesus Christ. Later, rabbis viewed Ruth as the ideal convert. She broke completely with her past to identify fully with the people and God of her new family.

MASTERY KEYS

Read this short book as a warm and inspiring story. Then contrast the picture it gives of life during the age of the judges with three other portraits of that time, found in Jdg. 17–21. Ruth reveals the presence of godly individuals during Israel's spiritually darkest days.

SPECIAL FEATURES

Ruth told Naomi, "Your people will be my people and your God my God" (1:16). The order is significant. Ruth identified herself with God's covenant people and through that people established her claim to relationship with God.

The book also mentions unusual customs. Ruth's request that Boaz cover her with his cloak does not suggest immorality but rather symbolizes the protection of marriage (3:9). Taking off a sandal and handing it to another person formally ratified an agreement two persons had discussed (4:6,7).

Medieval woodcut by Hans Holbein the Younger illustrates Ruth gleaning in Boaz's field. Boaz is asking the foreman of his harvesters, "Whose young woman is that?" (Ruth 2:5).

RUTH: A READING AND STUDY GUIDE		
Chapter	**Content Summary**	**Related Articles**
1	Naomi's family moves to Moab in a time of famine. Her sons marry but die, and Naomi decides to return home to Israel. Ruth, one of her daughters-in-law, chooses to go with her.	Marriage Covenant Naomi
2	Ruth gathers grain in the fields of Boaz. He is kind to her, aware of her good reputation. Naomi directs her to return to Boaz's fields the next day.	Boaz Gleaning
3	Ruth asks Boaz to fulfill the role of the kinsman-redeemer and marry her.	Kinsman
4	Boaz negotiates with a nearer relative for the right to marry Ruth. He weds Ruth. Their first son becomes the grandfather of David.	

Ship

Samson

Shield

Spear

Sheep

Scribe

Scroll

Seal

Shepherd

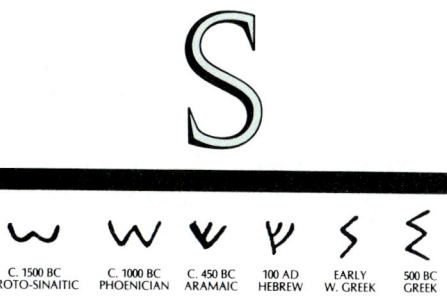

C. 1500 BC
PROTO-SINAITIC

C. 1000 BC
PHOENICIAN

C. 450 BC
ARAMAIC

100 AD
HEBREW

EARLY
W. GREEK

500 BC
GREEK

Sabbath [Heb., *shabat*; "rest," "cessation of activity"]. (1) The seventh day of the Hebrew week, a holy day set aside to honor the Lord (Ex. 20:8-11); (2) a special festival day that shared characteristics of the weekly Sabbath (Lev. 16:31; 23:24, 32,39); (3) every seventh year, during which crops were not to be planted (Lev. 25:2-6; 26:34,35,43). *See also* Feasts; Sabbath Year.

ORIGIN OF THE SABBATH

The Sabbath is modeled on the creation week's seventh day, which God blessed and made holy (Gen. 2:1-3). While some have attempted to trace the roots of the Sabbath to Babylonia's "evil days," the differences between those days and the Hebrew Sabbath are far more striking than the similarities.

On the way to Mount Sinai, Moses commanded Israel to treat the Sabbath as a holy day (Ex. 16:23). Sabbath law was later woven into the Mosaic legislation, where it is frequently repeated. The importance of this day is seen in God's command to stone a Sabbath-breaker (Num. 15:32-36) and in the prophets' exhortations to keep the Sabbath as God intended (Isa. 56:2; Jer. 17:19-27; Ezek. 44:24).

SIGNIFICANCE OF THE SABBATH

The Sabbath, which divided the 28-day Hebrew lunar month into four equal parts,

Each time a person today reads a passage in the Bible, he or she enters another world, an era when soldiers carried swords and shields, and when trading ships plied the Mediterranean. It was a time when men like Samson made strange vows and faced wild animals that now live only in Africa; when a scribe was the only copier, a scroll the only book and a seal the only authoritative signature. It was also a time when a psalmist said, "The Lord is my shepherd," when a prophet proclaimed, "We all like sheep have gone astray." Later Jesus called himself "the good shepherd who lays down his life for the sheep." In one of his most beloved parables, Jesus told of searching for one lost sheep, and after finding it, putting it on his shoulders and going home rejoicing.

had deep religious import as a memorial. As a holy day of rest, the Sabbath served to remind each generation of Israelites of their roots and their identity as God's covenant people. The Sabbath commemorated not only the seventh day of the creation week but also God's deliverance of Israel from slavery in Egypt (Deut. 5:15). The Sabbath also served as a symbol of God's covenant with Israel. As such, keeping the Sabbath was a measure of Israel's commitment to its relationship with the Lord (Ex. 31:12-17; Isa. 58:13,14).

The Hebrew people observed the Sabbath by resting from ordinary labor. Every Israelite with his slaves and even his animals was to refrain from work so that all might "be refreshed" (Ex. 23:10-12). God cared for the physical as well as the spiritual state of his people.

JESUS AND THE SABBATH

By the first century, the general prohibition against work on the Sabbath had been greatly expanded. The Mishna, a repository of Hebrew oral tradition, lists some 39 major forbidden activities: plowing, sowing, harvesting, constructing or tearing down buildings, spinning, weaving, sewing, hunting, butchering, hammering, cooking, baking, writing, making a fire or putting one out, etc. Many of these were reasonable inferences from Torah, but the tendency of Judaism to extend the Law by adding further restrictions brought Jesus into conflict with the Pharisees. By their definition, plucking a few kernels of grain to eat from a roadside stalk was work, as was healing on the Sabbath (Mt. 12:1-14; Lk. 13:10-16). Jesus answered their criticism by referring to the humanitarian aspect of Sabbath legislation. Since God created the Sabbath to provide man with rest, it clearly was "lawful to do good on the Sabbath" (Mt. 12:12). As Lord of the Sabbath (Mk. 2:28), Jesus reaffirmed its purpose as a time for spiritual and physical renewal, reclaiming it from those zealous legalists who unwit-

879

tingly shifted its focus from God to lists of detailed dos and don'ts.

SABBATH IN THE CHRISTIAN ERA

As significant as the Sabbath is in the OT, it was not retained by the church. The early Christians met on the first day of the week, the day that Jesus rose from the dead (Jn. 20:1). Other significant NT events took place on the first day as well. Six of Jesus' eight post-resurrection appearances took place on the first day. Many think the day of Pentecost, when the Holy Spirit came upon Jesus' followers, was also Sunday. Thus the first day of the week became the Christians' special day. Writing in the second century, Ignatius says Christians "have come to the possession of a new hope, no longer observing the Sabbath, but living in observance of the Lord's Day, on which also our life has sprung up again by Him and by His death." Justin Martyr, in A.D. 150, describes the church's worship "on the day called Sunday." The resurrection, so central in Christian faith, marks a great shift, not only from OT times but also from OT practices.

Even so, there are vital lessons to be learned from the Sabbath. The Christian day of worship, like the Jewish, is a day to remember what God has done for us as his people. It is not a day to load down with obligations, but a day for spiritual and physical refreshment. Both Sabbath and Sunday are invitations to rest, renewing not only ourselves but also our awareness of our personal relationship with the Lord. *See also* Rest; Sunday.

Sabbath day's journey The distance a person was allowed to walk on the Sabbath day according to Pharisaic rules (Acts 1:12).

The Exodus generation was told to gather two days' supply of manna on Friday and not to search for manna on the seventh day. "Everyone is to stay where he is on the seventh day; no one is to go out" (Ex. 16:29). Later, rabbis took this verse out of context, teaching that no person could journey away from home on the Sabbath. But what constituted a journey? The rabbis' answer was drawn from Num. 35:5, which stated that a town's pasturelands extended 3,000 feet (914 meters) beyond the town. From this, the rabbis deduced that any journey of more than 3,000 feet would take a person "out" and was therefore forbidden.

Archaeologists have found boundary stones placed outside some excavated cities in Israel marking the lawful limits of the Sabbath day's journey. *See also* Sabbath.

sabbath year A year of rest for the land, during which no new crops were to be planted. Any crops that grew spontaneously were to be made available to the poor or left for animals (Lev. 25:1-7). Also during the sabbath year, all outstanding debts were to be canceled (Deut. 15:1-18).

Despite the promise that God would cause the land to produce enough the sixth year to supply Israel for three years (Lev. 25:20-22), the sabbath year was not observed in ancient Israel (Lev. 26:35; 2 Chr. 36:21). Nehemiah insisted that sabbath-year legislation be honored in Judea after the return from Babylon (Neh. 10:31). Josephus reports that Julius Caesar did not require the Jews to pay the annual tribute due the Romans during the sabbath year, since the Jews did not plant crops or gather produce during it. Technically, seventh-year legislation still applies in modern Israel. However, Israelis have followed the practice of leasing their lands to non-Jews during the sabbath year, so that lost crops will not hurt their nation's economy. *See also* Poor.

sackbut (KJV) A harp-like musical instrument (Dan. 3:5,7,10,15). Modern versions have "lyre." *See also* Music.

sackcloth Coarse, dark clothing worn as a sign of mourning (Gen. 37:34; Ps. 35:13), earnest prayer (2 Ki. 19:1,2; Dan. 9:3), or repentance (1 Ki. 21:27; Mt. 11:21). *See also* Mourn; Repent.

sacrament A Christian rite which is believed to convey grace to the worshiper.

The word "sacrament" is not found in the Bible. Catholic and Greek Orthodox believers identify seven sacraments: baptism, confirmation, eucharist (the Lord's Supper), penance, the sacrament of the

Sackcloth was cheap material woven from goat or camel hair and commonly used to make grain bags (Gen. 42:25). Its use for garments of mourning or repentance continued into NT times (Mt. 11:21).

880

Priests make a burnt offering on the altar of the tabernacle. The head of a family brought the sacrificial animal, skinned and cut it up, after which it was burned up by the priests (Lev. 1).

sick, orders, and marriage. Reformed and Lutheran Protestants identify only baptism and the Lord's Supper as sacraments.

Catholic doctrine holds that the sacraments are a means of conveying God's grace. The sacrament operates objectively, not depending on the faith of the believer as long as his or her attitude presents no obstacle. Reformed and Lutheran Protestants believe the two sacraments they recognize serve, with the Word of God, as witnesses to Christ and his promise of forgiveness of sins. The efficacy of these two sacraments depends on the faith exercised by the believer. *See also* Memorial.

Other Protestants view the Lord's Supper and baptism as ordinances rather than sacraments; that is, these practices commanded by Christ serve as testimonies to his work for us but are not a means through which God's grace is given. *See also* Baptism; Lord's Supper.

sacred (1) Any object, person, or time that is set apart and dedicated to the sole service of God, such as Aaron's garments (Ex. 29:29), sacrifices (Lev. 22:2), religious assemblies (Lev. 23:3), etc.; (2) objects dedicated to pagan deities, such as sacred stones (2 Chr. 14:3). While OT religion identifies a number of sacred things, the NT calls only the believer, God's living temple, sacred (1 Cor. 3:17). Paul suggests that while Christians are free to consider one day more sacred than others, believers are also free not to do so (Rom. 14:5). *See also* Holy; Sanctify.

sacrifices and offerings (1) Prescribed rituals in which animals or other possessions of worshipers are presented to God in expiation of sin or as gifts expressing thanksgiving (Lev. 3:3; Num. 6:17). (2) Metaphorically, anything offered to God, as in Ps. 51:17, ''The sacrifices of God are a broken spirit; a broken and contrite heart, O God, you will not despise.''

OLD TESTAMENT

We can trace the biblical practice of making sacrifices back to God's killing of an animal to provide coverings for Adam and Eve after their sin (Gen. 3:21). Later, Cain is rebuked because in bringing fruits of the soil to offer God rather than an animal of the flock, as his brother Abel did, Cain failed to ''do what is right'' (Gen. 4:3-7). Thus, Scripture suggests that early man's practice of bringing animal sacrifices was rooted in a tradition established immediately after man's Fall. Animal sacrifices continued to be the norm, as illustrated by the offerings of Noah (Gen. 8:20,21) and Abraham and the other patriarchs (Gen. 12:8; 13:4; 26:25), long before Moses' Law was established.

The Law, however, formalized the practice, identifying a number of personal and community animal sacrifices to be made by God's covenant people. ''The life of a creature is in the blood,'' Lev. 17:11 explains, ''and I have given it to you to make atonement . . . for one's life.'' At the time the Law was given, the priesthood was established for the purpose of offering sacrifices on behalf of the Israelite community. Sacrifice, sin, and atonement are all intimately linked in the thought and theology of the OT. *See also* Atonement; Sin.

During the wilderness years and the era of the judges, sacrifices and offerings were to be made only at the tabernacle. After David established Jerusalem as Israel's capital, and particularly after Solomon's Temple was constructed there, sacrifices were to be made only at that site (Deut. 12:5,6,13,14). The symbolism affirms Israel's God as the one God and indicates that there is only one way of approach to him.

It would be wrong, however, to conclude that Israel's religion was merely a matter of ritual. The prophets thundered against a people who in effect mocked God by following the prescribed rituals while their hearts were far from him and their lives corrupt with injustice. Worship and morality, sacrifice and social concern, ritual and reality must be united or the ritual becomes meaningless. Through Isaiah, God warned a nation whose religion had deteriorated into ritual alone:

When you come to meet with me,
  who has asked this of you,
    this trampling of my courts?
Stop bringing meaningless offerings!
  Your incense is detestable to me.
New Moons, Sabbaths and convocations—
  I cannot bear your evil assemblies.
Your New Moon festivals and your appointed
  feasts my soul hates.
They have become a burden to me;
  I am weary of bearing them.
When you spread out your hands in prayer,
  I will hide my eyes from you;
even if you offer many prayers,
  I will not listen.
Your hands are full of blood;
  wash and make yourselves clean.
Take your evil deeds
  out of my sight!
Stop doing wrong,
  learn to do right!
Seek justice,
  encourage the oppressed.
Defend the cause of the fatherless
  plead the case of the widow. (Isa. 1:12-17)

With words like these, the prophets reminded Israel that sacrifices and offerings were intended as expressions of worship to God. Apart from a faith in God, exhibited by one's commitment to a godly

Stone figurine of a Mesopotamian man carrying a sacrificial lamb (Mari, 2460–2290 B.C.). During the patriarchal period, sacrifices and offerings were made by the patriarchs themselves (for example, Gen. 8:20; 12:8; 22:13; 28:18).

Facing page: Animals brought for sacrifice had to be physically perfect. They were collected for inspection in pens near the tabernacle and then on the Temple Mount.

life, the sacrifices of the OT were of no value to the individual or to God (Jer. 7:20-26; Amos 5:21-27; Mic. 6:6-8).

SACRIFICE IN THE GOSPELS

Jesus said nothing against the OT sacrifices (Lk. 5:14). He did, however, like the OT prophets, condemn ritual alone. Twice he alluded to Micah 6:6-8, which reminded Israel that God requires justice and mercy and that, without these things, even thousands of sacrifices would not please him. In each situation, Jesus challenged his critics to "go and learn what this means: 'I desire mercy, not sacrifice' " (Mt. 9:13; 12:7). God's priority is not on the ritual act but on love for God and for neighbor (Mk. 12:33,34).

At the same time, Jesus was deeply aware that the OT sacrifices symbolized the death he himself must die, fulfilling all that was implied in the deaths of the thousands of lambs whose blood bathed Jewish altars (Jn. 1:29,36).

JESUS' DEATH AS A SACRIFICE

In the NT Epistles, both Paul and the writer of Hebrews interpret Jesus' death on Calvary as the offering of a blood sacrifice (Heb. 10:1-18). Paul speaks of Christ as our Passover Lamb, calling up the image of the blood sprinkled on the Jews' doorways that freed their homes from the threat of death in Egypt (1 Cor. 5:7), and the predominance of the lamb as an offering in the OT sacrificial system. In

INDIVIDUAL SACRIFICES

Name	Elements	Procedure	Significance
Burnt offering Lev. 1; 6:8-13	Bull, ram, he-goat or male dove or young pigeon (for poor) without defect	Offerer laid hand(s) on head of the sacrifice, killed it on north side of the altar. He then cut up and washed the sacrifice. Priest poured the blood at side of the altar and burned the whole animal. The priest received the animal skin.	This voluntary offering signifies complete surrender to God. With the fellowship offering, it signifies devotion and commitment (2 Chr. 29:31-35).
Grain offering (KJV: Meat) Lev. 2; 6:14-23	Fine flour, baked bread, or crushed grain made with olive oil and salt; never any yeast or honey; incense	The food was prepared by offerer and brought to the altar. Priest burned a "memorial portion" (handful) of the offering and kept the rest as his food.	This voluntary offering accompanied most burnt and fellowship offerings.
Fellowship offering (KJV: Peace) Lev. 3; 7:11-36	Any animal without defect from herd or flock; variety of breads	Offerer laid hands on head of the sacrifice and killed it at the door to the outer tabernacle or Temple court. Priest collected the blood, threw it against the altar. Choice parts were burned. Part of the animal was given to the priest. The offerer and his family ate the rest as a communal meal.	The communal meal symbolized fellowship with God. This voluntary offering could be thanks for a blessing bestowed, a ritual expression of a vow, or a freewill offering to be brought to one of three required religious convocations.
Sin offering Lev. 4:1–5:13 6:24-30 12:6-8 14:12-14	Suitable animal without defect: • Young bull for high priest and congregation • Male goat for leader • Female goat or lamb for common person • Dove or pigeon for the poor • Tenth of an ephah of fine flour for the very poor	Offerer laid hand(s) on animal's head, then killed it on north side of the altar. Priest poured blood on horns of the altar and at its base. The choice parts were burned. The priest received what was edible, except in the case of a bull.	This mandatory offering was made by a person who sinned unintentionally or was ritually unclean. The worshiper identified himself with the sacrifice before it was killed for his atonement.
Guilt offering Lev. 5:14–6:7 7:1-6 14:12-18	Ram or lamb without defect and of proper value	Offerer first made full restoration plus one-fifth, then laid hand(s) on animal's head and killed it on north side of the altar. Priest poured the blood on the ground around the altar. Choice parts were burned. The priest received what was edible.	This mandatory offering was made when a person deprived another of his rights, as by theft or leprosy; in the latter case, God had been deprived of the leper's worship while he or she was unclean.

Elevation of the Cross by Peter Paul Rubens, part of the altar at Our Lady's Cathedral, Antwerp, Belgium. Jesus died a sacrificial death: he offered up his life to God as a substitute for all humanity (Rom. 3:23-25; Phil. 2:8).

sacrifice for sin, the NT both relies on and explains the symbolism of the OT sacrifice. Throughout human history, the death of sacrificial animals gave evidence that the forgiveness of sin requires the shedding of blood (Heb. 9:22). In OT times God accepted the death of an animal as a covering for sin. But the NT gives a fuller revelation: Jesus died a sacrificial death. He offered up his life in place of the lives of sinful human beings. God accepted that sacrifice and so offers a full pardon to all who put their trust in his Son.

Thus, Jesus in his death and resurrection fulfills the greatest prophecy of Isaiah, penned hundreds of years before Christ's birth:

It was the Lord's will to crush him and cause
him to suffer,
and though the Lord makes his life a
guilt offering,
he will see his offspring and prolong his days,
and the will of the Lord will prosper in
his hand.
After the suffering of his soul,
he will see the light of life and be
satisfied;
by his knowledge my righteous servant will
justify many,
and he will bear their iniquities.
(Isa. 53:10,11)

CHRISTIAN SELF-SACRIFICE

While the NT takes the language of sacrifice literally when applying it to Christ's death, the same language is used metaphorically when applied to Christian living. Believers are to present themselves to God as "living sacrifices" (Rom. 12:1), consecrating themselves to his service. Paul sees his approaching death as a libation—a drink offering used to enhance the odor of a burnt offering (Phil. 2:17). Even the gifts given by the Philippians to support Paul in his ministry are acceptable sacrifices, fragrant and pleasing to God because of their intent (Phil. 4:18).

We can do nothing to add to the efficacy of Christ's sacrifice of himself for us. But we can express our gratitude for his self-giving by freely giving of ourselves to him and to other members of the community of faith.

Rom. 3:25 Paul says that, by making Jesus the atoning sacrifice, God was enabled to forgive justly those who believe in his Son. Paul goes on in Rom. 5:8,9 to say that we are justified "by his blood."

Hebrews 8–10 make Scripture's definitive statement about Christ's sacrifice. The OT tabernacle and sacrificial system were "a copy and shadow" of reality (8:5). The gifts and sacrifices offered there cleansed externally but were unable to transform the worshiper or clear his conscience. Although inadequate, the blood of OT sacrifices did foreshadow the work of Christ. Christ, offering up his own life as symbolized by his blood, "obtained eternal redemption" for us. His blood is able to bring about the required transformation of the believer, bringing us not only forgiveness but inner renewal. His sacrifice was so efficacious that "once for all" Jesus was able to "do away with sin by the sacrifice of himself" (9:26). "We have been made holy through the sacrifice of the body of Jesus Christ once for all" (10:10) and through him have been guaranteed full forgiveness (10:11-18).

In interpreting the death of Jesus as a

sacrilege (KJV) (1) Taking something that has been set apart as sacred for secular or personal use (Rom. 2:22, KJV, where it translates the Greek *hierosyleō*—to "rob temples"); (2) intentional desecration of something holy or sacred (Mk. 13:14, where the RSV reads "desolating sacrilege"). *See also* Abomination of Desolation.

Sadducees [Heb., *sadiqim;* "righteous ones"]. A party or school of thought in Judaism from the second century B.C. to first century A.D. The Sadducees are mentioned by name only a dozen times in the NT, where they are portrayed as opponents of the Pharisees, who nevertheless joined them in an effort to be rid of Jesus.

Information on the Sadducees comes only from the dozen brief mentions in the NT and hostile sources: from Josephus, who admired the Pharisees; and from the Talmud, written by rabbis from the Pharisaic school of thought. Josephus says the Sadducees were the party of the well-to-do, the party of the aristocratic priesthood, who led the movement to introduce Greek ways to Judea. Certainly, a large block in the Jewish Sanhedrin was made up of Sadducees (Acts 23:6-11).

The sources agree concerning certain doctrines of the Sadducees. The Sadducees denied the possibility of life after death and scoffed at the common belief in resurrection (Mk. 12:18). They also rejected the existence of angels or spirits (Acts 23:8). The Sadducees believed in the total freedom of the human will, uninfluenced by fate or God's providence. The Sadducees held that only the five books of Moses were authoritative, and rejected the traditional interpretations of the Law so dear to the Pharisees.

No writings of the Sadducees exist. Perhaps these were suppressed by the heirs of the Pharisees, the authors of the extensive early rabbinic literature that we still have today. Without such sources, nothing certain can be said about the motives, the ideals, or the role of members of this movement.

saint [Heb., *qadosh,* "one set apart"; *hasid,* "devoted to God." Gk., *hagioi;* "holy ones"]. A person set apart to God by virtue of a personal relationship with him.

In both Testaments, "saints" are people who belong to God (Ps. 16:3; Rom. 1:7; 2 Cor. 8:4). Paul's Epistles were addressed to saints, meaning believers, in various NT cities. While the word does not necessarily imply extraordinarily holy character, there is a moral obligation implicit in any saint's personal relationship with God. This obligation is stated clearly in Eph. 5:1-3:

Be imitators of God, therefore, as dearly loved children and live a life of love, just as Christ loved us and gave himself up for us as a fragrant offering and sacrifice to God. But among you there must not be even a hint of sexual immorality, or of any kind of impurity, or of greed, because these are improper for God's holy people [saints].

In Christian history certain heroic followers of Christ, first martyrs and then others, were revered as saints. The Roman Catholic Church has developed the practice of canonization, by which the Church declares a particular individual to be a saint if his or her life meets certain specifications of holiness.

salt A common seasoning, valued in biblical times for its many uses.

Salt was vital to a people whose diet was mainly cereals and vegetables. Israelites obtained salt by evaporating the waters of the Dead Sea, which are seven times saltier than normal seawater. Salt was also mined from a great ledge of rock salt that lay in a valley nearby.

Salt was used to flavor foods, and rock salt was spread lightly on soil as a fertilizer. Salt solutions were used medicinally, as in washing a newborn infant (Ezek. 16:4). The importance of salt in NT times is illustrated by the Roman army giving a salt allowance to its officers and men. Our word "salary" is derived from that allowance, the *salarium.*

Symbolically, salt implies purity, loyalty, and either desolation or fruitfulness. As a required part of many OT sacrifices (Lev. 2:13; Ezek. 43:24), salt is associated with purity. Thus, Elisha used salt to purify a poisonous spring (2 Ki. 2:19-22). Jesus' reference to "salting with fire" is usually taken as a reference to purification (Mk. 9:49).

Salt's intimate link with loyalty is seen in many passages. Binding relationships were established by giving a gift of salt at a shared meal, a practice still observed in Arab lands. Biblical references to a "covenant of salt" (Num. 18:19; 2 Chr. 13:5) indicate a formal commitment to lifelong loyalty.

The OT also speaks of sowing the ruins of a defeated city with salt (Jdg. 9:45). Too much salt in soil makes it barren (Deut. 29:23). The act of sprinkling salt on an enemy's land was usually symbolic, cursing the site with permanent desolation.

The NT reports Jesus' announcement to his disciples, "You are the salt of the earth," and his warning that salt can "lose its saltiness" (Mt. 5:13). He was apparently referring to rock salt (rather than the purified salt obtained from evaporation), used as fertilizer. As our lives reflect our personal relationship with God the Father, we "fertilize" others, stimulating their spiritual growth, enabling them to taste and see the goodness of our God. But the rock salt of Jesus' day could lose its saltiness. Minerals were leached from it by moisture, and the salt deteriorated under high heat. Without saltiness, what remained had no value to anyone.

Salt mounds precipitate naturally on the surface of the Dead or Salt Sea, so called because of its 25-35 percent salinity level, caused solely by evaporation.

Salt Sea The Dead Sea in the southern Jordan Valley, whose waters are seven times as salty as earth's oceans (Deut. 3:17; Josh. 15:5).

Salt, Valley of A valley in the Dead Sea area where rock salt was mined. David won battles there against the Edomites (2 Sam. 8:13; *see* 2 Ki. 14:7; 2 Chr. 25:11). The exact location is uncertain. *See also* Salt.

salutation (KJV) (1) Oral greeting given when meeting another person; (2) a greeting included at the beginning of a letter (Gal. 1:3,4; 1 Pet. 1:2; 2 Jn. 3) or a closing expression (1 Cor. 16:21; Col. 4:18; 2 Th. 3:17).

Greetings in the Middle East were often highly expressive. They might include words, hugs, kisses, kissing the hand, or kneeling, depending on the status of the person being greeted and one's relationship to him or her.

Among biblical phrases used in salutation are: "God be gracious to you" (Gen. 43:29); "May my lord [the king] live forever" (1 Ki. 1:31); "Go in peace" (1 Sam. 1:17); "Greetings" (Mt. 26:49); "Peace be with you" (Lk. 24:36). These brief salutations do not reflect the lengthy string of honorifics with which the Pharisees loved to be greeted in the marketplace (Mt. 23:7).

salvation Deliverance from slavery or some great distress achieved by someone, notably God, acting on behalf of the endangered person or nation.

In the OT, nearly all 353 references to salvation (*yasha'*) are related to a concrete, historical situation, such as a natural disaster or enemy invasion. In the NT, most references to salvation (*sōtēria*) focus on God's action in Christ delivering believers from the hostile power of sin, death, and Satan. The NT's 24 uses of *sōtēr*, Savior, all refer to Jesus (16 times) or to God the Father (8 times). Common elements in the salvation passages of OT and NT include (1) human beings in danger and distress, (2) the action of a divine or human savior, which (3) wins release and changes the condition of the endangered for the better.

OLD TESTAMENT

In the OT, "save" and "salvation" are down-to-earth, not abstract, terms. Only a few passages even hint at a spiritual salvation from sin (Pss. 51:14; 79:9; Ezek. 37:23). At the same time, the OT makes it clear that God is the believer's only hope for aid (Ps. 33:16-19; Isa. 30:15; 45:22). Salvation is the direct outcome of a covenant relationship with God. *See also* Covenant.

NEW TESTAMENT

In the NT, the image of salvation explains both the spiritual condition of human beings and the meaning of Christ's incarnation. In Eph. 2:1-10, Paul analyzes each element in the concept of salvation.

• *Man's distressed state* All human beings are "dead in transgressions and sins," following "the ways of this world and of the ruler of the kingdom of the air, the spirit who is now at work in those who are disobedient." In this dreadful condition, human beings gratify "the cravings of our sinful nature . . . following its desires and thoughts." All are "by nature objects of [God's] wrath."

• *God's action as deliverer* Because God had "great love for us," he acted in Christ to save us. This action is an expression of grace, appropriated through faith, and "not from yourselves, it is the gift of God."

• *Man's new, improved situation* God's action in Christ "made us alive," and even "seated us . . . in the heavenly realms in Christ Jesus." As God's workmanship, we are now shaped to "do good works, which God prepared in advance for us to do."

Salvation then is God's work, by which he completely changes the moral condition of the believer, not only releasing him or her from sin and the prospect of facing divine wrath, but even making the believer able to do truly good works.

THREE TENSES OF SALVATION

The salvation work accomplished for us by Jesus has three dimensions. (1) According to Scripture, it is proper to speak of salvation as a historical reality. We have been saved by what God has done for us in Jesus (2 Tim. 1:9; Tit. 3:5). (2) It is also proper to speak of salvation as a present, ongoing experience. The risen Christ is actively at work in us through his Spirit, delivering us from the grip of our sin nature and enabling us to be and do good (Rom. 5:10; 6:5-14; 2 Cor. 3:18). (3) Finally, it is proper to speak of salvation as a future hope. When Jesus returns we will be perfected at last, with every hint of sin removed (Rom. 8:18-39; 1 Cor. 15:12-58).

These three tenses of salvation assure us that Christ has met all our spiritual needs. "Salvation accomplished" releases us from wrath and the dread penalty of sin. "Salvation experienced" releases us from the need to sin and enables us to live righteous lives. "Salvation expected" is our hope of resurrection to true and perfect holiness.

HUMAN ELEMENT IN SALVATION

Scripture makes it clear that the work of salvation is God's work, accomplished on our behalf by Jesus Christ. Man's part in salvation is to receive the grace given to us. This grace is received by faith alone, and faith is to be understood as an active trust in God rather than mere intellectual assent to statements about him. *See also* Atonement; Death of Christ; Resurrection; Righteousness.

Samaritan OT: (1) Inhabitant of the northern kingdom of Israel (2 Ki. 17:29, KJV); NT: (2) inhabitant of the district of Samaria, which lay between Judea and Galilee (Mt. 10:5; Lk. 9:52; Acts 8:25). *See also* IDENTIQUICK: PLACES.

When Assyria overran the Northern Kingdom in 722 B.C., much of the population was deported, and other nationalities were resettled in Israel. Sargon claimed in Assyrian annals that he carried away 27,290 from Samaria, Israel's capital, and then "the city I rebuilt—I made it greater than it was before. People of lands which I had conquered I settled therein."

The new inhabitants worshiped their own gods, but when the then-sparsely populated areas became infested with dangerous wild beasts, they appealed to the king of Assyria to send them Israelite priests to instruct them on how to worship the "god of that country." The result was a syncretistic religion, in which national groups "worshiped the Lord, but they also served their own gods in accordance with the customs of the nations from which they had been brought" (2 Ki. 17:33).

Later, in the Persian period, Samaria served as the administrative center of the district that included Judea. When a small colony of Jews returned from Babylonian captivity in 538 B.C., the Samaritans offered to help them rebuild the Temple, claiming "We seek your God and have been sacrificing to him since the time of Esarhaddon king of Assyria, who brought us here" (Ezra 4:2). The offer was rejected decisively:

The lasting hostility of the Jews toward the Samaritans only accentuated their identity. To this day a Samaritan community in Nablus (left) has maintained its own customs, scriptures, and alphabet.

The mixed race, having only a corrupt form of the true religion of Moses, had "no part" with the returned captives of Judah.

Samaritans of the NT era were so despised by the Jews that the Samaritan woman expressed surprise that Jesus would even ask her for a drink. "Jews do not associate with Samaritans," John comments (Jn. 4:9). Mutual hostility is also reflected in Lk. 9:52,53. Jesus and his disciples were not welcomed in a Samaritan village "because he was heading for Jerusalem."

The 13th-century stone mezuzah or doorpost displays, in Samaritan script, portions of Deuteronomy.

The existing attitudes add power to Jesus' story of the Good Samaritan, who showed love for his "neighbor" by stopping to help a Jew who would normally despise him (Lk. 10:25-37). *See also* Good Samaritan.

Samson [SAM-suhn; "distinguished"]. Listed among the judges, Samson possessed legendary physical strength, which was matched by his weak moral character. Despite his personal exploits, Samson failed to free his people from domination by the Philistines, 1095–1075 B.C. **Father:** Manoah. **Children:** None. **Scripture:** Jdg. 13–16.

BACKGROUND

When Samson was born, the Israelite tribes nearest the coast had been subject to the Philistines for some 40 years (Jdg. 13:1). The Philistines were also established in much of the tribal territory of Dan and Judah.

The two races intermingled, despite their enmity. The Israelite Samson could court a Philistine woman, join them at wedding festivities, and gamble over a riddle (Jdg. 14). Yet the Philistines clearly dominated. Their pressure had forced most of the tribe of Dan to move far to the north (Jdg. 18). When Samson battled the Philistines, he had no weapons but used his bare hands or snatched up the handy jawbone of a donkey (Jdg. 15:13-17). Under pressure from the Philistines, Samson's own people begged him to surrender, saying, "Don't you realize that the Philistines are rulers over us?" (15:11). Scripture and archaeology testify that this dominance was in part because the Philistines knew the secret of working iron and kept this technology from the Israelites. *See also* Iron.

This had been the situation when the angel of the Lord announced to Manoah and his wife that they would have a son, who was to be brought up as a Nazirite (a person specially dedicated to God) from birth. *See also* Nazirite.

Three dominant themes appear in the extended report of Samson's life. (1) The Spirit of God was active in Samson, the source of his amazing physical strength (Jdg. 13:25; 14:6,19; 15:14). (2) Samson's strength enabled him to perform great exploits. (3) Samson's moral weaknesses led to personal tragedy. These moral weaknesses appear constantly. Samson was enraged at a personal insult (Jdg. 14:19,20), but apparently not by the condition of his people. He violated each of the three conditions of the Nazirite vow: he touched the dead body of the lion he killed (14:8,9); he joined in a feast (a *mishteh*, a "drinking bout") before his wedding (14:10); and he let his hair be cut (16:19). Samson's uncontrolled sex drive moved him to demand a Philistine bride (14:1-4), violating the Law's prohibition against marrying pagans. His weakness for women is revealed not only in reports of his spending the night with prostitutes (16:1,2) but also in the dominating passion he had for Delilah, who gladly betrayed him for a vast sum of money (16:4-21).

With his hair cut off and his strength drained, Samson was blinded, chained, and set to do the work of an animal in Philistia. His last act, performed after his hair had grown back, was to beg God for strength to "get revenge on the Philistines for my two eyes" (16:28). As Samson pushed with all his might against the pillars that held up the Philistine temple where he stood as an object of ridicule, his strength returned. The temple collapsed, killing Samson and with him "many

more'' Philistines than he had killed during his lifetime.

LEARNING FROM SAMSON'S LIFE

Though Samson had received great gifts from the Spirit of God, he fell far short of holiness. Today, too, great spiritual gifts are not to be confused with personal holiness. Samson had amazing physical strength. Yet it was his body, dominated by sensual desire, that betrayed him. Often the very area in which a person is most gifted proves to be his or her weakness. Samson had every spiritual advantage as a child. He failed not because he lacked a godly environment, but because he chose not to respond to his parents' guidance. Likewise, people today are responsible for their own choices. Parents may influence, but do not determine, their children's successes or failures. Samson put his personal desires ahead of any concern for his people. A life lived only for self is sure to end in disappointment, if not disaster.

Samuel, First and Second Books of

Two historical books that tell the story of Israel's transition from a loose, oppressed confederation of tribes to a strong, united nation. The story is told by recounting the exploits of three men: Samuel, Israel's last judge (1063–1043 B.C.); Saul, her first, flawed king (1043–1010 B.C.); and David, the gifted and godly ruler honored as Israel's greatest king (1010–970 B.C.).

BACKGROUND AND AUTHORSHIP

The two books, originally one in the Hebrew Bible, trace the emergence of a powerful united tenth-century Hebrew kingdom from a loose collection of Israelite tribes that had grown progressively

weaker through the age of the judges. The books, which resemble the political literature of other lands dating much earlier than David, lay a firm foundation for defense of the dynasty established by the founder and his son Solomon.

Though named for the prophet Samuel, these accounts must have been written after his death, since Samuel died before David's triumphs. The text adds explanatory notes (1 Sam. 9:9) and speaks of events that affected Israel "ever since." Yet the material is generally presented in a powerful, straightforward way, often with details suggesting eyewitness reports. This has led scholars to agree that the author, whoever he was, used sources to shape his report of history, probably including "the records of Samuel the seer" (1 Chr. 29:29).

There is no agreement as to when the books were written, although some conservative scholars have argued that one or both of the prophets who served David —Nathan or Gad—may have been the author(s). Regardless of who actually wrote this account, these books graphically portray one of the most important and fas-

This bound prince, a fragment of a sculptured stone vase (2500 B.C.), evokes the image of Samson, who wore his uncut hair in seven braids and was tied up by Delilah in an attempt to subdue him (Jdg. 16).

"Samuel took the horn of oil and anointed [David] in the presence of his brothers, and from that day on the Spirit of the Lord came upon David in power" (1 Sam. 16:13). Detail of a 12th-century illuminated manuscript.

	STRUCTURE OF **1 & 2 SAMUEL**	
I.	Samuel, the last judge	1 Sam. 1–7
II.	Saul, the first king	1 Sam. 8–31
III.	David, founder of a dynasty	2 Sam. 1–24
	A. His triumphs	1–10
	B. His transgression	11
	C. His troubles	12–24

After God routed the Philistines at Mizpah, Samuel set up a memorial stone and "named it Ebenezer ['stone of help'], saying, 'Thus far the Lord has helped us'" (1 Sam. 7:12). Fresco from a third-century A.D. synagogue at Dura Europus, Syria.

1 SAMUEL: A READING AND STUDY GUIDE

Chapter	Content Summary	Related Articles
1	Childless Hannah vows to give her first child to God. Samuel is born as an answer to prayer and dedicated to serve God under Eli the priest at the tabernacle.	Hannah Vow Tabernacle
2	Hannah praises God. Eli's sons violate God's commands. A prophet warns Eli that God will judge his family.	Priest Eli
3	God calls Samuel to a prophetic ministry while he is still a child.	Prophet
4	The Philistines attack and capture the ark of God. Eli's sons are killed, and Eli dies.	Ark of the Covenant Philistines
5	The Philistines suffer plagues due to the presence of God's ark.	Plague Dagon
6	The ark is returned to Israel, but God strikes some 70 Israelites dead because they treated it disrespectfully.	
7	Some 20 years later, Samuel leads Israel in religious revival and defeats the Philistines at Mizpah.	Judge
8	In Samuel's old age, the Israelites demand a king, in order to "be like all the other nations."	King
9	God shows Samuel that he intends to make Saul, a young Benjamite, Israel's first king.	Saul
10	Samuel anoints Saul privately. Later, he is publicly made king.	Urim and Thummim Lots
11	Saul's first act is to rescue a besieged Israelite city. He is enthusiastically reaffirmed by the Israelites.	Ammonites
12	Samuel's farewell speech warns against the dangers of monarchy and emphasizes the need to obey God.	Obedience
13	Saul disobeys the prophet's instruction to wait and officiates at a sacrifice, intruding on the priest's office. Samuel confronts and rebukes him.	Sacrifices and Offerings Priest
14	Jonathan, Saul's son, leads an attack on a Philistine outpost, routing the enemy army. He unwittingly eats honey and violates a vow made by his father.	Jonathan Vow

Chapter	Content Summary	Related Articles
15	Saul disobeys a direct command of God through Samuel. God refuses to establish Saul's dynasty.	Amalekites Rebellion
16	Samuel is directed to the family of Jesse in Bethlehem, where he secretly anoints young David to become king.	David Anoint
17	David courageously defeats the giant Goliath.	
18	Saul becomes jealous of David but hides his feelings. He gives David both military command and his daughter.	Michal David
19	Saul tries to kill David, but David escapes with the help of his wife.	
20	David and Jonathan swear friendship and promise to care for each other's children. David is forced to flee.	
21	David finds food and a weapon, the sword of Goliath, at Nob. David goes to Philistia and fakes madness.	
22	Saul kills the priests who aided David.	Abiathar
23	David, joined by others, rescues the city of Keilah from the Philistines. Saul then pursues David.	
24	David spares Saul's life, and Saul temporarily turns back from pursuing him.	David
25	A wise wife, Abigail, saves her husband's property and keeps David from taking revenge.	Abigail
26	David again spares Saul's life, and the king again turns back from pursuing him.	
27	David becomes discouraged and settles briefly in the land of the Philistines.	Philistines
28	Saul, desperate because he has lost all touch with God, goes to a spiritist at Endor. Samuel's ghost appears and announces that Saul and his sons will die.	Medium
29	The Philistines, preparing for battle with Israel, will not permit David to accompany them.	
30	David's men return home to find their town razed by Amalekites. David's men pursue and rescue their families.	Amalekites
31	Saul is mortally wounded in battle with the Philistines. He commits suicide rather than permit himself to be captured.	

cinating periods of sacred history, the progression from Samuel, the last judge, through Saul to David, Israel's greatest king.

SAMUEL, THE MAN

Samuel [SAM-yoo-uhl; "name of God"] was born in answer to his mother's prayer and dedicated to serve God from early childhood (1 Sam. 1,2). Samuel, whose parents were Levites (1 Chr. 6:26,33), was called to a prophetic ministry as a child (1 Sam. 3). He was young when Israel experienced a disastrous defeat at Aphek (1 Sam. 4–6), but he later led his people to a victory at Mizpah, which halted Philistine encroachment during his lifetime (1 Sam.

7). After the military victory, Samuel was recognized as Israel's "judge," a role that incorporated military, political, judicial, and spiritual leadership. In Samuel's old age, he was pressured to appoint a king. Grudgingly, Samuel gave in and was directed by God to anoint Saul as Israel's first monarch (1 Sam. 8–11). Samuel was bitterly disappointed in Saul, who turned out to have serious personality flaws (1 Sam. 13–15). Before his death, however, Samuel was led by God to anoint the young David as Saul's successor (1 Sam. 16).

Samuel was a godly man, who never used his leadership position to enrich himself or to oppress anyone (1 Sam. 12:1-4). Yet, like his mentor Eli, Samuel was un-

2 SAMUEL: A READING AND STUDY GUIDE

Chapter	Content Summary	Related Articles
1	David hears of the death of Saul and Jonathan and laments them.	Lament
2	David is anointed king over Judah. Abner, Saul's army commander, supports one of Saul's sons in the north.	Abner
3	Abner determines to go over to David. But Abner is murdered by Joab, David's army commander.	
4	Saul's son Ish-Bosheth, David's rival, is murdered.	Murder
5	David becomes king over a united Israel. He conquers Jerusalem to serve as his capital, and defeats Philistia.	Jerusalem
6	David brings God's ark to Jerusalem, establishing it as Israel's center of worship and government.	Ark of the Covenant
7	God promises David that he will be succeeded by one of his offspring who will reign over an eternal kingdom.	Covenant Messiah
8	David's victories and several key officials are noted.	
9	David seeks out a crippled son of Jonathan to help.	Mephibosheth
10	David defeats the Ammonites.	
11	David sins with Bathsheba and plots to have her husband, Uriah, killed.	Bathsheba
12	Nathan the prophet confronts David with his sin, and the king repents.	Nathan
13	Lust and incest create hatred within David's family, a consequence of his own earlier sin. Absalom kills a brother who raped his sister, Tamar.	Absalom
14	Absalom returns from exile but is not seen by David.	
15	Absalom conspires with several of David's officials to rebel against his father, forcing David to flee for his life.	
16	Ziba comes to David's aid but lies about his master Mephibosheth. Shimei curses David.	
17	David's friends delay pursuit, enabling David to raise an army.	Ahithophel
18	In the ensuing battle, Absalom is killed against David's express orders. David mourns for his rebel son.	Mourn
19	Joab rebukes the king, who then returns to Jerusalem.	
20	Some in Israel, led by Sheba, continue the rebellion, but are put down immediately by Joab.	
21	The Gibeonites, many of whom Saul killed in violation of a treaty made by Joshua, demand the death of seven of Saul's male descendants.	
22	David records a song of praise written when he was delivered "from all his enemies."	Deliver Psalms
23	David's last words are recorded. The names of his war heroes are listed and some of their exploits recounted.	
24	At some time during his reign, David sins by counting his fighting men. His people are struck with a plague. David ends the plague by building an altar and offering sacrifices.	

able to influence his sons to imitate his own personal integrity and commitment (1 Sam. 8:3). This, plus Saul's shortcomings, discouraged Samuel during his declining years.

THEOLOGICAL CONTRIBUTIONS

The major contribution of 1 and 2 Samuel is historical. Yet 1 Samuel reports the establishment of the Davidic covenant, God's promise to David that one of his descendants would rule an eternal kingdom. This covenant promise has been, and will be, fulfilled in Jesus Christ, a biological descendant of David through his mother Mary as well as a legal descendant through her husband, Joseph.

MASTERY KEYS

Aside from these books' historical value in describing the roots of the Hebrew kingdom, many insights can be gained from a study of the lives of Samuel, Saul, and David. There are no more powerful warnings in Scripture against jealousy than the image of Saul persecuting David, no more powerful warning against lust than the tragedy of David's affair with Bathsheba, no more encouraging reminder of the power of forgiveness than we see in David's confession of his sin (see Ps. 51). To master the spiritual message of 1 and 2 Samuel, read them not just as history but as a true, personal story—through which God speaks to every heart.

SPECIAL FEATURES

Who really killed Goliath—David (1 Sam. 17) or Elhanan (2 Sam. 21:19)? The answer is found in 1 Chr. 20:5. Elhanan killed the brother of Goliath. "Brother" was apparently lost in transmission of the text.

What about the witch of Endor (1 Sam. 28)? Did this person (Heb., 'ob; "medium" or "spiritist") actually have power to bring Samuel up from the grave? No, the text makes it clear that the woman was astonished when the real Samuel appeared and spoke to King Saul (v.12).

sanctify, sanctification To make holy, to set apart. In OT Israel, people were to "sanctify themselves" before taking part in worship (Lev. 11:44) and before special encounters with God (Ex. 19:22; Josh. 3:5). Scripture speaks of sanctifying ("consecrating" or "making holy") priests (Lev. 22:31,32), the firstborn (Ex. 13:2), the Temple (2 Chr. 29:5), the Sabbath (Gen. 2:3; Deut. 5:12), the altar (Ex. 29:37), and the anointing oil used in worship (Lev. 8:10). All these were "set apart" in some way, dedicated to the service of God. The message conveyed by the strict separation of the secular and the sacred was clear: God is unique, and his people must commit themselves fully and only to him.

New Testament sanctification is distinctly different. Rather than a strict separation of secular and sacred, "sanctify" now pictures God's invasion of the secular. Through Jesus, ordinary human beings are set apart to serve God in their daily lives. Christ, alive in his people in every situation, enables believers to glorify God by living their lives in a Christ-like way.

Several NT passages help clarify the sanctification of believers. Sanctification is made possible by the blood that Christ shed (Heb. 10:29). In one sense, all believers have been sanctified through Christ and are set apart to God for holiness (Acts 20:32; 26:18; Rom. 15:16; 1 Cor. 6:11). In another sense, each is to have a growing experience of sanctification, actually becoming holy in what he or she says and does (Jn. 17:17; 2 Cor. 3:18; 1 Th. 5:23). Thus in the NT, "sanctification" is a powerful word of hope, assuring believers that a truly good life has now become possible.

The NT also offers this promise: We will experience sanctification "through the sanctifying work of the Spirit" (2 Th. 2:13; 1 Pet. 1:2) and through God's Word (Jn. 17:17). As we rely on the Spirit of God and obey the Word which God has spoken, the Lord will help us become the kind of person he wants each of us to be.

Only one NT verse refers to an unbeliever as sanctified (1 Cor. 7:14). An unbelieving spouse is "set apart" by the believing partner—perhaps "set apart" in the sense of being brought into contact with the holy.

SANCTIFICATION IN THEOLOGY

Christians have disagreed on just how sanctification is worked out in personal experience.

One tradition holds that sanctification involves complete freedom from sin in this life, and is accompanied by a perfect love for God. ("Sin" here is understood in a limited sense, as the conscious choice of known wrong.) However, the "perfection" that this tradition teaches is not a release from human imperfections or ignorance—even the most spiritual person can make mistakes.

In other traditions, sanctification is understood more in terms of a struggle between the sin so deeply rooted in human nature and the new nature given by God. The promise of sanctification is not one of complete release on earth, but rather a promise that, despite sin's powerful pull, the Holy Spirit enables the believer to choose the good. Through a series of such choices, the believer can grow to be more like Christ.

Despite these differences, Christians agree that God calls us to live holy lives, and together we believe in the exciting

893

Sea defenses built by Herod the Great once towered over this stretch of sand at Ashkelon. God promised to make Abraham's descendants "like the sand of the sea, which cannot be counted" (Gen. 31:12).

Below left: A Greek sandalmaker sits at a bench surrounded by tools and unfinished footwear. Sandals were the common footwear in biblical times, though laced and strapped boots were worn by soldiers.
Below right: These leather sandals were among the remains of the Jewish Zealot occupation of the fortress of Masada (A.D. 73).

prospects of personal transformation now and ultimate transformation at the resurrection (2 Cor. 3:18; *see* 1 Cor. 15:35-57). *See also* Holy; Resurrection.

sanctuary A holy place, which God's people set apart to meet with and worship God. In the Bible, the term most often refers to Israel's tabernacle or Temple. The writer of the Epistle to the Hebrews says that the earthly sanctuary copies or reflects heavenly realities (Heb. 8:5). *See also* Tabernacle; Temple.

sand Fine particles of stone. Sand was an impressive reality in the Middle East, flung along the Mediterranean coast and spread endlessly throughout the vast deserts. Thus, sand serves appropriately as a metaphor for a great quantity, as in God's promise to the patriarchs, "Your descendants [will be] like the sand of the sea, which cannot be counted" (Gen. 32:12; *see* Heb. 11:12), and in David's praise of God's thoughts, which "outnumber the grains of sand" (Ps. 139:18). Jesus referred to another characteristic of sand, instability, when he warned against building one's house on sand rather than on solid rock (Mt. 7:24-27).

sandal Footwear; a type of shoe worn throughout the biblical period, consisting of wood, leather, or fiber soles held in

place by leather thongs. The sandals of the wealthy often had heel caps or sides that came up over the arch of the foot. Because sandals were largely or partially open to the dust, guests entering a house customarily removed them and received a foot bath. *See also* Footwashing.

The Bible mentions several customs and symbols associated with sandals. In the time of the judges, an agreement was formalized when one party took off a sandal and handed it to the other (Ruth 4:7,8). References to tossing a sandal upon Edom in Pss. 60:8 and 108:9 suggest Edom will become a servant of Israel (*see* Mt. 3:11). Finally, the unconcern of the rich for the poor in Amos's time is symbolized by their readiness to sell a debtor into servitude for no more money than it would take to buy a pair of luxury sandals (Amos 2:6; 8:6).

Sanhedrin (1) The council of 71 members that had supreme executive, legislative, and judicial power over the Jewish faith and life-style, within limits imposed by Rome. Jesus, Peter, John, Stephen, and Paul all appeared before this council (Mt. 26:59; Mk. 14:55; Acts 4:15; 5:21; 6:12; 22:30). (2) A lower court or local council of from 7 to 23 members (Mt. 5:22; Mk. 13:9).

Tradition roots the Sanhedrin in the body of 70 elders appointed by Moses (Num. 11:16-25), a council supposedly reconstituted by Ezra after the Exile. A group of elders did function under the Seleucid Empire (198–167 B.C.) and played a significant role after the Maccabean revolt (167 B.C.). Julius Caesar confirmed the power of the Sanhedrin over all Judea. Though this power was limited during the rule of Herod the Great (37–4 B.C.), under Roman procurators (A.D. 6–66) the Sanhedrin functioned as the internal government of Judea. The Romans, of course, had the right to override any action taken by the Sanhedrin. In particular, Rome retained the sole right to impose the death penalty, but did in some cases, such as sacrilege, allow local bodies to carry out the death penalty.

Most believe that the Sanhedrin was originally dominated by the Sadducees, a group usually equated with the chief priests and wealthy nobility. However, about 75 years before Christ's birth, Pharisees and scribes were added to the council. Their influence was encouraged by Herod, who wanted to counter his rivals in the aristocracy. At the time of Jesus' trial and the early church period, the Sanhedrin was composed of both Pharisees and Sadducees, with the high priest serving as president of the body (*see* Acts 23:2).

In view of what is known of the rather strict procedures to be followed when the Sanhedrin tried capital cases, many writers have concluded that the trial of Jesus was conducted illegally. *See also* Sadducees; Trial of Jesus.

sapphire *See* Breastplate.

Sarah [SAIR-uh; "princess"]. The half-sister and wife of Abraham who gave birth to Isaac in her old age, 2100 B.C. Sarah is commended several times in later OT and NT texts. **Scripture:** Gen. 12–23.

BACKGROUND

Sarah accompanied her husband, Abraham, when he set out from his homeland for Canaan in response to God's call. And when famine struck Canaan, she traveled with him to Egypt. Because of her beauty, Abraham feared the Egyptians might kill him and take her into the Pharaoh's harem. He asked her to pretend to be his sister; she went along with it. They tried the same ruse years later in another land.

Each time God had to intervene to protect her (Gen. 12:10-20; 20:1-18).

Sarah suffered greatly because she was childless. Despairing of ever having children, she urged Abraham to take her servant Hagar as a secondary wife. According to ancient custom, the child Hagar bore would be considered Sarah's. But when Hagar conceived, she showed contempt for Sarah, stimulating her embittered mistress to treat her harshly. *See also* Hagar.

However, God repeated his promise that Abraham would have a son by Sarah (Gen. 17:15,16). He even changed her name from "Sarai" to "Sarah" as a sign of this promise.

At age 90, Sarah choked back a laugh when she overheard an angel of the Lord promise Abraham she would bear a child within the year (Gen. 18:1-15). Rebuked by the angel, Sarah denied laughing, but within a year she did give birth to a son, Isaac. *See also* Isaac.

The hostility between Hagar and Sarah grew, and Sarah urged Abraham to expel both Hagar and her son, Ishmael. This violated the clearly defined cultural standards of morality. But in this case, God himself told Abraham to listen to his wife and promised he would care for Abraham's older son. *See also* Ishmael.

Sarah died at age 127 and was buried with great ceremony in a cave at Machpelah, where Abraham's body was later laid.

LEARNING FROM SARAH'S LIFE

Sarah's barrenness seems to have made her a bitter and vindictive woman. Tradition demanded that she "bear children" for Abraham by her maid Hagar. But she found no satisfaction in Hagar's pregnancy, which proved Abraham's potency

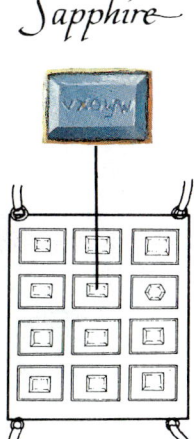

Sapphire

When the OT speaks of the sapphire, it is probably the deep-blue lapis lazuli that is meant.

Interior of the rock-cut tombs of some members of the Sanhedrin, the ruling council of Jews in NT times. Jesus was buried in a tomb donated by a prominent council member, Joseph of Arimathea.

Gypsum statues of a Mesopotamian man and woman (Tell Asmar, 2700–2500 B.C.). Sarah shared Abraham's journey to the land of Canaan, and in the Lord's promise of many descendants.

and suggested their childlessness was Sarah's fault. Furthermore, Sarah was hardly a gracious mistress. She treated the provocative Hagar harshly and later urged Abraham to expel Hagar and her child. Yet for all her faults, Sarah is held up as an example of faith in Isa. 51:2 and Heb. 11:11 and commended in 1 Pet. 3:6 as a model of those who "do what is right and do not give way to fear."

The apparent contrast between the Sarah we meet in Genesis and the Sarah portrayed by later writers serves as a reminder. Genesis shows us a Sarah under stress, not the Sarah who was Abraham's faithful wife for a century. We know little of this Sarah, and even less of her daily relationship with God. The fact that Scripture commends rather than censures her suggests that Sarah had more positive qualities than we might suspect.

sardonyx A red and white stone, used by the Romans in signet rings. The sardonyx appears only in Rev. 21:20. Some take the stone to be onyx (RSV) or agate (JB). *See also* Jewels and Precious Stones.

Satan [SAY-tuhn; "adversary"]. The powerful angelic being portrayed in Scripture as the determined enemy of God and of human beings. While Satan has great in-

fluence, he, a created being, is in no way equal to God.

OLD TESTAMENT

Satan is introduced in Gen. 3, where through a serpent he successfully tempts Eve to disobey God, thus corrupting the human race. He appears again in Job 1, which suggests his ability to supernaturally influence events on earth. Satan also is seen as a personal being in 1 Chr. 21:1 and Zech. 3:1,2.

Some commentators believe Satan is the object of Isa. 14:12-15, which describes the fall from heaven of a proud ruler determined to "raise [his] throne above all the stars of God." The same commentators also see Satan in Ezek. 28:11-19, where the focus shifts from a "ruler" of Tyre to a "king" described as a "model of perfection" until "wickedness was found in [him]." The text describes this individual as "a guardian cherub" who was "on the holy mount of God" until pride led to sin. According to one view, these passages explain Satan's origin as a highly ranked angel, whose sin introduced evil into the universe and made him an implacable enemy of God and a malicious adversary of God's people.

NEW TESTAMENT

The NT has much more to say about Satan, who is mentioned by this name 36 times and referred to as the devil (*diabolos*, "slanderer") 33 more. The NT also has other names and descriptive phrases for Satan:

- "accuser of our brothers" (Rev. 12:10)
- "that ancient serpent" (Rev. 12:9)
- Abaddon ("destroyer" Rev. 9:11)
- Apollyon ("destroyer" Rev. 9:11)
- Beelzebub (Mt. 12:24)
- Belial (2 Cor. 6:15)
- "your enemy" (1 Pet. 5:8)
- "the evil one" (Mt. 13:19)
- "the father of lies" (Jn. 8:44)
- "the god of this age" (2 Cor. 4:4)
- "the great dragon" (Rev. 12:9)
- "a murderer" (Jn. 8:44)
- "the one who leads the whole world astray" (Rev. 12:9)
- "prince of this world" (Jn. 12:31)
- "ruler of the kingdom of the air" (Eph. 2:2)
- "the spirit at work in those who are disobedient" (Eph. 2:2)
- "the tempter" (Mt. 4:3)

Together, NT passages provide a grim picture of Satan's character and activities.

Satan is portrayed as one who shapes the *kosmos*, the world's system of thought and values. He induces mankind to follow the sinful passions of corrupted human nature, causing people to believe lies and blinding their minds to the light of the Gospel. Satan also stimulates active opposition to God's work in the world by directly attacking Christians and stirring up persecution. Satan even worked through Judas's natural inclinations to encourage his betrayal of Christ.

While Satan is a single individual, he has the allegiance of other spirit beings who joined him in his rebellion against God. Many believe the demons of the Gospels are these fallen angels. *See also* Angel; Demon.

SATAN AND CHRIST

Satan is a created being; Christ is God. Satan's rebellion may be permitted temporarily, but as a created being, he has limited powers, and his doom is certain. The NT states that Christ came into the world "to destroy [render inoperative] the devil's work" (1 Jn. 3:8). Christ demonstrated his superiority by resisting Satan's temptations (Mt. 4:1-11; Lk. 4:1-13) and by casting out demons (Mk. 3:22-27). By his death and resurrection, Christ shattered the power of Satan over mankind (Col. 2:14,15; Heb. 2:14,15). While Satan continues to be active in human affairs, Christians are encouraged to "resist the devil, and he will flee from you" (Jas. 4:7; *see* 1 Pet. 5:8,9; Eph. 4:25-27). We are reminded that "the one who is in you is greater than the one who is in the world" (1 Jn. 4:4). While believers are to take Satan seriously, Christians are not to fear the evil one but to place complete trust in Jesus Christ.

SATAN'S DOOM

While the origin of Satan may be shrouded in uncertainty, his ultimate doom is clearly predicted. Jesus spoke of Satan's eventual defeat (Lk. 10:18) and described "eternal fire" that has been prepared for the devil and his angels (Mt. 25:41). Revelation speaks of a time at history's end during which Satan will be bound for a thousand years, then briefly loosed, and finally cast into a "lake of burning sulfur" to be "tormented day and night for ever and ever" (Rev. 20:7-10).

Temptation of Christ by Duccio di Buoninsegna portrays the common medieval image of Satan. Jesus responds, "Away from me, Satan!" (Mt. 4:10).

While some object to the doctrine of a personal devil, Scripture unhesitatingly affirms his existence. Yet while Satan's powers are great, Scripture never permits us to blame this malignant being for our own failures or sins. Satan cannot make us act against our will.

satrap The title of a governor of a province or a district in the Persian Empire (Esth. 3:12; Dan. 6:1).

satyr (KJV) A goat, goat idol, or goat demon (Lev. 17:7; 2 Chr. 11:15; Isa. 13:21). In Greek mythology, a creature that was half man, half goat. The Israelites were warned not to worship such beings.

Saul [SAWL; "asked of God"]. The first, flawed king of Israel, whose failure to trust and obey God led to his replacement by David, 1050–1010 B.C. **Father:** Kish. **Wives:** Ahinoam, Rizpah. **Children:** Jonathan, Malki-Shua, Abinadab, Esh-Baal (Ish-Bosheth), Armoni, Mephibosheth, Merab, Michal. **Scripture:** 1 Sam. 9–31.

BACKGROUND

For centuries Israel had been little more than a loose association of separate tribes, oppressed by a series of foreign enemies. Now the tribes held only a fraction of the Promised Land. The Ammonites threatened from across the Jordan and the Philistines, who controlled the Mediterranean coast, were so dominant that they had established an outpost within the Jordan Valley. The Philistine dominance was technological as well as military: They had the secret of smelting iron. Israelites had no iron weapons; they even had to go to the Philistines to have iron farm implements sharpened (1 Sam. 13:19-22). Frustrated by this situation, the people of Israel demanded that Samuel, the last of the OT judges, set up a monarchy—and God led Samuel to the tall, young Benjamite, Saul. *See also* King; Philistines.

The servants and herds of donkeys in 1 Sam. 9 mark Saul's family as wealthy. Yet they would have been influential only within the small tribe of Benjamin. Saul himself, though handsome and tall, was unassuming. He had no political plans when he met Samuel and was anointed king. *See also* Anoint; Samuel.

EFFECTS OF SAUL'S RULE

Saul was little more than a war-chief recognized by Israel's twelve tribes. He led his people to victories over their major enemies, but Saul failed to break the Philistines' monopoly on iron and failed to unify the tribes politically. His capacity for organization seems limited to setting up three core groups of 1,000 warriors each, and he depended on a militia drawn from the people when war threatened. While Saul put down pagan practices in Israel, he led no spiritual revival. His own flawed relationship with God prevented him from having a greater impact on his people.

SAUL'S SPIRITUAL JOURNEY

Saul began well. As Saul journeyed home after being anointed, the Spirit of the Lord "came upon" him (1 Sam. 10:6). In the OT, this phrase indicates a special endowment of power to accomplish a task assigned by God. Saul responded well to his first challenge as king. He led Israel to victory over the Ammonites and explicitly credited God with the triumph.

Soon, however, Saul's flaws were revealed. Three incidents are significant:

1. *1 Sam. 13.* When a major Philistine army invaded Israel's holdings, Saul was told by Samuel to wait until the old prophet came to offer sacrifice. But as Saul watched his citizen-army desert day by day, he grew impatient. In disobedience, he offered the sacrifice himself. In Israel prophets spoke for God: To disobey Samuel was to disobey God. And OT Law forbade anyone but a priest from offering sacrifice. Saul could not see beyond the enemy; he had no clear vision of God or God's power to deliver. His unbelief was expressed in disobedience.

2. *1 Sam. 15.* Samuel conveyed God's command to utterly destroy another enemy, the Amalekites. Saul led the expedition but spared both king and cattle. Saul's

A jealous and disturbed King Saul prepares to hurl his spear at David, the object of his envy (1 Sam. 18:6-11); detail from a 13th-century French illumination.

first excuse (the cattle were to be an offering to God) led to Samuel's famous reply: "To obey is better than sacrifice." At last Saul admitted the truth: "I was afraid of the people and gave in to them." Saul no longer led but followed. Having lost sight of God, Saul completely lost his bearings.

The next chapters report God's withdrawal of special empowerment and Saul's bouts with depression (1 Sam. 16:14-23). A young David was introduced in Saul's court to soothe the king with harp music. But when David killed Goliath and won the admiration of Saul's people, the king became jealous (1 Sam. 17–19). As David performed other exploits and demonstrated leadership qualities, Saul's jealousy turned to fear. Soon the hostile and guilt-ridden king determined to take David's life. Many incidents, such as casting his spear at his own son and the execution of priests who had unknowingly helped David escape him (1 Sam. 21,22), reveal how far Saul had strayed from his early promise. The willful choice to disobey God makes us vulnerable to our baser passions.

3. *1 Sam. 28.* At the end of Saul's 42-year reign, the Philistines gathered an army to invade Israelite territory. A terrified Saul begged for divine guidance but received no word from the Lord. Finally, he crept in disguise to a spiritist, one whose occult practices the king himself had banned. Both were stunned when the now-dead Samuel appeared, announcing that Saul would surely die and Israel would be defeated in the coming battle. This last desperate act of disobedience sums up Saul's career. When the king turned his back on the Lord, he set out on a road leading to personal and national disaster.

LEARNING FROM SAUL'S LIFE

Saul stands as a warning and example to believers of every age. The tests Saul failed remind us: (1) God is greater than our circumstances. We need to remain aware of his great power and respond to him rather than to obstacles in our situation. (2) God's opinion, not the opinion of others, should be most important to us. Fear of others must not keep us from being obedient. (3) When God is silent we must wait, rather than seek aid from other sources.

We can also profit by a study of Saul's relationships with three persons: Samuel, Jonathan, and David. What flaws are revealed by his responses to each? What responses should Saul have made in each situation?

Saul is graphically portrayed in Scripture not to frighten us, but to encourage. By studying Saul's life, we can learn how to avoid Saul's failures by responding properly to God in difficult situations. When we obey God, we can trust God to preserve us from the tragic fate of this flawed king. *See also* David; Jonathan.

Detail of The Suicide of Saul *by Pieter Bruegel (A.D. 1562). Saul and three of his sons died the day the Philistines soundly defeated the Israelites on Mount Gilboa (1 Sam. 31).*

Savior One who delivers another from some physical or spiritual plight. The OT portrays God as Israel's Savior from foreign enemies. In such expressions as "God our Savior" (Ps. 65:5), "savior" is not so much a name as a descriptive term, stressing that God is one who intervenes with saving acts.

In the NT, "Savior" is applied to the Father (1 Tim. 1:1; Tit. 1:3), but more often

refers to Jesus (Jn. 4:42; Phil. 3:20; Tit. 3:6). In his death and resurrection, Jesus became "the Savior of the world" (1 Jn. 4:14). His saving act rescues all who believe from every consequence of sin. *See also* Salvation.

savor (KJV) As a noun, a pleasant aroma or taste (Gen. 8:21; 2 Cor. 2:14,15). As a verb, to enjoy such a sensation.

saw A tool with a notched blade used to cut wood or stone (1 Ki. 7:9; Isa. 10:15). The Egyptians used bronze saws with an abrasive compound to cut granite.

Saws in ancient times cut only when the blade was pulled through an object, not in both directions. Carpenters used small handsaws with pistol grip handles, and often held the object being sawed between their toes.

The saw also served as an instrument of torture (Heb. 11:37). Tradition reports that Isaiah was executed by being sawn in two.

scales (1) The thin, horny overlapping plates that cover the bodies of many fish and some reptiles (Lev. 11:9-12). "Something like scales" fell from the eyes of the apostle Paul when he was healed of the blindness that struck him on the road to Damascus (Acts 9:18). "Scale armor" was made by sewing small, scale-like metal plates to a garment (1 Sam. 17:5). *See also* Armor. (2) Balances used in weighing money, grain, or other commodities (Isa. 46:6; Rev. 6:5). Old Testament Law demands, "Use honest scales and honest weights" (Lev. 19:36). Yet the Israelites frequently resorted to "cheating with dishonest scales" (Amos 8:5), and were rebuked regularly by the prophets. (3) As a verb, "scale" means to climb up or over. David cries, "With my God I can scale a wall" (Ps. 18:29). The usual image is military, of soldiers assaulting and climbing the stone walls of a city under attack.

scapegoat A goat released in the wilderness on the Day of Atonement, symbolically carrying the guilt of God's covenant people away from the faith community.

Mentioned only in Lev. 16, the scapegoat was one of a pair; the other was killed as a sacrifice. In a similar ceremony, a recovered leper released a bird, which symbolically carried away his disease, before he was pronounced ritually clean (Lev. 14:1-7).

scarlet A bright red color, derived from the bodies of worms which infest the holly plant. The shades of this color vary widely and could not be controlled in ancient dyeing. Because of this, it is impossible to distinguish accurately between scarlet and crimson as these terms are used in Scripture.

Isaiah uses the two in parallel form: "Though your sins are like scarlet, they shall be as white as snow; though they are red as crimson, they shall be like wool" (Isa. 1:18).

Scarlet appears to be one of three primary colors (with blue and purple) in the furnishing of Israel's tabernacle (Ex. 25:4). These were royal colors. In irony, the soldiers dressed Jesus in the scarlet robe of a king (Mt. 27:28).

Scarlet garments were generally expensive and thus well-made. That is why the good wife and mother can relax when it snows: The scarlet clothing of her children will keep them warm (Prov. 31:21; see 2 Sam. 1:24).

When Rahab hung a scarlet cord from the window of her Jericho home, it served the same function as the blood of the Passover lamb: God's destruction bypassed her. The color was probably chosen because its brightness would be visible to the attacking Israelites, but early church scholars saw it as a picture of Christ's saving blood. *See also* Crimson.

Above: Fourth-century A.D. stone statue of the Good Shepherd. This was a popular image in the early church for Jesus as Savior, the one who laid down his life for the sheep (Jn. 10:11-18).

Right: Once a year the high priest, representing the whole nation, symbolically placed the people's sins on a male goat. Burdened with these sins, the scapegoat was sent into the desert (Lev. 16).

Below: Ashurnasirpal watches as tribute paid to him is weighed on a pair of scales; detail from the so-called Bassam Obelisk (Nimrud, 865 B.C.).

scepter A short staff or rod carried by kings and other leaders as symbols of authority (Ezek. 19:11). The symbolism of an "iron scepter," or "rod of iron," suggests complete domination (Ps. 2:9; *see* Rev. 2:27; 12:5; 19:15). The scepter is a messianic symbol in Gen. 49:10 and Num. 24:17, picked up in Heb. 1:8. In contrast, the fragile reed (Gk., *kalamos*) given Jesus by the soldiers who ridiculed him after his trial mocked the royalty of this supposed "King of the Jews" (Mt. 27:29).

schemes Plans. In Scripture, the meaning is always negative, an effort to gain some personal objective in an underhanded or dishonest way. The NT characterizes Satan as scheming, using two Greek words: *noēma*, "thoughts and purposes" (2 Cor. 2:11), and *methodeia*, "craftiness" (Eph. 6:11). Each of these passages warns and encourages the believer. Christians have the mind of Christ, and thus the ability to recognize Satan's thoughts and purposes. And we have the armor of God to protect us from the devil's crafty attacks (Eph. 6:10,11).

school A place of instruction. The first schools may have been established in Sumeria, where as early as 2500 B.C. scribes were trained. Archaeologists have found word lists, bilingual dictionaries, and fragments containing students' writing exercises in Ur and other early Mesopotamian cities. For the role of schools in Hebrew culture, *see* Education.

Acts 19:9 (KJV and NASB) refers to Paul's teaching in the school of Tyrannus in Ephesus, and according to one Greek text he lectured there from 11 A.M. to 4 P.M. each day. Other versions speak of it as a lecture hall. Probably it was used for secular instruction in the cooler morning hours, but was available later for Paul's use.

schoolmaster (KJV) A slave assigned to supervise an under-age child. In Gal. 3:24,25, Paul says that the Law had this role in the OT era, but now that Christ has come the believer has the position of an older son, who is directly responsible to his father. Instead of schoolmaster, other versions use custodian (RSV), guardian (JB) or tutor (NEB). The NIV translates the word as "put in charge." *See also* Law.

scoff To mock, deride. A "scoffer," however, is not just one who occasionally teases, but is an arrogant person, hard-

ened against God and his revelation, ever willing to ridicule the Lord and the godly. Scoffers "follow their own evil desires" and "deliberately forget" the lessons God has communicated to humankind in his mighty acts and by his Word (2 Pet. 3:3,5).

scorn An English word used to translate Hebrew and Greek terms with a wide variety of meanings: "to laugh," "to treat with contempt," "to treat as a fool," "to reproach by blaming," "to ridicule," "to mock," "to show disrespect," "to verbally abuse." While the connotation is usually negative, Heb. 12:2 turns it around: Jesus "endured the cross, scorning its shame." That is, he thought little of it—it could not compare to "the joy set before him." *See also* Contempt; Despise.

scorpion An arachnid whose curved tail is tipped with a poisonous barb. A dozen varieties of scorpions are found in Palestine. While the sting of a scorpion is painful, it is not fatal to a healthy human. Symbolically, scorpions stand for something that is painful or to be feared (1 Ki. 12:11; Rev. 9:3,5).

Left: Hollow copper scepters found at Nahal Mishmar, a cave in the Judean desert (4th millennium B.C.). Above: Drawing copied from the tomb of Tutankhamen shows this pharaoh holding the crook and the flail, the royal scepters of Egypt and symbols of the authority granted by the god Osiris.

In Scripture the scorpion is a symbol of danger (Deut. 8:15; Ezek. 2:6) and punishment (1 Chr. 10:11, 14; Rev. 9:3, 10).

scourge To beat, whip, or flog. The image is often a metaphor for divine punishment (Isa. 10:26 KJV, RSV). *See also* Whip.

scribe (1) A person employed in composing or recording private, public, and religious documents (2 Ki. 22:8; 1 Chr. 24:6; Jer. 32:12). (2) After the Exile and in the NT, one who is dedicated to the study and teaching of the Scriptures (Neh. 8:1; *see* Ezra 7:10).

As professional students of the Law, the scribes were responsible for preserving various legal decisions applying the Mosaic Code, and thus were responsible for the "traditions of men" that Jesus criticized (Mk. 7:6-9). Yet the scribes as a class served an important function in carefully preserving and transmitting the OT text itself, and in applying the OT Scriptures to the lives of Jewish believers.

As teachers of the Law, scribes instructed groups of students, apprentices who were expected to master what was taught and to transmit it in exact form to the next generation. By NT times, members of every social class, from the priests to merchants to tentmakers and even day laborers, might study and become recognized as experts in God's Law.

The apocryphal book of Ecclesiasticus, dating from the period between OT and NT, praises the scribe in these famous verses:

If the great Lord is willing,
*   he will be filled with the spirit of*
*   understanding;*
he will pour forth words of wisdom
*   and give thanks to the Lord in prayer.*
He will direct his counsel and knowledge
*   aright,*
*   and meditate on his secrets.*
He will reveal instruction in his teaching,
*   and will glory in the law of the*
*   Lord's covenant.*
Many will praise his understanding,
*   and it will never be blotted out;*
his memory will not disappear,
*   and his name will live through all*
*   generations.*
Nations will declare his wisdom,
*   and the congregation will proclaim his*
*   praise;*
if he lives long, he will leave a name
*   greater than a thousand,*
and if he goes to rest, it is enough for him.
(Ecclesiasticus 39:6-11)

Scribes also served on the Sanhedrin, which administered justice in Judea. Josephus suggests that the scribes sided with the Pharisees, although the two groups were distinct from each other. But the phrase "scribes of the Pharisees" (Acts

23:9 RSV), implies that certain scribes were associated with various Jewish parties. *See also* Disciple; Pharisees; Rabbi; Sanhedrin.

Scripture [Gk., *gramma*, "document"; *graphē*, "writings"]. The Law (Rom. 4:3); the body of Moses' writings (Jn. 5:39); or the entire collection of sacred writings (2 Tim. 3:16). Peter indicates that the writings of the apostle Paul were quickly accepted in the early church as equal to "the other Scriptures" (2 Pet. 3:16).

In most cases the phrase "the Scriptures" in the NT refers to the OT. Both Testaments consistently reflect the conviction expressed in 2 Tim. 3:16 that "all Scripture is God-breathed." *See also* Bible; Inspiration.

scroll A document, written on a strip of treated leather or papyrus, which was stored by being rolled up on a pair of rods. The Book of Isaiah found among the Dead Sea Scrolls was recorded on a scroll 24 feet (7.4 meters) long and 10 inches (25.4 centimeters) wide, consisting of 17 pieces of skin sewn together. Documents were not arranged in page (codex) form until after the NT era. *See also* Book; Papyrus.

King Jehoiakim was so offended by Jeremiah's prophecy that he sliced one of the prophet's scrolls with a knife and threw the pieces in the fire (Jer. 36). Ezekiel was told to eat a scroll, which "tasted as sweet as honey" (Ezek. 3:1-3). And as Jesus stood before his hometown synagogue, he unrolled the scroll of Isaiah and read from chapter 61 (Lk. 4:16-21).

sea (1) A large body of water (Gen. 9:2; Josh. 1:4); (2) in prophecy, sometimes a symbol for the mass of humanity (Dan. 7:2; Rev. 13:1). Figuratively, the turbulent waters of the sea suggest uncertainty and insecurity (Jas. 1:6). Isaiah says the wicked are "like the tossing sea, which cannot rest, whose waves cast up mire and mud. There is no peace . . . for the wicked" (Isa. 57:20,21).

Four major seas are mentioned in Scripture: (1) The Red Sea (1 Ki. 9:26). In Exodus, the "Red Sea" is literally the "Sea of Reeds," probably a large lake lying along the route of the Exodus. (2) The Mediterranean Sea, though it is not named as such in Scripture. It is called the Great Sea, the Western Sea, and the Sea of the Philistines (Josh. 23:4; Deut. 34:2; *see* Ex. 23:31). (3) The Dead Sea, a lake with no outlet lying in Palestine's rift valley, also called the "Salt Sea" (Num. 34:12) or the "Sea of the Arabah" (Deut. 3:17). (4) The

Sea of Galilee, a large freshwater lake (Mk. 1:16). This body of water is also called the Sea of Tiberius and the Sea (or Lake) of Kinnereth.

The Sea of Galilee was an important source of fish to the Hebrews. As many as 330 fishing boats worked the large lake in NT times. However, the Hebrews were not a sea-going people, so the Mediterranean, the area's major body of water, plays an insignificant role in the biblical narrative.

Only four events in Scripture, besides Paul's travels, are directly related to ocean travel. Hiram of Tyre floated rafts of timbers to be used in Solomon's Temple along the coast (1 Ki. 5:9). King Hiram also joined with Solomon in outfitting a trading fleet that sailed successfully from the Red Sea port of Ezion Geber. Jehoshaphat tried a similar venture with Israel's King Ahaziah, but their ships were wrecked (2 Chr. 20:35-37). The final, familiar incident is Jonah's attempt to run from God by taking a ship from Joppa to Tarshish (Jon. 1:1-3).

Several factors explain Israel's indifference to the sea. The Mediterranean coast of Palestine was controlled for much of the OT period by the Philistines. Even when the Hebrew people had access, there were no sheltered areas along the coastline where ports might be developed. In addition, the Hebrew economy was based on agriculture. The Jews were not traders during the OT era and so had little need to develop ocean-going skills. Finally, the sea itself was controlled by the Phoeni-

The Gulf of Aqaba, which opens to the Red Sea, lies at the southeastern corner of the Negev. On the northern shore of the gulf, at Ezion Geber, Solomon built a fleet of trading ships and sent them to southern Arabia and/or East Africa (1 Ki. 9:26-28; 2 Chr. 8:17; 9:10,11).

cians of Tyre and Sidon, and later by the Carthaginians. Had Israel attempted to become a maritime power, these peoples would hardly have permitted it.

In Revelation, "sea" is used in its literal sense (7:3; 18:17), to represent the glory of God (4:6; 15:2), and figuratively of the mass of wicked humanity (13:1). John's portrait of God's new heaven and earth states that "there was no longer any sea" (Rev. 21:1).

The "sea of brass," an enormous bronze bowl mounted on twelve bronze oxen, contained water for the priests' ritual washing. This is one artist's conception of what it may have looked like.

sea of brass, molten sea (KJV) A large, cast bronze water bowl placed in the courtyard of Solomon's Temple (1 Ki. 7:23-26; 2 Chr. 4:1-5). The molten sea was used to fill ten smaller portable lavers, in which the priests washed. The volume of water held in Solomon's molten sea was either 10,000 gallons (1 Ki. 7:26) or 15,000 gallons (2 Chr. 4:5). *See also* Laver; Wash.

Sea of Galilee *See* Galilee, Sea of.

seal A device usually engraved with the owner's symbol, name, and/or title, used to establish the ownership of an item or to authenticate a document or decree.

Seals had four major uses:

1. *As symbols of authority.* When Mordecai used the king's seal to stamp the decree he devised, that decree had royal and binding authority (Esth. 8:8-10).

2. *As signs of ownership.* A person's seal was an extension of himself and might be used to mark an object of his own (Gen. 38:18,25). The sign of circumcision functioned as a "confirming seal" of the righteousness Abraham had gained by faith (Rom. 4:11). Symbolically, the Holy Spirit is the seal of God's ownership of the believer, and thus our guarantee of redemption (Eph. 1:13).

3. *As marks of authenticity.* Seals demonstrated that a document was originated by a certain individual. In this sense, Paul's converts served as the "seal of my apostleship" (1 Cor. 9:2).

4. *As means of securing a document or container* (Jer. 32:10; Mt. 27:66). A sealed

book could be read only by first opening or breaking the seal. To say that a prophecy is sealed (Dan. 12:9; Rev. 5:1) indicates that its full meaning is hidden until the time comes for the seal to be broken. In contrast, Daniel's reference to a given number of years set by God to "seal up vision and prophecy" (Dan. 9:24) means, in our idiom, "to close the book on," or to fulfill, prophecy.

The earliest seals were carved, hardened clay cylinders. These were rolled over wax or soft clay to make their impression. Most seals mentioned in the Bible were personal seals, engraved on small semi-precious stones that were usually less than an inch long. The name and title of the owner were engraved in reverse, so they could be easily read when the seal was pressed into wax or soft clay. Such seals might be worn on a string around the neck, or placed in a setting and worn as a ring.

Archaeologists have found well over a thousand impressions of Hebrew seals on jars and other artifacts, as well as some 200 actual seals. In addition, hundreds of clay *bullae* have been recovered. These are hardened clay impressions made by seals, which originally were small balls of clay used to fasten strings or ribbons wrapped around documents. One of the most fascinating finds is the impression of a seal which reads "Barakiah son of Neriah the scribe." Barakiah appears to be a longer name for Baruch, the son of Neriah, who served as Jeremiah's friend and secretary and to whom the prophet dictated his great OT book (Jer. 36:32).

seat (1) A place where a person sits; a stool, throne, chair. (2) A position occupied by a person in authority (Ps. 47:8; Dan. 7:9; Mt. 27:19). (3) Figuratively, a characterization of a moral position, as in "the seat of mockers" (Ps. 1:1).

The "most important seats in the synagogues" (Mt. 23:6) were reserved for the elders of the congregation or honored

Right: Impression of Babylonian cylinder seal from the time of Sargon I (about 2500 B.C.). The bearded hero Gilgamesh, with the help of the half-man, half-bull Engidu, slays a wild bull and a lion.

guests, and were placed facing the congregation.

At a banquet the seat closest to the host was the place of honor. Guests were seated in order of their social status (Lk. 14:7-11).

The "judgment seat" was the platform from which a person acting as a judge announced his decision (Mt. 27:19; 2 Cor. 5:10).

"Moses' seat" (Mt. 23:2) was the chair of honor in the synagogue where one sat to teach from the scroll of the Law. Jesus used this phrase when speaking of the scribes, those experts in the OT Law whose interpretations of the Law were accepted by the Jewish people. *See also* Judgment Seat.

Second Coming The physical, personal return of Jesus Christ to earth. The phrase "second coming" is not in the Bible, but the NT mentions the event about 300 times, commonly with the Greek word *parousia* (as in 1 Cor. 15:23; 1 Th. 2:19; 3:13; Jas. 5:7,8; 2 Pet. 1:16; 3:3-7; 1 Jn. 2:28). Christians believe the promise of the angel who announced at Jesus' ascension: "This same Jesus, who has been taken from you into heaven, will come back in the same way you have seen him go into heaven" (Acts 1:11).

The OT implies a second coming of the Messiah, portraying him as both a suffering Savior and one who will establish justice on earth (Isa. 53). Such texts as Zech. 14:4,5 seem to describe Jesus' reappearance, for they speak of a day when the Messiah will stand on the Mount of Olives, which "will be split in two from east to west," and "the LORD my God will come, and all the holy ones with him."

What the OT implies, the NT explicitly teaches (Mt. 19:28; 23:39; 24:1-51; Mk. 13:24-37; Lk. 12:35-48; 21:25-28; Rom. 11:25-27; 1 Cor. 11:26; 15:51-58; 1 Th. 4:13-18; 2 Th. 1:7-10; 2 Pet. 3:10-12; Rev. 16:15; 19:11-21). These passages associate a number of events with Jesus' Second Coming: a terrible tribulation; an angelic gathering of the saved; and a divine judgment on ungodliness through war, famine, earthquakes. An evil empire will be established, then destroyed, followed by the dissolution of the present universe in roaring flames. While these events are drawn in clear and decisive language, the NT gives no sequence of events. And we cannot be sure how long a time span these events cover. It seems wise, then, not to speak too dogmatically about how the elements in Scripture's portrait of the Second Coming fit together.

What does the NT say about the time of Jesus' Second Coming? Christ said, "No one knows about that day or hour, not even the angels in heaven, nor the Son, but only the Father" (Mt. 24:36). Since we cannot place Christ's return in any given century or decade, Christians are told to "keep watch." Jesus taught, "You also must be ready, because the Son of Man

Two images of Jesus Christ at his Second Coming. On the left, Christ is the victorious rider called "Faithful and True" who wages war against the armies of the beast (Rev. 19:11-21). On the right, Christ is the bridegroom who meets his own people in the air (1 Th. 4:16,17).

will come at an hour when you do not expect him" (Mt. 24:42-44). *See also* Future; Rapture.

second death A phrase found in Rev. 20:14, referring to the "lake of fire" to which Satan and the lost are condemned at the final judgment, to be "tormented day and night for ever and ever" (Rev. 20:10). *See also* Hell.

The first death is physical death at the end of one's life on earth.

sect A faction or party within a larger religious group. The Pharisees functioned as a sect within Judaism (Lk. 5:30; Acts 26:5). For some time Christians were considered a Jewish sect (Acts 24:5,14). This identification was important to the early spread of the Gospel: The Romans considered Judaism an ancient and honorable religion, and thus gave early Christians a rather free rein to practice and propagate their faith.

seed The fertilized egg of a plant (Gen. 1:11; Mk. 4:3); the sperm of a male human or animal (Gen. 38:9). Figuratively, seed in Scripture stands for (1) a person's descendants (Gen. 12:7, KJV), and (2) specifically the Messiah, Jesus, the particular descendant in whom God's covenant promises to Abraham are fulfilled (Gal. 3:16).

In Israel's agricultural economy, planting and harvest were familiar activities. Seeds play a prominent part in three of Jesus' parables (Mt. 13:3-9,18-32,36-43). Jesus compared his death to a seed which, planted in the ground, "dies" as a separate entity, but multiplies itself through the plant it generates (Jn. 12:24).

seedtime The time when crops were planted. In Palestine, late October or early November was seedtime for grains. Garden vegetables were planted between January and March. *See also* Agriculture.

seek (1) Gk., *zēteō*, "to give attention and priority to," "to desire," "to choose to follow" (Mt. 6:33; 7:8; Lk. 19:10; 1 Cor. 7:27; 10:24). According to these texts, we are to give priority to God and his Kingdom, and to the good of others rather than ourselves, even as Jesus came to give priority to and save the lost. (2) Gk., *ekzēteō*, "to make a concerted effort" (Acts 15:17; Rom. 3:11; Heb. 12:17; 1 Pet. 1:10). Hebrews teaches that God "rewards those who earnestly seek him" (11:6).

seer A person thought to receive divine messages through visions or dreams; a prophet. A note in 1 Sam. 9:9 reads: "The prophet of today used to be called a seer." *See also* Prophet.

selah A liturgical or musical notation found 71 times in the Psalms and three times in Habakkuk. The specific meaning of *selah* remains uncertain. The most likely explanations: (1) a liturgical note calling for worshipers to lift up their voices or hands; (2) a liturgical note calling for worshipers to fall silent and "think about that"; (3) a musical notation calling for the singers or orchestra to play more loudly; (4) a cry like "Hallelujah" or "Amen."

self-control Power over one's own actions; moderation; good sense. In the NT self-control, especially mastery of one's passions, is viewed as one of the virtues that flows from a relationship with Christ, mediated by the indwelling Holy Spirit.

Proverbs states that a man who controls his temper is better than one who takes a city (16:32). That is, power over others is meaningless unless a person is able to control himself. A related proverb turns the thought around: A man lacking in self-control is as vulnerable to others as a "city whose walls are broken down" (Prov. 25:28).

The NT calls self-control a fruit of the Spirit (Gal. 5:22,23), and lists it among the qualities to be sought in spiritual leaders (1 Tim. 3:2; Tit. 1:8).

sensual/sensuality Abandoning oneself to the pleasures of the flesh. Sensuality (Gk., *aselgeia*) often appears in lists of negative traits which characterize pagans or the wicked. The Greek word occurs three times in Peter's discussion of false teachers: they follow "shameful" ways (2 Pet. 2:2); they resemble the men of Lot's day who lived "filthy" lives (2 Pet. 2:7); and they appeal to people's "lustful" desires (2 Pet. 2:18).

Paul engages in some helpful wordplay in Eph. 4:19, speaking of the unbelieving "Gentiles." "Having lost all sensitivity [Gk., *apalgeō*], they have given themselves over to sensuality [Gk., *aselgeia*]." They may indulge their senses, but that only hardens them, making them less sensitive, "with a continual lust for more."

Scripture does not view sexual impulses as inherently evil. But human beings, created in the image of God, are to exercise control over their physical nature rather than be dominated by it.

separate/separation OT: (1) Isolation from any thing or activity that would make a person ritually or morally unclean (Lev. 15:31; 2 Cor. 6:17); (2) a distinction between two things or groups physically or conceptually set apart from each other (Gen. 1:18; Mk. 10:9). NT: (3) God's act at history's end isolating the good from the evil, and sending each group to its appointed destiny (Mt. 13:49; 25:32).

Separation in OT faith was rooted in the distinction God made between Israel and other nations. Various laws called for Israel's separation from what was ritually "unclean." This served to remind Israel that their covenant with the Lord made them special. By NT times the concept of separation had been applied to justify the isolation of the Jew from significant social relationships with non-Jews. *See also* Clean and Unclean.

Yet NT writers do not emphasize the OT ideal of ritual separation. While Christians are not to establish yoked relationships with unbelievers (2 Cor. 6:14-17), Paul urges them not to isolate themselves from unbelievers. "I have written you in my letter not to associate with sexually immoral people," he writes, but then he clarifies, "not at all meaning the people of this world who are immoral, or the greedy and swindlers, or idolaters. In that case you would have to leave this world" (1 Cor. 5:9,10). Paul goes on to warn about associating with other (so-called) Christians who are ruled by these sins.

God has scattered his church throughout the world, to represent and witness to him. While the Christian is to be morally and spiritually separated, NT separation depends on maintaining a vital personal relationship with God, not on physical isolation from others. The Christian is to walk in this world as Jesus walked, living a human life in union with God (1 Jn. 2:6).

Septuagint [Gk., "seventy," often abbreviated by the Roman numeral LXX]. An early translation of the Hebrew OT into Greek. The name reflects the tradition that the translation was the work of 70 Jewish elders, working in Alexandria during the reign of Ptolemy II Philadelphius (284–247 B.C.). Many Jews, scattered throughout the Greek-speaking world, had lost their knowledge of Hebrew. The Septuagint allowed them to read their Scriptures in their new language.

While the LXX generally renders the books of Moses carefully and accurately, some other OT books are translated freely, as if they deserved less respect than the Pentateuch.

Scholars find the LXX translation helpful in studying the Hebrew text. The meaning of obscure ancient Hebrew words becomes clearer in light of their Greek counterpart. New Testament writers rely frequently on the LXX when quoting from the OT. In addition, a number of words and phrases in the LXX are picked up and used by NT writers, indicating that the LXX was influential in shaping the language of biblical faith in the Greek-speaking world.

The LXX was also one of several factors that paved the way for the spread of Christianity through the Mediterranean world. Most of the Roman Empire spoke Greek, a result of Alexander's conquests. The LXX enabled Christian missionaries to preach Christ as the fulfillment of OT prophecies.

Winged creature, carved in bone, from 7th century B.C., Hazor, Israel. Isaiah described the seraphim as six-winged angelic beings (Isa. 6:2).

sepulcher A tomb, a place where a dead body is buried. *See also* Burial; Burial of Jesus.

seraphim [Heb., "burning ones"]. An order of angelic beings named only in Isa. 6. Humanoid in form, except for three pairs of wings, the seraphim continually worship God, crying "Holy, Holy, Holy" (Ezek. 1:5-28; *compare* Rev. 4:6-8). Isaiah's scene suggests that the seraphim are associated with divine judgment on sin, which is one aspect of God's holiness. *See also* Angel.

Sermon on the Mount The first and longest discourse of Jesus, reported in Mt. 5–7. Parallel material is found in Lk. 6:20-49. Both Gospels place this sermon in Jesus' first year of public ministry, during which he emphasized the "Gospel of the Kingdom" (*see* Mt. 4:17). Matthew emphasizes the fact that Jesus spoke with complete authority (5:21-48; 7:28,29), having been identified as the Son of God (3:16,17).

Christians have interpreted the Sermon on the Mount in various ways. Some view it as Christ's statement of the way of salvation. Others see the sermon as an eschatological document, the constitution of a literal Kingdom Jesus will one day establish. In view of the biblical concept of "kingdom," it is best to understand this sermon as Christ's statement of those principles of relationship with God and others which enable believers of any era to experience God's active and sovereign involvement in their lives. *See also* Kingdom of God.

Some of the most familiar of Jesus' sayings are found in these chapters, including the Beatitudes (5:3-12); the call to love our enemies (5:43-48); the Lord's Prayer (6:9-13); Christ's encouragement not to worry (6:25-34); his invitation to ask, seek, and knock (7:7-12); and the story of the wise and foolish builders (7:24-27). *See also* Beatitudes; Lord's Prayer.

serpent Snake, reptile. The biblical attitude toward these creatures is established in Gen. 3, where Satan uses the form of a serpent to deceive Eve. This resulted in man's Fall and sin's corruption of the human race; it also brought judgment to the serpent, who was doomed to "crawl on your belly" for all time (Gen. 3:14).

While some pagan peoples associated snakes with their gods and goddesses, biblical passages generally view snakes negatively. The snakes mentioned by name in the Bible are poisonous (adder, asp, cobra). Only the coming of Messiah will neutralize the serpent's deadly poison (Isa. 11:8; 65:25). Jesus concluded his scathing condemnation of the teachers of the Law and Pharisees who opposed him by describing them as a "brood of vipers" who surely will not "escape being condemned to hell" (Mt. 23:33). Revelation describes the devil as "that ancient serpent" (12:9; 20:2). *See also* Adder; Asp; Bronze Serpent; Viper.

servant A person who performs tasks at the direction of another. To be called the servant of a king or of God implies a high rather than menial position. One of the OT titles of the Messiah is "Servant of the Lord." One of the Christian's proudest claims is to be a bond-servant (Gk., *doulos*) of Christ. *See also* Slave.

OLD TESTAMENT

Two of the several Hebrew words for service or serving are particularly important. *'Abad* means "to work" or "to serve." It covers a wide range of activities, from menial service to a significant mission undertaken for a king. It also covers a variety of relationships, from the forced labor demanded by a conqueror to the eager service offered a ruler by a loyal subject. The noun of this stem, *'ebed*, can mean either servant or slave, depending on the context. It is also used to identify one who worships a god. A "servant of Baal" was one who worshiped that pagan deity, and a "servant of the Lord" was a worshiper of Yahweh (*see* Jer. 2:19,20).

Sharat also means "to serve." But this word is special, reserved for significant service rendered to a person of highest rank by someone who has a close relationship with the person being served. This is the word used in Ps. 103:21, "Praise the Lord, all his heavenly hosts, you his servants who do his will."

The Mount of the Beatitudes near Bethsaida with a view of the Sea of Galilee. This hill is the traditional site of Jesus' Sermon on the Mount.

Two kitchen servants, one slicing meat and the other grinding spices; detail of a relief from a Roman family mausoleum at Igel, Germany (100–300 A.D.).

THE SERVANT OF THE LORD

Several passages in Isaiah speak of God's servant (*'ebed*). One set portrays a servant who has failed, usually identified as Israel (41:8-10; 42:18,19; 44:1-3; 45:4; 48:20). The other set of servant passages speaks of God's Messiah (Anointed One), who will be obedient and through his obedience will accomplish humanity's redemption. *See also* Messiah.

Isa. 41:1-9. God's servant will be filled with the Spirit. God will lead and protect him. The servant will establish justice on earth. He himself will be the key that unlocks the chains of mankind's long captivity.

Isa. 49:1-6. God's servant has a divine commission, and is on a mission to display God's glory. Though he appears to be a failure, he will bring salvation to all.

Isa. 50:4-10. God's servant is in constant touch with the Lord, and is completely obedient. Obedience leads to suffering, yet God will work through the suffering and will vindicate his servant fully. Those who fear the Lord will respond to the word of God's servant.

Isa. 52:13–53:12. God's servant will be rejected by men. Yet he will be put to death for human transgressions, and through the punishment that he receives, mankind will find peace. God's human sheep have all gone astray. So God has chosen to lay all man's iniquity on the shoulders of his servant. Though the servant must die, he will be restored to see the results of what he accomplished in pouring out his life and bearing man's sin.

There is no clearer prophetic picture in the OT of the ministry and death of Jesus the Messiah. At the same time, there is no clearer example of the nature of servant-hood. A servant of God is moved by an honest desire to do God's will even when this involves suffering, and is characterized by humility and concern for others.

NEW TESTAMENT

The NT uses two primary Greek words for "servant." A *doulos,* a slave or bond-servant, completely subjects his will to another. Christians are God's bondslaves, called to submit fully to the will of God. A *diakonos* is a helper or minister. While *doulos* emphasizes submission to another's will, *diakonos* focuses attention on the needs the servant can meet. In this second sense, Christians should serve one another, being sensitive to needs and willing to meet them. *See also* Deacon.

THE NT'S CALL TO SERVANTHOOD

Jesus identified himself as the OT's Servant of the Lord (*compare* Lk. 22:37 *with* Isa. 53:12; Acts 3:13,26; 4:27,30), who "did not come to be served, but to serve [*diakoneō*], and to give his life as a ransom for many" (Mt. 20:28). In this, Christ provided an example Christians are to follow. We are both to serve the Lord as a *doulos* (Rom. 12:11; Col. 3:24), and to serve others as a *diakonos.* As Peter says, "Each one should use whatever gift he has received to serve others, faithfully administering God's grace in its various forms. . . . If anyone serves, he should do it with the strength God provides, so that in all things God may be praised through Jesus Christ" (1 Pet. 4:10,11).

Servant of the Lord *See* Servant.

seven/seventy Seven is established as a special or sacred number in the creation account (Gen. 2:2,3). This is the day God

909

rested and set aside. The number itself came to represent rest, completion, or perfection. *See also* Sabbath.

Seven gave structure to the Hebrew week, and frequently appeared in OT ritual, in the number of animals sacrificed on special occasions, and in various ritual repetitions (*see* Lev. 4:6; 2 Ki. 5:10). Similarly, the number 70 has great significance, reflected in the 70 who entered Egypt in the time of Joseph (Gen. 46:27), the 70 elders of Moses' day (Ex. 24:1), and even in the 70 years which is man's normal life span (Ps. 90:10). The NT notes that at one point Jesus sent out 70 (or 72, NIV) disciples to preach (Lk. 10:1-16). The early church selected seven men to serve as deacons in Jerusalem (Acts 6:1-7). While the repetition of such numbers is noteworthy, it is wrong to give them too much significance, or to assume that such numbers are mystical rather than historically accurate. *See also* Number.

Seven Words from the Cross Jesus' statements during his crucifixion, as reported by the four Gospels. These "seven words from the cross" frequently serve as the text for Good Friday services.

1. Addressed to God: "Father, forgive them, for they do not know what they are doing" (Lk. 23:34).
2. Addressed to a thief, dying on a nearby cross: "I tell you the truth, today you will be with me in paradise" (Lk. 23:43).
3. Addressed to his mother, Mary, and the disciple John: "Dear woman, here is your son. . . . Here is your mother" (Jn. 19:26,27).
4. Addressed to God: "My God, my God, why have you forsaken me?" (Mt. 27:46).
5. An exclamation: "I am thirsty" (Jn. 19:28).
6. An exultant shout: "It is finished!" (Jn. 19:30).
7. Addressed to God: "Father, into your hands I commit my spirit" (Lk. 23:46).

seventy weeks "Seventy sevens" of years (490), a period of time specified in Dan. 9:24-27 "to finish transgression, to put an end to sin, to atone for wickedness, to bring in everlasting righteousness, to seal up [fulfill] vision and prophecy and to anoint the most holy." The prophecy in Daniel indicates that the "seventy sevens" begin at the time of the issuing of the

decree to restore and rebuild Jerusalem. The Anointed One (the Messiah) is to appear in 483 years, but will be "cut off [killed] and have nothing." After this the final seven years will come, but only after the appearance of a ruler who will desolate Jerusalem. The final seven years will be marked by desolating world-wide wars.

Premillennial students of prophecy frequently follow an interpretation similar to one set forth by Sir Robert Anderson, who calculated the 483 years (69 sevens) to be 173,880 days, based on the Hebrew 360-day calendar. Figuring from 445 B.C. when Nehemiah was given authorization to rebuild Jerusalem, Anderson computed the end of the period to come in A.D. 33 when the Messiah was to be "cut off," referring to Jesus' crucifixion. The "desolation" of Jerusalem occurred in A.D. 70, according to Anderson, when the Roman army under Titus sacked the city. The final prophetic 70th "week" is still in the future, awaiting the events of Mt. 24. Only then will the fulfillment of Dan. 9:24 be complete.

sex, sexual intercourse The intimate activity of a male and female associated with reproduction. There is no specific word for "sex" in the Bible. But a number of expressions, such as "know," and "lie with," indicate sexual intercourse. Despite the indirect vocabulary, sex plays a significant role in many biblical stories, intercourse is carefully regulated in OT Law, and a clear attitude toward human sexuality is evident in the Scriptures.

SCRIPTURE'S VIEW

The creation story ascribes the origin of sex to God, who created human beings male and female and, before the Fall, encouraged Adam and Eve to "be fruitful and increase in number" (Gen. 1:28). In Gen. 2:24 Adam and Eve are united sexually, to become one in their shared life on earth. The rest of Scripture reflects the positive attitude toward sex within marriage implied in early Genesis. Sex is a source of joy and pleasure for a loving couple. It is a powerful unifying experience, deepening the bond of commitment that is to exist between husband and wife. Sex is also the means by which a union miraculously produces new life, blending the genetic contribution of husband and wife to produce a unique, new human being who is neither his nor hers but truly theirs. In each of these functions, sex is viewed as a good and gracious gift of God.

THE DISTORTION OF SEX

Sex has a powerful impact on the human

personality itself. The Bible insists that marriage is the only context within which sexual intercourse can be either beneficial or right. Human beings are called on to accept this fact, and to exercise self-control rather than to be controlled by sexual passions.

Society is only now beginning to understand the tragic distortion of the human personality that takes place when incest, rape, or other sexual crimes are committed. Yet many stories in the Bible illustrate how failure to exercise sexual self-control leads to personal and interpersonal disaster. Among such stories are Shechem's rape of Dinah and the subsequent murder of all in his Hivite city by Dinah's brothers (Gen. 34); David's passion for Bathsheba, which led him to arrange for the death in battle of her husband, Uriah (2 Sam. 11); and Amnon's rape of his half-sister Tamar, and his own murder by her brother, Absalom (2 Sam. 13). In each of these incidents, sex, which God intended to promote love and unity, was misused. In its misuse, sex spawned hatred, injustice, and even more terrible sins. Within marriage sex can promote harmony. Outside of marriage sex is harmful as well as wrong.

Sexual intercourse played a significant role in pagan religions during OT times. These religions assumed that fertility of the land was linked to sex acts by their deities, and that their gods were excited by witnessing human sex acts. Ritual prostitution and sexual orgies were elements in most of the religions of Canaan. The Book of Romans traces degrading sexual perversions to the darkening of the minds of those who refuse to acknowledge the true God, and goes on to link sexual perversions with every kind of wickedness (Rom. 1:18-27).

It is the unmistakable position of Scripture that sexuality, a powerful positive force enriching human experience within the bond of marital commitment, is as powerful a negative force distorting and corrupting human experience outside of that bond. Thus it is doubly important for individuals and for society to take a stand with Scripture, and prohibit those sexual acts which God's Word proscribes. Sexual activities which are clearly and specifically condemned in the Bible include: adultery and fornication (Ex. 20:14; 22:16); prostitution (Lev. 18:6-18; Deut. 23:17,18); homosexuality (Lev. 18:22; 20:13; Rom. 1:26,27); incest (Lev. 18:6-18; Deut. 27:20); and bestiality (Lev. 18:23; 20:15,16). *See also* Adultery; Homosexuality; Prostitution.

SEXUALITY IN THE NT

The OT never trivializes sex by using graphic or earthy terminology for sexual organs or sex acts. The same sensitivity to the mystery of human sexuality is maintained in the NT, in such phrases as Paul's reference to "parts that are unpresentable" and thus "treated with special modesty" (1 Cor. 12:23), to the statement in Hebrews that the marriage "bed" is undefiled (Heb. 13:4). At the same time, NT writers are not embarrassed by human sexuality. Paul, who chose not to marry, is well aware that sex is important within marriage. He tells married couples not to deprive each other of sex, "except by mutual consent and for a [limited] time" (1 Cor. 7:5) when they feel a need to concentrate on prayer. Young widows and virgins moved by strong sexual urges should not hesitate to marry (1 Cor. 7:36-40; 1 Tim. 5:11-15). Paul even goes so far as to call the teachings of those who forbid people to marry "doctrines of devils" (1 Tim. 4:1-3, KJV). Paul does, however, encourage be-

Bronze belt buckle cast with an embracing couple (second century B.C.).

lievers to consider celibacy as a valid alternative life-style to marriage. *See also* Celibacy. God created married love to be received with thanksgiving. While giving unrestricted rein to sexual desires is sinful and harmful as well, the full enjoyment of our sexual nature within marriage is beneficial and right.

shackles *See* Fetters.

Shaddai A Hebrew term used in a common name for God. El Shaddai, which may mean "god of mountains," appears 48 times in the OT, suggesting great power and authority. *See also* God.

shadow A darkened area, in the shape of any solid object which is placed between the sun or another source of light and another surface. In Scripture, "shadow" is used (1) literally (Jon. 4:6; Acts 5:15); (2) figuratively, of something insubstantial and fleeting, like the days of our life (1 Chr. 29:15; Ps. 109:23); also of a secure hiding place, as in "refuge in the shadow of your [God's] wings" (Ps. 36:7); (3) theologically, for a hint or foreshadowing of better things to come. New Testament writers considered the religion of Israel a "copy and shadow" of greater spiritual realities revealed in Jesus (Col. 2:17; Heb. 8:5; 10:1).

shame OT: (1) Public disgrace and humiliation (Ps. 25:1-3); (2) the subjective feeling of humiliation associated with awareness of sin or the reaping of sin's consequences (Ezra 9:6). NT: (3) The above, but also a sense of humiliation caused by ridicule (Mk. 8:34-38).

Shame in the OT is often associated with defeat at the hands of foreign enemies during times when Israel forsook God. Thus the psalmist says,

My times are in your hands;
    deliver me from my enemies
    and from those who pursue me. . . .
Let me not be put to shame, O Lord,
    for I have cried out to you.

(Ps. 31:15,17)

This OT meaning of "shame" is carried over into the NT in passages like Rom. 9:33 and 10:11. These verses promise that those who trust God will "never be put to shame" [i.e., fail, and be exposed by failure to public humiliation]. At the same time, the Greek word (*aischynomai*) introduces the concept of a shame which some feel when exposed to ridicule and deri-

sion. Believers may well be exposed to ridicule, but are not to "be ashamed to testify about our Lord" (2 Tim. 1:8).

Another Greek word, *entrepō*, describes inner humiliation a person feels when he or she falls short and behaves in an unworthy manner. In such cases it is failure to live up to one's own standards that causes shame (2 Th. 3:14).

Shame is a complex concept in Scripture. The word may be used to describe the objective situation in which a person is exposed to ruin, or the subjective emotion felt by an individual when belittled by others or when he or she feels like a failure. Scripture, however, offers an antidote to shame in all its aspects: a vital relationship with God. The OT assures Israel that the individual or the nation that trusts and obeys God will be preserved. The NT invites us to care so much about the good opinion of our Lord that we will be unmoved by what others think of us. Finally, full commitment to God will motivate us to do what is right, and thus preserve us from the hidden humiliation of acting against our conscience.

shave To cut or remove hair from one's face, head, or body. Hebrew men wore beards, unlike Egyptians and Romans. While beards and hair were carefully trimmed, these were shaved only in unusual circumstances. Old Testament Law commanded a person cured of an infectious skin disease to shave off all his hair and bathe (Lev. 14:8,9). Isaiah picks up the image of a ritual cleansing when he calls Assyria a razor which God will use to shave all the hair from Israel (Isa. 7:20). The nation has been defiled by sin, and must be cleansed. Likewise, the hair of any female prisoner of war an Israelite desired to marry was to be shaved as part of her ritual purification (Deut. 21:12). Finally, any person who made a Nazirite vow was to shave his or her head after the vow was completed, and offer the hair to God (Num. 6:5-21). *See also* Barber; Razor.

sheaf A tied bundle of grain stalks. The Israelites used hand sickles to cut grain stalks near the ground. Several stalks were tied into a bundle by the reaper or a person working behind him (Jer. 9:22). The first sheaves of each harvest were brought to the Lord as a firstfruit offering (Lev. 23:10). *See also* Firstfruits.

sheep The small, domesticated animal that represented the wealth and livelihood of

many Israelites. Mentioned some 500 times in the Bible, sheep provided the Hebrews with milk to drink, with wool for clothing, and with meat to eat. The lamb, a young sheep, is the animal most frequently offered in sacrifice to God. *See also* Lamb.

Figuratively, sheep suggest defenselessness and helplessness (Mt. 9:36), as well as a tendency to go astray (Isa. 53:6). In both Testaments sheep represent human beings, and the shepherd represents a loving God. The interplay between the sheep and shepherd serves to highlight facets of the relationship between human beings and God. *See also* Shepherd.

sheepfold A stone or brush enclosure in which sheep were kept at night. Sheepfolds in Israel generally had only one door, though they were constructed to hold several flocks of sheep.

Sheep Gate A gate in the east end of the north wall of Jerusalem, constructed when that wall was rebuilt by Nehemiah in 444 B.C. The gate was still used in Jesus' time

(Jn. 5:2). Since its location is near the Temple, some scholars have suggested that this was where sheep were brought in for the ritual sacrifices.

sheet A large piece of linen cloth (Acts 10:11). The Greek word specifies the material, but does not suggest its use. In Peter's story, the sheet appears almost as a tablecloth. Linen sheets were also used as garments and as sails. The OT describes the hammering of gold and bronze into sheets of metal (Ex. 39:3; Num. 16:38).

shekel (1) A unit of weight, about .4 ounce or 11.4 grams. (2) A coin, named for the weight of metal it contained. Like other silver coins named in the NT, the shekel was the equivalent of a day's pay for a laborer. *See also* Coins; Money.

shekinah [Heb., "that which dwells"]. A Hebrew term indicating the special or visible presence of God.

God expressed his presence in the cloudy/fiery pillar of the Exodus (Ex. 14:19,20), in the cloud that covered the tabernacle (Ex. 24:15-18), and in the cloud that filled Solomon's Temple (2 Chr. 7:1). These fiery manifestations have been called God's "shekinah presence" or "shekinah glory." Some would add the fire that burnt Elijah's sacrifice or the fiery chariot that took him to heaven; the brightness that eclipsed Mount Sinai, and later the Mount of Transfiguration, and shone on the faces of Moses and Jesus.

In Ezek. 8–11, the prophet observes the glory of God move from its place over the ark of the covenant, to the threshold of the Temple, and on out of the city. God refused to identify himself with a place where he was no longer honored, and

Flock of sheep on the coastal plain near the town of Gezer. Sheep serve as a powerful image in Scripture.

Above: Silver shekel from Tyre in Phoenicia (97–96 B.C.). When kings in Phoenicia and Palestine began minting coins in the 5th century B.C., merchants no longer needed to weigh small amounts of silver because the royal stamp verified each silver coin as a shekel's worth.

Left: Two Egyptian laborers bind sheaves of grain in this line drawing of a relief.

abandoned it to destruction by Babylonian invaders.

And might there have been a hint of shekinah glory in the bright white form that descended on Jesus "like a dove" at his baptism (Mt. 3:16)? The Spirit of God had returned to Israel in the person of Jesus, Immanuel, "God with us" (Mt. 1:23).

" And Jesus answered him,
The first of all the commandments is,
Hear, O Israel:
The Lord our God is one Lord. "

MARK 12:29 (KJV)

Because of its emphasis on the unity of God, the Shema is considered the Jewish confession of faith.

Shema [Heb., "Hear you. . ."]. The first words of Deut. 6:4, which give the title to the classic confession of Hebrew faith. The Shema was written on bits of paper and inserted in phylacteries and *mezuzahs*, and recited in the synagogues. The passages that compose the Shema are Deut. 6:4-9; Num. 15:37-41; and Deut. 11:13-21. Jesus quoted the Shema in identifying the Law's greatest command (Mk. 12:29,30).

Sheol The grave; the place and/or state of the dead. English translations render this Hebrew word as "the grave," as "death," and at times as "hell." *Sheol* is roughly equivalent to *hades* in the NT. In biblical imagery, *Sheol* and *hades* are located down, under the surface of the earth, in contrast to heaven, the abode of God, which is located up above.

By NT times the belief that *Sheol* was divided into compartments occupied by the righteous and the wicked was firmly established. This view is reflected in Jesus' story of the rich man and Lazarus (Lk. 16:19-31). *See also* Hades; Heaven; Hell; Resurrection.

shepherd A person who cares for sheep. Figuratively, (1) human leaders who care for God's human flock (Ezek. 34); (2) the Lord, to whom believers can relate as "my shepherd" (Ps. 23); and (3) Jesus Christ, who as the Good Shepherd gave his life for the sheep (Jn. 10:1-18).

GOD AS "MY SHEPHERD"

Clear analogies between actual sheep and their shepherds lie at the root of Scripture's sheep-shepherd imagery.

Sheep were a valued economic resource in Israel, known and named individually by the shepherds responsible for their care. To be called one of God's sheep was to be affirmed as someone truly important to God. Yet sheep are a relatively helpless animal, vulnerable to wild animals and prone to go astray. To call God "my shepherd" casts the Lord as a person who accepts responsibility to care for and protect the believer—one whom the believer can trust as fully as sheep could trust the shepherd who owned and cared for them.

David, the psalmist who became Israel's greatest king, was a shepherd. Even as a lad he killed a bear and lion that threatened the family flock. It was out of David's intimate knowledge of the shepherd/sheep relationship that he penned the Bible's most famous and comforting expression of trust in a loving God:

The Lord is my shepherd, I shall not be in
*   want.*
* He makes me lie down in green pastures,*
he leads me beside quiet waters,
* he restores my soul.*
He guides me in paths of righteousness
*   for his name's sake.*
Even though I walk
*   through the valley of the shadow of*
*   death,*
I will fear no evil,
* for you are with me;*
your rod and your staff,
* they comfort me.*

(Ps. 23:1-4)

The prophets pick up these images. Isaiah says of God: "He tends his flock like a shepherd: He gathers the lambs in his arms and carries them close to his heart; he gently leads those that have young" (Isa. 40:11). Jeremiah looks forward to history's end and says, "He who scattered Israel will gather them and will watch over his flock like a shepherd" (Jer. 31:10). Micah says of the coming Messiah, "He will stand and shepherd his flock in the strength of the Lord, in the majesty of the name of the Lord his God. And they will live securely, for then his greatness will reach to the ends of the earth. And he will be their peace" (Mic. 5:4).

The NT develops the analogy further in Jn. 10, which casts Jesus as the Good Shepherd. The voice of the good shepherd is recognized by his sheep, who listen to

him (v.4). The good shepherd "calls his own sheep by name and leads them out" (v.3). He goes ahead of his flock to lead them and the sheep follow [obey] him because they know his voice (v.4). They will never follow a stranger but will turn away from him (v.5). While a thief comes to steal and kill sheep, Jesus has come "that they [his sheep] may have life, and have it to the full" (v.10). Only the true shepherd has the good of the sheep at heart.

As the Good Shepherd, Jesus "lays down his life for the sheep" (v.11). Mere hired hands to whom the sheep have no personal value abandon them when the wolf comes. Because Jesus cares for his sheep, and has a personal relationship with each of them, he will lay down his life for the sheep (vv.14,15). Jesus lays down his life freely, voluntarily, and "of my own accord." Then Jesus will "take it [his life] up again" (vv.17,18). Thus, Jesus used the familiar imagery of sheep and shepherd to explain his coming death: As a good shepherd Jesus interposed himself between his sheep and deadly danger,

and willingly died that the sheep he valued might "have life, and have it to the full." Truly, as the writer of Hebrews says looking back on the cross and resurrection, Jesus is "that great Shepherd of the sheep" (Heb. 13:20).

HUMAN LEADERS AS SHEPHERDS

Two prophets of the Exile, Jeremiah and Ezekiel, describe Israel's leaders as "shepherds who only take care of themselves." Ezekiel 34 condemns Israel's spiritual leaders, who consumed all the sheep's produce, yet did not strengthen the weak, heal the sick, bind up the injured, or search for the lost. Instead, they ruled harshly and brutally. So God promised through Ezekiel that the human shepherds would be held accountable. One day the sovereign Lord will "myself search for my sheep and take care of them." Jeremiah too pronounces "woe to the shepherds who are destroying and scattering the sheep of my pasture" (23:1). Through Jeremiah, God promises, "I will give you shepherds after my own heart" (3:15).

While the image of sheep and shepherds

The Angel Announcing the Birth of Jesus to the Shepherds *by Govaert Flinck* (A.D. 1615–1660).

915

is primarily employed in Scripture to enrich our understanding of personal relationship with God, it also may serve as a model for spiritual leaders. Christian elders are to "be shepherds of the church of God" (Acts 20:28; 1 Pet. 5:2). As shepherds, spiritual leaders are to serve rather than use God's flock, to strengthen the weak, heal the sick, bind up the injured, and search for the lost, willingly giving of themselves for the benefit of those God has called them to serve.

Far right: Two Roman soldiers with shields and spears, carved in relief on a monument erected by Emperor Trajan (A.D. 109).

shewbread *See* Showbread.

shibboleth [Heb., "a stream in flood"]. A test applied by Jephthah's forces to identify Ephraimites after a battle described in Jdg. 12. The Ephraimites spoke a dialect that had no "sh" sound, and thus were easily detected when they tried to say "shibboleth." The word has come to mean any password or distinguishing mark or habit.

Right: Sumerian warriors advance together protected by large metal shields; detail from a larger relief celebrating the victory of the king of Lagash (about 2450 B.C.).

shield Defensive armor held in front of a soldier to ward off arrows or sword strokes. The Hebrew used the *meginah*, a small round shield, and the *sinah*, a large shield that covered the whole body. These larger shields could be held over the head for protection when attacking a walled city. The smaller *meginah* was usually carried by archers, while spearmen carried the larger *sinah* (1 Chr. 12:8; 2 Chr. 11:12; 14:8).

Metal shields seem to have had only ceremonial use in OT times (1 Ki. 10:16,17; 14:26,27). Shields actually used by soldiers were made of wood or wicker, covered with toughened animal hide. This explains the reference in Ezek. 39:9 to the shields of a defeated army being collected and burned. Some shields did have a metal boss at the center for added protection. But even the *scutum*, the shield used by the Roman legions, was made of leather.

This leather could be soaked in water as an added defense against burning arrows. Paul uses this image in Eph. 6:16, describing the "shield of faith, with which you can extinguish all the flaming arrows of the evil one."

Because they were made of perishable material, no Israelite shields have been found by archaeologists. The various shield shapes and sizes are well known, however, being pictured on the war memorials of Egyptians, Assyrians, Babylonians, and Romans.

In Hebrew poetry the shield serves as a powerful symbol of the security a believer can find in the Lord. As David wrote, "The Lord is my strength and my shield; my heart trusts in him, and I am helped" (Ps. 28:7).

ship A seagoing vessel intended to transport freight and/or persons.

Ships do not play a prominent part in sacred history. The Israelites were not a seagoing people, and Canaan had no rivers navigable by larger vessels. Yet ships aided the settlement of the Mediterranean and the spread of such cultural inventions as the alphabet. In NT times large freighters up to 180 feet (55 meters) long and 50 feet (15 meters) wide operated on the Mediterranean. These vessels also carried deck and steerage passengers. The ship taking Paul to Rome had 276 persons on board. The historian Josephus tells of a wreck he experienced in a ship carrying 600 persons. *See also* Boat.

shittim wood (KJV) *See* Acacia.

shoes *See* Sandal.

shophar [Heb.]. *See* Trumpet.

shoulder The part of an animal or human body between the neck and foreleg or upper arm. Figuratively, the shoulder suggests the bearing of heavy personal or spiritual burdens (Isa. 10:27; 14:25; Mt. 23:4). Those who "would not put their shoulders to the work" refused to do their share (Neh. 3:5).

shovel *See* Censer.

showbread (KJV) A dozen loaves of unleavened bread which were arranged in two rows of six on a low table within the tabernacle, and later the Temple (Lev. 24:5-9; Ex. 25:23-30). The NIV speaks of bread of the Presence, instead of showbread. The showbread was replaced each Sabbath. Old loaves were to be eaten only by the priests (*but see* 1 Sam. 21:5,6; Mt. 12:3,4). The showbread has been taken to symbolize Christ as the Bread of Life (Jn. 6).

shrine (1) A box or container in which sacred objects are placed; (2) any place where sacred objects are placed, or which is set aside for worship. The term is used of places where pagans or straying Israelites gathered to worship pagan deities.

In Ephesus, Paul got into serious trouble because his preaching disturbed the lucrative business of the local silversmiths who made shrines of the goddess Artemis (Acts 19:24).

shroud The large strip of cloth used to cover or wrap a dead body. Metaphorically, of dark and dreadful experiences (Job 19:8).

Many have believed that the Shroud of Turin, a 14 foot × 3.5 foot (4.3 meters by 1 meter) strip of cloth which bears the mysterious image of a crucified man, was the burial cloth in which the body of Jesus Christ was wrapped. The Roman Catholic Church has officially repudiated this view, after a carbon-14 dating of the cloth placed it much later than the first century.

sickness Affliction with physical or mental illness; a state of being defective or unwell. Hebrew words for sickness indicate a state of weakness in contrast to a state of health and wholeness. In the OT sickness is often a symbol of a national decline caused by sin (Isa. 1:4-7). It also serves as a figure for anguish caused by guilt (Ps. 38:5: "My wounds fester and are loathsome because of my sinful folly"). Greek words also suggest bodily weakness. Paul uses the

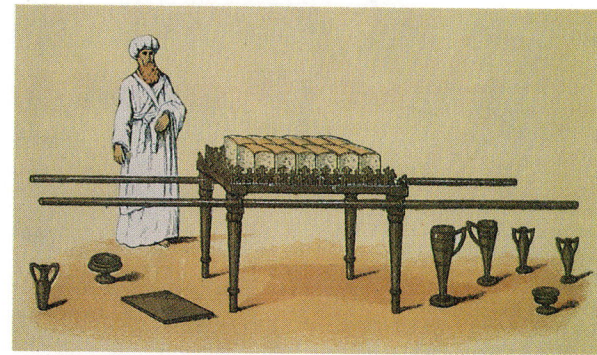

High priest attending the table of the showbread. The Hebrew phrase for showbread means "bread set before the face [of God]" (Ex. 25:30).

1. *Ceremonial barge of the Egyptian noble Huy, the viceroy of Nubia, painted on the walls of his tomb.*
2. *Egyptian cargo ship, loaded with goods from the land of Punt (eastern Sudan): incense, ebony, ivory, white gold, myrrh trees, scented woods, panther skins, greyhounds, baboons, and monkeys. Drawing from 15th-century B.C. relief at Thebes.*
3. *Line drawing of Egyptian boatwrights bending a boat into a curve.*
4. *The ship as a symbol of life: a vessel with lowered sails enters its port; on a relief from the mausoleum of a wealthy Pompeian man (A.D. 100–150).*
5. *Roman coin bearing a Greek inscription and figure of a galley with two sailors; from the time of Nero (A.D. 54–68).*

3

4

2

5

6. *Model of an Egyptian supply ship on which the captain is shown harassing his Canaanite crew (19th century B.C.). Moses warned the Israelites that if they disobeyed God, he might allow the Egyptians to forcibly take them back in ships (Deut. 28:68).*
7. *Small Egyptian boat from the time of the Old Empire (2686–2180 B.C.). It differs from larger boats of that era in its high stern and lack of oars.*
8. *Roman ships at sea during a storm (third century A.D.). The vessel on the left has standard sail rigging, the one on the right a bowsprit sail.*
9. *This model steering oar, found in an Egyptian tomb of the Middle Kingdom, is decorated with lotus and eye motifs.*
10. *Cross-sectional view of a Greek trireme, a three-tiered, oar-driven warship.*
11. *Phoenician warship escaping from Sidon after an attack by Assyrian King Sennacherib; line drawing from a relief at his palace in Nineveh (about 690 B.C.).*
12. *Two-banked warship shows the Phoenician innovation of a sharp projection on the stern below water level.*
13. *Raft of inflated skins is used to transport stone; line drawing of a relief in the palace of Sennacherib (about 690 B.C.).*
14. *Roman warship of the first century A.D. incised in green jasper. The inscription refers to Salacia, wife of the Roman sea god Neptune.*
15. *Athenian-styled vase painted about 475 B.C. with a scene from The*

Continued on page 920.

7

6

8

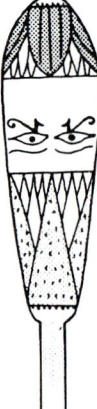

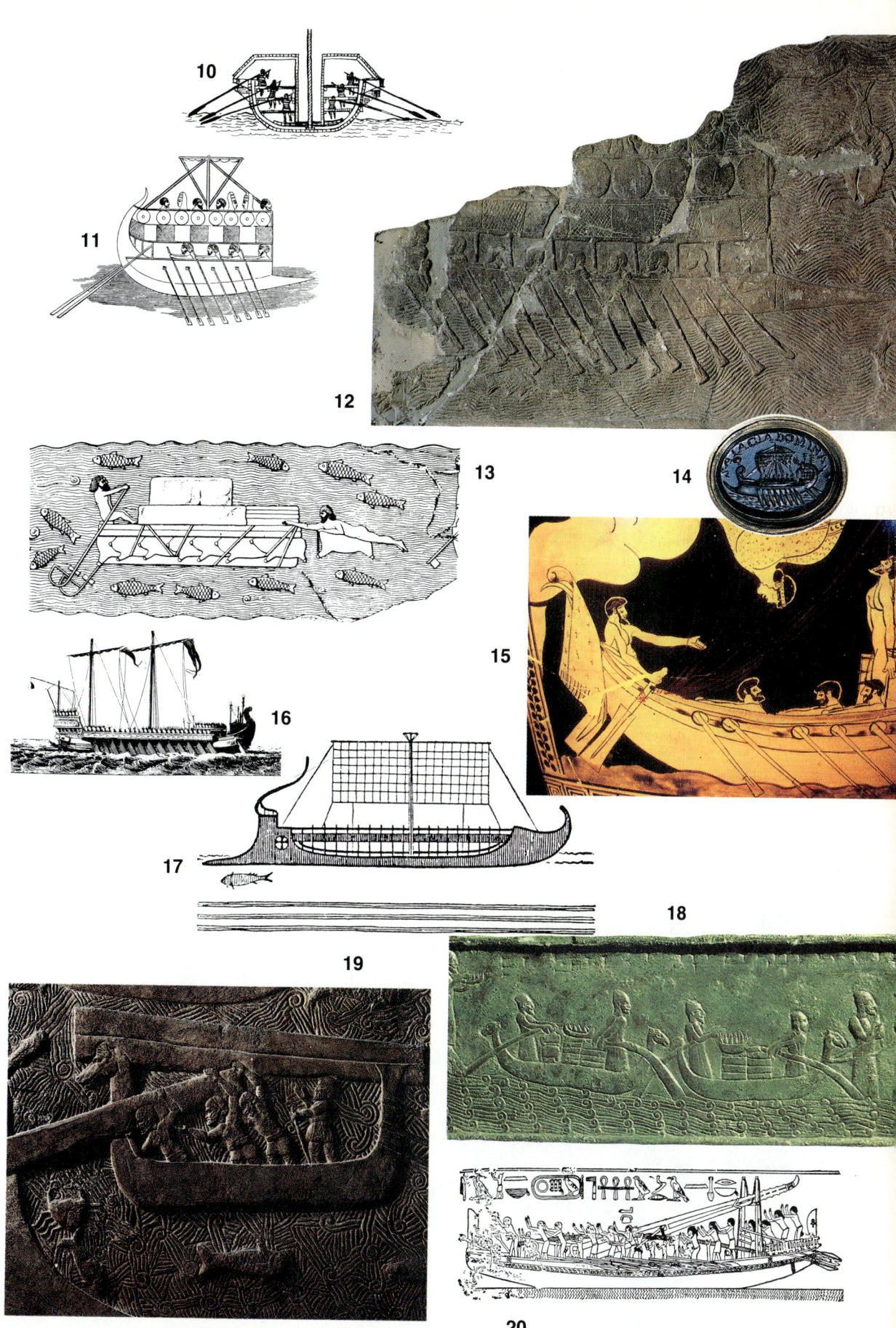

10

11

12

13

14

15

16

17

18

19

20

vocabulary of sickness to speak of human frailty (Rom. 8:3).

SICKNESS AND SIN IN THE OT

The primary link between sickness and sin is established in the account of the Fall. When Adam and Eve sinned, the principle of death was introduced into human experience. Here "death" means not only the cessation of biological life, but also all the debilitating weaknesses which human beings inherit. Sickness is at heart an aspect of the divine judgment on sin. See also Death.

Even more, the OT assumes that there is a direct link between God and specific incidents of sickness. This is partly because the OT views God as Sovereign, the ultimate cause of all things. But even more, the OT understands the Lord to be a covenant-keeping God, and God had made certain commitments related to health and well-being. In the Mosaic covenant, God promised that if his people carefully followed his laws, he would keep them "free from every disease" (Deut. 7:15; see Ex. 23:25,26). On the other hand, should Israel disobey, "severe and lingering illness" was one of the rods which God would use to discipline (Deut. 28:59).

The OT also associates physical recovery with forgiveness. The same God who "forgives all your sins" is the one who "heals all your diseases" (Ps. 103:3). A return to God restores the OT believer to fellowship with him, and to physical health and well-being (see Hos. 5:13–6:3).

While some sickness experienced by God's OT saints came as a punishment for sin and was removed when God's people repented, not all sickness was divine discipline. Even an intimate relationship with God is no guarantee of physical well-being. In reality human beings are frail, and all of us are subject to physical deterioration. Thus the OT believer did not hesitate to apply medicines and regularly turned to prayer and fasting when a loved one became ill (Ps. 35:13,14).

Modern medicine, exploring relation-

ships between sin and sickness, has found that a person who lives by his or her values, and is at peace within, is less likely to become ill, and if ill has a greater chance of recovery. The human immune system is inhibited by bad moral choices and by the distortion of the personality such choices cause.

SICKNESS AND SIN IN THE NT

By NT times the link between sin and sickness was accepted as absolute in popular thought. What was merely one cause of sickness had been accepted as the only cause. Yet when Jesus' disciples asked him whose sin had caused a certain man to be blind from birth, Christ answered, "Neither this man nor his parents sinned" (Jn. 9:1-3). The man's physical condition was not the result of personal sin at all. Similarly, Jesus identified a woman who had suffered a crippling affliction for some 18 years as a "daughter of Abraham," i.e., a woman of faith (Lk. 13:10-16; see Rom. 4:11,12). In her case the cause was probably demonic oppression, an attack against one of God's own by forces hostile to him.

In the Epistles, Paul, greatly troubled by a chronic illness that many believe to be a disfiguring eye disease, tells how he begged God to heal him. God refused, telling Paul that his physical weakness was intended to promote greater dependence on the Lord, who would display his power by working through a disabled instrument. Paul then rejoiced in his weakness. Because of it, he would experience Christ's powerful presence in a more complete way.

Thus, Scripture offers no single explanation for human illness. God may bring sickness as punishment. Sickness may simply be a consequence of human frailty. Sickness may be caused by demonic attack. Sickness may even be a gift of God, intended to enrich us spiritually. Clearly it would be wrong for anyone to torment himself when sick, wondering what he had done wrong to deserve punishment. It would be wrong when tragedy strikes another to assume that the sickness is punishment for some hidden sin. Human beings are frail, and subject to sickness along with many other ills. How much then we need to rely on God, if not for healing, at least to redeem our situation and to strengthen us spiritually even as he did the apostle Paul. See also Disease; Healing; Health; Medicine; Physician.

sickle A curved, sharpened blade mounted on a short handle; a hand-tool used for

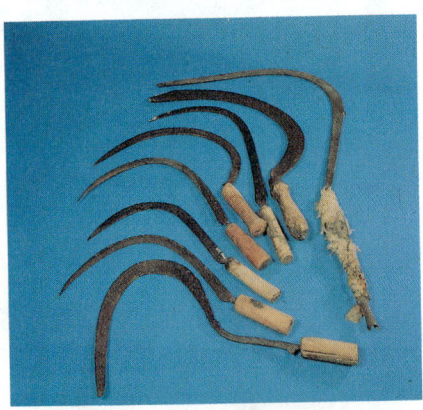

cutting grain. The earliest sickles were of flint. Later sickles had metal blades. In a powerful metaphor, Revelation pictures avenging angels harvesting earth at history's end, using sharp sickles to gather the wicked and throw them "into the great winepress of God's wrath" (14:19).

siege A military tactic, in which a walled city was surrounded by an attacking army. The purpose of the siege was to isolate the city and starve its citizens into surrender (2 Ki. 6:24,25), or breach its walls by direct attack (Ezek. 4:2; Hab. 1:10).

Invading armies mounted a variety of attacks against walled cities. Battering rams were used to shatter a city's gates. Fires were set at the base of its walls to weaken the sandstone blocks of which they were built. Sappers tunneled under the walls to weaken their foundations. Direct attacks on the walls were launched from wheeled towers. The Babylonians and Assyrians built earthen ramps up to the walls from which to mount their as-

Above: Egyptian soldiers besiege a fortress; line drawing taken from an existing relief.
Left: Assyrian archers storm a fortress while a wheeled siege tower moves toward its walls (Nimrud, about 865 B.C.). Isaiah prophesied that God would "besiege Ariel" (Jerusalem) because of Israel's lip service in worship (29:2,3,13).

saults. General assaults were made by infantry who mounted tall scaling ladders, supported by archers who attempted to clear the walls of defenders.

By NT times the Romans had added a variety of machines, including giant spring-wound devices for shooting arrows, and catapults that hurled fire or boulders. Catapults were also used to hurl dead bodies of people and animals over city walls in an attempt to spread plague and further weaken defenders.

Within a besieged city, defenders attempted to counter these strategies. Assaults were met with arrows, rocks, and boiling oil. Fiery arrows were shot at siege towers, and the defenders used chains and grappling irons to snatch at the attackers' battering rams. However, as the war memorials erected by Assyrians and Babylonians demonstrate, the advantage lay with the attackers. In time even the strongest city would surely be taken, and its citizens killed or taken captive.

Boar-headed battering ram rolls toward a city gate while archers provide cover; detail of bronze door covering from the palace of Shalmaneser III at Balawat, Assyria (858–824 B.C.). The city of Samaria resisted an Assyrian siege for three years—the longest in biblical history—before succumbing in 722 B.C. (2 Ki. 17:5,6).

sign An indication. Biblically, an identifying mark of God's presence or purpose.

Biblical signs include: (1) natural phenomena, such as the rainbow which served as a sign of God's promise not to destroy life with another flood (Gen. 9:12-17); (2) circumcision, which served as a sign of descent from Abraham and participation in the covenant God made with him (Gen. 17:11); (3) a tribal standard (Num. 2:2), the mark God placed on Cain (Gen. 4:15), or any other object or mark intended to convey a particular message; (4) the death of Eli's sons (1 Sam. 2:34) and of Hananiah (Jer. 28), or any other event foretold by a prophet which served to authenticate him as a messenger from God; (5) miraculous interventions, such as the plagues God brought upon Egypt prior to the Exodus (Ex. 8:23; see Jn. 4:54). In Christ's later ministry he refused to perform miraculous signs on demand for his enemies, for his many miracles of healing had both established his credentials and expressed God's love for his people (Mk. 8:11,12; see Jn. 10:41). See also Miracle.

signet A ring bearing an engraved stone or, after the fifth century B.C., an engraved gold band. The signet bore the name and title of the wearer and served as a sign of authority. Pressed into wax or clay, the signet sealed documents with an identifying mark, establishing the ownership of items so marked. The importance of the signet ring is implied in Jer. 22:24, where God declares that "'even if you, Jehoiachin son of Jehoiakim king of Judah, were a signet ring on my right hand, I would still pull you off'" (see Hag. 2:23). See also Ring; Seal.

Two Hebrew signet rings from the 8th–7th centuries B.C. Twice in the Scriptures the Lord God used a signet ring as a metaphor for an Israelite ruler (Jer. 22:24; Hag. 2:23).

Silas [SI-luhs; "asked" or "wood"]. Also known in the KJV and RSV as Silvanus [sil-VANE-uhs; "wood"], a leader in the Jerusalem church who later traveled as a missionary with both Paul and Peter. **Scripture:** Acts 15–18.

BACKGROUND

Acts 15 identifies Silas as a leader of the Jerusalem church. He was sent to Antioch to confirm in person the decision of the first church council that Gentile Christians were not subject to Jewish (OT) Law. Later Silas joined Paul on his second missionary journey, sharing that apostle's imprisonment in Philippi and his flight from Thessalonica. In some translations of the Epistles Silas is called by his Roman name, Silvanus. He is mentioned by Paul in 2 Cor. 1:19; 1 Th. 1:1; and 2 Th. 1:1. In 1 Th. 1:1 he is linked with Paul and Timothy in a way that, given the use of "we" throughout the book, may suggest that he was considered a major contributor. Later Silas rejoined Peter, whom he must have known well from their years together in leadership of the Jerusalem church. Peter says in his first letter that he wrote "with the help of Silas" (1 Pet. 5:12). The Greek phrase suggests that Silas expressed Pe-

ter's thoughts in Silas's words, serving as a secretary, but also actively participating in the writing process.

LEARNING FROM SILAS'S LIFE

Silas might be called the "silent partner of the apostles." A leader in his own right, and known for his faithfulness, Silas still is what most would consider a minor figure in church history. Yet his choice by the Jerusalem church as an envoy, his selection by Paul as a companion, and his commendation by Peter as a faithful brother who served him as a scribe, all indicate that Silas had an important role in the early church, and contributed greatly to the ministry of the NT's two "greats," Peter and Paul. The quality of the lives of "silent partners" like Silas wins the respect of those who know them. And their quiet, behind-the-scenes ministry is vital to the success of their more famous brothers and sisters.

silk Cloth woven from the threads in the cocoon of a Chinese moth.

A type of silk was produced from an eastern Mediterranean moth, stimulating a silk industry in Sidon. Chinese silk was not introduced in the West until Roman times, and is mentioned only in Rev. 18:12. The cloth identified as silk in some versions of the OT may have been the local product from Sidon. But the Hebrew words translated "silk" in the KJV of Ezek. 16:10 are rendered "fine linen" in most modern versions.

silver A lustrous white precious metal, which served with gold as a standard of wealth in biblical times.

Silver is mentioned some 300 times in the OT. It was used in ornaments and jewelry, pagan cult objects were made or overlaid with it (Acts 19:24), and Israel used silver utensils in both tabernacle (Ex. 26:19; Num. 7:13) and Temple (1 Ki. 7:51; 2 Chr. 2:7). The primary use of silver in biblical times was as a medium of exchange. An agreed-on amount of silver was carefully weighed out and exchanged for grain, land, or another commodity (Gen. 23:16). About 600 B.C. silver was cast in coins. Frequently "silver" in Scripture simply means "money" (Isa. 13:17; Acts 20:33). *See also* Coin; Money.

The process of refining silver by heating it to remove impurities is a frequent figure of God's purification of his people (Zech. 13:9; Mal. 3:3).

silversmith A person who refines and works silver (Zech. 13:9; Mal. 3:2,3). Both Testaments mention smiths who used their talents to create idols for pagan worship (Isa. 40:19; Acts 19:24). *See also* Shrine.

sin Rebellion against God; falling short of or deviation from standards established by God. The NT particularly portrays sin as a corruption of human nature that makes man hostile to God, captive to baser passions and desires, and unwilling to submit to God's known will. By understanding the biblical doctrine of sin, we can better appreciate the salvation God offers us in Jesus Christ. Sin has shattered human beings' relationship with God and lies at the root of the distortions in human society and in people's relationships with others.

Some describe "sin" singular as man's condition or state and "sins" plural as

Silver ingots and objects from Shiloh, the religious center for the Israelite tribes through the period of the judges. There silver devoted to God would have been stored in the tabernacle treasury.

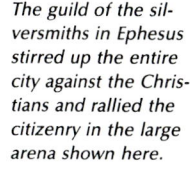

The guild of the silversmiths in Ephesus stirred up the entire city against the Christians and rallied the citizenry in the large arena shown here.

responsible choices made by individuals. Sins bring guilt, but both sin in general and particular sins bring human beings before the throne of divine justice. *See also* Judgment; Judgment Day.

BIBLE WORDS FOR SIN

Three key Hebrew terms express the OT's view of sin. Each is rooted in the conviction that God has established certain standards for humankind. The divine standard may be directly revealed, as in Mosaic Law, but a consciousness of standards is also woven into human nature itself, as demonstrated by man's establishment of his own standards where God's are not known (Rom. 2:14,15).

Of the Hebrew words for sin, *hata'* appears most frequently (some 580 times). It means to fall short of the divine standards. *'Avon*, often rendered "iniquity" or "guilt," means to twist the divine standards or to deviate from them. *Pesha'*, translated "transgression" or "rebellion," is human revolt against God's standards or his expressed will.

Psalm 51, David's public confession of his sin with Bathsheba, makes it clear that human beings are personally responsible for sinful choices. Yet the psalm implies a truth later developed in the NT: The pull toward what is wrong is rooted in a distortion of human nature itself. David knows he has been "sinful from the time my mother conceived me" (Ps. 51:5). While God does forgive sins, the ultimate remedy for the human condition, as David illustrates, calls for God to "create in me a pure heart" (Ps. 51:10).

The NT identifies many specific sins, such as murder, theft, and adultery. Its vocabulary of sin also includes general terms like guilt, injustice, lawlessness, offense, unrighteousness, wickedness, and many others. However, two major Greek words express the core concept of sin in the NT. *Adikia* is "wrongdoing," "unrighteousness," or "injustice." Sins of *adikia* are conscious human choices that cause harm to other persons in violation of God's standards. It is somewhat akin to the Hebrew *'avon*. *Hamartia*, the other NT term, most closely incorporates the meaning of *hata'*, the idea of "missing the mark." In the NT Epistles, *hamartia* is used in a distinctive theological sense, drawing attention not to human acts but to human nature. There, "sin" portrays man's nature itself as warped and often malignant.

SIN IN CHRISTIAN TRADITIONS

Christian traditions have differed somewhat in interpreting the Bible's teaching on sins. Some, like Calvinist theologian A. A. Hodge, view sins inclusively, treating as sin "any and every want of conformity with the moral law of God, whether of excess or defect, whether of omission or commission. Sin is any want of conformity of the moral states . . . as well as actions of the human soul with the Law of God." Others view sins more narrowly, as in the Wesleyan tradition, whose founder, John Wesley, wrote that "nothing is sin, strictly speaking, but a voluntary transgression of the known will of God."

Yet all Christian traditions agree that human beings are sinners, and that sin involves the corruption of the nature of all the offspring of Adam.

SIN AS HUMAN CHOICE

Sins are human choices that in some way violate the divine standards and for which the individual is fully responsible. The psalmist expects God to "call him [the wicked person] to account for his wickedness" (Ps. 10:15). The prophet Ezekiel warns that, in the coming invasion of Judah by Babylon, "the soul [person] who sins is the one who will die" (Ezek. 18:4). The same prophet announced, "You must bear the consequences of your [sins]" (23:35). Sacred history illustrates this reality. For instance, the Exodus generation, by refusing to obey God, had to wander in the wilderness until all the adults responsible for the choice to disobey had died (Num. 14). Saul's sins destroyed his chances to found a dynasty (1 Sam. 28:16-19). The experience of generation after generation shows that sins bring punishment from God.

The theme of personal responsibility was also emphasized in Israel's sacrificial system. Even one who sinned unintentionally and later learned of his failure to live up to the divine standards was to bring a sacrifice and seek forgiveness. In offering the sacrifice, the worshiper laid his hands on the head of the animal, admitting his guilt by identifying himself with the one to be slain. *See also* Forgive; Guilt; Sacrifices.

The NT continues to underline responsibility for sinful acts. The doctrine of coming judgment implies that each of us is responsible to God for our choices and that we must give an account of them to God (Mt. 12:36; Heb. 4:13; 13:17; 1 Pet. 4:5).

SIN AS A STATE OR CONDITION

While sins are acts for which individuals

King David catches sight of Bathsheba bathing. The account of David's adultery with her and the murder of her husband illustrates sin as deliberate wrongdoing (1 Sam. 11,12).

are personally responsible, the NT develops the thought that "sin" also describes the general human condition. Both man's essential nature and his individual acts fall short of and deviate from the standard God established in the original creation.

Both Testaments trace this deviation back to the disobedience of Adam and Eve in Eden (Gen. 3; Rom. 5:12-17). As a consequence of that original sin, Adam's own created nature was warped. Furthermore, all human beings have inherited from Adam this fallen and sinful nature.

The NT particularly describes man's nature in desperate terms. By nature, we are enemies of God (Rom. 5:10); subject to biological and spiritual death (Rom. 5:12-14); vulnerable to the influence of Satan and other hostile spiritual beings (Eph. 2:2); slaves to the "cravings" of our sinful human nature and subject to God's wrath and eternal punishment (Eph. 2:3).

Evidence of humanity's lost condition abounds. People's basic hostility to God is demonstrated not so much in atheism as in religion. Rejecting God's self-revelation in nature and tradition, humanity has turned to a host of counterfeits in a futile effort to satisfy inner spiritual hunger. Also, man's subjection to sinful passions is demonstrated daily, not only in the crime and injustice that corrupt human society, but also in the selfishness that distorts interpersonal relationships. As Jesus said, the sinful heart of man (human nature) is the source of sinful acts (*see* Mt. 15:16-20).

THE DIVINE REMEDY

God deals with sins, those choices that violate his standards and make individuals subject to punishment, by offering forgiveness in Jesus Christ. When God forgives sins, he neither ignores them nor lightly dismisses human guilt. Rather, God considers the sacrifice of Christ a propitiation (satisfactory payment) for the sins of humankind.

By his self-sacrifice, Christ also made it possible for God to deal with man's sinful state and condition. Believers, united to Jesus by faith, die with him and are raised with him (Rom. 6). God then implants a new nature within the believer, recreating that which Adam lost (2 Cor. 5:17; Col. 3:10). For now, the old pull toward sin continues to exist, alongside a new and righteous nature. But the existence of the new nature opens up new possibilities, enabling the Christian to live a truly righteous life now. Then, in the resurrection, our old, sinful nature will be gone, and we will be fully restored to original holiness. *See also* Resurrection.

SIN AND THE GOSPEL

The biblical doctrine of sin does not teach that human beings are as bad as they can be. Jesus pointed out that even the evil often do good to those who are good to them (Lk. 6:32-34). Rather, the biblical doctrine teaches that human beings are as "bad off" as they can be.

Those sinful acts that trouble the conscience and cause so much unhappiness are expressions of a warped and distorted nature. No matter how much we struggle to control our actions, there is nothing we can do about the nature from which they issue.

925

However, the picture that Scripture paints of sin and its consequences is actually a good word from God. It is good because it turns our eyes away from ourselves and our futile efforts to be good and challenges us to search for a remedy. It is good because it teaches us that we can have hope only if we surrender all hope in ourselves and instead place our hope in God. A biblical understanding of sin provides a powerful motivation to look to Jesus Christ and to rely only on him for both forgiveness and renewal. *See also* Grace; Salvation.

sin offering An offering to be brought to God by an Israelite when he or she became aware of committing an unintentional sin. *See also* Sacrifice.

Below: Terrain in the southern Sinai peninsula is today still much as the Israelites experienced it on their trek through this wilderness. Inset: The Sinai peninsula is the triangular region that serves as a land bridge between Asia and Africa.

Sinai (1) The arid 24,000 square-mile (62,000 square-kilometer) peninsula between Africa and Palestine; (2) Mount Sinai, where God called Moses as Israel's deliverer and later revealed the Mosaic Law. The OT also calls this mountain "Horeb" and "the mountain of God."

In Bible times the peninsula was divided into five districts, referred to in the OT as the wildernesses of Shur, Sin, Sinai, Paran, and Zin. Although dry, the Sinai has been home to small village settlements and Bedouins for many thousands of years. As early as the 2600s B.C., some 500 years before Abraham, the Egyptians mined turquoise there.

Scholars have suggested several candidates for Mount Sinai. The traditional and most likely site is *Jebel Musa*, a 7,363-foot (2,244-meter) granite mountain that dominates the plain below.

Mount Sinai is significant for two special divine revelations. Here God revealed the name Yahweh to Moses (Ex. 3:1–4:17). Later God led the people of Israel back to Sinai, where he gave them the Ten Commandments and his Law (Ex. 19:20). *See also* Covenant; Ten Commandments; Yahweh.

The apostle Paul, aware of the fuller revelation of the grace mediated to us through Christ, sees Sinai as a symbol of bondage to the Mosaic code (Gal. 4:21-31). His analogy shows no disrespect for the

earlier revelation (Rom. 7:12). Paul does, however, contrast the freedom Christians are granted to be truly good with the inability of Sinai's Law to produce holiness. *See also* Free; Law.

sincere Without pretense, honest, unadulterated. Several different Greek words are translated "sincere" in various English versions. Together they suggest honest expression of a person's true thoughts, motives, and feelings—without hypocrisy, simple, and genuine.

The sincere person is genuine at all times, a person fully committed to God who can be trusted by all. "Love must be sincere," Paul told the Romans (12:9), and writing to Timothy, he calls for a "sincere faith" (1 Tim. 1:5). Perhaps recalling that the Lord's most scathing remarks were leveled at the hypocrisy of the Pharisees, Peter urges followers of Jesus toward the opposite of hypocrisy and to "have sincere love for your brothers," loving them "deeply, from the heart" (1 Pet. 1:22). "Therefore, rid yourselves of all . . . hypocrisy" (1 Pet. 2:1).

Gladness and sincerity were marks of the early church in Jerusalem (Acts 2:46), and these two characteristics attracted others to the Lord.

singing Producing musical notes with the voice; vocalizing words in musical tones. Singing played an important role in Hebrew and Greek culture as well as in worship. *See also* Music.

sister (1) A female sibling; (2) a female relative or person from the same community (Gen. 20:12); (3) at times, a term of endearment that does not imply a sibling relationship (Song 4:9); (4) in the NT, a Christian woman, emphasizing the intimate family relationship that exists between those who have God as their common Father (Rom. 16:1).

While a number of biblical women are well-known in their own right, others are notable primarily as sisters of famous persons. Among well-known sisters of the Bible are: Miriam, the sister of Moses; Sarah, the half-sister and wife of Abraham; and Tamar, the sister of Absalom. In the NT, the sisters Mary and Martha were close friends and supporters of Jesus.

Sivan *See* Calendar.

six hundred sixty-six (666) Symbolic number representing the name of the first "beast" of Rev. 13, who is generally taken to be the Antichrist. The identification of a name with a number reflects the fact that in the Hebrew and Greek languages numbers were indicated by letters of the alphabet. This made possible the play on names with numbers, called *gematria*. The names of caesars Nero, Caligula, and Domitian were all proposed, in John's day, to identify the beast. Since that time, many erroneous identifications of the Antichrist have been made using such a system, and books have been written to "prove" that the Antichrist was a variety of historical figures, from Napoleon to Mussolini to John F. Kennedy.

Scholars today are divided on their interpretation of 666. Some still "calculate" the name with historical bearing, but others believe that John's numeric symbol would have been recognizable to his readers as a consistent falling short of the thrice-repeated number of perfection, 777. In this case, 666 simply symbolizes the beast and false religion.

skin (1) The outer layer of a human's or an animal's body. The first mention of animal hides is found in Gen. 3:21, where God made coverings of animal skins for Adam and Eve.

(2) Animal hides that were treated and then sewn together served as bottles for water, milk, or wine in biblical times. Such containers are intended when the text speaks of a "skin" of some liquid (Jdg. 4:19; Mt.9:16,17). *See also* Wineskin

Regarding human skin, Leviticus 13 deals extensively with infectious skin diseases, called "leprosy" in older English

Pigskin floats buoy Assyrian soldiers as they swim across a river. Animal skins cover the circle-framed boat called a coracle (Nimrud, about 865 B.C.).

Right: Goatskin "bottle" of Bedouins (Arabic nomads) in the Sinai and line drawing of man bearing a full one. Animal skins were sewn up tightly to carry water or wine (Gen. 21:14; Josh. 9:4; 1 Sam. 1:24). Far right: A Babylonian mother gives her child a drink from a waterskin; detail of a relief from Nineveh, about 690 B.C.

versions. Such diseases made an Israelite ritually unclean *See also* Leprosy. .

A number of biblical expressions containing "skin" have become proverbial. Among them are: "nothing but skin and bones" (Job 19:20); "the skin of my teeth" (Job 19:20); and "Can the Ethiopian change his skin, or the leopard its spots?" (Jer. 13:23).

skirt An article of clothing mentioned in the OT. However, the meaning of the Hebrew terms for this word is uncertain. In modern versions, "skirt" refers to clothing intended to cover only the lower part of the body or just the hem of a garment (Jer 13:22,26). In OT references, the lifting of skirts caused shame, as one's nakedness is revealed (Isa. 47:2; Nah. 3:5). Covering a widowed relative with the corner of one's skirt symbolized possession or protection through marriage (Ruth 3:9).

sky (1) The upper atmosphere (2 Sam. 22:12; Prov. 23:5); (2) the visible universe beyond earth (Gen. 1:8). Often the term "the heavens" in the NT is simply a reference to the sky.

slander (1) To speak critically of another person (Lev. 19:16); (2) in a judicial setting, to accuse falsely (Ex. 20:16). That both Testaments repeatedly list slander among major sins should encourage us to be especially sensitive to what we say about others (Mt. 15:19; Mk. 7:22; 2 Cor. 12:20; Eph. 4:31; 1 Pet. 2:1).

928

slave, slavery (1) A person who is legally the property of another person and is thus subject to the will of his or her master. (2) Figuratively, moral bondage to the baser emotions and motivations that drive human behavior.

SLAVERY IN BIBLE TIMES

Slavery existed but was not common in Israel during the OT era. A person might become a slave through capture in war (Num. 31:7-9), by birth to slave parents (Ex. 21:4), or by purchase. A convicted thief might be sold for funds needed to make restitution (Ex. 22:3). A debtor unable to pay what he owed might be sold into slavery or might sell his children to satisfy his creditor (Ex. 21:7; 2 Ki. 4:1). A person might also sell himself voluntarily in order to escape poverty (Lev. 25:39-53).

After six years of service, an Israelite was bound to free a fellow Israelite whom he had purchased as a slave, unless the slave freely chose to remain in his service (Deut. 15:16,17). While OT Law accepted the concept that slaves are the property of their owners, the Mosaic code protected slaves from harsh treatment (Ex. 20:10; 21:7-11,26,27).

Slavery was more prevalent in NT times in the Roman world beyond Palestine, where slaves were a definite economic asset. The Romans employed thousands of slaves on great rural estates and in their luxury villas. Most of these slaves were captives taken in war. Slaves also filled important staff positions in running the Empire. In the first century, a high percentage of the professionals in the Roman Empire, such as teachers and doctors, were slaves.

By the first century, humanitarian laws also protected slaves in the Empire. Strikingly, records of the era indicate that hundreds of thousands of slaves were freed by their masters, a situation that became so common that the Empire finally imposed a tax of five percent of the value of each slave to be freed. However, the typical free man was hardly better off financially than a slave and, in fact, was less certain of obtaining the necessities of life.

SLAVERY IN THE BIBLE

Both Testaments call for decent treatment of slaves by their masters. The NT also calls on slaves to serve their masters wholeheartedly, as if serving Christ himself (Eph. 6:5; Col. 3:22). In making these statements, Scripture treats slavery as a reality and does not confront the morality of ownership of one person by another. Nevertheless, the NT's command that masters treat their Christian slaves as brothers and sisters (Phlm. 16) undermines the slave system, for a person who is valued as a brother or sister can no longer be viewed as mere property. It is just this perspective that led to the outlawing of slavery first in England and later in the United States.

"SLAVERY" IN THEOLOGY

The Greek language has two distinct terms for service. One, *diakoneō*, simply suggests rendering aid or helping another person. The other, *douleuō*, means to serve as a slave, implying subjection. The slave is not free to do as he chooses but must act according to the will of his master. However well treated a slave might be, the essential fact of subjection remains. This is the basis of more than one illustration used by Jesus in his teaching (Mt. 6:24; Lk. 17:7-10).

Jesus also applied the terminology of slavery to the human condition. "Everyone who sins is a slave of sin," Jesus told the Pharisees (Jn. 8:34). He went on to say that a person can be freed from the dominating influence of sin only "if the Son sets you free" (Jn. 8:36). Paul picks up this thought. He describes mankind's condition as slavery to the dominating power of sin (Rom. 6:16; 7:7-25).

The NT writers argue that a person must offer himself as a servant to God, choosing not to "live the rest of his earthly life for evil human desires, but rather for the will of God" (1 Pet. 4:2), in order to find freedom from sin. Such submission is not only beneficial but right. "You are not

The Assyrians used gangs of slaves to transport a huge stone bull to Sennacherib's palace at Nineveh (about 700 B.C.). Inset: List of slaves inscribed in Sumerian pictographs on a terra-cotta tablet (about 2500 B.C.). The symbol of the hand denotes the slave-owner.

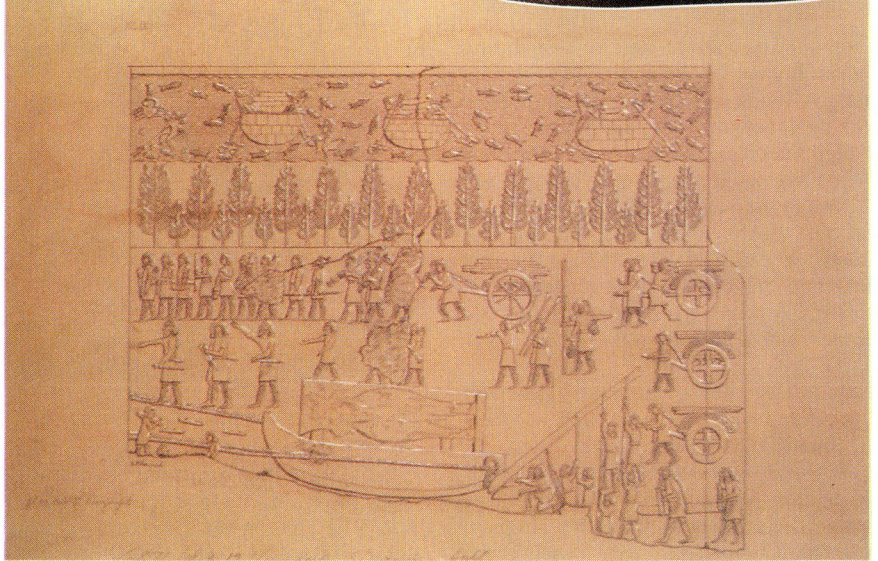

Right: Egyptian san-
dal soles painted with
a Nubian and an Asi-
atic prisoner fettered
at the elbows.
Foreign slaves in
Bible times were
commonly acquired
through military con-
quest, even in Israel
(Num. 31:25-47; Josh.
9:23; 1 Ki. 9:21).

pad. He then swung the stone around to
build momentum. Releasing one of the
straps, he allowed the stone to fly free
toward its target.

While primitive, the weapon was quite
powerful. Round stones found at biblical
sites and identified as slingstones are two
to three inches in diameter. Skilled warriors could "sling a stone at a hair and not
miss" (Jdg. 20:16). Given the effectiveness
of the weapon, David's victory over Goliath was not as surprising as many might
assume (1 Sam. 17).

slothful (KJV) *See* Lazy.

smith A craftsman who works in metal
(Jdg. 17:4; Isa. 40:19). For a description of
a smith at work, *see* Isa. 44:12. *See also*
Goldsmith; Iron; Metals; Silversmith.

snake *See* Serpent.

snare A trap. In biblical times, hunters
would often use a looped cord rigged with
a slip knot to tighten on the leg of an
animal or bird. The creature, trying to get
at the bait set by the hunter, would step
into the loop by accident (Pss. 91:3; 124:7).
Another form of snare caught the neck in

your own; you were bought at a price" (1
Cor. 6:19,20). Jesus has a right to our
allegiance because with his own blood he
purchased our release from slavery to sin.

Thus, Paul takes great pride in identifying himself as a "slave" (*doulos*) of Jesus
Christ (Rom. 1:1; Gal. 1:10; Phil. 1:1; Tit.
1:1). In becoming a slave to Christ, Paul
found the secret of freedom from domination by sin. Only in choosing to be God's
slave can a person achieve his full potential as a human being. *See also* Servant.

"David triumphed
over [Goliath] with a
sling and a stone;
without a sword in
his hand he struck
down the Philistine
and killed him" (1
Sam. 17:50). Relief of
a Hittite slingman,
Tell Halaf, Turkey.

sleep (1) The natural state of rest during
which human beings and animals remain
relatively unaware of their surroundings;
(2) a trance or coma-like state, called
"deep sleep," sometimes induced by God
when speaking to a human being (Gen.
15:12); figuratively, (3) mental dullness or
laziness (Prov. 20:13), and (4) biological
death (Job 14:12; 1 Cor. 15:51). This last
use is significant, for it suggests that
death, like sleep, is only a temporary state
from which a person awakes.

sling A weapon for hurling stones with
power and accuracy, used both by shepherds and the military.

The sling was made of two long straps
of leather attached to a flat pad. The
slinger held the end of the two straps in
one hand and placed a stone loosely in the

the loop and sprang upward, strangling
the bird or animal (Amos 3:5).

Snares and traps provided biblical writers with vivid pictures of spiritual temptation. The gods of the Canaanites were a
snare to Israel, enticing God's people to

practice paganism (Deut. 7:16; Jdg. 2:3). The Psalms often speak of enemies "setting a snare" to trap the godly (Pss. 119:110; 140:5). However, Isaiah warns that the coming Day of the Lord will be "terror and pit and snare" for the rebellious peoples of the earth (Isa. 24:17).

Several NT references also use the imagery of the trap (Lk. 21:34; Jn. 8:6; Rom. 11:9; 1 Tim. 3:7; 6:9; 2 Tim. 2:26).

snow Frozen flakes of water crystal formed in the upper atmosphere. Palestine is a hot land, yet snow is not uncommon in Israel's highlands. Mount Hermon is snow-capped most of the year and is visible from many parts of the land. However, only 2 Sam. 23:20 refers to actual snowfall. In other references, snow serves as a symbol of whiteness, purity, and of refreshing coolness.

soap Probably lye, a detergent solution produced by filtering water through ashes. Lye was not used so much to clean dirty garments as to treat the raw fibers in new clothing. The prophets mention soap figuratively as a purifying agent (Jer. 2:22; Mal. 3:2). *See also* Fuller (KJV).

Sodom and Gomorrah Two of five "cities of the plain," a fertile area in Abraham's time, lying at the southern end of the Dead Sea.

Abraham's nephew, Lot, allured by the wealth of the area, chose to settle in Sodom when he separated from his uncle. But Lot failed to consider the moral corruption of the population, illustrated by the attempted homosexual rape by the men of Sodom of angelic messengers sent to Lot (Gen. 19:1-5). Because of their wickedness (Gen. 18:22), the cities were destroyed in a firestorm of divine judgment, probably through the agency of an earthquake and ignition of deposits of highly flammable bitumen found in the area.

Sodom and Gomorrah are synonymous in Scripture with vice and depravity, and the prophets speak the name of these cities as a curse when describing a morally corrupt generation of Israelites (Isa. 1:10; Jer. 23:14; Ezek. 16:46,48). Sodom also serves as an example of God's commitment to judge sin (Isa. 13:29; Amos 4:11; Mt. 10:15; 2 Pet. 2:6; Jude 7). The fall of Sodom and Gomorrah, along with the Flood, epitomize the biblical conviction that God is holy and surely will punish those who persist in wickedness.

sodomy A general term for unnatural sex acts, specifically homosexuality. The name is taken from an incident reported in Gen. 19:1-11, when the men of Sodom surrounded the home of Lot and insisted he send out two visitors whom they wished to use sexually. *See also* Homosexuality.

soldier A person on active military duty or a person who has been trained to serve as a fighter.

In early Israel, all adult males served in the militia, called out to defend the land when attacked. Israel's first king, Saul, developed a small force of personal guards (1 Sam. 13:1,2), but it was David who developed a national army (2 Sam. 24). Later, a professional army served as the

Snow on Mount Hermon, part of the Lebanon Range at the northernmost limit of ancient Israel. Though relatively rare in Israel, snow served as a common standard for whiteness (for example, Ps. 51:7; Isa. 1:18; Mt. 28:3).

935

Foreign soldiers, such as these from Nubia and Asia Minor shown in relief, served in the Egyptian army. Two foreigners, Uriah the Hittite and Zelek the Ammonite, were members of King David's elite force of "mighty men" (2 Sam. 23:8-39).

core of forces in both Israel and Judah.

The soldiers mentioned in the NT were members of the Roman army. Roman soldiers and their auxiliary forces enlisted for a period of 20 years. They were recruited from various sections of the Empire, but assigned to duty away from their homelands. John the Baptist suggests that at least some of the soldiers assigned to Judea extorted money (Lk. 3:14). In contrast, centurions (officers) in the Roman army are portrayed in the NT as fair and even admirable men (Acts 10). *See also* Army; Centurion; War.

solemn assembly *See* Congregation.

Two Roman soldiers depicted in attack stance, on a column from the praetorium of Mogontiacum (Mainz, Germany).

Solomon [SAHL-uh-muhn; probably "peaceful"]. The son and successor of David and king of Israel's united kingdom, 970–931 B.C. The Solomonic era marked the height of Israel's material glory. Solomon's greatest achievement was the construction of the Temple in Jerusalem. **Parents:** David, Bathsheba. **Son and successor in Judah:** Rehoboam. **Scripture:** 1 Ki. 1–11; 2 Chr. 1–9; *see* Mt. 6:29; 12:42.

BACKGROUND

On David's death, his son Solomon inherited the area's largest and most powerful kingdom. Solomon continued to hold the lands his father had conquered by maintaining a strong standing army and by weaving a network of treaties with surrounding nations. Solomon's expanded kingdom gave him control of the major land trade routes that ran through Damascus, while his close association with King Hiram of Tyre led to joint trading ventures at sea.

Trade brought Solomon vast wealth. In addition, his income, not including trade revenue and taxes, amounted to 25 tons of gold annually (2 Chr. 9:13), much of which Solomon lavishly spent on public works. Among his building projects were the Jerusalem Temple, a magnificent palace, and reinforcement of strategic cities such as Megiddo. Despite Israel's wealth, Solomon's projects placed a strain on the economy. Taxes were raised, and thousands of Israelites were forced to spend time as workmen and supervisors. This created a general dissatisfaction, which led ten tribes to revolt after Solomon's death.

Solomon proved an able administrator, refining the centralized systems introduced by David (1 Ki. 4:7-19). He was also politically sensitive, dealing effectively with several problems he inherited from his father (1 Ki. 2:1-12). He showed restraint in dealing with his half-brother Adonijah, who had attempted a coup while David was still living. But when Adonijah asked permission to marry a young woman who had cared for David during his last years, Solomon saw an attempt to establish a future claim to his throne and acted decisively to execute Adonijah for treason (1 Ki. 2:13-46).

Solomon himself was famous for his intellectual achievements. He was renowned as a botanist, who catalogued plant life, and a zoologist, who gathered data on characteristics of birds, animals, and insects (1 Ki. 4:29-34). In addition he is said to have spoken "three thousand proverbs and his songs [psalms] numbered a thousand and five." Tradition assigns Solomon authorship of the Song of Songs, Ecclesiastes, and many of the sayings preserved in the Book of Proverbs.

LEARNING FROM SOLOMON'S LIFE

The biblical text pays close attention to Solomon's spiritual journey. Asked by God to choose any gift, Solomon pleased the Lord by requesting a discerning heart "to govern your people and to distinguish between right and wrong" (1 Ki. 3:9-15). The greatest moment in Solomon's spiritual life may have been at the dedication of the Temple he had constructed in Jerusalem. His prayer of dedication (1 Ki. 8:22-61) reveals both humility and a deep sensitivity to the love that moved God to make—and to keep—his covenant with Israel. God responded to this prayer of Solomon, too, and promised that Solomon would never lack a descendant qualified to sit on Israel's throne (1 Ki. 9:5)—a promise originally given to David and ultimately fulfilled in Christ.

However, as Solomon grew more confident in his rule, he made a tragic mistake (1 Ki. 11:1-13). As was customary in OT times, Solomon sealed many of the treaties he made with foreign rulers by marrying a member of their royal house. This was a dual violation of God's Law, which forbad marriage to foreign women and also decreed that a king of God's people must not "take many wives" (Deut. 17:17). Ultimately Solomon had some 700 wives and 300 concubines. His passion for many of these women led him to permit them to erect shrines to their pagan gods and god-

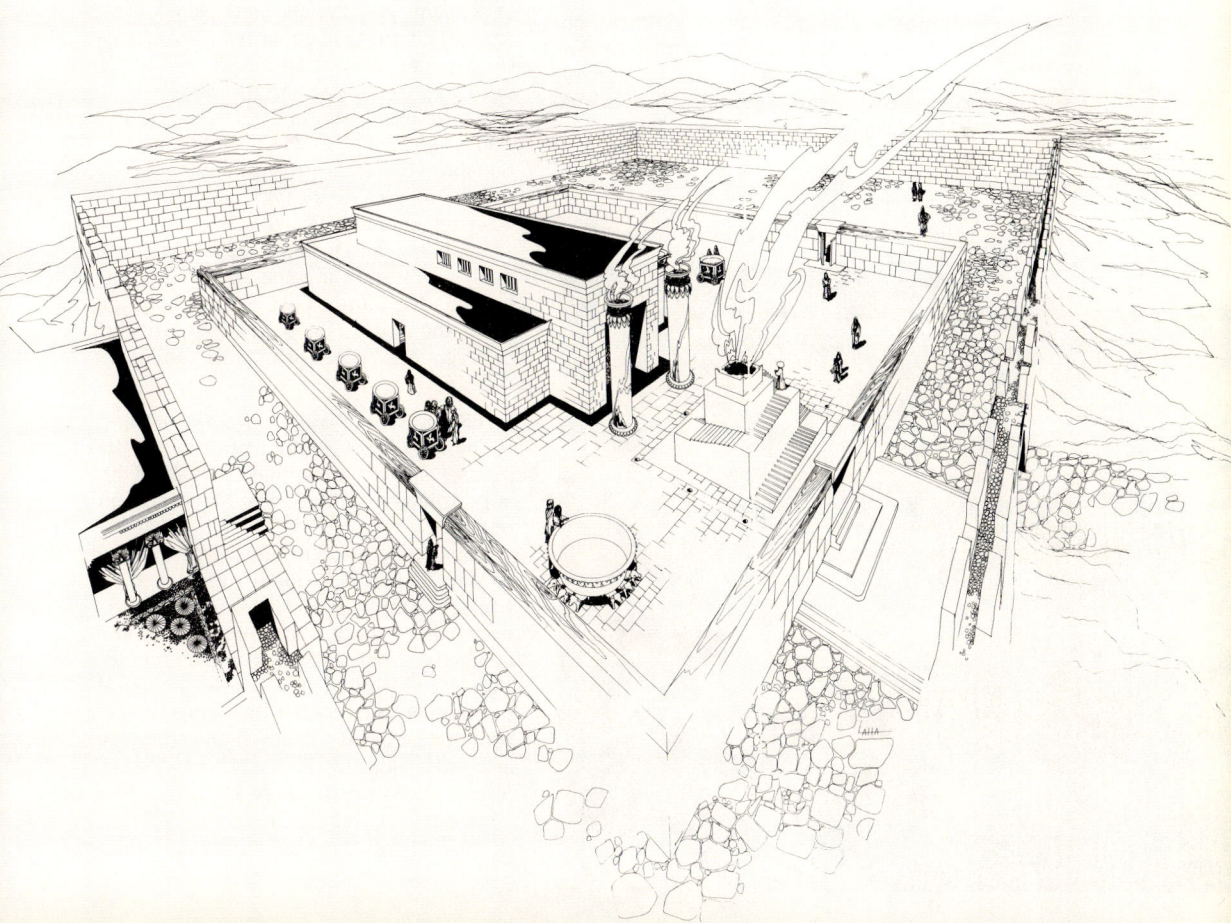

Reconstruction of Solomon's Temple and its courts. In the inner court are ten lavers, the molten sea (lower center), and the altar for burnt offerings (center). Solomon's palace (left) overlooked the Temple courts.

desses. As Solomon grew old, "his wives turned his heart after other gods, and his heart was not fully devoted to the Lord" (1 Ki. 11:4). This loss of spiritual bearings is reflected in the Book of Ecclesiastes, in which the author meditates on the futility of life. In this unique book, the old king seeks by wisdom to search out the meaning of life, but limits himself to what can be observed "under the sun." Isolated by his own choices from that intimate fellowship with God that sustained him in his youth, Solomon—despite his wealth, intellect, pleasures, and accomplishments—could find no meaning or purpose to life. *See also* Ecclesiastes.

The lesson from Solomon's life is an important one. No matter how blessed or talented an individual may be, life will be empty apart from a relationship with God. Solomon also serves to illustrate a warning God had given to Israel: "Be careful . . . when you build fine houses and settle down, and when your herds and flocks grow large and your silver and gold increase," for then there is danger that "your heart will become proud and you will forget the Lord your God" (Deut. 8:11-14).

Solomon, Song of *See* Song of Songs.

Solomon's Porch A raised platform on Herod's Temple featuring a double row of columns, constructed at the east end of the Temple's outer court (Jn. 10:23; Acts 3:11). Also called Solomon's Portico or Colonnade.

son OT [Heb., *ben*]. (1) A parent's male child (Gen. 16:15); (2) a descendant, however many generations removed (1 Chr. 1:5); (3) offspring of either sex (Gen. 3:16); (4) a polite form of address ("my son") used by a superior to an inferior (1 Sam. 3:6). The term "son of" (or "sons of") is also used in the OT (5) to define a relationship (Ex. 4:22), (6) to identify group membership (1 Ki. 20:35), and (7) to characterize generally (Ps. 89:6,22 KJV).

NT [Gk., *huios*]. Same as the Hebrew uses, but adding the special reference to Jesus as the Son of God, Son of Man, or just "the Son" (Jn. 5:20). Figuratively, believers are "sons [people] of the light" (Lk. 16:8).

JESUS: SON OF MAN, SON OF GOD

The two most significant uses of the phrase "son of" are applied to Jesus, who is portrayed as both Son of Man and Son of God.

Jesus often spoke of himself as the Son of Man. The title, frequently employed by Ezekiel, simply meant "human" and is used where the prophet emphasizes the distinctions between God and mankind. Daniel uses "son of man" in eschatological passages to convey that the being he saw coming from heaven with divine authority and power looked human (Dan. 7:13,14). Jesus builds on both these OT uses when

speaking of himself as the Son of Man. By this phrase, Christ affirms complete identification of himself with human beings and at the same time identifies himself as the Messiah through whom God will bring righteousness and peace.

The phrase "Son of God" when applied to Jesus affirms his deity. Christ is the Son of God in a unique sense, being his "one and only Son" who existed with God and as God from the beginning (Jn. 1:1-14). This distinctive relationship was announced at Jesus' baptism (Mk. 1:11), acknowledged by Satan during the temptation (Mt. 4:1-11), fearfully admitted by demons Christ confronted (Mk. 1:23-25; 3:11,12), taught by Christ while on earth (Mk. 13:32), and proven by Jesus' resurrection from the dead (Rom. 1:4).

Together these two descriptions of Jesus express the Christian conviction that Jesus is both fully God and truly human. *See also* Deity; God; Incarnation.

CHRISTIANS AS SONS OF GOD

The phrase "sons of God," when applied to Christians, encompasses both male and female believers. It goes beyond the concept of "children of God," reflecting a distinctive concept in Roman law. One who has been recognized as a "son" is not only a member of the family by birth or adoption, but has also reached an age at which he or she has achieved "full rights" (Gal. 4:5). All the rights and privileges, as well as the responsibilities, of being adult children of one's father are experienced by those who have come to God through Jesus. *See also* Adoption; Family; Father.

While all human beings are children of God in the limited sense of being his creations, only those with faith in Jesus are acknowledged as his sons (Jn. 1:12; 1 Jn. 3:1,2). *See also* Children.

song A musical composition. In OT times, songs were frequently intended as mne-

"SON(S) OF" IN THE BIBLE		
Phrase	**In Reference to**	**Meaning**
Sons of Aaron	Descendants of Aaron	Priests
Son of Abraham (Lk. 19:9)	Zacchaeus	Man of faith
Sons of Belial (1 Sam. 10:27, KJV)	Enemies of Saul	"Troublemakers" (NIV) or wicked people
Son of David	Jesus	The Messiah; anointed descendant of David
Son of fatness (Isa. 5:1, KJV)	Fields, land	Fertile soil
Son of God	Jesus	Anointed by God; One with the Father
Sons of God	Angels (Job 1,2) Israelites Christians	Specially created beings Specially chosen people Those in special relationship with God through Jesus
Sons of Israel/Jacob	Descendants of Jacob (Israel)	Israelites; Jews
Sons of Levi	Descendants of Levi	Levites, the Temple stewards
Sons of light (Jn. 12:36)	Disciples	Followers of Jesus
Son of perdition (Jn. 17:12, KJV)	Judas	One "doomed to destruction" (NIV)
Sons of the prophets	OT prophets (1 Sam. 10:5; Amos 7:14) Disciples (Acts 3:25, RSV)	Members of a prophets' "guild"? Heirs or adherents of the prophets
Sons of Thunder (Mk. 3:17)	James and John, sons of Zebedee	Quick-tempered men?
Sons of Zion	Inhabitants of the city of Zion	Jerusalem's citizens

monic devices to help God's people remember what God had done or how to
relate to him (Ex. 15:1; Deut. 31:30). Songs
were sung either by individuals or by the
entire congregation as praise to God (Pss.
28:7; 98:4; Jon. 2:9). The NT mentions
"spiritual songs" that members of the
early church sang, along with psalms and
hymns (Eph. 5:19; Col. 3:16). *See also*
Music.

song of ascents, song of degrees The
title given to each of Psalms 120–134.
The Hebrew word translated "degree"
(*ma'alah*) means ascent level, or step. The
usual explanation for this title is that pilgrims sang these psalms on their way
(ascent) to Jerusalem for the religious festivals held there. Some rabbis held that the
15 psalms correspond to the 15 steps that
led into the Temple. Still others take the
title as a musical term indicating the tune
to which the psalms should be sung. Yet

others see the "ascent" as a technical
poetic term (like "sonnet" or "limerick"),
describing the relationship of each verse of
these psalms to the preceding verse.

Song of Songs A romantic love poem that
tradition and its first verse assign to Solomon, 970–930 B.C. The book has puzzled
many, as it seems to lack theological orientation and language.

BACKGROUND

The debate about this OT book focuses
on whether it is simply a poem celebrating
love between a man and a woman or if it
contains a hidden "spiritual" message.
The debate has led to three major interpretations.

(1) Jewish rabbis and many church fathers saw the book as an allegory. To the
rabbis, the book symbolized the relationship between God and his covenant people; however, the early Christians saw a
symbolic representation of the relationship
between Christ and the Church. In this
latter view, chapters 1–3 describe the mutual love of Christ and the Church, chapter
5 the Church's graces, and so on. *See also*
Allegory.

(2) In the Middle Ages, interpreters began to view the Song of Songs as a type;
that is, the love that existed between the
king and his beloved is intended to reflect
the love of Christ for the Church and the
Church's response. *See also* Type.

(3) More recently, the work has been
viewed as a poetic love story. Some versions, such as the NIV, adopt this view
and include headings that set off a dramatic structure reflected in changes of
Hebrew gender and voice. According to
this interpretation, the book celebrates the
joys of romantic love, an appropriate and
healthy expression of God's gift of sexuality to humankind. *See also* Sex.

This last interpretation seems to fit the

SONG OF SONGS: A READING AND STUDY GUIDE

Chapter	Content Summary	Related Articles
1:1–2:7	Beloved and lover praise each other for the qualities they admire.	Beauty Solomon
2:8–3:11	The beloved praises her lover, using images from nature.	Nature; Sex, Sexual Intercourse
4:1–5:1	The lover praises his beloved's beauty.	
5:2–6:3	The lover leaves, leaving the beloved lonely and distraught.	Desire
6:4–8:14	The lover returns and the two are married, as friends celebrate their happiness.	Dance Marriage

"How beautiful you are, my darling!
  Oh, how beautiful!
    Your eyes are doves" (Song 1:15)
Figurine from
Yokneam (10th or 9th
century B.C.).

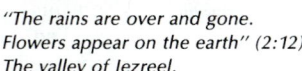

"The rains are over and gone.
Flowers appear on the earth" (2:12)
The valley of Jezreel.

"The fig tree forms its early fruit" (2:13).

"I went down to the
grove of nut trees
to look at the new
growth in the valley"
(6:11).
Fruit trees in bloom
in spring time.

"Catch for us the
  foxes,
the little foxes that
ruin the vineyards"
(2:15).
Mosaic floor from
Beth Shean (5th cen-
tury A.D.).

"Let us go early to the vineyards
. . . there I will give you my love" (7:12).
Vineyards in Judea, north of Jerusalem.

Hebrew text best. As such, the Song is the story of a wanderer who discovers his love in a rural area. He then disappears, only to return in royal splendor to claim his bride. On the one hand, this interpretation does not seem to fit what we know of Solomon's passionate relationship with so many different wives and concubines. Then again, it may be a poem expressing Solomon's romantic yearning for the ideal relationship that is possible only in monogamous marriage.

MASTERY KEYS

Write the following speakers in the margin of your Bible, then read the Song as a dramatic poem:

Beloved	Lover	Friends
1:2-4a		1:4b
1:5-7	1:8-11	
1:12-14	1:15	
1:16	1:17	
2:1	2:2	
2:3-13	2:14,15	
2:16–3:11	4:1-15	
4:16	5:1a,b	5:1c
5:2-8		5:9
5:10-16		6:1
6:2,3	6:4-12	6:13a
	6:13b–7:9a	
7:9b–8:4		8:5a
8:5b-7		8:8,9
8:10-12	8:13	
8:14		

Sons of Thunder *See* Boanerges.

soothsayer One who foretells the future using occult means (Isa. 3:2). The Law pointedly forbade involvement with any occult practice (Deut. 18:9-13). *See also* Magic; Medium; Occult.

sop (KJV) (1) A morsel or bit of bread torn from a flat loaf and used to scoop up food from the main dish (Ruth 2:14); (2) a bite of the most tasty food served at a feast, handed to a guest by the host (Jn. 13:25,26)—this act expresses warmth and friendship and is a mark of special honor even in biblical lands today.

When Jesus reached out to Judas with a morsel chosen from the Passover platter, the act showed that Christ was still unwilling to treat his betrayer as an enemy. The act also underlines the hardness of Judas's heart; even this special act of friendship could not move Judas to change his mind. *See also* Judas.

sorcerer A person who claims supernatural powers and who uses magic. In the ancient world, the powers of a sorcerer were generally thought to flow from evil rather than beneficial supernatural sources. Sorcery is mentioned in both Testaments (Ex. 7:11; Isa. 47:9; Acts 8:9-13; 13:8-11), always in negative terms. Like all other occult practices, sorcery is forbidden to God's people. *See also* Magic; Medium; Occult.

There are several sorcerers named in Scripture. In the OT, Moses and Aaron confronted Pharaoh's sorcerers, named Jannes and Jambres in Jewish tradition (2 Tim. 3:8). These "magicians" were only partially successful in their attempts to duplicate the miracles performed by God's servants (Ex. 7:11,12). In the NT, Peter rebuked an ex-sorcerer, Simon, when Simon tried to purchase the right to give the gift of the Holy Spirit. Peter revealed that Simon, while claiming to be a believer, was still bound by sin and needed to set his heart right with God (Acts 8:9-25). Paul and Barnabas also confronted a sorcerer, Bar-Jesus (Elymas), on the isle of Cyprus (Acts 13:4-12).

sorceress *See* Witch.

sorrow The mental stress and anguish, or physical pain, associated with some affliction.

Hebrew has 15 different terms for sorrow. Some draw attention to emotional distress (Ps. 13:2; Isa. 51:11; Jer. 31:13), others to physical pain (Isa. 53:3,4). Greek does not make the delicate distinctions of Hebrew, and uses one word (*lypē*) for "grief," "pain," "distress"—any sort of physical or emotional stress.

Paul distinguishes between "godly" and "worldly" sorrow (2 Cor. 7:8-11). A hurt that leads a person to turn to God in repentance is good. Such a person "becomes sorrowful as God intended" and is not harmed by his or her distress. However, "worldly sorrow" focuses on the experience rather than God and produces nothing but regret.

Paul's point is important. Any situation, no matter how painful, can be redeemed by taking it to God. A sorrow that turns our hearts toward God is strengthening. A sorrow that fails to turn our hearts to God is worldly, since we then deal with our grief just as people who have no relationship with God deal with theirs. Only regret and bitterness are produced by a worldly approach to our sorrows.

soul [Heb., *nepesh*; Gk., *psyche*]. (1) The individual self, each person's unique "I"; (2) the personal pronoun, "I," "me," "myself"; (3) life as experienced by the individual rather than as an abstract concept. Most modern versions use a variety of words, such as "life," "self," and "being," to translate the Hebrew *nepesh*.

The OT views human beings as whole persons and does not break man's nature into parts. The terms used in speaking of human beings—which include soul, spirit, flesh, heart, and others—are elements in a biblical "vocabulary of perspective." In the vocabulary of perspective, "flesh" describes the whole person in view of his or her experience on this earth; "heart" describes the whole person as a conscious self, aware of emotions and other inner states; "soul" is the essential self, the distinctive identity of the person. Thus, "soul" frequently serves as a personal pronoun: The anguished soul is a person in anguish (Ps. 6:3), and to "lift up" one's soul to God means simply that a person focuses all his attention on the Lord (Ps. 25:1).

In the NT, "soul" generally retains its Hebrew meanings. It also denotes the existence of a person after death (Lk. 9:25; 12:4; 21:19). *See also* Body; Man; Spirit.

MISUNDERSTOOD PASSAGES

Many passages containing "soul" have been misinterpreted. For instance:

• *Ezekiel 18:20.* Ezekiel warns that "the soul who sins is the one who will die." This is no reference to eternal punishment, except by consequence of physical death. Rather, Ezekiel was informing the people of Judah that evil persons would be killed in the coming Babylonian invasion of Judah, while the godly and penitent would be spared. The passage suggests that God actively protects those who live in covenant relationship with him in times of national peril.

• *Matthew 16:26; Mark 8:37.* Jesus rhetorically asked, "What can a man give in exchange for his soul?" Here the word means an individual's essential self. Christ's point is that a person who refuses to surrender to God in order to hold on to his old self, loses the "reborn" self he or she might become. Only in being a true disciple of Jesus can a human being achieve his or her potential.

• *Revelation 6:9; 20:4.* In his vision of heaven, John saw the "souls" of the dead. These were not disembodied fragments, but the believers themselves.

south A compass point to one's right when facing the rising sun.

The most common Hebrew word for "south" is *negeb*, which means dry or parched land. This makes sense, since the Sinai desert region lies south of Palestine. Politically, the major power to Israel's south was always Egypt, although desert tribes such as the Amalekites also raided Israel from the south. *See also* Negev.

The OT frequently mentions "north and south" together as an indication of the whole world (Ps. 89:12; Ezek. 20:47). Although there was some criss-crossing, the major routes of travel through Palestine ran north and south.

The springs at Ein Avdat oasis in the Negev Desert, which stretches across all of southern Palestine.

In a detailed prophecy, Daniel mentions a "king of the south" who would arise to do battle with a "king of the north" (Dan. 11). This was fulfilled in the power struggle after the death of Alexander the Great, as Ptolemy seized power in Egypt and Antiochus in Syria. Ptolemy IV Philopater defeated Antiochus III in 217 B.C. at Raphia, just south of Gaza.

sovereignty of God God's absolute right to govern all things as he chooses, without any limitations imposed by circumstances or human choices.

While the Bible does not use the term "sovereignty," it clearly teaches the concept of God's complete dominion over the universe. God has the same control over his creation and creatures that the potter has over his clay (Isa. 45:9-19; Rom. 9:19-21). As the psalmist proclaims, "Our God is in heaven; he does whatever pleases him" (Ps. 115:3). God's complete freedom enables him to guarantee the future redemption of the universe and the destiny of those who trust Christ. Only because God is sovereign can "neither the present nor the future, nor any powers, neither height nor depth, nor anything else in all creation . . . separate us from the love of God that is in Christ Jesus our Lord" (Rom. 8:38).

Both philosophers and theologians have struggled with the concept of God's absolute sovereignty. Some argue that a good God who had all power would never allow the human tragedies and pain that mar the universe. Others are concerned with the relationship between God's sovereignty and human freedom. The answer to both concerns is that God has chosen to extend a limited freedom to human beings. By sinning, mankind has misused that freedom. Thus, human suffering is a consequence of human rather than divine choices. That same limited freedom enables human beings to act in harmony with or against God's revealed will. But no human choice can thwart any of God's purposes or determine any divine choice. *See also* Freedom.

Paul raises this issue in Rom. 9. The Jews of his day believed that descent from Abraham, with obedience to Moses' Law, obligated God to them, so that they were in fact saved by good works. Paul shows from Israel's history that God has always acted sovereignly. He chose Isaac rather than Ishmael to inherit the covenant promises. He chose Jacob over his older twin Esau "before the twins were born or had

Farmer sowing seed; medieval woodcut from the Augsburger Kalendar *(1487).*

done anything good or bad" (Rom. 9:11). Paul's point in this chapter is not to teach an election to salvation with or without human will but to prove conclusively that God's choices are sovereign, not caused or limited by anything that human beings do. God acts as he does simply because he chooses to. Thus, God "works out everything in conformity with the purpose of his will" (Eph. 1:11).

The biblical vision of a totally sovereign God alienates some, but it need not concern the believer who remembers one thing. The way power is exercised depends on the character of the person holding it. And the God of Scripture, who has all power, is a God of love, justice, grace, and goodness. God will never do anything that violates his own character; thus, he and he alone can be trusted with the freedom of action he alone has.

Two of several teachings in Scripture help us appreciate the way God has chosen to exercise his freedom to act. First, God has chosen to provide salvation. His sovereignty is no threat to us but rather the basis of our hope. Second, God superintends the results of believers' choices. Peter discusses the case in which a believer does right but suffers for it (1 Pet. 3:10-22). He points out that Jesus found himself in this same situation. Jesus did only good, yet he suffered on Calvary. But look at the outcome, Peter says. Through Jesus' suffering, he brought us to God! Our sovereign God was able to take an injustice and transform it into redemption for humankind. So when we suffer for doing right, Peter says, we are to remember that God can use our suffering to create something beautiful and good.

sow, sowing To scatter grain seeds on the ground when planting a crop.

In the ancient world, the farmer generally carried seed in a leather sack slung around a shoulder. He took handfuls of the grain and, with a practiced motion, scattered it quite evenly on the ground. The farmer then used a plow to scratch the surface of the soil and cover the seed. Jesus' parable of the sower (Mt. 13:3-8; Mk. 4:3-8; Lk. 8:5-15) illustrates the process and gives insight into some of the everyday hazards faced by farmers in the ancient world.

span A measure of length, equal to half a cubit. Depending on the cubit used, a span was either about 8.7 inches (22 centimeters) or 10.2 inches (26 centimeters). *See also* Weights and Measures.

sparrow (1) A general word for any small, clean (edible) bird, including young doves and pigeons (Gen. 15:10); (2) specifically, the sparrow as we know it today (Ps. 84:3).

Children in Arab lands still catch small birds, pluck them, and tie several together for sale. This practice may be referred to in Jesus' illustration of sparrows bunched together for sale in the market. These would bring only the smallest of coins (Mt. 10:29-31; Lk. 12:6,7). A God who noted the fall of even these tiny bits of life would surely watch over human beings, who are of infinitely greater worth.

spear A thrusting weapon, created by attaching a sharpened head to a stout wooden staff. Spearmen fought behind large body shields, attempting to stab their enemies. Some ancient fishermen also used spears (Job 41:7).

Before about 1500 B.C. the spear head was shaped with a prong at its base. The shaft was split, the prong inserted, and the shaft tightly bound. Later spear heads

were made with sockets into which the shaft might fit. Often the base of the shaft was fitted with a metal point also, so the weapon could be thrust upright into the ground. Saul's general, Abner, killed Asahel, one of David's men, with the butt of his spear (2 Sam. 2:23).

Saul, encamped with his army, slept with his spear nearby, "stuck in the ground near his head" (1 Sam. 26:7). One night David crept in and took Saul's spear but did not kill the king (1 Sam. 26:12-22).

The prophets predict a time of peace when people "will beat . . . their spears into pruning hooks [vine-tending tools]" (Isa. 2:4; Mic. 4:3). But the Lord also delivers a reverse challenge to enemy nations: "Beat . . . your pruning hooks into spears" (Joel 3:10).

spices Fragrant vegetable substances, usually dried and powdered, used to add flavor to foods or aroma to incense. Spices were used to perfume oils, to scent cosmetics, to flavor foods and wines, and were mixed together to make various kinds of incense. Spices were also sprinkled on the graveclothes in which a body was wrapped for burial.

Spices were very expensive, luxury items in biblical Israel. Scripture lists them among other treasures held by Israel's kings (1 Ki. 10:25; 2 Ki. 20:13). The incense burned at the tabernacle and Temple included several spices (Ex. 30:23,34; 1 Chr. 9:29,30). Among spices mentioned in Scripture are: aloes, cinnamon, calamus, cassia, galbanum, myrrh, nard, onycha, and stacte.

spies Agents sent to obtain information about a potential enemy. As a test, Joseph accused his brothers of being spies when

Spearmen in relief on the sides of a doorway at Arslantash in Turkey (745–725 B.C.).

This highly realistic relief of a house sparrow is a plaster model found in Egypt (332–100 B.C.).

they came to Egypt to buy grain (Gen. 42). Envoys from Babylon who visited Judah in Hezekiah's time were certainly spies, taking back a detailed report of Israel's treasures (2 Ki. 20:12).

Spies figured prominently in two critical events in Israel's early history. Twelve Hebrew spies ventured into Canaan from the Sinai wilderness, but only Joshua and Caleb believed that God would enable Israel to conquer the formidable foes (Num. 13,14). A generation later, Joshua sent two spies into Jericho whose lives were saved by Rahab (Josh. 2).

spikenard (KJV) A costly spice used to perfume oils, which were often sealed in alabaster jars (Jn. 12:3). "Pure nard" was imported from India. *See also* Nard.

Above: Woman spinning depicted in stone relief, 8th–7th centuries B.C. "In her hand she holds the distaff and grasps the spindle with her fingers" (Prov. 31:19). Below: A woman unravels flax fibers while a man spins them together; line drawing of a wall painting in the tomb of Khnumhotep (2050–1800 B.C.).

spinning Drawing out and twisting natural fibers such as cotton, flax, and wool into thread, which was then woven into cloth. *See also* Weaving.

In biblical times women spun by hand, winding wool or flax around a distaff, which was held under the arm or thrust into the ground. The threads were drawn out by hand and wrapped around a spindle, which was then rotated to twist the thread (*see* illustration).

spirit [Heb., *ruah*, "breath"; Gk., *pneuma*, "wind"]. (1) Of God, that supernatural power that gives shape to the creation (Gen. 1:2) and infuses human beings with

life and power to do his will (Gen. 2:7; Jdg. 3:10; 6:34). (2) Of the third person of the Trinity, a descriptive title. *See also* Holy Spirit. (3) Of supernatural beings, an angel (Heb. 1:7, KJV) or a demon (Mt. 8:16; Mk. 1:23; Lk. 11:24). *See also* Angel; Demon. (4) Of human beings, a term that emphasizes the capacity of human beings to be conscious of and to relate to God. *See also* Soul.

Terms such as "soul," "flesh," and "spirit" define the perspective from which human nature is viewed. In the NT especially, *pneuma* views human beings as persons who are aware of and can respond to God (Mt. 5:3; Mk. 8:12; Lk. 1:47; Jn. 13:21; Rom. 1:9; 8:16; Gal. 6:18; Eph. 4:23).

spiritist *See* Wizard.

spirits in prison A phrase in 1 Pet. 3:19, best understood as a reference to those who died in the Flood because they rejected the warning God gave them through Noah.

Contemporary commentators have argued that "spirits in prison" are angels because the plural form of "spirit" with one exception refers to such supernatural beings. These fallen angels are either the "sons of God" in Gen. 6:1-4 or those in 2 Pet. 2:4 who are held for judgment in the dungeons of Tartarus, the place of doom, in Greek thought, below Hades. *See also* Hades; Hell.

spiritual Having to do with the spirit, characterized by the spirit, usually God's Spirit.

According to the NT, the Law is spiritual, but because lost human beings are unspiritual, it brings condemnation rather than hope (Rom. 7:14). The blessings God gives Christians are spiritual rather than material (Eph. 1:3). The resurrection body is spiritual rather than natural (1 Cor. 15:44-46). Complete surrender to God is spiritual worship (Rom. 12:1). Believers, who are being built into a spiritual house, are priests, called to offer God spiritual sacrifices (1 Pet. 2:5).

spiritual gifts [Gk., *charismata*]. Special endowments granted by the Holy Spirit that enable believers to serve others in the community of faith. At times, Christians use the term "spiritual gift" in speaking of divine enablement for any kind of ministry.

THE CONCEPT OF SPIRITUAL GIFTS

Even in the OT, God gave certain people the ability to serve him in special ways. God filled Bezalel "with the Spirit of God, with skill, ability, and knowledge in all kinds of crafts" to shape articles for the tabernacle (Ex. 31:3; *see* 31:6; Jdg. 3:10; 14:6). There is no specific word meaning "spiritual gift" in either Testament. However, the NT uses the Greek term *charisma*, "grace gift," to speak of God's enabling Christians to minister to one another.

Four NT passages deal specifically with spiritual gifts (Rom. 12; 1 Cor. 12; Eph. 4; and 1 Pet. 4:10). Three of them place gifts squarely in the context of ministry within the Body of Christ. These passages teach that each believer has a gift, a special capacity to contribute to the well-being and growth of other believers. There are different gifts that God distributes sovereignly within the Body (1 Cor. 12:6,7). When Christians live together in love, actively seeking to serve and help one another, these gifts are exercised and the whole Body is strengthened. Thus, Peter says, "Each one should use whatever gift he has received to serve others, faithfully administering God's grace in its various forms" (1 Pet. 4:10). God's grace (*charis*) is evidenced tangibly in the Body through the gifts of the Spirit (*charismata*).

It is important to note that each NT passage on spiritual gifts focuses our attention on the Christian community. Gifts are exercised within the context of a caring, loving fellowship with the purpose of building individuals and congregations to spiritual maturity (Eph. 4:12-16).

QUESTIONS ON SPIRITUAL GIFTS

Many Christians have practical questions concerning spiritual gifts.

1. *Are all spiritual gifts listed in the Bible?* Some limit *charismata* to specific gifts mentioned in Rom. 12; 1 Cor. 12; and Eph. 4. Others believe these lists are representative rather than exhaustive and that there are many ways in which a Christian can contribute to others that should be considered spiritual gifts.

2. *Where do spiritual gifts operate?* While some associate the exercise of spiritual gifts with institutional roles in the modern church, every NT context in which gifts are discussed emphasizes Christian interpersonal relationships. Spiritual gifts function in any time or place where Christians gather to share their faith and serve one another.

3. *How does a person discover his or her spiritual gift?* Gifts operate in an interpersonal context. So, as a Christian builds close and caring relationships with other believers, the gifts are discovered as they function. We learn of our spiritual gift when we see how God uses us to minister to others and when others recognize certain qualities in us. In effect, we discover our spiritual gifts by using them.

4. *Are the obviously supernatural gifts (speaking in tongues, healing, etc.) intended to operate in the local church today?* This question has led to debate and division in the contemporary church. Some Christians ar-

SPIRITUAL GIFTS IDENTIFIED IN THE NT

Scripture Reference	For Ministry in Word	For Ministry in Deed
Rom. 12:6-8	Prophecy Teaching	Service Showing mercy Giving (monetary) Encouragement Leadership
1 Cor. 12:4-11, 28-30	Apostolic proclamation Prophecy Discernment of prophecy ("of spirits") Teaching Spiritual wisdom Spiritual knowledge Speaking in "tongues" Interpreting "tongues"	Faith Healing Miraculous powers Helping Administration
Eph. 4:7-12*	Apostolic proclamation Prophecy "Pastoring" and/or teaching Evangelism	

* The text speaks of persons God has given to the Church to equip believers for their ministering work and does not specifically identify their roles as spiritual gifts.

gue that 1 Cor. 13:8 implies that the more spectacular gifts of the Spirit were set aside after the NT canon (Scripture) was complete. Other Christians are convinced that the obviously supernatural gifts are intended for today. The debate has all too often separated Christian brothers and sisters and led to rifts in many congregations. The very fact that we have these strong differences of opinion suggests that we should not take sides hastily. Certainly God is free to work as he chooses in this age as in any other. Surely, too, our understanding of the matter is incomplete.

SIGNIFICANCE OF SPIRITUAL GIFTS

It is all too easy to focus on differences, ignoring the significant truths about spiritual gifts that all Christians affirm. We agree that spiritual gifts are from God the Spirit, who alone enables us to minister to others. We agree that each Christian is spiritually significant. Each of us has a vital role to fill in the Body of Christ because of the Spirit's endowment. As we live with others, united in a fellowship of love, God uses each believer to enrich others.

spirituality The quality or state of being spiritual; characterized by spiritual rather than materialistic attitudes and concerns; being in harmony with and close to God. Biblical spirituality as displayed in the OT, as modeled by Jesus, and as experienced by God's NT people, is essentially living a human life in union with God.

The goal of OT religion was holiness, understood as living in this world by the Law of God. In the Hebrew religion, even the rabbi supported himself by working at a trade. The ideal was not study as an end in itself but that the Word of God might be a light to the daily path.

Jesus lived in our world as a true human being, yet demonstrated his oneness with the Father by actively seeking to do the will of God daily. Jesus was unaffected by materialism, committed to prayer, comfortable in the company of sinners, ever ready to heal the sick and hurting as well as to confront hypocrisy and evil. Jesus was deeply involved, always compassionate, ever reaching out to others with the love of God. Anyone who wonders what true spirituality involves need only to walk with Jesus as the Gospels trace his journeys in Galilee and Judea.

True spirituality for the Christian is to live our human life as Jesus lived his, responsive to the will of God and to the needs of others. As James puts it, "Religion that God our Father accepts as pure and faultless is this: to look after orphans and widows in their distress and to keep oneself from being polluted by the world" (Jas. 1:27). Rather than viewing spirituality as withdrawal from this world, or limiting spiritual disciplines to prayer, we need to grasp the Christian ideal and draw strength from our relationship with Jesus to live each day compassionately, kindly, in humility, gentleness, and patience, showing concern for believer and unbeliever alike.

spoil Plunder taken in war. In ancient warfare, a victorious army and its individual soldiers had the right to take any possessions of a defeated enemy that could be carried away. *See also* Booty.

Roman soldiers carry off spoils from the Temple in Jerusalem after they overran the city in A.D. 70. This relief from the Arch of Titus in Rome is the only depiction of the Temple's articles extant today.

944

Partial model of stables excavated at Megiddo. These are considered to be storerooms by some archaeologists, who argue that horses were kept in open enclosures.

spot (1) A location (Lk. 19:5). (2) A discoloration or blemish on the skin. White or reddish spots on the skin indicated various infectious skin diseases, which made an Israelite ritually unclean (Lev. 13:2,4). In some English versions, "spot" is also used of defects that disqualified animals from use as sacrifices (Num. 19:2 KJV). (3) Figuratively, to be "without spot" is to be morally unblemished or unstained and thus qualified for fellowship with God. Peter uses the ancient imagery to describe Jesus as "a lamb without blemish or defect," whose sacrifice of himself was acceptable to God (1 Pet. 1:19).

spring *See* Fountain.

sprinkle (1) A Middle Eastern expression of mourning, shown by tearing clothing and sprinkling dust on the head (Job 2:12; Ezek. 27:30). (2) As a technical theological term, a ceremonial act associated with the cleansing of ritually unclean objects and persons. Priests performed such ritual cleansings, most often using blood, but at times sprinkling objects with water or olive oil (Lev. 14:48-52; Num. 19:18-20). According to Heb. 9:13, the ceremonial act sanctified those who were ceremonially unclean so that they became outwardly clean. Isaiah picks up the image describing the ministry of the suffering Savior, who would "sprinkle many nations" (Isa. 52:15). Jesus symbolically sprinkles the believer with his own blood, cleansing us not outwardly but inwardly (Heb. 9:14).

stable A place where animals were lodged and fed. A stable might be a building, a cave, or simply an open enclosure.

The OT says that Solomon built 4,000 stalls for his war-horses (2 Chr. 9:25). Some archaeologists have identified remains of buildings at Megiddo, a city that Solomon strengthened, as stables. If this was their function, the stables at Megiddo had stalls for 450 horses, with attached sheds large enough for 150 horses.

The stable where Jesus was born was associated with an inn. Given the number of limestone caves around Bethlehem and their use in biblical times, Christ probably was laid in a manger (feed trough) in a cave where animals were sheltered from the cold (Lk. 2:7).

stacte The gum of the storax tree, *Styrax officinalis*, and an ingredient of the holy incense (Ex. 30:34). This small tree, with white flowers and green, hairy fruit, grows abundantly on lower hills and rocky places from Lebanon through Judea. *See also* Incense.

staff *See* Rod.

stairs A series of steps used for moving from one level to another.

Few homes in Palestine were more than a single story high. However, in most homes the flat roof served as an extra room for work and recreation. Wooden

These stone stairs in Jerusalem date to the Byzantine era and are reminiscent of the many stairways built into the streets of hilly Jerusalem in Bible times.

945

stairs built against the outside wall gave access to the roof.

Stone stair steps led up to the Temple (Neh. 9:4), and broad steps were built into the streets of hilly Jerusalem (Neh. 12:37). One famous flight of first-century stairs still survives in Jerusalem. Jesus and his disciples almost surely went down these very stone steps on the way to Gethsemane the night before his crucifixion.

stall *See* Stable.

standard *See* Banner.

star (1) In Bible times, understood as any luminous heavenly body other than sun and moon. The biblical term includes planets, comets, and meteors. (2) Metaphorically, an angelic being or power (Job 38:7; Rev. 1:16,20). (3) Frequently, a pagan deity, described in the aggregate as "starry hosts" (2 Ki. 17:16; Zeph. 1:5).

Only a few familiar constellations are named in the OT: Ursa Major or the Bear

A woodcut print by Gustav Doré pictures the Magi traveling in the direction of the Star of Bethlehem (Mt. 2:1,2).

(Job 9:9; 38:32), Orion (Job 9:9; 38:31; Amos 5:8), and the Pleiades (Job 9:9; 38:31; Amos 5:8). Other references to groups of stars are obscure. It is understandable that landlocked Israel should have less interest

in mapping the skies than would the ancient world's seagoing races.

However, the Israelites were impressed with the austere beauty of the lights that spanned the heavens. The distant and mysterious stars were viewed with some awe, for they declared the glory of the God who made them and by their very existence praised their Maker (Pss. 19:1-4; 148:1-6).

The OT phrase "as numerous as the stars in the sky" suggests a vast amount, beyond man's ability to count or comprehend (Gen. 22:17; Ex. 32:13; Deut. 10:22; 1 Chr. 27:23; Neh. 9:23). This imagery is striking in that with the naked eye just over a thousand stars are visible from any given point on earth. Galileo's telescope, invented in 1610, revealed a few more than 3,000. Only today, aided by giant telescopes and radio telescopes, have astronomers come to realize that there are 100 billion stars in our galaxy—and that there may be 100 billion galaxies in God's universe! The biblical imagery is far more appropriate than even the writers themselves could have imagined.

Star of Bethlehem A heavenly body whose appearance marked the birth of Jesus (Mt. 2:1-12). Many believe the Bethlehem star is foretold in Num. 24:17 and Isa. 60:3. The significance of the star was recognized by astrologers from the east, who came to honor the birth of the Jewish ruler-to-be. *See also* Magi.

Various explanations of the star have been offered. Some have suggested it was a comet (Halley's comet appeared in 11 B.C., which does not fit the probable date of Christ's birth). Some have suggested a planetary conjunction of Jupiter, Saturn, and Venus that took place in 7 B.C. Others have suggested a supernova, which would generate more light than all the other stars in the sky for a brief period and then gradually dim. Chinese astronomers did record an exploding star about the time the Star of Bethlehem would have appeared. Whatever the case, Matthew's Gospel indicates that the guiding star was a supernatural phenomenon, prompted by God.

stater (NASB) *See* Drachma; Shekel.

statute A law or decree. The Hebrew root word means "to engrave" or "to write." Depending on the context, it may indicate an obligation established by God (Ex. 15:25), behavior required by a human ruler

946

Detail from a 12th-century limoges-enamel chest depicts the stoning of Stephen outside the walls of Jerusalem. On his knees Stephen prays, "Lord, do not hold this sin against them," while to the left Saul sits watching (Acts 7:54–8:1).

(Gen. 47:26), or even an established custom (1 Sam. 30:25; Ezek. 20:18).

Stephen [STEE-ven; "crown"]. A deacon in Jerusalem and history's first Christian martyr, A.D. 33. **Scripture:** Acts 6,7.

BACKGROUND

Two incidents in the life of the Jerusalem church feature Stephen. He was one of seven men chosen to supervise distribution of food to widows in the Christian community (Acts 6:1-7). The text, however, sets Stephen apart from the others, as "a man full of faith and of the Holy Spirit" (v. 5).

Acts then describes Stephen's ministry as an evangelist, "full of God's grace and power" (6:8). His effectiveness provoked his opponents because "they could not stand up against his wisdom or the Spirit by whom he spoke" (6:10). Stephen was falsely accused before the Sanhedrin, which was then the Jewish supreme court. In his defense, Stephen reviewed the history of the Jewish people and demonstrated that the covenant people had consistently rebelled against each fresh revelation of God's will. Stephen concluded his indictment by charging his judges with betraying and murdering the Righteous One, the Messiah whom the prophets of earlier ages predicted would come. Furious, Stephen's hearers abandoned all pretext of a judicial proceeding and dragged Stephen outside the city, where they stoned him to death. A young Saul looked on with approval. Stephen's death unleashed a great persecution that forced many believers to flee Jerusalem.

LEARNING FROM STEPHEN'S LIFE

The word "martyr" means "witness." In Christianity it has come to mean a person who witnesses to his faith in Christ by giving his life rather than deny his Lord. One of the most powerful evidences of the truth of Christianity is found in the steadfastness and joy believers have experienced despite facing an agonizing death. The experience of Stephen suggests the reason. This first martyr saw a vision of Jesus, and while dying, cried out, "Lord Jesus, receive my spirit" (Acts 7:59). God had promised, "When you pass through the waters, I will be with you" (Isa. 43:2). As the martyrs of church history have discovered, the person who keeps his or her hope fixed on Jesus will experience Christ's living presence in time of greatest need.

steward A person with responsibility to manage the property and supervise the servants of another (Gen. 43:16). Modern versions sometimes use the term "manager" or "agent." Peter applies the image to Christians, who are responsible to administer (manage) the spiritual gifts God has given to each one (1 Pet. 4:10). Christ's parables emphasize that believers are responsible to God for managing their lives and wealth. The same parables point out that one day we will give an accounting to God and receive his commendation—or reproof—at that time (Mt. 25:14-30).

947

stiff-necked An idiomatic phrase meaning "proud," "unyielding," and thus "rebellious." Many different generations of Israelites are characterized in the OT as stiff-necked, arrogant, hardened, and rebellious (Deut. 10:16; 2 Ki. 17:14; Jer. 17:23; 19:15; Acts 7:51).

stocks An instrument of punishment used in later OT and in NT times (Jer. 20:2,3; Acts 16:24). Stocks were constructed of wooden logs shaped to hold the feet of a prisoner. Some stocks also immobilized a person's neck and hands.

Stoic philosophers Proponents of doctrines first systematically propounded in Greece by Zeno, about 335–263 B.C.

The Stoic god was a pantheistic divine fire. Each individual had a spark of the divine which returned to the omnipresent fire at death.

The Stoics believed that human beings must discover the "natural order of things" in the universe and learn to live therein. According to Stoic thinking, one must do what is necessary to fit into the place assigned him at birth, thus cooperating with the divine Reason (Logos) that ordered the universe. The gods were interpreted allegorically.

In ethics, duty was more important than love or desire; a state of passionlessness (*apatheia*) was prized. The individual must act out of a virtue that is disinterested in its benefits or consequences. The Stoics did insist, however, that human beings were responsible for their actions and passions but not for things beyond their control (fate).

By the first century, Stoicism had become concerned only with moral conduct. The Bible mentions Stoicism only in Acts 17:18, as Paul encounters the Athenian philosophers at the Areopagus (Mars' Hill). Their reaction (17:32) reflects in part Stoicism's disbelief in personal existence after death.

stone Hardened, non-metallic mineral of which rock is composed.

Palestine is a rocky land, filled with large and small limestone fragments. Stone served as the primary building material in this area. Many implements and early weapons were fashioned of stone, and heaps of stone were set up to mark the sites of significant events (Gen. 31:46; Josh. 4:9; 1 Sam. 7:12) or to serve as landmarks (2 Sam. 20:8).

While private homes were constructed

of rough stones, many public buildings in Israel were fashioned of cut stone blocks. Blocks used in constructing the second Temple were cut from quarries near Jerusalem. *See also* Mason.

Stone pillars often stood at pagan worship sites. Offerings were poured over the pillars, which represented the pagan deities. In times of apostasy, the Israelites "also set up for themselves high places, sacred stones, and Asherah poles" (1 Ki. 14:23).

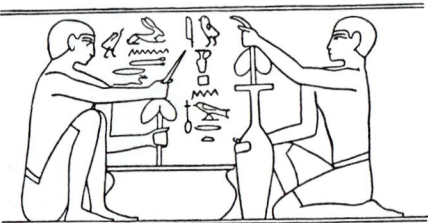

stonecutter *See* Mason.

stoning The method of execution used in Israel to punish capital offenses. *See also* Punish.

Moses' Law specified, "The people of the community are to stone" the guilty (Lev. 20:2). This reflects an important OT concept. In Israel all members of the community were responsible for maintaining the rule of God's Law. Actual participation in the act of execution underlined this personal responsibility (Josh. 7:25).

It is perhaps significant that while capital punishment is prescribed in OT Law, few legal executions are mentioned in Scripture. Joshua 7, which reports the stoning of Achan, provides an example of careful judicial examination leading to the stoning of an Israelite. In contrast, most stonings reported in Scripture were unjustified. Rehoboam's supervisor of forced labor was stoned as an act of rebellion, which helped precipitate the division of Solomon's kingdom (1 Ki. 12). Innocent Naboth was stoned as the victim of a plot by Queen Jezebel (1 Ki. 21). Stephen, a deacon in the Jerusalem church, was dragged out of the courtroom before his trial was over and stoned by an infuriated mob that included his judges (Acts 7). *See also* Achan; Stephen; Trial.

Moses and Jesus were both threatened with stoning by unruly mobs (Ex. 17:4; Jn. 8:59; 10:31). The apostle Paul was actually stoned and left for dead outside of the city of Lystra (Acts 14:8-20; 2 Cor. 11:25).

stool A three- or four-legged backless seat. The Hebrew word is commonly rendered "chair" (2 Ki. 4:10). Stools were common pieces of furniture in Bible times. However, there were also special stools.

The "delivery stool" mentioned in Ex. 1:16 was probably an arrangement of stones or blocks set side by side, on which a woman sat to give birth. The "footstool" is associated with the thrones of ancient rulers and is a symbol of power or authority (Isa. 66:1; Heb. 10:13).

store city Cities in which provisions and military equipment were stockpiled for use during famines or foreign invasion. In later Israel, the term referred to collection points where taxes were paid in the form of commodities like grain and wine (1 Ki. 4:7,22,23).

In Egypt the Hebrew slaves constructed the store cities of Pithom and Rameses (Tanis) (Ex. 1:11). Solomon built a number of store cities (1 Ki. 9:19; 2 Chr. 8:4,6). The ruins of large facilities that may have been storage buildings have been excavated at Lachish and other biblical sites.

storehouse (1) The Temple treasury, where tithes, gifts, and booty were kept (Mal. 3:10). (2) Any building constructed for the storage of grains, taxes, or military supplies (Gen. 41:56; 1 Chr. 27:25). (3) In some English versions, rooms in the Temple or a person's home where valuables

were kept (Neh. 10:38,39; Mt. 13:52). (4) Figuratively, of God's ability to provide bountifully for the needs of his people (Deut. 28:12). *See also* Store City.

storeroom *See* Storehouse.

stranger (1) A foreigner, a non-Israelite, either traveling through Israel or a resident alien. (2) A person who is not known (Mt. 25:35, "I was a stranger and you invited me in").

Old Testament Law guarded the rights and defined the responsibilities of aliens who took up residence in Israel. *See also* Alien.

strangle To kill by choking. Because strangling takes a life without shedding the blood, the Israelites were commanded not to eat the meat of strangled animals (Lev. 17:12).

The command underlines the significance of blood as an OT symbol of life-force. The blood of animals was reserved for sacrificial offerings and thus was not to be consumed by man (Lev. 17:11,12). Abhorrence of eating blood was so deeply ingrained in Jewish thought that it even affected the Jerusalem council of Acts 15. These early church leaders, all Jewish Christians, ruled that Gentile Christians were not subject to the Law of Moses. Yet they still requested that Gentile believers not eat the meat of strangled animals, lest they alienate their Jewish brothers and sisters (Acts 15:20). *See also* Blood.

straw *See* Stubble.

street In the Roman world, a street (Latin, *strata*) was a paved way. The Greek *rhumē*, used in identifying the "Straight Street" in Damascus (Acts 9:11), simply means alley, although archaeologists believe that that

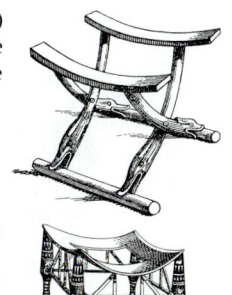

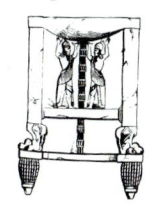

Above: Two Egyptian and two Assyrian stools.

Left: Solomon divided all of Israel —except his own tribe's territory of Judah—into twelve taxation districts and required each to supply one month's provisions for his court (1 Ki. 4). He also established store cities throughout his kingdom.

Clay model of an Egyptian granary, a storehouse for grain. Joseph filled the storehouses of Egypt with surplus grain to prepare for a seven-year famine (Gen. 41:48,49).

Broad, paved street in Ephesus, called the "Sacred Way" because it led from the theater out of the city to the temple of Artemis.

particular street was paved in the first century. Most city streets were narrow, pressed in by the walls of the houses and shops that lined them. Frequently, streets were only wide enough to permit the passage of a single pack animal or two or three people abreast.

Major cities had larger, broad streets as well. The Greek word for the more open street is *plateia*. Jesus envisioned the "hypocrites" standing on the corners of these broad thoroughfares and praying aloud (Mt. 6:5).

In another illustration, Jesus told of a king (representing God) who sent his servants out into the city to recruit guests for his banquet when those who had been invited (representing Israel) refused. He sent his servants not only to the *plateia*, where many pedestrians would be passing by, but also to the *rhumē*, the alleys, to make sure that everyone had an opportunity to hear and respond to the royal invitation (Lk. 14:15-24).

strength The power of a person or of God, however that power might be measured: in physical prowess, wealth, available force, wisdom, etc. Some English versions use the words "power" and "might."

Scripture expresses the conviction that, measured against the overwhelming power of God, all human strengths are insignificant. Many beautiful expressions of faith are constructed around this idea. David sang, "Look to the Lord and his strength" (1 Chr. 16:11). Isaiah echoed the psalmist in proclaiming, "The Lord is my strength and my song" (Isa. 12:2; *see* Ps. 118:14). In his great "comfort" chapter,

Isaiah affirmed, "He gives strength to the weary," and, "Those who hope in the Lord will renew their strength" (Isa. 40:29,31). "The Sovereign Lord is my strength," said Habakkuk when times were tough (Hab. 3:19). In the NT, Paul adds, "I can do everything through him who gives me strength" (Phil. 4:13).

striker (KJV) The Greek word suggests a violent, pugnacious, or over-competitive individual. This characteristic, so clearly in contrast with Christian ideals, disqualifies a person from Christian leadership (1 Tim. 3:3; Tit. 1:7).

stripes Blows administered with a whip as punishment. Jewish law limited the number of blows that could be given to 39 (Deut. 25:2,3; 2 Cor. 11:24). *See also* Whip. Isaiah 53:5 (KJV) declares that "with his [Christ's] stripes we are healed," signifying the punishment Jesus bore on our behalf.

strong drink (KJV) Any intoxicating drink other than wine. Wine was typically diluted with water when drunk at meals or celebrations. *See also* Beer; Drunkenness; Wine.

stronghold (1) Any fortified or secure location (1 Sam. 23:14); (2) figuratively, that in which a person trusts (Ps. 27:1, "The Lord is the stronghold of my life—of whom shall I be afraid?").

stubble Dried grain stalks left in the fields or on the threshing floors after grain has been harvested; frequently synonymous with straw and chaff. In Egypt, straw was mixed with mud when making bricks (Ex. 5:12). The chemicals released made the bricks harder.

In most of the Middle East, straw was used as animal feed (Gen. 24:25; 1 Ki. 4:28). Straw is highly flammable, and God's judgment is frequently likened to "a crackling fire consuming stubble" (Joel 2:5; *see* Isa. 5:24).

stumble (1) To trip or lose one's balance while walking or running (Prov. 4:12); (2) to walk unsteadily from weakness or age (Isa. 40:30; 59:10).

Each image is used figuratively in the OT, but the ethical fall that links stumbling with sin predominates. The wicked trip over their sins, performing acts that cause them to "stumble and fall" (Ps. 27:2; Jer. 50:32). Sin also causes spiritual blindness.

With "no acknowledgment of God in the land," people and prophets "stumble day and night" (Hos. 4:1-5). On the other hand, those who love God's Law find peace, "and nothing can make them stumble" (Ps. 119:165). People stumble, Peter says, "because they disobey [God's] message" (1 Pet. 2:8).

The less frequent figure, of stumbling along because of weakness, is more closely linked with trust than with sin. A person who trusts his own resources will soon exhaust them, for "even youths grow tired and weary, and young men stumble and fall; but those who hope in the Lord will renew their strength" and soar (Isa. 40:30,31).

stumbling block Any obstacle that causes a person to stumble. While the obstacle may be literal (Lev. 19:14), the term is most often used figuratively of any object, such as wealth (Ezek. 7:19) or idols (Ezek. 14:3,4), that causes a person to sin. In the NT, a Christian who exercises his freedom with no consideration for the convictions of the less spiritually mature puts a stumbling block in his brother's way (Rom. 14:13; 1 Cor. 8:9; 2 Cor. 6:3). *See also* Convictions; Freedom; Rights.

The cross proved a stumbling block to the Jews. The Greek word, *skandalon*, sometimes referred to the trigger of a trap.

The trigger that caused Israel's failure to respond to God's fresh revelation in Christ was their preconceived notion about how God must act, which made them blind to the meaning and manner of Jesus' death (Rom. 9:32,33; 11:9; 1 Cor. 1:23).

submission Subjection or obedience to another person or authority, whether forced (Lk. 10:17) or willing (Jas. 4:7). The NT refers to submission 41 times, always in the context of a relationship—with God, with society, or with other believers.

SITUATIONAL SUBMISSION

Scripture calls on believers to submit to governing authorities (Rom. 13:1; 1 Pet. 2:13). Slaves are urged to submit even to harsh masters (Tit. 2:9; 1 Pet. 2:18). This can be called situational submission: The believer is to do what is expected of a good person in his or her society. Situational submission makes no judgment about the morality of the society's institutions but rather calls on Christians to live within the framework of the world as it is, not as it might or should be. However, the principle of situational submission is a general one and does not apply when a Christian is commanded by governing authorities to perform an act that violates God's Word. The example of the early church, where thousands died rather than obey a govern-

Aerial view of Masada clearly indicates the impregnability of this stronghold that Herod built. Here the Jewish Zealots made a seven-year stand before Roman forces stormed the fortress from a great earthen ramp in A.D. 73.

mental command to offer incense at the emperor's shrine, makes this clear. When the two authorities conflict, "We must obey God rather than men!" (Acts 5:29).

INTERPERSONAL SUBMISSION

Christians are told, "Submit to one another out of reverence for Christ" (Eph. 5:21). Here submission is eagerness to put others first, to yield out of love. Submission of the younger to the older is particularly appropriate (1 Pet. 5:5), as is submission to those who serve full time in leadership (1 Cor. 16:15,16). However, the concept of mutual submission predominates in the NT, which teaches Christians, "Look not only to your own interests, but also to the interests of others" (Phil. 2:4; 1 Cor. 10:24,33; see Rom. 12:10). Jesus himself established this principle, saying that the person who chose to be a servant would be "great among you" (Mt. 20:26,27).

SUBMISSION TO LEADERS

Voluntary submission to leaders in the church is taught and implied in the NT (Heb. 13:17). However, this submission is not intended to release the believer from his or her personal responsibility to Jesus Christ as Lord.

SUBMISSION TO SPOUSES

Many Christians have struggled with Eph. 5:22—"Wives, submit to your husbands as to the Lord." Surely the idea that women must simply do as they are told is not implied here. Whether we take the verse to teach a situational or interpersonal submission, we need to interpret it in the total context. The preceding verse commands us to "submit to one another out of reverence for Christ" (Eph. 5:21).

Christian submission holds no implication of inferiority. Luke reminds us that Jesus returned to Nazareth with Mary and Joseph and "was obedient to them" (Lk. 2:51). Jesus chose to submit to his mother and Joseph, as was appropriate for a twelve-year-old, although he was the Son of God. Submission did not make Jesus inferior, nor can it make us inferior. In reality, the path of submission is a highway to greatness in God's Kingdom.

suburb (KJV) The uncultivated pasturelands surrounding cities (Lev. 25:34; Josh. 21:2). The OT also speaks of "daughter" villages around major cities and towns (Num. 21:25; 32:42; 2 Chr. 28:18; Neh. 11:25-31)—a rough equivalent of modern suburbs. The NIV regularly calls these "surrounding settlements." See also City.

success The accomplishment of an intended task; the fulfilling of a purpose. Biblical success is not measured by wealth, as our society tends to measure it, but by carrying a project through to its conclusion. Thus, Abraham's servant asked God, "Give me success today" (Gen. 24:12), meaning, "Let me find the bride I was sent to fetch for Isaac."

suffer, suffering To undergo something painful or unpleasant, whether a physical injury, emotional pain, grief, or loss.

OLD TESTAMENT

The Hebrew vocabulary is full of words for suffering: pain, grief, sorrow, mental and physical stress, agony, labor pains. The OT's repeated use of such words brings home to us the fact that human beings are subject to suffering all the days of this life. Why? The OT never directly answers this, but three themes are significant.

1. *Suffering and sin.* Suffering is first of all a consequence of sin. This is illustrated in the Fall, after which Adam and Eve experienced both physical pains, in the labor Adam had to exert to wrest a living from the now-cursed soil and in Eve's childbirth, and mental anguish as they saw one of their sons murder another. The story establishes the biblical perspective that suffering is a consequence of man's broken relationship with God and the foolish choices that human beings make. *See also* Evil; Sin.

2. *Suffering and salvation.* One of the great mysteries introduced in the OT is that God suffers for human sin. The thought is most clearly developed in Isa. 53, which portrays the Messiah as "a man of sorrows, and familiar with suffering" (v. 3). God causes his servant to suffer (v. 10); however, after "the suffering of his soul" (v. 11), the servant is vindicated and the divine purpose disclosed. The servant has suffered for God's straying sheep. He has borne their iniquity and justified many.

3. *Suffering and childbirth.* The OT's frequent association of suffering with childbirth is significant (Gen. 3:16). But just as childbirth ends not in death but in the introduction of a new life into the world, so human suffering is intended to renew rather than destroy (see Rom. 8:18-25).

4. *Job, a test case.* The Book of Job explores the particularly difficult problem of why the righteous suffer. Job is described as blameless and upright (1:8). His suffering cannot be ascribed to personal sins,

even though his three "comforters" struggle to convict him. Job is truly a victim. His suffering is caused by the vindictiveness of Satan, who seeks to embarrass God by causing Job to curse the Lord.

Job, however, refuses to deny God, even though he struggles with the unfairness of his plight. Ultimately, God visits Job, not to explain himself, but simply to reveal to Job the vastness of the gap between himself and human beings. Job immediately grasps the point. Rather than contend with God or charge God with unfair treatment, all Job can do is to trust and worship him. With the lesson learned, God gives Job twice as much as he had and blesses him all the rest of his long life. *See also* Job, Book of.

The story illustrates the childbirth theme. We suffer and hurt, and often what happens to us seems unfair. But we must trust God to have a purpose in all that happens and to bring fresh new life through the pain.

NEW TESTAMENT

The NT picks up on the themes introduced in the OT and amplifies two of them. God has not abandoned man to suffer alone. In Christ, God has come alongside to suffer with us and for us. At the same time, the NT is specific about some of the positive ends God seeks to achieve through the suffering of the believer.

1. *God suffers with and for us.* Christ's incarnation made him vulnerable to suffering (Heb. 2:18; 5:8-10). Yet Christ then went further, willingly accepting the intense physical and spiritual pain of crucifixion in order to redeem humankind. Any theology of suffering must note, first, that Christ's suffering was intentional. What happened to Jesus was an expression of "God's set purpose and foreknowledge" (Acts 2:23; *see* 1 Pet. 1:11). Second, Christ's suffering was purposeful, intended for our salvation (1 Pet. 3:18).

2. *God supervises the suffering of believers.* Peter examines the situation in which a Christian suffers despite doing good (1 Pet. 3:8-18), pointing out that God supervises the consequences of our choices (vv. 8-12), so that normally the believer will be blessed when he or she does what is good (v. 13). Sometimes, however, a believer suffers despite doing what is right (v. 14a). When this happens, the Christian is not to be afraid but should remember that Christ is Lord, exercising sovereign control (vv. 14b,15). The Christian is to keep a positive attitude and a clear conscience (vv. 16,17) while suffering. The Christian must also remember that Jesus suffered unjustly. The God who used Jesus' suffering to win our salvation will use our suffering in a positive, redemptive way (v. 18).

In this passage, the "childbirth" image of the OT is given explicit formulation. God does have a purpose in allowing the suffering of his children. We may not know what that purpose is, but we can be sure that in the end the pain we experience will bring forth newness and joy.

3. *Some of God's purposes in Christian suffering can be explained.* The NT, unlike the OT, does explain several of the purposes God has in mind in permitting believers to suffer. Suffering can build our character (Rom. 5:2-4), but only undeserved suffering has this value (1 Pet. 2:19; 4:15). It can also build our relationship with Christ (Phil. 3:10; 1 Pet. 4:1,13), as we share his commitment to doing the will of God.

GUIDELINES FOR SUFFERERS

No pain is enjoyable, and God does not expect us to delight in suffering. God does, however, expect us to develop a Christian perspective and to respond appropriately. That perspective includes the conviction that God has permitted our pain, stands beside us in our suffering, and intends the experience for our good.

Peter, who deals extensively with suffering in his first letter, gives us several guidelines for responding when suffering comes: (1) Follow Christ's example, entrusting yourself to God rather than railing at those who cause your pain (1 Pet. 2:23-25). (2) Do not surrender to fear or terror (1 Pet. 3:14). (3) Focus on the fact that Christ is Lord and maintain such a positive attitude that others are amazed (1 Pet. 3:15,16). (4) Keep on doing what is right, to maintain a clear conscience (1 Pet. 3:16; 4:19). (5) Finally, rejoice, not that you are suffering, but that in suffering "you participate in the sufferings of Christ, so that you may be overjoyed when his glory is revealed" (1 Pet. 4:13).

We suffer only for a little while. Our destiny is to share his eternal glory (1 Pet. 5:10).

suicide Self-murder. The word is not found in the Bible, but there are several instances of persons killing themselves to avoid what they perceived as even harsher consequences. Saul killed himself to avoid being captured by the Philistines (1 Sam. 31:4,5). Ahithophel, who abandoned

Ceiling painting from the tomb of Rameses VI illustrates the night and day journey of the sun goddess Nut. She swallowed the sun each night —shown by yellow dots—then it was born anew each morning.

David to counsel Absalom, killed himself when he realized that Absalom's rebellion would fail (2 Sam. 17:23). A later king of Israel, Zimri, set his palace on fire and perished in the flames (1 Ki. 16:18). And Judas, who could not live with himself after betraying Jesus, attempted to escape from his own conscience by hanging himself (Mt. 27:5). While no specific prohibition against suicide is found in OT Law, rabbinical interpretation appropriately viewed the Gen. 9:5,6 prohibition against shedding man's blood as a ruling against self-murder as well as the killing of others.

Sukkoth, Feast of The Hebrew Festival of Booths. *See also* Feasts, Fasts, and Festivals; Tabernacles, Feast of.

sulfur A combustible mineral substance found in major deposits in the Near East. *See also* Brimstone.

sun (1) The earth's source of light and heat (Deut. 33:14). Literally, the star Sol, around which our earth orbits. Like all other natural phenomena, the sun was created by God (Gen. 1:16) and remains

under his control (Josh. 10:13; Isa. 38:8). (2) A figure for God's reign and blessing. For example, "The Lord God is a sun and shield" (Ps. 84:11). The context makes it clear that here the sun stands for God as the source of blessing and of all good things.

Scripture reflects what we know from astronomical investigation: that the sun marks the hours and seasons by its movements (Gen. 1:14-16) and directions by its rising and setting (Deut. 11:30; Isa. 45:6). Truly it was created by God to "rule over the day" (Ps. 136:8).

At the end of time in the New Jerusalem, the source of light will change: "The city does not need the sun or the moon to shine on it, for the glory of God gives it light" (Rev. 21:23).

Worship of the sun as a deity, or as the personification of a deity, was common in Egypt, Assyria, and Babylon. The OT prohibits worship of any heavenly body (Deut. 4:19), yet sun worship found its way into Israel with other pagan practices (2 Ki. 21:5; Ezek. 8:16).

Sunday The Christian day of worship,

commemorating the resurrection of Jesus on the first day of the week. *See also* Lord's Day; Sabbath.

superscription The Romans customarily prepared a wooden sign that was carried in front of a person about to be executed, identifying his crime. Such a wooden plaque was nailed over Jesus' head. The slight variation in the wording reported in Mt. 27:37; Mk. 15:26; Lk. 23:38; and Jn. 19:19 may reflect nuances of the three languages in which the inscription on the cross was written. John's is the most complete: "Jesus of Nazareth, the King of the Jews."

"Superscription" also refers to the titles of psalms, indicating author, occasion, and/or musical style.

superstition Misdirected religious feelings or actions (Acts 17:22; 25:19 KJV). The biblical concept varies from the modern notion of superstition as beliefs and actions based on ignorant or unenlightened notions about the supernatural. Thus, most modern versions substitute "religious" where the KJV has "superstitious."

supper *See* Eating; Food.

Supper, Lord's *See* Lord's Supper.

supplication A specific request to God to meet a particular need. *See also* Prayer.

surety (KJV) A sworn pledge or a guarantee, such as a possession left by a debtor with the lender that insures repayment. Jesus is described as the "guarantee" (or surety) of God's new covenant promises to us (Heb. 7:22). Because of Jesus' permanent priesthood, "he is able to save completely those who come to God through him" (Heb. 7:25, NIV). *See also* Borrow.

survivor *See* Remnant.

swaddle To wrap an infant in bandage-like strips of cloth, intended to ensure normal development of the limbs. Throughout the biblical period, a newborn baby would be placed in a folded square of cloth, and then wrapped in swaddling bands that restricted movement. The figurative reference to swaddling an infant in Ezek. 16:4 shows that the practice was an indication of responsible and loving parenthood (*see* Lk. 2:7,12).

swear To make a binding commitment. *See also* Oath.

sweat Perspiration; in Scripture, a symbol of painful and unrewarding toil (Gen. 3:19) or of intense anguish. Describing Jesus' experience in Gethsemane, Luke writes, "Being in anguish, he prayed more earnestly, and his sweat was like drops of blood falling to the ground" (Lk. 22:44). Many take this to mean only that the drops of sweat that fell from Jesus were as large as drops of blood. However, ancient and modern medicine have described the phenomenon of blood passing through intact capillaries and coloring sweat when a person is under extreme stress, a process called "diapedesis."

swine *See* Boar; Pig.

sword A hand-held weapon with a hilt (handle) and a long blade. Although swords are mentioned frequently in the OT, they were not the principal weapon in ancient warfare.

Two types of swords were used in the Middle East. One was straight, with a triangular blade sharpened on both sides and at the point. This was the type used in Israel. The weapon was primarily used for thrusting. The distinction between swords and knives of the OT period is made simply on the basis of size. *See also* Knife.

The other type of sword was curved. It was sharpened only on one edge, with the other edge thickened to add weight. With this sword, a warrior would slash at an opponent. Recovered blades and illustrations carved into monuments show a variety of shapes for the curved blade. In NT

Above: Bronze sword from the 13th century B.C., found in northern Iran. The Israelites used straight-edged swords such as this rather than the curved type.

Left: As was the custom in her day, Mary wrapped her son Jesus in swaddling cloths (Lk. 2:7). Roman relief of a swaddled newborn baby.

times, Roman infantry used a short sword; the cavalry, a longer one.

"Sword" is frequently used figuratively in the Bible. In Rom. 13:4, it stands for the coercive force available to human government to ensure a citizen's obedience. In Mt. 10:34; Rom. 8:35; and Heb. 11:37 the sword symbolizes war or persecution. Frequently the sword stands for the power of God, bringing about the judgment of sinners (Isa. 66:16). God's Word is described as "sharper than any double-edged sword"; it penetrates to man's innermost being (Heb. 4:12) and is essential equipment for spiritual warfare (Eph. 6:17; *see* Rev. 1:16). *See also* Armor.

An early Christian symbol for Christ, found in the catacombs in Rome (A.D. 331). It combines the Greek letters X and P, which are the first two in the word Christ—XPICTOC.

sycamore-fig A common tree in Palestine that produces several crops of fig-like fruit each year. The tree must be carefully cultivated, as each fruit must be punctured at a particular stage of its development if it is to ripen and be edible. David appointed an agricultural supervisor to be in charge of the olive and sycamore-fig trees, suggesting how important this fruit was to Israel's economy in the tenth century B.C. (1 Chr. 27:28). Amos, the prophet of Tekoa, cultivated fields of this tree about 760 B.C. (Amos 7:14). In NT times the diminutive Zacchaeus found it easy to scramble up into the sycamore-fig's low branches to see Jesus (Lk. 19:4). The shady tree was often planted along roadways in Palestine.

symbol Something that represents or stands for something else, often a visible sign of that which is invisible, especially of a concept or truth. A symbol conveys the reality of an idea to the believer.

The Bible has a wealth of symbols. Adam, though presented as a historical figure, also symbolizes all of humanity, created in God's image but now subject to sin. Abraham serves as a symbol of faith, and all who believe are considered his children. The OT priesthood, the prophet, and the king all convey realities that are fully revealed in Christ. In both OT and NT blood symbolizes the life of the individual and substitutionary sacrifice. The pile of stones erected beside the Jordan was a symbolic reminder to Israelites of later generations that God had brought his people into the Promised Land by his personal intervention. And the cross, per-

The Egyptian goddess of the sycamore fig tree entertains high priest Userhat, his wife, and mother in a garden. She supports a small fig tree on her head.

956

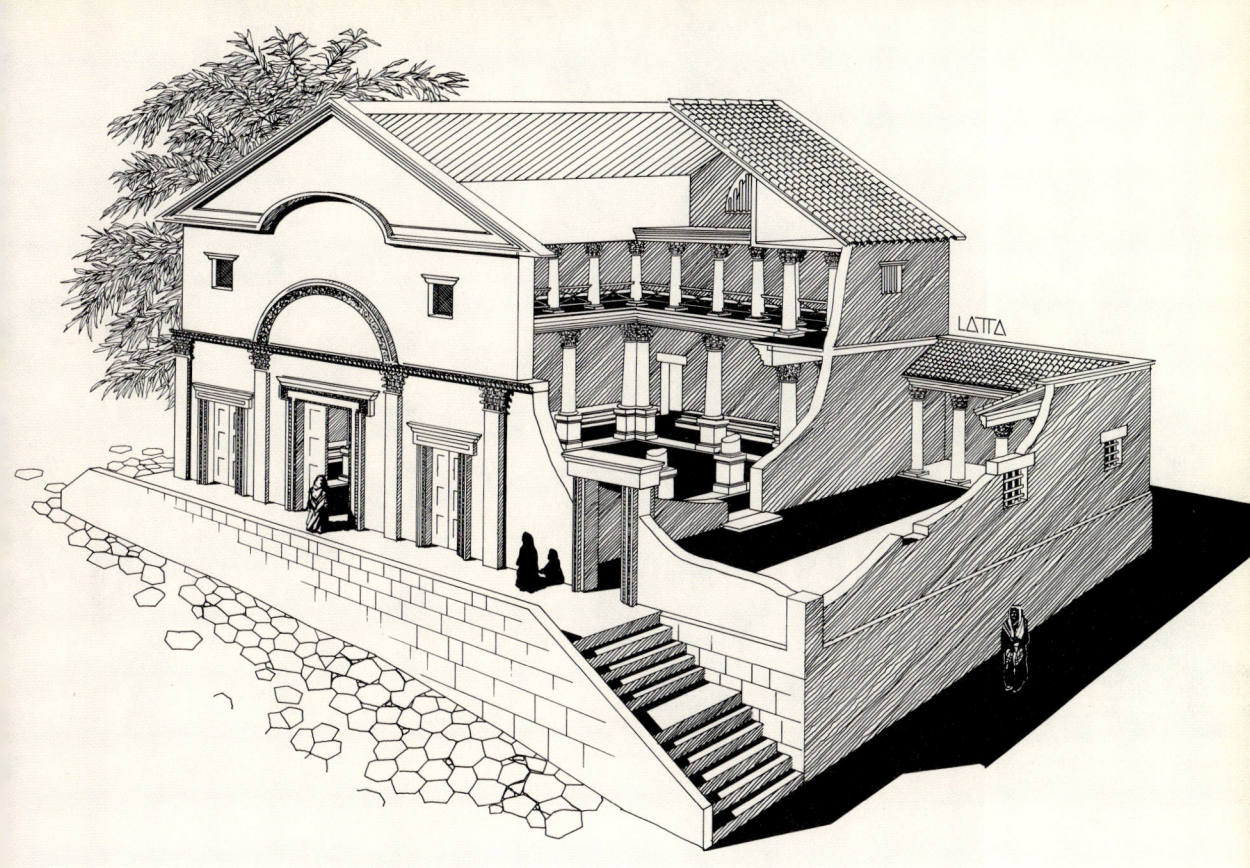

haps Christianity's ultimate symbol, powerfully portrays the Good News that Jesus died for us, that we might be forgiven and raised to new life in him.

Actions, too, can be symbolic, as was Jeremiah's purchase of a field then held by the Babylonians. That act uniquely conveyed the reality of his prophetic promise that the people of Judah, about to be torn from their homeland, would one day return. The Lord's Supper is a symbolic and holy act, by which we participate in the reality of Christ's death for us. The books of Daniel and Revelation are written in the apocalyptic literary form, which makes much use of symbols.

It is tempting to multiply biblical symbols, finding hidden meaning in colors, numbers, names, events, people, objects, and actions that may perhaps be there but not in a clear and compelling way. It is far better to limit our identification of biblical symbols to those things that unquestionably portray spiritual realities and do so in such a clear and powerful way that those realities are impressed on our hearts.

synagogue (1) A gathering or congregation of Jewish people for study and prayer; (2) the building erected for such meetings.

The synagogue movement originated during the Babylonian Captivity. The Jewish people in Babylon were isolated from the Temple and its altar, so small groups began to meet for prayer and study of their ancient Scriptures. When Jews finally returned to Judah and rebuilt the Temple, men like Ezra continued to study and teach the OT (Neh. 8). Some Jews remained in Babylon, and others migrated to other major cities of Mesopotamia and the Middle East. Thus, the synagogue movement, which had taken root in captivity, continued to flourish in Palestine and in the scattered Jewish communities.

The synagogue served the social as well as religious needs of the community. One task of the ruler of the synagogue was to distribute funds to those in need. Local courts were held in the synagogue, and synagogues sponsored the schools where children were taught to read and to memorize Scripture. *See also* Education.

It was common practice in the synagogue to invite qualified visitors to read from and comment on the Scriptures. Luke pictures Jesus given just such an honor in his home synagogue in Nazareth (Lk. 4:14-21). The biblical text speaks several times of Jesus going to the synagogue on the Sabbath (Mt. 12:9; Mk. 1:21; Lk. 6:6). It is believed that the foundation of

Typical synagogue of the first and second centuries A.D., with the large inner room where the men gathered and, above, the balcony for the women. This particular reconstruction is patterned after the synagogue excavated at Capernaum.

957

Remains of the synagogue at Bir'am in northern Galilee. Some 46 first-century A.D. synagogues have been discovered in Israel, most of which are in Galilee.

the very synagogue near Capernaum where Jesus taught (Jn. 6:59) has now been found under the ruins of a synagogue dating from the fifth century A.D.

By NT times, synagogues existed throughout the Roman Empire, in the pockets of Jewish population in many major cities. In some areas, Judaism had also become popular among Gentiles, who were attracted to the Jewish vision of God and of morality. *See also* God-fearers.

The apostle Paul and other early Christian missionaries took advantage of the opportunity to speak in these synagogues when they entered first-century cities. In this way they introduced the Gospel not only to the Jewish community, but also to large numbers of Gentiles.

A number of early synagogues have now been excavated. The typical first-century synagogue featured an entrance with doors facing Jerusalem. Benches along one wall were probably seats for the elders, while the rest of the congregation sat on mats spread on the floor. Men and women were seated apart. The congregation faced a portable "ark," which contained the holy scrolls. A platform was placed nearby for the person who read from the Law or who preached.

The synagogue service consisted of five distinct parts. (1) The congregation listened to the *Shema* (Deut. 6:4-9; 11:13-21; Num. 15:37-41). (2) Synagogue prayers were recited. (3) A portion of the Law was read aloud and expounded. (4) A portion of the prophets was read aloud and expounded. (A clear picture of this portion of the synagogue service is found in the description of Jesus reading Isaiah and teaching from it in the Nazareth synagogue, Lk. 4:16-22). (5) The service concluded with a benediction.

The Synagogue of Freedmen (Libertines, KJV) was founded in Jerusalem by ex-Jewish prisoners of war who had been freed and given Roman citizenship (Acts 6:9). At the time of its destruction in A.D. 70, Jerusalem reportedly had 394 synagogues (or 480, according to another tradition).

The reference in Rev. 2:9 and 3:9 to a "synagogue of Satan" is obscure. It may have been a Judaizing element within the church, a synagogue particularly opposed to Christianity, or one which tolerated the worship of other gods. In favor of the last option, archaeologists have unearthed ancient synagogues with small statues or pictures of pagan gods. *See also* Judaizers.

Syria Modern name of biblical Aram. *See also* Aram.

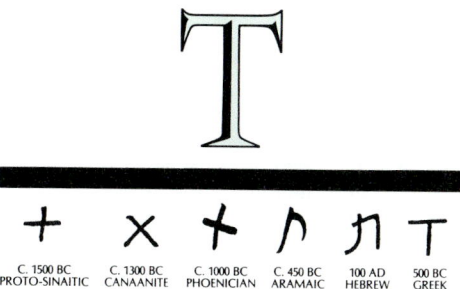

C. 1500 BC
PROTO-SINAITIC   C. 1300 BC
CANAANITE   C. 1000 BC
PHOENICIAN   C. 450 BC
ARAMAIC   100 AD
HEBREW   500 BC
GREEK

tabernacle The portable worship center first erected by the Exodus generation at Mount Sinai. The tabernacle was brought into Canaan by the victorious Israelites and set up at Shiloh (Josh. 18:1; 19:51). It remained there through much of the period of the judges (1 Sam. 4:4), but when Shiloh was threatened by the Philistines, the tabernacle was moved to Nob (1 Sam. 21:1-6).

When Solomon completed his Temple, the tabernacle and its furnishings were installed there as sacred relics (1 Ki. 8:4). This is the last mention of the tabernacle in the sacred writings.

DESIGN OF THE TABERNACLE

Detailed instructions for building the tabernacle and its furnishings were given to Moses by God (Ex. 25–30). The tabernacle stood in an enclosure of curtains that were hung on a metal framework 150 feet (46 meters) long, 75 feet (23 meters) wide, and 7½ feet (2.3 meters) high. The tabernacle itself was a large tent, covered with several layers of expensive fabrics and skins, which stood inside this enclosure.

The tabernacle proper was 45 feet (13.7 meters) long and 15 feet (4.6 meters) wide. It was divided into two unequal rooms, separated by a heavy woven curtain or veil. The outer room was holy, to be entered only by priests. It contained three pieces of furniture: a solid gold oil-fed lamp, which was the only source of light in the heavily curtained room; an altar where incense was burned; and a low table, on which fresh loaves of bread were placed each Sabbath. The inner room was Israel's Holy of Holies, the place on earth where God met with man. It contained only one piece of furniture, the ark of the covenant. This room could be entered only by the high priest and then once a year on the Day of Atonement. The high priest entered only to sprinkle blood on the cover of the ark, which was known as the "mercy seat."

There was only one entrance into the tabernacle court, at the east end. Anyone entering immediately confronted the altar of burnt offering, where sacrifices of all types were offered to God. According to the Law, this was the only place where sacrifices could be made. Just beyond the altar, set off to one side, was the laver, where the priests washed after offering sacrifices and before entering the tabernacle proper.

When the Israelites set up camp in the wilderness, the tabernacle was placed in the center of the camp. Later, when Israel settled in Canaan, the tabernacle was set up at Shiloh, a place accessible to all the Israelite tribes.

SIGNIFICANCE OF THE TABERNACLE

The tabernacle and its furnishings have great symbolic and theological significance. Essentially, the tabernacle showed that God is willing to meet with human beings here on earth. As symbols, both tabernacle and Temple foreshadow the ultimate meeting of God with man in Jesus' incarnation.

This symbolic meaning is made plain in frequent OT references to the tabernacle as the "tent of meeting." The first tent of meeting, described in Ex. 33:7-11, was a small tent set up outside Israel's camp.

Priests and worshipers crowd the courtyard in front of the tricolored curtain of the tabernacle.

The cloudy-fiery pillar, the visible sign of God's presence, hung over this tent, and Moses went there to speak with God. Israelites were invited to come to the tent of meeting to "inquire of the Lord," although only Moses could enter. When the tabernacle was dedicated, the title "tent of meeting" was transferred to it, and the pillar of fire that signified God's presence hung over that tent.

Apart from the tabernacle's role as a symbol of God's willingness to meet with human beings, each aspect of the construction has symbolic implications. Thus, Moses was told to be sure to construct it "according to the pattern shown you on the mountain" (Ex. 25:40). The NT picks up this thought, saying that the tabernacle was "a copy and shadow of what is in heaven" (Heb. 8:5).

Some of the symbolism can be deduced from our theology. For instance, there was only one entrance into the tabernacle court, as there is only one way by which human beings can come to God (Jn. 14:6). A person entering the tabernacle door could not avoid the altar of brass, which speaks both of God's judgment on sin and of his willingness to accept a substitutionary sacrifice (Lev. 1:3-9; 17:11).

Some of the tabernacle symbolism can be deduced from specific Scriptures. For instance, the table of incense represents prayer (Ps. 141:2; Rev. 5:8). The veil that divided the two rooms in the tabernacle symbolizes the fact that before Christ died there was no direct access to God for the believer (Lev. 16:2; Heb. 9:8). The tearing

of the veil when Jesus died (Mt. 27:51) reflects the new reality: We can now come boldly to the throne of grace and find both mercy and help (Heb. 4:16; 7:25).

A more subtle symbolism is pointed out in Heb. 10:1-18. The very fact that the sacrifices of the old covenant were performed daily showed that they were ineffective. They could only cleanse a person temporarily and outwardly. But when Christ offered himself up as a sacrifice, his one act "made perfect forever those who are being made holy" (v. 14).

It is clear from Heb. 9:5 that many if not

The tabernacle proper was made of an acacia-wood frame hung with linen curtains woven with blue, scarlet, and purple yarn. Over this was stretched a tent made of goat hair curtains covered with skins and hides. The altar was the focal point of the curtained enclosure around this Israelite tent-shrine. Inset: Only on the Day of Atonement could the high priest, dressed in linen garments, enter the Most Holy Place of the tabernacle in order to sprinkle blood on the ark of the Testimony (Lev. 16).

all aspects of tabernacle construction and worship have symbolic implications. There is, however, little value in the imaginative approach some have taken to drawing spiritual meanings for each tiny detail. The tabernacle, like the Temple which replaced it, was a shadow of heavenly realities, revealed fully in Jesus Christ. In that light, the significance of the shadow fades.

Tabernacles, Feast of One of the three major religious festivals of Israel, for which Jewish men were required to journey to Jerusalem. Tabernacles was a harvest festival, celebrated for eight days in September/October. Also called Feast of Booths and Feast of Ingathering. *See also* Feasts, Festivals, and Fasts.

table (1) A flat surface, commonly on legs, used for eating; (2) figuratively, a term referring to hospitality. In the wilderness, a table was simply a skin spread on the ground (Ps. 23:5). In most homes, it was an ordinary piece of wood furniture (2 Ki. 4:10), but in the homes of the wealthy a table was often an ornate stone setting.

Several colloquial expressions involve tables. To eat at someone's table implies that he meets your living expenses (Neh. 5:17). "The Lord's table" implies that Jesus is the host, who invites us to remember him as we eat (1 Cor. 11:23-26).

Table of Nations *See* Nations, Table of.

tabret (KJV) *See* Tambourine.

tackle The rigging of a ship (Isa. 33:23), or other nautical equipment (Acts 27:19).

talebearer (KJV) *See* Gossip.

talent A monetary unit, worth over a thousand dollars. Like other monetary units of biblical times, the talent represents a certain weight of silver or gold. *See also* Money; Weights and Measures.

Talitha Koum (*Talitha Cumi*, KJV) Aramaic for "Little girl, arise" (Mk. 5:41). Jesus used these words to recall the daughter of Jairus to life.

Talmud [Heb., "teaching," "a lesson"]. The name for two ancient commentaries on OT laws, one of which was developed in Palestine and one in Babylon. Each is a collection of the insights of thousands of rabbis, whose oral and written teachings were given from about 200 B.C. to A.D. 500. It was compiled A.D. 250–500.

Josephus credits the Pharisees with passing on "certain regulations handed down by former generations and not recorded in the Laws of Moses." Such traditional interpretations were intended to "hedge" the Law, defining its meaning so specifically that no Jew would transgress out of ignorance. Another function of the Talmud was to apply the Law to the changing social conditions experienced by Jews who lived in very different circumstances from the agricultural society envisioned in the books of Moses. However, in Jesus' time, these oral interpretations were accorded the force of the Law but at times went against the intent of the Law itself—a problem that Jesus repeatedly addressed (Mt. 15:2-9).

One-legged stone table excavated at the so-called "Burnt House" in Jerusalem (A.D. 70). The mosaic floor and fine pottery bowl indicate the wealth of this priest's home.

tamarisk An evergreen shrub or small tree indigenous to desert as well as well-watered areas in Palestine. The tamarisk was appreciated for the shade it provided (1 Sam. 22:6) and valued as a burial spot (1 Sam. 31:13).

The tamarisk has a feathery appearance with its slender branches and needle-like leaves. Several species grow in Palestine, especially in dry areas like Beersheba, where Abraham planted one (Gen. 21:33).

961

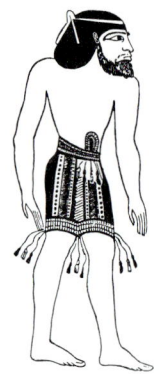

Semitic captive of Pharaoh Neco wears a loin cloth with tassels, such as the Israelites were instructed to wear on the corners of their garments (Num. 15:38).

Tambourine-playing women sit in a tent. Traces of pink and light green paint are still visible on this second century A.D. figurine found at Salamiya, Syria.

tambourine, tambril [Heb., *top*]. A small hand drum, played while chanting God's praises (Ex. 15:20; Ps. 81:2). *See also* Music.

Tammuz A pagan nature deity worshiped as early as the third millennium B.C. in Mesopotamia. The cult involved mourning as winter brought the death of the god, symbolized by dying vegetation, and rejoicing as spring's renewal of plants and trees symbolized the god's return to life. Ezekiel 8:14 pictures a group of women engaging in mourning rites for Tammuz in the Jerusalem Temple itself, revealing how far the people of Judah had departed from the OT faith at the time of the Babylonian invasion of 586 B.C.

tanning Treating the hides of animals to make them soft and pliable; transforming raw skins into leather.

Hides were scraped to remove hair and fragments of flesh or fat. They were then treated in various solutions of plant extracts and lime to soften the skins. In Israel, tanners were somewhat ostracized both for the stench created by the curing hides and because the tanner dealt with dead bodies, leaving him in a ceremonial state of "uncleanness." Tanners were forced to live and work outside of cities and towns. That Peter was staying with Simon the tanner in Acts 9:43 may indicate that Christians were already trying to reach out to outcasts.

The technology for tanning was known in Egypt long before Moses. Tanned hides served as coverings for Israel's tabernacle (Ex. 36:14,19) and as clothing, wineskins, and waterskins.

tar *See* Bitumen.

tares (KJV) A weed called darnel, which looks like wheat in its early stages. As the darnel grows, it is easily distinguished from wheat, but by then its roots are interwoven with the wheat. The counterfeit cannot be destroyed without endangering the real wheat plants. Jesus' parable of the wheat and the tares (Mt. 13:24-30) was easily understood by his listeners, many of whom probably struggled with this very problem in their own fields.

taskmaster (KJV) A foreman; one who oversees the work of others. The early chapters of Exodus refer frequently to the Egyptian "slave drivers" (Ex. 1:11; 3:7; 5:6,10). The Hebrew word implies oppression. However, a more common word, regularly translated "overseer," refers merely to supervision of a project.

tassel A fringe or cord attached to the cloaks worn by the Jews as a reminder of their relationship with God (Num. 15:37-41; Deut. 22:12). The Israelites were told to wear this symbolic decoration, which served as a mnemonic device, "to look at and so you will remember all the commands of the Lord. . . . Then you will remember to obey all my commands and will be consecrated to your God" (Num. 15:37-41). *See also* Fringe.

taste (1) One of the five senses, capable of distinguishing the flavor of substances placed on the tongue (2 Sam. 19:35). (2) Figuratively, to consciously experience something.

Figurative uses predominate in Scripture. The psalmist invites the listener to "taste and see that the Lord is good" (Ps. 34:8). The Book of Hebrews speaks of

Wall painting of Egyptian leatherworkers tanning hides (tomb of Rekhmira, 15th century B.C.). The Hebrew and Greek words for tanning translate literally "to redden," referring to the darkening which the process produces.

Christ tasting death (Heb. 2:9) and believers who "have tasted the heavenly gift" (Heb. 6:4). In this latter verse, admittedly a controversial text, the general use of the term "taste" indicates that these people have actually experienced Christ and thus are true believers and not, as some suggest, Jews who have come in contact with the Gospel but have not accepted it.

tax collector A person employed by a tax contractor to collect taxes or tolls on behalf of the Roman government. *See also* Taxes. The contractors themselves were generally foreigners in the region who then hired native inhabitants as collectors. Luke 19:2 implies that Zacchaeus was the contractor for Jericho.

Tax collectors were scorned in Jesus' time because they served the interests of the Romans and because they frequently charged much more than was due (Lk. 3:12,13; 19:8). Considering the oppressive taxes levied in Judea and Galilee, it is no wonder tax collectors were despised.

Moreover, because tax collectors had repeated contact with Gentiles, they were regarded as ceremonially unclean and classified among the worst sinners.

Jesus, however, commended the tax collectors for their willingness to believe him—unlike the self-righteous Pharisees (Mt. 9:9-13; 11:19; 21:31,32; Mk. 2:13-17; Lk. 5:27-32; 7:29-35; 15:1,2; 18:9-14; 19:1-10).

taxes Charges assessed by a governing body on those over whom it exercises authority. In the biblical era, taxes imposed on the Jewish people were in addition to the sacred tithe they were required to pay into the Temple. *See also* Tithe.

OLD TESTAMENT

The Law imposed a tax for the upkeep of the tabernacle and later the Temple (Ex. 30:11-16). This "temple tax" was still paid in the time of Christ by men over 20 (Mt. 17:24).

With the introduction of the monarchy, Israel entered an era of royal taxation. David imposed a ten-percent tax on produce and livestock (1 Sam. 8:15,17). Duties were also imposed on imported goods (1 Ki. 10:15). Another source of royal revenue was the tribute paid by nations Israel had defeated (2 Sam. 8:6; 2 Ki. 3:4). In a sense, the one month of military service David demanded was a tax on time (1 Chr. 27:1). The heavy taxes Solomon imposed led to the breakup of his kingdom after he died.

After the Captivity, the small Jewish community that returned to Judah paid taxes to the Persian Empire through the provincial governor and was also responsible to support the local Persian administrator. According to Neh. 5:1-5, these taxes were so heavy that many Jews were forced to mortgage their lands or even sell their children as slaves.

NEW TESTAMENT

In Jesus' time, the Jews paid taxes under the Roman system. This system sold the right to collect taxes, giving the contract to the highest bidder. *See also* Tax Collector.

Tax collectors imposed four kinds of duties: a tax on land, a poll tax levied on each individual, a tax on personal property, and a tax on imports and commodities, which was collected not only at ports and borders but also as a farmer's goods were brought into a city or transported on public roads. Josephus tells us that the people of Jerusalem were also forced to pay a house tax.

Herod levied additional taxes, such as a tax on fishing rights, a salt tax, and taxes on oil, clothing, and other commodities. However, the tax system was inconsistent: Those living in the districts of Judea and Galilee paid different kinds of taxes. When Jesus was an adult, the Jews probably paid 30 percent of their income in government taxes, in addition to the 10–20 percent religious tithe called for in the OT.

TAXES AND JESUS' MINISTRY

An understanding of the taxes the Jewish people paid and how they were col-

Collection of delinquent taxes by Egyptian treasury officials: Seated scribes keep record while deputies forcibly bring in the taxpayers. The hieroglyphics read, "Seizing the town rulers for a reckoning." King Solomon imposed heavy taxes through his twelve district governors (1 Ki. 4).

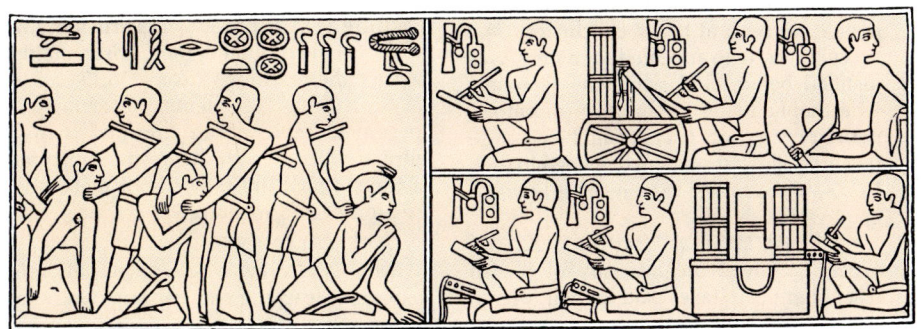

Seven persons gather around the table of a Roman tax collector; relief on funeral stela (A.D. 100–300). Jesus called Matthew to be his disciple while Matthew sat at his tax collection booth (Mt. 9:9).

lected in the first century gives fascinating insights into several incidents reported in the Gospels.

• *The calling of Levi* (Mt. 9:9-11; Mk. 2:14-16; Lk. 5:27-30). Early in his ministry, Jesus saw Levi sitting in his tax booth. This suggests Levi was collecting a value tax on goods brought along the roadway or entering the city. Jesus invited this despised collaborator to become one of his disciples and later even attended a dinner Levi held for his tax-collector friends. This scandalized the religious Jews, who not only resented the heavy taxes but condemned tax collectors for doing business with Gentiles. Yet it set the tone of Jesus' ministry. Christ came to minister to all in his society, high and low, rich and poor, socially acceptable and outcast. Christ would allow no social pressure to isolate him from anyone who might respond to his message of spiritual renewal.

• *The "publican" and Pharisee* (Lk. 18:9-14). In portraying a tax collector and Pharisee at prayer in the Temple, Jesus chose social extremes. How stunned the crowd must have been at Jesus' conclusion. The tax collector, who appealed for mercy, was justified before God while the Pharisee, who thanked God for his own moral superiority, was not. There could be no more powerful illustration of man's need to seek God's mercy rather than rely on his own good works.

• *"Render to Caesar"* (Mt. 22:15-22; Mk. 12:13-17). Given the intensity of Jewish resentment over taxes paid to their foreign

rulers, the Pharisees and Herodians set what must have seemed a perfect trap. "Is it right to pay taxes to Caesar or not?" they asked Jesus. A "No" and Jesus could be reported to the Roman governor, who would surely execute him for inciting a tax rebellion. A "Yes" and Christ's reputation with his countrymen would be ruined. Christ's response contains more than a bit of irony. Because he did not even have a coin, Jesus had to ask his enemies for the denarius he used to escape their snare. Caesar's picture was on the coin. Christ's response—let Caesar have what is his, but what counts is to give God his due.

As the NT Epistles point out, taxes are one of many annoyances faced by human beings in this life. The Christian pays the taxes due in order to support human government, for our quality of life is better under a government than without one (Rom. 13:1-7). Yet however burdensome taxes may be, they are irrelevant to the real issues of life: the honor we owe God and the priority he has in our lives.

teaching (1) The process of instruction (Jn. 6:59); (2) the content of the Christian faith, as in "the teaching" (Rom. 16:17; 2 Th. 3:6). In both Testaments, "teaching" is portrayed more as an informal than a formal process, with the desired outcome a transformed life rather than mere possession of information.

OLD TESTAMENT

Various Hebrew words reflect different aspects of teaching and learning. One suggests training as well as education, with the goal being obedience to God's will (Deut. 31:12,13). Another indicates practical instruction on how a person should conduct himself in real-life situations (Prov. 3:1,2). The main verb for "to know" involves the ability to distinguish, while the related noun, "knowledge," can mean either the skill needed to accomplish technical tasks or moral discernment (Ps. 119:66). Another word, used often in Proverbs, means "to discipline," to correct in such a way that a person learns from his experiences (Prov. 3:11,12). From these terms we get a picture of OT teaching focused on the goal of holy living. The processes through which holiness is taught involve verbal instruction, but they also presuppose a close relationship with a teacher who can exemplify a godly way of life.

Another vital feature of teaching and learning in the OT era was participation by the learner in the religious life of the community. A child's earliest experience of sacrifice, sharing in the Passover meal, hearing the songs and psalms of praise at annual festivals, and listening to stories of the Exodus and of Israel's heroes were all intended to teach faith and obedience to God's Law.

NEW TESTAMENT

Jesus' ministry with his disciples followed general patterns of first-century instruction and discipleship: The student lived with, listened to, questioned, and imitated his teacher. Jesus stated the desired outcome of this kind of instruction: "Everyone who is fully trained will be like his teacher" (Lk. 6:40). In the end, Jesus challenged his disciples to "go and make [more] disciples of all nations," in the process "teaching them to obey everything" Christ had commanded (Mt. 28:19,20).

The Epistles also emphasize the practical outcome of Christian teaching, producing a life "in accord with sound doctrine" (Tit. 2:1). Christian truth must be communicated in such a way that it shapes the individual's values, attitudes, and ultimately his or her whole way of life. Paul promotes the teaching process in his letter to Titus, using several distinct words. The pastor is to "teach" such things as temperance, self-control, and love (2:2,3); to "train" members to love, to be kind, to be self-controlled and pure (2:4,5); to "encourage" youth to be self-controlled (2:6); and to "set an example" of good living

(2:7,8). After extolling the grace of God, which "teaches us to say 'No' to ungodliness and worldly passions," the apostle sums up: "These . . . are the things you should teach [the Greek word means to speak out]. Encourage [*parakaleō*, the word used for the Holy Spirit, our 'Counselor,' in Jn. 14:26] and rebuke [again, the Spirit's ministry of 'convicting' from Jn. 16:8] with all authority" (Tit. 2:12-15). *See also* Disciple; Education; Example; Nurture.

Tebeth *See* Calendar.

teeth The hard, bone-like structures set in human and animal jaws and used for chewing food.

Teeth are a favorite image in Scripture, expressing ferocity and destructiveness among other things (Job 29:17; Ps. 124:6). Thus, to "break the teeth of the wicked" is to render them harmless (Ps. 3:7). "Gnashing teeth" indicates anger or hostility in such passages as Ps. 35:16, but anguish and pain in passages where it is linked with weeping (Mt. 8:12). In the KJV, the image of clean teeth indicates famine (Amos 4:6). The NIV interprets the phrase as "empty stomachs." The expression in OT Law calling for "an eye for an eye, a tooth for a tooth" (Ex. 21:24; Mt. 5:38,39) in personal injury cases is not as grim as it may seem. The regulation actually limits the damages a person can call for when injured and thus effectively prevents escalation of injury cases into violent family feuds.

Roman guardian teaches his young charge; detail from a child's sarcophagus (second century A.D.). Jews were unique in requiring all boys to attend schools paid for by a tax on all parents.

Et-Tell, the mound of ruins which some identify with the Canaanite town of Ai. The name "Ai" means "ruin" in Hebrew, which is equivalent to the Arabic word tell. The Israelites captured and destroyed Ai in their conquest of Canaan (Josh. 8).

tell An Arabic word for a mound or hill; used as an archaeological term. A mound of earth and debris marking the site of an ancient city or settlement is often designated by the prefix "Tell."

temperance In most KJV references, "self-control." In modern versions, a sober and responsible approach to life (1 Tim. 3:2; Tit. 2:2). *See also* Self-control.

temple A place of worship, typically viewed in pagan religions as the house in which a god or gods lived. In ancient times, such gods (idols of stone or metal) might be fed regular meals and even dressed for different occasions by the priests who served them.

Solomon's prayer at the dedication of the Jerusalem Temple expresses the OT conviction that the true God is too great to dwell in any house built by human hands. Yet God chose to be present in Israel's Temple in a special way and to meet with his worshipers there (2 Chr. 6,7).

In the NT, believers are called God's "temple," emphasizing that through the Holy Spirit God has actually taken up residence within the Christian. As God's "temples," Christians are exhorted to live holy lives, appropriate to the nature of the God who has bonded himself to them (1 Cor. 6:18-20).

Temple, Jerusalem The Jewish worship center, first built by Solomon, which stood on the Temple mount in Jerusalem.

The first Temple was erected there by Solomon in the 960s B.C., fulfilling a dream of his father, David. Solomon's Temple was destroyed by the Babylonians when they razed Jerusalem in 587 B.C. A second, much smaller Temple was erected on the same site by Zerubbabel when a small Jewish contingent returned to their homeland from Babylon. This structure, known as the Second Temple, was completed in 516/515 B.C. The Second Temple was greatly expanded and beautified by Herod the Great, a project which took 46 years to complete. The Romans destroyed this Second Temple in A.D. 70.

The site on which both Temples were constructed had great historic significance. Tradition identifies it with Mount Moriah, where Abraham came to sacrifice Isaac (Gen. 22:2), and where David purchased a threshing floor from Araunah to build an altar and sacrifice to God (2 Sam. 24:18-25).

The prophet Ezekiel predicted that a third Temple would stand in the same place in the time of the Messiah, although that site is currently occupied by the Mosque of Omar, considered the second most holy place in Islam. Whether or not this will be fulfilled literally is debated. Ezekiel's Temple is described in great detail in Ezek. 40–48.

ORIGINS OF THE TEMPLE

God promised through Moses that he would choose a particular location as "a dwelling place for his name" (Deut. 12:11). Only here would Israel be allowed to sacrifice (Deut. 12:13,14). Here, too, males would come three times a year to celebrate the major festivals of faith that God set forth in his Law. *See also* Feasts, Festivals, and Fasts.

The Temple was to supersede Israel's tabernacle, which during the wilderness years and the era of the judges had been the place for sacrifice and celebration. In this and in the Temple design, which copied that of the tabernacle, the Temple had a powerful symbolic role in Israel's faith. Israel's God was one, and the people who worshiped him were one. The emphasis on one place of worship taught both the unity of God and the unity of God's people, a unity based not on race but on loyalty to the God of the covenant. *See also* Altar; Lampstand; Laver; Sacrifice; Showbread; Tabernacle.

SOLOMON'S TEMPLE

David dedicated his last years to collecting a vast fortune in gold, silver, and other materials to be used in constructing a Temple (1 Chr. 29:1-9). David also organized the rituals to be celebrated there. Building began in Solomon's fourth year as king, 967/966 B.C., and was completed seven years later. Solomon employed hundreds of thousands of workmen and contracted with Hiram of Tyre for supplies and skilled craftsmen.

When the Temple was dedicated, a visible expression of "the glory of the Lord" descended from heaven and "filled the temple" (2 Chr. 7:1-3). In the centuries that followed, the Temple often fell into disrepair, and its treasures were carried off by foreign invaders (2 Ki. 12:5; 14:13,14; 24:13; 2 Chr. 24:7; 28:24). Just before the final Babylonian invasion of Judah, the prophet Ezekiel had a vision. In it he saw the glory of God, that visible expression of divine presence, lift from above the mercy seat in the Holy of Holies, leave the Temple, and depart from Jerusalem (Ezek. 8–11). The symbolism was overwhelmingly clear. God had abandoned his covenant people to their enemies. The Temple that had represented his supportive presence was now nothing more than a beautiful but empty heap of stones.

THE SECOND TEMPLE

Smaller than Solomon's structure, the Second Temple was constructed by the small company of Jews who returned to their homeland after the Persians conquered the Babylonian Empire. By royal decree, the government of the Persian province in which Judah lay financed its construction (Ezra 6:8-12). It was furnished with many articles that had been taken from the original Temple (Ezra 1:7).

The Temple area was expanded and heavily fortified in the following centuries. The Roman general Pompey besieged the Temple in 63 B.C. for three months before finally breaking down its ramparts. According to Josephus, 12,000 Jews died in the fighting.

Shortly after this, Herod the Great was confirmed by Rome as king of the Jews, and he began an ambitious expansion and beautification project. Josephus tells us that Herod, who was an Idumean, wanted to assure himself of a permanent memorial. The expansion was needed to accommodate the tens of thousands of Jews who visited Jerusalem for the annual religious festivals. (They also brought Herod increased income.) The rebuilding project began in 20/19 B.C., Herod's 18th year of reign. Detailed descriptions in Josephus's writings have made it possible to create models of the Temple as it must have appeared at its completion.

The expanded Temple was undoubtedly one of the wonders of the ancient world. Even the Roman commanders who put down the stubborn Jewish freedom fighters in A.D. 70 hesitated before destroying it. But they knew that the Temple might serve as a rallying point for yet another Jewish rebellion. A commemorative arch

Ruins of the temple of Artemis, patron deity of Sardis in Asia Minor.

Following page: King Solomon's magnificent Temple took seven years to build. He conscripted 30,000 laborers from Israel to quarry and dress stone and to cut timber, and employed Phoenician craftsmen, such as Huram the bronzeworker, to make the pillars, furnishings, and decorations (1 Ki. 5:13-18; 7:13-51).

Our only full description of Herod the Great's impressive complex of courtyards and terraces comes from the Jewish historian Josephus. These two models depict possible interpretations of what the Temple looked like in Jesus' day.

in Rome shows soldiers carrying off the Temple treasures.

THE SECOND TEMPLE IN THE NT

The Second Temple played a prominent role in Jesus' ministry and early church history. Jesus taught on the portico of the Second Temple, and he predicted its destruction (Mt. 24:2). The early Christians assembled at the Temple for worship (Acts 2:46). Peter performed a notable miracle there, healing a man crippled from birth (Acts 3:1-11). Later, Paul, returning to Jerusalem after years of missionary work among the Gentiles, underwent purification rites at the Temple (Acts 21:26). He was recognized and wrongly accused of bringing Gentiles into the inner court, which was reserved for Jews only. Only the intervention of a squad of soldiers, dashing into the crowd from the Fortress Antonia (which stood beside the Temple), saved his life (Acts 21:27-36).

None of the NT books mentions the destruction of the Temple, although some were written after A.D. 70. Yet this destruction was cataclysmic for Israel, which now had no place to offer the sacrifices or offerings required in the OT.

tempt, temptation (1) To induce or entice a person to sin (Jas. 1:13, "God cannot be tempted by evil, nor does he tempt anyone"); (2) to arouse desire in, to attract (Heb. 2:18, as Jesus "suffered when he was tempted," so he is "able to help those who are being tempted"). In this second sense, temptations are inner pressures caused by the interaction of circumstances and the limitations inherent in our humanity. But temptations are also opportunities. When we feel attracted to wrong, we have the opportunity to choose what is right and so to be strengthened spiritually.

TEMPTATION AND TESTING

The original meaning of the English

"tempt" was "to test." No test is real unless there is some pressure to make the wrong choice. But Scripture makes it clear that God does not try to incite us to do evil. He may allow us to be tested by circumstances, but he provides the resources necessary to win out.

Four biblical passages help us understand temptation. Two of the passages treat temptation as enticement to sin. Two of the passages treat situational temptations, in which pressures are created by our humanity itself.

1. *Eve's temptation* (Gen. 3). The passage shows Satan's strategies for weakening human defenses. The result: Adam and Eve introduced sin into the human race.

2. *Jesus' temptation* (Mt. 4; Lk. 4). Satan tries three times to incite Jesus to sin. Jesus, quoting Scripture, refuses. The story provides a paradigm of human vulnerability (we are susceptible to various hungers, greed, and pride). But it also reveals resources available to the believer to defeat the tempter (notably, God's Word). *See also* Temptation of Jesus.

3. *"He is able to help . . ."* (Heb. 2:14-18). This passage emphasizes Jesus' flesh-and-blood human nature, telling us that he felt the same pressures we experience. Though he "suffered when he was tempted," he did not surrender to the pressures (Heb. 5:7-10).

4. *"God is tempting me"?* (Jas. 1:13-15). No, James says, God does not tempt us. The pull toward sin we experience when tempted comes from our fallen human nature, not from God. Often the temptation situation itself is not evil; the evil lies within us. The passage goes on to say that God gives only good gifts, perhaps a reminder of 1 Cor. 10:13: "No temptation has seized you except what is common to man. And God is faithful; he will not let you be tempted beyond what you can bear. But when you are tempted, he will also provide a way out so that you can stand up under it." *See also* Test.

temptation of Jesus Satan's attempt to entice Jesus to sin at the beginning of his earthly ministry (Mt. 4:1-11; Lk. 4:1-13).

Theologically, the temptation of Jesus served to establish both his humanity and his complete commitment to God. This, in turn, established Jesus' qualifications to teach others how to live in intimate union with God.

Experientially, the temptation account alerts us to areas of human vulnerability and provides us with a model of victory to follow. Basic to Jesus' response to temptation was his recall of biblical principles and his commitment to live according to the Word of God. A believer who seeks to overcome temptations needs to be a student of the Word, committed to obey it.

1. *Stones into bread.* Satan reminded a hungry Jesus, who had fasted for 40 days, that as the Son of God he could turn stones into bread. Jesus recalled Deut. 8:3: "Man does not live on bread alone." Human beings are vulnerable to physical needs and desires. Yet human beings are not mere animals, and our physical needs must not dominate us. We are created in the image of God and can choose to respond to him despite pressures from our physical nature.

2. *Leap from the Temple.* The Greek construction tells us that the wording "if you are the Son of God" here does not so much express doubt about Jesus' sonship but assumes it to issue a challenge: "Since you are God's Son. . . ." Satan challenged Jesus to show his power by leaping from the high point of the Temple Mount. Satan misapplied Scripture to assert that angels would catch Jesus before he could be hurt. In response, Jesus quoted Deut. 6:16, "Do not put the Lord your God to the test." The passage recalls a day when the Exodus generation demanded a miracle, saying, "Is the Lord among us or not?" (Ex. 17:7). Human beings are vulnerable to doubt and unbelief. The principle Jesus dramatically reaffirmed is central to both Testaments: The people of God must live by faith, without depending on visible signs of God's loving presence.

3. *Bow down to Satan.* The enticement is

Terrain in the Judean wilderness, where Jesus fasted 40 days and was tempted by the devil.

not in the act of worship, but in the prize promised. Satan would give Jesus "all the kingdoms of the world and their splendor," if Jesus would but bow to Satan. The splendor hardly tempted Jesus—but think of all the good he could do as ruler of this world: Wars would cease; crime and injustice would be no more. Yet the path to Jesus' Kingdom led first to a cross. Jesus quoted Deut. 6:13: "Worship the Lord your God, and serve him only." Jesus would live by the will of God, whatever the inducement to step from that pathway. Human beings are vulnerable to their better as well as their baser natures. We may be tempted to do wrong in an effort to win some great good. Jesus reminds us that no end justifies wrong means. The people of God must do God's work in God's way.

The three temptations of Jesus, then, provide a paradigm of human vulnerability and point the way to victory. We are to live as spiritual rather than merely physical beings. We are to live by faith, not by sight. And we are to live daily by the will of God and avoid doing wrong even for "noble ends."

Ten Commandments   *See* Commandments, Ten.

tent (1) A portable structure of cloth or skin, spread over poles and anchored to the ground with pegs (Isa. 54:2). Frequently reed mats served as tent walls and would be rolled up to permit cooling by the breeze. (2) Figuratively, any dwelling. "Went unto their tents" (1 Ki. 8:66, KJV) is translated by the NIV, "went home." (3) Also figuratively, the mortal body as a temporary residence of the individual personality (2 Cor. 5:1; 2 Pet. 1:13). The image reflects Job's portrayal of death as pulling up the cords of one's tent (Job 4:21).

Tents served as home for the Hebrew patriarchs (Gen. 18:1; 31:25) and for the many nomadic peoples of biblical times (Jdg. 6:5; Jer. 35:7). Apparently husbands and wives often resided in separate tents (Gen. 24:67; 31:33). The Israelites lived in tents on the journey from Egypt (Ex. 16:16; Num. 16:26). Once they were in Canaan,

Two stylized idols found in Palestine (third millennium B.C.). The teraphim *referred to in various OT passages are associated with private worship, divination, and protection (Gen. 31:30-35; Jdg. 18; Ezek. 21:21).*

Israelites put up tents near the Tent of Meeting or tabernacle. The typical Israelite tent used a post-and-peg construction covered in goat hair material.

many slept outside in tents during the hot summer months. Shepherds used tents when in the fields with their flocks (Isa. 38:12), and armies slept in tents when on the march (2 Ki. 7:7).

Hebrews makes much of the fact that the patriarchs lived in tents. Apparently, they saw themselves as temporary visitors rather than permanent residents on this earth. They kept their eyes fixed on their true homeland, "the city with foundations, whose architect and builder is God" (Heb. 11:9,10). *See also* Tentmaker.

tentmaker A tradesman, probably better understood as "leatherworker." Acts 18:3 indicates that Paul was a tentmaker, and that he worked with Aquila and Priscilla in this trade. On several occasions, Paul mentioned that he worked with his own hands (Acts 20:34; 1 Cor. 4:12) to support himself. This, along with his preaching, kept him busy "night and day" (1 Th. 2:9; 2 Th. 3:8). Some modern Christians take Paul's example as a basis for self-supported missionary efforts. "Tentmaking" in this sense involves carrying on a ministry while earning a living at a trade. Yet the Bible also presents the idea of missionaries and church leaders supported by other Christians (2 Cor. 11:8,9; Gal. 6:6; 1 Tim. 5:17,18).

Tent of Meeting (NIV) *See* Tabernacle.

teraphim (KJV) Figures or images associated with pagan worship and the occult practice of divination. The Hebrew word is typically translated "household gods" or "idols." Teraphim are reported in all periods of OT history, showing the persistence of pagan practices in Israel (Gen. 31:19; Jdg. 17:5; 1 Sam. 15:23; 2 Ki. 23:24; Ezek. 21:21; Zech. 10:2). Teraphim are specifically condemned in most contexts where they are mentioned. *See also* Divination; Idol.

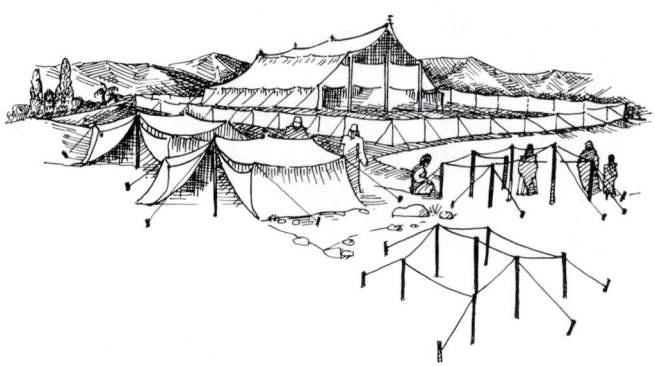

terror Fear, dread. In English versions, each of these terms is used to translate a number of different Hebrew and Greek words. *See also* Fear.

test A trial intended to ascertain value or quality (Ex. 16:4; Deut. 8:16); circumstances that try or prove a person's qualities (Jas. 1:12).

Both Testaments indicate that God tests human beings. Therefore, the Bible makes a careful distinction between testing and temptation. Hebrew words for testing include *nasah,* which frequently describes a difficult situation; *sarap,* which means to "smelt" or "refine," suggesting that testing is intended for purification (Pss. 17:3; 26:2); and *bahan,* for a test focused on some specific quality, intended to demonstrate whether that quality exists (Zech. 13:9; Mal. 3:10). Such tests are not intended to cause human beings to fail. Rather, the tests are intended to enable us to prove to ourselves and others the existence of a quality which, without the test, might never be displayed.

In the NT, two word groups are translated "to test." One is *peirazō,* sometimes the same word translated "to tempt" (Mt. 19:3; 2 Cor. 13:5). The context will determine whether or not the one designing the test intends the individual to fail—and thus whether it is a "tempting" or a "testing." The verb *dokimazō* means to prove the existence of a given quality. Thus, Christians are encouraged to "test and approve what God's will is" as our minds are renewed to match God's thinking (Rom. 12:2); and candidates for leadership are to be time-tested, so that the qualities necessary for leadership will be displayed to the church and community (1 Tim. 3:10).

The testing and trials that human beings experience are painful. But the testimony of Scripture is that God intends such experiences for our good. *See also* Tempt.

testament (KJV) (1) Most often, a covenant; a formal commitment by one person to another to perform certain acts; in the NT, the new covenant which Jesus instituted by his death and resurrection (Mt. 26:28; 2 Cor. 3:6). *See also* Covenant. (2) In Heb. 9:16,17 (KJV), a will; a written document specifying the distribution of a person's possessions, which is to take effect only after his or her death.

testify (1) To give evidence at some legal proceeding of what one has seen or learned about (Lev. 5:1; Deut. 8:19). (2)

Figuratively, to perform an act that may serve as evidence for or against a person (Jer. 14:7), or to speak out as a witness to some spiritual reality (Jn. 5:32-36; 1 Jn. 5:7). *See also* Witness.

testimony The evidence given by a witness; in the OT specifically (1) the tablet on which the Ten Commandments were written (Ex. 31:18); (2) the laws of God themselves (Ps. 119:36,88 KJV); (3) specific commands given by Moses (Deut. 4:45 KJV); or (4) evidence given by a witness in court (Deut. 17:6). In the NT, (1) the oral witness of John the Baptist to Jesus (Jn. 1:32); (2) the display of God's power expressed in Jesus' miracles (Jn. 5:36,37); (3) the witness of the Holy Spirit to the reality of Jesus (1 Jn. 5:9,10); and (4) the NT revelation itself (1 Cor. 2:1; 1 Jn. 5:11).

Testimony, Ark of the *See* Ark of the Covenant.

tetrarch A title given the ruler of a small district, a "petty prince." While of lower status than a king, a tetrarch under the Romans exercised royal authority within his district and was often granted the courtesy title "king" (Mk. 6:14; *see* Lk. 3:1). The word originally referred to the ruler of one-fourth of a realm, but by NT times, its meaning was broadened.

thank offering A type of fellowship offering; a voluntary offering presented to God by an individual worshiper (Lev. 7:12; 22:29). *See also* Sacrifices and Offerings.

thanks, thanksgiving OT: To acknowledge God's goodness by expressing praise or by bringing a sacrifice (Lev. 7:12; Ps. 107:1). NT: [Gk., *eucharistia*] An attitude or display of gratitude, usually to God (only three times in the NT is "thanksgiving" directed to people). We give thanks to God (a) in the Lord's Supper, for the body and blood of Christ (Mt. 26:26; 1 Cor. 11:24); (b) for blessings God has provided (1 Cor. 15:57; 2 Cor. 4:15); and (c) for those who have come to know Jesus (Eph. 1:16; Phil. 1:3; 1 Th. 2:13).

Paul challenged the Philippians—and us—to present requests to God "with thanksgiving." He promised, "The peace of God, which transcends all understanding, will guard your hearts and minds in Christ Jesus" (Phil. 4:6,7). *See also* Prayer; Thank Offering.

Lion statue on pedestal along the Via Egnatia, the ancient Macedonian road Paul traveled on between Neapolis and Thessalonica (Acts 16:11,12; 17:1).

the Fall were by angels, who spoke in God's name. If they were visitations by God, they were distinct from Christ in his incarnation, in that a theophany only appears to be a human being, while in the incarnation God actually took on a human nature. *See also* Incarnation.

Thessalonians, First and Second Epistles to the Paul wrote two letters to the newly established church at Thessalonica. The first, a warmly personal epistle, reviews truths he taught there and clarifies their uncertainty about the destiny of Christians who die before Jesus returns. The second letter also focuses on eschatology but describes an outbreak of evil to occur prior to the end. It assures the Thessalonians that the wicked who were persecuting them would ultimately be punished.

BACKGROUND

Paul, with Timothy and Silas (Silvanus), visited Thessalonica early in Paul's second missionary journey. The city was the capital of the Roman province of Macedonia and was an important naval base. Thessalonica had a large Jewish population, which had apparently attracted a number of Gentile God-fearers. When many of these Gentile adherents to Judaism joined Paul, the Jews became intensely jealous. They stirred up so much trouble that Paul and his team were forced to leave the city, leaving behind a congregation of very new believers (Acts 17:1-9).

Paul was deeply concerned about these new converts, who were being persecuted by those who had forced him to leave the city (1 Th. 3:3,5; 2 Th. 1:4,5; 3:2). So, Paul sent Timothy to revisit Thessalonica (1 Th. 3:2), and when the young minister returned, Paul wrote these two letters. Each reviews truths that Paul had taught in his brief time in Thessalonica, but which he had not had time to explain thoroughly (note the recurrence of "you know" in 1 Th. 1:5; 2:1,2,5,9-11; 3:3,4; 4:1,2,6,11; 5:2). The letters focus on the future for the believer (1 Th. 1:10; 2:19; 3:13; 4:13-18; 5:1-10,23) and the future for those who do not believe (2 Th. 1:5-10; 2:1-12).

AUTHORSHIP

The letters were probably written in A.D. 50/51. Most believe that 1 Thessalonians was written before any of Paul's other NT Epistles. While some have questioned Pauline authorship of 2 Thessalonians, both letters were accepted by the early church as authentic. Any differences in style or

theology The study of God. Christian theology is the study of God as he has revealed himself in creation, the Scriptures (his written Word), and in Christ (his living Word). The word "theology" does not appear in either Testament.

theophany An appearance by God, taking on some form (usually a human form) in order to be visible to human beings.

Genesis implies that God took a visible form to "walk" with Adam and Eve in the Garden of Eden (Gen. 3:8). There are several incidents in the OT where the text seems to imply that human beings did see God in human guise. The Lord spoke to Abraham through one of three visitors (Gen. 18). After wrestling all night with a man who then blessed him, Jacob said, "I saw God face to face" (Gen. 32:30). The "angel of the Lord" in the OT is at times identified as the Lord himself (Jdg. 6:11-14) and is understood by those he visits to be God (Jdg. 13:22). *See also* Angel of the Lord.

974   It is possible that such visitations after

word choice are easily explained by their differing subject matter.

THEOLOGICAL CONTRIBUTIONS

Paul includes a beautiful description of the resurrection of the believer at Christ's return (1 Th. 4:13-18). This was written specifically to reassure those who were concerned about believers who had recently died. Paul says that the dead in Christ will rise from the grave to join the living at Christ's return, and together they will "be with the Lord forever."

The second Epistle corrects another misunderstanding about eschatology. Many in the young church took the persecutions they were suffering as evidence that Jesus was about to appear. Some stopped working to wait for the great event. In this letter, Paul links his teaching about the future to the OT's prediction that a "man of sin [lawlessness]" will appear (2 Th. 2:1-4; *see* Dan. 11:36). This Antichrist will set himself up in God's Temple and proclaim himself to be God. His claim will be

1 & 2 THESSALONIANS: A READING AND STUDY GUIDE

Chapter	Content Summary	Related Articles
	1 Thessalonians	
1	Paul thanks God for the Thessalonians' response to the Gospel and their evangelization of Macedonia.	Holy Spirit Evangelist
2	Paul reviews his ministry among them and reminds them of the relationship he had with "each one."	Gospel Family
3	Paul reviews Timothy's encouraging report.	Prayer
4	Paul calls for continued holiness and commitment, and explains the Christian's resurrection hope.	Sex
5	Paul calls for the church to keep on ministering and for each individual to work and pray hard.	Salvation Sanctify
	2 Thessalonians	
1	Paul explains the meaning of Christ's return for the wicked: punishment with "everlasting destruction."	Second Coming Hell
2	Paul says that before this happens a "man of lawlessness" will appear and proclaim himself to be God. Christians are to "stand firm" in the faith.	Antichrist Future Truth
3	Paul calls on the church to discipline the idle, for the prospect of Jesus' return is no license for laziness.	Work Example

In Paul's day Thessalonica was governed by "politarchs," six of whom are named in this Greek inscription from a Roman arch at Thessalonica (A.D. 143).

supported by miraculous signs worked by Satan himself, and he will win the allegiance of all who have not believed in Jesus. Since none of this has happened, Paul says, the Thessalonians ought to return to work and to evangelization (2 Th. 3:6-15). *See also* Antichrist.

MASTERY KEYS

As you read, make a list of those things that Paul says the Thessalonians "know." How does what Paul says clarify or further explain these "known" ideas? In 1 Thessalonians underline what Paul says the future holds for believers. In 2 Thessalonians underline what Paul says the future holds for unbelievers and this world.

thief A person who takes the property of another. Although some thieves used violence (Jn. 10:10), most used surprise to "break in and steal" (Mt. 6:19; *see* Ex. 22:2). A "thief in the night" (1 Th. 5:2; 2 Pet. 3:10) would sneak up quietly, suddenly. This is the way the Lord will return—suddenly, unexpectedly. The two thieves who died on crosses next to Jesus were probably highwaymen, who attacked and killed or injured their victims —and thus deserved the death penalty.

thigh The upper part of the leg. The right thigh of many sacrificial animals was to be eaten by the priests and their families (Lev. 7:32-34; 10:14). Hebrew men strapped their swords to their thighs (Jdg. 3:16). To strike an enemy "hip and thigh" (Jdg. 15:8 KJV) was to do great damage, while to strike one's own thigh was symbolic of shame or frustration (Jer. 31:19; Ezek. 21:12 KJV).

The thigh also had early covenantal significance: A person making a binding promise did so with a hand resting under the other person's thigh (Gen. 24:2,9; 47:29). Jacob wrestled all night with God, resisting until the angel of the Lord touched Jacob's thigh and dislocated his hip. (The KJV's "hollow of his thigh" refers to the hip socket.) Genesis comments, "Therefore to this day the Israelites do not eat the tendon attached to the socket of the hip" (Gen. 32:22-32). One interesting but doubtful interpretation of this event suggests that the dislocation caused Jacob to stop struggling and instead cling to his opponent for support. A clinging Jacob became Israel, "a prince with God."

thistle One of any number of thorny plants. *See also* Brier.

Thomas [TOM-uhs; "twin"]. One of Jesus' original twelve disciples, called Didymus, which also means "twin." Thomas is best known for the doubt he expressed concerning Jesus' resurrection. **Scripture:** Jn. 11:16; 14:1-6; 20:24-29.

BACKGROUND

Where Peter was rash and impetuous, Thomas seemed cautious and hesitant. He always seemed willing to express his uncertainty. When Jesus made an obscure statement about leaving for his Father's house, it was Thomas who spoke the question on everyone's mind (Jn. 14:5). After Thomas missed seeing the resurrected Jesus when he appeared to the other disciples (Jn. 20:19-24), Thomas made the statement which won him his "doubting" nickname: "Unless I see the nail marks in his hands and put my finger where the nails were, and put my hand into his side, I will not believe it" (Jn. 20:25).

LEARNING FROM THOMAS'S LIFE

Thomas was not a convinced skeptic. He was a true believer, whose hope was mixed with uncertainty. In fact, Thomas did not require the evidence he demanded. When Jesus did appear and speak to Thomas, Thomas dropped to his knees and confessed, "My Lord and my God!" (Jn. 20:28). Thomas stopped doubting and believed.

Many believers know times of uncertainty. At such times, hope is diluted by doubt, and we may even list the evidence we require before we will fully commit to Jesus. It is helpful to note that Jesus was not angry with Thomas, and even offered him the proof Thomas thought he needed. It was then that Thomas discovered what all Christians come to know: What we need is not proof, but rather a simple word from Christ that speaks to our heart. Thomas saw and believed. We believe without seeing (Jn. 20:29).

Tradition tells us that Thomas turned to the east, even reaching India, where he served as a missionary. The doubter had become a man of faith.

thorn in the flesh A figurative reference to some serious illness or disease suffered by the apostle Paul (2 Cor. 12:7). The word for "thorn" here means a "sharp stake" and indicates a truly serious problem. Some argue that the "thorn" is not an illness but some kind of persecution or rejection.

In context, Paul describes this thorn as "a messenger of Satan" that God permitted to keep Paul from becoming conceited over revelations he had received from the Lord. Paul came to appreciate his "thorn" as a reminder that he must always rely on the Lord.

There have been many suggestions as to what illness constituted Paul's thorn. Some advance the theory that Paul's infirmity was a disfiguring eye disease, reflected in the close of the Galatian letter. There Paul apparently took the pen from his secretary, and says, "See what large letters I use as I write to you with my own hand!" (Gal. 6:11).

thorns Spine-bearing plants common to the Near East. A number of different Hebrew words describe the briers, brambles, nettles, spiny hedges, and thistles that fall into this category. There is no agreement about the specific plants indicated by these words, and translators generally take them as synonyms, using the English term which seems to them to best fit the context. There is similar uncertainty about the Greek vocabulary.

This makes it impossible to identify the plant that was used to weave the "crown of thorns" the Roman soldiers placed on Jesus' head (Mt. 27:29). Yet the thorns were strangely appropriate. The Bible first mentions thorns as being a result of Adam's sin (Gen. 3:18), and continues to use these plants as symbols of evil (Prov. 22:5; Mt. 7:16; 13:22). Thus, symbolically, Jesus bore the weight of our sin on his head. *See also* Brier.

thorns, crown of *See* Crown; Thorns.

thousand Ten hundreds. Though the Hebrew word often denotes the specific number (Josh. 3:4; 1 Sam. 4:2), it also has two broader meanings. It can refer to a subdivision of an Israelite clan or tribe, possibly a military unit (Num. 1:16; 31:14). Figuratively, it can indicate an indeterminate number or period of time, as in Ps. 90:4: "For a thousand years in your sight are like a day that has just gone by" (*see* 2 Pet. 3:8). Some understand the reference in Rev. 20:3 to a thousand-year reign of Christ to be just such a figurative use in the Greek, while others take it literally. *See also* Millennium.

thresh To separate the edible grains of ripe cereal crops from stalks and husks. In biblical times, dried wheat, barley, or rye stalks were spread on flat, open spaces called "threshing floors." These were usually on the tops or sides of high hills where strong winds blew. The dried stalks were first crushed, using wooden flails or weighted sleds drawn back and forth over the threshing floor by animals (Deut. 25:4; 1 Chr. 21:20-23; Isa. 28:28). The crushed stalks were then tossed into the air by the farmer. The heavier grain fell in a heap, while the wind blew the chaff and lighter straw away.

John the Baptist used threshing as an image of God's impending judgment. God will separate the grain from the chaff, "gathering the wheat into his barn and burning up the chaff with unquenchable fire" (Mt. 3:12). *See also* Chaff.

throne (1) The ceremonial seat occupied by a king (1 Ki. 1:46). (2) Symbolically, earthly royal power (2 Sam. 3:10), and also God's overarching sovereignty (Ps. 45:6). Since one function of the king was judicial, the image of a king taking his throne may suggest judgment (Mt. 25:31-46; Rev. 20:11).

The gilded throne of Pharaoh Tutankhamen illustrates the symbolic authority of a royal seat. The wooden throne is overlaid with gold, silver, blue ceramic, calcite, and glass.

Glazed tiles fully covered the palace walls of King Darius the Great of Persia (Susa, about 500 B.C.). The archer (below) and the winged lion with ram's horns and griffin's legs (right) are fine examples of the life-size art on the palace walls.

A number of references use the throne symbol to identify Jesus as the Messiah, that descendant of David who is the rightful inheritor of authority over Israel (Lk. 1:32; Acts 2:30; Heb. 1:5-9; *compare* Heb. 8:1 *with* 2 Sam. 7:12-16). Jesus also shares the Father's throne, a fact that establishes his deity (Heb. 1:8; Rev. 3:21).

thumb The innermost of the five fingers, which opposes the other four and enables a person to grasp objects. Hebrew uses the same term for the "thumb of the hand" and the "thumb of the foot," the big toe.

In Israelite rituals, blood of sacrificial animals was often placed on ear, thumb, and big toe (Lev. 8:23; 14:14). Some see in this act a symbolic dedication of the ears to hearing, and the body to doing, the will of God. In warfare, a captor might cut off an enemy's thumbs and big toes, rendering him unable to grasp a weapon or to travel easily (Jdg. 1:6).

Thummim *See* Urim and Thummim.

thunder The loud, explosive sound caused during storms by the expansion of air suddenly heated by the discharge of electricity as lightning bolts.

Scripture associates thunder with one of the judgments God brought on Egypt (Ex.

9) and with God's presence atop Mount Sinai (Ex. 19). Psalm 29 vividly portrays a thunderstorm as the voice of God, an indication of his great power and majesty. Thunder is frequently associated with acts of divine judgment, and especially so in the Book of Revelation (4:5; 6:1; 8:5; 9:9; 10:3,4; 11:19; 14:2; 16:18; 19:6).

Jesus nicknamed James and John "Sons of Thunder" (Boanerges), perhaps for their fiery tempers. It was they who wanted to call fire from heaven to destroy an unresponsive Samaritan village (Mk. 3:17; Lk. 9:54).

Thunder, Sons of *See* Boanerges; Thunder.

tile Flat, thin squares of baked clay that were frequently painted bright colors and used to decorate buildings. Archaeologists have recovered tiles that served as facing on the entrances to Babylon. In NT times, the homes of wealthier individuals might have tile roofs (Lk. 5:19).

timbrel (KJV, RSV) A percussion instrument; a hand drum. Modern versions use the word "tambourine." *See also* Music.

time A moment of occurrence, duration of an event, or the duration between events. The Hebrew OT has no general word for an abstract sense of time, nor specific terms for the categories "past," "present," or "future" as we use them. However, we can distinguish a view of time from individual contexts in both Testaments. The NT uses two Greek words to distinguish its dimensions.

OLD TESTAMENT
The OT understands this universe as a creation of God. As such, the universe reflects something of his nature, expressed in the regularity and consistency of repeated events whose patterns are expressed in days, weeks, months, and years. While human beings experience these rhythms, the universe is not trapped in endlessly repeated cycles of events. Human beings experience "appointed times," special moments of God's planning. Israel's annual religious festivals included celebrations of God's active intervention in history.

The OT also treats the past and future as realities, although they lie beyond the capacity of the living to experience. Because

Above right: This Egyptian device, like the sundial, used shadows to track intervals in the sun's passing. Because of its east-west orientation, however, it had to be turned around at noon. Right: Portable sundial.

God has an endless life span and is able to experience all of time, we can speak confidently about the past and future as he has revealed them to us.

NEW TESTAMENT
The NT contains several different time-related words. The two basic Greek words for time are *chronos*, which indicates a measured period of time, and *kairos*, which focuses attention on the quality or content of a specific period. Thus, Christ died at the "right time" (*kairos*), making the present an "acceptable time" (*kairos*), rich in opportunity for salvation (Rom. 5:6; 2 Cor. 6:2; *see* Eph. 1:10).

SEGMENTS OF MEASURED TIME
A number of biblical terms measure the passage of time (*see* chart). Note that the Hebrew year was lunar, based on months that stretched from new moon to new moon. This meant that the Jews probably followed the Babylonian pattern and used some regular plan to add an extra month or partial month every few years so the lunar year would correspond with the seasons of the solar year. *See also* Age; Calendar; Day; Hour; New; Old.

This tower near the ancient marketplace at Athens once housed a clock, which was fed with flowing water that filled a measure in a given time, like sand in an hourglass. It was built when Athens was under Roman control.

TIME MEASUREMENTS IN THE BIBLE

Term	Period	Explanation
Hour	1/24 of a day	No equal division of day in the OT. By NT times Jews divided day and night into 12-hour periods.
Day	24 hours	Though "day" is used loosely in the Bible for the hours from sunrise to sunset, the standard day was counted sunset to sunset (Gen. 1:5). Romans designated it midnight to midnight.
Night	12 hours	The Israelites/Jews divided the night into three "watches"; the Romans, four.
Week	7 days	In Hebrew, literally "a seven"; Israel is the first ancient culture known to have a 7-day week.
Month	30 days	Literally, "moon" in Hebrew; first day of the month always fell on a new moon. Lunar months necessitated addition of an extra month every two or three years to match seasons of solar year.
Year	12 months	Civil new year: first day of first month; Sacred new year: first day of seventh month; Sabbatical year: every seventh year; Jubilee: every fiftieth year

Timothy, First and Second Epistles to

Personal letters written by the apostle Paul to Timothy, his young friend and companion in ministry. Each Epistle is warm and positive in tone, rich in advice and encouragement. These letters, with the letter to Titus, are commonly called the Pastoral Epistles. The early church considered both 1 and 2 Timothy the work of the apostle Paul, although various modern critics have argued that a disciple of Paul wrote these in the name of or under the direction of Paul. *See also* Pastoral Epistles.

BACKGROUND

These two letters were written near the end of Paul's life: 1 Timothy during Paul's first Roman imprisonment about A.D. 64, and 2 Timothy during his second imprisonment and just before his execution, in A.D. 67 or 68. The two letters share many of Paul's final concerns about the churches he founded. Frequent references to false teachers make it clear that Paul sensed that the church was in more danger from threats from within than from persecution by outsiders. Paul urges Timothy to counter the internal danger with sound teaching, by giving an example of godliness, and by training local leaders who will guide their congregations effectively.

TIMOTHY

Timothy joined Paul's missionary team on the apostle's second journey (Acts 16:1). Paul's exhortation to Timothy not to let anyone look down on him because of his youth (1 Tim. 4:12) suggests either that Timothy had a shy and retiring nature or reflects that culture's prizing of age in leadership. Yet Paul's commendation of Timothy to the Philippians conveys this young disciple's strengths and commitment. Paul says, "I hope . . . to send Timothy to you soon. . . . I have no one else like him, who takes a genuine interest in your welfare. For everyone looks out for his own interests, not those of Jesus Christ. But you know that Timothy has proved himself, because as a son with his father he has served with me in the work of the gospel" (Phil. 2:19-22).

Timothy may well represent many young Christians who remain uncertain and hesitant despite a history of faithful service. He also represents a reality in the church: The leaders of each generation must pass the ministry on to others, who in turn will train still others to take up the burden of leadership. Timothy might appear young, but an early commitment to Christ and a genuine concern for others had effectively equipped him for ministry.

THEOLOGICAL CONTRIBUTIONS

These letters discuss false teachers, how to combat them, and how to select godly Christian leaders. Each of these is important in practical theology—the application of God's truth to guide our lives as his people.

Paul points out that false teachers are recognized by their motives, methods, and results. The best way to combat false teaching is to concentrate on teaching sound doctrine and on living righteous lives. These books carefully describe the qualifications of Christian leaders. The description matches perfectly with the Christian life-style that these leaders are supposed to teach others. *See also* False Prophets and Teachers.

There is much overlap in these two letters. It helps to read the two letters together, comparing Paul's treatment of the following themes:

- *Holiness and purity* (1 Tim. 1:3-7; 2 Tim. 1:3-12).
- *Sound doctrine* (1 Tim. 1:8-11; 2 Tim. 1:13,14).
- *Timothy's ministry* (1 Tim. 1:18–2:7; 2 Tim. 2:1-7).
- *Godly living* (1 Tim. 2:8-10; 2 Tim. 2:14-19).
- *Limits* (1 Tim. 2:11-15; 2 Tim. 2:20,21).
- *Leadership* (1 Tim. 3:1-15; 2 Tim. 2:22-26).
- *Falseness* (1 Tim. 4:1-5; 2 Tim. 3:1-9).
- *Ministry* (1 Tim. 4:11-16; 2 Tim. 3:10-17).

- *Practicing religion* (1 Tim. 5:1-8; 2 Tim. 4:1-5).

tithe The contribution of one-tenth of one's crops and livestock required in the OT for sacred purposes.

The practice of tithing was well established in the ancient Middle East, where the tenth was generally viewed as the king's portion and served as royal income. Abraham paid a tithe to Melchizedek, a local monarch, who blessed him (Gen. 14:18-20). In Israel, the tithe was established for the support of the Levites and priests, who served God but had been given no land of their own. *See also* Taxes.

OLD TESTAMENT

The tithe, assessed on all crops produced and animals born in Israel, was to be brought to the Jerusalem Temple (or to the tabernacle in earlier times). It was paid in kind, unless the person paying lived too far away to transport commodities conveniently. Then the tithe could be paid in money, but in such a case one-fifth had to be added to the cash price (Lev. 27:30-33;

1 & 2 TIMOTHY: A STUDY AND TEACHING GUIDE

Chapter	Content Summary	Related Articles
	1 Timothy	
1	Paul warns against those who misunderstand the goal of Christian teaching. Paul, himself the chief of sinners, understands the Gospel of grace.	Law Sin Grace
2	Paul urges prayer for governments, that Christians may live and worship in peace. He calls women to submit and learn quietly in the church.	Government, human Submission Woman
3	Paul sets forth qualifications for spiritual leaders who must exemplify certain qualities.	Leader Elder
4	Paul gives Timothy specific instructions on what to teach and how to minister to others.	Teaching Youth
5	Paul continues with advice on how to focus ministry to various groups within the church.	Widow
6	Paul concludes with warnings against a love of money. He charges Timothy to pursue righteousness, godliness, and faith.	Money Righteousness
	2 Timothy	
1	Paul encourages Timothy to be faithful to Christ, even if this includes suffering for the Gospel.	Gospel Suffer
2	Paul exhorts Timothy to endure as a soldier, strive as a worker, and pursue purity.	Creed False prophets and teachers
3	Paul warns Timothy of coming apostasy, and charges him to live a godly life guided by the Scriptures.	Apostasy Bible
4	Paul continues his charge: Timothy is to preach the Word, to endure hardship, and continue to evangelize.	Word

Num. 18:21-32; Deut. 12:5-18; 14:22-29).

The Levites, the tribe God had set apart to serve him at the Temple, received the tithe. They in turn gave a tithe to the priests. The tithe thus was intended for the support of those dedicated to maintain the worship of God in Israel.

Every third year the tithe was paid into a local storehouse. From there it was distributed not only to the Levites but also to the poor and needy. This third-year tithe may have been in addition to the regular tithe paid into the Temple.

UNDERLYING CONCEPTS

A complex but beautiful web of concepts underlies the OT practice of tithing. God had set aside the tribe of Levi to serve him. Rather than give Levi territory when Israel conquered Canaan, God himself determined to be their portion. Since the tithe that supported the priests and Levites was paid only on products of the land and God controlled the fruitfulness of Israel, the tithe was seen as God's gift to his priests and Levites. Yet all Israel participated with God in honoring his servants, since the people were the agents through whom his gift was given.

The tithe permitted all Israel to express trust in God and permitted God to demonstrate his faithfulness. Through lack of trust some generations withheld the tithe. To such persons God says through Malachi, "Bring the whole tithe into the storehouse, that there may be food in my house. Test me in this . . . and see if I will not throw open the floodgates of heaven and pour out so much blessing that you will not have room enough for it" (Mal. 3:10).

When the law on tithing was observed, Israel's trust in the Lord was both demonstrated and strengthened, as God gave his people adequate evidence of his faithfulness in the blessings he provided.

FREEWILL OFFERINGS

Giving in the OT goes beyond the tithe. The OT also speaks of the "voluntary contribution." This is a gift that flows from love, not an expression of duty or an effort to win divine blessing. Freewill offerings were most often called for to meet some special need for construction or repair of Israel's worship center (Ex. 36; 2 Chr. 35; Ezra 1:4).

The Jewish people were also exhorted to be generous to the poor and lend freely even when there was no expectation of repayment. Giving to meet the needs of others as well as to support worship was to be woven into the life-style of God's OT people. Thus the tithe was one way in which the people of Israel might use their money to express their love for God and to show his love to others.

NEW TESTAMENT

Tithing is mentioned only eight times in the NT. Each is a reference either to OT or contemporary Jewish practice. While the principles expressed in tithing may have application to Christians, there is no NT indication that a tithe is required. This is partly because the tithe was a unique expression of God's ownership of the land in Israel, and of the unique relationship that the Lord had with the Levites—but it is also because the NT lays out new principles of giving. *See also* Giving.

The "tittle" is a stroke on the Hebrew letter dalet *that distinguishes it from the* resh.

tittle (KJV) A tiny brush stroke made when adding a mark that distinguished certain Hebrew letters from others. Jesus refers to this brush stroke in Mt. 5:18: "Not the least stroke of a pen, will by any means disappear from the Law until everything is accomplished."

Titus, Epistle to A brief, personal letter to a Gentile friend and co-worker of Paul. This Epistle, one of Paul's last letters, contains advice to Titus, who was ministering on the island of Crete. Along with 1 and 2 Timothy, it is classified as a Pastoral Epistle. *See also* Pastoral Epistles.

BACKGROUND

The letter was written from Rome shortly before Paul's execution, probably in A.D. 67 or 68. Titus was one of the second generation of Christian leaders. Paul realized that this generation would soon be left to guide the Christian movement alone. He wanted to pass on valuable advice before he died.

TITUS: A READING AND STUDY GUIDE

Chapter	Content Summary	Related Articles
1	Paul describes the type of person to be appointed an elder. He emphasizes the need for good leaders.	Elder False prophets and teachers
2	Paul reminds Titus that he must teach the Cretans a Christian lifestyle appropriate to Christian doctrine.	Teaching Worldly
3	Paul reminds Titus to teach subjection to rulers and to be sure that those who have been justified are committed to a life of doing good works.	Government, human Justification Works, good

Titus is identified in other NT Epistles as an uncircumcised Greek convert (Gal. 2:3). Traveling as part of Paul's team on the third missionary journey, Titus was sent on a difficult mission to Corinth (2 Cor. 7). His success there may have convinced Paul to dispatch him to another difficult area, Crete. Titus's assignment to deal with troubled churches suggests that Paul viewed him as a particularly effective and wise companion. This letter to Titus reveals none of the concern shown in similar letters to Timothy, whom Paul continually exhorted and encouraged. *See also* Timothy, First and Second Epistles to.

Paul does, however, give Titus guidance. The believers on Crete must be taught to select leaders wisely and must commit themselves to a disciplined life, dedicated to doing good. These things are especially important because of the "mere talkers and deceivers" (1:10) who actively try to infiltrate the church and corrupt Christianity.

THEOLOGICAL CONTRIBUTIONS

Paul is particularly concerned with practical theology: the application of sound doctrine to produce godliness. Particularly fascinating is Paul's description of "teaching" in ch. 2. Teaching is not so much a process of transmitting sound doctrine as it is a process of developing a life-style that is in harmony with sound doctrine. Thus, teaching is not just talking; it is training (2:4), encouraging (2:6), setting an example (2:7), rebuking (2:15), and, throughout the chapter, teaching "to do." *See also* Teaching.

MASTERY KEYS

Focus on the life-style that Paul says is in accord with "sound doctrine." We often study orthodox doctrine. Look here for the description of an "orthodox life."

SPECIAL FEATURES

Titus puts "good works" in clear perspective. Those "having been justified" by Christ are to "be careful to devote themselves to doing what is good" (3:7,8). Good works express faith but can never replace faith as a basis for relationship with God. *See also* Works, Good.

tomb *See* Burial; Burial of Jesus.

tongue (1) The movable muscular structure in the mouth (Jdg. 7:5); (2) a language or dialect (Isa. 28:11); (3) figuratively, one's speech (Ps. 57:4; Jer. 9:5). The predominant figurative usage is negative, picturing the tongue as a weapon used against others or as an instrument of lying, backbiting, and deceit.

James 3:1-12 highlights our difficulty in controlling the tongue. It is inconsistent to use our tongue to speak well of God and at the same time to speak ill of human beings who are made in his image—but this is all too common. James says, "If anyone is never at fault in what he says, he is a perfect [spiritually mature] man, able to keep his whole body in check" (3:2).

tongues, confusion of God's sudden act of imposing different languages on humanity at the tower of Babel, described in Gen. 11:1-9.

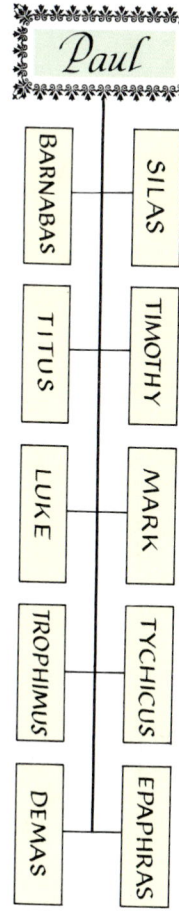

Paul and his Helpers

Paul

BARNABAS — SILAS

TITUS — TIMOTHY

LUKE — MARK

TROPHIMUS — TYCHICUS

DEMAS — EPAPHRAS

Medieval woodcut depicts the building of the "city with a tower that reaches the heavens" (Gen. 11:4). The city was called Babel, which sounds like the Hebrew for "confused," because there God confused the language of the whole world.

tongues, gift of The ability given by the Holy Spirit either to speak in an unlearned foreign language or to make ecstatic utterances unrelated to any human language.

Though a few OT prophets may have spoken ecstatically (*see* 1 Sam. 10:5-13), the phenomenon is distinctive in the NT, where it is mentioned in Acts and 1 Corinthians. In each case tongues is associated with the ministry of the Holy Spirit to and through Christians.

THE GIFT OF TONGUES IN ACTS

Acts 2:1-12 reports that at Pentecost, following Jesus' resurrection and ascension, the Holy Spirit was poured out on Christ's disciples. This was accompanied by unusual signs: a sound like rushing wind, what appeared to be flames of fire resting on each one, and the enablement by the Spirit to "speak in other tongues." The context makes it clear that here "tongues" were foreign languages, intelligible as the language of their homeland to the many foreign Jews visiting Jerusalem to celebrate Pentecost.

Two other Acts passages mention tongues (Acts 10:46; 19:6). In each case, the phenomenon took place at the time of conversion. The act of speaking in tongues by the Roman centurion Cornelius was cited by Peter as proof that the Gospel was for Gentiles as well as Jews (Acts 11:15-18). In Acts 19, the converts were Jews who had responded to John the Baptist's message but had not yet heard of Christ. In this case, the Holy Spirit "came upon" the converts in power at their baptism. Because there is no evidence to the contrary, it is reasonable to assume that on these occasions they also spoke in known languages. *See also* Baptism of the Spirit.

TONGUES IN 1 CORINTHIANS

In this passage, "tongues" seem to indicate an ecstatic utterance in no known human language. Paul claims this ability for himself, identifying it as one of the gifts given by the Holy Spirit. God also gave a gift for interpreting tongues, so the church might understand what a tongues-speaker was saying.

In Greek culture, those with ecstatic experiences were considered especially close to the gods. Thus, epilepsy was called the "divine disease"; a seizure indicated that a person was inspired. Against this background, it is understandable that the Corinthians were especially impressed with the gift of tongues, and that to some this gift became the ultimate test of spirituality. Paul does not deny the validity of the gift of tongues, but he does correct the misunderstandings.

In 1 Cor. 12, Paul places the gift of tongues in perspective. Paul notes that the Holy Spirit gives different gifts to different individuals. Each believer has a gift, and each is to use it in ministering to others. The distribution of gifts is based on God's sovereign choice, so that no gift is more "spiritual" than another. The Corinthians needed to realize that Christ's Church is a Body: Each part is needed to make a healthy whole. Thus, the gift of tongues was only one gift among many given to the Church, and, as with the other gifts, not everyone had this gift.

In 1 Cor. 13, Paul teaches that love, not one's gift, is the real indication of Christian spirituality.

In 1 Cor. 14, Paul goes on to regulate how the gift of tongues is to be used when Christians meet together. He argues that in public meetings prophecy—speaking God's Word in ordinary language—has priority. According to 1 Cor. 14:27,28, tongues could be used, but no more than three persons should speak in tongues during one meeting, and then only one at a time and only if a person with the gift of interpreting tongues was present. Since "the spirits of prophets are subject to the control of prophets" (14:32), no one can use the excuse that he or she could not help jumping up to speak in tongues when the Spirit moved. Paul makes it clear that the church is not to forbid speaking in tongues but insists that everything "be done in a fitting and orderly way" (14:39,40).

INTERPRETATIONS

Three major positions have been taken based on the biblical data and Christian experience.

1. *Limited to the apostolic era.* When the canon of Scripture was completed, tongues and other supernatural gifts were stilled (1 Cor. 13:8). Those who claim to speak in tongues today are deceived.

2. *Given as evidence of a special coming of the Holy Spirit upon the believer.* Christians are to pray for the Spirit and for this gift, which is evidence of his presence. The Christian who speaks in tongues thus has a different relationship with the Holy Spirit than other believers have. The lack of spiritual power in the modern church is rooted in the failure of Christians to seek this special relationship with the Holy Spirit.

3. *Given as one of many gifts.* The Holy Spirit remains free today to give any spiritual gift, including the gift of tongues.

However, tongues is but one of many spiritual gifts and should not be given priority or special honor over other gifts. Neither the presence nor absence of the gift should be made a requirement for Christian fellowship. Each believer has a special relationship with the Holy Spirit established at his or her conversion. Believers are to look expectantly to the Spirit for both gifts and spiritual power. While some who claim to speak in tongues today may be deceived, that gift as described in Scripture is a genuine work of the Spirit of God. No Christian should rule out the possibility that God may choose to work through the genuine, scriptural gift in the lives of believers.

tongues of fire The Acts 2 description of tongue-like flames that rested on Christ's disciples at Pentecost and that served as a sign of God's gift of the Holy Spirit to the Church. *See also* Holy Spirit.

tooth *See* Teeth.

Tophet, Topheth A district or place set aside for child sacrifice. A Topheth excavated near ancient Carthage has revealed the remains of thousands of children, usually between birth and age four, who had been burned alive as sacrifices.

Such a district existed in Israel, in the Valley of Hinnom southeast of Jerusalem (Jer. 7:31,32). Two of Israel's kings, Ahaz

"What seemed to be tongues of fire . . . separated and came to rest on each of them. All of them were filled with the Holy Spirit and began to speak in other tongues as the Spirit enabled them" (Acts 2:3,4).

The Hinnom Valley lies beneath Mount Zion in Jerusalem. God judged the people of Judah for their great evil here: "They have built the high places of Topheth in the Valley of Ben Hinnom to burn their sons and daughters in the fire—something I did not command, nor did it enter my mind" (Jer. 7:31).

985

(2 Ki. 16:3) and Manasseh (2 Ki. 21:6), offered their own children as sacrifices. Josiah desecrated the Topheth's "sacred" grounds "so no one could use it to sacrifice his son or daughter in the fire" (2 Ki. 23:10). In a possible reference to Josiah's decisive action, Jeremiah predicted that because of Judah's idolatry God would treat Jerusalem as Josiah had treated Hinnom's Topheth (Jer. 19:12-14). *See also* Child Sacrifice; Molech.

A Jewish man carries an encased Torah scroll in front of the Western Wall of the Temple Mount during Sukkoth, the Feast of Booths.

Torah [Heb., "guidance," "instruction"]. (1) God's instructions to Israel at Sinai; (2) the OT in all its aspects—Israel's history, Law, moral teaching and exhortations, poetry, praise, proverbs, and its call to worship God and love others. Though *torah* is often translated "Law" in English versions, the original concept is comprehensive, encompassing the whole way of life "taught" by God to Israel, not simply the legal code. Only after Bible times did *torah* come to designate the Pentateuch (written Torah) as well as rabbinic precepts and commentary (oral Torah). Thus Torah can refer to all of Jewish tradition.

torment Extreme pain or anguish. The Greek word (*basanos*) was originally used of torture intended to elicit information, but later took the general sense of torment. The NT uses this word for demon-caused illnesses (Mt. 8:6) and for the experience of the wicked dead (Lk. 16:23,28). The Book of Revelation frequently uses it in connection with divine judgment on the living as well as eternal punishment (9:5; 14:10,11; 18:7,10,15; 20:10).

tower (1) A tall, usually circular structure erected for defense along city walls (2 Chr. 14:7), or within a city as a last line of defense (Jdg. 9:46). Figuratively, God is a "strong tower against the foe" (Ps. 61:3). (2) A structure erected in fields from

which family members could guard ripening crops from animals and birds (Isa. 5:2; Mk. 12:1). (3) A high hill or rocky crag, as well as a man-made structure, from which a person might watch for approaching enemies (Hab. 2:1, KJV).

Above: Defenders of a walled city watching from towers; detail of a bas relief from the palace of Assyrian King Sargon II (Khorsabad, 8th century B.C.).
Left: This tower, today called the Citadel of David, rises from the foundations of the original Phasael Tower constructed by Herod the Great to protect his palace.

town Any settlement that lacks defensive walls and thus must depend on larger walled cities for defense and sale of locally produced goods. *See also* Village.

trade The buying and selling of goods and services, especially of their transport for sale over long distances.

LOCAL TRADE TO 750 B.C.

From about 1300 to 750 B.C., Israel's economy was largely self-contained. Trade took place within the Hebrew community, and a few luxury goods were imported. But the tiny Hebrew kingdom had little of value to export.

Trade goods during this period were food stuffs, such as grain, olive oil, wine, and fish. The varied climate of Palestine made it possible to grow a wide variety of foods, which were traded between districts. During this era, women generally made the family clothing, and someone in the family fashioned the clay pots, which had many uses in the home. Most men had some skill in necessary crafts, although some skilled craftsmen, such as scribes and metalworkers, undoubtedly specialized and bartered their services to others for goods. Some probably gathered salt from the deposits found at the southern end of the Jordan Valley, and still others gathered firewood and brought it to sell in the larger cities. While spices and other foreign products were imported, the Hebrew people had not at this time developed their own trading class, and life was centered on the land and what it produced. During this period, trade was conducted either by barter or by weighing out gold or silver.

About 750 B.C., something of an economic revolution took place in the kingdom of Israel and was reflected to some extent in Judah. Under the aggressive and successful Jeroboam II, Israel experienced a period of expansion. Military victories won control of trade routes once dominated by Syria. But the wealth that flowed into Israel was concentrated in the old aristocracy and a new merchant class. These demanded luxury imports and also began to buy up land to create great estates. The dispossessed poor moved into the cities, where they were further exploited. Society became polarized between rich and poor. During this period, Amos wrote scathing rebukes of Israel's wealthy class.

In Judah, too, something of an industrial revolution was taking place. The invention of the potter's wheel made it possible to

Trade ship of Queen Hatshepsut of Egypt arrives at Punt—often identified with the biblical Ophir (1 Chr. 29:4)—to load cargo of gold, spices, myrrh plants, ebony wood, and various animals. Limestone relief at Thebes, 15th century B.C.

mass-produce pottery vessels for sale. A specialized clothing industry grew up. Increasingly, families concentrated on trades, using their skills in dyeing, weaving, leatherworking, metalworking, etc., to earn a living. Various districts in cities were set aside for the bakers, the potters, and others who now sold their services and goods to their neighbors. The two Hebrew nations were gradually changing. No longer the agricultural people envisioned in OT Law, Hebrew life and society were becoming more complex.

During this entire period, only Solomon had pushed international trade. Under his rule, Israel became a middleman, trading horses and chariots between Egypt and the kingdoms to the north. Solomon also controlled the ancient trade routes and collected heavy taxes from merchants. He mined and smelted copper, which he sold as a trade item to the sea-going peoples of the Mediterranean. Solomon also entered into a profitable joint trading venture with Hiram, king of Tyre. After his death and the division of his kingdom, no ruler of Israel could recapture Solomon's international vision.

THE IMPACT OF CAPTIVITIES

The Assyrian deportation of Israel in 722 B.C. and the Babylonian Captivity of Judah in 586 B.C. set a new direction for the Jewish people. They no longer had a land on which to base their economy. So, in Babylon and the many other cities to which the Jews dispersed, they developed other skills. Many became craftsmen. Even the tiny group of Jews who returned to Palestine after 70 years in Babylon had its goldsmiths and perfume-makers (Neh.

3:8), who settled in a distinct district in the rebuilt Jerusalem.

Scattered through the Mediterranean world, many Jews became active in trade and banking. The development of financial institutions and services during this period was facilitated by the introduction around 650 B.C. of coined money. In the first century B.C., Jews actually controlled the financial district of Alexandria, the largest city in Egypt and second largest in the Roman Empire.

TRADE IN JESUS' TIME

In Galilee and Judea, Jews continued to carry on active trade. Fishermen dried or salted their catch from Galilee and transported it to Jerusalem. Yet Rome had created an explosion in international trade and commerce. The Roman navy had put down piracy on the Mediterranean. Large vessels carried tons of produce and goods between the Empire's cities. On land a network of highways made travel easy and relatively inexpensive. All this stimulated both trade and travel, opening a wide door for enterprising Jews. *See also* Boats; Roads; Travel.

Jerusalem in Jesus' day reflected the new direction. Crops and farming were still important, as many of Jesus' illustrations drawn from nature show. Yet archaeologists have learned that some of the finest glass and most beautiful luxury dishes of that time were crafted by the Jews of Jerusalem. The NT also reflects the city's international flavor, describing Jew-

Camels were instrumental in establishing long-distance trade. They carried spices and incense from Palestine to Egypt (Gen. 37:25) and the queen of Sheba's luggage from southern Arabia to Jerusalem (1 Ki. 10:2).

ish men and women of every Mediterranean nation who came in pilgrimage to Jerusalem (Acts 2:9-11). Trade, the introduction of coinage, and the scattering of the Jewish people throughout the ancient world had transformed the tiny agricultural nation of the OT into an international community.

tradition Customs and practices rooted in the past. The "traditions of the elders" (Mk. 7:3-13) mentioned in the NT are largely rulings of earlier rabbis (teachers of OT Law) who applied the Law to changing social conditions. The rabbis' goal was to protect Jews against unwittingly violating a divine commandment. In the first century, the traditions accepted by the Pharisees were viewed as an oral law equal in force to God's written Law. Many even believed the oral law had actually been given by Moses at the same time as the written code.

Jesus was attacked for ignoring some of the traditions the Pharisees held dear (Mk. 2:13-17). But Christ criticized such traditions, implying that many of them actually led men to violate the Law's intent (Mk. 15:1-9).

In Christianity, tradition refers to teachings developed after the NT and the close of the apostolic age. Belief that tradition is part of God's revelation is a major difference between Roman Catholic and Protestant Christians, because the latter accept Scripture alone as the repository of special revelation.

train *See* Disciple.

trance An altered state of consciousness and perception. The Greek word translated "trance" (*ekstasis*) means to "stand outside" one's normal self. While no explanation of trances has been provided by modern psychology, the phenomenon is known from the ancient literature of many societies (*see* Gen. 15:12; 2 Ki. 6:18; Acts 10:10; 22:17).

Transfiguration An event reported in three of the Gospels in which Jesus' "face shone like the sun, and his clothes became as white as the light" (Mt. 17:1-13; Mk. 9:2-8; Lk. 9:28-36). The Transfiguration was witnessed by three disciples: Peter, James, and John. Other miraculous signs accompanied it: Moses and Elijah appeared, a bright cloud covered them, and a voice speaking from the cloud said, "This is my Son, whom I love; with him I am well pleased. Listen to him!"

Elijah, destined to appear before the restoration of all things (Mk. 9:12; *see* Mal. 4:5,6), represents the prophets, Moses the Law. The bright cloud seems symbolic of the old covenant given at Sinai through Moses. The voice from heaven had said much the same thing at Jesus' baptism (Mt. 3:17). The words harken back to Ps. 2:7, a coronation hymn, and Isa. 42:1, the introduction of God's suffering servant.

Second Peter refers to this event as proof of the truth of the Gospel—historical evidence that past, present, and future are summed up in the person of Jesus Christ (1:16-18).

transformation (1) A supernatural change worked in the character or nature of the believer (Rom. 12:2; 2 Cor. 3:18; Phil. 3:21); (2) a superficial change intended to disguise one's true nature (2 Cor. 11:13-15 KJV).

Satan and his followers often appear as "angels of light" in an attempt to deceive and disrupt the church. This is merely a change in appearance, since no created being has the power to radically change his character or nature. In fact, Paul uses the word *metaschēmatizomai* to describe the devil's masquerading (2 Cor. 11:14), as opposed to *metamorphoomai* for a Christian's thoroughgoing metamorphosis of character: "being transformed into his [Jesus'] likeness with ever-increasing glory, which comes from the Lord, who is the Spirit" (2 Cor. 3:18). Christians also cooperate in this process by searching out

in Scripture the divine values, attitudes, and behavior that will renew our minds (Rom. 12:2). Even here, however, the word is passive. We cannot change ourselves; it is a work of God. God is working in us even now, and because of the active intervention of his Spirit, we can learn to live Christ-like lives.

In Phil. 3:21, Paul speaks of the Christian hope of ultimate transformation. One day we will be completely like Jesus, for when Christ returns, he "will transform our lowly bodies so that they will be like his glorious body."

transgression A conscious violation of the known will of God. The Hebrew word means "rebellion," indicating an act that violates the duty a subordinate owes to a

A transfigured Jesus stands between Moses and Elijah in this 13th-century mosaic from Constantinople.

superior (Ps. 32:1; Isa. 58:1). The NT word also denotes a deliberate violation of the Law (Rom. 4:15; 5:14; Gal. 3:19).

Transjordan Land east of the Jordan River deeded to three Israelite tribes when Israel conquered Canaan, about 1390 B.C.

The area is a large plateau, of 2,000 to 3,000 feet elevation, suitable for grazing herds of animals. Before Israel's conquest, it was occupied by the Ammonites and Moabites. Afterward, it became home to the tribes of Reuben, Gad, and Manasseh. The area is referred to in the OT as the land "beyond the Jordan."

travail (KJV) Extreme pain or suffering, as in childbirth; or constant, unrewarded labor. *See also* Suffer; Work.

travel To go from one place to another; to make a journey.

For most of the biblical period, the Hebrew people were not great travelers. Genesis reports Abraham's journey from Ur to Canaan. But this journey was directed by God, and Abraham's intention was to find a land in which to dwell. Later, Genesis tells of the family's move to Egypt, and Exodus tells of the people's return. Yet the goal of these travels was to settle down. We find no hint of a desire to travel for adventure or to establish trade. Other peoples engaged in trade by sea or led camel caravans down the Arabian Peninsula. However, the OT portrays the Hebrews as a people wedded to their land. The Hebrew ideal was to live one's life in the land God had given and to enjoy its yield.

TRAVEL WITHIN ISRAEL

Throughout the biblical period, most who traveled within Palestine did so on foot. There were major highways along which trade moved from north to south, notably the "way of the sea" (Isa. 9:1) along the Mediterranean coast. There were also several east/west routes that connected with the "King's Highway," which ran along the high plateau beyond the Jordan. Most who did travel, however, moved along the network of tracks and trails that connected small villages and towns, feeding into broader paths that led toward Jerusalem. For the most part, the travelers walked, and if they had goods to carry, they loaded them on sure-footed donkeys. These goods were primarily agricultural products, to be sold in nearby towns. Manufactured goods for sale were the products of "cottage industries" and,

even in the first century, were sold within a few miles of where they were made.

People might travel to visit relatives (Lk. 1:39). In fact, the oral law of Jesus' time guaranteed the right of a wife to visit her parents! But the primary motive for longer journeys within Israel was undoubtedly religious. Three of the festivals held at the Jerusalem Temple called for all Hebrew males to attend. While universal attendance was never achieved, many thousands did set out on each of these occasions to participate in the festive worship. *See also* Feasts, Festivals, and Fasts.

In the first century, travel from Galilee to Jerusalem was considered a four-day journey. Along the way, the travelers slept in the open or stayed with friends. The ancient principle of hospitality was deeply ingrained in Jewish culture, and travelers could expect to be taken into someone's home if night fell (Jdg. 19:15; Mt. 10:11). The inns at Bethlehem (Lk. 2:7) and on the road between Jerusalem and Jericho (Lk. 10:34) were on major routes and were exceptions rather than the rule.

TRAVEL OUTSIDE ISRAEL

The Assyrian and Babylonian captivities caused a radical change in the Jewish experience. After 500 B.C., far more Jews lived outside Israel than in it. By the first century A.D., nearly every major city in the Roman Empire and the Parthian Empire to the east had a significant Jewish population. Some estimate that as many as one in ten persons in the Roman Empire was a Jew, and in the Parthian Empire as many as one in five.

As the Roman Empire expanded and brought stability to the West, travel increased. In 67 B.C., Pompey cleared the Mediterranean of pirates, making ocean voyages relatively safe. The Roman policy of linking cities and provinces with paved roads, carefully maintained and guarded, also made travel easier, as did the use of a universal language, Greek, and the placing of a common value on silver coins.

The worldwide Jewish population had always maintained ties with Jerusalem, even sending back the annual half-shekel tax imposed on every Jewish male for the support of the Temple. In the first century, with travel relatively safe, thousands of Jews went to worship in Jerusalem during one of the three major festivals. Visitors often stayed for months or even years in one of the "houses of study" maintained for them. Acts 2 gives us a picture of the cosmopolitan crowds that gathered at such

The natural harbor at Dor made it a valuable port in Palestine throughout ancient times, until it was superseded by Herod's planned port of Caesarea Maritima (*30–20 B.C.*).

times, speaking of "God-fearing Jews from every nation under heaven" present for the feast of Pentecost, and listing "Parthians, Medes and Elamites; residents of Mesopotamia, Judea and Cappadocia, Pontus and Asia, Phrygia and Pamphylia, Egypt and the parts of Libya near Cyrene; visitors from Rome; Cretans and Arabs" (Acts 2:5,9-11).

Not only did Jews from these lands travel to Jerusalem, but sages and teachers were sent out from the Jewish homeland to them. These sages typically traveled in pairs and might serve as judges as well as instructors in the Jewish life-style. This practice no doubt helped prepare the way for Paul and other early Christian missionaries, who on entering any city went first to the Jewish community.

Not all travel was for religious purposes, however. In the first century, the world was on the move. The unusual mobility during this age is illustrated by the wide distribution of trade goods and an inscription on one tombstone that boasts that the

deceased man had traveled to Rome some 600 times during his lifetime! It was not unusual for a couple like Priscilla and Aquila to move from Rome to Corinth to Ephesus and back again to Rome (*see* Acts 18:1-3,18-28; Rom. 16:3,5; 1 Cor. 16:19). Nor was it unusual for the early church's missionaries to take to the road to spread the Gospel message while traveling Empire-wide.

LIFE ON THE ROAD

Yet travel was still filled with discomfort and danger. Travelers still relied in large part on hospitality when seeking a place to stay. Therefore, the NT describes Paul staying in private homes (Acts 16:12-15; 17:5; 21:16; 28:7,14; Phlm. 22). Because they had to walk, most travelers carried a minimum of baggage: simply a sack with a change or two of clothing and a purse worn at the belt or tied around the neck. Only the rich, like the Ethiopian eunuch, rode on horses or in chariots (Acts 8:28). Travel by sea was aboard ocean vessels

Gold-gilded, fan-shaped decoration from the tomb of Tut-ankhamen demon-strates the wealth of Egypt's pharaohs. If the tomb of an unim-portant king was so magnificent, one wonders what the tombs of greater kings might have held had they not been plundered (1 Ki. 10:14-29; 14:25,26).

built to carry cargo, but it was faster and easier than land travel. However, ship passengers had to provide their own mat-tresses, food, and cookware, and they stayed on deck. The months between May and October were relatively safe, but put-ting to sea at any time held danger, and many trading vessels were sunk by sud-den storms.

Paul sums up the experience of the first-century frequent traveler clearly: "I was shipwrecked, I spent a night and a day in the open sea, I have been constantly on the move. I have been in danger from rivers, in danger from bandits . . . in dan-ger in the city, in danger in the country, in danger at sea. . . . I have known hunger and thirst and have often gone without food; I have been cold and naked" (2 Cor. 11:25-27). See also Boats; Roads; Trade.

treasure, treasury Any collection of ob-jects of value; a place where valuables are stored.

In Scripture, "treasure" refers to collec-tions of gold, silver, and precious spices. It also refers to arsenals and provisions for war (Ex. 1:11 KJV), of stored grain (Jer. 41:8 KJV), of wisdom (Prov. 2:4), of Israel as God's treasure (Ex. 19:5), and of the Gos-pel (2 Cor. 4:7).

Similarly a treasury may contain any col-lection of valuables, and not just gold or silver. In Ezra 5:17, the treasury is the place where royal records are stored. In Ex. 1:11, it is a city equipped as an arsenal and mil-itary supply base. In Ezra 2:69, the treasury is a fund for rebuilding the Temple, and in Jn. 8:20, it is one of 13 trumpet-shaped of-fering boxes placed in the Temple courts. Figuratively, the sky is God's treasury, where he stores up rain (Deut. 28:12). The heart of a good man is a treasury, too, in which good words are stored (Mt. 12:35).

This flexible use of "treasure" provides the background for one of Jesus' most

often-quoted exhortations. His listeners would understand perfectly when Christ called on them not to lay up treasures on earth, but to lay up treasures in heaven (Mt. 6:19-21). Christ was not speaking only of money-making. Instead, Christ called on his listeners to treasure nothing on earth as much as they treasure those things that are of value to God.

treaty See Covenant.

tree Palestine had many trees in early bib-lical times. Aside from trees that produced crops—such as the olive, the fig, the sycamore-fig, and various fruit trees—the primary trees of the region were decidu-ous oaks and, in the hill country, ever-greens and the Aleppo pine.

The OT associates trees with pagan and Hebrew worship. Pagans erected asherah poles at outdoor worship sites. These were images carved from trees or perhaps living trees planted and honored as sacred. Of-ten the Hebrews followed the pagan prac-tice and worshiped God, in violation of the Mosaic Law, at outdoor sites where there were sacred groves (asherot). This is one of the practices that godly kings like Hezekiah tried to root out during religious reawakenings (2 Ki. 18:4).

Trees were valued for their beauty and shade as well as their fruit (Gen. 2:9; Lev. 23:40). The majestic cedar of Lebanon rep-resented strength (Ezek. 31:3; Dan. 4:10-12), and the tree with roots sunk deeply into the ground is frequently used in OT poetry as a symbol of vital spiritual life (Ps. 1:3; see Isa. 65:22). Fruit-bearing trees, particularly the olive, are symbolic of Canaan as a productive and blessed land (Lev. 26:4; see Jdg. 9:8-13). The great value placed on fruit trees is illustrated in Deu-teronomy's rule for the conduct of war: "When you lay siege to a city . . . do not destroy its trees by putting an ax to them, because you can eat their fruit. Do not cut them down. Are the trees of the field people, that you should besiege them? However, you may cut down trees that you know are not fruit trees and use them to build siege works until the city at war with you falls" (Deut. 20:19,20).

Through the centuries the land of Israel has been gradually denuded of its trees. Today modern Israel and Jordan are ac-tively engaged in several successful refor-estation projects.

tree of life A tree planted in Eden whose fruit, according to Gen. 3:22, would enable Adam and Eve to "live forever." After the

Fall, the two were expelled from Eden, and the way back to the tree of life was guarded by armed cherubim (Gen. 3:24). The Book of Revelation picks up the tree of life image, symbolizing everlasting life for the believer (2:7; 22:2,14,19).

It is best to understand Adam and Eve's expulsion from Eden as a divine gift. How tragic it would have been had they eaten from the life-giving tree and been doomed to live on through the centuries to see the full extent of the misery their act brought to the human race.

tree of the knowledge of good and evil
The name given in Gen. 2:9 to a tree planted in Eden, the fruit of which Adam and Eve were commanded not to eat. The two violated the divine command and, through this act of disobedience, sin entered the human race (Rom. 5:12-14). The significance of the name is the subject of much theological debate. As completeness is frequently expressed in Hebrew by paired extremes, some suggest the name indicates full and complete moral awareness. Tragically, human beings were

plunged by Adam and Eve's act into a state in which that knowledge was to be gained by experience. God grasps the full reality of good and evil yet never does evil. Finite humanity can only truly grasp the meaning of what is experienced. In a sense, human history, marred as it is by brutality, wars, injustice, and holocausts, is still plumbing the depths of the knowledge of good and evil that Eve mistakenly thought so desirable.

trespass To violate the rights of others, whether God or man.

A person who violated the property rights of others was to restore what had been taken, plus an added amount as a penalty, and make a trespass offering to the Lord. When a person sinned unintentionally against God, he was to make a trespass offering to remove his guilt. *See also* Restitution; Sacrifices and Offerings.

trespass offering *See* Sacrifices and Offerings.

trial A difficult situation experienced by believers. *See also* Tempt; Test.

A legal proceeding to test one's guilt or innocence. *See also* Court; Trial of Jesus.

trial of Jesus The proceedings before Jewish and Roman courts that led to Jesus' crucifixion. The trial of Jesus is reported in Mt. 26:57–27:26; Mk. 14:53–15:20; Lk. 22:54–23:25; Jn. 18:12–19:16.

Jesus was arrested by a mob at night to avoid intervention by the people of Jerusalem, many of whom viewed him as the Messiah. Jesus was taken to Annas, the father-in-law of the current high priest. The Sanhedrin assembled in his home for an illegal nighttime trial. False witnesses obtained by Jesus' judges gave conflicting evidence against him. Since OT Law insisted that witnesses must agree, this evidence was insufficient for conviction. Finally, Annas asked Jesus directly if he were the Son of God. Jesus said, "Yes." The assembly took this as blasphemy, which under OT Law was punishable by death.

The Sanhedrin reassembled at dawn to

The tree of life is an image known in mythological traditions of the ancient Near East as a sacred tree of fertility and immortality. Here it is depicted on the palace walls of Ashurnasirpal II (885–860 B.C.) at Nimrud.

Bronze juryman's ticket from Athens (mid-fourth century B.C.). It identifies the owner, Aristophon, and his assignment to a particular trial.

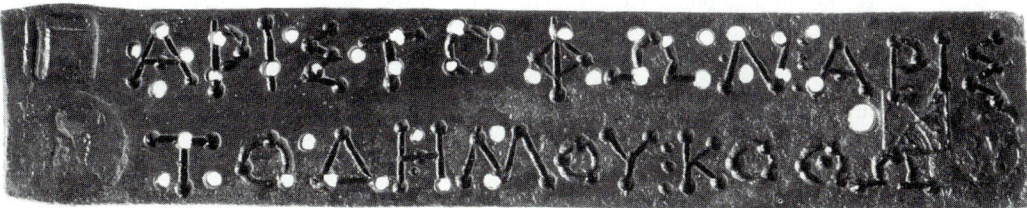

According to tradition, the trial of Jesus before the Roman prefect Pontius Pilate took place on the squared-stone floor of the Antonia Fortress, adjoining the Temple Mount. Here Jesus was sentenced to death by crucifixion.

render an official verdict. Jesus was condemned to death. But only a Roman court had authority to confirm the death sentence. So Jesus was taken to Pilate, the Roman governor. Since a claim of deity was not illegal under Roman law, the Jewish leaders invented three new charges (Lk. 23:2). They claimed Jesus had "subverted the nation," had forbidden the payment of taxes to Caesar, and that he claimed to be a king.

Only this last charge merited examination. When Jesus explained that his Kingdom was "not of this world," Pilate dismissed even this charge. But the outraged Jews shouted that Jesus had claimed to be God and deserved death. This frightened Pilate, and he examined Jesus again.

Hoping for a way out of his dilemma, Pilate sent Jesus to Herod, who ruled Christ's Galilean homeland. But Herod sent Christ back to Pilate when he would perform no miracles for him.

Again Pilate tried to release the prisoner, this time offering the mob a choice. He would free one prisoner: either Jesus or a noted criminal named Barabbas. Incited by the priests, the mob chose Barabbas.

Finally, the Jewish leaders exerted the ultimate pressure: They threatened to report to Caesar that Pilate released a man claiming to be a king. Surely Caesar would wonder why Pilate permitted any man to live who claimed royal authority. At this, Pilate gave in and ordered the execution of Jesus.

Legal scholars have examined the biblical record and pointed out a number of irregularities that would have made the trial illegal under the Sanhedrin's own rules. Among them are the nighttime trial and the rendering of a guilty verdict and condemnation to death at the same meeting, without a required 24-hour wait. Even the striking of Jesus during the nighttime

pre-trial hearing was illegal (Jn. 18:22; Acts 23:3). Another error was the revision of the charges against Jesus when the case passed to Pilate.

The Gospel records make it clear that such details were of little concern to the Jewish leaders; they were determined to see Jesus dead and ready to adopt any means to gain that end.

What is also clear from the NT is that God sovereignly used this tragic miscarriage of justice for his own purposes. The court that convicted Jesus did not know it, but sin, so glaringly revealed in this, history's supreme injustice, provided the one overwhelming reason for the crucifixion to take place. Jesus died, not as victim, but as victor; not as captive, but as liberator.

tribes (1) Family divisions of the people of Israel (Ex. 31:2; Deut. 1:23). (2) Infrequently, other ethnic groups (Rev. 7:9). *See also* Israel.

Tribes of Israel *See* Israel, Tribes of.

tribulation (KJV) OT: (1) Pressures from enemies or circumstances, often as divine judgment (Isa. 8:22; Jer. 14:8). NT: (2) Deep emotional and spiritual distress caused by pressures from within or without (2 Cor. 1:4). (3) As a technical theological term, a period of time near history's end (Mt. 24:21,29; Mk. 13:19,24). Some modern versions abandon the use of "tribulation" and substitute "distress" or "trouble."

IN CHRISTIAN EXPERIENCE

Christians are to expect troubles and pressure in this life (Jn. 15:18-27; 16:33; 1 Th. 3:3,4; 2 Th. 1:4; *see* 2 Cor. 4:8-12). The NT encourages us by pointing out that such experiences develop faith and Christian maturity (1 Pet. 1:6-9; Jas. 1:2-4). *See also* Suffer.

THE "GREAT TRIBULATION"

The OT abounds with images of a period of intense tribulation associated with the appearance of the Messiah. This is all part of the OT's repeated emphasis on the coming Day of the Lord (Deut. 4:30,31; Isa. 2:12,19; 13:6,9; Jer. 30:7; Ezek. 30:3; Dan. 12:1; Joel 1:15). *See also* Day of the Lord.

In his "Olivet Discourse," Jesus picked up the OT image, speaking of a coming "great distress [tribulation], unequaled from the beginning of the world until now—and never to be equaled again" (Mt.

24:21). Jesus specifically links this time with elements of Dan. 9:25-27. Based on an interpretation of that OT passage, some see the "great tribulation" as a seven-year period of time just prior to the return of Jesus to earth. *See also* Future; Seventy Weeks.

tribute Compulsory annual contributions in money or commodities demanded from one nation by another.

It was customary for rulers to exchange gifts (1 Ki. 5:10,11; 9:11), but the payment of tribute was a mark of national subordination. David received tribute from the Moabites and from Syria (2 Sam. 8:2,6). Solomon was paid tribute by all the states bordering Israel (1 Ki. 4:21). Jehoshaphat received tribute from the Philistines and Arabs (2 Chr. 17:11), and Uzziah from the Ammonites (2 Chr. 26:8). On the other hand, a number of the kings of Israel and Judah were forced to pay tribute money to Assyria (2 Ki. 15:17-30; 16:7-18; 2 Ki. 17:4).

The receipt or payment of tribute is an accurate indicator of the relative strength of Israel or Judah at any given time in OT history.

Trinity The Christian doctrine that God exists as three co-equal Persons—Father, Son, and Holy Spirit. This cardinal belief developed in the early church through three centuries of struggle against various heresies and was formulated by the First Council of Constantinople in A.D. 381. The word "trinity" is not found in either Testament. However, Scripture witnesses in a variety of ways to the Christian conviction.

Intimations of the Trinity are found in the OT, even in the Shema (Deut. 6:4,5), Israel's great affirmation of monotheism. Here the word for "one" is *'ehad,* which is used of a single bunch of grapes which in turn is divisible into distinguishable individual grapes, rather than *yahid,* which means uniquely one. The Hebrew word for God, *elohim,* is a plural noun, generally

Above: Nubians bring tribute to Pharaoh Thutmose IV: Gold cast into portable rings, ebony logs, giraffe tails (for fly whisks), a basket of fruit, leopard skins, and monkeys. Tomb painting from Thebes (1425–1417 B.C.). Left: Asiatic elephant and monkey, part of tribute being brought to Shalmaneser III, king of Assyria (Nimrud, about 830 B.C.). The fact that Solomon could exact tribute from bordering nations indicates the strength of Israel (1 Ki. 4:21).

taken as a plural of majesty. Genesis records that God spoke to himself and said, "Let us make man in our image" (Gen. 1:26). Both of these references suggest the existence of distinct persons within the Godhead. In addition, OT prophecies suggest that the Messiah will be God as well as man (Jer. 23:5,6; 33:14-16).

According to the NT, Jesus unequivocally claimed to be one with the Father. This essential unity identifies him as God from the very beginning. The same NT documents add that Jesus accepted worship from men, something unthinkable to Jews. The NT also refers to the Holy Spirit as a personal being. And in the formula given by Jesus, Christians are baptized "in the name of the Father and of the Son and of the Holy Spirit" (Mt. 28:19). *See also* Holy Spirit; Incarnation.

Christians have struggled to understand the mystery of how one God could exist in three persons. They have also struggled to illustrate the principle from nature. Some use the analogy of an egg, which is one with three parts: shell, white, and yolk. Others note that as water can exist as liquid, vapor, and ice, so the one God can exist as three personal beings sharing one substance or essence. Yet all such analogies fall short of portraying the trinitarian reality. Ultimately, Christians base their belief in the Trinity not on any ability to understand or explain the concept, but rather on the evidence of Scripture that our one God is Father, Son, and Holy Spirit.

trumpet In Hebrew culture, a curved ram's horn, fashioned into a musical instrument. Loud notes blown on the trumpet (Heb., *shōphar*) signaled special ritual events (Num. 29:1; Ps. 98:6), and called the people to assemble to resist foreign invaders (Jdg. 3:27). *See also* Horn; Music; Shophar.

Trumpets, Feast of *See* Feasts, Festivals, and Fasts.

trust *See* Believe.

truth (1) Something in accord with reality and therefore accurate, reliable, and, in the case of God, trustworthy. (2) In the NT especially, God's unveiling of reality through natural and special revelation (Rom. 1:17-20; Eph. 1:13; Col. 1:5). (3) Reality that can be experienced. The one who practices God's Word will "know the truth" and discover for himself that "the truth will make you free" (Jn. 8:31,32).

OLD TESTAMENT

The essential thought in both Testaments is that the truth is utterly reliable because it is in accord with reality. By contrast, the false is unreliable because it distorts reality. God is a God of truth, reliable because his words and his deeds match. Similarly, a man of truth is a person whose words and deeds correspond. No wonder God "desires truth in the inner parts" (Ps. 51:6).

It is also no wonder that the OT frequently praises God for this quality of trustworthiness. Scripture regularly describes God as "faithful" and "true."

PAUL'S EPISTLES

Paul argues that God has revealed truth to human beings in nature as well as in Scripture. Nature cannot reveal the whole truth, but it does communicate enough truth to provide a basis for man to respond to God. That mankind has not acknowledged God or thanked him is compelling evidence of human sinfulness (Rom. 1:17-32).

Now, however, the truth of the Gospel has been revealed (Gal. 2:5). Those who serve Christ describe reality; those who respond to the Gospel "obey the truth" (Gal. 5:7). Paul stresses that since this truth is also experienced, those who minister must both speak and live the truth. Paul frequently demands that leaders be examples, so that learners will see the truth in them as well as hear the truth from them (1 Tim. 4:12,13; 2 Tim. 3:10,11).

JOHN'S WRITINGS

Over half of the NT's references to truth appear in John's writings. John reports Jesus' statement that true disciples must continue in his words. Only such persons will "know the truth [by personally experiencing the reality God has revealed], and the truth [experienced] will make [them] free" (Jn. 8:31,32).

Jesus expressed a parallel thought in Jn. 17:17, praying that his followers will be sanctified by the truth and adding, "Your word is truth." Scripture's revelation of reality strips away all our illusions and shows us the values, attitudes, and way of life that are of ultimate value. Only a grasp of reality as it is revealed in God's Word can guide us to a truly healthy and holy way of life.

This thought is applied in 1 Jn. 1:5-9 to the problem of sin in the Christian's life. John says that maintaining fellowship with God depends on living by the truth. The person who denies his sins or sinfulness is deceived and "the truth is not in" him. Only by facing reality, recognizing sin in our lives as sin, and dealing with it by confession, can we maintain fellowship with God and with other believers. *See also* Confess.

While there are a number of ordinary uses of "true" and "truth" in the Bible, a grasp of this underlying concept—truth's correspondence with reality—will deepen the reader's understanding of many passages in which these words are used in significant, theological ways.

tumor An unnatural swelling on some part of the body (Deut. 28:27). Many commentators believe the tumors of 1 Sam. 5:6, which afflicted the Philistines who captured God's ark, were painful hemorrhoids. Others think they were symptoms of plague.

turban A headdress formed by wrapping or winding a cloth around the head.

The turban is frequently mentioned as the headdress of priests (Ex. 28:4,37,39; Lev. 8:9; Ezek. 44:18; Zech. 3:5). Ezekiel, a priest as well as a prophet, normally wore a turban (Ezek. 24:17), but Ezek. 24:23 suggests that turbans were normal dress for most men of his time.

turtledove (KJV) Any variety of small, ritually clean pigeon-like birds. *See also* Dove; Pigeon.

tutor (KJV) *See* Guardian.

Twelve, the *See* Disciple.

type A representative figure, institution, or event reported in the OT that foreshadows a NT person, institution, or event.

Clear biblical examples of types are Adam as a type of Christ, the second Adam (Rom. 5:14), and Melchizedek, a type of Christ as high priest (Heb. 7:11-28).

Some interpreters take almost every person, event, and institution of the OT as a "type" of some aspect of NT revelation. Others set severe limits, admitting nothing in the OT as a type unless it is so specified in the NT. Overemphasizing typology may at times rob OT themes of their historical significance, as NT concepts are "read into" them. Yet quite frequently, the NT does point out correspondences between the Testaments. Just as "Moses lifted up the snake in the desert," so Jesus was lifted up on the cross. By faith, when the people looked at the snake, they were

Small, pleated turban with tassel, fashioned from limestone, was made to fit on a figurine from a palace at Ebla in Syria (2400–2250 B.C.).

healed of serpents' venom. Likewise, when by faith we look to Jesus, we are healed of the poison of sin (Jn. 3:14,15; *see* Num. 21:8,9). Furthermore, Jesus is the ultimate king symbolized by David and the ultimate prophet symbolized by Moses. While there are many such correspondences, it is not necessary to label them "types" to gain insight from them. *See also* Symbol.

This Phoenician mask, painted red and black, was found in a tomb in Achzib, south of Tyre (8th–7th centuries B.C.).

Tyre The leading city of Phoenicia during the first millennium B.C. Tyre was located on the coast of modern Lebanon about 50 miles north of Jerusalem. The city was a major Mediterranean trading and sea power in biblical times, constructed partly on the mainland and partly on an island a thousand yards offshore. The island boasted two excellent harbors. Although viewed as impregnable, the city was taken in 332 B.C. by Alexander the Great, who tore down the mainland city and used its materials to construct a causeway out to the island.

Biblical Tyre was established about 1200 B.C. The city prospered and played a significant role in Bible history. When David negotiated with Hiram of Tyre about 985 B.C. for cedars and craftsmen (2 Sam. 5:11; 1 Chr. 14:1), the city was already the center of a trading empire. The bonds between Israel and Tyre were even closer in the reign of Solomon (970–930 B.C.), as Tyre continued to supply skilled metalworkers and materials used in building the Jerusalem Temple and the king's palace (1 Ki. 5:2-18; 7:13,14). Solomon also entered joint trading ventures with Hiram's skilled seamen to bring back distant riches and luxuries (1 Ki. 9:26-28; 10:11,12; 2 Chr. 8:17,18; 9:21,22).

About this time, expansionist Tyre began a program of colonization along the Mediterranean coast. Among the cities founded by the men of Tyre was Carthage, which centuries later became the dominant sea power in the Mediterranean and the greatest challenge to the emerging Roman republic.

Tyre's influence on the Hebrew kingdoms was far from beneficial. In the ninth century B.C., Ethbaal became king of Tyre. His daughter Jezebel married Ahab of Israel, and the two engaged in a determined effort to replace the worship of the Lord with a particularly virulent form of Baal-worship. The well-known stories of Elijah and Elisha come from this period and reflect the intense religious persecution that took place. Tyre's malodorous influence was also felt in Judah, through Jezebel's daughter Athaliah. She had married into Judah's royal family and later murdered her own grandchildren in an effort to obtain the throne (2 Ki. 11). Furthermore, the enduring hostility of Tyre toward God's people is reflected in a number of OT prophecies predicting that city's downfall (Isa. 23; Ezek. 27,28; Joel 3:4-8; Amos 1:9,10; Zech. 9:2-4).

Tyre continued as a dominant and wealthy trading power for many centuries. Secure on its island, protected by its powerful fleet, the city withstood a five-year Assyrian siege around 700 B.C., and a 13-year siege by Nebuchadnezzar about 120 years later. However, Tyre ultimately submitted to the Babylonians, and the city was finally destroyed by Alexander.

Tyre was later rebuilt and survived as a republic until it was incorporated into the Roman Empire in 20 B.C. It played no significant role in history after that.

In the NT, Tyre is mentioned as the home district of some of Jesus' followers (Mk. 3:8). Jesus visited the area and cast a demon out of a woman's daughter (Mk. 7:24). He obviously had the many OT prophecies against Tyre in mind when he compared that ancient city to the Jewish towns in which he was ministering. If Jesus' miracles had been done in Tyre and its neighboring city Sidon, even those evil cities would have been moved to repentance (Lk. 10:13).

The weakened condition of the rebuilt Tyre is evident in Acts 12:20-23. Tyre and Sidon depended on food from Galilean grainfields and so sued for peace with King Herod Agrippa I.

U

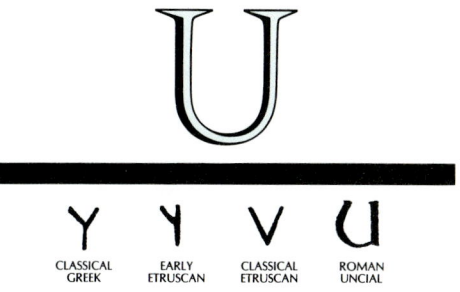

CLASSICAL GREEK   EARLY ETRUSCAN   CLASSICAL ETRUSCAN   ROMAN UNCIAL

Ugarit *See* Ras Shamra.

unbelief A failure to respond to God with trust; not just doubt but an act of rejection. *See also* Doubt.

In the NT, "unbeliever" is a general term for a non-Christian. Believers are not to avoid contact with unbelievers (1 Cor. 5:9-13), although Christians are warned against establishing a "yoked" relationship with them (2 Cor. 6:14). However, "unbelief" is a strongly negative term. It is the response of a "sinful, unbelieving heart that turns away from the living God" (Heb. 3:12). *See also* Believe; Separate.

uncircumcised Literally, (1) a person who had not undergone the rite of circumcision, in which the flap of skin at the end of the penis was removed. Circumcision was a sign of the covenant God made with Abraham, and all male descendants of Abraham through Isaac and Jacob were to be circumcised. *See also* Circumcision.

Figuratively, "uncircumcised" is used to designate (2) any non-Jew (Rom. 2:26) and also (3) rebellious and disobedient Israelites (Jer. 6:10 KJV). References to "uncircumcised ears" or "uncircumcised hearts" are intended to represent an individual's spiritual condition.

In Rom. 2:25-27, Paul uses circumcision and uncircumcision to portray spiritual conditions. The sinning Jew is spiritually uncircumcised and thus set outside the true people of God, whatever his physical state. In other letters, Paul notes that all human beings are invited to receive salvation in Jesus Christ, so that fleshly circumcision and uncircumcision are meaningless categories. All who believe are united in a single community of faith (1 Cor. 7:19; Gal. 5:6; 6:15; Eph. 2:11-22; Col. 3:11).

unclean Morally and/or physically polluted, and thus ritually disqualified from participation in Israel's OT worship (Lev. 15:31). Individuals could be defiled by an act, animal, or condition (Lev. 5:2; 11; Num. 5:2).

The prophets applied this concept to the moral teachings of God's Law, announcing that idolatry and injustice also made God's people unclean (Isa. 6:5). Jesus expanded the thought, pointing out that people are made unclean not by what they eat, but by what is in their hearts (Mt. 15:11-20).

The OT distinction between clean and unclean foods was abandoned by the church (Rom. 14:14), but the image was retained to suggest the impact of moral failures on one's relationship with the Lord (2 Cor. 6:17).

The use of "unclean" in 1 Cor. 7:14 implies only that the children of nonbelievers have no opportunity for daily contact with persons of faith, while children with even one Christian parent are, through that parent, in the presence of God. *See also* Clean and Unclean.

unction (KJV) *See* Anoint.

undefiled (KJV) Clean; not tainted by moral evil; pure (Heb. 7:26; 13:4). *See also* Clean and Unclean.

understanding Good judgment; the capacity to distinguish between conflicting views of reality. In Scripture, understanding is a moral rather than strictly intellectual concept. A person of understanding has grasped the moral message of Scripture and is committed to living in accord with the divine revelation.

OLD TESTAMENT

The key Hebrew word most often translated "understanding" means making distinctions between options. It is closely linked with sound judgment. This in turn is intimately linked with revelation, for by obeying God's commands Israel discovered and demonstrated the Lord's "wisdom and understanding" (Deut. 4:6). The man of understanding keeps God's Law (Ps. 119:34).

NEW TESTAMENT

The Greek words for "understanding" are used in ways that reflect the OT perspective. They indicate comprehension, usually of spiritual principles; organizing and interpreting what is known; and general mental orientation.

Apart from God's revelation, human beings have no capacity to understand ultimate truth and reality. The person of understanding will accept his limitations and orient his mind to the truths revealed in Scripture. He will commit himself not simply to master truth intellectually, but to work through the implication of truth for his life. The person of understanding is the one who is able to use revealed truth to accurately assess complex life situations. He or she goes on to choose the wise and the godly way.

ungodliness A pagan-like disregard of God in thought and action.

unicorn (KJV) A mythical beast characterized as a horse with a single horn growing from the center of its forehead.

What the KJV translators called a unicorn (and many modern versions translate "wild ox") is probably the oryx. This large white antelope with two long, straight horns fits the characteristics of the beast mentioned in Num. 24:8; Deut. 33:17; and Job 39:9,10. The gait of the oryx is horse-like, and it often prances playfully. Some speculate that the myth of the unicorn, reflected on many medieval tapestries, was inspired by glimpses of the oryx from the side (the two horns would then look like one).

The translators of the King James Version mistakenly used the "unicorn" as the English equivalent of the oryx.

unity The quality of being one in spirit, sentiment, and purpose. In Scripture, Christian unity is not organizational but interpersonal, an expression of a mutual love that grows out of our awareness that we share a relationship with God through Jesus Christ.

IMPLICATIONS OF UNITY

The NT calls for Christians to be of one mind, bonded together in the worship of God and in concern for one another's interests (Rom. 12:4-9; Phil. 2:1-4). In Acts, Luke often describes the church's actions as *homothymadon*. Usually translated "together," the word gives a sense of common purpose and united action. (Literally, the word indicates "same passion.") This is how the church meets and prays and decides things—together. Other Greek writings show us that *homothymadon* does not mean there are no differences of opin-

ion. But people in such a group put aside their differences because they share a common goal. Paul expresses the church's goal in this way:

May the God who gives endurance and encouragement give you a spirit of unity among yourselves as you follow Christ Jesus, so that with one heart [homothymadon] and mouth you may glorify the God and Father of our Lord Jesus Christ.

(Rom. 15:5,6)

JESUS' PRAYER

In what is often called Jesus' "high priestly prayer," Christ asked that future believers might "be brought to complete unity to let the world know that you sent me and have loved them even as you have loved me" (Jn. 17:23).

How this unity is to be seen by the world has been a matter of discussion for years, but there is no question that the NT repeatedly expresses concern for the unity of the Body, which is the Church (*see* Phil. 1:27; 1 Pet. 3:8-12).

unknown god A term found only in Acts 17:23, as a quotation from the dedication inscribed on an altar in pagan Athens. The inscription, common on Athenian altars, may reflect the philosophical tradition that doubts the possibility of human beings gaining any real knowledge of God. Paul used this inscription as a point of contact with his audience of Greek philosophers, announcing that he would tell them about the true God whom they worshiped as unknown.

unknown tongue (KJV) (1) A foreign language unknown to the speaker; (2) an ecstatic utterance. The word "unknown" is not in the Greek text of 1 Cor. 14, nor is it found in modern English versions. The phrase refers to the spiritual gift of tongues-speaking. *See also* Spiritual Gifts; Tongues.

unlearned (KJV) Untrained (Jn. 7:15; Acts 4:13; 1 Cor. 14:16); ignorant (2 Pet. 3:16).

unleavened bread Bread baked from dough made without yeast or leaven. The Israelites were to eat only unleavened bread during the seven days following Passover (Ex. 12:15-20; 13:3-7). The practice was a reminder of Israel's hasty departure from Egypt in the days of the Exodus.

Baked cereal offerings burned on the altar were also to be made of unleavened bread (Lev. 2:4; 6:17). *See also* Feasts, Festivals, and Fasts; Leaven.

Left: Jesus reclining at the table with the Twelve in the "large upper room, furnished and ready" (Mk. 14:15). Detail of a Greek illuminated manuscript, The Four Gospels (12th century A.D.).
Below: The Coenaculum on Mount Zion—at the southwest corner of Jerusalem—is the traditional site of the Upper Room where Jesus and his disciples shared their last meal together.

unpardonable sin *See* Forgive.

untimely birth (KJV) A spontaneous abortion before a fetus reached full term. In the OT, each context indicates a stillborn child (Job 3:16; Ps. 58:8; Eccl. 6:3). In 1 Cor. 15:8, Paul intends a premature live birth. Unlike the other apostles, Paul had not been a disciple of Jesus—he had been just the opposite, persecuting the early church. Thus, Paul was an apostle "born out of due time."

upper room The place in Jerusalem where Jesus shared the Last Supper with his disciples (Mk. 14:14,15; Lk. 22:11,12). Such a room was traditionally set aside in the homes of well-to-do individuals to entertain guests. Many take this to be the same room in which Christ's disciples met after Jesus' ascension, and where they were gathered when the Spirit came upon the church at Pentecost (Acts 2).

Early Christian writers report that the upper room still stood a century after Jesus' crucifixion, despite the Roman destruction of Jerusalem in A.D. 70. The "upper room" in Jerusalem that Christian pilgrims are shown today dates from the Middle Ages. *See also* Lord's Supper.

Ur of the Chaldees The Mesopotamian city from which Abraham migrated about 2100 B.C.

Most scholars believe Ur was located in southern Mesopotamia, although some have speculated that it might have been located in the north.

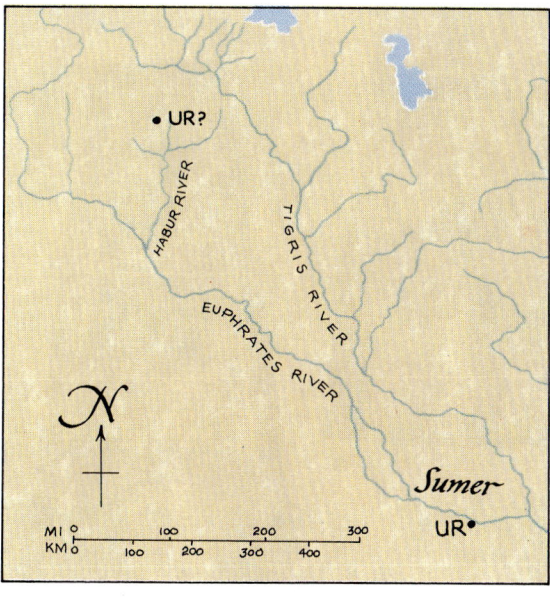

Two different sites for Abraham's Ur have been suggested. One is in the north, near Haran. The other is in the south, deep in Mesopotamia near the Persian Gulf. The latter location is supported by the defining phrase "of the Chaldees [Babylonians]."

Excavations were conducted at the southern site between 1922 and 1934. The impressive finds captivated the imagination of that generation and showed that Abraham left a highly developed society to venture to Canaan, a distant frontier territory.

Ur was dominated by a giant three-stage ziggurat, reaching some 70 feet above the flat plain below. On it were shrines to Nannar, the city's god. The city was enclosed by oval walls some 30 feet high, which protected not only the city but two harbors. Streets were carefully laid out. House walls faced the streets, and homes featured an inner courtyard onto which their rooms faced. Among the more spectacular finds from Ur's early period are beautifully worked gold jewelry and objects, gold-inlaid musical instruments, and colorful mosaics illustrating civil and military life. In addition, a number of clay tablets were recovered, including a Sumerian dictionary and a mathematical text recording cube roots. There were also business records, which show that the people of Ur were actively involved in international trade.

The splendid city that Abraham knew and left behind was reduced to ruins about 1740 B.C. In obeying God and leaving Ur's culture behind, Abraham won a future for his descendants that surely would have been denied them had he remained in the ill-fated city.

Urim and Thummim Gems or stones placed in the breastpiece of the Hebrew high priest. When the people needed special guidance from God, these were consulted. Either the stones were cast like lots, or a "yes," "no," or "wait" marker was drawn out. *See also* Guidance; Lots.

usury Any interest charged on borrowed money, not (as today) excessive interest.

Old Testament Law prohibited Israelites from charging interest on money lent to their countrymen (Deut. 23:19,20). In the agricultural society on which the Law was based, a person would borrow only to survive when crops failed, not to purchase new or luxury items. Interest-free lending was one of the mechanisms by which Israel dealt with the problem of poverty. Thus, Ps. 15:5 includes "lends his money without usury" among attributes of the righteous person.

Foreigners, generally merchants or traders conducting business in Israel, could be charged interest on borrowed money (Deut. 23:20). This was a normal business expense for them. But Israel's economy had changed so much by Jesus' time that he could speak freely (and without censure) of bankers paying interest on deposits (Mt. 25:27). However, Jesus' teachings still reflected the OT's call to be generous toward the needy (Lk. 6:34). *See also* Borrow; Interest; Pledge; Poor; Surety.

utterance (KJV) *See* Spiritual Gifts.

1002

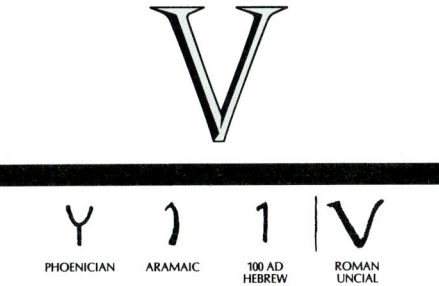

V

PHOENICIAN   ARAMAIC   100 AD HEBREW   ROMAN UNCIAL

valley (or **vale** KJV) Any depression lying between two higher points of land.

Hebrew words translated "vale" or "valley" define geographic features more precisely than the English terms. Among them are words that indicate (1) a broad, depressed plain (Deut. 34:3; Josh. 11:8); (2) a deep ravine (Josh. 15:8; Ezek. 39:11); (3) a ravine formed by rushing waters, but dry except during the rainy season (Jdg. 16:4); and (4) a broad valley lying between ranges of hills or mountains (Josh. 7:24; Ps. 60:6).

vanity (KJV) Emptiness, futility; sometimes pride. "Vanity of vanities," writes the Preacher of Ecclesiastes; "all is vanity" (Eccl. 1:2 KJV). The Hebrew word denotes a breath or vapor, yet the OT sometimes uses it for "worthless" idols—the point being that they are insubstantial and temporary. Ecclesiastes applies this thought to the whole scope of human activity "under the sun" (that is, apart from God). Without God's Spirit breathing through our lives, all we do is "Meaningless! Meaningless! . . . Utterly meaningless!" (Eccl. 1:2 NIV). *See also* Ecclesiastes.

veil (1) The multi-colored curtain that separated the Holy of Holies from the holy place in Israel's tabernacle and Temple (Ex. 26:31-33). Only the high priest could pass this barrier and then only on the Day of Atonement when carrying sacrificial blood. At the moment of Christ's death, the Temple veil was torn from top to bottom (Mt. 27:51; Mk. 15:38), symbolizing the free access to God that Christ's death won for believers (Heb. 6:19,20; 7:25).

(2) The cloth with which Middle Eastern women modestly cover their faces (*see* Isa. 47:2). The veil might even disguise a woman's identity (Gen. 38:14). In the NT, Paul uses this imagery in saying that the Gospel is veiled, or hidden, from Israel (2 Cor. 3:14,15). He also seems to exhort that women should wear veils when praying or prophesying (1 Cor. 11:4-16). *See also* Covering the Head.

Moses veiled his face after speaking with God (Ex. 34:33). His face became radiant from his encounter with God, and, as Paul explains it, Moses did not want the Israelites to see that splendor fade. By contrast, Christians need not fear exposing their true selves to others, for God's Spirit is at work within, progressively transforming us to display more and more of God's splendor (2 Cor. 3:12-18).

vengeance The act or motive of punishing another in retaliation for wrongdoing.

The Bible prohibits individuals from taking revenge on those who injure them

Woman wearing a veil and walking wrap. An Israelite woman wore a veil at the time of her wedding (Gen. 24:65-67; Song 4:1,3; 6:7).

The valley of Kidron is specified in Hebrew as a nahal, a ravine wet only in the rainy season. It begins north of Jerusalem and passes between the Mount of Olives and the Temple Mount on its way to the Dead Sea.

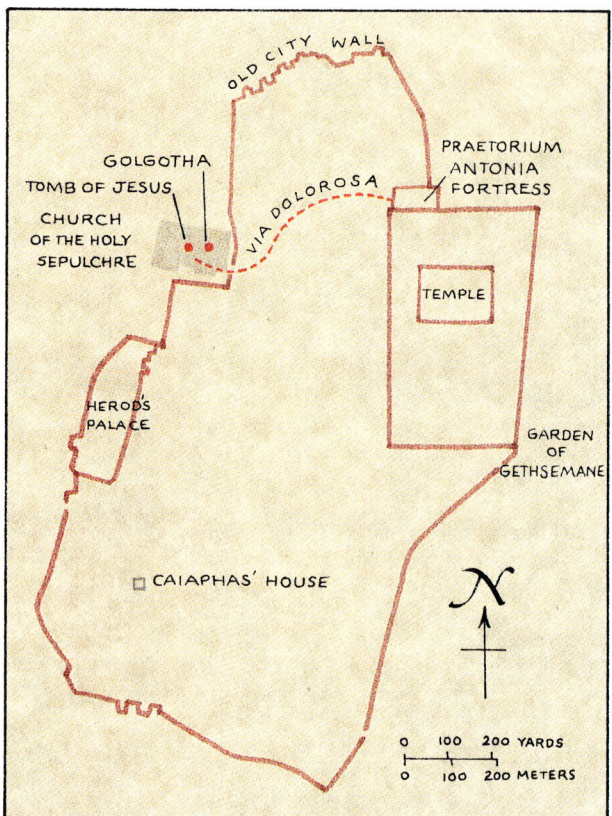

The traditional Via Dolorosa in Jerusalem has long been a devotional practice for Christian pilgrims seeking to follow the route Jesus took to Golgotha.

aspect of God's nature is powerfully expressed in Nah. 1:2,3:

The Lord is a jealous and avenging God;
the Lord takes vengeance and is filled
with wrath.
The Lord takes vengeance on his foes
and maintains his wrath against his
enemies.
The Lord is slow to anger and great in
power;
the Lord will not leave the guilty
unpunished.

Via Dolorosa ["The way of sorrows"]. According to tradition, the route Jesus followed from Pilate's judgment hall to Calvary.

The path is marked by 14 "stations of the cross," intended to commemorate events of that fateful day. These 14 stations are frequently used by Roman Catholic Christians to focus their devotions. Not all the events they observe are mentioned in Scripture. The stations are:

1. Christ is condemned in Pilate's hall.
2. Christ is forced to take up the cross.
3. Christ stumbles and falls.
4. Christ meets his mother.
5. Simon is forced to carry Jesus' cross (Mt. 27:32).
6. Christ's face is wiped by Veronica.
7. Christ falls again.
8. Christ meets the women of Jerusalem (Lk. 23:27-31).
9. Christ falls a third time.
10. Christ's clothing is taken away (Mt. 27:35).
11. Christ is nailed to the cross (Lk. 23:33).
12. Christ dies (Mt. 27:50).
13. Christ's body is taken from the cross (Mt. 27:59).
14. Christ's body is placed in a tomb (Mt. 27:60).

The city of Jerusalem was demolished by the Romans in A.D. 70 and again in A.D. 135. Its streets were obliterated, so the modern route of sorrows is unlikely to trace Christ's final journey accurately.

vial (KJV) Usually a flask or small bottle (1 Sam. 10:1), but in Rev. 5:8 and 21:9, a shallow basin.

(Lev. 19:18). However, it is not wrong to use the judicial system to seek redress. Both Testaments indicate that, while personal revenge is wrong, God as moral ruler of his universe must punish wrongdoers. It is in this moral context that the Lord is presented as a "God who avenges" (Ps. 94:1). As the NT quotes, "It is mine to avenge; I will repay" (Rom. 12:19; *see* Deut. 32:35). *See also* Avenger of Blood; Courts; Crime and Punishment.

In the OT, vengeance is normally directed toward those who reject God or persecute his people (Deut. 32:41,43). Similarly, the NT word means both vengeance and punishment. In nearly every NT instance, the time of punishment is specified as history's end. In the present time, God is displaying kindness, providing an opportunity for all to repent (Rom. 2:4). Then, when Christ appears, God will "pay back trouble to those who trouble" his own, and "will punish those who do not know God and do not obey the gospel" (2 Th. 1:6,8).

To have an adequate concept of the God revealed in Scripture, the believer must appreciate God's commitment to absolute justice as well as to love and mercy. This

victory OT: God's deliverance of his covenant people from physical foes (Deut. 20:4). NT: God's ultimate salvation of his people from sin and all its consequences.

Both Testaments link victory with a work of God on behalf of those who trust him. God's final victory is described in 1 Cor. 15:54-57—a passage filled with exultation, as Paul looks forward to the day when the perishable will be clothed with imperishability, and death will be "swallowed up in victory."

village A small unwalled cluster of dwellings. At times, in the Hebrew text, villages are called "daughters" of nearby cities, which they supplied with food. If the area were invaded by an enemy, villagers would take shelter behind the walls of the nearby "mother" city.

Remains of many hundreds of small unwalled settlements have been found in Israel. Most of these were occupied only before the Babylonian Captivity.

vine, vineyard The plant on which grapes grow; an area devoted to growing grapes. Isaiah describes the preparation of a hillside plot where grapes could be grown and processed (Isa. 5:1,2). The juice of mature grapes was extracted in a stone winepress by barefoot workers who sang as they danced on the year's crop (Isa. 16:10; Jer. 25:30; Hos. 2:15). The product was stored in jars or new goatskin bags, where it was permitted to ferment. Grapes

were also sun-dried, and the raisins thus produced were pressed together to form cakes. *See also* Wine.

The vine, which made such an important economic contribution to Israelite life, served as a symbol of peace and prosperity. The OT portrays Israel as a vine God planted (Ps. 80:8-18; Isa. 5:1-7; Jer. 2:21; Hos. 10:1). Isaiah's powerful imagery emphasizes that God expected the vine he planted in a choice plot to produce the fruit of righteousness and justice. Instead, Israel produced the bitter fruit of injustice.

Several of Christ's parables feature vineyards (Mt. 20:1-16; 21:28-32,33-41; Lk. 13:6-9). And in a powerful figure, Jesus described himself as the "true vine" (Jn. 15:1-8). Believers are like branches; they cannot bear fruit unless they remain united to the vine. God is compared to a gardener who tends the Christian, pruning when necessary to make life more productive. Jesus went on to explain that the Christian experiences union with him when the believer keeps Christ's commands (Jn. 15:10).

vinegar Sour or overly fermented wine. While vinegar was used as a relish with other foods (Ruth 2:14), it was a poor substitute for wine (Ps. 69:21).

The only mention of vinegar in the NT is in connection with Jesus' crucifixion. The offer of sour wine mixed with gall was intended as a kindness, to deaden suffering (Mt. 27:34). However, Jesus refused

Curved rows of flourishing grapevines in Israel. From ancient times the climate and terrain of the Syro-Palestine region has favored viticulture, and certain vineyards were especially notable (Num. 13:23,24; Jer. 48:32; Ezek. 27:18).

Above: Roman soldier offers Jesus a sponge soaked in wine vinegar. This fermented drink was a cheap refreshment and was part of soldiers' rations. Scene carved on an ivory altar (Germany, 11th century A.D.).

Above right: Because of the poisonous bite of some vipers, these snakes served as a symbol of evil (Job 20:16; Isa. 30:6; 59:5; Mt. 3:7; 12:34; Lk. 20:9-16).

this treatment as the soldiers prepared to crucify him. Later, he was offered a sponge dipped in vinegar to moisten his lips (Mt. 27:48; Mk. 15:36; Jn. 19:29,30).

violence The use of force to destroy or to harm.

In both Testaments, human violence implies a wicked acting out of aggression against others, or a disposition toward harming others if this will help the individual get his or her own way. The Hebrew word indicates willfully destructive acts or violent upheavals of nature (Gen. 6:11). The violent person is called ruthless and destructive.

The NT describes violent people as dangerous (Mt. 8:28), directing wicked acts against others (Rom. 1:29-31; 1 Tim. 1:13).

Paul requires that overseers (elders) of the church be "not violent." The Greek word he uses refers to "bullies" who try to impose their will on others (1 Tim. 3:3-7; Tit. 1:7).

viper Any poisonous snake. Shipwrecked on the island of Malta, Paul was bitten by a viper, but the apostle just "shook the snake off into the fire and suffered no ill effects." This made the islanders think he was a god (Acts 28:3-6). *See also* Serpent.

virgin OT: (1) *betulah,* a technical term for a woman who has not had sexual relations (Ex. 22:16); (2) *'almah,* a young woman of marriageable age, whether married or not. This Hebrew word occurs only seven times in the OT (Gen. 24:43; Ex. 2:8; Ps. 68:25; Prov. 30:19; Song 1:3; 6:8; Isa. 7:14). NT: (3) *parthenos,* the normal Greek word for one who is a "virgin."

Through Isaiah, God promised to give his people a sign: An *'almah* would bear a child. That Hebrew word itself can mean any young woman, not necessarily a virgin. The double meaning may be intentional, since the prophecy was fulfilled twice. Very likely, it was Isaiah's wife who would bear the child, and before the boy came of age, Assyria would be threatening. Sure enough, about twelve years later, Assyria swept away the Northern Kingdom of Israel (Isa. 7:1–8:4). Thus, in this immediate fulfillment, the *'almah* would be a young married woman, not a virgin.

But the NT focuses on a second fulfillment, the birth of the Messiah. Interestingly, the translators of the Septuagint chose *parthenos* as their rendering of *'almah.* This Greek word leaves little question: It would be a virgin, one with no sexual relations, who would conceive in some miraculous way. Matthew quotes this verse —using *parthenos*—in reporting the birth of Jesus. The context of the passage makes it clear: Mary was a virgin when Jesus was conceived in her womb; it was a miracle of God (Mt. 1:18-25; *see* Lk. 1:34).

virtue In older Bible versions, moral worth or excellence.

vision A revelation from God received while the prophet or seer is in a dream-like state (Gen. 46:2; Dan. 10:7; Lk. 1:22).

Acts reports several revelatory visions (9:10; 10:3,9-23; 18:9). Often such visions were avenues through which God provided special guidance. Lack of visions suggested that a given generation was forced to struggle without divine guidance (1 Sam. 3:1). Visions were typically given to recognized prophets (Num. 12:6). However, the mere fact of an unusual experience did not validate God as the source of the vision, as Satan often deceived through false visions and false prophets. *See also* Dream; Prophet.

voice The making of sound through human vocal cords; or God's verbal communication with people.

The theological significance of the "voice of God" is established in Heb. 3,4, which equate refusal to obey the voice of God with unbelief. Christians are told, "Today, if you hear his voice, do not harden your hearts" (Heb. 3:15; *see* Ps. 95:7,8). This emphasis suggests that God communicates to each generation of believers. While God's will is expressed in the Scriptures, God also speaks in a fresh manner to each new generation. The Israelites, for instance, had the Law, God's written truth from their earliest days as a nation. But they also had prophets, God's contemporary voice to his people age after age. The Holy Spirit serves today as God's contemporary voice to Christians.

When Christians experience guidance from the Spirit, they must test their subjective perceptions of what the Spirit is saying against Scripture's objective revelation of God's will. God will not contradict himself. Where experience and Scripture conflict, one must rely on Scripture. *See also* Holy Spirit; Lead.

vow A promise made to God but never to other human beings.

A vow was an expression of devotion that went beyond the normal requirements laid down in the OT Law. While voluntarily made, a vow became a sacred duty once spoken aloud (Deut. 23:21-23). Almost anything might be promised to God and could be redeemed by a money equivalent, plus one-fifth of its value. One unique feature of vows reflects the role of women in OT society. A husband could veto his wife's vow, and a father could veto a vow of his daughter. But the veto had to be uttered when the husband or father first heard of it (Num. 30:3-15).

vulture A large scavenger bird that lives on carrion.

The Hebrew and Greek words can mean "eagle," a large bird of prey, as well as "vulture." What linked these birds was their size and the fact that both were ritually unclean, not to be eaten by the Jews. Several kinds of large vultures are found in various parts of Israel. *See also* Eagle.

Nekhbet, the vulture goddess of Egypt, hovers protectively, holding the shen, *the symbol of infinity, in her talons. About 1490 B.C., from the temple of Hatshepsut. As scavengers, vultures were considered unclean by the Israelites (Dt. 14:12; Prov. 30:17; Mt. 24:28).*

Wheat

Washing

Widow

Women
in the
Bible

Wolf

Well

Weaving

Wine

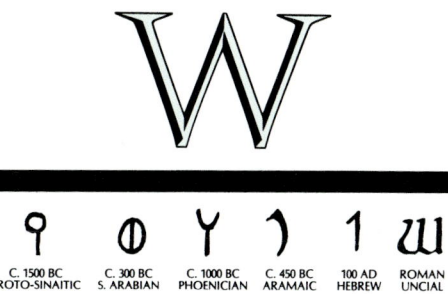

W

q Φ Y) 1 ɰ

C. 1500 BC PROTO-SINAITIC   C. 300 BC S. ARABIAN   C. 1000 BC PHOENICIAN   C. 450 BC ARAMAIC   100 AD HEBREW   ROMAN UNCIAL

wadi An Arabic word for a ravine or valley cut by a stream that is dry except during the rainy season. Some versions call wadis "brooks" or "torrents." The foolish builder in Jesus' story tried to build his house in a wadi. When the rains came, the dry stream bed filled with rushing waters. These undercut the stone structure the foolish man built, collapsing his house (Mt. 7:24-27; Lk. 6:47-49).

wafer Flat, thin bread, prepared by beating unleavened dough. Some wafers were sweetened with honey (Ex. 16:31), but wafers offered to God in Israel's sacrificial system were simply spread with olive oil (Lev. 2:4; Num. 6:15).

wages Payment made for one's work. The Hebrew and Greek terms are sometimes translated "reward" and "hire" in English versions.

In early Israel each family worked its own land. By the time of Isaiah, a working class, called "wage earners," had developed (Isa. 19:10). Wages were often bartered as there was not a set standard. Thus, Jacob bartered his wages from Laban (Gen. 30:25–31:55), and the landowner bartered with the laborers to fix a daily wage (Mt. 20:1-16). The Law commanded that wages be paid on a daily basis (Lev. 19:13; Deut. 24:14,15).

In the Jewish society of Christ's day, many members of the working class depended on day labor to earn a living. It was no shame to be a member of the working class. Jesus focuses on God's character in a parable about daily wages (Mt. 20:1-16) and alludes to day labor in others (Lk. 15:17,19; Jn. 10:13).

In Roman society, labor was looked on as menial, and the working class was considered contemptible by many. Yet in Christian churches wage earners worshiped both with land owners and slaves. Moreover, Paul contrasts the relationship of a worker and his employer with the believer's relationship with God. The Lord is not an employer who pays wages. If God paid us what we earned, that payment would be death (Rom. 6:23). But God has chosen to relate to human beings as a loving Father, and so offers us eternal life as a free gift (Rom. 4:4-12). *See also* Gift.

wagon *See* Cart.

wail A loud, agonizing cry associated with death or destruction. It was Jewish custom

*Throughout the Bible, **women** play major roles. Jesus praised a **widow** who gave two coins, and the Jewish nation was indebted to an Egyptian princess who rescued the baby Moses. Other women brought shame, like Salome, the daughter of Herodias, who caused the execution of John the Baptist. It was a woman who **washed** the feet of Jesus, a woman by a **well** who gave refreshment to Abraham's servant, and a woman, Mary, who asked Jesus for help when the **wine** supply was low. Women worked hard in Bible times, carrying **water** jugs to and from the town well, **weaving** wool, and making flour from **wheat** to bake their bread.*

Dry, cracked riverbed or wadi in northern Sinai. The prophet Jeremiah used the wadi (Heb., nahal) as a metaphor for deceit, because it was an undependable source of water (15:18).

to wail loudly when a person died. Some even hired professional mourners to accompany the family to the grave site. *See also* Funeral.

walk (1) Literally, to travel on foot. (2) Figuratively, one's spiritual or moral journey.

Walking was the main mode of transportation in Bible times. Some rode on horses or donkeys or in animal-drawn carts, but these were not common, and carts usually hauled goods, not passengers. Footpaths connected houses and villages. Roads criss-crossed Palestine, going up and down the hilly terrain. Walking was tiring, hot work, which was why the Law limited travel on the Sabbath. Nevertheless, walking was the way to get from one place to another; therefore, it is not surprising that images of walking appear frequently in Scripture.

In the OT, the references to walking are many, especially in a figurative sense. The psalmist fears that his feet will slip (Pss. 66:9; 73:2). Therefore, he appreciates God's Word, a "light unto my path" (Ps. 119:105 KJV). Deuteronomy speaks of believers "walking in [God's] ways" (Deut. 8:6). Here walking is more than plodding the paths of Palestine. It is a picture of life itself: God's commands become "ways" or roads that get us where we want to go. It is dangerous to step elsewhere.

The NT picks up this imagery. Paul reminds the Colossians that they used to walk in ways determined by man's earthly

[sin] nature (Col. 3:7). John writes, "Whoever claims to live in him must walk as Jesus did" (1 Jn. 2:6). *See also* Travel.

walls (1) Stone or brier enclosures surrounding a field or a corral for cattle (Isa. 5:5; Mt. 21:33). (2) House walls, typically made from rough stone or brick, coated inside with smoothed mud (Hab. 2:11). (3) Walls of public buildings, which were often made of great blocks of stone, hewn smooth and carefully fitted together (1 Ki. 5:15-17). (4) Large, defensive walls built to protect cities from attack. From the early third millennium B.C. until the relative peace of the Roman Empire under Julius Caesar, Middle Eastern cities were nearly always enclosed by fortified stone walls. And though their size and design varied widely, city walls were invariably massive, averaging 15 feet (4.5 meters) thick and 25 feet (7.6 meters) high. The walls of some cities in biblical history are particularly memorable: Jericho (Josh. 6:20), Beth Shan (1 Sam. 31:10-12), Babylon (Jer. 51:44,58), Damascus (Jer. 49:27; Acts 9:25), Tyre (Ezek. 26:4-12), and especially Jerusalem (2 Sam. 5:9; 1 Ki. 3:1,2; 2 Chr. 25:23; 36:19; Neh. 2:11–6:16; 12:27-43). *See also* Fortifications.

want (1) To desire, wish for; (2) a serious lack of resources, even basic necessities.

The familiar 23rd Psalm reflects the second sense: "The Lord is my Shepherd, I shall not be in want." However, the NT of most modern versions uses "want" almost exclusively in the first sense, to express a desire or wish. *See also* Desire.

war Armed conflict between peoples or nations.

War was a terrible reality in the ancient world. Palestine has always served as a battleground for the great empires surrounding it. In biblical times, the nations of Egypt, Assyria, and Babylon regularly fought in and around Israel's land.

OLD TESTAMENT

1. *God's involvement in Israel's wars*. God was involved in Israel's wars as in every other aspect of his people's experience. In general God is not portrayed as the cause of wars, but he does use wars for judicial purposes (Deut. 7:1,2,16; 20:16,17).

The conquest of Canaan was intended to be a war of extermination. Israel fought not only to wrest their Promised Land from the Canaanites, but as an instrument of divine judgment on peoples committed to evil. Extermination of these peoples was both righteous and necessary to protect God's own covenant people from moral and spiritual corruption (Gen. 15:16; Deut. 7:3-6). *See also* Canaan.

The wars of survival and expansion illustrate another aspect of God's involvement in Israel's wars. God promised to do battle for his people, but only when Israel was faithful to him (Ex. 14:14; Deut. 1:30; 3:22; Neh. 4:20; *see* Pss. 118:10-14; 124:1-3).

A third aspect of God's involvement is seen during the era when war served as an instrument of Israel's and Judah's national policy. God used the Assyrian and Babylonian armies to discipline his own people and to punish them for their many sins. The prophets proclaimed God's ultimate control of international affairs and his specific intention to use foreign nations to chastise his covenant people (Isa. 63:10; Jer. 21:1-10; Amos 3:14,15; Hab. 1:5-12). For extended passages on God's control of international politics, *see* Isa. 13–23; Jer. 46–51; Ezek. 25–32; Amos 1,2.

After the Babylonian Captivity, Judah was repopulated but remained a subject state in a series of powerful empires. A semblance of independence was won in a popular uprising under the Maccabees in 165 B.C. After this, various factions fought bitter battles, trying to establish dominance. Rebellions against Rome in A.D. 70 and again in A.D. 135 led to the razing of Jerusalem.

2. *Rules of warfare*. Biblical law governed Israel's conduct of war, establishing far more humane rules of warfare than were practiced by other nations (Deut. 20). God promised to be with his people when they faced "an army greater than yours" (v. 1). A priest was to address the army and to encourage trust in the Lord. Then army officers were to announce exemptions for any citizen soldier just married or any who had just dedicated a house or planted a vineyard. Anyone who was "afraid or fainthearted" (v. 8) was encouraged to go home, lest he adversely affect the morale of the army.

When an Israelite army attacked a city, that city was to be given an opportunity to surrender. Only if a city fought could it be plundered or its citizens killed. When laying siege to a city, Israel's army was not to cut down fruit trees to build its siege equipment.

3. *War vs. peace*. The OT prophets foresaw a time of blessing and international peace (Isa. 2:3-5; Mic. 4:1-5; Zech. 14). In that day, humankind "will beat their swords into plowshares and their spears into pruning hooks. Nation will not take up sword against nation, nor will they train for war anymore" (Isa. 2:4,5). Yet this and similar passages suppose that God himself is present in the person of his Messiah and will impose peace only after winning a worldwide war (Isa. 13:4; 24:21-23; 29:5-8; *see* Zech. 14:5).

NEW TESTAMENT

The NT has little to say about war. Jesus warned that future history would continue to be marred by wars and rumors of wars (Mt. 24:6; Lk. 21:9). John the Baptist and Paul both referred to the military, but neither condemned a military career. In fact, Paul uses military analogies to remind believers they are engaged in spiritual warfare and must be as disciplined as soldiers in their commitment (Eph. 6:10-20; 2 Tim. 2:3,4; *see* 1 Pet. 2:11).

James shows that wars originate in

ISRAEL'S WARS

Type of War	Fighters	Approximate Dates (B.C.)	References
War of Conquest	All adult males	1390–1350	Joshua
Wars of Survival	Volunteer militia	1350–1010	Judges
Wars of Expansion	Professional army	1010–930	1,2 Samuel 1 Chronicles
Instrument of National Policy	Professional army	930–722 (Israel) 930–586 (Judah)	1,2 Kings 2 Chr. 10–27
Wars of Rebellion	Volunteer militia (Maccabeans & Zealots)	165–A.D. 135	1 Maccabees Acts 5:36,37

1. Assyrian troops pursue Arabian warriors; relief at Nineveh, about 645 B.C. Gideon led a small band of Israelites in victory over the Midianites, a desert tribe from northwestern Arabia (Jdg. 7).

2. Egyptian archers from the Middle Kingdom era (2040–1786 B.C.) perform a war dance. They carry bows with a double-convex shape. Invading Hyksos warriors probably later introduced the powerful composite bow—a glued bow of wood, sinew, and horn —into Egypt (1786–1550 B.C.).

3. Relief of a Hittite archer found at Tell Halaf (Gozen), Syria (9th century B.C.). Archers were the most technically skilled of warriors and played a crucial role in ancient warfare because they could engage the enemy from a distance while being protected by full-length shields.

4. Assyrian soldiers behead Elamite captives; detail of a relief from the palace of Ashurbanipal at Nineveh (about 650 B.C.). The Assyrians, who generally followed a policy of deporting conquered peoples (2 Ki. 17:6,24), were ruthless toward officials whom they held responsible for rebelling.

5,6. Artist's reconstruction of the assault on the gate of Lachish, based on a series of reliefs (for example, inset) from the palace of Assyrian King Sennacherib at Nineveh (about 701 B.C.). The painting shows in proper perspective the double walls, city gate, siege ramp and battering rams, as well as the opposing forces hurling projectiles. Sennacherib recorded in his annals how he attacked the towns of Judah: "I conquered them by means of well-stamped earth ramps and battering rams brought near to the walls, combined with the attack by foot soldiers using tunnels, breaches, as well as trench works."

7. In this stone relief (early second century A.D.) a Roman legionary battles with a barbarian. Josephus wrote that Roman warriors fought as if their weapons were permanently attached to them.

8. The troops of Pharaoh Rameses III battle and defeat invading bands of "Sea Peoples"; drawings copied from bas reliefs at Thebes, Egypt. Three successive Egyptian

continued on page 1014

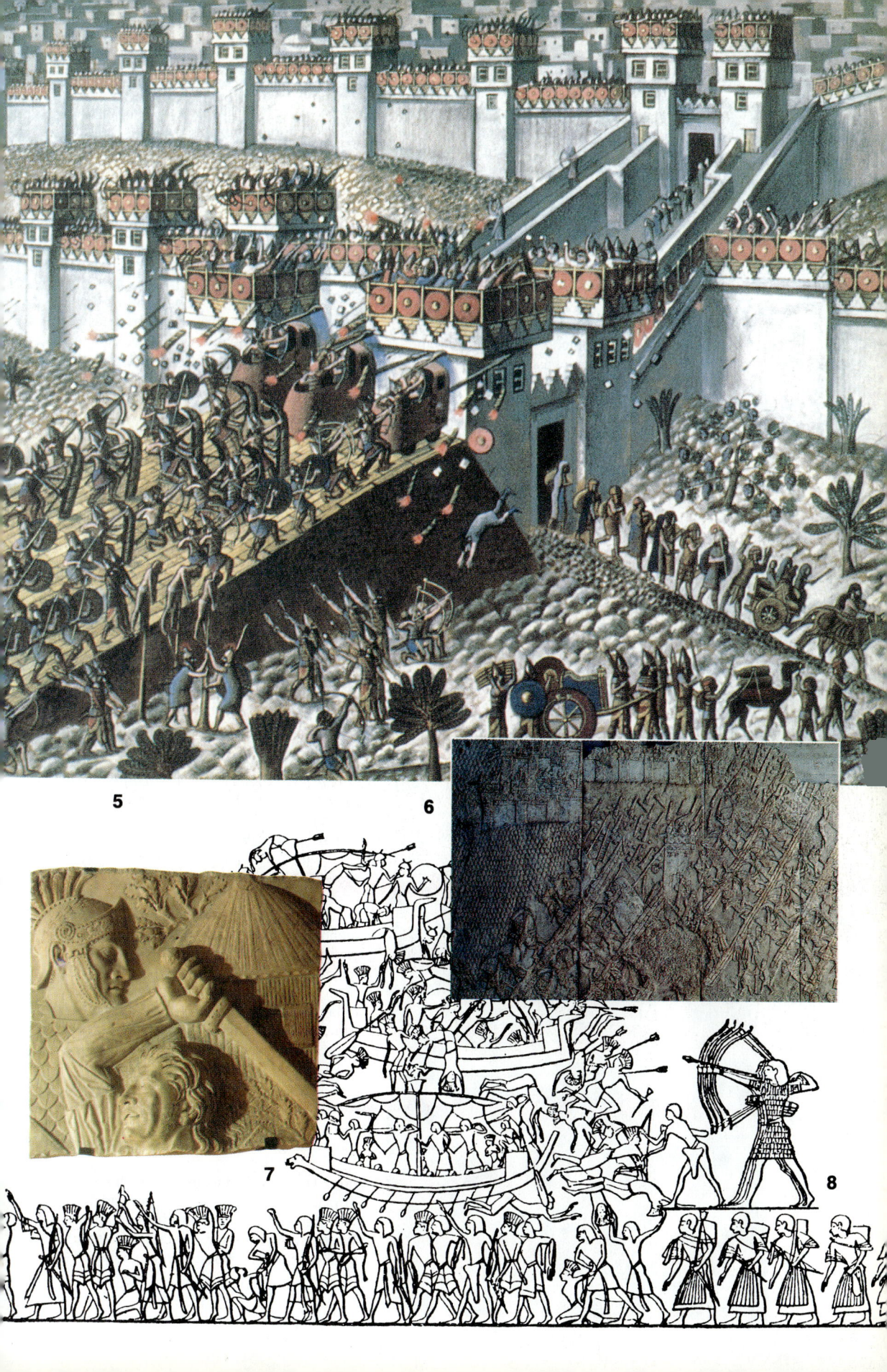

5

6

7

8

man's sinful nature (Jas. 4:1-3). But even this does not speak to the question of whether or not it is right for the Christian citizen to participate in a war. Those who take a pacifist stand generally base their conviction on Jesus' statements about peacemaking and nonretribution in one's personal conduct.

wash To cleanse with water. Washing was necessary in hot, dry Israel. Even when one's whole body could not be cleansed, it was common practice to wash the hands. Hosts would also wash the feet of visitors to cleanse the dust of travel (Lk. 7:44). *See also* Footwashing.

Washing also had ceremonial significance in Israel's religion. A person who was ritually defiled was required to wash his or her body and clothing (Lev. 13:6; Num. 19:7,8). After such a ritual bath, the person would be "clean," qualified to take part in Israel's worship services. The writer of Hebrews uses this imagery of cleansing, noting that Jesus has done for the heart what OT ritual did for man's outward body (Heb. 10:22).

By Christ's time the practice of ritual washing had been extended to include ceremonies not prescribed in the OT. When the Pharisees criticized Jesus and his disciples for not washing their hands

before eating, they were referring to this ritual washing, not a normal cleansing of the hands (Mt. 15:2; Mk. 7:4; Lk. 11:38).

Affluent homes would often have a *mikvah* or pool where ritual baths might be taken. Many Jerusalem Jews had also adopted the Greek and Roman practice of bathing in large public baths for ordinary cleanliness. *See also* Baptism.

watch, watchman (1) A person or group on guard against approaching enemies (2 Sam. 18:24). Watchmen were posted on high hills and the tops of city walls, where they could see the enemy a long way off. The NT warns believers to be on guard against those who cause dissension (Rom. 16:17). (2) A particular period of time during which a sentry is assigned to be on duty (Mt. 14:25). (3) A person or group camping in a field to guard ripening crops against birds and animals (Isa. 5:2). As a verb, (4) to wait in order to observe (Dan. 7:11); (5) to be careful to observe or do something (Ps. 39:1).

Metaphorically, God keeps watch over his people (Ps. 121:3-5), giving the believer a sense of confidence and peace. Similarly God calls the spiritual leaders of his people "watchmen" and assigns them to guard his people against internal and external enemies (Ezek. 3:17; Heb. 13:17).

watches of the night Measures for reckoning the passage of time at night.

The Jews divided the night into three roughly equal watches: a beginning or evening watch (Lam. 2:19), a middle watch (Jdg. 7:19), and a morning watch (Ex. 14:24; 1 Sam. 11:11). The Roman system, which divided the day into twelve hours and the night into four watches, is used in the Gospels. Thus, when Jesus met his disciples while walking the stormy waters of the Sea of Galilee during the fourth watch, it was between 3 and 6 A.M. (Mt. 14:25; Mk. 6:48). Believers are urged to be ready for Christ's return "even if he comes in the second or third watch of the night," between 9 P.M. and 3 A.M. when most people are sleeping (Lk. 12:38).

watchtower Any elevated natural or manmade structure on which a watchman might be posted. *See also* Tower; Watch.

water H_2O in liquid form, on which the life of plants, animals, and man depends.

Water is an essential resource in Canaan. While parts of ancient Israel had many springs, the land boasted no major rivers

like the Nile or Euphrates to support a large population. Life in Palestine depended on heavy fall and spring rains. When these failed, the people faced serious drought.

Because water was so precious, the people developed a number of strategies to preserve and use it. Farmers terraced hillsides, hewing channels in the rock to guide water from springs to their fields. Each home in more arid regions had its own system of cisterns to preserve the water that fell during the rainy seasons. Cities maintained giant underground cisterns that could hold hundreds of thousands of gallons of water, thus enabling its citizens to survive under siege. Some 700 years before Christ, Hezekiah's engineers

tunneled through rock to give Jerusalem access to water. In Jesus' time, a complicated system of aqueducts and channels carried water to Jerusalem (*see* Jer. 2:13).

Water was important in Israel not only for drinking but also for ceremonial purposes. Many violations of OT ceremonial law called for a ritual washing of one's body and clothing. *See also* Wash.

Symbolically, water speaks of abundance and blessing. God leads his people beside quiet waters, where there is always plenty to drink (Ps. 23:2). When the Messiah comes, "water will gush forth in the wilderness and streams in the desert. The burning sand will become a pool, the thirsty ground bubbling springs" (Isa. 35: 6,7). A central feature in John's vision of

Above: Aqueduct that brought water to the Roman colony of Antioch in Pisidia. Roman engineers designed impressive, gravity-driven water systems to supply major cities across the whole Empire.
Above left: Entrance of the tunnel that brings water from the spring of Gihon to the Pool of Siloam, which used to lie within Jerusalem's walls. It was constructed by King Hezekiah (728–697 B.C.) to ensure the water supply to Jerusalem in time of siege.
Left: Man transfers water from one level to another by means of a triangular bucket attached to a long beam. The beam is weighted and carefully balanced on a central stand so that the bucket rises easily. This kind of water-sweep is still used in parts of the Middle East.

heaven is "the river of the water of life, as clear as crystal, flowing from the throne of God" (Rev. 22:1). God himself is seen as a perpetually bubbling "spring of living water" (Jer. 2:13), an image that is applied in the NT to the Holy Spirit (Jn. 7:38).

While it is true that "deep waters" frequently imply danger and that the waters of the Genesis Flood brought judgment (Ps. 18:16; 2 Pet. 3:6), water itself is predominantly viewed in a positive way, as a source of life, a provision for cleansing, and a gift given by God to his covenant people. Thus, the pollution of the waters described in Revelation symbolizes divine judgment and the withdrawal of providential blessing from earth and its population (Rev. 8:11; 11:6).

Above: Drawing of Egyptian water-bearers.
Right: Terra-cotta jug from Cyprus decorated with a black gazelle (7th century B.C.). Jugs like this were used to carry water from a well to larger storage jars.

water jars (**water pots** KJV) Pottery jars that held water. In cities and towns, women often carried water from a community well or cistern in pottery jars set on their heads or shoulders (Gen. 24:15-18). A household might keep its water in a large stone or pottery jar that could hold 20 to 30 gallons (75 to 115 liters) (Jn. 2:6). Evaporation cooled the water and the room in which these giants jars stood.

water of cleansing, purification, separation Water mixed with the ashes of a sacrificed heifer, used in Israel's purification rites (Num. 19).

water that brings a curse, water of bitterness Water to be drunk by the wife of a jealous husband (Num. 5:11-31). An innocent woman would be unharmed by this water mixed with ink, while the drink would cause painful swelling in the guilty. *See also* Jealousy.

wave offering That portion of sacrifices and offerings which was not burned but could be eaten by the priests and their families (Ex. 29:24-26; Lev. 8:27-29). These pieces were waved before the altar, symbolizing their presentation to the Lord.

way (1) A path or road customarily followed by travelers; (2) a pattern in nature and animal behavior (Job 38:35; Prov. 30:19); (3) man's moral conduct (Pss. 1:6; 119:30; 1 Cor. 4:17; Jas. 5:20); (4) human experience in general (Job 3:23; Ps. 37:5); and (5) God's will, judgments, purposes, and sovereign determinations (Deut. 10:12; Pss. 18:30; 86:11; Mk. 12:14).

Two distinctive uses of "way" are found in the NT. The early Christian movement became known as "The Way" (Acts 9:2; 19:9,23; 22:4; 24:14,22). Jesus presented himself as "the way and the truth and the life," the only one through whom human beings can come to the Father (Jn. 14:4-6).

weakness Physical, mental, economic, or spiritual limitation or inability.

Paul experienced a limiting disability which he called a weakness (2 Cor. 12:7-10). The NT speaks of weak faith (Rom. 14:1,2), a weak and faulty conscience (1 Cor. 8:7-13), and the "weak and useless" OT Law (Heb. 7:18). This last is no criticism of the Law in itself but of human nature. Paul explains that the Law was unable to make men righteous because "it was weakened by the sinful nature" (Rom. 8:3). The image is that of an anchor that does not hold because the sea bed is too hard for the anchor to gain a grip.

The Bible typically contrasts man's weakness with God's strength. Because "the Spirit helps us in our weakness" (Rom. 8:26), those who rely on Christ are empowered by God to overcome normal human frailties. *See also* Strength.

wealth (1) Valuables of any sort: precious metals, gems, spices, clothing, herds, land, crops, etc. (2) Prosperity, an abundance of necessities, enabling an individual to take life easy. (3) To the rich, luxury items such as fine linen clothing, ivory inlaid furniture, etc.

OLD TESTAMENT
God promised to bless his covenant people with prosperity if they were faithful to

him (Deut. 7:12-15). In normal times, the godly individual could expect similar material blessings (Ps. 112:1-6). As Prov. 10:22 says, "The blessing of the Lord brings wealth, and he adds no trouble to it."

At the same time, the OT recognizes that wealth can be dangerous to one's spiritual well-being. Moses reminded Israel to praise God when prosperous, lest "when you build fine houses and settle down, and when your herds and flocks grow large and your silver and gold increase and all you have is multiplied, then your heart will become proud and you will forget the Lord your God. . . . Remember the Lord your God, for it is he who gives you the ability to produce wealth, and so confirms his covenant" (Deut. 8:12-14,18).

Other homilies warning of the dangers of wealth are found throughout the OT. Too often, the rich escape justice (Hos. 12:8). Wealth, like life, is fleeting (Ps. 49:12). Riches are less important than understanding (Ps. 49:16-20). Wealth can so deaden a person's sense of dependence on God that it becomes a snare, endangering the soul (Ps. 52:5-7). Whatever riches can buy, they cannot purchase salvation (Ps. 49:6-12).

Thus, while prosperity can be a blessing from God, the wealthy person must be especially aware of its potential danger and focus on developing his or her relationship with God.

JESUS' TEACHING

By Jesus' time the Jewish people had largely forgotten the warnings of the OT and saw wealth as an unmixed blessing. Many assumed that a wealthy person was proved righteous by the very fact that he had been blessed with riches. Thus, Jesus' statement that it was difficult for a rich man to enter God's Kingdom stunned even his disciples (Mt. 19:24-30).

In various stories and illustrations, Jesus expressed his own perspective on wealth. The story of the rich fool drew attention to the fleeting nature of this life. How useless it is to store up wealth on earth when one may die at any moment. Early wealth will be of no value then. The believer will see the wisdom of being rich toward God (Lk. 12:13-21).

The story of the rich man and the beggar Lazarus caps this theme. The rich man, who ignored the impoverished Lazarus at his gate, found himself in torment while the beggar was welcomed to paradise by Father Abraham himself. Wealth or poverty does not determine one's eternal destiny (Lk. 16:19-31). Furthermore, it is difficult to keep one's focus on heaven, and some who hear God's Word permit it to wither when they are distracted by the "worries of this life and the deceitfulness of wealth" (Mt. 13:18-23).

Jesus' famous reference to the lilies of the field carries his teaching even further. Believers should not be anxious even about necessities. God, their heavenly Father, knows and will meet their needs. Thus, the believer is free to concentrate on God and his Kingdom, laying up treasures in heaven rather than on earth (Mt. 6:19-34).

A final illustration puts Jesus' teaching into sharper perspective. Christ told of a manager about to be fired who called in his employer's creditors and permitted them to falsify their accounts. He did this so that when he lost his job "people will welcome me into their houses." Jesus commended the manager, not for his dishonesty, but for his insight into an important fact: Money is to be used to prepare for the future; wealth has no value in and of itself. The Christian who applies this parable will begin to see his wealth as an opportunity to prepare for his welcome into "eternal dwellings" and will not fall into any of the traps riches set (Lk. 16:1-15).

THE EPISTLES

The Epistles pick up and develop Jesus' perspective. A desire for riches is a root from which every kind of evil can grow. Godliness, not money, is important (1 Tim. 6:3-10). Those who are rich are encouraged to be generous and willing to share; in this way they build a firm foundation for life in the coming age (1 Tim. 6:17-19). Christians are commanded not to

Gold, shell-shaped bowl from the Canaanite-period palace at Megiddo (14th century B.C.). The Book of Proverbs teaches that the accumulation of wealth should not be sought for its own sake (15:16; 22:16; 28:20,22).

be partial toward the rich (Jas. 2:1-11). James also issues a dire warning against the rich (5:1-6). In contrast, love generated by a relationship with Christ will motivate believers to use their material possessions to help others in need (1 Jn. 3:16-20).

In the context of the NT's spirit of love and generosity, the possession of wealth is not so much a blessing in itself, but a gift which enables the Christian to be a blessing to others. Neither wealth nor poverty is a measure of spiritual worth or of God's loving concern. The Christian must continue to trust God for everything in his or her daily life and use possessions to express faith. *See also* Money.

wean To gradually accustom a child to other foods, withdrawing its dependence on the mother's milk. In biblical times, children typically were not weaned until they were two or even three years old (1 Sam. 1:23). Weaning was apparently an important milestone in the family marked by a feast hosted by the father (Gen. 21:8).

weapons The weapons systems of biblical warfare fall into several categories: short-range weapons, used in hand-to-hand combat (the ax, mace, sword, and spear); long-range weapons (the sling, bow and arrow, and javelin); defensive weaponry (shields of various shapes and sizes, and mail made of metal scales sewn to cloth); and, later, chariots (first, light mobile platforms used by archers, then heavy assault vehicles intended to batter foot soldiers).

Strong walls defended strategic cities, and cistern systems supplied water in time of siege. With the growth of great empires to the north, siege weapons began to appear, including battering rams used to weaken walls or city gates, giant mobile towers which gradually pushed up against the walls, and earthen ramps enabling invaders to run up to and over city walls. Defenders used rocks, boiling oil, and chains rigged to entangle battering rams, as well as bows and arrows against besieging armies.

We can identify three types of conflicts: raids, in which a relatively small group entered another people's territory to obtain plunder (1 Sam. 27:8; 2 Ki. 13:20); battles, in which massed armies faced one another in hand-to-hand combat (1 Sam. 28:4; 2 Ki. 3:6; 2 Chr. 13:3); and sieges, in which a large invading force surrounded a nation's walled cities and either starved out the citizens or broke through the walls (1 Ki. 20:1; 2 Ki. 16:5). The Assyrians and Babylonians, who perfected siege warfare, typically deported the citizens of defeated lands to some other territory in order to destroy national identity and a people's will to resist.

See also Armor; Arrows; Bow; Chariot; Javelin; Shield; Siege; Sling; Spear; Sword.

weather *See* Agriculture.

weaving Criss-crossing threads in such a way as to produce cloth.

The craft of weaving was highly developed at a very early date. Cloth woven in Ebla around 2500 B.C. was prized as a trade item. Egyptian wall paintings dating as early as 2000 B.C. trace in step-by-step

Below: Reconstruction of an Israelite vertical loom, showing weights tied to the bottom of the yarn strands. This was the common loom in Palestine in Bible times.
Lower right: Egyptian weaver's comb used to push close the weft or horizontal threads as they are woven on a loom.
Right: Two women at a wool basket. A painting from an Athenian box for toilet articles (470–460 B.C.)

fashion the stripping of fibers from flax plants, the creation of threads, and their weaving into linen cloth. The Israelites possessed some skill in weaving as early as the Exodus, for they dyed and wove the fabrics used in the tabernacle and in priestly dress (Ex. 26,28).

Weaving was done on three types of looms. A ground loom was constructed by driving parallel rows of pegs into the ground. Threads tied between the pegs served as the warp of the cloth. A hand loom was a smaller wooden square. An upright loom was created by driving two poles into the ground, with a third pole, called the weaver's beam, balanced atop them. Threads were weighted with stones and hung from the beam. These threads served as the warp of the cloth. By progressively wrapping the newly woven material around the beam, very long strips of cloth could be created. In early Israel, the women of each family wove the wool and rough linen cloth.

web (1) A gossamer pattern spun by spiders, or a cobweb (Job 8:14,15). (2) The fabric being woven in a loom (Jdg. 16:13,14 KJV).

wedding *See* Marriage.

week Seven consecutive days. The seventh day of the week, which according to Jewish reckoning lasted from Friday evening to Saturday evening, was the Sabbath. *See also* Calendar; Lord's Day; Sabbath; Sunday; Time.

Weeks, Feast of A harvest festival just 50 days after Passover, also known as Pentecost or Firstfruits. This was the second of three great Jewish religious festivals that all Jewish men in Israel were required to attend. *See also* Feasts, Festivals, and Fasts; Pentecost.

weep To cry aloud, as an expression of strong emotions. Joseph wept with joy when reunited with his brothers (Gen. 45:14). At times weeping is associated with repentance and prayer (Jdg. 20:26; Neh. 8:9; Esth. 4:3). Most often weeping expresses distress and anguish (Isa. 15:3; Jer. 31:15).

weights and measures Established standards for determining amounts of mass or distance. Precise measurements were not possible during most of the biblical era. Instead, weights and measures were approximations; general rather than specific, rough estimates rather than attuned to universal standards, local rather than international. Still, inexact measurement made little difference in rural, agricultural societies.

The emergence of great empires and

strong national powers made standardization of weights and measures increasingly important. Royal architects required a standard cubit. Tax collectors, who often received revenue in the form of produce, required standard containers for measurement of grains, olive oil, and wine.

Gradually variance in weights and measures was reduced. The weights and measures shown on these pages represent the standardized (but still imprecise) calibrations of the Old and New Testament worlds.

In early biblical times, gold and silver, bronze, or other mediums of exchange were weighed out in payment for goods or services. (Coinage was a relatively late

Left: Wooden tomb model of a weaver's house in which women prepare, spin, and weave flax on a horizontal loom (Egypt, 1990–1780 B.C.).

These 7th-century B.C. weights found in Jerusalem are each inscribed with their value in shekels.

BIBLICAL WEIGHTS AND MEASURES

Units	Approx. Equivalents
Weights	
Old Testament	
Talent (60 minas)	75 lbs. (34.2 kg.)
Mina (50 shekels)	1.2 lbs. (0.6 kg.)
Shekel (common)	0.4 oz. (11.4 g.)
(royal)	0.44 oz. (12.5 g.)
Pim (⅔ shekel)	0.25 oz. (7 g.)
Beka (½ shekel)	0.22 oz. (6.2 g.)
Gerah (1/20 shekel)	0.02 oz. (0.57 g.)
New Testament	
Talent (125 litra)	88 lbs. (40 kg.)
Pound (1 litra)	11.4 oz. (327 g.)
Lengths	
Old Testament	
Cubit (short)	17.5 in. (44.4 cm.)
(long)	20.4 in. (51.8 cm.)
Span (½ cubit)	9.0 in. (23 cm.)
Handbreadth/palm	3.0 in. (7.6 cm.)
New Testament	
Mile (8 stadion)	1618 yds. (1478 m.)
Stadion/furlong	202 yds. (185 m.)
Fathom	6 ft. (1.8 m.)
Cubit (Roman)	17.5 in. (44.4 cm.)
(Jewish)	20.6 in. (52.5 cm.)
Liquid Measures	
Old Testament	
Cor/Kor (10 baths)	55 gal. (216 liters)
Bath	5.5 gal. (21.6 l.)
Hin (⅙ bath)	3.8 qt. (3.6 l.)
Log (1/72 bath)	0.5 pt. (0.3 l.)
New Testament	
Gallon/firkin	10.4 gal. (39.4 l.)
(batos or metrētēs)	
Dry Measures	
Old Testament	
Homer or cor/kor	200 qt. (220 l.)
Letek (½ homer)	100 qt. (110 l.)
Ephah	20 qt. (22 l.)
Seah	7.7 qt. (7.3 l.)
Omer (1/10 ephah)	2 qt. (2.2 l.)
Cab/Kab (¼ seah)	1.1 qt. (1.2 l.)
New Testament	
Measure (koros)	14.9 bu. (525 l.)
Measure (saton)	11.1 qt. (12.3 l.)
Bushel (modios)	8 qt. (8.75 l.)
Quart (choinix)	1 qt. (1.1 l.)

Although this table is based on the best available information, it is not mathematically precise and at some points the equivalents are uncertain.

Top right: Duck-shaped stone weight with royal inscription guaranteeing its 5 mina weight (Ur, about 2100 B.C.). The prophet Amos chastised Israelite merchants for "skimping the measure, boosting the price and cheating with dishonest scales" (8:5).
Right: Bull- and lion-shaped weights from Ras Shamra (1400–1200 B.C.), in bronze and lead, respectively.

invention; _see_ Money.) Hundreds of small stone weights, many with symbols indicating their value, have been recovered by archaeologists. Merchants carried such weights with them, and the OT warns the Israelites not to defraud by using two sets of weights—a light weight for buying and a heavy weight for selling (Deut. 25:15; Amos 8:5). The actual weights of recovered stones used as standards for such units as the _pim_ or _shekel_ vary slightly. By taking an average, archaeologists have established an approximate value for each.

Originally, the cubit, the basic measure of length, was simply the length of a man's forearm, and the span was the width of a hand. Distance was measured by the number of days required to travel it. The basic measure of farm land, though rendered "acre" in English versions, was simply the amount of land a team of oxen could plow in one day.

Measurements of capacity were equally imprecise. The Hebrew _hin_ was a pot and the _ephah_ a basket, the actual size of which differed by locality. The _bath_, the standard OT liquid measure, was the amount of liquid held by a large clay jar, but very difficult to relate to NT liquid measures such as the _kor_.

Similarly, the modern equivalents of measures of volume, distance, and area have been determined by careful study of recovered artifacts and from data given in Scripture and other ancient documents. (For detailed information regarding any one specific weight or measure, see that entry.)

well A shaft dug to reach underground water. In some English versions, wells are confused with cisterns and springs.

Wells were especially important in arid areas of biblical lands. Wells were constructed in pasturelands, as a source of water for herds (Gen. 29:1-8), and near towns. In areas of blowing sand, wells

were bell-shaped, with a small opening that could be covered with a flat rock.

It was difficult to force shafts through rocky soil with inadequate tools. Yet some ancient wells reached a depth of over 100 feet (30 meters). It seemed easier to some to fight over wells than to go to the work of digging them (Gen. 26:17-22). The Israelites who conquered Canaan benefited from wells they did not dig as well as vineyards and olive groves they did not plant (Deut. 6:11).

Frequently wells were named. The prefix "Beer-" in biblical place names means "the well of."

Women who came to city wells often stopped to socialize. The woman of Samaria whom Jesus met and talked with at the well outside of Sychar came there alone, suggesting perhaps that her immorality made her something of an outcast in her village (Jn. 4:5-26).

west In Palestine, the direction of the sea and the sunset. It is also the direction from which rain-bearing clouds come. Other than these three features, the "west" had no particular significance to the Hebrew people.

whale (KJV) The whale is not mentioned in the OT. Where the KJV has whale, later English versions accurately read "great fish" (Jon. 1:17), "monster in the seas" (Ezek. 32:2, NIV), or "sea monster" (Job 7:12, RSV). *See also* Leviathan.

wheat An annual grass producing a grain used for food in biblical times as in our own.

Wheat is mentioned 52 times in the Bible. Along with barley, it was one of the grains ground to make flour used in bread, the staple food of the ancients. Wheat was harvested in Palestine April through June. The land produced rich harvests, not only feeding the Israelites but frequently providing a surplus that could be exported to other nations (1 Ki. 5:11; 2 Chr. 2:10; Amos 8:5).

Symbolically, wheat is used in Scripture to illustrate the goodness of God (Ps. 147:14) and the principle that the death of "self" brings forth spiritual life (Jn. 12:24; *compare* 1 Cor. 15:35-38). *See also* Barley; Bread; Corn; Grain; Sow; Thresh.

wheel A circular frame or solid disk that turns on a central axis and is used to move vehicles (Ex. 14:25) or as a machine (Eccl. 12:6).

WHEELED VEHICLES

Clay models of wheeled carts and of potters' wheels indicate that the solid wheel was in use in the flat Mesopotamian valley as early as 3500 B.C. Wheels with rims and spokes were common by the middle of the second millennium B.C. The chariot mentioned in Joseph's story (Gen. 41:43), dating about 1900 B.C., was probably one of the light, spoke-wheeled vehicles favored by the Egyptians. In contrast, the Assyrians and Canaanites favored heavy war chariots, whose sturdy wheels

Left: Samaritan woman portrayed in relief on a medieval ivory container (7th century A.D.). She had a life-changing talk with Jesus at Jacob's Well outside her hometown of Sychar.

Above: Loading wheat on a ship for transport down the Nile River; tomb painting from Thebes, 1500–1300 B.C. Joseph's brothers came to Egypt in search of wheat during a drought-caused famine in Canaan (Gen. 42).
Inset: Stalks of wheat, a cereal grass of the genus Triticum.

Above: Spoked wheels on a cart; detail of an Assyrian relief (about 701 B.C.). Left: Clay model of a war chariot with solid wheels (Cyprus, 7th century B.C.).

Egyptian whip with several thongs. Jesus was scourged with a whip that had pieces of lead or bone tied in each thong.

rolled noisily as the armies mounted their attacks (Jer. 47:3; Nah. 3:2). Because wheeled vehicles were primarily used in warfare, they came to symbolize speed and power (Ezek. 1:17-20; Dan. 7:9). *See also* Chariot.

Wheeled vehicles were seldom used to transport goods in Israel (*see* 2 Sam. 6:3). Much of that land is hilly, and sure-footed donkeys, capable of carrying amazingly heavy loads, were more practical.

WHEELED MACHINES

As early as 3500 B.C., a round platform that could be rotated by one's feet was used by potters when shaping clay vessels. *See also* Potter. The only other specific use of the wheel as a machine is found in Eccl. 12:6, which suggests that a rope wound around a wheel was used to lower a bucket into a well and then to draw it up filled with water.

However, archaeology suggests that the wheel was adopted to other uses. Heavy, wheel-shaped stones were used in the first stage of pressing olives. These were rolled over the fruit after the olives were placed in special round stone troughs, designed so the oil would drain from a carved spout. Furthermore, oxen were hitched to long poles that extended from a central rotating hub for threshing or grinding. And in the first century, giant stone wheels, set in stone tracks, were used to block the opening of hillside tombs (Mt. 27:60). *See also* Burial.

whip An instrument of punishment, consisting of a handle with a rawhide lash or lashes attached. Jesus made a whip of cords, which he used to drive money-changers from the Jerusalem Temple (Jn. 2:15).

Beatings given with a whip are called floggings or scourgings in English versions. The whip or scourge often serves as a metaphor in the OT for divine judgment (Ps. 39:10; Isa. 28:15,18). A relatively mild form of beating could be ordered as punishment by various courts: Jewish law limited the number of strokes that could be given with a whip to 39 (2 Cor. 11:23-25). Pilate intended to give Jesus such a beating and then release him (Lk. 23:14-22). But the outcry at Pilate's announcement and pressure exerted by the religious leaders forced Pilate to reverse himself and reluctantly order a severe beating and crucifixion.

Severe beatings that could lead to death were administered by whips that had metal spikes or sharp rocks woven into the cords. Beaten with this brutal type of scourge before his crucifixion, Jesus was so weakened by the loss of blood that he was unable to carry his cross (Mt. 27:26,32).

whirlwind Any violent storm that is capable of producing damage. The biblical whirlwind is not, as some suppose, a tornado or swirling motion; it is just a powerful storm. The whirlwind serves as an apt metaphor for an enemy sweeping down on an unprepared people (Isa. 5:28; Jer. 4:13). Scripture associates the whirlwind with divine judgment on sin, as in Hosea's warning to idolatrous Israel that "a whirlwind will sweep them away" (Hos. 4:19; *see* Zech. 7:14).

whore (KJV) *See* Prostitute.

wicked, wickedness Evil expressed in the harm a person does to others; criminal acts.

All sin involves some violation of divine standards. However, the words typically translated "wicked" and "wickedness" focus attention on those sinful acts that violate God's standards for the treatment of others. Among these acts are violence, oppression, fraud, theft, extortion, and dishonesty. Thus, wickedness not only causes individuals harm but distorts the very fabric of society itself.

widow A woman whose husband has died.

OLD TESTAMENT

Because widowed women were particularly vulnerable and powerless in the ancient world, the OT Law singles them out and calls for their protection. God promises to respond if a widow cries out to him; he will punish those who harm her. Citizens of Israel were to take up the cause of the widow (Deut. 10:18). Job defends his claim to be a good man partly on the basis of his favorable treatment of widows, whose eyes he never let "grow weary" and whom he aided with gifts of food and clothing (Job 31:16-20).

OT Law also made specific provision for meeting the needs of the widow through food stored in each community as Israel's third-year tithe (Deut. 24:19-21; 26:12,13) and in the other provisions made for the upkeep of the poor. *See also* Poor.

Because of the concern shown in the Mosaic Law, the psalmist celebrates God as one who "sustains the fatherless and the widow" (Ps. 146:9).

THE GOSPELS

Jesus criticized some of the Pharisees who opposed him for making a show of their piety while they devoured widows' houses (Mk. 12:40). This may have been a form of soliciting funds for their teaching services. Jesus' story of a persistent widow probably drew on the all-too-common experience of first-century women who were left alone when their husbands died (Lk. 18:1-5). Although the OT clearly calls for active intervention on the side of the widow, this may have been the exception rather than the rule in first-century Judea.

THE EARLY CHURCH

The tithes established in the OT for Israel were not applied by the young Christian church, which took shape as small groups of believers scattered through the Roman Empire. However, the concern for widows seen in the OT is also seen in the church. Acts 6 describes a new system through which the needs of Christian widows in Jerusalem were met. James, writing in that same early period, restates the OT ideal when he identifies true and undefiled religion with the care of orphans and widows (Jas. 1:27). *See also* Give.

Paul's later Epistles suggest that widows who had relatives were to be cared for by their families. But Paul also writes of a corps of widows who served as active Christian workers (1 Tim. 5:3-16; Tit. 2:3-5). Younger widows were urged to remarry, but those over 60, with a reputation for faith and effectiveness in their own homes, were enlisted in this widows' corps supported by the church. They gave their time to help and to train younger Christian women to live the faith in their homes.

wife A married woman, the spouse of a husband. Marriage and family were cen-

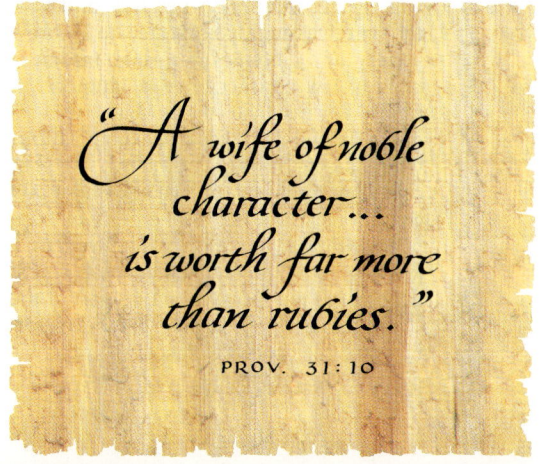

"*A wife of noble character... is worth far more than rubies.*"

PROV. 31:10

tral to the Hebrew concept of life. God had commanded Adam and Eve to be fruitful and multiply. Marriage was thus an obligation as well as a gift. *See also* Marriage.

Because marriage was assumed in Hebrew society to be the desirable state for both men and women, widows and divorcees were expected to remarry. Tradition protected the rights of the wife and guaranteed that if the wife was divorced she would receive back the dowry and other resources she brought into the marriage. These rights could be enforced in court. The husband could divorce his wife simply by writing a bill of divorce. But the wife could also demand a divorce, and, by the first century, the courts would compel him to give her the required bill. *See also* Divorce.

We gain insight into the life of the Jewish wife and mother not only from Scripture but also from early Jewish writings that discuss the rights and duties of the wife. According to the literature, the wife was responsible to grind flour, bake, launder, cook, nurse her children, make the beds, and spin wool. Married women did not shop at the market; this was one of the husband's duties. If she brought a maid-servant when she entered the marriage, her duties were lessened. Women were not responsible to help in the fields, but many wives did so voluntarily. Wives also might operate a home workshop, sell its products, and keep the income (Prov. 31:10-31).

Another major responsibility of the wife was to care for guests. As travelers expected to find lodging in a private home, this was frequently a significant task. Women were also responsible to prepare their children for school—and at times to go with them to make sure they arrived. The wife also had the privilege of "raising the shoe" in discipline, an act parallel to the father's use of the rod (Prov. 22:15).

It is true that in significant ways a wife was legally inferior to her husband. Yet the wife was highly respected in Hebrew society, and rabbinic interpretations of the biblical law granted her a number of rights. For instance, the husband was required to maintain weekly sexual relations with his wife throughout the marriage but could not force her to have sex under any conditions. He was to leave her well supplied with food and money if he went on a journey. Tradition mandated that a husband could not move from one part of the country to another without his wife's permission. Nor could a husband forbid his

wife to visit her parents, even if they lived at a distance. These and similar rulings, though they come to us from about the first century A.D., accurately reflect the deference paid to wives in Hebrew culture. The wife was a person who deserved love and respect.

A similar attitude is reflected in the NT, which urges men to "be considerate as you live with your wives, and treat them with respect as the weaker partner and as heirs with you of the gracious gift of life" (1 Pet. 3:7). The ideal wife of the NT, who lived in a society that encouraged no other occupation for women than homemaker, is pictured in Tit. 2:4,5. Good wives "love their husbands and children," are "self-controlled and pure," remain busy at home, are kind, and are subject to their husbands.

wilderness Any desolate and unpopulated or sparsely populated area.

Several Hebrew words are found where English versions have "wilderness." *Midbar* is unsettled land, ranging from grasslands suitable as cattle range to empty desert. Such lands are generally dangerous, for an individual must face wild animals or hostile nomadic tribesmen without community support. The Greek *erēmos* has the same general meaning. Other words emphasize the arid nature of deserts containing little but rocks and burning sand.

The most significant "wilderness" mentioned in Scripture is the desolate land of the Sinai peninsula where Israel was forced to wander for some 38 years during the Exodus. *See also* Desert; Exodus.

will (1) A legal document appointing a person one's heir (Gal. 3:15). According to

Greek custom such a document could not be revoked once it had been ratified. (2) A legal document directing the disposal of a person's estate, to take effect only after his death (Heb. 9:16,17). (3) The voluntary desire or active choice of a living person, either human or God. Broadly conceived, the will indicates the power of choice and deliberate action, or the intention that is expressed in taking an action.

MAN'S VOLITION

In the OT, human will is expressed as intentional action by a variety of verbs: "to choose," "to love," "to desire," "to determine," etc. But biblical Hebrew makes no effort to distinguish will from intellect, feeling, or emotion as we today analyze personality. "Will" was an objective reality of action, not an analysis of inner thought. The NT reflects the same perspective; two Greek verbs express choice and inclination, intention and fixed purpose.

Scripture presents human beings as responsible agents who deliberate, choose, and act, and who can respond to the revealed will of God.

GOD'S WILL

Given the flexibility of the terms used in Scripture to express desire and choice, the concept of the "will of God" is quite complex. Among distinguishable meanings are:

1. *The will of God is his revealed expectation for human moral behavior.* In this sense, the will of God is expressed in the standards impressed on human nature itself, but more specifically found in biblical revelation (Acts 20:27). Human beings are to respond to this revelation of God's will by choosing to obey it (Mt. 7:21; Jn. 7:17).

2. *The will of God is an expression of his*

Stele with relief of two men settling a contract (Ras Shamra, 1300–1100 B.C.).

desires for humanity and especially for believers. God does not want anyone to perish (2 Pet. 3:9), even though the Bible clearly teaches that some persons will. God wants believers to be holy (1 Th. 4:3), although some will resist and go their own way. This weaker use of "God's will" does not suggest that he is unable to do what he wishes, but that God has chosen to give human beings freedom, even though the choices they make may hurt them and him deeply. When Christians understand what God wants for his human family, they will be able to pray according to God's will and thus in harmony with his purposes (1 Jn. 5:14).

3. *The will of God is his sovereign determi-*

Gorge at Ein Avdat in the Wilderness of Zin, part of the Negev Desert. The Israelites traveled through this region several times during their wandering.

nation of events, his absolute choice of what surely will come to pass. Among those things that God is said to have absolutely determined: that he will grant new birth to those who believe (Jn. 1:13; 1 Pet. 1:23); that all who believe will have eternal life (Jn. 6:38-40); that Jesus would die a sacrificial death to win man's salvation (Acts 4:28); that human beings who believe will be rescued from this present evil age by Jesus (Gal. 1:4); and that each member of the Godhead would have a distinct part in planning and carrying out Christ's rescue mission (Eph. 1:3-14).

4. *The will of God is his plan for each believer's life, or the divine control over the believer's personal destiny* (Rom. 8:28-39; *see* Mt. 26:39; Lk. 22:42). In this sense the will of God is something that believers are to discern as they live their lives day by day, experiencing the guidance of the Holy Spirit.

Each of these aspects of God's will calls for an appropriate response from human beings. As we learn his expectations for human behavior from the Scriptures, we are to accept them as standards to live by. As we read the Bible and discern God's values and desires, we are to let them shape both us and our prayers. As we discover God's purposes in Christ, we are to respond with trust. And as we realize that God has a plan for our individual lives, we should actively seek the guidance of his Holy Spirit. In each of these ways, we acknowledge God for who he is and confess that we can find fulfillment not in demanding our own way but in doing his

"Beside the streams of Babylon we sat and wept at the memory of Zion. On the willows there, we hung our harps" (Ps. 137:1,2 JB).

The prevailing wind came off the Mediterranean in winter and from the desert in the summer. But even in summertime, a breeze from the west often moderated the midday heat and left a heavy dew at night.

will. *See also* Guide; Holy Spirit; Lead; Predestine.

willow A tree or shrub of the genus *Salix*, which have flexible twigs and long narrow leaves and which grow along streams and lakes. The specific species of willow in-

tended by the Hebrew *'ereb* is uncertain. The "fresh thongs" with which Samson was bound by Delilah were probably willow branches, although the NIV takes them as bowstrings (Jdg. 16:7).

wind Stirring of the air, whether by nature or breath. Winds are a natural phenomenon associated with storms.

THE WIND AND ISRAEL'S CLIMATE
Winds played an important part in determining weather conditions in ancient as in modern Israel. The north wind is cool and invigorating, blowing over Palestine primarily in June and October. Then, the wind swings to the northwest in November, bringing winter rains (Prov. 25:23).

Spring winds from the south are hot and include the oven-like sirocco that sweeps in from the desert. Jesus quoted the common wisdom in Lk. 12:54,55 when he said to the crowd, "When you see a cloud rising in the west, immediately you say, 'It's going to rain,' and it does. And when the south wind blows, you say, 'It's going to be hot,' and it is."

Westerly winds in Palestine carry moisture from the Mediterranean. Winds generally blow from some quarter of the west from November to February, and bring the moisture needed to grow crops.

MEDITERRANEAN SEA

SEA OF GALILEE

NORTHWEST *Winter Rains* PROV. 25:23

NORTH *Cool Wind* JOB 37:21,22

WEST *Winter Showers* (NOV.-FEB.) 1 KI. 18:44 LK. 12:54

Jerusalem

DEAD SEA

EAST *Desert Winds Hot, Violent* (FEB.-JUNE) HOS. 13:15 JOB 1:19

SOUTH *Hot, Dry* (SUMMER) LK. 12:55 ISA. 21:1

East winds pass over the desert and are spoken of in Scripture as "scorching" (Jon. 4:8), making vegetation shrivel (Ezek. 19:12). These violent east winds blow intermittently in Palestine from February to July.

WINDS IN FIGURES OF SPEECH

Winds served as symbols of mystery and of the brevity of human life. In a powerful metaphor, Solomon complains that all man's efforts to discover meaning in life are futile, "a chasing after the wind" (Eccl. 2:11,17). Men themselves are like chaff or smoke, so fragile that a wind can blow them away (Pss. 1:4; 18:42; 68:2). God controls the winds (Pss. 78:26; 104:4), but human beings have no knowledge of where winds come from or where they go (Eccl. 1:6; Jn. 3:8). Against this background Jesus' power over the stormy winds that whipped up deadly waves on the Sea of Galilee totally astounded his disciples (Mk. 4:41).

The word for spirit in both Hebrew (*ruah*) and Greek (*pneuma*) also means "wind." Thus Jesus was punning with Nicodemus when he said that spiritual birth was just as mysterious as the origin of wind (Jn. 3:5-8). And it is appropriate that the Holy Spirit came on the disciples at Pentecost with "a sound like the blowing of a violent wind" (Acts 2:2).

window An opening in a building that lets in light and air.

Most houses in Palestine were of one or two stories, constructed of rock or mud bricks. Window spaces could be left in their walls, but there was no good material to use to fill these spaces. By the first century A.D., glass was available and also flat sheets of translucent stone. But the high cost made these options only for the affluent.

In most houses, windows were few and tended to be small. This was not too great a burden, however, as most daylight and evening hours were spent outside in the common courtyard shared with other families or on the flat roof of the home.

Some homes did have larger windows. These were closed off during the winter, but during the summer, one could sit on the wide clay window sill and enjoy the late afternoon breeze. Eutychus, a young man listening to Paul speak, dozed off on one of these broad window seats and fell out the window to his death—and resuscitation (Acts 20:9-12). Typically, larger windows were fitted with wooden lattices, for protection against burglars.

The KJV image of God throwing open the windows of heaven to pour out blessings (Mal. 3:10) actually portrays opening sluice-gates, an image drawn from irrigation.

wine Fermented grape juice. Wine was an important product in Israel, and it was served at celebrations (2 Chr. 2:10,15; Ezek. 27:18).

OLD TESTAMENT

Yayin is the common Hebrew word for wine. *Tirosh* is new wine, not an unfermented drink but one made from the first squeezings of the grapes. The OT associates wine with divine blessing and celebration (Deut. 7:13; 11:14; Jdg. 9:13; Ps. 104:15; Isa. 24:9; Amos 9:13,14). Worshipers at the tabernacle and later the Temple offered

Left: In Egypt's Old Empire, wine was wrung out of sacks that were twisted as far as was possible. Later, wine was made by treading the grapes.
Below: Egyptian laborers harvesting and treading grapes for winemaking; detail of a wall painting from the tomb of Nakht at Thebes (about 1420 B.C.).

wine to God (Ex. 29:40; Lev. 23:13; Num. 15:7). At the same time, the OT contains many warnings against the misuse of wine (Prov. 20:1; 21:17; 23:31-35; Isa. 5:11; Hab. 2:5). It sternly condemns drunkenness and associated sins.

Seven to ten percent alcohol, wines of biblical times were frequently mixed with spices or herbs. Rabbinical writers identify several ways in which wines were mixed, one of which featured honey and pepper. These mixed wines were more intoxicating than ordinary wine (Prov. 9:2,5).

The alcohol content of wine made it useful as an antiseptic when poured on injuries (Lk. 10:34), as a sedative for the distressed (Prov. 31:6), as a stimulant for the faint (2 Sam. 16:2), and to deaden pain when mixed with gall (Mt. 27:34; Mk. 15:23).

NEW TESTAMENT

Paul recommended that Timothy drink wine for medicinal purposes (1 Tim. 5:23), and Jesus gave his blessing to its celebratory use by turning water into wine at a wedding in Galilee (Jn. 2:1-10; *see* Mt. 11: 18,19). At the Passover meal which Christians call the Last Supper, Jesus used a cup of wine to establish the memorial celebration of his self-sacrifice on the cross (Mt. 26:27-29; Lk. 22:20). However, because ancient writers always describe wine being diluted by two to ten parts water to each part of wine, it is likely that the wine drunk by the average person was diluted too.

The NT is negative toward excessive drinking. Wine is never forbidden, but drunkenness is condemned as pagan (Eph. 5:18; 1 Pet. 4:3). Those considered for Christian leadership must "not [be] given to drunkenness" (1 Tim. 3:3; Tit. 1:7). Paul calls on Christians to expect the Holy Spirit to lift their life out of the ordinary, so they will have no need for the artificial "high" produced by wine and other alcoholic drinks (Eph. 5:18). *See also* Drunkenness; Strong Drink.

winepress A stone vat in which the juice of grapes is pressed. Each vineyard typi-

Right: Juice collection vat or pit (Mark 12:1), in which any remaining grape skins would sink to the bottom. The new wine could then be scooped out and poured into clay jars or skins for further fermentation. Below: Treading or "pressing" grapes; scene from a Byzantine mosaic floor from Beth Shan, Israel. The grape harvest was a time of special joy, accompanied with singing and shouting (Isa. 16:10; Jer. 48:33).

cally had its winepress, in the form of a square basin. Grapes were heaped up in the winepress and then crushed by men and women who leaped and danced on the crop (Jer. 48:33). The juices flowed out of the vat and were collected in clay jars or new wineskins.

The flood of red juices serves as an image of divine judgment (Isa. 63:2,3; Joel 3:13). In the last book of the NT, Christ is portrayed in his return as treading "the winepress of the fury of the wrath of God Almighty" (Rev. 19:15).

wineskin A bag containing wine, and usually made from the treated skin of a goat. Wineskins were made from whole, tanned animal hides with the openings sewn shut.

Jesus' comment that "no one pours new wine into old wineskins" reflects the well-known fact that old skins would burst under the pressure created by fermentation (Mt. 9:17; Mk. 2:22; Lk. 5:37,38). Jesus' point was that the fresh revelation he brought Israel from God was not intended to fit the framework of OT faith. Christ's comment in Luke, "No one after drinking old wine wants the new" (5:39), reflects the thought that new wine must have time to ferment and develop its own unique character before its worth can be told. Thus, his listeners should not make a hasty judgment in favor of Judaism, but withhold judgment until the nature of Christ's revelation is made clear.

wing The feathered forelimb of a bird. The flight of birds has always attracted man and at times evoked envy. In Scripture, wings frequently signify freedom and strength. Thus, the distraught psalmist sighs, "Oh, that I had the wings of a dove! I would fly away and be at rest" (Ps. 55:6). And Isaiah promises that those who hope in the Lord will find renewed strength and will "soar on wings like eagles" (Isa. 40:31).

At times, wings symbolize safety and comfort. Ruth chose to be sheltered under the wings of the God of Israel (Ruth 2:12; see Ps. 17:8), and Jesus wept over a Jerusalem unwilling to do so (Mt. 23:37).

In the ancient world, wings are also identified with power or holiness. Many monuments from Assyria and Babylon feature carved winged lions. In Daniel's vision of world powers, one kingdom was represented by a lion with wings (Dan. 7:4). Furthermore, biblical cherubim and seraphim, who stand before the throne of God and cry "Holy, Holy, Holy," are also described as winged beings (Isa. 6:2; Ezek. 10:5-14).

Egyptian laborers winnow wheat by tossing it into the air with wooden scoops.

winnow The process of separating grain from chaff. *See also* Chaff; Thresh.

wisdom The ability to discern right choices. While the ability to make wise choices depends on possession of relevant knowledge, wisdom in Scripture refers to the distinct mental process of weighing and judging alternatives.

OLD TESTAMENT
The OT presents wisdom as a practical matter, hailing the skill of artists (Ex. 36:1-4) and even suggesting that wisdom includes financial savvy (Prov. 8:18). However, wisdom's primary focus is moral. A reverential awe of God and respect for his Word is the foundation of biblical wisdom (Prov. 1:7; 2:6). A person who approaches each decision in life with a trust in the Lord and who acknowledges God rather than leaning on his own understanding is wise. "You will understand what is right and just and fair—every good path," says Proverbs. "Wisdom will save you from the ways of wicked men, from men whose words are perverse" (Prov. 2:9,12).

WISDOM LITERATURE
Job, Proverbs, Ecclesiastes, and several psalms (19,37,104,107,147,148) are known as "wisdom literature." These give practical advice, making observations on wise and foolish choices human beings make.

NEW TESTAMENT
In the Greek world, "wisdom" was related to philosophical speculation. Not so in the NT, which portrays the world's "wisdom" as of less value than the "foolishness" of God (1 Cor. 1–3). Paul points out that man is naturally unable to grasp spiritual realities. Human beings must rely on revelation for true understanding.

Paul reinforces the OT emphasis on wisdom as the application of God's revelation to life rather than mere knowledge. Only by applying our knowledge of what God has willed "through all spiritual wisdom and understanding" will Christians be able to "live a life worthy of the Lord and . . . please him in every way" (Col. 1:9,10).

While the OT frequently portrays wisdom in terms of contrasting actions, James describes its qualities. The wisdom that comes from above is "pure; then peace-loving, considerate, submissive, full of mercy and good fruit, impartial and sincere" (Jas. 3:17). The person who displays these qualities in every situation is both godly and wise.

wise men The "wise men" of the nativity story are called *magoi*, a term borrowed from Persian. That the wise men were "from the east" (Mt. 2:1) indicates they were probably members of a scholarly class that had existed in Mesopotamia from before the time of Daniel. The legend that says there were three wise men— kings with specific names—has no historical foundation. *See also* Magi.

witch (KJV) A person supposed to have the ability to manipulate evil powers by magic. The "witch of Endor" (1 Sam. 28) was a medium who claimed contact with the spirit world. Witchcraft, with other occult practices, is condemned in both OT (Deut. 18:9-12) and NT (Gal. 5:19-21). *See also* Magic; Medium; Occult.

Bill of sale for a house in Mesopotamia. A list of witnesses makes up the last three lines (about 2550 B.C.). Genesis 23 records the sale of the cave of Machpelah to Abraham in front of many witnesses.

witness (1) A person who gives testimony concerning something about which he has personal knowledge (Deut. 19:15; Acts 1:8). (2) An object that serves as a memorial of some significant event. This might be a stone pillar (Gen. 31:44-52), the Law itself (Deut. 31:26), or an altar (Josh. 22:26-34; Isa. 19:19,20).

Early commercial transactions were conducted in front of witnesses who could testify later to any conditions (Gen. 23; Ruth 4:9). Later, written contracts served this purpose (Jer. 32:11,12).

The OT Law required the testimony of two or more witnesses before a defendant in a capital case could be convicted (Num. 35:30; Deut. 19:15; 1 Ki. 21:10,13). This principle undoubtedly applied in other cases as well (Mt. 18:16). More importantly, OT Law obligated anyone who witnessed a serious crime to come forward with his information and take the role of a prosecutor (Lev. 24:11; Num. 15:33; Deut. 13:6-11). That requirement is significant, for God, as a witness to man's acts, must thus take the role of prosecutor of human beings for their sins (Jer. 29:23; Mic. 1:2; Mal. 2:14).

The Law is very strict with false witnesses and wrongful accusations. If a witness's testimony is found to be false, he is to pay the penalty that would have been inflicted on the defendant (Ex. 20:16; Deut. 5:20; 19:16-21).

witness of the Spirit The active testimony given by the Holy Spirit within a human personality, authenticating the Gospel message about Jesus and related truths. John 15:26,27 describes this ministry of the Holy Spirit: "When the Counselor comes, whom I will send to you from the Father, the Spirit of truth who goes out from the Father, he will testify about me. And you also must testify." (*See also* Jn. 14:26; 16:7-15; 1 Jn. 2:20-22.)

This phrase can also refer to the Spirit testifying to the believer that he or she is indeed born of God (Rom. 8:16).

wizard (KJV) A person who practices magic, sorcery, or engages in other occult practices. *See also* Magic.

woe Grief, sorrow, or an exclamation expressing grief or announcing judgment. Jesus uttered such a cry when denouncing Korazin and Bethsaida (Mt. 11:21), the rich (Lk. 6:24-26), the religious leaders who opposed him (Lk. 11:42-52), and his betrayer, Judas (Mk. 14:21). *See also* Curse.

wolf A large, flesh-eating, dog-like animal.

Wolves in Bible lands grew to a length of some 4 feet (1.2 meters) and weighed up to 100 pounds (45.3 kilograms). While not mentioned in any narrative passage of

"Beware of false prophets, which come to you in sheep's clothing, but inwardly they are ravenous wolves" (Mt. 7:15 RSV). Two terracotta wolves tear at a ram (Boeotia, 6th century B.C.).

OT or NT, the wolf is referred to metaphorically. Jesus viewed false prophets as savage wolves dressed in sheep's clothing, outwardly harmless but capable of tearing their prey apart (Mt. 7:15). Isaiah speaks of God's coming rule as a peaceable kingdom, in which "the wolf will live with the lamb" (Isa. 11:6; *see* 65:25). Even the wolf's violent nature will change.

woman A female human being.

OLD TESTAMENT

The creation story establishes Scripture's perception that men and women are partners in personhood. Each is created in the image of God; together they share dominion over the earth (Gen. 1:27,28). The formation of Eve from Adam's rib (or "side") symbolizes this identity, as expressed in Adam's exclamation that Eve was "bone of my bones and flesh of my flesh" (Gen. 2:23). Eve's identification as a "suitable helper ['*ezer*]" for Adam (Gen. 2:18,20) does not imply inferiority, for God himself is called the believer's help (*'ezer*) in Ps. 33:20.

1. *Women in the social order*. According to Gen. 3:16, one consequence of sin for the woman was that her "desire will be for [her] husband, and he will rule over [her]." This prediction of hierarchy in the social order is reflected in the structure of nations, of the family, and of women's role in society. Yet tension exists throughout the OT between the ideal of equality in creation and women's role in the social order.

On the one hand, a woman's legal position under OT Law was definitely weaker than a man's. A jealous man might insist that his wife take a test for faithfulness (Num. 5:11-31), but there is no similar test for husbands; polygamy was permitted. The husband could write a bill of divorce and put away his wife (Deut. 24:1-4). A husband or father could cancel a wife or daughter's vow (Num. 30:1-15). A daughter sold into servitude by her father (Ex. 21:7) was not freed in six years, as a male would be (Lev. 25:40). When dedicated to God, a woman's value was set at about half the value of a man the same age (Lev. 27:1-8). *See also* Divorce; Marriage; Vow; Wife.

The patriarchal character of Hebrew society is shown in many other ways as well. Property was inherited by males. Men were required to attend three annual festivals; women could attend but were not required to. The father presented sacrifices and offerings on behalf of the family, except for the sacrifice a woman offered after the birth of a child (Lev. 12:6). Women alone, as shown in the many laws intended to protect widows and orphans, were socially powerless and thus had to be given special consideration and protection.

In Israel's culture, women prepared and cooked the food, carried water, made clothing, worked with the men at harvest time, and trained their daughters to do "women's work."

Yet despite women's weaker position in

the social order, the OT still reflects something of the basic sense of shared identity with men as persons. Sons in the family were not higher than their mother; children were to treat their mother with respect equal to that given the father (Ex. 20:12; Deut. 21:18-21). In the case of adultery, both male and female were to be stoned (Deut. 22:22). In the case of secluded rape, the rapist was to be executed (Deut. 22:23-27). When no male heir sur-

Figurine of two female musicians, terracotta with residue of pink paint (Syria, second century A.D.).

vived, women could inherit property. In these and many other ways, women were given greater respect in Hebrew society than in other ancient cultures.

The cultures of the Egyptians, Philistines, Babylonians, and others generally put women in a degraded role. Often, women were treated as property of their husbands—like his slaves or herds. By contrast, a distinctive sense of the value of women pervades the Hebrew Scriptures.

2. *Personhood in family and society.* The creation account establishes the identity of men and women as persons. The story of the Fall places women in the weaker position in a hierarchical society dominated by men. Male domination is seen in male roles in the family, in the selection of only males to serve as priests, and in the predominance of male leaders in political and religious affairs. It is important, however, to note that within this structure women had abundant opportunity to find fulfill-

ment through the full exercise of every human capacity.

The clearest example of this in terms of the home is found in Prov. 31:10-31. The wife supervised a staff of workers (vv. 15,27). She was the buyer of resources for her many enterprises (v. 13). She sold what her household produced (vv. 18,24) and invested her profits (v. 16). She gave to the needy (v. 20) and was respected for her wisdom (vv. 26-31). In essence, she conducted "business," just as men did.

It is also noteworthy that women were not automatically disqualified by their sex from political or spiritual leadership. While leadership roles were generally filled by men in Israel's patriarchal society, the gifts of exceptional women were recognized. Deborah was both a political and religious leader (Jdg. 4). She, with Miriam (Ex. 15:20), Isaiah's wife (Isa. 8:3), and others were recognized as prophets. Both Sarah and Rahab are honored in Heb. 11 as models of OT faith.

It is undoubtedly true that women had a less significant role than men in the OT social order. But it is also true that the OT affirms the personhood of women and that women had both more honor and more opportunity in Israel than in other ancient societies.

NEW TESTAMENT
To what extent has Christ restored fallen humanity? How is restoration in Christ to be expressed in the shared life of the Christian community? Particularly, does it make a difference in how men and women relate to each other in the church?

1. *Jesus and women in the Gospels.* A Jewish woman's religious role in the first century A.D. was undoubtedly limited. Only men could receive advanced training in the Scripture and hope for recognition as rabbis. Only men could be counted to reach the quorum necessary to start a synagogue. Men and women were seated apart in the synagogue, and women were expected to be silent during religious services.

Against this background, several of the things Jesus did were stunning. He welcomed women as learners (Lk. 10:38-42). Apparently, several women even traveled with Jesus and the disciples (Lk. 8:1-3). Jesus is often pictured in the Gospels talking with women, commending their faith, and using them in illustrations. In all this, Christ displays a most unusual and open attitude toward women.

2. *The early church and women.* The openness Christ displayed to women is re-

flected in the activities of the early church. Women were among the disciples gathered in the upper room when all were filled by the Spirit (Acts 1:14; 2:1). Both men and women in the early church were persecuted for their faith (Acts 8:3; 9:2); both shared their faith in Christ with others when persecution drove the Christians from Jerusalem (Acts 8:1,4). Women participated in the prayer meeting held for Peter (Acts 12:1-17) and in open church meetings (1 Cor. 11:2-16). Women served as prophets (Acts 2:17; 21:9; 1 Cor. 11:2-16). Phoebe was a deacon of the church at Cenchrea (Rom. 16:1,2). Priscilla was an active partner in Christian work with her husband and is given priority when the pair is named (Acts 18:26). Euodia and Syntyche were "women who have contended at my [Paul's] side in the cause of the gospel, along with Clement and the rest of my fellow workers" (Phil. 4:3). Together these and other references to women in the NT suggest active participation by women in the life of the early church.

In fact, this participation more or less fits the changing role of women in the Greco-Roman city of the first century. The ruins of Pompeii (A.D. 79) attest that women ran estates and businesses of every kind (see Acts 16:14). Women were members of men's clubs. As many as five to ten percent of the patrons, who endowed such clubs or met their expenses, were women. A study of Judaism in western Asia Minor under the Romans shows that inscriptions ranging from the first century B.C. to the sixth century A.D. refer to women with such titles as "head of the synagogue," "leader," "elder," or "mother of the synagogue." These suggest that, outside of Judea in the urban culture of the Hellenistic world, Jewish women served in leadership roles that may not have been permitted in Judea itself.

Certainly the NT portrait of women active in the young church fits the emerging picture of women active in first-century urban society.

3. *Passages that restrict women's role in the church.* Two key NT texts restrict the activity of women in the church assembly. These passages are the focus of much debate in contemporary Christianity.

(1) 1 Cor. 14:34,35—Women are to "remain silent in the churches" and "are not allowed to speak." The passage should be interpreted narrowly, since 1 Cor. 11:5 specifically speaks of women both praying and prophesying in the church. Thus, the

interpretive key must be the context in 1 Cor. 14. That context (vv. 26-40) has to do with weighing statements made by members as prophetic revelations. In context, it seems that Paul is saying that women are not to participate in the process of weighing the utterances of prophets.

(2) 1 Tim. 2:11-15—"A woman should learn in quietness and full submission. I do not permit a woman to teach or to have authority over a man; she must be silent." Paul explains this by referring to the creation order (Eve was made second) and to the Fall (she sinned first).

"Quietness" and "silence" in 1 Timothy both translate *hēsychia*. It suggests attentiveness and receptiveness. The link between "teach" and "have authority" should probably be taken together to mean "authoritative teaching." According to Paul, this role is not compatible with the woman's role of *hēsychia*, attentive listening and learning. Paul shows a sensitivity to Greco-Roman culture, in which the authority of a tutor or guardian-teacher was a distinctively male role. In contrast, Greco-Roman society had no such restrictions on women prophets, so that their participation in Christian worship would not have caused offense (see 1 Cor. 11:2-16).

If this interpretation of these two passages is accurate, the restrictions on women's role in the church are minor. They are kept only from determining the church's authoritative teaching or evaluating the utterances of prophets.

TODAY'S CHURCH

A tension persists in understanding the role of women in the modern church. Surely both creation and the redemption

Above: Clay figurine of a woman holding a round object (9th–7th centuries B.C.). Above left: Head of a woman with an Egyptian hairdo (1550–1200 B.C.).

Four maidservants assist a lady in her adornment (second–third centuries A.D.).

won by Christ testify to a full equality of women and men as persons. Building on this reality, Christian leaders like the Wesleys and General Booth of The Salvation Army opened every role in church leadership to women.

Others, concerned about the NT passages that limit women's roles, even though the area of limitation is narrow, have retained the hierarchical approach reflected in the OT social order and applied it to Christian family and church leadership.

Whatever position a person may take, and there are many between these extremes, it should be clear that neither OT nor NT supports male authoritarianism. The NT especially challenges us to make opportunities in home, church, and society for women to exercise every gift and capacity that they have been given by God.

womb The uterus, that place in a woman's body which holds and protects a developing fetus.

Various OT passages depict the womb as the place in which the individual is formed and portray God watching over the developmental process. Thus, the psalmist says to God, "You created my inmost being; you knit me together in my mother's womb," and identifies this shaping of the fetus as one of God's "wonderful" works (Ps. 139:13,14). Jeremiah adds his testimony, recounting God's words to him: "Before I formed you in the womb I knew you, before you were born I set you apart" (Jer. 1:5). Luke reports that the unborn John the Baptist "leaped" in his mother Elizabeth's womb at the sound of Mary's voice (Lk. 1:44).

The biblical language is in fullest harmony with modern medical science, which has shown that the chromosome pattern of the unborn child is distinctly and uniquely his or hers from the moment of conception. That Scripture portrays God as actively and intimately involved in the formation of the unborn individual underlines the sanctity of every life, before and after birth.

wool The fleece of sheep and the fabric made from it. Treated wool is white and serves as a symbol of purity in Isa. 1:18 (*see* Ps. 147:16).

word (1) Ordinary speech or talk. (2) Theologically, an identification—"the word of the Lord"—a particular message as a divine revelation (Ps. 18:30). (3) The active expression of God's will exercised in creation (Ps. 33:4-11). (4) A name—"the Word"—ascribed to Christ as pre-existent deity (Jn. 1:1,14).

The phrase "the word of the Lord" and similar expressions occur hundreds of times in the OT. In each case, the formula expresses the conviction of the biblical writer that God is the source of the message the writer brings. This OT word from God established the moral order of the universe and gave human beings guidance for their everyday lives. The same word from God revealed Israel's identity as a covenant people and unveiled God's plans for the future.

Two different Greek words are translated "word" in the NT. *Rhēma*, found only 70 times, is used of specific utterances (Mt. 4:4). *Logos*, found over 300 times, has commonplace meanings in the NT, such as "speech," "book," "treatise," or even "subject matter." But *logos* is also a powerful theological term, picking up the OT sense of the revelatory word (Lk. 3:2). *Logos* also expresses the active presence of God, as in the transforming "word" that Jesus spoke to heal the sick and drive out demons. In Acts and the Epistles, *logos* serves as a synonym for the Gospel itself, summing up the meaning of Christ (Acts 6:7; Eph. 1:13). In this and other uses, the NT views the "word" as an active, living expression of God's presence with his people and in the world. Thus, the written Word is both objective and subjective, historical and existential. In the Word, the believer not only hears about God, but meets him.

John begins his Gospel with the affirmation that the *logos* was God and was with God from eternity, and that Jesus is this *logos* made flesh (Jn. 1:1,14). The use of *logos* may have several roots. John may have purposed to ground a contemporary

belief in the logical order of the universe, which was perceived in Greek philosophy, in the existence of a personal God. More likely his metaphor served as a bridge to Hellenistic culture for the personification of wisdom (Prov. 8; *compare* Wisdom of Solomon 9; Mt. 11:28-30) or to personalize the OT's concept of the "word of God." Jesus the living Word becomes the place of meeting, where God's hidden glory is unveiled and the Father becomes known. Jesus is the ultimate revelation of God (*see* Heb. 1:1-3) and the living "bridge" between God and human beings (Jn. 14:6; 1 Tim. 2:5).

Balls of wool with knitting needles from Egypt (14th century B.C.).

work Effort exerted in some purposeful activity; one's occupation. God is portrayed

Assyrian workmen carrying picks and shovels in a relief from Sennacherib's palace at Nineveh (about 690 B.C.). The wise author of Ecclesiastes writes, "That everyone may eat and drink, and find satisfaction in all his work—this is the gift of God" (Eccles. 3:13).

in Gen. 1 doing work and finding satisfaction in his work. God gave Adam meaningful work to do before the Fall (Gen. 2:15), and the NT calls on each Christian to work to earn his own living (2 Th. 3:10).

OLD TESTAMENT

Different Hebrew words explore various aspects of human labor. One set of words (especially *'abad*) portrays work as accomplishment that brings satisfaction or as significant service. Such work generally earns an appropriate reward and is fulfilling for the person who does it.

Another set of words views work as a consequence of the Fall. Part of God's curse on sin was that men would be forced to win their living by "painful toil" (Gen. 3:17). Several words (especially *yaga'*) describe forced or futile labor, which wearies the one who toils without bringing commensurate reward.

The NT also has different words for work. The most common (*ergon*) indicates business and achievement. *Kopos*, though, is toil, hard work—Paul describes his ministry as such a labor (1 Th. 2:9). Elsewhere he insists that Christians "must work" (*kopiatō*) to support themselves and have something to share with others (Eph. 4:28).

Paul chose, for the sake of the churches, to support himself by tentmaking on many of his missionary ventures because he did

not want to make himself a burden (1 Cor. 9:1-14; 2 Cor. 11:7-9). Like Paul, believers are expected to work hard, to meet their own needs, and to help those less fortunate (2 Th. 3:6-15).

works, good Moral or righteous acts performed by human beings. The NT makes it clear that no acts performed by humans merit God's favor. Salvation cannot be earned but must be received as a gift. Thus, Paul writes in Eph. 2:8,9, "It is by grace you have been saved, through faith —and this not from yourselves, it is the gift of God—not by works, so that no one can boast."

At the same time, the NT insists that those who have received Christ as Savior are to be people "zealous" for good works (Tit. 2:14 KJV). Paul concludes his Ephesians statement about grace with this balancing comment: Those who have received God's grace are "God's workmanship, created in Christ Jesus to do good works, which God prepared in advance for us to do" (Eph. 2:10).

Moral and righteous acts are never a way to earn salvation, but they are fruit that salvation is expected to produce (Jas. 2:14-26). *See also* Righteous.

works of God (1) Deeds performed by God, especially his intervening on behalf of human beings (Jdg. 2:7,10) or in judgment (Isa. 5:16-30). (2) Things made by God (Ps. 145:4).

world (1) The earth (Isa. 23:17; Rev. 13:3); (2) the current age; (3) the collective population of earth; (4) the structure and order of society.

This fourth meaning comes through in the NT use of *kosmos* (some 200 times). Though it can mean the whole creation, the earth as man's habitation, or all humanity, it has a special theological meaning developed by Paul and especially by John. *Kosmos* views human society as an interwoven system created by a web of sinful human desires, illusory beliefs, and surging passions. As such, the world is a dark place (Eph. 6:12). It is under the control of Satan (1 Jn. 5:19), and it operates on principles that are contrary to those of God (Col. 2:20; 1 Jn. 2:16; *see* 1 Cor. 2:12; 3:19; 11:32; Eph. 2:2; Jas. 1:27; 4:4; 1 Jn. 2:15-17).

worldly Partaking in the values, desires, perceptions, attitudes, and behavior that characterize unredeemed human cultures.

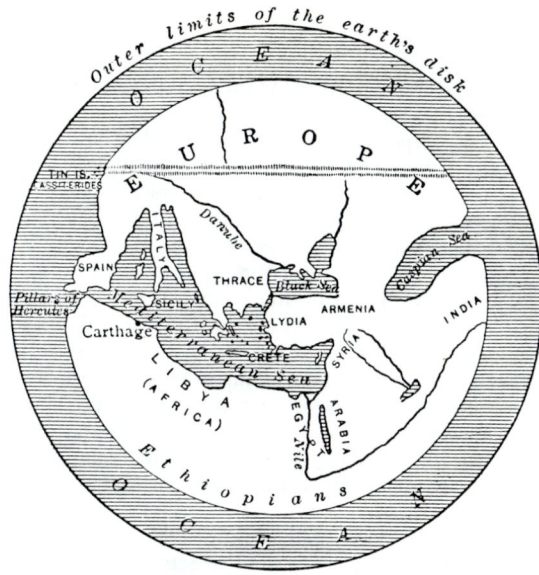

Above: Map of the world by Hecataeus, about 517 B.C. Place names were translated into English in the past century.
Right: Depiction of the world at the time of Sargon of Agade (about 2300 B.C.) on a tablet from the 7th century B.C. Babylon is at the center of a circular world surrounded by water.

The worldly person is one who is squeezed into the mold of the *kosmos*, in contrast to one whose whole world view has been transformed by God (Rom. 12:2). Worldliness is not necessarily a matter of participating in questionable activities or adopting certain styles of dress or appearance, as some Christians in every generation have supposed. It is rather the acceptance of the values and assumptions of a society that has no place for God. *See also* World.

wormwood A shrub-like plant of the aster family, noted for its bitterness. Wormwood, called "gall" in many modern versions, stands as a metaphor in the OT for extreme sorrow (Prov. 5:4; Lam. 3:19,20; Amos 5:7) and for divine judgment (Jer. 9:15). In Rev. 8:11, "Wormwood" is the symbolic name of a star that falls and kills millions by poisoning earth's waters.

worry *See* Anxiety.

worship That attitude and those corporate and personal acts of reverence that are the appropriate response of human beings to God's self-revelation.

OLD TESTAMENT
The OT shows people responding to God in many ways. The ancient Israelite showed his reverence for God by giving thanks, by praising, by making required and voluntary donations, by maintaining ritual purity, and by obeying the Law's moral precepts, as well as by taking part in the worship rituals established in the Law.

Specific acts of worship in OT times can be categorized as corporate ritual, corporate nonritual, individual ritual, and individual nonritual.

1. *Corporate ritual worship.* This originally took place at the tabernacle and later the Temple. The system of sacrifices and offerings and the annual festivals and fasts were all part of the corporate worship of Israel. Corporate worship revolved around both family and community. The family met as a unit for the Passover meal and together lived outdoors in rude lean-tos during the Feast of Tabernacles. The family also shared the meat of several of the sacrifices offered by the father and in that act met at God's table as his guests. Three times a year, all adult men met at Israel's worship center to celebrate the Lord together. There the prescribed rituals were performed, with shared sorrow on the Day of Atonement and with shared shouts of joy at other festivals. With the ritual, there were prayers (Num. 6:24-26) and (later) choral and instrumental music

(1 Chr. 16:4-6). *See also* Feasts, Festivals, and Fasts.

While God ordained the ritual by which he was to be worshiped—and that ritual was to be performed exactly as he ordained—corporate ritual worship was unacceptable unless it was a true expression of the community's heart for God. This was demonstrated not through the ritual, but by committing oneself to the moral and ethical precepts in Israel's Law (Ps. 50:12-15; Isa. 1:11-17; Amos 5:21-24). A true heart for God was also expressed in the worshiper's joy. Many of the psalms chanted or sung in public worship capture the sense of joy the true believer found in his or her relationship with the Lord. This is perhaps best exemplified by David, who leaped and danced before the Lord "with all his might" as he led the procession bringing the ark of God to Jerusalem (2 Sam. 6:14-16). The contrary attitude is exemplified by the people of Malachi's day, who found ritual worship a "burden" (Mal. 1:13).

Ritual worship in Israel, then, was never intended to deteriorate into ritualism. It was a way for faithful generations to express their appreciation to God for himself

Worshiping figure from Larsa, Mesopotamia, is portrayed kneeling humbly before the god Amurru. The English word "worship" in the OT translates the Hebrew word meaning "to bow down" or "to prostrate oneself."

—and in the process to find deep personal joy.

2. *Corporate nonritual worship.* During the Babylonian Captivity, the synagogue gathering was introduced. The practice of assembling on the Sabbath for study of the Law, praise, and prayers was maintained by the Jews scattered throughout the ancient world and by the relative few who returned to Israel. As long as the restored Jerusalem Temple stood, the synagogue's corporate nonritual worship existed alongside the ritual worship conducted at the Temple. Since the Temple's destruction in A.D. 70, the synagogue has been the main center of Jewish worship. *See also* Synagogue.

3. *Individual ritual worship.* Old Testament Law calls for individual acts of ritual worship. Those who sinned unintentionally were to offer specified sacrifices. Observing rules of uncleanness and cleansing was part of the individual's ritual expression of reverence for God. Individuals were also able to express their appreciation to the Lord in personal vows and voluntary offerings.

4. *Individual nonritual worship.* The OT contains many examples of personal worship apart from sacrifices and vows. Abraham's servant praised God for answering his prayers (Gen. 24:26,27). Jacob erected a pillar to commemorate his vision of God (Gen. 28:10-22). Hannah's psalm of praise is among the most beautiful expressions of personal nonritual worship (1 Sam. 2:1-10). The primary models for personal worship are the Psalms, in which the most intimate of human emotions are freely expressed to God and in which the most exalted expressions of praise to God can be found. The believer who wishes to learn how to worship can train himself or herself by daily reading and praying the Psalms.

NEW TESTAMENT

The NT has several words for worship, expressing different shades of meaning. The most common, *proskyneō,* means "to bow down" and is used in a variety of spiritual and physical, public and private ways. *Sebomai* (Rom. 1:25) means "to fear or show reverence." It is used mostly in non-Jewish contexts, characterizing pagan worship—though it was used on occasion for Christian worship. *Latreuō* generally connotes the act of Israel's ritual worship, particularly the "service" performed by priests and Levites. But serving God in the NT also involves obeying him in daily life, presenting our bodies as living sacrifices,

frequently begins his letters with praise (Eph. 1:3-10) and often includes expressions of praise within his prayers (Eph. 3:20,21). Paul encourages worship, as in his exhortation to pray about everything "with thanksgiving" (Phil. 4:6).

worthy Having value; deserving. There is a comparative quality here. One is worthy to do something or get something. Thus John the Baptist exclaimed that he was not worthy to untie Jesus' sandals (Mk. 1:7). That is, his worth did not match up. Paul urges Christians to live lives worthy of our calling—that is, appropriate to God's treatment of us (Eph. 4:1; Col. 1:10).

"Worthy" takes on an absolute sense only when we deal with absolute worth —in the person of Jesus. "Worthy is the Lamb," the Revelation chorus sings, "to receive power and wealth and wisdom and strength and honor and glory and praise!" (Rev. 5:12).

wrath of God God's response to sin and evil and the manifestation of that response.

The Bible avoids depicting wrath as malice or vindictiveness. Instead, God's wrath must be understood against the background of his holiness and righteousness, which cause him to punish wickedness and evil.

Biblical illustrations of God's wrath abound. The Lord destroyed wicked Sodom and Gomorrah (Gen. 19). He judged Egypt by the plagues that led to the Exodus deliverance (Ex. 7–11). God expelled his own people from their land when they pursued other gods and abandoned justice (Deut. 28; 2 Chr. 36; Isa. 1). All these are examples of the wrath of a holy God. Jesus demonstrated God's wrath when he became furious and drove the tradesmen from the Jerusalem Temple (Jn. 2:13-17).

The NT Epistles speak frequently of the wrath of God and warn that those who refuse his grace in Jesus will one day be punished (Rom. 1:18; 2:5; Eph. 2:3; Col. 3:6). Paul affirms that it is the right thing for God to "punish those who do not know God and do not obey the gospel of our Lord Jesus. They will be punished with everlasting destruction and shut out from the presence of the Lord" (2 Th. 1:8,9). Eternal punishment is the ultimate expression of divine wrath, and its awesome proportions cause it to be described metaphorically as a "lake of burning sulfur" (Rev. 20:10).

Female figure portrayed with hands clasped at her waist in devotion. Her posture illustrates worship in Ps. 131: "My heart is not proud, O Lord, my eyes are not haughty; . . . but I have stilled and quieted my soul; like a weaned child with its mother" (vv. 1,2).

as Paul said, "which is [our] spiritual worship" (Rom. 12:1).

1. *Corporate nonritual worship.* The ritual elements of OT worship are absent from the worship of the church, with the exception of the communion service. The services of the church as portrayed in the NT seem both informal and spontaneous. Brief descriptions of the church at worship in Acts 2,4; 1 Cor. 14; and elsewhere indicate that services included teaching, singing, prayer, praise, thanksgiving, exhortation, rebuking, encouragement, prophecy, and the exercise of other gifts of the Spirit. The NT also contains various creedal statements (Phil. 2:6-11) and benedictions (Heb. 13:20,21) that may have been part of a developing liturgy.

Perhaps the most unusual aspect of the NT's portrayal of corporate worship appears in Revelation, where the great congregation of heaven utters many expressions of praise (4:8,11; 5:9-14; 7:9-17; 11:16-18; 12:10-12; 15:3,4; 16:5-7; 19:1-8).

2. *Individual personal worship.* Individual personal worship is both expressed and encouraged in the NT Epistles, although not to the extent found in the OT. Paul

Two wrestlers form the bronze handle of a Roman-period lid. Paul writes in Eph. 6:12: "We wrestle not against flesh and blood, but against principalities, against powers, against the rulers of the darkness of this world."

While the doctrine of the wrath of God is terrible from a merely human perspective, we must never forget that God has taken every possible step to enable men and women to escape it. In Jesus, God himself experienced the full fury of his own wrath, bearing our sins on Calvary so that we might be forgiven. This overwhelming act of love helps us to realize that God's attitude toward us is one of compassion and grace, not hostility and anger. As we respond to the love of God, we find a forgiveness and a welcome that assures us we have been delivered from the punishment that we deserve. *See also* Anger; Propitiation.

wrestle, wrestling A hand-to-hand struggle won by throwing or forcing the opponent to the ground. Figuratively, intense effort (Eph. 6:12).

The best-known wrestling match in Scripture is Jacob's bout with an angel of God (Gen. 32:22-32). The most common type of wrestling in the Middle East was belt wrestling, in which each wrestler took hold of his opponent's tightly wrapped belt. The image of "girding up the loins"— our "tightening the belt"—was a colloquial way of saying, "Prepare for action."

A number of OT references may allude to belt wrestling, most clearly in Isa. 11:5, which describes the Messiah about to appear to struggle for justice. The text says, "Righteousness will be his belt and faithfulness the sash around his waist."

writing Symbols or characters representing human language; the act of making these symbols or composing the thoughts to be symbolized.

Writing was introduced in Mesopotamia and Egypt in the fourth millennium B.C. A number of writing systems were developed, but each was supplanted by the alphabet system developed in Syria-Palestine in the second millennium. An alphabet was in use in Syria-Palestine probably by 1800 B.C., and distinct Semitic

dialects, including Hebrew, existed by 1400 B.C. These early alphabets contained only consonants, unlike the Greek alphabet, which also had vowels.

Various writing materials are mentioned in the Bible or have been discovered by archaeologists. Stone inscriptions are common (Ex. 31:18; Josh. 8:32), and frequently longer texts were written on walls prepared with a coating of plaster (Deut. 27:1-3). Ink made from soot was applied with brushes. Other writing surfaces included wood covered with a wax coating (Hab. 2:2), and even thin silver or copper plates. A stylus of iron or flint (Jer. 17:1) was used to inscribe these surfaces. By far the most common writing surfaces, however, were parchment—the dried, scraped hide of an animal—and paper, made from the pith of the papyrus reed. *See also* Paper.

In ancient cultures, as in our own, records were kept (Josh. 18:8,9), deeds were prepared (Jer. 32:10), divorce decrees issued (Deut. 24:1,3), personal and official letters sent (2 Sam. 11:14; 1 Ki. 21:8; Ezra 4–7), and in Israel careful genealogical records were maintained (Neh. 7:5-73). Special care was taken to accurately preserve the sacred books that contained Israel's heritage.

The OT contains several indications that Israel was a literate society. In the time of the judges, a "young man" of Succoth, captured by chance, was able to write down the names of 77 elders in his city (Jdg. 8:14). Archaeologists have also unearthed what seem to be practice tablets used by children to practice writing (*see*

Isa. 10:19; 29:11). The great power and vividness of the prophets' writings suggest a complex and highly developed language, implying a literate people as well as a highly educated class.

Even so, a professional class of scribes made an occupation of writing, at least from the kingdom period. These men served in the government but most likely drew up deeds and other documents as well. Baruch, a scribe, served Jeremiah as a secretary and wrote down that prophet's oracles (Jer. 36:2,4; *see* 1 Chr. 2:55). Even Paul dictated his letters (Rom. 16:22; Gal. 6:11; 2 Th. 3:17).

Archaeologists have unearthed libraries filled with religious, historical, medical, magical, and other treatises, as well as typical business documents. These affirm that writing was essential in these cultures, not only to preserve their heritage but also to conduct the business of daily life. Modern scholars find these libraries an invaluable source of background information for biblical study.

Above: Egyptian pupil's slate for practicing writing (1580–1085 B.C.). Top: This monument of Darius I (522–486 B.C.), cut in a cliff 300 feet above the road at Bisitun, Iran, is also an important ancient "document." It is made up of four parts: a bas relief (A), showing rebels submitting to the Persian king; and three inscriptions, in Persian (B), Babylonian (C), and Elamite (D). Together these texts enabled Sir Henry Rawlinson to decipher cuneiform script.

1041

X

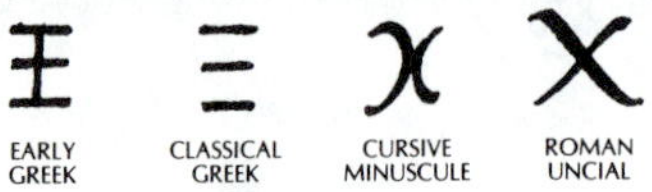

EARLY GREEK   CLASSICAL GREEK   CURSIVE MINUSCULE   ROMAN UNCIAL

Xerxes [ZERK-sees]. Known in some versions as Ahasuerus, Xerxes I ruled Persia 486–465 B.C. His efforts to invade Europe were thrown back by the Greek city-states. In Scripture, he is the ruler who married Esther. **Scripture:** Book of Esther; Ezra 4:6. A different Xerxes is mentioned in Dan. 9:1 as the father of Darius.

The Book of Esther tells the story of an early attempt to wipe out the Jewish people, and how they were saved by Esther, Xerxes' young Jewish queen. Parallels between the biblical account and writings of the Greek historian Herodotus support this identification. Each tells of a feast held in Xerxes' third year, which Herodotus explains was in preparation for the invasion of Greece. Xerxes did cross the Hellespont and conquer Athens in 480 B.C. But the Persian fleet was wiped out at Salamis, and in 479 B.C. the Persian army was thrown back at Plataea. Xerxes then returned home, where Herodotus reports that he spent his seventh year with his harem. The Bible says Ahasuerus spent his seventh year selecting a queen from young virgins assembled throughout his empire. Xerxes was assassinated during the 20th year of his rule.

The winged disc above the sphinxes is the emblem of Ahuramazda, the Persian god of creation. Xerxes frequently credited this god for his accession to the throne and aid in controlling his vast empire. Enameled brick panel from Susa, 6th century B.C. Inset: A Persian inscription depicting the signet of King Xerxes I (486–465 B.C.)

1042

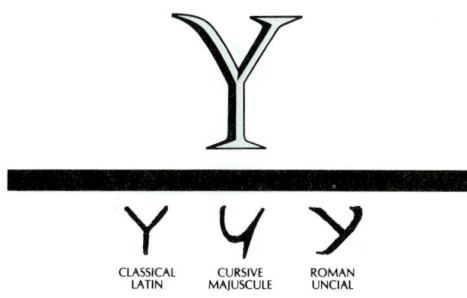

Y

CLASSICAL
LATIN

CURSIVE
MAJUSCULE

ROMAN
UNCIAL

Yahweh The probable pronunciation of the Hebrew letters YHWH, which form the personal name of God in the OT. It is usually translated "the LORD." (The small capital letters in many versions indicate that this name is used.) The name is a form of the Hebrew verb "to be" and probably has the meaning of "The One Who Is Always Present."

year *See* Calendar; Time.

yeast *See* Leaven.

YHWH *See* Yahweh.

yoke (1) A piece of wood shaped to fit over the neck of load-pulling animals to link them together (Num. 19:2). (2) A pair of work animals, such as oxen (1 Sam. 11:7; Lk. 14:19). (3) Figuratively, a heavy burden or slavery (Ex. 6:6; 1 Tim. 6:1). (4) Also figuratively, a linkage emotionally or socially with another.

The NT applies the image of the yoke in several ways. The Jerusalem Council and Paul viewed the Law as a yoke, a crushing burden "neither we nor our fathers have been able to bear" (Acts 15:10). Paul calls up the negative image of being "yoked together with unbelievers" (2 Cor. 6:14). Just as the Law prohibited plowing with an ox and donkey yoked together (Deut. 22:10), Christians and non-Christians cannot be linked in any significant relationship demanding harmony of purpose and ideals.

The most unusual use of the image is by Jesus, who calls the weary and burdened to "take my yoke upon you and learn from me, for I am gentle and humble in heart, and you will find rest for your souls. For my yoke is easy and my burden is light" (Mt. 11:29,30). In harness with Jesus, we become his partner as he shares his strength with us, easing the weight we once had to pull alone.

yokefellow A partner or co-worker (Phil. 4:3).

Yom Kippur *See* Atonement, Day of.

youth One's early life, especially the time after infancy and before marriageable age. Youth was considered a time of physical vigor. Yet youth was also the age of immaturity, when a person lacked the wisdom others had gained through experience.

However, neither youth's advantages nor limitations are decisive. Isaiah reminds us that "even youths grow tired and weary, and young men stumble and fall; but those who hope in the Lord will renew their strength" (Isa. 40:30,31). And the psalmist says: "I have more insight than all my teachers, for I meditate on your statutes. I have more understanding than the elders, for I obey your precepts" (Ps. 119:99,100). Paul advised the young Timothy, "Don't let anyone look down on you because you are young, but set an example for the believers in speech, in life, in love, in faith and in purity" (1 Tim. 4:12). *See also* Age.

This 6th-century B.C. ostracon or potsherd from Arad contains the earliest reference outside of the Bible to Solomon's Temple. The bottom line reads: byt yhwh or "House of Yahweh."

Marble bust of Caligula (Gaius Caesar) in his youth, about age 16 (Rome, A.D. 28). He was only 27 when he became emperor.

Wooden yoke from ancient Israel. The yoke is used in the Scriptures to symbolize hardship or servitude (1 Ki. 12:1-11; Jer. 27,28; Lam. 1:14; 3:27).

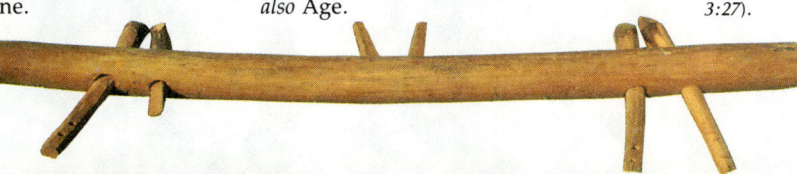

Z

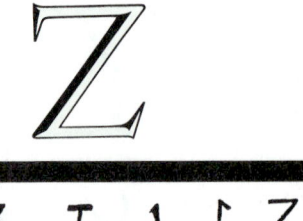

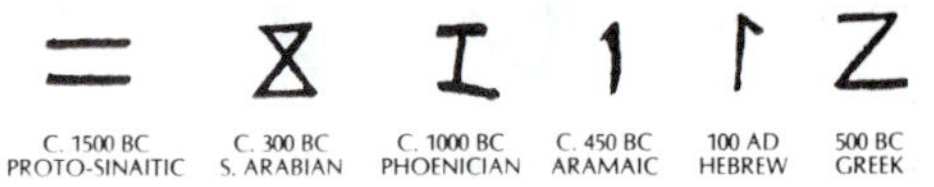

C. 1500 BC
PROTO-SINAITIC

C. 300 BC
S. ARABIAN

C. 1000 BC
PHOENICIAN

C. 450 BC
ARAMAIC

100 AD
HEBREW

500 BC
GREEK

zeal A passionate devotion to a person, belief, or cause. The Hebrew and Greek words can also mean "jealousy." *See also* Jealousy.

God's zeal, as his devotion to both his covenant people and to righteousness, is often expressed in judgment against evil (Deut. 29:20). But it will also be expressed when he introduces the glorious reign of his Messiah (Isa. 9:6,7).

The NT describes the pious Jew's pas-

sionate commitment to his religion as an indication of zeal, but a zeal not based on knowledge (Rom. 10:2; *see* Phil. 3:6). Paul himself was consumed by this passion for OT traditions before his conversion (Gal. 1:14).

Zeal is commendable in Christians, whose faith is to be far more than intellectual assent to a set of doctrinal statements. Paul exhorts the believers in Rome, "Never be lacking in zeal, but keep your

Christ Cleansing the Temple by El Greco. Jesus' action fulfilled the prophecy of Ps. 69:9: "Zeal for your house consumes me."

spiritual fervor" (Rom. 12:11). Yet he warns the Galatians, "It is fine to be zealous, provided the purpose is good" (Gal. 4:18).

zealot A person of Jesus' time who believed in armed resistance against the Romans who occupied the Jewish homeland. A number of splinter parties in Judaism undoubtedly shared this ideology, which expressed itself in disastrous rebellions against Rome in the late A.D. 60s and again in the A.D. 130s.

One of Christ's disciples, Simon, was nicknamed "the Zealot" (Lk. 6:15; Acts 1:13), possibly indicating his involvement in this radical movement.

Zebulun, tribe of *See* Israel, Tribes of.

Zechariah, Book of A book of OT prophecy, recording messages directed to the Jews who had returned to Judah after captivity in Babylon. Its immediate impact was to support the call of Haggai to complete the reconstruction of the Jerusalem Temple. Its long-term effect was to stimulate hope in coming generations, who would be ruled by a series of Gentile world empires.

BACKGROUND

Only a few thousand of the Jews scattered through the Babylonian Empire responded when the new ruler, Cyrus the Great, allowed captive peoples to return to their national homelands (538 B.C.). Those who returned were highly motivated and immediately laid the foundation for a new Temple. But for the next 18 years the Temple lay incomplete as the Jews struggled simply to survive in a land that had reverted to wilderness during the 70 years of their captivity.

Then in 520 B.C., Haggai appeared, calling his contemporaries back to God. A few months later the young Zechariah [ZEK-uh-RI-uh; "Yahweh remembers"], a descendant of Iddo, a leader of one of Judah's priestly families, uttered his first prophecies. Reinvigorated by the ministry of these two prophets, the Jews quickly completed work on the Temple and through Haggai received God's promise of immediate material blessing. *See also* Haggai.

The material in the first eight chapters of Zechariah dates from 520 to 518 B.C., those exciting days when enthusiasm for God was at its height (1:1,7; 7:1). But while Haggai's ministry focused on the present, Zechariah looked into the future. In a series of symbolic visions, he foresaw a future that parallels what Daniel envisioned. Even though the Jews faced the dreary prospect of centuries under the power of Gentiles, God intended to fulfill his ancient promises. In chapters 9 through 14, Zechariah describes the ultimate worldwide triumph of God through

Jewish Zealots held out against the Romans at Masada for seven years (A.D. 66–73) and then killed one another rather than surrender, before the rocktop fortress was finally overrun.

the Jewish Messiah. *See also* Daniel; Messiah.

AUTHORSHIP

Because the material in chs. 1–8 and 9–14 differs so greatly, some scholars have questioned Zechariah's unity. Moreover, chs. 1–8 are dated prophecies; 9–14 are not. In response, some conservative scholars have argued that the two sections might well have been written years apart, at the beginning and near the end of Zechariah's life. However, the book is organized in a sophisticated literary form called *chiasmus*, in which themes and counter-themes are skillfully balanced. This suggests not only that a single author

composed the work in this form, but also that the entire book was probably written about the same time.

THEOLOGICAL CONTRIBUTIONS

The Book of Zechariah, like Daniel and Revelation, contains apocalyptic visions. More significantly, it is rich in messianic material. Zechariah foresees the symbolic crowning of the Messiah (3:1-10), his entry into Jerusalem on the back of a donkey (9:9), Israel's mourning for a Messiah that the inhabitants of Jerusalem themselves have pierced (12:10-13), the shepherd sent by God struck and the sheep scattered (13:7-9), and the rejected shepherd being valued at 30 pieces of silver (11:12). But ultimately Zechariah foresees a day when

ZECHARIAH: A READING AND STUDY GUIDE

Chapter	Content Summary	Related Articles
	I. The Eight Visions of Zechariah	
1	Zechariah calls Judah to return to God. First vision: The world is at rest and Jerusalem still captive. Yet God cares and will bless. Second vision: Each coming Gentile world empire will be thrown down.	Vision Angel Future Horn
2	Third vision: God surveys Jerusalem in order to erect a wall of fire around it.	
3	Fourth vision: The high priest is cleansed and restored, symbolizing a coming high priest who will remove Israel's sin.	Priest Branch Messiah
4	Fifth vision: God promises resources needed to finish the Temple.	
5	Sixth vision: A flying scroll symbolizes judgment on those who disobey God's Law. Seventh vision: Wickedness, personified by a woman in a basket, is removed from the land of Judah.	Judgment Disobedience Wicked
6	Eighth vision: The high priest is crowned, symbolizing future unification of priesthood/kingship in Messiah.	King
	II. Questions Concerning Fasting	
7,8	Fasts commemorating Jerusalem's fall to Babylon will be replaced by celebration when God blesses his people.	Fast Jerusalem
	III. The Coming Intervention of God on Earth	
9	Jerusalem's enemies will be judged, and the Lord will appear to save the flock of his people.	Lord
10	Deceitful leaders are rebuked. God will redeem, restore, and regather his scattered people.	Redeem
11	The good shepherd God sends to Judah will be rejected, valued at only 30 pieces of silver.	Shepherd Prophet
12	God will shield Jerusalem when enemies invade. Then the inhabitants will "look on me, the one they have pierced" and recognize their Messiah.	
13	Deceitful spiritual leaders and false prophets will be rejected. After the true shepherd dies, his sheep will be scattered. Yet the Jews will be recalled to their homeland.	Prophet
14	The Lord himself will come and reign over the earth.	

"the Lord will be king over the whole earth" (14:9).

Strikingly, the themes that appeared in the pre-exilic prophets—of Israel scattered and regathered, of the world gathered against God's people to make war, and of divine intervention leading to the establishment of Messiah's throne—are present here in a prophecy written after the return from captivity. What previous prophets had envisioned was only partly fulfilled in Israel's captivity and return. Zechariah pointed out that these themes would still be played out in the future.

SPECIAL FEATURES

The Jews had instituted fasts in mourning over the destruction of Jerusalem and the Temple. The people ask whether these should be continued (7:3). God answers through Zechariah, "No." The Jews are not to look backward, but forward. God intends to bless Jerusalem. He will bring his people back, save them, and make them a blessing. The days that were once set aside for mourning will "become joyful and glad occasions and happy festivals for Judah" (8:19). Until that time, God's people are simply to "love truth and peace" and fulfill the word God uttered through the prophets. "Administer true justice; show mercy and compassion to one another. Do not oppress the widow or the fatherless, the alien or the poor. In your hearts do not think evil of each other" (7:8-10).

Zedekiah *See* IDENTIQUICK:PEOPLE.

Zephaniah, Book of The brief, three-chapter OT book of prophecy, dating from the time of Josiah (640–609 B.C.). Zephaniah predicts a universal divine judgment to come.

BACKGROUND

Zephaniah [ZEF-uh-NI-uh; "God has preserved"] was the great-great-grandson of godly King Hezekiah (1:1). His obvious concern with Judah's degeneration into idolatry (1:4-6) suggests he wrote before the powerful religious reforms Josiah instituted in 621 B.C. Zephaniah's message is simple and clear: God will punish sin in his people and in the surrounding nations. Punishment will come at a time designated "the great day of the Lord" (1:14), which Zephaniah senses is imminent. *See also* Josiah.

Like the other prophets, Zephaniah concludes on a note of hope. Judah will accept correction; God will take away her punish-

ment; and the Jewish people will be gathered. "At that time I will bring you home" (3:20).

THEOLOGICAL CONTRIBUTIONS

Zephaniah contributes to the OT portrait of "the day of the Lord." Here he clearly refers to a coming time when God will personally intervene to judge sin. *See also* Day of the Lord.

SPECIAL FEATURES

The book speaks specifically to those who think "the Lord will do nothing, either good or bad" (1:12). God is moral ruler of the universe and accepts his responsibility to punish the wicked.

This Babylonian Chronicle for the years 605–594 B.C. records the appointment of Zedekiah as king of Judah after the capture of Jerusalem in March 597 B.C. and also the exile of Judeans to Babylon.

ZEPHANIAH: A READING AND STUDY GUIDE

Chapter	Content Summary	Related Articles
1	God will "sweep everything away" in judgment when the day of the Lord comes.	Day of the Lord Jealousy
2	God calls individuals to "seek the Lord" and humility, and then turns to announce judgment on foreign nations.	Righteousness Judgment
3	The future of Jerusalem is bright, for God will save and restore a remnant of his people.	Remnant Love

The Greek god Zeus, flanked by his messenger, Hermes (left), and Aphrodite (right), the goddess of love and beauty.

Zeus The chief deity in the Greek pantheon, usually represented as the sky god with a thunderbolt. The pagan people of Lystra, where there was a temple to Zeus, thought Barnabas was Zeus, while Paul was taken as his spokesman, the god Hermes (Acts 14:8-20)—a misperception that the missionaries soon set straight.

ziggurat [ZIG-er-aht; "summit"]. A massive, step-like brick hill. Ziggurats were

created by Mesopotamian peoples as sites on which to build temples to their principal deities. Many believe the Tower of Babel was a ziggurat. *See also* Babel.

Zion [ZI-uhn; "citadel," "fortress"?]. Originally Zion was the southernmost of the hilltops of Jerusalem. That fortified stronghold was taken by David (2 Sam. 5:6-10; 1 Chr. 11:4-9) and became known as the "City of David." After Solomon built the Jerusalem Temple on a site north of the citadel, the name Zion was extended to incorporate the Temple Mount (Pss. 2:6; 78:68,69). The name continued to be extended, becoming a metaphor for all Jerusalem as the religious capital of Israel, and later as a metaphor for Israel and all its inhabitants (Isa. 28:16; 40:9; 60:11-14; Jer. 31:12; Zech. 9:13). This figurative use of Zion to represent the people of God is further extended in Heb. 12:22 and Rev. 14:1 to encompass God's people of all ages.

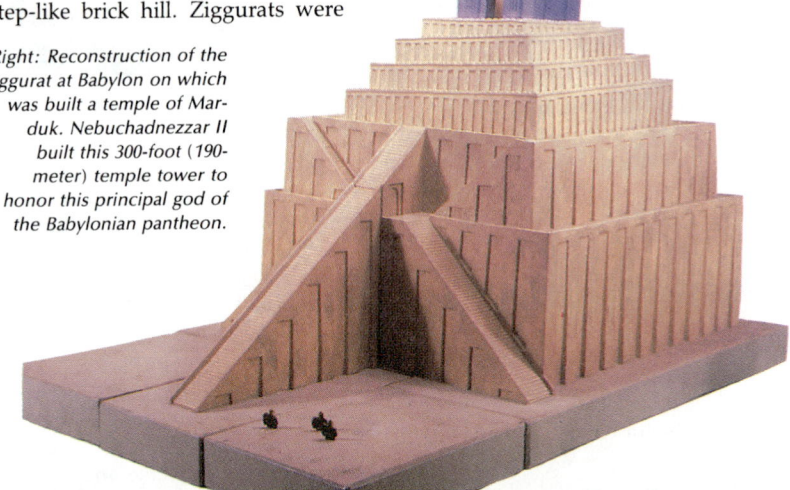

Right: Reconstruction of the ziggurat at Babylon on which was built a temple of Marduk. Nebuchadnezzar II built this 300-foot (190-meter) temple tower to honor this principal god of the Babylonian pantheon.

Cylinder seal, with impression, depicts Mesopotamians building ziggurats (2600–2350 B.C.). At the top a god was thought to appear.

IDENTIQUICK™
PEOPLE + PLACES + MAPS

1050

IDENTIQUICK™ PEOPLE
All the people in the Bible, with pronunciation guide, Scripture references, and full identification

1105

IDENTIQUICK™ PLACES
All the places in the Bible keyed to maps to provide their accurate location, with pronunciation guide, Scripture references, and full identification

1140

IDENTIQUICK™ MAPS

Exclusively prepared maps of the Bible lands accompanied by articles linking historical developments with geography

identiquick™
PEOPLE

AN INTRODUCTION TO THE PEOPLE OF THE BIBLE

This section provides an alphabetical listing of the people mentioned in the Bible. The information provided includes:

1. Names of Bible people as they appear in the NIV translation, with alternate spellings as they appear in other popular versions.
2. A guide to pronouncing each name, with the syllable(s) to be accented in capital letters.
3. The meaning of each name when it is known.
4. Approximate dates at which persons were mentioned in Bible history.
5. A brief description, indicating the person's role in the story of the Bible.
6. Scripture references where further information about each can be found.
7. Other names by which an individual may be known in the Bible.

Major Bible persons are also treated at length in the main body of this Bible dictionary, where suggestions are provided for studying and teaching their lives. An asterisk following a name or number indicates that an entry for this person may be found in the main section.

The pronunciation guide reflects a consensus of scholarly opinion. Each pronunciation is intended to be comfortable for the English speaker. While pronunciations do not reproduce exactly the way the names were pronounced in Hebrew or Greek, they still reflect Hebrew and Greek emphases.

Names, especially Hebrew names, were often intended to communicate something important about an individual's character or calling. While the meaning of many names remains uncertain, those given here represent a consensus of scholarly opinion.

It is not possible to determine the exact date of prominence of many persons who are mentioned in the Bible. This is particularly true of those found only in genealogies or the early chapters of Genesis. The dates which are given are estimates only, based on an individual's relationship to well-known Bible characters. In most cases, dates given are rounded off to the nearest quarter century in which an individual played his or her adult role in Bible history. However, the dates of kings of Israel and Judah represent their years on the throne.

For a discussion of biblical dates see the entry Chronology of the Bible in the main section of the dictionary.

A

AARON* [AIR-uhn] 1450 B.C. The older brother and companion of Moses during the Exodus, and Israel's first high priest. Ex. 4–40; Lev.; Num.; Deut. 9,10. **Parents:** Amram and Jochebed. **Siblings:** Moses and Miriam. **Wife:** Elisheba. **Sons:** Nadab, Abihu, Eleazar, Ithamar.

ABADDON [uh-BAD-uhn; "destroyer, destruction"] Hebrew name for the king of the abyss in Rev. 9:11. Apollyon is the Greek form of the name.

ABAGTHA [uh-BAG-thuh; "happy, prosperous"] 475 B.C. One of the seven stewards who served Ahasuerus. Esth. 1:10.

ABDA [AB-duh; "servant; worshiper"; shortened form of Obadiah]
1. 975 B.C. Father of Adoniram, a chief official of Solomon in charge of forced labor. 1 Ki. 4:6.
2. 450 B.C. A chief Levite in Jerusalem after the Exile. Neh. 11:17. Called Obadiah in 1 Chr. 9:16.

ABDEEL [AB-dee-el; "servant of God"] 625 B.C. Father of Shelemiah, servant under Jehoiakim instructed to arrest Baruch and Jeremiah. Jer. 36:26.

ABDI [AB-di; shortened form of "servant of Yahweh"]
1. 1075 B.C. Grandfather of Ethan, one of David's ministers of music at the tabernacle. 1 Chr. 6:44.
2. 750 B.C. Father of Kish, a Levite who served at the Temple in Hezekiah's time. 2 Chr. 29:12.
3. 450 B.C. A Jew who took a foreign wife after the Exile. Ezra 10:26.

ABDIEL [AB-dee-el; "servant of God"] B.C. (date unknown). Ancestral head of a family, listed only in the genealogy of Gad. 1 Chr. 5:15.

ABDON [AB-dahn; "service, servile"]
1. B.C. (date unknown). A Benjamite who lived in Jerusalem. 1 Chr. 8:23.
2. 1075 B.C. A wealthy but minor judge who led Israel for a period of eight years. Jdg. 12:13-15.
3. 1075 B.C. Firstborn son of Jeiel and Maacah, and brother of Ner, Saul's father. 1 Chr. 8:30.
4. 625 B.C. An official of Josiah. 2 Chr. 34:20. Called Acbor in 2 Ki. 22:12.

ABEDNEGO [uh-BED-nuh-goh; "servant of Nego" (a Babylonian god)] 600 B.C. New name given to Azariah upon entering the service of Nebuchadnezzar. He was one of the three Jewish companions of Daniel who refused to worship Nebuchadnezzar's idol. They were then thrown into a blazing furnace but were miraculously delivered. Dan. 1:7; 2:49; 3:12-30.

ABEL* [AY-buhl; possibly "breath, vapor," or "son"] B.C. (date unknown). The godly second son of Adam murdered by his brother Cain. Gen. 4. **Parents:** Adam and Eve. No descendants recorded.

ABI [AY-bi; "my father"] 750 B.C. Mother of Hezekiah. 2 Ki. 18:2. Called Abijah in 2 Chr. 29:1.

ABI-ALBON [AY-bi-AL-buhn; "father of strength"] 1000 B.C. A military leader, one of David's thirty mighty men. 2 Sam. 23:31. Called Abiel in 1 Chr. 11:32.

ABIASAPH [uh-BI-uh-saf; "my father has gathered"] B.C. (date unknown). A Levite clan leader whose descendants served as gatekeepers and musicians of the tabernacle. Ex. 6:24. Called Ebiasaph in 1 Chr. 6:23,37; 9:19.

ABIATHAR* [uh-BI-uh-thahr; "father of abundance"] 1000 B.C. Sole survivor when Saul massacred his father and 84 other priests; chaplain and later joint high priest under King David. 1 Sam. 22,23; 2 Sam. 15,17; 1 Ki. 1-4; 1 Chr. 15,18,27. **Father:** Ahimelech. **Son:** Ahimelech.

ABIDA [uh-BI-duh; "father of knowledge"] 2000 B.C. KJV: Abidah. Fourth of the five sons of Midian, the son of Abraham. Gen. 25:4.

ABIDAN [uh-BI-duhn; "father is judge"] 1450 B.C. Leader of the tribe of Benjamin in Moses' time. Num. 1:11.

ABIEL [AY-bee-el; "father is God"]
1. 1100 B.C. Ancestor of Saul in 1 Sam. 9:1. Probably same as Jeiel, father of Kish, in 1 Chr. 8:29; 9:35.
2. 1000 B.C. A military commander, one of David's thirty mighty men. 1 Chr. 11:32. Called Abi-Albon in 2 Sam. 23:31.

ABIEZER [AY-bih-EE-zuhr; "father is help"]
1. B.C. (date unknown). A descendant of Manasseh and ancestral head of his own clan. Josh. 17:2; Jdg. 8:2; 1 Chr. 7:18. Called Iezer in Num. 26:30.
2. 1000 B.C. A Benjamite military leader, one of David's thirty mighty men. 2 Sam. 23:27.

ABIGAIL [AB-uh-gayl; "father rejoices"]
1.* 1000 B.C. Wise wife of Nabal, who saved his household from David and later married David. 1 Sam. 25,27,30; 2 Sam. 2,3. **Son by David:** Kileab.
2. 1000 B.C. A sister of David and mother of Amasa 1. 2 Sam. 17:25; 1 Chr. 2:16,17.

ABIHAIL [AB-uh-hayl; "father is strength"]
1. 1475 B.C. Father of Zuriel, a clan leader of the tribe of Levi. Num. 3:35.

2. B.C. (date unknown). Wife of Abishur, listed in the genealogy of Jerahmeel, a descendant of Judah. 1 Chr. 2:29.
3. 975 B.C. Wife of Jerimoth, son of David, and mother of Mahalath, wife of Rehoboam. 2 Chr. 11:18. **Father:** Eliab, brother of David.
4. B.C. (date unknown). A descendant of Gad listed only in the genealogy of Gad in 1 Chr. 5:14.
5. 500 B.C. Father of Esther and uncle of Mordecai. Esth. 2:15; 9:29.

ABIHU* [uh-BI-hoo; "father is he"] 1450 B.C. Second of the four sons of Aaron, notable for approaching God's altar with "unauthorized fire." He was consumed by fire from God. Ex. 6:23; Lev. 10; Num. 3:1-4.

ABIHUD [uh-BI-hud; "father is majesty"] 1825 B.C. Third of the nine sons of Bela, firstborn son of Benjamin. 1 Chr. 8:3. Possibly a mistranslation of "father of Ehud."

ABIJAH [uh-BI-jah; "my father is Yahweh"] KJV, RSV: Abiah, Abia.
1. 1825 B.C. Seventh of the nine sons of Beker, son of Benjamin in 1 Chr. 7:8.
2. B.C. (date unknown). Wife of Hezron, descendant of Judah, in 1 Chr. 2:24.
3. 1050 B.C. Son of Samuel and corrupt judge of Israel. 1 Sam. 8:1-5.
4. 1000 B.C. Head of the eighth of twenty-four priestly divisions established by David; Zechariah, father of John the Baptist, belonged to this priestly division. 1 Chr. 24:10; Lk. 1:5.
5. 925 B.C. The son of Jeroboam I, king of Israel who died in childhood. 1 Ki. 14:1-8.
6.* Ruled 913–910 B.C. Second king of Judah. 1 Ki. 15; 2 Chr. 13. Also called Abijam. **Parents:** Rehoboam and Maacah, daughter of Absalom. **Sons:** 22, including Asa.
7. 750 B.C. Mother of Hezekiah. 2 Chr. 29:1. Called Abi, a shortened form of Abijah, in 2 Ki. 18:2.
8. 525 B.C. Head of a family of priests who returned to Judah with Zerubbabel after the Exile. Neh. 12:1,4,17.
9. 450 B.C. A priest who signed the covenant renewal with God in Nehemiah's time, probably with the name of the family's ancestral head. See Abijah 8. Neh. 10:7.

ABIJAM [uh-BI-juhm; "father of the sea (or west)"] Ruled 913–910 B.C. Son and successor of Rehoboam, king of Judah; an ancestor of Christ. 1 Ki. 15; 2 Chr. 13. See Abijah 6.

ABIMAEL [uh-BIM-ay-el; "my father is God"] B.C. (date unknown). Ninth of the thirteen sons of Joktan, a descendant of Shem found only in the genealogy of Gen. 10:28.

ABIMELECH [uh-BIM-uh-lek; "my father is king"] A title of Philistine kings.
1. 2050 B.C. A Philistine king of Gerar who established a treaty with Abraham. Gen. 20:1-18; 21:22-34.
2. 1950 B.C. Also a king of Gerar, possibly the successor of Abimelech 1. He formed an alliance with Abraham's son Isaac. Gen. 26:1-33.
3.* Ruled 1129–1126 B.C. Notable as assassin of 70 of his brothers to establish himself as king. Jdg. 9. **Father:** Gideon.
4. 1025 B.C. Achish king of Gath in David's time is referred to as Abimelech in Ps. 34.
5. 975 B.C. A priest in David's time. In the KJV, 1 Chr. 18:16. The name should be Ahimelech, son of Abiathar. See Ahimelech 3.

ABINADAB [uh-BIN-uh-dab; "father is generous"]
1. 1025 B.C. A man from Kireath Jearim, at whose house the ark was kept for twenty years after its return by the Philistines. 1 Sam. 7:1; 2 Sam. 6:3.
2. 1025 B.C. The second son of Jesse and one of David's six older brothers. 1 Sam. 16:8; 17:3; 1 Chr. 2:13.

3. 1025 B.C. One of Saul's sons, slain in battle by the Philistines. 1 Sam. 31:2; 1 Chr. 8:33.
4. 950 B.C. Father of one of Solomon's district governors, Ben-Abinadab. 1 Ki. 4:11.

ABINOAM [uh-BIN-oh-am; "father is delight"] 1250 B.C. The father of Barak, the general who served under Deborah, the judge. Jdg. 4:6,12; 5:1,12.

ABIRAM [uh-BI-ruhm; "father is exalted"]
1. 1450 B.C. A Reubenite who was one of the leaders of a rebellion against Moses and Aaron. Num. 16:1,12,24-27; 26:9.
2. 850 B.C. Firstborn son of Hiel of Bethel, who rebuilt Jericho in the time of Ahab. He died in accordance with the prophetic curse spoken by Joshua at the fall of Jericho (see Josh. 6:26). 1 Ki. 16:34.

ABISHAG [AB-ih-shag; possibly "my father was a wanderer"] 975 B.C. A beautiful young Shunammite woman brought to King David to care for him shortly before he died. 1 Ki. 1:3,15; 2:17-22.

ABISHAI* [uh-BEE-shi; meaning uncertain] 1000 B.C. Loyal battle companion of David. 1 Sam. 26; 2 Sam. 2,3,10,16,18–21,23; 1 Chr. 2,11,18,19. **Mother:** Jeruiah, sister of David. **Brothers:** Joab, Asahel.

ABISHALOM [uh-BISH-uh-lohm; "father of peace"] 975 B.C. Father (or grandfather) of Maacah, wife of Rehoboam and mother of Abijah. 1 Ki. 15:2,10. Also called Absalom, another form of the name, in 2 Chr. 11:20,21, and Uriel in 2 Chr. 13:2. May be the same as Absalom, son of David.

ABISHUA [uh-BISH-oo-uh; "father of deliverance"]
1. 1825 B.C. Fourth of the nine sons born to Bela, firstborn son of Benjamin, in 1 Chr. 8:4.
2. B.C. (date unknown). A descendant of Aaron and an ancestor of Ezra the scribe. 1 Chr. 6:5,50; Ezra 7:5.

ABISHUR [uh-BI-shur; "father is a wall"(?)] B.C. (date unknown). A Judahite listed only in the genealogy of Jerahmeel, descendant of Judah, in 1 Chr. 2:28,29.

ABITAL [uh-BI-tuhl; "father is the dew"] 1000 B.C. A wife of David and mother of Shephatiah. 2 Sam. 3:4; 1 Chr. 3:3.

ABITUB [uh-BI-tub; "my father is good"] B.C. (date unknown). Listed only in the genealogy of Benjamin in 1 Chr. 8:11.

ABIUD [uh-BI-ud; possibly form of Abihud "father is majesty"] 525 B.C. Son of Zerubbabel and an ancestor of Christ. Mt. 1:13.

ABNER* [AB-nuhr; "father is a lamp"] 1025 B.C. Commander of Saul's armies. 1 Sam. 17,20; 2 Sam. 2,3.

ABRAHAM* [AY-bruh-ham; "father of a multitude"] Known as Abram [AY-bruhm; "exalted father"] until his name was changed by God. He was the key figure in Israel's history about 2100 B.C.; the OT's prime example of faith. Gen. 11:26–25:11. **Father:** Terah. **Brothers:** Nahor, Haran. **Wives:** Sarah, Keturah. **Concubine:** Hagar. **Children:** by Sarah, Isaac; by Hagar, Ishmael; by Keturah, Zimran, Kokshan, Medan, Midian, Ishbak, Shuah.

ABSALOM [AB-suh-luhm; "father of peace"]
1.* Notable as rebellious son of David who threatened his father's throne about 975 B.C. 2 Sam. 13–20. **Parents:** David and Maacah. **Children:** three unnamed sons, and Tamar, his daughter.
2. 975 B.C. Father (or possibly grandfather) of Maacah, wife of Rehoboam and mother of Abijah. 2 Chr. 11:20,21. Called Abishalom,

another form of the name, in 1 Ki. 15:2,10. Called Uriel in 2 Chr. 13:2. May be the same as Absalom 1, the son of David.

ACBOR [AK-bohr; "mouse"] KJV, RSV, NASB: Achbor.
1. The father of the Edomite King Baal-Hanan. Gen. 36:38,39.
2. 625 B.C. Father of Elnathan. Jer. 26:22; 36:12.
3. 625 B.C. An official sent by Josiah to speak to the prophetess Huldah concerning the rediscovered Book of the Law. 2 Ki. 22:12. Also called Abdon in 2 Chr. 34:20. Probably the same as Acbor 2.

ACHAICUS [uh-KAY-uh-kuhs; "belonging to Achaia," a Roman province, possibly indicating he was a slave] A.D. 55. One of three men from the church in Corinth who came to visit Paul in Ephesus. 1 Cor. 16:17.

ACHAN* [AY-kuhn; "troubler"] 1400 B.C. An Israelite who violated God's command by taking loot from Jericho, causing a military defeat at Ai. Josh. 7,8. **Father:** Carmi.

ACHIM (KJV, RSV, NASB). See Akim.

ACHISH [AY-kish; "the king gives" or "serpent charmer"(?)]
1. 1025 B.C. A ruler of Gath, a city in Philistia, to whom David fled to escape Saul. David and his men were given the city of Ziklag by Achish. 1 Sam. 21:10-15; 27; 29:2-10. **Father:** Maoch. Called Abimelech in Ps. 34, heading.
2. 975 B.C. Also a ruler of Gath, to whom two of Shimei's slaves fled. His father is identified as Maacah, but he is likely the same as Achish 1. 1 Ki. 2:39,40.

ACSAH [AK-suh; "anklet"] KJV, RSV, NASB: Achsah; 1 Chr. 2:49, KJV: Achsa. 1400 B.C. A daughter of Caleb, whom he gave as a wife to Othniel, the son of her uncle, Kenaz, for capturing Kireath Sepher. Josh. 15:16,17.

ADAH [AY-duh; "adorned"]
1. B.C. (date unknown). One of Lamech's two wives, and mother of Jabal and Jubal. Gen. 4:19-23.
2. 1950 B.C. A wife of Esau, daughter of Elon the Hittite. Gen. 36:2.

ADAIAH [uh-DAY-uh; "Yahweh has adorned"]
1. 1675 B.C. Father of Jedidah, the mother of Josiah. 2 Ki. 22:1.
2. B.C. (date unknown). A Levite, ancestor of Asaph, the minister of music at the Temple in David's time. 1 Chr. 6:41. Called Iddo in 1 Chr. 6:21.
3. B.C. (date unknown). Listed only in the genealogy of Benjamin in 1 Chr. 8:21.
4. 850 B.C. Father of Maaseiah, a military commander who helped Jehoiada overthrow Athaliah. 2 Chr. 23:1.
5. 525 B.C. Ancestor of Maaseiah, a descendant of Judah who settled in Jerusalem after the Exile. Neh. 11:5.
6. 450 B.C. A priest who settled in Jerusalem after the Exile. 1 Chr. 9:12; Neh. 11:12.
7. 450 B.C. A Jew who took a foreign wife in Ezra's time. Ezra 10:29.
8. 450 B.C. Also one who took a foreign wife after the Exile. Ezra 10:39.

ADALIA [uh-DAYL-yah] 475 B.C. Fifth of the ten sons of Haman put to death by the Jews during the reign of Ahasuerus. Esth. 9:8.

ADAM* [AD-uhm; "human being" or "humanity"] The first man, directly created by God in his own image and given dominion on earth. Gen. 1-5. **Wife:** Eve. **Children:** Cain, Abel, Seth, and "other sons and daughters."

ADBEEL [AD-bee-el; "languishing for God"] 2025 B.C. The third of Ishmael's twelve sons. Gen. 25:13.

ADDAR [AD-dahr; possibly "honor"] 1850 B.C. First of the nine sons of Bela, son of Benjamin, in 1 Chr. 8:3. Probably the same as Ard.

ADDI [AD-i; "my witness" or "pleasure"] B.C. (date unknown). An ancestor of Jesus, through Joseph. Lk. 3:28.

ADER (KJV). See Eder.

ADIEL [AY-dee-el; "God is an ornament"]
1. 1025 B.C. Father of Azmaveth, an overseer of the royal treasuries of David. 1 Chr. 27:25.
2. 700 B.C. A Simeonite clan leader who lived in Hezekiah's time. 1 Chr. 4:36.
3. 450 B.C. A priest whose son, Maasai, resettled in Jerusalem after the Exile. 1 Chr. 9:12.

ADIN [AY-din; "ornament"]
1. B.C. (date unknown). Ancestral head of a family of Jews who returned to Judah after the Exile. Ezra 2:15; Neh. 7:20.
2. 450 B.C. A Jewish leader who sealed the covenant renewal in Nehemiah's time, probably with the name of the family's ancestral head. Neh. 10:16. See Adin 1.

ADINO THE EZNITE (KJV, NASB). See Josheb-Basshebeth.

ADLAI [AD-lay; "lax, weary"(?)] 1025 B.C. Father of Shaphat, an overseer of David's herds. 1 Chr. 27:29.

ADMATHA [ad-MAY-thuh] 475 B.C. One of the seven nobles of Persia and Media who advised Ahasuerus to banish Queen Vashti. Esth. 1:14.

ADNA [AD-nuh; "pleasure"]
1. 525 B.C. Father of a priestly family who returned with Zerubbabel from Exile. Neh. 12:15.
2. 450 B.C. A Jew who took a foreign wife after the Exile. Ezra 10:30.

ADNAH [AD-nuh; "pleasure"]
1. 1000 B.C. A man of Manasseh who joined David's army at Ziklag. 1 Chr. 12:20.
2. 875 B.C. A commander in the army of Jehoshaphat. 2 Chr. 17:14.

ADONI-BEZEK [uh-DOH-ni-BEH-zek; "lord of Bezek"] 1400 B.C. Title of a king who ruled the town of Bezek, defeated in battle and taken captive by Israelites of the tribes of Judah and Simeon. Jdg. 1:5-7.

ADONIJAH [AD-oh-NI-juh; "Yahweh is Lord"]
1.* 975 B.C. David's oldest surviving son, set aside when Solomon was proclaimed king by David. Solomon later had him executed. 1 Ki. 1,2. **Parents:** David and Haggith. **Siblings:** Amnon. **Significant half-brothers:** Absalom, Solomon.
2. 875 B.C. One among the Levites sent by Jehoshaphat to teach the Law throughout Judah. 2 Chr. 17:8.
3. 450 B.C. A Jewish leader who sealed the covenant renewal in the time of Nehemiah, probably with the name of the family's ancestral head. Neh. 10:16. See Adonikam.

ADONIKAM [ad-uh-NI-kuhm; "my lord has risen"] B.C. (date unknown). Ancestral head of a family that returned to Judah after the Exile. Ezra 2:13; 8:13; Neh. 7:18.

ADONIRAM [ad-oh-ni-ruhm; "my lord is exalted"] KJV, RSV: Adoram; 2 Chr. 10:18, KJV, RSV: Hadoram. 975 B.C. Chief official in charge of forced labor under David, Solomon, and Rehoboam. He was stoned to death during the Israelite revolt against Rehoboam. 2 Sam. 20:24; 1 Ki. 4:6; 12:18.

ADONI-ZEDEK [uh-DOH-ni-ZEH-dek; "lord of righteousness"] 1400 B.C. KJV: Adoni-Zedec. King of Jerusalem who made a pact with four other Amorite kings to attack the Gibeonites for allying with Israel. Joshua and the Israelites defeated the Amorite armies and put the five kings to death. Josh. 10:1-26.

ADRAMMELECH [uh-DRAM-muh-lek; "the lord is king" or "Adad is king"]
1. 725 B.C. A deity of the Sepharvites, a people transplanted in Samaria by the Assyrians, to whom they sacrificed their children. 2 Ki. 17:31.
2. 675 B.C. Son of Sennacherib, king of Assyria; he and his brother Sharezer murdered their father in the temple of Nisroch. 2 Ki. 19:37; Isa. 37:38.

ADRIEL [AY-dree-el; "my help is God"] 1025 B.C. The man to whom Saul gave his daughter Merab in marriage. 1 Sam. 18:19; 2 Sam. 21:8. **Sons:** Five, all of whom David later handed over to the Gibeonites for execution.

AENEAS [eh-NEE-uhs; "praise"] A.D. 35. A paralytic in Lydda who was healed by Peter. Acts 9:33,34.

AGABUS [AG-uh-buhs; possibly "locust"] A.D. 45. A Christian prophet from Jerusalem who, at Antioch, predicted a severe famine throughout the Roman Empire. Later, at Caesarea, he accurately prophesied Paul's arrest in Jerusalem and surrender to the Roman authorities. Acts 11:28; 21:10.

AGAG [AY-gag; "high" or "warlike"; this may have been a title given to Amalekite kings]
1. B.C. (date unknown). A powerful king mentioned by Balaam in his third oracle to the Moabite King Balak. Num. 24:7.
2. 1025 B.C. The king of the Amalekites who Saul spared in direct disobedience of the Lord's command through Samuel. As a result, Samuel told Saul he was to be rejected as king by God; Samuel himself put Agag to death. 1 Sam. 15:8-33.

AGEE [AG-ee; "fugitive"] 1025 B.C. Father of the valiant Shammah, a military commander and one of David's mighty men. 2 Sam. 23:11.

AGRIPPA* [uh-GRIP-uh] Ruled A.D. 50-100. Agrippa II, the ruler of Galilee to whom the new Roman governor, Festus, turned for advice about an imprisoned Paul, in A.D. 59. Acts 25:13-26; 26:1-32. **Father:** Herod Agrippa I.

AGUR [AY-guhr; possibly "hireling" or "gatherer"] B.C. (date unknown). Son of Jakeh and author of Proverbs 30.

AHAB [AY-hab; "father is brother"]
1.* One of Israel's most wicked, yet most successful kings, who ruled the northern kingdom 874-853 B.C. 1 Ki. 16-21; 2 Chr. 18-22. **Father:** Omri. **Wife:** Jezebel. **Sons:** Ahaziah, Jehoram. **Daughter:** Athaliah.
2. 600 B.C. A false prophet among the Jews in Babylon during the Exile. Jer. 29:21-23.

AHARAH [uh-HAR-uh; "brother's follower"] 1850 B.C. Third of the five sons of Benjamin listed in 1 Chr. 8:1. Called Ahiram in Num. 26:38. Possibly the same as Aher in 1 Chr. 7:12 and Ehi in Gen. 46:21.

AHARHEL [uh-HAR-hel; "brother of Rachel"] B.C. (date unknown). A clan leader listed only in the genealogy of Judah in 1 Chr. 4:8.

AHASBAI [uh-HAS-bi; "blooming"] 1025 B.C. Father of Eliphelet, a military commander listed among David's thirty mighty men in 2 Sam. 23:34. The parallel passage reads "Eliphal son of Ur" (1 Chr. 11:35).

AHASUERUS (KJV) [uh-HAZ-yoo-EE-ruhs]
1. 575 B.C. Father of Darius the Mede mentioned in Dan. 9:1.

2. Notable in history as Xerxes I, who ruled Persia from 486–465 B.C.; and in Scripture known as the ruler who married Esther. Esther; Ezra. 4:6.

AHAZ [Ay-haz; "he grasped"]
1. 950 B.C. Son of Micah, great grandson of Saul. 1 Chr. 8:35,36; 9:42.
2.* 742–725 B.C. Evil eleventh king of Judah who burned a son as a human sacrifice. 2 Ki. 16; 2 Chr. 28; Isa. 7. **Father:** Jotham. **Wife:** Abijah. **Son:** Hezekiah.

AHAZIAH [AY-huh-ZI-uh; "Yahweh sustains"]
1. The evil ninth king of Israel who ruled from 853–852 B.C. He consulted Baal-Zebub rather than the Lord when he was injured. 1 Ki. 22; 2 Ki. 1; 2 Chr. 20. **Parents:** Ahab and Jezebel. **Children:** none.
2.* Evil sixth king of Judah who ruled in 841 BC. 2 Ki. 8,9; 2 Chr. 22. He is called Jehoahaz in 2 Chr. 21:16,17 where he is identified as the youngest son of Jehoram. **Parents:** Jehoram and Athaliah. **Grandparents:** Ahab and Jezebel. **Sister:** Jehosheba. **Surviving son:** Joash.

AHBAN [AH-bahn; "brother of intelligence"] B.C. (date unknown). A Judahite, listed only in the genealogy of Jerahmeel. 1 Chr. 2:29.

AHER [AY-huhr; "another"(?)] B.C. (date unknown). A Benjamite; ancestor of the Hushites. 1 Chr. 7:12. Possibly a shortened form of Ahiram.

AHI [AY-hi; "my brother"]
1. B.C. (date unknown). Son of Shomer, listed only in the genealogy of Asher in 1 Chr. 7:34. Possibly a mistranslation of "his brother Shomer."
2. B.C. (date unknown). Head of a family, listed in the genealogy of Gad in 1 Chr. 5:15.

AHIAH [uh-HI-uh; "Yahweh is brother"] 450 B.C. KJV: Ahijah. A Jewish leader who sealed the covenant renewal in Nehemiah's day. Neh. 10:26.

AHIAM [uh-HI-uhm] 1000 B.C. One of David's thirty mighty warriors. 2 Sam. 23:33; 1 Chr. 11:35.

AHIAN [uh-HI-uhn; "brotherly"] B.C. (date unknown). Listed only in the genealogy of Manasseh in 1 Chr. 7:19.

AHIEZER [AY-hi-EE-zuhr; "brother is help"]
1. 1450 B.C. Leader of the tribe of Dan in Moses' day. Num. 1:12.
2. 1000 B.C. Benjamite military leader and kinsman of Saul, he defected to David's army at Ziklag. 1 Chr. 12:3.

AHIHUD [uh-HI-hud; "brother is majesty"]
1. B.C. (date unknown). Son of Gera, a descendant of Benjamin. 1 Chr. 8:7.
2. 1400 B.C. Leader from the tribe of Asher appointed by Moses to help divide the land upon entering Canaan. Num. 34:27.

AHIJAH [uh-HI-juh; "Yahweh is brother"] KJV: Ahiah. Probably a shortened form of Ahimelech.
1. B.C. (date unknown). A son of Jerahmeel, a descendant of Judah. 1 Chr. 2:25.
2. 1025 B.C. Son of Ahitub and a priest with Saul's army in charge of the ark at Gibeah. Likely the same as Ahimelech 2, son of Ahitub 1. 1 Sam. 14:3,18.
3. 1000 B.C. A military commander, one of David's thirty mighty men listed in 1 Chr. 11:36. Parallel text in 2 Sam. 23:34 reads: "Eliam son of Ahithophel."
4. 1000 B.C. A Levite in charge of the Temple treasuries in David's day, according to the KJV and RSV. The name should probably be read as "an adjective," as in the NIV translation. 1 Chr. 26:20.

5. 950 B.C. A secretary for Solomon. 1 Ki. 4:3. **Brother:** Elihoreph.
6. 925 B.C. The prophet of Shiloh who foretold the division of the kingdom of Israel between the reigns of Solomon and Jeroboam. He later predicted the death of Jeroboam's son, and the end of Jeroboam's dynasty. 1 Ki. 11:29-39; 14:1-18.
7. 925 B.C. Father of Baasha, who became king of Israel after killing Nadab, son of Jeroboam. 1 Ki. 15:27,33.
8. B.C. (date unknown). KJV: Ahiah. A descendant of Benjamin deported to Manahath, listed in 1 Chr. 8:7. Possibly a scribal error, duplicating v. 4.
9. (KJV). See Ahiah.

AHIKAM [uh-HI-kuhm; "my brother has risen"] 625 B.C. An official of Josiah, sent to speak to the prophetess Huldah concerning the rediscovered Book of the Law. Ahikam later preserved the life of Jeremiah during the reign of Jehoiakim. 2 Ki. 22:12,14; Jer. 26:24; 40:5-16. **Son:** Gedaliah, later governor of Jerusalem.

AHILUD [uh-HI-luhd; "a brother born"(?)] 1025 B.C. Father of Jehoshaphat, official recorder under David and Solomon. Probably same as Ahilud, father of Baana, one of Solomon's twelve district governors. 2 Sam. 8:16; 20:24; 1 Ki. 4:3,12.

AHIMAAZ [uh-HIM-ay-az; "brother is wrath"(?)]
1. 1050 B.C. Father of Ahinoam, Saul's wife. 1 Sam. 14:50.
2. 975 B.C. Son of Zadok the high priest who remained loyal to David during Absalom's revolt. 2 Sam. 15:27,36; 17:17,20; 18:19-29.
3. 950 B.C. One of Solomon's twelve district governors. He married Solomon's daughter, Basemath. 1 Ki. 4:15.

AHIMAN [uh-HI-muhn; "brother of fortune"]
1. 1400 B.C. Descendant of Anak, among the Canaanites driven from Hebron by Caleb. Num. 13:22; Josh. 15:14.
2. 450 B.C. A gatekeeper at the Temple in Jerusalem after the Exile. 1 Chr. 9:17.

AHIMELECH [uh-HIM-eh-lek; "my brother is king"]
1. 1025 B.C. A Hittite with David as he fled from Saul. 1 Sam. 26:6.
2. The priest at Nob who aided David. In response to this aid, Saul executed all the priests at Nob, as well as their entire households. Abiathar, a son of Ahimelech, alone escaped. 1 Sam. 21:1-9; 22:9-20. Probably the same as Ahijah 2; both identified as a son of Ahitub 1.
3. 975 B.C. Son of Abiathar, and grandson of Ahimelech 2. 2 Sam. 8:17; 1 Chr. 24:6. In KJV called Abimelech in 1 Chr. 18:16.

AHIMOTH [uh-HI-moth; "brother is death"] A Levite from whom Samuel is descended. 1 Chr. 6:25.

AHINADAB [uh-HIN-uh-dab; "brother is noble"] 950 B.C. One of Solomon's twelve district governors. 1 Ki. 4:14.

AHINOAM [uh-HIN-oh-am; "brother is delight"]
1. 1025 B.C. Wife of Saul and daughter of Ahimaaz. 1 Sam. 14:50.
2. 1000 B.C. One of David's wives and mother of his firstborn son, Amnon. 1 Sam. 25:43; 27:3; 30:5; 2 Sam. 3:2.

AHIO [uh-HI-oh; "his brother"]
1. B.C. (date unknown). Listed only in the genealogy of Benjamin in 1 Chr. 8:14.
2. 1075 B.C. Eighth of the ten sons of Jeiel and Maacah and an uncle of Saul. 1 Chr. 8:31; 9:37.
3. 1000 B.C. A son of Abinadab who with his brother Uzzah helped move the ark from his father's house in Kireath Jearim to Jerusalem. 2 Sam. 6:3,4; 1 Chr. 13:7.

AHIRA [uh-HI-ruh; "brother is evil"] 1450 B.C. Leader of the tribe of Naphtali in Moses' day. Num. 1:15; 2:29; 10:27.

AHIRAM [uh-HI-ruhm; "brother is exalted"] 1850 B.C. Also Aharah, in 1 Chr. 8:1. Third of the five sons of Benjamin listed in Num. 26:38. Possibly the same as Aher in 1 Chr. 7:12 and Ehi in Gen. 46:21.

AHISAMACH [uh-HIS-uh-mahk; "brother supports"] 1475 B.C. A Danite, father of Oholiab, a craftsman who helped build the tabernacle and its furnishings. Ex. 31:6; 35:34; 38:23.

AHISHAHAR [uh-HISH-uh-hahr; "brother of the dawn"] B.C. (date unknown). Listed only in the genealogy of Benjamin in 1 Chr. 7:10.

AHISHAR [uh-HI-shahr; "brother has sung"] 950 B.C. A chief official of Solomon in charge of the palace. 1 Ki. 4:6.

AHITHOPHEL [uh-HITH-oh-fel; "brother of foolishness"]
1. 1025 B.C. Father of Eliam, a military commander, one of David's thirty mighty men listed in 2 Sam. 23:34.
2.* 975 B.C. The brilliant advisor of David, who joined David's son Absalom in a revolt against his father. 2 Sam. 15–17. Some think he is the grandfather of Bathsheba (compare 2 Sam. 23:34, 2 Sam. 11:3) who joined Absalom because of David's adultery with that young wife (2 Sam. 11,12). See also Ahithophel 1.

AHITUB [uh-HI-tub; "brother is good"]
1. 1050 B.C. Descendant of Aaron, father of Ahimelech 2 (see also Ahijah 2) the priest of Nob. 1 Sam. 14:3; 22:9.
2. 1050 B.C. Father of Zadok, the high priest in David's day (but probably Zadok's grandfather as indicated by 1 Chr. 9:11). 2 Sam. 8:17; 1 Chr. 6:7,8,52; 9:11; Ezra 7:2; Neh. 11:11. Possibly the same as Ahitub 1.
3. B.C. (date unknown). A Levite, also father of Zadok, descended from Ahitub 2. 1 Chr. 6:11,12.

AHLAI [AH-li]
1. B.C. (date unknown). Daughter of Sheshan; listed only in the genealogy of Jerahmeel, a descendant of Judah. 1 Chr. 2:31.
2. 1025 B.C. Father of Zabad, one of David's mighty men. 1 Chr. 12:41.

AHOAH [uh-HO-uh] 1825 B.C. Possibly an error for "Ahijah" in v.7. Sixth of the nine sons of Bela, firstborn son of Benjamin. 1 Chr. 8:4.

AHOLIAB (KJV). See Oholiab.

AHOLIBAMAH (KJV). See Oholibamah.

AHUMAI [uh-HOO-mi] B.C. (date unknown). Clan leader listed only in the genealogy of Judah in 1 Chr. 4:2.

AHUZZAM [uh-HUZ-uhm; "possessor"] B.C. (date unknown). KJV: Ahuzam. Listed only in the genealogy of Judah in 1 Chr. 4:6.

AHUZZATH [uh-HUZ-ath; "held fast"] 2025 B.C. Personal advisor of Abimelech, king of the Philistines, at the time of his treaty with Isaac. Gen. 26:26-31.

AHZAI [UH-zi; possibly a corruption of Ahaziah, "Yahweh sustains"] B.C. (date unknown). KJV: Ahasai. Ancestor of Amashsai, a priest in Nehemiah's time. Neh. 11:13. Possibly the same as Jahzerah in 1 Chr. 9:12.

AIAH [AY-yuh; "vulture"] KJV: Ajah.
1. 1975 B.C. Son of Zibeon and brother of Anah who lived in the land of Seir during Esau's time. Gen. 36:24.
2. 1075 B.C. Father of Rizpah, Saul's concubine. 2 Sam. 3:7; 21:8-11.

AKAN [AY-kan; "intelligent"(?)] 1925 B.C. RSV: Jaakan. KJV: Jakan. A son of Ezer, a Horite chief in the land of Seir when Esau settled there. Gen. 36:27; 1 Chr. 1:42.

AKIM [AY-kim; "woes"(?); possibly a shortened form of Jehoiakim] B.C. (date unknown). KJV, RSV: Achim. An ancestor of Jesus through Joseph. Mt. 1:14.

AKKUB [AK-ub; "pursuer"(?)]
1. B.C. (date unknown). Ancestral head of a family of gatekeepers after the Exile. Ezra 2:42; Neh. 7:45.
2. B.C. (date unknown). Ancestral head of a family of Temple servants after the Exile. Ezra 2:45.
3. 450 B.C. A gatekeeper at the Temple in Jerusalem, after the Exile. 1 Chr. 9:17; Neh. 11:19; 12:25.
4. 450 B.C. A Levite who in Jerusalem instructed the people in the Law with Ezra. Neh. 8:7.
5. B.C. (date unknown). A descendant of Zerubbabel listed in the genealogy of the royal line of David after the Exile. 1 Chr. 3:24.

ALEMETH [AL-uh-meth; "hidden"] KJV: Alameth.
1. 1825 B.C. Last of the nine sons of Beker, son of Benjamin. 1 Chr. 7:8.
2. B.C. (date unknown). A descendant of Jonathan, son of Saul. His father is given as Jehoaddah in 1 Chr. 8:36 and Jadah in 1 Chr. 9:42.

ALEXANDER [al-ig-ZAN-duhr; "defender of man"]
1.* "The Great." King of Macedon from 336–323 B.C., who conquered the Persian Empire and, in the process, spread Greek culture and language throughout the eastern world. **Parents:** Philip II of Macedon and Olympias of Epirus.
2. A.D. 30. A member of the Sanhedrin and kinsman of Annas the high priest. Acts 4:6.
3. A.D. 50. A son of Simon, the man from Cyrene who was forced by soldiers to carry the cross for Jesus. Mk. 15:21.
4. A.D. 55. A Jewish spokesman at the time of the riot in Ephesus. Acts 19:33,34.
5. A.D. 65. A false teacher who Paul had ejected from the early church, probably for teaching early Gnosticism. 1 Tim. 1:20.
6. A.D. 65. A metalworker who opposed the message of Paul. 2 Tim. 4:14. Possibly the same as Alexander 5.

ALIAH (KJV, RSV). *See* Alvah.

ALIAN (KJV, RSV). *See* Alvan.

ALLON [AL-luhn; "large tree"] Listed only in the genealogy of Simeon. 1 Chr. 4:37. KJV indicates the name in Josh. 19:33, properly rendered "large tree in Zaanannim" in NIV.

ALMODAD [al-MO-dad; "agitator" or El-modad, "God is friend"] B.C. (date unknown). A son of Joktan descended from Shem. Gen. 10:26; 1 Chr. 1:20.

ALPHAEUS [al-FEE-uhs; "leader"]
1. A.D. 1. Father of Levi the tax collector, who became Matthew, one of the twelve apostles. Mk. 2:14.
2. A.D. 1. Father of the apostle James (the Less), not to be identified with the better-known James, son of Zebedee. Possibly the same as Alphaeus 1, which would make James and Matthew brothers. Mt. 10:3; Mk. 3:18; Lk. 6:15; Acts 1:13.

ALVAH [AL-vuh; "sublime"(?)] B.C. (date unknown). KJV, RSV: Aliah (1 Chr. 1:51). A chief of Edom descended from Esau. Gen. 36:40; 1 Chr. 1:51.

ALVAN [AL-vun; "sublime"(?)] 1950 B.C. KJV, RSV: Alian (1 Chr. 1:40). Firstborn son of Shobal, a Horite chief in the land of Seir when Esau settled there. Gen. 36:23; 1 Chr. 1:40.

AMAL [AY-mahl; "laborer"] B.C. (date unknown). Listed only in the genealogy of Asher. 1 Chr. 7:35.

AMALEK [AM-uh-lek; "warlike"] 1900 B.C. Son of Eliphaz and his concubine Timna, and grandson of Esau. He is the ancestral source of the Amalekites.* The name is also used of the nomadic people and the land they inhabited. Gen. 36:12,16; 1 Chr. 1:36.

AMARIAH [am-uh-RI-uh; "Yahweh has said"]
1. 1100 B.C. Grandfather (or possibly great-grandfather) of Zadok, the high priest in David's time. 1 Chr. 6:7,52; Ezra 7:3.
2. B.C. (date unknown). Descendant of Amariah 1, listed in the genealogy of Levi. 1 Chr. 6:11.
3. B.C. (date unknown). A descendant of Kohath, son of Levi. 1 Chr. 23:19; 24:23.
4. 875 B.C. High priest during Jehoshaphat's reign. 2 Chr. 19:11.
5. B.C. (date unknown). Ancestor of Zephaniah the prophet. Zeph. 1:1.
6. 725 B.C. A Levite who helped distribute offerings among the priests in Hezekiah's time. 2 Chr. 31:15.
7. 525 B.C. Head of a priestly family that returned with Zerubbabel to Judah after the Exile. It is likely that his name as ancestral father of the family was used to seal the covenant renewal with God in Nehemiah's time. Neh. 10:3; 12:2,13.
8. 450 B.C. A Judahite who took a foreign wife after the Exile. Ezra 10:42.
9. B.C. (date unknown). An ancestor of Athaiah, one of those who stayed in Jerusalem after the Exile. Neh. 11:4.

AMASA [uh-MAS-uh; "burden-bearer"(?)]
1. 975 B.C. The appointed commander of Absalom's army and, after Absalom's death, David's army, replacing Joab. Shortly thereafter, Joab murdered him. 2 Sam. 17:25; 19:13; 20:4-13; 1 Chr. 2:17. **Mother:** Abigail, sister of David.
2. 750 B.C. An Israelite leader who opposed enslavement of captured men of Judah. 2 Chr. 28:12.

AMASAI [uh-MAS-i; "burden-bearer"(?)]
1. B.C. (date unknown). A Levite, ancestor of Heman, a Temple minister of music in David's time. 1 Chr. 6:25,35; 2 Chr. 29:12.
2. 1000 B.C. Chief of David's thirty mighty men, possibly the same as Abishai, the brother of Joab; or possibly the same as Amasa 1. 1 Chr. 12:18.
3. 1000 B.C. A priest who blew the trumpet before the ark as it was brought by David to Jerusalem. 1 Chr. 15:24.

AMASHSAI [uh-MASH-si] KJV: Amashai. 450 B.C. A priest who resided in Jerusalem in Nehemiah's time. Neh. 11:13.

AMASIAH [am-ah-SI-uh; "Yahweh bears"] 875 B.C. A Judahite military commander under Jehoshaphat. 2 Chr. 17:16.

AMAZIAH [AM-uh-ZI-uh; "Yahweh is mighty"]
1. 1000 B.C. A Levite, one of David's Temple musicians. 1 Chr. 6:45.
2.* Ruled 796–767 B.C. The eighth king of Judah, who began well but turned from God and ultimately was assassinated. **Parents:** Joash and Jehoaddin. **Son:** Uzziah. 2 Ki. 14; 2 Chr. 25.

3. 775 B.C. The priest at Bethel who opposed Amos. Amos uttered a prophetic curse against him. Amos 7:10-17.
4. 725 B.C. A Simeonite clan leader in Hezekiah's day. 1 Chr. 4:34.

AMI [AY-mi; "faithful"] 950 B.C. A servant of Solomon whose descendants returned to Judah after the Exile. Ezra 2:57. Called Amon in parallel text in Neh. 7:59.

AMITTAI [uh-MIT-i; "truthful"] 775 B.C. Father of Jonah the prophet. 2 Ki. 14:25; Jon. 1:1.

AMMIEL [AM-ee-el; "God is kinsman"]
1. 1450 B.C. A Danite sent by Moses to explore Canaan. Num. 13:12.
2. 1025 B.C. Father of Makir, who aided David as he fled from Absalom. 2 Sam. 9:4,5; 17:27.
3. 1025 B.C. The father of Bathsheba, wife of David and mother of Solomon. 1 Chr. 3:5. Identified as Eliam in 2 Sam. 11:3.
4. 1000 B.C. The sixth of the eight sons of Obed-Edom, all of whom were gatekeepers in David's day. 1 Chr. 26:5.

AMMIHUD [uh-MI-hud; "my kinsman is glorious"]
1. 1450 B.C. Leader of the tribe of Ephraim in Moses' day. Num. 1:10; 7:26.
2. 1400 B.C. A Simeonite appointed by Moses to help divide the land of Canaan. Num. 34:20.
3. 1400 B.C. Leader from the tribe of Naphtali appointed by Moses to help divide the land of Canaan. Num. 34:28.
4. 1025 B.C. Father of Talmai, king of Geshur to whom Absalom fled after killing his half-brother Amnon. 2 Sam. 13:37.
5. 450 B.C. Descendant of Perez the son of Judah, who resettled in Jerusalem after the Exile. 1 Chr. 9:4.

AMMINADAB [uh-MIN-uh-dab; "my kinsman is noble"] KJV NT: Aminadab.
1. B.C. (date unknown). A descendant of Kohath, son of Levi, identified as father of Korah in 1 Chr. 6:22. Elsewhere Izhar is so listed.

2. 1500 B.C. Father of Nahshon and his sister Elisheba, the wife of Aaron. Leader of the tribe of Judah in Moses' day and ancestor of David. Ex. 6:23; Num. 1:7; Ruth 4:19,20; Mt. 1:4; Lk. 3:33.

3. 1000 B.C. A descendant of Aaron. Head of Levite family who carried the ark when David brought it to Jerusalem. 1 Chr. 15:10,11.

AMMISHADDAI [am-mi-SHAD-i; "Almighty is kinsman"] 1500 B.C. Father of Ahiezer, leader of the tribe of Dan in Moses' day. Num. 1:12.

AMMIZABAD [uh-MIZ-uh-bad; "my kinsman has given"] 975 B.C. Son of Benaiah, captain of David's bodyguard. He served as commander of his father's division. 1 Chr. 27:6.

AMNON [AM-nahn; "faithful"]
1. B.C. (date unknown). Listed only in the genealogy of Judah in 1 Chr. 4:20.
2. 1000 B.C. Firstborn son of David, by Ahinoam, who raped his half-sister Tamar. In revenge, Absalom killed him; this initiated the split that eventually resulted in Absalom's rebellion against David. 2 Sam. 3:2; 13:1-39; 1 Chr. 3:1.

AMOK [AY-muhk; "deep"] 525 B.C. A priest who returned to Judah with Zerubbabel after the Exile; ancestor of Eber, a priest in Joiakim's time. Neh. 12:7,20.

AMON [UH-muhn; "trustworthy"]
1. B.C. (date unknown). The Egyptian deity of Thebes. Jer. 46:25. KJV renders the name "the multitude of No."
2. 950 B.C. A servant of Solomon whose descendants returned to Judah with Zerubbabel after the Exile. Neh. 7:59. Called Ami in Ezra 2:57.
3. 875 B.C. Governor of the city of Samaria during Ahab's reign. 1 Ki. 22:26.
4. Ruled 642–640 B.C. Son of Manasseh and also his successor; he reigned for two years, then was assassinated by his own officials. 2 Ki. 21:18-26; 2 Chr. 33:21-25.

AMOS [AY-muhs; "burden-bearer"]
1.* 775 B.C. A prophet during the reigns of Uzziah and Jeroboam II whose prophetic message is contained in the Book of Amos.
2. B.C. (date unknown). An ancestor of Christ. Lk. 3:25.

AMOZ [AY-mahz; "strong"] 775 B.C. Father of Isaiah the prophet. 2 Ki. 19:2,20; Isa. 1:1.

AMPLIATUS [AM-plee-AY-tuhs; "large"] A.D. 55. KJV: Amplias. A Roman Christian to whom Paul sent greetings. Rom. 16:8.

AMRAM [AM-ram; "the kinsman is exalted"]
1. 1525 B.C. A descendant of Levi and father of Moses, Aaron, and Miriam. Ex. 6:18,20; Num. 26:58,59. **Wife:** Jochebed.
2. 450 B.C. A Jew who took a foreign wife in Ezra's day. Ezra 10:34.

AMRAPHEL [AM-rah-fel; meaning uncertain] 2100 B.C. A king of Shinar, who was among a coalition of kings who defeated the kings of Sodom and Gomorrah, and were thereafter defeated by Abraham and his allies. Gen. 14.

AMZI [AM-zi; "my strength"]
1. B.C. (date unknown). Ancestor of Ethan, a Levite who served as a minister of music at the Temple in David's time. 1 Chr. 6:46.
2. B.C. (date unknown). Ancestor of Adaiah, a priest who settled in Jerusalem in Nehemiah's time. Neh. 11:12.

ANAH [AY-nuh]
1. 1975 B.C. The second of Zibeon the Horite's two sons and father of Oholibamah, one of Esau's wives. In Gen. 36:2,14, KJV mistak-

enly identifies Anah as Zibeon's daughter. Gen. 36:2,14,24-29; 1 Chr. 1:40. Probably the same as Beeri, father of Judith (Gen. 26:34); Beeri is likely a nickname ("man of the springs") for Anah, who "discovered the hot springs in the desert" (Gen. 36:24 NIV).
2. 1950 B.C. The uncle of Anah 1 and a Horite chief in Esau's time. Gen. 36:20,29; 1 Chr. 1:38.

ANAIAH [uh-NI-uh; "Yahweh has answered"]
1. 450 B.C. One who stood with Ezra as he read the Law before the people. Neh. 8:4.
2. 450 B.C. A leader who sealed the covenant renewal with God in Nehemiah's time. Neh. 10:22. Possibly the same as Anaiah 1.

ANAK [AY-nak; "long-necked"] B.C. (date unknown). Ancestral source of the Anakites.* Num. 13:22,28,33.

ANAMMELECH [uh-NAM-uh-lek] A deity of the Sepharvites to whom they sacrificed their children. 2 Ki. 17:31.

ANAN [AY-nuhn; "cloud"] 450 B.C. A leader who sealed the covenant renewal with God in Nehemiah's time. Neh. 10:26.

ANANI [uh-NAY-ni; "my cloud"(?)] B.C. (date unknown). A descendant of Zerubbabel, listed in the genealogy of the royal line of David after the Exile. 1 Chr. 3:24.

ANANIAH [AN-uh-NI-uh; "Yahweh has covered"(?)] 500 B.C. Grandfather of Azariah, who helped reconstruct the walls of Jerusalem in Nehemiah's time. Neh. 3:23.

ANANIAS [AN-uh-NI-hus; "protected by Yahweh"]
1.* A.D. 30. An early believer who was struck dead with his wife Sapphira for plotting to deceive the early church. Acts 5:1-11.
2. A.D. 35. A Christian in Damascus, noted for healing Saul after he was stricken with blindness. Acts 9:10-19; 22:12.
3. A.D. 60. High priest at Paul's trial before the Sanhedrin in Jerusalem. Acts 23:2; 24:1.

ANATH [AY-nath] 1225 B.C. Father of Shamgar, a minor judge of Israel. Jdg. 3:31; 5:6.

ANATHOTH [AN-uh-thath]
1. 1800 B.C. Eighth of the nine sons of Beker, son of Benjamin. 1 Chr. 7:8.
2. 450 B.C. A Jewish leader who sealed the covenant renewal with God in Nehemiah's time. Neh. 10:19.

ANDREW* [AN-droo; "manly"] A.D. 25. One of Jesus' earliest followers and one of the twelve disciples. **Father:** John, also called Jonah (Mt. 16:17). **Brother:** Peter, with whom he operated a fishing business from their home in Capernaum, in partnership with James and John who also became Jesus' disciples. The church historian Eusebius says Andrew later ministered in Scythia, an area in southern Russia north of the Black Sea. Mt. 4:18-22; Mk. 1:16-18; Jn. 1:40.

ANDRONICUS [an-DRON-uh-kuhs; "conqueror"] A.D. 55. A male relative Paul greets in Rom. 16:7.

ANER [AY-nuhr; "sprout" or "waterfall"(?)] 2100 B.C. One of the three Amorite brothers, allied with Abraham against the attackers of Sodom and Gomorrah who had taken Lot captive. Gen. 14:13,24. **Brothers:** Mamre and Eshcol.

ANIAM [uh-NI-uhm; "lamentation of the people"] B.C. (date unknown). Listed only in the genealogy of Manasseh in 1 Chr. 7:19.

ANNA* [AN-uh; "grace"] 5 B.C. Asherite prophetess notable for her recognition of the baby Jesus as the Messiah. Lk. 2:36-38.

ANNAS* [AN-uhs; "grace"] High priest from A.D. 6 to A.D. 15, he first saw and questioned Jesus after his arrest. Caiaphas, the acting high priest at the time, was his son-in-law. Jn. 18:13,24; Acts 4:6.

ANTHOTHIJAH [AN-thoh-THI-jah; "belonging to Anathoth"(?)] B.C. (date unknown). KJV: Antothijah. Listed only in the genealogy of Benjamin in 1 Chr. 8:24.

ANTIPAS [AN-ti-puhs] A.D. 80. A Christian martyr from the church in Pergamum. Rev. 2:13.

ANUB [AY-nub; "ripe"] B.C. (date unknown). Listed only in the genealogy of Judah in 1 Chr. 4:8.

APELLES [uh-PEL-eez] A.D. 55. A Christian Paul greets in Rom. 16:10 as one "tested and approved in Christ."

APHIAH [uh-FI-uh; "striving"(?)] B.C. (date unknown). A Benjamite, ancestor of Saul. 1 Sam. 9:1.

APHSES (KJV). See Happizzez.

APOLLOS [uh-PAH-lohs; "a destroyer"(?)] A.D. 50. A scholarly Jew converted to Christianity, who became an influential teacher in the early church at Corinth. Acts 18:24-28; 1 Cor. 1:12; 3:4-6,22.

APOLLYON [uh-PÁHL-ee-ahn; "the destroyer, destruction"] Greek name of Abaddon, the angel of the Abyss and king of the locusts released when the fifth angel sounds his trumpet in Rev. 9:11.

APPAIM [AP-ay-im; "faces; nostrils"] B.C. (date unknown). Listed only in the genealogy of Jerahmeel, descendant of Judah. 1 Chr. 2:30,31.

APPHIA [AF-ee-uh] A.D. 60. A Christian woman addressed by Paul in the greeting of his letter to Philemon. Phlm. 2.

AQUILA* [AK-wih-luh; "eagle"] A.D. 50. An early Christian who, with his wife Priscilla, was a friend and faithful supporter of Paul. Acts 18.

ARA [AR-uh] B.C. (date unknown). Listed only in the genealogy of Asher. 1 Chr. 7:38.

ARAD [AIR-ad; "fugitive"] B.C. (date unknown). Listed only in the genealogy of Benjamin in 1 Chr. 8:15.

ARAH [AIR-uh; "wanderer, traveler"]
1. B.C. (date unknown). Listed only in the genealogy of Asher. 1 Chr. 7:39.
2. B.C. (date unknown). Ancestor of a family that returned to Judah with Zerubbabel after the Exile. Ezra 2:5; Neh. 6:18; 7:10.

ARAM [AIR-uhm; "high, exalted"]
1.* B.C. (date unknown). Last of the five sons of Shem and ancestral source of the Arameans. Gen. 10:22,23; 1 Chr. 1:17. The name is frequently used to refer to the people or the land of the Arameans.
2. 2000 B.C. Son of Kemuel, the nephew of Abraham. Gen. 22:21.
3. B.C. (date unknown). Listed only in the genealogy of Asher in 1 Chr. 7:34.

ARAN [AIR-ahn; "wild goat"] 1950 B.C. Son of Dishan the Horite chief. Gen. 36:28.

ARAUNAH [uh-RAH-nuh; possibly "noble"] 1000 B.C. KJV, RSV: Ornan (1 Chronicles). The Jebusite whose threshing floor David purchased as the site of an altar to end a plague that had stricken Israel. Later Solomon would build the Temple on this site. 2 Sam. 24:15-25; 1 Chr. 21:18-28; 2 Chr. 3:1.

ARBA [AR-buh; "four"] Ancestor of Anak (possibly indicating the people), and founder of Kireath Arba (Hebron). Josh. 14:15; 15:13; 21:11.

ARCHELAUS [ahr-kuh-LAY-uhs; "people's chief"] 4 B.C.–A.D. 6. Son of Herod the Great, he succeeded his father as ethnarch of Judea. Mt. 2:22. **Brothers:** Herod Antipas and Philip.

ARCHIPPUS [ahr-KIP-uhs; "chief groom"] A.D. 60. A Christian Paul encourages in Col. 4:17 and addresses in his letter to Philemon. Possibly the owner of Onesimus, the runaway slave. Phlm. 2.

ARD [AHRD] 1825 B.C. Last of the ten sons of Benjamin and ancestral father of his own clan. Gen. 46:21; Num. 26:40. Probably same as Addar, son of Bela, in 1 Chr. 8:3.

ARDON [AHR-dahn; "descendant"(?)] B.C. (date unknown). Listed only in the genealogy of Judah. 1 Chr. 2:18.

ARELI [uh-REE-li] 1850 B.C. Last of the seven sons of Gad and ancestral head of his own clan. Gen. 46:16; Num. 26:17.

ARETAS [AHR-uh-tuhs; "goodness, excellence"] A.D. 35. Aretus IV, the Nabatean king over the governor of Damascus, who tried to capture Paul. 2 Cor. 11:32.

ARGOB [AHR-gahb; "a mound"] 750 B.C. An Israelite official assassinated with Pekahiah by Pekah. 2 Ki. 15:25.

ARIDAI [AIR-uh-di] 475 B.C. Ninth of the ten sons of Haman put to death by the Jews during the reign of Ahasuerus. Esth. 9:9.

ARIDATHA [AHR-uh-DAY-thuh] 475 B.C. Sixth of the ten sons of Haman slain by the Jews during Ahasuerus's reign. Esth. 9:8.

ARIEH [AIR-yah; "lion of Yahweh?)"] 750 B.C. An official slain with Pekahiah by Pekah. 2 Ki. 15:25.

ARIEL [AIR-ee-el; "lion of God"] 450 B.C. One of those sent by Ezra to retrieve Temple servants from Iddo, leader at Casiphia. Ezra 8:16.

ARIOCH [AHR-ee-ahk; possibly "lion-like"]
1. 2100 B.C. King of Ellasar and member of a coalition of kings that attacked Sodom and Gomorrah, taking Lot captive. Abraham defeated them and rescued Lot. Gen. 14:1,9.
2. 600 B.C. Commander of Nebuchadnezzar's guard, who was instructed by the king to execute the wise men of Babylon. Dan. 2:14,15,24,25.

ARISAI [AHR-uh-si] 475 B.C. Eighth of the ten sons of Haman put to death by the Jews during Ahasuerus's reign. Esth. 9:9.

ARISTARCHUS [AIR-uhs-TAHR-kuhs; "best ruler"] A.D. 55. A Christian from Thessalonica who was a traveling companion and prisoner with Paul. Acts 19:29; 20:4; 27:2; Col. 4:10; Phlm. 24.

ARISTOBULUS [air-is-TOB-yuh-luhs; "best advisor"] A.D. 55. A Roman whose household Paul greets in Rom. 16:10.

ARMONI [ahr-MOH-nee] 1000 B.C. Son of Saul and his concubine Rizpah. 2 Sam. 21:8.

ARNAN [AHR-nuhn; "joyous"(?)] B.C. (date unknown). A descendant of Zerubbabel listed in the genealogy of the royal line of David after the Exile. 1 Chr. 3:21.

ARODI [AIR-oh-dee] 1900 B.C. KJV, RSV: Arod (Num. 26:17). Sixth of the seven sons of Gad. Gen. 46:16; Num. 26:17.

ARPHAXAD [ahr-FAKS-ad] B.C. (date unknown). RSV OT: Arpachshad. A son of Shem and an ancestor of Christ, through Joseph. Gen. 10:22,24; Lk. 3:36.

ARTAXERXES* [AHR-tuh-ZERK-sees] The name of four Persian kings. Artaxerxes I Longimanus is the subject of the biblical references, who reigned 464–424 B.C. Notable for authorizing the rebuilding of Jerusalem's walls under Nehemiah. Ezra 4:7; 7:1–8:1; Neh. 2:1; 5:14.

ARTEMAS [AHR-teh-muhs; possibly contracted form of Artemidorus, "gift of Artemis," the Greek goddess] A.D. 65. A Christian companion of Paul's mentioned in his letter to Titus. Tit. 3:12.

ARTEMIS* [AHR-teh-mis] KJV: Diana (the Roman name of Artemis). A goddess worshiped throughout the Hellenic world. Her temple at Ephesus was one of the seven wonders of the ancient world. Acts 19:23-35.

ARZA [AHR-zuh] 900 B.C. The steward of Elah in whose house Elah was slain by Zimri, his successor. 1 Ki. 16:9.

ASA [AY-suh; "healer"]
1.* 910–869 B.C. The third king of Judah, and its first godly ruler. 1 Ki. 15:9-33; 2 Chr. 14–16. **Father:** Abijah. **Wife:** Azubah. **Son and successor:** Jehoshaphat.
2. B.C. (date unknown). Ancestor of Berekiah, a Levite who lived in Jerusalem after the Exile. 1 Chr. 9:16.

ASAHEL [AS-uh-hel; "God has made"]
1. 1025 B.C. Brother of Joab and Abishai, the sons of Zuruiah, David's sister. One of David's mighty men, killed by Abner. 2 Sam. 2:18-23,30,32; 3:27,30; 23:24; 1 Chr. 2:16; 11:26; 27:7. **Son:** Zebadiah.
2. 875 B.C. A Levite sent by Jehoshaphat to teach the Law to the people throughout Judah. 2 Chr. 17:8.
3. 725 B.C. A supervisor overseeing collection of tithes and contributions to the Temple in Hezekiah's time. 2 Chr. 31:13.
4. 450 B.C. One of the men who opposed Ezra's plan to purge the Jews of foreign wives. Ezra 10:15.

ASAIAH [uh-ZAY-uh; "Yahweh has made"]
1. 1000 B.C. A Levite, son of Haggiah, who helped David return the ark to Jerusalem. 1 Chr. 6:30; 15:6,11.
2. 725 B.C. A clan leader of the Simeonites in Hezekiah's time. 1 Chr. 4:36.
3. 625 B.C. KJV: Asahiah. Josiah's attendant, among those sent to speak to the prophetess Huldah concerning the rediscovered Book of the Law. 2 Ki. 22:12,14.
4. 450 B.C. A Shilonite who resettled with his sons in Jerusalem after the Exile. 1 Chr. 9:5. Called Maaseiah in Neh. 11:5.

ASAPH [AY-saf; "collector"]
1. B.C. (date unknown). A descendant of Korah and father of Kore, whose descendants were Temple gatekeepers in David's time. Most likely a scribal error for Abiasaph. 1 Chr. 26:1.
2. 1000 B.C. A Levite, a chief minister of music with his sons at the Temple in David's time. He was the author of Psalms 50 and 73–83. 1 Chr. 6:39; 15:17,19.
3. B.C. (date unknown). A descendant of Shemaiah, a Levite who resettled in Jerusalem after the Exile. 1 Chr. 9:15.
4. 725 B.C. Father of Joah, a recorder for Hezekiah. 2 Ki. 18:18,37; Isa. 36:3.
5. 450 B.C. Keeper of the king's forests in Judah to whom Artaxerxes sent a letter requesting timber needed by Nehemiah to rebuild Jerusalem. Neh. 2:8.

ASAREL [AS-uh-rel] B.C. (date unknown). KJV: Asareel. Listed only in the genealogy of Judah in 1 Chr. 4:16.

ASARELAH [AS-uh-REH-luh] 1000 B.C. RSV: Asharelah. A son of Asaph who minis-

tered with music in the Temple. 1 Chr. 25:2. Called Jesarelah in 25:14.

ASENATH [AS-en-ath; "belonging to Neit," a deity] 1875 B.C. Egyptian wife of Joseph and mother of Manasseh and Ephraim. Gen. 41:45,50; 46:20.

ASHBEL [ASH-bel; "man of Baal"(?)] 1850 B.C. Third of the ten sons of Benjamin in Gen. 46:21. Also listed in Num. 26:38; 1 Chr. 8:1.

ASHER [ASH-uhr; "happy"] 1900 B.C. KJV NT: Aser. Second son of Jacob and Zilpah, the maidservant of his first wife, Leah. Ancestral head of the tribe of Asher. Gen. 30:13; 35:26; 46:17; 49:20; 1 Chr. 2:2; Lk. 2:36; Rev. 7:6.

ASHERAH* [uh-SHEER-uh] Canaanite goddess of fertility and originally the consort of El, but in biblical times of Baal. Known also in Scripture as Ashtoreth and by the plural form Ashtoroth. Ex. 34:13; 2 Ki. 23:4-15.

ASHHUR [ASH-uhr; "happy"(?)] B.C. (date unknown). KJV: Ashur. A descendant of Judah, and leader of the people of Tekoa. 1 Chr. 2:24; 4:5.

ASHIMA [uh-SHI-muh] A deity whose idol the people of Hamath fashioned and worshiped after they were resettled in Samaria by Assyria. 2 Ki. 17:30.

ASHKENAZ [ASH-keh-nahz] B.C. (date unknown). KJV: Aschenaz (1 Chr. 1:6). First son of Gomer and a great-grandson of Noah. Gen. 10:3; 1 Chr. 1:6.

ASHPENAZ [ASH-peh-naz] 600 B.C. Chief of Nebuchadnezzar's court officials, made responsible for the training and instruction of Israelite youths, among them Daniel and his companions. Dan. 1:3.

ASHTORETH [ASH-tuh-reth; "goddess"] Plural Ashtaroth, in KJV and RSV. A fertility goddess worshiped by the Canaanites; the consort of Baal. Jdg. 2:13; 1 Ki. 11:5,33.

ASHURBANIPAL [ash-uhr-BAHN-uh-pahl; "Asshur has created an heir"] 669–626 B.C. RSV: Osnapper; KJV: Asnapper. Son of Esarhaddon, and last of the great kings of Assyria. Ezra 4:10.

ASHVATH [ASH-vath; "fashioned"(?)] B.C. (date unknown). Listed only in the genealogy of Asher. 1 Chr. 7:33.

ASIEL [AS-ee-el] B.C. (date unknown). An ancestor of Jehu, a Simeonite clan leader in Hezekiah's time. 1 Chr. 4:35.

ASNAH [AS-nah] B.C. (date unknown). Ancestral head of a family of Temple servants who returned to Judah with Zerubbabel after the Exile. Ezra 2:50.

ASPATHA [as-PAY-thuh; "horse-given"(?)] 475 B.C. Third of the ten sons of Haman slain by the Jews in Ahasuerus's time. Esth. 9:7.

ASRIEL [AS-ree-el] 1400 B.C. KJV: Ashriel (1 Chr. 7:14). A descendant of Manasseh and ancestral head of his own clan. Num. 26:31; Josh. 17:2; 1 Chr. 7:14.

ASSHUR [ASH-uhr; "level plain"(?)] B.C. (date unknown). Second of the five sons of Shem, possibly the ancestral source of the Assyrians. Gen. 10:22; 1 Chr. 1:17.

ASSIR [AS-uhr; "captive"]
1. B.C. (date unknown). A Levite, son or descendant of Korah. Ex. 6:24; 1 Chr. 6:22.
2. B.C. (date unknown). Son of Ebiasaph and great-grandson of Assir 1 in 1 Chr. 6:23,37.

ASYNCRITUS [uh-SING-krih-tuhs; "incomparable"] A.D. 55. A Roman Christian to whom Paul sends greetings. Rom. 16:14.

ATARAH [AT-uh-ruh; "crown"] B.C. (date unknown). A wife of Jerahmeel and mother of Onam in the genealogy of Judah in 1 Chr. 2:26.

ATER [AY-tuhr; "bound"]
1. B.C. (date unknown). Ancestral head of a family that returned to Judah with Zerubbabel after the Exile. Ezra 2:16; Neh. 7:21.
2. B.C. (date unknown). Ancestor of a family of gatekeepers who returned to Judah with Zerubbabel, probably same as Ater 1. Ezra 2:42; Neh. 7:45.
3. 450 B.C. A leader who sealed the covenant renewal with God in Nehemiah's time, possibly with the name of his family's ancestral head. Neh. 10:17.

ATHAIAH [uh-THAY-uh; "Yahweh is helper"] 450 B.C. A Judahite who lived in Jerusalem after the Exile. Neh. 11:4.

ATHALIAH [ATH-uh-LI-uh; "Yahweh is great"]
1. B.C. (date unknown). Third of the six sons of Jeroham, a Benjamite who lived in Jerusalem. 1 Chr. 8:26.
2.* 841–835 B.C. An evil queen who murdered her grandchildren to secure the throne. She was the only woman to reign over Judah. Daughter of Ahab and Jezebel and wife of Jehoram, king of Judah. Mother of Ahaziah. 2 Ki. 8,11; 2 Chr. 22,23.
3. 475 B.C. Father of Jeshaiah, head of a family of Elamites who returned to Judah with Ezra after the Exile. Ezra 8:7.

ATHLAI [ATH-li; shortened form of Athaliah, "Yahweh is great"] 450 B.C. A descendant of Bebai who took a foreign wife in Ezra's time. Ezra 10:28.

ATTAI [AT-ti; "timely"]
1. B.C. (date unknown). Listed only in the genealogy of Jerahmeel, a descendant of Judah. 1 Chr. 2:35,36.
2. 1000 B.C. A Gadite warrior who joined David at Ziklag. 1 Chr. 12:11.
3. 900 B.C. Second of the four sons of Rehoboam and Maacah, daughter of Absalom. 2 Chr. 11:20.

AUGUSTUS CAESAR* [uh-GUST-uhs; "august"] 63 B.C.–A.D. 14. Title of Octavian, nephew and successor of Julius Caesar. Christ was born during his reign. Lk. 2:1.

AZALIAH [AZ-uh-LI-uh; "Yahweh has set aside"] 650 B.C. Father of Shaphan, the secretary of Josiah. 2 Ki. 22:3; 2 Chr. 34:8.

AZANIAH [AZ-uh-NI-uh; "Yahweh has heard"] 475 B.C. Father of Jeshua, a Levite who sealed the covenant renewal with God in Nehemiah's time. Neh. 10:9.

AZAREL [AZ-uh-rel; "God has helped"] KJV: Azareel; Azarael (Neh. 12:36).
1. 1000 B.C. A Korahite who joined David's army at Ziklag. 1 Chr. 12:6.
2. 1000 B.C. A son of Heman and a Temple musician in David's time. 1 Chr. 25:18. Called Uzziel in 1 Chr. 25:4.

3. 1000 B.C. Son of Jeroham and officer of the tribe of Dan in David's time. 1 Chr. 27:22.
4. 475 B.C. Father of Amashsai, a priest who resettled in Jerusalem after the Exile. Neh. 11:13.
5. 450 B.C. A descendant of Binnui who took a foreign wife in Ezra's time. Ezra 10:41.
6. 450 B.C. A priest who played music at the dedication of the walls of Jerusalem in Nehemiah's time. Neh. 12:36.

AZARIAH [AZ-uh-RI-uh; "Yahweh has helped"]
1. B.C. (date unknown). Listed only in the genealogy of Judah in 1 Chr. 2:8.
2. B.C. (date unknown). Ancestor of Samuel the prophet listed in the genealogy of Heman the musician in David's time. 1 Chr. 6:36.
3. B.C. (date unknown). Listed only in the genealogy of Jerahmeel, a descendant of Judah, in 1 Chr. 2:38,39.
4. B.C. (date unknown). Ancestor of Zadok the high priest listed in the genealogy of Ezra the scribe. Ezra 7:3. He is excluded from the list of high priests in 1 Chr. 6:7.
5. 975 B.C. Son of Ahimaaz and grandson of Zadok the high priest. Grandfather of Azariah 6. 1 Chr. 6:9.
6. 950 B.C. A descendant of Zadok the high priest and chief priest in Solomon's time. 1 Ki. 4:2; 1 Chr. 6:10,11.
7. 950 B.C. Son of Nathan and chief official of Solomon in charge of the twelve district governors. 1 Ki. 4:5. Possibly Solomon's nephew.
8. 900 B.C. Son of Oded and prophet during the reign of Asa. 2 Chr. 15:1-8.
9. 850 B.C. A son of Jehoshaphat, king of Judah, killed by his brother Jehoram. 2 Chr. 21:2. Note: In the same verse, KJV and RSV also call Azariahu son of Jehoshaphat by its shortened form. See Azariahu.
10. 850 B.C. A military commander, son of Jeroham, who helped Jehoiada overthrow Athaliah and place Joash on the throne of Judah. 2 Chr. 23:1.
11. 850 B.C. Another military commander, a son of Obed, who aided Jehoiada. 2 Chr. 23:1.
12. 792–740 B.C. The tenth king of Judah. Also called Uzziah. 2 Ki. 14:21; 15:1-8; 1 Chr. 3:12. **Parents:** Amaziah and Jecoliah. Jotham was his son and successor.
13. 775 B.C. The high priest who opposed Uzziah king of Judah. 2 Chr. 26:17-20.
14. 750 B.C. An Israelite leader who opposed enslavement of captured men of Judah. 2 Chr. 28:12.
15. 750 B.C. Father of Joel, a Levite who helped purify the Temple in Hezekiah's time. 2 Chr. 29:12.
16. 725 B.C. A Levite, son of Jehallelel, who helped purify the Temple during the reign of Hezekiah. 2 Chr. 29:12.
17. 725 B.C. A descendant of Zadok and high priest in Hezekiah's time. 2 Chr. 31:10,13. Possibly the same as Azariah 15.
18. 600 B.C. Son of Hilkiah, high priest in Josiah's time, and ancestor of Ezra. 1 Chr. 6:13,14; Ezra 7:1.
19. 600 B.C. Original name of Abednego, one of the three companions of Daniel who refused to worship the idol of Nebuchadnezzar. Dan. 1:7; 2:17,49; 3:12-30.
20. 575 B.C. A son of Hoshaiah who ignored the advice of Jeremiah. Jer. 43:2. Called Jezaniah in Jer. 42:1.
21. 525 B.C. One of those who returned to Judah with Zerubbabel after the Exile. Neh. 7:7. Probably the same as Azariah 20; called Seraiah in Ezra 2:2.
22. 450 B.C. A son of Maaseiah who helped rebuild the walls of Jerusalem in Nehemiah's time. Neh. 3:23,24.
23. 450 B.C. A Levite who in Jerusalem instructed the people in the Law with Ezra. Neh. 8:7.
24. 450 B.C. A priest who sealed the cove-

nant renewal with God in Nehemiah's time. Neh. 10:2. The name is likely that of a family's ancestral head, perhaps Ezra in Neh. 12:1,13 (not Ezra the scribe).
25. 450 B.C. A leader of Judah at the time of the dedication of the walls of Jerusalem in Nehemiah's time. Neh. 12:33.
26. 450 B.C. Head of a priestly family who settled in Jerusalem after the Exile; son Azariah 18. 1 Chr. 9:11. Properly called Seraiah, as in 1 Chr. 6:14; Neh. 11:11.

AZARIAHU [AZ-uh-RI-uh-hoo; "God has helped"] 850 B.C. KJV, RSV: Azariah. A son of Jehoshaphat killed by his brother Jehoram, successor of Jehoshaphat. 2 Chr. 21:2.

AZAZ [AY-zaz; "powerful"] B.C. (date unknown). Listed only in the genealogy of Reuben in 1 Chr. 5:8.

AZAZIAH [AZ-uh-ZI-uh; "Yahweh is strong"]
1. 1025 B.C. Father of Hoshea, officer over the tribe of Ephraim in David's day. 1 Chr. 27:20.
2. 1000 B.C. A Levite who played the harp as the ark was brought back to Jerusalem by David. 1 Chr. 15:21.
3. 725 B.C. A supervisor overseeing collection of tithes and contributions to the Temple in Hezekiah's time. 2 Chr. 31:13.

AZBUK [AZ-buk] 475 B.C. Father of Nehemiah (a contemporary of the governor of the same name), who helped rebuild the wall of Jerusalem. Neh. 3:16.

AZEL [AY-zel; "noble"] B.C. (date unknown). A descendant of Jonathan, son of Saul, listed in 1 Chr. 8:37,38; 9:43,44.

AZGAD [AZ-gad; "Gad is strong"]
1. B.C. (date unknown). Ancestral head of a family whose descendants returned from Exile with Zerubbabel and, a later group, with Ezra. Ezra 2:12; 8:12; Neh. 7:17.
2. 450 B.C. A Jewish leader who sealed, probably with the name of his family's ancestral father (see Azgad 1), the covenant renewal with God in Nehemiah's time. Neh. 10:15.

AZIEL [AY-zee-el; "God is power"] 1000 B.C. Shortened form of Jaaziel (1 Chr. 15:18). A Levite who played the lyre as the ark was returned to Jerusalem by David. 1 Chr. 15:20.

AZIZA [ah-ZI-zuh; "strong"] 450 B.C. A Jew who took a foreign wife during the Exile. Ezra 10:27.

AZMAVETH [AZ-muh-veth; "strength of death"]
1. 1000 B.C. A military leader, one of David's thirty mighty men. 2 Sam. 23:31; 1 Chr. 11:33.
2. 1000 B.C. Father of Jeziel and Pelet, warriors who joined David at Ziklag. 1 Chr. 12:3. Probably same as Azmaveth 1.
3. 1000 B.C. A chief official of David, in charge of the royal storehouses. 1 Chr. 27:25.
4. A descendant of Jonathan, son of Saul, in 1 Chr. 9:42.

AZOR [AY-zor] B.C. (date unknown). An ancestor of Jesus listed only in Matthew's genealogy of Jesus. Mt. 1:13,14.

AZRIEL [AZ-ree-el; "God is helper"]
1. 1000 B.C. Father of Jerimoth, officer of the tribe of Naphtali in David's time. 1 Chr. 27:19.
2. 750 B.C. A family head of the tribe of Manasseh, taken into captivity by Tiglath-Pileser, king of Assyria. 1 Chr. 5:24-26.
3. 625 B.C. Father of Seraiah, who was sent by Jehoiakim to arrest Jeremiah and Baruch. Jer. 36:26.

AZRIKAM [AZ-rih-kam; "help has risen"]
1. B.C. (date unknown). A Benjamite descended from Jonathan, son of Saul. 1 Chr. 8:38; 9:44.

2. 750 B.C. A chief official of Ahaz in charge of the palace. 2 Chr. 28:7.
3. B.C. (date unknown). Ancestor of Shemaiah, a Levite who resettled in Jerusalem after the Exile. 1 Chr. 9:14; Neh. 11:15.
4. B.C. (date unknown). A descendant of Zerubbabel listed in the royal line of David. 1 Chr. 3:23.

AZUBAH [uh-ZOO-buh; "forsaken"]
1. B.C. (date unknown). First wife of Caleb, son of Hezron, listed in the genealogy of Judah in 1 Chr. 2:18,19.
2. 900 B.C. Mother of Jehoshaphat, king of Judah. 1 Ki. 22:42.

AZZAN [AZ-zuhn] 1450 B.C. Father of Paltiel, leader from the tribe of Isaachar appointed by Moses to help divide the land upon entering Canaan. Num. 34:26.

AZZUR [AZ-uhr; "helper"] KJV: Azur (Jer. 28; Ezek. 11:1).
1. 625 B.C. Father of Hananiah, the false prophet who opposed Jeremiah. Jer. 28.
2. 575 B.C. Father of Jaazariah, a Jewish leader seen by Ezekiel in a vision. Ezek. 11:1.
3. 450 B.C. A leader who sealed the covenant renewal with God, probably with the name of his family's ancestral father. Neh. 10:17.

B

BAAL [BAY-uhl; "master, lord"]
1.* The title of a Canaanite deity, the central figure in Canaanite worship in biblical times. The name also refers to local gods of the Canaanites, whose power and worship involved a particular location. Num. 25:1-5; 1 Ki. 16:31,32; 18:18-26,40; 2 Ki. 10:18-28; Jer. 19:5.
2. B.C. (date unknown). Listed only in the genealogy of Reuben in 1 Chr. 5:5.
3. B.C. (date unknown). Fourth of the ten sons of Jeiel and a brother of Kish, ancestor of Saul. 1 Chr. 8:30; 9:36.

BAAL-HANAN [BAY-uhl HAY-nuhn; "Baal is gracious"]
1. A pre-Israelite king of Edom. Gen. 36:38,39.
2. 1000 B.C. A Gederite, regional overseer of David's olive and sycamore trees. 1 Chr. 27:28.

BAALIS [BAY-uhl-is; "lord of joy"(?)] 575 B.C. King of the Ammonites after the fall of Jerusalem. Jer. 40:14.

BAAL-ZEBUB [BAY-uhl ZEE-bub; "lord of the flies"] The Philistine god of Ekron that Ahaziah attempted to consult. 2 Ki. 1:2-17. *See also* Beelzebub.

BAANA [BAY-ah-nuh; "son of oppression"]
1. 950 B.C. A son of Ahilud and one of Solomon's twelve district governors. 1 Ki. 4:12.
2. 950 B.C. A son of Hushai and one of Solomon's twelve district governors. 1 Ki. 4:16.
3. 475 B.C. Father of Zadok, who helped repair the wall of Jerusalem in Nehemiah's time. Neh. 3:4.

BAANAH [BAY-ah-nuh; "son of oppression"]

1. 1050 B.C. Father of Heled, one of David's military elite known as his thirty mighty men. 2 Sam. 23:29; 1 Chr. 11:30.
2. 1000 B.C. A military leader noted, with his brother Recab, for the murder of Ish-Bosheth, the son and successor of Saul. 2 Sam. 4:2-12.
3. 525 B.C. One who returned with Zerubbabel from Exile. Ezra 2:2; Neh. 7:7.
4. 450 B.C. A leader who sealed the covenant renewal with God in Nehemiah's time, probably with the name of a family ancestor (*see* Baanah 3). Neh. 10:27.

BAARA [BAY-ah-ruh] B.C. (date unknown). A divorced wife of Shaharaim, listed only in the genealogy of Benjamin in 1 Chr. 8:8.

BAASEIAH [BAY-uh-SEE-yuh; "Yahweh is bold" or "work of the Lord"] B.C. (date unknown). An ancestor of Asaph, a chief minister of music at the Temple in David's time. 1 Chr. 6:40.

BAASHA [BAY-ah-shuh; "boldness"(?)] 908–886 B.C. The killer of Nadab, he took the throne to become the third king of Israel. 1 Ki. 15:16–16:13; 2 Chr. 16:1-6.

BAKBAKKAR [bak-BAK-uhr; "searcher"] 450 B.C. A Levite who resettled in Jerusalem after the Exile. 1 Chr. 9:15. Called Bakbukiah in Neh. 11:17.

BAKBUK [BAK-buk; "wasted" or "flask"] B.C. (date unknown). Ancestor of a family of Temple servants who returned to Judah after the Exile. Ezra 2:51; Neh. 7:53.

BAKBUKIAH [BAK-buh-KI-uh; "wasted by Yahweh" or "Yahweh's flask"]
1. 525 B.C. A Levite who returned to Judah with Zerubbabel. Neh. 12:9.
2. 475 B.C. A Levite gatekeeper who guarded the Temple storehouse. Neh. 12:25.
3. 450 B.C. A Levite who resettled in Jerusalem after the Exile. Neh. 11:17. Called Bakbakkar in 1 Chr. 9:15. Possibly the same as Bakbukiah 2.

BALAAM* [BAY-luhm; possibly "devourer"] 1400 B.C. A famous pagan practitioner of the occult hired by King Balak of Moab to curse Israel. Num. 22–24; 31:8,16. **Father:** Beor.

BALADAN [BAL-uh-duhn] 750 B.C. Father of Merodach-Baladan, king of Babylon. 2 Ki. 20:12; Isa. 39:1.

BALAK [BAY-lak; "devastator"] 1400 B.C. KJV NT: Balac. The king of Moab at the time when Israel entered Canaan; he tried to prevent Israel's progress by hiring Balaam to curse Israel. Num. 22–24; Rev. 2:14. **Father:** Zippor.

BANI [BAY-ni; "posterity"]
1. B.C. (date unknown). A Levite whose descendant, Ethan, was a chief minister of music in David's time. 1 Chr. 6:46.
2. 1000 B.C. RSV, KJV have Bani as one of David's mighty men, in 2 Sam. 23:36; the NIV has "son of Hagri" as is found in the parallel text in 1 Chr. 11:38.
3. B.C. (date unknown). A Judahite whose descendant, Uthai, resettled in Jerusalem after the Exile. 1 Chr. 9:4.
4. B.C. (date unknown). Ancestral head of a family that returned to Judah with Zerubbabel after the Exile. Ezra 2:10; 10:29. Called Binnui in Neh. 7:15.
5. B.C. (date unknown). Another named Bani whose descendants took foreign wives after the Exile. Ezra 10:34. Possibly the same as Bani 4.
6. 475 B.C. Father of Rehum, a Levite who helped repair the wall of Jerusalem in Nehemiah's time. Neh. 3:17.
7. 475 B.C. A descendant of Asaph and father of Uzzi, chief officer of the Levites in Jerusalem. Neh. 11:22.

8. 450 B.C. A Levite who with Ezra instructed the people in the Law. Neh. 8:7; 9:4.
9. 450 B.C. A Levite involved in leading worship before the people. Neh. 9:4,5.
10. 450 B.C. A Levite who sealed the covenant renewal with God in Nehemiah's time. Neh. 10:13. Possibly the same as Bani 7 or 8.
11. 450 B.C. A Jewish leader who sealed the covenant renewal with God after the Exile, probably with the name of the family's ancestral head. Neh. 10:14.

BARABBAS* [buh-RAB-uhs; "father's son" or "son of Abba"] A.D. 30. The criminal that Pilate released at the crowd's insistence instead of Jesus, who was crucified in his place. Mt. 27:16-26; Mk. 15:7-15; Lk. 23:18; Jn. 18:40.

BARAK [BAIR-uhk; "lightning"] 1225 B.C. KJV, RSV: Bedan (1 Sam. 12:11). The general who, under Deborah the judge, defeated the forces of the Canaanite king Jabin. Jdg. 4,5; 1 Sam. 12:11. **Father:** Abinoam.

BARAKEL [BAHR-uh-kel; "God blesses"] B.C. (date unknown). KJV, RSV: Barachel. Father of Elihu, one who argued with Job. Job 32:2,6.

BARIAH [buh-RI-uh; "fugitive"] B.C. (date unknown). A descendant of Zerubbabel in the royal line of David after the Exile. 1 Chr. 3:22.

BAR-JESUS [BAHR-JEE-suhs; "son of Jesus"] A.D. 45. A Jewish sorcerer and false prophet on Cyprus stricken with temporary blindness when Paul denounced him. Acts 13:6-11. Also called Elymas.

BARKOS [BAHR-kuhs] B.C. (date unknown). An ancestor of a family of Temple servants that returned to Judah with Zerubbabel. Ezra 2:53; Neh. 7:55.

BARNABAS* [BAHR-nuh-buhs; "son of encouragement"] A.D. 35. A Jewish Christian who traveled extensively with Paul on his missionary journeys, and a significant leader in the early church. Acts 4:36,37; 9:26,27; 11:22-30; 13:1-7; 15:22-26,36-40; Gal. 2:1,9-13. His original name was Joseph (KJV: Joses), but he was renamed by the apostles. Mark was his cousin (Col. 4:10).

BARSABBAS [bahr-SAHB-uhs; "son of Saba" or "son of the Sabbath"] KJV: Barsabas.
1. A.D. 30. Nickname of Joseph, one of the two men proposed to replace Judas Iscariot as the twelfth apostle; Matthias was selected. Acts 1:23. Also known as Justus.
2. A.D. 50. Nickname of Judas, sent with Paul and Barnabas to Antioch by the church in Jerusalem. Acts 15:22.

BARTHOLOMEW* [bahr-THAHL-uh-myoo; "son of Talmai"] A.D. 25. One of the "unknown" among the twelve disciples of Jesus, who appears only in lists which name them all. Mt. 10:3; Mk. 3:18; Lk. 6:14; Acts 1:13. Some suggest he is Nathanael of John 1:45-51.

BARTIMAEUS [BAHR-tuh-MAY-uhs; "son of Timaeus"] A.D. 25. A blind beggar at Jericho healed by Jesus. Mk. 10:46-52.

BARUCH [BAIR-uhk; "blessed"]
1.* 600 B.C. The friend and secretary of the prophet Jeremiah. Jer. 32,36,43,45. **Father:** Neriah. **Brother:** Seraiah, an official in the royal court.
2. 475 B.C. Father of Maaseiah, a Judahite who resettled in Jerusalem after the Exile. Neh. 11:5.
3. 450 B.C. One who helped rebuild the wall of Jerusalem in Nehemiah's time. Neh. 3:20.
4. 450 B.C. A priest who signed the covenant renewal with God in Nehemiah's time. Neh. 10:6. Probably the same as Baruch 3.

BARZILLAI [bahr-ZIL-i; "of iron"]
1. 1050 B.C. Father of Adriel, the husband of Merab, daughter of Saul. 2 Sam. 21:8.
2. 1000 B.C. An old and wealthy Gileadite who aided David as he fled from Absalom. 2 Sam. 17:27; 19:31-39. His sons were provided for by David. 2 Ki. 2:7.
3. 975 B.C. Ancestor of a family of priests who could not prove their priestly ancestry. Ezra 2:61; Neh. 7:63. He took his name from Barzillai 2, whose daughter he married.

BASEMATH [BAS-uh-math; "fragrant"] KJV: Bashemath; Basmath (1 Ki. 4:15).
1. 1950 B.C. A Canaanite wife of Esau, daughter of Elon the Hittite. Gen. 26:34. Probably the same as Adah, daughter of Elon the Hittite.
2. 1925 B.C. Another wife of Esau, daughter of Abraham's son Ishmael. Gen. 36:3,4,10,13. Called Mahalath in Gen. 28:6-9.
3. 925 B.C. A daughter of Solomon and wife of Ahimaaz, one of Solomon's district governors. 1 Ki. 4:15.

BATHSHEBA* [bath-SHEE-bah; "daughter of an oath" or "seventh daughter"(?)] 1000 B.C. KJV, RSV: Bathshua (1 Chr. 3:5). The woman with whom King David committed adultery and later married. 2 Sam. 11,12; 1 Ki. 1:11-31; 2:13-25; 1 Chr. 3:5. **Father:** Ammiel. **Husbands:** Uriah and David. **Sons by David:** Shammua, Shobab, Nathan, and Solomon, David's successor as king of Israel.

BATHSHUA (KJV, RSV) [bath-SHOO-uh; "daughter of abundance"] 1875 B.C. NIV: "daughter of Shua" (1 Chr. 2:3). A Canaanite woman, wife of Judah and mother of Er, Onan, and Shelah. 1 Chr. 2:3. Called Shua in Gen. 38:2,12.

BAZLUTH [BAZ-luth] B.C. (date unknown). KJV, RSV: Bazlith (Neh. 7:54). Ancestral head of a family of Temple servants that returned to Judah with Zerubbabel after the Exile. Ezra 2:52; Neh. 7:54.

BEALIAH [BEE-uh-LI-uh; "Yahweh is lord"] 1000 B.C. A Benjamite and kinsman of Saul who defected to David's army at Ziklag. 1 Chr. 12:5.

BEBAI [BEE-bi; "fatherly"]
1. B.C. (date unknown). Ancestral head of a family that returned to Judah after the Exile. Ezra 2:11; 8:11; 10:28; Neh. 7:16.
2. 450 B.C. A Jewish leader who sealed the covenant renewal with God in Nehemiah's time, probably with the name of his family's ancestral head (see Bebai 1). Neh. 10:15.

BECORATH [beh-KOHR-ath; "firstborn"] B.C. (date unknown). KJV: Bechorath. A Benjamite, ancestor of Saul. 1 Sam. 9:1.

BEDAD [BEE-dad; "alone"] B.C. (date unknown). Father of Hadad, a pre-Israelite king of Edom. Gen. 36:35.

BEDAN [BEE-dan] B.C. (date unknown). Listed only in the genealogy of Manasseh in 1 Chr. 7:17.

BEDEIAH [beh-DEE-yuh; "servant of Yahweh"] 450 B.C. A descendant of Bani who took a foreign wife after the Exile. Ezra 10:35.

BEELIADA [BEE-uh-LI-ah-duh; "the lord knows"] 1000 B.C. A son of David. 1 Chr. 14:7. Called Eliada in 2 Sam. 5:16; 1 Chr. 3:8.

BEELZEBUB* [bee-EL-zeh-buhb; "lord of the flies"] RSV: Beelzebul; KJV: Baal-zebub. The name by which the prince of demons was known in Jesus' time. Mt. 12:24-27; Lk. 11:15-19. The name is probably derived from the Philistine deity Baal-Zebub.

BEERA [BEER-uh; "well"] B.C. (date unknown). Listed only in the genealogy of Asher in 1 Chr. 7:37.

BEERAH [BEER-uh; "well"] 750 B.C. A Reubenite leader taken into captivity by Tiglath-Pileser, king of Assyria. 1 Chr. 5:6.

BEERI [BEER-ee; "man of the springs"]
1. 1975 B.C. Father of Judith, a wife of Esau. Gen. 26:34. Probably the same as Anah, father of Oholibamah (probably another name for Judith), in Gen. 36:24,25. He "discovered hot springs" (NIV), thus Beeri is likely a nickname.
2. 725 B.C. Father of Hosea the prophet. Hos. 1:1.

BEKER [BEE-kuhr; "youth" or "young camel"] KJV, RSV: Becher.
1. 1850 B.C. The second son of Benjamin listed in Gen. 46:21; 1 Chr. 7:6,8.
2. B.C. (date unknown). A descendant of Ephraim listed in Num. 26:35. Called Bered in 1 Chr. 7:20.

BEL [BEL; "lord"] Alternate name of Marduk (Merodach), chief god of Babylon. Isa. 46:1; Jer. 50:2; 51:44.

BELA [BEE-luh; "consumer"] KJV: Belah.
1. 1850 B.C. Firstborn son of Benjamin, listed in Gen. 46:21; 1 Chr. 7:6,7; 8:1,3.
2. B.C. (date unknown). A pre-Israelite king of Edom, listed in Gen. 36:32,33.
3. B.C. (date unknown). A clan leader listed only in the genealogy of Reuben in 1 Chr. 5:8.

BELIAL* [BEE-lee-uhl; "worthlessness, lawlessness"] In the KJV OT, a word denoting wickedness (Jdg. 19:22; 1 Sam. 30:22). In NT times, it had become a proper name used to identify Satan. 2 Cor. 6:15.

BELSHAZZAR [bel-SHAZ-uhr; "Bel protect the king"] Son of Nabonidus and co-regent of Babylon from 550-539 B.C., notable as king for whom Daniel interpreted writing on the wall of the palace. Dan. 5.

BELTESHAZZAR [BEL-tuh-SHAZ-uhr; "protect his life"] 600 B.C. Babylonian name given to Daniel upon entrance into the service of Nebuchadnezzar. Dan. 1:7. See Daniel.

BEN-ABINADAB [BEN-ah-BIN-uh-dab; KJV: "son of Abinadab"] 950 B.C. One of Solomon's twelve district governors, married to Taphath, daughter of Solomon. 1 Ki. 4:11.

BENAIAH [beh-NAY-yuh; "Yahweh has built"]
1. 1025 B.C. Father of Jehoiada, successor of Ahithophel. 1 Chr. 27:34.
2. 1000 B.C. The son of Jehoiada the priest, notable as the slayer of Adonijah and Joab upon Solomon's command. He served as commander of David's bodyguard and, after Joab's death, as commander of Israel's army under Solomon. 2 Sam. 20:23; 23:20-22; 1 Ki. 1:8,10,26,36; 2:25,29-35,46; 4:4. **Son:** Ammizabad.
3. 1000 B.C. Benaiah the Pirathonite, one of the military elite known as David's thirty mighty men. 2 Sam. 23:30; 1 Chr. 27:14.
4. 1000 B.C. A Temple musician who played the lyre. 1 Chr. 15:18,20.
5. 1000 B.C. A priest assigned to blow the trumpet before the ark. 1 Chr. 15:24; 16:6. Probably the same as Benaiah 4.
6. 925 B.C. Descendant of Asaph and grandfather of Jahaziel, a priest in Jehoshaphat's time. 2 Chr. 20:14.
7. 725 B.C. A Simeonite clan leader in the time of Hezekiah. 1 Chr. 4:36.
8. 725 B.C. A supervisor overseeing collection of tithes and contributions to the Temple in Hezekiah's time. 2 Chr. 31:13.
9. 625 B.C. Father of Pelatiah, a Jewish

leader seen in a vision by Ezekiel. Ezek. 11:1-3,13.
10, 11, 12, and 13. 450 B.C. Four Jews listed among those who took foreign wives after the Exile. Ezra 10:25,30,35,43.

BEN-AMMI [ben-AM-ee; "son of my people"] 2025 B.C. KJV: Ammon. Son of Lot by his younger daughter and ancestral father of the Ammonites. Gen. 19:38.

BEN-DEKER [ben-DEE-kuhr; KJV: "son of Dekar"] 950 B.C. One of Solomon's twelve district governors. 1 Ki. 4:9.

BEN-GEBER [ben-GEE-buhr; KJV: "son of Geber"] 950 B.C. One of Solomon's twelve district governors, over the territory of Ramoth Gilead. 1 Ki. 4:13.

BEN-HADAD [ben-HAY-dad; "son of Hadad"] Dynastic name of Syrian kings.
1. 875 B.C. Ben-Hadad I, a king of Syria with whom King Asa established a treaty. 1 Ki. 15:18-20. Son of Tabrimmon.
2. 850 B.C. Ben-Hadad II, also a Syrian king, probably son of Ben-Hadad 1. He was defeated by Ahab. 1 Ki. 20; 2 Ki. 6:24; 8:7-15.
3. 800 B.C. The son and successor of Hazael who had killed Ben-Hadad II and usurped the throne. With his father, Ben-Hadad III oppressed Israel during the reign of Jehoahaz. He was defeated three times by Jehoash, son of Jehoahaz. 2 Ki. 13:3,24,25.

BEN-HAIL [ben-HAYL; "son of strength"] 875 B.C. An official sent by King Jehoshaphat to teach the Law throughout Judah. 2 Chr. 17:7.

BEN-HANAN [ben-HAY-nuhn; "son of grace"] B.C. (date unknown). Listed only in the genealogy of Judah in 1 Chr. 4:20.

BEN-HESED [BEN-HEH-sed; "son of loving-kindness"] 950 B.C. KJV: "son of Hesed." One of Solomon's twelve district governors. 1 Ki. 4:10.

BEN-HUR [ben-HUHR; KJV: "son of Hur"] 950 B.C. One of the twelve district governors under Solomon. 1 Ki. 4:8.

BENINU [buh-NI-noo; "our son"] 450 B.C. A Levite who sealed the covenant renewal with God in Nehemiah's time. Neh. 10:13.

BENJAMIN [BEN-juh-min; "son of my right hand"]
1. 1875 B.C. Jacob's youngest son; as Rachel was dying in childbirth, she named him Ben-Oni ("child of my sorrow"), but afterwards Jacob called him Benjamin. He was the ancestral source of the tribe of Benjamin. Gen. 35:18,24; 42-45; 46:21; 49:27. **Brother:** Joseph. **Half-brothers:** (see Jacob).
2. B.C. (date unknown). Listed only in the genealogy of the tribe of Benjamin in 1 Chr. 7:10.
3. 450 B.C. A descendant of Harim who took a foreign wife after the Exile. Ezra 10:32.
4. 450 B.C. One who helped rebuild the wall of Jerusalem in Nehemiah's time. Neh. 3:23.
5. 450 B.C. One who helped dedicate the reconstructed wall of Jerusalem. Neh. 12:34. Possibly the same as Benjamin 4.

BENO [BEE-noh; "his son"] B.C. (date unknown). A Levite listed among the descendants of Merari in 1 Chr. 24:26,27.

BEN-ONI [ben-OH-nee; "son of my trouble"] 1875 B.C. Name given by Rachel to her second son, changed to Benjamin by his father Jacob after Rachel's death. Gen. 35:18.

BEN-ZOHETH [ben-ZO-heth; "son of Zoheth"] B.C. (date unknown). Listed only in the genealogy of Judah in 1 Chr. 4:20.

1059

BEOR [BEE-ohr; "shepherd"]
1. B.C. (date unknown). Father of Bela, who reigned as a pre-Israelite king of Edom. Gen. 36:32.
2. 1425 B.C. Father of Baalam, the seer hired by Balak to curse the Israelites. Num. 22:5.

BERA [BEER-uh] 2100 B.C. The king of Sodom defeated in battle; Abram came to his aid. Gen. 14.

BERACAH [BAIR-uh-kah; "blessing"] 1000 B.C. KJV: Berachah. A Benjamite and kinsman of Saul who joined David's army at Ziklag. 1 Chr. 12:3.

BERAIAH [buh-RAY-yuh; "Yahweh has created"] B.C. (date unknown). Listed only in the genealogy of Benjamin in 1 Chr. 8:21.

BERAKIAH [BAIR-uh-KI-uh; "Yahweh has blessed"] B.C. (date unknown). KJV: Barachias; RSV: Barachiah. Father of Zechariah, a righteous man slain by the Jews. Mt. 23:35. Probably the same as Berekiah 4, father of Zechariah the prophet.

BERED [BEER-ed] B.C. (date unknown). A son of Ephraim. 1 Chr. 7:20. Probably the same as Beker in Num. 26:35.

BEREKIAH [BAIR-uh-KI-uh; "Yahweh has blessed"] KJV, RSV: Berechiah.
1. 1025 B.C. Father of Asaph, a chief minister of music in David's time. 1 Chr. 6:39; 15:17.
2. 1000 B.C. A doorkeeper for the ark in David's time. 1 Chr. 15:23.
3. 750 B.C. A leader in Ephraim, son of Meshillemoth, who opposed the enslavement of Jews from Judah during the reign of Ahaz. 2 Chr. 28:12.
4. 550 B.C. KJV: Barachias. Father of Zechariah the prophet. Zech. 1:1,7. Probably the same as Berakiah, father of Zechariah referred to in Mt. 23:35.
5. 500 B.C. A son of Zerubbabel listed only in the genealogy of the royal line of David after the Exile. 1 Chr. 3:20.
6. 475 B.C. Father of Meshullam, who helped repair the walls of Jerusalem. Neh. 3:4,30; 6:18.
7. 450 B.C. A Levite who resettled near Jerusalem after the Exile. 1 Chr. 9:16.

BERI [BEER-ee; "wisdom"] B.C. (date unknown). Listed only in the genealogy of Asher in 1 Chr. 7:36.

BERIAH [buh-RI-uh; "misfortune"]
1. 1850 B.C. Last of the four sons of Asher listed in Gen. 46:17; Num. 26:44,45.
2. 1825 B.C. A son of Ephraim listed in 1 Chr. 7:23.
3. B.C. (date unknown). Head of a family of Benjamites that lived in Aijalon. 1 Chr. 8:13,16.
4. B.C. (date unknown). Listed only in the genealogy of the Levites descended from Gershon, son of Levi. 1 Chr. 23:10,11.

BERNICE [buhr-NI-see; "victorious"] A.D. 50. Daughter of Agrippa I, she was married to Marcus, son of Tiberius Julius Alexander, and after his death, to her uncle Herod. However, at the time of their arrival at Caesarea, she was living incestuously with her brother, Agrippa II. Acts 25:13,23; 26:30.

BESAI [BEE-si; "downtrodden"] B.C. (date unknown). Ancestral father of a family of Temple servants that returned to Judah with Zerubbabel. Ezra 2:49; Neh. 7:52.

BESODEIAH [BEZ-uh-DEE-yuh; "in the confidence of Yahweh"] 475 B.C. Father of Meshullam, who helped rebuild the wall of Jerusalem. Neh. 3:6.

BETHUEL [be-THOO-uhl; "dweller in God"] 2050 B.C. A son of Abraham's brother Nahor, and the father of Rebekah and Laban. Gen. 22:22,23; 24:15,50.

BEZAI [BEE-zi]
1. B.C. (date unknown). Ancestral head of a family who returned to Judah with Zerubbabel after the Exile. Ezra 2:17; Neh. 7:23.
2. 450 B.C. A Jewish leader who sealed the covenant renewal in Nehemiah's time, probably with the name of his family's ancestral head. (see Bezai 1). Neh. 10:18.

BEZALEL [BEZ-uh-lel; "protected by God"] KJV: Bezaleel.
1.* 1450 B.C. A Judahite chosen by God to serve as chief designer and craftsman of the tabernacle and its furnishings. Ex. 31:1-5; 35:30—36:2; 37:1.
2. 450 B.C. One who took a foreign wife after the Exile. Ezra 10:30.

BEZER [BEE-zuhr; "strong" or "gold"] B.C. (date unknown). Listed only in the genealogy of Asher in 1 Chr. 7:37.

BICRI [BIK-ri; "youth, firstborn"] B.C. (date unknown). KJV, RSV: Bichri. A Benjamite, the father or ancestor of Sheba, who rebelled against David. 2 Sam. 20. Possibly the same as Beker, son of Benjamin (1 Chr. 7:6,8).

BIDKAR [BID-kahr] 850 B.C. The chariot officer of Jehu, king of Judah. 2 Ki. 9:25.

BIGTHA [BIG-thuh; "gift of fortune"(?)] 475 B.C. One of the seven stewards who served Xerxes. Esth. 1:10.

BIGTHANA [BIG-thuh-nuh; "gift of fortune"(?)] 475 B.C. KJV, RSV: Bigthan (Esth. 2:21). An official who conspired to assassinate Xerxes, and was executed. Esth. 2:21; 6:2. Possibly the same as Bigtha.

BIGVAI [BIG-vi]
1. B.C. (date unknown). Ancestral head of a family who returned to Judah with Zerubbabel after the Exile. Ezra 2:2,14; 8:14; Neh. 7:7,19.
2. 450 B.C. Leader of a family who sealed the covenant renewal with God in Nehemiah's time, probably with the name of the family's ancestral head (see Bigvai 1). Neh. 10:16.

BILDAD [BIL-dad] B.C. (date unknown). One of the three friends of Job who came to contend with Job concerning the justice of God. Job 2:11; 8,18,25.

BILGAH [BIL-guh; "brightness"]
1. 1000 B.C. Head of the fourteenth of the twenty-four priestly divisions in David's time. 1 Chr. 24:14.
2. 525 B.C. Head of a priestly family who returned to Judah with Zerubbabel after the Exile. Neh. 12:5,18.

BILGAI [BIL-gi; "cheerfulness"] 450 B.C. Head of a priestly family who sealed the covenant renewal with God in Nehemiah's time. Neh. 10:8. Possibly the name used was that of an ancestor (see Bilgah 2).

BILHAH [BIL-hah] 1925 B.C. Maidservant given to Rachel by Laban; she was given to Jacob as a concubine when Rachel believed herself to be barren. Bilhah was the mother of Dan and Naphtali by Jacob. Gen. 29:29; 30:3,4,7; 35:22,25; 37:2; 46:25.

BILHAN [BIL-han]
1. 1925 B.C. A son of Ezer, a Horite chief living in the land of Seir when Esau settled there. Gen. 36:27; 1 Chr. 1:42.
2. B.C. (date unknown). Son of Jediael listed in the genealogy of Benjamin in 1 Chr. 7:10.

BILSHAN [BIL-shan; "inquirer" or "their Lord"] 525 B.C. Head of a family who returned to Judah with Zerubbabel after the Exile. Ezra 2:2; Neh. 7:7.

BIMHAL [BIM-hal; "circumcised"] B.C. (date unknown). Listed only in the genealogy of Asher in 1 Chr. 7:33.

BINEA [BIN-ee-uh] B.C. (date unknown). A descendant of Jonathan, son of Saul. 1 Chr. 8:37; 9:43.

BINNUI [BIN-noo-i; "built, building"] KJV: Bavai; RSV: Bavvai (Neh 3:18).
1. B.C. (date unknown). Ancestor of some who took foreign wives in Ezra's time. Ezra 10:38.
2. B.C. (date unknown). Ancestral head of a family that returned to Judah with Zerubbabel after the Exile. Called Bani in Ezra 2:10. Neh. 7:15.
3. 525 B.C. A Levite who returned to Judah with Zerubbabel after the Exile. Neh. 12:8.
4. 450 B.C. Father of Noadiah, a Levite who helped weigh the sacred Temple articles of gold and silver in Ezra's time. Ezra 8:33.
5. 450 B.C. A descendant of Pahath-Moab who took a foreign wife after the Exile. Ezra 10:30.
6. 450 B.C. A Levite who helped repair the walls of Jerusalem and sealed the covenant renewal with God in Nehemiah's time. Neh. 3:18,24; 10:9.

BIRSHA [BUHR-shuh] 2100 B.C. King of Gomorrah who rebelled against Kedorlaomer, king of Elam, in the time of Abram. Gen. 14:2.

BIRZAITH [buhr-ZAY-uhth; "well of olives"] B.C. (date unknown). KJV: Birzavith. Son of Malkiel and great-grandson of Asher in 1 Chr. 7:31. It is possible the name of a town founded by Malkiel is intended.

BISHLAM [BISH-luhm; "peaceful"] 475 B.C. One of three men who wrote a letter to Artaxerxes against the Jews. Ezra 4:7.

BITHIAH [bih-THI-uh; "daughter of Yahweh"] B.C. (date unknown). A daughter of Pharaoh who married Mered, a Judahite. 1 Chr. 4:18.

BIZTHA [BIZ-thuh; "eunuch"(?)] 475 B.C. One of the seven stewards who served under Xerxes. Esth. 1:10.

BLASTUS [BLAST-uhs; "bud," "sprout"] A.D. 50. A personal servant of Herod Agrippa I. Acts 12:20.

BOANERGES* [BOH-uh-NUHR-jeez; "sons of thunder"] 25 B.C. Nickname given to James and John by Jesus. Mk. 3:17.

BOAZ* [BOH-az; "quickness; strength"] 1100 B.C. The "kinsman redeemer" who married Ruth and became the grandfather of King David. Ruth 2–4; 1 Chr. 2:11,12. **Father:** Salmon. **Son:** Obed.

BOHAN [BO-han] B.C. (date unknown). One of Reuben's sons for whom is named a boundary marker, the Stone of Bohan, between the lands of the tribes of Judah and Benjamin. Josh. 15:6; 18:17.

BOKERU [BO-kuh-roo] B.C. (date unknown). KJV, RSV: Bocheru. A Benjamite descended from Jonathan, son of Saul. 1 Chr. 8:38; 9:44.

BUKKI [BUHK-i; "proven"]
1. 1400 B.C. Danite leader appointed by Moses to help divide the land upon entering Canaan. Num. 34:22.
2. B.C. (date unknown). Descendant of Aaron and ancestor of Ezra the scribe. 1 Chr. 6:5,51; Ezra 7:4.

BUKKIAH [buh-KI-uh; "Yahweh has proven"] 1000 B.C. A son of Heman and a musician at the Temple. 1 Chr. 25:4,13.

BUNAH [BOO-nuh; "intelligence"] B.C. (date unknown). Second son of Jerahmeel, listed in the genealogy of Judah in 1 Chr. 2:25.

BUNNI [BUHN-i]
1. B.C. (date unknown). Ancestor of Shema-

iah the Levite, who resettled in Jerusalem after the Exile. Neh. 11:15.

2. 450 B.C. A Levite involved in worship of the Lord at the time of Ezra's reading of the Law before the people. Neh. 9:4.

3. 450 B.C. A Jewish leader who sealed the covenant renewal with God after the Exile, possibly using the name of his family's ancestral head. Neh. 10:15.

BUZ [BUZ; "contempt"]
1. 2050 B.C. The second son of Nahor, brother of Abraham. Gen. 22:21.
2. B.C. (date unknown). Listed only in the genealogy of Gad in 1 Chr. 5:14.

BUZI [BUZ-i; "contempt"] 625 B.C. The father of Ezekiel the prophet. Ezek. 1:3.

C

CAESAR* [SEE-zuhr] Title of Roman emperors derived from Julius Caesar. Mt. 22:17-21; Lk. 2:1; 3:1; 23:2; Acts 17:7. *See* Claudius, Augustus, and Tiberius.

CAIAPHAS* [KAY-uh-fuhs] A.D. 30. High priest who presided at Jesus' illegal trial before the Sanhedrin. Mt. 26:3,57-66; Jn. 11:49. **Father-in-law:** Annas.

CAIN* [KAYN; "to acquire"] The farmer son of Adam and Eve who killed his brother Abel when his own offering of produce was rejected by God. Gen. 4; 1 Jn. 3:12.

CAINAN [KAY-nuhn]
1. B.C. (date unknown). Son of Enos and great-grandson of Adam, listed in the genealogy of Christ in Lk. 3:37 KJV. Called Kenan in RSV and NIV in Gen. 5:9-14; 1 Chr. 1:2; Lk. 3:37.
2. B.C. (date unknown). Son of Arphaxad listed only in the genealogy of Christ in Lk. 3:36.

CALCOL [KAL-kahl; "sustaining"] B.C. (date unknown). KJV: Chalcol (1 Ki. 4:31). One of the wise sons of Mahol, listed as a son of Zerah in the genealogy of Judah. 1 Ki. 4:31; 1 Chr. 2:6.

CALEB [KAY-leb; "dog" or "rabid"]
1. B.C. (date unknown). A son of Hezron, descendant of Judah. 1 Chr. 2:9,18,19, 42-50.
2.* 1400 B.C. The righteous son of Jephunneh sent by Moses to spy out the land of Canaan. He survived the forty years in the wilderness to enter the Promised Land. Num. 13:6,30; 14; Josh. 14,15; 1 Chr. 4:15. **Nephew and son-in-law:** Othniel. Possibly a descendant of Caleb 1.

CANAAN [KAY-nuhn; "merchant" or "lowly"] B.C. (date unknown). A son of Ham and grandson of Noah, he is the ancestral father of the Canaanites.* Gen. 9:18-27; 10:6,15-18.

CANDACE [KAN-duh-see] A.D. 35. Title of the queen of Ethiopia whose treasurer, the Ethiopian eunuch, was baptized by Philip. Acts 8:27.

CARCAS [KAHR-kuhs; "vulture"(?)] 475 B.C. RSV: Carkas. One of the seven stewards of Ahasuerus. Esth. 1:10.

CARMI [KAHR-mi; "fruitful" or "vineyard"(?)]
1. 1850 B.C. Last of the four sons of Reuben who went with him to Egypt. Gen. 46:9; Ex. 6:14.
2. 1425 B.C. The father of Achan, a Judahite who stole some of the things devoted to God from Jericho, bringing judgment on Israel. Josh. 7:1,18; 1 Chr. 4:1. Called Achar (which means "disaster") in 1 Chr. 2:7.

CARPUS [KAHR-puhs; "fruit"] A.D. 65. A resident of Troas with whom Paul left his cloak. 2 Tim. 4:13.

CARSHENA [kahr-SHEE-nuh] 475 B.C. One of the seven nobles of Persia and Media who advised Ahasuerus. Esth. 1:14.

CASTOR [KAS-tuhr] One of the twin sons of Zeus and Leda in classical mythology. They came to be represented as the twins of the constellation Gemini and were considered protectors of those at sea. Acts 28:11.

CEPHAS [SEE-fuhs; "rock"] A.D. 25. The Aramaic equivalent of Peter, the name given to Simon by Christ. He was a fisherman who became a prominent apostle and a leader of the early church. Jn. 1:42; 1 Cor. 1:12; 3:22; 9:5. *See* Peter.

CHLOE [KLOH-ee; "tender shoot"] A.D. 55. A woman, some of whose household reported to Paul on problems in the Corinthian church. 1 Cor. 1:11.

CHRIST* [KRIST; "anointed one"] A name that indicated an individual anointed by God to a royal, priestly, or prophetic ministry, and was associated with the Messiah. Mt. 1:18; 16:16-20; Mk. 14:61; Jn. 4:25.

CLAUDIA [KLAW-dee-uh] A.D. 65. A Christian woman in Rome whose greeting Paul transmits to Timothy in 2 Tim. 4:21.

CLAUDIUS [KLAW-dee-uhs] A.D. 41-54. The Roman Caesar who expelled the Jews from Rome for rioting. Acts 11:28; 18:2.

CLAUDIUS LYSIAS [KLAW-dee-uhs-LIS-ee-uhs] A.D. 60. Commander of the Roman garrison in Jerusalem who arrested Paul to prevent his death at the hands of a mob. Acts 23:26.

CLEMENT [KLEM-uhnt; "mild; merciful"] A.D. 60. A Christian at Philippi who Paul identifies as a fellow worker in Phil. 4:3.

CLEOPAS [KLEE-uh-puhs; "renowned father"] A.D. 30. One of the two disciples Jesus met along the road to Emmaus after his resurrection. Lk. 24:13-35. Possibly the same as Clopas.

CLOPAS [KLOH-puhs] A.D. 30. KJV: Cleophas. One who stood below the cross at the crucifixion. Jn. 19:25. His wife's name was Mary, but was neither Mary Magdalene nor Jesus' mother.

COL-HOZEH [kahl-HOH-zuh; "all seeing"]
1. B.C. (date unknown). A Judahite, ancestor of Maaseiah, who resided in Jerusalem after the Exile. Neh. 11:5.
2. 475 B.C. Father of Shallun, who helped rebuild the wall of Jerusalem in Nehemiah's time. Neh. 3:15. Possibly the same as Col-Hozeh 1.

CONANIAH [KOH-nuh-NI-uh; "Yahweh has founded"]
1. 725 B.C. KJV: Cononiah (2 Chr. 31:12,13). A Levite in charge of tithes and contributions at the Temple during Hezekiah's reign. 2 Chr. 31:12,13. **Brother:** Shimei.

2. 625 B.C. A chief Levite during Josiah's reign. 2 Chr. 35:9.

CORNELIUS* [kohr-NEEL-ee-uhs] A.D. 40. Roman centurion at Caesarea whose entire household was converted to Christianity. Acts 10.

COSAM [KOH-suhm; "diviner"] B.C. (date unknown). An ancestor of Christ listed in Lk. 3:28.

COZBI [KAHZ-bee; "voluptuousness"] 1400 B.C. A Midianite woman slain by Phinehas, grandson of Aaron. Num. 25.

CRESCENS [KRES-uhnz; "increasing"] A.D. 65. A companion of Paul during his imprisonment in Rome who left for Galatia. 2 Tim. 4:10.

CRISPUS [KRIS-puhs; "curled"] A.D. 55. Ruler of a Jewish synagogue in Corinth who was converted with his household to Christianity. Acts 18:8; 1 Cor. 1:14.

CUSH [KOOSH]
1. B.C. (date unknown). Firstborn son of Ham, son of Noah, and ancestral source of the Cushites. Gen. 10:6-8; 1 Chr. 1:8-10.
2. 1000 B.C. A Benjamite and enemy of David, mentioned only in the title of Ps. 7.

CUSHAN-RISHATHAIM [KOOSH-an-RISH-uh-THAY-uhm] 1382-1374 B.C. KJV: Chushan-rishathaim. A king of Mesopotamia who ruled over Israel for eight years during the period of the judges. Jdg. 3:8.

CUSHI [KOOSH-i]
1. B.C. (date unknown). Ancestor of Jehudi and an official who brought the scroll of Jeremiah's prophecies to Jehoiakim, king of Judah. Jer. 36:14.
2. 675 B.C. Father of Zephaniah the prophet. Zeph. 1:1.

CUZA [KOO-zuh] A.D. 25. KJV, RSV: Chuza. Manager of Herod's household. Lk. 8:3. **Wife:** Joanna, a woman healed miraculously by Jesus.

CYRUS* [SI-ruhs] 558-529 B.C. Cyrus II, "the Great," founder of the Medo-Persian Empire. He was the ruler who allowed the Jews to return to Judah from Exile in Babylon, and aided in the rebuilding of the Temple. Isaiah referred to Cyrus by name in his prophecies two centuries earlier (Isa. 44:28-45:1,13). 2 Chr. 36:20-23; Ezra 1:1-8; Dan. 6:28; 10:1.

D

DAGON* [DAY-gahn; "grain" or "cloudy," "rainy"] Chief god of the Philistines. Jdg. 16:23; 1 Sam. 5:1-7; 1 Chr. 10:10.

DALPHON [DAL-fahn] 475 B.C. Second of the ten sons of Haman put to death by the Jews. Esth. 9:7.

DAMARIS [DAM-uh-ris; "heifer"(?)] A.D. 50. A woman in Athens converted to Christianity. Acts 17:34.

DAN [DAN; "he has vindicated"] 1900 B.C. Fifth son of Jacob, and first by Bilhah, maidservant of Rachel. Ancestral father of the tribe of Dan. Gen. 30:6; 35:25; 46:23; 49:16,17.

DANIEL [DAN-yuhl; "God is my judge"]
1. B.C. (date unknown). A wise man referred to by Ezekiel. Ezek. 14:14,20; 28:3. Possibly the prophet (see Daniel 2), a contemporary of Ezekiel, is indicated.
2. 975 B.C. Son of David and Abigail. 1 Chr. 3:1. Called Kileab in 2 Sam. 3:3.
3.* 600 B.C. The prophet whose life and prophecies are recorded in the Book of Daniel. He was taken into Exile by Nebuchadnezzar to be trained as an administrator. Through interpreting a dream that troubled Nebuchadnezzar, Daniel gained a position of importance in Babylon and remained an influential figure through the reigns of Cyrus and Darius.
4. 450 B.C. A descendant of Ithamar and head of a priestly family who returned to Judah with Ezra after the Exile. Ezra 8:2; Neh. 10:6.

DARDA [DAHR-duh; "full of wisdom" or "thistle"(?)] KJV, RSV: Dara (1 Chr. 2:6).
1. B.C. (date unknown). One of the wise sons of Mahol who Solomon was said to surpass in wisdom. 1 Ki. 4:31.
2. B.C. (date unknown). A son of Zerah listed in the genealogy of Judah in 1 Chr. 2:6. Probably the same as Darda 1.

DARIUS [duh-RI-uhs] The name of three Persian kings.
1.* 539–538 B.C. Darius the Mede, who according to the Book of Daniel became king after Belshazzar. Probably another name for Gubaru, made governor of Babylon by Cyrus the Great; or perhaps another name for Cyrus himself. He was notable as the king who reluctantly threw Daniel in the lions' den. Dan. 5:31; 6.
2. 522–486 B.C. Darius the Great, a powerful ruler noted for aiding in the reconstruction of the Temple, as decreed by Cyrus. Ezra 5:6; Hag. 1:1; Zech. 1:1.
3. 424–405 B.C. Darius II, during whose reign the names of chief Jewish priests were recorded. Neh. 12:22.

DARKON [DAHR-kahn] 950 B.C. A servant of Solomon from whom descended a family that returned to Judah after the Exile. Ezra 2:56; Neh. 7:58.

DATHAN [DAY-thuhn] 1450 B.C. A Reubenite leader and one of the two sons of Eliab who, with Korah and On, led a rebellion against Moses. Num. 16; 26:9; Deut. 11:6; Ps. 106:17.

DAVID* [DAY-vid; "beloved"] Reigned 1010–970 B.C. Israel's greatest king who wholeheartedly loved the Lord. David defeated Israel's enemies, expanded the nation's borders, and established Jerusalem as its political and religious center. His military, political, and religious innovations initiated Israel's golden age and unified the Hebrew people as never before. David is Scripture's ideal king; the model for God's Messiah, who was to be born of David's family line and ultimately rule God's never-ending Kingdom. 1 and 2 Sam.; 1 Chr.

DEBIR [DEE-buhr; "back part" or "oracle"(?)] 1400 B.C. King of Eglon and member of a coalition of five Amorite kings defeated by Joshua in battle. Josh. 10.

DEBORAH [DEB-uhr-uh; "honey bee"]
1. 2025 B.C. The nurse of Rebekah, wife of Isaac. Gen. 35:8.
2.* 1225 B.C. A prophetess who led Israel during the era of the judges. Under her command, Barak led an army against the Canaanite king Jabin and defeated his forces, freeing

Israel of foreign oppression for a period of forty years. Jdg. 4,5.

DEDAN [DEE-duhn]
1. B.C. (date unknown). Second son of Raamah, great-grandson of Noah, listed in the Table of Nations in Gen. 10:7. Ancestral father of the Dedanites.
2. 2000 B.C. A son of Jokshan and grandson of Abraham. Gen. 25:3.

DELAIAH [duh-LAY-uh; "Yahweh has raised up"] KJV: Dalaiah (1 Chr. 3:24).
1. 1000 B.C. Head of the twenty-third division of the priests in David's time. 1 Chr. 24:18.
2. B.C. (date unknown). Ancestor of a family that could not prove Israelite ancestry upon return from Exile. Ezra 2:60; Neh. 7:62.
3. 600 B.C. An official of Jehoiakim who advised against burning the scroll containing Jeremiah's prophecies. Jer. 36:12,25.
4. B.C. (date unknown). Listed only in the genealogy of the royal line of David after the Exile. 1 Chr. 3:24.
5. 475 B.C. Father or ancestor of Shemaiah, who was bribed to deceive Nehemiah. Neh. 6:10. Possibly the same as Delaiah 2.

DELILAH [duh-LI-luh; "small, dainty"] 1075 B.C. The woman who tricked Samson into revealing his secret source of strength and handed him over to the Philistines. Jdg. 16:4-22.

DEMAS [DEE-muhs] A.D. 60. A friend and servant of Paul during his imprisonment in Rome who later deserted him. Col. 4:14; 2 Tim. 4:10; Phlm. 24.

DEMETRIUS [duh-MEE-tree-uhs; "belonging to Demeter"]
1. A.D. 55. A silversmith who instigated a riot in Ephesus against Paul and his fellow Christians. Acts 19:23-41.
2. A.D. 90. A Christian praised by John in 3 Jn. 12.

DEUEL [DOO-uhl; "knowledge of God" or "God knows"] 1475 B.C. KJV: Reuel (Num. 2:14). Father of Eliasaph, leader of the Gadite tribe in Moses' time. Num. 1:14; 2:14.

DIBLAIM [DIB-lay-uhm; "two cakes"] 775 B.C. Father of Gomer, the adulterous wife of Hosea the prophet. Hos. 1:3.

DIBRI [DIB-ri; "wordy"(?)] 1475 B.C. A Danite whose daughter, Shelomith, married an Egyptian; her son was stoned to death for blasphemy. Lev. 24:10,11.

DIDYMAS [DID-uh-muhs; "twin"] A.D. 25. The name by which Thomas was commonly called. He was the disciple who refused to believe in Jesus Christ's resurrection until he had seen Christ for himself. Jn. 11:16; 20:24-29.

DIKLAH [DIK-luh; "place of palms"] B.C. (date unknown). A son of Joktan listed in the genealogy of Shem, son of Noah. Gen. 10:27; 1 Chr. 1:21.

DINAH [DI-nuh; "justice"] 1900 B.C. The daughter of Jacob and Leah who was violated by Shechem, son of Hamor. Gen. 34.

DIONYSIUS [DI-uh-NI-suhs] A.D. 50. A member of the Areopagus court in Athens who converted to Christianity. Acts 17:34.

DIOTREPHES [di-AH-truh-feez; "nourished by Zeus"] A.D. 90. A leader of a church who refused to receive John and the disciples. 3 Jn. 9,10.

DISHAN [DI-shan; "antelope" or "mountain goat"] 1950 B.C. A son of Seir and a Horite chief in Esau's time. Gen. 36:21,28,30.

DISHON [DI-shahn; "antelope" or "mountain goat"]
1. 1950 B.C. A son of Seir and a Horite chief. Gen. 36:21,26,30.
2. 1950 B.C. Son of Anah and a Horite chief; his sister Oholibamah married Esau. Gen. 36:25.

DODAI [DOH-di; "beloved"] 1025 B.C. KJV, RSV: Dodo (2 Sam. 23:9,10). Commander of a division of David's army and father of Eleazar, who was one of the three chiefs of David's military elite called the thirty mighty men. 2 Sam. 23:9,10; 1 Chr. 27:4.

DODAVAHU [doh-duh-VAY-hoo; "beloved of Yahweh"] 875 B.C. KJV: Dodavah. Father of Eliezer, who prophesied against Jehoshaphat. 2 Chr. 20:37.

DODO [DOH-doh; "beloved"]
1. 1175 B.C. Grandfather of Tola, a judge who led Israel for twenty-three years. Jdg. 10:1.
2. 1025 B.C. A man from Bethlehem and the father of Elhanan, one of David's mighty men. 2 Sam. 23:24; 1 Chr. 11:26.

DOEG [DOH-eg; "anxious"] 1000 B.C. An Edomite, Saul's head shepherd who informed Saul that Ahimelech, the priest of Nob, had aided David. At Saul's command, Doeg killed all the priests of Nob and their families. 1 Sam. 21:7; 22:9-19.

DORCAS* [DOHR-kuhs; Greek translation of Tabitha, meaning "gazelle"] A.D. 35. A woman disciple in Joppa who died and was miraculously brought back to life by Peter. Acts 9:36-42. See also Tabitha.

DRUSILLA [droo-SIL-uh] A.D. 60. A Jewess, the daughter of Herod Agrippa I and wife of Felix, Roman governor of Judea, who presided over the trial of Paul at Caesarea. Acts 24:24.

DUMAH [DOO-muh; "silence"] 2025 B.C. Sixth of the twelve sons of Ishmael, son of Abraham and Hagar. Gen. 25:14.

E

EBAL [EE-bahl; "bare"] 1950 B.C. Third of the five sons of Shobal, a Horite chief and son of Seir. Gen. 36:23; 1 Chr. 1:40.

EBED [EE-bed; "servant"]
1. 1150 B.C. Father of Gaal, a resident of Shechem who conspired against Abimelech. Jdg. 9:26-35.
2. 450 B.C. A descendant of Adin who returned to Judah with Ezra after the Exile. Ezra 8:6.

EBED-MELECH [EE-bed-MEL-ehk; "king's servant"] 600 B.C. An Ethiopian who served under Zedekiah; he freed Jeremiah from imprisonment in a cistern. Jer. 38:7-13; 39:15-18.

EBER [EE-buhr; "cross over" or "other side"]
1. B.C. (date unknown). Son of Shelah and an ancestor of Abraham. Gen. 10:21,25; 11:14-17; 1 Chr. 1:18-25.
2. B.C. (date unknown). Head of a family listed only in the genealogy of Gad in 1 Chr. 5:13.
3. B.C. (date unknown). Head of a family of Benjamites who lived in Aijalon. 1 Chr. 8:12.
4. B.C. (date unknown). Another head of a Benjamite family listed in 1 Chr. 8:22.
5. 500 B.C. Head of a priestly family in Joiakim's time, after the Exile. Neh. 12:20.

EBIASAPH [uh-BI-uh-saf; "my father has gathered"] B.C. (date unknown). A Levite, ancestor of Heman the musician. 1 Chr. 6:23,37; 9:19. Called Abiasaph in Ex. 6:24.

EDEN [EE-duhn; "delight"]
1. 725 B.C. A Levite who helped purify the Temple in Hezekiah's time. 2 Chr. 29:12.
2. 700 B.C. A Levite who helped distribute offerings among the priests during Hezekiah's reign. 2 Chr. 31:15. Probably the same as Eden 1.

EDER [EE-duhr; "helper"] KJV: Ader (1 Chr. 8:15).
1. B.C. (date unknown). Listed only in the genealogy of Benjamin in 1 Chr. 8:15.
2. B.C. (date unknown). A Levite descended from Merari. 1 Chr. 23:23; 24:30.

EDOM* [EE-duhm; "red"] 1950 B.C. Name given to Esau, firstborn son of Isaac, because he sold his inheritance for some red stew. Gen. 25:30.

EGLAH [EG-luh; "calf"] 1000 B.C. A wife of David and mother of Ithream. 2 Sam. 3:5; 1 Chr. 3:3.

EGLON [EG-lahn; "circle"] 1334–1316 B.C. A king of Moab who ruled over Israel for eighteen years during the period of the judges. Jdg. 3:12-25.

EHI [EE-hi] 1825 B.C. Sixth of the ten sons of Benjamin listed in Gen. 46:21. The same as Ahiram in Num. 26:38 and Aharah in 1 Chr. 8:1. Possibly the same as Aher.

EHUD [EE-hud]
1. 1316–1235 B.C. The judge who slew King Eglon and delivered Israel from Moabite oppression. Jdg. 3:15-31.
2. B.C. (date unknown). A descendant of Benjamin, listed in 1 Chr. 7:10; 8:6. Possibly the same as Ehud 1.

EKER [EE-kuhr; "root"] B.C. (date unknown). Listed only in the genealogy of Judah in 1 Chr. 2:27.

ELA [EE-luh] 975 B.C. KJV: Elah. Father of Shimei, one of Solomon's twelve district governors. 1 Ki. 4:18.

ELAH [EE-luh; "oak"]
1. B.C. (date unknown). A chief of Edom descended from Esau. Gen. 36:41; 1 Chr. 1:52.
2. 1375 B.C. Second of the three sons of Caleb the son of Jephunneh. He was one of the men sent by Moses to spy out the land of Canaan. 1 Chr. 4:15.
3. 886–885 B.C. The fourth king of the northern kingdom of Israel, he was son and successor of Baasha. 1 Ki. 16:8-14.
4. 775 B.C. Father of Hoshea, who assassinated Pekah and became the last king of Israel. 2 Ki. 15:30; 17:1.
5. B.C. (date unknown). A Benjamin who resettled in Jerusalem after the Exile. 1 Chr. 9:8.

ELAM [EE-luhm; "highland"]
1. B.C. (date unknown). Firstborn son of Shem. The name probably indicates a people,

listed in the table of nations. Gen. 10:22; 1 Chr. 1:17.
2. B.C. (date unknown). A resident of Jerusalem listed only in the genealogy of Benjamin in 1 Chr. 8:24.
3. 1000 B.C. Fifth of the seven sons of Meshelemiah, who was a grandson of Asaph and a gatekeeper in David's time. 1 Chr. 26:3.
4. B.C. (date unknown). Ancestral head of a family that returned to Judah with Zerubbabel after the Exile. Ezra 2:7; 8:7; Neh. 7:12.
5. B.C. (date unknown). Ancestral head of another family that returned from the Exile with Zerubbabel. Ezra 2:31; Neh. 7:34.
6. B.C. (date unknown). Ancestor of some who took foreign wives after the Exile. Ezra 10:26. Probably the same as either Elam 4 or 5.
7. 450 B.C. A Jewish leader who sealed the covenant renewal with God in Nehemiah's time, probably with the name of the family's ancestral father (see Elam 4 and 5). Neh. 10:14.
8. 450 B.C. A Levite in the choir at the dedication of the wall of Jerusalem in Nehemiah's time. Neh. 12:42.

ELASAH [EL-uh-suh; "God has made"]
1. 600 B.C. A son of Shaphan who delivered Jeremiah's letter to the exiles in Babylon. Jer. 29:3.
2. 450 B.C. A descendant of Pashhur who took a foreign wife after the Exile. Ezra 10:22.

ELDAAH [el-DAY-uh] 1975 B.C. A son of Midian and grandson of Abraham. Gen. 25:4; 1 Chr. 1:33.

ELDAD [EL-dad; "God has loved" or "God is a friend"] 1450 B.C. One of two elders who, although not at the tabernacle, received the power to prophesy. Num. 11:26,27.

ELEAD [EL-ee-ad; "God has testified"] 1800 B.C. A son of Ephraim who was slain by men of Gath. 1 Chr. 7:21.

ELEADAH [EL-ee-AY-duh; "God has adorned"] B.C. (date unknown). KJV: Eladah. Listed only in the genealogy of Ephraim in 1 Chr. 7:20.

ELEASAH [EL-ee-AY-suh; "God has made"]
1. B.C. (date unknown). Listed only in the genealogy of Jerahmeel, a descendant of Judah. 1 Chr. 2:40.
2. B.C. (date unknown). A Benjamite descended from Saul. 1 Chr. 8:37; 9:43.

ELEAZAR [EL-ee-AY-zuhr; "God has helped"]
1. B.C. (date unknown). Great grandson of Levi, listed in 1 Chr. 23:21,22.
2. 1400 B.C. The third of the four sons of Aaron who became high priest after his father's death. Son: Phinehas. Ex. 6:23-25; Lev. 10:6-16; Num. 3:2-4; 20:23-29.
3. 1000 B.C. Son of Abinadab, at whose house the ark was kept for twenty years. 1 Sam. 7:1.
4. 1000 B.C. One of the Three, the leaders of David's military elite known as the thirty mighty men. 2 Sam. 23:9,10.
5. 450 B.C. A descendant of Phinehas who helped weigh out the sacred Temple articles in Ezra's time. Ezra 8:33.
6. 450 B.C. A descendant of Parosh who took a foreign wife after the Exile. Ezra 10:25.
7. 450 B.C. A priest in the choir at the dedication of the wall of Jerusalem in Nehemiah's time. Neh. 12:42.
8. B.C. (date unknown). An ancestor of Christ through Joseph, listed in the genealogy in Mt. 1:15.

ELHANAN [el-HAY-nuhn; "God is gracious"]
1. 1000 B.C. A warrior who killed Lahmi, the brother of Goliath. 2 Sam. 21:19; 1 Chr. 20:5.

2. 1000 B.C. A military commander, one of David's mighty men. 2 Sam. 23:24; 1 Chr. 11:26.

ELI* [EE-li; shortened form of "Yahweh is exalted"] 1120–1080 B.C. The high priest who trained Samuel during his childhood. His failure to restrain the sins of his sons brought judgment upon Israel, resulting in the death of Eli and his two sons and the capture of the ark by the Philistines. 1 Sam. 1–4.

ELIAB [ee-LI-uhb; "God is father"]
1. 1475 B.C. A Reubenite, father of Dathan and Abiram, who rebelled against Moses. Num. 16:1,12.
2. 1450 B.C. Leader of the tribe of Zebulun at the time of the Exodus. Num. 1:9.
3. B.C. (date unknown). An ancestor of Samuel listed in the genealogy of Levi in 1 Chr. 6:27. Called Elihu in 1 Sam. 1:1, and Eliel in 1 Chr. 6:34.
4. 1025 B.C. Firstborn son of Jesse and brother of David. Daughter: Abihail, wife of Rehoboam. 1 Sam. 16:6; 17:13,28; 1 Chr. 2:13; 2 Chr. 11:18.
5. 1000 B.C. A Gadite who joined David's army at Ziklag. 1 Chr. 12:9.
6. 1000 B.C. A Levite minister of music in David's time. 1 Chr. 15:18,20; 16:5.

ELIADA [ee-LI-ah-duh; "God knows"]
1. 1000 B.C. A son of David. 2 Sam. 5:16; 1 Chr. 3:8. Called Beeliada in 1 Chr. 14:7.
2. 950 B.C. Father of Rezon, a Syrian king and enemy of Solomon. 1 Ki. 11:23.
3. 875 B.C. Benjamite military commander under Jehoshaphat. 2 Chr. 17:17.

ELIAHBA [ee-LI-ah-buh; "God hides"] 1000 B.C. A military commander and one of David's mighty men. 2 Sam. 23:32; 1 Chr. 11:33.

ELIAKIM [ee-LI-uh-kim; "God raises up"]
1. B.C. (date unknown). Ancestor of Christ listed in Luke's genealogy in Lk. 3:30.
2. 700 B.C. Palace administrator under Hezekiah at the time of the siege of Jerusalem by the Assyrians under Sennacherib. 2 Ki. 18:18,26,37; 19:2; Isa. 22:20–24; 36:3,11,22; 37:2.
3. 609–598 B.C. The son of Josiah, whose name was changed to Jehoiakim when he was made king of Judah by Pharaoh Neco. 2 Ki. 23:34; 2 Chr. 36:4.
4. 450 B.C. A priest who sang in the choir at the dedication of the wall of Jerusalem, after the Exile. Neh. 12:41.
5. B.C. (date unknown). An ancestor of Christ through Joseph. Mt. 1:13.

ELIAM [ee-LI-um; "God is kinsman"]
1. Father of Bathsheba. 2 Sam. 11:3. Called Ammiel in 1 Chr. 3:5.
2. Son of Ahithophel and one of David's military elite known as his thirty mighty men. 2 Sam. 23:34. Called Ahijah in 1 Chr. 11:36.

ELIASAPH [ee-LI-uh-saf; "God has added"]
1. 1450 B.C. Leader of the tribe of Gad at the time of the Exodus. Num. 1:14.
2. 1450 B.C. A Levite clan leader of the Gershonites in Moses' time. Num. 3:24.

ELIASHIB [ee-LI-uh-shib; "God restores"]
1. 1000 B.C. Head of the eleventh of the twenty-four priestly divisions in David's time. 1 Chr. 24:12.
2. 475 B.C. High priest who angered Nehemiah by providing living quarters for Tobiah within the Temple storerooms. Ezra 10:6; Neh. 3:1,20,21; 12:10,22,23; 13:4-9.
3. 450 B.C. A Levite singer who took a foreign wife after the Exile. Ezra 10:24.
4. 450 B.C. A descendant of Zattu married to a foreign woman in Ezra's time. Ezra 10:27.
5. 450 B.C. A descendant of Bani who was guilty of intermarriage after the Exile. Ezra 10:36.

6. B.C. (date unknown). A descendant of Zerubbabel listed in the royal line of David. 1 Chr. 3:24.

ELIATHAH [ee-LI-ah-thuh; "God has come"] 1000 B.C. A son of Heman who served as a minister of music. 1 Chr. 25:4,27.

ELIDAD [ee-LI-dad; "God has loved"] 1400 B.C. A leader from the tribe of Benjamin appointed by Moses to help divide the land of Canaan. Num. 34:21.

ELIEHOENAI [ee-LI-uh-HO-ee-ni; "toward Yahweh are my eyes"] KJV: Elihoenai (Ezra 8:4); Elioenai (1 Chr. 26:3).
1. 975 B.C. A son of Meshelemiah who served as a gatekeeper in David's time. 1 Chr. 26:3.
2. 450 B.C. A descendant of Pahath-Moab who returned to Judah with Ezra after the Exile. Ezra 8:4.

ELIEL [ee-LI-uhl; "my God is God"]
1. B.C. (date unknown). Head of a family of the half-tribe of Manasseh. 1 Chr. 5:24.
2. B.C. (date unknown). A Levite listed in the genealogy of Heman the Temple musician. 1 Chr. 6:34. Called Eliab in 1 Chr. 6:27 and Elihu in 1 Sam. 1:1.
3 and 4. B.C. (date unknown). Two listed in the genealogy of Benjamin in 1 Chr. 8:20,22.
5. 1000 B.C. A Mahavite, one of David's military elite known as his mighty men. 1 Chr. 11:46.
6. 1000 B.C. Another who was one of David's mighty men. 1 Chr. 11:47.
7. 1000 B.C. A Gadite military commander who joined David's army at Ziklag. 1 Chr. 12:11. Possibly the same as Eliel 5 or 6.
8. 1000 B.C. A chief Levite from Hebron who helped David bring the ark to Jerusalem. 1 Chr. 15:9,11.
9. 725 B.C. A supervisor under Conaniah the Levite who oversaw storage of offerings to the Temple in Hezekiah's time. 2 Chr. 31:13.

ELIENAI [el-eh-EE-ni; possibly "toward Yahweh are my eyes"] B.C. (date unknown). Listed only in the genealogy of Benjamin in 1 Chr. 8:20.

ELIEZER [el-eh-EE-zuhr; "God is help"]
1. 2100 B.C. Head servant of Abraham. Gen. 15:2.
2. 1825 B.C. A son of Beker, the second son of Benjamin. 1 Chr. 7:8.
3. 1450 B.C. Second son of Moses by his wife Zipporah. Ex. 18:4; 1 Chr. 23:15; 17; 26:25.
4. 1000 B.C. A priest who blew a trumpet before the ark as it was brought to Jerusalem by David. 1 Chr. 15:24.
5. 1000 B.C. Officer over the tribe of Reuben in David's day. 1 Chr. 27:16.
6. 850 B.C. One who prophesied against Jehoshaphat. 2 Chr. 20:37.
7. B.C. (date unknown). An ancestor of Christ listed in Luke's genealogy. Lk. 3:29.
8. 450 B.C. A leader sent by Ezra to retrieve Levites from Casiphia to serve in the Temple in Jerusalem. Ezra 8:16.
9. 450 B.C. A priest who took a foreign wife after the Exile. Ezra 10:18.
10. 450 B.C. A Levite who married a foreign woman after the Exile. Ezra 10:23.
11. 450 B.C. A descendant of Harim who was found guilty of intermarriage. Ezra 10:31.

ELIHOREPH [el-uh-HOHR-uhf; "God's autumn"(?)] 950 B.C. An official of Solomon, Elihoreph and his brother Ahijah were secretaries. 1 Ki. 4:3.

ELIHU [el-LI-hoo; "he is my God"]
1. B.C. (date unknown). A young man who argued with Job and his three friends. Job 32–37.
2. B.C. (date unknown). An ancestor of the prophet Samuel. 1 Sam. 1:1. Called Eliab in 1 Chr. 6:27 and Eliel in 1 Chr. 6:34.
3. 1000 B.C. A warrior of Manasseh who joined David's army at Ziklag. 1 Chr. 12:20.
4. 1000 B.C. A descendant of Obed-Edom and a gatekeeper in David's time. 1 Chr. 26:7,8.
5. 1000 B.C. Oldest brother of David and officer over the tribe of Judah. 1 Chr. 27:18. Called Eliab in 1 Sam. 16:6; 1 Chr. 2:13.

ELIJAH [ee-LI-juh; "Yahweh is my God"] KJV: Elias (NT), Eliah (1 Chr. 8:27; Ezra 10:26).
1.* 875 B.C. The most prominent prophet of his time, Elijah confronted the evil King Ahab and Queen Jezebel when they tried to establish Baal worship as Israel's religion. With Enoch, one of the only two persons who were taken to heaven without dying. 1 Ki. 17–19, 21; 2 Ki. 1,2.
2. B.C. (date unknown). Listed only in the genealogy of Benjamin in 1 Chr. 8:27.
3. 450 B.C. A priest who took a foreign wife after the Exile. Ezra 10:21.
4. 450 B.C. A descendant of Elam who also married a foreign woman after the Exile. Ezra 10:26.

ELIKA [el-LI-kuh] 1000 B.C. A military leader, one of David's mighty men. 2 Sam. 23:25.

ELIMELECH [el-LIM-uh-lek; "God is king"] 1100 B.C. Husband of Naomi and father-in-law of Ruth. Ruth 1:2,3; 2:1,3; 4:3,9.

ELIOENAI [EL-ee-oh-EE-ni; "toward Yahweh are my eyes"]
1. 1825 B.C. Fourth of the nine sons of Beker, son of Benjamin. 1 Chr. 7:8.
2. B.C. (date unknown). A clan leader listed only in the genealogy of Simeon in 1 Chr. 4:36.
3. 450 B.C. A priest who married a foreign wife after the Exile. Ezra 10:22.
4. 450 B.C. A descendant of Pashur who took a foreign wife after the Exile. Ezra 10:27.
5. 450 B.C. A priest in the choir at the dedication of the wall of Jerusalem in Nehemiah's time. Neh. 12:41.
6. B.C. (date unknown). A descendant of Zerubbabel listed in the genealogy of the royal line of David after the Exile. 1 Chr. 3:23,24.

ELIPHAL [el-LI-fuhl; "God has judged"] 1000 B.C. A military leader listed among David's mighty men, in 1 Chr. 11:35. Called Eliphelet in 2 Sam. 23:34.

ELIPHAZ [EL-uh-faz; "God is victorious"(?)]
1. B.C. (date unknown). One of the three friends who contended with Job concerning God's justice. Job 4,15,22; 42:7-9.
2. 1925 B.C. The son of Esau by his wife Adah. Gen. 36:4,11,16; 1 Chr. 1:35,36.

ELIPHELEHU [uh-LIF-uh-LEE-hoo; "may God distinguish him"] 1000 B.C. KJV: Elipheleh. A Levite appointed to play the harp before the ark as it was brought by David to Jerusalem. 1 Chr. 15:18,21.

ELIPHELET [uh-LIF-uh-let; "God is deliverance"] KJV: Eliphalet (2 Sam. 5:16; 1 Chr. 14:7).
1. 1000 B.C. A military commander, one of David's mighty men. 2 Sam. 23:34. Called Eliphal in 1 Chr. 11:35.
2 and 3. 975 B.C. Two sons of David born in Jerusalem. 2 Sam. 5:16; 1 Chr. 3:6,8; 14:7. The first is called Elpelet in 1 Chr. 14:5.
4. B.C. (date unknown). A descendant of Jonathan, son of Saul, listed in 1 Chr. 8:39.
5. 450 B.C. A descendant of Adonikam who returned to Judah with Ezra. Ezra 8:13.
6. 450 B.C. A descendant of Hashum who took a foreign wife after the Exile. Ezra 10:33.

ELISHA* [ee-LI-shuh; "God is salvation"] KJV: Eliseus (Lk. 4:27). 850 B.C. The successor of Elijah and leading prophet in Israel, the northern kingdom, during the reigns of Joram, Jehu, Jehoahaz, and Joash. **Father:** Shaphat of Abel Meholah. 2 Ki. 1–9,13.

ELISHAH [el-LI-shuh; "God is salvation"] B.C. (date unknown). A great-grandson of Noah listed in the Table of Nations, in Gen. 10:4.

ELISHAMA [ee-LISH-ah-muh; "God has heard"]
1. 1450 B.C. Leader of the tribe of Ephraim at the time of the Exodus, and grandfather of Joshua. Num. 1:10; 1 Chr. 7:26.
2. B.C. (date unknown). Listed only in the genealogy of Jerahmeel, a descendant of Judah. 1 Chr. 2:41.
3. 975 B.C. A son of David born in Jerusalem. 2 Sam. 5:16; 1 Chr. 3:8; 14:7.
4. 875 B.C. A priest who taught the Law throughout Judah during Jehoshaphat's reign. 2 Chr. 17:8.
5. 600 B.C. Grandfather of Ishmael, who assassinated Gedaliah, the governor of Judah. 2 Ki. 25:25; Jer. 41:1.
6. 600 B.C. A secretary who served under Jehoiakim. Jer. 36:12,20,21.

ELISHAPHAT [ee-LISH-uh-fat; "God has judged"] 850 B.C. A military commander who conspired with Jehoiada the priest to overthrow Athaliah. 2 Chr. 23:1.

ELISHEBA [ee-LISH-uh-buh; "God is an oath"] 1450 B.C. The wife of Aaron and mother of Nadab, Abihu, Eleazar, and Ithamar. Ex. 6:23.

ELISHUA [el-uh-SHOO-uh; "God is salvation"] KJV, RSV: Elishama (1 Chr. 3:6). 975 B.C. A son of David born in Jerusalem. 2 Sam. 5:15; 1 Chr. 3:6; 14:5.

ELIUD [ee-LI-uhd; "God my praise"] B.C. (date unknown). An ancestor of Christ descended from Zerubbabel. Mt. 1:14,15.

ELIZABETH [ee-LIZ-uh-beth; "God is my oath"] 5 B.C. KJV: Elisabeth. The righteous mother of John the Baptist. She was barren until an angel foretold the birth of her son. **Husband:** Zechariah the priest. Lk. 1.

ELIZAPHAN [ee-LIZ-uh-fan/el-uh-ZAY-fan; "God has protected"]
1. 1450 B.C. A Kohathite clan leader of the Levites at the time of the Exodus. Num. 3:30; 1 Chr. 15:8; 2 Chr. 29:13. Called Elzaphan in Ex. 6:22; Lev. 10:4.
2. 1400 B.C. Leader from the tribe of Zebulun appointed by Moses to help divide the land of Canaan. Num. 34:25.

ELIZUR [el-LI-zuhr; "God is a rock"] 1450 B.C. Leader of the tribe of Reuben at the time of the Exodus. Num. 1:5.

ELKANAH [el-KAY-nuh; "God has taken possession"]
1. B.C. (date unknown). A Levite, grandson of Korah, listed in Ex. 6:24; 1 Chr. 6:23,25,36.

2. B.C. (date unknown). An ancestor of Samuel listed in the genealogy of Levi in 1 Chr. 6:26,35.
3. 1100 B.C. A Levite from the hill country of Ephraim who was the father of Samuel the judge. 1 Sam. 1; 2:11,20; 1 Chr. 6:27,34. **Wives:** Hannah, mother of Samuel, and Peninnah.
4. 1000 B.C. A Korahite who joined David's army at Ziklag. 1 Chr. 12:6.
5. 1000 B.C. A Levite who served as doorkeeper for the ark. 1 Chr. 15:23. Possibly the same as Elkanah 4.
6. 750 B.C. An official in Judah who was second in authority only to King Ahaz. He was killed when the Israelites defeated Judah in battle. 2 Chr. 28:7.
7. B.C. (date unknown). Ancestor of Berekiah, a Levite who resettled in Jerusalem after the Exile. 1 Chr. 9:16.

ELMADAM [el-MAY-duhm] KJV: Elmodam. B.C. (date unknown). An ancestor of Christ. Lk. 3:28.

ELNAAM [el-NAY-uhm; "God is pleasant, delightful"] 1025 B.C. Father of Jerivai and Joshaviah, two of the military elite known as David's mighty men. 1 Chr. 11:46.

ELNATHAN [el-NAY-thuhn; "God has given"]
1. 600 B.C. A servant of Jehoiakim who brought Uriah out of Egypt. Father of Nehushta, the mother of Jehoiachin. 2 Ki. 24:8; Jer. 26:22; 36:12,25.
2, 3, and 4. 450 B.C. Two Jewish leaders and one scholar sent by Ezra to retrieve Levites from Casiphia for service in the Temple. Ezra 8:16.

ELON [EE-lahn; "oak; terebinth"]
1. 1950 B.C. A Hittite, father of Basemath, a wife of Esau. Gen. 26:34; 36:2.
2. 1850 B.C. Son of Zebulun and ancestral source of his own clan. Gen. 46:14; Num. 26:26.
3. 1100 B.C. A judge who ruled in Israel for ten years. Jdg. 12:11,12.

ELPAAL [el-PAY-uhl; "God has wrought"] B.C. (date unknown). Listed only in the genealogy of Benjamin in 1 Chr. 8:11,12,18.

ELPELET [el-PAY-let; "God is deliverance"] 975 B.C. KJV: Elpalet. A son of David born in Jerusalem. 1 Chr. 14:5. Called Eliphelet in 2 Sam. 5:16; 1 Chr. 3:6.

ELUZAI [ee-LOO-zi; "God is my strength"] 1000 B.C. A kinsman of Saul who defected to David's army at Ziklag. 1 Chr. 12:5.

ELYMAS [EL-uh-muhs; "sorcerer"] A.D. 50. Nickname of Bar-Jesus, a Jewish false prophet at Paphos who was stricken with blindness for opposing Paul. Acts 13:6-11.

ELZABAD [el-ZAY-bad; "God has given"]
1. 1000 B.C. A Gadite who joined David at Ziklag. 1 Chr. 12:12.
2. 975 B.C. A Levite who served as a gatekeeper at the Temple. 1 Chr. 26:7.

ELZAPHAN [el-ZAY-fan; "God has protected"] 1450 B.C. A son of Uzziel and kinsman of Moses and Aaron. Ex. 6:22; Lev. 10:4. Called Elizaphan in Num. 3:30.

ENAN [EE-nuhn; possibly "fountain" or "spring"] 1475 B.C. Father of Ahira, leader of the tribe of Naphtali at the time of the Exodus. Num. 1:15; 2:29; 7:78,83; 10:27.

ENOCH [EE-nuhk; possibly "initiated"]
1. B.C. (date unknown). Son of Cain. Gen. 4:17.
2. B.C. (date unknown). A righteous man who lived before the flood; only he and Elijah were taken directly to heaven without dying. The

author of the Book of Jude quoted from the author of the apocalyptic Book of Enoch. Gen. 5:18-24; Heb. 11:5; Jude 14.

ENOS [EE-nahs; "man, mankind"] B.C. (date unknown). An ancestor of Christ. Lk. 3:38. Same as Enosh.

ENOSH [EE-nahsh; "man; mankind"] KJV: Enos. B.C. (date unknown). A son of Seth, the son of Adam. Gen. 4:26; 5:6-11. See Enos.

EPAPHRAS [EP-uh-fras/eh-PAF-ruhs; contracted form of Epaphroditus, "handsome, charming"] A.D. 60. A Christian leader at the Colossian church and a fellow prisoner with Paul in Rome. Col. 1:7; 4:12; Phlm. 23.

EPAPHRODITUS [eh-PAF-roh-DI-tuhs; "handsome, charming"] A.D. 60. A Christian who brought Paul a gift from the church at Philippi. Phil. 2:25; 4:18.

EPENETUS [eh-PEE-nuh-tuhs; "praised"] A.D. 55. KJV, RSV: Epaenetus. One who was greeted by Paul in his letter to the church at Rome and referred to as the first convert in Asia. Rom. 16:5.

EPHAH [EE-fah]
1. B.C. (date unknown). A grandson of Abraham and a son of Midian. Gen. 25:4; 1 Chr. 1:33.
2. B.C. (date unknown). One of Caleb's concubines and the mother of three of Caleb's sons. 1 Chr. 2:46.
3. B.C. (date unknown). One of Jahdai's sons listed in 1 Chr. 2:47.

EPHAI [EE-fi] 625 B.C. The father of some who remained in Judah under Gedaliah at the time of the Exile. Jer. 40:8.

EPHER [EE-fuhr; "young deer"]
1. 1975 B.C. Second of the five sons of Midian and grandson of Abraham. Gen. 25:4; 1 Chr. 1:33.
2. B.C. (date unknown). Listed only in the genealogy of Judah in 1 Chr. 4:17.
3. 750 B.C. Head of a Manasseh family taken into exile by Tiglath-Pileser, king of Assyria. 1 Chr. 5:24.

EPHLAL [EF-lal] B.C. (date unknown). Listed only in the genealogy of Jerahmeel, a descendant of Judah. 1 Chr. 2:37.

EPHOD [EE-fahd] B.C. (date unknown). Father of Hanniel, a leader in the tribe of Manasseh who was appointed by Moses to help divide the land of Canaan. Num. 34:23.

EPHRAIM [EE-free-uhm/EF-ray-uhm; "fruitful"] 1850 B.C. Second son of Joseph and his Egyptian wife, Asenath. Ancestral source of one of the twelve tribes of Israel. Gen. 41:52; 46:20; 48. **Brother:** Manasseh.

EPHRATH [EF-rath] B.C. (date unknown). Second wife of Caleb, listed in the genealogy of Judah in 1 Chr. 2:19. Same as Ephrathah.

EPHRATHAH [EF-rath-uh] B.C. (date unknown). KJV: Ephratah. Wife of Caleb, and mother of Hur. 1 Chr. 2:50; 4:4. See Ephrath.

EPHRON [EE-frahn; "fawn"(?)] 2025 B.C. A Hittite from whom Abraham purchased a cave in which to bury his wife Sarah. Gen. 23:8-17; 25:9.

ER [UHR; "watcher"]
1. 1875 B.C. The firstborn son of Judah and first husband of Tamar. Gen. 38:3-7; 46:12; 1 Chr. 2:3.
2. B.C. (date unknown). A son or descendant of Shelah, the son of Judah. 1 Chr. 4:21.
3. B.C. (date unknown). An ancestor of Christ, listed in Luke's genealogy. Lk. 3:28.

ERAN [EE-ran] B.C. (date unknown). A descendant of Ephraim and ancestral head of the Eranites. Num. 26:36.

ERASTUS [uh-RAS-tuhs; "beloved"]
1. A.D. 55. A Christian sent by Paul with Timothy to Macedonia. Acts 19:22.
2. A.D. 55. Director of public works in Corinth who sent greetings to the church in Rome in Rom. 16:23.
3. A.D. 65. A Christian whom Paul left behind in Corinth. 2 Tim. 4:20. Possibly the same as Erastus 1 and/or 2.

ERI [EE-ri; "watchful"] 1875 B.C. Fifth of the seven sons of Gad, son of Jacob. Gen. 46:16; Num. 26:16.

ESARHADDON [eh-suhr-HAD-uhn; "Assur has given a brother"] 680–669 B.C. The son and successor of Sennacherib, king of Assyria. 2 Ki. 19:37; Ezra 4:2; Isa. 37:38. **Brothers:** Adrammelech and Sharezer.

ESAU* [EE-saw; "hairy"] 1950 B.C. The older twin brother of Jacob, who "despised his birthright" and traded away the Abrahamic Covenant for a bowl of stew. **Father:** Isaac. **Mother:** Rebekah. His descendants through his six wives later became known as the Edomites. Gen. 25–27, 36. Same as Edom.

ESH-BAAL [ESH-bay-uhl; "servant of Baal"] 1005–1003 B.C. Last of the four sons of Saul, notable as his successor, murdered by Recab and Baanah. 1 Chr. 8:33; 9:39. Same as Ish-Bosheth.

ESHBAN [ESH-ban] 1925 B.C. Son of Dishon, a Horite chief in the land of Seir. Gen. 36:26; 1 Chr. 1:41.

ESHCOL [ESH-kahl; "cluster of grapes"] 2100 B.C. An Amorite who with his brothers Mamre and Aner helped Abraham defeat the armies of a coalition of kings and rescue Lot. Gen. 14:13,24.

ESHEK [EE-shek; "oppressor"] B.C. (date unknown). A descendant of Jonathan, son of Saul, listed in the genealogy of Benjamin in 1 Chr. 8:39.

ESHTEMOA [ESH-tuh-MOH-uh; "listening post"]
1. B.C. (date unknown). Son of Ishbah listed only in the genealogy of Judah. 1 Chr. 4:17. Possibly the reference indicates Ishbah was the lord of the city of Eshtemoa.
2. B.C. (date unknown). Son of Hodiah listed only in the genealogy of Judah in 1 Chr. 4:19.

ESHTON [ESH-tuhn] B.C. (date unknown). Listed only in the genealogy of Judah in 1 Chr. 4:11,12.

ESLI [ES-li] B.C. (date unknown). An ancestor of Christ, listed in Luke's genealogy in Lk. 3:25.

ESTHER* [ES-tuhr; "star"] 475 B.C. A Benjamite girl notable for being chosen as the wife of King Xerxes, and whose story is related in the Book of Esther.* She revealed to Ahasuerus, king of Persia, the plans of Haman to massacre the Jews and thus delivered her people from destruction. Esth. 1–10.

ETAM [EE-tuhm; possibly "lair of wild beasts"] B.C. (date unknown). Listed only in the genealogy of Judah in 1 Chr. 4:3. Possibly the name of a town is intended.

ETHAN [EE-thuhn; "enduring"]
1. B.C. (date unknown). A wise man surpassed by Solomon in wisdom, listed as a descendant of Judah. Author of Psalm 89. 1 Ki. 4:31; 1 Chr. 2:6,8.
2. B.C. (date unknown). A Levite listed in the genealogy of Asaph the minister of music in 1 Chr. 6:42.

3. 1000 B.C. A chief minister of music with Asaph and Heman, appointed in David's time. 1 Chr. 6:44; 15:17,19.

ETHBAAL [ETH-bay-uhl; "with Baal" or "man of Baal"] 875 B.C. King of Sidon and father of Jezebel, wife of Ahab. 1 Ki. 16:31.

ETHNAN [ETH-nuhn; "hire" or "gift"] B.C. (date unknown). Listed in the genealogy of Judah in 1 Chr. 4:7.

ETHNI [ETH-ni; "gift"] B.C. (date unknown). A Levite who was an ancestor of Asaph the minister of music in David's time. 1 Chr. 6:41.

EUBULUS [yoo-BYOO-luhs; "well advised" or "good counsel"] A.D. 65. A Christian who with Paul sent greetings to Timothy. 2 Tim. 4:21.

EUNICE [YOO-nis; "good victory"] A.D. 30. The pious mother of Timothy. 2 Tim. 1:5.

EUODIA [yoo-OH-dee-uh; "prosperous journey; success"] A.D. 60. KJV: Euodias (a clear mistake since a woman is indicated). A prominent Christian woman of Philippi. Phil. 4:2.

EUTYCHUS [YOO-tuh-kuhs; "fortunate"] A.D. 55. A young man of Troas who fell to his death and was miraculously restored to life by Paul. Acts 20:9-12.

EVE* [EEV; "life giver"(?)] B.C. (date unknown). The first woman and wife of Adam, Eve was deceived by Satan and disobeyed God, eating from the tree of knowledge. **Named sons:** Cain, Abel, Seth. Gen. 2,3.

EVI [EE-vi; "desire"] 1400 B.C. A king of Midian defeated in battle and put to death by the Israelites. Num. 31:8; Josh. 13:21.

EVIL-MERODACH [EE-vuhl MAIR-uh-dahk; "man of (the god) Marduk"] 562–560 B.C. Son and successor of Nebuchadnezzar as king of the Babylonian Empire who released Jehoiachin from prison. 2 Ki. 25:27-30; Jer. 52:31-34.

EZBAI [EZ-bi; "shining, beautiful"] 1000 B.C. Father of Naarai, one of the military elite known as David's mighty men. 1 Chr. 11:37. The parallel text in 2 Sam. 23:35 has "Paarai the Arbite."

EZBON [EZ-bahn]
1. 1875 B.C. Fourth of the seven sons of Gad listed in Gen. 46:16.
2. 1825 B.C. Firstborn son of Bela, son of Benjamin. 1 Chr. 7:7.

EZEKIEL* [ee-ZEE-kee-uhl; "God strengthens"] 575 B.C. A major prophet whose prophetic message is recorded in the Book of Ezekiel.* He was among the aristocracy taken with Jehoiachin into exile in Babylon. Ezekiel's prophetic message among the exiles foretold the fall of Jerusalem. After Jerusalem fell, he stopped prophesying for 13 years. Then he returned to his ministry with a new message, one of hope and consolation that looked forward to the coming of the Messiah. Ezek. 1–48. **Father:** Buzi.

EZER [EE-zuhr; "help"] KJV: Ezar (1 Chr. 1:38).
1. 1975 B.C. A Horite chief who lived in the land of Seir in Esau's time. Gen. 36:21,27,30; 1 Chr. 1:38,42.
2. 1800 B.C. A son of Ephraim slain by men of Gath when he was caught stealing livestock. 1 Chr. 7:21.
3. B.C. (date unknown). Listed only in the genealogy of Judah in 1 Chr. 4:4.
4. 1000 B.C. Chief of the Gadites who joined David's army at Ziklag. 1 Chr. 12:9.
5. 450 B.C. A Levite, son of Jeshua, who helped repair the wall of Jerusalem in Nehemiah's time. Neh. 3:19.

6. 450 B.C. A priest in the choir at the dedication of the wall of Jerusalem. Neh. 12:42.

EZRA [EZ-ruh; "Yahweh helps"]
1. A priest who returned to Judah with Zerubbabel after the Exile. Neh. 12:1,13. Same as Azariah in Neh. 10:2.
2.* 450 B.C. A priest and scribe known as the traditional author of the Books of Ezra and Nehemiah. Ezra led the second return of exiles to Judah, in 458 B.C., and taught the Law during the revival stimulated by Nehemiah. Ezra.

EZRAH [EZ-ruh; "Yahweh helps"] B.C. (date unknown). KJV: Ezra. Listed only in the genealogy of Judah in 1 Chr. 4:17.

EZRI [EZ-ri; "my help"] 975 B.C. Overseer of farm workers who cultivated the royal lands in David's time. 1 Chr. 27:26.

F

FELIX [FEE-liks; "happy"] A.D. 60. Roman governor of Judea before whom Paul was tried in Caesarea. For the last two years of his rule, he kept Paul in prison without passing judgment on the case. Acts 23:23–24:27.

FESTUS [FES-tuhs] A.D. 60. Appointed to succeed Felix as governor of Judea, he continued the trial of Paul. Upon Paul's appeal to Caesar, Festus ordered him sent to Rome for trial. Acts 24:27; 25; 26:24-32.

FORTUNATUS [FOHR-choo-NAH-tuhs; "fortunate"] A.D. 55. A Christian from the church at Corinth who visited Paul in Rome. 1 Cor. 16:17.

G

GAAL [GAY-uhl; possibly "scarab"] 1125 B.C. A man of Shechem who incited a rebellion against Abimelech and was defeated. Jdg. 9:26-41.

GABBAI [GAB-i; "collector"] 450 B.C. A Benjamite who resettled in Jerusalem after the Exile. Neh. 11:8.

GABRIEL* [GAY-bree-uhl; "God is great"] The angelic messenger whose four appearances in the Bible record were each connected with the coming of the Messiah. Dan. 8:16; 9:21; Lk. 1:19,26.

GAD [GAD; "fortune"]
1. 1875 B.C. Seventh son of Jacob, his first by Leah's maidservant, Zilpah. Ancestral

source of one of the twelve tribes of Israel. Gen. 30:11; 46:16; 49:19. **Brother:** Asher.
2. 1000 B.C. A prophet who served and advised David. According to 1 Chronicles 29:29, he is said to have recorded the events of David's reign. 1 Sam. 22:5; 2 Sam. 24:11-19; 1 Chr. 21:9-19; 2 Chr. 29:25.

GADDI [GAD-i; "my fortune"] 1450 B.C. Leader of the tribe of Manasseh sent by Moses to explore the land of Canaan. Num. 13:11.

GADDIEL [GAD-ee-uhl; "fortune of God"] 1450 B.C. Leader of the tribe of Zebulun chosen by Moses to explore the land of Canaan. Num. 13:10.

GADI [GAD-i; "my fortune"] 775 B.C. Father of Menahem, who assassinated Shallum and succeeded him as king of Israel. 2 Ki. 15:14,17.

GAHAM [GAY-ham] 2050 B.C. A son of Nahor, brother of Abraham. Gen. 22:24.

GAHAR [GAY-hahr; (date unknown). Ancestral head of a family of Temple servants that returned to Judah with Zerubbabel after the Exile. Ezra 2:47. Called Gaher in Neh. 7:49.

GAHER [GAY-hahr; B.C. (date unknown). KJV, RSV: Gahar. Ancestor of Temple servants who accompanied Zerubbabel. Neh. 7:49. See Gahar.

GAIUS [GAY-yuhs]
1. A.D. 55. A Christian companion of Paul from Macedonia, seized by the crowd during the riot in Ephesus. Acts 19:29.
2. A.D. 55. A Christian from Derbe who traveled with Paul. Acts 20:4. An alternate reading suggests he was of Doberus, a Macedonian town, in which case he is likely the same as Gaius 1.
3. A.D. 55. A Christian at Corinth, in whose home Paul stayed when he wrote his letter to the Romans. Rom. 16:23.
4. A.D. 50. A Corinthian Christian whom Paul baptized. 1 Cor. 1:14. Likely the same as Gaius 3.
5. A.D. 90. One to whom 3 John is addressed. 3 Jn. 1.

GALAL [GAY-lal; "rolling"]
1. 450 B.C. A Levite who resettled in Jerusalem after the Exile. 1 Chr. 9:15.
2. B.C. (date unknown). Ancestor of Obadiah (called Abda in Neh. 11:17), a Levite who settled in Jerusalem after the Exile. 1 Chr. 9:16; Neh. 11:17.

GALLIO [GAL-ee-oh] A.D. 50. Proconsul of Achaia who at court in Corinth refused to try Paul on issues of Jewish law. Acts 18:12-17.

GAMALIEL [guh-MAY-lee-uhl; "God is my reward or recompense"]
1. 1450 B.C. Leader of the tribe of Manasseh at the time of the Exodus. Num. 1:10; 7:54-59.
2.* A.D. 35. A well-respected Pharisee whom Paul claimed as his teacher in the Law. At the hearing of Peter and the apostles before the Sanhedrin, Gamaliel wisely persuaded the Sanhedrin to release the apostles for "if their purpose or activity is of human origin, it will fail." Acts 5:33-40; 22:3.

GAMUL [GAY-mul; "weaned"(?)] 1000 B.C. Appointed head of the twenty-second division of priests in David's time. 1 Chr. 24:17.

GAREB [GAIR-eb; "scabrous"] 1000 B.C. A military commander, one of David's mighty men. 2 Sam. 23:38; 1 Chr. 11:40.

GATAM [GAY-tuhm; "burnt valley"(?)] 1875 B.C. A son of Eliphaz, the firstborn son of Esau, and an Edomite chief. Gen. 36:11,16.

GAZEZ [GAY-ziz; "shearer"]
1. A son of Caleb, descendant of Judah, listed in the genealogy of the clans of Caleb in 1 Chr. 2:46.
2. B.C. (date unknown). A grandson of Caleb listed in the genealogy of Judah in 1 Chr. 2:46.

GAZZAM [GAZ-uhm] B.C. (date unknown). Ancestor of a family of Temple servants that returned to Judah with Zerubbabel after the Exile. Ezra 2:48; Neh. 7:51.

GEBER [GEE-buhr; "man; strong one"] 950 B.C. One of Solomon's twelve district governors, over the district of Gilead. 1 Ki. 4:19.

GEDALIAH [ged-uh-LI-uh; "Yahweh is great"]
1. 1000 B.C. Son of Jeduthun and a minister of music at the Temple in David's time. 1 Chr. 25:3,9.
2. B.C. (date unknown). Ancestor of Zephaniah the prophet. Zeph. 1:1.
3. 600 B.C. One of the officials of Zedekiah who threw Jeremiah into a cistern to die. Jer. 38:1-6.
4.* Reigned 587 B.C. Governor of Judah appointed by Nebuchadnezzar, king of Babylon, after the fall of Jerusalem. He was assassinated by Ishmael, son of Nethaniah, after two months in office. 2 Ki. 25:22-25; Jer. 39:14; 40:5–41:18. **Father:** Ahikam.
5. 450 B.C. A priest who took a foreign wife after the Exile. Ezra 10:18.

GEDOR [GEE-dohr; "wall"]
1. B.C. (date unknown). Son of Penuel listed only in the genealogy of Judah in 1 Chr. 4:4. Possibly the town of Gedor is intended, and Penuel was its founder.
2. B.C. (date unknown). A descendant of Judah, in 1 Chr. 4:18. Possibly the reference is to Jared as founder or civic leader of a town called Gedor in Judah.
3. 1075 B.C. A Benjamite, son of Jeiel and younger brother of Ner, grandfather of Saul. 1 Chr. 8:31; 9:37.

GEHAZI* [guh-HAY-zi; "valley of vision"] 850 B.C. The servant of Elisha who because of his dishonesty was stricken with leprosy. 2 Ki. 4:12-37; 5:19-27; 8:4,5.

GEMALLI [guh-MAL-i; "camel driver"(?)] 1475 B.C. Father of Ammiel, the leader from the tribe of Dan sent by Moses to explore the land of Canaan. Num. 13:12.

GEMARIAH [gem-uh-RI-uh; "Yahweh has accomplished"]
1. 600 B.C. An official of Jehoiakim from whose room Baruch read Jeremiah's scroll. Gemariah was among those who urged the king not to burn Jeremiah's scroll of prophecies. Jer. 36:10-25. **Father:** Shaphan the scribe.
2. 600 B.C. One of the emissaries of King Zedekiah who delivered Jeremiah's message to those in exile in Babylon. Jer. 29:3. **Father:** Hilkiah.

GENUBATH [guh-NOO-bath] 925 B.C. Son of Hadad the Edomite and the sister-in-law of the Pharaoh of Egypt. 1 Ki. 11:20.

GERA [GEER-uh]
1. 1850 B.C. A son of Benjamin, listed in Gen. 46:21.
2 and 3. 1825 B.C. Two sons of Bela, firstborn son of Benjamin, listed in 1 Chr. 8:3-7.
4. 1350 B.C. A Benjamite, father of Ehud, the judge who delivered Israel from the Moabites. Jdg. 3:15. Possibly an ancestor of or the same as Gera 1, 2, or 3.
5. 1000 B.C. Father (or ancestor) of Shimei, the Benjamite from Bahurim who during the revolt of Absalom cursed David and later repented. 2 Sam. 16:5; 19:16-18; 1 Ki. 2:8.

GERSHOM [GUHR-shuhm; sounds like Heb. "an alien there"]
1. 1450 B.C. Firstborn son of Moses and Zipporah. Ex. 2:22; 18:3.
2. B.C. (date unknown). Father or ancestor of Jonathan, whose family improperly served as priests for the Danites. Son or descendant of Moses (KJV: Manasseh). Jdg. 18:30. Likely same as Gershom 1.
3. 450 B.C. A descendant of Phinehas who returned to Judah with Ezra. Ezra 8:2.

GERSHON [GUHR-shuhn] 1875 B.C. KJV: Gershom (1 Chronicles). Firstborn son of Levi. Gen. 46:11; Ex. 6:16,17; 1 Chr. 6.

GESHAN [GESH-uhn] B.C. (date unknown). KJV: Gesham. Listed only in the genealogy of Judah in 1 Chr. 2:47.

GESHEM [GESH-uhm; "rainstorm"] 450 B.C. KJV: Gashmu (Neh. 6:6). An Arab who was one of the enemies of Nehemiah and opposed the reconstruction of the wall of Jerusalem. Neh. 2:19; 6:1-7. He has been identified historically by some as an Arabian king, Gashm.

GETHER [GEE-thuhr] B.C. (date unknown). A son of Aram and grandson of Shem, son of Noah, listed in the table of nations. Gen. 10:23.

GEUEL [GOO-uhl] 1450 B.C. A leader from the tribe of Gad chosen by Moses to explore the land of Canaan. Num. 13:15.

GIBBAR [GIB-ahr; "mighty"] B.C. (date unknown). Ancestral head of a family that returned to Judah with Zerubbabel after the Exile. Ezra 2:20.

GIBEA [GIB-ee-uh; "hill; highlander"] B.C. (date unknown). Grandson of Caleb listed only in the genealogy of Judah in 1 Chr. 2:49.

GIDDALTI [guh-DAL-ti; "I have magnified (God)"] 1000 B.C. A son of Heman and minister of music at the Temple in David's time. 1 Chr. 25:4,29.

GIDDEL [GID-uhl; "very great"]
1. 950 B.C. A Temple servant of Solomon. Some of his descendants returned to Judah with Zerubbabel. Ezra 2:56; Neh. 7:58.
2. B.C. (date unknown). Ancestor of some Temple servants who returned to Judah with Zerubbabel after the Exile. Ezra 2:47; Neh. 7:49.

GIDEON* [GID-ee-uhn; "hewer" (i.e., great warrior)] Ruled 1169–1129 B.C. KJV: Gedeon (Heb. 11:32). A major judge who delivered Israel from the Midianites. Jdg. 6–8. Also called Jerub-Baal. **Sons:** Abimelech and seventy others.

GIDEONI [gid-ee-OH-nee; "hewer"] 1450 B.C. Father of Abidan, leader of the tribe of Benjamin at the time of the Exodus. Num. 1:11.

GILALAI [guh-LAY-li] 450 B.C. A priest who played music at the dedication of the wall of Jerusalem in Nehemiah's time. Neh. 12:36.

GILEAD [GIL-ee-ad]
1. 1825 B.C. Grandson of Manasseh and ancestral source of the Gileadite clan. Num. 26:29,30.
2. 1125 B.C. Father of Jephthah the judge. Jdg. 11:1,2.
3. B.C. (date unknown). Listed only in the genealogy of Gad in 1 Chr. 5:14.

GINATH [GI-nath] 900 B.C. Father of Tibni, who contended with Omri to become the sixth king of Israel and was slain. 1 Ki. 16:21,22.

GINNETHON [GIN-uh-thahn] KJV: Ginnetho; RSV: Ginnethoi (Neh. 12:4).
1. 525 B.C. A chief priest who returned to

Judah with Zerubbabel after the Exile. Neh. 12:4,16.
2. 450 B.C. A priest who sealed the covenant renewal with God, possibly with the name of his family's ancestor (see Ginnethon 1). Neh. 10:6.

GISHPA [GISH-puh] 450 B.C. KJV: Gispa. A Levite who, with Ziha, was in charge of the Temple servants in Nehemiah's time. Neh. 11:21.

GOG [GAHG]
1. B.C. (date unknown). Listed only in the genealogy of Reuben in 1 Chr. 5:4.
2.* B.C. (date unknown). Chief prince of Meshach and Tubal from the land of Magog; leader of a great army against Israel in the prophecies of Ezekiel. Ezek. 38,39. Symbolically used of a nation in Rev. 20:8.

GOLIATH [goh-LI-uhth]
1. 1025 B.C. The Gittite giant notable as the Philistine champion whom David slew with a stone from his sling. 1 Sam. 17; 21:9; 22:10.
2. 1000 B.C. Another giant identified as a Gittite, slain by Elhanan. Possibly the son of Goliath 1; however, the parallel text in 1 Chr. 20:5 has "Lahmi, brother of Goliath." 2 Sam. 21:19.

GOMER [GOH-muhr]
1. B.C. (date unknown). Firstborn son of Japheth listed in the Table of Nations. Possibly a nation or people is indicated. Gen. 10:2,3.
2. 750 B.C. The adulterous wife of the prophet Hosea who became a symbol for Israel's unfaithfulness to God. Hos. 1:2-8.

GUNI [GOO-ni]
1. 1850 B.C. Second of the four sons of Naphtali, listed among the descendants of Jacob. Gen. 46:24; Num. 26:48.
2. B.C. (date unknown). Listed only in the genealogy of Gad in 1 Chr. 5:15.

H

HAAHASHTARI [HAY-uh-HASH-tuh-ri; "the Ahashtarites"] B.C. (date unknown). A family listed only in the genealogy of Judah in 1 Chr. 4:6.

HABAKKUK* [huh-BAK-uhk; "embracer" or "wrestler"] 600 B.C. One of the minor prophets, whose words are recorded in the Book of Habakkuk. His prophecy called for judgment upon Judah because of its corruption, and stressed the importance of living by faith. Hab. 1:1; 3:1.

HABAZZINIAH [HAB-uh-zuh-NI-uh] 650 B.C. KJV: Habazinah. Grandfather of Jaazaniah the Recabite, who when offered wine by Jeremiah refused to drink. Jer. 35:3.

HACALIAH [HAK-uh-LI-uh] 475 B.C. KJV: Hachaliah. Father of Nehemiah. Neh. 1:1; 10:1.

HACMONI [HAK-moh-ni; "wise"] B.C. (date unknown). KJV, RSV: Hachmoni. Family of Jehiel, who cared for the sons of King David.

1 Chr. 27:32. The name should probably be rendered "Hacmonite" as in 1 Chr. 11:11.

HADAD [HAY-dad; "thunderer," (weather deity)] KJV: Hadar (Gen. 25:15; 36:39); RSV: Hadar (Gen. 36:39).
1. B.C. (date unknown). Eighth son of Ishmael, son of Abraham and Hagar. Gen. 25:15.
2. B.C. (date unknown). A pre-Israelite king, successor of Husham, listed in the genealogy of the rulers of Edom in Gen. 36:35,36.
3. B.C. (date unknown). Also a king listed in the genealogy of the rulers of Edom; successor of Baal-Hanan. Gen. 36:39.
4. 950 B.C. An Edomite of the royal line who was an enemy of Solomon. 1 Ki. 11:14-25.

HADADEZER [HAY-dad-EE-zuhr/HAD-uh-DEE-zuhr; "Hadad is help"] 1000 B.C. KJV: Hadarezer (2 Sam. 10; 1 Chr. 18:19). King of Zobah defeated by David. 2 Sam. 8:3-12; 10:15-19; 1 Chr. 18:3-10; 19:16,19.

HADAD RIMMON [HAY-dad RIM-uhn; a fusion of two weather deities, Hadad and Rimmon] Formerly considered a place name, as in the KJV, it is now thought by many scholars to refer to a vegetation deity. Zech. 12:11.

HADASSAH [huh-DAS-uh; "myrtle"] 475 B.C. Either the original Hebrew name of Esther or a title given to her, in which case the name was derived from the Akkadian, meaning "bride," a title of the goddess Ishtar. Esth. 2:7.

HADLAI [HAD-li] 775 B.C. Father of Amasa, an Ephraimite leader in Pekah's time. 2 Chr. 28:12.

HADORAM [huh-DOHR-uhm; "Hadad is exalted"]
1. B.C. (date unknown). A son of Joktan listed in the Table of Nations in Gen. 10:27. Ancestral source of an unidentified Arabian tribe.
2. 975 B.C. Son of Tou, king of Hamath; he brought a gift from his father to David after the defeat of their mutual enemy, Hadadezer, king of Zobah. 1 Chr. 18:10. Called Joram in 2 Sam. 8:10.

HAGAB [HAY-gab; "locust"] B.C. (date unknown). Ancestor of a family of Temple servants who returned to Judah with Zerubbabel. Ezra 2:46.

HAGABA [HAG-uh-buh; "locust"] B.C. (date unknown). Ancestor of exiles who accompanied Zerubbabel to Judah. Neh. 7:48. Called Hagabah in Ezra 2:45.

HAGABAH [HAG-uh-buh; "locust"] B.C. (date unknown). Ancestor of some Temple servants. Ezra 2:45. See also Hagaba.

HAGAR* [HAY-gahr; "flight"] 2075 B.C. The Egyptian maidservant who at the suggestion of Sarah became the concubine of Abraham. She gave birth to Ishmael, which began an enduring antagonism between her and Sarah. Eventually, after the birth of Isaac, Sarah compelled Abraham to send Hagar and Ishmael away. Gen. 16,21; Gal. 4:24,25.

HAGGAI* [HAG-i; "born on a feast day"] 525 B.C. One of the minor prophets, whose words are recorded in the Book of Haggai. His message was directed toward those Jews who returned from Exile in Babylonia, an exhortation to complete the rebuilding of the Temple with the promise of God's blessing. Ezra 5:1; 6:14; Hag. 1,2.

HAGGEDOLIM [HAG-uh-DOH-lim; "the great men"] 475 B.C. KJV: "One of the great men." Father of Zabdiel, a priest who resettled in Jerusalem after the Exile. Neh. 11:14. The term is perhaps better rendered by the KJV.

HAGGI [HAG-i; "born on a feast day"] 1875 B.C. Second of the seven sons of Gad. Gen. 46:16; Num. 26:15.

HAGGIAH [hah-GI-uh; "feast of Yahweh"] B.C. (date unknown). A descendant of Merari listed only in the genealogy of Levi in 1 Chr. 6:30.

HAGGITH [HAG-ith; "born on a feast day"] 1000 B.C. A wife of David, mother of Adonijah. 2 Sam. 3:4; 1 Ki. 1:5.

HAGRI [HAG-ri] 1025 B.C. KJV: Haggeri (1 Chr. 11:38). Father of Mibhar, a military commander listed among the mighty men of David. 1 Chr. 11:38. "Son of Hagri" in 2 Sam. 23:36 is rendered "Bani the Gadite" in the KJV and RSV.

HAKKATAN [HAK-uh-tan; "the little one"] 475 B.C. A descendant of Azgad; his son, Johanan, returned to Judah with Ezra after the Exile. Ezra 8:12.

HAKKOZ [HAK-ahz; "thorn"] KJV: Koz.
1. 1000 B.C. Head of the seventh division of priests in David's time. 1 Chr. 24:10.
2. B.C. (date unknown). Ancestral father of priests who were unable to demonstrate their Israelite descent. Ezra 2:61; Neh. 7:63.
3. B.C. (date unknown). Ancestor of Meremoth, who helped rebuild the wall of Jerusalem in Nehemiah's time. Neh. 3:4,21.
All three occurrences of the name may denote the same person.

HAKUPHA [huh-KOO-fuh; "crooked"] B.C. (date unknown). Ancestor of some Temple servants who returned to Judah with Zerubbabel after the Exile. Ezra 2:51; Neh. 7:53.

HALLOHESH [hah-LOH-hesh; "the whisperer"] 475 B.C. KJV: Halohesh (Neh. 3:12). A Jewish leader whose son, Shallum, helped rebuild the wall of Jerusalem. Hallohesh is among those who sealed the covenant renewal with God after the Exile. Neh. 3:12; 10:24.

HAM* [HAM] B.C. (date unknown). Second of the three sons of Noah; Ham's son, Canaan, was cursed by Noah to become the slave of Shem. Gen. 5:32; 7:13; 9:18-27.

HAMAN* [HAY-muhn] 475 B.C. The nobleman elevated by King Xerxes who plotted to massacre the Jewish population in Babylon. Esther revealed the plan of Haman to destroy the Jews; as a result, Haman was executed. Esth. 3–9.

HAMMEDATHA [HAM-uh-DAY-thuh] 500 B.C. Father of Haman, high official of King Xerxes. Esth. 3:1; 8:5; 9:24.

HAMMOLEKETH [hah-MOHL-uh-keth; "the queen"] B.C. (date unknown). RSV: Hammolecheth. Listed only in the genealogy of Manasseh in 1 Chr. 7:18.

HAMMUEL [HAM-yoo-uhl] B.C. (date unknown). KJV: Hamuel. Listed only in the genealogy of Simeon in 1 Chr. 4:26.

HAMOR [HAY-mohr; "ass"] 1925 B.C. Hivite ruler and father of Shechem, who raped Dinah, the daughter of Jacob. He and his son were killed in revenge by Simeon and Levi. Gen. 33:19–34:26; Josh. 24:32; Jdg. 9:28.

HAMUL [HAY-muhl; "spared"] 1850 B.C. Son of Perez and grandson of Judah. Gen. 46:12; Num. 26:21.

HAMUTAL [huh-MOO-tuhl] 650 B.C. Wife of Josiah and mother of Jehoahaz and Zedekiah. 2 Ki. 23:31; 24:18.

HANAMEL [HAN-uh-mehl; "grace of God"] 600 B.C. KJV: Hanameel. Jeremiah's cousin

from whom the prophet bought a field at Anathoth. Jer. 32:6-12.

HANAN [HAY-nuhn; "grace"]
1. B.C. (date unknown). Listed only in the genealogy of Benjamin in 1 Chr. 8:23.
2. 1000 B.C. A military commander, one of David's mighty men. 1 Chr. 11:43.
3. B.C. (date unknown). A descendant of Jonathan, son of Saul, listed in the genealogy of Benjamin in 1 Chr. 8:38; 9:44.
4. B.C. (date unknown). Ancestor of a family of Temple servants that returned to Judah with Zerubbabel after the Exile. Ezra 2:46; Neh. 7:49.
5. 625 B.C. Son of Igdaliah, "the man of God"; the sons of Hanan had a room in the Temple. Jer. 35:4.
6. 450 B.C. A Levite who with Ezra instructed the people in the meaning of the Law. Neh. 8:7.
7. 450 B.C. A Levite who sealed the covenant renewal with God in Nehemiah's time. Neh. 10:10. Possibly the same as Hanan 6.
8 and 9. 450 B.C. Two Jewish leaders who sealed the covenant renewal with God after the Exile. Neh. 10:22,26.
10. 425 B.C. Son of Zaccur appointed by Nehemiah as an assistant treasurer in the Temple. Neh. 13:13.

HANANI [huh-NAY-nee; "gracious"]
1. 975 B.C. A son of Heman, seer and minister of music for David. 1 Chr. 25:4,25.
2. 900 B.C. A seer who prophesied against Asa and was thrown in prison. He was father of Jehu, a prophet during the reigns of Baasha and Jehoshaphat. 1 Ki. 16:1,7; 2 Chr. 16:7-10; 19:2.
3. 450 B.C. A priest who took a foreign wife after the Exile. Ezra 10:20.
4. 450 B.C. A brother of Nehemiah who brought news to him in Babylon concerning the Jews who had returned to Jerusalem after the Exile. Between his two terms as governor, Nehemiah put his brother in charge of Jerusalem. Neh. 1:2; 7:2.
5. 450 B.C. A priest and musician at the dedication of the wall of Jerusalem in Nehemiah's time. Neh. 12:36.

HANANIAH [HAN-uh-NI-uh; "Yahweh is gracious"]
1. B.C. (date unknown). Listed only in the genealogy of Benjamin in 1 Chr. 8:24.
2. 975 B.C. A son of Heman and a musician in David's time. 1 Chr. 25:4,23.
3. 775 B.C. A royal official and military commander under Uzziah. 2 Chr. 26:11.
4. 650 B.C. Grandfather of Irijah, captain of the guard at the Benjamin Gate who imprisoned Jeremiah the prophet at the time of the fall of Jerusalem. Jer. 37:13.
5. 600 B.C. Father of Zedekiah, an official of King Jehoiakim. Jer. 36:12.
6. 600 B.C. A false prophet during the reign of Zedekiah who opposed Jeremiah, predicting that Babylonian oppression of Judah would end. He died that same year, in accordance with Jeremiah's prophecy. Jer. 28.
7. 600 B.C. One of Daniel's three Jewish friends taken with him to Babylon. Hananiah's name was changed to Shadrach upon entering Nebuchadnezzar's service. Dan. 1:6-19. See also Shadrach.
8. 500 B.C. A son of Zerubbabel listed in the genealogy of the royal line of Judah after the Exile. 1 Chr. 3:19,21.
9. 500 B.C. Head of a priestly family in Joiakim's time. Neh. 12:12.
10. 450 B.C. A Jew who took a foreign wife after the Exile. Ezra 10:28.
11. 450 B.C. A perfume maker who helped repair the wall of Jerusalem in Nehemiah's time. Neh. 3:8.
12. 450 B.C. Another who helped rebuild the wall of Jerusalem after the Exile. Neh. 3:30.

13. 450 B.C. "Commander of the citadel" whom Nehemiah, along with his brother, put in charge of Jerusalem. Neh. 7:2. Due to an uncertainty in the Hebrew, it is possible Hananiah is another name for Hanani, brother of Nehemiah.

14. 450 B.C. A Jewish leader who sealed the covenant renewal with God in Nehemiah's time. Neh. 10:23.

15. 450 B.C. A priest who played the trumpet at the dedication of the wall of Jerusalem. Neh. 12:41.

HANNAH* [HAN-nuh; "grace"] 1125 B.C. The wife of Elkanah and mother of Samuel. At the tabernacle, Hannah prayed fervently for a son, whom she vowed she would dedicate to the Lord. Shortly after the birth of her son, she gave Samuel to Eli the priest to serve in the tabernacle. 1 Sam. 1–2:11,18-21.

HANNIEL [HAN-ee-uhl; "God is gracious"] KJV: Haniel (1 Chr. 7:39).
1. 1400 B.C. The leader from the tribe of Manasseh appointed by Moses to help divide the land of Canaan. Num. 34:23.
2. B.C. (date unknown). Listed only in the genealogy of Asher in 1 Chr. 7:39.

HANOCH [HAY-nahk] KJV: Henoch (1 Chr. 1:33).
1. 1950 B.C. Third of the five sons of Midian, son of Abraham. Gen. 25:4; 1 Chr. 1:33.
2. 1900 B.C. Firstborn son of Reuben, eldest son of Jacob. Gen. 46:9; Num. 26:5.

HANUN [HAY-nuhn; "gracious"]
1. 1000 B.C. Son and successor of Nahash, king of the Ammonites. When David sent a delegation of men to express sympathy for the death of Nahash, Hanun mistreated them. This resulted in a war in which the Ammonites were defeated. 2 Sam. 10; 1 Chr. 19.
2. 450 B.C. One who helped repair the wall of Jerusalem in Nehemiah's time. Neh. 3:13.
3. 450 B.C. Son of Zalaph; he was another who worked on the walls of Jerusalem. Neh. 3:30.

HAPPIZZEZ [HAP-uh-zehz] 1000 B.C. KJV: Aphses. Head of the eighteenth division of priests in David's time. 1 Chr. 24:15.

HARAN [HAIR-uhn]
1. 2100 B.C. A younger brother of Abraham and the father of Lot. Gen. 11:26-31.
2. B.C. (date unknown). Firstborn son of Caleb and his concubine, Ephah, listed in the genealogy of Judah. 1 Chr. 2:46.
3. B.C. (date unknown). A descendant of Gershon, son of Levi. 1 Chr. 23:9.

HARBONA [hahr-BOH-nuh] 475 B.C. KJV: Harbonah (Esth. 7:9). One of the seven eunuchs who served King Xerxes. Esth. 1:10; 7:9.

HAREPH [HAHR-ef] B.C. (date unknown). Founder of Beth Gader listed in the genealogy of Judah in 1 Chr. 2:51.

HARHAIAH [hahr-HAY-uh; "Yahweh protects"] 475 B.C. Father of Uzziel, who helped reconstruct the wall of Jerusalem. Neh. 3:8.

HARHAS [HAHR-hahs; possibly "splendor"] 675 B.C. Grandfather of Shallum, husband of the prophetess Huldah. 2 Ki. 22:14. Called Hasrah in 2 Chr. 34:22.

HARHUR [HAHR-huhr] B.C. (date unknown). Ancestor of a family of Temple servants that returned to Judah with Zerubbabel after the Exile. Ezra 2:51; Neh. 7:53.

HARIM [HAIR-uhm; "consecrated"]
1. 1000 B.C. Head of the third division of priests in David's time. 1 Chr. 24:8.
2. B.C. (date unknown). Ancestral head of a family that returned to Judah with Zerubbabel after the Exile. Ezra 2:32; Neh. 7:35.
3. B.C. (date unknown). Ancestral head of a priestly family that returned from Exile. Ezra 2:39; 10:21; Neh. 7:42; 10:5; 12:15. Possibly the same as Harim 1.
4. B.C. (date unknown). Ancestor of some who took foreign wives after the Exile. Ezra 10:31. Probably the same as Harim 2.
5. 450 B.C. A Jewish leader who sealed the covenant renewal with God in Nehemiah's time, possibly with the name of a family ancestor (compare Harim 2). Neh. 10:27.

HARIPH [HAIR-if]
1. B.C. (date unknown). Ancestral head of a family that returned to Judah with Zerubbabel. Neh. 7:24.
2. 450 B.C. A Jewish leader who sealed the covenant renewal in Nehemiah's time, possibly with the name of a family ancestor (compare Hariph 1). Neh. 10:19.

HARNEPHER [HAHR-nuh-fuhr] B.C. (date unknown). Listed only in the genealogy of Asher in 1 Chr. 7:36.

HAROEH [huh-ROH-uh; "the seer"] B.C. (date unknown). A descendant of Caleb listed in the genealogy of Judah in 1 Chr. 2:52.

HARSHA [HAHR-shuh] B.C. (date unknown). Ancestral head of a family of Temple servants that returned with Zerubbabel to Judah. Ezra 2:52; Neh. 7:54.

HARUM [HAIR-uhm] B.C. (date unknown). Listed only in the genealogy of Judah in 1 Chr. 4:8.

HARUMAPH [huh-ROO-mahf; "slit-nose" (?)] 475 B.C. Father of Jedaiah, who helped in the rebuilding of Jerusalem in Nehemiah's time. Neh. 3:10.

HARUZ [HAIR-uhz] 700 B.C. Father of Meshullemeth, wife of Manasseh and mother of Amon. 2 Ki. 21:19.

HASADIAH [HAS-uh-DI-uh; "Yahweh is kind"] 425 B.C. A son of Zerubbabel. 1 Chr. 3:20.

HASHABIAH [HASH-uh-BI-uh; "Yahweh has taken account"]
1. B.C. (date unknown). Listed in the genealogy of Ethan, one of the chief ministers of music in David's time. 1 Chr. 6:45.
2. 975 B.C. A son of Jeduthun (also called Ethan) and head of the twelfth division of musicians in David's time. 1 Chr. 25:3,19.
3. 975 B.C. A Hebronite, one of David's officials. 1 Chr. 26:30.
4. 975 B.C. A son of Kemuel and an officer over the tribe of Levi in David's time. 1 Chr. 27:17.
5. 625 B.C. A chief Levite during the reign of Josiah. 2 Chr. 35:9.

6. B.C. (date unknown). Ancestor of Shemaiah, a Levite who resettled in Jerusalem after the Exile. 1 Chr. 9:14; Neh. 11:15.
7. B.C. (date unknown). Ancestor of Uzzi, chief officer of the Levites in Jerusalem in Nehemiah's time. Neh. 11:22.
8. 500 B.C. Head of a priestly family while Joiakim was high priest. Neh. 12:21.
9. 450 B.C. A Levite who returned with Ezra to Judah after the Exile. He was one of those who sealed the covenant renewal with God. Ezra 8:19,24; Neh. 10:11; 12:24.
10. 450 B.C. Ruler over half the district of Keilah who carried out repairs in his district during the rebuilding of Jerusalem's wall. Neh. 3:17.

HASHABNAH [huh-SHAB-nuh] 450 B.C. A Jewish leader who sealed the covenant renewal with God in Nehemiah's time. Neh. 10:25.

HASHABNEIAH [HASH-uhb-NEE-uh] KJV: Hashabniah.
1. 475 B.C. Father of Hattush, who helped repair the wall of Jerusalem in Nehemiah's time. Neh. 3:10.
2. 450 B.C. One of the Levites who led Israel in prayer previous to the covenant renewal. Neh. 9:5.

HASHBADDANAH [hash-BAD-duh-nuh] 450 B.C. KJV: Hashbadana. One who stood to the left of Ezra the scribe at the reading of the Law before the people. Neh. 8:4.

HASHEM [HAY-shehm] 1000 B.C. A Gizonite, one of the military elite known as David's thirty mighty men. 1 Chr. 11:34.

HASHUBAH [huh-SHOO-buh; "consideration" (?)] 425 B.C. A son of Zerubbabel, governor of Judah. 1 Chr. 3:20.

HASHUM [HAY-shuhm]
1. B.C. (date unknown). Ancestral head of a family that returned to Judah with Zerubbabel after the Exile. Ezra 2:19; Neh. 7:22.
2. B.C. (date unknown). Ancestor of some who took foreign wives after the Exile. Ezra 10:33. Possibly the same as Hashum 1.
3. 450 B.C. One who stood to the left of Ezra the scribe at the reading of the Law. Neh. 8:4.
4. 450 B.C. A Jewish leader who sealed the covenant renewal with God, probably with the name of a family ancestor (compare Hashum 1). Neh. 10:18.

HASRAH [HAZ-ruh] 675 B.C. Grandfather of Shallum, who was husband of the prophetess Huldah. 2 Chr. 34:22. Called Harhas in 2 Ki. 22:14.

HASSENAAH [has-uh-NAY-uh] B.C. (date unknown). Ancestor of some who rebuilt the Fish Gate in Nehemiah's time. Neh. 3:3. Probably the same as Senaah.

HASSENUAH [HAS-uh-NOO-uh] B.C. (date unknown). KJV: Hasenuah (1 Chr. 9:7), Senuah (Neh. 11:9). Ancestor of Sallu, a Benjamite who resettled in Jerusalem after the Exile. 1 Chr. 9:7; Neh. 11:9.

HASSHUB [HASH-uhb; "considerate" (?)] KJV: Hashub (Nehemiah).
1. 475 B.C. Father of Shemaiah, a Levite who resettled in Jerusalem after the Exile. 1 Chr. 9:14; Neh. 11:15.
2 and 3. 450 B.C. Two who helped rebuild the wall of Jerusalem. Neh. 3:11,23.
4. 450 B.C. One who sealed the covenant renewal with God in Nehemiah's time. Neh. 10:23. Possibly the same as Hasshub 2 or 3.

HASSOPHERETH [hah-SAHF-uh-reth] 950 B.C. KJV: Sophereth. A servant of Solomon whose descendants returned to Judah with Zerubbabel. Ezra 2:55. Called Sophereth in the parallel text in Neh. 7:57.

HASUPHA [huh-SOO-fuh] 950 B.C. KJV: Hashupha (Neh. 7:46). A servant of Solomon, whose descendants returned to Judah after the Exile. Ezra 2:43; Neh. 7:46.

HATHACH [HAY-thak] 475 B.C. KJV: Hatach. One of King Xerxes' eunuchs, assigned to attend Esther. Esth. 4:5-9.

HATHATH [HAY-thath] 1350 B.C. Son of Othniel the judge listed in 1 Chr. 4:13.

HATIPHA [huh-TI-fuh; "seized, captive"] B.C. (date unknown). Ancestor of some Temple servants who returned to Judah with Zerubbabel. Ezra 2:54; Neh. 7:45.

HATITA [huh-TI-tuh] B.C. (date unknown). Ancestral head of a family of Temple gatekeepers that returned from the Exile with Zerubbabel. Ezra 2:42; Neh. 7:45.

HATTIL [HAT-uhl] 950 B.C. A servant of Solomon whose descendants returned to Judah after the Exile. Ezra 2:57; Neh. 7:59.

HATTUSH [HAT-uhsh]
1. 525 B.C. A chief priest who returned to Judah with Zerubbabel. Neh. 12:2.
2. 450 B.C. A descendant of Shecaniah, son of Zerubbabel; he returned to Judah with Ezra. 1 Chr. 3:22; Ezra 8:2.
3. 450 B.C. Son of Hashabneiah, who helped repair the walls of Jerusalem. Neh. 3:10. Possibly the same as Hattush 1.
4. 450 B.C. A priest who sealed the covenant renewal with God in Nehemiah's time, possibly with the name of his family ancestor (compare Hattush 1). Neh. 10:4.

HAVILAH [HAV-uh-luh; "sandy"]
1. B.C. (date unknown). A son of Cush listed in the Table of Nations in Gen. 10:7.
2. B.C. (date unknown). A descendant of Shem listed in the Table of Nations in Gen. 10:29.

HAZAEL [HAY-zee-uhl; "God sees"] 850 B.C. An official of Ben-Hadad, king of Syria. He murdered the ill king and usurped the throne. His reign led to the Syrian oppression of Israel during the reigns of Jehu and Jehoahaz. 1 Ki. 19:15-17; 2 Ki. 8:8-15; 13:3,22-25.

HAZAIAH [ha-ZAY-yuh; "Yahweh sees"] B.C. (date unknown). Ancestor of Maaseiah, a Judahite who resettled in Jerusalem after the Exile. Neh. 11:5.

HAZARMAVETH [hay-zuhr-MAY-veth; "court of death"] B.C. (date unknown). A descendant of Shem listed in the Table of Nations in Gen. 10:26. Ancestral source of a people who settled in southern Arabia.

HAZIEL [HAY-zee-uhl; "God sees"] B.C. (date unknown). A family head listed in the genealogy of Gershon, son of Levi, in 1 Chr. 23:9.

HAZO [HAY-zoh] 2075 B.C. A son of Nahor, the brother of Abraham. Gen. 22:22.

HAZZELELPONI [HAZ-uh-lehl-POH-ni] B.C. (date unknown). KJV: Hazelelponi. Daughter of Etam listed only in the genealogy of Judah in 1 Chr. 4:3.

HAZZOBEBAH [HAZ-oh-BEE-buh] KJV, RSV: Zobebah. B.C. (date unknown). Listed only in the genealogy of Judah in 1 Chr. 4:8.

HEBER [HEE-buhr; "companion"]
1. 1850 B.C. A grandson of Asher. Gen. 46:17; 1 Chr. 7:31,32.
2. 1225 B.C. A Kenite descended from Hobab, Moses' brother-in-law. His wife, Jael, killed Sisera, commander of a Canaanite army. Jdg. 4:11,17; 5:24.
3. B.C. (date unknown). Listed only in the genealogy of Judah in 1 Chr. 4:18.

4. B.C. (date unknown). Listed only in the genealogy of Benjamin in 1 Chr. 8:17.

HEBRON [HEB-ruhn; "league, association"]

1. 1850 B.C. A grandson of Levi. Ex. 6:18; Num. 3:19.
2. B.C. (date unknown). Listed only in the genealogy of the clans of Caleb, a descendant of Judah. 1 Chr. 2:42,43.

HEGAI [HEHG-i] 475 B.C. KJV: Hege. Eunuch of King Xerxes put in charge of the king's harem. Esth. 2:3,8,15.

HELAH [HEE-luh; "necklace"(?)] B.C. (date unknown). A wife of Ashhur listed in the genealogy of Judah in 1 Chr. 4:5,7.

HELDAI [HEL-di]
1. 975 B.C. KJV, RSV: Helem (Zech. 6:14). A descendant of Othniel and commander of the twelfth division of David's army. 1 Chr. 27:15. Probably the same as Heled, one of David's thirty mighty men.
2. 525 B.C. One who brought gold and silver to the Jews who returned to Judah from the Exile in Babylon. Zech. 6:10,14.

HELED [HEE-lehd] 1000 B.C. KJV, RSV: Heleb (2 Sam. 23:29). A military commander, one of David's thirty mighty men. 2 Sam. 23:29; 1 Chr. 11:30. Probably the same as Heldai 1.

HELEK [HEE-lehk; "portion, lot"] B.C. (date unknown). Ancestral head of a clan in the tribe of Manasseh. Num. 26:30.

HELEM [HEE-luhm] B.C. (date unknown). Listed only in the genealogy of Asher in 1 Chr. 7:35.

HELEZ [HEE-lehz]
1. 1000 B.C. A military commander, one of David's thirty mighty men. 2 Sam. 23:26; 1 Chr. 11:27; 27:10.
2. B.C. (date unknown). Listed only in the genealogy of Jerahmeel, a descendant of Judah. 1 Chr. 2:39.

HELI [HEE-li] 25 B.C. Father of Joseph listed in the genealogy of Christ in Lk. 3:23.

HELKAI [HEL-ki; shortened form of Helkiah, "Yahweh is my portion"] 500 B.C. Head of a priestly family when Joiakim was high priest among the Jews who returned to Judah after the Exile. Neh. 12:15.

HELON [HEE-lahn; "strength, valor"] 1475 B.C. Father of Eliab, leader of the tribe of Zebulun at the time of the Exodus. Num. 1:9.

HEMAN [HEE-muhn; "faithful"]
1. B.C. (date unknown). A wise man whom Solomon was said to exceed in wisdom. 1 Ki. 4:31; 1 Chr. 2:6. Author of Ps. 88.
2. 1000 B.C. Levite seer who served as one of David's chief ministers of music in the Temple. 1 Chr. 6:33; 15:17-19; 16:41,42; 25:1-6.

HEMDAN [HEM-dan] 1925 B.C. KJV: Amram (1 Chr. 1:41); RSV: Hamran (1 Chr. 1:41). Firstborn son of Dishon, a Horite chief in Esau's time. Gen. 36:26; 1 Chr. 1:41.

HEN [HEN; "favor"] 525 B.C. RSV: Josiah. A son of Zephaniah. Zech. 6:14. Likely the same as Josiah in v. 10. According to the NIV, the word may possibly be rendered "the gracious one."

HENADAD [HEN-uh-dad; "favor of Hadad" (weather deity)] B.C. (date unknown). Ancestral head of a Levite family that helped rebuild the Temple after the Exile. Ezra 3:9; Neh. 3:18,24; 10:9.

HEPHER [HEE-fuhr]
1. B.C. (date unknown). A descendant of Gilead and ancestral source of a clan in the tribe of Manasseh. Num. 26:32,33; 27:1; Josh. 17:2,3.
2. B.C. (date unknown). Listed in the genealogy of Judah in 1 Chr. 4:6.
3. 1000 B.C. A military commander, one of David's thirty mighty men. 1 Chr. 11:36.

HEPHZIBAH [HEF-zib-uh; "my delight is in her"] 725 B.C. Wife of Hezekiah and mother of Manasseh, fourteenth king of Judah. 2 Ki. 21:1.

HERESH [HEER-esh] 450 B.C. A Levite who resettled in Jerusalem after the Exile. 1 Chr. 9:15. The name is omitted in the parallel text in Neh. 11:15-17.

HERMAS [HUHR-muhs] A.D. 55. A Christian greeted by Paul in his letter to the Romans. Rom. 16:14.

HERMES [HUHR-meez]
1. A deity in the Greek pantheon, messenger of the gods. Acts 14:12. Called Mercurius in KJV.
2. A.D. 55. A Roman Christian to whom Paul sends greetings. Rom. 16:14.

HERMOGENES [huhr-MAHJ-uh-neez; "born of Hermes"] A.D. 65. One who deserted Paul. 2 Tim. 1:15.

HEROD [HAIR-uhd]
1.* 37–4 B.C. Herod the Great, the infamous king of Judea who slaughtered the children of Bethlehem in an attempt to kill the infant Messiah. Mt. 2; Lk. 1:5.
2. 4 B.C.–A.D. 39. Herod Antipas, the son of Herod the Great and tetrarch of Galilee and Perea during Jesus' ministry. His marriage to his brother Philip's wife, Herodias, was strongly opposed by John the Baptist, who was eventually beheaded by Antipas. He was the Herod who mocked Christ before returning him to Pilate. Mt. 14:1-11; Mk. 6:14-28; Lk. 3:19,20; 23:6-15. See also Antipas.
3. A.D. 25. Herod Philip, son of Herod the Great and Mariamne; first husband of Herodias and father of Salome. Mt. 14:3; Mk. 6:17. See also Philip 1.
4. 4 B.C.–A.D. 34. Herod Philip, son of Herod the Great and Cleopatra of Jerusalem; tetrarch of Iturea and Traconitis. He married Salome, daughter of Herodias. Lk. 3:1. See also Philip 2.
5. A.D. 37–44. Herod Agrippa I, son of Aristobulus and grandson of Herod the Great; he was the king of Judea who persecuted the early church. He put James son of Zebedee to death and imprisoned Peter. He was stricken by an angel of the Lord and died. Acts 12. See also Agrippa.
6.* A.D. 50–100. Herod Agrippa II, son and successor of Agrippa I. He was consulted by Festus during the trial of Paul. Acts 24:35. See also Agrippa.

HERODIAS [huh-ROH-dee-uhs] A.D. 25. Daughter of Aristobulus, the son of Herod the

Great. She left her first husband, Herod Philip, for his brother Herod Antipas. She is known for arranging the execution of John the Baptist, who denounced the remarriage as immoral. Mt. 14:3-6; Mk. 6:17-22; Lk. 3:19.

HERODION [huh-ROH-dee-uhn] A.D. 55. A relative Paul greets in Rom. 16:11.

HEZEKIAH [HEZ-uh-KI-uh; "Yahweh is my strength"] KJV: Hizkiah (Zeph. 1:1), Hizkijah (Neh. 10:17).
1.* 728–697 B.C. The pious king of Judah who brought about extensive religious reforms, restoring the Temple of Jerusalem and eliminating idolatrous practices in Judah. 2 Ki. 18–20; 2 Chr. 29–32; Isa. 36–39.
2. B.C. (date unknown). Ancestor of Zephaniah the prophet. Zeph. 1:1.
3. 525 B.C. Head of a family that returned to Judah with Zerubbabel after the Exile. Ezra 2:16; Neh. 7:21.
4. 450 B.C. One who sealed the covenant renewal with God in Nehemiah's time, possibly with the name of an ancestor (compare Hezekiah 3). Neh. 10:17.

HEZION [HEZ-ee-uhn] 950 B.C. Grandfather of Ben-Hadad, the king of Syria (Aram) who formed a treaty with King Asa. 1 Ki. 15:18.

HEZIR [HEZ-uhr]
1. 1000 B.C. Head of the seventeenth division of priests in David's time. 1 Chr. 24:15.
2. 450 B.C. A Jewish leader who sealed the covenant renewal with God in Nehemiah's time. Neh. 10:20.

HEZRO [HEZ-roh] 1000 B.C. KJV: Hezroni. A military commander, one of David's thirty mighty men. 2 Sam. 23:35; 1 Chr. 11:37.

HEZRON [HEZ-ruhn]
1. 1875 B.C. Third of the four sons of Reuben, who was the firstborn son of Jacob. Gen. 46:9; Ex. 6:14; 1 Chr. 5:3.
2. 1825 B.C. Son of Perez and grandson of Judah, son of Jacob. Gen. 46:12; Ruth 4:18; 1 Chr. 2:9,21,24. He is listed in the genealogies of Christ in Mt. 1:3 and Lk. 3:33.

HIDDAI [HID-i] 1000 B.C. A military commander, one of David's thirty mighty men. 2 Sam. 23:30. Called Hurai in the parallel text in 1 Chr. 11:32.

HIEL [HI-uhl] 875 B.C. A man from Bethel who rebuilt Jericho at the cost of the lives of his eldest and youngest sons, in accordance with Joshua's prophecy (Josh. 6:26). It is likely Hiel sacrificed his sons. 1 Ki. 16:34.

HILKIAH [hil-KI-uh; "Yahweh is my portion"]
1. B.C. (date unknown). A Levite listed in the genealogy of Ethan, a chief minister of music in David's time. 1 Chr. 6:45.
2. 975 B.C. Son of Hosah, a Levite and Temple gatekeeper in David's time. 1 Chr. 26:11.
3. 725 B.C. Father of Eliakim, palace administrator during the reign of Hezekiah. 2 Ki. 18:18; Isa. 22:20; 36:3.
4. 625 B.C. High priest who discovered the lost Book of the Law in the Temple during the reign of King Josiah. 2 Ki. 22; 23:4,24; 1 Chr. 6:13; 2 Chr. 34.
5. 625 B.C. A priest of Anathoth, father of Jeremiah the prophet. Jer. 1:1.
6. 600 B.C. Father of Gemariah, an ambassador to Babylon in the time of Zedekiah. Jer. 29:3.
7. 525 B.C. A chief priest who returned to Judah with Zerubbabel after the Exile. Neh. 12:7,21.
8. 475 B.C. Father of a priest who settled in Jerusalem in Nehemiah's time. 1 Chr. 9:11; Neh. 11:11.
9. 450 B.C. One who stood to the right of Ezra the scribe as he read the Law to the people. Neh. 8:4.

HILLEL [HIL-ehl] 1100 B.C. Father of Abdon, a minor judge. Jdg. 12:13,15.

HIRAH [HI-ruh] 1900 B.C. A man from Adullam with whom Judah stayed. Gen. 38:1,12.

HIRAM [HI-ruhm; shortened form of Ahiram, "my brother is exalted"] 975 B.C. King of Tyre who was an ally of David and Solomon. He supplied materials for the building of the Temple. 2 Sam. 5:11; 1 Ki. 5,9.

HIZKI [HIZ-ki; shortened form of Hezekiah] B.C. (date unknown). Listed only in the genealogy of Benjamin in 1 Chr. 8:17.

HIZKIAH [hiz-KI-uh; "Yahweh is my strength"] B.C. (date unknown). KJV: Hezekiah. A descendant of Zerubbabel listed in the genealogy of the royal line of David. 1 Chr. 3:23.

HOBAB [HOH-bahb; "beloved"] 1450 B.C. Son of Reuel the Midianite, and Moses' brother-in-law. He served as a guide to the Israelites during the Exodus. Num. 10:29; Jdg. 4:11.

HOBAIAH [hoh-BI-uh; "Yahweh has hidden"] B.C. (date unknown). KJV, RSV: Habaiah (Ezra 2:61). Ancestral head of a family of priests that returned to Judah with Zerubbabel after the Exile. Ezra 2:61; Neh. 7:63.

HOD [HAHD; "majesty"] B.C. (date unknown). Listed only in the genealogy of Asher in 1 Chr. 7:37.

HODAVIAH [HAHD-uh-VI-uh; "honorer of Yahweh"] KJV: Hodaiah (1 Chr. 3:24). KJV, RSV: Henadad (Ezra 3:9); Hoderah (Neh. 7:43).
1. B.C. (date unknown). Ancestor of a Levite family that returned to Judah with Zerubbabel. Ezra 2:40; 3:9; Neh. 7:43.
2. 750 B.C. Head of a family in the tribe of Manasseh. 1 Chr. 5:24.
3. B.C. (date unknown). Ancestor of Sallu, a Benjamite who resettled in Jerusalem after the Exile. 1 Chr. 9:7. Omitted from the parallel text in Neh. 11:7.
4. B.C. (date unknown). Descendant of Zerubbabel listed in the genealogy of the royal line after the Exile. 1 Chr. 3:24.

HODESH [HOH-desh; "new moon"] B.C. (date unknown). Third wife of Shaharaim, listed only in the genealogy of Benjamin in 1 Chr. 8:9.

HODIAH [hoh-DI-uh; "splendor of Yahweh"] KJV: Hodijah (Nehemiah).
1. B.C. (date unknown). Listed only in the genealogy of Judah in 1 Chr. 4:19. Incorrectly rendered as "his wife" in the KJV.
2. 450 B.C. A Levite who interpreted for the people while Ezra the scribe read from the Law. Neh. 8:7; 9:5.
3 and 4. 450 B.C. Two Levites who sealed the covenant renewal with God in Nehemiah's time. Neh. 10:10,13. Either may be the same as Hodiah 2.
5. 450 B.C. A Jewish leader who sealed the covenant renewal with God in Nehemiah's time. Neh. 10:18.

HOGLAH [HAHG-luh; "partridge"] 1400 B.C. One of the daughters of Zelophehad, a descendant of Manasseh, who petitioned Moses and received their father's land as an inheritance. Num. 26:33; 27:1; 36:11; Josh. 17:3.

HOHAM [HOH-ham] 1400 B.C. King of Hebron who joined four other Amorite kings to attack Gibeon for making a treaty with the Israelites. They were defeated by Joshua on the day the sun stood still. Josh. 10.

HOMAM [HOH-mam] 1950 B.C. KJV: Hemam; RSV: Heman (Gen. 36:22). A son of Lotan, a Horite chief in Esau's time. Gen. 36:22; 1 Chr. 1:39.

HOPHNI [HAHF-ni] 1100 B.C. One of the two unholy sons of Eli, who served as priests at the tabernacle. For their sins both died on the same day, in accordance with a prophecy given to Eli. 1 Sam. 1:3; 2–4. **Brother:** Phinehas.

HOPHRA [HAHF-ruh] 589–570 B.C. Egyptian Pharaoh who marched against Nebuchadnezzar to aid Zedekiah, who was under siege in Jerusalem. However, Hophra immediately withdrew, and as a result, Nebuchadnezzar's army again laid siege to Jerusalem, which eventually resulted in its fall (Jer. 37:5-8). Hophra's death was prophesied by Jeremiah. Jer. 44:30.

HORAM [HOH-ram] 1400 B.C. A king of Gezer who was defeated by Joshua. Josh. 10:33.

HORI [HOHR-i]
1. 1950 B.C. Firstborn son of Lotan and grandson of Seir, the Horite chief. Gen. 36:22.
2. 1475 B.C. Father of Shaphat, the Simeonite leader sent by Moses to explore the land of Canaan. Num. 13:5.

HOSAH [HOH-zuh; "refuge"] 1000 B.C. A chief Temple gatekeeper in the time of David. 1 Chr. 16:38; 26:10,11,16.

HOSEA* [hoh-ZAY-uh; "Yahweh has saved"] 750 B.C. KJV: Osee (Rom. 9:25). One of the minor prophets, whose words are recorded in the Book of Hosea. In his message to Israel, his adulterous wife, Gomer, became a symbol for Israel's unfaithfulness to God. Hos. 1–14; Rom. 9:25. **Father:** Beeri. **Children:** Jezreel, Lo-Ruhamah, Lo-Ammi.

HOSHAIAH [hoh-SHAY-yuh; "Yahweh has saved"]
1. 625 B.C. Father of Azariah (also called Jezaniah), an army officer who requested that Jeremiah seek the will of God for the remnant of Judah after Jerusalem fell. Jer. 42:1; 43:2.
2. 450 B.C. A Jewish leader at the dedication of the rebuilt walls of Jerusalem in Nehemiah's time. Neh. 12:32.

HOSHAMA [HOSH-ah-muh; shortened form of "Yahweh has heard"] 550 B.C. A son or grandson of Jehoiachin, listed only in the genealogy of the royal line after the Exile. 1 Chr. 3:18.

HOSHEA [hoh-SHEE-uh; "may Yahweh save"]
1. 1450 B.C. An Ephraimite leader whose given name was changed by Moses to Joshua. Notable as the righteous leader of Israel who, after the death of Moses, led Israel into the Promised Land. Num. 13:8,16. See also Joshua 1.
2. 1000 B.C. Officer over the tribe of Ephraim in David's day. 1 Chr. 27:20.
3. 732–723 B.C. The last king of Israel, who assassinated Pekah and took the throne. Shalmanezer, king of Assyria, imprisoned Hoshea and laid siege to Samaria for three years before the capital of Israel fell to Assyrian forces. 2 Ki. 15:30; 17:1-6; 18:1,9,10.
4. 450 B.C. A Jewish leader who sealed the covenant renewal with God in Nehemiah's time. Neh. 10:23.

HOTHAM [HOH-thuhm] KJV: Hothan (1 Chr. 11:44).
1. B.C. (date unknown). Listed only in the genealogy of Asher in 1 Chr. 7:32.
2. 1025 B.C. Father of Shama and Jeiel, two members of the military elite known as David's thirty mighty men. 1 Chr. 11:44.

HOTHIR [HOH-thuhr; "abundance"] 975 B.C. A son of Heman, and a Temple musician in David's time. 1 Chr. 25:4,28.

HUBBAH [HUB-buh] B.C. (date unknown). KJV, RSV: Jehubbah. Listed only in the genealogy of Asher in 1 Chr. 7:34.

HUL [HUL] B.C. (date unknown). A son of Aram and grandson of Shem, listed in the Table of Nations in Gen. 10:23.

HULDAH [HUL-duh; "weasel"(?)] 625 B.C. The prophetess consulted about the Book of the Law after its rediscovery during the reign of Josiah. 2 Ki. 22:14-20; 2 Chr. 34:22-28.

HUPHAM [HOO-fuhm; "coast-inhabitant"] B.C. (date unknown). Ancestral head of a Benjamite clan. Num. 26:39. Called Huppim in Gen. 46:21 and 1 Chr. 7:12.

HUPPAH [HUP-uh; "protection"] 1000 B.C. Head of the thirteenth division of priests in David's time. 1 Chr. 24:13.

HUPPIM [HUP-ihm; "coast people"] B.C. (date unknown). A son of Benjamin listed in Gen. 46:21. *See also* Hupham.

HUR [HUHR]
1. 1500 B.C. Son (or descendant) of Caleb, son of Hezron, and grandfather of Bezalel, chief craftsman of the tabernacle and its furnishings. Ex. 31:2; 1 Chr. 2:19,20; 4:1,4.
2. 1450 B.C. One who with Aaron held up the hands of Moses until the Amalekites were defeated. Ex. 17:10-12; 24:14.
3. 1400 B.C. One of five kings of Midian defeated by Moses and the Israelites. Num. 31:8; Josh. 13:21.
4. 475 B.C. Father of Rephaiah, who helped repair the wall of Jerusalem in Nehemiah's time. Neh. 3:9.

HURAI [HYOOR-i] 1000 B.C. A military commander, one of David's thirty mighty men. 1 Chr. 11:32. Called Hiddai in 2 Sam. 23:30.

HURAM [HYOOR-uhm] KJV, RSV: Hiram (1 Kings).
1. 1825 B.C. A son of Bela, who was the firstborn son of Benjamin. 1 Chr. 8:5.
2. 950 B.C. A skilled metalworker who cast the two bronze pillars, Boaz and Jakin, at the entrance to the Temple in Solomon's time. 1 Ki. 7:13-45; 2 Chr. 4:11. Also called Huram-Abi.

HURAM-ABI [HYOOR-uhm-AY-bi; "master Huram"] 950 B.C. KJV: "Huram, my father." A craftsman who undertook work on the Temple for Solomon. 2 Chr. 2:13; 4:16. *See also* Huram 2.

HURI [HYOOR-i] B.C. (date unknown). Listed only in the genealogy of Gad in 1 Chr. 5:14.

HUSHAH [HOO-shuh] B.C. (date unknown). Listed in the genealogy of Judah in 1 Chr. 4:4.

HUSHAI [HOO-shi]
1. 975 B.C. The Arkite, notable as the friend of David who misled Absalom into following his advice rather than the counsel of Ahithophel. Hushai's deception eventually led to the death of Absalom. 2 Sam. 15:32-37; 16:15–17:16.
2. 975 B.C. Father of Baana, one of Solomon's twelve district governors. 1 Ki. 4:16. Probably the same as Hushai 1.

HUSHAM [HOO-shuhm] B.C. (date unknown). A pre-Israelite king of Edom, descended from Esau. Gen. 36:34,35.

HUSHIM [HOO-shim]
1. 1875 B.C. Son of Dan and a grandson of Jacob. Gen. 46:23. Called Shuham in Num. 26:42.
2. B.C. (date unknown). A wife divorced by Shaharaim, listed only in the genealogy of Benjamin in 1 Chr. 8:8,11.

HYMENAEUS [HI-muh-NEE-uhs] A.D. 65. A false teacher condemned by Paul in his letters to Timothy. His heretical teaching was likely an early form of gnosticism. 1 Tim. 1:20; 2 Tim. 2:17.

I

IBHAR [IB-hahr; "God chooses"] 975 B.C. A son born to David in Jerusalem. 2 Sam. 5:15.

IBNEIAH [ib-NEE-yuh; "Yahweh builds up"] 450 B.C. A Benjamite who resettled in Jerusalem after the Exile. 1 Chr. 9:8.

IBNIJAH [ib-NI-juh; "Yahweh builds up"] B.C. (date unknown). Ancestor of Elah, a Benjamite who resettled in Jerusalem after the rebuilding of the wall. 1 Chr. 9:8.

IBRI [ib-REE; "a Hebrew"] 1000 B.C. A descendant of Merari, listed among the Levites in David's time. 1 Chr. 24:27.

IBSAM [IB-sam; "fragrant"] B.C. (date unknown). KJV: Jibsam. Listed only in the genealogy of Issachar in 1 Chr. 7:2.

IBZAN [IB-zan; "swift"(?)] Ruled 1078–1072 B.C. A minor judge from Bethlehem who ruled in Israel for a period of seven years. Jdg. 12:8-10.

ICHABOD [IK-uh-bahd; "no glory"] 1050 B.C. Son of Phinehas and grandson of Eli, born shortly after their deaths. His mother named him as she was dying in delivery, saying, "The glory has departed from Israel," because the Philistines had captured the ark of the covenant. 1 Sam. 4:21; 14:3. **Brother:** Ahitub.

IDBASH [ID-bash; "honey-sweet"] B.C. (date unknown). Listed in the genealogy of Judah in 1 Chr. 4:3.

IDDO [ID-oh; "beloved" or "adorned" (**1,2**), "timely" (**3**)].
1. B.C. (date unknown). A descendant of Gershon, son of Levi. 1 Chr. 6:21. Probably the same as Adaiah in 1 Chr. 6:41.
2. 1000 B.C. Officer over the tribe of Manasseh within the territory of Gilead. 1 Chr. 27:21.
3. 975 B.C. Father of Ahinadab, a district governor who married Taphath, a daughter of Solomon. 1 Ki. 4:14.
4. 900 B.C. A seer whom the Chronicler refers to as a source of information concerning the reigns of Solomon, Rehoboam, and Abijah. 2 Chr. 9:29; 12:15; 13:22.
5. 575 B.C. Grandfather of Zechariah the prophet. Ezra 5:1; Zech. 1:1.
6. 525 B.C. A chief priest who returned to Judah with Zerubbabel after the Exile. Neh. 12:4,16.
7. 450 B.C. Leader of the Levites at Casiphia from whom Ezra gathered servants to serve at the Temple in Jerusalem. Ezra 8:17.

IEZER [i-EE-zuhr; shortened form of Abiezer] B.C. (date unknown). KJV: Jeezer. Ancestral head of a clan of Manasseh. Num. 26:30. Probably the same as Abiezer in Joshua's time.

IGAL [I-gal; "may God redeem"] KJV: Igeal (1 Chr. 3:22).
1. 1450 B.C. A leader from the tribe of Issachar sent by Moses to explore the land of Canaan. Num. 13:7.
2. 1000 B.C. Son of Nathan from Zobah and one of the military elite known as David's thirty mighty men. 2 Sam. 23:36. In the parallel text in 1 Chr. 11:38, the name is given as "Joel the brother of Nathan."
3. B.C. (date unknown). A descendant of Zerubbabel listed in the genealogy of the royal line after the Exile. 1 Chr. 3:22.

IGDALIAH [IG-duh-LI-uh; "Yahweh is great"] B.C. (date unknown). Ancestor of some who had a room in the Temple in Jeremiah's time. He is called "the man of God," probably indicating he was a prophet. Jer. 35:4.

IKKESH [IK-esh; "crooked"] 1025 B.C. A man from Tekoa, father of Ira, one of David's thirty mighty men. 2 Sam. 23:26; 1 Chr. 11:28; 27:9.

ILAI [I-li] 1000 B.C. A military commander, one of David's thirty mighty men. 1 Chr. 11:29. Called Zalmon in 2 Sam. 23:28.

IMLAH [IM-luh; "fulness"(?)] 900 B.C. Father of Micaiah, a prophet who predicted the death of Ahab. 1 Ki. 22:8,9; 2 Chr. 18:7,8.

IMMANUEL [ih-MAN-yoo-el; "with us is God"] Name given to the child to be born of the virgin in Isaiah's prophecies; subsequently given to Jesus at his birth. Isa. 7:14; 8:8,10; Mt. 1:23.

IMMER [IM-uhr; "lamb"]
1. 1000 B.C. Head of the sixteenth division of priests in David's time. 1 Chr. 24:14.
2. B.C. (date unknown). Ancestral head of a priestly family that returned to Judah with Zerubbabel after the Exile. Ezra 2:37; 10:20; Neh. 7:40.
3. B.C. (date unknown). Ancestor of Amashsai, a priest who resettled in Jerusalem after the Exile. 1 Chr. 9:12; Neh. 11:13.
4. 625 B.C. Father of Pashhur, a chief officer in the Temple who had Jeremiah beaten and put in stocks. Jer. 20:1. If the relationship is ancestral, he is probably the same as Immer 1.

IMNA [IM-nuh] B.C. (date unknown). Listed only in the genealogy of Asher in 1 Chr. 7:35.

IMNAH [IM-nuh] KJV: Jimnah (Gen. 46:17); Jimna (Num. 26:44).
1. 1875 B.C. Firstborn son of Asher. Gen. 46:17; Num. 26:44; 1 Chr. 7:30.
2. 725 B.C. A Levite, chief gatekeeper at the East Gate in Hezekiah's time. 2 Chr. 31:14.

IMRAH [IM-ruh] B.C. (date unknown). Listed only in the genealogy of Asher in 1 Chr. 7:36.

IMRI [IM-ri]
1. B.C. (date unknown). Ancestor of Uthai, a Judahite who resettled in Jerusalem after the Exile. 1 Chr. 9:4.
2. 475 B.C. Father of Zaccur, who helped rebuild the wall of Jerusalem in Nehemiah's time. Neh. 3:2.

IPHDEIAH [if-DEE-yuh; "Yahweh redeems"] KJV: Iphedeiah. Listed only in the genealogy of Benjamin in 1 Chr. 8:25.

IR [EER] B.C. (date unknown). Descendant of Benjamin and ancestral source of the Huppites and Shuppites. 1 Chr. 7:12.

IRA [I-ruh]
1. 1000 B.C. A Jairite, of the tribe of Manasseh. Although not of Levitic descent, he is called David's priest. 2 Sam. 20:26.

2. 1000 B.C. Son of Ikkesh and one of the military elite known as David's thirty mighty men. 2 Sam. 23:26; 1 Chr. 11:28; 27:9.

3. 1000 B.C. The Ithrite, also a military commander listed among David's thirty mighty men. 2 Sam. 23:38; 1 Chr. 11:40.

IRAD [I-rad] B.C. (date unknown). Son of Enoch and grandson of Cain. Gen. 4:18.

IRAM [I-ram] B.C. (date unknown). A chief of Edom descended from Esau. Gen. 36:43.

IRI [I-ri] B.C. (date unknown). Listed in the genealogy of Benjamin in 1 Chr. 7:7. Possibly the same as Ir.

IRIJAH [i-RI-juh; "Yahweh sees"] 600 B.C. Captain of the guard at the Benjamin Gate in Jerusalem; he arrested Jeremiah on the charge that he was deserting to the Babylonians. Jer. 37:13,14.

IR NAHASH [ur-NAY-hash] B.C. (date unknown). KJV: Ir-nahash; RSV: Irnahash. Probably a mistranslation of "the city of Nahash." 1 Chr. 4:12.

IRU [I-roo] 1425 B.C. A son of Caleb, the spy sent by Moses to explore Canaan. 1 Chr. 4:15.

ISAAC* [I-zik; "laughing" or "he laughed"] 2066 B.C. The son of Abraham who inherited the covenant promises. Gen. 21–28. **Mother:** Sarah. **Wife:** Rebekah. **Children:** Esau, Jacob.

ISAIAH* [I-ZAY-yuh; "Yahweh is salvation"] 739–701 B.C. KJV: Esaias (Mt. 3:3). A prophet who ministered in Jerusalem during the rule of kings Uzziah, Jotham, Ahaz, and Hezekiah; author of the Book of Isaiah. 2 Ki. 19,20; 2 Chr. 26,32; Isaiah. **Father:** Amoz. **Wife:** unnamed prophetess. **Children:** Shear-Jashub, Maher-shalal-hash-baz.

ISCAH [IZ-kuh] 2075 B.C. Daughter of Haran and sister of Milcah, the wife of Nahor. Gen. 11:29.

ISCARIOT [is-KAIR-ee-uht; possibly "man of Kerioth"] See also Judas Iscariot; Simon Iscariot.

ISHBAH [ISH-buh] B.C. (date unknown). Listed only in the genealogy of Judah in 1 Chr. 4:17.

ISHBAK [ISH-bak] 2000 B.C. A son of Abraham by Keturah, his second wife. Gen. 25:2.

ISHBI-BENOB [ISH-bi-BEE-nahb; "dweller at Nob"] 1000 B.C. A Philistine warrior who threatened to kill King David but was slain by Abishai son of Zeruiah. 2 Sam. 21:16.

ISH-BOSHETH [ish-BOSH-eth; "man of shame"] 1000 B.C. A son of Saul who was made king of Israel by Abner. 2 Sam. 2. Also called Esh-Baal in 1 Chr. 8:33. See also Ishvi.

ISHHOD [ISH-hahd] B.C. (date unknown). KJV: Ishod. Listed only in the genealogy of Manasseh in 1 Chr. 7:18.

ISHI [ISH-i; "my husband"]
1. B.C. (date unknown). Listed only in the genealogy of Jerahmeel a descendant of Judah. 1 Chr. 2:31.
2. B.C. (date unknown). Listed only in the genealogy of Judah in 1 Chr. 4:20.
3. B.C. (date unknown). Ancestor of some Simeonites who drove the Amalekites from the hill country of Seir. 1 Chr. 4:42,43.
4. 750 B.C. Head of a family of the tribe of Manasseh taken into Exile by Tiglath-Pileser, king of Assyria. 1 Chr. 5:24.

ISHIJAH [ish-I-juh] 450 B.C. RSV: Isshijah. A descendant of Harim who took a foreign wife after the Exile. Ezra 10:31.

ISHMA [ISH-muh] B.C. (date unknown). Listed only in the genealogy of Judah in 1 Chr. 4:3.

ISHMAEL [ISH-may-uhl; "God heard"]
1.* 2050 B.C. The son of Abraham by Hagar, the maidservant of Sarah. After their expulsion from Abraham's household, Hagar and Ishmael fled into the desert, where God "heard the boy" and provided for his survival. He too received God's promise to become a great nation, but not within the Abrahamic covenant. Gen. 16,17; 21:9-21; 25:12-18.
2. B.C. (date unknown). A Benjamite descended from Jonathan, son of Saul. 1 Chr. 8:38.
3. 900 B.C. Father of Zebadiah, who was appointed as a judge by Jehoshaphat over all matters concerning the king. 2 Chr. 19:11.
4. 850 B.C. A military commander who aided Jehoiada in overthrowing Athaliah and instating Joash, son of Ahaziah, as king of Judah. 2 Chr. 23:1.
5. 575 B.C. A member of the royal line who assassinated Gedaliah, the governor of Judah appointed by Nebuchadnezzar after the fall of Jerusalem. 2 Ki. 25:23-26; Jer. 40:7–41:16.
6. 450 B.C. A priest who took a foreign wife after the Exile. Ezra 10:22.

ISHMAIAH [ish-MAY-uh; "Yahweh hears"] KJV: Ismaiah (1 Chr. 12:4).
1. 1000 B.C. A Gibeonite who joined David at Ziklag and was a leader of David's thirty mighty men. 1 Chr. 12:4.
2. 1000 B.C. Officer over the tribe of Zebulun in David's time. 1 Chr. 27:19.

ISHMERAI [ISH-muh-ri; "guard, protector"] B.C. (date unknown). Listed only in the genealogy of Benjamin in 1 Chr. 8:18.

ISHPAH [ISH-puh] B.C. (date unknown). Listed only in the genealogy of Benjamin in 1 Chr. 8:16.

ISHPAN [ISH-pan] B.C. (date unknown). A descendant of Benjamin, listed in 1 Chr. 8:22.

ISHTAR [ISH-tahr] Babylonian and Assyrian goddess of love and fertility. She was associated with the vegetation deity Tammuz. Unnamed in the Bible, she was referred to by her title as "Queen of Heaven" in Jer. 7:18; 44:17-19.

ISHVAH [ISH-vuh] 1875 B.C. KJV: Ishuah (Gen. 46:17), Isuah (1 Chr. 7:30). Second of the four sons of Asher. Gen. 46:17; 1 Chr. 7:30.

ISHVI [ISH-vi; "equal"] KJV: Ishuai (1 Chr. 7:30), Isui (Gen. 46:17), Jesui (Num. 26:44), Ishui (1 Sam. 14:49).
1. 1875 B.C. Third of the four sons of Asher. Gen. 46:17; Num. 26:44; 1 Chr. 7:30.
2. Ruled 1005–1003 B.C. Alternate name of Ish-Bosheth, son and successor of Saul. 1 Sam. 14:49. See also Ish-Bosheth; Esh-Baal.

ISMAKIAH [IZ-muh-KI-uh; "Yahweh sustains"] 725 B.C. KJV, RSV: Ismachiah. A supervisor with Conaniah, official of Hezekiah in charge of tithes and offerings. 2 Chr. 31:13.

ISRAEL* [IZ-ree-uhl; "God perseveres" or "he struggles with God"(?)] Name given by God to Jacob, ancestral father of the Israelites. Gen. 32:28; 35:10; 1 Ki. 18:31. See also Jacob.

ISSACHAR [IS-uh-kahr]
1. 1900 B.C. Fifth of the six sons born to Jacob by his first wife, Leah, and ancestral source of one of the twelve tribes of Israel. Gen. 30:18; 35:23; 46:13; 49:14.
2. 975 B.C. Seventh son of Obed-Edom and Temple gatekeeper in David's time. 1 Chr. 26:5.

ISSHIAH [ish-I-uh] KJV: Ishiah (1 Chr. 7:3), Jesiah (1 Chr. 12:6; 23:20).
1. B.C. (date unknown). Listed only in the genealogy of Issachar in 1 Chr. 7:3.
2. B.C. (date unknown). Listed only in the genealogy of Levi in 1 Chr. 24:21.
3. B.C. (date unknown). Listed in the genealogies of Levi in 1 Chr. 23:20; 24:25.
4. 1000 B.C. A military commander, one of David's thirty mighty men. 1 Chr. 12:6.

ITHAI [ITH-i] 1000 B.C. KJV, RSV: Ittai (2 Sam. 23:29). A military commander, one of David's thirty mighty men. 2 Sam. 23:29; 1 Chr. 11:31.

ITHAMAR [ITH-uh-mahr] 1400 B.C. Last of the four sons of Aaron. Ex. 6:23. Eli was descended from him.

ITHIEL [ITH-ee-uhl; "God is with me"(?)]
1. B.C. (date unknown). A man to whom the proverbs of Agur were directed. Prov. 30:1. Some scholars believe the name should be read as the verb "to be weary." See also Ucal.
2. B.C. (date unknown). Ancestor of a Benjamite who resettled in Jerusalem after the reconstruction of the walls. Neh. 11:7.

ITHMAH [ITH-muh] 1000 B.C. A Moabite, one of the military elite known as David's thirty mighty men. 1 Chr. 11:46.

ITHRAN [ITH-ran]
1. 1900 B.C. A son of Dishon, a Horite chief in Esau's time. Gen. 36:26.
2. B.C. (date unknown). Listed only in the genealogy of Asher in 1 Chr. 7:37. Possibly the same as Jether in v. 38. See also Jether 3.

ITHREAM [ITH-ree-uhm] 975 B.C. Son of David by his wife Eglah. 2 Sam. 3:5.

ITTAI [IT-i] 975 B.C. A Philistine military leader who served David during Absalom's rebellion. 2 Sam. 15:19-22; 18:2,5,12.

IZHAR [IZ-hahr; "shine forth"(?)] B.C. (date unknown). KJV: Izehar (Num. 3:19). A descendant of Kohath, son of Levi. Ex. 6:18-21; Num. 3:19.

IZLIAH [iz-LI-uh] B.C. (date unknown). KJV: Jezliah. Listed in the genealogy of Benjamin in 1 Chr. 8:18.

IZRAHIAH [IZ-ruh-HI-uh; "Yahweh shines forth"] B.C. (date unknown). Listed only in the genealogy of Issachar in 1 Chr. 7:3.

IZRI [IZ-ri] 1000 B.C. Head of the fourth division of priests in David's time. 1 Chr. 25:11.

IZZIAH [iz-I-uh; "Yahweh purifies"] 450 B.C. KJV: Jeziah. A descendant of Parosh who took a foreign wife after the Exile. Ezra 10:25.

J

JAAKOBAH [JAY-uh-KOH-buh; probably "may God protect"] 725 B.C. A Simeonite leader who helped defeat the Hamites and Amalekites during the reign of Hezekiah. 1 Chr. 4:36.

JAALA [JAY-ah-luh; perhaps "ibex" or "mountain goat"] 950 B.C. KJV, RSV: Jaalah (Ezra 2:56). A servant of Solomon, whose descendants returned to Judah with Zerubbabel. Ezra 2:56; Neh. 7:58.

JAARE-OREGIM [JAY-uh-ree-OHR-uh-jim] 975 B.C. Father of Elhanan, who killed Goliath the Gittite, according to 2 Sam. 21:19. In 1 Chr. 20:5, the parallel text reads "son of Jair killed Lahmi the brother of Goliath." This is the preferred reading.

JAARESHIAH [JAIR-uh-SHI-uh] B.C. (date unknown). KJV: Jaresiah. Listed only in the genealogy of Benjamin in 1 Chr. 8:27.

JAASIEL [jay-AY-zee-uhl; "God does" or "God makes"] KJV: Jasiel.
1. 1000 B.C. A Mezobaite; listed among the military elite known as David's thirty mighty men. 1 Chr. 11:47.
2. 1000 B.C. Son of Abner and officer over the tribe of Benjamin in David's time. 1 Chr. 27:21. Possibly the same as Jaasiel 1.

JAASU [JAY-uh-soo; "maker" or "doer"] 450 B.C. KJV: Jaasau. One who took a foreign wife after the Exile. Ezra 10:37.

JAAZANIAH [jay-AZ-uh-NI-uh; "Yahweh hears"]
1. 600 B.C. Son of Shaphan; an Israelite elder seen by Ezekiel in a vision offering incense to an idol. Ezek. 8:11.
2. 600 B.C. Son of Azzur and an Israelite leader seen giving false advice in one of Ezekiel's visions. Ezek. 11:1.
3. 575 B.C. A military leader who joined Gedaliah after he was made governor by Nebuchadnezzar. 2 Ki. 25:23; Jer. 40:8. Probably the same as Azariah 20, also called Jezaniah in Jer. 42:1.
4. 575 B.C. A Recabite who refused to drink when offered wine by Jeremiah the prophet. Jer. 35:3.

JAAZIAH [JAY-uh-ZI-uh; "Yahweh strengthens"] B.C. (date unknown). Ancestor of some Levites in David's time. 1 Chr. 24:26,27.

JAAZIEL [jay-AY-zee-uhl; "God strengthens"] 1000 B.C. A Levite who played the lyre as the ark of the covenant was brought by David to Jerusalem. 1 Chr. 15:18. Called Aziel in v. 20.

JABAL [JAY-buhl] B.C. (date unknown). Son of Lamech by his wife Adah, said to be "the father of those who live in tents and raise livestock." Gen. 4:20.

JABESH [JAY-besh; "dry"] 752 B.C. Father of Shallum, who murdered Zechariah, king of Israel, and succeeded him as king. 2 Ki. 15:10-14.

JABEZ [JAY-bez] B.C. (date unknown). A descendant of Judah, an honorable man who called upon and received God's blessing. 1 Chr. 4:9,10.

JABIN [JAY-bin; "intelligent" or "discerning"]
1. 1400 B.C. King of Hazor who led Canaanite kings against the Israelites; defeated and executed by Joshua. Josh. 11:1-11.
2. 1225 B.C. Another Canaanite king of Hazor, probably a descendant of Jabin 1. He oppressed Israel for twenty years until Deborah and Barak defeated his army. Jdg. 4; Ps. 83:9.

JACAN [JAY-kuhn] B.C. (date unknown). KJV: Jachan. Ancestral head of a Gadite family. 1 Chr. 5:13.

JACOB [JAY-kuhb; "supplanter"]
1.* 1950 B.C. The son of Isaac and Rebekah and twin brother of Esau. He bought Esau's birthright and later deceived his father and received the blessing meant for Esau. Gen. 25–50. *See also* Israel.
2. 25 B.C. Father of Joseph, the husband of Mary, mother of Jesus. Mt. 1:15.

JADA [JAY-duh; "caring"] B.C. (date unknown). Listed only in the genealogy of Judah. 1 Chr. 2:28,32.

JADAH [JAY-duh; "honeycomb"(?)] B.C. (date unknown). KJV, RSV: Jarah. A descendant of Jonathan, son of Saul. 1 Chr. 9:42. Called Jehoaddah in 1 Chr. 8:36.

JADDAI [JAD-i; "beloved"] 450 B.C. KJV: Jadau. One who took a foreign wife after the Exile. Ezra 10:43.

JADDUA [JAD-oo-uh; "known"]
1. 450 B.C. A Jewish leader who sealed the covenant renewal with God in Nehemiah's time. Neh. 10:21.
2. 400 B.C. Great-grandson of Eliashib, the high priest in Nehemiah's time. Jaddua was high priest during the reign of Darius the Persian. According to Josephus, he was high priest at the time of Alexander the Great's entrance into Jerusalem in 331 B.C., but this is unlikely. Neh. 12:22.

JADON [JAY-dahn] 450 B.C. A man from Meronoth who helped repair the wall of Jerusalem in Nehemiah's time. Neh. 3:7.

JAEL [JAY-el; "mountain goat"] 1225 B.C. Wife of Heber the Kenite; she killed Sisera, commander of the army of Jabin, king of Hazor. Jdg. 4:17-22; 5:24.

JAHATH [JAY-hath; shortened form of "God will snatch up"]
1. B.C. (date unknown). Listed only in the genealogy of Judah in 1 Chr. 4:2.
2. B.C. (date unknown). A Levite, ancestor of Asaph, the chief minister of music in David's time. 1 Chr. 6:43. Called Jehath in 1 Chr. 6:20.
3. B.C. (date unknown). A descendant of Gershon, son of Levi. 1 Chr. 23:10. Possibly the same as Jahath 2.
4. 975 B.C. A Levite family in the time of David. 1 Chr. 24:22.
5. 625 B.C. A Levite who supervised the reconstruction of the Temple during the reign of Josiah. 2 Chr. 34:12.

JAHAZIEL [juh-HAY-zee-uhl; "God sees"]
1. 1000 B.C. A Benjamite who joined the army of David at Ziklag. 1 Chr. 12:4.
2. 1000 B.C. A priest who blew the trumpet before the procession as David brought the ark of the covenant to Jerusalem. 1 Chr. 16:6.

3. 975 B.C. A Levite family in the time of David. 1 Chr. 23:19; 24:23.
4. 875 B.C. A priest descended from Asaph; he prophesied before King Jehoshaphat, promising victory over the Moabite and Ammonite invaders. 2 Chr. 20:14-17.
5. 475 B.C. Father of Shecaniah, a descendant of Zattu who returned to Judah with Ezra. Ezra 8:5.

JAHDAI [JAH-di; "leader" or "Yahweh leads"] B.C. (date unknown). Listed in the genealogy of the clans of Caleb, a descendant of Judah. 1 Chr. 2:47.

JAHDIEL [JAH-dee-uhl; "God gives joy"] 750 B.C. Head of a Manassehite family taken into exile by Tiglath-Pileser, king of the Assyrians. 1 Chr. 5:24.

JAHDO [JAH-doh] B.C. (date unknown). Listed only in the genealogy of Gad in 1 Chr. 5:14.

JAHLEEL [JAH-lee-uhl; "God waits"] 1875 B.C. Last of the three sons of Zebulun, son of Jacob. Gen. 46:14; Num. 26:26.

JAHMAI [JAH-mi; "Yahweh protects"] B.C. (date unknown). Listed only in the genealogy of Issachar in 1 Chr. 7:2.

JAHZEEL [JAH-zee-uhl; "God apportions"] B.C. (date unknown). Ancestral head of one of the clans of Naphtali. Num. 26:48. Same as Jaziel, son of Naphtali, in Gen. 46:24; 1 Chr. 7:13.

JAHZEIAH [JAH-zee-yuh; "Yahweh sees"] 450 B.C. KJV: Jahaziah. One who opposed Ezra's reform requiring the Israelites to divorce their foreign wives. Ezra 10:15.

JAHZERAH [JAH-zuh-ruh] B.C. (date unknown). Ancestor of Maasai, a priest who resettled in Jerusalem after the Exile. 1 Chr. 9:12. Called Ahzai in Neh. 11:13.

JAHZIEL [JAH-zee-uhl; "God apportions"] 1875 B.C. KJV, RSV: Jahzeel (Gen. 46:24). Firstborn son of Naphtali, listed in Gen. 46:24; 1 Chr. 7:13.

JAIR [JAIR; "may he shine forth" or "he enlightens"]
1. 1400 B.C. A descendant of Manasseh; he captured towns of the Amorites and named them Havvoth Jair, "settlements of Jair." Num. 32:41; Deut. 3:14; Josh. 13:30; 1 Chr. 2:22,23.
2. 1100 B.C. A Gileadite who led Israel for twenty-two years. Possibly a descendant of Jair 1. Jdg. 10:3-5.
3. 975 B.C. Father of Elhanan, who killed Lahmi, the brother of Goliath. 1 Chr. 20:5. Also called Jaare-Oregim.
4. 525 B.C. A Benjamite, father of Mordecai, the righteous uncle of Esther. Esth. 2:5.

JAIRUS [JAIR-uhs; "he will enlighten"] A.D. 30. A synagogue ruler whose daughter Jesus raised from the dead. Mk. 5:21-43; Lk. 8:40-56. He is unnamed in the parallel text in Mt. 9:18-26.

JAKEH [JAY-kuh] B.C. (date unknown). Father of Agur, author of Prov. 30.

JAKIM [JAY-kim; "he will establish"]
1. B.C. (date unknown). Listed only in the genealogy of Benjamin in 1 Chr. 8:19.
2. 975 B.C. Head of the twelfth division of priests in David's day. 1 Chr. 24:12.

JAKIN [JAY-kin; "he will establish"] KJV, RSV: Jachin.
1. 1900 B.C. A son of Simeon and grandson of Jacob. Gen. 46:10; Num. 26:12. Called Jarib in 1 Chr. 4:24.
2. 975 B.C. Head of the twenty-first division of priests in David's day. 1 Chr. 24:17.
3. 450 B.C. A priest who resettled in Jerusalem after the Exile. 1 Chr. 9:10; Neh. 11:10.

JALAM [JAY-luhm; "young man"(?)] 1925 B.C. KJV: Jaalam. Son of Esau by his wife Oholibamah. Gen. 36:5,14,18.

JALON [JAY-lahn] B.C. (date unknown). Listed only in the genealogy of Judah in 1 Chr. 4:17.

JAMBRES [JAM-breez] 1450 B.C. Traditionally, one of the Egyptian sorcerers who imitated Moses' miracles before Pharaoh. The name is found only in 2 Tim. 3:8 (compare Ex. 7:11,22; 8:7,18). See also Jannes.

JAMES [JAYMZ; Gk. form of Jacob]
1. A.D. 1. Father of the apostle Judas (not to be confused with Judas Iscariot). Lk. 6:16; Acts 1:13.
2. A.D. 25. Son of Zebedee and brother of John. One of the twelve apostles, he was put to death by Herod Agrippa I, thus fulfilling Christ's prophecy (Mk. 10:39). Mt. 4:21; 10:2; Acts 12:2.
3. A.D. 25. Son of Alphaeus and one of the apostles. Mt. 10:3; Acts 1:13. Possibly the brother of Matthew, who is also called "son of Alphaeus."
4. A.D. 30. James the younger, son of Mary and brother of Joses. Mt. 27:56; Mk. 15:40; 16:1. Possibly the same as James 2.
5. * A.D. 30. The Lord's brother, he became a believer and a leader in the early church after Christ's resurrection. Mt. 13:55; Mk. 6:3; Acts 15:13; 21:18; Gal. 1:19; 2:9. Author of the Book of James.

JAMIN [JAY-min]
1. 1900 B.C. A son of Simeon and grandson of Jacob. Gen. 46:10; Num. 26:12.
2. B.C. (date unknown). A grandson of Jerahmeel listed in the genealogy of Judah in 1 Chr. 2:27.
3. 450 B.C. A Levite who helped Ezra instruct the people in the Law. Neh. 8:7.

JAMLECH [JAM-lek; "may God give dominion"] B.C. (date unknown). A clan leader listed only in the genealogy of Simeon in 1 Chr. 4:34.

JANAI [JAY-ni; "may God answer"] B.C. (date unknown). KJV: Jaanai. A Gadite chief listed in the genealogy of Gad in 1 Chr. 5:12.

JANNAI [JAN-i] B.C. (date unknown). KJV: Janna. A descendant of Zerubbabel, listed in the genealogy of Jesus in Lk. 3:24.

JANNES [JAN-ez; "he who seduces"(?)] 1450 B.C. One of the Egyptian sorcerers who opposed Moses before Pharaoh. The magicians are unnamed in the OT (compare Ex. 7:11,22). In referring to this name, Paul draws on Jewish tradition. 2 Tim. 3:8. See also Jambres.

JAPHETH [JAY-feth; "may God enlarge"] B.C. (date unknown). Son of Noah and brother of Shem and Ham. Gen. 5:32; 9:18-27; 10:2.

JAPHIA [ja-FI-uh]
1. 1400 B.C. Amorite king of Lachish defeated and executed by Joshua. Josh. 10:3.
2. 975 B.C. A son of David, born in Jerusalem. 2 Sam. 5:15; 1 Chr. 3:7.

JAPHLET [JAF-luht] B.C. (date unknown). Listed only in the genealogy of Asher in 1 Chr. 7:32,33.

JARED [JAIR-uhd; "descent"] B.C. (date unknown). KJV: Jered (1 Chr. 1:2). Father of Enoch and an ancestor of Noah. Gen. 5:15-20; 1 Chr. 1:2; Lk. 3:37.

JARHA [JAR-hah] B.C. (date unknown). An Egyptian servant who married the daughter of Sheshan, listed in the genealogy of Judah in 1 Chr. 2:34,35.

JARIB [JAIR-uhb; "he contends"]
1. B.C. (date unknown). A son or descendant of Simeon. 1 Chr. 4:24. Called Jakin in Gen. 46:10.
2. 450 B.C. A Jewish leader sent by Ezra to Iddo at Casiphia to retrieve Levites for service at the Temple. Ezra 8:16.
3. 450 B.C. A descendant of Jeshua the high priest who took a foreign wife after the Exile. Ezra 10:18.

JAROAH [juh-ROH-uh] B.C. (date unknown). A Gadite listed in the genealogy of Gad in 1 Chr. 5:14.

JASHAR [JAY-shahr; "upright"] B.C. (date unknown). KJV: Jasher. Author of the Book of Jashar, twice quoted in the OT. Josh. 10:13; 2 Sam. 1:18. Likely, a poetic book compiling nationalistic songs from Israel's early history. Jashar may be a poetic name for Israel itself.

JASHEN [JAY-shuhn] 1025 B.C. Father of two or more of David's mighty men. 2 Sam. 23:32. Called "Hashem the Gizonite" in 1 Chr. 11:34.

JASHOBEAM [juh-SHOH-bee-uhm]
1. 1000 B.C. Chief of the Three, who led David's thirty mighty men. 1 Chr. 11:11. Called Josheb-Basshebeth, a Tahkemonite, in 2 Sam. 23:8. The text appears corrupt; most scholars believe the original to have read "Ishbaal the Hacmonite."
2. 1000 B.C. A Korahite of the tribe of Benjamin; he joined David at Ziklag. 1 Chr. 12:6.
3. 975 B.C. A Judahite, son of Zabdiel; in charge of the first division of David's army. 1 Chr. 27:2. Possibly the same as Jashobeam 1.

JASHUB [JAY-shuhb; "may he return"] KJV: Job (Gen. 46:13); RSV: Iob (Gen. 46:13).
1. 1875 B.C. A son of Issachar and grandson of Jacob. Gen. 46:13; Num. 26:24; 1 Chr. 7:1.
2. 450 B.C. Listed among those who took foreign wives after the Exile. Ezra 10:29.

JASON [JAY-suhn; "healing"]
1. A.D. 50. A Thessalonian Christian charged with fostering sedition by allowing Paul and Silas to stay in his house. Acts 17:5-9.
2. A.D. 55. One of Paul's relatives, who sent greetings to the church in Rome through Paul. Rom. 16:21. Possibly the same as Jason 1.

JATHNIEL [JATH-nee-el] 975 B.C. Fourth son of Meshelemiah, a chief Temple gatekeeper appointed in David's day. 1 Chr. 26:2.

JAVAN [JAY-vuhn] B.C. (date unknown). Fourth son of Japheth, son of Noah, listed in the Table of Nations. Gen. 10:2,4. The name corresponds etymologically to Ionia and is associated with the Greeks and Macedonians.

JAZIZ [JAY-ziz] 1000 B.C. A Hagrite who oversaw the flocks of King David. 1 Chr. 27:31.

JEATHERAI [jee-ATH-uh-ri] B.C. (date unknown). KJV: Jeaterai. Listed only in the genealogy of Levi in 1 Chr. 6:21.

JEBEREKIAH [juh-BAIR-uh-KI-uh; "Yahweh blesses"] 725 B.C. KJV, RSV: Jeberechiah. Father of Zechariah, who served as a witness to one of Isaiah's prophecies. Isa. 8:2.

JECOLIAH [JEK-uh-LI-uh] 825 B.C. KJV: Jecholiah. Mother of Azariah (also called Uzziah), tenth king of Judah. 2 Ki. 15:2; 2 Chr. 26:3.

JECONIAH [JEK-uh-NI-uh] 597 B.C. Alternate name of Jehoiachin, king of Judah. Mt. 1:11,12. See also Jehoiachin.

JEDAIAH [jeh-DAY-yuh; "Yahweh has favored" (**3,7**) or "Yahweh knows"]
1. 1000 B.C. Head of the second division of priests in David's day. 1 Chr. 24:7.

2. B.C. (date unknown). Ancestral head of a family of priests that returned to Judah with Zerubbabel. Jeshua the high priest was descended from him. Ezra 2:36; Neh. 7:39.
3. B.C. (date unknown). Ancestor of Ziza, a Simeonite chief in the days of Hezekiah. 1 Chr. 4:37.
4 and 5. 525 B.C. Two priests who returned to Judah with Zerubbabel after the Exile. Neh. 12:6,7,19,21.
6. 525 B.C. One who brought gold and silver to Jerusalem from Babylon. Zech. 6:10,14. Possibly the same as either Jedaiah 4 or 5.
7. 450 B.C. Son of Harumaph; he helped repair the wall of Jerusalem in Nehemiah's time. Neh. 3:10.
8. 450 B.C. A priest who resettled in Jerusalem after the Exile. Neh. 9:10; Neh. 11:10.

JEDIAEL [jeh-DI-uhl; "God knows"]
1. B.C. (date unknown). Son or descendant of Benjamin listed in 1 Chr. 7:6,10,11.
2. 1000 B.C. A military commander, one of David's thirty mighty men. 1 Chr. 11:45. Also listed among the mighty men is his brother Joha.
3. 1000 B.C. A man of Manasseh who joined David at Ziklag. 1 Chr. 12:20. Possibly the same as Jediael 2.
4. 975 B.C. A son of Meshelemiah, and a Temple gatekeeper. 1 Chr. 26:2.

JEDIDAH [jeh-DI-duh; "beloved"] 650 B.C. Mother of Josiah, sixteenth king of Judah. 2 Ki. 22:1.

JEDIDIAH [JED-uh-DI-uh; "beloved of Yahweh"] 950 B.C. The name God gave to Solomon at his birth, through Nathan the prophet. 2 Sam. 12:25.

JEDUTHUN [jeh-DOO-thuhn]
1. 1000 B.C. A Levite descended from Merari. A chief minister of music in David's day. 1 Chr. 9:16; 25:1-6; Neh. 11:17. Also called Ethan in 1 Chr. 6:44; 15:17.
2. 1025 B.C. Father of Obed-Edom, a chief gatekeeper in David's day. 1 Chr. 16:38.

JEHALLELEL [jeh-HAL-uh-lel; "may God shine forth"] KJV: Jehaleleel (1 Chr. 4:16); Jehalelel (2 Chr. 29:12).
1. B.C. (date unknown). Listed only in the genealogy of Judah in 1 Chr. 4:16.
2. 725 B.C. Father of Azariah, a Levite who helped purify the Temple in Hezekiah's time. 2 Chr. 29:12.

JEHATH [JEE-hath; "God will snatch up"] KJV, RSV: Jahath. B.C. (date unknown). Listed in the genealogy of Levi, in 1 Chr. 6:20. Called Jahath in 1 Chr. 6:43.

JEHDEIAH [jeh-DEE-yuh; "may Yahweh rejoice"]
1. 975 B.C. Listed among the Levites who served during the time of David. 1 Chr. 24:20.
2. 975 B.C. An official of David in charge of the king's donkeys. 1 Chr. 27:30.

JEHEZKEL [jeh-HEZ-kel; "God strengthens"] 975 B.C. KJV: Jehezekel. Head of the twentieth division of priests in David's day. 1 Chr. 24:16.

JEHIAH [jeh-HI-uh; "Yahweh lives"] 1000 B.C. A gatekeeper for the ark of the covenant as it was brought by David to Jerusalem. 1 Chr. 15:24.

JEHIEL [jeh-HI-uhl; "God lives"]
1. 1000 B.C. A Levite assigned to play the lyre before the ark of the covenant as it was brought to Jerusalem. 1 Chr. 15:18,20; 16:5.
2. 1000 B.C. Listed among the Levites descended from Gershon; he oversaw the treasury provided for the building of the Temple. 1 Chr. 23:8; 29:8. Called Jehieli in 1 Chr. 26:21.
3. 975 B.C. Caretaker of King David's sons. 1 Chr. 27:32.

4. 850 B.C. One of the younger brothers of Jehoram, son of Jehoshaphat; he was put to death when Jehoram succeeded his father as king of Judah. 2 Chr. 21:2.

5. 725 B.C. A descendant of Heman the seer; he served at the Temple during the reign of Hezekiah. 2 Chr. 29:14; 31:13.

6. 625 B.C. A chief administrator at the Temple during the reign of Josiah. 1 Chr. 35:8.

7. 475 B.C. Father of Obadiah, a descendant of Joab who returned to Judah with Ezra. Ezra 8:9.

8. 475 B.C. Father of Shecaniah, who supported Ezra's reform requiring the divorce of foreign wives. Ezra 10:2-4.

9. 450 B.C. A priest who took a foreign wife after the Exile. Ezra 10:21.

10. 450 B.C. A descendant of Elam; he also took a foreign wife after the Exile. Ezra 10:26. Probably the same as Jehiel 8.

JEHIELI [jeh-HI-uh-li] 975 B.C. A Levite in charge of the treasuries of the Temple in David's day. 1 Chr. 26:21. Same as Jehiel 2.

JEHIZKIAH [JEE-hiz-KI-uh; "Yahweh strengthens"] 750 B.C. An Ephraimite leader who with Oded the prophet opposed the enslavement of those taken prisoner in battle with Judah. 2 Chr. 28:12.

JEHOADDAH [juh-HOH-uh-duh] B.C. (date unknown). KJV: Jehoadah. A descendant of Jonathan son of Saul, listed in the genealogy of Benjamin in 1 Chr. 8:36. Called Jadah in 1 Chr. 9:42 (KJV, RSV: Jarah).

JEHOADDIN [juh-HOH-uh-din; "Yahweh is delight"(?)] 825 B.C. RSV (2 Ki. 14:2), KJV: Jehoaddan. Mother of Amaziah, son and successor of Joash, king of Judah. 2 Ki. 14:2; 2 Chr. 25:1.

JEHOAHAZ [juh-HOH-uh-haz; "Yahweh has grasped"]
1. 814–798 B.C. Son and successor of Jehu, king of Israel. 2 Ki. 13:1-9. **Son:** Jehoash.
2. 608 B.C. Son and successor of Josiah, king of Judah. He reigned for only three months until taken captive by Pharaoh Neco, who put his brother Jehoiakim on the throne in his place. 2 Ki. 23:30-34; 2 Chr. 36:1-4. Called Shallum in 1 Chr. 3:15 and Jer. 22:11.

JEHOASH [juh-HOH-ash; "Yahweh has given"] 798–782 B.C. KJV, RSV: Joash. Son and successor of Jehoahaz, eleventh king of Israel. He consulted Elisha on the prophet's deathbed, and Elisha prophesied that three times during his reign Jehoash would defeat Syria. 2 Ki. 13:9-25; 2 Chr. 25:17-25; Amos 1:1. Called Joash in Hos. 1:1. **Son and successor:** Jeroboam II.

JEHOHANAN [jeh-hoh-HAY-nuhn; "Yahweh is gracious"] RSV (2 Chr. 28:12), KJV (2 Chr. 28:12; Ezra 10:6): Johanan.
1. 975 B.C. Sixth of the seven sons of Meshelemiah listed among the Temple gatekeepers in 1 Chr. 26:3.
2. 875 B.C. A chief military commander under Jehoshaphat king of Judah. 2 Chr. 17:15.
3. 875 B.C. Father of Ishmael, a military commander who helped Jehoiada overthrow Athaliah to make Joash king of Judah. 2 Chr. 23:1. Probably the same as Jehohanan 2.
4. 775 B.C. Father of Azariah, a leader in Ephraim who opposed the enslavement of captives from Judah. 2 Chr. 28:12.
5. 500 B.C. Head of the priestly family of Amariah in the time of Joiakim the high priest. Neh. 12:13.
6. 450 B.C. High priest in Ezra's time. Ezra 10:6. Same as Johanan in Neh. 12:22,23 and Jonathan in Neh. 12:11.
7. 450 B.C. A descendant of Bebai; he took a foreign wife after the Exile. Ezra 10:28.
8. 450 B.C. Son of Tobiah, an enemy of Nehemiah who tried to disrupt the reconstruction of Jerusalem's walls. Neh. 6:18.

9. 450 B.C. A priest who took part in the dedication of the wall of Jerusalem in Nehemiah's time. Neh. 12:42.

JEHOIACHIN [jeh-HOY-ah-chin; "Yahweh will establish"] 597 B.C. KJV, RSV (Jer. 24:1; 29:2): Jeconiah; KJV, RSV (Jer. 22:24,28; 37:1): Coniah. The nineteenth king of Judah, son and successor of Jehoiakim. He reigned for only three months before he was taken by Nebuchadnezzar into captivity in Babylon. 2 Ki. 24:8-17; 2 Chr. 36:8-10; Jer. 22:24-30; 52:31-34. **Mother:** Nehushta. **Uncle and successor:** Zedekiah.

JEHOIADA [jeh-HOY-ah-duh; "Yahweh knows"]
1. 1000 B.C. Father of Benaiah, loyal officer in charge of David's bodyguard who later led Solomon's army. 2 Sam. 8:18; 23:20-23; 1 Chr. 11:22-24.
2. 1000 B.C. A leader descended from Aaron who joined David at Hebron. 1 Chr. 12:27.
3. 975 B.C. Son of Benaiah and an adviser of David. 1 Chr. 27:34. Possibly the name is reversed by a scribal error, in which case it should read "Benaiah son of Jehoiada" (compare Jehoiada 1).
4. 850 B.C. The priest who engineered the overthrow of Athaliah and put the child Joash on the throne. 2 Ki. 11,12; 2 Chr. 23,24. **Wife:** Jehosheba. **Son:** Zechariah.
5. 600 B.C. A chief priest replaced by Zephaniah at the Temple in Jerusalem. Jer. 29:26.

JEHOIAKIM [jeh-HOY-ah-kim; "Yahweh raises up" or "Yahweh will establish"] 609–598 B.C. The nineteenth king of Judah, his name was changed from Eliakim by Pharaoh Neco, who made him king in place of Jehoahaz. 2 Ki. 23:34–24:6; 2 Chr. 36:4-8; Jer. 22:18; 26:21-23; 36. **Father:** Josiah. **Mother:** Zebidah. **Brother:** Zedekiah. **Son and successor:** Jehoiachin.

JEHOIARIB [jeh-HOY-ah-rib; "Yahweh contends"]
1. 975 B.C. Head of the first division of priests in David's time. 1 Chr. 24:7.
2. 450 B.C. A priest who resettled in Jerusalem after the Exile. 1 Chr. 9:10. The parallel text in Neh. 11:10 has "the son of Joiarib."

JEHONADAB [jeh-HAHN-uh-dab; "Yahweh is noble" or "Yahweh is liberal"] 850 B.C. A Recabite who joined Jehu king of Israel in destroying the family of Ahab. 2 Ki. 10:15-23. Possibly the same as Jonadab son of Recab in Jer. 35:6-19.

JEHONATHAN [jeh-HAHN-uh-thuhn; "Yahweh has given"]
1. 875 B.C. A Levite sent by Jehoshaphat to teach the Law throughout Judah. 2 Chr. 17:8.
2. 500 B.C. Head of a priestly family in the days of Joiakim the high priest. Neh. 12:18.

JEHORAM [juh-HOHR-uhm; "Yahweh is exalted"]
1. 853–841 B.C. Son and successor of Jehoshaphat; he married Athaliah, a daughter of Ahab. His wife corrupted him and led him away from the ways of his righteous father. He was afflicted with an incurable disease, as prophesied by Elijah. 2 Ki. 8:16-24; 1 Chr. 3:11; 2 Chr. 21. **Son and successor:** Ahaziah. **Daughter:** Jehosheba.
2. 850 B.C. A priest sent by King Jehoshaphat to teach the Law to the people of Judah. 2 Chr. 17:8.

JEHOSHAPHAT [juh-HAHSH-uh-fat; "Yahweh has judged"]
1. 975 B.C. Son of Ahilud, official recorder of David and Solomon. 2 Sam. 8:16; 20:24; 1 Ki. 4:3.
2. 950 B.C. Son of Paruah and one of Solomon's twelve district governors. 1 Ki. 4:17.

3.* Reigned 872–848 B.C. Son and successor of Asa, third king of Judah. Although he erred in allying himself with Ahab king of Israel, he was one of the pious kings of Judah and brought about a restoration of the Mosaic faith during his reign. 1 Ki. 22; 2 Chr. 17:1–21:3. **Son and successor:** Jehoram.
4. 875 B.C. Father of Jehu, the tenth king of Israel. 2 Ki. 9:2,14.

JEHOSHEBA [juh-HAHSH-uh-buh; "Yahweh is abundance"] 850 B.C. KJV, RSV: Jehoshabeath (2 Chr. 22:11). Sister of King Ahaziah; she hid Joash in the Temple when Athaliah seized the throne and put to death the royal princes. After six years, her husband, Jehoiada the priest, made Joash king. 2 Ki. 11:2; 2 Chr. 22:11. **Father:** Jehoram.

JEHOZABAD [juh-HOH-zuh-bad; "Yahweh gives"]
1. 975 B.C. Second son of Obed-Edom, and a Temple gatekeeper in David's day. 1 Chr. 26:4.
2. 875 B.C. A Benjamite military commander who served under Jehoshaphat. 2 Chr. 17:18.
3. 800 B.C. An official of King Joash who conspired against and murdered the king at Beth Millo. 2 Ki. 12:21; 2 Chr. 24:26.

JEHOZADAK [juh-HOH-zuh-dak; "Yahweh is righteous"] 575 B.C. KJV: Josedech (Hag. 1:1; Zech. 6:11). Father of Jeshua (Joshua), high priest when the Jews returned to Judah with Zerubbabel. 1 Chr. 6:14,15; Hag. 1:1; Zech. 6:11. Called Jozadak in Ezra and Nehemiah.

JEHU [JEE-hoo; "he is Yahweh"]
1. B.C. (date unknown). Listed only in the genealogy of Judah in 1 Chr. 2:38.
2. 1000 B.C. A Benjamite who defected from Saul's army to David. 1 Chr. 12:3.
3. 900 B.C. Son of Hanani; he prophesied against Baasha, third king of Israel. He later opposed Jehoshaphat's alliance with Ahab. 1 Ki. 16:1-7,12; 2 Chr. 19:2,3.
4.* 841–814 B.C. A military commander anointed king of Israel by both Elijah and Elisha. Jehu rebelled against Joram and killed both Joram and Ahaziah, king of Judah. Then he had the rest of Ahab's family put to death and ended Baal worship in Israel. 1 Ki. 19:16,17; 2 Ki. 9,10; 2 Chr. 22. **Son and successor:** Jehoahaz.
5. 725 B.C. Head of a Simeonite family during the reign of Hezekiah. 1 Chr. 4:35.

JEHUCAL [juh-HOO-kuhl; possibly "Yahweh is powerful"] 600 B.C. KJV, RSV: Jucal (Jer. 38:1). An official of Zedekiah who threw Jeremiah the prophet into a cistern to die. Jer. 37:3; 38:1.

JEHUDI [juh-HOO-di] 600 B.C. Official sent to retrieve the scroll of Jeremiah's prophecies and read it before King Jehoiakim. Jer. 36:14,21-23.

JEIEL [jeh-I-uhl] KJV: Jehiel (1 Chr. 9:35; 11:44); RSV: Jeuel (2 Chr. 29:13).
1. B.C. (date unknown). Head of a clan of Reubenites listed in 1 Chr. 5:7.
2. 1125 B.C. Father of Ner and great-grandfather of King Saul. 1 Chr. 8:29; 9:35.
3. 1000 B.C. A military commander, he and his brother Shama were both listed among David's thirty mighty men. 1 Chr. 11:44.
4. 1000 B.C. A Levite, appointed gatekeeper and musician for the ark of the covenant as it was brought by David to Jerusalem. 1 Chr. 15:18,21; 16:5.
5. 1000 B.C. Another Levite appointed to play music before the ark of the covenant. 1 Chr. 16:5.
6. B.C. (date unknown). A descendant of Asaph and ancestor of Jahaziel, who prophesied before King Jehoshaphat. 2 Chr. 20:14.

7. 775 B.C. Secretary of Uzziah king of Judah. 2 Chr. 26:11.
8. 725 B.C. A Levite descended from Elizaphan who helped purify the Temple in Hezekiah's time. 2 Chr. 29:13.
9. 650 B.C. A chief Levite in Josiah's day. 2 Chr. 35:9.
10. 450 B.C. A Jew who took a foreign wife after the Exile. Ezra 10:43.

JEKAMEAM [JEK-uh-MEE-uhm] 975 B.C. A Levite listed among the Kohathites in David's day. 1 Chr. 23:19; 1 Chr. 24:23.

JEKAMIAH [JEK-uh-MI-uh; "may Yahweh establish"] KJV: Jecamiah (1 Chr. 3:18).
1. B.C. (date unknown). Listed only in the genealogy of Judah in 1 Chr. 2:41.
2. 550 B.C. A son of Jehoiachin listed in the genealogy of the royal line in 1 Chr. 3:18.

JEKUTHIEL [juh-KOO-thee-uhl] B.C. (date unknown). Listed only in the genealogy of Judah in 1 Chr. 4:18.

JEMIMAH [juh-MI-muh; "little dove"(?)] B.C. (date unknown). A daughter of Job, born in the latter part of his life. Job 42:14.

JEMUEL [JEM-yoo-uhl] 1900 B.C. Firstborn son of Simeon, listed in Gen. 46:10. Called Nemuel in Num. 26:12; 1 Chr. 4:24.

JEPHTHAH* [JEF-thuh; "he opens"] 1085–1079 B.C. KJV: Jephthae (Heb. 11:32). A Gileadite notable as the judge who delivered Israel from the Ammonites. He ruled for six years. Jdg. 11:1–12:7; Heb. 11:32.

JEPHUNNEH [juh-FUN-uh]
1. 1475 B.C. Father of Caleb the spy. Num. 13:6; 1 Chr. 4:15.
2. B.C. (date unknown). Listed only in the genealogy of Asher in 1 Chr. 7:38.

JERAH [JEER-uh; "moon"] B.C. (date unknown). A descendant of Shem, listed in the Table of Nations in Gen. 10:26. Probably the ancestral source of an Arabian tribe.

JERAHMEEL [juh-RAH-mee-uhl; "may God have mercy"]
1. B.C. (date unknown). One of the three "sons of Hezron" through whom the genealogy of Judah is traced. 1 Chr. 2:9,25-27.
2. 975 B.C. A Levite in David's time. 1 Chr. 24:29.
3. 600 B.C. One commanded by King Jehoiakim to arrest Baruch and Jeremiah; in the NIV and RSV, he is called a "son of the king." Jer. 36:26.

JERED [JEER-ed] B.C. (date unknown). Father of Gedor listed only in the genealogy of Judah in 1 Chr. 4:18.

JEREMAI [JAIR-uh-mi] 450 B.C. A descendant of Hashum who took a foreign wife after the Exile. Ezra 10:33.

JEREMIAH [JAIR-uh-MI-uh; possibly "Yahweh lifts up"] KJV: Jeremias (Mt. 16:14).
1. 1000 B.C. A Benjamite warrior who joined David's army at Ziklag. 1 Chr. 12:4.
2 and 3. 1000 B.C. Two Gadite warriors who also joined David at Ziklag. 1 Chr. 12:10,13.
4. 875 B.C. Father of Hamutal, the mother of Jehoahaz, eleventh king of Israel. 2 Ki. 23:31; 24:18.
5. 750 B.C. Head of a family of the tribe of Manasseh, taken into exile by Tiglath-Pileser, king of Assyria. 1 Chr. 5:24.
6.* 625 B.C. The prophet during the last years of the kingdom of Judah who predicted the fall of Jerusalem and subsequent return of the Jews after seventy years in Babylon. His words are recorded in the books of Jeremiah and Lamentations. 2 Chr. 35:25; 36:21,22; Ezra 1:1; Jer. 1–52; Mt. 2:17; 16:14; 27:9.
7. 600 B.C. A Recabite, father of Jaazaniah. Jer. 35:3.
8. 525 B.C. A priest who returned to Judah with Zerubbabel after the Exile. Neh. 12:1,12.
9. 450 B.C. A priest who sealed the covenant renewal with God after the Exile. Neh. 10:2. Possibly the same as Jeremiah 8.
10. 450 B.C. A Jewish leader who took part in the dedication of the wall of Jerusalem in Nehemiah's time. Neh. 12:34.

JEREMOTH [JAIR-uh-mahth; "swollen"] KJV: Jerimoth (1 Chr. 7:8; 24:30); Ramoth (Ezra 10:29); RSV: Jerimoth (1 Chr. 24:30).
1. B.C. (date unknown). A son or descendant of Beker, son of Benjamin, listed in 1 Chr. 7:8.
2. B.C. (date unknown). Listed only in the genealogy of Benjamin in 1 Chr. 8:14.
3. 975 B.C. A Levite who lived in the time of David. 1 Chr. 23:23.
4, 5, and 6. 450 B.C. Three who took foreign wives after the Exile. Ezra 10:26,27,29.

JERIAH [juh-RI-uh; "Yahweh sees"(?)] 975 B.C. KJV, RSV: Jerijah (1 Chr. 26:31,32). A Levite, firstborn of the descendants of Hebron in the time of David. 1 Chr. 23:19; 24:23; 26:31,32.

JERIBAI [JAIR-uh-bi] 1000 B.C. One of the two sons of Elnaam listed among David's thirty mighty men. 1 Chr. 11:46.

JERIEL [JEER-ee-uhl; "God sees"(?)] B.C. (date unknown). Listed in the genealogy of Issachar in 1 Chr. 7:2.

JERIMOTH [JAIR-uh-mahth; "swollen"] KJV (1 Chr. 23:23; 25:22); RSV (1 Chr. 23:23; 25:22; 27:19): Jeremoth.
1. 1850 B.C. Fourth of the five sons of Bela, son of Benjamin, listed in 1 Chr. 7:7.
2. 1000 B.C. A Benjamite who joined David's army at Ziklag. 1 Chr. 12:5.
3. 975 B.C. A Levite descended from Mushi who lived in the time of David. 1 Chr. 23:23; 24:30.
4. 975 B.C. A son of Heman the seer and a minister of music appointed for the Temple in David's day. 1 Chr. 25:4,22.
5. 975 B.C. Officer over the tribe of Naphtali in David's time. 1 Chr. 27:19.
6. 950 B.C. A son of David and father of Mahalath, wife of King Rehoboam. 2 Chr. 11:18.
7. 725 B.C. A Levite under Conaniah, supervisor of offerings at the Temple in Hezekiah's time. 2 Chr. 31:13.

JERIOTH [JAIR-ee-ahth; "tents"] B.C. (date unknown). A wife of Caleb, son of Hezron, listed in the genealogy of Judah in 1 Chr. 2:18.

JEROBOAM* [JAIR-uh-BOH-uhm; "may the people increase"]
1. 930–909 B.C. Jeroboam I; the first king of

Israel following the division of the kingdom. He led Israel into the idolatry that would inevitably bring an end to the kingdom. 1 Ki. 11:26–14:20; 2 Chr. 10,13. **Father:** Nebat. **Son and successor:** Nadab.
2. 793–753 B.C. Jeroboam II; the thirteenth king of Israel during the divided monarchy. 2 Ki. 14:16-29; Amos 7:9-11.

JEROHAM [juh-ROH-ham]
1. 1125 B.C. A Levite; father of Elkanah, the husband of Hannah and father of Samuel. 1 Sam. 1:1; 1 Chr. 6:27,34.
2. B.C. (date unknown). Listed only in the genealogy of Benjamin in 1 Chr. 8:27.
3. B.C. (date unknown). Ancestor of a Benjamite who resettled in Jerusalem after the Exile. 1 Chr. 9:8.
4. 475 B.C. Father of Adaiah, a priest who resettled in Jerusalem after the Exile. 1 Chr. 9:12; Neh. 11:12.
5. 1000 B.C. Father of two Benjamite warriors who joined David at Ziklag. 1 Chr. 12:7.
6. 975 B.C. Father of Azarel, officer over the tribe of Dan in David's time. 1 Chr. 27:22.
7. 850 B.C. Father of Azariah, a military commander who helped Jehoiada overthrow Athaliah and put Joash on the throne. 2 Chr. 23:1.

JERUB-BAAL [JAIR-uhb-BAY-uhl; "let Baal contend"] 1169–1129 B.C. Name given to Gideon the judge after his destruction of the altar of Baal. Jdg. 6–8. See also Gideon.

JERUB-BESHETH [JAIR-uhb-BEH-sheth; "let shame contend"] 1169–1129 B.C. Alternate form of Jerub-Baal, substituting the word "shame" for "Baal" in order to avoid pronouncing the name of the false deity. 2 Sam. 11:21. See also Gideon.

JERUSHA [juh-ROO-shuh; "possession"] 775 B.C. KJV, RSV: Jerushah (2 Chr. 27:1). Wife of Uzziah and mother of Jotham, king of Judah. 2 Ki. 15:33; 2 Chr. 27:1.

JESARELAH [JES-uh-REE-luh] 975 B.C. KJV, RSV: Jesharelah. A son of Asaph and a minister of music appointed to the Temple in David's day. 1 Chr. 25:14. Called Asarelah in v. 2.

JESHAIAH [jeh-SHAY-yuh; "Yahweh has saved"] KJV: Jesaiah (1 Chr. 3:21).
1. B.C. (date unknown). A descendant of Moses and ancestor of Shelomith, who served as one of the officials in charge of the treasury in David's time. 1 Chr. 26:25.
2. 975 B.C. A son of Jeduthun and a minister of music appointed to the Temple in David's time. 1 Chr. 25:3,15.
3. B.C. (date unknown). Ancestor of a Benjamite who resettled in Jerusalem after the Exile. Neh. 11:7.
4. 450 B.C. A descendant of Elam who returned to Judah with Ezra after the Exile. Ezra 8:7.
5. 450 B.C. A Levite descended from Merari who returned to Judah with Ezra. Ezra 8:19.
6. B.C. (date unknown). A descendant of Zerubbabel in the genealogy of the royal line after the Exile. 1 Chr. 3:21.

JESHEBEAB [juh-SHEB-ee-ab] 975 B.C. Head of the fourteenth division of priests in David's day. 1 Chr. 24:13.

JESHER [JEH-shuhr; "uprightness"(?)] B.C. (date unknown). Son of Caleb, son of Hezron, listed only in the genealogy of Judah in 1 Chr. 2:18.

JESHISHAI [jeh-SHISH-i; "aged"(?)] B.C. (date unknown). Listed only in the genealogy of Gad in 1 Chr. 5:14.

JESHOHAIAH [JESH-uh-HAY-yuh; "Yahweh humbles"] 725 B.C. A Simeonite leader during the reign of Hezekiah. 1 Chr. 4:36.

JESHUA [JESH-oo-uh; "Yahweh is salvation"] KJV: Jeshuah (1 Chr. 24:11).

1. 975 B.C. Head of the ninth division of priests in David's time. 1 Chr. 24:11; Ezra 2:36; Neh. 7:39.

2. 725 B.C. A priest who helped distribute contributions among his fellow priests in Hezekiah's time. 2 Chr. 31:15.

3. B.C. (date unknown). A descendant of Pahath-Moab and ancestor of some who returned to Judah with Zerubbabel. Ezra 2:6; Neh. 7:11.

4. 525 B.C. The high priest who returned to Judah with Zerubbabel after the Exile. Ezra 2:2; 3:2-8; 5:2; 10:18; Neh. 7:7; 12:1,7,10. **Father:** Jozadak. **Son:** Joiakim. Called Joshua in Haggai and Zechariah.

5. 525 B.C. A Levite descended from Hodaviah; he returned to Judah with Zerubbabel and instructed the people in the Law. Ezra 2:40; 7:43; 9:4,5; 12:8,24.

6. 475 B.C. Father of Jozabad, a Levite in Ezra's time. Ezra 8:33.

7. 475 B.C. Father of Ezer and ruler of Mizpah in Nehemiah's time. Neh. 3:19.

8. 450 B.C. A Levite who sealed the covenant renewal with God in Nehemiah's time, possibly with the name of his family ancestor (compare Jeshua 5). Neh. 10:9.

JESHURUN [JESH-uh-ruhn; "upright"] KJV: Jesurun (Isa. 44:2). Name used of Israel in Moses' personification of its national history and relationship with God. Deut. 32:15; 33:5,26; Isa. 44:2.

JESIMIEL [jeh-SIM-ee-uhl; "may God establish"] 725 B.C. Head of a Simeonite family during the reign of Hezekiah, king of Judah. 1 Chr. 4:36.

JESSE [JES-ee] 1050 B.C. Father of King David and an ancestor of Jesus Christ. He was a wealthy man of Bethlehem who had eight sons and two daughters. Ruth 4:17,22; 1 Sam. 16:1-13; 17:12-19.

JESUS [JEE-zuhs; Gk. form of Joshua, "Yahweh is salvation"]

1.* 4 B.C.–A.D. 30. The Son of God incarnate. His name, Jesus, from a Hebrew word meaning "savior" or "Yahweh saves." His title, Christ, meaning Messiah or "Anointed one." Born in Bethlehem, raised in Nazareth, he centered his ministry in Capernaum near the Sea of Galilee. Sentenced by Pontius Pilate to crucifixion. Three days later he rose from the tomb, and 40 days later he ascended into heaven. **Parents:** Mary and Joseph (adoptive father). **Other family members:** James, Joseph, Simon, Judas and unnamed sisters.

2. A.D. 60. A Christian with Paul who sent greetings to the church at Colosse. Col. 4:11. Also called Justus.

JETHER [JEE-thuhr; "abundance"] KJV, RSV: Ithra (2 Sam. 17:25).

1. B.C. (date unknown). Listed only in the genealogy of Jerahmeel, a descendant of Judah. 1 Chr. 2:32.

2. B.C. (date unknown). Listed only in the genealogy of Judah in 1 Chr. 4:17.

3. B.C. (date unknown). Listed only in the genealogy of Asher in 1 Chr. 7:38.

4. 1150 B.C. Oldest son of Gideon the judge. Jdg. 8:20.

5. 1000 B.C. Husband of Abigail, David's sister, and father of Amasa, the commander of Absalom's army who was killed by Joab. 2 Sam. 17:25; 1 Ki. 2:5,32; 1 Chr. 2:17.

JETHETH [JEE-theth] B.C. (date unknown). An Edomite chief descended from Esau. Gen. 36:40.

JETHRO [JETH-roh; "excellence"] 1500 B.C. Priest of Midian and father of Zipporah, the wife of Moses. Moses was tending Jethro's flocks when he saw the burning bush. Ex. 3:1; 4:18; 18:1-27. Called Reuel in Ex. 2:18; Num. 10:29.

JETUR [JEE-tuhr] 2025 B.C. One of the sons of Ishmael, the son of Abraham and Hagar. Gen. 25:15. Ancestral source of an Ishmaelite tribe (1 Chr. 5:19).

JEUEL [JOO-uhl] 450 B.C. KJV: Jeiel (Ezra 8:13).

1. A Judahite who resettled in Jerusalem after the Exile. 1 Chr. 9:6.

2. 450 B.C. A descendant of Adonikam who returned to Judah with Ezra. Ezra 8:13.

JEUSH [JEE-uhsh] KJV: Jehush (1 Chr. 8:39).

1. 1925 B.C. A son of Esau by his wife Oholibamah. Gen. 36:5,14,18.

2. B.C. (date unknown). Listed only in the genealogy of Benjamin in 1 Chr. 7:10.

3. 975 B.C. Head of a Levite family descended from Gershon. 1 Chr. 23:10,11.

4. 900 B.C. A son of Rehoboam, the son and successor of Solomon. 2 Chr. 11:19.

5. B.C. (date unknown). A descendant of Jonathan, son of Saul, in 1 Chr. 8:39.

JEUZ [JEE-uhz] B.C. (date unknown). Listed only in the genealogy of Benjamin in 1 Chr. 8:10.

JEZANIAH [JEZ-uh-NI-uh; "Yahweh hears"] 600 B.C. RSV: Azariah. Army officer who sought but disregarded the advice of Jeremiah the prophet after the death of Gedaliah. Jer. 42:1. Called Jaazaniah in 2 Ki. 25:23; Jer. 40:8. Probably the same as Azariah in Jer. 43:2.

JEZEBEL [JEZ-uh-bel; "unexalted" or "unhusbanded"]

1.* 875 B.C. The wicked wife of King Ahab who slaughtered the Lord's prophets and promoted Baal worship in Israel. 1 Ki. 16:31; 18–21; 2 Ki. 9. **Father:** Ethbaal, king of Phoenicia. **Daughter:** Athaliah.

2. A.D. 90. A false prophetess who misled some at the church in Thyatira. Rev. 2:20. Possibly the name is used figuratively.

JEZER [JEE-zuhr] 1875 B.C. A son of Naphtali and ancestral head of a clan. Gen. 46:24; Num. 26:49.

JEZIEL [JEE-zee-uhl; "God unites"(?)] 1000 B.C. A Benjamite; one of the two sons of Azmaveth who joined David's army at Ziklag. 1 Chr. 12:3.

JEZRAHIAH [JEZ-ruh-HI-uh] 450 B.C. Leader of the choirs at the dedication of the walls of Jerusalem in Nehemiah's time. Neh. 12:42.

JEZREEL [JEZ-ree-uhl; "God sows"]

1. B.C. (date unknown). Listed only in the genealogy of Judah in 1 Chr. 4:3.

2. 700 B.C. Symbolic name given to the firstborn son of Hosea, as a sign of the impending judgment of Jehu and his house for the bloodshed at Jezreel. Hos. 1:4.

JIDLAPH [JID-laf] 2075 B.C. A son of Nahor the brother of Abraham. Gen. 22:22.

JOAB [JOH-ab; "Yahweh is father"]

1. 1000 B.C. Son of Zeruiah the sister of David; notable as the ruthless commander of David's army who murdered Abner and Amasa. He also killed Absalom, thus ending the rebellion against David. 2 Sam. 2:13-32; 3:22-31; 14,18–20; 1 Ki. 2. **Brothers:** Abishai and Asahel.

2. B.C. (date unknown). Listed only in the genealogy of Judah in 1 Chr. 4:14.

3. B.C. (date unknown). A descendant of Pahath-Moab and ancestor of some who returned to Judah with Zerubbabel and Ezra. Ezra 2:6; 8:9; Neh. 7:11.

JOAH [JOH-uh; "Yahweh is brother"]

1. B.C. (date unknown). Listed only in the genealogy of Levi in 1 Chr. 6:21.

2. 975 B.C. Third son of Obed-Edom and head of a family of Temple gatekeepers in David's time. 1 Chr. 26:4.

3. 725 B.C. A Levite who helped purify the Temple during the reign of Hezekiah. 2 Chr. 29:12.

4. 700 B.C. An official of Hezekiah who spoke with the Assyrian commander while Jerusalem lay under siege. 2 Ki. 18:18-37; Isa. 36:3-22.

5. 625 B.C. An official of Josiah sent to help repair the Temple. 2 Chr. 34:8.

JOAHAZ [JOH-uh-haz; "Yahweh has grasped"] 625 B.C. Father of Joah, Josiah's recorder. 2 Chr. 34:8.

JOANAN [joh-AY-nuhn] B.C. (date unknown). KJV: Joanna. A descendant of Zerubbabel listed in the genealogy of Christ in Lk. 3:27.

JOANNA [joh-AN-uh; probably feminine form of John] A.D. 30. Wife of Cuza, manager of Herod Antipas's household; she helped support Jesus' ministry. She was among the women who discovered the tomb to be empty and brought news to the apostles of Christ's resurrection. Lk. 8:3; 24:10.

JOASH [JOH-ash; "Yahweh has given"] KJV, RSV: Jehoash (2 Ki. 11,12).

1. 1850 B.C. A son of Beker and grandson of Benjamin. 1 Chr. 7:8.

2. B.C. (date unknown). Listed only in the genealogy of Judah in 1 Chr. 4:22.

3. 1100 B.C. An Abiezrite, father of Gideon the judge. Jdg. 6:11,29-31.

4. 1000 B.C. A Benjamite who, with his brother, Ahiezer, joined David's army at Ziklag. 1 Chr. 12:3.

5. 975 B.C. An official of David in charge of the supplies of olive oil. 1 Chr. 27:28.

6. 850 B.C. A son of Ahab who held Micaiah the prophet prisoner while Ahab went to war against Ramoth Gilead. 1 Ki. 22:26; 2 Chr. 18:25.

7.* 835–796 B.C. The eighth king of Judah, crowned as a child after the overthrow of Athaliah, daughter of Jezebel. Under the guidance of Jehoiada the priest, he repaired the Temple and removed Baal worship. After the death of Jehoiada, he reinstated idolatry. 2 Ki. 11:2,21; 12; 1 Chr. 3:11; 2 Chr. 24. **Father:** Ahaziah. **Mother:** Zibeah. **Son and successor:** Amaziah.

JOB* [JOHB; meaning uncertain] B.C. (date unknown). The righteous man whose sufferings are the central issue of the Book of Job. A native of Uz, Job's trials took place during the early patriarchal period. His endurance of hardship by faith in God, which led to his eventual restoration, serves as a model of human suffering and redemption. Job 1–42; Ezek. 14:14,20; James 5:11.

JOBAB [JOH-bab]
1. B.C. (date unknown). Last of the sons of Joktan listed in the Table of Nations. Gen. 10:29; 1 Chr. 1:23. May refer to an unknown Arabian tribe.
2. A pre-Israelite king of Edom. Gen. 36:33,34; 1 Chr. 1:44,45.
3. 1400 B.C. King of the town of Madon who joined with other Canaanite kings to battle Joshua. Josh. 11:1.
4 and 5. B.C. (dates unknown). Two listed only in the genealogy of Benjamin in 1 Chr. 8:9,18.

JOCHEBED [JAHK-uh-bed; "Yahweh is glory"] 1525 B.C. Wife of Amram and mother of Moses and Aaron. Ex. 6:20; Num. 26:59.

JODA [JOH-duh] B.C. (date unknown). KJV: Judah. A descendant of Zerubbabel and ancestor of Christ. Lk. 3:26.

JOED [JOH-ed; "Yahweh is witness"] B.C. (date unknown). Ancestor of Sallu, a Benjamite who resettled in Jerusalem after the Exile. Neh. 11:7.

JOEL [JOH-uhl; "Yahweh is God"] KJV: Vashni (1 Chr. 6:28).
1. B.C. (date unknown). Listed only in the genealogy of Issachar in 1 Chr. 7:3.
2. B.C. (date unknown). Listed only in the genealogy of Reuben in 1 Chr. 5:4,8.
3. B.C. (date unknown). A Gadite chief who lived in Bashan. 1 Chr. 5:12.
4. B.C. (date unknown). Ancestor of Samuel listed in the genealogy of Heman the seer in 1 Chr. 6:36.
5. 1050 B.C. Firstborn son of Samuel. Appointed as judges, Samuel's sons became corrupt, which led to the selection of King Saul to rule over Israel. 1 Sam. 8:2; 1 Chr. 6:28,33; 15:17. **Brother:** Abijah.
6. 1000 B.C. A Benjamite who joined David at Ziklag. 1 Chr. 4:35.
7. 1000 B.C. A military commander, one of David's thirty mighty men. 1 Chr. 11:38.
8. 1000 B.C. A Levite, leader of the Gershonites in David's time. 1 Chr. 15:7,11.
9. 975 B.C. A Gershonite appointed by David to serve as a Temple treasurer. 1 Chr. 23:8; 26:22. Probably the same as Joel 8.
10. 975 B.C. Officer over the tribe of Manasseh in David's day. 1 Chr. 27:20.
11.* B.C. (date unknown). A minor prophet whose words are recorded in the Book of Joel. Joel 1:1; Acts 2:16.
12. 725 B.C. A Levite who helped purify the Temple in Hezekiah's time. 2 Chr. 29:12.
13. 450 B.C. A descendant of Nebo who took a foreign wife after the Exile. Ezra 10:43.
14. 450 B.C. Chief officer of the Benjamites who resettled in Jerusalem after the Exile. Neh. 11:9.

JOELAH [joh-EE-luh] 1000 B.C. A Benjamite, one of the two sons of Jeroham who joined David's army at Ziklag. 1 Chr. 12:7.

JOEZER [joh-EE-zuhr; "Yahweh is help"] 1000 B.C. A warrior who joined David at Ziklag. 1 Chr. 12:6.

JOGLI [JAHG-li] 1425 B.C. Father of Bukki, leader from the tribe of Dan appointed by Moses to help divide the land of Canaan. Num. 34:22.

JOHA [JOH-uh]
1. B.C. (date unknown). Listed only in the genealogy of Benjamin in 1 Chr. 8:16.
2. 1000 B.C. A military commander, one of David's thirty mighty men. 1 Chr. 11:45.

JOHANAN [joh-HAY-nuhn; "Yahweh is gracious"]
1. 1000 B.C. A Benjamite and kinsman of Saul who defected to David's army at Ziklag. 1 Chr. 12:4.
2. 1000 B.C. A Gadite who also joined David at Ziklag. 1 Chr. 12:12.
3. 950 B.C. Great-grandson of Zadok, priest of David and Solomon. 1 Chr. 6:9,10.
4. 625 B.C. Firstborn son of Josiah; he did not become successor to the throne. 1 Chr. 3:15.
5. 575 B.C. A military officer who warned Gedeliah of a plot to assassinate him. Later, this Johanan rejected Jeremiah's advice and led the Israelites to Egypt. 2 Ki. 25:23; Jer. 40:8,13-16; 41:11–43:7.
6. 450 B.C. A descendant of Azgad who returned to Judah with Ezra. Ezra 8:12.
7. 400 B.C. Grandson of Eliashib the high priest and a high priest during the reign of Darius the Persian. Neh. 12:22,23. Called Jonathan in Neh. 12:11.
8. B.C. (date unknown). A descendant of Zerubbabel listed in the genealogy of the royal line in 1 Chr. 3:24.

JOHN [JAHN; shortened form of Jehohanan] KJV: Jona (Jn. 1:42); Jonas (Jn. 21:15-17).
1. A.D. 1. Father of Peter the apostle. Jn. 1:42; 21:15-17. Also called Jonah.
2.* A.D. 25. John the Baptist, son of Zechariah and Elizabeth. Notable as the forerunner of Jesus, sent to prepare Israel for the Messiah. Mt. 3; 11:2-18; 14:1-12; Lk. 1:13-17,57-63; Jn. 1:6-40.
3.* A.D. 25. Son of Zebedee and brother of James, notable as a prominent member of the twelve apostles. Author of the Gospel of John, the three Epistles of John, and Revelation. Mt. 4:21; 10:2; Acts 1:13; Gal. 2:9.
4. A.D. 30. John called Mark, one of the twelve apostles. Author of the Gospel of Mark. Acts 12:12,25; 15:37-39. See Mark.
5. A.D. 35. A relative of Annas the priest present at the trial of Peter and John before the Sanhedrin. Acts 4:6.

JOIADA [JOY-uh-duh; "Yahweh knows"] Jehoiada, KJV (Neh. 3:6), RSV (Neh. 13:28).
1. 450 B.C. Son of Paseah; he helped repair the wall of Jerusalem in Nehemiah's time. Neh. 3:6.
2. 425 B.C. Son of Eliashib in the line of high priests following the return to Judah after the Exile. Neh. 12:10,11,22; 13:28.

JOIAKIM [JOY-uh-kim; shortened form of Jehoiakim] 500 B.C. Son of Jeshua and high priest following his father; his son Eliashib was high priest in Ezra's time. Neh. 12:10,12,26.

JOIARIB [JOY-uh-rib; shortened form of Jehoiarib]
1. B.C. (date unknown). Ancestor of Sallu, a Benjamite who resettled in Jerusalem after the Exile. Neh. 11:5.
2. 525 B.C. A priest who returned to Judah with Zerubbabel after the Exile. Neh. 12:6,19.
3. 450 B.C. A priest whose son resettled in Jerusalem. Neh. 11:10. Possibly same as Joiarib 2. In the parallel text in 1 Chr. 9:10, Jehoiarib is listed among the priests who resettled in Jerusalem.
4. 450 B.C. A man of learning who was sent by Ezra to retrieve Levites to serve at the Temple in Jerusalem. Ezra 8:16.

JOKIM [JOH-kim; "Yahweh raises up"] B.C. (date unknown). A descendant of Shelah, son of Judah, listed in 1 Chr. 4:22.

JOKSHAN [JAHK-shan] 2000 B.C. A son of Abraham by his second wife, Keturah. Gen. 25:2,3.

JOKTAN [JAHK-tan] B.C. (date unknown). A descendant of Shem listed in the Table of Nations. Gen. 10:25-29. Ancestral source of several Arabian tribes.

JONADAB [JOH-nuh-dab; "Yahweh is noble" or "Yahweh is liberal"]
1. 1000 B.C. Son of Shimeah, David's brother, and sly friend of David's son Amnon. He devised the plan for Amnon to seduce his half-sister, Tamar. 2 Sam. 13:3-5,32-35.
2. B.C. (date unknown). Son of Recab and ancestor of the Recabites whose commands to abstain from wine and to live as nomads were faithfully followed by his descendants. Jer. 35:6-19.

JONAH [JOH-nuh; "dove"] KJV, RSV: Bar-Jona (Mt. 16:17).
1.* 775 B.C. The prophet from Gath Hepher whose story is recorded in the Book of Jonah. He was compelled by God to go to Nineveh where he delivered his message of judgment that caused its people to repent. 2 Ki. 14:25; Jon. 1–4; Mt. 12:39-41; Lk. 11:29-32.
2. A.D. 1. Father of the apostle Peter. Mt. 16:17.

JONAM [JOH-nuhm] B.C. (date unknown). KJV: Jonan. Listed only in the genealogy of Jesus in Lk. 3:30.

JONATHAN [JAHN-uh-thuhn; "Yahweh has given"]
1. B.C. (date unknown). Listed only in the genealogy of Jerahmeel, a descendant of Judah. 1 Chr. 2:32,33.
2. B.C. (date unknown). A descendant of Moses who became the household priest for Micah. His descendants continued to serve as idolatrous priests for the Danites until the fall of Israel to Assyria. Jdg. 17:7–18:6; 18:17-31.
3. 1025 B.C. Uncle of David who served the king as counselor and scribe. 1 Chr. 27:32.
4.* 1025 B.C. The eldest son of Saul and a close friend of David. He was slain with Saul in battle against the Philistines. 1 Sam. 13:16–14:49; 18–20; 23:16-18; 31:2; 2 Sam. 1. **Son:** Mephibosheth.
5. 1000 B.C. Son of Abiathar, a high priest in David's time. 2 Sam. 15:27,36; 17:17-20; 1 Ki. 1:42-48.
6. 1000 B.C. A military commander, one of David's thirty mighty men. 2 Sam. 23:32; 1 Chr. 11:34.
7. 975 B.C. Son of Shimea, David's brother, who killed a giant of Gath, a champion for the Philistines. 2 Sam. 21:21; 1 Chr. 20:7.
8. 975 B.C. Son of Uzziah who was in charge of town storehouses in David's time. 1 Chr. 27:25.
9. 600 B.C. Secretary of Zedekiah the king of Judah in whose house Jeremiah the prophet was temporarily imprisoned. Jer. 37:15,20; 38:26.
10. 575 B.C. A son of Kareah and a military officer in the time of Gedaliah, governor of Judah. Jer. 40:8. **Brother:** Johanan. Does not appear in RSV.
11. 500 B.C. Head of a priestly family in the days of Joiakim the high priest. Neh. 12:14.
12. 475 B.C. Father of Ebed, a descendant of Adin who returned to Judah with Ezra. Ezra 8:6.
13. 450 B.C. Father of Zechariah, a priest who took part in the dedication of the wall of Jerusalem in Nehemiah's time. Neh. 12:35.
14. 450 B.C. Son of Asahel who opposed Ezra's plan to divorce the foreign wives taken by the Jews after the Exile. Ezra 10:15.
15. 400 B.C. Descendant of Jeshua the high priest. Neh. 12:11. Called Johanan in Neh. 12:22,23. Some believe he is also the Jehohanan or Johanan (KJV) in Ezra 10:6. See Jehohanan.

JORAH [JOHR-uh] B.C. (date unknown). Ancestral head of a family that returned to Judah with Zerubbabel after the Exile. Ezra 2:18. Called Hariph in Neh. 7:24.

JORAI [JOHR-i] B.C. (date unknown). Listed only in the genealogy of Gad in 1 Chr. 5:13.

JORAM [JOHR-uhm; "Yahweh is exalted"] KJV, RSV: Jehoram (2 Ki. 1:17; 3).
1. B.C. (date unknown). Ancestor of Shelomith, a Levite who served as treasurer in King David's time. 1 Chr. 26:25.
2. 1000 B.C. Son of Tou, king of Hamath, who congratulated David for his victory over Hadadezer. 2 Sam. 8:10. Called Hadoram in 1 Chr. 18:10.
3. 852–841 B.C. Son of Ahab; notable as the successor of his brother Ahaziah as king of Israel. 2 Ki. 1:17; 3; 9:14-29.
4. 853–841 B.C. Alternate name of Jehoram, the son and successor of Jehoshaphat, king of Judah. He is listed in the genealogy of Christ in Mt. 1:8. See Jehoram.

JORIM [JOHR-im; "Yahweh is exalted"] B.C. (date unknown). Listed only in the genealogy of Christ in Lk. 3:29.

JORKEAM [JOHR-kee-uhm] B.C. (date unknown). KJV: Jorkoam. Listed only in the genealogy of Judah in 1 Chr. 2:44. Possibly a place name, identified by some as Jokdeam (Josh. 15:56).

JOSECH [JOH-zek] B.C. (date unknown). KJV: Joseph. A descendant of Zerubbabel listed only in the genealogy of Christ in Lk. 3:26.

JOSEPH [JOH-suhf; "may (God) add"]
1.* 1900 B.C. The son of Jacob and Rachel who was sold into slavery by his brothers. By interpreting a dream of the Pharaoh, he rose to a position of power in Egypt. When famine came to Judah, he was able to deliver his family from starvation. Gen. 30:24,25; 37; 39–50.
2. 1475 B.C. Father of Igal, a leader from the tribe of Issachar sent by Moses to spy out the land of Canaan. Num. 13:7.
3. 975 B.C. A son of Asaph, one of the chief ministers of music in David's time. 1 Chr. 25:2,9.
4. B.C. (date unknown). A descendant of David listed in the genealogy of Christ in Lk. 3:30.
5. 500 B.C. Head of a family of priests in the days of Joiakim, son of Jeshua the high priest. Neh. 12:14.
6. 450 B.C. A Jew who took a foreign wife after the Exile. Ezra 10:42.
7. B.C. (date unknown). A descendant of Zerubbabel listed in the genealogy of Christ in Lk. 3:24.
8.* A.D. 1. The carpenter husband of Mary, mother of Jesus. When he discovered Mary was pregnant prior to their marriage, he planned to divorce her quietly, until an angel in a dream assured him the child was conceived through the Holy Spirit. Mt. 1:16–2:23; Lk. 1:27; 2:4,5,16.
9. A.D. 25. A brother of Jesus. Mt. 13:55. Called Joses in Mk. 6:3.
10. A.D. 30. Joseph of Arimathea, a Jew in whose tomb Jesus was buried after the crucifixion. Mk. 15:42-46; Jn. 19:38-42.
11. A.D. 35. Joseph called Barsabbas, one of the two Christians who were considered to replace Judas Iscariot as twelfth apostle. Matthias was chosen instead. Acts 1:23.
12. A.D. 35. The given name of Barnabas. Acts 4:36. See Barnabas.

JOSES [JOH-seez] RSV: Joseph (Mt. 27:56).
1. A.D. 25. A brother of Jesus. Mk. 6:3. Called Joseph in Mt. 13:55.
2. A.D. 30. Brother of James the younger, whose mother Mary was present at the crucifixion. Mk. 15:40,47.

JOSHAH [JAHSH-uh; "Yahweh's gift"] 725 B.C. A clan leader listed only in the genealogy of Simeon in 1 Chr. 4:34.

JOSHAPHAT [JAHSH-uh-fat; "Yahweh has judged"] KJV: Jehoshaphat (1 Chr. 15:24).
1. 1000 B.C. A military commander, one of David's thirty mighty men. 1 Chr. 11:43.
2. 1000 B.C. A priest who blew the trumpet before the ark as it was brought by David to Jerusalem. 1 Chr. 15:24.

JOSHAVIAH [JAHSH-uh-VI-uh] 1000 B.C. One of the two sons of Elnaam who are listed among the military elite known as David's thirty mighty men. 1 Chr. 11:46.

JOSHBEKASHAH [JAHSH-buh-KAY-shuh] 975 B.C. A son of Heman the seer; one of David's chief ministers of music. 1 Chr. 25:4,24.

JOSHEB-BASSHEBETH [JOH-shuhb-bah-SHEE-buhth] 1000 B.C. Not found in KJV. Chief of the Three, who were over David's thirty mighty men. 2 Sam. 23:8. Called Jashobeam in 1 Chr. 11:11.

JOSHIBIAH [JAHSH-uh-BI-uh; "Yahweh causes to dwell"] 750(?) B.C. Father of Jehu, a Simeonite clan leader. 1 Chr. 4:35.

JOSHUA [JAHSH-oo-uh; "Yahweh is salvation"] KJV: Jehoshua (Num. 13:16); Jesus, (Acts 7:45; Heb. 4:8); Jose (Lk. 3:29); RSV: Jesus (Lk. 3:29).
1.* 1450 B.C. The righteous son of Nun who led Israel in the conquest of Canaan after the death of Moses. Moses changed his name to Joshua from Hoshea. Ex. 17:9-14; Num. 13:8,16; Deut. 31:7,14,23; Josh. 1–24.
2. 1075 B.C. One who owned a field in Beth Shemesh. 1 Sam. 6:14-18.
3. 625 B.C. Governor of Jerusalem during the reign of Josiah. 2 Ki. 23:8.
4. 525 B.C. Alternate name of Jeshua, the high priest at the time of the return from exile in Babylonia. Hag. 1; Zech. 3. See Jeshua 4.
5. B.C. (date unknown). Listed in the genealogy of Jesus in Lk. 3:29.

JOSIAH [joh-SI-uh; "Yahweh supports"] KJV: Josias (Mt. 1:10,11).
1.* 640–609 B.C. The pious king of Judah during whose reign the Book of the Law was rediscovered. He removed idolatry from Judah and renewed the covenant relationship with God. 2 Ki. 22:1–23:30; 1 Chr. 3:14,15; 2 Chr. 34,35; Mt. 1:10,11. **Father:** Amon. **Sons:** Jehoahaz, Jehoiakim, Zedekiah, and Johanan.
2. 525 B.C. Son of Zephaniah; a contemporary of Zechariah the prophet. Zech. 6:10. Probably the same as Hen in v. 14.

JOSIPHIAH [JAHS-uh-FI-uh; "Yahweh adds"] 450 B.C. Father of Shelomith, leader of the descendants of Bani who returned to Judah with Ezra. Ezra 8:10.

JOTHAM [JAH-thuhm; "Yahweh is perfect"]
1. B.C. (date unknown). Listed only in the genealogy of Judah in 1 Chr. 2:47.
2. 1125 B.C. The youngest of the seventy sons of Gideon; he escaped when Abimelech murdered their brothers. Jdg. 9:5-21,57.
3. 750–735 B.C. The son and successor of Uzziah king of Judah. He continued in the pious ways of his father. **Mother:** Jerusha. 2 Ki. 15:5,7,32-38; 2 Chr. 27:1-9.

JOZABAD [JAHZ-uh-bad; "Yahweh has bestowed"] KJV: Jozachar (2 Ki. 12:21); RSV: Jozacar (2 Ki. 12:21).
1. 1000 B.C. A Benjamite who defected from Saul to David at Ziklag. 1 Chr. 12:4.
2 and 3. 1000 B.C. Two military commanders of Manasseh who joined David. 1 Chr. 12:20.

4. 800 B.C. An official who with Jehozabad assassinated Joash at Beth Millo. 2 Ki. 12:21. Called Zabad in 2 Chr. 24:26.
5. 725 B.C. A Levite under Conaniah who was in charge of offerings to the Temple during the reign of Hezekiah. 2 Chr. 31:13.
6. 625 B.C. A chief Levite in the time of Josiah. 2 Chr. 35:9.
7. 450 B.C. A Levite who helped weigh the sacred articles of silver and gold. Ezra 8:33.
8. 450 B.C. A priest who took a foreign wife after the Exile. Ezra 10:22.
9. 450 B.C. A Levite who took a foreign wife after the Exile. Ezra 10:23.
10. 450 B.C. A Levite who instructed the people in the Law. Neh. 8:7.
11. 450 B.C. A chief Levite who settled in Jerusalem after the Exile. Neh. 11:16. May be the same as Jozabad 7, 9, or 10.

JOZADAK [JAHZ-uh-dak; "Yahweh is righteous"] 575 B.C. Father of Jeshua, the high priest at the time of the first return from exile in Babylon. Ezra 3:2,8. Called Jehozadak in Hag. 1:1; Zech. 6:11.

JUBAL [JOO-bahl] B.C. (date unknown). Son of Lamech, called "father of all who play the harp and flute." Gen. 4:21.

JUDAH [JOO-duh; "praise"]
1. 1900 B.C. Fourth of the six sons of Jacob and Leah; ancestral source of the tribe of Judah, to which David and Jesus belonged. Gen. 29:35; 35:23; 37:26; 38,43,44,46; 1 Chr. 2:1,3; 4:21.
2. B.C. (date unknown). Listed only in the genealogy of Jesus in Lk. 3:30.
3. 525 B.C. A Levite who returned to Judah with Zerubbabel after the Exile. Neh. 12:8.
4. 450 B.C. A Levite who took a foreign wife after the Exile. Ezra 10:23.
5. 450 B.C. A Benjamite who resettled in Jerusalem after the Exile. Neh. 11:9.
6. 450 B.C. One involved in the dedication of the wall of Jerusalem in Nehemiah's time. Neh. 12:34.
7. 450 B.C. A priest who played music at the dedication of the rebuilt wall of Jerusalem after the Exile. Neh. 12:36.

JUDAS [JOO-duhs; "praise"] New Testament form of Judah.
1. 5 B.C. Judas the Galilean, instigator of a rebellion against Rome when Quirinius was governor. Acts 5:37.
2. A.D. 25. A brother of Jesus, notable as the author of Jude. Mt. 13:55; Mk. 6:3. See Jude.
3. A.D. 25. Son of James, one of the twelve apostles. Lk. 6:16; Acts 1:13. Possibly the same as Thaddaeus.
4.* A.D. 30. Judas Iscariot, the apostle who betrayed Christ for thirty silver pieces. Afterwards, seized by remorse, Judas hanged himself. Mt. 26:14-25,47-50; 27:3-10; Acts 1:16-25. **Father:** Simon Iscariot.
5. A.D. 35. One at whose house Saul of Tarsus (Paul) stayed after he was blinded on the road to Damascus. There Ananias restored his sight. Acts 9:11.
6. A.D. 50. Judas called Barsabbas; a prophet at the church in Jerusalem sent with Silas to Antioch. Acts 15:22-32. Also known as Justus.

JUDE* [JOOD; variant form of Judah] A.D. 65. Younger brother of Jesus, the author of the Book of Jude. He humbly identifies himself only as the brother of James. Jude 1. Called Judas in Mt. 13:55 and Mk. 6:3.

JUDITH [JOO-dith] 1950 B.C. Daughter of Beeri the Hittite and a wife of Esau. Gen. 26:34. Probably the same as Oholibamah, daughter of Anah the Horite.

JULIA [JOOL-yuh; feminine form of Julius] A.D. 55. A woman at the church in Rome greeted by Paul. Rom. 16:15.

JULIUS [JOOL-yuhs] A.D. 60. A centurion who brought Paul to Rome to stand trial. Acts 27.

JUNIAS [JOO-nee-uhs] A.D. 55. KJV: Junia. A Christian who at one time was imprisoned with Paul; he is greeted by Paul in Rom. 16:7.

JUSHAB-HESED [JOO-shuhb-HEE-suhd; "loving-kindness is returned"] 500 B.C. A son of Zerubbabel listed in the genealogy of the royal line after the Exile. 1 Chr. 3:20.

JUSTUS [JUS-tuhs; "just"]
1. A.D. 35. Latin name of Joseph, who was also called Barsabbas. Acts 1:23.
2. A.D. 55. *See* Titius Justus.
3. A.D. 60. Latin name of Jesus, a Christian companion of Paul who sent greetings to the church in Colosse. Col. 4:11.

K

KADMIEL [KAD-mee-uhl; "God is ancient"(?)]
1. 525 B.C. Head of a family of Levites that returned to Judah with Zerubbabel after the Exile. Ezra 2:40; 3:9; Neh. 7:43; 12:8.
2. 450 B.C. A Levite, among those who led the people in worship in Nehemiah's time. Neh. 9:4,5; 12:24.
3. 450 B.C. A Levite who sealed the covenant renewal with God in Nehemiah's time. Neh. 10:9. Possibly same as Kadmiel 1 or 2.

KALLAI [KAL-i; "swift"(?)] 500 B.C. Head of a priestly family during the time of Joiakim the high priest. Neh. 12:20.

KAREAH [kuh-REE-uh; "bald head"] 625 B.C. KJV: Careah (2 Ki. 25:23). Father of Johanan and Jonathan, two military leaders who allied themselves with Gedaliah after the fall of Jerusalem. 2 Ki. 25:23; Jer. 40:8–41:16.

KEDAR [KEE-duhr; "powerful" or "dark, swarthy"] B.C. (date unknown). Second of the sons of Ishmael. Gen. 25:13. Possibly the ancestral source of the North Arabian tribe of the same name (*for example* Isa. 21:16,17; Jer. 49:28).

KEDEMAH [KED-uh-muh; "eastward"] B.C. (date unknown). Last of the sons of Ishmael, listed in Gen. 25:15. Head of an Ishmaelite tribe.

KEDORLAOMER [KED-ohr-lay-OH-muhr] 2100 B.C. KJV, RSV: Chedorlaomer. King of Elam who led a coalition of kings that defeated the kings of Sodom and Gomorrah. Lot was among those taken captive in Sodom; Abram came to his rescue, and in a night raid defeated Kedorlaomer and his allies. Gen. 14.

KEILAH [kuh-I-luh] B.C. (date unknown). Listed only in the genealogy of the clans of Judah in 1 Chr. 4:19.

KELAIAH [kuh-LAY-yuh] 450 B.C. A Levite who took a foreign wife after the Exile. Ezra 10:23. Also called Kelita.

KELAL [KEE-lal; "perfection"] 450 B.C. KJV, RSV: Chelal. A descendant of Pahath-Moab who took a foreign wife after the Exile. Ezra 10:30.

KELITA [kuh-LI-tuh; possibly "dwarf"]
1. 450 B.C. A Levite listed among those guilty of intermarriage with foreign women in Ezra's time. Ezra 10:23. Also called Kelaiah.
2. 450 B.C. A Levite who with Ezra instructed the people in the Law. Neh. 8:7.
3. 450 B.C. A Levite who sealed the covenant renewal with God in Nehemiah's time. Neh. 10:10.

It is likely that all are the same individual.

KELUB [KEE-lub] KJV, RSV: Chelub.
1. B.C. (date unknown). Listed only in the genealogy of Judah in 1 Chr. 4:11.
2. 1025 B.C. Father of Ezri, an official of David in charge of the field workers on royal farmlands. 1 Chr. 27:26.

KELUHI [KEL-uh-hi] 450 B.C. KJV: Chelluh; RSV: Cheluhi. A Jew listed among those who married foreign women after the Exile. Ezra 10:35.

KEMUEL [KEM-yoo-uhl]
1. 2050 B.C. A son of Nahor, brother of Abraham, and father of Aram. Gen. 22:21.
2. 1400 B.C. A leader from the tribe of Ephraim appointed by Moses to help divide the land of Canaan. Num. 34:24.
3. 1000 B.C. Father of Hashabiah, officer over the tribe of Levi in David's day. 1 Chr. 27:17.

KENAANAH [kuh-NAY-uh-nuh] KJV, RSV: Chenaanah.
1. B.C. (date unknown). Listed only in the genealogy of Benjamin in 1 Chr. 7:10.
2. 875 B.C. Father of Zedekiah, a false prophet who opposed Micaiah the prophet in Ahab's time. 1 Ki. 22:11,24; 2 Chr. 18:10,23.

KENAN [KEE-nuhn] B.C. (date unknown). KJV: Cainan (Gen. 5:9-14). Son of Enosh listed in the genealogy of Adam's line before the Flood. Gen. 5:9-14; 1 Chr. 1:2. Called Cainan in Lk. 3:37.

KENANI [kuh-NAY-ni] 450 B.C. KJV, RSV: Chenani. A Levite who led the Israelites in confession at the covenant renewal in Nehemiah's time. Neh. 9:4.

KENANIAH [KEN-uh-NI-uh; "establish by Yahweh"] KJV, RSV: Chenaniah.
1. 1000 B.C. A Levite who led the choirs in the procession before the ark as it was brought to Jerusalem by David. 1 Chr. 15:22,27.
2. 975 B.C. A Levite who served as an official of David. 1 Chr. 26:29.

KENAZ [KEE-naz; "hunting"]
1. 1875 B.C. A grandson of Esau and an Edomite chief. Gen. 36:11,15,42.
2. 1425 B.C. Younger brother of Caleb the spy and father of Othniel the judge. Jdg. 1:13; 3:9-11; 1 Chr. 4:13.
3. 1400 B.C. Grandson of Caleb the spy. 1 Chr. 4:15.

KERAN [KEER-uhn] 1925 B.C. KJV, RSV: Cheran. A son of Dishon, who was a Horite chief and brother of Oholibamah, one of Esau's wives. Gen. 36:26.

KEREN-HAPPUCH [KAIR-uhn-HAP-uhk; "horn of antimony" (eye shadow)] B.C. (date unknown). Youngest of the three daughters of Job born in the latter part of his life. Job 42:14.

KEROS [KEER-ahs; "fortress"] B.C. (date unknown). Ancestral head of a family of Temple servants that returned to Judah with Zerubbabel after the Exile. Ezra 2:44; Neh. 7:47.

KESED [KEH-sed] 2050 B.C. KJV, RSV: Chesed. A son of Nahor, brother of Abraham. Gen. 22:22.

KETURAH [keh-TOOR-uh; "incense"] 2025 B.C. Second wife of Abraham, possibly taken after the death of Sarah. In 1 Chronicles, she is called his concubine. Gen. 25:1-4; 1 Chr. 1:32,33.

KEZIAH [keh-ZI-uh; "cassia"] B.C. (date unknown). Second of the three daughters of Job born during the latter part of his life. Job 42:14.

KILEAB [KIL-ee-ab] 975 B.C. KJV, RSV: Chileab. A son of David and Abigail, born in Hebron. 2 Sam. 3:3.

KILION [KIL-ee-uhn; "pining"] B.C. (date unknown). KJV, RSV: Chilion. Son of Elimelech and Naomi; his brother, Mahlon, was the husband of Ruth. Ruth 1:2,5.

KIMHAM [KIM-ham] 1000 B.C. KJV, RSV: Chimham. A kinsman or son of Barzillai; he accompanied David in his return to Jerusalem after Absalom's death, and remained there in Barzillai's stead. 2 Sam. 19:37-40.

KISH [KISH; "bow" or "power"] KJV: Cis. (Acts 13:21).
1. 1100 B.C. A son of Jeiel listed in the genealogy of Benjamin. Perhaps the uncle of Kish, father of Saul. 1 Chr. 8:30; 9:36.
2. 1075 B.C. A Benjamite; father of King Saul. Although Abiel is said to be Kish's father, this is likely an ancestral relationship. Ner was probably his actual father, and thus Kish was the brother of Abner. 1 Sam. 9:1-5; 14:51; 1 Chr. 9:39.
3. B.C. (date unknown). Listed in the genealogies of Levi in 1 Chr. 23:21,22; 24:29.
4. 725 B.C. A Levite who helped purify the Temple in Hezekiah's time. 2 Chr. 29:12.
5. B.C. (date unknown). A Benjamite; ancestor of Mordecai, the uncle of Esther. Esth. 2:5.

KISHI [KISH-i] 1025 B.C. A Levite, father of Ethan (also called Jeduthun), one of the three chief ministers of music in David's time. 1 Chr. 6:44. Called Kushaiah in 1 Chr. 15:17.

KISLON [KIZ-lahn] 1400 B.C. KJV, RSV: Chislon. Father of Elidad, a leader from the tribe of Benjamin appointed by Moses to help divide the land of Canaan. Num. 34:21.

KITTIM [KIT-im] B.C. (date unknown). A Japhethite listed in the Table of Nations, in Gen. 10:4. Possibly the ancestral source of the inhabitants of Cyprus.

KOHATH [KOH-hath] 1875 B.C. One of the three sons of Levi; Moses and Aaron were among his descendants. Gen. 46:11; Ex. 6:16-18; 1 Chr. 6.

KOLAIAH [koh-LAY-yuh; "voice of Yahweh"]
1. 625 B.C. Father of Ahab, a false prophet among the exiles in Babylon. Jer. 29:21.
2. B.C. (date unknown). Ancestor of Sallu, a Benjamite who resettled in Jerusalem after the Exile. Neh. 11:7.

KORAH [KOHR-uh; "bald"] KJV: Core (Jude 11).
1. 1900 B.C. A son of Esau by his wife Oholibamah. Gen. 36:5,14,18.
2. 1875 B.C. A grandson of Esau and an Edomite chief. Gen. 36:16.
3. B.C. (date unknown). Listed only in the genealogy of Judah in 1 Chr. 2:43.
4.* 1450 B.C. A Levite descended from Kohath who was the leader of a rebellion against Moses. The earth opened up and swallowed Korah along with the other leaders of the rebellion. Ex. 6:21-24; Num. 16; 26:9-11; Jude 11.

KORE [KOHR-ee; "quail"(?)]
1. 1000 B.C. A son of Asaph whose descendants served as Temple gatekeepers. 1 Chr. 9:19; 26:1.

2. 725 B.C. A Levite in charge of distributing freewill offerings given at the Temple in Hezekiah's time. 2 Chr. 31:14.

KOZ [KAHZ; "thorn"] B.C. (date unknown). KJV: Coz. Listed in the genealogy of Judah in 1 Chr. 4:8.

KUSHAIAH [koo-SHAY-yuh; "bow of Yahweh"] 1025 B.C. Father of Ethan (also called Jeduthun), a chief minister of music in David's day. 1 Chr. 15:17. Called Kishi in 1 Chr. 6:44.

L

LAADAH [LAY-uh-duh] B.C. (date unknown). Listed in the genealogy of Judah in 1 Chr. 4:21.

LABAN* [LAY-buhn; "white"] 2000 B.C. The brother of Rebekah and father of Rachel and Leah. Jacob worked for him for seven years in order to marry Rachel, but Laban tricked him by substituting Leah at the wedding festival. Thereafter, Jacob served another seven years as the bride price for Rachel, whom he also married. Gen. 25:20; 27:43; 29–31. **Father:** Bethuel. **Grandfather:** Nahor.

LADAN [LAY-duhn] KJV: Laadan.
1. B.C. (date unknown). An Ephraimite, ancestor of Joshua the son of Nun. 1 Chr. 7:26.
2. B.C. (date unknown). A descendant of Gershon. 1 Chr. 23:7-9; 26:21. Called Libni in 1 Chr. 6:17,20.

LAEL [LAY-uhl; "belonging to God"] 1475 B.C. Father of Eliasaph, leader of the Gershonites at the time of the Exodus. Num. 3:24.

LAHAD [LAY-had] B.C. (date unknown). Listed in the genealogy of Judah in 1 Chr. 4:2.

LAHMI [LAH-mi] 975 B.C. Brother of Goliath; he too was a Philistine giant, slain in battle by Elhanan. 1 Chr. 20:5. The parallel text in 2 Sam. 21:19 is apparently corrupt due to scribal error.

LAISH [LAY-ish; "lion"] 1050 B.C. Father of Paltiel, to whom Saul gave his daughter, Michal, although he had previously promised her to David. 1 Sam. 25:44; 2 Sam. 3:15.

LAMECH [LAY-mek; "strong youth"(?)]
1.* B.C. (date unknown). A descendant of Cain and the first recorded polygamist. Gen. 4:18-24.
2. B.C. (date unknown). Father of Noah. Gen. 5:25-31.

LAPPIDOTH [LAP-uh-dahth; "flames, torches"(?)] 1225 B.C. KJV: Lapidoth. Husband of Deborah the prophetess who became judge over Israel. Jdg. 4:4.

LAZARUS [LAZ-uh-ruhs; shortened form of "God has helped"]
1. Name of the beggar in Christ's parable of the rich man and poor man in the afterlife. It is the only instance where a name is used in Christ's parables. Lk. 16:19-31.
2.* A.D. 30. The brother of Martha and Mary whom Jesus raised from the dead. Jn. 11,12.

LEAH* [LEE-uh; "wild cow"(?)] 1950 B.C. The older daughter of Laban who by Laban's

deception on the wedding night became Jacob's first wife in place of her sister, Rachel. Gen. 29–31.

LEBANA [luh-BAY-nuh; "white"] B.C. (date unknown). Ancestral head of a family of Temple servants that returned to Judah with Zerubbabel after the Exile. Neh. 7:48. Called Lebanah in Ezra 2:45.

LEBANAH [luh-BAH-nuh; "white"] B.C. (date unknown). Ancestor of Temple servants. Ezra 2:45. See Lebana.

LECAH [LEE-kuh; "walking"] B.C. (date unknown). Listed only in the genealogy of Judah in 1 Chr. 4:21.

LEMUEL [lem-YOO-uhl; "devoted to God"] B.C. (date unknown). A king who is identified as the author of Proverbs 31:1-9. According to tradition, he is thought to be Solomon or possibly Hezekiah; he is otherwise unknown. King of Massa according to RSV.

LEVI [LEE-vi; "joined"]
1. 1900 B.C. Third son of Jacob by his wife Leah. Ancestral source of one of the twelve tribes of Israel. With Simeon he took part in the slaughter of the Shechemites. Gen. 29:34; 34:25-31; 1 Chr. 6.
2 and 3. B.C. (dates unknown). Two ancestors of Christ descended from David. Lk. 3:24,29.
4. A.D. 30. The tax collector who became Matthew the apostle. Mk. 2:14-17; Lk. 5:27-32. See Matthew.

LIBNI [LIB-ni; "white"(?)]
1. B.C. (date unknown). A descendant of Gershon, son of Levi, and ancestral head of his own clan. Ex. 6:17; 1 Chr. 6:17,20. Called Ladan in 1 Chr. 23:7-9.
2. B.C. (date unknown). A descendant of Merari listed in the genealogy of Levi in 1 Chr. 6:29.

LIKHI [LIK-hi] B.C. (date unknown). Listed only in the genealogy of Manasseh in 1 Chr. 7:19.

LINUS [LI-nuhs] A.D. 65. A Christian who with Paul sent greetings to Timothy. 2 Tim. 4:21.

LO-AMMI [LOH-AM-i; "not my people"] 725 B.C. Symbolic name given to the second son of the prophet Hosea, as a sign of God's rejection of the Northern Kingdom. Hos. 1:9.

LOIS [LOH-is; possibly "better"] A.D. 1. Pious grandmother of Timothy. 2 Tim. 1:5.

LO-RUHAMAH [LOH-roo-HAH-muh; "not loved" or "not pitied"] 725 B.C. Symbolic name of Hosea's daughter, indicating God's refusal to forgive the sins of the Israelites. Hos. 1:6-8; 2:23.

LOT* [LAHT; "covering"] 2100 B.C. The nephew of Abraham who settled near Sodom; he escaped from the judgment that fell upon Sodom and Gomorrah, but his wife perished. Through his daughters, he is the ancestral source of the Moabites and Ammonites. Gen. 13,19.

LOTAN [LOH-tan] 1975 B.C. A Horite chief who lived in the land of Seir in Esau's time. Gen. 36:20,22,29.

LUCIUS [LOO-shuhs; "light"]
1. A.D. 45. A Christian from Cyrene, and one of the leaders of the early church at Antioch. Acts 13:1.
2. A.D. 55. A Christian who sent his greetings in Paul's letter to the Roman church. Rom. 16:21. Paul calls him "my relative," although this may be a figurative designation. Possibly same as Lucius 1.

LUD [LUD] B.C. (date unknown). A son of Shem, and ancestral source of a Semitic nation, probably Lydia. Gen. 10:22.

LUKE* [shortened form of Lucas; "light"] A.D. 50. The author of the books of Luke and Acts. He was a physician and a missionary who accompanied Paul in his journeys. Col. 4:14; 2 Tim. 4:11; Phlm. 24.

LYDIA [LID-ee-uh] A.D. 50. A business woman from Thyatira who was converted by Paul in Philippi. Acts 16:14,15,40.

LYSANIAS [lih-SAY-nee-uhs] A.D. 25. Tetrarch of Abilene at the time John the Baptist began his ministry. Lk. 3:1.

LYSIAS [LIS-ee-uhs] A.D. 60. Military tribune in command of the Jerusalem garrison who arrested Paul when a mob sought his life. A Greek who had paid dearly for his Roman citizenship, he discovered that Paul was freeborn and immediately altered his treatment of the apostle. Acts 21:31–23:30; 24:7,22. See also Claudius Lysias.

M

MAACAH [MAY-uh-kuh; "oppression"] KJV: Maachah, except Maacah (1 Sam. 3:3); Michaiah (2 Chr. 13:2); RSV: Micaiah (2 Chr. 13:2).
1. 2050 B.C. A son of Nahor by his concubine, Reumah. Ancestral source of the Maacathites. Gen. 22:24.
2. B.C. (date unknown). Concubine of Caleb, Hezron's son. 1 Chr. 2:48.
3. B.C. (date unknown). Wife of Makir listed in the genealogy of Manasseh in 1 Chr. 7:15,16.
4. 1125 B.C. Wife of Jeiel, ancestor of Saul. 1 Chr. 8:29; 9:35.
5. 1025 B.C. Father of Hanan, one of David's thirty mighty men. 1 Chr. 11:43.
6. 1000 B.C. A wife of David and mother of Absalom. 2 Sam. 3:3; 1 Chr. 3:2. **Father:** Talmai, king of Geshur.
7. 1025 B.C. Father of Achish, Philistine king of Gath. 1 Ki. 2:39. Called Maoch in 1 Sam. 27:2.
8. 1000 B.C. Father of Shephatiah, officer over the tribe of Simeon in David's day. 1 Chr. 27:16.
9. 950 B.C. Favorite wife of Rehoboam and mother of Abijah, king of Judah. Deposed as queen mother by her grandson, Asa, because she made an Asherah pole. 1 Ki. 15:2,10,13; 2 Chr. 11:20-22; 13:2. Probably the daughter of Uriel and granddaughter of Absalom.

MAADAI [MAY-uh-di; "Yahweh is an ornament"] 450 B.C. One who took a foreign wife after the Exile. Ezra 10:34.

MAADIAH [MAY-uh-DI-uh; "Yahweh is an ornament"] 525 B.C. KJV, RSV: Moadiah (Neh. 12:17). Head of a priestly family that returned to Jerusalem with Zerubbabel after the Exile. Neh. 12:5,17.

MAAI [MAY-i; "compassionate"] 450 B.C. A musician who took part in the dedication of the wall of Jerusalem in Nehemiah's time. Neh. 12:36.

MAASAI [MAY-uh-si; "work of Yahweh"] 450 B.C. KJV: Maasiai. A priest who resettled in Jerusalem after the Exile. 1 Chr. 9:12. Called Amashsai in Neh. 11:13.

MAASEIAH [MAY-uh-SEE-yuh; "work of Yahweh"]

1. 1000 B.C. A Levite who played the lyre as David brought the ark to Jerusalem. 1 Chr. 15:18,20.

2. 850 B.C. A military commander who helped Jehoiada overthrow Queen Athaliah. 2 Chr. 23:1.

3. 800 B.C. A military officer who served under Uzziah, king of Judah. 2 Chr. 26:11.

4. 725 B.C. A son of King Ahab slain in battle with Pekah, king of Israel. 2 Chr. 28:7.

5. 625 B.C. Governor of Jerusalem who helped Josiah repair and purify the Temple. 2 Chr. 34:8.

6. 625 B.C. Father of Zephaniah, a priest during the reign of Zedekiah. Jer. 21:1; 29:25; 37:3.

7. 625 B.C. Father of Zedekiah, a false prophet among the exiles in Babylon. Jer. 29:21.

8. 600 B.C. A doorkeeper who had a room in the Temple during the reign of Zedekiah. Jer. 35:4.

9. 475 B.C. Father of Azariah, who helped repair the wall of Jerusalem. Neh. 3:23.

10, 11, and 12. 450 B.C. Three priests who took foreign wives in Ezra's time. Ezra 10:18,21,22.

13. 450 B.C. A descendant of Pahath-Moab; he too took a foreign wife. Ezra 10:30.

14. 450 B.C. One who stood to Ezra's right as he read the Law before the people. Neh. 8:4.

15. 450 B.C. A Levite who instructed the people in the Law. Neh. 8:7.

16. 450 B.C. A Jewish leader who sealed the covenant renewal with God in Nehemiah's time. Neh. 10:25.

17. 450 B.C. A Judahite who resettled in Jerusalem after the Exile. Neh. 11:5.

18. 450 B.C. An ancestor of Sallu, a Benjamite who resettled in Jerusalem in Ezra's time. Neh. 11:7.

19 and 20. 450 B.C. Two priests in the choir at the dedication of the wall of Jerusalem in Nehemiah's time. Neh. 12:41,42.

MAATH [MAY-ath; "small"] B.C. (date unknown). A descendant of Zerubbabel listed in the genealogy of Jesus in Lk. 3:26.

MAAZ [MAY-az] B.C. (date unknown). Listed in the genealogy of Jerahmeel, a descendant of Judah. 1 Chr. 2:27.

MAAZIAH [MAY-uh-ZI-uh]

1. 975 B.C. Head of the twenty-fourth division of priests in David's day. 1 Chr. 24:18.

2. 450 B.C. A priest who sealed the covenant renewal with God in Nehemiah's time. Neh. 10:8.

MACBANNAI [mak-BAN-i] 1000 B.C. KJV: Machbanai; RSV: Machbannai. A Gadite warrior who joined David's army at Ziklag. 1 Chr. 12:13.

MACBENAH [mak-BEE-nuh] B.C. (date unknown). KJV, RSV: Machbenah. Listed in the genealogy of the clans of Caleb, a descendant of Judah. 1 Chr. 2:49. Possibly a place, identified by some as Cabbon (Josh. 15:40).

MACNADEBAI [mak-NAD-uh-bi] 450 B.C. KJV, RSV: Machnadebai. One who took a foreign wife after the Exile. Ezra 10:40.

MADAI [MAY-di] B.C. (date unknown). A son of Japheth listed in the Table of Nations. Gen. 10:2; 1 Chr. 1:5. Ancestral source of the Medes.

MAGDIEL [MAG-dee-uhl] B.C. (date unknown). An Edomite chief descended from Esau. Gen. 36:43; 1 Chr. 1:54.

MAGOG [MAY-gahg] B.C. (date unknown). A son of Japheth listed in the Table of Nations. Gen. 10:2. Ancestor of a people inhabiting a northern land. Josephus identified the name with the Scythians. "Magog" appears in Rev. 20:8 as a symbolic name of the ungodly nations opposed to the people of God.

MAGOR-MISSABIB
[MAY-gohr-MIS-uh-bib; "terror on every side"] 600 B.C. Symbolic name given to Pashhur the priest by Jeremiah. Jer. 20:3.

MAGPIASH [MAG-pee-ash; "moth killer"(?)] 450 B.C. A Jewish leader who sealed the covenant renewal with God in Nehemiah's time. Neh. 10:20.

MAHALALEEL [muh-HAL-uh-LEE-uhl; "God is praise" or "God shines forth"] B.C. (date unknown). KJV: Malaleel. Ancestor of Noah listed in the genealogy of Christ. Lk. 3:37. Called Mahalalel in Gen. 5:12-17.

MAHALALEL [muh-HAL-uh-lel; "God is praise" or "God shines forth"] KJV: Mahalaleel (Gen. 5:12-17), Maleleel (Lk. 3:37); RSV: Mahalaleel (Lk. 3:37).

1. B.C. (date unknown). Listed in the genealogy of Adam's line prior to the Flood. Gen. 5:12-17.

2. B.C. (date unknown). Ancestor of Athaiah, a Judahite who resettled in Jerusalem after the Exile. Neh. 11:4.

MAHALATH [MAY-huh-lath]

1. 1925 B.C. Daughter of Ishmael and third wife of Esau. Gen. 28:9.

2. 925 B.C. Wife of Rehoboam and daughter of David's son, Jerimoth. 2 Chr. 11:18.

MAHARAI [MAY-huh-ri; "impetuous"(?)] 1000 B.C. A military leader from the town of Netophah; one of David's mighty men. 2 Sam. 23:28; 1 Chr. 11:30; 27:13.

MAHATH [MAY-hath; "snatching"(?)]

1. B.C. (date unknown). Listed in the genealogy of Heman the seer. 1 Chr. 6:35.

2. 725 B.C. A Levite who served in the Temple in Hezekiah's time. 2 Chr. 29:12; 31:13.

MAHAZIOTH [muh-HAY-zee-ahth; "visions"] 975 B.C. A son of Heman the seer and a minister of music in David's time. 1 Chr. 25:4,30.

MAHER-SHALAL-HASH-BAZ
[MAY-huhr-SHAL-uhl-HASH-baz; "the spoil speeds, the prey hastens"] 725 B.C. Symbolic name given to one of Isaiah's sons as a sign that Syria and the Northern Kingdom would soon be destroyed by Assyria. Isa. 8:1,3.

MAHLAH [MAH-luh; "weak, sickly"] KJV: Mahalah (1 Chr. 7:18).

1. 1800 B.C. Great-grandson of Manasseh who traced his lineage through his mother, Hammolecheth. 1 Chr. 7:18.

2. 1400 B.C. A daughter of Zelophehad, a descendant of Manasseh. With her sisters, she petitioned Moses and received her father's inheritance. Num. 26:33; Num. 27:1-7.

MAHLI [MAH-li; "weak, sickly"] KJV: Mahali (Ex. 6:19).

1. B.C. (date unknown). A descendant of Merari, son of Levi. Ex. 6:19; 1 Chr. 23:21; 24:26.

2. B.C. (date unknown). Listed in the genealogies of Levi. 1 Chr. 6:47; 23:23; 24:30.

MAHLON [MAH-luhn] 1100 B.C. Son of Elimelech and Naomi; he was the first husband of Ruth. Ruth 1:2,5; 4:9.

MAHOL [MAY-hahl; "dance"] B.C. (date unknown). Father or ancestor of four wise men who were exceeded in wisdom by Solomon. 1 Ki. 4:31. "Sons of Mahol" may not indicate a person at all, but is perhaps an appellation

indicating their membership in the religious guild of musicians.

MAHSEIAH [mah-SEE-yuh; "Yahweh is a refuge"] 650 B.C. KJV: Maaseiah. Paternal grandfather of Seraiah and Baruch the scribe. Jer. 32:12; 51:59.

MAKI [MAY-ki] 1475 B.C. KJV, RSV: Machi. Father of Geuel, leader from the tribe of Gad sent to spy out the land of Canaan. Num. 13:15.

MAKIR [MAY-keer; "sold"] KJV, RSV: Machir.

1. 1825 B.C. Firstborn son of Manasseh, son of Jacob. Gen. 50:23; Num. 26:29; 1 Chr. 7:14-17.

2. 975 B.C. A man of Lo Debar in whose house Jonathan's son Mephibosheth lived. 2 Sam. 9:4,5; 17:27.

MALACHI* [MAL-uh-ki; "my messenger" or "angel"] 450 B.C. A minor prophet whose words are recorded in the Book of Malachi, the last book of the OT. His message concerned the spiritual laxity that had developed among the returned exiles. Mal. 1–4.

MALCAM [MAL-kam; "their king"] B.C. (date unknown). Listed only in the genealogy of Benjamin in 1 Chr. 8:9.

MALCHUS [MAL-kuhs; "ruler"] A.D. 30. The high priest's servant, whose ear was cut off by Peter. Jn. 18:10.

MALKIEL [MAL-kee-uhl; "God is king"] KJV, RSV: Malchiel. A descendant of Gad. Gen. 46:17; Num. 26:45.

MALKIJAH [mal-KI-juh; "Yahweh is king"] KJV, RSV: Malchiah (Jeremiah).

1. B.C. (date unknown). Listed in the genealogy of Asaph, the chief minister of music in David's day. 1 Chr. 6:40.

2. 975 B.C. Head of the fifth division of priests in David's day. 1 Chr. 24:9.

3. 600 B.C. Father of Pashhur, one of the officials of Zedekiah who threw Jeremiah into a cistern to die. Jer. 21:1; 38:1.

4. 600 B.C. Son of Zedekiah and owner of the cistern into which Jeremiah's enemies cast the prophet. Jer. 38:6.

5. B.C. (date unknown). Ancestor of Adaiah, a priest who resettled in Jerusalem in Nehemiah's time. 1 Chr. 9:12; Neh. 11:12.

6 and 7. 450 B.C. Two who took foreign wives after the Exile; both were descendants of Parosh. Ezra 10:25.

8. 450 B.C. A descendant of Harim, listed among those who took foreign wives. He contributed to the rebuilding of Jerusalem's wall. Ezra 10:31; Neh. 3:11.

9. 450 B.C. A Recabite who helped repair the wall of Jerusalem. Neh. 3:14.

10. 450 B.C. A goldsmith also involved in the wall's reconstruction. Neh. 3:31.

11. 450 B.C. One who stood to Ezra's left at the reading of the Law. Neh. 8:4.

12. 450 B.C. A priest who sealed the covenant renewal with God in Nehemiah's time. Neh. 10:3. Possibly the same as Malkijah 5.

13. 450 B.C. A priest who sang in the choir at the dedication of the wall of Jerusalem. Neh. 12:42. Possibly the same as Malkijah 11 or 12.

MALKIRAM [mal-KI-ruhm; "my king is exalted"] 575 B.C. KJV, RSV: Malchiram. A son of Jehoiachin, listed in the genealogy of the royal line after the Exile. 1 Chr. 3:18.

MALKI-SHUA [MAL-kih-SHOO-uh; "the king saves"] 1025 B.C. KJV: Malchishua, except Melchishua (1 Sam. 14:49); RSV: Malchishua. Third son of Saul, killed with his father in battle against the Philistines. 1 Sam. 14:49; 31:2; 1 Chr. 8:33; 10:2. **Mother:** Ahinoam. **Brothers:** Jonathan, Abinadab, and Ish-Bosheth.

MALLOTHI [MAL-uh-thi; "Yahweh has spoken"] 975 B.C. A son of Heman and head of the nineteenth division of Temple singers. 1 Chr. 25:4,26.

MALLUCH [MAL-uhk; "counselor"]
1. B.C. (date unknown). A Levite; ancestor of Ethan, a chief minister of music in David's day. 1 Chr. 6:44.
2. 525 B.C. A priest who returned to Judah with Zerubbabel after the Exile. Neh. 12:2,14.
3 and 4. 450 B.C. Two who took foreign wives after the Exile. Ezra 10:29,32.
5. 450 B.C. A priest who sealed the covenant renewal with God in Nehemiah's time, possibly with the name of a family ancestor (see Malluch 2). Neh. 10:4.
6. 450 B.C. A Jewish leader who sealed the covenant renewal with God after the Exile. Neh. 10:27.

MAMRE [MAM-ree; "strength"] 2100 B.C. An Amorite allied with Abram; he and his brothers helped Abram defeat Kedorlaomer and his allies, who had taken Lot prisoner. Gen. 14:13,24.

MANAEN [MAN-ee-uhn; "comforter"] A.D. 45. One of the prophets and teachers at the church at Antioch who "set apart" Saul and Barnabas for missionary work. Acts 13:1.

MANAHATH [MAN-uh-hath] 1950 B.C. Son of a Horite chief who lived in the land of Seir in Esau's time. Gen. 36:23.

MANASSEH [muh-NAS-uh; "one who causes forgetfulness"] KJV: Manasses. Mt. 1:10.
1. 1850 B.C. Firstborn son of Joseph. Adopted by Jacob as a full heir with his brother, Ephraim, he thereby became ancestor of one of the twelve tribes of Israel. Gen. 41:51; 48; Num. 26:28-34; Mt. 1:10.
2.* 697–642 B.C. Son and successor of Hezekiah; he did not follow in his father's pious ways, but led Israel back into idolatry. After being taken into exile, he repented and was restored to the throne of Judah. 2 Ki. 21:1-18; 2 Chr. 33:1-23. **Mother:** Hephzibah. **Son and successor:** Amon.
3 and 4. 450 B.C. Two who took foreign wives after the Exile. Ezra 10:30,33.

MANOAH [muh-NOH-uh; "rest"] 1125 B.C. A Danite, father of Samson. Jdg. 13.

MAOCH [MAY-ahk; "poor"] 1025 B.C. Father of Achish, the Philistine king of Gath with whom David and his men took refuge from Saul. 1 Sam. 27:2. Called Maacah in 1 Ki. 2:39.

MAON [MAY-ahn; "dwelling"] B.C. (date unknown). Listed in the genealogy of Judah in 1 Chr. 2:45.

MARA [MAHR-uh; "bitter"] B.C. (date unknown). Name assumed by Naomi after the death of her husband and sons. Ruth 1:20.

MARDUK [MAHR-dook] KJV, RSV: Merodach. A god of Babylon who became the chief deity of the Babylonian pantheon in the time of Hammurabi. Jer. 50:2.

MARESHAH [muh-REE-shuh]
1. B.C. (date unknown). Listed only in the genealogy of the clans of Caleb, a descendant of Judah, in 1 Chr. 2:42.
2. B.C. (date unknown). Listed only in the genealogy of Judah in 1 Chr. 4:21.

MARK* [MAHRK; "large hammer"] A.D. 45. KJV: Marcus (Col. 4:10; 1 Pet. 5:13). Son of Mary of Jerusalem, notable as a traveling companion of Paul and his cousin Barnabus. Traditional author of the Gospel bearing his name. Acts 12:12,25; 15:37-39; Col. 4:10; 2 Tim. 4:11; 1 Pet. 5:13. His Jewish name was John.

MARSENA [mahr-SEE-nuh] 475 B.C. One of the seven nobles of Persia and Media who advised King Xerxes. Esth. 1:14.

MARTHA* [MAHR-thuh; "lady"] A.D. 30. Older sister of Mary and Lazarus, who lived in Bethany. Lk. 10:38-42; Jn. 11:1-45; 12:2.

MARY [MAIR-ee; Gk. form of Miriam]
1.* A.D. 1. The young Jewish virgin chosen by God to bear the Messiah, Jesus Christ. At the time, she was betrothed to Joseph, a carpenter of Nazareth, who intended to quietly divorce her, until he was visited by an angel in a dream, revealing the divine origin of Mary's pregnancy. Scripture portrays Mary as a humble and obedient individual, whose heart was devoted to God. Mt. 1:18-25; Lk. 1:26-56; 2; Acts 1:14.
2. A.D. 20. Mother of Mark; Peter went to her house after his miraculous escape from prison. Acts 12:12.
3. A.D. 30. Sister of Martha and Lazarus; she anointed Jesus with expensive perfume shortly before his death. Lk. 10:39-42; Jn. 11:1-45; 12:1-8.
4. A.D. 30. Mary Magdalene; so called after the name of her native city, Magdala. She was healed of demon possession by Jesus, and became one of his followers. Jesus appeared to her first after his resurrection. Mt. 27:56,61; Lk. 8:2; Jn. 20:1,11-18.
5. A.D. 30. Mother of James the younger and Joseph, also called Joses. Mt. 27:56; Mk. 15:40,47. Referred to as "the other Mary" in Mt. 27:61; 28:1. Probably the same as Mary the wife of Clopas (Jn. 19:25).
6. A.D. 55. A Roman Christian to whom Paul sent greetings. Rom. 16:6.

MASSA [MAS-uh; "burden"] 2025 B.C. A son of Ishmael, and ancestral source of a North Arabian tribe. Gen. 25:14.

MATRED [MAY-trid; "expulsion"] B.C. (date unknown). Mother of Mehetabel, the wife of Hadad, king of Edom. Gen. 36:39.

MATRI [MAY-tri; "rainy"] B.C. (date unknown). RSV: Matrites. Ancestral head of the Benjamite clan from which Saul was selected to become king of Israel. 1 Sam. 10:21.

MATTAN [MAT-uhn; "gift"]
1. 850 B.C. Priest of Baal slain during the overthrow of Queen Athaliah. 2 Ki. 11:18; 2 Chr. 23:17.
2. 625 B.C. Father of Shephatiah, one of the officials of Zedekiah who threw Jeremiah into a cistern to die. Jer. 38:1.

MATTANIAH [MAT-uh-NI-uh; "gift of Yahweh"]
1. 975 B.C. A son of Heman and head of the ninth division of Temple singers appointed by David. 1 Chr. 25:4,16.
2. B.C. (date unknown). A descendant of Asaph and ancestor of Jahaziel, who prophesied before King Jehoshaphat. 2 Chr. 20:14.
3. B.C. (date unknown). A descendant of Asaph and ancestor of Zechariah, a priest at the dedication of the wall of Jerusalem in Nehemiah's time. Neh. 12:35.
4. B.C. (date unknown). Also a Levite descended from Asaph; his descendants settled in Jerusalem after the Exile. 1 Chr. 9:15; Neh. 11:17,22. Possibly the same as Mattaniah 3.
5. 725 B.C. Another Levite descended from Asaph; he helped purify the Temple in Hezekiah's time. 2 Chr. 29:13.
6. 597–587 B.C. Last king of Judah, whose name was changed by Nebuchadnezzar when he made Mattaniah king in place of his nephew, Jehoiachin. 2 Ki. 24:17. **Father:** Josiah. **Brothers:** Jehoahaz and Jehoiakim. See Zedekiah 4.
7. 525 B.C. A Levite who returned to Judah with Zerubbabel after the Exile. Neh. 12:8.
8. 500 B.C. Grandfather of Hanan, assistant to

those in charge of the Temple storerooms in Nehemiah's time. Neh. 13:13. Possibly the same as Mattaniah 7.
9. 500 B.C. A Temple gatekeeper in the time of Joiakim the high priest. Neh. 12:25.
10, 11, 12, and 13. 450 B.C. Four who took foreign wives after the Exile. Ezra 10:26,27,30,37.

MATTATHA [MAT-uh-thuh; "gift"] B.C. (date unknown). A descendant of David listed in the genealogy of Jesus in Lk. 3:31.

MATTATHIAS [MAT-uh-THI-uhs; "gift of Yahweh"]
1 and 2. B.C. (dates unknown). Two descendants of Zerubbabel listed in the genealogy of Jesus in Lk. 3:25,26.

MATTATTAH [MAT-uh-tuh] 450 B.C. KJV: Mattathah. A Jew who put away his foreign wife in the time of Ezra. Ezra 10:33.

MATTENAI [MAT-uh-ni; "gift of Yahweh"]
1. 500 B.C. A priest during the time of Joiakim the high priest. Neh. 12:19.
2 and 3. Two who took foreign wives after the Exile. Ezra 10:33,37.

MATTHAN [MATH-an; "gift"] 50 B.C. Grandfather of Joseph the carpenter, husband of Mary, in the genealogy of Jesus in Mt. 1:15. Possibly the same as Matthat in Lk. 3:24.

MATTHAT [MATH-at; "gift"]
1. B.C. (date unknown). Listed in the genealogy of Jesus in Lk. 3:29.
2. 50 B.C. Grandfather of Joseph in Luke's genealogy of Jesus. Lk. 3:24. See Matthan.

MATTHEW* [MATH-yoo; shortened form of "gift of Yahweh"] A.D. 25. One of the twelve apostles and traditionally accepted as the author of the Gospel bearing his name. Also called Levi, he was a tax collector before his call. Mt. 9:9-13; 10:3; Acts 1:13. See Levi.

MATTHIAS [muh-THI-uhs; shortened form of "gift of Yahweh"] A.D. 30. A Christian chosen to become the twelfth apostle in place of Judas Iscariot. Acts 1:21-26. He was likely one of the seventy disciples of Christ during his ministry (Lk. 10:1).

MATTITHIAH [MAT-uh-THI-uh; "gift of Yahweh"]
1. 1000 B.C. A Levite who played the harp before the ark as it was brought to Jerusalem by David. 1 Chr. 15:18,21; 16:5.
2. 975 B.C. A son of Jeduthun and head of the fourteenth division of Temple singers in David's day. 1 Chr. 25:3,21. Possibly the same as Mattithiah 1.
3. 450 B.C. A Levite in charge of baking the bread offerings for the Temple in Nehemiah's time. 1 Chr. 9:31.
4. 450 B.C. A descendant of Nebo; he took a foreign wife after the Exile. Ezra 10:43.
5. 450 B.C. One who stood to Ezra's right at the reading of the Law. Neh. 8:4. Possibly the same as Mattithiah 3.

MEBUNNAI [meh-BUN-i] 1000 B.C. A military leader, one of David's thirty mighty men. 2 Sam. 23:27. Called Sibbecai the Hushathite in 2 Sam. 21:18; 1 Chr. 11:29; 20:4; 27:11.

MEDAD [MEE-dad; "loved"(?)] 1450 B.C. An Israelite elder who prophesied in the wilderness camp in Moses' time. Num. 11:26,27.

MEDAN [MEE-dan] 2000 B.C. A son of Abraham by Keturah. Gen. 25:2.

MEHETABEL [muh-HET-uh-bel; "God is doing good"] KJV: Mehetabeel (Neh. 6:10).
1. B.C. (date unknown). Wife of Hadad, a pre-Israelite king of Edom. Gen. 36:39.

2. 500 B.C. Grandfather of Shemaiah, a traitor hired by Tobiah and Sanballat to tempt Nehemiah into committing sacrilege. Neh. 6:10.

MEHIDA [muh-HI-duh; "famous" (date unknown). Ancestral head of a family of Temple servants that returned to Judah with Zerubbabel after the Exile. Ezra 2:52; Neh. 7:54.

MEHIR [MEE-huhr] B.C. (date unknown). Listed only in the genealogy of Judah in 1 Chr. 4:11.

MEHUJAEL [meh-HOO-jee-uhl; "God is smiting"] B.C. (date unknown). A descendant of Cain. Gen. 4:18.

MEHUMAN [meh-HOO-muhn] 475 B.C. One of the seven eunuchs who served King Xerxes. Esth. 1:10.

MELATIAH [MEL-uh-TI-uh; "Yahweh has delivered"] 450 B.C. A man from Gibeon who helped repair the wall of Jerusalem in Nehemiah's time. Neh. 3:7.

MELCHIZEDEK* [mel-KIZ-uh-dek; "king of righteousness"] 2100 B.C. KJV NT: Melchisedec. Priest-king of Jerusalem who blessed Abram after his defeat of Kedorlaomer and his allies. Abram gave him one tenth of all he owned. The author of Hebrews used Melchizedek as a symbolic representation of Christ. Gen. 14:18-20; Ps. 110:4; Heb. 5-7.

MELEA [MEE-lee-uh] B.C. (date unknown). A descendant of David listed in the genealogy of Christ in Lk. 3:31.

MELECH [MEE-lek; "king"] B.C. (date unknown). A descendant of Jonathan, son of Saul. 1 Chr. 8:35; 9:41.

MELKI [MEL-ki; "my king"] KJV, RSV: Melchi.

1 and 2. B.C. (dates unknown). Two ancestors of Christ listed in Luke's genealogy. Lk. 3:24,28.

MEMUCAN [meh-MOO-kuhn] 475 B.C. One of the seven nobles of Persia and Media who advised King Xerxes (Ahasuerus). It was upon his advice that Xerxes divorced Queen Vashti and selected a new queen. Esth. 1:14-21.

MENAHEM [MEN-uh-hem; "comforter"] 752–742 B.C. The brutal king of Israel who assassinated Shallum and seized the throne. 2 Ki. 15:14-22. **Father:** Gadi. **Son and successor:** Pekahiah.

MENNA [MEN-uh] B.C. (date unknown). KJV: Menan. A descendant of David, listed only in the genealogy of Christ in Lk. 3:31.

MEONOTHAI [mee-AHN-uh-thi; "my dwelling"] 1350 B.C. Son of Othniel the judge, listed only in the genealogy of Judah in 1 Chr. 4:13,14.

MEPHIBOSHETH [meh-FIB-oh-sheth; "he scatters shame," i.e., "idol breaker"]
1.* 1000 B.C. Lame son of Jonathan, son of Saul. After the death of Jonathan, David gave Mephibosheth Saul's estate, and thereafter he ate at the king's table. 2 Sam. 4:4; 9:6-13; 16:1-4; 19:24-30. Called Merib-Baal in 1 Chr. 9:40.
2. 1000 B.C. A son of Saul by his concubine Rizpah. David delivered him over to the Gibeonites, enemies of Saul, who put him to death. 2 Sam. 21:8.

MERAB [MEER-ab; "increase"] 1025 B.C. Older daughter of Saul, promised to David, but instead given in marriage to Adriel of Meholah. Her five sons were handed over to the Gibeonites to be killed. 1 Sam. 14:49; 18:17-19; 2 Sam. 21:8. The KJV mistakenly

reads "Michal," who was the younger sister of Merab, in 2 Sam. 21:8.

MERAIAH [muh-RAY-yuh] 500 B.C. Head of a priestly family in the time of Joiakim the high priest. Neh. 12:12.

MERAIOTH [muh-RAY-ahth]
1. 1100 B.C. Descendant of Aaron, grandfather of Ahitub, and great-grandfather of Zadok, David's high priest. Listed in the genealogy of Ezra. 1 Chr. 6:6,7,52; Ezra 7:3.
2. B.C. (date unknown). Ancestor of Azariah, a priest who resettled in Jerusalem in Nehemiah's time. 1 Chr. 9:11; Neh. 11:11.

MERARI [muhr-AHR-i; "bitter" (?)] 1875 B.C. Son of Levi, and ancestral head of the Merarite clan. Gen. 46:11; Num. 3:17,33-37; 1 Chr. 6.

MERED [MEER-ed; "rebel"] B.C. (date unknown). Listed only in the genealogy of Judah in 1 Chr. 4:17,18.

MEREMOTH [MAIR-uh-mahth] KJV, RSV: Meraioth (Neh. 12:15).
1. 525 B.C. A priest who returned to Judah with Zerubbabel after the Exile. Neh. 12:3,15.
2. 450 B.C. A priest who helped weigh the sacred articles of silver and gold. Ezra 8:33; Neh. 3:4,21.
3. 450 B.C. One who took a foreign wife after the Exile. Ezra 10:36.
4. 450 B.C. A priest who sealed the covenant renewal with God in Nehemiah's time. Neh. 10:5. Possibly the same as Meremoth 1 or 2.

MERES [MEER-ez; "worthy"] 475 B.C. One of the seven nobles of Persia and Media who advised King Xerxes. Esth. 1:14.

MERIB-BAAL [MAIR-ib-BAY-uhl; "Baal contends"] 1000 B.C. Original name of Mephibosheth, son of Jonathan, to whom David showed kindness. 1 Chr. 8:34; 9:40.

MERODACH-BALADAN
[MAIR-uh-dak-BAL-uh-duhn; "Marduk has given a son"] 725 B.C. KJV: Berodach-baladan (2 Ki. 20:12). Babylonian king who sent a gift to Hezekiah during his sickness. He strongly opposed Assyrian influence in Babylon. His embassy to Judah was undoubtedly sent to encourage Hezekiah to revolt against Assyria. 2 Ki. 20:12-19; Isa. 39:1-8.

MESHA [MEE-shuh]
1. B.C. (date unknown). Listed as the firstborn son of Caleb in the genealogy of the clans of Caleb in 1 Chr. 2:42.
2. B.C. (date unknown). Listed only in the genealogy of Benjamin in 1 Chr. 8:9.
3. 850 B.C. King of Moab who rebelled against Ahaziah, son of King Ahab. Suffering defeat at the hands of Ahaziah and his allies, Mesha sacrificed his firstborn son, which caused the Israelite army to withdraw. 2 Ki. 3.

MESHACH [MEE-shak] 600 B.C. Babylonian name given to Mishael, one of the three companions of Daniel who refused to bow down to Nebuchadnezzar's idol. They were then thrown into a blazing furnace but were miraculously delivered. Dan. 1:7; 2:49; 3.

MESHECH [MEE-shek; "long; tall"] KJV, RSV: Mash (Gen. 10:23).
1. B.C. (date unknown). A son of Japheth listed in the Table of Nations, in Gen. 10:2. Ancestral source of a people who lived in central Asia Minor, but were driven by the Assyrians into the mountainous region southeast of the Black Sea.
2. B.C. (date unknown). A son of Aram listed in the Table of Nations, in Gen. 10:23. Possibly the ancestor of a people living near Mount Masius in northern Mesopotamia.

MESHELEMIAH [muh-SHEL-uh-MI-uh; "Yahweh repays"] B.C. (date unknown). A

Levite, one of the chief Temple gatekeepers appointed by David. 1 Chr. 9:21; 26:1,2,9. Called Shelemiah in 1 Chr. 26:14.

MESHEZABEL [muh-SHEZ-uh-bel; "God delivers"] KJV: Meshezabeel.
1. 500 B.C. Grandfather of one who helped rebuild the wall of Jerusalem in Nehemiah's time. Neh. 3:4.
2. 475 B.C. A Judahite, father of Pethahiah. Neh. 11:24.

3. 450 B.C. A Jewish leader who sealed the covenant renewal with God in Nehemiah's time. Neh. 10:21.

MESHILLEMITH [muh-SHIL-uh-mith] B.C. (date unknown). A descendant of Immer and ancestor of a priest who resettled in Jerusalem after the Exile. 1 Chr. 9:12. Called Meshillemoth in Neh. 11:13.

MESHILLEMOTH [muh-SHIL-uh-mahth]
1. B.C. (date unknown). Ancestor of Amashsai, a priest who lived in Jerusalem in Nehemiah's time. Neh. 11:13. See Meshillemith.
2. 775 B.C. Father of Berekiah, an Ephraimite leader who opposed the enslavement of prisoners from Judah. 2 Chr. 28:12.

MESHOBAB [muh-SHOH-bab] 725 B.C. A Simeonite leader who lived in the time of Hezekiah. 1 Chr. 4:34.

MESHULLAM [muh-SHOO-luhm; "reconciliation" or "friendship"]
1. B.C. (date unknown). Listed only in the genealogy of Benjamin in 1 Chr. 8:17.
2. B.C. (date unknown). Head of a Gadite family who lived in Bashan. 1 Chr. 5:13.
3. B.C. (date unknown). Ancestor of Maasai, a priest who resettled in Jerusalem after the Exile. 1 Chr. 9:12.
4. 675 B.C. Grandfather of Shaphan, secretary of King Josiah. 2 Ki. 22:3.
5. 650 B.C. A descendant of Zadok, David's high priest, and father of Hilkiah, the high priest in Josiah's day. 1 Chr. 9:11; Neh. 11:11. Called Shallum in 1 Chr. 6:12,13; Ezra 7:2.
6. 625 B.C. A Levite who supervised the restoration of the Temple in Josiah's time. 2 Chr. 34:12.
7. 500 B.C. Son of Zerubbabel, listed in the genealogy of the royal line after the Exile. 1 Chr. 3:19.
8 and 9. 500 B.C. Two priests in the days of Joiakim the high priest. Neh. 12:13,16.
10. 500 B.C. A Levite who served as a gatekeeper in the time of Joiakim. Neh. 12:25.
11. 475 B.C. Father of Sallu, a Benjamite who resettled in Jerusalem after the Exile. 1 Chr. 9:7; Neh. 11:7.
12. 450 B.C. A Benjamite who settled in Jerusalem in Nehemiah's time. 1 Chr. 9:8.
13. 450 B.C. A Jewish leader who returned to Judah with Ezra. Ezra 8:16.

14. 450 B.C. One who opposed Ezra's proposal to divorce foreign wives among the Jews returned from exile. Ezra 10:15.
15. 450 B.C. A Jew who took a foreign wife after the Exile. Ezra 10:29.
16. 450 B.C. A priest who made repairs on the wall of Jerusalem in Nehemiah's time. His daughter married Jehohanan, son of Tobiah, an enemy of Nehemiah. Neh. 3:4,30; 6:18.
17. 450 B.C. One who helped repair the wall of Jerusalem after the Exile. Neh. 3:6.
18. 450 B.C. One who stood to Ezra's left at the reading of the Law. Neh. 8:4.
19. 450 B.C. A priest who sealed the covenant renewal with God in Nehemiah's time. Neh. 10:7.
20. 450 B.C. A Jewish leader who sealed the covenant renewal with God. Neh. 10:20. Possibly the same as Meshullam 13.
21. 450 B.C. A Jewish leader involved in the dedication of Jerusalem's wall. Neh. 12:33.

MESHULLEMETH [muh-SHOO-luh-meth; "reconciliation" or "friendship"] 675 B.C. A wife of King Manasseh and mother of Amon. 2 Ki. 21:19.

METHUSELAH [muh-THOO-zuh-luh; "man of the javelin"] B.C. (date unknown). KJV NT: Mathusala. Longest-living human recorded in the Bible; ancestor of Moses. Gen. 5:21-27; Lk. 3:37.

METHUSHAEL [muh-THOO-shee-uhl; "man of God"(?)] KJV: Methusael. A descendant of Cain and father of Lamech. Gen. 4:18.

MEUNIM [me-YOO-nim] B.C. (date unknown). KJV: Mehunim (Ezra 2:50). Ancestral head of a family of Temple servants that returned to Judah with Zerubbabel after the Exile. Ezra 2:50; Neh. 7:52.

ME-ZAHAB [MEH-zay-hab] B.C. (date unknown). KJV, RSV: Mezahab. Grandfather of Mehetabel, wife of Hadad, a pre-Israelite king of Edom. Gen. 36:39; 1 Chr. 1:50.

MIBHAR [MIB-hahr; "choice"] 1000 B.C. A military leader, one of David's mighty men. 1 Chr. 11:38.

MIBSAM [MIB-suhm; "sweet odor"]
1. 2025 B.C. A son of Ishmael, and ancestral source of one of the twelve Ishmaelite tribes. Gen. 25:13; 1 Chr. 1:29.
2. B.C. (date unknown). Listed only in the genealogy of Simeon in 1 Chr. 4:25.

MIBZAR [MIB-zahr; "fortress"] B.C. (date unknown). An Edomite chief descended from Esau. Gen. 36:42; 1 Chr. 1:53.

MICA [MI-kuh; shortened form of "who is like Yahweh?"] KJV: Micha (2 Sam. 9:12; Nehemiah); Micah (1 Ch 9:15).
1. 975 B.C. Son of Mephibosheth, the lame son of Jonathan. 2 Sam. 9:12. Called Micah in 1 Chr. 8:34,35; 9:40,41.
2. B.C. (date unknown). A descendant of Asaph and ancestor of Uzzi, chief officer of the Levites in Jerusalem after the Exile. 1 Chr. 9:15; Neh. 11:17,22. Called Micaiah in Neh. 12:35.
3. 450 B.C. A Levite who sealed the covenant renewal with God in Nehemiah's time, possibly with the name of a family ancestor (see Mica 2). Neh. 10:11.

MICAH [MI-kuh; shortened form of Micaiah] KJV: Michah (1 Chr. 23:20; 24:24,25).
1. B.C. (date unknown). An Ephraimite who hired a Levite as priest in his household shrine. An army of Danites enlisted the Levite to serve as their priest and stole Micah's idolatrous objects of worship. Jdg. 17,18.
2. B.C. (date unknown). Listed only in the genealogy of Reuben in 1 Chr. 5:5.
3. 975 B.C. Son of Mephibosheth and great-grandson of Saul. 1 Chr. 8:34,35; 9:40,41. Called Mica in 2 Sam. 9:12.

4. 975 B.C. A Levite listed among the Kohathites in David's time. 1 Chr. 23:20; 24:24,25.
5. 725 B.C. Micah of Moresheth, the prophet in the days of Hezekiah whose words are recorded in the Book of Micah. Jer. 26:18; Mic. 1:1.
6. 650 B.C. Father of Abdon, an official of Josiah sent to inquire of Huldah the prophetess. 2 Chr. 34:20. Called Micaiah in 2 Ki. 22:12.

MICAIAH [mih-KAY-yuh; "who is like Yahweh?"] KJV: Michaiah, except 1 and 2.
1. 875 B.C. A prophet who contradicted the favorable predictions of four hundred false prophets and foretold the death of Ahab in Ramoth Gilead. 1 Ki. 22; 2 Chr. 18. **Father:** Imlah.
2. 875 B.C. An official of Jehoshaphat sent to teach the Law throughout Judah. 2 Chr. 17:7.
3. B.C. (date unknown). A descendant of Asaph and ancestor of Zechariah, a Levite who took part in the dedication of Jerusalem's wall. Neh. 12:35. Same as Mica 2.
4. 650 B.C. Father of Acbor, an official of Josiah sent to inquire of the prophetess Huldah. 2 Ki. 22:12. Called Micah, father of Abdon, in 2 Chr. 34:20.
5. 600 B.C. A contemporary of Jeremiah who witnessed Jeremiah's prophecies and reported him to the officials of Jehoiakim. Jer. 36:11-13.
6. 450 B.C. A priest who sang at the dedication of Jerusalem's wall in Nehemiah's time. Neh. 12:41.

MICHAEL [MI-kuhl; "who is like God?"]
1. The archangel who is the prince and protector of the Jewish people. Dan. 10:13,21; 12:1; Jude 9; Rev. 12:7.
2. 1475 B.C. Father of Sether, the leader from the tribe of Asher sent by Moses to spy out the land of Canaan. Num. 13:13.
3. B.C. (date unknown). Listed only in the genealogy of Issachar in 1 Chr. 7:3.
4 and 5. B.C. (dates unknown). Two listed only in the genealogy of Gad in 1 Chr. 5:13,14.
6. B.C. (date unknown). Ancestor of Asaph, a chief minister of music in David's time. 1 Chr. 6:40.
7. B.C. (date unknown). Listed only in the genealogy of Benjamin in 1 Chr. 8:16.
8. 1000 B.C. A man of Manasseh who joined David at Ziklag. 1 Chr. 12:20.
9. 1000 B.C. Father of Omri, officer of the tribe of Issachar in David's day. 1 Chr. 27:18.
10. 850 B.C. A son of Jehoshaphat, king of Judah. 2 Chr. 21:2-4.
11. 525 B.C. Father of Zebadiah, head of a family that returned to Judah with Ezra. Ezra 8:8.

MICHAL* [MI-kuhl; "who is like God?"] 1025 B.C. The younger daughter of Saul and first wife of David. She saved David's life when Saul sought to kill him. Saul gave Michal to Paltiel while David was in hiding, but when David became king, he took her back. She had no children. 1 Sam. 18:20–19:17; 25:44; 2 Sam. 3:13; 6:16-23.

MICRI [MIK-ri] B.C. (date unknown). KJV, RSV: Michri. Ancestor of Elah, a Benjamite who resettled in Jerusalem after the Exile. 1 Chr. 9:8.

MIDIAN [MID-ee-uhn] 2000 B.C. A son of Abraham by Keturah and ancestral source of the Midianites. Gen. 25:2,4.

MIJAMIN [MIJ-uh-min; "of the right hand," i.e., fortunate] KJV: Miamin (Ezra 10:25; Neh. 12:5); KJV, RSV: Miniamin (Neh.12:41).
1. 975 B.C. Head of the sixth division of priests in David's day. 1 Chr. 24:9.
2. 525 B.C. A priest who returned to Judah

with Zerubbabel after the Exile. Neh. 12:5. Called Miniamin in Neh. 12:17,41.
3. 450 B.C. One who took a foreign wife after the Exile. Ezra 10:25.
4. 450 B.C. A priest who sealed the covenant renewal with God in Nehemiah's time. Neh. 10:7. Possibly the same as Mijamin 2.
5. 450 B.C. A priest who played the trumpet at the dedication of the wall of Jerusalem in Nehemiah's time. Neh. 12:41. Possibly the same as Mijamin 4.

MIKLOTH [MIK-lahth]
1. 1100 B.C. A son of Jeiel listed in the genealogy of Saul in 1 Chr. 8:32; 9:37,38.
2. 975 B.C. Leader of the division of David's army that served during the second month. 1 Chr. 27:4.

MIKNEIAH [mik-NEE-yuh; "Yahweh possesses"] 1000 B.C. A Levite who played the harp before the ark as it was brought by David to Jerusalem. 1 Chr. 15:18,21,

MILALAI [MIL-uh-li] 450 B.C. A Levite musician at the dedication of Jerusalem's wall in Nehemiah's time. Neh. 12:36.

MILCAH [MIL-kuh; "counsel"]
1. 2075 B.C. Wife of Nahor and daughter of Haran, Abraham's brothers. Gen. 11:29; 22:20-23. **Granddaughter:** Rebekah.
2. 1400 B.C. One of the daughters of Zelophehad who were given their father's land as inheritance by Moses. Num. 26:33; 27:1.

MINIAMIN [MIN-yuh-min; "of the right hand"]
1. 725 B.C. A priest who helped distribute Temple offerings. 2 Chr. 31:15.
2. 525 B.C. A priest who returned to Judah with Zerubbabel after the Exile. Neh. 12:17,41. Called Mijamin in Neh. 12:5.

MIRIAM [MEER-ee-uhm; "loved by Yahweh" or "plump"(?)]
1. 1450 B.C. The sister of Moses and Aaron; with Aaron, she opposed Moses' leadership in the wilderness and was temporarily stricken with leprosy. Ex. 15:20,21; Num. 12; 20:1. **Father:** Amram.
2. B.C. (date unknown). Listed in the genealogy of Judah in 1 Chr. 4:17.

MIRMAH [MUHR-muh] B.C. (date unknown). KJV: Mirma. Listed only in the genealogy of Benjamin in 1 Chr. 8:10.

MISHAEL [MISH-ee-uhl; "who is what God is?"]
1. 1450 B.C. A kinsman of Moses and Aaron instructed to remove the bodies of Aaron's sons, Nadab and Abihu, after they sinned and were struck dead before the sanctuary. Ex. 6:22; Lev. 10:4.
2. 600 B.C. Original name of Meshach, one of the three Jewish friends of Daniel taken with him to Babylon. Dan. 1:6,7,19; 2:17. See Meshach.
3. 450 B.C. One who stood to Ezra's left at the reading of the Law. Neh. 8:4.

MISHAM [MI-sham] B.C. (date unknown). Listed only in the genealogy of Benjamin in 1 Chr. 8:12.

MISHMA [MISH-muh]
1. 2025 B.C. A son of Ishmael and ancestral source of a tribe. Gen. 25:14.
2. B.C. (date unknown). Listed in the genealogy of Simeon in 1 Chr. 4:25,26.

MISHMANNAH [MISH-man-uh] 1000 B.C. A Gadite leader who joined David's army at Ziklag. 1 Chr. 12:10.

MISPAR [MIS-pahr] B.C. (date unknown). KJV: Mizpar. Ancestral head of a family that returned to Jerusalem with Zerubbabel after the Exile. Ezra 2:2. Called Mispereth in Neh. 7:7.

MISPERETH [MIS-puhr-eth] B.C. (date unknown). Ancestor of a post-exilic family. Neh. 7:7. See Mispar.

MITHREDATH [MITH-ruh-dath; "gift of Mithra"]
1. 525 B.C. Treasurer of Cyrus, king of Persia; he gave to Sheshbazzar the sacred articles of gold and silver required for the Temple of Jerusalem. Ezra 1:8.
2. 450 B.C. An official of the Trans-Euphrates province who opposed the rebuilding of Jerusalem during the reign of Artaxerxes. Ezra 4:7.

MIZRAIM [MIZ-ray-uhm] B.C. (date unknown). RSV: Egypt. A son of Ham listed in the Table of Nations, in Gen. 10:6,13. Probably the ancestral source of the Egyptians.

MIZZAH [MIZ-uh; "terror"(?)] 1875 B.C. A grandson of Esau and Basemath, and an Edomite chief. Gen. 36:13,17.

MNASON [NAY-suhn] A.D. 60. A Christian from Cyprus, at whose house in Jerusalem Paul and his companions stayed. Acts 21:16.

MOAB [MOH-ab; "from my father"] 2025 B.C. Son of Lot by incest with his eldest daughter. Ancestral source of the Moabites. Gen. 19:37.

MOADIAH [mo-uh-DI-uh] 525 B.C. KJV, RSV: Maadiah (Neh. 12:5). A priest who returned to Judah with Zerubbabel after the Exile. Neh. 12:5,17.

MOLECH* [MAHL-ek; possibly "ruler"] KJV: Milcom (1 Ki. 11:5; 2 Ki. 23:13); Malcham (Zeph. 1:5). Pagan deity of the Ammonites whose worship involved child sacrifice. The primary site of Molech worship in the Valley of Ben Hinnom, or Gehenna, became a symbolic image of Hell. Lev. 18:21; 20:2-5; 1 Ki. 11:5-7; 2 Ki. 23:10,13; Jer. 32:35; Zeph. 1:5. Called Moloch in Acts 7:43.

MOLID [MOH-lid] B.C. (date unknown). Listed only in the genealogy of Judah in 1 Chr. 2:29.

MOLOCH [MOL-uhk] See Molech.

MORDECAI [MOHR-duh-ki]
1. B.C. 525. A Jew who returned to Judah with Zerubbabel after the Exile. Ezra 2:2; Neh. 7:7.
2.* 475 B.C. A Benjamite deported to Babylon with Jehoiachin; he was the man whose cousin, Esther, became wife of King Xerxes. He uncovered Haman's plot to destroy the Jews and persuaded Esther to petition the king for the lives of her people. Mordecai was thereafter raised to a position of power in Babylon. Esth. 2–10.

MOSES* [MOH-zuhs; "drawn-out" or "born"] B.C. 1450. The great leader who by God's power brought the people of Israel out of bondage in Egypt, delivered to them the Law at Sinai, and finally led them to the Promised Land. The authorship of the first five books of the OT—known as the Pentateuch—is attributed to him. Exodus, Leviticus, Numbers, Deuteronomy.

MOZA [MOH-zuh]
1. B.C. (date unknown). A son of Caleb listed in the genealogy of Judah, in 1 Chr. 2:46.
2. B.C. (date unknown). A Benjamite descended from Jonathan, son of Saul. 1 Chr. 8:36,37; 9:42,43.

MUPPIM [MUP-im] 1825 B.C. A son or descendant of Benjamin. Gen. 46:21. Called Shupham in Num. 26:39, and Shephuphan in 1 Chr. 8:5.

MUSHI [MOO-shi] B.C. (date unknown). Son of Merari and ancestral head of a Levite clan. Ex. 6:19; Num. 3:20; 1 Chr. 23:21,23.

N

NAAM [NAY-uhm; "pleasant"] B.C. 1425. A son of Caleb the spy, listed only in the genealogy of Judah in 1 Chr. 4:15.

NAAMAH [NAY-uh-muh; "pleasant"]
1. B.C. (date unknown). Daughter of Lamech and Zillah. Gen. 4:22.
2. 950 B.C. Ammonite mother of Rehoboam, son and successor of Solomon. 1 Ki. 14:21,31; 2 Chr. 12:13.

NAAMAN [NAY-uh-muhn; "pleasantness"]
1. 1825 B.C. A son of Bela, firstborn son of Benjamin. Gen. 46:21; Num. 26:40; 1 Chr. 8:4. Ancestral source of the Naamite clan.
2.* 850 B.C. Syrian commander healed of leprosy by Elisha the prophet. Because of his deceit in accepting a gift from Naaman, Gehazi, Elisha's servant, was inflicted with Naaman's disease. 2 Ki. 5; Lk. 4:27.
3. B.C. (date unknown). Listed in the genealogy of Benjamin in 1 Chr. 8:7.

NAARAH [NAY-uh-ruh; "girl"] B.C. (date unknown). A wife of Ashhur, leader of the town of Tekoa. 1 Chr. 4:5,6.

NAARAI [NAY-uh-ri] 1000 B.C. A military commander, one of David's mighty men. 1 Chr. 11:37. Called Paarai the Arbite in 2 Sam. 23:35.

NABAL [NAY-buhl; "foolish"] 1025 B.C. A wealthy Carmelite who denied hospitality to David and his men. Abigail, Nabal's wife, delivered food to David, thus preventing bloodshed. Ten days later, Nabal died. 1 Sam. 25.

NABOTH [NAY-bahth; "a sprout"] 875 B.C. A Jezreelite who refused to sell his vineyard to King Ahab. Jezebel arranged to have Naboth killed. 1 Ki. 21:1-19; 2 Ki. 9:21-26.

NACON [NAY-kahn] 1000 B.C. KJV: Nachon. Owner of a threshing floor near which Uzzah was struck dead for touching the ark. 2 Sam. 6:6. Called Kidon in 1 Chr. 13:9.

NADAB [NAY-dab; "liberal"]
1. 1450 B.C. Firstborn son of Aaron who was consumed by fire for offering "unauthorized fire" before the Lord. Ex. 6:23; Lev. 10:1,2. **Mother:** Elisheba.
2. B.C. (date unknown). Listed only in the genealogy of Judah in 1 Chr. 2:28-30.
3. 1100 B.C. A son of Jeiel and probably a grand-uncle of Saul. 1 Chr. 8:30; 9:36.
4. 909–908 B.C. The son and successor of Jeroboam I; Baasha killed King Nadab in the second year of his reign and usurped the throne. 1 Ki. 15:25-31.

NAGGAI [NAG-i] KJV: Nagge. Listed only in the genealogy of Jesus in Lk. 3:25.

NAHAM [NAY-ham; "comfort"] B.C. (date unknown). Listed only in the genealogy of Judah in 1 Chr. 4:19.

NAHAMANI [NAY-huh-MAY-ni; "compassionate"] 525 B.C. One of the Jewish leaders who returned to Judah with Zerubbabel after the Exile. Neh. 7:7.

NAHARAI [NAY-uh-ri] 1000 B.C. KJV: Nahari (2 Sam. 23:37). A military commander from the city of Beeroth and one of David's thirty mighty men. 2 Sam. 23:37; 1 Chr. 11:39.

NAHASH [NAY-hash; "serpent"]
1. 1050 B.C. Ammonite king who besieged Jabesh Gilead and was subsequently defeated by Saul. 1 Sam. 11:1-3; 12:12.
2. 1000 B.C. Ammonite king who befriended David. 2 Sam. 10:2; 17:27; 1 Chr. 19:1,2. **Sons:** Hanun and Shobi.
3. 1000 B.C. Father of Abigail and Zeruiah, sisters of David. Possibly an alternate name for Jesse, or the former husband of Jesse's wife. 2 Sam. 17:25.

NAHATH [NAY-hath]
1. 1875 B.C. A grandson of Esau and an Edomite chief. Gen. 36:13,17.
2. B.C. (date unknown). An ancestor of Samuel, listed in the genealogy of Levi in 1 Chr. 6:26.
3. 725 B.C. A Levite who served in the Temple during the reign of Hezekiah. 2 Chr. 31:13.

NAHBI [NAH-bi] 1450 B.C. Leader from the tribe of Naphtali sent by Moses to explore the land of Canaan. Num. 13:14.

NAHOR [NAY-hohr] KJV: Nachor (Josh. 24:2; Lk. 3:34).
1. B.C. (date unknown). Ancestor of Abraham. Gen. 11:22-25; Lk. 3:34.
2. 2150 B.C. Brother of Abraham; he married Milcah, daughter of his brother Haran. Gen. 11:26-29; 22:20-23. **Granddaughter:** Rebekah.

NAHSHON [NAH-shahn] 1450 B.C. KJV: Nahshon (Ex. 6:23); KJV NT: Naasson. Brother-in-law of Aaron and leader of the tribe of Judah at the time of the Exodus. Ancestor of David and Christ. Ex. 6:23; Num. 1:7; 1 Chr. 2:10,11; Mt. 1:4; Lk. 3:32.

NAHUM [NAY-hum; "comforter"] KJV: Naum (Lk. 3:25).
1.* 650 B.C. A minor prophet from the city of Elkosh; his words are recorded in the Book of Nahum. In his poetic oracle, he prophesied that Nineveh, the capital of Assyria, would be overthrown, and bring to an end that powerful and oppressive nation. Nah. 1:1.
2. B.C. (date unknown). A descendant of Zerubbabel and ancestor of Christ. Lk. 3:25.

NAOMI* [nay-OH-mee; "pleasantness" or "my joy"] 1125 B.C. The mother-in-law of Ruth; her husband, Elimelech, and two sons died, so she returned from Moab to Bethlehem, accompanied by Ruth. She asked Ruth to call her "Mara," which means "bitterness," in contrast to the meaning of "Naomi." Ruth 1–4.

NAPHISH [NAY-fish] 2025 B.C. A son of Ishmael and ancestral head of an Ishmaelite tribe (1 Chr. 5:19). Gen. 25:15; 1 Chr. 1:31.

NAPHTALI [NAF-tuh-li; "wrestle"] 2000 B.C. Sixth son of Jacob and ancestral source of one of the twelve tribes of Israel. Gen. 30:8; 46:24; 49:21; 1 Chr. 7:13.

NARCISSUS [nahr-SIS-uhs] A.D. 55. Head of a household, some of whom were Christians. Rom. 16:11.

NATHAN [NAY-thuhn; "gift"]
1. B.C. (date unknown). Listed only in the genealogy of Judah in 1 Chr. 2:36.
2. 1025 B.C. A man from Zobah and father of Igal, one of David's mighty men. 2 Sam. 23:36. In the parallel text in 1 Chr. 11:38 he is the brother of Joel.

3.* 1000 B.C. The court prophet who rebuked David for his adultery with Bathsheba and the murder of her husband, Uriah the Hittite. He later helped prevent Adonijah from seizing the throne. 2 Sam. 7:1-17; 12:1-15,25; 1 Ki. 1:8-45; 1 Chr. 29:29.

4. 975 B.C. A son born to David in Jerusalem. 2 Sam. 5:14; 1 Chr. 3:5; Zech. 12:12; Lk. 3:31.

5. 975 B.C. Father of Azariah and Zabud, two of Solomon's officials. 1 Ki. 4:5. Possibly the same as Nathan 3 or 4.

6. 450 B.C. A Jewish leader sent by Ezra to Iddo at Casiphia to retrieve Levites for the Temple. Ezra 8:16.

7. 450 B.C. One who took a foreign wife after the Exile. Ezra 10:39

NATHANAEL* [nuh-THAN-ee-uhl; "God has given"] A.D. 30. A Galilean called to become a disciple of Christ. Jn. 1:45-51; 21:2. Some identify him with Bartholomew.

NATHAN-MELECH [NAY-thuhn-MEL-ek; "king's gift"] 625 B.C. An official during the reign of Josiah, king of Judah. 2 Ki. 23:11.

NEARIAH [NEE-uh-RI-uh]
1. 725 B.C. A Simeonite leader who invaded the hill country of Seir in the time of Hezekiah. 1 Chr. 4:42.
2. B.C. (date unknown). A descendant of Zerubbabel listed in the genealogy of the royal line. 1 Chr. 3:22,23.

NEBAI [NEE-bi] 450 B.C. A Jewish leader who sealed the covenant renewal with God in Nehemiah's time. Neh. 10:19.

NEBAIOTH [neh-BAY-yahth] 2025 B.C. KJV: Nebajoth. Firstborn son of Ishmael and ancestral head of a North Arabian tribe (Isa. 60:7). Gen. 25:13.

NEBAT [NEE-bat] 950 B.C. Father of Jeroboam I. 1 Ki. 11:26; 12:2,15.

NEBO [NEE-boh; "to announce" or "height"]
1. A Babylonian deity, god of wisdom, mentioned with Bel (Marduk) in Isaiah's prophecy of Babylon's fall. Isa. 46:1.
2. B.C. (date unknown). Ancestor of some who took foreign wives after the Exile. Ezra 10:43. Possibly a reference to a city.

NEBO-SARSEKIM [NEE-boh-SAHR-suh-kim] 600 B.C. An official of Nebuchadnezzar present at the fall of Jerusalem. Jer. 39:3. KJV and RSV have the names "Samgar-nebo" and "Sarsechim" instead.

NEBUCHADNEZZAR*
[NEB-uh-kuhd-NEZ-urh; "may Nebo protect my boundary"] 605–562 B.C. KJV, RSV variant: Nebuchadrezzar. Son of Nabopolassar and father of Evil-Merodach. The powerful king of Babylon who captured Jerusalem and deported the Jews to Babylon. The Book of Daniel tells of his period of madness, which lasted seven years, until he acknowledged the sovereignty of the Lord and was restored. 2 Ki. 24,25; 2 Chr. 36; Dan. 1–4.

NEBUSHAZBAN [NEB-uh-SHAZ-ban; "Nebo deliver me"] 600 B.C. KJV: Nebushasban. A chief Babylonian officer instructed by Nebuchadnezzar to free Jeremiah following his seizure at the fall of Jerusalem. Jer. 39:13.

NEBUZARADAN [NEB-uh-zahr-AY-duhn; "Nebo has given offspring"] 600 B.C. Commander of the imperial guard under Nebuchadnezzar; he led the Babylonian army at the fall of Jerusalem, and took the Jews into exile. 2 Ki. 25:8-20; Jer. 39:9-14; 52:12-30.

NECO [NEE-koh] 609–595 B.C. KJV: Necho (2 Chronicles); Nechoh (2 Kings). Pharaoh who killed King Josiah at Megiddo; later he made Jehoiakim king of Judah in place of Jehoahaz. He was subsequently defeated by

Nebuchadnezzar, in 605 B.C. 2 Ki. 23:29-35; 2 Chr. 35:20–36:4; Jer. 46:2.

NEDABIAH [NED-uh-BI-uh; "Yahweh is willing"] 550 B.C. A son of Jehoiachin, listed in the genealogy of the royal line after the Exile. 1 Chr. 3:18.

NEHEMIAH [NEE-uh-MI-uh; "Yahweh comforts"]
1. 525 B.C. One who returned to Judah with Zerubbabel. Ezra 2:2; Neh. 7:7.
2.* 450 B.C. The righteous governor who led the Jews in the rebuilding of Jerusalem's wall. His words are recorded in the Book of Nehemiah. Neh. 1–13. Possibly the same as Sheshbazzar.
3. 450 B.C. Son of Azbuk; he helped repair the wall of Jerusalem. Neh. 3:16.

NEHUM [NEE-hum] 525 B.C. One who returned to Judah with Zerubbabel after the Exile. Neh. 7:7. Called Rehum in Ezra 2:2.

NEHUSHTA [neh-HUSH-tuh] 625 B.C. Wife of Jehoiakim and mother of Jehoiachin. 2 Ki. 24:8.

NEKODA [neh-KOH-duh]
1. B.C. (date unknown). Ancestral head of a family of Temple servants that returned to Judah after the Exile. Ezra 2:48; Neh. 7:50.
2. B.C. (date unknown). Ancestor of some of the returned exiles who were unable to prove Israelite descent. Ezra 2:60; Neh. 7:62.

NEMUEL [NEM-yoo-uhl]
1. 1875 B.C. A son of Simeon and ancestral head of a clan. Num. 26:12; 1 Chr. 4:24. Called Jemuel in Gen. 46:10 and Ex. 6:15.
2. 1425 B.C. A Reubenite; brother of Dathan and Abiram, who rebelled against Moses. Num. 26:9.

NEPHEG [NEE-feg; "sprout"]
1. B.C. (date unknown). A Levite listed in the family record of Moses and Aaron. Ex. 6:21.
2. 975 B.C. A son of David born in Jerusalem. 2 Sam. 5:15.

NEPHUSSIM [neh-FOO-sim] KJV: Nephusim, RSV: Nephisim (Ezra 2:50); KJV: Nephishesim, RSV: Nephushesim (Neh. 7:52). Ancestor of some Temple servants who returned to Judah after the Exile. Ezra 2:50; Neh. 7:52. Probably the same as Naphish.

NER [NUHR; "light" or "lamp"]
1. 1100 B.C. Grandfather of King Saul. 1 Chr. 8:33.
2. 1100 B.C. Father of Abner. Uncle or grand-uncle of Saul. 1 Sam. 14:50,51; 26:5,14. He may be the same as Ner 1.

NEREUS [NEER-ee-uhs] A.D. 55. A Roman Christian greeted by Paul. Rom. 16:15.

NERGAL [NUHR-gahl] Akkadian deity of pestilence and death, worshiped by men of Cuthah who were deported to Samaria by the Assyrians. 2 Ki. 17:30.

NERGAL-SHAREZER
[NUHR-gahl-shahr-EE-zuhr; "may Nergal protect the king"] 600 B.C. A Babylonian official present at the fall of Jerusalem. Probably identical to Neriglissar, who later assassinated his brother-in-law, Evil-Merodach, Nebuchadnezzar's son and successor. Neriglissar thereafter seized the throne and reigned from 559–556 B.C. Jer. 39:3,13.

NERI [NEER-i; shortened form of Neriah] B.C. (date unknown). Listed only in the genealogy of Jesus in Lk. 3:27.

NERIAH [nuh-RI-uh; "Yahweh is light"] 625 B.C. A man of Judah whose sons, Baruch and Seraiah, served Jeremiah the prophet. Jer. 32:12,16; 51:59.

NETHANEL [nuh-THAN-uhl; "gift of God"] KJV: Nethaneel.
1. 1450 B.C. Leader of the tribe of Issachar at the time of the Exodus. Num. 1:8.
2. 1025 B.C. Fourth son of Jesse and older brother of David. 1 Chr. 2:14.
3. 1000 B.C. A priest who blew the trumpet before the ark as it was brought by David to Jerusalem. 1 Chr. 15:24.
4. 1000 B.C. A Levite; father of Shemaiah the scribe. 1 Chr. 24:6.
5. 975 B.C. Fifth son of Obed-Edom and a Temple gatekeeper appointed by David. 1 Chr. 26:4.
6. 875 B.C. An official under Jehoshaphat sent to teach the Law throughout Judah. 2 Chr. 17:7.
7. 625 B.C. A chief Levite who provided offerings for the Passover celebration in Josiah's time. 2 Chr. 35:9.
8. 500 B.C. Head of a priestly family in the time of Joiakim the high priest. Neh. 12:21.
9. 450 B.C. A priest who took a foreign wife after the Exile. Ezra 10:22.
10. 450 B.C. A Levite who played music at the dedication of the wall of Jerusalem in Nehemiah's time. Neh. 12:36.

NETHANIAH [NETH-uh-NI-uh; "gift of Yahweh"]
1. 975 B.C. A son of Asaph and a Temple singer. 1 Chr. 25:2,12
2. 875 B.C. A Levite who instructed people in the Law in Jehoshaphat's time. 2 Chr. 17:8.
3. 600 B.C. Father of Jehudi, an official of Jehoiakim. Jer. 36:14.
4. 575 B.C. Father of Ishmael, the military officer who murdered Gedaliah, governor of Judah. 2 Ki. 25:23,25; Jer. 40:8–41:18.

NEZIAH [neh-ZI-uh; "faithful"] B.C. (date unknown). Ancestral head of a family of Temple servants that returned to Judah with Zerubbabel after the Exile. Ezra 2:54; Neh. 7:56.

NIBHAZ [NIB-haz] A deity worshiped by the Avvites resettled in Samaria after the deportation of the Israelites in 722 B.C. 2 Ki. 17:31.

NICANOR [ni-KAY-nohr; "conqueror"] A.D. 35. One of the seven disciples chosen to oversee distribution of food in the Christian community in Jerusalem. Acts 6:5.

NICODEMUS* [NIK-uh-DEE-muhs; "conqueror of the people"] A.D. 30. A Pharisee and member of the Sanhedrin who secretly spoke with Jesus; he helped prepare the body of Christ for burial. Jn. 3:1-21; 7:50-52; 19:39.

NICOLAS [NIK-uh-luhs; "conqueror of the people"] A.D. 35. RSV: Nicolaus. A convert from Antioch, one of the seven appointed to distribute food to the poor. Acts 6:5.

NIGER [NI-juhr; "black"] A.D. 45. Surname of Simeon, one of the prophets and teachers of the church at Antioch. Acts 13:1. Possibly the same as Simon the Cyrene.

NIMROD* [NIM-rahd] B.C. (date unknown). Renowned warrior and hunter listed among the Hamites in the Table of Nations; he established a kingdom in Babylonia, later extended into Assyria. Founder of many ancient cities, among them, Erech, Babel, Akkad, and Nineveh. Gen. 10:8-12; Mic. 5:6.

NIMSHI [NIM-shi] 900 B.C. Grandfather of Jehu, king of Israel. 1 Ki. 19:16; 2 Ki. 9:2,14,20.

NISROCH [NIS-rahk] Assyrian deity in whose temple King Sennacherib of Assyria was assassinated by two of his sons. 2 Ki. 19:37; Isa. 37:38. Historical identification is uncertain; possibly a corruption of the original name.

NOADIAH [NOH-uh-DI-uh; "Yahweh assembles"]
1. 450 B.C. A Levite who helped weigh out the sacred articles for the Temple. Ezra 8:33.
2. 450 B.C. A prophetess who opposed Nehemiah. Neh. 6:14.

NOAH [NOH-uh; "rest" or "comfort"]
1.* B.C. (date unknown). The righteous man who built the ark; he and his family alone survived the Genesis Flood. Gen. 5:28-32; 6:8–9:29; Mt. 24:38,39; Heb. 11:7.
2. 1400 B.C. One of the daughters of Zelophehad given their father's land as inheritance. Num. 26:33; 27:1.

NOBAH [NOH-buh] 1400 B.C. A man of Manasseh who captured Kenath and renamed it Nobah after himself. Num. 32:42.

NODAB [NOH-dab] B.C. (date unknown). Ancestral head of an Arabian tribe defeated by the tribes of Reuben, Gad, and Manasseh. 1 Chr. 5:19. Possibly the same as Kedamah, son of Ishmael.

NOGAH [NOH-guh; "splendor"] 975 B.C. A son born to David in Jerusalem. 1 Chr. 3:7; 14:6.

NOHAH [NOH-hah; "rest"] 1850 B.C. A son of Benjamin, according to 1 Chr. 8:2. Omitted from his list of sons in Gen. 46:21.

NUN [NUN; "fish"] 1475 B.C. An Ephraimite; father of Joshua. Ex. 33:11; Josh. 1:1; 1 Chr. 7:27.

NYMPHA [NIM-fuh] A.D. 60. KJV: Nymphas. A Christian whose house served as a church. Col. 4:15. It is uncertain whether the name refers to a man or a woman.

O

OBADIAH [OH-buh-DI-uh; "servant of Yahweh"]
1. B.C. (date unknown). Listed only in the genealogy of Issachar in 1 Chr. 7:3.
2. 1000 B.C. A Gadite commander who joined David at Ziklag. 1 Chr. 12:9.
3. 1000 B.C. Father of Ishmaiah, officer of the tribe of Zebulun in David's day. 1 Chr. 27:19.
4. 875 B.C. An official of Jehoshaphat sent throughout Judah to instruct the people in the Law. 2 Chr. 17:7.
5. 875 B.C. Devout follower of Yahweh in charge of Ahab's palace. During Queen Jezebel's persecutions, he hid 100 prophets of God in two caves. He feared for his life when asked by Elijah to relay a message to King Ahab. 1 Ki. 18:1-16.
6. B.C. (date unknown). A descendant of Jonathan, son of Saul, listed in the genealogy of Benjamin in 1 Chr. 8:38; 9:44.
7. 625 B.C. A Levite who supervised the restoration of the Temple in Josiah's time. 2 Chr. 34:12.

8. 500 B.C. A chief gatekeeper who served in the days of Joiakim. Neh. 12:25.
9.* Sixth century B.C. (or ninth). A minor prophet whose prophecy against Edom is recorded in the Book of Obadiah, the shortest book in the OT. Obad. 1.
10. B.C. (date unknown). A descendant of Zerubbabel listed in the genealogy of the royal line of Judah. 1 Chr. 3:21.
11. 450 B.C. A Levite descended from Jeduthun the minister of music. 1 Chr. 9:16. Called Abda in Neh. 11:17.
12. 450 B.C. Head of a family that returned to Judah with Zerubbabel. Ezra 8:9.
13. 450 B.C. A priest who sealed the covenant renewal with God in Nehemiah's time. Neh. 10:5.

OBAL [OH-buhl] B.C. (date unknown). KJV, RSV: Ebal (1 Chr. 1:22). Son of Joktan listed in the Table of Nations; ancestral source of an Arabian tribe. Gen. 10:28; 1 Chr. 1:22.

OBED [OH-bed; "worshiper" or "servant"]
1. 1075 B.C. Son of Ruth and Boaz, and grandfather of David. Ruth 4:17,21,22; 1 Chr. 2:12.
2. B.C. (date unknown). Listed only in the genealogy of Judah in 1 Chr. 2:37,38.
3. 1000 B.C. A military commander, one of David's thirty mighty men. 1 Chr. 11:47.
4. 975 B.C. A grandson of Obed-Edom and a Temple gatekeeper. 1 Chr. 26:7.
5. 875 B.C. Father of Azariah, a military commander who helped Jehoiada overthrow Queen Athaliah. 2 Chr. 23:1.

OBED-EDOM [OH-bed-EE-duhm; "servant of Edom"]
1. 1000 B.C. A man of Gath in whose house the ark of the Lord remained for three months. 2 Sam. 6:10-12; 1 Chr. 13:13,14; 1 Chr. 15:25.
2. 1000 B.C. Son of Jeduthun and a chief gatekeeper appointed by David. 1 Chr. 15:18,24; 16:5,38; 26:4-8.
3. 800 B.C. Temple treasurer in the time of Amaziah, king of Judah. 2 Chr. 25:24.

OBIL [OH-bil; "camel driver"] 975 B.C. An Ishmaelite; overseer of King David's camels. 1 Chr. 27:30.

OCRAN [AHK-ruhn; "trouble"] 1450 B.C. RSV: Ochran. Father of Pagiel, leader of the tribe of Asher at the time of the Exodus. Num. 1:13.

ODED [OH-ded; "restorer"]
1. 925 B.C. Father of Azariah, a prophet who encouraged Asa to seek the Lord. 2 Chr. 15:1-8. The KJV mistakenly makes Oded himself the prophet.
2. 750 B.C. A prophet who opposed the enslavement of captives Pekah took in his war with Ahaz, king of Judah. 2 Chr. 28:9-11.

OG [AHG] 1400 B.C. Amorite king of Bashan defeated by the Israelites under Moses. He was the last of the giant Rephaites. Num. 21:33-35; Deut. 3:1-13.

OHAD [OH-had] 1875 B.C. A son of Simeon. Gen. 46:10; Ex. 6:15.

OHEL [OH-hel; "tent"] 500 B.C. A son of Zerubbabel listed in the genealogy of the royal line after the Exile. 1 Chr. 3:20.

OHOLIAB [oh-HOHL-lee-ab; "father's tent"] 1450 B.C. KJV: Aholiab. A Danite craftsman appointed to assist Bezalel in the construction of the tabernacle and its furnishings. Ex. 31:6; 35:34–36:2.

OHOLIBAMAH [oh-HOH-lih-BAH-muh; "tent of the high place"] KJV: Aholibamah.
1. 1950 B.C. Horite wife of Esau. Gen. 36:14,25. Possibly the same as Judith, in Gen. 26:34.

2. B.C. (date unknown). An Edomite chief descended from Esau. Gen. 36:41.

OLYMPAS [oh-LIM-puhs] A.D. 55. A Roman Christian to whom Paul sent greetings. Rom. 16:15.

OMAR [OH-mahr] 1875 B.C. A son of Eliphaz and grandson of Esau. Gen. 36:11,15.

OMRI [AHM-ree]
1. B.C. (date unknown). Listed in the genealogy of Benjamin in 1 Chr. 7:8.
2. 975 B.C. Officer over the tribe of Issachar in David's day. 1 Chr. 27:18.
3. 885–874 B.C. The commander of King Elah's army who became king of Israel after Zimri murdered Elah. Founder of Samaria, capital of the Northern Kingdom. 1 Ki. 16:16-29. **Son and successor:** Ahab.
4. B.C. (date unknown). Ancestor of Uthai, a Judahite who resettled in Jerusalem after the Exile. 1 Chr. 9:4.

ON [AHN; "strength"] 1450 B.C. A Reubenite leader who joined Korah in a rebellion against Moses. Num. 16:1.

ONAM [OH-nam; "vigorous"]
1. 1950 B.C. A son of Shobal, a Horite chief who lived in the land of Seir in Esau's time. Gen. 36:23.
2. B.C. (date unknown). Listed in the genealogy of Judah in 1 Chr. 2:26,28.

ONAN [OH-nan; "vigorous"] 1875 B.C. Second son of Judah, slain by the Lord for his disobedience. Gen. 38:4,8,9; 46:12.

ONESIMUS* [oh-NES-ih-muhs; "profitable"] A.D. 60. A slave on whose behalf Paul wrote a letter to his master, Philemon. Col. 4:9; Phlm. 10.

ONESIPHORUS [on-uh-SIF-uh-ruhs; "profit-bringer"] A.D. 65. A Christian who ministered to Paul during his imprisonment in Rome. 2 Tim. 1:16; 4:19.

OPHIR [OH-fuhr; "rich"] B.C. (date unknown). A son of Joktan, listed in the Table of Nations; ancestral source of the people who inhabited Ophir. Gen. 10:29.

OPHRA [AHF-ruh; "fawn"] 1350 B.C. KJV, RSV: Ophrah. A grandson of Othniel, listed in the genealogy of Judah. 1 Chr. 4:14.

OREB [OHR-eb; "raven"] 1175 B.C. A Midianite leader put to death by Ephraimites led by Gideon. Jdg. 7:25; 8:3; Ps. 83:11.

OREN [OHR-en; "fir tree"] B.C. (date unknown). A son of Jerahmeel, listed in genealogy of Judah. 1 Chr. 2:25.

ORPAH [OHR-puh] 1100 B.C. Moabite wife of Kilion, son of Naomi and Elimelech. She returned to her home after the death of her husband. Ruth 1:4,14.

OTHNI [AHTH-ni] 975 B.C. A son of Shemaiah and grandson of Obed-Edom; he served as a Temple gatekeeper. 1 Chr. 26:7.

OTHNIEL [AHTH-nee-uhl; "God is might"(?)] 1374–1334 B.C. The first judge of Israel following the death of Joshua. Caleb, his uncle, gave him his daughter Acsah when he recaptured Debir. Josh. 15:17,18; Jdg. 1:13,14; 3:7-11; 1 Chr. 4:13.

OZEM [OH-zuhm]
1. B.C. (date unknown). Son of Jerahmeel, listed in the genealogy of Judah in 1 Chr. 2:25.
2. 1025 B.C. Sixth son of Jesse and older brother of David. 1 Chr. 2:15.

OZNI [AHZ-ni] 1875 B.C. Ancestral head of a Gadite clan. Num. 26:16. Same as Ezbon, son of Gad, in Gen. 46:16.

P

PAARAI [PAY-uh-ri] 1000 B.C. A military commander, one of David's thirty mighty men. 2 Sam. 23:35. Called Naarai in 1 Chr. 11:37.

PADON [PAY-dahn; "redemption"] B.C. (date unknown). Ancestral head of a family of Temple servants that returned to Judah with Zerubbabel. Ezra 2:44; Neh. 7:47.

PAGIEL [PAY-gee-uhl] 1450 B.C. Leader of the tribe of Asher at the time of the Exodus. Num. 1:13; 7:72-77.

PAHATH-MOAB [PAY-hath-MOH-ab; "ruler of Moab"]
1. B.C. (date unknown). Ancestral head of a family that returned to Judah with Zerubbabel; the name may be a title. Ezra 2:6; 8:4; Neh. 3:11.
2. 450 B.C. A Jewish leader who sealed the covenant renewal with God in Nehemiah's time, probably with the name of his family ancestor (see Pahath-Moab 1). Neh. 10:14.

PALAL [PAY-lal; "judge"] 450 B.C. One who helped rebuild the wall of Jerusalem in Nehemiah's time. Neh. 3:25.

PALLU [PAL-oo; "distinguished"] 1900 B.C. KJV: Phallu (Gen. 46:9). Second son of Reuben, the firstborn son of Jacob. Gen. 46:9; Ex. 6:14; Num. 26:5.

PALTI [PAL-ti; "Yahweh delivers"] 1400 B.C. Leader from the tribe of Benjamin sent by Moses to explore Canaan. Num. 13:9.

PALTIEL [PAL-tee-uhl; "God delivers"] KJV: Phalti, and RSV: Palti (1 Sam. 25:44); KJV: Phaltiel (2 Sam. 3:15).
1. 1400 B.C. Leader from the tribe of Issachar appointed to help divide the land of Canaan. Num. 34:26.
2. 1025 B.C. A Benjamite to whom Saul gave his daughter Michal, although she was already David's wife. She was later taken away from Paltiel and restored to David. 1 Sam. 25:44; 2 Sam. 3:15.

PARMASHTA [pahr-MASH-tuh] 475 B.C. One of the ten sons of Haman slain by the Jews. Esth. 9:9.

PARMENAS [PAHR-muh-nuhs; "steadfast"] A.D. 35. One of the seven disciples appointed to distribute food among the poor. Acts 6:5.

PARNACH [PAHR-nak; "gifted"(?)] 1425 B.C. Father of Elizaphan, leader from the tribe of Zebulun appointed to divide the land of Canaan. Num. 34:25.

PAROSH [PAIR-ahsh] KJV: Pharosh (Ezra 8:3).
1. B.C. (date unknown). Ancestral head of a post-exilic family. Ezra 2:3; 8:3; 10:25; Neh. 3:25.
2. 450 B.C. A Jewish leader who sealed the covenant renewal with God in Nehemiah's time, probably with the name of a family ancestor (see Parosh 1). Neh. 10:14.

PARSHANDATHA [pahr-shan-DAY-thuh] 475 B.C. A son of Haman put to death by the Jews in the citadel of Susa. Esth. 9:7.

PARUAH [puh-ROO-uh; "blooming"] 975 B.C. Father of Jehoshaphat, one of Solomon's district governors. 1 Ki. 4:17.

PASACH [PAY-sak] B.C. (date unknown). Listed only in the genealogy of Asher in 1 Chr. 7:33.

PASEAH [puh-SEE-uh; "limping"] KJV: Phaseah (Ezra 2:49; Neh. 7:51)
1. B.C. (date unknown). Listed only in the genealogy of Judah in 1 Chr. 4:12.
2. B.C. (date unknown). Ancestral head of a family of Temple servants that returned to Judah with Zerubbabel. Ezra 2:49; Neh. 7:51.
3. 475 B.C. Father of Joiada, one of the rebuilders of the wall of Jerusalem in Nehemiah's time. Neh. 3:6.

PASHHUR [PASH-hur] KJV: Pashur.
1. B.C. (date unknown). Ancestral head of a priestly family that returned to Judah after the Exile. Ezra 2:38; 10:22; Neh. 7:41.
2. 625 B.C. Father of Gedaliah, one of the officials of Zedekiah who threw Jeremiah into a cistern. Jer. 38:1. Possibly the same as Pashhur 3 or 4.
3. 600 B.C. A priest who put Jeremiah in stocks; he was denounced by Jeremiah, who named him "Magor-Missabib," which means "terror on every side." Jer. 20:1-6.
4. 600 B.C. An official of Zedekiah sent to inquire of Jeremiah; later he was among the officials who threw Jeremiah into a cistern to die. Jer. 21:1; 38:1.
5. B.C. (date unknown). Ancestor of Adaiah, a priest who resettled in Jerusalem after the Exile. 1 Chr. 9:12; Neh. 11:12. Probably the same as Pashhur 4.
6. 450 B.C. A priest who sealed the covenant renewal with God in Nehemiah's time, possibly with the name of his family ancestor (see Pashhur 1). Neh. 10:3.

PATROBAS [PAT-ruh-buhs; "paternal"] A.D. 55. A Roman Christian to whom Paul sent greetings. Rom. 16:14.

PAUL* [PAWL; "little"] A.D. 35. Notable as a Pharisee who mercilessly persecuted the early Christians until his miraculous conversion on the road to Damascus. Thereafter, he became the apostle to the Gentiles. Author of thirteen NT Epistles. Acts 7:57,58; 8:1-3; 9; 13–28. His Hebrew name is Saul.

PEDAHEL [PED-uh-hel; "God has redeemed"] 1400 B.C. Leader from the tribe of Naphtali appointed to help assign inheritances within the land of Canaan. Num. 34:28.

PEDAHZUR [peh-DAH-zuhr; "the rock has redeemed"] 1475 B.C. Father of Gamaliel, leader of the tribe of Manasseh at the time of the Exodus. Num. 1:10.

PEDAIAH [puh-DAY-yuh; "Yahweh has redeemed"]
1. 1000 B.C. Father of Joel, officer over half the tribe of Manasseh in David's day. 1 Chr. 27:20.
2. 650 B.C. Father of Zebidah, the mother of Jehoiakim. 2 Ki. 23:36.
3. 550 B.C. A son of Jehoiachin; he is listed as the father of Zerubbabel in the genealogy of the royal line after the Exile, but elsewhere his brother Shealtiel is given as Zerubbabel's father (compare Ezra 3:2; Neh. 12:1). 1 Chr. 3:18,19.
4. B.C. (date unknown). Ancestor of Sallu, a Benjamite who resettled in Jerusalem after the Exile. Neh. 11:7.
5. 450 B.C. One who helped rebuild Jerusalem's wall. Neh. 3:25.
6. 450 B.C. One who stood to the left of Ezra at the reading of the Law. Neh. 8:4.

7. 425 B.C. A Levite put in charge of the storerooms of food by Nehemiah. Neh. 13:13. Possibly the same as Pedaiah 5 or 6.

PEKAH [PEE-kuh; "he opens" or "he sees"] 752–732 B.C. A powerful military officer during the reign of Pekahiah who assassinated the king and seized the throne of Israel. An ill-fated alliance with Rezin, king of Syria, against Tiglath-Pileser resulted in successive defeats at the hands of the Assyrians. He was assassinated by his successor, Hoshea. 2 Ki. 15:25-31; 16:5; 2 Chr. 28:6; Isa. 7:1.

PEKAHIAH [PEH-kuh-HI-uh; "Yahweh opens" or "Yahweh sees"] 742–740 B.C. Son and successor of Menahem, king of Israel. He was assassinated by Pekah. 2 Ki. 15:22-26.

PELAIAH [puh-LAY-yuh; "Yahweh is marvelous"]
1. 450 B.C. A Levite who interpreted for the people as Ezra read the Law. Neh. 8:7.
2. 450 B.C. A Levite who sealed the covenant renewal with God in Nehemiah's time. Neh. 10:10. Possibly the same as Pelaiah 1.
3. B.C. (date unknown). A descendant of Zerubbabel, listed only in the genealogy of the royal line after the Exile. 1 Chr. 3:24.

PELALIAH [PEL-uh-LI-uh; "Yahweh judges"] B.C. (date unknown). Ancestor of a priest who resettled in Jerusalem after the Exile. Neh. 11:12.

PELATIAH [PEL-uh-TI-uh; "Yahweh delivers"]
1. 725 B.C. A leader of the Simeonites who destroyed the remaining Amalekites in the hill country of Seir. 1 Chr. 4:42.
2. 600 B.C. A leader in Jerusalem seen by Ezekiel giving "wicked advice." As Ezekiel prophesied, Pelatiah fell dead as a sign of the Lord's judgment of Israel's leaders. Ezek. 11:1-13.
3. B.C. (date unknown). A descendant of Zerubbabel listed in the genealogy of the royal line after the Exile. 1 Chr. 3:21.
4. 450 B.C. A Jewish leader who sealed the covenant renewal with God in Nehemiah's time. Neh. 10:22.

PELEG [PEE-leg; "division" or "channel"] B.C. (date unknown). KJV: Phalec. A descendant of Shem and an ancestor of Abraham. So named because "in his time the earth was divided." Gen. 10:25; 11:16-19; Lk. 3:35.

PELET [PEE-let; "deliverance"]
1. B.C. (date unknown). A Judahite, listed in the genealogy of the clans of Caleb in 1 Chr. 2:47.
2. 1000 B.C. A Benjamite, one of the two sons of Azmaveth who joined David's army at Ziklag. 1 Chr. 12:3.

PELETH [PEE-leth; "swiftness"]
1. 1475 B.C. Father of On, one of the Reubenites who rebelled against Moses. Num. 16:1.
2. B.C. (date unknown). Listed only in the genealogy of Judah in 1 Chr. 2:33.

PENINNAH [peh-NIN-uh; "coral"] 1125 B.C. One of the two wives of Elkanah; she had children while Hannah remained childless. 1 Sam. 1:2-7.

PENUEL [peh-NOO-uhl; "face of God"]
1. B.C. (date unknown). Listed only in the genealogy of Judah in 1 Chr. 4:4.
2. B.C. (date unknown). Listed only in the genealogy of Benjamin in 1 Chr. 8:25.

PERESH [PEER-esh] B.C. (date unknown). Listed in the genealogy of Manasseh. 1 Chr. 7:16.

PEREZ [PEER-ez; "bursting forth"] 1850 B.C. KJV OT: Pharez; KJV NT: Phares. One of the twin sons born to Judah by his daughter-in-law, Tamar. He was an ancestor of Christ. Gen. 38:29; 46:12; Mt. 1:3.

PERIDA [puh-RI-duh; "divided"] B.C. (date unknown). A servant of Solomon and ancestor of a family that returned to Judah with Zerubbabel. Neh. 7:57. Called Peruda in Ezra 2:55.

PERSIS [PUHR-sis; "Persian woman"] A.D. 55. A Christian woman at the church in Rome greeted by Paul as a dear friend who "has worked very hard in the Lord." Rom. 16:12.

PERUDA [puh-ROO-duh] B.C. (date unknown). One whose descendants returned to Judah after the Exile. Ezra 2:55. See Perida.

PETER* [PEE-tuhr; "rock"] A.D. 30. The prominent apostle who denied Christ three times; he later became a leader in the early church and according to tradition, suffered martyrdom under Nero. Author of the two Epistles that bear his name. His original name was Simon, which Christ changed to Peter, or Cephas in Aramaic. **Brother:** Andrew. Mt. 16:13-23; 26:32-46,69-75; Jn. 21; Acts 1–5; 9:32–12; 15.

PETHAHIAH [PETH-uh-HI-uh; "Yahweh opens up"]
1. 975 B.C. Head of the nineteenth division of priests appointed by David. 1 Chr. 24:16.
2. 450 B.C. A Levite who took a foreign wife after the Exile. Ezra 10:23.
3. 450 B.C. A Levite who led the people in a public confession at the ceremony of covenant renewal. Neh. 9:5. Probably the same as Pethahiah 2.
4. 450 B.C. A Judahite who was the agent of King Artaxerxes "in all affairs relating to the people." Neh. 11:24.

PETHUEL [puh-THOO-uhl] B.C. (date unknown). Father of Joel the prophet. Joel 1:1.

PEULLETHAI [pee-UHL-uh-thi] 975 B.C. KJV: Peulthai. Eighth son of Obed-Edom and a gatekeeper appointed by David. 1 Chr. 26:5.

PHANUEL [fuh-NOO-uhl] 75 B.C. An Asherite, father of Anna the prophetess. Lk. 2:36.

PHARAOH* [FAIR-oh; "great house"] Royal title of Egyptian rulers. See Hophra, Neco.

PHICOL [FI-kahl] 2050 B.C. KJV: Phichol. Philistine commander in charge of Abimelech's army in the time of Abraham and Isaac. Gen. 21:22-32; 26:26. Many scholars believe this is a title, like Abimelech, and the events described involve two persons.

PHILEMON* [fi-LEE-muhn; "friendship"] A.D. 60. An important Christian to whom Paul wrote the Epistle bearing this name. In his letter to Philemon, Paul exhorts him to accept Onesimus back, not as a slave, but as "a brother in the Lord." Phlm. 1.

PHILETUS [fi-LEE-tuhs; "beloved"] A.D. 65. A heretical teacher in the church at Ephesus. 2 Tim. 2:17.

PHILIP [FIL-ip; "lover of horses"]
1. A.D. 25. Herod Philip I, first husband of Herodias, who later married Philip's half-brother, Antipas, resulting in a scandal. He was the father of Salome, who asked for the head of John the Baptist. Mt. 14:3; Mk. 6:17. **Parents:** Herod the Great and Mariamne. See Herod.*
2. 4 B.C.–A.D. 34. Herod Philip II, tetrarch of Iturea and Trachonitis. Unlike that of his brothers, his reign was peaceful and benevolent. He came to be loved by the people under his rule. Lk. 3:1. **Parents:** Herod the Great and Cleopatra of Jerusalem. **Wife:** Salome. See Herod.*
3.* A.D. 30. One of the twelve apostles; like Andrew and Peter, he was from the town of Bethsaida. Mt. 10:3; Jn. 1:43-48; 6:5-7; 12:21,22; 14:8,9; Acts 1:13.

4. A.D. 35. Notable as Philip the evangelist, one of the seven deacons of the church at Jerusalem. He became an important missionary to the Samaritans and Gentiles. Acts 6:5; 8:4-13,26-40; 21:8. **Children:** four daughters who were prophetesses.

PHILOLOGUS [fi-LAHL-uh-guhs; "lover of learning"] A.D. 55. A Roman Christian greeted by Paul. Rom. 16:15.

PHINEHAS [FIN-ee-uhs; "mouth of brass"]
1.* 1400 B.C. Righteous and zealous son of Eleazar, son of Aaron. Ex. 6:25; Num. 25:7-13; Josh. 22:13-34.
2. 1100 B.C. One of the wicked sons of Eli against whom Samuel prophesied. They were slain when the Philistines captured the ark of the Lord. 1 Sam. 1:3; 2:12-17,22-36; 3:11-13; 4:4,11-22. **Brother:** Hophni. **Sons:** Ichabod and Ahitub.
3. 475 B.C. Father of Eleazar, a priest who helped weigh out the sacred articles of the Temple. Ezra 8:33.

PHLEGON [FLEG-ahn; "burning"] A.D. 55. A Roman Christian to whom Paul sent greetings. Rom. 16:14.

PHOEBE* [FEE-bee; "radiant"] A.D. 55. KJV: Phebe. A deaconess at the church at Cenchrea, near Corinth. She may have carried Paul's letter to the church in Rome. Rom. 16:1,2.

PHYGELUS [fi-JEL-uhs; "fugitive"] A.D. 65. KJV: Phygellus. One who deserted Paul in Asia. 2 Tim. 1:15.

PILATE* [PI-luht; "javelin-carrier"] A.D. 26–36. Roman procurator of Judea before whom Christ was brought for trial. Although he found Christ innocent, he yielded to pressure from the Jews and ordered Christ's crucifixion. Mt. 27; Lk. 13:1; 23; Jn. 18:29–19:38. See also Pontius.

PILDASH [PIL-dash] 2050 B.C. Sixth son of Nahor, brother of Abraham. Gen. 22:22.

PILHA [PIL-hah] KJV: Pileha. 450 B.C. A Jewish leader who sealed the covenant renewal with God in Nehemiah's time. Neh. 10:24.

PILTAI [PIL-ti; "Yahweh delivers"] 500 B.C. Head of a priestly family in the time of Joiakim the high priest. Neh. 12:17.

PINON [PI-nahn] B.C. (date unknown). An Edomite chief descended from Esau. Gen. 36:41.

PIRAM [PI-ruhm] 1400 B.C. Amorite king of Jarmuth, among the kings who joined Adoni-Zedek in an attack on Gibeon. The Amorites were defeated by Joshua. Josh. 10:3.

PISPAH [PIS-puh] B.C. (date unknown). RSV: Pispa. Listed only in the genealogy of Asher in 1 Chr. 7:38.

PITHON [PI-thahn] 950 B.C. A great-grandson of Jonathan, son of Saul. 1 Chr. 8:35; 9:41.

POKERETH-HAZZEBAIM [PAHK-uh-reth-HAZ-uh-BAY-uhm; "binder of gazelle"] RSV: Pochereth-Hazzebaim; KJV: "Pochereth of Zebaim." Ancestral head of a family that returned to Judah with Zerubbabel. Ezra 2:57; Neh. 7:59.

POLLUX [PAHL-uks] With Castor, one of the twin gods, sons of Zeus; they became astral deities, the twins of the constellation, Gemini, and were patrons of sailors. Acts 28:11.

PONTIUS [PAHN-shuhs] A.D. 26–36. Roman family name of Pilate, procurator of Judea in the time of Christ. Lk. 3:1; Acts 4:27. See Pilate.

PORATHA [pohr-AY-thuh] 475 B.C. One of the ten sons of Haman slain by the Jews at the citadel of Suza. Esth. 9:8.

PORCIUS [POHR-shee-uhs] See Festus.

POTIPHAR [PAHT-i-fuhr; "whom (the sun god) Re has given"] 1875 B.C. Egyptian captain of the guard who bought Joseph. The false accusation of his wife prompted Potiphar to throw Joseph into prison. Gen. 37:36; 39.

POTIPHERA [pah-TIF-uhr-uh; "given by the sun god"] 1900 B.C. Egyptian priest of On and father of Asenath, wife of Joseph. Gen. 41:45,50.

PRISCILLA* [prih-SIL-uh] A.D. 55. RSV: Prisca (Rom. 16:3). A Christian woman who served with Paul in Corinth; she and her husband, Aquila, led a house church in Ephesus. Acts 18:2,18,26; Rom. 16:3.

PROCORUS [PRAH-kohr-uhs] A.D. 35. KJV, RSV: Prochorus. One of the seven appointed to oversee the daily distribution of food in the Jerusalem church. Acts 6:5.

PUAH [POO-uh] RSV: Puvah (Gen. 46:13, Num. 26:23); KJV: Phuvah (Gen. 46:13).
1. 1875 B.C. A son of Issachar and head of a clan. Gen. 46:13; Num. 26:23.
2. 1525 B.C. A Hebrew midwife who refused to obey the command of Pharaoh to kill Hebrew male infants. Ex. 1:15-21.
3. 1150 B.C. Father of Tola, a minor judge who led Israel for twenty-three years. Judg. 10:1.

PUBLIUS [PUB-lee-uhs] A.D. 60. The chief official on Malta who showed hospitality to Paul after his shipwreck. Paul healed his father. Acts 28:7.

PUDENS [POO-denz; "modest"] A.D. 65. A Christian who with Paul sent greetings to Timothy. 2 Tim. 4:21.

PUL [PUL or POOL] See Tiglath-Pileser.

PURAH [PYOOR-uh] 1175 B.C. KJV: Phurah. Servant who accompanied Gideon in his night reconnaissance of the Midianite camp. Jdg. 7:10,11.

PUT [PUT] KJV: Phut. A son of Ham listed in the Table of Nations, in Gen. 10:6. Generally identified with the nation of Libya.

PUTIEL [POO-tee-uhl] 1425 B.C. Father-in-law of Eleazar, son of Aaron. Ex. 6:25.

PYRRHUS [PEER-uhs; "fiery red"] A.D. 25. Father of Sopater, a companion of Paul. Acts 20:4.

Q

QUARTUS [KWOHR-tus; "fourth"] A.D. 55. A Christian in Corinth who sent greetings to the Roman church through Paul. Rom. 16:23.

QUIRINIUS [kwih-RIN-ee-uhs] 5 B.C. KJV: Cyrenius. Roman governor of Syria at the time of Jesus' birth. Lk. 2:2.

R

RAAMAH [RAY-uh-muh; possibly "thunder" or "trembling"] B.C. (date unknown). A descendant of Ham, listed in the Table of Nations. Gen. 10:7. Possibly the ancestral source of a tribe that dwelt in southwest Arabia.

RAAMIAH [RAY-uh-MI-uh; "Yahweh has thundered"(?)] 525 B.C. One of the twelve Israelite leaders who returned to Judah with Zerubbabel after the Exile. Neh. 7:7. Same as Reelaiah in Ezra 2:2.

RACHEL* [RAY-chuhl; "ewe"] 1925 B.C. KJV: Rahel (Jer. 31:15). Daughter of Laban and younger sister of Leah; both sisters became wives of Jacob. Gen. 29–31; 33; 35:16-20. **Sons:** Joseph and Benjamin.

RADDAI [RAD-i] 1025 B.C. Son of Jesse and an older brother of David. 1 Chr. 2:14.

RAHAB [RAY-hab; "broad"] KJV: Rachab (Mt. 1:5).
1.* 1400 B.C. A prostitute in Jericho who preserved the lives of Joshua's spies. After the destruction of Jericho, she and her family joined the Israelites. She is listed in the genealogy of Christ. Josh. 2; 6:17-25; Mt. 1:5; Heb. 11:31; Jas. 2:25.
2. Name of a mythical sea monster, poetically ascribed to Egypt. Isa. 30:7; 51:9; Job 9:13; Pss. 87:4; 89:10

RAHAM [RAY-ham; "mercy, love"] B.C. (date unknown). A Judahite listed only in the genealogy of the clans of Caleb. 1 Chr. 2:44.

RAKEM [RAY-kuhm] B.C. (date unknown). Listed only in the genealogy of Manasseh in 1 Chr. 7:16.

RAM [RAM] KJV: Aram (Lk. 3:33); RSV: Arni (Lk. 3:33).
1. B.C. (date unknown). Head of the family of Elihu, who contended with Job. Job 32:2.
2. B.C. (date unknown). An ancestor of David and Christ. Ruth 4:19; 1 Chr. 2:9,10; Lk. 3:33.
3. B.C. (date unknown). Firstborn son of Jerahmeel, a descendant of Judah. 1 Chr. 2:25,27.

RAMIAH [ruh-MI-uh; "Yahweh is high"] 450 B.C. One who took a foreign wife after the Exile. Ezra 10:25.

RAPHA [RAY-fuh] KJV, RSV: "Giant" (2 Samuel).
1. B.C. (date unknown). Ancestor of the Philistine giants defeated in battle by Israel in David's time. 2 Sam. 21:16-22; 1 Chr. 20:6-8.
2. 1825 B.C. Listed as the last son of Benjamin, in 1 Chr. 8:2; omitted from list of his sons in Gen. 46:21.

RAPHAH [RAY-fuh] B.C. (date unknown). KJV: Rapha. A descendant of Saul through Jonathan. 1 Chr. 8:37. Called Rephaiah in 1 Chr. 9:43.

RAPHU [RAY-foo; "healed"] 1475 B.C. Father of Palti, leader from the tribe of Benjamin sent to spy out the land of Canaan. Num. 13:9.

REAIAH [ree-AY-yuh; "Yahweh has seen"] KJV: Reaia (1 Chr. 5:5).
1. B.C. (date unknown). Listed in the genealogy of Judah in 1 Chr. 4:2.
2. B.C. (date unknown). Listed in the genealogy of Reuben in 1 Chr. 5:5.
3. B.C. (date unknown). Ancestral head of a family of Temple servants that returned to Judah with Zerubbabel. Ezra 2:47; Neh. 7:50.

REBA [REE-buh] 1400 B.C. One of the five Midianite kings killed in battle by the Israelites under Moses. Num. 31:8; Josh. 13:21.

REBEKAH* [ruh-BEK-uh] 1925 B.C. KJV, RSV: Rebecca (Rom. 9:10). Daughter of Bethuel, Abraham's nephew; the wife of Isaac and mother of the twins Jacob and Esau. Gen. 22:23; 24–27; 49:31; Rom. 9:10.

RECAB [REE-kab; "horseman"] KJV, RSV: Rechab.
1. B.C. (date unknown). Ancestor of Jehonadab, an ally of Jehu against the house of Ahab. Founder of the Recabites, who foreswore wine and lived as nomads. 2 Ki. 10:15,23; 1 Chr. 2:55; Jer. 35.
2. 1000 B.C. A Benjamite from Beeroth who with his brother, Baanah, assassinated Ish-Bosheth, son of Saul. The traitors expected a reward but instead were executed by David. 2 Sam. 4:2-12.
3. 475 B.C. Father of Malkijah, who helped repair the wall of Jerusalem. Neh. 3:14. If the relationship is ancestral, he is probably the same as Recab 1.

REELAIAH [REE-uh-LAY-yuh] 525 B.C. One who returned to Judah with Zerubbabel. Ezra 2:2. Called Raamiah in Neh. 7:7.

REGEM [REE-guhm; "friend"] B.C. (date unknown). A Judahite, listed only in the genealogy of the clans of Caleb in 1 Chr. 2:47.

REGEM-MELECH [REE-guhm-MEH-lek; "royal friend"] 525 B.C. One of a delegation sent to ask the Temple priests whether fasting to commemorate the Temple's destruction should be continued. Zech. 7:2. Possibly a personal name is not intended, and this should be translated "friend of the king."

REHABIAH [REE-huh-BI-uh; "Yahweh has made wide"] 1425 B.C. Son of Eliezer and grandson of Moses. 1 Chr. 23:17; 24:21; 26:25.

REHOB [REE-hahb; "broad; open"]
1. 1025 B.C. Father of Hadadezer, the king of Zobah defeated in battle by David. 2 Sam. 8:3,12.
2. 450 B.C. A Levite who sealed the covenant renewal with God in Nehemiah's time. Neh. 10:11.

REHOBOAM* [REE-huh-BOH-uhm] 931–913 B.C. KJV NT: Roboam. The son and successor of Solomon; the kingdom of Israel became divided during his reign when Israel rebelled against his heavy taxation. Ten of the tribes formed the northern kingdom of Israel under Jeroboam I, and only the tribes of Judah and Benjamin remained under the rule of Rehoboam. 1 Ki. 12; 14:21-31; 2 Chr. 10–12. **Mother:** Naamah. **Son and Successor:** Abijah.

REHUM [REE-hum; "merciful"]
1. 525 B.C. One of the leaders who accompanied Zerubbabel in the return to Judah after the Exile. Ezra 2:2. Called Nehum in Neh. 7:7.
2. 525 B.C. A chief priest who returned to Judah with Zerubbabel. Neh. 12:3.
3. 450 B.C. A Persian officer who co-authored a letter to Artaxerxes opposing the rebuilding of Jerusalem by the Jews; with Artaxerxes's permission, he forced the Jews to stop the reconstruction until the decree was later overturned. Ezra 4:6-23.

4. 450 B.C. One who helped repair the wall of Jerusalem. Neh. 3:17.
5. 450 B.C. A Jewish leader who sealed the covenant renewal with God in Nehemiah's time. Neh. 10:25.

REI [REE-i; "friendly"] 975 B.C. A loyal friend of David when Adonijah attempted to seize the throne. 1 Ki. 1:8.

REKEM [REE-kuhm; "friendship"]
1. 1400 B.C. One of the five kings of Midian killed in battle with the Israelites under Moses. Num. 31:8; Josh. 13:21.
2. B.C. (date unknown). A descendant of Caleb listed in the genealogy of Judah in 1 Chr. 2:43,44.

REMALIAH [REM-uh-LI-uh; "Yahweh adorns"] 775 B.C. Father of Pekah, king of Israel. 2 Ki. 15:25.

REPHAEL [REF-ay-el; "God heals"] 975 B.C. A son of Shemaiah and grandson of Obed-Edom; he served as a tabernacle gatekeeper in David's time. 1 Chr. 26:7.

REPHAH [REE-fuh; "healing" or "support"] B.C. (date unknown). Listed only in the genealogy of Ephraim in 1 Chr. 7:25.

REPHAIAH [reh-FAY-yuh; "Yahweh heals"]
1. B.C. (date unknown). Listed only in the genealogy of Issachar in 1 Chr. 7:2.
2. B.C. (date unknown). A descendant of Saul through Jonathan. 1 Chr. 9:43. Called Raphah in 1 Chr. 8:37.
3. 725 B.C. A Simeonite leader who fought against the Amalekites in Hezekiah's time. 1 Chr. 4:42.
4. B.C. (date unknown). A descendant of David listed in the genealogy of the royal line after the Exile. 1 Chr. 3:21.
5. 450 B.C. One who helped repair the wall of Jerusalem in Nehemiah's time. Neh. 3:9.

REPHAN [REE-fan] KJV: Remphan. A pagan astral deity worshiped by the Israelites; associated with the planet Saturn. Acts 7:43.

RESHEPH [REE-shef; "flame"] B.C. (date unknown). Listed only in the genealogy of Ephraim in 1 Chr. 7:25.

REU [REE-oo; "friendship"] B.C. (date unknown). KJV: Ragau (Lk. 3:35). A descendant of Shem and ancestor of Abraham. Gen. 11:18-21; Lk. 3:35.

REUBEN* [ROO-ben; "see, a son"] 1900 B.C. Firstborn son of Jacob, by his wife Leah, and ancestral source of one of the twelve tribes of Israel. Because of an illicit affair with Bilhah, Jacob's concubine, Reuben lost his birthright. Gen. 29:32; 35:22,23; 37:21-29; 49:3,4.

REUEL [ROO-uhl; "friend of God"] KJV: Raguel (Num. 10:29).
1. 1925 B.C. A son of Esau by Basemath, daughter of Ishmael. Gen. 36:4,10-17.
2. 1500 B.C. A Midianite priest who gave his daughter Zipporah to Moses in marriage. Moses was tending the flock of Reuel when he saw the burning bush. Ex. 2:18; Num. 10:29. Also called Jethro.
3. B.C. (date unknown). A Benjamite; ancestor of one who resettled in Jerusalem after the Exile. 1 Chr. 9:8.

REUMAH [ROO-muh] 2075 B.C. The concubine of Nahor, brother of Abraham. Gen. 22:24.

REZIN [REE-zin]
1. 750 B.C. A king of Syria who warred against Jotham and Ahaz. He was put to death by Tiglath-Pileser, king of Assyria, at the fall of Damascus. 2 Ki. 15:37; 16:5-9; Isa. 7:1-8.
2. B.C. (date unknown). Ancestor of a family

of Temple servants that returned to Judah after the Exile. Ezra 2:48; Neh. 7:50.

REZON [REE-zuhn; "prince"] 950 B.C. A man of Zobah who became king of Damascus and founded a dynasty of Syrian rulers. He was an intractable enemy of Israel during the reign of Solomon. 1 Ki. 11:23-25. Probably the same as Hezion in 1 Ki. 15:18.

RHESA [REE-suh] 500 B.C. Son of Zerubbabel in Luke's genealogy of Jesus. Lk. 3:27.

RHODA [ROH-duh; "rose"] A.D. 45. A servant girl at the house of Mary, mother of Mark. Acts 12:13.

RIBAI [RI-bi] 1025 B.C. A Benjamite from Gibeah; father of Ithai, one of David's mighty men. 2 Sam. 23:29; 1 Chr. 11:31.

RIMMON [RIM-ahn; "pomegranate"]
1. Syrian deity, known to the Assyrians as "Ramanu," a title of Hadad the storm god which means "the thunderer." 2 Ki. 5:18.
2. 1025 B.C. A Benjamite of Beeroth, and father of Recab and Baanah, the murderers of Ish-Bosheth, son of Saul. 2 Sam. 4:2-9.

RINNAH [RIN-uh; "praise to God"] B.C. (date unknown). Listed only in the genealogy of Judah in 1 Chr. 4:20.

RIPHATH [RI-fath] B.C. (date unknown). KJV, RSV: Diphath (1 Chr. 1:6). A descendant of Japheth listed in the Table of Nations. Gen. 10:3; 1 Chr. 1:6. Possibly an ancestral source of the Ripheans, an ancient name for the Paphlagonians on the south coast of the Black Sea.

RIZIA [rih-ZI-uh] B.C. (date unknown). KJV: Rezia. Listed only in the genealogy of Asher in 1 Chr. 7:39.

RIZPAH [RIZ-pah; "hot stone"] 1025 B.C. A concubine of Saul; Ish-Bosheth accused his kinsman Abner of incest with her, which could be interpreted as a claim to the throne. In anger, Abner transferred his allegiance to David. Later, when two of her sons were put to death by the Gibeonites, her devoted vigil by their bodies led David to bury their bones with those of Saul and Jonathan in Kish's tomb. 2 Sam. 3:7; 21:8-14.

RODANIM [ROH-duh-nim] B.C. (date unknown). KJV, RSV (Gen. 10:4): Dodanim. A descendant of Japheth listed in the Table of Nations. Gen. 10:4; 1 Chr. 1:7. Probably a reference to the inhabitants of the isle of Rhodes.

ROHGAH [ROH-guh] B.C. (date unknown). Listed only in the genealogy of Asher in 1 Chr. 7:34.

ROMAMTI-EZER [roh-MAM-tih-EE-zuhr; "highest help"] 975 B.C. Son of Heman the seer and head of the twenty-fourth division of Temple singers. 1 Chr. 25:4,31.

ROSH [RAHSH; "head"] 1825 B.C. A son or grandson of Benjamin. Gen. 46:21.

RUFUS [ROO-fuhs; "red"]
1. A.D. 50. A brother of Alexander and son of Simon of Cyrene, the man who carried the cross for Christ. Mk. 15:21.
2. A.D. 55. A Christian who with his mother received greetings from Paul in his letter to the Roman church. Rom. 16:13. Possibly the same as Rufus 1.

RUTH* [ROOTH] 1100 B.C. The Moabite wife of Mahlon, a son of Elimelech and Naomi of Bethlehem. Following the deaths of their husbands, Ruth and Naomi left Moab and returned to Bethlehem. There, Ruth married her kinsman, Boaz. Her story is told in the OT book bearing her name. Ruth 1–4; Mt. 1:5

S

SABTA [SAB-tuh] B.C. (date unknown). A Hamite listed in the Table of Nations. 1 Chr. 1:9. Called Sabtah in Gen. 10:7.

SABTAH [SAB-tuh] B.C. (date unknown). A son of Cush and ancestral source of an unidentified Arabian people. Gen. 10:7. See Sabta.

SABTECA [SAB-tuh-kuh] B.C. (date unknown). KJV: Sabtecha. Last of the sons of Cush listed in the Table of Nations. 1 Chr. 1:9. Called Sabtecah in Gen. 10:7.

SABTECAH [SAB-tuh-kuh] B.C. (date unknown). KJV: Sabtechah. A Hamite and ancestral source of an unidentified Arabian people. Gen. 10:7. See Sabteca.

SACAR [SAY-kahr] RSV: Sachar.
1. 1025 B.C. Father of Ahiam, one of David's thirty mighty men. 1 Chr. 11:35. Called Sharar in 2 Sam. 23:33.
2. 975 B.C. A son of Obed-Edom and a gatekeeper in David's day. 1 Chr. 26:4.

SAKIA [suh-KI-uh] B.C. (date unknown). KJV: Shachia; RSV: Sachia. Listed only in the genealogy of Benjamin in 1 Chr. 8:10.

SALLAI [SAL-i] 450 B.C. A Benjamite who resettled in Jerusalem after the Exile. Neh. 11:8.

SALLU [SAL-oo] KJV, RSV (Neh. 12:20): Sallai.
1. 525 B.C. A priest who returned to Judah with Zerubbabel after the Exile. Neh. 12:7,20.
2. 450 B.C. A Benjamite listed among the residents of Jerusalem after the reconstruction of its wall in Nehemiah's time. 1 Chr. 9:7; Neh. 11:7.

SALMA [SAL-muh; "strength"] B.C. (date unknown). A descendant of Caleb and founder of Bethlehem. 1 Chr. 2:51,54.

SALMON [SAL-muhn; "clothing"] B.C. (date unknown). Ancestor of Boaz, the second husband of Ruth, in the Davidic line. Ruth 4:20,21; 1 Chr. 2:11; Mt. 1:4,5; Lk. 3:32.

SALOME [suh-LOH-mee; feminine of Solomon]
1. A.D. 30. A Galilean follower of Jesus; she was present at the crucifixion. Mk. 15:40,41; 16:1. Probably the wife of Zebedee and mother of James and John (compare Mt. 27:56).
2. A.D. 30. Daughter of Herodias and Herod Philip who at the prompting of her mother, asked Herod Antipas for the head of John the Baptist (Mt. 14:3-11; Mk. 6:16-28). She later became the wife of her uncle Philip the tetrarch, and thereafter, her cousin Aristobulus. Her name does not appear in the Bible.

SALU [SAY-loo] 1425 B.C. Father of Zimri, a Simeonite leader slain with a Midianite woman by Phinehas. Num. 25:14.

SAMLAH [SAM-luh; "garment"] B.C. (date unknown). A pre-Israelite king of Edom; a native of Masrekah. Gen. 36:36,37.

SAMSON* [SAM-suhn; "sun's man" or "distinguished"] 1095-1075 B.C. An Israelite judge for twenty years. A Nazirite possessed of heroic strength, his moral weakness ultimately led to his downfall. Jdg. 13–16; Heb. 11:32.
Father: Manoah.

SAMUEL* [SAM-yoo-uhl; "name of God" or "God hears"] 1063-1043 B.C. Son of Elkanah and Hannah, notable as a prophet and the last judge of Israel. He anointed Saul and later David as king over Israel. 1 Sam. 1:20-28; 3, 4; 7–13; 15, 16; 28:3-16; 1 Chr. 6:27,28.
Sons: Joel and Abijah.

SANBALLAT [san-BAL-uht; "Sin (the god) has given life"] 450 B.C. A Samaritan from Beth-Horon who with Tobiah and Geshem opposed the rebuilding of Jerusalem's wall in Nehemiah's time. According to Egyptian papyri, he became governor of Samaria. Neh. 2:10,19; 6:1-14; 13:28.

SAPH [SAF] 975 B.C. A descendant of Philistine giants who was slain by Sibbecai the Hushathite at Gob. 2 Sam. 21:18. Called Sippai in 1 Chr. 20:4.

SAPPHIRA [suh-FI-ruh; "beautiful; sapphire"] A.D. 35. Wife of Ananias; both were struck dead by God for deceptively withholding money from the church. Acts 5:1-10.

SARAH* [SAIR-uh; "princess"] 2100 B.C. The wife and half-sister of Abraham; her name was changed from Sarai by God when he promised that she would bear a son who would become a great nation. She was barren, but in accordance with God's promise to Abraham, she gave birth to Isaac in her old age. Gen. 17:15–18:15; 20:1–21:12; 23:1,2.
Father: Terah.

SARAI [SAY-ri; "Yahweh is prince"(?)] 2100 B.C. Original name of Sarah, changed by God at the forming of the covenant of circumcision with Abraham. Gen. 11:29–12:20; 16:1-9; 17:15. See Sarah.

SARAPH [SAIR-uhf] B.C. (date unknown). A Judahite who ruled in Moab and Jashubi Lehem. 1 Chr. 4:22.

SARGON [SAHR-gahn; "the king is legitimate"] 722-705 B.C. Sargon II, son of Tiglath-Pileser and successor of his brother, Shalmaneser V, king of Assyria. He conquered Samaria and deported the Israelites. Mentioned by name only in Isa. 20:1.

SATAN* [SAY-tuhn; "adversary"] The powerful angelic being portrayed in Scripture as the enemy of God and humanity. Through the serpent, he tempted Eve to disobey God, leading to the Fall. He also sought and failed to tempt Christ to sin. Satan will continue to exercise his evil dominion in the world until the final judgment. Job 1,2; Mk. 1:13; Lk. 22:3,31; Rom. 16:20; Rev. 12:9; 20:2,7. He is also known as "the devil."

SAUL [SAWL; "asked"]
1.* 1043-1010 B.C. A Benjamite, the son of Kish anointed by Samuel to become the first king of Israel. For his failure to obey the Lord, he was rejected by God. David's growing renown drove Saul to seek his life, and David fled from the king, eventually escaping to the land of the Philistines. David did not return until after Saul died in battle against the Philistines at Mount Gilboa. 1 Sam. 9–29,31.
Sons by Ahinoam: Jonathan, Malki-Shua, Abinadab, and Esh-Baal.
2. A.D. 35. Hebrew name of the apostle Paul. Acts 7:58–8:3; 9:1-30; 13. See Paul.

SCEVA [SEE-vuh] A.D. 25. A Jewish priest in Ephesus whose sons attempted to invoke the name of Jesus to cast out evil spirits. Acts 19:14.

SEBA [SEE-buh] B.C. (date unknown). A son of Cush listed in the Table of Nations, in Gen. 10:7. Ancestral source of the Sabeans, a people in south Arabia.

SECUNDUS [seh-KUN-duhs; "second"] A.D. 55. A Thessalonian Christian and companion of Paul during part of his third missionary journey. Acts 20:4.

SEGUB [SEE-gub]
1. B.C. (date unknown). A son of Hezron listed only in the genealogy of Judah in 1 Chr. 2:21,22.
2. 850 B.C. Youngest son of Heil, the rebuilder of Jericho. He died, possibly sacrificed by his father when his father set up the city gates, thus fulfilling Joshua's prophetic curse (Josh. 6:26). 1 Ki. 16:34.

SEIR [SEER] B.C. (date unknown). A Horite and ancestral source of the inhabitants of the land of Seir. Gen. 36:20.

SELED [SEE-led] B.C. (date unknown). Listed in the genealogy of Jerahmeel, a descendant of Judah. 1 Chr. 2:30.

SEMAKIAH [SEM-uh-KI-uh; "Yahweh has sustained"] 975 B.C. KJV, RSV: Semachiah. A Levite who served as a tabernacle gatekeeper in David's time. 1 Chr. 26:7.

SEMEIN [SEM-ee-in] B.C. (date unknown). KJV: Semei. Listed in the genealogy of Christ in Lk. 3:26.

SENAAH [suh-NAY-uh] B.C. (date unknown). Ancestor of a family that returned to Judah with Zerubbabel after the Exile. Ezra 2:35; Neh. 7:38. Called Hassenaah in Neh. 3:3. The name may refer to an unknown place.

SENNACHERIB [suh-NAK-uhr-ib; "Sin (the moon-god) has increased the brothers"] 705–681 B.C. Son and successor of Sargon II, king of Assyria. Rebellion was widespread throughout the kingdom during his reign. After he crushed Babylon under Merodach-Baladan, he turned against a coalition of rebels in the west, among them Hezekiah, king of Judah. Sennacherib took the fortified cities of Judah and besieged Jerusalem, but his army was miraculously destroyed. Sometime after his return to Ninevah, Sennacherib was assassinated by his sons Adrammelech and Sharezer. 2 Ki. 18:13–19:17; 2 Chr. 32:1-22; Isa. 36,37. **Son and successor:** Esarhaddon.

SEORIM [see-OHR-im] 975 B.C. Head of the fourth division of priests in David's day. 1 Chr. 24:8.

SERAH [SEER-uh; "extension"] B.C. (date unknown). KJV, RSV: Sarah (Num. 26:46). A daughter of Asher. Gen. 46:17; Num. 26:46.

SERAIAH [suh-RAY-yuh; "Yahweh is prince" or "Yahweh has prevailed"]
1. 1375 B.C. Son of Kenaz and brother of Othniel the judge. 1 Chr. 4:13,14.
2. B.C. (date unknown). Listed in the genealogy of Simeon in 1 Chr. 4:35.
3. 1000 B.C. Secretary of David. 2 Sam. 8:17. Also called Sheva (2 Sam. 20:25), Shisha (1 Ki. 4:3), and Shavsha (1 Chr. 18:16).
4. 600 B.C. High priest when Nebuchadnezzar took Jerusalem. He was taken to Riblah and put to death. Ancestor of Jeshua the high priest and Ezra the scribe. 2 Ki. 25:18-21; 1 Chr. 6:14; Ezra 7:1; Jer. 52:24-27.
5. 600 B.C. An official of Jehoiakim instructed to arrest Baruch and Jeremiah. Jer. 36:26.
6. 600 B.C. Son of Neriah and brother of Baruch; he was an army officer who went with

Zedekiah to Babylon in the king's fourth year. Jeremiah gave Seraiah a scroll prophesying the fall of Babylon. Jer. 51:59-64.
7. 575 B.C. Army officer who allied with Gedaliah at Mizpah; he fled to Egypt after Gedaliah's death. 2 Ki. 25:23; Jer. 40:8.
8. 525 B.C. One who returned to Judah with Zerubbabel after the Exile. Ezra 2:2. Called Azariah in Neh. 7:7. Possibly the same as Seraiah 9.
9. 525 B.C. Head of a priestly family among those who returned to Judah with Zerubbabel. Neh. 12:1,12.
10. 450 B.C. A priest who sealed the covenant renewal with God in Nehemiah's time, possibly with the name of a family ancestor (see Seraiah 9). Neh. 10:2.
11. 450 B.C. A priest descended from Zadok; he resettled in Jerusalem after the Exile. Neh. 11:11. Possibly the same as Seraiah 10.

SERED [SEER-ed] 1875 B.C. Eldest son of Zebulun and ancestral head of a clan. Gen. 46:14; Num. 26:26.

SERGIUS PAULUS [SUHR-jee-uhs-PAWL-us] A.D. 45. Roman proconsul of Cyprus converted to Christianity when he saw Paul strike Elymas with blindness. Acts 13:7,8.

SERUG [SEER-ug] B.C. (date unknown). KJV: Saruch (Lk. 3:35). A descendant of Shem and ancestor of Abraham. Gen. 11:20-23; Lk. 3:35.

SETH [SETH; "restitution" or "substitute"] B.C. (date unknown). KJV: Sheth (1 Chr. 1:1). Third son of Adam and Eve; the Messianic line descends from him. Gen. 4:25,26; 1 Chr. 1:1; Lk. 3:38.

SETHUR [SEE-thuhr; "hidden"] 1450 B.C. Leader from the tribe of Asher sent by Moses to spy out the land of Canaan. Num. 13:13.

SHAAPH [SHAY-af]
1. B.C. (date unknown). A son of Caleb by his concubine, Maacah; ancestor of the inhabitants of Madmannah. 1 Chr. 2:49.
2. B.C. (date unknown). A Judahite listed only in the genealogy of the clans of Caleb. 1 Chr. 2:47.

SHAASHGAZ [shay-ASH-gaz] 475 B.C. Eunuch of King Xerxes in charge of the concubines, including Esther. Esth. 2:14.

SHABBETHAI [SHAB-uh-thi; "sabbath-born"]
1. 450 B.C. A Levite involved in the dispute concerning Ezra's requirement that Jews divorce their foreign wives. It is uncertain from the text whether he opposed or supported Ezra. Ezra 10:15.
2. 450 B.C. A Levite who interpreted the Law for the people. Neh. 8:7. Possibly the same as Shabbethai 1.
3. 450 B.C. A chief Levite who resettled in Jerusalem after the reconstruction of its wall. Neh. 11:16. Possibly the same as Shabbethai 1.

SHADRACH [SHAD-rak] 600 B.C. Babylonian name given to Hananiah upon entering the service of Nebuchadnezzar. Notable as one of the three Jewish friends of Daniel thrown into a blazing furnace for refusing to bow down to Nebuchadnezzar's idol. They were miraculously delivered. Dan. 1:7; 2:49; 3:12-30.

SHAGEE [SHAY-gee; "wandering"] 1025 B.C. KJV: Shage. Father of Jonathan, one of David's thirty mighty men. 1 Chr. 11:34.

SHAHARAIM [SHAY-huh-RAY-im; "double dawn"] B.C. (date unknown). A Benjamite who lived in Moab. 1 Chr. 8:8.

SHALLUM [SHAL-uhm; "recompense"]
1. 1850 B.C. Son of Shaul and grandson of Simeon. 1 Chr. 4:25.
2. B.C. (date unknown). Listed only in the genealogy of Jerahmeel, a descendant of Judah. 1 Chr. 2:40,41.
3. 775 B.C. Father of Jehizkiah, an Ephraimite leader during Pekah's reign. 2 Chr. 28:12.
4. 752 B.C. Son of Jabesh and a king of Israel. After killing Zechariah, he seized the throne and reigned for only a month until he himself was assassinated by Menahem. 2 Ki. 15:10-15.
5. 675 B.C. A descendant of Zadok in the high priestly line. Father of Hilkiah, high priest during the reign of Josiah, and an ancestor of Ezra. 1 Chr. 6:12,13; Ezra 7:2. Possibly the same as Meshullam in 1 Chr. 9:11.
6. 625 B.C. Keeper of the king's wardrobe during Josiah's reign, and husband of the prophetess Huldah. 2 Ki. 22:14; 2 Chr. 34:22.
7. 625 B.C. Uncle of Jeremiah and father of Hanamel, whose field at Anathoth Jeremiah bought. Jer. 32:7. Possibly the same as Shallum 6.
8. 625 B.C. Father of Maaseiah, a doorkeeper who had a room in the Temple in Jehoiakim's time. Jer. 35:4.
9. 609–608 B.C. Another name for Jehoahaz, son and successor of Josiah, king of Judah. 1 Chr. 3:15; Jer. 22:11. See Jehoahaz.
10. B.C. (date unknown). Ancestral head of a family of gatekeepers that returned to Judah after the Exile. Ezra 2:42; Neh. 7:45.
11. 450 B.C. A chief gatekeeper at the Temple in Jerusalem after the Exile. 1 Chr. 9:17, 19,31.
12. 450 B.C. A gatekeeper listed among the Levites who took foreign wives after the Exile. Ezra 10:24. Possibly the same as Shallum 11.
13. 450 B.C. A descendant of Binnui; he also took a foreign wife after the Exile. Ezra 10:42.
14. 450 B.C. Son of Hallohesh who with his daughters helped repair the wall of Jerusalem in Nehemiah's time. Neh. 3:12.

SHALLUN [SHAL-uhn] 450 B.C. RSV: Shallum. One who helped repair the wall of Jerusalem in Nehemiah's day. Neh. 3:15.

SHALMAI [SHAL-mi] B.C. (date unknown). RSV: Shamlai (Ezra 2:46). Ancestor of a family of Temple servants that returned to Judah with Zerubbabel. Ezra 2:46; Neh. 7:48.

SHALMAN [SHAL-muhn] B.C. (date unknown). One who sacked Beth Arbel, mentioned only in Hos. 10:14. It has been suggested that he was either Shalmaneser, king of Assyria, or the Moabite king Salmanu, mentioned in the records of Tiglath-Pileser.

SHALMANESER [SHAL-muh-NEE-zuhr; "Sulman (the god) is chief"] 727–722 B.C. Shalmaneser V, son and successor of Tiglath-

Pileser, king of Assyria. He received tribute from Hoshea until his rebellion. Thereafter, Shalmaneser laid siege to Samaria, but apparently died before its fall. Sargon, his successor, conquered the city and deported the Israelites. 2 Ki. 17:3-6; 18:9.

1094

SHAMA [SHAY-muh; "he has heard"] 1000 B.C. A son of Hotham; he and his brother were members of the military elite known as David's mighty men. 1 Chr. 11:44.

SHAMGAR [SHAM-gahr] B.C. (date unknown). A minor judge who "struck down six hundred Philistines with an oxgoad." Jdg. 3:31; 5:6. He may have been from Beth-Anath.

SHAMHUTH [SHAM-huth] 975 B.C. Commander of the fifth division of David's army. 1 Chr. 27:8.

SHAMIR [SHAY-muhr; "sharp point; thorn"] 1000 B.C. A Levite family in David's time. 1 Chr. 24:24.

SHAMMA [SHAM-uh] B.C. (date unknown). Listed only in the genealogy of Asher in 1 Chr. 7:37.

SHAMMAH [SHAM-uh; "desolation, waste"]
1. 1875 B.C. An Edomite chief; son of Reuel and grandson of Esau. Gen. 36:13,17.
2. 1025 B.C. Third son of Jesse and older brother of David. Father of Jonadab, Amnon's friend. 1 Sam. 16:9; 17:13. Also called Shimea (1 Chr. 2:13; 20:7), and Shimeah (2 Sam. 13:3,32).
3. 1000 B.C. One of the Three, the leaders of the military elite known as David's thirty mighty men; father of Jonathan, one of the thirty. 2 Sam. 23:11,12,33. Called Shagee in 1 Chr. 11:34.
4. 1000 B.C. Another member of David's thirty mighty men. 2 Sam. 23:25. Called Shammoth in 1 Chr. 11:27.

SHAMMAI [SHAM-i]
1. B.C. (date unknown). A Judahite listed in the genealogy of Jerahmeel. 1 Chr. 2:28,32.
2. B.C. (date unknown). Listed only in the genealogy of the clans of Caleb, a descendant of Judah, in 1 Chr. 2:44,45.
3. B.C. (date unknown). Listed in the genealogy of Judah in 1 Chr. 4:17.

SHAMMOTH [SHAM-ahth] 1000 B.C. One of David's mighty men. 1 Chr. 11:27. Called Shammah in 2 Sam. 23:25.

SHAMMUA [SHAM-moo-uh; "renowned"] KJV: Shammuah (2 Sam. 5:14); KJV, RSV: Shimea (1 Chr. 3:5).
1. 1450 B.C. Leader from the tribe of Reuben sent by Moses to spy out the land of Canaan. Num. 13:4.
2. 975 B.C. A son of David and Bathsheba born in Jerusalem; brother of Solomon. 2 Sam. 5:14; 1 Chr. 3:5.
3. B.C. (date unknown). Ancestor of a Levite who resettled in Jerusalem after the Exile. Neh. 11:17. Called Shemaiah in 1 Chr. 9:16.
4. 500 B.C. Head of a priestly family in the time of Joiakim. Neh. 12:18.

SHAMSHERAI [SHAM-shuh-ri] B.C. (date unknown). Listed only in the genealogy of Benjamin in 1 Chr. 8:26.

SHAPHAM [SHAY-fuhm] 750 B.C. A chief Gadite who lived in Bashan. 1 Chr. 5:12.

SHAPHAN [SHAY-fuhn; "rock badger"]
1. 650 B.C. Father of Ahikam and grandfather of Gedaliah the governor. 2 Ki. 22:12; Jer. 26:24; 40:5,11.
2. 625 B.C. Secretary of Josiah who brought to the king the rediscovered Book of the Law. 2 Ki. 22:3-14; 25:22; 2 Chr. 34:8-21; Jer. 36:10-12. Possibly the same as Shaphan 1.
3. 625 B.C. Father of Elasah, who took Jeremiah's letter to the exiles in Babylon. Jer. 29:3. Possibly the same as Shaphan 1 or 2.
4. 625 B.C. Father of Jaazaniah, one of the seventy idolators in the Temple seen by Ezekiel in a vision. Ezek. 8:11.

SHAPHAT [SHAF-at; "judged"]

1. 1450 B.C. Leader from the tribe of Simeon sent by Moses to explore the land of Canaan. Num. 13:5.
2. 975 B.C. An official of David in charge of royal herds in the valleys. 1 Chr. 27:29.
3. 875 B.C. Father of Elisha the prophet. 1 Ki. 19:16,19.
4. B.C. (date unknown). A descendant of Zerubbabel listed in the genealogy of the royal line after the Exile. 1 Chr. 3:22.
5. 750 B.C. A Gadite chief who lived in Bashan. 1 Chr. 5:12.

SHARAI [SHAIR-i] 450 B.C. One who took a foreign wife after the Exile. Ezra 10:40.

SHARAR [SHAIR-ahr] 1000 B.C. Father of Ahiam, a member of the military elite known as David's mighty men. 2 Sam. 23:33. Called Sacar in 1 Chr. 11:35.

SHAREZER [shuh-REE-zuhr; "he has protected the king"]
1. 675 B.C. A son of Sennacherib, king of Assyria. With his brother Adrammelech, he murdered his father in 681 B.C. 2 Ki. 19:37; Isa. 37:38.
2. 525 B.C. One sent by the people of Bethel to consult the priests and prophets in Jerusalem regarding the practice of ritual fasting. Zech. 7:2.

SHASHAI [SHAY-shi; "noble"] 450 B.C. Among the descendants of Binnui who divorced their foreign wives in Ezra's time. Ezra 10:40.

SHASHAK [SHAY-shak] B.C. (date unknown). Listed only in the genealogy of Benjamin. 1 Chr. 8:14,25.

SHAUL [SHAWL; variant of Saul] KJV: Saul (Gen. 36:37,38).
1. 1875 B.C. A son of Simeon by a Canaanite woman. Gen. 46:10; Num. 26:13; 1 Chr. 4:24.
2. B.C. (date unknown). A pre-Israelite king of Edom. Gen. 36:37,38.
3. B.C. (date unknown). A Kohathite listed in the genealogy of Levi, in 1 Chr. 6:24.

SHAVSHA [SHAV-shuh] 975 B.C. Secretary of King David. 1 Chr. 18:16. *See* Seraiah 3.

SHEAL [SHEE-uhl; "request"] 450 B.C. One who took a foreign wife after the Exile. Ezra 10:29.

SHEALTIEL [shee-AL-tee-uhl] 550 B.C. KJV: Salathiel (1 Chr. 3:17 and NT). Eldest son of Jehoiachin, and father of Zerubbabel. His brother Pedaiah is given as the father of Zerubbabel in 1 Chr. 3:19; it has been suggested that the childless Shealtiel adopted Zerubbabel or that he was born as the result of a Levirate marriage. Ezra 3:2; Hag. 1:1; Mt. 1:12; Lk. 3:27.

SHEARIAH [SHEE-uh-RI-uh; "Yahweh considers"] A Benjamite descended from Jonathan, son of Saul. 1 Chr. 8:38; 9:44.

SHEAR-JASHUB [SHEER-JAH-shub; "a remnant shall return"] 725 B.C. Symbolic name of Isaiah's firstborn son, foreshadowing the restoration of the Jews after the Exile. Isa. 7:3.

SHEBA [SHEE-buh; "oath"]
1. B.C. (date unknown). A Hamite listed in the Table of Nations. Gen. 10:7.
2. B.C. (date unknown). A descendant of Shem and probably the ancestral source of the Sabeans, inhabitants of the country of Sheba located in South Arabia. Gen. 10:28.
3. B.C. (date unknown). Eldest son of Jokshan, descended from Abraham and Keturah. Gen. 25:3. Also associated with the Sabeans, possibly through intermarriage of his descendants.
4. 975 B.C. A Benjamite who instigated a brief rebellion against David; when he took refuge

from Joab in Abel Beth Maacah, he was beheaded by its inhabitants. 2 Sam. 20.
5. 750 B.C. Head of a Gadite family that lived in Bashan during the time of Jotham. 1 Chr. 5:13.

SHEBANIAH [sheb-uh-NI-uh]
1. 1000 B.C. A priest who blew the trumpet before the ark of the covenant as it was brought by David to Jerusalem. 1 Chr. 15:24.
2. 450 B.C. A Levite involved in the ceremony of covenant renewal in Nehemiah's time. Neh. 9:4,5.
3. 450 B.C. A priest who sealed the covenant renewal with God. Neh. 10:4.
4 and 5. 450 B.C. Two Levites who also put their seals upon the renewed covenant with Nehemiah. Neh. 10:10,12. Either may be the same as Shebaniah 2.

SHEBER [SHEE-buhr; "breach"(?)] B.C. (date unknown). A son of Caleb by his concubine Maacah, in the genealogy of Judah in 1 Chr. 2:48.

SHEBNA [SHEB-nuh; "youthfulness"(?)] 725 B.C. Secretary of Hezekiah whom Eliakim replaced as palace administrator. Isaiah denounced him for his pride and predicted his downfall. 2 Ki. 18:18–19:2; Isa. 22:15-21; 36:3–37:2.

SHECANIAH [SHEK-uh-NI-uh; "dweller with Yahweh"] KJV: Shechaniah.
1. 975 B.C. Head of the tenth division of priests in David's day. 1 Chr. 24:11.
2. 725 B.C. A priest who helped distribute contributions among his priestly brethren. 2 Chr. 31:15.
3. 525 B.C. A priest who returned to Judah with Zerubbabel. Neh. 12:3,14.
4. B.C. (date unknown). Ancestor of Hattush, a descendant of David who returned to Judah with Ezra. Ezra 8:3.
5. B.C. (date unknown). A descendant of Zerubbabel listed in the royal line of David after the Exile. 1 Chr. 3:21,22. Probably the same as Shecaniah 4.
6. 475 B.C. Father of Shemaiah, who helped repair the wall of Jerusalem. Neh. 3:29.
7. 450 B.C. Head of a family that returned to Judah with Ezra. Ezra 8:5.
8. 450 B.C. One who supported Ezra's reform requiring the divorce of foreign wives among the Jews. Ezra 10:2-5.
9. 450 B.C. Father-in-law of Tobiah the Ammonite, an enemy of Nehemiah. Neh. 6:18.

SHECHEM [SHEK-uhm; "shoulder"]
1. 1900 B.C. Son of Hamor the Hivite who violated Dinah, daughter of Jacob. He and the men of his city were killed in revenge by her brothers, Simeon and Levi. Gen. 33:19; 34.
2. B.C. (date unknown). A descendant of Manasseh and head of a clan. Num. 26:31; Josh. 17:2.
3. B.C. (date unknown). Listed only in the genealogy of Manasseh in 1 Chr. 7:19.

SHEDEUR [SHED-ee-uhr; "shedder of light"] 1475 B.C. Father of Elizur, leader of the tribe of Reuben at the time of the Exodus. Num. 1:5.

SHEERAH [SHEE-uh-ruh; "blood relationship"] B.C. (date unknown). KJV: Sherah. Descendant of Ephraim; she was responsible for the building of three towns. 1 Chr. 7:24.

SHEHARIAH [SHEH-huh-RI-uh] B.C. (date unknown). Listed in the genealogy of Benjamin in 1 Chr. 8:26.

SHELAH [SHEE-luh][KJV: Salah (Gen. 10:24; 11:12-15); Sala (Lk. 3:35); Shiloni (Neh. 11:5); RSV: the Shilonite (Neh. 11:5).
1. B.C. (date unknown). A descendant of Shem and an ancestor of Abraham. Gen. 10:24; 11:12-15; 1 Chr. 1:18,24; Lk. 3:35.

2. 1850 B.C. Third son of Judah by the Canaanite daughter of Shua, promised but never given in marriage to Tamar. Gen. 38:5,11-26; Num. 26:20; 1 Chr. 4:21.

3. B.C. (date unknown). Ancestor of a Judahite who resettled in Jerusalem after the Exile. Neh. 11:5. Probably the same as Shelah 2.

SHELEMIAH [SHEL-uh-MI-uh; "Yahweh is recompense"]

1. 975 B.C. A gatekeeper selected to guard the East Gate entrance to the sanctuary in David's time. 1 Chr. 26:14. Called Meshelemiah in 1 Chr. 26:1,2.

2. 650 B.C. Grandfather of Jehudi, sent by the officials of Jehoiakim to retrieve the scroll of Jeremiah's prophecies. Jer. 36:14.

3. 625 B.C. Father of Jehucal, one of Zedekiah's officials who threw Jeremiah into a cistern. Jer. 37:3; 38:1.

4. 625 B.C. Father of Irijah, captain of the guard at Benjamin Gate, who arrested Jeremiah. Jer. 37:13.

5. 600 B.C. One sent by King Jehoiakim to arrest Baruch and Jeremiah. Jer. 36:26.

6. 475 B.C. Father of Hananiah, who rebuilt a section of Jerusalem's wall in Nehemiah's time. Neh. 3:30.

7 and 8. 450 B.C. Two of Binnui's descendants who put away their foreign wives in Ezra's time. Ezra 10:39,41.

9. 425 B.C. A priest appointed as a Temple treasurer by Nehemiah. Neh. 13:13.

SHELEPH [SHEE-lef] B.C. (date unknown). A descendant of Shem listed in the Table of Nations. Gen. 10:26. Ancestral source of a South Arabian tribe.

SHELESH [SHEE-lesh] B.C. (date unknown). Listed only in the genealogy of Asher in 1 Chr. 7:35.

SHELOMI [shuh-LOH-mi; "peace"] 1425 B.C. Father of Ahihud, leader from the tribe of Asher appointed to help assign inheritances in Canaan. Num. 34:27.

SHELOMITH [shuh-LOH-mith; "peaceful"] RSV: Shelomoth (1 Chr. 26:25-28).

1. 1475? B.C. Mother of a blasphemer who was stoned to death. Lev. 24:11.

2. B.C. (date unknown). A Levite descended from Izhar. 1 Chr. 23:18. Called Shelomoth in 1 Chr. 24:22.

3. 975 B.C. A descendant of Eliezer, son of Moses, who was made treasurer of the valuable equipment in the Temple. 1 Chr. 26:25-28.

4. 900 B.C. Son or daughter of King Rehoboam and his wife Maacah. 2 Chr. 11:20.

5. 500 B.C. Daughter of Zerubbabel listed in the genealogy of the royal line after the Exile. 1 Chr. 3:19.

6. 450 B.C. Head of a family that returned to Judah with Ezra. Ezra 8:10.

SHELOMOTH [shuh-LOH-mahth; "peaceful"] KJV: Shelomith (1 Chr. 23:9).

1. 1000 B.C. A Gershonite, head of a family listed in the divisions of the Levites in David's day. 1 Chr. 23:9.

2. B.C. (date unknown). Listed in the genealogy of Levi in 1 Chr. 24:22. See Shelomith 2.

SHELUMIEL [shuh-LOO-mee-uhl; "God is peace"] 1450 B.C. Leader of the tribe of Simeon at the time of the Exodus. Num. 1:6.

SHEM [SHEM; "name" or "renown"] B.C. (date unknown). Son of Noah and ancestral source of the Semitic race. Gen. 5:32; 9:23-27; 10:21,22; 11:10,11. **Brothers:** Ham and Japheth.

SHEMA [SHEE-muh; "fame; rumor"]

1. B.C. (date unknown). A descendant of Caleb listed in the genealogy of Judah in 1 Chr. 2:43,44.

2. B.C. (date unknown). Listed only in the genealogy of Reuben in 1 Chr. 5:8.

3. B.C. (date unknown). Head of a Benjamite family who lived in Aijalon and helped defeat the Philistine inhabitants of Gath. 1 Chr. 8:13.

4. 450 B.C. One who stood to Ezra's right at the reading of the Law. Neh. 8:4.

SHEMAAH [shuh-MAY-uh; "fame"] 1025 B.C. A Benjamite from Gibeah; his two sons joined David at Ziklag. 1 Chr. 12:3.

SHEMAIAH [shuh-MAY-yuh; "Yahweh hears"]

1. B.C. (date unknown). Ancestor of a Simeonite who lived during the reign of Hezekiah. 1 Chr. 4:37.

2. B.C. (date unknown). Listed only in the genealogy of Reuben in 1 Chr. 5:4.

3. 1000 B.C. A chief Levite who assisted David in bringing the ark of the covenant to Jerusalem. 1 Chr. 15:8,11.

4. 975 B.C.. A Levite scribe who recorded the divisions of the priests in David's day. 1 Chr. 24:6.

5. 975 B.C. Firstborn son of Obed-Edom and head of a family of tabernacle gatekeepers in David's time. 1 Chr. 26:4,6,7.

6. 925 B.C. A prophet who told Rehoboam not to go to war against the ten northern tribes of Israel after their rebellion. 1 Ki. 12:22-24; 2 Chr. 11:2-4; 12:5-8,15.

7. 875 B.C. A Levite sent by Jehoshaphat to teach the Law throughout Judah. 2 Chr. 17:8.

8. 725 B.C. A Levite who helped purify the Temple in Hezekiah's time. 2 Chr. 29:14.

9. 725 B.C. An assistant to Kore, a Levite in charge of distributing offerings among the towns of the priests. 2 Chr. 31:15.

10. 625 B.C. A chief Levite who with his brothers contributed to the Passover celebration during Josiah's religious revival. 2 Chr. 35:9.

11. 625 B.C. Father of Uriah, a prophet killed by Jehoiakim. Jer. 26:20.

12. 625 B.C. Father of Delaiah, an official of Jehoiakim, who urged the king not to burn the scroll of Jeremiah. Jer. 36:12.

13. 600 B.C. A false prophet among the exiles and an opponent of Jeremiah. Jer. 29:24-32.

14. B.C. (date unknown). A Levite descended from Asaph. Neh. 12:36.

15. 525 B.C. A priest who returned to Judah with Zerubbabel after the Exile. Neh. 10:8; 12:6,18.

16. 475 B.C. Father of Obadiah, a Levite who resettled in Jerusalem in Nehemiah's time. 1 Chr. 9:16. Called Shammua in Neh. 11:17.

17. 450 B.C. A Levite who resettled in Jerusalem after the Exile. 1 Chr. 9:14; Neh. 11:15.

18. 450 B.C. One who returned to Judah with Ezra after the Exile. Ezra 8:13.

19. 450 B.C. One sent as part of a delegation to Iddo to retrieve Levites to serve at the Temple in Jerusalem. Ezra 8:16.

20. 450 B.C. A priest who took a foreign wife after the Exile. Ezra 10:21.

21. 450 B.C. Another required to put away his foreign wife in Ezra's time. Ezra 10:31.

22. 450 B.C. Son of Shecaniah, keeper of the East Gate of Jerusalem; he helped rebuild the wall in Nehemiah's time. Neh. 3:29.

23. 450 B.C. A false prophet hired by Tobiah and Sanballat to frighten Nehemiah into committing an act of sacrilege. Neh. 6:10-13.

24. 450 B.C. A priest who sealed the covenant renewal with God in Nehemiah's time, possibly with the name of a family ancestor (*see* Shemaiah 15). Neh. 10:8.

25. 450 B.C. A Jewish leader who participated in the dedication of the wall of Jerusalem in Nehemiah's time. Neh. 12:34.

26. 450 B.C. A Levite musician in the procession at the dedication of Jerusalem's wall in Nehemiah's time. Neh. 12:35.

27. 450 B.C. A priest in one of the choirs at the dedication of the wall. Neh. 12:42.

28. B.C. (date unknown). A descendant of Zerubbabel listed in the genealogy of the royal line after the Exile. 1 Chr. 3:22.

SHEMARIAH [SHEM-uh-RI-uh; "Yahweh keeps"] KJV: Shamariah (2 Chr. 11:19).

1. 1000 B.C. A Benjamite warrior who defected to David at Ziklag. 1 Chr. 12:5.

2. 900 B.C. A son of Rehoboam, king of Judah, by his wife Mahalath. 2 Chr. 11:19.

3 and 4. 450 B.C. Two who took foreign wives after the Exile. Ezra 10:32,41.

SHEMEBER [shem-EE-buhr] 2100 B.C. King of Zeboiim allied with the kings of Sodom and Gomorrah; they were defeated by Kedorlaomer and his allies, who captured Lot. Gen. 14:2.

SHEMED [SHEE-med; "dstruction"] B.C. (date unknown). KJV: Shamed. Builder of the towns of Ono and Lod, listed in the genealogy of Benjamin. 1 Chr. 8:12.

SHEMER [SHEE-muhr; "watch"] KJV: Shamer (1 Chr. 6:46).

1. A Levite descended from Merari; ancestor of Ethan, a chief minister of music in David's day. 1 Chr. 6:46.

2. 875 B.C. Owner of a hill that Omri, king of Israel, bought; Omri then built the city of Samaria, named after its original owner, upon that site. 1 Ki. 16:24.

SHEMIDA [shuh-MI-duh] B.C. (date unknown). KJV: Shemidah (1 Chr. 7:19). Ancestral head of a clan of Manasseh. Num. 26:32; 1 Chr. 7:19.

SHEMIRAMOTH [shuh-MEER-uh-mahth]

1. 1000 B.C. A Levite who played the lyre while the ark of the covenant was brought to Jerusalem by David. 1 Chr. 15:18,20; 16:5.

2. 875 B.C. A Levite sent by King Jehoshaphat to teach the Law in the cities of Judah. 2 Chr. 17:8.

SHEMUEL [SHEM-yoo-uhl; variant form of Samuel] 1400 B.C. Leader from the tribe of Simeon appointed to help assign inheritances in the land of Canaan. Num. 34:20.

SHENAZZAR [shuh-NAZ-uhr] 550 B.C. KJV: Shenazar. A son of Jehoiachin, listed in the genealogy of the royal line after the Exile. 1 Chr. 3:18.

SHEPHATIAH [SHEF-uh-TI-uh; "Yahweh is judge"]

1. 1000 B.C. A Benjamite who joined David at Ziklag. 1 Chr. 12:5.

2. 975 B.C. A son born to David in Hebron, by his wife Abital. 2 Sam. 3:4; 1 Chr. 3:3.

3. 975 B.C. Officer over the tribe of Simeon in David's time. 1 Chr. 27:16.

4. 950 B.C. A servant of Solomon whose descendants returned to Judah with Zerubbabel. Ezra 2:57; Neh. 7:59.

5. 850 B.C. A son of Jehoshaphat and younger brother of Jehoram. 2 Chr. 21:2.

6. B.C. (date unknown). Ancestral head of a family whose members returned to Judah with Zerubbabel and Ezra. Ezra 2:4; 8:8; Neh. 7:9.

7. B.C. (date unknown). Ancestor of a Judahite who resettled in Jerusalem in Nehemiah's time. Neh. 11:4.

8. 600 B.C. One of the officials of Zedekiah who threw Jeremiah into a cistern to die. Jer. 38:1.

9. 475 B.C. Father of Meshullam, a Benjamite who resettled in Jerusalem after the Exile. 1 Chr. 9:8.

SHEPHO [SHEE-foh] 1950 B.C. KJV: Shephi (1 Chr. 1:40). A son of Shobal, a Horite chief in Esau's time. Gen. 36:23; 1 Chr. 1:40.

SHEPHUPHAN [sheh-FOO-fan] 1825 B.C. A grandson of Benjamin and ancestral source of the Shuppites (1 Chr. 7:12,15). 1 Chr. 8:5. Called Shupham in Num. 26:39; possibly the same as Muppim in Gen. 46:21.

SHEREBIAH [SHAIR-uh-BI-uh]
1. 525 B.C. A Levite who returned to Judah with Zerubbabel after the Exile. Neh. 12:8.
2. 450 B.C. Head of a Levite family that were recruited from Iddo by Ezra to serve at the Temple in Jerusalem. Ezra 8:18,24; Neh. 8:7; 9:4,5.
3. 450 B.C. A Levite who sealed the covenant renewal with God in Nehemiah's time. Neh. 10:12. Possibly the same as Sherebiah 1 or 2.
4. 450 B.C. A chief Levite in the time of Eliashib the high priest. Neh. 12:24. Probably the same as Sherebiah 2.

SHERESH [SHEER-esh] B.C. (date unknown). Listed only in the genealogy of Manasseh in 1 Chr. 7:16.

SHESHAI [SHEE-shi] 1450 B.C. A giant descended from Anak; he was driven out of Hebron by Caleb, son of Jephunneh. Num. 13:22; Josh. 15:14; Jdg. 1:10.

SHESHAN [SHEE-shan] B.C. (date unknown). A descendant of Judah who had no sons; he gave his daughter to his Egyptian slave to continue his line. 1 Chr. 2:31,34,35.

SHESHBAZZAR [shesh-BAZ-uhr] 525 B.C. A prince of Judah who brought the sacred Temple vessels to Jerusalem when Cyrus decreed the rebuilding of the Temple. He was appointed governor over Judah. Ezra 1:8,11; 5:14,16. Possibly the Persian name of Zerubbabel.

SHETH [SHETH; "tumult"(?)] B.C. (date unknown). A descriptive name given to the Moabites in Balaam's fourth oracle. Num. 24:17.

SHETHAR [SHEE-thahr] 475 B.C. One of the seven nobles of Persia and Media who advised King Xerxes. Esth. 1:14.

SHETHAR-BOZENAI [SHEE-thahr-BAHZ-uh-ni] 525 B.C. A Persian official who with Tattenai sent a letter to King Darius in opposition to the rebuilding of the Temple. However, Darius returned a decree requiring they assist the Jews in the rebuilding. Ezra 5:3,6; 6:6,13.

SHEVA [SHEE-vuh]
1. B.C. (date unknown). Son of Caleb by his concubine, Maacah; listed only in the genealogy of Judah in 1 Chr. 2:49.
2. 1000 B.C. David's secretary. 2 Sam. 20:25. See Seraiah 3.

SHILHI [SHIL-hi] 925 B.C. Grandfather of Jehoshaphat, king of Judah. 1 Ki. 22:42.

SHILLEM [SHIL-uhm] 1875 B.C. KJV, RSV: Shallum (1 Chr. 7:13). Fourth son of Naphtali, son of Jacob, and ancestral head of a clan. Gen. 46:24; Num. 26:49; 1 Chr. 7:13.

SHILSHAH [SHIL-shuh] B.C. (date unknown). Listed only in the genealogy of Asher in 1 Chr. 7:37.

SHIMEA [SHIM-ee-uh; "fame" or "God has heard"] KJV: Shimma (1 Chr. 2:13).
1. B.C. (date unknown). A descendant of Merari listed only in the genealogy of Levi in 1 Chr. 6:30.
2. 1075 B.C. A Levite descended from Gershon and grandfather of Asaph, a chief minister of music in David's day. 1 Chr. 6:39.
3. 1025 B.C. Third son of Jesse and older brother of David. 1 Chr. 2:13; 20:7. Also called Shammah (1 Sam. 16:9), and Shimeah (2 Sam. 13:3,32; 21:21). **Son:** Jonadab.

SHIMEAH [SHIM-ee-uh; "fame" or "God has heard"] RSV: Shimei (2 Sam. 21:21).
1. 1075 B.C. A relative of King Saul who lived in Jerusalem. 1 Chr. 8:32. Called Shimeam in 1 Chr. 9:38.

2. 1025 B.C. A brother of David. 2 Sam. 13:3,32; 21:21.

SHIMEAM [SHIM-ee-uhm; "fame" or "God has heard"] 1075 B.C. Son of Mikloth, an uncle of Kish, father of Saul. 1 Chr. 9:38. See Shimeah 1.

SHIMEATH [SHIM-ee-ath; "fame"] 825 B.C. Ammonite mother of one of the officials who murdered Joash, king of Judah. 2 Ki. 12:21; 2 Chr. 24:26.

SHIMEI [SHIM-ee-i; "Yahweh hear me"]
1. 1850 B.C. A son of Gershon, son of Levi; ancestral head of a Levite clan. Ex. 6:17; Num. 3:18; 1 Chr. 23:7,10; Zech. 12:13.
2. B.C. (date unknown). Listed only in the genealogy of Simeon in 1 Chr. 4:26,27.
3. B.C. (date unknown). Listed only in the genealogy of Reuben in 1 Chr. 5:4.
4. B.C. (date unknown). A descendant of Merari in the genealogy of Levi. 1 Chr. 6:29.
5. B.C. (date unknown). Listed in the genealogy of Heman, a chief minister of music in David's day. 1 Chr. 6:42. Possibly the same as Shimei 1.
6. B.C. (date unknown). Listed in the genealogy of Benjamin in 1 Chr. 8:21.
7. B.C. (date unknown). A Levite descended from Gershon. 1 Chr. 23:9. Possibly the same as Shimei 5.
8. B.C. (date unknown). A descendant of Kish and ancestor of Mordecai. Esth. 2:5.
9. 975 B.C. A Benjamite and kinsman of Saul who cursed David as he fled from Absalom. He later begged for mercy from David and received it, but when Solomon became king, he instructed Shimei never to leave Jerusalem. Shimei left the city to retrieve two runaway slaves, and upon his return Solomon had him put to death. 2 Sam. 16:5-13; 19:16-23; 1 Ki. 2:8,9,36-46.
10. 975 B.C. An officer of David who remained loyal to him when Adonijah attempted to seize the throne. 1 Ki. 1:8.
11. 975 B.C. A son of Jeduthun and head of the tenth division of ministers of music in David's time. 1 Chr. 25:3,17.
12. 975 B.C. Overseer of King David's vineyards. 1 Chr. 27:27.
13. 950 B.C. A Benjamite, one of Solomon's twelve district governors. 1 Ki. 4:18. Possibly the same as Shimei 10.
14. 725 B.C. A Levite descendant of Heman; he helped purify the Temple in Hezekiah's time. 2 Chr. 29:14.
15. 725 B.C. Brother of Conaniah and next in rank in charge of the Temple treasury. 2 Chr. 31:12,13. Possibly the same as Shimei 14.
16. 525 B.C. Grandson of Jehoiachin, listed in the genealogy of the royal line after the Exile. 1 Chr. 3:19.
17. 450 B.C. A Levite who took a foreign wife after the Exile. Ezra 10:23.
18 and 19. 450 B.C. Two more who took foreign wives after the Exile. Ezra 10:33,38.

SHIMEON [SHIM-ee-uhn; "hearing" or "(God) has heard"] 450 B.C. One who put away his foreign wife in Ezra's time. Ezra 10:31.

SHIMON [SHI-muhn] B.C. (date unknown). Listed only in the genealogy of Judah in 1 Chr. 4:20.

SHIMRATH [SHIM-rath; "watch"] B.C. (date unknown). Listed only in the genealogy of Benjamin in 1 Chr. 8:21.

SHIMRI [SHIM-ri; "(Yahweh) watches"]
1. B.C. (date unknown). Listed in the genealogy of Simeon in 1 Chr. 4:37.
2. 1025 B.C. Father of Jediael, one of David's mighty men. 1 Chr. 11:45.
3. 975 B.C. Son of Hosah the Merarite; he was among the tabernacle gatekeepers in David's time. 1 Chr. 26:10.
4. 725 B.C. A Levite who helped purify the Temple in Hezekiah's day. 2 Chr. 29:13.

SHIMRITH [SHIM-rith; "watch"] 825 B.C. Moabite mother of one of the officials who murdered Joash, king of Judah. 2 Chr. 24:26. Called Shomer in 2 Ki. 12:21.

SHIMRON [SHIM-rahn; "a guard"] 1875 B.C. KJV: Shimrom (1 Chr. 7:1). Fourth son of Issachar, and ancestral head of a clan. Gen. 46:13; Num. 26:24.

SHIMSHAI [SHIM-shi] 450 B.C. A Persian secretary who with Rehum wrote a letter to Artaxerxes, king of Persia, opposing the rebuilding of Jerusalem's walls. Ezra 4:8-23.

SHINAB [SHI-nab] 2100 B.C. King of Admah who with his allies rebelled against Kedorlaomer and was defeated. Gen. 14:2.

SHIPHI [SHI-fi] 750 B.C. Father of Ziza, a Simeonite who lived in the days of Hezekiah. 1 Chr. 4:37.

SHIPHRAH [SHIF-ruh; "beauty"] 1525 B.C. A Hebrew midwife who disobeyed the Pharaoh's order to kill the male children born to the Israelites. Ex. 1:15-21.

SHIPHTAN [SHIF-tan; "judge"] 1425 B.C. Father of Kemuel, an Ephraimite leader appointed by Moses to help divide the land of Canaan. Num. 34:24.

SHISHA [SHI-shuh] 975 B.C. Father of Solomon's secretaries, Elihoreph and Ahijah. 1 Ki. 4:3. See Seraiah 3.

SHISHAK [SHI-shak] 925 B.C. Egyptian Pharaoh and founder of the twenty-second dynasty; he sheltered Jeroboam when he fled from Solomon. In Rehoboam's fifth year, he overran Judah and attacked Jerusalem, carrying off the treasures stored in the palace and Temple. 1 Ki. 11:40; 14:25; 2 Chr. 12:2-9.

SHITRAI [SHI-tri] 975 B.C. A Sharonite in charge of the flocks that grazed in Sharon. 1 Chr. 27:29.

SHIZA [SHI-zuh] 1025 B.C. A Reubenite, father of Adina, one of David's thirty mighty men. 1 Chr. 11:42.

SHOBAB [SHOH-bab]
1. B.C. (date unknown). A son of Caleb, a descendant of Judah. 1 Chr. 2:18.
2. 975 B.C. A son born to David in Jerusalem. 2 Sam. 5:14; 1 Chr. 3:5; 14:4.

SHOBACH [SHOH-bak] 975 B.C. Syrian commander of Hadadezer's army, defeated and killed in battle against King David. 2 Sam. 10:16-18. Called Shophach in 1 Chr. 19:16-18.

SHOBAI [SHOH-bi] B.C. (date unknown). Ancestral head of a family of Temple gatekeepers that returned to Judah after the Exile. Ezra 2:42; Neh. 7:45.

SHOBAL [SHOH-buhl]
1. 1975 B.C. A Horite chief living in the land of Seir in Ezra's time. Gen. 36:20,23,29.

2. B.C. (date unknown). A Judahite descended from Caleb; founder of Kireath Jearim or ancestor of its inhabitants. 1 Chr. 2:50-52.

3. B.C. (date unknown). Ancestral source of the clans of the Zorathites listed in the genealogy of Judah in 1 Chr. 4:1,2. Probably the same as Shobal 2.

SHOBEK [SHOH-bek] 450 B.C. A Jewish leader who sealed the covenant renewal with God in Nehemiah's time. Neh. 10:24.

SHOBI [SHOH-bi] 975 B.C. A son of Nahash, king of the Ammonites; he brought food to David as he fled from Absalom. 2 Sam. 17:27.

SHOHAM [SHOH-ham] 1000 B.C. Head of a family of Levites who served in David's time. 1 Chr. 24:27.

SHOMER [SHOH-muhr; "keeper; watcher"] KJV: Shamer (1 Chr. 7:34).
1. B.C. (date unknown). Listed only in the genealogy of Asher in 1 Chr. 7:32,34.
2. 825 B.C. A Moabite woman, mother of Jehozabad, one of the conspirators who killed Joash, king of Judah. 2 Ki. 12:21. Called Shimrith in 2 Chr. 24:26.

SHOPHACH [SHOH-fak] 975 B.C. General of the Syrian army, slain by David. 1 Chr. 19:16-18. See Shobach.

SHUA [SHOO-uh; "prosperity"] KJV: Shuah (Gen. 38:2,12).
1. 1925 B.C. Canaanite whose daughter married Judah, son of Jacob. Gen. 38:2,12.
2. B.C. (date unknown). Daughter of Heber, listed only in the genealogy of Asher. 1 Chr. 7:32.

SHUAH [SHOO-uh; "depression"] 2000 B.C. A son of Abraham by Keturah. Gen. 25:2.

SHUAL [SHOO-uhl; "fox" or "jackal"] B.C. (date unknown). Listed only in the genealogy of Asher in 1 Chr. 7:36.

SHUBAEL [SHOO-bay-uhl; "God's captive"] KJV, RSV: Shebuel (1 Chr. 23:16; 25:4; 26:24).
1. B.C. (date unknown). A Levite descendant of Amram. 1 Chr. 24:20.
2. 1000 B.C. A Levite descended from Gershom, son of Moses; officer in charge of the treasuries in David's time. 1 Chr. 23:16; 26:24.
3. 975 B.C. A son of Heman and head of the thirteenth division of singers in David's time. 1 Chr. 25:4,20.

SHUHAH [SHOO-huh; "depression"] B.C. (date unknown). KJV: Shuah. Listed only in the genealogy of the clans of Judah in 1 Chr. 4:11.

SHUHAM [SHOO-ham] 1875 B.C. A son of Dan and ancestral source of the Shuhamite clan. Num. 26:42. Called Hushim in Gen. 46:23.

SHUNI [SHOO-ni] 1875 B.C. A son of Gad and ancestral head of a clan. Gen. 46:16; Num. 26:15.

SHUPHAM [SHOO-fam] 1825 B.C. RSV: Shephupham. A son or grandson of Benjamin. Num. 26:39. Called Shephuphan in 1 Chr. 8:5. See Muppim.

SHUPPIM [SHUP-im] 975 B.C. A gatekeeper in the days of David. 1 Chr. 26:16.

SHUTHELAH [SHOO-thuh-luh]
1. 1850 B.C. A son of Ephraim and ancestral source of the clans of Ephraim. Num. 26:35,36; 1 Chr. 7:20.
2. B.C. (date unknown). Another descended from Ephraim, son of Joseph. 1 Chr. 7:21.

SIA [SI-uh] B.C. (date unknown). Ancestral head of a family of post-exilic family of Temple servants. Neh. 7:47. Called Siaha in Ezra 2:44.

SIAHA [SI-uh-huh] B.C. (date unknown). Ancestor of a family of Temple servants that returned to Judah with Zerubbabel. Ezra 2:44. See Sia.

SIBBECAI [SIB-uh-ki; "Yahweh intervenes"] KJV: Sibbechai (2 Sam. 21:18). A Hushathite warrior, one of David's mighty men. He slew Saph, a Philistine giant. 2 Sam. 21:18; 1 Chr. 11:29; 27:11. Called Mebunnai in 2 Sam. 23:27.

SIHON [SI-hahn] 1425 B.C. An Amorite king who denied the Israelites passage through his territory on their way from Egypt to Palestine. When he led his army against Israel, he was slain; thereafter his territory was taken and inhabited by the Israelites. Num. 21:21-34; Deut. 2:24-37.

SILAS* [SI-luhs; form of Silvanus or Saul] A.D. 50. KJV, RSV: Silvanus (1 Th. 1:1; 2 Th. 1:1; 2 Cor. 1:19). A Christian chosen by the Jerusalem church to accompany Paul and Barnabus to Antioch; after Paul and Barnabus separated, Silas traveled with Paul throughout most of his second missionary journey. Acts 15:22-40; 16:16–17:15; 2 Cor. 1:19.

SIMEON [SIM-ee-uhn; "he hears" or "hearing"] RSV: Symeon (Acts 13:1).
1. 1900 B.C. Second son of Jacob by Leah and head of one of the twelve tribes of Israel. With Levi, he slew the people of Shechem in revenge for the violation of his sister Dinah. Gen. 29:33; 34:25-30; 49:5-7.
2. B.C. (date unknown). A descendant of David and an ancestor of Jesus Christ. Lk. 3:30.
3. 5 B.C. A devout Jew in Jerusalem who recognized the child Jesus as the Messiah. Lk. 2:25-35.
4. A.D. 45. One of the prophets and teachers at the church in Antioch; also called Niger. Acts 13:1.

SIMON [SI-muhn; "he hears" or "hearing"]
1. A.D. 1. Father of Judas Iscariot, the betrayer of Christ. Jn. 6:71; 13:2,26.
2.* A.D. 25. Given name of the apostle Peter. Mt. 4:18; 16:17; Mk. 3:16. See Peter.
3. A.D. 25. Simon the Zealot, notable as one of the twelve apostles. Mt. 10:4; Lk. 6:15. The KJV and RSV mistakenly call him the Canaanite or Cananaean (Mt. 10:4).
4. A.D. 25. A brother of Christ. Mt. 13:55; Mk. 6:3.
5. A.D. 25. A Pharisee in whose house Jesus' feet were anointed. Lk. 7:36-50.
6. A.D. 30. A leper in Bethany in whose house Jesus was anointed with perfume shortly before his crucifixion. Mt. 26:6; Mk. 14:3.
7. A.D. 30. A man from Cyrene who was forced to carry the cross to the place of Christ's crucifixion. He was the father of Alexander and Rufus, probably members of the Roman church. Mk. 15:21; Lk. 23:26.
8. A.D. 35. Simon Magus, a renowned sorcerer in Samaria who tried to buy the miraculous powers of the apostles Peter and John. Acts 8:9-24.
9. A.D. 35. A tanner with whom Peter stayed while he was in Joppa. Acts 9:43; 10:6,32.

SIPPAI [SIP-i] 1000 B.C. A Philistine champion descended from the giant Raphaites; he was slain in combat by Sibbecai. 1 Chr. 20:4. Called Saph in 2 Sam. 21:18.

SISERA [SIS-uhr-uh]
1. 1225 B.C. Commander of the army of Jabin, Canaanite king of Hazor who oppressed Israel. Sisera fled after his defeat at the hands of Deborah and Barak, taking refuge in the tent of Jael. He was killed by Jael in his sleep. Jdg. 4; 5:20-30.

2. B.C. (date unknown). Ancestral head of a family of Temple servants that returned to Judah with Zerubbabel after the Exile. Ezra 2:53; Neh. 7:55.

SISMAI [SIS-mi] B.C. (date unknown). KJV: Sisamai. Listed only in the genealogy of Judah in 1 Chr. 2:40.

SITHRI [SITH-ri; "Yahweh is protection"] B.C. (date unknown). KJV: Zithri. A Kohathite Levite listed in the family record of Moses and Aaron. Ex. 6:22.

SO [SOH] 725 B.C. A king of Egypt, to whom Hoshea appealed when he rebelled against Assyria. He has been identified with Sabaeo; Sib'e, an Egyptian general; Osorkon IV; and Tefnakht. Some believe the name is a reference to the city of Sais, Tefnakht's native city. 2 Ki. 17:4.

SOCO [SOC-oh; "thorny"] B.C. (date unknown). KJV: Socho. A descendant of Judah and a son of Heber. 1 Chr. 4:18. Possibly the name of a town in Judah is intended.

SODI [SOH-di] 1475 B.C. Father of Gaddiel, leader from the tribe of Zebulun sent to spy out the land of Canaan. Num. 13:10.

SOLOMON* [SAHL-uh-muhn; "peaceable"] 970–930 B.C. The son of David and Bathsheba, renowned for his wisdom. He succeeded David as king and led Israel into a period of great prosperity. He built the Temple but later in life he was led into idolatry by his foreign wives. Traditionally accepted as the author of Ecclesiastes, many of the Proverbs, the Song of Songs, and two Psalms (72, 127). 2 Sam. 12:24,25; 1 Ki. 1–11; 1 Chr. 28:5–2 Chr. 9:31; Mt. 1:6,7.

SOPATER [SOH-pah-tuhr] A.D. 55. A man from Berea who accompanied Paul from Greece to Jerusalem. Acts 20:4. Possibly the same as Sosipater.

SOPHERETH [SAHF-uh-reth] 950 B.C. A servant of Solomon whose descendants returned to Judah after the Exile. Neh. 7:57. Called Hassophereth in Ezra 2:55.

SOSIPATER [soh-SIP-uh-tuhr; "defending one's father"] A.D. 55. One who sent greetings to the Roman church through Paul. Paul calls him "my relative," meaning he was a Jew. Rom. 16:21. He may be the same as Sopater.

SOSTHENES [SAHS-thuh-neez]
1. A.D. 55. Ruler of the synagogue at Corinth when the Jews took Paul to court. When the case was dismissed against Paul, Sosthenes was seized and beaten by the crowd in an act of anti-Semitism. Acts 18:17.
2. A.D. 55. A Christian mentioned in the salutation of 1 Corinthians. He may be identical to Sosthenes 1, having been converted after the incident in Corinth. 1 Cor. 1:1.

SOTAI [SOH-ti] 950 B.C. Ancestral head of a family of Solomon's servants that returned to Judah with Zerubbabel. Ezra 2:55; Neh. 7:57.

STACHYS [STAY-kis; "head of grain"] A.D. 55. A Christian at Rome greeted by Paul as his "dear friend." Rom. 16:9.

STEPHANUS [STEF-uh-nuhs; "crown"] A.D. 60. A Christian convert from Achaia whose household was baptized by Paul at Corinth. He was among the delegation from the church of Corinth who visited Paul in Ephesus. 1 Cor. 1:16; 16:15-18.

STEPHEN* [STEE-vuhn; "crown"] A.D. 35. First and foremost of the seven deacons appointed by the Jerusalem church; his teaching and the miraculous signs he performed drew the hostile attention of certain Jews, and he was taken before the Sanhedrin. His defense, recorded in Acts 7, so enraged them that they immediately dragged Stephen from the city and stoned him. He thus became the first Christian martyr and precipitated Saul's persecution of the church. Acts 6:5–8:2.

SUAH [SOO-uh] B.C. (date unknown). Listed only in the genealogy of Asher in 1 Chr. 7:36.

SUSANNA [soo-ZAN-uh; "lily"] A.D. 25. A follower of Christ who helped support him during his ministry. Lk. 8:3.

SUSI [SOO-si] 1475 B.C. Father of Gaddi, leader from the tribe of Manasseh sent by Moses to spy out the land of Canaan. Num. 13:11.

SYNTYCHE [SIN-tih-kee; "fortunate"] A.D. 65. A Christian woman in the church at Philippi whose disagreement with Euodia came to the attention of Paul. In Philippians 4:2,3, he exhorts the women to "agree with each other in the Lord." Phil. 4:2,3.

T

TABALIAH [TAB-uh-LI-uh; "Yahweh has purified"(?)] 975 B.C. KJV, RSV: Tebaliah. A tabernacle gatekeeper in David's day. 1 Chr. 26:11.

TABBAOTH [TAB-ay-ahth; "rings"] B.C. (date unknown). Ancestral head of a family of Temple servants that returned to Judah with Zerubbabel after the Exile. Ezra 2:43; Neh. 7:46.

TABEEL [TAY-bee-uhl; "God is good"] KJV: Tabeal (Isa. 7:6).
1. 775 B.C. Father of a man who Rezin, king of Damascus, and Pekah, king of Israel, planned to set up as a puppet king of Judah after deposing Ahaz. Isa. 7:6.
2. 450 B.C. An official in Samaria who took part in sending a letter to Artaxerxes in opposition to the rebuilding of Jerusalem's walls. Ezra 4:7.

TABITHA [TAB-ih-thuh; "gazelle"] A.D. 35. A Christian woman in Joppa known for her charitable acts; Peter raised her from the dead. Acts 9:36-42. The Greek form of her name is Dorcas.

TABRIMMON [tab-RIM-ahn; "Rimmon (the deity) is good"] 925 B.C. KJV: Tabrimon. Son of Hezion and father of Ben-Hadad I, king of Syria. 1 Ki. 15:18.

TAHAN [TAY-han]
1. B.C. (date unknown). Ancestral head of an Ephraimite clan. Num. 26:35.
2. B.C. (date unknown). A descendant of Ephraim, listed in 1 Chr. 7:25.

TAHASH [TA-hash] 2050 B.C. A son of Abraham's brother Nahor by his concubine, Reumah. Gen. 22:24.

TAHATH [TAY-hath]
1. B.C. (date unknown). A Kohathite listed in the genealogy of Levi in 1 Chr. 6:24,37.
2 and 3. B.C. (dates unknown). Two listed in the genealogy of Ephraim in 1 Chr. 7:20.

TAHPENES [TAH-puh-neez] 975 B.C. An Egyptian queen in the time of David and Solomon; she raised Genubath, son of her sister and Hadad the Edomite. 1 Ki. 11:19,20.

TAHREA [TAH-ree-uh] B.C. (date unknown). Son of Micah and descendant of Saul. 1 Chr. 9:41. Called Tarea in 1 Chr. 8:35.

TALMAI [TAL-mi]
1. 1400 B.C. One of the three sons of Anak and head of a clan driven out of Hebron by Caleb. Num. 13:22; Josh. 15:14; Jdg. 1:10.
2. 1025 B.C.. King of Geshur and father of Maacah, the wife of David and mother of Absalom. After Absalom killed Amnon, he took refuge in Geshur with his grandfather, Talmai. 2 Sam. 3:3; 13:37.

TALMON [TAL-mahn]
1. B.C. (date unknown). Ancestral head of a family of gatekeepers that returned to Judah with Zerubbabel. Ezra 2:42; Neh. 7:45.
2. 450 B.C. A gatekeeper among the Levites who resettled in Jerusalem in Ezra's day. 1 Chr. 9:17; Neh. 11:19; 12:25.

TAMAR [TAY-mahr; "palm tree"] KJV NT: Thamar.
1. 1850 B.C. The widow of Judah's son, Er, who posed as a prostitute for Judah. She bore Judah twin sons, Perez and Zerah. Tamar is listed in the genealogy of Jesus. Gen. 38:6-30; Ruth 4:12; Mt. 1:3.
2. 975 B.C. The daughter of David violated by her half-brother, Amnon. Her brother Absalom killed Amnon in revenge, and thereafter fled to Geshur. 2 Sam. 13; 1 Chr. 3:9.
3. 950 B.C. The daughter of Absalom. 2 Sam. 14:27.

TAMMUZ* [TAM-uhz] A Sumerian vegetation deity, husband and brother of Ishtar (Ashtoreth), goddess of fertility. Similar to the cults of Adonis and the Egyptian god Osiris, his death and entrance into the underworld symbolized the death of nature at the onset of winter, at which time an annual rite of mourning was held. Ezekiel describes a variation of this rite. Ezek. 8:14.

TANHUMETH [tan-HOO-meth; "comfort"] 625 B.C. Father of Seraiah, a military commander who joined Gedaliah at Mizpah. 2 Ki. 25:23; Jer. 40:8.

TAPHATH [TAY-fath] 950 B.C. Daughter of Solomon and wife of Ben-Abinadab, one of Solomon's district governors. 1 Ki. 4:11.

TAPPUAH [TAP-poo-uh] B.C. (date unknown). A descendant of Caleb listed in the genealogy of Judah in 1 Chr. 2:43.

TAREA [TAIR-ee-uh] B.C. (date unknown). Son of Micah and great-grandson of Jonathan, son of Saul. 1 Chr. 8:35. See Tahrea.

TARSHISH [TAHR-shish]
1. B.C. (date unknown). A son of Javan listed in the Table of Nations, in Gen. 10:4. Ancestral source of a Mediterranean people, possibly the inhabitants of Tartessus, an ancient city in southwest Spain (compare Jon. 1:3).
2. B.C. (date unknown). Listed only in the genealogy of Benjamin in 1 Chr. 7:10.
3. 475 B.C. One of the seven nobles of Persia and Media who advised King Xerxes. Esth. 1:14.

TARTAK [TAHR-tak] A deity worshiped by the Avvites, transplanted in Samaria after 722 B.C. 2 Ki. 17:31.

TATTENAI [TAT-uh-ni] 500 B.C. KJV: Tatnai. A Persian governor of the territory west of the Euphrates ordered by King Darius to help the Jews rebuild the Temple. Ezra 5:3–6:13.

TEBAH [TEE-buh] 2050 B.C. Eldest son of Abraham's brother Nahor, by his concubine, Reumah. Gen. 22:24.

TEHINNAH [tuh-HIN-uh; "supplication"] B.C. (date unknown). Founder of the city of Ir Nahash, listed only in the genealogy of Judah in 1 Chr. 4:12.

TELAH [TEE-luh] B.C. (date unknown). Listed only in the genealogy of Ephraim in 1 Chr. 7:25.

TELEM [TEE-lem] 450 B.C. A gatekeeper who took a foreign wife after the Exile. Ezra 10:24.

TEMA [TEE-muh; "south"] 2025 B.C. A son of Ishmael and ancestral source of the inhabitants of Tema in northern Arabia. Gen. 25:15.

TEMAH [TEE-muh] B.C. (date unknown). KJV: Thamah (Ezra 2:53); Tamah (Neh. 7:55). Ancestor of a family of Temple servants that returned to Judah after the Exile. Ezra 2:53; Neh. 7:55.

TEMAN [TEE-muhn; "south"]
1. 1875 B.C. A grandson of Esau and an Edomite chief. Gen. 36:11,15; 1 Chr. 1:36.
2. B.C. (date unknown). An Edomite chief descended from Esau. Gen. 36:42.

TEMENI [TEM-uh-ni; "fortunate"] B.C. (date unknown). Listed only in the genealogy of Judah in 1 Chr. 4:6.

TERAH [TEER-uh] 2200 B.C. KJV NT: Thara. Father of Abraham, Nahor, and Haran. Gen. 11:24-32; Lk. 3:34.

TERESH [TEER-esh] 475 B.C. A bodyguard of Xerxes who conspired to assassinate the king. He was executed after Mordecai discovered and revealed the plot. Esth. 2:21; 6:2.

TERTIUS [TUHR-shee-uhs; "third"] A.D. 55. The person to whom Paul dictated his letter to the Romans. Rom. 16:22.

TERTULLUS [tuhr-TUL-uhs; diminutive of Tertius] A.D. 60. Lawyer hired by the Jews to present their case against Paul before Felix, the Roman governor of Judea. Acts 24:1-8.

THADDAEUS [THAD-ee-uhs] A.D. 30. One of the twelve apostles. Mt. 10:3; Mk. 3:18. Possibly the same as Judas the son of James, in Lk. 6:16; Jn. 14:22; Acts 1:13.

THEOPHILUS [thee-AHF-uh-luhs; "loved by God"] A.D. 60. The person, otherwise unknown, to whom Luke dedicated his Gospel and the Book of Acts. Lk. 1:3; Acts 1:1.

THEUDAS [THYOO-duhs; "gift of God" (?)] B.C. (date unknown). Leader of a short-lived rebellion, used as an example by Gamaliel in his speech cautioning the Sanhedrin to use tolerance in reaction to the apostles. Acts 5:36.

THOMAS* [TAHM-uhs; "twin"] A.D. 25. The apostle who refused to believe in the resurrection until he saw Christ with his own eyes. Mt. 10:3; Jn. 11:16; 14:1-6; 20:24-29; Acts 1:13. Didymus is the Greek form of his name.

TIBERIUS [ti-BEER-ee-us] Claudius Caesar Augustus, Roman emperor from A.D. 14, when he succeeded Augustus, to A.D. 37. Lk. 3:1.

TIBNI [TIB-ni] 885–880 B.C. One who challenged Omri for the throne of Israel after the death of Zimri. Tibni was killed and Omri became king. 1 Ki. 16:21,22.

TIDAL [TI-duhl] 2000 B.C. King of Goiim who with the kings of Shinar, Ellasar, and Elam waged war with five kings of the area surrounding the Dead Sea. Tidal and his allies plundered Sodom and Gomorrah and captured Lot; Abram defeated them and rescued Lot. Gen. 14:1-17.

TIGLATH-PILESER [TIG-lath-pih-LEE-zuhr] 744–727 B.C. Tiglath-Pileser III, notable as the king of Assyria who initiated a resurgence of the Assyrian Empire. He conquered Babylon and greatly extended the territory under his influence. When Pekah and Rezin attacked Judah, Ahaz appealed to Tiglath-Pileser for help. He came and sacked Damascus, deporting its inhabitants. 2 Ki. 15:19, 20,29; 16:7-10; 1 Chr. 5:6,26; 2 Chr. 28:16-21. Also called Pul. **Son and successor:** Shalmaneser V.

TIKVAH [TIK-vuh; "hope"]
1. 650 B.C. Father of Shallum, husband of Huldah the prophetess. 2 Ki. 22:14. Called Tokhath in 2 Chr. 34:22.
2. 475 B.C. Father of Jahzeiah, who disputed Ezra's reform requiring the divorce of foreign wives among the Jews. Ezra 10:15.

TILON [TI-lahn] B.C. (date unknown). Listed only in the genealogy of Judah in 1 Chr. 4:20.

TIMAEUS [tih-MAY-uhs] A.D. 1. Father of Bartimaeus, a blind beggar of Jericho healed by Christ. Mk. 10:46.

TIMNA [TIM-nuh; "restraining"] KJV: Timnah (Gen. 36:40).
1. 1900 B.C. Concubine of Eliphaz, son of Esau. Gen. 36:12; 1 Chr. 1:36.
2. 1975 B.C. Sister of Lotan, a Horite chief who lived in the land of Seir in Esau's time. Gen. 36:22.
3. B.C. (date unknown). An Edomite chief descended from Esau. Gen. 36:40; 1 Chr. 1:51.

TIMON [TI-mahn] A.D. 35. One of the seven deacons chosen by the church in Jerusalem to minister to the poor. Acts 6:5.

TIMOTHY* [TIM-uh-thee; "honored by God" or "honoring God"] A.D. 50. KJV: Timotheus (Acts and 1 Corinthians). A youthful companion of Paul who traveled extensively with the apostle during his missionary journeys. Recipient of the two Epistles bearing his name. Acts 16:1-3; 17:14,15; 20:4; 1 Cor. 4:17; 1 Tim.1-6; 2 Tim.1-4. **Mother:** Eunice. **Grandmother:** Lois.

TIRAS [TI-ruhs] B.C. (date unknown). A son of Japheth listed in the Table of Nations. Gen. 10:2. Josephus and others believed his descendants to be the Thracians; some have identified him with the piratical Tarusha in the Aegian Sea.

TIRHAKAH [tuhr-HAY-kuh] 700 B.C. A king of Egypt and Ethiopia who promised but failed to deliver aid to Hezekiah against Sennacherib, king of Assyria. 2 Ki. 19:9; Isa. 37:9.

TIRHANAH [tuhr-HAY-nuh] B.C. (date unknown). A Judahite, son of Caleb, by his concubine Maacah. 1 Chr. 2:48.

TIRIA [TEER-ee-uh] B.C. (date unknown). Listed only in the genealogy of Judah. 1 Chr. 4:16.

TIRZAH [TUHR-zuh] 1400 B.C. Youngest of the daughters of Zelophehad; they petitioned Moses and received their father's inheritance. Num. 26:33; 27:1-8; 36.

TITIUS JUSTUS [TIT-ee-us JUS-tuhs] A.D. 55. A Christian in Corinth with whom Paul stayed. Acts 18:7.

TITUS* [TI-tuhs] A.D. 55. A Greek converted to Christianity; he became a resourceful servant of the apostle Paul, who entrusted him with difficult missions in Corinth and Crete. 2 Cor. 2:13; 7:6-15; 8:6,16-24; Tit. 1–3.

TOAH [TOH-uh] B.C. (date unknown). A Levite and ancestor of Samuel. 1 Chr. 6:34. Called Nahath in 1 Chr. 6:26 and Tohu in 1 Sam. 1:1.

TOB-ADONIJAH [TAHB-AD-oh-NI-juh; "the Lord Yahweh is good"] 875 B.C. A Levite sent to teach the Law throughout Judah during the reign of Jehoshaphat. 2 Chr. 17:8.

TOBIAH [toh-BI-uh; "Yahweh is good"]
1. B.C. (date unknown). Ancestor of some who returned to Judah with Zerubbabel but could not prove their Israelite descent. Ezra 2:60; Neh. 7:62.
2. 450 B.C. An Ammonite official who with Sanballat opposed Nehemiah's reconstruction of Jerusalem. Eliashib the high priest improperly gave Tobiah a room in the Temple, and during his second term as governor, Nehemiah threw him out of the house of God. Neh. 2:10,19; 4:1-8; 6; 13:4-8.

TOBIJAH [tob-BI-juh; "Yahweh is good"]
1. 875 B.C. A Levite sent by Jehoshaphat to teach the Law in the towns of Judah. 2 Chr. 17:8.
2. 525 B.C. A Jewish exile among those who brought gold and silver from Babylon used to make a crown for the high priest. Zech. 6:10-14.

TOGARMAH [toh-GAHR-muh] B.C. (date unknown). Listed among the Japhethites in the Table of Nations. Gen. 10:3. Ancestral source of a nation north of Palestine among the allies of Magog (compare Ezek. 27:14; 38:6).

TOHU [TOH-hoo] B.C. (date unknown). A Kohathite ancestor of Samuel. 1 Sam. 1:1. See Toah.

TOKHATH [TAHK-hath] 650 B.C. KJV: Tikvath. Father of Shallum, the husband of Huldah the prophetess. 2 Chr. 34:22. Called Tikvah in 2 Ki. 22:14.

TOLA [TOH-luh]
1. 1875 B.C. Firstborn son of Issachar, among those who went into Egypt with Jacob. Gen. 46:13; Num. 26:23; 1 Chr. 7:1,2.
2. 1100 B.C. A minor judge from the tribe of Issachar who led Israel for twenty-three years. Jdg. 10:1,2.

TOU [TOH-oo] 1000 B.C. KJV: Toi (2 Sam. 8:9,10). King of Hamath who sent his son to congratulate David on his victory over Hadadezer, their mutual enemy. 2 Sam. 8:9,10; 1 Chr. 18:9,10.

TROPHIMUS [TRAHF-ih-muhs; "nourishing"] A.D. 55. A Christian convert from Ephesus who was one of Paul's traveling companions. He was a Gentile, and some Asian Jews mistakenly supposed he had entered the Temple in Jerusalem with Paul. The riot that followed resulted in Paul's arrest and imprisonment. Acts 20:4; 21:29; 2 Tim. 4:20.

TRYPHENA [tri-FEE-nuh; "dainty"] A.D. 55. A Christian woman greeted by Paul in his letter to the Romans. Rom. 16:12.

TRYPHOSA [tri-FOH-suh; "delicate"] A.D. 55. A Roman Christian who with Tryphena was greeted by Paul as "women who work hard in the Lord." Rom. 16:12.

TUBAL [TOO-bahl] B.C. (date unknown). A son of Japheth listed in the Table of Nations, in Gen. 10:2. Ancestral source of a people in Asia Minor (Ezek. 27:13; 38:2,3); referred to as Tabal in Assyrian inscriptions.

TUBAL-CAIN [TOO-bahl-CAYN] B.C. (date unknown). A son of Lamech and a master metalworker. Gen. 4:22.

TYCHICUS [TIK-ih-kuhs; "fortuitous"] A.D. 60. An Asian Christian who traveled with Paul and served as his messenger during Paul's imprisonment in Rome. Acts 20:4; Eph. 6:21; Col. 4:7; 2 Tim.4:12.

TYRANNUS [tuh-RAN-uhs; "tyrant"] A.D. (date unknown). An Ephesian in whose school Paul taught daily for two years. Tyrannus may have been a Greek rhetorician or Jewish rabbi, or perhaps merely the founder of the school. Acts 19:9.

U

UCAL [OO-kuhl; meaning uncertain] B.C. (date unknown). One of the two men to whom Agur addressed his sayings. Possibly the word is a verb rather than a name, meaning "to be faint." Prov. 30:1.

UEL [OO-uhl; "will of God"] 450 B.C. One who took a foreign wife after the Exile. Ezra 10:34.

ULAM [OO-lam; "first"]
1. B.C. (date unknown). Listed only in the genealogy of Manasseh in 1 Chr. 7:16,17.
2. B.C. (date unknown). A Benjamite descended from Jonathan, son of Saul; his sons are described as "brave warriors who could handle the bow." 1 Chr. 8:39,40.

ULLA [UL-uh] B.C. (date unknown). Listed only in the genealogy of Asher in 1 Chr. 7:39.

UNNI [UN-i] RSV: Unno (Neh. 12:9)
1. 1000 B.C. A Levite who played the lyre in the procession before the ark of the covenant. 1 Chr. 15:18,20.
2. 525 B.C. A Levite who returned to Judah with Zerubbabel after the Exile. Neh. 12:9.

UR [UHR; "flame"] 1025 B.C. Father of Eliphal, one of David's mighty men. 1 Chr. 11:35.

URBANUS [uhr-BAY-nuhs; "pleasant, urbane"] A.D. 55. KJV: Urbane. A Roman Christian to whom Paul sent greetings. Rom. 16:9.

URI [YOOR-i; "fiery" or "enlightened"]
1. 1475 B.C. Father of Bezalel, the head craftsman chosen and empowered by God to build the tabernacle and its furnishings. Ex. 31:2; 1 Chr. 2:20.
2. 1000 B.C. Father of Geber, district governor over Gilead in Solomon's time. 1 Ki. 4:19.
3. 450 B.C. A Levite gatekeeper who took a foreign wife after the return from the Exile. Ezra 10:24.

URIAH [yoor-I-uh; "Yahweh is light"] KJV: Urijah.
1. 1000 B.C. The righteous husband of Bathsheba and a Hittite officer in David's army. David arranged his death in battle and thereafter married Bathsheba. 2 Sam. 11:2–12:10; 23:39.
2. 750 B.C. A chief priest during the reign of Ahaz; at the king's command, he constructed an Assyrian altar in the Temple. 2 Ki. 16:10-16.
3. 750 B.C. A priest in Ahaz's time who served as a witness to a prophecy of Isaiah. Isa. 8:2. Probably the same as Uriah 2.
4. 600 B.C. A prophet from Kiriath Jearim and a contemporary of Jeremiah; he was put to death by Jehoiakim. Jer. 26:20-23.

5. 475 B.C. Father of Meremoth, a priest who helped Ezra weigh out the sacred articles for the Temple. Ezra 8:33; Neh. 3:4,21.

6. 450 B.C. One who stood to Ezra's right at the reading of the Law. Neh. 8:4.

URIEL [YOOR-ee-el; "God is light"]
1. 1000 B.C. A Kohathite Levite during the time of David. 1 Chr. 6:24; 1 Chr. 15:5,11.
2. 975 B.C. A man from Gibeah whose daughter, Maacah, was the mother of Abijah, king of Judah. 2 Chr. 13:2.

UTHAI [OO-thi]
1. 450 B.C. A Judahite who resettled in Jerusalem after the Exile. 1 Chr. 9:4.
2. 450 B.C. Head of a family that returned with Ezra to Judah. Ezra 8:14.

UZ [UZ] KJV: Huz (Gen. 22:21).
1. B.C. (date unknown). Firstborn son of Aram listed in the Table of Nations. Gen. 10:23; 1 Chr. 1:17.
2. 2050 B.C. Firstborn son of Nahor and Milcah. Gen. 22:21.
3. 2050 B.C. A son of Dishan, a Horite chief who lived in the land of Seir in Esau's time. Gen. 36:28.

UZAI [UZ-i] 475 B.C. Father of Palal, who helped rebuild the walls of Jerusalem in Nehemiah's time. Neh. 3:25.

UZAL [OO-zuhl] A son of Joktan listed among the semites in the Table of Nations. Gen. 10:27. Founder of Uzal, possibly the ancient name of Sanaa, the capital of Yemen (see Ezek. 27:19).

UZZA [UZ-uh; "strength"]
1. B.C. (date unknown). Listed only in the genealogy of Benjamin in 1 Chr. 8:7.
2. B.C. (date unknown). Ancestor of a family of Temple servants that returned to Judah after the Exile. Ezra 2:49; Neh. 7:51.

UZZAH [UZ-uh; "strength"] KJV: Uzza (1 Chr. 6:29).
1. B.C. (date unknown). A Levite descendant of Merari. 1 Chr. 6:29.
2. 1000 B.C. A son of Abinadab, struck dead by God when he touched the ark. 2 Sam. 6:3-8; 1 Chr. 13:7-11.

UZZI [UZ-i; "my strength"]
1. B.C. (date unknown). A descendant of Issachar. 1 Chr. 7:2,3.
2. B.C. (date unknown). A descendant of Benjamin. 1 Chr. 7:7.
3. B.C. (date unknown). A priest in the line of Eleazar, son of Aaron. 1 Chr. 6:6,51; Ezra 7:4.
4. B.C. (date unknown). Ancestor of a Benjamite who resettled in Jerusalem in Ezra's time. 1 Chr. 9:8.
5. 500 B.C. Head of a priestly family in the time of Joiakim the high priest. Neh. 12:19.
6. 450 B.C. A descendant of Asaph and chief officer of the Levites in Jerusalem. Neh. 11:22.
7. 450 B.C. A Levite involved in the dedication of the wall of Jerusalem. Neh. 12:42.

UZZIA [uh-ZI-uh; "Yahweh is my strength"] 1000 B.C. A military commander from Ashtaroth; one of David's thirty mighty men. 1 Chr. 11:44.

UZZIAH [uh-ZI-uh; "Yahweh is my strength"] KJV NT: Ozias.
1. 1000 B.C. Father of Jonathan, an overseer of King David. 1 Chr. 27:25.
2. B.C. (date unknown). A Levite descended from Kohath. 1 Chr. 6:24.
3. 790–739 B.C. The son and successor of Amaziah, king of Judah. A pious king, in his later years his pride led him to commit sacrilege, and he was immediately stricken with leprosy. 2 Ki. 15:13,30-34; 2 Chr. 26; Mt. 1:9. Also called Azariah in 2 Ki. 15:1.
4. 475 B.C. Father of Athaiah, a Judahite who resettled in Jerusalem in Nehemiah's time. Neh. 11:4.

5. 450 B.C. A priest who put away his foreign wife in the time of Ezra. Ezra 10:21.

UZZIEL [uh-ZI-uhl; "God is my strength"]
1. B.C. (date unknown). Listed in the genealogy of Benjamin. 1 Chr. 7:7.
2. B.C. (date unknown). A Kohathite Levite and ancestor of the Uzzielites. Ex. 6:18,22; Lev. 10:4; 1 Chr. 15:10; 23:20.
3. 975 B.C. A son of Heman the king's seer and a minister of music in David's time. 1 Chr. 25:4. Called Azarel in v. 18.
4. 725 B.C. A Simeonite leader among those who invaded the land of Seir and destroyed the remaining Amalekites. 1 Chr. 4:42.
5. 725 B.C. A Levite who helped purify the Temple in Hezekiah's time. 2 Chr. 29:14.
6. 450 B.C. A goldsmith who helped rebuild Jerusalem's wall in Nehemiah's time. Neh. 3:8.

V

VAIZATHA [VI-zuh-thuh] 475 B.C. KJV: Vajezatha. One of the ten sons of Haman slain by the Jews in the citadel of Susa. Esth. 9:9.

VANIAH [vuh-NI-uh] 450 B.C. A descendant of Bani listed among those who took a foreign wife after the Exile. Ezra 10:34.

VASHTI [VASH-ti; "beautiful woman"] 475 B.C. The queen of Persia divorced by King Xerxes for her refusal to present herself before the nobles on the seventh day of a banquet. Her deposal led to the selection of Esther as queen. Esth. 1; 2:1-4.

VOPHSI [VAHF-si] 1475 B.C. Father of Nahbi, leader from the tribe of Naphtali sent to explore the land of Canaan. Num. 13:14.

W, X, Y

XERXES* [ZERK-seez] 485–464 B.C. KJV, RSV: Ahasuerus. Xerxes I, The son and successor of Darius the Great; he launched a campaign against Greece but suffered successive defeats, which led to the decline of the Persian Empire. He was the king of Persia who divorced Vashti and married Esther. Ezra 4:6; Esth. 1–10; Dan. 9:1. **Son and successor:** Artaxerxes I.

Z

ZAAVAN [ZAY-uh-van; "fearful"(?)] 1950 B.C. KJV: Zavan (1 Chr. 1:42). A son of Ezer, a Horite chief in Esau's time. Gen. 36:27; 1 Chr. 1:42.

ZABAD [ZAY-bad; "gift" or "endowment"]
1. B.C. (date unknown). Listed only in the genealogy of Ephraim in 1 Chr. 7:21.
2. B.C. (date unknown). A Judahite listed only in the genealogy of Jerahmeel in 1 Chr. 2:36,37.
3. 1000 B.C. A military commander, one of David's thirty mighty men. 1 Chr. 11:41. Possibly the same as Zabad 2.
4. 800 B.C. An official of Joash involved in planning and executing the assassination of the king. Amaziah later had him executed. 2 Chr. 24:25,26; 25:3. Called Jozabad in 2 Ki. 12:21.
5, 6, and 7. 450 B.C. Three who pledged to divorce their foreign wives in accordance with Ezra's marriage reforms. Ezra 10:27,33,43.

ZABBAI [ZAB-i]
1. 475 B.C. Father of Baruch, who helped rebuild Jerusalem's wall in Nehemiah's time. Neh. 3:20.
2. 450 B.C. One who took a foreign wife after the Exile. Ezra 10:28.

ZABDI [ZAB-di; "Yahweh has given"]
1. B.C. (date unknown). Listed only in the genealogy of Benjamin in 1 Chr. 8:19.
2. 975 B.C. An overseer in charge of King David's royal wine cellars. 1 Chr. 27:27.
3. B.C. (date unknown). A Levite descended from Asaph. Neh. 11:17. Also called Zicri (1 Chr. 9:15) and Zaccur (1 Chr. 25:2,10; Neh. 12:35).

ZABDIEL [ZAB-dee-uhl; "God has given"]
1. 1025 B.C. A Judahite, father of Jashobeam, one of the three chiefs of David's mighty men and leader of the first division of his army. 1 Chr. 27:2.
2. 450 B.C. Chief officer of the priests who resettled in Jerusalem after the Exile. Neh. 11:14.

ZABUD [ZAY-buhd; "bestowed"] 950 B.C. A priest and personal advisor to King Solomon. 1 Ki. 4:5. Possibly the son of Nathan the prophet.

ZACCAI [ZAK-i] B.C. (date unknown). Ancestral head of a family that returned to Judah with Zerubbabel. Ezra 2:9; Neh. 7:14.

ZACCHAEUS [za-KEE-uhs; "pure"] A.D. 30. A wealthy and dishonest tax collector in Jericho who became a disciple of Christ. Thereafter he gave half of his possessions to the poor and repaid fourfold those he had cheated. Lk. 19:1-10.

ZACCUR [ZAK-uhr; "remembered"] KJV: Zacchur (1 Chr. 4:26); Zabbud (Ezra 8:14).

1. 1475 B.C. Father of Shammua, leader from the tribe of Reuben sent by Moses to explore the land of Canaan. Num. 13:4.

2. B.C. (date unknown). Listed in the genealogy of Simeon in 1 Chr. 4:26.

3. B.C. (date unknown). A Levite descended from Merari. 1 Chr. 24:27.

4. 975 B.C. A son of Asaph and head of the third division of ministers of music. 1 Chr. 25:2,10; Neh. 12:35. *See* Zabdi 3.

5. 450 B.C. One who returned to Judah with Ezra after the Exile. Ezra 8:14.

6. 450 B.C. One who helped reconstruct the wall of Jerusalem under Nehemiah. Neh. 3:2.

7. 450 B.C. A Levite who sealed the covenant renewal with God in Nehemiah's time. Neh. 10:12.

8. 450 B.C. Father of Hanan, made assistant to the Temple treasurers by Nehemiah. Neh. 13:13.

ZADOK [ZAY-dahk; "righteous"] KJV: Sadoc (Mt. 1:14).

1. 1000 B.C. Son of Ahitub and father of Ahimaaz; he was a high priest of David who demonstrated an unswerving loyalty to the king. 2 Sam. 8:17; 15:24-36; 1 Ki. 1:8,32-45; 1 Chr. 12:28; 27:17.

2. 800 B.C. Father of Jerusha, the mother of Jotham, king of Judah. 2 Ki. 15:33; 2 Chr. 27:1.

3. B.C. (date unknown). An Aaronite and descendant of Zadok, the high priest in David's time. 1 Chr. 6:12; 9:11; Ezra 7:2.

4. 450 B.C. One who helped repair the wall of Jerusalem in Nehemiah's time. Neh. 3:4.

5. 450 B.C. A priest who also helped with Jerusalem's reconstruction under Nehemiah. Neh. 3:29.

6. 450 B.C. A Jewish leader who sealed the covenant renewal with God in Nehemiah's time. Neh. 10:21. Probably the same as 4.

7. 425 B.C. A scribe among those put in charge of the Temple treasuries by Nehemiah. Neh. 13:13.

8. B.C. (date unknown). A descendant of Zerubbabel and ancestor of Christ. Mt. 1:14.

ZAHAM [ZAY-ham] 900 B.C. A son of King Rehoboam and David's granddaughter Mahalath. 2 Chr. 11:19.

ZALAPH [ZAY-laf] 475 B.C. Father of Hanun, a rebuilder of Jerusalem's wall in Nehemiah's time. Neh. 3:30.

ZALMON [ZAL-muhn] 1000 B.C. An Ahohite, among the military elite known as David's mighty men. 2 Sam. 23:28. Called Ilai in 1 Chr. 11:29.

ZALMUNNA [zal-MUN-uh; "deprived of shade (protection)"] 1175 B.C. A king of Midian who with Zebah was pursued and put to death by Gideon, thus ending the Midianite oppression of Israel. Jdg. 8:5-21; Ps. 83:11. *See also* Zebah.

ZANOAH [zuh-NO-uh] B.C. (date unknown). Son of Jekuthiel and grandson of Mered by his Judean wife, listed in the genealogy of Judah in 1 Chr. 4:18.

ZAPHENATH-PANEAH [ZAF-uh-nath-puh-NEE-uh; "the god speaks and he lives" or "sustainer of the land"(?)] 1875 B.C. Name given by Pharaoh to Joseph after he interpreted the Pharaoh's dream. Gen. 41:45. *See* Joseph.

ZATTU [ZAT-oo] KJV: Zatthu (Neh. 10:14).

1. B.C. (date unknown). Ancestral head of a family whose members returned to Judah with Zerubbabel and Ezra after the Exile. Ezra 2:8; 8:5; 10:27; Neh. 7:13.

2. 450 B.C. A Jewish leader who sealed the covenant renewal with God in Nehemiah's time, probaby with the name of his family ancestor (*see* Zattu 1). Neh. 10:14.

ZAZA [ZAY-zuh] B.C. (date unknown). A Judahite listed only in the genealogy of Jerahmeel in 1 Chr. 2:33.

ZEBADIAH [ZEB-uh-DI-uh; "Yahweh has bestowed"]

1 and 2. B.C. (dates unknown). Two listed in the genealogy of Benjamin in 1 Chr. 8:15,17.

3. 1000 B.C. A Benjamite warrior, son of Jeroham from Gedor; he and his brother Joelah joined David's army at Ziklag. 1 Chr. 12:7.

4. 975 B.C. Third son of Meshelemiah and a tabernacle gatekeeper. 1 Chr. 26:2.

5. 975 B.C. Son of Asahel, the brother of Joel; leader of the fourth division of David's army. 1 Chr. 27:7.

6. 875 B.C. A Levite sent by King Jehoshaphat to teach the Law throughout the towns of Judah. 2 Chr. 17:8.

7. 850 B.C. Leader of the tribe of Judah in Jehoshaphat's day who was made judge of all matters pertaining to the king. 2 Chr. 19:11.

8. 450 B.C. Head of a family group descended from Shephatiah; they returned to Judah from exile with Ezra. Ezra 8:8.

9. 450 B.C. An Immerite priest who took a foreign wife after the Exile. Ezra 10:20.

ZEBAH [ZEE-buh; "sacrifice"] A Midianite king allied with Zalmunna; they invaded and oppressed Israel until both were defeated and put to death by Gideon. Jdg. 8:5-21; Ps. 83:11.

ZEBEDEE [ZEB-uh-dee; "gift of Yahweh" (?)] A.D. 1. A wealthy fisherman on the sea of Galilee, husband of Salome, and father of the apostles James and John. Andrew and Peter were their partners in the business. Zebedee was likely a resident of Capernaum. Mt. 4:21; Mk. 1:19,20; Lk. 5:9,10.

ZEBIDAH [zuh-BI-duh; "given"] 625 B.C. KJV: Zebudah. Mother of Jehoiakim, king of Judah. 2 Ki. 23:36.

ZEBINA [zuh-BI-nuh; "purchased"] 450 B.C. A Jew who took a foreign wife after the Exile. Ezra 10:43.

ZEBUL [ZEE-buhl; "dwelling"] 1125 B.C. Governor of the city of Shechem; he informed Abimelech of a revolt of townsmen led by Gaal. Abimelech came and routed the rebels. Jdg. 9:28-41.

ZEBULUN [ZEB-yoo-luhn; "dwelling" or "honor"] 2000 B.C. Sixth son of Jacob by his first wife, Leah; ancestral source of one of the twelve tribes of Israel. Gen. 30:20; 46:14; 49:13.

ZECHARIAH [ZEK-uh-RI-uh; "Yahweh remembers"] KJV: Zachariah (2 Kings); KJV NT: Zacharias.

1. B.C. (date unknown). Listed only in the genealogy of Reuben in 1 Chr. 5:7.

2. 1100 B.C. A son of Jeiel and a relative of Saul. 1 Chr. 9:37. Called Zeker in 1 Chr. 8:31.

3. 1000 B.C. A Levite musician who played the lyre as the ark was brought to Jerusalem by David. 1 Chr. 15:18,20; 16:5.

4. 1000 B.C. A priest who blew the trumpet in the procession before the ark. 1 Chr. 15:24.

5. 1000 B.C. The head of a Levite family descended from Isshiah, listed among the divisions of the Levites in David's day. 1 Chr. 24:25. Possibly the same as Zechariah 3.

6. 975 B.C. Firstborn son of Meshelemiah and head of a division of Temple gatekeepers. 1 Chr. 26:2,14.

7. 975 B.C. Fourth son of Hosah the Merarite; also a Levite gatekeeper. 1 Chr. 26:11.

8. 975 B.C. Officer over the tribe of Manasseh within the territory of Gilead in David's time. 1 Chr. 27:21.

9. 875 B.C. An official sent by King Jehoshaphat to teach the Law in the towns of Judah. 2 Chr. 17:7.

10. 875 B.C. A Levite descended from Asaph and father of Jahaziel, who prophesied before Jehoshaphat. 2 Chr. 20:14.

11. 850 B.C. A son of Jehoshaphat put to death when his brother Jehoram ascended to the throne of Judah. 2 Chr. 21:2.

12. 800 B.C. Son of Jehoiada the priest. He prophesied against Joash for turning to idolatry after Jehoiada's death; Joash therefore ordered his execution. 2 Chr. 24:20.

13. 775 B.C. A mentor who led King Uzziah to seek God during the early years of his reign. 2 Chr. 26:5.

14. 775 B.C. Father of Abijah, the mother of King Hezekiah. 2 Ki. 18:2; 2 Chr. 29:1.

15. 753 B.C. Son and successor of Jeroboam II, king of Israel. He reigned in Samaria only six months before he was assassinated by Shallum, who usurped the throne. 2 Ki. 14:29; 15:8-12.

16. 750 B.C. Son of Jeberekiah who served as a reliable witness for the prophet Isaiah. Isa. 8:2.

17. 725 B.C. A Levite descended from Asaph; he took part in the purification of the Temple in Hezekiah's time. 2 Chr. 29:13.

18. 625 B.C. A Kohathite Levite who served as a supervisor during the reconstruction of the Temple in Josiah's time. 2 Chr. 34:12.

19. 625 B.C. A priestly administrator of the Temple who contributed to the Passover celebration in Josiah's time. 2 Chr. 35:8.

20. B.C. (date unknown). Ancestor of a priest who resettled in Jerusalem after the Exile. Neh. 11:12.

21. B.C. (date unknown). Ancestor of Athaiah, a Judahite who resettled in Jerusalem in Nehemiah's time. Neh. 11:4.

22. B.C. (date unknown). Ancestor of another descendent of Judah who resettled in Jerusalem. Neh. 11:5.

23.* 525 B.C. Zechariah the prophet, notable as a post-exilic priest whose prophetic visions are recorded in the Book of Zechariah. A contemporary of Haggai and Zerubbabel, his message sought to counter the present spiritual apathy and despair in Jerusalem, and offered hope to the Jews as they awaited the coming of the Messiah. Neh. 12:16; Zech. 1-14.

24. B.C. (date unknown). A prophet, son of Berekiah, said by Christ to have been killed between the altar and the Temple. Mt. 23:35; Lk. 11:51. Most likely identical to either Zechariah 12 or 23.

25. 500 B.C. Head of a priestly family in the days of Joiakim the high priest. Neh. 12:16.

26 and 27. 450 B.C.. Two Jewish leaders who returned to Judah with Ezra after the Exile. Ezra 8:3,11.

28. 450 B.C. A Jewish leader sent by Ezra as part of a delegation to retrieve Levites from Casiphia to serve in the Temple. Ezra 8:16. Possibly the same as either Zechariah 26 or 27.

29. 450 B.C. One who took a foreign wife after the Exile. Ezra 10:26.

30. 450 B.C. One who stood to Ezra's left at the public reading of the Law. Neh. 8:4.

31. 450 B.C. A Temple gatekeeper descended from Meshelemiah; he or his descendants resettled in Jerusalem after the Exile. 1 Chr. 9:21. Possibly the same as Zechariah 6.

32. 450 B.C. A Levite descended from Asaph, among the musicians at the dedication of Jerusalem's wall in Nehemiah's time. Neh. 12:35.

33. 450 B.C. A priest who blew the trumpet at the dedication of the wall. Neh. 12:41.

34. 5 B.C. A priest notable as the father of John the Baptist. In his old age, the angel Gabriel appeared to him and foretold the birth of his son. Because he doubted the words of Gabriel, he was stricken dumb until after the birth and naming of the infant John. Lk. 1:5-25,57-79.

ZEDEKIAH [ZED-uh-KI-uh; "Yahweh is my righteousness"] KJV: Zidkijah (Neh. 10:1).
1. 850 B.C. Son of Kenaanah; one of the four hundred false prophets who, in opposition to the prophet Micaiah, assured Ahab he would be victorious against Syria. 1 Ki. 22:11,24; 2 Chr. 18:10,23.
2. 600 B.C. A false prophet among the exiles in Babylon; Jeremiah prophesied that he would be put to death by Nebuchadnezzar. Jer. 29:21-23.
3. 600 B.C. An official under Jehoiakim, king of Judah. Jer. 36:12.
4. 597–586 B.C. The son of Josiah and Hamutal who became the last king of Judah. His original name, Mattaniah, was changed when Nebuchadnezzar made him king in place of his nephew, Jehoiachin. He rebelled against Nebuchadnezzar, who came and sacked Jerusalem, taking the Jews into captivity in Babylon. 2 Ki. 24:17—25:7; 1 Chr. 3:15,16; Jer. 21; 34; 37:1–39:7.
5. 450 B.C. A priest who sealed the covenant renewal with God in Nehemiah's time. Neh. 10:1.

ZEEB [ZEE-eb; "wolf"] 1175 B.C. A Midianite leader captured and put to death by the Ephraimites led by Gideon. Jdg. 7:25; 8:3; Ps. 83:11.

ZEKER [ZEE-kuhr; "fame" or "remembrance"] 1100 B.C. KJV: Zacher; RSV: Zecher. A son of Jeiel listed in the genealogy of Saul the Benjamite. 1 Chr. 8:31. See Zechariah 2.

ZELEK [ZEE-luhk; "fissure"] 1000 B.C. An Ammonite listed among the military elite known as David's mighty men. 2 Sam. 23:37; 1 Chr. 11:39.

ZELOPHEHAD [zeh-LOH-fuh-had] 1450 B.C. A Manassehite who had no sons; his daughters were given his inheritance by Moses. Num. 26:33; 27:1-11; 36:1-13.

ZEMIRAH [zuh-MI-ruh] B.C. (date unknown). A son or descendant of Beker, son of Benjamin. 1 Chr. 7:8.

ZENAS [ZEE-nuhs] A.D. 65. A Christian missionary in Crete skilled in Roman or Jewish law; Paul asked Titus to aid Zenas and his companion Apollos on their way to see Paul in Nicopolis. Tit. 3:13.

ZEPHANIAH [ZEF-uh-NI-uh; "Yahweh has hidden" or "Yahweh has treasured"]
1. B.C. (date unknown). A Kohathite Levite listed in the genealogy of Heman, a chief minister of music in David's day. 1 Chr. 6:36.
2. 625 B.C. A minor prophet, whose words are recorded in the Book of Zephaniah. His primary message concerned the impending judgment of Judah, but promised the restoration of a remnant. Zeph. 1–3.
3. 600 B.C. A chief priest in Jerusalem during the reign of Zedekiah. When the city fell to Nebuchadnezzar, he was arrested and executed at Riblah. 2 Ki. 25:18-21; Jer. 21:1; 29:25-32.
4. 550 B.C. Father of Josiah and Hen, who returned to Judah after the Exile. Zech. 6:10,14.

ZEPHO [ZEE-foh; "watch"] 1875 B.C. KJV, RSV: Zephi (1 Chr. 1:36). A grandson of Esau and an Edomite chief. Gen. 36:11,15; 1 Chr. 1:36.

ZEPHON [ZEE-fahn; "watching"(?)] 1875 B.C. KJV, RSV: Ziphion (Gen. 46:16). Firstborn son of Gad, among those who traveled with Jacob into Egypt. Gen. 46:16; Num. 26:15.

ZERAH [ZEER-uh; "shining" or "risen"(?)] KJV NT: Zara.
1. 1875 B.C. A grandson of Esau and an Edomite chief. Gen. 36:13,17.

2. 1825 B.C. A son of Judah by Tamar and twin brother of Perez. Gen. 38:30; 46:12; Num. 26:20; 1 Chr. 2:4,6; Mt. 1:3.
3. B.C. (date unknown). A descendant of Simeon and ancestor of a clan. Num. 26:13; 1 Chr. 4:24. Possibly the same as Zohar, son of Simeon.
4. B.C. (date unknown). Father of Bela, a pre-Israelite king of Edom. Gen. 36:33.
5. B.C. (date unknown). A Gershonite Levite, ancestor of Asaph, a chief minister of music in David's time. 1 Chr. 6:21,41.
6. 900 B.C. A Cushite (Ethiopian) king who led a powerful army against Asa and was defeated. 2 Chr. 14:9-15.

ZERAHIAH [ZAIR-uh-HI-uh; "Yahweh has come forth"]
1. B.C. (date unknown). A Levite listed in the high priestly line; an ancestor of Ezra the scribe. 1 Chr. 6:6,51; Ezra 7:4.
2. 475 B.C. Father of Eliehoenai, who returned to Judah with Ezra. Ezra 8:4.

ZERESH [ZEER-esh; "gold"] 475 B.C. Wife of Haman; she was among those who suggested he build a gallows upon which to hang Mordecai. Haman himself was later hanged on the gallows prepared for Mordecai. Esth. 5:10-14; 6:13.

ZERETH [ZEER-eth; "brilliance"(?)] B.C. (date unknown). Listed only in the genealogy of Judah. 1 Chr. 4:7.

ZERI [ZEER-i] 975 B.C. A son of Jeduthun and head of a division of Temple singers. 1 Chr. 25:3. Called Izri in v. 11.

ZEROR [ZEER-ohr] B.C. (date unknown). A Benjamite, ancestor of Saul. 1 Sam. 9:1.

ZERUAH [zuh-ROO-uh; "leprous"] 950 B.C. Mother of Jeroboam I. 1 Ki. 11:26.

ZERUBBABEL [zuh-RUB-uh-buhl; "seed of Babylon"] 525 B.C. KJV NT: Zorobabel. The prince of Judah who led the first return of the Jews to Judah after the Exile. Against strong opposition, he oversaw the work of rebuilding the Temple, completed and dedicated during the reign of Darius the Great, in 516 B.C. 1 Chr. 3:19; Ezra 2:1,2; 3:1–4:5; 5; Neh. 7:7; 12:1,47; Mt. 1:12,13. Possibly the same as Sheshbazzar.

ZERUIAH [zuh-ROO-yuh] 1025 B.C. David's sister and mother of Joab, Abishai, and Asahel, three important military leaders in David's army. 1 Sam. 26:6; 1 Chr. 2:16.

ZETHAM [ZEE-thuhm; "olive tree"] B.C. (date unknown). A Gershonite Levite descended from Ladan; he served as a Temple treasurer in David's time. 1 Chr. 23:8; 26:22.

ZETHAN [ZEE-thuhn; "olive tree"] B.C. (date unknown). Listed only in the genealogy of Benjamin in 1 Chr. 7:10.

ZETHAR [ZEE-thahr; "victor"(?)] 475 B.C. One of the seven eunuchs who served King Xerxes. Esth. 1:10.

ZEUS* [ZOOS] Sky deity, head of the Olympian gods in the Greek pantheon. Identical to the Roman god Jupiter. The people of Lystra called Barnabas "Zeus," believing him to be the manifestation of the god, and then prepared to make the appropriate sacrifices to the deity. Acts 14:12, 13.

ZIA [ZI-uh; "trembling"(?)] B.C. (date unknown). Listed only in the genealogy of Gad in 1 Chr. 5:13.

ZIBA [ZI-buh; "plant"] 1000 B.C. A servant of Saul instructed by King David to cultivate the lands of Saul for Mephibosheth, the lame son of Jonathan. Ziba later falsely accused Mephibosheth of treason, and was given the

lands of his master. When Mephibosheth protested his innocence, David divided the lands of Saul evenly between the two. 2 Sam. 9:1-13; 16:1-4; 19:17,26-30.

ZIBEON [ZIB-ee-uhn; "hyena"] 1975 B.C. Grandfather of Oholibamah, one of the wives of Esau. Gen. 36:2,14,20,24.

ZIBIA [ZIB-ee-uh; "gazelle"] B.C. (date unknown). Listed only in the genealogy of Benjamin in 1 Chr. 8:9.

ZIBIAH [ZIB-ee-uh; "gazelle"] 850 B.C. Mother of Joash, king of Judah. 2 Ki. 12:1.

ZICRI [ZIK-ri; "remembered"] KJV, RSV: Zichri.
1. B.C. (date unknown). A Levite listed in the family record of Moses and Aaron. Ex. 6:21.
2, 3, and 4. B.C. (dates unknown). Three men listed in the genealogy of Benjamin in 1 Chr. 8:19,23,27.
5. 1025 B.C. Father of Shelomith, a Levite official in David's time. 1 Chr. 26:25.
6. 1000 B.C. Father of Eliezer, officer over the tribe of Reuben. 1 Chr. 27:16.
7. 975 B.C. Son of Asaph and ancestor of a Levite who resettled in Jerusalem after the Exile. 1 Chr. 9:15. See Zabdi 2.
8. 900 B.C. Father of Amasiah, commander of an army of Judahites under Jehoshaphat. 2 Chr. 17:16.
9. 875 B.C. Father of Elishaphat, a military commander who aided Jehoiada in the overthrow of Athaliah. 2 Chr. 23:1.
10. 750 B.C. An Ephraimite warrior who killed Maaseiah, son of King Ahaz. 2 Chr. 28:7.
11. 500 B.C. Head of a priestly family in the time of Joiakim the high priest. Neh. 12:17.
12. 475 B.C. Father of Joel, chief officer over the Benjamites in Nehemiah's time. Neh. 11:9.

ZIHA [ZI-huh]
1. B.C. (date unknown). Ancestor of a family of Temple servants that returned to Judah with Zerubbabel. Ezra 2:43; Neh. 7:46.
2. 450 B.C. Overseer of the Temple servants in Nehemiah's time. Neh. 11:21. The name may indicate the family descended from Ziha 1.

ZILLAH [ZIL-uh; "shadow; protection"] B.C. (date unknown). One of the wives of Lamech and mother of Tubal-Cain. Gen. 4:19-23.

ZILLETHAI [ZIL-uh-thi; "shadow; protection"] KJV: Zilthai.
1. B.C. (date unknown). Listed only in the genealogy of Benjamin in 1 Chr. 8:20.
2. 1000 B.C. A military leader of the tribe of Manasseh; he joined David's army at Ziklag. 1 Chr. 12:20.

ZILPAH [ZIL-puh] 1925 B.C. The maidservant of Leah, whom she gave to Jacob as a wife. Mother of Gad and Asher. Gen. 29:24; 30:9-12.

ZIMMAH [ZIM-uh]
1. B.C. (date unknown). A Levite descended from Gershon. 1 Chr. 6:20,42.
2. 750 B.C. Father of Joah, a Gershonite Levite who helped purify the Temple in Hezekiah's time. 2 Chr. 29:12. If the relationship to Joah is ancestral, he is possibly the same as Zimmah 1.

ZIMRAN [ZIM-ran; "fame"(?)] 2000 B.C. Firstborn son of Abraham by Keturah. Gen. 25:2.

ZIMRI [ZIM-ri] KJV, RSV Zabdi (Joshua).
1. 1400 B.C. A Simeonite leader who was slain by Phinehas, grandson of Aaron, for his adultery with a Midianite woman. Num. 25:6-14.
2. B.C. (date unknown). Ancestral head of a Judahite family. Josh. 7:1,17,18; 1 Chr. 2:6.
3. B.C. (date unknown). A Benjamite de-

scended from Jonathan, son of Saul. 1 Chr. 8:36; 9:42.

4. 885 B.C. A military officer of Elah who killed the king and his entire family, seizing the throne of Israel. He reigned in the capital at Tirzah only seven days. 1 Ki. 16:9-20.

ZIPH [ZIF]
1. B.C. (date unknown). Grandson of Caleb, a descendant of Judah. 1 Chr. 2:42.
2. B.C. (date unknown). Listed only in the genealogy of Judah. 1 Chr. 4:16.

ZIPHAH [ZIF-uh] B.C. (date unknown). A Judahite; son of Jehallelel. 1 Chr. 4:16.

ZIPPOR [ZIP-ohr; "bird"] 1425 B.C. Father of Balak, a Moabite king who opposed the Israelites in Moses' time. Num. 22:2.

ZIPPORAH [zih-POHR-uh; "bird"] 1475 B.C. Daughter of Jethro (Reuel), a priest of Midian. She was given in marriage to Moses, and gave birth to Gershom and Eliezer. Ex. 2:21,22; 4:25; 18:1-6.

ZIZA [ZI-zuh] KJV, RSV: Zizah (1 Chr. 23:11); KJV, RSV: Zina (1 Chr. 23:10).
1. B.C. (date unknown). A Levite listed in the genealogy of the Gershonites. 1 Chr. 23:10,11.

2. 900 B.C. Son of Rehoboam and Maacah. 2 Chr. 11:20.
3. 725 B.C. A Simeonite leader who lived in the time of Hezekiah. 1 Chr. 4:37.

ZOHAR [ZOH-hahr]
1. 2025 B.C. Father of Ephron, a Hittite who sold Abraham a field with a cave to use as a burial site. Gen. 23:8; 25:9.
2. 1875 B.C. A son of Simeon among those who went to Egypt with Jacob. Gen. 46:10; Ex. 6:15. Probably the same as Zerah 3.
3. B.C. (date unknown). Listed only in the genealogy of Judah in 1 Chr. 4:7.

ZOHETH [ZOH-heth] B.C. (date unknown). Listed in the genealogy of Judah in 1 Chr. 4:20.

ZOPHAH [ZOH-fuh] B.C. (date unknown). Listed only in the genealogy of Asher in 1 Chr. 7:35,36.

ZOPHAI [ZOH-fi] B.C. (date unknown). A Levite descended from Kohath. 1 Chr. 6:26. Called Zuph in v. 35.

ZOPHAR [ZOH-fuhr] B.C. (date unknown). One of the three friends of Job who came to commiserate and contend with Job in his suffering. Job 2:11; 11; 20; 42:9.

ZUAR [ZOO-uhr; "little"] 1475 B.C. Father of Eliab, leader of the tribe of Issachar at the time of the Exodus. Num. 1:8.

ZUPH [ZUF; "honeycomb"] B.C. (date unknown). An ancestor of Elkanah and Samuel; he may have been a Levite by profession or called an Ephraimite because he lived in the hill country of Ephraim. 1 Sam. 1:1; 1 Chr. 6:35. *See* Zophai.

ZUR [ZUHR; "rock"]
1. 1425 B.C. A Midianite king whose daughter was slain by Phinehas, grandson of Aaron. He himself was later killed in battle with Israel. Num. 25:15; 31:8.
2. 1100 B.C. A Benjamite listed in the genealogy of Saul. 1 Chr. 8:30.

ZURIEL [ZUHR-ee-uhl; "God is a rock"] 1450 B.C. Leader of the Merarite clans at the time of the Exodus. Num. 3:35.

ZURISHADDAI [ZUHR-ih-SHAD-i; "the Almighty is a rock"] 1475 B.C. Father of Shelumiel, leader of the tribe of Simeon at the time of the Exodus. Num. 1:6.

identiquick™
PLACES

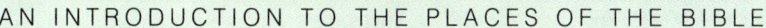
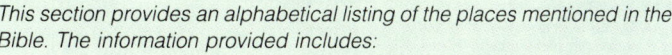

AN INTRODUCTION TO THE PLACES OF THE BIBLE

This section provides an alphabetical listing of the places mentioned in the Bible. The information provided includes:

1. *Names of Bible places as they appear in the NIV translation, with alternate spellings as they appear in other popular versions.*
2. *A guide to pronouncing each name, with the syllable(s) to be accented in capital letters.*
3. *The meaning of each name when it is known.*
4. *Cross-reference coordinates for those places identified in the map section.*
5. *A brief description, indicating the place's role in the story of the Bible.*
6. *Scripture references where further information about each can be found.*
7. *Other names by which a place may be known in the Bible.*

Places in this section are identified by a map (a Roman numeral) and by coordinates within that map. The Roman numeral will refer you to a map in the following section of maps (I–XIII), and the coordinates will help you pinpoint the place on the map.

It is not possible to determine the exact location of many places mentioned in the Bible. This is particularly true of those found only in lists, such as in the Book of Joshua. In most cases these places are given a general location near a city or site that can be identified with more certainty.

Some major Bible places are also treated at length in the main body of this dictionary. An asterisk following a name or number indicates this.

The pronunciation guide reflects a consensus of scholarly opinion. Each pronunciation is intended to be comfortable for the English speaker. While pronunciations do not reproduce exactly the way the names were pronounced in Hebrew or Greek, they still reflect Hebrew and Greek emphases.

Names, especially Hebrew names, were often intended to communicate something important about a place's character or role in historical events. While the meaning of many names remains uncertain, those given here represent the most likely meanings.

A

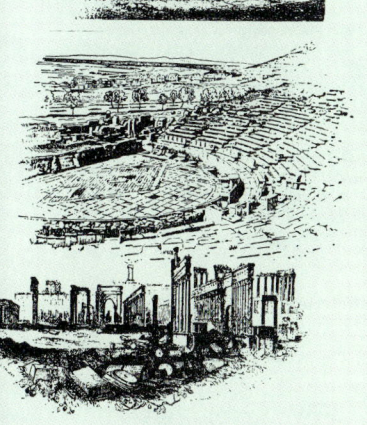

ABANA [uh-BAN-uh; "stony"] A river that flows through Damascus from its source about 23 miles (37 km) to the NW in the Anti-Lebanon Mountains. Its modern name is Barada. 2 Ki. 5:12.

ABARIM [AB-uh-reem; "region beyond"] A mountainous region in NW Moab that includes Mt. Nebo [**IV,** D1], overlooking the Dead Sea and Jordan Valley. God sent Moses there to look upon the land of Canaan before his death. Num. 27:12; Deut. 32:49; Jer. 22:20.

ABDON [AB-dahn; possibly "servile"] Hebron, KJV; Ebron, RSV. A Levitical town in Asher assigned to the Gershonites. Identified with the ruins of Abdeh, about 15 miles (24 km) S of Tyre [**VII,** B1]. Josh. 19:28; 21:30; 1 Chr. 6:74.

ABEL [AY-buhl; "meadow"] Shortened form of Abel Beth Maacah in 2 Sam. 20:18.

ABEL BETH MAACAH [AY-buhl BETH MAY-uh-kuh; "meadow (or brook) of the house of Maacah"] A town of Naphtali located in N Palestine located about 4 miles (6.5 km) W of the city of Dan [**VIII,** A2]. The rebel Sheba, son of Bicri, took refuge in the city to escape Joab, but was beheaded by its inhabitants. Later, the city was captured by Ben-Hadad, and thereafter fell to Tiglath-Pileser, in 733 B.C. Identified with modern Abil el-Qamh. 2 Sam. 20:14-18; 1 Ki. 15:20; 2 Ki. 15:29. *See* Abel; Abel-Maim.

ABEL KERAMIM [AY-buhl KAIR-uh-mim; "meadow of vineyards"] "Plain of the vineyards," KJV. A location SW of Rabbah [**VII,** C2], marking the extent of the territory devastated by Jephthah in his military campaign against the Ammonites. Identified with a site located about 37 miles (60 km) E of Jerusalem, and occupied from about 3000 to 500 B.C. Jdg. 11:33.

ABEL MAIM [AY-buhl MAY-ahm; "meadow of waters"] Variant form of Abel Beth Maacah. 2 Chr. 16:4.

ABEL MEHOLAH [AY-buhl meh-HOH-luh; "meadow of dancing"] **VIII,** B2. A town usually placed in the Jordan Valley S of Beth Shan, the home of Elisha the prophet. The exact site is uncertain. Jdg. 7:22; 1 Ki. 4:12; 19:16,19-21.

ABEL MIZRAIM [AY-buhl MIZ-ray-uhm; "meadow of Egypt"] Name given to the threshing floor of Atad by the Canaanites after they

1105

saw the funeral procession of Jacob stop to mourn at the site. The name is a pun: *'abel* sounds like *'ebel*, which in Hebrew means "mourning." Gen. 50:11.

ABEL SHITTIM [AY-buhl SHI-tim; "meadow of the acacias"] The last Israelite encampment before crossing the Jordan, located on the plains of Moab E of the Jordan. Possibly modern Tell Kefrein, about 14 miles (22 km) E of Jericho [**V**, C2]. Num. 33:49. *See* Shittim.

ABILENE [AB-ih-leen; "meadow" or "brook"] A Syrian tetrarchy, taking its name from its principal city, Abila, about 18 miles (29 km) NW of Damascus [**I**, A2]. Lk. 3:1.

ACCO [AK-oh] Accho, KJV. [**I**, A1; **VI**]. An important seaport about 25 miles (40 km) S of Tyre. It was allotted to the Asherites, who failed to drive out its Canaanite inhabitants. Of strategic import from ancient times, the city appears in many early Egyptian sources, from the Execration Texts (about 1900 B.C.) to the Amarna Letters (about 1350 B.C.). Acco probably lay within the territory ceded to Hiram king of Tyre by Solomon (1 Ki. 9:10-13), and remained a Phoenician city for much of its history. During the Hellenistic period, its name was changed to Ptolemais. Acco's population may have reached 100,000 before the city fell to Rome in 65 B.C. Modern Acre. Jdg. 1:31. *See* Ptolemais.

ACHAIA [uh-KAY-uh] **XIII**, B3. In NT times, a Roman province that included all of Greece S of Thessaly. Corinth was its capital. Acts 18:12; 19:21; 2 Cor. 1:1.

ACHOR [AY-kor; "trouble"] Valley on the N boundary of Judah where Achan was stoned to death. The exact site between Jerusalem [**VII**, C1] and Jericho [**VI**, D3] is uncertain. Josh. 7:24-26; 15:7; Isa. 65:10; Hos. 2:15.

ACSHAPH [AK-shaf; "sorcery"] Achshaph, KJV, RSV. [**V**, A2]. An ancient Canaanite royal city conquered by Joshua and allotted to Asher. Possibly located about 7 miles (11 km) SE of Acco. Josh. 11:1; 12:20; 19:24,25.

ACZIB [AK-zib; "lie, deception"] Achzib, KJV, RSV.
1. A town in the W foothills of Judah, about 3 miles (5 km) W of Adullam [**VI**, D2]. Josh. 15:44; Mic. 1:14. Probably to be identified with Kezib in Gen. 38:5 and Cozeba in 1 Chr. 4:22.
2. A Canaanite city in Asher, identified with modern ez-Zib, located on the Mediterranean coast about 9 miles (15 km) N of Acco [**I**, A1]. It became known as Ekdippa during the Hellenistic period. Josh. 19:29; Jdg. 1:31.

ADADAH [AD-uh-duh] A town in the S desert region of Judah, W of Edom. Josh. 15:22.

ADAM [AD-uhm; "red" or "made"] A town near Zarethan on the E bank of the Jordan River, where the waters of the Jordan backed up, allowing the Israelites under Joshua to cross on dry land. Possibly a site near the confluence of the Jabbok and Jordan rivers. Josh. 3:16.

ADAMAH [AD-uh-muh; "red ground"] A fortified city of Naphtali in the time of Joshua. Exact location uncertain. Josh. 19:36. *See* Madon.

ADAMI NEKEB [AD-uh-mi NEK-eb] Adami, KJV. A town of Naphtali at the border of Zebulun. Possibly a site located about 4.5 miles (7 km) SW of Tiberias [**XI**, B3]. Josh. 19:33.

ADDAN [AD-uhn] An unidentified city in Babylonia; some of its inhabitants, upon returning from exile, were unable to demonstrate their Israelite ancestry. Ezra 2:59. Called Addon in Neh. 7:61.

ADDAR [AD-dar; "height" or "threshing floor"] Adar, KJV. A place on the S border of Judah, near Kadesh Barnea [**III**, B4]. Josh. 15:3. With nearby Nezron called Hazar Addar in Num. 34:4.

ADDON [AD-uhn] *See* Addan.

ADITHAIM [AD-uh-THAY-uhm] A town in the SW foothills of Judah. Josh. 15:36. Location unidentified.

ADMAH [AD-muh; "red earth"] One of the Cities of the Plain. Admah was destroyed in the divine judgment that fell upon its neighbor cities, Sodom and Gomorrah [**I**, C2]. Gen. 10:19; 14:2,8; Deut. 29:23; Hos. 11:8.

ADORAIM [AD-uh-RAY-uhm] A city of Judah fortified by Rehoboam. 2 Chr. 11:9. Identified with modern Dura, 5 miles (8 km) SW of Hebron [**V**, C2].

ADRAMYTTIUM [AD-ruh-MIT-ee-uhm]. An ancient port city of Mysia, a Roman province in NW Asia Minor. Acts 27:2-5. Its original site is now known as Karatash, near Edremit.

ADRIATIC [AY-dree-AT-ic] **SEA**, Adria, KJV, RSV. [**XIII**, A2]. The gulf between Italy and the Dalmatian Coast, named after the town of Adria near the mouth of the Po River. The use of the name was extended by NT times to include the Mediterranean between Crete and Sicily. Acts 27:27.

ADULLAM [uh-DULL-um; "refuge"] **VI**, D2; **X**. An ancient Canaanite royal city midway between Jerusalem and Lachish. With Socoh, it controlled a principal pass into the hill country of Judah, and thus was fortified by Rehoboam. Destroyed by Sennacherib, Adullam was again occupied after the Exile. Shortly after leaving Gath, David hid with his men in one of the limestone caves near the city. Gen. 38:1; Josh. 12:15; 1 Sam. 22:1; 2 Sam. 23:13; Neh. 11:30.

ADUMMIM [uh-DUM-im; "red spots"(?)] A pass on the road between Jerusalem and Jericho [**V**, C2], on the border between Judah and Benjamin. Probably the intended site of Jesus' parable of the Good Samaritan (Lk. 10:30-35). Josh. 15:7; 18:17.

AENON [EE-nahn; "springs"] A place near Salim, where springs supplied water for John the Baptist to baptize his converts. Possibly a site in the Jordan Valley 8 miles (13 km) S of Beth Shan [**VII**, C1], or perhaps near modern Salim, about 3.5 miles (5.5 km) E of Shechem [**X**, A2]. Jn. 3:23.

AHAVA [uh-HAH-vuh] A canal named after an area by which it flowed; here Ezra assembled the returning exiles before their journey to Jerusalem. Ezra 8:15,21,31.

AHLAB [AH-luhb; "fruitful"] A town of Asher from which the Israelites failed to expel the Canaanite inhabitants. Jdg. 1:31. Identified with a place 4 miles (6.5 km) NE of Tyre [**VII**, B1].

AI [AY-ie; "ruin" (?)] [**V**, C2].
1.* The city at which Joshua's forces met defeat after the victory at Jericho, about 1400 B.C. Located E of Bethel, its site is usually identified at the ancient ruins of Et Tell (shown on map). However, this site is problematic, for it appears to have been unoccupied at the time of the conquest. Also there was apparently no occupation of the city after about 1050 B.C., although natives of Ai are said to have returned to Judah after the Exile. An alternative site, Khirbet Nisya, has been proposed, and has several advantages over the traditional site. It is located 11 miles (18 km) N of Jerusalem, a little SW of Et Tell. Gen. 12:8; Josh. 7,8; Ezra 2:28.
2. An Ammonite city, near Heshbon. Jer. 49:3.

AIATH [IE-ath] Alternate, fem. form of the city Ai. Isa. 10:28.

AIJA [IE-juh] Alternate form of the city Ai in Neh. 11:31.

AIJALON [AY-juh-lahn; "place of the deer"] Ajalon, KJV (Josh. 10:12; 19:42; 2 Chr. 28:18).
1. [**V**, **VI**, D2]. A Canaanite town assigned to the tribe of Dan, and thereafter designated as a Levitical city. It overlooks the Valley of Aijalon, mentioned by Joshua (Josh. 10:12). Aijalon was captured and occupied by the Philistines during the reign of Ahaz. Josh. 19:42; 21:24; 1 Sam. 14:31; 2 Chr. 28:18. Identified as modern Yalo E of Emmaus.
2. A town in Zebulun, where Elon the judge was buried. Location unknown. Jdg. 12:12.
3. A Levitical city in the territory of Ephraim. 1 Chr. 6:69. Possibly the same as Elon, or Aijalon 1.

AIN [AYN; "spring" or "fountain"]
1. A place W of Riblah [**VII**, B2], on the NE border of the Promised Land. Location uncertain. Num. 34:11.
2. A town in the S desert region of Judah, later allotted to Simeon, and thereafter made a Levitical city. Josh. 15:32; 19:7; 21:16. Called En Rimmon in Neh. 11:29. Ashan is substituted for Ain in 1 Chr. 6:59.

AKELDAMA* [uh-KEL-duh-muh; "field of blood"] Aceldama, KJV. The potter's field bought with the money given Judas to betray Christ. Traditionally, the site has been identified with the Potter's House (Jer. 18:2-12; *compare* Zech. 11:13), located S of Jerusalem in the Valley of Hinnom [**XII**, D2]. Acts 1:19.

AKKAD [ah-KAD; "fortress"] Accad, KJV, RSV. Ancient Mesopotamian city built by Nimrod, in N Babylonia. Generally identified with Agade, which became the capital city of the conqueror Sargon I, founder of the dynasty of Akkad. Its location is uncertain. Gen. 10:10.

ALEMETH [AL-uh-meth; "hidden"] A Levitical city in the territory of Benjamin, about 2.5 miles (4 km) E of Gibeah [**VII**, C1]. 1 Chr. 6:60. Called Almon in Josh. 21:18. Modern Almit.

ALEXANDRIA [AL-eg-ZAN-dree-uh; "city of Alexander"] **XIII**, D3. Egyptian seaport founded by Alexander the Great about 331 B.C., on a narrow strip of land between the Mediterranean and Lake Mareotis, W of the Nile. The lighthouse of Pharos near Alexandria was one of the seven wonders of the ancient world. Alexandria served for centuries as the Greek and Roman capital of Egypt. Acts 27:6; 28:11-13.

ALLON BACUTH [AL-ahn BAK-uhth; "oak of weeping"] Burial place of Deborah, the nurse of Rebekah, under an oak near Bethel. Gen. 35:8.

ALMON [AL-muhn] *See* Alemeth.

ALMON DIBLATHAIM [AL-muhn DIB-luh-THAY-uhm; "hiding place of the two cakes of figs"] A campsite of the Israelites during their wilderness wanderings, shortly before they entered the land of Canaan. Lying between Dibon Gad and the mountains of Abarim, in Moab, its precise location is uncertain. Num. 33:47. Probably the same as Beth-Diblathaim.

ALOTH [AY-lahth] Bealoth, RSV. A town or district of Israel included with Asher in the territory under the governorship of Baana in Solomon's time. 1 Ki. 4:16.

ALUSH [AY-lush] A campsite of the Israelites during the Exodus, between Dophkah and Rephidim. Num. 33:13,14.

AMAD [AY-mad] A town in the territory of Asher. Josh. 19:26.

AMAM [AY-mam] A town in the S desert of Judah, exact location unknown. Josh. 15:26.

AMANA [uh-MAN-uh] A mountain in the Anti-Lebanon range beside the Abana River. Song 4:8.

AMMAH [AHM-uh; "source"] A hill near Giah not far from the wilderness of Gibeon. Joab ended his pursuit of Abner at this site after the death of his brother, Asahel. 2 Sam. 2:24-28.

AMMON [AM-uhn; "people"(?)] **IV; VI; VII,** C2; **VIII.** Land of the Ammonites in central Transjordan, SE of Gilead and bounded by the Arnon River to the S. The W border of Ammon generally conformed to the upper course of the Jabbok, which runs N before turning toward the Jordan. Originally, Ammon extended as far as the Jordan, but by the time of Moses, Sihon, king of the Amorites, held the W portion of Ammon, which was thereafter taken by Israel. The capital of Ammon was Rabbah, modern Amman. Num. 21:24; Deut. 2:19-21,37; 2 Sam. 11:1.

AMPHIPOLIS [am-FIP-oh-liss; "surrounded city"] **XIII,** A3. A city of Thrace founded in 436 B.C. by the Athenians and later made capital of a Roman district of Macedonia; its name may be derived from the position of the city surrounded on three sides inside a bend of the Strymon River, 3 miles (5 km) from where it issues into the Aegean Sea. Act. 17:1.

ANAB [AY-nab; "grapes"] A town of the Anakites in the hill country of Judah, taken by Joshua. Possibly Khirbet Anab located about 13 miles (21 km) SW of Hebron [**V,** C2]. Josh. 11:21; 15:50.

ANAHARATH [uh-NAY-huh-rath] A town of Issachar, in the Valley of Jezreel. Modern en-Naura, 2 miles (3 km) S of Endor [**VII,** C1]. Josh. 19:19.

ANANIAH [AN-uh-NIE-uh; "Yahweh protects"] A town resettled by Benjamites upon their return to Judah after the Exile. Neh. 11:32. Possibly the same as Bethany in the NT.

ANATHOTH [AN-uh-thahth; sounds like Hebrew for "answer"; possibly plural of goddess Anath] A Levitical town in the territory of Benjamin, near present-day Anata, about 2.5 miles (4 km) NE of Jerusalem [**VII,** C1]. Native city of the prophet Jeremiah, Anathoth was resettled by Benjamites after the Exile. Josh. 21:18; 1 Ki. 2:26; Neh. 11:32; Jer. 1:1; 11:21.

ANEM [AY-nem] A Levitical city in the territory of Issachar. 1 Chr. 6:73. Called En Gannim in the parallel list in Josh. 21:29.

ANER [AY-nair] An unidentified city in Manasseh given to the Kohathite Levites. 1 Chr. 6:70.

ANIM [AY-nim; "springs"] A town near Eshtemoa in the S hill country of Judah. Josh. 15:50. Identified with the ruins of el-Ghuwein about 11 miles (18 km) S of Hebron [**V,** A2].

ANTIOCH* [AN-tee-ahk]
1. [**XIII,** C7]. Syrian Antioch; capital of Syria and third city of the Roman Empire, built on

the bank of the Orontes, about 15 miles (24 km) from where the river empties into the Mediterranean. In Antioch of Syria, followers of Christ first became known as "Christians." Acts 11:19-27; 15:22-30.
2. [**XIII,** B5]. Pisidian Antioch; a city in Phrygia near Pisidia, so-named to distinguish it from other cities of the same name. In A.D. 25, Pisidian Antioch was made capital of the Roman Province of Galatia. Acts 13:14-52.

ANTIPATRIS [an-TIP-uh-tris] **XI,** D1. City rebuilt by Herod the Great in 9 B.C. on the site of the ancient Philistine city of Aphek [**I,** B1]. Its ruins lie in the Plain of Sharon, NE of Joppa. Acts 23:31.

APHEK [AY-fek; "strength"] Aphik, KJV, RSV (Jdg. 1:31).
1. [**I,** B1; **V; VI; VIII**]. A Philistine royal city on the Plain of Sharon NE of Joppa, whose king was defeated by Joshua. Strategically located on the Great Trunk Road, its name appears in several ancient Egyptian sources. Possibly the campsite of the Philistines before their defeat of the Israelite army and capture of the ark. Josh. 12:18; 1 Sam. 4:1; 29:1. Antipatris was later built on the site. See Antipatris.
2. A city in N Canaan still held by the Canaanites in Joshua's old age; identified with modern Afqa, NE of Beirut. Josh. 13:4.
3. A coastal city of Asher; the Israelites failed to expel its native Canaanite inhabitants. Identified with a site about 5 miles (8 km) S of Acco [**I,** A1] near the source of the River Naaman. Josh. 19:30; Jdg. 1:31.
4. A town possibly located in the Golan about 3 miles (5 km) E of the Sea of Galilee, on the Via Maris between Beth Shan and Damascus. It may have been here that Ben-Hadad and his army fled after his defeat by Ahaz. 1 Ki. 20:26-30; 2 Ki. 13:17.

APHEKAH [uh-FEE-kuh] An unidentified town in the hill country of Judah. Josh. 15:53.

APOLLONIA [AP-uh-LOH-nee-uh; "city of Apollo"] **XIII,** A3. A Macedonian city located about 28 miles (45 km) SW of Amphipolis on the Egnatian Way. Acts 17:1.

APPIUS [AP-ee-uhs] Appii forum, KJV. [**XIII,** A1]. The Forum of Appius was a town on the Appian Way, about 40 miles (65 km) SE of Rome. Acts 28:15.

AR [AR; possibly "city"] A chief city of Moab, E of the Dead Sea, located near the Arnon River. In Moses' time, it bordered on the territory of the Amorites to the N. Its exact location is uncertain. Num. 21:15,28; Deut. 2:9; Isa. 15:1.

ARAB [AIR-uhb; "ambush"] A town in the hill country of Judah. Josh. 15:52.

ARABAH [AIR-uh-buh; "desert; plain"] Usually "plain," KJV. The great rift valley running over 200 miles (320 km) N to S through Palestine from Mt. Hermon to the Gulf of Aqaba. Containing the Sea of Galilee, Jordan River, and the Dead Sea, the Arabah is actually part of a fault line extending from N Syria to the SE coast of Africa. In modern usage, the Arabah is limited to the region between the Dead Sea and the Gulf of Aqaba. The "Sea of Arabah" is an alternate name for the Dead Sea. Deut. 1:7; 3:17; Josh. 18:18.

ARABIA* [uh-RAY-bee-uh; "desert"] Large peninsula in SW Asia, bounded on the W by the Red Sea, S by the Indian Ocean, and E by the Persian Gulf. It is an arid land historically inhabited by many nomadic peoples. 2 Chr. 9:14; Jer. 25:24; Gal. 1:17; 4:25.

ARAD [AIR-ad; "wild ass"]
1. [**VI,** E3]. A town in the region of the Negev where the Kenites settled during the time of

the Judges. Its site is most likely Tell Arad, about 17 miles (27 km) S of Hebron. Jdg. 1:16.
2. [**III,** B4]. A fortified city in the Negev whose Canaanite king attacked the Israelites under Moses, and was defeated. Possibly located at Tell Malhata, about 8 miles (13 km) SW of 1. Num. 21:1-3; Josh. 12:14.

ARAH [AIR-uh] Mearah, KJV, RSV. A place in the vicinity of Sidon. Jos. 13:4.

ARAM* [AIR-uhm; "high; exalted"] **VII; VIII,** A2-B2. An ancient country of indefinite extent, formed of a collection of city-states. Among those mentioned in the OT are Damascus, Zobah, Geshur, Maacah, Beth Eden, and Beth Rehob. The territory of Aram was largely confined to the plains NE of Palestine and SW of the Euphrates. The Aramean kingdoms were absorbed into the Assyrian Empire by Tiglath-Pileser III. Jdg. 3:10; 1 Ki. 11:25; 1 Ki. 20.

ARAM MAACAH [AIR-uhm MAY-uh-kuh] See Maacah.

ARAM NAHARAIM [AIR-uhm NAY-huh-RAY-uhm; "Aram of the two rivers"] A region in NW Mesopotamia, located between the upper Euphrates and the Habor River. Cushan-Rishathaim, king of Aram Naharaim, held power over Israel for eight years during the period of the Judges. Gen. 24:10; Jdg. 3:8-10; 1 Chr. 19:6. See Paddan Aram.

ARARAT* [AIR-uh-rat] **II,** A6. A mountainous region in Armenia, surrounding Lake Van. Noah's ark came to rest on the mountains of Ararat. In Jer. 51:27, the prophet refers to a nation in the vicinity of Lake Van, known as Urartu in Assyrian inscriptions. Gen. 8:4; 2 Ki. 19:37.

AREOPAGUS* [AIR-ee-AHP-uh-gus; "the hill of Ares"] A rocky hill NW of the Acropolis in Athens [**XIII,** B3]; original site where the Council of the Areopagus held its meetings. In NT times, its members usually heard trials at the Stoa Basileios ("royal porch") in the Athenian marketplace, called the agora. Acts 17:19-34.

ARGOB [AR-gahb; "region of clods"] **IV,** B2. A region in Bashan extending as far S and E as Salecah and Edrei, territorially defining the kingdom of Og, Rephaite king of Bashan. Its NW limit bordered on the Aramean kingdoms of Geshur and Maacah, and seems to indicate that the Argob comprised the arable land along the tributaries of the Yarmuk River, which feeds into the Jordan S of the Sea of Galilee. It contained 60 fortified cities, which all fell to the Israelites under Moses. The territory was given to the tribe of Manasseh. Later the Argob became one of Solomon's territorial districts. Deut. 3:4-14; 1 Ki. 4:13.

ARIEL [AIR-ee-uhl; "lion of God"] Poetic name given to Jerusalem in Isa. 29:1,2,7.

ARIMATHEA [AIR-uh-muth-EE-uh] Arimathaea, KJV. [**XI,** D1]. Native city of Joseph, who buried Jesus' body in his own new-cut tomb. The location is uncertain, but is generally identified with modern Rentis, about 20 miles (32 km) NW of Jerusalem. Mt. 27:57; Mk. 15:43; Lk. 23:51; Jn. 19:38. Possibly same as Ramathaim, the birthplace of Samuel.

ARMAGEDDON* [AHR-muh-GED-uhn; "Mount Megiddo"(?)] Site where the kings of the East gather for the final battle between good and evil. Rev. 16:16.

ARNON [AHR-nahn; "rushing stream"] **I,** C2; **IV; VI.** A river, now dry most of the year, that flows westward from the hills of N Arabia into the Dead Sea, opposite En Gedi. It marked the boundary between the Moabites and Amorites in the time of Moses, and later became the S boundary of the territory of

Reuben. Num. 21:13; Jdg. 11:18–26; 2 Ki. 10:32,33.

AROER [uh-ROH-uhr; "naked"]
1. [**IV**, E2; **VI**; **VIII**]. A city on the N bank of the Arnon River, in the territory of Sihon, king of the Amorites, taken by the Israelites under Moses. It was fortified by the Gadites, and later assigned to Reuben. Aroer was conquered by Hazael, king of Syria, in the time of Jehu. Its modern name is Arair. Num. 32:34; Josh. 12:2; 13:9; 2 Ki. 10:33; Isa. 17:2.
2. A town near Rabbah, capital of Ammon, that was assigned to Gad. Conquered by Jephthah when he subdued the Ammonites. Site unknown. Josh. 13:25; Jdg. 11:33.
3. A town in S Judah, about 12 miles (19 km) SE of Beersheba. 1 Sam. 30:28.

ARPAD [AHR-pad] Arphad, KJV (Isa. 36:19). [**IX**, B3]. A city and Aramean province in N Syria, near Hamath. Conquered by Tiglath-Pileser III, king of Assyria, in 740 B.C., and again by Sargon II in 720 B.C., after a short-lived rebellion with Hamath, Damascus, and Samaria. Isa. 36:19; Jer. 49:23.

ARUBBOTH [uh-RUB-uhth; "windows"(?)] Aruboth, KJV. A town or administrative district of Israel under Ben-Hesed, a governor of King Solomon. Site uncertain. 1 Ki. 4:10.

ARUMAH [uh-ROO-muh; "heights"(?)] A town in central Palestine where Abimelech stayed. Probably a site about 5 miles (8 km) SE of Shechem [**I**, B1]. Jdg. 9:41.

ARVAD [AHR-vad] **II**; **VII**, A2. A Phoenician city built on an island 2 miles (3 km) from the Syrian coast, about 125 miles (200 km) N of Tyre, opposite Cyprus. Its inhabitants were of Canaanite descent (*see* Gen. 10:8). Site of the modern city of Ruwad. Ezek. 27:8,11.

ASHAN [AY-shan] A town in the W foothills of Judah, reassigned to Simeon, and then made a priestly city; perhaps located about 1.5 miles (2.5 km) NW of Beersheba [**I**, C1]. Josh. 15:42; 19:7; 1 Chr. 6:59. Possibly same as Bor Ashan.

ASHDOD [ASH-dahd; "fortress"(?)] **V**; **VI**, D2; **VII**; **VIII**; **X**. One of five chief Philistine cities, on the great coastal road about 3 miles (5 km) from the coast of S Palestine, W of Jerusalem. The ark of the covenant was placed in the temple of Dagon in Ashdod after its capture by the Philistines, but was moved after the city was stricken with plague. Allotted to Judah, it was not conquered by the Israelites until the time of Uzziah. The city was later sacked by Sargon II, following a short-lived rebellion against Assyria. After the Exile, the inhabitants of Ashdod were among those who opposed the rebuilding of Jerusalem's walls under Nehemiah. Josh. 13:3; 15:46,47; 1 Sam. 5:1-8; 6:17; Neh. 4:7; 13:23,24; Isa. 20:1; Amos 3:9. Known as Azotus in NT times.

ASHER [ASH-uhr; "happy"]
1. [**VI**, A3-B3]. Region in Canaan allotted to the tribe of Asher at the time of the conquest. The territory in NW Palestine extended from the Mediterranean to the W Galilean hills, and from Mt. Carmel as far N as Sidon. Bordered on the W by Naphtali and Zebulun, and on the S by Manasseh, the Asherites failed to expel the Canaanite inhabitants from their land, most of which remained under the kingdom of Phoenicia. Josh. 19:24-31,34; Jdg. 1:31,32.
2. A border town in the territory of Manasseh may be referred to in Josh. 17:7, possibly located 11 miles (18 km) NE of Shechem [**I**, B1] on the road to Beth Shan. However, this may be a reference to the territory of Asher.

ASHKELON [ASH-kuh-lahn] **I**; **VI**; **VIII**; C1; **X**. An ancient Canaanite city first settled in Neolithic times, it fell to Joshua at the time of the conquest. The Judahites temporarily held the city during the time of the Judges, as evidenced by the Stele of Merneptah, dated about 1220 B.C. It was later conquered by the Philistines and became one of the five principal Philistine cities in Palestine. Ashkelon became subject to Assyria during the reign of Tiglath-Pileser III, and fell to the Babylonian king Nebuchadnezzar in 604 B.C. It belonged to Tyre in Persian times, and became a free Hellenistic city in 104 B.C. Herod the Great was born here. Ashkelon is located on the Mediterranean coast about 12 miles (19 km) N of Gaza. Josh. 13:3; Jdg. 14:19; Jer. 47:5; Amos 1:6-8; Zeph. 2:4,7.

ASHNAH [ASH-nuh]
1. A town in the W foothills of Judah, near Zorah, possibly located about 3 miles (5 km) NE of Beth Shemesh [**VI**, D2]. Josh. 15:33.
2. Also a town of Judah, S of 1, near Libnah. Jos. 15:43.

ASHTAROTH [ASH-tuh-rahth] **IV**, B2; **VI**. Ancient royal city of the kingdom of Og, Rephaite king of Bashan, located E of the Sea of Galilee. It was conquered and given to the tribe of Manasseh, and later to the Gershonites as a Levitical city. Deut. 1:4; Josh. 12:4; 1 Chr. 6:71. *See* Ashteroth Karnaim.

ASHTEROTH KARNAIM [ASH-tuh-rahth kahr-NAY-uhm] **I**, B2. A city inhabited by the Rephaites, conquered by Kedorlaomer and his allies in the time of Abram. Probably the same as Ashtaroth, situated in the N Transjordan near Karnaim. Gen. 14:5.

ASIA* [AY-zhuh; "eastern"] **XIII**, B4-B5. In the NT, the name of a Roman province comprising the W and SW end of Asia Minor. Its capital was Ephesus. Acts 19, 20; 2 Tim. 1:15; Rev. 1:4.

ASSHUR [ASH-uhr] Assur, KJV. [**II**; **IX**, B3]. Ancient capital city of Assyria. Its ruins lie about 56 miles (90 km) S of Nineveh, on the W bank of the Tigris River in N Mesopotamia. In Balaam's prophecy, the name is used to indicate the nation of Assyria. Gen. 2:14; Num. 24:22,24; Ezek. 27:23.

ASSOS [AS-ohs] **XIII**, B4. A seaport of Mysia, on the N coast of the Gulf of Adrammytium, N of the isle of Lesbos and 20 miles (32 km) S of Troas. Acts 20:13,14.

ASSYRIA* [uh-SEER-ee-uh] **II**, B5-B6; **IX(a)**. An ancient and powerful kingdom of Mesopotamia, notable as the great nation that defeated the northern kingdom of Israel and deported its people, in 722 B.C. The Assyrian Empire was located N of Babylonia, in the region of the upper Tigris and Euphrates rivers, bounded on the W by the Syrian desert and on the N and E by the Armenian and Persian hills. Assyrian power reached its zenith in the 8th–7th centuries B.C., its territorial control extending throughout the Fertile Crescent, in the E from Elam to Media, and in the W from Cilicia to Egypt. Its capital was originally Asshur, and later Nineveh. Gen. 10:11; 2 Ki. 15–19; Ezek. 16:28.

ASWAN [AZ-wahn] **IX**, C2. Ancient Syene, an Egyptian city situated on the E bank of the Nile, at the first cataract of the river. Located about 550 miles (885 km) S of Cairo, near the border of Cush, it marked the effective boundary of Egypt in ancient times. Ezek. 29:10; 30:6.

ATAD [AY-tad; "thorn"] The "threshing floor of Atad," E of the Jordan where Joseph and his brothers held a seven-day ceremony of mourning for Jacob. The Canaanites witnessed the event and renamed the site Abel Mizraim. Gen. 50:10,11.

ATAROTH [AT-uh-rahth; "crowns"]
1. [**IV**, D1]. A town in the Transjordan, inhabited and fortified by the Gadites. The Moabite Stone lists this city among those taken by Mesha, king of the Moabites, in the time of Ahab and Ahaziah. Identified with a site 8 miles (13 km) NW of Dibon. Num. 32:3,34.
2. A town on the S border of Ephraim; probaby the same as Ataroth Addar. Josh. 16:2.
3. A town on the E border of Ephraim, in the Jordan Valley. Josh. 16:7.

ATAROTH ADDAR [AT-uh-rahth AD-dar; "crown of Addar"] A town on the border between Ephraim and Benjamin. Location uncertain. Josh. 16:5, 18:13.

ATHACH [AY-thak] A village in the S territory of Judah in David's time. 1 Sam. 30:30.

ATHENS* [ATH-uhnz; "city of Athena"] **IX**; **XIII**, B3. Principal city of the ancient Greek state of Attica and the modern capital of Greece. The city was built about 5 miles (8 km) from the Mediterranean coast, around a rocky hill known as the Acropolis, atop which lie Athens's famous monuments, most notably the Parthenon. Following the Athenian victories over the Persians at Marathon (490 B.C.) and a decade later at Salamis, Athens reached the height of its cultural and political influence under Pericles (459–431 B.C.). Although conquered by Rome, its culture and learning spread throughout the Roman world. Acts 17:16-34; 1 Th. 3:1.

ATROTH BETH JOAB [AT-rahth beth JOH-ab] Ataroth, KJV. An unknown site whose Judahite inhabitants were descendants of Caleb. 1 Chr. 2:54.

ATROTH SHOPHAN [AT-rahth SHOH-fan] A city E of the Jordan, rebuilt by the Gadites. Num. 32:35. The KJV treats this as two locations, Atroth and Shophan.

ATTALIA [AT-uh-LIE-uh] A seaport of Pamphylia, near Perga [**XIII**, B5], founded by Attalus Philadelphus, king of Pergamum (159–138 B.C.), and later bequeathed to Rome. Acts 14:25,26. Modern Adalia.

AVEN [AY-ven; "emptiness, wickedness"] A valley in Syria, near Damascus; a place of heathen worship. Amos 1:5.

AVITH [AY-vith] Royal city of Hadad, a pre-Israelite king of Edom. Gen. 36:35.

AVVA [AV-uh] Ava, KJV. A city conquered by Assyria; some of its inhabitants were resettled in Samaria following the deportation of the Jews. 2 Ki. 17:24. Probably same as Ivvah.

AVVIM [AV-im] Avim, KJV. A town in the territory of Benjamin. Josh. 18:23.

AYYAH [IE-yuh] Gaza, KJV. A town of the tribe of Ephraim. 1 Chr. 7:28.

AZEKAH [uh-ZEE-kuh] **V**, C1; **X**. A city in the western foothills of Judah, about 4 miles (6.5 km) SW of Beth Shemesh. Joshua pursued the Amorites as far as Azekah on the day the sun stood still. It was fortified by Rehoboam, and reoccupied after the Exile. Josh. 10:10,11; 1 Sam. 17:1; Neh. 11:30; Jer. 34:7.

AZEL [AY-zuhl; "noble" or "slope"] A place near Jerusalem [**VII**, C1]. Zech. 14:5.

AZMAVETH [AZ-muh-veth; "strength of death"] A town about 5 miles (8 km) NE of Jerusalem [**VII**, C1]; hometown of some who returned to Judah after the Exile. Ezra 2:24; Neh. 12:29. Also called Beth Azmaveth, Neh. 7:28.

AZMON [AZ-mahn; "strong"] **III**, B4. A town in the Negev, located on the SW border of Judah, between Hazar Addar and the Wadi of Egypt. Num. 34:4; Josh. 15:4.

AZNOTH TABOR [AZ-nahth TAY-bor; "slopes (ears) of Tabor"] A place near Mt. Tabor, on the S boundary of Naphtali. Josh. 19:34.

AZOTUS [uh-ZOH-tus] **XI**, E1. Greek name for Ashdod, by which the city was known during NT times. Acts 8:40. See Ashdod.

B

BAALAH [BAY-uh-luh; "owner" or "mistress"]
1. Baalah of Judah is an alternate name for Kiriath Jearim, in Josh. 15:9-11; 1 Chr. 13:6.
2. A Simeonite city in the S desert country of Judah. Josh. 15:29. Same as Balah in Josh. 19:3, and Bilhah, in 1 Chr. 4:29.
3. A mountain in Judah between Ekron and Jabneel [**VI**, D2]. Josh. 15:11.

BAALATH [BAY-uh-lath; "mistress"] Baal, KJV, RSV (1 Chr. 4:33).
1. A Simeonite border town. Also called Baalath Beer, in Josh. 19:8.
2. A border town in the territory of Dan. Josh. 19:44.
3. A store city rebuilt by Solomon, near Gezer [**VII**, C1]. 1 Ki. 9:18. Probably same as 2.

BAALATH BEER [BAY-uh-lath BEER; "mistress of a well"] An unidentified town in the territory of Simeon; also called the "Ramah in the Negev." Josh. 19:8. See Baalath 1.

BAAL GAD [BAY-uhl GAD; "lord is fortune"] A town in the Valley of Lebanon, at the foot of Mt. Hermon [**VI**, A4], marking the N extreme of the territory taken in Joshua's conquests. Josh. 11:17.

BAAL HAMON [BAY-uhl HAY-muhn; "lord of abundance"] An unidentified place where King Solomon had a vineyard. Song 8:11.

BAAL HAZOR [BAY-uhl HAY-zor; "lord of the enclosure"] A location on the border of Ephraim where Absalom had Amnon killed. Probably a site about 5 miles (8 km) NE of Bethel [**V**, C2]. 2 Sam. 13:23.

BAAL HERMON [BAY-uhl HER-muhn; "lord of Hermon"] A place of Canaanite worship on the slopes of Mt. Hermon [**VI**, A4], on the N boundary of Manasseh E of the Jordan. "Mount Baal Hermon" may refer to the particular slope of the Hermon range containing the sacred site. Jdg. 3:3; 1 Chr. 5:23.

BAAL MEON [BAY-uhl MEE-ahn] An Amorite city E of the Jordan and N of Moab. It was taken and rebuilt by the Reubenites, but eventually fell to the Moabites. Identified with the ruins of Main, about 3.5 miles (5.5 km) SW of Medeba [**VIII**, B2]. Num. 32:38; Ezek. 25:9. Also called Beth Meon (Jer. 48:23), Beth Baal Meon (Josh. 13:17), and Beon (Num. 32:3).

BAAL PEOR [BAY-uhl PEE-or; "lord of Peor"] Moabite town that was the worship center of a local Baal cult. Deut. 4:3; Hos. 9:10. See Beth Peor.

BAAL PERAZIM [BAY-uhl PAIR-uh-zim; "lord of the breach"] Place where King David defeated the Philistines, near the Valley of Rephaim. 2 Sam. 5:20. Called Mt. Perazim in Isa. 28:21.

BAAL SHALISHAH [BAY-uhl SHAL-ih-shuh; "lord of Shalishah"] Baal-shalisha, KJV. A town in the time of Elisha, possibly a site

about 12 miles (19 km) SW of the city of Samaria [**X**, A2]. 2 Ki. 4:42.

BAAL TAMAR [BAY-uhl TAY-mar; "lord of palms"] A place in Benjamin, near Bethel and Gibeah [**VII**, C1]. Here the Israelites launched an ambush against the pursuing Benjamites. Jdg. 20:33. Location unknown.

BAAL ZEPHON [BAY-uhl ZEF-ahn; "lord of the North"] A place "directly opposite" the site where the Israelites camped before crossing the Red Sea. Ex. 14:2,9; Num. 33:7. Exact location unknown.

BABEL* [BAY-buhl, or BAB-uhl; sounds like Hebrew for "confusion"]
1. A great city built in the plain of Shinar. Within its walls, its inhabitants began construction on a temple "that reaches to the heavens." The Lord intervened, confusing the languages of its builders, and scattering them over the earth. Gen. 11:1-9.
2. The "Tower of Babel," as it is commonly known, was a structure built in the city of Babel—possibly a ziggurat, which was common to many of the ancient cities of Mesopotamia. The use of burnt clay bricks and bitumen (tar), as described in Gen. 11:3, is attested from early times. Identified by some with the ziggurat Esagila in Babylon, or its prototype, modified by several periods of reconstruction during the history of the city. A text of Sharkalisharri, king of Agade (biblical Akkad), records his restoration of an earlier temple-tower at Babylon, around 2250 B.C. Others identify the site with the vitrified remains of the tower at Borsippa (modern Birs Nimrud), about 7 miles (11 km) SW of Babylon. However, the actual Babel, with its tower, very possibly dates back into Neolithic times, and may be lost forever in human prehistory. Gen. 11:1-9.

BABYLON* [BAB-ih-lahn] **II**, C6; **IX**. An ancient city on the Euphrates River in S Mesopotamia, notable as the capital of the Babylonian Empire. The name is commonly thought to derive from the Akkadian *Babilu*, meaning "gate of God," but actually may be a Semitic pronunciation of the Hurrian "*Papil*." At the height of its power, Babylon was an extraordinarily large and wealthy city, known for the magnificence of its great temples. The famous hanging gardens of Babylon, constructed by Nebuchadnezzar, were regarded as one of seven wonders of the ancient world. 2 Ki. 24,25; Ezra 5:12-17; Isa. 39:1-17; Jer. 27–29, 50–52; Dan. 2:48. As is often the case, the name of the capital city is often used in the Bible to indicate all of Babylonia.

BABYLONIA [BAB-ih-LOH-nee-uh] **II**, C6; **IX(b)**. Ancient empire of S Mesopotamia, between the Tigris and Euphrates rivers. It was bounded on the N by Assyria, the E by Elam, and the S and W by the Arabian Desert. During the period of the Chaldean Dynasty (626–539 B.C.), Babylonian control extended to encompass Assyria and all of Syria-Palestine. See Babylon.

BACA [BAY-kuh; "weeping" or "balsam trees"] A valley in Palestine which served as a route to approach Zion (Jerusalem [**VII**, C1]). Possibly a reference to the Valley of Rephaim. The valley is used symbolically by the Psalmist to describe a transformation from sorrow to joy as one approaches God. Ps. 84:6.

BAHURIM [bah-HOOR-im] A town in Benjamin near the Mount of Olives [**XII**, C3], on the road from Jerusalem to Jericho. 2 Sam. 3:16; 16:5; 17:18.

BALAH [BAY-luh] A city allotted to Simeon from within the territory of Judah. Josh. 19:3. Same as Baalah 2 and Bilhah.

BAMAH [BAY-muh; "high place"] Presumably a prominent location of idolatrous worship; as a generic term it refers to any such place. Ezekiel plays upon the syllables of the word, *ba* ("go") and *mah* ("what"), in Ezek. 20:29.

BAMOTH [BAY-mahth] Shortened form of Bamoth Baal in Num. 21:19,20.

BAMOTH BAAL [BAY-mahth BAY-uhl; "high places of Baal"] A Reubenite town in the Transjordan, N of the Arnon River. Possibly located just S of Mt. Nebo [**IV**, D1]. It appears on the Moabite Stone as Beth Bamoth, among the cities captured by Mesha. Num. 22:41; Josh. 13:17. Called Bamoth in Num. 21:19,20.

BASHAN [BAY-shan; "smooth, fertile"] **IV**, B2. A fertile tableland E of the Sea of Galilee, and N of the Yarmuk River. It extended as far N as Mt. Hermon and as far E as Salecah in Hauran. Occupied by the Rephaites from the Patriarchal period, much of the territory was within the kingdom of Og at the time of the conquest under Moses. Israel defeated Og at Edrei and assigned the region to the tribe of Manasseh as part of its portion E of the Jordan. Following the Israelite monarchy, the region was lost to the Arameans, and later was incorporated into the Assyrian Empire by Tiglath-Pileser III. The Bashan roughly coincided with the district of Karnaim during the Persian period, and Batanea in Greco-Roman times. Deut. 3:1-14; Josh. 13:30,31; Isa. 2:13. See Havvoth Jair.

BATH RABBIM [bath RAB-im; "daughter of multitudes"] A city gate of Heshbon [**IV**, D1], near two pools which are compared to the eyes of the Shulammite in Song 7:4.

BEALOTH [BEE-uh-lahth; "mistresses" or "possessors"] A town in the extreme S of Judah. Josh. 15:24. Possibly same as Baalath Beer.

BEAUTIFUL GATE [**XII**, C3]. A gate of Jerusalem where Peter and John healed a lame man. Probably the gate on the E side of Herod's Temple, made of Corinthian bronze and renowned for its magnificence. Acts 3:2.

BEER [BEER; "a well"]
1. A campsite of the Israelites during their wilderness wanderings, located in the Transjordan N of the Arnon River. Num. 21:16. Possibly same as Beer Elim.
2. A place to which Jotham fled to escape his brother Abimelech; its location is unknown. Jdg. 9:21.

BEER ELIM [BEER EE-lim; "well of Elim"] A Moabite border town. Location unknown. Isa. 15:8. See Beer 1.

BEER LAHAI ROI [BEER luh-HIGH roy; "well of the living one who sees me"] Lahairoi, KJV (Gen. 24:62; 25:11). A well where the angel of the Lord appeared to Hagar. Its location in the Negev is uncertain. Possibly a site NW of Kadesh Barnea, near the W border of Palestine. Gen. 16:14; 24:62; 25:11.

BEEROTH [BEE-uh-rahth; "wells"] One of the four cities of the Gibeonites, assigned to the tribe of Benjamin. Possibly located about 2 miles (3 km) W of Gibeah [**VII**, C1]. Josh. 9:17; 18:25; 2 Sam. 4:2,3; Ezra 2:25.

BEERSHEBA [beer-SHEE-buh; "well of the seven"] **I**, C1; **III**; **VI**, E2; **VII**; **VIII**; **X**. The chief city of the Negev in S Judah, allotted to the tribe of Simeon. For all practical purposes, it was the S limit of Israelite territory, thus giving rise to the expression "from Dan to Beersheba" to indicate the whole of Israel.

Abraham dug a well at Beersheba, which

was seized by the servants of Abimelech, king of Gerar. Following this, Abraham and Abimelech met at Beersheba to form a treaty in which Abraham would be given deed to the well. The name of the site was derived from the seven lambs Abraham gave to the king of Gerar as a witness to their covenant. God appeared to Hagar, Isaac, and Jacob at Beersheba.

Ancient Beersheba is identified with Tell es-Saba, about 2 miles (3 km) E of the modern city. No remains from Patriarchal times have been found, and very possibly lie beneath the site of the modern city. There are several wells in the vicinity. Gen. 21:14,22-34; Gen. 26:23-33; Josh. 15:28; Jdg. 20:1; Neh. 11:27,30.

BE ESHTERAH [bee-ESH-tuhr-uh; "temple of Ashtaroth"] Alternate name for Ashtaroth, in Josh. 21:27.

BELA [BEE-luh; "destruction"] A neighboring city of Sodom and Gomorrah [**I**, C2], preserved at Lot's request from the destruction that fell upon the cities of the plain. Gen. 14:2,8. It is identical to Zoar.

BENE BERAK [BEN-eh BEER-ak; "sons of lightning"] A town in the territory of Dan, located about 5 miles (8 km) SE of Joppa [**VI**, D2]. Josh. 19:45.

BENE JAAKAN [BEN-eh JAY-uh-kahn; "sons of Jaakan"] **III**, B4. A campsite of the Israelites during the period of the Exodus. Possibly located at modern Birein, N of Kadesh Barnea. Num. 33:31,32. The NIV refers to the same location as "the wells of the Jaakanites" in Deut. 10:6.

BEN HINNOM [ben HIN-ahm] Usually "son of Hinnom," KJV, RSV. *See* Hinnom.

BENJAMIN [BEN-juh-min] **VI**, D3. The tribe of Benjamin was allotted territory in central Palestine, bounded by Judah to the S and Ephraim to the N. It touched the Jordan near Jericho, extending down to the Dead Sea along its E boundary, and bordered on Dan to the W, from Beth Horon to Kireath Jearim. Josh. 18:11-20.

BERACAH [BAIR-uh-kuh; "blessing"] Berachah, KJV. A valley in the Judean desert W of the Dead Sea, running from a point S of Bethlehem SE toward En Gedi [**VI**, E3]. 2 Chr. 20:26.

BEREA [buh-REE-uh] Beroea, RSV. [**XIII**, A3]. A city in S Macedonia, on the E slope of the Olympus range, about 50 miles (80 km) W of Thessalonica. Modern Verria. Acts 17:10-15; 20:4.

BERED [BEER-ed] A place in the extreme S of Judah. Gen. 16:14.

BEROTHAH [buh-ROH-thuh; "wells"(?)] **VII**, B2. A town lying between Damascus and Hamath, identified with modern Bereitan, N of Damascus. Ezek. 47:16. Probably same as Berothai, in 2 Sam. 8:8, and Cun, in 1 Chr. 18:8.

BEROTHAI [buh-ROH-thie] An Aramean city under Hadadezer, king of Zobah. It was conquered by David. 2 Sam. 8:8. Called Cun in 1 Chr. 18:8. *See* Berothah.

BESOR [BEE-sor] A ravine SW of Ziklag, running NW into the Mediterranean, S of Gaza. 1 Sam. 30:9,21.

BETEN [BEE-ten; "hollow"] A city allotted to Asher; its location is uncertain. Josh. 19:25.

BETH ANATH [beth AY-nath; "house of Anath"] Bethanath, KJV. A fortified city of Naphtali, whose Canaanite inhabitants were enslaved by the Israelites. Josh. 19:38; Jdg.

1:33. Several sites in Galilee have been proposed.

BETH ANOTH [BETH AY-nahth; "house of (the Canaanite goddess) Anoth"] A town in the hill country of Judah, located about 4 miles (6 km) NE of Hebron [**V**, C2]. Josh. 15:59.

BETHANY [BETH-uh-nee; "house of unripe figs"] Bethabara, KJV (Jn. 1:28).
1. [**XI**, E2]. A village on the E slope of the Mount of Olives, notable as the hometown of Mary, Martha, Lazarus, and Simon the Leper. Here Christ raised Lazarus from the dead, and near here he ascended to heaven. Located about 2 miles (3 km) E of Jerusalem, at the site of the present-day village of al-Azariyeh, an Arabic derivation of the Latin *Lazarium*. Mk. 14:3-9.
2. A place on the E side of the Jordan where John baptized. Site unknown. Jn. 1:28.

BETH ARABAH [BETH AIR-uh-buh; "house of the desert"] A town on the boundary between Judah and Benjamin, probably to be identified with Rujm et-Bahr, at the N end of the Dead Sea. Josh. 15:6,61; 18:18,22.

BETH ARBEL [BETH AR-buhl; "house of Arbel"] A town whose destruction by Shalman (Salamanu, king of Moab) is used as an illustration in Hos. 10:14. Usually identified with modern Irbid, located about 19 miles (30 km) SW of the Sea of Galilee. Others believe Shalman refers to Shalmaneser V, and identify Beth Arbel with Arbela in Galilee, NW of Tiberias [**XI**, B3].

BETH ASHBEA [BETH ASH-bee-uh] "House of Ashbea," KJV. Home of a family of linen workers. Location unknown. 1 Chr. 4:21.

BETH AVEN [BETH AY-ven; "house of wickedness"]
1. A Canaanite city on the N boundary of Benjamin, located near Ai and to the E of Bethel [**V**, C2]. Josh. 7:2; 18:12; 1 Sam. 13:5; 14:23.
2. Derogatory name used by Hosea in reference to Bethel ("house of God"), which had become the center of Jeroboam's idolatrous cult. Hos. 4:15; 5:8; 10:5. *See* Bethel.

BETH AZMAVETH [BETH AZ-muh-veth; "house of the strength of death"] A town in Benjamin, about 4 miles (6.5 km) W of Gibeon [**V**, C2]. Descendants of its residents returned to Judah with Zerubbabel. Neh. 7:28. Called Azmaveth in Ezra 2:24.

BETH BAAL MEON [beth BAY-uhl MEE-ahn; "house of Baal Meon"] *See* Baal Meon.

BETH BARAH [BETH BAR-uh; "house of the ford"] Beth-barah, KJV. A place located near a ford across the Jordan. Site unknown. Jdg. 7:24.

BETH BIRI [BETH BEER-ee; "house of my creator"] Beth-birei, KJV. *See* Beth Lebaoth.

BETH CAR [BETH KAR; "house of the lamb"] An unidentified place W of Mizpah, below which the stone named Ebenezer was raised. 1 Sam. 7:11.

BETH DAGON [BETH DAY-gahn; "house of (the Philistine god) Dagon"]
1. A town in the W foothills of Judah; possibly modern Khirbet Dajun, 5 miles (8 km) NW of Lydda (ancient Lod) [**XI**, D1], listed among the cities that fell to Sennacherib. Josh. 15:41.
2. A town on the boundary between Asher and Zebulun. Josh. 19:27.

BETH DIBLATHAIM [BETH DIB-luh-THAY-uhm; "house of the cakes of figs"] A town of Moab, mentioned on the Moabite Stone. Jer. 48:22. Probably the same as Almon Diblathaim.

BETH EDEN [BETH EE-duhn; "house of delight"] "House of Eden," KJV. An Aramean state located between the Euphrates and one of its tributaries, the Balih. It was called Bit-Adini in Assyrian inscriptions. Beth Eden fell to Assyria and its people were deported. Amos 1:5. Simply called Eden in 2 Ki. 19:12 and Ezek. 27:23.

BETH EKED [BETH EE-ked; "Shearing house," KJV.] A town on the road between Jezreel and Samaria. At "Beth Eked of the Shepherds," Jehu slaughtered 42 of Ahaziah's kinsmen. Identified with a site about 6 miles (9 km) SW of Dothan [**I**, B1]. 2 Ki. 10:12,14.

BETHEL [BETH-uhl; "house of God"]
1. [**V**, C2. **VI**; **VIII**, B1; **X**.] An ancient Canaanite city originally known as Luz, situated on an important N-S route through the hill country of central Palestine. Near the city, Abram erected an altar, and Jacob later renamed the city "Bethel." Deborah, the nurse of Rebekah, died and was buried here.

Located on the N border of Benjamin, the city was captured by Joshua, but subsequently lost again to the Canaanites. It was thereafter taken and occupied by the Ephraimites. The ark of God was kept at Bethel before its removal to Shiloh. After the division of the kingdom, Bethel became the center of Jeroboam's idolatrous cult, instituted to rival the Temple in Jerusalem. It continued as an Israelite royal sanctuary into the time of the prophets, who condemned the city for its idolatry. Not until the time of Josiah was the altar of Jeroboam destroyed. Bethel was reinhabited after the Exile.

Its site is generally identified with Beitin (shown on map). However, problems identifying nearby Et Tell with Ai, which Bethel was closely associated, also bring into the question the traditional identification of Bethel. The ancient site may be located at Bireh, a little to the SW, which shows evidence of occupation extending back to the Chalcolithic period. Gen. 12:8; 13:3; 35; Josh. 8; Jdg. 20:18-31; 1 Ki. 12:28-33; 2 Ki. 23:15-19; Neh. 11:31; Amos 5:5,6.
2. *See* Bethuel.

BETH EMEK [BETH EE-mek; "house of the valley"] A place near the boundary of Asher. Possibly a site about 5 miles (8 km) NE of Acco [**I**, A1]. Josh. 19:27.

BETHESDA* [beh-THEZ-duh; "house of grace"] Beth-zatha, RSV. [**XII**, B3]. A pool surrounded by five colonnades, located near the Sheep Gate in the NE corner of Jerusalem. Here the sick gathered, hoping to be healed by its waters. Jn. 5:2.

BETH EZEL [BETH EE-zuhl; "a house adjoining"] A town of Judah, possibly modern Deir el-Asel, located in a valley about 5.5 miles (9 km) W of Jezreel [**VIII**, B2]. Mic. 1:11.

BETH GADER [BETH GAY-der; "house of the wall"] A town of Judah founded by Hareph, a descendant of Caleb. 1 Chr. 2:51. Possibly the same as Geder.

BETH GAMUL [BETH GAY-mul; "house of recompense"] A town of Moab, located about 5 miles (8 km) E of Aroer [**IV**, E2]. Jer. 48:23.

BETH GILGAL [BETH GIL-gal; "house of Gilgal," KJV.] A town near Jerusalem. Neh. 12:29. Probably the same as Gilgal 2.

BETH HAGGAN [BETH HAG-uhn; "house of the garden"] "Garden house," KJV. A town on the road S of Jezreel; identified with En Gannim [**VI**, C3], modern Jenin. 2 Ki. 9:27.

BETH HAKKEREM [BETH ha-KEER-uhm; "house of the vineyard"] Bethhaccerem, KJV (Neh. 3:14). A town that served as a vantage point near Jerusalem. Jer. 6:1. Probably Ramet Rahel, located on a hill midway between Jerusalem and Bethlehem [**VII**, C1].

BETH HARAM [BETH HAIR-uhm; "house of the heights"] Beth-aram, KJV. A Gadite town, identified with a site in the Transjordan, about 8 miles (13 km) NE of the mouth of the Jordan River. Josh. 13:27. Same as Beth Haran, in Num. 32:36.

BETH HARAN [BETH HAIR-uhn] See Beth Haram.

BETH HOGLAH [BETH HAHG-luh; "house of a partridge"] A Benjamite town in the Jordan Valley, located on the N border of Judah. Josh. 15:6; 18:19,21. Identified with Ain Hajlah, about 4 miles (6.5 km) SE of Jericho [**V**, C2].

BETH HORON [BETH HOR-ahn; "house of (the Canaanite god) Horon"] **V**, C2. Twin towns built in the hills of Ephraim by Sheerah, a granddaughter of Ephraim. Called Upper and Lower Beth Horon because of the wide variance in their elevations, they were situated along the Valley of Aijalon, which served as an important pass from the Jerusalem hills to the plains of Joppa. For this reason, the cities were fortified by Solomon, and many armies passed by the cities in OT times. The higher city, Beit Ur el-Foka is about 800 ft. (244 m) higher than Beit Ur el-Tahta, and lies a little over a mile (about 2 km) SE of the lower city. Josh. 10:10; 16:3,5; 21:22; 1 Sam. 13:18.

BETH JESHIMOTH [BETH JESH-uh-mahth; "house of deserts"] An Amorite town near the S end of the plains of Moab, located about 3 miles (5 km) E of the Dead Sea's NE corner. It became a town of Reuben, but eventually fell into the hands of the Moabites. Num. 33:49; Josh. 12:3; 13:20; Ezek. 25:9.

BETH LEBAOTH [BETH luh-BAY-uhth; "house of lionesses"] A town in S Judah assigned to the tribe of Simeon. Josh. 19:6. Called Lebaoth, in Josh. 15:32, and Beth Biri, in 1 Chr. 4:31.

BETHLEHEM [BETH-luh-hem; "house of bread"]
1. [**I**; **VII**, C1; **XI**, E2]. A Judean town about 6 miles (9 km) SW of Jerusalem, notable as the birthplace of Jesus. In patriarchal times, it was known as Ephrath, and later became known as Bethlehem in Judah or Bethlehem Ephrathah to distinguish it from the Zebulunite city of the same name. The Amarna Letters refer to it as Bit-Lahmi, in a report of the city's capture by the Habiru in the 14th century.

David was born and raised in Bethlehem, and it was here that Samuel anointed him the successor of King Saul. In accordance with Micah's prophecy, the Messiah, a descendent of David, was also born in Bethlehem. A tradition going back to the 2nd century A.D. identifies the site of his birth with a cave that once served as the stable of an inn near Bethlehem. The Church of the Nativity now marks the ancient site, believed by many to be the authentic birthplace of the Savior. Gen. 35:19; Ruth 1:1,2; 1 Sam. 16:13-15; 2 Sam. 23:14-16; Mic. 5:2; Mt. 2.
2. A town of Zebulun, identified with modern Beit Lahm, 7 miles (11 km) NW of Nazareth [**XI**, B2]. Josh. 19:15.

BETH MARCABOTH [BETH MAHR-kuh-bahth; "house of chariots"] A Simeonite town in the extreme S of Judah. Josh. 19:5; 1 Chr. 4:31. Possibly the same as Madmannah, in Josh. 15:31.

BETH MEON [BETH MEE-ahn] See Baal Meon.

BETH MILLO [BETH MIL-oh; "house of fullness" indicating a mound or rampart] Millo, KJV. A fortification in or near Shechem [**I**, B1], possibly to be identified with the tower of Shechem. Jdg. 9:6,20; 2 Ki. 12:20.

BETH NIMRAH [BETH NIM-rah; "house of the leopard"] **VI**, D4. A fortified city of Gad E of the Jordan. Identified with a site located along the Wadi Nimrin, N of the plains of Moab. Num. 32:36; Josh. 13:27. Called Nimrah, in Num. 32:3.

BETH OPHRAH [BETH AHF-ruh; "house of dust"] Aphrah, KJV, Beth-le-aphra, RSV. An unidentified town in SW Palestine. Mic. 1:10.

BETH PAZZEZ [BETH PAZ-ez] A town of Issachar, site unknown. Josh. 19:21.

BETH PELET [BETH PEE-let; "house of escape"] Beth-palet and Beth-phelet, KJV. A town in the Negev of Judah, resettled after the Exile. Josh. 15:27; Neh. 11:26.

BETH PEOR [BETH PEE-or; "house of Peor"] **IV**, D1. A city of Sihon, king of the Amorites, assigned to the tribe of Reuben. Moses' burial place was in the valley near Beth Peor, which is located just E of Mt. Pisgah and N of Mt. Nebo. Deut. 3:29; 4:46; 34:6; Josh. 13:20. Probably identical to Baal Peor.

BETHPHAGE [beth-FAY-jee; "house of unripe figs"] A village on the Mount of Olives, near Bethany. The colt was retrieved from this town for Christ's entry into Jerusalem on Palm Sunday. Mt. 21:1; Mk. 11:1; Lk. 19:29.

BETH RAPHA [BETH RAY-fuh] A town founded by Eshton, a descendant of Judah. 1 Chr. 4:12.

BETH REHOB [BETH REE-hahb; "place of a street"(?)] An Aramean city-state located W of Mt. Hermon, near Dan. Jdg. 18:28; 2 Sam. 10:6. Probably the same as Rehob, in Num. 13:21.

BETHSAIDA [beth-say-ih-duh; "house of fishing"]
1. [**XI**, B3]. A town a short distance N of the Sea of Galilee, E of the Jordan, it was later enlarged and given the name Julian by Philip the tetrarch. Near here, Jesus fed the 5000. Mt. 11:21; Mk. 8:22; Lk. 9:10.
2. A fishing village on the shore of the Sea of Galilee, and the home of Peter, Andrew, and Philip. It may have been the fishing district of 1, although the Bible closely associates the town with Capernaum in Gennesaret, farther W. Sites on both sides of the Jordan have been proposed. Mk. 6:45-54; Jn. 1:44; 12:21.

BETH SHAN [BETH SHAN; "house of quiet"] Also Beth-Shean, KJV, RSV. [**I**, B2; **V**, B2; **VI**, C3; **VII**, C1]. An important city of Manasseh within the territory of Issachar, from which the Canaanites could not be driven. Originally founded before 3000 B.C., the Canaanite town became the site of an Egyptian garrison from the 15th to 12th centuries B.C. Thereafter the Philistines occupied it into the time of the Israelite monarchy. After Saul was killed at the battle of Mt. Gilboa, his body was hung from the wall of Beth Shan. Beth Shan apparently came under Israelite control during David's reign, but was later sacked by Shishak during the reign of Rehoboam. The city was abandoned until its refounding in Hellenistic times, when it became known as Scythopolis.

The ruins of Beth Shan, modern Tell el-Husn, are located at the junction of the Jordan and Jezreel valleys, about 14 miles (22 km) S of the Dead Sea. Nearby is the present-day village of Beisan, which preserves the name of the ancient city. The ruins have been thoroughly excavated. Along with 13 inscribed monuments and carved reliefs from the time of Egyptian occupation, two temples from the

11th century B.C. have been uncovered and are identified with the temples of Dagon and Ashtaroth, in which Saul's head and armor were displayed. Josh. 17:11,12; Jdg. 1:27; 1 Sam. 31:8-12; 1 Chr. 10:10.

BETH SHEMESH [BETH SHEM-esh; "house of the sun"]
1. [**VI**, D2; **VIII**]. An important border town in NW Judah, about 15 miles (24 km) W of Jerusalem. Strategically situated in the Valley of Sorek, defending a route from the plain of Philistia into the hill country of Judah, it was a fortified Canaanite stronghold before the Israelites captured it in the time of the Judges. The ark of the covenant was returned to Beth Shemesh by the Philistines after they were stricken with plague.

Its fortifications were strengthened by David, but the city was later destroyed, probably during the invasion of Shishak about 918 B.C. A century later, Joash of Israel defeated Amaziah of Judah near the city. It was captured by the Philistines during the reign of Ahaz, but Tiglath-Pileser III regained Beth Shemesh for Judah following Ahaz's urgent appeal for help. Beth Shemesh was finally destroyed by Nebuchadnezzar in the 6th century B.C., never to be reoccupied. Josh. 15:10; 1 Sam. 6:12-20; 2 Ki. 14:11; 2 Chr. 25:21. Called Ir Shemesh in Josh. 19:41.
2. A town on the boundary between Issachar and Naphtali, near the Jordan River. Possibly located about 2 miles (3 km) S of the Sea of Galilee. Josh. 19:38.
3. A fortified town of Naphtali, possibly to be identified with a site in the upper Galilee, about 14 miles (22 km) W of Hazor [**V**, A2], although it may be the same as 2. During the period of the Judges, its Canaanite inhabitants successfully resisted expulsion by the Israelites. Jdg. 1:33.

BETH SHITTAH [BETH SHI-tuh; "house of the acacia"] A town in the Jordan Valley, between Zererah and Jezreel [**VIII**, B2]. Jdg. 7:22.

BETH TAPPUAH [BETH TAP-yoo-uh; "house of apples"] A town in the hill country of Judah; identified with modern Taffuh, about 5 miles (8 km) NW of Hebron [**V**, C2]. Josh. 15:53. Same as Tappuah.

BETH TOGARMAH [BETH toh-GAR-muh] "House of Togarmah," KJV. A nation in the far north, which supplied horses to Tyre, and soldiers to Gog. It is attested in ancient Hittite and Akkadian texts as a city and district located on the border of Tubal, between the upper courses of the Halys and Euphrates rivers. It was called Til-garimmu in the annals of Sargon and Sennacherib. Ezek. 27:14; 38:6.

BETHUEL [beh-THOO-uhl; "abode of God"] A town of Simeon. 1 Chr. 4:30. Also called Bethul (Josh. 19:4), Bethel (1 Sam. 30:27), and Kesil (Josh. 15:30).

BETHUL [BETH-uhl] See Bethuel.

BETH ZUR [BETH ZOOR; "house of rock"] **X**, B2. A city in the hills of Judea, fortified by Rehoboam. Later known as Bethsura, an important fortress during the time of the Maccabees. Josh. 15:58; 1 Chr. 2:45; Neh. 3:16. Modern Beit Sur, 4 miles (6.5 km) N of Hebron.

BETONIM [BET-uh-nim] A town of Gad in the Transjordan, probably modern Batneh, about 16 miles (26 km) NE of Jericho [**V**, C2]. Josh. 13:26.

BEULAH [BYOO-luh; "married"] A poetic name for the land of Israel, looking forward to its future blessed condition in relationship with God. Isa. 62:4.

BEZEK [BEE-zek]
1. A city whose Canaanite and Perizzite inhabitants were defeated by Joshua. Jdg. 1:4. It may be located at the ruins of Bezkah, about 20 miles (32 km) NE of Jerusalem [**VII**, C1].
2. A place S of Mt. Gilboa, where Saul gathered his forces to attack the Philistines at Jabesh Gilead. Located about 6.5 miles (10 km) NE of Tirzah [**V**, B2]. 1 Sam. 11:8.

BEZER [BEE-zuhr; "stronghold"] **VI**, D4. A levitical city of Reuben located on the desert plateau E of the Dead Sea, and designated as a city of refuge. It was later captured by the Moabites, and fortified by Mesha, king of Moab, about 830 B.C. Identified with a site several miles E of Mt. Nebo. Deut. 4:43; Josh. 21:36. Called Bozrah in Jer. 48:24.

BILEAM [BIL-ee-uhm] A Levitical city in the territory of Manasseh. 1 Chr. 6:70. Probably the same as Ibleam.

BITHRON [BITH-rahn; "ravine" or "morning"] "Forenoon," RSV. A valley leading E from the Jordan toward Mahanaim [**I**, B2], probably the gorge of the Jabbok River. 2 Sam. 2:29. The translation is uncertain, and perhaps is meant to indicate that Abner and his men "continued through the whole *morning* and came to Mahanaim."

BITHYNIA [bih-THIN-ee-uh] **XIII**, A5-A6. A region of NW Asia Minor, bordering on the Black Sea to the N and the Marmara Sea to the W. It remained a largely independent kingdom until bequeathed to Rome by its last king in 74 B.C. Shortly thereafter Bithynia was united with Pontus to the E to form a single Roman province. Acts 16:7; 1 Pet. 1:1.

BIZIOTHIAH [BIZ-ee-oh-THIE-uh] Bizjothjah, KJV. A town in the Negev region of Judah. Josh. 15:28. Possibly a textual corruption that should read "and its settlements" (*compare* Neh. 11:27).

BOHAN [BOH-han] The "stone of Bohan" was a boundary marker on the border between Judah and Benjamin, NE of Jerusalem [**VII**, C1]. Josh. 15:6; 18:17.

BOKIM [BOH-kim; "weepers"] Bochim, KJV, RSV. A place near Gilgal [**V**, C2] where the angel of the Lord pronounced judgment on the Israelites. Jdg. 2:1-5.

BOR ASHAN [BOR AY-shan; "smoking pit"] Chor-ashan, KJV. A town in SW Judah, to which David sent plunder after defeating the Amalekites. 1 Sam. 30:30. Likely the same as Ashan.

BOZEZ [BOH-zez] A rocky crag to one side of the pass Jonathan used to reach the Philistine outpost in Micmash [**X**, A2]. 1 Sam. 14:4. *See* Seneh.

BOZKATH [BAHZ-kath; "craggy"] Bozcath, KJV (2 Ki. 22:1). A city in the W foothills of Judah, near Lachish [**V**, C1]; hometown of Josiah's mother. Josh. 15:39.

BOZRAH [BAHZ-ruh; "fortress"]
1. [**VIII**, C2]. An ancient and heavily fortified city of Edom. At times, it probably served as the nation's capital. Identified with modern Buseirah, SE of the Dead Sea and N of Petra (biblical Sela). Gen. 36:33; Isa. 34:6; Jer. 49:13,22; Amos 1:12.
2. A city of Moab, probably identical to Bezer. Jer. 48:24.

BUBASTIS [boo-BAS-tis] Pibeseth, KJV, RSV. A city in the E Delta region of Egypt, located NE of Memphis, near On (Heliopolis) [**III**, C1]. Pharaoh Sheshonq, the biblical Shishak, ruled Egypt from his palace in Bubastis. Ezek. 30:17.

BUZ [BUZ] A kingdom near Tema and Dedan [**IX**, C3], in the NW region of the Arabian Peninsula. Jer. 25:23.

C

CABBON [KAB-ahn; "surround"(?)] A town in the W foothills of Judah, in the vicinity of the Amorite cities of Eglon and Lachish [**V**, C1]. Josh. 15:40.

CABUL [KAY-bul; "barren" or "worthless"]
1. [**VI**, B3]. A border town of Asher, identified with modern Kabul, a village located about 9 miles (14.5 km) SE of Acco. Josh. 19:27.
2. A district of N Galilee containing 20 towns, given to Hiram king of Tyre by Solomon. The region was so-named as an indication of Hiram's displeasure with the villages of the region, and the parallel passage in 2 Chr. 8:2 suggests that he may have returned the towns to Solomon, who rebuilt them. 1 Ki. 9:13.

CAESAREA* [ses-uh-REE-uh] **XI**, C1; **XIII**. A magnificent port city on the coast of Palestine, about 23 miles (37 km) S of Mt. Carmel. Built by Herod the Great over a period of twelve years, (23–13 B.C.), it became the Roman metropolis of Judea. During his term as procurator of Judea, Pilate occupied the governor's residence in Caesarea. Acts 8:40; 10:1; 25.

CAESAREA PHILIPPI [ses-uh-REE-uh FIH-lip-eye] **XI**, A3. A city in N Palestine, located on the S slopes of Mt. Hermon, near the primary source of the Jordan River. An ancient site of Baal worship, with the coming of the Greeks it became a cult center for the god Pan, after which the city became known as Paneas. Augustus Caesar gave the town to Herod the Great, who built a temple there dedicated to the Roman emperor. Herod's son, Philip the tetrarch, renamed the city Caesarea Philippi. It is likely that the city was not far from the site of Christ's transfiguration. Now known as Banias. Mt. 16:13; Mk. 8:27. Possibly the same as Baal Gad.

CALAH [KAY-luh] **II**; **IX**, B3. An ancient city established by Nimrod, settled in prehistoric times and already falling into decline by the time of Hammurabi, about 1792–1750 B.C. It was rebuilt by Shalmaneser I in the 13th century B.C., and later replaced Asshur as capital of Assyria, during the reign of Ashurnasirpal II (about 883–859 B.C.). The modern site is Nimrud, located about 18 miles (29 km) S of Nineveh, on the E bank of the Tigris River. Gen. 10:11,12.

CALEB EPHRATHAH [KAY-leb EF-rah-thuh] Place where Hezron died, according to 1 Chr. 2:24. The RSV translation treats this as two persons rather than a location.

CALNEH [KAL-neh]
1. An ancient city founded by Nimrod in the land of Shinar. Its exact location in S Mesopotamia is uncertain. Some scholars believe the Hebrew translation of the name should be read as the phrase "all of them." Gen. 10:10. Possibly the same as Calneh in Amos 6:2 and Calno in Isa. 10:9.
2. A place mentioned with Hamath and Gath in N Mesopotamia; despite the discrepancy in location, this may be the same as 1, or perhaps a site whose name was derived from the city in Shinar. It may be identical to Kullan Koy, about 6 miles (9.5 km) SE of Arpad [**IX**,

B3]. Amos 6:2. Probably the same as Calno in Isa. 10:9 and Canneh in Ezek. 27:23.

CALNO [KAL-noh] A city mentioned, with Carchemish, among the conquests of Assyria. Isa. 10:9. Probably the same as Calneh 2.

CALVARY* [KAL-vuh-ree; "skull"] **XII**, B2. A place outside Jerusalem where Christ was crucified. Called the Place of the Skull in the NIV. Mt. 27:33; Jn. 19:17. *See* Golgotha.

CANA [KAY-nuh; "reeds"] **XI**, B2. A village of Galilee where Christ performed his first miracle. Located in the hill country W of the lake, it is identified by some with a site about 4 miles (6 km) NE of Nazareth. However, a more likely location is Khirbet Kana, about 9 miles (14 km) N of Nazareth (shown on map). Jn. 2:1,11; 4:46; 21:2.

CANAAN* [KAY-nuhn] Ancient name of Palestine, the land given to Abraham and his descendants. Gen. 10:19; 12:5; Num. 34:1-12.

CANNEH [KAN-eh; "distinguished"] A city mentioned with Haran and Eden for its trade with Tyre. Possibly same as Calneh 2. Some identify it with a site on the S coast of Arabia, the location of present-day Canne. Ezek. 27:23.

CAPERNAUM* [kuh-PER-nay-uhm; "village of Nahum"] **XI**, B3. An important city in NT times, located on the NW shore of the Sea of Galilee. After Jesus left Nazareth, Capernaum became the headquarters of his ministry in Galilee. It is identified with Tell Hum. Mt. 4:13; Lk. 4:23,31; Jn. 6:17-24,59.

CAPHTOR [KAF-tor] Island or seacoast region from which the Philistines originally came. Generally identified with Crete [**XIII**, C4] and the surrounding Aegean islands. Deut. 2:23; Jer. 47:4; Amos 9:7.

CAPPADOCIA [KAP-uh-DOH-shuh] **XIII**, B6-B7. A large Roman province in E Asia Minor. It was bounded on the N by Pontus, on the E by Armenia and Syria, on the S by Cilicia, and on the W by Lycaonia and Galatia. Acts 2:9; 1 Pet. 1:1.

CARCHEMISH [KAR-kuh-mish] **II**,B4; **IX(b)**. An ancient capital of the Hittites, located on the W bank of the Euphrates in N Syria. The Hittite Empire fell in 717 B.C. with its capture by Sargon II of Assyria. In 605 B.C., Carchemish was the site of a decisive battle between Nebuchadnezzar and Pharaoh Neco, whose army occupied the city. The defeat of Neco at the hands of the Babylonians decided the fate of all of W Asia. Modern Jerablus. 2 Chr. 35:20; Isa. 10:9; Jer. 46:2.

CARMEL [KAR-muhl; "garden" or "orchard"]
1. [**V**; **XI**, B1]. A mountain range extending about 13 miles (21 km) SE from a point on the Mediterranean coast just S of the Bay of Acre. To the S of the range lies the Plain of Sharon and to the N flows the River Kishon through the plain of Esdraelon. At the NW promontory, Mt. Carmel reaches a height of 470 ft. (143 m); farther S is its summit at 1742 ft. (531 m) above sea level. Notable as the site of Elijah's confrontation with the 850 prophets of Baal. Josh. 12:22; 1 Ki. 18; Jer. 46:18; Amos 9:3.
2. [**VII**, C1]. An ancient town in the hill country of Judah, identified with a site 8 miles (13 km) SE of Hebron. Home of Nabal, who refused hospitality to David. Modern Kermel. Josh. 15:55; 1 Sam. 25:2-7,40.

CASIPHIA [kuh-SIF-ee-uh] An unidentified town in Babylon from which Ezra retrieved Levites to serve in the Temple in Jerusalem. Ezra 8:17.

CAUDA [KAW-duh] Clauda, KJV. An island about 50 miles (80 km) S of the SW coast of Crete [**XIII**, C4]. Modern Gavdhos. Acts 27:16.

CENCHREA [SENG-kree-uh] **XIII**, B3. A town which served as the E harbor for the city of Corinth, located about 7 miles (11 km) to the W. Phoebe was a deaconess of the church at Cenchrea. Acts 18:18; Rom. 16:1.

CHALDEA [kal-DEE-uh] **IX(b)**. A small region at the head of the Persian Gulf, inhabited by the Chaldeans, a people distinct from the Arameans. Appearing in the early 1st millennium B.C. as Kaldu in Assyrian texts, they spread into S Babylonia, occupying Ur "of the Chaldeans." Later, during the time of the Chaldean kings in Babylon, the name became synonymous with all Babylonia. Gen. 11:28; Ezra 5:12; Ezek. 23:15,16. *See* Chaldeans.

CILICIA [sih-LIS-ee-uh] **XIII**, B6. In NT times, a Roman province in SE Asia Minor, bounded on the N by the Taurus Mountains and extending S to the Mediterranean. Geographically two regions, the western territory was known as Cilicia Tracheia, a rough, mountainous area; to the E was Cilicia Pedias, a fertile plain which controlled the only land route between Syria and Asia Minor. The great highway crossed the Taurus Mountains by way of the majestic pass known as the Cilician Gates. The chief city of the province was Tarsus, the birthplace of the apostle Paul. Acts 6:9; 15:41; 21:39; 27:5.

CITY OF DAVID.* The Jebusite fortress of Zion (ancient Jerusalem), captured by David and made his royal city. 2 Sam. 5:6-9; 1 Chr. 11:5-7.

CITY OF SALT. A city in the S desert region of Judah, probably near En Gedi [**VI**, E3]. Josh. 15:62.

CNIDUS [NIGH-dus; "'age'"] A city in SW Asia Minor, situated at the end of a long peninsula projecting between the islands of Cos and Rhodes. Acts 27:7.

COLOSSE [kuh-LAH-see] Colossae, RSV. [**XIII**, B5]. An ancient city of Phrygia, located on the Lycus River about 11 miles (18 km) SE of Laodicea. By NT times the city was in decline, eclipsed by the neighboring cities of Laodicea and Hierapolis. Col. 1:2. *See* Colossians.

CORINTH [KOR-inth; "ornament"] **XIII**, B3. Important commercial city of ancient Greece, ideally situated on the W end of the isthmus between the Peloponnesus and the mainland. N-S land routes passed through the city, and much of the traffic between Rome and the East was brought to its harbors, to be transported across the isthmus. This permitted sea trade connecting the Adriatic and Aegean seas while avoiding the treacherous journey around the S capes of the Peloponnesus.

In a locality first settled as early as the 6th millennium B.C., the present-day site of Corinth had its beginnings in the 7th century B.C.. It quickly grew to become a prosperous and influential city-state. The city established early the international trade of its famed Corinthian bronze and ceramics, its wealth and power reaching a zenith during the rule of Periander, about 625–583 B.C. Thereafter it began to decline under the pressure of Athenian influence, and came under the dominion of Macedonia during most of the 3rd and 4th centuries B.C.. In 196 B.C., the city received limited autonomy from Rome, only to rebel against Roman rule 50 years later. As a result, Corinth was destroyed in 146 B.C., remaining a ruin only sparsely inhabited for the next century. In 46 B.C., Julius Caesar declared Corinth a Roman colony. By his command the city was rebuilt and repopulated with freed slaves and poor people gathered from every corner of the Mediterranean world. Corinth was made the capital of Achaia,

and rapidly regained its prominence, growing to enormous proportions. Acts 18; 1 Cor. 1:2; 2 Cor. 1:1,23.

CORNER GATE. A gate near the NW corner of the wall of Jerusalem, S of the Ephraim Gate and W of the palace. 2 Ki. 14:13; 2 Chr. 26:9; Jer. 31:38.

COS [KAHS] **XIII**, C4. A small island off the coast of Asia Minor with a large Jewish community; its capital city bore the same name. Acts 21:1.

CRETE [KREET] **IX**; **XIII**, C4. A large island in the Mediterranean, SE of the Greek mainland, about 160 miles (258 km) long and up to 30 miles (48 km) in width. Archaeology on Crete has uncovered the history and remains of the ancient Minoan civilization, which arose, flourished, and declined on the island during the Bronze Age (about 2600–1125 B.C.). The island of Crete was made a Roman province in the 1st century B.C. Acts 27:7-13,21; Tit. 1:5. Probably same as Caphtor, the original homeland of the Philistines.

CUN [KUHN] Chun, KJV. A town in Syria. 1 Chr. 18:8. Same as Berothah, in Ezek. 47:16, and Berothai, in 2 Sam. 8:8.

CUSH [KUSH; "black"] Usually Ethiopia, KJV, RSV.
1. A land along the course of the Gihon River, one of the four rivers of the Garden of Eden. Presumably an area in or near Mesopotamia. Gen. 2:13. *See* Gihon.
2. The land along the middle Nile S of Egypt, corresponding to Nubia. Biblical Ethiopians came from Cush, which should not be confused with modern Ethiopia. Esth. 1:1; Isa. 18:1; Ezek. 29:10; 30:4-9.

CUSHAN [KOO-shan] A name referred to in Hab. 3:7. Possibly the same as Cush or, more likely, another name for the land of Midian. Moses' wife is called a Cushite in Num. 12:1, possibly indicating she was from Cushan, or Midian.

CUTHAH [KOO-thuh] **II**, C6. An ancient and important city of Babylonia; its ruins lie about 16 miles (26 km) NE of Babylon. The city's residents were deported to Samaria by Sargon, and were apparently numerous, for the inhabitants of Samaria were thereafter referred to as Cutheans. The city contained a temple dedicated to Nergal, god of the underworld. 2 Ki. 17:24,30.

CYPRUS [SIE-prus] **II**; **IX**; **XIII**, C6. A large island in NE Mediterranean, about 60 miles (96 km) W of the Syrian coast and 40 miles (64 km) S of the coast of Cilicia (modern Turkey). It was made a province in 27 B.C., and thereafter was governed by a proconsul (*compare* Acts 13:6-12). Barnabas was a native of Cyprus. Isa. 23:1,12; Ezek. 27:6; Acts 4:36; 11:19,20; 13:4. Also called Kittim, in the OT.

CYRENE [sie-REE-neh] **XIII**, D3. A Libyan city near the coast of N Africa, settled by Greek colonists in the 7th century B.C. Chief city of the Roman province of Cyrenaica. Simon, the man forced to carry the cross for Jesus, was a native of this city. Mt. 27:32; Acts 2:10; 6:9.

D

DABBESHETH [DAB-uh-sheth; "camel hump"] A border town of Zebulun; location uncertain. Josh. 19:11.

DABERATH [DAB-uh-rath] Dabareh, KJV (Josh. 21:28). A Levitical city on the border between Issachar and Zebulun. Josh. 19:12. Identified with modern Daburiyeh, on the NW slope of Mt. Tabor [**VI**, B3].

DALMANUTHA [DAL-muh-NOO-thuh] A village on the W coast of the Sea of Galilee, identified with the NT town of Magdala; its ruins lie near modern Mejdel, about 3 miles (5 km) N of Tiberias [**XI**, B3]. Mk. 8:10. Called Magadan in Mt. 15:39.

DALMATIA [dal-MAY-shuh; "deceitful"] A mountainous region on the E shore of the Adriatic Sea [**XIII**, A2]. In NT times, it was part of the province of Illyricum. 2 Tim. 4:10.

DAMASCUS* [duh-MAS-kus] **I**, A2; **II**; **VII**, B2; **VIII**; **XIII**. Ancient city of Syria, situated in a desert oasis owed to the abundant water supplied by the Abana and Pharpar rivers. Its position at the crossroads of the Great Trunk Road and the King's Highway, connecting the lands of the Near East, made Damascus a great commercial city. It reached the height of its wealth and influence as the capital of an Aramean kingdom in the 10th–8th centuries B.C. Tiglath-Pileser III ended Damascus's period as an independent power, destroying the city in 732 B.C. and deporting its inhabitants. Damascus was thereafter stripped of its political importance and reduced to a secondary city within the Assyrian province of Hamath.

Damascus flourished after Syria was made a Roman province in 64 B.C., dramatically increasing in size, although it was still less important than Antioch. After A.D. 33, the city was apparently absorbed within the territory of the Nabatean king Aretas. Shortly after Paul's conversion on the road to Damascus, the apostle began to preach in its many synagogues. Strong opposition from the Jewish community in Damascus eventually forced Paul to escape over the city wall. He later returned to the city, where a strong Christian community had already been firmly established. Gen. 14:15; 2 Sam. 8:6; 1 Ki. 15:18; 2 Ki. 16:9-12; Acts 9; 22:4-12; 2 Cor. 11:32.

DAN [DAN]
1. [**VI**; **VII**; **VIII**, A2]. City in the extreme N of Palestine, originally known as Laish. It was renamed after its capture by the Danites, who had migrated to the N. For all practical purposes, it was the N limit of Israelite occupation, thus giving rise to the phrase, "from Dan to Beersheba" to describe the territory of Israel from N to S. Jeroboam I set up a golden calf idol in the city, making Dan a royal sanctuary of his idolatrous cult. Identified with a site at the S foot of Mt. Hermon. Josh. 19:47; Jdg. 18:29; 1 Sam. 3:20; 1 Ki. 12:29,30.
2. [**VI**, D2]. The territory assigned to the tribe of Dan, bounded by Judah to the S, Benjamin to the W, and Ephraim and Manasseh to the N. They were unable to drive the Philistines and Amorites from their territory, and many Danites migrated N, settling near the source of the Jordan. Josh. 19:40-48.

DAN JAAN [DAN JAY-uhn] A place between Gilead and Sidon. Possibly a suburb of Dan [**VIII**, A2]. 2 Sam. 24:6.

DANNAH [DAN-uh] A town in the hill country of Judah, near Socoh and Debir. Josh. 15:49.

DEAD SEA. [**I**; **III**; **IV**; **V**; **VI**, D3-E3; **VII**; **X**]. Name adopted in the 2nd century A.D. for the large lake at the mouth of the Jordan River, typically referred to in the Bible as the Salt Sea. *See* Salt Sea; Arabah.

DEBIR [deh-BEER]
1. [**V**, D2]. A Canaanite city in the hill country of Judah, twice captured by Israel, and later designated a Levitical city. Several locations near Hebron have been suggested as the site of the city, but Khirbet Rabud, about 8 miles (13 km) SW of Hebron is the most probable. Josh. 10:38,39; 15:15,49; 1 Chr. 6:58. Also called Kiriath Sepher and Kiriath Sannah.
2. A border town of Gad, E of the Jordan, near Mahanaim. Josh. 13:26. Possibly the same as Lo Debar.
3. A town on the boundary between Judah and Benjamin, near the Valley of Achor; probably on the road between Jerusalem and Jericho. Josh. 15:7.

DECAPOLIS [deh-KAP-oh-lis; "ten cities"] **XI**, B3-C3. A district containing ten cities with large Greek populations, all but Scythopolis situated E of the Jordan. The Hellenized cities gained autonomy under Pompey in 63 B.C., and later formed a loose league for trade and mutual defense. Pliny the Elder identified the cities comprising the Decapolis as: Scythopolis (the OT Beth Shan), Hippos, Gadara, Pella, Philadelphia (the OT Rabbah), Gerasa, Dion, Canatha (the OT Kenath), Raphana, and Damascus. Lists differ, and more cities were eventually added to the district. Mt. 4:25; Mk. 5:20; 7:31.

DEDAN [DEE-dan] **IX**, C3. Rhodes, RSV (Ezek. 27:15). An oasis town and the surrounding region in NW Arabia, near Edom. The oasis of Dedan is probably the modern el-Ela, about 50 miles (80 km) SW of Tema. The Dedanites were known as traders whose caravans ranged across the wilderness of Arabia. Jer. 25:23; Ezek. 25:13; 27:15.

DERBE [DER-bee] **XIII**, B6. A city in the province of Lycaonia, in SE Asia Minor, located about 45 miles (76 km) SE of Iconium. Acts 14:6,20; 20:4.

DIBLAH [DIB-luh] Diblath, KJV. An unidentified location in the extreme N of Israel. Probably the same as Riblah, about 50 miles (80 km) S of Hamath [**VII**, A2]. Ezek. 6:14.

DIBON [DIE-bahn]
1. [**IV**, D1; **VI**]. A fortified Amorite town, located N of the Arnon River, and about 13 miles (21 km) E of the Dead Sea. After its capture, it was rebuilt by the Gadites, but allotted by Moses to Reuben. Later, the town fell to Mesha, king of Moab, who set up the famous Moabite Stone at this site. Its ruins lie near modern Dhiban. Num. 21:30; 32:34; Josh. 13:17; Jer. 48:18,22. Possibly same as Dimon.
2. A town in Judah, resettled by some who accompanied Zerubbabel in his return from exile. Neh. 11:25. Possibly same as Dimonah, in Josh. 15:22.

DIBON GAD [DIE-bahn GAD] A campsite of the Israelites during their wilderness wanderings. Num. 33:45,46. Probably the same as Dibon 1.

DILEAN [DIL-ee-uhn] A town in the W foothills of Judah. Josh. 15:38.

DIMNAH [DIM-nuh] A Levitical town in the territory of Zebulun, W of the Sea of Galilee. Josh. 21:35. Possibly the same as Rimmono, in 1 Chr. 6:77.

DIMON [DIE-mahn] A city of Moab, near the Arnon River. Isa. 15:9. Possibly the same as Dibon 1.

DIMONAH [dih-MOH-nuh] A town in the S wilderness of Judah. Josh. 15:22. Probably the same as Dibon 2.

DINHABAH [DIN-huh-buh; "give judgment"] Royal city of Bela, a pre-Israelite king of Edom. Location unknown. Gen. 36:32.

DIZAHAB [DIZ-uh-hab; "possessing gold"] A place E of the Arabah, near the site where Moses gave his farewell speech to Israel. Its exact location is unknown. Deut. 1:1.

DOPHKAH [DAHF-kuh] An Israelite campsite in the Wilderness of Sinai, between Rephidim and the Red Sea. Num. 33:12–13.

DOR [DOR] **V**, B1; **VI**. An ancient Canaanite town on the coast of Palestine, now known as Tantura, about 8 miles (13 km) N of Caesarea. After Joshua defeated the king of Dor, the city was allotted to the Manassites, but they failed to drive out its Canaanite inhabitants. Josh. 12:23; 17:11; 1 Chr. 7:29. Also called Naphoth and Naphoth Dor.

DOTHAN [DOH-thuhn; "two wells"] **I**, B1; **VI**; **VII**. An ancient city in the territory of Manasseh, about 13 miles (21 km) N of the city of Samaria, near Mt. Gilboa. Dothan was situated in a fertile valley between Mt. Carmel and the hills of Samaria. This valley served as an important pass from the Jezreel Valley to the coastal plain. At Dothan, Joseph was sold into slavery. Gen. 37:17; 2 Ki. 6:13.

DUMAH [DOO-muh; "silence"]
1. A town in the hilll country of Judah, identified with modern ed-Domeh, about 6 miles (9.5 km) SW of Hebron [**V**, C2]. Josh. 15:52.
2. A symbolic name for Edom or possibly a reference to the oasis town of Dumah, in the Arabian desert E of Edom. Isa. 21:11.

DUNG GATE. A gate of Jerusalem in Nehemiah's time, located in the SW corner of the wall. Neh. 2:13; 3:14; 12:31.

E

EAST GATE. A gate on the eastern side of the Temple. 1 Chr. 26:14; 2 Chr. 31:14.

EBAL [EE-buhl] **V**, B2; **XI**. A mountain rising 3077 ft. (938 m) above sea level and located just N of Shechem, opposite Mt. Gerizim. A large Israelite altar has recently been discovered on its summit, and may be the altar built by Joshua. Modern Jebel Eslamiyeh. Deut. 11:29; 27:4,13; Josh. 8:30-35.

EBENEZER [EB-uh-NEE-zer; "stone of help"]
1. Site of the Israelite encampment before the Battle of Shiloh (about 1080 B.C.), in which the ark of the covenant was captured by the Philistines. It is probably located at Izbet Sartah, a small town E of Aphek [**I**, B1], on the road to Shiloh, occupied only for about two centuries, about 1200–1000 B.C. 1 Sam. 4:1; 5:1.
2. A stone erected by Samuel between Shen and Mizpah [**VIII**, B1] to commemorate the victory of Israel over the Philistines. 1 Sam. 7:12.

EBEZ [EE-bez] Abez, KJV. A town in N Palestine, allotted to the tribe of Issachar. Josh. 19:20.

ECBATANA [ek-BAT-uh-nuh; "fortress" or "place of assembly"] Achmetha, KJV. [**IX**, B4]. Capital of the Median Empire. Cyrus the Persian captured it in 550 B.C., after which it became the summer residence of the kings of Persia. It fell to Alexander the Great in 330 B.C. The remains of the city lie near the site of modern Hamadan, halfway between Tehran and Baghdad. Ezra 6:2.

EDEN* [EE-duhn; "delight"]
1. The garden created by God as a home for Adam and Eve, the first man and woman.

After the Fall, Adam and Eve were banished from the garden.
According to Gen. 2:10, from Eden flowed a river with four headstreams: the Pishon, Gihon, Tigris, and Euphrates, the latter two located in Mesopotamia. Many theories have been proposed concerning the location of the garden of Eden, ranging from Armenia—where the Tigris and Euphrates originate—to the head of the Persian Gulf in S Mesopotamia. No locality is without difficulties, and it may be that the geographical features have changed, making identification impossible. Gen. 2:4–3:24.
2. An Aramean kingdom in Mesopotamia, known from Assyrian sources as Bit-Adini. After its fall to Sennacherib III of Assyria, the region's inhabitants were deported to Kir. 2 Ki. 19:12; Isa. 37:12; Ezek. 27:23. See Beth Eden.

EDER [EE-duhr; "flock"]
1. A town in the S desert region of Judah, near Edom. Possibly a site about 4.5 miles (7.2 km) S of Gaza [**VI**, E1]. Josh. 15:21.
2. See Migdal Eder.

EDOM* [EE-duhm; "red"] **III**, B5-C5; **IV**; **VI**; **VII**; **VIII**. The rough mountainous territory S of Moab and largely E of the Arabah, extending about 100 miles (160 km) from the Zered river valley, at the base of the Dead Sea, to the Gulf of Aqabah. Its inhabitants, the Edomites, were descendants of Esau (or Edom). Its chief cities were Sela, Bozra, and Teman. Num. 20:14-21; Josh. 15:1,21; 2 Sam. 8:13,14; 2 Ki. 8:20-22; Jer. 49:7-22. See Idumea.

EDREI [ED-ree-ie; "strong"(?)]
1. [**IV**, B2; **VI**]. A royal city of Og, king of Bashan, and the site of his defeat in battle against the Israelites. After its capture, the town was assigned to the tribe of Manasseh. Identified with Dera, located midway between Damascus and Rabbah, on the S tributary of the Yarmuk River, which feeds into the Sea of Galilee. Num. 21:33; Deut. 3:1,10; Josh. 13:12,31.
2. A fortified city of Naphtali, N of the Sea of Galilee. Exact location unknown. Josh. 19:37.

EGLAIM [EG-lay-uhm] An unidentified location in Moab. Isa. 15:8.

EGLATH SHELISHIYAH [EG-lath SHEL-uh-SHY-uh] "A heifer of three years old," KJV. A place in Moab, near Zoar. Its exact location is unknown. Isa. 15:5; Jer. 48:34.

EGLON [EG-lahn] **V**, D1. An Amorite royal city conquered by Joshua. Tell el-Hesi is the preferred site, located in the lowlands of Judah, about 7 miles (11 km) SW of Lachish. Josh. 10; 15:39.

EGYPT* [EE-jipt; derived from Ha-ku-ptah, a name of Memphis] **II**; **III**, A1-E1; **IX**; **XIII**. Land in the NE corner of Africa, along the course of the lower Nile and its delta on the Mediterranean. The country was from its early history divided into two lands, Upper and Lower Egypt. Upper Egypt extended almost 600 miles (965 km) along the Nile Valley, from Cairo to Aswan; Lower Egypt commanded the Nile Delta, N of Cairo—a region about 125 miles (200 km) long and 115 miles (185 km) wide. Egypt was the seat of an ancient civilization that during its periods of ascendancy spread its influence throughout the Mediterranean and Near East. In this land the Israelites lived for 430 years, until the time of the Exodus. Gen. 12:10-20; 39–41; Ex. 1–14; 1 Ki. 14:25-28; Isa. 11:11; Jer. 42–46.

EGYPT, WADI OF [**III**, B3; **VII**]. A desert stream bed that marked the border between Canaan and Egypt. It is identified with the Wadi el-Arish. Num. 34:5; Josh. 15:4,47.

EKRON [EK-rahn] **VI**, D2. Northernmost of the five chief Philistine cities, located near the

N boundary of Judah. The city, one of the largest in Israel, was assigned to Dan but conquered by Judah, which then lost it to the Philistines. Ekron was temporarily recaptured in the time of Samuel, but had again fallen to the Philistines by Saul's time. Later the city became a tributary of Assyria. The god of Ekron was Baal-Zebub. Its identification is disputed, but Khirbet Muqanna now appears to be the most likely site, about 13 miles (21 km) E of Ashdod. Josh. 13:3; 15:45,46; 19:43; 1 Sam. 5:10; 7:14; 2 Ki. 1:2-16.

ELAH [EE-luh; "oak"] A valley that provided passage from the plain of Philistia into the hill country of Judah. David slew Goliath here. Generally identified with the Wadi es-Sant, along which the probable sites of Gath and Azekah are situated. 1 Sam. 17:2,19; 21:9.

ELAM [EE-luhm] **II**, D7; **IX**. Region E of the Tigris River, incorporating the plain of Khuzistan and the Zagros Mountains, inhabited from early times. Its civilization was closely associated with the cultures of Mesopotamia, and its control of the trade routes to the E made Elam the object of many invasions by Mesopotamian kings. About 2000 B.C. there arose a powerful Elamite dynasty, which conquered Ur and several other cities of ancient Babylonia, dominating the region until the time of Hammurabi of Babylon. Kedorlaomer probably ruled as king of Elam early in this period of expansion.

Elam resisted the later rise of Assyrian power during the early 1st millennium B.C., and supported the Chaldean rebellion led by Merodach-Baladan. Ashurbanipal of Assyria ended Elamite power with an invasion in 640 B.C. Under Cyrus, Elam became a Persian province, with its capital at the ancient city of Susa. Gen. 14; Isa. 21:2; Jer. 49:34-39; Dan. 8:2; Acts 2:9.

ELATH [EE-lath; "palm grove"] Also Eloth, KJV, RSV. **III**, C4]. A port city in Edom, located at the N extremity of the Gulf of Aqabah, also known as the Gulf of Elath. It lies near Ezion Geber, Solomon's seaport on the Red Sea, from which he carried on trade with the kingdoms of Arabia, possibly ranging as far as India. Under Israelite dominion during the period of the monarchy, Elath fell under Edomite control in Jehoram's time. Reconquered by Amaziah, it was lost again in the days of Ahaz, never to be recovered. It may be identified with the port Aila in Roman times, modern Aqabah (shown on map). However, it is also possible that Elath is Tell el-Kheleifeh, about 2.5 miles (4 km) W of Aqabah, which has also been identified with Ezion Geber. Some theories hold that the place name changed during its history. Deut. 2:8; 1 Ki. 9:26; 2 Ki. 14:22; 16:6; 2 Chr. 26:2. See Ezion Geber.

EL BETHEL [EL BETH-uhl; "God of Bethel"] Site of an altar erected by Jacob at Bethel, so-named because it was there that God revealed himself to Jacob. Gen. 35:7.

ELEALAH [EE-lee-AY-luh; "God ascends"] A Reubenite town E of the Jordan, located 1.5 miles (2.5 km) N of Heshbon [**IV**, D1]. It later fell into the hands of the Moabites. Identified with modern el-Al. Num. 32:3,37; Isa. 15:4; Jer. 48:34.

EL ELOHE ISRAEL [EL ee-LOH-heh IZ-ray-el] An altar set up by Jacob, outside the city of Shechem. Gen. 33:20.

ELIM [EE-lim; "oaks"] Second resting place of the Israelites after they crossed the Red Sea during the Exodus. Probably located in the Sinai Peninsula near the Gulf of Suez, its exact location is uncertain. Ex. 16:1; Num. 33:9,10.

ELISHAH [ee-LIE-shuh] A land somewhere in the Mediterranean; from its coasts Tyre was supplied with purple dye. Possibly Cyprus. Ezek. 27:7.

ELKOSH [EL-kahsh] Birthplace of Nahum the prophet. Its location is unknown. Nah. 1:1.

ELLASAR [el-AY-sar] **II**, C6. A kingdom allied with Kedorlaomer, king of Elam, in Abraham's time. It is possibly to be identified with Larsa, an ancient Sumerian city located at the site of modern Senkereh in lower Mesopotamia. Gen. 14:1,9.

ELON [EE-lahn; "oak"] An unidentified city in the tribe of Dan. Josh. 19:43. Probably the same as Elon Bethhanan.

ELON BETHHANAN [EE-lahn beth-HAY-nuhn; "oak of the house of grace"] A town in the district governed by Ben-Hesed during the reign of Solomon. 1 Ki. 4:9. See Elon.

EL PARAN [EL PAIR-uhn] **I**, E1. Southernmost Horite location conquered by Kedorlaomer and his allies. It may be an ancient name for Elath, an Edomite seaport on the N tip of the Gulf of Aqabah, bordering on the wilderness of Paran. Gen. 14:6.

ELTEKEH [EL-teh-kuh] Elteke, RSV [Jos. 21:23]. A Levitical town in the territory of Dan. It is listed among the conquests of Sennacherib, about 701 B.C. Possibly located at a site about 15 miles (24 km) NE of Ashdod [**VI**, D2]. Josh. 19:44; 21:23.

ELTEKON [EL-teh-kahn] A city in the hill country of Judah, possibly located in the vicinity of Hebron. Josh. 15:59.

ELTOLAD [el-TOH-lad] A town in S Judah, given to the Simeonites. Possibly located about 13 miles (21 km) SE of Beersheba [**I**, C1]. Josh. 15:30; 19:4. Called Tolad in 1 Chr. 4:29.

EMEK KEZIZ [EE-mek keh-ZIZ; "valley of Keziz," KJV.] An unidentified location listed among the towns of Benjamin. Josh. 18:21.

EMMAUS [eh-MAY-us] **XI**, E2. A village about 7 miles (11 km) from Jerusalem; its exact site is uncertain. Two disciples were met by Christ on the road to Emmaus, following the resurrection.

Some identify Emmaus with a site about 16 miles (26 km) W of Jerusalem, but this is too far distant. Possibly el-Qubeibah, about 7 miles (11 km) NW of Jerusalem, is the site of the NT village (shown on map). Lk. 24:13.

ENAIM [eh-NAY-im; "two fountains"] A town on the road to Timnah. Translated as "open place" in the KJV. Gen. 38:14,21. Probably the same as Enam.

ENAM [EE-nuhm; "two fountains"] A town in the lowlands of Judah. Its location is uncertain. Josh. 15:34. Probably a variant of Enaim.

ENDOR [EN-dor; "fountain of habitation"] **VII**, C1. A town in the territory of Issachar, inhabited by the Manassites. Here Saul consulted a witch to summon forth the spirit of Samuel from the dead. Identified with modern Indur, about 4 miles (6.5 km) S of Mt. Tabor. Josh. 17:11; 1 Sam. 28:7; Ps. 83:10.

EN EGLAIM [en EG-lay-uhm; "spring of the two calves"] An unidentified site on the NW shore of the Dead Sea, where according to prophecy the waters will one day yield fish. Ezek. 47:10.

EN GANNIM [en GAN-im; "spring of gardens"]
1. A town in the W foothills of Judah. Josh. 15:34.
2. [**VI**, C3]. A town of the tribe of Issachar, assigned to the Gershonite Levites. Probably to be identified with modern Jenin, located at the S end of the triangular plain of Esdraelon. Josh. 19:21; 21:29. Called Anem in 1 Chr. 6:73, and Beth Haggan in 2 Ki. 9:27.

EN GEDI [en GEH-dee; "spring of the goat"] **VI**, E3. A town of Judah, located near the W coast of the Dead Sea, about 35 miles (56 km) SE of Jerusalem, near modern Ain Jidi. An oasis fed by warm springs, David and his men took refuge there while fleeing Saul. Josh. 15:62; 1 Sam. 24:1; 2 Chr. 20:2; Song 1:14. Called Hazezon Tamar in Gen. 14:7.

EN HADDAH [en HAD-uh; "swift fountain"] A border town of Issachar. Josh. 19:21.

EN HAKKORE [en HAK-or-ee; "spring of him who called"] A spring near Lehi, from which Samson drank after slaying a thousand Philistines. Jdg. 15:19.

EN HAZOR [en HAY-zor; "spring of the village"] A fortified city of Naphtali, not to be identified with the royal city of Hazor also located in Naphtali. Josh. 19:37.

EN MISHPAT [en MISH-pat; "spring of judgment"] Ancient name for Kadesh Barnea, conquered by Kedorlaomer in the time of Abraham. Gen. 14:7.

ENOCH [EE-nahk] A town built by Cain and named after his son. Gen. 4:17.

EN RIMMON [en RIM-ahn; "spring of the pomegranate"] A village of Judah, reoccupied after the Exile. Possibly identical to "Ain and Rimmon" (Josh. 15:32; 19:7) through the fusion of those two sites or as the result of a scribal error. Identified with Umm er-Rammamin, located about 10 miles (16 km) NE of Beersheba [**I**, C1]. Neh. 11:29. See Rimmon.

EN ROGEL [en ROH-guhl; "spring of the fuller"] **XII**, D3. A spring outside of Jerusalem, near the Valley of Hinnom, on the border between Judah and Benjamin. Here Adonijah held a sacrificial feast when he attempted to seize the throne. It is now known as Bir Aiyub, or the "well of Job." Josh. 15:7; 2 Sam. 17:17; 1 Ki. 1:9.

EN SHEMESH [en SHEM-esh; "spring of the sun"] A spring on the border of Judah and Benjamin, located about 3 miles (5 km) E of Jerusalem [**VII**, C1], on the road to Jericho. Modern Ain el-Hod. Josh. 15:7; 18:17.

EN TAPPUAH [en TAP-yoo-uh; "apple spring"] A spring on the border between Manasseh and Ephraim. Josh. 17:7. See Tappuah.

EPHES DAMMIM [EE-fes DAM-im; "boundary of blood"] A place between Socoh and Azekah [**V**, C1] where the Philistines camped before battle with the Israelites under Saul. David slew Goliath near this site. 1 Sam. 17:1. Called Pas Dammim in 1 Chr. 11:13.

EPHESUS [EF-eh-sus] **XIII**, B4. Largest and most important trading port in the Roman province of Asia, situated at the mouth of the Cayster River on the shore of the Aegean. By NT times, it was in a state of decline, due to the silting of its harbor, and its control of trade in the region had diminished. Paul lived there for over two years during his third missionary journey, making it central to the evangelization of the entire province.

The famous temple of Artemis was built at a sacred site of an ancient Anatolian fertility goddess, about 1.5 miles (2.5 km) NE of the city; the magnificent structure ranked as one of the seven wonders of the ancient world. It was widely represented on Roman coins, and was reputed to be four times the size of the Roman Parthenon. The great theater in Ephesus, into which the rioting mob carried Paul's traveling companions, had a capacity of about 24,000. It remains largely intact to this day, at the end of the impressive marble boulevard that led from Mt. Pion to the ancient harbor, now several miles inland. Acts 18:18–19:41; Eph. 1:1; Rev. 2:1-7. See Ephesians.

EPHRAIM [EE-free-uhm; "fruitful"]
1. [**VI**, C2-D3]. Territory assigned to the tribe of Ephraim at the time of the conquest. Ideally extending from the Jordan to the Mediterranean Sea, Ephraim was bounded on the N by Manasseh and on the S by Dan and Benjamin. Josh. 16:5-10.
2. The "forest of Ephraim" was the site of a battle between the armies of David and Absalom, in which the king's rebellious son was slain. It may have been a region in the forested hill country of Gilead, E of the Jordan (Josh. 17:14-18). 2 Sam. 18:6.
3. A gate on the N wall of Jerusalem previous to the Exile, later rebuilt by Nehemiah. 2 Ki. 14:13; Neh. 12:39.
4. [**XI**, D2]. A village near the desert where Jesus took refuge after he raised Lazarus from the dead. Identified with modern et-Taiyibeh, about 4 miles (7 km) NE of Bethel. Jn. 11:54. Possibly the same as Ophrah 1.

EPHRATAH [EF-ruh-tuh] Ephrathah, RSV. Ancient name of Bethlehem of Judah, or the district surrounding the city. Jesse, father of David, was an Ephrathite from Bethlehem (1 Sam. 17:12). Ruth 4:11. Called Ephrathah in Ps. 132:6, and Bethlehem Ephrathah in Mic. 5:2. Probably identical to Ephrath.

EPHRATH [EF-rath] Burial place of Rachel. Elsewhere the site of Rachel's tomb is set in the territory of Benjamin (1 Sam. 10:2; Jer. 31:15). Some believe the phrase "that is, Bethlehem" (Gen. 35:19) may have been later added to the text. Gen. 35:16,19; 48:7.

EPHRATHAH [EF-rath-uh] See Ephratah.

EPHRON [EE-frahn]
1. A mountain on the N boundary of Judah, about 5 miles (8 km) NW of Jerusalem [**VII**, C1]. Josh. 15:9.
2. A town in the vicinity of Bethel, taken from Jeroboam by Ahijah. 2 Chr. 13:19. Possibly the same as Ophrah 1 or Ephraim 4.

ERECH [EER-ek] Archevites, KJV (Ezra 4:9). [**II**, C6; **IX**]. An ancient Sumerian city-state, known as Uruk in Babylonian sources. It is identified with modern Warka in S Mesopotamia, situated along the Euphrates between Babylon and Ur. The city was inhabited from the 4th millennium B.C. until its decline during the Hellenistic period. According to the Epic of Gilgamesh, the legendary hero was its fifth king. The earliest known example of a ziggurat was discovered at Erech. Gen. 10:10; Ezra 4:9,10.

ESEK [EE-sek; "dispute"] A well in the Valley of Gerar [**I**, C1], dug by Esau but claimed by the Philistines living there. Gen. 26:20.

ESHAN [EE-shan; "support"] Eshean, KJV. A town of Judah located in the Hebron hills. Possibly a site about 10 miles (16 km) SW of Hebron [**V**, C2], near Dumah. Josh. 15:52.

ESHCOL [ESH-kahl; "cluster of grapes"] A valley just N of Hebron [**V**, C2], famous for its vineyards. Num. 13:23,24; 32:9.

ESHTAOL [ESH-tay-uhl] A town in the NW foothills of Judah, allotted to the tribe of Dan. Probably about 13 miles (21 km) W of Jerusalem [**VII**, C1], near Zorah. Samson grew up and was buried between Zorah and Eshtaol. Later, Danites from Zorah and Eshtaol migrated to the area in N Naphtali, capturing the city of Laish and renaming it Dan. Josh. 15:33; 19:41; Jdg. 16:31; 18:2-11.

ESHTEMOA [ESH-teh-MOH-uh] A priestly city located about 9 miles (14 km) S of Hebron [**V**, C2]. Modern es-Samoa. Josh. 21:14; 1 Sam. 30:28. Same as Eshtemoh.

ESHTEMOH [ESH-teh-moh] A town in the hill country of Judah, identified with Eshtemoa. Josh. 15:50.

ETAM [EE-tuhm; "lair"]
1. A cave in W Judah, in which Samson hid from the Philistines. Jdg. 15:8,11.
2. A town in S Judah, belonging to the tribe of Simeon. Tentatively identified with modern Aitun, about 11 miles (18 km) SW of Hebron [**V**, C2]. 1 Chr. 4:32.
3. A town fortified by Rehoboam, located in the hill country of Judah, about 1.5 miles (2.5 km) SW of Bethlehem [**VII**, C1]. 2 Chr. 11:6.

ETHAM [EE-thuhm; "fortress"(?)] A place "on the edge of the wilderness," where the Israelites camped after leaving Succoth, possibly located N of the Gulf of Suez. The Desert of Etham through which they traveled for three days apparently extended E of the Red Sea's western gulf. Ex. 13:20; Num. 33:6-8.

ETHER [EE-th-uh-er]
1. A town in the foothills of Judah, between Libnah and Ashan. Possibly to be identified with a site near modern Beit-Jibrin. Josh. 15:42.
2. A town in the S of Judah, near Ashan. Josh. 19:7. Called Token in 1 Chr. 4:32. Possibly the same as 1.

ETHIOPIA [ee-thee-OH-pee-uh; "burnt face"] See Cush.

ETH KAZIN [eth KAY-zin] Ittah-kazin, KJV. A place on the border of Zebulun, near Gath Hepher. Josh. 19:13.

EUPHRATES [yoo-FRAY-teez] **II**; **VII**; **IX** B3-C4; **XIII**. The longest river in W Asia, extending 1780 miles (2890 km), from the Taurus Mountains in Turkey to the head of the Persian Gulf. Its primary tributary, the Murad Su, flows W from mountains of Armenia, joining the Karasu, which has its source in the Anti-Taurus Mountains. Many of Mesopotamia's ancient cities were located along the river, including Babylon, Carchemesh, Cuthah, Larsa (possibly biblical Ellasar), Erech, and Ur. In the Bible, it is often referred to as "the great river" or simply "the River." Gen. 2:14; 15:18; Deut. 1:7; Jer. 46:2,6,10.

EZEL [EE-zel; "departure"] "Yonder stone heap," RSV. A stone that marked the site of David and Jonathan's final parting. 1 Sam. 20:19.

EZEM [EE-zem; "mighty"] A town in the Negev, near Edom; assigned to the tribe of Simeon. Possibly a site about 15 miles (24 km) SE of Beersheba [**I**, C1]. Josh. 15:29; 19:3; 1 Chr. 4:29.

EZION GEBER [EE-zee-uhn GEE-buhr] **VII**, D1. A place near Elath, located at the tip of the Gulf of Aqabah. First mentioned as a stopping-place of the Israelites during the Exodus; it was possibly no more than an oasis at the time. Later, Solomon made it the port for his fleet, which traded with Ophir and the nations of Arabia. Jehoshaphat also built a sea-going fleet, which was destroyed in a storm at Ezion Geber. Some identify it with Tell el-Kheleifeh, about 2.5 miles (4 km) W of Aqaba (shown on map). Others propose that the Solomonic port was on the island of Jaziret Phara'on, about 10 miles (16 km) S of Tell el-Kheleifeh. Such an island base was a common Phoenician practice, and may have been adopted by Solomon, whose fleet was built with the aid of Hiram, king of Tyre. Num. 33:35,36; 1 Ki. 9:26; 22:48; 2 Chr. 20:36,37.

F

FAIR HAVENS. [**XIII**, C4]. An anchorage on the S coast of Crete, near Lasea. Because it was an open bay, it could not provide a secure harbor during the winter. Acts 27:8-12.

FISH GATE. An ancient gate of Jerusalem, on the N wall. 2 Chr. 33:14; Neh. 12:39.

FOUNTAIN GATE. Gate at the SE corner of ancient Jerusalem's walls, rebuilt during the time of Nehemiah. Neh. 2:14; 3:15; 12:37.

G

GAASH [GAY-ash; "quaking"] A mountain in the hill country of Ephraim, S of Timnath Serah, where Joshua was buried. Josh. 24:30; 2 Sam. 23:30.

GABBATHA [GAB-uh-thuh; "height"] Aramaic name of the "Stone Pavement," the site from which Pontius Pilate ordered Christ's crucifixion. It has been identified with a Roman pavement made of large slabs of stone, believed to have been the courtyard of the Tower of Antonia [**XII**, B2-B3] in the E part of Jerusalem. Jn. 19:13.

GAD [GAD; "fortune"] **VI**, C4-D4. The territory of Gad lay E of the Jordan, with Manasseh to the N and Reuben to the S. The Gadites received the portion of the Amorite kingdom of Sihon N of Heshbon. The Jabbok was the N boundary of Gad, except for the inclusion of the E Jordan Valley up to the Sea of Galilee, and a fertile tract NE of Mahanaim, extending N to Ramoth Gilead. The land of Gad in S Gilead was a region of conflict between Israel and Aram, until the deportation of the Gadites by Tiglath-Pileser III. Num. 32:20-36; Josh. 13:24-28; 2 Ki. 15:29; 1 Chr. 5:25,26.

GADARA [GAD-uh-ruh; "walls"] **XI**, B3. A city in the Transjordan, located about 6 miles (10 km) SE of the Sea of Galilee. It was a Greek city, a member of the Decapolis, and served as the capital of the Roman province of Perea. It was the nearest major city to the site by the E shore of the Sea of Galilee where Christ cast out the demon called Legion. Mt. 8:28.

GALATIA [guh-LAY-shuh] **XIII**, B6. A region in N central Asia Minor, settled in the 3rd century B.C. by the Celtic tribes from ancient Gaul, from whom the region derived its name. In 25 B.C., Galatia was bequeathed to Rome upon the death of its last king, Amyntas. Caesar Augustus then established the Roman province of Galatia, annexing portions of Pontus, Phrygia, Lycaonia, Pisidia, Paphlagonia, and Isauria. Acts 16:6; 18:23; Gal. 1:2; 1 Pet. 1:1.

GALEED [guh-LEED; "witness heap"] Hebrew name given to the pile of stones raised by Jacob and Laban in the hill country of Gilead, as a memorial to their covenant. Gen. 31:47,48. Called Jegar Sahadutha in Aramaic.

GALILEE [GAL-ih-lee; "circle" or "district"]
1. [**XI**, A2-B2]. A region in N Palestine, and a district in NT times, measuring about 44 miles (70 km) long and 25 miles (40 km) wide. It was bounded on the W by the Phoenician plain, from Lebanon to Mt. Carmel, and on the E by the Jordan Valley, both above and below the Sea of Galilee. In the S, Galilee extended to the line of mountains bordering the Jezreel Valley, and in OT times extended N to Dan. A slender valley, running E of Acco, divides the territory into two parts, Upper and Lower Galilee. The rugged Upper Galilee is actually the S exten-

sion of the Lebanon range, and rises to almost 4000 ft. (1220 m) above sea level. Lower Galilee remains under 2000 ft. (610 m), its low hills alternating with fertile plains.

The N position of Galilee fostered cultural mixing of the Jews with the Gentiles, who maintained a strong presence in the region. With the deportation of the Israelites and the influx of foreign immigrants after the fall of Samaria, the Israelite population became a minority. Because of this, the land was referred to as "Galilee of the Gentiles" (Mt. 4:15) and was held in contempt by the S orthodox Jews. Nonetheless, it was at Nazareth in Galilee that Jesus lived until age 30, and he selected his disciples from among the Galileans. Most of Christ's ministry was in Galilee among the culturally and religiously corrupt rather than among the Judeans, whose arrogance and prejudice hindered their reception of the gospel message. 2 Ki. 15:29; Isa. 9:1; Mt. 4:15-25; Jn. 4:43-54; 7.

2. [IV; V; VI; XI, B3]. The Sea of Galilee, a large fresh-water lake to the E of central Galilee. The lake is formed by a depression in the Jordan Valley, and is about 13 miles (21 km) in length by 8 miles (13 km) in width. The Jordan, flowing S from Lake Huleh, enters the N end of the sea and flows out near the S tip, descending sharply on its course toward the Dead Sea. The lake, surrounded by high hills, lies about 690 feet (211 m) below sea level. Its fresh, clear waters provide an abundance of fish, and in NT times supported a prosperous fishing industry. Four of Christ's disciples were fishermen on the Sea of Galilee, until called to become "fishers of men." Mt. 4:18-22; Mk. 7:31; see Lk. 8:22-40. Also called Gennesaret and Kinnereth.

GALLIM [GAL-im; "heaps"] Hometown of Paltiel, to whom Saul gave his daughter Michal, though she was already the wife of David. 1 Sam. 25:44; Isa. 10:30.

GAMMAD [GAM-uhd; "valorous"(?)] Gammadim, KJV; Gamad, RSV. A city whose men guarded the towers of Tyre. Possibly Kumidi, in N Syria, mentioned in the Amarna Letters. However, some believe this was merely an epithet applied to the warriors of Tyre. Ezek. 27:11.

GAREB [GAIR-eb; "scabrous"] A hill near Jerusalem, exact site uncertain. Jer. 31:39.

GATH [GATH; "winepress"] V; VI; VII, C1. With Gaza, Ashdod, Ekron, and Ashkelon, one of the five chief cities of the Philistines, all located near the coast of S Palestine. Among its inhabitants were the Anakites, from whom were descended the Gittite giants, most notably Goliath. David twice took refuge in the city to escape Saul, entering the service of Achish, king of Gath. Later, Gath was made subject to Israel, during the reign of David. Hazael, king of Syria, captured the city, but Gath was reconquered by Uzziah. Gath may have been destroyed by Sargon II about 715 B.C.; by the time of Amos, it was a ruin, and thereafter is no longer mentioned among the lists of Philistine cities. The site of the city is much debated, but Tell es Safi, located in the Valley of Elah about 12 miles (19 km) SE of Ashdod, is the preferred location. Josh. 11:22; 1 Sam. 5:8,9; 17:23; 21:10-15; 27:2-12; 2 Ki. 12:17; 2 Chr. 26:6.

GATH HEPHER [GATH HEE-fuhr; "winepress of digging"] Gittah-hepher, KJV (Josh. 19:13). [VIII, B2]. A town on the border of Zebulunite territory, notable as the hometown of the prophet Jonah. Located 3 miles (5 km) NE of Nazareth [XI, B2], near the village of Meshhed in Galilee, the traditional site of Jonah's tomb. 2 Ki. 14:25.

GATH RIMMON [GATH RIM-ahn; "winepress of the pomegranate"]
1. A Danite town, with Aijalon given to the Kohathite Levites. Identified with a site 4.5 miles (7 km) NE of Joppa [VI, D2]. Josh. 19:45; 21:24.
2. A Levitical town in the territory of Manasseh, W of the Jordan. Josh. 21:25. Probably the same as Bileam, in 1 Chr. 6:70.

GAZA [GAH-zuh; "strong"] I; III; V; VI, E1; VII; VIII. Southernmost of the five principal cities of Philistia, located at the site of the modern city, about 3 miles (5 km) from the coast of S Palestine. An ancient Canaanite city until its conquest by the Philistines, it became subject to Israel in the time of King David. Sennacherib gave some of the cities of Judah to his subject, Sillibel, king of Gaza, following the siege of Jerusalem. Alexander the Great conquered Gaza in 332 B.C., and in 96 B.C. the city was destroyed by Alexander Jannaeus, who slaughtered its inhabitants. Gaza was rebuilt farther to the S, extending to the shore of the Mediterranean, and by NT times the old site may have been abandoned. Gen. 10:19; Deut. 2:23; Jdg. 16; 2 Ki. 18:8; Acts 8:26.

GEBA [GEE-buh; "hill"] Gaba, KJV (Josh. 18:24; Ezra 2:26); Gibeah, KJV (1 Sam. 13:16). [X, A2]. A Benjamite town near Micmash, assigned to the Levites. Here Jonathan, with only his armor-bearer, defeated a Philistine outpost. In the time of the divided kingdom, it became the N extreme of Judah. Located at modern Jeba, about 6 miles (10 km) NE of Jerusalem. Neh. 11:31.

GEBAL [GEE-buhl; "hill, mountain"]
1. [II; VII, B2]. An ancient and prosperous seaport of N Phoenicia, situated on a bluff overlooking the Mediterranean, about 42 miles (68 km) N of Sidon. Inhabited since Neolithic times, in the 3rd millennium it became an important trading port with Egypt. During the period of Phoenician expansion, Gebal flourished, becoming so famous for its extensive trade in papyrus scrolls that the Greeks called the city Byblos (that is, "book"). Some evidence suggests that the first linear alphabet arose here. Stonemasonry and shipbuilding were also among its industries. 1 Ki. 5:18; Ezek. 27:9.
2. A mountainous region between Petra and the S end of the Dead Sea, in N Edom. Ps. 83:7.

GEBIM [GEE-bim; "ditches"] A Benjamite town, located just N of Jerusalem, near Nob. Its exact location has not been identified. Isa. 10:31.

GEDER [GEE-duhr; "wall"] A Canaanite royal city, near Debir. Location unknown. Josh. 12:13.

GEDERAH [geh-DEER-uh; "walled" or "sheepfold"] A town in the lowlands W of Jerusalem, inhabited by potters. Generally identified with modern Jedeira, about 4 miles (6 km) W of Aijalon [VI, D2]. Josh. 15:36; 1 Chr. 4:23.

GEDEROTH [GED-uhr-ahth; "walls" or "sheepfolds"] A town in the W foothills of Judah, captured by the Philistines in the time of Ahaz. Possibly modern Qatra, about 4 miles (6.5 km) SW of Ekron [VI, D2]. Josh. 15:41; 2 Chr. 28:18.

GEDEROTHAIM [GED-uh-roh-THAY-uhm; "two walls" or "two sheepfolds"] Probably a variant of Gederah. If it is a distinct city, the location is perhaps a site about 4 miles (6 km) E of Azekah [V, C1]. Josh. 15:36.

GEDOR [GEE-dor; "wall"]
1. A town in the hills of Judah, probably located about 7 miles (11 km) N of Hebron [V, C2]. Possibly inhabited by the family of Penuel. Josh. 15:58; 1 Chr. 4:4.

2. A city founded by Jered, a Judahite. Possibly located between the Socoh and Zanoah in the W foothills. 1 Chr. 4:18. It may be the same as Gederothaim.
3. A location on the edge of the territory occupied by the Simeonites in S Judah. 1 Chr. 4:39. Possibly Gerar.
4. Hometown of two Benjamite warriors who served under David. 1 Chr. 12:7.

GE HARASHIM [geh HAR-uh-shim; "valley of craftsmen"] Charashim, KJV. A valley in Judah, bordering the Plain of Sharon, E of Joppa [VI, D2]. It was inhabited by craftsmen of the Kenizzite clan. Benjamites settled there after the Exile. 1 Chr. 4:14. Called Valley of the Craftsmen in Neh. 11:35.

GELILOTH [geh-LIE-lahth; fem. plural of Gilgal: "circles"] "Borders," KJV, and "region about," RSV (Josh. 22:10, 11).
1. A landmark or small region on the S border of Benjamin, E of Jerusalem [VI, D3]. Josh. 18:17. Possibly the same as Gilgal, in Josh. 15:7.
2. Area W of the Jordan where the Israelite tribes of the Transjordan built an altar. It may be Gilgal, where Joshua set up a circle of stones, or the region around it, E of Jericho. The possibility remains that no place is indicated, as in the KJV and RSV translations. Josh. 22:10,11.

GENNESARET [geh-NES-uh-ret]
1. "The land of Gennesaret" was a plain stretching 3 miles (5 km) along the NW shore of the Sea of Galilee [XI, B3], and extending a mile inland. This fertile region produced an abundance of crops and wild trees. Present-day el Ghuweir. Mt. 14:34; Mk. 6:53. See Kinnereth.
2. The "Lake of Gennesaret" is a name for the Sea of Galilee, derived from the plain along its shore (see 1). Lk. 5:1. See Galilee.

GERAR [geh-RAR]
1. [I, C1; VI; VIII]. Ancient city located in the Negev in SW Palestine; both Abraham and Isaac journeyed to Gerar and formed treaties with its king, Abimelech. It later became a part of Philistia. During the divided kingdom period, Asa pursued the Cushites as far as Gerar, destroying the surrounding villages. Until recently believed to be Tell Jemmeh; its excavation revealed occupation only as early as the 16th century B.C. It is now identified with Tell Abu Hureirah, between Gaza and Beersheba, a site that prospered during the age of the Patriarchs. Gen. 10:19; 20; 26; 2 Chr. 14:13,14.
2. The "Valley of Gerar," identified with the Wadi Es-Sariah, near 1. Gen. 26:17.

GERASA [geh-RAH-suh] An important city, in NT times a member of the Decapolis. The reference to the city probably indicates that Gerasa was the chief city of the district in which Christ's healing of the demoniac occurred. Its ruins lie near the modern village of Jerash, about 30 miles (48 km) E of the Jordan, midway between the Sea of Galilee and the Dead Sea. Mk. 5:1; LK. 8:26,37.

GERIZIM [GAIR-uh-zim] V, C2; XI. A mountain on the S side of the pass in which the ancient city of Shechem was located, on the main N-S road through central Palestine. It rises to a height of 2849 ft. (868 m) above sea level, opposite Mt. Ebal. The Samaritans erected a temple on the hill to rival the Temple in Jerusalem, but it was destroyed during the time of the Maccabees. "This mountain" in Jn. 4:20 refers to Mt. Gerizim, where Samaritan worship continued in NT times. Modern Nablus now lies in the valley below. Deut. 11:29; 27:12; Josh. 8:33; Jdg. 9:7.

GERUTH KIMHAM [GAIR-ooth KIM-ham; "inn of Kimham"] "Habitation of Chimbam," KJV; Geruth-chimham, RSV. An unidentified place near Bethlehem [**VII**, C1], on the road to Egypt. It apparently retained the name of the son of Barzillai for centuries after the time of David. Jer. 41:17.

GESHUR [GESH-uhr; "bridge"]
1. [**VII**, B2-C2]. A small Aramean kingdom in upper Bashan, situated SW of Maacah and NW of the Argob. Although within the territory allotted to Manasseh E of the Jordan, the people of Geshur were not driven out by Israel. The daughter of Talmai, king of Geshur, became a wife of David. Her son, Absalom, escaped to Geshur after the murder of Amnon. Josh. 12:5; 13:11-13; 2 Sam. 14:23,32; 1 Chr. 2:23.
2. A region S of Philistia in S Palestine and Sinai. David led raids against the Geshurites while serving Achish, king of Gath. Josh. 13:2; 1 Sam. 27:8.

GETHSEMANE* [geth-SEM-uh-nee; "oil press"] **XII**, B3. The garden where Jesus was betrayed, on the night before his crucifixion. Gethsemane was an olive grove on the slopes of the Mount of Olives, located just E of Jerusalem, across the Kidron Valley. Mt. 26:36; Mk. 14:32 (*compare* Jn. 18:1).

GEZER [GEZ-uhr; "portion"] **V; VI; VII**, C1; **X.** A chief city of Palestine, located at a strategic point near the junction of major routes through central Palestine, W of the Valley of Aijalon. An ancient Canaanite city conquered by Joshua, by 1200 B.C. the city had succumbed to the Philistine invasion of S Palestine. Gezer later fell to an Egyptian Pharaoh, who gave it to his daughter on her marriage to Solomon. Excavations have revealed extensive fortifications from the Solomonic period (*see* 1 Ki. 9:17). Gezer (then called Gazara) served as an important military fortress during the time of the Maccabees. Josh. 12:12; 16:3,10; 1 Ki. 9:15-17; 1 Chr. 14:16.

GIAH [GIE-uh] An unidentified place near Gibeon [**V**, C2], in the territory of Benjamin. 2 Sam. 2:24.

GIBBETHON [GIB-uh-thahn; "height" or "mound"] **VIII**, B1. A Levitical town of the tribe of Dan. During its occupation by the Philistines, Baasha assassinated Nadab, king of Israel, at Gibbethon. It was conquered by Sargon, king of Assyria, in 712 B.C. Identified with a site about 6 miles (10 km) W of Gezer. Josh. 19:44; 21:23; 1 Ki. 15:27; 16:15,17.

GIBEAH [GIB-ee-uh; "hill"] Gibeath, KJV (Josh. 18:28). "Hill of God," KJV, "Gibeath-elohim," RSV (1 Sam. 10:5).
1. A town in the hill country of Judah, possibly a site about 12 miles (19 km) SW of Jerusalem [**VII**, C1]. Josh. 15:57.
2. [**VII**, C1]. A city of Benjamin, located about 3 miles (5 km) N of Jerusalem. During the period of the Judges, the crime committed by its men led to a war between Israel and the Benjamites, ending in the destruction of the town and the virtual annihilation of the tribe. It appears later in the OT as the birthplace of Saul, and capital during his reign. Excavations have uncovered the remains of Saul's fortress at Gibeah. 1 Sam. 14:2,16; 15:34; Hos. 10:9.
3. A town in the hill country of Ephraim, allotted to Phinehas, son of Aaron. It was the burial place of Eleazar the priest. Josh. 24:33.
4. Gibeah of God, where Saul was filled with the spirit of the Lord. 1 Sam. 10:5-10. Possibly the same as Geba.

GIBEATH HAARALOTH [GIB-ee-ath hay-AHR-uh-lahth; "hill of foreskins," KJV.] Place where the Israelites under Joshua were circumcised. Josh. 5:3.

GIBEON [GIB-ee-uhn; "hill"] **V**, C2; **VI; X.** The ancient Canaanite city whose Hivite inhabitants through a deception gained a peace treaty with Joshua. The Gibeonite cities of Kephirah, Beeroth, and Kireath Jearim were also preserved from destruction, but the Gibeonites were thereafter compelled to serve as laborers for the Israelites. Because of the covenant formed with Israel, a coalition of Amorite kings attacked Gibeon, but were defeated by Joshua on the day the sun stood still.

Identified with El Jib, about 6 miles (10 km) NW of Jerusalem. Excavation has uncovered the pool of Gibeon, 36 ft. (11 m) in diameter and 30 ft. (9 m) deep, cut through solid rock. A system of tunnels cut through stone led to an underground cistern room, fed directly by a spring. Other archaeological finds indicate that Gibeon was the center of a large wine-making industry. Josh. 9,10; 2 Sam. 2:12-24; 1 Ki. 3:5; Neh. 3:7; Jer. 41:12,16.

GIDOM [GIE-duhm; "desolation"] A place to which the routed Benjamites were pursued by the tribes of Israel, possibly E of Bethel. Jdg. 20:45.

GIHON [GIE-hahn; "stream" or "bursting forth"]
1. One of the four rivers flowing from Eden. It may indicate the Nile or the Ganges, or perhaps a lesser river of Mesopotamia, presuming present geography can account for the description. Gen. 2:13.
2. [**XII**, C3]. A spring in the Valley of Kidron, E of Jerusalem. The Jebusites cut a water shaft that led into the city. Later, Hezekiah blocked it off, and cut a new tunnel to supply water to the pool of Siloam. Solomon was anointed king beside the spring. 1 Ki. 1:33-45; 2 Chr. 32:30; 33:14.

GILBOA [gil-BOH-uh; "bubbling fountain"(?)] A semi-circular ridge of hills in the territory of Issachar, rising to a height of about 1700 ft. (520 m) above sea level. Located E of the Jezreel Valley, the battle of Mt. Gilboa, in which Saul and his sons died, took place on its W slopes. 1 Sam. 28:4; 31:1-9.

GILEAD [GIL-ee-ad; "rugged"]
1. [**IV**, C1]. A mountainous region E of the Jordan, rising to an altitude of about 3000 ft. (915 m) above sea level. Gilead extends from below the Yarmuk River in the N to the Dead Sea in the S, bordering on Ammon and the Arabian desert to the E. The hill country of Gilead was divided into two parts by the Jabbok River, its N portion belonging to Manasseh and S Gilead to Gad. The term, used loosely, includes the territory of Reuben, N of the Arnon River; and sometimes denotes the whole Transjordan occupied by Israel (Jdg. 20:1; 2 Ki. 10:33; 15:29). The heavily wooded territory was famous for its production of a curative balm (Jer. 8:22; 46:11). Gilead fell to Hazael, Aram's king, and later to Tiglath-Pileser, who deported its inhabitants. Gen. 31:21-25; Deut. 3:10-16; Jdg. 10:3-12:7; 2 Sam. 2:9.
2. A mountain on the edge of the Jezreel Valley, S of the hill of Moreh. Jdg. 7:3. Possibly another name for Mt. Gilboa.
3. A city in the region of Gilead; either Jabesh Gilead or Ramoth Gilead. Hos. 6:8.

GILGAL [GIL-gal; "circle" or "rolling"]
1. A place inhabited by Canaanites, identified by some with a site 2.5 miles (4 km) SE of Shechem [**I**, B1]. Deut. 11:30.
2. [**V**, C2]. First campsite of the Israelites after crossing the Jordan; Joshua set up a circle of twelve stones here to commemorate the entrance of the Israelites into the Promised Land. It served as a base of operations in Joshua's military campaigns. Gilgal apparently grew into a prominent city, for it was here that Saul was confirmed as king. It also became a center of idolatrous practices, unless the references by Amos and Hosea refer to Gilgal 4. Possibly located about 1 mile (1.5 km) NE of OT Jericho. Josh. 4:19,20; 10; 1 Sam. 11:12-15; 13:4-15; Amos 4:4; Hos. 4:15.

3. A town or region between Dor and Tirzah, whose king was defeated by Joshua. Possibly located on the Plain of Sharon about 3 miles (5 km) N of Aphek [**I**, B1]. Josh. 12:23.
4. A place on the N border of Judah. Josh. 15:7. See Geliloth 1.
5. A place through which Elijah and Elisha passed on the way to Bethel. Possibly a town in the hill country of Ephraim, about 7 miles (11 km) N of Bethel [**V**, C2]. 2 Ki. 2:1; 4:38.

GILOH [GIE-loh] A town in the hill country of Judah, the home of Ahithophel, counselor of David who rebelled with Absalom. Possibly located about 5 miles (8 km) NW of Hebron [**V**, C2]. Josh. 15:51; 2 Sam. 15:12.

GIMZO [GIM-zoh; "sycamore"] A town captured by the Philistines during the reign of Ahaz. Identified with modern Jimzu, 3 miles (5 km) SW of Lydda (ancient Lod) [**VI**, D2]. 2 Chr. 28:18.

GITTAIM [GIT-ay-uhm; "two wine-spresses"] **X**, A1. A Benjamite town to which the Beerothites fled from King Saul. It was resettled after the Exile. Probably a site about 4 miles (6.5 km) S of Lydda. 2 Sam. 4:3; Neh. 11:33.

GOAH [GO-uh] Goath, KJV. A boundary of the rebuilt city of Jerusalem according to prophecy. Jer. 31:39.

GOB [GAHB; "cistern"] The site of two battles between David and the Philistines, possibly identical to Gath or Gezer. 2 Sam. 21:18,19.

GOIIM [GOY-im] "Nations," KJV. Kingdom of Tidal, an ally of Kedorlaomer. Probably to be identified with a region in Syria. Gen. 14:1,9. Identical to Goyim in Josh. 12:23.

GOLAN [GOH-lan; "round"(?)] **VI**, B4. A Manassite city of refuge E of the Jordan, and a district of the Bashan. Gaulinitis, or Golan, was a fertile plateau, made a separate district of the Bashan in the Hellenistic period. The town from which the surrounding region gained its name is possibly to be identified with modern Jaulan, located about 17 miles (27 km) E of the Sea of Galilee. Deut. 4:43; Josh. 20:8; 21:27.

GOLGOTHA* [GAHL-guh-thuh; "the skull"] **XII**, C2. The place where Jesus Christ was crucified. It lay outside the city walls of Jerusalem in NT times, and was visible from some distance. A tradition dating back to the 4th century A.D. identifies Golgotha with the site of the Church of the Holy Sepulchre. Recent excavations indicate the site did in fact lay outside the wall of Jerusalem in the time of Christ. However, little evidence exists to verify its authenticity. Mt. 27:33; Mk. 15:22; Jn. 19:17.

GOMORRAH [guh-MOR-uh; "submersion"] **I**, C2. A city in the Valley of Siddim at the S end of the Dead Sea, notorious for its depravity. With Sodom and the lesser cities of the plain, Gomorrah was destroyed by God, as an act of judgment on the immorality of its inhabitants. Gen. 10:19; 14; 18:20; 19. *See* Cities of the Plain; Sodom.

GOSHEN [GOH-shen; "mound of earth"]
1. [**III**, B1-B2]. A region in Egypt where the household of Jacob settled; the land provided rich pastures for the grazing of livestock. Equated with the "district of Rameses" (*compare* Gen. 47:6,11), Goshen is identified with the region of the E Nile Delta where the cities of Pithom and Rameses once stood. It continued to be inhabited by the Israelites until the time of the Exodus, and was partly shielded from the plagues that fell on Egypt. Gen. 46:28-47; Ex. 8:22; 9:26.

2. A region of S Palestine subdued by Joshua, possibly taking its name from 3. Josh. 10:41; 11:16.

3. A town in the S hill country of Judah, possibly a site about 18 miles (28 km) SW of Hebron [**V**, C2]. Josh. 15:51.

GOYIM [GOY-im] "Nations," KJV; Goiim, RSV. *See* Gilgal 2; Goiim.

GOZAN [GOH-zan] **II**, B5; **IX**. An ancient city on the S bank of the Habor River, a tributary of the Euphrates. Its original settlement extends back as early as the 5th millennium B.C. Gozan, or Guzana, was the capital of the small Aramean city-state in NW Mesopotamia during the 10th and 9th centuries. By 808 B.C., it was subject to Assyria, and thereafter became one of the primary areas to which the Israelites were deported by the kings of Assyria. Excavations of its ruins have unearthed cuneiform texts of the 7th and 8th centuries, containing Hebrew names, very likely of deportees. 2 Ki. 17:6; 18:11; 1 Chr. 5:26; Isa. 37:12.

GREAT SEA. Biblical name for the Mediterranean.

GREECE* [GREES] A country in SE Europe, between Italy and Asia Minor, consisting of a mountainous peninsula and associated archipelagoes to the S. It was a region of self-governing city-states, which flourished through sea trade and established Greek colonies from Spain to the Black Sea. Philip II of Macedon conquered the S peninsula, unifying the strife-ridden republics of Greece. The "king of Greece" mentioned in Dan. 8:21 is probably Philip's son, Alexander the Great, who conquered Persia and established the Greek Empire. The resultant spread of Greek language and culture, known as Hellenism, provided a homogenizing and civilizing influence throughout the known world. Dan. 10:20; Acts 20:2.

GUDGODAH [gud-GOH-duh; "cleft" or "incision"] *See* Hor Haggidgad.

GUR [GER; "lion cub"(?)] A hill or town near Ibleam [**VI**, C3]; here Ahaziah was mortally wounded by the Jehu's men. 2 Ki. 9:27.

GUR BAAL [guhr BAY-uhl; "dwelling of Baal" or "sojourn of Baal"] A town in the S desert region of Judah, inhabited by Arabs. 2 Chr. 26:7. Possibly the same as Jagur.

H

HABOR [HAY-bor; "fertile"] **II**, B5. Modern Habur, a river that rises in the fertile region between the upper Euphrates and Tigris rivers, and flows about 200 miles (320 km) S until it unites with the Euphrates. Many very ancient ruins lie along its course, among them Tell Halaf, identified with Gozan, capital of a region to which many of the Israelites were deported by Assyria. 2 Ki. 17:6; 18:11.

HADASHAH [huh-DASH-uh; "new"] A village in the W foothills of Judah. Josh. 15:37.

HADES [HAY-deez] Hell, KJV. The Greek name for the place where the souls of the dead reside. It is the NT equivalent of "Sheol." Mt. 16:18; Rev. 1:18; 20:13,14.

HADID [HAY-did; "sharp"] A Benjamite town located about 3 miles (5 km) NE of Lydda (ancient Lod) [**VI**, D2]. Ezra 2:33; Neh. 11:34.

HADRACH [HAD-rak] A city-state in N Syria, first mentioned in the inscription of Zacar, king of Hamath, about 800 B.C. It appears as Hatarikka in Assyrian documents of the time. Zech 9:1.

HAELEPH [HAY-lef] Eleph, KJV. A town near Jerusalem, in the territory of Benjamin. Location uncertain. Josh. 18:28.

HAKILAH [huh-KIE-luh; "gloomy"] Hachilah, KJV, RSV. A hill in the wilderness SE of Hebron [**V**, C2], where David took refuge from Saul. 1 Sam 23:19; 26:1-3.

HALAH [HAY-luh] A city and district of Assyria to which the Israelites were deported. Possibly along the Habor River, SE of Gozan [**II**, B5], or the Assyrian Halahhu, NE of Nineveh [**II**, B5]. 2 Ki. 17:6; 1 Chr. 5:26.

HALAK [HAY-lak; "smooth" or "bald"] A mountain marking the S limit of the territory conquered by Joshua. Probably Jebel Halaq, W of the Scorpion Pass in central Negev. Josh. 11:17; 12:7.

HALHUL [HAL-huhl] A Judean town about 4 miles (6.5 km) N of Hebron [**V**, C2]. It still retains its ancient name. Josh. 15:58.

HALI [HAY-li; "ornament"] A town near the border of Asher, possibly about 6 miles (10 km) W of Hannathon [**VI**, B3]. Josh. 19:25.

HAM [HAM]
1. [**I**, B2]. A city whose inhabitants, the Zuzites, were conquered by Kedorlaomer and his allies. Located in the central Transjordan, it may be modern Ham, about 25 miles (40 km) SW of Ashtaroth. Gen. 14:5.
2. A poetic name for Egypt. Pss. 78:51; 105:23,27.

HAMATH [HAY-math; "fortification"] **II**; **VII**, A2; **IX**. Ancient city on the E bank of the Orontes in N Syria. In David's time, it was the capital of an Aramean-Hittite kingdom to the N of Damascus, extending up to the Euphrates. King Tou of Hamath became an ally, and possibly a subject, of David. Solomon temporarily controlled Hamath, and the city was later conquered by Jeroboam II of Israel. After the city fell to Sargon, about 721 B.C., the kingdom of Hamath was made a province of Assyria. It is known today as Hama. 2 Sam. 8:9; 2 Ki. 14:28; 17:24,30; 2 Chr. 8:4; Amos 6:2.

HAMATH ZOBAH [HAY-math ZOH-buh] A city captured by Solomon. Possibly a reference to a Syrian city of Hamath in Zobah, or the nations of Hamath and Zobah. 2 Chr. 8:3.

HAMMATH [HAM-uhth; "hot spring"] **VI**, B3. A fortified town of Naphtali, located at Hammam Tabariyeh, the site of the hot spring on the W shore of the Sea of Galilee, about 1 mile (2 km) S of Tiberias [**XI**, B3]. Josh. 19:35. Probably identical to Hammoth Dor in Josh. 21:32, and Hammon in 1 Chr. 6:76.

HAMMON [HAM-uhn; "hot spring"]
1. A border town of Asher, identified with a site near the Mediterranean coast about 10 miles (16 km) S of Tyre [**VII**, B1]. Josh. 19:28.
2. A Levitical city of Naphtali. 1 Chr. 6:76. *See* Hammath.

HAMMOTH DOR [HAM-uhth DOR; "hot springs of Dor"] A Levitical city of Naphtali, probably identical to the fortified town of Hammath. Josh. 21:32.

HAMON GOG [HAY-muhn GAHG; "multitude of Gog"] A valley used as a mass burial place for the armies of Gog, according to the prophecy of Ezekiel. Ezek. 39:11,15.

HAMONAH [huh-MOH-nuh; "multitude"] According to prophecy, a town in the valley of Hamon Gog. Ezek. 39:16.

HANANEL [HAN-uh-nel; "God is gracious"] Hananeel, KJV. A tower on the N wall of Jerusalem, between the Fish Gate and Sheep Gate. Neh. 3:1; 12:39; Zech. 14:10.

HANES [HAY-neez] A city of Egypt, often identified with Heracleopolis Magna, about 50 miles (80 km) S of Memphis. However, a site in the Nile delta region seems to better fit the parellelism of the verse; possibly Heracleopolis Parva in the E Delta. Isa. 30:4.

HANNATHON [HAN-uh-thahn; "dedicated to grace"] **VI**, B3. A border town of Zebulun, probably to be identified with a site 6 miles (10 km) N of Nazareth. An ancient city of some importance, it was mentioned twice in the Amarna Letters, and later among the conquests of Tiglath-Pileser III. Josh. 19:14.

HAPHARAIM [HAF-uh-RAY-uhm; "two pits"] Haphraim, KJV. A town in the territory of Issachar, listed among the towns conquered by Shishak, king of Egypt. Two possible sites have been proposed: one just S of Mt. Carmel, about 6 miles (10 km) NW of Megiddo [**V**, B2]; and another, modern et-Taiyiba, about 7 miles (11 km) NW of Beth Shan [**VII**, C1]. Josh. 19:19.

HARA [HAIR-uh; "hill country"] A place in Assyria to which Israelites E of the Jordan were deported by Tiglath-Pileser III, about 732 B.C. Possibly Haran or an unknown site; however, comparison with parallel references suggests the text may be corrupt (*see* 2 Ki. 17:6; 18:11). 1 Chr. 5:26.

HARADAH [huh-RAY-duh; "fear"] One of the Israelite campsites during the Exodus. Site unknown. Num. 33:24,25.

HARAN [HAIR-uhn; Assyr. "highway"] Charran, KJV NT. [**II**, B4; **IX**]. An ancient city in N Mesopotamia, situated on the banks of the Balih River, along the main trade route from Nineveh to Aleppo. Abram and his father lived here after leaving Ur. After Terah's death, Abram left the city and migrated to Canaan. His brother Nahor remained, and his daughter, Rebekah, became the wife of Isaac. Later, Jacob fled to Haran to escape Esau. He married Rachel and Leah, the daughters of Laban, while he lived there.

Haran was a cult center of the moon god Sin from Patriarchal times. It became subject to Assyria, and for some centuries served as a provincial capital. After the city rebelled, it was destroyed in 763 B.C., but Sargon II and his successors rebuilt the city and restored its temple. After the fall of Nineveh in 612 B.C., it became the last capital of Assyria, until it was taken by the Babylonians in 609 B.C. However, it remained an important commercial city, and continued as a center of pagan moon worship for several centuries after Christ. Gen. 11:31–12:5; 27:43; Isa. 37:12.

HARIM [HAIR-im; "consecrated"] Hometown of some Israelites who returned to Judah after the Exile. Possibly located about 3.5 miles (5.5 km) S of Azekah [**V**, C1]. Ezra 2:32,39; Neh. 7:35,42.

HARMON [HAR-muhn] "The palace," KJV. An unknown location to which the people of Samaria were to be exiled. Amos 4:3.

HAROD [HAIR-uhd; "trembling"] A spring identified as modern Ain Jalud, located at the foot of Mt. Gilboa about 1.5 miles (2.5 km) SE of Jezreel [**VIII**, B2]. Jdg. 7:1.

HAROSHETH HAGGOYIM [hah-ROH-sheth hah-GOY-im] "Harosheth of the Nations," KJV, Harosheth-ha-goiim, RSV. Hometown of Sisera, commander of the army of Jabin, king of Hazor. Possibly to be identified with a site located on the bank of the Kishon

River about 16 miles (26 km) NW of Megiddo [**V**, B2]. Jdg. 4:2,13,16.

HASHMONAH [hash-MOH-nuh; "fruitfulness"] An unidentified place where the Israelites camped during the Exodus. Num. 33:29,30.

HAURAN [HOHR-uhn; "black land"] A fertile plain E of the Jordan and the Sea of Galilee, SE of Mt. Hermon and Damascus, and N of Gilead and Ammon; an area largely corresponding to the Bashan. When the region was conquered, it became an Assyrian district. During the Greco-Roman period, the district was known as Auranitis, and became the breadbasket of Palestine, its rich volcanic soil ideal for wheat production. Now a part of Syria, it is once again known as Hauran. Ezek. 47:16,18.

HAVILAH [HAV-ih-luh; "circle" or "district"]
1. A land through which the Pishon River winds, said to have an abundance of gold. Location unknown. Gen. 2:11.
2. A region inhabited by the Ishmaelites and Amalekites, most likely located in NW Arabia. Gen. 25:18; 1 Sam. 15:7.

HAVVOTH JAIR [HAV-uhth JAIR] A region in Gilead and the Bashan, E of the Jordan. It contained 60 fortified towns, which were captured by Jair, and thereafter became a part of the inheritance of Manasseh. The region was later taken by the Arameans. Num. 32:41; Jdg. 10:4; 1 Chr. 2:23.

HAZAR ADDAR [HAY-zar AD-ar] A location on the S boundary of Canaan, E of Azmon [**III**, B4]. Num. 34:4. *See* Hazor 3, Hazor Hadattah, and Addar.

HAZAR ENAN [HAY-zar EE-nuhn; "village of fountains"] A place marking the NE corner of Canaan, between Damascus and Hamath. Num. 34:9,10; Ezek. 47:17.

HAZAR GADDAH [HAY-zar GAD-uh; "village of fortune"] A town in the extreme S of Judah. Location uncertain. Josh. 15:27.

HAZAR SHUAL [HAY-zar SHOO-uhl; "village of the jackal"] A town in S Judah given to the Simeonites. It was repopulated after the Exile. Possibly located about 2 miles (3 km) SE of Beersheba [**I**, C1]. Josh. 15:28; 19:3; Neh. 11:27.

HAZAR SUSAH [HAY-zar SOO-zuh; "village of horses"] A Simeonite town located in the Negev in S Palestine. Site uncertain. Josh. 19:5. Called Hazar Susim in 1 Chr. 4:31.

HAZAR SUSIM [HAY-zar SOO-zim] *See* Hazar Susah.

HAZAZON TAMAR [HAZ-uh-zahn TAY-mar] **I**, C1. Ancient name of En Gedi, on the W shore of the Dead Sea. However, some identify it with Tamar, on the road S to Elath. 2 Chr. 20:2. Called Hazezon Tamar in Gen. 14:7.

HAZER HATTICON [HAY-zer HAT-ih-kahn] Hazar-hatticon, KJV. A location on the border of Hauran, near Damascus. Location unknown. Ezek. 47:16.

HAZEROTH [HAZ-uh-rahth; "villages"] **III**, D4. Stopping place during the Exodus where Aaron and Miriam opposed Moses. Possibly to be identified with Ain Hadra, about 40 miles (65 km) NE of Mt. Sinai (Jebel Musa). Num. 11:35; 12:16; 33:17,18; Deut. 1:1.

HAZEZON TAMAR [HAZ-uh-zahn TAY-mar] *See* Hazazon Tamar.

HAZOR [HAY-zor; "enclosure"]
1. [**I; II; V**, A2; **VI; VII**]. A Canaanite royal city in N Palestine, ruled by King Jabin, who led a coalition of northern kings against Joshua.

After defeating the Canaanite forces, Joshua burned Hazor to the ground. During the time of the Judges, another Jabin who ruled in Hazor oppressed Israel, and was defeated by Deborah and Barak.

Allotted to Naphtali, the city was later fortified by Solomon, and a citadel dates from the time of Ahab. A heavy layer of ashes, in places up to a yard thick, marks the city's final destruction by Tiglath-Pileser III, about 732 B.C. Thereafter, Hazor served as little more than a military outpost.

Located about 10 miles (16 km) NW of the Sea of Galilee, the ruins of the upper city date from the 3rd millennium B.C. The lower city of the 2nd millennium occupied an area exceeding 150 acres, making Hazor the largest city built in Palestine during OT times, with up to 40,000 inhabitants. However, following its destruction by Joshua, the lower city was never rebuilt. Josh. 11:1,10-13; 19:36; Jdg. 4; 1 Ki. 9:15; 2 Ki. 15:29.
2. An unidentified town in the Negev of Judah. Josh. 15:23.
3. Alternate name for Kerioth Hezron, in Josh. 15:25.
4. A kingdom near Kedar in Arabia, against which Jeremiah uttered a prophetic oracle. Jer. 49:28-33.
5. A town resettled by Benjamites after the Exile, possibly to be identified with a site about 4 miles (6.5 km) NW of Jerusalem [**IX**, B3]. Neh. 11:33.

HAZOR HADATTAH [HAY-zor huh-DAT-uh; "new Hazor"] A town in the S desert region of Judah. The KJV translates the term as two separate locations. Josh. 15:25. Possibly the same as Hazor 3 or Hazar Addar.

HEBRON [HEB-ruhn; "confederacy"] **I; III; V**, C2; **VI; VII**, C1; **VIII; X**. An important city in S Palestine, located in the hill country of Judah about 19 miles (31 km) S of Jerusalem. The city is near the ridge of the hills, and at an altitude of 3040 ft. (927 m) above sea level, Hebron is the highest town in Palestine. The archaeological record shows almost continuous occupation at Hebron from the Early Bronze Age to modern times. It may be the oldest unwalled city in the world to possess that distinction.

According to tradition, it was founded seven years before Zoan (that is, Tanis) in Egypt (Num. 13:22). It became a campsite of Abram, who lived at the oaks of Mamre near the city. The cave of Machpelah at Mamre became the patriarchal burial place. At the time of the conquest, it was a royal city of the Anakites, known as Kiriath Arba. Joshua took the city, but prior to his death, it had reverted to the Anakites. Caleb recaptured Hebron, which was designated a city of refuge.

Its inhabitants aided David while he was a fugitive, and after Saul's death, David was anointed king of Judah in Hebron. David reigned here for seven years until the transfer of the capital to Jerusalem. Later, Absalom engineered his rebellion from Hebron. During the reign of Rehoboam, it was refortified as a S defense of Jerusalem. Hebron appears among the cities named on royal jar-handle stamps of Judah, suggesting its importance as an administrative center during the OT kingdom period. It was resettled after the Exile, and later became a city of the Edomites, within the province of Idumea. Gen. 13:18; 23; Num. 13:22; Josh. 10; 2 Sam. 2:1-11; 3:27; 15:7-10.

HELAM [HEE-luhm] **VII**, C2. A place E of the Jordan where David defeated the army of Hadadezer, Aramean king of Zobah. Possibly identical to modern Alma, about 22 miles (35 km) NE of Ramoth Gilead. 2 Sam. 10:16,17.

HELBAH [HEL-buh; "fertile"] A town in the territory of Asher whose Canaanite inhabitants

were not driven out by the Israelites. Jdg. 1:31. Possibly the same as Ahlab, identified with el-Mahalib, 4 miles (6.5 km) N of Tyre [**VII**, B1].

HELBON [HEL-buhn; "fat" or "fertile"] A town near Damascus that exported wine to Tyre. Identified with modern Helbun, about 13 miles (21 km) N of Damascus [**I**, A2]. Ezek. 27:18.

HELECH [HEE-lek; "strength"] "Thine army," KJV. If a place is indicated, it may be the same as the Assyrian *Hilakku*, which referred to Cilicia in SE Asia Minor. Ezek. 27:11.

HELEPH [HEE-lef] A place on the S boundary of Naphtali, possibly a site about 3 miles (5 km) NE of Mt. Tabor [**VI**, B3]. Josh. 19:33.

HELIOPOLIS [hee-lee-AH-poh-lis] Greek name for the Egyptian city of On. Ezek. 30:17. *See* On.

HELKATH [HEL-kath; "field" or "portion"] A town near the S border of Asher, dedicated to the Levites of the Gershonite clan. Possibly a 2nd millennium site about 13 miles (21 km) S of Acco [**I**, A1], near the Kishon River; or perhaps another site about 5 miles (8 km) farther S. Josh. 19:25; 21:31. Called Hukok in 1 Chr. 6:75.

HELKATH HAZZURIM [HEL-kath HAZ-er-im; "field of daggers" or "field of hostilities" (?)] A flat area near the pool of Gibeon where Joab's warriors fought to the death against the men of Abner. 2 Sam. 2:16.

HENA [HEE-nuh] A city that fell to Sennacherib, king of Assyria. Possibly modern Anah on the Euphrates about 20 miles (32 km) NW of Babylon [**II**, C6]. 2 Ki. 18:34; 19:13.

HEPHER [HEE-fer; "pit" or "well"] A Canaanite royal city, defeated by Joshua. The region surrounding it formed a district of Israel during the reign of Solomon. Identified with a site located on the Plain of Sharon about 8.5 miles (13 km) E of Socoh [**VI**, C2]. Josh. 12:17; 1 Ki. 4:10.

HEPHZIBAH [HEF-zih-buh; "my delight is in her"] A poetic name given to the restored Israel in the prophetic writings of Isaiah. Isa. 62:4.

HERES [HEER-ez; "sun"] Har-heres, RSV.
1. A mountain near Aijalon. Jdg. 1:35.
2. A pass E of Jericho by which Gideon returned to Succoth from the site of his victory over the Midianite kings, Zebah and Zalmunna. The KJV translation reads "before the sun was up" rather than "by the Pass of Heres," which appears in the NIV. Location uncertain. Jdg. 8:13.

HERETH [HEER-eth] Hareth, KJV. A forest of Judah in which David took refuge. 1 Sam. 22:5.

HERMON [HER-muhn; "sacred" or "sanctuary"] **VI**, A4; **VII**. The S end of the Anti-Lebanon Range, marking the N extreme of the territory conquered by Moses and Joshua E of the Jordan. The range is about 18 miles (29 km) in length, separated from the N Anti-Lebanons by the gorge of the River Barada (OT Abana). Its highest peak rises 9232 ft. (2814 m) above sea level, making it easily the tallest mountain in Palestine. The runoff from its snow-covered peaks provides the principal source of water for the Jordan River. Like many of Palestine's taller mountains, it was regarded as a sacred place by the local Canaanite inhabitants (*see* Baal Hermon). Because of its close proximity to Caesarea Philippi, Mt. Hermon is the probable site of the Transfiguration of Christ. Deut. 3:8,9; Josh. 12:1,5; Ps. 42:6; Song 4:8. *See* Sirion; Senir; and Siyon.

HESHBON [HESH-bahn] **IV**, D1; **VI**. A large Moabite city, located in the Transjordan, about 47 miles (75 km) due E of Jerusalem. Sihon, king of the Amorites, captured Heshbon and made it his capital. The Israelites under Moses defeated Sihon and conquered the city, which was allotted to the tribe of Reuben. Later, it came into the possession of the Gadites, and was made a Levitical city. By the time of the prophets, it had been retaken by Moab. Excavation of Tell Hesban has found little evidence of occupation prior to the Iron Age. It is possible that one of the nearby Bronze Age sites was the city of Sihon's time. Num. 21:25-34; Josh. 13:21; Jdg. 11:26; Jer. 48:34,45.

HESHMON [HESH-mahn; "fruitful"] An unidentified town in S Judah, near Beersheba. Josh. 15:27.

HETHLON [HETH-lahn] A route from the Mediterranean coast to Lebo Hamath. The Hethlon road may well have taken its name from a city of Hethlon, identified with modern Heitela, NE of Tripoli. The road presumably ran along the el-Kabir River just N of the Lebanon Mountains, then turned S to Lebo Hamath. Ezek. 47:15; 48:1.

HEZRON [HEZ-rahn] A town on the S border of Judah, near Kadesh Barnea. Josh. 15:3. See Hazar Addar.

HIERAPOLIS [HIE-uhr-AHP-oh-lis; "sacred city"] A town in the Lycus River Valley, located in the Roman province of Asia about 6 miles (9.5 km) S of Laodicea [**XIII**, B5]. Its name derived from its function as a cult center of the goddess Leto, mother of Artemis. The hot springs near Hierapolis made it a popular spa resort of the Romans. The church at Hierapolis may have been established while Paul was at Ephesus, possibly by Epaphras. Col. 4:13.

HILEN [HIE-len] See Holon.

HINNOM [HIN-ahm] **XII**, D2. A valley that runs along the western and southern perimeter of Jerusalem, joining the Kidron Valley SE of the city. Within the Hinnom Valley was Topheth, notorious site of idolatrous worship, in which children were sacrificed in the fire, until it was destroyed by Josiah. By Jesus' time, the valley was used as a place to burn rubbish, and became a figurative name for hell in Christ's teachings. Some believe it to be the site of Akeldama, also known as the "potter's field." Josh. 15:8; 2 Ki. 23:10; 2 Chr. 28:3; 33:6; Jer. 19:1-6. See Gehenna.

HOBAH [HOH-buh] A place N of Damascus to which Abraham pursued the forces of Kedorlaomer. Location uncertain. Gen. 14:15.

HOLON [HOH-lahn]
1. A Levitical town in the hill country of Judah, possibly located about 11 miles (17 km) NW of Hebron [**V**, C2]. Josh. 15:51; 21:15.
2. A town on the plain of Moab, site unknown. Jer. 48:21.

HOR [HOR; "mountain"]
1. A mountain in the southernmost region of Judah, on the border of Edom; the site of Aaron's death and burial. It is traditionally identified with Jebel Haroun, a peak about 4382 ft. (1336 m) high, just W of Petra (biblical Sela), however this would seem to lie within Edom. Several other sites have been suggested. Num. 20:22-27; 21:4; 33:37-41. See Moserah.
2. A mountain on the N boundary of Canaan, between the Mediterranean and Lebo Hamath. Presumably one of the N peaks of the Lebanon Mountains. Num. 34:7.

HOREB [HOR-eb; "desert"] The "mountain of God" where Moses saw the burning bush

and received the Law. It was also at Mt. Horeb that the Lord appeared to Elijah. It is geographically identical to Mt. Sinai. Ex. 3:1; 17:6; Deut. 1:2,6; 1 Ki. 19. See Sinai.

HOREM [HOR-em; "consecrated"] A fortified city of Naphtali, possibly modern Hurah about 3 miles (5 km) NE of Beth Shemesh [**VI**, D2]. Josh. 19:38.

HORESH [HOR-esh; "forest"] "Wood," KJV. A place on the hill of Hakilah in the Desert of Ziph. Here David and about 600 of his men took refuge from Saul. Possibly to be identified with a site about 5 miles (8 km) S of Hebron [**V**, C2]. 1 Sam. 23:15-19.

HOR HAGGIDGAD [HOR hah-GID-gad; "cavern of Gidgad"] A campsite of the Israelites during the Exodus. Num. 33:32. Probably the same as Gudgodah, in Deut. 10:7.

HORMAH [HOR-muh; "devoted" or "destruction"]
1. [**VI**, E2]. A Canaanite royal city near Ziklag in the S of Judah, and closely associated with Canaanite Arad. Originally called Zephath, its name was changed to Hormah after its destruction by the Israelites. It apparently changed hands more than once between Judah and Simeon. Probably to be identified with a site located about 8 miles (13 km) SE of Beersheba. Num. 21:3; Josh. 12:14; 15:30; 19:4; Jdg. 1:17.
2. A place in the S of Canaan to which the Canaanites pursued the Israelites. It may be the same as 1. Num. 14:45; Deut. 1:44.

HORONAIM [HOR-uh-NAY-uhm; "two caves"] A town near Zoar in S Moab. Location uncertain. 2 Sam. 13:34; Isa. 15:5.

HORSE GATE. A gate of Jerusalem E of the palace. Here Athaliah was put to death, by order of Jehoiada the priest. 2 Chr. 23:15; Neh. 3:28.

HOSAH [HOH-zuh; "refuge"] A town on the N border of Asher, possibly located about 4 miles (6.5 km) SE of Tyre [**VII**, B1]. Josh. 19:29.

HUKKOK [HUH-kahk] A place on the border of Naphtali, generally identified with modern Yaquq, about 6 miles (9.5 km) W of Capernaum [**XI**, B3]. Josh. 19:34.

HUKOK [HUH-kahk] A Levitical city of Asher. 1 Chr. 6.75. See Helkath.

HUMTAH [HUM-tuh] An unidentified town in the hill country of Judah, near Hebron. Josh. 15:54.

I

IBLEAM [IB-lee-uhm] **VI**, C3. A Manassite town bordering on the territory of Issachar, from which the men of Israel failed to drive its Canaanite inhabitants. An ancient city, it was listed among the conquests of Thutmose III, in the 15th century B.C. The ruins of Ibleam are identified with a site about 12 miles (19 km) SE of Megiddo. Josh. 17:11; Jdg. 1:27; 2 Ki. 9:27. Probably the same as Bileam, in 1 Chr. 6:70.

ICONIUM [ie-KOH-nee-um] **XIII**, B6. An ancient Phrygian city in S central Asia Minor, situated in a well-watered, fertile region on the SW edge of the Anatolian Plateau. By the 3rd century B.C., it was an independent Hellenistic city, although a significant portion of the population retained Phrygian culture and beliefs. It was probably among them that the Jewish

leaders stirred up opposition to the apostle Paul on his first visit to the city, about A.D. 47. It is now known as Konya. Acts 14:1-6,21; 2 Tim. 3:11.

IDALAH [ID-uh-luh] A town allotted to the tribe of Zebulun, possibly located about 5.5 miles (9 km) SW of Hannathon [**VI**, B3]. Josh. 19:15.

IDUMEA [id-yoo-MEE-uh] **X**, B1-B2. Greek form of Edom; in NT times, it referred to the region of S Judah occupied by the Edomites following the fall of Jerusalem in 587 B.C. Pressure from the Nabateans caused the Edomites to migrate heavily into the territory. Under the Seleucids, Idumea absorbed the district of Ashdod. About 126 B.C., John Hyrcanus subdued the Idumeans, and converted them to Judaism by force. It came under the governorship of Herod the Great, and in A.D. 41 was included in the kingdom of Agrippa I. Its border with Judea lay just N of Lachish and Hebron, running E to the central Dead Sea. Below this line, the territory of Idumea extended as far S as Beersheba. Mk. 3:8.

IIM [IE-im; "heaps" or "ruins"] A town in the Negev of Judah, near Edom. Josh. 15:29.

IJON [IE-jahn; "heap" or "ruin"] A town in Naphtali, conquered by Ben-Hadad during the reign of Baasha, and later by Tiglath-Pileser, about 732 B.C. Its inhabitants were subsequently deported to Assyria. Possibly to be identified with a site in the valley of Merg Ayun, about 19 miles (30 km) N of Lake Huleh. 1 Ki. 15:20; 2 Ki. 15:29; 2 Chr. 16:4.

ILLYRICUM [ih-LEER-ih-kum] **XIII**, A2-A3. A mountainous region across the Adriatic Sea from Italy, divided into the Roman provinces of Dalmatia and Pannonia in the 1st century A.D. Rom. 15:19.

IMMER [IM-uhr; "lamb"] An unidentified town in Babylonia, from which returned some exiles who could not prove their Israelite ancestry. Ezra 2:59; Neh. 7:61.

INDIA [IN-dee-uh] **IX**, C6. A country which marked the E extremity of the Persian Empire under King Xerxes. In Esther, the name refers to a Persian province in the NW corner of the Indian peninsula, along the Indus River and its tributaries. Esth. 1:1; 8:9.

IPHTAH [IF-tuh] Jiphtah, KJV. A town in the W foothills of Judah, possibly about 7 miles (11 km) NW of Hebron [**V**, C2]. Josh. 15:43.

IPHTAH EL [IF-tuh EL] Jiphtah-el, KJV. A valley on the border between Asher and Zebulun. Josh. 19:14,27.

IR NAHASH [eer NAY-hash; "city of the serpent"] A town of Judah founded by Tehinnah. Site uncertain. 1 Chr. 4:12.

IRON [EER-ahn] Yiron, RSV. A fortified town of Naphtali, probably modern Yarun, about 10 miles (16 km) W of Lake Huleh. Josh. 19:38

IRPEEL [EER-pee-uhl; "God heals"] A town of Benjamin, possibly located about 6 miles (10 km) N of Jerusalem [**VII**, C1]. Josh. 18:27.

IR SHEMESH [eer SHEM-esh; "city of the sun"] A city of Dan; probably an alternate name for Beth Shemesh, in Josh. 19:41.

ISRAEL[*] [IZ-ray-uhl] **VII**, C1-C2; **VIII**, B1-B2. Nation whose tribes traced their ancestry to the twelve sons of Jacob. The ten northern tribes, led by Ephraim, constituted the nation of Israel following the division of the kingdom. It was also known as Samaria, after its capital city, and Ephraim, after its principal tribe.

ISSACHAR [IS-uh-kar] **VI**, B3-C3. A tribe of Israel whose allotted territory was bounded by Zebulun and Naphtali on the N and Manasseh on the S, extending E to the Jordan River. The fertile Valley of Jezreel, an area of frequent conflict with the Canaanites, comprised much of its territory. Josh. 17:11; 19:17-23.

ITALY [IT-uh-lee] **XIII**, A1-B2. Long peninsular country that juts into the Mediterranean from the S coast of Europe. Rome was its capital. Acts 18:2; Heb. 13:24.

ITHLAH [ITH-luh] Jethlah, KJV. A town in the tribal territory of Dan, possibly about 3 miles (5 km) SE of Aijalon [**VI**, D2]. Josh. 19:42.

ITHNAN [ITH-nahn] An unidentified town in the extreme S of Judah. Josh. 15:23.

ITUREA [IT-oor-EE-uh] Ituraea, KJV. A region NE of Palestine, named after the Itureans, a tribe descended from Jetur, son of Ishmael (1 Chr. 5:19). Under the Romans, it was added to the territory ruled by Herod the Great. Thereafter, it became part of the tetrarchy of his son Philip. The geographical location and dimensions of the region are very uncertain; some suggest that it is identical to NT Trachonitis. Lk. 3:1.

IVVAH [IV-uh] Ivah, KJV. A city conquered by the Assyrians prior to Sennacherib's siege of Jerusalem. 2 Ki. 18:34; Isa. 37:13. See Avva.

IYE ABARIM [IE-yuh AB-uh-rim; "ruins of Abarim"] Ije-abarim, KJV. Site on the border of Moab where the Israelites encamped during their wilderness wanderings, possibly located along the Zered River. Num. 21:11; 33:44.

IYIM [IE-yim] Iim, KJV. A shortened form of Iye Abarim, in Num. 33:45.

J

JAAR [JAR; "forest"] "The wood," KJV. Possibly another name for Kireath Jearim, where the ark remained for 20 years before it was brought to Jerusalem. Ps. 132:6.

JABBOK [JAB-uhk; "flowing"] **I; IV**, C1-C2; **VI**. A major river in the Transjordan that flows NE in an arc and then turns due W, turning SW shortly before it joins the Jordan River, roughly midway between the Dead Sea and the Sea of Galilee. It served as the N border to the territory under Sihon, king of the Amorites, and the northern arc of the river defined the W boundary of Ammon. The gorge cut by the Jabbok divides the Gilead plateau into two parts; following the Israelite conquest, the N half was allotted to Manasseh and the S half to Gad. A ford of the Jabbok was the site where Jacob wrestled the angel and was given the name of Israel. Modern Zerqa. Gen. 32:22-30; Num. 21:21-25; Josh. 12:2.

JABESH [JAY-besh] A shortened form of Jabesh Gilead.

JABESH GILEAD [JAY-besh GIL-ee-ad; "dry place of Gilead"] **VI; VII**, C2. A town of Gilead, in the territory of Manasseh, E of the Jordan. During the period of the Judges, its inhabitants refused to join in the punitive war against the Benjamites, for which the men of the town were put to death. Early in Saul's reign, it was besieged by the king of Ammon. Saul came to its rescue, defeating the Ammo-

nite army. The citizens of Jabesh Gilead remembered his aid, and later rescued the bodies of Saul and his sons from the walls of Beth Shan, burying the remains in Jabesh. It is probably located about 10 miles (16 km) SE of Beth Shan, along the Wadi Yabis, which very likely derived its name from the ancient city. Jdg. 21; 1 Sam. 11; 31:11-13

JABEZ [JAY-bez] An unidentified town of Judah, inhabited by scribes descended from Caleb. 1 Chr. 2:55.

JABNEEL [JAB-nee-uhl; "God builds"]
1. [**VI**, D2; **XI**] A town on the N border of Judah, situated on the Via Maris about 4 miles (6.5 km) from the Mediterranean coast. Called Jabneh in 2 Chr. 26:6, it was among the Philistine cities that fell to Uzziah, king of Judah. Captured by Simon Maccabeus in 147 B.C., the city, then called Jamnia, remained a Jewish city until it fell to Pompey in 64 B.C., when it became an autonomous city. After Jerusalem fell in A.D. 70, Jabneel became the seat of the Sanhedrin. Modern Yabneh, located about 9 miles (14 km) NE of Ashdod. Josh. 15:11.
2. A border town of Naphtali, about 7 miles (11 km) S of Tiberias [**XI**, B3]. Josh. 19:33.

JABNEH [JAB-neh] See Jabneel 1.

JACOB'S WELL. A well near Sychar where Jesus met the Samaritan woman. A tradition from OT times identifies it with the portion of land near Shechem, purchased by Jacob and later given to his son Joseph (Gen. 33:19; 48:22). It is modern Bir Yakub, located at the base of Mt. Gerizim [**V**, C2]. Jn. 4:6.

JAGUR [JAY-ger] An unidentified town in the extreme S of Judah. Josh. 15:21. See Gurbaal.

JAHAZ [JAY-haz] **IV**, D2. A stronghold N of the Arnon River, where Sihon, king of the Amorites, attacked and was defeated by the Israelites in Moses' time. Allotted to Reuben, it was made a Levitical city. During the period of the divided kingdom, Mesha, king of Moab, took the city, and it remained under Moabite control throughout the time of the prophets. It has been tentatively identified with a site on the edge of the desert, NE of Dibon. Num. 21:23; Josh. 13:18; 21:36; Isa. 15:4. Also called Jahzah.

JAHZAH [JAH-zuh] Jahazah, KJV (Jer. 48:21). An alternate form of Jahaz. 1 Chr. 6:78; Jer. 48:21.

JANIM [JAY-nim] Janum, KJV. A town in the hill country of Judah, possibly a site about 3 miles (5 km) E of Hebron [**V**, C2]. Josh. 15:53.

JANOAH [juh-NOH-uh; "resting"] Janohah, KJV (Josh. 16:6,7).
1. A border town of Ephraim, identified with Khirbet Yanun, located in the E Samaria Hills, about 6 miles (9.5 km) SE of Shechem [**I**, B1]. Josh. 16:6,7.
2. A town of Naphtali conquered by Tiglath-Pileser during the reign of Pekah. Site uncertain. 2 Ki. 15:29.

JAPHIA [JAF-ee-uh] A border town of Zebulun, called Yapu in the Amarna Letters, and known as Iafa after the Exile. After its fortification by Josephus, the city fell to a Roman siege in A.D. 67 and its inhabitants were slaughtered. Modern Yafa, less than 2 miles (3 km) SW of Nazareth [**XI**, B2]. Josh. 19:12.

JARMUTH [JAR-muth; "height"]
1. [**V**, C1; **X**]. A Canaanite royal city in Judah, whose Amorite king joined Adoni-Zedek in the attack upon Gibeon and was defeated. Rebuilt and occupied after the Exile, its ruins have been identified in the foothills of Judah, about 3 miles (5 km) S of Beth Shemesh. Josh. 10; 12:11; 15:35; Neh. 11:29.

2. A Levitical city in the territory of Issachar. Josh. 21:29.

JASHUBI LEHEM [juh-SHOO-bee LEE-hem] A place inhabited by the descendants of Shelah, a Judahite. The text appears corrupt; in the RSV it reads "and returned to Lehem," and in the KJV the name is treated as a person. 1 Chr. 4:22.

JATTIR [JAT-uhr] A Levitical town in the hills of Judah, identified with a site about 13 miles (21 km) SW of Hebron [**V**, C2]. Josh. 15:48; 21:14; 1 Sam. 30:27.

JAZER [JAY-zer] Jaazer, KJV (Num. 21:32; 32:35). [**IV**, C1]. A town in the Amorite kingdom of Sihon, captured by Israel in the time of Moses. Rebuilt by Gad, it later became a Levitical city. Eventually Jazer fell to the Moabites. Its ruins are located in S Gilead to the W of Rabbah, although the exact site is disputed. Num. 32:1-3,35; Josh. 21:39; 2 Sam 24:5; Isa. 16:8,9.

JEARIM [JEE-uh-rim] A mountain on the N border of Judah, with the town of Kesalon atop it. Possibly a hill located midway between Beth Shemesh [**VI**, D2] and Kiriath Jearim [**VI**, D3]. Josh. 15:10.

JEBUS [JEE-buhs] A name of Jerusalem, whose Canaanite inhabitants were known as the Jebusites. Although it was taken and set on fire during the time of the Judges, the Israelites failed to retain control of the city. David conquered the Jebusite stronghold, gaining entry to the city by a water tunnel (2 Sam. 5:6-10). He made it his capital, and it became known as the City of David. The Jebusite stronghold was situated on Mt. Zion, the SE hill of Jerusalem. It is identical to the fortress of Zion. Jdg. 19:10,11; 1 Chr. 11:4. See City of David; Jerusalem.

JEGAR SAHADUTHA [JEE-gar say-huh-DOO-thuh; "witness heap"] Aramaic equivalent of Galeed. Gen 31:47.

JEHOSHAPHAT [jeh-HAHSH-uh-fat; "Yahweh has judged"] A valley in the prophecy of Joel where the nations shall receive final judgment by the Lord. Tradition identifies it with the Kidron Valley, E of Jerusalem, but it is very likely a symbolic term rather than a geographical reference. Joel 3:2,12.

JEKABZEEL [jeh-KAB-zee-uhl] A town of Judah SW of Eshtemoa, resettled after the Exile. Neh. 11:25. See Kabzeel.

JERICHO* [JAIR-ih-koh; "moon city" (?)] **I; IV; V**, C2; **VI; XI**, E2. A city in the Jordan Valley about 17 miles (27 km) NE of Jerusalem, founded as early as 8000 B.C. Situated in a flourishing oasis, fed by a perennial spring, OT Jericho also became known as the "City of Palms." In biblical history, it is notable as the ancient city conquered by Joshua and the Israelites following their entrance into the land of Canaan. After its fall, the walled city remained in ruins until the time of Ahab. It was finally abandoned at the time of the Babylonian Captivity.

The NT Jericho was on the road from the fords of the lower Jordan to Jerusalem, a little S of the ancient site. Herod the Great built much of the NT city as a winter residence, and died there in 4 B.C. Nearby are the traditional sites of Jesus' baptism in the Jordan, and his temptations in the mountains to the W of the city.

Extensive excavations have gone on at Jericho for over a century. Between 1930 and 1936, John Garstang undertook a major excavation that uncovered evidence of a massive destruction of Jericho's walls by fire and earthquake, which he dated to the 15th century B.C. This was popularly accepted as the city destroyed by Joshua. However, later redating of the site by Kathleen Kenyon rejected Garstang's findings and found little evidence for occupation of the site between 1500–1200 B.C., possibly washed away by the elements during its long abandonment. Although most scholars accept Kenyon's conclusions, dispute continues concerning the dating of the city's levels, and a recent reassessment of the data has returned in support of Garstang's original dating. Josh. 2; 5:13–6:21; 18:12,21; 1 Ki. 16:34; Mk. 10:46-52; Lk. 10:30.

JERUEL [jeh-ROO-uh; "founded by God"] A wilderness area where Jehoshaphat witnessed the destruction of the armies of Ammon, Moab, and Edom. Apparently identical to the Desert of Tekoa, extending W of the city to the Dead Sea, N of En Gedi [**VI**, E3]. 2 Chr. 20:16.

JERUSALEM* [jeh-ROO-suh-lem; "city of peace"] **II; V; VI; VII,** C1; **VIII; IX; X; XI,** E2; **XII; XIII.** The capital of the Davidic kingdom and the religious center of Israel. Solomon constructed the Temple there as the sole worship center of the God of Israel. After the division of the kingdom, Jerusalem remained the capital of the southern kingdom of Judah until the city's destruction by Nebuchadnezzar in 586 B.C. After the return from exile, the Temple was rebuilt, and a century later Jerusalem's walls were restored under the leadership of Nehemiah.

Jesus spent the last week of his ministry at Jerusalem and at week's end he was crucified outside its walls. The Scriptures contain over 800 references to the city of Jerusalem. *See* Salem; Jebus; Zion; City of David.

JESHANAH [JESH-uh-nuh; "old"] "Old Gate," KJV, RSV in Nehemiah.
1. A town near Bethel, taken from Jeroboam by Abijah, king of Judah. Probably a site about 4 miles (6 km) N of Bethel [**V**, C2]. 2 Chr. 13:19. Possibly the same as Shen in 1 Sam. 7:12.
2. Jeshanah Gate, a gate in the NW corner of Jerusalem in Nehemiah's time. Neh. 3:6; 12:39.

JESHIMON [juh-SHIE-muhn; "waste" or "desert"] The E wilderness region of the Judean hills, SE of Hebron. 1 Sam. 23:19,24; 26:1-3.

JESHUA [JESH-oo-uh; "Yahweh is salvation"] A post-exilic town in S Judah. Possibly located about 11 miles (18 km) E of Beersheba [**I**, C1]. Neh. 11:26.

JEZREEL [JEZ-ree-uhl; "God sows"]
1. [**VI; VIII,** B2]. A city in N Palestine, situated in the Jezreel Valley. Although within the territory of Issachar, it was allotted to Manasseh. Ahab built his palace in Jezreel, and his son and successor, Joram, also lived here. The entire household of Ahab was put to death in the city by Jehu. At his command, Jezebel was thrown from the window of the palace in Jezreel. It has been identified as modern Zer'in. Josh. 19:18; 1 Ki. 21:1; 2 Ki. 9:15,30-37.
2. The SE part of the great plain that divides Galilee from Samaria. A very fertile region, it lies NW of Mt. Gilboa, extending from the city of Jezreel to Beth Shan. In a looser sense, the name is applied to the entire lowland region, stretching from the Jordan Valley to Mt. Carmel, and encompassing the Valley of Megiddo, now known as the Plain of Esdraelon. The entire valley was the only natural E-W route through Palestine, and was the site of numerous battles throughout history. Josh. 17:16; Jdg. 6:33; 1 Sam. 29:1; Hos. 1:4,5.
3. A town in the hill country of Judah; hometown of Ahinoam, one of David's wives. Hosh. 15:56; 1 Sam. 25:43; 2 Sam. 3:2.

JOGBEHAH [jahg-BEE-huh; "height"] **VI,** D4. A town E of the Jordan refortified by the Gadites. Modern Jubeihah, about 7 miles (11 km) NW of Rabbah. Num. 32:35; Jdg. 8:11.

JOKDEAM [JAHK-dee-uhm] A town in the hills of Judah, possibly located about 4 miles (6.5 km) S of Hebron [**V**, C2]. Josh. 15:56.

JOKMEAM [JAHK-mee-uhm] Jokneam, KJV (1 Ki. 4:12). A Levitical city in the hill country of Ephraim, possibly located about 3 miles (5 km) W of the Jordan, opposite the mouth of the Jabbok River. 1 Ki. 4:12; 1 Chr. 6:68. Probably the same as Kibzaim in Josh. 21:22.

JOKNEAM [JAHK-nee-uhm] **V,** B2; **VII.** A Canaanite royal city on or near Mt. Carmel, among the cities given to the Merarite Levites from the tribe of Zebulun. Identified with a site about 7 miles (11 km) NW of Megiddo [**VI,** B3]. Josh. 12:22; 19:11; 21:34.

JOKTHEEL [JAHK-thee-uhl]
1. A town near Lachish in the foothills of Judah. Josh. 15:38.
2. The Edomite city of Sela in the Valley of Salt, conquered and renamed Joktheel by Amaziah, king of Judah, generally identified with the ruins of an Edomite stronghold on a plateau 1000 ft. (305 m) above the Nabatean capital of Petra [**VIII,** D2]. 2 Ki. 14:7. *See* Sela.

JOPPA [JAH-puh; "beautiful"] **VI,** D2; **VII; VIII; X; XI;** D1. Ancient fortified city on the coast of Palestine, about 35 miles (56 km) NW of Jerusalem. The city was allotted to Dan, but was not captured until the time of David. Joppa fell to Sennacherib about 701 B.C., and in the mid-5th century B.C. came under the control of Sidon. Because it possessed the only natural harbor in Palestine S of the Bay of Acre, it was for centuries the seaport of Jerusalem.

In NT times, Joppa was the hometown of Simon the tanner and Tabitha (or Dorcas) whom Peter raised from the dead. In A.D. 67, the city was destroyed by the Romans. Now known as Jaffa. 2 Chr. 2:16; Ezra 3:7; Jon. 1:3; Acts 9:36–10:23.

JORDAN* [JOR-duhn; "descending"] **I; IV,** A1-D1; **VI; VII; X; XI,** A3-E3; **XIII.** The major river of Palestine, which flows through the rift valley from Mt. Hermon in the N to the Dead Sea. It is the lowest river in the world, descending rapidly from Lake Huleh, at about 7 ft. (2 m) above sea level, winding some 66 miles (105 km) S to empty into the Dead Sea, where the water's surface is about 1292 ft. (394 m) below sea level.

The Jordan River provided the E boundary of the Promised Land, separating Canaan from the region to the E, now known as the Transjordan. The fords of the Jordan were the sites of many battles in OT times. In NT times, John the Baptist preached beside the river, and baptized Jesus Christ in its waters. Gen. 13:10,11; Num. 34:12; Josh. 3; Jdg. 12:5,6; Mt. 3.

JOTBAH [JAHT-buh; "pleasantness"] Hometown of Meshullemeth, mother of Amon, later conquered by Tiglath-Pileser III. Called Jotapata in the Roman period, it is identified with a site in Lower Galilee, about 3 miles (5 km) N of Hannathon [**VI,** B3]. 2 Ki. 21:19.

JOTBATHAH [jaht-BATH-uh; "pleasantness"] Jotbath, KJV (Deut. 10:7). [**III,** C4]. A stopping-place during the wilderness wandering of the Israelites under Moses. It was located in the Desert of Paran, possibly at Tabeh on the W shore of the Gulf of Aqabah, about 7 miles (11 km) SW of Elath. Num. 33:33,34; Deut. 10:7.

JUDAH* [JOO-duh; "praise"]
1. [**VI,** D3-F1]. A large territory in S Palestine, allotted to the tribe of Judah. Its border lay S of Dan and Benjamin, running from the N end of the Dead Sea to the Mediterranean, originally passing just S of Jerusalem. The territory extended as far S as Kadesh Barnea, bounded on the E by Edom and the Dead Sea, and on the W by the Wadi of Egypt (modern Wadi el-Arish) and the Mediterranean. In practice, however, the coastal plains were dominated by the Philistines throughout most of Israelite history. For their aid in taking possession of the land, the tribe of Judah donated to the Simeonites a portion of their territory in the Negev. Josh. 15; 19:1-9. Jdg. 1:1-20.
2. [**VIII,** C1]. The S kingdom, formed by the tribes of Judah and Benjamin following the division of Israel, became known as Judah. Its kings were all Judahites in the Davidic line. Judah remained an independent nation until its fall in 586 B.C., when its inhabitants were taken into captivity in Babylonia. 1 Ki. 12:19-24; 1 Chr. 3:10-16.

JUDEA* [joo-DEE-uh] **X; XI,** E1-E2. **XIII.** Sometime after the return from exile, Judah was made a province in the Persian Empire, called Judea. Under the Persians, the district of Judea was generally administered by a Jewish governor. The Maccabean revolt, beginning in 187 B.C., resulted in the establishment of an independent Jewish state. Civil war broke out between the sons of Jannaeus, and Rome was eventually invited to intervene. In 63 B.C., Pompey entered Jerusalem, and Judea became a Roman tributary. Following the banishment of Archelaus in A.D. 6, Judea was annexed to the Roman province of Syria. Thereafter, procurators were charged with its governance, officially residing in Caesarea. They were subject to the proconsul of Syria in Antioch.

Judean territory roughly encompassed a region about 50–55 miles (80–88 km) square, from the Mediterranean to the Dead Sea, and from Joppa in the N to the vicinity of Hebron. The boundaries varied, and portions of the coastal plain were frequently under the control of the Philistine cities of Ashkelon, Ashdod, and Gaza. Mt. 2:1; 19:1; Lk. 1:5; Acts 8:1-3; 9:31.

JUTTAH [JUT-uh; "extended"] A town in the hill country of Judah, given to the Aaronites as a priestly city. Modern Yatta, about 5 miles (8 km) S of Hebron [**V,** C2]. Josh. 15:55; 21:16; 1 Chr. 6:59.

K

KABZEEL [KAB-zee-uhl; "God gathers"] **VI,** E2. A town in the extreme S of Judah, near Edom. Possibly about 7 miles (11 km) NE of Beersheba. Josh. 15:21; 2 Sam. 23:20. Probably same as Jekabzeel in Neh. 11:25.

KADESH [KAY-desh] A shortened form of Kadesh Barnea.

KADESH BARNEA* [KAY-desh bar-NEE-uh; "holy"] **I; III,** B4; **VII.** Site of an oasis in the NE corner of the Sinai Peninsula. It was located on the S border of Palestine, at the intersection of the Way of Shur and the road running N from Elath into central Palestine. It became the primary station on the route of the Exodus, where the rebellious Israelites were condemned by God to wander in the desert for 40 years. Identified with a site in the Negev about 50 miles (80 km) SW of Beersheba; Ain el Qudeirat is its primary spring, although Ain

Qedeis preserves the original name (shown on map). Gen. 14:7; 20:1; Num. 13:26; 20; Deut. 1:2,19; Josh. 15:3. Also called En Mishpat.

KAIN [KAYN; "smith"] Cain, KJV. A town in the hills of Judah, possibly located about 3 miles (5 km) SE of Hebron [**V,** C2]. Josh. 15:57.

KAMON [KAY-muhn] Camon, KJV. A town in Gilead where the judge Jair was buried. Possibly a site about 5 miles (8 km) SE of Gadara [**XI,** B3]. Judg. 10:5.

KANAH [KAY-nuh; "reeds"]
1. A ravine on the border between Ephraim and Manasseh, identified with the Wadi Kanah, which flows W from a spot S of Shechem into the Mediterranean, about 4 miles (6.5 km) N of Joppa [**VI,** D2]. Josh. 16:8; 17:9.
2. A border town of Asher in NW Palestine, probably modern Kana, about 7 miles (11 km) SE of Tyre [**VII,** B1]. Josh. 19:28.

KARKA [KAR-kuh; "floor"] Karkaa, KJV. An unidentified location on the S border of Judah. Josh. 15:3.

KARKOR [KAR-kor] A place in the Transjordan where Gideon defeated the remnant of the army of Zebah and Zalmunna, the two kings of Midian. Site uncertain. Jdg. 8:10.

KARNAIM [kar-NAY-uhm; "two peaks"] "Horns," KJV. [**VIII,** B2]. Capital of the Bashan under Aramean and Assyrian rule, following the decline of nearby Ashtaroth. Identified with Sheikh Saad, NE of Ashtaroth. Amos 6:13.

KARTAH [KAR-tuh; "city"] A Levitical city in the territory of Zebulun. Site uncertain. Josh. 21:34; 1 Chr. 6:77.

KARTAN [KAR-tan; "city"] A town of Naphtali given to the Gershonite Levites. Possibly a site in Upper Galilee, about 9 miles (14.5 km) NW of Hazor [**V,** A2]. Josh. 21:32. Called Kiriathaim in 1 Chr. 6:76.

KATTATH [KAT-ath; "small"] A town in Zebulun. Josh. 19:15. Possibly the same as Kitron, in Jdg. 1:30.

KEBAR [KEE-bar] Chebar, KJV, RSV. A river or canal in Babylonia, beside which Ezekiel saw visions. Possibly the Habor River, or the Babylonian *nari kabari*, the "great canal," near Nippur. Ezek. 1:1,3; 10:15-22.

KEDAR [KEE-dar; "dark" or "powerful"] A nomadic tribe of Ishmaelites who dwelt in the desert of N Arabia, E of Palestine. Both Ashurbanipal and Nebuchadnezzar conducted military campaigns against the Kedarites. In the Persian period, the kings of Kedar controlled the region between Egypt and S Palestine. Geshem, one of Nehemiah's enemies (Neh. 6:1-6), may have been Gashmu, a king of Kedar and contemporary of Nehemiah. Ps. 120:5; Isa. 21:16,17; Jer. 49:28.

KEDEMOTH [KED-uh-mahth; "eastern parts" or "ancient places"] A town in the Transjordan, N of the Arnon; in Moses' time, it was near the E border of Sihon's territory. Kedemoth was made a Levitical city within the inheritance of Reuben. Possibly a site located about 7 miles (11 km) SE of Medeba [**VIII,** B2]. Deut. 2:26; Josh. 13:18; 21:37.

KEDESH [KEE-desh; "sacred place"]
1. [**V,** A2; **VI; VIII**]. A royal city of the Canaanites defeated by Joshua in his northern campaign. Allotted to the tribe of Naphtali and was made a city of refuge. Tiglath-Pileser III, king of Assyria, conquered the city and deported its inhabitants during the reign of Pekah. Iden-

tified with Tell Qades in upper Galilee, about 4 miles (6 km) NW of Lake Huleh. Josh. 12:22; 19:37; 20:7; 2 Ki. 15:29.
2. Home of Barak, where the forces of Naphtali and Zebulun gathered to fight the army of Jabin, Jdg. 4:6. Possibly the same as 1, or a site about 3 miles (5 km) S of Tiberias [**XI,** B3], in lower Galilee.
3. A town of Issachar given to the Gershonite clan of the Levites. Possibly the Kedesh referred to in Jdg. 4:11, near the tent of Heber the Kenite, where Sisera was slain. 1 Chr. 6:72. Called Kishion in Josh. 21:28.
4. A town in S Judah, near Edom. Josh. 15:23. Possibly another name for Kadesh Barnea.

KEHELATHAH [kee-huh-LAY-thuh; "assembly"] A place in the Desert of Paran where the Israelites camped during the Exodus. Num. 33:22,23.

KEILAH [kee-IE-luh; "fortress"] **X,** B1. A fortified city strategically located in the foothills of Judah. The Philistines attacked the city during the reign of Saul, but David came to its rescue. It was reoccupied after the Exile. Identified with a site about 8 miles (13 km) NW of Hebron. Josh. 15:44; 1 Sam. 23:1-13; Neh. 31:17,18.

KENATH [KEE-nath; "possession"] A city in the territory of Manasseh E of the Jordan, captured by Nobah the Manassite and renamed after himself. Later, it was captured by the Arameans. As Canatha, it became the easternmost of the ten cities of the Decapolis. Identified with Kanawat, about 62 miles (100 km) E of the Sea of Galilee. Num. 32:42; 1 Chr. 2:23. *See* Nobah.

KEPHAR AMMONI [KEE-far AM-uh-nee; "village of the Ammonites"] Chephar-haammonai, KJV; Chephar-ammoni, RSV. A town in the inheritance of Benjamin. Possibly located about 3 miles (5 km) N of Bethel [**V,** C2]. Josh. 18:24.

KEPHIRAH [keh-FI-ruh; "village"] Chephirah, KJV, RSV. A city of the Gibeonites, allotted to Benjamin. Natives of Kephirah returned to Judah after the Exile. Located about 1.5 miles (2.5 km) N of Kireath Jearim [**VI,** D3]. Josh. 9:17; 18:26; Ezra 2:25.

KERIOTH [KAIR-ee-ahth; "cities"] A fortified city of Moab, possibly el-Qereiyat, about 3 miles (5 km) SE of Ataroth [**IV,** D1], although some identity it with Ar of Moab. According to the Moabite Stone, it was a cult center of Chemosh. Jer. 48:24; Amos 2:2.

KERIOTH HEZRON [KAIR-ee-ahth HEZ-ruhn] Kerioth and Hezron, KJV. A town in the Negev of Judah. Possibly located about 10 miles (16 km) S of Hebron [**V,** C2], near Arad. Josh. 15:25. Same as Hazor 3.

KERITH [KAIR-ith; "gorge"] Cherith, KJV, RSV. A ravine E of the Jordan where Elijah was fed by ravens. 1 Ki. 17:3,5.

KERUB [KAIR-ub] Cherub, KJV, RSV. An unidentified place in Babylonia; some Jews who returned to Judah from there could not establish their Israelite ancestry. Ezra 2:59; Neh. 7:61.

KESALON [KES-uh-lahn] Chesalon, KJV, RSV. A town on the slopes of Mt. Jearim, located on the N border of Judah, about 9 miles (15 km) W of Jerusalem [**VII,** C1]. Josh. 15:10.

KESIL [KEE-sil; "fool"] Chesil, KJV, RSV. A town in the extreme S of Judah. Josh. 15:30. *See* Bethuel.

KESULLOTH [keh-SUL-ahth; "loins"] Chesulloth, KJV, RSV. A town in the territory of Issachar, N of Jezreel. Modern Iksal, about 3

miles (5 km) SE of Nazareth [**XI,** B2]. Josh. 19:18.

KEZIB [KEE-zib] Probably an alternate form of Aczib, in Gen. 38:5. *See* Aczib 1.

KIBROTH HATTAAVAH [KIB-rahth hah-TAY-uh-vah; "graves of craving"] A campsite of the Israelites one day's journey from the Desert of Sinai; so-named because here the people demanded meat and received plague-carrying quail that caused many deaths. Possibly Ruweis el-Ebeirig, NE of Mt. Sinai (Jebel Musa). Num. 11:34,35; 33:16,17; Deut. 9:22.

KIBZAIM [kib-ZAY-uhm; "two heaps"] A Levitical city of Ephraim. Josh. 21:22. Probably the same as Jokmeam in 1 Chr. 6:68.

KIDON [KIE-dahn] Chidon, KJV, RSV. The "floor of Kidon" was the site where Uzzah touched the ark of God and was struck dead. Because of this, the place was renamed Perez Uzzah. 1 Chr. 13:9. Called Nacon in 2 Sam. 6:6.

KIDRON [KID-ruhn; "gloomy"] Cedron, KJV (Jn. 18:1). [**XII,** A3-D3]. A river valley, modern Wadi en-Nar, which runs along the E side of Jerusalem, between the hill of Ophel (Temple Mt.) and the Mount of Olives, to join the Valley of Hinnom SE of the city. From there, the wadi winds through the desert of Judea until it reaches the Dead Sea. The river bed remains dry throughout the year, except during the winter torrents. On the W side of the valley lies the Gihon spring. 2 Sam. 15:23; 2 Ki. 23:4-12; Jn. 18:1. Possibly the same as the Valley of Jehoshaphat in Joel 3:2,12.

KILMAD [KIL-mad] Chilmad, KJV, RSV. A place in Mesopotamia that traded with Tyre. Location unknown. Ezek. 27:23.

KINAH [KIE-nuh] A town in the extreme S of Judah, near the border of Edom. Site uncertain. Josh. 15:22.

KING'S HIGHWAY [**I; III,** A5-C4]. A major trade route from the Gulf of Aqabah up through the Transjordan to Damascus, in use well before 2000 B.C. This was the road by which Kedorlaomer and his allies approached Sodom and Gomorrah. Its use continued into Roman times. Num. 20:17; 21:22.

KING'S VALLEY. The Valley of Shaveh, E of Jerusalem, where Abram met Melchizedek. Here, Absalom raised a pillar as a monument to himself. Gen. 14:17; 2 Sam. 18:18.

KINNERETH [KIN-uh-reth; "harps"] Often Chinnereth, Chinneroth, or Cinneroth, in the KJV and RSV.
1. The ancient name of the Sea of Galilee, in NT times also called the Lake of Gennesaret. Num. 34:11; Deut. 3:17.
2. An ancient fortified city of Naphtali, located on the NW shore of the Sea of Galilee. Mentioned in the lists of cities conquered by Thutmose III of Egypt, in the 15th century B.C. Josh. 19:35.
3. A fertile plain that surrounds the city of Kinnereth, known as the Plain of Gennesaret in Roman times. 1 Ki. 15:20.

KIOS [KEE-ahs] Chios, KJV, RSV. An island in the Mediterranean about 12 miles (19 km) W of Smyrna [**XIII,** B4]. Acts 20:15.

KIR [KEER; "city" or "wall"]
1. A place to which the inhabitants of Damascus were deported by Tiglath-Pileser, king of Assyria. In Amos 9:7, the prophet either predicts their eventual return to Syria, or refers to a previous homeland occupied by the Arameans of Damascus. Possibly near Elam, its site is unknown. 2 Ki. 16:9; Isa. 22:6; Amos 1:5; 9:7.
2. Shortened form of Kir Haraseth, in Isa. 15:1.

KIR HARESETH [keer HAR-uh-seth; "wall of pottery" or "new city"] Kir-haraseth, Kir-haresh, Kir-heres are variants of the name that appear in the KJV and RSV translations. [**VII; VIII,** C2]. A fortified city in S Moab, and Moabite capital when it was besieged by the kings of Judah, Israel, and Edom in the mid-9th century B.C. The siege was broken when King Mesha sacrificed his son upon the wall of the city. Identified with modern el-Kerak, about 50 miles (80 km) SE of Jerusalem. 2 Ki. 3:25; Isa. 16:7,11; Jer. 48:31,36.

KIRIATH [KEER-ee-ath; "city"] A city of the tribe of Benjamin. Josh. 18:28. Probably identical to Kiriath Jearim.

KIRIATHAIM [KEER-ee-uh-THAY-uhm; "double city"] Also Kirjathaim, KJV.
1. [**I; VI,** E4]. A city of Moab, conquered and rebuilt by the Reubenites. The city was later recaptured by the Moabites, and rebuilt by Mesha. Possibly modern el-Qereiyat, just S of Ataroth (shown on map). Num. 32:37; Josh. 13:19; Jer. 48:1,23. Possibly the same as Shaveh Kiriathaim.
2. A town of Naphtali given to the Gershonite Levites. 1 Chr. 6:76. *See* Kartan.

KIRIATH ARBA [KEER-ee-ath AR-buh; "fourth city"] Also Kirjath-arba, KJV. Ancient name of Hebron, taken from a great leader of the Anakites, a Canaanite people inhabiting the city until the time of its conquest by Caleb. Gen. 23:2; 35:27; Josh. 14:15; Neh. 11:25.

KIRIATH BAAL [KEER-ee-ath BAY-uhl; "city of Baal"] Kirjath-baal, KJV. An early name of Kiriath Jearim, in Josh. 15:60; 18:14.

KIRIATH HUZOTH [KEER-ee-ath HUH-zahht; "city of streets"] Kirjath-huzoth, KJV. An unidentified town in Moab where Balak took Balaam, probably near Bamoth Baal. Num. 22:39. Possibly the same as Kiriathaim or Kerioth.

KIRIATH JEARIM [KEER-ee-ath JEER-uhm; "city of forests"] Kirjath-jearim, KJV. [**VI,** D3]. A fortified city of the Gibeonites, on the border between Judah and Benjamin. Kiriath Baal and Baalah were earlier names of the city, indicating it was formerly a Canaanite high place. After the ark of the covenant was returned from the Philistines, it was moved from Beth Shemesh to Kireath Jearim, where it remained for 20 years in the house of Abinadab. It was the hometown of Uriah the prophet, a contemporary of Jeremiah. Its ancient site is probably to be identified with a hill just NW of the present-day village of Abu Ghosh, about 9 miles (15 km) NW of Jerusalem. Josh. 9:17; 15:9,60; 1 Sam. 6:21–7:2; 2 Chr. 1:4; Jer. 26:20.

KIRIATH SANNAH [KEER-ee-ath SAN-uh; "city of instruction"] Kirjath-sannah, KJV. A town in the hill country of Judah, assigned to the Levites. Josh. 15:49. Same as Debir 1, and Kiriath Sepher.

KIRIATH SEPHER [KEER-ee-ath SEE-fer; "city of books"] Former name of Debir, used in Josh. 15:15,16; Jdg. 1:11,12. *See* Kiriath Sannah.

KISHION [KISH-ee-ahn] Kishon, KJV (Josh. 21:28). A city of Issachar, given to the Levites of the Gershonite clan. It may be a site located less than 2 miles (3 km) S of Mt. Tabor [**VI,** B3]. Josh. 19:20; 21:28. *See* Kedesh 3.

KISHON [KISH-ahn; "curving"] **V,** B2. A river which flows from Mt. Gilboa NW through the Valley of Jezreel, to enter the Mediterranean Sea just N of Mt. Carmel. It is fed by numerous tributaries in the hills of N Samaria and lower Galilee. Only the last 6 miles of the river, continuously fed by runoff from the Car-

mel range, flows throughout the year, often flooding onto the surrounding plain during the rainy season. Such a flooding of the Kishon brought victory over the army of Sisera, whose chariots, deployed upon the plain, became bogged down and useless. Jdg. 4:7,13; 5:21; 1 Ki. 18:40. Called the "waters of Megiddo" in Jdg. 5:19.

KISLOTH TABOR [KIS-lahth TAY-bor; "loins of Tabor"] Chisloth-tabor, KJV, RSV. A border town of Zebulun near Mt. Tabor [**VI,** B3]. Josh. 19:12. Probably the same as Kesulloth.

KITLISH [KIT-lish] Kithlith, KJV; Chitlish, RSV. A town in the lowlands of Judah, possibly about 5 miles (8 km) SW of Lachish [**V,** C1]. Josh. 15:40.

KITRON [KIT-ruhn] A town from which the Zebulunites failed to expel the Canaanites. Possibly a site located W of Mt. Carmel, about 10 miles (16 km) S of Acco [**I,** A1]. Jdg. 1:30. Possibly the same as Kattath, in Josh. 19:15.

KITTIM [KIT-im] Also Chittim, KJV. OT name for Cyprus, possibly derived from the ancient city of Kition. Gen. 10:4. *See* Cyprus; Elishah.

KOA [KOH-uh] Possibly the territory of a people E of the Tigris, to be identified with the Qutu in Assyrian texts. The Sutu, often mentioned with the Qutu in these sources, may be the "Shoa" that precedes Koa in Ezek. 23:23.

KORAZIN [KOR-uh-zin] Chorazin, KJV, RSV. [**XI,** B3]. A town on the Sea of Galilee, condemned by Christ for its failure to repent. Identified with modern Kerazeh, about 2 miles (3 km) N of Capernaum. Mt. 11:21; Lk. 10:13.

KUE [KWEE] "Linen yarn," KJV. **IX (a).** A kingdom identified as E Cilicia in SE Asia Minor; its king paid tribute to Tiglath-Pileser III of Assyria. A source of fine horses in Solomon's day. 1 Ki. 10:28.

L

LABAN [LAY-buhn; "white"] An unknown place, apparently in the territory of Moab, E of the Jordan. Deut. 1:1.

LACHISH* [LAY-kish] **V,** C1; **VI; VIII; X.** A large fortified city in the W foothills of Judah. Appearing as Lakisu in the Amarna Letters, it served as an important stronghold of the Canaanites during the 2nd millennium B.C., until its conquest by Joshua. Lachish was later rebuilt by Rehoboam as part of his defenses against Egyptian aggression. Later, Amaziah, king of Judah, fled from a rebellion in Jerusalem to Lachish, and was killed inside its walls.
A relief on the wall of Sennacherib's palace at Nineveh portrays the Assyrian siege and capture of Lachish in 701 B.C. For some time thereafter, it was under an Assyrian governor, and its walls were again rebuilt. By 587 B.C., Azekah and Lachish were the last strongholds defending Judah against Nebuchadnezzar of Babylon. Found in the gatehouse during excavation at Lachish were 21 ostraca (inscribed potsherds), known as the Lachish Letters, written shortly before the destruction of the city. They provide a fascinating insight into that critical period of the Israelite nation. Two of the letters make references to a prophet, very possibly Jeremiah.
Lachish was revived after the Exile, and continued to be inhabited through the Persian

and Hellenistic periods, until its abandonment about 150 B.C. Josh. 10; 2 Ki. 14:19; 18:14-17; 19:8; Neh. 11:30; Jer. 34:7.

LAHMAS [LAH-muhs] Lahmam, KJV, RSV. A city in the W foothills of Judah, possibly located about 2.5 miles (4 km) E of Lachish [**V,** C1] Josh. 15:40.

LAISH [LAY-ish] An ancient Canaanite city in N Palestine conquered by the tribe of Dan during the period of the Judges. Many of the Danites migrated there, and the city's name was changed to Dan. Excavation has uncovered a layer of ash corresponding to the end of the Late Bronze Age that may mark its conquest by the Danites. Jdg. 18:7-29. Also called Leshem in Josh. 19:47. *See* Dan.

LAISHAH [LAY-ih-shuh] Laish, KJV. A city of Benjamin, in the path of the Assyrians' approach to Jerusalem from the N. Possibly a site about 2.5 miles (4 km) N of Jerusalem [**VII,** C1]. Isa. 10:30.

LAKKUM [LAK-uhm] A town of Naphtali, possibly modern Mansura, a site at the S end of the Sea of Galilee, W of the Jordan. Josh. 19:33.

LAODICEA [LAY-uh-dih-SEE-uh] **XIII,** B5. A city located on the banks of the Lycus River in the province of Phrygia; last of the seven churches of Asia referred to in Rev. 2–3. It was founded in the 3rd century B.C. by Antiochus, who named the city after his wife, Laodice. Situated on a major crossroads, the city enjoyed great prosperity—so much so that, with the aid of its large banking community, the city was able to refuse aid from Rome after its devastation by an earthquake in A.D. 60. Laodicea was known for its black wool industry, as well as the manufacture of an eye salve called collyrium, both clearly alluded to in Rev 3:18. Its self-sufficiency was compromised only by its limited water supply, so that water provided by hot springs had to be brought some distance by aqueduct, arriving lukewarm. The city was eventually abandoned, its extensive ruins known in Turkish as Eski Hissar, or "old castle." Col. 4:13-16; Rev. 3:14-18.

LASEA [lah-SEE-uh] A seaport on the S coast of Crete [**XIII,** C4], probably a site about 5 miles (8 km) E of the harbor, Fair Havens. Acts. 27:8.

LASHA [LASH-uh] A place near Sodom and Gomorrah, marking the SE extent of Canaanite territory in Patriarchal times. Gen. 10:19.

LASHARON [lah-SHAIR-uhn] A Canaanite royal city conquered by Joshua. Possibly ancient Sarona, located about 6.5 miles (10 km) SW of Tiberias [**XI,** B3]. However, some translations (NEB) read this as "the king of Aphek in Sharon." Josh. 12:18. *See* Aphek 1.

LEBANON [LEB-uh-nahn; "white"]
1. The name of a mountain range, more loosely applied to the surrounding region, which has become a republic in modern times. The Lebanon range rises abruptly from the Mediterranean coast of Syria, running almost 100 miles (160 km) NE from Tyre to Kadash on the Orontes. Its name is derived from its white limestone cliffs and snow-laden peaks.
The Lebanon range has many prominent peaks, the highest of which is Qurnet es-Sauda, E of Tripoli, exceeding 3050 ft (1000 m) at its apex. West of the Lebanon ridge lies the narrow coastal plain of Phoenicia, and its ancient sea-trading city-states, Byblos (biblical Gebal), Sidon, and Tyre. The wealth of Lebanon's forests was much exploited by the Phoenician traders. Hiram of Tyre provided Solomon with huge quantities of the renowned

cedars of Lebanon for use in the construction of the Temple and other building projects. Deut. 1:7; Jdg. 3:3; 1 Ki. 5:6-14; Jer. 22:6,20-23.
2. Between the Lebanon and the Anti-Lebanon mountain ranges lies the Valley of Lebanon. Flanked by high peaks, it receives little rain, but is well watered by the Litani and Orontes rivers, which flow SW and NE respectively from near the center of the valley. Near its S terminus, the sources of the Jordan originate on the slopes of Mt. Hermon. In classical times, it became known as Coelesyria ("hollow Syria"), and is now called el-Buqeia, which simply means "the valley." Josh. 11:17; 12:7.

LEBAOTH [leh-BAY-ahth] See Beth Lebaoth.

LEB KAMAI [leb KAY-mie] Chaldea, RSV. A cryptogram for Chaldea. Jer. 51:1.

LEBO HAMATH [LEE-boh HAY-math] "Entrance of Hamath," KJV, RSV. [**VII**, B2]. A city on the N boundary of the Promised Land. Mentioned as Rabah in Egyptian sources, and as Labu in Assyrian inscriptions, it is identified with Lebwe, located at the N end of the Valley of Lebanon, near the head of the Orontes River. The actual territory of Israel extended as far N as Lebo Hamath only during the reigns of David, Solomon, and Jeroboam II. Num. 34:8; 1 Ki. 8:65; 2 Ki. 14:25; Ezek. 47:15,20; 48:1.

LEBONAH [leh-BOH-nuh] A place on the road between Bethel and Shechem. Identified with modern Lubban, about 3 miles (5 km) NW of Shiloh [**VI**, D3]. Jdg. 21:19.

LEHI [LEE-hi; "jawbone"] Jashubi-lehem, KJV. A place in the W foothills of Judah, where Samson slew a thousand Philistines with a jawbone. Site uncertain. Jdg. 15:9-19. See Ramath Lehi.

LESHEM [LESH-em] Alternate form of Laish in Josh. 19:47. See Dan.

LIBNAH [LIB-nuh; "whiteness"]
1. A stopping-place of the Israelites during the Exodus. Site uncertain. Num. 33:20,21. Possibly the same as Laban.
2. A Canaanite royal city in the W foothills of Judah, conquered by Joshua in his southern campaign. Assigned to the priests, the city revolted during the reign of Jehoram, king of Judah. At some point, Judah regained control of it, and during the reign of Hezekiah, the heavily fortified city withstood the siege of Sennacherib. It may have been at this time that 185,000 of his men died overnight (Isa. 37). The site of Libnah is commonly identified with Tell es-Safi, about 4.5 miles (7 km) S of Azekah [**V**, C1]. The white limestone cliffs of the area may have given the city its name. However, more recently, this site has been called into question; several alternate sites to the SE have been proposed, but the actual location of Libnah remains uncertain. Josh. 10:29-39; 15:42; 2 Ki. 8:22; 19:8.

LIBYA [LIB-ee-uh] Lubim, KJV OT. [**IX**, B1-C2]. Greek term for the land and people in N Africa to the W of Egypt, derived from the Egyptian "Libu." The Lehabites of Gen. 10:13 were possibly its inhabitants. 2 Chr. 12:3; Nah. 3:9 Acts 2:10. See Put.

LOD [LAHD] [**VI**, D2; **X**.] A town built or rebuilt by the Benjamite Shemed on a crossroads of two major trade routes. Lod was located in the Plain of Sharon, about 11 miles (18 km) SE of Joppa. It was reinhabited after the Exile, and came to be known as Lydda in NT times. 1 Chr 8:12; Ezra 2:33; Neh 7:37; 11:35. See Lydda.

LO DEBAR [loh deh-BAR; "barren"] A town E of the Jordan, probably identical to Debir 2. 2 Sam. 9:4,5; 17:27; Amos 6:13.

LUHITH [LOO-hith] A place in Moab, built on a hill. Possibly between Rabbah and Zoar. Isa. 15:5; Jer. 48:5.

LUZ [LUHZ; "almond tree"]
1. Ancient name of the city of Bethel. Gen. 28:19; Josh. 16:2.
2. A city in the land of the Hittites, built by a man from Luz in Canaan. Jdg. 1:26.

LYCAONIA [LIK-ay-OH-nee-uh] An inland district of central Asia Minor, containing the cities of Lystra and Derbe. Lycaonia was apportioned among the Roman provinces in the 1st century B.C.; the NT use refers to the portion within the province of Galatia, bounded on the S by Pamphylia and Cilicia, on the W by Cappadocia, and on the E by Phrygia and Pisidia. See Acts 14:6,11.

LYCIA [LISH-ee-uh] A small, mountainous district on the SW coast of Asia Minor, where the land bulges into the Mediterranean E of Rhodes [**XIII**, C4-C5]. The Lycians were conquered by Persia in 546 B.C., and later were largely Hellenized under Greek influence. In 167 B.C., Lycia was freed by Rome, and remained largely independent until A.D. 42, when the region was annexed by Claudius into the province of Pamphylia. However, Lycia apparently regained its freedom in A.D. 69. Its primary seaports were Myra and Patara. Acts 27:5.

LYDDA [LID-uh] **XI**, D1. Greek name of the OT city of Lod, located about 11 miles (18 km) SE of Joppa. In post-exilic times, the city came under the control of the governor of Samaria, but was returned to the Jews in 145 B.C. Here Peter healed the paralytic. Acts 9:32-38.

LYDIA [LID-ee-uh] **IX**, A2-B2; **IX** (b). A country in W Asia Minor, bounded on the N by Mysia, on the E by Phrygia, and on the S by Caria; its territory consisted largely of fertile river valleys. Croesus, the last king of Lydia, dominated all of Asia Minor until his defeat by Cyrus, who captured Sardis, the capital, in 546 B.C. It became a part of the kingdom of Pergamum, before it was added to the Roman province of Asia in 133 B.C. Jer. 46:9; Ezek. 27:10; 30:5.

LYSTRA [LIS-truh] **XIII**, B6. A small, backward town of Lycaonia, in central Asia Minor, established as a Roman colony by Augustus, about 6 B.C. Zeus and Hermes were linked in a local cult, which developed around a legend that the two gods once visited the city. This explains their abrupt identification of Paul and Barnabas with the two gods. A temple of Zeus has been found at the site but has yet to be excavated. Timothy was a native of Lystra. Acts 14:6-21; 16:1,2; 2 Tim. 3:11.

M

MAACAH [MAY-uh-kuh] **VII**, B2. A small Aramean kingdom SW of Mt. Hermon, bordering on the territory of Manasseh E of the Jordan. Following David's victory over the Aramean forces at Helam, Maacah became a tributary of Israel. It was eventually absorbed by the Aramean kingdom of Damascus. Josh. 12:5; 13:11-13; 2 Sam. 10:6-8.

MAARATH [MAY-uh-rath] A town in the hill country of Judah, about 7 miles (11 km) N of Hebron [**V**, C2]. Josh. 15:59.

MACEDONIA* [MAS-uh-DOH-nee-uh] **IX**; **XIII**, A3-B3. A Greek kingdom established as early as the 7th century B.C. Under Philip II of Macedon (359–336 B.C.), the mountain tribes of Macedonia were unified and exercised dominion over the whole of mainland Greece. His son, Alexander the Great, overthrew Persia and founded the largest Near Eastern empire then known, which maintained dynastic rule throughout the E Mediterranean until the rise of Roman power.
Macedonia was made a Roman province in 148 B.C. In NT times, it extended from the Aegean Sea to the Adriatic, N of the province of Achaia and SW of Thrace. It was crossed from W to E by the great Egnatian Way. Thessalonica was its capital. Acts 16:9-12; 19:21-29; 2 Cor. 7:5; 1 Th. 1:7,8.

MACHPELAH [mak-PEE-luh; "double"] A field containing the cave bought by Abraham from the Hittites as a burial place for his wife Sarah. Abraham, Isaac, Rebekah, Leah, and Jacob were all buried there. It was located at Mamre, just N of Hebron. The modern city of el-Khalil has incorporated the site of the cave. Once covered by a Christian church, a Moslem mosque now stands over the cave. Gen. 23:9,17-19; 25:9; 49:30; 50:13.

MADMANNAH [mad-MAN-uh; "manure pile"] A town in the W foothills of Judah, near Ziklag [**VI**, E2]. Josh. 15:31. Possibly the same as Beth Marcaboth in Josh. 19:5.

MADMEN [MAD-men; "manure pile"] A town of Moab; its name sounds like the Hebrew for "silence." Possibly a site located about 2.5 miles (4 km) NW of Rabbah [**VII**, C2]. Jer. 48:2.

MADMENAH [mad-MEE-nuh; "manure pile"] A town of Benjamin, N of Jerusalem. Site uncertain. Isa. 10:31.

MADON [MAY-dahn] A Canaanite royal city in N Palestine, conquered by Joshua. Possibly a site about 5 miles (8 km) NW of Tiberias [**XI**, B3], or perhaps Khirbet Madin, 3 miles (5 km) farther S. Josh. 11:1; 12:19. It may be the same as Adamah.

MAGADAN [MAG-uh-dan] Magdala, KJV. A place on the W shore of the Sea of Galilee, probably Magdala, or the area about the town. Mt. 15:39. Called Dalmanutha in Mk. 8:10.

MAGBISH [MAG-bish] Hometown of some who returned to Judah after the Exile. Location uncertain. Ezra 2:30.

MAGDALA [MAG-duh-luh] **XI**, B3. A small town on the W shore of the Sea of Galilee, between Tiberias and Capernaum. Home of Mary Magdalene. Jn. 19:25; 20:1,18. See Magadan; Dalmanutha.

MAHANAIM [MAY-huh-NAY-uhm; "two camps"] **I**, B2; **VI**; **VII**. An ancient town in central Gilead, situated near the Jabbok River, on the border between Gad and E Manasseh. Jacob gave the place its name after he met angels there, providing him assurance that God was with him. For two years, Mahanaim was the capital of Ish-Bosheth, the son of Saul. David later took refuge there during the rebellion of his son, Absalom. The exact location is still disputed, although a site along the Jabbok, some distance from the Jordan, is probable. Gen. 32:1-20; Josh. 13:26,30; 2 Sam. 2:8-12,29; 17:24-27.

MAHANEH DAN [may-HAN-uh DAN; "camp of Dan"]
1. A place between Zorah and Eshtaol, which are both located about 2 miles (3 km) NE of Beth Shemesh [**VI**, D2], separated by the Valley of Kesalon. Jdg. 13:25.

2. A place W of Kiriath Jearim where the Danites camped on their way to Laish. Possibly the same as 1, although the two sites described appear to be several miles apart. Or perhaps Mahaneh Day lay in the Kesalon Valley, which is between Zorah and Eshtaol, but farther E, near Kireath Jearim. It could be that this site derived its name from 1; as both were apparently temporary settlements, it is unlikely either will ever be identified. Jdg. 18:12.

MAKAZ [MAY-kaz] A town of Judah, possibly located about 6 miles (9.5 km) NW of Beth Shemesh [**VI**, D2]. 1Ki. 4:9.

MAKHELOTH [mak-HEE-lahth; "assemblies"] A place where the Israelites camped during the Exodus. The site is uncertain. Num. 33:25,26.

MAKKEDAH [mak-EE-duh; "place of shepherds"] **V**, C1. A royal city of the Canaanites, conquered by Joshua. The five Amorite kings who attacked Gibeon and were defeated by Joshua took refuge in a cave at Makkedah, but were found and put to death. It fell to Pharaoh Sheshonq I (the biblical Shishak) during the reign of Rehoboam. The site may be located about midway between Lachish and Hebron. Josh. 10:10-29; 15:41.

MALTA [MAWL-tuh] Melita, KJV. [**XIII**, C1]. A Mediterranean island located in a strategic position below Sicily, about 90 miles (145 km) SW of Syracuse. As part of the Roman Empire, Malta was placed under a procurator, who was called the "chief official." This was Publius at the time when Paul was shipwrecked on the island. Acts 28:1.

MAMRE [MAM-ree; "strength"] **I**, C1. A grove near Hebron, named after Mamre the Amorite. Here Abraham built an altar and just to the SE was the cave of Machpelah, which became the family burial place. Identified with Ramet el-Khalil, about 2 miles (3 km) N of Hebron. Gen. 13:18; 23:17-19.

MANAHATH [MAN-uh-hath] A city to which some of the Benjamites were deported. 1 Chr. 8:6.

MANASSEH [muh-NAS-uh] Manasses, KJV. [**VI**, C2-A5]. A tribe of Israel whose territory extended to both sides of the Jordan River. E of the Jordan, Manasseh encompassed the Bashan and half of Gilead, from the Jabbok River to Mt. Hermon. The W portion of Manasseh lay N of Ephraim and S of the territories of Asher, Zebulun, and Issachar, stretching from the Jordan to the Mediterranean Sea. This large region contained a number of Canaanite fortresses that strongly resisted the Manassite settlement of the land. Josh. 17:1-13.

MAON [MAY-ahn; "habitation"] A town in the hill country of Judah, situated in the Desert of Maon, where David took refuge from Saul. Identified with a site about 9 miles (14 km) S of Hebron [**V**, C2]. Josh. 15:55; 1 Sam. 23:24,25; 25:1,2.

MARAH [MAIR-uh; "bitter"] **III**, D2. A place in the Desert of Shur which Moses and the Israelites reached three days after crossing the Red Sea.The water there was too bitter to drink. Possibly modern Ain Hawarah, about 47 miles (75 km) SSE of Suez. Ex. 15:23; Num. 33:8,9.

MARALAH [MAIR-uh-luh] Mareal, RSV. A town on the W border of Zebulun. Site uncertain. Josh. 19:11.

MARESHAH [muh-REE-shuh; "head place"(?)] **VI**; **X**, B1. A Canaanite city in the lowlands of Judah, guarding a pass to Hebron. Fortified by Rehoboam, a large Cushite

army was defeated here by Asa, and driven back to Gerar. The city became the Edomite capital following their infiltration of S Judah after the fall of Jerusalem in 586 B.C. The invading Parthians destroyed Mareshah, then called Marisa, in 40 B.C. Josh. 15:44; 2 Chr. 14:9,10; Mic. 1:15.

MAROTH [MAIR-ahth; "bitterness"] A town probably located in the W foothills of Judah, mentioned only in Mic. 1:12. Possibly the same as Maarath.

MASHAL [MAY-shal] Alternate form of Mishal, in 1 Chr. 6:74.

MASREKAH [mas-REE-kuh] Home of Samlah, a pre-Israelite king of Edom. Site uncertain. Gen. 36:36.

MASSAH [MAS-uh; "testing"] A place in the wilderness of Sin near Rephidim. Here the Israelites put God to the test, demanding in response, God instructed Moses to strike the rock at Horeb with his staff, bringing forth water. Ex. 17:7; Deut. 6:16; Ps. 95:8. Also called Meribah.

MATTANAH [MAT-uh-nuh; "gift"] A campsite of the Israelites, in the Transjordan, N of the Arnon River. The exact site is unknown. Num. 21:18,19.

MECONA [meh-KOH-nuh] Mekona, KJV. An unidentified town in S Judah, near Ziklag; it was inhabited by the Israelites after the Exile. Neh. 11:28.

MEDEBA [MED-uh-buh; "waters of quiet"] **IV**; **VI**; **VIII**, B2. A city of Sihon the Amorite, E of the Jordan, taken by Israel and assigned to the tribe of Reuben. The city changed hands frequently during its history. According to the Moabite Stone, Omri conquered Medeba, which was later lost to Mesha, king of Moab. Jeroboam II subsequently captured the city, but by the time of Isaiah, it was once again under Moabite dominion. In Hellenistic times, it marked the N limit of the Nabatean kingdom. In 1890, excavation uncovered the Medeba Map, a mosaic map of Palestine dating from the 6th century A.D. Modern Madaba is located about 6 miles (10 km) S of Heshbon. Num. 21:30; Josh. 13:9,16; 1 Chr. 19:7; Isa. 15:2.

MEDIA [MEE-dee-uh] **II**, B7; **IX (b)**. Ancient country of Asia, bounded on the N by the Caspian Sea, on the E by Parthia, on the W by Assyria and Armenia, and on the S by Elam and Persia. The inhabitants of the region were called the Medes or Medians, and were closely associated with the Persians. In 550 B.C., Cyrus captured Ecbatana, capital of Media, and assumed the title "king of the Medes." The combined empire of Persia and Media conquered Babylon, initiating the period of Persian world dominance. Ezra 6:2; Esth. 1:3,14; Isa. 21:2; Dan. 8:20. See Medes.

MEGIDDO* [meh-GID-oh] **I**; **V**, B2; **VI**; **VIII**, B1. An important walled city guarding the principal pass through the Carmel mountain range, connecting the plain of Megiddo (modern plain of Esdraelon) with the coastal plain. Megiddo's great strategic value was derived from this key placement along the main road from Egypt to Syria. Thus, from ancient times, it was the site of battles. The most thoroughly recorded battle of antiquity occurred at Megiddo, when Thutmose III of Egypt defeated a coalition of Asiatic kings there, about 1468 B.C.

Joshua defeated Megiddo in the conquest of Canaan, but its inhabitants were not driven out by the Manassites, to whom the city was allotted. Deborah and Barak later defeated the army of Sisera in a battle near "the waters of Megiddo," indicating the headwaters of

the Kishon River. Solomon refortified the city, which became a central city in one of his twelve districts of Israel. In 609 B.C., Josiah was killed in a battle on the plain of Megiddo, during his attempt to halt the march of Pharaoh Neco N to Carchemish. This event probably marks the final destruction of the city. Josh. 12:21; 17:11; Jdg. 5:19; 2 Ki. 9:27; 23:29,30; Zech. 12:11. See Armageddon.

MEHOLAH [meh-HCH-luh] Shortened form of Abel Meholah, in 1 Sam. 18:19.

ME JARKON [mee JAR-kuhn] A city in the territory of Dan, near Joppa. Possibly a site on the stream Nahr el-Auja, which flows into the Mediterranean about 4 miles (6.5 km) N of Joppa [**VI**, D2]. Josh. 19:46.

MEMPHIS [MEM-fis] Usually Noph, KJV, RSV. [**II; III**, C1; **IX**]. Ancient city founded by Mene, first Pharaoh of all Egypt; it became the Egyptian capital during the period of the Old Kingdom (2680–2180) with Thebes and Rameses, Memphis was also a royal city during the period of the New Kingdom (1552–1069) and remained important until its conquest by Alexander the Great in 332 B.C. After the fall of Jerusalem and the death of governor Gedaliah, many Jews fled to Egypt, establishing a colony at Memphis.

Today, little remains of the original site except the necropolis and the ancient pyramids constructed nearby, hinting at the lost splendor of this once great city. It was situated on the W bank of the Nile, about 13 miles (21 km) S of Cairo, the modern capital of Egypt. Isa. 19:13; Jer. 46:14,19; Hos. 9:6.

MEPHAATH [MEF-ay-ahth] A Reubenite city assigned to the Levites. Later, the town was captured by the Moabites. Possibly a site S of Rabbah and NE of Heshbon. Josh. 13:18; 21:37; Jer. 48:21.

MERATHAIM [MAIR-uh-THAY-uhm; "double rebellion"] A symbolic name for Babylon in Jer. 50:21.

MERIBAH [MAIR-ih-buh; "quarreling"]
1. A place in the wilderness where Moses struck the rock at Horeb to bring forth water. Ex. 17:1-7. See Massah.
2. Meribah Kadesh; a second place where, nearly 39 years later, the Israelites demanded water. In response, Moses struck the rock twice rather than merely speaking to the rock. A river gushed forth, but the Lord told Moses he would not enter the land of Canaan because of this act of disobedience. Num. 20:1-13; Deut. 32:51; Ezek. 47:19. It is the same as Kadesh Barnea.

MERIBAH KADESH [MAIR-ih-buh KAY-desh] See Meribah 2.

MEROM [MEER-ahm; "high place"] **V**, A2. An ancient city near the "Waters of Merom," the site of the battle in which Joshua defeated the northern kings of Canaan, under Jabin, king of Hazor. It is possibly to be identified with the modern village of Meiron, situated near the foot of Jebel Jarmuk (shown on map). It lies near the source of the Wadi Ammud, which flows SE into the Sea of Galilee. A site, about 4 miles (6.5 km) W of Lake Huleh has also been proposed. Josh. 11:5,7.

MERONOTH [meh-RAHN-ahth] A place near Gibeon. Site uncertain. Neh. 3:7.

MEROZ [MEER-ahz] A town in Galilee whose inhabitants did not join Deborah and Barak in their campaign against Jabin, king of Hazor. It was apparently near the site of the battle at the Kishon River, possibly a site about 7.5 miles (12 km) S of Kedesh in Naphtali [**VI**, A3-B3]. Jdg. 5:23.

MESHA [MEE-shuh] A place marking the boundary of the land occupied by the descendants of Joktan. Probably located in S Arabia. Gen. 10:30. *See* Sephar.

MESHECH [MEE-shek; "tall"] **IX**, A3. The territory of a tribe of central Asia Minor, called the Mushki in Assyrian inscriptions. In the 8th century B.C., Mita, king of the Mushki was a powerful enemy of Sargon. He was likely the King Midas of Phrygia in Greek traditions. Ps. 120:5; Ezek. 32:26; 38:2,3. *See* Tubal.

MESOPOTAMIA [MES-oh-poh-TAY-mee-uh; "between two rivers"] The land between the Tigris and Euphrates rivers, a name derived from the OT Aram Naharaim, the region E of the upper Euphrates. By NT times, Mesopotamia had come to describe the whole Tigris-Euphrates Valley, corresponding to modern Iraq. Acts 2:9; 7:2.

METHEG AMMAH [MEE-theg AM-uh; "the bridle of the mother city"(?)] Possibly a place near Gath, or a figurative name for Gath itself (*compare* 1 Chr. 18:1). 2 Sam. 8:1.

MICMASH [MIK-mash] Michmash, KJV. [**X**, A2]. A town of Benjamin, located on the pass between Bethel and Jericho. Here the Philistines camped to prepare for battle against Saul. The city was resettled by Benjamites after the Exile. Identified with a site about 7 miles (11 km) NE of Jerusalem. Modern Mukhmas. 1 Sam. 13:2-23; 14:5,31; Ezra 2:27; Neh. 11:31; Isa. 10:28.

MICMETHATH [mik-MEE-thath] An unidentified place on the border between Ephraim and Manasseh, E of Shechem. Josh. 16:6; 17:7.

MIDDIN [MID-uhn; "judgment"] A city in the wilderness of Judah, just W of the Dead Sea. Josh. 15:61.

MIDIAN [MID-ee-uhn] **III**, D4-D5. A region in the desert of NW Arabia inhabited by the Midianites, a group of semi-nomadic tribes descended from Midian, son of Abraham and Keturah. After he fled from Egypt, Moses spent 40 years in Midian, which at that time apparently extended as far as the S and E parts of the Sinai Peninsula. By the time of the conquest E of the Jordan, Midian was allied with the Moabites and Amorites against Israel. Over two centuries later, Israel came under Midianite oppression, until Gideon defeated and killed their two kings, Zebah and Zalmunna. Archaeological evidence left by the Midianites is scanty at best, and little can be said about these people who roamed the desert wastes E of the Jordan and the Arabah. Ex. 2:11–4:20; Num. 22:4,7; 31:1-24; Jdg. 7, 8. *See* Midianites

MIGDAL EDER [MIG-duhl EE-duhr; "tower of the Eder"] Edar, KJV; Eder, RSV. A watchtower between Hebron and Bethlehem. Jacob once camped here. Identified with Siyar el-Ghanam, about 5 miles (8 km) S of Jerusalem [**VII**, C1]. Gen. 35:21.

MIGDAL EL [MIG-duhl EL; "tower of God"] A fortified city in Naphtali, possibly about 3 miles (5 km) N of Kedesh [**V**, A2]. Josh. 19:38.

MIGDAL GAD [MIG-duhl GAD; "tower of Gad"] A town in the W foothills of Judah, possibly located about 3 miles (5 km) SE of Lachish [**V**, C1]. Josh. 15:37.

MIGDOL [MIG-duhl; "tower" or "fortress"] "Tower of Syene, KJV, in Ezekiel.
1. An Egyptian fort in the E Nile Delta, W of the Sea of Reeds. Its exact site is uncertain. Ex. 14:2; Num. 33:7.
2. A city in NE Egypt where the Jews took refuge in the days of Jeremiah. Possibly to be

identified with Tell el-Her. Jer. 44:1; Ezek. 29:10.

MIGRON [MIG-rahn]
1. A town of Benjamin on the outskirts of Gibeah, S of Micmash. 1 Sam.14:2.
2. Also a Benjamite town, on the Assyrian path toward Jerusalem from the N. Isa. 10:28. Possibly the same as 1, although a village N of Micmash seems to be indicated.

MILETUS [mie-LEE-tuhs] **XIII**, B4. An Ionian city on the W coast of Asia Minor, about 37 miles (60 km) S of Ephesus. The city flourished during the 8th–6th centuries B.C. as the capital of Ionia, establishing many colonies about the Black Sea. The city was destroyed by Persia in 494 B.C., during the Ionian Revolt. Due to the silting up of its harbor, at the mouth of the Meander River, Miletus was in a state of decline in NT times. It now lies about 5 miles (8 km) from the Mediterranean coast. Acts 20:15,17; 2 Tim. 4:20.

MINNI [MIN-nee] A nation in Armenia, S of Lake Urmia, inhabited by a warlike people frequently mentioned in Assyrian sources between the 9th and 7th centuries B.C. Sargon of Assyria defeated the Minni in 719 B.C. They later came under the control of the Medes. Jer. 51:27.

MINNITH [MIN-ith] An Ammonite town devastated by Jephthah, possibly located about 4 miles (6.5 km) NE of Heshbon [**IV**, D1]. Jdg. 11:33; Ezek. 27:17.

MISHAL [MISH-uhl] Misheal, KJV (Josh. 19:26). A Levitical town of Asher, possibly located about 5 miles (8 km) SE of Acco [**I**, A1]. Josh. 19:26; 21:30. Called Mashal in 1 Chr. 6:74.

MISREPHOTH MAIM [MIZ-reh-fahth MAY-im; "hot springs"] A place S of Sidon to which Joshua pursued the Canaanite forces defeated by the Waters of Merom. It may be Khirbet el-Mushreifeh just S of the promontory midway between Acco and Tyre [**VII**, B1]. Josh. 11:8; 13:6.

MITHCAH [MITH-kuh; "sweetness"] Mithkah, RSV. An unidentified encampment of the Israelites during the Exodus. Num. 33:28,29.

MITYLENE [MIT-uh-LEE-nee; "purity"] **XIII**, B4. The chief city of Lesbos, an island in the Aegean Sea off the W coast of Asia Minor. Acts 20:14.

MIZAR [MIE-zar; "small"] A hill E of the Jordan, probably within sight of Mt. Hermon. Ps. 42:6.

MIZPAH [MIZ-puh; "watchtower"] Mizpeh, KJV, RSV, in Joshua.
1. A place in Gilead where Jacob and Laban raised a mound of stones as a witness to their covenant. Exact site unknown. Gen. 31:49.
2. A region at the foot of Mt. Hermon (Josh. 11:3), called the Valley of Mizpah in Josh. 11:8. In Joshua's time, the territory was inhabited by the Hivites.
3. An unidentified town in the W foothills of Judah. Josh. 15:38.
4. [**VIII**, B1]. A town of Benjamin, near Gibeon; Saul's inauguration as king took place here. It was later fortified by Asa, king of Judah. The residence of governor Gedaliah was at Mizpah after the fall of Jerusalem. The cistern built by Asa was filled with the bodies of those slain by Ishmael, the murderer of Gedaliah. Two possible sites are proposed: the traditional site, Nebi Samwil, located 4 miles (6.5 km) NW of Jerusalem, and Tell en-Nasbeh, on a hill about 8 miles (13 km) N of Jerusalem, which is supported by archaeological evidence (shown on map). Excavation has uncovered a prosperous city there that flourished during the divided kingdom. A

seal bearing the inscription "belonging to Jaazaniah" (*see* 2 Ki. 25:23) also supports its identification with Mizpah of Benjamin. Josh. 18:26; 1 Sam. 10:17-25; 1 Ki. 15:22.
5. A town in Gilead, E of the Jordan, where the Israelites assembled under Jephthah to go to war against Ammon. Jdg. 10:17; 11:11,29,34. Possibly the same as 1, it may also be identical to Ramath Mizpah in Josh. 13:26.
6. A town of Moab; some identify it with the Moabite capital, Kir Hareseth [**VIII**, C2]. 1 Sam. 22:3.

MOAB [MOH-ab] **III**; **IV**, D1-D2; **VI**; **VII**; **VIII**. Nation in the Transjordan, inhabited by the descendants of Moab. Its territory at the time of the conquest lay S of the Arnon River and N of the Zered, bounded by the Dead Sea to the W and the Arabian Desert to the E. Before this, the Moabites also possessed the territory that comprised the kingdom of Sihon, king of the Amorites, and at several times during Israelite history, the Moabites extended their territory to the N, seizing and occupying towns beyond the Arnon.

In Moses' time, Balak, king of Moab, hired Balaam to curse the Israelites as they passed through the kingdom on their way to the Promised Land. In the time of the Judges, Eglon, king of Moab, oppressed Israel for a period of 18 years. Moab became a tributary nation under David and Solomon, but regained its independence after Solomon's death. The Moabites were again subdued by Omri, and remained under Israelite domination until the rebellion of Mesha, about 850 B.C. The Moabite Stone records his revolt against Israel and the capture of many cities in Reubenite territory. Moab became a tributary of Assyria, and thereafter successively came under the control of the Babylonians, Persians, and Nabateans. Num. 21:10-20; 22–25; Jdg. 3:12-30; Ruth 1; 2 Ki. 3; Isa. 15, 16; Jer. 48.

MOLADAH [MAHL-uh-duh; "generation"] A town in the extreme S of Judah, allotted to the Simeonites. It was resettled by Judahites after the Exile. Possibly a site about 8 miles (13 km) SE of Beersheba [**I**, C1]. Josh. 15:26; 19:2; Neh. 11:26.

MOREH [MOR-uh; "teacher" or "diviner"]
1. Abraham's first stopping-place in Canaan, where he set up an altar. Located near Shechem, the great tree of Moreh may have been a sacred oak tree before Abraham's arrival. Gen. 12:6; .Deut. 11:30.
2. A hill in the territory of Issachar near where the Midianites gathered to fight the Israelites under Gideon. Identified with present-day Jebel Dahi in the Valley of Jezreel, S of Mt. Tabor [**VI**, B3]. Jdg. 7:1.

MORESHETH [MOR-uh-sheth; "possession"] "Morasthite," KJV. The hometown of Micah the prophet, possibly located about 6 miles (10 km) NE of Lachish [**V**, C1]. Jer. 26:18; Mic. 1:1. Also called Moresheth Gath, in Mic. 1:14.

MORESHETH GATH [MOR-uh-sheth GATH; "possession of Gath"] Identical to Moresheth, the birthplace of Micah, so-called because of its proximity to the Philistine territory of Gath. Mic. 1:14.

MORIAH [mor-IE-uh]
1. [**I**, C1]. The "land of Moriah" was the mountainous region where Abraham was instructed by God to offer up Isaac as a burnt sacrifice. It was three days' journey from Beersheba. Some identify it with the site of Jerusalem, although Samaritan tradition associates it with Mt. Gerizim. Gen. 22:2.
2. Mount Moriah was the site of Solomon's Temple at Jerusalem, on the threshing floor of Araunah. 2 Chr. 3:1.

MOSERAH [moh-SEER-uh; "bond"] Mosera, KJV. A place in the wilderness where the Israelites camped, probably on more than one occasion. Here Aaron is said to have died, although elsewhere Mt. Hor is reported as the site of his death and burial (Num. 20:22-29; 33:37-39). For this reason, many believe it was near to Mt. Hor, although its exact location remains unknown. Deut. 10:6. Also called Moseroth.

MOSEROTH [moh-SEER-ahth; "bonds"] Plural form of Moserah, in Num. 33:30,31.

MOZAH [MOH-zuh; "unleavened"] A town assigned to the tribe of Benjamin, possibly located about 5 miles (8 km) NW of Jerusalem [**VII**, C1]. Josh. 18:26.

MYRA [MIE-ruh] **XIII**, C5. A chief seaport of Lycia, located on the Andracus River in SW Asia Minor, about 4 miles (6.5 km) from the Mediterranean. Modern Dembre. Acts 27:5.

MYSIA [MIS-ee-uh] A region in NW Asia Minor, bounded by the Aegean to the W, the Hellespont and Propontis to the N, Bithynia and Phrygia to the E, and Lydia to the S. Cities of Mysia included Troas, Assos, Adramyttium, and Pergamum. Previously a part of the kingdom of Pergamum, Mysia fell to Rome in 133 B.C., and was thereafter incorporated into the province of Asia [**XIII**, B4]. Acts 16:7,8.

N

NAAMAH [NAY-uh-muh; "pleasant"] An unidentified town in the W foothills of Judah. Zophar, one of Job's friends, is called "the Naamathite," but this is undoubtedly a reference to another city. Josh. 15:41.

NAARAH [NAY-uh-ruh; "youthful"] Naarath, KJV. A city on the S border of Ephraim, possibly located about 5 miles (8 km) NW of Jericho [**V**, C2]. Josh. 16:7. Also called Naaran, in 1 Chr. 7:28.

NAARAN [NAY-uh-ruhn] See Naarah.

NAHALAL [NAY-huh-lal] Nahallal, KJV (Josh. 19:15). A Levitical city in the territory of Zebulun; the Israelites failed to expel its Canaanite inhabitants, but eventually subjected them to forced labor. The site is uncertain, but may be near modern Nahalal, about 5 miles (8 km) W of Nazareth [**XI**, B2]. Josh. 19:15; 21:35. Called Nahalol in Jdg. 1:30.

NAHALIEL [nuh-HAY-lee-uhl; "valley of God"] A valley N of the Arnon where the Israelites camped on their way to Mt. Pisgah in the Transjordan. Possibly the modern Wadi Zerqa Main, which flows into the Dead Sea about 10 miles (16 km) S of the Jordan's mouth. Num. 21:19.

NAHALOL [NAY-huh-lahl] See Nahalal.

NAHOR [NAY-hor] A city mentioned in Gen. 24:10. It may be the N Mesopotamian city that appears as Nahur in Mari texts from the 18th century B.C. Alternatively, this may merely be a reference to the city in which Nahor lived. In either case, it was near Haran [**II**, B4].

NAIN [NAYN; possibly "pleasant"] **XI**, B2. A city in S Galilee, situated on the NW slope of the hill of Moreh. Modern Nein now occupies the site of its ruins, about 5 miles (8 km) SE of Nazareth. In Nain, Jesus raised a widow's son from the dead. Lk. 7:11.

NAIOTH [NAY-yahth; "habitation"] A place in or near Ramah of Benjamin, where David sought sanctuary from Saul. It may have been the domicile of Samuel, who lived in Ramah. 1 Sam. 19:18–20:1.

NAPHOTH [NAY-fahth] Shortened form of Naphoth Dor, in Josh. 17:11.

NAPHOTH DOR [NAY-fahth DOR; "heights of Dor"] Region or borders of Dor, KJV. Alternate form of Dor, or the region surrounding the city. Josh. 11: 2; 12:23; 1 Ki. 4:11.

NAPHTALI [NAF-tuh-lie; "wrestle"] **VI**, A3-B3. The territory allotted to the tribe of this name lay in N Palestine, E of Asher and W of the upper Jordan and the Sea of Galilee. To the S, it bordered on Zebulun and Issachar, and it extended N as far as Mt. Hermon. Naphtali was a mountainous and fertile region, encompassing most of Galilee. The Canaanites held many strongholds in the area, most notably Hazor, the largest Canaanite city. Eventually, the Israelites overcame Hazor, enslaving the Canaanites of Beth Shemesh and Beth Anath. Ben-Hadad I, the king of Aram, conquered much of Naphtali during the reign of Baasha, and in 734 B.C. Tiglath-Pileser III annexed the region, deporting its Israelite inhabitants. Josh. 19:32-39; 1 Ki. 15:20; Isa. 9:1.

NAZARETH [NAZ-uh-reth; "watch-tower"(?)] **XI**, B2. The town in lower Galilee where Jesus lived until the age of 30. It was an unimportant town located in the territory of Zebulun, overlooking the plain of Esdraelon. Although situated near several of the important trade routes of Palestine, the town itself was surrounded on three sides by high hills, giving it the appearance of isolation. This, with the poor reputation of Galileans, led to the scorn with which the strict Jews viewed Nazareth (see Jn. 1:46). Jesus was twice rejected by the people of Nazareth, prompting his statement that "only in his hometown . . . is a prophet without honor" (Mt. 13:53-58). The ancient site lies near the modern town of Nazareth, or En-Nasira. Mt. 4:13; Lk. 1:26; 2:4,51; 4:13-30.

NEAH [NEE-uh] A border town of Zebulun, location unknown. Josh. 19:13. See Neiel.

NEAPOLIS [nee-AP-oh-lis; "new city"] A town of Macedonia, on the N shore of the Aegean Sea. It served as the port of Philippi. Identified with modern Kavalla, about 10 miles (16 km) SE of Philippi [**XIII**, A4]. Acts 16:11.

NEBAIOTH [nuh-BAY-yahth] An Arabian tribe mentioned with Kedar; possibly to be identified with the later Nabataeans. Isa. 60:7.

NEBALLAT [neh-BAL-uht] **X**, A1. A town of Benjamin repopulated after the return from Exile. Modern Beit Nabala, about 4 miles (6.5 km) NE of Lydda. Neh. 11:34.

NEBO [NEE-boh]
1. A city of Moab conquered by the Israelites and allotted to the tribe of Reuben. Located on or near Mt. Nebo, it was recaptured by Mesha, king of Moab, in the mid-9th century B.C. Num. 32:3,38; Jer. 48:1,22.
2. [**III**; **IV**, D1; **VI**] Mt. Nebo, a mountain in the Abarim, from which Moses surveyed the Promised Land before his death. Probably Jebel en Neba, about 8 miles (13 km) E of the mouth of the Jordan. Deut. 32:49; 34:1.
3. A town mentioned with Bethel and Ai, inhabited by the Israelites at the time of the Exile. Possibly a site about 7 miles (11 km) NW of Hebron [**V**, C2]. Ezra. 2:29; Neh. 7:33.

NEGEV [NEG-ev; "dry"] "South," KJV; Negeb, RSV. [**I**, D1; **V**]. The S desert region of Palestine, forming a large triangle which stretches from the Gulf of Aqabah in the S to Gaza on the W and the Dead Sea on the E. It is crossed by important trade routes to Arabia and Egypt, and was historically an area of copper mining and smelting activities.

Settlement in the Negev has fluctuated sharply throughout history, extending back to Paleolithic times. During the Patriarchal period, there is evidence that a flourishing society arose in the area around Beersheba, completely destroyed in the 19th century B.C. The Negev was inhabited by the Amalekites at the time the Israelites arrived in the land during the Exodus. Allotted to Judah, much of the region was given to the Simeonites. In post-exilic times, the Nabateans resettled the Negev in large numbers, creating a semi-urban civilization there that lasted through NT times. Gen. 13:1-3; 24:62; Josh. 15:19,21; Jdg. 1:9; 1 Sam. 27:10; 30; Ps. 126:4.

NEIEL [nee-IE-uhl] A town on the E border of Asher, probably a site about 8.5 miles (14 km) E of Acco [**I**, A1]. Josh. 19:27. Possibly same as Neah.

NEPHTOAH [nef-TOH-uh; "an opening"] The site of a spring located on the border between Judah and Benjamin. Generally identified with the modern village of Lifta, about 2.5 miles (4 km) NW of Jerusalem [**VII**, C1]. Josh. 15:9; 18:15.

NETAIM [neh-TAY-uhm; "plants," KJV.] A place in Judah occupied by royal potters. 1 Chr. 4:23.

NETOPHAH [neh-TOH-fuh] A village of Judah, located about 2.5 miles (4 km) SE of Bethlehem [**VII**, C1]. Its inhabitants were called the Netophathites (see 2 Sam. 23:28,29; 1 Chr. 2:54). Ezra 2:22; Neh. 7:26.

NEZIB [NEE-zib] A town in the foothills of Judah, located about 7 miles (11 km) NW of Hebron [**VII**, C1]. Josh. 15:43.

NIBSHAN [NIB-shan] A town in the desert of Judah, W of the Dead Sea. Several sites SE of the Jerusalem hills have been suggested. Josh. 15:62.

NICOPOLIS [nih-KAHP-oh-lis; "city of victory"] **XIII**, B3. The capital of Epirus in W Greece, situated on a peninsula in the Gulf of Arta. Located at the site of his military encampment prior to the battle at Actium, 4 miles (6.5 km) to the N, Augustus built the city to celebrate his victory over Mark Antony in 31 B.C. Tit. 3:12.

NILE* [NILE] "River" or "brooks," KJV. [**II**; **III**, A1-E1; **IX**]. Great river of Egypt that flows nearly 2500 miles (4000 km) N from its beginning at Lake Victoria in central Africa to the Mediterranean Sea. In the OT Hebrew, it is called simply "the river." Gen. 41:1-32; Ex. 2:3-10; 7:15–8:11; Isa. 19:7,8.

NIMRAH [NIM-ruh] Shortened form of Beth Nimrah. Num. 32:3.

NIMRIM [NIM-rim; possibly "basins of clear water"] The waters of Nimrim, mentioned by the prophets in conjunction with the overthrow of Moab. It is generally identified with the Wadi en-Numeirah, about 10 miles (16 km) S of the Dead Sea. Isa. 15:6; Jer. 48:34.

NINEVEH* [NIN-uh-vuh] **II**, B5; **IX(a)**. Ancient city founded by Nimrod in N Mesopotamia, and capital of the Assyrian Empire 705–612 B.C. It was to Nineveh that God sent the prophet Jonah, to warn the people of the city's impending destruction. The people repented, forestalling the overthrow of Nineveh for nearly two centuries.

The impressive ruins of Nineveh lie on the E bank of the Tigris, identified with the associated tells of Kuyunjiq and Nebi Yunus ("Prophet Jonah") in N Iraq. Occupied from prehistoric times, it became an alternative royal residence to Asshur and Calah by the reign of Tiglath-Pileser I (1114–1076 B.C.). Following the death of Sargon II, Sennacherib rebuilt Nineveh and made it capital of all Assyria. The Assyrian Empire reached its greatest extent under the kings who ruled from Nineveh, and with its fall to the Babylonians in 612 B.C., the empire was brought to an end. Nineveh has remained a ruin to this day. Gen. 10:11; 2 Ki. 19:36; Jon. 3; 4:11; Nah. 1–3.

NOB [NAHB] **X**, A2. A priestly city in Benjamin where David sought aid during his flight from Saul. Because they helped the fugitive David, Saul slaughtered the chief priest, Ahimelech, the 85 priests of Nob, and their entire households. The town, located 2.5 miles (4 km) N of Jerusalem, was reinhabited after the Exile. 1 Sam. 21:1-9; 22:6-19; Neh. 11:32; Isa. 10:32.

NOBAH [NOH-buh]
1. Name given to Kenath, after the Manassite leader who captured the city. Num. 32:42. *See* Kenath.
2. A place lying W of the caravan route used by Gideon to launch a surprise attack upon the Midianite army at Karkor. It is presumably located in Gilead, in the vicinity of Jogbehah. Jdg. 8:11.

NOD [NAHD; "wandering"] An unknown land E of Eden, to which Cain was banished after the murder of Abel. A region of nomadic habitation seems to be suggested. Gen. 4:16.

NOPHAH [NOH-fuh] "Fire spread," RSV. A place in Moab, within the kingdom of Sihon the Amorite in the time of Moses. Location unknown. Num. 21:30.

O

OBOTH [OH-bahth; "waterskins"]. A place between Punon and Iye Abarim, where the Israelites encamped during their wilderness wanderings. Possibly Ain el-Weiba, located in the Arabah, roughly 35 miles (56 km) S of the Dead Sea. Num. 21:10,11; 33:43,44.

OLIVES, MOUNT OF. Also Olivet, KJV. [**XII**, C3]. Central summit of a N-S ridge of hills, lying just E of Jerusalem, across the Kidron Valley. It rises to a height of 2660 ft. (811 m), and was once covered with dense olive groves. It played an important role in the last week of Christ's ministry. He entered Jerusalem by the road that descended the mount; here, the crowds spread their garments before him, praising God at the coming of the Messiah. Later, in the Garden of Gethsemane, located on its W slope, Christ was betrayed. A secondary summit of the Mount of Olives is traditionally identified as the site of Christ's ascension. 2 Sam. 15:30; Zech. 14:4; Lk. 19:28-44; 21:37-39; Acts 1:12.

ON [AHN; "sun"] **II; III**, C1. An ancient Egyptian city situated in the Nile Delta, about 19 miles (31 km) N of Memphis. From early times, it was the cult center of Re, the sun god. The pharaohs of Egypt adorned the temple of Re with numerous obelisks, monolithic pillars terminating in a pyramidal point. Jeremiah referred to these when he prophesied that Nebuchadnezzar would "demolish the sacred pillars" of On (Jer. 43:13). Only one remains standing today to mark the site of the ruined temple of the sun-god. Gen. 41:45,50. Also called Heliopolis.

ONO [OH-noh] **X**, A1. A town in the territory of Dan, given to Benjamin because it was rebuilt by Shemed the Benjamite. It was reoccupied after the Exile. Identified with Kefr Ana, located in the plain, about 6 miles (10 km) SE of Joppa. 1 Chr. 8:12; Ezra 2:33; Neh. 6:2; 11:35.

OPHEL [OH-fel; "hill"] **XII**, C3. A hill NE of the City of David, situated on the SE corner of ancient Jerusalem. The construction of Jerusalem undertaken by Jotham and Manasseh placed Ophel within the city's walls. The hill now lies outside the SE corner of modern Jerusalem. 2 Chr. 27:3; 33:14; Neh. 11:21.

OPHIR [OH-fuhr; "rich"] A country from which Solomon obtained large amounts of gold and other exotic goods. Ophir's location is uncertain, possibly to be identified with Oman in SE Arabia or Somaliland on the E coast of Africa. 1 Ki. 9:28; 10:11; Job 22:24; Ps. 45:9.

OPHNI [AHF-ni] A city of Benjamin, located about 3 miles (5 km) NW of Bethel [**V**, C2]. Its name was changed to Ophnah sometime after the Exile. Josh. 18:24.

OPHRAH [AHF-ruh; "fawn"]
1. A town of Benjamin, identified with et-Tayibeh, on a high hill about 6 miles (9.5 km) S of Shiloh [**VI**, D3]. Josh. 18:23; 1 Sam. 13:17. The same as Ephron in 2 Chr. 13:19, and possibly the same as Ephraim in Jn. 11:54.
2. Ophrah of the Abiezrites, a town of Manasseh notable as the home of Gideon. He raised an altar here after the angel of God appeared to him, and later Gideon's ephod was put in the city. Possibly the ancient mound at Afula, located about 4 miles (7 km) NW of Jezreel [**VIII**, B2], or et-Tayibeh, midway between Mt. Tabor and Beth Shan [**XI**, C3]. Several sites have been suggested. Jdg. 6:11,24; 8:27; 9:5.

OREB [OR-eb; "raven"] A rock near Beth Barah, named after the Midianite leader who was put to death here in the time of Gideon. Jdg. 7:25.

P

PADDAN [PAD-uhn] Shortened form of Paddan Aram in Gen. 48:7.

PADDAN ARAM [PAD-uhn AIR-uhm; "plain of Aram"] **II**, B4-B5. The region in N Mesopotamia surrounding Haran, between the Habor River and the upper course of the Euphrates. Jacob lived there while he was with Laban. Gen. 25:20; 28:2-7. Identical to Aram Naharaim.

PAMPHYLIA [pam-FIL-ee-uh] **XIII**, B5-C6. A small lowland region in S central Asia Minor, extending along the Mediterranean coast about 75 miles (120 km) and encompassing territory up to 30 miles (48 km) inland, to the Taurus Mountains. It is bounded by Cilicia to the E, Lycia to the SW, and Pisidia to the N. In NT times, it was part of the Roman province of Galatia, until A.D. 43, when Claudius formed the province of Lycia-Pamphylia. Its capital was Perga. Acts 13:13; 14:24; 15:38.

PAPHOS [PAF-ohs] **XIII**, C6. Two cities in SW Cyprus were known by this name, distinguished as Old and New Paphos. Old Paphos, an ancient Phoenician city, lay about 10 miles (16 km) SE of New Paphos, the city mentioned in Acts. New Paphos was the center of Roman rule on Cyprus, which was annexed in 58 B.C. Modern Baffa. Acts 13:6,13.

PARAH [PAIR-uh; "cow"] A town of Benjamin, identified with Farah, about 5 miles (8 km) N of Jerusalem [**VII**, C1]. Josh. 18:23.

PARAN [PAIR-uhn]
1. [**I**; **III**, C4]. A desert region of uncertain boundaries, located in the E central part of the Sinai Peninsula. It was bounded on the E by the Arabah and the Gulf of Aqabah. At its N extreme, it overlapped the Wilderness of Zin, and Kadesh Barnea was included within both regions. During the Exodus, the Israelites twice camped in this wilderness after leaving Mt. Sinai. Gen. 21:21; Num. 10:12; 12:16; 1 Ki. 11:18. *See* El Paran.
2. Mt. Paran; possibly a peak in the rugged range W of the Gulf of Aqabah. Deut. 33:2; Hab. 3:3

PARVAIM [par-VAY-uhm] A place from which Solomon imported gold for the Temple. Possibly Farwa in Yemen or Sak el-Farwein in S Arabia. 2 Chr. 3:6.

PAS DAMMIM [pas DAM-im; "place of bloodshed"] Place where the Philistines gathered to fight the Israelites under David. 2 Sam. 23:9 *See* Ephes Dammim.

PATARA [PAT-uh-ruh] **XII**, C5. A seaport of SW Lycia, near the mouth of the Xanthus. Its position made the port a useful starting point for sea passage to Phoenicia or Egypt. It was famous for its oracle of Apollo. Acts 21:1.

PATHROS [PATH-rohs] The Hebrew name for Upper Egypt, the territory of the Nile River Valley S of the delta, between Cairo and Aswan. After the fall of Jerusalem, some Jews fled to Pathros to form a Jewish colony (Jer. 44:1,15). The Pathrusim, mentioned in Gen. 10:14, were apparently its ancient inhabitants. Ezek. 29:14; 30:14.

PATMOS [PAT-muhs] **XIII**, B4. A small rocky island lying off the SW coast of Asia Minor, about 35 miles (56 km) W of Miletus, used by the Romans as a place of exile for criminals. The apostle John was banished to this island about A.D. 95, and wrote the Book of Revelation during the months he lived here. Modern Patino. Rev. 1:9.

PAU [POW] Pai, KJV, RSV (1 Chr. 1:50). Royal city of Hadad, a pre-Israelite King of Edom. Location unknown. Gen. 36:39.

PEKOD [PEE-kahd; sounds like "punishment"] A small Aramean tribe in S Babylonia, E of the lower Tigris. Referred to in Assyrian records as the *Puqudu*, they were a subject state of Assyria during the 8th–7th centuries B.C. Jer. 50:21; Ezek. 23:23.

PELUSIUM [peh-LOO-se-uhm; "city of mud"] Sin, KJV. Greek name for the Egyptian city of Sin. Identified with the site of a fortress, located about a mile (1.5 km) from the Mediterranean in the NE Nile Delta. Ezek. 30:15,16

PENIEL [peh-NIE-uhl; "face of God"] Penuel, KJV, RSV except Gen. 32:30. [**VI, VIII**, B2]. A place in the Transjordan E of Succoth where Jacob wrestled with the angel of God. Gideon destroyed the tower built at Peniel, after the townspeople refused to supply his men with provisions. Jeroboam later rebuilt the city. Peniel is possibly to be identified with a site located on the Jabbok, about 4 miles (6.5 km) E of Succoth. Gen. 32:30,31; Jdg. 8:8,17; 1 Ki. 12:25.

PEOR [PEE-or; "opening"] A mountain in Moab, near the town of Baal Peor. It was a high peak located N of the Dead Sea, opposite Jericho, from which Balaam could view the encampment of the Israelites. Exact site uncertain. Num. 23:28; 25:18; Josh. 22:17. *See* Baal Peor; Beth Peor.

PERATH [PEER-ath] Euphrates, KJV, RSV. A place where Jeremiah was instructed to go and hide in a crevice in the rocks. Jer. 13:4-7. Possibly the same as the Euphrates.

PERAZIM [PAIR-uh-zim; "breaches"] A mountain of Palestine mentioned in Isa. 28:21. Probably the same as Baal Perazim in 2 Sam. 5:20.

PEREZ UZZAH [PAIR-ez UZ-uh; "breach of Uzzah"] Name given to the place where Uzzah was struck dead upon touching the ark of the covenant. Located between Jerusalem and Kiriath Jearim [**VI**, D3], the exact site is unknown. 2 Sam. 6:8; 1 Chr. 13:11.

PERGA [PER-guh] **XIII**, B5. The principal city of the Roman province of Pamphylia, in S. Asia Minor. It was situated on the River Cestris about 8 miles (13 km) from the Mediterranean. The origin of the city is uncertain, but at some point it was colonized by the Greeks and thereafter became a worship center of Artemis. Acts 13:13,14; 14:25.

PERGAMUM [PER-guh-mum] Pergamos, KJV. [**IX; XIII**, B4]. A city in Mysia, located in the Caicus Valley about 15 miles (24 km) from the Aegean Sea. In the 3rd century B.C., it became the capital of the kingdom of Pergamum, which was bequeathed to Rome in 133 B.C. Thereafter, Pergamum became the chief city of the Roman province of Asia, and was the center of a complex of pagan cults, particularly emperor worship. For this reason, Revelation calls Pergamum the place "where Satan has his throne." Rev. 1:11; 2:12-17.

PERSIA* [PER-zhuh] **IX**. A country inhabited by an Indo-European tribe that migrated S from the hills of Russia, entering the Iranian plateau by the beginning of the 1st millennium B.C. By the 7th century B.C. they had established a kingdom, known as Persis, with its capital at Anshan, NW of Susa. It was bounded on the W by Elam, on the E by Carmania, on the N by Media, and on the S by the Persian Gulf.
Cyrus II of Persia became king at Anshan in 559 B.C. Nine years later, he conquered Ecbatana, and killed Astyages, king of Media. Successively subjecting Anatolia and Lydia, Cyrus moved on Babylon, and in 539 B.C., with the fall of Babylon, he established the Persian Empire, which would remain the premier world power until its defeat by Alexander the Great in 331 B.C. At its greatest extent, the Persian Empire stretched from Thrace and Libya in the W to the Indus River in the E—a territory almost 3000 miles (4800 km) in width. To the N, it bordered the Black Sea, the Caucasus Mountains, the Caspian and Aral seas. N to S, its longest expanse reached nearly 1500 miles, from the Jaxartes River to the Arabian Sea. 2 Chr. 36:20-23; Ezra 1,4; Esth. 1:1-3; Dan. 8:20; 10:13,20.

PETHOR [PEE-thor; "soothsayer"] A city in N Mesopotamia, in which Balaam lived. Identified with the Pitru of Hittite texts, it was located on the Sajur near where it joins the Euphrates. Num. 22:5; Deut. 23:4.

PHARPAR [FAR-par] A river of Damascus, possibly the present-day Awaj, which flows E from its source on the E slopes of Mt. Hermon, and passes about 10 miles (16 km) S of Damascus [**VII**, B2] before emptying into the Lake Bahret Hijaneh. 2 Ki. 5:12.

PHILADELPHIA [FIL-uh-DEL-fee-uh; "brotherly love"] **XIII**, B5. A city of Lydia, named after Attalus II Philadelphus, king of Pergamum (159–138 B.C.). Situated on the Cogamus River, a tributary of the Hermus, it lies in an area of frequent seismic activity. The city was devastated by an earthquake in A.D. 17, and tormented by recurrent quakes for

some time thereafter. Philadelphia was the site of one of the seven churches of Asia. Modern Alasehir. Rev. 3:7-13.

PHILIPPI [FIL-ih-pie] **XIII**, A4. In NT times, a Roman colony and chief city of a district of Macedonia, in N Greece. It is strategically situated on the Egnatian Way, in the plain E of Mt. Pangaeus. Its harbor, Neapolis, is located on the coast of the Aegean 8 miles (13 km) to the S.
Originally known as Krenides, the city was captured and fortified by Philip of Macedon about 360 B.C., and renamed for him. It was annexed by Rome in 168 B.C. and in 42 B.C. the famous battle of Philippi took place just W of the city, in which Antony and Octavian (later Augustus Caesar) overcame the forces of Brutus and Cassius. Visited by Paul on his second missionary journey, it was the first European city to receive the Gospel of Christ. Acts 16:12; 20:6; Phil. 1:1; 1 Th. 2:2. See Philippians.

PHILISTIA [fih-LIS-tee-uh] **VII**, C1; **VIII**. The plain extending S of Mt. Carmel along the Mediterranean coast in S Palestine. It was the nucleus of the territory inhabited by the Philistines, containing the five principal cities of the Philistines: Gaza, Ashkelon, Ashdod, Ekron, and Gath. Ex. 15:14; Ps. 60:8; Isa. 11:14; Joel 3:4. See Philistines.

PHOENICIA* [fih-NEE-shuh] Phenice, KJV; Canaan, KJV, RSV (Isa. 23:11). [**VII**, B1-B2, **VIII**]. The territory inhabited by the Phoenicians, NE of Palestine. It encompassed the territory from the Lebanon Range and Upper Galilee to the Mediterranean, and extended from Mt. Carmel to Arvad. Phoenicia is referred to in the OT by the name of its principal city-states, Sidon and Tyre. Mk. 7:26; Acts 11:19. See Phoenicians.

PHOENIX [FEE-niks] Phenice, KJV. [**XIII**, C3]. A town and harbor on the S coast of Crete, identified with modern Loutro, W of Fair Havens. However, there is some difficulty with this identification, since Loutro faces E, and Luke describes the harbor as "facing both southwest and northwest." The W bay opposite Loutro once offered more shelter than it now does, and it still retains the name of Phineka. Acts 27:12.

PHRYGIA [FRIJ-ee-uh] **IX**, B2. An inland territory of SW Asia Minor. Under the Romans, portions of Phrygia were within the imperial provinces of Asia and Galatia. Acts 16:6; 18:23.

PI HAHIROTH [PIE huh-HIE-ruhth] Last campsite of the Israelites before they crossed the Red Sea during the Exodus. Described as "between Migdol and the sea," its exact location is unknown. Ex. 14:2,9; Num. 33:7,8.

PIRATHON [PEER-uh-thahn] Hometown of Abdon, an Ephraimite judge of Israel. Possibly modern Ferata, located about 7.5 miles (12 km) W of Shechem [**V**, B2]. Jdg. 12:13,15.

PISGAH [PIZ-guh; "cleft"] A peak or ridge in the mountains of Abarim, located in Moab near the NE shore of the Dead Sea. Its wider usage probably refers to the entire ridge of the Abarim Mountains; as a particular peak, it is probably to be identified with Ras es Siyaghah, slightly lower and just NW of Mt. Nebo [**IV**, D1]. Num. 21:20; 23:14; Deut. 3:27; 34:1; Josh. 13:20.

PISHON [PIE-shahn] Pison, KJV. One of the four rivers of Eden, said to flow through the entire land of Havilah. Its location is much disputed. Gen. 2:11.

PISIDIA [pih-SID-ee-uh] A small province in S central Asia Minor, bounded by Lycaonia to

the N and E, Pamphylia to the S, and Asia to the N and W. A mountainous and lawless region, it was incorporated into the Roman province of Galatia. Acts 14:24.

PISIDIAN ANTIOCH [pih-SID-ee-uhn AN-tee-ahk] See Antioch 2.

PITHOM [PIE-thuhm; "mansion of the god Atum"] **III**, B2. A store city in Lower Egypt, built by the Israelites during their years of slavery in Egypt. Located in the vicinity of Rameses, some believe Pithom to be the sacred name of Succoth, while others identify Pithom with Tell er-Rataba, about 10 miles (16 km) W of Succoth (shown on map). Ex. 1:11.

PONTUS [PAHN-tuhs; "sea"] **XIII**, A5-A6. A province in N Asia Minor, situated on the S shore of the Black Sea, or Pontus Euxinus. A rugged region of mountain ranges broken by deep valleys, W Pontus was combined with Bithynia to form a Roman province following the defeat of the kingdom of Mithridates in 63 B.C.. Aquila was among the Jews native to Pontus. Acts 18:2, 1 Pet. 1:1.

PTOLEMAIS [TAHL-uh-MAY-is] **XI**, B2. A seaport in N Palestine, between Tyre and Caesarea. Acts 21:7. See Acco.

PUNON [POO-nahn] **III**, B5. A place in the wilderness where the Israelites camped shortly after leaving Sinai. Probably to be identified with modern Feinan, a copper mining site E of the Arabah, about 25 miles (40 km) S of the Dead Sea. Num. 33:42,43.

PUT [PUT] Often Libya, KJV. A nation in Africa associated with Egypt and Ethiopia. Probably a reference to certain tribes of Libya. Jer. 46:9; Ezek. 30:5; 38:5; Nah. 3:9.

PUTEOLI [POOT-ee-OH-lee; "little wells"] **XIII**, A1. An important seaport on the W shore of S Italy, located on the N side of the Bay of Naples. Modern Pozzuoli. Acts 28:13.

R

RAAMAH [RAY-uh-muh; "trembling"] A tribe or region in SW Arabia, whose merchants traded with Tyre. Ezek. 27:22.

RABBAH [RAB-uh; "great" or "citadel"] Rabbath, KJV (Deut. 3:11).
1. [**IV; VI; VII**, C2; **VIII**]. The capital city of Ammon, known as "Rabbah of the Ammonites." Situated on the King's Highway, at the headwaters of the Jabbok River, it is now known as Amman, the capital of Jordan. First mentioned as the resting place of King Og's iron bedstead, David later besieged and captured the city in his war against the Ammonite king Hanun, consigning its inhabitants to forced labor. Rabbah regained its independence during the divided kingdom, and several prophecies against the city and its people appear thereafter in the oracles of the prophets. Conquered and rebuilt by Ptolemy II Philadelphus (285–246 B.C.), Rabbah was renamed Philadelphia, and after the Roman conquest it became a member of the Decapolis. Deut. 3:11; Josh. 13:25; 2 Sam. 11:1; 12:26-31; Jer. 49:2,3.
2. A town in the hill country of Judah, mentioned with Kiriath Jearim. Site uncertain. Josh. 15:60.

RABBITH [RAB-ith; "great"] A town of Issachar, possibly modern Rama, about 7 miles (11 km) N of Tirzah [**V**, B2]. Josh. 19:20.

RACAL [RAY-kuhl; "trade"] Rachal, KJV. A town in S Judah to which David sent plunder from Ziklag. 1 Sam. 30:29. Possibly the same as Carmel 2.

RAKKATH [RAK-uhth] A fortified city of Naphtali, on the W shore of the Sea of Galilee, between Hammath and Kinnereth. Traditionally identified with Tiberias, it is more likely an ancient site less than 2 miles (3 km) N of Tiberias [**XI**, B3]. Josh. 19:35.

RAKKON [RAK-ahn] A town in the territorial inheritance assigned to Dan, possibly a site about 6 miles (9.5 km) N of Joppa [**VI**, D2]. Josh. 19:46.

RAMAH [RAH-muh; "height"] Ramath, KJV (Jos. 19:8).
1. A city assigned to Benjamin. It was fortified by Baasha, king of Israel, but immediately torn down by King Asa, who used its building stones and timber to build up Geba and Mizpah. Here, Nebuzaradan gathered the Israelite captives after the fall of Jerusalem. He released Jeremiah before taking the rest of his prisoners into exile. It was later resettled by Jews who returned to Judah from Babylon. Probably er-Ram, located about 6 miles (10 km) N of Jerusalem [**VII**, C1]. Josh. 18:25; 1 Ki. 15:17-22; Neh. 11:33; Jer. 40:1.
2. A town of Simeon, in the extreme S of Judah, also called Baalath Beer. Site unknown. Josh. 19:8. The same as Ramoth Negev, in 1 Sam. 30:27.
3. A border town of Asher, possibly Ramiyeh, about 13 miles (21 km) SE of Tyre [**VII**, B1], although this identification is disputed by many. Josh. 19:29.
4. A fortified town of Naphtali, probably to be identified with a site near the modern village of er-Rama, situated on a pass through the mountains of Galilee about 16 miles (26 km) E of Acco [**I**, A1]. Josh. 19:36.
5. The hometown of Samuel in Ephraim. 1 Sam. 1:19; 8:4; 19:19-23. Called Ramathaim in 1 Sam. 1:1. See Arimathea.
6. Shortened form of Ramoth Gilead. 2 Ki. 8:29; 2 Chr. 22:6.

RAMATHAIM [RAH-muh-THAY-uhm] Ramathaim-zophim, KJV, RSV. Alternate form of Ramah 2 in 1 Sam. 1:1. See Arimathea.

RAMATH LEHI [RAY-muhth LEE-hie; "heights of the jawbone"] Place in Judah where Samson threw away the jawbone with which he had killed a thousand Philistines. Jdg. 15:17. See Lehi.

RAMATH MIZPAH [RAY-muhth MIZ-puh; "heights of the watchtower"] Ramath Mizpeh, KJV. A border town of Gad E of the Jordan. Probably the same as Mizpah 5, about 15 miles (24 km) NW of Rabbah [**VII**, C2]. Josh. 13:26. See Ramoth Gilead.

RAMESES [RAM-zeez; "estate of Rameses"] Raamses, KJV, RSV (Ex. 1:11).
1. The "land of Rameses" refers to the district in the E Nile Delta where the city of Rameses was later built (see 2). Here Jacob and his household settled. Gen. 47:11. See Goshen.
2. [**III**, B2]. A store city in the Nile Delta, on which the Hebrew slaves labored prior to the Exodus. Its site was previously identified with Tanis, but it has been rejected in favor of Qantir, located 19 miles (30 km) S of Tanis. It is presumed to be identical to Pi-Ramesse, the royal residence of Ramesses II, Pharaoh of Egypt during the 13th century B.C. Many scholars use this to support a late date for the Exodus; however, the name may be used retrospectively, as in 1. Recent excavation has also uncovered occupation at Rameses, as well as Tell er-Retabah (a probable location of biblical Pithom), from the period of the 18th Dynasty (about 1550–1300 B.C.). Ex. 1:11; 12:37.

RAMOTH [RAY-mahth; "heights" or "high places"]
1. Shortened form of Ramoth Gilead. Deut. 4:43; 2 Ki. 8:29.
2. A Levitical city in Issachar. 1 Chr. 6:73. Called Remeth in Josh. 19:21, and Jarmuth in Josh. 21:29.

RAMOTH GILEAD [RAY-muhth GIL-ee-ad; "heights of Gilead"] **VII**, C2; **VIII**. A chief fortified city of Gad, designated as a city of refuge by Moses. It was the administrative center of one of Solomon's twelve districts. After the division of Israel, Ramoth Gilead, located near the border of Israel and Aram, became a prize between the two nations and changed hands several times. King Ahab was slain trying to recapture Ramoth Gilead, and his son was likewise wounded in an attempt to take the city. Several sites have been suggested for Ramoth Gilead, such as the site of Ramath Mizpah, but Tell Ramith is preferred. 1 Ki. 22; 2 Ki. 8:28–9:14.

RAMOTH NEGEV [RAY-muhth NEG-ev; "heights of Negev"] "South Ramoth," KJV. Ramoth of the Negeb, RSV. See Ramah 2.

RECAH [REE-kuh] Rechah, KJV. A town of Judah, location unknown. 1 Chr. 4:12.

RED SEA.* [**IX**, C3]. In modern geography, a narrow sea that divides NE Africa from Arabia, and extends SSE about 1300 miles (2100 km), from Suez to the Gulf of Aden. It forms part of the great rift valley that runs along the Jordan and Lebanon valleys. The two N branches of the Red Sea are known as the Gulf of Suez and the Gulf of Aqabah, to the W and E of the Sinai Peninsula, respectively.

In the OT, the term "yam suph" is translated Red Sea, but it is now generally recognized by scholars to be a derivation of the Egyptian word for papyrus, and should be translated as the "sea of reeds." As such the term is applicable to any body of water producing the papyrus reeds common to the Egyptian delta region. Accepting the traditional route of the Exodus, yam suph indicates the Bitter Lakes region between the Gulf of Suez and the Nile Delta. Lake Timsah, Menzaleh, and Sirbonis have also been proposed as the Reed Sea crossed by the Israelites during the Exodus. The latter is to be rejected since it lies along the way to the land of the Philistines (see Ex. 13:17,18). Its wider use extended to the gulfs of the Red Sea as well. Ex. 10:19; 13:17–15:22; 23:31; Num. 14:25; 21:4; 1 Ki. 9:26.

REHOB [REE-hahb; "open place"]
1. The N limit reached by the spies who searched out the land of Canaan. Num. 13:21; 2 Sam. 10:8. It is identical to Beth Rehob.
2. A border town in N Asher, possibly in the vicinity of Aczib. Josh. 19:28.
3. Another town of Asher, possibly located on the plain about 5 miles (8 km) E of Acco [**I**, A1]. The site with which it is identified was a very large Bronze Age city, and shows Phoenician and Asherite occupation during the Iron Age. Josh. 19:30. Either 2 or 3 was given to the Gershonite Levites (Josh. 21:31).

REHOBOTH [reh-HOH-buhth; "open places"]
1. A well dug by Isaac in the Valley of Gerar, generally identified with Ruheibeh, about 19 miles (31 km) SW of Beersheba [**I**, C1]. Gen. 26:22.
2. Native city of the Edomite king Shaul, located "on the river," probably indicating it was on the banks of the Zered, the N boundary of Edom. Gen. 36:37.

REHOBOTH IR [reh-HOH-buhth EER; "open places of the city"] An unidentified city built by Nimrod in Assyria. It is possibly another name for Asshur. An alternate reading interprets the name as a description rather than a proper noun, referring to the city squares of Nineveh. Gen. 10:11.

REKEM [REK-uhm; "friendship"] A town of Benjamin, location uncertain. Josh. 18:27.

REMETH [REM-uhth; "height"] A town in the territory of Issachar. Josh. 19:21. See Jarmuth and Ramoth 2.

REPHAIM [REF-ay-uhm; "giants"] A fertile valley SW of Jerusalem and NW of Bethlehem, where David defeated the Philistines. Josh. 15:8; 2 Sam. 5:18,22; Isa. 17:5.

REPHIDIM [REF-ih-dim] **III**, D3. A place where the Israelites camped between the Desert of Sin and Mt. Sinai. The people complained because no water was available there, so God instructed Moses to strike the rock and bring forth water. The place was thereafter named Massah and Meribah. Following this event, Joshua met the Amalekites in battle at Rephidim, securing victory with divine aid. Possibly located at Wadi Refayid or Wadi Feiran, NW of Jebel Musa, the traditional site of Mt. Sinai. Ex. 17:1-16; 19:2; Num. 33:14,15.

RESEN [REE-zuhn] A city built by Nimrod in N Mesopotamia, between Calah and Nineveh. Site uncertain. Gen. 10:12.

REUBEN [ROO-ben] **VI**, D4-D5. The territorial inheritance of Reuben, E of the Jordan, S of Gad, and N of the Arnon River. It was a region well suited to the pastoral life-style of the Reubenites. In the time of Saul, they joined the Gadites and Manassites in their assault on the Hagrites to the E of Gilead, but by the time of Moabite incursion into Reubenite territory under Mesha, the tribe was apparently much diminished in strength. The Moabite Stone celebrating Mesha's conquests in the region mentions Gad but contains no reference to Reuben. The remaining Reubenites were deported with the other tribes of the Transjordan by Tiglath-Pileser III of Assyria. Josh. 13:15-23; 1 Chr. 5:10,18-22,25,26.

REZEPH [REE-zef] A Syrian city defeated by the Assyrians. It was an important caravan center between the Euphrates and Hamath. Identified with modern Rasafa, located W of the Euphrates, about 125 miles (200 km) E of Hamath [**VII**, A2]. 2 Ki. 19:12.

RHEGIUM [REE-jee-uhm; "break"] **XIII**, B1. A port located at the S tip of Italy, opposite Messina in Sicily. A Greek colony founded in 720 B.C., Rhegium was a safe haven in the difficult waters of the strait. It was common to wait in port for a favorable S wind before attempting passage. Modern Reggio. Acts 28:13.

RHODES [ROHDZ; "rose"] **XIII**, C4-C5. A large island in the Aegean, 10 miles (16 km) off the SW coast of Asia Minor. The island is about 42 miles (68 km) long and 15 miles (24 km) wide, lying on the main sea route from Greece to Syria and Palestine. The city of Rhodes was situated on the NE corner of the isle. The famous Colossus of Rhodes stood at the entrance to its harbor. The huge bronze statue of Apollo was among the seven wonders of the ancient world.

After the conquests of Alexander opened up the E to trade, Rhodes became the leading Greek republic. The city cultivated a cooperative relationship with Rome during its rise to power, and was given territory in Caria and Lycia. Rhodes later fell from favor with Rome, resulting in the loss of its mainland dependents and the declaration of Delos as a free port. This effectively destroyed Rhodes's economic ascendancy, and by NT times its importance was gone. Ezek. 27:15; Acts 21:1.

RIBLAH [RIB-luh]
1.   A place on the E boundary of the land of Canaan. Num. 34:11.
2.   [**VII**, B2; **IX**] A Syrian city in the land of Hamath, near the headwaters of the Orontes River, on the main route from Egypt to the Euphrates. It was a stronghold of Pharaoh Neco after his defeat of Josiah at Megiddo. At Riblah, he deposed Jehoahaz and appointed Jehoiakim king of Judah in his place. When Nebuchadnezzar crushed the Egyptians at Carchemish in 605 B.C., he established a military base here as well. Following the failure of his rebellion against Babylon, Zedekiah was blinded and his sons were executed at Riblah. Identified with the modern village of Ribleh, located about 50 miles (80 km) S of Hamath. 2 Ki. 23:33; Jer. 52:9,10,26,27. Possibly the same as Diblah in Ezek. 6:14.

RIMMON   [RIM-ahn;   "pomegranate"] Remmon-methoar, KJV (Josh. 19:13).
1.   A town in the S of Judah, allotted to the Simeonites. Identified with Khirbet er-Ramamim, about 10 miles (16 km) N of Beersheba [**I**, C1]. Josh. 15:32; 19:7; 1 Chr. 4:32. *See* En Rimmon.
2.   A border town of Zebulun, possibly to be identified with a site about 6.5 miles (10 km) N of Nazareth [**XI**, B2]. Josh. 19:13. Probably the same as Dimnah in Josh. 21:35 and Rimmono in 1 Chr. 6:77.
3.   A rocky hill near Gibeah where 600 Benjamites took refuge for four months. Probably to be identified with the limestone outcropping upon which the modern village of Rammon is situated, about 3.5 miles (5.5 km) E of Bethel [**V**, C2]. Jdg. 20:45,47; 21:13.

RIMMONO [rih-MOH-noh] A Levitical city of Zebulun. 1 Chr. 6:77. *See* Rimmon 2.

RIMMON PEREZ [RIM-ahn PAIR-ez; "pomegranate of the pass"] Rimmon-parez, KJV. A campsite of the Israelites during the Exodus. As the name suggests, it was probably a pass between cliffs where pomegranate trees grew. Possibly modern Nakt el-Biyar, W of Elath [**III**, C4]. Num. 33:19,20.

RISSAH [RIS-uh; "ruins" or "dew"] A campsite of the Israelites during the Exodus. Site uncertain. Num. 33:21,22.

RITHMAH [RITH-muh] A place where the Israelites encamped after leaving the Desert of Sinai, located between Hazeroth and Rimmon Perez. Site unknown. Num. 33:18,19.

ROGELIM [ROH-guh-lim] A town in Gilead, possibly located about 25 miles (40 km) N of Mahanaim [**I**, B2]. Hometown of Barzillai the Gileadite. 2 Sam. 17:27; 19:31.

ROME [ROHM] **XIII**, A1. Notable as the capital city of the Roman Empire, situated at the first ford from the mouth of the Tiber River, halfway up the W coast of Italy. Traditionally founded on the Palatine Hill in 753 B.C., it grew to encompass the seven hills of Rome. It was ruled by kings until 510 B.C., after which a republic was established, lasting until 31 B.C., when Augustus Caesar became its first emperor. Augustus began massive reconstructions on Rome in the 1st century A.D., and claimed to have "found the city built of brick and left it built of marble." The magnificent and elaborately constructed temples and public buildings of Rome contrasted sharply with the crowded multi-story tenements that housed the general populace, whose numbers exceeded 1 million by NT times.
In the 3rd century B.C., Rome began the expansion which would, over the next three centuries, unite most of the civilized world under a single government. When Jesus was born in Bethlehem, Judea was but a tiny district in the huge Roman Empire, stretching from Hispania (modern Spain and Portugal)

to the Caspian Sea. Although the empire created by Rome provided an ideal condition for the rapid spread of Christianity, it also fostered idolatry and, under Nero and later emperors, persecuted the early church. As a result, the city became a symbol of paganism and worldly power in opposition to the Gospel of Christ (*compare* Rev. 17,18). Acts 18:2; 25:25; 28:14-16; Rom. 1:7,15. *See* Roman Empire.

RUMAH [ROO-muh] Hometown of Zebidah, the mother of Jehoiakim. Possibly Khirbet al-Rumah, about 6.5 miles (10 km) N of Nazareth [**XI**, B2]. 2 Ki. 23:36.

S

SALAMIS [SAL-uh-mis] **XIII**, C6. A large port city on the E coast of Cyprus, with a large Jewish population and several Jewish synagogues in NT times. According to tradition, Barnabas was stoned to death in Salamis during the reign of Nero. Acts 13:4.

SALECAH [SAL-uh-kuh] **VII**, C2. Salcah and Salchah, KJV. A city marking the E extreme of the Bashan, within the territory of Manasseh E of the Jordan. At some later point, it became the N limit of the land inhabited by the Gadites. Identified with modern Salkhad, on the S slopes of the Hauran. Deut. 3:10; Josh. 12:5; 1 Chr. 5:11.

SALEM [SAY-luhm; "peace"] **I**, C1. City ruled by the priest-king Melchizedek, near the Valley of Shaveh. Usually identified with ancient Jerusalem. Gen. 14:18; Ps. 76:2; Heb. 7:1,2.

SALIM [SAY-lim; "peace"] A place near the waters of Aenon, where John the Baptist baptized. Jn. 3:23. *See* Aenon.

SALMONE [Sal-MOH-nee; "peace"] A promontory at the E shore of Crete, now known as Cape Sidero. Acts 27:7.

SALT, CITY OF. *See* City of Salt.

SALT SEA. OT name for the saltwater lake into which the Jordan River empties in S Palestine. The mineral content of its waters is too high to support life, and for this reason the lake has been commonly known as the Dead Sea since the 2nd century A.D. The great rift valley, which runs along a geologic fault from Syria to Nyasa Lake in E Africa, reaches its lowest point at the surface of the sea, averaging about 1400 ft. (427 m) below sea level. The maximum depth of the Salt Sea is about 1420 ft. (433 m) at the SE corner, below the mountains of Moab. Gen. 14:3; Num. 34:3,12; Deut. 3:17. *See* Dead Sea; Kinnereth 1.

SALT, VALLEY OF. A valley in which both David and Amaziah defeated the Edomites in battle. Possibly a plain S of the Dead Sea, or the Wadi el-Milh just E of Beersheba [**VI**, E2]. 2 Sam. 8:13; 2 Ki. 14:7.

SAMARIA [suh-MAIR-ee-uh; "watch-tower"]
1.   [**VIII**; **X**, A2; **XI**]. The capital of the northern kingdom from 879 B.C. It was built by Omri on a high hill commanding the major N-S route through Palestine. He spent six years on the construction of his new capital, continued by Ahab, who built a temple to the Sidonian god Baal-Melqart for Jezebel, and expanded and beautified the palace. Excavations at Samaria have uncovered Ahab's palace "inlaid with ivory" (1 Ki. 22:39), a well-crafted two-story

structure, with hundreds of ivory plaques and fragments in an adjacent storeroom. During Ahab's reign, Ben-Hadad of Aram unsuccessfully assaulted Samaria. In 722 B.C., the city finally fell to the Assyrians after a three-year siege, bringing to an end Israel's existence as an independent nation.
Its people were deported, after which the city was rebuilt and placed under an Assyrian governor. In Nehemiah's time, its Persian governor was Sanballat, who opposed the rebuilding of Jerusalem's walls. Alexander the Great conquered Samaria in 332 B.C., during his conquest of Palestine.
It became a large fortification in Maccabean times, subsequently destroyed by John Hyrcanus. Herod the Great extensively rebuilt the city, and changed its name to Sebaste. Within the city, he constructed a magnificent pagan temple, dedicated to Augustus. Samaria is the traditional site of John the Baptist's tomb. 1 Ki. 16:24-32; 20:1–22:40; 2 Ki. 6:20–7:20; 17:1-6.
2.   [**X**; **XI**, C2-D2]. An alternate name for the kingdom of Israel, after the capital city founded by Omri. Following the fall of the northern kingdom in 722 B.C., Samaria became a district in central Palestine, S of Galilee and N of Judea. It covered a territory of about 40 miles (64 km) in length and 35 miles (56 km) in width, extending from Bethel and Beth Horon in the S to Mt. Carmel and the Jezreel Valley in the N, and from the Jordan to the coastal plain. 1 Ki. 18:2; 2 Ki. 17:24-29; Ezra 4:17; Lk. 17:11; Acts 8:1-14. *See* Samaritans.

SAMGAR [SAM-gar] Samgar-nebo, KJV, RSV. The hometown of Nergal-Sharezer, as translated in the NIV. Samgar is treated as part of the name of a Babylonian officer in the KJV and RSV. Some take it to be the title of Nergal-Sharezer. Jer. 39:3.

SAMOS [SAM-ohs; "lofty"] An island in the Aegean Sea, about 1 mile (1.5 km) off the coast of SW Asia Minor. Colonized by the Ionians in the 11th century B.C., it became a prosperous and important maritime city-state. Under the Romans, Samos was part of the province of Asia until it gained its freedom from Augustus in 17 B.C. Acts 20:15.

SAMOTHRACE [SAM-oh-thrays] **XIII**, A4. A small mountainous island located in the Aegean, about 31 miles (50 km) off the S coast of Thrace. Center of a mystery cult of the Cabiri, twin fertility gods of ancient origin. Acts. 16:11.

SANSANNAH   [san-SAN-uh;   "palm branch"] A town in the S of Judah. Possibly a site about 10 miles (16 km) NE of Beersheba [**I**, C1]. Josh. 15:31. Probably the same as Hazar Susah.

SARDIS [SAR-dis] **XIII**, B5. A city in the province of Asia, situated on a spur of Mt. Tmolus above the Hermus Valley, at the junction of the royal highways linking Ephesus, Pergamum, and Smyrna with central Asia Minor. It was the Lydian capital under Croesus, who became legendary for his wealth, largely derived from the gold in the Pactolus, a river which flowed through the city. In a surprise attack, Cyrus the Persian conquered the heavily fortified city, about 549 B.C. Sardis fell again in 214 B.C., this time to the Romans, who used similar tactics in their assault. Under Roman rule the city declined, and its devastation in an earthquake in A.D. 17, sealed the fate of the once great city; Sardis never recovered. The church in Sardis apparently shared in the character of the city, relying on its past reputation but inwardly decaying. Rev. 1:11; 3:1-5.

SARID [SAIR-id; "survivor"] A village on the boundary of Zebulun, probably modern Tell Shadud, about 5 miles (8 km) SW of Nazareth [**XI**, B2]. Josh. 19:10,12.

SEBA [SEE-buh] A land inhabited by the Sabeans (Isa. 45:14), and closely related to Sheba. Its site is uncertain, possibly a site in SW Arabia or in E Africa, on the shore of the Red Sea. Ps. 72:10; Isa. 43:3.

SEBAM [SEE-buhm] Shebam, KJV. Alternate form of Sibmah, in Num. 32:3.

SECACAH [see-KAY-kuh] A town in the desert of Judah, possibly one of several proposed sites W of the Dead Sea, near the Valley of Achor. Josh. 15:61.

SECU [SEE-koo] Sechu, KJV. A village with a large cistern, near Ramah 1. Site uncertain. 1 Sam. 19:22.

SEIR [SEER]
1. [**I**, D2]. A mountainous region E of the Arabah, ranging in elevation from about 600 to 6000 ft. (180 to 1800 m) above sea level. Inhabited by the Horites, Esau—also called Edom—settled here, and the land later became known as Edom, after the patriarch. Gen. 14:6; 33; 36; Deut. 2.
2. A mountain ridge on the border of Judah, W of Kiriath Jearim. Josh. 15:10.

SEIRAH [SEER-uh; possibly "wooded"] Seirath, KJV. A place in the hill country of Ephraim to which Ehud escaped after killing Eglon, king of Moab. Jdg. 3:26.

SELA [SEE-luh; "rock" or "cliff"]
1. A place on the border of Amorite territory in the time of the Judges. Site uncertain. Jdg. 1:36.
2. [**VII**; **VIII**, D2]. The capital of Edom, conquered by Amaziah and renamed Joktheel. Traditionally identified with the Iron Age ruins built on the rock formation known as Umm el-Biyyara, which rises 1000 ft. (305 m) above the Nabatean city of Petra (shown on map). More recently proposed as the ancient site is modern es-Sela, about 2.5 miles (4 km) NW of Bozra. 2 Ki. 14:7; Isa. 16:1; 42:11.

SELA HAMMAHLEKOTH [SEE-luh huh-MAH-leh-kahth; "rock of parting"] A crag near the Desert of Maon, where Saul broke off his pursuit of David. 1 Sam. 23:28.

SELEUCIA [suh-LOO-see-uh] **XIII**, C7. The port of Syrian Antioch, situated on the coast about 5 miles (8 km) N of the mouth of the Orontes. Founded by Seleucus Nicator in 301 B.C., it changed hands several times between the Seleucids and Ptolemies over the next two centuries. When Pompey established the Roman province of Syria in 64 B.C., he made Seleucia a free city. Strategically located, it became the base of Rome's Syrian fleet. With Barnabas, Paul sailed from Seleucia to nearby Cyprus on their first missionary journey, and in all probability, he used the port on several other occasions, although the city is not specifically named (see Acts 14:26; 15:30,39). Acts 13:4.

SENEH [SEE-nuh] A cliff S of the mountain pass between Micmash and Geba, about 7 miles (11 km) NE of Jerusalem [**VII**, C1]. It was opposite the cliff called Bozez. 1 Sam. 14:4.

SENIR [suh-NEER] Also Shenir, KJV. The Amorite name for Mt. Hermon, possibly referring to a specific peak in the mountain range. Deut. 3:9; Song 4:8; Ezek. 27:5.

SEPHAR [SEE-far] A place in the Table of Nations, marking the E limit of the region inhabited by the sons of Joktan. Presumably located in S Arabia, the exact site is unknown. Gen. 10:30.

SEPHARAD [seh-FAR-ad] A place to which Jews from Jerusalem were exiled. Possibly Shaparda, a country allied to Media, in the annals of Sargon II; or more likely, a reference to Sardis, capital of Lydia, which had a large Jewish community in Persian times, when it was known as Sfarda. Obad. 20. See Sardis.

SEPHARVAIM [SEF-ar-VAY-uhm] A city conquered by the Assyrians, who deported its inhabitants to Samaria. Previously thought to be Sippar in Babylonia, it is now believed to be a Syrian city, possibly Shabara, between Damascus and Hamath [**VII**, A2]. The latter identification better fits the context of Rabshaka's speech. 2 Ki. 17:24,31; Isa. 37:13.

SHAALABBIN [SHAY-uh-LAB-in; "haunt of foxes"] A town in Dan, W of Jerusalem. Josh. 19:42. Same as Shaalbim.

SHAALBIM [SHAY-al-bim; "haunt of foxes"] An Amorite city in the territory of Dan, later included within Solomon's second administrative district. Identified with modern Selbit, about 3 miles (5 km) NW of Aijalon [**VI**, D2]. Jdg. 1:35; 1 Ki. 4:9. Called Shaalabbin in Josh. 19:42.

SHAALIM [SHAY-uh-lim] Shalim, KJV. A district Saul traversed in search of his father's donkeys. 1 Sam. 9:4.

SHAARAIM [SHAY-uh-RAY-uhm] Sharaim, KJV (Jos 15:36).
1. A town in the W foothills of Judah. The Valley of Elah (modern Wadi es-Sant) down which the Philistines fled, from Azekah toward Gath, was called the Shaaraim road, suggesting a position of the town somewhere along this valley. The site is unidentified. Josh. 15:36; 1 Sam. 17:52.
2. Alternate form of Sharuhen in 1 Chr. 4:31.

SHAHAZUMAH [SHAY-huh-ZOO-muh] Shahazimah, KJV. A town on the N border of Issachar, possibly located about 5 miles (8 km) SE of Mt. Tabor [**VI**, B3]. Josh. 19:22.

SHALISHA [shuh-LISH-uh; "the third"] Shalishah, RSV. A region in or near the hill country of Ephraim through which Saul passed in search of his father's donkeys. 1 Sam. 9:4. Possibly the same as Baal Shalishah, in 2 Ki. 4:42.

SHALLEKETH [SHAL-uh-keth] Shallecheth, KJV, RSV. The W gate of the temple of Solomon at Jerusalem. 1 Chr. 26:16.

SHAMIR [shah-MEER]
1. A town in the hill country of Judah, probably a site about 13 miles (21 km) SW of Hebron [**V**, C2]. Josh. 15:48.
2. A town in the hill country of Ephraim, where the judge Tola lived and was buried. Its location is unknown; some identify it with the ancient site of Samaria [**X**, A2]. Jdg. 10:1,2.

SHAPHIR [shah-FEER; "pleasant"] A city against which Micah prophesied. Probably located in SW Palestine, its exact site is uncertain. Mic. 1:11.

SHARON [SHAIR-uhn; "plain"(?)] Largest coastal plain of Palestine, stretching about 50 miles (80 km) from Mt. Carmel to the vicinity of Joppa [**VI**, D2]. The lowland region was renowned in ancient times for its beauty and fertility. 1 Chr. 27:29; Isa. 33:9; 35:2; Song 2:1; Acts 9:35.

SHARUHEN [shuh-ROO-hen] An ancient town in SW Palestine, assigned to the Simeonites. Generally identified with a site about 15 miles (24 km) S of Gaza [**VI**, E1]. Josh. 19:6. Probably the same as Shaaraim in 1 Chr. 4:31, and Shilhim in Josh. 15:32.

SHAVEH [SHAY-vuh; "plain"] A valley near Salem (that is, Jerusalem) where Abram met the king of Sodom after defeating Kedorlaomer. Possibly the broad upper section of the Valley of Hinnom [**XII**, D2]. Gen. 14:17.

SHAVEH KIRIATHAIM [SHAY-vuh KEER-ee-uh-THAY-uhm; "the plain of Kiriathaim"] A plain in the Transjordan near the city of Kiriathaim in Moab. Kedorlaomer defeated the Emites here. Gen. 14:5.

SHEBA [SHEE-buh; "oath"]
1. According to the NIV translation, a shortened form of Beersheba. Josh. 19:2.
2. A mountainous country in SW Arabia. Sheba became a commercial power through caravan trade in the exotic goods of Arabia. In the 10th century, the queen of Sheba journeyed to Jerusalem to test the wisdom of Solomon, and very likely to obtain a trade agreement from the Israelite king. 1 Ki. 10:1-13; Job 6:19; Ezek. 27:22,23.

SHECHEM [SHEK-uhm; "shoulder"] **I**, B1; **V**; **VI**; **VIII**; **X**, A2. An ancient and important fortified city, situated between Mt. Ebal and Mt. Gerizim at the intersection of the major trade routes through central Palestine. Abram built his first altar at Shechem, and when Jacob returned to Canaan from Haran, he settled down there, buying property outside the town. There followed the incident in which Dinah was defiled by Shechem, the Hivite prince, and in revenge the Shechemite men were slaughtered by Levi and Simeon.

At the time of the conquest, it was allotted to Ephraim, and was made a city of refuge. At Shechem, Joshua led Israel in the covenant renewal, with the Israelites gathered on the opposing mountains of Ebal and Gerizim. During the period of the Judges, Abimelech established himself as king of Shechem after slaying his 70 brothers. When the Shechemites later rebelled, Abimelech destroyed the city, and burned down the temple-tower of Baal-Berith, in which the town's citizens had taken refuge.

Shechem became the first capital of the northern kingdom, but the capital was moved shortly thereafter. The city was destroyed by the Assyrians, and remained little more than a village for several centuries. Sometime after the Exile it was rebuilt, and became a chief Samaritan center before its destruction by John Hyrcanus, about 108 B.C. Near the site of Shechem, Jesus met the Samaritan woman, by Jacob's well. Today, the village of Nablus lies near the ancient ruins. Gen. 12:6,7; 34; 37:12-16; Josh. 24; Jdg. 9; 1 Ki. 12:25.

SHEMA [SHEE-muh; "fame; rumor"] A town in the S of Judah, located in the Negev. Josh. 15:26.

SHEN [SHEN; "tooth" or "pointed"] Jeshanah, RSV. A place near which Samuel raised a monument. 1 Sam. 7:12. See Jeshanah 1.

SHEPHAM [SHEF-uhm] A place on the E border of the Promised Land, between Hazar Enan and Riblah. Exact site unknown. Num. 34:10,11.

SHEPHER [SHEF-er; "beauty"] Shapher, KJV. A mountain where the Israelites camped during the Exodus. Site uncertain. Num. 33:23,24.

SHESHACH [SHEE-shak] A cryptogram for Babylon in Jer. 25:26; 51:41.

SHIBAH [SHEE-buh; "oath" or "seven"] Shebah, KJV. A well dug by Isaac, from which the town of Beersheba derived its name. Gen. 26:33.

SHIHOR [SHIE-hor] Usually Sihor, KJV. A river marking the SW boundary of Palestine, E of Egypt. Possibly the River of Egypt (modern Wadi el Arish) or more likely an E branch of the Nile. Josh. 13:3; 1 Chr. 13:5; Jer. 2:18.

SHIHOR LIBNATH [SHIE-hor LIB-nath] A stream on the SW boundary of Asher. Possibly the Nahr ez-Zerqa, which flows into the Mediterranean S of Mt. Carmel. Josh. 19:26.

SHIKKERON [SHIK-uh-rahn] Shicron, KJV. A place on the N boundary of Judah, between Ekron and Mt. Baalah. Probably a site located about 11 miles (18 km) SE of Ashdod [**VI**, D2]. Josh. 15:11.

SHILHIM [SHIL-him] A town in the S of Judah. Josh. 15:32. See Sharuhen.

SHILOAH [shie-LOH-uh; "sent"] An open water channel that flowed along the SE slopes of Jerusalem, carrying water from the spring of Gihon to the lower pool of Siloam. It predated the construction of the tunnel made by Hezekiah. Isa. 8:6. See Siloam.

SHILOH [SHIE-loh] **V**; **VI**, D3. A city in Ephraim, notable as the worship center of Israel during the period of the Judges. After the initial conquest of Canaan, Joshua gathered the Israelites at Shiloh and set up the tabernacle. It housed the ark of the covenant until its capture by the Philistines in the time of Samuel. Consequently, Shiloh's importance as a religious center waned. By the time of Jeremiah, Shiloh had fallen into ruins, only sparsely inhabited. Its modern name is Seilun. Josh. 18:1-10; 22:12; Jdg. 18:31; 1 Sam 1:24; 4:4; 1 Ki. 14:2-4; Ps. 78:60; Jer. 7:12-14.

SHIMRON [SHIM-rahn; "guard"] **V**, B2. A Canaanite royal city in N Palestine, defeated by Joshua, and later allotted to Zebulun. Possibly to be identified with Semuniyeh, located about 6 miles (10 km) W of Nazareth [**XI**, B2]. Josh 11:1; 19:15. Called Shimron Meron in Josh. 12:20.

SHIMRON MERON [SHIM-rahn MEER-ahn] See Shimron.

SHINAR [SHIE-nar] The plains containing the great cities of Babylon, Erech, Akkad, and Calneh. Identified with the land of S Mesopotamia, later known as Babylonia or Chaldea. Gen. 10:10; 11:2; 14:1,9.

SHION [SHIE-ahn] Shihon, KJV. A border town of Issachar, possibly to be identified with a site about 3 miles (5 km) NW of Mt. Tabor [**VI**, B3]. Josh. 19:19.

SHITTIM [SHI-tim; "acacia trees"] **III**; **IV**, D1. Shortened form of Abel Shittim; it was the last campsite of the Israelites before crossing the Jordan into the Promised Land. Num. 25:1; Josh. 2:1; Mic. 6:5.

SHOA [SHOH-uh] A nation allied with the Babylonians and Assyrians against Judah in the prophecy of Ezekiel. Possibly to be identified with the Sutu in Assyrian documents, a Semitic tribe which migrated from the Syrian desert to the area E of Baghdad [**II**, C6]. Ezek. 23:23. See Koa.

SHUAL [SHOO-uhl; "fox"] A town or district in the vicinity of Ophrah. 1 Sam. 13:17.

SHUNEM [SHOO-nuhm] A city allotted to the tribe of Issachar, located about 3 miles (5 km) N of Jezreel [**VIII**, B2], near Mt. Gilboa. It was the home of the Shunammite woman whose son Elisha raised from the dead. Josh. 19:18; 1 Sam 28:4; 2 Ki. 4:8.

SHUR [SHOOR; "wall"] **III**, B2-C3. A wilderness region in NW Sinai, through which passed the way of Shur, a caravan route from S Palestine to Egypt. Gen. 20:1; Ex. 15:22; 1 Sam. 15:7; 27:8.

SIBMAH [SIB-muh] Shibmah, KJV (Num. 32:35). A town in the Amorite kingdom of Sihon, captured by the Israelites and allotted to the tribe of Reuben. It was later taken by Moab. Usually identified with a site about 3 miles (5 km) W of Heshbon [**IV**, D1]. Num. 32:38; Josh. 13:19; Isa. 16:8,9. Called Sebam in Num 32:3.

SIBRAIM [sib-RAY-uhm; "twofold hope"] A place on Ezekiel's N boundary of Canaan, between Damascus and Hamath. Site uncertain. Ezek. 47:16.

SIDDIM [SID-im; "salt" or "tilled fields"] A fertile valley probably located at the S end of the Dead Sea, and possibly now submerged by the sea's S extension, below the Lisan Peninsula. Described as "full of tar pits," it was the battleground where the forces of the cities of the plain were defeated by Kedorlaomer and his allies. Gen. 14:3-10.

SIDON [SIE-duhn] **II**; **VII**, B1; **VIII**; **IX**; **XIII**. The earliest and most prominent Phoenician port city, founded on the coast of Lebanon, about 25 miles (40 km) N of Tyre. In the late 2nd millennium B.C., Sidon overcame its Egyptian dependency and became a wealthy seafaring kingdom, establishing colonies as far distant as Malta. Its early preeminence among the cities of Phoenicia was such that in the OT "Sidonian" was used to indicate all Phoenicia.

Sidon became a corrupting religious influence from the time the Israelites settled in Canaan. Ethbaal, king of Sidon, was the father of Jezebel. Her marriage to King Ahab proved disastrous, resulting in the slaughter of Yahweh's priests and institutionalization of Baal and Ashtoreth worship throughout Israel.

Sidonian expansion was halted with the rise of Assyrian power, after which followed centuries of subjugation and revolt, in which the city was destroyed and rebuilt several times. Under the Romans, Sidon was given local autonomy, which continued into NT times. Gen. 10:19; Jdg. 1:31; 10:6; Ezek. 28:21-25; Mt. 11:21,22; 15:21-28. See Phoenicians.

SILLA [SIL-uh] An unknown place near Beth Millo, where Joash king of Judah was assassinated. 2 Ki. 12:20.

SILOAM [sih-LOH-uhm; "sent"]
1. [**XII**, D3]. A pool at the S end of the City of David, originally fed by an open channel (the "waters of Shiloah" in Isa. 8:6), which brought water S from the spring of Gihon. Later, Hezekiah blocked the Gihon spring, diverting its flow into an underground water tunnel and upper pool he constructed. Thereafter, the lower pool apparently served as a reservoir for the overflow from Hezekiah's newer pool (modern Birket Silwan). By Christian times, the name Siloam had become transferred to the upper pool as well; it is uncertain to which pool Christ directed the blind man. Neh. 3:15; Jn. 9:7,11.
2. A tower on the Ophel ridge near the pool of Siloam. Lk. 13:4.

SIMEON [SIM-ee-uhn; "hearing"] **VI**, E1-F2. A tribe of Israel given land in the extreme S of Judah. Beersheba, Ziklag, and Hormah were among the cities within its territory. Josh. 19:1-9; Jdg. 1:1-3,17.

SIN [SIN; "clay"] A desert between Elim and Mt. Sinai. Ex. 16:1; Num. 33:11,12.

SINAI [SIE-nie]
1. [**III**, B3-E4]. The triangular peninsula formed by the gulfs of Aqabah and Suez, through which the Israelites traveled during the Exodus. The Sinai Peninsula extends about 150 miles (241 km), from the Egyptian frontier to SW Canaan, and stretches about 250 miles (400 km) from the Mediterranean to the S tip of the peninsula. Little settlement took place in Sinai, although it was extensively

mined by the Egyptians from the 3rd millennium onward. Ex. 19:1,2; Num. 1:1; Jdg. 5:5.
2. [**III**, D3]. "The mountain of God" upon which God gave Moses the Ten Commandments. Jebel Musa is the preferred site, following a tradition that dates back about 1500 years. Several other mountains have been proposed, but with little in general to recommend them. Ex. 19:3-25; 34; Gal. 4:24,25. See Horeb.

SINIM [SIN-im] A region from which scattered Israelites would be gathered. Probably to be identified with Aswan [**IX**, C2]. Isa. 49:12. See Aswan.

SIPHMOTH [SIF-mahth; "fruitful"] An unidentified town in the S of Judah, to which David sent some of the plunder from the Amalekites who destroyed Ziklag. 1 Sam. 30:28.

SIRAH [SEE-ruh] A well near Hebron. Probably Ain Sarah, located about 1.5 miles (2.5 km) NW of Hebron [**V**, C2]. 2 Sam. 3:26.

SIRION [SEER-ee-ahn; "breastplate"] Name given to Mt. Hermon by the Sidonians, and probably used to indicate the entire Anti-Lebanon range. Deut. 3:9; Ps. 29:6.

SITNAH [SIT-nuh; "opposition"] Second well dug by Isaac in the Valley of Gerar; he abandoned it after a dispute in which the herdsmen of Gerar claimed it as their own. Site uncertain. Gen. 26:21.

SIYON [SIE-yuhn; "lofty"] Sion, KJV; Sirion, RSV. A name for Mt. Hermon; probably a form of the Phoenician name, Sirion. Deut. 4:48.

SMYRNA [SMUHR-nuh; "myrrh"] **XIII**, B4. A port city in the Roman province of Asia, at the head of the gulf into which the Hermus River empties. An early Greek colony of great prosperity, it was referred to in ancient times as the "first of Asia." Destroyed by the Lydians in 627 B.C., it virtually ceased to exist for three centuries until it was refounded and "came to life again" (see Rev. 2:8). Its resurgence was facilitated by alliance with Rome and, under the Roman Empire, Smyrna once again achieved prominence. It became a center of Caesar worship, a cult responsible for much of the persecution of the early church. The "crown of Smyrna," possibly a reference to the magnificent public buildings that encircled the summit of Mt. Pagos, is well-known from literary sources, and is alluded to by John. Rev. 1:11; 2:8-11.

SOCO [SOH-koh; "brambles"]
1. A city of Judah founded by Heber. 1 Chr. 4:18.
2. A city in Judah fortified by Rehoboam. 2 Chr. 11:7. Possibly the same as Socoh 1 or 2.
3. A city of Judah, captured by the Philistines during the reign of King Ahaz. 2 Chr. 28:18. The same as Socoh 1.

SOCOH [SOH-koh; "brambles"]
1. A city in the W foothills of Judah, located SW of Azekah [**V**, C1]. In the time of Saul, it was captured by the Philistines, who encamped between Socoh and Azekah before the battle in which David slew Goliath. Josh. 15:35; 1 Sam. 17:1.
2. A town in the hill country of Judah, identified with a site 10 miles (16 km) SW of Hebron [**V**, C2]. Josh. 15:48.
3. [**VI**, C2]. A city in one of Solomon's administrative districts; identified with present-day Tell er-Ras, in the Plain of Sharon, about 10 miles (16 km) NW of Samaria. 1 Ki. 4:10.

SODOM [SAH-duhm] **I**, C2. The most frequently mentioned of the five cities of the plain, situated in the fertile, well-watered Valley of Siddim. The cities of the plain rebelled and were conquered by a coalition of kings led by the Elamite Kedorlaomer. Lot, who had settled at Sodom, was taken captive, but was rescued by Abraham.

Sodom was notorious for its immorality; only Lot and his family were delivered from the fiery destruction which God brought upon Sodom and the entire region.

Located in the vicinity of the Dead Sea, the exact site of Sodom is uncertain. Many scholars believe the cities of the plain are now submerged beneath the shallow S end of the Dead Sea. It is an area abounding in salt, bitumen, and sulfur, which figure in the destruction described in Genesis. Recent exploration of the area has found no evidence of the cities.

Five sites SE of the Dead Sea have also been proposed as the biblical cities of the plain. Bordering the Arabah, each of the five sites is situated beside a flowing spring, and dates from the late 3rd millennium B.C. Several of the sites were destroyed in a conflagration that has left a thick layer of ash over the surface of the ruins. One of the sites, Safi, is identified as Zoar on the Medeba Map, from the 6th century A.D. Gen. 14; 18:16-30; Mt. 11:23,24.

SOLOMON'S COLONNADE. A double porch at the E end of the Jerusalem Temple's outer court. Only the platform upon which it was constructed survives today. Jn. 10:23; Acts 3:11; 5:12.

SOREK [SOR-ek; "vine"] A valley in which Delilah lived. Identified with the Wadi es-Sarar, which runs from W of Jerusalem to the Mediterranean, S of Joppa. Jdg. 16:4.

SPAIN [SPAYN] The large peninsula of Europe at the W end of the Mediterranean, first colonized by the Phoenicians, and then by the Greeks. Carthage gained a foothold in Spain, which was used by Hannibal as a launching platform for his invasion of Italy in the Second Punic War. Rome eventually extinguished the Carthaginian presence in Spain, after which it remained a part of the Roman Empire. It is uncertain whether Paul's plan to reach Spain in his missionary journeys ever materialized. Rom. 15:24.

SUCCOTH [SUK-ahth; "shelters"]
1. [III, B2]. The first stopping place of the Israelites after their departure from Rameses during the Exodus. Possibly to be identified with Tell el-Maskhuta in the Wadi Tumilat. Ex. 12:37; 13:20. Identified by some with Pithom.
2. [I, B2]. An ancient town E of the Jordan where Jacob built a house for himself and his livestock. It was later assigned to the tribe of Gad and, in the time of the Judges, its inhabitants denied aid to Gideon and his men. Located in the Jordan Valley near Zarethan, it is possibly to be identified with Deir Alla. Gen. 33:17; Josh. 13:27; Jdg. 8:5-16.

SUPH [SOOF] Red Sea, KJV. An unknown place or region opposite the campsite in the Transjordan where Moses explained the Law to the Israelites. Deut. 1:1.

SUPHAH [SOO-fuh] Red Sea, KJV. An unknown place associated with the border of Moab. Num. 21:14.

SUR [SOOR] A gate in the city of Jerusalem, probably leading from the king's palace to the Temple area. The parallel passage in 2 Chr. 23:5 calls it the Foundation Gate. 2 Kl. 11:6.

SUSA [SOO-suh; "lily"(?)] Shushan, KJV. [II, C7; IX]. The ancient capital of Elam, occupied continuously from about 3500 B.C. until its abandonment in the 13th century A.D. In 640 B.C., the city was devastated by Ashurbanipal, who deported some of its inhabitants to Samaria. Susa regained its importance as one of

the capitals of the Persian Empire during the reign of Darius the Great, who built his palace there. This palace became the winter residence of later Persian kings. Its ruins are located in SW Iran, about 150 miles (241 km) N of the Persian Gulf. Ezra 4:9; Neh. 1:1; Esth. 1:2-5; 9:6-18; Dan. 8:2.

SYCHAR [SIE-kar] **XI**, D2. A town in Samaria, located near Mt. Ebal and Mt. Gerizim; not far from this village, Jesus met the woman at Jacob's well. Commonly identified with the modern Arab village of Askar, located about half a mile N of Jacob's well, near Shechem. Jn. 4:5.

SYRACUSE [SEER-uh-kyooz] **XIII**, B1. A Greek city on the island of Sicily, founded in 734 B.C. by Corinthian colonists. A large harbor contributed greatly to its prosperity and, by the end of the 5th century, it was the most prominent city on the island. Acts 28:12.

SYRIA [SEER-ee-uh] **XIII**, C7. The central territory of the Seleucid kingdom, made a Roman province by Pompey in 64 B.C. In NT times, it was bounded by the Taurus Mountains to the N, the upper Euphrates to the E, and extended as far S as the NE Sinai Peninsula, encompassing Palestine. Mt. 4:24; Acts 15:23,41; Gal. 1:21. See Aram.

SYRTIS [SUHR-tis] Name given to the shallow waters of the wide bay on the N coast of Africa. The Greater Syrtis lies W of Cyrene, known today as the Gulf of Sidra. The Lesser Syrtis, to the E of Carthage, is now the Gulf of Gabes. Acts 27:17.

T

TAANACH [TAY-uh-nak] **V**, B2; **VI**. An ancient city whose Canaanite king was defeated by Joshua. It was made a Levitical city of Manasseh, but the Israelites failed to displace the Canaanite inhabitants. The battle in which Deborah and Barak defeated Sisera took place at Taanach. Pharaoh Sheshonq I, the biblical Shishak, captured the city in 926 B.C., during his campaign against Palestine. It was thereafter only sparsely occupied. The ruins of Taanach lie at the S end of the plain of Esdraelon, about 5 miles (8 km) SW of Megiddo. Josh. 12:21; 21:25; Jdg. 5:19; 1 Ki. 4:12.

TAANATH SHILOH [TAY-uh-nath SHIE-loh; "approach to Shiloh"(?)] A border town of Ephraim, W of Micmethath. Possibly to be identified with a site about 7 miles (11 km) SE of Shechem [I, B1]. Josh. 16:6.

TABBATH [TAB-uhth] A place near Abel Meholah, to which Gideon pursued the routed Midianites. Possibly to be identified with Ras Abu Tabat, located E of the Jordan, about 7 miles (11 km) N of Succoth [I, B2]. Jdg. 7:22.

TABERAH [TAB-uhr-uh; "burning"] A place in the Desert of Paran where fire from the Lord consumed some on the outskirts of the Israelite camp as a punishment for their complaints. Num. 11:3; Deut. 9:22.

TABOR [TAY-bor]
1. A Levitical town on the border between Issachar and Zebulun, presumably located on or near Mt. Tabor. Josh. 19:22; Jdg. 8:18; 1 Chr. 6:77.
2. [VI, B3]. A mountain in the Jezreel Valley, rising steeply to a height of about 1900 ft. (580 m) above sea level. Here Barak gathered his army for the battle against Sisera. In Hosea's

time, its summit was the site of an idolatrous shrine, possibly dating back to ancient times. An ancient tradition holds Mt. Tabor as the site of Christ's transfiguration, although this is unlikely. Jdg. 4:6,12,14; Ps. 89:12; Hos. 5:1.
3. The "great tree of Tabor" was a site somewhere in the territory of Benjamin, possibly a well-known sacred tree or grove. It is mistakenly referred to as the "plain of Tabor" in the KJV translation. 1 Sam. 10:3.

TADMOR [TAD-mor] Tamar, RSV (1 Ki. 9:18). [VII, B3; IX]. An oasis town in the Syrian desert on the major trade road from Damascus to Haran. Solomon probably captured the city during his operations in Syria, and fortified it to strengthen his control of the N region of his empire. In later history, it became known to the Greeks and Romans as Palmyra, a wealthy and important commercial center. Excavation has revealed impressive ruins from the Roman period. Known to the Arabs as Tudmur, it is located about 120 miles (193 km) NE of Damascus. 2 Chr. 8:4. There is some question whether the Tadmor of 1 Ki. 9:18 refers to the Syrian city or to Tamar, in SE Judah.

TAHATH [TAY-hath] A desert encampment of the Israelites during the Exodus. Num. 33:26,27.

TAHPANHES [tah-PAN-eez] Also Tehaphnehes, KJV, RSV (Ezek. 30:18). [IX, C2]. An Egyptian fortress city on the E edge of the Nile Delta. Following the fall of Jerusalem and the assassination of Gedaliah, some of the Jews fled to the city, bringing Jeremiah by force. Its site is identified with Modern Tell Dafneh, on the edge of Lake Menzaleh. Jer. 43:7-13; Ezek. 30:18.

TAHTIM HODSHI [TAH-tim HAHD-shee] A town or region in the N of David's kingdom. Following the Septuagint, the RSV translation reads "to Kadesh in the land of the Hittites," a reference to Kadesh on the Orontes [VII, B2]. 2 Sam. 24:6.

TAMAR [TAY-mar; "palm tree"] A place at the SE corner of Palestine in Ezekiel's prophecy. Identified with the Roman Thamara, modern Kurnub, about 20 miles (32 km) SW of the Dead Sea, on the road between Hebron and Elath. Ezek. 47:18,19; 48:28. See Tadmor.

TAPPUAH [TAP-yoo-uh]
1. A town in the foothills of Judah, possibly located about 4 miles (6.5 km) N of Hebron [V, C2]. Josh. 12:17; 15:34. It may be the same as Beth Tappuah.
2. A town on the N boundary of Ephraim, possibly modern Sheikh Abu Zarad, about 8 miles (13 km) S of Shechem [I, B1]. Josh. 16:8; 17:8.

TARALAH [TAR-uh-luh; "strength"] A town allotted to the tribe of Benjamin, possibly located about 5 miles (8 km) N of Jerusalem [VII, C1]. Josh. 18:27.

TARSHISH [TAR-shish] The name in a generic sense is conected to metals and their refining; its use in the OT refers to a distant land rich in metals. Most scholars identify the name with Tartessus, a city in SW Spain, possibly located near the mouth of the Baetis River, an area rich in silver, copper, and lead. The biblical references speak frequently of the "ships of Tarshish," which may have been a term applied to the type of deep sea-going vessels used in the transport of refined metals. Ps. 72:10; Jer. 10:9; Ezek 27:12,25; Jon. 1:3; 4:2.

TARSUS [TAR-suhs] **IX; XIII**, B6. An ancient city situated on the banks of the Cydnus River, about 10 miles (16 km) from the coast of SE Asia Minor. The wealth of the city was secured by its position S of the Cilician Gates, a gorge through which passed the great trade route between Syria and Asia Minor. Roman expansion allowed Tarsus to gain a measure of independence under the Seleucids, which led to the subsequent Hellenization of the city. It was made capital of the province of Cilicia about 67 B.C., and became a leading center of Greek learning. In Roman times, its population may have reached 500,000.

Paul was born in Tarsus, among the minority of Jews who held Roman citizenship. It was an ideal environment for his education, where Western culture and learning conjoined with the thought and religion of the East. Acts 9:11,30; 11:25.

TEBAH [TEE-buh] Betah, KJV, RSV (2 Sam. 8:8); Tibhath, KJV, RSV (1 Chr. 18:8). A city in the Aramean kingdom of Zobah, conquered by David. Location unknown. 2 Sam 8:8; 1 Chr. 18:8.

TEKOA [teh-KOH-uh] **VIII; X**, B2. A town in the hill country of Judah, situated on the edge of the Judean Desert. Amos the prophet was a shepherd of Tekoa at the time of his calling. The town was resettled after the Exile. Its ruins are located about 10 miles (16 km) S of Jerusalem. 2 Sam. 14:2-4; 2 Chr. 11:6; Neh. 3:5,27; Amos 1:1.

TELAIM [teh-LAY-uhm; "lambs"] A town where Saul gathered his forces before he attacked the Amalekites, probably situated in the extreme S of Judah. 1 Sam. 15:4. Possibly the same as Telem.

TEL ASSAR [tel AS-uhr; "mound of Asshur"] Thelasar, KJV (2 Ki 19:12). A city inhabited by the "people of Eden," conquered by the Assyrians. Identification uncertain. 2 Ki. 19:12; Isa. 37:12.

TEL AVIV [TEL uh-VEEV] Tel Abib, KJV, RSV. A location in Babylonia, near the Kebar River, where Ezekiel stayed among the Jewish exiles. Not to be confused with the modern city of Tel Aviv in Palestine. Ezek 3:15.

TELEM [TEE-lem; "a lamb"] An unidentified town in the S of Judah. Josh. 15:24. See Telaim.

TEL HARSHA [tel HAR-shuh] Tel-harsa and Tel-haresha, KJV. A Babylonian town where Jews resided in exile. Some of these Jews, upon returning to Jerusalem after the Exile, could not demonstrate their Israelite descent. Ezra 2:59; Neh. 7:61.

TEL MELAH [tel MEE-luh; "hill of salt"] A city in Babylonia mentioned in Ezra 2:59; Neh. 7:61. Possibly located on the low salt tract near the Persian Gulf.

TEMA [TEE-muh; "south"] **IX**, C3. An oasis in NW Arabia, on the intersection of important caravan routes, midway between Damascus and Mecca. Identified with modern Teima, to which Nabonidus retired while his son Belshazzar was regent in Babylon. Job 6:18-20; Isa. 21:14; Jer. 25:23.

TEMAN [TEE-muhn; "south"] An important city in Edom; its inhabitants were known for their wisdom. The prophets declared the coming destruction of Teman in their oracles against Edom. Possibly modern Tawilan, about 3 miles (5 km) E of Petra [**VIII**, D2]; in some instances it may have been used to denote an entire region of Edom. Jer. 49:7,20; Ezek. 25:13; Amos 1:12.

TERAH [TAIR-uh] Tarah, KJV. An Israelite encampment during the Exodus. Num. 33:27,28.

THEBES [THEEBZ; "city of (the god) Amun"] No, KJV. [**IX**, C2]. An ancient city in Upper Egypt, located on both banks of the

Nile, 330 miles (528 km) S of Cairo. It rose to prominence in the early 2nd millennium B.C. From Thebes came the 18th Dynasty kings that expelled the foreign Hyksos and reunited the Egyptian Empire, establishing the age of the New Kingdom. The capital was soon moved back to Memphis, but Thebes remained the S capital of Egypt, and cult center of the god Amun. The magnificent city was sacked in 663 B.C. by the Assyrians, who carried away as plunder the wealth of a thousand years. On the E bank of the Nile was the city proper and the huge temple precincts of the god Amun. On the W bank lay the funerary temples of the kings, and beyond them, the Valley of the Kings, in which the tomb of Tutankhamen was discovered. Jer. 46:25; Ezek. 30:14-16; Nah. 3:8.

THEBEZ [THEE-bez] **VI**, C3. A city in Ephraim, where Abimelech was mortally wounded. Identified with modern Tubas, about 3 miles (5 km) NE of Tirzah, along the road to Beth Shan. Jdg. 9:50; 2 Sam. 11:21.

THESSALONICA [THES-uh-lah-NIE-kuh] **XIII**, A3. The chief city and principal port of Macedonia, located on the Egnatian Way, at the N tip of the Thermaic Gulf. The city was given its freedom for its support of Antony and Octavian during the civil war that followed Julius Caesar's death. This gave the city the right to self-government, among other things. The officials of the city Luke calls "politarchs" in the original text, a term historians once thought to be in error. It has since been confirmed as a common title for magistrates throughout Macedonia. Modern Salonica. Acts 17:1,13; Acts 20:4; Phil. 4:16. See Thessalonians.

THREE TAVERNS. A village at a road junction on the Appian Way, about 33 miles (53 km) S of Rome [**XIII**, A1]. Acts 28:15.

THYATIRA [THIE-uh-TIE-ruh] **XIII**, B4. A city in the Roman province of Asia, on the road from Pergamum to Sardis. For centuries a garrison town, in Roman times it became a busy commercial center, with more trade guilds than have been identified in any other Asian city. Membership in these guilds was essential to social and financial success in the trading community of Thyatira, but often involved acts of pagan worship and immorality. It is likely that the teaching of the woman known as "Jezebel" advocated compromise with the paganism of the city. Acts 16:14; Rev. 2:18-24.

TIBERIAS [tie-BEER-ee-us]
1. An alternate name of the Sea of Galilee, in Jn. 6:1; 21:1.
2. [**XI**, B3]. A city on the W coast of the Sea of Galilee, named in honor of Emperor Tiberius by Herod Antipas, who founded the city about A.D. 21. Tiberias was a popular Roman resort, with hot springs just S of the city. Said to have occupied the site of Rakkath, the town of Naphtali (Josh. 19:35). Jewish rumor held that it was built over a graveyard. Therefore it was declared unclean, and Jews refused to enter the city. Ironically, it became the chief center of rabbinical learning in the centuries following the fall of Jerusalem. Jn. 6:23.

TIGRIS* [TIE-gris] Hiddekel, KJV (Gen. 2:14). [**II**, A5-D7; **IX**]. The lesser of the two great rivers of Mesopotamia, rising in the mountains of Armenia and flowing SE for 1150 miles (1850 km) to join the river Euphrates just 40 miles (64 km) N of the Persian Gulf, into which the combined river empties. A wide and shallow river, it is subject to flooding during the rainy seasons. Its principal tributaries to the E are the Great Zab, the Little Zab, and the Diyala. Nineveh, Calah, Baghdad, and Asshur are among the ancient cities along its banks. Dan. 10:4.

TIMNAH [TIM-nuh; "allotted portion"] Often Timnath, KJV; Timnathah, KJV (Josh. 19:43).
1. A town in the hill country of Judah. Probably the place where Judah went to have his sheep sheared. Identified with present-day Tibneh, about 4 miles (6 km) SE of Beth Shemesh [**VI**, D2]. Gen 38:12-14; Josh. 15:57.
2. A Danite city on the N border of Judah, where Samson's wife lived. It was located in an area of conflict between the Philistines and Israelites. Possibly a site about 5 miles (8 km) S of Gezer [**VII**, C1], although some identify it with the location of 1. Josh. 15:10; Jdg. 14:1-5; 2 Chr. 28:18.

TIMNATH HERES [TIM-nath HEER-ez; "portion of the sun"] A place in the hill country of Ephraim. It was the personal inheritance of Joshua, and became the site of his burial. The name may indicate the site was originally a place of idolatrous worship, perhaps explaining the adoption of a variant form of the name, Timnath Serah. Samaritan tradition identifies its site with Kafr Haris, about 10 miles (16 km) S of Shechem, but modern scholars usually place it at Khirbet Tibneh, about 17 miles (28 km) SW of Shechem [**I**, B1]. Jdg. 2:9.

TIMNATH SERAH [TIM-nath SEER-uh; "extra portion"] Alternate name of the place where Joshua was buried. Josh. 19:50; 24:30.

TIPHSAH [TIF-suh; "ford"]
1. [**VII**, A3]. A city on the NE boundary of Solomon's kingdom, probably Thapsacus, at an important crossing on the middle Euphrates River. This caravan town was situated on the great E-W trade route through the Fertile Crescent. 1 Ki. 4:24.
2. A town apparently near Tirzah whose inhabitants were brutally slaughtered by Menahem. Possibly Tafsah, about 6.5 miles (10.5 km) SW of Shechem [**I**, B1]. 2 Ki. 15:16.

TIRZAH [TEER-zuh] **V**, B2; **VIII**. A Canaanite royal city conquered by Joshua. Tirzah became the capital of the northern kingdom during the latter years of Jeroboam I, and remained so until the sixth year of Omri's reign, after which the capital was transferred to the newly constructed city of Samaria. It is probably to be identified with a site located about 7 miles (11 km) NE of Shechem, where the archaeological data closely corresponds to the biblical chronology of Tirzah. Evidence of habitation at the site dates from the 4th millennium to the 7th century B.C., when the city was destroyed. Josh. 12:24; 1 Ki. 15:21,33; 16:6-23.

TISHBE [TISH-bee] "The inhabitants," KJV; Tishbeh, RSV. [**VIII**, B2]. A town in Gilead, the home of Elijah the prophet. Traditionally identified with el-Istib, about 7.5 miles (12 km) N of the Jabbok, to the W of Mahanaim. 1 Ki. 17:1.

TOB [TAHB; "good"] A fertile district of S Hauran in the Transjordan, between Gilead and the Syrian desert. Jephthah took refuge here from his half-brothers, until he was called to lead Israel against the Ammonites. It may be the Dubu in the Amarna Letters, an Aramean state E of the Jordan. Some associate it with Al-Tabiya, 10 miles (15 km) S of Gadara [**XI**, B3]. Jdg. 11:3-5; 2 Sam. 10:6-8.

TOKEN [TOH-ken; "a measure"] A town in the territory of Simeon. 1 Chr. 4:32.

TOLAD [TOH-lad] A town of Simeon. 1 Chr. 4:29. The same as Eltolad in Josh. 15:30.

TOPHEL [TOH-fuhl] A place in the Arabah, identified by some with the modern Arab village of el-Tafileh, about 14 miles (23 km) SE of the Dead Sea. Deut. 1:1.

TOPHETH* [TOH-feth] Also Tophet, KJV; "a burning place," RSV (Isa 30:33). A place in the Valley of Hinnom [**XII, D2**] where child sacrifices were offered to Molech. Isaiah used Topheth as a symbol of the destruction God would bring upon the Assyrians. Two kings of Judah sacrificed sons at Topheth, Ahaz and Manasseh, before Josiah destroyed the idolatrous site during his religious reforms. 2 Ki. 23:10; Isa. 30:33; Jer. 7:31,32; 19:6-14. *See* Gehenna; Hinnom.

TRACONITIS [TRAK-uh-NIGHT-uhs; "rough region"] A district in the tetrarchy of Philip, bordering on Iturea to the S and Damascus to the N. Identified with modern al-Laja, a plateau of volcanic rock, wild and infertile. According to the Jewish historian Josephus, it was infested with outlaws. Lk. 3:1.

TRANSJORDAN.* A non-biblical term for the plateau region E of the Jordan, the Dead Sea, and the Arabah and W of the Arabian Desert.

TROAS [TROH-az] **XIII, B4.** Originally Alexandria Troas, founded on the coast of Mysia about 300 B.C., following Alexander's conquest of Asia Minor. It became a leading seaport, by NT times known simply as Troas, a name derived from its proximity to the ruins of ancient Troy, about 10 miles (16 km) to the SW.

The apostle Paul visited this important city on several occasions. In Troas, he had the vision of "a man of Macedonia," calling him to preach in Europe. Here also Paul raised Eutychus, who was killed in a fall from a window. Act. 16:8-12; 20:5,6; 2 Cor. 2:12.

TYRE* [TIE-uhr; "rock"] **VI; VII; B1; VIII; XI, A2; XIII.** An ancient and important Phoenician seaport, situated on the coast NW of Palestine, about 5 miles (8 km) S of the Litani River. The city included the mainland port and an island, just offshore.

Tyre may have originated as a Sidonian colony, and for its early history was dominated by the older city. With the decline of Egyptian power over the region, Tyre became an independent maritime state, and came to dominate the Phoenician coast by the time of the Israelite monarchy. Hiram, king of Tyre, was an ally and trading partner of David and Solomon. He rebuilt and fortified Tyre, constructing a large harbor on the S side of the island. The city established colonies as far distant as Spain, and in the 9th century founded the city of Carthage on the N coast of Africa. Tyre came under Assyrian domination for the next two centuries, but by the end of the 7th century it had regained its autonomy. Ezekiel's prophecies against the city date from this time, during which Tyre reached the height of its wealth and power. Not long after, the city fell to Nebuchadnezzar after a 13-year siege, about 587–574 B.C., resulting in the destruction of the mainland city. The island port later fell to Alexander the Great, about 332 B.C., after the construction of a causeway to the island.

The city was rebuilt in Roman times, and Jesus visited the region of Tyre and Sidon during his ministry. A small Christian community had been established there by the time of Paul. Josh. 19:29; 2 Sam. 5:11; 1 Ki. 5; 9:11,12; Isa. 23; Ezek. 26–28; Mk. 7:24-31. *See* Phoenicians.

U

ULAI [YOO-lie] A river or irrigation canal of Elam, near Susa. Classical Greek writers called it Eulaeus, but topographical changes make any modern identification uncertain. It has been suggested that the present-day Lower Karun and Upper Kherbah rivers were once a single stream running into the delta N of the Persian Gulf. Dan. 8:2,16.

UMMAH [UHM-uh] A town in the territory of Asher, near Aphek. Josh. 19:30. Possibly the same as Acco, which later became Ptolamais.

UPHAZ [YOO-faz] A place famous for its fine gold. Perhaps a textual error for Ophir. Jer. 10:9.

UR* [ER] **II, D6; IX.** The native city of Abraham, traditionally identified with Tell el-Muqayyar in S Babylonia. From here, Terah, Abraham's father, moved his family to Haran in NW Mesopotamia. One of the great cities of ancient times, its occupation dates back to about 4000 B.C. Abraham lived there during the period of the Third Dynasty (about 2112–2004 B.C.), when the city was at the height of its power and prosperity. The Third Dynasty ended with the destruction of Ur by foreign invaders, described in an ancient epic poem lamenting the overthrow of the city. Ur was periodically rebuilt over the next two millennia, but never recovered its former glory. It came to be known as "Ur of the Chaldeans" after the Chaldean settlement of S Babylonia at the end of the 2nd millennium B.C. The city was finally abandoned about 300 B.C.

Extensive excavations at Ur have uncovered impressive remains of the ancient city, dominated by the great ziggurat, dedicated to the moon god. Gen. 11:28-31; 15:7; Neh. 9:7.

UZ [UHZ]
1. The land in which Job lived. Traditionally identified with Hauran, E of the Sea of Galilee and S of Damascus. Others support an identification with the region E of Edom in N Arabia. Job 1:1.
2. A land against which Jeremiah prophesied, closely associated with Edom. Jer. 25:20; Lam. 4:21. Possibly the same as 1.

UZZEN SHEERAH [UHZ-uhn SHEER-uh] Uzzen-sherah, KJV. A town established by Sheerah, granddaughter of Ephraim. Located near Upper and Lower Beth Horon, it is probably to be identified with modern Beit Sira, about 13 miles (21 km) NW of Jerusalem [**VII, C1**]. 1 Chr. 7:24.

V

VALLEY GATE. A gate in the SW wall of Jerusalem, opening toward the Valley of Hinnom. Neh. 2:13.

W

WAHEB [WAY-heb] An unknown place near the Arnon River. The KJV translation reads "What he did in the Red Sea" whereas the RSV and NIV render the same "Waheb in Suphah." Num. 21:14.

WATER GATE. A gate of Jerusalem before which the people gathered to hear Ezra read the Law. Located on the E side of Jerusalem, the exact site is uncertain. Neh. 8:1,3.

Y

YAUDI [YAH-oo-dee] Judah, KJV, RSV. A form of Judah in 2 Ki. 14:28.

Z

ZAANAN [ZAY-uh-nan; sounds like "come out"] An unidentified town in the W foothills of Judah. Mic. 1:11. Probably the same as Zenan.

ZAANANNIM [ZAY-uh-NAN-im] Zaanaim, KJV, RSV (Jdg. 4:11). A place on the S border of Naphtali, where Heber the Kenite pitched his tent. Here Jael killed Sisera, the commander of Jabin's army. Possibly to be identified with Khan et-Tuggar, located about 3 miles (5 km) NW of Mt. Tabor [**VI, B3**]. Josh. 19:33.

ZAHAR [ZAY-har; "white"] KJV, RSV. A city that provided Damascus with wool. Ezek. 27:18.

ZAIR [ZAIR; "small" or "narrow"] An unidentified place, where King Jehoram fought the rebelling Edomites. Possibly the same as Zior, although a place in or near Edom seems more likely. 2 Ki. 8:21.

ZALMON [ZAL-muhn; "terrace"(?)] Salmon, KJV (Ps. 68:14).
1. A forested mountain near Shechem where Abimelech and his men gathered wood to burn down the tower of Shechem. Possibly the S peak of Mt. Gerizim, now called Jebel Sulman. Jdg. 9:48.
2. A mountain, perhaps identical to 1, although it is often identified with Mt. Hauran, Jebel ed-Druz. Ps. 68:14.

ZALMONAH [zal-MOH-nuh; "dark"] A desert encampment of the Israelites during their wilderness wanderings. It lay between Mt. Hor and Punon. Num. 33:41,42.

ZANOAH [zuh-NOH-uh]
1. [**X, B1**]. A town in the W foothills of Judah, whose residents rebuilt the Dung Gate after the Exile. Khirbet Zanu, about 2 miles (3 km) SE of Beth Shemesh. Josh. 15:34; Neh. 3:13; 11:30.
2. A town in the hill country of Judah, probably located about 6 miles (9.5 km) SW of Hebron [**V, C2**]. Josh. 15:56.

ZAPHON [ZAY-fahn; "north"] A city E of the Jordan, allotted to the tribe of Gad. Here the Ephraimites confronted Jephthah after his defeat of the Ammonites, resulting in a battle. Several sites in the Jordan Valley N of Succoth have been suggested. Josh. 13:27; Jdg. 12:1; Ps. 48:2. Called Shophan in Num. 32:35.

ZAREPHATH [ZAIR-uh-fath; "dyeing" or "refinement"] Sarepta, KJV NT. [**VIII, A2**]. A small Phoenician town within the domain of Sidon. It was conquered successively by Sennacherib and Esarhaddon of Assyria, and the latter awarded the city to Tyre. Elijah stayed with a widow and her son in Zarephath, through the period of drought and famine. In NT times, it was known by the Greek name, Sarepta. It was located on the coast of Palestine, about 8 miles (13 km) S of Sidon. 1 Ki. 17:9,10; Obad. 20; Lk. 4:26.

ZARETHAN [ZAIR-uh-than; "cooling"(?)] Also Zaretan, Zarthan, Zartanah, Zeredathah, KJV; Zeredah, RSV (2 Chr. 4:17). A town located in the Jordan Valley, near Adam. Tell es-Saidiyeh E of the Jordan, several miles NW of Succoth, is the preferred site. Excavation there uncovered pre-Solomonic copper and bronze working activities. However, the identification is uncertain, and several locations E and W of the Jordan have been proposed. Josh. 3:16; 1 Ki. 4:12; 7:46. Possibly the same as Zererah.

ZEBOIIM [zeh-BOY-uhm; "gazelles"(?)] Zeboim, KJV (Hos. 11:8). [**I,** C2]. One of the Cities of the Plain, destroyed with Sodom and Gomorrah. Gen. 10:19; 14:2,8. *See also* Sodom. *See* Cities of the Plain.

ZEBOIM [zeh-BOH-uhm; "hyena"(?)]
1. A valley E of Micmash [**X,** A2] in Benjamite territory. 1 Sam. 13:18.
2. A Benjamite town resettled in post-exilic times. Probably located N of Lydda [**XI,** D1], its exact site is uncertain. Neh. 11:34.

ZEBULUN [ZEB-yoo-luhn; "dwelling"] **VI,** B3. The tribal inheritance of Zebulun lay primarily in S Galilee, SE of Asher, SW of Naphtali, and N of Manasseh and Issachar. Its SW extent reached the Kishon River near Jokneam, but stopped far short of the Palestinian coast; nor did the territory reach the Jordan River to the E. It was a small but fertile region, encompassing a portion of the Jezreel Valley. At least a part of Zebulun was apparently annexed into the Assyrian Empire following the invasion of Galilee by Tiglath-Pileser III (Isa. 9:1). Josh. 19:10-16; Jdg. 1:30.

ZEDAD [ZEE-dad; "mountainside"] A place on the N border of the Promised Land, generally identified with Sadad, located about 65 miles (105 km) NE of Damascus [**I,** A2]. Num. 34:8; Ezek. 47:15.

ZELA [ZEE-luh] A town in Benjamin where Saul and Jonathan were buried in the tomb of Saul's father, Kish. Possibly Khirbet Salah, about 2.5 miles (4 km) NW of Jerusalem [**VII,** C1]. 2 Sam. 21:14. Called Zelah in Josh. 18:28.

ZELAH [ZEE-luh] *See* Zela.

ZELZAH [ZEL-zuh] A place on the border of Benjamin. Exact site uncertain. 1 Sam. 10:2.

ZEMARAIM [ZEM-uh-RAY-uhm]
1. A town in the territory of Benjamin. Several sites E of Bethel have been proposed. Josh. 18:22.
2. A mountain in Ephraim, from which Abijah, king of Judah, spoke against Jeroboam. It may have been located near the town of Zemaraim. 2 Chr. 13:4.

ZENAN [ZEE-nan] A town in the lowlands of Judah, possibly located about 4 miles (6 km) NW of Lachish [**V,** C1]. Josh. 15:37. *See* Zaanan.

ZEPHATH [ZEE-fath; "watchtower"] A Canaanite city destroyed by the men of Judah and Simeon, who renamed it Hormah [**VI,** E2]. Jdg. 1:17.

ZEPHATHAH [ZEF-uh-thuh; "watchtower"] A valley near Mareshah [**X,** B1] where Asa took up battle positions against the army of Zerah the Cushite. 2 Chr. 14:10.

ZEPHON [ZEE-fahn] Shortened form of Baal Zephon in Num. 33:7.

ZER [ZER] A fortified city of Naphtali; its exact site is uncertain. Josh. 19:35.

ZERED [ZEER-ed] Zared, KJV (Num. 21:12). [**I; IV,** E1-F2; **VI**]. A river valley on the boundary between Edom and Moab. Probably to be identified with the Wadi el-Hesa, which runs into the Dead Sea from the SE. Num. 21:12; Deut. 2:13,14.

ZEREDAH [ZAIR-eh-duh; "ambush"] Zareda, KJV. The hometown of Jeroboam the Ephraimite. It was located in the hill country of Ephraim, about 15 miles (24 km) SW of Shechem [**I,** B1]. 1 Ki. 11:26.

ZERERAH [ZAIR-eh-ruh] Zererath, KJV. A place in the Jordan Valley toward which the Midianites fled from Gideon. Jdg. 7:22. Possibly the same as Zarethan.

ZERETH SHAHAR [ZEER-eth SHAY-har; "splendor of the dawn"] A town in Reubenite territory, possibly located on the shore of the Dead Sea about 20 miles (32 km) SW of Medeba [**VIII,** B2]. Josh. 13:19.

ZIDDIM [ZID-im; "flanks"] A fortified city of Naphtali, possibly to be identified with modern Hattin, about 5 miles (8 km) NW of Tiberias [**XI,** B3]. Josh. 19:35.

ZIKLAG [ZIK-lag] **VI,** E2; **VII; X.** A town in the S desert region of Judah, allotted to the Simeonites. It came under the control of Achish, king of Gath, who gave the town to David during the time he served as a vassal of the Philistine king. From there, David and his men went on raids against the nomadic tribes in the Negev. At one point, it was burned down by the Amalekites, whom David pursued and defeated, recovering the captives and plunder from Ziklag. The city was resettled after the Exile. Possibly to be identified with a site about 12.5 miles (20 km) NW of Beersheba. Josh. 19:5; 1 Sam. 27:6-12; 30; Neh. 11:28.

ZIN [ZIN] **III,** B4. A desert region overlapping the ideal S border of the Promised Land. It was bounded on the S by the Desert of Paran and the E by Edom. Kadesh Barnea lay on the border of the Zin and Paran deserts. Num. 20:1; 27:14; 34:3,4.

ZION[*] [ZIE-uhn; "fortress"(?)] Another name for the Jebusite stronghold, and the SE hill of Jerusalem upon which it stood. The use of the name was progressively expanded to include the Temple, and eventually all of Jerusalem. It came to be applied figuratively to the nation of Judah and the whole of the Israelite people. Through this process of change, the name also developed a religious connotation, emphasizing Jerusalem as the city of God, and the Israelites as God's people. In NT times, the spiritual significance of the name is further extended to indicate the church of God and his spiritual kingdom. 2 Sam 5:7; Ps. 48:2,11,12; Isa. 40:9; 60:14; Heb. 12:22; 1 Pet. 2:4-6.

ZIOR [ZIE-or; "smallness"] A town in the hill country of Judah, identified with modern Si'ir,

about 5 miles (8 km) NE of Hebron [**V,** C2]. Josh. 15:54.

ZIPH [ZIF]
1. A town in the S of Judah, near Edom. Possibly a site located about 15 miles (24 km) S of Hormah [**VI,** E2]. Josh. 15:24.
2. A town in the hill country of Judah, identified with Tell Zif, 4 miles (6.5 km) SE of Hebron [**V,** C2], within a barren wilderness region known as the Desert of Ziph. Josh. 15:55; 1 Sam. 23:14-24.

ZIPHRON [ZIF-rahn] An unidentified place on the ideal N border of the Promised Land, near Hazar Enan. Num. 34:9.

ZIZ [ZIZ] A pass that leads from the W shore of the Dead Sea near En Gedi to the Desert of Jeruel. Identified with the Wadi Hasasa, about 6 miles (10 km) N of En Gedi [**VI,** E3]. 2 Chr. 20:16.

ZOAN [ZOH-an] **III,** B2; **IX(a).** The ancient Egyptian city of Dja'net, classical Tanis, in the NE Nile Delta, built—or more likely, rebuilt—seven years after Hebron. By the 20th Dynasty (1198-1069 B.C.), it was an important trading port with Phoenicia, and with the founding of the 21st Dynasty, it became the effective capital of Egypt, remaining so for the next 500 years. Previous identification of Tanis/Zoan with either the Hyksos capital, Avaris, or the city of Rameses, is now unlikely. The extensive ruins of Tanis are situated near the S shore of Lake Menzaleh. Num. 13:22; Ps. 78:12,43; Isa 19:11-13.

ZOAR [ZOR; "small"] **I,** C2. A city near Sodom and Gomorrah, located near the base of the Dead Sea. Previously called Bela, its name was changed after it was spared, at Lot's request, the destruction that fell on the other cities of the plain. Possibly to be identified with es-Safi, near the SE corner of the Dead Sea. Gen. 14; Isa. 15:5. *See* Sodom; Cities of the Plain.

ZOBAH [ZOH-buh] Zoba, KJV. [**VII,** B2]. A powerful kingdom in central Syria, between Damascus and Hamath. Saul fought against Zobah, and David defeated its king, Hadadezer. In the process, he captured the cities of Zobah, and returned to Judah with a great quantity of bronze as booty. 1 Sam. 14:47; 2 Sam. 8:3-12; 10:6-19; 1 Ki. 11:23,24.

ZOHELETH [ZOH-huh-leth; "serpent"] Serpent's Stone, RSV. A stone beside En Rogel where Adonijah prepared a feast during his attempt to seize the throne of David. 1 Ki. 1:9.

ZOPHIM [ZOH-fim; "watchers"] A field on the top of Pisgah, where Balaam viewed the Israelite encampment below; exact site uncertain. Num. 23:14.

ZORAH [ZOR-uh] A town in the W foothills of Judah, allotted to Dan. It was the hometown of Manoah, the father of Samson. The city was later fortified by Rehoboam, and was reoccupied after the Exile. Zorah is identified with a site along the Valley of Sorek, about 2 miles (3 km) N of Beth Shemesh [**VI,** D2]. Josh. 15:33; Jdg. 13:2,25; 16:31; 18:2,11; Neh. 11:29.

ZUPH [ZOOF; "honeycomb"] A district in Ephraim or N Benjamin through which Saul passed in search of his father's donkeys. 1 Sam. 9:5.

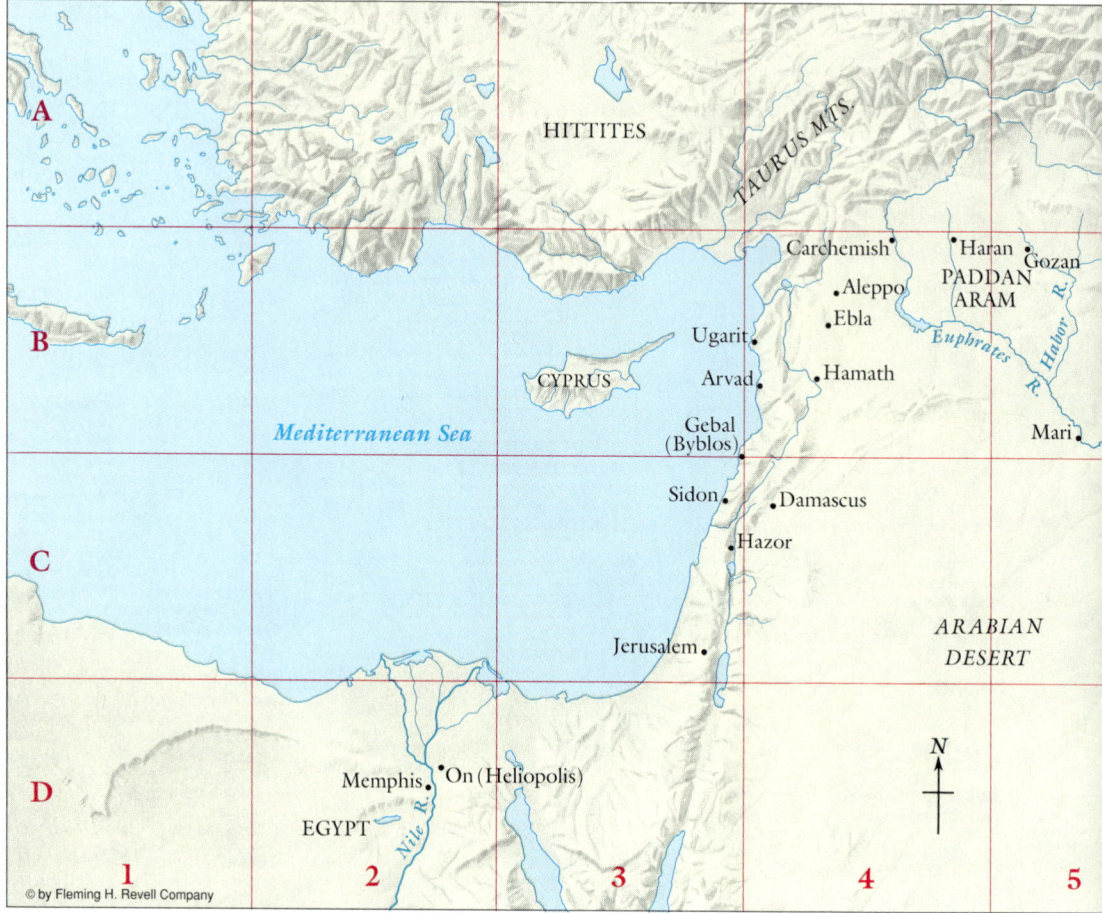

Map showing the Mediterranean Sea region with locations including: HITTITES, TAURUS MTS, Carchemish, Haran, Gozan, Aleppo, PADDAN ARAM, Ugarit, Ebla, Euphrates R., Habor R., CYPRUS, Arvad, Hamath, Mari, Gebal (Byblos), Sidon, Damascus, Hazor, Jerusalem, ARABIAN DESERT, On (Heliopolis), Memphis, EGYPT, Nile R. Grid references A–D and 1–5.

MAP
1

The Days of the Patriarchs

A little more than 2,000 years before Jesus was born, Abraham left Sumerian Ur with his father's large family group. He traveled northwest some 600 miles along one of two well-established trade routes that paralleled the Tigris and Euphrates rivers. Most of the family settled at Paddan Aram, in NW Mesopotamia. Following the death of his father, Abraham led his wife and servants and his nephew Lot, with their extensive flocks and herds, southwest another 400 miles to Canaan, the Promised Land.

About 250 years earlier, the large, fortified city-states which had dominated that land had been destroyed in war. Among these cities had been Ebla, with a population of some 260,000 people. But when Abraham traveled the King's Highway from Paddan Aram to Damascus, Canaan was sparsely settled. Amorites, Canaanites, Hittites, and others lived in scattered unwalled villages or were nomadic herders.

In 2150 B.C. Palestine was far greener than it is today. Forests and grasses covered the hillsides, where bears and lions lived. During the following centuries this natural cover would be destroyed by a growing population that cut down the forests and by marching armies that devastated the fields.

Abraham may have crossed into Canaan just below the Sea of Galilee, along one branch of the Great Trunk Road that split from the King's Highway at Damascus. Traveling up into the highlands, Abraham built an altar at Shechem to offer God thanks. According to the Book of Genesis, he stopped briefly at Bethel and then moved southward into the Negev. This district, lying south of the Dead Sea, was arid, with half of it receiving only about two inches of rainfall a year. But near Gerar, where the annual rainfall of six inches was supplemented by wells, the nomadic peoples who moved their tents and

MTS. OF ARARAT

Lake Van

Caspian Sea

Lake Urmia

Nineveh

Calah

ASSYRIA

Asshur

Nuzi

MEDIA

ZAGROS MTS.

Tigris R.

Euphrates R.

Baghdad

Babylon • Cuthah

Nippur

Susa

BABYLONIA

Ellasar (Larsa)

Erech

Ur

ELAM

| 0 | 50 | 100 | 150 | 200 Mi. |

| 0 | 50 | 100 | 150 | 200 Km. |

Persian Gulf

6   7

MAP II

1   2

major trade route

Damascus

A

Mediterranean Sea

Hazor

Acco

Ashtaroth Karnaim

Yarmuk R.

Megiddo

Ham

B

Dothan

Beth Shan

Jordan R.

Shechem   Succoth

Mahanaim

Aphek

Jabbok R.

Salem (Mt. Moriah)

Jericho

Bethlehem

Ashkelon

Hebron (Mamre)

Dead Sea

Kiriathaim

Gaza

Hazazon Tamar

Arnon R.

C

Gerar

Beersheba (Patriarchal)

Possible location of Sodom, Gomorrah, Admah, Zeboiim

Zoar

Zered Brook

NEGEV

SEIR

D Kadesh Barnea

N

DESERT OF PARAN

E El Paran

| 0 | 10 | 20 | 30 | 40 | 50 Mi. |

| 0 | 10 | 20 | 30 | 40 | 50 Km. |

Gulf of Aqaba

© by Fleming H. Revell Company

flocks with the seasons were able to grow crops.

It was in the south that the patriarchs lived most of their lives, although there were occasional retreats into Egypt in times of famine.

In Jacob's time, around 1950 B.C., the land began to change. The central highlands saw a revival of walled cities, at places like Bethel, Shechem, and Dothan. During the next 500 years a distinct Canaanite culture would develop, marked not only by material prosperity but also by spiritual and moral depravity.

Before this Canaanite culture reached its peak, however, God led the descendants of Abraham into Egypt. There the 70 persons who entered Egypt multiplied despite their bondage. When the Israelites finally returned to Canaan, they would shatter Canaanite power and take by force the land promised to their forefather Abraham. *See* Abraham; Canaan.

Tracing the Exodus

Both the date and the route of the Exodus are hotly debated by biblical scholars and archaeologists. Most of the places named so carefully in the biblical text cannot be pinpointed today. Yet there is no doubt that the Bible describes a mass movement of Israelite slaves out of Egypt, led by Moses.

The Exodus began from the city Rameses (modern Tell ed-Daba') and proceeded to Suc-

coth (modern Tell Maskhuta). From there, the Israelites could have followed a major highway along the Mediterranean shore to the land of the Philistines, but that route was guarded by a series of Egyptian forts. So the Israelites turned south into the desert, a route which brought them to a series of marshy lakes linked by defensive canals over 200 feet wide at ground level and 65 feet wide at the bottom. This was

- •   city or campsite
- —— route of the Exodus
- ••••• alternate route
- – – – Israelite route to Canaan
- —— major trade route

the Yam Suph [sea of (papyrus) reeds, *not* the "Red Sea"] that blocked the Israelites' progress. And now they were pursued by an Egyptian chariot army.

Here the Lord miraculously opened a passage through the waters of one of these lakes. That passage was wide enough for the frightened mass of Israelites to pass through in a single night. Here, too, the Lord trapped the pursuing Egyptians and caused the waters to return to their place.

Safe now on the southern side of Egypt's watery defensive line, the Israelites set out down the Sinai peninsula for Mount Sinai, which is traditionally identified with modern Jebel Musa, a rugged granite peak towering silently over the arid plains below. It was at Sinai that God gave Israel his Law. Here the tabernacle was constructed and the religion of Israel given its distinctive form. And here the loosely structured tribal groups were reorganized. *See* Sinai.

After more than a year on the plains before Sinai, the Israelites moved on, to approach Canaan, their Promised Land, from the south. But at Kadesh Barnea the Israelites rebelled, refusing to obey God's command to attack Canaan. Turned back by the Lord, the Israelites spent the next 38 years circling in the desert between Kadesh Barnea and Ezion Geber.

Finally, when all the rebellious generation had died, Moses led the Israelites north. After pitched battles with the Edomites and Moabites, a new and obedient generation of Israelites stood poised across the Jordan from Jericho. There Moses died. And from there the new leader, Joshua, launched the conquest of the land which God had promised centuries before to Abraham, Isaac, and Jacob, and to their descendants. *See* Exodus; Sinai.

MAP
IV

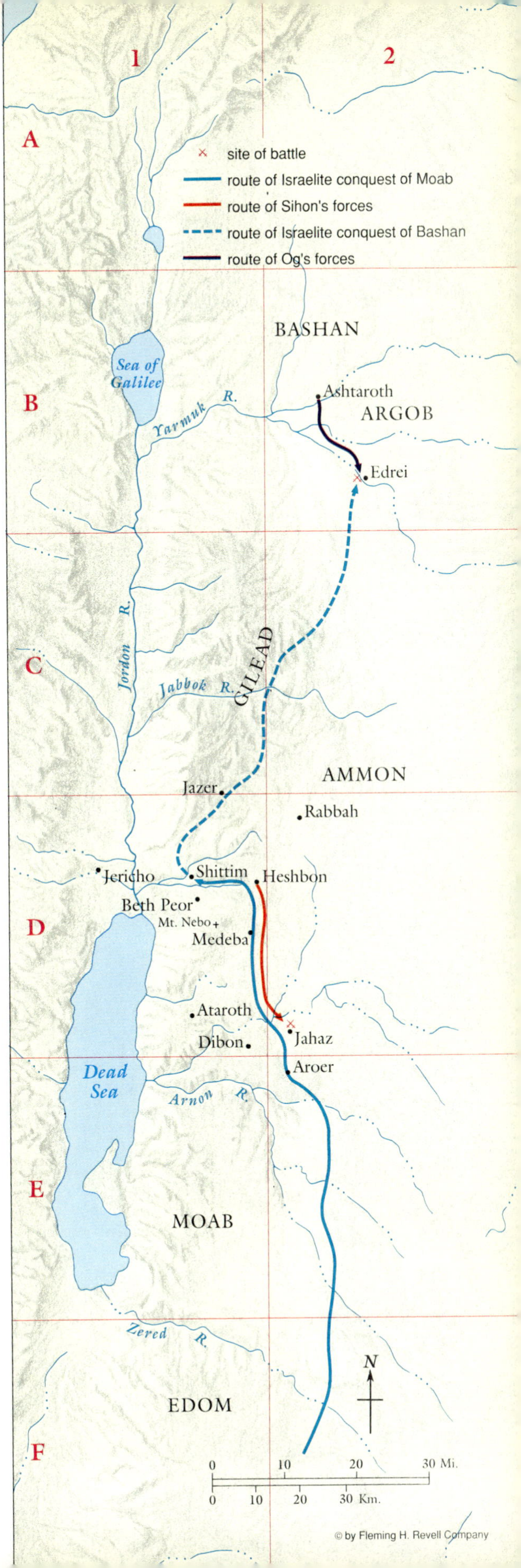

×   site of battle
——   route of Israelite conquest of Moab
——   route of Sihon's forces
- - -   route of Israelite conquest of Bashan
——   route of Og's forces

BASHAN

Sea of Galilee

Ashtaroth

ARGOB

Yarmuk R.

Edrei

Jordan R.

GILEAD

Jabbok R.

AMMON

Jazer

Rabbah

Jericho   Shittim   Heshbon

Beth Peor

Mt. Nebo

Medeba

Ataroth

Dibon   Jahaz

Aroer

Dead Sea

Arnon R.

MOAB

Zered R.

EDOM

N

0   10   20   30 Mi.

0   10   20   30 Km.

Canaan, Conquest, and the Judges

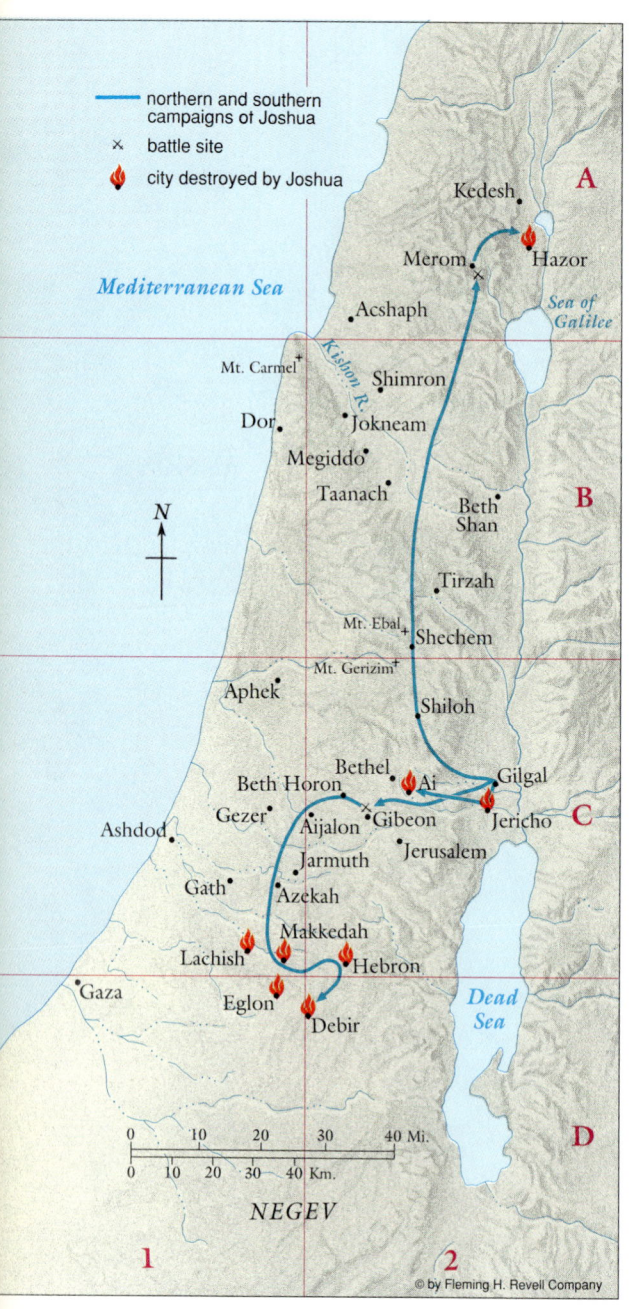

northern and southern campaigns of Joshua

× battle site

city destroyed by Joshua

Mediterranean Sea

Kedesh

A

Merom Hazor

Acshaph

Sea of Galilee

Mt. Carmel

Shimron

Dor

Jokneam

Megiddo

Taanach

Beth Shan

B

Tirzah

Mt. Ebal Shechem

Mt. Gerizim

Aphek

Shiloh

Bethel

Beth Horon Ai Gilgal

Gezer Aijalon Gibeon Jericho C

Ashdod Jarmuth Jerusalem

Gath Azekah

Lachish Makkedah

Hebron Dead Sea

Gaza Eglon

Debir

N

0 10 20 30 40 Mi.

0 10 20 30 40 Km.

NEGEV

1 2

Canaan was again a land of heavily fortified, independent walled cities when Joshua led the Israelites into Canaan. In a series of battles, four of which are reported in the Book of Joshua, the Israelites shattered the forces of these Canaanite city-states and permanently established themselves in Palestine's highlands. The course of the conquest, condensed in the Bible, is shown on the inset map on the next page. Many believe it took up to seven years for Israel to subdue the Canaanites.

At this point the land was divided among the tribes and clans of Israel, with the major cities in each territory identified. In addition, 48 cities scattered throughout the tribal areas were given to the Levites.

However, Joshua did not drive all the Canaanites from the Promised Land. Many were entrenched in lowland areas, where their iron chariots gave them military superiority. The task of rooting out the enemies who remained was left to the individual Israelite tribes.

The Book of Judges picks up the story. Only Palestine's central highlands remained under permanent Israelite control. Even when Canaanite groups were subdued, the Israelites frequently disobeyed God's command to destroy them totally. Instead, the Canaanites were put to work as forced labor.

This policy contributed to the religious, moral, and political stagnation of the next centuries. Attracted by the sensuous elements in Canaan's fertility religions, the Israelites repeatedly abandoned the God of the Covenant and turned to idolatry.

It would be a mistake to think of Israel during this period as a single nation. The tribes existed as a loose confederation, held together by a common heritage, language, and faith. The judges who arose to serve as deliverers and then rulers exercised authority only in their own districts, over one or several of the tribes, but not over them all. For the hundreds of years that the era of the judges lasted, Israel occupied parts of the Promised Land but was not in any sense a nation. *See* Chronology; Conquest; Jericho.

MAP V

MAP VI

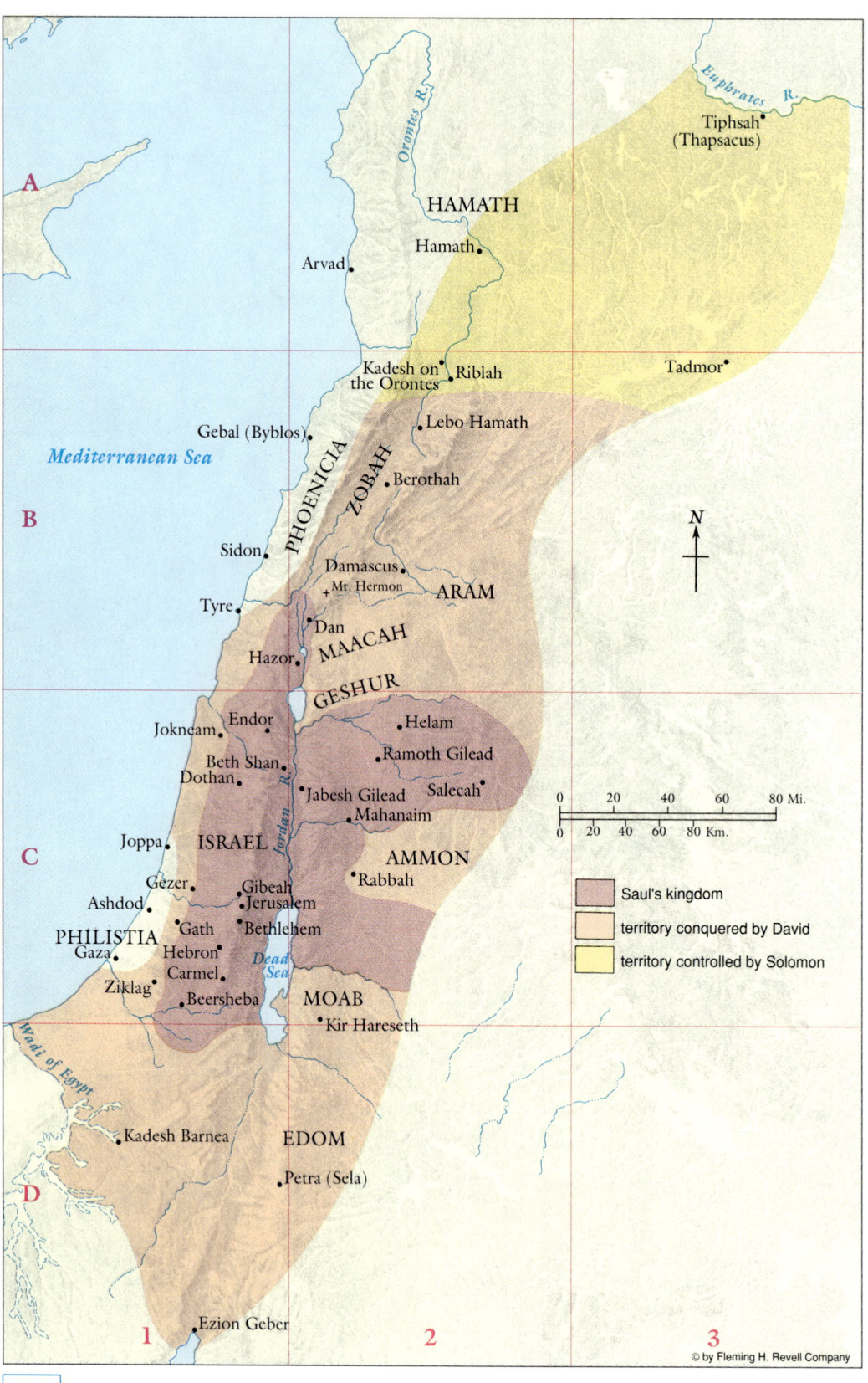

A

HAMATH

Tiphsah
(Thapsacus)

Hamath

Arvad

Mediterranean Sea

Euphrates R.

Orontes R.

Kadesh on
the Orontes • Riblah

Tadmor•

Gebal (Byblos)•

PHOENICIA

ZOBAH

•Lebo Hamath

•Berothah

B

Sidon•

Damascus•
+Mt. Hermon

Tyre•

•Dan

Hazor•

MAACAH

GESHUR

ARAM

N

Jokneam•

•Endor

Beth Shan•

Dothan•

•Helam

•Ramoth Gilead

•Jabesh Gilead

Mahanaim•

•Salecah

Jordan R.

Joppa•

ISRAEL

C

Gezer•

Ashdod•

PHILISTIA

Gaza•

Ziklag•

•Gibeah
•Jerusalem

•Gath

•Bethlehem

Hebron•

Carmel•

•Beersheba

AMMON

•Rabbah

Dead
Sea

MOAB

•Kir Hareseth

0   20   40   60   80 Mi.
0 20 40 60 80 Km.

■ Saul's kingdom

■ territory conquered by David

■ territory controlled by Solomon

Wadi of Egypt

•Kadesh Barnea

EDOM

•Petra (Sela)

D

•Ezion Geber

1   2   3

© by Fleming H. Revell Company

MAP
VII

The Kingdom United and Divided

Israel's first king, Saul, was able to defeat many enemies, but he lacked the spiritual and organizational qualities needed to bond the Israelite tribes together into a single nation. Those qualities belonged to his successor, David. Not only did David defeat all the surrounding nations, expanding the territory Israel controlled some ten times, but he also established Jerusalem as the political and religious center of the nation and set up an effective system that enabled him to govern the whole land.

David's son and successor, Solomon, built on the foundation David established. He constructed the Jerusalem Temple, which served as the focal point of united Israel's religion. He strengthened his country's military forces and further developed the central government's bureaucracy. Solomon also made maximum use of the trade routes Israel now controlled to add to the wealth of his kingdom.

However, after Solomon's death in 931 B.C., the nation broke apart into two hostile kingdoms, known as Israel and Judah.

Seriously weakened by the rift, both Israel and Judah lost much of the territory that David and Solomon had controlled.

The next 200 years saw periods of relative prosperity as well as times of crushing defeat for both Israel and Judah. Then in 722 B.C., the northern kingdom of Israel collapsed under pressure from the mighty Assyrian Empire. Israel's capital, Samaria, was destroyed, and its people—along with 200,000 citizens of Judah—were carried away by the Assyrians, to be resettled elsewhere.

Judah survived for a time as an independent nation. Under Josiah the nation even expanded southward for a time. However, after the Babylonians replaced Assyria as the dominant world power, Judah quickly fell. In 586 B.C. the final conquest was accomplished. Jerusalem was destroyed, the majority of the population was taken to Babylon, and the tiny group that remained was frightened into a flight to Egypt.

With the destruction of Judah, the land God promised to his covenant people fell under the domination of the Gentiles. *See* Assyria; Babylon; Jerusalem.

10th century B.C.:
- Israel
- Judah

Expansion, mid-8th century B.C.:
- Israel
- Judah

Mediterranean Sea

Sidon
Zarephath
Tyre
Kedesh
Damascus
ARAM
Dan
PHOENICIA
A

Gath Hepher
Megiddo
Jezreel
Karnaim
Ramoth Gilead
Abel Meholah
Tishbe
Samaria
Shechem
Tirzah
Peniel
B

Joppa
Aphek
Bethel
ISRAEL
AMMON
Rabbah
Gibbethon
Beth Shemesh
Ashdod
Mizpah
Jerusalem
Medeba
Ashkelon
Lachish
Tekoa
Gaza
Gerar
Hebron
Dead Sea
Aroer
Beersheba
Kir Hareseth
MOAB
JUDAH
C
Bozrah
EDOM
Petra (Sela)
N
D
Gulf of Aqaba

0   20   40   60 Mi.
0   20   40   60 Km.

© by Fleming H. Revell Company

1   2

MAP VIII

Persian Empire ▢

A

MACEDONIA
THRACE
Byzantium
Black Sea
CAUCASUS MTS.
Caspian Sea

LYDIA
Pergamum
Helys R.
MESHECH
ARMENIA

Delphi
Athens
Sparta
IONIA
PHRYGIA
Tarsus
Gozan
L. Van
L. Urmia
Calah
Arpad
Haran
Asshur
Ecbatana

B

CRETE
CYPRUS
Hamath
Riblah
Tadmor
Tigris R.
Euphrates R.
Susa

Mediterranean Sea
Sidon
Jerusalem
Babylon
Erech
Ur

LIBYA
Tahpanhes
Memphis
N
EGYPT
ARABIAN DESERT
PERSIS

Tema
Dedan

C

0 100 200 300 400 Mi.
0 100 200 300 400 Km.

Thebes
Nile R.
Red Sea
Aswan

© by Fleming H. Revell Company

1   2   3   4

MAP
IX

The Remnant Returns

When the Persians took over the Babylonian Empire in 539 B.C., Cyrus the Great reversed the earlier deportation policy. Cyrus issued decrees permitting the return of all captives to their national homelands.

Only some 50,000 Jews took advantage of this decree and set out to return to Palestine. The first returnees did not occupy Jerusalem but rather chose the areas of Judah that were more suitable for agriculture.

Finally after 18 years, a new but smaller temple was rebuilt on the site of Solomon's magnificent edifice. Then, 80 years later, Nehemiah supervised a rebuilding of the walls of Jerusalem.

After that, the people of Judah settled down to wait. That wait stretched on and on, for years, then decades, then centuries.

Judah waited while the Greeks under Alexander supplanted the Persians (330 B.C.). Judah waited as control of the land passed to the Ptolemys after Alexander's death, and then in 198 B.C. to the rival Seleucids. Judah waited

Assyrian Empire ▫

KUE
Nineveh
Asshur
Jerusalem   Babylon   ELAM
Zoan (Tanis)

Aral Sea
Iaxartes R.
Oxus R.
PARTHIA
CARMANIA
Indus R.
INDIA
Arabian Sea

5   6

Babylonian Empire ▫

LYDIA
Carchemish   Nineveh   MEDIA
Jerusalem   Babylon
Ur
CHALDEA

MAP
X

Post-Exilic Judea

1   2

Jordan R.

Samaria
Shechem

A   SAMARIA

Joppa

N

Ono
Lod   Neballat   Bethel
Gittaim   Micmash
Gibeon   Geba
Gezer
Jerusalem   Nob

Ashdod

Jarmuth   JUDEA
Azekah   Adullam   Tekoa
Keilah
Ashkelon   Mareshah   Beth Zur   Dead
Lachish   Sea
Zanoah   Hebron

B
0   10   20   30 Mi.

Ziklag
0   10   20   30 Km.

IDUMEA
Beersheba

through the upheaval of the Maccabean revolt, a rebellion stimulated in the 160s B.C. by the efforts of Antiochus IV to wipe out Judaism. Judah waited during a fleeting, fantasy independence. Judah waited through the bloody decades that followed until, with Roman support, Herod the Great established his authority over the home-land of the Jews. Judah waited, until the ap-pointed time came, and a child promised by the prophets of old was born in Bethlehem. *See* Alexander; Maccabees; Persia.

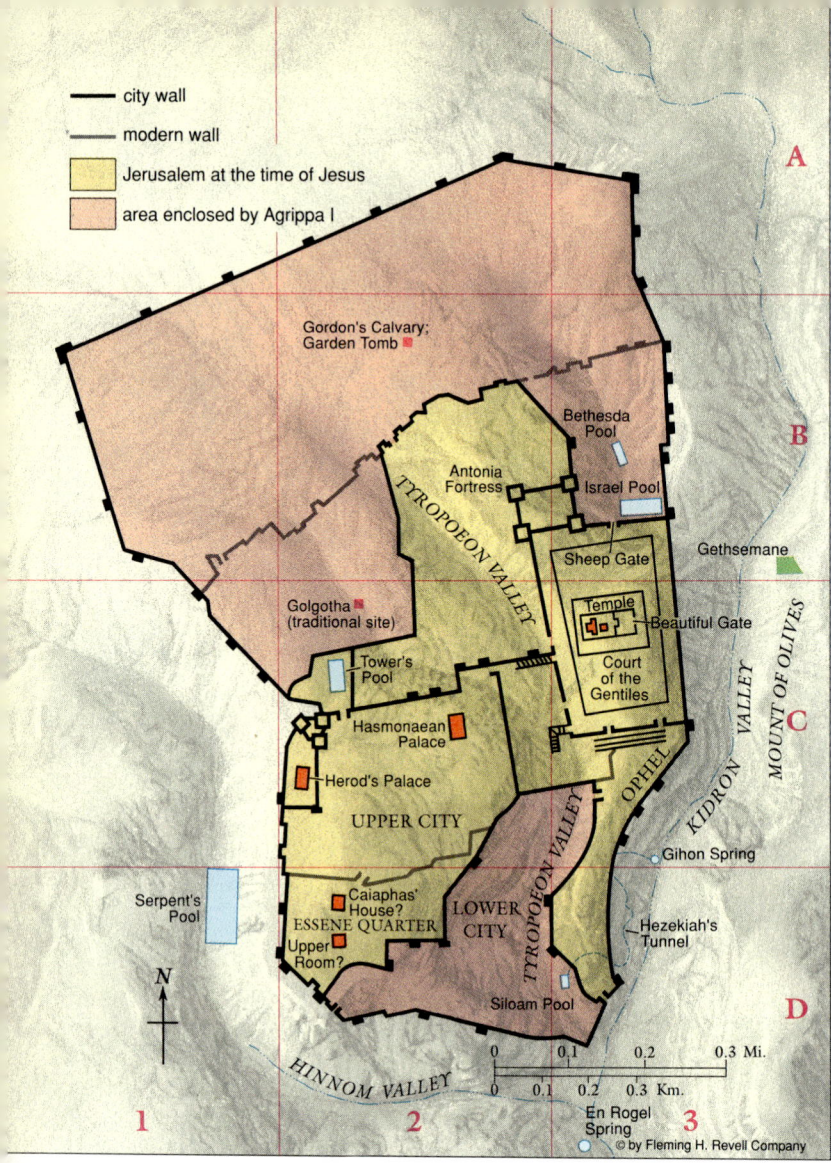

The Land Jesus Knew

When Jesus was born, the kingdom of Herod the Great had known peace for a generation. The Jews, though restive under Roman and Herod's rule, concentrated their attention on the duties of daily life and the mysteries of their ancient religion. Taxes were heavy. Yet the land was productive. Terraced farms supplied food to Palestine's major cities, the Sea of Galilee supported a thriving fishing industry, and thousands were occupied with Herod's many building projects.

When Jesus was about 30, he began his public ministry. Herod the Great was long dead, the various districts of his kingdom given to his sons or directly controlled by the Romans. Most of the ministry of Jesus reported in the Gospels took place in Galilee, where a son of Herod ruled. Jesus moved from Nazareth and centered his ministry in Capernaum, then an active and prosperous fishing village and also an important administrative center.

Jesus also journeyed to Jerusalem and Judea, sometimes taking the route through Samaria preferred by Galileans (Jn. 4), a route disdained by those who lived in Judah. Since all Jewish males were to appear in Jerusalem three times a year at established religious festivals, Christ must have made this journey many times.

The last third of each of the four Gospels focuses on events that took place in Judea, in and around Jerusalem. The holy city of the Jews, beautified by Herod, held many spectacular buildings, but it was dominated by the greatly expanded Second Temple. It is possible to locate many of the events of Jesus' last week on a map of the city as it then was. Even so, the critical locations—where Jesus was crucified and where his body was buried—remain uncertain.

Tyre

•Caesarea
Philippi

A

L. Huleh

N

GALILEE

0 2 4 6 8 Mi.
0 2 4 6 8 Km.

Korazin•
•Capernaum
•Bethsaida

•Ptolemais (Acco)

Cana•

Magdala•

Sea of
Galilee

Mt. Carmel +

B *Mediterranean
Sea*

Nazareth•

Tiberius•

Nain•

•Gadara

Caesarea•

Scythopolis•
(Beth Shan)

DECAPOLIS

C

SAMARIA

Sebaste•
(Samaria)

Mt. Ebel +
Mt. Gerizim +

•Sychar

Jordan R.

Antipatris (Aphek)•

D
Joppa•

Arimathea•

PEREA

Lydda (Lod)•

Ephraim•

Jamnia (Jabneel)•

Jericho•

•Emmaus

Azotus (Ashdod)•

Jerusalem•
•Bethany

E

•Bethlehem

JUDEA

Dead Sea

1

2

3

© by Fleming H. Revell Company

MAP
XII

MAP
XIII

The World of the

Augustus (31 B.C.–A.D. 14) brought peace and stability to the Roman Empire. The land and sea routes that linked major cities were secured and made safe for travel. Sixty thousand miles of highways were built and maintained, making movement easy. Vigorous trade took place. Pilgrims and businessmen as well as politicians and soldiers could travel safely. A common language, *koine* (common) Greek, was spoken. Generally, most people had adopted the ideals and values of Greek culture. Religiously the Romans adopted a stance of tolerance. Many different religions were recognized as *licit* (legal), and could be freely practiced and promoted within the empire. Laws were enforced, taxes were collected, and criminals were dealt with effectively, though often brutally.

The cities of the first century were cosmopolitan. Added to the base population already existing in any area were often companies of retired Roman soldiers and transported citizens. Most cities of the empire also had large Jewish

5   6   7

Black Sea

BITHYNIA
AND PONTUS

Sangarius R.

GALATIA   CAPPADOCIA

Halys R.

L. Tuz

Antioch
(Pisidian)

Iconium

Lystra

Derbe   CILICIA

Tarsus   Euphrates R.

Perga   PAMPHYLIA   Antioch
(Syrian)

Seleucia   Aleppo

Myra

Salamis   SYRIA

CYPRUS

Paphos

Sidon   Damascus

Tyre

Caesarea   Jordan R.

JUDEA   Jerusalem

Alexandria

EGYPT

Paul's First Missionary Journey

Paul's Second Missionary Journey

Paul's Third Missionary Journey

First Century

populations. The Jews, who were in many ways model, hard-working citizens, had settled in Asian and Mesopotamian cities after the Assyrian and Babylonian captivities. By the time of Christ, as many as a million Jews were living in Egypt. Jewish communities were also established in Asia Minor and in Greece, and a large Jewish colony was located in Rome. Some have estimated that, in the first century, one in ten persons in the Roman Empire was either a Jew or a Gentile adherent to Jewish religion.

When the new Christian faith reached out beyond Palestine, conditions in the empire were ideal for its spread. The common language, the ease of travel, the established patterns of trade and communication, the core of Gentiles as well as Jews familiar with the Old Testament's God and its prophecies, the tolerance of the Romans to religious and philosophical ideas, all these together created a climate in which the new faith spread quickly through the Roman world.

Photo and Illustration Credits

The publisher gratefully acknowledges the cooperation of these sources, whose illustrations appear in the present work. Following each source is the page number and, where necessary, the position on the page where the illustration is located.

AGNES SCOTT COLLEGE, DECA-TUR, GA: 162, 696, 704 (bottom).

AMERICAN NUMISMATIC SOCI-ETY, NEW YORK: 373 (bottom).

ANTWERP CATHEDRAL, BEL-GIUM: 564, 884.

ARCHER, DR. GLEASON L.: 8 (top), 36 (bottom), 44 (left), 97 (top rt.), 109 (rt.), 112 (bottom), 182 (bottom left), 290 (bottom left), 317 (top rt.), 750 (rt. middle), 822, 849, 913 (rt.).

ASHMOLEAN MUSEUM, OXFORD, ENGLAND: 423.

BEERS, V. GILBERT: 14 (bottom), 27, 49 (left), 59 (bottom), 62, 71, 117 (left), 201 (top rt.), 245.

BIBLICAL MUSEUM, AMSTERDAM: 85, 212, 213, 716 (#12), 816, 881, 883, 900 (rt.), 959, 970 (bottom).

BLATT, DANIEL: 3, 30, 34, 35 (bottom), 38 (top), 48 (top), 50 (bottom), 80, 122, 131 (top left), 135 (bottom), 141 (top rt.) 146, 149, 169 (bottom), 170 (cntr.), 180 (top), 181 (cntr.), 183 (top), 184 (left cntr.), 190 (rt.), 191 (rt.), 192 (rt.), 225 (left), 226 (top left), 227 (top rt. & cntr. rt.), 229 (top rt.), 273 (top left), 283 (top rt.), 286, 290–291 (bottom), 310 (top), 315 (cntr.), 338 (bottom), 381 (rt.), 387 (bottom), 391 (left), 394 (left cntr.), 402, 404 (rt.), 413 (top), 421 (left), 430 (rt.), 482 (top & bottom), 484 (top left), 485, 494 (bottom), 510 (rt.), 532–533, 554 (left), 580 (bottom), 589 (bottom), 590, 591 (bottom), 593 (bottom), 604, 622 (top), 632, 641 (top), 649 (top left), 658 (top), 668 (bottom rt.), 694 (top), 697 (left), 708, 718, 742 (bottom), 747 (top left), 750 (top left & rt.), 752, 753, 787 (top), 795, 796 (bottom), 800 (left), 802 (top rt.), 805, 807 (top rt.), 808 (bottom), 814 (bottom rt.), 818 (top-rt.), 823, 839 (top), 867 (bottom), 894 (top), 903 (bottom rt.), 913 (top), 920 (top), 926 (bottom), 930 (bottom), 951 (top rt.), 966, 986 (top & bottom left), 991, 1003 (bottom), 1004 (bottom left), 1005, 1010 (bottom left), 1018 (left), 1024–1025, 1026 (rt.), 1043 (bottom), 1049 (cntr.).

BRISSON, JAMES F.: 1 (top), 6, 10 (inset), 13, 17, 18, 24, 28, 30 (bottom), 31 (bottom), 36 (top), 37 (bottom), 38 (time), 49 (bottom rt.), 53 (top), 56 (left), 57 (top), 69 (rt.), 73, 81 (top), 83 (rt. inset), 88 (bottom), 94 (left), 95, 100 (bottom), 105 (inset), 117 (top), 120 (bottom rt.), 131 (inset rt.), 133 (bottom rt.), 139 (top left), 145 (rt. cntr.), 179 (rt. cntr.), 182, 187, 189 (rt.), 191 (inset), 195, 201 (inset), 202 (rt.), 209 (bottom), 223 (top & cntr.), 234, 236 (inset), 242, 251, 274 (rt.), 279 (bottom rt.), 283 (bottom inset), 304–305 (top), 317 (top), 319 (rt.), 325 (top), 329 (rt.), 334, 340 (top), 351 (inset), 356 (left inset), 366 (top), 406 (top left), 410 (top and bottom), 412, 429 (rt.), 430 (left), 433, 439 (bottom), 454 (inset), 455 (top), 458 (top), 476 (left), 483, 487 (left), 490 (left), 510 (top), 513, 528, 536 (top & left), 539 (top), 540 (bottom), 548 (left), 591 (left), 595, 602 (top), 603 (rt.), 611 (top), 615, 617 (bottom left), 635 (bottom), 657 (top), 658 (bottom), 691, 720 (top), 724, 725 (rt.), 733 (rt.), 734 (rt.), 742 (top), 745, 749, 752 (top), 773 (top), 791 (middle), 840 (top), 842 (top), 851, 868 (rt.), 879, 895 (top rt.), 914, 926 (top), 949 (left), 959 (top), 983 (top), 999, 1001 (bottom rt.), 1003, 1004, 1009 (top), 1023, 1026 (bottom), 1042 (top), 1043 (top), 1044 (top).

BRITISH LIBRARY, LONDON: 151, 163, 262–263, 426, 477 (top rt.), 478 (rt.), 555, 832 (top).

BRITISH MUSEUM, LONDON: 29, 53 (bottom), 105 (top), 106 (top), 141 (bottom), 169 (top left), 173, 181 (bottom), 188, 193, 194 (bottom left), 199 (bottom rt.), 200, 205 (top rt.), 210, 261, 267, 273 (bottom left), 276 (inset), 283 (cntr.), 284, 289 (rt.), 302 (left), 306 (top), 314 (top left), 317 (bottom), 318 (bottom left & cntr.), 320 (top), 327 (top), 330 (#4 & 11), 339 (top & bottom), 345, 367, 381 (left), 382, 389 (top), 393 (cntr.), 398 (left), 403 (rt.), 407, 419 (#9 & 11), 422 (bottom), 434, 441 (bottom), 443 (bottom), 451 (bottom), 452 (top), 455 (top, bottom left), 462 (bottom), 463 (top rt.), 466 (top & bottom), 472 (rt.), 474, 487 (rt.), 488 (top), 496 (bottom), 507, 519, 527, 529, 543, 551 (left), 566 (bottom rt.), 608 (top left), 622 (bottom left), 623 (bottom left), 642, 650 (bottom left), 652, 655 (bottom), 660 (rt.), 667 (top), 674 (rt.), 683, 685 (middle rt., bottom rt., bottom left and left), 688, 702, 703 (top rt.), 704 (top left), 708 (rt.), 712 (left), 716 (#1), 717 (#4, 11), 720, 726 (bottom rt.), 730 (top rt.), 735 (bottom rt.), 744, 751 (top rt.) 791 (bottom left), 814 (top), 819, 838 (top), 888, 894 (far left), 900 (bottom left), 904 (rt.), 919 (#12, 14, 15, 18), 921 (bottom), 922 (top), 927, 928 (rt.), 929 (bottom), 930 (bottom rt.), 948 (left), 975 (bottom), 995, 1001 (bottom rt.), 1002, 1012 (top left, lower middle, bottom), 1012–1013, 1015 (bottom), 1018 (top rt., bottom rt.), 1035 (bottom), 1037 (rt.), 1040 (left), 1047 (top rt.).

THE BROOKLYN MUSEUM: 25 (top rt.), 26, 65 (top), 303, 307, 510 (bottom left); GIFT OF HAGOP KEVORKIAN FOUN-DATION: 137 (top rt.), 993 (left); GIFT OF NEW HERMES FOUNDATION: 497; DICK S. RAMSAY FUND: 67; CHARLES EDWIN WIL-BOUR FUND: 43, 68, 74, 83 (top), 508 (rt.), 755 (top).

THE CLEVELAND MUSEUM OF ART, MR. AND MRS. WILLIAM H. MARLATT FUND: 500.

CORNING MUSEUM OF GLASS, CORNING, NY: 146 (left), 167 (left cntr.), 270 (top middle), 301 (bottom), 331 (#10), 353, 385 (bottom), 436 (top left & rt.), 748 (left), 802 (bottom rt.).

DEE, D. JAMES, ICON: 678.

R. R. DONNELLEY & SONS CO., CARTOGRAPHIC SERVICES CEN-TER; MAPS: 1140–1153.

DOVER PUBLICATIONS: *Ancient Egyptian Designs for Artists and Craftspeople,* Eva Wilson, 1986: 136 (rt.), 918 (#9); *Animals: 1419 Copyright-Free Illustrations,* Jim Harter, 1979: 161 (top rt.), 265 (top), 492

(top left), 536 (bottom), 643 (top rt.), 712 (top left), 766, 774 (top left), 1000, 1006 (top right); *Bible Stories Coloring Book,* 1973: 2, 186 (top), 313 (top), 352, 403 (top rt.), 614, 840 (bottom), 852 (top), 925, 983 (bottom); *The Complete Woodcuts of Albrecht Dürer,* Dr. Willi Kurth, ed., 1963: 75, 715; *The Doré Bible Illustrations,* 1974: 158, 238, 361, 471 (top), 653 (bottom), 740 (bottom), 841 (far left), 845, 848 (bottom left), 946, 985 (top); *Handbook of Plant and Floral Ornament,* Richard C. Hatton, 1960: 508 (left), 633 (bottom rt.); *Historic Costumes in Pictures,* Braun and Schneider, 1975: 230 (#1, 6, 8, 13), 231 (#3, 5, 11, 16, 18), 435 (top left), 636 (top); *An Introduction to a History of Woodcut,* Vol. 1, Arthur M. Hind, 1963: 877; *An Introduction to a History of Woodcut,* Vol. 2, 1963: 298; *Jewelry: A Pictorial Archive of Woodcuts and Engravings,* Harold J. Hart, ed., 1977: 318 (cntr. rt.), 867 (cntr. lower rt., cntr. lower left, and cntr. bottom); *Life in Ancient Egypt,* Adolf Erman, 1971: 239, 247 (bottom), 392 (top rt.), 420 (bottom rt.), 468 (bottom left), 481 (Egyptian), 583 (left), 838 (left), 901 (top rt.), 902 (bottom left & rt.), 918 (#2, 3, 7), 920 (left), 942 (bottom), 949 (top rt.), 963, 1012 (upper middle), 1013 (bottom), 1022 (bottom rt.); *The New Testament: A Pictorial Archive from Nineteenth Century Sources,* Don Rice, ed., 1986: 46, 61, 606, 729 (top rt.), 783; *Plants of the Bible,* Harold N. and Alma L. Moldenke, 1952: 249 (left), 269 (bottom); *Rings for the Finger,* George Frederick Kunz, 1973: 867 (cntr. upper left & cntr. upper rt.); *Symbols, Signs and Signets,* Ernst Lehner, 1950: 330 (#5), 540 (top left, both), 956 (left), 1042 (bottom rt.).

ENGEL, BILL: 177, 509 (top), 640, 699 (top).

FOGG ART MUSEUM, HARVARD UNIVERSITY, FRIENDS OF THE FOGG: 185 (top).

GEORGE FORSYTHE and KURT WEITZMAN, *The Monastery of St. Catherine at Sinai: The Church and Fortress of Justinian,* University of Michigan Press, 1973: 709

FRANZ, GORDON: 90, 139 (rt.), 205 (top left), 278 (top rt.), 486, 490 (rt.), 772 (bottom), 917, 960.

THE FRICK COLLECTION, NEW YORK (COPYRIGHT): 897.

HAIGHT, JO: 32 (bottom), 33 (bottom), 137 (top rt.), 145 (bottom), 167 (top left), 198 (left), 201 (bottom), 221 (bottom), 233 (bottom), 241, 265 (bottom), 266, 269 (rt.), 311 (top), 326 (bottom), 331 (#9), 376, 449 (top), 504 (#1, 4, 5), 505 (#8, 9, 12, 13), 602 (left), 621 (bottom rt.), 717 (#5), 756 (rt.).

HAIGHT, ROGER: 331 (#7).

HARPER & ROW, PUBLISHERS, INC.: Illustration from *The Conquest of Civilization* by James Henry Breasted. Copyright 1926. Reprinted by permission of the publisher, 685 (top rt.).

ISRAEL GOVERNMENT TOURIST OFFICE: 81 (bottom middle), 183 (left cntr.), 314 (rt. cntr.).

KIBBUTZ GINOSAR, ISRAEL: 413 (cntr.).

KROEGER, CATHERINE: 651.

LA SOR, WILLIAM S.: 59 (top), 83 (bottom left), 88 (cntr.), 91 (top), 109 (top), 275 (top rt.), 296 (bottom), 351 (bottom), 444 (bottom), 458, 488 (bottom), 524, 777 (rt.), 923 (bottom), 1015 (top rt.).

LESSING, ERICH: 92 (top), 97 (bottom), 115, 132, 134 (bottom), 138 (top), 155, 172 (bottom), 174 (top), 222, 236 (cntr.), 296, 297, 323 (top left), 343, 356 (bottom rt.), 399 (bottom), 411, 413 (bottom), 419 (#10), 453 (bottom), 454 (top), 460, 469, 471 (bottom), 476 (rt.), 484 (bottom), 517, 583 (bottom rt.) 587, 629, 633 (top), 673 (top), 687 (left middle), 698 (top left), 699 (bottom rt.), 717 (#3), 727 (bottom), 738 (top), 759 (bottom), 760 (top), 761, 765 (top left, rt.), 787 (bottom), 806 (top left), 807 (bottom left), 808 (top left), 821, 830, 853, 868 (bottom left), 869, 902 (top left), 908 (bottom), 911, 918 (#4), 945 (bottom rt. & bottom), 950, 954, 962 (bottom), 971, 980, 987, 994, 1015 (top left).

LESSING, ERICH, ALEPPO MUSEUM: 168 (top), 259, 273 (bottom rt.), 323, 504 (#2), 634 (top rt.), 847 (left), 882, 997, 1020 (bottom rt.), 1025 (top rt.); ARCHAEOLOGICAL MUSEUM, ISTANBUL, 340 (cntr.), 484 (bottom left), 558, 900 (top left), 916 (top); BATHS OF DIOCLETIAN, ROME: 127, 777 (left); BIBLIOTHEQUE NATIONALE, PARIS: 335; BONNAT MUSEUM, BAYONNE, FRANCE, 842 (top left); BRITISH MUSEUM: 8 (bottom), 12, 92 (bottom, 104 (top left), 138 (top), 312, 355, 416, 419 (#9), 456, 462, 734 (bottom left), 760 (left), 774 (bottom rt.), 911, 1022 (top rt.); THE BRONFMAN ARCHAEOLOGICAL MUSEUM, JERUSALEM: 998; CATACOMBS OF ST. CALIXTUS, ROME: 644; CATACOMBS OF ST. PRISCILLA, ROME: 406 (bottom), 811; CATHEDRAL SAN MARCO, VENICE: 594; CATHEDRAL OF SAN MATTEO, SALERNO, ITALY: 746 (left), 847 (rt.); DAGON COLLECTION, HAIFA: 9 (bottom), 270 (top rt.), 708 (rt.), 808 (top rt.), 972 (rt.), 1036; DAMASCUS MUSEUM: 57 (left & rt. bottom), 322, 426 (left); EGYPTIAN MUSEUM, CAIRO: 124 (rt.), 514, 781 (top), 856, 992; EGYPTIAN MUSEUM, LEIDEN, 231 (#10), 331 (#12), 380, 841 (left); FORUM ROMANUM, ROME: 765, (bottom left), 873 (top rt.) 944; GIMEL-LES-CASCADES, FRANCE: 947; GRAPHISCHE SAMMLUNG ALBERTINA, VIENNA: 649 (top rt.), 811; GROTTE VATICANE, ROME: 569, 764 (bottom rt.); HAARETZ MUSEUM, TEL AVIV: 436 (bottom), 504 (#6), 697 (middle rt. & bottom rt.), 808 (middle rt.), 814 (bottom left), 846, 872 (top rt.), 1016 (rt.); HECHT MUSEUM, UNIV. OF HAIFA, ISRAEL: 78 (top), 120 (left), 164, 167 (rt. middle), 174 (bottom rt.), 302 (top left), 324 (left), 341 (cntr. rt.), 479 (top), 516, 535 (lower left), 728 (top), 750 (bottom rt.), 767 (rt.), 808 (middle), 848 (rt.), 1033 (bottom); HESSISCHES LANDESMUSEUM, DARMSTADT, GERMANY; 289 (rt.), 1006 (left); HITTITE MUSEUM, ANKARA, 996 (left); HOLY LAND HOTEL, JERUSALEM, 934 (bottom); HOTEL-DIEU, BEAUNE, FRANCE: 562; COLLECTIONS OF ISRAEL DEPT. OF ANTIQUITIES & MUSEUMS, JERUSALEM: 78, 135 (rt.), 167 (far left), 174, 246, 249 (top left), 256, 272, 311 (bottom), 324 (left), 477 (bottom), 613 (top), 619, 660 (left), 667 (bottom rt.) 770 (left), 789, 807 (middle), 1033 (top rt.); Collections of I.D.A.M., at the Israel Museum: 116 (top left & rt.), 167 (far rt.), 168 (bottom left), 248 (cntr. rt.), 268 (bottom), 481 (left), 603 (top left), 721 (left), 808 (top left), 901 (top

left); Collections of I.D.A.M., at the Rockefeller Museum: 274 (left cntr.), 285, 419 (#12), 1017. IRAQ MUSEUM, BAGHDAD: 140 (top rt.), 896, 1020 (top rt.); COLLECTION OF THE ISRAEL MUSEUM, JERUSALEM: 270 (top left), 278 (top left), 463 (bottom rt.), 593 (top rt.); KLOSTERNEUBURG ABBEY, AUSTRIA: 612 (top rt.), 769; KUNSTHISTORISCHES MUSEUM, VIENNA: 11, 72, (left), 118 (top left), 125 (top), 142 (bottom), 161 (top), 206 (top), 224 (left), 230 (#2, 15), 342 (left), 354 (rt.), 418 (#6), 463 (left), 539 (bottom), 540 (rt.), 566 (bottom left), 780 (bottom rt.), 899, 1040 (top rt.); LIBRARY OF THE CATHEDRAL, GERONA, SPAIN, 389 (bottom); MUSEE DU BARDO, TUNIS, 208; MUSEE ARCHEOLOGIQUE, DIJON, FRANCE: 839 (left); MUSEE D'ART ET DE HISTOIRE, METZ: 321 (rt.), 359 (bottom left), 501, 955 (bottom); MUSEE DE CLUNY, PARIS: 1021 (left); MUSEE LAPIDAIRE CHRETIEN, ARLES: 134 (top), 253, 557, 690 (left), 775, 1049 (top); MUSEE DU LOUVRE, PARIS: 107 (bottom), 108, 119, 176, 202 (bottom rt.), 205 (bottom rt.), 209 (top), 219, 225 (rt.), 230 (#7, 14), 231 (#12), 260, 273 (bottom rt.), 279 (cntr.), 309 (top, bottom left), 356 (rt. cntr.), 372, 373 (top inset), 375, 419 (#8), 449 (bottom), 465 (left & rt.), 472 (bottom), 540 (rt.), 613 (bottom), 617 (top), 623 (top rt.), 638 (rt.), 643 (bottom left), 674 (left), 680, 690 (rt.), 703 (bottom rt.), 714 (rt.), 716 (#14), 717 (#16), 729 (bottom rt.), 733 (bottom cntr.), 740 (rt.), 747 (left), 770 (rt.), 774 (bottom left), 793 (bottom left), 818 (bottom left), 841 (bottom rt.), 859, 867 (left), 872 (middle left), 873 (top left), 889 (top left), 902 (cntr. top), 916 (bottom), 919 (#19), 929 (top), 942 (top left), 955 (top rt.), 965, 978 (bottom left & top), 986 (rt.), 1013 (bottom left), 1021 (rt.), 1022 (left), 1030, 1031, 1035 (top), 1038, 1041 (bottom rt.), 1042 (center); MUSEE MUNICIPALE, SENS: 404 (bottom rt.); MUSEO ARCHEOLOGICO, AQUILEIA, ITALY: 759 (top); MUSEO DELL'ARCIVESCOVADO, RAVENNA, ITALY: 574; MUSEO EGIZIO, TURIN: 583 (bottom left), 930 (top left), 949 (bottom); MUSEO LATERANENSE, ROME: 758; MUSEO NAZIONALE, NAPLES: 231 (#17), 686, 754 (top rt.), 872 (bottom), 873 (middle rt., bottom left), 875 (rt.); MUSEO NAZIONALE ROMANO, ROME: 301 (top), 875 (rt.), 876 (rt.); MUSEO OSTIENSE, OSTIA, ITALY: 206 (bottom left), 359 (top left), 566 (lower left), 673 (rt.), 684 (top left), 689; MUSEUM AND ARCHIVES, WELS, UPPER AUSTRIA: 142 (top); MUSEUM OF CARTHAGO, CARTHAGE, TUNISIA: 391 (rt.); MUSEUM OF ORIENTAL ANTIQUITIES, ISTANBUL: 39, 82, 450 (top left), 941 (top), 1014; MUSEUM STUDIUM BIBLICUM, FRANCISCANUM, JERUSALEM: 327 (left), 559, 634 (bottom left); NATIONAL ARCHAEOLOGICAL MUSEUM, ATHENS: 110 (top); NATIONAL ARCHAEOLOGICAL MUSEUM, NAPLES, 110 (rt.), 873 (middle left); NATIONAL LIBRARY, ATHENS: 184 (bottom rt.), 575, 634 (top left), 756 (top left), 1001 (top left); NATIONAL MARITIME MUSEUM, HAIFA: 359 (bottom rt.), 643 (cntr.), 918 (#5, 6), NATIONAL MUSEUM, DAMASCUS, SYRIA: 962 (top), 1032; NATIONAL MUSEUM OF ARCHAEOLOGY, BEIRUT: 91 (bottom), 791 (bottom); NORBERT SCHIMMEL, NEW YORK: 161 (bottom), 612 (bottom), 748 (top left), 932 (top); NY CARLSBERG GLYPTOTHEK, COPENHAGEN: 717 (#6), 918 (#8); O.O.LANDESMUSEUM, LINZ, AUSTRIA: 771; PALATINE LIBRARY, PARMA, ITALY: 394 (top), 631; REIFENBERG COLLECTION, ISRAEL MUSEUM, JERUSALEM: 657; RHEINSCHES LANDESMUSEUM, TRIER: 326 (top), 741, 784, 837, 909, 964, 1034; ROMISCH-GERMANISCHES ZENTRALMUSEUM, MAINZ: 872 (top left), 932 (bottom); STAATLICHE MUSEEN, EAST BERLIN: 121, 726 (top left, top rt.); TREASURY OF THE CATHEDRAL, CHARTRES, FRANCE: 491; TREASURY OF THE

CATHEDRAL, MILANO: 576; VICTORIA & ALBERT MUSEUM, LONDON: 275 (top left), 401.

UNIVERSITY OF LONDON, INSTITUTE OF ARCHAEOLOGY: 503.

METROPOLITAN MUSEUM OF ART, NEW YORK CITY (all rights reserved): 25 (top left), 35 (top), 107 (top), 116 (far rt. & bottom), 178 (top), 179 (top), 231 (#9), 254 (bottom left), 341 (top rt.), 354 (bottom left), 371, 384, 392 (bottom), 393 (inset), 400 (top), 418 (#1), 444 (top), 618 (left), 661, 693, 731, 842–843 (bottom), 1027 (bottom); CARNAVON COLLECTION, Gift of Edward S. Harkness, 1926: 418 (#4), 422 (top); EGYPTIAN EXPEDITION, 1919–1920: 1019 (top left); EGYPTIAN EXPEDITION, ROGERS FUND, 1930: 124 (top), 130, 196–197 (bottom), 330 (#6), 638 (left), 870, 918 (#1), 956 (bottom), 1007; EGYPTIAN EXPLORATION FUND, 1901: 418 (#2); FLETCHER FUND, 1927: 383, 717 (#15); GIFT OF HELEN MILLER GOULD, 1910: 418 (#3); GIFT OF EDWARD S. HARKNESS, 1916–1917: 196 (cntr. left); JOINT EXPEDITION OF THE METROPOLITAN MUSEUM OF ART AND THE GERMAN STATE MUSEUMS TO CTESIPHON, 1931–1932: ROGERS FUND, 1932: 136; MUSEUM EXCAVATIONS, 1922–1923: ROGERS FUND, 1923: 66 (bottom); MUSEUM EXCAVATIONS, 1934–1935: ROGERS FUND, 1935, 848 (top); ROGERS FUND: 902 (top rt.); ROGERS FUND, 1907: 941 (left); ROGERS FUND 1914: 841 (top); ROGERS FUND 1924: 439 (top); ROGERS FUND 1930: 386–387 (top), 405; ROGERS FUND 1931: 156–157 (top); ROGERS FUND 1933: 386 (bottom); ROGERS FUND 1940: 419 (#14); ROGERS FUND 1959: 110 (top).

OTTO MULLER VERLAG, SALZBURG, distributed by Illuminations of Hildegard of Bingen: 475.

MUSEE DU LOUVRE, PARIS: 93 (top), 94 (bottom), 268–269, 437, 438, 579, 834, 915, 919 (#19), 989, 1043 (middle rt.).

MUSEUM OF FINE ARTS, BOSTON, H.L. PIERCE FUND: 521 (top).

MUSEUM OF FINE ARTS, SPRINGFIELD, MA: 796 (top).

THE NATIONAL GALLERY, LONDON: 207, 276 (top).

NATIONAL GALLERIES OF SCOTLAND: 677.

NATIONAL GALLERY OF ART, WASHINGTON, D.C.: CHESTER DALE COLLECTION: 646–647; AILSA MELLON BRUCE FUND: 276, 700 (top), 711; GIFT OF AVALON FOUNDATION: 820; ANDREW W. MELLON COLLECTION: 70; SAMUEL H. KRESS COLLECTION: 129, 336–337, 385 (top), 410 (top), 572, 669, 670, 732, 827, 1044; ROSENWALD COLLECTION: 290 (top), 354 (bottom left); WIDENER COLLECTION: 453 (top), 628, 764 (top left).

ALAN ODDIE/PHOTO EDIT: 292, 342 (rt.).

ORIENTAL INSTITUTE, UNIVERSITY OF CHICAGO: 9 (top), 54, 94 (top rt.), 119, 125 (cntr.), 148, 165, 170 (top), 174 (bottom left), 204 (bottom rt.), 224 (rt.), 231 (#4), 248 (bottom left), 330 (#1, 2, 3, 13, 14), 348 (top), 418 (#5), 470, 481 (bottom rt.), 493, 535 (left), 566 (top), 655 (left), 684 (top rt.), 716 (#2), 746 (rt.), 772 (top), 774 (top), 799, 806 (top rt.), 945 (top), 1048 (bottom & middle).

PETERSEN, WILLIAM: 419 (#13).

1155